Paradise Lost | *A Concordance*

Paradise Lost | A Concordance

Compiled by GLADYS W. HUDSON, *Baylor University*

GALE RESEARCH COMPANY • BOOK TOWER, DETROIT, MICHIGAN 48226

Also published by Gale

An O'Neill Concordance—J. Russell Reaver
Concordance to Beowulf—Albert Stanburrough Cook
A Zola Dictionary—J. G. Patterson
The Waverley Dictionary—May Rogers
A Ballade of the Scottysshe Kynge—John Skelton

Library of Congress Catalog Number 74-127413

Contents

Preface

The development of modern technology has opened possibilities for relatively quick and highly accurate studies which in the past would have been laborious tasks requiring years for completion. Recognition of the need for a complete, accurate and usable concordance for John Milton's *Paradise Lost* led to the consideration of the computer as a means of producing such a volume. Although numerous problems had to be solved and many decisions made, the time and effort expended were negligible compared with what would have been required by the old-fashioned "cut and paste" method or the "index card" method used before the availability of computers.

Selection of Text

Selection of an appropriate text seemed to be of prime importance. Milton's seventeenth-century English has undergone numerous changes, and most modern editions of *Paradise Lost* have, to varying degrees, been modernized. In order that the concordance in its final form might be useful as both a literary and a linguistic tool, the second edition of *Paradise Lost,* published in 1674, was chosen as the text to be used. The text of this edition was obtained from the excellent photographic facsimile edition of *John Milton's Complete Poetic Works,* edited by Harris Francis Fletcher and published by The University of Illinois Press.

The first edition, published in 1667, contained a number of errors which Milton himself corrected for the second edition. In addition, Milton divided two of the original books so that the second edition consists of twelve, rather than ten, books. This plan is now the standard arrangement for printing *Paradise Lost.* Since this is the form which Milton evidently preferred, it seemed appropriate that this form be used.

Retention of Milton's spelling, though it is often archaic, provides for language studies which would be impossible in a modernized version. Variant readings of lines are not included in the concordance, as the variations between individual copies of the second edition are largely minor changes in spelling, punctuation, spacing and page numbers. Some changes in words and insertions were made between the first and second editions, but since most of these are obviously corrections of printing errors, amending of faulty rhythmic patterns, or limited additions of lines due to the division of two of the books, it was decided not to consider them for this work.

A few minor changes were made in the text for the sake of clarity. In a few places two words were printed without an intervening space. The space was inserted in the concordance so the computer would not, for example, read CALLIN as one word. In one instance the letter *l* was used by the printer where an exclamation point was obviously called for. In another place a space was left in a word where an apostrophe was obviously intended but failed to print. In one line, an *f* was used in place of the old style *ſ,* probably because of foul case. Only such minor corrections as these were made in the text.

Limitations of a Computer Concordance

The computer, although a willing and obedient slave, does have a few limitations which affect the work. The most obvious one is that lower case letters are not readily available. Milton's use of capital letters, while perhaps interesting, is not vital to the study of the poem. The loss of lower case letters does not seem to be a problem of any magnitude.

Punctuation posed another problem. The Honeywell 1200 will produce every necessary punctuation mark except the exclamation point. It was finally decided that a period would be substituted for the exclamation point. Such a substitution should be easily detected by the user, and is certainly preferable to omission of all punctuation.

The only other loss is that of the old style *ſ,* a loss which everyone who has struggled with its ambiguity will probably consider salutary.

Since so few copies of the second edition are readily available, page numbers as reference data were considered meaningless. Referencing is, therefore, limited to book and line numbers. This makes possible location of the line in any edition. The first column is the book number, and the second is the line number.

Special Problems

Milton made frequent use of hyphenated words and expressions. The listing of such words as a single unit only would present the disadvantage of losing the second element as a prime listing should it happen to be a term in which some interest might lie. The listing of the elements separately would cause loss of the compound. It was finally decided to list each hyphenated expression as a unit, and in addition, to list each second element in its own right. The hyphenated expression itself will appear close enough in the list to the logical location of the first element that an additional listing for the first element does not seem necessary. In only one instance did Milton use a hyphenated expression in which the first word is on one line and the second on the following line. The computer could not conveniently reference such a circumstance. In Book 10, lines 581-582, the expression WIDE-ENCROACHING is divided. The concordance lists two separate words for this expression.

Apostrophes were the next problem. Milton's frequent contractions for metric purposes as well as his occasional use of the apostrophe for both plurals and possessives offer many ambiguous situations. For example, GODS might be a plural word or it might be a singular possessive case, while GOD'S is also used in each of these senses. Since the computer is unable to make such distinctions in meaning, all appearances of GODS are listed together, and all appearances of GOD'S are grouped in a separate listing.

Since the computer must rely on actual spelling for sorting, singular and plural forms of the same word or various tenses of a single verb cannot appear in a single listing. The opposite difficulty was encountered with homographs. Such words as MIGHT and LIGHT may have two or more meanings which are unrelated, but all meanings will of necessity appear in the same list.

Several expressions which Milton spelled variously as one or two words were treated as one word and appear in the listing as one expression. Intensive pronouns, although omitted from the indexing, are treated as one word so that SELF and SELVES do not appear when used in this manner, but do appear in other instances. Other such expressions are:

FOR EVER	NO WHERE	WHAT EVER
IN STEAD	TO MORROW	WHEN EVER
MEAN WHILE	WHAT E'RE	WHICH E'RE
ME THOUGHT	WHAT ERE	

Omitted Index Words

Although the computer would accurately list every appearance of every word, however insignificant, page after page of references for words such as articles, common pronouns, prepositions, and auxiliary verbs could serve no useful purpose. A list of words was prepared and the computer was instructed not to list these references. Homographs again entered the picture. The auxiliary verb MAY was considered insignificant, but the name of the month was not. A signal, therefore, was placed in the data to show the computer that MAY should be retained the one time when it was the name of the month. A similar situation arose in one instance when Milton spelled the verb HASTE without the final E.

The following words have been omitted from the concordance:

&	BIN	DIDST	HADST	HERS
A	BOTH	DO	HAST	HER SELF
AM	BUT	DON	HATH	HIM
AN	BY	DONE	HAV	HIMSELF
AND	CAN	DOST	HAVE	HIS
ARE	CANNOT	DOTH	HAVING	HOW
AT	CANST	EACH	HE	I
BE	COULD	EITHER	HEE	I'
BECAUSE	COULD'ST	FOR	HEER	IF
BEEN	COULDST	FROM	HER	IN
BEEST	DID	HAD	HERE	INTO

IS	NO	T'	THOU	WHETHER
IT	NOR	TH'	THOUGH	WHICH
ITH'	NOT	THAT	THROUGH	WHO
ITS	NOW	THE	THUS	WHOM
IT SELF	OF	THEE	THY	WHOSE
MAI'ST	ON	THEIR	THY SELF	WHY
MAIST	OR	THEIRS	TO	WITH
MAY	OUR	THEM	TOO	WOULD
MAY'ST	OURS	THEMSELVES	US	WOULDST
MAYST	OUR SELVES	THEMSELVS	WAS	YE
ME	SHAL	THER	WAST	YEE
MEE	SHALL	THERE	WE	YOU
MIGHTST	SHALT	THESE	WEE	YOUR
MINE	SHE	THEY	WERE	YOURS
MUST	SHEE	THINE	WERT	YOUR SELVES
MY	SHOULD	THIR	WHAT	
MY SELF	SHOULDST	THIS	WHEN	
NEITHER	SO	THOSE	WHERE	

The words AS, LIKE, and THAN which would ordinarily be considered insignificant were retained to facilitate the study of Milton's similes. This same purpose also dictated the retention of THEN, as Milton nearly always substituted this spelling for THAN.

Frequency Listing

At the end of the concordance appears a listing of all words in *Paradise Lost,* including those omitted from the concordance, in the order of the frequency of their appearance. Omitted index words are indicated by an asterisk. Although only one listing under a particular index word is made in the concordance for a line in which a single word appears two or more times, each appearance in that line is counted for the frequency listing.

Acknowledgments

Much gratitude is due to Professor Jack Herring, Director of the Armstrong Browning Library and Professor of English at Baylor University who encouraged me to undertake this project and provided advice on some of the editing problems. The whole project would have been impossible without the many patient hours spent writing and testing the computer program by my husband, Jack W. Hudson, Director of Management Information Systems, Baylor University.

We also acknowledge with gratitude the advice and help of all the personnel of the Data Processing Center of Baylor University who aided us in the project, and the kind cooperation of the University of Illinois Press in allowing us to use the text of their edition of *Paradise Lost.*

Gladys W. Hudson

Baylor University
Waco, Texas
June 1, 1970

Paradise Lost | A Concordance

Based on the second edition, 1674, as reproduced photographically in John Milton's Complete Poetic Works, *edited by Harris Francis Fletcher and published by The University of Illinois Press. References apply to any modern edition, however.*

	Book	*Line*
AARON		
MOSES AND AARON) SENT FROM GOD TO CLAIME . . .	12	170
AARONS		
IN AARONS BREST-PLATE, AND A STONE BESIDES . . .	3	598
ABANDON		
ABANDON FEAR; TO STRENGTH AND COUNSEL JOIND . .	6	494
ABANDOND		
ABANDOND AT THE TERROR OF THY POWER	6	134
TO SORROW ABANDOND, BUT WORSE FELT WITHIN, . . .	10	717
ABARIM		
OF SOUTHMOST ABARIM; IN HESEBON	1	408
ABASH'T		
TO WHOM THUS HALF ABASH'T ADAM REPLI'D.	8	595
TILL ADAM, THOUGH NOT LESS THEN EVE ABASH'T, . .	9	1065
ABASHT		
THEY HEARD, AND WERE ABASHT, AND UP THEY SPRUNG .	1	331
INVINCIBLE: ABASHT THE DEVIL STOOD, ...	4	846
BOLD OR LOQUACIOUS, THUS ABASHT REPLI'D. . . .	10	161
ABASSIN		
NOR WHERE ABASSIN KINGS THIR ISSUE GUARD, . . .	4	280
ABATED		
WHICH NOW ABATED, FOR THE CLOUDS WERE FLED, . . .	11	841
ABBANA		
OF ABBANA AND PHARPHAR, LUCID STREAMS.	1	469
ABDIEL		
ABDIEL, THEN WHOM NONE WITH MORE ZEALE ADOR'D . .	5	805
SO SPAKE THE SERAPH ABDIEL FAITHFUL FOUND, . .	5	896
ABDIEL THAT SIGHT ENDUR'D NOT, WHERE HE STOOD . .	6	111
TO WHOM IN BRIEF THUS ABDIEL STERN REPLI'D. . .	6	171
NOR STOOD UNMINDFUL ABDIEL TO ANNOY	6	369
ABHOR		
ABHOR TO JOYN; AND BY IMPRUDENCE MIXT, ...	11	686
ABHORR		
THAT WHAT IN SLEEP THOU DIDST ABHORR TO DREAM, .	5	120
ABHORR'D		
THEY WORSE ABHORR'D. SATAN BEHELD THIR PLIGHT, .	6	607
ABHORRD		
WITHIN UNSEEN. FARR LESS ABHORRD THAN THESE . .	2	659
ABHORRE		
TO DO WHAT ELSE THOUGH DAMND I SHOULD ABHORRE. .	4	392
ABHORRED		
IN THIS ABHORRED DEEP TO UTTER WOE;	2	87
ABHORRED STYX THE FLOOD OF DEADLY HATE, ...	2	577
ABHORR'ST		
TO WHOM THUS MICHAEL. JUSTLY THOU ABHORR'ST . . .	12	79

	Book	*Line*
ABIDE		
AMONG THE NATIONS ROUND, AND DURST ABIDE	1	385
HOW DEARLY I ABIDE THAT BOAST SO VAINE, ...	4	87
UNDER HIS GREAT VICE-GERENT REIGN ABIDE	5	609
ABIDES		
IMPRESST THE EFFULGENCE OF HIS GLORIE ABIDES, . .	3	388
WHERE HE ABIDES, THINK THERE THY NATIVE SOILE. .	11	292
ABJECT		
ABJECT AND LOST LAY THESE, COVERING THE FLOOD, .	1	312
OR IN THIS ABJECT POSTURE HAVE YE SWORN	1	322
THE TRODDEN HERB, OF ABJECT THOUGHTS AND LOW, . .	9	572
THEREFORE SO ABJECT IS THIR PUNISHMENT, ...	11	520
ABJURE		
HER LOSS, AND OTHER PLEASURES ALL ABJURE: . . .	8	480
ABLE		
SOM OTHER ABLE, AND AS WILLING, PAY	3	211
VERNAL DELIGHT AND JOY, ABLE TO DRIVE	4	155
FOR GOD'S, YET ABLE TO MAKE GODS OF MEN:	5	70
THAT I MUST LEAVE YE, SONS; O WERE I ABLE . . .	10	819
BEARE THINE OWN FIRST, ILL ABLE TO SUSTAINE . .	10	950
WITH SPIRITUAL ARMOUR, ABLE TO RESIST	12	491
ABODE		
ADAMS ABODE, THOSE LOFTIE SHADES HIS BOWRE. . .	3	734
BETTER ABODE, AND MY AFFLICTED POWERS	4	939
UP TO THE HEAV'N OF HEAV'NS HIS HIGH ABODE, . .	7	553
ABOLISH		
ABOLISH HIS OWN WORKS. THIS WOULD SURPASS . . .	2	370
ABOLISH THY CREATION, AND UNMAKE, ...	3	163
US TO ABOLISH, LEAST THE ADVERSARY	9	947
ABOLISHT		
WE SHOULD BE QUITE ABOLISHT AND EXPIRE.	2	93
ABOMINABLE		
ABOMINABLE, INUTTERABLE, AND WORSE	2	626
ABOMINABLE, ACCURST, THE HOUSE OF WOE, ...	10	465
ABOMINATIONS		
ABOMINATIONS; AND WITH CURSED THINGS	1	389
ABORTIVE		
THREATENS HIM, PLUNG'D IN THAT ABORTIVE GULF. . .	2	441
ABORTIVE, MONSTROUS, OR UNKINDLY MIXT, ...	3	456
ABORTIVE, TO TORMENT ME ERE THIR BEING, ...	11	769
ABOUND		
IN FUTURE DAYES, IF MALICE SHOULD ABOUND, ...	6	502
FROM GOD, AND OVER WRAUTH GRACE SHALL ABOUND. .	12	478
ABOUNDANCE		
TO US, IN SUCH ABOUNDANCE LIES OUR CHOICE, . . .	9	620
ABOUNDED		
LOVE HATH ABOUNDED MORE THEN GLORY ABOUNDS, . .	3	312
ABOUNDS		
LOVE HATH ABOUNDED MORE THEN GLORY ABOUNDS, . .	3	312

ABOUT

POUR FORTH THIR POPULOUS YOUTH ABOUT THE HIVE 1 770
OF SOME NEW RACE CALL'D MAN, ABOUT THIS TIME 2 348
WITH MORTAL STING: ABOUT HER MIDDLE ROUND 2 653
ABOUT HIM ALL THE SANCTITIES OF HEAVEN 3 60
DRAWN ROUND ABOUT THEE LIKE A RADIANT SHRINE, 3 379
HE BRINGS, AND ROUND ABOUT HIM, NOR FROM HELL 4 21
ALONE AS THEY. ABOUT THEM FRISKING PLAYD 4 340
BY WORD OR ACTION MARKT: ABOUT THEM ROUND 4 401
ABOUT HIM EXERCIS'D HEROIC GAMES 4 551
TO WED HER ELM; SHE SPOUS'D ABOUT HIM TWINES 5 216
IN SONG AND DANCE ABOUT THE SACRED HILL, 5 619
MELODIOUS HYMNS ABOUT THE SOVRAN THRONE 5 656
ABOUT THE GREAT RECEPTION OF THIR KING, 5 769
AGAINST US FROM ABOUT HIS THRONE, AND JUDG'D 6 426
AND FROM ABOUT HIM FIERCE EFFUSION ROWLD 6 765
ABOUT HIS CHARIOT NUMBERLESS WERE POUR'D 7 197
AND FROM ABOUT HER SHOT DARTS OF DESIRE 8 62
INCITED, DANCE ABOUT HIM VARIOUS ROUNDS? 8 125
STOOD ON MY FEET; ABOUT ME ROUND I SAW 8 261
ABOVE, OR ROUND ABOUT THEE OR BENEATH. 8 318
ABOUT HER, AS A GUARD ANGELIC PLAC'T. 8 559
THRICE FUGITIVE ABOUT TROY WALL; OR RAGE 9 16
PLEASURES ABOUT ME, SO MUCH MORE I FEEL 9 120
ABOUT HER GLOWD, OFT STOOPING TO SUPPORT 9 427
ABOUT THE MOSSIE TRUNK I WOUND ME SOON, 9 589
ABOUT HIM. BUT TO ADAM IN WHAT SORT 9 816
ABOUT THIR SPIRITS HAD PLAID, AND INMOST POWERS 9 1048
AND HONOUR FROM ABOUT THEM, NAKED LEFT 9 1057
ABOUT THE MOTHER TREE, A PILLARD SHADE 9 1106
ABOUT THE NEW-ARRIV'D, IN MULTITUDES 10 26
AND ALL ABOUT FOUND DESOLATE; FOR THOSE 10 420
FARR TO THE INLAND RETIR'D, ABOUT THE WALLS 10 423
HE SATE, AND ROUND ABOUT HIM SAW UNSEEN: 10 448
PITCHT ABOUT SECHEM, AND THE NEIGHBOURING PLAINE 12 136

ABOVE

ABOVE TH' AONIAN MOUNT, WHILE IT PURSUES 1 15
TO SET HIMSELF IN GLORY ABOVE HIS PEERS, 1 39
WITH HEAD UP-LIFT ABOVE THE WAVE, AND EYES 1 193
ABOVE HIS EQUALS. FAREWEL HAPPY FIELDS 1 249
OF RIOT ASCENDS ABOVE THEIR LOFTIEST TOWRS, 1 499
THIR DREAD COMMANDER: HE ABOVE THE REST 1 589
ABOVE THEM ALL TH' ARCH ANGEL: BUT HIS FACE 1 600
AND PLUNGE US IN THE FLAMES? OR FROM ABOVE 2 172
OF HIM WHO RULES ABOVE; SO WAS HIS WILL 2 351
ABOVE HIS FELLOWS, WITH MONARCHAL PRIDE 2 428
OF HAZARD MORE, AS HE ABOVE THE REST 2 455
FOR HIM WHO SITS ABOVE AND LAUGHS THE WHILE 2 731
SAVE HE WHO REIGNS ABOVE, NONE CAN RESIST. 2 814
BUT WHAT OW I TO HIS COMMANDS ABOVE 2 856
NOW HAD THE ALMIGHTY FATHER FROM ABOVE, 3 56
HIGH THRON'D ABOVE ALL HIGHTH, BENT DOWN HIS EYE, 3 58
ELECT ABOVE THE REST; SO IS MY WILL: 3 184
TO MORTAL MEN, ABOVE WHICH ONLY SHON 3 268
THUS THEY IN HEAV'N, ABOVE THE STARRY SPHEAR, 3 416
SO HIGH ABOVE THE CIRCLING CANOPIE 3 556
HE STAYD NOT TO ENQUIRE: ABOVE THEM ALL 3 571
I FELL, HOW GLORIOUS ONCE ABOVE THY SPHEARE; 4 39
SHADE ABOVE SHADE, A WOODIE THEATRE 4 141
HE HELD IT VAIN; AWE FROM ABOVE HAD QUELLD 4 860
UNSPEAKABLE, WHO FIRST ABOVE THESE HEAVENS 5 156
ABOVE ALL HILLS. AS WHEN BY NIGHT THE GLASS 5 261
WILDE ABOVE RULE OR ART; ENORMOUS BLISS. 5 297
SINCE BY DESCENDING FROM THE THRONES ABOVE, 5 363
OF THINGS ABOVE HIS WORLD, AND OF THIR BEING 5 455
IN PLACE THY SELF SO HIGH ABOVE THY PEERES. 5 812
THIR PERFET RANKS; FOR HIGH ABOVE THE GROUND 6 71
GAVE THEM ABOVE THIR FOES, NOT TO HAVE SINND, 6 402
IN HEAV'N AND HELL THY POWER ABOVE COMPARE, 6 705
FOLLOWING, ABOVE TH' OLYMPIAN HILL I SOARE, 7 3
ABOVE THE FLIGHT OF PEGASEAN WING. 7 4
STANDING ON EARTH, NOT RAPT ABOVE THE POLE, 7 23
THINGS ABOVE EARTHLY THOUGHT, WHICH YET CONCERND 7 82
THY HEARING, SUCH COMMISSION FROM ABOVE 7 118
THE WATERS UNDERNEATH FROM THOSE ABOVE 7 268
AND LET FOWLE FLIE ABOVE THE EARTH, WITH WINGS 7 389
RISING, THE CRUMBL'D EARTH ABOVE THEM THREW 7 468
INVISIBLE ELSE ABOVE ALL STARRS, THE WHEELE 8 135
LEAVE THEM TO GOD ABOVE, HIM SERVE AND FEARE; 8 168
ABOVE, OR ROUND ABOUT THEE OR BENEATH. 8 318
O BY WHAT NAME, FOR THOU ABOVE ALL THESE, 8 357
ABOVE MANKINDE, OR AUGHT THEN MANKINDE HIGHER, 8 358
LIGHT ABOVE LIGHT, FOR THEE ALONE, AS SEEMS, 9 105
COMPARE ABOVE ALL LIVING CREATURES DEARE, 9 228
FOULD ABOVE FOULD A SURGING MAZE, HIS HEAD 9 499
TO ME SO FRIENDLY GROWN ABOVE THE REST 9 564
WHEREIN GOD SET THEE ABOVE HER MADE OF THEE, 10 149
ABOVE ALL CATTLE, EACH BEAST OF THE FIELD; 10 176
ABOVE THE REST STILL TO RETAIN; THEY ALL 10 532
HIS WILL WHO REIGNS ABOVE, TO AGGRAVATE 10 549
PRAYING, FOR FROM THE MERCIE-SEAT ABOVE 11 2
STRENGTH ADDED FROM ABOVE, NEW HOPE TO SPRING 11 138
OR OF THE THRONES ABOVE, SUCH MAJESTIE 11 232
PRINCE ABOVE PRINCES, GENTLY HAST THOU TOULD 11 298
AND JUDGMENT FROM ABOVE: HIM OLD AND YOUNG 11 668
ABOVE THE HIGHEST HILLS: THEN SHALL THIS MOUNT 11 829
ABOVE HIS BRETHREN, TO HIMSELF ASSUMING 12 65

ABOVE (CONTINUED)

ABOVE THE CLOUDS WILL PINE HIS ENTRAILS GROSS, 12 77
ABOVE ALL NAMES IN HEAV'N; AND THENCE SHALL COME, 12 458

ABRAHAM

WHOM FAITHFUL ABRAHAM DUE TIME SHALL CALL, 12 152
PROMISD TO ABRAHAM AND HIS SEED: THE REST 12 260
FROM ABRAHAM, SON OF ISAAC, AND FROM HIM 12 268
JUST ABRAHAM AND HIS SEED: NOW FIRST I FINDE 12 273
FORETOLD TO ABRAHAM, AS IN WHOM SHALL TRUST 12 328

ABRAHAMS

NOT ONELY TO THE SONS OF ABRAHAMS LOINES 12 447
OF ABRAHAMS FAITH WHEREVER THROUGH THE WORLD; 12 449

ABROAD

AGAINST A WAKEFUL FOE, WHILE I ABROAD 2 463

ABRUPT

OVER THE VAST ABRUPT, ERE HE ARRIVE 2 409

ABSENCE

OFT IN HER ABSENCE MIMIC FANSIE WAKES 5 110
OR WE CAN BID HIS ABSENCE, TILL THY SONG 7 107
THEE SATIATE, TO SHORT ABSENCE I COULD YIELD. 9 248
THY ABSENCE FROM MY SIGHT, BUT TO AVOID 9 294
THE PAIN OF ABSENCE FROM THY SIGHT. BUT STRANGE 9 861

ABSENT

SHALL ENTER HEAVEN LONG ABSENT, AND RETURNE, 3 261
FOR I THAT DAY WAS ABSENT, AS BEFELL, 8 229
THOSE TWO; THE THIRD BEST ABSENT IS CONDEMN'D, 10 82

ABSENTS

GO; FOR THY STAY, NOT FREE, ABSENTS THEE MORE; 9 372
ABSENTS THEE, OR WHAT CHANCE DETAINS? COME FORTH. 10 108

ABSOLUTE

FIXT FATE, FREE WILL, FOREKNOWLEDG ABSOLUTE, 2 560
THIR WILL, DISPOS'D BY ABSOLUTE DECREE 3 115
ABSOLUTE RULE; AND HYACINTHIN LOCKS 4 301
AND THROUGH ALL NUMBERS ABSOLUTE, THOUGH ONE; 8 421
HER LOVELINESS, SO ABSOLUTE SHE SEEMS 8 547
OF ABSOLUTE PERFECTION, THEREIN MAN 10 483
BUT PRAYER AGAINST HIS ABSOLUTE DECREE 11 311
DOMINION ABSOLUTE; THAT RIGHT WE HOLD 12 68

ABSOLUTELY

COMMAND ME ABSOLUTELY NOT TO GO, 9 1156

ABSOLV'D

ABSOLV'D, IF UNFORBID THOU MAIST UNFOULD 7 94

ABSOLVE

IMPUTED SHALL ABSOLVE THEM WHO RENOUNCE 3 291
FORC'T I ABSOLVE: ALL MY EVASIONS VAIN, 10 829

ABSTAIN

OUR MAKER BIDS INCREASE, WHO BIDS ABSTAIN 4 748
OF KNOWLEDGE WITHIN BOUNDS; BEYOND ABSTAIN 7 120
THOUGH TO DELUDE THEM SENT, COULD NOT ABSTAIN, 10 557
CONVERSING, LOOKING, LOVING, TO ABSTAIN 10 993

ABSTAIN'D

MUCH PLEASURE WE HAVE LOST, WHILE WE ABSTAIN'D 9 1022

ABSTINENCE

THAT SACRED FRUIT, SACRED TO ABSTINENCE, 9 924

ABSTRACT

ABSTRACT AS IN A TRANSE METHOUGHT I SAW, 8 462

ABSTRACTED

THAT SPACE THE EVIL ONE ABSTRACTED STOOD 9 463

ABSTRUSE

ENTRING ON STUDIOUS THOUGHTS ABSTRUSE, WHICH EVE 8 40

ABSTRUSEST

ABSTRUSEST THOUGHTS, FROM FORTH HIS HOLY MOUNT 5 712

ABUNDANCE

FOR US TOO LARGE, WHERE THY ABUNDANCE WANTS 4 730
ABUNDANCE, FIT TO HONOUR AND RECEIVE 5 315

ABUNDANT

COMMUNICATED, MORE ABUNDANT GROWES, 5 72
REPTIL WITH SPAWN ABUNDANT, LIVING SOULE: 7 388

ABUNDANTLY

ABUNDANTLY HIS GIFTS HATH ALSO POUR'D 8 220

ABUS'D

WITH MONSTROUS SHAPES AND SORCERIES ABUS'D 1 479

ABUSE

TO WORST ABUSE, OR TO THIR MEANEST USE. 4 204
AND LOOK FOR ADORATION TO TH' ABUSE 5 800

ABYSS
DOVE-LIKE SATST BROODING ON THE VAST ABYSS 1 21
CAELESTIAL SPIRITS IN BONDAGE, NOR TH' ABYSS 1 658
THE DARK UNBOTTOM'D INFINITE ABYSS 2 405
BY HARALDS VOICE EXPLAIN'D: THE HOLLOW ABYSS 2 518
CHANCE GOVERNS ALL. INTO THIS WILDE ABYSS, 2 910
INTO THIS WILD ABYSS THE WARIE FIEND 2 917
OR SPIRIT OF THE NETHERMOST ABYSS 2 956
AND SPIRITS OF THIS NETHERMOST ABYSS, 2 969
OVER THE DARK ABYSS, WHOSE BOILING GULF 2 1027
HEAPT ON HIM THERE, NOR YET THE MAIN ABYSS 3 83
TO WING THE DESOLATE ABYSS, AND SPIE 4 936
THEY VIEW'D THE VAST IMMEASURABLE ABYSS 7 211
COVER'D TH' ABYSS: BUT ON THE WATRIE CALME 7 234
OVER THE VEXT ABYSS, FOLLOWING THE TRACK 10 314
WITH THIS PORTENTOUS BRIDGE THE DARK ABYSS. 10 371
O CONSCIENCE, INTO WHAT ABYSS OF FEARS 10 842
TILL TIME STAND FIXT: BEYOND IS ALL ABYSS, 12 555

ABYSSE
TH' UNTRACTABLE ABYSSE, PLUNG'D IN THE WOMB 10 476

ACANTHUS
ACANTHUS, AND EACH ODOROUS BUSHIE SHRUB 4 696

ACCARON
AND ACCARON AND GAZA'S FRONTIER BOUNDS. 1 466

ACCENT
AND WITH PERSWASIVE ACCENT THUS BEGAN. 2 118
THUS HER REPLY WITH ACCENT SWEET RENEWD. 9 321

ACCEPT
ACCEPT THIS DARK OPPROBRIOUS DEN OF SHAME, 2 58
SO HARDIE AS TO PROFFER OR ACCEPT 2 425
REFUSING TO ACCEPT AS GREAT A SHARE 2 452
IN THOSE WHO, WHEN THEY MAY, ACCEPT NOT GRACE. 3 302
ACCEPT YOUR MAKERS WORK; HE GAVE IT ME, 4 380
OF BLOWING MYRRH AND BALME; IF THOU ACCEPT 9 629
THOU DIDST ACCEPT THEM; WILT THOU ENJOY THE GOOD, 10 758
ACCEPT ME, AND IN MEE FROM THESE RECEAVE 11 37
WHAT WE RECEIVE, WOULD EITHER NOT ACCEPT 11 505

ACCEPTABLE
SO FIT, SO ACCEPTABLE, SO DIVINE, 10 139
SAID HEE, WITH ONE THRICE ACCEPTABLE STROKE 10 855

ACCEPTANCE
FINDES NO ACCEPTANCE, NOR CAN FIND, FOR HOW 5 531
PERMISSIVE, AND ACCEPTANCE FOUND, WHICH GAIN'D 8 435
OF NEW ACCEPTANCE, HOPEFUL TO REGAINE 10 972
FROM HEAV'N ACCEPTANCE; BUT THE BLOODIE FACT 11 457
ACCEPTANCE OF LARGE GRACE, FROM SERVIL FEAR 12 305

ACCEPTED
FOOD NOT OF ANGELS, YET ACCEPTED SO, 5 465
ACCEPTED, FEARLESS IN HIS RIGHTEOUS CAUSE, 6 804
ALL THY REQUEST FOR MAN, ACCEPTED SON, 11 46

ACCESS
ATTENDED: ALL ACCESS WAS THRONG'D, THE GATES 1 761
WITH ARMED WATCH, THAT RENDER ALL ACCESS 2 130
ACCESS DENI'D; AND OVER HEAD UP GREW 4 137
ACCESS IN EVERY VERTUE, IN THY SIGHT 9 310
AT FIRST, AS ONE WHO SOUGHT ACCESS, BUT FEARD 9 511
AND GIV'ST ACCESS, THOUGH SECRET SHE RETIRE. 9 810
INSTRUCTED THAT TO GOD IS NO ACCESS 12 239

ACCESSIBLE
ACCESSIBLE FROM EARTH, ONE ENTRANCE HIGH; 4 546

ACCESSORIES
ALIKE, TO SERPENTS ALL AS ACCESSORIES 10 520

ACCLAIM
WITH DEAFNING SHOUT, RETURN'D THEM LOUD ACCLAIM. 2 520

ACCLAIME
BACK FROM PURSUIT THY POWERS WITH LOUD ACCLAIME 3 397
THIR MIGHTY CHIEF RETURND: LOUD WAS TH' ACCLAIME: 10 455

ACCLAMATION
FOLLOWD WITH ACCLAMATION AND THE SOUND 7 558

ACCLAMATIONS
WITH JOY AND ACCLAMATIONS LOUD, THAT ONE 6 23

ACCOMPANI'D
ACCOMPANI'D THEN WITH HIS OWN COMPLEAT 5 352

ACCOMPANIED
SILENCE ACCOMPANIED, FOR BEAST AND BIRD, 4 600
BEST WITH THY SELF ACCOMPANIED, SEEK'ST NOT 8 428
ACCOMPANIED TO HEAVEN GATE, FROM WHENCE 10 88
ACCOMPANIED, WITH DAMPS AND DREADFUL GLOOM, 10 848

ACCOMPLISH'D
SO EV'N AND MORN ACCOMPLISH'D THE SIXT DAY: 7 550

ACCOMPLISHING
ACCOMPLISHING GREAT THINGS, BY THINGS DEEMD WEAK 12 567

ACCOMPLISH'T
YET WITH REVENGE ACCOMPLISH'T AND TO HELL 3 160

ACCOMPLISHT
DAUGHTER OF GOD AND MAN, ACCOMPLISHT EVE, 4 660

ACCORD
TO UNION, AND FIRM FAITH, AND FIRM ACCORD, 2 36
AS IF (WHICH MIGHT INDUCE US TO ACCORD) 2 503

ACCORDING
HATH HONOURD ME ACCORDING TO HIS WILL. 6 816
ACCORDING TO HIS DOOM: HE WOULD HAVE SPOKE, 10 517
BY WHICH ALL CAUSES ELSE ACCORDING STILL 10 806

ACCOST
YET THUS, UNMOVD WITH FEAR, ACCOST HIM SOON. 4 822

ACCOSTES
O'RE SEA AND LAND: HIM SATAN THUS ACCOSTES; 3 653

ACCOUNT
ACCOUNT MEE MAN; I FOR HIS SAKE WILL LEAVE 3 238
AND COUNTRY WHEREOF HERE NEEDS NO ACCOUNT, 4 235
AND OF THIR DOINGS GOD TAKES NO ACCOUNT. 4 622
BUT COME, FOR THOU, BE SURE, SHALT GIVE ACCOUNT 4 841
AS IS MOST JUST; THIS I MY GLORIE ACCOUNT, 6 726
OR MUCH MORE GRIEVOUS PAIN? YE HAVE TH' ACCOUNT 10 501

ACCOUNTABLE
FREE, AND TO NONE ACCOUNTABLE, PREFERRING 2 255
ACCOUNTABLE MADE HASTE TO MAKE APPEAR 10 29

ACCURST
ACCURST, AND IN A CURSED HOUR HE HIES. 2 1055
BE THEN HIS LOVE ACCURST, SINCE LOVE OR HATE, 4 69
O ALIENATE FROM GOD, O SPIRIT ACCURST, 5 877
AMONG TH' ACCURST, THAT WITHERD ALL THIR STRENGTH, 6 850
OF HIS CREATION; JUSTLY THEN ACCURST, 10 168
BECAUSE THOU HAST DONE THIS, THOU ART ACCURST 10 175
ABOMINABLE, ACCURST, THE HOUSE OF WOE, 10 465
ACCURST OF BLESSED, HIDE ME FROM THE FACE 10 723
A SHAMEFUL AND ACCURST, NAILD TO THE CROSS 12 413

ACCUSATION
THUS THEY IN MUTUAL ACCUSATION SPENT 9 1187

ACCUS'D
TO JUDGEMENT HE PROCEEDED ON TH' ACCUS'D 10 164
CURS'D HIS CREATION, DEATH AS OFT ACCUS'D 10 852

ACCUSE
SO WERE CREATED, NOR CAN JUSTLY ACCUSE 3 112
THOU HADST: WHOM HAST THOU THEN OR WHAT TO ACCUSE, 4 67
ACCUSE NOT NATURE, SHE HATH DON HER PART; 8 561
SHEE FIRST HIS WEAK INDULGENCE WILL ACCUSE. 9 1186
MY SELF THE TOTAL CRIME, OR TO ACCUSE 10 127
THOUGH OF REBELLION OTHERS HE ACCUSE. 12 37

ACCUSER
THE TEMPTER ERE TH' ACCUSER OF MAN-KIND, 4 10
AND THOU TH' ACCUSER. THUS IT SHALL BEFALL 9 1182

ACCUSTOMD
FORTH ISSUING AT TH' ACCUSTOMD HOUR STOOD ARMD 4 779
LESS PURE, ACCUSTOMD TO IMMORTAL FRUITS? 11 285

ACHERON
SAD ACHERON OF SORROW, BLACK AND DEEP; 2 578

ACHIEV'D
SOM ADVANTAGIOUS ACT MAY BE ACHIEV'D 2 363
HAD BEEN ACHIEV'D, WHEREOF ALL HELL HAD RUNG, 2 723

ACHIEVD
HATH BIN ACHIEVD OF MERIT, YET THIS LOSS 2 21
SUBDUING NATIONS, AND ACHIEVD THEREBY 11 792

ACHIEVE
THE SERPENT, BY WHAT MEANS HE SHALL ACHIEVE 12 234

ACHILLES
OF STERN ACHILLES ON HIS FOE PURSU'D 9 15

ACKNOWLDG'D
ALLEGEANCE TO TH' ACKNOWLDG'D POWER SUPREAM? 4 956

ACKNOWLEDG'D
ACKNOWLEDG'D AND DEPLOR'D, IN ADAM WRAUGHT 10 939
TAUGHT THEM, BUT THEY HIS GIFTS ACKNOWLEDG'D NONE. 11 612

ACKNOWLEDGE
ACKNOWLEDGE HIM THY GREATER, SOUND HIS PRAISE 5 172
BUT GRATEFUL TO ACKNOWLEDGE WHENCE HIS GOOD 7 512
THE MORE SHE WILL ACKNOWLEDGE THEE HER HEAD, 8 574

ACKNOWLEDGE (CONTINUED)
ACKNOWLEDGE MY REDEEMER EVER BLEST. 12 573

ACQUAINT
TO MY ASSOCIATE POWERS, THEM TO ACQUAINT . . . 10 395

ACQUITTANCE
FORBEARANCE NO ACQUITTANCE ERE DAY END. 10 53

ACQUITTED
WITH ME? HOW CAN THEY THEN ACQUITTED STAND . . 10 827

ACT
BELIAL, IN ACT MORE GRACEFUL AND HUMANE; 2 109
SOM ADVANTAGIOUS ACT MAY BE ACHIEV'D 2 363
BY ACT OF GRACE MY FORMER STATE; HOW SOON . . . 4 94
TO ACT OR NOT, NECESSITIE AND CHANCE 7 172
WITH ACT INTELLIGENTIAL; BUT HIS SLEEP 9 190
FLUCTUATS DISTURBD, YET COMELY AND IN ACT . . . 9 668
MOTION, EACH ACT WON AUDIENCE ERE THE TONGUE, . . 9 674
MEANWHILE THE HAINOUS AND DESPIGHTFULL ACT . . . 10 1
TO OBSERVE THE SEQUEL, SAW HIS GUILEFUL ACT . . 10 334
TRIUMPHAL WITH TRIUMPHAL ACT HAVE MET, ... 10 390
TO THE RECEPTION OF THIR MATTER ACT, ... 10 807
AND ONE BAD ACT WITH MANY DEEDS WELL DONE . . . 11 256
BY FAITH NOT VOID OF WORKES: THIS GOD-LIKE ACT . . 12 427
IN SIN FOR EVER LOST FROM LIFE; THIS ACT . . . 12 429
SECULAR POWER, THOUGH FEIGNING STILL TO ACT . . 12 517

ACTION
BY WORD OR ACTION MARKT: ABOUT THEM ROUND 4 401
OF GESTURE OR LEST ACTION OVERAWD 9 460

ACTIONS
FROM ALL HER WORDS AND ACTIONS MIXT WITH LOVE . . 8 602
MUCH REASON, AND IN THIR ACTIONS OFT APPEERS. . . 9 559
HIS THOUGHTS, HIS LOOKS, WORDS, ACTIONS ALL INFECT, 10 608

ACTIVE
EACH IN THIR SEVERAL ACTIVE SPHEARS ASSIGND, . . . 5 477
ACTIVE WITHIN BEYOND THE SENSE OF BRUTE. 9 96

ACTS
HOLY MEMORIALS, ACTS OF ZEALE AND LOVE 5 593
THESE ACTS OF HATEFUL STRIFE, HATEFUL TO ALL, . . 6 264
IN MIGHT THOUGH WONDROUS AND IN ACTS OF WARR, . . 6 377
EYE WITNESSES OF HIS ALMIGHTIE ACTS, ... 6 883
IMMEDIATE ARE THE ACTS OF GOD, MORE SWIFT . . . 7 176
CREATION AND THE SIX DAYES ACTS THEY SUNG, . . . 7 601
SO MUCH DELIGHTS ME AS THOSE GRACEFUL ACTS, . . . 8 600
WE ARE BY DOOM TO PAY; RATHER SUCH ACTS 10 1026
FIRST SEEN IN ACTS OF PROWESS EMINENT 11 789

ACTUAL
ONCE ACTUAL, NOW IN BODY, AND TO DWELL 10 587

ADAM
ADAM THE GOODLIEST MAN OF MEN SINCE BORNE 4 323
GRIP'T IN EACH PAW: WHEN ADAM FIRST OF MEN . . . 4 408
WHEN ADAM THUS TO EVE: FAIR CONSORT, TH' HOUR . . 4 610
ADAM FROM HIS FAIR SPOUSE, NOR EVE THE RITES . . . 4 742
WHEN ADAM WAK'T, SO CUSTOMD, FOR HIS SLEEP . . . 5 3
ON ADAM, WHOM IMBRACING, THUS SHE SPAKE. 5 27
RELATED, AND THUS ADAM ANSWERD SAD. 5 94
CONVERSE WITH ADAM, IN WHAT BOWRE OR SHADE . . . 5 230
ADAM DISCERND, AS IN THE DORE HE SAT 5 299
EARTHS INMOST WOMB, MORE WARMTH THEN ADAM NEEDS; . 5 302
BERRIE OR GRAPE: TO WHOM THUS ADAM CALL'D. . . . 5 307
TO WHOM THUS EVE. ADAM, EARTHS HALLOWD MOULD, . . 5 321
NEERER HIS PRESENCE ADAM THOUGH NOT AWD, ... 5 358
ADAM, I THEREFORE CAME, NOR ART THOU SUCH . . . 5 372
IN ADAM, NOT TO LET TH' OCCASION PASS 5 453
O ADAM, ONE ALMIGHTIE IS, FROM WHOM 5 469
THUS ADAM MADE REQUEST, AND RAPHAEL 5 561
ALL THY DOMINION, ADAM, IS NO MORE 5 751
ADAM BY DIRE EXAMPLE TO BEWARE 7 42
IN PARADISE TO ADAM OR HIS RACE, ... 7 45
WITH BLESSEDNESS. WHENCE ADAM SOON REPEAL'D . . . 7 59
THUS ADAM HIS ILLUSTRIOUS GUEST BESOUGHT: 7 109
THIS SAID, HE FORMD THEE, ADAM, THEE O MAN . . . 7 524
ADAM RELATING, THE SOLE AUDITRESS; 8 51
TO WHOM THUS ADAM CLEERD OF DOUBT, REPLI'D. . . . 8 179
AND SAID, THY MANSION WANTS THEE, ADAM, RISE, . . 8 296
OF THY ASSOCIATES, ADAM, AND WILT TASTE 8 401
THUS FARR TO TRY THEE, ADAM, I WAS PLEAS'D, . . . 8 437
TO WHOM THUS HALF ABASH'T ADAM REPLI'D. 8 595
SO SAYING, HE AROSE; WHOM ADAM THUS 8 644
FROM THE THICK SHADE, AND ADAM TO HIS BOWRE. . . 8 653
ADAM, WELL MAY WE LABOUR STILL TO DRESS 9 205
TO WHOM MILD ANSWER ADAM THUS RETURN'D. 9 226
ADAM, MISSTHOUGHT OF HER TO THEE SO DEAR? 9 289
TO WHOM WITH HEALING WORDS ADAM REPLYD. 9 290
SO SPAKE DOMESTICK ADAM IN HIS CARE 9 318
TO WHOM THUS ADAM FERVENTLY REPLI'D. 9 342
ABOUT HIM. BUT TO ADAM IN WHAT SORT 9 816
AND ADAM WEDDED TO ANOTHER EVE, ... 9 828
ADAM SHALL SHARE WITH ME IN BLISS OR WOE: 9 831
FROM NECTAR, DRINK OF GODS. ADAM THE WHILE . . . 9 838

ADAM (CONTINUED)
HAST THOU NOT WONDERD, ADAM, AT MY STAY? 9 856
ON TH' OTHER SIDE, ADAM, SOON AS HE HEARD . . . 9 888
SO ADAM, AND THUS EVE TO HIM REPLI'D. 9 960
ADAM, FROM WHOSE DEARE SIDE I BOAST ME SPRUNG, . 9 965
ON MY EXPERIENCE, ADAM, FREELY TASTE, ... 9 988
ORIGINAL; WHILE ADAM TOOK NO THOUGHT, ... 9 1004
TILL ADAM THUS 'GAN EVE TO DALLIANCE MOVE, . . . 9 1016
TILL ADAM, THOUGH NOT LESS THEN EVE ABASH'T, . . 9 1065
ADAM, ESTRANG'D IN LOOK AND ALTERD STILE, . . . 9 1132
WHAT WORDS HAVE PAST THY LIPS, ADAM SEVERE, . . 9 1144
TO WHOM THEN FIRST INCENST ADAM REPLI'D, . . . 9 1162
APPROACHING, THUS TO ADAM CALL'D ALOUD. 10 102
WHERE ART THOU ADAM, WONT WITH JOY TO MEET . . . 10 103
WHENCE ADAM FAULTRING LONG, THUS ANSWER'D BRIEF. . 10 115
TO WHOM THUS ADAM SORE BESET REPLI'D. 10 124
ON ADAM LAST THUS JUDGEMENT HE PRONOUNC'D. . . . 10 197
THE GROWING MISERIES, WHICH ADAM SAW 10 715
FOR THIS WE MAY THANK ADAM; BUT HIS THANKS . . . 10 736
THUS ADAM TO HIMSELF LAMENTED LOUD 10 845
FORSAKE ME NOT THUS, ADAM, WITNESS HEAV'N . . . 10 914
ACKNOWLEDG'D AND DEPLOR'D, IN ADAM WRAUGHT . . . 10 939
ADAM, BY SAD EXPERIMENT I KNOW 10 967
BUT ADAM WITH SUCH COUNSEL NOTHING SWAY'D, . . . 10 1010
TO ADAM WHAT SHALL COME IN FUTURE DAYES, ... 11 114
THE EARTH, WHEN ADAM AND FIRST MATRON EVE . . . 11 136
ADAM OBSERV'D, AND WITH HIS EYE THE CHASE . . . 11 191
TO FIND WHERE ADAM SHELTERD, TOOK HIS WAY, . . . 11 223
NOT UNPERCEAV'D OF ADAM, WHO TO EVE, ... 11 224
ADAM BOWD LOW, HEE KINGLY FROM HIS STATE . . . 11 249
ADAM, HEAV'NS HIGH BEHEST NO PREFACE NEEDS: . . . 11 251
HE ADDED NOT, FOR ADAM AT THE NEWES 11 263
ADAM BY THIS FROM THE COLD SUDDEN DAMP 11 293
ADAM, THOU KNOW'ST HEAV'N HIS, AND ALL THE EARTH. 11 335
TO WHOM THUS ADAM GRATEFULLY REPLI'D. 11 370
OUR SECOND ADAM IN THE WILDERNESS, ... 11 383
THAT ADAM NOW ENFORC'T TO CLOSE HIS EYES, . . . 11 419
ADAM, NOW OPE THINE EYES, AND FIRST BEHOLD . . . 11 423
MUCH AT THAT SIGHT WAS ADAM IN HIS HEART . . . 11 448
THESE TWO ARE BRETHREN, ADAM, AND TO COME . . . 11 454
DRIE-EY'D BEHOLD? ADAM COULD NOT, BUT WEPT, . . 11 495
I YIELD IT JUST, SAID ADAM, AND SUBMIT. 11 526
OF ADAM, SOON ENCLIN'D TO ADMIT DELIGHT, . . . 11 596
TO WHOM THUS ADAM OF SHORT JOY BEREFT. 11 628
ADAM WAS ALL IN TEARS, AND TO HIS GUIDE 11 674
HOW DIDST THOU GRIEVE THEN, ADAM, TO BEHOLD . . 11 754
WHEREAT THE HEART OF ADAM ERST SO SAD 11 868
IF ADAM AUGHT PERHAPS MIGHT INTERPOSE; 12 4
WHERETO THUS ADAM FATHERLY DISPLEAS'D. 12 63
HERE ADAM INTERPOS'D. O SENT FROM HEAV'N, . . . 12 270
HE CEAS'D, DISCERNING ADAM WITH SUCH JOY . . . 12 372
HE ENDED; AND THUS ADAM LAST REPLY'D. 12 552
DESCENDED, ADAM TO THE BOWRE WHERE EVE 12 607
SO SPAKE OUR MOTHER EVE, AND ADAM HEARD 12 624

ADAMANT
NINEFOLD, AND GATES OF BURNING ADAMANT 2 436
CAME TOWRING, ARMD IN ADAMANT AND GOLD; 6 110
OF TENFOLD ADAMANT, HIS AMPLE SHIELD 6 255
OF THIS ROUND WORLD: WITH PINNS OF ADAMANT . . . 10 318

ADAMANTINE
IN ADAMANTINE CHAINS AND PENAL FIRE, ... 1 48
THREE IRON, THREE OF ADAMANTINE ROCK, ... 2 646
THESE ADAMANTINE GATES; AGAINST ALL FORCE 2 853
HIS ADAMANTINE COAT GIRD WELL, AND EACH 6 542

ADAM'S
AND RAPHAEL NOW TO ADAM'S DOUBT PROPOS'D 8 64

ADAMS
BY WONDROUS BIRTH: BE THOU IN ADAMS ROOM 3 285
THE HEAD OF ALL MANKIND, THOUGH ADAMS SON. . . . 3 286
ADAMS ABODE, THOSE LOFTIE SHADES HIS BOWRE. . . . 3 734
THE ANGEL ENDED, AND IN ADAMS EARE 8 1
THY UTMOST REACH OR ADAMS: ROUND THE TREE . . . 9 591
AND CARNAL FEAR THAT DAY DIMM'D ADAMS EYE, . . . 11 212
MICHAEL FROM ADAMS EYES THE FILME REMOV'D . . . 11 412

ADD
FALSE FUGITIVE, AND TO THY SPEED ADD WINGS, . . . 2 700
BUT WITH NO FRIENDLY VOICE, AND ADD THY NAME . . . 4 36
SATAN, AND COULDST THOU FAITHFUL ADD? O NAME, . . 4 950
TO ADD MORE SWEETNESS, AND THEY THUS BEGAN, . . . 5 152
WITHOUT COPARTNER? SO TO ADD WHAT WANTS 9 821
AND ALL THE RULE, ONE EMPIRE; ONELY ADD 12 581
DEEDS TO THY KNOWLEDGE ANSWERABLE, ADD FAITH, . . 12 582
ADD VERTUE, PATIENCE, TEMPERANCE, ADD LOVE, . . . 12 583

ADDE
THAT TO CORPOREAL SUBSTANCES COULD ADDE 8 109

ADDED
SEVERE IN YOUTHFUL BEAUTIE, ADDED GRACE 4 845
THIR SNAKIE FOULDS, AND ADDED WINGS. FIRST CREPT 7 484
SUFFICIENT PENALTIE, WHY HAST THOU ADDED . . . 10 753
HE ADDED NOT, AND FROM HER TURN'D, BUT EVE . . . 10 909
STRENGTH ADDED FROM ABOVE, NEW HOPE TO SPRING . . 11 138

ADDED (CONTINUED)
HE ADDED NOT, FOR ADAM AT THE NEWES 11 263

ADDER
TO WHOM THE WILIE ADDER, BLITHE AND GLAD. 9 625

ADDITION
BUT WITH ADDITION STRANGE; YET BE NOT SAD. . . . 5 116
TH' ADDITION OF HIS EMPIRE, HOW IT SHEW'D 7 555

ADDRESS
ADDRESS, AND TO BEGIRT TH' ALMIGHTY THRONE . . . 5 868

ADDRESS'D
ADDRESS'D HIS WAY, NOT WITH INDENTED WAVE, . . . 9 496

ADDRESSD
TO MICHAEL THUS HIS HUMBLE WORDS ADDRESSD. . . . 11 295

ADDREST
THEY ENDED PARLE, AND BOTH ADDREST FOR FIGHT . . 6 296
FLOURISHD, SINCE MUTE, TO SOM GREAT CAUSE ADDREST, 9 672
WHICH WITH BLAND WORDS AT WILL SHE THUS ADDREST. . 9 855

ADES
ORCUS AND ADES, AND THE DREADED NAME 2 964

ADHERE
THIR LIGHTER WINGS. TO WHOM THESE MOST ADHERE, . 2 906
FATHER AND MOTHER, AND TO HIS WIFE ADHERE; . . . 8 498

ADHERENTS
AND THY ADHERENTS: HOW HAST THOU DISTURB'D . . . 6 266
AND HIS ADHERENTS, THAT WITH SO MUCH EASE . . . 10 622

ADJOURNE
A DAY ENTIRE, AND NIGHTS DUE COURSE ADJOURNE, . . 12 264

ADJOYND
ADJOYND, FROM EACH THING MET CONCEAVES DELIGHT, . 9 449

ADJUDG'D
MUST HAVE BIN LOST, ADJUDG'D TO DEATH AND HELL . 3 223
WHICH OF THOSE REBELL SPIRITS ADJUDG'D TO HELL . 4 823
AS BATTEL HATH ADJUDG'D, FROM THIS NEW WORLD . . 10 377

ADMIRATION
OF HIS GREAT FATHER. ADMIRATION SEIS'D 3 271
OR OPEN ADMIRATION HIM BEHOLD 3 672
WITH ADMIRATION, AND DEEP MUSE TO HEARE 7 52
REASONING TO ADMIRATION, AND WITH MEE 9 872

ADMIR'D
TH' UNDAUNTED FIEND WHAT THIS MIGHT BE ADMIR'D, . 2 677
ADMIR'D, NOT FEAR'D; GOD AND HIS SON EXCEPT, . . 2 678
TH' INVENTION ALL ADMIR'D, AND EACH, HOW HEE . . 6 498
MUCH HEE THE PLACE ADMIR'D, THE PERSON MORE. . . 9 444
WHERE UNIVERSALLY ADMIR'D; BUT HERE 9 542
THOUGH KEPT FROM MAN, AND WORTHY TO BE ADMIR'D, . 9 746
FOR IN THOSE DAYES MIGHT ONELY SHALL BE ADMIR'D, . 11 689

ADMIRE
AND DIG'D OUT RIBS OF GOLD. LET NONE ADMIRE . . . 1 690
USELESS BESIDES, REASONING I OFT ADMIRE, ... 8 25
RATHER ADMIRE; OR IF THEY LIST TO TRY 8 75

ADMIRING
WERE ALWAYS DOWNWARD BENT, ADMIRING MORE 1 681
ADMIRING ENTER'D, AND THE WORK SOME PRAISE 1 731
BUT AS IN GAZE ADMIRING: OFT HE BOWD 9 524
I ALSO ERR'D IN OVERMUCH ADMIRING 9 1178
LONG HEE ADMIRING STOOD, TILL SIN, HIS FAIRE . . . 10 352

ADMIR'ST
FOR WHAT ADMIR'ST THOU, WHAT TRANSPORTS THEE SO, . 8 567

ADMIT
WOULD NOT ADMIT; THINE AND OF ALL THY SONS 8 637
WOULDST THOU ADMIT FOR HIS CONTEMPT OF THEE . . 10 763
EVE, EASILY MAY FAITH ADMIT, THAT ALL 11 141
OF ADAM, SOON ENCLIN'D TO ADMIT DELIGHT, ... 11 596

ADMITTING
ADMITTING MOTION IN THE HEAV'NS, TO SHEW 8 115

ADMONISH
SHALL THEM ADMONISH, AND BEFORE THEM SET . . . 11 813

ADMONISH'D
I WARN'D THEE, I ADMONISH'D THEE, FORETOLD . . . 9 1171

ADMONISHMENT
IMMORTAL THANKS, AND HIS ADMONISHMENT 7 77

ADMONISHT
ADMONISHT BY HIS EAR, AND STRAIT WAS KNOWN 3 647

ADONIS
WHILE SMOOTH ADONIS FROM HIS NATIVE ROCK 1 450
OR OF REVIV'D ADONIS, OR RENOWND 9 440

ADOPTED
HER DOWR TH' ADOPTED CLUSTERS, TO ADORN 5 218

ADORATION
WITH SOLEMN ADORATION DOWN THEY CAST 3 351
OBSERVING NONE, BUT ADORATION PURE 4 737
AND LOOK FOR ADORATION TO TH' ABUSE 5 800
IN ADORATION AT HIS FEET I FELL 8 315

ADOR'D
THIR ALTARS BY HIS ALTAR, GODS ADOR'D 1 384
BOTH TURND, AND UNDER OP'N SKIE ADOR'D 4 721
ONCE FAWN'D, AND CRING'D, AND SERVILLY ADOR'D . . 4 959
ABDIEL, THEN WHOM NONE WITH MORE ZEALE ADOR'D . . 5 805
A GODDESS AMONG GODS, ADOR'D AND SERV'D 9 547

ADORE
TO ADORE THE CONQUEROUR? WHO NOW BEHOLDS . . . 1 323
AND DEVILS TO ADORE FOR DEITIES: 1 373
HIS ODIOUS OFFRINGS, AND ADORE THE GODS 1 475
ADORE HIM, WHO TO COMPASS ALL THIS DIES, ... 3 342
ADORE THE SON, AND HONOUR HIM AS MEE. 3 343
WHILE THEY ADORE ME ON THE THRONE OF HELL, . . . 4 89
DIRECTED IN DEVOTION, TO ADORE 7 514
TELL ME, HOW MAY I KNOW HIM, HOW ADORE, ... 8 280
ADORE THEE, AUTHOR OF THIS UNIVERSE, ... 8 360
SENT FROM WHOSE SOVRAN GOODNESS I ADORE. 8 647
BY GIFT, AND THY CELESTIAL BEAUTIE ADORE 9 540
OF GLORY, AND FARR OFF HIS STEPS ADORE. 11 333

ADORERS
OF HIS ADORERS: HEE TO BE AVENG'D, ... 9 143

ADORING
LOWLY THEY BOW'D ADORING, AND BEGAN 5 144

ADORN
HER DOWR TH' ADOPTED CLUSTERS, TO ADORN 5 218
MADE SO ADORN FOR THY DELIGHT THE MORE, ... 8 576

ADORN'D
OFT TO THE IMAGE OF A BRUTE, ADORN'D 1 371
AND THIS IMPERIAL SOV'RANTY, ADORN'D 2 446
WITH OPAL TOWRS AND BATTLEMENTS ADORN'D 2 1049
BROUGHT HER IN NAKED BEAUTY MORE ADORN'D, ... 4 713
I SAW THEE FIRST AND WEDDED THEE, ADORN'D . . . 9 1030

ADORND
WITH GLISTERING SPIRES AND PINNACLES ADORND, . . 3 550
TO WHOM THUS EVE WITH PERFET BEAUTY ADORND. . . 4 634
THIS CONTINENT OF SPACIOUS HEAV'N, ADORND . . . 6 474
DISTANT SO HIGH, WITH MOVING FIRES ADORND . . . 7 87
SPANGLING THE HEMISPHERE: THEN FIRST ADORND . . 7 384
SUCH AS I SAW HER IN MY DREAM, ADORND 8 482
TO PALES, OR POMONA THUS ADORND, ... 9 393
HERS IN ALL REAL DIGNITIE: ADORND 10 151
THEE LASTLY NUPTIAL BOWRE, BY MEE ADORND . . . 11 280

ADORNE
OF CHOICEST FLOURS A GARLAND TO ADORNE 9 840

ADORNS
ADORNS HIM, COLOUR'D WITH THE FLORID HUE 7 445

ADRAMELEC
VANQUISH'D ADRAMELEC, AND ASMADAI, ... 6 365

ADRIA
FLED OVER ADRIA TO TH' HESPERIAN FIELDS, ... 1 520

ADRIFT
WITH ALL HIS VERDURE SPOIL'D, AND TREES ADRIFT . 11 832

ADULTERIE
RAPE OR ADULTERIE, WHERE PASSING FAIRE 11 717

ADULTEROUS
BY THEE ADULTEROUS LUST WAS DRIV'N FROM MEN . . 4 753

ADUST
AND VAPOUR AS THE LIBYAN AIR ADUST, ... 12 635

ADUSTED
CONCOCTED AND ADUSTED THEY REDUC'D 6 514

ADVANC'D
WITH DIADEM AND SCEPTER HIGH ADVANC'D 4 90
TEN THOUSAND THOUSAND ENSIGNES HIGH ADVANC'D, . . 5 588
WITH JUBILIE ADVANC'D; AND AS THEY WENT, ... 6 884

ADVANCE
THAT DAR'ST, THOUGH GRIM AND TERRIBLE, ADVANCE . 2 682
RISING OR FALLING STILL ADVANCE HIS PRAISE. . . 5 191
WHEN TO ADVANCE, OR STAND, OR TURN THE SWAY . . 6 234

ADVANCE (CONTINUED)
OR SHEE FROM WEST HER SILENT COURSE ADVANCE . . 8 163
DETERMIN'D TO ADVANCE INTO OUR ROOM 9 148
SEE WITH WHAT HEAT THESE DOGS OF HELL ADVANCE . . 10 616
SAFE TOWARDS CANAAN FROM THE SHOAR ADVANCE . . . 12 215

ADVANCING
ADVANCING, SOW'D THE EARTH WITH ORIENT PEARLE, . 5 2

ADVANC'T
IN ARMS NOT WORSE, IN FORESIGHT MUCH ADVANC'T, . 1 119
TH' IMPERIAL ENSIGN, WHICH FULL HIGH ADVANC'T . . 1 536
ADVANC'T IN VIEW, THEY STAND, A HORRID FRONT . . 1 563
INTO OUR ROOM OF BLISS THUS HIGH ADVANC'T . . . 4 359
FAR WAS ADVANC'T ON WINGED SPEED, AN HOST . . . 5 744
SATAN WITH VAST AND HAUGHTIE STRIDES ADVANC'T, . 6 109
IN CUBIC PHALANX FIRM ADVANC'T ENTIRE, ... 6 399
AND SONS OF MEN, WHOM GOD HATH THUS ADVANC'T, . . 7 626
HOMEWARD RETURNING, HIGH IN FRONT ADVANC'T, . . 12 632

ADVANTAGE
TH' ADVANTAGE, AND DESCENDING TREAD US DOWN . . 1 327
WILL COVET MORE. WITH THIS ADVANTAGE THEN . . . 2 35
YOURS BE TH' ADVANTAGE ALL, MINE THE REVENGE. . . 2 987
AND NO ADVANTAGE GAINE. WHAT IF THE SUN . . . 8 122
HIS WISH AND BEST ADVANTAGE, US ASUNDER, . . . 9 258
THE GODS ARE FIRST, AND THAT ADVANTAGE USE . . . 9 718

ADVANTAGES
SUCH HIGH ADVANTAGES THIR INNOCENCE 6 401
TO THIR OWN VILE ADVANTAGES SHALL TURNE 12 510

ADVANTAGIOUS
SOM ADVANTAGIOUS ACT MAY BE ACHIEV'D 2 363

ADVENT'ROUS
HEROIC ARDOR TO ADVENT'ROUS DEEDS 6 66

ADVENTROUS
INVOKE THY AID TO MY ADVENTROUS SONG, ... 1 13
IN CONFUS'D MARCH FORLORN, TH' ADVENTROUS BANDS . 2 615
BOLD DEED THOU HAST PRESUM'D, ADVENTROUS EVE, . . 9 921
ADVENTROUS WORK, YET TO THY POWER AND MINE . . . 10 255

ADVENTURE
DREADED NOT MORE TH' ADVENTURE THEN HIS VOICE . . 2 474
ON BOLD ADVENTURE TO DISCOVER WIDE 2 571
LITTLE INFERIOUR, BY MY ADVENTURE HARD 10 468

ADVENTURER
EACH HOUR THEIR GREAT ADVENTURER FROM THE SEARCH . 10 440

ADVERSARIE
TRANSPORTS OUR ADVERSARIE, WHOM NO BOUNDS . . . 3 81
OR SHALL THE ADVERSARIE THUS OBTAIN 3 156
THE ADVERSARIE. NOR THINK THOU WITH WIND . . . 6 282
TO A FELL ADVERSARIE, HIS HATE OR SHAME: . . . 10 906
THE ADVERSARIE SERPENT, AND BRING BACK 12 312

ADVERSARY
MEAN WHILE THE ADVERSARY OF GOD AND MAN, ... 2 629
US TO ABOLISH, LEAST THE ADVERSARY 9 947

ADVERSE
HIS UTMOST POWER WITH ADVERSE POWER OPPOS'D . . 1 103
TO US IS ADVERSE. WHO BUT FELT OF LATE 2 77
USEFUL OF HURTFUL, PROSPEROUS OF ADVERSE . . . 2 259
THE ADVERSE LEGIONS, NOR LESS HIDEOUS JOYN'D . . 6 206
ADVERSE, THAT THEY SHALL FEAR WE HAVE DISARMD . . 6 490
ADVERSE TO LIFE: THEN FOUNDED, THEN CONGLOB'D . . 7 239
AS WHEN TWO POLAR WINDS BLOWING ADVERSE . . . 10 289
WITH ADVERSE BLAST UP-TURNS THEM FROM THE SOUTH . 10 701
PROSPEROUS OR ADVERSE: SO SHALT THOU LEAD . . . 11 364

ADVICE
BY MY ADVICE; SINCE FATE INEVITABLE 2 197

ADVIS'D
THIS WAS THAT CAUTION GIV'N THEE; BE ADVIS'D. . . 5 523
THIS TUMULT, AND PERMITTED ALL, ADVIS'D: . . . 6 674

ADVISE
WE NOW DEBATE; WHO CAN ADVISE, MAY SPEAK. . . . 2 42
ALL THOUGHTS OF WARR: YE HAVE WHAT I ADVISE. . . 2 283
FADED SO SOON. ADVISE IF THIS BE WORTH 2 376
AS MAY ADVISE HIM OF HIS HAPPIE STATE, ... 5 234
LET US ADVISE, AND TO THIS HAZARD DRAW 5 729
THY DISOBEDIENCE. WELL THOU DIDST ADVISE, . . . 5 888
YET NOT FOR THY ADVISE OR THREATS I FLY 5 889
TENDING TO WILDE. THOU THEREFORE NOW ADVISE . . 9 212
FOR GOD IS ALSO IN SLEEP, AND DREAMS ADVISE, . . 12 611

ADVISING
ADVISING PEACE: FOR SUCH ANOTHER FIELD 2 292

ADVOCATE
INTERPRET FOR HIM, MEE HIS ADVOCATE 11 33

AEGAEAN
ON LEMNOS TH' AEGAEAN ILE: THUS THEY RELATE, . . 1 746

AEGYPT
THIR KINGS, WHEN AEGYPT WITH ASSYRIA STROVE . . 1 721
BORDERS ON AEGYPT AND THE ARABIAN SHOARE; . . . 3 537
FROM MEDIA POST TO AEGYPT, THERE FAST BOUND. . . 4 171

AEGYPTIAN
BRIGHT TEMPLE, TO AEGYPTIAN THEB'S HE FLIES. . . 5 274

AEQUATOR
CULMINATE FROM TH' AEQUATOR, AS THEY NOW . . . 3 617

AEQUINOCTIAL
HANGS IN THE CLOUDS, BY AEQUINOCTIAL WINDS . . . 2 637

AEREAL
UP HITHER LIKE AEREAL VAPOURS FLEW 3 445
AEREAL MUSIC SEND: NOR KNEW I NOT 5 548
THE MID AEREAL SKIE: OTHERS ON GROUND 7 442
WITH TERROR THROUGH THE DARK AEREAL HALL. . . . 10 667

AERIE
CAN EXECUTE THIR AERIE PURPOSES, ... 1 430
THIR STATE AFFAIRS. SO THICK THE AERIE CROWD . . 1 775
HIS UNCOUTH WAY, OR SPREAD HIS AERIE FLIGHT . . 2 407
PRICK FORTH THE AERIE KNIGHTS, AND COUCH THIR
SPEARS 2 536
THROWS HIS STEEP FLIGHT IN MANY AN AERIE WHEELE, . 3 741
BENT ALL ON SPEED, AND MARKT HIS AERIE GATE; . . 4 568
WAS AERIE LIGHT FROM PURE DIGESTION BRED, . . . 5 4
SHE FORMS IMAGINATIONS, AERIE SHAPES, ... 5 105
MORE AERIE, LAST THE BRIGHT CONSUMMATE FLOURE . . 5 481
THE BIRD OF JOVE, STOOPT FROM HIS AERIE TOUR, . . 11 185

AETNA
OF THUNDRING AETNA, WHOSE COMBUSTIBLE 1 233
A GOD, LEAP'D FONDLY INTO AETNA FLAMES, ... 3 470

AFER
NOTUS AND AFER BLACK WITH THUNDROUS CLOUDS . . . 10 702

AFFABLE
THE AFFABLE ARCH-ANGEL, HAD FOREWARN'D 7 41
GENTLE TO ME AND AFFABLE HATH BEEN 8 648

AFFAIRES
IF YOUR JOYNT POWER PREVAILES, TH' AFFAIRES OF HELL 10 408

AFFAIRS
THIR STATE AFFAIRS. SO THICK THE AERIE CROWD . . 1 775

AFFECT
TOO MEAN PRETENSE, BUT WHAT WE MORE AFFECT, . . 6 421
AS MIGHT AFFECT THE EARTH WITH COLD AND HEAT . . 10 653

AFFECTING
AFFECTING GOD-HEAD, AND SO LOOSING ALL, ... 3 206
AFFECTING ALL EQUALITY WITH GOD, ... 5 763
SUCH TROUBLE BROUGHT, AFFECTING TO SUBDUE . . . 12 81

AFFECTS
AFFECTS ME EQUALLY; NOR CAN I LIKE 5 97

AFFIRM
ALL WHAT WE AFFIRM OR WHAT DENY, AND CALL . . . 5 107
NOT THAT I SO AFFIRM, THOUGH SO IT SEEM 8 117

AFFLICTED
AND REASSEMBLING OUR AFFLICTED POWERS, ... 1 186
BETTER ABODE, AND MY AFFLICTED POWERS 4 939
EXHAUSTED, SPIRITLESS, AFFLICTED, FALL'N. . . . 6 852
WHOM THUS AFFLICTED WHEN SAD EVE BEHELD, . . . 10 863

AFFLICTING
WITH HEAV'NS AFFLICTING THUNDER, AND BESOUGHT . . 2 166

AFFLICTION
THAT WITNESS'D HUGE AFFLICTION AND DISMAY . . . 1 57

AFFLICTS
THIS MOST AFFLICTS ME, THAT DEPARTING HENCE, . . 11 315

AFFORD
WHAT COULD BE LESS THEN TO AFFORD HIM PRAISE, . . 4 46
OUR HEAV'NLY STRANGER; WELL WE MAY AFFORD . . . 5 316
ANOTHER RIB AFFORD, YET LOSS OF THEE 9 912
BE WANTING, BUT AFFORD THEE EQUAL AID, ... 10 271

AFFORDS
THIS DAY AFFORDS, DECLARING THEE RESOLVD, . . . 9 968

AFFRAID
ALL TH' HOST OF HEAV'N; BACK THEY RECOILD AFFRAID 2 759
AFFRAID, BEING NAKED, HID MY SELF. TO WHOM . . 10 117
WHAT MAN CAN DO AGAINST THEM, NOT AFFRAID, . . . 12 493

AFFRIGHTED
AFFRIGHTED; BUT STRICT FATE HAD CAST TOO DEEP . . 6 869

AFFRONT
AND WITH THIR DARKNESS DURST AFFRONT HIS LIGHT. . 1 391
IF SUCH AFFRONT I LABOUR TO AVERT 9 302

AFFRONTS
TEMPTING AFFRONTS US WITH HIS FOUL ESTEEM . . . 9 328

AFLOAT
AFLOAT, WHEN WITH FIERCE WINDS ORION ARM'D . . . 1 305

AFRESH
AFRESH WITH CONSCIOUS TERROURS VEX ME ROUND, . . 2 801

AFRIC
OR WHOM BISERTA SENT FROM AFRIC SHORE 1 585

AFTER
LONG AFTER KNOWN IN PALESTINE, AND NAM'D . . . 1 80
SHOT AFTER US IN STORM, OREBLOWN HATH LAID . . . 1 172
AFTER THE TOYL OF BATTEL TO REPOSE 1 319
THIR SEATS LONG AFTER NEXT THE SEAT OF GOD, . . 1 383
WHOM HE HAD VANQUISHT. AFTER THESE APPEAR'D . . 1 476
FOR WHO CAN YET BELEEVE, THOUGH AFTER LOSS, . . 1 631
FREQUENT AND FULL. AFTER SHORT SILENCE THEN . . 1 797
OF ALL HIS AIM, AFTER SOME DIRE REVENGE. . . . 2 128
NOT PEACE: AND AFTER HIM THUS MAMMON SPAKE. . . 2 228
AFTER THE TEMPEST: SUCH APPLAUSE WAS HEARD . . . 2 290
DREW AFTER HIM THE THIRD PART OF HEAV'NS SONS . . 2 692
BUT HEE ONCE PAST, SOON AFTER WHEN MAN FELL, . . 2 1023
PAV'D AFTER HIM A BROAD AND BEAT'N WAY 2 1026
DRAW AFTER HIM THE WHOLE RACE OF MANKIND, . . . 3 161
LIGHT AFTER LIGHT WELL US'D THEY SHALL ATTAIN, . 3 196
AND AFTER ALL THIR TRIBULATIONS LONG 3 336
LONG AFTER, NOW UNPEOPL'D, AND UNTROD; 3 497
WHO AFTER CAME FROM EARTH, SAYLING ARRIV'D, . . 3 520
SUCH WONDER SEIS'D, THOUGH AFTER HEAVEN SEEN, . . 3 552
THEY SAT THEM DOWN, AND AFTER NO MORE TOIL . . . 4 327
AFTER SOFT SHOWERS; AND SWEET THE COMING ON . . 4 646
GLISTRING WITH DEW, NOR FRAGRANCE AFTER SHOWERS, . 4 653
AFTER HIS CHARGE RECEIVD; BUT FROM AMONG . . . 5 248
TASTE AFTER TASTE UPHELD WITH KINDLIEST CHANGE, . 5 336
LONG AFTER TO BLEST MARIE, SECOND EVE. 5 387
AFTER SHORT PAUSE ASSENTING, THUS BEGAN. . . . 5 562
DREW AFTER HIM THE THIRD PART OF HEAV'NS HOST: . 5 710
INTERPRETED) WHICH NOT LONG AFTER, HE 5 762
BURNT AFTER THEM TO THE BOTTOMLESS PIT. 6 866
KNOW THEN, THAT AFTER LUCIFER FROM HEAV'N . . . 7 131
WAVE ROWLING AFTER WAVE, WHERE WAY THEY FOUND, . 7 298
AND FRUIT TREE YIELDING FRUIT AFTER HER KIND; . . 7 311
AND EVERY BIRD OF WING AFTER HIS KINDE; 7 394
AFTER THIR KINDES; I BRING THEM TO RECEAVE . . . 8 343
AS ONE INTENDED FIRST, NOT AFTER MADE 8 555
THE SUN WAS SUNK, AND AFTER HIM THE STARR . . . 9 48
HIM AFTER LONG DEBATE, IRRESOLUTE 9 87
FOR WHAT GOD AFTER BETTER WORSE WOULD BUILD? . . 9 102
RECOMFORTED, AND AFTER THOUGHTS DISTURBD . . . 9 918
AS MEET IS, AFTER SUCH DELICIOUS FARE; 9 1028
HEE AFTER EVE SEDUC'T, UNMINDED SLUNK 10 332
THAT I MUST AFTER THEE WITH THIS THY SON; . . . 10 363
IN SIGHT OF GOD? HIM AFTER ALL DISPUTES 10 828
THAT AFTER WRETCHED LIFE MUST BE AT LAST . . . 10 985
HIS FINAL REMEDIE, AND AFTER LIFE 11 62
THOUGH AFTER SLEEPLESS NIGHT; FOR SEE THE MORN, . 11 173
AFTER SHORT BLUSH OF MORN; NIGH IN HER SIGHT . . 11 184
FULFIL OR GRAV'N IN METTLE. AFTER THESE, . . . 11 573
AS AFTER THIRST, WHICH MADE THIR FLOWING SHRINK . 11 846
AND AFTER HIM, THE SURER MESSENGER, ... 11 856
TO HARAN, AFTER HIM A CUMBROUS TRAIN 12 131
MORE HARD'ND AFTER THAW, TILL IN HIS RAGE . . . 12 194
NOR AFTER RESURRECTION SHALL HE STAY 12 436

AFTER-BANDS
BIND US WITH AFTER-BANDS, WHAT PROFITS THEN . . . 9 761

AFTERNOONS
NOONTIDE REPAST, OR AFTERNOONS REPOSE. 9 403

AFTER-TIMES
WIDER BY FARR THEN THAT OF AFTER-TIMES 3 529

AGAIN
TH' EVENT IS FEAR'D; SHOULD WE AGAIN PROVOKE . . 2 82
SHOULD INTERMITTED VENGEANCE ARM AGAIN 2 173
THEN CROWN'D AGAIN THIR GOLD'N HARPS THEY TOOK, . 3 365
IF OUR PROPOSALS ONCE AGAIN WERE HEARD 6 618
THAT WISHT THE MOUNTAINS NOW MIGHT BE AGAIN . . 6 842
AGAIN, GOD SAID, LET THER BE FIRMAMENT 7 261
AGAIN TH' ALMIGHTIE SPAKE: LET THERE BE LIGHTS . 7 339
TO LIVE AGAIN IN THESE WILDE WOODS FORLORN? . . 9 910
EARTH TREMBL'D FROM HER ENTRAILS, AS AGAIN . . . 9 1000
LEAST IT AGAIN DISSOLVE AND SHOWR THE EARTH? . . 11 883
THE EARTH AGAIN BY FLOOD, NOR LET THE SEA . . . 11 893

AGAINST
AGAINST THE THRONE AND MONARCHY OF GOD 1 42

AGAINST (CONTINUED)
HIS TEMPLE RIGHT AGAINST THE TEMPLE OF GOD . . . 1 402
HE ALSO AGAINST THE HOUSE OF GOD WAS BOLD: . . . 1 470
AGAINST THE HIGHEST, AND FIERCE WITH GRASPED ARMS 1 667
FORMOST TO STAND AGAINST THE THUNDERERS AIM . . 2 28
AGAINST THE TORTURER; WHEN TO MEET THE NOISE . . 2 64
WITH UPRIGHT WING AGAINST A HIGHER FOE. 2 72
IF WE WERE WISE, AGAINST SO GREAT A FOE 2 202
BANDED AGAINST HIS THRONE, BUT TO REMAINE . . . 2 320
AGAINST A WAKEFUL FOE, WHILE I ABROAD 2 463
CONJUR'D AGAINST THE HIGHEST, FOR WHICH BOTH THOU 2 693
AGAINST THY ONLY SON? WHAT FURY O SON, ... 2 728
AGAINST THY FATHERS HEAD? AND KNOW'ST FOR WHOM; . 2 730
IN BOLD CONSPIRACY AGAINST HEAV'NS KING, ... 2 751
THESE ADAMANTINE GATES; AGAINST ALL FORCE . . . 2 853
MADE HEAD AGAINST HEAV'NS KING, THOUGH OVERTHROWN. 2 992
ON EVEN GROUND AGAINST HIS MORTAL FOE, ... 3 179
AGAINST THE HIGH SUPREMACIE OF HEAV'N, ... 3 205
DIRECT AGAINST WHICH OP'ND FROM BENEATH, ... 3 526
WARRING IN HEAV'N AGAINST HEAV'NS MATCHLESS KING: 4 41
NAY CURS'D BE THOU; SINCE AGAINST HIS THY WILL . 4 71
AGAINST THE EASTERN GATE OF PARADISE 4 542
AGAINST A RUMORD WARR, THE SMUTTIE GRAINE . . . 4 817
SINGLE AGAINST THEE WICKED, AND THENCE WEAK. . . 4 856
WHAT THOU AND THY GAY LEGIONS DARE AGAINST; . . 4 942
WITH ENVIE AGAINST THE SON OF GOD, THAT DAY . . 5 662
AGAINST THEE ARE GON FORTH WITHOUT RECALL; . . . 5 885
AGAINST REVOLTED MULTITUDES THE CAUSE 6 31
AGAINST TH' OMNIPOTENT TO RISE IN ARMS; 6 136
AGAINST HIS WORTHIER, AS THINE NOW SERVE THEE, . 6 180
ARMIE AGAINST ARMIE NUMBERLESS TO RAISE 6 224
AGAINST US FROM ABOUT HIS THRONE, AND JUDG'D . . 6 426
AGAINST UNEQUAL ARMES TO FIGHT IN PAINE, . . . 6 454
AGAINST UNPAIND, IMPASSIVE; FROM WHICH EVIL . . 6 455
AGAINST SUCH HELLISH MISCHIEF FIT TO OPPOSE. . . 6 636
AGAINST GOD AND MESSIAH, OR TO FALL 6 796
YET ENVIED; AGAINST MEE IS ALL THIR RAGE, . . . 6 813
OR I ALONE AGAINST THEM, SINCE BY STRENGTH . . . 6 820
AS A DESPITE DON AGAINST THE MOST HIGH, ... 6 906
AGAINST A SOLEMN DAY, HARNEST AT HAND, ... 7 202
TO LESSEN THEE, AGAINST HIS PURPOSE SERVES . . . 7 614
AGAINST THE CHARM OF BEAUTIES POWERFUL GLANCE. . 8 533
AGAINST TEMPTATION: THOU THY SELF WITH SCORNE . . 9 299
AGAINST HIS WILL HE CAN RECEAVE NO HARME. . . . 9 350
IMPART AGAINST HIS WILL IF ALL BE HIS? 9 728
AGAINST HIS BETTER KNOWLEDGE, NOT DECEAV'D, . . 9 998
AGAINST HIS MAKER; NO DECREE OF MINE 10 43
AGAINST THE DAY OF BATTEL, TO A FIELD, ... 10 275
CONSTANT, MATURE, PROOF AGAINST ALL ASSAULTS, . . 10 882
AGAINST A FOE BY DOOM EXPRESS ASSIGN'D US, . . . 10 926
AGAINST GOD ONELY, I AGAINST GOD AND THEE, . . . 10 931
AGAINST US THIS DECEIT: TO CRUSH HIS HEAD . . . 10 1035
AGAINST OUR SELVES, AND WILFUL BARRENNESS, . . . 10 1042
RELUCTANCE AGAINST GOD AND HIS JUST YOKE . . . 10 1045
AGAINST THE SYRIAN KING, WHO TO SURPRIZE . . . 11 218
BUT PRAYER AGAINST HIS ABSOLUTE DECREE 11 311
NO MORE AVAILES THEN BREATH AGAINST THE WINDE, . 11 312
AND TESTIFI'D AGAINST THIR WAYES; HEE OFT . . . 11 721
AGAINST INVADERS; THEREFORE COOLD IN ZEALE . . . 11 801
IN A DARK AGE, AGAINST EXAMPLE GOOD, ... 11 809
AGAINST ALLUREMENT, CUSTOM, AND A WORLD 11 810
SIN AGAINST LAW TO FIGHT; THAT WHEN THEY SEE . . 12 289
THE LAW THAT IS AGAINST THEE, AND THE SINS . . . 12 416
WHAT MAN CAN DO AGAINST THEM, NOT AFFRAID, . . . 12 493
THOUGH TO THE DEATH, AGAINST SUCH CRUELTIES . . 12 494
WHO AGAINST FAITH AND CONSCIENCE CAN BE HEARD . . 12 529

AGAPE
DAZLES THE CROUD, AND SETS THEM ALL AGAPE. . . . 5 357

AGAST
WITH SHUDDRING HORROR PALE, AND EYES AGAST . . . 2 616

AGE
WHAT IN AN AGE THEY WITH INCESSANT TOYLE 1 698
THAT NAME, UNLESS AN AGE TOO LATE, OR COLD . . . 9 44
THIS IS OLD AGE; BUT THEN THOU MUST OUTLIVE . . 11 538
OF MIDDLE AGE ONE RISING, EMINENT 11 665
IN A DARK AGE, AGAINST EXAMPLE GOOD, ... 11 809
AND ALL THE PROPHETS IN THIR AGE THE TIMES . . . 12 243

AGEN
A DOVE SENT FORTH ONCE AND AGEN TO SPIE 11 857

AGENTS
OF HIGHEST AGENTS, DEEMD HOWEVER WISE. 9 683

AGES
AGES OF HOPELESS END; THIS WOULD BE WORSE. . . . 2 186
OF ALL PAST AGES TO THE GENERAL DOOM 3 328
HIS GOOD TO WORLDS AND AGES INFINITE. 7 191
NEW HEAV'N AND EARTH SHALL TO THE AGES RISE, . . 10 647
WHO OF ALL AGES TO SUCCEED, BUT FEELING 10 733
OR MONUMENT TO AGES, AND THEREON 11 326
THE BURD'N OF MANY AGES, ON ME LIGHT 11 767
NEW HEAV'NS, NEW EARTH, AGES OF ENDLESS DATE . . 12 549

AGGRAVATE
THE FIEND BY EASIE ASCENT, OR AGGRAVATE 3 524
HIS WILL WHO REIGNS ABOVE, TO AGGRAVATE 10 549

AGGREGATED
CATHAIAN COAST. THE AGGREGATED SOYLE 10 293

AGITATION
KINDL'D THROUGH AGITATION TO A FLAME, 9 637

AGONIE
HERE IN PERPETUAL AGONIE AND PAIN, 2 861
THY PRESENCE, AGONIE OF LOVE TILL NOW 9 858
OF HEART-SICK AGONIE, ALL FEAVOROUS KINDS, 11 482

AGRA
TO AGRA AND LAHOR OF GREAT MOGUL 11 391

AH
AH WHEREFORE. HE DESERVD NO SUCH RETURN 4 42
AH GENTLE PAIR, YEE LITTLE THINK HOW NIGH 4 366
ME NOW YOUR CURSE. AH, WHY SHOULD ALL MANKIND 10 822

AHAZ
AHAZ HIS SOTTISH CONQUEROUR, WHOM HE DREW 1 472

AIALON
AND THOU MOON IN THE VALE OF AIALON, 12 266

AID
INVOKE THY AID TO MY ADVENTROUS SONG, 1 13
OF REBEL ANGELS, BY WHOSE AID ASPIRING 1 38
SUBLIM'D WITH MINERAL FURY, AID THE WINDS, 1 235
AND JOIN HIM NAM'D ALMIGHTY TO THY AID, 6 294
ALL LIKE HIMSELF REBELLIOUS, BY WHOSE AID 7 140
PERFET WITHIN, NO OUTWARD AID REQUIRE; 8 642
AID US, THE WORK UNDER OUR LABOUR GROWS, 9 208
ANGELS, NOR THINK SUPERFLUOUS OTHERS AID. 9 308
BE WANTING, BUT AFFORD THEE EQUAL AID, 10 271
WHEREON I LIVE, THY GENTLE LOOKS, THY AID, 10 919
OF HIM SO LATELY PROMIS'D TO THY AID 12 542

AIDE
HAPPIE FOR MAN, SO COMING; HE HER AIDE 3 232
(SO CALL THAT OPPOSITE FAIR STARR) HER AIDE 3 727
THY FIERCEST, WHEN IN BATTEL TO THY AIDE 4 927
HIS PUISSANCE, TRUSTING IN TH' ALMIGHTIE'S AIDE, 6 119
FORTHWITH ON ALL SIDES TO HIS AIDE WAS RUN 6 335
BY NATURE AS IN AIDE, AND CLOS'D MINE EYES. 8 459
TO OTHER SPEEDIE AIDE MIGHT LEND AT NEED; 9 260
HIS COUNSEL WHOM SHE HAD DISPLEAS'D, HIS AIDE; 10 944
BUT CALL IN AIDE, WHICH MAKES A BLOODY FRAY; 11 651
IN SHARP CONTEST OF BATTEL FOUND NO AIDE 11 800

AIDED
REMAINS THEE, AIDED BY THIS HOST OF FRIENDS, 6 38

AIERIE
THIR AIERIE CARAVAN HIGH OVER SEA'S 7 428

AIM
IF HE OPPOS'D; AND WITH AMBITIOUS AIM 1 41
HIS INMOST COUNSELS FROM THIR DESTIND AIM. 1 168
FORMOST TO STAND AGAINST THE THUNDERERS AIM 2 28
OF ALL HIS AIM, AFTER SOME DIRE REVENGE. 2 128

AIM'D
UPLIFTED IMMINENT ONE STROKE THEY AIM'D 6 317
LET IT; I RECK NOT, SO IT LIGHT WELL AIM'D, 9 173

AIME
LEVEL'D HIS DEADLY AIME; THIR FATALL HANDS 2 712

AIMES
VAINE HOPES, VAINE AIMES, INORDINATE DESIRES 4 808

AIM'ST
TO WHOM TH' ARCHANGEL. DEXTROUSLY THOU AIM'ST; 11 884

AIR
ALOFT, INCUMBENT ON THE DUSKY AIR 1 226
OF COLD OLYMPUS RUL'D THE MIDDLE AIR 1 516
TEN THOUSAND BANNERS RISE INTO THE AIR 1 545
LOOKS THROUGH THE HORIZONTAL MISTY AIR 1 595
THICK SWARM'D, BOTH ON THE GROUND AND IN THE AIR, 1 767
OR SUMMERS NOON-TIDE AIR, WHILE THUS HE SPAKE. 2 309
PURGE OFF THIS GLOOM; THE SOFT DELICIOUS AIR, 2 400
PART ON THE PLAIN, OR IN THE AIR SUBLIME 2 528
REND UP BOTH ROCKS AND HILLS, AND RIDE THE AIR 2 540
WHERE ARMIES WHOLE HAVE SUNK: THE PARCHING AIR 2 594
IN SECRET, RIDING THROUGH THE AIR SHE COMES 2 663
TO JOYN THIR DARK ENCOUNTER IN MID AIR; 2 718
WING SILENTLY THE BUXOM AIR, IMBALM'D 2 842
OF NEITHER SEA, NOR SHORE, NOR AIR, NOR FIRE, 2 912
OR IN THE EMPTIER WASTE, RESEMBLING AIR, 2 1045
IN THE DUN AIR SUBLIME, AND READY NOW 3 72
UNCERTAIN WHICH, IN OCEAN OR IN AIR. 3 76
I THROUGH THE AMPLE AIR IN TRIUMPH HIGH 3 254

AIR (CONTINUED)
OF GLIMMERING AIR LESS VEXT WITH TEMPEST LOUD: 3 429
INTO THE DEVIOUS AIR; THEN MIGHT YE SEE 3 489
THROUGH THE PURE MARBLE AIR HIS OBLIQUE WAY 3 564
IMPRESS THE AIR, AND SHEWS THE MARINER 4 558
CELESTIAL VOICES TO THE MIDNIGHT AIR, 4 682
THE GOD THAT MADE BOTH SKIE, AIR, EARTH AND HEAV'N 4 722
BUT SOMTIMES IN THE AIR, AS WEE, SOMTIMES 5 79
WINNOWS THE BUXOM AIR; TILL WITHIN SOARE 5 270
EARTH AND THE SEA FEED AIR, THE AIR THOSE FIRES 5 417
THIR MARCH WAS, AND THE PASSIVE AIR UPBORE 6 72
TORMENTED ALL THE AIR; ALL AIR SEEMD THEN 6 244
EMBOWELD WITH OUTRAGIOUS NOISE THE AIR, 6 587
MAIN PROMONTORIES FLUNG, WHICH IN THE AIR 6 654
SO HILLS AMID THE AIR ENCOUNTERD HILLS 6 664
DISPARTED, AND BETWEEN SPUN OUT THE AIR, 7 241
TRANSPARENT, ELEMENTAL AIR, DIFFUS'D 7 265
THEY SUMM'D THIR PENNS, AND SOARING TH' AIR SUBLIME 7 421
OVER HIS WORKS, ON EARTH, IN SEA, OR AIR, 7 629
AND BEARES THEE SOFT WITH THE SMOOTH AIR ALONG, 8 166
EASIER THEN AIR WITH AIR, IF SPIRITS EMBRACE, 8 626
ORGANIC, OR IMPULSE OF VOCAL AIR, 9 530
HIS NOSTRIL WIDE INTO THE MURKIE AIR, 10 280
WHOLSOM AND COOL, AND MILD, BUT WITH BLACK AIR 10 847
THE AIR ATTRITE TO FIRE, AS LATE THE CLOUDS 10 1073
WATERING THE GROUND, AND WITH OUR SIGHS THE AIR 10 1090
WATERING THE GROUND, AND WITH THIR SIGHS THE AIR 10 1102
OF FLIGHT PURSU'D IN TH' AIR AND ORE THE GROUND 11 202
AND VAPOUR AS THE LIBYAN AIR ADUST, 12 635

AIRE
SHADOW FROM BODY OPAQUE CAN FALL, AND THE AIRE, 3 619
THE CUMBROUS ELEMENTS, EARTH, FLOOD, AIRE, FIRE, 3 715
THAT LANTSKIP; AND OF PURE NOW PURER AIRE 4 153
EARTH, AIRE, AND SEA. THEN LET US NOT THINK HARD 4 432
WITH SUDDEN BLAZE DIFFUS'D, INFLAMES THE AIRE: 4 818
TO SETTLE HERE ON EARTH, OR IN MID AIRE; 4 940
THE PENDULOUS ROUND EARTH WITH BALLANC'T AIRE 4 1000
AIRE, AND YE ELEMENTS THE ELDEST BIRTH 5 180
STREAME IN THE AIRE, AND FOR DISTINCTION SERVE 5 590
NOW WAV'D THIR FIERIE SWORDS, AND IN THE AIRE 6 304
RECEIVE, NO MORE THEN CAN THE FLUID AIRE: 6 349
CAME FLYING, AND IN MID AIRE ALOUD THUS CRI'D. 6 536
AN EARTHLIE GUEST, AND DRAWN EMPYREAL AIRE, 7 14
ALL SPACE, THE AMBIENT AIRE WIDE INTERFUS'D 7 89
HER ANNUAL VOIAGE, BORN ON WINDES; THE AIRE 7 431
WITH FISH REPLENISHT, AND THE AIRE WITH FOWLE, 7 447
CONSUMMATE LOVLY SMIL'D; AIRE, WATER, EARTH, 7 502
OVER THE FISH AND FOWLE OF SEA AND AIRE, 7 521
OVER FISH OF THE SEA, AND FOWLE OF THE AIRE, 7 533
ANGELIC HARMONIES: THE EARTH, THE AIRE 7 560
SENT FROM HER THROUGH THE WIDE TRANSPICUOUS AIRE, 8 141
FROM WHERE I FIRST DREW AIRE, AND FIRST BEHELD 8 284
AND OVER FIELDS AND WATERS, AS IN AIRE 8 301
OR LIVE IN SEA, OR AIRE, BEAST, FISH, AND FOWLE. 8 341
THIR ELEMENT TO DRAW THE THINNER AIRE. 8 348
WITH VARIOUS LIVING CREATURES, AND THE AIRE 8 370
AND INTO ALL THINGS FROM HER AIRE INSPIR'D 8 476
WHERE HOUSES THICK AND SEWERS ANNOY THE AIRE, 9 446
HER GRACEFUL INNOCENCE, HER EVERY AIRE 9 459
YET LORDS DECLAR'D OF ALL IN EARTH OR AIRE? 9 658
PRINCE OF THE AIRE; THEN RISING FROM HIS GRAVE 10 185
CAPTIVITY LED CAPTIVE THROUGH THE AIRE, 10 188
BEFORE HIM NAKED TO THE AIRE, THAT NOW 10 212
DOMINION EXERCISE AND IN THE AIRE, 10 400
SEA, AIRE, AND SHOAR, THE THUNDER WHEN TO ROWLE 10 666
AS A DISTEMPER, GROSS TO AIRE AS GROSS, 11 53
ON BIRD, BEAST, AIRE, AIRE SUDDENLY ECLIPS'D 11 183
AND WILDE, HOW SHALL WE BREATH IN OTHER AIRE 11 284
LAND, SEA, AND AIRE, AND EVERY KINDE THAT LIVES, 11 337
TO WHAT THOU HAST, AND FOR THE AIRE OF YOUTH 11 542
HIMSELF AND HIS RASH ARMIE, WHERE THIN AIRE 12 76
WITH VICTORY, TRIUMPHING THROUGH THE AIRE 12 452
THE SERPENT, PRINCE OF AIRE, AND DRAG IN CHAINES 12 454
OR WORKS OF GOD IN HEAV'N, AIRE, EARTH, OR SEA, 12 579

AIRES
THE BIRDS THIR QUIRE APPLY; AIRES, VERNAL AIRES, 4 264
JOYOUS THE BIRDS; FRESH GALES AND GENTLE AIRES 8 515
THE SEASON, PRIME FOR SWEETEST SENTS AND AIRES: 9 200
FROM NOON, AND GENTLE AIRES DUE AT THIR HOUR 10 93

AIRIE
OF AIRIE THREATS TO AW WHOM YET WITH DEEDS 6 283
TO JOURNIE THROUGH THE AIRIE GLOOM BEGAN, 7 246

ALABLASTER
OF ALABLASTER, PIL'D UP TO THE CLOUDS, 4 544

ALACRITIE
WITH FRESH ALACRITIE AND FORCE RENEW'D 2 1012

ALADULE
THE REALM OF ALADULE, IN HIS RETREATE 10 435

ALAS
THE PUNISHMENT ALL ON THY SELF; ALAS, 10 949
ALAS, BOTH FOR THE DEED AND FOR THE CAUSE. 11 461

ALCAIRO
NOR GREAT ALCAIRO SUCH MAGNIFICENCE 1 718

ALCHIMIST
OF SOOTY COAL THE EMPIRIC ALCHIMIST 5 440

ALCHYMIE
PUT TO THIR MOUTHS THE SOUNDING ALCHYMIE 2 517

ALCIDES
AS WHEN ALCIDES FROM OECHALIA CROWN'D 2 542

ALCINOUS
ALCINOUS REIGN'D, FRUIT OF ALL KINDES, IN COATE, . 5 341
ALCINOUS, HOST OF OLD LAERTES SON, ... 9 441

ALEIAN
DISMOUNTED, ON TH' ALEIAN FIELD I FALL 7 19

ALGIERS
MAROCCO AND ALGIERS, AND TREMISEN; 11 404

ALIEN
ALIEN FROM HEAV'N, WITH PASSIONS FOUL OBSCUR'D: . 4 571

ALIENATE
O ALIENATE FROM GOD, O SPIRIT ACCURST, ... 5 877

ALIENATED
OF ALIENATED JUDAH. NEXT CAME ONE 1 457
NOW ALIENATED, DISTANCE AND DISTASTE, ... 9 9
RETIRING, BY HIS OWN DOOM ALIENATED, ... 10 378

ALIGHTED
SATAN ALIGHTED WALKS: A GLOBE FARR OFF 3 422

ALIGHTS
DOWN HE ALIGHTS AMONG THE SPORTFUL HERD 4 396

ALIKE
WARR THEREFORE, OPEN OR CONCEAL'D, ALIKE 2 187
OF HAZARD AS OF HONOUR, DUE ALIKE 2 453
NOT ALL PARTS LIKE, BUT ALL ALIKE INFORMD 3 593
TO ME ALIKE, IT DEALS ETERNAL WOE. 4 70
ALL SEASONS AND THIR CHANGE, ALL PLEASE ALIKE. . 4 640
NO INGRATEFUL FOOD: AND FOOD ALIKE THOSE PURE . . 5 407
SHOULD WIN IN ARMS, IN BOTH DISPUTES ALIKE . . . 6 123
DISTINCT ALIKE WITH MULTITUDE OF EYES, ... 6 847
TEDIOUS ALIKE: OF FELLOWSHIP I SPEAK 8 389
ALIKE, TO SERPENTS ALL AS ACCESSORIES 10 520
ALIKE IS HELL, OR PARADISE, OR HEAVEN, ... 10 598
AND WHAT THOU FEARST, ALIKE DESTROYES ALL HOPE . 10 838
GOD IS AS HERE, AND WILL BE FOUND ALIKE 11 350
THE SPIRIT OF GOD, PROMISD ALIKE AND GIV'N . . . 12 519

ALIMENTAL
FROM ALL HIS ALIMENTAL RECOMPENCE 5 424

ALIVE
THE ONE JUST MAN ALIVE; BY HIS COMMAND 11 818

ALL
BROUGHT DEATH INTO THE WORLD, AND ALL OUR WOE, . 1 3
BEFORE ALL TEMPLES TH' UPRIGHT HEART AND PURE, . 1 18
HAD CAST HIM OUT FROM HEAV'N, WITH ALL HIS HOST . 1 37
A DUNGEON HORRIBLE, ON ALL SIDES ROUND 1 61
THAT COMES TO ALL; BUT TORTURE WITHOUT END . . . 1 67
ALL IS NOT LOST; THE UNCONQUERABLE WILL, ... 1 106
HATH LOST US HEAV'N, AND ALL THIS MIGHTY HOST . . 1 136
THOUGH ALL OUR GLORY EXTINCT, AND HAPPY STATE . . 1 141
LEVIATHAN, WHICH GOD OF ALL HIS WORKS 1 201
HOW ALL HIS MALICE SERV'D BUT TO BRING FORTH . . 1 217
AND LEAVE A SINGED BOTTOM ALL INVOLV'D 1 236
AND WHAT I SHOULD BE, ALL BUT LESS THEN HE . . . 1 257
OF BATTEL WHEN IT RAG'D, IN ALL ASSAULTS 1 277
HE CALL'D SO LOUD, THAT ALL THE HOLLOW DEEP . . . 1 314
LIKE NIGHT, AND DARKEN'D ALL THE LAND OF NILE: . 1 343
ON THE FIRM BRIMSTONE, AND FILL ALL THE PLAIN; . 1 350
IN AMOROUS DITTYES ALL A SUMMERS DAY, ... 1 449
BOTH HER FIRST BORN AND ALL HER BLEATING GODS. . 1 489
OR IN DODONA, AND THROUGH ALL THE BOUNDS 1 518
ALL THESE AND MORE CAME FLOCKING; BUT WITH LOOKS . 1 522
SERAPHIC ARMS AND TROPHIES: ALL THE WHILE 1 539
ALL IN A MOMENT THROUGH THE GLOOM WERE SEEN . . . 1 544
WARR'D ON BY CRANES: THOUGH ALL THE GIANT BROOD . 1 576
AND ALL WHO SINCE, BAPTIZ'D OR INFIDEL 1 582
WHEN CHARLEMAIN WITH ALL HIS PEERAGE FELL 1 586
ALL HER ORIGINAL BRIGHTNESS, NOR APPEAR'D 1 592
ABOVE THEM ALL TH' ARCH ANGEL: BUT HIS FACE . . . 1 600
WITH ALL HIS PEERS: ATTENTION HELD THEM MUTE. . . 1 618
THAT ALL THESE PUISSANT LEGIONS, WHOSE EXILE . . 1 632
FOR MEE BE WITNESS ALL THE HOST OF HEAV'N, . . . 1 635
EQUAL'D IN ALL THIR GLORIES, TO INSHRINE 1 719
BY ALL HIS ENGINS, BUT WAS HEADLONG SENT 1 750
ATTENDED: ALL ACCESS WAS THRONG'D, THE GATES . . 1 761
CAR'D NOT TO BE AT ALL; WITH THAT CARE LOST . . . 2 48
WENT ALL HIS FEAR; OF GOD, OR HELL, OR WORSE . . 2 49
ARM'D WITH HELL FLAMES AND FURY ALL AT ONCE . . . 2 61

ALL (CONTINUED)
BUT ALL WAS FALSE AND HOLLOW; THOUGH HIS TONGUE . 2 112
OF ALL HIS AIM, AFTER SOME DIRE REVENGE. 2 128
WITH ARMED WATCH, THAT RENDER ALL ACCESS 2 130
BY FORCE, AND AT OUR HEELS ALL HELL SHOULD RISE . 2 135
ALL INCORRUPTIBLE WOULD ON HIS THRONE 2 138
TH' ALMIGHTY VICTOR TO SPEND ALL HIS RAGE, . . . 2 144
HIS RED RIGHT HAND TO PLAGUE US? WHAT IF ALL . . 2 174
VIEWS ALL THINGS AT ONE VIEW? HE FROM HEAV'NS HIGHTH 2 190
ALL THESE OUR MOTIONS VAIN, SEES AND DERIDES; . . 2 191
THEN WISE TO FRUSTRATE ALL OUR PLOTS AND WILES. . 2 193
AND PUBLISH GRACE TO ALL, ON PROMISE MADE 2 238
THE SENSIBLE OF PAIN. ALL THINGS INVITE 2 278
ALL THOUGHTS OF WARR: YE HAVE WHAT I ADVISE. . . 2 283
THE SOUND OF BLUSTRING WINDS, WHICH ALL NIGHT LONG 2 286
THITHER LET US BEND ALL OUR THOUGHTS, TO LEARN . 2 354
ALL AS OUR OWN, AND DRIVE AS WE WERE DRIVEN, . . 2 366
BUT FROM THE AUTHOR OF ALL ILL COULD SPRING . . . 2 381
TO MINGLE AND INVOLVE, DONE ALL TO SPITE 2 384
SPARKL'D IN ALL THIR EYES; WITH FULL ASSENT . . . 2 388
ALL CIRCUMSPECTION, AND WE NOW NO LESS 2 414
THE WEIGHT OF ALL AND OUR LAST HOPE RELIES. . . . 2 416
THE PERILOUS ATTEMPT: BUT ALL SAT MUTE, ... 2 420
BARR'D OVER US PROHIBIT ALL EGRESS. 2 437
THROUGH ALL THE COASTS OF DARK DESTRUCTION SEEK . 2 464
DELIVERANCE FOR US ALL: THIS ENTERPRIZE 2 465
THE MONARCH, AND PREVENTED ALL REPLY, ... 2 467
THIR RISING ALL AT ONCE WAS AS THE SOUND 2 476
LOOSE ALL HER VIRTUE; LEAST BAD MEN SHOULD BOAST . 2 483
HEARD FARR AND WIDE, AND ALL THE HOST OF HELL . . 2 519
VAIN WISDOM ALL, AND FALSE PHILOSOPHIE: 2 565
OF ANCIENT PILE; ALL ELSE DEEP SNOW AND ICE, . . 2 591
AT CERTAIN REVOLUTIONS ALL THE DAMN'D 2 597
IN SWEET FORGETFULNESS ALL PAIN AND WOE, ... 2 608
ALL IN ONE MOMENT, AND SO NEER THE BRINK; 2 609
ALL TASTE OF LIVING WIGHT, AS ONCE IT FLED . . . 2 613
WHERE ALL LIFE DIES, DEATH LIVES, AND NATURE BREEDS, ... 2 624
PERVERSE, ALL MONSTROUS, ALL PRODIGIOUS THINGS, . 2 625
HAD BEEN ACHIEV'D, WHEREOF ALL HELL HAD RUNG, . . 2 723
OF ALL THE SERAPHIM WITH THEE COMBIN'D 2 750
ALL ON A SUDDEN MISERABLE PAIN 2 752
ALL TH' HOST OF HEAV'N; BACK THEY RECOILD AFFRAID 2 759
THROUGH ALL THE EMPYREAN: DOWN THEY FELL 2 771
DISTORTED, ALL MY NETHER SHAPE THUS GREW 2 784
FROM ALL HER CAVES, AND BACK RESOUNDED DEATH. . . 2 789
MEE OVERTOOK HIS MOTHER ALL DISMAID, ... 2 792
BOTH HIM AND THEE, AND ALL THE HEAV'NLY HOST . . 2 824
THIS UNCOUTH ERRAND SOLE, AND ONE FOR ALL 2 827
IMMEASURABLY, ALL THINGS SHALL BE YOUR PREY. . . 2 844
THESE ADAMANTINE GATES; AGAINST ALL FORCE 2 853
SAD INSTRUMENT OF ALL OUR WOE, SHE TOOK; 2 872
WHICH BUT HER SELF NOT ALL THE STYGIAN POWERS . . 2 875
CHANCE GOVERNS ALL. INTO THIS WILDE ABYSS, . . . 2 910
BUT ALL THESE IN THIR PREGNANT CAUSES MIXT . . . 2 913
WITH ALL HER BATTERING ENGINES BENT TO RASE . . . 2 923
A VAST VACUITIE: ALL UNAWARES 2 932
OF STUNNING SOUNDS AND VOICES ALL CONFUS'D . . . 2 952
AND TUMULT AND CONFUSION ALL IMBROILD, ... 2 966
ALL USURPATION THENCE EXPELL'D, REDUCE 2 983
YOURS BE TH' ADVANTAGE ALL, MINE THE REVENGE. . . 2 987
KEEP RESIDENCE; IF ALL I CAN WILL SERVE, ... 2 999
OF FIGHTING ELEMENTS, ON ALL SIDES ROUND 2 1015
SHINE INWARD, AND THE MIND THROUGH ALL HER POWERS 3 52
IRRADIATE, THERE PLANT EYES, ALL MIST FROM THENCE 3 53
HIGH THRON'D ABOVE ALL HIGHTH, BENT DOWN HIS EYE, 3 58
ABOUT HIM ALL THE SANCTITIES OF HEAVEN 3 60
PRESCRIB'D, NO BARRS OF HELL, NOR ALL THE CHAINS . 3 82
THROUGH ALL RESTRAINT BROKE LOOSE HE WINGS HIS WAY 3 87
ALL HE COULD HAVE; I MADE HIM JUST AND RIGHT, . . 3 98
SUCH I CREATED ALL TH' ETHEREAL POWERS 3 100
THEY TRESPASS, AUTHORS TO THEMSELVES IN ALL . . . 3 122
ALL HEAV'N, AND IN THE BLESSED SPIRITS ELECT . . 3 136
MOST GLORIOUS, IN HIM ALL HIS FATHER SHON 3 139
OF ALL THINGS MADE, AND JUDGEST ONELY RIGHT. . . 3 155
ALL HAST THOU SPOK'N AS MY THOUGHTS ARE, ALL . . 3 171
ALL HIS DELIV'RANCE, AND TO NONE BUT ME. 3 182
BUT YET ALL IS NOT DON; MAN DISOBEYING, ... 3 203
AFFECTING GOD-HEAD, AND SO LOOSING ALL, ... 3 206
DWELS IN ALL HEAVEN CHARITIE SO DEARE? 3 216
HE ASK'D, BUT ALL THE HEAV'NLY QUIRE STOOD MUTE, . 3 217
AND NOW WITHOUT REDEMPTION ALL MANKIND 3 222
TO VISIT ALL THY CREATURES, AND TO ALL 3 230
WELL PLEAS'D, ON ME LET DEATH WRECK ALL HIS RAGE; 3 241
ALL THAT OF ME CAN DIE, YET THAT DEBT PAID, . . . 3 246
WHILE BY THEE RAIS'D I RUIN ALL MY FOES, ... 3 258
ALL HEAV'N, WHAT THIS MIGHT MEAN, AND WHITHER TEND 3 272
TO ME ARE ALL MY WORKS, NOR MAN THE LEAST 3 277
THE HEAD OF ALL MANKIND, THOUGH ADAMS SON. . . . 3 286
AS IN HIM PERISH ALL MEN, SO IN THEE 3 287
HIS CRIME MAKES GUILTIE ALL HIS SONS, THY MERIT . 3 290
GOD-LIKE FRUITION, QUITTED ALL TO SAVE 3 307
ANOINTED UNIVERSAL KING; ALL POWER 3 317
ALL KNEES TO THEE SHALL BOW, OF THEM THAT BIDE . 3 321
THY DREAD TRIBUNAL: FORTHWITH FROM ALL WINDES . . 3 326
OF ALL PAST AGES TO THE GENERAL DOOM 3 328
THEN ALL THY SAINTS ASSEMBL'D, THOU SHALT JUDGE . 3 330

ALL (CONTINUED)

AND AFTER ALL THIR TRIBULATIONS LONG	3	336
GOD SHALL BE ALL IN ALL. BUT ALL YE GODS,	3	341
ADORE HIM, WHO TO COMPASS ALL THIS DIES,	3	342
NO SOONER HAD TH' ALMIGHTY CEAS'T, BUT ALL	3	344
ETERNAL KING; THEE AUTHOR OF ALL BEING,	3	374
THEE NEXT THEY SANG OF ALL CREATION FIRST,	3	383
HEE HEAV'N OF HEAVENS AND ALL THE POWERS THEREIN	3	390
OF ALL THINGS TRANSITORIE AND VAIN, WHEN SIN	3	446
BOTH ALL THINGS VAIN, AND ALL WHO IN VAIN THINGS	3	448
ALL WHO HAVE THIR REWARD ON EARTH, THE FRUITS	3	451
ALL TH' UNACCOMPLISHT WORKS OF NATURES HAND,	3	455
WHITE, BLACK AND GREY, WITH ALL THIR TRUMPERIE.	3	475
THE SPORT OF WINDS: ALL THESE UPWHIRLD ALOFT	3	493
ALL THIS DARK GLOBE THE FIEND FOUND AS HE PASS'D,	3	498
OF ALL THIS WORLD AT ONCE. AS WHEN A SCOUT	3	543
ALL NIGHT; AT LAST BY BREAK OF CHEARFUL DAWNE	3	545
AT SIGHT OF ALL THIS WORLD BEHELD SO FAIRE.	3	554
HE STAYD NOT TO ENQUIRE: ABOVE THEM ALL	3	571
NOT ALL PARTS LIKE, BUT ALL ALIKE INFORMD	3	593
BUT ALL SUN-SHINE, AS WHEN HIS BEAMS AT NOON	3	616
THAT RUN THROUGH ALL THE HEAV'NS, OR DOWN TO TH' EARTH	3	651
WHERE ALL HIS SONS THY EMBASSIE ATTEND;	3	658
ALL THESE HIS WONDROUS WORKS, BUT CHIEFLY MAN,	3	663
ALL THESE HIS WORKS SO WONDROUS HE ORDAIND,	3	665
IN WHICH OF ALL THESE SHINING ORBES HATH MAN	3	668
BUT ALL THESE SHINING ORBES HIS CHOICE TO DWELL;	3	670
WORLDS, AND ON WHOM HATH ALL THESE GRACES POWRD;	3	674
THAT BOTH IN HIM AND ALL THINGS, AS IS MEET,	3	675
TO SERVE HIM BETTER: WISE ARE ALL HIS WAYES.	3	680
THE SHARPEST SIGHTED SPIRIT OF ALL IN HEAV'N;	3	691
FOR WONDERFUL INDEED ARE ALL HIS WORKS,	3	702
PLEASANT TO KNOW, AND WORTHIEST TO BE ALL	3	703
OF THIS NEW WORLD; AT WHOSE SIGHT ALL THE STARRS	4	34
HOW DUE. YET ALL HIS GOOD PROV'D ILL IN ME,	4	48
OR FROM WITHOUT, TO ALL TEMPTATIONS ARM'D.	4	65
BUT HEAV'NS FREE LOVE DEALT EQUALLY TO ALL?	4	68
ALL HOPE EXCLUDED THUS, BEHOLD IN STEAD	4	105
FARWEL REMORSE: ALL GOOD TO ME IS LOST;	4	109
AS HE SUPPOS'D, ALL UNOBSERV'D, UNSEEN.	4	130
ALL SADNESS BUT DESPAIR: NOW GENTLE GALES	4	156
ALL PATH OF MAN OR BEAST THAT PAST THAT WAY:	4	177
AT ONE SLIGHT BOUND HIGH OVER LEAP'D ALL BOUND	4	181
TO ALL DELIGHT OF HUMAN SENSE EXPOS'D	4	206
ALL TREES OF NOBLEST KIND FOR SIGHT, SMELL, TASTE;	4	217
AND ALL AMID THEM STOOD THE TREE OF LIFE,	4	218
FLOURS OF ALL HUE, AND WITHOUT THORN THE ROSE:	4	256
WAS GATHERD, WHICH COST CERES ALL THAT PAIN	4	271
SAW UNDELIGHTED ALL DELIGHT, ALL KIND	4	286
IN NAKED MAJESTIE SEEMD LORDS OF ALL,	4	290
SIN-BRED, HOW HAVE YE TROUBL'D ALL MANKIND	4	315
ALL BEASTS OF TH' EARTH, SINCE WILDE, AND OF ALL CHASE	4	341
TO MAKE THEM MIRTH US'D ALL HIS MIGHT, AND WREATHD	4	346
YOUR CHANGE APPROACHES, WHEN ALL THESE DELIGHTS	4	367
AND SEND FORTH ALL HER KINGS; THERE WILL BE ROOM,	4	383
TURND HIM ALL EARE TO HEAR NEW UTTERANCE FLOW,	4	410
SOLE PARTNER AND SOLE PART OF ALL THESE JOYES,	4	411
DEARER THY SELF THEN ALL; NEEDS MUST THE POWER	4	412
IN ALL THIS HAPPINESS, WHO AT HIS HAND	4	417
THIS ONE, THIS EASIE CHARGE, OF ALL THE TREES	4	421
OVER ALL OTHER CREATURES THAT POSSESS	4	431
FREE LEAVE SO LARGE TO ALL THINGS ELSE, AND CHOICE	4	434
FOR WEE TO HIM INDEED ALL PRAISES OWE,	4	444
FROM THIR OWN MOUTHS; ALL IS NOT THEIRS IT SEEMS:	4	513
BENT ALL ON SPEED, AND MARKT HIS AERIE GATE;	4	568
HAD IN HER SOBER LIVERIE ALL THINGS CLAD;	4	599
WERE SLUNK, ALL BUT THE WAKEFUL NIGHTINGALE;	4	602
SHE ALL NIGHT LONG HER AMOROUS DESCANT SUNG;	4	603
OF NIGHT, AND ALL THINGS NOW RETIR'D TO REST	4	611
OUR EYE-LIDS; OTHER CREATURES ALL DAY LONG	4	616
AND THE REGARD OF HEAV'N ON ALL HIS WAIES;	4	620
WITH THEE CONVERSING I FORGET ALL TIME,	4	639
ALL SEASONS AND THIR CHANGE, ALL PLEASE ALIKE.	4	640
BUT WHEREFORE ALL NIGHT LONG SHINE THESE, FOR WHOM	4	657
THIS GLORIOUS SIGHT, WHEN SLEEP HATH SHUT ALL EYES?	4	658
IN NATURE AND ALL THINGS, WHICH THESE SOFT FIRES	4	667
THIR STELLAR VERTUE ON ALL KINDS THAT GROW	4	671
ALL THESE WITH CEASLESS PRAISE HIS WORKS BEHOLD	4	679
ALL THINGS TO MANS DELIGHTFUL USE; THE ROOFE	4	692
IRIS ALL HUES, ROSES, AND GESSAMIN	4	698
ENDOWD WITH ALL THIR GIFTS, AND O TOO LIKE	4	715
AND MUTUAL LOVE, THE CROWN OF ALL OUR BLISS	4	728
PURE, AND COMMANDS TO SOM, LEAVES FREE TO ALL.	4	747
IN PARADISE OF ALL THINGS COMMON ELSE.	4	752
RELATIONS DEAR, AND ALL THE CHARITIES	4	756
OR ALL AT ONCE; MORE GLORIE WILL BE WONN,	4	853
CAME NOT ALL HELL BROKE LOOSE? IS PAIN TO THEM	4	918
THY BLASTING VOLIED THUNDER MADE ALL SPEED	4	928
A FAITHFUL LEADER, NOT TO HAZARD ALL	4	933
COLLECTING ALL HIS MIGHT DILATED STOOD,	4	986
OF HEAV'N PERHAPS, OR ALL THE ELEMENTS	4	993
WHEREIN ALL THINGS CREATED FIRST HE WEIGHD,	4	999
IN COUNTERPOISE, NOW PONDERS ALL EVENTS,	4	1001
O SOLE IN WHOM MY THOUGHTS FIND ALL REPOSE,	5	28
IF NONE REGARD; HEAV'N WAKES WITH ALL HIS EYES,	5	44
IN WHOSE SIGHT ALL THINGS JOY, WITH RAVISHMENT	5	46

ALL (CONTINUED)

HER OFFICE HOLDS; OF ALL EXTERNAL THINGS,	5	103
ALL WHAT WE AFFIRM OR WHAT DENY, AND CALL	5	107
SO ALL WAS CLEARD, AND TO THE FIELD THEY HASTE.	5	136
DISCOVERING IN WIDE LANTSKIP ALL THE EAST	5	142
ON EARTH JOYN ALL YE CREATURES TO EXTOLL	5	164
AND NOURISH ALL THINGS, LET YOUR CEASLESS CHANGE	5	183
JOYN VOICES ALL YE LIVING SOULS, YE BIRDS,	5	197
IN THEM AT ONCE TO RUIN ALL MANKIND.	5	228
ALL JUSTICE: NOR DELAID THE WINGED SAINT	5	247
THROUGH ALL TH' EMPYREAL ROAD; TILL AT THE GATE	5	253
ABOVE ALL HILLS. AS WHEN BY NIGHT THE GLASS	5	261
OF TOWRING EAGLES, TO ALL THE FOWLES HE SEEMS	5	271
A PHOENIX, GAZ'D BY ALL, AS THAT SOLE BIRD	5	272
THE CIRCUIT WIDE. STRAIT KNEW HIM ALL THE BANDS	5	287
ALL SEASONS, RIPE FOR USE HANGS ON THE STALK;	5	323
ALCINOUS REIGN'D, FRUIT OF ALL KINDES, IN COATE,	5	341
PERFECTIONS, IN HIMSELF WAS ALL HIS STATE,	5	353
DAZLES THE CROUD, AND SETS THEM ALL AGAPE.	5	357
ALL AUTUMN PIL'D, THOUGH SPRING AND AUTUMN HERE	5	394
ALL PERFET GOOD UNMEASUR'D OUT, DESCENDS,	5	399
THAT ONE CELESTIAL FATHER GIVES TO ALL.	5	403
THE SUN THAT LIGHT IMPARTS TO ALL, RECEIVES	5	423
FROM ALL HIS ALIMENTAL RECOMPENCE	5	424
ALL THINGS PROCEED, AND UP TO HIM RETURN,	5	470
IF NOT DEPRAV'D FROM GOOD, CREATED ALL	5	471
SUCH TO PERFECTION, ONE FIRST MATTER ALL,	5	472
YOUR BODIES MAY AT LAST TURN ALL TO SPIRIT,	5	497
MY SELF AND ALL TH' ANGELIC HOST THAT STAND	5	535
TO MOTION, MEASURES ALL THINGS DURABLE	5	581
FORTHWITH FROM ALL THE ENDS OF HEAV'N APPEERD	5	586
HEAR ALL YE ANGELS, PROGENIE OF LIGHT,	5	600
ALL KNEES IN HEAV'N, AND SHALL CONFESS HIM LORD:	5	608
ALL SEEMD WELL PLEAS'D, ALL SEEM'D, BUT WERE NOT ALL	5	617
OF PLANETS AND OF FIXT IN ALL HER WHEELES	5	621
DESIROUS; ALL IN CIRCLES AS THEY STOOD,	5	631
EXCESS, BEFORE TH' ALL BOUNTEOUS KING, WHO SHOWRD	5	640
ALL BUT THE UNSLEEPING EYES OF GOD TO REST,	5	647
WIDE OVER ALL THE PLAIN, AND WIDER FARR	5	648
THEN ALL THIS GLOBOUS EARTH IN PLAIN OUT SPRED,	5	649
ALTERNATE ALL NIGHT LONG: BUT NOT SO WAK'D	5	657
WITH ALL HIS LEGIONS TO DISLODGE, AND LEAVE	5	669
OF ALL THOSE MYRIADS WHICH WE LEAD THE CHIEF;	5	684
AND ALL WHO UNDER ME THIR BANNERS WAVE,	5	687
WHO SPEEDILY THROUGH ALL THE HIERARCHIES	5	692
OR TAINT INTEGRITIE; BUT ALL OBEY'D	5	704
IN FULL RESPLENDENCE, HEIR OF ALL MY MIGHT,	5	720
WITH SPEED WHAT FORCE IS LEFT, AND ALL IMPLOY	5	730
ILLUSTRATES, WHEN THEY SEE ALL REGAL POWER	5	739
ALL THY DOMINION, ADAM, IS NO MORE	5	751
THEN WHAT THIS GARDEN IS TO ALL THE EARTH,	5	752
AND ALL THE SEA, FROM ONE ENTIRE GLOBOSE	5	753
AFFECTING ALL EQUALITY WITH GOD,	5	763
FOR THITHER HE ASSEMBL'D ALL HIS TRAIN,	5	767
ALL POWER, AND US ECLIPST UNDER THE NAME	5	776
OF KING ANOINTED, FOR WHOM ALL THIS HASTE	5	777
BY NONE, AND IF NOT EQUAL ALL, YET FREE,	5	791
EXPECTED, LEAST OF ALL FROM THEE, INGRATE	5	811
ONE OVER ALL WITH UNSUCCEEDED POWER.	5	821
OR ALL ANGELIC NATURE JOIND IN ONE,	5	834
ALL THINGS, EV'N THEE, AND ALL THE SPIRITS OF HEAV'N	5	837
HIS LAWS OUR LAWS, ALL HONOUR TO HIM DONE	5	844
FORSAK'N OF ALL GOOD; I SEE THY FALL	5	878
ALL NIGHT THE DREADLESS ANGEL UNPURSU'D	6	1
SHOT THROUGH WITH ORIENT BEAMS; WHEN ALL THE PLAIN	6	15
THEN VIOLENCE: FOR THIS WAS ALL THY CARE	6	35
TO DARKEN ALL THE HILL, AND SMOAK TO ROWL	6	57
REACHING BEYOND ALL LIMIT AT ONE BLOW	6	140
ALL ARE NOT OF THY TRAIN; THERE BE WHO FAITH	6	143
FROM ALL: MY SECT THOU SEEST, NOW LEARN TOO LATE	6	147
TO HEAV'NLY SOULES HAD BIN ALL ONE; BUT NOW	6	165
HALF SUNK WITH ALL HIS PINES. AMAZEMENT SEIS'D	6	198
AND INEXTINGUISHABLE RAGE; ALL HEAV'N	6	217
RESOUNDED, AND HAD EARTH BIN THEN, ALL EARTH	6	218
OF ALL THIR REGIONS; HOW MUCH MORE OF POWER	6	223
TORMENTED ALL THE AIR; ALL AIR SEEMD THEN	6	244
AND VISAGE ALL ENFLAM'D FIRST THUS BEGAN.	6	261
THESE ACTS OF HATEFUL STRIFE, HATEFUL TO ALL,	6	264
FROM ALL HER CONFINES. HEAV'N THE SEAT OF BLISS	6	273
ALL HIS RIGHT SIDE; THEN SATAN FIRST KNEW PAIN,	6	327
AND ALL HIS ARMOUR STAIND ERE WHILE SO BRIGHT.	6	334
FORTHWITH ON ALL SIDES TO HIS AIDE WAS RUN	6	335
ALL HEART THEY LIVE, ALL HEAD, ALL EYE, ALL EARE,	6	350
ALL INTELLECT, ALL SENSE, AND AS THEY PLEASE,	6	351
ENTER'D, AND FOUL DISORDER; ALL THE GROUND	6	388
WHICH ALL SUBDUES, AND MAKES REMISS THE HANDS	6	458
ALL PATIENCE. HE WHO THEREFORE CAN INVENT	6	464
TH' INVENTION ALL ADMIR'D, AND EACH, HOW HEE	6	498
SO ALL ERE DAY-SPRING, UNDER CONSCIOUS NIGHT	6	521
IN ORDER, QUIT OF ALL IMPEDIMENT;	6	548
THAT ALL MAY SEE WHO HATE US, HOW WE SEEK	6	559
WHAT WE PROPOUND, AND LOUD THAT ALL MAY HEAR.	6	567
NOT LONG, FOR SUDDEN ALL AT ONCE THIR REEDS	6	582
BUT SOON OBSCUR'D WITH SMOAK, ALL HEAV'N APPEERD,	6	585
AND ALL HER ENTRAILS TORE, DISGORGING FOULE	6	588
SUCH AS WE MIGHT PERCEIVE AMUS'D THEM ALL,	6	623

ALL (CONTINUED)

ALL DOUBT OF VICTORIE, ETERNAL MIGHT	6	630
AND ALL HIS HOST DERIDED, WHILE THEY STOOD	6	633
THEY PLUCKT THE SEATED HILLS WITH ALL THIR LOAD,	6	644
THEY SAW THEM WHELM'D, AND ALL THIR CONFIDENCE	6	651
UPON CONFUSION ROSE: AND NOW ALL HEAV'N	6	669
THIS TUMULT, AND PERMITTED ALL, ADVIS'D:	6	674
ALL POWER ON HIM TRANSFERR'D: WHENCE TO HIS SON	6	678
IMMENSE I HAVE TRANSFUS'D, THAT ALL MAY KNOW	6	704
OF ALL THINGS, TO BE HEIR AND TO BE KING	6	708
THAT SHAKE HEAV'NS BASIS, BRING FORTH ALL MY WARR,	6	712
FROM ALL HEAV'NS BOUNDS INTO THE UTTER DEEP:	6	716
SHON FULL, HE ALL HIS FATHER FULL EXPREST	6	720
FULFILL'D, WHICH TO FULFIL IS ALL MY BLISS.	6	729
THOU SHALT BE ALL IN ALL, AND I IN THEE	6	732
FOR EVER, AND IN MEE ALL WHOM THOU LOV'ST:	6	733
IMAGE OF THEE IN ALL THINGS; AND SHALL SOON,	6	736
HAD WONDROUS, AS WITH STARRS THIR BODIES ALL	6	754
HEE IN CELESTIAL PANOPLIE ALL ARMD	6	760
UNDER THIR HEAD IMBODIED ALL IN ONE.	6	779
TO ALL HIS HOST ON EITHER HAND THUS SPAKE.	6	800
YET ENVIED; AGAINST MEE IS ALL THIR RAGE,	6	813
IN BATTEL WHICH THE STRONGER PROVES, THEY ALL,	6	819
THEY MEASURE ALL, OF OTHER EXCELLENCE	6	821
ALL BUT THE THRONE IT SELF OF GOD. FULL SOON	6	834
PLAGUES; THEY ASTONISHT ALL RESISTANCE LOST,	6	838
ALL COURAGE; DOWN THIR IDLE WEAPONS DROP'D;	6	839
AMONG TH' ACCURST, THAT WITHERD ALL THIR STRENGTH,	6	850
TO MEET HIM ALL HIS SAINTS, WHO SILENT STOOD	6	882
WHICH WOULD BE ALL HIS SOLACE AND REVENGE.	6	905
OF ALL TASTES ELSE TO PLEASE THIR APPETITE,	7	49
ALL SPACE, THE AMBIENT AIRE WIDE INTERFUS'D	7	89
THROUGH ALL ETERNITIE SO LATE TO BUILD	7	92
ALL LIKE HIMSELF REBELLIOUS, BY WHOSE AID	7	140
IMMENSE, AND ALL HIS FATHER IN HIM SHON.	7	196
FOR CHAOS HEARD HIS VOICE: HIM ALL HIS TRAINE	7	221
THIS UNIVERSE, AND ALL CREATED THINGS:	7	227
APPEER'D NOT: OVER ALL THE FACE OF EARTH	7	278
PROLIFIC HUMOUR SOFT'NING ALL HER GLOBE,	7	280
ALL BUT WITHIN THOSE BANKS, WHERE RIVERS NOW	7	305
WENT UP AND WATERD ALL THE GROUND, AND EACH	7	334
REGENT OF DAY, AND ALL TH' HORIZON ROUND	7	371
CEAS'D WARBLING, BUT ALL NIGHT TUN'D HER SOFT LAYES:	7	436
IN ALL THE LIVERIES DECT OF SUMMERS PRIDE	7	478
STREAKING THE GROUND WITH SINUOUS TRACE; NOT ALL	7	481
THE SERPENT SUTTL'ST BEAST OF ALL THE FIELD,	7	495
NOW HEAV'N IN ALL HER GLORIE SHON, AND ROWLD	7	499
OF ALL YET DON; A CREATURE WHO NOT PRONE	7	506
OF ALL HIS WORKS: THEREFORE THE OMNIPOTENT	7	516
BEAST OF THE FIELD, AND OVER ALL THE EARTH,	7	522
AND FREELY ALL THIR PLEASANT FRUIT FOR FOOD	7	540
GAVE THEE, ALL SORTS ARE HERE THAT ALL TH' EARTH YIELDS,	7	541
HERE FINISH'D HEE, AND ALL THAT HE HAD MADE	7	548
VIEW'D, AND BEHOLD ALL WAS ENTIRELY GOOD;	7	549
THE HEAV'NS AND ALL THE CONSTELLATIONS RUNG,	7	562
AUTHOR AND END OF ALL THINGS, AND FROM WORK	7	591
AS RESTING ON THAT DAY FROM ALL HIS WORK,	7	593
AND DULCIMER, ALL ORGANS OF SWEET STOP,	7	596
ALL SOUNDS ON FRET BY STRING OR GOLDEN WIRE	7	597
AND ALL HER NUMBERD STARRS, THAT SEEM TO ROWLE	8	19
ONE DAY AND NIGHT; IN ALL THIR VAST SURVEY	8	24
INTO ALL EYES TO WISH HER STILL IN SIGHT.	8	63
INVISIBLE ELSE ABOVE ALL STARRS, THE WHEELE	8	135
GOD HATH BID DWELL FARR OFF ALL ANXIOUS CARES,	8	185
SPEAKING OR MUTE ALL COMLINESS AND GRACE	8	222
BIRDS ON THE BRANCHES WARBLING; ALL THINGS SMIL'D,	8	265
BEFORE MINE EYES ALL REAL, AS THE DREAM	8	310
SAID MILDELY, AUTHOR OF ALL THIS THOU SEEST	8	317
NOT ONELY THESE FAIR BOUNDS, BUT ALL THE EARTH	8	338
POSSESS IT, AND ALL THINGS THAT THEREIN LIVE,	8	340
O BY WHAT NAME, FOR THOU ABOVE ALL THESE,	8	357
AND ALL THIS GOOD TO MAN, FOR WHOSE WELL BEING	8	361
THOU HAST PROVIDED ALL THINGS: BUT WITH MEE	8	363
OR ALL ENJOYING, WHAT CONTENTMENT FIND?	8	366
REPLENISHT, AND ALL THESE AT THY COMMAND	8	371
ALL RATIONAL DELIGHT, WHEREIN THE BRUTE	8	391
WORS THEN CAN MAN WITH BEAST, AND LEAST OF ALL.	8	397
FROM ALL ETERNITIE, FOR NONE I KNOW	8	406
ALL HUMAN THOUGHTS COME SHORT, SUPREAM OF THINGS;	8	414
AND THROUGH ALL NUMBERS ABSOLUTE, THOUGH ONE;	8	421
THAT WHAT SEEMD FAIR IN ALL THE WORLD, SEEMD NOW	8	472
AND INTO ALL THINGS FROM HER AIRE INSPIR'D	8	476
HER LOSS, AND OTHER PLEASURES ALL ABJURE:	8	480
WITH WHAT ALL EARTH OR HEAVEN COULD BESTOW	8	483
GRACE WAS IN ALL HER STEPS, HEAV'N IN HER EYE,	8	488
GIVER OF ALL THINGS FAIRE, BUT FAIREST THIS	8	493
OF ALL THY GIFTS, NOR ENVIEST. I NOW SEE	8	494
THE MORE DESIRABLE, OR TO SAY ALL,	8	505
I LED HER BLUSHING LIKE THE MORN: ALL HEAV'N,	8	511
THUS I HAVE TOLD THEE ALL MY STATE, AND BROUGHT	8	521
IN ALL THINGS ELSE DELIGHT INDEED, BUT SUCH	8	524
COMMOTION STRANGE, IN ALL ENJOYMENTS ELSE	8	531
ALL HIGHER KNOWLEDGE IN HER PRESENCE FALLS	8	551
OCCASIONALLY; AND TO CONSUMMATE ALL,	8	556
AND TO REALITIES YIELD ALL HER SHOWS:	8	575
BEYOND ALL OTHER, THINK THE SAME VOUTSAF'T	8	581

ALL (CONTINUED)

IN PROCREATION COMMON TO ALL KINDES	8	597
FROM ALL HER WORDS AND ACTIONS MIXT WITH LOVE	8	602
BE STRONG, LIVE HAPPIE, AND LOVE, BUT FIRST OF ALL	8	633
WOULD NOT ADMIT; THINE AND OF ALL THY SONS	8	637
AND ALL THE BLEST: STAND FAST; TO STAND OR FALL	8	640
AND ALL TEMPTATION TO TRANSGRESS REPEL.	8	643
DEPREST, AND MUCH THEY MAY, IF ALL BE MINE,	9	46
CONSIDER'D EVERY CREATURE, WHICH OF ALL	9	84
THE SERPENT SUTTLEST BEAST OF ALL THE FIELD.	9	86
IN THEE CONCENTRING ALL THIR PRECIOUS BEAMS	9	106
IS CENTER, YET EXTENDS TO ALL, SO THOU	9	108
CENTRING RECEAV'ST FROM ALL THOSE ORBS; IN THEE,	9	109
NOT IN THEMSELVES, ALL THIR KNOWN VERTUE APPEERS	9	110
OF GROWTH, SENSE, REASON, ALL SUMM'D UP IN MAN,	9	113
OF CONTRARIES; ALL GOOD TO ME BECOMES	9	122
FOR WHOM ALL THIS WAS MADE, ALL THIS WILL SOON	9	132
THIR MORNING INCENSE, WHEN ALL THINGS THAT BREATH,	9	194
FOR WHILE SO NEAR EACH OTHER THUS ALL DAY	9	220
COMPARE ABOVE ALL LIVING CREATURES DEARE,	9	228
OFSPRING OF HEAV'N AND EARTH, AND ALL EARTHS LORD,	9	273
O WOMAN, BEST ARE ALL THINGS AS THE WILL	9	343
OF ALL THAT HE CREATED, MUCH LESS MAN,	9	346
ON WHAT THOU HAST OF VERTUE, SUMMON ALL,	9	374
AND ALL THINGS IN BEST ORDER TO INVITE	9	402
SHE MOST, AND IN HER LOOK SUMMS ALL DELIGHT.	9	454
FIERCE HATE HE RECOLLECTS, AND ALL HIS THOUGHTS	9	471
OF PLEASURE, BUT ALL PLEASURE TO DESTROY,	9	477
THE WOMAN, OPPORTUNE TO ALL ATTEMPTS,	9	481
THEE ALL THINGS LIVING GAZE ON, ALL THINGS THINE	9	539
CREATED MUTE TO ALL ARTICULAT SOUND;	9	557
THEE, SERPENT, SUTTLEST BEAST OF ALL THE FIELD	9	560
EASIE TO MEE IT IS TO TELL THEE ALL	9	569
ALL OTHER BEASTS THAT SAW, WITH LIKE DESIRE	9	592
CONSIDERD ALL THINGS VISIBLE IN HEAV'N,	9	604
OR EARTH, OR MIDDLE, ALL THINGS FAIR AND GOOD;	9	605
BUT ALL THAT FAIR AND GOOD IN THY DIVINE	9	606
OF PROHIBITION, ROOT OF ALL OUR WOE;	9	645
OF ALL THESE GARDEN TREES YE SHALL NOT EATE,	9	657
YET LORDS DECLAR'D OF ALL IN EARTH OR AIRE?	9	658
THE TEMPTER ALL IMPASSIOND THUS BEGAN.	9	678
ON OUR BELIEF, THAT ALL FROM THEM PROCEEDS;	9	719
THEM NOTHING: IF THEY ALL THINGS, WHO ENCLOS'D	9	722
IMPART AGAINST HIS WILL IF ALL BE HIS?	9	728
AND YET UNKNOWN, IS AS NOT HAD AT ALL.	9	757
HERE GROWS THE CURE OF ALL, THIS FRUIT DIVINE,	9	776
SIGHING THROUGH ALL HER WORKS GAVE SIGNS OF WOE,	9	783
THAT ALL WAS LOST. BACK TO THE THICKET SLUNK	9	784
O SOVRAN, VERTUOUS, PRECIOUS OF ALL TREES	9	795
OF THY FULL BRANCHES OFFER'D FREE TO ALL;	9	802
IN KNOWLEDGE, AS THE GODS WHO ALL THINGS KNOW;	9	804
OUR GREAT FORBIDDER, SAFE WITH ALL HIS SPIES	9	815
SO DEAR I LOVE HIM THAT WITH HIM ALL DEATHS	9	832
RAN THROUGH HIS VEINS, AND ALL HIS JOYNTS RELAX'D;	9	891
DOWN DROP'D, AND ALL THE FADED ROSES SHED:	9	893
OF ALL GODS WORKS, CREATURE IN WHOM EXCELL'D	9	897
SET OVER ALL HIS WORKS, WHICH IN OUR FALL,	9	941
WITH ALL PERFECTIONS, SO ENFLAME MY SENSE	9	1031
OF ALL THIR VERTUE: SILENT, AND IN FACE	9	1063
OF ALL OUR GOOD, SHAM'D, NAKED, MISERABLE,	9	1139
OMNISCIENT, WHO IN ALL THINGS WISE AND JUST,	10	7
ALL WERE WHO HEARD, DIM SADNESS DID NOT SPARE	10	23
HOW ALL BEFELL: THEY TOWARDS THE THRONE SUPREAM	10	28
AND FLATTER'D OUT OF ALL, BELIEVING LIES	10	42
ALL JUDGEMENT, WHETHER IN HEAV'N, OR EARTH, OR HELL.	10	57
RESPLENDENT ALL HIS FATHER MANIFEST	10	66
CONVICT BY FLIGHT, AND REBEL TO ALL LAW	10	83
EDEN AND ALL THE COAST IN PROSPECT LAY.	10	89
HOWEVER INSUPPORTABLE, BE ALL	10	134
HERS IN ALL REAL DIGNITIE: ADORND	10	151
ABOVE ALL CATTLE, EACH BEAST OF THE FIELD;	10	176
AND DUST SHALT EAT ALL THE DAYES OF THY LIFE.	10	178
SHALT EATE THEREOF ALL THE DAYS OF THY LIFE;	10	202
ALL, THOUGH ALL-KNOWING, WHAT HAD PAST WITH MAN	10	227
OF MERIT HIGH TO ALL TH' INFERNAL HOST,	10	259
THE SAVOUR OF DEATH FROM ALL THINGS THERE THAT LIVE:	10	269
AND CHAINS THEY MADE ALL FAST, TOO FAST THEY MADE	10	319
BY EVE, THOUGH ALL UNWEETING, SECONDED	10	335
THINE NOW IS ALL THIS WORLD, THY VERTUE HATH WON	10	372
OF ALL THINGS PARTED BY TH' EMPYREAL BOUNDS,	10	380
AMPLY HAVE MERITED OF ME, OF ALL	10	388
ALL YOURS, RIGHT DOWN TO PARADISE DESCEND;	10	398
CHIEFLY ON MAN, SOLE LORD OF ALL DECLAR'D,	10	401
MY HOLD OF THIS NEW KINGDOM ALL DEPENDS,	10	406
AND ALL ABOUT FOUND DESOLATE; FOR THOSE	10	420
FLOWN TO THE UPPER WORLD; THE REST WERE ALL	10	422
OF TURKISH CRESCENT, LEAVES ALL WASTE BEYOND	10	434
WAS LEFT HIM, OR FALSE GLITTER: ALL AMAZ'D	10	452
BOTH HIS BELOVED MAN AND ALL HIS WORLD,	10	489
TO RULE, AS OVER ALL HE SHOULD HAVE RUL'D.	10	493
ON ALL SIDES, FROM INNUMERABLE TONGUES	10	507
TO FORKED TONGUE, FOR NOW WERE ALL TRANSFORM'D	10	519
ALIKE, TO SERPENTS ALL AS ACCESSORIES	10	520
ABOVE THE REST STILL TO RETAIN; THEY ALL	10	532
WHERE ALL YET LEFT OF THAT REVOLTED ROUT	10	534
SECOND OF SATAN SPRUNG, ALL CONQUERING DEATH,	10	591

ALL (CONTINUED)
WHICH HERE, THOUGH PLENTEOUS, ALL TO LITTLE SEEMS 10 600
HIS THOUGHTS, HIS LOOKS, WORDS, ACTIONS ALL INFECT, 10 608
ALL KINDS, AND FOR DESTRUCTION TO MATURE 10 612
OF PASSION, I TO THEM HAD QUITTED ALL, 10 627
RIGHTEOUS ARE THY DECREES ON ALL THY WORKS; 10 644
AND FISH WITH FISH; TO GRAZE THE HERB ALL LEAVING, 10 711
ALL THAT I EAT OR DRINK, OR SHALL BEGET, 10 728
WHO OF ALL AGES TO SUCCEED, BUT FEELING 10 733
MINE OWN THAT BIDE UPON ME, ALL FROM MEE 10 738
ALL I RECEAV'D, UNABLE TO PERFORME 10 750
PURSUES ME STILL, LEAST ALL I CANNOT DIE, 10 783
ALL OF ME THEN SHALL DIE: LET THIS APPEASE 10 792
FOR THOUGH THE LORD OF ALL BE INFINITE, 10 794
BY WHICH ALL CAUSES ELSE ACCORDING STILL 10 806
NOR I ON MY PART SINGLE, IN MEE ALL 10 817
TO WASTE IT ALL MY SELF, AND LEAVE YE NONE, 10 820
ME NOW YOUR CURSE. AH, WHY SHOULD ALL MANKIND 10 822
BUT ALL CORRUPT, BOTH MIND AND WILL DEPRAV'D, 10 825
IN SIGHT OF GOD? HIM AFTER ALL DISPUTES 10 828
FORC'T I ABSOLVE: ALL MY EVASIONS VAIN, 10 829
OF ALL CORRUPTION, ALL THE BLAME LIGHTS DUE; 10 833
THEN ALL THE WORLD MUCH HEAVIER, THOUGH DIVIDED 10 836
AND WHAT THOU FEARST, ALIKE DESTROYES ALL HOPE 10 838
BEYOND ALL PAST EXAMPLE AND FUTURE, 10 840
ALL THINGS WITH DOUBLE TERROR: ON THE GROUND 10 850
THY INWARD FRAUD, TO WARN ALL CREATURES FROM THEE 10 871
CONSTANT, MATURE, PROOF AGAINST ALL ASSAULTS, 10 882
AND UNDERSTOOD NOT ALL WAS BUT A SHEW 10 883
RATHER THEN SOLID VERTU, ALL BUT A RIB 10 884
AND TRESSES ALL DISORDERD, AT HIS FEET 10 911
THERE WITH MY CRIES IMPORTUNE HEAVEN, THAT ALL 10 933
ON ME, SOLE CAUSE TO THEE OF ALL THIS WOE, 10 935
AS ONE DISARM'D, HIS ANGER ALL HE LOST, 10 945
THE PUNISHMENT ALL ON THY SELF; ALAS, 10 949
THAT ON MY HEAD ALL MIGHT BE VISITED, 10 955
WHICH HIS OWN HAND MANURING ALL THE TREES 11 28
AND PROPITIATION, ALL HIS WORKS ON MEE 11 34
ALL MY REDEEMD MAY DWELL IN JOY AND BLISS, 11 43
ALL THY REQUEST FOR MAN, ACCEPTED SON, 11 46
OBTAIN, ALL THY REQUEST WAS MY DECREE: 11 47
DISTEMPERD ALL THINGS, AND OF INCORRUPT 11 56
BUT LET US CALL TO SYNOD ALL THE BLEST 11 67
FILLD ALL THE REGIONS: FROM THIR BLISSFUL BOWRS 11 77
GOOD BY IT SELF, AND EVIL NOT AT ALL. 11 89
BEWAILING THIR EXCESS, ALL TERROR HIDE. 11 111
WIDE WAVING, ALL APPROACH FARR OFF TO FRIGHT, 11 121
AND GUARD ALL PASSAGE TO THE TREE OF LIFE: 11 122
TO SPIRITS FOULE, AND ALL MY TREES THIR PREY, 11 124
HAD, LIKE A DOUBLE JANUS, ALL THIR SHAPE 11 129
EVE, EASILY MAY FAITH ADMIT, THAT ALL 11 141
KNEEL'D AND BEFORE HIM HUMBL'D ALL MY HEART, 11 150
EVE RIGHTLY CALL'D, MOTHER OF ALL MANKIND, 11 159
MOTHER OF ALL THINGS LIVING, SINCE BY THEE 11 160
MAN IS TO LIVE, AND ALL THINGS LIVE FOR MAN. 11 161
RATHER BELONGS, DISTRUST AND ALL DISPRAISE: 11 166
THAT I WHO FIRST BROUGHT DEATH ON ALL, AM GRAC'T 11 168
ALL UNCONCERN'D WITH OUR UNREST, BEGINS 11 174
GOODLIEST OF ALL THE FORREST, HART AND HINDE; 11 189
THAT ALL HIS SENSES BOUND; EVE, WHO UNSEEN 11 265
YET ALL HAD HEARD, WITH AUDIBLE LAMENT 11 266
FAMILIAR TO OUR EYES, ALL PLACES ELSE 11 305
OF HIM WHO ALL THINGS CAN, I WOULD NOT CEASE 11 309
ADAM, THOU KNOW'ST HEAV'N HIS, AND ALL THE EARTH. 11 335
ALL TH' EARTH HE GAVE THEE TO POSSESS AND RULE, 11 339
ALL GENERATIONS, AND HAD HITHER COME 11 344
FROM ALL THE ENDS OF TH' EARTH, TO CELEBRATE 11 345
TO SHEW HIM ALL EARTHS KINGDOMES AND THIR GLORY. 11 384
SUNK DOWN AND ALL HIS SPIRITS BECAME INTRANST; 11 420
ON THE CLEFT WOOD, AND ALL DUE RITES PERFORM'D. 11 440
TO HIS GRIM CAVE, ALL DISMAL; YET TO SENSE 11 469
NUMBERS OF ALL DISEAS'D, ALL MALADIES 11 480
OF HEART-SICK AGONIE, ALL FEAVOROUS KINDS, 11 482
OBTUSE, ALL TASTE OF PLEASURE MUST FORGOE, 11 541
INSTINCT THROUGH ALL PROPORTIONS LOW AND HIGH 11 562
JUST MEN THEY SEEMD, AND ALL THIR STUDY BENT 11 577
LOVES HARBINGER APPEERD; THEN ALL IN HEAT 11 589
WITH FEAST AND MUSICK ALL THE TENTS RESOUND. 11 592
HERE NATURE SEEMS FULFILLD IN ALL HER ENDS. 11 602
YET EMPTY OF ALL GOOD WHEREIN CONSISTS 11 616
SHALL YIELD UP ALL THIR VERTUE, ALL THIR FAME 11 623
THROUGH ALL THE PLAIN, AND REFUGE NONE WAS FOUND. 11 673
ADAM WAS ALL IN TEARS, AND TO HIS GUIDE 11 674
ALL NOW WAS TURN'D TO JOLLITIE AND GAME, 11 714
BUT ALL IN VAIN: WHICH WHEN HE SAW, HE CEAS'D 11 726
WIDE HOVERING, ALL THE CLOUDS TOGETHER DROVE 11 739
RODE TILTING O'RE THE WAVES, ALL DWELLINGS ELSE 11 747
FLOOD OVERWHELMD, AND THEM WITH ALL THIR POMP 11 748
ALL LEFT, IN ONE SMALL BOTTOM SWUM IMBARK'T. 11 753
THE END OF ALL THY OFSPRING, END SO SAD, 11 755
HIS CHILDREN, ALL IN VIEW DESTROYD AT ONCE; 11 761
ALL WOULD HAVE THEN GON WELL, PEACE WOULD HAVE
CROWND 11 781
SHALL WITH THIR FREEDOM LOST ALL VERTU LOOSE 11 798
SO ALL SHALL TURN DEGENERATE, ALL DEPRAV'D, 11 806
AND SHELTERD ROUND, BUT ALL THE CATARACTS 11 824
RAINE DAY AND NIGHT, ALL FOUNTAINS OF THE DEEP 11 826
BEYOND ALL BOUNDS, TILL INUNDATION RISE 11 828

ALL (CONTINUED)
WITH ALL HIS VERDURE SPOIL'D, AND TREES ADRIFT 11 832
THE ANCIENT SIRE DESCENDS WITH ALL HIS TRAIN; 11 862
WITH ALL THE CREATURES, AND THIR SEED PRESERVE. 11 873
FROM HIM, AND ALL HIS ANGER TO FORGET. 11 878
THE WHOLE EARTH FILL'D WITH VIOLENCE, AND ALL FLESH 11 888
SHALL HOLD THIR COURSE, TILL FIRE PURGE ALL THINGS
NEW, 11 900
NOT UNDERSTOOD, TILL HOARSE, AND ALL IN RAGE, 12 58
FROM ALL THE REST, OF WHOM TO BE INVOK'D, 12 112
ALL NATIONS SHALL BE BLEST; HE STRAIGHT OBEYS, 12 126
NOT WANDRING POOR, BUT TRUSTING ALL HIS WEALTH 12 133
GIFT TO HIS PROGENIE OF ALL THAT LAND; 12 138
THIS PONDER, THAT ALL NATIONS OF THE EARTH 12 147
FROGS, LICE AND FLIES MUST ALL HIS PALACE FILL 12 177
WITH LOATH'D INTRUSION, AND FILL ALL THE LAND; 12 178
BOTCHES AND BLAINES MUST ALL HIS FLESH IMBOSS, 12 180
AND ALL HIS PEOPLE; THUNDER MIXT WITH HAILE, 12 181
DARKNESS MUST OVERSHADOW ALL HIS BOUNDS, 12 187
LAST WITH ONE MIDNIGHT STROKE ALL THE FIRST-BORN 12 189
ALL NIGHT HE WILL PURSUE, BUT HIS APPROACH 12 206
GOD LOOKING FORTH WILL TROUBLE ALL HIS HOST 12 209
AND ALL THE PROPHETS IN THIR AGE THE TIMES 12 243
OF MEE AND ALL MANKIND; BUT NOW I SEE 12 276
HIS DAY, IN WHOM ALL NATIONS SHALL BE BLEST, 12 277
ALL PROPHECIE, THAT OF THE ROYAL STOCK 12 325
ALL NATIONS, AND TO KINGS FORETOLD, OF KINGS 12 329
WITH ALL HIS SACRED THINGS, A SCORN AND PREY 12 341
PROCLAIMING LIFE TO ALL WHO SHALL BELIEVE 12 407
OF ALL MANKINDE, WITH HIM THERE CRUCIFI'D, 12 417
TO TEACH ALL NATIONS WHAT OF HIM THEY LEARN'D 12 440
ALL NATIONS THEY SHALL TEACH; FOR FROM THAT DAY 12 446
SO IN HIS SEED ALL NATIONS SHALL BE BLEST. 12 450
THROUGH ALL HIS REALME, AND THERE CONFOUNDED LEAVE; 12 455
ABOVE ALL NAMES IN HEAV'N; AND THENCE SHALL COME, 12 458
SHALL ALL BE PARADISE, FAR HAPPIER PLACE 12 464
THAT ALL THIS GOOD OF EVIL SHALL PRODUCE, 12 470
TO GUIDE THEM IN ALL TRUTH, AND ALSO ARME 12 490
TO EVANGELIZE THE NATIONS, THEN ON ALL 12 499
TO SPEAK ALL TONGUES, AND DO ALL MIRACLES, 12 501
WHO ALL THE SACRED MYSTERIES OF HEAV'N 12 509
TO ALL BELEEVERS; AND FROM THAT PRETENSE, 12 520
ON ALL WHO IN THE WORSHIP PERSEVERE 12 532
TILL TIME STAND FIXT: BEYOND IS ALL ABYSS, 12 555
MERCIFULL OVER ALL HIS WORKS, WITH GOOD 12 565
OF WISDOME; HOPE NO HIGHER, THOUGH ALL THE STARRS 12 576
THOU KNEWST BY NAME, AND ALL TH' ETHEREAL POWERS, 12 577
ALL SECRETS OF THE DEEP, ALL NATURES WORKS, 12 578
AND ALL THE RICHES OF THIS WORLD ENJOYDST, 12 580
AND ALL THE RULE, ONE EMPIRE; ONELY ADD 12 581
OF ALL THE REST: THEN WILT THOU NOT BE LOATH 12 585
PORTENDING GOOD, AND ALL HER SPIRITS COMPOS'D 12 596
(FOR BY THE WOMANS SEED) ON ALL MANKIND. 12 601
ART ALL THINGS UNDER HEAV'N, ALL PLACES THOU, 12 618
I CARRY HENCE; THOUGH ALL BY MEE IS LOST, 12 621
BY MEE THE PROMIS'D SEED SHALL ALL RESTORE. 12 623
TO THIR FIXT STATION, ALL IN BRIGHT ARRAY 12 627
THEY LOOKING BACK, ALL TH' EASTERN SIDE BEHELD 12 641
THE WORLD WAS ALL BEFORE THEM, WHERE TO CHOOSE 12 646

ALLARM
INSTANT WITHOUT DISTURB THEY TOOK ALLARM, 6 549

ALLARM'D
PROVE CHAFF. ON TH' OTHER SIDE SATAN ALLARM'D 4 985

ALLARMD
LEAST ENTRING ON THE CANAANITE ALLARMD 12 217

ALLARME
AND WITH PERPETUAL INRODES TO ALLARME, 2 103
WITHOUT OUR HAZARD, LABOUR, OR ALLARME, 10 491

ALLAY
DECEAV'D; THEY FONDLY THINKING TO ALLAY 10 564

ALLAY'D
YET SCARCE ALLAY'D STILL EYES THE CURRENT STREAME, 7 67

ALLAYD
HYSTORIAN, WHO THUS LARGELY HAST ALLAYD 8 7

ALL-BEARING
WHATEVER EARTH ALL-BEARING MOTHER YIELDS 5 338

ALL-CHEARING
DAYS, MONTHS, & YEARS, TOWARDS HIS ALL-CHEARING
LAMP 3 581

ALLEDG'D
THE FIRST IN FLIGHT FROM PAIN, HAD'ST THOU ALLEDG'D 4 921

ALLEGEANCE
ALLEGEANCE TO TH' ACKNOWLDG'D POWER SUPREAM? 4 956

ALLEGIANCE
OF TRUE ALLEGIANCE, CONSTANT FAITH OR LOVE, 3 104

ALLIES
YON FLOURIE ARBORS, YONDER ALLIES GREEN, 4 626

ALL-KNOWING
ALL, THOUGH ALL-KNOWING, WHAT HAD PAST WITH MAN 10 227

ALLOTTED
ALLOTTED THERE; AND OTHER SUNS PERHAPS 8 148

ALLOW
VIGOUR DIVINE WITHIN THEM, CAN ALLOW 6 158

ALL-POWERFUL
AND BY COMMAND OF HEAV'NS ALL-POWERFUL KING 2 851

ALL-RULING
AND HIGH PERMISSION OF ALL-RULING HEAVEN 1 212
THICK CLOUDS AND DARK DOTH HEAV'NS ALL-RULING SIRE 2 264

ALL-SEEING
OF GOD ALL-SEEING, OR DECEAVE HIS HEART 10 6

ALLUR'D
WHOSE ANNUAL WOUND IN LEBANON ALLUR'D 1 447
ALLUR'D HIS EYE: THITHER HIS COURSE HE BENDS 3 573
THE STARRIE FLOCK, ALLUR'D THEM, AND WITH LYES 5 709

ALLURD
ALLURD THEM; THENCE FROM CUPS TO CIVIL BROILES. 11 718

ALLUREMENT
AGAINST ALLUREMENT, CUSTOM, AND A WORLD 11 810

ALLURING
OF THAT ALLURING FRUIT, URG'D ME SO KEENE. 9 588

ALLUSION
OF LUCIFER, SO BY ALLUSION CALLD, 10 425

ALMANSOR
THE KINGDOMS OF ALMANSOR, FEZ AND SUS, 11 403

ALMIGHTIE
ALMIGHTIE, THINE THIS UNIVERSAL FRAME, 5 154
O ADAM, ONE ALMIGHTIE IS, FROM WHOM 5 469
OF HEAV'NS ALMIGHTIE. THOU TO ME THY THOUGHTS 5 676
TOGETHER BOTH WITH NEXT TO ALMIGHTIE ARME, 6 316
HAD NOT TH' ALMIGHTIE FATHER WHERE HE SITS 6 671
MY BOW AND THUNDER, MY ALMIGHTIE ARMS 6 713
EYE WITNESSES OF HIS ALMIGHTIE ACTS, 6 883
IN PRESENCE OF TH' ALMIGHTIE FATHER, PLEAS'D 7 11
OBTAINE; THOUGH TO RECOUNT ALMIGHTIE WORKS 7 112
SO SPAKE TH' ALMIGHTIE, AND TO WHAT HE SPAKE 7 174
AGAIN TH' ALMIGHTIE SPAKE: LET THERE BE LIGHTS 7 339
WHAT HE ALMIGHTIE STYL'D, FIX NIGHTS AND DAYS 9 137
ANTAGONIST OF HEAV'NS ALMIGHTIE KING) 10 387
SOONER OR LATER; WHICH TH' ALMIGHTIE SEEING, 10 613

ALMIGHTIE'S
HIS PUISSANCE, TRUSTING IN TH' ALMIGHTIE'S AIDE, 6 119
WHEN SUCH WAS HEARD DECLAR'D THE ALMIGHTIE'S WILL; 7 181

ALMIGHTIES
MORE OF TH' ALMIGHTIES WORKS, AND CHIEFLY MAN 4 566
INNUMERABLE BEFORE TH' ALMIGHTIES THRONE 5 585

ALMIGHTY
WITH VAIN ATTEMPT. HIM THE ALMIGHTY POWER 1 44
OF FORCE BELIEVE ALMIGHTY, SINCE NO LESS 1 144
WE SHALL BE FREE; TH' ALMIGHTY HATH NOT BUILT 1 259
MATCHLESS, BUT WITH TH' ALMIGHTY, AND THAT STRIFE 1 623
OF HIS ALMIGHTY ENGIN HE SHALL HEAR 2 65
TH' ALMIGHTY VICTOR TO SPEND ALL HIS RAGE, 2 144
NOT MORE ALMIGHTY TO RESIST OUR MIGHT 2 192
(FOR WHAT COULD ELSE) TO OUR ALMIGHTY FOE 2 769
UNLESS TH' ALMIGHTY MAKER THEM ORDAIN 2 915
NOW HAD THE ALMIGHTY FATHER FROM ABOVE, 3 56
WONDRING; BUT SOON TH' ALMIGHTY THUS REPLY'D: 3 273
NO SOONER HAD TH' ALMIGHTY CEAS'T, BUT ALL 3 344
MADE VISIBLE, TH' ALMIGHTY FATHER SHINES, 3 386
ADDRESS, AND TO BEGIRT TH' ALMIGHTY THRONE 5 868
AND JOIN HIM NAM'D ALMIGHTY TO THY AID, 6 294
WHERETO TH' ALMIGHTY ANSWER'D, NOT DISPLEAS'D. 8 398
TH' ALMIGHTY THUS PRONOUNCD HIS SOVRAN WILL. 11 83

ALMOST
OF AMPLITUDE ALMOST IMMENSE, WITH STARR'S 7 620
SPEED ALMOST SPIRITUAL; MEE THOU THINKST NOT SLOW, 8 110

ALOFT
ALOFT, INCUMBENT ON THE DUSKY AIR 1 226
AS MANY MILES ALOFT: THAT FURIE STAY'D, 2 938
AND FLOURS ALOFT SHADING THE FOUNT OF LIFE, 3 357
THE SPORT OF WINDS: ALL THESE UPWHIRLD ALOFT 3 493
HIS MOUNTED SCALE ALOFT: NOR MORE; BUT FLED 4 1014
BRANDISHT ALOFT THE HORRID EDGE CAME DOWN 6 252
ALOFT BY ANGELS BORN, HIS SIGN IN HEAV'N: 6 776
CRESTED ALOFT, AND CARBUNCLE HIS EYES; 9 500

ALONE
ALONE THE DREADFUL VOYAGE; TILL AT LAST 2 426
ALONE TH' ANTAGONIST OF HEAV'N, NOR LESS 2 509
ALONE, BUT LONG I SAT NOT, TILL MY WOMB 2 778
ALONE, AND WITHOUT GUIDE, HALF LOST, I SEEK 2 975
SON OF MY BOSOM, SON WHO ART ALONE 3 169
WALK'D UP AND DOWN ALONE BENT ON HIS PREY, 3 441
ALONE, FOR OTHER CREATURE IN THIS PLACE 3 442
ALONE THUS WANDRING. BRIGHTEST SERAPH TELL 3 667
INVISIBLE, EXCEPT TO GOD ALONE, 3 684
FROM THY EMPYREAL MANSION THUS ALONE, 3 699
HE MARKD AND MAD DEMEANOUR, THEN ALONE, 4 129
ANY, BUT GOD ALONE, TO VALUE RIGHT 4 202
ALONE AS THEY. ABOUT THEM FRISKING PLAYD 4 340
AND WISDOM, WHICH ALONE IS TRULY FAIR. 4 491
THUS TALKING HAND IN HAND ALONE THEY PASS'D 4 689
BUT WHEREFORE THOU ALONE? WHEREFORE WITH THEE 4 917
I THEREFORE, I ALONE FIRST UNDERTOOK 4 935
AND ON, METHOUGHT, ALONE I PASS'D THROUGH WAYS 5 50
THE FLAMING SERAPH FEARLESS, THOUGH ALONE 5 875
TO THEE NOT VISIBLE, WHEN I ALONE 6 145
FOUND WORTHY NOT OF LIBERTIE ALONE, 6 420
OR I ALONE AGAINST THEM, SINCE BY STRENGTH 6 820
AND SOLITUDE; YET NOT ALONE, WHILE THOU 7 28
NOT WORDS ALONE PLEAS'D HER. O WHEN MEET NOW 8 57
EARTH SITTING STILL, WHEN SHE ALONE RECEAVES 8 89
WHAT HAPPINESS, WHO CAN ENJOY ALONE, 8 365
OF HAPPINESS, OR NOT? WHO AM ALONE 8 405
THOU IN THY SECRESIE ALTHOUGH ALONE, 8 427
AND FINDE THEE KNOWING NOT OF BEASTS ALONE, 8 438
KNEW IT NOT GOOD FOR MAN TO BE ALONE, 8 445
LIGHT ABOVE LIGHT, FOR THEE ALONE, AS SEEMS, 9 105
FROM THEE ALONE, WHICH ON US BOTH AT ONCE 9 303
ALONE, WITHOUT EXTERIOR HELP SUSTAIND? 9 336
THUS EARLIE, THUS ALONE; HER HEAV'NLY FORME 9 457
OCCASION WHICH NOW SMILES, BEHOLD ALONE 9 480
MIGHT TEMPT ALONE, AND IN HER EARS THE SOUND 9 736
IRRATIONAL TILL THEN. FOR US ALONE 9 766
THIS MY ATTEMPT, I WOULD SUSTAIN ALONE 9 978
POSSESSION OF THE GARDEN; HEE ALONE, 11 222
ALONE FULFILL THE LAW; THY PUNISHMENT 12 404

ALONG
AND TO THE FIERCE CONTENTION BROUGHT ALONG 1 100
FOUR WAYS THIR FLYING MARCH, ALONG THE BANKS 2 574
HENCE THEN, AND EVIL GO WITH THEE ALONG 6 275
I SEND ALONG, RIDE FORTH, AND BID THE DEEP 7 166
AND BEARES THEE SOFT WITH THE SMOOTH AIR ALONG, 8 166
INSEPARABLE MUST WITH MEE ALONG: 10 250

ALOOF
WHILE THE PROMISCUOUS CROUD STOOD YET ALOOF? 1 380

ALOOFF
ALOOFF THE VULGAR CONSTELLATIONS THICK, 3 577

ALOUD
VAUNTING ALOUD, BUT RACKT WITH DEEP DESPARE: 1 126
TH' APOCALYPS, HEARD CRY IN HEAVEN ALOUD, 4 2
THOU FOLLOWING CRYD'ST ALOUD, RETURN FAIRE EVE; 4 481
GABRIEL FROM THE FRONT THUS CALLD ALOUD. 4 865
CAME FLYING, AND IN MID AIRE ALOUD THUS CRI'D. 6 536
I OVERJOYD COULD NOT FORBEAR ALOUD. 8 490
APPROACHING, THUS TO ADAM CALL'D ALOUD. 10 102

ALPE
O'RE MANY A FROZEN, MANY A FIERIE ALPE, 2 620

ALREADIE
ALREADIE BY THY REASONING THIS I GUESS, 8 85
ALREADIE IN PART, THOUGH HID IN GLOOMIEST SHADE, 10 716
SHALL MEET, ALREADIE LINKT AND WEDLOCK-BOUND 10 905
ON ME ALREADIE LOST, MEE THEN THY SELF 10 929

ALREADY
ALREADY KNOWN WHAT HE FOR NEWS HAD THOUGHT 6 20
ALREADY DONE, TO HAVE DISPEOPL'D HEAV'N 7 151
SHOULDST PROPAGAT, ALREADY INFINITE; 8 420
WHICH HE PRESUMES ALREADY VAIN AND VOID, 10 50

ALSO
IN SION ALSO NOT UNSUNG, WHERE STOOD 1 442
HE ALSO AGAINST THE HOUSE OF GOD WAS BOLD: 1 470
IN COURTS AND PALACES HE ALSO REIGNS 1 497
MEN ALSO, AND BY HIS SUGGESTION TAUGHT, 1 685
OUR TORMENTS ALSO MAY IN LENGTH OF TIME 2 274
I ALSO; AT WHICH TIME THIS POWERFUL KEY 2 774
WHEN WILL AND REASON (REASON ALSO IS CHOICE) 3 108
THIR NATURE ALSO TO THY NATURE JOYN; 3 282
WITH THEE THY MANHOOD ALSO TO THIS THRONE; 3 314
THE SAME WHOM JOHN SAW ALSO IN THE SUN: 3 623
THOSE BLOSSOMS ALSO, AND THOSE DROPPING GUMMS, 4 630
AND STARRIE POLE: THOU ALSO MAD'ST THE NIGHT, 4 724
AMBROSIA; ON THAT TREE HE ALSO GAZ'D; 5 57
PARTAKE THOU ALSO; HAPPIE THOUGH THOU ART, 5 75
(FOR WEE HAVE ALSO OUR EEVNING AND OUR MORN, 5 628
THEE ALSO FROM OBEDIENCE, THAT WITH HIM 6 902
THIS ALSO THY REQUEST WITH CAUTION ASKT 7 111

ALSO (CONTINUED)
THEE ALSO HAPPIER, SHALL NOT BE WITHHELD 7 117
WITH HIS GREAT FATHER (FOR HE ALSO WENT 7 588
ABUNDANTLY HIS GIFTS HATH ALSO POUR'D 8 220
THIR LANGUAGE AND THIR WAYES, THEY ALSO KNOW, . . 8 373
IN OUTWARD ALSO HER RESEMBLING LESS 8 543
THY PRAISE HEE ALSO WHO FORBIDS THY USE, . . . 9 750
HAVE ALSO TASTED, AND HAVE ALSO FOUND 9 874
THOU THEREFORE ALSO TASTE, THAT EQUAL LOT . . . 9 881
I ALSO ERR'D IN OVERMUCH ADMIRING 9 1178
THORNS ALSO AND THISTLES IT SHALL BRING THEE FORTH 10 203
NOW ALSO EVIDENCE, BUT STRAIGHT I FELT 10 361
TRUE IS, MEE ALSO HE HATH JUDG'D, OR RATHER . . 10 494
IS HIS WRAUTH ALSO? BE IT, MAN IS NOT SO, . . . 10 795
REACH ALSO OF THE TREE OF LIFE, AND EAT, . . . 11 94
THE WORLD: IN SPIRIT PERHAPS HE ALSO SAW . . . 11 406
T' WHOM MICHAEL THUS, HEE ALSO MOV'D, REPLI'D, . 11 453
OF TEARS AND SORROW A FLOUD THEE ALSO DROWN'D, . 11 757
THE CONQUERD ALSO, AND ENSLAV'D BY WARR 11 797
THIS ALSO SHALL THEY GAIN BY THIR DELAY 12 223
TO GUIDE THEM IN ALL TRUTH, AND ALSO ARME . . . 12 490
TO WHOM THUS ALSO TH' ANGEL LAST REPLI'D: . . . 12 574
HER ALSO I WITH GENTLE DREAMS HAVE CALM'D . . . 12 595
FOR GOD IS ALSO IN SLEEP, AND DREAMS ADVISE, . . 12 611

ALT
IN MOTION OR IN ALT: HIM SOON THEY MET 6 532
IN PARADISE, AND ON A HILL MADE ALT, ... 11 210

ALTAR
THIR ALTARS BY HIS ALTAR, GODS ADOR'D 1 384
HIS RIGHTEOUS ALTAR, BOWING LOWLY DOWN 1 434
GODS ALTAR TO DISPARAGE AND DISPLACE 1 473
OR ALTAR SMOAK'D; YET WHO MORE OFT THEN HEE . . 1 493
OUR ENVIED SOVRAN, AND HIS ALTAR BREATHES . . . 2 244
FROM TH' EARTHS GREAT ALTAR SEND UP SILENT PRAISE 9 195
WITH INCENSE, WHERE THE GOLDEN ALTAR FUM'D, . . 11 18
ITH' MIDST AN ALTAR AS THE LAND-MARK STOOD . . . 11 432
MEN WHO ATTEND THE ALTAR, AND SHOULD MOST . . . 12 354

ALTARS
THIR ALTARS BY HIS ALTAR, GODS ADOR'D 1 384
IN TEMPLES AND AT ALTARS, WHEN THE PRIEST . . . 1 494
SO MANY GRATEFUL ALTARS I WOULD REARE 11 323

ALTER
COULD ALTER HIGH DECREES, I TO THAT PLACE . . . 10 953

ALTERATION
STRANGE ALTERATION. SIN AND DEATH AMAIN . . . 2 1024
STRANGE ALTERATION IN ME, TO DEGREE 9 599

ALTER'D
NOR ALTER'D HIS OFFENCE; YET GOD AT LAST . . . 10 171

ALTERD
ALTERD HER CHEEK. ON WHOM THE ANGEL HAILE . . . 5 385
ADAM, ESTRANG'D IN LOOK AND ALTERD STILE, . . . 9 1132

ALTERNATE
ALTERNATE ALL NIGHT LONG: BUT NOT SO WAK'D . . . 5 657

ALTERNE
THE LESS BY NIGHT ALTERNE: AND MADE THE STARRS, . 7 348

ALTHOUGH
THOU IN THY SECRESIE ALTHOUGH ALONE, ... 8 427

ALWAYES
THERE ALWAYES, BUT DRAWN UP TO HEAV'N SOMTIMES . 3 517
HAD IN REMEMBRANCE ALWAYES WITH DELIGHT; 3 704
FIRST, HIGHEST, HOLIEST, BEST, THOU ALWAYES SEEKST 6 724
TO GLORIFIE THY SON, I ALWAYES THEE, ... 6 725
BUT THE HOT HELL THAT ALWAYES IN HIM BURNES, . . 9 467
IS LOST, WHICH ALWAYES WITH RIGHT REASON DWELLS . 12 84

ALWAYS
WERE ALWAYS DOWNWARD BENT, ADMIRING MORE . . . 1 681

AMAIN
WHAT WHEN WE FLED AMAIN, PURSU'D AND STROOK . . 2 165
STRANGE ALTERATION. SIN AND DEATH AMAIN . . . 2 1024
SENT UP AMAIN; AND NOW THE THICK'ND SKIE . . . 11 742

AMAINE
UP TO THE TROPIC CRAB; THENCE DOWN AMAINE . . . 10 675

AMALTHEA
HID AMALTHEA AND HER FLORID SON 4 278

AMARA
MOUNT AMARA, THOUGH THIS BY SOM SUPPOS'D . . . 4 281

AMARANT
THIR CROWNS INWOVE WITH AMARANT AND GOLD, . . . 3 352
IMMORTAL AMARANT, A FLOUR WHICH ONCE 3 353

AMARANTIN
OF AMARANTIN SHADE, FOUNTAIN OR SPRING, ... 11 78

AMAZ'D
AS WE EREWHILE, ASTOUNDED AND AMAZ'D, ... 1 281
BACK STEPT THOSE TWO FAIRE ANGELS HALF AMAZ'D . . 4 820
YET MORE AMAZ'D UNWARIE THUS REPLY'D. 9 614
MISLEADS TH' AMAZ'D NIGHT-WANDERER FROM HIS WAY . 9 640
THE FATAL TRESPASS DON BY EVE, AMAZ'D, ... 9 889
WAS LEFT HIM, OR FALSE GLITTER: ALL AMAZ'D . . . 10 452

AMAZE
UP LIFTING BORE THEM IN THIR HANDS: AMAZE, . . . 6 646
AND OFT SUPPORTED SO AS SHALL AMAZE 12 496

AMAZEMENT
UNDER AMAZEMENT OF THIR HIDEOUS CHANGE. 1 313
OUT OF THY HEAD I SPRUNG: AMAZEMENT SEIS'D . . . 2 758
HALF SUNK WITH ALL HIS PINES. AMAZEMENT SEIS'D . 6 198

AMAZONIAN
THEY GATHERD, BROAD AS AMAZONIAN TARGE, ... 9 1111

AMBER
ROWLS O'RE ELISIAN FLOURS HER AMBER STREAM; . . 3 359
AMBER, AND COLOURS OF THE SHOWRIE ARCH. 6 759

AMBIENT
SO BEAUTEOUS, OP'NING TO THE AMBIENT LIGHT. . . 6 481
ALL SPACE, THE AMBIENT AIRE WIDE INTERFUS'D . . 7 89

AMBIGUOUS
AMBIGUOUS WORDS AND JEALOUSIES, TO SOUND . . . 5 703
SO SCOFFING IN AMBIGUOUS WORDS HE SCARCE, . . . 6 568
AS PLANTS: AMBIGUOUS BETWEEN SEA AND LAND . . . 7 473

AMBITION
TO REIGN IS WORTH AMBITION THOUGH IN HELL: . . . 1 262
OR CLOS AMBITION VARNISHT O'RE WITH ZEAL. . . . 2 485
TILL PRIDE AND WORSE AMBITION THREW ME DOWN . . 4 40
AMBITION. YET WHY NOT? SOM OTHER POWER . . . 4 61
IN MISERIE; SUCH JOY AMBITION FINDES. 4 92
BUT WHAT WILL NOT AMBITION AND REVENGE 9 168
HEE WITH A CREW, WHOM LIKE AMBITION JOYNS . . . 12 38
OF LUCRE AND AMBITION, AND THE TRUTH 12 511

AMBITIOUS
IF HE OPPOS'D; AND WITH AMBITIOUS AIM 1 41
OF PRESENT PAIN, THAT WITH AMBITIOUS MIND . . . 2 34
BEFORE THY FELLOWS, AMBITIOUS TO WIN 6 160
OF PROUD AMBITIOUS HEART, WHO NOT CONTENT . . . 12 25

AMBROSIA
AMBROSIA; ON THAT TREE HE ALSO GAZ'D; 5 57

AMBROSIAL
AMBROSIAL ODOURS AND AMBROSIAL FLOWERS, ... 2 245
THUS WHILE GOD SPAKE, AMBROSIAL FRAGRANCE FILL'D . 3 135
HIGH EMINENT, BLOOMING AMBROSIAL FRUIT 4 219
OF LIFE AMBROSIAL FRUTAGE BEAR, AND VINES . . . 5 427
NOW WHEN AMBROSIAL NIGHT WITH CLOUDS EXHAL'D . . 5 642
WITH PLANT, FRUIT, FLOUR AMBROSIAL, GEMMS & GOLD, 6 475
NEW GATHERD, AND AMBROSIAL SMELL DIFFUS'D. . . . 9 852
YOUR TRIBES, AND WATER FROM TH' AMBROSIAL FOUNT? . 11 279

AMBUSH
OR AMBUSH FROM THE DEEP. WHAT IF WE FIND . . . 2 344
SUCH AMBUSH HID AMONG SWEET FLOURS AND SHADES . . 9 408

AMENDS
THIS TURN HATH MADE AMENDS; THOU HAST FULFILL'D . 8 491
THE SERPENTS HEAD; PITEOUS AMENDS, UNLESS . . . 10 1032

AMERC'T
MILLIONS OF SPIRITS FOR HIS FAULT AMERC'T . . . 1 609

AMERICAN
COLUMBUS FOUND TH' AMERICAN SO GIRT 9 1116

AMIABLE
HUNG AMIABLE, HESPERIAN FABLES TRUE, ... 4 250
TO MAKE HER AMIABLE: ON SHE CAME, ... 8 484
HOLY, DIVINE, GOOD, AMIABLE, OR SWEET. 9 899

AMIABLIE
LESS WINNING SOFT, LESS AMIABLIE MILDE, ... 4 479

AMID
IN HURDL'D COTES AMID THE FIELD SECURE, ... 4 186
AND ALL AMID THEM STOOD THE TREE OF LIFE, . . . 4 218
AMID THE SUNS BRIGHT CIRCLE WHERE THOU SITST, . . 4 578
SO HILLS AMID THE AIR ENCOUNTERD HILLS 6 664
SO EASILY OBEYD AMID THE CHOICE 7 48
AMID THE WATERS, AND LET IT DIVIDE 7 262
AMID THE GARDEN BY THE TREE OF LIFE, ... 8 326
TO BE RETURND BY NOON AMID THE BOWRE, ... 9 401
AMID THE TREE NOW GOT, WHERE PLENTY HUNG 9 594
UNSEEN AMID THE THRONG: SO VIOLENCE 11 671

AMIDST
- THOUGH WITHOUT NUMBER STILL AMIDST THE HALL 1 791
- OF DARKNESS DO WE DREAD? HOW OFT AMIDST 2 263
- ETERNAL ANARCHIE, AMIDST THE NOISE 2 896
- AMIDST THE GLORIOUS BRIGHTNESS WHERE THOU SIT'ST 3 376
- OR PILOT FROM AMIDST THE CYCLADES 5 264
- AMIDST AS FROM A FLAMING MOUNT, WHOSE TOP 5 598
- THOUGH SINGLE. FROM AMIDST THEM FORTH HE PASSD, 5 903
- (SO CALL HIM, BRIGHTER ONCE AMIDST THE HOST 7 132
- AMIDST HIS CIRCLING SPIRES, THAT ON THE GRASS 9 502
- BUT OF THE FRUIT OF THIS FAIR TREE AMIDST 9 661
- AMIDST IN THUNDER UTTER'D THUS HIS VOICE. 10 33
- TO SAVE HIMSELF AND HOUSHOLD FROM AMIDST 11 820

AMITIE
- AND MUTUAL AMITIE SO STREIGHT, SO CLOSE, 4 376
- COLLATERAL LOVE, AND DEEREST AMITIE. 8 426

AMITY
- WITH SECRET AMITY THINGS OF LIKE KINDE 10 248

AMMIRAL
- OF SOME GREAT AMMIRAL, WERE BUT A WAND, 1 294

AMMON
- WHOM GENTILES AMMON CALL AND LYBIAN JOVE, 4 277

AMMONIAN
- AMMONIAN JOVE, OR CAPITOLINE WAS SEEN, 9 508

AMMONITE
- TO HIS GRIM IDOL. HIM THE AMMONITE 1 396

AMONG
- NOR HAD THEY YET AMONG THE SONS OF EVE 1 364
- AMONG THE NATIONS ROUND, AND DURST ABIDE 1 385
- IN CLUSTERS; THEY AMONG FRESH DEWS AND FLOWERS 1 771
- AMONG HIS ANGELS; AND HIS THRONE IT SELF 2 68
- PRONOUNC'D AMONG THE GODS, AND BY AN OATH, 2 352
- ASTONISHT: NONE AMONG THE CHOICE AND PRIME 2 423
- OTHERS AMONG THE CHIEF MIGHT OFFER NOW 2 469
- AMONG THEMSELVES, AND LEVIE CRUEL WARRES, 2 501
- TO THAT NEW WORLD OF LIGHT AND BLISS, AMONG 2 867
- AND BE THY SELF MAN AMONG MEN ON EARTH, 3 283
- AMONG THE SPIRITS BENEATH, WHOM I SEDUC'D 4 83
- DOWN HE ALIGHTS AMONG THE SPORTFUL HERD 4 396
- AMONG SO MANY SIGNES OF POWER AND RULE 4 429
- AMONG OUR OTHER TORMENTS NOT THE LEAST, 4 510
- AMONG THE BESTIAL HERDS TO RAUNGE, BY THEE 4 754
- TASTE THIS, AND BE HENCEFORTH AMONG THE GODS 5 77
- REASON AS CHIEF; AMONG THESE FANSIE NEXT 5 102
- AMONG THE GROVES, THE FOUNTAINS, AND THE FLOURS 5 126
- AMONG SWEET DEWES AND FLOURS; WHERE ANY ROW 5 212
- AFTER HIS CHARGE RECEIVD; BUT FROM AMONG 5 248
- EASTWARD AMONG THOSE TREES, WHAT GLORIOUS SHAPE 5 309
- BY LIVING STREAMS AMONG THE TREES OF LIFE, 5 652
- AMONG THE SONS OF MORN, WHAT MULTITUDES 5 716
- HAD AUDIENCE, WHEN AMONG THE SERAPHIM 5 804
- AMONG THE FAITHLESS, FAITHFUL ONLY HEE; 5 897
- AMONG INNUMERABLE FALSE, UNMOV'D, 5 898
- AMONG THOSE FRIENDLY POWERS WHO HIM RECEAV'D 6 22
- AMONG THE MIGHTIEST, BENT ON HIGHEST DEEDS, 6 112
- AMONG THE CONSTELLATIONS WARR WERE SPRUNG, 6 312
- FROM FAR WITH THUNDRING NOISE AMONG OUR FOES 6 487
- SO THEY AMONG THEMSELVES IN PLEASANT VEINE 6 628
- HYMNS OF HIGH PRAISE, AND I AMONG THEM CHIEF. 6 745
- AMONG THEM HE ARRIV'D; IN HIS RIGHT HAND 6 835
- AMONG TH' ACCURST, THAT WITHERD ALL THIR STRENGTH, 6 850
- AMONG TH' ANGELIC POWERS, AND THE DEEP FALL 6 898
- OF ANGELS, THEN THAT STARR THE STARRS AMONG) 7 133
- AMONG THE TREES IN PAIRS THEY ROSE, THEY WALK'D: 7 459
- THIR SEASONS: AMONG THESE THE SEAT OF MEN, 7 623
- ROSE, AND WENT FORTH AMONG HER FRUITS AND FLOURS, 8 44
- UP HITHER, FROM AMONG THE TREES APPEER'D 8 313
- AMONG UNEQUALS WHAT SOCIETIE 8 383
- AMONG THE BEASTS NO MATE FOR THEE WAS FOUND. 8 594
- TO MEE SHALL BE THE GLORIE SOLE AMONG 9 135
- SUCH AMBUSH HID AMONG SWEET FLOURS AND SHADES 9 408
- AMONG THICK-WOV'N ARBORETS AND FLOURS 9 437
- AMONG THE PLEASANT VILLAGES AND FARMES 9 448
- IN THIS ENCLOSURE WILD, THESE BEASTS AMONG, 9 543
- A GODDESS AMONG GODS, ADOR'D AND SERV'D 9 547
- AMONG THE TREES ON ILES AND WOODIE SHORES. 9 1118
- AND FROM HIS PRESENCE HID THEMSELVES AMONG 10 100
- YOU TWO THIS WAY, AMONG THESE NUMEROUS ORBS 10 397
- AMONG THE HEATHEN OF THIR PURCHASE GOT, 10 579
- FROM HIS TRANSCENDENT SEAT THE SAINTS AMONG, 10 614
- DAUGHTER OF SIN, AMONG TH' IRRATIONAL, 10 708
- TAKE TO THEE FROM AMONG THE CHERUBIM 11 100
- CELESTIAL, WHETHER AMONG THE THRONES, OR NAM'D 11 296
- STOOD VISIBLE, AMONG THESE PINES HIS VOICE 11 321
- AT LENGTH A REVEREND SIRE AMONG THEM CAME, 11 719
- AMONG THE BUILDERS; EACH TO OTHER CALLS 12 57
- HIS PRESENCE FROM AMONG THEM, AND AVERT 12 108
- AMONG THEM TO SET UP HIS TABERNACLE, 12 247
- AMONG WHOM GOD WILL DEIGNE TO DWELL ON EARTH 12 281
- AMONG THEM; HOW CAN GOD WITH SUCH RESIDE? 12 284
- WILL REIGN AMONG THEM, AS OF THEE BEGOT; 12 286

AMONG (CONTINUED)
- BUT FIRST AMONG THE PRIESTS DISSENSION SPRINGS, 12 353
- HIS FAITHFUL, LEFT AMONG TH' UNFAITHFUL HERD, 12 481

AMONGST
- AMONGST INNUMERABLE STARRS, THAT SHON 3 565

AMOROUS
- IN AMOROUS DITTYES ALL A SUMMERS DAY, 1 449
- AND SWEET RELUCTANT AMOROUS DELAY. 4 311
- SHE ALL NIGHT LONG HER AMOROUS DESCANT SUNG; 4 603
- THE SPIRIT OF LOVE AND AMOROUS DELIGHT. 8 477
- DISPORTING, TILL THE AMOROUS BIRD OF NIGHT 8 518
- OF AMOROUS INTENT, WELL UNDERSTOOD 9 1035
- OPPRESS'D THEM, WEARIED WITH THIR AMOROUS PLAY. 9 1045
- SOFT AMOROUS DITTIES, AND IN DANCE CAME ON: 11 584
- ROVE WITHOUT REIN, TILL IN THE AMOROUS NET 11 586

AMOURS
- CASUAL FRUITION, NOR IN COURT AMOURS 4 767

AMPHISBAENA
- SCORPION AND ASP, AND AMPHISBAENA DIRE, 10 524

AMPLE
- WITHIN, HER AMPLE SPACES, O'RE THE SMOOTH 1 725
- I THROUGH THE AMPLE AIR IN TRIUMPH HIGH 3 254
- TRANSFUS'D ON THEE HIS AMPLE SPIRIT RESTS. 3 389
- THAT MADE US, AND FOR US THIS AMPLE WORLD 4 413
- AND ON HER AMPLE SQUARE FROM SIDE TO SIDE 5 393
- OF TENFOLD ADAMANT, HIS AMPLE SHIELD 6 255
- A BROAD AND AMPLE RODE, WHOSE DUST IS GOLD 7 577
- AND GAZ'D A WHILE THE AMPLE SKIE, TILL RAIS'D 8 258

AMPLER
- DIMM ERST, DILATED SPIRITS, AMPLER HEART, 9 876

AMPLEST
- STRETCHT OUT TO THE AMPLEST REACH OF PROSPECT LAY. 11 380

AMPLIER
- NOW AMPLIER KNOWN THY SAVIOUR AND THY LORD, 12 544

AMPLITUDE
- OF AMPLITUDE ALMOST IMMENSE, WITH STARR'S 7 620

AMPLY
- SO AMPLY, AND WITH HANDS SO LIBERAL 8 362
- AMPLY HAVE MERITED OF ME, OF ALL 10 388

AMRAMS
- OF AMRAMS SON IN EGYPTS EVILL DAY 1 339

AMUS'D
- COLLECTED STOOD WITHIN OUR THOUGHTS AMUS'D, 6 581
- SUCH AS WE MIGHT PERCEIVE AMUS'D THEM ALL, 6 623

ANARCH
- THUS SATAN; AND HIM THUS THE ANARCH OLD 2 988

ANARCHIE
- ETERNAL ANARCHIE, AMIDST THE NOISE 2 896
- THROUGH HIS WILDE ANARCHIE, SO HUGE A ROUT 6 873
- WIDE ANARCHIE OF CHAOS DAMP AND DARK 10 283

ANCESTOR
- TO WHOM OUR GENERAL ANCESTOR REPLI'D. 4 659
- MY HEAD, ILL FARE OUR ANCESTOR IMPURE, 10 735
- THE BALME OF LIFE. TO WHOM OUR ANCESTOR. 11 546

ANCESTORS
- AND CHAOS, ANCESTORS OF NATURE, HOLD 2 895

ANCHOR
- WITH FIXED ANCHOR IN HIS SKALY RIND 1 206

ANCHORS
- OR PINNACE ANCHORS IN A CRAGGY BAY 2 289

ANCIENT
- BY ANCIENT TARSUS HELD, OR THAT SEA-BEAST 1 200
- IN ANCIENT GREECE; AND IN AUSONIAN LAND 1 739
- (IF ANCIENT AND PROPHETIC FAME IN HEAV'N 2 346
- NEERER OUR ANCIENT SEAT; PERHAPS IN VIEW 2 394
- OF ANCIENT PILE; ALL ELSE DEEP SNOW AND ICE, 2 591
- CHAOS AND ANCIENT NIGHT, I COME NO SPY, 2 970
- ERECT THE STANDARD THERE OF ANCIENT NIGHT; 2 986
- FIRST FROM THE ANCIENT WORLD THOSE GIANTS CAME 3 464
- SEEM'D THIR PETITION, THEN WHEN TH' ANCIENT PAIR 11 10
- IN FABLES OLD, LESS ANCIENT YET THEN THESE, 11 11
- THE ANCIENT SIRE DESCENDS WITH ALL HIS TRAIN; 11 862

ANCIENTLY
- WE MEAN TO HOLD WHAT ANCIENTLY WE CLAIM 5 723

ANDROMEDA
- ANDROMEDA FARR OFF ATLANTIC SEAS 3 559

ANGEL

SO SPAKE TH' APOSTATE ANGEL, THOUGH IN PAIN, . . . 1 125
SAID THEN THE LOST ARCH-ANGEL, THIS THE SEAT . . 1 243
HIS LEGIONS, ANGEL FORMS, WHO LAY INTRANS'T . . 1 301
LESS THEN ARCH ANGEL RUIND, AND TH' EXCESS . . . 1 593
ABOVE THEM ALL TH' ARCH ANGEL: BUT HIS FACE . . 1 600
ART THOU THAT TRAITOR ANGEL, ART THOU HEE, . . . 2 689
THAT MIGHTY LEADING ANGEL, WHO OF LATE 2 991
SAW WITHIN KENN A GLORIOUS ANGEL STAND, ... 3 622
HE DREW NOT NIGH UNHEARD, THE ANGEL BRIGHT, . . 3 645
TH' ARCH-ANGEL URIEL, ONE OF THE SEAV'N 3 648
FOR NEITHER MAN NOR ANGEL CAN DISCERN 3 682
FAIR ANGEL, THY DESIRE WHICH TENDS TO KNOW . . . 3 694
ME SOME INFERIOUR ANGEL, I HAD STOOD 4 59
OF GOD OR ANGEL, FOR THEY THOUGHT NO ILL: . . . 4 320
WHAT DAY THE GENIAL ANGEL TO OUR SIRE 4 712
THUS HE IN SCORN. THE WARLIKE ANGEL MOV'D, . . . 4 902
INSULTING ANGEL, WELL THOU KNOWST I STOOD . . . 4 926
TO WHOM THE WARRIOUR ANGEL, SOON REPLI'D. . . . 4 946
TO ENTERTAIN OUR ANGEL GUEST, AS HEE 5 328
ALTERD HER CHEEK. ON WHOM THE ANGEL HAILE . . . 5 385
TO WHOM THE ANGEL. THEREFORE WHAT HE GIVES . . . 5 404
THE ANGEL, NOR IN MIST, THE COMMON GLOSS . . . 5 435
TO WHOM THE ANGEL. SON OF HEAV'N AND EARTH, . . 5 519
IF NOT THE FIRST ARCH-ANGEL, GREAT IN POWER, . . . 5 660
SO SPAKE THE FALSE ARCH-ANGEL, AND INFUS'D . . . 5 694
SO SPAKE THE FERVENT ANGEL, BUT HIS ZEALE . . . 5 849
ALL NIGHT THE DREADLESS ANGEL UNPURSU'D 6 1
AT FIRST, THAT ANGEL SHOULD WITH ANGEL WARR, . . . 6 92
FROM FLIGHT, SEDITIOUS ANGEL, TO RECEAVE . . . 6 152
TH' ARCH-ANGEL TRUMPET; THROUGH THE VAST OF HEAVEN 6 203
THE GREAT ARCH-ANGEL FROM HIS WARLIKE TOILE . . 6 257
BY THOUSANDS, ANGEL ON ARCH-ANGEL ROWL'D; . . . 6 594
THE AFFABLE ARCH-ANGEL, HAD FOREWARN'D 7 41
AND THUS THE GODLIKE ANGEL ANSWERD MILDE. . . . 7 110
THE ANGEL ENDED, AND IN ADAMS EARE 8 1
BEFORE THE ANGEL, AND OF HIM TO ASK 8 53
FROM MAN OR ANGEL THE GREAT ARCHITECT 8 72
INTELLIGENCE OF HEAV'N, ANGEL SERENE, ... 8 181
TO WHOM THE ANGEL WITH CONTRACTED BROW. 8 560
TO WHOM THE ANGEL WITH A SMILE THAT GLOW'D . . . 8 618
SO PARTED THEY, THE ANGEL UP TO HEAV'N 8 652
NO MORE OF TALK WHERE GOD OR ANGEL GUEST . . . 9 1
SUBJECTED TO HIS SERVICE ANGEL WINGS, ... 9 155
AND FROM THE PARTING ANGEL OVER-HEARD 9 276
HENCEFORTH OF GOD OR ANGEL, EARST WITH JOY . . . 9 1081
SATAN IN LIKENESS OF AN ANGEL BRIGHT 10 327
IN SHEW PLEBEIAN ANGEL MILITANT 10 442
HE ENDED; AND TH' ARCH-ANGEL SOON DREW NIGH, . . 11 238
WHOM THUS THE ANGEL INTERRUPTED MILDE. 11 286
BUT HIM THE GENTLE ANGEL BY THE HAND 11 421
DISMAI'D, AND THUS IN HASTE TO TH' ANGEL CRI'D. . 11 449
TRUE OPENER OF MINE EYES, PRIME ANGEL BLEST, . . 11 598
SAID TH' ANGEL, WHO SHOULD BETTER HOLD HIS PLACE . 11 635
BY TH' ANGEL, ON THY FEET THOU STOODST AT LAST, . 11 759
AND SCARCE TO TH' ANGEL UTTERDST THUS THY PLAINT. 11 762
THOUGH PRESENT IN HIS ANGEL, WHO SHALL GOE . . . 12 201
CONDUCTED BY HIS ANGEL TO THE LAND 12 259
HIS PLACE OF BIRTH A SOLEMN ANGEL TELLS 12 364
BE SURE THEY WILL, SAID TH' ANGEL; BUT FROM HEAV'N 12 485
TO WHOM THUS ALSO TH' ANGEL LAST REPLI'D: . . . 12 574
IN EITHER HAND THE HASTNING ANGEL CAUGHT . . . 12 637

ANGELIC

CHIEF OF TH' ANGELIC GUARDS, AWAITING NIGHT; . . . 4 550
WHILE THUS HE SPAKE, TH' ANGELIC SQUADRON BRIGHT . 4 977
HERE, HAPPIE CREATURE, FAIR ANGELIC EVE, ... 5 74
FLEW THROUGH THE MIDST OF HEAV'N; TH' ANGELIC
QUIRES 5 251
WHOM THUS THE ANGELIC VERTUE ANSWERD MILDE. . . 5 371
MY SELF AND ALL TH' ANGELIC HOST THAT STAND . . 5 535
(SUCH ARE THE COURTS OF GOD) TH' ANGELIC THRONG . 5 650
OR ALL ANGELIC NATURE JOIND IN ONE, ... 5 834
WHERE ERST WAS THICKEST FIGHT, TH' ANGELIC THRONG, 6 308
AMONG TH' ANGELIC POWERS, AND THE DEEP FALL . . 6 898
ANGELIC HARMONIES: THE EARTH, THE AIRE 7 560
ABOUT HER, AS A GUARD ANGELIC PLAC'T. 8 559
TH' ANGELIC NAME, AND THINNER LEFT THE THRONG . . 9 142
ANGELIC, BUT MORE SOFT, AND FEMININE, ... 9 458
TH' ANGELIC GUARDS ASCENDED, MUTE AND SAD . . . 10 18
TO SOUND AT GENERAL DOOM. TH' ANGELIC BLAST . . 11 76

ANGELICAL

WITH NOTES ANGELICAL TO MANY A HARP 2 548
BETWIXT TH' ANGELICAL AND HUMAN KINDE: 3 462

ANGELS

OF REBEL ANGELS, BY WHOSE AID ASPIRING 1 38
AT ONCE AS FAR AS ANGELS KENN HE VIEWS 1 59
SO NUMBERLESS WERE THOSE BAD ANGELS SEEN . . . 1 344
TEARS SUCH AS ANGELS WEEP, BURST FORTH: AT LAST . 1 620
WHERE SCEPTER'D ANGELS HELD THIR RESIDENCE, . . . 1 734
AMONG HIS ANGELS; AND HIS THRONE IT SELF . . . 2 68
OF ANGELS WATCHING ROUND? HERE HE HAD NEED . . . 2 413
GOD AND GOOD ANGELS GUARD BY SPECIAL GRACE. . . 2 1033
THE SUMMONING ARCH-ANGELS TO PROCLAIME 3 325
BAD MEN AND ANGELS, THEY ARRAIGND SHALL SINK . . 3 331
THE MULTITUDE OF ANGELS WITH A SHOUT 3 345

ANGELS (CONTINUED)

THOU DROV'ST OF WARRING ANGELS DISARRAID. . . . 3 396
ANGELS ASCENDING AND DESCENDING, BANDS 3 511
WAFTED BY ANGELS, OR FLEW O'RE THE LAKE 3 521
ON HIGH BEHESTS HIS ANGELS TO AND FRO 3 533
BACK STEPT THOSE TWO FAIRE ANGELS HALF AMAZ'D . . 4 820
ANGELS, FOR YEE BEHOLD HIM, AND WITH SONGS . . . 5 161
OF ANGELS UNDER WATCH; AND TO HIS STATE, . . . 5 288
FOOD NOT OF ANGELS, YET ACCEPTED SO, ... 5 465
WITH ANGELS MAY PARTICIPATE, AND FIND 5 494
OF ANGELS BY IMPERIAL SUMMONS CALL'D, ... 5 584
HEAR ALL YE ANGELS, PROGENIE OF LIGHT, ... 5 600
WITH ANGELS FOOD, AND RUBIED NECTAR FLOWS . . . 5 633
MILLIONS OF FIERCE ENCOUNTRING ANGELS FOUGHT . . 6 220
SO SPAKE THE PRINCE OF ANGELS; TO WHOM THUS . . 6 281
OF ANGELS, CAN RELATE, OR TO WHAT THINGS . . . 6 298
BY ANGELS MANY AND STRONG, WHO INTERPOS'D . . . 6 336
ANGELS CONTENTED WITH THIR FAME IN HEAV'N . . . 6 375
MICHAEL AND HIS ANGELS PREVALENT 6 411
UP ROSE THE VICTOR ANGELS, AND TO ARMS 6 525
WHICH GOD HATH IN HIS MIGHTY ANGELS PLAC'D) . . 6 638
ALOFT BY ANGELS BORN, HIS SIGN IN HEAV'N: . . . 6 776
YE ANGELS ARM'D, THIS DAY FROM BATTEL REST; . . 6 802
OF ANGELS, THEN THAT STARR THE STARRS AMONG) . . 7 133
THEN FROM THE GIANT ANGELS; THEE THAT DAY . . . 7 605
MORE ANGELS TO CREATE, IF THEY AT LEAST 9 146
ANGELS, NOR THINK SUPERFLUOUS OTHERS AID. . . . 9 308
GUILTLESS OF FIRE HAD FORMD, OR ANGELS BROUGHT. . 9 392
BY ANGELS NUMBERLESS, THY DAILY TRAIN. 9 548
BUT TO BE GODS, OR ANGELS DEMI-GODS. 9 937
ASSEMBL'D ANGELS, AND YE POWERS RETURN'D . . . 10 34
HIS MIGHTIE ANGELS GAVE THEM SEVERAL CHARGE, . . 10 650
SOME SAY HE BID HIS ANGELS TURNE ASCANSE . . . 10 668
WITH MEN AS ANGELS WITHOUT FEMININE, ... 10 893
AS HOW WITH PECCANT ANGELS LATE THEY SAW; . . . 11 70
NOT THAT MORE GLORIOUS, WHEN THE ANGELS MET . . 11 213
OF SQUADROND ANGELS HEAR HIS CAROL SUNG, . . . 12 367

ANGER

THE VASSALS OF HIS ANGER, WHEN THE SCOURGE . . . 2 90
THEM IN HIS ANGER, WHOM HIS ANGER SAVES 2 158
HIS ANGER, AND PERHAPS THUS FARR REMOV'D 2 211
I OFFER, ON MEE LET THINE ANGER FALL; 3 237
OF ANGER SHALL REMAIN, BUT PEACE ASSUR'D, . . . 3 263
CAN EQUAL ANGER INFINITE PROVOK'T. 4 916
ANGER AND JUST REBUKE, AND JUDGEMENT GIV'N, . . . 9 10
AND ANGER WOULDST RESENT THE OFFER'D WRONG, . . . 9 300
BEGAN TO RISE, HIGH PASSIONS, ANGER, HATE, . . . 9 1123
ANGER, AND OBSTINACIE, AND HATE, AND GUILE. . . 10 114
AS ONE DISARM'D, HIS ANGER ALL HE LOST, . . . 10 945
FROM HIM, AND ALL HIS ANGER TO FORGET. 11 878

ANGERS

FOR ANGERS SAKE, FINITE TO INFINITE 10 802

ANGOLA

OF CONGO, AND ANGOLA FARDEST SOUTH; 11 401

ANGRIE

FOR THOUGH I FLED HIM ANGRIE, YET RECALL'D . . . 11 330

ANGRY

BUT SEE THE ANGRY VICTOR HATH RECALL'D 1 169
FROM HEAV'N, THEY FABL'D, THROWN BY ANGRY JOVE . 1 741
LET THIS BE GOOD, WHETHER OUR ANGRY FOE 2 152
WHEN ANGRY MOST HE SEEM'D AND MOST SEVERE, . . . 10 1095

ANGUISH

ANGUISH AND DOUBT AND FEAR AND SORROW AND PAIN . 1 558
PAIN FOR A WHILE OR ANGUISH, AND EXCITE 2 567
GNASHING FOR ANGUISH AND DESPITE AND SHAME . . . 6 340
THAT KEPT THIR WATCH; THENCE FULL OF ANGUISH
DRIV'N, ... 9 62
NOT THY CONTEMPT, BUT ANGUISH AND REGRET . . . 10 1018
FAMIN AND ANGUISH WILL AT LAST CONSUME 11 778

ANIMAL

TH' ANIMAL SPIRITS THAT FROM PURE BLOOD ARISE . . 4 805
TO VITAL SPIRITS ASPIRE, TO ANIMAL, ... 5 484

ANIMALS

WHILE OTHER ANIMALS UNACTIVE RANGE, ... 4 621

ANIMATE

WHICH TWO GREAT SEXES ANIMATE THE WORLD, ... 8 151
OF CREATURES ANIMATE WITH GRADUAL LIFE 9 112

ANNEXT

BUT JUSTICE, AND SOME FATAL CURSE ANNEXT . . . 12 99

ANNIHILATING

CANNOT BUT BY ANNIHILATING DIE; 6 347

ANNOY

NOR STOOD UNMINDFUL ABDIEL TO ANNOY 6 369
WHERE HOUSES THICK AND SEWERS ANNOY THE AIRE, . . 9 446

ANNUAL
WHOSE ANNUAL WOUND IN LEBANON ALLUR'D 1 447
HER ANNUAL VOIAGE, BORN ON WINDES; THE AIRE 7 431
THIS ANNUAL HUMBLING CERTAIN NUMBER'D DAYS, 10 576

ANNULS
ANNULS THY DOOM, THE DEATH THOU SHOULDST HAVE DY'D, 12 428

ANOINTED
ANOINTED UNIVERSAL KING; ALL POWER 3 317
HIM HAVE ANOINTED, WHOM YE NOW BEHOLD 5 605
MESSIAH KING ANOINTED, COULD NOT BEARE 5 664
OF KING ANOINTED, FOR WHOM ALL THIS HASTE 5 777
THESE TIDINGS CARRIE TO TH' ANOINTED KING; 5 870
TO HONOUR HIS ANOINTED SON AVENG'D 6 676
GOD AND MESSIAH HIS ANOINTED KING. 6 718
ANOINTED KING MESSIAH MIGHT BE BORN 12 359

ANON
WITH SCATTER'D ARMS AND ENSIGNS, TILL ANON 1 325
OF DEPTH IMMEASURABLE: ANON THEY MOVE 1 549
ANON OUT OF THE EARTH A FABRICK HUGE 1 710
BY PLACE OR CHOICE THE WORTHIEST; THEY ANON 1 759
REFREIN'D HIS TONGUE BLASPHEMOUS; BUT ANON 6 360
HEAV'N WITNESS THOU ANON, WHILE WE DISCHARGE 6 564
RUSTIC, OF GRASSIE SORD; THITHER ANON 11 433
TO COUNCIL IN THE CITIE GATES: ANON 11 661
ANON DRIE GROUND APPEERS, AND FROM HIS ARKE 11 861
THE SERPENTS HEAD; WHEREOF TO THEE ANON 12 150

ANOTHER
ADVISING PEACE: FOR SUCH ANOTHER FIELD 2 292
ERR NOT) ANOTHER WORLD, THE HAPPY SEAT 2 347
ANOTHER PART IN SQUADRONS AND GROSS BANDS, 2 570
NOW LATELY HEAVEN AND EARTH, ANOTHER WORLD 2 1004
ANOTHER SIDE, UMBRAGEOUS GROTS AND CAVES 4 257
SMOOTH LAKE, THAT TO ME SEEMD ANOTHER SKIE. 4 459
COMES THIS WAY MOVING; SEEMS ANOTHER MORN 5 310
THE SECRETS OF ANOTHER WORLD, PERHAPS 5 569
ANOTHER NOW HATH TO HIMSELF INGROSS'T 5 775
STOOD RANKT OF SERAPHIM ANOTHER ROW 6 604
ANOTHER WORLD, OUT OF ONE MAN A RACE 7 155
WITNESS THIS NEW-MADE WORLD, ANOTHER HEAV'N 7 617
AND ADAM WEDDED TO ANOTHER EVE, 9 828
SHOULD GOD CREATE ANOTHER EVE, AND I 9 911
ANOTHER RIB AFFORD, YET LOSS OF THEE 9 912
AND NOW PREPARE THEE FOR ANOTHER SIGHT. 11 555
BUT NOW PREPARE THEE FOR ANOTHER SCENE. 11 637
DEPOPULATION; THEE ANOTHER FLOUD, 11 756
THAT GOD VOUTSAFES TO RAISE ANOTHER WORLD 11 877

ANOTHERS
IMPARADIS'T IN ONE ANOTHERS ARMS 4 506
THIR OWN FAITH NOT ANOTHERS: FOR ON EARTH 12 528

ANOUGH
YET NOT ANOUGH HAD PRACTISD TO DECEIVE 4 124
ANOUGH IS LEFT BESIDES TO SEARCH AND KNOW. 7 125
ANOUGH TO BEARE; THOSE NOW, THAT WERE DISPENST 11 766
MORE THEN ANOUGH, THAT TEMPERANCE MAY BE TRI'D: 11 805

ANOW
MAN HAD NOT HELLISH FOES ANOW BESIDES, 2 504

ANSWER
IN HIS UPRIGHTNESS ANSWER THUS RETURND. 3 693
MADE ANSWER. MIGHTIE FATHER, THOU THY FOES 5 735
I HAVE RECEAV'D, TO ANSWER THY DESIRE 7 119
THIS HAPPIE LIGHT, WHEN ANSWER NONE RETURN'D, 8 285
THIS ANSWER FROM THE GRATIOUS VOICE DIVINE. 8 436
TO WHOM MILD ANSWER ADAM THUS RETURN'D. 9 226
NOT UNAMAZ'D SHE THUS IN ANSWER SPAKE. 9 552
TO ANSWER, AND RESOUND FARR OTHER SONG. 10 862

ANSWERABLE
IF ANSWERABLE STYLE I CAN OBTAINE 9 20
DEEDS TO THY KNOWLEDGE ANSWERABLE, ADD FAITH, 12 582

ANSWER'D
AND HIM THUS ANSWER'D SOON HIS BOLD COMPEER. 1 127
THUS ANSWER'D. LEADER OF THOSE ARMIES BRIGHT, 1 272
ANSWER'D. I KNOW THEE, STRANGER, WHO THOU ART, 2 990
TO WHOM THUS RAPHAEL ANSWER'D HEAV'NLY MEEK. 8 217
WHERETO TH' ALMIGHTY ANSWER'D, NOT DISPLEAS'D. 8 398
HE CEAS'D, I LOWLY ANSWER'D. TO ATTAINE 8 412
ANSWER'D. LET IT SUFFICE THEE THAT THOU KNOW'ST 8 620
EXPRESS'D, AND THUS DIVINELY ANSWER'D MILDE. 10 67
WHENCE ADAM FAULTRING LONG, THUS ANSWER'D BRIEF. 10 115
WELL PLEAS'D, BUT ANSWER'D NOT; FOR NOW TOO NIGH 12 625

ANSWERD
SOON LEARND, NOW MILDER, AND THUS ANSWERD SMOOTH. 2 816
TO WHICH THE FIEND THUS ANSWERD FROWNING STERN. 4 924
RELATED, AND THUS ADAM ANSWERD SAD. 5 94
WHOM THUS THE ANGELIC VERTUE ANSWERD MILDE. 5 371
ENCOMPASS'D ROUND WITH FOES, THUS ANSWERD BOLD. 5 876
THUS ANSWERD. ILL FOR THEE, BUT IN WISHT HOURE 6 150
AND THUS THE GODLIKE ANGEL ANSWERD MILDE. 7 110

ANSWERD (CONTINUED)
WHOM THUS THE MEAGER SHADOW ANSWERD SOON. 10 264
WHOM THUS THE PRINCE OF DARKNESS ANSWERD GLAD. 10 383
WHOM THUS THE SIN-BORN MONSTER ANSWERD SOON. 10 596
THIR MAKERS IMAGE, ANSWERD MICHAEL, THEN 11 515

ANSWERING
PLEAS'D IT RETURND AS SOON WITH ANSWERING LOOKS 4 464
TO WHOM THUS ZEPHON, ANSWERING SCORN WITH SCORN. 4 834
AND CLOUDIE IN ASPECT THUS ANSWERING SPAKE. 6 450
AND THUS THE FILIAL GODHEAD ANSWERING SPAKE. 6 722
ANSWERING HIS GREAT IDEA. UP HE RODE 7 557

ANTAGONIST
ALONE TH' ANTAGONIST OF HEAV'N, NOR LESS 2 509
ANTAGONIST OF HEAV'NS ALMIGHTIE KING) 10 387

ANTARTIC
DOWNWARD AS FARR ANTARTIC; AND IN LENGTH 9 79

ANTIPATHIE
DEATH INTRODUC'D THROUGH FIERCE ANTIPATHIE: 10 709

ANXIOUS
GOD HATH BID DWELL FARR OFF ALL ANXIOUS CARES, 8 185

ANY
THERE REST, IF ANY REST CAN HARBOUR THERE, 1 185
THESE PAST, IF ANY PASS, THE VOID PROFOUND 2 438
THAT DISMAL WORLD, IF ANY CLIME PERHAPS 2 572
HIM COUNTERFET, IF ANY EYE BEHELD. 4 117
ANY, BUT GOD ALONE, TO VALUE RIGHT 4 202
AMONG SWEET DEWES AND FLOURS; WHERE ANY ROW 5 212
IN BOWRE AND FIELD HE SOUGHT, WHERE ANY TUFT 9 417
IF ANY BE, OF TASTING THIS FAIR FRUIT, 9 972

AONIAN
ABOVE TH' AONIAN MOUNT, WHILE IT PURSUES 1 15

APACE
SHALL LEAD THIR LIVES, AND MULTIPLIE APACE, 12 17

APART
OTHERS APART SAT ON A HILL RETIR'D, 2 557

APATHIE
PASSION AND APATHIE, AND GLORY AND SHAME, 2 564

APE
SO WELL CONVERSE, NOR WITH THE OX THE APE; 8 396

APOCALYPS
TH' APOCALYPS, HEARD CRY IN HEAVEN ALOUD, 4 2

APOLOGIE
CAME PROLOGUE, AND APOLOGIE TO PROMPT, 9 854

APOSTASIE
APOSTASIE, BY WHAT BEFELL IN HEAVEN 7 43

APOSTAT
TH' APOSTAT, AND MORE HAUGHTY THUS REPLI'D. 5 852
TH' APOSTAT IN HIS SUN-BRIGHT CHARIOT SATE 6 100
APOSTAT, STILL THOU ERRST, NOR END WILT FIND 6 172
OF SPIRITS APOSTAT AND THIR COUNSELS VAINE 7 610

APOSTATE
SO SPAKE TH' APOSTATE ANGEL, THOUGH IN PAIN, 1 125

APOSTATES
TO THOSE APOSTATES, LEAST THE LIKE BEFALL 7 44

APOSTLES
POWRD FIRST ON HIS APOSTLES, WHOM HE SENDS 12 498

APPAID
SO ONELY CAN HIGH JUSTICE REST APPAID. 12 401

APPARENT
APPARENT QUEEN UNVAILD HER PEERLESS LIGHT, 4 608
OR TO EACH OTHER, BUT APPARENT GUILT, 10 112

APPARITION
WHOSE INWARD APPARITION GENTLY MOV'D 8 293
A GLORIOUS APPARITION, HAD NOT DOUBT 11 211

APPEAR
CELESTIAL VERTUES RISING, WILL APPEAR 2 15
DROPT MANNA, AND COULD MAKE THE WORSE APPEAR 2 113
BEFORE THIR EYES IN SUDDEN VIEW APPEAR 2 890
ACCOUNTABLE MADE HASTE TO MAKE APPEAR 10 29
BEFORE THEE SHALL APPEAR; THAT THOU MAYST KNOW 11 475

APPEARANCE
MEER SERPENT IN APPEARANCE, FORTH WAS COME, 9 413

APPEARANCES
HIS BRIGHT APPEARANCES, OR FOOT STEP-TRACE? 11 329

APPEAR'D
AND SUCH APPEAR'D IN HUE, AS WHEN THE FORCE . . 1 230
WHOM HE HAD VANQUISHT. AFTER THESE APPEAR'D . . 1 476
DOWN CAST AND DAMP, YET SUCH WHEREIN APPEAR'D . . 1 523
APPEAR'D, AND SERRIED SHIELDS IN THICK ARRAY . . 1 548
ALL HER ORIGINAL BRIGHTNESS, NOR APPEAR'D . . . 1 592
WHERE OBVIOUS DUTIE EREWHILE APPEAR'D UNSAUGHT: . 10 106

APPEARD
WHERE ONELY WHAT THEY NEEDS MUST DO, APPEARD, . . 3 105
BEFORE HIS EYES APPEARD, SAD, NOYSOM, DARK, . . 11 478

APPEARS
AS WHEN TO WARN PROUD CITIES WARR APPEARS . . . 2 533
OF LIGHT APPEARS, AND FROM THE WALLS OF HEAV'N . 2 1035
CROOKED BY NATURE, BENT, AS NOW APPEARS, . . . 10 885
SO LAW APPEARS IMPERFET, AND BUT GIV'N 12 300

APPEAS'D
IN GLORY AS OF OLD, TO HIM APPEAS'D 10 226
MAYST COVER: WELL MAY THEN THY LORD APPEAS'D . . 11 257
DISTENDED AS THE BROW OF GOD APPEAS'D, ... 11 880

APPEASE
THIR SINFUL STATE, AND TO APPEASE BETIMES . . . 3 186
HE TO APPEASE THY WRAUTH, AND END THE STRIFE . . 3 406
AND TEMPT NOT THESE; BUT HAST'N TO APPEASE . . . 5 846
THEM FULLY SATISFIED, AND THEE APPEASE. 10 79
ALL OF ME THEN SHALL DIE: LET THIS APPEASE . . . 10 792
BY PRAYER TH' OFFENDED DEITIE TO APPEASE, . . . 11 149
CANNOT APPEASE, NOR MAN THE MORAL PART 12 298

APPEER
OF SERVILE POMP. OUR GREATNESS WILL APPEER . . 2 257
FARR OFF THE FLYING FIEND: AT LAST APPEER . . . 2 643
SHALT IN THE SKY APPEER, AND FROM THEE SEND . . 3 324
DARK WITH EXCESSIVE BRIGHT THY SKIRTS APPEER, . . 3 380
WITHIN THESE HALLOWD LIMITS THOU APPEER, . . . 4 964
INTO ONE PLACE, AND LET DRY LAND APPEER. . . . 7 278
IMMEDIATELY THE MOUNTAINS HUGE APPEER 7 285
AND PAVEMENT STARRS, AS STARRS TO THEE APPEER, . 7 578
SHALL I APPEER? SHALL I TO HIM MAKE KNOWN . . . 9 817
INHOSPITABLE APPEER AND DESOLATE, ... 11 306
AND NOW THE TOPS OF HILLS AS ROCKS APPEER; . . . 11 852
LONGER ON EARTH THEN CERTAINE TIMES TO APPEER . . 12 437
APPEER OF RESPIRATION TO THE JUST, ... 12 540

APPEERANCES
TO SAVE APPEERANCES, HOW GIRD THE SPHEAR . . . 8 82

APPEER'D
HIS LOOK SUSPENCE, AWAITING WHO APPEER'D . . . 2 418
FARR IN TH' HORIZON TO THE NORTH APPEER'D . . . 6 79
ON HIS GREAT EXPEDITION NOW APPEER'D, ... 7 193
APPEER'D NOT: OVER ALL THE FACE OF EARTH . . . 7 278
WITH THOUSAND THOUSAND STARRES, THAT THEN APPEER'D 7 383
THE GRASSIE CLODS NOW CALV'D, NOW HALF APPEER'D . 7 463
OF COMMONALTIE: SWARMING NEXT APPEER'D 7 489
UP HITHER, FROM AMONG THE TREES APPEER'D . . . 8 313
AND OF THIR VAIN CONTEST APPEER'D NO END. . . . 9 1189
AND SHAPE STARR BRIGHT APPEER'D, OR BRIGHTER, CLAD 10 450

APPEERD
DIVINE COMPASSION VISIBLY APPEERD, ... 3 141
PATRON OR INTERCESSOR NONE APPEERD, ... 3 219
AT TOP WHEREOF, BUT FARR MORE RICH APPEERD . . . 3 504
APPEERD, WITH GAY ENAMELD COLOURS MIXT; 4 149
A SHAPE WITHIN THE WATRY GLEAM APPEERD 4 461
FORTHWITH FROM ALL THE ENDS OF HEAV'N APPEERD . . 5 586
AS NOT OF POWER, AT ONCE; NOR ODDS APPEERD . . . 6 319
NOW WHEN FAIR MORN ORIENT IN HEAV'N APPEERD . . 6 524
A WHILE, BUT SUDDENLY AT HEAD APPEERD 6 556
BUT SOON OBSCUR'D WITH SMOAK, ALL HEAV'N APPEERD, 6 585
BEFORE THE HILLS APPEERD, OR FOUNTAIN FLOW'D, . . 7 8
NOR THAT WHICH ON THE FLAMING MOUNT APPEERD . . 11 216
ON THIS MOUNT HE APPEERD, UNDER THIS TREE . . . 11 320
LOVES HARBINGER APPEERD; THEN ALL IN HEAT . . . 11 589

APPEERING
DELOS OR SAMOS FIRST APPEERING KENNS 5 265
LEAST BY SOME FAIRE APPEERING GOOD SURPRIS'D . . 9 354

APPEERS
WORTH WAITING, SINCE OUR PRESENT LOT APPEERS . . 2 223
AND NOW A STRIPLING CHERUBE HE APPEERS, ... 3 636
WHICH FROM HIS DARKSOM PASSAGE NOW APPEERS, . . 4 232
FOR AUGHT APPEERS, AND ON THIR ORBS IMPOSE . . . 8 30
NOT IN THEMSELVES, ALL THIR KNOWN VERTUE APPEERS . 9 110
MUCH REASON, AND IN THIR ACTIONS OFT APPEERS, . . 9 559
ANON DRIE GROUND APPEERS, AND FROM HIS ARKE . . 11 861

APPERE
WHO SLEW HIS BROTHER; STUDIOUS THEY APPERE . . . 11 609

APPERTAINE
ORDAINE THEM LAWES; PART SUCH AS APPERTAINE . . 12 230

APPERTAINS
KINGDOM AND POWER AND GLORIE APPERTAINS, ... 6 815

APPETENCE
OF LUSTFUL APPETENCE, TO SING, TO DANCE, ... 11 619

APPETITE
MORE EASIE, WHOLSOM THIRST AND APPETITE 4 330
SO QUICK'ND APPETITE, THAT I, METHOUGHT, ... 5 85
TRUE APPETITE, AND NOT DISRELISH THIRST 5 305
OF ALL TASTES ELSE TO PLEASE THIR APPETITE, . . . 7 49
HER TEMPERANCE OVER APPETITE, TO KNOW 7 127
AND GOVERN WELL THY APPETITE, LEAST SIN 7 546
TEMPTING, STIRR'D IN ME SUDDEN APPETITE 8 308
GRATEFUL TO APPETITE, MORE PLEAS'D MY SENSE . . . 9 580
AN EAGER APPETITE, RAIS'D BY THE SMELL 9 740
TO SENSUAL APPETITE, WHO FROM BENEATHE 9 1129
THIR APPETITE WITH GUST, INSTEAD OF FRUIT . . . 10 565
TO SERVE UNGOVERN'D APPETITE, AND TOOK 11 517

APPLAUDED
THEY LED HIM HIGH APPLAUDED, AND PRESENT . . . 6 26

APPLAUSE
AFTER THE TEMPEST: SUCH APPLAUSE WAS HEARD . . . 2 290
HOARCE MURMUR ECHO'D TO HIS WORDS APPLAUSE . . . 5 873
THIR UNIVERSAL SHOUT AND HIGH APPLAUSE 10 505
AS IN THIR CRIME. THUS WAS TH' APPLAUSE THEY
MEANT, ... 10 545

APPLE
YOUR WONDER, WITH AN APPLE; HE THEREAT 10 487

APPLES
OF TASTING THOSE FAIR APPLES, I RESOLV'D . . . 9 585

APPLI'D
(FOR TIME, THOUGH IN ETERNITIE, APPLI'D 5 580
PUT FORTH, AND TO A NARROW VENT APPLI'D 6 583

APPLY
THE BIRDS THIR QUIRE APPLY; AIRES, VERNAL AIRES, . 4 264
SINCE TO EACH MEANING SAVOUR ME APPLY, ... 9 1019

APPLY'D
TO SATAN FIRST IN SIN HIS DOOM APPLY'D, ... 10 172

APPOINT
AT MY RIGHT HAND; YOUR HEAD I HIM APPOINT; . . . 5 606

APPOINTED
EACH HAD HIS PLACE APPOINTED, EACH HIS COURSE, . 3 720
APPOINTED, WHICH DECLARES HIS DIGNITIE, ... 4 619
WHICH WE IN OUR APPOINTED WORK IMPLOYD 4 726
FREELY OUR PART; YEE WHO APPOINTED STAND . . . 6 565
WITHIN APPOINTED BOUNDS BE HEAV'N AND EARTH, . . 7 167
APPOINTED TO SIT THERE, HAD LEFT THIR CHARGE, . . 10 421
WHICH I MUST KEEP TILL MY APPOINTED DAY . . . 11 550

APPOINTS
VENGEANCE IS HIS, OR WHOSE HE SOLE APPOINTS; . . 6 808

APPREHEND
HUMAN DESIRES CAN SEEK OR APPREHEND? 5 518
THIS YET I APPREHEND NOT, WHY TO THOSE 12 280

APPREHENDED
OR SEX, AND APPREHENDED NOTHING HIGH: 9 574

APPREHENSION
MY SUDDEN APPREHENSION: BUT IN THESE 8 354
IN APPREHENSION THEN IN SUBSTANCE FEEL 11 775

APPROACH
DAY, OR THE SWEET APPROACH OF EV'N OR MORN, . . 3 42
APPROACH NOT, BUT WITH BOTH WINGS VEIL THIR EYES. 3 382
MEETS HIS APPROACH, AND TO THE HEART INSPIRES . . 4 154
NO EVIL THING APPROACH OR ENTER IN; 4 563
WITH FIRST APPROACH OF LIGHT, WE MUST BE RIS'N, . 4 624
YET WITH SUBMISS APPROACH AND REVERENCE MEEK, . . 5 359
A VAST CIRCUMFERENCE: AT HIS APPROACH 6 256
APPROACH NOT MEE, AND WHAT I WILL IS FATE. . . . 7 173
O'RE OTHER CREATURES; YET WHEN I APPROACH . . . 8 546
DISTURBD NOT, WAITING CLOSE TH' APPROACH OF MORN. 9 191
DISPLEAS'D THAT I APPROACH THEE THUS, AND GAZE . 9 535
WIDE WAVING, ALL APPROACH FARR OFF TO FRIGHT, . . 11 121
ALL NIGHT HE WILL PURSUE, BUT HIS APPROACH . . . 12 206

APPROACH'D
LISTENS DELIGHTED. EEVNING NOW APPROACH'D . . . 5 627
CONGRATULANT APPROACH'D HIM, WHO WITH HAND . . . 10 458

APPROACHD
HE SCARCE HAD ENDED, WHEN THOSE TWO APPROACHD . . 4 874
WHILE THE GREAT VISITANT APPROACHD, THUS SPAKE. . 11 225

APPROACHES
YOUR CHANGE APPROACHES, WHEN ALL THESE DELIGHTS . 4 367

APPROACHING
APPROACHING GROSS AND HUGE; IN HOLLOW CUBE 6 552
BUT LONG ERE OUR APPROACHING HEARD WITHIN 8 242
APPROACHING TWO AND TWO, THESE COWRING LOW 8 350
APPROACHING, THUS TO ADAM CALL'D ALOUD. 10 102
DESOLATE WHERE SHE SATE, APPROACHING NIGH, 10 864

APPROACHT
AND BEAUTIE, NOT APPROACHT BY STRONGER HATE, 9 491

APPROPRIATING
BY SPIRITUAL, TO THEMSELVES APPROPRIATING 12 518

APPROV'D
TO STAND APPROV'D IN SIGHT OF GOD, THOUGH WORLDS 6 36
AND WITH OBSEQUIOUS MAJESTIE APPROV'D 8 509
AND EASILY APPROV'D; WHEN THE MOST HIGH 10 31
WILL BE AVENG'D, AND TH' OTHERS FAITH APPROV'D 11 458

APPROVE
OF OTHERS, WHO APPROVE NOT TO TRANSGRESS 4 880
APPROVE THE BEST, AND FOLLOW WHAT I APPROVE. 8 611
WOULDST THOU APPROVE THY CONSTANCIE, APPROVE 9 367
LET NONE HENCEFORTH SEEK NEEDLESS CAUSE TO APPROVE 9 1140
NAY DIDST PERMIT, APPROVE, AND FAIR DISMISS. 9 1159

APT
BUT APT THE MIND OR FANCIE IS TO ROAVE 8 188

APTER
ON EARTH, MADE HEREBY APTER TO RECEIVE 4 672

ARABIAN
BORDERS ON AEGYPT AND THE ARABIAN SHOARE; 3 537

ARABIE
OF ARABIE THE BLEST, WITH SUCH DELAY 4 163

ARABLE
PART ARABLE AND TILTH, WHEREON WERE SHEAVES 11 430

ARAM
TO PADAN-ARAM IN THE FIELD OF LUZ, 3 513

ARAYING
ARAYING COVER'D FROM HIS FATHERS SIGHT. 10 223

ARBITER
BY WHICH HE REIGNS: NEXT HIM HIGH ARBITER 2 909
TWILIGHT UPON THE EARTH, SHORT ARBITER 9 50

ARBITRARY
AND STRIPES, AND ARBITRARY PUNISHMENT 2 334

ARBITRATOR
AND HEAV'NS HIGH ARBITRATOR SIT SECURE 2 359

ARBITREMENT
FREE IN THINE OWN ARBITREMENT IT LIES. 8 641

ARBITRESS
SITS ARBITRESS, AND NEERER TO THE EARTH 1 785

ARBORETS
AMONG THICK-WOV'N ARBORETS AND FLOURS 9 437

ARBOROUS
BUT FIRST FROM UNDER SHADIE ARBOROUS ROOF, 5 137

ARBORS
YON FLOURIE ARBORS, YONDER ALLIES GREEN, 4 626

ARBOUR
THEY CAME, THAT LIKE POMONA'S ARBOUR SMIL'D 5 378
THE WOODBINE ROUND THIS ARBOUR, OR DIRECT 9 216

ARCADIAN
CHARM'D WITH ARCADIAN PIPE, THE PASTORAL REED 11 132

ARCH
LESS THEN ARCH ANGEL RUIND, AND TH' EXCESS 1 593
ABOVE THEM ALL TH' ARCH ANGEL: BUT HIS FACE 1 600
INTESTINE WAR IN HEAV'N, THE ARCH FOE SUBDU'D 6 259
AMBER, AND COLOURS OF THE SHOWRIE ARCH. 6 759

ARCHANGEL
TO WHOM TH' ARCHANGEL. DEXTROUSLY THOU AIM'ST; 11 884
THOUGH BENT ON SPEED, SO HEER THE ARCHANGEL PAUS'D 12 2
SO SPAKE TH' ARCHANGEL MICHAEL, THEN PAUS'D, 12 466
TH' ARCHANGEL STOOD, AND FROM THE OTHER HILL 12 626

ARCH-ANGEL
SAID THEN THE LOST ARCH-ANGEL, THIS THE SEAT 1 243
TH' ARCH-ANGEL URIEL, ONE OF THE SEAV'N 3 648
IF NOT THE FIRST ARCH-ANGEL, GREAT IN POWER, 5 660
SO SPAKE THE FALSE ARCH-ANGEL, AND INFUS'D 5 694
TH' ARCH-ANGEL TRUMPET; THROUGH THE VAST OF HEAVEN 6 203
THE GREAT ARCH-ANGEL FROM HIS WARLIKE TOILE 6 257

ARCH-ANGEL (CONTINUED)
BY THOUSANDS, ANGEL ON ARCH-ANGEL ROWL'D; 6 594
THE AFFABLE ARCH-ANGEL, HAD FOREWARN'D 7 41
HE ENDED; AND TH' ARCH-ANGEL SOON DREW NIGH, 11 238

ARCHANGELIC
HE CEAS'D; AND TH' ARCHANGELIC POWER PREPAR'D 11 126

ARCH-ANGELS
THE SUMMONING ARCH-ANGELS TO PROCLAIME 3 325

ARCH-CHIMIC
TH' ARCH-CHIMIC SUN SO FARR FROM US REMOTE 3 609

ARCHED
AND LEVEL PAVEMENT: FROM THE ARCHED ROOF 1 726
THIR DOWNIE BREST; THE SWAN WITH ARCHED NECK 7 438

ARCH-ENEMY
BEELZEBUB. TO WHOM TH' ARCH-ENEMY, 1 81

ARCH-FELLON
ON TH' OTHER SIDE: WHICH WHEN TH' ARCH-FELLON SAW 4 179

ARCH-FIEND
WHERETO WITH SPEEDY WORDS TH' ARCH-FIEND REPLY'D. 1 156
SO STRETCHT OUT HUGE IN LENGTH THE ARCH-FIEND LAY 1 209

ARCHITECT
AND SOME THE ARCHITECT: HIS HAND WAS KNOWN 1 732
DIVINE THE SOV'RAN ARCHITECT HAD FRAM'D. 5 256
FROM MAN OR ANGEL THE GREAT ARCHITECT 8 72
THOU ART THIR AUTHOR AND PRIME ARCHITECT: 10 356

ARCHITRAVE
WITH GOLDEN ARCHITRAVE; NOR DID THERE WANT 1 715

ARCHT
OVER THE FOAMING DEEP HIGH ARCHT, A BRIDGE 10 301

ARDENT
HER LONG WITH ARDENT LOOK HIS EYE PURSU'D 9 397

ARDOR
HEROIC ARDOR TO ADVENT'ROUS DEEDS 6 66
WITH ARDOR TO ENJOY THEE, FAIRER NOW 9 1032

ARDORS
THOUSAND CELESTIAL ARDORS, WHERE HE STOOD 5 249

ARGENT
THOSE ARGENT FIELDS MORE LIKELY HABITANTS, 3 460

ARGESTES
BOREAS AND CAECIAS AND ARGESTES LOUD 10 699

ARGO
AND MORE ENDANGER'D, THEN WHEN ARGO PASS'D 2 1017

ARGOB
IN ARGOB AND IN BASAN, TO THE STREAM 1 398

ARGU'D
OF GOOD AND EVIL MUCH THEY ARGU'D THEN, 2 562
THAT ARGU'D FEAR; EACH ON HIMSELF RELI'D, 6 238

ARGUE
ARGUE THY INEXPERIENCE WHAT BEHOOVES 4 931
TO ARGUE IN THEE SOMTHING MORE SUBLIME 10 1014
SO MANY LAWS ARGUE SO MANY SINS 12 283

ARGUES
THE FORMER VAIN TO HOPE ARGUES AS VAIN 2 234
NOT TO KNOW MEE ARGUES YOUR SELVES UNKNOWN, 4 830
ARGUES NO LEADER BUT A LYAR TRAC'T, 4 949
THIR DISTANCE ARGUES AND THIR SWIFT RETURN 8 21

ARGUING
NONE ARGUING STOOD, INNUMERABLE HANDS 6 508

ARGUMENT
THAT TO THE HIGHTH OF THIS GREAT ARGUMENT 1 24
O ARGUMENT BLASPHEMOUS, FALSE AND PROUD, 5 809
VARIOUS, WITH BOASTFUL ARGUMENT PORTRAID, 6 84
DEATHS HARBINGER: SAD TASK, YET ARGUMENT 9 13
WARRS, HITHERTO THE ONELY ARGUMENT 9 28
NOR SKILLD NOR STUDIOUS, HIGHER ARGUMENT 9 42
IMPOSSIBLE IS HELD, AS ARGUMENT 10 800

ARGUS
OF ARGUS, AND MORE WAKEFUL THEN TO DROUZE, 11 131

ARIEL
ARIEL AND ARIOC, AND THE VIOLENCE 6 371

ARIES
HIS ZENITH, WHILE THE SUN IN ARIES ROSE; 10 329

ARIGHT
NOT UNINVENTED THAT, WHICH THOU ARIGHT 6 470
AND PERSON, HAD'ST THOU KNOWN THY SELF ARIGHT. . 10 156
TO WORSHIP GOD ARIGHT, AND KNOW HIS WORKS . . . 11 578

ARIMASPIAN
PURSUES THE ARIMASPIAN, WHO BY STELTH 2 945

ARIOC
ARIEL AND ARIOC, AND THE VIOLENCE 6 371

ARISE
AWAKE, ARISE, OR BE FOR EVER FALL'N. 1 330
TH' ANIMAL SPIRITS THAT FROM PURE BLOOD ARISE . . 4 805
USEFUL, WHENCE HAPLY MENTION MAY ARISE 8 200
WHENCE HEAVIE PERSECUTION SHALL ARISE 12 531

ARISES
WHILE DAY ARISES, THAT SWEET HOUR OF PRIME. . . 5 170

ARK
WHO MOURN'D IN EARNEST, WHEN THE CAPTIVE ARK . . 1 458
SHALL BUILD A WONDROUS ARK, AS THOU BEHELDST, . . 11 819
SELECT FOR LIFE SHALL IN THE ARK BE LODG'D, . . 11 823
HE LOOKD, AND SAW THE ARK HULL ON THE FLOUD, . . 11 840
THE ARK NO MORE NOW FLOTES, BUT SEEMS ON GROUND . 11 850
OF HIM WHO BUILT THE ARK, WHO FOR THE SHAME . . 12 102
AN ARK, AND IN THE ARK HIS TESTIMONY, ... 12 251
THE CLOUDED ARK OF GOD TILL THEN IN TENTS . . . 12 333
THIR CITIE, HIS TEMPLE, AND HIS HOLY ARK . . . 12 340

ARKE
FORTHWITH FROM OUT THE ARKE A RAVEN FLIES, . . . 11 855
ANON DRIE GROUND APPEERS, AND FROM HIS ARKE . . 11 861

ARM
WHO FROM THE TERROUR OF THIS ARM SO LATE 1 113
SHOULD INTERMITTED VENGEANCE ARM AGAIN 2 173
BEYOND HIS POTENT ARM, TO LIVE EXEMPT 2 318
FALLACIOUS HOPE, OR ARM TH' OBDURED BREST . . . 2 568
THESE ELEMENTS, AND ARM HIM WITH THE FORCE . . . 6 222
AS ONELY IN HIS ARM THE MOMENT LAY 6 239
THOU CANST, WHO ART SOLE WONDER, MUCH LESS ARM . 9 533
OF THY VICTORIOUS ARM, WELL-PLEASING SON, . . . 10 634

ARM'D
INNUMERABLE FORCE OF SPIRITS ARM'D 1 101
AFLOAT, WHEN WITH FIERCE WINDS ORION ARM'D . . . 1 305
OF PIONERS WITH SPADE AND PICKAX ARM'D 1 676
WONT RIDE IN ARM'D, AND AT THE SOLDANS CHAIR . . 1 764
ARM'D WITH HELL FLAMES AND FURY ALL AT ONCE . . 2 61
WITH SPLENDOR, ARM'D WITH POWER, IF AUGHT PROPOS'D 2 447
VOLUMINOUS AND VAST, A SERPENT ARM'D 2 652
THEN SHINING HEAV'NLY FAIR, A GODDESS ARM'D . . 2 757
OF SPIRITS THAT IN OUR JUST PRETENSES ARM'D . . 2 825
LIGHT-ARM'D OR HEAVY, SHARP, SMOOTH, SWIFT OR SLOW, 2 902
OR FROM WITHOUT, TO ALL TEMPTATIONS ARM'D. . . . 4 65
SUCH HAST THOU ARM'D, THE MINSTRELSIE OF HEAV'N, . 6 168
INVULNERABLE, IMPENITRABLY ARM'D: 6 400
OMNISCIENT THOUGHT. TRUE IS, LESS FIRMLY ARM'D, . 6 430
CAME SHADOWING, AND OPPREST WHOLE LEGIONS ARM'D, . 6 655
AS LIKELIEST WAS, WHEN TWO SUCH FOES MET ARM'D; . 6 688
WITH MOUNTAINS AS WITH WEAPONS ARM'D, WHICH MAKES 6 697
YE ANGELS ARM'D, THIS DAY FROM BATTEL REST; . . 6 802
OF MAN, WITH STRENGTH ENTIRE, AND FREE WILL ARM'D, 10 9
HATH WISELIER ARM'D HIS VENGEFUL IRE THEN SO . . 10 1023

ARMD
FORTH ISSUING AT TH' ACCUSTOMD HOUR STOOD ARMD . 4 779
CAME TOWRING, ARMD IN ADAMANT AND GOLD; 6 110
THOUGH HUGE, AND IN A ROCK OF DIAMOND ARMD, . . 6 364
ARMD WITH THY MIGHT, RID HEAV'N OF THESE REBELL'D, 6 737
HEE IN CELESTIAL PANOPLIE ALL ARMD 6 760
THOUGH NOT AS SHEE WITH BOW AND QUIVER ARMD, . . 9 390
BURSTING THIR BRAZEN DUNGEON, ARMD WITH ICE . . 10 697

ARME
FROM MY PREVAILING ARME, THOUGH HEAVENS KING . . 4 973
THIS SAID HE PAUS'D NOT, BUT WITH VENTROUS ARME . 5 64
TOGETHER BOTH WITH NEXT TO ALMIGHTIE ARME, . . . 6 316
OUR YET UNWOUNDED ENEMIES, OR ARME 6 466
ARME, WARRIOURS, ARME FOR FIGHT, THE FOE AT HAND, 6 537
TO GUIDE THEM IN ALL TRUTH, AND ALSO ARME . . . 12 490

ARMED
HAD TO IMPOSE: HE THROUGH THE ARMED FILES 1 567
WITH ARMED WATCH, THAT RENDER ALL ACCESS 2 130
INVINCIBLE, LEAD FORTH MY ARMED SAINTS 6 47
SO PONDERING, AND FROM HIS ARMED PEERS 6 127
A NUMEROUS HOST, IN STRENGTH EACH ARMED HAND . . 6 231
LOOKD ROUND, AND SCOUTS EACH COAST LIGHT-ARMED
SCOURE, ... 6 529

ARMES
CHARIOTS AND FLAMING ARMES, AND FIERIE STEEDS . . 6 17
OF TRUTH, IN WORD MIGHTIER THEN THEY IN ARMES; . 6 32
PRODIGIOUS POWER HAD SHEWN, AND MET IN ARMES . . 6 247
DOWN CLOV'N TO THE WASTE, WITH SHATTERD ARMES . . 6 361

ARMES (CONTINUED)
O NOW IN DANGER TRI'D, NOW KNOWN IN ARMES . . . 6 418
THE REMEDIE; PERHAPS MORE VALID ARMES, ... 6 438
SORE TOILD, HIS RIV'N ARMES TO HAVOC HEWN, . . . 6 449
AGAINST UNEQUAL ARMES TO FIGHT IN PAINE, . . . 6 454
THE REST IN IMITATION TO LIKE ARMES 6 662
IN MALABAR OR DECAN SPREDS HER ARMES 9 1103
HIS ARMES CLUNG TO HIS RIBS, HIS LEGGS ENTWINING . 10 512
CLAD TO MEET MAN; OVER HIS LUCID ARMES 11 240
UNTRAIND IN ARMES, WHERE RASHNESS LEADS NOT ON. . 12 222
DEFEATING SIN AND DEATH, HIS TWO MAINE ARMES, . . 12 431
WITH DREADFUL FACES THRONG'D AND FIERIE ARMES: . 12 644

ARMIE
ARMIE OF FIENDS, FIT BODY TO FIT HEAD; 4 953
ARMIE AGAINST ARMIE NUMBERLESS TO RAISE 6 224
HIS ARMIE, CIRCUMFUS'D ON EITHER WING, ... 6 778
HIMSELF AND HIS RASH ARMIE, WHERE THIN AIRE . . 12 76

ARMIES
THUS ANSWER'D. LEADER OF THOSE ARMIES BRIGHT, . 1 272
WAG'D IN THE TROUBL'D SKIE, AND ARMIES RUSH . . 2 534
WHERE ARMIES WHOLE HAVE SUNK: THE PARCHING AIR . 2 594
GO MICHAEL OF CELESTIAL ARMIES PRINCE, ... 6 44
HAVE RAIS'D INCESSANT ARMIES TO DEFEAT 6 138
IT SOUNDED, AND THE FAITHFUL ARMIES RUNG . . . 6 204
ON THE SWIFT FLOUDS: AS ARMIES AT THE CALL . . . 7 295
OF TRUMPET (FOR OF ARMIES THOU HAST HEARD) . . . 7 296
WHERE ARMIES LIE ENCAMPT, COME FLYING, LUR'D . . 10 276

ARMING
ARMING TO BATTEL, AND IN STEAD OF RAGE 1 553
MY OBVIOUS BREAST, ARMING TO OVERCOM 11 374

ARMOR
THIR ARMOR HELP'D THIR HARM, CRUSH'T IN AND BRUIS'D 6 656

ARMORIC
BEGIRT WITH BRITISH AND ARMORIC KNIGHTS; . . . 1 581

ARMORIE
OF MICHAEL FROM THE ARMORIE OF GOD 6 321

ARMOUR
WAS NEVER, ARMS ON ARMOUR CLASHING BRAY'D . . . 6 209
AND ALL HIS ARMOUR STAIND ERE WHILE SO BRIGHT, . 6 334
WITH SHIVERD ARMOUR STROW'N, AND ON A HEAP . . 6 389
IN JOINTED ARMOUR WATCH: ON SMOOTH THE SEALE, . . 7 409
WITH SPIRITUAL ARMOUR, ABLE TO RESIST 12 491

ARMOURIE
CELESTIAL ARMOURIE, SHIELDS, HELMES, AND SPEARES, 4 553

ARMOURY
FROM THE ARMOURY OF GOD, WHERE STAND OF OLD . . 7 200

ARMS
WHO DURST DEFIE TH' OMNIPOTENT TO ARMS. 1 49
THE FORCE OF THOSE DIRE ARMS? YET NOT FOR THOSE, . 1 94
IN ARMS NOT WORSE, IN FORESIGHT MUCH ADVANC'T, . 1 119
WITH RALLIED ARMS TO TRY WHAT MAY BE YET . . . 1 269
WITH SCATTER'D ARMS AND ENSIGNS, TILL ANON . . . 1 325
SERAPHIC ARMS AND TROPHIES: ALL THE WHILE . . . 1 539
OF DREADFUL LENGTH AND DAZLING ARMS, IN GUISE . . 1 564
AGAINST THE HIGHEST, AND FIERCE WITH GRASPED ARMS 1 667
MILLIONS THAT STAND IN ARMS, AND LONGING WAIT . . 2 55
TURNING OUR TORTURES INTO HORRID ARMS 2 63
WHEN HE WHO MOST EXCELS IN FACT OF ARMS, . . . 2 124
THUS SITTING, THUS CONSULTING, THUS IN ARMS? . . 2 164
OF THOSE BRIGHT CONFINES, WHENCE WITH NEIGHBOURING
ARMS 2 395
WITH BRIGHT IMBLAZONRIE, AND HORRENT ARMS. . . . 2 513
TILL THICKEST LEGIONS CLOSE; WITH FEATS OF ARMS . 2 537
UNBROK'N, AND IN PROUD REBELLIOUS ARMS 2 691
TO BE INVULNERABLE IN THOSE BRIGHT ARMS, . . . 2 812
IMPARADIS'T IN ONE ANOTHERS ARMS 4 506
TO BOAST WHAT ARMS CAN DOE, SINCE THINE NO MORE . 4 1008
HER MARIAGEABLE ARMS, AND WITH HER BRINGS . . . 5 217
OF OUR OMNIPOTENCE, AND WITH WHAT ARMS 5 722
REBELLIOUS, THEM WITH FIRE AND HOSTILE ARMS . . 6 50
SHOULD WIN IN ARMS, IN BOTH DISPUTES ALIKE . . . 6 123
AGAINST TH' OMNIPOTENT TO RISE IN ARMS; 6 136
WAS NEVER, ARMS ON ARMOUR CLASHING BRAY'D . . . 6 209
STOOD THEY OR MOV'D, IN STATURE, MOTION, ARMS . . 6 302
UP ROSE THE VICTOR ANGELS, AND TO ARMS 6 525
THE MATIN TRUMPET SUNG: IN ARMS THEY STOOD . . . 6 526
THE SOONER FOR THIR ARMS, UNARM'D THEY MIGHT . . 6 595
RAGE PROMPTED THEM AT LENGTH, AND FOUND THEM ARMS 6 635
THIR ARMS AWAY THEY THREW, AND TO THE HILLS . . 6 639
MY BOW AND THUNDER, MY ALMIGHTIE ARMS 6 713
THEY FELT THEMSELVS NOW CHANGING; DOWN THIR ARMS, 10 541
CONCOURS IN ARMS, FIERCE FACES THREATNING WARR, . 11 641
PART WIELD THIR ARMS, PART COURB THE FOAMING STEED, 11 643
WITH CARCASSES AND ARMS TH' ENSANGUIND FIELD . . 11 654

ARNON
OF UTMOST ARNON. NOR CONTENT WITH SUCH 1 399

AROAR
FROM AROAR TO NEBO, AND THE WILD 1 407

AROSE
A GROWING BURDEN. MEAN WHILE WARR AROSE, 2 767
NOT BURD'ND NATURE, SUDDEN MIND AROSE 5 452
THE DOUBTS THAT IN HIS HEART AROSE: AND NOW 7 60
THE SIXT, AND OF CREATION LAST AROSE 7 449
EEV'NING AROSE IN EDEN, FOR THE SUN 7 582
SO SAYING, HE AROSE; WHOM ADAM THUS 8 644

AROUND
THIR EMBRYON ATOMS; THEY AROUND THE FLAG 2 900

ARRAIGND
BAD MEN AND ANGELS, THEY ARRAIGND SHALL SINK 3 331

ARRAY
APPEAR'D, AND SERRIED SHIELDS IN THICK ARRAY 1 548
WITH HORSE AND CHARIOTS RANKT IN LOOSE ARRAY; 2 887
OF BIRDS IN ORDERLY ARRAY ON WING 6 74
PRESENTED STOOD IN TERRIBLE ARRAY 6 106
AND WITH FIERCE ENSIGNES PIERC'D THE DEEP ARRAY 6 356
STAND STILL IN BRIGHT ARRAY YE SAINTS, HERE STAND 6 801
HEAV'N-FALL'N, IN STATION STOOD OR JUST ARRAY, 10 535
SINGLE OR IN ARRAY OF BATTEL RANG'D 11 644
TO THIR FIXT STATION, ALL IN BRIGHT ARRAY 12 627

ARRAYD
SUCH AS IN HIGHEST HEAV'N, ARRAYD IN GOLD 6 13

ARRAYING
ARRAYING WITH REFLECTED PURPLE AND GOLD 4 596

ARREEDE
BUT MARK WHAT I ARREEDE THEE NOW, AVANT; 4 962

ARRIV'D
WHO AFTER CAME FROM EARTH, SAYLING ARRIV'D, 3 520
THUS AT THIR SHADIE LODGE ARRIV'D, BOTH STOOD 4 720
THIS EEVNING FROM THE SUN'S DECLINE ARRIV'D 4 792
OF HEAV'N ARRIV'D, THE GATE SELF-OPEND WIDE 5 254
AMONG THEM HE ARRIV'D; IN HIS RIGHT HAND 6 835
THE FILIAL POWER ARRIV'D, AND SATE HIM DOWN 7 587
WHERE GOD RESIDES, AND ERE MID-DAY ARRIV'D 8 112
FROM EARTH ARRIV'D AT HEAVEN GATE, DISPLEAS'D 10 22
ABOUT THE NEW-ARRIV'D, IN MULTITUDES 10 26
TOO SOON ARRIV'D, SIN THERE IN POWER BEFORE, 10 586

ARRIVE
OVER THE VAST ABRUPT, ERE HE ARRIVE 2 409
POSSESSES LATELY, THITHER TO ARRIVE 2 979
AND TO THE END PERSISTING, SAFE ARRIVE. 3 197

ARROGATE
WILL ARROGATE DOMINION UNDESERV'D 12 27

ARROW
HIS DEADLY ARROW; NEITHER VAINLY HOPE 2 811

ARROWS
BUT RATLING STORM OF ARROWS BARBD WITH FIRE. 6 546
HIS ARROWS, FROM THE FOURFOLD-VISAG'D FOURE, 6 845

ART
AND STRENGTH AND ART ARE EASILY OUT-DONE 1 696
WITH WOND'ROUS ART FOUND OUT THE MASSIE ORE, 1 703
NOR WANT WE SKILL OR ART, FROM WHENCE TO RAISE 2 272
THE HAPPY ILE; WHAT STRENGTH, WHAT ART CAN THEN 2 410
WHENCE AND WHAT ART THOU, EXECRABLE SHAPE, 2 681
ART THOU THAT TRAITOR ANGEL, ART THOU HEE, 2 689
WHAT THING THOU ART, THUS DOUBLE-FORM'D, AND WHY 2 741
THOU ART MY FATHER, THOU MY AUTHOR, THOU 2 864
ANSWER'D. I KNOW THEE, STRANGER, WHO THOU ART, 2 990
THAT FARR BE FROM THEE, FATHER, WHO ART JUDG 3 154
SON OF MY BOSOM, SON WHO ART ALONE 3 169
IN VAIN, THOUGH BY THIR POWERFUL ART THEY BINDE 3 602
THE FIRST ART WONT HIS GREAT AUTHENTIC WILL 3 656
AND HERE ART LIKELIEST BY SUPREAM DECREE 3 659
BUT RATHER TO TELL HOW, IF ART COULD TELL, 4 236
FLOURS WORTHY OF PARADISE WHICH NOT NICE ART 4 241
WHOSE IMAGE THOU ART, HIM THOU SHALL ENJOY 4 472
WHOM FLI'ST THOU? WHOM THOU FLI'ST, OF HIM THOU ART, 4 482
ASSAYING BY HIS DEVILISH ART TO REACH 4 801
WHERE THOU ART WEIGH'D, AND SHOWN HOW LIGHT, HOW WEAK, 4 1012
PARTAKE THOU ALSO; HAPPIE THOUGH THOU ART, 5 75
WILDE ABOVE RULE OR ART; ENORMOUS BLISS. 5 297
ADAM, I THEREFORE CAME, NOR ART THOU SUCH 5 372
ATTEND: THAT THOU ART HAPPIE, OWE TO GOD; 5 520
THITHER TO COME, AND WITH CALUMNIOUS ART 5 770
THEE WHAT THOU ART, AND FORMD THE POW'RS OF HEAV'N 5 824
PROUD, ART THOU MET? THY HOPE WAS TO HAVE REACHT 6 131
THEY FOUND, THEY MINGL'D, AND WITH SUTTLE ART, 6 513
IF RIGHTLY THOU ART CALL'D, WHOSE VOICE DIVINE 7 2
FOR THOU ART HEAV'NLIE, SHEE AN EMPTY DREAME. 7 39
WHO ART TO LEAD THY OFSPRING, AND SUPPOSEST 8 86

ART (CONTINUED)
THOU IN THY SELF ART PERFET, AND IN THEE 8 415
THY MATE, WHO SEES WHEN THOU ART SEEN LEAST WISE. 8 578
FOR SUCH THOU ART, FROM SIN AND BLAME ENTIRE: 9 292
BUT WITH SUCH GARDNING TOOLS AS ART YET RUDE, 9 391
THOU CANST, WHO ART SOLE WONDER, MUCH LESS ARM 9 533
HOW ART THOU LOST, HOW ON A SUDDEN LOST, 9 900
BONE OF MY BONE THOU ART, AND FROM THY STATE 9 915
MY OWN IN THEE, FOR WHAT THOU ART IS MINE; 9 957
EVE, NOW I SEE THOU ART EXACT OF TASTE, 9 1017
WHERE ART THOU ADAM, WONT WITH JOY TO MEET 10 103
SO DREADFUL TO THEE? THAT THOU ART NAKED, WHO 10 121
BECAUSE THOU HAST DONE THIS, THOU ART ACCURST 10 175
FOR DUST THOU ART, AND SHALT TO DUST RETURNE. 10 208
NOW HAD THEY BROUGHT THE WORK BY WONDROUS ART 10 312
THOU ART THIR AUTHOR AND PRIME ARCHITECT: 10 356
CHILDLESS THOU ART, CHILDLESS REMAINE: 10 989
THY HUSBAND, HIM TO FOLLOW THOU ART BOUND; 11 291
CREATED, AS THOU ART, TO NOBLER END 11 605
ART ALL THINGS UNDER HEAV'N, ALL PLACES THOU, 12 618
WHO FOR MY WILFUL CRIME ART BANISHT HENCE. 12 619

ARTICK
IN TH' ARTICK SKY, AND FROM HIS HORRID HAIR 2 710

ARTICULAT
CREATED MUTE TO ALL ARTICULAT SOUND; 9 557

ARTIFICE
THE SKILL OF ARTIFICE OR OFFICE MEAN, 9 39

ARTIFICER
ARTIFICER OF FRAUD; AND WAS THE FIRST 4 121

ARTILLERY
WITH HEAV'NS ARTILLERY FRAUGHT, COME RATTLING ON 2 715

ARTIST
THROUGH OPTIC GLASS THE TUSCAN ARTIST VIEWS 1 288

ARTS
OF ARTS THAT POLISH LIFE, INVENTERS RARE, 11 610

AS
AT ONCE AS FAR AS ANGELS KENN HE VIEWS 1 59
AS ONE GREAT FURNACE FLAM'D, YET FROM THOSE FLAMES 1 62
AS FAR REMOV'D FROM GOD AND LIGHT OF HEAV'N 1 73
AS FROM THE CENTER THRICE TO TH' UTMOST POLE. 1 74
AS FAR AS GODS AND HEAV'NLY ESSENCES 1 138
THEN SUCH COULD HAV OREPOW'RD SUCH FORCE AS OURS) 1 145
OR DO HIM MIGHTIER SERVICE AS HIS THRALLS 1 149
AS BEING THE CONTRARY TO HIS HIGH WILL 1 161
WHICH OFT TIMES MAY SUCCEED, SO AS PERHAPS 1 166
LAY FLOATING MANY A ROOD, IN BULK AS HUGE 1 196
AS WHOM THE FABLES NAME OF MONSTROUS SIZE, 1 197
DEEMING SOME ISLAND, OFT, AS SEA-MEN TELL, 1 205
WITH SOLID, AS THE LAKE WITH LIQUID FIRE; 1 229
AND SUCH APPEAR'D IN HUE, AS WHEN THE FORCE 1 230
AS GODS, AND BY THIR OWN RECOVER'D STRENGTH, 1 240
AS WE EREWHILE, ASTOUNDED AND AMAZ'D, 1 281
THICK AS AUTUMNAL LEAVES THAT STROW THE BROOKS 1 302
IF SUCH ASTONISHMENT AS THIS CAN SIEZE 1 317
TO SLUMBER HERE, AS IN THE VALES OF HEAV'N? 1 321
UPON THE WING, AS WHEN MEN WONT TO WATCH 1 332
INNUMERABLE. AS WHEN THE POTENT ROD 1 338
TILL, AS A SIGNAL GIV'N, TH' UPLIFTED SPEAR 1 347
AT THIR GREAT EMPERORS CALL, AS NEXT IN WORTH 1 378
TO BESTIAL GODS; FOR WHICH THIR HEADS AS LOW 1 435
TURNS ATHEIST, AS DID ELY'S SONS, WHO FILL'D 1 495
AZAZEL AS HIS RIGHT, A CHERUBE TALL: 1 534
OF FLUTES AND SOFT RECORDERS; SUCH AS RAIS'D 1 551
THIR VISAGES AND STATURE AS OF GODS, 1 570
MET SUCH IMBODIED FORCE, AS NAM'D WITH THESE 1 574
OF GLORY OBSCUR'D; AS WHEN THE SUN NEW RIS'N 1 594
THIR GLORY WITHERD. AS WHEN HEAVENS FIRE 1 612
TEARS SUCH AS ANGELS WEEP, BURST FORTH: AT LAST 1 620
AS THIS PLACE TESTIFIES, AND THIS DIRE CHANGE 1 625
AS STOOD LIKE THESE, COULD EVER KNOW REPULSE? 1 630
MONARCH IN HEAV'N, TILL THEN AS ONE SECURE 1 638
SO AS NOT EITHER TO PROVOKE, OR DREAD 1 644
A NUMEROUS BRIGAD HASTEN'D. AS WHEN BANDS 1 675
A THIRD AS SOON HAD FORM'D WITHIN THE GROUND 1 705
AS IN AN ORGAN FROM ONE BLAST OF WIND 1 708
AS FROM A SKY. THE HASTY MULTITUDE 1 730
AND SAT AS PRINCES, WHOM THE SUPREME KING 1 735
BRUSHT WITH THE HISS OF RUSSLING WINGS. AS BEES 1 768
AS NOT BEHIND IN HATE; IF WHAT WAS URG'D 2 120
AND UTTER DISSOLUTION, AS THE SCOPE 2 127
THE VICTORS WILL. TO SUFFER, AS TO DOE, 2 199
THE FORMER VAIN TO HOPE ARGUES AS VAIN 2 234
AS HE OUR DARKNESS, CANNOT WE HIS LIGHT 2 269
AS SOFT AS NOW SEVERE, OUR TEMPER CHANG'D 2 276
TH' ASSEMBLY, AS WHEN HOLLOW ROCKS RETAIN 2 285
AS MAMMON ENDED, AND HIS SENTENCE PLEAS'D, 2 291
DREW AUDIENCE AND ATTENTION STILL AS NIGHT 2 308
US HERE, AS WITH HIS GOLDEN THOSE IN HEAV'N, 2 328
ALL AS OUR OWN, AND DRIVE AS WE WERE DRIVEN, 2 366
SO HARDIE AS TO PROFFER OR ACCEPT 2 425

AS (CONTINUED)

THEN UNKNOWN DANGERS AND AS HARD ESCAPE. 2 444
REFUSING TO ACCEPT AS GREAT A SHARE 2 452
OF HAZARD AS OF HONOUR, DUE ALIKE 2 453
OF HAZARD MORE, AS HE ABOVE THE REST 2 455
THIR RISING ALL AT ONCE WAS AS THE SOUND 2 476
WITH AWFUL REVERENCE PRONE; AND AS A GOD 2 478
AS WHEN FROM MOUNTAIN TOPS THE DUSKY CLOUDS 2 488
AS IF (WHICH MIGHT INDUCE US TO ACCORD) 2 503
PURSUES, AS INCLINATION OR SAD CHOICE 2 524
AS AT TH' OLYMPIAN GAMES OR PYTHIAN FIELDS; 2 530
AS WHEN TO WARN PROUD CITIES WARR APPEARS 2 533
AS WHEN ALCIDES FROM OECHALIA CROWN'D 2 542
WITH STUBBORN PATIENCE AS WITH TRIPLE STEEL. 2 569
A GULF PROFOUND AS THAT SERBONIAN BOG 2 592
AND WISH AND STRUGGLE, AS THEY PASS, TO REACH 2 606
ALL TASTE OF LIVING WIGHT, AS ONCE IT FLED 2 613
AS WHEN FARR OFF AT SEA A FLEET DESCRI'D 2 636
FOR EACH SEEM'D EITHER; BLACK IT STOOD AS NIGHT, 2 670
FIERCE AS TEN FURIES, TERRIBLE AS HELL, 2 671
THE MONSTER MOVING ONWARD CAME AS FAST 2 675
WITH HORRID STRIDES, HELL TREMBLED AS HE STRODE. 2 676
EACH CAST AT TH' OTHER, AS WHEN TWO BLACK CLOUDS 2 714
SURROUND ME, AS THOU SAWST, HOURLY CONCEIV'D 2 796
AT THY RIGHT HAND VOLUPTUOUS, AS BESEEMS 2 869
SWARM POPULOUS, UNNUMBER'D AS THE SANDS 2 903
AS IN A CLOUDY CHAIR ASCENDING RIDES 2 930
AS MANY MILES ALOFT: THAT FURIE STAY'D, 2 938
AS WHEN A GRYFON THROUGH THE WILDERNESS 2 943
WANDRING THIS DARKSOME DESART, AS MY WAY, 2 973
AS FROM HER OUTMOST WORKS A BROK'D FOE 2 1039
THIS PENDANT WORLD, IN BIGNESS AS A STARR 2 1052
OF GOD, AS WITH A MANTLE DIDST INVEST 3 10
HARMONIOUS NUMBERS; AS THE WAKEFUL BIRD 3 38
STOOD THICK AS STARRS, AND FROM HIS SIGHT RECEIV'D 3 61
NOT MEE. THEY THEREFORE AS TO RIGHT BELONGD, 3 111
AS IF PREDESTINATION OVER-RUL'D 3 114
ALL HAST THOU SPOK'N AS MY THOUGHTS ARE, ALL 3 171
AS MY ETERNAL PURPOSE HATH DECREED: 3 172
AND I WILL PLACE WITHIN THEM AS A GUIDE 3 194
SOM OTHER ABLE, AND AS WILLING, PAY 3 211
FILIAL OBEDIENCE: AS A SACRIFICE 3 269
AS IN HIM PERISH ALL MEN, SO IN THEE 3 287
AS FROM A SECOND ROOT SHALL BE RESTOR'D, 3 288
AS MANY AS ARE RESTOR'D, WITHOUT THEE NONE. 3 289
RECEIVE NEW LIFE. SO MAN, AS IS MOST JUST, 3 294
THY MERITS; UNDER THEE AS HEAD SUPREAM 3 319
ADORE THE SON, AND HONOUR HIM AS MEE. 3 343
LOUD AS FROM NUMBERS WITHOUT NUMBER, SWEET 3 346
AS FROM BLEST VOICES, UTTERING JOY, HEAV'N RUNG 3 347
AS WHEN A VULTUR ON IMAUS BRED, 3 431
FIT RETRIBUTION, EMPTIE AS THIR DEEDS; 3 454
NOT IN THE NEIGHBOURING MOON, AS SOME HAVE DREAMD; 3 459
ALL THIS DARK GLOBE THE FIEND FOUND AS HE PASS'D, 3 498
THE WORK AS OF A KINGLY PALACE GATE 3 505
THE STAIRS WERE SUCH AS WHEREON JACOB SAW 3 510
TO DARKNESS, SUCH AS BOUND THE OCEAN WAVE. 3 539
OF ALL THIS WORLD AT ONCE. AS WHEN A SCOUT 3 543
DISPENSES LIGHT FROM FARR; THEY AS THEY MOVE 3 579
WITH RADIANT LIGHT, AS GLOWING IRON WITH FIRE; 3 594
BUT ALL SUN-SHINE, AS WHEN HIS BEAMS AT NOON 3 616
CULMINATE FROM TH' AEQUATOR, AS THEY NOW 3 617
GLAD WAS THE SPIRIT IMPURE AS NOW IN HOPE 3 630
NOT OF THE PRIME, YET SUCH AS IN HIS FACE 3 637
LIKE HONOUR TO OBTAIN, AND AS HIS EYE 3 660
THAT BOTH IN HIM AND ALL THINGS, AS IS MEET, 3 675
NUMBERLESS, AS THOU SEEST, AND HOW THEY MOVE; 3 719
HIS DAY, WHICH ELSE AS TH' OTHER HEMISPHERE 3 725
AS TO SUPERIOR SPIRITS IS WONT IN HEAVEN, 3 737
AS GREAT MIGHT HAVE ASPIR'D, AND ME THOUGH MEAN 4 62
DRAWN TO HIS PART; BUT OTHER POWERS AS GREAT 4 63
VOWS MADE IN PAIN, AS VIOLENT AND VOID. 4 97
THIS KNOWS MY PUNISHER; THEREFORE AS FARR 4 103
FROM GRANTING HEE, AS I FROM BEGGING PEACE: 4 104
AS MAN ERE LONG, AND THIS NEW WORLD SHALL KNOW. 4 113
AS HE SUPPOS'D, ALL UNOBSERV'D, UNSEEN. 4 130
AS WITH A RURAL MOUND THE CHAMPAIN HEAD 4 134
A SILVAN SCENE, AND AS THE RANKS ASCEND 4 140
THOSE BALMIE SPOILES. AS WHEN TO THEM WHO SAILE 4 159
AS ONE CONTINU'D BRAKE, THE UNDERGROWTH 4 175
LIGHTS ON HIS FEET. AS WHEN A PROWLING WOLFE, 4 183
OR AS A THIEF BENT TO UNHOORD THE CASH 4 188
THAT MOUNTAIN AS HIS GARDEN MOULD HIGH RAIS'D 4 226
NOT EQUAL, AS THIR SEX NOT EQUAL SEEMD; 4 296
SHEE AS A VAIL DOWN TO THE SLENDER WASTE 4 304
AS THE VINE CURLES HER TENDRILS, WHICH IMPLI'D 4 307
YIELDED THEM, SIDE-LONG AS THEY SAT RECLINE 4 333
STILL AS THEY THIRSTED SCOOP THE BRIMMING STREAM; 4 336
WANTED, NOR YOUTHFUL DALLIANCE AS BESEEMS 4 338
ALONE AS THEY. ABOUT THEM FRISKING PLAYD 4 340
WHEN SATAN STILL IN GAZE, AS FIRST HE STOOD, 4 356
AS NOW IS ENTERD; YET NO PURPOS'D FOE 4 373
WHICH I AS FREELY GIVE; HELL SHALL UNFOLD, 4 381
MELT, AS I DOE, YET PUBLIC REASON JUST, 4 389
NOW OTHER, AS THIR SHAPE SERVD BEST HIS END 4 398
THEN AS A TYGER, WHO BY CHANCE HATH SPI'D 4 403
HIS COUCHANT WATCH, AS ONE WHO CHOSE HIS GROUND 4 406
AS LIBERAL AND FREE AS INFINITE, 4 415

AS (CONTINUED)

PURE AS TH' EXPANSE OF HEAV'N; I THITHER WENT 4 456
AS I BENT DOWN TO LOOK, JUST OPPOSITE, 4 460
PLEAS'D IT RETURND AS SOON WITH ANSWERING LOOKS 4 464
SMIL'D WITH SUPERIOR LOVE, AS JUPITER 4 499
STILL AS IT ROSE, IMPOSSIBLE TO CLIMBE. 4 548
ON A SUN BEAM, SWIFT AS A SHOOTING STARR 4 556
A SPIRIT, ZEALOUS, AS HE SEEM'D, TO KNOW 4 565
THE VIGILANCE HERE PLAC'T, BUT SUCH AS COME 4 580
LABOUR AND REST, AS DAY AND NIGHT TO MEN 4 613
MEAN WHILE, AS NATURE WILLS, NIGHT BIDS US REST. 4 633
AND WHEN WE SEEK, AS NOW, THY GIFT OF SLEEP. 4 735
DEFAMING AS IMPURE WHAT GOD DECLARES 4 746
PRESENT, OR PAST, AS SAINTS AND PATRIARCHS US'D. 4 762
OUR CIRCUIT MEETS FULL WEST. AS FLAME THEY PART 4 784
ILLUSIONS AS HE LIST, PHANTASMS AND DREAMS, 4 803
DISCOVERD AND SURPRIZ'D. AS WHEN A SPARK 4 814
YOUR MESSAGE, LIKE TO END AS MUCH IN VAIN? 4 833
AS WHEN THOU STOODST IN HEAV'N UPRIGHT AND PURE; 4 837
BUT STILL THY WORDS AT RANDOM, AS BEFORE, 4 930
AND SEALE THEE SO, AS HENCEFORTH NOT TO SCORNE 4 966
WITH PORTED SPEARS, AS THICK AS WHEN A FIELD 4 980
TO TRAMPLE THEE AS MIRE: FOR PROOF LOOK UP, 4 1010
AS THROUGH UNQUIET REST: HE ON HIS SIDE 5 11
MILDE, AS WHEN ZEPHYRUS ON FLORA BREATHES, 5 16
IF DREAM'D, NOT AS I OFT AM WONT, OF THEE, 5 32
I ROSE AS AT THY CALL, BUT FOUND THEE NOT; 5 48
AND AS I WONDRING LOOKT, BESIDE IT STOOD 5 54
FORBIDD'N HERE, IT SEEMS, AS ONELY FIT 5 69
BUT SOMTIMES IN THE AIR, AS WEE, SOMTIMES 5 79
REASON AS CHIEF; AMONG THESE FANSIE NEXT 5 102
KISS'D AS THE GRACIOUS SIGNS OF SWEET REMORSE 5 134
SOON AS THEY FORTH WERE COME TO OPEN SIGHT 5 138
FOUNTAINS AND YEE, THAT WARBLE, AS YE FLOW, 5 195
DISPERSE IT, AS NOW LIGHT DISPELS THE DARK. 5 208
GO THEREFORE, HALF THIS DAY AS FRIEND WITH FRIEND 5 229
AS MAY ADVISE HIM OF HIS HAPPIE STATE, 5 234
ON GOLDEN HINGES TURNING, AS BY WORK 5 255
ABOVE ALL HILLS. AS WHEN BY NIGHT THE GLASS 5 261
A PHOENIX, GAZ'D BY ALL, AS THAT SOLE BIRD 5 272
WANTOND AS IN HER PRIME, AND PLAID AT WILL 5 295
ADAM DISCERND, AS IN THE DORE HE SAT 5 299
TO ENTERTAIN OUR ANGEL GUEST, AS HEE 5 328
GOD HATH DISPENST HIS BOUNTIES AS IN HEAV'N. 5 330
WHAT ORDER, SO CONTRIV'D AS NOT TO MIX 5 334
AS TO A SUPERIOR NATURE, BOWING LOW, 5 360
AS MAY NOT OFT INVITE, THOUGH SPIRITS OF HEAV'N 5 374
AS DOTH YOUR RATIONAL; AND BOTH CONTAIN 5 409
ETHEREAL, AND AS LOWEST FIRST THE MOON; 5 418
AS MAY COMPARE WITH HEAVEN; AND TO TASTE 5 432
AS FROM THE MINE. MEAN WHILE AT TABLE EVE 5 443
AS THAT MORE WILLINGLY THOU COULDST NOT SEEM 5 466
AS NEERER TO HIM PLAC'T OR NEERER TENDING 5 476
IF I REFUSE NOT, BUT CONVERT, AS YOU, 5 492
ETHEREAL, AS WEE, OR MAY AT CHOICE 5 499
HOLD, AS YOU YOURS, WHILE OUR OBEDIENCE HOLDS; 5 537
BECAUSE WEE FREELY LOVE, AS IN OUR WILL 5 539
AS MAY EXPRESS THEM BEST, THOUGH WHAT IF EARTH 5 574
AS YET THIS WORLD WAS NOT, AND CHAOS WILDE 5 577
AS HEAV'NS GREAT YEAR BRINGS FORTH, TH' EMPYREAL HOST 5 583
AMIDST AS FROM A FLAMING MOUNT, WHOSE TOP 5 598
UNITED AS ONE INDIVIDUAL SOULE 5 610
THAT DAY, AS OTHER SOLEMN DAYES, THEY SPENT 5 618
DESIROUS; ALL IN CIRCLES AS THEY STOOD, 5 631
SOON AS MIDNIGHT BROUGHT ON THE DUSKIE HOURE 5 667
UNDER HIM REGENT, TELLS, AS HE WAS TAUGHT, 5 698
HIS COUNT'NANCE, AS THE MORNING STARR THAT GUIDES 5 708
INNUMERABLE AS THE STARRS OF NIGHT, 5 745
HIGH ON A HILL, FAR BLAZING, AS A MOUNT 5 757
MONARCHIE OVER SUCH AS LIVE BY RIGHT 5 795
SUCH AS HE PLEASD, AND CIRCUMSCRIB'D THIR BEING? 5 825
AS BY HIS WORD THE MIGHTY FATHER MADE 5 836
NONE SECONDED, AS OUT OF SEASON JUDG'D, 5 850
WE KNOW NO TIME WHEN WE WERE NOT AS NOW; 5 859
HE SAID, AND AS THE SOUND OF WATERS DEEP 5 872
SUCH AS IN HIGHEST HEAV'N, ARRAYD IN GOLD 6 13
THIR NIMBLE TREAD, AS WHEN THE TOTAL KIND 6 73
UNANIMOUS, AS SONS OF ONE GREAT SIRE 6 95
HIGH IN THE MIDST EXALTED AS A GOD 6 99
AS BOTH THIR DEEDS COMPAR'D THIS DAY SHALL PROVE. 6 170
AGAINST HIS WORTHIER, AS THINE NOW SERVE THEE. 6 180
FROM MEE RETURND, AS ERST THOU SAIDST, FROM FLIGHT, 6 187
HIS MASSIE SPEAR UPSTAID; AS IF ON EARTH 6 195
AND CLAMOUR SUCH AS HEARD IN HEAV'N TILL NOW 6 208
AS EACH DIVIDED LEGION MIGHT HAVE SEEMD 6 230
EACH WARRIOUR SINGLE AS IN CHIEF, EXPERT 6 233
AS ONELY IN HIS ARM THE MOMENT LAY 6 239
SURCEAS'D, AND GLAD AS HOPING HERE TO END 6 258
UNNAM'D IN HEAV'N, NOW PLENTEOUS, AS THOU SEEST 6 263
OF SUCH COMMOTION, SUCH AS TO SET FORTH 6 310
AS NOT OF POWER, AT ONCE; NOR ODDS APPEERD 6 319
SANGUIN, SUCH AS CELESTIAL SPIRITS MAY BLEED, 6 333
VITAL IN EVERY PART, NOT AS FRAIL MAN 6 345
ALL INTELLECT, ALL SENSE, AND AS THEY PLEASE, 6 351
ASSUME, AS LIKES THEM BEST, CONDENSE OR RARE. 6 353
TILL NOW NOT KNOWN, BUT KNOWN AS SOON CONTEMND, 6 432
OF EVIL THEN SO SMALL AS EASIE THINK 6 437

AS (CONTINUED)

AS ONE HE STOOD ESCAP'T FROM CRUEL FIGHT, 6 448
ENJOYMENT OF OUR RIGHT AS GODS; YET HARD 6 452
THESE THINGS, AS NOT TO MIND FROM WHENCE THEY GROW 6 477
SUCH IMPLEMENTS OF MISCHIEF AS SHALL DASH 6 488
DO AS YOU HAVE IN CHARGE, AND BRIEFLY TOUCH 6 566
THOUGH STANDING ELSE AS ROCKS, BUT DOWN THEY FELL 6 593
HAVE EASILY AS SPIRITS EVADED SWIFT 6 596
AS THEY WOULD DANCE, YET FOR A DANCE THEY SEEMD 6 615
SUCH AS WE MIGHT PERCEIVE AMUS'D THEM ALL, 6 623
LIGHT AS THE LIGHTNING GLIMPS THEY RAN, THEY FLEW, 6 642
TWO DAYES, AS WE COMPUTE THE DAYES OF HEAV'N, 6 685
AS LIKELIEST WAS, WHEN TWO SUCH FOES MET ARM'D; 6 688
WITH MOUNTAINS AS WITH WEAPONS ARM'D, WHICH MAKES 6 697
THERE LET THEM LEARN, AS LIKES THEM, TO DESPISE 6 717
AS IS MOST JUST; THIS I MY GLORIE ACCOUNT, 6 726
THY TERRORS, AS I PUT THY MILDNESS ON, 6 735
HAD WONDROUS, AS WITH STARRS THIR BODIES ALL 6 754
AND AS YE HAVE RECEIVD, SO HAVE YE DON 6 805
OF HIS FIERCE CHARIOT ROWLD, AS WITH THE SOUND 6 829
GLOOMIE AS NIGHT; UNDER HIS BURNING WHEELES 6 832
BEFORE HIM, SUCH AS IN THIR SOULES INFIX'D 6 837
THROWN ON THEM AS A SHELTER FROM HIS IRE. 6 843
THE OVERTHROWN HE RAIS'D, AND AS A HEARD 6 856
WITH JUBILIE ADVANC'D; AND AS THEY WENT, 6 884
AS A DESPITE DON AGAINST THE MOST HIGH, 6 906
LEAST FROM THIS FLYING STEED UNREIN'D, (AS ONCE 7 17
SO UNIMAGINABLE AS HATE IN HEAV'N, 7 54
DRIV'N BACK REDOUNDED AS A FLOOD ON THOSE 7 57
BEFORE HIS MEMORIE, AS ONE WHOSE DROUTH 7 66
OUR KNOWING, AS TO HIGHEST WISDOM SEEMD, 7 83
BUT KNOWLEDGE IS AS FOOD, AND NEEDS NO LESS 7 126
WISDOM TO FOLLY, AS NOURISHMENT TO WINDE. 7 130
SO TOLD AS EARTHLY NOTION CAN RECEAVE. 7 179
OUTRAGEOUS AS A SEA, DARK, WASTEFUL, WILDE, 7 212
AND SURGING WAVES, AS MOUNTAINS TO ASSAULT 7 214
DIVIDING: FOR AS EARTH, SO HE THE WORLD 7 269
THE EARTH WAS FORM'D, BUT IN THE WOMB AS YET 7 276
SO HIGH AS HEAV'D THE TUMID HILLS, SO LOW 7 288
AS DROPS ON DUST CONGLOBING FROM THE DRIE; 7 292
ON THE SWIFT FLOUDS: AS ARMIES AT THE CALL 7 295
ROSE AS IN DANCE THE STATELY TREES, AND SPRED 7 324
AND LET THEM BE FOR LIGHTS AS I ORDAINE 7 343
AND SOWD WITH STARRS THE HEAV'N THICK AS A FIELD: 7 358
HITHER AS TO THIR FOUNTAIN OTHER STARRS 7 364
THIR BROOD AS NUMEROUS HATCH, FROM THE EGG THAT
SOON 7 418
FLOATS, AS THEY PASS, FANN'D WITH UNNUMBER'D
PLUMES: 7 432
AS FROM HIS LAIRE THE WILDE BEAST WHERE HE WONNS 7 457
HIS HINDER PARTS, THEN SPRINGS AS BROKE FROM BONDS, 7 465
THE LIBBARD, AND THE TYGER, AS THE MOALE 7 467
AS PLANTS: AMBIGUOUS BETWEEN SEA AND LAND 7 473
THESE AS A LINE THIR LONG DIMENSION DREW, 7 480
HER MOTIONS, AS THE GREAT FIRST-MOVERS HAND 7 500
AND BRUTE AS OTHER CREATURES, BUT ENDU'D 7 507
IS YET DISTINCT BY NAME, THENCE, AS THOU KNOW'ST 7 536
AND PAVEMENT STARRS, AS STARRS TO THEE APPEER, 7 578
WHICH NIGHTLY AS A CIRCLING ZONE THOU SEEST 7 580
AS RESTING ON THAT DAY FROM ALL HIS WORK, 7 593
THEN AS NEW WAK'T THUS GRATEFULLY REPLI'D. 8 4
WITH WONDER, BUT DELIGHT, AND, AS IS DUE, 8 11
AS TRIBUTE SUCH A SUMLESS JOURNEY BROUGHT 8 36
YET WENT SHE NOT, AS NOT WITH SUCH DISCOURSE 8 48
NOT UNATTENDED, FOR ON HER AS QUEEN 8 60
IS AS THE BOOK OF GOD BEFORE THEE SET, 8 67
TO THE TERRESTRIAL MOON BE AS A STARR 8 142
ENLIGHTNING HER BY DAY, AS SHE BY NIGHT 8 143
AS CLOUDS, AND CLOUDS MAY RAIN, AND RAIN PRODUCE 8 146
OF OTHER CREATURES, AS HIM PLEASES BEST, 8 169
FOR I THAT DAY WAS ABSENT, AS BEFELL, 8 229
FOR STATE, AS SOVRAN KING, AND TO ENURE 8 239
INDUC'D ME. AS NEW WAK'T FROM SOUNDEST SLEEP 8 253
AS THITHERWARD ENDEVORING, AND UPRIGHT 8 260
AND OVER FIELDS AND WATERS, AS IN AIRE 8 301
BEFORE MINE EYES ALL REAL, AS THE DREAM 8 310
TO THEE AND TO THY RACE I GIVE; AS LORDS 8 339
AS THUS HE SPAKE, EACH BIRD AND BEAST BEHOLD 8 349
I NAM'D THEM, AS THEY PASS'D, AND UNDERSTOOD 8 352
AS WITH A SMILE MORE BRIGHT'ND, THUS REPLI'D. 8 368
SUCH AS I SEEK, FIT TO PARTICIPATE 8 390
AND NO SUCH COMPANIE AS THEN THOU SAW'ST 8 446
AS WITH AN OBJECT THAT EXCELS THE SENSE, 8 456
BY NATURE AS IN AIDE, AND CLOS'D MINE EYES. 8 459
ABSTRACT AS IN A TRANSE METHOUGHT I SAW, 8 462
SUCH AS I SAW HER IN MY DREAM, ADORND 8 482
AS US'D OR NOT, WORKS IN THE MIND NO CHANGE, 8 525
AS ONE INTENDED FIRST, NOT AFTER MADE 8 555
ABOUT HER, AS A GUARD ANGELIC PLAC'T. 8 559
LESS EXCELLENT, AS THOU THY SELF PERCEAV'ST. 8 566
SO MUCH DELIGHTS ME AS THOSE GRACEFUL ACTS, 8 600
AS FLESH TO MIX WITH FLESH, OR SOUL WITH SOUL. 8 629
WITH MAN, AS WITH HIS FRIEND, FAMILIAR US'D 9 2
DOWNWARD AS FARR ANTARTIC; AND IN LENGTH 9 79
AS FROM HIS WIT AND NATIVE SUTTLETIE 9 93
MORE JUSTLY, SEAT WORTHIER OF GODS, AS BUILT 9 100
LIGHT ABOVE LIGHT, FOR THEE ALONE, AS SEEMS, 9 105
OF SACRED INFLUENCE: AS GOD IN HEAV'N 9 107

AS (CONTINUED)

TORMENT WITHIN ME, AS FROM THE HATEFUL SIEGE 9 121
AS I, THOUGH THEREBY WORSE TO ME REDOUND: 9 128
FOLLOW, AS TO HIM LINKT IN WEAL OR WOE, 9 133
DESCEND TO? WHO ASPIRES MUST DOWN AS LOW 9 169
AS HIGH HE SOARD, OBNOXIOUS FIRST OR LAST 9 170
NOW WHEN AS SACRED LIGHT BEGAN TO DAWNE 9 192
LABOUR, AS TO DEBARR US WHEN WE NEED 9 236
WILL KEEP FROM WILDERNESS WITH EASE, AS WIDE 9 245
AS WE NEED WALK, TILL YOUNGER HANDS ERE LONG 9 246
AS ONE WHO LOVES, AND SOME UNKINDNESS MEETS, 9 271
AS IN A SHADIE NOOK I STOOD BEHIND, 9 277
AS WEE, NOT CAPABLE OF DEATH OR PAINE, 9 283
AS NOT SECURE TO SINGLE OR COMBIN'D. 9 339
O WOMAN, BEST ARE ALL THINGS AS THE WILL 9 343
NOT KEEPING STRICTEST WATCH, AS SHE WAS WARND. 9 363
THOUGH NOT AS SHEE WITH BOW AND QUIVER ARMD, 9 390
BUT WITH SUCH GARDNING TOOLS AS ART YET RUDE, 9 391
REPEATED, SHEE TO HIM AS OFT ENGAG'D 9 400
AS ONE WHO LONG IN POPULOUS CITY PENT, 9 445
PRONE ON THE GROUND, AS SINCE, BUT ON HIS REARE, 9 497
AT FIRST, AS ONE WHO SOUGHT ACCESS, BUT FEARD 9 511
AS WHEN A SHIP BY SKILFUL STEARSMAN WROUGHT 9 513
VERES OFT, AS OFT SO STEERS, AND SHIFTS HER SAILE; 9 515
OF RUSLING LEAVES, BUT MINDED NOT, AS US'D 9 519
BUT AS IN GAZE ADMIRING: OFT HE BOWD 9 524
I WAS AT FIRST AS OTHER BEASTS THAT GRAZE 9 571
AS WAS MY FOOD, NOR AUGHT BUT FOOD DISCERN'D 9 573
AS LEAVES A GREATER STORE OF FRUIT UNTOUCHT, 9 621
BRIGHT'NS HIS CREST, AS WHEN A WANDRING FIRE, 9 634
NEW PART PUTS ON, AND AS TO PASSION MOV'D, 9 667
RAIS'D, AS OF SOM GREAT MATTER TO BEGIN. 9 669
AS WHEN OF OLD SOM ORATOR RENOUND 9 670
SOMTIMES IN HIGHTH BEGAN, AS NO DELAY 9 675
OP'ND AND CLEERD, AND YE SHALL BE AS GODS, 9 708
KNOWING BOTH GOOD AND EVIL AS THEY KNOW. 9 709
THAT YE SHOULD BE AS GODS, SINCE I AS MAN, 9 710
AS THEY, PARTICIPATING GOD-LIKE FOOD? 9 717
AND YET UNKNOWN, IS AS NOT HAD AT ALL. 9 757
REGARDED, SUCH DELIGHT TILL THEN, AS SEEMD, 9 787
AND HIGHT'ND AS WITH WINE, JOCOND AND BOON, 9 793
AND THY FAIR FRUIT LET HANG, AS TO NO END 9 798
IN KNOWLEDGE, AS THE GODS WHO ALL THINGS KNOW; 9 804
AS YET MY CHANGE, AND GIVE HIM TO PARTAKE 9 818
BUT FIRST LOW REVERENCE DON, AS TO THE POWER 9 835
AS REAPERS OFT ARE WONT THIR HARVEST QUEEN. 9 842
THIS TREE IS NOT AS WE ARE TOLD, A TREE 9 863
OR NOT RESTRAIND AS WEE, OR NOT OBEYING, 9 868
NOT DEAD, AS WE ARE THREATN'D, BUT THENCEFORTH 9 870
FOR BLISS, AS THOU HAST PART, TO ME IS BLISS, 9 879
MAY JOYNE US, EQUAL JOY, AS EQUAL LOVE; 9 882
ON TH' OTHER SIDE, ADAM, SOON AS HE HEARD 9 888
SO HAVING SAID, AS ONE FROM SAD DISMAY 9 917
LIVES, AS THOU SAIDST, AND GAINES TO LIVE AS MAN 9 933
TO US, AS LIKELY TASTING TO ATTAINE 9 935
CONSORT WITH THEE, DEATH IS TO MEE AS LIFE; 9 954
HAD SO ENOBL'D, AS OF CHOICE TO INCURR 9 992
EARTH TREMBL'D FROM HER ENTRAILS, AS AGAIN 9 1000
AS WITH NEW WINE INTOXICATED BOTH 9 1008
AS WANTONLY REPAID; IN LUST THEY BURNE: 9 1015
AS MEET IS, AFTER SUCH DELICIOUS FARE; 9 1028
SOON AS THE FORCE OF THAT FALLACIOUS FRUIT, 9 1046
AS FROM UNREST, AND EACH THE OTHER VIEWING, 9 1052
HOW DARK'ND; INNOCENCE, THAT AS A VEILE 9 1054
CONFOUNDED LONG THEY SATE, AS STRUCK'N MUTE, 9 1064
AND BROWN AS EVENING: COVER ME YE PINES, 9 1088
BUT LET US NOW, AS IN BAD PLIGHT, DEVISE 9 1091
THERE SIT NOT, AND REPROACH US AS UNCLEAN, 9 1098
BUT SUCH AS AT THIS DAY TO INDIANS KNOWN 9 1102
THEY GATHERD, BROAD AS AMAZONIAN TARGE, 9 1111
THUS FENC'T, AND AS THEY THOUGHT, THIR SHAME IN
PART 9 1119
WITH ME, AS I BESOUGHT THEE, WHEN THAT STRANGE 9 1135
REMAIND STILL HAPPIE, NOT AS NOW, DESPOILD 9 1138
OF WANDRING, AS THOU CALL'ST IT, WHICH WHO KNOWS 9 1146
BUT MIGHT AS ILL HAVE HAPP'ND THOU BEING BY, 9 1147
FRAUD IN THE SERPENT, SPEAKING AS HE SPAKE; 9 1150
AS GOOD HAVE GROWN THERE STILL A LIVELESS RIB. 9 1154
BEING AS I AM, WHY DIDST NOT THOU THE HEAD 9 1155
GOING INTO SUCH DANGER AS THOU SAIDST? 9 1157
AND AM I NOW UPBRAIDED, AS THE CAUSE 9 1168
ENTRANCE UNSEEN. SOON AS TH' UNWELCOME NEWS 10 21
BECAUSE NOT YET INFLICTED, AS HE FEAR'D, 10 51
JUSTICE SHALL NOT RETURN AS BOUNTIE SCORN'D. 10 54
JUSTICE WITH MERCIE, AS MAY ILLUSTRATE MOST 10 78
AND GAV'ST ME AS THY PERFET GIFT, SO GOOD, 10 138
WERE SUCH AS UNDER GOVERNMENT WELL SEEM'D, 10 154
AS VITIATED IN NATURE: MORE TO KNOW 10 169
THOUGH IN MYSTERIOUS TERMS, JUDG'D AS THEN BEST: 10 173
AS WHEN HE WASH'D HIS SERVANTS FEET SO NOW 10 215
AS FATHER OF HIS FAMILIE HE CLAD 10 216
OR AS THE SNAKE WITH YOUTHFUL COATE REPAID; 10 218
IN GLORY AS OF OLD, TO HIM APPEAS'D 10 226
OR TRANSMIGRATION, AS THIR LOT SHALL LEAD. 10 261
OF MORTAL CHANGE ON EARTH. AS WHEN A FLOCK 10 273
SOLID OR SLIMIE, AS IN RAGING SEA 10 286
AS WHEN TWO POLAR WINDS BLOWING ADVERSE 10 289
AS WITH A TRIDENT SMOTE, AND FIX'T AS FIRM 10 295

AS (CONTINUED)
AS DELOS FLOATING ONCE; THE REST HIS LOOK 10 296
AND WITH ASPHALTIC SLIME; BROAD AS THE GATE, 10 298
THY TROPHIES, WHICH THOU VIEW'ST AS NOT THINE OWN, 10 355
AS BATTEL HATH ADJUDG'D, FROM THIS NEW WORLD 10 377
AS WHEN THE TARTAR FROM HIS RUSSIAN FOE 10 431
AT LAST AS FROM A CLOUD HIS FULGENT HEAD 10 449
AS LORDS, A SPACIOUS WORLD, TO OUR NATIVE HEAVEN 10 467
TO RULE, AS OVER ALL HE SHOULD HAVE RUL'D. 10 493
ALIKE, TO SERPENTS ALL AS ACCESSORIES 10 520
DOWN FELL BOTH SPEAR AND SHIELD, DOWN THEY AS FAST, 10 542
AS IN THIR CRIME. THUS WAS TH' APPLAUSE THEY MEANT, 10 545
HUNGER AND THIRST CONSTRAINING, DRUGD AS OFT, 10 568
INTO THE SAME ILLUSION, NOT AS MAN 10 571
THAT LAUGH, AS IF TRANSPORTED WITH SOME FIT 10 626
SUNG HALLELUIA, AS THE SOUND OF SEAS, 10 642
AS SORTED BEST WITH PRESENT THINGS. THE SUN 10 651
AS MIGHT AFFECT THE EARTH WITH COLD AND HEAT 10 653
AS DEEP AS CAPRICORNE, TO BRING IN CHANGE 10 677
FROM COLD ESTOTILAND, AND SOUTH AS FARR 10 686
THE SUN, AS FROM THYESTEAN BANQUET, TURN'D 10 688
FROM SERRALIONA; THWART OF THESE AS FIERCE 10 703
ON MEE AS ON THIR NATURAL CENTER LIGHT 10 740
IN THIS DELICIOUS GARDEN? AS MY WILL 10 746
AS IN MY MOTHERS LAP? THERE I SHOULD REST 10 778
IMPOSSIBLE IS HELD, AS ARGUMENT 10 800
THAT DEATH BE NOT ONE STROAK, AS I SUPPOS'D, 10 809
ON MEE, MEE ONELY, AS THE SOURSE AND SPRING 10 832
THROUGH THE STILL NIGHT, NOT NOW, AS ERE MAN FELL, 10 846
CURS'D HIS CREATION, DEATH AS OFT ACCUS'D 10 852
BEFITS THEE WITH HIM LEAGU'D, THY SELF AS FALSE 10 868
CROOKED BY NATURE, BENT, AS NOW APPEARS, 10 885
WELL IF THROWN OUT, AS SUPERNUMERARIE 10 887
WITH MEN AS ANGELS WITHOUT FEMININE, 10 893
AS SOME MISFORTUNE BRINGS HIM, OR MISTAKE, 10 900
AS JOYN'D IN INJURIES, ONE ENMITIE 10 925
AS ONE DISARM'D, HIS ANGER ALL HE LOST, 10 945
UNWARIE, AND TOO DESIROUS, AS BEFORE, 10 947
HIS FULL WRAUTH WHOSE THOU FEELST AS YET LEST PART, 10 951
RESTOR'D BY THEE, VILE AS I AM, TO PLACE 10 971
AS IN OUR EVILS, AND OF EASIER CHOICE. 10 978
HAD ENTERTAIND, AS DI'D HER CHEEKS WITH PALE. 10 1009
OR IF THOU COVET DEATH, AS UTMOST END 10 1020
RESOLV'D, AS THOU PROPOSEST; SO OUR FOE 10 1038
THE AIR ATTRITE TO FIRE, AS LATE THE CLOUDS 10 1073
BESEECHING HIM, SO AS WE NEED NOT FEAR 10 1082
MADE ONE WITH ME AS I WITH THEE AM ONE. 11 44
AS A DISTEMPER, GROSS TO AIRE AS GROSS, 11 53
AND MORTAL FOOD, AS MAY DISPOSE HIM BEST 11 54
AS HOW WITH PECCANT ANGELS LATE THEY SAW; 11 70
AS I SHALL THEE ENLIGHTEN, INTERMIX 11 115
SO PREVALENT AS TO CONCERNE THE MIND 11 144
AS RAPHAEL, THAT I SHOULD MUCH CONFIDE, 11 235
NOT IN HIS SHAPE CELESTIAL, BUT AS MAN 11 239
AS IN A GLISTERING ZODIAC HUNG THE SWORD, 11 247
AS FROM HIS FACE I SHALL BE HID, DEPRIVD 11 316
GOD IS AS HERE, AND WILL BE FOUND ALIKE 11 350
AS ONCE THOU SLEPST, WHILE SHEE TO LIFE WAS FORMD. 11 369
ITH' MIDST AN ALTAR AS THE LAND-MARK STOOD 11 432
UNCULL'D, AS CAME TO HAND; A SHEPHERD NEXT 11 436
WHEREAT HEE INLIE RAG'D, AND AS THY TALK'D, 11 444
SOME, AS THOU SAW'ST, BY VIOLENT STROKE SHALL DIE, 11 471
WITH VOWS, AS THIR CHIEF GOOD, AND FINAL HOPE. 11 493
CREATED, AS THOU ART, TO NOBLER END 11 605
DID, AS THOU SAWST, RECEAVE, TO WALK WITH GOD 11 707
MARRYING OR PROSTITUTING, AS BEFELL, 11 716
CONVERSION AND REPENTANCE, AS TO SOULS 11 724
CAME SEAVENS, AND PAIRS, AND ENTERD IN, AS TAUGHT 11 735
AND SUNK THEE AS THY SONS; TILL GENTLY REARD 11 758
THOUGH COMFORTLESS, AS WHEN A FATHER MOURNS 11 760
SHALL BUILD A WONDROUS ARK, AS THOU BEHELDST, 11 819
WRINKL'D THE FACE OF DELUGE, AS DECAI'D; 11 843
AS AFTER THIRST, WHICH MADE THIR FLOWING SHRINK 11 846
HIS SLUCES, AS THE HEAV'N HIS WINDOWS SHUT. 11 849
AND NOW THE TOPS OF HILLS AS ROCKS APPEER; 11 852
AS PRESENT, HEAV'NLY INSTRUCTER, I REVIVE 11 871
DISTENDED AS THE BROW OF GOD APPEAS'D, 11 880
OR SERVE THEY AS A FLOURIE VERGE TO BINDE 11 881
AS ONE WHO IN HIS JOURNEY BATES AT NOONE, 12 1
AND MAN AS FROM A SECOND STOCK PROCEED. 12 7
WITH WARR AND HOSTILE SNARE SUCH AS REFUSE 12 31
BEFORE THE LORD, AS IN DESPITE OF HEAV'N, 12 34
AS MOCKT THEY STORM; GREAT LAUGHTER WAS IN HEAV'N 12 59
WHO OFT AS UNDESERVEDLY ENTHRALL 12 94
THUS WILL THIS LATTER, AS THE FORMER WORLD, 12 105
AS TO FORSAKE THE LIVING GOD, AND FALL 12 118
IN PROSPECT, AS I POINT THEM; ON THE SHOARE 12 143
TO STOP THIR OVERGROWTH, AS INMATE GUESTS 12 166
HUMBLES HIS STUBBORN HEART, BUT STILL AS ICE 12 193
AS ON DRIE LAND BETWEEN TWO CHRISTAL WALLS, 12 197
ORDAINE THEM LAWES; PART SUCH AS APPERTAINE 12 230
SEAVEN LAMPS AS IN A ZODIAC REPRESENTING 12 255
WILL REIGN AMONG THEM, AS OF THEE BEGOT; 12 286
FROM WHOM AS OFT HE SAVES THEM PENITENT 12 319
FORETOLD TO ABRAHAM, AS IN WHOM SHALL TRUST 12 328
SUCH FOLLOW HIM, AS SHALL BE REGISTERD 12 335
GOD, AS TO LEAVE THEM, AND EXPOSE THIR LAND, 12 339

AS (CONTINUED)
TO DAVID, STABLISHT AS THE DAYES OF HEAV'N. 12 347
SURCHARG'D, AS HAD LIKE GRIEF BIN DEW'D IN TEARS, 12 373
AS OF A DUEL, OR THE LOCAL WOUNDS 12 387
OUT OF HIS GRAVE, FRESH AS THE DAWNING LIGHT, 12 423
HIS DEATH FOR MAN, AS MANY AS OFFERD LIFE 12 425
AS AT THE WORLDS GREAT PERIOD; AND OUR SIRE 12 467
AND OFT SUPPORTED SO AS SHALL AMAZE 12 496
AS DID THIR LORD BEFORE THEM. THUS THEY WIN 12 502
THEY DIE; BUT IN THIR ROOM, AS THEY FOREWARNE, 12 507
AS IN HIS PRESENCE, EVER TO OBSERVE 12 563
GLIDING METEOROUS, AS EV'NING MIST 12 629
FIERCE AS A COMET; WHICH WITH TORRID HEAT, 12 634
AND VAPOUR AS THE LIBYAN AIR ADUST, 12 635
LED THEM DIRECT, AND DOWN THE CLIFF AS FAST 12 639

ASCALON
OF PALESTINE, IN GATH AND ASCALON 1 465

ASCANSE
SOME SAY HE BID HIS ANGELS TURNE ASCANSE 10 668

ASCEND
HATH EMPTIED HEAV'N, SHALL FAIL TO RE-ASCEND 1 633
THE SIGNAL TO ASCEND, SIT LINGRING HERE 2 56
THAT IN OUR PROPER MOTION WE ASCEND 2 75
A SILVAN SCENE, AND AS THE RANKS ASCEND 4 140
ASCEND TO HEAV'N, BY MERIT THINE, AND SEE 5 80
THAT SINGING UP TO HEAVEN GATE ASCEND, 5 198
IMPROV'D BY TRACT OF TIME, AND WINGD ASCEND 5 498
BY STEPS WE MAY ASCEND TO GOD. BUT SAY, 5 512
ASCEND MY CHARIOT, GUIDE THE RAPID WHEELES 6 711
INTO THE CLOUDS, THIR TOPS ASCEND THE SKIE: 7 287
BY WHICH TO HEAV'NLY LOVE THOU MAIST ASCEND, 8 592
BUT THAT FROM US OUGHT SHOULD ASCEND TO HEAV'N 11 143
THY MORTAL PASSAGE WHEN IT COMES. ASCEND 11 366
ASCEND, I FOLLOW THEE, SAFE GUIDE, THE PATH 11 371
IF SO I MAY ATTAIN. SO BOTH ASCEND 11 376
THE POWER OF THE MOST HIGH; HE SHALL ASCEND 12 369
THEN TO THE HEAV'N OF HEAV'NS HE SHALL ASCEND 12 451

ASCENDED
ASCENDED, AT HIS RIGHT HAND VICTORIE 6 762
WHILE THE BRIGHT POMP ASCENDED JUBILANT. 7 564
TH' ANGELIC GUARDS ASCENDED, MUTE AND SAD 10 18
ASCENDED HIS HIGH THRONE, WHICH UNDER STATE 10 445

ASCENDING
IN WEALTH AND LUXURIE. TH' ASCENDING PILE 1 722
ASCENDING, WHILE THE NORTH WIND SLEEPS, O'RESPREAD 2 489
AS IN A CLOUDY CHAIR ASCENDING RIDES 2 930
ASCENDING BY DEGREES MAGNIFICENT 3 502
ANGELS ASCENDING AND DESCENDING, BANDS 3 511
TO TH' OCEAN ILES, AND IN TH' ASCENDING SCALE 4 354
THE GLORIOUS TRAIN ASCENDING: HE THROUGH HEAV'N, 7 574

ASCENDS
OF RIOT ASCENDS ABOVE THEIR LOFTIEST TOWRS, 1 499
BUT NEITHER BREATH OF MORN WHEN SHE ASCENDS 4 650

ASCENT
WE SUNK THUS LOW? TH' ASCENT IS EASIE THEN; 2 81
OF HEAV'NS ASCENT THEY LIFT THIR FEET, WHEN LOE 3 486
THE FIEND BY EASIE ASCENT, OR AGGRAVATE 3 524
NOW TO TH' ASCENT OF THAT STEEP SAVAGE HILL 4 172
CONSPICUOUS FARR, WINDING WITH ONE ASCENT 4 545
PROPORTIONAL ASCENT, WHICH CANNOT BE 9 936
TO HIM WITH SWIFT ASCENT HE UP RETURND, 10 224

ASCENTION
IN OPEN SHEW, AND WITH ASCENTION BRIGHT 10 187

ASCRIBE
WHICH ELSE TO SEVERAL SPHEARS THOU MUST ASCRIBE, 8 131

ASHES
THE WORLD SHALL BURN, AND FROM HER ASHES SPRING 3 334
CHEWD BITTER ASHES, WHICH TH' OFFENDED TASTE 10 566

ASHTAROTH
OF BAALIM AND ASHTAROTH, THOSE MALE, 1 422

ASIA
BRIDGING HIS WAY, EUROPE WITH ASIA JOYN'D, 10 310

ASIDE
WITH KISSES PURE: ASIDE THE DEVIL TURND 4 502
ENTERD SO FAIRE, SHOULD TURN ASIDE TO TREAD 11 630

ASK
MIGHT IN THAT NOISE RESIDE, OF WHOM TO ASK 2 957
ASK RIDDANCE, IF WE MEAN TO TREAD WITH EASE; 4 632
WHY ASK YE, AND SUPERFLUOUS BEGIN 4 832
OR NOT, WHO ASK WHAT BOLDNESS BROUGHT HIM HITHER 4 908
PROCEEDED THUS TO ASK HIS HEAV'NLY GUEST. 7 69
TO ASK, NOR LET THINE OWN INVENTIONS HOPE 7 121
BEFORE THE ANGEL, AND OF HIM TO ASK 8 53
TO ASK OR SEARCH I BLAME THEE NOT, FOR HEAV'N 8 66

ASK (CONTINUED)
OF SOMTHING NOT UNSEASONABLE TO ASK 8 201
BEAR WITH ME THEN, IF LAWFUL WHAT I ASK; 8 614

ASKANCE
EY'D THEM ASKANCE, AND TO HIMSELF THUS PLAIND. 4 504
WHOM THE GRAND FOE WITH SCORNFUL EYE ASKANCE 6 149

ASK'D
HE ASK'D, BUT ALL THE HEAV'NLY QUIRE STOOD MUTE, 3 217
AND THY REQUEST THINK NOW FULFILL'D, THAT ASK'D 7 635

ASKE
WHAT WEE, NOT TO EXPLORE THE SECRETS ASKE 7 95

ASKT
THAT BE ASSUR'D, WITHOUT LEAVE ASKT OF THEE: 2 685
AND SUCH I HELD THEE; BUT THIS QUESTION ASKT 4 887
IN THAT DARK DURANCE: THUS MUCH WHAT WAS ASKT. 4 899
THIS ALSO THY REQUEST WITH CAUTION ASKT 7 111

ASLEEP
NOW LAID PERHAPS ASLEEP SECURE OF HARME. 4 791
BEAUTIE, WHICH WHETHER WAKING OR ASLEEP, 5 14
AND FELL ASLEEP; BUT O HOW GLAD I WAK'D 5 92
WEARIED I FELL ASLEEP: BUT NOW LEAD ON; 12 614

ASLOPE
FRUIT OF THY WOMB: ON MEE THE CURSE ASLOPE 10 1053

ASMADAI
VANQUISH'D ADRAMELEC, AND ASMADAI, 6 365

ASMODEUS
THEN ASMODEUS WITH THE FISHIE FUME, 4 168

ASP
SCORPION AND ASP, AND AMPHISBAENA DIRE, 10 524

ASPECT
ASPECT HE ROSE, AND IN HIS RISING SEEM'D 2 301
HIS WORDS HERE ENDED, BUT HIS MEEK ASPECT 3 266
SLOWLY DESCENDED, AND WITH RIGHT ASPECT 4 541
TO WHOM THE SON WITH CALM ASPECT AND CLEER 5 733
IN BATTAILOUS ASPECT, AND NEERER VIEW 6 81
TWO PLANETS RUSHING FROM ASPECT MALIGNE 6 313
AND CLOUDIE IN ASPECT THUS ANSWERING SPAKE. 6 450
IN THAT ASPECT, AND STILL THAT DISTANCE KEEPES 7 379
NOT TO INCUR; BUT SOON HIS CLEER ASPECT 8 336
BENT THIR ASPECT, AND WHOM THEY WISH'D BEHELD, 10 454

ASPECTS
THIR PLANETARIE MOTIONS AND ASPECTS 10 658

ASPERSES
FOR HEE WHO TEMPTS, THOUGH IN VAIN, AT LEAST ASPERSES 9 296

ASPHALTIC
AND WITH ASPHALTIC SLIME; BROAD AS THE GATE, 10 298

ASPHALTICK
AND ELEALE TO TH' ASPHALTICK POOL. 1 411

ASPHALTUS
WITH NAPHTHA AND ASPHALTUS YEILDED LIGHT 1 729

ASPHODEL
PANSIES, AND VIOLETS, AND ASPHODEL, 9 1040

ASPIR'D
AS GREAT MIGHT HAVE ASPIR'D, AND ME THOUGH MEAN 4 62
THAT TO THE HIGHT OF DEITIE ASPIR'D; 9 167

ASPIRE
TO VITAL SPIRITS ASPIRE, TO ANIMAL, 5 484
O EXECRABLE SON SO TO ASPIRE 12 64
BEYOND WHICH WAS MY FOLLY TO ASPIRE. 12 560

ASPIRER
ASPIRER, BUT THIR THOUGHTS PROV'D FOND AND VAIN 6 90

ASPIRES
THUS HIGH UPLIFTED BEYOND HOPE, ASPIRES 2 7
AND IGNOMINIE, YET TO GLORIE ASPIRES 6 383
DESCEND TO? WHO ASPIRES MUST DOWN AS LOW 9 169

ASPIRING
OF REBEL ANGELS, BY WHOSE AID ASPIRING 1 38
TH' ASPIRING DOMINATIONS: THOU THAT DAY 3 392
EQUAL WITH GODS; ASPIRING TO BE SUCH, 4 526
THE HIGHTH OF THY ASPIRING UNOPPOS'D, 6 132
TOOK ENVIE, AND ASPIRING TO HIS HIGHTH, 6 793
OF THOSE TOO HIGH ASPIRING, WHO REBELLD 6 899

ASPRAMONT
JOUSTED IN ASPRAMONT OR MONTALBAN, 1 583

ASSAIES
FROM HARD ASSAIES AND ILL SUCCESSES PAST 4 932

ASSAILD
AND WITH REBOUNDING SURGE THE BARRS ASSAILD, 10 417

ASSASSIN-LIKE
ONE MAN, ASSASSIN-LIKE HAD LEVIED WARR, 11 219

ASSAULT
HEAV'N, WHOSE HIGH WALLS FEAR NO ASSAULT OR SIEGE, 2 343
CROSS-BARRD AND BOLTED FAST, FEAR NO ASSAULT, 4 190
FEARLESS ASSAULT, AND TO THE BROW OF HEAV'N 6 51
BOTH BATTELS MAINE, WITH RUINOUS ASSAULT 6 216
AND SURGING WAVES, AS MOUNTAINS TO ASSAULT 7 214
BY SLY ASSAULT; AND SOMWHERE NIGH AT HAND 9 256
OR DARING, FIRST ON MEE TH' ASSAULT SHALL LIGHT. 9 305

ASSAULTING
ASSAULTING; OTHERS FROM THE WALL DEFEND 11 657

ASSAULTS
OF BATTEL WHEN IT RAG'D, IN ALL ASSAULTS 1 277
BORN THROUGH THE HOLLOW DARK ASSAULTS HIS EARE 2 953
CONSTANT, MATURE, PROOF AGAINST ALL ASSAULTS, 10 882
SATANS ASSAULTS, AND QUENCH HIS FIERIE DARTS, 12 492

ASSAY
AND MAN THERE PLAC'T, WITH PURPOSE TO ASSAY 3 90
THY MERITED REWARD, THE FIRST ASSAY 6 153
WHOSE TASTE, TOO LONG FORBORN, AT FIRST ASSAY 9 747

ASSAY'D
SOFT WORDS TO HIS FIERCE PASSION SHE ASSAY'D: 10 865

ASSAYD
THRICE HE ASSAYD, AND THRICE IN SPIGHT OF SCORN, 1 619
WITH SPATTERING NOISE REJECTED: OFT THEY ASSAYD, 10 567

ASSAYING
ASSAYING BY HIS DEVILISH ART TO REACH 4 801

ASSEMBL'D
THEN ALL THY SAINTS ASSEMBL'D, THOU SHALT JUDGE 3 330
FOR THITHER HE ASSEMBL'D ALL HIS TRAIN, 5 767
ASSEMBL'D ANGELS, AND YE POWERS RETURN'D 10 34

ASSEMBLE
TO UTTER IS NOT SAFE. ASSEMBLE THOU 5 683
ASSEMBLE, AND HARANGUES ARE HEARD, BUT SOON 11 663

ASSEMBLIES
FREQUENTED THIR ASSEMBLIES, WHERESO MET, 11 722

ASSEMBLY
TH' ASSEMBLY, AS WHEN HOLLOW ROCKS RETAIN 2 285
IN HEAV'N, WHEN AT TH' ASSEMBLY, AND IN SIGHT 2 749
HE SAT; AND IN TH' ASSEMBLY NEXT UPSTOOD 6 446

ASSENT
SPARKL'D IN ALL THIR EYES; WITH FULL ASSENT 2 388

ASSENTING
AFTER SHORT PAUSE ASSENTING, THUS BEGAN. 5 562

ASSERT
I MAY ASSERT ETERNAL PROVIDENCE, 1 25
OF THOSE IMPERIAL TITLES WHICH ASSERT 5 801
THIR DEITIES TO ASSERT, WHO WHILE THEY FEEL 6 157

ASSESSOR
TH' ASSESSOR OF HIS THRONE HE THUS BEGAN. 6 679

ASSIDUOUS
TO WEARIE HIM WITH MY ASSIDUOUS CRIES: 11 310

ASSIG'N'D
THEREFORE TO MEE THIR DOOM HE HATH ASSIG'N'D; 6 817

ASSIGN'D
GOD HATH ASSIGN'D US, NOR OF ME SHALT PASS 9 231
AGAINST A FOE BY DOOM EXPRESS ASSIGN'D US, 10 926

ASSIGND
EACH IN THIR SEVERAL ACTIVE SPHEARS ASSIGND, 5 477

ASSIMILATE
TASTING CONCOCT, DIGEST, ASSIMILATE, 5 412

ASSIST
ASSIST US: BUT IF MUCH CONVERSE PERHAPS 9 247

ASSOCIATE
OF HIS ASSOCIATE; HEE TOGETHER CALLS, 5 696
SOLE EVE, ASSOCIATE SOLE, TO ME BEYOND 9 227
TO MY ASSOCIATE POWERS, THEM TO ACQUAINT 10 395

ASSOCIATES		
TH' ASSOCIATES AND COPARTNERS OF OUR LOSS	1	265
OF THY ASSOCIATES, ADAM, AND WILT TASTE	8	401
ASSUME		
CAN EITHER SEX ASSUME, OR BOTH; SO SOFT	1	424
ME FROM ATTEMPTING. WHEREFORE DO I ASSUME	2	450
NOR SHALT THOU BY DESCENDING TO ASSUME	3	303
I GIVE THEE, REIGN FOR EVER, AND ASSUME	3	318
WHO CAN IN REASON THEN OR RIGHT ASSUME	5	794
ASSUME, AS LIKES THEM BEST, CONDENSE OR RARE.	6	353
SCEPTER AND POWER, THY GIVING, I ASSUME,	6	730
THENCEFORTH THE FORM OF SERVANT TO ASSUME,	10	214
ASSUMING		
ABOVE HIS BRETHREN, TO HIMSELF ASSUMING	12	65
ASSUR'D		
COULD HAVE ASSUR'D US; AND BY WHAT BEST WAY,	2	40
THAT BE ASSUR'D, WITHOUT LEAVE ASKT OF THEE:	2	685
OF ANGER SHALL REMAIN, BUT PEACE ASSUR'D,	3	263
OF GALILEO, LESS ASSUR'D, OBSERVES	5	262
ASSUR'D ME, AND STILL ASSURE: THOUGH WHAT THOU TELLST	5	553
WHAT NEXT I BRING SHALL PLEASE THEE, BE ASSUR'D,	8	449
PERNICIOUS TO THY PEACE, CHIEFLY ASSUR'D	9	981
AT THIS LAST SIGHT, ASSUR'D THAT MAN SHALL LIVE	11	872
ASSURE		
ASSUR'D ME, AND STILL ASSURE: THOUGH WHAT THOU TELLST	5	553
ASSURES		
ASSURES ME THAT THE BITTERNESS OF DEATH	11	157
ASSYRIA		
THIR KINGS, WHEN AEGYPT WITH ASSYRIA STROVE	1	721
ASSYRIAN		
THE WAY HE WENT, AND ON TH' ASSYRIAN MOUNT	4	126
FROM THIS ASSYRIAN GARDEN, WHERE THE FIEND	4	285
ASTARTE		
ASTARTE, QUEEN OF HEAV'N, WITH CRESCENT HORNS;	1	439
ASTHMA'S		
DROPSIES, AND ASTHMA'S, AND JOINT-RACKING RHEUMS.	11	488
ASTONIED		
ASTONIED STOOD AND BLANK, WHILE HORROR CHILL	9	890
ASTONISHMENT		
IF SUCH ASTONISHMENT AS THIS CAN SIEZE	1	317
ASTONISHT		
LYE THUS ASTONISHT ON TH' OBLIVIOUS POOL,	1	266
ASTONISHT; NONE AMONG THE CHOICE AND PRIME	2	423
PLAGUES; THEY ASTONISHT ALL RESISTANCE LOST,	6	838
ASTORETH		
CAME ASTORETH, WHOM THE PHOENICIANS CALL'D	1	438
ASTOUNDED		
AS WE EREWHILE, ASTOUNDED AND AMAZ'D,	1	281
ASTRACAN		
BY ASTRACAN OVER THE SNOWIE PLAINES	10	432
ASTREA		
BETWIXT ASTREA AND THE SCORPION SIGNE,	4	998
ASTRONOMER		
ASTRONOMER IN THE SUN'S LUCENT ORBE	3	589
ASUNDER		
HIS WISH AND BEST ADVANTAGE, US ASUNDER,	9	258
ATABALIPA		
OF ATABALIPA, AND YET UNSPOIL'D	11	409
ATCHIEV'D		
THOU HAST ATCHIEV'D OUR LIBERTIE, CONFIN'D	10	368
WITH PERIL GREAT ATCHIEV'D. LONG WERE TO TELL	10	469
THUS FAME SHALL BE ATCHIEV'D, RENOWN ON EARTH,	11	698
ATCHIEVING		
DETERRD NOT FROM ATCHIEVING WHAT MIGHT LEADE	9	696
ATHEIST		
TURNS ATHEIST, AS DID ELY'S SONS, WHO FILL'D	1	495
THE ATHEIST CREW, BUT WITH REDOUBL'D BLOW	6	370
ATHEISTS		
OF THESE FAIR ATHEISTS, AND NOW SWIM IN JOY,	11	625
ATHENS		
IN ATHENS OR FREE ROME, WHERE ELOQUENCE	9	671
ATHWART		
THY MISCREATED FRONT ATHWART MY WAY	2	683
ATLANTEAN		
WITH ATLANTEAN SHOULDERS FIT TO BEAR	2	306
ATLANTIC		
ANDROMEDA FARR OFF ATLANTIC SEAS	3	559
ATLANTICK		
ATLANTICK SISTERS, AND THE SPARTAN TWINS	10	674
ATLAS		
LIKE TENERIFF OR ATLAS UNREMOV'D:	4	987
OR THENCE FROM NIGER FLOOD TO ATLAS MOUNT	11	402
ATOM		
AN ATOM, WITH THE FIRMAMENT COMPAR'D	8	18
ATOMS		
THIR EMBRYON ATOMS; THEY AROUND THE FLAG	2	900
ATROPHIE		
AND MOON-STRUCK MADNESS, PINING ATROPHIE,	11	486
ATTACH'D		
AND CHARMING SYMPHONIES ATTACH'D THE HEART	11	595
ATTACK		
NO EQUAL, RAUNGING THROUGH THE DIRE ATTACK	6	248
ATTAIN		
LIGHT AFTER LIGHT WELL US'D THEY SHALL ATTAIN,	3	196
YET WHAT THOU CANST ATTAIN, WHICH BEST MAY SERVE	7	115
THIS TO ATTAIN, WHETHER HEAV'N MOVE OR EARTH,	8	70
TH' OFFENCE, THAT MAN SHOULD THUS ATTAIN TO KNOW?	9	726
IF SO I MAY ATTAIN. SO BOTH ASCEND	11	376
ATTAIND		
AND LIFE MORE PERFET HAVE ATTAIND THEN FATE	9	689
THIS HAVING LEARNT, THOU HAST ATTAIND THE SUMME	12	575
ATTAINE		
HE CEAS'D, I LOWLY ANSWER'D. TO ATTAINE	8	412
TO US, AS LIKELY TASTING TO ATTAINE	9	935
OF THY PERFECTION, HOW SHALL I ATTAINE,	9	964
ATTAINES		
SERV'D BY MORE NOBLE THEN HER SELF, ATTAINES	8	34
ATTAINS		
THAT WHOSO EATS THEREOF, FORTHWITH ATTAINS	9	724
CANAAN HE NOW ATTAINS, I SEE HIS TENTS	12	135
ATTEMPT		
WITH VAIN ATTEMPT. HIM THE ALMIGHTY POWER	1	44
WHICH TEMPTED OUR ATTEMPT, AND WROUGHT OUR FALL.	1	642
THE PERILOUS ATTEMPT; BUT ALL SAT MUTE,	2	420
BUT FATE WITHSTANDS, AND TO OPPOSE TH' ATTEMPT	2	610
BEGINS HIS DIRE ATTEMPT, WHICH NIGH THE BIRTH	4	15
THY EMPIRE? EASILY THE PROUD ATTEMPT	7	609
NOT THAT THEY DURST WITHOUT HIS LEAVE ATTEMPT,	8	237
TH' ATTEMPT IT SELF, INTENDED BY OUR FOE.	9	295
THIS MY ATTEMPT, I WOULD SUSTAIN ALONE	9	978
OR HERE TH' ATTEMPT, THOU COULDST NOT HAVE DISCERND	9	1149
NO EVIL DURST ATTEMPT THEE, BUT I RUE	9	1180
HINDER'D NOT SATAN TO ATTEMPT THE MINDE	10	8
ATTEMPTED		
AND WHERE THIR WEAKNESS, HOW ATTEMPTED BEST,	2	357
NOT SEEING THEE ATTEMPTED, WHO ATTEST?	9	369
ATTEMPTING		
ATTEMPTING, OR TO SIT IN DARKNESS HERE	2	377
ME FROM ATTEMPTING. WHEREFORE DO I ASSUME	2	450
ATTEMPTS		
THE WOMAN, OPPORTUNE TO ALL ATTEMPTS,	9	481
ATTEND		
WHERE ALL HIS SONS THY EMBASSIE ATTEND;	3	658
THE CLOUDS THAT ON HIS WESTERN THRONE ATTEND:	4	597
ATTEND: THAT THOU ART HAPPIE, OWE TO GOD;	5	520
OR IN THIR PEARLIE SHELLS AT EASE, ATTEND	7	407
BUT THY RELATION NOW; FOR I ATTEND,	8	247
OF RENDRING UP, AND PATIENTLY ATTEND	11	551
THOU THEREFORE GIVE DUE AUDIENCE, AND ATTEND.	12	12
MEN WHO ATTEND THE ALTAR, AND SHOULD MOST	12	354
ATTENDANCE		
ATTENDANCE NONE SHALL NEED, NOR TRAIN, WHERE NONE	10	80
ATTENDANT		
ATTENDANT ON THIR LORD: HEAV'N OP'ND WIDE	7	205
SURPRISE THEE, AND HER BLACK ATTENDANT DEATH.	7	547
WITH THIR ATTENDANT MOONS THOU WILT DESCRIE	8	149

ATTENDED
ATTENDED: ALL ACCESS WAS THRONG'D, THE GATES 1 761
WHEN THOU ATTENDED GLORIOUSLY FROM HEAV'N 3 323
ATTENDED WITH TEN THOUSAND THOUSAND SAINTS, 6 767

ATTENDS
GLAD TO BE OFFER'D, HE ATTENDS THE WILL 3 270
ATTENDS THEE, AND EACH WORD, EACH MOTION FORMES, 8 223
WHICH OFT, THEY SAY, SOME EVIL SPIRIT ATTENDS 9 638
BUT THAT SUCCESS ATTENDS HIM; IF MISHAP, 10 239

ATTENTION
WITH ALL HIS PEERS: ATTENTION HELD THEM MUTE. 1 618
DREW AUDIENCE AND ATTENTION STILL AS NIGHT 2 308
OF HER ATTENTION GAIND, WITH SERPENT TONGUE 9 529
SAY, FOR SUCH WONDER CLAIMS ATTENTION DUE. 9 566
SILENCE, AND WITH THESE WORDS ATTENTION WON. 10 459
SOON RAIS'D, AND HIS ATTENTION THUS RECALL'D. 11 422

ATTENTIVE
ATTENTIVE, AND WITH MORE DELIGHTED EARE, 5 545
THE STORIE HEARD ATTENTIVE, AND WAS FILL'D 7 51
TO BETTER HOPES HIS MORE ATTENTIVE MINDE 10 1011

ATTEST
ATTEST THIR JOY, THAT HILL AND VALLEY RINGS. 2 495
NOT SEEING THEE ATTEMPTED, WHO ATTEST? 9 369

ATTIRE
FIRST WHEELD THIR COURSE; EARTH IN HER RICH ATTIRE 7 501

ATTONEMENT
ATTONEMENT FOR HIMSELF OR OFFERING MEET, 3 234

ATTRACT
SHEE WAS INDEED, AND LOVELY TO ATTRACT 10 152

ATTRACTED
ATTRACTED BY THY BEAUTY STILL TO GAZE. 5 47

ATTRACTION
OF CONJUGAL ATTRACTION UNREPROV'D, 4 493
BY THIS NEW FELT ATTRACTION AND INSTINCT. 10 263

ATTRACTIVE
I PLEAS'D, AND WITH ATTRACTIVE GRACES WON 2 762
FOR SOFTNESS SHEE AND SWEET ATTRACTIVE GRACE, 4 298
BY HIS ATTRACTIVE VERTUE AND THIR OWN 8 124
ATTRACTIVE, HUMAN, RATIONAL, LOVE STILL; 8 587

ATTRIBUTE
THE SWIFTNESS OF THOSE CIRCLES ATTRIBUTE, 8 107

ATTRIBUTED
WITH GLORIE ATTRIBUTED TO THE HIGH 8 12
LESS ATTRIBUTED TO HER FAITH SINCERE, 9 320

ATTRIBUTES
TO TEACH THEE THAT GOD ATTRIBUTES TO PLACE 11 836

ATTRIBUTING
BY ATTRIBUTING OVERMUCH TO THINGS 8 565

ATTRITE
THE AIR ATTRITE TO FIRE, AS LATE THE CLOUDS 10 1073

ATTUNE
BREATHING THE SMELL OF FIELD AND GROVE, ATTUNE 4 265

AUDACIOUS
AUDACIOUS NEIGHBOURHOOD, THE WISEST HEART 1 400
AUDACIOUS, BUT THAT SEAT SOON FAILING, MEETS 2 931

AUDIBLE
YET ALL HAD HEARD, WITH AUDIBLE LAMENT 11 266

AUDIBLY
PRESENT) THUS TO HIS SON AUDIBLY SPAKE. 7 518

AUDIENCE
DREW AUDIENCE AND ATTENTION STILL AS NIGHT 2 308
THE THRONGING AUDIENCE. IN DISCOURSE MORE SWEET 2 555
HAD AUDIENCE, WHEN AMONG THE SERAPHIM 5 804
URANIA, AND FIT AUDIENCE FIND, THOUGH FEW. 7 31
HASTE TO THY AUDIENCE, NIGHT WITH HER WILL BRING 7 105
MOTION, EACH ACT WON AUDIENCE ERE THE TONGUE, 9 674
HE ENDED, AND THE HEAV'NLY AUDIENCE LOUD 10 641
THOU THEREFORE GIVE DUE AUDIENCE, AND ATTEND. 12 12

AUDITRESS
ADAM RELATING, THE SOLE AUDITRESS; 8 51

AUGHT
THEN AUGHT DIVINE OR HOLY ELSE ENJOY'D 1 683
FELL LONG BEFORE; NOR AUGHT AVAIL'D HIM NOW 1 748
WITH SPLENDOR, ARM'D WITH POWER, IF AUGHT PROPOS'D 2 447
IF AUGHT DISTURB'D THIR NOYSE, INTO HER WOOMB, 2 657
MIGHT HAP TO MOVE NEW BROILES: BE THIS OR AUGHT 2 837

AUGHT (CONTINUED)
OR AUGHT BY ME IMMUTABLIE FORESEEN, 3 121
COMPAR'D WITH AUGHT ON EARTH, MEDAL OR STONE; 3 592
AUGHT WHEREOF HEE HATH NEED, HEE WHO REQUIRES 4 419
HAVE GATHERED AUGHT OF EVIL OR CONCEALD, 5 207
SUPERIOR, NOR OF VIOLENCE FEAR'D AUGHT; 5 905
UNSOUND AND FALSE; NOR IS IT AUGHT BUT JUST, 6 121
IF I CONJECTURE AUGHT, NO DRIZLING SHOWR, 6 545
AUGHT, NOT SURPASSING HUMAN MEASURE, SAY. 7 640
FOR AUGHT APPEERS, AND ON THIR ORBS IMPOSE 8 30
ABOVE MANKINDE, OR AUGHT THEN MANKINDE HIGHER, 8 358
TO THEM MADE COMMON AND DIVULG'D, IF AUGHT 8 583
NEITHER HER OUT-SIDE FORMD SO FAIR, NOR AUGHT 8 596
THY JUDGEMENT TO DO AUGHT, WHICH ELSE FREE WILL 8 636
IF I COULD JOY IN AUGHT, SWEET INTERCHANGE 9 115
OR AUGHT THAT MIGHT HIS HAPPIE STATE SECURE, 9 347
AS WAS MY FOOD, NOR AUGHT BUT FOOD DISCERN'D 9 573
RATHER THEN DEATH OR AUGHT THEN DEATH MORE DREAD 9 969
IF ADAM AUGHT PERHAPS MIGHT INTERPOSE; 12 4

AUGMENT
HIS GLORY TO AUGMENT. THE BOLD DESIGN 2 386
BOTH TO AND FRO, THIR SORROW TO AUGMENT, 2 605
BY TINCTURE OR REFLECTION THEY AUGMENT 7 367
A LONG DAYS DYING TO AUGMENT OUR PAINE, 10 964

AUGMENTED
PRECIPITATE THEE WITH AUGMENTED PAINE. 6 280
AUGMENTED, OP'ND EYES, NEW HOPES, NEW JOYES, 9 985

AURAN
FROM AURAN EASTWARD TO THE ROYAL TOWRS 4 211

AURORA'S
OF LEAVES AND FUMING RILLS, AURORA'S FAN, 5 6

AUSONIAN
IN ANCIENT GREECE; AND IN AUSONIAN LAND 1 739

AUSTEER
WITH SWEET AUSTEER COMPOSURE THUS REPLY'D, 9 272

AUSTERELY
WHATEVER HYPOCRITES AUSTERELY TALK 4 744

AUTHENTIC
THE FIRST ART WONT HIS GREAT AUTHENTIC WILL 3 656
ON HIM WHO HAD STOLE JOVES AUTHENTIC FIRE. 4 719

AUTHOR
BUT FROM THE AUTHOR OF ALL ILL COULD SPRING 2 381
THOU ART MY FATHER, THOU MY AUTHOR, THOU 2 864
ETERNAL KING; THEE AUTHOR OF ALL BEING, 3 374
MY AUTHOR AND DISPOSER, WHAT THOU BIDST 4 635
THE AUTHOR NOT IMPAIR'D, BUT HONOURD MORE? 5 73
IN HONOUR TO THE WORLDS GREAT AUTHOR RISE, 5 188
AUTHOR OF EVIL, UNKNOWN TILL THY REVOLT, 6 262
AUTHOR AND END OF ALL THINGS, AND FROM WORK 7 591
SAID MILDELY, AUTHOR OF ALL THIS THOU SEEST 8 317
ADORE THEE, AUTHOR OF THIS UNIVERSE, 8 360
THE GOOD BEFALL'N HIM, AUTHOR UNSUSPECT, 9 771
IDLELY, WHILE SATAN OUR GREAT AUTHOR THRIVES 10 236
THOU ART THIR AUTHOR AND PRIME ARCHITECT: 10 356

AUTHORITIE
AUTHORITIE USURPT, FROM GOD NOT GIV'N: 12 66

AUTHORITY
AUTHORITY AND REASON ON HER WAITE, 8 554

AUTHORS
THEY TRESPASS, AUTHORS TO THEMSELVES IN ALL 3 122

AUTHOUR
OUR AUTHOUR. HEAV'NLY STRANGER, PLEASE TO TASTE 5 397

AUTORITIE
WHENCE TRUE AUTORITIE IN MEN; THOUGH BOTH 4 295

AUTUMN
IN AUTUMN THWARTS THE NIGHT, WHEN VAPORS FIR'D 4 557
ALL AUTUMN PIL'D, THOUGH SPRING AND AUTUMN HERE 5 394

AUTUMNAL
THICK AS AUTUMNAL LEAVES THAT STROW THE BROOKS 1 302

AUXILIAR
MIXT WITH AUXILIAR GODS; AND WHAT RESOUNDS 1 579

AVAIL
WHAT CAN IT THEN AVAIL THOUGH YET WE FEEL 1 153
THEN SHALL THEY SEEK TO AVAIL THEMSELVES OF NAMES, 12 515

AVAIL'D
FELL LONG BEFORE; NOR AUGHT AVAIL'D HIM NOW 1 748

AVAILE
BUT TO CONVINCE THE PROUD WHAT SIGNS AVAILE, 6 789

AVAILE (CONTINUED)
WHAT MAY NO LESS PERHAPS AVAILE US KNOWN, 7 85

AVAILES
RUIN MUST NEEDS ENSUE; FOR WHAT AVAILES 6 456
NO MORE AVAILES THEN BREATH AGAINST THE WINDE, 11 312

AVANT
BUT MARK WHAT I ARREEDE THEE NOW, AVANT; 4 962

AVENG'D
TO HONOUR HIS ANOINTED SON AVENG'D 6 676
OF HIS ADORERS: HEE TO BE AVENG'D, 9 143
WITH ODDS WHAT WARR HATH LOST, AND FULLY AVENG'D 10 374
WILL BE AVENG'D, AND TH' OTHERS FAITH APPROV'D 11 458

AVENGD
MANKIND WITH HER FAIRE LOOKS, TO BE AVENGD 4 718

AVENGERS
BY HIS AVENGERS, SINCE NO PLACE LIKE THIS 10 241

AVENGING
ERE THIS AVENGING SWORD BEGIN THY DOOME, 6 278
GLORIE TO HIM WHOSE JUST AVENGING IRE 7 184

AVERSE
THE MOST AVERSE, THEE CHIEFLY, WHO FULL OFT 2 763
TRAVELLING EAST, AND WITH HER PART AVERSE 8 138
ON THE EIGHTH RETURN'D, AND ON THE COAST AVERSE 9 67

AVERT
IF SUCH AFFRONT I LABOUR TO AVERT 9 302
HIS PRESENCE FROM AMONG THEM, AND AVERT 12 108

AVOID
EXPOS'D A MATRON TO AVOID WORSE RAPE. 1 505
THY ABSENCE FROM MY SIGHT, BUT TO AVOID 9 294

AVOIDE
SEEK NOT TEMPTATION THEN, WHICH TO AVOIDE 9 364

AVOIDED
AVOIDED PINCHING COLD AND SCORCHING HEATE? 10 691

AW
OF AIRIE THREATS TO AW WHOM YET WITH DEEDS 6 283
PRESENCE DIVINE. REJOYCING, BUT WITH AW 8 314

AWAITING
AWAITING WHAT COMMAND THIR MIGHTY CHIEF 1 566
HIS LOOK SUSPENCE, AWAITING WHO APPEER'D 2 418
CHIEF OF TH' ANGELIC GUARDS, AWAITING NIGHT; 4 550
AWAITING NEXT COMMAND. TO WHOM THIR CHIEF 4 864

AWAITS
O EVE, SOME FURDER CHANGE AWAITS US NIGH, 11 193
AWAITS THE GOOD, THE REST WHAT PUNISHMENT? 11 710

AWAK'D
AWAK'D SHOULD BLOW THEM INTO SEVENFOLD RAGE 2 171

AWAKE
AWAKE, ARISE, OR BE FOR EVER FALL'N. 1 330
ROUSE AND BESTIR THEMSELVES ERE WELL AWAKE. 1 334
HER HAND SOFT TOUCHING, WHISPERD THUS. AWAKE 5 17
AWAKE, THE MORNING SHINES, AND THE FRESH FIELD 5 20
TO THE NIGHT-WARBLING BIRD, THAT NOW AWAKE 5 40
STILL GLORIOUS BEFORE WHOM AWAKE I STOOD; 8 464

AWAK'NING
AWAK'NING, THUS TO HIM IN SECRET SPAKE. 5 672

AWAK'T
I FIRST AWAK'T, AND FOUND MY SELF REPOS'D 4 450
OF WRAUTH AWAK'T: NOR WITH LESS DREAD THE LOUD 6 59

AWARE
ARE EVER CLEER. WHEREOF HEE SOON AWARE, 4 119
SO WARND HE THEM AWARE THEMSELVES, AND SOON 6 547

AWAY
THIR ARMS AWAY THEY THREW, AND TO THE HILLS 6 639

AW'D
AW'D BY THE ROD OF MOSES SO TO STAND 12 198

AWD
NEERER HIS PRESENCE ADAM THOUGH NOT AWD, 5 358

AWE
SUCH WAS THIR AWE OF MAN. IN SHADIE BOWER 4 705
HE HELD IT VAIN; AWE FROM ABOVE HAD QUELLD 4 860
AND PIOUS AWE, THAT FEARD TO HAVE OFFENDED. 5 135
BUILD IN HER LOVELIEST, AND CREATE AN AWE 8 558
WHY THEN WAS THIS FORBID? WHY BUT TO AWE, 9 703
DEVOURD EACH OTHER; NOR STOOD MUCH IN AWE 10 712

AWFUL
OF SOVRAN POWER, WITH AWFUL CEREMONY 1 753
WITH AWFUL REVERENCE PRONE; AND AS A GOD 2 478
AND FELT HOW AWFUL GOODNESS IS, AND SAW 4 847
HEAV'NS AWFUL MONARCH? WHEREFORE BUT IN HOPE 4 960
SO AWFUL, THAT WITH HONOUR THOU MAIST LOVE 8 577
THY AWFUL BROW, MORE AWFUL THUS RETIR'D. 9 537

AWRY
BLOWS THEM TRANSVERSE TEN THOUSAND LEAGUES AWRY 3 488

AXLE
IN MUTINIE HAD FROM HER AXLE TORN 2 926
REVOLVD ON HEAV'NS GREAT AXLE, AND HER REIGN 7 381
ON HER SOFT AXLE, WHILE SHE PACES EEV'N, 8 165
FROM THE SUNS AXLE; THEY WITH LABOUR PUSH'D 10 670

AY
TH' OMNIPOTENT. AY ME, THEY LITTLE KNOW 4 86
TO PERPETUITIE; AY ME, THAT FEAR 10 813

AZAZEL
AZAZEL AS HIS RIGHT, A CHERUBE TALL: 1 534

AZORES
BENEATH TH' AZORES; WHITHER THE PRIME ORB, 4 592

AZOTUS
REAR'D IN AZOTUS, DREADED THROUGH THE COAST 1 464

AZURE
ON HEAVENS AZURE, AND THE TORRID CLIME 1 297
WITH SPOTS OF GOLD AND PURPLE, AZURE AND GREEN: 7 479
CARNATION, PURPLE, AZURE, OR SPECT WITH GOLD, 9 429

BAALIM
OF BAALIM AND ASHTAROTH, THOSE MALE, 1 422

BABEL
OF BABEL, AND THE WORKS OF MEMPHIAN KINGS 1 694
THE BUILDERS NEXT OF BABEL ON THE PLAIN 3 466

BABELS
NEW BABELS, HAD THEY WHEREWITHALL, WOULD BUILD: 3 468

BABILON
THE ROOF WAS FRETTED GOLD. NOT BABILON, 1 717

BABYLON
LEFT IN CONFUSION, BABYLON THENCE CALL'D. 12 343
RETURND FROM BABYLON BY LEAVE OF KINGS 12 348

BACCHUS
YOUNG BACCHUS FROM HIS STEPDAME RHEA'S EYE; 4 279
OF BACCHUS AND HIS REVELLERS, THE RACE 7 33

BACK
BACK TO THE GATES OF HEAV'N; THE SULPHUROUS HAIL 1 171
PERIODS OF TIME, THENCE HURRIED BACK TO FIRE. 2 603
THY KING AND LORD? BACK TO THY PUNISHMENT, 2 699
ALL TH' HOST OF HEAV'N; BACK THEY RECOILD AFFRAID 2 759
FROM ALL HER CAVES, AND BACK RESOUNDED DEATH. 2 789
BACK FROM PURSUIT THY POWERS WITH LOUD ACCLAIME 3 397
HIS BACK WAS TURND, BUT NOT HIS BRIGHTNESS HID; 3 624
AND LIKE A DEVILLISH ENGINE BACK RECOILES 4 17
BENDING TO LOOK ON ME, I STARTED BACK, 4 462
IT STARTED BACK, BUT PLEAS'D I SOON RETURND, 4 463
THEN THAT SMOOTH WATRY IMAGE; BACK I TURND, 4 480
BACK STEPT THOSE TWO FAIRE ANGELS HALF AMAZ'D 4 820
SEAVENFOLD, AND SCOURGE THAT WISDOM BACK TO HELL, 4 914
BACK TO TH' INFERNAL PIT I DRAG THEE CHAIND, 4 965
AND WITH RETORTED SCORN HIS BACK HE TURN'D 5 906
BACK ON THY FOES MORE GLORIOUS TO RETURN 6 39
HE BACK RECOILD; THE TENTH ON BENDED KNEE 6 194
BACK TO HIS CHARIOT; WHERE IT STOOD RETIR'D 6 338
BUT FIRM BATTALION; BACK WITH SPEEDIEST SAIL 6 534
OUR OVERTURE, AND TURN NOT BACK PERVERSE; 6 562
OF THUNDER; BACK DEFEATED TO RETURN 6 606
DRIV'N BACK REDOUNDED AS A FLOOD ON THOSE 7 57
LIGHT BACK TO THEM, IS OBVIOUS TO DISPUTE. 8 158
BITTER ERE LONG BACK ON IT SELF RECOILES; 9 172
TO INTERCEPT THY WAY, OR SEND THEE BACK 9 410
THAT ALL WAS LOST. BACK TO THE THICKET SLUNK 9 784
BUT LEAST THE DIFFICULTIE OF PASSING BACK 10 252
DESIROUS TO RESIGNE, AND RENDER BACK 10 749
COMES THUNDRING BACK WITH DREADFUL REVOLUTION 10 814
BLOWN STIFLING BACK ON HIM THAT BREATHS IT FORTH: 11 313
WITH GLORY AND SPOILE BACK TO THIR PROMIS'D LAND. 12 172
RETURN THEM BACK TO EGYPT, CHOOSING RATHER 12 219
THE ADVERSARIE SERPENT, AND BRING BACK 12 312
THE SPACE OF SEVENTIE YEARS, THEN BRINGS THEM BACK, 12 345
THEY LOOKING BACK, ALL TH' EASTERN SIDE BEHELD 12 641

BACKS
EMERGENT, AND THIR BROAD BARE BACKS UPHEAVE 7 286

BACKSIDE
FLY O'RE THE BACKSIDE OF THE WORLD FARR OFF 3 494

BACKWARD
DRIVN BACKWARD SLOPE THIR POINTING SPIRES, AND ROWLD 1 223
STROOK THEM WITH HORROR BACKWARD, BUT FAR WORSE 6 863

BACTRIAN
RETIRES, OR BACTRIAN SOPHI FROM THE HORNES 10 433

BAD
SO NUMBERLESS WERE THOSE BAD ANGELS SEEN 1 344
TO THAT BAD EMINENCE; AND FROM DESPAIR 2 6
LOOSE ALL HER VIRTUE; LEAST BAD MEN SHOULD BOAST 2 483
HIS MOTHER BAD, AND THUS BESPAKE HER SIRE. 2 849
BAD MEN AND ANGELS, THEY ARRAIGND SHALL SINK 3 331
THE BARRS OF HELL, ON ERRAND BAD NO DOUBT: 4 795
BAD INFLUENCE INTO TH' UNWARIE BREST 5 695
IN SERPENT, INMATE BAD, AND TOWARD EVE 9 495
IN RECOMPENCE (FOR SUCH COMPLIANCE BAD 9 994
BAD FRUIT OF KNOWLEDGE, IF THIS BE TO KNOW, 9 1073
BUT LET US NOW, AS IN BAD PLIGHT, DEVISE 9 1091
ON HIS BAD ERRAND, MAN SHOULD BE SEDUC'T 10 41
WITH THAT BAD WOMAN? THUS WHAT THOU DESIR'ST 10 837
AND ONE BAD ACT WITH MANY DEEDS WELL DONE 11 256
TO THEE AND TO THY OFSPRING; GOOD WITH BAD 11 358
WHERE GOOD WITH BAD WERE MATCHT, WHO OF THEMSELVES 11 685
STILL TEND FROM BAD TO WORSE, TILL GOD AT LAST 12 106
PART GOOD, PART BAD, OF BAD THE LONGER SCROWLE, 12 336
TO GOOD MALIGNANT, TO BAD MEN BENIGNE, 12 538

BAIT
WHICH GREW IN PARADISE, THE BAIT OF EVE 10 551

BAL
MIXT DANCE, OR WANTON MASK, OR MIDNIGHT BAL, 4 768

BALEFUL
TORMENTS HIM; ROUND HE THROWS HIS BALEFUL EYES 1 56
INTO THE BURNING LAKE THIR BALEFUL STREAMS; 2 576

BALLANCE
THIR COURSE, IN EVEN BALLANCE DOWN THEY LIGHT 1 349
AND THAT CRYSTALLINE SPHEAR WHOSE BALLANCE WEIGHS 3 482

BALLANC'T
THE PENDULOUS ROUND EARTH WITH BALLANC'T AIRE 4 1000
AND EARTH SELF BALLANC'T ON HER CENTER HUNG. 7 242

BALLS
WHEREOF TO FOUND THIR ENGINS AND THIR BALLS 6 518

BALME
SHALL BREATHE HER BALME. BUT FIRST WHOM SHALL WE SEND 2 402
GROVES WHOSE RICH TREES WEPT ODOROUS GUMMS AND BALME, 4 248
AND FLOURING ODOURS, CASSIA, NARD, AND BALME; 5 293
OF BLOWING MYRRH AND BALME; IF THOU ACCEPT 9 629
THE BALME OF LIFE. TO WHOM OUR ANCESTOR. 11 546

BALMIE
THOSE BALMIE SPOILES. AS WHEN TO THEM WHO SAILE 4 159
WHAT DROPS THE MYRRHE, AND WHAT THE BALMIE REED, 5 23
IN BALMIE SWEAT, WHICH WITH HIS BEAMES THE SUN 8 255
RAPT IN A BALMIE CLOUD WITH WINGED STEEDS 11 706

BAND
FORTHWITH FROM EVERY SQUADRON AND EACH BAND 1 356
FROM EVERY BAND AND SQUARED REGIMENT 1 758
GENTLY WITH MIRTLE BAND, MINDLESS THE WHILE, 9 431
ONE WAY A BAND SELECT FROM FORAGE DRIVES 11 646

BANDED
BANDED AGAINST HIS THRONE, BUT TO REMAINE 2 320
WERE BANDED TO OPPOSE HIS HIGH DECREE; 5 717
THE BANDED POWERS OF SATAN HASTING ON 6 85
SOON BANDED; OTHERS FROM THE DAWNING HILLS 6 528

BANDS
A NUMEROUS BRIGAD HASTEN'D. AS WHEN BANDS 1 675
ANOTHER PART IN SQUADRONS AND GROSS BANDS, 2 570
IN CONFUS'D MARCH FORLORN, TH' ADVENTROUS BANDS 2 615
POURD OUT BY MILLIONS HER VICTORIOUS BANDS 2 997
ANGELS ASCENDING AND DESCENDING, BANDS 3 511
SINGING THIR GREAT CREATOR: OFT IN BANDS 4 684
THE CIRCUIT WIDE. STRAIT KNEW HIM ALL THE BANDS 5 287
DISPERST IN BANDS AND FILES THIR CAMP EXTEND 5 651
BIND US WITH AFTER-BANDS, WHAT PROFITS THEN 9 761
HE ERR'D NOT, FOR BY THIS THE HEAV'NLY BANDS 11 208

BANE
DESERVE THE PRECIOUS BANE. AND HERE LET THOSE 1 692
SHOULD PROVE A BITTER MORSEL, AND HIS BANE, 2 808
WHO CAME THIR BANE, THOUGH WITH THEM BETTER PLEAS'D 4 167
BANE, AND IN HEAV'N MUCH WORSE WOULD BE MY STATE. 9 123
SPREADING THIR BANE; THE BLASTED STARRS LOOKT WAN, 10 412

BANISHMENT
PERPETUAL BANISHMENT. YET LEAST THEY FAINT 11 108

BANISHT
AND BANISHT FROM MANS LIFE HIS HAPPIEST LIFE, 4 317
LOST SIGHT OF HIM; ONE OF THE BANISHT CREW 4 573
HEAV'N-BANISHT HOST, LEFT DESERT UTMOST HELL 10 437
WHO FOR MY WILFUL CRIME ART BANISHT HENCE. 12 619

BANK
THAT TO THE FRINGED BANK WITH MYRTLE CROWND, 4 262
ON THE SOFT DOWNIE BANK DAMASKT WITH FLOURS: 4 334
ON THE GREEN BANK, TO LOOK INTO THE CLEER 4 458
BANK THE MID SEA: PART SINGLE OR WITH MATE 7 403
ON A GREEN SHADIE BANK PROFUSE OF FLOURS 8 286
IMBORDERD ON EACH BANK, THE HAND OF EVE: 9 438
HER HAND HE SEIS'D, AND TO A SHADIE BANK, 9 1037

BANKS
WAS FAIR DAMASCUS, ON THE FERTIL BANKS 1 468
FOUR WAYS THIR FLYING MARCH, ALONG THE BANKS 2 574
ALL BUT WITHIN THOSE BANKS, WHERE RIVERS NOW 7 305

BANNE
MUCH MORE TO TASTE IT UNDER BANNE TO TOUCH. 9 925

BANNERD
THAT WITH EXTENDED WINGS A BANNERD HOST 2 885

BANNERS
TEN THOUSAND BANNERS RISE INTO THE AIR 1 545
AND ALL WHO UNDER ME THIR BANNERS WAVE, 5 687

BANQUET
THE SUN, AS FROM THYESTEAN BANQUET, TURN'D 10 688

BAPTIZ'D
AND ALL WHO SINCE, BAPTIZ'D OR INFIDEL 1 582
BAPTIZ'D, SHALL THEM WITH WONDROUS GIFTS ENDUE 12 500

BAPTIZING
BAPTIZING IN THE PROFLUENT STREAM, THE SIGNE 12 442

BAR
TH' INTRICATE WARDS, AND EVERY BOLT AND BAR 2 877

BARBARIC
SHOWRS ON HER KINGS BARBARIC PEARL AND GOLD, 2 4

BARBAROUS
RHENE OR THE DANAW, WHEN HER BARBAROUS SONS 1 353
BUT DRIVE FARR OFF THE BARBAROUS DISSONANCE 7 32

BARBD
BUT RATLING STORM OF ARROWS BARBD WITH FIRE. 6 546

BARCA
OF BARCA OR CYRENE'S TORRID SOIL, 2 904

BARD
OF THAT WILDE ROUT THAT TORE THE THRACIAN BARD 7 34

BARE
CAME SINGLY WHERE HE STOOD ON THE BARE STRAND, 1 379
WITH SINGED TOP THIR STATELY GROWTH THOUGH BARE 1 614
ON THE BARE OUTSIDE OF THIS WORLD, THAT SEEM'D 3 74
EMERGENT, AND THIR BROAD BARE BACKS UPHEAVE 7 286
HE SCARCE HAD SAID, WHEN THE BARE EARTH, TILL THEN 7 313
DESERT AND BARE, UNSIGHTLY, UNADORND, 7 314
SHORN OF HIS STRENGTH, THEY DESTITUTE AND BARE 9 1062
FROM OUT OF CHAOS TO THE OUT SIDE BARE 10 317
AND THERE TAKE ROOT AN ILAND SALT AND BARE, 11 834

BARK
SEA-FARING MEN OREWATCHT, WHOSE BARK BY CHANCE 2 288
KINDLES THE GUMMIE BARK OF FIRR OR PINE, 10 1076

BARK'D
A CRY OF HELL HOUNDS NEVER CEASING BARK'D 2 654
AND KENNEL THERE, YET THERE STILL BARK'D AND HOWL'D, 2 658

BARR
SPIRITUAL SUBSTANCE WITH CORPOREAL BARR. 4 585
HIS WILL WHO BOUND US? LET HIM SURER BARR 4 897

BARR'D
BARR'D OVER US PROHIBIT ALL EGRESS. 2 437
WEST FROM ORONTES TO THE OCEAN BARR'D 9 80
BARR'D OF HIS RIGHT; YET AT HIS BIRTH A STARR 12 360

BARRD
CROSS-BARRD AND BOLTED FAST, FEAR NO ASSAULT, 4 190
THE FACIL GATES OF HELL TOO SLIGHTLY BARRD. 4 967

BARREN
BUT IN HIS WAY LIGHTS ON THE BARREN PLAINES 3 437
HIS BARREN LEAVES. THEM THUS IMPLOID BEHELD 5 219
MORE PLENTY THEN THE SUN THAT BARREN SHINES, 8 94

BARRENNESS
AGAINST OUR SELVES, AND WILFUL BARRENNESS, 10 1042

BARRICADO'D
THE DISMAL GATES, AND BARRICADO'D STRONG; 8 241

BARRS
PRESCRIB'D, NO BARRS OF HELL, NOR ALL THE CHAINS 3 82
THE BARRS OF HELL, ON ERRAND BAD NO DOUBT: 4 795
OF MEMBRANE, JOYNT, OR LIMB, EXCLUSIVE BARRS: 8 625
AND WITH REBOUNDING SURGE THE BARRS ASSAILD, 10 417

BASAN
IN ARGOB AND IN BASAN, TO THE STREAM 1 398

BASE
EXALTED FROM SO BASE ORIGINAL, 9 150
CIRCULAR BASE OF RISING FOULDS, THAT TOUR'D 9 498

BASER
HER MISCHIEF, AND PURGE OFF THE BASER FIRE 2 141

BASES
BASES AND TINSEL TRAPPINGS, GORGIOUS KNIGHTS 9 36

BASEST
TO BASEST THINGS. REVENGE, AT FIRST THOUGH SWEET, 9 171

BASIS
THAT SHAKE HEAV'NS BASIS, BRING FORTH ALL MY WARR, 6 712

BATES
AS ONE WHO IN HIS JOURNEY BATES AT NOONE, 12 1

BATH'D
OTHERS ON SILVER LAKES AND RIVERS BATH'D 7 437

BATHING
VEX'D SCYLLA BATHING IN THE SEA THAT PARTS 2 660

BATTAILOUS
IN BATTAILOUS ASPECT, AND NEERER VIEW 6 81

BATTALION
THE WHOLE BATTALION VIEWS, THIR ORDER DUE, 1 569
BUT FIRM BATTALION; BACK WITH SPEEDIEST SAIL 6 534

BATTEL
RAIS'D IMPIOUS WAR IN HEAV'N AND BATTEL PROUD 1 43
IN DUBIOUS BATTEL ON THE PLAINS OF HEAV'N, 1 104
OF BATTEL WHEN IT RAG'D, IN ALL ASSAULTS 1 277
AFTER THE TOYL OF BATTEL TO REPOSE 1 319
BOW'D DOWN IN BATTEL, SUNK BEFORE THE SPEAR 1 436
ARMING TO BATTEL, AND IN STEAD OF RAGE 1 553
DESPERATE REVENGE, AND BATTEL DANGEROUS 2 107
TO BATTEL IN THE CLOUDS, BEFORE EACH VAN 2 535
BY DOOM OF BATTEL; AND COMPLAIN THAT FATE 2 550
STRIVE HERE FOR MAISTRIE, AND TO BATTEL BRING 2 899
OF THAT FIRST BATTEL, AND HIS FLIGHT TO HELL: 4 12
THY FIERCEST, WHEN IN BATTEL TO THY AIDE 4 927
IN BATTEL, WHAT OUR POWER IS, OR OUR RIGHT. 5 728
GABRIEL, LEAD FORTH TO BATTEL THESE MY SONS 6 46
OF BATTEL NOW BEGAN, AND RUSHING SOUND 6 97
ON THE ROUGH EDGE OF BATTEL ERE IT JOYN'D, 6 108
OF BATTEL: WHEREAT MICHAEL BID SOUND 6 202
OF BATTEL, OPEN WHEN, AND WHEN TO CLOSE 6 235
THE BATTEL HUNG; TILL SATAN, WHO THAT DAY 6 246
AND NOW THIR MIGHTIEST QUELLD, THE BATTEL SWERV'D, 6 386
TO FINAL BATTEL DREW, DISDAINING FLIGHT, 6 798
YE ANGELS ARM'D, THIS DAY FROM BATTEL REST; 6 802
IN BATTEL WHICH THE STRONGER PROVES, THEY ALL, 6 819
AGAINST THE DAY OF BATTEL, TO A FIELD, 10 275
AS BATTEL HATH ADJUDG'D, FROM THIS NEW WORLD 10 377
SINGLE OR IN ARRAY OF BATTEL RANG'D 11 644
IN SHARP CONTEST OF BATTEL FOUND NO AIDE 11 800

BATTELS
BATTELS AND REALMS: IN THESE HE PUT TWO WEIGHTS 4 1002
BOTH BATTELS MAINE, WITH RUINOUS ASSAULT 6 216
IN BATTELS FEIGN'D; THE BETTER FORTITUDE 9 31
WERE LONG TO TELL, HOW MANY BATTELS FOUGHT, 12 261

BATTERIE
LAY SEIGE, ENCAMPT; BY BATTERIE, SCALE, AND MINE, 11 656

BATTERING
WITH ALL HER BATTERING ENGINES BENT TO RASE 2 923

BATTLE
TO OVERCOME IN BATTLE, AND SUBDUE 11 691

BATTLEMENTS
SHEER O'RE THE CHRYSTAL BATTLEMENTS; FROM MORN 1 742
WITH OPAL TOWRS AND BATTLEMENTS ADORN'D 2 1049

BAUM
NEW RUB'D WITH BAUM, EXPATIATE AND CONFER 1 774

BAY
OR PINNACE ANCHORS IN A CRAGGY BAY 2 289
FORTHWITH THE SOUNDS AND SEAS, EACH CREEK AND BAY 7 399

BEACH
NATHLESS HE SO ENDUR'D, TILL ON THE BEACH 1 299
DEEP TO THE ROOTS OF HELL THE GATHER'D BEACH 10 299

BEADS
AND FLUTTERD INTO RAGGS, THEN RELIQUES, BEADS, 3 491

BEAKED
UPLIFTED; AND SECURE WITH BEAKED PROW 11 746

BEAM
SECURE, AND AT THE BRIGHTNING ORIENT BEAM 2 399
EXTEND HIS EV'NING BEAM, THE FIELDS REVIVE, 2 493
OR OF TH' ETERNAL COETERNAL BEAM 3 2
BY HIS MAGNETIC BEAM, THAT GENTLY WARMS 3 583
ON A SUN BEAM, SWIFT AS A SHOOTING STARR 4 556
RETURND ON THAT BRIGHT BEAM, WHOSE POINT NOW RAISD 4 590
THE LATTER QUICK UP FLEW, AND KICKT THE BEAM; 4 1004
FROM THE SUNS BEAM MEET NIGHT, HER OTHER PART 8 139

BEAMES
IN BALMIE SWEAT, WHICH WITH HIS BEAMES THE SUN 8 255

BEAMING
OF BEAMING SUNNIE RAIES, A GOLDEN TIAR 3 625

BEAMS
SHORN OF HIS BEAMS, OR FROM BEHIND THE MOON 1 596
BIND THIR RESPLENDENT LOCKS INWREATH'D WITH BEAMS, 3 361
THE FULL BLAZE OF THY BEAMS, AND THROUGH A CLOUD 3 378
WHICH NOW THE RISING SUN GUILDS WITH HIS BEAMS. 3 551
BUT ALL SUN-SHINE, AS WHEN HIS BEAMS AT NOON 3 616
O SUN, TO TELL THEE HOW I HATE THY BEAMS 4 37
ON WHICH THE SUN MORE GLAD IMPRESS'D HIS BEAMS 4 150
HIS ORIENT BEAMS, ON HERB, TREE, FRUIT, AND FLOUR, 4 644
SHOT THROUGH WITH ORIENT BEAMS: WHEN ALL THE PLAIN 6 15
BRISTL'D WITH UPRIGHT BEAMS INNUMERABLE 6 82
HER GATHER'D BEAMS, GREAT PALACE NOW OF LIGHT. 7 363
HIS BEAMS, UNACTIVE ELSE, THIR VIGOUR FIND. 8 97
IN THEE CONCENTRING ALL THIR PRECIOUS BEAMS 9 106
LEAVE COLD THE NIGHT, HOW WE HIS GATHER'D BEAMS 10 1070

BEAR
OUR DOOM; WHICH IF WE CAN SUSTAIN AND BEAR, 2 209
WITH ATLANTEAN SHOULDERS FIT TO BEAR 2 306
SUFFICE, OR WHAT EVASION BEAR HIM SAFE 2 411
BEAR HIS SWIFT ERRANDS OVER MOIST AND DRY, 3 652
IN PARADISE THAT BEAR DELICIOUS FRUIT 4 422
BEAR ON YOUR WINGS AND IN YOUR NOTES HIS PRAISE; 5 199
OF LIFE AMBROSIAL FRUTAGE BEAR, AND VINES 5 427
OR IN THIR GLITTERING TISSUES BEAR IMBLAZ'D 5 592
BEAR WITH ME THEN, IF LAWFUL WHAT I ASK; 8 614
THAT SHINE, YET BEAR THIR BRIGHT OFFICIOUS LAMPS, 9 104
OR BEAR WHAT TO MY MINDE FIRST THOUGHTS PRESENT, 9 213
THAT BURDEN HEAVIER THEN THE EARTH TO BEAR 10 835
GRIEVOUS TO BEAR: BUT THAT CARE NOW IS PAST, 11 776
SHALL LEAVE THEM TO ENJOY; FOR TH' EARTH SHALL BEAR 11 804

BEARDED
HER BEARDED GROVE OF EARS, WHICH WAY THE WIND 4 982
ROUGH, OR SMOOTH RIN'D, OR BEARDED HUSK, OR SHELL 5 342

BEARE
INSEPARABLIE THINE, TO HIM SHALT BEARE 4 473
MESSIAH KING ANOINTED, COULD NOT BEARE 5 664
UNIVERSAL REPROACH, FAR WORSE TO BEARE 6 34
FIND PASTIME, AND BEARE RULE; THY REALM IS LARGE. 8 375
UNSEEMLY TO BEARE RULE, WHICH WAS THY PART 10 155
THE MISERIE, I DESERV'D IT, AND WOULD BEARE 10 726
I BEARE THEE, AND UNWEETING HAVE OFFENDED, 10 916
BEARE THINE OWN FIRST, ILL ABLE TO SUSTAINE 10 950
BY MODERATION EITHER STATE TO BEARE, 11 363
ANOUGH TO BEARE; THOSE NOW, THAT WERE DISPENST 11 766

BEARES
AND BEARES THEE SOFT WITH THE SMOOTH AIR ALONG, 8 166
MOSES IN FIGURE BEARES, TO INTRODUCE 12 241

BEARING
WHATEVER EARTH ALL-BEARING MOTHER YIELDS 5 338
PAINS ONELY IN CHILD-BEARING WERE FORETOLD, 10 1051
HIS NAME AND OFFICE BEARING, WHO SHALL QUELL 12 311

BEARS
OF LIBRA TO THE FLEECIE STARR THAT BEARS 3 558
DANDL'D THE KID; BEARS, TYGERS, OUNCES, PARDS, 4 344
TO REST, AND WHAT THE GARDEN CHOICEST BEARS 5 368

BEARST
AND MY DISPLEASURE BEARST SO ILL. IF PRAYERS 10 952

BEARTH
HELP TO DISBURDEN NATURE OF HER BEARTH. 9 624

BEAST

BY ANCIENT TARSUS HELD, OR THAT SEA-BEAST 1 200
ALL PATH OF MAN OR BEAST THAT PAST THAT WAY: 4 177
SILENCE ACCOMPANIED, FOR BEAST AND BIRD, 4 600
BEAST, BIRD, INSECT, OR WORM DURST ENTER NONE; 4 704
CATTEL AND CREEPING THINGS, AND BEAST OF THE EARTH, 7 452
AS FROM HIS LAIRE THE WILDE BEAST WHERE HE WONNS 7 457
THE SERPENT SUTTL'ST BEAST OF ALL THE FIELD, 7 495
BY FOWL, FISH, BEAST, WAS FLOWN, WAS SWUM, WAS WALKT 7 503
BEAST OF THE FIELD, AND OVER ALL THE EARTH, 7 522
OR LIVE IN SEA, OR AIRE, BEAST, FISH, AND FOWLE. 8 341
IN SIGNE WHEREOF EACH BIRD AND BEAST BEHOLD 8 342
AS THUS HE SPAKE, EACH BIRD AND BEAST BEHOLD 8 349
MUCH LESS CAN BIRD WITH BEAST, OR FISH WITH FOWLE 8 395
WORS THEN CAN MAN WITH BEAST, AND LEAST OF ALL. 8 397
TO CATTEL AND EACH BEAST; WHICH WOULD NOT BE 8 582
THE SERPENT SUTTLEST BEAST OF ALL THE FIELD. 9 86
INTO A BEAST, AND MIXT WITH BESTIAL SLIME, 9 165
FROM EVERY BEAST, MORE DUTEOUS AT HER CALL, 9 521
THEE, SERPENT, SUTTLEST BEAST OF ALL THE FIELD 9 560
SHALL THAT BE SHUT TO MAN, WHICH TO THE BEAST 9 691
FOR BEASTS IT SEEMS: YET THAT ONE BEAST WHICH FIRST 9 769
ABOVE ALL CATTLE, EACH BEAST OF THE FIELD; 10 176
FEED FIRST, ON EACH BEAST NEXT, AND FISH, AND FOWLE, 10 604
BEAST NOW WITH BEAST GAN WAR, AND FOWLE WITH FOWLE, 10 710
ON BIRD, BEAST, AIRE, AIRE SUDDENLY ECLIPS'D 11 183
DOWN FROM A HILL THE BEAST THAT REIGNS IN WOODS, 11 187
FOR MAN AND BEAST: WHEN LOE A WONDER STRANGE, 11 733
OF EVERY BEAST, AND BIRD, AND INSECT SMALL 11 734
NO SOONER HEE WITH THEM OF MAN AND BEAST 11 822
WITH MAN THEREIN OR BEAST; BUT WHEN HE BRINGS 11 895
HE GAVE US ONELY OVER BEAST, FISH, FOWL 12 67

BEASTS

ALL BEASTS OF TH' EARTH, SINCE WILDE, AND OF ALL CHASE 4 341
AND FINDE THEE KNOWING NOT OF BEASTS ALONE, 8 438
AMONG THE BEASTS NO MATE FOR THEE WAS FOUND. 8 594
PROCEEDING, WHICH IN OTHER BEASTS OBSERV'D 9 94
IN THIS ENCLOSURE WILD, THESE BEASTS AMONG, 9 543
TO BEASTS, WHOM GOD ON THIR CREATION-DAY 9 556
I WAS AT FIRST AS OTHER BEASTS THAT GRAZE 9 571
ALL OTHER BEASTS THAT SAW, WITH LIKE DESIRE 9 592
THIS INTELLECTUAL FOOD, FOR BEASTS RESERV'D? 9 768
FOR BEASTS IT SEEMS: YET THAT ONE BEAST WHICH FIRST 9 769
THIR NAKEDNESS WITH SKINS OF BEASTS, OR SLAIN, 10 217
OF BEASTS, BUT INWARD NAKEDNESS, MUCH MORE 10 221
HUNTING (AND MEN NOT BEASTS SHALL BE HIS GAME) 12 30

BEAT

LIES DARK AND WILDE, BEAT WITH PERPETUAL STORMS 2 588
THAT BEAT OUT LIFE; HE FELL, AND DEADLY PALE 11 446

BEATEN

AND LIKE A WEATHER-BEATEN VESSEL HOLDS 2 1043

BEATIFIC

IN VISION BEATIFIC: BY HIM FIRST 1 684

BEATITUDE

BEATITUDE PAST UTTERANCE; ON HIS RIGHT 3 62

BEAT'N

PAV'D AFTER HIM A BROAD AND BEAT'N WAY 2 1026

BEAUTEOUS

FENC'D UP THE VERDANT WALL; EACH BEAUTEOUS FLOUR, 4 697
SO BEAUTEOUS, OP'NING TO THE AMBIENT LIGHT. 6 481
YET THEY A BEAUTEOUS OFSPRING SHALL BEGET; 11 613

BEAUTIE

SEVERE IN YOUTHFUL BEAUTIE, ADDED GRACE 4 845
BEAUTIE, WHICH WHETHER WAKING OR ASLEEP, 5 14
AND BEAUTIE, NOT APPROACHT BY STRONGER HATE, 9 491
BY GIFT, AND THY CELESTIAL BEAUTIE ADORE 9 540
FOR NEVER DID THY BEAUTIE SINCE THE DAY 9 1029

BEAUTIES

AGAINST THE CHARM OF BEAUTIES POWERFUL GLANCE. 8 533
SEMBLANCE, AND IN THY BEAUTIES HEAV'NLY RAY 9 607

BEAUTY

HOW BEAUTY IS EXCELLD BY MANLY GRACE 4 490
BOTH OF HER BEAUTY AND SUBMISSIVE CHARMS 4 498
TO WHOM THUS EVE WITH PERFET BEAUTY ADORND. 4 634
BROUGHT HER IN NAKED BEAUTY MORE ADORN'D, 4 713
ATTRACTED BY THY BEAUTY STILL TO GAZE. 5 47
THY YOUTH, THY STRENGTH, THY BEAUTY, WHICH WILL CHANGE 11 539

BEAVIE

A BEAVIE OF FAIR WOMEN, RICHLY GAY 11 582

BECAME

A HELP, BECAME THY SNARE; TO MEE REPROACH 11 165
SUNK DOWN AND ALL HIS SPIRITS BECAME INTRANST: 11 420

BECAM'ST

BECAM'ST ENAMOUR'D, AND SUCH JOY THOU TOOK'ST 2 765
EXPRESS, AND THOU BECAM'ST A LIVING SOUL. 7 528

BECOM

THE GLORY OF THAT GLORY, WHO NOW BECOM 10 722
ERWHILE PERPLEXT WITH THOUGHTS WHAT WOULD BECOM 12 275

BECOME

BECOME OUR ELEMENTS, THESE PIERCING FIRES 2 275
BUT I SHOULD ILL BECOME THIS THRONE, O PEERS, 2 445
AND WHAT ARE GODS THAT MAN MAY NOT BECOME 9 716
HATH EAT'N OF THE FRUIT, AND IS BECOME, 9 869
THAT ERROUR NOW, WHICH IS BECOME MY CRIME, 9 1181
BUT STILL REJOYC'T, HOW IS IT NOW BECOME 10 120
O SONS, LIKE ONE OF US MAN IS BECOME 11 84

BECOMES

ONE OF OUR NUMBER THUS REDUC'T BECOMES, 5 843
OF CONTRARIES; ALL GOOD TO ME BECOMES 9 122
TILL I PROVIDED DEATH; SO DEATH BECOMES 11 61
IMPUTED BECOMES THEIRS BY FAITH, HIS MERITS 12 409

BED

ESPOUSED EVE DECKT FIRST HER NUPTIAL BED, 4 710
WHOSE BED IS UNDEFIL'D AND CHASTE PRONOUNC'T, 4 761
CAPACIOUS BED OF WATERS: THITHER THEY 7 290
(THOUGH HIGHER OF THE GENIAL BED BY FAR, 8 598

BEDROPT

BEDROPT WITH BLOOD OF GORGON, OR THE ISLE 10 527

BEDS

FROM BEDS OF RAGING FIRE TO STARVE IN ICE 2 600
IN BEDS AND CURIOUS KNOTS, BUT NATURE BOON 4 242

BEDWARD

OR BEDWARD RUMINATING: FOR THE SUN 4 352

BEE

HOW NATURE PAINTS HER COLOURS, HOW THE BEE 5 24
THE FEMALE BEE THAT FEEDS HER HUSBAND DRONE 7 490

BEELZEBUB

BEELZEBUB. TO WHOM TH' ARCH-ENEMY, 1 81
SO SATAN SPAKE, AND HIM BEELZEBUB 1 271
WHICH WHEN BEELZEBUB PERCEIV'D, THEN WHOM, 2 299
HATCHING VAIN EMPIRES. THUS BEELZEBUB 2 378

BEERSABA

TO BEERSABA, WHERE THE HOLY LAND 3 536

BEES

BRUSHT WITH THE HISS OF RUSSLING WINGS. AS BEES 1 768

BEEVES

A HERD OF BEEVES, FAIRE OXEN AND FAIRE KINE 11 647

BEFALL

SAW HIM DISFIGUR'D, MORE THEN COULD BEFALL 4 127
TO THOSE APOSTATES, LEAST THE LIKE BEFALL 7 44
BEFALL THEE SEVER'D FROM ME; FOR THOU KNOWST 9 252
AND THOU TH' ACCUSER. THUS IT SHALL BEFALL 9 1182
AND MORE THAT SHALL BEFALL, INNUMERABLE 10 896
HENCEFORTH TO BE FORETOLD WHAT SHALL BEFALL 11 771
PURE, AND IN MIND PREPAR'D, IF SO BEFALL, 12 444

BEFALL'N

THE GOOD BEFALL'N HIM, AUTHOR UNSUSPECT, 9 771
MANKIND? THIS MISCHIEF HAD NOT THEN BEFALL'N, 10 895
THY HATRED FOR THIS MISERIE BEFALL'N, 10 928
O TEACHER, SOME GREAT MISCHIEF HATH BEFALL'N 11 450

BEFALLN

BEFALLN US UNFORESEEN, UNTHOUGHT OF, KNOW 2 821

BEFEL

THE DISCORD WHICH BEFEL, AND WARR IN HEAV'N 6 897

BEFELL

APOSTASIE, BY WHAT BEFELL IN HEAVEN 7 43
FOR I THAT DAY WAS ABSENT, AS BEFELL, 8 229
HOW ALL BEFELL: THEY TOWARDS THE THRONE SUPREAM 10 28
MARRYING OR PROSTITUTING, AS BEFELL, 11 716

BEFITS

BEFITS THEE WITH HIM LEAGU'D, THY SELF AS FALSE 10 868

BEFORE

BEFORE ALL TEMPLES TH' UPRIGHT HEART AND PURE, 1 18
BOW'D DOWN IN BATTEL, SUNK BEFORE THE SPEAR 1 436
FELL LONG BEFORE; NOR AUGHT AVAIL'D HIM NOW 1 748
HARD LIBERTY BEFORE THE EASIE YOKE 2 256
TO BATTEL IN THE CLOUDS, BEFORE EACH VAN 2 535
YET UNCONSUM'D. BEFORE THE GATES THERE SAT 2 648
STRANGE HORROR SEISE THEE, AND PANGS UNFELT BEFORE. 2 703
BEFORE MINE EYES IN OPPOSITION SITS 2 803
BEFORE THIR EYES IN SUDDEN VIEW APPEAR 2 890

BEFORE (CONTINUED)
WHOSE FOUNTAIN WHO SHALL TELL? BEFORE THE SUN, 3 8
BEFORE THE HEAVENS THOU WERT, AND AT THE VOICE 3 9
BEFORE HIS DECENT STEPS A SILVER WAND. 3 644
THE GOOD BEFORE HIM, BUT PERVERTS BEST THINGS 4 203
OR WHERE THE SONS OF EDEN LONG BEFORE 4 213
GAMBOLD BEFORE THEM, TH' UNWIELDY ELEPHANT 4 345
BUT STILL THY WORDS AT RANDOM, AS BEFORE, 4 930
INNUMERABLE BEFORE TH' ALMIGHTIES THRONE 5 585
EXCESS, BEFORE TH' ALL BOUNTEOUS KING, WHO SHOWRD 5 640
NIGHTLY BEFORE HIM, SAW WITHOUT THIR LIGHT 5 714
NATIVES AND SONS OF HEAV'N POSSEST BEFORE 5 790
KNOW NONE BEFORE US, SELF-BEGOT, SELF-RAIS'D 5 860
EMPYREAL, FROM BEFORE HER VANISHT NIGHT, 6 14
BEFORE THE SEAT SUPREAM; FROM WHENCE A VOICE 6 27
OF HIDEOUS LENGTH; BEFORE THE CLOUDIE VAN, 6 107
BEFORE THY FELLOWS, AMBITIOUS TO WIN 6 160
BEFORE HIM POWER DIVINE HIS WAY PREPAR'D; 6 780
BEFORE HIM, SUCH AS IN THIR SOULES INFIX'D 6 837
DROVE THEM BEFORE HIM THUNDER-STRUCK, PURSU'D 6 858
BEFORE THE HILLS APPEERD, OR FOUNTAIN FLOW'D, 7 8
BEFORE HIS MEMORIE, AS ONE WHOSE DROUTH 7 66
GOD MADE, AND EVERY HERB, BEFORE IT GREW 7 336
DAWN, AND THE PLEIADES BEFORE HIM DANC'D 7 374
AND WHAT BEFORE THY MEMORIE WAS DON 7 637
BEFORE THE ANGEL, AND OF HIM TO ASK 8 53
IS AS THE BOOK OF GOD BEFORE THEE SET, 8 67
THAT WHICH BEFORE US LIES IN DAILY LIFE, 8 193
OF EARTH BEFORE SCARCE PLEASANT SEEMD. EACH TREE 8 306
BEFORE MINE EYES ALL REAL, AS THE DREAM 8 310
TO COME AND PLAY BEFORE THEE, KNOW'ST THOU NOT 8 372
STILL GLORIOUS BEFORE WHOM AWAKE I STOOD; 8 464
SWEETNESS INTO MY HEART, UNFELT BEFORE, 8 475
BEFORE ME; WOMAN IS HER NAME, OF MAN 8 496
WHEN SATAN WHO LATE FLED BEFORE THE THREATS 9 53
BEFORE HAD BIN CONTRIVING, THOUGH PERHAPS 9 139
TO SUCH DISPORT BEFORE HER THROUGH THE FIELD, 9 520
HEE BOULDER NOW, UNCALL'D BEFORE HER STOOD; 9 523
TASTE SO DIVINE, THAT WHAT OF SWEET BEFORE 9 986
BEFORE THEE; AND NOT REPENTING, THIS OBTAINE 10 75
BEFORE MY JUDGE, EITHER TO UNDERGOE 10 126
BEFORE HIS VOICE, OR WAS SHEE MADE THY GUIDE, 10 146
CONFESSING SOON, YET NOT BEFORE HER JUDGE 10 160
BEFORE HIM NAKED TO THE AIRE, THAT NOW 10 212
TOO SOON ARRIV'D, SIN THERE IN POWER BEFORE, 10 586
UNWARIE, AND TOO DESIROUS, AS BEFORE, 10 947
WOULD SPEED BEFORE THEE, AND BE LOUDER HEARD, 10 954
BEFORE THE PRESENT OBJECT LANGUISHING 10 996
BEFORE HIM REVERENT, AND THERE CONFESS 10 1088
BEFORE HIM REVERENT, AND BOTH CONFESS'D 10 1100
THE RACE OF MANKIND DROWND, BEFORE THE SHRINE 11 13
BEFORE THE FATHERS THRONE: THEM THE GLAD SON 11 20
WITH INCENSE, I THY PRIEST BEFORE THEE BRING, 11 25
BEFORE THEE RECONCIL'D, AT LEAST HIS DAYS 11 39
KNEEL'D AND BEFORE HIM HUMBL'D ALL MY HEART, 11 150
TWO BIRDS OF GAYEST PLUME BEFORE HIM DROVE: 11 186
BEFORE THEE SHALL APPEAR; THAT THOU MAYST KNOW 11 475
BEFORE HIS EYES APPEARD, SAD, NOYSOM, DARK, 11 478
BEFORE HIM, TOWNS, AND RURAL WORKS BETWEEN, 11 639
SHALL THEM ADMONISH, AND BEFORE THEM SET 11 813
BEFORE THE LORD, AS IN DESPITE OF HEAV'N, 12 34
BEFORE THEM IN A CLOUD, AND PILLAR OF FIRE, 12 202
OF TWO BRIGHT CHERUBIM, BEFORE HIM BURN 12 254
UNSEEN BEFORE IN HEAV'N PROCLAIMS HIM COM, 12 361
AS DID THIR LORD BEFORE THEM. THUS THEY WIN 12 502
LAY SLEEPING RAN BEFORE, BUT FOUND HER WAK'T; 12 608
THE BRANDISHT SWORD OF GOD BEFORE THEM BLAZ'D 12 633
THE WORLD WAS ALL BEFORE THEM, WHERE TO CHOOSE 12 646

BEG
I BEG, AND CLASP THY KNEES; BEREAVE ME NOT, 10 918
HUMBLY OUR FAULTS, AND PARDON BEG, WITH TEARS 10 1089
LIFE OFFER'D, OR SOON BEG TO LAY IT DOWN, 11 506

BEGAN
BREAKING THE HORRID SILENCE THUS BEGAN. 1 83
AND SUMMONS READ, THE GREAT CONSULT BEGAN. 1 798
AND WITH PERSWASIVE ACCENT THUS BEGAN. 2 118
AND WITH DISDAINFUL LOOK THUS FIRST BEGAN. 2 680
BEGAN TO BLOOM, BUT SOON FOR MANS OFFENCE 3 355
THEN MUCH REVOLVING, THUS IN SIGHS BEGAN. 4 31
BUT WITH SLY CIRCUMSPECTION, AND BEGAN 4 537
IMPETUOUS WINDS: HE THUS BEGAN IN HASTE. 4 560
THIR PHALANX, AND BEGAN TO HEMM HIM ROUND 4 979
LOWLY THEY BOW'D ADORING, AND BEGAN 5 144
TO ADD MORE SWEETNESS, AND THEY THUS BEGAN. 5 152
NO FEAR LEST DINNER COOLE; WHEN THUS BEGAN 5 396
AFTER SHORT PAUSE ASSENTING, THUS BEGAN. 5 562
SO SPAKE THE SOVRAN VOICE, AND CLOUDS BEGAN 6 56
OF BATTEL NOW BEGAN, AND RUSHING SOUND 6 97
AND VISAGE ALL ENFLAM'D FIRST THUS BEGAN. 6 261
NOW NIGHT HER COURSE BEGAN, AND OVER HEAV'N 6 406
AND IN THE MIDST THUS UNDISMAI'D BEGAN. 6 417
TH' ASSESSOR OF HIS THRONE HE THUS BEGAN. 6 679
AND THE THIRD SACRED MORN BEGAN TO SHINE 6 748
OF HEAV'N AND EARTH CONSPICIOUS FIRST BEGAN, 7 63
HOW FIRST BEGAN THIS HEAV'N WHICH WE BEHOLD 7 86
TO JOURNIE THROUGH THE AIRIE GLOOM BEGAN, 7 246

BEGAN (CONTINUED)
HOW FIRST THIS WORLD AND FACE OF THINGS BEGAN, 7 636
FOR MAN TO TELL HOW HUMAN LIFE BEGAN 8 250
NOW WHEN AS SACRED LIGHT BEGAN TO DAWNE 9 192
AND EVE FIRST TO HER HUSBAND THUS BEGAN. 9 204
HIS FRAUDULENT TEMPTATION THUS BEGAN. 9 531
SOMTIMES IN HIGHTH BEGAN, AS NO DELAY 9 675
THE TEMPTER ALL IMPASSIOND THUS BEGAN. 9 678
THUS TO HER SELF SHE PLEASINGLY BEGAN. 9 794
BEGAN TO CAST LASCIVIOUS EYES, SHE HIM 9 1014
BEGAN TO RISE, HIGH PASSIONS, ANGER, HATE, 9 1123
SIN OPENING, WHO THUS NOW TO DEATH BEGAN. 10 234
ON HIS PALE HORSE: TO WHOM SIN THUS BEGAN. 10 590
SIROCCO, AND LIBECCHIO. THUS BEGAN 10 706
PRESENTING, THUS TO INTERCEDE BEGAN. 11 21
BEGAN TO BUILD A VESSEL OF HUGE BULK, 11 729
BEGAN TO PARCH THAT TEMPERATE CLIME; WHEREAT 12 636

BEG'D
HUMBLY THIR FAULTS, AND PARDON BEG'D, WITH TEARS 10 1101

BEGET
HIS SINGLE IMPERFECTION, AND BEGET 8 423
DOUBT MIGHT BEGET OF DIABOLIC POW'R 9 95
ALL THAT I EAT OR DRINK, OR SHALL BEGET, 10 728
WHEREFORE DIDST THOU BEGET ME? I SOUGHT IT NOT 10 762
YET THEY A BEAUTEOUS OFSPRING SHALL BEGET; 11 613

BEGGING
FROM GRANTING HEE, AS I FROM BEGGING PEACE: 4 104

BEGIN
WHY ASK YE, AND SUPERFLUOUS BEGIN 4 832
ERE THIS AVENGING SWORD BEGIN THY DOOME, 6 278
HEE FROM THE EAST HIS FLAMING RODE BEGIN, 8 162
RAIS'D, AS OF SOM GREAT MATTER TO BEGIN. 9 669
SUCH PROOF, CONCLUDE, THEY THEN BEGIN TO FAILE. 9 1142
MUST SUFFER CHANGE, DISDAIN'D NOT TO BEGIN 10 213
HOLDS ON THE SAME, FROM WOMAN TO BEGIN. 11 633
THUS THOU HAST SEEN ONE WORLD BEGIN AND END; 12 6

BEGINNING
IN THE BEGINNING HOW THE HEAV'NS AND EARTH 1 9
HIS JOURNIES END AND OUR BEGINNING WOE. 3 633
FROM THE BEGINNING, THAT POSTERITIE 7 638
IS HARD; FOR WHO HIMSELF BEGINNING KNEW? 8 251
PLEAS'D ME LONG CHOOSING, AND BEGINNING LATE; 9 26

BEGINS
A GLIMMERING DAWN; HERE NATURE FIRST BEGINS 2 1037
BEGINS HIS DIRE ATTEMPT, WHICH NIGH THE BIRTH 4 15
HATH FINISHT HALF HIS JOURNEY, AND SCARCE BEGINS 5 559
WHICH NOW THE SKIE WITH VARIOUS FACE BEGINS 10 1064
ALL UNCONCERN'D WITH OUR UNREST, BEGINS 11 174
FROM MANS EFFEMINATE SLACKNESS IT BEGINS, 11 634

BEGIRT
BEGIRT WITH BRITISH AND ARMORIC KNIGHTS; 1 581
ADDRESS, AND TO BEGIRT TH' ALMIGHTY THRONE 5 868

BEGOT
INGENDRING WITH ME, OF THAT RAPE BEGOT 2 794
THIS DAY I HAVE BEGOT WHOM I DECLARE 5 603
KNOW NONE BEFORE US, SELF-BEGOT, SELF-RAIS'D 5 860
BUT NATURAL NECESSITY BEGOT. 10 765
WILL REIGN AMONG THEM, AS OF THEE BEGOT; 12 286

BEGOTTEN
THINE OWN BEGOTTEN, BREAKING VIOLENT WAY 2 782
ONELY BEGOTTEN SON, SEEST THOU WHAT RAGE 3 80
BEGOTTEN SON, DIVINE SIMILITUDE, 3 384
EQUAL TO HIM BEGOTTEN SON, BY WHOM 5 835
AND THOU MY WORD, BEGOTTEN SON, BY THEE 7 163
OUR OWN BEGOTTEN, AND OF OUR LOINES TO BRING 10 983

BEGUIL'D
BEGUIL'D BY FAIR IDOLATRESSES, FELL 1 445
WHERE NO ILL SEEMS; WHICH NOW FOR ONCE BEGUIL'D 3 689
OF ENEMIE HATH BEGUIL'D THEE, YET UNKNOWN, 9 905
THE SERPENT ME BEGUIL'D AND I DID EATE. 10 162
FOOL'D AND BEGUIL'D, BY HIM THOU, I BY THEE, 10 880

BEGUN
IN CHAOS, AND THE WORK BEGUN, HOW SOON 7 93
HAD LIVELY SHADOWD: HERE HAD NEW BEGUN 8 311
OUR DAYES WORK BROUGHT TO LITTLE, THOUGH BEGUN 9 224
FROM THIS DAY ONWARD, WHICH I FEEL BEGUN 10 811

BEHALF
AND SILENCE WAS IN HEAV'N: ON MANS BEHALF 3 218
OR IN BEHALF OF MAN, OR TO INVADE 11 102

BEHELD
THE SOJOURNERS OF GOSHEN, WHO BEHELD 1 309
(FAR OTHER ONCE BEHELD IN BLISS) CONDEMN'D 1 607
HIS ONELY SON; ON EARTH HE FIRST BEHELD 3 64
AT SIGHT OF ALL THIS WORLD BEHELD SO FAIRE. 3 554
HIM COUNTERFET, IF ANY EYE BEHELD. 4 117

BEHELD (CONTINUED)
WHICH THEY BEHELD, THE MOONS RESPLENDENT GLOBE 4 723
HUNG OVER HER ENAMOUR'D, AND BEHELD 5 13
WITH HIM I FLEW, AND UNDERNEATH BEHELD 5 87
HIS BARREN LEAVES. THEM THUS IMPLOID BEHELD 5 219
THEY WORSE ABHORR'D. SATAN BEHELD THIR PLIGHT, 6 607
SON IN WHOSE FACE INVISIBLE IS BEHELD 6 681
HIS COUNT'NANCE TOO SEVERE TO BE BEHELD 6 825
ETERNAL FATHER FROM HIS THRONE BEHELD 7 137
EXHALING FIRST FROM DARKNESS THEY BEHELD; 7 255
FROM WHERE I FIRST DREW AIRE, AND FIRST BEHELD 8 284
WITH RAVISHMENT BEHELD, THERE BEST BEHELD 9 541
UNITED I BEHELD; NO FAIR TO THINE 9 608
AND RAPTURE SO OFT BEHELD? THOSE HEAV'NLY SHAPES 9 1082
BENT THIR ASPECT, AND WHOM THEY WISH'D BEHELD, 10 454
WHOM THUS AFFLICTED WHEN SAD EVE BEHELD, 10 863
HIS EYES HE OP'ND, AND BEHELD A FIELD, 11 429
THEY LOOKING BACK, ALL TH' EASTERN SIDE BEHELD 12 641

BEHELDST
BUT HEE THE SEVENTH FROM THEE, WHOM THOU BEHELDST 11 700
SHALL BUILD A WONDROUS ARK, AS THOU BEHELDST, 11 819

BEHEMOTH
BEHEMOTH BIGGEST BORN OF EARTH UPHEAV'D 7 471

BEHEST
RIS'N ON MID-NOON; SOM GREAT BEHEST FROM HEAV'N 5 311
MICHAEL, THIS MY BEHEST HAVE THOU IN CHARGE, 11 99
ADAM, HEAV'NS HIGH BEHEST NO PREFACE NEEDS: 11 251

BEHESTS
ON HIGH BEHESTS HIS ANGELS TO AND FRO 3 533
BEHESTS OBEY, WORTHIEST TO BE OBEY'D, 6 185
BUT US HE SENDS UPON HIS HIGH BEHESTS 8 238

BEHIND
BEHIND HIM CAST; THE BROAD CIRCUMFERENCE 1 286
TO IDOLS FOUL. THAMMUZ CAME NEXT BEHIND, 1 446
SHORN OF HIS BEAMS, OR FROM BEHIND THE MOON 1 596
AS NOT BEHIND IN HATE; IF WHAT WAS URG'D 2 120
CIRCL'D HIS HEAD, NOR LESS HIS LOCKS BEHIND 3 626
NO SPOT OR BLAME BEHIND: WHICH GIVES ME HOPE 5 119
PORTENDING HOLLOW TRUCE; AT EACH BEHIND 6 578
URG'D THEM BEHIND; HEADLONG THEMSELVES THEY THREW 6 864
AS IN A SHADIE NOOK I STOOD BEHIND, 9 277
HABITUAL HABITANT; BEHIND HER DEATH 10 588

BEHINDE
LEADS THEE, I SHALL NOT LAG BEHINDE, NOR ERRE 10 266
BEHINDE THEM, WHILE TH' OBDURAT KING PURSUES: 12 205

BEHOLD
SIGNS OF REMORSE AND PASSION TO BEHOLD 1 605
BEHOLD A WONDER. THEY BUT NOW WHO SEEMD 1 777
BORDERING ON LIGHT; WHEN STRAIT BEHOLD THE THRONE 2 959
WEIGHS HIS SPREAD WINGS, AT LEASURE TO BEHOLD 2 1046
BEHOLD MEE THEN, MEE FOR HIM, LIFE FOR LIFE 3 236
WHOM ELSE NO CREATURE CAN BEHOLD; ON THEE 3 387
OR OPEN ADMIRATION HIM BEHOLD 3 672
ALL HOPE EXCLUDED THUS, BEHOLD IN STEAD 4 105
O HELL. WHAT DOE MINE EYES WITH GRIEF BEHOLD, 4 358
ALL THESE WITH CEASLESS PRAISE HIS WORKS BEHOLD 4 679
SO SUDDEN TO BEHOLD THE GRIESLIE KING; 4 821
WHOM TO BEHOLD BUT THEE, NATURES DESIRE, 5 45
ANGELS, FOR YEE BEHOLD HIM, AND WITH SONGS 5 161
HASTE HITHER EVE, AND WORTH THY SIGHT BEHOLD 5 308
HIM HAVE ANOINTED, WHOM YE NOW BEHOLD 5 605
SON, THOU IN WHOM MY GLORY I BEHOLD 5 719
WHO IS OUR EQUAL: THEN THOU SHALT BEHOLD 5 866
AND ONWARD MOVE EMBATTELLD; WHEN BEHOLD 6 550
FORTHWITH (BEHOLD THE EXCELLENCE, THE POWER 6 637
NOR MULTITUDE, STAND ONELY AND BEHOLD 6 810
HOW FIRST BEGAN THIS HEAV'N WHICH WE BEHOLD 7 86
FOLLOW'D IN BRIGHT PROCESSION TO BEHOLD 7 222
DELECTABLE BOTH TO BEHOLD AND TASTE; 7 539
VIEW'D, AND BEHOLD ALL WAS ENTIRELY GOOD; 7 549
THENCE TO BEHOLD THIS NEW CREATED WORLD 7 554
WHEN I BEHOLD THIS GOODLY FRAME, THIS WORLD 8 15
IN SIGNE WHEREOF EACH BIRD AND BEAST BEHOLD 8 342
AS THUS HE SPAKE, EACH BIRD AND BEAST BEHOLD 8 349
WHEN OUT OF HOPE, BEHOLD HER, NOT FARR OFF, 8 481
FARR OTHERWISE, TRANSPORTED I BEHOLD, 8 529
HARMONIE TO BEHOLD IN WEDDED PAIR 8 605
SUCH PLEASURE TOOK THE SERPENT TO BEHOLD 9 455
OCCASION WHICH NOW SMILES, BEHOLD ALONE 9 480
A GOODLY TREE FARR DISTANT TO BEHOLD 9 576
FIXT ON THE FRUIT SHE GAZ'D, WHICH TO BEHOLD 9 735
BE SURE THEN. HOW SHALL I BEHOLD THE FACE 9 1080
ARE TO BEHOLD THE JUDGMENT, BUT THE JUDG'D, 10 81
TO PARADISE FIRST TENDING, WHEN BEHOLD 10 326
OF GOD, WHOM TO BEHOLD WAS THEN MY HIGHTH 10 724
FOR I BEHOLD THEM SOFTN'D AND WITH TEARS 11 110
GLADLY BEHOLD THOUGH BUT HIS UTMOST SKIRTS 11 332
ADAM, NOW OPE THINE EYES, AND FIRST BEHOLD 11 423
OF TERROUR, FOUL AND UGLY TO BEHOLD, 11 464
DRIE-EY'D BEHOLD? ADAM COULD NOT, BUT WEPT, 11 495
LONG HAD NOT WALKT, WHEN FROM THE TENTS BEHOLD 11 581

BEHOLD (CONTINUED)
WHICH NOW DIRECT THINE EYES AND SOON BEHOLD. 11 711
HOW DIDST THOU GRIEVE THEN, ADAM, TO BEHOLD 11 754
AND NOW WHAT FURTHER SHALL ENSUE, BEHOLD. 11 839
MOUNT HERMON, YONDER SEA, EACH PLACE BEHOLD 12 142

BEHOLDERS
BEHOLDERS RUDE, AND SHALLOW TO DISCERNE 9 544

BEHOLDING
HIM GOD BEHOLDING FROM HIS PROSPECT HIGH, 3 77
BEHOLDING SHALL CONFESS THAT HERE ON EARTH 5 329
TO MARK THIR DOINGS, THEM BEHOLDING SOON, 12 50

BEHOLDS
TO ADORE THE CONQUEROUR? WHO NOW BEHOLDS 1 323
WHEREIN PAST, PRESENT, FUTURE HE BEHOLDS, 3 78
WHICH OF US WHO BEHOLDS THE BRIGHT SURFACE 6 472
GRATEFUL TO HEAV'N, OVER HIS HEAD BEHOLDS 11 864

BEHOOF
TO YOUR BEHOOF, IF I THAT REGION LOST, 2 982

BEHOOVES
ARGUE THY INEXPERIENCE WHAT BEHOOVES 4 931

BEHOVES
HALF FLYING; BEHOVES HIM NOW BOTH OARE AND SAILE. 2 942

BEING
STRENGTH UNDIMINISHT, OR ETERNAL BEING 1 154
AS BEING THE CONTRARY TO HIS HIGH WILL 1 161
THEN MISERABLE TO HAVE ETERNAL BEING: 2 98
THOUGH FULL OF PAIN, THIS INTELLECTUAL BEING, 2 147
WIDE GAPING, AND WITH UTTER LOSS OF BEING 2 440
FORTHWITH HIS FORMER STATE AND BEING FORGETS, 2 585
MY BEING GAV'ST ME; WHOM SHOULD I OBEY 2 865
FOUND WORTHIEST TO BE SO BY BEING GOOD, 3 310
ETERNAL KING; THEE AUTHOR OF ALL BEING, 3 374
HIS FLESH, HIS BONE; TO GIVE THEE BEING I LENT 4 483
OF THINGS ABOVE HIS WORLD, AND OF THIR BEING 5 455
REASON RECEIVES, AND REASON IS HER BEING, 5 487
OUR BEING ORDAIN'D TO GOVERN, NOT TO SERVE? 5 802
SUCH AS HE PLEASD, AND CIRCUMSCRIB'D THIR BEING? 5 825
THY MAKING, WHILE THE MAKER GAVE THEE BEING? 5 858
THINK ONELY WHAT CONCERNES THEE AND THY BEING; 8 174
MY FANCY TO BELIEVE I YET HAD BEING, 8 294
AND ALL THIS GOOD TO MAN, FOR WHOSE WELL BEING 8 361
THAT GAVE THEE BEING, STILL SHADES THEE AND PROTECTS. 9 266
HIS VIOLENCE THOU FEARST NOT, BEING SUCH, 9 282
BUT MIGHT AS ILL HAVE HAPP'ND THOU BEING BY, 9 1147
BEING AS I AM, WHY DIDST NOT THOU THE HEAD 9 1155
AFFRAID, BEING NAKED, HID MY SELF. TO WHOM 10 117
CONCURD NOT TO MY BEING, IT WERE BUT RIGHT 10 747
THE RACE UNBLEST, TO BEING YET UNBEGOT. 10 988
ABORTIVE, TO TORMENT ME ERE THIR BEING, 11 769
TWINN'D, AND FROM HER HATH NO DIVIDUAL BEING: 12 85
HIGHLY BELOV'D, BEING BUT THE MINISTER 12 308

BELATED
OR FOUNTAIN SOME BELATED PEASANT SEES, 1 783

BELCH'D
BELCH'D FIRE AND ROWLING SMOAK; THE REST ENTIRE 1 671

BELCHING
STOOD OPEN WIDE, BELCHING OUTRAGEOUS FLAME 10 232

BELCHT
FROM THOSE DEEP THROATED ENGINS BELCHT, WHOSE ROAR 6 586

BELEEFE
OF DAY AND NIGHT; WHICH NEEDS NOT THY BELEEFE, 8 136

BELEEVE
FOR WHO CAN YET BELEEVE, THOUGH AFTER LOSS, 1 631
WHICH THAT THOU MAYST BELEEVE, AND BE CONFIRMD 11 355
AND HIS SALVATION, THEM WHO SHALL BELEEVE 12 441

BELEEVERS
TO ALL BELEEVERS; AND FROM THAT PRETENSE, 12 520

BELIAL
BELIAL CAME LAST, THEN WHOM A SPIRIT MORE LEWD 1 490
OF BELIAL, FLOWN WITH INSOLENCE AND WINE. 1 502
BELIAL, IN ACT MORE GRACEFUL AND HUMANE; 2 109
THUS BELIAL WITH WORDS CLOATH'D IN REASONS GARB 2 226
TO WHOM THUS BELIAL IN LIKE GAMESOM MOOD, 6 620

BELIEF
ON OUR BELIEF, THAT ALL FROM THEM PROCEEDS; 9 719
HARD TO BELIEF MAY SEEM; YET THIS WILL PRAYER, 11 146

BELIEVE
OF FORCE BELIEVE ALMIGHTY, SINCE NO LESS 1 144
MY FANCY TO BELIEVE I YET HAD BEING, 8 294
QUEEN OF THIS UNIVERSE, DOE NOT BELIEVE 9 684

BELIEVE (CONTINUED)
(CANST THOU BELIEVE?) SHOULD BE SO STUPID GROWN, 12 116
PROCLAIMING LIFE TO ALL WHO SHALL BELIEVE 12 407

BELIEVES
NOT KNOWING TO WHAT LAND, YET FIRM BELIEVES: 12 127

BELIEVING
AND FLATTER'D OUT OF ALL, BELIEVING LIES 10 42

BELIEVST
BELIEVST SO MAIN TO OUR SUCCESS, I BRING; 6 471

BELIKE
BELIKE THROUGH IMPOTENCE, OR UNAWARE, 2 156

BELLEROPHON
BELLEROPHON, THOUGH FROM A LOWER CLIME) 7 18

BELLONA
GREAT THINGS WITH SMALL) THEN WHEN BELLONA STORMS, 2 922

BELLOW
TO BELLOW THROUGH THE VAST AND BOUNDLESS DEEP. 1 177

BELLOWING
AND UNCOUTH PAINE FLED BELLOWING. ON EACH WING 6 362

BELLY
UPON THY BELLY GROVELING THOU SHALT GOE, 10 177
A MONSTROUS SERPENT ON HIS BELLY PRONE, 10 514

BELONG
IF BETTER THOU BELONG NOT TO THE DAWN, 5 167
ILL WORTHIE I SUCH TITLE SHOULD BELONG 11 163

BELONGD
NOT MEE. THEY THEREFORE AS TO RIGHT BELONGD, 3 111

BELONGS
THE PUNISHMENT TO OTHER HAND BELONGS, 6 807
CONVICTION TO THE SERPENT NONE BELONGS. 10 84
MAN I DECEAV'D: THAT WHICH TO MEE BELONGS, 10 496
RATHER BELONGS, DISTRUST AND ALL DISPRAISE: 11 166

BELOV'D
EFFULGENCE OF MY GLORIE, SON BELOV'D, 6 680
SUPREAM, THAT THOU IN MEE THY SON BELOV'D 10 70
HIGHLY BELOV'D, BEING BUT THE MINISTER 12 308

BELOVED
BOTH HIS BELOVED MAN AND ALL HIS WORLD, 10 489

BELOW
THAT STONE, OR LIKE TO THAT WHICH HERE BELOW 3 600
HERE SLEEP BELOW WHILE THOU TO FORESIGHT WAK'ST, 11 368

BELUS
BELUS OR SERAPIS THIR GODS, OR SEAT 1 720

BEND
TO SPEAK; WHEREAT THIR DOUBL'D RANKS THEY BEND 1 616
THITHER LET US BEND ALL OUR THOUGHTS, TO LEARN 2 354
OF THUNDER HEARD REMOTE. TOWARDS HIM THEY BEND 2 477
MIGHT YIELD THEM EASIER HABITATION, BEND 2 573
POSSESSES THEE TO BEND THAT MORTAL DART 2 729
WILL YE SUBMIT YOUR NECKS, AND CHUSE TO BEND 5 787
SHALL BEND THE KNEE, AND IN THAT HONOUR DUE 5 817
FROM INNOCENCE. NOW THEREFORE BEND THINE EARE 11 30

BENDED
HE BACK RECOILD; THE TENTH ON BENDED KNEE 6 194
AND BENDED DOLPHINS PLAY: PART HUGE OF BULK 7 410
THE BENDED TWIGS TAKE ROOT, AND DAUGHTERS GROW 9 1105

BENDING
BENDING TO LOOK ON ME, I STARTED BACK, 4 462
BENDING HIS EARE; PERSWASION IN ME GREW 11 152

BENDS
ALLUR'D HIS EYE: THITHER HIS COURSE HE BENDS 3 573
OF CERES RIPE FOR HARVEST WAVING BENDS 4 981

BENEATH
THAT WERE AN IGNOMINY AND SHAME BENEATH 1 115
BENEATH GIBRALTER TO THE LYBIAN SANDS. 1 355
YOUR DUNGEON STRETCHING FAR AND WIDE BENEATH; 2 1003
THEE SION AND THE FLOWRIE BROOKS BENEATH 3 30
BENEATH THY SENTENCE; HELL HER NUMBERS FULL 3 332
DIRECT AGAINST WHICH OP'ND FROM BENEATH, 3 526
TOOK LEAVE, AND TOWARD THE COAST OF EARTH BENEATH, 3 739
AMONG THE SPIRITS BENEATH, WHOM I SEDUC'D 4 83
BENEATH HIM WITH NEW WONDER NOW HE VIEWS 4 205
CLUSTRING, BUT NOT BENEATH HIS SHOULDERS BROAD: 4 303
BENEATH TH' AZORES; WHITHER THE PRIME ORB, 4 592
HUMBL'D BY SUCH REBUKE, SO FARR BENEATH 6 342
WIDE THE CELESTIAL SOILE, AND SAW BENEATH 6 510
ABOVE, OR ROUND ABOUT THEE OR BENEATH. 8 318

BENEATH (CONTINUED)
AND THESE INFERIOUR FARR BENEATH ME SET? 8 382
BENEATH WHAT OTHER CREATURES ARE TO THEE? 8 411
BENEATH MAGELLAN. AT THAT TASTED FRUIT 10 687

BENEATHE
TO SENSUAL APPETITE, WHO FROM BENEATHE 9 1129

BENEDICTION
FOLLOW'D WITH BENEDICTION. SINCE TO PART, 8 645
HIS BENEDICTION SO, THAT IN HIS SEED 12 125

BENEFIT
THE BENEFIT: CONSIDER FIRST, THAT GREAT 8 90
NEGLECT NOT, AND THE BENEFIT IMBRACE 12 426

BENEVOLENT
BENEVOLENT AND FACIL THUS REPLI'D. 8 65

BENGALA
CLOSE SAILING FROM BENGALA, OR THE ILES 2 638

BENIGNE
THY WORDS, CREATOR BOUNTEOUS AND BENIGNE, 8 492
TO WHOM THUS MICHAEL WITH REGARD BENIGNE. 11 334
TO GOOD MALIGNANT, TO BAD MEN BENIGNE, 12 538

BENT
WERE ALWAYS DOWNWARD BENT, ADMIRING MORE 1 681
WITH ALL HER BATTERING ENGINES BENT TO RASE 2 923
HIGH THRON'D ABOVE ALL HIGHTH, BENT DOWN HIS EYE, 3 58
WIDE INTERRUPT CAN HOLD; SO BENT HE SEEMS 3 84
WALK'D UP AND DOWN ALONE BENT ON HIS PREY, 3 441
OR AS A THIEF BENT TO UNHOORD THE CASH 4 188
AS I BENT DOWN TO LOOK, JUST OPPOSITE, 4 460
BENT ALL ON SPEED, AND MARKT HIS AERIE GATE; 4 568
HITHERWARD BENT (WHO COULD HAVE THOUGHT?) ESCAP'D 4 794
TO MAKE US LESS, BENT RATHER TO EXALT 5 829
AMONG THE MIGHTIEST, BENT ON HIGHEST DEEDS, 6 112
FOR SIN, ON WARR AND MUTUAL SLAUGHTER BENT. 6 506
AND FULL OF WRAUTH BENT ON HIS ENEMIES. 6 826
IN MEDITATED FRAUD AND MALICE, BENT 9 55
SO BENT, THE MORE SHALL SHAME HIM HIS REPULSE. 9 384
BENT THIR ASPECT, AND WHOM THEY WISH'D BEHELD, 10 454
CROOKED BY NATURE, BENT, AS NOW APPEARS, 10 885
DIRECT TO TH' EASTERN GATE WAS BENT THIR FLIGHT. 11 190
LIFE MUCH, BENT RATHER HOW I MAY BE QUIT 11 548
JUST MEN THEY SEEMD, AND ALL THIR STUDY BENT 11 577
THE BENT OF NATURE; WHICH HE THUS EXPRESS'D. 11 597
THOUGH BENT ON SPEED, SO HEER THE ARCHANGEL PAUS'D 12 2

BENUMM
OF THAT FORGETFUL LAKE BENUMM NOT STILL, 2 74

BENUMM'D
OUR LIMBS BENUMM'D, ERE THIS DIURNAL STARR 10 1069

BEREAV'D
HIS MALICE, AND WITH RAPINE SWEET BEREAV'D 9 461

BEREAVD
BEREAVD OF HAPPINESS THOU MAIST PARTAKE 6 903

BEREAVE
I BEG, AND CLASP THY KNEES; BEREAVE ME NOT, 10 918

BEREAVING
BEREAVING SENSE, BUT ENDLESS MISERIE 10 810

BEREFT
TO WHOM THUS ADAM OF SHORT JOY BEREFT. 11 628

BERIL
OF BERIL, AND CAREERING FIRES BETWEEN; 6 756

BERRIE
BERRIE OR GRAPE: TO WHOM THUS ADAM CALL'D. 5 307
FROM MANY A BERRIE, AND FROM SWEET KERNELS PREST 5 346

BESAUGHT
FELL HUMBLE, AND IMBRACING THEM, BESAUGHT 10 912
AND TERROR CEASE; HE GRANTS WHAT THEY BESAUGHT 12 238

BESEECH
TO MORTAL EARE IS DREADFUL; THEY BESEECH 12 236

BESEECHING
BESEECHING OR BESIEGING. THIS REPORT, 5 869
BESEECHING HIM, SO AS WE NEED NOT FEAR 10 1082

BESEEMS
AT THY RIGHT HAND VOLUPTUOUS, AS BESEEMS 2 869
WANTED, NOR YOUTHFUL DALLIANCE AS BESEEMS 4 338

BESET
ENVIRON'D WINS HIS WAY; HARDER BESET 2 1016
TO WHOM THUS ADAM SORE BESET REPLI'D. 10 124
AND THEREFORE HATED, THEREFORE SO BESET 11 702

BESIDE
- AND AS I WONDRING LOOKT, BESIDE IT STOOD — 5 54
- SATE EAGLE-WING'D, BESIDE HIM HUNG HIS BOW — 6 763

BESIDES
- FOR ONE RESTRAINT, LORDS OF THE WORLD BESIDES? — 1 32
- THAT SPARKLING BLAZ'D, HIS OTHER PARTS BESIDES — 1 194
- SMOTE ON HIM SORE BESIDES, VAULTED WITH FIRE; — 1 298
- WITH WHAT BESIDES, IN COUNSEL OR IN FIGHT, — 2 20
- BESIDES WHAT HOPE THE NEVER-ENDING FLIGHT — 2 221
- MAN HAD NOT HELLISH FOES ANOW BESIDES, — 2 504
- IN AARONS BREST-PLATE, AND A STONE BESIDES — 3 598
- NOT UNDERSTOOD, THIS GIFT THEY HAVE BESIDES, — 6 626
- ANOUGH IS LEFT BESIDES TO SEARCH AND KNOW. — 7 125
- USELESS BESIDES, REASONING I OFT ADMIRE, — 8 25
- SHALL BE THE EXECRATION; SO BESIDES — 10 737
- AND IN PERFORMING END US; WHAT BESIDES — 11 300
- BUT IS THERE YET NO OTHER WAY, BESIDES — 11 527

BESIEGING
- BESEECHING OR BESIEGING. THIS REPORT, — 5 869

BESMEAR'D
- FIRST MOLOCH, HORRID KING BESMEAR'D WITH BLOOD — 1 392

BESMEARD
- OF HORSES LED, AND GROOMS BESMEARD WITH GOLD — 5 356

BESOUGHT
- WITH HEAV'NS AFFLICTING THUNDER, AND BESOUGHT — 2 166
- WHILE PARDON MAY BE FOUND IN TIME BESOUGHT. — 5 848
- THUS ADAM HIS ILLUSTRIOUS GUEST BESOUGHT: — 7 109
- WITH ME, AS I BESOUGHT THEE, WHEN THAT STRANGE — 9 1135

BESPAKE
- HIS MOTHER BAD, AND THUS BESPAKE HER SIRE. — 2 849
- WHICH GABRIEL SPYING, THUS BESPAKE THE FIEND. — 4 1005

BEST
- WHAT SHALL BE RIGHT: FARDEST FROM HIM IS BEST — 1 247
- THAT RICHES GROW IN HELL; THAT SOYLE MAY BEST — 1 691
- DEFI'D THE BEST OF PANIM CHIVALRY — 1 765
- COULD HAVE ASSUR'D US; AND BY WHAT BEST WAY, — 2 40
- WE WARR, IF WARR BE BEST, OR TO REGAIN — 2 230
- OF ORDER, HOW IN SAFETY BEST WE MAY — 2 280
- AND WHERE THIR WEAKNESS, HOW ATTEMPTED BEST, — 2 357
- WHILE HERE SHALL BE OUR HOME, WHAT BEST MAY EASE — 2 458
- THE GOOD BEFORE HIM, BUT PERVERTS BEST THINGS — 4 203
- AND BY HER YIELDED, BY HIM BEST RECEIVD, — 4 309
- NOW OTHER, AS THIR SHAPE SERVD BEST HIS END — 4 398
- WHICH GOD LIKES BEST, INTO THIR INMOST BOWRE — 4 738
- TO HIS PROUD FAIR, BEST QUITTED WITH DISDAIN. — 4 770
- BEST WITH THE BEST, THE SENDER NOT THE SENT, — 4 852
- HEAV'NS LAST BEST GIFT, MY EVER NEW DELIGHT, — 5 19
- BEST IMAGE OF MY SELF AND DEARER HALF, — 5 95
- SPEAK YEE WHO BEST CAN TELL, YE SONS OF LIGHT, — 5 160
- WHAT CHOICE TO CHUSE FOR DELICACIE BEST, — 5 333
- AS MAY EXPRESS THEM BEST, THOUGH WHAT IF EARTH — 5 574
- THIS ONELY TO CONSULT HOW WE MAY BEST — 5 779
- ASSUME, AS LIKES THEM BEST, CONDENSE OR RARE. — 6 353
- FIRST, HIGHEST, HOLIEST, BEST, THOU ALWAYES SEEKST — 6 724
- YET WHAT THOU CANST ATTAIN, WHICH BEST MAY SERVE — 7 115
- ORDAIN'D FOR USES TO HIS LORD BEST KNOWN. — 8 106
- OF OTHER CREATURES, AS HIM PLEASES BEST, — 8 169
- BEST WITH THY SELF ACCOMPANIED, SEEK'ST NOT — 8 428
- SEEMS WISEST, VERTUOUSEST, DISCREETEST, BEST; — 8 550
- APPROVE THE BEST, AND FOLLOW WHAT I APPROVE. — 8 611
- FROM DUST: SPITE THEN WITH SPITE IS BEST REPAID. — 9 178
- THEN COMMUNE HOW THAT DAY THEY BEST MAY PLY — 9 201
- HOW WE MIGHT BEST FULFILL THE WORK WHICH HERE — 9 230
- FOR SOLITUDE SOMTIMES IS BEST SOCIETIE, — 9 249
- HIS WISH AND BEST ADVANTAGE, US ASUNDER, — 9 258
- WITH ME, BEST WITNESS OF THY VERTUE TRI'D. — 9 317
- O WOMAN, BEST ARE ALL THINGS AS THE WILL — 9 343
- AND ALL THINGS IN BEST ORDER TO INVITE — 9 402
- FROM HER BEST PROP SO FARR, AND STORM SO NIGH. — 9 433
- WITH RAVISHMENT BEHELD, THERE BEST BEHELD — 9 541
- GREAT ARE THY VERTUES, DOUBTLESS, BEST OF FRUITS. — 9 745
- BEST GUIDE; NOT FOLLOWING THEE, I HAD REMAIND — 9 808
- O FAIREST OF CREATION, LAST AND BEST — 9 896
- SUCH RECOMPENCE BEST MERITS) FROM THE BOUGH — 9 995
- WHAT BEST MAY FROM THE PRESENT SERVE TO HIDE — 9 1092
- THOSE TWO; THE THIRD BEST ABSENT IS CONDEMN'D, — 10 82
- THOUGH IN MYSTERIOUS TERMS, JUDG'D AS THEN BEST: — 10 173
- THERE BEST, WHERE MOST WITH RAVIN I MAY MEET; — 10 599
- AS SORTED BEST WITH PRESENT THINGS. THE SUN — 10 651
- OUT OF MY SIGHT, THOU SERPENT, THAT NAME BEST — 10 867
- AND MORTAL FOOD, AS MAY DISPOSE HIM BEST — 11 54
- SAFEST THY LIFE, AND BEST PREPAR'D ENDURE — 11 365
- CHOICEST AND BEST; THEN SACRIFICING, LAID — 11 438
- HIS BEST OF MAN, AND GAVE HIM UP TO TEARS — 11 497
- TO WHOM THUS MICHAEL. JUDG NOT WHAT IS BEST — 11 603
- HENCEFORTH I LEARNE, THAT TO OBEY IS BEST, — 12 561

BESTIAL
- TO BESTIAL GODS; FOR WHICH THIR HEADS AS LOW — 1 435
- AND TOWARDS THE GATE ROULING HER BESTIAL TRAIN, — 2 873
- AMONG THE BESTIAL HERDS TO RAUNGE, BY THEE — 4 754

BESTIAL (CONTINUED)
- INTO A BEAST, AND MIXT WITH BESTIAL SLIME, — 9 165

BESTIR
- ROUSE AND BESTIR THEMSELVES ERE WELL AWAKE. — 1 334

BESTIRS
- BESTIRS HER THEN, AND FROM EACH TENDER STALK — 5 337

BESTOW
- OUR GIVERS THIR OWN GIFTS, AND LARGE BESTOW — 5 317
- WITH WHAT ALL EARTH OR HEAVEN COULD BESTOW — 8 483

BESTOW'D
- MORE THEN ENOUGH; AT LEAST ON HER BESTOW'D — 8 537

BESTOWD
- ON WHOM THE GREAT CREATOR HATH BESTOWD — 3 673
- FROM LARGE BESTOWD, WHERE NATURE MULTIPLIES — 5 318
- BESTOWD, THE HOLY SALUTATION US'D — 5 386

BESTROWN
- AND BROKEN CHARIOT WHEELS, SO THICK BESTROWN — 1 311

BESTROWNE
- THAT LIE BESTROWNE UNSIGHTLY AND UNSMOOTH, — 4 631

BESTUCK
- BESTUCK WITH SLANDROUS DARTS, AND WORKS OF FAITH — 12 536

BETAKE
- WHITHER SHALL I BETAKE ME, WHERE SUBSIST? — 10 922

BETHEL
- DOUBL'D THAT SIN IN BETHEL AND IN DAN, — 1 485

BETHINK
- LET SUCH BETHINK THEM, IF THE SLEEPY DRENCH — 2 73

BETIDE
- MUST REASCEND, WHAT WILL BETIDE THE FEW — 12 480

BETIMES
- THIR SINFUL STATE, AND TO APPEASE BETIMES — 3 186

BETOK'NING
- BETOK'NING PEACE FROM GOD, AND COV'NANT NEW. — 11 867

BETOOK
- BETOOK THEM, AND THE NEIGHBOURING HILLS UPTORE; — 6 663
- BETOOK HER TO THE GROVES, BUT DELIA'S SELF — 9 388
- THIS SAID, THEY BOTH BETOOK THEM SEVERAL WAYES, — 10 610

BETRAID
- WHICH MARRD HIS BORROW'D VISAGE, AND BETRAID — 4 116

BETTER
- BETTER TO REIGN IN HELL, THEN SERVE IN HEAV'N. — 1 263
- NEW WARR, PROVOK'T; OUR BETTER PART REMAINS — 1 645
- FOR TREASURES BETTER HID. SOON HAD HIS CREW — 1 688
- THE BETTER REASON, TO PERPLEX AND DASH — 2 114
- CHAINS AND THESE TORMENTS? BETTER THESE THEN WORSE — 2 196
- TO SERVE HIM BETTER: WISE ARE ALL HIS WAYES. — 3 680
- WHO CAME THIR BANE, THOUGH WITH THEM BETTER PLEAS'D — 4 167
- YOUR NUMEROUS OFSPRING; IF NO BETTER PLACE, — 4 385
- WHICH TAUGHT THEE YET NO BETTER, THAT NO PAIN — 4 915
- BETTER ABODE, AND MY AFFLICTED POWERS — 4 939
- IF BETTER THOU BELONG NOT TO THE DAWN, — 5 167
- BUT WHAT IF BETTER COUNSELS MIGHT ERECT — 5 785
- THE BETTER FIGHT, WHO SINGLE HAST MAINTAIND — 6 30
- MAY SERVE TO BETTER US, AND WORSE OUR FOES, — 6 440
- OF SPIRITS MALIGNE A BETTER RACE TO BRING — 7 189
- THAT BETTER MIGHT WITH FARR LESS COMPASS MOVE, — 8 33
- IN BATTELS FEIGN'D; THE BETTER FORTITUDE — 9 31
- FOR WHAT GOD AFTER BETTER WORSE WOULD BUILD? — 9 102
- WERE BETTER, AND MOST LIKELIE IF FROM MEE — 9 365
- AGAINST HIS BETTER KNOWLEDGE, NOT DECEAV'D, — 9 998
- WITH TRAVAIL DIFFICULT, NOT BETTER FARR — 10 593
- TO BETTER HOPES HIS MORE ATTENTIVE MINDE — 10 1011
- SOM BETTER SHROUD, SOM BETTER WARMTH TO CHERISH — 10 1068
- WHAT BETTER CAN WE DO, THEN TO THE PLACE — 10 1086
- TO BETTER LIFE SHALL YEELD HIM, WHERE WITH MEE — 11 42
- BETTER END HEER UNBORN. WHY IS LIFE GIV'N — 11 502
- MUCH BETTER SEEMS THIS VISION, AND MORE HOPE — 11 599
- SAID TH' ANGEL, WHO SHOULD BETTER HOLD HIS PLACE — 11 635
- O VISIONS ILL FORESEEN. BETTER HAD I — 11 763
- UP TO A BETTER COV'NANT, DISCIPLIN'D — 12 302

BETWEEN
- BETWEEN THE CHERUBIM; YEA, OFTEN PLAC'D — 1 387
- RIS'N, AND WITH HIDEOUS OUTCRY RUSH'D BETWEEN. — 2 726
- HELL AND THE GULF BETWEEN, AND SATAN THERE — 3 70
- REAR'D HIGH THIR FLOURISHT HEADS BETWEEN, AND WROUGHT — 4 699
- SAILES BETWEEN WORLDS AND WORLDS, WITH STEDDIE WING — 5 268
- OF NECTAROUS DRAUGHTS BETWEEN, FROM MILKIE STREAM, — 5 306
- TELLS THE SUGGESTED CAUSE, AND CASTS BETWEEN — 5 702
- DESTRUCTION TO THE REST: THIS PAUSE BETWEEN — 6 162

BETWEEN (CONTINUED)
OR EQUAL WHAT BETWEEN US MADE THE ODDS, 6 441
OF BERIL, AND CAREERING FIRES BETWEEN; 6 756
MYRIADS BETWEEN TWO BRAZEN MOUNTAINS LODG'D 7 201
DISPARTED, AND BETWEEN SPUN OUT THE AIR, 7 241
BETWEEN HER WHITE WINGS MANTLING PROUDLY, ROWES 7 439
AS PLANTS: AMBIGUOUS BETWEEN SEA AND LAND 7 473
REFRESHMENT, WHETHER FOOD, OR TALK BETWEEN, 9 237
HIGH OVERARCH'T, AND ECHOING WALKS BETWEEN; 9 1107
NO GROUND OF ENMITIE BETWEEN US KNOWN, 9 1151
BETWEEN THEE AND THE WOMAN I WILL PUT 10 179
ENMITIE, AND BETWEEN THINE AND HER SEED; 10 180
THOUGH DISTANT FROM THEE WORLDS BETWEEN, YET FELT 10 362
IS ENMITY, WHICH HE WILL PUT BETWEEN 10 497
BETWEEN US TWO LET THERE BE PEACE, BOTH JOYNING, 10 924
BEFORE HIM, TOWNS, AND RURAL WORKS BETWEEN, 11 639
AS ON DRIE LAND BETWEEN TWO CHRISTAL WALLS, 12 197
DARKNESS DEFENDS BETWEEN TILL MORNING WATCH; 12 207
A MERCIE-SEAT OF GOLD BETWEEN THE WINGS 12 253

BETWIXT
BETWIXT DAMIATA AND MOUNT CASIUS OLD, 2 593
THROUGH BOSPORUS BETWIXT THE JUSTLING ROCKS: 2 1018
BETWIXT TH' ANGELICAL AND HUMAN KINDE: 3 462
BETWIXT THEM LAWNS, OR LEVEL DOWNS, AND FLOCKS 4 252
BETWIXT THESE ROCKIE PILLARS GABRIEL SAT 4 549
BETWIXT ASTREA AND THE SCORPION SIGNE, 4 998
BETWIXT THE CENTAURE AND THE SCORPION STEARING 10 328
BETWIXT THE WORLD DESTROY'D AND WORLD RESTOR'D, 12 3

BEWAILING
BEWAILING THIR EXCESS, ALL TERROR HIDE. 11 111

BEWARE
FROM WHAT POINT OF HIS COMPASS TO BEWARE 4 559
YET MUTABLE; WHENCE WARNE HIM TO BEWARE 5 237
AT THY REQUEST, AND THAT THOU MAIST BEWARE 6 894
ADAM BY DIRE EXAMPLE TO BEWARE 7 42
DEATH IS THE PENALTIE IMPOS'D, BEWARE, 7 545
THE WEAL OR WOE IN THEE IS PLAC'T; BEWARE. 8 638
BUT BID HER WELL BEWARE, AND STILL ERECT, 9 353

BEYOND
AND HORONAIM, SEONS REALM, BEYOND 1 409
A SHOUT THAT TORE HELLS CONCAVE, AND BEYOND 1 542
BY FONTARABBIA. THUS FAR THESE BEYOND 1 587
BEYOND THE INDIAN MOUNT, OR FAERIE ELVES, 1 781
THUS HIGH UPLIFTED BEYOND HOPE, ASPIRES 2 7
BEYOND THUS HIGH, INSATIATE TO PURSUE 2 8
BEYOND HIS POTENT ARM, TO LIVE EXEMPT 2 318
BEYOND THIS FLOOD A FROZEN CONTINENT 2 587
BEYOND COMPARE THE SON OF GOD WAS SEEN 3 138
BEYOND TH' HORIZON; THEN FROM POLE TO POLE 3 560
THE PLACE HE FOUND BEYOND EXPRESSION BRIGHT, 3 591
BEYOND THE CAPE OF HOPE, AND NOW ARE PAST 4 160
THY GOODNESS BEYOND THOUGHT, AND POWER DIVINE: 5 159
REACHING BEYOND ALL LIMIT AT ONE BLOW 6 140
STOOD SCOFFING, HIGHTHN'D IN THIR THOUGHTS BEYOND 6 629
OF KNOWLEDGE WITHIN BOUNDS; BEYOND ABSTAIN 7 120
BEYOND ALL OTHER, THINK THE SAME VOUTSAF'T 8 581
BEYOND THE EARTHS GREEN CAPE AND VERDANT ISLES 8 631
MAEOTIS, UP BEYOND THE RIVER OB; 9 78
ACTIVE WITHIN BEYOND THE SENSE OF BRUTE. 9 96
SOLE EVE, ASSOCIATE SOLE, TO ME BEYOND 9 227
BEYOND HIS HOPE, EVE SEPARATE HE SPIES, 9 424
BEYOND A ROW OF MYRTLES, ON A FLAT, 9 627
THAT LAY IN WAIT; BEYOND THIS HAD BIN FORCE, 9 1173
BEYOND THIS DEEP; WHATEVER DRAWES ME ON, 10 245
BEYOND PETSORA EASTWARD, TO THE RICH 10 292
OF TURKISH CRESCENT, LEAVES ALL WASTE BEYOND 10 434
SUCCESSFUL BEYOND HOPE, TO LEAD YE FORTH 10 463
BEYOND THE POLAR CIRCLES; TO THEM DAY 10 681
HIS SENTENCE BEYOND DUST AND NATURES LAW, 10 805
BEYOND ALL PAST EXAMPLE AND FUTURE, 10 840
BEYOND ALL BOUNDS, TILL INUNDATION RISE 11 828
TILL TIME STAND FIXT: BEYOND IS ALL ABYSS, 12 555
BEYOND WHICH WAS MY FOLLY TO ASPIRE. 12 560

BICKERING
OF SMOAK AND BICKERING FLAME, AND SPARKLES DIRE; 6 766

BID
WHO NOW IS SOVRAN CAN DISPOSE AND BID 1 246
THEN OF THIR SESSION ENDED THEY BID CRY 2 514
OR NATURE; GOD AND NATURE BID THE SAME, 6 176
OF BATTEL: WHEREAT MICHAEL BID SOUND 6 202
OR WE CAN BID HIS ABSENCE, TILL THY SONG 7 107
I SEND ALONG, RIDE FORTH, AND BID THE DEEP 7 166
EASIE, E'RE GOD HAD BID THE GROUND BE DRIE, 7 304
GOD HATH BID DWELL FARR OFF ALL ANXIOUS CARES, 8 185
SUNG SPOUSAL, AND BID HASTE THE EEVNING STARR 8 519
BUT BID HER WELL BEWARE, AND STILL ERECT, 9 353
SOME SAY HE BID HIS ANGELS TURNE ASCANSE 10 668
WAS BID TURN REINES FROM TH' EQUINOCTIAL RODE 10 672
THEY LIGHT THE NUPTIAL TORCH, AND BID INVOKE 11 590

BIDDING
TILL AT HIS SECOND BIDDING DARKNESS FLED, 3 712

BIDDING (CONTINUED)
IF PATIENTLY THY BIDDING THEY OBEY, 11 112
THEREFORE TO HIS GREAT BIDDING I SUBMIT. 11 314

BIDE
ALL KNEES TO THEE SHALL BOW, OF THEM THAT BIDE 3 321
MINE OWN THAT BIDE UPON ME, ALL FROM MEE 10 738

BIDS
WHAT E'RE HIS WRATH, WHICH HE CALLS JUSTICE, BIDS, 2 733
MEAN WHILE, AS NATURE WILLS, NIGHT BIDS US REST. 4 633
OUR MAKER BIDS INCREASE, WHO BIDS ABSTAIN 4 748
OF THESE FAIR SPREADING TREES; WHICH BIDS US SEEK 10 1067

BIDST
MY AUTHOR AND DISPOSER, WHAT THOU BIDST 4 635

BIGGEST
BEHEMOTH BIGGEST BORN OF EARTH UPHEAV'D 7 471

BIGNESS
IN BIGNESS TO SURPASS EARTHS GIANT SONS 1 778
THIS PENDANT WORLD, IN BIGNESS AS A STARR 2 1052

BILL
THE SECOND TIME RETURNING, IN HIS BILL 11 859

BILLOWS
IN BILLOWS, LEAVE I' TH' MIDST A HORRID VALE. 1 224

BIND
BIND THIR RESPLENDENT LOCKS INWREATH'D WITH BEAMS, 3 361
LOP OVERGROWN, OR PRUNE, OR PROP, OR BIND, 9 210
BIND US WITH AFTER-BANDS, WHAT PROFITS THEN 9 761

BINDE
IN VAIN, THOUGH BY THIR POWERFUL ART THEY BINDE 3 602
FLATLY UNJUST, TO BINDE WITH LAWS THE FREE, 5 819
SUCH PROHIBITIONS BINDE NOT. BUT IF DEATH 9 760
OR SERVE THEY AS A FLOURIE VERGE TO BINDE 11 881
BUT FORCE THE SPIRIT OF GRACE IT SELF, AND BINDE 12 525

BIRD
HARMONIOUS NUMBERS; AS THE WAKEFUL BIRD 3 38
SILENCE ACCOMPANIED, FOR BEAST AND BIRD, 4 600
WITH THIS HER SOLEMN BIRD AND THIS FAIR MOON, 4 648
WITH THIS HER SOLEMN BIRD, NOR WALK BY MOON, 4 655
BEAST, BIRD, INSECT, OR WORM DURST ENTER NONE; 4 704
TO THE NIGHT-WARBLING BIRD, THAT NOW AWAKE 5 40
A PHOENIX, GAZ'D BY ALL, AS THAT SOLE BIRD 5 272
AND EVERY BIRD OF WING AFTER HIS KINDE; 7 394
IN SIGNE WHEREOF EACH BIRD AND BEAST BEHOLD 8 342
AS THUS HE SPAKE, EACH BIRD AND BEAST BEHOLD 8 349
WITH BLANDISHMENT, EACH BIRD STOOP'D ON HIS WING. 8 351
MUCH LESS CAN BIRD WITH BEAST, OR FISH WITH FOWLE 8 395
DISPORTING, TILL THE AMOROUS BIRD OF NIGHT 8 518
ON BIRD, BEAST, AIRE, AIRE SUDDENLY ECLIPS'D 11 183
THE BIRD OF JOVE, STOOPT FROM HIS AERIE TOUR, 11 185
OF EVERY BEAST, AND BIRD, AND INSECT SMALL 11 734

BIRDS
THE BIRDS THIR NOTES RENEW, AND BLEATING HERDS 2 494
THE BIRDS THIR QUIRE APPLY; AIRES, VERNAL AIRES, 4 264
WITH CHARM OF EARLIEST BIRDS; PLEASANT THE SUN 4 642
WITH CHARM OF EARLIEST BIRDS, NOR RISING SUN 4 651
OF BIRDS ON EVERY BOUGH; SO MUCH THE MORE 5 8
JOYN VOICES ALL YE LIVING SOULS, YE BIRDS, 5 197
OF BIRDS IN ORDERLY ARRAY ON WING 6 74
FROM BRANCH TO BRANCH THE SMALLER BIRDS WITH SONG 7 433
BIRDS ON THE BRANCHES WARBLING; ALL THINGS SMIL'D, 8 265
JOYOUS THE BIRDS; FRESH GALES AND GENTLE AIRES 8 515
WALKS, AND THE MELODIE OF BIRDS; BUT HERE 8 528
TWO BIRDS OF GAYEST PLUME BEFORE HIM DROVE; 11 186

BIRTH
BY WONDROUS BIRTH: BE THOU IN ADAMS ROOM 3 285
BEGINS HIS DIRE ATTEMPT, WHICH NIGH THE BIRTH 4 15
AIRE, AND YE ELEMENTS THE ELDEST BIRTH 5 180
HAD CIRCL'D HIS FULL ORBE, THE BIRTH MATURE 5 862
HIS GENERATION, AND THE RISING BIRTH 7 102
OP'NING HER FERTIL WOOMB TEEM'D AT A BIRTH 7 454
PRODUCTIVE IN HERB, PLANT, AND NOBLER BIRTH 9 111
OUT OF THE GROUND WAST TAKEN, KNOW THY BIRTH, 10 207
AT ONCE, BY MY FOREKNOWLEDGE GAINING BIRTH 11 768
BARR'D OF HIS RIGHT; YET AT HIS BIRTH A STARR 12 360
HIS PLACE OF BIRTH A SOLEMN ANGEL TELLS 12 364

BIRTH-DAY
BIRTH-DAY OF HEAV'N AND EARTH; WITH JOY AND SHOUT 7 256

BIRTHRIGHT
WITH HIS ENORMOUS BROOD, AND BIRTHRIGHT SEIS'D 1 511
BY MERIT MORE THEN BIRTHRIGHT SON OF GOD, 3 309

BIRTHS
PRODUCE PRODIGIOUS BIRTHS OF BODIE OR MIND. 11 687

BISERTA
OR WHOM BISERTA SENT FROM AFRIC SHORE 1 585

BITTER
ARE BROUGHT: AND FEEL BY TURNS THE BITTER CHANGE . 2 598
SHOULD PROVE A BITTER MORSEL, AND HIS BANE, . . 2 808
THAT SLUMBERD, WAKES THE BITTER MEMORIE 4 24
AND SHUN THE BITTER CONSEQUENCE: FOR KNOW, . . . 8 328
BITTER ERE LONG BACK ON IT SELF RECOILES; . . . 9 172
CHEWD BITTER ASHES, WHICH TH' OFFENDED TASTE . . 10 566

BITTERNESS
ASSURES ME THAT THE BITTERNESS OF DEATH 11 157

BITUMINOUS
NEER THAT BITUMINOUS LAKE WHERE SODOM FLAM'D; . . 10 562
THE PLAIN, WHEREIN A BLACK BITUMINOUS GURGE . . 12 41

BIZANCE
IN MOSCO, OR THE SULTAN IN BIZANCE, ... 11 395

BLACK
AND BLACK GEHENNA CALL'D THE TYPE OF HELL. . . . 1 405
BLACK FIRE AND HORROR SHOT WITH EQUAL RAGE . . . 2 67
SAD ACHERON OF SORROW, BLACK AND DEEP; 2 578
FOR EACH SEEM'D EITHER; BLACK IT STOOD AS NIGHT, . 2 670
EACH CAST AT TH' OTHER, AS WHEN TWO BLACK CLOUDS . 2 714
WHITE, BLACK AND GREY, WITH ALL THIR TRUMPERIE. . 3 475
THE BLACK TARTAREOUS COLD INFERNAL DREGS . . . 7 238
SURPRISE THEE, AND HER BLACK ATTENDANT DEATH. . . 7 547
LIKE A BLACK MIST LOW CREEPING, HE HELD ON . . . 9 180
NOTUS AND AFER BLACK WITH THUNDROUS CLOUDS . . . 10 702
WHOLSOM AND COOL, AND MILD, BUT WITH BLACK AIR . 10 847
MEANWHILE THE SOUTHWIND ROSE, AND WITH BLACK WINGS 11 738
THE PLAIN, WHEREIN A BLACK BITUMINOUS GURGE . . 12 41

BLACKEST
WITH BLACKEST INSURRECTION, TO CONFOUND 2 136
TO BLACKEST GRAIN, AND INTO STORE CONVEY'D: . . 6 515

BLAINES
BOTCHES AND BLAINES MUST ALL HIS FLESH IMBOSS, . 12 180

BLAM'D
EACH OTHER, BLAM'D ENOUGH ELSEWHERE, BUT STRIVE . 10 959

BLAME
THAT REACHES BLAME, BUT RATHER MERITS PRAISE . . 3 697
FARR BE IT, THAT I SHOULD WRITE THEE SIN OR BLAME, 4 758
NO SPOT OR BLAME BEHIND: WHICH GIVES ME HOPE . . 5 119
TO ASK OR SEARCH I BLAME THEE NOT, FOR HEAV'N . . 8 66
FOR SUCH THOU ART, FROM SIN AND BLAME ENTIRE: . . 9 292
TO WHOM SOON MOV'D WITH TOUCH OF BLAME THUS EVE. . 9 1143
I SHOULD CONCEAL, AND NOT EXPOSE TO BLAME . . 10 130
OF ALL CORRUPTION, ALL THE BLAME LIGHTS DUE; . . 10 833
BUT RISE, LET US NO MORE CONTEND, NOR BLAME . . 10 958

BLAM'ST
TO LOVE THOU BLAM'ST ME NOT, FOR LOVE THOU SAIST . 8 612

BLANC
PRESENTED WITH A UNIVERSAL BLANC 3 48
SOLSTITIAL SUMMERS HEAT. TO THE BLANC MOONE . . 10 656

BLAND
AND TEMPERAT VAPORS BLAND, WHICH TH' ONLY SOUND . 5 5
WHICH WITH BLAND WORDS AT WILL SHE THUS ADDREST. . 9 855
THAT WITH EXHILERATING VAPOUR BLAND 9 1047

BLANDISHMENT
WITH BLANDISHMENT, EACH BIRD STOOP'D ON HIS WING. 8 351

BLANK
ASTONIED STOOD AND BLANK, WHILE HORROR CHILL . . 9 890

BLASPHEAM'D
BE QUESTIOND AND BLASPHEAM'D WITHOUT DEFENCE. . . 3 166

BLASPHEM'D
FOR THIS HE SHALL LIVE HATED, BE BLASPHEM'D, . . 12 411

BLASPHEMOUS
O ARGUMENT BLASPHEMOUS, FALSE AND PROUD. . . . 5 809
REFREIN'D HIS TONGUE BLASPHEMOUS; BUT ANON . . . 6 360

BLAST
AS IN AN ORGAN FROM ONE BLAST OF WIND 1 708
LIKE CHANGE ON SEA AND LAND, SIDERAL BLAST, . . 10 693
WITH ADVERSE BLAST UP-TURNS THEM FROM THE SOUTH . 10 701
TO SOUND AT GENERAL DOOM. TH' ANGELIC BLAST . . 11 76

BLASTED
STANDS ON THE BLASTED HEATH. HE NOW PREPAR'D . . 1 615
OF RAMIEL SCORCHT AND BLASTED OVERTHREW. . . . 6 372
SPREADING THIR BANE; THE BLASTED STARRS LOOKT WAN, 10 412

BLASTING
THY BLASTING VOLIED THUNDER MADE ALL SPEED . . . 4 928

BLAZ'D
THAT SPARKLING BLAZ'D, HIS OTHER PARTS BESIDES . 1 194
BLAZ'D OPPOSITE, WHILE EXPECTATION STOOD . . . 6 306
WHEN THE GREAT ENSIGN OF MESSIAH BLAZ'D 6 775
BLAZ'D FORTH UNCLOUDED DEITIE; HE FULL 10 65
THE BRANDISHT SWORD OF GOD BEFORE THEM BLAZ'D . . 12 633

BLAZE
OF MIGHTY CHERUBIM; THE SUDDEN BLAZE 1 665
THE FULL BLAZE OF THY BEAMS, AND THROUGH A CLOUD . 3 378
WITH SUDDEN BLAZE DIFFUS'D, INFLAMES THE AIRE: . 4 818
REFLECTING BLAZE ON BLAZE, FIRST MET HIS VIEW: . 6 18
WILL DAZLE NOW THIS EARTHLY, WITH THIR BLAZE . . 9 1083
AT THAT SO SUDDEN BLAZE THE STYGIAN THRONG . . 10 453

BLAZING
OF STARRY LAMPS AND BLAZING CRESSETS FED . . . 1 728
SOMETIMES TOWARDS HEAV'N AND THE FULL-BLAZING SUN, 4 29
HIGH ON A HILL, FAR BLAZING, AS A MOUNT 5 757
THAT OPEN'D WIDE HER BLAZING PORTALS, LED . . . 7 575
HOVERING AND BLAZING WITH DELUSIVE LIGHT, . . . 9 639
FROM YONDER BLAZING CLOUD THAT VEILS THE HILL . . 11 229

BLEATING
BOTH HER FIRST BORN AND ALL HER BLEATING GODS. . 1 489
THE BIRDS THIR NOTES RENEW, AND BLEATING HERDS . 2 494
HIS VASTNESS: FLEEC'T THE FLOCKS AND BLEATING ROSE, 7 472
EWES AND THIR BLEATING LAMBS OVER THE PLAINE, . . 11 649

BLEED
SANGUIN, SUCH AS CELESTIAL SPIRITS MAY BLEED, . . .6 333

BLESS
SO DISINHERITED HOW WOULD YE BLESS 10 821

BLESS'D
AND SAW THAT IT WAS GOOD, AND BLESS'D THEM, SAYING, 7 395
FEMALE FOR RACE; THEN BLESS'D MANKINDE, AND SAID, 7 530
NOW RESTING, BLESS'D AND HALLOWD THE SEAV'NTH DAY, 7 592

BLESSED
ALL HEAV'N, AND IN THE BLESSED SPIRITS ELECT . . 3 136
CAST OUT FROM GOD AND BLESSED VISION, FALLS . . 5 613
HEAV'NS BLESSED PEACE, AND INTO NATURE BROUGHT . 6 267
ACCURST OF BLESSED, HIDE ME FROM THE FACE . . . 10 723
HIS BLESSED COUNT'NANCE; HERE I COULD FREQUENT, . 11 317
SHALL IN HIS SEED BE BLESSED; BY THAT SEED . . 12 148

BLESSEDNESS
WITH BLESSEDNESS. WHENCE ADAM SOON REPEAL'D . . 7 59

BLEST
HIS FAMINE SHOULD BE FILL'D, AND BLEST HIS MAWE . 2 847
ENCOMPASS'D SHALL RESOUND THEE EVER BLEST, . . . 3 149
AS FROM BLEST VOICES, UTTERING JOY, HEAV'N RUNG . 3 347
OF ARABIE THE BLEST, WITH SUCH DELAY 4 163
BLEST PAIR; AND O YET HAPPIEST IF YE SEEK . . . 4 774
LONG AFTER TO BLEST MARIE, SECOND EVE. 5 387
IN HEAV'N GOD EVER BLEST, AND HIS DIVINE . . . 6 184
AND ALL THE BLEST: STAND FAST; TO STAND OR FALL . 8 640
IN PARADISE, OF OPERATION BLEST 9 796
BUT LET US CALL TO SYNOD ALL THE BLEST . . . 11 67
OF GOD HIGH-BLEST, OR TO INCLINE HIS WILL, . . 11 145
TRUE OPENER OF MINE EYES, PRIME ANGEL BLEST, . . 11 598
ALL NATIONS SHALL BE BLEST; HE STRAIGHT OBEYS, . 12 126
PLAINLIER SHALL BE REVEALD. THIS PATRIARCH BLEST, 12 151
HIS DAY, IN WHOM ALL NATIONS SHALL BE BLEST, . . 12 277
SO IN HIS SEED ALL NATIONS SHALL BE BLEST. . . 12 450
HOW SOON HATH THY PREDICTION, SEER BLEST, . . . 12 553
ACKNOWLEDGE MY REDEEMER EVER BLEST. 12 573

BLEW
TO THE BRIGHT MINISTER THAT WATCHD, HEE BLEW . . 11 73
O'RE THE BLEW FIRMAMENT A RADIANT WHITE, . . . 11 206

BLIND
BLIND THAMYRIS AND BLIND MAEONIDES, ... 3 35
BUT HARD BE HARD'ND, BLIND BE BLINDED MORE, . . 3 200
OF PAINFUL SUPERSTITION AND BLIND ZEAL, ... 3 452

BLINDED
BUT HARD BE HARD'ND, BLIND BE BLINDED MORE, . . 3 200

BLISS
(FAR OTHER ONCE BEHELD IN BLISS) CONDEMN'D . . . 1 607
THEN TO DWELL HERE, DRIV'N OUT FROM BLISS,
CONDEMN'D 2 86
THIR FRAIL ORIGINAL, AND FADED BLISS, ... 2 375
CREATED VAST AND ROUND, A PLACE OF BLISS . . . 2 832
TO THAT NEW WORLD OF LIGHT AND BLISS, AMONG . . 2 867
BECAUSE THOU HAST, THOUGH THRON'D IN HIGHEST BLISS 3 305
AND WHERE THE RIVER OF BLISS THROUGH MIDST OF HEAVN 3 358
REGARDLESS OF THE BLISS WHEREIN HEE SAT 3 408
HIS SAD EXCLUSION FROM THE DORES OF BLISS. . . . 3 525
INTO OUR ROOM OF BLISS THUS HIGH ADVANC'T . . . 4 359
OF BLISS ON BLISS, WHILE I TO HELL AM THRUST, . . 4 508
AND MUTUAL LOVE, THE CROWN OF ALL OUR BLISS . . 4 728
WHOSE DWELLING GOD HATH PLANTED HERE IN BLISS? . 4 884

BLISS (CONTINUED)
- THE FALL OF OTHERS FROM LIKE STATE OF BLISS; 5 241
- WILDE ABOVE RULE OR ART; ENORMOUS BLISS. 5 297
- FULL TO THE UTMOST MEASURE OF WHAT BLISS 5 517
- FROM WHAT HIGH STATE OF BLISS INTO WHAT WOE. 5 543
- BY WHOM IN BLISS IMBOSOM'D SAT THE SON, 5 597
- PURSUING DRIVE THEM OUT FROM GOD AND BLISS, 6 52
- FROM ALL HER CONFINES. HEAV'N THE SEAT OF BLISS 6 273
- FULFILL'D, WHICH TO FULFIL IS ALL MY BLISS. 6 729
- WHERE NOW HE SITS AT THE RIGHT HAND OF BLISS. 6 892
- AND WARR SO NEER THE PEACE OF GOD IN BLISS 7 55
- TO THE GARDEN OF BLISS, THY SEAT PREPAR'D. 8 299
- MY STORIE TO THE SUM OF EARTHLY BLISS 8 522
- CONJUGAL LOVE, THEN WHICH PERHAPS NO BLISS 9 263
- DESPOILD OF INNOCENCE, OF FAITH, OF BLISS. 9 411
- ADAM SHALL SHARE WITH ME IN BLISS OR WOE: 9 831
- FOR BLISS, AS THOU HAST PART, TO ME IS BLISS, 9 879
- MINE NEVER SHALL BE PARTED, BLISS OR WOE. 9 916
- WHO MIGHT HAVE LIV'D AND JOYD IMMORTAL BLISS, 9 1166
- WITH PITIE, VIOLATED NOT THIR BLISS. 10 25
- THERE DWELL AND REIGN IN BLISS, THENCE ON THE EARTH 10 399
- BUT UP AND ENTER NOW INTO FULL BLISS. 10 503
- ALL MY REDEEMD MAY DWELL IN JOY AND BLISS, 11 43
- HIGH IN SALVATION AND THE CLIMES OF BLISS, 11 708
- HIS FAITHFUL, AND RECEAVE THEM INTO BLISS, 12 462
- TO BRING FORTH FRUITS JOY AND ETERNAL BLISS. 12 551

BLISSFUL
- RESTORE US, AND REGAIN THE BLISSFUL SEAT, 1 5
- IN BLISSFUL SOLITUDE; HE THEN SURVEY'D 3 69
- JUST O'RE THE BLISSFUL SEAT OF PARADISE, 3 527
- A HEAV'N ON EARTH, FOR BLISSFUL PARADISE 4 208
- ON TO THIR BLISSFUL BOWER; IT WAS A PLACE 4 690
- INTO THE BLISSFUL FIELD, THROUGH GROVES OF MYRRHE, 5 292
- INTO HIS BLISSFUL BOSOM REASSUM'D 10 225
- FILLD ALL THE REGIONS: FROM THIR BLISSFUL BOWRS 11 77

BLITHE
- TO WHOM THE WILIE ADDER, BLITHE AND GLAD. 9 625
- THUS EVE WITH COUNTNANCE BLITHE HER STORIE TOLD; 9 886
- OF GODDESSES, SO BLITHE, SO SMOOTH, SO GAY, 11 615

BLOOD
- FIRST MOLOCH, HORRID KING BESMEAR'D WITH BLOOD 1 392
- RAN PURPLE TO THE SEA, SUPPOS'D WITH BLOOD 1 451
- LUR'D WITH THE SMELL OF INFANT BLOOD, TO DANCE 2 664
- TH' ANIMAL SPIRITS THAT FROM PURE BLOOD ARISE 4 805
- AND LIFE-BLOOD STREAMING FRESH; WIDE WAS THE WOUND, 8 467
- BEDROPT WITH BLOOD OF GORGON, OR THE ISLE 10 527
- HOPEFUL AND CHEERFUL, IN THY BLOOD WILL REIGNE 11 543
- WHO HAVING SPILT MUCH BLOOD, AND DON MUCH WASTE 11 791
- TO BLOOD UNSHED THE RIVERS MUST BE TURND, 12 176

BLOODIE
- FOR DEATH, THE FOLLOWING DAY, IN BLOODIE FIGHT. 10 278
- FROM HEAV'N ACCEPTANCE; BUT THE BLOODIE FACT 11 457

BLOODY
- BUT CALL IN AIDE, WHICH MAKES A BLOODY FRAY; 11 651

BLOOM
- OR SIGHT OF VERNAL BLOOM, OR SUMMERS ROSE, 3 43
- BEGAN TO BLOOM, BUT SOON FOR MANS OFFENCE 3 355
- SITS ON THE BLOOM EXTRACTING LIQUID SWEET. 5 25
- TO VISIT HOW THEY PROSPER'D, BUD AND BLOOM, 8 45

BLOOMING
- HIGH EMINENT, BLOOMING AMBROSIAL FRUIT 4 219

BLOSSOMS
- BLOSSOMS AND FRUITS AT ONCE OF GOLDEN HUE 4 148
- THOSE BLOSSOMS ALSO, AND THOSE DROPPING GUMMS, 4 630
- THIR BLOSSOMS: WITH HIGH WOODS THE HILLS WERE CROWND, 7 326

BLOT
- THAT HE RELENTS, NOT TO BLOT OUT MANKIND, 11 891
- PALPABLE DARKNESS, AND BLOT OUT THREE DAYES; 12 188

BLOTTED
- BE NO MEMORIAL BLOTTED OUT AND RAS'D 1 362

BLOUD
- GROAND OUT HIS SOUL WITH GUSHING BLOUD EFFUS'D. 11 447
- THE BLOUD OF BULLS AND GOATS, THEY MAY CONCLUDE 12 292
- SOME BLOUD MORE PRECIOUS MUST BE PAID FOR MAN, 12 293

BLOW
- AWAK'D SHOULD BLOW THEM INTO SEVENFOLD RAGE 2 171
- HOV'RING A SPACE, TILL WINDS THE SIGNAL BLOW 2 717
- MOZAMBIC, OFF AT SEA NORTH-EAST WINDES BLOW 4 161
- HIS PRAISE YE WINDS, THAT FROM FOUR QUARTERS BLOW, 5 192
- ETHEREAL TRUMPET FROM ON HIGH GAN BLOW: 6 60
- REACHING BEYOND ALL LIMIT AT ONE BLOW 6 140
- THE ATHEIST CREW, BUT WITH REDOUBL'D BLOW 6 370
- BLOW MOIST AND KEEN, SHATTERING THE GRACEFUL LOCKS 10 1066

BLOWING
- SONOROUS METTAL BLOWING MARTIAL SOUNDS: 1 540
- OF BLOWING MYRRH AND BALME; IF THOU ACCEPT 9 629
- AS WHEN TWO POLAR WINDS BLOWING ADVERSE 10 289
- DRIVN BY A KEEN NORTH-WINDE, THAT BLOWING DRIE 11 842

BLOW'N
- WHEN FROM THE BOUGHES A SAVORIE ODOUR BLOW'N, 9 579
- BLOW'N VAGABOND OR FRUSTRATE: IN THEY PASSD 11 16

BLOWN
- BLOWN UP WITH HIGH CONCEITS INGENDRING PRIDE. 4 809
- HER BOSOM SMELLING SWEET: AND THESE SCARCE BLOWN, 7 319
- BLOWN STIFLING BACK ON HIM THAT BREATHS IT FORTH: 11 313

BLOWS
- BLOWS THEM TRANSVERSE TEN THOUSAND LEAGUES AWRY 3 488
- OUR TENDED PLANTS, HOW BLOWS THE CITRON GROVE, 5 22

BLUSH
- AFTER SHORT BLUSH OF MORN; NIGH IN HER SIGHT 11 184

BLUSHING
- I LED HER BLUSHING LIKE THE MORN: ALL HEAV'N, 8 511

BLUSTER
- THIR CORNERS, WHEN WITH BLUSTER TO CONFOUND 10 665

BLUSTRING
- THE SOUND OF BLUSTRING WINDS, WHICH ALL NIGHT LONG 2 286
- OF CHAOS BLUSTRING ROUND, INCLEMENT SKIE; 3 426

BOARD
- TO MANY A ROW OF PIPES THE SOUND-BOARD BREATHS. 1 709
- SHE GATHERS, TRIBUTE LARGE, AND ON THE BOARD 5 343

BOAST
- WHO BOAST IN MORTAL THINGS, AND WOND'RING TELL 1 693
- MORE UNEXPERT, I BOAST NOT; THEM LET THOSE 2 52
- LOOSE ALL HER VIRTUE; LEAST BAD MEN SHOULD BOAST 2 483
- FAR OFF AND FEARLESS, NOR WITH CAUSE TO BOAST, 4 14
- HOW DEARLY I ABIDE THAT BOAST SO VAINE, 4 87
- TO BOAST WHAT ARMS CAN DOE, SINCE THINE NO MORE 4 1008
- (UNANSWERD LEAST THOU BOAST) TO LET THEE KNOW; 6 163
- ADAM, FROM WHOSE DEARE SIDE I BOAST ME SPRUNG, 9 965
- OF THAT DEFENDED FRUIT; BUT LET HIM BOAST 11 86

BOASTED
- THIR BOASTED PARENTS; TITAN HEAV'NS FIRST BORN 1 510

BOASTFUL
- VARIOUS, WITH BOASTFUL ARGUMENT PORTRAID, 6 84

BOASTING
- THEN TO SUBMIT, BOASTING I COULD SUBDUE 4 85

BODIE
- TO REACH, AND FEED AT ONCE BOTH BODIE AND MIND? 9 779
- AND SIN? THE BODIE PROPERLY HATH NEITHER. 10 791
- PRODUCE PRODIGIOUS BIRTHS OF BODIE OR MIND. 11 687

BODIES
- YOUR BODIES MAY AT LAST TURN ALL TO SPIRIT, 5 497
- OR HOLLOW'D BODIES MADE OF OAK OR FIRR 6 574
- HAD WONDROUS, AS WITH STARRS THIR BODIES ALL 6 754
- FOR OF CELESTIAL BODIES FIRST THE SUN 7 354
- SO MANY NOBLER BODIES TO CREATE, 8 28
- THAT BODIES BRIGHT AND GREATER SHOULD NOT SERVE 8 87
- OR BY COLLISION OF TWO BODIES GRINDE 10 1072

BODY
- SHADOW FROM BODY OPAQUE CAN FALL, AND THE AIRE, 3 619
- MAN HATH HIS DAILY WORK OF BODY OR MIND 4 618
- ARMIE OF FIENDS, FIT BODY TO FIT HEAD; 4 953
- TILL BODY UP TO SPIRIT WORK, IN BOUNDS 5 478
- WHATEVER PURE THOU IN THE BODY ENJOY'ST 8 622
- ONCE ACTUAL, NOW IN BODY, AND TO DWELL 10 587

BOG
- A GULF PROFOUND AS THAT SERBONIAN BOG 2 592
- ORE BOG OR STEEP, THROUGH STRAIT, ROUGH, DENSE, OR RARE, 2 948

BOGGIE
- QUENCHT IN A BOGGIE SYRTIS, NEITHER SEA, 2 939

BOGGS
- TO BOGGS AND MIRES, AND OFT THROUGH POND OR POOLE, 9 641

BOGS
- ROCKS, CAVE, LAKES, FENS, BOGS, DENS, AND SHADES OF DEATH, 2 621

BOILES
- NOW ROWLING, BOILES IN HIS TUMULTUOUS BREST, 4 16
- BOILES OUT FROM UNDER GROUND, THE MOUTH OF HELL; 12 42

BOILING
OVER THE DARK ABYSS, WHOSE BOILING GULF 2 1027

BOLD
AND THENCE IN HEAV'N CALL'D SATAN, WITH BOLD WORDS 1 82
AND HIM THUS ANSWER'D SOON HIS BOLD COMPEER. 1 127
HE ALSO AGAINST THE HOUSE OF GOD WAS BOLD: 1 470
(THOUGH LIKE A COVER'D FIELD, WHERE CHAMPIONS BOLD 1 763
I LAUGH, WHEN THOSE WHO AT THE SPEAR ARE BOLD 2 204
HIS GLORY TO AUGMENT. THE BOLD DESIGN 2 386
ON BOLD ADVENTURE TO DISCOVER WIDE 2 571
IN BOLD CONSPIRACY AGAINST HEAV'NS KING, 2 751
YET NOT REJOYCING IN HIS SPEED, THOUGH BOLD, 4 13
OR LESS BE LOST. THY FEAR, SAID ZEPHON BOLD, 4 854
TO QUESTION THY BOLD ENTRANCE ON THIS PLACE; 4 882
AT SUCH BOLD WORDS VOUCHT WITH A DEED SO BOLD: 5 66
THUS FARR HIS BOLD DISCOURSE WITHOUT CONTROULE 5 803
ENCOMPASS'D ROUND WITH FOES, THUS ANSWERD BOLD. 5 876
LEAST HEE INCENST AT SUCH ERUPTION BOLD, 8 235
THE ENEMIE, THOUGH BOLD, WILL HARDLY DARE, 9 304
THEN VOLUBLE AND BOLD, NOW HID, NOW SEEN 9 436
SHE SCARSE HAD SAID, THOUGH BRIEF, WHEN NOW MORE
BOLD 9 664
BOLD DEED THOU HAST PRESUM'D, ADVENTROUS EVE, 9 921
BOLD OR LOQUACIOUS, THUS ABASHT REPLI'D. 10 161
TO HIS BOLD RIOT; DREADFUL WAS THE DIN 10 521

BOLDER
THEE I RE-VISIT NOW WITH BOLDER WING, 3 13
SELF-LEFT. LEAST THEREFORE HIS NOW BOLDER HAND 11 93

BOLDEST
WHERE BOLDEST; THOUGH TO SIGHT UNCONQUERABLE? 6 118

BOLDLY
T' WHOM SATAN TURNING BOLDLY, THUS. YE POWERS 2 968
AND BOLDLY VENTURE TO WHATEVER PLACE 4 891

BOLDNESS
OR NOT, WHO ASK WHAT BOLDNESS BROUGHT HIM HITHER 4 908

BOLT
TH' INTRICATE WARDS, AND EVERY BOLT AND BAR 2 877
THE THUNDERER OF HIS ONLY DREADED BOLT. 6 491

BOLTED
CROSS-BARRD AND BOLTED FAST, FEAR NO ASSAULT, 4 190
AND QUIVER WITH THREE-BOLTED THUNDER STOR'D, 6 764

BOND
THE BOND OF NATURE DRAW ME TO MY OWNE, 9 956

BONDAGE
CAELESTIAL SPIRITS IN BONDAGE, NOR TH' ABYSS 1 658
IN STRICTEST BONDAGE, THOUGH THUS FAR REMOV'D, 2 321

BONDS
EXILE, OR IGNOMINY, OR BONDS, OR PAIN, 2 207
HIS HINDER PARTS, THEN SPRINGS AS BROKE FROM BONDS, 7 465

BONE
HIS FLESH, HIS BONE; TO GIVE THEE BEING I LENT 4 483
BONE OF MY BONE, FLESH OF MY FLESH, MY SELF 8 495
BONE OF MY BONE THOU ART, AND FROM THY STATE 9 915
GIANTS OF MIGHTIE BONE, AND BOULD EMPRISE; 11 642

BONES
NOR FOUNDED ON THE BRITTLE STRENGTH OF BONES, 1 427

BOOK
CUT OFF, AND FOR THE BOOK OF KNOWLEDG FAIR 3 47
IS AS THE BOOK OF GOD BEFORE THEE SET, 8 67

BOOKS
BY THIR REBELLION, FROM THE BOOKS OF LIFE. 1 363

BOON
IN BEDS AND CURIOUS KNOTS, BUT NATURE BOON 4 242
AND HIGHT'ND AS WITH WINE, JOCOND AND BOON, 9 793

BOOTIE
THIR BOOTIE; SCARCE WITH LIFE THE SHEPHERDS FLYE, 11 650

BORDER
THE UTMOST BORDER OF HIS KINGDOM, LEFT 2 361
SO ON HE FARES, AND TO THE BORDER COMES, 4 131

BORDERING
IMPREGNABLE; OFT ON THE BORDERING DEEP 2 131
BORDERING ON LIGHT; WHEN STRAIT BEHOLD THE THRONE 2 959

BORDERS
BORDERS ON AEGYPT AND THE ARABIAN SHOARE; 3 537
WITH BORDERS LONG THE RIVERS. THAT EARTH NOW 7 328

BORDRING
WITH THESE CAME THEY, WHO FROM THE BORDRING FLOOD 1 419

BORE
SOON RECOLLECTING, WITH HIGH WORDS, THAT BORE 1 528
BORE HIM SLOPE DOWNWARD TO THE SUN NOW FALL'N 4 591
DEFENCE, WHILE OTHERS BORE HIM ON THIR SHIELDS 6 337
THICK-RAMMD, AT TH' OTHER BORE WITH TOUCH OF FIRE 6 485
UP LIFTING BORE THEM IN THIR HANDS: AMAZE, 6 646
BORE UP HIS BRANCHING HEAD; SCARSE FROM HIS MOULD 7 470
HEE WITH OLYMPIAS, THIS WITH HER WHO BORE 9 509
BUT CONFIDENCE THEN BORE THEE ON, SECURE 9 1175

BOREAS
BOREAS AND CAECIAS AND ARGESTES LOUD 10 699

BORN
TITANIAN, OR EARTH-BORN, THAT WARR'D ON JOVE, 1 198
BOTH HER FIRST BORN AND ALL HER BLEATING GODS. 1 489
THIR BOASTED PARENTS; TITAN HEAV'NS FIRST BORN 1 510
HELL-BORN, NOT TO CONTEND WITH SPIRITS OF HEAV'N. 2 687
AND HOURLY BORN, WITH SORROW INFINITE 2 797
INHABITANT OF HEAV'N, AND HEAV'NLIE-BORN, 2 860
BORN THROUGH THE HOLLOW DARK ASSAULTS HIS EARE 2 953
HAIL HOLY LIGHT, OFSPRING OF HEAV'N FIRST-BORN, 3 1
HITHER OF ILL-JOYND SONS AND DAUGHTERS BORN 3 463
CREATURES OF OTHER MOULD, EARTH-BORN PERHAPS, 4 360
AND FOR THE TESTIMONIE OF TRUTH HAST BORN 6 33
BORN EEVN OR HIGH, FOR THIS DAY WILL POUR DOWN, 6 544
ALOFT BY ANGELS BORN, HIS SIGN IN HEAV'N: 6 776
HER ANNUAL VOIAGE, BORN ON WINDES; THE AIRE 7 431
BEHEMOTH BIGGEST BORN OF EARTH UPHEAV'D 7 471
AND OPS, ERE YET DICTAEAN JOVE WAS BORN, 10 584
WHOM THUS THE SIN-BORN MONSTER ANSWERD SOON. 10 596
WHICH MUST BE BORN TO CERTAIN WOE, DEVOURD 10 980
TURCHESTAN-BORN; NOR COULD HIS EYE NOT KEN 11 396
THOUGH NOT OF WOMAN BORN; COMPASSION QUELL'D 11 496
LAST WITH ONE MIDNIGHT STROKE ALL THE FIRST-BORN 12 189
ANOINTED KING MESSIAH MIGHT BE BORN 12 359

BORNE
THROUGH UTTER AND THROUGH MIDDLE DARKNESS BORNE 3 16
ADAM THE GOODLIEST MAN OF MEN SINCE BORNE 4 323
OF OLD OLYMPUS DWELL'ST, BUT HEAV'NLIE BORNE, 7 7
OR ONE SHORT SIGH OF HUMANE BREATH, UP-BORNE 11 147
LIV'D IGNORANT OF FUTURE, SO HAD BORNE 11 764

BORROW'D
TH' INFECTION WHEN THIR BORROW'D GOLD COMPOS'D 1 483
WHICH MARRD HIS BORROW'D VISAGE, AND BETRAID 4 116

BORROWD
WITH BORROWD LIGHT HER COUNTENANCE TRIFORM 3 730

BORROWING
HIS MIRROR, WITH FULL FACE BORROWING HER LIGHT 7 377

BOSOM
SHOOTS FARR INTO THE BOSOM OF DIM NIGHT 2 1036
SON OF MY BOSOM, SON WHO ART ALONE 3 169
THY BOSOM, AND THIS GLORIE NEXT TO THEE 3 239
THEE FROM MY BOSOM AND RIGHT HAND, TO SAVE, 3 279
HER BOSOM SMELLING SWEET: AND THESE SCARCE BLOWN, 7 319
INTO HIS BLISSFUL BOSOM REASSUM'D 10 225

BOSOM'D
THAT OPEN NOW THIR CHOICEST BOSOM'D SMELLS 5 127

BOSPORUS
THROUGH BOSPORUS BETWIXT THE JUSTLING ROCKS: 2 1018

BOSSY
CORNICE OR FREEZE, WITH BOSSY SCULPTURES GRAV'N, 1 716

BOTCHES
BOTCHES AND BLAINES MUST ALL HIS FLESH IMBOSS, 12 180

BOTTOM
AND LEAVE A SINGED BOTTOM ALL INVOLV'D 1 236
TRANSFIX US TO THE BOTTOM OF THIS GULFE. 1 329
HARSH THUNDER, THAT THE LOWEST BOTTOM SHOOK 2 882
HIS TROUBL'D THOUGHTS, AND FROM THE BOTTOM STIRR 4 19
THE BOTTOM OF THE MOUNTAINS UPWARD TURN'D, 6 649
UP FROM THE BOTTOM TURN'D BY FURIOUS WINDES 7 213
DOWN SUNK A HOLLOW BOTTOM BROAD AND DEEP, 7 289
ALL LEFT, IN ONE SMALL BOTTOM SWUM IMBARK'T. 11 753

BOTTOMLESS
TO BOTTOMLESS PERDITION, THERE TO DWELL 1 47
BURNT AFTER THEM TO THE BOTTOMLESS PIT. 6 866

BOUGH
OF BIRDS ON EVERY BOUGH; SO MUCH THE MORE 5 8
BUT I WILL HASTE AND FROM EACH BOUGH AND BREAK, 5 326
A BOUGH OF FAIREST FRUIT THAT DOWNIE SMIL'D, 9 851
SUCH RECOMPENCE BEST MERITS) FROM THE BOUGH 9 995

BOUGHES
NECTARINE FRUITS WHICH THE COMPLIANT BOUGHES 4 332
THIR PAMPERD BOUGHES, AND NEEDED HANDS TO CHECK 5 214
WHEN FROM THE BOUGHES A SAVORIE ODOUR BLOW'N, 9 579

BOUGHS

YIELD NECTAR, THOUGH FROM OFF THE BOUGHS EACH MORN	5	428
YE CEDARS, WITH INNUMERABLE BOUGHS	9	1089

BOUGHT

SHORT INTERMISSION BOUGHT WITH DOUBLE SMART.	4	102
KNOWLEDGE OF GOOD BOUGHT DEAR BY KNOWING ILL.	4	222
REIGNS HERE AND REVELS; NOT IN THE BOUGHT SMILE	4	765
OF PARADISE, DEARE BOUGHT WITH LASTING WOES.	10	742

BOULD

GIANTS OF MIGHTIE BONE, AND BOULD EMPRISE;	11	642

BOULDER

HEE BOULDER NOW, UNCALL'D BEFORE HER STOOD;	9	523

BOUND

WITHIN HEAV'NS BOUND, UNLESS HEAV'NS LORD SUPREAM	2	236
ILLIMITABLE OCEAN WITHOUT BOUND,	2	892
THE POWERS OF DARKNESS BOUND. THOU AT THE SIGHT	3	256
TO DARKNESS, SUCH AS BOUND THE OCEAN WAVE.	3	539
FROM MEDIA POST TO AEGYPT, THERE FAST BOUND.	4	171
AT ONE SLIGHT BOUND HIGH OVER LEAP'D ALL BOUND	4	181
HIS WILL WHO BOUND US? LET HIM SURER BARR	4	897
FOR ON SOM MESSAGE HIGH THEY GUESSD HIM BOUND.	5	290
AND AT HIS CHARIOT WHEELES TO DRAG HIM BOUND	6	358
HER DARK FOUNDATIONS, AND TOO FAST HAD BOUND.	6	870
HALF YET REMAINES UNSUNG BUT NARROWER BOUND	7	21
WHO CAN IMPAIR THEE, MIGHTY KING, OR BOUND	7	608
BOUND ON A VOYAGE UNCOUTH AND OBSCURE,	8	230
BOUND WITH GORGONIAN RIGOR NOT TO MOVE.	10	297
TO STUFF THIS MAW, THIS VAST UNHIDE-BOUND CORPS.	10	601
SHALL MEET, ALREADIE LINKT AND WEDLOCK-BOUND	10	905
THAT ALL HIS SENSES BOUND; EVE, WHO UNSEEN	11	265
THY HUSBAND, HIM TO FOLLOW THOU ART BOUND;	11	291
THE THRONE HEREDITARIE, AND BOUND HIS REIGN	12	370

BOUNDLESS

TO BELLOW THROUGH THE VAST AND BOUNDLESS DEEP.	1	177
IT SEEM'D, NOW SEEMS A BOUNDLESS CONTINENT	3	423
BOUNDLESS THE DEEP, BECAUSE I AM WHO FILL	7	168

BOUNDS

AND ACCARON AND GAZA'S FRONTIER BOUNDS.	1	466
OR IN DODONA, AND THROUGH ALL THE BOUNDS	1	518
HELL BOUNDS HIGH REACHING TO THE HORRID ROOF,	2	644
WHAT READIEST PATH LEADS WHERE YOUR GLOOMIE BOUNDS	2	976
TRANSPORTS OUR ADVERSARIE, WHOM NO BOUNDS	3	81
WHOSE SNOWIE RIDGE THE ROVING TARTAR BOUNDS,	3	432
SO WIDE THE OP'NING SEEMD, WHERE BOUNDS WERE SET	3	538
SO MINDED, HAVE ORELEAPT THESE EARTHIE BOUNDS	4	583
WHY HAST THOU, SATAN, BROKE THE BOUNDS PRESCRIB'D	4	878
UNLICENC'T FROM HIS BOUNDS IN HELL PRESCRIB'D;	4	909
TILL BODY UP TO SPIRIT WORK, IN BOUNDS	5	478
OF SURFET WHERE FULL MEASURE ONELY BOUNDS	5	639
FROM ALL HEAV'NS BOUNDS INTO THE UTTER DEEP:	6	716
WITH TERRORS AND WITH FURIES TO THE BOUNDS	6	859
OF KNOWLEDGE WITHIN BOUNDS; BEYOND ABSTAIN	7	120
WITHIN APPOINTED BOUNDS BE HEAV'N AND EARTH,	7	167
AND SAID, THUS FARR EXTEND, THUS FARR THY BOUNDS,	7	230
NOT ONELY THESE FAIR BOUNDS, BUT ALL THE EARTH	8	338
HELL COULD NO LONGER HOLD US IN HER BOUNDS,	10	365
OF ALL THINGS PARTED BY TH' EMPYREAL BOUNDS,	10	380
THROUGH HEAV'NS WIDE BOUNDS; FROM THEM I WILL NOT HIDE	11	68
HIS PRESENCE TO THESE NARROW BOUNDS CONFIN'D	11	341
BEYOND ALL BOUNDS, TILL INUNDATION RISE	11	828
SURPASS HIS BOUNDS, NOR RAIN TO DROWN THE WORLD	11	894
DARKNESS MUST OVERSHADOW ALL HIS BOUNDS,	12	187
WITH EARTHS WIDE BOUNDS, HIS GLORY WITH THE HEAV'NS.	12	371

BOUNTEOUS

HAIL UNIVERSAL LORD, BE BOUNTEOUS STILL	5	205
EXCESS, BEFORE TH' ALL BOUNTEOUS KING, WHO SHOWRD	5	640
THY WORDS, CREATOR BOUNTEOUS AND BENIGNE,	8	492

BOUNTIE

HIS BOUNTIE, FOLLOWING OUR DELIGHTFUL TASK	4	437
THEN EVER, BOUNTIE OF THIS VERTUOUS TREE.	9	1033
JUSTICE SHALL NOT RETURN AS BOUNTIE SCORN'D.	10	54

BOUNTIES

GOD HATH DISPENST HIS BOUNTIES AS IN HEAV'N.	5	330
THESE BOUNTIES WHICH OUR NOURISHER, FROM WHOM	5	398

BOUNTY

VARIED HIS BOUNTY SO WITH NEW DELIGHTS.	5	431

BOW

EXTORT FROM ME. TO BOW AND SUE FOR GRACE	1	111
ALL KNEES TO THEE SHALL BOW, OF THEM THAT BIDE	3	321
TOWARDS EITHER THRONE THEY BOW, AND TO THE GROUND	3	350
THEN IN FAIR EVENING CLOUD, OR HUMID BOW,	4	151
AND BY MY SELF HAVE SWORN TO HIM SHALL BOW	5	607
MY BOW AND THUNDER, MY ALMIGHTIE ARMS	6	713
SATE EAGLE-WING'D, BESIDE HIM HUNG HIS BOW	6	763
THOUGH NOT AS SHEE WITH BOW AND QUIVER ARMD,	9	390

BOW (CONTINUED)

A DEWIE CLOUD, AND IN THE CLOUD A BOW	11	865
HIS TRIPLE-COLOUR'D BOW, WHEREON TO LOOK	11	897

BOW'D

BOW'D DOWN IN BATTEL, SUNK BEFORE THE SPEAR	1	436
LOWLY THEY BOW'D ADORING, AND BEGAN	5	144

BOWD

BUT AS IN GAZE ADMIRING: OFT HE BOWD	9	524
ADAM BOWD LOW, HEE KINGLY FROM HIS STATE	11	249

BOWELS

RIFL'D THE BOWELS OF THIR MOTHER EARTH	1	687
MY BOWELS, THIR REPAST; THEN BURSTING FORTH	2	800
OF MINE OWN BROOD, THAT ON MY BOWELS FEED:	2	863

BOWER

ON TO THIR BLISSFUL BOWER; IT WAS A PLACE	4	690
SUCH WAS THIR AWE OF MAN. IN SHADIE BOWER	4	705
DAZ'LING THE MOON; THESE TO THE BOWER DIRECT	4	798

BOWERS

PLANTED, WITH WALKS, AND BOWERS, THAT WHAT I SAW	8	305
THESE PATHS & BOWERS DOUBT NOT BUT OUR JOYNT HANDS	9	244

BOWING

HIS RIGHTEOUS ALTAR, BOWING LOWLY DOWN	1	434
THUS SAID, HE TURND, AND SATAN BOWING LOW,	3	736
AS TO A SUPERIOR NATURE, BOWING LOW,	5	360
SO SAID, HE O'RE HIS SCEPTER BOWING, ROSE	6	746

BOWRE

ADAMS ABODE, THOSE LOFTIE SHADES HIS BOWRE.	3	734
WHICH GOD LIKES BEST, INTO THIR INMOST BOWRE	4	738
CONVERSE WITH ADAM, IN WHAT BOWRE OR SHADE	5	230
OF HIS COOLE BOWRE, WHILE NOW THE MOUNTED SUN	5	300
THIS SPACIOUS GROUND, IN YONDER SHADIE BOWRE	5	367
TO VISIT THEE; LEAD ON THEN WHERE THY BOWRE	5	375
MY PLEADED REASON. TO THE NUPTIAL BOWRE	8	510
FROM THE THICK SHADE, AND ADAM TO HIS BOWRE.	8	653
TO BE RETURND BY NOON AMID THE BOWRE,	9	401
IN BOWRE AND FIELD HE SOUGHT, WHERE ANY TUFT	9	417
THEE LASTLY NUPTIAL BOWRE, BY MEE ADORND	11	280
DESCENDED, ADAM TO THE BOWRE WHERE EVE	12	607

BOWRS

IMBROUND THE NOONTIDE BOWRS: THUS WAS THIS PLACE,	4	246
O WOODS, O FOUNTAINS, HILLOCKS, DALES AND BOWRS,	10	860
FILLD ALL THE REGIONS: FROM THIR BLISSFUL BOWRS	11	77

BOYLING

A VARIOUS MOULD, AND FROM THE BOYLING CELLS	1	706
UNDER YON BOYLING OCEAN, WRAPT IN CHAINS;	2	183

BRACE

FIRST HUNTER THEN, PURSU'D A GENTLE BRACE,	11	188

BRAKE

AS ONE CONTINU'D BRAKE, THE UNDERGROWTH	4	175
IN FORREST WILDE, IN THICKET, BRAKE, OR DEN;	7	458
IN EVERY BUSH AND BRAKE, WHERE HAP MAY FINDE	9	160

BRANCH

FROM BRANCH TO BRANCH THE SMALLER BIRDS WITH SONG	7	433

BRANCHES

OUR WALK AT NOON, WITH BRANCHES OVERGROWN,	4	627
WITH BRANCHES LOPT, IN WOOD OR MOUNTAIN FELL'D)	6	575
THIR BRANCHES HUNG WITH COPIOUS FRUIT; OR GEMM'D	7	325
BIRDS ON THE BRANCHES WARBLING; ALL THINGS SMIL'D,	8	265
FOR HIGH FROM GROUND THE BRANCHES WOULD REQUIRE	9	590
OF THY FULL BRANCHES OFFER'D FREE TO ALL;	9	802

BRANCHING

CEDAR, AND PINE, AND FIRR, AND BRANCHING PALM,	4	139
SHADED WITH BRANCHING PALME, EACH ORDER BRIGHT,	6	885
BORE UP HIS BRANCHING HEAD; SCARSE FROM HIS MOULD	7	470

BRAND

WAV'D OVER BY THAT FLAMING BRAND, THE GATE	12	643

BRANDISHING

FORTH ISSU'D, BRANDISHING HIS FATAL DART	2	786

BRANDISHT

BRANDISHT ALOFT THE HORRID EDGE CAME DOWN	6	252
THE BRANDISHT SWORD OF GOD BEFORE THEM BLAZ'D	12	633

BRASS

AND THRICE THREEFOLD THE GATES; THREE FOLDS WERE BRASS,	2	645
BRASS, IRON, STONIE MOULD, HAD NOT THIR MOUTHES	6	576
LABOURING, TWO MASSIE CLODS OF IRON AND BRASS	11	565

BRAUNCHING

BRAUNCHING SO BROAD AND LONG, THAT IN THE GROUND	9	1104

BRAY'D
WAS NEVER, ARMS ON ARMOUR CLASHING BRAY'D 6 209

BRAZEN
OP'NING THIR BRAZEN FOULDS DISCOVER WIDE 1 724
OF BRAZEN CHARIOTS RAG'D; DIRE WAS THE NOISE 6 211
MYRIADS BETWEEN TWO BRAZEN MOUNTAINS LODG'D 7 201
OF HUGE EXTENT SOMTIMES, WITH BRAZEN EYES 7 496
BURSTING THIR BRAZEN DUNGEON, ARMD WITH ICE 10 697
THE BRAZEN THROAT OF WARR HAD CEAST TO ROAR, 11 713

BREACH
HER MURAL BREACH, RETURNING WHENCE IT ROWLD. 6 879
THOSE NOTES TO TRAGIC; FOUL DISTRUST, AND BREACH 9 6

BREAD
IN THE SWEAT OF THY FACE SHALT THOU EAT BREAD, 10 205
MY BREAD; WHAT HARM? IDLENESS HAD BIN WORSE; 10 1055
AND FAMISH HIM OF BREATH, IF NOT OF BREAD? 12 78

BREADED
HIS BREADED TRAIN, AND OF HIS FATAL GUILE 4 349

BREADTH
WITHOUT DIMENSION, WHERE LENGTH, BREADTH, & HIGHTH, 2 893
LIKE DISTANT BREADTH TO TAURUS WITH THE SEAV'N 10 673
MEASUR'D BY CUBIT, LENGTH, AND BREADTH, AND HIGHTH, 11 730

BREAK
SCORNING SURPRIZE. OR COULD WE BREAK OUR WAY 2 134
ALL NIGHT; AT LAST BY BREAK OF CHEARFUL DAWNE 3 545
WHO WOULD NOT, FINDING WAY, BREAK LOOSE FROM HELL, 4 889
BUT I WILL HASTE AND FROM EACH BOUGH AND BREAK, 5 326
FOR NOW, AND SINCE FIRST BREAK OF DAWNE THE FIEND, 9 412

BREAKE
IS NOW AN IRON ROD TO BRUISE AND BREAKE 5 887

BREAKING
BREAKING THE HORRID SILENCE THUS BEGAN. 1 83
THINE OWN BEGOTTEN, BREAKING VIOLENT WAY 2 782

BREAKS
DISLOYAL BREAKS HIS FEALTIE, AND SINNS 3 204
MEE DISOBEYES, BREAKS UNION, AND THAT DAY 5 612

BREAST
ON OUR FIRST FATHER, HALF HER SWELLING BREAST 4 495
MY OBVIOUS BREAST, ARMING TO OVERCOM 11 374

BREATH
WHAT IF THE BREATH THAT KINDL'D THOSE GRIM FIRES 2 170
WILL SLACK'N, IF HIS BREATH STIR NOT THIR FLAMES. 2 214
SWEET IS THE BREATH OF MORN, HER RISING SWEET, 4 641
BUT NEITHER BREATH OF MORN WHEN SHE ASCENDS 4 650
THE BREATH OF LIFE; IN HIS OWN IMAGE HEE 7 526
THIR MORNING INCENSE, WHEN ALL THINGS THAT BREATH, 9 194
LEAST THAT PURE BREATH OF LIFE, THE SPIRIT OF MAN 10 784
HORRID, IF TRUE. YET WHY? IT WAS BUT BREATH 10 789
OR ONE SHORT SIGH OF HUMANE BREATH, UP-BORNE 11 147
AND WILDE, HOW SHALL WE BREATH IN OTHER AIRE 11 284
NO MORE AVAILES THEN BREATH AGAINST THE WINDE, 11 312
AND FAMISH HIM OF BREATH, IF NOT OF BREAD? 12 78

BREATH'D
DELIBERATE VALOUR BREATH'D, FIRM AND UNMOV'D 1 554
SILENT YET SPAKE, AND BREATH'D IMMORTAL LOVE 3 267
OF INSTRUMENTAL HARMONIE THAT BREATH'D 6 65
DUST OF THE GROUND, AND IN THY NOSTRILS BREATH'D 7 525
REGENERATE GROW INSTEAD, THAT SIGHS NOW BREATH'D 11 5

BREATHD
IN EDEN ON THE HUMID FLOURS, THAT BREATHD 9 193
WITHOUT THE VENT OF WORDS, WHICH THESE HE BREATHD. 12 374

BREATHE
SHALL BREATHE HER BALME. BUT FIRST WHOM SHALL WE
SEND 2 402
BREATHE FORTH ELIXIR PURE, AND RIVERS RUN 3 607
BREATHE SOFT OR LOUD; AND WAVE YOUR TOPS, YE PINES, 5 193
FORTH ISSUING ON A SUMMERS MORN TO BREATHE 9 447

BREATHES
OUR ENVIED SOVRAN, AND HIS ALTAR BREATHES 2 244
MILDE, AS WHEN ZEPHYRUS ON FLORA BREATHES, 5 16
SPIRITS ODOROUS BREATHES: FLOURS AND THIR FRUIT 5 482

BREATHING
BREATHING UNITED FORCE WITH FIXED THOUGHT 1 560
BREATHING THE SMELL OF FIELD AND GROVE, ATTUNE 4 265

BREATHS
TO MANY A ROW OF PIPES THE SOUND-BOARD BREATHS. 1 709
LIKE GENTLE BREATHS FROM RIVERS PURE, THENCE RAISE 4 806
BLOWN STIFLING BACK ON HIM THAT BREATHS IT FORTH; 11 313

BREATH'ST
HELL-DOOM'D, AND BREATH'ST DEFIANCE HERE AND SCORN 2 697

BRED
THAT BRED THEM THEY RETURN, AND HOWLE AND GNAW 2 799
AS WHEN A VULTUR ON IMAUS BRED, 3 431
SIN-BRED, HOW HAVE YE TROUBL'D ALL MANKIND 4 315
WAS AERIE LIGHT FROM PURE DIGESTION BRED, 5 4
BRED OF UNKINDLY FUMES, WITH CONSCIOUS DREAMS 9 1050
AT EEV'N, WHICH I BRED UP WITH TENDER HAND 11 276
HAD BRED; THEN PURG'D WITH EUPHRASIE AND RUE 11 414
BRED ONELY AND COMPLETED TO THE TASTE 11 618
BRED UP IN IDOL-WORSHIP; O THAT MEN 12 115

BREDTH
HE VIEWS IN BREDTH, AND WITHOUT LONGER PAUSE 3 561

BREEDING
DIVINITIE WITHIN THEM BREEDING WINGS 9 1010

BREEDS
WHERE ALL LIFE DIES, DEATH LIVES, AND NATURE
BREEDS, 2 624

BREST
FALLACIOUS HOPE, OR ARM TH' OBDURED BREST 2 568
NOW ROWLING, BOILES IN HIS TUMULTUOUS BREST, 4 16
EACH SHOULDER BROAD, CAME MANTLING O'RE HIS BREST 5 279
BAD INFLUENCE INTO TH' UNWARIE BREST 5 695
PEACE AND COMPOSURE, AND WITH OPEN BREST 6 560
AND BREST, (WHAT COULD WE MORE?) PROPOUNDED TERMS 6 612
THIR DOWNIE BREST; THE SWAN WITH ARCHED NECK 7 438
THOUGHTS, WHICH HOW FOUND THEY HARBOUR IN THY BREST 9 288
SUPERIOR SWAY; FROM THUS DISTEMPERD BREST, 9 1131
WHAT THOUGHTS IN MY UNQUIET BREST ARE RIS'N, 10 975
HOME TO MY BREST, AND TO MY MEMORIE 11 154

BREST-PLATE
IN AARONS BREST-PLATE, AND A STONE BESIDES 3 598

BRESTS
IN HEAV'NLY BRESTS? THESE, THESE AND MANY MORE 9 730

BRETHREN
HIS BRETHREN, RANSOMD WITH HIS OWN DEAR LIFE. 3 297
THESE TWO ARE BRETHREN, ADAM, AND TO COME 11 454
MAKE THEY BUT OF THIR BRETHREN, MEN OF MEN? 11 680
OVER HIS BRETHREN, AND QUITE DISPOSSESS 12 28
ABOVE HIS BRETHREN, TO HIMSELF ASSUMING 12 65
TILL BY TWO BRETHREN (THOSE TWO BRETHREN CALL 12 169

BRIAREOS
BRIAREOS OR TYPHOON, WHOM THE DEN 1 199

BRICK
OF BRICK, AND OF THAT STUFF THEY CAST TO BUILD 12 43

BRIDAL
ON HIS HILL TOP, TO LIGHT THE BRIDAL LAMP. 8 520

BRIDGE
TAMELY ENDUR'D A BRIDGE OF WONDROUS LENGTH 2 1028
OVER THE FOAMING DEEP HIGH ARCHT, A BRIDGE 10 301
OF THAT STUPENDIOUS BRIDGE HIS JOY ENCREAS'D. 10 351
WITH THIS PORTENTOUS BRIDGE THE DARK ABYSS. 10 371

BRIDGING
BRIDGING HIS WAY, EUROPE WITH ASIA JOYN'D, 10 310

BRIEF
AND BRIEF RELATED WHOM THEY BROUGHT, WHERE FOUND, 4 875
TO WHOM IN BRIEF THUS ABDIEL STERN REPLI'D. 6 171
SHE SCARSE HAD SAID, THOUGH BRIEF, WHEN NOW MORE
BOLD 9 664
WHENCE ADAM FAULTRING LONG, THUS ANSWER'D BRIEF. 10 115

BRIEFLY
DO AS YOU HAVE IN CHARGE, AND BRIEFLY TOUCH 6 566

BRIGAD
A NUMEROUS BRIGAD HASTEN'D. AS WHEN BANDS 1 675

BRIGADS
WITH RAPID WHEELS, OR FRONTED BRIGADS FORM. 2 532

BRIGHT
MYRIADS THOUGH BRIGHT: IF HE WHOM MUTUAL LEAGUE, 1 87
THUS ANSWER'D. LEADER OF THOSE ARMIES BRIGHT, 1 272
DILATED OR CONDENS'T, BRIGHT OR OBSCURE, 1 429
TO WHOSE BRIGHT IMAGE NIGHTLY BY THE MOON 1 440
EACH IN HIS HIERARCHIE, THE ORDERS BRIGHT. 1 737
OF THOSE BRIGHT CONFINES, WHENCE WITH NEIGHBOURING
ARMS 2 395
WITH BRIGHT IMBLAZONRIE, AND HORRENT ARMS. 2 513
LIKEST TO THEE IN SHAPE AND COUNT'NANCE BRIGHT, 2 756
TO BE INVULNERABLE IN THOSE BRIGHT ARMS, 2 812
BRIGHT EFFLUENCE OF BRIGHT ESSENCE INCREATE. 3 6
NOW IN LOOSE GARLANDS THICK THROWN OFF, THE BRIGHT 3 362
DARK WITH EXCESSIVE BRIGHT THY SKIRTS APPEER, 3 380
OF GUARDIANS BRIGHT, WHEN HE FROM ESAU FLED 3 512
VIEWLESS, AND UNDERNEATH A BRIGHT SEA FLOW'D 3 518

BRIGHT (CONTINUED)
SO WONDROUSLY WAS SET HIS STATION BRIGHT. 3 587
THE PLACE HE FOUND BEYOND EXPRESSION BRIGHT, 3 591
HE DREW NOT NIGH UNHEARD, THE ANGEL BRIGHT, 3 645
IN SIGHT OF GOD'S HIGH THRONE, GLORIOUSLY BRIGHT, 3 655
IN THAT BRIGHT EMINENCE, AND WITH HIS GOOD 4 44
NOT SPIRITS, YET TO HEAV'NLY SPIRITS BRIGHT 4 361
AMID THE SUNS BRIGHT CIRCLE WHERE THOU SITST, 4 578
RETURND ON THAT BRIGHT BEAM, WHOSE POINT NOW RAISD 4 590
WHILE THUS HE SPAKE, TH' ANGELIC SQUADRON BRIGHT 4 977
WITH THY BRIGHT CIRCLET, PRAISE HIM IN THY SPHEARE 5 169
BRIGHT TEMPLE, TO AEGYPTIAN THEB'S HE FLIES. 5 274
MORE AERIE, LAST THE BRIGHT CONSUMMATE FLOURE 5 481
UNDER THIR HIERARCHS IN ORDERS BRIGHT 5 587
BY HIM CREATED IN THIR BRIGHT DEGREES, 5 838
COVERD WITH THICK EMBATTELD SQUADRONS BRIGHT, 6 16
IN SILENCE THIR BRIGHT LEGIONS, TO THE SOUND 6 64
TH' APOSTAT IN HIS SUN-BRIGHT CHARIOT SATE 6 100
AND ALL HIS ARMOUR STAIND ERE WHILE SO BRIGHT. 6 334
WHICH OF US WHO BEHOLDS THE BRIGHT SURFACE 6 472
STAND STILL IN BRIGHT ARRAY YE SAINTS, HERE STAND 6 801
SHADED WITH BRANCHING PALME, EACH ORDER BRIGHT, 6 885
FOLLOW'D IN BRIGHT PROCESSION TO BEHOLD 7 222
INVESTED WITH BRIGHT RAYES, JOCOND TO RUN 7 372
SHEDDING SWEET INFLUENCE: LESS BRIGHT THE MOON, 7 375
WITH THIR BRIGHT LUMINARIES THAT SET AND ROSE, 7 385
WHILE THE BRIGHT POMP ASCENDED JUBILANT. 7 564
THAT BODIES BRIGHT AND GREATER SHOULD NOT SERVE 8 87
THE LESS NOT BRIGHT, NOR HEAV'N SUCH JOURNIES RUN, 8 88
OR BRIGHT INFERRS NOT EXCELLENCE: THE EARTH 8 91
YET NOT TO EARTH ARE THOSE BRIGHT LUMINARIES 8 98
THUS I PRESUMPTUOUS; AND THE VISION BRIGHT, 8 367
THAT SHINE, YET BEAR THIR BRIGHT OFFICIOUS LAMPS, 9 104
INSUFFERABLY BRIGHT. O MIGHT I HERE 9 1084
SO SPAKE THE FATHER, AND UNFOULDING BRIGHT 10 63
IN OPEN SHEW, AND WITH ASCENTION BRIGHT 10 187
SATAN IN LIKENESS OF AN ANGEL BRIGHT 10 327
OF THAT BRIGHT STARR TO SATAN PARAGOND. 10 426
AND SHAPE STARR BRIGHT APPEER'D, OR BRIGHTER, CLAD 10 450
TO THOSE BRIGHT ORDERS UTTERD THUS HIS VOICE. 10 615
TO THE BRIGHT MINISTER THAT WATCHD, HEE BLEW 11 73
FOR SWIFT DESCENT, WITH HIM THE COHORT BRIGHT 11 127
THE FIELD PAVILION'D WITH HIS GUARDIANS BRIGHT; 11 215
IN THIR BRIGHT STAND, THERE LEFT HIS POWERS TO SEISE 11 221
HIS BRIGHT APPEARANCES, OR FOOT STEP-TRACE? 11 329
OF TWO BRIGHT CHERUBIM, BEFORE HIM BURN 12 254
TO THIR FIXT STATION, ALL IN BRIGHT ARRAY 12 627

BRIGHTER
(SO CALL HIM, BRIGHTER ONCE AMIDST THE HOST 7 132
AND SHAPE STARR BRIGHT APPEER'D, OR BRIGHTER, CLAD 10 450

BRIGHTEST
BUT MERCY FIRST AND LAST SHALL BRIGHTEST SHINE. 3 134
YET DAZLE HEAV'N, THAT BRIGHTEST SERAPHIM 3 381
ALONE THUS WANDRING. BRIGHTEST SERAPH TELL 3 667
THE STARRIE HOST, RODE BRIGHTEST, TILL THE MOON 4 606
SPRING BOTH, THE FACE OF BRIGHTEST HEAV'N HAD CHANGD 5 644

BRIGHT'ND
AS WITH A SMILE MORE BRIGHT'ND, THUS REPLI'D. 8 368

BRIGHTNESS
CLOTH'D WITH TRANSCENDENT BRIGHTNESS DIDST OUT-SHINE 1 86
ALL HER ORIGINAL BRIGHTNESS, NOR APPEAR'D 1 592
AMIDST THE GLORIOUS BRIGHTNESS WHERE THOU SIT'ST 3 376
HIS BACK WAS TURND, BUT NOT HIS BRIGHTNESS HID; 3 624
OR UNDIMINISHT BRIGHTNESS, TO BE KNOWN 4 836
BRIGHTNESS HAD MADE INVISIBLE, THUS SPAKE. 5 599

BRIGHTNING
SECURE, AND AT THE BRIGHTNING ORIENT BEAM 2 399

BRIGHT'NS
BRIGHT'NS HIS CREST, AS WHEN A WANDRING FIRE, 9 634

BRIM
WITH WHEELS YET HOV'RING O'RE THE OCEAN BRIM, 5 140

BRIMMING
STILL AS THEY THIRSTED SCOOP THE BRIMMING STREAM; 4 336

BRIMSTONE
ON THE FIRM BRIMSTONE, AND FILL ALL THE PLAIN; 1 350

BRINDED
AND RAMPANT SHAKES HIS BRINDED MAIN; THE OUNCE, 7 466

BRING
OUT OF OUR EVIL SEEK TO BRING FORTH GOOD, 1 163
HOW ALL HIS MALICE SERV'D BUT TO BRING FORTH 1 217
OF FUTURE DAYES MAY BRING, WHAT CHANCE, WHAT CHANGE 2 222
OF TERNATE AND TIDORE, WHENCE MERCHANTS BRING 2 639
AND BRING YE TO THE PLACE WHERE THOU AND DEATH 2 840
BUT THEE, WHOM FOLLOW? THOU WILT BRING ME SOON 2 866

BRING (CONTINUED)
STRIVE HERE FOR MAISTRIE, AND TO BATTEL BRING 2 899
HIS MALICE, AND THY GOODNESS BRING TO NAUGHT, 3 158
TO PRAY, REPENT, AND BRING OBEDIENCE DUE. 3 190
INDEBTED AND UNDON, HATH NONE TO BRING: 3 235
INTERPRETER THROUGH HIGHEST HEAV'N TO BRING, 3 657
THAT BRING TO MY REMEMBRANCE FROM WHAT STATE 4 38
AND I WILL BRING THEE WHERE NO SHADOW STAIES 4 470
SUCH WHERE YE FIND, SEISE FAST, AND HITHER BRING. 4 796
OR WITH REPOSE; AND SUCH DISCOURSE BRING ON, 5 233
AND WHAT THY STORES CONTAIN, BRING FORTH AND POURE 5 314
TASTES, NOT WELL JOYND, INELEGANT, BUT BRING 5 335
BELIEVST SO MAIN TO OUR SUCCESS, I BRING; 6 471
THAT SHAKE HEAV'NS BASIS, BRING FORTH ALL MY WARR, 6 712
HASTE TO THY AUDIENCE, NIGHT WITH HER WILL BRING 7 105
OF SPIRITS MALIGNE A BETTER RACE TO BRING 7 189
LET TH' EARTH BRING FORTH FOUL LIVING IN HER KINDE, 7 451
IMBU'D, BRING TO THIR SWEETNESS NO SATIETIE. 8 216
AFTER THIR KINDES; I BRING THEM TO RECEAVE 8 343
WHAT NEXT I BRING SHALL PLEASE THEE, BE ASSUR'D, 8 449
OF HESPERUS, WHOSE OFFICE IS TO BRING 9 49
TO HIDE ME, AND THE DARK INTENT I BRING. 9 162
MY CONDUCT, I CAN BRING THEE THITHER SOON. 9 630
THOUGH THREAT'ND, WHICH NO WORSE THEN THIS CAN BRING. 9 715
BY THY CONCEPTION; CHILDREN THOU SHALT BRING 10 194
THORNS ALSO AND THISTLES IT SHALL BRING THEE FORTH 10 203
DECREPIT WINTER, FROM THE SOUTH TO BRING 10 655
AS DEEP AS CAPRICORNE, TO BRING IN CHANGE 10 677
OUR OWN BEGOTTEN, AND OF OUR LOINES TO BRING 10 983
WITH INCENSE, I THY PRIEST BEFORE THEE BRING, 11 25
OUR FRAILTIE CAN SUSTAIN, THY TIDINGS BRING, 11 302
CORRUPTION TO BRING FORTH MORE VIOLENT DEEDS. 11 428
IN MEATS AND DRINKS, WHICH ON THE EARTH SHALL BRING 11 473
SHALL BRING ON MEN. IMMEDIATELY A PLACE 11 477
NATIONS, AND BRING HOME SPOILS WITH INFINITE 11 692
THE ADVERSARIE SERPENT, AND BRING BACK 12 312
TO BRING FORTH FRUITS JOY AND ETERNAL BLISS. 12 551

BRINGING
AND BRINGING FORTH, SOON RECOMPENC'T WITH JOY, 10 1052
BY HIS OWN NATION, SLAINE FOR BRINGING LIFE; 12 414

BRINGS
RECEIVE THY NEW POSSESSOR: ONE WHO BRINGS 1 252
DIRECTED NO MEAN RECOMPENCE IT BRINGS 2 981
HE BRINGS, AND ROUND ABOUT HIM, NOR FROM HELL 4 21
HER MARIAGEABLE ARMS, AND WITH HER BRINGS 5 217
TO US PERHAPS HE BRINGS, AND WILL VOUTSAFE 5 312
AS HEAV'NS GREAT YEAR BRINGS FORTH, TH' EMPYREAL HOST 5 583
BUT OF THE TREE WHOSE OPERATION BRINGS 8 323
NOT HERS WHO BRINGS IT NIGHTLY TO MY EAR. 9 47
HATH TASTED, ENVIES NOT, BUT BRINGS WITH JOY 9 770
AS SOME MISFORTUNE BRINGS HIM, OR MISTAKE, 10 900
AN OLIVE LEAFE HE BRINGS, PACIFIC SIGNE: 11 860
WITH MAN THEREIN OR BEAST; BUT WHEN HE BRINGS 11 895
THE SPACE OF SEVENTIE YEARS, THEN BRINGS THEM BACK, 12 345
ENDEAVOUR PEACE: THIR STRIFE POLLUTION BRINGS 12 355

BRINK
ALL IN ONE MOMENT, AND SO NEER THE BRINK; 2 609
STOOD ON THE BRINK OF HELL AND LOOK'D A WHILE, 2 918
AND AT THE BRINK OF CHAOS, NEER THE FOOT 10 347

BRISTL'D
BRISTL'D WITH UPRIGHT BEAMS INNUMERABLE 6 82

BRITISH
BEGIRT WITH BRITISH AND ARMORIC KNIGHTS; 1 581

BRITTLE
NOR FOUNDED ON THE BRITTLE STRENGTH OF BONES, 1 427

BROAD
BEHIND HIM CAST; THE BROAD CIRCUMFERENCE 1 286
THE STEDFAST EARTH. AT LAST HIS SAIL-BROAD VANNES 2 927
PAV'D AFTER HIM A BROAD AND BEAT'N WAY 2 1026
INTO A LIMBO LARGE AND BROAD, SINCE CALLD 3 495
CLUSTRING, BUT NOT BENEATH HIS SHOULDERS BROAD: 4 303
EACH SHOULDER BROAD, CAME MANTLING O'RE HIS BREST 5 279
MADE HORRID CIRCLES; TWO BROAD SUNS THIR SHIELDS 6 305
EMERGENT, AND THIR BROAD BARE BACKS UPHEAVE 7 286
DOWN SUNK A HOLLOW BOTTOM BROAD AND DEEP, 7 289
PASTURING AT ONCE, AND IN BROAD HERDS UPSPRUNG. 7 462
A BROAD AND AMPLE RODE, WHOSE DUST IS GOLD 7 577
TO STARR OR SUN-LIGHT, SPREAD THIR UMBRAGE BROAD 9 1087
SOME TREE WHOSE BROAD SMOOTH LEAVES TOGETHER SOWD, 9 1095
BRAUNCHING SO BROAD AND LONG, THAT IN THE GROUND 9 1104
THEY GATHERD, BROAD AS AMAZONIAN TARGE, 9 1111
AND WITH ASPHALTIC SLIME; BROAD AS THE GATE, 10 298
FORFEIT TO DEATH; FROM HENCE A PASSAGE BROAD, 10 304
BY SIN AND DEATH A BROAD WAY NOW IS PAV'D 10 473

BROIDERD
BROIDERD THE GROUND, MORE COLOUR'D THEN WITH STONE 4 702

BROILES
MIGHT HAP TO MOVE NEW BROILES: BE THIS OR AUGHT 2 837
ENCROACHT ON STILL THROUGH OUR INTESTINE BROILES 2 1001
THOU AND THY WICKED CREW; THERE MINGLE BROILES, 6 277
ALLURD THEM; THENCE FROM CUPS TO CIVIL BROILES. 11 718

BROK'D
AS FROM HER OUTMOST WORKS A BROK'D FOE 2 1039

BROKE
WHO FIRST BROKE PEACE IN HEAV'N AND FAITH, TILL THEN 2 690
THROUGH ALL RESTRAINT BROKE LOOSE HE WINGS HIS WAY 3 87
WHY HAST THOU, SATAN, BROKE THE BOUNDS PRESCRIB'D 4 878
CAME NOT ALL HELL BROKE LOOSE? IS PAIN TO THEM 4 918
GREAT THINGS BY SMALL, IF NATURES CONCORD BROKE, 6 311
HIS HINDER PARTS, THEN SPRINGS AS BROKE FROM BONDS, 7 465
FIRST TO HIMSELF HE INWARD SILENCE BROKE. 9 895
INCHANTING DAUGHTER, THUS THE SILENCE BROKE. 10 353
BROKE OFF THE REST; SO MUCH OF DEATH HER THOUGHTS 10 1008
BROKE UP, SHALL HEAVE THE OCEAN TO USURP 11 827
GREATLY REJOYC'D, AND THUS HIS JOY BROKE FORTH. 11 869

BROKEN
AND BROKEN CHARIOT WHEELS, SO THICK BESTROWN 1 311

BROK'N
WHEN THE FIERCE FOE HUNG ON OUR BROK'N REAR 2 78

BROOD
WITH HIS ENORMOUS BROOD, AND BIRTHRIGHT SEIS'D 1 511
WARR'D ON BY CRANES: THOUGH ALL THE GIANT BROOD 1 576
OF MINE OWN BROOD, THAT ON MY BOWELS FEED: 2 863
THIR BROOD AS NUMEROUS HATCH, FROM THE EGG THAT SOON 7 418

BROODING
DOVE-LIKE SATST BROODING ON THE VAST ABYSS 1 21
HIS BROODING WINGS THE SPIRIT OF GOD OUTSPRED, 7 235

BROOK
DELIGHT THEE MORE, AND SILOA'S BROOK THAT FLOW'D 1 11
OF OLD EUPHRATES TO THE BROOK THAT PARTS 1 420
LETS HER WILL RULE; RESTRAINT SHE WILL NOT BROOK, 9 1184
OF LUSTRE FROM THE BROOK, IN MEMORIE, 11 325

BROOKING
OF PREFACE BROOKING THROUGH HIS ZEAL OF RIGHT. 9 676

BROOKS
THICK AS AUTUMNAL LEAVES THAT STROW THE BROOKS 1 302
THEE SION AND THE FLOWRIE BROOKS BENEATH 3 30
HOW FROM THAT SAPHIRE FOUNT THE CRISPED BROOKS, 4 237
BROOKS NOT THE WORKS OF VIOLENCE AND WARR. 6 274

BROTHER
OF FATHER, SON, AND BROTHER FIRST WERE KNOWN. 4 757
WHO SLEW HIS BROTHER; STUDIOUS THEY APPERE 11 609
HIS BROTHER; FOR OF WHOM SUCH MASSACHER 11 679

BROTHERS
FOR ENVIE THAT HIS BROTHERS OFFERING FOUND 11 456

BROUGHT
BROUGHT DEATH INTO THE WORLD, AND ALL OUR WOE, 1 3
AND TO THE FIERCE CONTENTION BROUGHT ALONG 1 100
ARE BROUGHT: AND FEEL BY TURNS THE BITTER CHANGE 2 598
HATH BROUGHT ME FROM THE QUIRES OF CHERUBIM 3 666
THAT BROUGHT THEM FORTH, BUT HID THIR CAUSES DEEP. 3 707
AND WHAT I WAS, WHENCE THITHER BROUGHT, AND HOW. 4 452
BROUGHT HER IN NAKED BEAUTY MORE ADORN'D, 4 713
OF JAPHET BROUGHT BY HERMES, SHE ENSNAR'D 4 717
AND BRIEF RELATED WHOM THEY BROUGHT, WHERE FOUND, 4 875
OR NOT, WHO ASK WHAT BOLDNESS BROUGHT HIM HITHER 4 908
THAT BROUGHT ME ON A SUDDEN TO THE TREE 5 51
SOON AS MIDNIGHT BROUGHT ON THE DUSKIE HOURE 5 667
HEAV'NS BLESSED PEACE, AND INTO NATURE BROUGHT 6 267
FLED IGNOMINIOUS, TO SUCH EVIL BROUGHT 6 395
BROUGHT FORTH THE TENDER GRASS, WHOSE VERDURE CLAD 7 315
HE BROUGHT THEE INTO THIS DELICIOUS GROVE, 7 537
AS TRIBUTE SUCH A SUMLESS JOURNEY BROUGHT 8 36
INTENDED THEE, FOR TRIAL ONELY BROUGHT, 8 447
SHE HEARD ME THUS, AND THOUGH DIVINELY BROUGHT, 8 500
THUS I HAVE TOLD THEE ALL MY STATE, AND BROUGHT 8 521
THAT BROUGHT INTO THIS WORLD A WORLD OF WOE, 9 11
OUR DAYES WORK BROUGHT TO LITTLE, THOUGH BEGUN 9 224
GUILTLESS OF FIRE HAD FORMD, OR ANGELS BROUGHT, 9 392
HIS FIERCENESS OF THE FIERCE INTENT IT BROUGHT: 9 462
WHAT HITHER BROUGHT US, HATE, NOT LOVE, NOR HOPE 9 475
BROUGHT TO THIR EARS, WHILE DAY DECLIN'D, THEY HEARD, 10 99
NOW HAD THEY BROUGHT THE WORK BY WONDROUS ART 10 312
THE EVIL ON HIM BROUGHT BY ME, WILL CURSE 10 734
BY DEATH BROUGHT ON OUR SELVES, OR CHILDLESS DAYS 10 1037
THAT I WHO FIRST BROUGHT DEATH ON ALL, AM GRAC'T 11 168
BUT THIS PRAEEMINENCE THOU HAST LOST, BROUGHT DOWN 11 347
A SWEATIE REAPER FROM HIS TILLAGE BROUGHT 11 434
NO SANCTITIE, IF NONE BE THITHER BROUGHT 11 837

BROUGHT (CONTINUED)
SUCH TROUBLE BROUGHT, AFFECTING TO SUBDUE 12 81
THEN THAT WHICH BY CREATION FIRST BROUGHT FORTH 12 472
WITH JOY THE TIDINGS BROUGHT FROM HEAV'N: AT LENGTH 12 504

BROW
OBTAINS THE BROW OF SOME HIGH-CLIMBING HILL, 3 546
TO WHOM THUS SATAN, WITH CONTEMPTUOUS BROW. 4 885
FEARLESS ASSAULT, AND TO THE BROW OF HEAV'N 6 51
TO WHOM THE ANGEL WITH CONTRACTED BROW. 8 560
THY AWFUL BROW, MORE AWFUL THUS RETIR'D. 9 537
DISTENDED AS THE BROW OF GOD APPEAS'D, 11 880

BROWES
SAT ON HIS FADED CHEEK, BUT UNDER BROWES 1 602

BROWN
AND BROWN AS EVENING: COVER ME YE PINES, 9 1088

BRUIS'D
THIR ARMOR HELP'D THIR HARM, CRUSH'T IN AND BRUIS'D 6 656

BRUISE
IS NOW AN IRON ROD TO BRUISE AND BREAKE 5 887
HER SEED SHALL BRUISE THY HEAD, THOU BRUISE HIS HEEL. 10 181
EEVN HEE WHO NOW FORETOLD HIS FATAL BRUISE, 10 191
MEE AND MANKINDE; I AM TO BRUISE HIS HEEL; 10 498
HIS SEED, WHEN IS NOT SET, SHALL BRUISE MY HEAD: 10 499
A WORLD WHO WOULD NOT PURCHASE WITH A BRUISE, 10 500
PART OF OUR SENTENCE, THAT THY SEED SHALL BRUISE 10 1031
HIS PROMISE, THAT THY SEED SHALL BRUISE OUR FOE; 11 155
IS MEANT THY GREAT DELIVERER, WHO SHALL BRUISE 12 149
AND SHADOWS, OF THAT DESTIND SEED TO BRUISE 12 233
NEEDS MUST THE SERPENT NOW HIS CAPITAL BRUISE 12 383
THIR FIGHT, WHAT STROKE SHALL BRUISE THE VICTORS HEEL, 12 385
SATAN, WHOSE FALL FROM HEAV'N, A DEADLIER BRUISE, 12 391
SHALL BRUISE THE HEAD OF SATAN, CRUSH HIS STRENGTH 12 430
THEN TEMPORAL DEATH SHALL BRUISE THE VICTORS HEEL, 12 433

BRUSE
HER SEED SHALL BRUSE THY HEAD, THOU BRUISE HIS HEEL. 10 181

BRUSH
WE BRUSH MELLIFLUOUS DEWES, AND FIND THE GROUND 5 429

BRUSHT
BRUSHT WITH THE HISS OF RUSSLING WINGS. AS BEES 1 768

BRUTAL
THE DEVIL ENTERD, AND HIS BRUTAL SENSE, 9 188
OF BRUTAL KIND, THAT DAILY ARE IN SIGHT? 9 565

BRUTE
OFT TO THE IMAGE OF A BRUTE, ADORN'D 1 371
MAIM'D HIS BRUTE IMAGE, HEAD AND HANDS LOPT OFF 1 459
AND BRUTE AS OTHER CREATURES, BUT ENDU'D 7 507
ALL RATIONAL DELIGHT, WHEREIN THE BRUTE 8 391
MY IMAGE, NOT IMPARTED TO THE BRUTE, 8 441
ACTIVE WITHIN BEYOND THE SENSE OF BRUTE. 9 96
TO BRUTE DENI'D, AND ARE OF LOVE THE FOOD, 9 240
BY TONGUE OF BRUTE, AND HUMAN SENSE EXPREST? 9 554
I OF BRUTE HUMAN, YEE OF HUMAN GODS. 9 712
SERPENT THOUGH BRUTE, UNABLE TO TRANSFERRE 10 165
MEE NOT, BUT THE BRUTE SERPENT IN WHOSE SHAPE 10 495

BRUTISH
THIR WANDRING GODS DISGUIS'D IN BRUTISH FORMS 1 481
VICTOR; THOUGH BRUTISH THAT CONTEST AND FOULE, 6 124
HIS IMAGE WHOM THEY SERV'D, A BRUTISH VICE, 11 518

BUD
TO VISIT HOW THEY PROSPER'D, BUD AND BLOOM, 8 45
FROM THE FIRST OP'NING BUD, AND GAVE YE NAMES, 11 277

BUILD
OF SOLOMON HE LED BY FRAUD TO BUILD 1 401
WITH HIS INDUSTRIOUS CREW TO BUILD IN HELL. 1 751
INCLINES, HERE TO CONTINUE, AND BUILD UP HERE 2 314
NEW BABELS, HAD THEY WHEREWITHALL, WOULD BUILD: 3 468
O FAIR FOUNDATION LAID WHEREON TO BUILD 4 521
THROUGH ALL ETERNITIE SO LATE TO BUILD 7 92
ON CLIFFS AND CEDAR TOPS THIR EYRIES BUILD: 7 424
THE MIGHTIE FRAME, HOW BUILD, UNBUILD, CONTRIVE 8 81
BUILD IN HER LOVELIEST, AND CREATE AN AWE 8 558
FOR WHAT GOD AFTER BETTER WORSE WOULD BUILD? 9 102
BEGAN TO BUILD A VESSEL OF HUGE BULK, 11 729
SHALL BUILD A WONDROUS ARK, AS THOU BEHELDST, 11 819
OF BRICK, AND OF THAT STUFF THEY CAST TO BUILD 12 43

BUILDED
WHAT THY HANDS BUILDED NOT, THY WISDOM GAIN'D 10 373

BUILDERS
THE BUILDERS NEXT OF BABEL ON THE PLAIN 3 466
AMONG THE BUILDERS; EACH TO OTHER CALLS 12 57

BUILDING
AND HEAR THE DIN; THUS WAS THE BUILDING LEFT 12 61

BUILDS
DELICIOUSLY, AND BUILDS HER WAXEN CELLS 7 491

BUILT
WE SHALL BE FREE; TH' ALMIGHTY HATH NOT BUILT 1 259
HER TEMPLE ON TH' OFFENSIVE MOUNTAIN, BUILT 1 443
BUILT LIKE A TEMPLE, WHERE PILASTERS ROUND 1 713
TO HAVE BUILT IN HEAV'N HIGH TOWRS; NOR DID HE SCAPE 1 749
THE SUBURB OF THIR STRAW-BUILT CITTADEL, 1 773
BUILT THIR FOND HOPES OF GLORIE OR LASTING FAME, 3 449
OF GREAT SELEUCIA, BUILT BY GRECIAN KINGS, 4 212
BUILT ON CIRCUMFLUOUS WATERS CALME, IN WIDE 7 270
THE MAKERS HIGH MAGNIFICENCE, WHO BUILT 8 101
MORE JUSTLY, SEAT WORTHIER OF GODS, AS BUILT 9 100
HE EFFECTED; MAN HE MADE, AND FOR HIM BUILT 9 152
HEROIC BUILT, THOUGH OF TERRESTRIAL MOULD, 9 485
OF HIM WHO BUILT THE ARK, WHO FOR THE SHAME 12 102
HIS LIVING TEMPLES, BUILT BY FAITH TO STAND, 12 527

BULK
LAY FLOATING MANY A ROOD, IN BULK AS HUGE 1 196
AND BENDED DOLPHINS PLAY: PART HUGE OF BULK 7 410
BEGAN TO BUILD A VESSEL OF HUGE BULK, 11 729

BULLION
SEVERING EACH KIND, AND SCUM'D THE BULLION DROSS: 1 704

BULLOCK
OFT SACRIFICING BULLOCK, LAMB, OR KID, 12 20

BULLS
INDULGENCES, DISPENSES, PARDONS, BULLS, 3 492
THE BLOUD OF BULLS AND GOATS, THEY MAY CONCLUDE 12 292

BULWARK
YOUR BULWARK, AND CONDEMNS TO GREATEST SHARE 2 29

BURDEN
A GROWING BURDEN. MEAN WHILE WARR AROSE, 2 767
INDEBTED AND DISCHARGD; WHAT BURDEN THEN? 4 57
SHALL TEND THEE, AND THE FERTIL BURDEN EASE 9 801
THAT BURDEN HEAVIER THEN THE EARTH TO BEAR 10 835
EACH OTHERS BURDEN IN OUR SHARE OF WOE; 10 961

BURD'N
THE BURD'N OF MANY AGES, ON ME LIGHT 11 767

BURD'ND
NOT BURD'ND NATURE, SUDDEN MIND AROSE 5 452

BURGHER
OF SOME RICH BURGHER, WHOSE SUBSTANTIAL DORES, 4 189

BURIED
UNDER THE WEIGHT OF MOUNTAINS BURIED DEEP, 6 652

BURN
FOR ONE OF SYRIAN MODE, WHEREON TO BURN 1 474
THE WORLD SHALL BURN, AND FROM HER ASHES SPRING 3 334
OF TWO BRIGHT CHERUBIM, BEFORE HIM BURN 12 254

BURN'D
HE LIGHTS, IF IT WERE LAND THAT EVER BURN'D 1 228
UNTERRIFI'D, AND LIKE A COMET BURN'D, 2 708

BURNE
AND FROM WITHIN THE GOLDEN LAMPS THAT BURNE 5 713
AS WANTONLY REPAID; IN LUST THEY BURNE; 9 1015

BURNES
BUT THE HOT HELL THAT ALWAYES IN HIM BURNES, 9 467

BURNING
WITH EVER-BURNING SULPHUR UNCONSUM'D: 1 69
CHAIN'D ON THE BURNING LAKE, NOR EVER THENCE 1 210
OVER THE BURNING MARLE, NOT LIKE THOSE STEPS 1 296
CHAIN'D ON THE BURNING LAKE? THAT SURE WAS WORSE. 2 169
NINEFOLD, AND GATES OF BURNING ADAMANT 2 436
INTO THE BURNING LAKE THIR BALEFUL STREAMS; 2 576
GLOOMIE AS NIGHT; UNDER HIS BURNING WHEELES 6 832

BURNISHT
OTHERS WHOSE FRUIT BURNISHT WITH GOLDEN RINDE 4 249
WITH BURNISHT NECK OF VERDANT GOLD, ERECT 9 501

BURNS
FROM EITHER END OF HEAV'N THE WELKIN BURNS. 2 538
BURNS FRORE, AND COLD PERFORMS TH' EFFECT OF FIRE. 2 595

BURNT
THIR PAINFUL STEPS O'RE THE BURNT SOYLE; AND NOW 1 562
BURNT AFTER THEM TO THE BOTTOMLESS PIT. 6 866

BURST
TEARS SUCH AS ANGELS WEEP, BURST FORTH: AT LAST 1 620
ON WHAT WAS PURE, TILL CRAMM'D AND GORG'D, NIGH BURST 10 632

BURSTING
MY BOWELS, THIR REPAST; THEN BURSTING FORTH 2 800
BURSTING WITH KINDLY RUPTURE FORTH DISCLOS'D 7 419
HIS BURSTING PASSION INTO PLAINTS THUS POUR'D: 9 98
BURSTING THIR BRAZEN DUNGEON, ARMD WITH ICE 10 697

BURTHENSOME
SO BURTHENSOME STILL PAYING, STILL TO OW; 4 53

BUSH
AND BUSH WITH FRIZL'D HAIR IMPLICIT: LAST 7 323
IN EVERY BUSH AND BRAKE, WHERE HAP MAY FINDE 9 160

BUSHES
OF SHRUBS AND TANGLING BUSHES HAD PERPLEXT 4 176

BUSHIE
ACANTHUS, AND EACH ODOROUS BUSHIE SHRUB 4 696

BUSHING
HALF SPI'D, SO THICK THE ROSES BUSHING ROUND 9 426

BUSIED
HOW BUSIED, IN WHAT FORM AND POSTURE COUCHT, 4 876
TO LURE HER EYE; SHEE BUSIED HEARD THE SOUND 9 518

BUSIEST
TENDED THE SICK BUSIEST FROM COUCH TO COUCH; 11 490

BUSINESS
BY RIGHT OF WARR, WHAT E'RE HIS BUSINESS BE 1 150
WHOSE EASIER BUSINESS WERE TO SERVE THIR LORD 4 943

BUSIRIS
BUSIRIS AND HIS MEMPHIAN CHIVALRY, 1 307

BUXOM
WING SILENTLY THE BUXOM AIR, IMBALM'D 2 842
WINNOWS THE BUXOM AIR; TILL WITHIN SOARE 5 270

CADENCE
HAD ROUS'D THE SEA, NOW WITH HOARSE CADENCE LULL 2 287
NOW WAS THE SUN IN WESTERN CADENCE LOW 10 92

CADMUS
HERMIONE AND CADMUS, OR THE GOD 9 506

CAECIAS
BOREAS AND CAECIAS AND ARGESTES LOUD 10 699

CAELESTIAL
CAELESTIAL SPIRITS IN BONDAGE, NOR TH' ABYSS 1 658

CALABRIA
CALABRIA FROM THE HOARCE TRINACRIAN SHORE: 2 661

CALAMITIE
WHICH INFINITE CALAMITIE SHALL CAUSE 10 907

CALAMITOUS
SUBDUES ME, AND CALAMITOUS CONSTRAINT 10 132

CALAMITY
HOW OVERCOME THIS DIRE CALAMITY, 1 189

CALCULATE
AND CALCULATE THE STARRS, HOW THEY WILL WEILD 8 80

CALF
THE CALF IN OREB: AND THE REBEL KING 1 484

CALL
AND CALL THEM NOT TO SHARE WITH US THEIR PART 1 267
AT THIR GREAT EMPERORS CALL, AS NEXT IN WORTH 1 378
THE REST SHALL HEAR ME CALL, AND OFT BE WARND 3 185
VOLATIL HERMES, AND CALL UP UNBOUND 3 603
(SO CALL THAT OPPOSITE FAIR STARR) HER AIDE 3 727
HIDE THIR DIMINISHT HEADS; TO THEE I CALL, 4 35
WHOM GENTILES AMMON CALL AND LYBIAN JOVE, 4 277
I ROSE AS AT THY CALL, BUT FOUND THEE NOT; 5 48
ALL WHAT WE AFFIRM OR WHAT DENY, AND CALL 5 107
SATAN, SO CALL HIM NOW, HIS FORMER NAME 5 658
THE PALACE OF GREAT LUCIFER, (SO CALL 5 760
THE MEANING, NOT THE NAME I CALL: FOR THOU 7 5
(SO CALL HIM, BRIGHTER ONCE AMIDST THE HOST 7 132
ON THE SWIFT FLOUDS: AS ARMIES AT THE CALL 7 295
NOT NOXIOUS, BUT OBEDIENT AT THY CALL. 7 498
FROM EVERY BEAST, MORE DUTEOUS AT HER CALL, 9 521
THEN AT CIRCEAN CALL THE HERD DISGUIS'D. 9 522
AND PALATE CALL JUDICIOUS; I THE PRAISE 9 1020
I CALL YE AND DECLARE YE NOW, RETURND 10 462
SCARCE TOLLERABLE, AND FROM THE NORTH TO CALL 10 654
BUT DEATH COMES NOT AT CALL, JUSTICE DIVINE 10 858

CALL (CONTINUED)
BUT LET US CALL TO SYNOD ALL THE BLEST 11 67
CALL EL DORADO: BUT TO NOBLER SIGHTS 11 411
BUT CALL IN AIDE, WHICH MAKES A BLOODY FRAY; 11 651
IN OTHER PART THE SCEPTER'D HARALDS CALL 11 660
AND CALL TO MIND HIS COV'NANT: DAY AND NIGHT, 11 898
TO CALL BY VISION FROM HIS FATHERS HOUSE, 12 121
(THINGS BY THIR NAMES I CALL, THOUGH YET UNNAM'D) 12 140
WHOM FAITHFUL ABRAHAM DUE TIME SHALL CALL, 12 152
TILL BY TWO BRETHREN (THOSE TWO BRETHREN CALL 12 169
TILL ISRAEL OVERCOME; SO CALL THE THIRD 12 267
BUT JOSHUA WHOM THE GENTILES JESUS CALL, 12 310

CALL'D
AND THENCE IN HEAV'N CALL'D SATAN, WITH BOLD WORDS 1 82
OF THAT INFLAMED SEA, HE STOOD AND CALL'D 1 300
HE CALL'D SO LOUD, THAT ALL THE HOLLOW DEEP 1 314
WAV'D ROUND THE COAST, UP CALL'D A PITCHY CLOUD 1 340
AND BLACK GEHENNA CALL'D THE TYPE OF HELL. 1 405
CAME ASTORETH, WHOM THE PHOENICIANS CALL'D 1 438
MEN CALL'D HIM MULCIBER; AND HOW HE FELL 1 740
OF SATAN AND HIS PEERS: THIR SUMMONS CALL'D 1 757
MUST WE RENOUNCE, AND CHANGING STILE BE CALL'D 2 312
OF SOME NEW RACE CALL'D MAN, ABOUT THIS TIME 2 348
NOR UGLIER FOLLOW THE NIGHT-HAG, WHEN CALL'D 2 662
IF SHAPE IT MIGHT BE CALL'D THAT SHAPE HAD NONE 2 667
OR SUBSTANCE MIGHT BE CALL'D THAT SHADOW SEEM'D, 2 669
AT FIRST, AND CALL'D ME SIN, AND FOR A SIGN 2 760
MULTITUDES LIKE THY SELF, AND THENCE BE CALL'D 4 474
ONE FATAL TREE THERE STANDS OF KNOWLEDGE CALL'D, 4 514
CLOSE AT MINE EAR ONE CALL'D ME FORTH TO WALK 5 36
HIS PRAISE, WHO OUT OF DARKNESS CALL'D UP LIGHT. 5 179
WITH PITTIE HEAV'NS HIGH KING, AND TO HIM CALL'D 5 220
BERRIE OR GRAPE: TO WHOM THUS ADAM CALL'D. 5 307
OF ANGELS BY IMPERIAL SUMMONS CALL'D, 5 584
THE MOUNTAIN OF THE CONGREGATION CALL'D; 5 766
HIS POTENTATES TO COUNCEL CALL'D BY NIGHT; 6 416
AND TO HIS MATES THUS IN DERISION CALL'D. 6 608
IF RIGHTLY THOU ART CALL'D, WHOSE VOICE DIVINE 7 2
OF CONGREGATED WATERS HE CALL'D SEAS: 7 308
WHILE THUS I CALL'D, AND STRAY'D I KNEW NOT
WHITHER. 8 283
FIRST FATHER, CALL'D BY THEE I COME THY GUIDE 8 298
OF SLEEP, WHICH INSTANTLY FELL ON ME, CALL'D 8 458
APPROACHING, THUS TO ADAM CALL'D ALOUD. 10 102
AND KNOW NOT THAT I CALL'D AND DREW THEM THITHER 10 629
EVE RIGHTLY CALL'D, MOTHER OF ALL MANKIND, 11 159
AND VALOUR AND HEROIC VERTU CALL'D; 11 690
DESTROYERS RIGHTLIER CALL'D AND PLAGUES OF MEN. 11 697
WITH GOD, WHO CALL'D HIM, IN A LAND UNKNOWN. 12 134
FROM CANAAN, TO A LAND HEREAFTER CALL'D 12 156
LEFT IN CONFUSION, BABYLON THENCE CALL'D. 12 343
WHY OUR GREAT EXPECTATION SHOULD BE CALL'D 12 378
BY NAME TO COME CALL'D CHARITIE, THE SOUL 12 584

CALLD
INTO A LIMBO LARGE AND BROAD, SINCE CALLD 3 495
FROM THESE, TWO STRONG AND SUTTLE SPIRITS HE CALLD 4 786
GABRIEL FROM THE FRONT THUS CALLD ALOUD. 4 865
OF LUCIFER, SO BY ALLUSION CALLD, 10 425
AND FABL'D HOW THE SERPENT, WHOM THEY CALLD 10 580

CALLING
WHILE THE CREATOR CALLING FORTH BY NAME 10 649
I HAVE IN VIEW, CALLING TO MINDE WITH HEED 10 1030

CALLOW
THIR CALLOW YOUNG, BUT FEATHERD SOON AND FLEDGE 7 420

CALLS
CALLS US TO PENANCE? MORE DESTROY'D THEN THUS 2 92
WHAT E'RE HIS WRATH, WHICH HE CALLS JUSTICE, BIDS, 2 733
CALLS US, WE LOSE THE PRIME, TO MARK HOW SPRING 5 21
OF HIS ASSOCIATE; HEE TOGETHER CALLS, 5 696
TO LABOUR CALLS US NOW WITH SWEAT IMPOS'D, 11 172
AMONG THE BUILDERS; EACH TO OTHER CALLS 12 57

CALL'ST
IN THIS INFERNAL VAILE FIRST MET THOU CALL'ST 2 742
ME FATHER, AND THAT FANTASM CALL'ST MY SON? 2 743
THE STRIFE WHICH THOU CALL'ST EVIL, BUT WEE STYLE 6 289
WHAT CALL'ST THOU SOLITUDE, IS NOT THE EARTH 8 369
OF WANDRING, AS THOU CALL'ST IT, WHICH WHO KNOWS 9 1146

CALM
THROUGH THE CALM FIRMAMENT; BUT UP OR DOWNE 3 574
FIRM PEACE RECOVERD SOON AND WONTED CALM. 5 210
TO WHOM THE SON WITH CALM ASPECT AND CLEER 5 733
THUS IN CALM MOOD HIS WORDS TO EVE HE TURND. 9 920
THIR INWARD STATE OF MIND, CALM REGION ONCE 9 1125

CALM'D
HER ALSO I WITH GENTLE DREAMS HAVE CALM'D 12 595

CALME
EACH PERTURBATION SMOOTH'D WITH OUTWARD CALME, 4 120
COVER'D TH' ABYSS: BUT ON THE WATRIE CALME 7 234
BUILT ON CIRCUMFLUOUS WATERS CALME, IN WIDE 7 270

CALMER
WAFTS ON THE CALMER WAVE BY DUBIOUS LIGHT 2 1042

CALMEST
BUT LIVE CONTENT, WHICH IS THE CALMEST LIFE: 6 461

CALUMNIOUS
THITHER TO COME, AND WITH CALUMNIOUS ART 5 770

CALV'D
THE GRASSIE CLODS NOW CALV'D, NOW HALF APPEER'D 7 463

CAMBALU
OF CAMBALU, SEAT OF CATHAIAN CAN 11 388

CAME
CAME LIKE A DELUGE ON THE SOUTH, AND SPREAD 1 354
CAME SINGLY WHERE HE STOOD ON THE BARE STRAND, 1 379
WITH THESE CAME THEY, WHO FROM THE BORDRING FLOOD 1 419
CAME ASTORETH, WHOM THE PHOENICIANS CALL'D 1 438
TO IDOLS FOUL. THAMMUZ CAME NEXT BEHIND, 1 446
OF ALIENATED JUDAH. NEXT CAME ONE 1 457
BELIAL CAME LAST, THEN WHOM A SPIRIT MORE LEWD 1 490
ALL THESE AND MORE CAME FLOCKING; BUT WITH LOOKS 1 522
WITH HUNDERDS AND WITH THOUSANDS TROOPING CAME 1 760
IN ORDER CAME THE GRAND INFERNAL PEERS, 2 507
MIDST CAME THIR MIGHTY PARAMOUNT, AND SEEMD 2 508
THE MONSTER MOVING ONWARD CAME AS FAST 2 675
FIRST FROM THE ANCIENT WORLD THOSE GIANTS CAME 3 464
OTHERS CAME SINGLE; HE WHO TO BE DEEMD 3 469
WHO AFTER CAME FROM EARTH, SAYLING ARRIV'D, 3 520
THIS WORLDS MATERIAL MOULD, CAME TO A HEAP: 3 709
CAME FURIOUS DOWN TO BE REVENG'D ON MEN, 4 4
SATAN, NOW FIRST INFLAM'D WITH RAGE, CAME DOWN, 4 9
WHO CAME THIR BANE, THOUGH WITH THEM BETTER PLEAS'D 4 167
WITH THEE IT CAME AND GOES: BUT FOLLOW ME, 4 469
THITHER CAME URIEL, GLIDING THROUGH THE EEVEN 4 555
THIS DAY AT HIGHTH OF NOON CAME TO MY SPHEARE 4 564
NOW CAME STILL EEVNING ON, AND TWILIGHT GRAY 4 598
CAME NOT ALL HELL BROKE LOOSE? IS PAIN TO THEM 4 918
EACH SHOULDER BROAD, CAME MANTLING O'RE HIS BREST 5 279
ADAM, I THEREFORE CAME, NOR ART THOU SUCH 5 372
THEY CAME, THAT LIKE POMONA'S ARBOUR SMIL'D 5 378
THEY CAME, AND SATAN TO HIS ROYAL SEAT 5 756
CAME SUMMOND OVER EDEN TO RECEIVE 6 75
CAME TOWRING, ARMD IN ADAMANT AND GOLD; 6 110
BRANDISHT ALOFT THE HORRID EDGE CAME DOWN 6 252
CAME FLYING, AND IN MID AIRE ALOUD THUS CRI'D. 6 536
CAME SHADOWING, AND OPPREST WHOLE LEGIONS ARM'D, 6 655
HE ONWARD CAME, FARR OFF HIS COMING SHON, 6 768
CELESTIAL EQUIPAGE; AND NOW CAME FORTH 7 203
AT ONCE CAME FORTH WHATEVER CREEPS THE GROUND, 7 475
WAS SET, AND TWILIGHT FROM THE EAST CAME ONE, 7 583
TELL, IF YE SAW, HOW CAME I THUS, HOW HERE? 8 277
AND LIVD: ONE CAME, METHOUGHT, OF SHAPE DIVINE, 8 295
TO MAKE HER AMIABLE: ON SHE CAME, 8 484
WITH GRATEFUL SMELL, FORTH CAME THE HUMAN PAIR 9 197
CAME PROLOGUE, AND APOLOGIE TO PROMPT, 9 854
CAME THE MILD JUDGE AND INTERCESSOR BOTH 10 96
HE CAME, AND WITH HIM EVE, MORE LOTH, THOUGH FIRST 10 109
CAME TO THE SEA, AND OVER HELLESPONT 10 309
DISGUIS'D HE CAME, BUT THOSE HIS CHILDREN DEAR 10 330
MET WHO TO MEET HIM CAME, HIS OFSPRING DEAR. 10 349
BY THIR GREAT INTERCESSOR, CAME IN SIGHT 11 19
UNCULL'D, AS CAME TO HAND; A SHEPHERD NEXT 11 436
MORE MEEK CAME WITH THE FIRSTLINGS OF HIS FLOCK 11 437
SOFT AMOROUS DITTIES, AND IN DANCE CAME ON: 11 584
AT LENGTH A REVEREND SIRE AMONG THEM CAME, 11 719
CAME SEAVENS, AND PAIRS, AND ENTERD IN, AS TAUGHT 11 735

CAMP
FORERUN THE ROYAL CAMP, TO TRENCH A FIELD, 1 677
DISPERST IN BANDS AND FILES THIR CAMP EXTEND 5 651
IN DOTHAN, COVER'D WITH A CAMP OF FIRE, 11 217

CAM'ST
HOW CAM'ST THOU SPEAKABLE OF MUTE, AND HOW 9 563

CANAAN
CANAAN HE NOW ATTAINS, I SEE HIS TENTS 12 135
FROM CANAAN, TO A LAND HEREAFTER CALL'D 12 156
SAFE TOWARDS CANAAN FROM THE SHOAR ADVANCE 12 215
HIS WHOLE DESCENT, WHO THUS SHALL CANAAN WIN. 12 269
OF LAW, HIS PEOPLE INTO CANAAN LEAD; 12 309
MEANWHILE THEY IN THIR EARTHLY CANAAN PLAC'T 12 315

CANAANITE
LEAST ENTRING ON THE CANAANITE ALLARMD 12 217

CANCELD
CANCELD FROM HEAV'N AND SACRED MEMORIE, 6 379

CANIE
WITH SAILS AND WIND THIR CANIE WAGGONS LIGHT: 3 439

CANOPIE
SO HIGH ABOVE THE CIRCLING CANOPIE 3 556

CAPABLE
DELIGHTED, OR NOT CAPABLE HER EARE 8 49
AS WEE, NOT CAPABLE OF DEATH OR PAINE, ... 9 283

CAPACIOUS
CAPACIOUS BED OF WATERS: THITHER THEY 7 290
I TURND MY THOUGHTS, AND WITH CAPACIOUS MIND . . 9 603

CAPARISONS
IMPRESES QUAINT, CAPARISONS AND STEEDS; 9 35

CAPE
THROUGH THE WIDE ETHIOPIAN TO THE CAPE 2 641
BEYOND THE CAPE OF HOPE, AND NOW ARE PAST . . . 4 160
BEYOND THE EARTHS GREEN CAPE AND VERDANT ISLES . 8 631

CAPITAL
AT PANDAEMONIUM, THE HIGH CAPITAL 1 756
SOM CAPITAL CITY; OR LESS THEN IF THIS FRAME . . 2 924
PERHAPS THY CAPITAL SEATE, FROM WHENCE HAD SPRED . 11 343
NEEDS MUST THE SERPENT NOW HIS CAPITAL BRUISE . . 12 383

CAPITOLINE
AMMONIAN JOVE, OR CAPITOLINE WAS SEEN, ... 9 508

CAPRICORNE
AS DEEP AS CAPRICORNE, TO BRING IN CHANGE 10 677

CAPTIVE
WHO MOURN'D IN EARNEST, WHEN THE CAPTIVE ARK . . . 1 458
HIS CAPTIVE MULTITUDE: FOR HE, BE SURE 2 323
SHALL LEAD HELL CAPTIVE MAUGRE HELL, AND SHOW . . 3 255
THEN WHEN I AM THY CAPTIVE TALK OF CHAINES, . . 4 970
OR CAPTIVE DRAG'D IN CHAINS, WITH HOSTILE FROWN . 6 260
CAPTIVITY LED CAPTIVE THROUGH THE AIRE, ... 10 188

CAPTIVITIE
THERE IN CAPTIVITIE HE LETS THEM DWELL 12 344

CAPTIVITY
CAPTIVITY LED CAPTIVE THROUGH THE AIRE, ... 10 188

CARAVAN
THIR AIERIE CARAVAN HIGH OVER SEA'S 7 428

CARBUNCLE
IF STONE, CARBUNCLE MOST OR CHRYSOLITE, ... 3 596
CRESTED ALOFT, AND CARBUNCLE HIS EYES; 9 500

CARCASS
DEATH LAST, AND WITH HIS CARCASS GLUT THE GRAVE: . 3 259

CARCASSES
WITH SENT OF LIVING CARCASSES DESIGN'D 10 277
WITH CARCASSES AND ARMS TH' ENSANGUIND FIELD . . 11 654

CAR'D
CAR'D NOT TO BE AT ALL; WITH THAT CARE LOST . . . 2 48

CARE
DEEP SCARS OF THUNDER HAD INTRENCHT, AND CARE . . 1 601
CAR'D NOT TO BE AT ALL; WITH THAT CARE LOST . . 2 48
DELIBERATION SAT AND PUBLIC CARE; 2 303
NEW TROUBLES; HIM THY CARE MUST BE TO FIND, . . 4 575
THEN VIOLENCE: FOR THIS WAS ALL THY CARE . . . 6 35
NOT EMULOUS, NOR CARE WHO THEM EXCELLS; 6 822
SO SPAKE DOMESTICK ADAM IN HIS CARE 9 318
CREATED; BUT HENCEFORTH MY EARLY CARE, ... 9 799
EACH THING ON EARTH; AND OTHER CARE PERHAPS . . 9 813
WHICH YOUR SINCEREST CARE COULD NOT PREVENT, . . 10 37
IF CARE OF OUR DESCENT PERPLEX US MOST, ... 10 979
OR HEAT SHOULD INJURE US, HIS TIMELY CARE . . . 10 1057
GRIEVOUS TO BEAR: BUT THAT CARE NOW IS PAST, . . 11 776

CAREERING
OF BERIL, AND CAREERING FIRES BETWEEN; 6 756

CAREFUL
SWAYES THEM; THE CAREFUL PLOWMAN DOUBTING STANDS . 4 983
MANY A DARK LEAGUE, REDUC'T IN CAREFUL WATCH . . 10 438

CARES
GOD HATH BID DWELL FARR OFF ALL ANXIOUS CARES, . 8 185

CARESSES
WITH CONJUGAL CARESSES, FROM HIS LIP 8 56

CARKASES
FROM THE SAFE SHORE THIR FLOATING CARKASES 1 310

CARMEL
MOUNT CARMEL; HERE THE DOUBLE-FOUNTED STREAM . . . 12 144

CARNAGE
OF CARNAGE, PREY INNUMERABLE, AND TASTE 10 268

CARNAL
NOT SUNK IN CARNAL PLEASURE, FOR WHICH CAUSE . . . 8 593

CARNAL (CONTINUED)
CARNAL DESIRE ENFLAMING, HEE ON EVE 9 1013
AND CARNAL FEAR THAT DAY DIMM'D ADAMS EYE. . . . 11 212
SPIRITUAL LAWES BY CARNAL POWER SHALL FORCE . . 12 521

CARNATION
CARNATION, PURPLE, AZURE, OR SPECT WITH GOLD, . . 9 429

CAROL
OF SQUADROND ANGELS HEAR HIS CAROL SUNG. . . . 12 367

CARR
HE CIRCL'D, FOUR TIMES CROSS'D THE CARR OF NIGHT . 9 65

CARREER
TO MORTAL COMBAT OR CARREER WITH LANCE) 1 766
DECLIN'D WAS HASTING NOW WITH PRONE CARREER . . 4 353

CARRIE
THESE TIDINGS CARRIE TO TH' ANOINTED KING; . . . 5 870

CARRY
I CARRY HENCE; THOUGH ALL BY MEE IS LOST, . . . 12 621

CASBEEN
TO TAURIS OR CASBEEN. SO THESE THE LATE . . . 10 436

CASH
OR AS A THIEF BENT TO UNHOORD THE CASH 4 188

CASIUS
BETWIXT DAMIATA AND MOUNT CASIUS OLD, ... 2 593

CASPIAN
OVER THE CASPIAN, THEN STAND FRONT TO FRONT . . 2 716

CASSIA
AND FLOURING ODOURS, CASSIA, NARD, AND BALME; . . 5 293

CAST
HAD CAST HIM OUT FROM HEAV'N, WITH ALL HIS HOST . 1 37
BEHIND HIM CAST; THE BROAD CIRCUMFERENCE . . . 1 286
DOWN CAST AND DAMP, YET SUCH WHEREIN APPEAR'D . 1 523
IN LOSS IT SELF; WHICH ON HIS COUNT'NANCE CAST . 1 526
WAITING REVENGE: CRUEL HIS EYE, BUT CAST . . . 1 604
OR CAST A RAMPART. MAMMON LED THEM ON, ... 1 678
DID NOT DISSWADE ME MOST, AND SEEM TO CAST . . 2 122
EACH CAST AT TH' OTHER, AS WHEN TWO BLACK CLOUDS . 2 714
CAST FORTH REDOUNDING SMOAK AND RUDDY FLAME. . . 2 889
WITH SOLEMN ADORATION DOWN THEY CAST 3 351
OF US OUT-CAST, EXIL'D, HIS NEW DELIGHT, . . . 4 106
CAST OUT FROM GOD AND BLESSED VISION, FALLS . . 5 613
OUR MINDS AND TEACH US TO CAST OFF THIS YOKE? . 5 786
AFFRIGHTED; BUT STRICT FATE HAD CAST TOO DEEP . . 6 869
BEGAN TO CAST LASCIVIOUS EYES, SHE HIM 9 1014
CAST ON THEMSELVES FROM THIR OWN MOUTHS. THERE STOOD 10 547
OF BRICK, AND OF THAT STUFF THEY CAST TO BUILD . 12 43

CASTALIAN
CASTALIAN SPRING, MIGHT WITH THIS PARADISE . . . 4 274

CASTS
CASTS PALE AND DREADFUL? THITHER LET US TEND . . 1 183
BUT FIRST HE CASTS TO CHANGE HIS PROPER SHAPE, . 3 634
TELLS THE SUGGESTED CAUSE, AND CASTS BETWEEN . . 5 702
TO TROUBLE HOLY REST; HEAV'N CASTS THEE OUT . . 6 272

CASUAL
CASUAL FRUITION, NOR IN COURT AMOURS 4 767
CASUAL DISCOURSE DRAW ON, WHICH INTERMITS . . . 9 223
HAD MELTED (WHETHER FOUND WHERE CASUAL FIRE . . 11 566

CATARACTS
OF HELL SHOULD SPOUT HER CATARACTS OF FIRE, . . . 2 176
AND SHELTERD ROUND, BUT ALL THE CATARACTS . . . 11 824

CATARRHS
CONVULSIONS, EPILEPSIES, FIERCE CATARRHS, . . . 11 483

CATCH
AND UPSTART PASSIONS CATCH THE GOVERNMENT . . . 12 88

CATCHT
CATCHT BY CONTAGION, LIKE IN PUNISHMENT, . . . 10 544

CATHAIAN
CATHAIAN COAST. THE AGGREGATED SOYLE 10 293
OF CAMBALU, SEAT OF CATHAIAN CAN 11 388

CATTEL
CATTEL AND CREEPING THINGS, AND BEAST OF THE EARTH, 7 452
THE CATTEL IN THE FIELDS AND MEDDOWES GREEN: . . 7 460
TO CATTEL AND EACH BEAST; WHICH WOULD NOT BE . . 8 582
OF CATTEL GRAZING: OTHERS, WHENCE THE SOUND . . 11 558
HIS CATTEL MUST OF ROT AND MURREN DIE, ... 12 179

CATTLE
ABOVE ALL CATTLE, EACH BEAST OF THE FIELD; . . . 10 176
WHERE CATTLE PASTUR'D LATE, NOW SCATTERD LIES . . 11 653

CAUGHT
CAUGHT IN A FIERIE TEMPEST SHALL BE HURL'D . . . 2 180
FAST CAUGHT, THEY LIK'D, AND EACH HIS LIKING CHOSE; 11 587
IN EITHER HAND THE HASTNING ANGEL CAUGHT . . . 12 637

CAUS'D
OUT OF THE FERTIL GROUND HE CAUS'D TO GROW . . . 4 216
TO US FOR FOOD AND FOR DELIGHT HATH CAUS'D . . . 5 400

CAUSE
NOR THE DEEP TRACT OF HELL, SAY FIRST WHAT CAUSE . 1 28
FAR OFF AND FEARLESS, NOR WITH CAUSE TO BOAST, . 4 14
TO THY DESERTED HOST THIS CAUSE OF FLIGHT, . . 4 922
TELLS THE SUGGESTED CAUSE, AND CASTS BETWEEN . . 5 702
AGAINST REVOLTED MULTITUDES THE CAUSE 6 31
UNDER THIR GOD-LIKE LEADERS, IN THE CAUSE . . . 6 67
IN NATURE NONE: IF OTHER HIDDEN CAUSE 6 442
ACCEPTED, FEARLESS IN HIS RIGHTEOUS CAUSE, . . . 6 804
WHEN, AND WHEREOF CREATED, FOR WHAT CAUSE, . . . 7 64
IMBRACING ROUND THIS FLORID EARTH, WHAT CAUSE . . 7 90
BUT WHO I WAS, OR WHERE, OR FROM WHAT CAUSE, . . 8 270
BUT IN DEGREE, THE CAUSE OF HIS DESIRE 8 417
EXTRACTED; FOR THIS CAUSE HE SHALL FORGOE . . . 8 497
NOT SUNK IN CARNAL PLEASURE, FOR WHICH CAUSE . . 8 593
WONDROUS INDEED, IF CAUSE OF SUCH EFFECTS. . . . 9 650
FLOURISHD, SINCE MUTE, TO SOM GREAT CAUSE ADDREST, 9 672
HATH BIN THE CAUSE, AND WONDERFUL TO HEARE: . . 9 862
LET NONE HENCEFORTH SEEK NEEDLESS CAUSE TO APPROVE 9 1140
AND AM I NOW UPBRAIDED, AS THE CAUSE 9 1168
WHICH INFINITE CALAMITIE SHALL CAUSE 10 907
ON ME, SOLE CAUSE TO THEE OF ALL THIS WOE, . . . 10 935
TO BE TO OTHERS CAUSE OF MISERY, ... 10 982
WHEREON FOR DIFFERENT CAUSE THE TEMPTER SET . . 11 382
ALAS, BOTH FOR THE DEED AND FOR THE CAUSE. . . 11 461
WITH CAUSE FOR EVILS PAST, YET MUCH MORE CHEER'D . 12 604

CAUSES
BUT ALL THESE IN THIR PREGNANT CAUSES MIXT . . . 2 913
THAT BROUGHT THEM FORTH, BUT HID THIR CAUSES DEEP. 3 707
THINGS IN THIR CAUSES, BUT TO TRACE THE WAYES . . 9 682
CAUSES IMPORT YOUR NEED OF THIS FAIR FRUIT. . . 9 731
BY WHICH ALL CAUSES ELSE ACCORDING STILL . . . 10 806

CAUSEY
THE CAUSEY TO HELL GATE; ON EITHER SIDE 10 415

CAUTION
WHAT MEANT THAT CAUTION JOIND, IF YE BE FOUND . . 5 513
THIS WAS THAT CAUTION GIV'N THEE; BE ADVIS'D. . . 5 523
THIS ALSO THY REQUEST WITH CAUTION ASKT 7 111

CAUTIOUS
FROM COMPASSING THE EARTH, CAUTIOUS OF DAY, . . . 9 59

CAVE
ROCKS, CAVE, LAKES, FENS, BOGS, DENS, AND SHADES OF
DEATH, ... 2 621
OF WATERS ISSU'D FROM A CAVE AND SPREAD 4 454
UNBARR'D THE GATES OF LIGHT. THERE IS A CAVE . . 6 4
TO HIS GRIM CAVE, ALL DISMAL; YET TO SENSE . . . 11 469

CAVES
FROM ALL HER CAVES, AND BACK RESOUNDED DEATH. . . 2 789
ANOTHER SIDE, UMBRAGEOUS GROTS AND CAVES . . . 4 257
MEAN WHILE THE TEPID CAVES, AND FENS AND SHOARES . 7 417
ROCKS, DENS, AND CAVES; BUT I IN NONE OF THESE . 9 118
TO SOM CAVES MOUTH, OR WHETHER WASHT BY STREAM . 11 569

CAVIL
THEN CAVIL THE CONDITIONS? AND THOUGH GOD . . . 10 759

CEAS'D
HE CEAS'D, AND NEXT HIM MOLOC, SCEPTER'D KING . . 2 43
HE CEAS'D, FOR BOTH SEEMD HIGHLY PLEASD, AND DEATH 2 845
HE CEAS'D; AND SATAN STAID NOT TO REPLY, . . . 2 1010
CEAS'D WARBLING, BUT ALL NIGHT TUN'D HER SOFT
LAYES: 7 436
HE CEAS'D, I LOWLY ANSWER'D. TO ATTAINE . . . 8 412
NOT SO REPULST, WITH TEARS THAT CEAS'D NOT FLOWING, 10 910
HE CEAS'D; AND TH' ARCHANGELIC POWER PREPAR'D . . 11 126
BUT ALL IN VAIN: WHICH WHEN HE SAW, HE CEAS'D . . 11 726
HE CEAS'D, DISCERNING ADAM WITH SUCH JOY . . . 12 372

CEASE
AND CANNOT CEASE TO BE, WE ARE AT WORST 2 100
TO PUNISH ENDLESS? WHEREFORE CEASE WE THEN? . . 2 159
CEASE I TO WANDER WHERE THE MUSES HAUNT 3 27
RETURNS OUR OWN. CEASE THEN THIS IMPIOUS RAGE, . 5 845
OF HIM WHO ALL THINGS CAN, I WOULD NOT CEASE . . 11 309
AND TERROR CEASE; HE GRANTS WHAT THEY BESAUGHT . 12 238

CEASES
PERHAPS HATH SPENT HIS SHAFTS, AND CEASES NOW . . 1 176

CEASING
A CRY OF HELL HOUNDS NEVER CEASING BARK'D . . . 2 654

CEASLESS
THESE YELLING MONSTERS THAT WITH CEASLESS CRY . . 2 795
ALL THESE WITH CEASLESS PRAISE HIS WORKS BEHOLD . 4 679
AND NOURISH ALL THINGS, LET YOUR CEASLESS CHANGE . 5 183
AND WORN WITH FAMIN, LONG AND CEASLESS HISS, . . 10 573

CEAS'T
HE SCARCE HAD CEAS'T WHEN THE SUPERIOUR FIEND . . 1 283
NO SOONER HAD TH' ALMIGHTY CEAS'T, BUT ALL . . . 3 344
WHEN VIOLENCE WAS CEAS'T, AND WARR ON EARTH, . . 11 780

CEAST
THE BRAZEN THROAT OF WARR HAD CEAST TO ROAR, . . 11 713

CEDAR
CEDAR, AND PINE, AND FIRR, AND BRANCHING PALM, . 4 139
ON CLIFFS AND CEDAR TOPS THIR EYRIES BUILD; . . 7 424
OF STATELIEST COVERT, CEDAR, PINE, OR PALME, . . 9 435
OF CEDAR, OVERLAID WITH GOLD, THEREIN 12 250

CEDARS
EARTH AND THE GARD'N OF GOD, WITH CEDARS CROWND . 5 260
YE CEDARS, WITH INNUMERABLE BOUGHS 9 1089

CEELING
LIKE A DARK CEELING STOOD; DOWN RUSH'D THE RAIN . 11 743

CELEBRATE
STRICT LAWS IMPOS'D, TO CELEBRATE HIS THRONE . . 2 241
FROM ALL THE ENDS OF TH' EARTH, TO CELEBRATE . . 11 345

CELEBRATED
WORTHIEST TO REIGN: HE CELEBRATED RODE 6 888

CELESTIAL
FOR THAT CELESTIAL LIGHT? BE IT SO, SINCE HE . . 1 245
CELESTIAL VERTUES RISING, WILL APPEAR 2 15
SO MUCH THE RATHER THOU CELESTIAL LIGHT 3 51
IMPURPL'D WITH CELESTIAL ROSES SMIL'D. 3 364
YOUTH SMIL'D CELESTIAL, AND TO EVERY LIMB . . . 3 638
CELESTIAL ARMOURIE, SHIELDS, HELMES, AND SPEARES, 4 553
CELESTIAL VOICES TO THE MIDNIGHT AIR, ... 4 682
TOUCH OF CELESTIAL TEMPER, BUT RETURNS 4 812
AND READ THY LOT IN YON CELESTIAL SIGN 4 1011
THOUSAND CELESTIAL ARDORS, WHERE HE STOOD . . . 5 249
THAT ONE CELESTIAL FATHER GIVES TO ALL. 5 403
CELESTIAL TABERNACLES, WHERE THEY SLEPT 5 654
GO MICHAEL OF CELESTIAL ARMIES PRINCE, ... 6 44
SANGUIN, SUCH AS CELESTIAL SPIRITS MAY BLEED, . . 6 333
WIDE THE CELESTIAL SOILE, AND SAW BENEATH . . . 6 510
HEE IN CELESTIAL PANOPLIE ALL ARMD 6 760
WITH THY CELESTIAL SONG. UP LED BY THEE . . . 7 12
CELESTIAL EQUIPAGE; AND NOW CAME FORTH 7 203
BY THE CELESTIAL QUIRES, WHEN ORIENT LIGHT . . . 7 254
FOR OF CELESTIAL BODIES FIRST THE SUN 7 354
IN THAT CELESTIAL COLLOQUIE SUBLIME, ... 8 455
CELESTIAL ROSIE RED, LOVES PROPER HUE, ... 8 619
OF MY CELESTIAL PATRONESS, WHO DEIGNES 9 21
BY GIFT, AND THY CELESTIAL BEAUTIE ADORE . . . 9 540
THAT TIME CELESTIAL VISAGES, YET MIXT 10 24
NOT IN HIS SHAPE CELESTIAL, BUT AS MAN 11 239
CELESTIAL, WHETHER AMONG THE THRONES, OR NAM'D . 11 296
HOW COMES IT THUS? UNFOULD, CELESTIAL GUIDE, . . 11 785

CELL
INTO HER PRIVATE CELL WHEN NATURE RESTS. . . . 5 109
MINE EYES HE CLOS'D, BUT OP'N LEFT THE CELL . . 8 460

CELLS
NIGH ON THE PLAIN IN MANY CELLS PREPAR'D, . . . 1 700
A VARIOUS MOULD, AND FROM THE BOYLING CELLS . . 1 706
DELICIOUSLY, AND BUILDS HER WAXEN CELLS 7 491

CELTIC
AND ORE THE CELTIC ROAM'D THE UTMOST ISLES. . . 1 521

CENSER
AND PRAYERS, WHICH IN THIS GOLDEN CENSER, MIXT . 11 24

CENSERS
FUMING FROM GOLDEN CENSERS HID THE MOUNT. . . . 7 600

CENTAURE
BETWIXT THE CENTAURE AND THE SCORPION STEARING . 10 328

CENTER
AS FROM THE CENTER THRICE TO TH' UTMOST POLE. . . 1 74
RANSACK'D THE CENTER, AND WITH IMPIOUS HANDS . . 1 686
BY CENTER, OR ECCENTRIC, HARD TO TELL, ... 3 575
FROM CENTER TO CIRCUMFERENCE, WHEREON 5 510
UPON HER CENTER POIS'D, WHEN ON A DAY 5 579
HAD TO HER CENTER SHOOK. WHAT WONDER? WHEN . . 6 219
HEAV'NS HIGHTH, AND WITH THE CENTER MIX THE POLE. 7 215
AND EARTH SELF BALLANC'T ON HER CENTER HUNG. . . 7 242
BE CENTER TO THE WORLD, AND OTHER STARRS . . . 8 123

CENTER (CONTINUED)
IS CENTER, YET EXTENDS TO ALL, SO THOU 9 108
ON MEE AS ON THIR NATURAL CENTER LIGHT 10 740

CENTER'D
ONE FOOT HE CENTER'D, AND THE OTHER TURN'D 7 228

CENTRIC
WITH CENTRIC AND ECCENTRIC SCRIBL'D O'RE, 8 83
OBLIQUE THE CENTRIC GLOBE: SOM SAY THE SUN 10 671

CENTRING
CENTRING RECEAV'ST FROM ALL THOSE ORBS; IN THEE, 9 109

CERASTES
CERASTES HORND, HYDRUS, AND ELLOPS DREAR, 10 525

CERBERIAN
WITH WIDE CERBERIAN MOUTHS FULL LOUD, AND RUNG 2 655

CEREMONIES
OF CONSCIENCE, WHICH THE LAW BY CEREMONIES 12 297

CEREMONY
OF SOVRAN POWER, WITH AWFUL CEREMONY 1 753

CERES
WAS GATHERD, WHICH COST CERES ALL THAT PAIN 4 271
OF CERES RIPE FOR HARVEST WAVING BENDS 4 981
VERTUMNUS, OR TO CERES IN HER PRIME, 9 395

CERTAIN
(CERTAIN TO BE REFUS'D) WHAT ERST THEY FEARD; 2 470
AT CERTAIN REVOLUTIONS ALL THE DAMN'D 2 597
WHICH HAD NO LESS PROV'D CERTAIN UNFOREKNOWN. 3 119
CERTAIN MY RESOLUTION IS TO DIE; 9 907
CERTAIN TO UNDERGOE LIKE DOOM, IF DEATH 9 953
THIS ANNUAL HUMBLING CERTAIN NUMBER'D DAYS, 10 576
WHICH MUST BE BORN TO CERTAIN WOE, DEVOURD 10 980

CERTAINE
LONGER ON EARTH THEN CERTAINE TIMES TO APPEER 12 437

CHAFF
PROVE CHAFF. ON TH' OTHER SIDE SATAN ALLARM'D 4 985

CHAIN
HUNG ORE MY REALM, LINK'D IN A GOLDEN CHAIN 2 1005
AND FAST BY HANGING IN A GOLDEN CHAIN 2 1051

CHAIN'D
CHAIN'D ON THE BURNING LAKE, NOR EVER THENCE 1 210
CHAIN'D ON THE BURNING LAKE? THAT SURE WAS WORSE. 2 169

CHAIND
BACK TO TH' INFERNAL PIT I DRAG THEE CHAIND, 4 965
THIR DEVILISH GLUT, CHAIND THUNDERBOLTS AND HAIL 6 589

CHAINES
THEN WHEN I AM THY CAPTIVE TALK OF CHAINES, 4 970
THE SERPENT, PRINCE OF AIRE, AND DRAG IN CHAINES 12 454

CHAINS
IN ADAMANTINE CHAINS AND PENAL FIRE, 1 48
UNDER YON BOYLING OCEAN, WRAPT IN CHAINS; 2 183
CHAINS AND THESE TORMENTS? BETTER THESE THEN WORSE 2 196
PRESCRIB'D, NO BARRS OF HELL, NOR ALL THE CHAINS 3 82
YET CHAINS IN HELL, NOT REALMS EXPECT: MEAN WHILE 6 186
OR CAPTIVE DRAG'D IN CHAINS, WITH HOSTILE FROWN 6 260
TO CHAINS OF DARKNESS, AND TH' UNDYING WORM, 6 739
AND CHAINS THEY MADE ALL FAST, TOO FAST THEY MADE 10 319

CHAIR
WONT RIDE IN ARM'D, AND AT THE SOLDANS CHAIR 1 764
AS IN A CLOUDY CHAIR ASCENDING RIDES 2 930

CHALDAEA
UR OF CHALDAEA, PASSING NOW THE FORD 12 130

CHAM
GIRT WITH THE RIVER TRITON, WHERE OLD CHAM, 4 276

CHAMPAIN
AS WITH A RURAL MOUND THE CHAMPAIN HEAD 4 134
THROUGH HEAV'NS WIDE CHAMPAIN HELD HIS WAY, TILL
MORN, 6 2

CHAMPIONS
(THOUGH LIKE A COVER'D FIELD, WHERE CHAMPIONS BOLD 1 763
OF THOSE HEAV'N-WARRING CHAMPIONS COULD BE FOUND 2 424
FOR HOT, COLD, MOIST, AND DRY, FOUR CHAMPIONS
FIERCE 2 898

CHANC'D
OF WHAT SO SELDOM CHANC'D, WHEN TO HIS WISH, 9 423
TILL ON A DAY ROAVING THE FIELD, I CHANC'D 9 575

CHANCE
WHETHER UPHELD BY STRENGTH, OR CHANCE, OR FATE, 1 133
OF FUTURE DAYES MAY BRING, WHAT CHANCE, WHAT CHANGE 2 222
TO FICKLE CHANCE, AND CHAOS JUDGE THE STRIFE: 2 233
SEA-FARING MEN OREWATCHT, WHOSE BARK BY CHANCE 2 288
AND OPPORTUNE EXCURSION WE MAY CHANCE 2 396
IF CHANCE THE RADIANT SUN WITH FAREWELL SWEET 2 492
FREE VERTUE SHOULD ENTHRALL TO FORCE OR CHANCE. 2 551
CHANCE GOVERNS ALL. INTO THIS WILDE ABYSS, 2 910
DOWN HAD BEEN FALLING, HAD NOT BY ILL CHANCE 2 935
OF DEMOGORGON; RUMOR NEXT AND CHANCE, 2 965
THEN AS A TYGER, WHO BY CHANCE HATH SPI'D 4 403
A CHANCE BUT CHANCE MAY LEAD WHERE I MAY MEET 4 530
TO ACT OR NOT, NECESSITIE AND CHANCE 7 172
IF CHANCE WITH NYMPHLIKE STEP FAIR VIRGIN PASS, 9 452
ABSENTS THEE, OR WHAT CHANCE DETAINS? COME FORTH. 10 108
IN COUNCIL SATE, SOLLICITOUS WHAT CHANCE 10 428

CHANG'D
IF THOU BEEST HE; BUT O HOW FALL'N, HOW CHANG'D 1 84
THOUGH CHANG'D IN OUTWARD LUSTRE; THAT FIXT MIND 1 97
A MIND NOT TO BE CHANG'D BY PLACE OR TIME. 1 253
OR CHANG'D AT LENGTH, AND TO THE PLACE CONFORMD 2 217
AS SOFT AS NOW SEVERE, OUR TEMPER CHANG'D 2 276
THRICE CHANG'D WITH PALE, IRE, ENVIE AND DESPAIR, 4 115
NOR CHANG'D HIS COURSE, BUT THROUGH THE SHAGGIE
HILL 4 224
OF COMPOSITION, STRAIT THEY CHANG'D THIR MINDS, 6 613
SO SPAKE THE SON, AND INTO TERROUR CHANG'D 6 824
AND EARTH BE CHANG'D TO HEAV'N, & HEAV'N TO EARTH, 7 160
LOVELIER, NOT THOSE THAT IN ILLYRIA CHANG'D 9 505
HE LOOK'D, AND SAW THE FACE OF THINGS QUITE
CHANG'D, 11 712

CHANGD
SPRING BOTH, THE FACE OF BRIGHTEST HEAV'N HAD
CHANGD 5 644

CHANGE
CAN ELSE INFLICT, DO I REPENT OR CHANGE, 1 96
THAT WE MUST CHANGE FOR HEAV'N, THIS MOURNFUL GLOOM 1 244
UNDER AMAZEMENT OF THIR HIDEOUS CHANGE. 1 313
ON HALF THE NATIONS, AND WITH FEAR OF CHANGE 1 598
AS THIS PLACE TESTIFIES, AND THIS DIRE CHANGE 1 625
OF FUTURE DAYES MAY BRING, WHAT CHANCE, WHAT CHANGE 2 222
ARE BROUGHT: AND FEEL BY TURNS THE BITTER CHANGE 2 598
OF FIERCE EXTREAMS, EXTREAMS BY CHANGE MORE FIERCE, 2 599
THEN SWEET, NOW SAD TO MENTION, THROUGH DIRE CHANGE 2 820
TILL THEY ENTHRALL THEMSELVES: I ELSE MUST CHANGE 3 125
BUT FIRST HE CASTS TO CHANGE HIS PROPER SHAPE, 3 634
BY CHANGE OF PLACE: NOW CONSCIENCE WAKES DESPAIR 4 23
YOUR CHANGE APPROACHES, WHEN ALL THESE DELIGHTS 4 367
ALL SEASONS AND THIR CHANGE, ALL PLEASE ALIKE. 4 640
FARTHEST FROM PAIN, WHERE THOU MIGHTST HOPE TO
CHANGE 4 892
AND VARIOUS: WONDRING AT MY FLIGHT AND CHANGE 5 89
AND NOURISH ALL THINGS, LET YOUR CEASLESS CHANGE 5 183
TASTE AFTER TASTE UPHELD WITH KINDLIEST CHANGE, 5 336
WEE OURS FOR CHANGE DELECTABLE, NOT NEED) 5 629
TO SWERVE FROM TRUTH, OR CHANGE HIS CONSTANT MIND 5 902
NOT HITHER SUMMOND, SINCE THEY CANNOT CHANGE 8 347
AS US'D OR NOT, WORKS IN THE MIND NO CHANGE, 8 525
VENIAL DISCOURSE UNBLAM'D: I NOW MUST CHANGE 9 5
NOW NOT, THOUGH SIN, NOT TIME, FIRST WRAUGHT THE
CHANGE, 9 70
AS YET MY CHANGE, AND GIVE HIM TO PARTAKE 9 818
OR COME I LESS CONSPICUOUS, OR WHAT CHANGE 10 107
MUST SUFFER CHANGE, DISDAIN'D NOT TO BEGIN 10 213
OF MORTAL CHANGE ON EARTH. AS WHEN A FLOCK 10 273
A GROVE HARD BY, SPRUNG UP WITH THIS THIR CHANGE, 10 548
AS DEEP AS CAPRICORNE, TO BRING IN CHANGE 10 677
LIKE CHANGE ON SEA AND LAND, SIDERAL BLAST, 10 693
O EVE, SOME FURDER CHANGE AWAITS US NIGH, 11 193
INCESSANT I COULD HOPE TO CHANGE THE WILL 11 308
THY YOUTH, THY STRENGTH, THY BEAUTY, WHICH WILL
CHANGE 11 539
SHALL CHANGE THIR COURSE TO PLEASURE, EASE, AND
SLOTH, 11 794

CHANGES
STRAIT COUCHES CLOSE, THEN RISING CHANGES OFT 4 405
THESE CHANGES IN THE HEAV'NS, THOUGH SLOW, PRODUC'D 10 692

CHANGING
MUST WE RENOUNCE, AND CHANGING STILE BE CALL'D 2 312
INTO THE WOOD FAST BY, AND CHANGING SHAPE 10 333
THEY FELT THEMSELVS NOW CHANGING; DOWN THIR ARMS, 10 541

CHANNELS
AND ON THE WASHIE OOSE DEEP CHANNELS WORE; 7 303

CHAOS
ROSE OUT OF CHAOS: OR IF SION HILL 1 10
FRIGHTED THE REIGN OF CHAOS AND OLD NIGHT. 1 543
TO FICKLE CHANCE, AND CHAOS JUDGE THE STRIFE: 2 233
AND CHAOS, ANCESTORS OF NATURE, HOLD 2 895
HEE RULES A MOMENT; CHAOS UMPIRE SITS, 2 907
OF CHAOS, AND HIS DARK PAVILION SPREAD 2 960

CHAOS (CONTINUED)
CHAOS AND ANCIENT NIGHT, I COME NO SPY, ... 2 970
HER FARDEST VERGE, AND CHAOS TO RETIRE 2 1038
I SUNG OF CHAOS AND ETERNAL NIGHT, ... 3 18
FROM CHAOS AND TH' INROAD OF DARKNESS OLD, . . . 3 421
OF CHAOS BLUSTRING ROUND, INCLEMENT SKIE; . . . 3 426
AS YET THIS WORLD WAS NOT, AND CHAOS WILDE . . . 5 577
HIS FIERY CHAOS TO RECEAVE THIR FALL. 6 55
NINE DAYES THEY FELL; CONFOUNDED CHAOS ROARD, . . . 6 871
IN CHAOS, AND THE WORK BEGUN, HOW SOON 7 93
FARR INTO CHAOS, AND THE WORLD UNBORN; 7 220
FOR CHAOS HEARD HIS VOICE: HIM ALL HIS TRAINE . . 7 221
OF CHAOS FARR REMOV'D, LEAST FIERCE EXTREAMES . . 7 272
FARR INTO CHAOS, SINCE THE FIEND PASS'D THROUGH, . 10 233
WIDE ANARCHIE OF CHAOS DAMP AND DARK 10 283
FROM OUT OF CHAOS TO THE OUT SIDE BARE 10 317
AND AT THE BRINK OF CHAOS, NEER THE FOOT . . . 10 347
DISPARTED CHAOS OVERBUILT EXCLAIMD, ... 10 416
OF UNORIGINAL NIGHT AND CHAOS WILDE, ... 10 477
THROUGH CHAOS HURLD, OBSTRUCT THE MOUTH OF HELL . 10 636

CHARACTER
THE CHARACTER OF THAT DOMINION GIV'N 8 545

CHARG'D
CHARG'D NOT TO TOUCH THE INTERDICTED TREE, ... 7 46
I CHARG'D THEE, SAYING: THOU SHALT NOT EATE
THEREOF, ... 10 200

CHARGE
INTO MY HAND WAS GIV'N, WITH CHARGE TO KEEP . . . 2 775
LAY WAVING ROUND; ON SOM GREAT CHARGE IMPLOY'D . 3 628
RESIGNS HER CHARGE, WHILE GOODNESS THINKS NO ILL . 3 688
THIS ONE, THIS EASIE CHARGE, OF ALL THE TREES . . 4 421
CHARGE AND STRICT WATCH THAT TO THIS HAPPIE PLACE 4 562
SO PROMIS'D HEE, AND URIEL TO HIS CHARGE . . . 4 589
THAT NEER HIM STOOD, AND GAVE THEM THUS IN CHARGE. 4 787
TO HIM WHO SENT US, WHOSE CHARGE IS TO KEEP . . 4 842
TO THY TRANSGRESSIONS, AND DISTURBD THE CHARGE . 4 879
AFTER HIS CHARGE RECEIVD; BUT FROM AMONG . . . 5 248
DO AS YOU HAVE IN CHARGE, AND BRIEFLY TOUCH . . 6 566
ERE SABBATH EEV'NING: SO WE HAD IN CHARGE. . . . 8 246
THIR EARTHY CHARGE: OF THESE THE VIGILANCE . . . 9 157
OFT HE TO HER HIS CHARGE OF QUICK RETURNE . . . 9 399
FROM UNSUCCESSFUL CHARGE, BE NOT DISMAID, . . . 10 35
WHEREOF I GAVE THEE CHARGE THOU SHOULDST NOT EAT? 10 123
APPOINTED TO SIT THERE, HAD LEFT THIR CHARGE, . . 10 421
HIS MIGHTIE ANGELS GAVE THEM SEVERAL CHARGE, . . 10 650
MICHAEL, THIS MY BEHEST HAVE THOU IN CHARGE, . . 11 99
FAIREST AND EASIEST OF THIS COMBROUS CHARGE, . . 11 549
STILL FOLLOW'D HIM; TO THEM SHALL LEAVE IN CHARGE 12 439

CHARIOT
AND BROKEN CHARIOT WHEELS, SO THICK BESTROWN . . 1 311
NOR STOP THY FLAMING CHARIOT WHEELS, THAT SHOOK . 3 394
RAPT IN A CHARIOT DRAWN BY FIERY STEEDS. . . . 3 522
TH' APOSTAT IN HIS SUN-BRIGHT CHARIOT SATE . . . 6 100
BACK TO HIS CHARIOT; WHERE IT STOOD RETIR'D . . . 6 338
AND AT HIS CHARIOT WHEELES TO DRAG HIM BOUND . . 6 358
CHARIOT AND CHARIOTER LAY OVERTURND 6 390
ASCEND MY CHARIOT, GUIDE THE RAPID WHEELES . . . 6 711
THE CHARIOT OF PATERNAL DEITIE, ... 6 750
OF HIS FIERCE CHARIOT ROWLD, AS WITH THE SOUND . . 6 829
MESSIAH HIS TRIUMPHAL CHARIOT TURND: 6 881
ABOUT HIS CHARIOT NUMBERLESS WERE POUR'D . . . 7 197
AND CRAZE THIR CHARIOT WHEELS: WHEN BY COMMAND . 12 210

CHARIOTER
CHARIOT AND CHARIOTER LAY OVERTURND 6 390

CHARIOTS
WITH HORSE AND CHARIOTS RANKT IN LOOSE ARRAY; . . 2 887
CHARIOTS AND FLAMING ARMES, AND FIERIE STEEDS . . 6 17
OF BRAZEN CHARIOTS RAG'D; DIRE WAS THE NOISE . . 6 211
CHARIOTS OF GOD, HALF ON EACH HAND WERE SEEN; . . 6 770
AND VERTUES, WINGED SPIRITS, AND CHARIOTS WING'D, 7 199

CHARITIE
DWELS IN ALL HEAVEN CHARITIE SO DEARE? 3 216
BY NAME TO COME CALL'D CHARITIE, THE SOUL . . . 12 584

CHARITIES
RELATIONS DEAR, AND ALL THE CHARITIES 4 756

CHARLEMAIN
WHEN CHARLEMAIN WITH ALL HIS PEERAGE FELL 1 586

CHARM
INTENT, WITH JOCOND MUSIC CHARM HIS EAR; 1 787
MORE TOLLERABLE; IF THERE BE CURE OR CHARM . . . 2 460
YET WITH A PLEASING SORCERIE COULD CHARM . . . 2 566
WITH CHARM OF EARLIEST BIRDS; PLEASANT THE SUN . 4 642
WITH CHARM OF EARLIEST BIRDS, NOR RISING SUN . . 4 651
AGAINST THE CHARM OF BEAUTIES POWERFUL GLANCE. . 8 533
BUT FONDLY OVERCOME WITH FEMAL CHARM. 9 999

CHARM'D
MOV'D ON IN SILENCE TO SOFT PIPES THAT CHARM'D . 1 561

CHARM'D (CONTINUED)
CHARM'D WITH ARCADIAN PIPE, THE PASTORAL REED . . 11 132

CHARMING
OF CHARMING SYMPHONIE THEY INTRODUCE 3 368
SO SMOOTHS HER CHARMING TONES, THAT GODS OWN EAR . 5 626
SO CHARMING LEFT HIS VOICE, THAT HE A WHILE . . 8 2
AND CHARMING SYMPHONIES ATTACH'D THE HEART . . . 11 595

CHARMS
(FOR ELOQUENCE THE SOUL, SONG CHARMS THE SENSE,) . 2 556
ECLIPSES AT THIR CHARMS. THE OTHER SHAPE, . . . 2 666
BOTH OF HER BEAUTY AND SUBMISSIVE CHARMS . . . 4 498

CHARYBDIS
CHARYBDIS, AND BY TH' OTHER WHIRLPOOL STEARD. . . 2 1020

CHASE
WITH SOLEMN TOUCHES, TROUBL'D THOUGHTS, AND CHASE 1 557
ALL BEASTS OF TH' EARTH, SINCE WILDE, AND OF ALL
CHASE 4 341
TO CHASE ME HENCE? ERRE NOT THAT SO SHALL END . 6 288
ADAM OBSERV'D, AND WITH HIS EYE THE CHASE . . . 11 191

CHASTE
WHOSE BED IS UNDEFIL'D AND CHASTE PRONOUNC'T, . . 4 761
DEUCALION AND CHASTE PYRRHA TO RESTORE 11 12

CHAST'NING
HOWEVER CHAST'NING, TO THE EVIL TURNE 11 373

CHAUMPING
CHAUMPING HIS IRON CURB: TO STRIVE OR FLIE . . . 4 859

CHEAP
HIS RIVALS, WINNING CHEAP THE HIGH REPUTE . . . 2 472

CHEAR'D
CHEAR'D WITH THE GRATEFUL SMELL OLD OCEAN SMILES. 4 165

CHEARD
SO CHEARD HE HIS FAIR SPOUSE, AND SHE WAS CHEARD, 5 129

CHEARFUL
HEAV'NS CHEARFUL FACE, THE LOWRING ELEMENT . . . 2 490
SURROUNDS ME, FROM THE CHEARFUL WAYES OF MEN . . 3 46
ALL NIGHT; AT LAST BY BREAK OF CHEARFUL DAWNE . . 3 545
THAT WONT TO BE MORE CHEARFUL AND SERENE . . . 5 123

CHEARING
DAYS, MONTHS, & YEARS, TOWARDS HIS ALL-CHEARING
LAMP 3 581

CHECK
THIR PAMPERD BOUGHES, AND NEEDED HANDS TO CHECK . 5 214

CHECK'D
YET HALF HIS STRENGTH HE PUT NOT FORTH, BUT CHECK'D 6 853

CHECKS
AND IN HER PALE DOMINION CHECKS THE NIGHT. . . . 3 732

CHEEK
SAT ON HIS FADED CHEEK, BUT UNDER BROWES . . . 1 602
IN CURLES ON EITHER CHEEK PLAID, WINGS HE WORE . 3 641
WITH TRESSES DISCOMPOS'D, AND GLOWING CHEEK, . . 5 10
ALTERD HER CHEEK. ON WHOM THE ANGEL HAILE . . . 5 385
BUT IN HER CHEEK DISTEMPER FLUSHING GLOWD. . . . 9 887

CHEEKS
HAD ENTERTAIND, AS DI'D HER CHEEKS WITH PALE. . . 10 1009

CHEER'D
WITH CAUSE FOR EVILS PAST, YET MUCH MORE CHEER'D . 12 604

CHEERFUL
HOPEFUL AND CHEERFUL, IN THY BLOOD WILL REIGNE . 11 543

CHEMOS
NEXT CHEMOS, TH' OBSCENE DREAD OF MOABS SONS, . . 1 406

CHERE
HE ENDED, AND HIS WORDS THIR DROOPING CHERE . . 6 496

CHERISH
SOM BETTER SHROUD, SOM BETTER WARMTH TO CHERISH . 10 1068

CHERISHING
THY CHERISHING, THY HONOURING, AND THY LOVE, . . 8 569

CHERSONESE
DOWN TO THE GOLDEN CHERSONESE, OR WHERE 11 392

CHERUB
HEE ON THE WINGS OF CHERUB RODE SUBLIME 6 771
CHERUB AND SERAPH, POTENTATES AND THRONES, . . . 7 198

CHERUBE
FALL'N CHERUBE, TO BE WEAK IS MISERABLE 1 157
CHERUBE AND SERAPH ROWLING IN THE FLOOD 1 324
AZAZEL AS HIS RIGHT, A CHERUBE TALL: 1 534
AND NOW A STRIPLING CHERUBE HE APPEERS, 3 636
SO SPAKE THE CHERUBE, AND HIS GRAVE REBUKE 4 844
PROUD LIMITARIE CHERUBE, BUT ERE THEN 4 971

CHERUBIC
CHERUBIC SONGS BY NIGHT FROM NEIGHBOURING HILLS 5 547
CHERUBIC WAVING FIRES: ON TH' OTHER PART 6 413
BY FOUR CHERUBIC SHAPES, FOUR FACES EACH 6 753
FROM ENTRANCE OR CHERUBIC WATCH, BY STEALTH 9 68
CHERUBIC WATCH, AND OF A SWORD THE FLAME 11 120

CHERUBIM
BETWEEN THE CHERUBIM; YEA, OFTEN PLAC'D 1 387
OF MIGHTY CHERUBIM; THE SUDDEN BLAZE 1 665
THE GREAT SERAPHIC LORDS AND CHERUBIM 1 794
TOWARD THE FOUR WINDS FOUR SPEEDY CHERUBIM 2 516
HATH BROUGHT ME FROM THE QUIRES OF CHERUBIM 3 666
AND FROM THIR IVORIE PORT THE CHERUBIM 4 778
WITH FLAMING CHERUBIM, AND GOLDEN SHIELDS; 6 102
ZOPHIEL, OF CHERUBIM THE SWIFTEST WING, 6 535
NOR STAID, BUT ON THE WINGS OF CHERUBIM 7 218
HIS ENTRANCE, AND FOREWARND THE CHERUBIM 9 61
TAKE TO THEE FROM AMONG THE CHERUBIM 11 100
OF WATCHFUL CHERUBIM; FOUR FACES EACH 11 128
OF TWO BRIGHT CHERUBIM, BEFORE HIM BURN 12 254
THE CHERUBIM DESCENDED; ON THE GROUND 12 628

CHEW
THE SAVOURIE PULP THEY CHEW, AND IN THE RINDE 4 335

CHEWD
CHEWD BITTER ASHES, WHICH TH' OFFENDED TASTE 10 566

CHIEF
O PRINCE, O CHIEF OF MANY THRONED POWERS, 1 128
THE CHIEF WERE THOSE WHO FROM THE PIT OF HELL 1 381
OBSCURE SOME GLIMPS OF JOY, TO HAVE FOUND THIR CHIEF 1 524
AWAITING WHAT COMMAND THIR MIGHTY CHIEF 1 566
AND PORCHES WIDE, BUT CHIEF THE SPACIOUS HALL 1 762
OTHERS AMONG THE CHIEF MIGHT OFFER NOW 2 469
ENDED REJOYCING IN THIR MATCHLESS CHIEF: 2 487
THE IRKSOM HOURS, TILL THIS GREAT CHIEF RETURN. 2 527
SMIT WITH THE LOVE OF SACRED SONG; BUT CHIEF 3 29
O SON, IN WHOM MY SOUL HATH CHIEF DELIGHT, 3 168
HIS CHIEF DELIGHT AND FAVOUR, HIM FOR WHOM 3 664
CHIEF OF TH' ANGELIC GUARDS, AWAITING NIGHT; 4 550
AWAITING NEXT COMMAND. TO WHOM THIR CHIEF 4 864
LESS HARDIE TO ENDURE? COURAGEOUS CHIEF, 4 920
REASON AS CHIEF; AMONG THESE FANSIE NEXT 5 102
OF ALL THOSE MYRIADS WHICH WE LEAD THE CHIEF; 5 684
EACH WARRIOUR SINGLE AS IN CHIEF, EXPERT 6 233
HYMNS OF HIGH PRAISE, AND I AMONG THEM CHIEF. 6 745
AND WORSHIP GOD SUPREAM, WHO MADE HIM CHIEF 7 515
HEROIC DEEM'D, CHIEF MAISTRIE TO DISSECT 9 29
THIR MIGHTY CHIEF RETURND: LOUD WAS TH' ACCLAIME: 10 455
IN TRIUMPH ISSUING FORTH THIR GLORIOUS CHIEF; 10 537
WITH VOWS, AS THIR CHIEF GOOD, AND FINAL HOPE. 11 493
WOMANS DOMESTIC HONOUR AND CHIEF PRAISE; 11 617

CHIEFLY
AND CHIEFLY THOU, O SPIRIT, THAT DOST PREFER 1 17
THE MOST AVERSE, THEE CHIEFLY, WHO FULL OFT 2 763
ALL THESE HIS WONDROUS WORKS, BUT CHIEFLY MAN, 3 663
AND DAILY THANKS, I CHIEFLY WHO ENJOY 4 445
MORE OF TH' ALMIGHTIES WORKS, AND CHIEFLY MAN 4 566
BUT CHIEFLY WHERE THOSE TWO FAIR CREATURES LODGE, 4 790
HIS LOSS; BUT CHIEFLY TO FIND HERE OBSERVD 4 849
CHIEFLY BY WHAT THY OWN LAST REASONING WORDS 9 379
CHIEFLY I SOUGHT, WITHOUT THEE CAN DESPISE. 9 878
PERNICIOUS TO THY PEACE, CHIEFLY ASSUR'D 9 981
CHIEFLY ON MAN, SOLE LORD OF ALL DECLAR'D, 10 401
THOU HAST REVEALD, THOSE CHIEFLY WHICH CONCERNE 12 272
CHIEFLY WHAT MAY CONCERN HER FAITH TO KNOW, 12 599

CHIL'D
HE PLUCKT, HE TASTED; MEE DAMP HORROR CHIL'D 5 65

CHILD-BEARING
PAINS ONELY IN CHILD-BEARING WERE FORETOLD, 10 1051

CHILDE
A SON, AND OF HIS SON A GRAND-CHILDE LEAVES, 12 153

CHILDERN
HIM OR HIS CHILDERN, EVIL HE MAY BE SURE, 11 772

CHILDLESS
CHILDLESS THOU ART, CHILDLESS REMAINE: 10 989
BY DEATH BROUGHT ON OUR SELVES, OR CHILDLESS DAYS 10 1037

CHILDREN
BY THY CONCEPTION; CHILDREN THOU SHALT BRING 10 194
DISGUIS'D HE CAME, BUT THOSE HIS CHILDREN DEAR 10 330

CHILDREN (CONTINUED)
HIS CHILDREN, ALL IN VIEW DESTROYD AT ONCE; 11 761

CHILDRENS
THIR CHILDRENS CRIES UNHEARD, THAT PAST THROUGH FIRE 1 395

CHILL
ASTONIED STOOD AND BLANK, WHILE HORROR CHILL 9 890

CHILLING
HEART-STROOK WITH CHILLING GRIPE OF SORROW STOOD, 11 264

CHIME
OF INSTRUMENTS THAT MADE MELODIOUS CHIME 11 559

CHIMERA'S
GORGONS AND HYDRA'S, AND CHIMERA'S DIRE. 2 628

CHIMIC
TH' ARCH-CHIMIC SUN SO FARR FROM US REMOTE 3 609

CHINESES
OF SERICANA, WHERE CHINESES DRIVE 3 438

CHIVALRY
BUSIRIS AND HIS MEMPHIAN CHIVALRY, 1 307
DEFI'D THE BEST OF PANIM CHIVALRY 1 765

CHOICE
A GENERATION, WHOM HIS CHOICE REGARD 1 653
BY PLACE OR CHOICE THE WORTHIEST; THEY ANON 1 759
DID FIRST CREATE YOUR LEADER, NEXT FREE CHOICE, 2 19
CHOICE IN OUR SUFFRAGE; FOR ON WHOM WE SEND, 2 415
ASTONISHT: NONE AMONG THE CHOICE AND PRIME 2 423
PURSUES, AS INCLINATION OR SAD CHOICE 2 524
WHEN WILL AND REASON (REASON ALSO IS CHOICE) 3 108
PASS'D FREQUENT, AND HIS EYE WITH CHOICE REGARD 3 534
BUT ALL THESE SHINING ORBES HIS CHOICE TO DWELL; 3 670
FREE LEAVE SO LARGE TO ALL THINGS ELSE, AND CHOICE 4 434
EACH PLANT AND JUCIEST GOURD WILL PLUCK SUCH CHOICE 5 327
WHAT CHOICE TO CHUSE FOR DELICACIE BEST, 5 333
ETHEREAL, AS WEE, OR MAY AT CHOICE 5 499
SO EASILY OBEYD AMID THE CHOICE 7 48
YET DREADFUL IN MINE EARE, THOUGH IN MY CHOICE 8 335
THOU TO THY SELF PROPOSEST, IN THE CHOICE 8 400
LET US DIVIDE OUR LABOURS, THOU WHERE CHOICE 9 214
TO US, IN SUCH ABOUNDANCE LIES OUR CHOICE, 9 620
HAD SO ENOBL'D, AS OF CHOICE TO INCURR 9 992
GOD MADE THEE OF CHOICE HIS OWN, AND OF HIS OWN 10 766
BY PARENTS, OR HIS HAPPIEST CHOICE TOO LATE 10 904
AS IN OUR EVILS, AND OF EASIER CHOICE. 10 978
THY CHOICE OF FLAMING WARRIOURS, LEAST THE FIEND 11 101

CHOICEST
THAT OPEN NOW THIR CHOICEST BOSOM'D SMELLS 5 127
TO REST, AND WHAT THE GARDEN CHOICEST BEARS 5 368
OF CHOICEST FLOURS A GARLAND TO ADORNE 9 840
CHOICEST AND BEST; THEN SACRIFICING, LAID 11 438

CHOOSE
LIKE CUMBROUS FLESH; BUT IN WHAT SHAPE THEY CHOOSE 1 428
BY OUR DELAY? NO, LET US RATHER CHOOSE 2 60
CHOOSE TO RESIDE, HIS GLORY UNOBSCUR'D, 2 265
BOTH WHAT THEY JUDGE AND WHAT THEY CHOOSE; FOR SO 3 123
BY DESTINIE, AND CAN NO OTHER CHOOSE? 5 534
OUR TASKE WE CHOOSE, WHAT WONDER IF SO NEAR 9 221
WHEN I AM PRESENT, AND THY TRIAL CHOOSE 9 316
THIR GOVERNMENT, AND THIR GREAT SENATE CHOOSE 12 225
THE WORLD WAS ALL BEFORE THEM, WHERE TO CHOOSE 12 646

CHOOSING
PLEAS'D ME LONG CHOOSING, AND BEGINNING LATE; 9 26
OF MANY WAYS TO DIE THE SHORTEST CHOOSING, 10 1005
RETURN THEM BACK TO EGYPT, CHOOSING RATHER 12 219

CHORAL
AND CHORAL SYMPHONIES, DAY WITHOUT NIGHT, 5 162
CHORAL OR UNISON: OF INCENSE CLOUDS 7 599

CHORDS
THIR STOPS AND CHORDS WAS SEEN: HIS VOLANT TOUCH 11 561

CHORUS
AND MORNING CHORUS SUNG THE SECOND DAY. 7 275

CHOSE
CHOSE FREELY WHAT IT NOW SO JUSTLY RUES. 4 72
HIS COUCHANT WATCH, AS ONE WHO CHOSE HIS GROUND 4 406
CHOSE RATHER; HEE, SHE KNEW WOULD INTERMIX 8 54
OF THOUGHTS REVOLV'D, HIS FINAL SENTENCE CHOSE 9 88
INTO THE THICKEST WOOD, THERE SOON THEY CHOSE 9 1100
YET WILLINGLY CHOSE RATHER DEATH WITH THEE: 9 1167
FAST CAUGHT, THEY LIK'D, AND EACH HIS LIKING CHOSE; 11 587

CHOSEN
THAT SHEPHERD, WHO FIRST TAUGHT THE CHOSEN SEED, 1 8
SOME I HAVE CHOSEN OF PECULIAR GRACE 3 183

CLAMOUR
AND CLAMOUR SUCH AS HEARD IN HEAV'N TILL NOW 6 208

CLANG
WITH CLANG DESPIS'D THE GROUND, UNDER A CLOUD 7 422
THE HAUNT OF SEALES AND ORCS, AND SEA-MEWS CLANG. 11 835

CLANNS
OF EACH HIS FACTION, IN THIR SEVERAL CLANNS, 2 901

CLARION
WALK'D FIRM; THE CRESTED COCK WHOSE CLARION SOUNDS 7 443

CLARIONS
OF TRUMPETS LOUD AND CLARIONS BE UPREARD 1 532

CLASH'D
CLASH'D ON THIR SOUNDING SHIELDS THE DIN OF WAR, 1 668

CLASHING
WAS NEVER, ARMS ON ARMOUR CLASHING BRAY'D 6 209

CLASP
I BEG, AND CLASP THY KNEES; BEREAVE ME NOT, 10 918

CLASPING
THE CLASPING IVIE WHERE TO CLIMB, WHILE I 9 217

CLAY
OF HEAV'N, THIS MAN OF CLAY, SON OF DESPITE, 9 176
DID I REQUEST THEE, MAKER, FROM MY CLAY 10 743

CLEAR
OF UTMOST HOPE. NOW CLEAR I UNDERSTAND 12 376

CLEARD
SO ALL WAS CLEARD, AND TO THE FIELD THEY HASTE. 5 136

CLEARER
WHICH THAT FALSE FRUIT THAT PROMIS'D CLEARER SIGHT 11 413

CLEER
CLEER VICTORY, TO OUR PART LOSS AND ROUT 2 770
CLEER SPRING, OR SHADIE GROVE, OR SUNNIE HILL, 3 28
INVITES; FOR I WILL CLEER THIR SENSES DARK, 3 188
IF METTAL, PART SEEMD GOLD, PART SILVER CLEER; 3 595
NO WHERE SO CLEER, SHARP'ND HIS VISUAL RAY 3 620
ARE EVER CLEER. WHEREOF HEE SOON AWARE, 4 119
ON THE GREEN BANK, TO LOOK INTO THE CLEER 4 458
TO WHOM THE SON WITH CALM ASPECT AND CLEER 5 733
ON THE CLEER HYALINE, THE GLASSIE SEA; 7 619
NOT TO INCUR; BUT SOON HIS CLEER ASPECT 8 336
AND THE CLEER SUN ON HIS WIDE WATRIE GLASS 11 844

CLEERD
TO WHOM THUS ADAM CLEERD OF DOUBT, REPLI'D. 8 179
OP'ND AND CLEERD, AND YE SHALL BE AS GODS, 9 708

CLEERE
WITHIN ME CLEERE, NOT ONELY TO DISCERNE 9 681
YE EATE THEREOF, YOUR EYES THAT SEEM SO CLEERE, 9 706

CLEEREST
THE HEMISPHERE OF EARTH IN CLEEREST KEN 11 379

CLEFT
ON THE CLEFT WOOD, AND ALL DUE RITES PERFORM'D. 11 440

CLEOMBROTUS
CLEOMBROTUS, AND MANY MORE TOO LONG, 3 473

CLIFF
THIR HIGHEST HEAV'N; OR ON THE DELPHIAN CLIFF, 1 517
THE REST WAS CRAGGIE CLIFF, THAT OVERHUNG 4 547
AT ONCE ON TH' EASTERN CLIFF OF PARADISE 5 275
LED THEM DIRECT, AND DOWN THE CLIFF AS FAST 12 639

CLIFFS
ON CLIFFS AND CEDAR TOPS THIR EYRIES BUILD: 7 424

CLIMAT
CLIMAT, OR YEARS DAMP MY INTENDED WING 9 45

CLIMATE
THAT NEVER WILL IN OTHER CLIMATE GROW, 11 274

CLIMB
THE CLASPING IVIE WHERE TO CLIMB, WHILE I 9 217

CLIMBE
SO SINCE INTO HIS CHURCH LEWD HIRELINGS CLIMBE. 4 193
STILL AS IT ROSE, IMPOSSIBLE TO CLIMBE. 4 548

CLIMBES
WHERE ENTRANCE UP FROM EDEN EASIEST CLIMBES, 11 119

CLIMBING
OBTAINS THE BROW OF SOME HIGH-CLIMBING HILL, 3 546

CLIMBING (CONTINUED)
CLIMBING, SAT THICKER THEN THE SNAKIE LOCKS 10 559

CLIMBS
IN AT THE WINDOW CLIMBS, OR O'RE THE TILES; 4 191

CLIMBST
IN THY ETERNAL COURSE, BOTH WHEN THOU CLIMBST, 5 173

CLIME
IS THIS THE REGION, THIS THE SOIL, THE CLIME, 1 242
ON HEAVENS AZURE, AND THE TORRID CLIME 1 297
THAT DISMAL WORLD, IF ANY CLIME PERHAPS 2 572
NOW MORN HER ROSIE STEPS IN TH' EASTERN CLIME 5 1
BELLEROPHON, THOUGH FROM A LOWER CLIME) 7 18
OF SEASONS TO EACH CLIME; ELSE HAD THE SPRING 10 678
BEGAN TO PARCH THAT TEMPERATE CLIME; WHEREAT 12 636

CLIMES
HIGH IN SALVATION AND THE CLIMES OF BLISS, 11 708

CLOATH
AND THOUGHT NOT MUCH TO CLOATH HIS ENEMIES: 10 219

CLOATH'D
THUS BELIAL WITH WORDS CLOATH'D IN REASONS GARB 2 226
CLOATH'D US UNWORTHIE, PITYING WHILE HE JUDG'D; 10 1059

CLOD
WITH THIS CORPOREAL CLOD; THEN IN THE GRAVE, 10 786

CLODS
THE GRASSIE CLODS NOW CALV'D, NOW HALF APPEER'D 7 463
LABOURING, TWO MASSIE CLODS OF IRON AND BRASS 11 565

CLOMB
SO CLOMB THIS FIRST GRAND THIEF INTO GODS FOULD: 4 192

CLOS
OR CLOS AMBITION VARNISHT O'RE WITH ZEAL. 2 485

CLOS'D
O FATHER, GRACIOUS WAS THAT WORD WHICH CLOS'D 3 144
PASS'D THROUGH HIM, BUT TH' ETHEREAL SUBSTANCE
CLOS'D 6 330
YAWNING RECEAVD THEM WHOLE, AND ON THEM CLOS'D, 6 875
BY NATURE AS IN AIDE, AND CLOS'D MINE EYES. 8 459
MINE EYES HE CLOS'D, BUT OP'N LEFT THE CELL 8 460

CLOSE
TO WORK IN CLOSE DESIGN, BY FRAUD OR GUILE 1 646
IN CLOSE RECESS AND SECRET CONCLAVE SAT 1 795
TILL THICKEST LEGIONS CLOSE; WITH FEATS OF ARMS 2 537
CLOSE SAILING FROM BENGALA, OR THE ILES 2 638
OF SMALLEST MAGNITUDE CLOSE BY THE MOON. 2 1053
HIS LITHE PROBOSCIS; CLOSE THE SERPENT SLY 4 347
AND MUTUAL AMITIE SO STREIGHT, SO CLOSE, 4 376
STRAIT COUCHES CLOSE, THEN RISING CHANGES OFT 4 405
NOR FAUNUS HAUNTED. HERE IN CLOSE RECESS 4 708
SQUAT LIKE A TOAD, CLOSE AT THE EARE OF EVE; 4 800
CLOSE AT MINE EAR ONE CALL'D ME FORTH TO WALK 5 36
SLEEPST THOU COMPANION DEAR, WHAT SLEEP CAN CLOSE 5 673
OF BATTEL, OPEN WHEN, AND WHEN TO CLOSE 6 235
DISTURBD NOT, WAITING CLOSE TH' APPROACH OF MORN. 9 191
CLOSE FOLLOWING PACE FOR PACE, NOT MOUNTED YET 10 589
THAT ADAM NOW ENFORC'T TO CLOSE HIS EYES, 11 419

CLOSING
JUST MET, AND CLOSING STOOD IN SQUADRON JOIND 4 863
SOON CLOSING, AND BY NATIVE VIGOUR HEAL'D. 6 436

CLOTH'D
CLOTH'D WITH TRANSCENDENT BRIGHTNESS DIDST
OUT-SHINE 1 86

CLOUD
WAV'D ROUND THE COAST, UP CALL'D A PITCHY CLOUD 1 340
THE STRONG REBUFF OF SOM TUMULTUOUS CLOUD 2 936
BUT CLOUD IN STEAD, AND EVER-DURING DARK 3 45
FATHER, TO SEE THY FACE, WHEREIN NO CLOUD 3 262
THE FULL BLAZE OF THY BEAMS, AND THROUGH A CLOUD 3 378
IN WHOSE CONSPICUOUS COUNT'NANCE, WITHOUT CLOUD 3 385
THEN IN FAIR EVENING CLOUD, OR HUMID BOW, 4 151
BE NOT DISHEART'ND THEN, NOR CLOUD THOSE LOOKS 5 122
FROM HENCE, NO CLOUD, OR, TO OBSTRUCT HIS SIGHT, 5 257
HER SHADOWIE CLOUD WITHDRAWS, I AM TO HASTE, 5 686
FROM MIDST A GOLDEN CLOUD THUS MILDE WAS HEARD. 6 28
THIS DAY, FEAR NOT HIS FLIGHT; SO THICK A CLOUD 6 539
SPHEAR'D IN A RADIANT CLOUD, FOR YET THE SUN 7 247
WITH CLANG DESPIS'D THE GROUND, UNDER A CLOUD 7 422
VEILD IN A CLOUD OF FRAGRANCE, WHERE SHE STOOD, 9 425
ETERNAL FATHER FROM HIS SECRET CLOUD, 10 32
AT LAST AS FROM A CLOUD HIS FULGENT HEAD 10 449
TO WHOM THE FATHER, WITHOUT CLOUD, SERENE. 11 45
MORE ORIENT IN YON WESTERN CLOUD THAT DRAWS 11 205
FROM YONDER BLAZING CLOUD THAT VEILS THE HILL 11 229
HAD NOT A CLOUD DESCENDING SNATCH'D HIM THENCE 11 670
RAPT IN A BALMIE CLOUD WITH WINGED STEEDS 11 706

CLOUD (CONTINUED)
A DEWIE CLOUD, AND IN THE CLOUD A BOW 11 865
THE FLUID SKIRTS OF THAT SAME WATRIE CLOUD, . . 11 882
OVER THE EARTH A CLOUD, WILL THEREIN SET . . . 11 896
A DARKSOM CLOUD OF LOCUSTS SWARMING DOWN . . . 12 185
BEFORE THEM IN A CLOUD, AND PILLAR OF FIRE, . . 12 202
BY DAY A CLOUD, BY NIGHT A PILLAR OF FIRE, . . . 12 203
THEN THROUGH THE FIREY PILLAR AND THE CLOUD . . 12 208
THE HEAV'NLY FIRES; OVER THE TENT A CLOUD . . . 12 256

CLOUDED
RISING IN CLOUDED MAJESTIE, AT LENGTH 4 607
THE CLOUDED ARK OF GOD TILL THEN IN TENTS . . . 12 333

CLOUDIE
OF HIDEOUS LENGTH: BEFORE THE CLOUDIE VAN, . . . 6 107
UNDER HER CLOUDIE COVERT BOTH RETIR'D, ... 6 409
AND CLOUDIE IN ASPECT THUS ANSWERING SPAKE. . . 6 450
WAS NOT; SHEE IN A CLOUDIE TABERNACLE 7 248
TRANSPLANTED FROM HER CLOUDIE SHRINE, AND PLAC'D . 7 360

CLOUDS
THICK CLOUDS AND DARK DOTH HEAV'NS ALL-RULING SIRE 2 264
AS WHEN FROM MOUNTAIN TOPS THE DUSKY CLOUDS . . 2 488
TO BATTEL IN THE CLOUDS, BEFORE EACH VAN . . . 2 535
HANGS IN THE CLOUDS, BY AEQUINOCTIAL WINDS . . . 2 637
EACH CAST AT TH' OTHER, AS WHEN TWO BLACK CLOUDS . 2 714
ON JUNO SMILES, WHEN HE IMPREGNS THE CLOUDS . . 4 500
OF ALABLASTER, PIL'D UP TO THE CLOUDS, ... 4 544
THE CLOUDS THAT ON HIS WESTERN THRONE ATTEND: . . 4 597
COULD NOT BUT TASTE. FORTHWITH UP TO THE CLOUDS . 5 86
WHETHER TO DECK WITH CLOUDS THE UNCOLOURD SKIE, . 5 189
NOW WHEN AMBROSIAL NIGHT WITH CLOUDS EXHAL'D . . 5 642
SO SPAKE THE SOVRAN VOICE, AND CLOUDS BEGAN . . 6 56
INTO THE CLOUDS, THIR TOPS ASCEND THE SKIE: . . 7 287
CHORAL OR UNISON: OF INCENSE CLOUDS 7 599
AS CLOUDS, AND CLOUDS MAY RAIN, AND RAIN PRODUCE . 8 146
NOTUS AND AFER BLACK WITH THUNDROUS CLOUDS . . 10 702
THE AIR ATTRITE TO FIRE, AS LATE THE CLOUDS . . 10 1073
WIDE HOVERING, ALL THE CLOUDS TOGETHER DROVE . . 11 739
WHICH NOW ABATED, FOR THE CLOUDS WERE FLED, . . 11 841
ABOVE THE CLOUDS WILL PINE HIS ENTRAILS GROSS, . 12 77
LAST IN THE CLOUDS FROM HEAV'N TO BE REVEALD . . 12 545

CLOUDY
AS IN A CLOUDY CHAIR ASCENDING RIDES 2 930
A CLOUDY SPOT. DOWN THITHER PRONE IN FLIGHT . . 5 266

CLOV'N
DOWN CLOV'N TO THE WASTE, WITH SHATTERD ARMES . . 6 361

CLUNG
HIS ARMES CLUNG TO HIS RIBS, HIS LEGGS ENTWINING . 10 512

CLUSTERS
IN CLUSTERS; THEY AMONG FRESH DEWS AND FLOWERS . 1 771
HER DOWR TH' ADOPTED CLUSTERS, TO ADORN 5 218

CLUSTRING
CLUSTRING, BUT NOT BENEATH HIS SHOULDERS BROAD: . 4 303
FORTH FLOURISH'T THICK THE CLUSTRING VINE, FORTH CREPT 7 320

COAL
OF SOOTY COAL THE EMPIRIC ALCHIMIST 5 440

COAST
HATH VEXT THE RED-SEA COAST, WHOSE WAVES ORETHREW 1 306
WAV'D ROUND THE COAST, UP CALL'D A PITCHY CLOUD . 1 340
REAR'D IN AZOTUS, DREADED THROUGH THE COAST . . 1 464
HE SCOURS THE RIGHT HAND COAST, SOM TIMES THE LEFT, 2 633
WHICH WAY THE NEEREST COAST OF DARKNESS LYES . . 2 958
A VIOLENT CROSS WIND FROM EITHER COAST 3 487
TOOK LEAVE, AND TOWARD THE COAST OF EARTH BENEATH, 3 739
UZZIEL, HALF THESE DRAW OFF, AND COAST THE SOUTH . 4 782
IN PONTUS OR THE PUNIC COAST, OR WHERE 5 340
LOOKD ROUND, AND SCOUTS EACH COAST LIGHT-ARMED SCOURE, ... 6 529
ON THE EIGHTH RETURN'D, AND ON THE COAST AVERSE . 9 67
EDEN AND ALL THE COAST IN PROSPECT LAY. . . . 10 89
CATHAIAN COAST. THE AGGREGATED SOYLE 10 293

COASTING
COASTING THE WALL OF HEAV'N ON THIS SIDE NIGHT . 3 71

COASTS
THROUGH ALL THE COASTS OF DARK DESTRUCTION SEEK . 2 464
GLAD WE RETURN'D UP TO THE COASTS OF LIGHT . . . 8 245

COAT
HIS ADAMANTINE COAT GIRD WELL, AND EACH 6 542

COATE
ALCINOUS REIGN'D, FRUIT OF ALL KINDES, IN COATE, . 5 341
OR AS THE SNAKE WITH YOUTHFUL COATE REPAID; . . 10 218

COATS
SHOW TO THE SUN THIR WAV'D COATS DROPT WITH GOLD, 7 406

COCK
WALK'D FIRM; THE CRESTED COCK WHOSE CLARION SOUNDS 7 443

COCYTUS
COCYTUS, NAM'D OF LAMENTATION LOUD 2 579

COETERNAL
OR OF TH' ETERNAL COETERNAL BEAM 3 2

COGITATION
HE SEEMD, OR FIXT IN COGITATION DEEP. 3 629

COHORT
FOR SWIFT DESCENT, WITH HIM THE COHORT BRIGHT . . 11 127

COLD
OF COLD OLYMPUS RUL'D THE MIDDLE AIR 1 516
BURNS FRORE, AND COLD PERFORMS TH' EFFECT OF FIRE. 2 595
FOR HOT, COLD, MOIST, AND DRY, FOUR CHAMPIONS FIERCE 2 898
THE BLACK TARTAREOUS COLD INFERNAL DREGS . . . 7 238
THAT NAME, UNLESS AN AGE TOO LATE, OR COLD . . . 9 44
CONDENSES, AND THE COLD INVIRONS ROUND, ... 9 636
DEATH WITH HIS MACE PETRIFIC, COLD AND DRY, . . 10 294
AS MIGHT AFFECT THE EARTH WITH COLD AND HEAT . . 10 653
FROM COLD ESTOTILAND, AND SOUTH AS FARR . . . 10 686
AVOIDED PINCHING COLD AND SCORCHING HEATE? . . . 10 691
OUTSTRETCHT HE LAY, ON THE COLD GROUND, AND OFT . 10 851
MY LABOUR WILL SUSTAIN ME; AND LEAST COLD . . 10 1056
LEAVE COLD THE NIGHT, HOW WE HIS GATHER'D BEAMS . 10 1070
ADAM BY THIS FROM THE COLD SUDDEN DAMP 11 293
A MELANCHOLLY DAMP OF COLD AND DRY 11 544

COLIC
INTESTIN STONE AND ULCER, COLIC PANGS, ... 11 484

COLLATERAL
COLLATERAL LOVE, AND DEEREST AMITIE. 8 426
OF HIGH COLLATERAL GLORIE: HIM THRONES AND POWERS, 10 86

COLLECTED
COLLECTED STOOD WITHIN OUR THOUGHTS AMUS'D, . . . 6 581
STOOD IN HIMSELF COLLECTED, WHILE EACH PART, . . 9 673

COLLECTING
COLLECTING ALL HIS MIGHT DILATED STOOD, ... 4 986

COLLEGUE
MERCIE COLLEGUE WITH JUSTICE, SENDING THEE . . . 10 59

COLLISION
OR BY COLLISION OF TWO BODIES GRINDE 10 1072

COLLOQUIE
IN THAT CELESTIAL COLLOQUIE SUBLIME, ... 8 455

COLOUR
OF COLOUR GLORIOUS AND EFFECT SO RARE? 3 612
THEY LIMB THEMSELVES, AND COLOUR, SHAPE OR SIZE . 6 352
LIKE HIS, AND COLOUR SERPENTINE MAY SHEW . . . 10 870

COLOUR'D
BROIDERD THE GROUND, MORE COLOUR'D THEN WITH STONE 4 702
ADORNS HIM, COLOUR'D WITH THE FLORID HUE . . . 7 445
HIS TRIPLE-COLOUR'D BOW, WHEREON TO LOOK . . . 11 897

COLOURD
OF MANY A COLOURD PLUME SPRINKL'D WITH GOLD, . . 3 642
BUT SAY, WHAT MEAN THOSE COLOURD STREAKS IN HEAVN, 11 879

COLOURS
WITH ORIENT COLOURS WAVING: WITH THEM ROSE . . . 1 546
APPEERD, WITH GAY ENAMELD COLOURS MIXT: 4 149
HOW NATURE PAINTS HER COLOURS, HOW THE BEE . . . 5 24
AND COLOURS DIPT IN HEAV'N; THE THIRD HIS FEET . 5 283
AMBER, AND COLOURS OF THE SHOWRIE ARCH. 6 759
OP'NING THIR VARIOUS COLOURS, AND MADE GAY . . . 7 318
LOADEN WITH FRUIT OF FAIREST COLOURS MIXT, . . . 9 577
CONSPICUOUS WITH THREE LIFTED COLOURS GAY, . . . 11 866

COLUMBUS
COLUMBUS FOUND TH' AMERICAN SO GIRT 9 1116

COLURE
FROM POLE TO POLE, TRAVERSING EACH COLURE; . . . 9 66

COM
HIM THROUGH THE SPICIE FORREST ONWARD COM . . . 5 298
HENCEFORTH WHAT IS TO COM I WILL RELATE, . . . 12 11
UNSEEN BEFORE IN HEAV'N PROCLAIMS HIM COM, . . . 12 361

COMBAT
TO MORTAL COMBAT OR CARREER WITH LANCE) 1 766
SHOULD COMBAT, AND THIR JARRING SPHEARS CONFOUND. 6 315

COMBATANTS
SO FROWND THE MIGHTY COMBATANTS, THAT HELL . . . 2 719

COMBIN'D
OF ALL THE SERAPHIM WITH THEE COMBIN'D 2 750
SO FITLY THEM IN PAIRS THOU HAST COMBIN'D; 8 394
AS NOT SECURE TO SINGLE OR COMBIN'D. 9 339

COMBROUS
FAIREST AND EASIEST OF THIS COMBROUS CHARGE, 11 549

COMBUSTIBLE
OF THUNDRING AETNA, WHOSE COMBUSTIBLE 1 233

COMBUSTION
WITH HIDEOUS RUINE AND COMBUSTION DOWN 1 46
DREADFUL COMBUSTION WARRING, AND DISTURB, 6 225

COME
WITH HEAV'NS ARTILLERY FRAUGHT, COME RATTLING ON 2 715
I COME NO ENEMIE, BUT TO SET FREE 2 822
CHAOS AND ANCIENT NIGHT, I COME NO SPY, 2 970
THE VIGILANCE HERE PLAC'T, BUT SUCH AS COME 4 580
BUT COME, FOR THOU, BE SURE, SHALT GIVE ACCOUNT 4 841
THOU SURELY HADST NOT COME SOLE FUGITIVE. 4 923
MAY COME AND GO, SO UNAPPROV'D, AND LEAVE 5 118
SOON AS THEY FORTH WERE COME TO OPEN SIGHT 5 138
THIR GLITTERING TENTS HE PASSD, AND NOW IS COME 5 291
TO PROPER SUBSTANCE; TIME MAY COME WHEN MEN 5 493
THITHER TO COME, AND WITH CALUMNIOUS ART 5 770
O FRIENDS, WHY COME NOT ON THESE VICTORS PROUD? 6 609
HEREAFTER, WHEN THEY COME TO MODEL HEAV'N 8 79
FIRST FATHER, CALL'D BY THEE I COME THY GUIDE 8 298
TO COME AND PLAY BEFORE THEE, KNOW'ST THOU NOT 8 372
ALL HUMAN THOUGHTS COME SHORT, SUPREAM OF THINGS; 8 414
THOU SEVER NOT: TRIAL WILL COME UNSOUGHT. 9 366
MEER SERPENT IN APPEARANCE, FORTH WAS COME, 9 413
MEE THUS, THOUGH IMPORTUNE PERHAPS, TO COME 9 610
BUT COME, SO WELL REFRESH'T, NOW LET US PLAY. 9 1027
FORETOLD SO LATELY WHAT WOULD COME TO PASS, 10 38
OR COME I LESS CONSPICUOUS, OR WHAT CHANGE 10 107
ABSENTS THEE, OR WHAT CHANCE DETAINS? COME FORTH. 10 108
WHERE ARMIES LIE ENCAMPT, COME FLYING, LUR'D 10 276
TO ADAM WHAT SHALL COME IN FUTURE DAYES, 11 114
PERMITS NOT; TO REMOVE THEE I AM COME, 11 260
ALL GENERATIONS, AND HAD HITHER COME 11 344
TO SHEW THEE WHAT SHALL COME IN FUTURE DAYES 11 357
THESE TWO ARE BRETHREN, ADAM, AND TO COME 11 454
THESE PAINFUL PASSAGES, HOW WE MAY COME 11 528
AND UTTER ODIOUS TRUTH, THAT GOD WOULD COME 11 704
AND FULL OF PEACE, DENOUNCING WRAUTH TO COME 11 815
SAVE WHEN THEY JOURNIE, AND AT LENGTH THEY COME, 12 258
ABOVE ALL NAMES IN HEAV'N; AND THENCE SHALL COME, 12 458
BY NAME TO COME CALL'D CHARITIE, THE SOUL 12 584
THE GREAT DELIVERANCE BY HER SEED TO COME 12 600

COMELY
FLUCTUATS DISTURBD, YET COMELY AND IN ACT 9 668

COMES
AND REST CAN NEVER DWELL, HOPE NEVER COMES 1 66
THAT COMES TO ALL; BUT TORTURE WITHOUT END 1 67
IN SECRET, RIDING THROUGH THE AIR SHE COMES 2 663
COMES UNPREVENTED, UNIMPLOR'D, UNSOUGHT, 3 231
SO ON HE FARES, AND TO THE BORDER COMES, 4 131
AND WITH THEM COMES A THIRD OF REGAL PORT, 4 869
COMES THIS WAY MOVING; SEEMS ANOTHER MORN 5 310
TO GRATEFUL TWILIGHT (FOR NIGHT COMES NOT THERE 5 645
HE COMES, AND SETTL'D IN HIS FACE I SEE 6 540
EARLY, AND TH' HOUR OF SUPPER COMES UNEARN'D. 9 225
COMES THUNDRING BACK WITH DREADFUL REVOLUTION 10 814
THE DAY OF HIS OFFENCE. WHY COMES NOT DEATH, 10 854
BUT DEATH COMES NOT AT CALL, JUSTICE DIVINE 10 858
THY MORTAL PASSAGE WHEN IT COMES. ASCEND 11 366
HOW COMES IT THUS? UNFOULD, CELESTIAL GUIDE, 11 785
COMES DOWN TO SEE THIR CITIE, ERE THE TOWER 12 51
HE COMES INVITED BY A YONGER SON 12 160
WHICH HEE, WHO COMES THY SAVIOUR, SHALL RECURE, 12 393

COMET
UNTERRIFI'D, AND LIKE A COMET BURN'D, 2 708
FIERCE AS A COMET; WHICH WITH TORRID HEAT, 12 634

COMFORTABLE
AND SENDS A COMFORTABLE HEAT FROM FARR, 10 1077

COMFORTER
HEE TO HIS OWN A COMFORTER WILL SEND, 12 486

COMFORTLESS
THOUGH COMFORTLESS, AS WHEN A FATHER MOURNS 11 760

COMFORTS
BY HIM WITH MANY COMFORTS, TILL WE END 10 1084

COMING
HAPPIE FOR MAN, SO COMING; HE HER AIDE 3 232
THE COMING OF THIR SECRET FOE, AND SCAP'D 4 7
THY COMING, AND THY SOFT IMBRACES, HEE 4 471
AFTER SOFT SHOWERS; AND SWEET THE COMING ON 4 646
RECEIVE HIM COMING TO RECEIVE FROM US 5 781

COMING (CONTINUED)
ERE WHILE THEY FIERCE WERE COMING, AND WHEN WEE, 6 610
WHEN COMING TOWARDS THEM SO DREAD THEY SAW 6 648
HE ONWARD CAME, FARR OFF HIS COMING SHON, 6 768
AND SPIRIT COMING TO CREATE NEW WORLDS. 7 209
HER NURSERIE; THEY AT HER COMING SPRUNG 8 46
SERPENT, WE MIGHT HAVE SPAR'D OUR COMING HITHER, 9 647
MY COMING SEEN FAR OFF? I MISS THEE HERE, 10 104
INVESTS HIM COMING? YET NOT TERRIBLE, 11 233
INCLIN'D NOT, BUT HIS COMING THUS DECLAR'D. 11 250
HE SHALL ENDURE BY COMING IN THE FLESH 12 405

COMLINESS
SPEAKING OR MUTE ALL COMLINESS AND GRACE 8 222

COMMAND
AWAITING WHAT COMMAND THIR MIGHTY CHIEF 1 566
MEAN WHILE THE WINGED HARALDS BY COMMAND 1 752
AND BY COMMAND OF HEAV'NS ALL-POWERFUL KING 2 851
AND EASILY TRANSGRESS THE SOLE COMMAND, 3 94
STAND READY AT COMMAND, AND ARE HIS EYES 3 650
AWAITING NEXT COMMAND. TO WHOM THIR CHIEF 4 864
OUR MAKER, AND OBEY HIM WHOSE COMMAND 5 551
TELL THEM THAT BY COMMAND, ERE YET DIM NIGHT 5 685
AT WHICH COMMAND THE POWERS MILITANT, 6 61
AT HIS COMMAND THE UPROOTED HILLS RETIR'D 6 781
IF THEY TRANSGRESS, AND SLIGHT THAT SOLE COMMAND, 7 47
FOR HASTE; SUCH FLIGHT THE GREAT COMMAND IMPRESS'D 7 294
SQUAR'D IN FULL LEGION (SUCH COMMAND WE HAD) 8 232
THE DAY THOU EAT'ST THEREOF, MY SOLE COMMAND 8 329
REPLENISHT, AND ALL THESE AT THY COMMAND 8 371
HIS GREAT COMMAND; TAKE HEED LEAST PASSION SWAY 8 635
GOD SO COMMANDED, AND LEFT THAT COMMAND 9 652
COMMAND ME ABSOLUTELY NOT TO GO, 9 1156
DEPARTING GAVE COMMAND, AND THEY OBSERV'D. 10 430
HIS EYE MIGHT THERE COMMAND WHEREVER STOOD 11 385
THE ONE JUST MAN ALIVE; BY HIS COMMAND 11 818
AND CRAZE THIR CHARIOT WHEELS: WHEN BY COMMAND 12 210

COMMANDED
PRETENDING SO COMMANDED TO CONSULT 5 768
GOD SO COMMANDED, AND LEFT THAT COMMAND 9 652

COMMANDER
THIR GREAT COMMANDER; GODLIKE SHAPES AND FORMS 1 358
THIR DREAD COMMANDER: HE ABOVE THE REST 1 589

COMMANDING
THAT THE MOST HIGH COMMANDING, NOW ERE NIGHT, 5 699
SATAN; AND THUS WAS HEARD COMMANDING LOUD. 6 557
MANS VOICE COMMANDING, SUN IN GIBEON STAND, 12 265

COMMANDS
THEN STRAIT COMMANDS THAT AT THE WARLIKE SOUND 1 531
BUT WHAT OW I TO HIS COMMANDS ABOVE 2 856
UNDAZL'D, FARR AND WIDE HIS EYE COMMANDS, 3 614
ENVIOUS COMMANDS, INVENTED WITH DESIGNE 4 524
PURE, AND COMMANDS TO SOM, LEAVES FREE TO ALL. 4 747
THE GREAT MESSIAH, AND HIS NEW COMMANDS, 5 691
THE DEITIE, AND DIVINE COMMANDS OBEI'D, 5 806

COMMANDST
WHAT THOU COMMANDST, AND RIGHT THOU SHOULDST BE
OBEYD: 9 570

COMMENDS
COMMENDS THEE MORE, WHILE IT INFERRS THE GOOD 9 754

COMMER
THOSE MIDDLE PARTS, THAT THIS NEW COMMER, SHAME, 9 1097

COMMISERATION
COMMISERATION; SOON HIS HEART RELENTED 10 940

COMMISSION
THY HEARING, SUCH COMMISSION FROM ABOVE 7 118

COMMIT
HOW NATURE WISE AND FRUGAL COULD COMMIT 8 26

COMMITTED
TO ME COMMITTED AND BY ME EXPOS'D. 10 957

COMMODIOUSLY
TO PASS COMMODIOUSLY THIS LIFE, SUSTAIN'D 10 1083

COMMON
COMMON REVENGE, AND INTERRUPT HIS JOY 2 371
IN PARADISE OF ALL THINGS COMMON ELSE. 4 752
THE ANGEL, NOR IN MIST, THE COMMON GLOSS 5 435
IN COMMON, RANG'D IN FIGURE WEDGE THIR WAY, 7 426
TO THEM MADE COMMON AND DIVULG'D, IF AUGHT 8 583
IN PROCREATION COMMON TO ALL KINDES 8 597
MADE COMMON AND UNHALLOWD ERE OUR TASTE; 9 931

COMMONALTIE
OF COMMONALTIE: SWARMING NEXT APPEER'D 7 489

COMMOTION
IN THIS COMMOTION, BUT THE STARRIE COPE 4 992
OF SUCH COMMOTION, SUCH AS TO SET FORTH 6 310
AND THIS PERVERSE COMMOTION GOVERND THUS, 6 706
COMMOTION STRANGE, IN ALL ENJOYMENTS ELSE 8 531

COMMUNE
THEN COMMUNE HOW THAT DAY THEY BEST MAY PLY 9 201

COMMUNICABLE
TO NONE COMMUNICABLE IN EARTH OR HEAVEN: 7 124

COMMUNICATED
COMMUNICATED, MORE ABUNDANT GROWES, 5 72
BY THEE COMMUNICATED, AND OUR WANT: 9 755

COMMUNICATING
COMMUNICATING MALE AND FEMAL LIGHT, 8 150

COMMUNICATION
SOCIAL COMMUNICATION, YET SO PLEAS'D, 8 429

COMMUNION
THEY EATE, THEY DRINK, AND IN COMMUNION SWEET 5 637
OF UNION OR COMMUNION, DEIFI'D; 8 431

COMPACT
COMPACT OF UNCTUOUS VAPOR, WHICH THE NIGHT 9 635

COMPANIE
AND NO SUCH COMPANIE AS THEN THOU SAW'ST 8 446

COMPANION
SLEEPST THOU COMPANION DEAR, WHAT SLEEP CAN CLOSE 5 673
THEE ONCE TO GAINE COMPANION OF HIS WOE. 6 907

COMPANIONS
THERE THE COMPANIONS OF HIS FALL, O'REWHELM'D 1 76
NOT TO BE OVERPOWERD, COMPANIONS DEARE, 6 419

COMPAR'D
COMPAR'D WITH AUGHT ON EARTH, MEDAL OR STONE; 3 592
AS BOTH THIR DEEDS COMPAR'D THIS DAY SHALL PROVE. 6 170
AN ATOM, WITH THE FIRMAMENT COMPAR'D 8 18
SO, IF GREAT THINGS TO SMALL MAY BE COMPAR'D, 10 306

COMPARE
COMPARE OF MORTAL PROWESS, YET OBSERV'D 1 588
WITH NOISES LOUD AND RUINOUS (TO COMPARE 2 921
BEYOND COMPARE THE SON OF GOD WAS SEEN 3 138
AS MAY COMPARE WITH HEAVEN; AND TO TASTE 5 432
AT HEAV'NS HIGH FEASTS TO HAVE FED: YET WHAT COMPARE? 5 467
IN HEAV'N AND HELL THY POWER ABOVE COMPARE, 6 705
COMPARE ABOVE ALL LIVING CREATURES DEARE, 9 228

COMPARISON
THOUGH, IN COMPARISON OF HEAV'N, SO SMALL, 8 92

COMPASS
ADORE HIM, WHO TO COMPASS ALL THIS DIES, 3 342
FROM WHAT POINT OF HIS COMPASS TO BEWARE 4 559
THAT BETTER MIGHT WITH FARR LESS COMPASS MOVE, 8 33

COMPASSES
HE TOOK THE GOLDEN COMPASSES, PREPAR'D 7 225

COMPASSING
FROM COMPASSING THE EARTH, CAUTIOUS OF DAY, 9 59
STILL FOLLOWING THEE, STILL COMPASSING THEE ROUND 11 352

COMPASSION
DIVINE COMPASSION VISIBLY APPEERD, 3 141
THOUGH NOT OF WOMAN BORN; COMPASSION QUELL'D 11 496

COMPASST
WITH TERRORS AND WITH CLAMORS COMPASST ROUND 2 862

COMPAST
IN DARKNESS, AND WITH DANGERS COMPAST ROUND, 7 27

COMPEER
AND HIM THUS ANSWER'D SOON HIS BOLD COMPEER. 1 127

COMPEERS
RIDE ON THY WINGS, AND THOU WITH THY COMPEERS, 4 974

COMPEL
WE SHOULD COMPEL THEM TO A QUICK RESULT. 6 619

COMPEL'D
EQUIVALENT OR SECOND, WHICH COMPEL'D 9 609

COMPELLD
MUST BE COMPELLD BY SIGNES AND JUDGEMENTS DIRE; 12 175

COMPELS
BY CONQUERING THIS NEW WORLD, COMPELS ME NOW 4 391

COMPLACENCE
MY SOLE COMPLACENCE. WELL THOU KNOW'ST HOW DEAR, 3 276
FROM PRONE, NOR IN THIR WAYES COMPLACENCE FIND. 8 433

COMPLAIN
BY DOOM OF BATTEL; AND COMPLAIN THAT FATE 2 550

COMPLAINT
BY MY COMPLAINT; BUT STRICT NECESSITIE 10 131
THUS TO DISBURD'N SOUGHT WITH SAD COMPLAINT. 10 719

COMPLEAT
ACCOMPANI'D THEN WITH HIS OWN COMPLEAT 5 352
AND IN HER SELF COMPLEAT, SO WELL TO KNOW 8 548

COMPLEATING
WEPT AT COMPLEATING OF THE MORTAL SIN 9 1003

COMPLETE
COMPLETE TO HAVE DISCOVER'D AND REPULST 10 10

COMPLETED
BRED ONELY AND COMPLETED TO THE TASTE 11 618

COMPLIANCE
AND SWEET COMPLIANCE, WHICH DECLARE UNFEIGN'D 8 603
IN RECOMPENCE (FOR SUCH COMPLIANCE BAD 9 994

COMPLIANT
NECTARINE FRUITS WHICH THE COMPLIANT BOUGHES 4 332

COMPLICATED
WITH COMPLICATED MONSTERS HEAD AND TAILE, 10 523

COMPOS'D
TH' INFECTION WHEN THIR BORROW'D GOLD COMPOS'D 1 483
FOR DIGNITY COMPOS'D AND HIGH EXPLOIT: 2 111
WHERETO WITH LOOK COMPOS'D SATAN REPLI'D. 6 469
PORTENDING GOOD, AND ALL HER SPIRITS COMPOS'D 12 596

COMPOSE
COMPOSE OUR PRESENT EVILS, WITH REGARD 2 281

COMPOSITION
OF COMPOSITION, STRAIT THEY CHANG'D THIR MINDS, 6 613

COMPOSURE
PEACE AND COMPOSURE, AND WITH OPEN BREST 6 560
WITH SWEET AUSTEER COMPOSURE THUS REPLY'D, 9 272

COMPREHEND
BUT WHAT CREATED MIND CAN COMPREHEND 3 705
CAN COMPREHEND, INCAPABLE OF MORE, 5 505
OR HEART OF MAN SUFFICE TO COMPREHEND? 7 114

COMPULSION
WITH WHAT COMPULSION AND LABORIOUS FLIGHT 2 80
COMPULSION THUS TRANSPORTED TO FORGET 9 474

COMPUTE
THIR STARRY DANCE IN NUMBERS THAT COMPUTE 3 580
TWO DAYES, AS WE COMPUTE THE DAYES OF HEAV'N, 6 685
OF HEAV'N AND EARTH CONSISTING, AND COMPUTE, 8 16

COM'ST
COM'ST THOU, ESCAP'D THY PRISON, AND TRANSFORM'D, 4 824

COMST
OMNIPOTENCE TO NONE. BUT WELL THOU COMST 6 159

CONCAVE
A SHOUT THAT TORE HELLS CONCAVE, AND BEYOND 1 542
UP TO THE FIERY CONCAVE TOURING HIGH. 2 635

CONCEAL
DID WISELY TO CONCEAL, AND NOT DIVULGE 8 73
I SHOULD CONCEAL, AND NOT EXPOSE TO BLAME 10 130

CONCEAL'D
PUT FORTH AT FULL, BUT STILL HIS STRENGTH CONCEAL'D, 1 641
WARR THEREFORE, OPEN OR CONCEAL'D, ALIKE 2 187

CONCEALD
NOR THOSE MYSTERIOUS PARTS WERE THEN CONCEALD, 4 312
HAVE GATHERED AUGHT OF EVIL OR CONCEALD, 5 207

CONCEALE
DEEP MALICE TO CONCEALE, COUCH'T WITH REVENGE: 4 123
WOULDST EASILY DETECT WHAT I CONCEALE. 10 136

CONCEALES
CONCEALES NOT FROM US, NAMING THEE THE TREE 9 751

CONCEAV'D
NOT WELL CONCEAV'D OF GOD, WHO THOUGH HIS POWER 9 945

CONCEAVE
FERMENTED THE GREAT MOTHER TO CONCEAVE, 7 281

CONCEAVES
ADJOYND, FROM EACH THING MET CONCEAVES DELIGHT, 9 449

CONCEITS
BLOWN UP WITH HIGH CONCEITS INGENDRING PRIDE. 4 809

CONCEIV'D
THAN FABLES YET HAVE FEIGN'D, OR FEAR CONCEIV'D, 2 627
WITH ME IN SECRET, THAT MY WOMB CONCEIV'D 2 766
SURROUND ME, AS THOU SAWST, HOURLY CONCEIV'D 2 796

CONCEIVING
AND FEWEL'D ENTRALS THENCE CONCEIVING FIRE, 1 234
DEEP MALICE THENCE CONCEIVING AND DISDAIN, 5 666
INSENSATE, HOPE CONCEIVING FROM DESPAIR. 6 787

CONCENTRING
IN THEE CONCENTRING ALL THIR PRECIOUS BEAMS 9 106

CONCEPTION
CONCEPTION; SULPHUROUS AND NITROUS FOAME 6 512
BY THY CONCEPTION; CHILDREN THOU SHALT BRING 10 194
IT LIES, YET ERE CONCEPTION TO PREVENT 10 987

CONCERN
WHAT NEERER MIGHT CONCERN HIM, HOW THIS WORLD 7 62
CHIEFLY WHAT MAY CONCERN HER FAITH TO KNOW, 12 599

CONCERN'D
CONCERN'D NOT MAN (SINCE HE NO FURTHER KNEW) 10 170

CONCERND
THINGS ABOVE EARTHLY THOUGHT, WHICH YET CONCERND 7 82

CONCERNE
AND RENDERS US IN THINGS THAT MOST CONCERNE 8 196
SO PREVALENT AS TO CONCERNE THE MIND 11 144
THOU HAST REVEALD, THOSE CHIEFLY WHICH CONCERNE 12 272

CONCERNES
NEERLY IT NOW CONCERNES US TO BE SURE 5 721
THINK ONELY WHAT CONCERNES THEE AND THY BEING; 8 174

CONCERNING
AND EATEN OF THE TREE CONCERNING WHICH 10 199

CONCLAVE
IN CLOSE RECESS AND SECRET CONCLAVE SAT 1 795

CONCLUDE
SUCH PROOF, CONCLUDE, THEY THEN BEGIN TO FAILE. 9 1142
THE BLOUD OF BULLS AND GOATS, THEY MAY CONCLUDE 12 292

CONCLUDES
OF REFUGE, AND CONCLUDES THEE MISERABLE 10 839

CONCOCT
TASTING CONCOCT, DIGEST, ASSIMILATE, 5 412

CONCOCTED
CONCOCTED AND ADUSTED THEY REDUC'D 6 514

CONCOCTIVE
OF REAL HUNGER, AND CONCOCTIVE HEATE 5 437

CONCORD
FIRM CONCORD HOLDS, MEN ONELY DISAGREE 2 497
MELODIOUS PART, SUCH CONCORD IS IN HEAV'N. 3 371
GREAT THINGS BY SMALL, IF NATURES CONCORD BROKE, 6 311
CONCORD AND LAW OF NATURE FROM THE EARTH, 12 29

CONCOURS
CONCOURS IN ARMS, FIERCE FACES THREATNING WARR, 11 641

CONCUPISCENCE
OF FOUL CONCUPISCENCE; WHENCE EVIL STORE; 9 1078

CONCURD
CONCURD NOT TO MY BEING, IT WERE BUT RIGHT 10 747

CONCURRING
SHOULD BE, AND, BY CONCURRING SIGNS, ERE NOW 2 831
CONCURRING TO NECESSITATE HIS FALL, 10 44

CONDEMN'D
(FAR OTHER ONCE BEHELD IN BLISS) CONDEMN'D 1 607
THEN TO DWELL HERE, DRIV'N OUT FROM BLISS, CONDEMN'D 2 86
AND THEY OUTCAST FROM GOD, ARE HERE CONDEMN'D 2 694
THOSE TWO; THE THIRD BEST ABSENT IS CONDEMN'D, 10 82
FOR ONE MANS FAULT THUS GUILTLESS BE CONDEMN'D, 10 823

CONDEMND
SEIS'D ON BY FORCE, JUDG'D, AND TO DEATH CONDEMND 12 412

CONDEMNE
CANST THOU WITH IMPIOUS OBLOQUIE CONDEMNE 5 813

CONDEMNING
THE FRUITLESS HOURS, BUT NEITHER SELF-CONDEMNING, 9 1188

CONDEMNS
YOUR BULWARK, AND CONDEMNS TO GREATEST SHARE 2 29

CONDENSE
ASSUME, AS LIKES THEM BEST, CONDENSE OR RARE. 6 353

CONDENSES
CONDENSES, AND THE COLD INVIRONS ROUND, 9 636

CONDENS'T
DILATED OR CONDENS'T, BRIGHT OR OBSCURE, 1 429

CONDESCENSION
THY CONDESCENSION, AND SHALL BE HONOUR'D EVER 8 649

CONDESCENTION
THIS FRIENDLY CONDESCENTION TO RELATE 8 9

CONDITION
HIS FALL'N CONDITION IS, AND TO ME OW 3 181
LIVE, IN WHAT STATE, CONDITION OR DEGREE, 8 176
IF THIS BE OUR CONDITION, THUS TO DWELL 9 322

CONDITIONS
THEN CAVIL THE CONDITIONS? AND THOUGH GOD 10 759

CONDUCT
UNDER THY CONDUCT, AND IN DREADFUL DEEDS 1 130
UNDER WHOSE CONDUCT MICHAEL SOON REDUC'D 6 777
MY CONDUCT, I CAN BRING THEE THITHER SOON. 9 630

CONDUCTED
CONDUCTED BY HIS ANGEL TO THE LAND 12 259

CONE
NOW HAD NIGHT MEASUR'D WITH HER SHADDOWIE CONE 4 776

CONFER
NEW RUB'D WITH BAUM, EXPATIATE AND CONFER 1 774

CONFERENCE
GIVEN HIM BY THIS GREAT CONFERENCE TO KNOW 5 454

CONFERRD
CONFERRD UPON US, AND DOMINION GIV'N 4 430

CONFESS
BEHOLDING SHALL CONFESS THAT HERE ON EARTH 5 329
ALL KNEES IN HEAV'N, AND SHALL CONFESS HIM LORD: 5 608
CONFESS HIM RIGHTFUL KING? UNJUST THOU SAIST 5 818
WHICH I ENJOY, AND MUST CONFESS TO FIND 8 523
BEFORE HIM REVERENT, AND THERE CONFESS 10 1088

CONFESS'D
BEFORE HIM REVERENT, AND BOTH CONFESS'D 10 1100

CONFESSING
CONFESSING SOON, YET NOT BEFORE HER JUDGE 10 160

CONFEST
GODS, YET CONFEST LATER THEN HEAV'N AND EARTH 1 509

CONFIDE
AS RAPHAEL, THAT I SHOULD MUCH CONFIDE, 11 235

CONFIDENCE
HIS CONFIDENCE TO EQUAL GOD IN POWER, 6 343
THEY SAW THEM WHELM'D, AND ALL THIR CONFIDENCE 6 651
JUST CONFIDENCE, AND NATIVE RIGHTEOUSNESS 9 1056
BUT CONFIDENCE THEN BORE THEE ON, SECURE 9 1175

CONFIN'D
TO SIT IN HATEFUL OFFICE HERE CONFIN'D, 2 859
STOOD RUL'D, STOOD VAST INFINITUDE CONFIN'D; 3 711
THOU HAST ATCHIEV'D OUR LIBERTIE, CONFIN'D 10 368
HIS PRESENCE TO THESE NARROW BOUNDS CONFIN'D 11 341

CONFIND
THY SELF A GODDESS, NOT TO EARTH CONFIND, 5 78

CONFINE
CONFINE WITH HEAV'N; OR IF SOM OTHER PLACE 2 977

CONFINES
OF THOSE BRIGHT CONFINES, WHENCE WITH NEIGHBOURING ARMS 2 395
FROM ALL HER CONFINES. HEAV'N THE SEAT OF BLISS 6 273
THE CONFINES MET OF EMPYREAN HEAV'N 10 321

CONFIRM
HE SPAKE: AND TO CONFIRM HIS WORDS, OUT-FLEW 1 663

CONFIRM'D
THAT SHOOK HEAV'NS WHOL CIRCUMFERENCE, CONFIRM'D. 2 353
A DEATH TO THINK. CONFIRM'D THEN I RESOLVE, . . 9 830

CONFIRMD
AND IN THIR STATE, THOUGH FIRM, STOOD MORE CONFIRMD. 11 71
WHICH THAT THOU MAYST BELEEVE, AND BE CONFIRMD . 11 355

CONFLAGRANT
FROM THE CONFLAGRANT MASS, PURG'D AND REFIN'D, . 12 548

CONFLICT
WITH VIOLENCE OF THIS CONFLICT, HAD NOT SOON . . 4 995
OF CONFLICT; OVER HEAD THE DISMAL HISS 6 212

CONFLICTING
CONFLICTING FIRE: LONG TIME IN EEVEN SCALE . . . 6 245

CONFORMD
OR CHANG'D AT LENGTH, AND TO THE PLACE CONFORMD . 2 217

CONFORMITIE
HOLIE AND PURE, CONFORMITIE DIVINE. 11 606

CONFOUND
WITH BLACKEST INSURRECTION, TO CONFOUND 2 136
SO DEEP A MALICE, TO CONFOUND THE RACE 2 382
SHOULD COMBAT, AND THIR JARRING SPHEARS CONFOUND. 6 315
THIR CORNERS, WHEN WITH BLUSTER TO CONFOUND . . 10 665
TO HUMANE LIFE, AND HOUSHOLD PEACE CONFOUND. . . 10 908

CONFOUNDED
CONFOUNDED THOUGH IMMORTAL: BUT HIS DOOM . . . 1 53
CONFUSION WORSE CONFOUNDED; AND HEAV'N GATES . . 2 996
NINE DAYES THEY FELL; CONFOUNDED CHAOS ROARD, . . 6 871
CONFOUNDED LONG THEY SATE, AS STRUCK'N MUTE, . . 9 1064
THROUGH ALL HIS REALME, AND THERE CONFOUNDED LEAVE; 12 455

CONFUS'D
IN CONFUS'D MARCH FORLORN, TH' ADVENTROUS BANDS . 2 615
OF STUNNING SOUNDS AND VOICES ALL CONFUS'D . . . 2 952
OF FIGHTING SERAPHIM CONFUS'D, AT LENGTH . . . 6 249

CONFUS'DLY
CONFUS'DLY, AND WHICH THUS MUST EVER FIGHT, . . 2 914

CONFUSION
TREBLE CONFUSION, WRATH AND VENGEANCE POUR'D, . . 1 220
IN OUR CONFUSION, AND OUR JOY UPRAISE 2 372
OF ENDLESS WARRS, AND BY CONFUSION STAND. . . . 2 897
AND TUMULT AND CONFUSION ALL IMBROIL'D, ... 2 966
CONFUSION WORSE CONFOUNDED; AND HEAV'N GATES . . 2 996
CONFUSION HEARD HIS VOICE, AND WILDE UPROAR . . 3 710
TO THIS UPROAR; HORRID CONFUSION HEAPT 6 668
UPON CONFUSION ROSE: AND NOW ALL HEAV'N 6 669
AND FELT TENFOLD CONFUSION IN THIR FALL 6 872
WITH SUCH CONFUSION: BUT THE EVIL SOON 7 56
OF HORRIBLE CONFUSION, OVER WHICH 10 472
RIDICULOUS, AND THE WORK CONFUSION NAM'D. . . . 12 62
LEFT IN CONFUSION, BABYLON THENCE CALL'D. . . . 12 343

CONGLOB'D
ADVERSE TO LIFE: THEN FOUNDED, THEN CONGLOB'D . . 7 239

CONGLOBING
AS DROPS ON DUST CONGLOBING FROM THE DRIE; . . . 7 292

CONGO
OF CONGO, AND ANGOLA FARDEST SOUTH; 11 401

CONGRATULANT
CONGRATULANT APPROACH'D HIM, WHO WITH HAND . . . 10 458

CONGREGATED
OF CONGREGATED WATERS HE CALL'D SEAS: 7 308

CONGREGATION
THE MOUNTAIN OF THE CONGREGATION CALL'D; . . . 5 766

CONJECTURE
OMINOUS CONJECTURE ON THE WHOLE SUCCESS: . . . 2 123
IF I CONJECTURE AUGHT, NO DRIZLING SHOWR, . . . 6 545
CONJECTURE, HE HIS FABRIC OF THE HEAV'NS . . . 8 76
BE MEANT, WHOM I CONJECTURE, OUR GRAND FOE . . . 10 1033

CONJUGAL
OF CONJUGAL ATTRACTION UNREPROV'D, ... 4 493
WITH CONJUGAL CARESSES, FROM HIS LIP 8 56
CONJUGAL LOVE, THEN WHICH PERHAPS NO BLISS . . . 9 263

CONJUNCTION
AND STRAIGHT CONJUNCTION WITH THIS SEX; FOR EITHER 10 898

CONJUR'D
CONJUR'D AGAINST THE HIGHEST, FOR WHICH BOTH THOU 2 693

CONNATURAL
OR SYMPATHIE, OR SOM CONNATURAL FORCE 10 246
TO DEATH, AND MIX WITH OUR CONNATURAL DUST? . . 11 529

CONNEXION
STILL MOVES WITH THINE, JOIN'D IN CONNEXION SWEET, 10 359

CONNIVING
A PLACE SO HEAV'NLY, AND CONNIVING SEEM 10 624

CONNUBIAL
MYSTERIOUS OF CONNUBIAL LOVE REFUS'D: 4 743

CONQUERD
THE CONQUERD ALSO, AND ENSLAV'D BY WARR 11 797

CONQUERING
BY CONQUERING THIS NEW WORLD, COMPELS ME NOW . . 4 391
SECOND OF SATAN SPRUNG, ALL CONQUERING DEATH, . . 10 591

CONQUEROR
YET EVER PLOTTING HOW THE CONQUEROR LEAST . . . 2 338

CONQUEROUR
BUT WHAT IF HE OUR CONQUEROUR, (WHOM I NOW . . . 1 143
TO ADORE THE CONQUEROUR? WHO NOW BEHOLDS . . . 1 323
AHAZ HIS SOTTISH CONQUEROUR, WHOM HE DREW . . . 1 472
THE SENTENCE OF THIR CONQUEROUR: THIS IS NOW . . 2 208

CONQUEROURS
OF TRIUMPH, TO BE STYL'D GREAT CONQUEROURS, . . 11 695

CONQUEST
MAY REAP HIS CONQUEST, AND MAY LEAST REJOYCE . . 2 339
WITH CONQUEST, FELT TH' ENVENOM'D ROBE, AND TORE . 2 543
JUDG'D THEE PERVERSE: THE EASIER CONQUEST NOW . . 6 37

CONSCIENCE
MY UMPIRE CONSCIENCE, WHOM IF THEY WILL HEAR, . . 3 195
BY CHANGE OF PLACE: NOW CONSCIENCE WAKES DESPAIR . 4 23
HER VERTUE AND THE CONSCIENCE OF HER WORTH, . . 8 502
O CONSCIENCE, INTO WHAT ABYSS OF FEARS 10 842
WHICH TO HIS EVIL CONSCIENCE REPRESENTED . . . 10 849
OF CONSCIENCE, WHICH THE LAW BY CEREMONIES . . . 12 297
ON EVERY CONSCIENCE; LAWS WHICH NONE SHALL FINDE . 12 522
WHO AGAINST FAITH AND CONSCIENCE CAN BE HEARD . . 12 529

CONSCIOUS
CONSCIOUS OF HIGHEST WORTH, UNMOV'D THUS SPAKE. . 2 429
AFRESH WITH CONSCIOUS TERROURS VEX ME ROUND, . . 2 801
SO ALL ERE DAY-SPRING, UNDER CONSCIOUS NIGHT . . 6 521
BRED OF UNKINDLY FUMES, WITH CONSCIOUS DREAMS . . 9 1050

CONSENT
CONSENT OR CUSTOME, AND HIS REGAL STATE 1 640
YIELDED WITH FULL CONSENT. THE HAPPIER STATE . . 2 24
WAKING THOU NEVER WILT CONSENT TO DO. 5 121
BUT MORE DESIRE TO HEAR, IF THOU CONSENT, . . . 5 555

CONSEQUENCE
AND SHUN THE BITTER CONSEQUENCE: FOR KNOW, . . . 8 328
SUCH FATAL CONSEQUENCE UNITES US THREE: 10 364

CONSIDER
THE BENEFIT: CONSIDER FIRST, THAT GREAT 8 90

CONSIDERATE
OF DAUNTLESS COURAGE, AND CONSIDERATE PRIDE . . 1 603

CONSIDER'D
CONSIDER'D EVERY CREATURE, WHICH OF ALL 9 84

CONSIDERD
CONSIDERD ALL THINGS VISIBLE IN HEAV'N, ... 9 604

CONSIST
JARR NOT WITH LIBERTY, BUT WELL CONSIST. . . . 5 793

CONSISTENCE
TREADING THE CRUDE CONSISTENCE, HALF ON FOOT, . . 2 941

CONSISTING
OF HEAV'N AND EARTH CONSISTING, AND COMPUTE, . . 8 16

CONSISTS
WHEREIN TRUE LOVE CONSISTS NOT; LOVE REFINES . . 8 589
YET EMPTY OF ALL GOOD WHEREIN CONSISTS 11 616

CONSOLATION
RECESS, AND ONELY CONSOLATION LEFT 11 304
THIS FURTHER CONSOLATION YET SECURE 12 620

CONSOLATIONS
WITH INWARD CONSOLATIONS RECOMPENC'T, ... 12 495

CONSORT
THE CONSORT OF HIS REIGN; AND BY THEM STOOD . . 2 963
LIKE CONSORT TO THY SELF CANST NO WHERE FIND. . . 4 448

CONSORT (CONTINUED)
WHEN ADAM THUS TO EVE: FAIR CONSORT, TH' HOUR . . 4 610
MALE HE CREATED THEE, BUT THY CONSORT 7 529
CANNOT BE HUMAN CONSORT; THEY REJOYCE 8 392
CONSORT WITH THEE, DEATH IS TO MEE AS LIFE; . . 9 954
HIS CONSORT LIBERTIE; WHAT, BUT UNBUILD 12 526

CONSORTED
THOUGH WANDRING. HE WITH HIS CONSORTED EVE . . 7 50

CONSPICIOUS
OF HEAV'N AND EARTH CONSPICIOUS FIRST BEGAN, . . 7 63

CONSPICUOUS
THEN MOST CONSPICUOUS, WHEN GREAT THINGS OF SMALL, 2 258
IN WHOSE CONSPICUOUS COUNT'NANCE, WITHOUT CLOUD . 3 385
CONSPICUOUS FARR, WINDING WITH ONE ASCENT . . . 4 545
LIKEN ON EARTH CONSPICUOUS, THAT MAY LIFT . . . 6 299
OR COME I LESS CONSPICUOUS, OR WHAT CHANGE . . . 10 107
CONSPICUOUS WITH THREE LIFTED COLOURS GAY, . . . 11 866

CONSPIRACY
IN BOLD CONSPIRACY AGAINST HEAV'NS KING, ... 2 751

CONSPIR'D
TH' EXCEPTED TREE, NOR WITH THE SNAKE CONSPIR'D, . 11 426

CONSTANCIE
WOULDST THOU APPROVE THY CONSTANCIE, APPROVE . . 9 367

CONSTANT
OF TRUE ALLEGIANCE, CONSTANT FAITH OR LOVE, . . 3 104
HIS CONSTANT LAMP, AND WAVES HIS PURPLE WINGS, . 4 764
SINGLE, IS YET SO JUST, MY CONSTANT THOUGHTS . . 5 552
TO SWERVE FROM TRUTH, OR CHANGE HIS CONSTANT MIND 5 902
CONSTANT, MATURE, PROOF AGAINST ALL ASSAULTS, . . 10 882

CONSTELLATIONS
ALOOFF THE VULGAR CONSTELLATIONS THICK, ... 3 577
AMONG THE CONSTELLATIONS WARR WERE SPRUNG, . . . 6 312
THE HEAV'NS AND ALL THE CONSTELLATIONS RUNG, . . 7 562
AND HAPPIE CONSTELLATIONS ON THAT HOURE 8 512
THIR COURSE THROUGH THICKEST CONSTELLATIONS HELD . 10 411

CONSTRAIND
WITH GODS TO SIT THE HIGHEST, AM NOW CONSTRAIND . 9 164
AT LENGTH GAVE UTTERANCE TO THESE WORDS CONSTRAIND. 9 1066

CONSTRAINING
HUNGER AND THIRST CONSTRAINING, DRUGD AS OFT, . . 10 568

CONSTRAINT
THE SECRETS OF YOUR REALM, BUT BY CONSTRAINT . . 2 972
SUBDUES ME, AND CALAMITOUS CONSTRAINT 10 132

CONSULT
CONSULT HOW WE MAY HENCEFORTH MOST OFFEND 1 187
AND SUMMONS READ, THE GREAT CONSULT BEGAN. . . . 1 798
PRETENDING SO COMMANDED TO CONSULT 5 768
THIS ONELY TO CONSULT HOW WE MAY BEST 5 779

CONSULTATION
DUE SEARCH AND CONSULTATION WILL DISCLOSE. . . . 6 445

CONSULTATIONS
THUS THEY THIR DOUBTFUL CONSULTATIONS DARK . . . 2 486

CONSULTING
THUS SITTING, THUS CONSULTING, THUS IN ARMS? . . 2 164
CONSULTING ON THE SUM OF THINGS, FORESEEN . . . 6 673
FORTH RUSH'D IN HASTE THE GREAT CONSULTING PEERS, 10 456

CONSUM'D
CONSUM'D WITH NIMBLE GLANCE, AND GRATEFUL STEAME; 11 442

CONSUME
WILL EITHER QUITE CONSUME US, AND REDUCE 2 96
TO WEIGH THY SPIRITS DOWN, AND LAST CONSUME . . 11 545
FAMIN AND ANGUISH WILL AT LAST CONSUME 11 778

CONSUMES
TO NOURISH, AND SUPERFLUOUS MOIST CONSUMES: . . 5 325

CONSUMMATE
MORE AERIE, LAST THE BRIGHT CONSUMMATE FLOURE . . 5 481
CONSUMMATE LOVLY SMIL'D; AIRE, WATER, EARTH, . . 7 502
OCCASIONALLY; AND TO CONSUMMATE ALL, ... 8 556

CONTAGION
IN THIS PERFIDIOUS FRAUD, CONTAGION SPRED . . . 5 880
CATCHT BY CONTAGION, LIKE IN PUNISHMENT, . . . 10 544

CONTAGIOUS
OF EVE, WHOSE EYE DARTED CONTAGIOUS FIRE. . . . 9 1036

CONTAIN
AND WHAT THY STORES CONTAIN, BRING FORTH AND POURE 5 314
NONE CAN THEN HEAV'N SUCH GLORIOUS SHAPE CONTAIN; 5 362

CONTAIN (CONTINUED)
AS DOTH YOUR RATIONAL; AND BOTH CONTAIN 5 409
IN MEASURE WHAT THE MIND MAY WELL CONTAIN, . . . 7 128

CONTAIND
MEAN, OR IN HER SUMMD UP, IN HER CONTAIND . . . 8 473

CONTAINE
NOR GLISTERING, MAY OF SOLID GOOD CONTAINE . . . 8 93
OF KNOWLEDGE, WHAT THIS VESSEL CAN CONTAINE; . . 12 559

CONTEMN
NOR THOU HIS MALICE AND FALSE GUILE CONTEMN; . . 9 306

CONTEMND
TILL NOW NOT KNOWN, BUT KNOWN AS SOON CONTEMND, . 6 432

CONTEMNES
AND EXCELLENT THEN WHAT THY MINDE CONTEMNES; . . 10 1015

CONTEMPLATION
FOR CONTEMPLATION HEE AND VALOUR FORMD, ... 4 297
IN CONTEMPLATION OF CREATED THINGS 5 511

CONTEMPT
DUE ENTRANCE HE DISDAIND, AND IN CONTEMPT, . . . 4 180
WOULDST THOU ADMIT FOR HIS CONTEMPT OF THEE . . 10 763
EVE, THY CONTEMPT OF LIFE AND PLEASURE SEEMS . . 10 1013
NOT THY CONTEMPT, BUT ANGUISH AND REGRET . . . 10 1018

CONTEMPTIBLY
AND REASON NOT CONTEMPTIBLY; WITH THESE 8 374

CONTEMPTUOUS
TO WHOM THUS SATAN, WITH CONTEMPTUOUS BROW. . . 4 885
CONTEMPTUOUS, AND HIS NEXT SUBORDINATE 5 671

CONTEND
THAT WITH THE MIGHTIEST RAIS'D ME TO CONTEND, . . 1 99
UPON THE WING, OR IN SWIFT RACE CONTEND, . . . 2 529
HELL-BORN, NOT TO CONTEND WITH SPIRITS OF HEAV'N. 2 687
UNDAUNTED. IF I MUST CONTEND, SAID HE, ... 4 851
SERVILITIE WITH FREEDOM TO CONTEND, ... 6 169
BUT RISE, LET US NO MORE CONTEND, NOR BLAME . . 10 958

CONTENDED
O FOUL DESCENT. THAT I WHO ERST CONTENDED . . . 9 163

CONTENDING
CONTENDING, AND SO DOUBTFUL WHAT MIGHT FALL. . . 2 203
EXPECT TO HEAR, SUPERNAL GRACE CONTENDING . . . 11 359
CONTENDING, AND REMOV'D HIS TENTS FARR OFF; . . 11 727

CONTENT
OF UTMOST ARNON. NOR CONTENT WITH SUCH 1 399
NOR SO CONTENT, HATH IN HIS THOUGHT TO TRY . . . 5 727
BUT LIVE CONTENT, WHICH IS THE CALMEST LIFE: . . 6 461
HERE LET US LIVE, THOUGH IN FALL'N STATE, CONTENT. 11 180
OF PROUD AMBITIOUS HEART, WHO NOT CONTENT . . . 12 25

CONTENTED
CONTENTED WITH REPORT HEAR ONELY IN HEAV'N: . . 3 701
ANGELS CONTENTED WITH THIR FAME IN HEAV'N . . . 6 375
CONTENTED THAT THUS FARR HATH BEEN REVEAL'D . . 8 177

CONTENTION
AND TO THE FIERCE CONTENTION BROUGHT ALONG . . . 1 100

CONTENTMENT
OR ALL ENJOYING, WHAT CONTENTMENT FIND? 8 366
THY LOVE, THE SOLE CONTENTMENT OF MY HEART . . . 10 973

CONTENTS
OF HARD CONTENTS, AND FULL OF FORCE URG'D HOME, . 6 622

CONTEST
NOT LIKELY TO PART HENCE WITHOUT CONTEST; . . . 4 872
VICTOR; THOUGH BRUTISH THAT CONTEST AND FOULE, . . 6 124
AND OF THIR VAIN CONTEST APPEER'D NO END. . . . 9 1189
I THUS CONTEST; THEN SHOULD HAVE BEEN REFUSD . . 10 756
IN SHARP CONTEST OF BATTEL FOUND NO AIDE . . . 11 800

CONTIGUOUS
WITH DREADFUL SHADE CONTIGUOUS, AND THE ORBES . . 6 828
CONTIGUOUS MIGHT DISTEMPER THE WHOLE FRAME: . . 7 273

CONTINENT
BEYOND THIS FLOOD A FROZEN CONTINENT 2 587
IT SEEM'D, NOW SEEMS A BOUNDLESS CONTINENT . . . 3 423
FROM HER MOIST CONTINENT TO HIGHER ORBES. . . . 5 422
THIS CONTINENT OF SPACIOUS HEAV'N, ADORND . . . 6 474
HELL AND THIS WORLD, ONE REALM, ONE CONTINENT . . 10 392

CONTINUAL
MAY HAVE DIVERTED FROM CONTINUAL WATCH 9 814

CONTINU'D
FROM HELL CONTINU'D REACHING TH' UTMOST ORBE . . 2 1029

CONTINU'D (CONTINUED)
AS ONE CONTINU'D BRAKE, THE UNDERGROWTH 4 175
THE SPACE OF SEVEN CONTINU'D NIGHTS HE RODE . . 9 63
CONTINU'D MAKING, AND WHO KNOWS HOW LONG . . . 9 138
IMPETUOUS, AND CONTINU'D TILL THE EARTH 11 744

CONTINUE
INCLINES, HERE TO CONTINUE, AND BUILD UP HERE . . 2 314
LONG TO CONTINUE, AND THIS HIGH SEAT YOUR HEAV'N . 4 371

CONTINU'ST
THAT THOU CONTINU'ST SUCH, OWE TO THY SELF, . . 5 521

CONTRACTED
TO WHOM THE ANGEL WITH CONTRACTED BROW. 8 560

CONTRACTION
BY QUICK CONTRACTION OR REMOVE; BUT NOW 6 597

CONTRADICTION
INSPIR'D WITH CONTRADICTION DURST OPPOSE . . . 6 155
STRANGE CONTRADICTION, WHICH TO GOD HIMSELF . . 10 799

CONTRARIE
MOV'D CONTRARIE WITH THWART OBLIQUITIES, . . . 8 132

CONTRARIES
OF CONTRARIES; ALL GOOD TO ME BECOMES 9 122

CONTRARY
AS BEING THE CONTRARY TO HIS HIGH WILL 1 161
TO FILL HIS EARE, WHEN CONTRARY HE HEARS . . . 10 506

CONTRIBUTE
ONELY TO SHINE, YET SCARCE TO CONTRIBUTE . . . 8 155

CONTRITE
FREQUENTING, SENT FROM HEARTS CONTRITE, IN SIGN . 10 1091
FREQUENTING, SENT FROM HEARTS CONTRITE, IN SIGN . 10 1103
HE SORROWS NOW, REPENTS, AND PRAYES CONTRITE, . . 11 90

CONTRITION
SOW'N WITH CONTRITION IN HIS HEART, THEN THOSE . 11 27

CONTRIV'D
WHAT ORDER, SO CONTRIV'D AS NOT TO MIX 5 334
SATAN, WHO IN THE SERPENT HATH CONTRIV'D . . . 10 1034
CONTRIV'D, AND OF PROVISIONS LAID IN LARGE . . . 11 732

CONTRIVE
CONTRIVE WHO NEED, OR WHEN THEY NEED, NOT NOW . . 2 53
THE MIGHTIE FRAME, HOW BUILD, UNBUILD, CONTRIVE . 8 81

CONTRIVING
FOR WHILE THEY SIT CONTRIVING, SHALL THE REST . . 2 54
BEFORE HAD BIN CONTRIVING, THOUGH PERHAPS . . . 9 139

CONTROULE
THUS FARR HIS BOLD DISCOURSE WITHOUT CONTROULE . 5 803

CONTUMACIE
OF CONTUMACIE WILL PROVOKE THE HIGHEST 10 1027

CONVERSATION
BY CONVERSATION WITH HIS LIKE TO HELP, ... 8 418

CONVERSE
THERE TO CONVERSE WITH EVERLASTING GROANS, . . . 2 184
CONVERSE WITH ADAM, IN WHAT BOWRE OR SHADE . . . 5 230
THOU WITH ETERNAL WISDOM DIDST CONVERSE, . . . 7 9
DESIRE WITH THEE STILL LONGER TO CONVERSE . . . 8 252
SO WELL CONVERSE, NOR WITH THE OX THE APE; . . . 8 396
HOW HAVE I THEN WITH WHOM TO HOLD CONVERSE . . . 8 408
ASSIST US: BUT IF MUCH CONVERSE PERHAPS 9 247
THY SWEET CONVERSE AND LOVE SO DEARLY JOYN'D, . . 9 909

CONVERSING
WITH THEE CONVERSING I FORGET ALL TIME, ... 4 639
I BY CONVERSING CANNOT THESE ERECT 8 432
CONVERSING, LOOKING, LOVING, TO ABSTAIN 10 993

CONVERSION
CONVERSION AND REPENTANCE, AS TO SOULS 11 724

CONVERT
IF I REFUSE NOT, BUT CONVERT, AS YOU, ... 5 492

CONVEX
OUR PRISON STRONG, THIS HUGE CONVEX OF FIRE, . . 2 434
OF THIS ROUND WORLD, WHOSE FIRST CONVEX DIVIDES . 3 419
IN CIRCUIT TO THE UTTERMOST CONVEX 7 266

CONVEY
WILL HE CONVEY UP THITHER TO SUSTAIN 12 75

CONVEYANCE
BY STRANGE CONVEYANCE FILL'D EACH HOLLOW NOOK, . 1 707
DESIRING; NOR RESTRAIN'D CONVEYANCE NEED 8 628

CONVEYANCE (CONTINUED)
BY SECRETEST CONVEYANCE. THOU MY SHADE 10 249

CONVEY'D
TO BLACKEST GRAIN, AND INTO STORE CONVEY'D: . . 6 515

CONVEYD
EACH ORB A GLIMPS OF LIGHT, CONVEYD SO FARR . . 8 156

CONVICT
CONVICT BY FLIGHT, AND REBEL TO ALL LAW 10 83

CONVICTION
CONVICTION TO THE SERPENT NONE BELONGS. 10 84
BUT TO MY OWN CONVICTION: FIRST AND LAST . . . 10 831

CONVINCE
BUT TO CONVINCE THE PROUD WHAT SIGNS AVAILE, . . 6 789

CONVOLV'D
AND WRITH'D HIM TO AND FRO CONVOLV'D; SO SORE . . 6 328

CONVOYD
IT SELF INSTINCT WITH SPIRIT, BUT CONVOYD . . . 6 752

CONVULSIONS
CONVULSIONS, EPILEPSIES, FIERCE CATARRHS, . . . 11 483

COOL
THE COOL, THE SILENT, SAVE WHERE SILENCE YIELDS . 5 39
WHOLSOM AND COOL, AND MILD, BUT WITH BLACK AIR . 10 847

COOLD
AGAINST INVADERS; THEREFORE COOLD IN ZEALE . . . 11 801

COOLE
OF COOLE RECESS, O'RE WHICH THE MANTLING VINE . . 4 258
TO RECOMMEND COOLE ZEPHYR, AND MADE EASE . . . 4 329
OF HIS COOLE BOWRE, WHILE NOW THE MOUNTED SUN . . 5 300
BE OVER, AND THE SUN MORE COOLE DECLINE. . . . 5 370
NO FEAR LEST DINNER COOLE; WHEN THUS BEGAN . . . 5 396
FANND WITH COOLE WINDS, SAVE THOSE WHO IN THIR
COURSE 5 655
SHELTERS IN COOLE, AND TENDS HIS PASTURING HERDS . 9 1109
THE EEVNING COOLE WHEN HE FROM WRAUTH MORE COOLE . 10 95

COPARTNER
WITHOUT COPARTNER? SO TO ADD WHAT WANTS . . . 9 821

COPARTNERS
TH' ASSOCIATES AND COPARTNERS OF OUR LOSS . . . 1 265

COPE
HOVERING ON WING UNDER THE COPE OF HELL 1 345
IN THIS COMMOTION, BUT THE STARRIE COPE 4 992
SO UNDER FIERIE COPE TOGETHER RUSH'D 6 215

COPIOUS
SHALL BE THE COPIOUS MATTER OF MY SONG 3 413
WITH COPIOUS HAND, REJOYCING IN THIR JOY. . . . 5 641
THIR BRANCHES HUNG WITH COPIOUS FRUIT; OR GEMM'D . 7 325

CORAL
OF CORAL STRAY, OR SPORTING WITH QUICK GLANCE . . 7 405

CORDIAL
LEANING HALF-RAIS'D, WITH LOOKS OF CORDIAL LOVE . 5 12
FROM THENCE A RIB, WITH CORDIAL SPIRITS WARME; . 8 466

CORMORANT
SAT LIKE A CORMORANT; YET NOT TRUE LIFE 4 196

CORN
CORN WINE AND OYLE; AND FROM THE HERD OR FLOCK, . 12 19

CORNER
THIS GARDEN, AND NO CORNER LEAVE UNSPI'D; . . . 4 529

CORNERS
THIR CORNERS, WHEN WITH BLUSTER TO CONFOUND . . 10 665

CORNICE
CORNICE OR FREEZE, WITH BOSSY SCULPTURES GRAV'N, . 1 716

CORNIE
THE SMELLING GOURD, UP STOOD THE CORNIE REED . . 7 321

CORONET
UNDER A CORONET HIS FLOWING HAIRE 3 640

CORPORAL
AND FROM THESE CORPORAL NUTRIMENTS PERHAPS . . . 5 496
BY LIK'NING SPIRITUAL TO CORPORAL FORMS, . . . 5 573

CORPOREAL
SPIRITUAL SUBSTANCE WITH CORPOREAL BARR. 4 585
AND CORPOREAL TO INCORPOREAL TURN. 5 413
THAT TO CORPOREAL SUBSTANCES COULD ADDE 8 109

CORPOREAL (CONTINUED)
WITH THIS CORPOREAL CLOD; THEN IN THE GRAVE, . . . 10 786

CORPS
TO STUFF THIS MAW, THIS VAST UNHIDE-BOUND CORPS. . 10 601

CORPULENCE
WONDROUS IN LENGTH AND CORPULENCE INVOLV'D 7 483

CORRESPOND
MAGNANIMOUS TO CORRESPOND WITH HEAV'N, ... 7 511
TH' EFFECTS TO CORRESPOND, OPENER MINE EYES, . . . 9 875

CORROSIVE
TO HEAL THE SCARR OF THESE CORROSIVE FIRES 2 401

CORRUPT
CORRUPT AND PESTILENT: NOW FROM THE NORTH . . . 10 695
BUT ALL CORRUPT, BOTH MIND AND WILL DEPRAV'D, . . 10 825
PEACE TO CORRUPT NO LESS THEN WARR TO WASTE. . . 11 784

CORRUPTED
OF MANKIND THEY CORRUPTED TO FORSAKE 1 368
BY HIM CORRUPTED? OR WILT THOU THY SELF 3 162
CORRUPTED. I AT FIRST WITH TWO FAIR GIFTS . . . 11 57

CORRUPTING
CORRUPTING EACH THIR WAY; YET THOSE REMOOV'D, . . 11 889

CORRUPTION
FOR EVER WITH CORRUPTION THERE TO DWELL; 3 249
OF ALL CORRUPTION, ALL THE BLAME LIGHTS DUE; . . 10 833
CORRUPTION TO BRING FORTH MORE VIOLENT DEEDS. . . 11 428

COST
TO DO HIM WANTON RITES, WHICH COST THEM WOE. . . 1 414
WAS GATHERD, WHICH COST CERES ALL THAT PAIN . . 4 271

COSTLIEST
OF COSTLIEST EMBLEM: OTHER CREATURE HERE 4 703

COTES
IN HURDL'D COTES AMID THE FIELD SECURE, ... 4 186

COUCH
ROUS'D FROM THE SLUMBER, ON THAT FIERY COUCH, . . 1 377
PRICK FORTH THE AERIE KNIGHTS, AND COUCH THIR SPEARS 2 536
THEY TO THIR GRASSIE COUCH, THESE TO THIR NESTS . 4 601
HE LED HER NOTHING LOATH; FLOURS WERE THE COUCH, . 9 1039
TENDED THE SICK BUSIEST FROM COUCH TO COUCH; . . 11 490

COUCHANT
HIS COUCHANT WATCH, AS ONE WHO CHOSE HIS GROUND . 4 406

COUCHES
STRAIT COUCHES CLOSE, THEN RISING CHANGES OFT . . 4 405

COUCH'T
DEEP MALICE TO CONCEALE, COUCH'T WITH REVENGE: . 4 123

COUCHT
COUCHT, AND NOW FILD WITH PASTURE GAZING SAT, . . 4 351
HOW BUSIED, IN WHAT FORM AND POSTURE COUCHT. . . 4 876

COUNCEL
A SOLEMN COUNCEL FORTHWITH TO BE HELD 1 755
HIS POTENTATES TO COUNCEL CALL'D BY NIGHT; . . . 6 416
FORTHWITH FROM COUNCEL TO THE WORK THEY FLEW, . . 6 507

COUNCIL
IN COUNCIL SATE, SOLLICITOUS WHAT CHANCE 10 428
TO COUNCIL IN THE CITIE GATES: ANON 11 661

COUNSEL
FULL COUNSEL MUST MATURE: PEACE IS DESPAIRD, . . . 1 660
WITH WHAT BESIDES, IN COUNSEL OR IN FIGHT, ... 2 20
SAY THEY WHO COUNSEL WARR, WE ARE DECREED, ... 2 160
AND PRINCELY COUNSEL IN HIS FACE YET SHON, ... 2 304
PLEADED HIS DEVILISH COUNSEL, FIRST DEVIS'D . . . 2 379
THE STYGIAN COUNSEL THUS DISSOLV'D; AND FORTH . . 2 506
ABANDON FEAR; TO STRENGTH AND COUNSEL JOIND . . . 6 494
THY COUNSEL IN THIS UTTERMOST DISTRESS, ... 10 920
HIS COUNSEL WHOM SHE HAD DISPLEAS'D, HIS AIDE; . 10 944
BUT ADAM WITH SUCH COUNSEL NOTHING SWAY'D, . . . 10 1010

COUNSEL'D
COUNSEL'D IGNOBLE EASE, AND PEACEFUL SLOATH, . . . 2 227
SO COUNSEL'D HEE, AND BOTH TOGETHER WENT 9 1099

COUNSELS
UNITED THOUGHTS AND COUNSELS, EQUAL HOPE 1 88
HIS INMOST COUNSELS FROM THIR DESTIND AIM. . . . 1 168
IF COUNSELS DIFFERENT, OR DANGER SHUN'D 1 636
MATUREST COUNSELS: FOR HIS THOUGHTS WERE LOW; . . 2 115
IN WHAT HE COUNSELS AND IN WHAT EXCELS 2 125
TO PEACEFUL COUNSELS, AND THE SETTL'D STATE . . . 2 279
IN US WHO SERVE, NEW COUNSELS, TO DEBATE 5 681

COUNSELS (CONTINUED)
BUT WHAT IF BETTER COUNSELS MIGHT ERECT 5 785
OF SPIRITS APOSTAT AND THIR COUNSELS VAINE . . . 7 610

COUNT
THY SELF THOUGH GREAT AND GLORIOUS DOST THOU COUNT, 5 833
THIS PARADISE I GIVE THEE, COUNT IT THINE . . . 8 319

COUNTENANCE
WITH BORROWD LIGHT HER COUNTENANCE TRIFORM . . . 3 730

COUNTERFET
HIM COUNTERFET, IF ANY EYE BEHELD. 4 117
TO COUNTERFET MANS VOICE, TRUE IN OUR FALL, . . 9 1069

COUNTERFETED
OF COUNTERFETED TRUTH THUS HELD THIR EARS. . . . 5 771

COUNTERPOISE
IN COUNTERPOISE, NOW PONDERS ALL EVENTS, ... 4 1001

COUNTERVIEW
IN COUNTERVIEW WITHIN THE GATES, THAT NOW . . . 10 231

COUNT'NANCE
IN LOSS IT SELF; WHICH ON HIS COUNT'NANCE CAST . 1 526
IN OTHERS COUNT'NANCE READ HIS OWN DISMAY . . . 2 422
LIKEST TO THEE IN SHAPE AND COUNT'NANCE BRIGHT, . 2 756
IN WHOSE CONSPICUOUS COUNT'NANCE, WITHOUT CLOUD . 3 385
HIS COUNT'NANCE, AS THE MORNING STARR THAT GUIDES 5 708
HIS COUNT'NANCE TOO SEVERE TO BE BEHELD 6 825
SO SPAKE OUR SIRE, AND BY HIS COUNT'NANCE SEEMD . 8 39
OF MAN, BUT FLED HIM, OR WITH COUNT'NANCE GRIM . 10 713
HIS BLESSED COUNT'NANCE; HERE I COULD FREQUENT, . 11 317

COUNTNANCE
THUS EVE WITH COUNTNANCE BLITHE HER STORIE TOLD; . 9 886

COUNTRY
AND COUNTRY WHEREOF HERE NEEDS NO ACCOUNT, . . . 4 235

COUNTS
TIME COUNTS NOT, THOUGH WITH SWIFTEST MINUTES WING'D. 10 91

COUPLE
FAIR COUPLE, LINKT IN HAPPIE NUPTIAL LEAGUE, . . 4 339

COURAGE
AND COURAGE NEVER TO SUBMIT OR YIELD: 1 108
NEW COURAGE AND REVIVE, THOUGH NOW THEY LYE . . 1 279
THIR FANTING COURAGE, AND DISPEL'D THIR FEARS. . 1 530
OF DAUNTLESS COURAGE, AND CONSIDERATE PRIDE . . 1 603
MISTRUSTFUL, GROUNDS HIS COURAGE ON DESPAIR . . 2 126
ALL COURAGE; DOWN THIR IDLE WEAPONS DROP'D; . . 6 839
AND STRENGTH, OF COURAGE HAUTIE, AND OF LIMB . . 9 484

COURAGEOUS
LESS HARDIE TO ENDURE? COURAGEOUS CHIEF, ... 4 920

COURB
PART WIELD THIR ARMS, PART COURB THE FOAMING STEED, 11 643

COURSE
THIR COURSE, IN EVEN BALLANCE DOWN THEY LIGHT . . 1 349
WHEELS HER PALE COURSE, THEY ON THIR MIRTH AND DANCE 1 786
WITH WINGED COURSE ORE HILL OR MOARIE DALE, . . 2 944
I TRAVEL THIS PROFOUND, DIRECT MY COURSE; . . . 2 980
ALLUR'D HIS EYE: THITHER HIS COURSE HE BENDS . . 3 573
EACH HAD HIS PLACE APPOINTED, EACH HIS COURSE, . 3 720
WELL PLEAS'D THEY SLACK THIR COURSE, AND MANY A LEAGUE 4 164
NOR CHANG'D HIS COURSE, BUT THROUGH THE SHAGGIE HILL 4 224
GABRIEL, TO THEE THY COURSE BY LOT HATH GIV'N . . 4 561
THOSE HAVE THIR COURSE TO FINISH, ROUND THE EARTH, 4 661
IN THY ETERNAL COURSE, BOTH WHEN THOU CLIMBST, . 5 173
FANND WITH COOLE WINDS, SAVE THOSE WHO IN THIR COURSE 5 655
BY OUR OWN QUICK'NING POWER, WHEN FATAL COURSE . 5 861
NOW NIGHT HER COURSE BEGAN, AND OVER HEAV'N . . 6 406
FIRST WHEELD THIR COURSE; EARTH IN HER RICH ATTIRE 7 501
THIR WANDRING COURSE NOW HIGH, NOW LOW, THEN HID, 8 126
OR SHEE FROM WEST HER SILENT COURSE ADVANCE . . 8 163
THIR COURSE THROUGH THICKEST CONSTELLATIONS HELD . 10 411
HIS COURSE INTENDED; ELSE HOW HAD THE WORLD . . 10 689
DARKNESS ERE DAYES MID-COURSE, AND MORNING LIGHT . 11 204
SHALL CHANGE THIR COURSE TO PLEASURE, EASE, AND SLOTH, ... 11 794
SHALL HOLD THIR COURSE, TILL FIRE PURGE ALL THINGS NEW, ... 11 900
A DAY ENTIRE, AND NIGHTS DUE COURSE ADJOURNE, . . 12 264

COURT
OF THAT INFERNAL COURT. BUT FAR WITHIN 1 792
CASUAL FRUITION, NOR IN COURT AMOURS 4 767

COURTS
IN COURTS AND PALACES HE ALSO REIGNS 1 497
(SUCH ARE THE COURTS OF GOD) TH' ANGELIC THRONG 5 650
TRIUMPHANT THROUGH MID HEAV'N, INTO THE COURTS 6 889

COVENANT
AND MAKES A COVENANT NEVER TO DESTROY 11 892

COVER
LONG UNDER DARKNESS COVER. BUT THESE THOUGHTS 1 659
AND BROWN AS EVENING: COVER ME YE PINES, 9 1088
AND GIRDED ON OUR LOYNS, MAY COVER ROUND 9 1096
MAYST COVER: WELL MAY THEN THY LORD APPEAS'D 11 257

COVER'D
(THOUGH LIKE A COVER'D FIELD, WHERE CHAMPIONS BOLD 1 763
COVER'D WITH PEARLY GRAIN: YET GOD HATH HERE 5 430
COVER'D TH' ABYSS: BUT ON THE WATRIE CALME 7 234
TO GUILTIE SHAME HEE COVER'D, BUT HIS ROBE 9 1058
ARAYING COVER'D FROM HIS FATHERS SIGHT. 10 223
IN DOTHAN, COVER'D WITH A CAMP OF FIRE, 11 217
DEEP UNDER WATER ROULD; SEA COVER'D SEA, 11 749

COVERD
COVERD WITH THICK EMBATTELD SQUADRONS BRIGHT, 6 16
COVERD, BUT NOT AT REST OR EASE OF MIND, 9 1120

COVERING
ABJECT AND LOST LAY THESE, COVERING THE FLOOD, 1 312
TO GIRD THIR WASTE, VAIN COVERING IF TO HIDE 9 1113

COVERS
COVERS HIS THRONE; FROM WHENCE DEEP THUNDERS ROAR 2 267

COVERT
WHETHER OF OPEN WARR OR COVERT GUILE, 2 41
SINGS DARKLING, AND IN SHADIEST COVERT HID 3 39
OF THICKEST COVERT WAS INWOVEN SHADE 4 693
UNDER HER CLOUDIE COVERT BOTH RETIR'D, 6 409
OF STATELIEST COVERT, CEDAR, PINE, OR PALME, 9 435

COVERTURES
VAIN COVERTURES; BUT WHEN HE SAW DESCEND 10 337

COVET
WILL COVET MORE. WITH THIS ADVANTAGE THEN 2 35
OR IF THOU COVET DEATH, AS UTMOST END 10 1020

COVETING
HAD IT BEEN ONELY COVETING TO EYE 9 923

COV'NANT
MY COV'NANT IN THE WOMANS SEED RENEWD; 11 116
BETOK'NING PEACE FROM GOD, AND COV'NANT NEW. 11 867
AND CALL TO MIND HIS COV'NANT: DAY AND NIGHT, 11 898
THE RECORDS OF HIS COV'NANT, OVER THESE 12 252
UP TO A BETTER COV'NANT, DISCIPLIN'D 12 302
REMEMBRING MERCIE, AND HIS COV'NANT SWORN 12 346

COWLES
COWLES, HOODS AND HABITS WITH THIR WEARERS TOST 3 490

COWRING
APPROACHING TWO AND TWO, THESE COWRING LOW 8 350

COY
YIELDED WITH COY SUBMISSION, MODEST PRIDE, 4 310

CRAB
UP TO THE TROPIC CRAB; THENCE DOWN AMAINE 10 675

CRAGGIE
THE REST WAS CRAGGIE CLIFF, THAT OVERHUNG 4 547

CRAGGY
OR PINNACE ANCHORS IN A CRAGGY BAY 2 289

CRAMM'D
ON WHAT WAS PURE, TILL CRAMM'D AND GORG'D, NIGH
BURST 10 632

CRANE
EASING THIR FLIGHT; SO STEARS THE PRUDENT CRANE 7 430

CRANES
WARR'D ON BY CRANES: THOUGH ALL THE GIANT BROOD 1 576

CRAZE
AND CRAZE THIR CHARIOT WHEELS: WHEN BY COMMAND 12 210

CREAMS
SHE TEMPERS DULCET CREAMS, NOR THESE TO HOLD 5 347

CREATE
INTENDED TO CREATE, AND THEREIN PLANT 1 652
DID FIRST CREATE YOUR LEADER, NEXT FREE CHOICE, 2 19
WE CAN CREATE, AND IN WHAT PLACE SO E'RE 2 260
HIS DARK MATERIALS TO CREATE MORE WORLDS, 2 916

CREATE (CONTINUED)
SELF-LOST, AND IN A MOMENT WILL CREATE 7 154
GOOD OUT OF EVIL TO CREATE, IN STEAD 7 188
AND SPIRIT COMING TO CREATE NEW WORLDS. 7 209
THY THUNDERS MAGNIFI'D; BUT TO CREATE 7 606
SO MANY NOBLER BODIES TO CREATE, 8 28
BUILD IN HER LOVELIEST, AND CREATE AN AWE 8 558
MORE ANGELS TO CREATE, IF THEY AT LEAST 9 146
SHOULD GOD CREATE ANOTHER EVE, AND I 9 911
MY SUBSTITUTES I SEND YE, AND CREATE 10 403
WITH SPIRITS MASCULINE, CREATE AT LAST 10 890

CREATED
CREATED HUGEST THAT SWIM TH' OCEAN STREAM: 1 202
GLORIES: FOR NEVER SINCE CREATED MAN, 1 573
TO BE CREATED LIKE TO US, THOUGH LESS 2 349
CREATED EVIL, FOR EVIL ONLY GOOD, 2 623
CREATED THING NAUGHT VALU'D HE NOR SHUN'D; 2 679
CREATED VAST AND ROUND, A PLACE OF BLISS 2 832
DIRECTLY TOWARDS THE NEW CREATED WORLD, 3 89
SUCH I CREATED ALL TH' ETHEREAL POWERS 3 100
SO WERE CREATED, NOR CAN JUSTLY ACCUSE 3 112
THOUGH LAST CREATED, THAT FOR HIM I SPARE 3 278
BY THEE CREATED, AND BY THEE THREW DOWN 3 391
CREATED THIS NEW HAPPIE RACE OF MEN 3 679
BUT WHAT CREATED MIND CAN COMPREHEND 3 705
FROM ME, WHOM HE CREATED WHAT I WAS 4 43
MANKIND CREATED, AND FOR HIM THIS WORLD. 4 107
THIS NEW CREATED WORLD, WHEREOF IN HELL 4 937
WHEREIN ALL THINGS CREATED FIRST HE WEIGHD, 4 999
CREATED PURE. BUT KNOW THAT IN THE SOULE 5 100
CREATED, OR SUCH PLACE HAST HERE TO DWELL, 5 373
FOR KNOW, WHATEVER WAS CREATED, NEEDS 5 414
IF NOT DEPRAV'D FROM GOOD, CREATED ALL 5 471
IN CONTEMPLATION OF CREATED THINGS 5 511
TO BE BOTH WILL AND DEED CREATED FREE; 5 549
BY HIM CREATED IN THIR BRIGHT DEGREES, 5 838
THEN WHO CREATED THEE LAMENTING LEARNE, 5 894
WHEN, AND WHEREOF CREATED, FOR WHAT CAUSE, 7 64
THIS UNIVERSE, AND ALL CREATED THINGS: 7 227
THUS GOD THE HEAV'N CREATED, THUS THE EARTH, 7 232
AND GOD CREATED THE GREAT WHALES, AND EACH 7 391
CREATED THEE, IN THE IMAGE OF GOD 7 527
MALE HE CREATED THEE, BUT THY CONSORT 7 529
WHEREVER THUS CREATED, FOR NO PLACE 7 535
THENCE TO BEHOLD THIS NEW CREATED WORLD 7 554
IS GREATER THEN CREATED TO DESTROY. 7 607
CREATED IN HIS IMAGE, THERE TO DWELL 7 627
(AND PURE THOU WERT CREATED) WE ENJOY 8 623
ARE HIS CREATED, OR TO SPITE US MORE, 9 147
OF ALL THAT HE CREATED, MUCH LESS MAN, 9 346
CREATED MUTE TO ALL ARTICULAT SOUND; 9 557
CREATED; BUT HENCEFORTH MY EARLY CARE, 9 799
FOR US CREATED, NEEDS WITH US MUST FAILE, 9 942
THE NEW CREATED WORLD, WHICH FAME IN HEAV'N 10 481
SO FAIR AND GOOD CREATED, AND HAD STILL 10 618
CREATED HIM ENDOWD, WITH HAPPINESS 11 58
TH' IMAGE OF GOD IN MAN CREATED ONCE 11 508
CREATED, AS THOU ART, TO NOBLER END 11 605

CREATING
OF GOD ORDAIN'D THEM, HIS CREATING HAND 9 344

CREATION
TO WASTE HIS WHOLE CREATION, OR POSSESS 2 365
ABOLISH THY CREATION, AND UNMAKE, 3 163
THEE NEXT THEY SANG OF ALL CREATION FIRST, 3 383
TO VISIT OFT THIS NEW CREATION ROUND; 3 661
WHEN THIS CREATION WAS? REMEMBERST THOU 5 857
EQUAL IN THEIR CREATION THEY WERE FORM'D, 6 690
CREATION, AND THE WONDERS OF HIS MIGHT. 7 223
THE SIXT, AND OF CREATION LAST AROSE 7 449
CREATION AND THE SIX DAYES ACTS THEY SUNG, 7 601
DESTRUCTION WITH CREATION MIGHT HAVE MIXT. 8 236
O FAIREST OF CREATION, LAST AND BEST 9 896
CREATION COULD REPEATE, YET WOULD BE LOATH 9 946
OF HIS CREATION; JUSTLY THEN ACCURST, 10 168
CURS'D HIS CREATION, DEATH AS OFT ACCUS'D 10 852
THEN THAT WHICH BY CREATION FIRST BROUGHT FORTH 12 472

CREATION-DAY
TO BEASTS, WHOM GOD ON THIR CREATION-DAY 9 556

CREATOR
FROM THIR CREATOR, AND TRANSGRESS HIS WILL 1 31
GOD THIR CREATOR, AND TH' INVISIBLE 1 369
ON WHOM THE GREAT CREATOR HATH BESTOWD 3 673
SINGING THIR GREAT CREATOR: OFT IN BANDS 4 684
MOV'D THE CREATOR IN HIS HOLY REST 7 91
YET NOT TILL THE CREATOR FROM HIS WORK 7 551
THE GREAT CREATOR FROM HIS WORK RETURND 7 567
CREATOR; SOMETHING YET OF DOUBT REMAINES, 8 13
THY WORDS, CREATOR BOUNTEOUS AND BENIGNE, 8 492
TO THE CREATOR, AND HIS NOSTRILS FILL 9 196
NOR CAN I THINK THAT GOD, CREATOR WISE, 9 938
FROM HIS CREATOR, AND THE MORE TO INCREASE 10 486
WHILE THE CREATOR CALLING FORTH BY NAME 10 649
CREATOR WISE, THAT PEOPL'D HIGHEST HEAV'N 10 889

CREATOUR
THE GREAT CREATOUR? BUT THIR SPITE STILL SERVES 2 385
TO WHOM THE GREAT CREATOUR THUS REPLY'D. 3 167
GOD AND HIS WORKS, CREATOUR HIM THEY SUNG, 7 259

CREAT'ST
THOU USEST, AND FROM THENCE CREAT'ST MORE GOOD. 7 616

CREATURE
THY CREATURE LATE SO LOV'D, THY YOUNGEST SON 3 151
WHOM ELSE NO CREATURE CAN BEHOLD; ON THEE 3 387
ALONE, FOR OTHER CREATURE IN THIS PLACE 3 442
WHAT THERE THOU SEEST FAIR CREATURE IS THY SELF, 4 468
NO CREATURE THENCE: IF SPIRIT OF OTHER SORT, 4 582
OF COSTLIEST EMBLEM: OTHER CREATURE HERE 4 703
HERE, HAPPIE CREATURE, FAIR ANGELIC EVE, 5 74
OF ALL YET DON; A CREATURE WHO NOT PRONE 7 506
CANST RAISE THY CREATURE TO WHAT HIGHTH THOU WILT 8 430
UNDER HIS FORMING HANDS A CREATURE GREW, 8 470
CONSIDER'D EVERY CREATURE, WHICH OF ALL 9 84
A CREATURE FORM'D OF EARTH, AND HIM ENDOW, 9 149
OF ALL GODS WORKS, CREATURE IN WHOM EXCELL'D 9 897
CREATURE SO FAIRE HIS RECONCILEMENT SEEKING, 10 943

CREATURES
WHAT CREATURES THERE INHABIT, OF WHAT MOULD, 2 355
OF CREATURES RATIONAL, THOUGH UNDER HOPE 2 498
A RACE OF UPSTART CREATURES, TO SUPPLY 2 834
TO VISIT ALL THY CREATURES, AND TO ALL 3 230
OF LIVING CREATURES NEW TO SIGHT AND STRANGE: 4 287
CREATURES OF OTHER MOULD, EARTH-BORN PERHAPS, 4 360
OVER ALL OTHER CREATURES THAT POSSESS 4 431
OUR EYE-LIDS; OTHER CREATURES ALL DAY LONG 4 616
MILLIONS OF SPIRITUAL CREATURES WALK THE EARTH 4 677
BUT CHIEFLY WHERE THOSE TWO FAIR CREATURES LODGE, 4 790
ON EARTH JOYN ALL YE CREATURES TO EXTOLL 5 164
HUGEST OF LIVING CREATURES, ON THE DEEP 7 413
INNUMEROUS LIVING CREATURES, PERFET FORMES, 7 455
AND BRUTE AS OTHER CREATURES, BUT ENDU'D 7 507
OF OTHER CREATURES, AS HIM PLEASES BEST, 8 169
DREAM NOT OF OTHER WORLDS, WHAT CREATURES THERE 8 175
CREATURES THAT LIVD, AND MOVD, AND WALK'D, OR FLEW, 8 264
AND YE THAT LIVE AND MOVE, FAIR CREATURES, TELL, 8 276
WITH VARIOUS LIVING CREATURES, AND THE AIRE 8 370
SAVE WITH THE CREATURES WHICH I MADE, AND THOSE 8 409
BENEATH WHAT OTHER CREATURES ARE TO THEE? 8 411
O'RE OTHER CREATURES; YET WHEN I APPROACH 8 546
OF CREATURES ANIMATE WITH GRADUAL LIFE 9 112
OF CREATURES WANTING VOICE, THAT DONE, PARTAKE 9 199
COMPARE ABOVE ALL LIVING CREATURES DEARE, 9 228
SOVRAN OF CREATURES, UNIVERSAL DAME. 9 612
US HIS PRIME CREATURES, DIGNIFI'D SO HIGH, 9 940
THY INWARD FRAUD, TO WARN ALL CREATURES FROM THEE 10 871
WITH ALL THE CREATURES, AND THIR SEED PRESERVE. 11 873

CREDIT
THE CREDIT OF WHOSE VERTUE REST WITH THEE, 9 649

CREDULOUS
LED EVE OUR CREDULOUS MOTHER, TO THE TREE 9 644

CREEK
FORTHWITH THE SOUNDS AND SEAS, EACH CREEK AND BAY 7 399

CREEP
A HIDEOUS PEAL: YET, WHEN THEY LIST, WOULD CREEP, 2 656
THE EARTH, AND STATELY TREAD, OR LOWLY CREEP; 5 201

CREEPING
CATTEL AND CREEPING THINGS, AND BEAST OF THE EARTH, 7 452
AND EVERY CREEPING THING THAT CREEPS THE GROUND. 7 523
LIKE A BLACK MIST LOW CREEPING, HE HELD ON 9 180

CREEPS
AND SWIMS OR SINKS, OR WADES, OR CREEPS, OR FLYES: 2 950
LAYES FORTH HER PURPLE GRAPE, AND GENTLY CREEPS 4 259
AT ONCE CAME FORTH WHATEVER CREEPS THE GROUND, 7 475
AND EVERY CREEPING THING THAT CREEPS THE GROUND. 7 523

CREET
SO JOVE USURPING REIGN'D: THESE FIRST IN CREET 1 514

CREPT
FORTH FLOURISH'T THICK THE CLUSTRING VINE, FORTH CREPT 7 320
SOUL LIVING, EACH THAT CREPT, WHICH PLENTEOUSLY 7 392
THIR SNAKIE FOULDS, AND ADDED WINGS. FIRST CREPT 7 484

CRESCENT
ASTARTE, QUEEN OF HEAV'N, WITH CRESCENT HORNS; 1 439
OF TURKISH CRESCENT, LEAVES ALL WASTE BEYOND 10 434

CRESSETS
OF STARRY LAMPS AND BLAZING CRESSETS FED 1 728

CREST
HIS STATURE REACHT THE SKIE, AND ON HIS CREST 4 988
THIS GREETING ON THY IMPIOUS CREST RECEIVE. 6 188

CREST (CONTINUED)
ON THE PROUD CREST OF SATAN, THAT NO SIGHT, 6 191
HIS TURRET CREST, AND SLEEK ENAMEL'D NECK, 9 525
BRIGHT'NS HIS CREST, AS WHEN A WANDRING FIRE, 9 634

CRESTED
WALK'D FIRM; THE CRESTED COCK WHOSE CLARION SOUNDS 7 443
CRESTED ALOFT, AND CARBUNCLE HIS EYES; 9 500

CREW
TO MORTAL MEN, HE WITH HIS HORRID CREW 1 51
A CREW WHO UNDER NAMES OF OLD RENOWN, 1 477
FOR TREASURES BETTER HID. SOON HAD HIS CREW 1 688
WITH HIS INDUSTRIOUS CREW TO BUILD IN HELL. 1 751
LOST SIGHT OF HIM; ONE OF THE BANISHT CREW 4 573
FAITHFUL TO WHOM? TO THY REBELLIOUS CREW? 4 952
DETERMIND, AND THY HAPLESS CREW INVOLV'D 5 879
EQUAL IN NUMBER TO THAT GODLESS CREW 6 49
THOU AND THY WICKED CREW; THERE MINGLE BROILES, 6 277
THE ATHEIST CREW, BUT WITH REDOUBL'D BLOW 6 370
INVINCIBLY; BUT OF THIS CURSED CREW 6 806
DISEASES DIRE, OF WHICH A MONSTROUS CREW 11 474
HEE WITH A CREW, WHOM LIKE AMBITION JOYNS 12 38

CRI'D
AND WAKING CRI'D, THIS IS THE GATE OF HEAV'N 3 515
CAME FLYING, AND IN MID AIRE ALOUD THUS CRI'D. 6 536
DISMAI'D, AND THUS IN HASTE TO TH' ANGEL CRI'D. 11 449

CRIES
THIR CHILDRENS CRIES UNHEARD, THAT PAST THROUGH FIRE 1 395
MENDS NOT HER SLOWEST PACE FOR PRAYERS OR CRIES. 10 859
THERE WITH MY CRIES IMPORTUNE HEAVEN, THAT ALL 10 933
TO WEARIE HIM WITH MY ASSIDUOUS CRIES: 11 310

CRIME
ONE NEXT HIMSELF IN POWER, AND NEXT IN CRIME, 1 79
THE FELLOWS OF HIS CRIME, THE FOLLOWERS RATHER 1 606
MANS MORTAL CRIME, AND JUST TH' UNJUST TO SAVE, 3 215
HIS CRIME MAKES GUILTIE ALL HIS SONS, THY MERIT 3 290
BOTH OF THY CRIME AND PUNISHMENT; HENCEFORTH 5 881
MISERIE, UNCREATED TILL THE CRIME 6 268
TO UNDERGOE WITH MEE ONE GUILT, ONE CRIME, 9 971
THAT ERROUR NOW, WHICH IS BECOME MY CRIME, 9 1181
MY SELF THE TOTAL CRIME, OR TO ACCUSE 10 127
AS IN THIR CRIME. THUS WAS TH' APPLAUSE THEY MEANT, 10 545
TO SATAN ONLY LIKE BOTH CRIME AND DOOM. 10 841
TH' EFFECTS WHICH THY ORIGINAL CRIME HATH WROUGHT 11 424
WHO FOR MY WILFUL CRIME ART BANISHT HENCE. 12 619

CRIMES
THAT WITH REITERATED CRIMES HE MIGHT 1 214

CRING'D
ONCE FAWN'D, AND CRING'D, AND SERVILLY ADOR'D 4 959

CRINGE
AND PRACTIS'D DISTANCES TO CRINGE, NOT FIGHT. 4 945

CRISPED
HOW FROM THAT SAPHIRE FOUNT THE CRISPED BROOKS, 4 237

CROCODILE
THE RIVER HORSE AND SCALIE CROCODILE. 7 474

CROCUS
CROCUS, AND HYACINTH WITH RICH INLAY 4 701

CRONIAN
UPON THE CRONIAN SEA, TOGETHER DRIVE 10 290

CROOKED
CROOKED BY NATURE, BENT, AS NOW APPEARS, 10 885

CROP
LABOURING THE SOILE, AND REAPING PLENTEOUS CROP, 12 18

CROPT
SWEET OF THY SELF, BUT MUCH MORE SWEET THUS CROPT, 5 68

CROSS
HE HAD TO CROSS. NOR WAS HIS EARE LESS PEAL'D 2 920
A VIOLENT CROSS WIND FROM EITHER COAST 3 487
A SHAMEFUL AND ACCURST, NAILD TO THE CROSS 12 413
BUT TO THE CROSS HE NAILES THY ENEMIES, 12 415

CROSS-BARRD
CROSS-BARRD AND BOLTED FAST, FEAR NO ASSAULT, 4 190

CROSS'D
HE CIRCL'D, FOUR TIMES CROSS'D THE CARR OF NIGHT 9 65
WHEN FIRST THIS TEMPTER CROSS'D THE GULF FROM HELL. 10 39

CROUD
WHILE THE PROMISCUOUS CROUD STOOD YET ALOOF? 1 380
DAZLES THE CROUD, AND SETS THEM ALL AGAPE. 5 357

CROWD
THIR STATE AFFAIRS. SO THICK THE AERIE CROWD . . 1 775
THEY SAW, BUT OTHER SIGHT INSTEAD, A CROWD . . . 10 538

CROWDED
TOST UP AND DOWN, TOGETHER CROWDED DROVE . . . 10 287

CROWN
THE LIKENESS OF A KINGLY CROWN HAD ON. 2 673
AND MUTUAL LOVE, THE CROWN OF ALL OUR BLISS . . 4 728
HER TRESSES, AND HER RURAL LABOURS CROWN, . . . 9 841

CROWN'D
AS WHEN ALCIDES FROM OECHALIA CROWN'D 2 542
THEN CROWN'D AGAIN THIR GOLD'N HARPS THEY TOOK, . 3 365
WITH PLEASANT LIQUORS CROWN'D: O INNOCENCE . . . 5 445
GIRT WITH OMNIPOTENCE, WITH RADIANCE CROWN'D . . 7 194

CROWND
O THOU THAT WITH SURPASSING GLORY CROWND, . . . 4 32
THAT TO THE FRINGED BANK WITH MYRTLE CROWND, . . 4 262
EARTH AND THE GARD'N OF GOD, WITH CEDARS CROWND . 5 260
ON FLOURS REPOS'D, AND WITH FRESH FLOURETS CROWND, 5 636
CROWND THEM WITH GLORY, AND TO THIR GLORY NAM'D . 5 839
THIR BLOSSOMS: WITH HIGH WOODS THE HILLS WERE
CROWND, ... 7 326
GLAD EEVNING AND GLAD MORN CROWND THE FOURTH DAY. 7 386
NOW LAND, NOW SEA, AND SHORES WITH FORREST CROWND, 9 117
ALL WOULD HAVE THEN GON WELL, PEACE WOULD HAVE
CROWND 11 781

CROWNS
THIR CROWNS INWOVE WITH AMARANT AND GOLD, . . . 3 352
NOW NEARER, CROWNS WITH HER ENCLOSURE GREEN, . . 4 133

CROWNST
SURE PLEDGE OF DAY, THAT CROWNST THE SMILING MORN 5 168

CRUCIFI'D
OF ALL MANKINDE, WITH HIM THERE CRUCIFI'D, . . . 12 417

CRUDE
TREADING THE CRUDE CONSISTENCE, HALF ON FOOT, . . 2 941
DEEP UNDER GROUND, MATERIALS DARK AND CRUDE, . . 6 478
TH' ORIGINALS OF NATURE IN THIR CRUDE 6 511

CRUEL
WAITING REVENGE: CRUEL HIS EYE, BUT CAST . . . 1 604
AMONG THEMSELVES, AND LEVIE CRUEL WARRES, . . . 2 501
AS ONE HE STOOD ESCAP'T FROM CRUEL FIGHT, . . . 6 448
WITH CRUEL EXPECTATION. YET ONE DOUBT 10 782
THAT CRUEL SERPENT: ON ME EXERCISE NOT 10 927
WITH CRUEL TOURNAMENT THE SQUADRONS JOINE; . . . 11 652

CRUELTIES
THOUGH TO THE DEATH, AGAINST SUCH CRUELTIES . . 12 494

CRUMBL'D
RISING, THE CRUMBL'D EARTH ABOVE THEM THREW . . 7 468

CRUSH
AGAINST US THIS DECEIT: TO CRUSH HIS HEAD . . . 10 1035
SHALL BRUISE THE HEAD OF SATAN, CRUSH HIS STRENGTH 12 430

CRUSHES
SHE CRUSHES, INOFFENSIVE MOUST, AND MEATHES . . 5 345

CRUSH'T
THIR ARMOR HELP'D THIR HARM, CRUSH'T IN AND BRUIS'D 6 656

CRY
THEN OF THIR SESSION ENDED THEY BID CRY 2 514
A CRY OF HELL HOUNDS NEVER CEASING BARK'D . . . 2 654
THESE YELLING MONSTERS THAT WITH CEASLESS CRY . . 2 795
TH' APOCALYPS, HEARD CRY IN HEAVEN ALOUD, . . . 4 2

CRY'D
O FATHER, WHAT INTENDS THY HAND, SHE CRY'D, . . 2 727
MADE TO DESTROY: I FLED, AND CRY'D OUT DEATH; . . 2 787

CRYD'ST
THOU FOLLOWING CRYD'ST ALOUD, RETURN FAIRE EVE; . 4 481

CRYSTAL
PART RISE IN CRYSTAL WALL, OR RIDGE DIRECT, . . 7 293

CRYSTALLIN
CRYSTALLIN OCEAN, AND THE LOUD MISRULE 7 271

CRYSTALLINE
AND THAT CRYSTALLINE SPHEAR WHOSE BALLANCE WEIGHS 3 482

CUBE
APPROACHING GROSS AND HUGE; IN HOLLOW CUBE . . . 6 552

CUBIC
IN CUBIC PHALANX FIRM ADVANC'T ENTIRE, ... 6 399

CUBIT
MEASUR'D BY CUBIT, LENGTH, AND BREADTH, AND HIGHTH, 11 730

CULMINATE
CULMINATE FROM TH' AEQUATOR, AS THEY NOW . . . 3 617

CUMBROUS
LIKE CUMBROUS FLESH; BUT IN WHAT SHAPE THEY CHOOSE 1 428
THE CUMBROUS ELEMENTS, EARTH, FLOOD, AIRE, FIRE, . 3 715
TO HARAN, AFTER HIM A CUMBROUS TRAIN 12 131

CUPS
MINISTERD NAKED, AND THIR FLOWING CUPS 5 444
ALLURD THEM; THENCE FROM CUPS TO CIVIL BROILES. . 11 718

CURB
UNDER TH' INEVITABLE CURB, RESERV'D 2 322
PART CURB THIR FIERIE STEEDS, OR SHUN THE GOAL . 2 531
CHAUMPING HIS IRON CURB: TO STRIVE OR FLIE . . . 4 859

CURE
AND THAT MUST END US, THAT MUST BE OUR CURE, . . 2 145
TO BE NO MORE; SAD CURE; FOR WHO WOULD LOOSE, . . 2 146
MORE TOLLERABLE; IF THERE BE CURE OR CHARM . . . 2 460
HERE GROWS THE CURE OF ALL, THIS FRUIT DIVINE, . 9 776
AND WHAT MAY ELSE BE REMEDIE OR CURE 10 1079

CURIOUS
IN BEDS AND CURIOUS KNOTS, BUT NATURE BOON . . . 4 242

CURLD
CURLD MANY A WANTON WREATH IN SIGHT OF EVE, . . 9 517
THAT CURLD MEGARA: GREEDILY THEY PLUCK'D . . . 10 560

CURLES
IN CURLES ON EITHER CHEEK PLAID, WINGS HE WORE . 3 641
AS THE VINE CURLES HER TENDRILS, WHICH IMPLI'D . 4 307

CURRENT
UPON THE RAPID CURRENT, WHICH THROUGH VEINS . . 4 227
THE CURRENT OF HIS FURY THUS OPPOS'D. 5 808
YET SCARCE ALLAY'D STILL EYES THE CURRENT STREAME, 7 67

CURRENTS
WITH CLAMOR THENCE THE RAPID CURRENTS DRIVE . . 11 853

CURS'D
NAY CURS'D BE THOU; SINCE AGAINST HIS THY WILL . 4 71
CURS'D IS THE GROUND FOR THY SAKE, THOU IN SORROW 10 201
CURS'D HIS CREATION, DEATH AS OFT ACCUS'D . . . 10 852

CURSE
HURL'D HEADLONG TO PARTAKE WITH US, SHALL CURSE . 2 374
A UNIVERSE OF DEATH, WHICH GOD BY CURSE 2 622
AND ON THE SERPENT THUS HIS CURSE LET FALL. . . 10 174
TILL THEN THE CURSE PRONOUNC'T ON BOTH PRECEDES, . 10 640
IS PROPAGATED CURSE. O VOICE ONCE HEARD . . . 10 729
THE EVIL ON HIM BROUGHT BY ME, WILL CURSE . . . 10 734
ME NOW YOUR CURSE. AH, WHY SHOULD ALL MANKIND . 10 822
FRUIT OF THY WOMB; ON MEE THE CURSE ASLOPE . . . 10 1053
BUT JUSTICE, AND SOME FATAL CURSE ANNEXT . . . 12 99
DON TO HIS FATHER, HEARD THIS HEAVIE CURSE, . . 12 103

CURSED
ABOMINATIONS; AND WITH CURSED THINGS 1 389
ACCURST, AND IN A CURSED HOUR HE HIES. 2 1055
TILL ON THOSE CURSED ENGINS TRIPLE-ROW 6 650
INVINCIBLY; BUT OF THIS CURSED CREW 6 806
THE SACRED FRUIT FORBIDD'N. SOM CURSED FRAUD . . 9 904
INTO THIS CURSED WORLD A WOFUL RACE, ... 10 984
TO A REPROACHFUL LIFE AND CURSED DEATH, ... 12 406

CURSES
OR MULTIPLIE, BUT CURSES ON MY HEAD? 10 732

CURST
POSTERITIE STANDS CURST: FAIR PATRIMONIE 10 818

CUSCO
AND CUSCO IN PERU, THE RICHER SEAT 11 408

CUSTODY
TO US ENSLAV'D, BUT CUSTODY SEVERE, ... 2 333
HAD FROM HIS WAKEFUL CUSTODY PURLOIND 2 946

CUSTOM
AGAINST ALLUREMENT, CUSTOM, AND A WORLD 11 810

CUSTOMD
WHEN ADAM WAK'T, SO CUSTOMD, FOR HIS SLEEP . . . 5 3

CUSTOME
CONSENT OR CUSTOME, AND HIS REGAL STATE 1 640

CUT
CUT OFF, AND FOR THE BOOK OF KNOWLEDG FAIR . . . 3 47
DESCENDING, AND IN HALF CUT SHEERE, NOR STAID, . 6 325

CUT (CONTINUED)
AT LOOPHOLES CUT THROUGH THICKEST SHADE: THOSE LEAVES 9 1110

CUTS
THAT CUTS US OFF FROM HOPE, AND FAVOURS ONELY . . 10 1043

CYCLADES
OR PILOT FROM AMIDST THE CYCLADES 5 264

CYCLE
CYCLE AND EPICYCLE, ORB IN ORB: 8 84

CYRENE'S
OF BARCA OR CYRENE'S TORRID SOIL, ... 2 904

CYTHEREA'S
PERPLEX'D THE GREEK AND CYTHEREA'S SON; 9 19

DAEMONIAC
DAEMONIAC PHRENZIE, MOAPING MELANCHOLIE 11 485

DAGON
DAGON HIS NAME, SEA MONSTER, UPWARD MAN 1 462

DAIES
TO WASTE ETERNAL DAIES IN WOE AND PAIN? 2 695
THEN THIS OF EDEN, AND FAR HAPPIER DAIES. . . . 12 465

DAILY
AND DAILY THANKS, I CHIEFLY WHO ENJOY 4 445
MAN HATH HIS DAILY WORK OF BODY OR MIND 4 618
THAT WHICH BEFORE US LIES IN DAILY LIFE, ... 8 193
THOSE THOUSAND DECENCIES THAT DAILY FLOW 8 601
BY ANGELS NUMBERLESS, THY DAILY TRAIN. 9 548
OF BRUTAL KIND, THAT DAILY ARE IN SIGHT? 9 565

DAIRIE
OR DAIRIE, EACH RURAL SIGHT, EACH RURAL SOUND; . 9 451

DALE
THE FLOWRY DALE OF SIBMA CLAD WITH VINES, ... 1 410
WITH WINGED COURSE ORE HILL OR MOARIE DALE, . . . 2 944
POWRD FORTH PROFUSE ON HILL AND DALE AND PLAINE, . 4 243
THROUGH WOOD, THROUGH WASTE, O'RE HILL, O'RE DALE HIS ROAM. 4 538
OF PLEASURE SITUATE IN HILL AND DALE) 6 641
HILL, DALE, AND SHADIE WOODS, AND SUNNIE PLAINES, 8 262

DALES
YE HILLS AND DALES, YE RIVERS, WOODS, AND PLAINES, 8 275
O WOODS, O FOUNTAINS, HILLOCKS, DALES AND BOWRS, . 10 860

DALILAH
OF PHILISTEAN DALILAH, AND WAK'D 9 1061

DALLIANCE
OF DALLIANCE HAD WITH THEE IN HEAV'N, AND JOYS . 2 819
WANTED, NOR YOUTHFUL DALLIANCE AS BESEEMS 4 338
HELD DALLIANCE WITH HIS FAIRE EGYPTIAN SPOUSE. . 9 443
TILL ADAM THUS 'GAN EVE TO DALLIANCE MOVE, . . . 9 1016

DAMAGE
MY DAMAGE FONDLY DEEM'D, I CAN REPAIRE 7 152

DAMASCO
DAMASCO, OR MAROCCO, OR TREBISOND, ... 1 584

DAMASCUS
WAS FAIR DAMASCUS, ON THE FERTIL BANKS 1 468

DAMASKT
ON THE SOFT DOWNIE BANK DAMASKT WITH FLOURS: . . . 4 334

DAME
SOVRAN OF CREATURES, UNIVERSAL DAME. 9 612

DAMIATA
BETWIXT DAMIATA AND MOUNT CASIUS OLD, ... 2 593

DAMNATION
HEAP ON HIMSELF DAMNATION, WHILE HE SOUGHT 1 215

DAMN'D
HIS OWN; FOR NEITHER DO THE SPIRITS DAMN'D 2 482
O SHAME TO MEN. DEVIL WITH DEVIL DAMN'D 2 496
AT CERTAIN REVOLUTIONS ALL THE DAMN'D 2 597

DAMND
TO DO WHAT ELSE THOUGH DAMND I SHOULD ABHORRE. . 4 392

DAMP
DOWN CAST AND DAMP, YET SUCH WHEREIN APPEAR'D . . 1 523
HE PLUCKT, HE TASTED; MEE DAMP HORROR CHIL'D . . 5 65
CLIMAT, OR YEARS DAMP MY INTENDED WING 9 45
WIDE ANARCHIE OF CHAOS DAMP AND DARK 10 283
ADAM BY THIS FROM THE COLD SUDDEN DAMP 11 293
A MELANCHOLLY DAMP OF COLD AND DRY 11 544

DAMPS
ACCOMPANIED, WITH DAMPS AND DREADFUL GLOOM, . . 10 848

DAMSELS
THE SYRIAN DAMSELS TO LAMENT HIS FATE 1 448

DAN
DOUBL'D THAT SIN IN BETHEL AND IN DAN, ... 1 485

DANAW
RHENE OR THE DANAW, WHEN HER BARBAROUS SONS . . 1 353

DANC'D
DANC'D HAND IN HAND. A WHILE DISCOURSE THEY HOLD; 5 395
DAWN, AND THE PLEIADES BEFORE HIM DANC'D 7 374

DANCE
WHEELS HER PALE COURSE, THEY ON THIR MIRTH AND DANCE 1 786
LUR'D WITH THE SMELL OF INFANT BLOOD, TO DANCE . 2 664
THIR STARRY DANCE IN NUMBERS THAT COMPUTE . . . 3 580
KNIT WITH THE GRACES AND THE HOURS IN DANCE . . 4 267
MIXT DANCE, OR WANTON MASK, OR MIDNIGHT BAL, . . 4 768
IN MYSTIC DANCE NOT WITHOUT SONG, RESOUND . . . 5 178
IN SONG AND DANCE ABOUT THE SACRED HILL, . . . 5 619
MYSTICAL DANCE, WHICH YONDER STARRIE SPHEARE . . 5 620
FORTHWITH FROM DANCE TO SWEET REPAST THEY TURN . 5 630
AS THEY WOULD DANCE, YET FOR A DANCE THEY SEEMD . 6 615
ROSE AS IN DANCE THE STATELY TREES, AND SPRED . . 7 324
INCITED, DANCE ABOUT HIM VARIOUS ROUNDS? . . . 8 125
NOISE, OTHER THEN THE SOUND OF DANCE OR SONG, . . 8 243
SOFT AMOROUS DITTIES, AND IN DANCE CAME ON: . . 11 584
OF LUSTFUL APPETENCE, TO SING, TO DANCE, . . . 11 619
TO LUXURIE AND RIOT, FEAST AND DANCE, ... 11 715

DANCK
SO SAYING, THROUGH EACH THICKET DANCK OR DRIE, . 9 179

DANC'T
TERRESTRIAL HEAV'N, DANC'T ROUND BY OTHER HEAV'NS 9 103

DANDL'D
DANDL'D THE KID; BEARS, TYGERS, OUNCES, PARDS, . 4 344

DANGER
IF COUNSELS DIFFERENT, OR DANGER SHUN'D 1 636
PONDERING THE DANGER WITH DEEP THOUGHTS; AND EACH 2 421
OF DIFFICULTY OR DANGER COULD DETERR 2 449
SO MUCH THE NEERER DANGER; GO AND SPEED; 2 1008
WHICH ELSE MIGHT WORK HIM DANGER OR DELAY: . . . 3 635
THROUGH WAYES OF DANGER BY HIMSELF UNTRI'D, . . 4 934
HIS DANGER, AND FROM WHOM, WHAT ENEMIE 5 239
O NOW IN DANGER TRI'D, NOW KNOWN IN ARMES . . . 6 418
THE WIFE, WHERE DANGER OR DISHONOUR LURKS, . . . 9 267
THE DANGER LIES, YET LIES WITHIN HIS POWER: . . 9 349
OF DANGER TASTED, NOR TO EVIL UNKNOWN 9 864
GOING INTO SUCH DANGER AS THOU SAIDST? 9 1157
THE DANGER, AND THE LURKING ENEMIE 9 1172
EITHER TO MEET NO DANGER, OR TO FINDE 9 1176

DANGEROUS
DESPERATE REVENGE, AND BATTEL DANGEROUS 2 107
WITH DANGEROUS EXPEDITION TO INVADE 2 342
WILD WORK IN HEAV'N, AND DANGEROUS TO THE MAINE. 6 698

DANGERS
OF HOPE IN FEARS AND DANGERS, HEARD SO OFT . . . 1 275
THEN UNKNOWN DANGERS AND AS HARD ESCAPE. . . . 2 444
IN DARKNESS, AND WITH DANGERS COMPAST ROUND, . . 7 27

DANG'ROUS
OR TRIE THEE NOW MORE DANG'ROUS TO HIS THRONE. . 10 382

DANITE
UNCOVER'D MORE, SO ROSE THE DANITE STRONG . . . 9 1059

DANK
THE DANK, AND RISING ON STIFF PENNONS, TOWRE . . 7 441

DAPHNE
OF DAPHNE BY ORONTES, AND TH' INSPIR'D 4 273

DAR'D
AND PERIL GREAT PROVOK'T, WHO THUS HATH DAR'D . . 9 922

DARE
THE STAIRS WERE THEN LET DOWN, WHETHER TO DARE . 3 523
WHAT THOU AND THY GAY LEGIONS DARE AGAINST; . . 4 942
THE ENEMIE, THOUGH BOLD, WILL HARDLY DARE, . . . 9 304

DARIEN
AT DARIEN, THENCE TO THE LAND WHERE FLOWES . . . 9 81

DARING
HIS DARING FOE, AT THIS PREVENTION MORE 6 129
OR DARING, FIRST ON MEE TH' ASSAULT SHALL LIGHT. . 9 305
WITH FOES FOR DARING SINGLE TO BE JUST, ... 11 703

DARK
AND MAD'ST IT PREGNANT; WHAT IN ME IS DARK . . . 1 22
LEFT HIM AT LARGE TO HIS OWN DARK DESIGNS, . . . 1 213
HIS EYE SURVAY'D THE DARK IDOLATRIES 1 456
ACCEPT THIS DARK OPPROBRIOUS DEN OF SHAME, . . . 2 58
THICK CLOUDS AND DARK DOTH HEAV'NS ALL-RULING SIRE 2 264
THE DARK UNBOTTOM'D INFINITE ABYSS 2 405
THROUGH ALL THE COASTS OF DARK DESTRUCTION SEEK . 2 464
THUS THEY THIR DOUBTFUL CONSULTATIONS DARK . . . 2 486
LIES DARK AND WILDE, BEAT WITH PERPETUAL STORMS . 2 588
NO REST: THROUGH MANY A DARK AND DREARIE VAILE . 2 618
TO JOYN THIR DARK ENCOUNTER IN MID AIR: 2 718
FROM OUT THIS DARK AND DISMAL HOUSE OF PAIN, . . 2 823
THE SECRETS OF THE HOARIE DEEP, A DARK 2 891
HIS DARK MATERIALS TO CREATE MORE WORLDS, . . . 2 916
BORN THROUGH THE HOLLOW DARK ASSAULTS HIS EARE . 2 953
OF CHAOS, AND HIS DARK PAVILION SPREAD 2 960
OVER THE DARK ABYSS, WHOSE BOILING GULF 2 1027
THE RISING WORLD OF WATERS DARK AND DEEP, . . . 3 11
THE DARK DESCENT, AND UP TO REASCEND, ... 3 20
BUT CLOUD IN STEAD, AND EVER-DURING DARK . . . 3 45
INVITES; FOR I WILL CLEER THIR SENSES DARK, . . 3 188
DARK WITH EXCESSIVE BRIGHT THY SKIRTS APPEER, . . 3 380
DARK, WASTE, AND WILD, UNDER THE FROWN OF NIGHT . 3 424
ALL THIS DARK GLOBE THE FIEND FOUND AS HE PASS'D, 3 498
THROUGH DARK AND DESART WAYES WITH PERIL GONE . . 3 544
HERE IN THE DARK SO MANY PRECIOUS THINGS . . . 3 611
AND O'RE THE DARK HER SILVER MANTLE THREW. . . . 4 609
IN THAT DARK DURANCE: THUS MUCH WHAT WAS ASKT. . 4 899
DISPERSE IT, AS NOW LIGHT DISPELS THE DARK. . . 5 208
NAMELESS IN DARK OBLIVION LET THEM DWELL. . . . 6 380
FAR IN THE DARK DISLODG'D, AND VOID OF REST, . . 6 415
DEEP UNDER GROUND, MATERIALS DARK AND CRUDE, . . 6 478
THESE IN THIR DARK NATIVITIE THE DEEP 6 482
HER DARK FOUNDATIONS, AND TOO FAST HAD BOUND. . . 6 870
OUTRAGEOUS AS A SEA, DARK, WASTEFUL, WILDE, . . 7 212
SHEE DISAPPEERD, AND LEFT ME DARK, I WAK'D . . . 8 478
TO ENTER, AND HIS DARK SUGGESTIONS HIDE 9 90
TO HIDE ME, AND THE DARK INTENT I BRING. . . . 9 162
WIDE ANARCHIE OF CHAOS DAMP AND DARK 10 283
WITH THIS PORTENTOUS BRIDGE THE DARK ABYSS. . . 10 371
MANY A DARK LEAGUE, REDUC'T IN CAREFUL WATCH . . 10 438
RAIS'D FROM THIR DARK DIVAN, AND WITH LIKE JOY . 10 457
THEN STIL AT HELS DARK THRESHOLD TO HAVE SATE
WATCH, ... 10 594
WITH TERROR THROUGH THE DARK AEREAL HALL. . . . 10 667
BEFORE HIS EYES APPEARD, SAD, NOYSOM, DARK, . . 11 478
LIKE A DARK CEELING STOOD; DOWN RUSH'D THE RAIN . 11 743
IN A DARK AGE, AGAINST EXAMPLE GOOD, ... 11 809

DARKEN
TO DARKEN ALL THE HILL, AND SMOAK TO ROWL . . . 6 57

DARKEN'D
LIKE NIGHT, AND DARKEN'D ALL THE LAND OF NILE: . 1 343

DARKENS
DARKENS THE STREETS, THEN WANDER FORTH THE SONS . 1 501

DARKER
GREW DARKER AT THIR FROWN, SO MATCHT THEY STOOD; . 2 720
IN DARKER VEILE) AND ROSEAT DEWS DISPOS'D . . . 5 646

DARKLING
SINGS DARKLING, AND IN SHADIEST COVERT HID . . . 3 39

DARK'N'D
PERPLEXES MONARCHS. DARK'N'D SO, YET SHON . . . 1 599

DARK'ND
SCOWLS ORE THE DARK'ND LANTSKIP SNOW, OR SHOWRE; . 2 491
HOW DARK'ND; INNOCENCE, THAT AS A VEILE 9 1054

DARKNESS
NO LIGHT, BUT RATHER DARKNESS VISIBLE 1 63
IN UTTER DARKNESS, AND THIR PORTION SET 1 72
AND WITH THIR DARKNESS DURST AFFRONT HIS LIGHT. . 1 391
LONG UNDER DARKNESS COVER. BUT THESE THOUGHTS . 1 659
THIS HORROR WILL GROW MILDE, THIS DARKNESS LIGHT, 2 220
OF DARKNESS DO WE DREAD? HOW OFT AMIDST . . . 2 263
AND WITH THE MAJESTY OF DARKNESS ROUND 2 266
AS HE OUR DARKNESS, CANNOT WE HIS LIGHT 2 269
ATTEMPTING, OR TO SIT IN DARKNESS HERE 2 377
IN DARKNESS, WHILE THY HEAD FLAMES THICK AND FAST 2 754
WHICH WAY THE NEEREST COAST OF DARKNESS LYES . . 2 958
TO HER ORIGINAL DARKNESS AND YOUR SWAY 2 984
THROUGH UTTER AND THROUGH MIDDLE DARKNESS BORNE . 3 16
THE POWERS OF DARKNESS BOUND. THOU AT THE SIGHT . 3 256
FROM CHAOS AND TH' INROAD OF DARKNESS OLD, . . . 3 421
TO DARKNESS, SUCH AS BOUND THE OCEAN WAVE. . . . 3 539
TILL AT HIS SECOND BIDDING DARKNESS FLED, . . . 3 712
LEAST TOTAL DARKNESS SHOULD BY NIGHT REGAINE . . 4 665
HIS PRAISE, WHO OUT OF DARKNESS CALL'D UP LIGHT. . 5 179
INTO UTTER DARKNESS, DEEP INGULFT, HIS PLACE . . 5 614
WHERE LIGHT AND DARKNESS IN PERPETUAL ROUND . . 6 6
OBSEQUIOUS DARKNESS ENTERS, TILL HER HOURE . . . 6 10
TO VEILE THE HEAV'N, THOUGH DARKNESS THERE MIGHT
WELL 6 11

DARKNESS (CONTINUED)
THY LEGIONS UNDER DARKNESS; BUT THOU SEEST . . . 6 142
INDUCING DARKNESS, GRATEFUL TRUCE IMPOS'D, . . . 6 407
PURSUE THESE SONS OF DARKNESS, DRIVE THEM OUT . . 6 715
TO CHAINS OF DARKNESS, AND TH' UNDYING WORM, . . 6 739
IN DARKNESS, AND WITH DANGERS COMPAST ROUND, . . 7 27
MATTER UNFORM'D AND VOID: DARKNESS PROFOUND . . 7 233
AND LIGHT FROM DARKNESS BY THE HEMISPHERE . . . 7 250
DIVIDED: LIGHT THE DAY, AND DARKNESS NIGHT . . . 7 251
EXHALING FIRST FROM DARKNESS THEY BEHELD; . . . 7 255
AND LIGHT FROM DARKNESS TO DIVIDE. GOD SAW, . . 7 352
WITH DARKNESS, THRICE THE EQUINOCTIAL LINE . . . 9 64
WHOM THUS THE PRINCE OF DARKNESS ANSWERD GLAD. . 10 383
DESCEND THROUGH DARKNESS, ON YOUR RODE WITH EASE . 10 394
FROM DARKNESS TO PROMOTE ME, OR HERE PLACE . . 10 745
DARKNESS ERE DAYES MID-COURSE, AND MORNING LIGHT . 11 204
DARKNESS MUST OVERSHADOW ALL HIS BOUNDS, . . . 12 187
PALPABLE DARKNESS, AND BLOT OUT THREE DAYES; . . 12 188
DARKNESS DEFENDS BETWEEN TILL MORNING WATCH; . . 12 207
ENLIGHTNER OF MY DARKNESS, GRACIOUS THINGS . . . 12 271
LIGHT OUT OF DARKNESS. FULL OF DOUBT I STAND. . 12 473

DARKSOM
WHICH FROM HIS DARKSOM PASSAGE NOW APPEERS, . . . 4 232
SATAN FROM HELL SCAP'T THROUGH THE DARKSOM GULF . 5 225
A DARKSOM CLOUD OF LOCUSTS SWARMING DOWN . . . 12 185

DARKSOME
WANDRING THIS DARKSOME DESART, AS MY WAY, ... 2 973

DARLING
IN HIS DISTURBANCE; WHEN HIS DARLING SONS . . . 2 373
THY DAUGHTER AND THY DARLING, WITHOUT END. . . . 2 870

DAR'ST
THAT DAR'ST, THOUGH GRIM AND TERRIBLE, ADVANCE . 2 682
YET LEUDLY DAR'ST OUR MINISTRING UPBRAID. . . . 6 182

DART
AND SHOOK A DREADFUL DART; WHAT SEEM'D HIS HEAD . 2 672
THY LINGRING, OR WITH ONE STROKE OF THIS DART . . 2 702
POSSESSES THEE TO BEND THAT MORTAL DART 2 729
FORTH ISSU'D, BRANDISHING HIS FATAL DART . . . 2 786
DEATH READY STANDS TO INTERPOSE HIS DART, . . . 2 854
AND OVER THEM TRIUMPHANT DEATH HIS DART 11 491
WITH DART AND JAV'LIN, STONES AND SULFUROUS FIRE; 11 658

DARTED
OF EVE, WHOSE EYE DARTED CONTAGIOUS FIRE. . . . 9 1036

DARTS
DARTS HIS EXPERIENC'T EYE, AND SOON TRAVERSE . . 1 568
OF FIERY DARTS IN FLAMING VOLIES FLEW, ... 6 213
AND FROM ABOUT HER SHOT DARTS OF DESIRE 8 62
SATANS ASSAULTS, AND QUENCH HIS FIERIE DARTS, . . 12 492
BESTUCK WITH SLANDROUS DARTS, AND WORKS OF FAITH . 12 536

DASH
THE BETTER REASON, TO PERPLEX AND DASH 2 114
SUCH IMPLEMENTS OF MISCHIEF AS SHALL DASH . . . 6 488
TO DASH THIR PRIDE, AND JOY FOR MAN SEDUC'T. . . 10 577

DATE
NEW HEAV'NS, NEW EARTH, AGES OF ENDLESS DATE . . 12 549

DAUGHTER
DEAR DAUGHTER, SINCE THOU CLAIM'ST ME FOR THY SIRE, 2 817
THY DAUGHTER AND THY DARLING, WITHOUT END. . . . 2 870
DAUGHTER OF GOD AND MAN, ACCOMPLISHT EVE, . . . 4 660
DAUGHTER OF GOD AND MAN, IMMORTAL EVE, ... 9 291
SOLE DAUGHTER OF HIS VOICE; THE REST, WE LIVE . . 9 653
INCHANTING DAUGHTER, THUS THE SILENCE BROKE. . . 10 353
FAIR DAUGHTER, AND THOU SON AND GRANDCHILD BOTH, . 10 384
DAUGHTER OF SIN, AMONG TH' IRRATIONAL, ... 10 708

DAUGHTERS
INFECTED SIONS DAUGHTERS WITH LIKE HEAT, . . . 1 453
HITHER OF ILL-JOYND SONS AND DAUGHTERS BORN . . 3 463
HIS SONS, THE FAIREST OF HER DAUGHTERS EVE. . . 4 324
THE BENDED TWIGS TAKE ROOT, AND DAUGHTERS GROW . 9 1105

DAUNTLESS
OF DAUNTLESS COURAGE, AND CONSIDERATE PRIDE . . 1 603
RATHER YOUR DAUNTLESS VERTUE, WHOM THE PAIN . . 9 694

DAVID
OF DAVID (SO I NAME THIS KING) SHALL RISE . . . 12 326
TO DAVID, STABLISHT AS THE DAYES OF HEAV'N, . . 12 347

DAVIDS
THE SCEPTER, AND REGARD NOT DAVIDS SONS, . . . 12 357

DAWN
A GLIMMERING DAWN; HERE NATURE FIRST BEGINS . . 2 1037
TO FIND THY PIERCING RAY, AND FIND NO DAWN; . . 3 24
IF BETTER THOU BELONG NOT TO THE DAWN, ... 5 167
DAWN, AND THE PLEIADES BEFORE HIM DANC'D . . . 7 374

DAWNE
ALL NIGHT; AT LAST BY BREAK OF CHEARFUL DAWNE 3 545
NOR LONG SHALL BE OUR LABOUR, YET ERE DAWNE, 6 492
NOW WHEN AS SACRED LIGHT BEGAN TO DAWNE 9 192
FOR NOW, AND SINCE FIRST BREAK OF DAWNE THE FIEND, 9 412

DAWNING
OF DAWNING LIGHT TURND THITHER-WARD IN HASTE 3 500
THOU TELLST, BY MORROW DAWNING I SHALL KNOW. 4 588
SOON BANDED; OTHERS FROM THE DAWNING HILLS 6 528
DAWNING THROUGH HEAV'N: FORTH RUSH'D WITH WHIRLWIND SOUND 6 749
SHALL LONG USURP; ERE THE THIRD DAWNING LIGHT 12 421
OUT OF HIS GRAVE, FRESH AS THE DAWNING LIGHT, 12 423

DAY
NINE TIMES THE SPACE THAT MEASURES DAY AND NIGHT 1 50
OF AMRAMS SON IN EGYPTS EVILL DAY 1 339
IN AMOROUS DITTYES ALL A SUMMERS DAY, 1 449
A SUMMERS DAY; AND WITH THE SETTING SUN 1 744
ONE DAY UPON OUR HEADS; WHILE WE PERHAPS 2 178
THAT DAY AND NIGHT FOR HIS DESTRUCTION WAITE. 2 505
HIS WRATH WHICH ONE DAY WILL DESTROY YE BOTH. 2 734
DAY, OR THE SWEET APPROACH OF EV'N OR MORN, 3 42
THIS MY LONG SUFFERANCE AND MY DAY OF GRACE 3 198
TH' ASPIRING DOMINATIONS: THOU THAT DAY 3 392
HIS DAY, WHICH ELSE AS TH' OTHER HEMISPHERE 3 725
THAT DAY I OFT REMEMBER, WHEN FROM SLEEP 4 449
THIS DAY AT HIGHTH OF NOON CAME TO MY SPHEARE 4 564
LABOUR AND REST, AS DAY AND NIGHT TO MEN 4 613
OUR EYE-LIDS; OTHER CREATURES ALL DAY LONG 4 616
BOTH DAY AND NIGHT: HOW OFTEN FROM THE STEEP 4 680
WHAT DAY THE GENIAL ANGEL TO OUR SIRE 4 712
MAKER OMNIPOTENT, AND THOU THE DAY, 4 725
WORKS OF DAY PASS'T, OR MORROWS NEXT DESIGNE, 5 33
MUCH FAIRER TO MY FANCIE THEN BY DAY: 5 53
AND CHORAL SYMPHONIES, DAY WITHOUT NIGHT, 5 162
SURE PLEDGE OF DAY, THAT CROWNST THE SMILING MORN 5 168
WHILE DAY ARISES, THAT SWEET HOUR OF PRIME. 5 170
GO THEREFORE, HALF THIS DAY AS FRIEND WITH FRIEND 5 229
THIS DAY TO BE OUR GUEST. BUT GOE WITH SPEED, 5 313
AND WE HAVE YET LARGE DAY, FOR SCARCE THE SUN 5 558
UPON HER CENTER POIS'D, WHEN ON A DAY 5 579
BY PRESENT, PAST, AND FUTURE) ON SUCH DAY 5 582
THIS DAY I HAVE BEGOT WHOM I DECLARE 5 603
MEE DISOBEYES, BREAKS UNION, AND THAT DAY 5 612
THAT DAY, AS OTHER SOLEMN DAYES, THEY SPENT 5 618
WITH ENVIE AGAINST THE SON OF GOD, THAT DAY 5 662
GRATEFUL VICISSITUDE, LIKE DAY AND NIGHT; 6 8
THAT SELF SAME DAY BY FIGHT, OR BY SURPRIZE 6 87
AS BOTH THIR DEEDS COMPAR'D THIS DAY SHALL PROVE. 6 170
THE BATTEL HUNG; TILL SATAN, WHO THAT DAY 6 246
WHO HAVE SUSTAIND ONE DAY IN DOUBTFUL FIGHT 6 423
(AND IF ONE DAY, WHY NOT ETERNAL DAYES?) 6 424
THIS DAY, FEAR NOT HIS FLIGHT; SO THICK A CLOUD 6 539
BORN EEVN OR HIGH, FOR THIS DAY WILL POUR DOWN, 6 544
YE ANGELS ARM'D, THIS DAY FROM BATTEL REST; 6 802
AND THE GREAT LIGHT OF DAY YET WANTS TO RUN 7 98
AGAINST A SOLEMN DAY, HARNEST AT HAND, 7 202
DIVIDED: LIGHT THE DAY, AND DARKNESS NIGHT 7 251
HE NAM'D. THUS WAS THE FIRST DAY EEV'N AND MORN: 7 252
BIRTH-DAY OF HEAV'N AND EARTH; WITH JOY AND SHOUT 7 256
AND MORNING CHORUS SUNG THE SECOND DAY. 7 275
SO EEV'N AND MORN RECORDED THE THIRD DAY. 7 338
THE DAY FROM NIGHT; AND LET THEM BE FOR SIGNES, 7 341
TO MAN, THE GREATER TO HAVE RULE BY DAY, 7 347
TO ILLUMINATE THE EARTH, AND RULE THE DAY 7 350
REGENT OF DAY, AND ALL TH' HORIZON ROUND 7 371
GLAD EEVNING AND GLAD MORN CROWND THE FOURTH DAY. 7 386
EV'NING AND MORN SOLEMNIZ'D THE FIFT DAY. 7 448
FREQUENT; AND OF THE SIXT DAY YET REMAIN'D; 7 504
THOU MAI'ST NOT; IN THE DAY THOU EAT'ST, THOU DI'ST; 7 544
SO EV'N AND MORN ACCOMPLISH'D THE SIXT DAY: 7 550
NOW RESTING, BLESS'D AND HALLOW'D THE SEAV'NTH DAY, 7 592
AS RESTING ON THAT DAY FROM ALL HIS WORK, 7 593
THEN FROM THE GIANT ANGELS; THEE THAT DAY 7 605
ONE DAY AND NIGHT; IN ALL THIR VAST SURVEY 8 24
SUCH RESTLESS REVOLUTION DAY BY DAY 8 31
WHERE GOD RESIDES, AND ERE MID-DAY ARRIV'D 8 112
OF DAY AND NIGHT; WHICH NEEDS NOT THY BELEEFE 8 136
IF EARTH INDUSTRIOUS OF HER SELF FETCH DAY 8 137
ENLIGHTNING HER BY DAY, AS SHE BY NIGHT 8 143
AND DAY IS YET NOT SPENT; TILL THEN THOU SEEST 8 206
FOR I THAT DAY WAS ABSENT, AS BEFELL, 8 229
THE DAY THOU EAT'ST THEREOF, MY SOLE COMMAND 8 329
FROM THAT DAY MORTAL, AND THIS HAPPIE STATE 8 331
TWIXT DAY AND NIGHT, AND NOW FROM END TO END 9 51
FROM COMPASSING THE EARTH, CAUTIOUS OF DAY, 9 59
THE INFERNAL POWERS, IN ONE DAY TO HAVE MARR'D 9 136
THEN COMMUNE HOW THAT DAY THEY BEST MAY PLY 9 201
LUXURIOUS BY RESTRAINT; WHAT WE BY DAY 9 209
FOR WHILE SO NEAR EACH OTHER THUS ALL DAY 9 220
TO BEASTS, WHOM GOD ON THIR CREATION-DAY 9 556
TILL ON A DAY ROAVING THE FIELD, I CHANC'D 9 575
HIS WORSHIPPERS; HE KNOWS THAT IN THE DAY 9 705
OUR INWARD FREEDOM? IN THE DAY WE EATE 9 762
THIS DAY AFFORDS, DECLARING THEE RESOLVD, 9 968

DAY (CONTINUED)
YEILD THEE, SO WELL THIS DAY THOU HAST PURVEY'D. 9 1021
FOR NEVER DID THY BEAUTIE SINCE THE DAY 9 1029
BUT SUCH AS AT THIS DAY TO INDIANS KNOWN 9 1102
ON HIS TRANSGRESSION, DEATH DENOUNC'T THAT DAY, 10 49
FORBEARANCE NO ACQUITTANCE ERE DAY END. 10 53
BROUGHT TO THIR EARS, WHILE DAY DECLIN'D, THEY HEARD, 10 99
O HEAV'N. IN EVIL STRAIT THIS DAY I STAND 10 125
AND TH' INSTANT STROKE OF DEATH DENOUNC'T THAT DAY 10 210
AGAINST THE DAY OF BATTEL, TO A FIELD, 10 275
FOR DEATH, THE FOLLOWING DAY, IN BLOODIE FIGHT. 10 278
BEYOND THE POLAR CIRCLES; TO THEM DAY 10 681
FIXD ON THIS DAY? WHY DO I OVERLIVE, 10 773
FROM THIS DAY ONWARD, WHICH I FEEL BEGUN 10 811
THE DAY OF HIS OFFENCE. WHY COMES NOT DEATH, 10 854
WAS MEANT BY DEATH THAT DAY, WHEN LO, TO THEE 10 1050
LABORIOUS, TILL DAY DROOP; WHILE HERE WE DWELL, 11 178
AND CARNAL FEAR THAT DAY DIMM'D ADAMS EYE. 11 212
QUIET THOUGH SAD, THE RESPIT OF THAT DAY 11 272
WHICH I MUST KEEP TILL MY APPOINTED DAY 11 550
RAINE DAY AND NIGHT, ALL FOUNTAINS OF THE DEEP 11 826
AND CALL TO MIND HIS COV'NANT: DAY AND NIGHT, 11 898
BY DAY A CLOUD, BY NIGHT A PILLAR OF FIRE, 12 203
ONE GREATER, OF WHOSE DAY HE SHALL FORETELL, 12 242
SHALL REST BY DAY, A FIERY GLEAME BY NIGHT, 12 257
A DAY ENTIRE, AND NIGHTS DUE COURSE ADJOURNE, 12 264
HIS DAY, IN WHOM ALL NATIONS SHALL BE BLEST, 12 277
ALL NATIONS THEY SHALL TEACH; FOR FROM THAT DAY 12 446
UNDER HER OWN WAIGHT GROANING TILL THE DAY 12 539

DAYES
OF FUTURE DAYES MAY BRING, WHAT CHANCE, WHAT CHANGE 2 222
THAT DAY, AS OTHER SOLEMN DAYES, THEY SPENT 5 618
(AND IF ONE DAY, WHY NOT ETERNAL DAYES?) 6 424
IN FUTURE DAYES, IF MALICE SHOULD ABOUND, 6 502
SECOND OMNIPOTENCE, TWO DAYES ARE PAST, 6 684
TWO DAYES, AS WE COMPUTE THE DAYES OF HEAV'N, 6 685
TWO DAYES ARE THEREFORE PAST, THE THIRD IS THINE; 6 699
NUMBER TO THIS DAYES WORK IS NOT ORDAIN'D 6 809
NINE DAYES THEY FELL; CONFOUNDED CHAOS ROARD, 6 871
TO HOARCE OR MUTE, THOUGH FALL'N ON EVIL DAYES, 7 25
ON EVIL DAYES THOUGH FALL'N, AND EVIL TONGUES; 7 26
FOR SEASONS, AND FOR DAYES, AND CIRCLING YEARS, 7 342
CREATION AND THE SIX DAYES ACTS THEY SUNG, 7 601
HIS SEASONS, HOURS, OR DAYES, OR MONTHS, OR YEARES: 8 69
OUR DAYES WORK BROUGHT TO LITTLE, THOUGH BEGUN 9 224
AND DUST SHALT EAT ALL THE DAYES OF THY LIFE. 10 178
TO ADAM WHAT SHALL COME IN FUTURE DAYES, 11 114
DARKNESS ERE DAYES MID-COURSE, AND MORNING LIGHT 11 204
DEFEATED OF HIS SEISURE MANY DAYES 11 254
TO SHEW THEE WHAT SHALL COME IN FUTURE DAYES 11 357
OF PEACEFUL DAYES PORTENDS, THEN THOSE TWO PAST; 11 600
FOR IN THOSE DAYES MIGHT ONELY SHALL BE ADMIR'D, 11 689
MY PART OF EVIL ONELY, EACH DAYES LOT 11 765
WITH LENGTH OF HAPPY DAYES THE RACE OF MAN; 11 782
SHAL SPEND THIR DAYES IN JOY UNBLAM'D, AND DWELL 12 22
PALPABLE DARKNESS, AND BLOT OUT THREE DAYES; 12 188
TO DAVID, STABLISHT AS THE DAYES OF HEAV'N. 12 347
THAT YE MAY LIVE, WHICH WILL BE MANY DAYES, 12 602

DAY-LABOUR
TO RESPIT HIS DAY-LABOUR WITH REPAST, 5 232

DAYS
SEE GOLDEN DAYS, FRUITFUL OF GOLDEN DEEDS, 3 337
DAYS, MONTHS, & YEARS, TOWARDS HIS ALL-CHEARING LAMP 3 581
A WHOLE DAYS JOURNY HIGH, BUT WIDE REMOTE 4 284
MAGNIFICENT, HIS SIX DAYS WORK, A WORLD; 7 568
WHAT HE ALMIGHTIE STYL'D, FIX NIGHTS AND DAYS 9 137
SHALT EATE THEREOF ALL THE DAYS OF THY LIFE; 10 202
THIS ANNUAL HUMBLING CERTAIN NUMBER'D DAYS, 10 576
EQUAL IN DAYS AND NIGHTS, EXCEPT TO THOSE 10 680
SINCE THIS DAYS DEATH DENOUNC'T, IF OUGHT I SEE, 10 962
A LONG DAYS DYING TO AUGMENT OUR PAINE, 10 964
BY DEATH BROUGHT ON OUR SELVES, OR CHILDLESS DAYS 10 1037
BEFORE THEE RECONCIL'D, AT LEAST HIS DAYS 11 39
WHERERE OUR DAYS WORK LIES, THOUGH NOW ENJOIND 11 177
SOME DAYS; HOW LONG, AND WHAT TILL THEN OUR LIFE, 11 198

DAY-SPRING
OF DAY-SPRING, AND THE SUN, WHO SCARCE UP RISEN 5 139
SO ALL ERE DAY-SPRING, UNDER CONSCIOUS NIGHT 6 521

DAZL'D
DAZL'D AND SPENT, SUNK DOWN, AND SOUGHT REPAIR 8 457

DAZLE
YET DAZLE HEAV'N, THAT BRIGHTEST SERAPHIM 3 381
WILL DAZLE NOW THIS EARTHLY, WITH THIR BLAZE 9 1083

DAZLES
DAZLES THE CROUD, AND SETS THEM ALL AGAPE. 5 357

DAZ'LING
DAZ'LING THE MOON; THESE TO THE BOWER DIRECT 4 798

DAZLING
OF DREADFUL LENGTH AND DAZLING ARMS, IN GUISE . . . 1 564

DEAD
CAN NEVER SEEK, ONCE DEAD IN SINS AND LOST; . . . 3 233
THE LIVING, AND FORTHWITH THE CITED DEAD . . . 3 327
IN GOLGOTHA HIM DEAD, WHO LIVES IN HEAV'N; . . . 3 477
NOT DEAD, AS WE ARE THREATN'D, BUT THENCEFORTH . 9 870
OF EGYPT MUST LIE DEAD. THUS WITH TEN WOUNDS . . 12 190
WITH GLORY AND POWER TO JUDGE BOTH QUICK AND DEAD, 12 460
TO JUDGE TH' UNFAITHFUL DEAD, BUT TO REWARD . . 12 461

DEADLIER
SATAN, WHOSE FALL FROM HEAV'N, A DEADLIER BRUISE, 12 391

DEADLY
ABHORRED STYX THE FLOOD OF DEADLY HATE, ... 2 577
LEVEL'D HIS DEADLY AIME; THIR FATALL HANDS . . . 2 712
HIS DEADLY ARROW; NEITHER VAINLY HOPE 2 811
THE DEADLY FORFEITURE, AND RANSOM SET. 3 221
WHERE WOUNDS OF DEADLY HATE HAVE PEIRC'D SO DEEP: 4 99
NOR YET ON HIM FOUND DEADLY, HE YET LIVES, . . . 9 932
THAT BEAT OUT LIFE; HE FELL, AND DEADLY PALE . 11 446

DEAFNING
WITH DEAFNING SHOUT, RETURN'D THEM LOUD ACCLAIM. . 2 520

DEAL
WHEN REASON HATH TO DEAL WITH FORCE, YET SO . . . 6 125
DEATHS MINISTERS, NOT MEN, WHO THUS DEAL DEATH . 11 676

DEALE
HIS PEOPLE, WHO DEFEND? WILL THEY NOT DEALE . . 12 483

DEALS
TO ME ALIKE, IT DEALS ETERNAL WOE. 4 70

DEALT
BUT HEAV'NS FREE LOVE DEALT EQUALLY TO ALL? . . . 4 68
WORS WITH HIS FOLLOWERS THEN WITH HIM THEY DEALT? 12 484

DEAR
DEAR DAUGHTER, SINCE THOU CLAIM'ST ME FOR THY SIRE, 2 817
AND MY FAIR SON HERE SHOWST ME, THE DEAR PLEDGE . 2 818
MY SOLE COMPLACENCE. WELL THOU KNOW'ST HOW DEAR, 3 276
HIS BRETHREN, RANSOMD WITH HIS OWN DEAR LIFE. . . 3 297
NO SOONER DID THY DEAR AND ONELY SON 3 403
OVER THE PROMIS'D LAND TO GOD SO DEAR, ... 3 531
KNOWLEDGE OF GOOD BOUGHT DEAR BY KNOWING ILL. . . 4 222
HENCEFORTH AN INDIVIDUAL SOLACE DEAR; 4 486
RELATIONS DEAR, AND ALL THE CHARITIES 4 756
SLEEPST THOU COMPANION DEAR, WHAT SLEEP CAN CLOSE 5 673
IS PROPAGATED SEEM SUCH DEAR DELIGHT 8 580
ADAM, MISSTHOUGHT OF HER TO THEE SO DEAR? . . . 9 289
SO DEAR I LOVE HIM THAT WITH HIM ALL DEATHS . . 9 832
DISGUIS'D HE CAME, BUT THOSE HIS CHILDREN DEAR . 10 330
MET WHO TO MEET HIM CAME, HIS OFSPRING DEAR. . 10 349

DEARE
DWELS IN ALL HEAVEN CHARITIE SO DEARE? 3 216
AND HEAVIER FALL: SO SHOULD I PURCHASE DEARE . . 4 101
NOT TO BE OVERPOWERD, COMPANIONS DEARE, ... 6 419
COMPARE ABOVE ALL LIVING CREATURES DEARE, . . . 9 228
ADAM, FROM WHOSE DEARE SIDE I BOAST ME SPRUNG, . 9 965
SHALL SEPARATE US, LINKT IN LOVE SO DEARE, . . . 9 970
FOR US HIS OFSPRING DEARE? IT CANNOT BE . . . 10 238
OF PARADISE, DEARE BOUGHT WITH LASTING WOES. . 10 742

DEARER
DEARER THY SELF THEN ALL; NEEDS MUST THE POWER . 4 412
BEST IMAGE OF MY SELF AND DEARER HALF, ... 5 95

DEAREST
HIS DEAREST MEDIATION THUS RENEWD. 3 226

DEARLY
SO DEARLY TO REDEEM WHAT HELLISH HATE 3 300
HOW DEARLY I ABIDE THAT BOAST SO VAINE, ... 4 87
THY SWEET CONVERSE AND LOVE SO DEARLY JOYN'D, . . 9 909

DEARTH
EATE FREELY WITH GLAD HEART; FEAR HERE NO DEARTH: 8 322
IN TIME OF DEARTH, A SON WHOSE WORTHY DEEDS . . 12 161

DEATH
BROUGHT DEATH INTO THE WORLD, AND ALL OUR WOE, . 1 3
WITH DREAD OF DEATH TO FLIGHT OR FOUL RETREAT, . 1 555
ROCKS, CAVE, LAKES, FENS, BOGS, DENS, AND SHADES OF
DEATH, ... 2 621
A UNIVERSE OF DEATH, WHICH GOD BY CURSE 2 622
WHERE ALL LIFE DIES, DEATH LIVES, AND NATURE
BREEDS, ... 2 624
MADE TO DESTROY: I FLED, AND CRY'D OUT DEATH; . . 2 787
FROM ALL HER CAVES, AND BACK RESOUNDED DEATH. . . 2 789
GRIM DEATH MY SON AND FOE, WHO SETS THEM ON, . . 2 804
AND BRING YE TO THE PLACE WHERE THOU AND DEATH . 2 840
HE CEAS'D, FOR BOTH SEEMD HIGHLY PLEASD, AND DEATH 2 845
DEATH READY STANDS TO INTERPOSE HIS DART, . . . 2 854

DEATH (CONTINUED)
STRANGE ALTERATION. SIN AND DEATH AMAIN . . . 2 1024
THE RIGID SATISFACTION, DEATH FOR DEATH. . . . 3 212
MUST HAVE BIN LOST, ADJUDG'D TO DEATH AND HELL . 3 223
WELL PLEAS'D, ON ME LET DEATH WRECK ALL HIS RAGE; 3 241
THOUGH NOW TO DEATH I YIELD, AND AM HIS DUE . . 3 245
DEATH HIS DEATHS WOUND SHALL THEN RECEIVE, AND
STOOP 3 252
DEATH LAST, AND WITH HIS CARCASS GLUT THE GRAVE: . 3 259
GIVING TO DEATH, AND DYING TO REDEEME, ... 3 299
THEREBY REGAIND, BUT SAT DEVISING DEATH 4 197
OUR DEATH THE TREE OF KNOWLEDGE GREW FAST BY, . . 4 221
SO NEER GROWS DEATH TO LIFE, WHAT ERE DEATH IS, . 4 425
GOD HATH PRONOUNC'T IT DEATH TO TASTE THAT TREE, . 4 427
CAN IT BE DEATH? AND DO THEY ONELY STAND . . . 4 518
DEATH IS THE PENALTIE IMPOS'D, BEWARE, ... 7 545
SURPRISE THEE, AND HER BLACK ATTENDANT DEATH. . . 7 547
SINNE AND HER SHADOW DEATH, AND MISERIE 9 12
AS WEE, NOT CAPABLE OF DEATH OR PAINE, ... 9 283
THOSE RIGID THREATS OF DEATH; YE SHALL NOT DIE: . 9 685
OF DEATH DENOUNC'T, WHATEVER THING DEATH BE, . . 9 695
YOUR FEARE IT SELF OF DEATH REMOVES THE FEARE. . 9 702
HUMAN, TO PUT ON GODS, DEATH TO BE WISHT, . . . 9 714
SUCH PROHIBITIONS BINDE NOT. BUT IF DEATH . . . 9 760
WAS DEATH INVENTED? OR TO US DENI'D 9 767
OF GOD OR DEATH, OF LAW OR PENALTIE? 9 775
AND KNEW NOT EATING DEATH: SATIATE AT LENGTH, . . 9 792
AND DEATH ENSUE? THEN I SHALL BE NO MORE, . . . 9 827
A DEATH TO THINK. CONFIRM'D THEN I RESOLVE, . . 9 830
DEFAC'T, DEFLOURD, AND NOW TO DEATH DEVOTE? . . 9 901
CERTAIN TO UNDERGOE LIKE DOOM, IF DEATH 9 953
CONSORT WITH THEE, DEATH IS TO MEE AS LIFE; . . 9 954
RATHER THEN DEATH OR AUGHT THEN DEATH MORE DREAD . 9 969
WERE IT I THOUGHT DEATH MENAC'T WOULD ENSUE . . 9 977
FARR OTHERWISE TH' EVENT, NOT DEATH, BUT LIFE . . 9 984
AND FEAR OF DEATH DELIVER TO THE WINDES. . . . 9 989
DIVINE DISPLEASURE FOR HER SAKE, OR DEATH. . . . 9 993
YET WILLINGLY CHOSE RATHER DEATH WITH THEE: . . 9 1167
ON HIS TRANSGRESSION, DEATH DENOUNC'T THAT DAY, . 10 49
AND TH' INSTANT STROKE OF DEATH DENOUNC'T THAT DAY 10 210
WITHIN THE GATES OF HELL SATE SIN AND DEATH, . . 10 230
SIN OPENING, WHO THUS NOW TO DEATH BEGAN. . . . 10 234
FOR DEATH FROM SIN NO POWER CAN SEPARATE. . . . 10 251
THE SAVOUR OF DEATH FROM ALL THINGS THERE THAT
LIVE: 10 269
FOR DEATH, THE FOLLOWING DAY, IN BLOODIE FIGHT. . 10 278
DEATH WITH HIS MACE PETRIFIC, COLD AND DRY, . . 10 294
FORFEIT TO DEATH; FROM HENCE A PASSAGE BROAD, . . 10 304
THROUGH SIN TO DEATH EXPOS'D BY MY EXPLOIT. . . 10 407
BY SIN AND DEATH A BROAD WAY NOW IS PAV'D . . . 10 473
TO SIN AND DEATH A PREY, AND SO TO US, ... 10 490
HABITUAL HABITANT; BEHIND HER DEATH 10 588
SECOND OF SATAN SPRUNG, ALL CONQUERING DEATH, . . 10 591
BOTH SIN, AND DEATH, AND YAWNING GRAVE AT LAST . 10 635
DEATH INTRODUC'D THROUGH FIERCE ANTIPATHIE: . . 10 709
NOW DEATH TO HEARE. FOR WHAT CAN I ENCREASE . . 10 731
WHY AM I MOCKT WITH DEATH, AND LENGTH'ND OUT . . 10 774
BUT I SHALL DIE A LIVING DEATH? O THOUGHT . . . 10 788
WRATH WITHOUT END ON MAN WHOM DEATH MUST END? . . 10 797
CAN HE MAKE DEATHLESS DEATH? THAT WERE TO MAKE . 10 798
THAT DEATH BE NOT ONE STROAK, AS I SUPPOS'D, . . 10 809
ON MY DEFENSLESS HEAD; BOTH DEATH AND I 10 815
CURS'D HIS CREATION, DEATH AS OFT ACCUS'D . . . 10 852
THE DAY OF HIS OFFENCE. WHY COMES NOT DEATH, . . 10 854
BUT DEATH COMES NOT AT CALL, JUSTICE DIVINE . . 10 858
SINCE THIS DAYS DEATH DENOUNC'T, IF OUGHT I SEE, . 10 962
BY DEATH AT LAST, AND MISERABLE IT IS 10 981
SO DEATH SHALL BE DECEAV'D HIS GLUT, AND WITH US
TWO 10 990
LET US SEEK DEATH, OR HE NOT FOUND, SUPPLY . . . 10 1001
THAT SHEW NO END BUT DEATH, AND HAVE THE POWER, . 10 1004
BROKE OFF THE REST; SO MUCH OF DEATH HER THOUGHTS 10 1008
OR IF THOU COVET DEATH, AS UTMOST END 10 1020
TO BE FORESTALL'D; MUCH MORE I FEAR LEAST DEATH . 10 1024
TO MAKE DEATH IN US LIVE: THEN LET US SEEK . . . 10 1028
BY DEATH BROUGHT ON OUR SELVES, OR CHILDLESS DAYS 10 1037
WAS MEANT BY DEATH THAT DAY, WHEN LO, TO THEE . . 10 1050
SHALL PERFET, AND FOR THESE MY DEATH SHALL PAY. . 11 36
NUMBERD, THOUGH SAD, TILL DEATH, HIS DOOM (WHICH I 11 40
TILL I PROVIDED DEATH; SO DEATH BECOMES 11 61
ASSURES ME THAT THE BITTERNESS OF DEATH 11 157
THAT I WHO FIRST BROUGHT DEATH ON ALL, AM GRAC'T . 11 168
FROM PENALTIE, BECAUSE FROM DEATH RELEAST . . . 11 197
SUFFICIENT THAT THY PRAYERS ARE HEARD, AND DEATH, 11 252
O UNEXPECTED STROKE, WORSE THEN OF DEATH. . . . 11 268
BUT HAVE I NOW SEEN DEATH? IS THIS THE WAY . . 11 462
TO WHOM THUS MICHAEL. DEATH THOU HAST SEEN . . 11 466
OF DEATH, AND MANY ARE THE WAYES THAT LEAD . . . 11 468
AND OVER THEM TRIUMPHANT DEATH HIS DART 11 491
TO DEATH, AND MIX WITH OUR CONNATURAL DUST? . . 11 529
GATHERD, NOT HARSHLY PLUCKT, FOR DEATH MATURE: . 11 537
HENCEFORTH I FLIE NOT DEATH, NOR WOULD PROLONG . 11 547
THOSE WERE OF HATE AND DEATH, OR PAIN MUCH WORSE, 11 601
DEATHS MINISTERS, NOT MEN, WHO THUS DEAL DEATH . 11 676
EXEMPT FROM DEATH; TO SHEW THEE WHAT REWARD . . 11 709
ON PENALTIE OF DEATH, AND SUFFERING DEATH, . . . 12 398
TO A REPROACHFUL LIFE AND CURSED DEATH, ... 12 406
SEIS'D ON BY FORCE, JUDG'D, AND TO DEATH CONDEMND 12 412

DEATH (CONTINUED)
BUT SOON REVIVES, DEATH OVER HIM NO POWER . . . 12 420
THY RANSOM PAID, WHICH MAN FROM DEATH REDEEMS, . 12 424
HIS DEATH FOR MAN, AS MANY AS OFFERD LIFE . . . 12 425
ANNULS THY DOOM, THE DEATH THOU SHOULDST HAVE DY'D, 12 428
DEFEATING SIN AND DEATH, HIS TWO MAINE ARMES, . . 12 431
THEN TEMPORAL DEATH SHALL BRUISE THE VICTORS HEEL, 12 433
OR THEIRS WHOM HE REDEEMS, A DEATH LIKE SLEEP, . 12 434
FOR DEATH, LIKE THAT WHICH THE REDEEMER DY'D. . . 12 445
THOUGH TO THE DEATH, AGAINST SUCH CRUELTIES . . 12 494
AND TO THE FAITHFUL DEATH THE GATE OF LIFE; . . 12 571

DEATHLESS
TO DEATHLESS PAIN? HOW GLADLY WOULD I MEET . . 10 775
CAN HE MAKE DEATHLESS DEATH? THAT WERE TO MAKE . 10 798

DEATHS
DEATH HIS DEATHS WOUND SHALL THEN RECEIVE, AND STOOP 3 252
DEATHS HARBINGER: SAD TASK, YET ARGUMENT . . . 9 13
SO DEAR I LOVE HIM THAT WITH HIM ALL DEATHS . . 9 832
REDEEM THEE QUITE FROM DEATHS RAPACIOUS CLAIME; . 11 258
DEATHS MINISTERS, NOT MEN, WHO THUS DEAL DEATH . 11 676
DISABL'D NOT TO GIVE THEE THY DEATHS WOUND: . . 12 392

DEBARR
LABOUR, AS TO DEBARR US WHEN WE NEED 9 236

DEBAS'D
I NOT; SO MUCH HATH HELL DEBAS'D, AND PAINE . . 9 487

DEBAS'T
TO SUCH UNSIGHTLY SUFFERINGS BE DEBAS'T 11 510

DEBATE
WE NOW DEBATE; WHO CAN ADVISE, MAY SPEAK. . . . 2 42
WELL HAVE YE JUDG'D, WELL ENDED LONG DEBATE, . . 2 390
IN US WHO SERVE, NEW COUNSELS, TO DEBATE . . . 5 681
THAT HE WHO IN DEBATE OF TRUTH HATH WON, . . . 6 122
HIM AFTER LONG DEBATE, IRRESOLUTE 9 87

DEBT
ALL THAT OF ME CAN DIE, YET THAT DEBT PAID, . . 3 246
THE DEBT IMMENSE OF ENDLESS GRATITUDE, ... 4 52

DECAI'D
WRINKL'D THE FACE OF DELUGE, AS DECAI'D; . . . 11 843

DECAN
IN MALABAR OR DECAN SPREDS HER ARMES 9 1103

DECEAV'D
O MUCH DECEAV'D, MUCH FAILING, HAPLESS EVE, . . 9 404
AGAINST HIS BETTER KNOWLEDGE, NOT DECEAV'D, . . 9 998
MAN I DECEAV'D: THAT WHICH TO MEE BELONGS, . . 10 496
DECEAV'D; THEY FONDLY THINKING TO ALLAY . . . 10 564
UNHAPPILIE DECEAV'D; THY SUPPLIANT 10 917
SO DEATH SHALL BE DECEAV'D HIS GLUT, AND WITH US TWO 10 990
BUT I WAS FARR DECEAV'D; FOR NOW I SEE . . . 11 783

DECEAVE
OF GOD ALL-SEEING, OR DECEAVE HIS HEART 10 6

DECEIT
BUT BY DECEIT AND LIES; THIS LET HIM KNOW, . . . 5 243
FRIENDLY TO MAN, FARR FROM DECEIT OR GUILE. . . 9 772
AGAINST US THIS DECEIT: TO CRUSH HIS HEAD . . . 10 1035

DECEIV'D
STIRD UP WITH ENVY AND REVENGE, DECEIV'D . . . 1 35
SELF-TEMPTED, SELF-DEPRAV'D: MAN FALLS DECEIV'D . 3 130

DECEIVE
WITH HIM, OR WHO DECEIVE HIS MIND, WHOSE EYE . . 2 189
TO RESPITE OR DECEIVE, OR SLACK THE PAIN . . . 2 461
YET NOT ANOUGH HAD PRACTISD TO DECEIVE 4 124

DECENCIES
THOSE THOUSAND DECENCIES THAT DAILY FLOW . . . 8 601

DECENT
BEFORE HIS DECENT STEPS A SILVER WAND. 3 644

DECEPTION
AND FALL INTO DECEPTION UNAWARE, ... 9 362

DECIDE
FIT TO DECIDE THE EMPIRE OF GREAT HEAV'N. . . . 6 303

DECISION
AND BY DECISION MORE IMBROILES THE FRAY 2 908

DECK
WHETHER TO DECK WITH CLOUDS THE UNCOLOURD SKIE, . 5 189

DECK'T
WITH FLOURETS DECK'T AND FRAGRANT SMELLS; BUT EVE 5 379

DECKT
ESPOUSED EVE DECKT FIRST HER NUPTIAL BED, . . . 4 710

DECLAR'D
HIS FAIR LARGE FRONT AND EYE SUBLIME DECLAR'D . . 4 300
MESSIAH WAS DECLAR'D IN SIGHT OF HEAV'N, . . . 5 765
WHEN SUCH WAS HEARD DECLAR'D THE ALMIGHTIE'S WILL; 7 181
AND GAZE, AND WORSHIP THEE OF RIGHT DECLAR'D . . 9 611
YET LORDS DECLAR'D OF ALL IN EARTH OR AIRE? . 9 658
CHIEFLY ON MAN, SOLE LORD OF ALL DECLAR'D, . . 10 401
INCLIN'D NOT, BUT HIS COMING THUS DECLAR'D. . 11 250
AND OF THIR DOINGS GREAT DISLIKE DECLAR'D, . . 11 720

DECLARE
IN THESE THY LOWEST WORKS, YET THESE DECLARE . . 5 158
THIS DAY I HAVE BEGOT WHOM I DECLARE 5 603
UPON HIS ENEMIES, AND TO DECLARE 6 677
AND SWEET COMPLIANCE, WHICH DECLARE UNFEIGN'D . . 8 603
I CALL YE AND DECLARE YE NOW, RETURND 10 462

DECLARES
APPOINTED, WHICH DECLARES HIS DIGNITIE, ... 4 619
DEFAMING AS IMPURE WHAT GOD DECLARES 4 746

DECLARING
THIS DAY AFFORDS, DECLARING THEE RESOLVD, . . . 9 968

DECLARST
THAT THOU IN ME WELL PLEAS'D, DECLARST THY WILL . 6 728

DECLIN'D
DECLIN'D WAS HASTING NOW WITH PRONE CARREER . . 4 353
BROUGHT TO THIR EARS, WHILE DAY DECLIN'D, THEY HEARD, ... 10 99

DECLINE
THIS EEVNING FROM THE SUN'S DECLINE ARRIV'D . . 4 792
BE OVER, AND THE SUN MORE COOLE DECLINE. . . . 5 370
YET SOMTIMES NATIONS WILL DECLINE SO LOW . . . 12 97

DECREE
SUBDUES US, AND OMNIPOTENT DECREE, ... 2 198
THIR WILL, DISPOS'D BY ABSOLUTE DECREE 3 115
THIR NATURE, AND REVOKE THE HIGH DECREE 3 126
AND HERE ART LIKELIEST BY SUPREAM DECREE 3 659
HEAR MY DECREE, WHICH UNREVOK'T SHALL STAND. . . 5 602
THY EYE-LIDS? AND REMEMBREST WHAT DECREE . . . 5 674
WERE BANDED TO OPPOSE HIS HIGH DECREE; 5 717
NOT MEERLY TITULAR, SINCE BY DECREE 5 774
THE JUST DECREE OF GOD, PRONOUNC'T AND SWORN, . . 5 814
AND IN WHOSE HAND WHAT BY DECREE I DOE, . . . 6 683
AGAINST HIS MAKER; NO DECREE OF MINE 10 43
FATHER ETERNAL, THINE IS TO DECREE, ... 10 68
HIS HAND TO EXECUTE WHAT HIS DECREE 10 772
OBTAIN, ALL THY REQUEST WAS MY DECREE: 11 47
FOR EVER, TO REMOVE HIM I DECREE, ... 11 96
BUT PRAYER AGAINST HIS ABSOLUTE DECREE 11 311

DECREED
SAY THEY WHO COUNSEL WARR, WE ARE DECREED, . . . 2 160
OR HIGH FOREKNOWLEDGE; THEY THEMSELVES DECREED . 3 116
AS MY ETERNAL PURPOSE HATH DECREED; 3 172
WITH HEAV'NLY SPOILS, OUR SPOILS: WHAT HE DECREED 9 151

DECREES
WILL NOT BE NOW VOUTSAF'T, OTHER DECREES . . . 5 884
RIGHTEOUS ARE THY DECREES ON ALL THY WORKS; . . 10 644
COULD ALTER HIGH DECREES, I TO THAT PLACE . . . 10 953

DECREPIT
DECREPIT WINTER, FROM THE SOUTH TO BRING . . . 10 655

DECT
IN ALL THE LIVERIES DECT OF SUMMERS PRIDE . . . 7 478

DEED
AT SUCH BOLD WORDS VOUCHT WITH A DEED SO BOLD: . 5 66
TO BE BOTH WILL AND DEED CREATED FREE; 5 549
NONE OF RETREAT, NO UNBECOMING DEED 6 237
BOLD DEED THOU HAST PRESUM'D, ADVENTROUS EVE, . . 9 921
HER DOING SEEM'D TO JUSTIFIE THE DEED; . . . 10 142
ALAS, BOTH FOR THE DEED AND FOR THE CAUSE. . . 11 461

DEEDS
UNDER THY CONDUCT, AND IN DREADFUL DEEDS . . . 1 130
TO VICE INDUSTRIOUS, BUT TO NOBLER DEEDS . . . 2 116
THIR SPECIOUS DEEDS ON EARTH, WHICH GLORY EXCITES, 2 484
THIR OWN HEROIC DEEDS AND HAPLESS FALL . . . 2 549
TO MEET SO GREAT A FOE; AND NOW GREAT DEEDS . . 2 722
PREVENTED SPARES TO TELL THEE YET BY DEEDS . . 2 739
THIR OWN BOTH RIGHTEOUS AND UNRIGHTEOUS DEEDS, . 3 292
SEE GOLDEN DAYS, FRUITFUL OF GOLDEN DEEDS, . . 3 337
FIT RETRIBUTION, EMPTIE AS THIR DEEDS; . . . 3 454
WORSE; OF WORSE DEEDS WORSE SUFFERINGS MUST ENSUE. 4 26
THE TYRANTS PLEA, EXCUS'D HIS DEVILISH DEEDS. . . 4 394
WHAT SEEMD BOTH SPEAR AND SHIELD: NOW DREADFUL DEEDS 4 990
ILL MATCHING WORDS AND DEEDS LONG PAST OR LATE. . 5 113

DEEDS (CONTINUED)
SHALL TEACH US HIGHEST DEEDS, BY PROOF TO TRY . . 5 865
HEROIC ARDOR TO ADVENT'ROUS DEEDS 6 66
AMONG THE MIGHTIEST, BENT ON HIGHEST DEEDS, . . 6 112
AS BOTH THIR DEEDS COMPAR'D THIS DAY SHALL PROVE. 6 170
OF VICTORIE; DEEDS OF ETERNAL FAME 6 240
OF AIRIE THREATS TO AW WHOM YET WITH DEEDS . . . 6 283
MEAN WHILE IN OTHER PARTS LIKE DEEDS DESERVD . . 6 354
O PARENT, THESE ARE THY MAGNIFIC DEEDS, ... 10 354
AND ONE BAD ACT WITH MANY DEEDS WELL DONE . . . 11 256
CORRUPTION TO BRING FORTH MORE VIOLENT DEEDS. . . 11 428
ON EACH HAND SLAUGHTER AND GIGANTIC DEEDS. . . . 11 659
RAISE OUT OF FRIENDSHIP HOSTIL DEEDS IN PEACE. . 11 796
IN TIME OF DEARTH, A SON WHOSE WORTHY DEEDS . . 12 161
AND PUISSANT DEEDS, A PROMISE SHALL RECEIVE . . 12 322
DEEDS TO THY KNOWLEDGE ANSWERABLE, ADD FAITH, . . 12 582

DEEM
OF FUTURE WE MAY DEEM HIM, THOUGH TILL NOW . . . 6 429
AND WITH MYSTERIOUS REVERENCE I DEEM) 8 599
WELL DEEM IN OUTWARD RITES AND SPECIOUS FORMES . 12 534

DEEM'D
HIS TRUST WAS WITH TH' ETERNAL TO BE DEEM'D . . 2 46
MY DAMAGE FONDLY DEEM'D, I CAN REPAIRE 7 152
HEROIC DEEM'D, CHIEF MAISTRIE TO DISSECT . . . 9 29

DEEMD
NOW IN THINE EYE SO FOUL, ONCE DEEMD SO FAIR . . 2 748
OTHERS CAME SINGLE; HE WHO TO BE DEEMD 3 469
OF HIGHEST AGENTS, DEEMD HOWEVER WISE. 9 683
ACCOMPLISHING GREAT THINGS, BY THINGS DEEMD WEAK . 12 567

DEEMING
DEEMING SOME ISLAND, OFT, AS SEA-MEN TELL, . . . 1 205

DEEP
NOR THE DEEP TRACT OF HELL, SAY FIRST WHAT CAUSE . 1 28
VAUNTING ALOUD, BUT RACKT WITH DEEP DESPARE: . . 1 126
OR DO HIS ERRANDS IN THE GLOOMY DEEP; 1 152
TO BELLOW THROUGH THE VAST AND BOUNDLESS DEEP. . 1 177
HE CALL'D SO LOUD, THAT ALL THE HOLLOW DEEP . . 1 314
DEEP SCARS OF THUNDER HAD INTRENCHT, AND CARE . . 1 601
FOR SINCE NO DEEP WITHIN HER GULF CAN HOLD . . . 2 12
INSULTING, AND PURSU'D US THROUGH THE DEEP, . . 2 79
IN THIS ABHORRED DEEP TO UTTER WOE; 2 87
IMPREGNABLE; OFT ON THE BORDERING DEEP 2 131
THE DEEP TO SHELTER US? THIS HELL THEN SEEM'D . 2 167
THROUGH LABOUR AND INDURANCE. THIS DEEP WORLD . 2 262
COVERS HIS THRONE; FROM WHENCE DEEP THUNDERS ROAR 2 267
A PILLAR OF STATE; DEEP ON HIS FRONT ENGRAVEN . . 2 302
OR AMBUSH FROM THE DEEP. WHAT IF WE FIND . . . 2 344
SO DEEP A MALICE, TO CONFOUND THE RACE 2 382
GREAT THINGS RESOLV'D, WHICH FROM THE LOWEST DEEP 2 392
PONDERING THE DANGER WITH DEEP THOUGHTS; AND EACH 2 421
WITH REASON HATH DEEP SILENCE AND DEMURR . . . 2 431
SAD ACHERON OF SORROW, BLACK AND DEEP; 2 578
OF ANCIENT PILE; ALL ELSE DEEP SNOW AND ICE, . . 2 591
NOW SHAVES WITH LEVEL WING THE DEEP, THEN SOARES . 2 634
INTO THIS DEEP, AND IN THE GENERAL FALL 2 773
TH' UNFOUNDED DEEP, AND THROUGH THE VOID IMMENSE . 2 829
THE SECRETS OF THE HOARIE DEEP, A DARK 2 891
TEN THOUSAND FADOM DEEP, AND TO THIS HOUR . . . 2 934
WIDE ON THE WASTEFUL DEEP; WITH HIM ENTHRON'D . . 2 961
FLED NOT IN SILENCE THROUGH THE FRIGHTED DEEP . . 2 994
THE RISING WORLD OF WATERS DARK AND DEEP, . . . 3 11
SHOOTS INVISIBLE VERTUE EVEN TO THE DEEP: . . . 3 586
HE SEEMD, OR FIXT IN COGITATION DEEP. 3 629
THAT BROUGHT THEM FORTH, BUT HID THIR CAUSES DEEP. 3 707
AND IN THE LOWEST DEEP A LOWER DEEP 4 76
WHERE WOUNDS OF DEADLY HATE HAVE PEIRC'D SO DEEP; 4 99
DEEP MALICE TO CONCEALE, COUCH'T WITH REVENGE: . 4 123
I FEAR, HATH VENTUR'D FROM THE DEEP, TO RAISE . 4 574
THESE THEN, THOUGH UNBEHELD IN DEEP OF NIGHT, . . 4 674
INTO UTTER DARKNESS, DEEP INGULFT, HIS PLACE . . 5 614
DEEP MALICE THENCE CONCEIVING AND DISDAIN, . . . 5 666
HE SAID, AND AS THE SOUND OF WATERS DEEP . . . 5 872
BUT WITH SWIFT WHEELE REVERSE, DEEP ENTRING SHAR'D 6 326
AND WITH FIERCE ENSIGNES PIERC'D THE DEEP ARRAY . 6 356
DEEP UNDER GROUND, MATERIALS DARK AND CRUDE, . . 6 478
THESE IN THIR DARK NATIVITIE THE DEEP 6 482
ON EVERY SIDE WITH SHADDOWING SQUADRONS DEEP, . . 6 554
FROM THOSE DEEP THROATED ENGINS BELCHT, WHOSE ROAR 6 586
UNDER THE WEIGHT OF MOUNTAINS BURIED DEEP, . . . 6 652
FROM ALL HEAV'NS BOUNDS INTO THE UTTER DEEP: . . 6 716
INTO THE WASTFUL DEEP; THE MONSTROUS SIGHT . . . 6 862
AFFRIGHTED; BUT STRICT FATE HAD CAST TOO DEEP . . 6 869
AMONG TH' ANGELIC POWERS, AND THE DEEP FALL . . . 6 898
WITH ADMIRATION, AND DEEP MUSE TO HEARE 7 52
OF NATURE FROM THE UNAPPARENT DEEP; 7 103
FELL WITH HIS FLAMING LEGIONS THROUGH THE DEEP . 7 134
I SEND ALONG, RIDE FORTH, AND BID THE DEEP . . . 7 166
BOUNDLESS THE DEEP, BECAUSE I AM WHO FILL . . . 7 168
SILENCE, YE TROUBL'D WAVES, AND THOU DEEP, PEACE, 7 216
SPRUNG FROM THE DEEP, AND FROM HER NATIVE EAST . 7 245
DOWN SUNK A HOLLOW BOTTOM BROAD AND DEEP, . . . 7 289
AND ON THE WASHIE OOSE DEEP CHANNELS WORE; . . . 7 303
HUGEST OF LIVING CREATURES, ON THE DEEP 7 413

DEEP (CONTINUED)
WITH NARROW SEARCH; AND WITH INSPECTION DEEP . . 9 83
THENCEFORTH TO SPECULATIONS HIGH OR DEEP . . . 9 602
BEYOND THIS DEEP; WHATEVER DRAWES ME ON, . . . 10 245
DEEP TO THE ROOTS OF HELL THE GATHER'D BEACH . . 10 299
OVER THE FOAMING DEEP HIGH ARCHT, A BRIDGE . . . 10 301
VOYAG'D TH' UNREAL, VAST, UNBOUNDED DEEP . . . 10 471
AS DEEP AS CAPRICORNE, TO BRING IN CHANGE . . . 10 677
I FIND NO WAY, FROM DEEP TO DEEPER PLUNG'D. . . 10 844
SO DEEP THE POWER OF THESE INGREDIENTS PIERC'D, . 11 417
DIRE WAS THE TOSSING, DEEP THE GROANS, DESPAIR . 11 489
DEEP UNDER WATER ROULD; SEA COVER'D SEA, . . . 11 749
RAINE DAY AND NIGHT, ALL FOUNTAINS OF THE DEEP . 11 826
WITH SOFT FOOT TOWARDS THE DEEP, WHO NOW HAD STOPT 11 848
ALL SECRETS OF THE DEEP, ALL NATURES WORKS, . . 12 578

DEEPER
THAT THEY MAY STUMBLE ON, AND DEEPER FALL; . . . 3 201
I FIND NO WAY, FROM DEEP TO DEEPER PLUNG'D. . . 10 844
AND FIX FARR DEEPER IN HIS HEAD THIR STINGS . . 12 432

DEEPEST
TO DEEPEST HELL, AND TO REPAIR THAT LOSS . . . 3 678
AND SO FROM HEAV'N TO DEEPEST HELL; O FALL . . . 5 542

DEEREST
COLLATERAL LOVE, AND DEEREST AMITIE. 8 426

DEFAC'T
DEFAC'T, DEFLOURD, AND NOW TO DEATH DEVOTE? . . 9 901
OR IF HIS LIKENESS, BY THEMSELVES DEFAC'T . . . 11 522

DEFAMING
DEFAMING AS IMPURE WHAT GOD DECLARES 4 746

DEFAULT
IMPUT'ST THOU THAT TO MY DEFAULT, OR WILL . . . 9 1145

DEFEAT
THAT WITH SAD OVERTHROW AND FOUL DEFEAT 1 135
HAVE RAIS'D INCESSANT ARMIES TO DEFEAT 6 138

DEFEATED
OF THUNDER: BACK DEFEATED TO RETURN 6 606
DEFEATED OF HIS SEISURE MANY DAYES 11 254

DEFEATING
DEFEATING SIN AND DEATH, HIS TWO MAINE ARMES, . . 12 431

DEFECT
THIS NOVELTIE ON EARTH, THIS FAIR DEFECT . . . 10 891

DEFECTIVE
IN UNITIE DEFECTIVE, WHICH REQUIRES 8 425

DEFECTS
OR SOLACE HIS DEFECTS. NO NEED THAT THOU . . . 8 419

DEFENCE
TO THEIR DEFENCE WHO HOLD IT: HERE PERHAPS . . . 2 362
BE QUESTIOND AND BLASPHEAM'D WITHOUT DEFENCE. . . 3 166
IN OUR DEFENCE, LEFT UNAWARES WE LOSE 5 731
DEFENCE, WHILE OTHERS BORE HIM ON THIR SHIELDS . 6 337
OUR SELVES WITH LIKE DEFENCE, TO ME DESERVES . . 6 467
SINGLE WITH LIKE DEFENCE, WHEREVER MET, ... 9 325

DEFEND
THAT LITTLE WHICH IS LEFT SO TO DEFEND, ... 2 1000
BOTH HARP AND VOICE; NOR COULD THE MUSE DEFEND . 7 37
ASSAULTING; OTHERS FROM THE WALL DEFEND . . . 11 657
HIS PEOPLE, WHO DEFEND? WILL THEY NOT DEALE . . 12 483

DEFENDED
OF THAT DEFENDED FRUIT; BUT LET HIM BOAST . . . 11 86

DEFENDS
DARKNESS DEFENDS BETWEEN TILL MORNING WATCH; . . 12 207

DEFENSIVE
DEFENSIVE SCARSE, OR WITH PALE FEAR SURPRIS'D, . 6 393

DEFENSLESS
ON MY DEFENSLESS HEAD; BOTH DEATH AND I 10 815

DEFERR
NOT TO DEFERR; HUNGER AND THIRST AT ONCE, . . . 9 586

DEFIANCE
HURLING DEFIANCE TOWARD THE VAULT OF HEAV'N, . . 1 669
HELL-DOOM'D, AND BREATH'ST DEFIANCE HERE AND SCORN 2 697
STAND FIRM, FOR IN HIS LOOK DEFIANCE LOURS. . . 4 873
SIEGE AND DEFIANCE: WRETCHED MAN. WHAT FOOD . . 12 74

DEFICIENCE
IS NO DEFICIENCE FOUND; NOT SO IS MAN, ... 8 416

DEFICIENT
NOTHING IMPERFET OR DEFICIENT LEFT 9 345

DEFI'D
DEFI'D THE BEST OF PANIM CHIVALRY 1 765
INCENS'T, AND THUS SECURELY HIM DEFI'D. 6 130
OF MOLOC FURIOUS KING, WHO HIM DEFI'D, 6 357

DEFIE
WHO DURST DEFIE TH' OMNIPOTENT TO ARMS. 1 49

DEFLOURD
DEFAC'T, DEFLOURD, AND NOW TO DEATH DEVOTE? 9 901

DEFORM
MORE DREADFUL AND DEFORM: ON TH' OTHER SIDE 2 706
SIGHT SO DEFORM WHAT HEART OF ROCK COULD LONG 11 494

DEFORMED
WITH MANY AN INRODE GOR'D; DEFORMED ROUT 6 387

DEFORMITIES
IN PART, FROM SUCH DEFORMITIES BE FREE, 11 513

DEGENERATE
SO ALL SHALL TURN DEGENERATE, ALL DEPRAV'D, 11 806

DEGRADE
MANS NATURE, LESS'N OR DEGRADE THINE OWNE. 3 304

DEGRADED
DEGRADED, WISDOM IN DISCOURSE WITH HER 8 552
DEGRADED, TO WHAT WRETCHED STATE RESERV'D. 11 501

DEGREE
DIFFERING BUT IN DEGREE, OF KIND THE SAME. 5 490
HIS NAME, AND HIGH WAS HIS DEGREE IN HEAV'N; 5 707
LIVE, IN WHAT STATE, CONDITION OR DEGREE, 8 176
BUT IN DEGREE, THE CAUSE OF HIS DESIRE 8 417
STRANGE ALTERATION IN ME, TO DEGREE 9 599
LEAST THOU NOT TASTING, DIFFERENT DEGREE 9 883
HIGHER DEGREE OF LIFE, INDUCEMENT STRONG 9 934

DEGREES
ASCENDING BY DEGREES MAGNIFICENT 3 502
INDU'D WITH VARIOUS FORMS VARIOUS DEGREES 5 473
OF HIERARCHIES, OF ORDERS, AND DEGREES; 5 591
IN THIR TRIPLE DEGREES, REGIONS TO WHICH 5 750
EQUALLY FREE; FOR ORDERS AND DEGREES 5 792
BY HIM CREATED IN THIR BRIGHT DEGREES, 5 838
NOT HERE, TILL BY DEGREES OF MERIT RAIS'D 7 157
THE POLES OF EARTH TWICE TEN DEGREES AND MORE 10 669

DEIFI'D
OF UNION OR COMMUNION, DEIFI'D; 8 431

DEIFIE
WITH SUPPLIANT KNEE, AND DEIFIE HIS POWER, 1 112

DEIGN
DEIGN TO DESCEND NOW LOWER, AND RELATE 7 84

DEIGN'D
RAPHAEL, THE SOCIABLE SPIRIT, THAT DEIGN'D 5 221
BY SUFFERANCE, AND THY WONTED FAVOUR DEIGN'D. 8 202

DEIGND
THOSE HAPPIE PLACES THOU HAST DEIGND A WHILE 5 364

DEIGNE
OPEN, AND HENCEFORTH OFT; FOR GOD WILL DEIGNE 7 569
AMONG WHOM GOD WILL DEIGNE TO DWELL ON EARTH 12 281

DEIGNES
OF MY CELESTIAL PATRONESS, WHO DEIGNES 9 21

DEIGNS
DEIGNS NONE TO EASE THY LOAD AND TASTE THY SWEET, 5 59

DEITIE
TH' INCENSED DEITIE, WHILE OFFERD GRACE 3 187
OF DEITIE OR EMPIRE, SUCH A FOE 5 724
THE DEITIE, AND DIVINE COMMANDS OBEI'D, 5 806
VISIBLY, WHAT BY DEITIE I AM, 6 682
THE CHARIOT OF PATERNAL DEITIE, 6 750
OF DEITIE SUPREAM, US DISPOSSEST, 7 142
THAT TO THE HIGHT OF DEITIE ASPIR'D; 9 167
DEITIE FOR THEE, WHEN FATE WILL NOT PERMIT. 9 885
BLAZ'D FORTH UNCLOUDED DEITIE; HE FULL 10 65
BY PRAYER TH' OFFENDED DEITIE TO APPEASE, 11 149
FRESH IN THIR MINDES, FEARING THE DEITIE, 12 15

DEITIES
AND DEVILS TO ADORE FOR DEITIES: 1 373
POWERS AND DOMINIONS, DEITIES OF HEAV'N, 2 11
THIR DEITIES TO ASSERT, WHO WHILE THEY FEEL 6 157

DEJECTION
OF SORROW AND DEJECTION AND DESPAIR 11 301

DELAID
ALL JUSTICE: NOR DELAID THE WINGED SAINT 5 247
SHOOK, BUT DELAID TO STRIKE, THOUGH OFT INVOK'T 11 492

DELAY
BY OUR DELAY? NO, LET US RATHER CHOOSE 2 60
WHICH ELSE MIGHT WORK HIM DANGER OR DELAY: 3 635
OF ARABIE THE BLEST, WITH SUCH DELAY 4 163
AND SWEET RELUCTANT AMOROUS DELAY. 4 311
AND LONGER WILL DELAY TO HEARE THEE TELL 7 101
SOMTIMES IN HIGHTH BEGAN, AS NO DELAY 9 675
WHICH WHEN THE LORD GOD HEARD, WITHOUT DELAY 10 163
THIS ALSO SHALL THEY GAIN BY THIR DELAY 12 223
IN MEE IS NO DELAY; WITH THEE TO GOE, 12 615

DELAY'D
SOLACE IN HER RETURN, SO LONG DELAY'D; 9 844

DELAYES
INVESTS THE SEA, AND WISHED MORN DELAYES: 1 208
O WELCOM HOUR WHENEVER. WHY DELAYES 10 771

DELECTABLE
WEE OURS FOR CHANGE DELECTABLE, NOT NEED) 5 629
DELECTABLE BOTH TO BEHOLD AND TASTE; 7 539

DELIA'S
OREAD OR DRYAD, OR OF DELIA'S TRAINE, 9 387
BETOOK HER TO THE GROVES, BUT DELIA'S SELF 9 388

DELIBERATE
DELIBERATE VALOUR BREATH'D, FIRM AND UNMOV'D 1 554

DELIBERATION
DELIBERATION SAT AND PUBLIC CARE; 2 303

DELICACIE
WHAT CHOICE TO CHUSE FOR DELICACIE BEST, 5 333

DELICACIES
NOR VEHEMENT DESIRE, THESE DELICACIES 8 526

DELICIOUS
PURGE OFF THIS GLOOM; THE SOFT DELICIOUS AIR, 2 400
OF EDEN, WHERE DELICIOUS PARADISE, 4 132
IF TRUE, HERE ONLY, AND OF DELICIOUS TASTE: 4 251
IN PARADISE THAT BEAR DELICIOUS FRUIT 4 422
ORDAIND BY THEE, AND THIS DELICIOUS PLACE 4 729
FRUIT OF DELICIOUS VINES, THE GROWTH OF HEAV'N, 5 635
HE BROUGHT THEE INTO THIS DELICIOUS GROVE, 7 537
SPOT MORE DELICIOUS THEN THOSE GARDENS FEIGN'D 9 439
AS MEET IS, AFTER SUCH DELICIOUS FARE; 9 1028
IN THIS DELICIOUS GARDEN? AS MY WILL 10 746

DELICIOUSLY
DELICIOUSLY, AND BUILDS HER WAXEN CELLS 7 491

DELIGHT
DELIGHT THEE MORE, AND SILOA'S BROOK THAT FLOW'D 1 11
BUT EVER TO DO ILL OUR SOLE DELIGHT, 1 160
IN HEAV'N THIS OUR DELIGHT; HOW WEARISOM 2 247
O SON, IN WHOM MY SOUL HATH CHIEF DELIGHT, 3 168
HIS CHIEF DELIGHT AND FAVOUR, HIM FOR WHOM 3 664
HAD IN REMEMBRANCE ALWAYES WITH DELIGHT; 3 704
OF US OUT-CAST, EXIL'D, HIS NEW DELIGHT, 4 106
VERNAL DELIGHT AND JOY, ABLE TO DRIVE 4 155
TO ALL DELIGHT OF HUMAN SENSE EXPOS'D 4 206
SAW UNDELIGHTED ALL DELIGHT, ALL KIND 4 286
OF HER LOOSE TRESSES HID: HE IN DELIGHT 4 497
DOLE WITH DELIGHT, WHICH IN THIS PLACE I SOUGHT; 4 894
HEAV'NS LAST BEST GIFT, MY EVER NEW DELIGHT, 5 19
TO US FOR FOOD AND FOR DELIGHT HATH CAUS'D 5 400
MY EXALTATION, AND MY WHOLE DELIGHT, 6 727
OR WANDER WITH DELIGHT, AND LOVE TO HAUNT 7 330
WITH WONDER, BUT DELIGHT, AND, AS IS DUE, 8 11
CAN SORT, WHAT HARMONIE OR TRUE DELIGHT? 8 384
ALL RATIONAL DELIGHT, WHEREIN THE BRUTE 8 391
THE SPIRIT OF LOVE AND AMOROUS DELIGHT. 8 477
IN ALL THINGS ELSE DELIGHT INDEED, BUT SUCH 8 524
MADE SO ADORN FOR THY DELIGHT THE MORE, 8 576
IS PROPAGATED SEEM SUCH DEAR DELIGHT 8 580
WITH WHAT DELIGHT COULD I HAVE WALKT THEE ROUND, 9 114
FOR NOT TO IRKSOM TOILE, BUT TO DELIGHT 9 242
HE MADE US, AND DELIGHT TO REASON JOYN'D. 9 243
THIR TENDANCE OR PLANTATION FOR DELIGHT, 9 419
ADJOYND, FROM EACH THING MET CONCEAVES DELIGHT, 9 449
SHE MOST, AND IN HER LOOK SUMMS ALL DELIGHT. 9 454
THOUGH IN MID HEAV'N, SOON ENDED HIS DELIGHT, 9 468
REGARDED, SUCH DELIGHT TILL THEN, AS SEEMD, 9 787
SO SAYING, WITH DELIGHT HE SNUFF'D THE SMELL 10 272
TOWARDS HER, HIS LIFE SO LATE AND SOLE DELIGHT, 10 941
DUE NOURISHMENT, NOT GLUTTONOUS DELIGHT, 11 533
OF ADAM, SOON ENCLIN'D TO ADMIT DELIGHT, 11 596
ESTABLISHT, SUCH DELIGHT HATH GOD IN MEN 12 245

DELIGHTED
ATTENTIVE, AND WITH MORE DELIGHTED EARE, 5 545
LISTENS DELIGHTED. EEVNING NOW APPROACH'D 5 627

DELIGHTED (CONTINUED)
DELIGHTED, AND WITH FREQUENT INTERCOURSE 7 571
DELIGHTED, OR NOT CAPABLE HER EARE 8 49
DELIGHTED, BUT DESIRING MORE HER STAY. 9 398

DELIGHTFUL
HIM FOLLOW'D RIMMON, WHOSE DELIGHTFUL SEAT 1 467
HIS BOUNTIE, FOLLOWING OUR DELIGHTFUL TASK 4 437
WHEN FIRST ON THIS DELIGHTFUL LAND HE SPREADS 4 643
ON THIS DELIGHTFUL LAND, NOR HERB, FRUIT, FLOURE, 4 652
ALL THINGS TO MANS DELIGHTFUL USE; THE ROOFE 4 692
FROM THIS DELIGHTFUL FRUIT, NOR KNOWN TILL NOW 9 1023

DELIGHTFULLY
DELIGHTFULLY, ENCREASE AND MULTIPLY, 10 730

DELIGHTS
YOUR CHANGE APPROACHES, WHEN ALL THESE DELIGHTS 4 367
UNLIMITED OF MANIFOLD DELIGHTS: 4 435
VARIED HIS BOUNTY SO WITH NEW DELIGHTS, 5 431
SO MUCH DELIGHTS ME AS THOSE GRACEFUL ACTS, 8 600

DELINEATE
OF HUMAN SENSE, I SHALL DELINEATE SO, 5 572

DELIVER
WILL VANISH AND DELIVER YE TO WOE, 4 368
AND FEAR OF DEATH DELIVER TO THE WINDES. 9 989

DELIVERANCE
DELIVERANCE FOR US ALL: THIS ENTERPRIZE 2 465
NO LESS THEN FOR DELIVERANCE WHAT WE OWE. 6 468
MANKINDS DELIVERANCE. BUT THE VOICE OF GOD 12 235
THE GREAT DELIVERANCE BY HER SEED TO COME 12 600

DELIVERER
DELIVERER FROM NEW LORDS, LEADER TO FREE 6 451
IS MEANT THY GREAT DELIVERER, WHO SHALL BRUISE 12 149
BUT SAY, IF OUR DELIVERER UP TO HEAV'N 12 479

DELIV'RANCE
ALL HIS DELIV'RANCE, AND TO NONE BUT ME. 3 182

DELOS
DELOS OR SAMOS FIRST APPEERING KENNS 5 265
AS DELOS FLOATING ONCE; THE REST HIS LOOK 10 296

DELPHIAN
THIR HIGHEST HEAV'N; OR ON THE DELPHIAN CLIFF, 1 517

DELUDE
THOUGH TO DELUDE THEM SENT, COULD NOT ABSTAIN, 10 557
WITH WHOSE STOL'N FRUIT MAN ONCE MORE TO DELUDE. 11 125

DELUGE
STILL URGES, AND A FIERY DELUGE, FED 1 68
CAME LIKE A DELUGE ON THE SOUTH, AND SPREAD 1 354
WRINKL'D THE FACE OF DELUGE, AS DECAI'D; 11 843

DELUSIVE
HOVERING AND BLAZING WITH DELUSIVE LIGHT, 9 639
THIS MORE DELUSIVE, NOT THE TOUCH, BUT TASTE 10 563

DEMEANOUR
HE MARKD AND MAD DEMEANOUR, THEN ALONE, 4 129
AND FIERCE DEMEANOUR SEEMS THE PRINCE OF HELL, 4 871
WITH GODDESS-LIKE DEMEANOUR FORTH SHE WENT; 8 59
TO WHOM THUS EVE WITH SAD DEMEANOUR MEEK. 11 162

DEMI-GODS
BUT TO BE GODS, OR ANGELS DEMI-GODS. 9 937

DEMOGORGON
OF DEMOGORGON; RUMOR NEXT AND CHANCE, 2 965

DEMURR
WITH REASON HATH DEEP SILENCE AND DEMURR 2 431

DEMURRE
THE LATTER I DEMURRE, FOR IN THIR LOOKS 9 558

DEMY-GODS
A THOUSAND DEMY-GODS ON GOLDEN SEAT'S, 1 796

DEN
BRIAREOS OR TYPHOON, WHOM THE DEN 1 199
ACCEPT THIS DARK OPPROBRIOUS DEN OF SHAME, 2 58
IN WOOD OR WILDERNESS, FORREST OR DEN; 4 342
IN FORREST WILDE, IN THICKET, BRAKE, OR DEN; 7 458
NOT YET IN HORRID SHADE OR DISMAL DEN, 9 185

DENI'D
ACCESS DENI'D; AND OVER HEAD UP GREW 4 137
TO BRUTE DENI'D, AND ARE OF LOVE THE FOOD, 9 240
WAS DEATH INVENTED? OR TO US DENI'D 9 767

DENID
THE FIRST AT LEST OF THESE I THOUGHT DENID 9 555

DENIES
BUT FIRST THE LAWLESS TYRANT, WHO DENIES 12 173

DENOUNC'D
HE ENDED FROWNING, AND HIS LOOK DENOUNC'D 2 106

DENOUNCE
FROM HALLOWD GROUND TH' UNHOLIE, AND DENOUNCE 11 106

DENOUNCING
AND FULL OF PEACE, DENOUNCING WRAUTH TO COME 11 815

DENOUNC'T
OF DEATH DENOUNC'T, WHATEVER THING DEATH BE, 9 695
ON HIS TRANSGRESSION, DEATH DENOUNC'T THAT DAY, 10 49
AND TH' INSTANT STROKE OF DEATH DENOUNC'T THAT DAY 10 210
OF TARDIE EXECUTION, SINCE DENOUNC'T 10 853
SINCE THIS DAYS DEATH DENOUNC'T, IF OUGHT I SEE, 10 962

DENS
ROCKS, CAVE, LAKES, FENS, BOGS, DENS, AND SHADES OF DEATH, 2 621
ROCKS, DENS, AND CAVES; BUT I IN NONE OF THESE 9 118

DENSE
ORE BOG OR STEEP, THROUGH STRAIT, ROUGH, DENSE, OR RARE, 2 948

DENY
ALL WHAT WE AFFIRM OR WHAT DENY, AND CALL 5 107

DEPART
THEN SCORND THOU DIDST DEPART, AND TO SUBDUE 6 40
HESPEREAN SETS, MY SIGNAL TO DEPART. 8 632
ERE THOU FROM HENCE DEPART, KNOW I AM SENT 11 356
TO LET HIS SOJOURNERS DEPART, AND OFT 12 192
GREATLY INSTRUCTED I SHALL HENCE DEPART, 12 557

DEPARTED
DEPARTED FROM THEE, AND THOU RESEMBL'ST NOW 4 839

DEPARTING
DEPARTING GAVE COMMAND, AND THEY OBSERV'D. 10 430
THIS MOST AFFLICTS ME, THAT DEPARTING HENCE, 11 315

DEPARTS
THE GRANDCHILDE WITH TWELVE SONS INCREAST, DEPARTS 12 155

DEPARTURE
DEPARTURE FROM THIS HAPPY PLACE, OUR SWEET 11 303

DEPEND
HIS PROVIDENCE, AND ON HIM SOLE DEPEND, 12 564

DEPENDENT
DEPENDENT MADE; SO GOD SHALL UNCREATE, 9 943

DEPENDS
MY HOLD OF THIS NEW KINGDOM ALL DEPENDS, 10 406

DEPLOR'D
ACKNOWLEDG'D AND DEPLOR'D, IN ADAM WRAUGHT 10 939

DEPLORE
TO FIND HER, OR FOR EVER TO DEPLORE 8 479

DEPOPULATION
DEPOPULATION; THEE ANOTHER FLOUD, 11 756

DEPORT
IN GATE SURPASS'D AND GODDESS-LIKE DEPORT, 9 389
IN WISE DEPORT, SPAKE MUCH OF RIGHT AND WRONG, 11 666

DEPRAV'D
SELF-TEMPTED, SELF-DEPRAV'D: MAN FALLS DECEIV'D 3 130
IF NOT DEPRAV'D FROM GOOD, CREATED ALL 5 471
BUT ALL CORRUPT, BOTH MIND AND WILL DEPRAV'D, 10 825
SO ALL SHALL TURN DEGENERATE, ALL DEPRAV'D, 11 806
THOUGH LATE REPENTING HIM OF MAN DEPRAV'D, 11 886

DEPRAV'ST
UNJUSTLY THOU DEPRAV'ST IT WITH THE NAME 6 174

DEPRECATION
AND HUMBLE DEPRECATION THUS REPLI'D. 8 378

DEPREST
DEPREST, AND MUCH THEY MAY, IF ALL BE MINE, 9 46

DEPRIV'D
THEE I HAVE MISST, AND THOUGHT IT LONG, DEPRIV'D 9 857

DEPRIVD
AS FROM HIS FACE I SHALL BE HID, DEPRIVD 11 316

DEPRIVES
DEPRIVES THEM OF THIR OUTWARD LIBERTIE, 12 100

DEPTH
OF DEPTH IMMEASURABLE: ANON THEY MOVE 1 549
FORESEEING OR PRESAGING, FROM THE DEPTH 1 627
IN HEIGHTH OR DEPTH, STILL FIRST AND LAST WILL REIGN 2 324
THE HIGHTH AND DEPTH OF THY ETERNAL WAYES . . . 8 413

DERIDED
AND ALL HIS HOST DERIDED, WHILE THEY STOOD . . . 6 633
OF THEM DERIDED, BUT OF GOD OBSERVD 11 817

DERIDES
ALL THESE OUR MOTIONS VAIN, SEES AND DERIDES; . . 2 191
ONE NIGHT OR TWO WITH WANTON GROWTH DERIDES . . 9 211

DERISION
JUSTLY HAST IN DERISION, AND SECURE 5 736
AND TO HIS MATES THUS IN DERISION CALL'D. . . . 6 608
OBSTRUCT HEAV'N TOWRS, AND IN DERISION SETS . . 12 52

DERIV'D
INTO THE PLANT SCIENTIAL SAP, DERIV'D 9 837
ON ME DERIV'D, YET I SHALL TEMPER SO 10 77
AND TO OUR SEED (O HAPLESS SEED.) DERIV'D. . . 10 965

DERIVE
NOR SINN'D THY SIN, YET FROM THAT DERIVE . . . 11 427
AND FROM REBELLION SHALL DERIVE HIS NAME, . . . 12 36

DESART
IMITATE WHEN WE PLEASE? THIS DESART SOILE . . . 2 270
WANDRING THIS DARKSOME DESART, AS MY WAY, . . . 2 973
THROUGH DARK AND DESART WAYES WITH PERIL GONE . . 3 544

DESCANT
SHE ALL NIGHT LONG HER AMOROUS DESCANT SUNG; . . 4 603

DESCEND
DESCEND FROM HEAV'N URANIA, BY THAT NAME . . . 7 1
DEIGN TO DESCEND NOW LOWER, AND RELATE 7 84
THEREFORE FROM THIS HIGH PITCH LET US DESCEND . . 8 198
DESCEND TO? WHO ASPIRES MUST DOWN AS LOW . . . 9 169
VAIN COVERTURES; BUT WHEN HE SAW DESCEND . . . 10 337
DESCEND THROUGH DARKNESS, ON YOUR RODE WITH EASE . 10 394
ALL YOURS, RIGHT DOWN TO PARADISE DESCEND; . . . 10 398
OR DOWN FROM HEAV'N DESCEND. SUCH WAS THIR SONG, 10 648
LET US DESCEND NOW THEREFORE FROM THIS TOP . . . 12 588
HE ENDED, AND THEY BOTH DESCEND THE HILL; . . . 12 606

DESCENDED
SLOWLY DESCENDED, AND WITH RIGHT ASPECT 4 541
DOWN HE DESCENDED STRAIT; THE SPEED OF GODS . . 10 90
WHEN GOD DESCENDED, AND PERHAPS ONCE MORE . . . 11 75
DOWN TO THE PLAIN DESCENDED: BY THIR GUISE . . . 11 576
DESCENDED, ADAM TO THE BOWRE WHERE EVE 12 607
THE CHERUBIM DESCENDED; ON THE GROUND 12 628

DESCENDING
TH' ADVANTAGE, AND DESCENDING TREAD US DOWN . . . 1 327
NOR SHALT THOU BY DESCENDING TO ASSUME 3 303
ANGELS ASCENDING AND DESCENDING, BANDS 3 511
SINCE BY DESCENDING FROM THE THRONES ABOVE, . . . 5 363
DESCENDING, AND IN HALF CUT SHEERE, NOR STAID, . . 6 325
PREVENIENT GRACE DESCENDING HAD REMOV'D 11 3
HAD NOT A CLOUD DESCENDING SNATCH'D HIM THENCE . 11 670
SHALL TREMBLE, HE DESCENDING, WILL HIMSELF . . . 12 228

DESCENDS
ALL PERFET GOOD UNMEASUR'D OUT, DESCENDS, ... 5 399
DESCENDS, THITHER WITH HEART AND VOICE AND EYES . 7 513
THE GOOD WHICH WE ENJOY, FROM HEAV'N DESCENDS; . 11 142
AND SLOW DESCENDS, WITH SOMTHING HEAV'NLY FRAUGHT. 11 207
THE ANCIENT SIRE DESCENDS WITH ALL HIS TRAIN; . . 11 862
BUT GOD WHO OFT DESCENDS TO VISIT MEN 12 48

DESCENT
I GIVE NOT HEAV'N FOR LOST. FROM THIS DESCENT . 2 14
UP TO OUR NATIVE SEAT: DESCENT AND FALL 2 76
THE DARK DESCENT, AND UP TO REASCEND, ... 3 20
O FOUL DESCENT. THAT I WHO ERST CONTENDED . . . 9 163
IF CARE OF OUR DESCENT PERPLEX US MOST, ... 10 979
FOR SWIFT DESCENT, WITH HIM THE COHORT BRIGHT . 11 127
HIS WHOLE DESCENT, WHO THUS SHALL CANAAN WIN. . 12 269

DESCENTS
TO ME INFERIOUR, INFINITE DESCENTS 8 410

DESCRIB'D
GODS LATEST IMAGE: I DESCRIB'D HIS WAY 4 567

DESCRIBE
SPEED, TO DESCRIBE WHOSE SWIFTNESS NUMBER FAILES. 8 38
UNSUNG; OR TO DESCRIBE RACES AND GAMES, ... 9 33

DESCRI'D
AS WHEN FARR OFF AT SEA A FLEET DESCRI'D . . . 2 636
SINCE URIEL REGENT OF THE SUN DESCRI'D 9 60
AND NOW THIR WAY TO EARTH THEY HAD DESCRI'D, . . 10 325

DESCRIE
EACH QUARTER, TO DESCRIE THE DISTANT FOE, . . . 6 530
WITH THIR ATTENDANT MOONS THOU WILT DESCRIE . . 8 149
NEW LAWS TO BE OBSERV'D; FOR I DESCRIE 11 228

DESCRIES
HIS TRAVELL'D STEPS; FARR DISTANT HE DESCRIES . . 3 501

DESCRY
OR IN VALDARNO, TO DESCRY NEW LANDS, ... 1 290

DESERT
TO HIM, OR POSSIBLY HIS LOVE DESERT 5 515
DESERT AND BARE, UNSIGHTLY, UNADORND, ... 7 314
BY LIVING SOULE, DESERT AND DESOLATE, ... 8 154
HEAV'N-BANISHT HOST, LEFT DESERT UTMOST HELL . . 10 437
WANDRING THAT WATRIE DESERT: I HAD HOPE 11 779
FROM HAMATH NORTHWARD TO THE DESERT SOUTH . . . 12 139
THROUGH THE WILDE DESERT, NOT THE READIEST WAY, . 12 216

DESERTED
TO THY DESERTED HOST THIS CAUSE OF FLIGHT, . . . 4 922
DESERTED, THEN OBLIGE THEE WITH A FACT 9 980
DESERTED: OTHERS TO A CITIE STRONG 11 655

DESERTS
OF WISDOM, SHE DESERTS THEE NOT, IF THOU . . . 8 563

DESERV'D
AND MANIFOLD IN SIN, DESERV'D TO FALL. 10 16
THE MISERIE, I DESERV'D IT, AND WOULD BEARE . . 10 726

DESERVD
AH WHEREFORE. HE DESERVD NO SUCH RETURN . . . 4 42
MEAN WHILE IN OTHER PARTS LIKE DEEDS DESERVD . . 6 354

DESERVE
DESERVE THE PRECIOUS BANE. AND HERE LET THOSE . 1 692

DESERVED
BY SACRED UNCTION, THY DESERVED RIGHT. 6 709

DESERVES
OUR SELVES WITH LIKE DEFENCE, TO ME DESERVES . . 6 467

DESERVING
DESERVING PARADISE. IF EVER, THEN, ... 5 446
FARR OTHER NAME DESERVING. BUT THE FIELD . . . 11 171

DESERVINGS
MY OWN DESERVINGS; BUT THIS WILL NOT SERVE; . . 10 727

DESIGN
TO WORK IN CLOSE DESIGN, BY FRAUD OR GUILE . . . 1 646
HIS GLORY TO AUGMENT. THE BOLD DESIGN 2 386
SATAN WITH THOUGHTS INFLAM'D OF HIGHEST DESIGN, . 2 630
WHETHER HIS FIRST DESIGN BE TO WITHDRAW 9 261

DESIGN'D
THEN THIS MORE SECRET NOW DESIGN'D, I HASTE . . 2 838
MANS FRIEND, HIS MEDIATOR, HIS DESIGN'D 10 60
WITH SENT OF LIVING CARCASSES DESIGN'D 10 277

DESIGNE
OF SENNAAR, AND STILL WITH VAIN DESIGNE 3 467
ENVIOUS COMMANDS, INVENTED WITH DESIGNE 4 524
WORKS OF DAY PASS'T, OR MORROWS NEXT DESIGNE, . . 5 33

DESIGNES
THIS NIGHT THE HUMAN PAIR, HOW HE DESIGNES . . . 5 227
LAUGH'ST AT THIR VAIN DESIGNES AND TUMULTS VAIN, . 5 737

DESIGNING
DESIGNING OR EXHORTING GLORIOUS WARR, ... 2 179

DESIGNS
LEFT HIM AT LARGE TO HIS OWN DARK DESIGNS, . . . 1 213

DESIRABLE
THE MORE DESIRABLE, OR TO SAY ALL, ... 8 505

DESIRE
WROUGHT STILL WITHIN THEM; AND NO LESS DESIRE . . 2 295
UNSPEAKABLE DESIRE TO SEE, AND KNOW 3 662
FAIR ANGEL, THY DESIRE WHICH TENDS TO KNOW . . . 3 694
MINE EYES TILL NOW, AND PIN'D WITH VAIN DESIRE, . 4 466
WHERE NEITHER JOY NOR LOVE, BUT FIERCE DESIRE, . 4 509
WITH MORE DESIRE TO KNOW, AND TO REJECT 4 523
WHOM TO BEHOLD BUT THEE, NATURES DESIRE, . . . 5 45
BUT MORE DESIRE TO HEAR, IF THOU CONSENT, . . . 5 555
PRESAGE OF VICTORIE AND FIERCE DESIRE 6 201
LED ON, YET SINLESS, WITH DESIRE TO KNOW . . . 7 61
I HAVE RECEAV'D, TO ANSWER THY DESIRE 7 119
AND FROM ABOUT HER SHOT DARTS OF DESIRE 8 62
DESIRE WITH THEE STILL LONGER TO CONVERSE . . . 8 252
BUT IN DEGREE, THE CAUSE OF HIS DESIRE 8 417
THY WISH EXACTLY TO THY HEARTS DESIRE. 8 451
NOR VEHEMENT DESIRE, THESE DELICACIES 8 526

DESIRE (CONTINUED)
TO SATISFIE THE SHARP DESIRE I HAD 9 584
ALL OTHER BEASTS THAT SAW, WITH LIKE DESIRE 9 592
SO SAVORIE OF THAT FRUIT, WHICH WITH DESIRE, 9 741
CARNAL DESIRE ENFLAMING, HEE ON EVE 9 1013
DESIRE OF WANDRING THIS UNHAPPIE MORN, 9 1136
AND WITH DESIRE TO LANGUISH WITHOUT HOPE, 10 995
WITH LIKE DESIRE, WHICH WOULD BE MESERIE 10 997

DESIRES
BY SIN TO FOUL EXORBITANT DESIRES; 3 177
VAINE HOPES, VAINE AIMES, INORDINATE DESIRES 4 808
HUMAN DESIRES CAN SEEK OR APPREHEND? 5 518
IMMEDIATELY INORDINATE DESIRES 12 87

DESIRING
DESIRING; NOR RESTRAIN'D CONVEYANCE NEED 8 628
DELIGHTED, BUT DESIRING MORE HER STAY. 9 398

DESIROUS
DESIROUS; ALL IN CIRCLES AS THEY STOOD, 5 631
WAITING DESIROUS HER RETURN, HAD WOVE 9 839
DESIROUS TO RESIGNE, AND RENDER BACK 10 749
UNWARIE, AND TOO DESIROUS, AS BEFORE, 10 947

DESIR'ST
WITH THAT BAD WOMAN? THUS WHAT THOU DESIR'ST 10 837
SO NOW OF WHAT THOU KNOWST NOT, WHO DESIR'ST 10 948

DESISTING
DESISTING, THOUGH UNWEARIED, UP RETURND 7 552

DESOLATE
TO WING THE DESOLATE ABYSS, AND SPIE 4 936
BY LIVING SOULE, DESERT AND DESOLATE, 8 154
AND ALL ABOUT FOUND DESOLATE; FOR THOSE 10 420
DESOLATE WHERE SHE SATE, APPROACHING NIGH, 10 864
INHOSPITABLE APPEER AND DESOLATE, 11 306

DESOLATION
THE SEAT OF DESOLATION, VOYD OF LIGHT, 1 181

DESPAIR
NOT IN DESPAIR, TO HAVE FOUND THEMSELVES NOT LOST 1 525
TO THAT BAD EMINENCE; AND FROM DESPAIR 2 6
THAT FOUGHT IN HEAV'N; NOW FIERCER BY DESPAIR: 2 45
MISTRUSTFUL, GROUNDS HIS COURAGE ON DESPAIR 2 126
IS FLAT DESPAIR: WE MUST EXASPERATE 2 143
BY CHANGE OF PLACE: NOW CONSCIENCE WAKES DESPAIR 4 23
THRICE CHANG'D WITH PALE, IRE, ENVIE AND DESPAIR, 4 115
ALL SADNESS BUT DESPAIR: NOW GENTLE GALES 4 156
INSENSATE, HOPE CONCEIVING FROM DESPAIR. 6 787
OF SORROW AND DEJECTION AND DESPAIR 11 301
DIRE WAS THE TOSSING, DEEP THE GROANS, DESPAIR 11 489

DESPAIRD
FULL COUNSEL MUST MATURE: PEACE IS DESPAIRD, 1 660
THINK NOTHING HARD, MUCH LESS TO BE DESPAIRD. 6 495

DESPAIRE
INFINITE WRAUTH, AND INFINITE DESPAIRE? 4 74
AND SHAME, AND PERTURBATION, AND DESPAIRE, 10 113
SHE ENDED HEER, OR VEHEMENT DESPAIRE 10 1007
OUT OF DESPAIRE, JOY, BUT WITH FEAR YET LINKT; 11 139

DESPAIRING
DESPAIRING, SEEKS TO WORK US WOE AND SHAME 9 255

DESPARATE
ON DESPARATE REVENG, THAT SHALL REDOUND 3 85

DESPARE
VAUNTING ALOUD, BUT RACKT WITH DEEP DESPARE: 1 126
IF NOT WHAT RESOLUTION FROM DESPARE. 1 191

DESPERATE
DESPERATE REVENGE, AND BATTEL DANGEROUS 2 107

DESPICABLE
OF DESPICABLE FOES. WITH THESE IN TROOP 1 437
NO DESPICABLE GIFT; SURMISE NOT THEN 11 340

DESPIGHTFULL
MEANWHILE THE HAINOUS AND DESPIGHTFULL ACT 10 1

DESPIS'D
THAT FOR THE GENERAL SAFETY HE DESPIS'D 2 481
NOR GOD, NOR MAN; IS KNOWLEDGE SO DESPIS'D? 5 60
DOUBL'D, WOULD RENDER THEM YET MORE DESPIS'D, 6 602
BY MEE, NOT YOU BUT MEE THEY HAVE DESPIS'D, 6 812
WITH CLANG DESPIS'D THE GROUND, UNDER A CLOUD 7 422

DESPISE
THERE LET THEM LEARN, AS LIKES THEM, TO DESPISE 6 717
CHIEFLY I SOUGHT, WITHOUT THEE CAN DESPISE. 9 878

DESPITE
GNASHING FOR ANGUISH AND DESPITE AND SHAME 6 340

DESPITE (CONTINUED)
AS A DESPITE DON AGAINST THE MOST HIGH, 6 906
OF HEAV'N, THIS MAN OF CLAY, SON OF DESPITE, 9 176
RANCOR AND PRIDE, IMPATIENCE AND DESPITE, 10 1044
BEFORE THE LORD, AS IN DESPITE OF HEAV'N, 12 34

DESPOILD
USELESS AND VAIN, OF FREEDOM BOTH DESPOILD, 3 109
DESPOILD OF INNOCENCE, OF FAITH, OF BLISS. 9 411
REMAIND STILL HAPPIE, NOT AS NOW, DESPOILD 9 1138

DESTIN'D
RESERV'D AND DESTIN'D TO ETERNAL WOE; 2 161
DESTIN'D TO THAT GOOD HOUR: NO LESS REJOYC'D 2 848
AND DESTIN'D MAN HIMSELF TO JUDGE MAN FALL'N. 10 62
DESTIN'D RESTORER OF MANKIND, BY WHOM 10 646

DESTIND
HIS INMOST COUNSELS FROM THIR DESTIND AIM. 1 168
OF DESTIND HABITATION; BUT THOU KNOW'ST 7 622
OF MIGHTIEST EMPIRE, FROM THE DESTIND WALLS 11 387
AND SHADOWS, OF THAT DESTIND SEED TO BRUISE 12 233

DESTINIE
BY DESTINIE, AND CAN NO OTHER CHOOSE? 5 534

DESTINY
O HAD HIS POWERFUL DESTINY ORDAIND 4 58

DESTITUTE
SHORN OF HIS STRENGTH, THEY DESTITUTE AND BARE 9 1062

DESTROY
WASTING THE EARTH, EACH OTHER TO DESTROY: 2 502
HIS WRATH WHICH ONE DAY WILL DESTROY YE BOTH. 2 734
MADE TO DESTROY: I FLED, AND CRY'D OUT DEATH; 2 787
IF HIM BY FORCE HE CAN DESTROY, OR WORSE, 3 91
THOUGH NOT DESTROY, THIR HAPPIE NATIVE SEAT; 6 226
NOT TO DESTROY, BUT ROOT THEM OUT OF HEAV'N: 6 855
IS GREATER THEN CREATED TO DESTROY. 7 607
OF PLEASURE, BUT ALL PLEASURE TO DESTROY, 9 477
THOUGH THREATNING, WILL IN EARNEST SO DESTROY 9 939
BOTH TO DESTROY, OR UNIMMORTAL MAKE 10 611
DESTRUCTION WITH DESTRUCTION TO DESTROY. 10 1006
AND MAKES A COVENANT NEVER TO DESTROY 11 892

DESTROY'D
FEAR TO BE WORSE DESTROY'D: WHAT CAN BE WORSE 2 85
CALLS US TO PENANCE? MORE DESTROY'D THEN THUS 2 92
SO EASILY DESTROY'D, AND STILL DESTROYES 3 301
BETWIXT THE WORLD DESTROY'D AND WORLD RESTOR'D, 12 3

DESTROYD
TO MY RELENTLESS THOUGHTS; AND HIM DESTROYD, 9 130
HIS CHILDREN, ALL IN VIEW DESTROYD AT ONCE; 11 761
OF WICKED SONS DESTROYD, THEN I REJOYCE 11 875
HOW MANY KINGS DESTROYD, AND KINGDOMS WON, 12 262

DESTROYER
BUT OUR DESTROYER, FOE TO GOD AND MAN? 4 749

DESTROYERS
DESTROYERS RIGHTLIER CALL'D AND PLAGUES OF MEN. 11 697

DESTROYES
SO EASILY DESTROY'D, AND STILL DESTROYES 3 301
AND WHAT THOU FEARST, ALIKE DESTROYES ALL HOPE 10 838

DESTROYING
FOR ONELY IN DESTROYING I FIND EASE 9 129
SAVE WHAT IS IN DESTROYING, OTHER JOY 9 478
NOT BY DESTROYING SATAN, BUT HIS WORKS 12 394

DESTRUCTION
IN HORRIBLE DESTRUCTION LAID THUS LOW, 1 137
TO OUR DESTRUCTION: IF THERE BE IN HELL 2 84
THROUGH ALL THE COASTS OF DARK DESTRUCTION SEEK 2 464
THAT DAY AND NIGHT FOR HIS DESTRUCTION WAITE. 2 505
BUT TO DESTRUCTION SACRED AND DEVOTE, 3 208
ON THOSE PROUD TOWRS TO SWIFT DESTRUCTION DOOM'D. 5 907
DESTRUCTION TO THE REST: THIS PAUSE BETWEEN 6 162
WIDE WASTING; SUCH DESTRUCTION TO WITHSTAND 6 253
DESTRUCTION WITH CREATION MIGHT HAVE MIXT. 8 236
ON MANS DESTRUCTION, MAUGRE WHAT MIGHT HAP 9 56
IN WO THEN; THAT DESTRUCTION WIDE MAY RANGE: 9 134
ALL KINDS, AND FOR DESTRUCTION TO MATURE 10 612
DESTRUCTION WITH DESTRUCTION TO DESTROY. 10 1006
BUT SELF-DESTRUCTION THEREFORE SAUGHT, REFUTES 10 1016

DETAIN
DETAIN FROM FOLLOWING THY ILLUSTRIOUS TRACK. 10 367

DETAIN'D
ESCAP'T THE STYGIAN POOL, THOUGH LONG DETAIN'D 3 14

DETAINE
HOW SUTTLY TO DETAINE THEE I DEVISE, 8 207

DIE (CONTINUED)
OF MANY WAYS TO DIE THE SHORTEST CHOOSING, 10 1005
LOOSE NO REWARD, THOUGH HERE THOU SEE HIM DIE, 11 459
SOME, AS THOU SAW'ST, BY VIOLENT STROKE SHALL DIE, 11 471
HIS CATTEL MUST OF ROT AND MURREN DIE, 12 179
THEY DIE; BUT IN THIR ROOM, AS THEY FOREWARNE, 12 507

DIES
WHERE ALL LIFE DIES, DEATH LIVES, AND NATURE BREEDS, 2 624
ADORE HIM, WHO TO COMPASS ALL THIS DIES, 3 342
HOW DIES THE SERPENT? HEE HATH EAT'N AND LIVES, 9 764
OF LIFE THAT SINN'D; WHAT DIES BUT WHAT HAD LIFE 10 790
OF PHARAO: THERE HE DIES, AND LEAVES HIS RACE 12 163
IN THIS HIS SATISFACTION; SO HE DIES, 12 419

DIET
NO INCONVENIENT DIET, NOR TOO LIGHT FARE; 5 495

DIETED
TILL DIETED BY THEE I GROW MATURE 9 803

DIFFERENT
IF COUNSELS DIFFERENT, OR DANGER SHUN'D 1 636
INSENSIBLY THREE DIFFERENT MOTIONS MOVE? 8 130
MANLIKE, BUT DIFFERENT SEX, SO LOVLY FAIRE, 8 471
LEAST THOU NOT TASTING, DIFFERENT DEGREE 9 883
WHEREON FOR DIFFERENT CAUSE THE TEMPTER SET 11 382
BUT ON THE HETHER SIDE A DIFFERENT SORT 11 574

DIFFERING
DIFFERING BUT IN DEGREE, OF KIND THE SAME. 5 490
FARR DIFFERING FROM THIS WORLD, THOU HAST REVEAL'D 7 71

DIFFICULT
THE WAY SEEMS DIFFICULT AND STEEP TO SCALE 2 71
WITH TRAVAIL DIFFICULT, NOT BETTER FARR 10 593
BUT IF THOU JUDGE IT HARD AND DIFFICULT, 10 992

DIFFICULTIE
BUT LEAST THE DIFFICULTIE OF PASSING BACK 10 252

DIFFICULTY
OF DIFFICULTY OR DANGER COULD DETERR 2 449
SO HE WITH DIFFICULTY AND LABOUR HARD 2 1021
MOV'D ON, WITH DIFFICULTY AND LABOUR HEE; 2 1022

DIFFIDENT
DO THOU BUT THINE, AND BE NOT DIFFIDENT 8 562
NOT DIFFIDENT OF THEE DO I DISSUADE 9 293

DIFFUS'D
SENSE OF NEW JOY INEFFABLE DIFFUS'D: 3 137
SUTABLE GRACE DIFFUS'D, SO WELL HE FEIGND; 3 639
WITH SUDDEN BLAZE DIFFUS'D, INFLAMES THE AIRE: 4 818
TRANSPARENT, ELEMENTAL AIR, DIFFUS'D 7 265
NEW GATHERD, AND AMBROSIAL SMELL DIFFUS'D. 9 852

DIFFUSE
INTO THIR VACANT ROOM, AND THENCE DIFFUSE 7 190

DIG'D
AND DIG'D OUT RIBS OF GOLD. LET NONE ADMIRE 1 690

DIGEST
TASTING CONCOCT, DIGEST, ASSIMILATE, 5 412

DIGESTION
WAS AERIE LIGHT FROM PURE DIGESTION BRED, 5 4

DIGGD
PART HIDD'N VEINS DIGGD UP (NOR HATH THIS EARTH 6 516

DIGNIFI'D
US HIS PRIME CREATURES, DIGNIFI'D SO HIGH, 9 940

DIGNITIE
APPOINTED, WHICH DECLARES HIS DIGNITIE, 4 619
AND OF OUR GOOD, AND OF OUR DIGNITIE 5 827
IN EVERY GESTURE DIGNITIE AND LOVE. 8 489
HERS IN ALL REAL DIGNITIE: ADORND 10 151

DIGNITIES
EXCELLING HUMAN, PRINCELY DIGNITIES, 1 359

DIGNITY
IN HEAV'N, WHICH FOLLOWS DIGNITY, MIGHT DRAW 2 25
FOR DIGNITY COMPOS'D AND HIGH EXPLOIT: 2 111

DIGRESSIONS
GRATEFUL DIGRESSIONS, AND SOLVE HIGH DISPUTE 8 55

DILATED
DILATED OR CONDENS'T, BRIGHT OR OBSCURE, 1 429
COLLECTING ALL HIS MIGHT DILATED STOOD, 4 986
DILATED AND INFURIATE SHALL SEND FORTH 6 486
DIMM ERST, DILATED SPIRITS, AMPLER HEART, 9 876

DIM
IN DIM ECLIPS DISASTROUS TWILIGHT SHEDS 1 597
SURPRIS'D THEE, DIM THINE EYES, AND DIZZIE SWUMM 2 753
SHOOTS FARR INTO THE BOSOM OF DIM NIGHT 2 1036
OR DIM SUFFUSION VEILD. YET NOT THE MORE 3 26
TELL THEM THAT BY COMMAND, ERE YET DIM NIGHT 5 685
NOW ERE DIM NIGHT HAD DISINCUMBERD HEAV'N, 5 700
YET ARE BUT DIM, SHALL PERFETLY BE THEN 9 707
ALL WERE WHO HEARD, DIM SADNESS DID NOT SPARE 10 23

DIMENSION
WITHOUT DIMENSION, WHERE LENGTH, BREADTH, & HIGHTH, 2 893
THESE AS A LINE THIR LONG DIMENSION DREW, 7 480

DIMENSIONS
AND IN THIR OWN DIMENSIONS LIKE THEMSELVES 1 793

DIMENTIONLESS
DIMENTIONLESS THROUGH HEAV'NLY DORES; THEN CLAD 11 17

DIMINISH
THEE TO DIMINISH, AND FROM THEE WITHDRAW 7 612

DIMINISHT
HIDE THIR DIMINISHT HEADS; TO THEE I CALL, 4 35

DIMINUTION
SO FARR REMOTE, WITH DIMINUTION SEEN. 7 369

DIMLY
TO US INVISIBLE OR DIMLY SEEN 5 157

DIMM
DIMM ERST, DILATED SPIRITS, AMPLER HEART, 9 876

DIMM'D
THUS WHILE HE SPAKE, EACH PASSION DIMM'D HIS FACE 4 114
AND CARNAL FEAR THAT DAY DIMM'D ADAMS EYE. 11 212

DIN
CLASH'D ON THIR SOUNDING SHIELDS THE DIN OF WAR, 1 668
WITH TUMULT LESS AND WITH LESS HOSTILE DIN, 2 1040
TO HIS BOLD RIOT: DREADFUL WAS THE DIN 10 521
AND HEAR THE DIN; THUS WAS THE BUILDING LEFT 12 61

DINN
AND SILENCE ON THE ODIOUS DINN OF WARR: 6 408

DINNER
FOR DINNER SAVOURIE FRUITS, OF TASTE TO PLEASE 5 304
NO FEAR LEST DINNER COOLE; WHEN THUS BEGAN 5 396

DINT
THOUGH TEMPER'D HEAV'NLY, FOR THAT MORTAL DINT, 2 813

DIPSAS
AND DIPSAS (NOT SO THICK SWARM'D ONCE THE SOIL 10 526

DIPT
AND COLOURS DIPT IN HEAV'N; THE THIRD HIS FEET 5 283
IN TIME OF TRUCE; IRIS HAD DIPT THE WOOFF; 11 244

DIRE
THE FORCE OF THOSE DIRE ARMS? YET NOT FOR THOSE, 1 94
TOO WELL I SEE AND RUE THE DIRE EVENT, 1 134
HOW OVERCOME THIS DIRE CALAMITY, 1 189
WAS NOT INGLORIOUS, THOUGH TH' EVENT WAS DIRE, 1 624
AS THIS PLACE TESTIFIES, AND THIS DIRE CHANGE 1 625
OF ALL HIS AIM, AFTER SOME DIRE REVENGE. 2 128
OF WHIRLWIND AND DIRE HAIL, WHICH ON FIRM LAND 2 589
GORGONS AND HYDRA'S, AND CHIMERA'S DIRE. 2 628
THEN SWEET, NOW SAD TO MENTION, THROUGH DIRE CHANGE 2 820
BEGINS HIS DIRE ATTEMPT, WHICH NIGH THE BIRTH 4 15
OF BRAZEN CHARIOTS RAG'D; DIRE WAS THE NOISE 6 211
NO EQUAL, RAUNGING THROUGH THE DIRE ATTACK 6 248
HURL'D TO AND FRO WITH JACULATION DIRE, 6 665
OF SMOAK AND BICKERING FLAME, AND SPARKLES DIRE; 6 766
ADAM BY DIRE EXAMPLE TO BEWARE 7 42
SO GLISTER'D THE DIRE SNAKE, AND INTO FRAUD 9 643
SCORPION AND ASP, AND AMPHISBAENA DIRE, 10 524
AND THE DIRE HISS RENEW'D, AND THE DIRE FORM 10 543
SATANS DIRE DREAD, AND IN HIS HAND THE SPEAR. 11 248
DISEASES DIRE, OF WHICH A MONSTROUS CREW 11 474
DIRE WAS THE TOSSING, DEEP THE GROANS, DESPAIR 11 489
MUST BE COMPELLD BY SIGNES AND JUDGEMENTS DIRE; 12 175

DIRECT
OF THIR GREAT SULTAN WAVING TO DIRECT 1 348
I TRAVEL THIS PROFOUND, DIRECT MY COURSE; 2 980
DIRECT AGAINST WHICH OP'ND FROM BENEATH, 3 526
SHOT UPWARD STILL DIRECT, WHENCE NO WAY ROUND 3 618
TO FIND WHO MIGHT DIRECT HIS WANDRING FLIGHT 3 631
DAZ'LING THE MOON; THESE TO THE BOWER DIRECT 4 798
SHOT DOWN DIRECT HIS FERVID RAIES TO WARME 5 301
WELL HAST THOU TAUGHT THE WAY THAT MIGHT DIRECT 5 508
HE SAID, AND ON HIS SON WITH RAYES DIRECT 6 719
PART RISE IN CRYSTAL WALL, OR RIDGE DIRECT, 7 293
TO GODS ETERNAL HOUSE DIRECT THE WAY, 7 576

DIRECT (CONTINUED)
THE WOODBINE ROUND THIS ARBOUR, OR DIRECT 9 216
DIRECT, OR BY OCCASION HATH PRESENTED 9 974
DIRECT TO TH' EASTERN GATE WAS BENT THIR FLIGHT. . 11 190
WHICH NOW DIRECT THINE EYES AND SOON BEHOLD. . . 11 711
LED THEM DIRECT, AND DOWN THE CLIFF AS FAST . . 12 639

DIRECTED
DIRECTED NO MEAN RECOMPENCE IT BRINGS 2 981
TO FIND THEE I DIRECTED THEN MY WALK; 5 49
DIRECTED IN DEVOTION, TO ADORE 7 514

DIRECTLY
DIRECTLY TOWARDS THE NEW CREATED WORLD, ... 3 89

DIS
HER SELF A FAIRER FLOURE BY GLOOMIE DIS 4 270

DISABL'D
DISABL'D NOT TO GIVE THEE THY DEATHS WOUND: . . 12 392

DISADVANTAGE
SOME DISADVANTAGE WE ENDUR'D AND PAINE, ... 6 431

DISAGREE
FIRM CONCORD HOLDS, MEN ONELY DISAGREE 2 497

DISAPPEER'D
TO THE SUBJECTED PLAINE; THEN DISAPPEER'D. 12 640

DISAPPEERD
SATAN WITH HIS REBELLIOUS DISAPPEERD, ... 6 414
SHEE DISAPPEERD, AND LEFT ME DARK, I WAK'D 8 478

DISARM'D
INGLORIOUS, OF HIS MORTALL STING DISARM'D. 3 253
STUPIDLY GOOD, OF ENMITIE DISARM'D, ... 9 465
AS ONE DISARM'D, HIS ANGER ALL HE LOST, ... 10 945

DISARMD
ADVERSE, THAT THEY SHALL FEAR WE HAVE DISARMD . . 6 490

DISARRAID
THOU DROV'ST OF WARRING ANGELS DISARRAID. 3 396

DISASTROUS
IN DIM ECLIPS DISASTROUS TWILIGHT SHEDS 1 597

DISBAND
DISBAND, AND WANDRING, EACH HIS SEVERAL WAY . . 2 523

DISBURDEN
HELP TO DISBURDEN NATURE OF HER BEARTH. 9 624

DISBURD'N
THUS TO DISBURD'N SOUGHT WITH SAD COMPLAINT. . . 10 719

DISBURD'ND
DISBURD'ND HEAV'N REJOIC'D, AND SOON REPAIRD . . . 6 878

DISBURD'NING
HER FERTIL GROWTH, AND BY DISBURD'NING GROWS . . . 5 319

DISCERN
HIS SWIFT PURSUERS FROM HEAV'N GATES DISCERN . . 1 326
FOR NEITHER MAN NOR ANGEL CAN DISCERN 3 682

DISCERN'D
OF MERCY AND JUSTICE IN THY FACE DISCERN'D, . . . 3 407
AS WAS MY FOOD, NOR AUGHT BUT FOOD DISCERN'D . . 9 573
THIR PARENT SOON DISCERN'D, THOUGH IN DISGUISE. . 10 331

DISCERND
WHERE HE FIRST LIGHTED, SOON DISCERND HIS LOOKS . 4 570
ADAM DISCERND, AS IN THE DORE HE SAT 5 299
OR HERE TH' ATTEMPT, THOU COULDST NOT HAVE DISCERND 9 1149

DISCERNE
HASTING THIS WAY, AND NOW BY GLIMPS DISCERNE . . 4 867
BEHOLDERS RUDE, AND SHALLOW TO DISCERNE 9 544
WITHIN ME CLEERE, NOT ONELY TO DISCERNE 9 681

DISCERNES
MEAN WHILE TH' ETERNAL EYE, WHOSE SIGHT DISCERNES 5 711

DISCERNING
HE CEAS'D, DISCERNING ADAM WITH SUCH JOY . . . 12 372

DISCERNS
HE SOON DISCERNS, AND WELTRING BY HIS SIDE . . . 1 78
AND KNOWS, AND SPEAKS, AND REASONS, AND DISCERNS, 9 765

DISCHARGD
INDEBTED AND DISCHARGD; WHAT BURDEN THEN? 4 57

DISCHARGE
HEAV'N WITNESS THOU ANON, WHILE WE DISCHARGE . . 6 564
US HAPLY TOO SECURE OF OUR DISCHARGE 11 196

DISCIPLES
TO HIS DISCIPLES, MEN WHO IN HIS LIFE 12 438

DISCIPLIN'D
UP TO A BETTER COV'NANT, DISCIPLIN'D 12 302

DISCIPLINE
WAS THIS YOUR DISCIPLINE AND FAITH INGAG'D, . . 4 954

DISCLOS'D
ROWLD INWARD, AND A SPACIOUS GAP DISCLOS'D . . . 6 861
BURSTING WITH KINDLY RUPTURE FORTH DISCLOS'D . . 7 419

DISCLOSE
DUE SEARCH AND CONSULTATION WILL DISCLOSE. . . . 6 445
YET THESE SUBJECT NOT; I TO THEE DISCLOSE . . . 8 607

DISCOMPOS'D
WITH TRESSES DISCOMPOS'D, AND GLOWING CHEEK, . . 5 10
TO OFFEND, DISCOUNT'NANC'T BOTH, AND DISCOMPOS'D; 10 110

DISCONSOLATE
DISMISS THEM NOT DISCONSOLATE; REVEALE 11 113

DISCONTENTED
AT LEAST DISTEMPERD, DISCONTENTED THOUGHTS, . . 4 807

DISCONTINUOUS
THE GRIDING SWORD WITH DISCONTINUOUS WOUND . . . 6 329

DISCORD
AND DISCORD WITH A THOUSAND VARIOUS MOUTHS. . . 2 967
HORRIBLE DISCORD, AND THE MADDING WHEELES . . . 6 210
THE DISCORD WHICH BEFEL, AND WARR IN HEAV'N . . 6 897
SAID THEN TH' OMNIFIC WORD, YOUR DISCORD END: . 7 217
MISTRUST, SUSPICION, DISCORD, AND SHOOK SORE . 9 1124
OUTRAGE FROM LIVELESS THINGS; BUT DISCORD FIRST . 10 707

DISCOUNT'NANC'T
LOOSES DISCOUNT'NANC'T, AND LIKE FOLLY SHEWES; . 8 553
TO OFFEND, DISCOUNT'NANC'T BOTH, AND DISCOMPOS'D; 10 110

DISCOURSE
THE THRONGING AUDIENCE. IN DISCOURSE MORE SWEET . 2 555
OR WITH REPOSE; AND SUCH DISCOURSE BRING ON, . . 5 233
DANC'D HAND IN HAND. A WHILE DISCOURSE THEY HOLD; 5 395
DISCURSIVE, OR INTUITIVE; DISCOURSE 5 488
THUS FARR HIS BOLD DISCOURSE WITHOUT CONTROULE . 5 803
YET WENT SHE NOT, AS NOT WITH SUCH DISCOURSE . . 8 48
AND SWEETER THY DISCOURSE IS TO MY EARE 8 211
DEGRADED, WISDOM IN DISCOURSE WITH HER 8 552
VENIAL DISCOURSE UNBLAM'D: I NOW MUST CHANGE . . 9 5
CASUAL DISCOURSE DRAW ON, WHICH INTERMITS . . . 9 223
SATE IN THIR SAD DISCOURSE, AND VARIOUS PLAINT, . 10 343

DISCOVER
SERV'D ONELY TO DISCOVER SIGHTS OF WOE, ... 1 64
OP'NING THIR BRAZEN FOULDS DISCOVER WIDE 1 724
ON BOLD ADVENTURE TO DISCOVER WIDE 2 571
LAW CAN DISCOVER SIN, BUT NOT REMOVE, ... 12 290

DISCOVER'D
COMPLETE TO HAVE DISCOVER'D AND REPULST 10 10
DISCOVER'D SOON THE PLACE OF HER RETIRE. . . . 11 267

DISCOVERD
DISCOVERD AND SURPRIZ'D. AS WHEN A SPARK . . . 4 814
WHICH TO OUR EYES DISCOVERD NEW AND STRANGE, . . 6 571

DISCOVERING
DISCOVERING IN WIDE LANTSKIP ALL THE EAST . . . 5 142

DISCOVERS
WHICH TO HIS EYE DISCOVERS UNAWARE 3 547

DISCREETEST
SEEMS WISEST, VERTUOUSEST, DISCREETEST, BEST; . . 8 550

DISCURSIVE
DISCURSIVE, OR INTUITIVE; DISCOURSE 5 488

DISDAIN
AND HIGH DISDAIN, FROM SENCE OF INJUR'D MERIT, . 1 98
DISDAIN FORBIDS ME, AND MY DREAD OF SHAME . . . 4 82
TO HIS PROUD FAIR, BEST QUITTED WITH DISDAIN. . 4 770
DEEP MALICE THENCE CONCEIVING AND DISDAIN, . . 5 666
THY LOOKS, THE HEAV'N OF MILDNESS, WITH DISDAIN, . 9 534

DISDAIN'D
DISDAIN'D, BUT MEANER THOUGHTS LEARND IN THIR
FLIGHT, ... 6 367
MUST SUFFER CHANGE, DISDAIN'D NOT TO BEGIN . . . 10 213
REJECTED MY FOREWARNING, AND DISDAIN'D 10 876

DISDAIND
DUE ENTRANCE HE DISDAIND, AND IN CONTEMPT, ... 4 180

DISDAINFUL
AND WITH DISDAINFUL LOOK THUS FIRST BEGAN. 2 680

DISDAINFULLY
DISDAINFULLY HALF SMILING THUS REPLI'D. 4 903

DISDAINING
TO FINAL BATTEL DREW, DISDAINING FLIGHT, 6 798

DISEAS'D
NUMBERS OF ALL DISEAS'D, ALL MALADIES 11 480

DISEASES
DISEASES DIRE, OF WHICH A MONSTROUS CREW 11 474

DISESPOUS'D
OF TURNUS FOR LAVINIA DISESPOUS'D, 9 17

DISFIGUR'D
SAW HIM DISFIGUR'D, MORE THEN COULD BEFALL 4 127

DISFIGURING
DISFIGURING NOT GODS LIKENESS, BUT THIR OWN, 11 521

DISGORGE
OF FOUR INFERNAL RIVERS THAT DISGORGE 2 575

DISGORGING
AND ALL HER ENTRAILS TORE, DISGORGING FOULE 6 588
SEE WHERE IT FLOWS, DISGORGING AT SEAVEN MOUTHES 12 158

DISGUIS'D
THIR WANDRING GODS DISGUIS'D IN BRUTISH FORMS 1 481
OR IN FRANCISCAN THINK TO PASS DISGUIS'D; 3 480
THEN AT CIRCEAN CALL THE HERD DISGUIS'D. 9 522
DISGUIS'D HE CAME, BUT THOSE HIS CHILDREN DEAR 10 330

DISGUISE
THIR PARENT SOON DISCERN'D, THOUGH IN DISGUISE. 10 331

DISGUISES
THESE TROUBLESOM DISGUISES WHICH WEE WEAR, 4 740

DISHEART'ND
BE NOT DISHEART'ND THEN, NOR CLOUD THOSE LOOKS 5 122

DISHEVELD
DISHEVELD, BUT IN WANTON RINGLETS WAV'D 4 306

DISHONEST
THEN WAS NOT GUILTIE SHAME, DISHONEST SHAME 4 313

DISHONOR
STICKS NO DISHONOR ON OUR FRONT, BUT TURNS 9 330

DISHONORABLE
OF NATURES WORKS, HONOR DISHONORABLE, 4 314

DISHONOUR
THE WIFE, WHERE DANGER OR DISHONOUR LURKS, 9 267
THE TEMPTED WITH DISHONOUR FOUL, SUPPOS'D 9 297

DISINCUMBERD
NOW ERE DIM NIGHT HAD DISINCUMBERD HEAV'N, 5 700

DISINHERITED
SO DISINHERITED HOW WOULD YE BLESS 10 821

DISINTHRONE
EITHER TO DISINTHRONE THE KING OF HEAV'N 2 229

DISJOINE
FORGET, NOR FROM THY FATHERS PRAISE DISJOINE. 3 415

DISJOYNE
DISJOYNE US, AND I THEN TOO LATE RENOUNCE 9 884

DISJOYNING
WHICH REASON JOYNING OR DISJOYNING, FRAMES 5 106

DISLIKE
THAT DURST DISLIKE HIS REIGN, AND ME PREFERRING, 1 102
GOOD REASON WAS THOU FREELY SHOULDST DISLIKE, 8 443
AND OF THIR DOINGS GREAT DISLIKE DECLAR'D, 11 720

DISLODG'D
FAR IN THE DARK DISLODG'D, AND VOID OF REST, 6 415

DISLODGE
WITH ALL HIS LEGIONS TO DISLODGE, AND LEAVE 5 669
LODGE AND DISLODGE BY TURNS, WHICH MAKES THROUGH HEAV'N 6 7

DISLODGING
DISLODGING FROM A REGION SCARCE OF PREY 3 433

DISLOYAL
DISLOYAL BREAKS HIS FEALTIE, AND SINNS 3 204

DISLOYAL (CONTINUED)
DISLOYAL ON THE PART OF MAN, REVOLT, 9 7

DISMAI'D
HIS HEART, NOT ELSE DISMAI'D. NOW DREW THEY NIGH 4 861
DISMAI'D, AND THUS IN HASTE TO TH' ANGEL CRI'D. 11 449

DISMAID
MEE OVERTOOK HIS MOTHER ALL DISMAID, 2 792
FROM UNSUCCESSFUL CHARGE, BE NOT DISMAID, 10 35

DISMAL
THE DISMAL SITUATION WASTE AND WILDE, 1 60
THAT DISMAL WORLD, IF ANY CLIME PERHAPS 2 572
FROM OUT THIS DARK AND DISMAL HOUSE OF PAIN, 2 823
OF CONFLICT; OVER HEAD THE DISMAL HISS 6 212
THAT UNDER GROUND, THEY FOUGHT IN DISMAL SHADE; 6 666
THE DISMAL GATES, AND BARRICADO'D STRONG; 8 241
NOT YET IN HORRID SHADE OR DISMAL DEN, 9 185
A DISMAL UNIVERSAL HISS, THE SOUND 10 508
OR IN SOME OTHER DISMAL PLACE WHO KNOWS 10 787
TO HIS GRIM CAVE, ALL DISMAL; YET TO SENSE 11 469

DISMAY
THAT WITNESS'D HUGE AFFLICTION AND DISMAY 1 57
IN OTHERS COUNT'NANCE READ HIS OWN DISMAY 2 422
SO HAVING SAID, AS ONE FROM SAD DISMAY 9 917
WHICH THEN NOT MINDED IN DISMAY, YET NOW 11 156

DISMISS
END, AND DISMISS THEE ERE THE MORNING SHINE. 7 108
DISMISS NOT HER, WHEN MOST THOU NEEDST HER NIGH, 8 564
NAY DIDST PERMIT, APPROVE, AND FAIR DISMISS. 9 1159
DISMISS THEM NOT DISCONSOLATE; REVEALE 11 113

DISMISS'D
SO SAYING HE DISMISS'D THEM, THEY WITH SPEED 10 410

DISMISSD
PURSUING WHOM HE LATE DISMISSD, THE SEA 12 195

DISMISSING
OF WHAT WE ARE AND WERE, DISMISSING QUITE 2 282

DISMIST
GLAD TO BE SO DISMIST IN PEACE. CAN THUS 11 507

DISMOUNTED
DISMOUNTED, ON TH' ALEIAN FIELD I FALL 7 19

DISOBEDIENCE
OF MANS FIRST DISOBEDIENCE, AND THE FRUIT 1 1
AND SOM ARE FALL'N, TO DISOBEDIENCE FALL'N, 5 541
THY DISOBEDIENCE. WELL THOU DIDST ADVISE, 5 888
BY SIN OF DISOBEDIENCE, TILL THAT HOUR 6 396
OF DISOBEDIENCE; FIRM THEY MIGHT HAVE STOOD, 6 911
AND DISOBEDIENCE: ON THE PART OF HEAV'N 9 8

DISOBEDIENT
THESE DISOBEDIENT; SORE HATH BEEN THIR FIGHT, 6 687
PROVE DISOBEDIENT, AND REPROV'D, RETORT, 10 761

DISOBEI'D
NOT TO HAVE DISOBEI'D; IN FIGHT THEY STOOD 6 403

DISOBEYES
FOR EVER HAPPIE: HIM WHO DISOBEYES 5 611
MEE DISOBEYES, BREAKS UNION, AND THAT DAY 5 612

DISOBEYING
BUT YET ALL IS NOT DON; MAN DISOBEYING, 3 203

DISOLUTION
WHEN THIS WORLDS DISOLUTION SHALL BE RIPE, 12 459

DISORDER
LIGHT SHON, AND ORDER FROM DISORDER SPRUNG: 3 713
ENTER'D, AND FOUL DISORDER; ALL THE GROUND 6 388

DISORDER'D
AND TO DISORDER'D RAGE LET LOOSE THE REINES, 6 696

DISORDERD
AND TRESSES ALL DISORDERD, AT HIS FEET 10 911

DISPARAGE
GODS ALTAR TO DISPARAGE AND DISPLACE 1 473

DISPARITIE
GIV'N AND RECEIV'D; BUT IN DISPARITIE 8 386

DISPARTED
DISPARTED, AND BETWEEN SPUN OUT THE AIR, 7 241
DISPARTED CHAOS OVERBUILT EXCLAIMD, 10 416

DISPATCH
OF THEOLOGIANS, BUT WITH KEEN DISPATCH 5 436
THE HANDS DISPATCH OF TWO GARDNING SO WIDE. 9 203

DISPATCHFUL
SO SAYING, WITH DISPATCHFUL LOOKS IN HASTE 5 331

DISPEL'D
THIR FANTING COURAGE, AND DISPEL'D THIR FEARS. . 1 530

DISPELS
DISPERSE IT, AS NOW LIGHT DISPELS THE DARK. . . 5 208

DISPENC'T
THIS IS DISPENC'T, AND WHAT SURMOUNTS THE REACH . 5 571

DISPENSE
FANNING THIR ODORIFEROUS WINGS DISPENSE 4 157

DISPENSES
INDULGENCES, DISPENSES, PARDONS, BULLS, ... 3 492
DISPENSES LIGHT FROM FARR; THEY AS THEY MOVE . . 3 579

DISPENST
GOD HATH DISPENST HIS BOUNTIES AS IN HEAV'N. . . 5 330
ANOUGH TO BEARE; THOSE NOW, THAT WERE DISPENST . 11 766

DISPEOPL'D
ALREADY DONE, TO HAVE DISPEOPL'D HEAV'N 7 151

DISPERS'D
LIGHTLY DISPERS'D, AND THE SHRILL MATIN SONG . . 5 7
HOWEVER SOME TRADITION THEY DISPERS'D 10 578

DISPERSE
PURGE AND DISPERSE, THAT I MAY SEE AND TELL . . 3 54
DISPERSE IT, AS NOW LIGHT DISPELS THE DARK. . . 5 208

DISPERST
DOWN THE SLOPE HILLS, DISPERST, OR IN A LAKE, . . 4 261
DISPERST IN BANDS AND FILES THIR CAMP EXTEND . . 5 651
AND GET THEMSELVES A NAME, LEAST FAR DISPERST . . 12 45

DISPLACE
GODS ALTAR TO DISPARAGE AND DISPLACE 1 473

DISPLAID
HIS PROUD IMAGINATIONS THUS DISPLAID. 2 10
FARR OTHER OPERATION FIRST DISPLAID, ... 9 1012

DISPLAYD
DISPLAYD ON THE OP'N FIRMAMENT OF HEAV'N. . . . 7 390

DISPLEAS'D
WHERETO TH' ALMIGHTY ANSWER'D, NOT DISPLEAS'D. . 8 398
DISPLEAS'D THAT I APPROACH THEE THUS, AND GAZE . 9 535
FROM EARTH ARRIV'D AT HEAVEN GATE, DISPLEAS'D . . 10 22
HIS COUNSEL WHOM SHE HAD DISPLEAS'D, HIS AIDE; . 10 944
WHERETO THUS ADAM FATHERLY DISPLEAS'D. 12 63

DISPLEASURE
DIVINE DISPLEASURE FOR HER SAKE, OR DEATH. . . . 9 993
AND MY DISPLEASURE BEARST SO ILL. IF PRAYERS . . 10 952
FROM HIS DISPLEASURE; IN WHOSE LOOK SERENE, . . 10 1094

DISPLODE
IN POSTURE TO DISPLODE THIR SECOND TIRE 6 605

DISPORT
TO SUCH DISPORT BEFORE HER THROUGH THE FIELD, . . 9 520
THERE THEY THIR FILL OF LOVE AND LOVES DISPORT . 9 1042

DISPORTING
DISPORTING, TILL THE AMOROUS BIRD OF NIGHT . . . 8 518

DISPOS'D
THIR WILL, DISPOS'D BY ABSOLUTE DECREE 3 115
IN DARKER VEILE) AND ROSEAT DEWS DISPOS'D . . . 5 646
THIR LORDS, WHOM GOD DISPOS'D, THE HOUSE OF GOD . 12 349

DISPOSE
WHO NOW IS SOVRAN CAN DISPOSE AND BID 1 246
WHEREVER PLAC'T, LET HIM DISPOSE; JOY THOU . . . 8 170
AND MORTAL FOOD, AS MAY DISPOSE HIM BEST . . . 11 54

DISPOSER
MY AUTHOR AND DISPOSER, WHAT THOU BIDST 4 635

DISPOSSESS
TO DISPOSSESS HIM, AND THY SELF TO REIGNE? . . . 4 961
OVER HIS BRETHREN, AND QUITE DISPOSSESS 12 28

DISPOSSEST
OF DEITIE SUPREAM, US DISPOSSEST, ... 7 142

DISPRAISE
ILLAUDABLE, NAUGHT MERITS BUT DISPRAISE 6 382
RATHER BELONGS, DISTRUST AND ALL DISPRAISE; . . 11 166

DISPROPORTIONS
SUCH DISPROPORTIONS, WITH SUPERFLUOUS HAND 8 27

DISPUTE
SHALT THOU GIVE LAW TO GOD, SHALT THOU DISPUTE . 5 822
GRATEFUL DIGRESSIONS, AND SOLVE HIGH DISPUTE . . 8 55
LIGHT BACK TO THEM, IS OBVIOUS TO DISPUTE. . . . 8 158

DISPUTES
SHOULD WIN IN ARMS, IN BOTH DISPUTES ALIKE . . . 6 123
HATH LEFT TO THIR DISPUTES, PERHAPS TO MOVE . . 8 77
IN SIGHT OF GOD? HIM AFTER ALL DISPUTES . . . 10 828

DISRELISH
TRUE APPETITE, AND NOT DISRELISH THIRST 5 305
WITH HATEFULLEST DISRELISH WRITH'D THIR JAWS . . 10 569

DISSECT
HEROIC DEEM'D, CHIEF MAISTRIE TO DISSECT 9 29

DISSEMBLER
SO SPAKE THE FALSE DISSEMBLER UNPERCEIVD; 3 681

DISSENSION
BUT FIRST AMONG THE PRIESTS DISSENSION SPRINGS, . 12 353

DISSENT
THY SLEEP DISSENT? NEW LAWS THOU SEEST IMPOS'D; . 5 679
SEEMD IN THY WORLD ERRONEOUS TO DISSENT 6 146
HADST THOU BIN FIRM AND FIXT IN THY DISSENT, . . 9 1160

DISSIPATION
FOULE DISSIPATION FOLLOW'D AND FORC'T ROUT; . . 6 598

DISSOLUTE
WORLDLIE OR DISSOLUTE, ON WHAT THIR LORDS . . . 11 803

DISSOLUTION
AND UTTER DISSOLUTION, AS THE SCOPE 2 127
TILL FINAL DISSOLUTION, WANDER HERE, ... 3 458
IMMEDIATE DISSOLUTION, WHICH WE THOUGHT 10 1049
FOR DISSOLUTION WROUGHT BY SIN, THAT FIRST . . . 11 55
MY DISSOLUTION. MICHAEL REPLI'D, ... 11 552

DISSOLV'D
THE STYGIAN COUNSEL THUS DISSOLV'D; AND FORTH . . 2 506

DISSOLVD
DISSOLVD ON EARTH, FLEET HITHER, AND IN VAIN, . . 3 457

DISSOLVE
YOUR MILITARY OBEDIENCE, TO DISSOLVE 4 955
INSENSIBLE, AND FORTHWITH TO DISSOLVE: 8 291
LEAST IT AGAIN DISSOLVE AND SHOWR THE EARTH? . . 11 883
IN GLORY OF THE FATHER, TO DISSOLVE 12 546

DISSONANCE
BUT DRIVE FARR OFF THE BARBAROUS DISSONANCE . . 7 32

DISSUADE
NOT DIFFIDENT OF THEE DO I DISSUADE 9 293

DISSWADE
DID NOT DISSWADE ME MOST, AND SEEM TO CAST . . . 2 122

DISSWADES
MY VOICE DISSWADES; FOR WHAT CAN FORCE OR GUILE . 2 188

DI'ST
THOU MAI'ST NOT; IN THE DAY THOU EAT'ST, THOU
DI'ST; 7 544

DISTANCE
THAT FROM HIS LORDLY EYE KEEP DISTANCE DUE, . . 3 578
IN THAT ASPECT, AND STILL THAT DISTANCE KEEPES . 7 379
THIR DISTANCE ARGUES AND THIR SWIFT RETURN . . . 8 21
IN EDEN, DISTANCE INEXPRESSIBLE 8 113
NOW ALIENATED, DISTANCE AND DISTASTE, ... 9 9
POWERFUL AT GREATEST DISTANCE TO UNITE 10 247
TO RECOMPENCE HIS DISTANCE, IN THIR SIGHT . . . 10 683

DISTANCES
AND PRACTIS'D DISTANCES TO CRINGE, NOT FIGHT. . . 4 945

DISTANT
THOUGH DISTANT FARR SOM SMALL REFLECTION GAINES . 3 428
HIS TRAVELL'D STEPS; FARR DISTANT HE DESCRIES . . 3 501
STARS DISTANT, BUT NIGH HAND SEEMD OTHER WORLDS, . 3 566
TO OBJECTS DISTANT FARR, WHEREBY HE SOON . . . 3 621
NOT DISTANT FAR FROM THENCE A MURMURING SOUND . . 4 453
EACH QUARTER, TO DESCRIE THE DISTANT FOE, . . . 6 530
NOT DISTANT FAR WITH HEAVIE PACE THE FOE . . . 6 551
DISTANT SO HIGH, WITH MOVING FIRES ADORND . . . 7 87
A GOODLY TREE FARR DISTANT TO BEHOLD 9 576
THOUGH DISTANT FROM THEE WORLDS BETWEEN, YET FELT 10 362
LIKE DISTANT BREADTH TO TAURUS WITH THE SEAV'N . 10 673

DISTASTE
NOW ALIENATED, DISTANCE AND DISTASTE, ... 9 9

DISTEMPER
CONTIGUOUS MIGHT DISTEMPER THE WHOLE FRAME: 7 273
BUT IN HER CHEEK DISTEMPER FLUSHING GLOWD. 9 887
AS A DISTEMPER, GROSS TO AIRE AS GROSS, 11 53

DISTEMPERD
AT LEAST DISTEMPERD, DISCONTENTED THOUGHTS, 4 807
SUPERIOR SWAY: FROM THUS DISTEMPERD BREST, 9 1131
DISTEMPERD ALL THINGS, AND OF INCORRUPT 11 56

DISTEMPERS
FOR HEAV'NLY MINDES FROM SUCH DISTEMPERS FOULE 4 118

DISTENDED
DISTENDED AS THE BROW OF GOD APPEAS'D, 11 880

DISTENDS
DISTENDS WITH PRIDE, AND HARDNING IN HIS STRENGTH 1 572

DISTILL'D
BY US OFT SEEN; HIS DEWIE LOCKS DISTILL'D 5 56

DISTINCT
DISTINCT WITH EYES, AND FROM THE LIVING WHEELS 6 846
DISTINCT ALIKE WITH MULTITUDE OF EYES, 6 847
IS YET DISTINCT BY NAME, THENCE, AS THOU KNOW'ST 7 536
HIGH AND REMOTE TO SEE FROM THENCE DISTINCT 9 812

DISTINCTION
STREAME IN THE AIRE, AND FOR DISTINCTION SERVE 5 590

DISTINGUISH
DISTINGUISH NOT: FOR SOON EXPECT TO FEEL 5 892

DISTINGUISHABLE
DISTINGUISHABLE IN MEMBER, JOYNT, OR LIMB, 2 668

DISTORTED
DISTORTED, ALL MY NETHER SHAPE THUS GREW 2 784

DISTRACT
UPON HIMSELF; HORROR AND DOUBT DISTRACT 4 18

DISTRESS
THY COUNSEL IN THIS UTTERMOST DISTRESS, 10 920
NOW AT HIS FEET SUBMISSIVE IN DISTRESS, 10 942
PRESAGING, SINCE WITH SORROW AND HEARTS DISTRESS 12 613

DISTRUST
THOSE NOTES TO TRAGIC; FOUL DISTRUST, AND BREACH 9 6
RATHER BELONGS, DISTRUST AND ALL DISPRAISE: 11 166

DISTURB
SHALL GRIEVE HIM, IF I FAIL NOT, AND DISTURB 1 167
OUR POWER SUFFICIENT TO DISTURB HIS HEAV'N, 2 102
WITH PURPOSE TO EXPLORE OR TO DISTURB 2 971
DREADFUL COMBUSTION WARRING, AND DISTURB, 6 225
INSTANT WITHOUT DISTURB THEY TOOK ALLARM, 6 549
OUR FEALTIE FROM GOD, OR TO DISTURB 9 262

DISTURBANCE
IN HIS DISTURBANCE; WHEN HIS DARLING SONS 2 373

DISTURBANCES
DISTURBANCES ON EARTH THROUGH FEMAL SNARES, 10 897

DISTURB'D
IF AUGHT DISTURB'D THIR NOYSE, INTO HER WOOMB, 2 657
AND THY ADHERENTS: HOW HAST THOU DISTURB'D 6 266

DISTURBD
TO THY TRANSGRESSIONS, AND DISTURBD THE CHARGE 4 879
AT LEAST HAD GON TO RACK, DISTURBD AND TORNE 4 994
HATH RAISD IN PARADISE, AND HOW DISTURBD 5 226
DISTURBD NOT, WAITING CLOSE TH' APPROACH OF MORN. 9 191
FLUCTUATS DISTURBD, YET COMELY AND IN ACT 9 668
RECOMFORTED, AND AFTER THOUGHTS DISTURBD 9 918

DITTIES
SOFT AMOROUS DITTIES, AND IN DANCE CAME ON: 11 584

DITTYES
IN AMOROUS DITTYES ALL A SUMMERS DAY, 1 449

DIURNAL
DIURNAL, OR THIS LESS VOLUBIL EARTH 4 594
WITHIN THE VISIBLE DIURNAL SPHEARE; 7 22
DIURNAL) MEERLY TO OFFICIATE LIGHT 8 22
NOCTURNAL AND DIURNAL RHOMB SUPPOS'D, 8 134
OUR LIMBS BENUMM'D, ERE THIS DIURNAL STARR 10 1069

DIVAN
RAIS'D FROM THIR DARK DIVAN, AND WITH LIKE JOY 10 457

DIVERS
RUNS DIVERS, WANDRING MANY A FAMOUS REALME 4 234
FLEW DIVERS, AND WITH POWER (THIR POWER WAS GREAT) 10 284

DIVERTED
MAY HAVE DIVERTED FROM CONTINUAL WATCH 9 814

DIVIDE
DIVIDE THE NIGHT, AND LIFT OUR THOUGHTS TO HEAVEN. 4 688
AMID THE WATERS, AND LET IT DIVIDE 7 262
HIGH IN TH' EXPANSE OF HEAVEN TO DIVIDE 7 340
AND LIGHT FROM DARKNESS TO DIVIDE. GOD SAW, 7 352
LET US DIVIDE OUR LABOURS, THOU WHERE CHOICE 9 214
AND HENCEFORTH MONARCHIE WITH THEE DIVIDE 10 379

DIVIDED
DIVIDED EMPIRE WITH HEAV'NS KING I HOLD 4 111
AND NOW DIVIDED INTO FOUR MAIN STREAMS, 4 233
AS EACH DIVIDED LEGION MIGHT HAVE SEEMD 6 230
FOR STRENGTH FROM TRUTH DIVIDED AND FROM JUST, 6 381
DIVIDED, AND TO EITHER FLANK RETIR'D. 6 570
DIVIDED: LIGHT THE DAY, AND DARKNESS NIGHT 7 251
THEN ALL THE WORLD MUCH HEAVIER, THOUGH DIVIDED 10 836
EGYPT, DIVIDED BY THE RIVER NILE; 12 157
DIVIDED, TILL HIS RESCU'D GAIN THIR SHOAR: 12 199

DIVIDES
OF THIS ROUND WORLD, WHOSE FIRST CONVEX DIVIDES 3 419
NOR STREIT'NING VALE, NOR WOOD, NOR STREAM DIVIDES 6 70

DIVIDING
DIVIDING: FOR AS EARTH, SO HE THE WORLD 7 269

DIVIDUAL
WITH THOUSAND LESSER LIGHTS DIVIDUAL HOLDS, 7 382
TWINN'D, AND FROM HER HATH NO DIVIDUAL BEING: 12 85

DIVIN'D
FOR I NO SOONER IN MY HEART DIVIN'D, 10 357

DIVINE
THEN AUGHT DIVINE OR HOLY ELSE ENJOY'D 1 683
OR IF OUR SUBSTANCE BE INDEED DIVINE, 2 99
OR FLOCKS, OR HEARDS, OR HUMAN FACE DIVINE; 3 44
DIVINE COMPASSION VISIBLY APPEERD, 3 141
IN WHOM THE FULNESS DWELS OF LOVE DIVINE, 3 225
BEGOTTEN SON, DIVINE SIMILITUDE, 3 384
LOVE NO WHERE TO BE FOUND LESS THEN DIVINE. 3 411
AND WORTHIE SEEMD, FOR IN THIR LOOKS DIVINE 4 291
IN THEM DIVINE RESEMBLANCE, AND SUCH GRACE 4 364
BUT HE THUS OVERJOY'D, O FRUIT DIVINE, 5 67
THY GOODNESS BEYOND THOUGHT, AND POWER DIVINE: 5 159
DIVINE THE SOV'RAN ARCHITECT HAD FRAM'D. 5 256
HIS LINEAMENTS DIVINE; THE PAIR THAT CLAD 5 278
DIVINE EFFULGENCE, WHOSE HIGH POWER SO FAR 5 458
DIVINE INSTRUCTER, I HAVE HEARD, THEN WHEN 5 546
AND IN THIR MOTIONS HARMONIE DIVINE 5 625
LIGHT'NING DIVINE, INEFFABLE, SERENE, 5 734
THE DEITIE, AND DIVINE COMMANDS OBEI'D, 5 806
IDOL OF MAJESTIE DIVINE, ENCLOS'D 6 101
VIGOUR DIVINE WITHIN THEM, CAN ALLOW 6 158
IN HEAV'N GOD EVER BLEST, AND HIS DIVINE 6 184
BEFORE HIM POWER DIVINE HIS WAY PREPAR'D; 6 780
IF RIGHTLY THOU ART CALL'D, WHOSE VOICE DIVINE 7 2
DIVINE INTERPRETER, BY FAVOUR SENT 7 72
OF MAJESTIE DIVINE, SAPIENCE AND LOVE 7 195
EQUAL HAVE I TO RENDER THEE, DIVINE 8 6
THOUGH PLEASANT, BUT THY WORDS WITH GRACE DIVINE 8 215
AND LIVD: ONE CAME, METHOUGHT, OF SHAPE DIVINE, 8 295
PRESENCE DIVINE. REJOYCING, BUT WITH AW 8 314
THIS ANSWER FROM THE GRATIOUS VOICE DIVINE. 8 436
BUT ALL THAT FAIR AND GOOD IN THY DIVINE 9 606
HERE GROWS THE CURE OF ALL, THIS FRUIT DIVINE, 9 776
YET OFT HIS HEART, DIVINE OF SOMTHING ILL, 9 845
OP'NING THE WAY, BUT OF DIVINE EFFECT 9 865
HOLY, DIVINE, GOOD, AMIABLE, OR SWEET. 9 899
TASTE SO DIVINE, THAT WHAT OF SWEET BEFORE 9 986
DIVINE DISPLEASURE FOR HER SAKE, OR DEATH. 9 993
SO FIT, SO ACCEPTABLE, SO DIVINE, 10 139
JUSTICE DIVINE NOT HAST'N TO BE JUST? 10 857
BUT DEATH COMES NOT AT CALL, JUSTICE DIVINE 10 858
PRESENCE DIVINE, AND TO MY SONS RELATE; 11 319
EXPRESS, AND OF HIS STEPS THE TRACK DIVINE. 11 354
RETAINING STILL DIVINE SIMILITUDE 11 512
HOLIE AND PURE, CONFORMITIE DIVINE. 11 606
THY MORTAL SIGHT TO FAILE; OBJECTS DIVINE 12 9

DIVINELY
OF RADIANT URIM, WORK DIVINELY WROUGHT, 6 761
SHE HEARD ME THUS, AND THOUGH DIVINELY BROUGHT, 8 500
SHEE FAIR, DIVINELY FAIR, FIT LOVE FOR GODS, 9 489
EXPRESS'D, AND THUS DIVINELY ANSWER'D MILDE. 10 67

DIVINITIE
DIVINITIE WITHIN THEM BREEDING WINGS 9 1010

DIVISIBLE
NOT LONG DIVISIBLE, AND FROM THE GASH 6 331

DIVULG'D
TO THEM MADE COMMON AND DIVULG'D, IF AUGHT 8 583

DIVULGE
DID WISELY TO CONCEAL, AND NOT DIVULGE 8 73

DIZZIE
SURPRIS'D THEE, DIM THINE EYES, AND DIZZIE SWUMM 2 753

DOCTRIN
DOCTRIN WHICH WE WOULD KNOW WHENCE LEARNT: WHO SAW 5 856

DOCTRINE
THIR DOCTRINE AND THIR STORY WRITTEN LEFT, 12 506

DODONA
OR IN DODONA, AND THROUGH ALL THE BOUNDS 1 518

DOE
THE VICTORS WILL. TO SUFFER, AS TO DOE, 2 199
O HELL. WHAT DOE MINE EYES WITH GRIEF BEHOLD, 4 358
MELT, AS I DOE, YET PUBLIC REASON JUST, 4 389
MOTHER OF HUMAN RACE: WHAT COULD I DOE, 4 475
WILL SAVE US TRIAL WHAT THE LEAST CAN DOE 4 855
TO BOAST WHAT ARMS CAN DOE, SINCE THINE NO MORE 4 1008
AND IN WHOSE HAND WHAT BY DECREE I DOE, 6 683
QUEEN OF THIS UNIVERSE, DOE NOT BELIEVE 9 684

DOGS
SEE WITH WHAT HEAT THESE DOGS OF HELL ADVANCE 10 616

DOING
DOING OR SUFFERING: BUT OF THIS BE SURE, 1 158
WHATEVER DOING, WHAT CAN WE SUFFER MORE, 2 162
IN DOING WHAT WE MOST IN SUFFERING FEEL? 2 340
HER DOING SEEM'D TO JUSTIFIE THE DEED; 10 142

DOINGS
AND OF THIR DOINGS GOD TAKES NO ACCOUNT, 4 622
AND OF THIR DOINGS GREAT DISLIKE DECLAR'D, 11 720
TO MARK THIR DOINGS, THEM BEHOLDING SOON, 12 50

DOLE
DOLE WITH DELIGHT, WHICH IN THIS PLACE I SOUGHT; 4 894

DOLEFUL
REGIONS OF SORROW, DOLEFUL SHADES, WHERE PEACE 1 65

DOLOROUS
THEY PASS'D, AND MANY A REGION DOLOROUS, 2 619
IMPLACABLE, AND MANY A DOLOROUS GROAN, 6 658

DOLPHINS
AND BENDED DOLPHINS PLAY: PART HUGE OF BULK 7 410

DOMESTIC
PERPETUAL FOUNTAIN OF DOMESTIC SWEETS, 4 760
WOMANS DOMESTIC HONOUR AND CHIEF PRAISE; 11 617

DOMESTICK
SO SPAKE DOMESTICK ADAM IN HIS CARE 9 318

DOMINATIONS
TH' ASPIRING DOMINATIONS: THOU THAT DAY 3 392
THRONES, DOMINATIONS, PRINCEDOMS, VERTUES, POWERS, 5 601
THRONES, DOMINATIONS, PRINCEDOMES, VERTUES, POWERS, 5 772
THRONES, DOMINATIONS, PRINCEDOMS, VERTUES, POWERS, 5 840
PRINCEDOMS, AND DOMINATIONS MINISTRANT 10 87
THRONES, DOMINATIONS, PRINCEDOMS, VERTUES, POWERS, 10 460

DOMINIC
DYING PUT ON THE WEEDS OF DOMINIC, 3 479

DOMINION
FROM YOUR DOMINION WON, TH' ETHEREAL KING 2 978
AND IN HER PALE DOMINION CHECKS THE NIGHT, 3 732
LOOK'ST FROM THY SOLE DOMINION LIKE THE GOD 4 33
CONFERRD UPON US, AND DOMINION GIV'N 4 430
ALL THY DOMINION, ADAM, IS NO MORE 5 751
HONOUR, DOMINION, GLORIE, AND RENOWNE, 6 422
SON, HEIR, AND LORD, TO HIM DOMINION GIV'N, 6 887
SUBDUE IT, AND THROUGHOUT DOMINION HOLD 7 532
THE CHARACTER OF THAT DOMINION GIV'N 8 545
WINGS GROWING, AND DOMINION GIV'N ME LARGE 10 244
DOMINION EXERCISE AND IN THE AIRE, 10 400
WILL ARROGATE DOMINION UNDESERV'D 12 27
DOMINION ABSOLUTE; THAT RIGHT WE HOLD 12 68

DOMINIONS
POWERS AND DOMINIONS, DEITIES OF HEAV'N, 2 11
THRONES, PRINCEDOMS, POWERS, DOMINIONS I REDUCE: 3 320

DONATION
BY HIS DONATION; BUT MAN OVER MEN 12 69

DOOM
CONFOUNDED THOUGH IMMORTAL: BUT HIS DOOM 1 53
OUR DOOM; WHICH IF WE CAN SUSTAIN AND BEAR, 2 209
BY DOOM OF BATTEL; AND COMPLAIN THAT FATE 2 550
OR PROUD RETURN THOUGH TO HIS HEAVIER DOOM, 3 159
BY DOOM SEVERE, HAD NOT THE SON OF GOD, 3 224

DOOM (CONTINUED)
OF ALL PAST AGES TO THE GENERAL DOOM 3 328
PERCEIVE THEE PURPOS'D NOT TO DOOM FRAIL MAN 3 404
THY SIN AND PLACE OF DOOM OBSCURE AND FOULE. 4 840
INSENSIBLY, FOR I SUSPEND THIR DOOM; 6 692
THEREFORE TO MEE THIR DOOM HE HATH ASSIG'N'D; 6 817
OF THIS FAIR FRUIT, OUR DOOM IS, WE SHALL DIE. 9 763
CERTAIN TO UNDERGOE LIKE DOOM, IF DEATH 9 953
OF RIGHT, THAT I MAY MITIGATE THIR DOOM 10 76
TO SATAN FIRST IN SIN HIS DOOM APPLY'D, 10 172
THENCE GATHERD HIS OWN DOOM, WHICH UNDERSTOOD 10 344
RETIRING, BY HIS OWN DOOM ALIENATED, 10 378
ACCORDING TO HIS DOOM; HE WOULD HAVE SPOKE, 10 517
BE IT SO, FOR I SUBMIT, HIS DOOM IS FAIR, 10 769
TO SATAN ONLY LIKE BOTH CRIME AND DOOM. 10 841
AGAINST A FOE BY DOOM EXPRESS ASSIGN'D US, 10 926
WE ARE BY DOOM TO PAY; RATHER SUCH ACTS 10 1026
NUMBERD, THOUGH SAD, TILL DEATH, HIS DOOM (WHICH I 11 40
TO SOUND AT GENERAL DOOM. TH' ANGELIC BLAST 11 76
ANNULS THY DOOM, THE DEATH THOU SHOULDST HAVE DY'D, 12 428

DOOM'D
AND KNOW NOT THAT THE KING OF HEAV'N HATH DOOM'D 2 316
HELL-DOOM'D, AND BREATH'ST DEFIANCE HERE AND SCORN 2 697
ON THOSE PROUD TOWRS TO SWIFT DESTRUCTION DOOM'D. 5 907
BUT MORTAL DOOM'D. HOW CAN HE EXERCISE 10 796

DOOMD
THOUGH THITHER DOOMD? THOU WOULDST THY SELF, NO
DOUBT, 4 890

DOOME
FATHER OF MERCIE AND GRACE, THOU DIDST NOT DOOME 3 401
ERE THIS AVENGING SWORD BEGIN THY DOOME, 6 278
NOR OF RENOWN LESS EAGER, YET BY DOOME 6 378
THEREFORE ETERNAL SILENCE BE THIR DOOME. 6 385

DOOR
IN GIBEAH, WHEN THE HOSPITABLE DOOR 1 504

DORE
ADAM DISCERND, AS IN THE DORE HE SAT 5 299
LIGHT ISSUES FORTH, AND AT THE OTHER DORE 6 9
TH' INFERNAL EMPIRE, THAT SO NEER HEAV'NS DORE 10 389
OF LOWEST ORDER, PAST; AND FROM THE DORE 10 443
SMEARD ROUND WITH PITCH, AND IN THE SIDE A DORE 11 731
WITH THIR FOUR WIVES; AND GOD MADE FAST THE DORE. 11 737

DORES
STOOD FIXT HER STATELY HIGHTH, AND STRAIT THE DORES 1 723
TH' INFERNAL DORES, AND ON THIR HINGES GRATE 2 881
HIS SAD EXCLUSION FROM THE DORES OF BLISS. 3 525
OF SOME RICH BURGHER, WHOSE SUBSTANTIAL DORES, 4 189
OPEN, YE HEAV'NS, YOUR LIVING DORES; LET IN 7 566
DIMENTIONLESS THROUGH HEAV'NLY DORES; THEN CLAD 11 17

DORIAN
IN PERFECT PHALANX TO THE DORIAN MOOD 1 550

DORIC
OF DORIC LAND; OR WHO WITH SATURN OLD 1 519
WERE SET, AND DORIC PILLARS OVERLAID 1 714

DOTHAN
IN DOTHAN, COVER'D WITH A CAMP OF FIRE, 11 217

DOUBL'D
DOUBL'D THAT SIN IN BETHEL AND IN DAN, 1 485
TO SPEAK; WHEREAT THIR DOUBL'D RANKS THEY BEND 1 616
DOUBL'D, WOULD RENDER THEM YET MORE DESPIS'D, 6 602

DOUBLD
THEN HEAV'N PERMITS, NOR MINE, THOUGH DOUBLD NOW 4 1009

DOUBLE
SHORT INTERMISSION BOUGHT WITH DOUBLE SMART. 4 102
TOO MUCH TO ONE, BUT DOUBLE HOW ENDUR'D, 5 783
BY US? WHO RATHER DOUBLE HONOUR GAINE 9 332
ALL THINGS WITH DOUBLE TERROR: ON THE GROUND 10 850
INSTEAD SHALL DOUBLE OURS UPON OUR HEADS. 10 1040
HAD, LIKE A DOUBLE JANUS, ALL THIR SHAPE 11 129
WHY ELSE THIS DOUBLE OBJECT IN OUR SIGHT 11 201

DOUBLE-FORM'D
WHAT THING THOU ART, THUS DOUBLE-FORM'D, AND WHY 2 741

DOUBLE-FOUNTED
MOUNT CARMEL; HERE THE DOUBLE-FOUNTED STREAM 12 144

DOUBT
ANGUISH AND DOUBT AND FEAR AND SORROW AND PAIN 1 558
WHAT FEAR WE THEN? WHAT DOUBT WE TO INCENSE 2 94
UPON HIMSELF; HORROR AND DOUBT DISTRACT 4 18
SOM DREADFUL THING NO DOUBT; FOR WELL THOU KNOWST 4 426
THE BARRS OF HELL, ON ERRAND BAD NO DOUBT: 4 795
PUTS ME IN DOUBT. LIVES THER WHO LOVES HIS PAIN? 4 888
THOUGH THITHER DOOMD? THOU WOULDST THY SELF, NO
DOUBT, 4 890

DOUBT (CONTINUED)
GRAVELY IN DOUBT WHETHER TO HOLD THEM WISE 4 907
HATH PAST IN HEAV'N, SOM DOUBT WITHIN ME MOVE, 5 554
BUT THAT I DOUBT, HOWEVER WITNESS HEAVEN, 6 563
ALL DOUBT OF VICTORIE, ETERNAL MIGHT 6 630
CREATOR; SOMETHING YET OF DOUBT REMAINES, 8 13
AND RAPHAEL NOW TO ADAM'S DOUBT PROPOS'D 8 64
INVALID THAT WHICH THEE TO DOUBT IT MOV'D; 8 116
TO WHOM THUS ADAM CLEERD OF DOUBT, REPLI'D. 8 179
AN OUTSIDE? FAIR NO DOUBT, AND WORTHY WELL 8 568
DOUBT MIGHT BEGET OF DIABOLIC POW'R 9 95
THESE PATHS & BOWERS DOUBT NOT BUT OUR JOYNT HANDS 9 244
BUT OTHER DOUBT POSSESSES ME, LEAST HARM 9 251
WATCHES, NO DOUBT, WITH GREEDY HOPE TO FIND 9 257
BUT THAT THOU SHOULDST MY FIRMNESS THEREFORE DOUBT 9 279
SERPENT, THY OVERPRAISING LEAVES IN DOUBT 9 615
WITH CRUEL EXPECTATION. YET ONE DOUBT 10 782
THE DOUBT, SINCE HUMANE REACH NO FURTHER KNOWS. 10 793
THE PENALTIE PRONOUNC'T, DOUBT NOT BUT GOD 10 1022
A GLORIOUS APPARITION, HAD NOT DOUBT 11 211
YET DOUBT NOT BUT IN VALLIE AND IN PLAINE 11 349
TO WHOM THUS MICHAEL. DOUBT NOT BUT THAT SIN 12 285
LIGHT OUT OF DARKNESS. FULL OF DOUBT I STAND. 12 473

DOUBTED
DOUBTED HIS EMPIRE, THAT WERE LOW INDEED, 1 114

DOUBTFUL
LIKE DOUBTFUL HUE: BUT HE HIS WONTED PRIDE 1 527
IS DOUBTFUL; THAT HE NEVER WILL IS SURE. 2 154
CONTENDING, AND SO DOUBTFUL WHAT MIGHT FALL. 2 203
THUS THEY THIR DOUBTFUL CONSULTATIONS DARK 2 486
WHAT DOUBTFUL MAY ENSUE, MORE IN THIS PLACE 5 682
WHO HAVE SUSTAIND ONE DAY IN DOUBTFUL FIGHT 6 423

DOUBTING
SWAYES THEM; THE CAREFUL PLOWMAN DOUBTING STANDS 4 983

DOUBTLESS
A GROWING EMPIRE; DOUBTLESS; WHILE WE DREAM, 2 315
GREAT ARE THY VERTUES, DOUBTLESS, BEST OF FRUITS. 9 745

DOUBTS
THE DOUBTS THAT IN HIS HEART AROSE: AND NOW 7 60

DOVE
A DOVE SENT FORTH ONCE AND AGEN TO SPIE 11 857

DOVE-LIKE
DOVE-LIKE SATST BROODING ON THE VAST ABYSS 1 21

DOWN
WITH HIDEOUS RUINE AND COMBUSTION DOWN 1 46
TH' ADVANTAGE, AND DESCENDING TREAD US DOWN 1 327
THIR COURSE, IN EVEN BALLANCE DOWN THEY LIGHT 1 349
HIS RIGHTEOUS ALTAR, BOWING LOWLY DOWN 1 434
BOW'D DOWN IN BATTEL, SUNK BEFORE THE SPEAR 1 436
DOWN CAST AND DAMP, YET SUCH WHEREIN APPEAR'D 1 523
THROUGH ALL THE EMPYREAN: DOWN THEY FELL 2 771
DRIV'N HEADLONG FROM THE PITCH OF HEAVEN, DOWN 2 772
SHALL DWELL AT EASE, AND UP AND DOWN UNSEEN 2 841
WHO HATES ME, AND HATH HITHER THRUST ME DOWN 2 857
FLUTTRING HIS PENNONS VAIN PLUMB DOWN HE DROPS 2 933
DOWN HAD BEEN FALLING, HAD NOT BY ILL CHANCE 2 935
TAUGHT BY THE HEAV'NLY MUSE TO VENTURE DOWN 3 19
HIGH THRON'D ABOVE ALL HIGHTH, BENT DOWN HIS EYE, 3 58
PLEAS'D, OUT OF HEAVEN SHALT LOOK DOWN AND SMILE, 3 257
WITH SOLEMN ADORATION DOWN THEY CAST 3 351
BY THEE CREATED, AND BY THEE THREW DOWN 3 391
WALK'D UP AND DOWN ALONE BENT ON HIS PREY, 3 441
THE STAIRS WERE THEN LET DOWN, WHETHER TO DARE 3 523
A PASSAGE DOWN TO TH' EARTH, A PASSAGE WIDE, 3 528
LOOKS DOWN WITH WONDER AT THE SUDDEN VIEW 3 542
DOWN RIGHT INTO THE WORLDS FIRST REGION THROWS 3 562
THAT RUN THROUGH ALL THE HEAV'NS, OR DOWN TO TH' EARTH 3 651
DOWN FROM TH' ECLIPTIC, SPED WITH HOP'D SUCCESS, 3 740
CAME FURIOUS DOWN TO BE REVENG'D ON MEN, 4 4
SATAN, NOW FIRST INFLAM'D WITH RAGE, CAME DOWN, 4 9
TILL PRIDE AND WORSE AMBITION THREW ME DOWN 4 40
URIEL ONCE WARND; WHOSE EYE PURSU'D HIM DOWN 4 125
DOWN THE STEEP GLADE, AND MET THE NEATHER FLOOD, 4 231
DOWN THE SLOPE HILLS, DISPERST, OR IN A LAKE, 4 261
SHEE AS A VAIL DOWN TO THE SLENDER WASTE 4 304
THEY SAT THEM DOWN, AND AFTER NO MORE TOIL 4 327
DOWN HE ALIGHTS AMONG THE SPORTFUL HERD 4 396
AS I BENT DOWN TO LOOK, JUST OPPOSITE, 4 460
TEMPER OR NOURISH, OR IN PART SHED DOWN 4 670
MY GUIDE WAS GON, AND I, ME THOUGHT, SUNK DOWN, 5 91
A CLOUDY SPOT. DOWN THITHER PRONE IN FLIGHT 5 266
SHOT DOWN DIRECT HIS FERVID RAIES TO WARME 5 301
THINK NOT I SHALL BE NICE. SO DOWN THEY SAT, 5 433
BRANDISHT ALOFT THE HORRID EDGE CAME DOWN 6 252
DOWN CLOV'N TO THE WASTE, WITH SHATTERD ARMES 6 361
BORN EEVN OR HIGH, FOR THIS DAY WILL POUR DOWN, 6 544
THOUGH STANDING ELSE AS ROCKS, BUT DOWN THEY FELL 6 593
TO THIR PREPAR'D ILL MANSION DRIVEN DOWN 6 738
ALL COURAGE; DOWN THIR IDLE WEAPONS DROP'D; 6 839
DOWN FROM THE VERGE OF HEAV'N, ETERNAL WRAUTH 6 865
THY TEMPRING; WITH LIKE SAFETIE GUIDED DOWN 7 15
DOWN FROM THE EMPYREAN TO FOREWARNE 7 73
DOWN SUNK A HOLLOW BOTTOM BROAD AND DEEP, 7 289
THE FILIAL POWER ARRIV'D, AND SATE HIM DOWN 7 587
DOWN TO THIS HABITABLE, WHICH RETURNES 8 157
PENSIVE I SATE ME DOWN; THERE GENTLE SLEEP 8 287
DAZL'D AND SPENT, SUNK DOWN, AND SOUGHT REPAIR 8 457
DESCEND TO? WHO ASPIRES MUST DOWN AS LOW 9 169
DOWN DROP'D, AND ALL THE FADED ROSES SHED: 9 893
THEY SATE THEM DOWN TO WEEP, NOR ONELY TEARES 9 1121
DOWN HE DESCENDED STRAIT; THE SPEED OF GODS 10 90
SAW SATAN FALL LIKE LIGHTNING DOWN FROM HEAV'N, 10 184
TOST UP AND DOWN, TOGETHER CROWDED DROVE 10 287
SMOOTH, EASIE, INOFFENSIVE DOWN TO HELL. 10 305
ALL YOURS, RIGHT DOWN TO PARADISE DESCEND; 10 398
THEN SUFFERD. TH' OTHER WAY SATAN WENT DOWN 10 414
WAS PLAC'T IN REGAL LUSTRE. DOWN A WHILE 10 447
EACH OTHER, TILL SUPPLANTED DOWN HE FELL 10 513
THEY FELT THEMSELVS NOW CHANGING; DOWN THIR ARMS, 10 541
DOWN FELL BOTH SPEAR AND SHIELD, DOWN THEY AS FAST, 10 542
THE SITHE OF TIME MOWES DOWN, DEVOUR UNSPAR'D, 10 606
OR DOWN FROM HEAV'N DESCEND. SUCH WAS THIR SONG, 10 648
UP TO THE TROPIC CRAB; THENCE DOWN AMAINE 10 675
INSENSIBLE, HOW GLAD WOULD LAY ME DOWN 10 777
TINE THE SLANT LIGHTNING, WHOSE THWART FLAME DRIV'N DOWN 10 1075
DOWN FROM A HILL THE BEAST THAT REIGNS IN WOODS, 11 187
DOWN FROM A SKIE OF JASPER LIGHTED NOW 11 209
HOW SHALL I PART, AND WHITHER WANDER DOWN 11 282
BUT THIS PRAEEMINENCE THOU HAST LOST, BROUGHT DOWN 11 347
DOWN TO THE GOLDEN CHERSONESE, OR WHERE 11 392
SUNK DOWN AND ALL HIS SPIRITS BECAME INTRANST: 11 420
LIFE OFFER'D, OR SOON BEG TO LAY IT DOWN, 11 506
TO WEIGH THY SPIRITS DOWN, AND LAST CONSUME 11 545
DOWN TO THE VEINS OF EARTH, THENCE GLIDING HOT 11 568
DOWN TO THE PLAIN DESCENDED: BY THIR GUISE 11 576
LIKE A DARK CEELING STOOD; DOWN RUSH'D THE RAIN 11 743
DOWN THE GREAT RIVER TO THE OP'NING GULF, 11 833
GRIEV'D AT HIS HEART, WHEN LOOKING DOWN HE SAW 11 887
COMES DOWN TO SEE THIR CITIE, ERE THE TOWER 12 51
AND LOOKING DOWN, TO SEE THE HUBBUB STRANGE 12 60
A DARKSOM CLOUD OF LOCUSTS SWARMING DOWN 12 185
LED THEM DIRECT, AND DOWN THE CLIFF AS FAST 12 639

DOWNE
THROUGH THE CALM FIRMAMENT; BUT UP OR DOWNE 3 574
WITH UNEXPERIENC'T THOUGHT, AND LAID ME DOWNE 4 457

DOWNFALL
THIS DOWNFALL; SINCE BY FATE THE STRENGTH OF GODS 1 116

DOWNIE
ON THE SOFT DOWNIE BANK DAMASKT WITH FLOURS: 4 334
SKIRTED HIS LOINES AND THIGHES WITH DOWNIE GOLD 5 282
THIR DOWNIE BREST; THE SWAN WITH ARCHED NECK 7 438
A BOUGH OF FAIREST FRUIT THAT DOWNIE SMIL'D, 9 851

DOWNS
BETWIXT THEM LAWNS, OR LEVEL DOWNS, AND FLOCKS 4 252

DOWNWARD
AND DOWNWARD FISH: YET HAD HIS TEMPLE HIGH 1 463
WERE ALWAYS DOWNWARD BENT, ADMIRING MORE 1 681
LOOK DOWNWARD ON THAT GLOBE WHOSE HITHER SIDE 3 722
BORE HIM SLOPE DOWNWARD TO THE SUN NOW FALL'N 4 591
THROUGHOUT THE FLUID MASS, BUT DOWNWARD PURG'D 7 237
DOWNWARD AS FARR ANTARTIC; AND IN LENGTH 9 79

DOWR
HER DOWR TH' ADOPTED CLUSTERS, TO ADORN 5 218

DRAFF
MY HELL-HOUNDS, TO LICK UP THE DRAFF AND FILTH 10 630

DRAG
BACK TO TH' INFERNAL PIT I DRAG THEE CHAIND, 4 965
AND AT HIS CHARIOT WHEELES TO DRAG HIM BOUND 6 358
THE SERPENT, PRINCE OF AIRE, AND DRAG IN CHAINES 12 454

DRAG'D
OR CAPTIVE DRAG'D IN CHAINS, WITH HOSTILE FROWN 6 260

DRAGON
THEN WHEN THE DRAGON, PUT TO SECOND ROUT, 4 3
NOW DRAGON GROWN, LARGER THEN WHOM THE SUN 10 529
THE RIVER-DRAGON TAM'D AT LENGTH SUBMITS 12 191

DRAIND
DRAIND THROUGH A LIMBEC TO HIS NATIVE FORME. 3 605
AND OF THIR WONTED VIGOUR LEFT THEM DRAIND, 6 851

DRAUGHTS
OF NECTAROUS DRAUGHTS BETWEEN, FROM MILKIE STREAM, 5 306

DRAW
IN HEAV'N, WHICH FOLLOWS DIGNITY, MIGHT DRAW 2 25

DRAW (CONTINUED)

DRAW AFTER HIM THE WHOLE RACE OF MANKIND, . . . 3 161
MUCH LESS THAT DURST UPON HIS OWN HEAD DRAW . . . 3 220
OR IN THICK SHADE RETIR'D, FROM HIM TO DRAW . . . 4 532
UZZIEL, HALF THESE DRAW OFF, AND COAST THE SOUTH . 4 782
LET US ADVISE, AND TO THIS HAZARD DRAW 5 729
STREAM, AND PERPETUAL DRAW THIR HUMID TRAINE. . . 7 306
REPAIRING, IN THIR GOLD'N URNS DRAW LIGHT. . . . 7 365
THIR ELEMENT TO DRAW THE THINNER AIRE. 8 348
CASUAL DISCOURSE DRAW ON, WHICH INTERMITS 9 223
IN FEMAL SEX, THE MORE TO DRAW HIS LOVE, ... 9 822
THE LINK OF NATURE DRAW ME: FLESH OF FLESH, . . . 9 914
THE BOND OF NATURE DRAW ME TO MY OWNE, ... 9 956
THE WAY, THOU LEADING, SUCH A SENT I DRAW . . . 10 267
OF WEAKNESS, NOT OF POWER. WILL HE, DRAW OUT, . 10 801

DRAWES

BEYOND THIS DEEP; WHATEVER DRAWES ME ON, . . . 10 245

DRAWN

MILLIONS OF FLAMING SWORDS, DRAWN FROM THE THIGHS 1 664
DRAWN ROUND ABOUT THEE LIKE A RADIANT SHRINE, . . 3 379
BY MODEL, OR BY SHADING PENCIL DRAWN. 3 509
THERE ALWAYES, BUT DRAWN UP TO HEAV'N SOMTIMES . 3 517
RAPT IN A CHARIOT DRAWN BY FIERY STEEDS. . . . 3 522
DRAWN TO HIS PART; BUT OTHER POWERS AS GREAT . . 4 63
OF POROUS EARTH WITH KINDLY THIRST UP DRAWN, . . 4 228
AN EARTHLIE GUEST, AND DRAWN EMPYREAL AIRE, . . 7 14
NOR CAN I MISS THE WAY, SO STRONGLY DRAWN . . 10 262
HIS VISAGE DRAWN HE FELT TO SHARP AND SPARE, . . 10 511
MORE TO THE PART SINISTER FROM ME DRAWN, . . . 10 886

DRAWS

DRAWS IN, AND AT HIS TRUNCK SPOUTS OUT A SEA. . . 7 416
MORE ORIENT IN YON WESTERN CLOUD THAT DRAWS . . 11 205

DRAW'ST

US'D TO THE YOAK, DRAW'ST HIS TRIUMPHANT WHEELS . 4 975

DREAD

ON DUTY, SLEEPING FOUND BY WHOM THEY DREAD, . . 1 333
NEXT CHEMOS, TH' OBSCENE DREAD OF MOABS SONS, . . 1 406
WITH DREAD OF DEATH TO FLIGHT OR FOUL RETREAT, . 1 555
THIR DREAD COMMANDER: HE ABOVE THE REST 1 589
SO AS NOT EITHER TO PROVOKE, OR DREAD 1 644
MORE GLORIOUS AND MORE DREAD THEN FROM NO FALL, . 2 16
OF DARKNESS DO WE DREAD? HOW OFT AMIDST . . . 2 263
THAN HELLS DREAD EMPEROUR WITH POMP SUPREAM, . . 2 510
THY DREAD TRIBUNAL: FORTHWITH FROM ALL WINDES . . 3 326
DISDAIN FORBIDS ME, AND MY DREAD OF SHAME . . . 4 82
OF WRAUTH AWAK'T: NOR WITH LESS DREAD THE LOUD . 6 59
WHEN COMING TOWARDS THEM SO DREAD THEY SAW . . . 6 648
I DREAD, AND TO ELUDE, THUS WRAPT IN MIST . . . 9 158
RATHER THEN DEATH OR AUGHT THEN DEATH MORE DREAD 9 969
AND TORMENT LESS THEN NONE OF WHAT WE DREAD, . . 10 998
SATANS DIRE DREAD, AND IN HIS HAND THE SPEAR, . 11 248
AND WHILE THE DREAD OF JUDGEMENT PAST REMAINS . 12 14

DREADED

REAR'D IN AZOTUS, DREADED THROUGH THE COAST . . 1 464
THEY DREADED WORSE THEN HELL: SO MUCH THE FEAR . 2 293
DREADED NOT MORE TH' ADVENTURE THEN HIS VOICE . . 2 474
ORCUS AND ADES, AND THE DREADED NAME 2 964
AND SECONDED THY ELSE NOT DREADED SPEAR. . . . 4 929
THE THUNDERER OF HIS ONLY DREADED BOLT. 6 491
THIR GUILT AND DREADED SHAME; O HOW UNLIKE . . . 9 1114

DREADFUL

UNDER THY CONDUCT, AND IN DREADFUL DEEDS . . . 1 130
CASTS PALE AND DREADFUL? THITHER LET US TEND . . 1 183
OF DREADFUL LENGTH AND DAZLING ARMS, IN GUISE . . 1 564
ALONE THE DREADFUL VOYAGE; TILL AT LAST . . . 2 426
AND SHOOK A DREADFUL DART; WHAT SEEM'D HIS HEAD . 2 672
MORE DREADFUL AND DEFORM: ON TH' OTHER SIDE . . 2 706
THY FATHERS DREADFUL THUNDER DIDST NOT SPARE, . . 3 393
SOM DREADFUL THING NO DOUBT; FOR WELL THOU KNOWST 4 426
WHAT SEEMD BOTH SPEAR AND SHIELD: NOW DREADFUL DEEDS 4 990
A DREADFUL INTERVALL, AND FRONT TO FRONT . . . 6 105
DREADFUL COMBUSTION WARRING, AND DISTURB, . . . 6 225
WITH DREADFUL SHADE CONTIGUOUS, AND THE ORBES . . 6 828
YET DREADFUL IN MINE EARE, THOUGH IN MY CHOICE . 8 335
SO DREADFUL TO THEE? THAT THOU ART NAKED, WHO . 10 121
TO HIS BOLD RIOT: DREADFUL WAS THE DIN . . . 10 521
AND SLEEP SECURE; HIS DREADFUL VOICE NO MORE . . 10 779
COMES THUNDRING BACK WITH DREADFUL REVOLUTION . 10 814
ACCOMPANIED, WITH DAMPS AND DREADFUL GLOOM, . . 10 848
TO MORTAL EARE IS DREADFUL; THEY BESEECH . . . 12 236
WITH DREADFUL FACES THRONG'D AND FIERIE ARMES; . 12 644

DREADLESS

ALL NIGHT THE DREADLESS ANGEL UNPURSU'D 6 1

DREAM

A GROWING EMPIRE; DOUBTLESS; WHILE WE DREAM, . . 2 315
TO FIND THIS BUT A DREAM. THUS EVE HER NIGHT . . 5 93
THIS UNCOUTH DREAM, OF EVIL SPRUNG I FEAR; . . . 5 98
OF OUR LAST EEVNINGS TALK, IN THIS THY DREAM, . . 5 115

DREAM (CONTINUED)

THAT WHAT IN SLEEP THOU DIDST ABHORR TO DREAM, . 5 120
DREAM NOT OF OTHER WORLDS, WHAT CREATURES THERE . 8 175
WHEN SUDDENLY STOOD AT MY HEAD A DREAM, ... 8 292
BEFORE MINE EYES ALL REAL, AS THE DREAM 8 310
SUCH AS I SAW HER IN MY DREAM, ADORND 8 482
AND LIVE FOR EVER, DREAM AT LEAST TO LIVE . . . 11 95
TO WHOM THUS MICHAEL. DREAM NOT OF THIR FIGHT, . 12 386

DREAM'D

SUCH NIGHT TILL THIS I NEVER PASS'D, HAVE DREAM'D, 5 31
IF DREAM'D, NOT AS I OFT AM WONT, OF THEE, . . . 5 32

DREAMD

NOT IN THE NEIGHBOURING MOON, AS SOME HAVE DREAMD; 3 459

DREAME

FOR THOU ART HEAV'NLIE, SHEE AN EMPTY DREAME. . . 7 39

DREAMING

DREAMING BY NIGHT UNDER THE OPEN SKIE, ... 3 514

DREAMS

OR DREAMS HE SEES, WHILE OVER-HEAD THE MOON . . 1 784
ILLUSIONS AS HE LIST, PHANTASMS AND DREAMS, . . 4 803
WILDE WORK PRODUCES OFT, AND MOST IN DREAMS, . . 5 112
BRED OF UNKINDLY FUMES, WITH CONSCIOUS DREAMS . . 9 1050
HER ALSO I WITH GENTLE DREAMS HAVE CALM'D . . 12 595
FOR GOD IS ALSO IN SLEEP, AND DREAMS ADVISE, . . 12 611

DREAR

CERASTES HORND, HYDRUS, AND ELLOPS DREAR, . . . 10 525

DREARIE

NO REST: THROUGH MANY A DARK AND DREARIE VAILE . 2 618

DREARY

SEEST THOU YON DREARY PLAIN, FORLORN AND WILDE, . 1 180

DREGS

THE BLACK TARTAREOUS COLD INFERNAL DREGS . . . 7 238

DREIND

FROM UNDERGROUND) THE LIQUID ORE HE DREIND . . . 11 570

DRENCH

LET SUCH BETHINK THEM, IF THE SLEEPY DRENCH . . 2 73

DRENCHT

THIS HILL; LET EVE (FOR I HAVE DRENCHT HER EYES) . 11 367

DRESS

ADAM, WELL MAY WE LABOUR STILL TO DRESS 9 205
IN GEMS AND WANTON DRESS; TO THE HARP THEY SUNG . 11 583
TO DRESS, AND TROULE THE TONGUE, AND ROULE THE EYE. 11 620

DREW

AHAZ HIS SOTTISH CONQUEROUR, WHOM HE DREW . . . 1 472
DREW AUDIENCE AND ATTENTION STILL AS NIGHT . . . 2 308
DREW AFTER HIM THE THIRD PART OF HEAV'NS SONS . . 2 692
FORTHWITH THE HUGE PORCULLIS HIGH UP DREW, . . . 2 874
HE DREW NOT NIGH UNHEARD, THE ANGEL BRIGHT, . . 3 645
ERE HE DREW NIGH, HIS RADIANT VISAGE TURND, . . 3 646
HIS HEART, NOT ELSE DISMAI'D. NOW DREW THEY NIGH 4 861
SO SAYING, HE DREW NIGH, AND TO ME HELD, . . . 5 82
DREW AFTER HIM THE THIRD PART OF HEAV'NS HOST: . 5 710
TO FINAL BATTEL DREW, DISDAINING FLIGHT, . . . 6 798
DREW MANY, WHOM THIR PLACE KNOWS HERE NO MORE; . 7 144
THESE AS A LINE THIR LONG DIMENSION DREW, . . . 7 480
FROM WHERE I FIRST DREW AIRE, AND FIRST BEHELD . 8 284
NEERER HE DREW, AND MANY A WALK TRAVERS'D . . . 9 434
RUDDIE AND GOLD: I NEARER DREW TO GAZE; 9 578
MEAN WHILE THE HOUR OF NOON DREW ON, AND WAK'D . 9 739
AND KNOW NOT THAT I CALL'D AND DREW THEM THITHER . 10 629
HE ENDED; AND TH' ARCH-ANGEL SOON DREW NIGH, . . 11 238
GAZ'D HOT, AND OF THE FRESH WAVE LARGELY DREW, . 11 845

DRI'D

SOON DRI'D, AND ON THE REAKING MOISTURE FED. . . 8 256

DRIE

AS DROPS ON DUST CONGLOBING FROM THE DRIE; . . . 7 292
EASIE, E'RE GOD HAD BID THE GROUND BE DRIE, . . . 7 304
SO SAYING, THROUGH EACH THICKET DANCK OR DRIE, . 9 179
DRIVN BY A KEEN NORTH-WINDE, THAT BLOWING DRIE . 11 842
ANON DRIE GROUND APPEERS, AND FROM HIS ARKE . . 11 861
AS ON DRIE LAND BETWEEN TWO CHRISTAL WALLS, . . 12 197

DRIE-EY'D

DRIE-EY'D BEHOLD? ADAM COULD NOT, BUT WEPT, . . 11 495

DRINK

HEAPS WITH UNSPARING HAND; FOR DRINK THE GRAPE . 5 344
THEY EATE, THEY DRINK, AND IN COMMUNION SWEET . . 5 637
AND DRINK THE LIQUID LIGHT, FIRM TO RETAINE . . 7 362
FROM NECTAR, DRINK OF GODS. ADAM THE WHILE . . . 9 838
ALL THAT I EAT OR DRINK, OR SHALL BEGET, . . . 10 728

DRINKS
HER WATRIE LABYRINTH, WHEREOF WHO DRINKS, ... 2 584
THUS WHEN WITH MEATS AND DRINKS THEY HAD SUFFIC'D, 5 451
IN MEATS AND DRINKS, WHICH ON THE EARTH SHALL BRING 11 473

DRINKST
IN WHAT THOU EATST AND DRINKST, SEEKING FROM THENCE 11 532

DRIVE
HERE FOR HIS ENVY, WILL NOT DRIVE US HENCE: . . 1 260
ALL AS OUR OWN, AND DRIVE AS WE WERE DRIVEN, . . 2 366
THE PUNIC HABITANTS, OR IF NOT DRIVE, ... 2 367
OF SERICANA, WHERE CHINESES DRIVE 3 438
VERNAL DELIGHT AND JOY, ABLE TO DRIVE 4 155
PURSUING DRIVE THEM OUT FROM GOD AND BLISS, . . 6 52
PURSUE THESE SONS OF DARKNESS, DRIVE THEM OUT . . 6 715
BUT DRIVE FARR OFF THE BARBAROUS DISSONANCE . . 7 32
UPON THE CRONIAN SEA, TOGETHER DRIVE 10 290
WITHOUT REMORSE DRIVE OUT THE SINFUL PAIR, . . . 11 105
WITH CLAMOR THENCE THE RAPID CURRENTS DRIVE . . 11 853

DRIVEN
ALL AS OUR OWN, AND DRIVE AS WE WERE DRIVEN, . . . 2 366
TO THIR PREPAR'D ILL MANSION DRIVEN DOWN . . . 6 738
HAD DRIVEN OUT TH' UNGODLY FROM HIS SIGHT . . . 7 185

DRIVES
WHOM HUNGER DRIVES TO SEEK NEW HAUNT FOR PREY, . 4 184
ONE WAY A BAND SELECT FROM FORAGE DRIVES . . . 11 646

DRIV'N
THEN TO DWELL HERE, DRIV'N OUT FROM BLISS,
CONDEMN'D 2 86
DRIV'N HEADLONG FROM THE PITCH OF HEAVEN, DOWN . 2 772
BY THEE ADULTEROUS LUST WAS DRIV'N FROM MEN . . 4 753
DRIV'N BACK REDOUNDED AS A FLOOD ON THOSE . . . 7 57
THAT KEPT THIR WATCH; THENCE FULL OF ANGUISH
DRIV'N, ... 9 62
ERE THIS HE HAD RETURN'D, WITH FURY DRIV'N . . 10 240
OF HIGH OLYMPUS, THENCE BY SATURN DRIV'N . . . 10 583
AND HORRORS HAST THOU DRIV'N ME; OUT OF WHICH . . 10 843
TINE THE SLANT LIGHTNING, WHOSE THWART FLAME DRIV'N
DOWN 10 1075

DRIVN
DRIVN BACKWARD SLOPE THIR POINTING SPIRES, AND
ROWLD 1 223
WHO JUSTLY HATH DRIVN OUT HIS REBELL FOES . . . 3 677
DRIVN BY A KEEN NORTH-WINDE, THAT BLOWING DRIE . 11 842

DRIZLING
IF I CONJECTURE AUGHT, NO DRIZLING SHOWR, ... 6 545

DRONE
THE FEMALE BEE THAT FEEDS HER HUSBAND DRONE . . 7 490

DROOP
LABORIOUS, TILL DAY DROOP; WHILE HERE WE DWELL, . 11 178

DROOPING
THUS DROOPING, OR WITH LINKED THUNDERBOLTS . . . 1 328
HE ENDED, AND HIS WORDS THIR DROOPING CHERE . . 6 496
HUNG DROOPING UNSUSTAIND, THEM SHE UPSTAIES . . 9 430

DROP
THE TEMPTING STREAM, WITH ONE SMALL DROP TO LOOSE 2 607
SO THICK A DROP SERENE HATH QUENCHT THIR ORBS, . 3 25
SO MAIST THOU LIVE, TILL LIKE RIPE FRUIT THOU DROP 11 535

DROP'D
ALL COURAGE; DOWN THIR IDLE WEAPONS DROP'D; . . 6 839
DOWN DROP'D, AND ALL THE FADED ROSES SHED: . . . 9 893
SOM NATURAL TEARS THEY DROP'D, BUT WIP'D THEM SOON; 12 645

DROPPING
THOSE BLOSSOMS ALSO, AND THOSE DROPPING GUMMS, . 4 630
OF EWE OR GOAT DROPPING WITH MILK AT EEVN, . . . 9 582

DROPS
FLUTTRING HIS PENNONS VAIN PLUMB DOWN HE DROPS . 2 933
WHAT DROPS THE MYRRHE, AND WHAT THE BALMIE REED, . 5 23
TWO OTHER PRECIOUS DROPS THAT READY STOOD, . . . 5 132
OR STARRS OF MORNING, DEW-DROPS, WHICH THE SUN . 5 746
AS DROPS ON DUST CONGLOBING FROM THE DRIE; . . . 7 292
SKIE LOWR'D AND MUTTERING THUNDER, SOM SAD DROPS . 9 1002
AND FROM THE WELL OF LIFE THREE DROPS INSTILL'D. . 11 416

DROPSIES
DROPSIES, AND ASTHMA'S, AND JOINT-RACKING RHEUMS. 11 488

DROPT
DROPT FROM THE ZENITH LIKE A FALLING STAR, . . . 1 745
DROPT MANNA, AND COULD MAKE THE WORSE APPEAR . . 2 113
SHOW TO THE SUN THIR WAV'D COATS DROPT WITH GOLD, 7 406

DROSS
SEVERING EACH KIND, AND SCUM'D THE BULLION DROSS: 1 704

DROSSIEST
METALS OF DROSSIEST ORE TO PERFET GOLD 5 442

DROUND
TO RAPTURE, TILL THE SAVAGE CLAMOR DROUND . . . 7 36

DROUSED
MY DROUSED SENSE, UNTROUBL'D, THOUGH I THOUGHT . 8 289

DROUTH
BEFORE HIS MEMORIE, AS ONE WHOSE DROUTH 7 66

DROUZE
OF ARGUS, AND MORE WAKEFUL THEN TO DROUZE, . . . 11 131

DROVE
TILL GOOD JOSIAH DROVE THEM THENCE TO HELL. . . 1 418
THAT DROVE HIM, THOUGH ENAMOURD, FROM THE SPOUSE . 4 169
HEE ON HIS IMPIOUS FOES RIGHT ONWARD DROVE, . . 6 831
DROVE THEM BEFORE HIM THUNDER-STRUCK, PURSU'D . . 6 858
TOST UP AND DOWN, TOGETHER CROWDED DROVE . . . 10 287
TWO BIRDS OF GAYEST PLUME BEFORE HIM DROVE: . . 11 186
WIDE HOVERING, ALL THE CLOUDS TOGETHER DROVE . . 11 739

DROV'ST
THOU DROV'ST OF WARRING ANGELS DISARRAID. . . . 3 396

DROWN
SURPASS HIS BOUNDS, NOR RAIN TO DROWN THE WORLD . 11 894

DROWN'D
OF TEARS AND SORROW A FLOUD THEE ALSO DROWN'D, . 11 757

DROWND
THE RACE OF MANKIND DROWND, BEFORE THE SHRINE . . 11 13

DRUDGE
AT THEE ORDAIN'D HIS DRUDGE, TO EXECUTE 2 732

DRUGD
HUNGER AND THIRST CONSTRAINING, DRUGD AS OFT, . . 10 568

DRUGS
THIR SPICIE DRUGS: THEY ON THE TRADING FLOOD . . 2 640

DRUMS
THOUGH FOR THE NOYSE OF DRUMS AND TIMBRELS LOUD . 1 394

DRY
THAT FELT UNUSUAL WEIGHT, TILL ON DRY LAND . . . 1 227
FOR HOT, COLD, MOIST, AND DRY, FOUR CHAMPIONS
FIERCE 2 898
NOR GOOD DRY LAND: NIGH FOUNDERD ON HE FARES, . . 2 940
BEAR HIS SWIFT ERRANDS OVER MOIST AND DRY, . . . 3 652
INTO ONE PLACE, AND LET DRY LAND APPEER, . . . 7 284
THE DRY LAND, EARTH, AND THE GREAT RECEPTACLE . . 7 307
DEATH WITH HIS MACE PETRIFIC, COLD AND DRY, . . 10 294
A MELANCHOLLY DAMP OF COLD AND DRY 11 544

DRYAD
OREAD OR DRYAD, OR OF DELIA'S TRAINE, ... 9 387

DUBIOUS
IN DUBIOUS BATTEL ON THE PLAINS OF HEAV'N, . . . 1 104
WAFTS ON THE CALMER WAVE BY DUBIOUS LIGHT . . . 2 1042

DUE
THE WHOLE BATTALION VIEWS, THIR ORDER DUE, . . . 1 569
OF HAZARD AS OF HONOUR, DUE ALIKE 2 453
TO HIM WHO REIGNS, AND SO MUCH TO HIM DUE . . . 2 454
THE KEY OF THIS INFERNAL PIT BY DUE, ... 2 850
TO PRAY, REPENT, AND BRING OBEDIENCE DUE. . . . 3 190
TO PRAYER, REPENTANCE, AND OBEDIENCE DUE, . . . 3 191
THOUGH NOW TO DEATH I YIELD, AND AM HIS DUE . . 3 245
THAT FROM HIS LORDLY EYE KEEP DISTANCE DUE, . . 3 578
WHERE HONOUR DUE AND REVERENCE NONE NEGLECTS, . . 3 738
HOW DUE. YET ALL HIS GOOD PROV'D ILL IN ME, . . 4 48
DUE ENTRANCE HE DISDAIND, AND IN CONTEMPT, . . . 4 180
AND EVE WITHIN, DUE AT HER HOUR PREPAR'D . . . 5 303
SHALL BEND THE KNEE, AND IN THAT HONOUR DUE . . 5 817
DUE SEARCH AND CONSULTATION WILL DISCLOSE. . . . 6 445
WITH MINISTERIES DUE AND SOLEMN RITES: 7 149
WITH WONDER, BUT DELIGHT, AND, AS IS DUE, . . . 8 11
WHICH MUST BE MUTUAL, IN PROPORTION DUE 8 385
SAY, FOR SUCH WONDER CLAIMS ATTENTION DUE. . . . 9 566
NOT WITHOUT SONG, EACH MORNING, AND DUE PRAISE . 9 800
FROM NOON, AND GENTLE AIRES DUE AT THIR HOUR . . 10 93
OF ALL CORRUPTION, ALL THE BLAME LIGHTS DUE; . . 10 833
FROM LOVES DUE RITES, NUPTIAL IMBRACES SWEET, . . 10 994
THEN DUE BY SENTENCE WHEN THOU DIDST TRANSGRESS, . 11 253
ON THE CLEFT WOOD, AND ALL DUE RITES PERFORM'D. . 11 440
DUE NOURISHMENT, NOT GLUTTONOUS DELIGHT, . . . 11 533
THOU THEREFORE GIVE DUE AUDIENCE, AND ATTEND. . . 12 12
WHOM FAITHFUL ABRAHAM DUE TIME SHALL CALL, . . . 12 152
A DAY ENTIRE, AND NIGHTS DUE COURSE ADJOURNE, . . 12 264
THE PENALTIE TO THY TRANSGRESSION DUE, ... 12 399
AND DUE TO THEIRS WHICH OUT OF THINE WILL GROW: . 12 400

DUEL
AS OF A DUEL, OR THE LOCAL WOUNDS 12 387

DULCET
OF DULCET SYMPHONIES AND VOICES SWEET, ... 1 712
SHE TEMPERS DULCET CREAMS, NOR THESE TO HOLD . . 5 347

DULCIMER
AND DULCIMER, ALL ORGANS OF SWEET STOP, ... 7 596

DULY
THIR ORISONS, EACH MORNING DULY PAID 5 145

DUMB
HIS GENTLE DUMB EXPRESSION TURND AT LENGTH 9 527

DUN
IN THE DUN AIR SUBLIME, AND READY NOW 3 72

DUNGEON
A DUNGEON HORRIBLE, ON ALL SIDES ROUND 1 61
THIS PLACE OUR DUNGEON, NOT OUR SAFE RETREAT . . 2 317
YOUR DUNGEON STRETCHING FAR AND WIDE BENEATH; . . 2 1003
AND DUNGEON OF OUR TYRANT: NOW POSSESS, ... 10 466
BURSTING THIR BRAZEN DUNGEON, ARMD WITH ICE . . 10 697

DURABLE
TO MOTION, MEASURES ALL THINGS DURABLE 5 581
AND DURABLE; AND NOW IN LITTLE SPACE 10 320

DURANCE
IN THAT DARK DURANCE: THUS MUCH WHAT WAS ASKT. . 4 899

DURING
BUT CLOUD IN STEAD, AND EVER-DURING DARK 3 45
HER EVER DURING GATES, HARMONIOUS SOUND 7 206

DURST
WHO DURST DEFIE TH' OMNIPOTENT TO ARMS, ... 1 49
THAT DURST DISLIKE HIS REIGN, AND ME PREFERRING, . 1 102
ROAMING TO SEEK THIR PREY ON EARTH, DURST FIX . . 1 382
AMONG THE NATIONS ROUND, AND DURST ABIDE . . . 1 385
AND WITH THIR DARKNESS DURST AFFRONT HIS LIGHT. . 1 391
MUCH LESS THAT DURST UPON HIS OWN HEAD DRAW . . 3 220
BEAST, BIRD, INSECT, OR WORM DURST ENTER NONE; . 4 704
FOR YOU, THERE SITTING WHERE YE DURST NOT SOARE; . 4 829
INSPIR'D WITH CONTRADICTION DURST OPPOSE . . . 6 155
NOT THAT THEY DURST WITHOUT HIS LEAVE ATTEMPT, . 8 237
NO EVIL DURST ATTEMPT THEE, BUT I RUE 9 1180

DUSK
VAPOUR, AND EXHALATION DUSK AND MOIST, ... 11 741

DUSKIE
FROM HILL OR STEAMING LAKE, DUSKIE OR GREY, . . . 5 186
SOON AS MIDNIGHT BROUGHT ON THE DUSKIE HOURE . . 5 667
IN DUSKIE WREATHES, RELUCTANT FLAMES, THE SIGNE . 6 58

DUSKY
ALOFT, INCUMBENT ON THE DUSKY AIR 1 226
AS WHEN FROM MOUNTAIN TOPS THE DUSKY CLOUDS . . 2 488

DUST
THAT RAIS'D US FROM THE DUST AND PLAC'T US HERE . 4 416
WHO FORMD US FROM THE DUST, AND PLAC'D US HERE . 5 516
AS DROPS ON DUST CONGLOBING FROM THE DRIE; . . . 7 292
DUST OF THE GROUND, AND IN THY NOSTRILS BREATH'D . 7 525
A BROAD AND AMPLE RODE, WHOSE DUST IS GOLD . . . 7 577
FROM DUST: SPITE THEN WITH SPITE IS BEST REPAID. . 9 178
AND DUST SHALT EAT ALL THE DAYES OF THY LIFE. . . 10 178
FOR DUST THOU ART, AND SHALT TO DUST RETURNE. . . 10 208
AND EQUAL TO REDUCE ME TO MY DUST, ... 10 748
THAT DUST I AM, AND SHALL TO DUST RETURNE: . . . 10 770
HIS SENTENCE BEYOND DUST AND NATURES LAW, . . . 10 805
IN DUST, OUR FINAL REST AND NATIVE HOME. . . . 10 1085
WHO KNOWS, OR MORE THEN THIS, THAT WE ARE DUST, . 11 199
ROWLING IN DUST AND GORE. TO WHICH OUR SIRE, . . 11 460
I MUST RETURN TO NATIVE DUST? O SIGHT 11 463
TO DEATH, AND MIX WITH OUR CONNATURAL DUST? . . 11 529

DUTEOUS
FROM EVERY BEAST, MORE DUTEOUS AT HER CALL, . . . 9 521

DUTIE
WHERE OBVIOUS DUTIE EREWHILE APPEAR'D UNSAUGHT: . 10 106

DUTY
ON DUTY, SLEEPING FOUND BY WHOM THEY DREAD, . . . 1 333

DWARFS
NOW LESS THEN SMALLEST DWARFS, IN NARROW ROOM . . 1 779

DWELL
TO BOTTOMLESS PERDITION, THERE TO DWELL 1 47
AND REST CAN NEVER DWELL, HOPE NEVER COMES . . . 1 66
THEN TO DWELL HERE, DRIV'N OUT FROM BLISS,
CONDEMN'D 2 86
DWELL NOT UNVISITED OF HEAV'NS FAIR LIGHT . . . 2 398

DWELL (CONTINUED)
SHALL DWELL AT EASE, AND UP AND DOWN UNSEEN . . 2 841
FOR EVER WITH CORRUPTION THERE TO DWELL; . . . 3 249
NEW HEAV'N AND EARTH, WHEREIN THE JUST SHALL DWELL, 3 335
BUT ALL THESE SHINING ORBES HIS CHOICE TO DWELL; . 3 670
THAT I WITH YOU MUST DWELL, OR YOU WITH ME . . . 4 377
CREATED, OR SUCH PLACE HAST HERE TO DWELL, . . . 5 373
WHO DWELL IN HEAV'N, WHOSE EXCELLENCE HE SAW . . 5 456
HERE OR IN HEAV'NLY PARADISES DWELL; 5 500
THOU FABLEST, HERE HOWEVER TO DWELL FREE, . . . 6 292
NAMELESS IN DARK OBLIVION LET THEM DWELL. . . . 6 380
IN HEAV'NLY SPIRITS COULD SUCH PERVERSENESS DWELL? 6 788
OF MEN INNUMERABLE, THERE TO DWELL, ... 7 156
SEEMD LIKE TO HEAV'N, A SEAT WHERE GODS MIGHT
DWELL, ... 7 329
CREATED IN HIS IMAGE, THERE TO DWELL 7 627
GOD HATH BID DWELL FARR OFF ALL ANXIOUS CARES, . 8 185
TO DWELL, UNLESS BY MAISTRING HEAV'NS SUPREAME; . 9 125
IF THIS BE OUR CONDITION, THUS TO DWELL 9 322
OR IS IT ENVIE, AND CAN ENVIE DWELL 9 729
THERE DWELL AND REIGN IN BLISS, THENCE ON THE EARTH 10 399
TO RANGE IN, AND TO DWELL, AND OVER MAN 10 492
ONCE ACTUAL, NOW IN BODY, AND TO DWELL 10 587
ALL MY REDEEMD MAY DWELL IN JOY AND BLISS, . . . 11 43
BUT LONGER IN THAT PARADISE TO DWELL, ... 11 48
LABORIOUS, TILL DAY DROOP; WHILE HERE WE DWELL, . 11 178
BUT LONGER IN THIS PARADISE TO DWELL 11 259
TO DWELL ON EEVEN GROUND NOW WITH THY SONS: . . 11 348
OF WICKEDNESS, WHEREIN SHALL DWELL HIS RACE . . 11 608
BY MEN WHO THERE FREQUENT, OR THEREIN DWELL. . . 11 838
BOTH HEAV'N AND EARTH, WHEREIN THE JUST SHALL
DWELL. 11 901
SHAL SPEND THIR DAYES IN JOY UNBLAM'D, AND DWELL . 12 22
SHALL DWELL TO SENIR, THAT LONG RIDGE OF HILLS. . 12 146
THE HOLY ONE WITH MORTAL MEN TO DWELL: 12 248
AMONG WHOM GOD WILL DEIGNE TO DWELL ON EARTH . . 12 281
LONG TIME SHALL DWELL AND PROSPER, BUT WHEN SINS . 12 316
THERE IN CAPTIVITIE HE LETS THEM DWELL 12 344
THE PROMISE OF THE FATHER, WHO SHALL DWELL . . . 12 487

DWELLING
HEAV'NS FUGITIVES, AND FOR THIR DWELLING PLACE . 2 57
HENCEFORTH; MY DWELLING HAPLY MAY NOT PLEASE . . 4 378
WHOSE DWELLING GOD HATH PLANTED HERE IN BLISS? . 4 884
THIR PLEASANT DWELLING PLACE. THRICE HAPPIE MEN, 7 625
TO THEE WHO HAST THY DWELLING HERE ON EARTH. . . 8 118

DWELLINGS
TO FUTURE MEN, AND IN THIR DWELLINGS PEACE: . . 7 183
TO VISIT OFT THE DWELLINGS OF JUST MEN 7 570
RODE TILTING O'RE THE WAVES, ALL DWELLINGS ELSE . 11 747

DWELLS
WHERE JOY FOR EVER DWELLS: HAIL HORROURS, HAIL . 1 250
THAT MAN MAY KNOW HE DWELLS NOT IN HIS OWN; . . 8 103
IS LOST, WHICH ALWAYES WITH RIGHT REASON DWELLS . 12 84

DWELL'ST
OF OLD OLYMPUS DWELL'ST, BUT HEAV'NLIE BORNE, . . 7 7

DWELS
DWELS IN ALL HEAVEN CHARITIE SO DEARE? 3 216
IN WHOM THE FULNESS DWELS OF LOVE DIVINE, . . . 3 225

DWELT
DWELT FROM ETERNITIE, DWELT THEN IN THEE, . . . 3 5
THRICE HAPPY ILES, BUT WHO DWELT HAPPY THERE . . 3 570
DWELT IN TELASSAR: IN THIS PLEASANT SOILE . . . 4 214
THAT DWELT WITHIN, WHOSE PRESENCE HAD INFUS'D . . 9 836

DY'D
ANNULS THY DOOM, THE DEATH THOU SHOULDST HAVE DY'D, 12 428
FOR DEATH, LIKE THAT WHICH THE REDEEMER DY'D. . . 12 445

DYE
HE WITH HIS WHOLE POSTERITIE MUST DYE, ... 3 209
DYE HEE OR JUSTICE MUST; UNLESS FOR HIM 3 210
FREELY PUT OFF, AND FOR HIM LASTLY DYE 3 240
TRANSGREST, INEVITABLY THOU SHALT DYE; 8 330

DYING
AND DYING RISE, AND RISING WITH HIM RAISE . . . 3 296
GIVING TO DEATH, AND DYING TO REDEEME, ... 3 299
DYING PUT ON THE WEEDS OF DOMINIC, ... 3 479
A LONG DAYS DYING TO AUGMENT OUR PAINE, ... 10 964
LIVING OR DYING, FROM THEE I WILL NOT HIDE . . . 10 974

EAGER
NOR OF RENOWN LESS EAGER, YET BY DOOME 6 378
AN EAGER APPETITE, RAIS'D BY THE SMELL 9 740

EAGERLY
THE GUARDED GOLD: SO EAGERLY THE FIEND 2 947

EAGLE
IN PROSPECT; THERE THE EAGLE AND THE STORK . . . 7 423

EAGLES

OF TOWRING EAGLES, TO ALL THE FOWLES HE SEEMS . . 5 271

EAGLE-WING'D

SATE EAGLE-WING'D, BESIDE HIM HUNG HIS BOW . . . 6 763

EAR

INTENT, WITH JOCOND MUSIC CHARM HIS EAR; . . . 1 787
TIMOROUS AND SLOTHFUL: YET HE PLEAS'D THE EAR, . 2 117
MINE EAR SHALL NOT BE SLOW, MINE EYE NOT SHUT, . 3 193
ADMONISHT BY HIS EAR, AND STRAIT WAS KNOWN . . . 3 647
CLOSE AT MINE EAR ONE CALL'D ME FORTH TO WALK . 5 36
SO SMOOTHS HER CHARMING TONES, THAT GODS OWN EAR . 5 626
NOT HERS WHO BRINGS IT NIGHTLY TO MY EAR. . . . 9 47
HOW MUCH MORE, IF WE PRAY HIM, WILL HIS EAR . . 10 1060

EARE

HE HAD TO CROSS. NOR WAS HIS EARE LESS PEAL'D . 2 920
BORN THROUGH THE HOLLOW DARK ASSAULTS HIS EARE . 2 953
TURND HIM ALL EARE TO HEAR NEW UTTERANCE FLOW. . 4 410
SQUAT LIKE A TOAD, CLOSE AT THE EARE OF EVE; . . 4 800
ATTENTIVE, AND WITH MORE DELIGHTED EARE, . . . 5 545
WORDS WHICH NO EARE EVER TO HEAR IN HEAV'N . . . 5 810
ALL HEART THEY LIVE, ALL HEAD, ALL EYE, ALL EARE, 6 350
THE ANGEL ENDED, AND IN ADAMS EARE 8 1
DELIGHTED, OR NOT CAPABLE HER EARE 8 49
AND SWEETER THY DISCOURSE IS TO MY EARE 8 211
YET DREADFUL IN MINE EARE, THOUGH IN MY CHOICE . 8 335
MORE GRATEFUL THEN HARMONIOUS SOUND TO THE EARE. . 8 606
O EVE, IN EVIL HOUR THOU DIDST GIVE EARE . . . 9 1067
TO FILL HIS EARE, WHEN CONTRARY HE HEARS . . . 10 506
FROM INNOCENCE. NOW THEREFORE BEND THINE EARE . 11 30
BENDING HIS EARE; PERSWASION IN ME GREW 11 152
FIRST FRUITS, THE GREEN EARE, AND THE YELLOW SHEAF, 11 435
TO MORTAL EARE IS DREADFUL; THEY BESEECH . . . 12 236

EARES

IN RHODOPE, WHERE WOODS AND ROCKS HAD EARES . . 7 35
GREAT THINGS, AND FULL OF WONDER IN OUR EARES, . 7 70

EARLIE

THUS EARLIE, THUS ALONE; HER HEAV'NLY FORME . . 9 457

EARLIEST

WITH CHARM OF EARLIEST BIRDS; PLEASANT THE SUN . 4 642
WITH CHARM OF EARLIEST BIRDS, NOR RISING SUN . . 4 651

EARLY

EARLY, AND TH' HOUR OF SUPPER COMES UNEARN'D. . . 9 225
CREATED; BUT HENCEFORTH MY EARLY CARE, ... 9 799
MY EARLY VISITATION, AND MY LAST 11 275

EARN

WHICH HE THROUGH HAZARD HUGE MUST EARN. BUT THEY 2 473

EARND

WHAT THINKST THOU OF OUR EMPIRE NOW, THOUGH EARND 10 592

EARNE

GLANC'D ON THE GROUND, WITH LABOUR I MUST EARNE . 10 1054
BY SUFFERING, AND EARNE REST FROM LABOUR WON, . . 11 375

EARNEST

WHO MOURN'D IN EARNEST, WHEN THE CAPTIVE ARK . . 1 458
THOUGH THREATNING, WILL IN EARNEST SO DESTROY . . 9 939
THIR EARNEST EYES THEY FIX'D, IMAGINING 10 553

EARNESTLY

THE FAITH THEY OWE; WHEN EARNESTLY THEY SEEK . . 9 1141

EARS

HER BEARDED GROVE OF EARS, WHICH WAY THE WIND . . 4 982
OF COUNTERFETED TRUTH THUS HELD THIR EARS. . . . 5 771
THEN TIME OR MOTION, BUT TO HUMAN EARS 7 177
MIGHT TEMPT ALONE, AND IN HER EARS THE SOUND . . 9 736
BROUGHT TO THIR EARS, WHILE DAY DECLIN'D, THEY
HEARD, ... 10 99
WOULD THUNDER IN MY EARS, NO FEAR OF WORSE . . . 10 780

EARST

AND POWERS THAT EARST IN HEAVEN SAT ON THRONES; . 1 360
HENCEFORTH OF GOD OR ANGEL, EARST WITH JOY . . . 9 1081

EARTH

IN THE BEGINNING HOW THE HEAV'NS AND EARTH . . . 1 9
GOT THEM NEW NAMES, TILL WANDRING ORE THE EARTH, . 1 365
ROAMING TO SEEK THIR PREY ON EARTH, DURST FIX . . 1 382
GODS, YET CONFEST LATER THEN HEAV'N AND EARTH . . 1 509
RIFL'D THE BOWELS OF THIR MOTHER EARTH 1 687
ANON OUT OF THE EARTH A FABRICK HUGE 1 710
SITS ARBITRESS, AND NEERER TO THE EARTH 1 785
OF MANKIND IN ONE ROOT, AND EARTH WITH HELL . . 2 383
THIR SPECIOUS DEEDS ON EARTH, WHICH GLORY EXCITES, 2 484
WASTING THE EARTH, EACH OTHER TO DESTROY: . . . 2 502
THE STEDFAST EARTH. AT LAST HIS SAIL-BROAD VANNES 2 927
NOW LATELY HEAVEN AND EARTH, ANOTHER WORLD . . 2 1004
HIS ONELY SON; ON EARTH HE FIRST BEHELD 3 64
THROUGH HEAV'N AND EARTH, SO SHALL MY GLORIE EXCEL, 3 133

EARTH (CONTINUED)

FOR WHICH BOTH HEAV'N AND EARTH SHALL HIGH EXTOLL 3 146
O THOU IN HEAV'N AND EARTH THE ONLY PEACE . . . 3 274
AND BE THY SELF MAN AMONG MEN ON EARTH, ... 3 283
IN HEAVEN, OR EARTH, OR UNDER EARTH IN HELL; . . 3 322
NEW HEAV'N AND EARTH, WHEREIN THE JUST SHALL DWELL, 3 335
NONE YET, BUT STORE HEREAFTER FROM THE EARTH . . 3 444
ALL WHO HAVE THIR REWARD ON EARTH, THE FRUITS . . 3 451
DISSOLVD ON EARTH, FLEET HITHER, AND IN VAIN, . . 3 457
THE PORTAL SHON, INIMITABLE ON EARTH 3 508
WHO AFTER CAME FROM EARTH, SAYLING ARRIV'D, . . 3 520
A PASSAGE DOWN TO TH' EARTH, A PASSAGE WIDE, . . 3 528
COMPAR'D WITH AUGHT ON EARTH, MEDAL OR STONE; . . 3 592
THAT RUN THROUGH ALL THE HEAV'NS, OR DOWN TO TH'
EARTH 3 651
BY HIS PERMISSIVE WILL, THROUGH HEAV'N AND EARTH: 3 685
THE CUMBROUS ELEMENTS, EARTH, FLOOD, AIRE, FIRE, . 3 715
THAT PLACE IS EARTH THE SEAT OF MAN, THAT LIGHT . 3 724
HENCE FILLS AND EMPTIES TO ENLIGHTEN TH' EARTH, . 3 731
TOOK LEAVE, AND TOWARD THE COAST OF EARTH BENEATH, 3 739
WO TO THE INHABITANTS ON EARTH. THAT NOW, . . . 4 5
WHEN GOD HATH SHOWRD THE EARTH; SO LOVELY SEEMD . 4 152
A HEAV'N ON EARTH, FOR BLISSFUL PARADISE . . . 4 208
OF POROUS EARTH WITH KINDLY THIRST UP DRAWN, . . 4 228
ALL BEASTS OF TH' EARTH, SINCE WILDE, AND OF ALL
CHASE 4 341
EARTH, AIRE, AND SEA. THEN LET US NOT THINK HARD 4 432
WITH EARTH AND OCEAN MEETS, THE SETTING SUN . . 4 540
ACCESSIBLE FROM EARTH, ONE ENTRANCE HIGH; . . . 4 546
DIURNAL, OR THIS LESS VOLUBIL EARTH 4 594
GLISTRING WITH DEW; FRAGRANT THE FERTIL EARTH . . 4 645
THOSE HAVE THIR COURSE TO FINISH, ROUND THE EARTH, 4 661
ON EARTH, MADE HEREBY APTER TO RECEIVE 4 672
MILLIONS OF SPIRITUAL CREATURES WALK THE EARTH . 4 677
THE GOD THAT MADE BOTH SKIE, AIR, EARTH AND HEAV'N 4 722
TO FILL THE EARTH, WHO SHALL WITH US EXTOLL . . 4 733
TO SETTLE HERE ON EARTH, OR IN MID AIRE; . . . 4 940
THE PENDULOUS ROUND EARTH WITH BALLANC'T AIRE . . 4 1000
ADVANCING, SOW'D THE EARTH WITH ORIENT PEARLE, . 5 2
THY SELF A GODDESS, NOT TO EARTH CONFIND, . . . 5 78
THE EARTH OUTSTRETCHT IMMENSE, A PROSPECT WIDE . 5 88
SHOT PARALEL TO THE EARTH HIS DEWIE RAY, . . . 5 141
ON EARTH JOYN ALL YE CREATURES TO EXTOLL . . . 5 164
OR WET THE THIRSTIE EARTH WITH FALLING SHOWERS, . 5 190
THE EARTH, AND STATELY TREAD, OR LOWLY CREEP; . . 5 201
RAPHAEL, SAID HEE, THOU HEAR'ST WHAT STIR ON EARTH 5 224
EARTH AND THE GARD'N OF GOD, WITH CEDARS CROWND . 5 260
BEHOLDING SHALL CONFESS THAT HERE ON EARTH . . 5 329
WHATEVER EARTH ALL-BEARING MOTHER YIELDS . . . 5 338
THE EARTH TO YIELD; UNSAVOURIE FOOD PERHAPS . . 5 401
THE GROSSER FEEDS THE PURER, EARTH THE SEA, . . 5 416
EARTH AND THE SEA FEED AIR, THE AIR THOSE FIRES . 5 417
TO WHOM THE ANGEL. SON OF HEAV'N AND EARTH, . . 5 519
AS MAY EXPRESS THEM BEST, THOUGH WHAT IF EARTH . 5 574
EACH TO OTHER LIKE, MORE THEN ON EARTH IS THOUGHT? 5 576
REIGND WHERE THESE HEAV'NS NOW ROWL, WHERE EARTH
NOW RESTS 5 578
THEN ALL THIS GLOBOUS EARTH IN PLAIN OUT SPRED, . 5 649
THEN WHAT THIS GARDEN IS TO ALL THE EARTH, . . . 5 752
HIS MASSIE SPEAR UPSTAID; AS IF ON EARTH . . . 6 195
RESOUNDED, AND HAD EARTH BIN THEN, ALL EARTH . . 6 218
LIKEN ON EARTH CONSPICUOUS, THAT MAY LIFT . . . 6 299
ETERNIZE HERE ON EARTH; BUT THOSE ELECT 6 374
PART HIDD'N VEINS DIGGD UP (NOR HATH THIS EARTH . 6 516
(FOR EARTH HATH THIS VARIETY FROM HEAV'N . . . 6 640
THUS MEASURING THINGS IN HEAV'N BY THINGS ON EARTH 6 893
STANDING ON EARTH, NOT RAPT ABOVE THE POLE, . . 7 23
OF HEAV'N AND EARTH CONSPICIOUS FIRST BEGAN, . . 7 63
IMBRACING ROUND THIS FLORID EARTH, WHAT CAUSE . . 7 90
TO NONE COMMUNICABLE IN EARTH OR HEAVEN: . . . 7 124
AND EARTH BE CHANG'D TO HEAV'N, & HEAV'N TO EARTH, 7 160
WITHIN APPOINTED BOUNDS BE HEAV'N AND EARTH, . . 7 167
THUS GOD THE HEAV'N CREATED, THUS THE EARTH, . . 7 232
AND EARTH SELF BALLANC'T ON HER CENTER HUNG. . . 7 242
BIRTH-DAY OF HEAV'N AND EARTH; WITH JOY AND SHOUT 7 256
DIVIDING: FOR AS EARTH, SO HE THE WORLD 7 269
THE EARTH WAS FORM'D, BUT IN THE WOMB AS YET . . 7 276
APPEER'D NOT: OVER ALL THE FACE OF EARTH . . . 7 278
THE DRY LAND, EARTH, AND THE GREAT RECEPTACLE . . 7 307
AND SAW THAT IT WAS GOOD, AND SAID, LET TH' EARTH 7 309
WHOSE SEED IS IN HER SELF UPON THE EARTH. . . . 7 312
HE SCARCE HAD SAID, WHEN THE BARE EARTH, TILL THEN 7 313
WITH BORDERS LONG THE RIVERS. THAT EARTH NOW . . 7 328
UPON THE EARTH, AND MAN TO TILL THE GROUND . . . 7 332
NONE WAS, BUT FROM THE EARTH A DEWIE MIST . . . 7 333
PLANT OF THE FIELD, WHICH E'RE IT WAS IN THE EARTH 7 335
TO GIVE LIGHT ON THE EARTH; AND IT WAS SO. . . . 7 345
TO ILLUMINATE THE EARTH, AND RULE THE DAY . . . 7 350
AND LET FOWLE FLIE ABOVE THE EARTH, WITH WINGS . 7 389
AND LET THE FOWLE BE MULTIPLY'D ON THE EARTH. . . 7 398
LET TH' EARTH BRING FORTH FOUL LIVING IN HER KINDE, 7 451
CATTEL AND CREEPING THINGS, AND BEAST OF THE EARTH, 7 452
EACH IN THEIR KINDE. THE EARTH OBEY'D, AND STRAIT 7 453
RISING, THE CRUMBL'D EARTH ABOVE THEM THREW . . 7 468
BEHEMOTH BIGGEST BORN OF EARTH UPHEAV'D 7 471
FIRST WHEELD THIR COURSE; EARTH IN HER RICH ATTIRE 7 501
CONSUMMATE LOVLY SMIL'D; AIRE, WATER, EARTH, . . 7 502
BEAST OF THE FIELD, AND OVER ALL THE EARTH, . . 7 522

EARTH (CONTINUED)
BE FRUITFUL, MULTIPLIE, AND FILL THE EARTH, 7 531
AND EVERY LIVING THING THAT MOVES ON THE EARTH. 7 534
GAVE THEE, ALL SORTS ARE HERE THAT ALL TH' EARTH YIELDS, 7 541
ANGELIC HARMONIES: THE EARTH, THE AIRE 7 560
POUDERD WITH STARRS. AND NOW ON EARTH THE SEVENTH 7 581
EARTH WITH HER NETHER OCEAN CIRCUMFUS'D, 7 624
OVER HIS WORKS, ON EARTH, IN SEA, OR AIR, 7 629
OF HEAV'N AND EARTH CONSISTING, AND COMPUTE, 8 16
THIR MAGNITUDES, THIS EARTH A SPOT, A GRAINE, 8 17
ROUND THIS OPACOUS EARTH, THIS PUNCTUAL SPOT, 8 23
REPEATED, WHILE THE SEDENTARIE EARTH, 8 32
THIS TO ATTAIN, WHETHER HEAV'N MOVE OR EARTH, 8 70
EARTH SITTING STILL, WHEN SHE ALONE RECEAVES 8 89
OR BRIGHT INFERRS NOT EXCELLENCE: THE EARTH 8 91
BUT IN THE FRUITFUL EARTH; THERE FIRST RECEAVD 8 96
YET NOT TO EARTH ARE THOSE BRIGHT LUMINARIES 8 98
TO THEE WHO HAST THY DWELLING HERE ON EARTH. 8 118
PLAC'D HEAV'N FROM EARTH SO FARR, THAT EARTHLY SIGHT, 8 120
THE PLANET EARTH, SO STEDFAST THOUGH SHE SEEM, 8 129
IF EARTH INDUSTRIOUS OF HER SELF FETCH DAY 8 137
THIS EARTH? RECIPROCAL, IF LAND BE THERE, 8 144
RISE ON THE EARTH, OR EARTH RISE ON THE SUN, 8 161
NOT OF EARTH ONELY BUT OF HIGHEST HEAV'N. 8 178
NOR LESS THINK WEE IN HEAV'N OF THEE ON EARTH 8 224
AND THOU ENLIGHT'ND EARTH, SO FRESH AND GAY, 8 274
OF EARTH BEFORE SCARCE PLEASANT SEEMD. EACH TREE 8 306
NOT ONELY THESE FAIR BOUNDS, BUT ALL THE EARTH 8 338
WHAT CALL'ST THOU SOLITUDE, IS NOT THE EARTH 8 369
WITH WHAT ALL EARTH OR HEAVEN COULD BESTOW 8 483
SHED THIR SELECTEST INFLUENCE; THE EARTH 8 513
TWILIGHT UPON THE EARTH, SHORT ARBITER 9 50
FROM COMPASSING THE EARTH, CAUTIOUS OF DAY, 9 59
O EARTH, HOW LIKE TO HEAV'N, IF NOT PREFERR'D 9 99
A CREATURE FORM'D OF EARTH, AND HIM ENDOW, 9 149
MAGNIFICENT THIS WORLD, AND EARTH HIS SEAT, 9 153
OFSPRING OF HEAV'N AND EARTH, AND ALL EARTHS LORD, 9 273
OR EARTH, OR MIDDLE, ALL THINGS FAIR AND GOOD; 9 605
YET LORDS DECLAR'D OF ALL IN EARTH OR AIRE? 9 658
I QUESTION IT, FOR THIS FAIR EARTH I SEE, 9 720
EARTH FELT THE WOUND, AND NATURE FROM HER SEAT 9 782
EACH THING ON EARTH; AND OTHER CARE PERHAPS 9 813
EARTH TREMBL'D FROM HER ENTRAILS, AS AGAIN 9 1000
WHEREWITH TO SCORNE THE EARTH; BUT THAT FALSE FRUIT 9 1011
FROM EARTH ARRIV'D AT HEAVEN GATE, DISPLEAS'D 10 22
NOR TROUBL'D AT THESE TIDINGS FROM THE EARTH, 10 36
ALL JUDGEMENT, WHETHER IN HEAV'N, OR EARTH, OR HELL. 10 57
MINE BOTH IN HEAV'N AND EARTH TO DO THY WILL 10 69
ON EARTH THESE THY TRANSGRESSORS, BUT THOU KNOWST, 10 72
TO FAN THE EARTH NOW WAK'D, AND USHER IN 10 94
MEANWHILE ERE THUS WAS SIN'D AND JUDG'D ON EARTH, 10 229
OF MORTAL CHANGE ON EARTH. AS WHEN A FLOCK 10 273
AND NOW THIR WAY TO EARTH THEY HAD DESCRI'D, 10 325
THAT THOU ON EARTH HADST PROSPER'D, WHICH THY LOOKS 10 360
THERE DWELL AND REIGN IN BLISS, THENCE ON THE EARTH 10 399
PLENIPOTENT ON EARTH, OF MATCHLESS MIGHT 10 404
THEN HEAV'N AND EARTH RENEWD SHALL BE MADE PURE 10 638
NEW HEAV'N AND EARTH SHALL TO THE AGES RISE, 10 647
AS MIGHT AFFECT THE EARTH WITH COLD AND HEAT 10 653
THE POLES OF EARTH TWICE TEN DEGREES AND MORE 10 669
PERPETUAL SMIL'D ON EARTH WITH VERNANT FLOURS, 10 679
MORTALITIE MY SENTENCE, AND BE EARTH 10 776
THAT BURDEN HEAVIER THEN THE EARTH TO BEAR 10 835
THIS NOVELTIE ON EARTH, THIS FAIR DEFECT 10 891
DISTURBANCES ON EARTH THROUGH FEMAL SNARES, 10 897
SEE FATHER, WHAT FIRST FRUITS ON EARTH ARE SPRUNG 11 22
RESIGNES HIM UP WITH HEAV'N AND EARTH RENEWD. 11 66
THE EARTH, WHEN ADAM AND FIRST MATRON EVE 11 136
ADAM, THOU KNOW'ST HEAV'N HIS, AND ALL THE EARTH, 11 335
ALL TH' EARTH HE GAVE THEE TO POSSESS AND RULE, 11 339
FROM ALL THE ENDS OF TH' EARTH, TO CELEBRATE 11 345
THE HEMISPHERE OF EARTH IN CLEEREST KEN 11 379
IN MEATS AND DRINKS, WHICH ON THE EARTH SHALL BRING 11 473
DOWN TO THE VEINS OF EARTH, THENCE GLIDING HOT 11 568
THUS FAME SHALL BE ATCHIEV'D, RENOWN ON EARTH, 11 698
IMPETUOUS, AND CONTINU'D TILL THE EARTH 11 744
WHEN VIOLENCE WAS CEAS'T, AND WARR ON EARTH, 11 780
SHALL LEAVE THEM TO ENJOY; FOR TH' EARTH SHALL BEAR 11 804
OF HEAV'N SET OPEN ON THE EARTH SHALL POWRE 11 825
LEAST IT AGAIN DISSOLVE AND SHOWR THE EARTH? 11 883
THE WHOLE EARTH FILL'D WITH VIOLENCE, AND ALL FLESH 11 888
THE EARTH AGAIN BY FLOOD, NOR LET THE SEA 11 893
OVER THE EARTH A CLOUD, WILL THEREIN SET 11 896
BOTH HEAV'N AND EARTH, WHEREIN THE JUST SHALL DWELL. 11 901
CONCORD AND LAW OF NATURE FROM THE EARTH, 12 29
THIS PONDER, THAT ALL NATIONS OF THE EARTH 12 147
AND WHEEL ON TH' EARTH, DEVOURING WHERE IT ROULS; 12 183
AMONG WHOM GOD WILL DEIGNE TO DWELL ON EARTH 12 281
LONGER ON EARTH THEN CERTAINE TIMES TO APPEER 12 437
WHETHER IN HEAV'N OR EARTH, FOR THEN THE EARTH 12 463
THIR OWN FAITH NOT ANOTHERS: FOR ON EARTH 12 528
NEW HEAV'NS, NEW EARTH, AGES OF ENDLESS DATE 12 549
OR WORKS OF GOD IN HEAV'N, AIRE, EARTH, OR SEA, 12 579

EARTH-BORN
TITANIAN, OR EARTH-BORN, THAT WARR'D ON JOVE, 1 198
CREATURES OF OTHER MOULD, EARTH-BORN PERHAPS, 4 360

EARTHIE
SO MINDED, HAVE ORELEAPT THESE EARTHIE BOUNDS 4 583

EARTHLIE
AN EARTHLIE GUEST, AND DRAWN EMPYREAL AIRE, 7 14

EARTHLY
TO ENTER, AND THESE EARTHLY FRUITS TO TASTE, 5 464
THINGS ABOVE EARTHLY THOUGHT, WHICH YET CONCERND 7 82
SO TOLD AS EARTHLY NOTION CAN RECEAVE. 7 179
PLAC'D HEAV'N FROM EARTH SO FARR, THAT EARTHLY SIGHT, 8 120
MY EARTHLY BY HIS HEAV'NLY OVERPOWERD, 8 453
MY STORIE TO THE SUM OF EARTHLY BLISS 8 522
WILL DAZLE NOW THIS EARTHLY, WITH THIR BLAZE 9 1083
MEANWHILE THEY IN THIR EARTHLY CANAAN PLAC'T 12 315

EARTHS
IN BIGNESS TO SURPASS EARTHS GIANT SONS 1 778
EARTHS INMOST WOMB, MORE WARMTH THEN ADAM NEEDS; 5 302
TO WHOM THUS EVE. ADAM, EARTHS HALLOWD MOULD, 5 321
OFFICIOUS, BUT TO THEE EARTHS HABITANT. 8 99
BEYOND THE EARTHS GREEN CAPE AND VERDANT ISLES 8 631
FROM TH' EARTHS GREAT ALTAR SEND UP SILENT PRAISE 9 195
OFSPRING OF HEAV'N AND EARTH, AND ALL EARTHS LORD, 9 273
AND HYACINTH, EARTHS FRESHEST SOFTEST LAP. 9 1041
TO SHEW HIM ALL EARTHS KINGDOMES AND THIR GLORY. 11 384
WITH EARTHS WIDE BOUNDS, HIS GLORY WITH THE HEAV'NS. 12 371

EARTHY
THIR EARTHY CHARGE: OF THESE THE VIGILANCE 9 157

EAS'D
HANDED THEY WENT; AND EAS'D THE PUTTING OFF 4 739
MINE EYES TRUE OP'NING, AND MY HEART MUCH EAS'D, 12 274

EASE
YOUR WEARIED VERTUE, FOR THE EASE YOU FIND 1 320
COUNSEL'D IGNOBLE EASE, AND PEACEFUL SLOATH, 2 227
THRIVE UNDER EVIL, AND WORK EASE OUT OF PAIN 2 261
WHILE HERE SHALL BE OUR HOME, WHAT BEST MAY EASE 2 458
THENCE MORE AT EASE THIR MINDS AND SOMWHAT RAIS'D 2 521
SHALL DWELL AT EASE, AND UP AND DOWN UNSEEN 2 841
THE GODS WHO LIVE AT EASE, WHERE I SHALL REIGN 2 868
OF MASSIE IRON OR SOLLID ROCK WITH EASE 2 878
THAT SATAN WITH LESS TOIL, AND NOW WITH EASE 2 1041
HIS FLIGHT PRECIPITANT, AND WINDES WITH EASE 3 563
WHAT FEIGN'D SUBMISSION SWORE: EASE WOULD RECANT 4 96
LEAPS O'RE THE FENCE WITH EASE INTO THE FOULD: 4 187
TO RECOMMEND COOLE ZEPHYR, AND MADE EASE 4 329
ASK RIDDANCE, IF WE MEAN TO TREAD WITH EASE; 4 632
TORMENT WITH EASE, AND SOONEST RECOMPENCE 4 893
DEIGNS NONE TO EASE THY LOAD AND TASTE THY SWEET, 5 59
THROUGH SPIRITS WITH EASE; NOR WONDER; IF BY FIRE 5 439
OR IN THIR PEARLIE SHELLS AT EASE, ATTEND 7 407
FOR ONELY IN DESTROYING I FIND EASE 9 129
WILL KEEP FROM WILDERNESS WITH EASE, AS WIDE 9 245
SHALL TEND THEE, AND THE FERTIL BURDEN EASE 9 801
COVERD, BUT NOT AT REST OR EASE OF MIND, 9 1120
DESCEND THROUGH DARKNESS, ON YOUR RODE WITH EASE 10 394
AND HIS ADHERENTS, THAT WITH SO MUCH EASE 10 622
INTO THY MOTHERS LAP, OR BE WITH EASE 11 536
SHALL CHANGE THIR COURSE TO PLEASURE, EASE, AND SLOTH, 11 794

EASIE
WE SUNK THUS LOW? TH' ASCENT IS EASIE THEN; 2 81
HARD LIBERTY BEFORE THE EASIE YOKE 2 256
WITH EASIE INTERCOURSE PASS TO AND FRO 2 1031
THE FIEND BY EASIE ASCENT, OR AGGRAVATE 3 524
MORE EASIE, WHOLSOM THIRST AND APPETITE 4 330
THIS ONE, THIS EASIE CHARGE, OF ALL THE TREES 4 421
ONE EASIE PROHIBITION, WHO ENJOY 4 433
OF EVIL THEN SO SMALL AS EASIE THINK 6 437
TO BE TH' INVENTER MISS'D, SO EASIE IT SEEMD 6 499
SO EASIE, AND OF HIS THUNDER MADE A SCORN, 6 632
EASIE, E'RE GOD HAD BID THE GROUND BE DRIE, 7 304
EASIE MY UNPREMEDITATED VERSE: 9 24
EASIE TO MEE IT IS TO TELL THEE ALL 9 569
INTO HER HEART TOO EASIE ENTRANCE WON: 9 734
EASIE IT MIGHT BE SEEN THAT I INTEND 10 58
SMOOTH, EASIE, INOFFENSIVE DOWN TO HELL. 10 305
OF EASIE THOROUGH-FARE. THEREFORE WHILE I 10 393

EASIER
SOME EASIER ENTERPRIZE? THERE IS A PLACE 2 345
MIGHT YIELD THEM EASIER HABITATION, BEND 2 573
WHOSE EASIER BUSINESS WERE TO SERVE THIR LORD 4 943
JUDG'D THEE PERVERSE: THE EASIER CONQUEST NOW 6 37
UNVANQUISHT, EASIER TO TRANSACT WITH MEE 6 286
EASIER THEN AIR WITH AIR, IF SPIRITS EMBRACE, 8 626
BE REAL, WHY NOT KNOWN, SINCE EASIER SHUNND? 9 699
AS IN OUR EVILS, AND OF EASIER CHOICE. 10 978

EASIEST
THE EASIEST RECOMPENCE, AND PAY HIM THANKS, 4 47
THE EASIEST WAY, NOR WITH PERPLEXING THOUGHTS 8 183
WHERE ENTRANCE UP FROM EDEN EASIEST CLIMBES, 11 119
FAIREST AND EASIEST OF THIS COMBROUS CHARGE, 11 549

EASILY
AND STRENGTH AND ART ARE EASILY OUT-DONE 1 696
AND EASILY TRANSGRESS THE SOLE COMMAND, 3 94
SO EASILY DESTROY'D, AND STILL DESTROYES 3 301
HAVE EASILY AS SPIRITS EVADED SWIFT 6 596
SO EASILY OBEYD AMID THE CHOICE 7 48
THY EMPIRE? EASILY THE PROUD ATTEMPT 7 609
AND EASILY APPROV'D; WHEN THE MOST HIGH 10 31
WOULDST EASILY DETECT WHAT I CONCEALE. 10 136
EVE, EASILY MAY FAITH ADMIT, THAT ALL 11 141

EASING
EASING THIR FLIGHT; SO STEARS THE PRUDENT CRANE 7 430
EASING THIR PASSAGE HENCE, FOR INTERCOURSE, 10 260

EAST
OR WHERE THE GORGEOUS EAST WITH RICHEST HAND 2 3
MOZAMBIC, OFF AT SEA NORTH-EAST WINDES BLOW 4 161
ONE GATE THERE ONLY WAS, AND THAT LOOK'D EAST 4 178
OF GOD THE GARDEN WAS, BY HIM IN THE EAST 4 209
BY SHORTER FLIGHT TO TH' EAST, HAD LEFT HIM THERE 4 595
TO MORROW ERE FRESH MORNING STREAK THE EAST 4 623
DISCOVERING IN WIDE LANTSKIP ALL THE EAST 5 142
IN INDIA EAST OR WEST, OR MIDDLE SHOARE 5 339
PURPLES THE EAST: STILL GOVERN THOU MY SONG, 7 30
SPRUNG FROM THE DEEP, AND FROM HER NATIVE EAST 7 245
FIRST IN HIS EAST THE GLORIOUS LAMP WAS SEEN, 7 370
TILL NIGHT, THEN IN THE EAST HER TURN SHE SHINES, 7 380
WAS SET, AND TWILIGHT FROM THE EAST CAME ONE, 7 583
TRAVELLING EAST, AND WITH HER PART AVERSE 8 138
HEE FROM THE EAST HIS FLAMING RODE BEGIN, 8 162
OR EAST OR WEST, WHICH HAD FORBID THE SNOW 10 685
AND ON THE EAST SIDE OF THE GARDEN PLACE, 11 118
ONE WAY THE SELF-SAME HOUR? WHY IN THE EAST 11 203
FROM HERMON EAST TO THE GREAT WESTERN SEA, 12 141

EASTERN
OF LOCUSTS, WARPING ON THE EASTERN WIND, 1 341
OF NIGHTS EXTENDED SHADE; FROM EASTERN POINT 3 557
AGAINST THE EASTERN GATE OF PARADISE 4 542
NOW MORN HER ROSIE STEPS IN TH' EASTERN CLIME 5 1
AT ONCE ON TH' EASTERN CLIFF OF PARADISE 5 275
DIRECT TO TH' EASTERN GATE WAS BENT THIR FLIGHT. 11 190
AND GUIDES THE EASTERN SAGES, WHO ENQUIRE 12 362
OUR LINGRING PARENTS, AND TO TH' EASTERN GATE 12 638
THEY LOOKING BACK, ALL TH' EASTERN SIDE BEHELD 12 641

EASTWARD
FROM AURAN EASTWARD TO THE ROYAL TOWRS 4 211
EASTWARD AMONG THOSE TREES, WHAT GLORIOUS SHAPE 5 309
BEYOND PETSORA EASTWARD, TO THE RICH 10 292
JORDAN, TRUE LIMIT EASTWARD; BUT HIS SONS 12 145

EAT
TEMPTING SO NIGH, TO PLUCK AND EAT MY FILL 9 595
FORTH REACHING TO THE FRUIT, SHE PLUCK'D, SHE EAT: 9 781
WITH LIBERAL HAND: HE SCRUPL'D NOT TO EAT 9 997
WHEREOF I GAVE THEE CHARGE THOU SHOULDST NOT EAT? 10 123
AND DUST SHALT EAT ALL THE DAYES OF THY LIFE. 10 178
IN THE SWEAT OF THY FACE SHALT THOU EAT BREAD, 10 205
ALL THAT I EAT OR DRINK, OR SHALL BEGET, 10 728
REACH ALSO OF THE TREE OF LIFE, AND EAT, 11 94
MUST EAT, AND ON THE GROUND LEAVE NOTHING GREEN: 12 186

EATE
THEY EATE, THEY DRINK, AND IN COMMUNION SWEET 5 637
FRUITS IN HER SOFT'ND SOILE, FOR SOME TO EATE 8 147
TO PLUCK AND EATE; WHEREAT I WAK'D, AND FOUND 8 309
TO TILL AND KEEP, AND OF THE FRUIT TO EATE: 8 320
EATE FREELY WITH GLAD HEART; FEAR HERE NO DEARTH: 8 322
OF ALL THESE GARDEN TREES YE SHALL NOT EATE, 9 657
OF EACH TREE IN THE GARDEN WE MAY EATE, 9 660
THE GARDEN, GOD HATH SAID, YE SHALL NOT EATE 9 662
YE EATE THEREOF, YOUR EYES THAT SEEM SO CLEERE, 9 706
OUR INWARD FREEDOM? IN THE DAY WE EATE 9 762
SHEE GAVE ME OF THE TREE, AND I DID EATE. 10 143
THE SERPENT ME BEGUIL'D AND I DID EATE. 10 162
I CHARG'D THEE, SAYING: THOU SHALT NOT EATE
THEREOF, 10 200
SHALT EATE THEREOF ALL THE DAYS OF THY LIFE; 10 202
UNBID, AND THOU SHALT EATE TH' HERB OF TH' FIELD, 10 204

EATEN
HATH TOLD THEE? HAST THOU EATEN OF THE TREE 10 122
AND EATEN OF THE TREE CONCERNING WHICH 10 199

EATING
AND KNEW NOT EATING DEATH: SATIATE AT LENGTH, 9 792
EATING HIS FILL, NOR EVE TO ITERATE 9 1005

EAT'N
HOW DIES THE SERPENT? HEE HATH EAT'N AND LIVES, 9 764

EAT'N (CONTINUED)
HATH EAT'N OF THE FRUIT, AND IS BECOME, 9 869

EATS
THAT WHOSO EATS THEREOF, FORTHWITH ATTAINS 9 724

EAT'ST
THOU MAI'ST NOT; IN THE DAY THOU EAT'ST, THOU
DI'ST; 7 544
THE DAY THOU EAT'ST THEREOF, MY SOLE COMMAND 8 329

EATST
IN WHAT THOU EATST AND DRINKST, SEEKING FROM THENCE 11 532

EBBE
FROM STANDING LAKE TO TRIPPING EBBE, THAT STOLE 11 847

EBBING
SOFT-EBBING; NOR WITHSTOOD THEM ROCK OR HILL, 7 300

ECBATAN
THE PERSIAN IN ECBATAN SATE, OR SINCE 11 393

ECCENTRIC
BY CENTER, OR ECCENTRIC, HARD TO TELL, 3 575
ECCENTRIC, INTERVOLV'D, YET REGULAR 5 623
WITH CENTRIC AND ECCENTRIC SCRIBL'D O'RE, 8 83

ECHO
WITH OTHER ECHO LATE I TAUGHT YOUR SHADES 10 861

ECHO'D
HOARCE MURMUR ECHO'D TO HIS WORDS APPLAUSE 5 873

ECHOING
OF ECHOING HILL OR THICKET HAVE WE HEARD 4 681
HIGH OVERARCH'T, AND ECHOING WALKS BETWEEN; 9 1107

ECLIPS
IN DIM ECLIPS DISASTROUS TWILIGHT SHEDS 1 597
AND PLANETS, PLANET-STROOK, REAL ECLIPS 10 413

ECLIPS'D
ON BIRD, BEAST, AIRE, AIRE SUDDENLY ECLIPS'D 11 183

ECLIPSES
ECLIPSES AT THIR CHARMS. THE OTHER SHAPE, 2 666

ECLIPST
ALL POWER, AND US ECLIPST UNDER THE NAME 5 776

ECLIPTIC
DOWN FROM TH' ECLIPTIC, SPED WITH HOP'D SUCCESS, 3 740

EDEN
WITH LOSS OF EDEN, TILL ONE GREATER MAN 1 4
SOMETIMES TOWARDS EDEN WHICH NOW IN HIS VIEW 4 27
OF EDEN, WHERE DELICIOUS PARADISE, 4 132
OF EDEN PLANTED; EDEN STRETCHED HER LINE 4 210
OR WHERE THE SONS OF EDEN LONG BEFORE 4 213
SOUTHWARD THROUGH EDEN WENT A RIVER LARGE, 4 223
OF EDEN STRIVE; NOR THAT NYSEIAN ILE 4 275
THE HAPPIER EDEN, SHALL ENJOY THIR FILL 4 507
BUT IN THE MOUNT THAT LIES FROM EDEN NORTH, 4 569
CAME SUMMOND OVER EDEN TO RECEIVE 6 75
WHAT WITHIN EDEN OR WITHOUT WAS DONE 7 65
EEV'NING AROSE IN EDEN, FOR THE SUN 7 582
IN EDEN, DISTANCE INEXPRESSIBLE 8 113
OF GABRIEL OUT OF EDEN, NOW IMPROV'D 9 54
FROM EDEN OVER PONTUS, AND THE POOLE 9 77
IN EDEN ON THE HUMID FLOURS, THAT BREATHD 9 193
AND EDEN WERE NO EDEN THUS EXPOS'D. 9 341
EDEN AND ALL THE COAST IN PROSPECT LAY. 10 89
WHERE ENTRANCE UP FROM EDEN EASIEST CLIMBES, 11 119
OF PARADISE OR EDEN: THIS HAD BEEN 11 342
MARCHING FROM EDEN TOWARDS THE WEST, SHALL FINDE 12 40
THEN THIS OF EDEN, AND FAR HAPPIER DAIES. 12 465
THROUGH EDEN TOOK THIR SOLITARIE WAY. 12 649

EDENS
OF PARADISE AND EDENS HAPPIE PLAINS, 5 143

EDGE
IN WORST EXTREAMS, AND ON THE PERILOUS EDGE 1 276
IN HIS OWN TEMPLE, ON THE GRUNSEL EDGE, 1 460
ON THE ROUGH EDGE OF BATTEL ERE IT JOYN'D, 6 108
BRANDISHT ALOFT THE HORRID EDGE CAME DOWN 6 252
NOR SOLID MIGHT RESIST THAT EDGE: IT MET 6 323

EDICT
LAW AND EDICT ON US, WHO WITHOUT LAW 5 798

EDIFICE
AN EDIFICE TOO LARGE FOR HIM TO FILL, 8 104

EDIFIE
THEY FIRST RE-EDIFIE, AND FOR A WHILE 12 350

EEVE
WATCHING WHERE SHEPHERDS PEN THIR FLOCKS AT EEVE . 4 185

EEVEN
THITHER CAME URIEL, GLIDING THROUGH THE EEVEN . . 4 555
WITNESS IF I BE SILENT, MORN OR EEVEN, ... 5 202
CONFLICTING FIRE: LONG TIME IN EEVEN SCALE . . . 6 245
TO DWELL ON EEVEN GROUND NOW WITH THY SONS: . . 11 348

EEV'N
HE NAM'D. THUS WAS THE FIRST DAY EEV'N AND MORN: 7 252
AND HEAV'N HE NAM'D THE FIRMAMENT: SO EEV'N . . 7 274
SO EEV'N AND MORN RECORDED THE THIRD DAY. . . . 7 338
ON HER SOFT AXLE, WHILE SHE PACES EEV'N, . . . 8 165
AT EEV'N, WHICH I BRED UP WITH TENDER HAND . . . 11 276

EEVN
BORN EEVN OR HIGH, FOR THIS DAY WILL POUR DOWN, . 6 544
OF EWE OR GOAT DROPPING WITH MILK AT EEVN, . . . 9 582
IN EEVN SCALE. BUT FALL'N HE IS, AND NOW . . . 10 47
EEVN HEE WHO NOW FORETOLD HIS FATAL BRUISE, . . 10 191
EEVN TO THE INMOST SEAT OF MENTAL SIGHT, . . . 11 418

EEV'NING
EEV'NING AROSE IN EDEN, FOR THE SUN 7 582
ERE SABBATH EEV'NING: SO WE HAD IN CHARGE. . . . 8 246

EEVNING
LEVELD HIS EEVNING RAYES: IT WAS A ROCK 4 543
NOW CAME STILL EEVNING ON, AND TWILIGHT GRAY . . 4 598
OF GRATEFUL EEVNING MILDE, THEN SILENT NIGHT . . 4 647
NOR GRATEFUL EEVNING MILD, NOR SILENT NIGHT . . 4 654
BY MORROW EEVNING, AND FROM LAND TO LAND . . . 4 662
THIS EEVNING FROM THE SUN'S DECLINE ARRIV'D . . 4 792
ORESHADES; FOR THESE MID-HOURS, TILL EEVNING RISE 5 376
LISTENS DELIGHTED. EEVNING NOW APPROACH'D . . . 5 627
(FOR WEE HAVE ALSO OUR EEVNING AND OUR MORN, . . 5 628
OR IF THE STARR OF EEVNING AND THE MOON 7 104
BOTH WHEN FIRST EEVNING WAS, AND WHEN FIRST MORN. 7 260
GLAD EEVNING AND GLAD MORN CROWND THE FOURTH DAY. 7 386
WITH EEVNING HARPS AND MATTIN, WHEN GOD SAID, . . 7 450
SUNG SPOUSAL, AND BID HASTE THE EEVNING STARR . . 8 519
THE EEVNING COOLE WHEN HE FROM WRAUTH MORE COOLE . 10 95
AND NOW OF LOVE THEY TREAT TILL TH' EEVNING STAR . 11 588

EEVNINGS
OF OUR LAST EEVNINGS TALK, IN THIS THY DREAM, . . 5 115

EFFECT
BURNS FRORE, AND COLD PERFORMS TH' EFFECT OF FIRE. 2 595
OF COLOUR GLORIOUS AND EFFECT SO RARE? 3 612
EFFECT SHALL END OUR WISH. MEAN WHILE REVIVE; . 6 493
HIS WORD, THE FILIAL GODHEAD, GAVE EFFECT. . . . 7 175
WHOSE VERTUE ON IT SELF WORKES NO EFFECT, . . . 8 95
OP'NING THE WAY, BUT OF DIVINE EFFECT 9 865

EFFECTED
WHAT FORCE EFFECTED NOT: THAT HE NO LESS 1 647
HE EFFECTED; MAN HE MADE, AND FOR HIM BUILT . . 9 152

EFFECTS
WONDROUS INDEED, IF CAUSE OF SUCH EFFECTS. . . . 9 650
TH' EFFECTS TO CORRESPOND, OPENER MINE EYES, . . 9 875
TH' EFFECTS WHICH THY ORIGINAL CRIME HATH WROUGHT 11 424

EFFECTUAL
MY WORD, MY WISDOM, AND EFFECTUAL MIGHT, ... 3 170

EFFEMINATE
FROM MANS EFFEMINATE SLACKNESS IT BEGINS, . . . 11 634

EFFICACIE
OF NOXIOUS EFFICACIE, AND WHEN TO JOYNE 10 660

EFFLUENCE
BRIGHT EFFLUENCE OF BRIGHT ESSENCE INCREATE. . . 3 6

EFFULGENCE
IMPRESST THE EFFULGENCE OF HIS GLORIE ABIDES, . . 3 388
DIVINE EFFULGENCE, WHOSE HIGH POWER SO FAR . . . 5 458
EFFULGENCE OF MY GLORIE, SON BELOV'D, ... 6 680

EFFUS'D
GROAND OUT HIS SOUL WITH GUSHING BLOUD EFFUS'D. . 11 447

EFFUSION
AND FROM ABOUT HIM FIERCE EFFUSION ROWLD 6 765

EGG
THIR BROOD AS NUMEROUS HATCH, FROM THE EGG THAT
SOON 7 418

EGRESS
BARR'D OVER US PROHIBIT ALL EGRESS. 2 437

EGYPT
EGYPT FROM SYRIAN GROUND, HAD GENERAL NAMES . . 1 421
FANATIC EGYPT AND HER PRIESTS, TO SEEK 1 480

EGYPT (CONTINUED)
FROM EGYPT MARCHING, EQUAL'D WITH ONE STROKE . . 1 488
EGYPT, DIVIDED BY THE RIVER NILE; 12 157
OF EGYPT MUST LIE DEAD. THUS WITH TEN WOUNDS . . 12 190
RETURN THEM BACK TO EGYPT, CHOOSING RATHER . . . 12 219

EGYPTIAN
HELD DALLIANCE WITH HIS FAIRE EGYPTIAN SPOUSE. . 9 443
HAILE MIXT WITH FIRE MUST REND TH' EGYPTIAN SKIE . 12 182

EGYPTS
OF AMRAMS SON IN EGYPTS EVILL DAY 1 339

EIGHTH
ON THE EIGHTH RETURN'D, AND ON THE COAST AVERSE . 9 67

EJECT
EJECT HIM TAINTED NOW, AND PURGE HIM OFF . . . 11 52

ELABORATE
ELABORATE, OF INWARD LESS EXACT. 8 539

ELDEST
AND TIME AND PLACE ARE LOST; WHERE ELDEST NIGHT . 2 894
SAT SABLE-VESTED NIGHT, ELDEST OF THINGS, . . . 2 962
AIRE, AND YE ELEMENTS THE ELDEST BIRTH 5 180

EL DORADO
CALL EL DORADO: BUT TO NOBLER SIGHTS 11 411

ELEALE
AND ELEALE TO TH' ASPHALTICK POOL. 1 411

ELECT
ALL HEAV'N, AND IN THE BLESSED SPIRITS ELECT . . 3 136
ELECT ABOVE THE REST; SO IS MY WILL: 3 184
WITH THESE THAT NEVER FADE THE SPIRITS ELECT . . 3 360
ETERNIZE HERE ON EARTH; BUT THOSE ELECT 6 374
AND OVERWHELM THIR WARR: THE RACE ELECT 12 214

ELECTION
THAT PROUD EXCUSE? YET HIM NOT THY ELECTION, . . 10 764

ELEGANT
AND ELEGANT, OF SAPIENCE NO SMALL PART, ... 9 1018

ELEMENT
HEAV'NS CHEARFUL FACE, THE LOWRING ELEMENT . . . 2 490
RETURN ME TO MY NATIVE ELEMENT: 7 16
THIR ELEMENT TO DRAW THE THINNER AIRE. 8 348

ELEMENTAL
TRANSPARENT, ELEMENTAL AIR, DIFFUS'D 7 265

ELEMENTS
BECOME OUR ELEMENTS, THESE PIERCING FIRES . . . 2 275
OF HEAV'N WERE FALLING, AND THESE ELEMENTS . . . 2 925
OF FIGHTING ELEMENTS, ON ALL SIDES ROUND . . . 2 1015
THE CUMBROUS ELEMENTS, EARTH, FLOOD, AIRE, FIRE, . 3 715
OF HEAV'N PERHAPS, OR ALL THE ELEMENTS 4 993
AIRE, AND YE ELEMENTS THE ELDEST BIRTH 5 180
TO BE SUSTAIND AND FED; OF ELEMENTS 5 415
THESE ELEMENTS, AND ARM HIM WITH THE FORCE . . . 6 222
THOSE PURE IMMORTAL ELEMENTS THAT KNOW 11 50

ELEPHANT
GAMBOLD BEFORE THEM, TH' UNWIELDY ELEPHANT . . . 4 345

ELEVATE
IN THOUGHTS MORE ELEVATE, AND REASON'D HIGH . . 2 558

ELEVATES
TO MISCHIEF SWIFT. HOPE ELEVATES, AND JOY . . . 9 633

ELISIAN
ROWLS O'RE ELISIAN FLOURS HER AMBER STREAM; . . 3 359

ELIXIR
BREATHE FORTH ELIXIR PURE, AND RIVERS RUN . . . 3 607

ELLOPS
CERASTES HORND, HYDRUS, AND ELLOPS DREAR, . . . 10 525

ELM
TO WED HER ELM; SHE SPOUS'D ABOUT HIM TWINES . . 5 216

ELOCUTION
GAVE ELOCUTION TO THE MUTE, AND TAUGHT 9 748

ELOQUENCE
(FOR ELOQUENCE THE SOUL, SONG CHARMS THE SENSE,) . 2 556
UNMEDITATED, SUCH PROMPT ELOQUENCE 5 149
IN ATHENS OR FREE ROME, WHERE ELOQUENCE 9 671

ELSE
CAN ELSE INFLICT, DO I REPENT OR CHANGE, ... 1 96
AND WHAT IS ELSE NOT TO BE OVERCOME? 1 109
THEN AUGHT DIVINE OR HOLY ELSE ENJOY'D 1 683

ELSE (CONTINUED)
RE-ENTER HEAV'N; OR ELSE IN SOME MILDE ZONE 2 397
OF ANCIENT PILE; ALL ELSE DEEP SNOW AND ICE, 2 591
(FOR WHAT COULD ELSE) TO OUR ALMIGHTY FOE 2 769
TILL THEY ENTHRALL THEMSELVES; I ELSE MUST CHANGE 3 125
WHOM ELSE NO CREATURE CAN BEHOLD; ON THEE 3 387
WHICH ELSE MIGHT WORK HIM DANGER OR DELAY: 3 635
HIS DAY, WHICH ELSE AS TH' OTHER HEMISPHERE 3 725
TO DO WHAT ELSE THOUGH DAMND I SHOULD ABHORRE. 4 392
FREE LEAVE SO LARGE TO ALL THINGS ELSE, AND CHOICE 4 434
IN PARADISE OF ALL THINGS COMMON ELSE. 4 752
HIS HEART, NOT ELSE DISMAI'D. NOW DREW THEY NIGH 4 861
AND SECONDED THY ELSE NOT DREADED SPEAR. 4 929
LONGER THY OFFERD GOOD, WHY ELSE SET HERE? 5 63
THOUGH STANDING ELSE AS ROCKS, BUT DOWN THEY FELL 6 593
WHAT MIGHT HAVE ELSE TO HUMAN RACE BIN HID; 6 896
OF ALL TASTES ELSE TO PLEASE THIR APPETITE, 7 49
US TIMELY OF WHAT MIGHT ELSE HAVE BIN OUR LOSS, 7 74
OPPRESSES ELSE WITH SURFET, AND SOON TURNS 7 129
INFORMD BY THEE MIGHT KNOW; IF ELSE THOU SEEKST 7 639
THINGS ELSE BY ME UNSEARCHABLE, NOW HEARD 8 10
HIS BEAMS, UNACTIVE ELSE, THIR VIGOUR FIND. 8 97
WHICH ELSE TO SEVERAL SPHEARS THOU MUST ASCRIBE, 8 131
INVISIBLE ELSE ABOVE ALL STARRS, THE WHEELE 8 135
IN ALL THINGS ELSE DELIGHT INDEED, BUT SUCH 8 524
COMMOTION STRANGE, IN ALL ENJOYMENTS ELSE 8 531
THY JUDGEMENT TO DO AUGHT, WHICH ELSE FREE WILL 8 636
INTENT NOW WHOLLY ON HER TASTE, NAUGHT ELSE 9 786
THIS HAPPIE TRIAL OF THY LOVE, WHICH ELSE 9 975
WITH FEATHERD CINCTURE, NAKED ELSE AND WILDE 9 1117
OF SEASONS TO EACH CLIME; ELSE HAD THE SPRING 10 678
HIS COURSE INTENDED; ELSE HOW HAD THE WORLD 10 689
BY WHICH ALL CAUSES ELSE ACCORDING STILL 10 806
AND WHAT MAY ELSE BE REMEDIE OR CURE 10 1079
WHAT ELSE BUT FAVOR, GRACE, AND MERCIE SHON? 10 1096
WHY ELSE THIS DOUBLE OBJECT IN OUR SIGHT 11 201
THY MESSAGE, WHICH MIGHT ELSE IN TELLING WOUND, 11 299
FAMILIAR TO OUR EYES, ALL PLACES ELSE 11 305
FIRST HIS OWN TOOLES; THEN, WHAT MIGHT ELSE BE WROUGHT 11 572
RODE TILTING O'RE THE WAVES, ALL DWELLINGS ELSE 11 747

ELSEWHERE
OUR FIRST ERUPTION, THITHER OR ELSEWHERE: 1 656
IMAGIND RATHER OFT THEN ELSEWHERE SEEN, 3 599
EACH OTHER, BLAM'D ENOUGH ELSEWHERE, BUT STRIVE 10 959

ELUDE
I DREAD, AND TO ELUDE, THUS WRAPT IN MIST 9 158

ELVES
BEYOND THE INDIAN MOUNT, OR FAERIE ELVES, 1 781

ELY'S
TURNS ATHEIST, AS DID ELY'S SONS, WHO FILL'D 1 495

ELYSIUM
PLATO'S ELYSIUM, LEAP'D INTO THE SEA, 3 472

EMBASSIE
WHERE ALL HIS SONS THY EMBASSIE ATTEND; 3 658

EMBATTELD
COVERD WITH THICK EMBATTELD SQUADRONS BRIGHT, 6 16

EMBATTELL'D
EMBATTELL'D IN HER FIELD: AND THE HUMBLE SHRUB, 7 322

EMBATTELLD
AND ONWARD MOVE EMBATTELLD; WHEN BEHOLD 6 550

EMBLAZON'D
OR TILTING FURNITURE, EMBLAZON'D SHIELDS, 9 34

EMBLEM
OF COSTLIEST EMBLEM: OTHER CREATURE HERE 4 703

EMBOLD'ND
THUS I EMBOLD'ND SPAKE, AND FREEDOM US'D 8 434

EMBOWELD
EMBOWELD WITH OUTRAGIOUS NOISE THE AIR, 6 587

EMBRAC'D
SO SAYING, SHE EMBRAC'D HIM, AND FOR JOY 9 990

EMBRACE
EASIER THEN AIR WITH AIR, IF SPIRITS EMBRACE, 8 626

EMBRACES
AND IN EMBRACES FORCIBLE AND FOULE 2 793

EMBRYON
THIR EMBRYON ATOMS; THEY AROUND THE FLAG 2 900
OF WATERS, EMBRYON IMMATURE INVOLV'D, 7 277

EMBRYO'S
EMBRYO'S AND IDIOTS, EREMITS AND FRIERS 3 474

EMERGENT
EMERGENT, AND THIR BROAD BARE BACKS UPHEAVE 7 286

EMINENCE
TO THAT BAD EMINENCE; AND FROM DESPAIR 2 6
IN THAT BRIGHT EMINENCE, AND WITH HIS GOOD 4 44
IN EMINENCE, AND OBSTACLE FIND NONE 8 624

EMINENT
IN SHAPE AND GESTURE PROUDLY EMINENT 1 590
HIGH EMINENT, BLOOMING AMBROSIAL FRUIT 4 219
RECORDED EMINENT. THUS WHEN IN ORBES 5 594
OF MIDDLE AGE ONE RISING, EMINENT 11 665
FIRST SEEN IN ACTS OF PROWESS EMINENT 11 789

EMINENTLY
SO EMINENTLY NEVER HAD BIN KNOWN. 9 976

EMMET
THE PARSIMONIOUS EMMET, PROVIDENT 7 485

EMPEDOCLES
EMPEDOCLES, AND HEE WHO TO ENJOY 3 471

EMPERORS
AT THIR GREAT EMPERORS CALL, AS NEXT IN WORTH 1 378

EMPEROUR
THAN HELLS DREAD EMPEROUR WITH POMP SUPREAM, 2 510
MIGHT INTERCEPT THIR EMPEROUR SENT, SO HEE 10 429

EMPIRE
DOUBTED HIS EMPIRE, THAT WERE LOW INDEED, 1 114
TO FOUND THIS NETHER EMPIRE, WHICH MIGHT RISE 2 296
A GROWING EMPIRE; DOUBTLESS; WHILE WE DREAM, 2 315
HIS EMPIRE, AND WITH IRON SCEPTER RULE 2 327
LIES THROUGH YOUR SPACIOUS EMPIRE UP TO LIGHT, 2 974
DIVIDED EMPIRE WITH HEAV'NS KING I HOLD 4 111
INTO HIS NEATHER EMPIRE NEIGHBOURING ROUND. 4 145
HONOUR AND EMPIRE WITH REVENGE ENLARG'D, 4 390
OF DEITIE OR EMPIRE, SUCH A FOE 5 724
FIT TO DECIDE THE EMPIRE OF GREAT HEAV'N. 6 303
OF HIS ETERNAL EMPIRE, BUT THE MORE 7 96
TH' ADDITION OF HIS EMPIRE, HOW IT SHEW'D 7 555
THY EMPIRE? EASILY THE PROUD ATTEMPT 7 609
TH' INFERNAL EMPIRE, THAT SO NEER HEAV'NS DORE 10 389
WHAT THINKST THOU OF OUR EMPIRE NOW, THOUGH EARND 10 592
OF MIGHTIEST EMPIRE, FROM THE DESTIND WALLS 11 387
TH' EMPIRE OF NEGUS TO HIS UTMOST PORT 11 397
SUBJECTION TO HIS EMPIRE TYRANNOUS: 12 32
AND ALL THE RULE, ONE EMPIRE; ONELY ADD 12 581

EMPIRES
HATCHING VAIN EMPIRES. THUS BEELZEBUB 2 378

EMPIRIC
OF SOOTY COAL THE EMPIRIC ALCHIMIST 5 440

EMPRESS
EMPRESS OF THIS FAIR WORLD, RESPLENDENT EVE, 9 568
EMPRESS, THE WAY IS READIE, AND NOT LONG, 9 626

EMPRISE
GIANTS OF MIGHTIE BONE, AND BOULD EMPRISE; 11 642

EMPTIE
FIT RETRIBUTION, EMPTIE AS THIR DEEDS; 3 454

EMPTIED
HATH EMPTIED HEAV'N, SHALL FAIL TO RE-ASCEND 1 633

EMPTIER
OR IN THE EMPTIER WASTE, RESEMBLING AIR, 2 1045

EMPTIES
HENCE FILLS AND EMPTIES TO ENLIGHTEN TH' EARTH, 3 731

EMPTINESS
OR EMPTINESS, OR FOND IMPERTINENCE, 8 195

EMPTY
FOR THOU ART HEAV'NLIE, SHEE AN EMPTY DREAME. 7 39
YET EMPTY OF ALL GOOD WHEREIN CONSISTS 11 616

EMPYREAL
AND THIS EMPYREAL SUBSTANCE CANNOT FAIL, 1 117
O PROGENY OF HEAV'N, EMPYREAL THRONES, 2 430
FARR OFF TH' EMPYREAL HEAV'N, EXTENDED WIDE 2 1047
FROM THY EMPYREAL MANSION THUS ALONE, 3 699
THROUGH ALL TH' EMPYREAL ROAD; TILL AT THE GATE 5 253
THUS TO TH' EMPYREAL MINISTER HE FRAM'D. 5 460
AS HEAV'NS GREAT YEAR BRINGS FORTH, TH' EMPYREAL HOST 5 583
EMPYREAL, FROM BEFORE HER VANISHT NIGHT, 6 14
SINCE NOW WE FIND THIS OUR EMPYREAL FORM 6 433
AN EARTHLIE GUEST, AND DRAWN EMPYREAL AIRE, 7 14
OF ALL THINGS PARTED BY TH' EMPYREAL BOUNDS, 10 380

EMPYREAN
THROUGH ALL THE EMPYREAN: DOWN THEY FELL 2 771
FROM THE PURE EMPYREAN WHERE HE SITS 3 57
THE STEDFAST EMPYREAN SHOOK THROUGHOUT, 6 833
DOWN FROM THE EMPYREAN TO FOREWARNE 7 73
SO SUNG THEY, AND THE EMPYREAN RUNG, 7 633
THE CONFINES MET OF EMPYREAN HEAV'N 10 321

EMULATE
INGAGING ME TO EMULATE, BUT SHORT 9 963

EMULATION
IN EMULATION OPPOSITE TO HEAV'N. 2 298

EMULOUS
NOT EMULOUS, NOR CARE WHO THEM EXCELLS; 6 822

ENAMEL'D
HIS TURRET CREST, AND SLEEK ENAMEL'D NECK, 9 525

ENAMELD
APPEERD, WITH GAY ENAMELD COLOURS MIXT: 4 149

ENAMOUR'D
BECAM'ST ENAMOUR'D, AND SUCH JOY THOU TOOK'ST 2 765
HUNG OVER HER ENAMOUR'D, AND BEHELD 5 13
ENAMOUR'D AT THAT SIGHT; BUT IN THOSE HEARTS 5 448

ENAMOURD
THAT DROVE HIM, THOUGH ENAMOURD, FROM THE SPOUSE 4 169

ENCAMP
ENCAMP THIR LEGIONS, OR WITH OBSCURE WING 2 132

ENCAMPING
ENCAMPING, PLAC'D IN GUARD THIR WATCHES ROUND, 6 412

ENCAMPT
WHERE ARMIES LIE ENCAMPT, COME FLYING, LUR'D 10 276
LAY SEIGE, ENCAMPT; BY BATTERIE, SCALE, AND MINE, 11 656
BY MEE ENCAMPT ON YONDER HILL, EXPECT 12 591

ENCLIN'D
SO STRICTLY, BUT MUCH MORE TO PITIE ENCLIN'D, 3 405
OF ADAM, SOON ENCLIN'D TO ADMIT DELIGHT, 11 596

ENCLINE
SO STRICTLY, BUT MUCH MORE TO PITIE ENCLINE: 3 402

ENCLOS'D
THE LUMINOUS INFERIOR ORBS, ENCLOS'D 3 420
IDOL OF MAJESTIE DIVINE, ENCLOS'D 6 101
OF FUTURE, IN SMALL ROOM LARGE HEART ENCLOS'D, 7 486
A CIRCUIT WIDE, ENCLOS'D, WITH GOODLIEST TREES 8 304
SO SPAKE THE ENEMIE OF MANKIND, ENCLOS'D 9 494
THEM NOTHING: IF THEY ALL THINGS, WHO ENCLOS'D 9 722

ENCLOSD
BY NILUS HEAD, ENCLOSD WITH SHINING ROCK, 4 283

ENCLOSE
FROM WING TO WING, AND HALF ENCLOSE HIM ROUND 1 617

ENCLOSURE
NOW NEARER, CROWNS WITH HER ENCLOSURE GREEN, 4 133
IN THIS ENCLOSURE WILD, THESE BEASTS AMONG, 9 543

ENCOMPASS'D
ENCOMPASS'D SHALL RESOUND THEE EVER BLEST. 3 149
ENCOMPASS'D ROUND WITH FOES, THUS ANSWERD BOLD. 5 876

ENCOUNTER
TO JOYN THIR DARK ENCOUNTER IN MID AIR; 2 718

ENCOUNTERD
SO HILLS AMID THE AIR ENCOUNTERD HILLS 6 664

ENCOUNTRING
MILLIONS OF FIERCE ENCOUNTRING ANGELS FOUGHT 6 220

ENCREAS'D
OF THAT STUPENDIOUS BRIDGE HIS JOY ENCREAS'D. 10 351

ENCREASE
DELIGHTFULLY, ENCREASE AND MULTIPLY, 10 730
NOW DEATH TO HEARE. FOR WHAT CAN I ENCREASE 10 731

ENCROACHING
ENCROACHING EVE PERHAPS, HAD FIRST THE RULE 10 582

ENCROACHMENT
BUT THIS USURPER HIS ENCROACHMENT PROUD 12 72

ENCROACHT
ENCROACHT ON STILL THROUGH OUR INTESTINE BROILES 2 1001

ENCUMBERD
ENCUMBERD, NOW HAD LEFT THEM, UP THEY ROSE 9 1051

END
THAT COMES TO ALL; BUT TORTURE WITHOUT END 1 67
OUR LABOUR MUST BE TO PERVERT THAT END, 1 164
MUST EXERCISE US WITHOUT HOPE OF END 2 89
AND THAT MUST END US, THAT MUST BE OUR CURE, 2 145
TO GIVE HIS ENEMIES THIR WISH, AND END 2 157
AGES OF HOPELESS END; THIS WOULD BE WORSE. 2 186
FROM EITHER END OF HEAV'N THE WELKIN BURNS. 2 538
AND FOUND NO END, IN WANDRING MAZES LOST. 2 561
HIS END WITH MINE INVOLVD; AND KNOWS THAT I 2 807
THY DAUGHTER AND THY DARLING, WITHOUT END. 2 870
LOVE WITHOUT END, AND WITHOUT MEASURE GRACE, 3 142
HIS END, AND FRUSTRATE THINE, SHALL HE FULFILL 3 157
AND TO THE END PERSISTING, SAFE ARRIVE. 3 197
HE TO APPEASE THY WRAUTH, AND END THE STRIFE 3 406
HIS JOURNIES END AND OUR BEGINNING WOE. 3 633
NOW OTHER, AS THIR SHAPE SERVD BEST HIS END 4 398
AND WITHOUT WHOM AM TO NO END, MY GUIDE 4 442
YOUR MESSAGE, LIKE TO END AS MUCH IN VAIN? 4 833
HIM FIRST, HIM LAST, HIM MIDST, AND WITHOUT END. 5 165
ORDAIND WITHOUT REDEMPTION, WITHOUT END. 5 615
WHO OUT OF SMALLEST THINGS COULD WITHOUT END 6 137
APOSTAT, STILL THOU ERRST, NOR END WILT FIND 6 172
SURCEAS'D, AND GLAD AS HOPING HERE TO END 6 258
TO CHASE ME HENCE? ERRE NOT THAT SO SHALL END 6 288
EFFECT SHALL END OUR WISH. MEAN WHILE REVIVE; 6 493
CAN END IT. INTO THEE SUCH VERTUE AND GRACE 6 703
AND GLADLIER SHALL RESIGN, WHEN IN THE END 6 731
IMMUTABLY HIS SOVRAN WILL, THE END 7 79
END, AND DISMISS THEE ERE THE MORNING SHINE. 7 108
ONE KINGDOM, JOY AND UNION WITHOUT END. 7 161
SAID THEN TH' OMNIFIC WORD, YOUR DISCORD END: 7 217
THERE WANTED YET THE MASTER WORK, THE END 7 505
VARIETIE WITHOUT END; BUT OF THE TREE 7 542
AUTHOR AND END OF ALL THINGS, AND FROM WORK 7 591
HER END WITHOUT LEAST MOTION, AND RECEAVES, 8 35
UNCHECKT, AND OF HER ROAVING IS NO END; 8 189
FOR WELL I UNDERSTAND IN THE PRIME END 8 540
TWIXT DAY AND NIGHT, AND NOW FROM END TO END 9 51
LOVE NOT THE LOWEST END OF HUMAN LIFE. 9 241
AND THY FAIR FRUIT LET HANG, AS TO NO END 9 798
AND OF THIR VAIN CONTEST APPEER'D NO END. 9 1189
FORBEARANCE NO ACQUITTANCE ERE DAY END. 10 53
OF MISCHIEF, AND POLLUTED FROM THE END 10 167
OF RICHEST TEXTURE SPRED, AT TH' UPPER END 10 446
O MISERABLE OF HAPPIE. IS THIS THE END 10 720
OF HAPPINESS: YET WELL, IF HERE WOULD END 10 725
WRATH WITHOUT END ON MAN WHOM DEATH MUST END? 10 797
TO END ME? SHALL TRUTH FAIL TO KEEP HER WORD, 10 856
OR END, THOUGH SHARP AND SAD, YET TOLERABLE, 10 977
THAT SHEW NO END BUT DEATH, AND HAVE THE POWER, 10 1004
OR IF THOU COVET DEATH, AS UTMOST END 10 1020
BY HIM WITH MANY COMFORTS, TILL WE END 10 1084
AND IN PERFORMING END US; WHAT BESIDES 11 300
BETTER END HEER UNBORN. WHY IS LIFE GIV'N 11 502
CREATED, AS THOU ART, TO NOBLER END 11 605
THE END OF ALL THY OFSPRING, END SO SAD, 11 755
AND WHETHER HERE THE RACE OF MAN WILL END 11 786
THUS THOU HAST SEEN ONE WORLD BEGIN AND END; 12 6
THE LAST, FOR OF HIS REIGN SHALL BE NO END. 12 330
ETERNITIE, WHOSE END NO EYE CAN REACH. 12 556
WITH MEDITATION ON THE HAPPIE END. 12 605

ENDANGER'D
FEARLESS, ENDANGER'D HEAV'NS PERPETUAL KING; 1 131
AND MORE ENDANGER'D, THEN WHEN ARGO PASS'D 2 1017

ENDEARING
NOR GENTLE PURPOSE, NOR ENDEARING SMILES 4 337

ENDEAVOUR
ENDEAVOUR PEACE: THIR STRIFE POLLUTION BRINGS 12 355

ENDED
HE ENDED FROWNING, AND HIS LOOK DENOUNC'D 2 106
AS MAMMON ENDED, AND HIS SENTENCE PLEAS'D, 2 291
WELL HAVE YE JUDG'D, WELL ENDED LONG DEBATE, 2 390
ENDED REJOYCING IN THIR MATCHLESS CHIEF: 2 487
THEN OF THIR SESSION ENDED THEY BID CRY 2 514
BUT ENDED FOUL IN MANY A SCALY FOULD 2 651
HIS WORDS HERE ENDED, BUT HIS MEEK ASPECT 3 266
HE SCARCE HAD ENDED, WHEN THOSE TWO APPROACHD 4 874
OF ONSET ENDED SOON EACH MILDER THOUGHT, 6 98
THEY ENDED PARLE, AND BOTH ADDREST FOR FIGHT 6 296
HE ENDED, AND HIS WORDS THIR DROOPING CHERE 6 496
HAD ENDED; WHEN TO RIGHT AND LEFT THE FRONT 6 569
THE ANGEL ENDED, AND IN ADAMS EARE 8 1
HEE ENDED, OR I HEARD NO MORE, FOR NOW 8 452
THOUGH IN MID HEAV'N, SOON ENDED HIS DELIGHT, 9 468
HE ENDED, AND HIS WORDS REPLETE WITH GUILE 9 733
HE ENDED, AND THE HEAV'NLY AUDIENCE LOUD 10 641
SHE ENDED WEEPING, AND HER LOWLIE PLIGHT, 10 937
SHE ENDED HEER, OR VEHEMENT DESPAIRE 10 1007
HE ENDED, AND THE SON GAVE SIGNAL HIGH 11 72
HAD ENDED NOW THIR ORISONS, AND FOUND 11 137
HE ENDED; AND TH' ARCH-ANGEL SOON DREW NIGH, 11 238
IN MANHOOD WHERE YOUTH ENDED; BY HIS SIDE 11 246
HE ENDED; AND THUS ADAM LAST REPLY'D. 12 552

ENTRANCE
AND WISDOME AT ONE ENTRANCE QUITE SHUT OUT. 3 50
DUE ENTRANCE HE DISDAIND, AND IN CONTEMPT, 4 180
ACCESSIBLE FROM EARTH, ONE ENTRANCE HIGH; 4 546
TO QUESTION THY BOLD ENTRANCE ON THIS PLACE; 4 882
HIS ENTRANCE, AND FOREWARND THE CHERUBIM 9 61
FROM ENTRANCE OR CHERUBIC WATCH, BY STEALTH 9 68
INTO HER HEART TOO EASIE ENTRANCE WON: 9 734
ENTRANCE UNSEEN. SOON AS TH' UNWELCOME NEWS 10 21
WHERE ENTRANCE UP FROM EDEN EASIEST CLIMBES, 11 119
MORE TERRIBLE AT TH' ENTRANCE THEN WITHIN. 11 470

ENTRING
BUT WITH SWIFT WHEELE REVERSE, DEEP ENTRING SHAR'D 6 326
ENTRING ON STUDIOUS THOUGHTS ABSTRUSE, WHICH EVE 8 40
LEAST ENTRING ON THE CANAANITE ALLARMD 12 217

ENTWIN'D
BUT FURTHER WAY FOUND NONE, SO THICK ENTWIN'D, 4 174

ENTWINING
HIS ARMES CLUNG TO HIS RIBS, HIS LEGGS ENTWINING 10 512

ENUR'D
THIR NOXIOUS VAPOUR, OR ENUR'D NOT FEEL, 2 216
AND PIOUS SORROW, EQUALLY ENUR'D 11 362

ENURE
FOR STATE, AS SOVRAN KING, AND TO ENURE 8 239

ENVENOM'D
WITH CONQUEST, FELT TH' ENVENOM'D ROBE, AND TORE 2 543

ENVIE
THRICE CHANG'D WITH PALE, IRE, ENVIE AND DESPAIR, 4 115
FOR ENVIE, YET WITH JEALOUS LEER MALIGNE 4 503
ENVIE THEM THAT? CAN IT BE SIN TO KNOW, 4 517
OR ENVIE, OR WHAT RESERVE FORBIDS TO TASTE? 5 61
WITH ENVIE AGAINST THE SON OF GOD, THAT DAY 5 662
TOOK ENVIE, AND ASPIRING TO HIS HIGHTH, 6 793
PROVOKES MY ENVIE, THIS NEW FAVORITE 9 175
ENJOY'D BY US EXCITES HIS ENVIE MORE; 9 264
OF GUILE, OF HATE, OF ENVIE, OF REVENGE; 9 466
OR IS IT ENVIE, AND CAN ENVIE DWELL 9 729
THOUGH OTHERS ENVIE WHAT THEY CANNOT GIVE; 9 805
FOR ENVIE THAT HIS BROTHERS OFFERING FOUND 11 456

ENVIED
OUR ENVIED SOVRAN, AND HIS ALTAR BREATHES 2 244
YET ENVIED; AGAINST MEE IS ALL THIR RAGE, 6 813

ENVIER
TO SET THE ENVIER OF HIS STATE, THE PROUD 6 89

ENVIES
WITH SATAN, HEE WHO ENVIES NOW THY STATE, 6 900
HATH TASTED, ENVIES NOT, BUT BRINGS WITH JOY 9 770

ENVIEST
OF ALL THY GIFTS, NOR ENVIEST. I NOW SEE 8 494

ENVIOUS
ENVIOUS COMMANDS, INVENTED WITH DESIGNE 4 524
AT LEAST OUR ENVIOUS FOE HATH FAIL'D, WHO THOUGHT 7 139
FLEW UP, NOR MISSD THE WAY, BY ENVIOUS WINDES 11 15

ENVIRON'D
ENVIRON'D WINS HIS WAY; HARDER BESET 2 1016

ENVY
STIRD UP WITH ENVY AND REVENGE, DECEIV'D 1 35
HERE FOR HIS ENVY, WILL NOT DRIVE US HENCE: 1 260
ENVY FROM EACH INFERIOR; BUT WHO HERE 2 26
WILL ENVY WHOM THE HIGHEST PLACE EXPOSES 2 27
THE SPIRIT MALIGNE, BUT MUCH MORE ENVY SEIS'D 3 553

ENVYING
ENVYING OUR HAPPINESS, AND OF HIS OWN 9 254
LONGING AND ENVYING STOOD, BUT COULD NOT REACH. 9 593

EPICYCLE
CYCLE AND EPICYCLE, ORB IN ORB: 8 84

EPIDAURUS
IN EPIDAURUS; NOR TO WHICH TRANSFORMD 9 507

EPILEPSIES
CONVULSIONS, EPILEPSIES, FIERCE CATARRHS, 11 483

EQUAL
UNITED THOUGHTS AND COUNSELS, EQUAL HOPE 1 88
IN EQUAL RUIN: INTO WHAT PIT THOU SEEST 1 91
HIS SPEAR, TO EQUAL WHICH THE TALLEST PINE 1 292
SHOULD FAVOUR EQUAL TO THE SONS OF HEAVEN; 1 654
EQUAL IN STRENGTH, AND RATHER THEN BE LESS 2 47
BLACK FIRE AND HORROR SHOT WITH EQUAL RAGE 2 67
OUR STRENGTH IS EQUAL, NOR THE LAW UNJUST 2 200
EXTOLL HIM EQUAL TO THE HIGHEST IN HEAV'N: 2 479

EQUAL (CONTINUED)
EQUAL TO GOD, AND EQUALLY ENJOYING 3 306
NOT EQUAL, AS THIR SEX NOT EQUAL SEEMD; 4 296
EQUAL WITH GODS; ASPIRING TO BE SUCH, 4 526
CAN EQUAL ANGER INFINITE PROVOK'T. 4 916
EQUAL TO OURS, THROUGHOUT THE SPACIOUS NORTH; 5 726
BY NONE, AND IF NOT EQUAL ALL, YET FREE, 5 791
IN FREEDOME EQUAL? OR CAN INTRODUCE 5 797
AND EQUAL OVER EQUALS TO LET REIGNE, 5 820
THAT EQUAL OVER EQUALS MONARCH REIGNE: 5 832
EQUAL TO HIM BEGOTTEN SON, BY WHOM 5 835
WHO IS OUR EQUAL: THEN THOU SHALT BEHOLD 5 866
EQUAL IN NUMBER TO THAT GODLESS CREW 6 49
NO EQUAL, RAUNGING THROUGH THE DIRE ATTACK 6 248
HIS CONFIDENCE TO EQUAL GOD IN POWER, 6 343
OR EQUAL WHAT BETWEEN US MADE THE ODDS, 6 441
EQUAL IN THEIR CREATION THEY WERE FORM'D, 6 690
EQUAL HAVE I TO RENDER THEE, DIVINE 8 6
ON MAN HIS EQUAL LOVE: SAY THEREFORE ON; 8 228
SECOND TO ME OR LIKE, EQUAL MUCH LESS. 8 407
THY EQUAL FEAR THAT MY FIRM FAITH AND LOVE 9 286
AND RENDER ME MORE EQUAL, AND PERHAPS, 9 823
THOU THEREFORE ALSO TASTE, THAT EQUAL LOT 9 881
MAY JOYNE US, EQUAL JOY, AS EQUAL LOVE; 9 882
SUPERIOR, OR BUT EQUAL, THAT TO HER 10 147
BE WANTING, BUT AFFORD THEE EQUAL AID, 10 271
EQUAL IN DAYS AND NIGHTS, EXCEPT TO THOSE 10 680
AND EQUAL TO REDUCE ME TO MY DUST, 10 748

EQUAL'D
HE TRUSTED TO HAVE EQUAL'D THE MOST HIGH, 1 40
FROM EGYPT MARCHING, EQUAL'D WITH ONE STROKE 1 488
EQUAL'D IN ALL THIR GLORIES, TO INSHRINE 1 719
THOSE OTHER TWO EQUAL'D WITH ME IN FATE, 3 33
SO WERE I EQUAL'D WITH THEM IN RENOWN, 3 34

EQUALD
WHOM REASON HATH EQUALD, FORCE HATH MADE SUPREAM 1 248

EQUALITIE
PATTERN OF JUST EQUALITIE PERHAPS 7 487
WITH FAIR EQUALITIE, FRATERNAL STATE, 12 26

EQUALITY
AFFECTING ALL EQUALITY WITH GOD, 5 763

EQUALLY
EQUAL TO GOD, AND EQUALLY ENJOYING 3 306
BUT HEAV'NS FREE LOVE DEALT EQUALLY TO ALL? 4 68
AFFECTS ME EQUALLY; NOR CAN I LIKE 5 97
EQUALLY FREE; FOR ORDERS AND DEGREES 5 792
AND PIOUS SORROW, EQUALLY ENUR'D 11 362

EQUALS
ABOVE HIS EQUALS. FAREWEL HAPPY FIELDS 1 249
HIS EQUALS, IF IN POWER AND SPLENDOR LESS, 5 796
AND EQUAL OVER EQUALS TO LET REIGNE, 5 820
THAT EQUAL OVER EQUALS MONARCH REIGNE: 5 832

EQUINOCTIAL
WITH DARKNESS, THRICE THE EQUINOCTIAL LINE 9 64
WAS BID TURN REINES FROM TH' EQUINOCTIAL RODE 10 672

EQUIPAGE
CELESTIAL EQUIPAGE; AND NOW CAME FORTH 7 203

EQUIVALENT
EQUIVALENT OR SECOND, WHICH COMPEL'D 9 609

ERCOCO
ERCOCO AND THE LESS MARITIM KINGS 11 398

E'RE
WE CAN CREATE, AND IN WHAT PLACE SO E'RE 2 260
EASIE, E'RE GOD HAD BID THE GROUND BE DRIE, 7 304

ERE
ROUSE AND BESTIR THEMSELVES ERE WELL AWAKE. 1 334
THERE WENT A FAME IN HEAV'N THAT HE ERE LONG 1 651
OVER THE VAST ABRUPT, ERE HE ARRIVE 2 409
SHOULD BE, AND, BY CONCURRING SIGNS, ERE NOW 2 831
ERE HE DREW NIGH, HIS RADIANT VISAGE TURND, 3 646
THE TEMPTER ERE TH' ACCUSER OF MAN-KIND, 4 10
AS MAN ERE LONG, AND THIS NEW WORLD SHALL KNOW. 4 113
TO MORROW ERE FRESH MORNING STREAK THE EAST 4 623
PROUD LIMITARIE CHERUBE, BUT ERE THEN 4 971
EACH IN THIR CHRYSTAL SLUCE, HEE ERE THEY FELL 5 133
TELL THEM THAT BY COMMAND, ERE YET DIM NIGHT 5 685
THAT THE MOST HIGH COMMANDING, NOW ERE NIGHT, 5 699
NOW ERE DIM NIGHT HAD DISINCUMBERD HEAV'N, 5 700
AND FLY, ERE EVIL INTERCEPT THY FLIGHT. 5 871
ON THE ROUGH EDGE OF BATTEL ERE IT JOYN'D, 6 108
ERE THIS AVENGING SWORD BEGIN THY DOOME, 6 278
AND ALL HIS ARMOUR STAIND ERE WHILE SO BRIGHT. 6 334
NOR LONG SHALL BE OUR LABOUR, YET ERE DAWNE, 6 492
SO ALL ERE DAY-SPRING, UNDER CONSCIOUS NIGHT 6 521
ERE WHILE THEY FIERCE WERE COMING, AND WHEN WEE, 6 610
LONG STRUGLING UNDERNEATH, ERE THEY COULD WIND 6 659

ERE (CONTINUED)		
END, AND DISMISS THEE ERE THE MORNING SHINE.	7	108
WHERE GOD RESIDES, AND ERE MID-DAY ARRIV'D	8	112
ERE MY REMEMBRANCE: NOW HEAR MEE RELATE	8	204
BUT LONG ERE OUR APPROACHING HEARD WITHIN	8	242
ERE SABBATH EEV'NING: SO WE HAD IN CHARGE.	8	246
AND BE SO MINDED STILL; I, ERE THOU SPAK'ST,	8	444
BITTER ERE LONG BACK ON IT SELF RECOILES;	9	172
AS WE NEED WALK, TILL YOUNGER HANDS ERE LONG	9	246
SATED AT LENGTH, ERE LONG I MIGHT PERCEAVE	9	598
MOTION, EACH ACT WON AUDIENCE ERE THE TONGUE,	9	674
MADE COMMON AND UNHALLOWD ERE OUR TASTE;	9	931
FORBEARANCE NO ACQUITTANCE ERE DAY END.	10	53
MEANWHILE ERE THUS WAS SIN'D AND JUDG'D ON EARTH,	10	229
ERE THIS HE HAD RETURN'D, WITH FURY DRIV'N	10	240
AND OPS, ERE YET DICTAEAN JOVE WAS BORN.	10	584
THROUGH THE STILL NIGHT, NOT NOW, AS ERE MAN FELL,	10	846
IT LIES, YET ERE CONCEPTION TO PREVENT	10	987
OUR LIMBS BENUMM'D, ERE THIS DIURNAL STARR	10	1069
OF PARADISE COULD HAVE PRODUC'T, ERE FALL'N	11	29
DARKNESS ERE DAYES MID-COURSE, AND MORNING LIGHT	11	204
ERE THOU FROM HENCE DEPART, KNOW I AM SENT	11	356
ABORTIVE, TO TORMENT ME ERE THIR BEING,	11	769
COMES DOWN TO SEE THIR CITIE, ERE THE TOWER	12	51
SHALL LONG USURP; ERE THE THIRD DAWNING LIGHT	12	421
EREBUS		
OF EREBUS. SHE OP'ND, BUT TO SHUT	2	883
ERECT		
ERECT THE STANDARD THERE OF ANCIENT NIGHT;	2	986
TWO OF FAR NOBLER SHAPE ERECT AND TALL,	4	288
GODLIKE ERECT, WITH NATIVE HONOUR CLAD	4	289
IS RISING, WHO INTENDS TO ERECT HIS THRONE	5	725
BUT WHAT IF BETTER COUNSELS MIGHT ERECT	5	785
WITH SANCTITIE OF REASON, MIGHT ERECT	7	508
I BY CONVERSING CANNOT THESE ERECT	8	432
BUT BID HER WELL BEWARE, AND STILL ERECT,	9	353
WITH BURNISHT NECK OF VERDANT GOLD, ERECT	9	501
SO GOODLY AND ERECT, THOUGH FAULTIE SINCE,	11	509
ERECTED		
MAMMON, THE LEAST ERECTED SPIRIT THAT FELL	1	679
ERELONG		
(ERELONG TO SWIM AT LARGE) AND LAUGH; FOR WHICH	11	626
THE WORLD ERELONG A WORLD OF TEARS MUST WEEPE.	11	627
EREMITS		
EMBRYO'S AND IDIOTS, EREMITS AND FRIERS	3	474
EREWHILE		
AS WE EREWHILE, ASTOUNDED AND AMAZ'D,	1	281
WHERE OBVIOUS DUTIE EREWHILE APPEAR'D UNSAUGHT:	10	106
ERR		
ERR NOT) ANOTHER WORLD, THE HAPPY SEAT	2	347
HOW FEW SOMTIMES MAY KNOW, WHEN THOUSANDS ERR.	6	148
ERRAND		
THIS UNCOUTH ERRAND SOLE, AND ONE FOR ALL	2	827
THE BARRS OF HELL, ON ERRAND BAD NO DOUBT:	4	795
ON HIS BAD ERRAND, MAN SHOULD BE SEDUC'T	10	41
ERRANDS		
OR DO HIS ERRANDS IN THE GLOOMY DEEP;	1	152
BEAR HIS SWIFT ERRANDS OVER MOIST AND DRY,	3	652
ON ERRANDS OF SUPERNAL GRACE. SO SUNG	7	573
ERR'D		
I ALSO ERR'D IN OVERMUCH ADMIRING	9	1178
HE ERR'D NOT, FOR BY THIS THE HEAV'NLY BANDS	11	208
ERRE		
ERRE NOT, MUCH LESS FOR THIS TO BE OUR LORD,	5	799
TO CHASE ME HENCE? ERRE NOT THAT SO SHALL END	6	288
IF IT PRESUME, MIGHT ERRE IN THINGS TOO HIGH,	8	121
MADE ERRE, WAS NOW EXHAL'D, AND GROSSER SLEEP	9	1049
LEADS THEE, I SHALL NOT LAG BEHINDE, NOR ERRE	10	266
ERRING		
ERRING; FOR HE WITH THIS REBELLIOUS ROUT	1	747
OF ERRING, FROM THE PATH OF TRUTH REMOTE:	6	173
ERRONEOUS		
SEEMD IN THY WORLD ERRONEOUS TO DISSENT	6	146
ERRONEOUS THERE TO WANDER AND FORLORNE.	7	20
FOUND SO ERRONEOUS, THENCE BY JUST EVENT	10	969
ERROR		
WITH MAZIE ERROR UNDER PENDANT SHADES	4	239
ERROUR		
WITH SERPENT ERROUR WANDRING, FOUND THIR WAY,	7	302
THAT ERROUR NOW, WHICH IS BECOME MY CRIME,	9	1181
ERRST		
APOSTAT, STILL THOU ERRST, NOR END WILT FIND	6	172

ERST		
(CERTAIN TO BE REFUS'D) WHAT ERST THEY FEARD;	2	470
FROM MEE RETURND, AS ERST THOU SAIDST, FROM FLIGHT,	6	187
WHERE ERST WAS THICKEST FIGHT, TH' ANGELIC THRONG,	6	308
O FOUL DESCENT. THAT I WHO ERST CONTENDED	9	163
DIMM ERST, DILATED SPIRITS, AMPLER HEART,	9	876
WHEREAT THE HEART OF ADAM ERST SO SAD	11	868
ERUPTION		
OUR FIRST ERUPTION, THITHER OR ELSEWHERE:	1	656
LEAST HEE INCENST AT SUCH ERUPTION BOLD,	8	235
ERWHILE		
ERWHILE PERPLEXT WITH THOUGHTS WHAT WOULD BECOM	12	275
ESAU		
OF GUARDIANS BRIGHT, WHEN HE FROM ESAU FLED	3	512
ESCAP'D		
HITHERWARD BENT (WHO COULD HAVE THOUGHT?) ESCAP'D	4	794
COM'ST THOU, ESCAP'D THY PRISON, AND TRANSFORM'D,	4	824
ESCAPE		
THEN UNKNOWN DANGERS AND AS HARD ESCAPE.	2	444
HEE FLED, NOT HOPING TO ESCAPE, BUT SHUN	10	339
ESCAP'T		
ESCAP'T THE STYGIAN POOL, THOUGH LONG DETAIN'D	3	14
AS ONE HE STOOD ESCAP'T FROM CRUEL FIGHT,	6	448
MAN IS NOT WHOM TO WARNE: THOSE FEW ESCAP'T	11	777
ESPI'D		
TILL I ESPI'D THEE, FAIR INDEED AND TALL,	4	477
ESPOUS'D		
MY FAIREST, MY ESPOUS'D, MY LATEST FOUND,	5	18
ESPOUSED		
ESPOUSED EVE DECKT FIRST HER NUPTIAL BED,	4	710
ESSENCE		
AND UNCOMPOUNDED IS THIR ESSENCE PURE,	1	425
OUR PURER ESSENCE THEN WILL OVERCOME	2	215
BRIGHT EFFLUENCE OF BRIGHT ESSENCE INCREATE.	3	6
THIS ESSENCE TO INCARNATE AND IMBRUTE,	9	166
ESSENCES		
AS FAR AS GODS AND HEAV'NLY ESSENCES	1	138
ESSENTIAL		
TO NOTHING THIS ESSENTIAL, HAPPIER FARR	2	97
ESSENTIAL POWERS, NOR BY HIS REIGN OBSCUR'D,	5	841
ESTABLISHT		
ESTABLISHT IN A SAFE UNENVIED THRONE	2	23
ESTABLISHT, SUCH DELIGHT HATH GOD IN MEN	12	245
ESTATE		
IN MEAN ESTATE LIVE MODERATE, TILL GROWN	12	351
ESTEEM		
GABRIEL, THOU HADST IN HEAV'N TH' ESTEEM OF WISE,	4	886
THEN SELF ESTEEM, GROUNDED ON JUST AND RIGHT	8	572
TEMPTING AFFRONTS US WITH HIS FOUL ESTEEM	9	328
ESTEEME		
OF OUR INTEGRITIE: HIS FOUL ESTEEME	9	329
ESTOTILAND		
FROM COLD ESTOTILAND, AND SOUTH AS FARR	10	686
ESTRANG'D		
ADAM, ESTRANG'D IN LOOK AND ALTERD STILE,	9	1132
ETERNAL		
I MAY ASSERT ETERNAL PROVIDENCE,	1	25
SUCH PLACE ETERNAL JUSTICE HAD PREPAR'D	1	70
TO WAGE BY FORCE OR GUILE ETERNAL WARR	1	121
STRENGTH UNDIMINISHT, OR ETERNAL BEING	1	154
TO UNDERGO ETERNAL PUNISHMENT?	1	155
ETERNAL SPIRITS; OR HAVE YE CHOS'N THIS PLACE	1	318
OF HEAV'N, AND FROM ETERNAL SPLENDORS FLUNG	1	610
HIS TRUST WAS WITH TH' ETERNAL TO BE DEEM'D	2	46
THEN MISERABLE TO HAVE ETERNAL BEING:	2	98
RESERV'D AND DESTIN'D TO ETERNAL WOE;	2	161
TO WASTE ETERNAL DAIES IN WOE AND PAIN?	2	695
ETERNAL ANARCHIE, AMIDST THE NOISE	2	896
OR OF TH' ETERNAL COETERNAL BEAM	3	2
I SUNG OF CHAOS AND ETERNAL NIGHT,	3	18
UNCHANGEABLE, ETERNAL, WHICH ORDAIN'D	3	127
AS MY ETERNAL PURPOSE HATH DECREED;	3	172
TH' ETERNAL REGIONS: LOWLY REVERENT	3	349
ETERNAL KING; THEE AUTHOR OF ALL BEING,	3	374
TO ME ALIKE, IT DEALS ETERNAL WOE.	4	70
LED ON TH' ETERNAL SPRING. NOT THAT FAIRE FIELD	4	268
TH' ETERNAL TO PREVENT SUCH HORRID FRAY	4	996
IN THY ETERNAL COURSE, BOTH WHEN THOU CLIMBST,	5	173
SO SPAKE TH' ETERNAL FATHER, AND FULFILLD	5	246

ETERNAL (CONTINUED)
MEAN WHILE TH' ETERNAL EYE, WHOSE SIGHT DISCERNES 5 711
HYMNING TH' ETERNAL FATHER: BUT THE SHOUT 6 96
HAD NOT TH' ETERNAL KING OMNIPOTENT 6 227
OF VICTORIE; DEEDS OF ETERNAL FAME 6 240
THEREFORE ETERNAL SILENCE BE THIR DOOME. 6 385
(AND IF ONE DAY, WHY NOT ETERNAL DAYES?) 6 424
ALL DOUBT OF VICTORIE, ETERNAL MIGHT 6 630
DOWN FROM THE VERGE OF HEAV'N, ETERNAL WRAUTH 6 865
HIS PUNISHMENT, ETERNAL MISERIE; 6 904
THOU WITH ETERNAL WISDOM DIDST CONVERSE, 7 9
OF HIS ETERNAL EMPIRE, BUT THE MORE 7 96
ETERNAL FATHER FROM HIS THRONE BEHELD 7 137
IN GODS ETERNAL STORE, TO CIRCUMSCRIBE 7 226
ETERNAL FATHER (FOR WHERE IS NOT HEE 7 517
TO GODS ETERNAL HOUSE DIRECT THE WAY, 7 576
THE HIGHTH AND DEPTH OF THY ETERNAL WAYES 8 413
ETERNAL FATHER FROM HIS SECRET CLOUD, 10 32
FATHER ETERNAL, THINE IS TO DECREE, 10 68
TO MEE, WHO WITH ETERNAL FAMIN PINE, 10 597
AM FOUND ETERNAL, AND INCORPORATE BOTH, 10 816
SAFE TO ETERNAL PARADISE OF REST. 12 314
TO BRING FORTH FRUITS JOY AND ETERNAL BLISS. 12 551

ETERNITIE
DWELT FROM ETERNITIE, DWELT THEN IN THEE, 3 5
(FOR TIME, THOUGH IN ETERNITIE, APPLI'D 5 580
THROUGH ALL ETERNITIE SO LATE TO BUILD 7 92
FROM ALL ETERNITIE, FOR NONE I KNOW 8 406
ETERNITIE, WHOSE END NO EYE CAN REACH. 12 556

ETERNITY
THOSE THOUGHTS THAT WANDER THROUGH ETERNITY, 2 148
ETERNITY SO SPENT IN WORSHIP PAID 2 248

ETERNIZE
ETERNIZE HERE ON EARTH; BUT THOSE ELECT 6 374
THIS OTHER SERV'D BUT TO ETERNIZE WOE; 11 60

ETHEREAL
HURLD HEADLONG FLAMING FROM TH' ETHEREAL SKIE 1 45
ETHEREAL TEMPER, MASSY, LARGE AND ROUND, 1 285
SIT UNPOLLUTED, AND TH' ETHEREAL MOULD 2 139
ETHEREAL VERTUES; OR THESE TITLES NOW 2 311
THIR SOFT ETHEREAL WARMTH, AND THERE TO PINE 2 601
FROM YOUR DOMINION WON, TH' ETHEREAL KING 2 978
OR HEAR'ST THOU RATHER PURE ETHEREAL STREAM, 3 7
SUCH I CREATED ALL TH' ETHEREAL POWERS 3 100
AND THIS ETHEREAL QUINTESSENCE OF HEAV'N 3 716
HE SPEEDS, AND THROUGH THE VAST ETHEREAL SKIE 5 267
ETHEREAL, AND AS LOWEST FIRST THE MOON; 5 418
ETHEREAL, AS WEE, OR MAY AT CHOICE 5 499
OF THIS OUR NATIVE HEAV'N, ETHEREAL SONS. 5 863
ETHEREAL TRUMPET FROM ON HIGH GAN BLOW: 6 60
PASS'D THROUGH HIM, BUT TH' ETHEREAL SUBSTANCE CLOS'D 6 330
ETHEREAL, FIRST OF THINGS, QUINTESSENCE PURE 7 244
THOUGH OF ETHEREAL MOULD: THEN FORM'D THE MOON 7 356
GO HEAVENLY GUEST, ETHEREAL MESSENGER, 8 646
TH' ETHEREAL PEOPLE RAN, TO HEAR AND KNOW 10 27
THOU KNEWST BY NAME, AND ALL TH' ETHEREAL POWERS, 12 577

ETHEREOUS
OF THIS ETHEREOUS MOULD WHEREON WE STAND, 6 473

ETHIOP
TRUE PARADISE UNDER THE ETHIOP LINE 4 282

ETHIOPIAN
THROUGH THE WIDE ETHIOPIAN TO THE CAPE 2 641

ETRURIAN
IN VALLOMBROSA, WHERE TH' ETRURIAN SHADES 1 303

EUBOIC
INTO TH' EUBOIC SEA. OTHERS MORE MILDE, 2 546

EUPHRASIE
HAD BRED; THEN PURG'D WITH EUPHRASIE AND RUE 11 414

EUPHRATES
OF OLD EUPHRATES TO THE BROOK THAT PARTS 1 420
HIM ON THIS SIDE EUPHRATES YET RESIDING, 12 114

EUROPE
BRIDGING HIS WAY, EUROPE WITH ASIA JOYN'D, 10 310
ON EUROPE THENCE, AND WHERE ROME WAS TO SWAY 11 405

EURUS
EURUS AND ZEPHIR WITH THIR LATERAL NOISE, 10 705

EURYNOME
OPHION WITH EURYNOME, THE WIDE- 10 581

EVADE
OF MISERIE, SO THINKING TO EVADE 10 1021

EVADED
HAVE EASILY AS SPIRITS EVADED SWIFT 6 596

EVANGELIZE
TO EVANGELIZE THE NATIONS, THEN ON ALL 12 499

EVASION
SUFFICE, OR WHAT EVASION BEAR HIM SAFE 2 411

EVASIONS
FORC'T I ABSOLVE: ALL MY EVASIONS VAIN, 10 829

EVE
NOR HAD THEY YET AMONG THE SONS OF EVE 1 364
TO NOON HE FELL, FROM NOON TO DEWY EVE, 1 743
HIS SONS, THE FAIREST OF HER DAUGHTERS EVE. 4 324
TO FIRST OF WOMEN EVE THUS MOVING SPEECH, 4 409
TO WHOM THUS EVE REPLI'D. O THOU FOR WHOM 4 440
THOU FOLLOWING CRYD'ST ALOUD, RETURN FAIRE EVE; 4 481
WHEN ADAM THUS TO EVE: FAIR CONSORT, TH' HOUR 4 610
TO WHOM THUS EVE WITH PERFET BEAUTY ADORND. 4 634
DAUGHTER OF GOD AND MAN, ACCOMPLISHT EVE, 4 660
ESPOUSED EVE DECKT FIRST HER NUPTIAL BED, 4 710
ADAM FROM HIS FAIR SPOUSE, NOR EVE THE RITES 4 742
SQUAT LIKE A TOAD, CLOSE AT THE EARE OF EVE; 4 800
HIS WONDER WAS TO FIND UNWAK'ND EVE 5 9
WHY SLEEPST THOU EVE? NOW IS THE PLEASANT TIME, 5 38
HERE, HAPPIE CREATURE, FAIR ANGELIC EVE, 5 74
TO FIND THIS BUT A DREAM. THUS EVE HER NIGHT 5 93
AND EVE WITHIN, DUE AT HER HOUR PREPAR'D 5 303
HASTE HITHER EVE, AND WORTH THY SIGHT BEHOLD 5 308
TO WHOM THUS EVE. ADAM, EARTHS HALLOWD MOULD, 5 321
WITH FLOURETS DECK'T AND FRAGRANT SMELLS; BUT EVE 5 379
LONG AFTER TO BLEST MARIE, SECOND EVE. 5 387
AS FROM THE MINE. MEAN WHILE AT TABLE EVE 5 443
THOUGH WANDRING. HE WITH HIS CONSORTED EVE 7 50
ENTRING ON STUDIOUS THOUGHTS ABSTRUSE, WHICH EVE 8 40
AND THY FAIRE EVE; HEAV'N IS FOR THEE TOO HIGH 8 172
AND EVE FIRST TO HER HUSBAND THUS BEGAN. 9 204
SOLE EVE, ASSOCIATE SOLE, TO ME BEYOND 9 227
TO WHOM THE VIRGIN MAJESTIE OF EVE, 9 270
DAUGHTER OF GOD AND MAN, IMMORTAL EVE, 9 291
AND MATRIMONIAL LOVE; BUT EVE, WHO THOUGHT 9 319
SO SPAKE THE PATRIARCH OF MANKINDE, BUT EVE 9 376
O MUCH DECEAV'D, MUCH FAILING, HAPLESS EVE, 9 404
EVE SEPARATE, HE WISH'D, BUT NOT WITH HOPE 9 422
BEYOND HIS HOPE, EVE SEPARATE HE SPIES, 9 424
IMBORDERD ON EACH BANK, THE HAND OF EVE: 9 438
THIS FLOURIE PLAT, THE SWEET RECESS OF EVE 9 456
IN SERPENT, INMATE BAD, AND TOWARD EVE 9 495
CURLD MANY A WANTON WREATH IN SIGHT OF EVE, 9 517
THE EYE OF EVE TO MARK HIS PLAY; HE GLAD 9 528
INTO THE HEART OF EVE HIS WORDS MADE WAY, 9 550
EMPRESS OF THIS FAIR WORLD, RESPLENDENT EVE, 9 568
SO TALK'D THE SPIRITED SLY SNAKE; AND EVE 9 613
LEAD THEN, SAID EVE. HEE LEADING SWIFTLY ROWLD 9 631
LED EVE OUR CREDULOUS MOTHER, TO THE TREE 9 644
TO WHOM THUS EVE YET SINLESS. OF THE FRUIT 9 659
THE GUILTIE SERPENT, AND WELL MIGHT, FOR EVE 9 785
AND ADAM WEDDED TO ANOTHER EVE, 9 828
THUS EVE WITH COUNTNANCE BLITHE HER STORIE TOLD; 9 886
THE FATAL TRESPASS DON BY EVE, AMAZ'D, 9 889
FROM HIS SLACK HAND THE GARLAND WREATH'D FOR EVE 9 892
SHOULD GOD CREATE ANOTHER EVE, AND I 9 911
THUS IN CALM MOOD HIS WORDS TO EVE HE TURND. 9 920
BOLD DEED THOU HAST PRESUM'D, ADVENTROUS EVE, 9 921
SO ADAM, AND THUS EVE TO HIM REPLI'D. 9 960
EATING HIS FILL, NOR EVE TO ITERATE 9 1005
CARNAL DESIRE ENFLAMING, HEE ON EVE 9 1013
TILL ADAM THUS 'GAN EVE TO DALLIANCE MOVE, 9 1016
EVE, NOW I SEE THOU ART EXACT OF TASTE, 9 1017
OF EVE, WHOSE EYE DARTED CONTAGIOUS FIRE. 9 1036
TILL ADAM, THOUGH NOT LESS THEN EVE ABASH'T, 9 1065
O EVE, IN EVIL HOUR THOU DIDST GIVE EARE 9 1067
SPEECH INTERMITTED THUS TO EVE RENEWD. 9 1133
TO WHOM SOON MOV'D WITH TOUCH OF BLAME THUS EVE. 9 1143
OF MINE TO THEE, INGRATEFUL EVE, EXPREST 9 1164
HEE IN THE SERPENT, HAD PERVERTED EVE, 10 3
HE CAME, AND WITH HIM EVE, MORE LOTH, THOUGH FIRST 10 109
SO HAVING SAID, HE THUS TO EVE IN FEW: 10 157
TO WHOM SAD EVE WITH SHAME NIGH OVERWHELM'D, 10 159
WHEN JESUS SON OF MARY SECOND EVE, 10 183
HEE AFTER EVE SEDUC'T, UNMINDED SLUNK 10 332
BY EVE, THOUGH ALL UNWEETING, SECONDED 10 335
WHICH GREW IN PARADISE, THE BAIT OF EVE 10 551
ENCROACHING EVE PERHAPS, HAD FIRST THE RULE 10 582
WHOM THUS AFFLICTED WHEN SAD EVE BEHELD, 10 863
HE ADDED NOT, AND FROM HER TURN'D, BUT EVE 10 909
TO WHOM THUS EVE, RECOVERING HEART, REPLI'D. 10 966
LABOURING HAD RAIS'D, AND THUS TO EVE REPLI'D. 10 1012
EVE, THY CONTEMPT OF LIFE AND PLEASURE SEEMS 10 1013
SO SPAKE OUR FATHER PENITENT, NOR EVE 10 1097
THE EARTH, WHEN ADAM AND FIRST MATRON EVE 11 136
WHICH THUS TO EVE HIS WELCOME WORDS RENEWD. 11 140
EVE, EASILY MAY FAITH ADMIT, THAT ALL 11 141
EVE RIGHTLY CALL'D, MOTHER OF ALL MANKIND, 11 159
TO WHOM THUS EVE WITH SAD DEMEANOUR MEEK. 11 162
SO SPAKE, SO WISH'D MUCH-HUMBL'D EVE, BUT FATE 11 181

EVE (CONTINUED)
PURSUING, NOT UNMOV'D TO EVE THUS SPAKE. 11 192
O EVE, SOME FURDER CHANGE AWAITS US NIGH, 11 193
NOT UNPERCEAV'D OF ADAM, WHO TO EVE, 11 224
EVE, NOW EXPECT GREAT TIDINGS, WHICH PERHAPS 11 226
THAT ALL HIS SENSES BOUND; EVE, WHO UNSEEN 11 265
LAMENT NOT EVE, BUT PATIENTLY RESIGNE 11 287
THIS HILL; LET EVE (FOR I HAVE DRENCHT HER EYES) 11 367
WHAT MISERIE TH' INABSTINENCE OF EVE 11 476
INDUCTIVE MAINLY TO THE SIN OF EVE. 11 519
WE MAY NO LONGER STAY: GO, WAKEN EVE; 12 594
DESCENDED, ADAM TO THE BOWRE WHERE EVE 12 607
SO SPAKE OUR MOTHER EVE, AND ADAM HEARD 12 624

EVEN
THIR COURSE, IN EVEN BALLANCE DOWN THEY LIGHT 1 349
EVEN TO THAT HILL OF SCANDAL, BY THE GROVE 1 416
ON EVEN GROUND AGAINST HIS MORTAL FOE, 3 179
SHOOTS INVISIBLE VERTUE EVEN TO THE DEEP: 3 586
EVEN TO MY MOUTH OF THAT SAME FRUIT HELD PART 5 83
IN HUMID EXHALATIONS, AND AT EVEN 5 425
EVEN SHAME, THE LAST OF EVILS; OF THE FIRST 9 1079

EVENING
THEN IN FAIR EVENING CLOUD, OR HUMID BOW, 4 151
OF HEAV'N THE STARRS THAT USHER EVENING ROSE: 4 355
JUST THEN RETURND AT SHUT OF EVENING FLOURS. 9 278
AND BROWN AS EVENING: COVER ME YE PINES, 9 1088

EVENT
SINCE THROUGH EXPERIENCE OF THIS GREAT EVENT 1 118
TOO WELL I SEE AND RUE THE DIRE EVENT, 1 134
WAS NOT INGLORIOUS, THOUGH TH' EVENT WAS DIRE, 1 624
TH' EVENT IS FEAR'D; SHOULD WE AGAIN PROVOKE 2 82
IN SAD EVENT, WHEN TO THE UNWISER SON 4 716
GIV'N ME TO QUELL THIR PRIDE, AND IN EVENT 5 740
FAVOUR FROM HEAV'N, OUR WITNESS FROM TH' EVENT. 9 334
OF THY PRESUM'D RETURN, EVENT PERVERSE. 9 405
FARR OTHERWISE TH' EVENT, NOT DEATH, BUT LIFE 9 984
FOUND SO ERRONEOUS, THENCE BY JUST EVENT 10 969
SUCH HAPPY INTERVIEW AND FAIR EVENT 11 593

EVENTS
IN COUNTERPOISE, NOW PONDERS ALL EVENTS, 4 1001

EVER
BUT EVER TO DO ILL OUR SOLE DELIGHT, 1 160
CHAIN'D ON THE BURNING LAKE, NOR EVER THENCE 1 210
HE LIGHTS, IF IT WERE LAND THAT EVER BURN'D 1 228
AS STOOD LIKE THESE, COULD EVER KNOW REPULSE? 1 630
CAN GIVE IT, OR WILL EVER? HOW HE CAN 2 153
YET EVER PLOTTING HOW THE CONQUEROR LEAST 2 338
I KNOW THEE NOT, NOR EVER SAW TILL NOW 2 744
CONFUS'DLY, AND WHICH THUS MUST EVER FIGHT, 2 914
ENCOMPASS'D SHALL RESOUND THEE EVER BLEST. 3 149
HARPS EVER TUN'D, THAT GLITTERING BY THIR SIDE 3 366
ARE EVER CLEER. WHEREOF HEE SOON AWARE, 4 119
THAT EVER SINCE IN LOVES IMBRACES MET, 4 322
BUT LET US EVER PRAISE HIM, AND EXTOLL 4 436
HEAV'NS LAST BEST GIFT, MY EVER NEW DELIGHT, 5 19
(WHOSE PRAISE BE EVER SUNG) TO MAN IN PART 5 405
DESERVING PARADISE. IF EVER, THEN, 5 446
WORDS WHICH NO EARE EVER TO HEAR IN HEAV'N 5 810
IN HEAV'N GOD EVER BLEST, AND HIS DIVINE 6 184
HER EVER DURING GATES, HARMONIOUS SOUND 7 206
THY CONDESCENSION, AND SHALL BE HONOUR'D EVER 8 649
THEN EVER, BOUNTIE OF THIS VERTUOUS TREE. 9 1033
MAYST EVER REST WELL PLEAS'D. I GO TO JUDGE 10 71
AS IN HIS PRESENCE, EVER TO OBSERVE 12 563
ACKNOWLEDGE MY REDEEMER EVER BLEST. 12 573

EVER-BURNING
WITH EVER-BURNING SULPHUR UNCONSUM'D: 1 69

EVER-DURING
BUT CLOUD IN STEAD, AND EVER-DURING DARK 3 45

EVERLASTING
THERE TO CONVERSE WITH EVERLASTING GROANS, 2 184
MAY HOPE WHEN EVERLASTING FATE SHALL YEILD 2 232
HEAV'NS EVERLASTING FRAME, WHILE O'RE THE NECKS 3 395
OPEN, YE EVERLASTING GATES, THEY SUNG, 7 565

EVER-THREATNING
STARLESS EXPOS'D, AND EVER-THREATNING STORMS 3 425

EVERY
FORTHWITH FROM EVERY SQUADRON AND EACH BAND 1 356
FROM EVERY BAND AND SQUARED REGIMENT 1 758
TH' INTRICATE WARDS, AND EVERY BOLT AND BAR 2 877
YOUTH SMIL'D CELESTIAL, AND TO EVERY LIMB 3 638
OF BIRDS ON EVERY BOUGH; SO MUCH THE MORE 5 8
WITH EVERY PLANT, IN SIGN OF WORSHIP WAVE. 5 194
WITHIN THEM EVERY LOWER FACULTIE 5 410
IMPEARLS ON EVERY LEAF AND EVERY FLOUER. 5 747
WITH REGAL SCEPTER, EVERY SOULE IN HEAV'N 5 816
VITAL IN EVERY PART, NOT AS FRAIL MAN 6 345
ON EVERY SIDE WITH SHADDOWING SQUADRONS DEEP, 6 554

EVERY (CONTINUED)
ONE SPIRIT IN THEM RUL'D, AND EVERY EYE 6 848
THEN HERBS OF EVERY LEAF, THAT SUDDEN FLOUR'D 7 317
GOD MADE, AND EVERY HERB, BEFORE IT GREW 7 336
GLOBOSE, AND EVERY MAGNITUDE OF STARRS, 7 357
AND EVERY BIRD OF WING AFTER HIS KINDE; 7 394
AND EVERY CREEPING THING THAT CREEPS THE GROUND. 7 523
AND EVERY LIVING THING THAT MOVES ON THE EARTH. 7 534
NUMEROUS, AND EVERY STARR PERHAPS A WORLD 7 621
OF EVERY TREE THAT IN THE GARDEN GROWES 8 321
IN EVERY GESTURE DIGNITIE AND LOVE. 8 489
CONSIDER'D EVERY CREATURE, WHICH OF ALL 9 84
IN EVERY BUSH AND BRAKE, WHERE HAP MAY FINDE 9 160
ACCESS IN EVERY VERTUE, IN THY SIGHT 9 310
HER GRACEFUL INNOCENCE, HER EVERY AIRE 9 459
FROM EVERY BEAST, MORE DUTEOUS AT HER CALL, 9 521
WARM'D BY THE SUN, PRODUCING EVERY KIND, 9 721
OF GRASSIE TERFE, AND PILE UP EVERY STONE 11 324
LAND, SEA, AND AIRE, AND EVERY KINDE THAT LIVES, 11 337
OF EVERY BEAST, AND BIRD, AND INSECT SMALL 11 734
ON EVERY CONSCIENCE; LAWS WHICH NONE SHALL FINDE 12 522

EVIDENCE
ILLUSTRIOUS EVIDENCE, EXAMPLE HIGH. 9 962
NOW ALSO EVIDENCE, BUT STRAIGHT I FELT 10 361

EVIDENT
AND IN OUR FACES EVIDENT THE SIGNES 9 1077

EVIL
OUT OF OUR EVIL SEEK TO BRING FORTH GOOD, 1 163
AND OUT OF GOOD STILL TO FIND MEANS OF EVIL; 1 165
EVIL TO OTHERS, AND ENRAG'D MIGHT SEE 1 216
NOR DID THEY NOT PERCEAVE THE EVIL PLIGHT 1 335
THRIVE UNDER EVIL, AND WORK EASE OUT OF PAIN 2 261
OF GOOD AND EVIL MUCH THEY ARGU'D THEN, 2 562
CREATED EVIL, FOR EVIL ONLY GOOD, 2 623
HYPOCRISIE, THE ONELY EVIL THAT WALKS 3 683
EVIL BE THOU MY GOOD; BY THEE AT LEAST 4 110
NO EVIL THING APPROACH OR ENTER IN; 4 563
BUT EVIL HAST NOT TRI'D: AND WILT OBJECT 4 896
THIS UNCOUTH DREAM, OF EVIL SPRUNG I FEAR; 5 98
YET EVIL WHENCE? IN THEE CAN HARBOUR NONE, 5 99
EVIL INTO THE MIND OF GOD OR MAN 5 117
HAVE GATHERED AUGHT OF EVIL OR CONCEALD, 5 207
AND FLY, ERE EVIL INTERCEPT THY FLIGHT. 5 871
AUTHOR OF EVIL, UNKNOWN TILL THY REVOLT, 6 262
HENCE THEN, AND EVIL GO WITH THEE ALONG 6 275
THY OFSPRING, TO THE PLACE OF EVIL, HELL, 6 276
THE STRIFE WHICH THOU CALL'ST EVIL, BUT WEE STYLE 6 289
FLED IGNOMINIOUS, TO SUCH EVIL BROUGHT 6 395
OF EVIL THEN SO SMALL AS EASIE THINK 6 437
AGAINST UNPAIND, IMPASSIVE; FROM WHICH EVIL 6 455
TO HOARCE OR MUTE, THOUGH FALL'N ON EVIL DAYES, 7 25
ON EVIL DAYES THOUGH FALL'N, AND EVIL TONGUES; 7 26
WITH SUCH CONFUSION: BUT THE EVIL SOON 7 56
GOOD OUT OF EVIL TO CREATE, IN STEAD 7 188
WHICH TASTED WORKS KNOWLEDGE OF GOOD AND EVIL, 7 543
TO MANIFEST THE MORE THY MIGHT: HIS EVIL 7 615
THAT SPACE THE EVIL ONE ABSTRACTED STOOD 9 463
FROM HIS OWN EVIL, AND FOR THE TIME REMAIND 9 464
WHICH OFT, THEY SAY, SOME EVIL SPIRIT ATTENDS 9 638
TO HAPPIER LIFE, KNOWLEDGE OF GOOD AND EVIL; 9 697
OF GOOD, HOW JUST? OF EVIL, IF WHAT IS EVIL 9 698
KNOWING BOTH GOOD AND EVIL AS THEY KNOW. 9 709
KNOWLEDGE OF GOOD AND EVIL IN THIS TREE, 9 723
OF KNOWLEDGE, KNOWLEDGE BOTH OF GOOD AND EVIL; 9 752
UNDER THIS IGNORANCE OF GOOD AND EVIL, 9 774
SO SAYING, HER RASH HAND IN EVIL HOUR 9 780
OF DANGER TASTED, NOR TO EVIL UNKNOWN 9 864
O EVE, IN EVIL HOUR THOU DIDST GIVE EARE 9 1067
BOTH GOOD AND EVIL, GOOD LOST, AND EVIL GOT, 9 1072
OF FOUL CONCUPISCENCE; WHENCE EVIL STORE; 9 1078
NO EVIL DURST ATTEMPT THEE, BUT I RUE 9 1180
AND LEFT TO HER SELF, IF EVIL THENCE ENSUE, 9 1185
O HEAV'N, IN EVIL STRAIT THIS DAY I STAND 10 125
THE EVIL ON HIM BROUGHT BY ME, WILL CURSE 10 734
WHICH TO HIS EVIL CONSCIENCE REPRESENTED 10 849
TO KNOW BOTH GOOD AND EVIL, SINCE HIS TASTE 11 85
HIS KNOWLEDGE OF GOOD LOST, AND EVIL GOT, 11 87
GOOD BY IT SELF, AND EVIL NOT AT ALL. 11 89
HOWEVER CHAST'NING, TO THE EVIL TURNE 11 373
MY PART OF EVIL ONELY, EACH DAYES LOT 11 765
HIM OR HIS CHILDERN, EVIL HE MAY BE SURE, 11 772
AND HEE THE FUTURE EVIL SHALL NO LESS 11 774
REGARDLESS WHETHER GOOD OR EVIL FAME. 12 47
THAT ALL THIS GOOD OF EVIL SHALL PRODUCE, 12 470
AND EVIL TURN TO GOOD; MORE WONDERFUL 12 471
STILL OVERCOMING EVIL, AND BY SMALL 12 566

EVILL
OF AMRAMS SON IN EGYPTS EVILL DAY 1 339
WILL PROVE NO SUDDEN, BUT A SLOW-PAC'T EVILL, 10 963

EVILS
COMPOSE OUR PRESENT EVILS, WITH REGARD 2 281
OF EVILS, AND EXCESSIVE, OVERTURNES 6 463
EVEN SHAME, THE LAST OF EVILS; OF THE FIRST 9 1079

EVILS (CONTINUED)
AS IN OUR EVILS, AND OF EASIER CHOICE. 10 978
TO EVILS WHICH OUR OWN MISDEEDS HAVE WROUGHT, . . 10 1080
WITH CAUSE FOR EVILS PAST, YET MUCH MORE CHEER'D . 12 604

EVINCE
AND THEREFORE WAS LAW GIVEN THEM TO EVINCE . . . 12 287

EV'N
FROM HEAV'N, FOR EV'N IN HEAV'N HIS LOOKS AND THOUGHTS 1 680
DAY, OR THE SWEET APPROACH OF EV'N OR MORN, . . 3 42
ALL THINGS, EV'N THEE, AND ALL THE SPIRITS OF HEAV'N 5 837
TILL EV'N, NOR THEN THE SOLEMN NIGHTINGAL . . . 7 435
SO EV'N AND MORN ACCOMPLISH'D THE SIXT DAY: . . 7 550
EV'N TO THE SEAT OF GOD. FOR SINCE I SAUGHT . . 11 148

EV'NING
AT EV'NING FROM THE TOP OF FESOLE, ... 1 289
EXTEND HIS EV'NING BEAM, THE FIELDS REVIVE, . . 2 493
EV'NING AND MORN SOLEMNIZ'D THE FIFT DAY. . . . 7 448
GLIDING METEOROUS, AS EV'NING MIST 12 629

EWE
OF EWE OR GOAT DROPPING WITH MILK AT EEVN, . . . 9 582

EWES
EWES AND THIR BLEATING LAMBS OVER THE PLAINE, . . 11 649

EXACT
FOR WINGS, AND SMALLEST LINEAMENTS EXACT . . . 7 477
ELABORATE, OF INWARD LESS EXACT. 8 539
EVE, NOW I SEE THOU ART EXACT OF TASTE, ... 9 1017
THE LAW OF GOD EXACT HE SHALL FULFILL 12 402

EXACTLY
THY WISH EXACTLY TO THY HEARTS DESIRE. 8 451

EXACTS
EXACTS OUR PARTING HENCE; AND SEE THE GUARDS, . . 12 590

EXALT
THEREFORE THY HUMILIATION SHALL EXALT 3 313
TO KEEP THEM LOW WHOM KNOWLEDGE MIGHT EXALT . . . 4 525
TO MAKE US LESS, BENT RATHER TO EXALT 5 829
BUT LEAST HIS HEART EXALT HIM IN THE HARME . . . 7 150

EXALTATION
TO THIS HIGH EXALTATION; SUDDENLY 5 90
MY EXALTATION, AND MY WHOLE DELIGHT, ... 6 727

EXALTED
EXALTED TO SUCH POWER, AND GAVE TO RULE, ... 1 736
SATAN EXALTED SAT, BY MERIT RAIS'D 2 5
HIGH IN THE MIDST EXALTED AS A GOD 6 99
EXALTED FROM SO BASE ORIGINAL, ... 9 150
HIS SEAT AT GODS RIGHT HAND, EXALTED HIGH . . . 12 457

EXAMPLE
BY THY EXAMPLE, BUT HAVE POWER AND RIGHT 4 881
NOR NUMBER, NOR EXAMPLE WITH HIM WROUGHT 5 901
BY TERRIBLE EXAMPLE THE REWARD 6 910
ADAM BY DIRE EXAMPLE TO BEWARE 7 42
ILLUSTRIOUS EVIDENCE, EXAMPLE HIGH. 9 962
BEYOND ALL PAST EXAMPLE AND FUTURE, ... 10 840
IN A DARK AGE, AGAINST EXAMPLE GOOD, ... 11 809
TAUGHT THIS BY HIS EXAMPLE WHOM I NOW 12 572

EXASPERATE
IS FLAT DESPAIR: WE MUST EXASPERATE 2 143

EXCEEDED
EXCEEDED HUMAN, AND HIS WARY SPEECH 5 459

EXCEEDING
O GLORIOUS TRIAL OF EXCEEDING LOVE, ... 9 961

EXCEL
THROUGH HEAV'N AND EARTH, SO SHALL MY GLORIE EXCEL, 3 133

EXCEL'D
EXCEL'D HER POWER; THE GATES WIDE OP'N STOOD, . . . 2 884

EXCELL
AND INWARD FACULTIES, WHICH MOST EXCELL, ... 8 542

EXCELL'D
OF ALL GODS WORKS, CREATURE IN WHOM EXCELL'D . . 9 897
AND FOR THEE, WHOSE PERFECTION FARR EXCELL'D . . 10 150

EXCELLD
HOW BEAUTY IS EXCELLD BY MANLY GRACE 4 490

EXCELLENCE
IN POWER AND EXCELLENCE, BUT FAVOUR'D MORE . . . 2 350
WHO DWELL IN HEAV'N, WHOSE EXCELLENCE HE SAW . . 5 456
FORTHWITH (BEHOLD THE EXCELLENCE, THE POWER . . 6 637

EXCELLENCE (CONTINUED)
THEY MEASURE ALL, OF OTHER EXCELLENCE 6 821
OR BRIGHT INFERRS NOT EXCELLENCE: THE EARTH . . 8 91
THAT EXCELLENCE THOUGHT IN THEE, AND IMPLIES, . . 10 1017

EXCELLENT
LESS EXCELLENT, AS THOU THY SELF PERCEAV'ST. . . 8 566
AND EXCELLENT THEN WHAT THY MINDE CONTEMNES; . . 10 1015

EXCELLING
EXCELLING HUMAN, PRINCELY DIGNITIES, ... 1 359

EXCELLS
WHEN HE WHO RULES IS WORTHIEST, AND EXCELLS . . 6 177
NOT EMULOUS, NOR CARE WHO THEM EXCELLS; 6 822

EXCELS
WHEN HE WHO MOST EXCELS IN FACT OF ARMS, ... 2 124
IN WHAT HE COUNSELS AND IN WHAT EXCELS 2 125
AS WITH AN OBJECT THAT EXCELS THE SENSE, ... 8 456

EXCEPT
SATAN EXCEPT, NONE HIGHER SAT, WITH GRAVE . . . 2 300
ADMIR'D, NOT FEAR'D; GOD AND HIS SON EXCEPT, . . 2 678
TO TEMPT OR PUNISH MORTALS, EXCEPT WHOM 2 1032
INVISIBLE, EXCEPT TO GOD ALONE, ... 3 684
HALF WHAT IN THEE IS FAIR, ONE MAN EXCEPT, . . . 9 545
EQUAL IN DAYS AND NIGHTS, EXCEPT TO THOSE . . . 10 680
ONE MAN EXCEPT, THE ONELY SON OF LIGHT 11 808

EXCEPTED
TH' EXCEPTED TREE, NOR WITH THE SNAKE CONSPIR'D, . 11 426

EXCESS
WHO NOW TRIUMPHS, AND IN TH' EXCESS OF JOY . . . 1 123
LESS THEN ARCH ANGEL RUIND, AND TH' EXCESS . . . 1 593
THE GREAT WORK-MAISTER, LEADS TO NO EXCESS . . . 3 696
THE MORE IT SEEMS EXCESS, THAT LED THEE HITHER . 3 698
EXCESS, BEFORE TH' ALL BOUNTEOUS KING, WHO SHOWRD 5 640
FRUITLESS TO MEE, THOUGH FRUIT BE HERE TO EXCESS, 9 648
BEWAILING THIR EXCESS, ALL TERROR HIDE. 11 111
A SPACE, TILL FIRMER THOUGHTS RESTRAIND EXCESS, . 11 498

EXCESSIVE
PREGNANT BY THEE, AND NOW EXCESSIVE GROWN . . . 2 779
DARK WITH EXCESSIVE BRIGHT THY SKIRTS APPEER, . . 3 380
OF EVILS, AND EXCESSIVE, OVERTURNES 6 463

EXCITE
PAIN FOR A WHILE OR ANGUISH, AND EXCITE 2 567
THIR RUINE. HENCE I WILL EXCITE THIR MINDS . . 4 522

EXCITES
THIR SPECIOUS DEEDS ON EARTH, WHICH GLORY EXCITES, 2 484
WHOSE LIQUID MURMUR HEARD NEW THIRST EXCITES, . . 7 68
ENJOY'D BY US EXCITES HIS ENVIE MORE; 9 264
OF MISCHIEF, GRATULATING, THUS EXCITES. 9 472

EXCLAIMD
DISPARTED CHAOS OVERBUILT EXCLAIMD, ... 10 416

EXCLUDE
AND NONE BUT SUCH FROM MERCY I EXCLUDE. 3 202
ON PURPOSE, HARD THOU KNOWST IT TO EXCLUDE . . . 4 584

EXCLUDED
ALL HOPE EXCLUDED THUS, BEHOLD IN STEAD 4 105

EXCLUSION
HIS SAD EXCLUSION FROM THE DORES OF BLISS. . . . 3 525

EXCLUSIVE
OF MEMBRANE, JOYNT, OR LIMB, EXCLUSIVE BARRS: . . 8 625

EXCURSION
AND OPPORTUNE EXCURSION WE MAY CHANCE 2 396
FARR ON EXCURSION TOWARD THE GATES OF HELL; . . 8 231

EXCUS'D
THE TYRANTS PLEA, EXCUS'D HIS DEVILISH DEEDS. . . 4 394

EXCUSE
THEN HAD THE SONS OF GOD EXCUSE TO HAVE BIN . . 5 447
TO HIM SHE HASTED, IN HER FACE EXCUSE 9 853
THAT PROUD EXCUSE? YET HIM NOT THY ELECTION, . . 10 764
THOUGH TO THE TYRANT THEREBY NO EXCUSE. 12 96

EXECRABLE
WHENCE AND WHAT ART THOU, EXECRABLE SHAPE, . . . 2 681
O EXECRABLE SON SO TO ASPIRE 12 64

EXECRATION
SHALL BE THE EXECRATION; SO BESIDES 10 737

EXECUTE
CAN EXECUTE THIR AERIE PURPOSES, ... 1 430
AT THEE ORDAIN'D HIS DRUDGE, TO EXECUTE 2 732
TO EXECUTE FIERCE VENGEANCE ON HIS FOES, ... 3 399

EXECUTE (CONTINUED)
HIS HAND TO EXECUTE WHAT HIS DECREE 10 772

EXECUTION
OF TARDIE EXECUTION, SINCE DENOUNC'T 10 853

EXEMPT
BEYOND HIS POTENT ARM, TO LIVE EXEMPT 2 318
NO VOICE EXEMPT, NO VOICE BUT WELL COULD JOINE 3 370
FOE NOT INFORMIDABLE, EXEMPT FROM WOUND, 9 486
SO SNATCHT WILL NOT EXEMPT US FROM THE PAINE 10 1025
AND FOR HIS MAKERS IMAGE SAKE EXEMPT? 11 514
EXEMPT FROM DEATH; TO SHEW THEE WHAT REWARD 11 709

EXERCIS'D
ABOUT HIM EXERCIS'D HEROIC GAMES 4 551

EXERCISE
MUST EXERCISE US WITHOUT HOPE OF END 2 89
DOMINION EXERCISE AND IN THE AIRE, 10 400
BUT MORTAL DOOM'D. HOW CAN HE EXERCISE 10 796
THAT CRUEL SERPENT: ON ME EXERCISE NOT 10 927

EXHALATION
ROSE LIKE AN EXHALATION, WITH THE SOUND 1 711
VAPOUR, AND MIST, AND EXHALATION HOT, 10 694
VAPOUR, AND EXHALATION DUSK AND MOIST, 11 741

EXHALATIONS
YE MISTS AND EXHALATIONS THAT NOW RISE 5 185
IN HUMID EXHALATIONS, AND AT EVEN 5 425

EXHAL'D
NOW WHEN AMBROSIAL NIGHT WITH CLOUDS EXHAL'D 5 642
MADE ERRE, WAS NOW EXHAL'D, AND GROSSER SLEEP 9 1049

EXHALE
NOR DOTH THE MOON NO NOURISHMENT EXHALE 5 421

EXHALING
EXHALING FIRST FROM DARKNESS THEY BEHELD; 7 255

EXHAUSTED
EXHAUSTED, SPIRITLESS, AFFLICTED, FALL'N. 6 852

EXHILERATING
THAT WITH EXHILERATING VAPOUR BLAND 9 1047

EXHORTING
DESIGNING OR EXHORTING GLORIOUS WARR, 2 179

EXIL'D
OF US OUT-CAST, EXIL'D, HIS NEW DELIGHT, 4 106

EXILE
THAT ALL THESE PUISSANT LEGIONS, WHOSE EXILE 1 632
EXILE, OR IGNOMINY, OR BONDS, OR PAIN, 2 207
PLAC'T IN A PARADISE, BY OUR EXILE 10 484

EXORBITANT
BY SIN TO FOUL EXORBITANT DESIRES; 3 177

EXPANDED
THEN WITH EXPANDED WINGS HE STEARS HIS FLIGHT 1 225

EXPANSE
INTO THE WILDE EXPANSE, AND THROUGH THE SHOCK 2 1014
PURE AS TH' EXPANSE OF HEAV'N; I THITHER WENT 4 456
THE FIRMAMENT, EXPANSE OF LIQUID, PURE, 7 264
HIGH IN TH' EXPANSE OF HEAVEN TO DIVIDE 7 340

EXPATIATE
NEW RUB'D WITH BAUM, EXPATIATE AND CONFER 1 774

EXPECT
FARR HEAVIER LOAD THY SELF EXPECT TO FEEL 4 972
DISTINGUISH NOT: FOR SOON EXPECT TO FEEL 5 892
YET CHAINS IN HELL, NOT REALMS EXPECT: MEAN WHILE 6 186
THE WILLINGER I GOE, NOR MUCH EXPECT 9 382
EVE, NOW EXPECT GREAT TIDINGS, WHICH PERHAPS 11 226
EXPECT TO HEAR, SUPERNAL GRACE CONTENDING 11 359
EXPECT WITH MORTAL PAINE: SAY WHERE AND WHEN 12 384
BY MEE ENCAMPT ON YONDER HILL, EXPECT 12 591

EXPECTATION
THIS SAID, HE SAT; AND EXPECTATION HELD 2 417
BLAZ'D OPPOSITE, WHILE EXPECTATION STOOD 6 306
OR FANSIED SO, THROUGH EXPECTATION HIGH 9 789
SUBLIME WITH EXPECTATION WHEN TO SEE 10 536
WITH CRUEL EXPECTATION. YET ONE DOUBT 10 782
WHY OUR GREAT EXPECTATION SHOULD BE CALL'D 12 378

EXPECTED
EXPECTED, LEAST OF ALL FROM THEE, INGRATE 5 811
MAY TEMPT IT, I EXPECTED NOT TO HEAR. 9 281
WITHOUT WRAUTH OR REVILING; WEE EXPECTED 10 1048

EXPECTING
ROUND THIR METROPOLIS, AND NOW EXPECTING 10 439
SO HAVING SAID, A WHILE HE STOOD, EXPECTING 10 504

EXPEDITE
TO EXPEDITE YOUR GLORIOUS MARCH; BUT I 10 474

EXPEDITION
WITH DANGEROUS EXPEDITION TO INVADE 2 342
WITH FURIOUS EXPEDITION; FOR THEY WEEND 6 86
ON HIS GREAT EXPEDITION NOW APPEER'D, 7 193

EXPEL
INCAPABLE OF STAIN WOULD SOON EXPEL 2 140

EXPELL'D
THUS TRAMPL'D, THUS EXPELL'D TO SUFFER HERE 2 195
ALL USURPATION THENCE EXPELL'D, REDUCE 2 983
SHALT LOOSE, EXPELL'D FROM HENCE INTO A WORLD 8 332

EXPERIENCE
SINCE THROUGH EXPERIENCE OF THIS GREAT EVENT 1 118
YET BY EXPERIENCE TAUGHT WE KNOW HOW GOOD, 5 826
TILL WARN'D, OR BY EXPERIENCE TAUGHT, SHE LEARNE, 8 190
THUS GROWN. EXPERIENCE, NEXT TO THEE I OWE, 9 807
ON MY EXPERIENCE, ADAM, FREELY TASTE, 9 988

EXPERIENC'T
DARTS HIS EXPERIENC'T EYE, AND SOON TRAVERSE 1 568

EXPERIMENT
ADAM, BY SAD EXPERIMENT I KNOW 10 967

EXPERT
EACH WARRIOUR SINGLE AS IN CHIEF, EXPERT 6 233

EXPIATE
TO EXPIATE HIS TREASON HATH NAUGHT LEFT, 3 207

EXPIATIONS
SAVE BY THOSE SHADOWIE EXPIATIONS WEAK, 12 291

EXPIRE
WE SHOULD BE QUITE ABOLISHT AND EXPIRE. 2 93

EXPLAIN'D
BY HARALDS VOICE EXPLAIN'D; THE HOLLOW ABYSS 2 518

EXPLODED
EXPLODED AND HAD SEIZ'D WITH VIOLENT HANDS, 11 669

EXPLODING
TURND TO EXPLODING HISS, TRIUMPH TO SHAME 10 546

EXPLOIT
FOR DIGNITY COMPOS'D AND HIGH EXPLOIT: 2 111
WITH MANY A VAIN EXPLOIT, THOUGH THEN RENOWND: 3 465
THROUGH SIN TO DEATH EXPOS'D BY MY EXPLOIT. 10 407

EXPLOITS
TO HUMAN SENSE TH' INVISIBLE EXPLOITS 5 565
AND GREAT EXPLOITS, BUT OF TRUE VERTU VOID; 11 790

EXPLORE
WITH PURPOSE TO EXPLORE OR TO DISTURB 2 971
WHAT WEE, NOT TO EXPLORE THE SECRETS ASKE 7 95

EXPLORES
EXPLORES HIS SOLITARY FLIGHT; SOM TIMES 2 632
AND THUS HIS OWN UNDAUNTED HEART EXPLORES. 6 113

EXPOS'D
EXPOS'D A MATRON TO AVOID WORSE RAPE. 1 505
IN HIS OWN STRENGTH, THIS PLACE MAY LYE EXPOS'D 2 360
STARLESS EXPOS'D, AND EVER-THREATNING STORMS 3 425
TO ALL DELIGHT OF HUMAN SENSE EXPOS'D 4 206
AND EDEN WERE NO EDEN THUS EXPOS'D. 9 341
THROUGH SIN TO DEATH EXPOS'D BY MY EXPLOIT. 10 407
TO ME COMMITTED AND BY ME EXPOS'D. 10 957

EXPOSE
MY SELF EXPOSE, WITH LONELY STEPS TO TREAD 2 828
I SHOULD CONCEAL, AND NOT EXPOSE TO BLAME 10 130
GOD, AS TO LEAVE THEM, AND EXPOSE THIR LAND, 12 339

EXPOSES
WILL ENVY WHOM THE HIGHEST PLACE EXPOSES 2 27

EXPRESLY
TO DO WHAT GOD EXPRESLY HATH FORBID, 9 356

EXPRESS
NOR FAIL'D THEY TO EXPRESS HOW MUCH THEY PRAIS'D, 2 480
MAY I EXPRESS THEE UNBLAM'D? SINCE GOD IS LIGHT, 3 3
AS MAY EXPRESS THEM BEST, THOUGH WHAT IF EARTH 5 574
EXPRESS, AND THOU BECAM'ST A LIVING SOUL. 7 528
EXPRESS THEY, BY LOOKS ONELY, OR DO THEY MIX 8 616
AGAINST A FOE BY DOOM EXPRESS ASSIGN'D US, 10 926

Word	Context	Book	Line
EXPRESS (CONTINUED)	EXPRESS, AND OF HIS STEPS THE TRACK DIVINE.	11	354
EXPRESS'D	SUBSTANTIALLY EXPRESS'D, AND IN HIS FACE	3	140
	EXPRESS'D, AND THUS DIVINELY ANSWER'D MILDE.	10	67
	THE BENT OF NATURE; WHICH HE THUS EXPRESS'D.	11	597
EXPRESSING	EXPRESSING WELL THE SPIRIT WITHIN THEE FREE,	8	440
	HIS IMAGE WHO MADE BOTH, AND LESS EXPRESSING	8	544
EXPRESSION	THE PLACE HE FOUND BEYOND EXPRESSION BRIGHT,	3	591
	HIS GENTLE DUMB EXPRESSION TURND AT LENGTH	9	527
EXPREST	SHON FULL, HE ALL HIS FATHER FULL EXPREST	6	720
	BY TONGUE OF BRUTE, AND HUMAN SENSE EXPREST?	9	554
	OF MINE TO THEE, INGRATEFUL EVE, EXPREST	9	1164
EXPULSION	SOLE VICTOR FROM TH' EXPULSION OF HIS FOES	6	880
EXPUNG'D	OF NATURES WORKS TO MEE EXPUNG'D AND RAS'D,	3	49
EXTEND	BY OUR REVOLT, BUT OVER HELL EXTEND	2	326
	EXTEND HIS EV'NING BEAM, THE FIELDS REVIVE,	2	493
	DISPERST IN BANDS AND FILES THIR CAMP EXTEND	5	651
	AND SAID, THUS FARR EXTEND, THUS FARR THY BOUNDS,	7	230
	SATISFI'D NEVER; THAT WERE TO EXTEND	10	804
EXTENDED	PRONE ON THE FLOOD, EXTENDED LONG AND LARGE	1	195
	THAT WITH EXTENDED WINGS A BANNERD HOST	2	885
	FARR OFF TH' EMPYREAL HEAV'N, EXTENDED WIDE	2	1047
	OF NIGHTS EXTENDED SHADE; FROM EASTERN POINT	3	557
EXTENDS	IS CENTER, YET EXTENDS TO ALL, SO THOU	9	108
	MOSES ONCE MORE HIS POTENT ROD EXTENDS	12	211
EXTENT	OF HUGE EXTENT SOMTIMES, WITH BRAZEN EYES	7	496
	NOT TO TH' EXTENT OF THIR OWN SPHEARE. BUT SAY	10	808
EXTENUATE	WHO CAN EXTENUATE THEE? NEXT, TO THE SON,	10	645
EXTERIOR	ALONE, WITHOUT EXTERIOR HELP SUSTAIND?	9	336
EXTERNAL	HER OFFICE HOLDS; OF ALL EXTERNAL THINGS,	5	103
EXTINCT	THOUGH ALL OUR GLORY EXTINCT, AND HAPPY STATE	1	141
	SHALL LIVE WITH HER ENJOYING, I EXTINCT;	9	829
EXTINGUISH	HER OLD POSSESSION, AND EXTINGUISH LIFE	4	666
EXTOLL	EXTOLL HIM EQUAL TO THE HIGHEST IN HEAV'N:	2	479
	FOR WHICH BOTH HEAV'N AND EARTH SHALL HIGH EXTOLL	3	146
	BUT LET US EVER PRAISE HIM, AND EXTOLL	4	436
	TO FILL THE EARTH, WHO SHALL WITH US EXTOLL	4	733
	ON EARTH JOYN ALL YE CREATURES TO EXTOLL	5	164
EXTOLL'D	THEE ONLY EXTOLL'D, SON OF THY FATHERS MIGHT,	3	398
EXTORT	EXTORT FROM ME. TO BOW AND SUE FOR GRACE	1	111
EXTRACTED	EXTRACTED; FOR THIS CAUSE HE SHALL FORGOE	8	497
EXTRACTING	SITS ON THE BLOOM EXTRACTING LIQUID SWEET.	5	25
EXTRAVAGANT	SOMEWHAT EXTRAVAGANT AND WILDE, PERHAPS	6	616
EXTREAMES	OF CHAOS FARR REMOV'D, LEAST FIERCE EXTREAMES	7	272
EXTREAMS	IN WORST EXTREAMS, AND ON THE PERILOUS EDGE	1	276
	OF FIERCE EXTREAMS, EXTREAMS BY CHANGE MORE FIERCE,	2	599
EXTREMES	TENDING TO SOME RELIEF OF OUR EXTREMES,	10	976
EY'D	EY'D THEM ASKANCE, AND TO HIMSELF THUS PLAIND.	4	504
EY'D (CONTINUED)	DRIE-EY'D BEHOLD? ADAM COULD NOT, BUT WEPT,	11	495
	THE MEN THOUGH GRAVE, EY'D THEM, AND LET THIR EYES	11	585
EYE	HIS EYE SURVAY'D THE DARK IDOLATRIES	1	456
	DARTS HIS EXPERIENC'T EYE, AND SOON TRAVERSE	1	568
	WAITING REVENGE: CRUEL HIS EYE, BUT CAST	1	604
	WITH HIM, OR WHO DECEIVE HIS MIND, WHOSE EYE	2	189
	NOW IN THINE EYE SO FOUL, ONCE DEEMD SO FAIR	2	748
	HIGH THRON'D ABOVE ALL HIGHTH, BENT DOWN HIS EYE,	3	58
	MINE EAR SHALL NOT BE SLOW, MINE EYE NOT SHUT.	3	193
	PASS'D FREQUENT, AND HIS EYE WITH CHOICE REGARD	3	534
	WHICH TO HIS EYE DISCOVERS UNAWARE	3	547
	ALLUR'D HIS EYE; THITHER HIS COURSE HE BENDS	3	573
	THAT FROM HIS LORDLY EYE KEEP DISTANCE DUE,	3	578
	UNDAZL'D, FARR AND WIDE HIS EYE COMMANDS,	3	614
	LIKE HONOUR TO OBTAIN, AND AS HIS EYE	3	660
	HIM COUNTERFET, IF ANY EYE BEHELD.	4	117
	URIEL ONCE WARND; WHOSE EYE PURSU'D HIM DOWN	4	125
	YOUNG BACCHUS FROM HIS STEPDAME RHEA'S EYE;	4	279
	HIS FAIR LARGE FRONT AND EYE SUBLIME DECLAR'D	4	300
	MINE EYE PURSU'D HIM STILL, BUT UNDER SHADE	4	572
	SUCH WHISPERING WAK'D HER, BUT WITH STARTL'D EYE	5	26
	FROM EITHER EYE, AND WIP'D THEM WITH HER HAIRE;	5	131
	THOU SUN, OF THIS GREAT WORLD BOTH EYE AND SOULE,	5	171
	MEAN WHILE TH' ETERNAL EYE, WHOSE SIGHT DISCERNES	5	711
	WHOM THE GRAND FOE WITH SCORNFUL EYE ASKANCE	6	149
	ALL HEART THEY LIVE, ALL HEAD, ALL EYE, ALL EARE,	6	350
	WHOSE EYE SO SUPERFICIALLY SURVEYES	6	476
	ONE SPIRIT IN THEM RUL'D, AND EVERY EYE	6	848
	EYE WITNESSES OF HIS ALMIGHTIE ACTS,	6	883
	LOAD'N WITH FAIREST FRUIT THAT HUNG TO THE EYE	8	307
	GRACE WAS IN ALL HER STEPS, HEAV'N IN HER EYE,	8	488
	HER LONG WITH ARDENT LOOK HIS EYE PURSU'D	9	397
	TO LURE HER EYE; SHEE BUSIED HEARD THE SOUND	9	518
	THE EYE OF EVE TO MARK HIS PLAY; HE GLAD	9	528
	SOLLICITED HER LONGING EYE; YET FIRST	9	743
	FAIR TO THE EYE, INVITING TO THE TASTE,	9	777
	HAD IT BEEN ONELY COVETING TO EYE	9	923
	OF EVE, WHOSE EYE DARTED CONTAGIOUS FIRE.	9	1036
	WAS KNOWN IN HEAV'N; FOR WHAT CAN SCAPE THE EYE	10	5
	ADAM OBSERV'D, AND WITH HIS EYE THE CHASE	11	191
	AND CARNAL FEAR THAT DAY DIMM'D ADAMS EYE.	11	212
	HIS EYE MIGHT THERE COMMAND WHEREVER STOOD	11	385
	TURCHESTAN-BORN; NOR COULD HIS EYE NOT KEN	11	396
	TO DRESS, AND TROULE THE TONGUE, AND ROULE THE EYE.	11	620
	ETERNITIE, WHOSE END NO EYE CAN REACH.	12	556
EYE-LIDS	OUR EYE-LIDS; OTHER CREATURES ALL DAY LONG	4	616
	THY EYE-LIDS? AND REMEMBREST WHAT DECREE	5	674
EYES	TORMENTS HIM; ROUND HE THROWS HIS BALEFUL EYES	1	56
	WITH HEAD UP-LIFT ABOVE THE WAVE, AND EYES	1	193
	OF NEW SUBJECTION; WITH WHAT EYES COULD WE	2	239
	SPARKL'D IN ALL THIR EYES; WITH FULL ASSENT	2	388
	WITH SHUDDRING HORROR PALE, AND EYES AGAST	2	616
	SURPRIS'D THEE, DIM THINE EYES, AND DIZZIE SWUMM	2	753
	BEFORE MINE EYES IN OPPOSITION SITS	2	803
	BEFORE THIR EYES IN SUDDEN VIEW APPEAR	2	890
	REVISIT'ST NOT THESE EYES, THAT ROWLE IN VAIN	3	23
	IRRADIATE, THERE PLANT EYES, ALL MIST FROM THENCE	3	53
	APPROACH NOT, BUT WITH BOTH WINGS VEIL THIR EYES.	3	382
	STAND READY AT COMMAND, AND ARE HIS EYES	3	650
	TO WITNESS WITH THINE EYES WHAT SOME PERHAPS	3	700
	O HELL. WHAT DOE MINE EYES WITH GRIEF BEHOLD,	4	358
	MINE EYES TILL NOW, AND PIN'D WITH VAIN DESIRE,	4	466
	SO SPAKE OUR GENERAL MOTHER, AND WITH EYES	4	492
	THIS GLORIOUS SIGHT, WHEN SLEEP HATH SHUT ALL EYES?	4	658
	IF NONE REGARD; HEAV'N WAKES WITH ALL HIS EYES,	5	44
	ALL BUT THE UNSLEEPING EYES OF GOD TO REST,	5	647
	WHICH TO OUR EYES DISCOVERD NEW AND STRANGE,	6	571
	AND WINGS WERE SET WITH EYES, WITH EYES THE WHEELS	6	755
	DISTINCT WITH EYES, AND FROM THE LIVING WHEELS	6	846
	DISTINCT ALIKE WITH MULTITUDE OF EYES,	6	847
	YET SCARCE ALLAY'D STILL EYES THE CURRENT STREAME,	7	67
	OF RAINBOWS AND STARRIE EYES. THE WATERS THUS	7	446
	OF HUGE EXTENT SOMTIMES, WITH BRAZEN EYES	7	496
	DESCENDS, THITHER WITH HEART AND VOICE AND EYES	7	513
	INTO ALL EYES TO WISH HER STILL IN SIGHT.	8	63
	STRAIT TOWARD HEAV'N MY WONDRING EYES I TURND,	8	257
	BEFORE MINE EYES ALL REAL, AS THE DREAM	8	310
	BY NATURE AS IN AIDE, AND CLOS'D MINE EYES.	8	459
	MINE EYES HE CLOS'D, BUT OP'N LEFT THE CELL	8	460
	CRESTED ALOFT, AND CARBUNCLE HIS EYES;	9	500
	YE EATE THEREOF, YOUR EYES THAT SEEM SO CLEERE,	9	706
	TO OPEN EYES, AND MAKE THEM GODS WHO TASTE;	9	866
	TH' EFFECTS TO CORRESPOND, OPENER MINE EYES,	9	875
	AUGMENTED, OP'ND EYES, NEW HOPES, NEW JOYES,	9	985
	BEGAN TO CAST LASCIVIOUS EYES, SHE HIM	9	1014
	SOON FOUND THIR EYES HOW OP'ND, AND THIR MINDS	9	1053
	FALSE IN OUR PROMIS'D RISING; SINCE OUR EYES	9	1070
	RAIND AT THIR EYES, BUT HIGH WINDS WORSE WITHIN	9	1122
	THIR EARNEST EYES THEY FIX'D, IMAGINING	10	553
	SPANGL'D WITH EYES MORE NUMEROUS THEN THOSE	11	130
	FAMILIAR TO OUR EYES, ALL PLACES ELSE	11	305

EYES (CONTINUED)
THIS HILL; LET EVE (FOR I HAVE DRENCHT HER EYES) . 11 367
MICHAEL FROM ADAMS EYES THE FILME REMOV'D . . . 11 412
THAT ADAM NOW ENFORC'T TO CLOSE HIS EYES, . . . 11 419
ADAM, NOW OPE THINE EYES, AND FIRST BEHOLD . . . 11 423
HIS EYES HE OP'ND, AND BEHELD A FIELD, . . . 11 429
BEFORE HIS EYES APPEARD, SAD, NOYSOM, DARK, . . 11 478
THE MEN THOUGH GRAVE, EY'D THEM, AND LET THIR EYES 11 585
TRUE OPENER OF MINE EYES, PRIME ANGEL BLEST, . . 11 598
WHICH NOW DIRECT THINE EYES AND SOON BEHOLD. . . 11 711
THEN WITH UPLIFTED HANDS, AND EYES DEVOUT, . . . 11 863
HIS HOLY EYES; RESOLVING FROM THENCEFORTH . . . 12 109
MINE EYES TRUE OP'NING, AND MY HEART MUCH EAS'D, . 12 274

EYRIES
ON CLIFFS AND CEDAR TOPS THIR EYRIES BUILD: . . . 7 424

EZEKIEL
EZEKIEL SAW, WHEN BY THE VISION LED 1 455

FABL'D
FROM HEAV'N, THEY FABL'D, THROWN BY ANGRY JOVE . 1 741
WITH LONG AND TEDIOUS HAVOC FABL'D KNIGHTS . . . 9 30
AND FABL'D HOW THE SERPENT, WHOM THEY CALLD . . 10 580

FABLE
IN FABLE OR ROMANCE OF UTHERS SON 1 580

FABLES
AS WHOM THE FABLES NAME OF MONSTROUS SIZE, . . . 1 197
THAN FABLES YET HAVE FEIGN'D, OR FEAR CONCEIV'D, . 2 627
HUNG AMIABLE, HESPERIAN FABLES TRUE, ... 4 250
IN FABLES OLD, LESS ANCIENT YET THEN THESE, . . 11 11

FABLEST
THOU FABLEST, HERE HOWEVER TO DWELL FREE, ... 6 292

FABRIC
CONJECTURE, HE HIS FABRIC OF THE HEAV'NS 8 76

FABRICK
ANON OUT OF THE EARTH A FABRICK HUGE 1 710
LONG HAD FORETOLD, A FABRICK WONDERFUL 10 482

FACE
ABOVE THEM ALL TH' ARCH ANGEL: BUT HIS FACE . . . 1 600
AND PRINCELY COUNSEL IN HIS FACE YET SHON, . . . 2 304
HEAV'NS CHEARFUL FACE, THE LOWRING ELEMENT . . . 2 490
OR FLOCKS, OR HEARDS, OR HUMAN FACE DIVINE; . . . 3 44
SUBSTANTIALLY EXPRESS'D, AND IN HIS FACE . . . 3 140
FATHER, TO SEE THY FACE, WHEREIN NO CLOUD . . . 3 262
OF MERCY AND JUSTICE IN THY FACE DISCERN'D, . . 3 407
NOT OF THE PRIME, YET SUCH AS IN HIS FACE . . . 3 637
THUS WHILE HE SPAKE, EACH PASSION DIMM'D HIS FACE 4 114
THY FACE, AND MORN RETURN'D, FOR I THIS NIGHT, . 5 30
SHADOWIE SETS OFF THE FACE OF THINGS; IN VAIN, . 5 43
SPRING BOTH, THE FACE OF BRIGHTEST HEAV'N HAD
CHANGD 5 644
HE COMES, AND SETTL'D IN HIS FACE I SEE 6 540
SON IN WHOSE FACE INVISIBLE IS BEHELD 6 681
INEFFABLY INTO HIS FACE RECEIV'D, ... 6 721
OBSEQUIOUS, HEAV'N HIS WONTED FACE RENEWD, . . . 6 783
APPEER'D NOT: OVER ALL THE FACE OF EARTH . . . 7 278
HER UNIVERSAL FACE WITH PLEASANT GREEN, ... 7 316
HIS MIRROR, WITH FULL FACE BORROWING HER LIGHT . 7 377
HOW FIRST THIS WORLD AND FACE OF THINGS BEGAN, . 7 636
TO HIM SHE HASTED, IN HER FACE EXCUSE 9 853
OF ALL THIR VERTUE: SILENT, AND IN FACE 9 1063
BE SURE THEN. HOW SHALL I BEHOLD THE FACE . . . 9 1080
IN THE SWEAT OF THY FACE SHALT THOU EAT BREAD, . 10 205
ACCURST OF BLESSED, HIDE ME FROM THE FACE . . . 10 723
WHICH NOW THE SKIE WITH VARIOUS FACE BEGINS . . 10 1064
AS FROM HIS FACE I SHALL BE HID, DEPRIVD . . . 11 316
WITH GOODNESS AND PATERNAL LOVE, HIS FACE . . . 11 353
HE LOOK'D, AND SAW THE FACE OF THINGS QUITE
CHANG'D, ... 11 712
WRINKL'D THE FACE OF DELUGE, AS DECAI'D; . . . 11 843

FACES
BY FOUR CHERUBIC SHAPES, FOUR FACES EACH 6 753
AND IN OUR FACES EVIDENT THE SIGNES 9 1077
OF WATCHFUL CHERUBIM; FOUR FACES EACH 11 128
CONCOURS IN ARMS, FIERCE FACES THREATNING WARR, . 11 641
WITH DREADFUL FACES THRONG'D AND FIERIE ARMES: . 12 644

FACIL
THE FACIL GATES OF HELL TOO SLIGHTLY BARRD. . . 4 967
BENEVOLENT AND FACIL THUS REPLI'D. 8 65
TOO FACIL THEN THOU DIDST NOT MUCH GAINSAY, . . 9 1158

FACT
WHEN HE WHO MOST EXCELS IN FACT OF ARMS, ... 2 124
PERHAPS THOU SHALT NOT DIE, PERHAPS THE FACT . . 9 928
DESERTED, THEN OBLIGE THEE WITH A FACT 9 980
FROM HEAV'N ACCEPTANCE; BUT THE BLOODIE FACT . . 11 457

FACTION
FROM FACTION; FOR NONE SURE WILL CLAIM IN HELL . 2 32

FACTION (CONTINUED)
OF EACH HIS FACTION, IN THIR SEVERAL CLANNS, . . 2 901

FACTIOUS
IN FACTIOUS OPPOSITION, TILL AT LAST 11 664
IN WEALTH AND MULTITUDE, FACTIOUS THEY GROW; . . 12 352

FACULTIE
WITHIN THEM EVERY LOWER FACULTIE 5 410

FACULTIES
ARE MANY LESSER FACULTIES THAT SERVE 5 101
AND INWARD FACULTIES, WHICH MOST EXCELL, ... 8 542

FADE
WITH THESE THAT NEVER FADE THE SPIRITS ELECT . . 3 360

FADED
SAT ON HIS FADED CHEEK, BUT UNDER BROWES 1 602
THIR FRAIL ORIGINAL, AND FADED BLISS, ... 2 375
FADED SO SOON. ADVISE IF THIS BE WORTH 2 376
BUT FADED SPLENDOR WAN; WHO BY HIS GATE 4 870
DOWN DROP'D, AND ALL THE FADED ROSES SHED: . . . 9 893

FADOM
TEN THOUSAND FADOM DEEP, AND TO THIS HOUR . . . 2 934

FAERIE
BEYOND THE INDIAN MOUNT, OR FAERIE ELVES, . . . 1 781

FAIL
AND THIS EMPYREAL SUBSTANCE CANNOT FAIL, ... 1 117
SHALL GRIEVE HIM, IF I FAIL NOT, AND DISTURB . . 1 167
HATH EMPTIED HEAV'N, SHALL FAIL TO RE-ASCEND . . 1 633
AND VENT'ROUS, IF THAT FAIL THEM, SHRINK AND FEAR 2 205
THERE FAIL WHERE VERTUE FAILS, OR WEAKEST PROVE . 6 117
HER SON. SO FAIL NOT THOU, WHO THEE IMPLORES: . 7 38
TO END ME? SHALL TRUTH FAIL TO KEEP HER WORD, . 10 856

FAIL'D
NOR FAIL'D THEY TO EXPRESS HOW MUCH THEY PRAIS'D, 2 480
AT LEAST OUR ENVIOUS FOE HATH FAIL'D, WHO THOUGHT 7 139

FAILD
AND SPIRITS, BOTH THEM WHO STOOD AND THEM WHO
FAILD; 3 101
SCARCE THUS AT LENGTH FAILD SPEECH RECOVERD SAD. 4 357
OR NATURE FAILD IN MEE, AND LEFT SOME PART . . . 8 534
WHETHER SUCH VERTUE SPENT OF OLD NOW FAILD . . . 9 145

FAILE
FOR US CREATED, NEEDS WITH US MUST FAILE, . . . 9 942
SUCH PROOF, CONCLUDE, THEY THEN BEGIN TO FAILE. . 9 1142
THY MORTAL SIGHT TO FAILE; OBJECTS DIVINE . . . 12 9

FAILES
SPEED, TO DESCRIBE WHOSE SWIFTNESS NUMBER FAILES. 8 38

FAILING
AUDACIOUS, BUT THAT SEAT SOON FAILING, MEETS . . 2 931
O MUCH DECEAV'D, MUCH FAILING, HAPLESS EVE, . . 9 404
WHOSE FAILING, WHILE HER FAITH TO ME REMAINES, . 10 129

FAILS
THERE FAIL WHERE VERTUE FAILS, OR WEAKEST PROVE . 6 117

FAINT
OREWEARIED, THROUGH THE FAINT SATANIC HOST . . . 6 392
OR FAINT RETREAT; WHEN THE GREAT SON OF GOD . . 6 799
PERPETUAL BANISHMENT. YET LEAST THEY FAINT . . 11 108
PATHS INDIRECT, OR IN THE MID WAY FAINT. . . . 11 631

FAIR
BEGUIL'D BY FAIR IDOLATRESSES, FELL 1 445
WAS FAIR DAMASCUS, ON THE FERTIL BANKS 1 468
DWELL NOT UNVISITED OF HEAV'NS FAIR LIGHT . . . 2 398
THE ONE SEEM'D WOMAN TO THE WASTE, AND FAIR, . . 2 650
NOW IN THINE EYE SO FOUL, ONCE DEEMD SO FAIR . . 2 748
THEN SHINING HEAV'NLY FAIR, A GODDESS ARM'D . . 2 757
AND MY FAIR SON HERE SHOWST ME, THE DEAR PLEDGE . 2 818
CUT OFF, AND FOR THE BOOK OF KNOWLEDG FAIR . . . 3 47
WITH JOY AND LOVE TRIUMPHING, AND FAIR TRUTH. . . 3 338
FAIR ANGEL, THY DESIRE WHICH TENDS TO KNOW . . . 3 694
(SO CALL THAT OPPOSITE FAIR STARR) HER AIDE . . 3 727
THEN IN FAIR EVENING CLOUD, OR HUMID BOW, . . . 4 151
HIS FAIR LARGE FRONT AND EYE SUBLIME DECLAR'D . . 4 300
FAIR COUPLE, LINKT IN HAPPIE NUPTIAL LEAGUE, . . 4 339
LIKE THIS FAIR PARADISE, YOUR SENSE, YET SUCH . . 4 379
WHAT THERE THOU SEEST FAIR CREATURE IS THY SELF, . 4 468
TILL I ESPI'D THEE, FAIR INDEED AND TALL, . . . 4 477
AND WISDOM, WHICH ALONE IS TRULY FAIR. 4 491
O FAIR FOUNDATION LAID WHEREON TO BUILD 4 521
WHEN ADAM THUS TO EVE: FAIR CONSORT, TH' HOUR . . 4 610
WITH THIS HER SOLEMN BIRD AND THIS FAIR MOON, . . 4 648
ADAM FROM HIS FAIR SPOUSE, NOR EVE THE RITES . . 4 742
TO HIS PROUD FAIR, BEST QUITTED WITH DISDAIN. . . 4 770
BUT CHIEFLY WHERE THOSE TWO FAIR CREATURES LODGE, 4 790
OF INTERDICTED KNOWLEDGE: FAIR IT SEEM'D, . . . 5 52

FAIR (CONTINUED)
AND O FAIR PLANT, SAID HE, WITH FRUIT SURCHARG'D, 5 58
HERE, HAPPIE CREATURE, FAIR ANGELIC EVE, 5 74
THEN WHEN FAIR MORNING FIRST SMILES ON THE WORLD, 5 124
SO CHEARD HE HIS FAIR SPOUSE, AND SHE WAS CHEARD, 5 129
THUS WONDROUS FAIR; THY SELF HOW WONDROUS THEN. 5 155
UNDECKT, SAVE WITH HER SELF MORE LOVELY FAIR 5 380
NOW WHEN FAIR MORN ORIENT IN HEAV'N APPEERD 6 524
TO ENTERTAIN THEM FAIR WITH OPEN FRONT 6 611
AND TOUCHT BY HER FAIR TENDANCE GLADLIER GREW. 8 47
AND YE THAT LIVE AND MOVE, FAIR CREATURES, TELL, 8 276
NOT ONELY THESE FAIR BOUNDS, BUT ALL THE EARTH 8 338
THAT WHAT SEEMD FAIR IN ALL THE WORLD, SEEMD NOW 8 472
AN OUTSIDE? FAIR NO DOUBT, AND WORTHY WELL 8 568
NEITHER HER OUT-SIDE FORMD SO FAIR, NOR AUGHT 8 596
IF CHANCE WITH NYMPHLIKE STEP FAIR VIRGIN PASS, 9 452
SHEE FAIR, DIVINELY FAIR, FIT LOVE FOR GODS, 9 489
HALF WHAT IN THEE IS FAIR, ONE MAN EXCEPT, 9 545
EMPRESS OF THIS FAIR WORLD, RESPLENDENT EVE, 9 568
OF TASTING THOSE FAIR APPLES, I RESOLV'D 9 585
OR EARTH, OR MIDDLE, ALL THINGS FAIR AND GOOD; 9 605
BUT ALL THAT FAIR AND GOOD IN THY DIVINE 9 606
UNITED I BEHELD; NO FAIR TO THINE 9 608
BUT OF THE FRUIT OF THIS FAIR TREE AMIDST 9 661
I QUESTION IT, FOR THIS FAIR EARTH I SEE, 9 720
CAUSES IMPORT YOUR NEED OF THIS FAIR FRUIT. 9 731
OF THIS FAIR FRUIT, OUR DOOM IS, WE SHALL DIE. 9 763
FAIR TO THE EYE, INVITING TO THE TASTE, 9 777
AND THY FAIR FRUIT LET HANG, AS TO NO END 9 798
IF ANY BE, OF TASTING THIS FAIR FRUIT, 9 972
SHE GAVE HIM OF THAT FAIR ENTICING FRUIT 9 996
NAY DIDST PERMIT, APPROVE, AND FAIR DISMISS. 9 1159
FAIR DAUGHTER, AND THOU SON AND GRANDCHILD BOTH, 10 384
THE FRUTAGE FAIR TO SIGHT, LIKE THAT WHICH GREW 10 561
SO FAIR AND GOOD CREATED, AND HAD STILL 10 618
BE IT SO, FOR I SUBMIT, HIS DOOM IS FAIR, 10 769
POSTERITIE STANDS CURST: FAIR PATRIMONIE 10 818
THIS NOVELTIE ON EARTH, THIS FAIR DEFECT 10 891
OF THESE FAIR SPREADING TREES; WHICH BIDS US SEEK 10 1067
CORRUPTED. I AT FIRST WITH TWO FAIR GIFTS 11 57
A BEAVIE OF FAIR WOMEN, RICHLY GAY 11 582
SUCH HAPPY INTERVIEW AND FAIR EVENT 11 593
FOR THAT FAIR FEMAL TROOP THOU SAWST, THAT SEEMD 11 614
OF THESE FAIR ATHEISTS, AND NOW SWIM IN JOY, 11 625
WITH FAIR EQUALITIE, FRATERNAL STATE, 12 26

FAIRE
AT SIGHT OF ALL THIS WORLD BEHELD SO FAIRE. 3 554
LED ON TH' ETERNAL SPRING. NOT THAT FAIRE FIELD 4 268
UNDER A PLATAN, YET METHOUGHT LESS FAIRE, 4 478
THOU FOLLOWING CRYD'ST ALOUD, RETURN FAIRE EVE; 4 481
MANKIND WITH HER FAIRE LOOKS, TO BE AVENGD 4 718
BACK STEPT THOSE TWO FAIRE ANGELS HALF AMAZ'D 4 820
IN PROSPECT FROM HIS THRONE, HOW GOOD, HOW FAIRE, 7 556
AND THY FAIRE EVE; HEAV'N IS FOR THEE TOO HIGH 8 172
INWARD AND OUTWARD BOTH, HIS IMAGE FAIRE: 8 221
WHAT E'RE I SAW. THOU SUN, SAID I, FAIRE LIGHT, 8 273
MANLIKE, BUT DIFFERENT SEX, SO LOVLY FAIRE, 8 471
GIVER OF ALL THINGS FAIRE, BUT FAIREST THIS 8 493
LEAST BY SOME FAIRE APPEERING GOOD SURPRIS'D 9 354
HELD DALLIANCE WITH HIS FAIRE EGYPTIAN SPOUSE. 9 443
FAIREST RESEMBLANCE OF THY MAKER FAIRE, 9 538
LONG HEE ADMIRING STOOD, TILL SIN, HIS FAIRE 10 352
CREATURE SO FAIRE HIS RECONCILEMENT SEEKING, 10 943
ENTERD SO FAIRE, SHOULD TURN ASIDE TO TREAD 11 630
A HERD OF BEEVES, FAIRE OXEN AND FAIRE KINE 11 647
RAPE OR ADULTERIE, WHERE PASSING FAIRE 11 717

FAIRER
A FAIRER PERSON LOST NOT HEAV'N; HE SEEMD 2 110
HER SELF A FAIRER FLOURE BY GLOOMIE DIS 4 270
MUCH FAIRER TO MY FANCIE THEN BY DAY: 5 53
WITH ARDOR TO ENJOY THEE, FAIRER NOW 9 1032

FAIREST
OF GOODLIEST TREES LOADEN WITH FAIREST FRUIT, 4 147
HIS SONS, THE FAIREST OF HER DAUGHTERS EVE. 4 324
MY FAIREST, MY ESPOUS'D, MY LATEST FOUND, 5 18
FAIREST OF STARRS, LAST IN THE TRAIN OF NIGHT, 5 166
THEN WOOD-NYMPH, OR THE FAIREST GODDESS FEIGN'D 5 381
LOAD'N WITH FAIREST FRUIT THAT HUNG TO THE EYE 8 307
GIVER OF ALL THINGS FAIRE, BUT FAIREST THIS 8 493
HER SELF, THOUGH FAIREST UNSUPPORTED FLOUR, 9 432
FAIREST RESEMBLANCE OF THY MAKER FAIRE, 9 538
LOADEN WITH FRUIT OF FAIREST COLOURS MIXT, 9 577
A BOUGH OF FAIREST FRUIT THAT DOWNIE SMIL'D, 9 851
O FAIREST OF CREATION, LAST AND BEST 9 896
FAIREST AND EASIEST OF THIS COMBROUS CHARGE, 11 549

FAITH
TO UNION, AND FIRM FAITH, AND FIRM ACCORD, 2 36
WHO FIRST BROKE PEACE IN HEAV'N AND FAITH, TILL
THEN 2 690
OF TRUE ALLEGIANCE, CONSTANT FAITH OR LOVE, 3 104
THE PROOF OF THIR OBEDIENCE AND THIR FAITH? 4 520
WAS THIS YOUR DISCIPLINE AND FAITH INGAG'D, 4 954
SHOULD YET REMAIN, WHERE FAITH AND REALTIE 6 115
ALL ARE NOT OF THY TRAIN; THERE BE WHO FAITH 6 143

FAITH (CONTINUED)
THE PLEDGE OF THY OBEDIENCE AND THY FAITH, 8 325
THY EQUAL FEAR THAT MY FIRM FAITH AND LOVE 9 286
NOT INCORRUPTIBLE OF FAITH, NOT PROOFF 9 298
LESS ATTRIBUTED TO HER FAITH SINCERE, 9 320
AND WHAT IS FAITH, LOVE, VERTUE UNASSAID 9 335
DESPOILD OF INNOCENCE, OF FAITH, OF BLISS. 9 411
OF INNOCENCE, OF FAITH, OF PURITIE, 9 1075
THE FAITH THEY OWE; WHEN EARNESTLY THEY SEEK 9 1141
WHOSE FAILING, WHILE HER FAITH TO ME REMAINES, 10 129
BY FAITH AND FAITHFUL WORKS, TO SECOND LIFE, 11 64
EVE, EASILY MAY FAITH ADMIT, THAT ALL 11 141
WILL BE AVENG'D, AND TH' OTHERS FAITH APPROV'D 11 458
JUSTICE AND TEMPERANCE, TRUTH AND FAITH FORGOT; 11 807
I SEE HIM, BUT THOU CANST NOT, WITH WHAT FAITH 12 128
LIKE HIM IN FAITH, IN WISDOM, AND RENOWN; 12 154
TO THEM BY FAITH IMPUTED, THEY MAY FINDE 12 295
TO FILIAL, WORKS OF LAW TO WORKS OF FAITH. 12 306
IMPUTED BECOMES THEIRS BY FAITH, HIS MERITS 12 409
BY FAITH NOT VOID OF WORKES: THIS GOD-LIKE ACT 12 427
OF ABRAHAMS FAITH WHEREVER THROUGH THE WORLD; 12 449
HIS SPIRIT WITHIN THEM, AND THE LAW OF FAITH 12 488
HIS LIVING TEMPLES, BUILT BY FAITH TO STAND, 12 527
THIR OWN FAITH NOT ANOTHERS; FOR ON EARTH 12 528
WHO AGAINST FAITH AND CONSCIENCE CAN BE HEARD 12 529
BESTUCK WITH SLANDROUS DARTS, AND WORKS OF FAITH 12 536
DEEDS TO THY KNOWLEDGE ANSWERABLE, ADD FAITH, 12 582
CHIEFLY WHAT MAY CONCERN HER FAITH TO KNOW, 12 599
BOTH IN ONE FAITH UNANIMOUS THOUGH SAD, 12 603

FAITHFUL
BUT WHEREFORE LET WE THEN OUR FAITHFUL FRIENDS, 1 264
A FAITHFUL LEADER, NOT TO HAZARD ALL 4 933
SATAN, AND COULDST THOU FAITHFUL ADD? O NAME, 4 950
FAITHFUL TO WHOM? TO THY REBELLIOUS CREW? 4 952
SO SPAKE THE SERAPH ABDIEL FAITHFUL FOUND, 5 896
AMONG THE FAITHLESS, FAITHFUL ONLY HEE; 5 897
IT SOUNDED, AND THE FAITHFUL ARMIES RUNG 6 204
AND FAITHFUL, NOW PROV'D FALSE. BUT THINK NOT HERE 6 271
FAITHFUL HATH BEEN YOUR WARFARE, AND OF GOD 6 803
OR THIS, OR WORSE, LEAVE NOT THE FAITHFUL SIDE 9 265
SO FAITHFUL LOVE UNEQUALD; BUT I FEEL 9 983
BY FAITH AND FAITHFUL WORKS, TO SECOND LIFE, 11 64
A NATION FROM ONE FAITHFUL MAN TO SPRING: 12 113
WHOM FAITHFUL ABRAHAM DUE TIME SHALL CALL, 12 152
HIS FAITHFUL, AND RECEAVE THEM INTO BLISS, 12 462
HIS FAITHFUL, LEFT AMONG TH' UNFAITHFUL HERD, 12 481
AND TO THE FAITHFUL DEATH THE GATE OF LIFE; 12 571

FAITHFULL
FOR HIS REVOLT, YET FAITHFULL HOW THEY STOOD, 1 611

FAITHFULNESS
O SACRED NAME OF FAITHFULNESS PROFAN'D. 4 951

FAITHLESS
HEE AND HIS FAITHLESS PROGENIE: WHOSE FAULT? 3 96
AMONG THE FAITHLESS, FAITHFUL ONLY HEE; 5 897

FALL
FAVOUR'D OF HEAV'N SO HIGHLY, TO FALL OFF 1 30
THERE THE COMPANIONS OF HIS FALL, O'REWHELM'D 1 76
WHICH TEMPTED OUR ATTEMPT, AND WROUGHT OUR FALL. 1 642
MORE GLORIOUS AND MORE DREAD THEN FROM NO FALL, 2 16
UP TO OUR NATIVE SEAT: DESCENT AND FALL 2 76
IMPENDENT HORRORS, THREATNING HIDEOUS FALL 2 177
CONTENDING, AND SO DOUBTFUL WHAT MIGHT FALL. 2 203
THIR OWN HEROIC DEEDS AND HAPLESS FALL 2 549
INTO THIS DEEP, AND IN THE GENERAL FALL 2 773
SOLE PLEDGE OF HIS OBEDIENCE: SO WILL FALL, 3 95
SUFFICIENT TO HAVE STOOD, THOUGH FREE TO FALL. 3 99
THIR FREEDOM, THEY THEMSELVES ORDAIN'D THIR FALL. 3 128
FALL CIRCUMVENTED THUS BY FRAUD, THOUGH JOYND 3 152
THAT THEY MAY STUMBLE ON, AND DEEPER FALL; 3 201
I OFFER, ON MEE LET THINE ANGER FALL; 3 237
SHADOW FROM BODY OPAQUE CAN FALL, AND THE AIRE, 3 619
THE LOWER STILL I FALL, ONELY SUPREAM 4 91
AND HEAVIER FALL: SO SHOULD I PURCHASE DEARE 4 101
LUXURIANT; MEAN WHILE MURMURING WATERS FALL 4 260
BUT SILENTLY A GENTLE TEAR LET FALL 5 130
THE FALL OF OTHERS FROM LIKE STATE OF BLISS; 5 241
TO LOVE OR NOT; IN THIS WE STAND OR FALL: 5 540
AND SO FROM HEAV'N TO DEEPEST HELL; O FALL 5 542
FORSAK'N OF ALL GOOD; I SEE THY FALL 5 878
HIS FIERY CHAOS TO RECEAVE THIR FALL. 6 55
TO FLIGHT, OR IF TO FALL, BUT THAT THEY RISE 6 285
AGAINST GOD AND MESSIAH, OR TO FALL 6 796
AND FELT TENFOLD CONFUSION IN THIR FALL 6 872
AMONG TH' ANGELIC POWERS, AND THE DEEP FALL 6 898
DISMOUNTED, ON TH' ALEIAN FIELD I FALL 7 19
AND ALL THE BLEST; STAND FAST; TO STAND OR FALL 8 640
SINCE HIGHER I FALL SHORT, ON HIM WHO NEXT 9 174
AND FALL INTO DECEPTION UNAWARE, 9 362
SET OVER ALL HIS WORKS, WHICH IN OUR FALL, 9 941
TO COUNTERFET MANS VOICE, TRUE IN OUR FALL, 9 1069
AND MANIFOLD IN SIN, DESERV'D TO FALL. 10 16
CONCURRING TO NECESSITATE HIS FALL, 10 44
AND ON THE SERPENT THUS HIS CURSE LET FALL. 10 174

FALL (CONTINUED)
SAW SATAN FALL LIKE LIGHTNING DOWN FROM HEAV'N, . 10 184
WITH WHAT PERMISSIVE GLORY SINCE HIS FALL . . . 10 451
REPAIRING WHERE HE JUDG'D US, PROSTRATE FALL . . 10 1087
O MISERABLE MANKIND, TO WHAT FALL 11 500
AS TO FORSAKE THE LIVING GOD, AND FALL 12 118
SATAN, WHOSE FALL FROM HEAV'N, A DEADLIER BRUISE, 12 391

FALLACIOUS
FALLACIOUS HOPE, OR ARM TH' OBDURED BREST 2 568
SOON AS THE FORCE OF THAT FALLACIOUS FRUIT, . . 9 1046

FALLIBLE
BUT PROVES NOT SO: THEN FALLIBLE, IT SEEMS, . . . 6 428

FALLING
OF HEAV'N RECEIV'D US FALLING, AND THE THUNDER, . 1 174
DROPT FROM THE ZENITH LIKE A FALLING STAR, . . . 1 745
OF HEAV'N WERE FALLING, AND THESE ELEMENTS . . . 2 925
DOWN HAD BEEN FALLING, HAD NOT BY ILL CHANCE . . 2 935
NOW FALLING WITH SOFT SLUMBROUS WEIGHT INCLINES . 4 615
OR WET THE THIRSTIE EARTH WITH FALLING SHOWERS, . 5 190
RISING OR FALLING STILL ADVANCE HIS PRAISE. . . 5 191
WHICH OF THEM RISING WITH THE SUN, OR FALLING, . 10 663

FALL'N
IF THOU BEEST HE; BUT O HOW FALL'N, HOW CHANG'D . 1 84
FROM WHAT HIGHTH FALL'N, SO MUCH THE STRONGER
PROV'D 1 92
FALL'N CHERUBE, TO BE WEAK IS MISERABLE 1 157
NO WONDER, FALL'N SUCH A PERNICIOUS HIGHTH. . . 1 282
AWAKE, ARISE, OR BE FOR EVER FALL'N. 1 330
IMMORTAL VIGOR, THOUGH OPPREST AND FALL'N, . . . 2 13
TERROR OF HEAV'N, THOUGH FALL'N; INTEND AT HOME, . 2 457
HIS FALL'N CONDITION IS, AND TO ME OW 3 181
NOT SO ON MAN; HIM THROUGH THEIR MALICE FALL'N, . 3 400
BORE HIM SLOPE DOWNWARD TO THE SUN NOW FALL'N . . 4 591
AND SOM ARE FALL'N, TO DISOBEDIENCE FALL'N, . . 5 541
THAT OF SO MANY MYRIADS FALL'N, YET ONE 6 24
EXHAUSTED, SPIRITLESS, AFFLICTED, FALL'N. . . . 6 852
TO HOARCE OR MUTE, THOUGH FALL'N ON EVIL DAYES, . 7 25
ON EVIL DAYES THOUGH FALL'N, AND EVIL TONGUES; . 7 26
IN EEVN SCALE. BUT FALL'N HE IS, AND NOW . . . 10 47
AND DESTIN'D MAN HIMSELF TO JUDGE MAN FALL'N. . . 10 62
HEAV'N-FALL'N, IN STATION STOOD OR JUST ARRAY, . 10 535
OF PARADISE COULD HAVE PRODUC'T, ERE FALL'N . . 11 29
HERE LET US LIVE, THOUGH IN FALL'N STATE, CONTENT. 11 180

FALLN
LATE FALLN HIMSELF FROM HEAV'N, IS PLOTTING NOW . 5 240

FALLS
SELF-TEMPTED, SELF-DEPRAV'D: MAN FALLS DECEIV'D . 3 130
PARTAKERS, AND UNCROPT FALLS TO THE GROUND. . . 4 731
CAST OUT FROM GOD AND BLESSED VISION, FALLS . . 5 613
ALL HIGHER KNOWLEDGE IN HER PRESENCE FALLS . . . 8 551

FALLST
AND WHEN HIGH NOON HAST GAIND, AND WHEN THOU
FALLST. 5 174

FALSE
BUT ALL WAS FALSE AND HOLLOW; THOUGH HIS TONGUE . 2 112
BY FALSE PRESUMPTUOUS HOPE, THE RANGED POWERS . . 2 522
VAIN WISDOM ALL, AND FALSE PHILOSOPHIE: 2 565
FALSE FUGITIVE, AND TO THY SPEED ADD WINGS, . . 2 700
BY SOME FALSE GUILE PERVERT; AND SHALL PERVERT . 3 92
SO SPAKE THE FALSE DISSEMBLER UNPERCEIVD; . . . 3 681
SO SPAKE THE FALSE ARCH-ANGEL, AND INFUS'D . . . 5 694
O ARGUMENT BLASPHEMOUS, FALSE AND PROUD. . . . 5 809
AMONG INNUMERABLE FALSE, UNMOV'D, ... 5 898
UNSOUND AND FALSE; NOR IS IT AUGHT BUT JUST, . . 6 121
AND FAITHFUL, NOW PROV'D FALSE. BUT THINK NOT HERE 6 271
NOR THOU HIS MALICE AND FALSE GUILE CONTEMN; . . 9 306
FROM HIS SURMISE PROV'D FALSE, FIND PEACE WITHIN, 9 333
SHE DICTATE FALSE, AND MISSINFORME THE WILL . . 9 355
WHEREWITH TO SCORNE THE EARTH: BUT THAT FALSE FRUIT 9 1011
TO THAT FALSE WORM, OF WHOMSOEVER TAUGHT . . . 9 1068
FALSE IN OUR PROMIS'D RISING; SINCE OUR EYES . . 9 1070
WAS LEFT HIM, OR FALSE GLITTER: ALL AMAZ'D . . . 10 452
BEFITS THEE WITH HIM LEAGU'D, THY SELF AS FALSE . 10 868
WHICH THAT FALSE FRUIT THAT PROMIS'D CLEARER SIGHT 11 413
HIS KINDRED AND FALSE GODS, INTO A LAND 12 122

FALSHOOD
THAT PRACTISD FALSHOOD UNDER SAINTLY SHEW, . . . 4 122
TOUCH'D LIGHTLY; FOR NO FALSHOOD CAN ENDURE . . 4 811
TO HELLISH FALSHOOD, SNARE THEM. BUT FOR THEE . 10 873

FALSITIES
BY FALSITIES AND LYES THE GREATEST PART 1 367

FAM'D
LIKE THOSE HESPERIAN GARDENS FAM'D OF OLD, . . . 3 568
AND HIS NEXT SON FOR WEALTH AND WISDOM FAM'D, . . 12 332

FAME
THERE WENT A FAME IN HEAV'N THAT HE ERE LONG . . 1 651

FAME (CONTINUED)
LEARN HOW THIR GREATEST MONUMENTS OF FAME, ... 1 695
(IF ANCIENT AND PROPHETIC FAME IN HEAV'N 2 346
BUILT THIR FOND HOPES OF GLORIE OR LASTING FAME, . 3 449
FAME IS NOT SILENT, HERE IN HOPE TO FIND . . . 4 938
OF VICTORIE; DEEDS OF ETERNAL FAME 6 240
ANGELS CONTENTED WITH THIR FAME IN HEAV'N . . . 6 375
VAIN GLORIOUS, AND THROUGH INFAMIE SEEKS FAME: . 6 384
THE NEW CREATED WORLD, WHICH FAME IN HEAV'N . . 10 481
CITY OF OLD OR MODERN FAME, THE SEAT 11 386
SHALL YIELD UP ALL THIR VERTUE, ALL THIR FAME . . 11 623
THUS FAME SHALL BE ATCHIEV'D, RENOWN ON EARTH, . 11 698
AND WHAT MOST MERITS FAME IN SILENCE HID. . . . 11 699
FAME IN THE WORLD, HIGH TITLES, AND RICH PREY, . 11 793
REGARDLESS WHETHER GOOD OR EVIL FAME. 12 47

FAMILIAR
FAMILIAR THE FIERCE HEAT, AND VOID OF PAIN; . . 2 219
PORTENTOUS HELD ME; BUT FAMILIAR GROWN, ... 2 761
WITH MAN, AS WITH HIS FRIEND, FAMILIAR US'D . . 9 2
FAMILIAR TO OUR EYES, ALL PLACES ELSE 11 305

FAMILIE
AS FATHER OF HIS FAMILIE HE CLAD 10 216

FAMILIES
LONG TIME IN PEACE BY FAMILIES AND TRIBES . . . 12 23

FAMIN
AND WORN WITH FAMIN, LONG AND CEASLESS HISS, . . 10 573
TO MEE, WHO WITH ETERNAL FAMIN PINE, ... 10 597
BY FIRE, FLOOD, FAMIN, BY INTEMPERANCE MORE . . 11 472
FAMIN AND ANGUISH WILL AT LAST CONSUME 11 778

FAMINE
HIS FAMINE SHOULD BE FILL'D, AND BLEST HIS MAWE . 2 847

FAMISH
AND FAMISH HIM OF BREATH, IF NOT OF BREAD? . . . 12 78

FAMOUS
RUNS DIVERS, WANDRING MANY A FAMOUS REALME . . . 4 234

FAN
OF LEAVES AND FUMING RILLS, AURORA'S FAN, . . . 5 6
TO FAN THE EARTH NOW WAK'D, AND USHER IN . . . 10 94

FANATIC
FANATIC EGYPT AND HER PRIESTS, TO SEEK 1 480

FANCIE
THE ORGANS OF HER FANCIE, AND WITH THEM FORGE . . 4 802
MUCH FAIRER TO MY FANCIE THEN BY DAY: 5 53
BUT APT THE MIND OR FANCIE IS TO ROAVE 8 188
OF FANCIE MY INTERNAL SIGHT, BY WHICH 8 461

FANCIES
HER VIRGIN FANCIES, POURING FORTH MORE SWEET, . . 5 296

FANCY
MY FANCY TO BELIEVE I YET HAD BEING, ... 8 294

FANN
NOW ON THE POLAR WINDES, THEN WITH QUICK FANN . . 5 269

FANN'D
FLOATS, AS THEY PASS, FANN'D WITH UNNUMBER'D
PLUMES: 7 432

FANND
FANND WITH COOLE WINDS, SAVE THOSE WHO IN THIR
COURSE 5 655

FANNING
FANNING THIR ODORIFEROUS WINGS DISPENSE 4 157

FANS
INSECT OR WORME; THOSE WAV'D THIR LIMBER FANS . . 7 476

FANSIE
REASON AS CHIEF; AMONG THESE FANSIE NEXT . . . 5 102
OFT IN HER ABSENCE MIMIC FANSIE WAKES 5 110
FANSIE AND UNDERSTANDING, WHENCE THE SOULE . . . 5 486
THEY SWIM IN MIRTH, AND FANSIE THAT THEY FEEL . . 9 1009

FANSIED
OR FANSIED SO, THROUGH EXPECTATION HIGH 9 789

FANTASM
ME FATHER, AND THAT FANTASM CALL'ST MY SON? . . 2 743

FANTING
THIR FANTING COURAGE, AND DISPEL'D THIR FEARS. . 1 530

FAR
AT ONCE AS FAR AS ANGELS KENN HE VIEWS 1 59
AS FAR REMOV'D FROM GOD AND LIGHT OF HEAV'N . . 1 73
AS FAR AS GODS AND HEAV'NLY ESSENCES 1 138

FAR (CONTINUED)
THE REST WERE LONG TO TELL, THOUGH FAR RENOWN'D, 1 507
BY FONTARABBIA. THUS FAR THESE BEYOND 1 587
(FAR OTHER ONCE BEHELD IN BLISS) CONDEMN'D 1 607
FAR ROUND ILLUMIN'D HELL: HIGHLY THEY RAG'D 1 666
THERE STOOD A HILL NOT FAR WHOSE GRIESLY TOP 1 670
OF THAT INFERNAL COURT. BUT FAR WITHIN 1 792
HIGH ON A THRONE OF ROYAL STATE, WHICH FAR 2 1
IN STRICTEST BONDAGE, THOUGH THUS FAR REMOV'D, 2 321
INFLAM'D WITH LUST THEN RAGE) AND SWIFTER FAR, 2 791
YOUR DUNGEON STRETCHING FAR AND WIDE BENEATH; 2 1003
FAR OFF AND FEARLESS, NOR WITH CAUSE TO BOAST, 4 14
TWO OF FAR NOBLER SHAPE ERECT AND TALL, 4 288
NOT DISTANT FAR FROM THENCE A MURMURING SOUND 4 453
DIVINE EFFULGENCE, WHOSE HIGH POWER SO FAR 5 458
FAR WAS ADVANC'T ON WINGED SPEED, AN HOST 5 744
HIGH ON A HILL, FAR BLAZING, AS A MOUNT 5 757
UNIVERSAL REPROACH, FAR WORSE TO BEARE 6 34
FAR OTHERWISE TH' INVIOLABLE SAINTS 6 398
FAR IN THE DARK DISLODG'D, AND VOID OF REST, 6 415
FROM FAR WITH THUNDRING NOISE AMONG OUR FOES 6 487
NOT DISTANT FAR WITH HEAVIE PACE THE FOE 6 551
STROOK THEM WITH HORROR BACKWARD, BUT FAR WORSE 6 863
(THOUGH HIGHER OF THE GENIAL BED BY FAR, 8 598
HER HUSBAND, FOR I VIEW FAR ROUND, NOT NIGH, 9 482
BUT SAY, WHERE GROWN THE TREE, FROM HENCE HOW FAR? 9 617
MY COMING SEEN FAR OFF? I MISS THEE HERE, 10 104
AND GET THEMSELVES A NAME, LEAST FAR DISPERST 12 45
SHALL ALL BE PARADISE, FAR HAPPIER PLACE 12 464
THEN THIS OF EDEN, AND FAR HAPPIER DAIES. 12 465

FARDEST
WHAT SHALL BE RIGHT: FARDEST FROM HIM IS BEST 1 247
HER FARDEST VERGE, AND CHAOS TO RETIRE 2 1038
OF CONGO, AND ANGOLA FARDEST SOUTH; 11 401

FARE
NO INCONVENIENT DIET, NOR TOO LIGHT FARE; 5 495
AS MEET IS, AFTER SUCH DELICIOUS FARE; 9 1028
OF EASIE THOROUGH-FARE. THEREFORE WHILE I 10 393
MY HEAD, ILL FARE OUR ANCESTOR IMPURE, 10 735

FARES
NOR GOOD DRY LAND: NIGH FOUNDERD ON HE FARES, 2 940
SO ON HE FARES, AND TO THE BORDER COMES, 4 131

FAREWEL
ABOVE HIS EQUALS. FAREWEL HAPPY FIELDS 1 249

FAREWELL
IF CHANCE THE RADIANT SUN WITH FAREWELL SWEET 2 492

FARING
SEA-FARING MEN OREWATCHT, WHOSE BARK BY CHANCE 2 288

FARMES
AMONG THE PLEASANT VILLAGES AND FARMES 9 448

FARR
THUS FARR AT LEAST RECOVER'D, HATH MUCH MORE 2 22
TO NOTHING THIS ESSENTIAL, HAPPIER FARR 2 97
SCOUT FARR AND WIDE INTO THE REALM OF NIGHT, 2 133
HIS ANGER, AND PERHAPS THUS FARR REMOV'D 2 211
HEARD FARR AND WIDE, AND ALL THE HOST OF HELL 2 519
FARR OFF FROM THESE A SLOW AND SILENT STREAM, 2 582
AS WHEN FARR OFF AT SEA A FLEET DESCRI'D 2 636
FARR OFF THE FLYING FIEND: AT LAST APPEER 2 643
WITHIN UNSEEN. FARR LESS ABHORRD THAN THESE 2 659
IF THAT WAY BE YOUR WALK, YOU HAVE NOT FARR; 2 1007
SHOOTS FARR INTO THE BOSOM OF DIM NIGHT 2 1036
FARR OFF TH' EMPYREAL HEAV'N, EXTENDED WIDE 2 1047
NOT FARR OFF HEAV'N, IN THE PRECINCTS OF LIGHT, 3 88
WITH HIS OWN FOLLY? THAT BE FROM THEE FARR, 3 153
THAT FARR BE FROM THEE, FATHER, WHO ART JUDG 3 154
FARR MORE THEN GREAT OR HIGH; BECAUSE IN THEE 3 311
SATAN ALIGHTED WALKS: A GLOBE FARR OFF 3 422
THOUGH DISTANT FARR SOM SMALL REFLECTION GAINES 3 428
HERE PILGRIMS ROAM, THAT STRAY'D SO FARR TO SEEK 3 476
FLY O'RE THE BACKSIDE OF THE WORLD FARR OFF 3 494
HIS TRAVELL'D STEPS; FARR DISTANT HE DESCRIES 3 501
AT TOP WHEREOF, BUT FARR MORE RICH APPEERD 3 504
WIDER BY FARR THEN THAT OF AFTER-TIMES 3 529
ANDROMEDA FARR OFF ATLANTIC SEAS 3 559
DISPENSES LIGHT FROM FARR; THEY AS THEY MOVE 3 579
TH' ARCH-CHIMIC SUN SO FARR FROM US REMOTE 3 609
UNDAZL'D, FARR AND WIDE HIS EYE COMMANDS, 3 614
TO OBJECTS DISTANT FARR, WHEREBY HE SOON 3 621
THIS KNOWS MY PUNISHER; THEREFORE AS FARR 4 103
HIS FARR MORE PLEASANT GARDEN GOD ORDAIND; 4 215
SO FARR THE HAPPIER LOT, ENJOYING THEE 4 446
CONSPICUOUS FARR, WINDING WITH ONE ASCENT 4 545
SEE FARR AND WIDE: IN AT THIS GATE NONE PASS 4 579
FARR BE IT, THAT I SHOULD WRITE THEE SIN OR BLAME, 4 758
FARR HEAVIER LOAD THY SELF EXPECT TO FEEL 4 972
OF FRUIT-TREES OVERWOODIE REACHD TOO FARR 5 213
TRANSCEND HIS OWN SO FARR, WHOSE RADIANT FORMS 5 457
WIDE OVER ALL THE PLAIN, AND WIDER FARR 5 648
THUS FARR HIS BOLD DISCOURSE WITHOUT CONTROULE 5 803

FARR (CONTINUED)
HOW PROVIDENT HE IS, HOW FARR FROM THOUGHT 5 828
FARR IN TH' HORIZON TO THE NORTH APPEER'D 6 79
I FLIE NOT, BUT HAVE SOUGHT THEE FARR AND NIGH. 6 295
HUMBL'D BY SUCH REBUKE, SO FARR BENEATH 6 342
FOR THEE I HAVE ORDAIN'D IT, AND THUS FARR 6 700
FARR SEPARATE, CIRCLING THY HOLY MOUNT 6 743
HE ONWARD CAME, FARR OFF HIS COMING SHON, 6 768
ILLUSTRIOUS FARR AND WIDE, BUT BY HIS OWN 6 773
BUT DRIVE FARR OFF THE BARBAROUS DISSONANCE 7 32
FARR DIFFERING FROM THIS WORLD, THOU HAST REVEAL'D 7 71
YET FARR THE GREATER PART HAVE KEPT, I SEE, 7 145
FARR INTO CHAOS, AND THE WORLD UNBORN; 7 220
AND SAID, THUS FARR EXTEND, THUS FARR THY BOUNDS, 7 230
OF CHAOS FARR REMOV'D, LEAST FIERCE EXTREAMES 7 272
OF LIGHT BY FARR THE GREATER PART HE TOOK, 7 359
SO FARR REMOTE, WITH DIMINUTION SEEN. 7 369
FROM HEAVEN GATE NOT FARR, FOUNDED IN VIEW 7 618
THAT BETTER MIGHT WITH FARR LESS COMPASS MOVE, 8 33
SO SPACIOUS, AND HIS LINE STRETCHT OUT SO FARR; 8 102
PLAC'D HEAV'N FROM EARTH SO FARR, THAT EARTHLY
SIGHT, 8 120
EACH ORB A GLIMPS OF LIGHT, CONVEYD SO FARR 8 156
CONTENTED THAT THUS FARR HATH BEEN REVEAL'D 8 177
GOD HATH BID DWELL FARR OFF ALL ANXIOUS CARES, 8 185
FARR ON EXCURSION TOWARD THE GATES OF HELL; 8 231
SURPASSEST FARR MY NAMING, HOW MAY I 8 359
AND THESE INFERIOUR FARR BENEATH ME SET? 8 382
THUS FARR TO TRY THEE, ADAM, I WAS PLEAS'D, 8 437
WHEN OUT OF HOPE, BEHOLD HER, NOT FARR OFF, 8 481
FARR OTHERWISE, TRANSPORTED I BEHOLD, 8 529
DOWNWARD AS FARR ANTARTIC; AND IN LENGTH 9 79
MAY FINDE US BOTH PERHAPS FARR LESS PREPAR'D, 9 381
FROM HER BEST PROP SO FARR, AND STORM SO NIGH. 9 433
A GOODLY TREE FARR DISTANT TO BEHOLD 9 576
THERE SWALLOW'D UP AND LOST, FROM SUCCOUR FARR. 9 642
FRIENDLY TO MAN, FARR FROM DECEIT OR GUILE. 9 772
FARR OTHERWISE TH' EVENT, NOT DEATH, BUT LIFE 9 984
FARR OTHER OPERATION FIRST DISPLAID, 9 1012
AND FOR THEE, WHOSE PERFECTION FARR EXCELL'D 10 150
REMOV'D FARR OFF; THEN PITTYING HOW THEY STOOD 10 211
FARR INTO CHAOS, SINCE THE FIEND PASS'D THROUGH, 10 233
SAGACIOUS OF HIS QUARRY FROM SO FARR. 10 281
TO FORTIFIE THUS FARR, AND OVERLAY 10 370
FARR TO THE INLAND RETIR'D, ABOUT THE WALLS 10 423
WITH TRAVAIL DIFFICULT, NOT BETTER FARR 10 593
FROM COLD ESTOTILAND, AND SOUTH AS FARR 10 686
TO ANSWER, AND RESOUND FARR OTHER SONG. 10 862
BY A FARR WORSE, OR IF SHE LOVE, WITHHELD 10 903
AND SENDS A COMFORTABLE HEAT FROM FARR, 10 1077
WIDE WAVING, ALL APPROACH FARR OFF TO FRIGHT, 11 121
FARR OTHER NAME DESERVING. BUT THE FIELD 11 171
OF GLORY, AND FARR OFF HIS STEPS ADORE. 11 333
CONTENDING, AND REMOV'D HIS TENTS FARR OFF; 11 727
BUT I WAS FARR DECEAV'D; FOR NOW I SEE 11 783
FARR LESS I NOW LAMENT FOR ONE WHOLE WORLD 11 874
AND FIX FARR DEEPER IN HIS HEAD THIR STINGS 12 432
OF SPIRIT AND TRUTH; THE REST, FARR GREATER PART, 12 533
A PARADISE WITHIN THEE, HAPPIER FARR. 12 587

FARTHEST
FARTHEST FROM PAIN, WHERE THOU MIGHTST HOPE TO
CHANGE 4 892

FARWEL
SO FARWEL HOPE, AND WITH HOPE FARWEL FEAR, 4 108
FARWEL REMORSE: ALL GOOD TO ME IS LOST; 4 109

FASHOND
THE RIB HE FORMD AND FASHOND WITH HIS HANDS; 8 469

FAST
FAST BY THE ORACLE OF GOD; I THENCE 1 12
THE MONSTER MOVING ONWARD CAME AS FAST 2 675
FAST BY HELL GATE, AND KEPT THE FATAL KEY, 2 725
IN DARKNESS, WHILE THY HEAD FLAMES THICK AND FAST 2 754
AND FAST BY HANGING IN A GOLDEN CHAIN 2 1051
IN PARADISE, FAST BY THE TREE OF LIFE 3 354
FROM MEDIA POST TO AEGYPT, THERE FAST BOUND. 4 171
CROSS-BARRD AND BOLTED FAST, FEAR NO ASSAULT, 4 190
OUR DEATH THE TREE OF KNOWLEDGE GREW FAST BY, 4 221
SUCH WHERE YE FIND, SEISE FAST, AND HITHER BRING. 4 796
WITHIN THE MOUNT OF GOD, FAST BY HIS THRONE, 6 5
FIT WELL HIS HELME, GRIPE FAST HIS ORBED SHIELD, 6 543
HER DARK FOUNDATIONS, AND TOO FAST HAD BOUND. 6 870
OUR PROMPT OBEDIENCE. FAST WE FOUND, FAST SHUT 8 240
AND ALL THE BLEST; STAND FAST; TO STAND OR FALL 8 640
THE SERPENT: HIM FAST SLEEPING SOON HE FOUND 9 182
FAST BY A FOUNTAIN, ONE SMALL THICKET PAST 9 628
AND CHAINS THEY MADE ALL FAST, TOO FAST THEY MADE 10 319
INTO THE WOOD FAST BY, AND CHANGING SHAPE 10 333
DOWN FELL BOTH SPEAR AND SHIELD, DOWN THEY AS FAST, 10 542
FAST CAUGHT, THEY LIK'D, AND EACH HIS LIKING CHOSE; 11 587
WITH THIR FOUR WIVES; AND GOD MADE FAST THE DORE. 11 737
FAST ON THE TOP OF SOM HIGH MOUNTAIN FIXT. 11 851
AND GATHERS GROUND FAST AT THE LABOURERS HEEL 12 631
LED THEM DIRECT, AND DOWN THE CLIFF AS FAST 12 639

FASTEN'D
- THEY FASTEN'D, AND THE MOLE IMMENSE WRAUGHT ON . 10 300

FAT
- THE INWARDS AND THIR FAT, WITH INCENSE STREW'D, . 11 439
- FROM A FAT MEDDOW GROUND; OR FLEECY FLOCK, . . . 11 648

FATAL
- THOUGH INACCESSIBLE, HIS FATAL THRONE: 2 104
- FAST BY HELL GATE, AND KEPT THE FATAL KEY, . . . 2 725
- FORTH ISSU'D, BRANDISHING HIS FATAL DART . . . 2 786
- THUS SAYING, FROM HER SIDE THE FATAL KEY, . . . 2 871
- HIS BREADED TRAIN, AND OF HIS FATAL GUILE . . . 4 349
- ONE FATAL TREE THERE STANDS OF KNOWLEDGE CALL'D, . 4 514
- BY OUR OWN QUICK'NING POWER, WHEN FATAL COURSE . 5 861
- THE FATAL TRESPASS DON BY EVE, AMAZ'D, ... 9 889
- EEVN HEE WHO NOW FORETOLD HIS FATAL BRUISE, . . 10 191
- SUCH FATAL CONSEQUENCE UNITES US THREE; 10 364
- BUT JUSTICE, AND SOME FATAL CURSE ANNEXT . . . 12 99

FATALL
- LEVEL'D HIS DEADLY AIME; THIR FATALL HANDS . . . 2 712
- HER HUSBAND SHEE, TO TASTE THE FATALL FRUIT, . . 10 4

FATE
- THIS DOWNFALL; SINCE BY FATE THE STRENGTH OF GODS 1 116
- WHETHER UPHELD BY STRENGTH, OR CHANCE, OR FATE, . 1 133
- THE SYRIAN DAMSELS TO LAMENT HIS FATE 1 448
- AND TRUST THEMSELVES TO FEAR NO SECOND FATE: . . 2 17
- BY MY ADVICE; SINCE FATE INEVITABLE 2 197
- MAY HOPE WHEN EVERLASTING FATE SHALL YEILD . . . 2 232
- WILL ONCE MORE LIFT US UP, IN SPIGHT OF FATE, . . 2 393
- BY DOOM OF BATTEL; AND COMPLAIN THAT FATE . . . 2 550
- OF PROVIDENCE, FOREKNOWLEDGE, WILL AND FATE, . . 2 559
- FIXT FATE, FREE WILL, FOREKNOWLEDG ABSOLUTE, . . 2 560
- BUT FATE WITHSTANDS, AND TO OPPOSE TH' ATTEMPT . 2 610
- WHEN EVER THAT SHALL BE; SO FATE PRONOUNC'D. . . 2 809
- THOSE OTHER TWO EQUAL'D WITH ME IN FATE, . . . 3 33
- THIR MAKER, OR THIR MAKING, OR THIR FATE, . . . 3 113
- SO WITHOUT LEAST IMPULSE OR SHADOW OF FATE, . . 3 120
- BY NATURE FREE, NOT OVER-RUL'D BY FATE 5 527
- AFFRIGHTED; BUT STRICT FATE HAD CAST TOO DEEP . 6 869
- APPROACH NOT MEE, AND WHAT I WILL IS FATE. . . 7 173
- AND LIFE MORE PERFET HAVE ATTAIND THEN FATE . . 9 689
- DEITIE FOR THEE, WHEN FATE WILL NOT PERMIT. . . 9 885
- NOT GOD OMNIPOTENT, NOR FATE, YET SO 9 927
- GOE WHITHER FATE AND INCLINATION STRONG . . . 10 265
- PROTESTING FATE SUPREAME; THENCE HOW I FOUND . 10 480
- SO SPAKE, SO WISH'D MUCH-HUMBL'D EVE, BUT FATE . 11 181

FATHER
- O FATHER, WHAT INTENDS THY HAND, SHE CRY'D, . . 2 727
- ME FATHER, AND THAT FANTASM CALL'ST MY SON? . . 2 743
- BUT THOU O FATHER, I FOREWARN THEE, SHUN . . . 2 810
- THOU ART MY FATHER, THOU MY AUTHOR, THOU . . . 2 864
- NOW HAD THE ALMIGHTY FATHER FROM ABOVE, ... 3 56
- MOST GLORIOUS, IN HIM ALL HIS FATHER SHON . . . 3 139
- WHICH UTTERING THUS HE TO HIS FATHER SPAKE. . . 3 143
- O FATHER, GRACIOUS WAS THAT WORD WHICH CLOS'D . 3 144
- THAT FARR BE FROM THEE, FATHER, WHO ART JUDG . . 3 154
- FATHER, THY WORD IS PAST, MAN SHALL FIND GRACE; 3 227
- FATHER, TO SEE THY FACE, WHEREIN NO CLOUD . . . 3 262
- OF HIS GREAT FATHER. ADMIRATION SEIS'D 3 271
- THEE FATHER FIRST THEY SUNG OMNIPOTENT, ... 3 372
- MADE VISIBLE, TH' ALMIGHTY FATHER SHINES, . . . 3 386
- FATHER OF MERCIE AND GRACE, THOU DIDST NOT DOOME 3 401
- ON OUR FIRST FATHER, HALF HER SWELLING BREAST . 4 495
- OF FATHER, SON, AND BROTHER FIRST WERE KNOWN. . 4 757
- SO SPAKE TH' ETERNAL FATHER, AND FULFILLD . . . 5 246
- THAT ONE CELESTIAL FATHER GIVES TO ALL. 5 403
- ORB WITHIN ORB, THE FATHER INFINITE, ... 5 596
- HONOURD BY HIS GREAT FATHER, AND PROCLAIMD . . 5 663
- MADE ANSWER. MIGHTIE FATHER, THOU THY FOES . . 5 735
- AS BY HIS WORD THE MIGHTY FATHER MADE 5 836
- TH' INCENSED FATHER, AND TH' INCENSED SON, . . 5 847
- FROM FATHER TO HIS SON? STRANGE POINT AND NEW. . 5 855
- HYMNING TH' ETERNAL FATHER: BUT THE SHOUT . . . 6 96
- HAD NOT TH' ALMIGHTIE FATHER WHERE HE SITS . . 6 671
- SHON FULL, HE ALL HIS FATHER FULL EXPREST . . . 6 720
- O FATHER, O SUPREAM OF HEAV'NLY THRONES, . . . 6 723
- BECAUSE THE FATHER, T' WHOM IN HEAV'N SUPREAM . 6 814
- AND TEMPLE OF HIS MIGHTIE FATHER THRON'D . . . 6 890
- IN PRESENCE OF TH' ALMIGHTIE FATHER, PLEAS'D . . 7 11
- ETERNAL FATHER FROM HIS THRONE BEHELD 7 137
- IMMENSE, AND ALL HIS FATHER IN HIM SHON. . . . 7 196
- ETERNAL FATHER (FOR WHERE IS NOT HEE 7 517
- WITH HIS GREAT FATHER (FOR HE ALSO WENT . . . 7 588
- FIRST FATHER, CALL'D BY THEE I COME THY GUIDE . 8 298
- FATHER AND MOTHER, AND TO HIS WIFE ADHERE; . . 8 498
- ETERNAL FATHER FROM HIS SECRET CLOUD, ... 10 32
- SO SPAKE THE FATHER, AND UNFOULDING BRIGHT . . 10 63
- RESPLENDENT ALL HIS FATHER MANIFEST 10 66
- FATHER ETERNAL, THINE IS TO DECREE, ... 10 68
- AS FATHER OF HIS FAMILIE HE CLAD 10 216
- SO SPAKE OUR FATHER PENITENT, NOR EVE 10 1097
- SEE FATHER, WHAT FIRST FRUITS ON EARTH ARE SPRUNG 11 22
- TO WHOM THE FATHER, WITHOUT CLOUD, SERENE. . . . 11 45
- THOUGH COMFORTLESS, AS WHEN A FATHER MOURNS . . 11 760

FATHER (CONTINUED)
- DON TO HIS FATHER, HEARD THIS HEAVIE CURSE, . . . 12 103
- THE PROMISE OF THE FATHER, WHO SHALL DWELL . . . 12 487
- IN GLORY OF THE FATHER, TO DISSOLVE 12 546

FATHERLY
- WHERETO THUS ADAM FATHERLY DISPLEAS'D. 12 63

FATHERS
- AGAINST THY FATHERS HEAD? AND KNOW'ST FOR WHOM; . 2 730
- THY FATHERS DREADFUL THUNDER DIDST NOT SPARE, . . 3 393
- THEE ONLY EXTOLL'D, SON OF THY FATHERS MIGHT, . . 3 398
- FORGET, NOR FROM THY FATHERS PRAISE DISJOINE. . . 3 415
- GO THEN THOU MIGHTIEST IN THY FATHERS MIGHT, . . 6 710
- ARAYING COVER'D FROM HIS FATHERS SIGHT. . . . 10 223
- BEFORE THE FATHERS THRONE: THEM THE GLAD SON . . 11 20
- TO CALL BY VISION FROM HIS FATHERS HOUSE, . . . 12 121

FAULT
- MILLIONS OF SPIRITS FOR HIS FAULT AMERC'T . . . 1 609
- HEE AND HIS FAITHLESS PROGENIE: WHOSE FAULT? . . 3 96
- FOREKNOWLEDGE HAD NO INFLUENCE ON THEIR FAULT, . 3 118
- FOR ONE MANS FAULT THUS GUILTLESS BE CONDEMN'D, . 10 823
- IMMOVEABLE TILL PEACE OBTAIN'D FROM FAULT . . . 10 938

FAULTIE
- SO GOODLY AND ERECT, THOUGH FAULTIE SINCE, . . . 11 509

FAULTRING
- WITH FAULTRING SPEECH AND VISAGE INCOMPOS'D . . 2 989
- MISGAVE HIM; HEE THE FAULTRING MEASURE FELT; . . 9 846
- WHENCE ADAM FAULTRING LONG, THUS ANSWER'D BRIEF. . 10 115

FAULTS
- HUMBLY OUR FAULTS, AND PARDON BEG, WITH TEARS . . 10 1089
- HUMBLY THIR FAULTS, AND PARDON BEG'D, WITH TEARS . 10 1101
- WHOSE FOUL IDOLATRIES, AND OTHER FAULTS 12 337

FAUNUS
- NOR FAUNUS HAUNTED. HERE IN CLOSE RECESS . . . 4 708

FAVOR
- WHAT ELSE BUT FAVOR, GRACE, AND MERCIE SHON? . . 10 1096

FAVORITE
- PROVOKES MY ENVIE, THIS NEW FAVORITE 9 175

FAVORS
- MOST FAVORS, WHO CAN PLEASE HIM LONG; MEE FIRST . 9 949

FAVOUR
- SHOULD FAVOUR EQUAL TO THE SONS OF HEAVEN: . . . 1 654
- HIS CHIEF DELIGHT AND FAVOUR, HIM FOR WHOM . . . 3 664
- THY FAVOUR, IN THIS HONOUR DONE TO MAN, ... 5 462
- IN FAVOUR AND PRAEEMINENCE, YET FRAUGHT 5 661
- DIVINE INTERPRETER, BY FAVOUR SENT 7 72
- BY SUFFERANCE, AND THY WONTED FAVOUR DEIGN'D. . 8 202
- FAVOUR FROM HEAV'N, OUR WITNESS FROM TH' EVENT, . 9 334
- THAT I WAS HEARD WITH FAVOUR; PEACE RETURND . . 11 153
- FAVOUR UNMERITED BY ME, WHO SOUGHT 12 278
- SUCH FAVOUR I UNWORTHIE AM VOUTSAFT, ... 12 622

FAVOURABLE
- O FAVOURABLE SPIRIT, PROPITIOUS GUEST, ... 5 507
- THE SOURSE OF LIFE; NEXT FAVOURABLE THOU, . . . 11 169

FAVOUR'D
- FAVOUR'D OF HEAV'N SO HIGHLY, TO FALL OFF . . . 1 30
- IN POWER AND EXCELLENCE, BUT FAVOUR'D MORE . . . 2 350

FAVOURS
- THAT CUTS US OFF FROM HOPE, AND FAVOURS ONELY . . 10 1043

FAWN'D
- ONCE FAWN'D, AND CRING'D, AND SERVILLY ADOR'D . . 4 959

FAWNES
- IN SOME PURLIEU TWO GENTLE FAWNES AT PLAY, . . . 4 404

FAWNING
- FAWNING, AND LICK'D THE GROUND WHEREON SHE TROD. . 9 526

FEALTIE
- DISLOYAL BREAKS HIS FEALTIE, AND SINNS 3 204
- FROM THEE THIR NAMES, AND PAY THEE FEALTIE . . . 8 344
- OUR FEALTIE FROM GOD, OR TO DISTURB 9 262

FEAR
- ANGUISH AND DOUBT AND FEAR AND SORROW AND PAIN . 1 558
- ON HALF THE NATIONS, AND WITH FEAR OF CHANGE . . 1 598
- AT ONCE WITH JOY AND FEAR HIS HEART REBOUNDS. . . 1 788
- AND TRUST THEMSELVES TO FEAR NO SECOND FATE: . . 2 17
- WENT ALL HIS FEAR: OF GOD, OR HELL, OR WORSE . . 2 49
- FEAR TO BE WORSE DESTROY'D: WHAT CAN BE WORSE . . 2 85
- WHAT FEAR WE THEN? WHAT DOUBT WE TO INCENSE . . 2 94
- AND VENT'ROUS, IF THAT FAIL THEM, SHRINK AND FEAR 2 205
- THEY DREADED WORSE THEN HELL; SO MUCH THE FEAR . 2 293
- HEAV'N, WHOSE HIGH WALLS FEAR NO ASSAULT OR SIEGE, 2 343

FEAR (CONTINUED)
THAN FABLES YET HAVE FEIGN'D, OR FEAR CONCEIV'D, 2 627
TORE THROUGH MY ENTRAILS, THAT WITH FEAR AND PAIN 2 783
SO FARWEL HOPE, AND WITH HOPE FARWEL FEAR, 4 108
CROSS-BARRD AND BOLTED FAST, FEAR NO ASSAULT, 4 190
I FEAR, HATH VENTUR'D FROM THE DEEP, TO RAISE 4 574
YET THUS, UNMOVD WITH FEAR, ACCOST HIM SOON. 4 822
OR LESS BE LOST. THY FEAR, SAID ZEPHON BOLD, 4 854
THIS UNCOUTH DREAM, OF EVIL SPRUNG I FEAR; 5 98
NO FEAR LEST DINNER COOLE; WHEN THUS BEGAN 5 396
THAT ARGU'D FEAR; EACH ON HIMSELF RELI'D, 6 238
DEFENSIVE SCARSE, OR WITH PALE FEAR SURPRIS'D, 6 393
THEN FIRST WITH FEAR SURPRIS'D AND SENSE OF PAINE 6 394
NOT LIABLE TO FEAR OR FLIGHT OR PAINE. 6 397
ADVERSE, THAT THEY SHALL FEAR WE HAVE DISARMD 6 490
ABANDON FEAR; TO STRENGTH AND COUNSEL JOIND 6 494
THIS DAY, FEAR NOT HIS FLIGHT; SO THICK A CLOUD 6 539
YET FELL; REMEMBER, AND FEAR TO TRANSGRESS. 6 912
EATE FREELY WITH GLAD HEART; FEAR HERE NO DEARTH: 8 322
HIS FRAUD IS THEN THY FEAR, WHICH PLAIN INFERRS 9 285
THY EQUAL FEAR THAT MY FIRM FAITH AND LOVE 9 286
HOW ARE WE HAPPIE, STILL IN FEAR OF HARM? 9 326
WHAT FEAR I THEN, RATHER WHAT KNOW TO FEARE 9 773
AND FEAR OF DEATH DELIVER TO THE WINDES. 9 989
WOULD THUNDER IN MY EARS, NO FEAR OF WORSE 10 780
TO PERPETUITIE; AY ME, THAT FEAR 10 813
FROM WHAT WE FEAR FOR BOTH, LET US MAKE SHORT, 10 1000
TO BE FORESTALL'D; MUCH MORE I FEAR LEAST DEATH 10 1024
BESEECHING HIM, SO AS WE NEED NOT FEAR 10 1082
OUT OF DESPAIRE, JOY, BUT WITH FEAR YET LINKT; 11 139
AND CARNAL FEAR THAT DAY DIMM'D ADAMS EYE. 11 212
THAT I SHOULD FEAR, NOR SOCIABLY MILD, 11 234
TRUE PATIENCE, AND TO TEMPER JOY WITH FEAR 11 361
AND FEAR OF GOD, FROM WHOM THIR PIETIE FEIGN'D 11 799
ACCEPTANCE OF LARGE GRACE, FROM SERVIL FEAR 12 305
AND LOVE WITH FEAR THE ONELY GOD, TO WALK 12 562

FEAR'D
OF KNOWLEDGE PAST OR PRESENT, COULD HAVE FEAR'D, 1 628
TH' EVENT IS FEAR'D; SHOULD WE AGAIN PROVOKE 2 82
ADMIR'D, NOT FEAR'D; GOD AND HIS SON EXCEPT, 2 678
SUPERIOR, NOR OF VIOLENCE FEAR'D AUGHT; 5 905
HER FORMER TRESPASS FEAR'D, THE MORE TO SOOTHE 9 1006
BECAUSE NOT YET INFLICTED, AS HE FEAR'D, 10 51
MY VOICE THOU OFT HAST HEARD, AND HAST NOT FEAR'D, 10 119

FEARD
(CERTAIN TO BE REFUS'D) WHAT ERST THEY FEARD; 2 470
AND PIOUS AWE, THAT FEARD TO HAVE OFFENDED. 5 135
FOUL ON HIMSELF; THEN WHEREFORE SHUND OR FEARD 9 331
AT FIRST, AS ONE WHO SOUGHT ACCESS, BUT FEARD 9 511
INSATIATE, I THUS SINGLE, NOR HAVE FEARD 9 536
NOT JUST, NOT GOD; NOT FEARD THEN, NOR OBEYD: 9 701

FEARE
LEAVE THEM TO GOD ABOVE, HIM SERVE AND FEARE; 8 168
YOUR FEARE IT SELF OF DEATH REMOVES THE FEARE. 9 702
WHAT FEAR I THEN, RATHER WHAT KNOW TO FEARE 9 773
NO DETRIMENT NEED FEARE, GOE AND BE STRONG. 10 409
WARR TERRIFIE THEM INEXPERT, AND FEARE 12 218

FEARES
WHY STAND WE LONGER SHIVERING UNDER FEARES, 10 1003

FEARING
THE PRESENT, FEARING GUILTIE WHAT HIS WRAUTH 10 340
FRESH IN THIR MINDES, FEARING THE DEITIE, 12 15

FEARLESS
FEARLESS, ENDANGER'D HEAV'NS PERPETUAL KING; 1 131
FEARLESS TO BE O'RMATCHT BY LIVING MIGHT. 2 855
FAR OFF AND FEARLESS, NOR WITH CAUSE TO BOAST, 4 14
THE FLAMING SERAPH FEARLESS, THOUGH ALONE 5 875
FEARLESS ASSAULT, AND TO THE BROW OF HEAV'N 6 51
ACCEPTED, FEARLESS IN HIS RIGHTEOUS CAUSE, 6 804
OF HEAVIER ON HIMSELF, FEARLESS RETURN'D. 9 57
FEARLESS UNFEARD HE SLEPT: IN AT HIS MOUTH 9 187
OFFENDED; FEARLESS OF REPROACH AND SCORN, 11 811

FEARS
OF HOPE IN FEARS AND DANGERS, HEARD SO OFT 1 275
THIR FANTING COURAGE, AND DISPEL'D THIR FEARS. 1 530
O CONSCIENCE, INTO WHAT ABYSS OF FEARS 10 842

FEARST
HIS VIOLENCE THOU FEARST NOT, BEING SUCH, 9 282
AND WHAT THOU FEARST, ALIKE DESTROYES ALL HOPE 10 838

FEAST
MINISTRING SPIRITS, TRAIND UP IN FEAST AND SONG; 6 167
AT JOUST AND TORNEAMENT; THEN MARSHAL'D FEAST 9 37
WITH FEAST AND MUSICK ALL THE TENTS RESOUND. 11 592
TO LUXURIE AND RIOT, FEAST AND DANCE, 11 715
WITH LARGE WINE-OFFERINGS POUR'D, AND SACRED FEAST, 12 21

FEASTS
HIS HOLY RITES, AND SOLEMN FEASTS PROFAN'D, 1 390

FEASTS (CONTINUED)
AT HEAV'NS HIGH FEASTS TO HAVE FED: YET WHAT COMPARE? 5 467

FEATHERD
SHADDOWD FROM EITHER HEELE WITH FEATHERD MAILE 5 284
THIR CALLOW YOUNG, BUT FEATHERD SOON AND FLEDGE 7 420
WITH FEATHERD CINCTURE, NAKED ELSE AND WILDE 9 1117

FEATS
TILL THICKEST LEGIONS CLOSE; WITH FEATS OF ARMS 2 537

FEATURE
SO SENTED THE GRIM FEATURE, AND UPTURN'D 10 279

FEAVOROUS
OF HEART-SICK AGONIE, ALL FEAVOROUS KINDS, 11 482

FED
STILL URGES, AND A FIERY DELUGE, FED 1 68
OF STARRY LAMPS AND BLAZING CRESSETS FED 1 728
WITH ODOURS; THERE YE SHALL BE FED AND FILL'D 2 843
ON HILLS WHERE FLOCKS ARE FED, FLIES TOWARD THE SPRINGS 3 435
RAN NECTAR, VISITING EACH PLANT, AND FED 4 240
TO BE SUSTAIND AND FED; OF ELEMENTS 5 415
AT HEAV'NS HIGH FEASTS TO HAVE FED: YET WHAT COMPARE? 5 467
SOON DRI'D, AND ON THE REAKING MOISTURE FED. 8 256

FEED
OF MINE OWN BROOD, THAT ON MY BOWELS FEED: 2 863
THEN FEED ON THOUGHTS, THAT VOLUNTARIE MOVE 3 37
EARTH AND THE SEA FEED AIR, THE AIR THOSE FIRES 5 417
AT FEED OR FOUNTAIN NEVER HAD I FOUND. 9 597
TO REACH, AND FEED AT ONCE BOTH BODIE AND MIND? 9 779
FEED FIRST, ON EACH BEAST NEXT, AND FISH, AND FOWLE, 10 604

FEEDS
THE GROSSER FEEDS THE PURER, EARTH THE SEA, 5 416
THE FEMALE BEE THAT FEEDS HER HUSBAND DRONE 7 490

FEEL
WHAT CAN IT THEN AVAIL THOUGH YET WE FEEL 1 153
IN WHICH THEY WERE, OR THE FIERCE PAINS NOT FEEL; 1 336
ON THIS SIDE NOTHING; AND BY PROOF WE FEEL 2 101
THIR NOXIOUS VAPOUR, OR ENUR'D NOT FEEL, 2 216
IN DOING WHAT WE MOST IN SUFFERING FEEL? 2 340
ARE BROUGHT: AND FEEL BY TURNS THE BITTER CHANGE 2 598
AND FEEL THY SOVRAN VITAL LAMP; BUT THOU 3 22
FARR HEAVIER LOAD THY SELF EXPECT TO FEEL 4 972
DISTINGUISH NOT; FOR SOON EXPECT TO FEEL 5 892
THIR DEITIES TO ASSERT, WHO WHILE THEY FEEL 6 157
AND FEEL THAT I AM HAPPIER THEN I KNOW. 8 282
WHAT INWARD THENCE I FEEL, NOT THEREFORE FOILD, 8 608
PLEASURES ABOUT ME, SO MUCH MORE I FEEL 9 120
WHY SHOULDST NOT THOU LIKE SENSE WITHIN THEE FEEL 9 315
MOTHER OF SCIENCE, NOW I FEEL THY POWER 9 680
WOULD NEVER FROM MY HEART; NO NO, I FEEL 9 913
SO FORCIBLE WITHIN MY HEART I FEEL 9 955
SO FAITHFUL LOVE UNEQUALD; BUT I FEEL 9 983
THEY SWIM IN MIRTH, AND FANSIE THAT THEY FEEL 9 1009
METHINKS I FEEL NEW STRENGTH WITHIN ME RISE, 10 243
FROM THIS DAY ONWARD, WHICH I FEEL BEGUN 10 811
HORRID TO THINK, HOW HORRIBLE TO FEEL. 11 465
IN APPREHENSION THEN IN SUBSTANCE FEEL 11 775

FEELING
WHO OF ALL AGES TO SUCCEED, BUT FEELING 10 733

FEELST
HIS FULL WRAUTH WHOSE THOU FEELST AS YET LEST PART, 10 951

FEET
OF UNBLEST FEET. HIM FOLLOWED HIS NEXT MATE, 1 238
SUFFICIENT? WHO SHALL TEMPT WITH WANDRING FEET 2 404
WITH HEAD, HANDS, WINGS OR FEET PURSUES HIS WAY, 2 949
THAT WASH THY HALLOWD FEET, AND WARBLING FLOW, 3 31
TO STOOP WITH WEARIED WINGS, AND WILLING FEET 3 73
OF HEAV'NS ASCENT THEY LIFT THIR FEET, WHEN LOE 3 486
LIGHTS ON HIS FEET. AS WHEN A PROWLING WOLFE, 4 183
O FRIENDS, I HEAR THE TREAD OF NIMBLE FEET 4 866
AND COLOURS DIPT IN HEAV'N; THE THIRD HIS FEET 5 283
THAT WHOM THEY HIT, NONE ON THIR FEET MIGHT STAND, 6 592
HER STATE WITH OARIE FEET: YET OFT THEY QUIT 7 440
STOOD ON MY FEET; ABOUT ME ROUND I SAW 8 261
IN ADORATION AT HIS FEET I FELL 8 315
WHOM HE SHALL TREAD AT LAST UNDER OUR FEET; 10 190
AS WHEN HE WASH'D HIS SERVANTS FEET SO NOW 10 215
AND TRESSES ALL DISORDERD, AT HIS FEET 10 911
NOW AT HIS FEET SUBMISSIVE IN DISTRESS, 10 942
BY TH' ANGEL, ON THY FEET THOU STOODST AT LAST, 11 759

FEIGN'D
THAN FABLES YET HAVE FEIGN'D, OR FEAR CONCEIV'D, 2 627
WHAT FEIGN'D SUBMISSION SWORE: EASE WOULD RECANT 4 96
THEN WOOD-NYMPH, OR THE FAIREST GODDESS FEIGN'D 5 381

FEIGN'D (CONTINUED)
IN BATTELS FEIGN'D; THE BETTER FORTITUDE 9 31
SPOT MORE DELICIOUS THEN THOSE GARDENS FEIGN'D 9 439
HATE STRONGER, UNDER SHEW OF LOVE WELL FEIGN'D, 9 492
AND FEAR OF GOD, FROM WHOM THIR PIETIE FEIGN'D 11 799

FEIGND
SUTABLE GRACE DIFFUS'D, SO WELL HE FEIGND; 3 639
MORE SACRED AND SEQUESTERD, THOUGH BUT FEIGND, 4 706

FEIGNING
SECULAR POWER, THOUGH FEIGNING STILL TO ACT 12 517

FEILDS
FEILDS AND INHABITANTS: HER SPOTS THOU SEEST 8 145

FELL
O HOW UNLIKE THE PLACE FROM WHENCE THEY FELL. 1 75
BEGUIL'D BY FAIR IDOLATRESSES, FELL 1 445
WHERE HE FELL FLAT, AND SHAM'D HIS WORSHIPERS: 1 461
FELL NOT FROM HEAVEN, OR MORE GROSS TO LOVE 1 491
WHEN CHARLEMAIN WITH ALL HIS PEERAGE FELL 1 586
MAMMON, THE LEAST ERECTED SPIRIT THAT FELL 1 679
MEN CALL'D HIM MULCIBER; AND HOW HE FELL 1 740
TO NOON HE FELL, FROM NOON TO DEWY EVE, 1 743
FELL LONG BEFORE; NOR AUGHT AVAIL'D HIM NOW 1 748
OTHERS WITH VAST TYPHOEAN RAGE MORE FELL 2 539
THROUGH ALL THE EMPYREAN: DOWN THEY FELL 2 771
FELL WITH US FROM ON HIGH: FROM THEM I GO 2 826
TO THAT SIDE HEAV'N FROM WHENCE YOUR LEGIONS FELL: 2 1006
BUT HEE ONCE PAST, SOON AFTER WHEN MAN FELL, 2 1023
FREELY THEY STOOD WHO STOOD, AND FELL WHO FELL. 3 102
THE FIRST SORT BY THIR OWN SUGGESTION FELL, 3 129
I FELL, HOW GLORIOUS ONCE ABOVE THY SPHEARE; 4 39
FELL NOT, BUT STAND UNSHAK'N, FROM WITHIN 4 64
WATERD THE GARDEN; THENCE UNITED FELL 4 230
MORE GRATEFUL, TO THIR SUPPER FRUITS THEY FELL, 4 331
SINCE SATAN FELL, WHOM FOLLIE OVERTHREW, 4 905
AND FELL ASLEEP; BUT O HOW GLAD I WAK'D 5 92
EACH IN THIR CHRYSTAL SLUCE, HEE ERE THEY FELL 5 133
AND TO THIR VIANDS FELL, NOR SEEMINGLY 5 434
WHICH HUNG NOT, BUT SO SWIFT WITH TEMPEST FELL 6 190
THOUGH STANDING ELSE AS ROCKS, BUT DOWN THEY FELL 6 593
FLEW OFF, AND INTO STRANGE VAGARIES FELL, 6 614
NOR LESS ON EITHER SIDE TEMPESTUOUS FELL 6 844
NINE DAYES THEY FELL; CONFOUNDED CHAOS ROARD, 6 871
YET FELL; REMEMBER, AND FEAR TO TRANSGRESS. 6 912
FELL WITH HIS FLAMING LEGIONS THROUGH THE DEEP 7 134
IN ADORATION AT HIS FEET I FELL 8 315
OF SLEEP, WHICH INSTANTLY FELL ON ME, CALL'D 8 458
EACH OTHER, TILL SUPPLANTED DOWN HE FELL 10 513
OF UGLY SERPENTS; HORROR ON THEM FELL, 10 539
DOWN FELL BOTH SPEAR AND SHIELD, DOWN THEY AS FAST, 10 542
WITH SOOT AND CINDERS FILL'D; SO OFT THEY FELL 10 570
THROUGH THE STILL NIGHT, NOT NOW, AS ERE MAN FELL, 10 846
TO A FELL ADVERSARIE, HIS HATE OR SHAME: 10 906
FELL HUMBLE, AND IMBRACING THEM, BESAUGHT 10 912
REPAIRING WHERE HE JUDG'D THEM PROSTRATE FELL 10 1099
THAT BEAT OUT LIFE; HE FELL, AND DEADLY PALE 11 446
WEARIED I FELL ASLEEP: BUT NOW LEAD ON; 12 614

FELL'D
SAW WHERE THE SWORD OF MICHAEL SMOTE, AND FELL'D 6 250
WITH BRANCHES LOPT, IN WOOD OR MOUNTAIN FELL'D) 6 575

FELLON
ON TH' OTHER SIDE: WHICH WHEN TH' ARCH-FELLON SAW 4 179

FELLOW
THEN OF OUR FELLOW SERVANT, AND INQUIRE 8 225

FELLOWS
THE FELLOWS OF HIS CRIME, THE FOLLOWERS RATHER 1 606
ABOVE HIS FELLOWS, WITH MONARCHAL PRIDE 2 428
BEFORE THY FELLOWS, AMBITIOUS TO WIN 6 160

FELLOWSHIP
TEDIOUS ALIKE: OF FELLOWSHIP I SPEAK 8 389
WHOSE FELLOWSHIP THEREFORE UNMEET FOR THEE 8 442

FELLOWSHIPS
IN FELLOWSHIPS OF JOY: THE SONS OF LIGHT 11 80

FELT
THAT FELT UNUSUAL WEIGHT, TILL ON DRY LAND 1 227
TO US IS ADVERSE. WHO BUT FELT OF LATE 2 77
WITH CONQUEST, FELT TH' ENVENOM'D ROBE, AND TORE 2 543
PRODIGIOUS MOTION FELT AND RUEFUL THROES. 2 780
AND FELT HOW AWFUL GOODNESS IS, AND SAW 4 847
AND FELT TENFOLD CONFUSION IN THIR FALL 6 872
TRANSPORTED TOUCH; HERE PASSION FIRST I FELT, 8 530
EARTH FELT THE WOUND, AND NATURE FROM HER SEAT 9 782
MISGAVE HIM; HEE THE FAULTRING MEASURE FELT; 9 846
NOT FELT, NOR SHALL BE TWICE, FOR NEVER MORE 9 859
BY THIS NEW FELT ATTRACTION AND INSTINCT. 10 263
NOW ALSO EVIDENCE, BUT STRAIGHT I FELT 10 361
THOUGH DISTANT FROM THEE WORLDS BETWEEN, YET FELT 10 362
HIS VISAGE DRAWN HE FELT TO SHARP AND SPARE, 10 511

FELT (CONTINUED)
THEY FELT THEMSELVS NOW CHANGING; DOWN THIR ARMS, 10 541
TO SORROW ABANDOND, BUT WORSE FELT WITHIN, 10 717
FELT LESS REMORSE: THEY FORTHWITH TO THE PLACE 10 1098

FEMAL
COMMUNICATING MALE AND FEMAL LIGHT, 8 150
IN FEMAL SEX, THE MORE TO DRAW HIS LOVE, 9 822
BUT FONDLY OVERCOME WITH FEMAL CHARM. 9 999
DISTURBANCES ON EARTH THROUGH FEMAL SNARES, 10 897
FOR THAT FAIR FEMAL TROOP THOU SAWST, THAT SEEMD 11 614

FEMALE
THE FEMALE BEE THAT FEEDS HER HUSBAND DRONE 7 490
FEMALE FOR RACE; THEN BLESS'D MANKINDE, AND SAID, 7 530

FEMININE
THESE FEMININE. FOR SPIRITS WHEN THEY PLEASE 1 423
ANGELIC, BUT MORE SOFT, AND FEMININE, 9 458
WITH MEN AS ANGELS WITHOUT FEMININE, 10 893

FENC'D
FENC'D UP THE VERDANT WALL; EACH BEAUTEOUS FLOUR, 4 697

FENCE
LEAPS O'RE THE FENCE WITH EASE INTO THE FOULD: 4 187

FENCELESS
IMMOVABLE OF THIS NOW FENCELESS WORLD 10 303

FENC'T
THUS FENC'T, AND AS THEY THOUGHT, THIR SHAME IN PART 9 1119

FENEL
THEN SMELL OF SWEETEST FENEL OR THE TEATS 9 581

FENS
ROCKS, CAVE, LAKES, FENS, BOGS, DENS, AND SHADES OF DEATH, 2 621
MEAN WHILE THE TEPID CAVES, AND FENS AND SHOARES 7 417

FERMENTED
FERMENTED THE GREAT MOTHER TO CONCEAVE, 7 281

FERRY
THEY FERRY OVER THIS LETHEAN SOUND 2 604

FERTIL
WAS FAIR DAMASCUS, ON THE FERTIL BANKS 1 468
OUT OF THE FERTIL GROUND HE CAUS'D TO GROW 4 216
GLISTRING WITH DEW; FRAGRANT THE FERTIL EARTH 4 645
HER FERTIL GROWTH, AND BY DISBURD'NING GROWS 5 319
OP'NING HER FERTIL WOOMB TEEM'D AT A BIRTH 7 454
SHALL TEND THEE, AND THE FERTIL BURDEN EASE 9 801

FERVENT
SO SPAKE THE FERVENT ANGEL, BUT HIS ZEALE 5 849

FERVENTLY
TO WHOM THUS ADAM FERVENTLY REPLI'D. 9 342

FERVID
SHOT DOWN DIRECT HIS FERVID RAIES TO WARME 5 301
THEN STAID THE FERVID WHEELES, AND IN HIS HAND 7 224

FESOLE
AT EV'NING FROM THE TOP OF FESOLE, 1 289

FESTIVALS
SO OFT IN FESTIVALS OF JOY AND LOVE 6 94
TRIUMPHS OR FESTIVALS, AND TO THEM PREACHD 11 723

FETCH
IF EARTH INDUSTRIOUS OF HER SELF FETCH DAY 8 137

FEW
THE PARADISE OF FOOLS, TO FEW UNKNOWN 3 496
HOW FEW SOMTIMES MAY KNOW, WHEN THOUSANDS ERR. 6 148
URANIA, AND FIT AUDIENCE FIND, THOUGH FEW. 7 31
SO HAVING SAID, HE THUS TO EVE IN FEW: 10 157
MAN IS NOT WHOM TO WARNE: THOSE FEW ESCAP'T 11 777
THIS SECOND SOURS OF MEN, WHILE YET BUT FEW; 12 13
MUST REASCEND, WHAT WILL BETIDE THE FEW 12 480

FEWEL'D
AND FEWEL'D ENTRALS THENCE CONCEIVING FIRE, 1 234

FEZ
THE KINGDOMS OF ALMANSOR, FEZ AND SUS, 11 403

FICKLE
TO FICKLE CHANCE, AND CHAOS JUDGE THE STRIFE: 2 233
TRIUMPH AND SAY; FICKLE THEIR STATE WHOM GOD 9 948

FIELD
AND SHOOK HIS THRONE. WHAT THOUGH THE FIELD BE LOST? 1 105

FIELD (CONTINUED)

FORERUN THE ROYAL CAMP, TO TRENCH A FIELD, 1 677
(THOUGH LIKE A COVER'D FIELD, WHERE CHAMPIONS BOLD 1 763
ADVISING PEACE: FOR SUCH ANOTHER FIELD 2 292
HERE WALK'D THE FIEND AT LARGE IN SPACIOUS FIELD. 3 430
TO PADAN-ARAM IN THE FIELD OF LUZ, 3 513
IN HURDL'D COTES AMID THE FIELD SECURE, 4 186
THE OPEN FIELD, AND WHERE THE UNPIERC'T SHADE 4 245
BREATHING THE SMELL OF FIELD AND GROVE, ATTUNE 4 265
LED ON TH' ETERNAL SPRING. NOT THAT FAIRE FIELD 4 268
WITH PORTED SPEARS, AS THICK AS WHEN A FIELD 4 980
AWAKE, THE MORNING SHINES, AND THE FRESH FIELD 5 20
SO ALL WAS CLEARD, AND TO THE FIELD THEY HASTE. 5 136
INTO THE BLISSFUL FIELD, THROUGH GROVES OF MYRRHE, 5 292
AND LEFT LARGE FIELD, UNSAFE WITHIN THE WIND 6 309
VICTOR AND VANQUISHT: ON THE FOUGHTEN FIELD 6 410
DISMOUNTED, ON TH' ALEIAN FIELD I FALL 7 19
EMBATTELL'D IN HER FIELD: AND THE HUMBLE SHRUB, 7 322
PLANT OF THE FIELD, WHICH E'RE IT WAS IN THE EARTH 7 335
AND SOWD WITH STARRS THE HEAV'N THICK AS A FIELD: 7 358
THE SERPENT SUTTL'ST BEAST OF ALL THE FIELD, 7 495
BEAST OF THE FIELD, AND OVER ALL THE EARTH, 7 522
THE SERPENT SUTTLEST BEAST OF ALL THE FIELD. 9 86
IN BOWRE AND FIELD HE SOUGHT, WHERE ANY TUFT 9 417
TO SUCH DISPORT BEFORE HER THROUGH THE FIELD, 9 520
THEE, SERPENT, SUTTLEST BEAST OF ALL THE FIELD 9 560
TILL ON A DAY ROAVING THE FIELD, I CHANC'D 9 575
ABOVE ALL CATTLE, EACH BEAST OF THE FIELD; 10 176
UNBID, AND THOU SHALT EATE TH' HERB OF TH' FIELD, 10 204
AGAINST THE DAY OF BATTEL, TO A FIELD, 10 275
HIM FOLLOW'D ISSUING FORTH TO TH' OPEN FIELD, 10 533
FARR OTHER NAME DESERVING. BUT THE FIELD 11 171
THE FIELD PAVILION'D WITH HIS GUARDIANS BRIGHT; 11 215
HIS EYES HE OP'ND, AND BEHELD A FIELD, 11 429
WITH CARCASSES AND ARMS TH' ENSANGUIND FIELD 11 654

FIELDS

ABOVE HIS EQUALS. FAREWEL HAPPY FIELDS 1 249
FLED OVER ADRIA TO TH' HESPERIAN FIELDS, 1 520
EXTEND HIS EV'NING BEAM, THE FIELDS REVIVE, 2 493
AS AT TH' OLYMPIAN GAMES OR PYTHIAN FIELDS; 2 530
AND FIELDS WERE FOUGHT IN HEAV'N; WHEREIN REMAIND 2 768
THOSE ARGENT FIELDS MORE LIKELY HABITANTS, 3 460
FORTUNATE FIELDS, AND GROVES AND FLOURIE VALES, 3 569
WHAT WONDER THEN IF FIELDS AND REGIONS HERE 3 606
THE CATTEL IN THE FIELDS AND MEDDOWES GREEN: 7 460
AND OVER FIELDS AND WATERS, AS IN AIRE 8 301

FIEND

WHERETO WITH SPEEDY WORDS TH' ARCH-FIEND REPLY'D. 1 156
SO STRETCHT OUT HUGE IN LENGTH THE ARCH-FIEND LAY 1 209
HE SCARCE HAD CEAS'T WHEN THE SUPERIOUR FIEND 1 283
FARR OFF THE FLYING FIEND: AT LAST APPEER 2 643
TH' UNDAUNTED FIEND WHAT THIS MIGHT BE ADMIR'D, 2 677
SHE FINISH'D, AND THE SUTTLE FIEND HIS LORE 2 815
INTO THIS WILD ABYSS THE WARIE FIEND 2 917
THE GUARDED GOLD: SO EAGERLY THE FIEND 2 947
HERE WALK'D THE FIEND AT LARGE IN SPACIOUS FIELD. 3 430
SO ON THIS WINDIE SEA OF LAND, THE FIEND 3 440
ALL THIS DARK GLOBE THE FIEND FOUND AS HE PASS'D, 3 498
THE FIEND BY EASIE ASCENT, OR AGGRAVATE 3 524
THERE LANDS THE FIEND, A SPOT LIKE WHICH PERHAPS 3 588
SO ENTERTAIND THOSE ODOROUS SWEETS THE FIEND 4 166
FROM THIS ASSYRIAN GARDEN, WHERE THE FIEND 4 285
SO SPAKE THE FIEND, AND WITH NECESSITIE, 4 393
SO STARTED UP IN HIS OWN SHAPE THE FIEND. 4 819
THE FIEND REPLI'D NOT, OVERCOME WITH RAGE; 4 857
TO WHICH THE FIEND THUS ANSWERD FROWNING STERN. 4 924
WHICH GABRIEL SPYING, THUS BESPAKE THE FIEND. 4 1005
IF THOU RESIST. THE FIEND LOOKT UP AND KNEW 4 1013
FOR NOW, AND SINCE FIRST BREAK OF DAWNE THE FIEND, 9 412
MUCH WONDRING HOW THE SUTTLE FIEND HAD STOLN 10 20
FARR INTO CHAOS, SINCE THE FIEND PASS'D THROUGH, 10 233
THY CHOICE OF FLAMING WARRIOURS, LEAST THE FIEND 11 101

FIENDS

ARMIE OF FIENDS, FIT BODY TO FIT HEAD; 4 953

FIERCE

AND TO THE FIERCE CONTENTION BROUGHT ALONG 1 100
AFLOAT, WHEN WITH FIERCE WINDS ORION ARM'D 1 305
IN WHICH THEY WERE, OR THE FIERCE PAINS NOT FEEL; 1 336
AGAINST THE HIGHEST, AND FIERCE WITH GRASPED ARMS 1 667
WHEN THE FIERCE FOE HUNG ON OUR BROK'N REAR 2 78
FAMILIAR THE FIERCE HEAT, AND VOID OF PAIN; 2 219
HEARD ON THE RUFUL STREAM; FIERCE PHLEGETON 2 580
OF FIERCE EXTREAMS, EXTREAMS BY CHANGE MORE FIERCE, 2 599
FIERCE AS TEN FURIES, TERRIBLE AS HELL, 2 671
FOR HOT, COLD, MOIST, AND DRY, FOUR CHAMPIONS
FIERCE 2 898
TO EXECUTE FIERCE VENGEANCE ON HIS FOES, 3 399
SPIRIT OF HAPPIE SORT: HIS GESTURES FIERCE 4 128
WHERE NEITHER JOY NOR LOVE, BUT FIERCE DESIRE, 4 509
AND FIERCE DEMEANOUR SEEMS THE PRINCE OF HELL, 4 871
AND IN FIERCE HOSTING MEET, WHO WONT TO MEET 6 93
PRESAGE OF VICTORIE AND FIERCE DESIRE 6 201
MILLIONS OF FIERCE ENCOUNTRING ANGELS FOUGHT 6 220
AND WITH FIERCE ENSIGNES PIERC'D THE DEEP ARRAY 6 356

FIERCE (CONTINUED)

ERE WHILE THEY FIERCE WERE COMING, AND WHEN WEE, 6 610
AND FROM ABOUT HIM FIERCE EFFUSION ROWLD 6 765
STOOD REIMBATTELL'D FIERCE, BY FORCE OR FRAUD 6 794
OF HIS FIERCE CHARIOT ROWLD, AS WITH THE SOUND 6 829
OF CHAOS FARR REMOV'D, LEAST FIERCE EXTREAMES 7 272
HIS FIERCENESS OF THE FIERCE INTENT IT BROUGHT; 9 462
FIERCE HATE HE RECOLLECTS, AND ALL HIS THOUGHTS 9 471
YET PARCHT WITH SCALDING THURST AND HUNGER FIERCE, 10 556
FROM SERRALIONA; THWART OF THESE AS FIERCE 10 703
DEATH INTRODUC'D THROUGH FIERCE ANTIPATHIE: 10 709
SHALL WITH A FIERCE REFLUX ON MEE REDOUND, 10 739
SOFT WORDS TO HIS FIERCE PASSION SHE ASSAY'D: 10 865
CONVULSIONS, EPILEPSIES, FIERCE CATARRHS, 11 483
CONCOURS IN ARMS, FIERCE FACES THREATNING WARR, 11 641
FIERCE AS A COMET; WHICH WITH TORRID HEAT, 12 634

FIERCELY

THAT JEALOUS OF THIR SECRETS FIERCELY OPPOS'D 10 478
IN SIGNAL OF REMOVE, WAVES FIERCELY ROUND; 12 593

FIERCENESS

HIS FIERCENESS OF THE FIERCE INTENT IT BROUGHT; 9 462

FIERCER

THAT FOUGHT IN HEAV'N; NOW FIERCER BY DESPAIR: 2 45

FIERCEST

STOOD UP, THE STRONGEST AND THE FIERCEST SPIRIT 2 44
THY FIERCEST, WHEN IN BATTEL TO THY AIDE 4 927
OF FIERCEST OPPOSITION IN MID SKIE, 6 314

FIERIE

CAUGHT IN A FIERIE TEMPEST SHALL BE HURL'D 2 180
A GLOBE OF FIERIE SERAPHIM INCLOS'D 2 512
PART CURB THIR FIERIE STEEDS, OR SHUN THE GOAL 2 531
O'RE MANY A FROZEN, MANY A FIERIE ALPE, 2 620
A LION NOW HE STALKES WITH FIERIE GLARE, 4 402
TURND FIERIE RED, SHARPNING IN MOONED HORNES 4 978
CHARIOTS AND FLAMING ARMES, AND FIERIE STEEDS 6 17
FROM SKIRT TO SKIRT A FIERIE REGION, STRETCHT 6 80
SO UNDER FIERIE COPE TOGETHER RUSH'D 6 215
NOW WAV'D THIR FIERIE SWORDS, AND IN THE AIRE 6 304
AND FIERIE FOAMING STEEDS; WHAT STOOD, RECOYLD 6 391
OF SPIRITOUS AND FIERIE SPUME, TILL TOUCHT 6 479
SATANS ASSAULTS, AND QUENCH HIS FIERIE DARTS, 12 492
WITH DREADFUL FACES THRONG'D AND FIERIE ARMES: 12 644

FIERY

LAY VANQUISHT, ROWLING IN THE FIERY GULFE 1 52
STILL URGES, AND A FIERY DELUGE, FED 1 68
THE FIERY SURGE, THAT FROM THE PRECIPICE 1 173
FROM OFF THE TOSSING OF THESE FIERY WAVES, 1 184
ROUS'D FROM THE SLUMBER, ON THAT FIERY COUCH, 1 377
UP TO THE FIERY CONCAVE TOURING HIGH, 2 635
RAPT IN A CHARIOT DRAWN BY FIERY STEEDS. 3 522
HIS FIERY CHAOS TO RECEAVE THIR FALL. 6 55
OF FIERY DARTS IN FLAMING VOLIES FLEW, 6 213
SHALL REST BY DAY, A FIERY GLEAME BY NIGHT, 12 257

FIFT

EV'NING AND MORN SOLEMNIZ'D THE FIFT DAY. 7 448

FIGHT

WITH WHAT BESIDES, IN COUNSEL OR IN FIGHT, 2 20
CONFUS'DLY, AND WHICH THUS MUST EVER FIGHT, 2 914
AND PRACTIS'D DISTANCES TO CRINGE, NOT FIGHT. 4 945
THE SEQUEL EACH OF PARTING AND OF FIGHT; 4 1003
THE BETTER FIGHT, WHO SINGLE HAST MAINTAIND 6 30
BY THOUSANDS AND BY MILLIONS RANG'D FOR FIGHT; 6 48
THAT SELF SAME DAY BY FIGHT, OR BY SURPRIZE 6 87
A LEGION; LED IN FIGHT, YET LEADER SEEMD 6 232
A STANDING FIGHT, THEN SOARING ON MAIN WING 6 243
THEY ENDED PARLE, AND BOTH ADDREST FOR FIGHT 6 296
WHERE ERST WAS THICKEST FIGHT, TH' ANGELIC THRONG, 6 308
NOT TO HAVE DISOBEI'D; IN FIGHT THEY STOOD 6 403
WHO HAVE SUSTAIND ONE DAY IN DOUBTFUL FIGHT 6 423
AS ONE HE STOOD ESCAP'T FROM CRUEL FIGHT, 6 448
AGAINST UNEQUAL ARMES TO FIGHT IN PAINE, 6 454
WHERE LODG'D, OR WHITHER FLED, OR IF FOR FIGHT, 6 531
ARME, WARRIOURS, ARME FOR FIGHT, THE FOE AT HAND, 6 537
THESE DISOBEDIENT; SORE HATH BEEN THIR FIGHT, 6 687
WHENCE IN PERPETUAL FIGHT THEY NEEDS MUST LAST 6 693
AND TO REBELLIOUS FIGHT RALLIED THIR POWERS 6 786
FOR DEATH, THE FOLLOWING DAY, IN BLOODIE FIGHT. 10 278
SIN AGAINST LAW TO FIGHT; THAT WHEN THEY SEE 12 289
THIR FIGHT, WHAT STROKE SHALL BRUISE THE VICTORS
HEEL. 12 385
TO WHOM THUS MICHAEL. DREAM NOT OF THIR FIGHT, 12 386

FIGHTING

OF FIGHTING ELEMENTS, ON ALL SIDES ROUND 2 1015
OF FIGHTING SERAPHIM CONFUS'D, AT LENGTH 6 249

FIGTREE

THE FIGTREE, NOT THAT KIND FOR FRUIT RENOWN'D, 9 1101

FIGURE
IN COMMON, RANG'D IN FIGURE WEDGE THIR WAY, 7 426
MOSES IN FIGURE BEARES, TO INTRODUCE 12 241

FILD
COUCHT, AND NOW FILD WITH PASTURE GAZING SAT, 4 351

FILES
HAD TO IMPOSE: HE THROUGH THE ARMED FILES 1 567
SO SAYING, ON HE LED HIS RADIANT FILES, 4 797
DISPERST IN BANDS AND FILES THIR CAMP EXTEND 5 651
FROM OFF THE FILES OF WARR; THERE THEY HIM LAID 6 339
NOR SERV'D IT TO RELAX THIR SERRIED FILES. 6 599

FILIAL
FILIAL OBEDIENCE: AS A SACRIFICE 3 269
SEVERE BUT IN TRUE FILIAL FREEDOM PLAC'T; 4 294
AND THUS THE FILIAL GODHEAD ANSWERING SPAKE. 6 722
HIS WORD, THE FILIAL GODHEAD, GAVE EFFECT. 7 175
THE FILIAL POWER ARRIV'D, AND SATE HIM DOWN 7 587
TO FILIAL, WORKS OF LAW TO WORKS OF FAITH. 12 306

FILL
ON THE FIRM BRIMSTONE, AND FILL ALL THE PLAIN; 1 350
THE HAPPIER EDEN, SHALL ENJOY THIR FILL 4 507
TO FILL THE EARTH, WHO SHALL WITH US EXTOLL 4 733
SHALL FILL THE WORLD MORE NUMEROUS WITH THY SONS 5 389
YOUR FILL WHAT HAPPINESS THIS HAPPIE STATE 5 504
BOUNDLESS THE DEEP, BECAUSE I AM WHO FILL 7 168
AND LAKES AND RUNNING STREAMS THE WATERS FILL; 7 397
BE FRUITFUL, MULTIPLIE, AND FILL THE EARTH, 7 531
AN EDIFICE TOO LARGE FOR HIM TO FILL, 8 104
OF SWEET REPAST; THEY SATIATE, AND SOON FILL, 8 214
TO THE CREATOR, AND HIS NOSTRILS FILL 9 196
TEMPTING SO NIGH, TO PLUCK AND EAT MY FILL 9 595
EATING HIS FILL, NOR EVE TO ITERATE 9 1005
THERE THEY THIR FILL OF LOVE AND LOVES DISPORT 9 1042
TO FILL HIS EARE, WHEN CONTRARY HE HEARS 10 506
OF NATURE, AND NOT FILL THE WORLD AT ONCE 10 892
FROGS, LICE AND FLIES MUST ALL HIS PALACE FILL 12 177
WITH LOATH'D INTRUSION, AND FILL ALL THE LAND; 12 178
GREATLY IN PEACE OF THOUGHT, AND HAVE MY FILL 12 558

FILL'D
TURNS ATHEIST, AS DID ELY'S SONS, WHO FILL'D 1 495
BY STRANGE CONVEYANCE FILL'D EACH HOLLOW NOOK, 1 707
FIRST, WHAT REVENGE? THE TOWRS OF HEAV'N ARE FILL'D 2 129
WITH ODOURS; THERE YE SHALL BE FED AND FILL'D 2 843
HIS FAMINE SHOULD BE FILL'D, AND BLEST HIS MAWE 2 847
THUS WHILE GOD SPAKE, AMBROSIAL FRAGRANCE FILL'D 3 135
KNOW YE NOT THEN SAID SATAN, FILL'D WITH SCORN, 4 827
THE STORIE HEARD ATTENTIVE, AND WAS FILL'D 7 51
THE HOLLOW UNIVERSAL ORB THEY FILL'D, 7 257
BUT SUDDENLY WITH FLESH FILL'D UP AND HEAL'D: 8 468
WITH SOOT AND CINDERS FILL'D; SO OFT THEY FELL 10 570
THE WHOLE EARTH FILL'D WITH VIOLENCE, AND ALL FLESH 11 888

FILLD
HE SCARCE HAD FINISHT, WHEN SUCH MURMUR FILLD 2 284
WITH JUBILEE, AND LOUD HOSANNA'S FILLD 3 348
WITH VANITY HAD FILLD THE WORKS OF MEN: 3 447
AND SHOOK HIS PLUMES, THAT HEAV'NLY FRAGRANCE FILLD 5 286
THUS FOIL'D THIR MIGHTIEST, OURS JOY FILLD, AND SHOUT, 6 200
FILLD ALL THE REGIONS: FROM THIR BLISSFUL BOWRS 11 77

FILLS
HENCE FILLS AND EMPTIES TO ENLIGHTEN TH' EARTH, 3 731
INNUMERABLE, AND THIS WHICH YEELDS OR FILLS 7 88
NOT THIS ROCK ONELY; HIS OMNIPRESENCE FILLS 11 336

FILME
MICHAEL FROM ADAMS EYES THE FILME REMOV'D 11 412

FILTH
MY HELL-HOUNDS, TO LICK UP THE DRAFF AND FILTH 10 630

FINAL
VICTORIOUS. THUS REPULS'D, OUR FINAL HOPE 2 142
OF HAPPINESS AND FINAL MISERY, 2 563
TILL FINAL DISSOLUTION, WANDER HERE, 3 458
TO FINAL BATTEL DREW, DISDAINING FLIGHT, 6 798
OF THOUGHTS REVOLV'D, HIS FINAL SENTENCE CHOSE 9 88
IN DUST, OUR FINAL REST AND NATIVE HOME. 10 1085
HIS FINAL REMEDIE, AND AFTER LIFE 11 62
WITH VOWS, AS THIR CHIEF GOOD, AND FINAL HOPE. 11 493

FINALLY
FOR SHOULD MAN FINALLY BE LOST, SHOULD MAN 3 150

FIND
AND OUT OF GOOD STILL TO FIND MEANS OF EVIL; 1 165
YOUR WEARIED VERTUE, FOR THE EASE YOU FIND 1 320
AT LENGTH FROM US MAY FIND, WHO OVERCOMES 1 648
OUR STRONGER, SOME WORSE WAY HIS WRATH MAY FIND 2 83
OR AMBUSH FROM THE DEEP. WHAT IF WE FIND 2 344
IN SEARCH OF THIS NEW WORLD, WHOM SHALL WE FIND 2 403

FIND (CONTINUED)
AND THROUGH THE PALPABLE OBSCURE FIND OUT 2 406
LEADS HIM PERPLEXT, WHERE HE MAY LIKELIEST FIND 2 525
THAT REST OR INTERMISSION NONE I FIND. 2 802
BUT GLAD THAT NOW HIS SEA SHOULD FIND A SHORE, 2 1011
TO FIND THY PIERCING RAY, AND FIND NO DAWN; 3 24
BY THE OTHER FIRST: MAN THEREFORE SHALL FIND GRACE, 3 131
THY SOVRAN SENTENCE, THAT MAN SHOULD FIND GRACE; 3 145
SAY HEAV'NLY POWERS, WHERE SHALL WE FIND SUCH LOVE, 3 213
FATHER, THY WORD IS PAST, MAN SHALL FIND GRACE; 3 227
AND SHALL GRACE NOT FIND MEANS, THAT FINDS HER WAY, 3 228
NAUGHT SEEKING BUT THE PRAISE OF MEN, HERE FIND 3 453
TO FIND WHO MIGHT DIRECT HIS WANDRING FLIGHT 3 631
THAT I MAY FIND HIM, AND WITH SECRET GAZE, 3 671
LIKE CONSORT TO THY SELF CANST NO WHERE FIND. 4 448
NEW TROUBLES; HIM THY CARE MUST BE TO FIND. 4 575
SUCH WHERE YE FIND, SEISE FAST, AND HITHER BRING. 4 796
HIS LOSS; BUT CHIEFLY TO FIND HERE OBSERVD 4 849
FAME IS NOT SILENT, HERE IN HOPE TO FIND 4 938
HIS WONDER WAS TO FIND UNWAK'ND EVE 5 9
O SOLE IN WHOM MY THOUGHTS FIND ALL REPOSE, 5 28
TO FIND THEE I DIRECTED THEN MY WALK; 5 49
TO FIND THIS BUT A DREAM. THUS EVE HER NIGHT 5 93
SOM SUCH RESEMBLANCES METHINKS I FIND 5 114
WE BRUSH MELLIFLUOUS DEWES, AND FIND THE GROUND 5 429
WITH ANGELS MAY PARTICIPATE, AND FIND 5 494
FINDES NO ACCEPTANCE, NOR CAN FIND, FOR HOW 5 531
APOSTAT, STILL THOU ERRST, NOR END WILT FIND 6 172
TO FIND HIMSELF NOT MATCHLESS, AND HIS PRIDE 6 341
SINCE NOW WE FIND THIS OUR EMPYREAL FORM 6 433
FOR GODS, AND TOO UNEQUAL WORK WE FIND 6 453
URANIA, AND FIT AUDIENCE FIND, THOUGH FEW. 7 31
HIS BEAMS, UNACTIVE ELSE, THIR VIGOUR FIND. 8 97
OR ALL ENJOYING, WHAT CONTENTMENT FIND? 8 366
FIND PASTIME, AND BEARE RULE; THY REALM IS LARGE. 8 375
FROM PRONE, NOR IN THIR WAYES COMPLACENCE FIND. 8 433
TO FIND HER, OR FOR EVER TO DEPLORE 8 479
WHICH I ENJOY, AND MUST CONFESS TO FIND 8 523
IN EMINENCE, AND OBSTACLE FIND NONE 8 624
FIND PLACE OR REFUGE; AND THE MORE I SEE 9 119
FOR ONELY IN DESTROYING I FIND EASE 9 129
WITH MYRTLE, FIND WHAT TO REDRESS TILL NOON: 9 219
WATCHES, NO DOUBT, WITH GREEDY HOPE TO FIND 9 257
FROM HIS SURMISE PROV'D FALSE, FIND PEACE WITHIN, 9 333
HE SOUGHT THEM BOTH, BUT WISH'D HIS HAP MIGHT FIND 9 421
OP'ND WE FIND INDEED, AND FIND WE KNOW 9 1071
BY SOME IMMEDIATE STROAK; BUT SOON SHALL FIND 10 52
I FIND NO WAY, FROM DEEP TO DEEPER PLUNG'D. 10 844
OR FIND SOME OTHER WAY TO GENERATE 10 894
HE NEVER SHALL FIND OUT FIT MATE, BUT SUCH 10 899
TO FIND WHERE ADAM SHELTERD, TOOK HIS WAY, 11 223
SUCH GRACE SHALL ONE JUST MAN FIND IN HIS SIGHT, 11 890

FINDE
AND FINDE THEE KNOWING NOT OF BEASTS ALONE, 8 438
IN EVERY BUSH AND BRAKE, WHERE HAP MAY FINDE 9 160
HIS MIDNIGHT SEARCH, WHERE SOONEST HE MIGHT FINDE 9 181
BUT IF THOU THINK, TRIAL UNSOUGHT MAY FINDE 9 370
MAY FINDE US BOTH PERHAPS FARR LESS PREPAR'D, 9 381
AND ON HIS QUEST, WHERE LIKELIEST HE MIGHT FINDE 9 414
EITHER TO MEET NO DANGER, OR TO FINDE 9 1176
HOW LITTLE WEIGHT MY WORDS WITH THEE CAN FINDE, 10 968
MARCHING FROM EDEN TOWARDS THE WEST, SHALL FINDE 12 40
JUST ABRAHAM AND HIS SEED: NOW FIRST I FINDE 12 273
TO THEM BY FAITH IMPUTED, THEY MAY FINDE 12 295
ON EVERY CONSCIENCE; LAWS WHICH NONE SHALL FINDE 12 522

FINDES
IN MISERIE; SUCH JOY AMBITION FINDES. 4 92
FINDES NO ACCEPTANCE, NOR CAN FIND, FOR HOW 5 531

FINDING
WHO WOULD NOT, FINDING WAY, BREAK LOOSE FROM HELL, 4 889

FINDS
AND SHALL GRACE NOT FIND MEANS, THAT FINDS HER WAY, 3 228

FIND'ST
THOU FIND'ST HIM FROM THE HEAT OF NOON RETIR'D, 5 231

FINDST
WHAT HIGHER IN HER SOCIETIE THOU FINDST 8 586

FINISH
THOSE HAVE THIR COURSE TO FINISH, ROUND THE EARTH, 4 661

FINISH'D
SHE FINISH'D, AND THE SUTTLE FIEND HIS LORE 2 815
SECRET THEY FINISH'D, AND IN ORDER SET, 6 522
HERE FINISH'D HEE, AND ALL THAT HE HAD MADE 7 548

FINISHER
O PROPHET OF GLAD TIDINGS, FINISHER 12 375

FINISHT
HE SCARCE HAD FINISHT, WHEN SUCH MURMUR FILLD 2 284
HAVE FINISHT HAPPIE IN OUR MUTUAL HELP 4 727
HATH FINISHT HALF HIS JOURNEY, AND SCARCE BEGINS 5 559

FINISHT (CONTINUED)
UNAIDED COULD HAVE FINISHT THEE, AND WHELMD 6 141

FINITE
FOR ANGERS SAKE, FINITE TO INFINITE 10 802

FINNS
OF FISH THAT WITH THIR FINNS AND SHINING SCALES 7 401

FIR'D
IN AUTUMN THWARTS THE NIGHT, WHEN VAPORS FIR'D 4 557

FIRE
IN ADAMANTINE CHAINS AND PENAL FIRE, 1 48
WITH FLOODS AND WHIRLWINDS OF TEMPESTUOUS FIRE, 1 77
HERE IN THE HEART OF HELL TO WORK IN FIRE, 1 151
WITH SOLID, AS THE LAKE WITH LIQUID FIRE; 1 229
AND FEWEL'D ENTRALS THENCE CONCEIVING FIRE, 1 234
GROVELING AND PROSTRATE ON YON LAKE OF FIRE, 1 280
SMOTE ON HIM SORE BESIDES, VAULTED WITH FIRE; 1 298
THIR CHILDRENS CRIES UNHEARD, THAT PAST THROUGH FIRE 1 395
THIR GLORY WITHERD. AS WHEN HEAVENS FIRE 1 612
BELCH'D FIRE AND ROWLING SMOAK; THE REST ENTIRE 1 671
THAT UNDERNEATH HAD VEINS OF LIQUID FIRE 1 701
BLACK FIRE AND HORROR SHOT WITH EQUAL RAGE 2 67
MIXT WITH TARTAREAN SULPHUR, AND STRANGE FIRE, 2 69
WHERE PAIN OF UNEXTINGUISHABLE FIRE 2 88
HER MISCHIEF, AND PURGE OFF THE BASER FIRE 2 141
OF HELL SHOULD SPOUT HER CATARACTS OF FIRE, 2 176
BY SUDDEN ONSET, EITHER WITH HELL FIRE 2 364
OUR PRISON STRONG, THIS HUGE CONVEX OF FIRE, 2 434
WHOSE WAVES OF TORRENT FIRE INFLAME WITH RAGE. 2 581
BURNS FRORE, AND COLD PERFORMS TH' EFFECT OF FIRE. 2 595
FROM BEDS OF RAGING FIRE TO STARVE IN ICE 2 600
PERIODS OF TIME, THENCE HURRIED BACK TO FIRE. 2 603
IMPENETRABLE, IMPAL'D WITH CIRCLING FIRE, 2 647
OF NEITHER SEA, NOR SHORE, NOR AIR, NOR FIRE, 2 912
INSTINCT WITH FIRE AND NITRE HURRIED HIM 2 937
SPRINGS UPWARD LIKE A PYRAMID OF FIRE 2 1013
WITH RADIANT LIGHT, AS GLOWING IRON WITH FIRE; 3 594
THE CUMBROUS ELEMENTS, EARTH, FLOOD, AIRE, FIRE, 3 715
ON HIM WHO HAD STOLE JOVES AUTHENTIC FIRE. 4 719
THROUGH SPIRITS WITH EASE; NOR WONDER; IF BY FIRE 5 439
HIS THUNDER ON THY HEAD, DEVOURING FIRE. 5 893
REBELLIOUS, THEM WITH FIRE AND HOSTILE ARMS 6 50
AND FLYING VAULTED EITHER HOST WITH FIRE. 6 214
CONFLICTING FIRE: LONG TIME IN EEVEN SCALE 6 245
THICK-RAMMD, AT TH' OTHER BORE WITH TOUCH OF FIRE 6 485
PROVIDE, PERNICIOUS WITH ONE TOUCH TO FIRE. 6 520
BUT RATLING STORM OF ARROWS BARBD WITH FIRE. 6 546
STOOD WAVING TIPT WITH FIRE; WHILE WE SUSPENSE, 6 580
GLAR'D LIGHTNING, AND SHOT FORTH PERNICIOUS FIRE 6 849
HELL THIR FIT HABITATION FRAUGHT WITH FIRE 6 876
GUILTLESS OF FIRE HAD FORMD, OR ANGELS BROUGHT. 9 392
BRIGHT'NS HIS CREST, AS WHEN A WANDRING FIRE, 9 634
OF EVE, WHOSE EYE DARTED CONTAGIOUS FIRE. 9 1036
THE AIR ATTRITE TO FIRE, AS LATE THE CLOUDS 10 1073
WHICH MIGHT SUPPLIE THE SUN: SUCH FIRE TO USE, 10 1078
IN DOTHAN, COVER'D WITH A CAMP OF FIRE, 11 217
HIS OFFRING SOON PROPITIOUS FIRE FROM HEAV'N 11 441
BY FIRE, FLOOD, FAMIN, BY INTEMPERANCE MORE 11 472
HAD MELTED (WHETHER FOUND WHERE CASUAL FIRE 11 566
WITH DART AND JAV'LIN, STONES AND SULFUROUS FIRE; 11 658
SHALL HOLD THIR COURSE, TILL FIRE PURGE ALL THINGS NEW, 11 900
HAILE MIXT WITH FIRE MUST REND TH' EGYPTIAN SKIE 12 182
BEFORE THEM IN A CLOUD, AND PILLAR OF FIRE, 12 202
BY DAY A CLOUD, BY NIGHT A PILLAR OF FIRE, 12 203

FIRES
'TWIXT UPPER, NETHER, AND SURROUNDING FIRES; 1 346
WHAT IF THE BREATH THAT KINDL'D THOSE GRIM FIRES 2 170
WITH WHAT IS PUNISH'T; WHENCE THESE RAGING FIRES 2 213
BECOME OUR ELEMENTS, THESE PIERCING FIRES 2 275
TO HEAL THE SCARR OF THESE CORROSIVE FIRES 2 401
THAT FIRES THE LENGTH OF OPHIUCUS HUGE 2 709
IN NATURE AND ALL THINGS, WHICH THESE SOFT FIRES 4 667
AND YEE FIVE OTHER WANDRING FIRES THAT MOVE 5 177
EARTH AND THE SEA FEED AIR, THE AIR THOSE FIRES 5 417
CHERUBIC WAVING FIRES: ON TH' OTHER PART 6 413
OF BERIL, AND CAREERING FIRES BETWEEN; 6 756
DISTANT SO HIGH, WITH MOVING FIRES ADORND 7 87
THE HEAV'NLY FIRES; OVER THE TENT A CLOUD 12 256

FIREY
THEN THROUGH THE FIREY PILLAR AND THE CLOUD 12 208

FIRM
ON THE FIRM BRIMSTONE, AND FILL ALL THE PLAIN; 1 350
DELIBERATE VALOUR BREATH'D, FIRM AND UNMOV'D 1 554
TO UNION, AND FIRM FAITH, AND FIRM ACCORD, 2 36
FIRM CONCORD HOLDS, MEN ONELY DISAGREE 2 497
OF WHIRLWIND AND DIRE HAIL, WHICH ON FIRM LAND 2 589
FIRM LAND IMBOSOM'D WITHOUT FIRMAMENT, 3 75
MEAN WHILE UPON THE FIRM OPACOUS GLOBE 3 418
OF FIRM AND FRAGRANT LEAF; ON EITHER SIDE 4 695
STAND FIRM, FOR IN HIS LOOK DEFIANCE LOURS. 4 873

FIRM (CONTINUED)
FIRM PEACE RECOVERD SOON AND WONTED CALM. 5 210
UNALTERABLY FIRM HIS LOVE ENTIRE 5 502
INDISSOLUBLY FIRM; NOR OBVIOUS HILL, 6 69
THAT WARR AND VARIOUS; SOMTIMES ON FIRM GROUND 6 242
IN CUBIC PHALANX FIRM ADVANC'T ENTIRE, 6 399
BUT FIRM BATTALION; BACK WITH SPEEDIEST SAIL 6 534
OF DISOBEDIENCE; FIRM THEY MIGHT HAVE STOOD, 6 911
OF THIS GREAT ROUND: PARTITION FIRM AND SURE, 7 267
AND DRINK THE LIQUID LIGHT, FIRM TO RETAINE 7 362
WALK'D FIRM; THE CRESTED COCK WHOSE CLARION SOUNDS 7 443
OF GODHEAD, FIXT FOR EVER FIRM AND SURE, 7 586
THY EQUAL FEAR THAT MY FIRM FAITH AND LOVE 9 286
FIRM WE SUBSIST, YET POSSIBLE TO SWERVE, 9 359
HADST THOU BIN FIRM AND FIXT IN THY DISSENT, 9 1160
AS WITH A TRIDENT SMOTE, AND FIX'T AS FIRM 10 295
AND IN THIR STATE, THOUGH FIRM, STOOD MORE CONFIRMD. 11 71
NOT KNOWING TO WHAT LAND, YET FIRM BELIEVES: 12 127

FIRMAMENT
HER STORES WERE OPEN'D, AND THIS FIRMAMENT 2 175
FIRM LAND IMBOSOM'D WITHOUT FIRMAMENT, 3 75
THROUGH THE CALM FIRMAMENT; BUT UP OR DOWNE 3 574
SILENCE WAS PLEAS'D: NOW GLOW'D THE FIRMAMENT 4 604
OVER THIR HEADS A CHRYSTAL FIRMAMENT, 6 757
AGAIN, GOD SAID, LET THER BE FIRMAMENT 7 261
THE FIRMAMENT, EXPANSE OF LIQUID, PURE, 7 264
AND HEAV'N HE NAM'D THE FIRMAMENT: SO EEV'N 7 274
THIR OFFICE IN THE FIRMAMENT OF HEAV'N 7 344
AND SET THEM IN THE FIRMAMENT OF HEAV'N 7 349
DISPLAYD ON THE OP'N FIRMAMENT OF HEAV'N. 7 390
AN ATOM, WITH THE FIRMAMENT COMPAR'D 8 18
O'RE THE BLEW FIRMAMENT A RADIANT WHITE, 11 206

FIRMER
A SPACE, TILL FIRMER THOUGHTS RESTRAIND EXCESS, 11 498

FIRMLY
OMNISCIENT THOUGHT. TRUE IS, LESS FIRMLY ARM'D, 6 430

FIRMNESS
SAVE WHAT BY FRUGAL STORING FIRMNESS GAINS 5 324
BUT THAT THOU SHOULDST MY FIRMNESS THEREFORE DOUBT 9 279

FIRR
CEDAR, AND PINE, AND FIRR, AND BRANCHING PALM, 4 139
OR HOLLOW'D BODIES MADE OF OAK OR FIRR 6 574
KINDLES THE GUMMIE BARK OF FIRR OR PINE, 10 1076

FIRST
OF MANS FIRST DISOBEDIENCE, AND THE FRUIT 1 1
THAT SHEPHERD, WHO FIRST TAUGHT THE CHOSEN SEED, 1 8
INSTRUCT ME, FOR THOU KNOW'ST; THOU FROM THE FIRST 1 19
SAY FIRST, FOR HEAV'N HIDES NOTHING FROM THY VIEW 1 27
NOR THE DEEP TRACT OF HELL, SAY FIRST WHAT CAUSE 1 28
WHO FIRST SEDUC'D THEM TO THAT FOUL REVOLT? 1 33
SAY, MUSE, THIR NAMES THEN KNOWN, WHO FIRST, WHO LAST, 1 376
FIRST MOLOCH, HORRID KING BESMEAR'D WITH BLOOD 1 392
BOTH HER FIRST BORN AND ALL HER BLEATING GODS. 1 489
THIR BOASTED PARENTS; TITAN HEAV'NS FIRST BORN 1 510
SO JOVE USURPING REIGN'D: THESE FIRST IN CREET 1 514
OUR FIRST ERUPTION, THITHER OR ELSEWHERE: 1 656
IN VISION BEATIFIC: BY HIM FIRST 1 684
DID FIRST CREATE YOUR LEADER, NEXT FREE CHOICE, 2 19
FIRST, WHAT REVENGE? THE TOWRS OF HEAV'N ARE FILL'D 2 129
THAT SO ORDAINS: THIS WAS AT FIRST RESOLV'D, 2 201
IN HEIGHTH OR DEPTH, STILL FIRST AND LAST WILL REIGN 2 324
PLEADED HIS DEVILISH COUNSEL, FIRST DEVIS'D 2 379
SHALL BREATHE HER BALME. BUT FIRST WHOM SHALL WE SEND 2 402
VIEW'D FIRST THIR LAMENTABLE LOT, AND FOUND 2 617
AND WITH DISDAINFUL LOOK THUS FIRST BEGAN. 2 680
WHO FIRST BROKE PEACE IN HEAV'N AND FAITH, TILL THEN 2 690
WHAT IT INTENDS; TILL FIRST I KNOW OF THEE, 2 740
IN THIS INFERNAL VAILE FIRST MET THOU CALL'ST 2 742
AT FIRST, AND CALL'D ME SIN, AND FOR A SIGN 2 760
WEAKNING THE SCEPTER OF OLD NIGHT: FIRST HELL 2 1002
A GLIMMERING DAWN; HERE NATURE FIRST BEGINS 2 1037
HIS ONELY SON; ON EARTH HE FIRST BEHELD 3 64
OUR TWO FIRST PARENTS, YET THE ONELY TWO 3 65
THE FIRST SORT BY THIR OWN SUGGESTION FELL, 3 129
BY THE OTHER FIRST: MAN THEREFORE SHALL FIND GRACE, 3 131
BUT MERCY FIRST AND LAST SHALL BRIGHTEST SHINE. 3 134
TO HEAV'N REMOV'D WHERE FIRST IT GREW, THERE GROWS, 3 356
THEE FATHER FIRST THEY SUNG OMNIPOTENT, 3 372
THEE NEXT THEY SANG OF ALL CREATION FIRST, 3 383
OF THIS ROUND WORLD, WHOSE FIRST CONVEX DIVIDES 3 419
FIRST FROM THE ANCIENT WORLD THOSE GIANTS CAME 3 464
THE TREPIDATION TALKT, AND THAT FIRST MOV'D; 3 483
DOWN RIGHT INTO THE WORLDS FIRST REGION THROWS 3 562
BUT FIRST HE CASTS TO CHANGE HIS PROPER SHAPE, 3 634
THE FIRST ART WONT HIS GREAT AUTHENTIC WILL 3 656
SATAN, NOW FIRST INFLAM'D WITH RAGE, CAME DOWN, 4 9

FIRST (CONTINUED)

OF THAT FIRST BATTEL, AND HIS FLIGHT TO HELL: 4 12
ARTIFICER OF FRAUD; AND WAS THE FIRST 4 121
SO CLOMB THIS FIRST GRAND THIEF INTO GODS FOULD: 4 192
BOTH WHERE THE MORNING SUN FIRST WARMLY SMOTE 4 244
WHEN SATAN STILL IN GAZE, AS FIRST HE STOOD, 4 356
GRIP'T IN EACH PAW: WHEN ADAM FIRST OF MEN 4 408
TO FIRST OF WOMEN EVE THUS MOVING SPEECH, 4 409
I FIRST AWAK'T, AND FOUND MY SELF REPOS'D 4 450
ON OUR FIRST FATHER, HALF HER SWELLING BREAST 4 495
BUT FIRST WITH NARROW SEARCH I MUST WALK ROUND 4 528
WHERE HE FIRST LIGHTED, SOON DISCERND HIS LOOKS 4 570
WITH FIRST APPROACH OF LIGHT, WE MUST BE RIS'N, 4 624
WHEN FIRST ON THIS DELIGHTFUL LAND HE SPREADS 4 643
ESPOUSED EVE DECKT FIRST HER NUPTIAL BED, 4 710
OF FATHER, SON, AND BROTHER FIRST WERE KNOWN. 4 757
THE FIRST IN FLIGHT FROM PAIN, HAD'ST THOU ALLEDG'D 4 921
I THEREFORE, I ALONE FIRST UNDERTOOK 4 935
TO SAY AND STRAIT UNSAY, PRETENDING FIRST 4 947
WHEREIN ALL THINGS CREATED FIRST HE WEIGHD, 4 999
THEN WHEN FAIR MORNING FIRST SMILES ON THE WORLD, 5 124
BUT FIRST FROM UNDER SHADIE ARBOROUS ROOF, 5 137
UNSPEAKABLE, WHO FIRST ABOVE THESE HEAVENS 5 156
HIM FIRST, HIM LAST, HIM MIDST, AND WITHOUT END. 5 165
DELOS OR SAMOS FIRST APPEERING KENNS 5 265
ETHEREAL, AND AS LOWEST FIRST THE MOON; 5 418
SUCH TO PERFECTION, ONE FIRST MATTER ALL, 5 472
IS HEARD NO MORE IN HEAV'N; HE OF THE FIRST, 5 659
IF NOT THE FIRST ARCH-ANGEL, GREAT IN POWER, 5 660
REFLECTING BLAZE ON BLAZE, FIRST MET HIS VIEW: 6 18
AT FIRST, THAT ANGEL SHOULD WITH ANGEL WARR, 6 92
OF MY REVENGE, FIRST SOUGHT FOR THOU RETURNST 6 151
THY MERITED REWARD, THE FIRST ASSAY 6 153
OF THIS RIGHT HAND PROVOK'T, SINCE FIRST THAT
TONGUE 6 154
AT FIRST I THOUGHT THAT LIBERTIE AND HEAV'N 6 164
AND VISAGE ALL ENFLAM'D FIRST THUS BEGAN. 6 261
ALL HIS RIGHT SIDE; THEN SATAN FIRST KNEW PAIN, 6 327
THEN FIRST WITH FEAR SURPRIS'D AND SENSE OF PAINE 6 394
PUREST AT FIRST, NOW GROSS BY SINNING GROWN. 6 661
FIRST, HIGHEST, HOLIEST, BEST, THOU ALWAYES SEEKST 6 724
FIRST SEEN, THEM UNEXPECTED JOY SURPRIZ'D, 6 774
OF HEAV'N AND EARTH CONSPICIOUS FIRST BEGAN, 7 63
HOW FIRST BEGAN THIS HEAV'N WHICH WE BEHOLD 7 86
ETHEREAL, FIRST OF THINGS, QUINTESSENCE PURE 7 244
HE NAM'D. THUS WAS THE FIRST DAY EEV'N AND MORN: 7 252
EXHALING FIRST FROM DARKNESS THEY BEHELD; 7 255
BOTH WHEN FIRST EEVNING WAS, AND WHEN FIRST MORN. 7 260
FOR OF CELESTIAL BODIES FIRST THE SUN 7 354
A MIGHTIE SPHEARE HE FRAM'D, UNLIGHTSOM FIRST, 7 355
FIRST IN HIS EAST THE GLORIOUS LAMP WAS SEEN, 7 370
SPANGLING THE HEMISPHERE: THEN FIRST ADORND 7 384
THIR SNAKIE FOULDS, AND ADDED WINGS. FIRST CREPT 7 484
FIRST WHEELD THIR COURSE; EARTH IN HER RICH ATTIRE 7 501
HOW FIRST THIS WORLD AND FACE OF THINGS BEGAN, 7 636
THE BENEFIT: CONSIDER FIRST, THAT GREAT 8 90
BUT IN THE FRUITFUL EARTH; THERE FIRST RECEAVD 8 96
FROM WHERE I FIRST DREW AIRE, AND FIRST BEHELD 8 284
FIRST FOUND ME, AND WITH SOFT OPPRESSION SEIS'D 8 288
FIRST MAN, OF MEN INNUMERABLE ORDAIN'D 8 297
FIRST FATHER, CALL'D BY THEE I COME THY GUIDE 8 298
TRANSPORTED TOUCH; HERE PASSION FIRST I FELT, 8 530
AS ONE INTENDED FIRST, NOT AFTER MADE 8 555
BE STRONG, LIVE HAPPIE, AND LOVE, BUT FIRST OF ALL 8 633
SINCE FIRST THIS SUBJECT FOR HEROIC SONG 9 25
NOW NOT, THOUGH SIN, NOT TIME, FIRST WRAUGHT THE
CHANGE, 9 70
THUS HE RESOLV'D, BUT FIRST FROM INWARD GRIEFE 9 97
AS HIGH HE SOARD, OBNOXIOUS FIRST OR LAST 9 170
TO BASEST THINGS. REVENGE, AT FIRST THOUGH SWEET, 9 171
AND EVE FIRST TO HER HUSBAND THUS BEGAN. 9 204
OR BEAR WHAT TO MY MINDE FIRST THOUGHTS PRESENT, 9 213
WHETHER HIS FIRST DESIGN BE TO WITHDRAW 9 261
OR DARING, FIRST ON MEE TH' ASSAULT SHALL LIGHT. 9 305
FIRST THY OBEDIENCE; TH' OTHER WHO CAN KNOW, 9 368
A FOE SO PROUD WILL FIRST THE WEAKER SEEK, 9 383
FOR NOW, AND SINCE FIRST BREAK OF DAWNE THE FIEND, 9 412
AT FIRST, AS ONE WHO SOUGHT ACCESS, BUT FEARD 9 511
THE FIRST AT LEST OF THESE I THOUGHT DENID 9 555
I WAS AT FIRST AS OTHER BEASTS THAT GRAZE 9 571
THE VERTUE OF THAT FRUIT, IN THEE FIRST PROV'D: 9 616
THE GODS ARE FIRST, AND THAT ADVANTAGE USE 9 718
SOLLICITED HER LONGING EYE; YET FIRST 9 743
WHOSE TASTE, TOO LONG FORBORN, AT FIRST ASSAY 9 747
FOR BEASTS IT SEEMS: YET THAT ONE BEAST WHICH FIRST 9 769
BUT FIRST LOW REVERENCE DON, AS TO THE POWER 9 835
THAT MORN WHEN FIRST THEY PARTED; BY THE TREE 9 848
FIRST TO HIMSELF HE INWARD SILENCE BROKE. 9 895
PROFAN'D FIRST BY THE SERPENT, BY HIM FIRST 9 930
MOST FAVORS, WHO CAN PLEASE HIM LONG; MEE FIRST 9 949
FARR OTHER OPERATION FIRST DISPLAID, 9 1012
I SAW THEE FIRST AND WEDDED THEE, ADORN'D 9 1030
EVEN SHAME, THE LAST OF EVILS; OF THE FIRST 9 1079
TO THAT FIRST NAKED GLORIE. SUCH OF LATE 9 1115
TO WHOM THEN FIRST INCENST ADAM REPLI'D, 9 1162
SHEE FIRST HIS WEAK INDULGENCE WILL ACCUSE. 9 1186
WHEN FIRST THIS TEMPTER CROSS'D THE GULF FROM HELL. 10 39
HE CAME, AND WITH HIM EVE, MORE LOTH, THOUGH FIRST 10 109

FIRST (CONTINUED)

TO SATAN FIRST IN SIN HIS DOOM APPLY'D, 10 172
FIRST LIGHTED FROM HIS WING, AND LANDED SAFE 10 316
TO PARADISE FIRST TENDING, WHEN BEHOLD 10 326
HIM FIRST MAKE SURE YOUR THRALL, AND LASTLY KILL. 10 402
ENCROACHING EVE PERHAPS, HAD FIRST THE RULE 10 582
FEED FIRST, ON EACH BEAST NEXT, AND FISH, AND
FOWLE, 10 604
HAD FIRST HIS PRECEPT SO TO MOVE, SO SHINE, 10 652
OUTRAGE FROM LIVELESS THINGS; BUT DISCORD FIRST 10 707
BUT TO MY OWN CONVICTION: FIRST AND LAST 10 831
BEARE THINE OWN FIRST, ILL ABLE TO SUSTAINE 10 950
SEE FATHER, WHAT FIRST FRUITS ON EARTH ARE SPRUNG 11 22
FOR DISSOLUTION WROUGHT BY SIN, THAT FIRST 11 55
CORRUPTED. I AT FIRST WITH TWO FAIR GIFTS 11 57
THE EARTH, WHEN ADAM AND FIRST MATRON EVE 11 136
THAT I WHO FIRST BROUGHT DEATH ON ALL, AM GRAC'T 11 168
SUBSCRIB'D NOT; NATURE FIRST GAVE SIGNS, IMPREST 11 182
FIRST HUNTER THEN, PURSU'D A GENTLE BRACE, 11 188
FROM THE FIRST OP'NING BUD, AND GAVE YE NAMES, 11 277
ADAM, NOW OPE THINE EYES, AND FIRST BEHOLD 11 423
FIRST FRUITS, THE GREEN EARE, AND THE YELLOW SHEAF, 11 435
IN HIS FIRST SHAPE ON MAN; BUT MANY SHAPES 11 467
FIRST HIS OWN TOOLES; THEN, WHAT MIGHT ELSE BE
WROUGHT 11 572
HYMEN, THEN FIRST TO MARRIAGE RITES INVOK'T; 11 591
FIRST SEEN IN ACTS OF PROWESS EMINENT 11 789
BUT FIRST THE LAWLESS TYRANT, WHO DENIES 12 173
JUST ABRAHAM AND HIS SEED: NOW FIRST I FINDE 12 273
BY JUDGES FIRST, THEN UNDER KINGS; OF WHOM 12 320
BUT FIRST A LONG SUCCESSION MUST ENSUE, 12 331
THEY FIRST RE-EDIFIE, AND FOR A WHILE 12 350
BUT FIRST AMONG THE PRIESTS DISSENSION SPRINGS, 12 353
THEN THAT WHICH BY CREATION FIRST BROUGHT FORTH 12 472
POWRD FIRST ON HIS APOSTLES, WHOM HE SENDS 12 498

FIRST-BORN

HAIL HOLY LIGHT, OFSPRING OF HEAV'N FIRST-BORN, 3 1
LAST WITH ONE MIDNIGHT STROKE ALL THE FIRST-BORN 12 189

FIRSTLINGS

MORE MEEK CAME WITH THE FIRSTLINGS OF HIS FLOCK 11 437

FIRST-MOVERS

HER MOTIONS, AS THE GREAT FIRST-MOVERS HAND 7 500

FIRST-PARENTS

WHILE TIME WAS, OUR FIRST-PARENTS HAD BIN WARND 4 6

FIRST-SEEN

FIRST-SEEN, OR SOME RENOWN'D METROPOLIS 3 549

FISH

AND DOWNWARD FISH: YET HAD HIS TEMPLE HIGH 1 463
OF FISH THAT WITH THIR FINNS AND SHINING SCALES 7 401
WITH FISH REPLENISHT, AND THE AIRE WITH FOWLE, 7 447
BY FOWL, FISH, BEAST, WAS FLOWN, WAS SWUM, WAS
WALKT 7 503
OVER THE FISH AND FOWLE OF SEA AND AIRE, 7 521
OVER FISH OF THE SEA, AND FOWLE OF THE AIRE, 7 533
OR LIVE IN SEA, OR AIRE, BEAST, FISH, AND FOWLE, 8 341
OF FISH WITHIN THIR WATRY RESIDENCE, 8 346
MUCH LESS CAN BIRD WITH BEAST, OR FISH WITH FOWLE 8 395
FEED FIRST, ON EACH BEAST NEXT, AND FISH, AND
FOWLE, 10 604
AND FISH WITH FISH; TO GRAZE THE HERB ALL LEAVING, 10 711
HE GAVE US ONELY OVER BEAST, FISH, FOWL 12 67

FISHIE

THEN ASMODEUS WITH THE FISHIE FUME, 4 168

FIT

WITH ATLANTEAN SHOULDERS FIT TO BEAR 2 306
FIT RETRIBUTION, EMPTIE AS THIR DEEDS; 3 454
HIS HABIT FIT FOR SPEED SUCCINCT, AND HELD 3 643
FIT FOR THE TUN SOM MAGAZIN TO STORE 4 816
ARMIE OF FIENDS, FIT BODY TO FIT HEAD; 4 953
FORBIDD'N HERE, IT SEEMS, AS ONELY FIT 5 69
THIR MAKER, IN FIT STRAINS PRONOUNC'T OR SUNG 5 148
ABUNDANCE, FIT TO HONOUR AND RECEIVE 5 315
WANTS HER FIT VESSELS PURE, THEN STREWS THE GROUND 5 348
FIT ENTERTAINMENT TO RECEIVE OUR KING 5 690
FIT TO DECIDE THE EMPIRE OF GREAT HEAV'N. 6 303
FIT WELL HIS HELME, GRIPE FAST HIS ORBED SHIELD, 6 543
AGAINST SUCH HELLISH MISCHIEF FIT TO OPPOSE. 6 636
HELL THIR FIT HABITATION FRAUGHT WITH FIRE 6 876
URANIA, AND FIT AUDIENCE FIND, THOUGH FEW. 7 31
SUCH AS I SEEK, FIT TO PARTICIPATE 8 390
TO SEE HOW THOU COULD'ST JUDGE OF FIT AND MEET: 8 448
THY LIKENESS, THY FIT HELP, THY OTHER SELF, 8 450
FIT VESSEL, FITTEST IMP OF FRAUD, IN WHOM 9 89
SHEE FAIR, DIVINELY FAIR, FIT LOVE FOR GODS, 9 489
SO FIT, SO ACCEPTABLE, SO DIVINE, 10 139
CAN FIT HIS PUNISHMENT, OR THEIR REVENGE. 10 242
THAT LAUGH, AS IF TRANSPORTED WITH SOME FIT 10 626
HE NEVER SHALL FIND OUT FIT MATE, BUT SUCH 10 899
FIT HAUNT OF GODS? WHERE I HAD HOPE TO SPEND, 11 271
INTO FIT MOULDS PREPAR'D; FROM WHICH HE FORMD 11 571

FIT (CONTINUED)
TO MEEK SUBMISSION: THOU AT SEASON FIT 12 597

FITLY
SO FITLY THEM IN PAIRS THOU HAST COMBIN'D; 8 394

FITTER
THE GROUND WHENCE HE WAS TAKEN, FITTER SOILE. 11 98
THE GROUND WHENCE THOU WAST TAK'N, FITTER SOILE. 11 262

FITTEST
FIT VESSEL, FITTEST IMP OF FRAUD, IN WHOM 9 89

FIVE
WHICH THE FIVE WATCHFUL SENSES REPRESENT, 5 104
AND YEE FIVE OTHER WANDRING FIRES THAT MOVE 5 177
HER OFFICE THEY PRESCRIB'D, TO TH' OTHER FIVE 10 657

FIX
ROAMING TO SEEK THIR PREY ON EARTH, DURST FIX 1 382
WHAT HE ALMIGHTIE STYL'D, FIX NIGHTS AND DAYS 9 137
AND FIX FARR DEEPER IN HIS HEAD THIR STINGS 12 432

FIX'D
THIR EARNEST EYES THEY FIX'D, IMAGINING 10 553

FIXD
FIXD ON THIS DAY? WHY DO I OVERLIVE, 10 773

FIXED
WITH FIXED ANCHOR IN HIS SKALY RIND 1 206
BREATHING UNITED FORCE WITH FIXED THOUGHT 1 560
HIS FIXED SEAT, OR FIXED SEAT HATH NONE, 3 669

FIXES
LAY PLEASANT, HIS GRIEVD LOOK HE FIXES SAD, 4 28

FIX'T
AS WITH A TRIDENT SMOTE, AND FIX'T AS FIRM 10 295

FIXT
THOUGH CHANG'D IN OUTWARD LUSTRE; THAT FIXT MIND 1 97
STOOD FIXT HER STATELY HIGHTH, AND STRAIT THE DORES 1 723
MEE THOUGH JUST RIGHT, AND THE FIXT LAWS OF HEAV'N 2 18
FIXT FATE, FREE WILL, FOREKNOWLEDG ABSOLUTE, 2 560
THEY PASS THE PLANETS SEVEN, AND PASS THE FIXT, 3 481
HE SEEMD, OR FIXT IN COGITATION DEEP. 3 629
OF SYMPATHIE AND LOVE; THERE I HAD FIXT 4 465
WITH THE FIXT STARRS, FIXT IN THIR ORB THAT FLIES, 5 176
OF PLANETS AND OF FIXT IN ALL HER WHEELES 5 621
OF GODHEAD, FIXT FOR EVER FIRM AND SURE, 7 586
THOUGHT HIM STILL SPEAKING, STILL STOOD FIXT TO HEAR; 8 3
FIXT ON THE FRUIT SHE GAZ'D, WHICH TO BEHOLD 9 735
HOWEVER I WITH THEE HAVE FIXT MY LOT, 9 952
HADST THOU BIN FIRM AND FIXT IN THY DISSENT, 9 1160
IN SYNOD UNBENIGNE, AND TAUGHT THE FIXT 10 661
FAST ON THE TOP OF SOM HIGH MOUNTAIN FIXT, 11 851
TILL TIME STAND FIXT: BEYOND IS ALL ABYSS, 12 555
TO THIR FIXT STATION, ALL IN BRIGHT ARRAY 12 627

FLAG
THIR EMBRYON ATOMS; THEY AROUND THE FLAG 2 900

FLAM'D
AS ONE GREAT FURNACE FLAM'D, YET FROM THOSE FLAMES 1 62
NEER THAT BITUMINOUS LAKE WHERE SODOM FLAM'D; 10 562

FLAME
CAST FORTH REDOUNDING SMOAK AND RUDDY FLAME. 2 889
OUR CIRCUIT MEETS FULL WEST. AS FLAME THEY PART 4 784
STOOD UP, AND IN A FLAME OF ZEALE SEVERE 5 807
IMPENDENT, RAGING INTO SUDDEN FLAME 5 891
SHALL YIELD US PREGNANT WITH INFERNAL FLAME, 6 483
WITH NICEST TOUCH. IMMEDIATE IN A FLAME, 6 584
OF SMOAK AND BICKERING FLAME, AND SPARKLES DIRE; 6 766
KINDL'D THROUGH AGITATION TO A FLAME, 9 637
STOOD OPEN WIDE, BELCHING OUTRAGEOUS FLAME 10 232
TINE THE SLANT LIGHTNING, WHOSE THWART FLAME DRIV'N DOWN 10 1075
CHERUBIC WATCH, AND OF A SWORD THE FLAME 11 120

FLAMES
AS ONE GREAT FURNACE FLAM'D, YET FROM THOSE FLAMES 1 62
SAVE WHAT THE GLIMMERING OF THESE LIVID FLAMES 1 182
HIS MIGHTY STATURE; ON EACH HAND THE FLAMES 1 222
ARM'D WITH HELL FLAMES AND FURY ALL AT ONCE 2 61
AND PLUNGE US IN THE FLAMES? OR FROM ABOVE 2 172
WILL SLACK'N, IF HIS BREATH STIR NOT THIR FLAMES. 2 214
IN DARKNESS, WHILE THY HEAD FLAMES THICK AND FAST 2 754
A GOD, LEAP'D FONDLY INTO AETNA FLAMES, 3 470
IN DUSKIE WREATHES, RELUCTANT FLAMES, THE SIGNE 6 58
FLASHING THICK FLAMES, WHEELE WITHIN WHEELE UNDRAWN, 6 751

FLAMING
HURLD HEADLONG FLAMING FROM TH' ETHEREAL SKIE 1 45
MILLIONS OF FLAMING SWORDS, DRAWN FROM THE THIGHS 1 664

FLAMING (CONTINUED)
NOR STOP THY FLAMING CHARIOT WHEELS, THAT SHOOK 3 394
HUNG HIGH WITH DIAMOND FLAMING, AND WITH GOLD. 4 554
AMIDST AS FROM A FLAMING MOUNT, WHOSE TOP 5 598
THE FLAMING SERAPH FEARLESS, THOUGH ALONE 5 875
CHARIOTS AND FLAMING ARMES, AND FIERIE STEEDS 6 17
WITH FLAMING CHERUBIM, AND GOLDEN SHIELDS; 6 102
OF FIERY DARTS IN FLAMING VOLIES FLEW, 6 213
FELL WITH HIS FLAMING LEGIONS THROUGH THE DEEP 7 134
HEE FROM THE EAST HIS FLAMING RODE BEGIN, 8 162
AND FLAMING MINISTERS TO WATCH AND TEND 9 156
THY CHOICE OF FLAMING WARRIOURS, LEAST THE FIEND 11 101
NOR THAT WHICH ON THE FLAMING MOUNT APPEERD 11 216
THIR MOTION, AT WHOSE FRONT A FLAMING SWORD, 12 592
WAV'D OVER BY THAT FLAMING BRAND, THE GATE 12 643

FLANK
DIVIDED, AND TO EITHER FLANK RETIR'D. 6 570

FLASHING
FLASHING THICK FLAMES, WHEELE WITHIN WHEELE UNDRAWN, 6 751

FLAT
WHERE HE FELL FLAT, AND SHAM'D HIS WORSHIPERS: 1 461
IS FLAT DESPAIR: WE MUST EXASPERATE 2 143
BEYOND A ROW OF MYRTLES, ON A FLAT, 9 627
HATH TOUCHT MY SENSE, FLAT SEEMS TO THIS, AND HARSH. 9 987

FLATLY
FLATLY UNJUST, TO BINDE WITH LAWS THE FREE, 5 819

FLATTER'D
AND FLATTER'D OUT OF ALL, BELIEVING LIES 10 42

FLAW
AND SNOW AND HAILE AND STORMIE GUST AND FLAW, 10 698

FLED
FLED OVER ADRIA TO TH' HESPERIAN FIELDS, 1 520
WHAT WHEN WE FLED AMAIN, PURSU'D AND STROOK 2 165
ALL TASTE OF LIVING WIGHT, AS ONCE IT FLED 2 613
MADE TO DESTROY: I FLED, AND CRY'D OUT DEATH; 2 787
I FLED, BUT HE PURSU'D (THOUGH MORE, IT SEEMS, 2 790
FLED NOT IN SILENCE THROUGH THE FRIGHTED DEEP 2 994
OF GUARDIANS BRIGHT, WHEN HE FROM ESAU FLED 3 512
TILL AT HIS SECOND BIDDING DARKNESS FLED, 3 712
LESS PAIN, LESS TO BE FLED, OR THOU THEN THEY 4 919
HIS MOUNTED SCALE ALOFT: NOR MORE; BUT FLED 4 1014
MURMURING, AND WITH HIM FLED THE SHADES OF NIGHT. 4 1015
AND UNCOUTH PAINE FLED BELLOWING. ON EACH WING 6 362
FLED IGNOMINIOUS, TO SUCH EVIL BROUGHT 6 395
WHERE LODG'D, OR WHITHER FLED, OR IF FOR FIGHT, 6 531
WHOM FLED WE THOUGHT, WILL SAVE US LONG PURSUIT 6 538
HEAV'N RUINING FROM HEAV'N AND WOULD HAVE FLED 6 868
WHEN SATAN WHO LATE FLED BEFORE THE THREATS 9 53
BY NIGHT HE FLED, AND AT MIDNIGHT RETURN'D 9 58
LIKELIEST SHE SEEMD, POMONA WHEN SHE FLED 9 394
HEE FLED, NOT HOPING TO ESCAPE, BUT SHUN 10 339
OF MAN, BUT FLED HIM, OR WITH COUNT'NANCE GRIM 10 713
FOR THOUGH I FLED HIM ANGRIE, YET RECALL'D 11 330
FLED AND PURSU'D TRANSVERSE THE RESONANT FUGUE. 11 563
WHICH NOW ABATED, FOR THE CLOUDS WERE FLED, 11 841

FLEDGE
ILLUSTRIOUS ON HIS SHOULDERS FLEDGE WITH WINGS 3 627
THIR CALLOW YOUNG, BUT FEATHERD SOON AND FLEDGE 7 420

FLEDST
FLIE THITHER WHENCE THOU FLEDST: IF FROM THIS HOURE 4 963

FLEECIE
OF LIBRA TO THE FLEECIE STARR THAT BEARS 3 558
TILL THE SUN PAINT YOUR FLEECIE SKIRTS WITH GOLD, 5 187

FLEEC'T
HIS VASTNESS: FLEEC'T THE FLOCKS AND BLEATING ROSE, 7 472

FLEECY
FROM A FAT MEDDOW GROUND; OR FLEECY FLOCK, 11 648

FLEET
AS WHEN FARR OFF AT SEA A FLEET DESCRI'D 2 636
DISSOLVD ON EARTH, FLEET HITHER, AND IN VAIN, 3 457

FLEETING
HEAVIE, THOUGH IN THIR PLACE. O FLEETING JOYES 10 741

FLEIGHTS
WHATEVER FLEIGHTS NONE WOULD SUSPICIOUS MARK, 9 92

FLESH
LIKE CUMBROUS FLESH; BUT IN WHAT SHAPE THEY CHOOSE 1 428
MADE FLESH, WHEN TIME SHALL BE, OF VIRGIN SEED, 3 284
TO GORGE THE FLESH OF LAMBS OR YEANLING KIDS 3 434
AND FROM WHOM I WAS FORMD FLESH OF THY FLESH, 4 441
HIS FLESH, HIS BONE; TO GIVE THEE BEING I LENT 4 483

FLESH (CONTINUED)
BUT SUDDENLY WITH FLESH FILL'D UP AND HEAL'D: . . 8 468
BONE OF MY BONE, FLESH OF MY FLESH, MY SELF . . 8 495
AND THEY SHALL BE ONE FLESH, ONE HEART, ONE SOULE. 8 499
AS FLESH TO MIX WITH FLESH, OR SOUL WITH SOUL. . 8 629
THE LINK OF NATURE DRAW ME: FLESH OF FLESH, . . 9 914
ONE FLESH; TO LOOSE THEE WERE TO LOOSE MY SELF. . 9 959
THE STONIE FROM THIR HEARTS, & MADE NEW FLESH . 11 4
THE WHOLE EARTH FILL'D WITH VIOLENCE, AND ALL FLESH 11 888
BOTCHES AND BLAINES MUST ALL HIS FLESH IMBOSS, . 12 180
FROM SHADOWIE TYPES TO TRUTH, FROM FLESH TO SPIRIT, 12 303
HE SHALL ENDURE BY COMING IN THE FLESH 12 405

FLEW
HE SPAKE: AND TO CONFIRM HIS WORDS, OUT-FLEW . . 1 663
UP HITHER LIKE AEREAL VAPOURS FLEW 3 445
WAFTED BY ANGELS, OR FLEW O'RE THE LAKE 3 521
FLEW UPWARD, SPIRITED WITH VARIOUS FORMS, . . . 3 717
THENCE UP HE FLEW, AND ON THE TREE OF LIFE . . . 4 194
THE LATTER QUICK UP FLEW, AND KICKT THE BEAM; . . 4 1004
WITH HIM I FLEW, AND UNDERNEATH BEHELD 5 87
FLEW THROUGH THE MIDST OF HEAV'N; TH' ANGELIC
QUIRES 5 251
OF FIERY DARTS IN FLAMING VOLIES FLEW, ... 6 213
FORTHWITH FROM COUNCEL TO THE WORK THEY FLEW, . . 6 507
FLEW OFF, AND INTO STRANGE VAGARIES FELL, . . . 6 614
LIGHT AS THE LIGHTNING GLIMPS THEY RAN, THEY FLEW, 6 642
CREATURES THAT LIVD, AND MOVD, AND WALK'D, OR FLEW, 8 264
FLEW DIVERS, AND WITH POWER (THIR POWER WAS GREAT) 10 284
FLEW UP, NOR MISSD THE WAY, BY ENVIOUS WINDES . . 11 15

FLIE
FLIE TO AND FRO, OR ON THE SMOOTHED PLANK, . . . 1 772
UNFAST'NS: ON A SUDDEN OP'N FLIE 2 879
ME MISERABLE. WHICH WAY SHALL I FLIE 4 73
WHICH WAY I FLIE IS HELL; MY SELF AM HELL; . . . 4 75
CHAUMPING HIS IRON CURB: TO STRIVE OR FLIE . . . 4 859
WISE TO FLIE PAIN, PROFESSING NEXT THE SPIE, . . 4 948
FLIE THITHER WHENCE THOU FLEDST: IF FROM THIS HOURE 4 963
I FLIE NOT, BUT HAVE SOUGHT THEE FARR AND NIGH. . 6 295
AND LET FOWLE FLIE ABOVE THE EARTH, WITH WINGS . 7 389
HENCEFORTH I FLIE NOT DEATH, NOR WOULD PROLONG . 11 547

FLIES
THE FORD, AND OF IT SELF THE WATER FLIES . . . 2 612
ON HILLS WHERE FLOCKS ARE FED, FLIES TOWARD THE
SPRINGS 3 435
WITH THE FIXT STARRS, FIXT IN THIR ORB THAT FLIES, 5 176
BRIGHT TEMPLE, TO AEGYPTIAN THEB'S HE FLIES. . . 5 274
FORTHWITH FROM OUT THE ARKE A RAVEN FLIES, . . . 11 855
FROGS, LICE AND FLIES MUST ALL HIS PALACE FILL . 12 177

FLIGHT
THAT WITH NO MIDDLE FLIGHT INTENDS TO SOAR . . . 1 14
THEN WITH EXPANDED WINGS HE STEARS HIS FLIGHT . . 1 225
WITH DREAD OF DEATH TO FLIGHT OR FOUL RETREAT, . 1 555
WITH WHAT COMPULSION AND LABORIOUS FLIGHT . . . 2 80
BESIDES WHAT HOPE THE NEVER-ENDING FLIGHT . . . 2 221
HIS UNCOUTH WAY, OR SPREAD HIS AERIE FLIGHT . . 2 407
EXPLORES HIS SOLITARY FLIGHT; SOM TIMES 2 632
HE SPREADS FOR FLIGHT, AND IN THE SURGING SMOAK . 2 928
IN THAT OBSCURE SOJOURN, WHILE IN MY FLIGHT . . 3 15
HIS FLIGHT PRECIPITANT, AND WINDES WITH EASE . . 3 563
TO FIND WHO MIGHT DIRECT HIS WANDRING FLIGHT . . 3 631
THROWS HIS STEEP FLIGHT IN MANY AN AERIE WHEELE, . 3 741
OF THAT FIRST BATTEL, AND HIS FLIGHT TO HELL: . . 4 12
BY SHORTER FLIGHT TO TH' EAST, HAD LEFT HIM THERE 4 595
WHICH THOU INCURR'ST BY FLYING, MEET THY FLIGHT . 4 913
THE FIRST IN FLIGHT FROM PAIN, HAD'ST THOU ALLEDG'D 4 921
TO THY DESERTED HOST THIS CAUSE OF FLIGHT, . . . 4 922
AND VARIOUS: WONDRING AT MY FLIGHT AND CHANGE . . 5 89
A CLOUDY SPOT. DOWN THITHER PRONE IN FLIGHT . . 5 266
AND FLY, ERE EVIL INTERCEPT THY FLIGHT. 5 871
FROM FLIGHT, SEDITIOUS ANGEL, TO RECEAVE . . . 6 152
FROM MEE RETURND, AS ERST THOU SAIDST, FROM FLIGHT, 6 187
THE RIDGES OF GRIM WARR; NO THOUGHT OF FLIGHT, . 6 236
TO FLIGHT, OR IF TO FALL, BUT THAT THEY RISE . . 6 285
DISDAIN'D, BUT MEANER THOUGHTS LEARND IN THIR
FLIGHT, ... 6 367
NOT LIABLE TO FEAR OR FLIGHT OR PAINE. 6 397
THIS DAY, FEAR NOT HIS FLIGHT; SO THICK A CLOUD . 6 539
TO FINAL BATTEL DREW, DISDAINING FLIGHT, . . . 6 798
ABOVE THE FLIGHT OF PEGASEAN WING. 7 4
FOR HASTE; SUCH FLIGHT THE GREAT COMMAND IMPRESS'D 7 294
EASING THIR FLIGHT; SO STEARS THE PRUDENT CRANE . 7 430
A LOWER FLIGHT, AND SPEAK OF THINGS AT HAND . . 8 199
CONVICT BY FLIGHT, AND REBEL TO ALL LAW . . . 10 83
INSPIR'D, AND WING'D FOR HEAV'N WITH SPEEDIER
FLIGHT 11 7
DIRECT TO TH' EASTERN GATE WAS BENT THIR FLIGHT. 11 190
OF FLIGHT PURSU'D IN TH' AIR AND ORE THE GROUND . 11 202

FLING
WITH SUCKT AND GLUTTED OFFAL, AT ONE FLING . . . 10 633

FLI'ST
WHOM FLI'ST THOU? WHOM THOU FLI'ST, OF HIM THOU
ART, ... 4 482

FLI'ST (CONTINUED)
MOON, THAT NOW MEETST THE ORIENT SUN, NOW FLI'ST . 5 175

FLOATING
LAY FLOATING MANY A ROOD, IN BULK AS HUGE . . . 1 196
FROM THE SAFE SHORE THIR FLOATING CARKASES . . . 1 310
AS DELOS FLOATING ONCE; THE REST HIS LOOK . . . 10 296
NO MORE WAS SEEN; THE FLOATING VESSEL SWUM . . . 11 745

FLOATS
FLOATS, AS THEY PASS, FANN'D WITH UNNUMBER'D
PLUMES: 7 432

FLOCK
THE STARRIE FLOCK, ALLUR'D THEM, AND WITH LYES . 5 709
OF GOATS OR TIMEROUS FLOCK TOGETHER THRONGD . . 6 857
OF MORTAL CHANGE ON EARTH. AS WHEN A FLOCK . . 10 273
MORE MEEK CAME WITH THE FIRSTLINGS OF HIS FLOCK . 11 437
FROM A FAT MEDDOW GROUND; OR FLEECY FLOCK, . . 11 648
CORN WINE AND OYLE; AND FROM THE HERD OR FLOCK, . 12 19

FLOCKING
ALL THESE AND MORE CAME FLOCKING; BUT WITH LOOKS . 1 522

FLOCKS
OR FLOCKS, OR HEARDS, OR HUMAN FACE DIVINE; . . 3 44
ON HILLS WHERE FLOCKS ARE FED, FLIES TOWARD THE
SPRINGS 3 435
WATCHING WHERE SHEPHERDS PEN THIR FLOCKS AT EEVE . 4 185
BETWIXT THEM LAWNS, OR LEVEL DOWNS, AND FLOCKS . 4 252
THOSE RARE AND SOLITARIE, THESE IN FLOCKS . . . 7 461
HIS VASTNESS: FLEEC'T THE FLOCKS AND BLEATING ROSE, 7 472
OF HERDS AND FLOCKS, AND NUMEROUS SERVITUDE; . . 12 132

FLOOD
PRONE ON THE FLOOD, EXTENDED LONG AND LARGE . . 1 195
BOTH GLORYING TO HAVE SCAP'T THE STYGIAN FLOOD . 1 239
ABJECT AND LOST LAY THESE, COVERING THE FLOOD, . 1 312
CHERUBE AND SERAPH ROWLING IN THE FLOOD . . . 1 324
WITH THESE CAME THEY, WHO FROM THE BORDRING FLOOD 1 419
ABHORRED STYX THE FLOOD OF DEADLY HATE, ... 2 577
BEYOND THIS FLOOD A FROZEN CONTINENT 2 587
THIR SPICIE DRUGS: THEY ON THE TRADING FLOOD . . 2 640
FROM PANEAS THE FOUNT OF JORDANS FLOOD 3 535
THE CUMBROUS ELEMENTS, EARTH, FLOOD, AIRE, FIRE, . 3 715
DOWN THE STEEP GLADE, AND MET THE NEATHER FLOOD, . 4 231
DRIV'N BACK REDOUNDED AS A FLOOD ON THOSE . . . 7 57
OR THENCE FROM NIGER FLOOD TO ATLAS MOUNT . . . 11 402
BY FIRE, FLOOD, FAMIN, BY INTEMPERANCE MORE . . 11 472
FLOOD OVERWHELMD, AND THEM WITH ALL THIR POMP . . 11 748
THE EARTH AGAIN BY FLOOD, NOR LET THE SEA . . . 11 893
WHILE YET THE PATRIARK LIV'D, WHO SCAP'D THE FLOOD, 12 117

FLOODS
WITH FLOODS AND WHIRLWINDS OF TEMPESTUOUS FIRE, . 1 77
OF TORRENT FLOODS, OR OF A NUMEROUS HOST. . . . 6 830

FLOORE
LEAST ON THE THRESHING FLOORE HIS HOPEFUL SHEAVES 4 984

FLORA
MILDE, AS WHEN ZEPHYRUS ON FLORA BREATHES, . . . 5 16

FLORID
HID AMALTHEA AND HER FLORID SON 4 278
IMBRACING ROUND THIS FLORID EARTH, WHAT CAUSE . . 7 90
ADORNS HIM, COLOUR'D WITH THE FLORID HUE . . . 7 445

FLOTED
FLOTED REDUNDANT: PLEASING WAS HIS SHAPE, . . . 9 503

FLOTES
THE ARK NO MORE NOW FLOTES, BUT SEEMS ON GROUND . 11 850

FLOUD
DEPOPULATION; THEE ANOTHER FLOUD, ... 11 756
OF TEARS AND SORROW A FLOUD THEE ALSO DROWN'D, . 11 757
OUT OF HIS PLACE, PUSHD BY THE HORNED FLOUD, . . 11 831
HE LOOKD, AND SAW THE ARK HULL ON THE FLOUD, . . 11 840

FLOUDS
ON THE SWIFT FLOUDS: AS ARMIES AT THE CALL . . . 7 295

FLOUER
IMPEARLS ON EVERY LEAF AND EVERY FLOUER. . . . 5 747

FLOUR
IMMORTAL AMARANT, A FLOUR WHICH ONCE 3 353
HIS ORIENT BEAMS, ON HERB, TREE, FRUIT, AND FLOUR, 4 644
FENC'D UP THE VERDANT WALL; EACH BEAUTEOUS FLOUR, 4 697
WITH PLANT, FRUIT, FLOUR AMBROSIAL, GEMMS & GOLD, 6 475
THIS GARDEN, STILL TO TEND PLANT, HERB AND FLOUR, 9 206
EACH FLOUR OF SLENDER STALK, WHOSE HEAD THOUGH GAY 9 428
HER SELF, THOUGH FAIREST UNSUPPORTED FLOUR, . . 9 432

FLOUR'D
THEN HERBS OF EVERY LEAF, THAT SUDDEN FLOUR'D . . 7 317

FLOURE
HER SELF A FAIRER FLOURE BY GLOOMIE DIS 4 270
ON THIS DELIGHTFUL LAND, NOR HERB, FRUIT, FLOURE, 4 652
MORE AERIE, LAST THE BRIGHT CONSUMMATE FLOURE . . 5 481

FLOURETS
WITH FLOURETS DECK'T AND FRAGRANT SMELLS; BUT EVE 5 379
ON FLOURS REPOS'D, AND WITH FRESH FLOURETS CROWND, 5 636
AND WITH FRESH FLOURETS HILL AND VALLEY SMIL'D. . 6 784

FLOURIE
FORTUNATE FIELDS, AND GROVES AND FLOURIE VALES, . 3 569
OR PALMIE HILLOC, OR THE FLOURIE LAP 4 254
YON FLOURIE ARBORS, YONDER ALLIES GREEN, . . . 4 626
AND ON THIR NAKED LIMBS THE FLOURIE ROOF . . . 4 772
SOFT ON THE FLOURIE HERB I FOUND ME LAID . . . 8 254
THIS FLOURIE PLAT, THE SWEET RECESS OF EVE . . . 9 456
OR SERVE THEY AS A FLOURIE VERGE TO BINDE . . . 11 881

FLOURING
AND FLOURING ODOURS, CASSIA, NARD, AND BALME; . . 5 293

FLOURISHD
FLOURISHD, SINCE MUTE, TO SOM GREAT CAUSE ADDREST, 9 672

FLOURISH'T
FORTH FLOURISH'T THICK THE CLUSTRING VINE, FORTH CREPT 7 320

FLOURISHT
REAR'D HIGH THIR FLOURISHT HEADS BETWEEN, AND WROUGHT 4 699

FLOURS
AND FLOURS ALOFT SHADING THE FOUNT OF LIFE, . . . 3 357
ROWLS O'RE ELISIAN FLOURS HER AMBER STREAM; . . 3 359
FLOURS WORTHY OF PARADISE WHICH NOT NICE ART . . 4 241
FLOURS OF ALL HUE, AND WITHOUT THORN THE ROSE: . . 4 256
OF ENNA, WHERE PROSERPIN GATHERING FLOURS . . . 4 269
ON THE SOFT DOWNIE BANK DAMASKT WITH FLOURS: . . 4 334
TO PRUNE THESE GROWING PLANTS, AND TEND THESE FLOURS, ... 4 438
UNDER A SHADE OF FLOURS, MUCH WONDRING WHERE . . 4 451
AMONG THE GROVES, THE FOUNTAINS, AND THE FLOURS . 5 126
AMONG SWEET DEWES AND FLOURS; WHERE ANY ROW . . 5 212
SPIRITS ODOROUS BREATHES: FLOURS AND THIR FRUIT . 5 482
ON FLOURS REPOS'D, AND WITH FRESH FLOURETS CROWND, 5 636
ROSE, AND WENT FORTH AMONG HER FRUITS AND FLOURS, 8 44
ON A GREEN SHADIE BANK PROFUSE OF FLOURS . . . 8 286
I MEAN OF TASTE, SIGHT, SMELL, HERBS, FRUITS, AND FLOURS, ... 8 527
IN EDEN ON THE HUMID FLOURS, THAT BREATHD . . . 9 193
JUST THEN RETURND AT SHUT OF EVENING FLOURS. . . 9 278
SUCH AMBUSH HID AMONG SWEET FLOURS AND SHADES . . 9 408
AMONG THICK-WOV'N ARBORETS AND FLOURS 9 437
OF CHOICEST FLOURS A GARLAND TO ADORNE 9 840
HE LED HER NOTHING LOATH; FLOURS WERE THE COUCH, . 9 1039
THOU THEREFORE ON THESE HERBS, AND FRUITS, AND FLOURS 10 603
PERPETUAL SMIL'D ON EARTH WITH VERNANT FLOURS, . 10 679
THAT MUST BE MORTAL TO US BOTH. O FLOURS, . . . 11 273
OFFER SWEET SMELLING GUMMS AND FRUITS AND FLOURS: 11 327
OF LOVE AND YOUTH NOT LOST, SONGS, GARLANDS, FLOURS, ... 11 594

FLOW
THAT WASH THY HALLOWD FEET, AND WARBLING FLOW, . 3 31
TURND HIM ALL EARE TO HEAR NEW UTTERANCE FLOW, . 4 410
FOUNTAINS AND YEE, THAT WARBLE, AS YE FLOW, . . 5 195
THOSE THOUSAND DECENCIES THAT DAILY FLOW . . . 8 601
OF LOOKS AND SMILES, FOR SMILES FROM REASON FLOW, 9 239

FLOW'D
DELIGHT THEE MORE, AND SILOA'S BROOK THAT FLOW'D . 1 11
VIEWLESS, AND UNDERNEATH A BRIGHT SEA FLOW'D . . 3 518
A STREAM OF NECTAROUS HUMOR ISSUING FLOW'D . . 6 332
BEFORE THE HILLS APPEERD, OR FOUNTAIN FLOW'D, . . 7 8
MAIN OCEAN FLOW'D, NOT IDLE, BUT WITH WARME . . 7 279

FLOWD
FLOWD FROM THIR LIPS, IN PROSE OR NUMEROUS VERSE, 5 150
A MILITARIE VEST OF PURPLE FLOWD 11 241

FLOWERS
IN CLUSTERS; THEY AMONG FRESH DEWS AND FLOWERS . 1 771
AMBROSIAL ODOURS AND AMBROSIAL FLOWERS, ... 2 245
THAT SHED MAY FLOWERS; AND PRESS'D HER MATRON LIP 4 501
WITH FLOWERS, GARLANDS, AND SWEET-SMELLING HERBS . 4 709

FLOWES
AT DARIEN, THENCE TO THE LAND WHERE FLOWES . . . 9 81

FLOWING
UNDER A CORONET HIS FLOWING HAIRE 3 640
NAKED MET HIS UNDER THE FLOWING GOLD 4 496
MINISTERD NAKED, AND THIR FLOWING CUPS 5 444
NOT SO REPULST, WITH TEARS THAT CEAS'D NOT FLOWING, 10 910
AS AFTER THIRST, WHICH MADE THIR FLOWING SHRINK . 11 846

FLOWN
OF BELIAL, FLOWN WITH INSOLENCE AND WINE. . . . 1 502
BY FOWL, FISH, BEAST, WAS FLOWN, WAS SWUM, WAS WALKT 7 503
FLOWN TO THE UPPER WORLD; THE REST WERE ALL . . 10 422

FLOWR
WARRIERS, THE FLOWR OF HEAV'N, ONCE YOURS, NOW LOST, ... 1 316

FLOWRIE
THEE SION AND THE FLOWRIE BROOKS BENEATH . . . 3 30

FLOWRY
THE FLOWRY DALE OF SIBMA CLAD WITH VINES, . . . 1 410

FLOWS
WITH ANGELS FOOD, AND RUBIED NECTAR FLOWS . . . 5 633
SEE WHERE IT FLOWS, DISGORGING AT SEAVEN MOUTHES . 12 158

FLUCTUATS
FLUCTUATS DISTURBD, YET COMELY AND IN ACT . . . 9 668

FLUID
RECEIVE, NO MORE THEN CAN THE FLUID AIRE: . . . 6 349
THROUGHOUT THE FLUID MASS, BUT DOWNWARD PURG'D . 7 237
THE FLUID SKIRTS OF THAT SAME WATRIE CLOUD, . . 11 882

FLUNG
OF HEAV'N, AND FROM ETERNAL SPLENDORS FLUNG . . 1 610
MAIN PROMONTORIES FLUNG, WHICH IN THE AIR . . . 6 654
FLUNG ROSE, FLUNG ODOURS FROM THE SPICIE SHRUB, . 8 517

FLUSHING
BUT IN HER CHEEK DISTEMPER FLUSHING GLOWD. . . . 9 887

FLUTES
OF FLUTES AND SOFT RECORDERS; SUCH AS RAIS'D . . 1 551

FLUTTERD
AND FLUTTERD INTO RAGGS, THEN RELIQUES, BEADS, . 3 491

FLUTTRING
FLUTTRING HIS PENNONS VAIN PLUMB DOWN HE DROPS . 2 933

FLY
FLY O'RE THE BACKSIDE OF THE WORLD FARR OFF . . 3 494
ONE STEP NO MORE THEN FROM HIMSELF CAN FLY . . . 4 22
SO WISE HE JUDGES IT TO FLY FROM PAIN 4 910
AND FLY, ERE EVIL INTERCEPT THY FLIGHT. 5 871
YET NOT FOR THY ADVISE OR THREATS I FLY 5 889

FLYE
THIR BOOTIE; SCARCE WITH LIFE THE SHEPHERDS FLYE, 11 650

FLYES
AND SWIMS OR SINKS, OR WADES, OR CREEPS, OR FLYES: 2 950

FLYING
FOUR WAYS THIR FLYING MARCH, ALONG THE BANKS . . 2 574
FARR OFF THE FLYING FIEND: AT LAST APPEER . . . 2 643
HALF FLYING; BEHOVES HIM NOW BOTH OARE AND SAILE. 2 942
WHICH THOU INCURR'ST BY FLYING, MEET THY FLIGHT . 4 913
HOMEWARD WITH FLYING MARCH WHERE WE POSSESS . . 5 688
AND FLYING VAULTED EITHER HOST WITH FIRE. . . . 6 214
CAME FLYING, AND IN MID AIRE ALOUD THUS CRI'D. . 6 536
LEAST FROM THIS FLYING STEED UNREIN'D, (AS ONCE . 7 17
FLYING, AND OVER LANDS WITH MUTUAL WING 7 429
WHERE ARMIES LIE ENCAMPT, COME FLYING, LUR'D . . 10 276

FOAM
HIM HAPLY SLUMBRING ON THE NORWAY FOAM 1 203

FOAME
CONCEPTION; SULPHUROUS AND NITROUS FOAME 6 512

FOAMING
AND FIERIE FOAMING STEEDS; WHAT STOOD, RECOYLD . 6 391
OVER THE FOAMING DEEP HIGH ARCHT, A BRIDGE . . . 10 301
PART WIELD THIR ARMS, PART COURB THE FOAMING STEED, 11 643

FOE
IRRECONCILEABLE, TO OUR GRAND FOE, ... 1 122
OR SATIATE FURY YIELD IT FROM OUR FOE. 1 179
BY FORCE, HATH OVERCOME BUT HALF HIS FOE. . . . 1 649
WITH UPRIGHT WING AGAINST A HIGHER FOE. 2 72
WHEN THE FIERCE FOE HUNG ON OUR BROK'N REAR . . 2 78
LET THIS BE GOOD, WHETHER OUR ANGRY FOE 2 152
IF WE WERE WISE, AGAINST SO GREAT A FOE 2 202
OUR SUPREAM FOE IN TIME MAY MUCH REMIT 2 210
MAY PROVE THIR FOE, AND WITH REPENTING HAND . . 2 369
AGAINST A WAKEFUL FOE, WHILE I ABROAD 2 463
TO MEET SO GREAT A FOE: AND NOW GREAT DEEDS . . 2 722
(FOR WHAT COULD ELSE) TO OUR ALMIGHTY FOE . . . 2 769
GRIM DEATH MY SON AND FOE, WHO SETS THEM ON, . . 2 804
AS FROM HER OUTMOST WORKS A BROK'D FOE 2 1039
ON EVEN GROUND AGAINST HIS MORTAL FOE, ... 3 179
THE COMING OF THIR SECRET FOE, AND SCAP'D . . . 4 7

FOE (CONTINUED)
ILL SENC'T FOR HEAV'N TO KEEP OUT SUCH A FOE 4 372
AS NOW IS ENTERD; YET NO PURPOS'D FOE 4 373
BUT OUR DESTROYER, FOE TO GOD AND MAN? 4 749
OF DEITIE OR EMPIRE, SUCH A FOE 5 724
HIS DARING FOE, AT THIS PREVENTION MORE 6 129
WHOM THE GRAND FOE WITH SCORNFUL EYE ASKANCE 6 149
INTESTINE WAR IN HEAV'N, THE ARCH FOE SUBDU'D 6 259
URIEL AND RAPHAEL HIS VAUNTING FOE, 6 363
EACH QUARTER, TO DESCRIE THE DISTANT FOE, 6 530
ARME, WARRIOURS, ARME FOR FIGHT, THE FOE AT HAND, 6 537
NOT DISTANT FAR WITH HEAVIE PACE THE FOE 6 551
AT LEAST OUR ENVIOUS FOE HATH FAIL'D, WHO THOUGHT 7 139
OF STERN ACHILLES ON HIS FOE PURSU'D 9 15
WHAT HATH BIN WARN'D US, WHAT MALICIOUS FOE 9 253
TO GOD OR THEE, BECAUSE WE HAVE A FOE 9 280
TH' ATTEMPT IT SELF, INTENDED BY OUR FOE. 9 295
IN NARROW CIRCUIT STRAIT'ND BY A FOE, 9 323
BUT HARM PRECEDES NOT SIN: ONELY OUR FOE 9 327
SOME SPECIOUS OBJECT BY THE FOE SUBORND, 9 361
A FOE SO PROUD WILL FIRST THE WEAKER SEEK, 9 383
FOE NOT INFORMIDABLE, EXEMPT FROM WOUND, 9 486
MATTER OF SCORNE, NOT TO BE GIVEN THE FOE, 9 951
WHATEVER WILES OF FOE OR SEEMING FRIEND. 10 11
AS WHEN THE TARTAR FROM HIS RUSSIAN FOE 10 431
AGAINST A FOE BY DOOM EXPRESS ASSIGN'D US, 10 926
BE MEANT, WHOM I CONJECTURE, OUR GRAND FOE 10 1033
RESOLV'D, AS THOU PROPOSEST; SO OUR FOE 10 1038
HIS PROMISE, THAT THY SEED SHALL BRUISE OUR FOE; 11 155

FOES
OF DESPICABLE FOES, WITH THESE IN TROOP 1 437
MAN HAD NOT HELLISH FOES ANOW BESIDES, 2 504
WHILE BY THEE RAIS'D I RUIN ALL MY FOES, 3 258
TO EXECUTE FIERCE VENGEANCE ON HIS FOES, 3 399
WHO JUSTLY HATH DRIVN OUT HIS REBELL FOES 3 677
MADE ANSWER. MIGHTIE FATHER, THOU THY FOES 5 735
ENCOMPASS'D ROUND WITH FOES, THUS ANSWERD BOLD. 5 876
BACK ON THY FOES MORE GLORIOUS TO RETURN 6 39
GAVE THEM ABOVE THIR FOES, NOT TO HAVE SINND, 6 402
MAY SERVE TO BETTER US, AND WORSE OUR FOES, 6 440
FROM FAR WITH THUNDRING NOISE AMONG OUR FOES 6 487
AND TO THIR FOES A LAUGHTER; FOR IN VIEW 6 603
THEY SHEW US WHEN OUR FOES WALK NOT UPRIGHT. 6 627
AS LIKELIEST WAS, WHEN TWO SUCH FOES MET ARM'D; 6 688
THIS SAW HIS HAPLESS FOES BUT STOOD OBDUR'D, 6 785
HEE ON HIS IMPIOUS FOES RIGHT ONWARD DROVE, 6 831
SOLE VICTOR FROM TH' EXPULSION OF HIS FOES 6 880
WITH FOES FOR DARING SINGLE TO BE JUST, 11 703
OVER HIS FOES AND THINE; THERE SHALL SURPRISE 12 453

FOIL
MANHOOD TO GOD-HEAD, WITH MORE STRENGTH TO FOIL 12 389

FOIL'D
THUS FOIL'D THIR MIGHTIEST, OURS JOY FILLD, AND SHOUT, 6 200

FOILD
WARR HATH DETERMIN'D US, AND FOILD WITH LOSS 2 330
WHAT INWARD THENCE I FEEL, NOT THEREFORE FOILD, 8 608

FOILE
OUR FOILE IN HEAV'N; HERE THOU SHALT MONARCH REIGN, 10 375

FOLDS
AND THRICE THREEFOLD THE GATES; THREE FOLDS WERE BRASS, 2 645

FOLLIE
SINCE SATAN FELL, WHOM FOLLIE OVERTHREW, 4 905
NEITHER OUR OWN BUT GIV'N; WHAT FOLLIE THEN 4 1007

FOLLOW
WHAT YET THEY KNOW MUST FOLLOW, TO ENDURE 2 206
NOR UGLIER FOLLOW THE NIGHT-HAG, WHEN CALL'D 2 662
BUT THEE, WHOM FOLLOW? THOU WILT BRING ME SOON 2 866
WITH THEE IT CAME AND GOES: BUT FOLLOW ME, 4 469
BUT FOLLOW STRAIT, INVISIBLY THUS LED? 4 476
APPROVE THE BEST, AND FOLLOW WHAT I APPROVE. 8 611
FOLLOW, AS TO HIM LINKT IN WEAL OR WOE, 9 133
THY HUSBAND, HIM TO FOLLOW THOU ART BOUND; 11 291
ASCEND, I FOLLOW THEE, SAFE GUIDE, THE PATH 11 371
SUCH FOLLOW HIM, AS SHALL BE REGISTERD 12 335

FOLLOW'D
HIM FOLLOW'D RIMMON, WHOSE DELIGHTFUL SEAT 1 467
FOULE DISSIPATION FOLLOW'D AND FORC'T ROUT; 6 598
FOLLOW'D IN BRIGHT PROCESSION TO BEHOLD 7 222
I FOLLOW'D HER, SHE WHAT WAS HONOUR KNEW, 8 508
FOLLOW'D WITH BENEDICTION. SINCE TO PART, 8 645
HIM FOLLOW'D ISSUING FORTH TO TH' OPEN FIELD, 10 533
STILL FOLLOW'D HIM; TO THEM SHALL LEAVE IN CHARGE 12 439

FOLLOWD
FOLLOWD WITH ACCLAMATION AND THE SOUND 7 558

FOLLOWED
OF UNBLEST FEET. HIM FOLLOWED HIS NEXT MATE, 1 238

FOLLOWERS
THE FELLOWS OF HIS CRIME, THE FOLLOWERS RATHER 1 606
WORS WITH HIS FOLLOWERS THEN WITH HIM THEY DEALT? 12 484

FOLLOWING
FOLLOWING HIS TRACK, SUCH WAS THE WILL OF HEAV'N, 2 1025
HIS BOUNTIE, FOLLOWING OUR DELIGHTFUL TASK 4 437
THOU FOLLOWING CRYD'ST ALOUD, RETURN FAIRE EVE; 4 481
FOLLOWING, ABOVE TH' OLYMPIAN HILL I SOARE, 7 3
BEST GUIDE; NOT FOLLOWING THEE, I HAD REMAIND 9 808
FOR DEATH, THE FOLLOWING DAY, IN BLOODIE FIGHT. 10 278
OVER THE VEXT ABYSS, FOLLOWING THE TRACK 10 314
DETAIN FROM FOLLOWING THY ILLUSTRIOUS TRACK. 10 367
CLOSE FOLLOWING PACE FOR PACE, NOT MOUNTED YET 10 589
STILL FOLLOWING THEE, STILL COMPASSING THEE ROUND 11 352

FOLLOWS
IN HEAV'N, WHICH FOLLOWS DIGNITY, MIGHT DRAW 2 25

FOLLY
RETIRE, OR TASTE THY FOLLY, AND LEARN BY PROOF, 2 686
WITH HIS OWN FOLLY? THAT BE FROM THEE FARR, 3 153
THY FOLLY; OR WITH SOLITARIE HAND 6 139
WISDOM TO FOLLY, AS NOURISHMENT TO WINDE. 7 130
LOOSES DISCOUNT'NANC'T, AND LIKE FOLLY SHEWES; 8 553
KEPT IN THAT STATE, HAD NOT THE FOLLY OF MAN 10 619
FOLLY TO MEE, SO DOTH THE PRINCE OF HELL 10 621
BEYOND WHICH WAS MY FOLLY TO ASPIRE. 12 560

FOMENT
OF VARIOUS INFLUENCE FOMENT AND WARME, 4 669
REFLECTED, MAY WITH MATTER SERE FOMENT, 10 1071

FOMENTED
FOMENTED BY HIS VIRTUAL POWER AND WARMD; 11 338

FOND
BUILT THIR FOND HOPES OF GLORIE OR LASTING FAME, 3 449
ASPIRER, BUT THIR THOUGHTS PROV'D FOND AND VAIN 6 90
OR EMPTINESS, OR FOND IMPERTINENCE, 8 195
FOND, WERE IT NOT IN HOPE OF THY REPLY; 8 209
SO MIGHT THE WRAUTH. FOND WISH. COULDST THOU SUPPORT 10 834
THUS OVER-FOND, ON THAT WHICH IS NOT THINE; 11 289

FONDLY
A GOD, LEAP'D FONDLY INTO AETNA FLAMES, 3 470
MY DAMAGE FONDLY DEEM'D, I CAN REPAIRE 7 152
BUT FONDLY OVERCOME WITH FEMAL CHARM. 9 999
DECEAV'D; THEY FONDLY THINKING TO ALLAY 10 564
AND IMMORTALITIE: THAT FONDLY LOST, 11 59

FONTARABBIA
BY FONTARABBIA. THUS FAR THESE BEYOND 1 587

FOOD
TO US FOR FOOD AND FOR DELIGHT HATH CAUS'D 5 400
THE EARTH TO YIELD; UNSAVOURIE FOOD PERHAPS 5 401
NO INGRATEFUL FOOD: AND FOOD ALIKE THOSE PURE 5 407
FOOD NOT OF ANGELS, YET ACCEPTED SO, 5 465
WITH ANGELS FOOD, AND RUBIED NECTAR FLOWS 5 633
BUT KNOWLEDGE IS AS FOOD, AND NEEDS NO LESS 7 126
MOIST NUTRIMENT, OR UNDER ROCKS THIR FOOD 7 408
AND FREELY ALL THIR PLEASANT FRUIT FOR FOOD 7 540
REFRESHMENT, WHETHER FOOD, OR TALK BETWEEN, 9 237
FOOD OF THE MIND, OR THIS SWEET INTERCOURSE 9 238
TO BRUTE DENI'D, AND ARE OF LOVE THE FOOD, 9 240
AS WAS MY FOOD, NOR AUGHT BUT FOOD DISCERN'D 9 573
AS THEY, PARTICIPATING GOD-LIKE FOOD? 9 717
THIS INTELLECTUAL FOOD, FOR BEASTS RESERV'D? 9 768
FOOD FOR SO FOULE A MONSTER, IN THY POWER 10 986
AND MORTAL FOOD, AS MAY DISPOSE HIM BEST 11 54
SIEGE AND DEFIANCE: WRETCHED MAN. WHAT FOOD 12 74

FOOL
OR POTENT TONGUE; FOOL, NOT TO THINK HOW VAIN 6 135

FOOL'D
FOOL'D AND BEGUIL'D, BY HIM THOU, I BY THEE. 10 880

FOOLS
THE PARADISE OF FOOLS, TO FEW UNKNOWN 3 496

FOOT
TREADING THE CRUDE CONSISTENCE, HALF ON FOOT, 2 941
TO WAIT THEM WITH HIS KEYS, AND NOW AT FOOT 3 485
HAD NEED FROM HEAD TO FOOT WELL UNDERSTAND; 6 625
ONE FOOT HE CENTER'D, AND THE OTHER TURN'D 7 228
WHERE TIGRIS AT THE FOOT OF PARADISE 9 71
AND AT THE BRINK OF CHAOS, NEER THE FOOT 10 347
HIS BRIGHT APPEARANCES, OR FOOT STEP-TRACE? 11 329
BOTH HORSE AND FOOT, NOR IDELY MUSTRING STOOD; 11 645
WITH SOFT FOOT TOWARDS THE DEEP, WHO NOW HAD STOPT 11 848
GREEN TREE OR GROUND WHEREON HIS FOOT MAY LIGHT; 11 858

FOOTED
THITHER BY HARPY-FOOTED FURIES HAIL'D, 2 596

FORAGE
ONE WAY A BAND SELECT FROM FORAGE DRIVES 11 646

FORAIGN
IN FORAIGN LANDS THIR MEMORIE BE LOST 12 46

FORBEAR
I OVERJOYD COULD NOT FORBEAR ALOUD. 8 490

FORBEARANCE
FORBEARANCE NO ACQUITTANCE ERE DAY END. 10 53

FORBID
FORBID WHO WILL, NONE SHALL FROM ME WITHHOLD 5 62
TO DO WHAT GOD EXPRESLY HATH FORBID, 9 356
WHY THEN WAS THIS FORBID? WHY BUT TO AWE, 9 703
OR EAST OR WEST, WHICH HAD FORBID THE SNOW 10 685

FORBIDDANCE
THE STRICT FORBIDDANCE, HOW TO VIOLATE 9 903

FORBIDDEN
OF THAT FORBIDDEN TREE, WHOSE MORTAL TAST 1 2
I KEEP, BY HIM FORBIDDEN TO UNLOCK 2 852
FORBIDDEN THEM TO TASTE: KNOWLEDGE FORBIDD'N? 4 515
IN THINGS TO US FORBIDDEN, IT MIGHT BE WISH'D, 9 1025
FOR THIS ONE TREE HAD BIN FORBIDDEN TEN. 9 1026
FOR ONE FORBIDDEN TREE A MULTITUDE 10 554

FORBIDDER
OUR GREAT FORBIDDER, SAFE WITH ALL HIS SPIES 9 815

FORBIDDING
FORBIDDING; AND AT ONCE WITH HIM THEY ROSE; 2 475
FORBIDS US THEN TO TASTE, BUT HIS FORBIDDING 9 753

FORBIDD'N
FORBIDDEN THEM TO TASTE: KNOWLEDGE FORBIDD'N? 4 515
FORBIDD'N HERE, IT SEEMS, AS ONELY FIT 5 69
THE SACRED FRUIT FORBIDD'N. SOM CURSED FRAUD 9 904
FORBIDD'N KNOWLEDGE BY FORBIDD'N MEANS. 12 279

FORBIDS
DISDAIN FORBIDS ME, AND MY DREAD OF SHAME 4 82
OR ENVIE, OR WHAT RESERVE FORBIDS TO TASTE? 5 61
THY PRAISE HEE ALSO WHO FORBIDS THY USE, 9 750
FORBIDS US THEN TO TASTE, BUT HIS FORBIDDING 9 753
IN PLAIN THEN, WHAT FORBIDS HE BUT TO KNOW, 9 758
FORBIDS US GOOD, FORBIDS US TO BE WISE? 9 759
THE LAW I GAVE TO NATURE HIM FORBIDS: 11 49

FORBORE
FORBORE, THEN THESE TO HER SATAN RETURN'D: 2 736
SO SAID HE, AND FORBORE NOT GLANCE OR TOY 9 1034

FORBORN
WHOSE TASTE, TOO LONG FORBORN, AT FIRST ASSAY 9 747

FORC'D
BE FORC'D TO SATISFIE HIS RAV'NOUS MAW. 10 991

FORCE
THE FORCE OF THOSE DIRE ARMS? YET NOT FOR THOSE, 1 94
INNUMERABLE FORCE OF SPIRITS ARM'D 1 101
TO WAGE BY FORCE OR GUILE ETERNAL WARR 1 121
OF FORCE BELIEVE ALMIGHTY, SINCE NO LESS 1 144
THEN SUCH COULD HAV OREPOW'RD SUCH FORCE AS OURS) 1 145
AND SUCH APPEAR'D IN HUE, AS WHEN THE FORCE 1 230
WHOM REASON HATH EQUALD, FORCE HATH MADE SUPREAM 1 248
BREATHING UNITED FORCE WITH FIXED THOUGHT 1 560
MET SUCH IMBODIED FORCE, AS NAM'D WITH THESE 1 574
HOW SUCH UNITED FORCE OF GODS, HOW SUCH 1 629
WHAT FORCE EFFECTED NOT: THAT HE NO LESS 1 647
BY FORCE, HATH OVERCOME BUT HALF HIS FOE. 1 649
O'RE HEAV'NS HIGH TOWRS TO FORCE RESISTLESS WAY, 2 62
BY FORCE, AND AT OUR HEELS ALL HELL SHOULD RISE 2 135
MY VOICE DISSWADES; FOR WHAT CAN FORCE OR GUILE 2 188
BY FORCE IMPOSSIBLE, BY LEAVE OBTAIN'D 2 250
BY FORCE OR SUTTLETY: THOUGH HEAV'N BE SHUT, 2 358
FREE VERTUE SHOULD ENTHRALL TO FORCE OR CHANCE. 2 551
THESE ADAMANTINE GATES; AGAINST ALL FORCE 2 853
WITH FRESH ALACRITIE AND FORCE RENEW'D 2 1012
IF HIM BY FORCE HE CAN DESTROY, OR WORSE, 3 91
OF FORCE TO ITS OWN LIKENESS: UP HE STARTS 4 813
WITH SPEED WHAT FORCE IS LEFT, AND ALL IMPLOY 5 730
BY FORCE, WHO REASON FOR THIR LAW REFUSE, 6 41
WHEN REASON HATH TO DEAL WITH FORCE, YET SO 6 125
THESE ELEMENTS, AND ARM HIM WITH THE FORCE 6 222
IF NOT TO REIGN: MEAN WHILE THY UTMOST FORCE, 6 293
THE SWORD OF SATAN WITH STEEP FORCE TO SMITE 6 324
OF HARD CONTENTS, AND FULL OF FORCE URG'D HOME, 6 622
STOOD REIMBATTELL'D FIERCE, BY FORCE OR FRAUD 6 794
SECURE FROM OUTWARD FORCE; WITHIN HIMSELF 9 348
SOON AS THE FORCE OF THAT FALLACIOUS FRUIT, 9 1046
THAT LAY IN WAIT; BEYOND THIS HAD BIN FORCE, 9 1173

FORCE (CONTINUED)
AND FORCE UPON FREE WILL HATH HERE NO PLACE. 9 1174
OR SYMPATHIE, OR SOM CONNATURAL FORCE 10 246
SEIS'D ON BY FORCE, JUDG'D, AND TO DEATH CONDEMND 12 412
SPIRITUAL LAWES BY CARNAL POWER SHALL FORCE 12 521
BUT FORCE THE SPIRIT OF GRACE IT SELF, AND BINDE 12 525

FORCIBLE
AND IN EMBRACES FORCIBLE AND FOULE 2 793
WITH WHAT MORE FORCIBLE WE MAY OFFEND 6 465
SO FORCIBLE WITHIN MY HEART I FEEL 9 955

FORCING
WINDS UNDER GROUND OR WATERS FORCING WAY 6 196

FORC'T
FORC'T HALLELUIAH'S; WHILE HE LORDLY SITS 2 243
FOULE DISSIPATION FOLLOW'D AND FORC'T ROUT; 6 598
TOILD OUT MY UNCOUTH PASSAGE, FORC'T TO RIDE 10 475
FORC'T I ABSOLVE: ALL MY EVASIONS VAIN, 10 829

FORD
THE FORD, AND OF IT SELF THE WATER FLIES 2 612
UR OF CHALDAEA, PASSING NOW THE FORD 12 130

FOREIN
THE GOODLY PROSPECT OF SOME FOREIN LAND 3 548

FOREKNEW
THIR OWN REVOLT, NOT I: IF I FOREKNEW, 3 117

FOREKNOWING
WHICH NEITHER HIS FOREKNOWING CAN PREVENT, 11 773

FOREKNOWLEDG
FIXT FATE, FREE WILL, FOREKNOWLEDG ABSOLUTE, 2 560

FOREKNOWLEDGE
OF PROVIDENCE, FOREKNOWLEDGE, WILL AND FATE, 2 559
OR HIGH FOREKNOWLEDGE; THEY THEMSELVES DECREED 3 116
FOREKNOWLEDGE HAD NO INFLUENCE ON THEIR FAULT, 3 118
AT ONCE, BY MY FOREKNOWLEDGE GAINING BIRTH 11 768

FORELAND
NIGH RIVERS MOUTH OR FORELAND, WHERE THE WIND 9 514

FORELOCK
ROUND FROM HIS PARTED FORELOCK MANLY HUNG 4 302

FORERUN
FORERUN THE ROYAL CAMP, TO TRENCH A FIELD, 1 677

FORERUNNERS
FORERUNNERS OF HIS PURPOSE, OR TO WARN 11 195

FORERUNNING
FORERUNNING NIGHT; WHEN AT THE HOLY MOUNT 7 584

FORESEEING
FORESEEING OR PRESAGING, FROM THE DEPTH 1 627
THUS TO HIS ONELY SON FORESEEING SPAKE. 3 79

FORESEEN
OR AUGHT BY ME IMMUTABLIE FORESEEN, 3 121
CONSULTING ON THE SUM OF THINGS, FORESEEN 6 673
O VISIONS ILL FORESEEN. BETTER HAD I 11 763

FORESIGHT
IN ARMS NOT WORSE, IN FORESIGHT MUCH ADVANC'T, 1 119
HERE SLEEP BELOW WHILE THOU TO FORESIGHT WAK'ST, 11 368

FORESTALL'D
TO BE FORESTALL'D; MUCH MORE I FEAR LEAST DEATH 10 1024

FORETASTED
IS NOT SO HAINOUS NOW, FORETASTED FRUIT, 9 929

FORETELL
ONE GREATER, OF WHOSE DAY HE SHALL FORETELL, 12 242

FORETOLD
TO SEARCH WITH WANDRING QUEST A PLACE FORETOLD 2 830
I WARN'D THEE, I ADMONISH'D THEE, FORETOLD 9 1171
FORETOLD SO LATELY WHAT WOULD COME TO PASS, 10 38
EEVN HEE WHO NOW FORETOLD HIS FATAL BRUISE, 10 191
LONG HAD FORETOLD, A FABRICK WONDERFUL 10 482
PAINS ONELY IN CHILD-BEARING WERE FORETOLD, 10 1051
HENCEFORTH TO BE FORETOLD WHAT SHALL BEFALL 11 771
A SON, THE WOMANS SEED TO THEE FORETOLD, 12 327
FORETOLD TO ABRAHAM, AS IN WHOM SHALL TRUST 12 328
ALL NATIONS, AND TO KINGS FORETOLD, OF KINGS 12 329
THE WOMANS SEED, OBSCURELY THEN FORETOLD, 12 543

FOR EVER
WHERE JOY FOR EVER DWELLS: HAIL HORROURS, HAIL 1 250
AWAKE, ARISE, OR BE FOR EVER FALL'N. 1 330
FOR EVER NOW TO HAVE THIR LOT IN PAIN, 1 608
OF RACKING WHIRLWINDS, OR FOR EVER SUNK 2 182

FOR EVER (CONTINUED)
THESE GATES FOR EVER SHUT, WHICH NONE CAN PASS . 2 776
LIFE IN MY SELF FOR EVER, BY THEE I LIVE, ... 3 244
FOR EVER WITH CORRUPTION THERE TO DWELL; 3 249
I GIVE THEE, REIGN FOR EVER, AND ASSUME 3 318
THENCEFORTH SHALL BE FOR EVER SHUT. MEAN WHILE . 3 333
FOR EVER HAPPIE: HIM WHO DISOBEYES 5 611
FOR EVER, AND IN MEE ALL WHOM THOU LOV'ST: 6 733
OF GODHEAD, FIXT FOR EVER FIRM AND SURE, ... 7 586
TO FIND HER, OR FOR EVER TO DEPLORE 8 479
FOR EVER, AND SEAL UP HIS RAVENOUS JAWES. 10 637
AND LIVE FOR EVER, DREAM AT LEAST TO LIVE 11 95
FOR EVER, TO REMOVE HIM I DECREE, ... 11 96
FOR EVER SHALL ENDURE; THE LIKE SHALL SING 12 324
IN SIN FOR EVER LOST FROM LIFE; THIS ACT 12 429

FOREWARN
BUT THOU O FATHER, I FOREWARN THEE, SHUN 2 810

FOREWARN'D
THE AFFABLE ARCH-ANGEL, HAD FOREWARN'D 7 41

FOREWARND
HIS ENTRANCE, AND FOREWARND THE CHERUBIM 9 61
WITH THY PERMISSION THEN, AND THUS FOREWARND . . . 9 378

FOREWARNE
DOWN FROM THE EMPYREAN TO FOREWARNE 7 73
THEY DIE; BUT IN THIR ROOM, AS THEY FOREWARNE, . 12 507

FOREWARNING
REJECTED MY FOREWARNING, AND DISDAIN'D 10 876

FORFEIT
HIS LAPSED POWERS, THOUGH FORFEIT AND ENTHRALL'D . 3 176
FORFEIT TO DEATH; FROM HENCE A PASSAGE BROAD, . . 10 304

FORFEITURE
THE DEADLY FORFEITURE, AND RANSOM SET. 3 221

FORGE
THE ORGANS OF HER FANCIE, AND WITH THEM FORGE . . 4 802
IN OTHER PART STOOD ONE WHO AT THE FORGE . . . 11 564

FORGET
NIGHTLY I VISIT: NOR SOMTIMES FORGET 3 32
FORGET, NOR FROM THY FATHERS PRAISE DISJOINE. . . 3 415
YET LET ME NOT FORGET WHAT I HAVE GAIN'D 4 512
WITH THEE CONVERSING I FORGET ALL TIME, ... 4 639
YET THAT WE NEVER SHALL FORGET TO LOVE 5 550
COMPULSION THUS TRANSPORTED TO FORGET 9 474
FROM HIM, AND ALL HIS ANGER TO FORGET. 11 878

FORGETFUL
OF THAT FORGETFUL LAKE BENUMM NOT STILL, ... 2 74
FORGETFUL WHAT FROM HIM I STILL RECEIVD, ... 4 54

FORGETFULNESS
IN SWEET FORGETFULNESS ALL PAIN AND WOE, ... 2 608

FORGETS
FORTHWITH HIS FORMER STATE AND BEING FORGETS, . . 2 585
FORGETS BOTH JOY AND GRIEF, PLEASURE AND PAIN. . 2 586

FORGIV'N
THY FRAILTIE AND INFIRMER SEX FORGIV'N, ... 10 956

FORGOE
EXTRACTED; FOR THIS CAUSE HE SHALL FORGOE 8 497
HOW CAN I LIVE WITHOUT THEE, HOW FORGOE 9 908
OBTUSE, ALL TASTE OF PLEASURE MUST FORGOE, ... 11 541

FORGOT
HAST THOU FORGOT ME THEN, AND DO I SEEM 2 747
JUSTICE AND TEMPERANCE, TRUTH AND FAITH FORGOT; . 11 807

FORKED
BUT HISS FOR HISS RETURND WITH FORKED TONGUE . . 10 518
TO FORKED TONGUE, FOR NOW WERE ALL TRANSFORM'D . 10 519

FORLORN
SEEST THOU YON DREARY PLAIN, FORLORN AND WILDE, . 1 180
IN CONFUS'D MARCH FORLORN, TH' ADVENTROUS BANDS . 2 615
TO LIVE AGAIN IN THESE WILDE WOODS FORLORN? . . 9 910
MY ONELY STRENGTH AND STAY: FORLORN OF THEE, . . 10 921

FORLORNE
TO YOU WHOM I COULD PITTIE THUS FORLORNE 4 374
ERRONEOUS THERE TO WANDER AND FORLORNE. 7 20

FORM
STOOD LIKE A TOWR; HIS FORM HAD YET NOT LOST . . 1 591
WITH RAPID WHEELS, OR FRONTED BRIGADS FORM. . . . 2 532
HOW BUSIED, IN WHAT FORM AND POSTURE COUCHT. . . . 4 876
SINCE NOW WE FIND THIS OUR EMPYREAL FORM 6 433
THENCEFORTH THE FORM OF SERVANT TO ASSUME, . . . 10 214
AND THE DIRE HISS RENEW'D, AND THE DIRE FORM . . 10 543
HENCEFORTH; LEAST THAT TOO HEAV'NLY FORM, PRETENDED 10 872

FORM'D
A THIRD AS SOON HAD FORM'D WITHIN THE GROUND . . 1 705
WHAT THING THOU ART, THUS DOUBLE-FORM'D, AND WHY . 2 741
EQUAL IN THEIR CREATION THEY WERE FORM'D, ... 6 690
THE EARTH WAS FORM'D, BUT IN THE WOMB AS YET . . 7 276
THOUGH OF ETHEREAL MOULD: THEN FORM'D THE MOON . 7 356
A CREATURE FORM'D OF EARTH, AND HIM ENDOW, . . . 9 149

FORMD
I FORMD THEM FREE, AND FREE THEY MUST REMAIN, . . 3 124
FOR CONTEMPLATION HEE AND VALOUR FORMD, ... 4 297
THE HAND THAT FORMD THEM ON THIR SHAPE HATH POURD. 4 365
AND FROM WHOM I WAS FORMD FLESH OF THY FLESH, . . 4 441
WHO FORMD US FROM THE DUST, AND PLAC'D US HERE . 5 516
THEE WHAT THOU ART, AND FORMD THE POW'RS OF HEAV'N 5 824
THAT WE WERE FORMD THEN SAIST THOU? AND THE WORK 5 853
THIS SAID, HE FORMD THEE, ADAM, THEE O MAN . . . 7 524
THE RIB HE FORMD AND FASHOND WITH HIS HANDS; . . 8 469
NEITHER HER OUT-SIDE FORMD SO FAIR, NOR AUGHT . . 8 596
GUILTLESS OF FIRE HAD FORMD, OR ANGELS BROUGHT. . 9 392
WHATEVER CAN TO SIGHT OR THOUGHT BE FORMD, . . . 9 898
AS ONCE THOU SLEPST, WHILE SHEE TO LIFE WAS FORMD. 11 369
INTO FIT MOULDS PREPAR'D; FROM WHICH HE FORMD . . 11 571

FORME
DRAIND THROUGH A LIMBEC TO HIS NATIVE FORME. . . 3 605
THUS EARLIE, THUS ALONE; HER HEAV'NLY FORME . . 9 457

FORMER
THE FORMER VAIN TO HOPE ARGUES AS VAIN 2 234
FORTHWITH HIS FORMER STATE AND BEING FORGETS, . . 2 585
BY ACT OF GRACE MY FORMER STATE; HOW SOON . . . 4 94
SATAN, SO CALL HIM NOW, HIS FORMER NAME 5 658
I THEN WAS PASSING TO MY FORMER STATE 8 290
HER FORMER TRESPASS FEAR'D, THE MORE TO SOOTHE . 9 1006
THUS WILL THIS LATTER, AS THE FORMER WORLD, . . 12 105

FORMES
INNUMEROUS LIVING CREATURES, PERFET FORMES, . . 7 455
ATTENDS THEE, AND EACH WORD, EACH MOTION FORMES, . 8 223
WELL DEEM IN OUTWARD RITES AND SPECIOUS FORMES . 12 534

FORMIDABLE
ON EITHER SIDE A FORMIDABLE SHAPE; 2 649

FORMING
UNDER HIS FORMING HANDS A CREATURE GREW, ... 8 470

FORMLESS
WON FROM THE VOID AND FORMLESS INFINITE. 3 12
I SAW WHEN AT HIS WORD THE FORMLESS MASS, ... 3 708

FORMOST
FORMOST TO STAND AGAINST THE THUNDERERS AIM . . 2 28

FORMS
HIS LEGIONS, ANGEL FORMS, WHO LAY INTRANS'T . . 1 301
THIR GREAT COMMANDER; GODLIKE SHAPES AND FORMS . 1 358
THIR WANDRING GODS DISGUIS'D IN BRUTISH FORMS . . 1 481
THUS INCORPOREAL SPIRITS TO SMALLEST FORMS . . . 1 789
FLEW UPWARD, SPIRITED WITH VARIOUS FORMS, . . . 3 717
SHE FORMS IMAGINATIONS, AERIE SHAPES, ... 5 105
TRANSCEND HIS OWN SO FARR, WHOSE RADIANT FORMS . 5 457
INDU'D WITH VARIOUS FORMS VARIOUS DEGREES . . . 5 473
BY LIK'NING SPIRITUAL TO CORPORAL FORMS, ... 5 573

FORREIN
OF FORREIN WORLDS: HE THROUGH THE MIDST UNMARKT, . 10 441

FORREST
A FORREST HUGE OF SPEARS: AND THRONGING HELMS . . 1 547
HATH SCATH'D THE FORREST OAKS, OR MOUNTAIN PINES, 1 613
WHOSE MIDNIGHT REVELS, BY A FORREST SIDE . . . 1 782
IN WOOD OR WILDERNESS, FORREST OR DEN; 4 342
HIM THROUGH THE SPICIE FORREST ONWARD COM . . . 5 298
IN FORREST WILDE, IN THICKET, BRAKE, OR DEN; . . 7 458
NOW LAND, NOW SEA, AND SHORES WITH FORREST CROWND, 9 117
GOODLIEST OF ALL THE FORREST, HART AND HINDE; . . 11 189

FORSAKE
OF MANKIND THEY CORRUPTED TO FORSAKE 1 368
FORSAKE ME NOT THUS, ADAM, WITNESS HEAV'N . . . 10 914
AS TO FORSAKE THE LIVING GOD, AND FALL 12 118

FORSAK'N
FORSAK'N OF ALL GOOD; I SEE THY FALL 5 878

FORSOOK
FOR THOSE THE RACE OF ISRAEL OFT FORSOOK 1 432
FORSOOK THEM, WHEN THEMSELVES THEY VILLIFI'D . . 11 516

FORTH
OUT OF OUR EVIL SEEK TO BRING FORTH GOOD, ... 1 163
HOW ALL HIS MALICE SERV'D BUT TO BRING FORTH . . 1 217
DARKENS THE STREETS, THEN WANDER FORTH THE SONS . 1 501
TEARS SUCH AS ANGELS WEEP, BURST FORTH: AT LAST . 1 620
PUT FORTH AT FULL, BUT STILL HIS STRENGTH
CONCEAL'D, ... 1 641

FORTH (CONTINUED)

POUR FORTH THIR POPULOUS YOUTH ABOUT THE HIVE 1 770
THE STYGIAN COUNSEL THUS DISSOLV'D; AND FORTH 2 506
PRICK FORTH THE AERIE KNIGHTS, AND COUCH THIR SPEARS 2 536
THREW FORTH, TILL ON THE LEFT SIDE OP'NING WIDE, 2 755
FORTH ISSU'D, BRANDISHING HIS FATAL DART 2 786
MY BOWELS, THIR REPAST; THEN BURSTING FORTH 2 800
CAST FORTH REDOUNDING SMOAK AND RUDDY FLAME. 2 889
BREATHE FORTH ELIXIR PURE, AND RIVERS RUN 3 607
THAT BROUGHT THEM FORTH, BUT HID THIR CAUSES DEEP. 3 707
POWRD FORTH PROFUSE ON HILL AND DALE AND PLAINE, 4 243
LAYES FORTH HER PURPLE GRAPE, AND GENTLY CREEPS 4 259
AND SEND FORTH ALL HER KINGS; THERE WILL BE ROOM, 4 383
FORTH ISSUING AT TH' ACCUSTOMD HOUR STOOD ARMD 4 779
HUNG FORTH IN HEAV'N HIS GOLDEN SCALES, YET SEEN 4 997
SHOT FORTH PECULIAR GRACES; THEN WITH VOICE 5 15
CLOSE AT MINE EAR ONE CALL'D ME FORTH TO WALK 5 36
SOON AS THEY FORTH WERE COME TO OPEN SIGHT 5 138
HER VIRGIN FANCIES, POURING FORTH MORE SWEET, 5 296
AND WHAT THY STORES CONTAIN, BRING FORTH AND POURE 5 314
HIS GOD-LIKE GUEST, WALKS FORTH, WITHOUT MORE TRAIN 5 351
AS HEAV'NS GREAT YEAR BRINGS FORTH, TH' EMPYREAL HOST 5 583
ABSTRUSEST THOUGHTS, FROM FORTH HIS HOLY MOUNT 5 712
AGAINST THEE ARE GON FORTH WITHOUT RECALL; 5 885
THOUGH SINGLE. FROM AMIDST THEM FORTH HE PASSD, 5 903
LIGHT ISSUES FORTH, AND AT THE OTHER DORE 6 9
SEEM TWILIGHT HERE; AND NOW WENT FORTH THE MORN 6 12
GABRIEL, LEAD FORTH TO BATTEL THESE MY SONS 6 46
INVINCIBLE, LEAD FORTH MY ARMED SAINTS 6 47
FORTH STEPPING OPPOSITE, HALF WAY HE MET 6 128
OF SUCH COMMOTION, SUCH AS TO SET FORTH 6 310
WITH HEAV'NS RAY, AND TEMPERD THEY SHOOT FORTH 6 480
DILATED AND INFURIATE SHALL SEND FORTH 6 486
PUT FORTH, AND TO A NARROW VENT APPLI'D 6 583
SINCE MICHAEL AND HIS POWERS WENT FORTH TO TAME 6 686
THAT SHAKE HEAV'NS BASIS, BRING FORTH ALL MY WARR, 6 712
DAWNING THROUGH HEAV'N: FORTH RUSH'D WITH WHIRLWIND SOUND 6 749
GLAR'D LIGHTNING, AND SHOT FORTH PERNICIOUS FIRE 6 849
YET HALF HIS STRENGTH HE PUT NOT FORTH, BUT CHECK'D 6 853
I SEND ALONG, RIDE FORTH, AND BID THE DEEP 7 166
AND PUT NOT FORTH MY GOODNESS, WHICH IS FREE 7 171
CELESTIAL EQUIPAGE; AND NOW CAME FORTH 7 203
ON GOLDEN HINGES MOVING, TO LET FORTH 7 207
PUT FORTH THE VERDANT GRASS, HERB YIELDING SEED, 7 310
BROUGHT FORTH THE TENDER GRASS, WHOSE VERDURE CLAD 7 315
FORTH FLOURISH'T THICK THE CLUSTRING VINE, FORTH CREPT 7 320
BURSTING WITH KINDLY RUPTURE FORTH DISCLOS'D 7 419
INTELLIGENT OF SEASONS, AND SET FORTH 7 427
LET TH' EARTH BRING FORTH FOUL LIVING IN HER KINDE, 7 451
AT ONCE CAME FORTH WHATEVER CREEPS THE GROUND, 7 475
ROSE, AND WENT FORTH AMONG HER FRUITS AND FLOURS, 8 44
WITH GODDESS-LIKE DEMEANOUR FORTH SHE WENT; 8 59
TO SEE THAT NONE THENCE ISSU'D FORTH A SPIE, 8 233
WITH GRATEFUL SMELL, FORTH CAME THE HUMAN PAIR 9 197
MEER SERPENT IN APPEARANCE, FORTH WAS COME, 9 413
FORTH ISSUING ON A SUMMERS MORN TO BREATHE 9 447
FORTH REACHING TO THE FRUIT, SHE PLUCK'D, SHE EAT: 9 781
AND FORTH TO MEET HER WENT, THE WAY SHE TOOK 9 847
BLAZ'D FORTH UNCLOUDED DEITIE; HE FULL 10 65
ABSENTS THEE, OR WHAT CHANCE DETAINS? COME FORTH, 10 108
IN SORROW FORTH, AND TO THY HUSBANDS WILL 10 195
THORNS ALSO AND THISTLES IT SHALL BRING THEE FORTH 10 203
FORTH RUSH'D IN HASTE THE GREAT CONSULTING PEERS, 10 456
SUCCESSFUL BEYOND HOPE, TO LEAD YE FORTH 10 463
HIM FOLLOW'D ISSUING FORTH TO TH' OPEN FIELD, 10 533
IN TRIUMPH ISSUING FORTH THIR GLORIOUS CHIEF; 10 537
WHILE THE CREATOR CALLING FORTH BY NAME 10 649
FORTH RUSH THE LEVANT AND THE PONENT WINDES 10 704
AND BRINGING FORTH, SOON RECOMPENC'T WITH JOY, 10 1052
AND SEND HIM FROM THE GARDEN FORTH TO TILL 11 97
SO SEND THEM FORTH, THOUGH SORROWING, YET IN PEACE: 11 117
HER ROSIE PROGRESS SMILING; LET US FORTH, 11 175
AND SEND THEE FROM THE GARDEN FORTH TO TILL 11 261
BLOWN STIFLING BACK ON HIM THAT BREATHS IT FORTH: 11 313
CORRUPTION TO BRING FORTH MORE VIOLENT DEEDS. 11 428
A DOVE SENT FORTH ONCE AND AGEN TO SPIE 11 857
GREATLY REJOYC'D, AND THUS HIS JOY BROKE FORTH. 11 869
GOD LOOKING FORTH WILL TROUBLE ALL HIS HOST 12 209
THEN THAT WHICH BY CREATION FIRST BROUGHT FORTH 12 472
TO BRING FORTH FRUITS JOY AND ETERNAL BLISS. 12 551

FORTHWITH

FORTHWITH UPRIGHT HE REARS FROM OFF THE POOL 1 221
FORTHWITH FROM EVERY SQUADRON AND EACH BAND 1 356
WHO FORTHWITH FROM THE GLITTERING STAFF UNFURLD 1 535
A SOLEMN COUNCEL FORTHWITH TO BE HELD 1 755
FORTHWITH HIS FORMER STATE AND BEING FORGETS, 2 585
FORTHWITH THE HUGE PORCULLIS HIGH UP DREW, 2 874
THY DREAD TRIBUNAL; FORTHWITH FROM ALL WINDES 3 326
THE LIVING, AND FORTHWITH THE CITED DEAD 3 327
COULD NOT BUT TASTE. FORTHWITH UP TO THE CLOUDS 5 86
FORTHWITH FROM ALL THE ENDS OF HEAV'N APPEERD 5 586
FORTHWITH FROM DANCE TO SWEET REPAST THEY TURN 5 630
FORTHWITH ON ALL SIDES TO HIS AIDE WAS RUN 6 335

FORTHWITH (CONTINUED)

FORTHWITH FROM COUNCEL TO THE WORK THEY FLEW, 6 507
FORTHWITH (BEHOLD THE EXCELLENCE, THE POWER 6 637
LET THER BE LIGHT, SAID GOD, AND FORTHWITH LIGHT 7 243
FORTHWITH THE SOUNDS AND SEAS, EACH CREEK AND BAY 7 399
KNEW NOT; TO SPEAK I TRI'D, AND FORTHWITH SPAKE, 8 271
INSENSIBLE, AND FORTHWITH TO DISSOLVE: 8 291
THAT WHOSO EATS THEREOF, FORTHWITH ATTAINS 9 724
FELT LESS REMORSE; THEY FORTHWITH TO THE PLACE 10 1098
FORTHWITH FROM OUT THE ARKE A RAVEN FLIES, 11 855
FORTHWITH A HIDEOUS GABBLE RISES LOUD 12 56

FORTIFIE

TO FORTIFIE THUS FARR, AND OVERLAY 10 370

FORTITUDE

IN BATTELS FEIGN'D; THE BETTER FORTITUDE 9 31
IS FORTITUDE TO HIGHEST VICTORIE, 12 570

FORTUNATE

FORTUNATE FIELDS, AND GROVES AND FLOURIE VALES, 3 569

FOUGHT

THAT FOUGHT AT THEB'S AND ILIUM, ON EACH SIDE 1 578
THAT FOUGHT IN HEAV'N; NOW FIERCER BY DESPAIR: 2 45
AND FIELDS WERE FOUGHT IN HEAV'N; WHEREIN REMAIND 2 768
SERVANT OF GOD, WELL DONE, WELL HAST THOU FOUGHT 6 29
MILLIONS OF FIERCE ENCOUNTRING ANGELS FOUGHT 6 220
MEMORIAL, WHERE THE MIGHT OF GABRIEL FOUGHT, 6 355
THAT UNDER GROUND, THEY FOUGHT IN DISMAL SHADE; 6 666
WERE LONG TO TELL, HOW MANY BATTELS FOUGHT, 12 261

FOUGHTEN

VICTOR AND VANQUISHT; ON THE FOUGHTEN FIELD 6 410

FOUL

WHO FIRST SEDUC'D THEM TO THAT FOUL REVOLT? 1 33
THAT WITH SAD OVERTHROW AND FOUL DEFEAT 1 135
TO IDOLS FOUL. THAMMUZ CAME NEXT BEHIND, 1 446
WITH DREAD OF DEATH TO FLIGHT OR FOUL RETREAT, 1 555
BUT ENDED FOUL IN MANY A SCALY FOULD 2 651
NOW IN THINE EYE SO FOUL, ONCE DEEMD SO FAIR 2 748
BY SIN TO FOUL EXORBITANT DESIRES; 3 177
ALIEN FROM HEAV'N, WITH PASSIONS FOUL OBSCUR'D: 4 571
ENTER'D, AND FOUL DISORDER; ALL THE GROUND 6 388
LET TH' EARTH BRING FORTH FOUL LIVING IN HER KINDE, 7 451
THOSE NOTES TO TRAGIC; FOUL DISTRUST, AND BREACH 9 6
O FOUL DESCENT. THAT I WHO ERST CONTENDED 9 163
THE TEMPTED WITH DISHONOUR FOUL, SUPPOS'D 9 297
TEMPTING AFFRONTS US WITH HIS FOUL ESTEEM 9 328
OF OUR INTEGRITIE; HIS FOUL ESTEEME 9 329
FOUL ON HIMSELF; THEN WHEREFORE SHUND OR FEARD 9 331
OF FOUL CONCUPISCENCE; WHENCE EVIL STORE; 9 1078
OF TERROUR, FOUL AND UGLY TO BEHOLD, 11 464
WHOSE FOUL IDOLATRIES, AND OTHER FAULTS 12 337

FOULD

BUT ENDED FOUL IN MANY A SCALY FOULD 2 651
LEAPS O'RE THE FENCE WITH EASE INTO THE FOULD: 4 187
SO CLOMB THIS FIRST GRAND THIEF INTO GODS FOULD: 4 192
FOULD ABOVE FOULD A SURGING MAZE, HIS HEAD 9 499

FOULDS

OP'NING THIR BRAZEN FOULDS DISCOVER WIDE 1 724
THIR SNAKIE FOULDS, AND ADDED WINGS. FIRST CREPT 7 484
THE SERPENT SLEEPING, IN WHOSE MAZIE FOULDS 9 161
CIRCULAR BASE OF RISING FOULDS, THAT TOUR'D 9 498
NEW REAPT, THE OTHER PART SHEEP-WALKS AND FOULDS; 11 431

FOULE

AND IN EMBRACES FORCIBLE AND FOULE 2 793
WHO TO THE FRAUDULENT IMPOSTOR FOULE 3 692
FOR HEAV'NLY MINDES FROM SUCH DISTEMPERS FOULE 4 118
THY SIN AND PLACE OF DOOM OBSCURE AND FOULE. 4 840
VICTOR; THOUGH BRUTISH THAT CONTEST AND FOULE, 6 124
AND ALL HER ENTRAILS TORE, DISGORGING FOULE 6 588
FOULE DISSIPATION FOLLOW'D AND FORC'T ROUT; 6 598
FOOD FOR SO FOULE A MONSTER, IN THY POWER 10 986
NO GROSS, NO UNHARMONEOUS MIXTURE FOULE, 11 51
TO SPIRITS FOULE, AND ALL MY TREES THIR PREY, 11 124

FOUND

WITH STENCH AND SMOAK: SUCH RESTING FOUND THE SOLE 1 237
ON DUTY, SLEEPING FOUND BY WHOM THEY DREAD, 1 333
HIS OWN AND RHEA'S SON LIKE MEASURE FOUND; 1 513
OBSCURE SOME GLIMPS OF JOY, TO HAVE FOUND THIR CHIEF 1 524
NOT IN DESPAIR, TO HAVE FOUND THEMSELVES NOT LOST 1 525
WORDS INTERWOVE WITH SIGHS FOUND OUT THIR WAY. 1 621
WITH WOND'ROUS ART FOUND OUT THE MASSIE ORE, 1 703
TO FOUND THIS NETHER EMPIRE, WHICH MIGHT RISE 2 296
OF THOSE HEAV'N-WARRING CHAMPIONS COULD BE FOUND 2 424
AND FOUND NO END, IN WANDRING MAZES LOST. 2 561
VIEW'D FIRST THIR LAMENTABLE LOT, AND FOUND 2 617
FOUND OUT FOR MANKIND UNDER WRAUTH, O THOU 3 275
A WORLD FROM UTTER LOSS, AND HAST BEEN FOUND 3 308
FOUND WORTHIEST TO BE SO BY BEING GOOD, 3 310
LOVE NO WHERE TO BE FOUND LESS THEN DIVINE. 3 411

FOUND (CONTINUED)
LIVING OR LIVELESS TO BE FOUND WAS NONE, 3 443
ALL THIS DARK GLOBE THE FIEND FOUND AS HE PASS'D, 3 498
THE PLACE HE FOUND BEYOND EXPRESSION BRIGHT, 3 591
FOR SIGHT NO OBSTACLE FOUND HERE, NOR SHADE, 3 615
BUT FURTHER WAY FOUND NONE, SO THICK ENTWIN'D, 4 174
I FIRST AWAK'T, AND FOUND MY SELF REPOS'D 4 450
IN SEARCH OF WHOM THEY SOUGHT: HIM THERE THEY FOUND 4 799
AND BRIEF RELATED WHOM THEY BROUGHT, WHERE FOUND, 4 875
THE REST IS TRUE, THEY FOUND ME WHERE THEY SAY; 4 900
MY FAIREST, MY ESPOUS'D, MY LATEST FOUND, 5 18
I ROSE AS AT THY CALL, BUT FOUND THEE NOT; 5 48
SPIRITUAL, MAY OF PUREST SPIRITS BE FOUND 5 406
IF YE BE FOUND OBEDIENT, AND RETAIN 5 501
WHAT MEANT THAT CAUTION JOIND, IF YE BE FOUND 5 513
THY REBELS, OR BE FOUND THE WORST IN HEAV'N. 5 742
WHILE PARDON MAY BE FOUND IN TIME BESOUGHT. 5 848
SO SPAKE THE SERAPH ABDIEL FAITHFUL FOUND, 5 896
WARR HE PERCEAV'D, WARR IN PROCINCT, AND FOUND 6 19
FOUND WORTHY NOT OF LIBERTIE ALONE, 6 420
ONCE FOUND, WHICH YET UNFOUND MOST WOULD HAVE
THOUGHT 6 500
THEY FOUND, THEY MINGL'D, AND WITH SUTTLE ART, 6 513
WHEREOF TO FOUND THIR ENGINS AND THIR BALLS 6 518
RAGE PROMPTED THEM AT LENGTH, AND FOUND THEM ARMS 6 635
ENDLESS, AND NO SOLUTION WILL BE FOUND: 6 694
WAVE ROWLING AFTER WAVE, WHERE WAY THEY FOUND, 7 298
WITH SERPENT ERROUR WANDRING, FOUND THIR WAY, 7 302
OUR PROMPT OBEDIENCE. FAST WE FOUND, FAST SHUT 8 240
SOFT ON THE FLOURIE HERB I FOUND ME LAID 8 254
FIRST FOUND ME, AND WITH SOFT OPPRESSION SEIS'D 8 288
TO PLUCK AND EATE; WHEREAT I WAK'D, AND FOUND 8 309
I FOUND NOT WHAT ME THOUGHT I WANTED STILL; 8 355
IS NO DEFICIENCE FOUND; NOT SO IS MAN, 8 416
PERMISSIVE, AND ACCEPTANCE FOUND, WHICH GAIN'D 8 435
AMONG THE BEASTS NO MATE FOR THEE WAS FOUND. 8 594
FOUND UNSUSPECTED WAY. THERE WAS A PLACE, 9 69
MOST OPPORTUNE MIGHT SERVE HIS WILES, AND FOUND 9 85
THE SERPENT: HIM FAST SLEEPING SOON HE FOUND 9 182
UNPRAIS'D: FOR NOTHING LOVELIER CAN BE FOUND 9 232
THOUGHTS, WHICH HOW FOUND THEY HARBOUR IN THY BREST 9 288
THOUGH INEFFECTUAL FOUND: MISDEEM NOT THEN, 9 301
AT FEED OR FOUNTAIN NEVER HAD I FOUND. 9 597
HAVE ALSO TASTED, AND HAVE ALSO FOUND 9 874
NOR YET ON HIM FOUND DEADLY, HE YET LIVES, 9 932
SOON FOUND THIR EYES HOW OP'ND, AND THIR MINDS 9 1053
COLUMBUS FOUND TH' AMERICAN SO GIRT 9 1116
NOT UNAGREEABLE, TO FOUND A PATH 10 256
AND ALL ABOUT FOUND DESOLATE; FOR THOSE 10 420
PROTESTING FATE SUPREAME; THENCE HOW I FOUND 10 480
AM FOUND ETERNAL, AND INCORPORATE BOTH, 10 816
TO MY JUST NUMBER FOUND. O WHY DID GOD, 10 888
FOUND SO ERRONEOUS, THENCE BY JUST EVENT 10 969
FOUND SO UNFORTUNATE; NEVERTHELESS, 10 970
LET US SEEK DEATH, OR HE NOT FOUND, SUPPLY 10 1001
HAD ENDED NOW THIR ORISONS, AND FOUND 11 137
GOD IS AS HERE, AND WILL BE FOUND ALIKE 11 350
FOR ENVIE THAT HIS BROTHERS OFFERING FOUND 11 456
HAD MELTED (WHETHER FOUND WHERE CASUAL FIRE 11 566
THROUGH ALL THE PLAIN, AND REFUGE NONE WAS FOUND. 11 673
IN SHARP CONTEST OF BATTEL FOUND NO AIDE 11 800
FOR ONE MAN FOUND SO PERFET AND SO JUST, 11 876
IN THE WIDE WILDERNESS, THERE THEY SHALL FOUND 12 224
RARELY BE FOUND: SO SHALL THE WORLD GOE ON, 12 537
LAY SLEEPING RAN BEFORE, BUT FOUND HER WAK'T; 12 608

FOUNDATION
O FAIR FOUNDATION LAID WHEREON TO BUILD 4 521

FOUNDATIONS
FROM THIR FOUNDATIONS LOOSNING TO AND FRO 6 643
HER DARK FOUNDATIONS, AND TOO FAST HAD BOUND. 6 870

FOUNDED
NOR FOUNDED ON THE BRITTLE STRENGTH OF BONES, 1 427
FOUNDED IN REASON, LOYAL, JUST, AND PURE, 4 755
ADVERSE TO LIFE: THEN FOUNDED, THEN CONGLOB'D 7 239
FROM HEAVEN GATE NOT FARR, FOUNDED IN VIEW 7 618
FOUNDED IN RIGHTEOUSNESS AND PEACE AND LOVE 12 550

FOUNDER'D
THE PILOT OF SOME SMALL NIGHT-FOUNDER'D SKIFF, 1 204

FOUNDERD
NOR GOOD DRY LAND: NIGH FOUNDERD ON HE FARES, 2 940

FOUNDST
FOUNDST EITHER SWEET REPAST, OR SOUND REPOSE; 9 407

FOUNT
AND FLOURS ALOFT SHADING THE FOUNT OF LIFE, 3 357
FROM PANEAS THE FOUNT OF JORDANS FLOOD 3 535
HOW FROM THAT SAPHIRE FOUNT THE CRISPED BROOKS, 4 237
YOUR TRIBES, AND WATER FROM TH' AMBROSIAL FOUNT? 11 279

FOUNTAIN
OR FOUNTAIN SOME BELATED PEASANT SEES, 1 783
WHOSE FOUNTAIN WHO SHALL TELL? BEFORE THE SUN, 3 8

FOUNTAIN (CONTINUED)
FOUNTAIN OF LIGHT, THY SELF INVISIBLE 3 375
ROSE A FRESH FOUNTAIN, AND WITH MANY A RILL 4 229
STOOD WHISPERING SOFT, BY A FRESH FOUNTAIN SIDE 4 326
SOME WANDRING SPIRIT OF HEAV'N, BY FOUNTAIN SIDE, 4 531
PERPETUAL FOUNTAIN OF DOMESTIC SWEETS, 4 760
TO HILL, OR VALLEY, FOUNTAIN, OR FRESH SHADE 5 203
BEFORE THE HILLS APPEERD, OR FOUNTAIN FLOW'D, 7 8
WITH TUFTS THE VALLIES AND EACH FOUNTAIN SIDE, 7 327
HITHER AS TO THIR FOUNTAIN OTHER STARRS 7 364
ROSE UP A FOUNTAIN BY THE TREE OF LIFE; 9 73
BY FOUNTAIN OR BY SHADIE RIVULET 9 420
AT FEED OR FOUNTAIN NEVER HAD I FOUND. 9 597
FAST BY A FOUNTAIN, ONE SMALL THICKET PAST 9 628
OF AMARANTIN SHADE, FOUNTAIN OR SPRING, 11 78
I HEARD, HERE WITH HIM AT THIS FOUNTAIN TALK'D: 11 322

FOUNTAINS
AMONG THE GROVES, THE FOUNTAINS, AND THE FLOURS 5 126
FOUNTAINS AND YEE, THAT WARBLE, AS YE FLOW, 5 195
O WOODS, O FOUNTAINS, HILLOCKS, DALES AND BOWRS, 10 860
RAINE DAY AND NIGHT, ALL FOUNTAINS OF THE DEEP 11 826

FOUNTED
MOUNT CARMEL; HERE THE DOUBLE-FOUNTED STREAM 12 144

FOUR
TOWARD THE FOUR WINDS FOUR SPEEDY CHERUBIM 2 516
FOUR WAYS THIR FLYING MARCH, ALONG THE BANKS 2 574
OF FOUR INFERNAL RIVERS THAT DISGORGE 2 575
FOR HOT, COLD, MOIST, AND DRY, FOUR CHAMPIONS
FIERCE 2 898
AND NOW DIVIDED INTO FOUR MAIN STREAMS, 4 233
HIS PRAISE YE WINDS, THAT FROM FOUR QUARTERS BLOW, 5 192
BY FOUR CHERUBIC SHAPES, FOUR FACES EACH 6 753
AT ONCE THE FOUR SPRED OUT THIR STARRIE WINGS 6 827
HE CIRCL'D, FOUR TIMES CROSS'D THE CARR OF NIGHT 9 65
OF WATCHFUL CHERUBIM; FOUR FACES EACH 11 128
WITH THIR FOUR WIVES; AND GOD MADE FAST THE DORE. 11 737

FOURE
HIS ARROWS, FROM THE FOURFOLD-VISAG'D FOURE, 6 845

FOURFOLD-VISAG'D
HIS ARROWS, FROM THE FOURFOLD-VISAG'D FOURE, 6 845

FOURFOOTED
OF THOSE FOURFOOTED KINDES, HIMSELF NOW ONE, 4 397

FOURTH
GLAD EEVNING AND GLAD MORN CROWND THE FOURTH DAY. 7 386

FOWL
BY FOWL, FISH, BEAST, WAS FLOWN, WAS SWUM, WAS
WALKT 7 503
OF RAVENOUS FOWL, THOUGH MANY A LEAGUE REMOTE, 10 274
HE GAVE US ONELY OVER BEAST, FISH, FOWL 12 67

FOWLE
AND LET FOWLE FLIE ABOVE THE EARTH, WITH WINGS 7 389
AND LET THE FOWLE BE MULTIPLY'D ON THE EARTH. 7 398
WITH FISH REPLENISHT, AND THE AIRE WITH FOWLE, 7 447
OVER THE FISH AND FOWLE OF SEA AND AIRE, 7 521
OVER FISH OF THE SEA, AND FOWLE OF THE AIRE, 7 533
OR LIVE IN SEA, OR AIRE, BEAST, FISH, AND FOWLE. 8 341
MUCH LESS CAN BIRD WITH BEAST, OR FISH WITH FOWLE 8 395
FEED FIRST, ON EACH BEAST NEXT, AND FISH, AND
FOWLE, 10 604
BEAST NOW WITH BEAST GAN WAR, AND FOWLE WITH FOWLE, 10 710

FOWLES
OF TOWRING EAGLES, TO ALL THE FOWLES HE SEEMS 5 271

FOYLD
WHICH BUT TH' OMNIPOTENT NONE COULD HAVE FOYLD, 1 273

FRAGRANCE
THUS WHILE GOD SPAKE, AMBROSIAL FRAGRANCE FILL'D 3 135
GLISTRING WITH DEW, NOR FRAGRANCE AFTER SHOWERS, 4 653
AND SHOOK HIS PLUMES, THAT HEAV'NLY FRAGRANCE FILLD 5 286
WITH FRAGRANCE AND WITH JOY MY HEART OREFLOW'D. 8 266
VEILD IN A CLOUD OF FRAGRANCE, WHERE SHE STOOD, 9 425

FRAGRANT
GLISTRING WITH DEW; FRAGRANT THE FERTIL EARTH 4 645
OF FIRM AND FRAGRANT LEAF; ON EITHER SIDE 4 695
WITH FLOURETS DECK'T AND FRAGRANT SMELLS; BUT EVE 5 379

FRAIL
THIR FRAIL ORIGINAL, AND FADED BLISS, 2 375
OF THIS FRAIL WORLD; BY WHICH THE SPIRITS PERVERSE 2 1030
BY ME UPHELD, THAT HE MAY KNOW HOW FRAIL 3 180
PERCEIVE THEE PURPOS'D NOT TO DOOM FRAIL MAN 3 404
TO WRECK ON INNOCENT FRAIL MAN HIS LOSS 4 11
VITAL IN EVERY PART, NOT AS FRAIL MAN 6 345

FRAILE
FRAILE IS OUR HAPPINESS, IF THIS BE SO, 9 340

FRAILTIE
THY FRAILTIE AND INFIRMER SEX FORGIV'N, 10 956
OUR FRAILTIE CAN SUSTAIN, THY TIDINGS BRING, 11 302

FRAM'D
CHOS'N BY THE SOVRAN PLANTER, WHEN HE FRAM'D 4 691
DIVINE THE SOV'RAN ARCHITECT HAD FRAM'D. 5 256
THUS TO TH' EMPYREAL MINISTER HE FRAM'D. 5 460
A MIGHTIE SPHEARE HE FRAM'D, UNLIGHTSOM FIRST, 7 355
BY HIS PRESCRIPT A SANCTUARY IS FRAM'D 12 249

FRAME
SOM CAPITAL CITY; OR LESS THEN IF THIS FRAME 2 924
HEAV'NS EVERLASTING FRAME, WHILE O'RE THE NECKS 3 395
ALMIGHTIE, THINE THIS UNIVERSAL FRAME, 5 154
CONTIGUOUS MIGHT DISTEMPER THE WHOLE FRAME: 7 273
WHEN I BEHOLD THIS GOODLY FRAME, THIS WORLD 8 15
THE MIGHTIE FRAME, HOW BUILD, UNBUILD, CONTRIVE 8 81

FRAMES
WHICH REASON JOYNING OR DISJOYNING, FRAMES 5 106

FRANCISCAN
OR IN FRANCISCAN THINK TO PASS DISGUIS'D; 3 480

FRATERNAL
WITH FAIR EQUALITIE, FRATERNAL STATE, 12 26

FRAUD
OF SOLOMON HE LED BY FRAUD TO BUILD 1 401
TO WORK IN CLOSE DESIGN, BY FRAUD OR GUILE 1 646
FALL CIRCUMVENTED THUS BY FRAUD, THOUGH JOYND 3 152
ARTIFICER OF FRAUD; AND WAS THE FIRST 4 121
IN THIS PERFIDIOUS FRAUD, CONTAGION SPRED 5 880
TO HIDE THE FRAUD. AT INTERVIEW BOTH STOOD 6 555
STOOD REIMBATTELL'D FIERCE, BY FORCE OR FRAUD 6 794
HE TRUSTED TO HAVE SEIS'D, AND INTO FRAUD 7 143
IN MEDITATED FRAUD AND MALICE, BENT 9 55
FIT VESSEL, FITTEST IMP OF FRAUD, IN WHOM 9 89
HIS FRAUD IS THEN THY FEAR, WHICH PLAIN INFERRS 9 285
CAN BY HIS FRAUD BE SHAK'N OR SEDUC'T; 9 287
SO GLISTER'D THE DIRE SNAKE, AND INTO FRAUD 9 643
THE SACRED FRUIT FORBIDD'N. SOM CURSED FRAUD 9 904
FRAUD IN THE SERPENT, SPEAKING AS HE SPAKE; 9 1150
MADE HAPPIE: HIM BY FRAUD I HAVE SEDUC'D 10 485
THY INWARD FRAUD, TO WARN ALL CREATURES FROM THEE 10 871

FRAUDULENT
WHO TO THE FRAUDULENT IMPOSTOR FOULE 3 692
HIS FRAUDULENT TEMPTATION THUS BEGAN. 9 531

FRAUGHT
WITH HEAV'NS ARTILLERY FRAUGHT, COME RATTLING ON 2 715
THITHER FULL FRAUGHT WITH MISCHIEVOUS REVENGE, 2 1054
IN FAVOUR AND PRAEEMINENCE, YET FRAUGHT 5 661
HELL THIR FIT HABITATION FRAUGHT WITH FIRE 6 876
AND TIDINGS FRAUGHT, TO HELL HE NOW RETURN'D, 10 346
AND SLOW DESCENDS, WITH SOMTHING HEAV'NLY FRAUGHT. 11 207

FRAY
AND BY DECISION MORE IMBROILES THE FRAY 2 908
TH' ETERNAL TO PREVENT SUCH HORRID FRAY 4 996
BUT CALL IN AIDE, WHICH MAKES A BLOODY FRAY; 11 651

FREE
WE SHALL BE FREE; TH' ALMIGHTY HATH NOT BUILT 1 259
DID FIRST CREATE YOUR LEADER, NEXT FREE CHOICE, 2 19
FREE, AND TO NONE ACCOUNTABLE, PREFERRING 2 255
FREE VERTUE SHOULD ENTHRALL TO FORCE OR CHANCE. 2 551
FIXT FATE, FREE WILL, FOREKNOWLEDG ABSOLUTE, 2 560
I COME NO ENEMIE, BUT TO SET FREE 2 822
SUFFICIENT TO HAVE STOOD, THOUGH FREE TO FALL. 3 99
NOT FREE, WHAT PROOF COULD THEY HAVE GIVN SINCERE 3 103
I FORMD THEM FREE, AND FREE THEY MUST REMAIN, 3 124
HADST THOU THE SAME FREE WILL AND POWER TO STAND? 4 66
BUT HEAV'NS FREE LOVE DEALT EQUALLY TO ALL? 4 68
AS LIBERAL AND FREE AS INFINITE, 4 415
FREE LEAVE SO LARGE TO ALL THINGS ELSE, AND CHOICE 4 434
PURE, AND COMMANDS TO SOM, LEAVES FREE TO ALL. 4 747
HAPPINESS IN HIS POWER LEFT FREE TO WILL, 5 235
LEFT TO HIS OWN FREE WILL, HIS WILL THOUGH FREE, 5 236
BY NATURE FREE, NOT OVER-RUL'D BY FATE 5 527
CAN HEARTS, NOT FREE, BE TRI'D WHETHER THEY SERVE 5 532
TO BE BOTH WILL AND DEED CREATED FREE; 5 549
BY NONE, AND IF NOT EQUAL ALL, YET FREE, 5 791
EQUALLY FREE; FOR ORDERS AND DEGREES 5 792
FLATLY UNJUST, TO BINDE WITH LAWS THE FREE, 5 819
THY SELF NOT FREE, BUT TO THY SELF ENTHRALL'D; 6 181
THOU FABLEST, HERE HOWEVER TO DWELL FREE, 6 292
DELIVERER FROM NEW LORDS, LEADER TO FREE 6 451
AND PUT NOT FORTH MY GOODNESS, WHICH IS FREE 7 171
THE TAWNIE LION, PAWING TO GET FREE 7 464
EXPRESSING WELL THE SPIRIT WITHIN THEE FREE, 8 440
VARIOUSLY REPRESENTING; YET STILL FREE 8 610
THY JUDGEMENT TO DO AUGHT, WHICH ELSE FREE WILL 8 636
FREE IN THINE OWN ARBITREMENT IT LIES. 8 641
BUT GOD LEFT FREE THE WILL, FOR WHAT OBEYES 9 351
REASON, IS FREE, AND REASON HE MADE RIGHT, 9 352

FREE (CONTINUED)
GO; FOR THY STAY, NOT FREE, ABSENTS THEE MORE; 9 372
IN ATHENS OR FREE ROME, WHERE ELOQUENCE 9 671
OF THY FULL BRANCHES OFFER'D FREE TO ALL; 9 802
SUPERIOR; FOR INFERIOR WHO IS FREE? 9 825
AND FORCE UPON FREE WILL HATH HERE NO PLACE. 9 1174
OF MAN, WITH STRENGTH ENTIRE, AND FREE WILL ARM'D, 10 9
HIS FREE WILL, TO HER OWN INCLINING LEFT 10 46
THEN BOTH OUR SELVES AND SEED AT ONCE TO FREE 10 999
IN PART, FROM SUCH DEFORMITIES BE FREE, 11 513
RESERVING, HUMAN LEFT FROM HUMAN FREE. 12 71
MAN TILL THEN FREE. THEREFORE SINCE HEE PERMITS 12 90
OVER FREE REASON, GOD IN JUDGEMENT JUST 12 92
FROM IMPOSITION OF STRICT LAWS, TO FREE 12 304

FREED
AND FREED FROM INTRICACIES, TAUGHT TO LIVE, 8 182
NOT LONGER THEN SINCE I IN ONE NIGHT FREED 9 140

FREEDOM
USELESS AND VAIN, OF FREEDOM BOTH DESPOILD, 3 109
THIR FREEDOM, THEY THEMSELVES ORDAIN'D THIR FALL. 3 128
SEVERE BUT IN TRUE FILIAL FREEDOM PLAC'T; 4 294
SERVILITIE WITH FREEDOM TO CONTEND, 6 169
THUS I EMBOLD'ND SPAKE, AND FREEDOM US'D 8 434
OUR INWARD FREEDOM? IN THE DAY WE EATE 9 762
FREEDOM AND PEACE TO MEN: THEY ON THE PLAIN 11 580
SHALL WITH THIR FREEDOM LOST ALL VERTU LOOSE 11 798
HIS OUTWARD FREEDOM: TYRANNIE MUST BE, 12 95

FREEDOME
IN FREEDOME EQUAL? OR CAN INTRODUCE 5 797

FREELY
FREELY THEY STOOD WHO STOOD, AND FELL WHO FELL. 3 102
FREELY VOUTSAFT; ONCE MORE I WILL RENEW 3 175
FREELY PUT OFF, AND FOR HIM LASTLY DYE 3 240
CHOSE FREELY WHAT IT NOW SO JUSTLY RUES. 4 72
WHICH I AS FREELY GIVE; HELL SHALL UNFOLD, 4 381
ON OTHER SURETY NONE; FREELY WE SERVE, 5 538
BECAUSE WEE FREELY LOVE, AS IN OUR WILL 5 539
FREELY OUR PART; YEE WHO APPOINTED STAND 6 565
AND FREELY ALL THIR PLEASANT FRUIT FOR FOOD 7 540
EATE FREELY WITH GLAD HEART; FEAR HERE NO DEARTH: 8 322
GOOD REASON WAS THOU FREELY SHOULDST DISLIKE, 8 443
GODDESS HUMANE, REACH THEN, AND FREELY TASTE. 9 732
ON MY EXPERIENCE, ADAM, FREELY TASTE, 9 988

FREEZE
CORNICE OR FREEZE, WITH BOSSY SCULPTURES GRAV'N, 1 716

FREQUENT
FREQUENT AND FULL. AFTER SHORT SILENCE THEN 1 797
PASS'D FREQUENT, AND HIS EYE WITH CHOICE REGARD 3 534
THOUGH WIDE, AND THIS HIGH TEMPLE TO FREQUENT 7 148
FREQUENT; AND OF THE SIXT DAY YET REMAIN'D; 7 504
DELIGHTED, AND WITH FREQUENT INTERCOURSE 7 571
HIS BLESSED COUNT'NANCE; HERE I COULD FREQUENT, 11 317
BY MEN WHO THERE FREQUENT, OR THEREIN DWELL. 11 838

FREQUENTED
FREQUENTED THIR ASSEMBLIES, WHERESO MET, 11 722

FREQUENTING
FREQUENTING, SENT FROM HEARTS CONTRITE, IN SIGN 10 1091
FREQUENTING, SENT FROM HEARTS CONTRITE, IN SIGN 10 1103

FRESH
IN CLUSTERS; THEY AMONG FRESH DEWS AND FLOWERS 1 771
WITH FRESH ALACRITIE AND FORCE RENEW'D 2 1012
ROSE A FRESH FOUNTAIN, AND WITH MANY A RILL 4 229
STOOD WHISPERING SOFT, BY A FRESH FOUNTAIN SIDE 4 326
TO MORROW ERE FRESH MORNING STREAK THE EAST 4 623
AWAKE, THE MORNING SHINES, AND THE FRESH FIELD 5 20
AND LET US TO OUR FRESH IMPLOYMENTS RISE 5 125
TO HILL, OR VALLEY, FOUNTAIN, OR FRESH SHADE 5 203
ON FLOURS REPOS'D, AND WITH FRESH FLOURETS CROWND, 5 636
AND WITH FRESH FLOURETS HILL AND VALLEY SMIL'D. 6 784
AND THOU ENLIGHT'ND EARTH, SO FRESH AND GAY, 8 274
AND LIFE-BLOOD STREAMING FRESH; WIDE WAS THE WOUND, 8 467
JOYOUS THE BIRDS; FRESH GALES AND GENTLE AIRES 8 515
LEUCOTHEA WAK'D, AND WITH FRESH DEWS IMBALMD 11 135
GAZ'D HOT, AND OF THE FRESH WAVE LARGELY DREW, 11 845
FRESH IN THIR MINDES, FEARING THE DEITIE, 12 15
OUT OF HIS GRAVE, FRESH AS THE DAWNING LIGHT, 12 423

FRESHEST
AND HYACINTH, EARTHS FRESHEST SOFTEST LAP. 9 1041

FRET
ALL SOUNDS ON FRET BY STRING OR GOLDEN WIRE 7 597

FRETTED
THE ROOF WAS FRETTED GOLD. NOT BABILON, 1 717

FRIE
WITH FRIE INNUMERABLE SWARME, AND SHOALES 7 400

FRIEND
GO THEREFORE, HALF THIS DAY AS FRIEND WITH FRIEND 5 229
WITH MAN, AS WITH HIS FRIEND, FAMILIAR US'D 9 2
WHATEVER WILES OF FOE OR SEEMING FRIEND. 10 11
MANS FRIEND, HIS MEDIATOR, HIS DESIGN'D 10 60

FRIENDLIEST
FRIENDLIEST TO SLEEP AND SILENCE, HE RESOLV'D 5 668

FRIENDLY
BUT WITH NO FRIENDLY VOICE, AND ADD THY NAME 4 36
AMONG THOSE FRIENDLY POWERS WHO HIM RECEAV'D 6 22
THIS FRIENDLY CONDESCENTION TO RELATE 8 9
BE GOOD AND FRIENDLY STILL, AND OFT RETURN. 8 651
TO ME SO FRIENDLY GROWN ABOVE THE REST 9 564
FRIENDLY TO MAN, FARR FROM DECEIT OR GUILE. 9 772

FRIENDS
BUT WHEREFORE LET WE THEN OUR FAITHFUL FRIENDS, 1 264
O FRIENDS, I HEAR THE TREAD OF NIMBLE FEET 4 866
REMAINS THEE, AIDED BY THIS HOST OF FRIENDS, 6 38
O FRIENDS, WHY COME NOT ON THESE VICTORS PROUD? 6 609
HE LEAVES HIS GODS, HIS FRIENDS, AND NATIVE SOILE 12 129

FRIENDSHIP
RAISE OUT OF FRIENDSHIP HOSTIL DEEDS IN PEACE. 11 796

FRIERS
EMBRYO'S AND IDIOTS, EREMITS AND FRIERS 3 474

FRIGHT
WIDE WAVING, ALL APPROACH FARR OFF TO FRIGHT, 11 121

FRIGHTED
FRIGHTED THE REIGN OF CHAOS AND OLD NIGHT. 1 543
FLED NOT IN SILENCE THROUGH THE FRIGHTED DEEP 2 994

FRINGED
THAT TO THE FRINGED BANK WITH MYRTLE CROWND, 4 262

FRISKING
ALONE AS THEY. ABOUT THEM FRISKING PLAYD 4 340

FRITH
PONDERING HIS VOYAGE; FOR NO NARROW FRITH 2 919

FRIZL'D
AND BUSH WITH FRIZL'D HAIR IMPLICIT: LAST 7 323

FRO
FLIE TO AND FRO, OR ON THE SMOOTHED PLANK, 1 772
BOTH TO AND FRO, THIR SORROW TO AUGMENT, 2 605
WITH EASIE INTERCOURSE PASS TO AND FRO 2 1031
ON HIGH BEHESTS HIS ANGELS TO AND FRO 3 533
AND WRITH'D HIM TO AND FRO CONVOLV'D; SO SORE 6 328
FROM THIR FOUNDATIONS LOOSNING TO AND FRO 6 643
HURL'D TO AND FRO WITH JACULATION DIRE, 6 665

FROGS
FROGS, LICE AND FLIES MUST ALL HIS PALACE FILL 12 177

FRONT
ADVANC'T IN VIEW, THEY STAND, A HORRID FRONT 1 563
A PILLAR OF STATE; DEEP ON HIS FRONT ENGRAVEN 2 302
THY MISCREATED FRONT ATHWART MY WAY 2 683
OVER THE CASPIAN, THEN STAND FRONT TO FRONT 2 716
HIS FAIR LARGE FRONT AND EYE SUBLIME DECLAR'D 4 300
GABRIEL FROM THE FRONT THUS CALLD ALOUD. 4 865
A DREADFUL INTERVALL, AND FRONT TO FRONT 6 105
VANGUARD, TO RIGHT AND LEFT THE FRONT UNFOULD; 6 558
HAD ENDED; WHEN TO RIGHT AND LEFT THE FRONT 6 569
TO ENTERTAIN THEM FAIR WITH OPEN FRONT 6 611
HIS STATURE, AND UPRIGHT WITH FRONT SERENE 7 509
STICKS NO DISHONOR ON OUR FRONT, BUT TURNS 9 330
THIR MOTION, AT WHOSE FRONT A FLAMING SWORD, 12 592
HOMEWARD RETURNING. HIGH IN FRONT ADVANC'T, 12 632

FRONTED
WITH RAPID WHEELS, OR FRONTED BRIGADS FORM. 2 532

FRONTIER
AND ACCARON AND GAZA'S FRONTIER BOUNDS. 1 466

FRONTIERES
PURSUING. I UPON MY FRONTIERES HERE 2 998

FRONTISPICE
WITH FRONTISPICE OF DIAMOND AND GOLD 3 506

FRORE
BURNS FRORE, AND COLD PERFORMS TH' EFFECT OF FIRE. 2 595

FROST
SEED TIME AND HARVEST, HEAT AND HOARY FROST 11 899

FROWN
NO SECOND STROKE INTEND, AND SUCH A FROWN 2 713
GREW DARKER AT THIR FROWN, SO MATCHT THEY STOOD; 2 720

FROWN (CONTINUED)
DARK, WASTE, AND WILD, UNDER THE FROWN OF NIGHT 3 424
OR CAPTIVE DRAG'D IN CHAINS, WITH HOSTILE FROWN 6 260

FROWND
SO FROWND THE MIGHTY COMBATANTS, THAT HELL 2 719

FROWNING
HE ENDED FROWNING, AND HIS LOOK DENOUNC'D 2 106
TO WHICH THE FIEND THUS ANSWERD FROWNING STERN. 4 924

FROZEN
POUR'D NEVER FROM HER FROZEN LOYNS, TO PASS 1 352
BEYOND THIS FLOOD A FROZEN CONTINENT 2 587
IMMOVABLE, INFIXT, AND FROZEN ROUND, 2 602
O'RE MANY A FROZEN, MANY A FIERIE ALPE, 2 620

FRUGAL
SAVE WHAT BY FRUGAL STORING FIRMNESS GAINS 5 324
HOW NATURE WISE AND FRUGAL COULD COMMIT 8 26

FRUIT
OF MANS FIRST DISOBEDIENCE, AND THE FRUIT 1 1
OF GOODLIEST TREES LOADEN WITH FAIREST FRUIT, 4 147
HIGH EMINENT, BLOOMING AMBROSIAL FRUIT 4 219
OTHERS WHOSE FRUIT BURNISHT WITH GOLDEN RINDE 4 249
IN PARADISE THAT BEAR DELICIOUS FRUIT 4 422
HIS ORIENT BEAMS, ON HERB, TREE, FRUIT, AND FLOUR, 4 644
ON THIS DELIGHTFUL LAND, NOR HERB, FRUIT, FLOURE, 4 652
AND O FAIR PLANT, SAID HE, WITH FRUIT SURCHARG'D, 5 58
BUT HE THUS OVERJOY'D, O FRUIT DIVINE, 5 67
EVEN TO MY MOUTH OF THAT SAME FRUIT HELD PART 5 83
ALCINOUS REIGN'D, FRUIT OF ALL KINDES, IN COATE, 5 341
SPIRITS ODOROUS BREATHES: FLOURS AND THIR FRUIT 5 482
FRUIT OF DELICIOUS VINES, THE GROWTH OF HEAV'N. 5 635
WITH PLANT, FRUIT, FLOUR AMBROSIAL, GEMMS & GOLD, 6 475
AND FRUIT TREE YIELDING FRUIT AFTER HER KIND; 7 311
THIR BRANCHES HUNG WITH COPIOUS FRUIT; OR GEMM'D 7 325
AND FREELY ALL THIR PLEASANT FRUIT FOR FOOD 7 540
LOAD'N WITH FAIREST FRUIT THAT HUNG TO THE EYE 8 307
TO TILL AND KEEP, AND OF THE FRUIT TO EATE: 8 320
LOADEN WITH FRUIT OF FAIREST COLOURS MIXT, 9 577
OF THAT ALLURING FRUIT, URG'D ME SO KEENE. 9 588
THE VERTUE OF THAT FRUIT, IN THEE FIRST PROV'D: 9 616
AS LEAVES A GREATER STORE OF FRUIT UNTOUCHT, 9 621
FRUITLESS TO MEE, THOUGH FRUIT BE HERE TO EXCESS, 9 648
INDEED? HATH GOD THEN SAID THAT OF THE FRUIT 9 656
TO WHOM THUS EVE YET SINLESS. OF THE FRUIT 9 659
BUT OF THE FRUIT OF THIS FAIR TREE AMIDST 9 661
HOW SHOULD YE? BY THE FRUIT? IT GIVES YOU LIFE 9 686
CAUSES IMPORT YOUR NEED OF THIS FAIR FRUIT. 9 731
FIXT ON THE FRUIT SHE GAZ'D, WHICH TO BEHOLD 9 735
SO SAVORIE OF THAT FRUIT, WHICH WITH DESIRE, 9 741
OF THIS FAIR FRUIT, OUR DOOM IS, WE SHALL DIE. 9 763
HERE GROWS THE CURE OF ALL, THIS FRUIT DIVINE, 9 776
FORTH REACHING TO THE FRUIT, SHE PLUCK'D, SHE EAT: 9 781
IN FRUIT SHE NEVER TASTED, WHETHER TRUE 9 788
AND THY FAIR FRUIT LET HANG, AS TO NO END 9 798
A BOUGH OF FAIREST FRUIT THAT DOWNIE SMIL'D, 9 851
HATH EAT'N OF THE FRUIT, AND IS BECOME, 9 869
THE SACRED FRUIT FORBIDD'N. SOM CURSED FRAUD 9 904
THAT SACRED FRUIT, SACRED TO ABSTINENCE, 9 924
IS NOT SO HAINOUS NOW, FORETASTED FRUIT, 9 929
IF ANY BE, OF TASTING THIS FAIR FRUIT, 9 972
SHE GAVE HIM OF THAT FAIR ENTICING FRUIT 9 996
WHEREWITH TO SCORNE THE EARTH: BUT THAT FALSE FRUIT 9 1011
FROM THIS DELIGHTFUL FRUIT, NOR KNOWN TILL NOW 9 1023
SOON AS THE FORCE OF THAT FALLACIOUS FRUIT, 9 1046
BAD FRUIT OF KNOWLEDGE, IF THIS BE TO KNOW, 9 1073
THE FIGTREE, NOT THAT KIND FOR FRUIT RENOWN'D, 9 1101
HER HUSBAND SHEE, TO TASTE THE FATALL FRUIT, 10 4
THE HIGH INJUNCTION NOT TO TASTE THAT FRUIT, 10 13
THIR PENANCE, LADEN WITH FRUIT LIKE THAT 10 550
THIR APPETITE WITH GUST, INSTEAD OF FRUIT 10 565
BENEATH MAGELLAN. AT THAT TASTED FRUIT 10 687
FRUIT OF THY WOMB: ON MEE THE CURSE ASLOPE 10 1053
OF THAT DEFENDED FRUIT; BUT LET HIM BOAST 11 86
WITH WHOSE STOL'N FRUIT MAN ONCE MORE TO DELUDE. 11 125
WHICH THAT FALSE FRUIT THAT PROMIS'D CLEARER SIGHT 11 413
SO MAIST THOU LIVE, TILL LIKE RIPE FRUIT THOU DROP 11 535
WHAT IT DEVOURS NOT, HERB, OR FRUIT, OR GRAINE, 12 184

FRUITFUL
SEE GOLDEN DAYS, FRUITFUL OF GOLDEN DEEDS, 3 337
MORE FRUITFUL, WHICH INSTRUCTS US NOT TO SPARE. 5 320
HAILE MOTHER OF MANKIND, WHOSE FRUITFUL WOMB 5 388
BE FRUITFUL, MULTIPLY, AND IN THE SEAS 7 396
BE FRUITFUL, MULTIPLIE, AND FILL THE EARTH, 7 531
BUT IN THE FRUITFUL EARTH; THERE FIRST RECEAVD 8 96

FRUITION
GOD-LIKE FRUITION, QUITTED ALL TO SAVE 3 307
CASUAL FRUITION, NOR IN COURT AMOURS 4 767

FRUITLESS
FRUITLESS IMBRACES: OR THEY LED THE VINE 5 215
FRUITLESS TO MEE, THOUGH FRUIT BE HERE TO EXCESS, 9 648
THE FRUITLESS HOURS, BUT NEITHER SELF-CONDEMNING, 9 1188

FRUITS
REAPING IMMORTAL FRUITS OF JOY AND LOVE, 3 67
ALL WHO HAVE THIR REWARD ON EARTH, THE FRUITS 3 451
BLOSSOMS AND FRUITS AT ONCE OF GOLDEN HUE 4 148
MORE GRATEFUL, TO THIR SUPPER FRUITS THEY FELL, 4 331
NECTARINE FRUITS WHICH THE COMPLIANT BOUGHES 4 332
FOR DINNER SAVOURIE FRUITS, OF TASTE TO PLEASE 5 304
THEN WITH THESE VARIOUS FRUITS THE TREES OF GOD 5 390
TO ENTER, AND THESE EARTHLY FRUITS TO TASTE, 5 464
ROSE, AND WENT FORTH AMONG HER FRUITS AND FLOURS, 8 44
FRUITS IN HER SOFT'ND SOILE, FOR SOME TO EATE 8 147
THEN FRUITS OF PALM-TREE PLEASANTEST TO THIRST 8 212
I MEAN OF TASTE, SIGHT, SMELL, HERBS, FRUITS, AND FLOURS, 8 527
GREAT ARE THY VERTUES, DOUBTLESS, BEST OF FRUITS. 9 745
THOU THEREFORE ON THESE HERBS, AND FRUITS, AND FLOURS 10 603
SEE FATHER, WHAT FIRST FRUITS ON EARTH ARE SPRUNG 11 22
FRUITS OF MORE PLEASING SAVOUR FROM THY SEED 11 26
LESS PURE, ACCUSTOMD TO IMMORTAL FRUITS? 11 285
OFFER SWEET SMELLING GUMMS AND FRUITS AND FLOURS: 11 327
FIRST FRUITS, THE GREEN EARE, AND THE YELLOW SHEAF, 11 435
TO BRING FORTH FRUITS JOY AND ETERNAL BLISS. 12 551

FRUIT-TREES
OF FRUIT-TREES OVERWOODIE REACHD TOO FARR 5 213

FRUSTRATE
THEN WISE TO FRUSTRATE ALL OUR PLOTS AND WILES. 2 193
HIS END, AND FRUSTRATE THINE, SHALL HE FULFILL 3 157
BE FRUSTRATE, DO, UNDO, AND LABOUR LOOSE. 9 944
BLOW'N VAGABOND OR FRUSTRATE: IN THEY PASSD 11 16

FRUTAGE
OF LIFE AMBROSIAL FRUTAGE BEAR, AND VINES 5 427
THE FRUTAGE FAIR TO SIGHT, LIKE THAT WHICH GREW 10 561

FUGITIVE
FALSE FUGITIVE, AND TO THY SPEED ADD WINGS, 2 700
THOU SURELY HADST NOT COME SOLE FUGITIVE. 4 923
THRICE FUGITIVE ABOUT TROY WALL; OR RAGE 9 16

FUGITIVES
HEAV'NS FUGITIVES, AND FOR THIR DWELLING PLACE 2 57

FUGUE
FLED AND PURSU'D TRANSVERSE THE RESONANT FUGUE. 11 563

FULFIL
FULFILL'D, WHICH TO FULFIL IS ALL MY BLISS. 6 729
FULFIL OR GRAV'N IN METTLE. AFTER THESE, 11 573

FULFILL
AND WORKS OF LOVE OR ENMITY FULFILL. 1 431
HIS END, AND FRUSTRATE THINE, SHALL HE FULFILL 3 157
THAT HIS GREAT PURPOSE HE MIGHT SO FULFILL, 6 675
HOW WE MIGHT BEST FULFILL THE WORK WHICH HERE 9 230
THE LAW OF GOD EXACT HE SHALL FULFILL 12 402
ALONE FULFILL THE LAW; THY PUNISHMENT 12 404

FULFILL'D
FULFILL'D, WHICH TO FULFIL IS ALL MY BLISS. 6 729
AND THY REQUEST THINK NOW FULFILL'D, THAT ASK'D 7 635
THIS TURN HATH MADE AMENDS; THOU HAST FULFILL'D 8 491

FULFILLD
SO SPAKE TH' ETERNAL FATHER, AND FULFILLD 5 246
HERE NATURE SEEMS FULFILLD IN ALL HER ENDS. 11 602

FULFILLING
BUT BY FULFILLING THAT WHICH THOU DIDST WANT, 12 396

FULGENT
AT LAST AS FROM A CLOUD HIS FULGENT HEAD 10 449

FULL
WITH GAY RELIGIONS FULL OF POMP AND GOLD, 1 372
TH' IMPERIAL ENSIGN, WHICH FULL HIGH ADVANC'T 1 536
PUT FORTH AT FULL, BUT STILL HIS STRENGTH CONCEAL'D, 1 641
FULL COUNSEL MUST MATURE: PEACE IS DESPAIRD, 1 660
FREQUENT AND FULL. AFTER SHORT SILENCE THEN 1 797
YIELDED WITH FULL CONSENT. THE HAPPIER STATE 2 24
THOUGH FULL OF PAIN, THIS INTELLECTUAL BEING, 2 147
SPARKL'D IN ALL THIR EYES; WITH FULL ASSENT 2 388
WITH WIDE CERBERIAN MOUTHS FULL LOUD, AND RUNG 2 655
TO WHOM THE GOBLIN FULL OF WRAUTH REPLY'D, 2 688
THE MOST AVERSE, THEE CHIEFLY, WHO FULL OFT 2 763
AND ME HIS PARENT WOULD FULL SOON DEVOUR 2 805
THITHER FULL FRAUGHT WITH MISCHIEVOUS REVENGE, 2 1054
BENEATH THY SENTENCE; HELL HER NUMBERS FULL 3 332
THE FULL BLAZE OF THY BEAMS, AND THROUGH A CLOUD 3 378
IN FULL HARMONIC NUMBER JOIND, THIR SONGS 4 687
OUR CIRCUIT MEETS FULL WEST. AS FLAME THEY PART 4 784
FULL ORB'D THE MOON, AND WITH MORE PLEASING LIGHT 5 42
FULL TO THE UTMOST MEASURE OF WHAT BLISS 5 517
THE FULL RELATION, WHICH MUST NEEDS BE STRANGE, 5 556
OF SURFET WHERE FULL MEASURE ONELY BOUNDS 5 639

FULL (CONTINUED)
IN FULL RESPLENDENCE, HEIR OF ALL MY MIGHT, 5 720
HAD CIRCL'D HIS FULL ORBE, THE BIRTH MATURE 5 862
OF HARD CONTENTS, AND FULL OF FORCE URG'D HOME, 6 622
SHON FULL, HE ALL HIS FATHER FULL EXPREST 6 720
AND FULL OF WRAUTH BENT ON HIS ENEMIES. 6 826
ALL BUT THE THRONE IT SELF OF GOD. FULL SOON 6 834
GREAT THINGS, AND FULL OF WONDER IN OUR EARES, 7 70
HIS MIRROR, WITH FULL FACE BORROWING HER LIGHT 7 377
LIMB'D AND FULL GROWN: OUT OF THE GROUND UP ROSE 7 456
SQUAR'D IN FULL LEGION (SUCH COMMAND WE HAD) 8 232
THAT KEPT THIR WATCH; THENCE FULL OF ANGUISH DRIV'N, 9 62
OF THY FULL BRANCHES OFFER'D FREE TO ALL; 9 802
FULL HAPPINESS WITH MEE, OR RATHER NOT, 9 819
AND FULL OF PEACE, NOW TOST AND TURBULENT: 9 1126
BLAZ'D FORTH UNCLOUDED DEITIE; HE FULL 10 65
BUT UP AND ENTER NOW INTO FULL BLISS. 10 503
HIS FULL WRAUTH WHOSE THOU FEELST AS YET LEST PART, 10 951
LAMENTING TURND FULL SAD; O WHAT ARE THESE, 11 675
AND FULL OF PEACE, DENOUNCING WRAUTH TO COME 11 815
WITH PURPOSE TO RESIGN THEM IN FULL TIME 12 301
LIGHT OUT OF DARKNESS. FULL OF DOUBT I STAND, 12 473

FULL-BLAZING
SOMETIMES TOWARDS HEAV'N AND THE FULL-BLAZING SUN, 4 29

FULLY
HOW FULLY HAST THOU SATISFI'D MEE, PURE 8 180
THEM FULLY SATISFIED, AND THEE APPEASE. 10 79
WITH ODDS WHAT WARR HATH LOST, AND FULLY AVENG'D 10 374

FULNESS
IN WHOM THE FULNESS DWELS OF LOVE DIVINE, 3 225

FUM'D
WITH INCENSE, WHERE THE GOLDEN ALTAR FUM'D, 11 18

FUME
THEN ASMODEUS WITH THE FISHIE FUME, 4 168
IS THE PRIME WISDOM, WHAT IS MORE, IS FUME, 8 194

FUMES
BRED OF UNKINDLY FUMES, WITH CONSCIOUS DREAMS 9 1050

FUMING
OF LEAVES AND FUMING RILLS, AURORA'S FAN, 5 6
FUMING FROM GOLDEN CENSERS HID THE MOUNT. 7 600

FURDER
NOW RIS'N, TO WORK THEM FURDER WOE OR SHAME; 10 555
O EVE, SOME FURDER CHANGE AWAITS US NIGH, 11 193

FURIE
AS MANY MILES ALOFT: THAT FURIE STAY'D, 2 938
THE HORRID SHOCK: NOW STORMING FURIE ROSE, 6 207
LEVEL'D, WITH SUCH IMPETUOUS FURIE SMOTE, 6 591

FURIES
THITHER BY HARPY-FOOTED FURIES HAIL'D, 2 596
FIERCE AS TEN FURIES, TERRIBLE AS HELL, 2 671
WITH TERRORS AND WITH FURIES TO THE BOUNDS 6 859
LET IN THESE WASTFUL FURIES, WHO IMPUTE 10 620

FURIOUS
CAME FURIOUS DOWN TO BE REVENG'D ON MEN, 4 4
WITH FURIOUS EXPEDITION; FOR THEY WEEND 6 86
OF MOLOC FURIOUS KING, WHO HIM DEFI'D, 6 357
UP FROM THE BOTTOM TURN'D BY FURIOUS WINDES 7 213
TORMENT, AND LOUD LAMENT, AND FURIOUS RAGE. 8 244
TOWARDS THE RETREATING SEA THIR FURIOUS TYDE. 11 854

FURNACE
AS ONE GREAT FURNACE FLAM'D, YET FROM THOSE FLAMES 1 62
SO WIDE THEY STOOD, AND LIKE A FURNACE MOUTH 2 888

FURNITURE
OR TILTING FURNITURE, EMBLAZON'D SHIELDS, 9 34

FURTHER
BUT FURTHER WAY FOUND NONE, SO THICK ENTWIN'D, 4 174
WHAT FURTHER WOULD BE LEARNT. LIVE WHILE YE MAY, 4 533
CONCERN'D NOT MAN (SINCE HE NO FURTHER KNEW) 10 170
THE DOUBT, SINCE HUMANE REACH NO FURTHER KNOWS. 10 793
AND TEACH US FURTHER BY WHAT MEANS TO SHUN 10 1062
AND NOW WHAT FURTHER SHALL ENSUE, BEHOLD. 11 839
THIS FURTHER CONSOLATION YET SECURE 12 620

FURY
OR SATIATE FURY YIELD IT FROM OUR FOE. 1 179
SUBLIM'D WITH MINERAL FURY, AID THE WINDS, 1 235
ARM'D WITH HELL FLAMES AND FURY ALL AT ONCE 2 61
AGAINST THY ONLY SON? WHAT FURY O SON, 2 728
THE CURRENT OF HIS FURY THUS OPPOS'D, 5 808
ERE THIS HE HAD RETURN'D, WITH FURY DRIV'N 10 240

FUTURE
OF FUTURE DAYES MAY BRING, WHAT CHANCE, WHAT CHANGE 2 222

FUTURE (CONTINUED)
WHEREIN PAST, PRESENT, FUTURE HE BEHOLDS, 3 78
BY PRESENT, PAST, AND FUTURE) ON SUCH DAY 5 582
OF FUTURE WE MAY DEEM HIM, THOUGH TILL NOW 6 429
IN FUTURE DAYES, IF MALICE SHOULD ABOUND, 6 502
TO FUTURE MEN, AND IN THIR DWELLINGS PEACE: 7 183
OF FUTURE, IN SMALL ROOM LARGE HEART ENCLOS'D, 7 486
NOT INSTANT, BUT OF FUTURE TIME. WITH JOY 10 345
BEYOND ALL PAST EXAMPLE AND FUTURE, 10 840
TO ADAM WHAT SHALL COME IN FUTURE DAYES, 11 114
TO SHEW THEE WHAT SHALL COME IN FUTURE DAYES 11 357
LIV'D IGNORANT OF FUTURE, SO HAD BORNE 11 764
AND HEE THE FUTURE EVIL SHALL NO LESS 11 774
O THOU WHO FUTURE THINGS CANST REPRESENT 11 870

GABBLE
FORTHWITH A HIDEOUS GABBLE RISES LOUD 12 56

GABRIEL
BETWIXT THESE ROCKIE PILLARS GABRIEL SAT 4 549
GABRIEL, TO THEE THY COURSE BY LOT HATH GIV'N 4 561
WHEN GABRIEL TO HIS NEXT IN POWER THUS SPAKE. 4 781
GABRIEL FROM THE FRONT THUS CALLD ALOUD. 4 865
TO WHOM WITH STERN REGARD THUS GABRIEL SPAKE. 4 877
GABRIEL, THOU HADST IN HEAV'N TH' ESTEEM OF WISE, 4 886
WHICH GABRIEL SPYING, THUS BESPAKE THE FIEND. 4 1005
GABRIEL, LEAD FORTH TO BATTEL THESE MY SONS 6 46
MEMORIAL, WHERE THE MIGHT OF GABRIEL FOUGHT, 6 355
OF GABRIEL OUT OF EDEN, NOW IMPROV'D 9 54

GAIN
WHAT REINFORCEMENT WE MAY GAIN FROM HOPE, 1 190
HAVOCK AND SPOIL AND RUIN ARE MY GAIN. 2 1009
OR WHOM HE WISHES MOST SHALL SELDOM GAIN 10 901
DIVIDED, TILL HIS RESCU'D GAIN THIR SHOAR: 12 199
THIS ALSO SHALL THEY GAIN BY THIR DELAY 12 223

GAIN'D
A LEPER ONCE HE LOST AND GAIN'D A KING, 1 471
YET LET ME NOT FORGET WHAT I HAVE GAIN'D 4 512
PERMISSIVE, AND ACCEPTANCE FOUND, WHICH GAIN'D 8 435
WHAT THY HANDS BUILDED NOT, THY WISDOM GAIN'D 10 373

GAIND
AND WHEN HIGH NOON HAST GAIND, AND WHEN THOU FALLST. 5 174
OF HER ATTENTION GAIND, WITH SERPENT TONGUE 9 529
THROUGH HER PERVERSNESS, BUT SHALL SEE HER GAIND 10 902

GAINE
THEE ONCE TO GAINE COMPANION OF HIS WOE. 6 907
AND NO ADVANTAGE GAINE. WHAT IF THE SUN 8 122
BY US? WHO RATHER DOUBLE HONOUR GAINE 9 332

GAINES
THOUGH DISTANT FARR SOM SMALL REFLECTION GAINES 3 428
LIVES, AS THOU SAIDST, AND GAINES TO LIVE AS MAN 9 933

GAINING
AT ONCE, BY MY FOREKNOWLEDGE GAINING BIRTH 11 768

GAINS
SAVE WHAT BY FRUGAL STORING FIRMNESS GAINS 5 324

GAINSAY
TOO FACIL THEN THOU DIDST NOT MUCH GAINSAY, 9 1158

GALAXIE
SEEN IN THE GALAXIE, THAT MILKIE WAY 7 579

GALES
ALL SADNESS BUT DESPAIR: NOW GENTLE GALES 4 156
JOYOUS THE BIRDS; FRESH GALES AND GENTLE AIRES 8 515

GALILEO
OF GALILEO, LESS ASSUR'D, OBSERVES 5 262

GAMBOLD
GAMBOLD BEFORE THEM, TH' UNWIELDY ELEPHANT 4 345

GAME
INFERNAL NOISE; WARR SEEM'D A CIVIL GAME 6 667
ALL NOW WAS TURN'D TO JOLLITIE AND GAME, 11 714
HUNTING (AND MEN NOT BEASTS SHALL BE HIS GAME) 12 30

GAMES
AS AT TH' OLYMPIAN GAMES OR PYTHIAN FIELDS; 2 530
ABOUT HIM EXERCIS'D HEROIC GAMES 4 551
UNSUNG; OR TO DESCRIBE RACES AND GAMES, 9 33

GAMESOM
TO WHOM THUS BELIAL IN LIKE GAMESOM MOOD, 6 620

'GAN
TILL ADAM THUS 'GAN EVE TO DALLIANCE MOVE, 9 1016

GAN
ETHEREAL TRUMPET FROM ON HIGH GAN BLOW: 6 60

GAN (CONTINUED)
BEAST NOW WITH BEAST GAN WAR, AND FOWLE WITH FOWLE, 10 710

GANGES
OF GANGES OR HYDASPES, INDIAN STREAMS; 3 436
GANGES AND INDUS: THUS THE ORB HE ROAM'D 9 82

GAP
ROWLD INWARD, AND A SPACIOUS GAP DISCLOS'D 6 861

GAPING
WIDE GAPING, AND WITH UTTER LOSS OF BEING 2 440

GAP'T
WITH HIDEOUS ORIFICE GAP'T ON US WIDE, 6 577

GARB
THUS BELIAL WITH WORDS CLOATH'D IN REASONS GARB 2 226

GARDEN
OF MANKIND, IN THE HAPPIE GARDEN PLAC'T, 3 66
OF GOD THE GARDEN WAS, BY HIM IN THE EAST 4 209
HIS FARR MORE PLEASANT GARDEN GOD ORDAIND; 4 215
THAT MOUNTAIN AS HIS GARDEN MOULD HIGH RAIS'D 4 226
WATERD THE GARDEN; THENCE UNITED FELL 4 230
FROM THIS ASSYRIAN GARDEN, WHERE THE FIEND 4 285
THIS GARDEN, AND NO CORNER LEAVE UNSPI'D; 4 529
SEARCH THROUGH THIS GARDEN, LEAVE UNSEARCHT NO NOOK, 4 789
TO REST, AND WHAT THE GARDEN CHOICEST BEARS 5 368
THEN WHAT THIS GARDEN IS TO ALL THE EARTH, 5 752
THIS GARDEN, PLANTED WITH THE TREES OF GOD, 7 538
TO THE GARDEN OF BLISS, THY SEAT PREPAR'D, 8 299
OF EVERY TREE THAT IN THE GARDEN GROWES 8 321
AMID THE GARDEN BY THE TREE OF LIFE, 8 326
THIS GARDEN, STILL TO TEND PLANT, HERB AND FLOUR, 9 206
OF ALL THESE GARDEN TREES YE SHALL NOT EATE, 9 657
OF EACH TREE IN THE GARDEN WE MAY EATE, 9 660
THE GARDEN, GOD HATH SAID, YE SHALL NOT EATE 9 662
NOW WALKING IN THE GARDEN, BY SOFT WINDES 10 98
I HEARD THEE IN THE GARDEN, AND OF THY VOICE 10 116
IN THIS DELICIOUS GARDEN? AS MY WILL 10 746
AND SEND HIM FROM THE GARDEN FORTH TO TILL 11 97
AND ON THE EAST SIDE OF THE GARDEN PLACE, 11 118
POSSESSION OF THE GARDEN; HEE ALONE, 11 222
AND SEND THEE FROM THE GARDEN FORTH TO TILL 11 261

GARDEN-PLOT
OF GROVE OR GARDEN-PLOT MORE PLEASANT LAY, 9 418

GARDENS
LIKE THOSE HESPERIAN GARDENS FAM'D OF OLD, 3 568
SPOT MORE DELICIOUS THEN THOSE GARDENS FEIGN'D 9 439

GARD'N
EARTH AND THE GARD'N OF GOD, WITH CEDARS CROWND 5 260

GARDNING
OF THIR SWEET GARDNING LABOUR THEN SUFFIC'D 4 328
THE HANDS DISPATCH OF TWO GARDNING SO WIDE. 9 203
BUT WITH SUCH GARDNING TOOLS AS ART YET RUDE, 9 391

GARLAND
OF CHOICEST FLOURS A GARLAND TO ADORNE 9 840
FROM HIS SLACK HAND THE GARLAND WREATH'D FOR EVE 9 892

GARLANDS
NOW IN LOOSE GARLANDS THICK THROWN OFF, THE BRIGHT 3 362
WITH FLOWERS, GARLANDS, AND SWEET-SMELLING HERBS 4 709
OF LOVE AND YOUTH NOT LOST, SONGS, GARLANDS, FLOURS, 11 594

GASH
NOT LONG DIVISIBLE, AND FROM THE GASH 6 331

GASTLY
GRINND HORRIBLE A GASTLY SMILE, TO HEAR 2 846
MANGL'D WITH GASTLY WOUNDS THROUGH PLATE AND MAILE, 6 368
OF GASTLY SPASM, OR RACKING TORTURE, QUALMES 11 481

GATE
FAST BY HELL GATE, AND KEPT THE FATAL KEY, 2 725
T' WHOM THUS THE PORTRESS OF HELL GATE REPLY'D; 2 746
AND TOWARDS THE GATE ROULING HER BESTIAL TRAIN, 2 873
THE WORK AS OF A KINGLY PALACE GATE 3 505
AND WAKING CRI'D, THIS IS THE GATE OF HEAV'N 3 515
THAT SCAL'D BY STEPS OF GOLD TO HEAV'N GATE 3 541
AT WISDOMS GATE, AND TO SIMPLICITIE 3 687
ONE GATE THERE ONLY WAS, AND THAT LOOK'D EAST 4 178
AGAINST THE EASTERN GATE OF PARADISE 4 542
BENT ALL ON SPEED, AND MARKT HIS AERIE GATE; 4 568
SEE FARR AND WIDE: IN AT THIS GATE NONE PASS 4 579
BUT FADED SPLENDOR WAN; WHO BY HIS GATE 4 870
THAT SINGING UP TO HEAVEN GATE ASCEND, 5 198
THROUGH ALL TH' EMPYREAL ROAD; TILL AT THE GATE 5 253
OF HEAV'N ARRIV'D, THE GATE SELF-OPEND WIDE 5 254
WALLOWING UNWEILDIE, ENORMOUS IN THIR GATE 7 411
FROM HEAVEN GATE NOT FARR, FOUNDED IN VIEW 7 618

GATE (CONTINUED)
IN GATE SURPASS'D AND GODDESS-LIKE DEPORT, 9 389
FROM EARTH ARRIV'D AT HEAVEN GATE, DISPLEAS'D 10 22
ACCOMPANIED TO HEAVEN GATE, FROM WHENCE 10 88
AND WITH ASPHALTIC SLIME; BROAD AS THE GATE, 10 298
THE CAUSEY TO HELL GATE; ON EITHER SIDE 10 415
THAT SCORN'D HIS INDIGNATION: THROUGH THE GATE, 10 418
DIRECT TO TH' EASTERN GATE WAS BENT THIR FLIGHT. 11 190
ONE OF THE HEAV'NLY HOST, AND BY HIS GATE 11 230
AND TO THE FAITHFUL DEATH THE GATE OF LIFE; 12 571
OUR LINGRING PARENTS, AND TO TH' EASTERN GATE 12 638
WAV'D OVER BY THAT FLAMING BRAND, THE GATE 12 643

GATES
BACK TO THE GATES OF HEAV'N: THE SULPHUROUS HAIL 1 171
HIS SWIFT PURSUERS FROM HEAV'N GATES DISCERN 1 326
ATTENDED: ALL ACCESS WAS THRONG'D, THE GATES 1 761
NINEFOLD, AND GATES OF BURNING ADAMANT 2 436
PUTS ON SWIFT WINGS, AND TOWARDS THE GATES OF HELL 2 631
AND THRICE THREEFOLD THE GATES; THREE FOLDS WERE BRASS, 2 645
YET UNCONSUM'D. BEFORE THE GATES THERE SAT 2 648
TO YONDER GATES? THROUGH THEM I MEAN TO PASS, 2 684
THESE GATES FOR EVER SHUT, WHICH NONE CAN PASS 2 776
THESE ADAMANTINE GATES; AGAINST ALL FORCE 2 853
EXCEL'D HER POWER; THE GATES WIDE OP'N STOOD, 2 884
CONFUSION WORSE CONFOUNDED; AND HEAV'N GATES 2 996
TO ENTERTAIN YOU TWO, HER WIDEST GATES, 4 382
HIS IRON GATES, IF HE INTENDS OUR STAY 4 898
THE FACIL GATES OF HELL TOO SLIGHTLY BARRD. 4 967
UNBARR'D THE GATES OF LIGHT. THERE IS A CAVE 6 4
HER EVER DURING GATES, HARMONIOUS SOUND 7 206
OPEN, YE EVERLASTING GATES, THEY SUNG, 7 565
FARR ON EXCURSION TOWARD THE GATES OF HELL; 8 231
THE DISMAL GATES, AND BARRICADO'D STRONG; 8 241
WITHIN THE GATES OF HELL SATE SIN AND DEATH, 10 230
IN COUNTERVIEW WITHIN THE GATES, THAT NOW 10 231
THEN BOTH FROM OUT HELL GATES INTO THE WASTE 10 282
WITHIN HELL GATES TILL NOW, THOU US IMPOW'RD 10 369
CITIES OF MEN WITH LOFTY GATES AND TOWRS, 11 640
TO COUNCIL IN THE CITIE GATES: ANON 11 661

GATH
OF PALESTINE, IN GATH AND ASCALON 1 465

GATHER'D
BE GATHER'D NOW YE WATERS UNDER HEAV'N 7 283
HER GATHER'D BEAMS, GREAT PALACE NOW OF LIGHT. 7 363
DEEP TO THE ROOTS OF HELL THE GATHER'D BEACH 10 299
LEAVE COLD THE NIGHT, HOW WE HIS GATHER'D BEAMS 10 1070

GATHERD
WAS GATHERD, WHICH COST CERES ALL THAT PAIN 4 271
NEW GATHERD, AND AMBROSIAL SMELL DIFFUS'D. 9 852
THEY GATHERD, BROAD AS AMAZONIAN TARGE, 9 1111
THENCE GATHERD HIS OWN DOOM, WHICH UNDERSTOOD 10 344
GATHERD, NOT HARSHLY PLUCKT, FOR DEATH MATURE: 11 537

GATHERED
HAVE GATHERED AUGHT OF EVIL OR CONCEALD, 5 207

GATHERING
OF ENNA, WHERE PROSERPIN GATHERING FLOURS 4 269

GATHERS
THAWS NOT, BUT GATHERS HEAP, AND RUIN SEEMS 2 590
SHE GATHERS, TRIBUTE LARGE, AND ON THE BOARD 5 343
AND GATHERS GROUND FAST AT THE LABOURERS HEEL 12 631

GAVE
EXALTED TO SUCH POWER, AND GAVE TO RULE, 1 736
WHICH TO OUR GENERAL SIRE GAVE PROSPECT LARGE 4 144
GAVE PROOF UNHEEDED; OTHERS ON THE GRASS 4 350
ACCEPT YOUR MAKERS WORK; HE GAVE IT ME, 4 380
THAT NEER HIM STOOD, AND GAVE THEM THUS IN CHARGE. 4 787
GAVE HEED, BUT WAXING MORE IN RAGE REPLI'D. 4 969
ON EACH HAND PARTING, TO HIS SPEED GAVE WAY 5 252
THY MAKING, WHILE THE MAKER GAVE THEE BEING? 5 858
GAVE THEM ABOVE THIR FOES, NOT TO HAVE SINND, 6 402
HIS WORD, THE FILIAL GODHEAD, GAVE EFFECT. 7 175
GAVE THEE, ALL SORTS ARE HERE THAT ALL TH' EARTH YIELDS, 7 541
GAVE SIGN OF GRATULATION, AND EACH HILL; 8 514
THAT GAVE THEE BEING, STILL SHADES THEE AND PROTECTS. 9 266
GAVE ELOCUTION TO THE MUTE, AND TAUGHT 9 748
SIGHING THROUGH ALL HER WORKS GAVE SIGNS OF WOE, 9 783
SHE GAVE HIM OF THAT FAIR ENTICING FRUIT 9 996
IN PANGS, AND NATURE GAVE A SECOND GROAN, 9 1001
AT LENGTH GAVE UTTERANCE TO THESE WORDS CONSTRAIND. 9 1066
WHEREOF I GAVE THEE CHARGE THOU SHOULDST NOT EAT? 10 123
SHEE GAVE ME OF THE TREE, AND I DID EATE. 10 143
DEPARTING GAVE COMMAND, AND THEY OBSERV'D. 10 430
HIS MIGHTIE ANGELS GAVE THEM SEVERAL CHARGE, 10 650
THE LAW I GAVE TO NATURE HIM FORBIDS: 11 49
HE ENDED, AND THE SON GAVE SIGNAL HIGH 11 72
SUBSCRIB'D NOT; NATURE FIRST GAVE SIGNS, IMPREST 11 182
FROM THE FIRST OP'NING BUD, AND GAVE YE NAMES, 11 277

GAVE (CONTINUED)
ALL TH' EARTH HE GAVE THEE TO POSSESS AND RULE, 11 339
HIS BEST OF MAN, AND GAVE HIM UP TO TEARS 11 497
HE GAVE US ONELY OVER BEAST, FISH, FOWL 12 67

GAV'ST
MY BEING GAV'ST ME; WHOM SHOULD I OBEY 2 865
AND THOU THIR NATURES KNOW'ST, & GAV'ST THEM NAMES, 7 493
AND GAV'ST ME AS THY PERFET GIFT, SO GOOD, 10 138

GAY
WITH GAY RELIGIONS FULL OF POMP AND GOLD, 1 372
APPEERD, WITH GAY ENAMELD COLOURS MIXT: 4 149
WHAT THOU AND THY GAY LEGIONS DARE AGAINST; 4 942
OP'NING THIR VARIOUS COLOURS, AND MADE GAY 7 318
THE SILENT HOURS, AND TH' OTHER WHOSE GAY TRAINE 7 444
AND THOU ENLIGHT'ND EARTH, SO FRESH AND GAY, 8 274
EACH FLOUR OF SLENDER STALK, WHOSE HEAD THOUGH GAY 9 428
A BEAVIE OF FAIR WOMEN, RICHLY GAY 11 582
OF GODDESSES, SO BLITHE, SO SMOOTH, SO GAY, 11 615
CONSPICUOUS WITH THREE LIFTED COLOURS GAY, 11 866

GAYEST
TWO BIRDS OF GAYEST PLUME BEFORE HIM DROVE: 11 186

GAZA'S
AND ACCARON AND GAZA'S FRONTIER BOUNDS. 1 466

GAZ'D
AMBROSIA; ON THAT TREE HE ALSO GAZ'D; 5 57
A PHOENIX, GAZ'D BY ALL, AS THAT SOLE BIRD 5 272
AND GAZ'D A WHILE THE AMPLE SKIE, TILL RAIS'D 8 258
FIXT ON THE FRUIT SHE GAZ'D, WHICH TO BEHOLD 9 735
GAZ'D HOT, AND OF THE FRESH WAVE LARGELY DREW, 11 845

GAZE
HERE MATTER NEW TO GAZE THE DEVIL MET 3 613
THAT I MAY FIND HIM, AND WITH SECRET GAZE, 3 671
WHEN SATAN STILL IN GAZE, AS FIRST HE STOOD, 4 356
ATTRACTED BY THY BEAUTY STILL TO GAZE. 5 47
HOSANNA TO THE HIGHEST; NOR STOOD AT GAZE 6 205
BUT AS IN GAZE ADMIRING: OFT HE BOWD 9 524
DISPLEAS'D THAT I APPROACH THEE THUS, AND GAZE 9 535
THEE ALL THINGS LIVING GAZE ON, ALL THINGS THINE 9 539
RUDDIE AND GOLD: I NEARER DREW TO GAZE; 9 578
AND GAZE, AND WORSHIP THEE OF RIGHT DECLAR'D 9 611

GAZING
COUCHT, AND NOW FILD WITH PASTURE GAZING SAT, 4 351

GEHENNA
AND BLACK GEHENNA CALL'D THE TYPE OF HELL. 1 405

GEMM'D
THIR BRANCHES HUNG WITH COPIOUS FRUIT; OR GEMM'D 7 325

GEMMES
IMBELLISHT, THICK WITH SPARKLING ORIENT GEMMES 3 507

GEMMS
WITH GEMMS AND GOLDEN LUSTRE RICH IMBLAZ'D, 1 538
WANTS NOT HER HIDDEN LUSTRE, GEMMS AND GOLD; 2 271
AND THESE THE GEMMS OF HEAV'N, HER STARRIE TRAIN: 4 649
WITH PLANT, FRUIT, FLOUR AMBROSIAL, GEMMS & GOLD, 6 475

GEMS
IN GEMS AND WANTON DRESS; TO THE HARP THEY SUNG 11 583

GENERAL
EGYPT FROM SYRIAN GROUND, HAD GENERAL NAMES 1 421
THAT FOR THE GENERAL SAFETY HE DESPIS'D 2 481
INTO THIS DEEP, AND IN THE GENERAL FALL 2 773
OF ALL PAST AGES TO THE GENERAL DOOM 3 328
WHICH TO OUR GENERAL SIRE GAVE PROSPECT LARGE 4 144
SO SPAKE OUR GENERAL MOTHER, AND WITH EYES 4 492
TO WHOM OUR GENERAL ANCESTOR REPLI'D. 4 659
TO SOUND AT GENERAL DOOM. TH' ANGELIC BLAST 11 76

GENERALS
YET TO THIR GENERALS VOYCE THEY SOON OBEYD 1 337

GENERATE
AND GOD SAID, LET THE WATERS GENERATE 7 387
OR FIND SOME OTHER WAY TO GENERATE 10 894

GENERATED
THE WATERS GENERATED BY THIR KINDES, 7 393

GENERATION
A GENERATION, WHOM HIS CHOICE REGARD 1 653
HIS GENERATION, AND THE RISING BIRTH 7 102

GENERATIONS
ALL GENERATIONS, AND HAD HITHER COME 11 344

GENIAL
WHAT DAY THE GENIAL ANGEL TO OUR SIRE 4 712
SATIATE WITH GENIAL MOISTURE, WHEN GOD SAID 7 282

GIVN (CONTINUED)
LIE VANQUISHT; THOU HAST GIVN ME TO POSSESS 3 243

GIV'ST
AND GIV'ST ACCESS, THOUGH SECRET SHE RETIRE. 9 810

GLAD
BUT GLAD THAT NOW HIS SEA SHOULD FIND A SHORE, 2 1011
GLAD TO BE OFFER'D, HE ATTENDS THE WILL 3 270
GLAD WAS THE SPIRIT IMPURE AS NOW IN HOPE 3 630
ON WHICH THE SUN MORE GLAD IMPRESS'D HIS BEAMS 4 150
MY GLORIE, MY PERFECTION, GLAD I SEE 5 29
AND FELL ASLEEP; BUT O HOW GLAD I WAK'D 5 92
SURCEAS'D, AND GLAD AS HOPING HERE TO END 6 258
HASTED WITH GLAD PRECIPITANCE, UPROWLD 7 291
GLAD EEVNING AND GLAD MORN CROWND THE FOURTH DAY. 7 386
GLAD WE RETURN'D UP TO THE COASTS OF LIGHT 8 245
EATE FREELY WITH GLAD HEART; FEAR HERE NO DEARTH: 8 322
THE EYE OF EVE TO MARK HIS PLAY; HE GLAD 9 528
TO WHOM THE WILIE ADDER, BLITHE AND GLAD. 9 625
WHOM THUS THE PRINCE OF DARKNESS ANSWERD GLAD. 10 383
INSENSIBLE, HOW GLAD WOULD LAY ME DOWN 10 777
BEFORE THE FATHERS THRONE: THEM THE GLAD SON 11 20
GLAD TO BE SO DISMIST IN PEACE. CAN THUS 11 507
O PROPHET OF GLAD TIDINGS, FINISHER 12 375

GLADE
DOWN THE STEEP GLADE, AND MET THE NEATHER FLOOD, 4 231
IN SOLITUDE LIVE SAVAGE, IN SOME GLADE 9 1085

GLADLIER
AND GLADLIER SHALL RESIGN, WHEN IN THE END 6 731
AND TOUCHT BY HER FAIR TENDANCE GLADLIER GREW. 8 47

GLADLY
GLADLY THE PORT, THOUGH SHROUDS AND TACKLE TORN; 2 1044
TO HAVE REPORTED; GLADLY THEN HE MIXT 6 21
GLADLY INTO THE WAYES OF GOD WITH MAN: 8 226
AND GLADLY OF OUR UNION HEARE THEE SPEAK, 9 966
TO DEATHLESS PAIN? HOW GLADLY WOULD I MEET 10 775
GLADLY BEHOLD THOUGH BUT HIS UTMOST SKIRTS 11 332
THEY GLADLY THITHER HASTE, AND BY A QUIRE 12 366

GLANC'D
GLANC'D ON THE GROUND, WITH LABOUR I MUST EARNE 10 1054

GLANCE
OF CORAL STRAY, OR SPORTING WITH QUICK GLANCE 7 405
AGAINST THE CHARM OF BEAUTIES POWERFUL GLANCE. 8 533
SO SAID HE, AND FORBORE NOT GLANCE OR TOY 9 1034
CONSUM'D WITH NIMBLE GLANCE, AND GRATEFUL STEAME; 11 442

GLAR'D
GLAR'D LIGHTNING, AND SHOT FORTH PERNICIOUS FIRE 6 849
GLAR'D ON HIM PASSING: THESE WERE FROM WITHOUT 10 714

GLARE
A LION NOW HE STALKES WITH FIERIE GLARE, 4 402

GLASS
THROUGH OPTIC GLASS THE TUSCAN ARTIST VIEWS 1 288
ABOVE ALL HILLS. AS WHEN BY NIGHT THE GLASS 5 261
AND THE CLEER SUN ON HIS WIDE WATRIE GLASS 11 844

GLASSIE
ON THE CLEER HYALINE, THE GLASSIE SEA; 7 619

GLAZ'D
THROUGH HIS GLAZ'D OPTIC TUBE YET NEVER SAW. 3 590

GLEAM
A SHAPE WITHIN THE WATRY GLEAM APPEERD 4 461

GLEAME
AND LONG HE WANDERD, TILL AT LAST A GLEAME 3 499
SHALL REST BY DAY, A FIERY GLEAME BY NIGHT, 12 257

GLIDE
YEE THAT IN WATERS GLIDE, AND YEE THAT WALK 5 200
GLIDE UNDER THE GREEN WAVE, IN SCULLES THAT OFT 7 402
OF MIDNIGHT VAPOR GLIDE OBSCURE, AND PRIE 9 159

GLIDES
RIS'N FROM A RIVER O'RE THE MARISH GLIDES, 12 630

GLIDING
THITHER CAME URIEL, GLIDING THROUGH THE EEVEN 4 555
DOWN TO THE VEINS OF EARTH, THENCE GLIDING HOT 11 568
GLIDING METEOROUS, AS EV'NING MIST 12 629

GLIMMERING
SAVE WHAT THE GLIMMERING OF THESE LIVID FLAMES 1 182
A GLIMMERING DAWN; HERE NATURE FIRST BEGINS 2 1037
OF GLIMMERING AIR LESS VEXT WITH TEMPEST LOUD: 3 429

GLIMPS
OBSCURE SOME GLIMPS OF JOY, TO HAVE FOUND THIR CHIEF 1 524

GLIMPS (CONTINUED)
HASTING THIS WAY, AND NOW BY GLIMPS DISCERNE 4 867
LIGHT AS THE LIGHTNING GLIMPS THEY RAN, THEY FLEW, 6 642
EACH ORB A GLIMPS OF LIGHT, CONVEYD SO FARR 8 156

GLISTER'D
SO GLISTER'D THE DIRE SNAKE, AND INTO FRAUD 9 643

GLISTERING
WITH GLISTERING SPIRES AND PINNACLES ADORND, 3 550
NOR GLISTERING, MAY OF SOLID GOOD CONTAINE 8 93
AS IN A GLISTERING ZODIAC HUNG THE SWORD, 11 247

GLISTRING
GLISTRING WITH DEW; FRAGRANT THE FERTIL EARTH 4 645
GLISTRING WITH DEW, NOR FRAGRANCE AFTER SHOWERS, 4 653

GLITTER
WAS LEFT HIM, OR FALSE GLITTER: ALL AMAZ'D 10 452

GLITTERING
WHO FORTHWITH FROM THE GLITTERING STAFF UNFURLD 1 535
HARPS EVER TUN'D, THAT GLITTERING BY THIR SIDE 3 366
OR GLITTERING STARR-LIGHT WITHOUT THEE IS SWEET. 4 656
THIR GLITTERING TENTS HE PASSD, AND NOW IS COME 5 291
OR IN THIR GLITTERING TISSUES BEAR IMBLAZ'D 5 592

GLOBE
RIVERS OR MOUNTAINS IN HER SPOTTY GLOBE. 1 291
A GLOBE OF FIERIE SERAPHIM INCLOS'D 2 512
MEAN WHILE UPON THE FIRM OPACOUS GLOBE 3 418
SATAN ALIGHTED WALKS: A GLOBE FARR OFF 3 422
ALL THIS DARK GLOBE THE FIEND FOUND AS HE PASS'D, 3 498
LOOK DOWNWARD ON THAT GLOBE WHOSE HITHER SIDE 3 722
WHICH THEY BEHELD, THE MOONS RESPLENDENT GLOBE 4 723
PROLIFIC HUMOUR SOFT'NING ALL HER GLOBE, 7 280
OBLIQUE THE CENTRIC GLOBE: SOM SAY THE SUN 10 671

GLOBES
NOT UNCONFORM TO OTHER SHINING GLOBES, 5 259
OF IRON GLOBES, WHICH ON THE VICTOR HOST 6 590

GLOBOSE
AND ALL THE SEA, FROM ONE ENTIRE GLOBOSE 5 753
GLOBOSE, AND EVERY MAGNITUDE OF STARRS, 7 357

GLOBOUS
THEN ALL THIS GLOBOUS EARTH IN PLAIN OUT SPRED, 5 649

GLOOM
THAT WE MUST CHANGE FOR HEAV'N, THIS MOURNFUL GLOOM 1 244
ALL IN A MOMENT THROUGH THE GLOOM WERE SEEN 1 544
PURGE OFF THIS GLOOM; THE SOFT DELICIOUS AIR, 2 400
INTO THIS GLOOM OF TARTARUS PROFOUND, 2 858
TO JOURNIE THROUGH THE AIRIE GLOOM BEGAN, 7 246
ACCOMPANIED, WITH DAMPS AND DREADFUL GLOOM, 10 848

GLOOMIE
WHAT READIEST PATH LEADS WHERE YOUR GLOOMIE BOUNDS 2 976
UNDER HIS GLOOMIE POWER I SHALL NOT LONG 3 242
HER SELF A FAIRER FLOURE BY GLOOMIE DIS 4 270
GLOOMIE AS NIGHT; UNDER HIS BURNING WHEELES 6 832

GLOOMIEST
ALREADIE IN PART, THOUGH HID IN GLOOMIEST SHADE, 10 716

GLOOMY
OR DO HIS ERRANDS IN THE GLOOMY DEEP; 1 152

GLORIE
THROUGH HEAV'N AND EARTH, SO SHALL MY GLORIE EXCEL, 3 133
FOR HIM, WHAT FOR THY GLORIE THOU HAST MADE? 3 164
THY BOSOM, AND THIS GLORIE NEXT TO THEE 3 239
IMPRESST THE EFFULGENCE OF HIS GLORIE ABIDES, 3 388
BUILT THIR FOND HOPES OF GLORIE OR LASTING FAME, 3 449
THAT GLORIE THEN, WHEN THOU NO MORE WAST GOOD, 4 838
OR ALL AT ONCE; MORE GLORIE WILL BE WONN, 4 853
MY GLORIE, MY PERFECTION, GLAD I SEE 5 29
THE STRIFE OF GLORIE; WHICH WE MEAN TO WIN, 6 290
AND IGNOMINIE, YET TO GLORIE ASPIRES 6 383
HONOUR, DOMINION, GLORIE, AND RENOWNE, 6 422
EFFULGENCE OF MY GLORIE, SON BELOV'D, 6 680
HAVE SUFFERD, THAT THE GLORIE MAY BE THINE 6 701
AS IS MOST JUST; THIS I MY GLORIE ACCOUNT, 6 726
FROM THE RIGHT HAND OF GLORIE WHERE HE SATE, 6 747
GRIEVING TO SEE HIS GLORIE, AT THE SIGHT 6 792
KINGDOM AND POWER AND GLORIE APPERTAINS, 6 815
ON HIGH: WHO INTO GLORIE HIM RECEAV'D, 6 891
GLORIE THEY SUNG TO THE MOST HIGH, GOOD WILL 7 182
GLORIE TO HIM WHOSE JUST AVENGING IRE 7 184
GLORIE AND PRAISE, WHOSE WISDOM HAD ORDAIN'D 7 187
THE KING OF GLORIE IN HIS POWERFUL WORD 7 208
UPLIFTED, IN PATERNAL GLORIE RODE 7 219
NOW HEAV'N IN ALL HER GLORIE SHON, AND ROWLD 7 499
WITH GLORIE ATTRIBUTED TO THE HIGH 8 12
TO MEE SHALL BE THE GLORIE SOLE AMONG 9 135
TO THAT FIRST NAKED GLORIE. SUCH OF LATE 9 1115
TOWARD THE RIGHT HAND HIS GLORIE, ON THE SON 10 64

GLORIE (CONTINUED)
OF HIGH COLLATERAL GLORIE: HIM THRONES AND POWERS, 10 86
OF SATAN (FOR I GLORIE IN THE NAME, 10 386
OF HUMAN GLORIE, AND FOR GLORIE DONE 11 694

GLORIES
GLORIES: FOR NEVER SINCE CREATED MAN, 1 573
EQUAL'D IN ALL THIR GLORIES, TO INSHRINE 1 719

GLORIFIE
THE WORKS OF GOD, THEREBY TO GLORIFIE 3 695
TO GLORIFIE THY SON, I ALWAYES THEE, 6 725
TO GLORIFIE THE MAKER, AND INFERR 7 116

GLORIOUS
AND HAZARD IN THE GLORIOUS ENTERPRIZE, 1 89
MORE GLORIOUS AND MORE DREAD THEN FROM NO FALL, 2 16
DESIGNING OR EXHORTING GLORIOUS WARR, 2 179
MOST GLORIOUS, IN HIM ALL HIS FATHER SHON 3 139
AMIDST THE GLORIOUS BRIGHTNESS WHERE THOU SIT'ST 3 376
OF COLOUR GLORIOUS AND EFFECT SO RARE? 3 612
SAW WITHIN KENN A GLORIOUS ANGEL STAND, 3 622
I FELL, HOW GLORIOUS ONCE ABOVE THY SPHEARE; 4 39
THE IMAGE OF THIR GLORIOUS MAKER SHON, 4 292
THIS GLORIOUS SIGHT, WHEN SLEEP HATH SHUT ALL EYES? 4 658
THESE ARE THY GLORIOUS WORKS, PARENT OF GOOD, 5 153
EASTWARD AMONG THOSE TREES, WHAT GLORIOUS SHAPE 5 309
NONE CAN THEN HEAV'N SUCH GLORIOUS SHAPE CONTAIN; 5 362
THE RUIN OF SO MANY GLORIOUS ONCE 5 567
THY SELF THOUGH GREAT AND GLORIOUS DOST THOU COUNT, 5 833
BACK ON THY FOES MORE GLORIOUS TO RETURN 6 39
VAIN GLORIOUS, AND THROUGH INFAMIE SEEKS FAME: 6 384
FIRST IN HIS EAST THE GLORIOUS LAMP WAS SEEN, 7 370
THE GLORIOUS TRAIN ASCENDING: HE THROUGH HEAV'N, 7 574
STILL GLORIOUS BEFORE WHOM AWAKE I STOOD; 8 464
O GLORIOUS TRIAL OF EXCEEDING LOVE, 9 961
MATTER OF GLORIOUS TRIAL; AND PERHAPS 9 1177
MINE WITH THIS GLORIOUS WORK, AND MADE ONE REALM 10 391
TO EXPEDITE YOUR GLORIOUS MARCH; BUT I 10 474
IN TRIUMPH ISSUING FORTH THIR GLORIOUS CHIEF; 10 537
OF THIS NEW GLORIOUS WORLD, AND MEE SO LATE 10 721
A GLORIOUS APPARITION, HAD NOT DOUBT 11 211
NOT THAT MORE GLORIOUS, WHEN THE ANGELS MET 11 213
WANDRING, SHALL IN A GLORIOUS TEMPLE ENSHRINE. 12 334

GLORIOUSLY
WHEN THOU ATTENDED GLORIOUSLY FROM HEAV'N 3 323
IN SIGHT OF GOD'S HIGH THRONE, GLORIOUSLY BRIGHT, 3 655

GLORY
TO SET HIMSELF IN GLORY ABOVE HIS PEERS, 1 39
THAT GLORY NEVER SHALL HIS WRATH OR MIGHT 1 110
THOUGH ALL OUR GLORY EXTINCT, AND HAPPY STATE 1 141
GLORY OF HIM THAT MADE THEM, TO TRANSFORM 1 370
OF GLORY OBSCUR'D: AS WHEN THE SUN NEW RIS'N 1 594
THIR GLORY WITHERD. AS WHEN HEAVENS FIRE 1 612
CHOOSE TO RESIDE, HIS GLORY UNOBSCUR'D, 2 265
HIS GLORY TO AUGMENT. THE BOLD DESIGN 2 386
SATAN, WHOM NOW TRANSCENDENT GLORY RAIS'D 2 427
THIR SPECIOUS DEEDS ON EARTH, WHICH GLORY EXCITES, 2 484
PASSION AND APATHIE, AND GLORY AND SHAME, 2 564
THE RADIANT IMAGE OF HIS GLORY SAT, 3 63
LOVE HATH ABOUNDED MORE THEN GLORY ABOUNDS, 3 312
O THOU THAT WITH SURPASSING GLORY CROWND, 4 32
SON, THOU IN WHOM MY GLORY I BEHOLD 5 719
MATTER TO MEE OF GLORY, WHOM THIR HATE 5 738
CROWND THEM WITH GLORY, AND TO THIR GLORY NAM'D 5 839
IN GLORY AS OF OLD, TO HIM APPEAS'D 10 226
WITH WHAT PERMISSIVE GLORY SINCE HIS FALL 10 451
THE GLORY OF THAT GLORY, WHO NOW BECOM 10 722
OF GLORY, AND FARR OFF HIS STEPS ADORE. 11 333
TO SHEW HIM ALL EARTHS KINGDOMES AND THIR GLORY. 11 384
WITH GLORY AND SPOILE BACK TO THIR PROMIS'D LAND. 12 172
WITH EARTHS WIDE BOUNDS, HIS GLORY WITH THE
HEAV'NS. 12 371
THEN ENTER INTO GLORY, AND RESUME 12 456
WITH GLORY AND POWER TO JUDGE BOTH QUICK AND DEAD, 12 460
TO GOD MORE GLORY, MORE GOOD WILL TO MEN 12 477
IN GLORY OF THE FATHER, TO DISSOLVE 12 546

GLORYING
BOTH GLORYING TO HAVE SCAP'T THE STYGIAN FLOOD 1 239

GLOSS
THE ANGEL, NOR IN MIST, THE COMMON GLOSS 5 435

GLOSSIE
SHON WITH A GLOSSIE SCURFF, UNDOUBTED SIGN 1 672

GLOW'D
SILENCE WAS PLEAS'D: NOW GLOW'D THE FIRMAMENT 4 604
TO WHOM THE ANGEL WITH A SMILE THAT GLOW'D 8 618

GLOWD
ABOUT HER GLOWD, OFT STOOPING TO SUPPORT 9 427
BUT IN HER CHEEK DISTEMPER FLUSHING GLOWD. 9 887

GLOWING
WITH RADIANT LIGHT, AS GLOWING IRON WITH FIRE; 3 594
WITH TRESSES DISCOMPOS'D, AND GLOWING CHEEK, 5 10

GLOZ'D
SO GLOZ'D THE TEMPTER, AND HIS PROEM TUN'D; 9 549

GLOZING
FOR MAN WILL HARK'N TO HIS GLOZING LYES, 3 93

GLUT
DEATH LAST, AND WITH HIS CARCASS GLUT THE GRAVE: 3 259
THIR DEVILISH GLUT, CHAIND THUNDERBOLTS AND HAIL 6 589
SO DEATH SHALL BE DECEAV'D HIS GLUT, AND WITH US
TWO 10 990

GLUTTED
WITH SUCKT AND GLUTTED OFFAL, AT ONE FLING 10 633

GLUTTONOUS
DUE NOURISHMENT, NOT GLUTTONOUS DELIGHT, 11 533

GNASHING
GNASHING FOR ANGUISH AND DESPITE AND SHAME 6 340

GNAW
THAT BRED THEM THEY RETURN, AND HOWLE AND GNAW 2 799

GO
HIGH HONOURD SITS? GO THEREFORE MIGHTY POWERS, 2 456
FELL WITH US FROM ON HIGH: FROM THEM I GO 2 826
SO MUCH THE NEERER DANGER; GO AND SPEED; 2 1008
MAY COME AND GO, SO UNAPPROV'D, AND LEAVE 5 118
GO THEREFORE, HALF THIS DAY AS FRIEND WITH FRIEND 5 229
GO MICHAEL OF CELESTIAL ARMIES PRINCE, 6 44
HENCE THEN, AND EVIL GO WITH THEE ALONG 6 275
GO THEN THOU MIGHTIEST IN THY FATHERS MIGHT, 6 710
GO HEAVENLY GUEST, ETHEREAL MESSENGER, 8 646
GO; FOR THY STAY, NOT FREE, ABSENTS THEE MORE; 9 372
GO IN THY NATIVE INNOCENCE, RELIE 9 373
COMMAND ME ABSOLUTELY NOT TO GO, 9 1156
MAYST EVER REST WELL PLEAS'D. I GO TO JUDGE 10 71
WE MAY NO LONGER STAY: GO, WAKEN EVE; 12 594
IS TO GO HENCE UNWILLING; THOU TO MEE 12 617

GOAL
PART CURB THIR FIERIE STEEDS, OR SHUN THE GOAL 2 531

GOAT
OF EWE OR GOAT DROPPING WITH MILK AT EEVN, 9 582

GOATS
OF GOATS OR TIMEROUS FLOCK TOGETHER THRONGD 6 857
THE BLOUD OF BULLS AND GOATS, THEY MAY CONCLUDE 12 292

GOBLIN
TO WHOM THE GOBLIN FULL OF WRAUTH REPLY'D, 2 688

GOD
FAST BY THE ORACLE OF GOD; I THENCE 1 12
AND JUSTIFIE THE WAYES OF GOD TO MEN. 1 26
AGAINST THE THRONE AND MONARCHY OF GOD 1 42
AS FAR REMOV'D FROM GOD AND LIGHT OF HEAV'N 1 73
LEVIATHAN, WHICH GOD OF ALL HIS WORKS 1 201
GOD THIR CREATOR, AND TH' INVISIBLE 1 369
THIR SEATS LONG AFTER NEXT THE SEAT OF GOD, 1 383
HIS TEMPLE RIGHT AGAINST THE TEMPLE OF GOD 1 402
HE ALSO AGAINST THE HOUSE OF GOD WAS BOLD: 1 470
WITH LUST AND VIOLENCE THE HOUSE OF GOD. 1 496
WENT ALL HIS FEAR: OF GOD, OR HELL, OR WORSE 2 49
SEDUCE THEM TO OUR PARTY, THAT THIR GOD 2 368
WITH AWFUL REVERENCE PRONE; AND AS A GOD 2 478
OF HEAVENLY GRACE: AND GOD PROCLAIMING PEACE, 2 499
A UNIVERSE OF DEATH, WHICH GOD BY CURSE 2 622
MEAN WHILE THE ADVERSARY OF GOD AND MAN, 2 629
ADMIR'D, NOT FEAR'D; GOD AND HIS SON EXCEPT, 2 678
AND THEY OUTCAST FROM GOD, ARE HERE CONDEMN'D 2 694
GOD AND GOOD ANGELS GUARD BY SPECIAL GRACE. 2 1033
MAY I EXPRESS THEE UNBLAM'D? SINCE GOD IS LIGHT, 3 3
OF GOD, AS WITH A MANTLE DIDST INVEST 3 10
HIM GOD BEHOLDING FROM HIS PROSPECT HIGH, 3 77
THUS WHILE GOD SPAKE, AMBROSIAL FRAGRANCE FILL'D 3 135
BEYOND COMPARE THE SON OF GOD WAS SEEN 3 138
BY DOOM SEVERE, HAD NOT THE SON OF GOD, 3 224
EQUAL TO GOD, AND EQUALLY ENJOYING 3 306
BY MERIT MORE THEN BIRTHRIGHT SON OF GOD, 3 309
BOTH GOD AND MAN, SON BOTH OF GOD AND MAN, 3 316
GOD SHALL BE ALL IN ALL. BUT ALL YE GODS, 3 341
HAIL SON OF GOD, SAVIOUR OF MEN, THY NAME 3 412
A GOD, LEAP'D FONDLY INTO AETNA FLAMES, 3 470
OVER THE PROMIS'D LAND TO GOD SO DEAR, 3 531
INVISIBLE, EXCEPT TO GOD ALONE, 3 684
THE WORKS OF GOD, THEREBY TO GLORIFIE 3 695
LOOK'ST FROM THY SOLE DOMINION LIKE THE GOD 4 33
WHEN GOD HATH SHOWRD THE EARTH; SO LOVELY SEEMD 4 152
ANY, BUT GOD ALONE, TO VALUE RIGHT 4 202
OF GOD THE GARDEN WAS, BY HIM IN THE EAST 4 209
HIS FARR MORE PLEASANT GARDEN GOD ORDAIND; 4 215

GOD (CONTINUED)

PASS'D UNDERNEATH INGULFT, FOR GOD HAD THROWN	4	225
HEE FOR GOD ONLY, SHEE FOR GOD IN HIM:	4	299
OF GOD OR ANGEL, FOR THEY THOUGHT NO ILL:	4	320
GOD HATH PRONOUNC'T IT DEATH TO TASTE THAT TREE,	4	427
MIND US OF LIKE REPOSE, SINCE GOD HATH SET	4	612
AND OF THIR DOINGS GOD TAKES NO ACCOUNT.	4	622
UNARGU'D I OBEY; SO GOD ORDAINS,	4	636
GOD IS THY LAW, THOU MINE: TO KNOW NO MORE	4	637
DAUGHTER OF GOD AND MAN, ACCOMPLISHT EVE,	4	660
THAT HEAV'N WOULD WANT SPECTATORS, GOD WANT PRAISE;	4	676
THE GOD THAT MADE BOTH SKIE, AIR, EARTH AND HEAV'N	4	722
WHICH GOD LIKES BEST, INTO THIR INMOST BOWRE	4	738
DEFAMING AS IMPURE WHAT GOD DECLARES	4	746
BUT OUR DESTROYER, FOE TO GOD AND MAN?	4	749
WHOSE DWELLING GOD HATH PLANTED HERE IN BLISS?	4	884
NOR GOD, NOR MAN; IS KNOWLEDGE SO DESPIS'D?	5	60
EVIL INTO THE MIND OF GOD OR MAN	5	117
EARTH AND THE GARD'N OF GOD, WITH CEDARS CROWND	5	260
OF GOD INSPIR'D, SMALL STORE WILL SERVE, WHERE STORE,	5	322
GOD HATH DISPENST HIS BOUNTIES AS IN HEAV'N.	5	330
THEN WITH THESE VARIOUS FRUITS THE TREES OF GOD	5	390
COVER'D WITH PEARLY GRAIN: YET GOD HATH HERE	5	430
THEN HAD THE SONS OF GOD EXCUSE TO HAVE BIN	5	447
INHABITANT WITH GOD, NOW KNOW I WELL	5	461
WONDER NOT THEN, WHAT GOD FOR YOU SAW GOOD	5	491
BY STEPS WE MAY ASCEND TO GOD. BUT SAY,	5	512
ATTEND: THAT THOU ART HAPPIE, OWE TO GOD;	5	520
GOD MADE THEE PERFET, NOT IMMUTABLE;	5	524
IN SIGHT OF GOD ENTHRON'D, OUR HAPPIE STATE	5	536
CAST OUT FROM GOD AND BLESSED VISION, FALLS	5	613
FROM THAT HIGH MOUNT OF GOD, WHENCE LIGHT & SHADE	5	643
ALL BUT THE UNSLEEPING EYES OF GOD TO REST,	5	647
(SUCH ARE THE COURTS OF GOD) TH' ANGELIC THRONG	5	650
WITH ENVIE AGAINST THE SON OF GOD, THAT DAY	5	662
AFFECTING ALL EQUALITY WITH GOD,	5	763
THE JUST DECREE OF GOD, PRONOUNC'T AND SWORN,	5	814
SHALT THOU GIVE LAW TO GOD, SHALT THOU DISPUTE	5	822
O ALIENATE FROM GOD, O SPIRIT ACCURST,	5	877
WITHIN THE MOUNT OF GOD, FAST BY HIS THRONE,	6	5
SERVANT OF GOD, WELL DONE, WELL HAST THOU FOUGHT	6	29
TO STAND APPROV'D IN SIGHT OF GOD, THOUGH WORLDS	6	36
PURSUING DRIVE THEM OUT FROM GOD AND BLISS,	6	52
OF GOD AND HIS MESSIAH. ON THEY MOVE	6	68
TO WIN THE MOUNT OF GOD, AND ON HIS THRONE	6	88
HIGH IN THE MIDST EXALTED AS A GOD	6	99
THE THRONE OF GOD UNGUARDED, AND HIS SIDE	6	133
PREFER, AND PIETIE TO GOD, THOUGH THEN	6	144
OF SERVITUDE TO SERVE WHOM GOD ORDAINS,	6	175
OR NATURE; GOD AND NATURE BID THE SAME,	6	176
IN HEAV'N GOD EVER BLEST, AND HIS DIVINE	6	184
OR SOM MORE SUDDEN VENGEANCE WING'D FROM GOD	6	279
OF MICHAEL FROM THE ARMORIE OF GOD	6	321
HIS CONFIDENCE TO EQUAL GOD IN POWER.	6	343
WHICH GOD HATH IN HIS MIGHTY ANGELS PLAC'D)	6	638
GOD AND MESSIAH HIS ANOINTED KING.	6	718
CHARIOTS OF GOD, HALF ON EACH HAND WERE SEEN:	6	770
AGAINST GOD AND MESSIAH, OR TO FALL	6	796
OR FAINT RETREAT; WHEN THE GREAT SON OF GOD	6	799
FAITHFUL HATH BEEN YOUR WARFARE, AND OF GOD	6	803
ALL BUT THE THRONE IT SELF OF GOD. FULL SOON	6	834
AND WARR SO NEER THE PEACE OF GOD IN BLISS	7	55
IMMEDIATE ARE THE ACTS OF GOD, MORE SWIFT	7	176
FROM THE ARMOURY OF GOD, WHERE STAND OF OLD	7	200
THUS GOD THE HEAV'N CREATED, THUS THE EARTH,	7	232
HIS BROODING WINGS THE SPIRIT OF GOD OUTSPRED,	7	235
LET THER BE LIGHT, SAID GOD, AND FORTHWITH LIGHT	7	243
SOJOURN'D THE WHILE. GOD SAW THE LIGHT WAS GOOD;	7	249
GOD AND HIS WORKS, CREATOUR HIM THEY SUNG,	7	259
AGAIN, GOD SAID, LET THER BE FIRMAMENT	7	261
THE WATERS FROM THE WATERS: AND GOD MADE	7	263
SATIATE WITH GENIAL MOISTURE, WHEN GOD SAID	7	282
EASIE, E'RE GOD HAD BID THE GROUND BE DRIE,	7	304
HER SACRED SHADES: THOUGH GOD HAD YET NOT RAIN'D	7	331
GOD MADE, AND EVERY HERB, BEFORE IT GREW	7	336
ON THE GREEN STEMM; GOD SAW THAT IT WAS GOOD,	7	337
AND GOD MADE TWO GREAT LIGHTS, GREAT FOR THIR USE	7	346
AND LIGHT FROM DARKNESS TO DIVIDE. GOD SAW,	7	352
AND GOD SAID, LET THE WATERS GENERATE	7	387
AND GOD CREATED THE GREAT WHALES, AND EACH	7	391
WITH EEVNING HARPS AND MATTIN, WHEN GOD SAID,	7	450
AND WORSHIP GOD SUPREAM, WHO MADE HIM CHIEF	7	515
CREATED THEE, IN THE IMAGE OF GOD	7	527
THIS GARDEN, PLANTED WITH THE TREES OF GOD,	7	538
OPEN, AND HENCEFORTH OFT; FOR GOD WILL DEIGNE	7	569
AND SONS OF MEN, WHOM GOD HATH THUS ADVANC'T,	7	626
IS AS THE BOOK OF GOD BEFORE THEE SET,	8	67
WHERE GOD RESIDES, AND ERE MID-DAY ARRIV'D	8	112
GOD TO REMOVE HIS WAYES FROM HUMAN SENSE,	8	119
LEAVE THEM TO GOD ABOVE, HIM SERVE AND FEARE;	8	168
GOD HATH BID DWELL FARR OFF ALL ANXIOUS CARES,	8	185
NOR TONGUE INELOQUENT; FOR GOD ON THEE	8	219
GLADLY INTO THE WAYES OF GOD WITH MAN:	8	226
FOR GOD WE SEE HATH HONOUR'D THEE, AND SET	8	227
OR ENEMIE, WHILE GOD WAS IN HIS WORK,	8	234
THIR NATURE, WITH SUCH KNOWLEDG GOD ENDU'D	8	353
NO MORE OF TALK WHERE GOD OR ANGEL GUEST	9	1

GOD (CONTINUED)

FOR WHAT GOD AFTER BETTER WORSE WOULD BUILD?	9	102
OF SACRED INFLUENCE: AS GOD IN HEAV'N	9	107
GOD HATH ASSIGN'D US, NOR OF ME SHALT PASS	9	231
OUR FEALTIE FROM GOD, OR TO DISTURB	9	262
TO GOD OR THEE, BECAUSE WE HAVE A FOE	9	280
DAUGHTER OF GOD AND MAN, IMMORTAL EVE,	9	291
OF GOD ORDAIN'D THEM, HIS CREATING HAND	9	344
BUT GOD LEFT FREE THE WILL, FOR WHAT OBEYES	9	351
TO DO WHAT GOD EXPRESLY HATH FORBID,	9	356
FOR GOD TOWARDS THEE HATH DONE HIS PART, DO THINE.	9	375
HERMIONE AND CADMUS, OR THE GOD	9	506
TO BEASTS, WHOM GOD ON THIR CREATION-DAY	9	556
FOR MANY ARE THE TREES OF GOD THAT GROW	9	618
GOD SO COMMANDED, AND LEFT THAT COMMAND	9	652
INDEED? HATH GOD THEN SAID THAT OF THE FRUIT	9	656
THE GARDEN, GOD HATH SAID, YE SHALL NOT EATE	9	662
IS OPEN? OR WILL GOD INCENSE HIS IRE	9	692
GOD THEREFORE CANNOT HURT YE, AND BE JUST;	9	700
NOT JUST, NOT GOD; NOT FEARD THEN, NOR OBEYD:	9	701
OF GOD OR DEATH, OF LAW OR PENALTIE?	9	775
THIS MAY BE WELL: BUT WHAT IF GOD HAVE SEEN,	9	826
SHOULD GOD CREATE ANOTHER EVE, AND I	9	911
NOT GOD OMNIPOTENT, NOR FATE, YET SO	9	927
NOR CAN I THINK THAT GOD, CREATOR WISE,	9	938
DEPENDENT MADE; SO GOD SHALL UNCREATE,	9	943
NOT WELL CONCEAV'D OF GOD, WHO THOUGH HIS POWER	9	945
TRIUMPH AND SAY; FICKLE THEIR STATE WHOM GOD	9	948
HENCEFORTH OF GOD OR ANGEL, EARST WITH JOY	9	1081
OF GOD ALL-SEEING, OR DECEAVE HIS HEART	10	6
TO SENTENCE MAN: THE VOICE OF GOD THEY HEARD	10	97
THE THICKEST TREES, BOTH MAN AND WIFE, TILL GOD	10	101
LOVE WAS NOT IN THIR LOOKS, EITHER TO GOD	10	111
WAS SHEE THY GOD, THAT HER THOU DIDST OBEY	10	145
WHEREIN GOD SET THEE ABOVE HER MADE OF THEE,	10	149
WHICH WHEN THE LORD GOD HEARD, WITHOUT DELAY	10	163
NOR ALTER'D HIS OFFENCE; YET GOD AT LAST	10	171
THE SON OF GOD TO JUDGE THEM TERRIFI'D	10	338
OF GOD, WHOM TO BEHOLD WAS THEN MY HIGHTH	10	724
THEN CAVIL THE CONDITIONS? AND THOUGH GOD	10	759
GOD MADE THEE OF CHOICE HIS OWN, AND OF HIS OWN	10	766
WHICH GOD INSPIR'D, CANNOT TOGETHER PERISH	10	785
STRANGE CONTRADICTION, WHICH TO GOD HIMSELF	10	799
IN SIGHT OF GOD? HIM AFTER ALL DISPUTES	10	828
TO MY JUST NUMBER FOUND. O WHY DID GOD,	10	888
AGAINST GOD ONELY, I AGAINST GOD AND THEE,	10	931
THE PENALTIE PRONOUNC'T, DOUBT NOT BUT GOD	10	1022
RELUCTANCE AGAINST GOD AND HIS JUST YOKE	10	1045
WHEN GOD DESCENDED, AND PERHAPS ONCE MORE	11	75
HAST THEE, AND FROM THE PARADISE OF GOD	11	104
OF GOD HIGH-BLEST, OR TO INCLINE HIS WILL,	11	145
EV'N TO THE SEAT OF GOD. FOR SINCE I SAUGHT	11	148
GOD IS AS HERE, AND WILL BE FOUND ALIKE	11	350
IN THE VISIONS OF GOD: IT WAS A HILL	11	377
TH' IMAGE OF GOD IN MAN CREATED ONCE	11	508
TO WORSHIP GOD ARIGHT, AND KNOW HIS WORKS	11	578
RELIGIOUS TITL'D THEM THE SONS OF GOD,	11	622
AND UTTER ODIOUS TRUTH, THAT GOD WOULD COME	11	704
DID, AS THOU SAWST, RECEAVE, TO WALK WITH GOD	11	707
WITH THIR FOUR WIVES; AND GOD MADE FAST THE DORE.	11	737
AND FEAR OF GOD, FROM WHOM THIR PIETIE FEIGN'D	11	799
OF THEM DERIDED, BUT OF GOD OBSERVD	11	817
TO TEACH THEE THAT GOD ATTRIBUTES TO PLACE	11	836
BETOK'NING PEACE FROM GOD, AND COV'NANT NEW.	11	867
THAT GOD VOUTSAFES TO RAISE ANOTHER WORLD	11	877
DISTENDED AS THE BROW OF GOD APPEAS'D,	11	880
SO WILLINGLY DOTH GOD REMIT HIS IRE,	11	885
BUT GOD WHO OFT DESCENDS TO VISIT MEN	12	48
AUTHORITIE USURPT, FROM GOD NOT GIV'N:	12	66
STAYES NOT ON MAN; TO GOD HIS TOWER INTENDS	12	73
OVER FREE REASON, GOD IN JUDGEMENT JUST	12	92
STILL TEND FROM BAD TO WORSE, TILL GOD AT LAST	12	106
AS TO FORSAKE THE LIVING GOD, AND FALL	12	118
FOR GODS. YET HIM GOD THE MOST HIGH VOUTSAFES	12	120
WITH GOD, WHO CALL'D HIM, IN A LAND UNKNOWN.	12	134
MOSES AND AARON) SENT FROM GOD TO CLAIME	12	170
TO KNOW THIR GOD, OR MESSAGE TO REGARD,	12	174
SUCH WONDROUS POWER GOD TO HIS SAINT WILL LEND,	12	200
GOD LOOKING FORTH WILL TROUBLE ALL HIS HOST	12	209
GOD FROM THE MOUNT OF SINAI, WHOSE GRAY TOP	12	227
MANKINDS DELIVERANCE. BUT THE VOICE OF GOD	12	235
INSTRUCTED THAT TO GOD IS NO ACCESS	12	239
ESTABLISHT, SUCH DELIGHT HATH GOD IN MEN	12	245
AMONG WHOM GOD WILL DEIGNE TO DWELL ON EARTH	12	281
AMONG THEM; HOW CAN GOD WITH SUCH RESIDE?	12	284
JUSTIFICATION TOWARDS GOD, AND PEACE	12	296
AND THEREFORE SHALL NOT MOSES, THOUGH OF GOD	12	307
PROVOKING GOD TO RAISE THEM ENEMIES:	12	318
THE CLOUDED ARK OF GOD TILL THEN IN TENTS	12	333
GOD, AS TO LEAVE THEM, AND EXPOSE THIR LAND,	12	339
THIR LORDS, WHOM GOD DISPOS'D, THE HOUSE OF GOD	12	349
OF GOD MOST HIGH; SO GOD WITH MAN UNITES.	12	382
OBEDIENCE TO THE LAW OF GOD, IMPOS'D	12	397
THE LAW OF GOD EXACT HE SHALL FULFILL	12	402
TO GOD MORE GLORY, MORE GOOD WILL TO MEN	12	477
FROM GOD, AND OVER WRAUTH GRACE SHALL ABOUND.	12	478
THE SPIRIT OF GOD, PROMISD ALIKE AND GIV'N	12	519
AND LOVE WITH FEAR THE ONELY GOD, TO WALK	12	562

GOD (CONTINUED)

OR WORKS OF GOD IN HEAV'N, AIRE, EARTH, OR SEA,	12	579
FOR GOD IS ALSO IN SLEEP, AND DREAMS ADVISE,	12	611
THE BRANDISHT SWORD OF GOD BEFORE THEM BLAZ'D	12	633

GODDESS

THEN SHINING HEAV'NLY FAIR, A GODDESS ARM'D	2	757
THY SELF A GODDESS, NOT TO EARTH CONFIND,	5	78
THEN WOOD-NYMPH, OR THE FAIREST GODDESS FEIGN'D	5	381
SAY GODDESS, WHAT ENSU'D WHEN RAPHAEL,	7	40
A GODDESS AMONG GODS, ADOR'D AND SERV'D	9	547
GODDESS HUMANE, REACH THEN, AND FREELY TASTE.	9	732

GODDESSES

OF GODDESSES, SO BLITHE, SO SMOOTH, SO GAY,	11	615

GODDESS-LIKE

WITH GODDESS-LIKE DEMEANOUR FORTH SHE WENT;	8	59
IN GATE SURPASS'D AND GODDESS-LIKE DEPORT,	9	389

GODHEAD

WITH WARBL'D HYMNS, AND TO HIS GODHEAD SING	2	242
AND THUS THE FILIAL GODHEAD ANSWERING SPAKE.	6	722
HIS WORD, THE FILIAL GODHEAD, GAVE EFFECT.	7	175
OF GODHEAD, FIXT FOR EVER FIRM AND SURE,	7	586
AND GROWING UP TO GODHEAD; WHICH FOR THEE	9	877

GOD-HEAD

AFFECTING GOD-HEAD, AND SO LOOSING ALL,	3	206
OF KNOWLEDG, NOR WAS GOD-HEAD FROM HER THOUGHT.	9	790
MANHOOD TO GOD-HEAD, WITH MORE STRENGTH TO FOIL	12	389

GODLESS

EQUAL IN NUMBER TO THAT GODLESS CREW	6	49
GODS INDIGNATION ON THESE GODLESS POURD	6	811

GOD-LIKE

AND GOD-LIKE IMITATED STATE; HIM ROUND	2	511
GOD-LIKE FRUITION, QUITTED ALL TO SAVE	3	307
HIS GOD-LIKE GUEST, WALKS FORTH, WITHOUT MORE TRAIN	5	351
UNDER THIR GOD-LIKE LEADERS, IN THE CAUSE	6	67
AS THEY, PARTICIPATING GOD-LIKE FOOD?	9	717
BY FAITH NOT VOID OF WORKES: THIS GOD-LIKE ACT	12	427

GODLIKE

THIR GREAT COMMANDER; GODLIKE SHAPES AND FORMS	1	358
GODLIKE ERECT, WITH NATIVE HONOUR CLAD	4	289
OF GODLIKE POWER: FOR LIKEST GODS THEY SEEMD,	6	301
AND THUS THE GODLIKE ANGEL ANSWERD MILDE.	7	110
SO SPAKE THE GODLIKE POWER, AND THUS OUR SIRE.	8	249

GOD'S

IN SIGHT OF GOD'S HIGH THRONE, GLORIOUSLY BRIGHT,	3	655
FOR GOD'S, YET ABLE TO MAKE GODS OF MEN:	5	70

GODS

THIS DOWNFALL; SINCE BY FATE THE STRENGTH OF GODS	1	116
AS FAR AS GODS AND HEAV'NLY ESSENCES	1	138
AS GODS, AND BY THIR OWN RECOVER'D STRENGTH,	1	240
THROUGH GODS HIGH SUFFERANCE FOR THE TRYAL OF MAN,	1	366
THIR ALTARS BY HIS ALTAR, GODS ADOR'D	1	384
TO BESTIAL GODS; FOR WHICH THIR HEADS AS LOW	1	435
GODS ALTAR TO DISPARAGE AND DISPLACE	1	473
HIS ODIOUS OFFRINGS, AND ADORE THE GODS	1	475
THIR WANDRING GODS DISGUIS'D IN BRUTISH FORMS	1	481
BOTH HER FIRST BORN AND ALL HER BLEATING GODS.	1	489
TH' IONIAN GODS, OF JAVANS ISSUE HELD	1	508
GODS, YET CONFEST LATER THEN HEAV'N AND EARTH	1	509
THIR VISAGES AND STATURE AS OF GODS,	1	570
MIXT WITH AUXILIAR GODS; AND WHAT RESOUNDS	1	579
HOW SUCH UNITED FORCE OF GODS, HOW SUCH	1	629
BELUS OR SERAPIS THIR GODS, OR SEAT	1	720
A THOUSAND DEMY-GODS ON GOLDEN SEAT'S,	1	796
TO LESS THEN GODS. ON TH' OTHER SIDE UP ROSE	2	108
PRONOUNC'D AMONG THE GODS, AND BY AN OATH,	2	352
SYNOD OF GODS, AND LIKE TO WHAT YE ARE,	2	391
THE GODS WHO LIVE AT EASE, WHERE I SHALL REIGN	2	868
GOD SHALL BE ALL IN ALL. BUT ALL YE GODS,	3	341
WHO IN GODS PRESENCE, NEEREST TO HIS THRONE	3	649
SO CLOMB THIS FIRST GRAND THIEF INTO GODS FOULD:	4	192
EQUAL WITH GODS; ASPIRING TO BE SUCH,	4	526
GODS LATEST IMAGE: I DESCRIB'D HIS WAY	4	567
MORE LOVELY THEN PANDORA, WHOM THE GODS	4	714
FOR GOD'S, YET ABLE TO MAKE GODS OF MEN:	5	70
AND WHY NOT GODS OF MEN, SINCE GOOD, THE MORE	5	71
TASTE THIS, AND BE HENCEFORTH AMONG THE GODS	5	77
WHAT LIFE THE GODS LIVE THERE, AND SUCH LIVE THOU.	5	81
SO SMOOTHS HER CHARMING TONES, THAT GODS OWN EAR	5	626
OF GODS MESSIAH; THOSE INDULGENT LAWS	5	883
A THIRD PART OF THE GODS, IN SYNOD MET	6	156
OF GODLIKE POWER: FOR LIKEST GODS THEY SEEMD,	6	301
TWO POTENT THRONES, THAT TO BE LESS THEN GODS	6	366
ENJOYMENT OF OUR RIGHT AS GODS; YET HARD	6	452
FOR GODS, AND TOO UNEQUAL WORK WE FIND	6	453
GODS INDIGNATION ON THESE GODLESS POURD	6	811
IN GODS ETERNAL STORE, TO CIRCUMSCRIBE	7	226
SEEMD LIKE TO HEAV'N, A SEAT WHERE GODS MIGHT DWELL,	7	329
TO GODS ETERNAL HOUSE DIRECT THE WAY,	7	576
MORE JUSTLY, SEAT WORTHIER OF GODS, AS BUILT	9	100
WITH GODS TO SIT THE HIGHEST, AM NOW CONSTRAIND	9	164
SHEE FAIR, DIVINELY FAIR, FIT LOVE FOR GODS,	9	489
A GODDESS AMONG GODS, ADOR'D AND SERV'D	9	547
OP'ND AND CLEERD, AND YE SHALL BE AS GODS,	9	708
THAT YE SHOULD BE AS GODS, SINCE I AS MAN,	9	710
I OF BRUTE HUMAN, YEE OF HUMAN GODS.	9	712
HUMAN, TO PUT ON GODS, DEATH TO BE WISHT,	9	714
AND WHAT ARE GODS THAT MAN MAY NOT BECOME	9	716
THE GODS ARE FIRST, AND THAT ADVANTAGE USE	9	718
IN KNOWLEDGE, AS THE GODS WHO ALL THINGS KNOW;	9	804
FROM NECTAR, DRINK OF GODS. ADAM THE WHILE	9	838
TO OPEN EYES, AND MAKE THEM GODS WHO TASTE;	9	866
OF ALL GODS WORKS, CREATURE IN WHOM EXCELL'D	9	897
BUT TO BE GODS, OR ANGELS DEMI-GODS.	9	937
DOWN HE DESCENDED STRAIT; THE SPEED OF GODS	10	90
OF MY PERFORMANCE: WHAT REMAINS, YE GODS,	10	502
FIT HAUNT OF GODS? WHERE I HAD HOPE TO SPEND,	11	271
DISFIGURING NOT GODS LIKENESS, BUT THIR OWN,	11	521
GODS IMAGE DID NOT REVERENCE IN THEMSELVES.	11	525
PATRONS OF MANKIND, GODS, AND SONS OF GODS,	11	696
FOR GODS. YET HIM GOD THE MOST HIGH VOUTSAFES	12	120
HIS KINDRED AND FALSE GODS, INTO A LAND	12	122
HE LEAVES HIS GODS, HIS FRIENDS, AND NATIVE SOILE	12	129
HIS SEAT AT GODS RIGHT HAND, EXALTED HIGH	12	457

GOE

THIS DAY TO BE OUR GUEST. BUT GOE WITH SPEED,	5	313
THE WILLINGER I GOE, NOR MUCH EXPECT	9	382
UPON THY BELLY GROVELING THOU SHALT GOE,	10	177
GOE WHITHER FATE AND INCLINATION STRONG	10	265
NO DETRIMENT NEED FEARE, GOE AND BE STRONG.	10	409
THOUGH PRESENT IN HIS ANGEL, WHO SHALL GOE	12	201
RARELY BE FOUND: SO SHALL THE WORLD GOE ON,	12	537
IN MEE IS NO DELAY; WITH THEE TO GOE,	12	615

GOES

WITH THEE IT CAME AND GOES: BUT FOLLOW ME,	4	469
THY GOING IS NOT LONELY, WITH THEE GOES	11	290

GOING

GOING INTO SUCH DANGER AS THOU SAIDST?	9	1157
THY GOING IS NOT LONELY, WITH THEE GOES	11	290

GOLD

WITH GAY RELIGIONS FULL OF POMP AND GOLD,	1	372
TH' INFECTION WHEN THIR BORROW'D GOLD COMPOS'D	1	483
THE RICHES OF HEAV'NS PAVEMENT, TROD'N GOLD,	1	682
AND DIG'D OUT RIBS OF GOLD. LET NONE ADMIRE	1	690
THE ROOF WAS FRETTED GOLD. NOT BABILON,	1	717
SHOWRS ON HER KINGS BARBARIC PEARL AND GOLD,	2	4
WANTS NOT HER HIDDEN LUSTRE, GEMMS AND GOLD;	2	271
THE GUARDED GOLD: SO EAGERLY THE FIEND	2	947
THIR CROWNS INWOVE WITH AMARANT AND GOLD,	3	352
WITH FRONTISPICE OF DIAMOND AND GOLD	3	506
THAT SCAL'D BY STEPS OF GOLD TO HEAV'N GATE	3	541
IF METTAL, PART SEEMD GOLD, PART SILVER CLEER;	3	595
POTABLE GOLD, WHEN WITH ONE VERTUOUS TOUCH	3	608
OF MANY A COLOURD PLUME SPRINKL'D WITH GOLD,	3	642
OF VEGETABLE GOLD; AND NEXT TO LIFE	4	220
ROWLING ON ORIENT PEARL AND SANDS OF GOLD,	4	238
NAKED MET HIS UNDER THE FLOWING GOLD	4	496
HUNG HIGH WITH DIAMOND FLAMING, AND WITH GOLD.	4	554
ARRAYING WITH REFLECTED PURPLE AND GOLD	4	596
TILL THE SUN PAINT YOUR FLEECIE SKIRTS WITH GOLD	5	187
SKIRTED HIS LOINES AND THIGHES WITH DOWNIE GOLD	5	282
OF HORSES LED, AND GROOMS BESMEARD WITH GOLD	5	356
METALS OF DROSSIEST ORE TO PERFET GOLD	5	442
IN PEARL, IN DIAMOND, AND MASSIE GOLD,	5	634
FROM DIAMOND QUARRIES HEW'N, AND ROCKS OF GOLD,	5	759
SUCH AS IN HIGHEST HEAV'N, ARRAYD IN GOLD	6	13
CAME TOWRING, ARMD IN ADAMANT AND GOLD;	6	110
WITH PLANT, FRUIT, FLOUR AMBROSIAL, GEMMS & GOLD,	6	475
SHOW TO THE SUN THIR WAV'D COATS DROPT WITH GOLD,	7	406
WITH SPOTS OF GOLD AND PURPLE, AZURE AND GREEN:	7	479
A BROAD AND AMPLE RODE, WHOSE DUST IS GOLD	7	577
CARNATION, PURPLE, AZURE, OR SPECT WITH GOLD,	9	429
WITH BURNISHT NECK OF VERDANT GOLD, ERECT	9	501
RUDDIE AND GOLD: I NEARER DREW TO GAZE;	9	578
OF CEDAR, OVERLAID WITH GOLD, THEREIN	12	250
A MERCIE-SEAT OF GOLD BETWEEN THE WINGS	12	253
HIS PLACE, TO OFFER INCENSE, MYRRH, AND GOLD;	12	363

GOLDEN

WITH GEMMS AND GOLDEN LUSTRE RICH IMBLAZ'D,	1	538
WITH GOLDEN ARCHITRAVE; NOR DID THERE WANT	1	715
A THOUSAND DEMY-GODS ON GOLDEN SEAT'S,	1	796
US HERE, AS WITH HIS GOLDEN THOSE IN HEAV'N.	2	328
HUNG ORE MY REALM, LINK'D IN A GOLDEN CHAIN	2	1005
AND FAST BY HANGING IN A GOLDEN CHAIN	2	1051
SEE GOLDEN DAYS, FRUITFUL OF GOLDEN DEEDS,	3	337
THE GOLDEN SUN IN SPLENDOR LIKEST HEAVEN	3	572
OF BEAMING SUNNIE RAIES, A GOLDEN TIAR	3	625
BLOSSOMS AND FRUITS AT ONCE OF GOLDEN HUE	4	148
OTHERS WHOSE FRUIT BURNISHT WITH GOLDEN RINDE	4	249
HER UNADORNED GOLDEN TRESSES WORE	4	305

GOLDEN (CONTINUED)

HERE LOVE HIS GOLDEN SHAFTS IMPLOIES, HERE LIGHTS	4	763
HUNG FORTH IN HEAV'N HIS GOLDEN SCALES, YET SEEN	4	997
ON GOLDEN HINGES TURNING, AS BY WORK	5	255
AND FROM WITHIN THE GOLDEN LAMPS THAT BURNE	5	713
THAT GOLDEN SCEPTER WHICH THOU DIDST REJECT	5	886
FROM MIDST A GOLDEN CLOUD THUS MILDE WAS HEARD.	6	28
WITH FLAMING CHERUBIM, AND GOLDEN SHIELDS;	6	102
OF GOLDEN PANOPLIE, REFULGENT HOST,	6	527
ON GOLDEN HINGES MOVING, TO LET FORTH	7	207
HE TOOK THE GOLDEN COMPASSES, PREPAR'D	7	225
AND TOUCH'T THIR GOLDEN HARPS, AND HYMNING PRAIS'D	7	258
ALL SOUNDS ON FRET BY STRING OR GOLDEN WIRE	7	597
FUMING FROM GOLDEN CENSERS HID THE MOUNT.	7	600
WITH INCENSE, WHERE THE GOLDEN ALTAR FUM'D,	11	18
AND PRAYERS, WHICH IN THIS GOLDEN CENSER, MIXT	11	24
DOWN TO THE GOLDEN CHERSONESE, OR WHERE	11	392

GOLD'N

THEN CROWN'D AGAIN THIR GOLD'N HARPS THEY TOOK,	3	365
REPAIRING, IN THIR GOLD'N URNS DRAW LIGHT,	7	365

GOLGOTHA

IN GOLGOTHA HIM DEAD, WHO LIVES IN HEAV'N;	3	477

GON

AT LEAST HAD GON TO RACK, DISTURBD AND TORNE	4	994
MY GUIDE WAS GON, AND I, ME THOUGHT, SUNK DOWN,	5	91
AGAINST THEE ARE GON FORTH WITHOUT RECALL;	5	885
HAD GON TO WRACK, WITH RUIN OVERSPRED,	6	670
HAD SHADOW'D THEM FROM KNOWING ILL, WAS GON,	9	1055
ALL WOULD HAVE THEN GON WELL, PEACE WOULD HAVE CROWND	11	781

GONE

THROUGH DARK AND DESART WAYES WITH PERIL GONE	3	544

GONFALONS

STANDARDS, AND GONFALONS TWIXT VAN AND REARE	5	589

GOOD

TO DO OUGHT GOOD NEVER WILL BE OUR TASK,	1	159
OUT OF OUR EVIL SEEK TO BRING FORTH GOOD,	1	163
AND OUT OF GOOD STILL TO FIND MEANS OF EVIL;	1	165
TILL GOOD JOSIAH DROVE THEM THENCE TO HELL.	1	418
OF ENDLESS PAIN? WHERE THERE IS THEN NO GOOD	2	30
LET THIS BE GOOD, WHETHER OUR ANGRY FOE	2	152
OUR OWN GOOD FROM OUR SELVES, AND FROM OUR OWN	2	253
OF GOOD AND EVIL MUCH THEY ARGU'D THEN,	2	562
CREATED EVIL, FOR EVIL ONLY GOOD,	2	623
DESTIN'D TO THAT GOOD HOUR: NO LESS REJOYC'D	2	848
NOR GOOD DRY LAND: NIGH FOUNDERD ON HE FARES,	2	940
GOD AND GOOD ANGELS GUARD BY SPECIAL GRACE.	2	1033
FOUND WORTHIEST TO BE SO BY BEING GOOD,	3	310
IN THAT BRIGHT EMINENCE, AND WITH HIS GOOD	4	44
HOW DUE. YET ALL HIS GOOD PROV'D ILL IN ME,	4	48
FARWEL REMORSE: ALL GOOD TO ME IS LOST;	4	109
EVIL BE THOU MY GOOD; BY THEE AT LEAST	4	110
THE GOOD BEFORE HIM, BUT PERVERTS BEST THINGS	4	203
KNOWLEDGE OF GOOD BOUGHT DEAR BY KNOWING ILL.	4	222
BE INFINITLY GOOD, AND OF HIS GOOD	4	414
THAT GLORIE THEN, WHEN THOU NO MORE WAST GOOD,	4	838
TO THEE NO REASON; WHO KNOWST ONLY GOOD,	4	895
LONGER THY OFFERD GOOD, WHY ELSE SET HERE?	5	63
AND WHY NOT GODS OF MEN, SINCE GOOD, THE MORE	5	71
THESE ARE THY GLORIOUS WORKS, PARENT OF GOOD,	5	153
TO GIVE US ONELY GOOD; AND IF THE NIGHT	5	206
ALL PERFET GOOD UNMEASUR'D OUT, DESCENDS,	5	399
IF NOT DEPRAV'D FROM GOOD, CREATED ALL	5	471
WONDER NOT THEN, WHAT GOD FOR YOU SAW GOOD	5	491
AND GOOD HE MADE THEE, BUT TO PERSEVERE	5	525
NOT LAWFUL TO REVEAL? YET FOR THY GOOD	5	570
YET BY EXPERIENCE TAUGHT WE KNOW HOW GOOD,	5	826
AND OF OUR GOOD, AND OF OUR DIGNITIE	5	827
FORSAK'N OF ALL GOOD; I SEE THY FALL	5	878
FOR WHICH TO THE INFINITLY GOOD WE OWE	7	76
GLORIE THEY SUNG TO THE MOST HIGH, GOOD WILL	7	182
GOOD OUT OF EVIL TO CREATE, IN STEAD	7	188
HIS GOOD TO WORLDS AND AGES INFINITE.	7	191
SOJOURN'D THE WHILE. GOD SAW THE LIGHT WAS GOOD;	7	249
AND SAW THAT IT WAS GOOD, AND SAID, LET TH' EARTH	7	309
ON THE GREEN STEMM; GOD SAW THAT IT WAS GOOD.	7	337
SURVEYING HIS GREAT WORK, THAT IT WAS GOOD:	7	353
AND SAW THAT IT WAS GOOD, AND BLESS'D THEM, SAYING,	7	395
BUT GRATEFUL TO ACKNOWLEDGE WHENCE HIS GOOD	7	512
WHICH TASTED WORKS KNOWLEDGE OF GOOD AND EVIL,	7	543
VIEW'D, AND BEHOLD ALL WAS ENTIRELY GOOD;	7	549
IN PROSPECT FROM HIS THRONE, HOW GOOD, HOW FAIRE,	7	556
THOU USEST, AND FROM THENCE CREAT'ST MORE GOOD.	7	616
NOR GLISTERING, MAY OF SOLID GOOD CONTAINE	8	93
KNOWLEDG OF GOOD AND ILL, WHICH I HAVE SET	8	324
AND ALL THIS GOOD TO MAN, FOR WHOSE WELL BEING	8	361
GOOD REASON WAS THOU FREELY SHOULDST DISLIKE,	8	443
KNEW IT NOT GOOD FOR MAN TO BE ALONE,	8	445
BE GOOD AND FRIENDLY STILL, AND OFT RETURN.	8	651
OF CONTRARIES; ALL GOOD TO ME BECOMES	9	122
IN WOMAN, THEN TO STUDIE HOUSHOLD GOOD,	9	233
AND GOOD WORKES IN HER HUSBAND TO PROMOTE.	9	234

GOOD (CONTINUED)

LEAST BY SOME FAIRE APPEERING GOOD SURPRIS'D	9	354
STUPIDLY GOOD, OF ENMITIE DISARM'D,	9	465
OR EARTH, OR MIDDLE, ALL THINGS FAIR AND GOOD;	9	605
BUT ALL THAT FAIR AND GOOD IN THY DIVINE	9	606
TO HAPPIER LIFE, KNOWLEDGE OF GOOD AND EVIL;	9	697
OF GOOD, HOW JUST? OF EVIL, IF WHAT IS EVIL	9	698
KNOWING BOTH GOOD AND EVIL AS THEY KNOW.	9	709
KNOWLEDGE OF GOOD AND EVIL IN THIS TREE,	9	723
OF KNOWLEDGE, KNOWLEDGE BOTH OF GOOD AND EVIL;	9	752
COMMENDS THEE MORE, WHILE IT INFERRS THE GOOD	9	754
FOR GOOD UNKNOWN, SURE IS NOT HAD, OR HAD	9	756
FORBIDS US GOOD, FORBIDS US TO BE WISE?	9	759
THE GOOD BEFALL'N HIM, AUTHOR UNSUSPECT,	9	771
UNDER THIS IGNORANCE OF GOOD AND EVIL,	9	774
HOLY, DIVINE, GOOD, AMIABLE, OR SWEET.	9	899
ONE HEART, ONE SOUL IN BOTH; WHEREOF GOOD PROOFF	9	967
WHOSE VERTUE, FOR OF GOOD STILL GOOD PROCEEDS,	9	973
BOTH GOOD AND EVIL, GOOD LOST, AND EVIL GOT,	9	1072
OF ALL OUR GOOD, SHAM'D, NAKED, MISERABLE,	9	1139
AS GOOD HAVE GROWN THERE STILL A LIVELESS RIB.	9	1154
AND GAV'ST ME AS THY PERFET GIFT, SO GOOD,	10	138
SO FAIR AND GOOD CREATED, AND HAD STILL	10	618
THE GOOD I SOUGHT NOT. TO THE LOSS OF THAT,	10	752
THOU DIDST ACCEPT THEM; WILT THOU ENJOY THE GOOD,	10	758
GOOD OR NOT GOOD INGRAFT, MY MERIT THOSE	11	35
TO KNOW BOTH GOOD AND EVIL, SINCE HIS TASTE	11	85
HIS KNOWLEDGE OF GOOD LOST, AND EVIL GOT,	11	87
GOOD BY IT SELF, AND EVIL NOT AT ALL.	11	89
THE GOOD WHICH WE ENJOY, FROM HEAV'N DESCENDS;	11	142
TO THEE AND TO THY OFSPRING; GOOD WITH BAD	11	358
WITH VOWS, AS THIR CHIEF GOOD, AND FINAL HOPE.	11	493
YET EMPTY OF ALL GOOD WHEREIN CONSISTS	11	616
WHERE GOOD WITH BAD WERE MATCHT, WHO OF THEMSELVES	11	685
AWAITS THE GOOD, THE REST WHAT PUNISHMENT?	11	710
IN A DARK AGE, AGAINST EXAMPLE GOOD,	11	809
REGARDLESS WHETHER GOOD OR EVIL FAME.	12	47
PART GOOD, PART BAD, OF BAD THE LONGER SCROWLE,	12	336
THAT ALL THIS GOOD OF EVIL SHALL PRODUCE,	12	470
AND EVIL TURN TO GOOD; MORE WONDERFUL	12	471
MUCH MORE, THAT MUCH MORE GOOD THEREOF SHALL SPRING,	12	476
TO GOD MORE GLORY, MORE GOOD WILL TO MEN	12	477
TO GOOD MALIGNANT, TO BAD MEN BENIGNE,	12	538
MERCIFULL OVER ALL HIS WORKS, WITH GOOD	12	565
PORTENDING GOOD, AND ALL HER SPIRITS COMPOS'D	12	596
WHICH HE HATH SENT PROPITIOUS, SOME GREAT GOOD	12	612

GOODLIEST

OF GOODLIEST TREES LOADEN WITH FAIREST FRUIT,	4	147
ADAM THE GOODLIEST MAN OF MEN SINCE BORNE	4	323
A CIRCUIT WIDE, ENCLOS'D, WITH GOODLIEST TREES	8	304
GOODLIEST OF ALL THE FORREST, HART AND HINDE;	11	189

GOODLY

THE GOODLY PROSPECT OF SOME FOREIN LAND	3	548
WHEN I BEHOLD THIS GOODLY FRAME, THIS WORLD	8	15
A GOODLY TREE FARR DISTANT TO BEHOLD	9	576
SO GOODLY AND ERECT, THOUGH FAULTIE SINCE,	11	509

GOODNESS

INFINITE GOODNESS, GRACE AND MERCY SHEWN	1	218
HIS MALICE, AND THY GOODNESS BRING TO NAUGHT,	3	158
SO SHOULD THY GOODNESS AND THY GREATNESS BOTH	3	165
RESIGNS HER CHARGE, WHILE GOODNESS THINKS NO ILL	3	688
THY GOODNESS INFINITE, BOTH WHEN WE WAKE,	4	734
AND FELT HOW AWFUL GOODNESS IS, AND SAW	4	847
THY GOODNESS BEYOND THOUGHT, AND POWER DIVINE:	5	159
AND PUT NOT FORTH MY GOODNESS, WHICH IS FREE	7	171
IN GOODNESS AND IN POWER PRAEEMINENT;	8	279
SENT FROM WHOSE SOVRAN GOODNESS I ADORE.	8	647
WITH GOODNESS AND PATERNAL LOVE, HIS FACE	11	353
O GOODNESS INFINITE, GOODNESS IMMENSE.	12	469

GOR'D

WITH MANY AN INRODE GOR'D; DEFORMED ROUT	6	387

GORDIAN

INSINUATING, WOVE WITH GORDIAN TWINE	4	348

GORE

ROWLING IN DUST AND GORE. TO WHICH OUR SIRE.	11	460

GORG'D

ON WHAT WAS PURE, TILL CRAMM'D AND GORG'D, NIGH BURST	10	632

GORGE

TO GORGE THE FLESH OF LAMBS OR YEANLING KIDS	3	434

GORGEOUS

OR WHERE THE GORGEOUS EAST WITH RICHEST HAND	2	3
VAILD WITH HIS GORGEOUS WINGS, UPSPRINGING LIGHT	5	250
THEN LIGHTED FROM HIS GORGEOUS THRONE, FOR NOW	6	103

GORGIOUS

BASES AND TINSEL TRAPPINGS, GORGIOUS KNIGHTS	9	36

GORGON
BEDROPT WITH BLOOD OF GORGON, OR THE ISLE 10 527

GORGONIAN
MEDUSA WITH GORGONIAN TERROR GUARDS 2 611
BOUND WITH GORGONIAN RIGOR NOT TO MOVE, 10 297

GORGONS
GORGONS AND HYDRA'S, AND CHIMERA'S DIRE. 2 628

GOSHEN
THE SOJOURNERS OF GOSHEN, WHO BEHELD 1 309

GOT
GOT THEM NEW NAMES, TILL WANDRING ORE THE EARTH, 1 365
AMID THE TREE NOW GOT, WHERE PLENTY HUNG 9 594
BOTH GOOD AND EVIL, GOOD LOST, AND EVIL GOT, 9 1072
AMONG THE HEATHEN OF THIR PURCHASE GOT, 10 579
HIS KNOWLEDGE OF GOOD LOST, AND EVIL GOT, 11 87

GOTTESQUE
WITH THICKET OVERGROWN, GOTTESQUE AND WILDE, 4 136

GOURD
EACH PLANT AND JUCIEST GOURD WILL PLUCK SUCH CHOICE 5 327
THE SMELLING GOURD, UP STOOD THE CORNIE REED 7 321

GOVERN
OUR BEING ORDAIN'D TO GOVERN, NOT TO SERVE? 5 802
PURPLES THE EAST: STILL GOVERN THOU MY SONG, 7 30
GOVERN THE REST, SELF-KNOWING, AND FROM THENCE 7 510
AND GOVERN WELL THY APPETITE, LEAST SIN 7 546

GOVERND
AND THIS PERVERSE COMMOTION GOVERND THUS, 6 706

GOVERNMENT
WERE SUCH AS UNDER GOVERNMENT WELL SEEM'D, 10 154
AND UPSTART PASSIONS CATCH THE GOVERNMENT 12 88
THIR GOVERNMENT, AND THIR GREAT SENATE CHOOSE 12 225

GOVERNS
CHANCE GOVERNS ALL. INTO THIS WILDE ABYSS, 2 910
THEM WHOM HE GOVERNS. THIS IS SERVITUDE, 6 178

GRACE
EXTORT FROM ME. TO BOW AND SUE FOR GRACE 1 111
INFINITE GOODNESS, GRACE AND MERCY SHEWN 1 218
AND PUBLISH GRACE TO ALL, ON PROMISE MADE 2 238
OF HEAVENLY GRACE: AND GOD PROCLAIMING PEACE, 2 499
GOD AND GOOD ANGELS GUARD BY SPECIAL GRACE. 2 1033
BY THE OTHER FIRST: MAN THEREFORE SHALL FIND GRACE, 3 131
LOVE WITHOUT END, AND WITHOUT MEASURE GRACE, 3 142
THY SOVRAN SENTENCE, THAT MAN SHOULD FIND GRACE; 3 145
YET NOT OF WILL IN HIM, BUT GRACE IN ME 3 174
SOME I HAVE CHOSEN OF PECULIAR GRACE 3 183
TH' INCENSED DEITIE, WHILE OFFERD GRACE 3 187
THIS MY LONG SUFFERANCE AND MY DAY OF GRACE 3 198
FATHER, THY WORD IS PAST, MAN SHALL FIND GRACE; 3 227
AND SHALL GRACE NOT FIND MEANS, THAT FINDS HER WAY, 3 228
IN THOSE WHO, WHEN THEY MAY, ACCEPT NOT GRACE. 3 302
FATHER OF MERCIE AND GRACE, THOU DIDST NOT DOOME 3 401
SUTABLE GRACE DIFFUS'D, SO WELL HE FEIGND; 3 639
BY ACT OF GRACE MY FORMER STATE; HOW SOON 4 94
FOR SOFTNESS SHEE AND SWEET ATTRACTIVE GRACE, 4 298
IN THEM DIVINE RESEMBLANCE, AND SUCH GRACE 4 364
HOW BEAUTY IS EXCELLD BY MANLY GRACE 4 490
SEVERE IN YOUTHFUL BEAUTIE, ADDED GRACE 4 845
CAN END IT. INTO THEE SUCH VERTUE AND GRACE 6 703
ON ERRANDS OF SUPERNAL GRACE. SO SUNG 7 573
AND GRACE THAT WON WHO SAW TO WISH HER STAY, 8 43
THOUGH PLEASANT, BUT THY WORDS WITH GRACE DIVINE 8 215
SPEAKING OR MUTE ALL COMLINESS AND GRACE 8 222
GRACE WAS IN ALL HER STEPS, HEAV'N IN HER EYE, 8 488
TO SERVE HIM, THY REWARD WAS OF HIS GRACE, 10 767
HEE WILL INSTRUCT US PRAYING, AND OF GRACE 10 1081
WHAT ELSE BUT FAVOR, GRACE, AND MERCIE SHON? 10 1096
PREVENIENT GRACE DESCENDING HAD REMOV'D 11 3
FROM THY IMPLANTED GRACE IN MAN, THESE SIGHS 11 23
GIV'N THEE OF GRACE, WHEREIN THOU MAY'ST REPENT, 11 255
EXPECT TO HEAR, SUPERNAL GRACE CONTENDING 11 359
SUCH GRACE SHALL ONE JUST MAN FIND IN HIS SIGHT, 11 890
ACCEPTANCE OF LARGE GRACE, FROM SERVIL FEAR 12 305
FROM GOD, AND OVER WRAUTH GRACE SHALL ABOUND. 12 478
BUT FORCE THE SPIRIT OF GRACE IT SELF, AND BINDE 12 525

GRACEFUL
BELIAL, IN ACT MORE GRACEFUL AND HUMANE; 2 109
SO MUCH DELIGHTS ME AS THOSE GRACEFUL ACTS, 8 600
HER GRACEFUL INNOCENCE, HER EVERY AIRE 9 459
BLOW MOIST AND KEEN, SHATTERING THE GRACEFUL LOCKS 10 1066

GRACES
I PLEAS'D, AND WITH ATTRACTIVE GRACES WON 2 762
WORLDS, AND ON WHOM HATH ALL THESE GRACES POWRD; 3 674
KNIT WITH THE GRACES AND THE HOURS IN DANCE 4 267
SHOT FORTH PECULIAR GRACES; THEN WITH VOICE 5 15
A POMP OF WINNING GRACES WAITED STILL, 8 61

GRACIOUS
O FATHER, GRACIOUS WAS THAT WORD WHICH CLOS'D 3 144
KISS'D AS THE GRACIOUS SIGNS OF SWEET REMORSE 5 134
RETURN'D AND GRACIOUS PURPOSE THUS RENEW'D. 8 337
THE GRACIOUS JUDGE WITHOUT REVILE REPLI'D. 10 118
AND GRACIOUS TEMPER HE BOTH HEARD AND JUDG'D 10 1047
ENLIGHTNER OF MY DARKNESS, GRACIOUS THINGS 12 271

GRAC'T
THAT I WHO FIRST BROUGHT DEATH ON ALL, AM GRAC'T 11 168

GRADUAL
MANS NOURISHMENT, BY GRADUAL SCALE SUBLIM'D 5 483
OF CREATURES ANIMATE WITH GRADUAL LIFE 9 112

GRAIN
SKIE-TINCTUR'D GRAIN. LIKE MAIA'S SON HE STOOD, 5 285
COVER'D WITH PEARLY GRAIN: YET GOD HATH HERE 5 430
TO BLACKEST GRAIN, AND INTO STORE CONVEY'D: 6 515
THE SMELL OF GRAIN, OR TEDDED GRASS, OR KINE, 9 450

GRAINE
AGAINST A RUMORD WARR, THE SMUTTIE GRAINE 4 817
THIR MAGNITUDES, THIS EARTH A SPOT, A GRAINE, 8 17
LIVELIER THEN MELIBOEAN, OR THE GRAINE 11 242
WHAT IT DEVOURS NOT, HERB, OR FRUIT, OR GRAINE, 12 184

GRAND
MOV'D OUR GRAND PARENTS IN THAT HAPPY STATE, 1 29
IRRECONCILEABLE, TO OUR GRAND FOE, 1 122
IN ORDER CAME THE GRAND INFERNAL PEERS, 2 507
SO CLOMB THIS FIRST GRAND THIEF INTO GODS FOULD: 4 192
WHOM THE GRAND FOE WITH SCORNFUL EYE ASKANCE 6 149
THERE KEPT THIR WATCH THE LEGIONS, WHILE THE GRAND 10 427
BE MEANT, WHOM I CONJECTURE, OUR GRAND FOE 10 1033

GRANDCHILD
FAIR DAUGHTER, AND THOU SON AND GRANDCHILD BOTH, 10 384

GRANDCHILDE
THE GRANDCHILDE WITH TWELVE SONS INCREAST, DEPARTS 12 155

GRAND-CHILDE
A SON, AND OF HIS SON A GRAND-CHILDE LEAVES, 12 153

GRANT
UNITED. BUT TO GRANT IT THEE UNJUST, 5 831

GRANTING
FROM GRANTING HEE, AS I FROM BEGGING PEACE: 4 104

GRANTS
AND TERROR CEASE; HE GRANTS WHAT THEY BESAUGHT 12 238

GRAPE
LAYES FORTH HER PURPLE GRAPE, AND GENTLY CREEPS 4 259
BERRIE OR GRAPE: TO WHOM THUS ADAM CALL'D. 5 307
HEAPS WITH UNSPARING HAND; FOR DRINK THE GRAPE 5 344

GRASING
GRASING THE TENDER HERB, WERE INTERPOS'D, 4 253

GRASPE
SAT HORROR PLUM'D; NOR WANTED IN HIS GRASPE 4 989

GRASPED
AGAINST THE HIGHEST, AND FIERCE WITH GRASPED ARMS 1 667

GRASPING
GRASPING TEN THOUSAND THUNDERS, WHICH HE SENT 6 836

GRASS
GAVE PROOF UNHEEDED; OTHERS ON THE GRASS 4 350
PUT FORTH THE VERDANT GRASS, HERB YIELDING SEED, 7 310
BROUGHT FORTH THE TENDER GRASS, WHOSE VERDURE CLAD 7 315
THE SMELL OF GRAIN, OR TEDDED GRASS, OR KINE, 9 450
AMIDST HIS CIRCLING SPIRES, THAT ON THE GRASS 9 502

GRASSIE
THEY TO THIR GRASSIE COUCH, THESE TO THIR NESTS 4 601
HAVE HEAP'D THIS TABLE. RAIS'D OF GRASSIE TERF 5 391
THE GRASSIE CLODS NOW CALV'D, NOW HALF APPEER'D 7 463
NOR NOCENT YET, BUT ON THE GRASSIE HERBE 9 186
OF GRASSIE TERFE, AND PILE UP EVERY STONE 11 324
RUSTIC, OF GRASSIE SORD; THITHER ANON 11 433

GRATE
TH' INFERNAL DORES, AND ON THIR HINGES GRATE 2 881

GRATEFUL
AND UNDERSTOOD NOT THAT A GRATEFUL MIND 4 55
CHEAR'D WITH THE GRATEFUL SMELL OLD OCEAN SMILES. 4 165
MORE GRATEFUL, TO THIR SUPPER FRUITS THEY FELL, 4 331
OF GRATEFUL EEVNING MILDE, THEN SILENT NIGHT 4 647
NOR GRATEFUL EEVNING MILD, NOR SILENT NIGHT 4 654
TO GRATEFUL TWILIGHT (FOR NIGHT COMES NOT THERE 5 645
GRATEFUL VICISSITUDE, LIKE DAY AND NIGHT; 6 8
INDUCING DARKNESS, GRATEFUL TRUCE IMPOS'D, 6 407

GRATEFUL (CONTINUED)
BUT GRATEFUL TO ACKNOWLEDGE WHENCE HIS GOOD 7 512
GRATEFUL DIGRESSIONS, AND SOLVE HIGH DISPUTE 8 55
MORE GRATEFUL THEN HARMONIOUS SOUND TO THE EARE. 8 606
WITH GRATEFUL MEMORIE: THOU TO MANKIND 8 650
WITH GRATEFUL SMELL, FORTH CAME THE HUMAN PAIR 9 197
GRATEFUL TO APPETITE, MORE PLEAS'D MY SENSE 9 580
SO MANY GRATEFUL ALTARS I WOULD REARE 11 323
CONSUM'D WITH NIMBLE GLANCE, AND GRATEFUL STEAME; 11 442
GRATEFUL TO HEAV'N, OVER HIS HEAD BEHOLDS 11 864

GRATEFULLY
THEN AS NEW WAK'T THUS GRATEFULLY REPLI'D. 8 4
TO WHOM THUS ADAM GRATEFULLY REPLI'D. 11 370

GRATIFIE
TO GRATIFIE MY SCORNFUL ENEMIES, 10 625

GRATIOUS
THIS ANSWER FROM THE GRATIOUS VOICE DIVINE. 8 436

GRATITUDE
THE DEBT IMMENSE OF ENDLESS GRATITUDE, 4 52

GRATULATING
OF MISCHIEF, GRATULATING, THUS EXCITES. 9 472

GRATULATION
GAVE SIGN OF GRATULATION, AND EACH HILL; 8 514

GRAVE
SATAN EXCEPT, NONE HIGHER SAT, WITH GRAVE 2 300
THE WOMB OF NATURE AND PERHAPS HER GRAVE, 2 911
THOU WILT NOT LEAVE ME IN THE LOATHSOM GRAVE 3 247
DEATH LAST, AND WITH HIS CARCASS GLUT THE GRAVE: 3 259
SO SPAKE THE CHERUBE, AND HIS GRAVE REBUKE 4 844
PRINCE OF THE AIRE; THEN RISING FROM HIS GRAVE 10 185
BOTH SIN, AND DEATH, AND YAWNING GRAVE AT LAST 10 635
WITH THIS CORPOREAL CLOD; THEN IN THE GRAVE, 10 786
THE MEN THOUGH GRAVE, EY'D THEM, AND LET THIR EYES 11 585
GREY-HEADED MEN AND GRAVE, WITH WARRIOURS MIXT, 11 662
OUT OF HIS GRAVE, FRESH AS THE DAWNING LIGHT, 12 423

GRAVELY
GRAVELY IN DOUBT WHETHER TO HOLD THEM WISE 4 907

GRAV'N
CORNICE OR FREEZE, WITH BOSSY SCULPTURES GRAV'N, 1 716
FULFIL OR GRAV'N IN METTLE. AFTER THESE, 11 573

GRAY
NOW CAME STILL EEVNING ON, AND TWILIGHT GRAY 4 598
HIS LONGITUDE THROUGH HEAV'NS HIGH RODE: THE GRAY 7 373
TO WITHERD WEAK AND GRAY; THY SENSES THEN 11 540
GOD FROM THE MOUNT OF SINAI, WHOSE GRAY TOP 12 227

GRAZE
GRAZE THE SEA WEED THIR PASTURE, AND THROUGH GROVES 7 404
I WAS AT FIRST AS OTHER BEASTS THAT GRAZE 9 571
AND FISH WITH FISH; TO GRAZE THE HERB ALL LEAVING, 10 711

GRAZED
LIK'NING HIS MAKER TO THE GRAZED OX, 1 486

GRAZING
OF CATTEL GRAZING: OTHERS, WHENCE THE SOUND 11 558

GREAT
THAT TO THE HIGHTH OF THIS GREAT ARGUMENT 1 24
AS ONE GREAT FURNACE FLAM'D, YET FROM THOSE FLAMES 1 62
SINCE THROUGH EXPERIENCE OF THIS GREAT EVENT 1 118
OF SOME GREAT AMMIRAL, WERE BUT A WAND, 1 294
OF THIR GREAT SULTAN WAVING TO DIRECT 1 348
THIR GREAT COMMANDER; GODLIKE SHAPES AND FORMS 1 358
AT THIR GREAT EMPERORS CALL, AS NEXT IN WORTH 1 378
NOR GREAT ALCAIRO SUCH MAGNIFICENCE 1 718
THE GREAT SERAPHIC LORDS AND CHERUBIM 1 794
AND SUMMONS READ, THE GREAT CONSULT BEGAN. 1 798
HEAV'NS PUREST LIGHT, YET OUR GREAT ENEMY 2 137
IF WE WERE WISE, AGAINST SO GREAT A FOE 2 202
THEN MOST CONSPICUOUS, WHEN GREAT THINGS OF SMALL, 2 258
THE GREAT CREATOUR? BUT THIR SPITE STILL SERVES 2 385
GREAT THINGS RESOLV'D, WHICH FROM THE LOWEST DEEP 2 392
REFUSING TO ACCEPT AS GREAT A SHARE 2 452
WITH TRUMPETS REGAL SOUND THE GREAT RESULT: 2 515
THE IRKSOM HOURS, TILL THIS GREAT CHIEF RETURN. 2 527
TO MEET SO GREAT A FOE: AND NOW GREAT DEEDS 2 722
GREAT THINGS WITH SMALL) THEN WHEN BELLONA STORMS, 2 922
TO WHOM THE GREAT CREATOUR THUS REPLY'D. 3 167
OF HIS GREAT FATHER. ADMIRATION SEIS'D 3 271
FARR MORE THEN GREAT OR HIGH; BECAUSE IN THEE 3 311
OR LONGITUDE, WHERE THE GREAT LUMINARIE 3 576
LAY WAVING ROUND; ON SOM GREAT CHARGE IMPLOY'D 3 628
THE FIRST ART WONT HIS GREAT AUTHENTIC WILL 3 656
ON WHOM THE GREAT CREATOR HATH BESTOWD 3 673
THE GREAT WORK-MAISTER, LEADS TO NO EXCESS 3 696
AS GREAT MIGHT HAVE ASPIR'D, AND ME THOUGH MEAN 4 62
DRAWN TO HIS PART; BUT OTHER POWERS AS GREAT 4 63

GREAT (CONTINUED)
OF GREAT SELEUCIA, BUILT BY GRECIAN KINGS, 4 212
SINGING THIR GREAT CREATOR; OFT IN BANDS 4 684
THOU SUN, OF THIS GREAT WORLD BOTH EYE AND SOULE, 5 171
VARIE TO OUR GREAT MAKER STILL NEW PRAISE. 5 184
IN HONOUR TO THE WORLDS GREAT AUTHOR RISE, 5 188
RIS'N ON MID-NOON; SOM GREAT BEHEST FROM HEAV'N 5 311
MEAN WHILE OUR PRIMITIVE GREAT SIRE, TO MEET 5 350
GIVEN HIM BY THIS GREAT CONFERENCE TO KNOW 5 454
TO WHOM OUR GREAT PROGENITOR. THY WORDS 5 544
HIS OTHER HALF IN THE GREAT ZONE OF HEAV'N. 5 560
AS HEAV'NS GREAT YEAR BRINGS FORTH, TH' EMPYREAL HOST 5 583
UNDER HIS GREAT VICE-GERENT REIGN ABIDE 5 609
IF NOT THE FIRST ARCH-ANGEL, GREAT IN POWER, 5 660
HONOURD BY HIS GREAT FATHER, AND PROCLAIMD 5 663
THE GREAT MESSIAH, AND HIS NEW COMMANDS, 5 691
THE GREAT HIERARCHAL STANDARD WAS TO MOVE; 5 701
OF THIR GREAT POTENTATE; FOR GREAT INDEED 5 706
THE PALACE OF GREAT LUCIFER, (SO CALL 5 760
ABOUT THE GREAT RECEPTION OF THIR KING, 5 769
THY SELF THOUGH GREAT AND GLORIOUS DOST THOU COUNT, 5 833
UNANIMOUS, AS SONS OF ONE GREAT SIRE 6 95
THE GREAT ARCH-ANGEL FROM HIS WARLIKE TOILE 6 257
FIT TO DECIDE THE EMPIRE OF GREAT HEAV'N. 6 303
GREAT THINGS BY SMALL, IF NATURES CONCORD BROKE, 6 311
THAT HIS GREAT PURPOSE HE MIGHT SO FULFILL, 6 675
OF ENDING THIS GREAT WARR, SINCE NONE BUT THOU 6 702
WHEN THE GREAT ENSIGN OF MESSIAH BLAZ'D 6 775
OR FAINT RETREAT; WHEN THE GREAT SON OF GOD 6 799
GREAT THINGS, AND FULL OF WONDER IN OUR EARES, 7 70
AND THE GREAT LIGHT OF DAY YET WANTS TO RUN 7 98
INTO HIS PLACE, AND THE GREAT SON RETURND 7 135
GREAT TRIUMPH AND REJOYCING WAS IN HEAV'N 7 180
ON HIS GREAT EXPEDITION NOW APPEER'D, 7 193
OF THIS GREAT ROUND: PARTITION FIRM AND SURE, 7 267
FERMENTED THE GREAT MOTHER TO CONCEAVE, 7 281
FOR HASTE; SUCH FLIGHT THE GREAT COMMAND IMPRESS'D 7 294
THE DRY LAND, EARTH, AND THE GREAT RECEPTACLE 7 307
AND GOD MADE TWO GREAT LIGHTS, GREAT FOR THIR USE 7 346
SURVEYING HIS GREAT WORK, THAT IT WAS GOOD: 7 353
HER GATHER'D BEAMS, GREAT PALACE NOW OF LIGHT. 7 363
REVOLVD ON HEAV'NS GREAT AXLE, AND HER REIGN 7 381
AND GOD CREATED THE GREAT WHALES, AND EACH 7 391
HER MOTIONS, AS THE GREAT FIRST-MOVERS HAND 7 500
ANSWERING HIS GREAT IDEA. UP HE RODE 7 557
THE GREAT CREATOR FROM HIS WORK RETURND 7 567
WITH HIS GREAT FATHER (FOR HE ALSO WENT 7 588
GREAT ARE THY WORKS, JEHOVAH, INFINITE 7 602
FROM MAN OR ANGEL THE GREAT ARCHITECT 8 72
THE BENEFIT: CONSIDER FIRST, THAT GREAT 8 90
WHICH TWO GREAT SEXES ANIMATE THE WORLD, 8 151
NOT OF MY SELF; BY SOME GREAT MAKER THEN, 8 278
HIS GREAT COMMAND; TAKE HEED LEAST PASSION SWAY 8 635
FROM TH' EARTHS GREAT ALTAR SEND UP SILENT PRAISE 9 195
RAIS'D, AS OF SOM GREAT MATTER TO BEGIN. 9 669
FLOURISHD, SINCE MUTE, TO SOM GREAT CAUSE ADDREST, 9 672
GREAT ARE THY VERTUES, DOUBTLESS, BEST OF FRUITS, 9 745
OUR GREAT FORBIDDER, SAFE WITH ALL HIS SPIES 9 815
GREAT JOY HE PROMIS'D TO HIS THOUGHTS, AND NEW 9 843
AND PERIL GREAT PROVOK'T, WHO THUS HATH DAR'D 9 922
IDLELY, WHILE SATAN OUR GREAT AUTHOR THRIVES 10 236
FLEW DIVERS, AND WITH POWER (THIR POWER WAS GREAT) 10 284
SO, IF GREAT THINGS TO SMALL MAY BE COMPAR'D, 10 306
GREAT JOY WAS AT THIR MEETING, AND AT SIGHT 10 350
EACH HOUR THEIR GREAT ADVENTURER FROM THE SEARCH 10 440
FORTH RUSH'D IN HASTE THE GREAT CONSULTING PEERS, 10 456
WITH PERIL GREAT ATCHIEV'D. LONG WERE TO TELL 10 469
BY THIR GREAT INTERCESSOR, CAME IN SIGHT 11 19
WHILE THE GREAT VISITANT APPROACHD, THUS SPAKE. 11 225
EVE, NOW EXPECT GREAT TIDINGS, WHICH PERHAPS 11 226
NONE OF THE MEANEST, SOME GREAT POTENTATE 11 231
THEREFORE TO HIS GREAT BIDDING I SUBMIT. 11 314
AND REVERENCE THEE THIR GREAT PROGENITOR. 11 346
TO AGRA AND LAHOR OF GREAT MOGUL 11 391
GUIANA, WHOSE GREAT CITIE GERYONS SONS 11 410
O TEACHER, SOME GREAT MISCHIEF HATH BEFALL'N 11 450
OF TRIUMPH, TO BE STYL'D GREAT CONQUEROURS, 11 695
AND OF THIR DOINGS GREAT DISLIKE DECLAR'D, 11 720
AND GREAT EXPLOITS, BUT OF TRUE VERTU VOID; 11 790
DOWN THE GREAT RIVER TO THE OP'NING GULF, 11 833
AS MOCKT THEY STORM; GREAT LAUGHTER WAS IN HEAV'N 12 59
FROM HERMON EAST TO THE GREAT WESTERN SEA, 12 141
IS MEANT THY GREAT DELIVERER, WHO SHALL BRUISE 12 149
THIR GOVERNMENT, AND THIR GREAT SENATE CHOOSE 12 225
OF GREAT MESSIAH SHALL SING. THUS LAWS AND RITES 12 244
WHY OUR GREAT EXPECTATION SHOULD BE CALL'D 12 378
AS AT THE WORLDS GREAT PERIOD; AND OUR SIRE 12 467
GREAT NUMBERS OF EACH NATION TO RECEAVE 12 503
ACCOMPLISHING GREAT THINGS, BY THINGS DEEMD WEAK 12 567
THE GREAT DELIVERANCE BY HER SEED TO COME 12 600
WHICH HE HATH SENT PROPITIOUS, SOME GREAT GOOD 12 612

GREATER
WITH LOSS OF EDEN, TILL ONE GREATER MAN 1 4
WHOM THUNDER HATH MADE GREATER? HERE AT LEAST 1 258
ACKNOWLEDGE HIM THY GREATER, SOUND HIS PRAISE 5 172
THE REBEL THRONES, BUT GREATER RAGE TO SEE 6 199

GREATER (CONTINUED)
YET FARR THE GREATER PART HAVE KEPT, I SEE, 7 145
TO MAN, THE GREATER TO HAVE RULE BY DAY, 7 347
OF LIGHT BY FARR THE GREATER PART HE TOOK, 7 359
RELATE THEE; GREATER NOW IN THY RETURN 7 604
IS GREATER THEN CREATED TO DESTROY. 7 607
GREATER SO MANIFOLD TO THIS ONE USE, 8 29
THAT BODIES BRIGHT AND GREATER SHOULD NOT SERVE 8 87
AS LEAVES A GREATER STORE OF FRUIT UNTOUCHT, 9 621
RELUCTANT, BUT IN VAINE, A GREATER POWER 10 515
ONE GREATER, OF WHOSE DAY HE SHALL FORETELL, 12 242
OF SPIRIT AND TRUTH; THE REST, FARR GREATER PART, 12 533

GREATEST
BY FALSITIES AND LYES THE GREATEST PART 1 367
LEARN HOW THIR GREATEST MONUMENTS OF FAME, 1 695
YOUR BULWARK, AND CONDEMNS TO GREATEST SHARE 2 29
POWERFUL AT GREATEST DISTANCE TO UNITE 10 247
OPHIUSA) BUT STILL GREATEST HEE THE MIDST, 10 528

GREATLY
THY SORROW I WILL GREATLY MULTIPLIE 10 193
GREATLY REJOYC'D, AND THUS HIS JOY BROKE FORTH. 11 869
GREATLY INSTRUCTED I SHALL HENCE DEPART, 12 557
GREATLY IN PEACE OF THOUGHT, AND HAVE MY FILL 12 558

GREATNESS
OF SERVILE POMP. OUR GREATNESS WILL APPEER 2 257
SO SHOULD THY GOODNESS AND THY GREATNESS BOTH 3 165
GREATNESS OF MIND AND NOBLENESS THIR SEAT 8 557

GRECIAN
OF GREAT SELEUCIA, BUILT BY GRECIAN KINGS, 4 212

GREECE
IN ANCIENT GREECE; AND IN AUSONIAN LAND 1 739
XERXES, THE LIBERTIE OF GREECE TO YOKE, 10 307

GREEDILY
GREEDILY SHE INGORG'D WITHOUT RESTRAINT, 9 791
THAT CURLD MEGARA: GREEDILY THEY PLUCK'D 10 560

GREEDY
WATCHES, NO DOUBT, WITH GREEDY HOPE TO FIND 9 257

GREEK
PERPLEX'D THE GREEK AND CYTHEREA'S SON; 9 19

GREEN
NOW NEARER, CROWNS WITH HER ENCLOSURE GREEN, 4 133
UNDER A TUFT OF SHADE THAT ON A GREEN 4 325
ON THE GREEN BANK, TO LOOK INTO THE CLEER 4 458
YON FLOURIE ARBORS, YONDER ALLIES GREEN, 4 626
SPRINGS LIGHTER THE GREEN STALK, FROM THENCE THE LEAVES 5 480
HER UNIVERSAL FACE WITH PLEASANT GREEN, 7 316
ON THE GREEN STEMM; GOD SAW THAT IT WAS GOOD. 7 337
GLIDE UNDER THE GREEN WAVE, IN SCULLES THAT OFT 7 402
THE CATTEL IN THE FIELDS AND MEDDOWES GREEN: 7 460
WITH SPOTS OF GOLD AND PURPLE, AZURE AND GREEN: 7 479
ON A GREEN SHADIE BANK PROFUSE OF FLOURS 8 286
BEYOND THE EARTHS GREEN CAPE AND VERDANT ISLES 8 631
FIRST FRUITS, THE GREEN EARE, AND THE YELLOW SHEAF, 11 435
GREEN TREE OR GROUND WHEREON HIS FOOT MAY LIGHT; 11 858
MUST EAT, AND ON THE GROUND LEAVE NOTHING GREEN: 12 186

GREETING
THIS GREETING ON THY IMPIOUS CREST RECEIVE. 6 188

GREW
SO SPEAKING AND SO THREATNING, GREW TENFOLD 2 705
GREW DARKER AT THIR FROWN, SO MATCHT THEY STOOD; 2 720
DISTORTED, ALL MY NETHER SHAPE THUS GREW 2 784
TO HEAV'N REMOV'D WHERE FIRST IT GREW, THERE GROWS, 3 356
ACCESS DENI'D; AND OVER HEAD UP GREW 4 137
THE MIDDLE TREE AND HIGHEST THERE THAT GREW, 4 195
OUR DEATH THE TREE OF KNOWLEDGE GREW FAST BY, 4 221
LAUREL AND MIRTLE, AND WHAT HIGHER GREW 4 694
GOD MADE, AND EVERY HERB, BEFORE IT GREW 7 336
AND TOUCHT BY HER FAIR TENDANCE GLADLIER GREW. 8 47
UNDER HIS FORMING HANDS A CREATURE GREW, 8 470
WHICH GREW IN PARADISE, THE BAIT OF EVE 10 551
THE FRUTAGE FAIR TO SIGHT, LIKE THAT WHICH GREW 10 561
BENDING HIS EARE; PERSWASION IN ME GREW 11 152

GREY
WHITE, BLACK AND GREY, WITH ALL THIR TRUMPERIE. 3 475
FROM HILL OR STEAMING LAKE, DUSKIE OR GREY, 5 186

GREY-HEADED
GREY-HEADED MEN AND GRAVE, WITH WARRIOURS MIXT, 11 662

GRIDING
THE GRIDING SWORD WITH DISCONTINUOUS WOUND 6 329

GRIEF
FORGETS BOTH JOY AND GRIEF, PLEASURE AND PAIN, 2 586
O HELL, WHAT DOE MINE EYES WITH GRIEF BEHOLD, 4 358

GRIEF (CONTINUED)
SURCHARG'D, AS HAD LIKE GRIEF BIN DEW'D IN TEARS, 12 373

GRIEFE
THUS HE RESOLV'D, BUT FIRST FROM INWARD GRIEFE 9 97

GRIESLIE
SO SPAKE THE GRIESLIE TERROUR, AND IN SHAPE, 2 704
SO SUDDEN TO BEHOLD THE GRIESLIE KING; 4 821

GRIESLY
THERE STOOD A HILL NOT FAR WHOSE GRIESLY TOP 1 670

GRIEV'D
GRIEV'D AT HIS HEART, WHEN LOOKING DOWN HE SAW 11 887

GRIEVD
LAY PLEASANT, HIS GRIEVD LOOK HE FIXES SAD, 4 28

GRIEVE
SHALL GRIEVE HIM, IF I FAIL NOT, AND DISTURB 1 167
HOW DIDST THOU GRIEVE THEN, ADAM, TO BEHOLD 11 754

GRIEVING
GRIEVING TO SEE HIS GLORIE, AT THE SIGHT 6 792

GRIEVOUS
OR MUCH MORE GRIEVOUS PAIN? YE HAVE TH' ACCOUNT 10 501
GRIEVOUS TO BEAR: BUT THAT CARE NOW IS PAST, 11 776
WOLVES SHALL SUCCEED FOR TEACHERS, GRIEVOUS WOLVES, 12 508

GRIM
TO HIS GRIM IDOL. HIM THE AMMONITE 1 396
WHAT IF THE BREATH THAT KINDL'D THOSE GRIM FIRES 2 170
THAT DAR'ST, THOUGH GRIM AND TERRIBLE, ADVANCE 2 682
GRIM DEATH MY SON AND FOE, WHO SETS THEM ON, 2 804
THE RIDGES OF GRIM WARR; NO THOUGHT OF FLIGHT, 6 236
SO SENTED THE GRIM FEATURE, AND UPTURN'D 10 279
OF MAN, BUT FLED HIM, OR WITH COUNT'NANCE GRIM 10 713
TO HIS GRIM CAVE, ALL DISMAL; YET TO SENSE 11 469

GRINDE
OR BY COLLISION OF TWO BODIES GRINDE 10 1072

GRINND
GRINND HORRIBLE A GASTLY SMILE, TO HEAR 2 846

GRIPE
FIT WELL HIS HELME, GRIPE FAST HIS ORBED SHIELD, 6 543
HEART-STROOK WITH CHILLING GRIPE OF SORROW STOOD, 11 264

GRIP'T
GRIP'T IN EACH PAW: WHEN ADAM FIRST OF MEN 4 408

GROAN
IMPLACABLE, AND MANY A DOLOROUS GROAN, 6 658
IN PANGS, AND NATURE GAVE A SECOND GROAN, 9 1001

GROAND
GROAND OUT HIS SOUL WITH GUSHING BLOUD EFFUS'D. 11 447

GROANE
UNDER WHAT TORMENTS INWARDLY I GROANE; 4 88

GROANING
UNDER HER OWN WAIGHT GROANING TILL THE DAY 12 539

GROANS
THERE TO CONVERSE WITH EVERLASTING GROANS, 2 184
DIRE WAS THE TOSSING, DEEP THE GROANS, DESPAIR 11 489

GROOMS
OF HORSES LED, AND GROOMS BESMEARD WITH GOLD 5 356

GROSS
FELL NOT FROM HEAVEN, OR MORE GROSS TO LOVE 1 491
ANOTHER PART IN SQUADRONS AND GROSS BANDS, 2 570
APPROACHING GROSS AND HUGE; IN HOLLOW CUBE 6 552
PUREST AT FIRST, NOW GROSS BY SINNING GROWN. 6 661
NO GROSS, NO UNHARMONEOUS MIXTURE FOULE, 11 51
AS A DISTEMPER, GROSS TO AIRE AS GROSS, 11 53
ABOVE THE CLOUDS WILL PINE HIS ENTRAILS GROSS, 12 77

GROSSER
THE GROSSER FEEDS THE PURER, EARTH THE SEA, 5 416
MADE ERRE, WAS NOW EXHAL'D, AND GROSSER SLEEP 9 1049

GROTS
ANOTHER SIDE, UMBRAGEOUS GROTS AND CAVES 4 257

GROUND
EGYPT FROM SYRIAN GROUND, HAD GENERAL NAMES 1 421
A THIRD AS SOON HAD FORM'D WITHIN THE GROUND 1 705
THICK SWARM'D, BOTH ON THE GROUND AND IN THE AIR, 1 767
UPLIFTED SPURNS THE GROUND, THENCE MANY A LEAGUE 2 929
ON EVEN GROUND AGAINST HIS MORTAL FOE, 3 179
TOWARDS EITHER THRONE THEY BOW, AND TO THE GROUND 3 350
OUT OF THE FERTIL GROUND HE CAUS'D TO GROW 4 216

GROUND (CONTINUED)
HIS COUCHANT WATCH, AS ONE WHO CHOSE HIS GROUND . 4 406
BROIDERD THE GROUND, MORE COLOUR'D THEN WITH STONE 4 702
PARTAKERS, AND UNCROPT FALLS TO THE GROUND. . . 4 731
WANTS HER FIT VESSELS PURE, THEN STREWS THE GROUND 5 348
THIS SPACIOUS GROUND, IN YONDER SHADIE BOWRE . . 5 367
WE BRUSH MELLIFLUOUS DEWES, AND FIND THE GROUND . 5 429
THIR PERFET RANKS; FOR HIGH ABOVE THE GROUND . . 6 71
WINDS UNDER GROUND OR WATERS FORCING WAY . . . 6 196
THAT WARR AND VARIOUS; SOMTIMES ON FIRM GROUND . 6 242
ENTER'D, AND FOUL DISORDER; ALL THE GROUND . . . 6 388
DEEP UNDER GROUND, MATERIALS DARK AND CRUDE, . . 6 478
THAT UNDER GROUND, THEY FOUGHT IN DISMAL SHADE; . 6 666
ON HEAV'NLY GROUND THEY STOOD, AND FROM THE SHORE 7 210
BUT THEY, OR UNDER GROUND, OR CIRCUIT WIDE . . . 7 301
EASIE, E'RE GOD HAD BID THE GROUND BE DRIE, . . 7 304
UPON THE EARTH, AND MAN TO TILL THE GROUND . . . 7 332
WENT UP AND WATERD ALL THE GROUND, AND EACH . . 7 334
WITH CLANG DESPIS'D THE GROUND, UNDER A CLOUD . . 7 422
THE MID AEREAL SKIE: OTHERS ON GROUND 7 442
LIMB'D AND FULL GROWN: OUT OF THE GROUND UP ROSE . 7 456
IN HILLOCKS; THE SWIFT STAG FROM UNDER GROUND . . 7 469
AT ONCE CAME FORTH WHATEVER CREEPS THE GROUND, . 7 475
STREAKING THE GROUND WITH SINUOUS TRACE; NOT ALL . 7 481
AND EVERY CREEPING THING THAT CREEPS THE GROUND. . 7 523
DUST OF THE GROUND, AND IN THY NOSTRILS BREATH'D . 7 525
INTO A GULF SHOT UNDER GROUND, TILL PART . . . 9 72
PRONE ON THE GROUND, AS SINCE, BUT ON HIS REARE, . 9 497
FAWNING, AND LICK'D THE GROUND WHEREON SHE TROD, . 9 526
FOR HIGH FROM GROUND THE BRANCHES WOULD REQUIRE . 9 590
BRAUNCHING SO BROAD AND LONG, THAT IN THE GROUND . 9 1104
NO GROUND OF ENMITIE BETWEEN US KNOWN, ... 9 1151
CURS'D IS THE GROUND FOR THY SAKE, THOU IN SORROW 10 201
TILL THOU RETURN UNTO THE GROUND, FOR THOU . . 10 206
OUT OF THE GROUND WAST TAKEN, KNOW THY BIRTH, . . 10 207
ALL THINGS WITH DOUBLE TERROR: ON THE GROUND . . 10 850
OUTSTRETCHT HE LAY, ON THE COLD GROUND, AND OFT . 10 851
GLANC'D ON THE GROUND, WITH LABOUR I MUST EARNE . 10 1054
WATERING THE GROUND, AND WITH OUR SIGHS THE AIR . 10 1090
WATERING THE GROUND, AND WITH THIR SIGHS THE AIR . 10 1102
THE GROUND WHENCE HE WAS TAKEN, FITTER SOILE. . . 11 98
FROM HALLOWD GROUND TH' UNHOLIE, AND DENOUNCE . . 11 106
OF FLIGHT PURSU'D IN TH' AIR AND ORE THE GROUND . 11 202
THE GROUND WHENCE THOU WAST TAK'N, FITTER SOILE. . 11 262
TO DWELL ON EEVEN GROUND NOW WITH THY SONS: . . 11 348
FROM A FAT MEDDOW GROUND; OR FLEECY FLOCK, . . . 11 648
THE ARK NO MORE NOW FLOTES, BUT SEEMS ON GROUND . 11 850
GREEN TREE OR GROUND WHEREON HIS FOOT MAY LIGHT; . 11 858
ANON DRIE GROUND APPEERS, AND FROM HIS ARKE . . 11 861
BOILES OUT FROM UNDER GROUND, THE MOUTH OF HELL; . 12 42
MUST EAT, AND ON THE GROUND LEAVE NOTHING GREEN; . 12 186
THE CHERUBIM DESCENDED; ON THE GROUND 12 628
AND GATHERS GROUND FAST AT THE LABOURERS HEEL . . 12 631

GROUNDED
THEN SELF ESTEEM, GROUNDED ON JUST AND RIGHT . . 8 572

GROUNDS
MISTRUSTFUL, GROUNDS HIS COURAGE ON DESPAIR . . 2 126

GROVE
ON THAT OPPROBRIOUS HILL, AND MADE HIS GROVE . . 1 403
EVEN TO THAT HILL OF SCANDAL, BY THE GROVE . . . 1 416
CLEER SPRING, OR SHADIE GROVE, OR SUNNIE HILL, . 3 28
BREATHING THE SMELL OF FIELD AND GROVE, ATTUNE . 4 265
TO SEEK HER THROUGH THE WORLD; NOR THAT SWEET GROVE 4 272
HER BEARDED GROVE OF EARS, WHICH WAY THE WIND . . 4 982
OUR TENDED PLANTS, HOW BLOWS THE CITRON GROVE, . 5 22
HE BROUGHT THEE INTO THIS DELICIOUS GROVE, . . . 7 537
OF GROVE OR GARDEN-PLOT MORE PLEASANT LAY, . . 9 418
A GROVE HARD BY, SPRUNG UP WITH THIS THIR CHANGE, 10 548

GROVELING
GROVELING AND PROSTRATE ON YON LAKE OF FIRE, . . 1 280
UPON THY BELLY GROVELING THOU SHALT GOE, . . . 10 177

GROVES
FORTUNATE FIELDS, AND GROVES AND FLOURIE VALES, . 3 569
GROVES WHOSE RICH TREES WEPT ODOROUS GUMMS AND
BALME, ... 4 248
AMONG THE GROVES, THE FOUNTAINS, AND THE FLOURS . 5 126
INTO THE BLISSFUL FIELD, THROUGH GROVES OF MYRRHE, 5 292
GRAZE THE SEA WEED THIR PASTURE, AND THROUGH GROVES 7 404
BETOOK HER TO THE GROVES, BUT DELIA'S SELF . . . 9 388

GROW
THAT RICHES GROW IN HELL; THAT SOYLE MAY BEST . . 1 691
FOR WHICH TO STRIVE, NO STRIFE CAN GROW UP THERE . 2 31
THIS HORROR WILL GROW MILDE, THIS DARKNESS LIGHT, 2 220
FOR NEVER CAN TRUE RECONCILEMENT GROW 4 98
OUT OF THE FERTIL GROUND HE CAUS'D TO GROW . . . 4 216
THIR STELLAR VERTUE ON ALL KINDS THAT GROW . . . 4 671
THESE THINGS, AS NOT TO MIND FROM WHENCE THEY GROW 6 477
FOR MANY ARE THE TREES OF GOD THAT GROW 9 618
GROW UP TO THIR PROVISION, AND MORE HANDS . . . 9 623
TILL DIETED BY THEE I GROW MATURE 9 803
THE BENDED TWIGS TAKE ROOT, AND DAUGHTERS GROW . 9 1105
REGENERATE GROW INSTEAD, THAT SIGHS NOW BREATH'D . 11 5

GROW (CONTINUED)
THAT NEVER WILL IN OTHER CLIMATE GROW, ... 11 274
IN WEALTH AND MULTITUDE, FACTIOUS THEY GROW; . . 12 352
AND DUE TO THEIRS WHICH OUT OF THINE WILL GROW; . 12 400

GROWES
COMMUNICATED, MORE ABUNDANT GROWES, ... 5 72
OF EVERY TREE THAT IN THE GARDEN GROWES 8 321

GROWING
A GROWING EMPIRE; DOUBTLESS; WHILE WE DREAM, . . 2 315
A GROWING BURDEN. MEAN WHILE WARR AROSE, . . . 2 767
TO PRUNE THESE GROWING PLANTS, AND TEND THESE
FLOURS, ... 4 438
THIR GROWING WORK: FOR MUCH THIR WORK OUTGREW . . 9 202
AND GROWING UP TO GODHEAD; WHICH FOR THEE . . . 9 877
WINGS GROWING, AND DOMINION GIV'N ME LARGE . . . 10 244
THE GROWING MISERIES, WHICH ADAM SAW 10 715
GROWING INTO A NATION, AND NOW GROWN 12 164

GROWN
PORTENTOUS HELD ME; BUT FAMILIAR GROWN, ... 2 761
PREGNANT BY THEE, AND NOW EXCESSIVE GROWN . . . 2 779
PUREST AT FIRST, NOW GROSS BY SINNING GROWN, . . 6 661
LIMB'D AND FULL GROWN: OUT OF THE GROUND UP ROSE . 7 456
TO ME SO FRIENDLY GROWN ABOVE THE REST 9 564
BUT SAY, WHERE GROWN THE TREE, FROM HENCE HOW FAR? 9 617
INCLINABLE NOW GROWN TO TOUCH OR TASTE, ... 9 742
THUS GROWN. EXPERIENCE, NEXT TO THEE I OWE, . . 9 807
AS GOOD HAVE GROWN THERE STILL A LIVELESS RIB. . 9 1154
NOW DRAGON GROWN, LARGER THEN WHOM THE SUN . . 10 529
(CANST THOU BELIEVE?) SHOULD BE SO STUPID GROWN, . 12 116
GROWING INTO A NATION, AND NOW GROWN 12 164
IN MEAN ESTATE LIVE MODERATE, TILL GROWN . . . 12 351

GROWS
TO HEAV'N REMOV'D WHERE FIRST IT GREW, THERE GROWS, 3 356
SO NEER GROWS DEATH TO LIFE, WHAT ERE DEATH IS, . 4 425
HER FERTIL GROWTH, AND BY DISBURD'NING GROWS . . 5 319
AID US, THE WORK UNDER OUR LABOUR GROWS, . . . 9 208
HERE GROWS THE CURE OF ALL, THIS FRUIT DIVINE, . 9 776

GROWTH
WITH SINGED TOP THIR STATELY GROWTH THOUGH BARE . 1 614
MORE HANDS THEN OURS TO LOP THIR WANTON GROWTH: . 4 629
HER FERTIL GROWTH, AND BY DISBURD'NING GROWS . . 5 319
FRUIT OF DELICIOUS VINES, THE GROWTH OF HEAV'N, . 5 635
OF GROWTH, SENSE, REASON, ALL SUMM'D UP IN MAN, . 9 113
ONE NIGHT OR TWO WITH WANTON GROWTH DERIDES . . 9 211

GRUNSEL
IN HIS OWN TEMPLE, ON THE GRUNSEL EDGE, ... 1 460

GRYFON
AS WHEN A GRYFON THROUGH THE WILDERNESS 2 943

GUARD
GOD AND GOOD ANGELS GUARD BY SPECIAL GRACE. . . 2 1033
NOR WHERE ABASSIN KINGS THIR ISSUE GUARD, . . . 4 280
ENCAMPING, PLAC'D IN GUARD THIR WATCHES ROUND, . 6 412
ABOUT HER, AS A GUARD ANGELIC PLAC'T. 8 559
AND GUARD ALL PASSAGE TO THE TREE OF LIFE: . . . 11 122

GUARDED
THE GUARDED GOLD: SO EAGERLY THE FIEND 2 947

GUARDIANS
OF GUARDIANS BRIGHT, WHEN HE FROM ESAU FLED . . 3 512
THE FIELD PAVILION'D WITH HIS GUARDIANS BRIGHT; . 11 215

GUARDS
MEDUSA WITH GORGONIAN TERROR GUARDS 2 611
CHIEF OF TH' ANGELIC GUARDS, AWAITING NIGHT; . . 4 550
THE WESTERN POINT, WHERE THOSE HALF-ROUNDING GUARDS 4 862
WHO GUARDS HER, OR WITH HER THE WORST ENDURES. . 9 269
TH' ANGELIC GUARDS ASCENDED, MUTE AND SAD . . . 10 18
EXACTS OUR PARTING HENCE; AND SEE THE GUARDS, . . 12 590

GUESS
ALREADIE BY THY REASONING THIS I GUESS, ... 8 85

GUESSD
FOR ON SOM MESSAGE HIGH THEY GUESSD HIM BOUND. . 5 290

GUEST
THIS DAY TO BE OUR GUEST. BUT GOE WITH SPEED, . 5 313
TO ENTERTAIN OUR ANGEL GUEST, AS HEE 5 328
HIS GOD-LIKE GUEST, WALKS FORTH, WITHOUT MORE TRAIN 5 351
STOOD TO ENTERTAIN HER GUEST FROM HEAV'N; NO VAILE 5 383
O FAVOURABLE SPIRIT, PROPITIOUS GUEST, ... 5 507
AN EARTHLIE GUEST, AND DRAWN EMPYREAL AIRE, . . 7 14
PROCEEDED THUS TO ASK HIS HEAV'NLY GUEST. . . . 7 69
THUS ADAM HIS ILLUSTRIOUS GUEST BESOUGHT: . . . 7 109
GO HEAVENLY GUEST, ETHEREAL MESSENGER, ... 8 646
NO MORE OF TALK WHERE GOD OR ANGEL GUEST . . . 9 1

GUESTS
TO STOP THIR OVERGROWTH, AS INMATE GUESTS . . . 12 166

GUESTS (CONTINUED)
TOO NUMEROUS; WHENCE OF GUESTS HE MAKES THEM SLAVES 12 167

GUIANA
GUIANA, WHOSE GREAT CITIE GERYONS SONS 11 410

GUIDE
ALONE, AND WITHOUT GUIDE, HALF LOST, I SEEK . . 2 975
AND I WILL PLACE WITHIN THEM AS A GUIDE 3 194
AND WITHOUT WHOM AM TO NO END, MY GUIDE 4 442
MY GUIDE WAS GON, AND I, ME THOUGHT, SUNK DOWN, . 5 91
ASCEND MY CHARIOT, GUIDE THE RAPID WHEELES . . 6 711
FIRST FATHER, CALL'D BY THEE I COME THY GUIDE . . 8 298
MY WANDRING, HAD NOT HEE WHO WAS MY GUIDE . . 8 312
LEADS UP TO HEAV'N, IS BOTH THE WAY AND GUIDE; . 8 613
WHICH WHEN SHE SAW, THUS TO HER GUIDE SHE SPAKE. . 9 646
BEST GUIDE; NOT FOLLOWING THEE, I HAD REMAIND . . 9 808
BEFORE HIS VOICE, OR WAS SHEE MADE THY GUIDE, . . 10 146
ASCEND, I FOLLOW THEE, SAFE GUIDE, THE PATH . . 11 371
ADAM WAS ALL IN TEARS, AND TO HIS GUIDE 11 674
HOW COMES IT THUS? UNFOULD, CELESTIAL GUIDE, . . 11 785
TO GUIDE THEM IN THIR JOURNEY, AND REMOVE . . . 12 204
THE ENEMIES OF TRUTH; WHO THEN SHALL GUIDE . . . 12 482
TO GUIDE THEM IN ALL TRUTH, AND ALSO ARME . . . 12 490
THIR PLACE OF REST, AND PROVIDENCE THIR GUIDE: . 12 647

GUIDED
THY TEMPRING; WITH LIKE SAFETIE GUIDED DOWN . . . 7 15
AND GUIDED BY HIS VOICE, NOR UNINFORMD 8 486

GUIDES
HIS COUNT'NANCE, AS THE MORNING STARR THAT GUIDES 5 708
AND GUIDES THE EASTERN SAGES, WHO ENQUIRE . . . 12 362

GUILDS
WHICH NOW THE RISING SUN GUILDS WITH HIS BEAMS. . 3 551
AND HENCE THE MORNING PLANET GUILDS HER HORNS; . 7 366

GUILE
TH' INFERNAL SERPENT; HE IT WAS, WHOSE GUILE . . 1 34
TO WAGE BY FORCE OR GUILE ETERNAL WARR 1 121
TO WORK IN CLOSE DESIGN, BY FRAUD OR GUILE . . . 1 646
WHETHER OF OPEN WARR OR COVERT GUILE, ... 2 41
MY VOICE DISSWADES; FOR WHAT CAN FORCE OR GUILE . 2 188
BY SOME FALSE GUILE PERVERT; AND SHALL PERVERT . 3 92
HIS BREADED TRAIN, AND OF HIS FATAL GUILE . . . 4 349
NOR THOU HIS MALICE AND FALSE GUILE CONTEMN; . . 9 306
OF GUILE, OF HATE, OF ENVIE, OF REVENGE; . . . 9 466
HE ENDED, AND HIS WORDS REPLETE WITH GUILE . . . 9 733
FRIENDLY TO MAN, FARR FROM DECEIT OR GUILE. . . 9 772
ANGER, AND OBSTINACIE, AND HATE, AND GUILE. . . 10 114

GUILEFUL
TO WHOM THE GUILEFUL TEMPTER THUS REPLY'D. . . . 9 567
TO OBSERVE THE SEQUEL, SAW HIS GUILEFUL ACT . . 10 334

GUILEFULLY
TO WHOM THE TEMPTER GUILEFULLY REPLI'D. 9 655

GUILT
TO UNDERGOE WITH MEE ONE GUILT, ONE CRIME, . . . 9 971
TOOK LARGELY, OF THIR MUTUAL GUILT THE SEALE, . . 9 1043
THIR GUILT AND DREADED SHAME; O HOW UNLIKE . . . 9 1114
OR TO EACH OTHER, BUT APPARENT GUILT, ... 10 112
THE GUILT ON HIM WHO MADE HIM INSTRUMENT . . . 10 166
OF WASHING THEM FROM GUILT OF SIN TO LIFE . . . 12 443

GUILTIE
HIS CRIME MAKES GUILTIE ALL HIS SONS, THY MERIT . 3 290
THEN WAS NOT GUILTIE SHAME, DISHONEST SHAME . . 4 313
THE GUILTIE SERPENT, AND WELL MIGHT, FOR EVE . . 9 785
TO GUILTIE SHAME HEE COVER'D, BUT HIS ROBE . . . 9 1058
THE PRESENT, FEARING GUILTIE WHAT HIS WRAUTH . . 10 340

GUILTLESS
GUILTLESS OF FIRE HAD FORMD, OR ANGELS BROUGHT. . 9 392
FOR ONE MANS FAULT THUS GUILTLESS BE CONDEMN'D, . 10 823
IF GUILTLESS? BUT FROM ME WHAT CAN PROCEED, . . 10 824

GUISE
OF DREADFUL LENGTH AND DAZLING ARMS, IN GUISE . . 1 564
DOWN TO THE PLAIN DESCENDED: BY THIR GUISE . . . 11 576

GULF
FOR SINCE NO DEEP WITHIN HER GULF CAN HOLD . . . 2 12
THREATENS HIM, PLUNG'D IN THAT ABORTIVE GULF. . . 2 441
A GULF PROFOUND AS THAT SERBONIAN BOG 2 592
OVER THE DARK ABYSS, WHOSE BOILING GULF 2 1027
HELL AND THE GULF BETWEEN, AND SATAN THERE . . . 3 70
SATAN FROM HELL SCAP'T THROUGH THE DARKSOM GULF . 5 225
INTO THIR PLACE OF PUNISHMENT, THE GULF 6 53
INTO A GULF SHOT UNDER GROUND, TILL PART . . . 9 72
WHEN FIRST THIS TEMPTER CROSS'D THE GULF FROM HELL. 10 39
NOR THIS UNVOYAGEABLE GULF OBSCURE 10 366
DOWN THE GREAT RIVER TO THE OP'NING GULF, . . . 11 833

GULFE
LAY VANQUISHT, ROWLING IN THE FIERY GULFE . . . 1 52

GULFE (CONTINUED)
TRANSFIX US TO THE BOTTOM OF THIS GULFE. . . . 1 329
STAY HIS RETURN PERHAPS OVER THIS GULFE 10 253

GUMMIE
KINDLES THE GUMMIE BARK OF FIRR OR PINE, . . . 10 1076

GUMMS
GROVES WHOSE RICH TREES WEPT ODOROUS GUMMS AND
BALME, ... 4 248
THOSE BLOSSOMS ALSO, AND THOSE DROPPING GUMMS, . 4 630
OFFER SWEET SMELLING GUMMS AND FRUITS AND FLOURS: 11 327

GURGE
THE PLAIN, WHEREIN A BLACK BITUMINOUS GURGE . . 12 41

GUSHING
GROAND OUT HIS SOUL WITH GUSHING BLOUD EFFUS'D. . 11 447

GUST
THIR APPETITE WITH GUST, INSTEAD OF FRUIT . . . 10 565
AND SNOW AND HAILE AND STORMIE GUST AND FLAW, . . 10 698

HABIT
HIS HABIT FIT FOR SPEED SUCCINCT, AND HELD . . . 3 643

HABITABLE
DOWN TO THIS HABITABLE, WHICH RETURNES 8 157

HABITANT
OFFICIOUS, BUT TO THEE EARTHS HABITANT. 8 99
HABITUAL HABITANT; BEHIND HER DEATH 10 588

HABITANTS
THE PUNIE HABITANTS, OR IF NOT DRIVE, ... 2 367
THOSE ARGENT FIELDS MORE LIKELY HABITANTS, . . . 3 460

HABITATION
MIGHT YIELD THEM EASIER HABITATION, BEND . . . 2 573
HELL THIR FIT HABITATION FRAUGHT WITH FIRE . . . 6 876
OF DESTIND HABITATION; BUT THOU KNOW'ST 7 622

HABITATIONS
AND TH' HABITATIONS OF THE JUST; TO HIM 7 186
UNSEEN, AND THROUGH THIR HABITATIONS WALKS . . . 12 49

HABITS
COWLES, HOODS AND HABITS WITH THIR WEARERS TOST . 3 490

HABITUAL
HABITUAL HABITANT; BEHIND HER DEATH 10 588

HAD'ST
THE FIRST IN FLIGHT FROM PAIN, HAD'ST THOU ALLEDG'D 4 921
AND PERSON, HAD'ST THOU KNOWN THY SELF ARIGHT. . 10 156

HAG
NOR UGLIER FOLLOW THE NIGHT-HAG, WHEN CALL'D . . 2 662

HAIL
BACK TO THE GATES OF HEAV'N: THE SULPHUROUS HAIL . 1 171
WHERE JOY FOR EVER DWELLS: HAIL HORROURS, HAIL . 1 250
OF WHIRLWIND AND DIRE HAIL, WHICH ON FIRM LAND . 2 589
HAIL HOLY LIGHT, OFSPRING OF HEAV'N FIRST-BORN, . 3 1
HAIL SON OF GOD, SAVIOUR OF MEN, THY NAME . . . 3 412
HAIL UNIVERSAL LORD, BE BOUNTEOUS STILL 5 205
THIR DEVILISH GLUT, CHAIND THUNDERBOLTS AND HAIL . 6 589
TH' INCLEMENT SEASONS, RAIN, ICE, HAIL AND SNOW, . 10 1063

HAIL'D
THITHER BY HARPY-FOOTED FURIES HAIL'D, ... 2 596

HAILE
HAILE WEDDED LOVE, MYSTERIOUS LAW, TRUE SOURCE . 4 750
ALTERD HER CHEEK. ON WHOM THE ANGEL HAILE . . . 5 385
HAILE MOTHER OF MANKIND, WHOSE FRUITFUL WOMB . . 5 388
AND SNOW AND HAILE AND STORMIE GUST AND FLAW, . . 10 698
IS PAST, AND WE SHALL LIVE. WHENCE HAILE TO THEE, 11 158
AND ALL HIS PEOPLE; THUNDER MIXT WITH HAILE, . . 12 181
HAILE MIXT WITH FIRE MUST REND TH' EGYPTIAN SKIE . 12 182
THE SEED OF WOMAN: VIRGIN MOTHER, HAILE, . . . 12 379

HAINOUS
IS NOT SO HAINOUS NOW, FORETASTED FRUIT, . . . 9 929
MEANWHILE THE HAINOUS AND DESPIGHTFULL ACT . . . 10 1

HAIR
IN TH' ARTICK SKY, AND FROM HIS HORRID HAIR . . 2 710
AND BUSH WITH FRIZL'D HAIR IMPLICIT: LAST . . . 7 323

HAIRE
UNDER A CORONET HIS FLOWING HAIRE 3 640
FROM EITHER EYE, AND WIP'D THEM WITH HER HAIRE; . 5 131

HAIRIE
OF A STEEP WILDERNESS, WHOSE HAIRIE SIDES . . . 4 135
AND HAIRIE MAIN TERRIFIC, THOUGH TO THEE . . . 7 497

HALF
ON HALF THE NATIONS, AND WITH FEAR OF CHANGE 1 598
FROM WING TO WING, AND HALF ENCLOSE HIM ROUND 1 617
BY FORCE, HATH OVERCOME BUT HALF HIS FOE. 1 649
TREADING THE CRUDE CONSISTENCE, HALF ON FOOT, 2 941
HALF FLYING; BEHOVES HIM NOW BOTH OARE AND SAILE. 2 942
ALONE, AND WITHOUT GUIDE, HALF LOST, I SEEK 2 975
BY THEE, AND MORE THEN HALF PERHAPS WILL REIGNE; 4 112
MY OTHER HALF: WITH THAT THY GENTLE HAND 4 488
AND MEEK SURRENDER, HALF IMBRACING LEAND 4 494
ON OUR FIRST FATHER, HALF HER SWELLING BREAST 4 495
HALF WAY UP HILL THIS VAST SUBLUNAR VAULT, 4 777
UZZIEL, HALF THESE DRAW OFF, AND COAST THE SOUTH 4 782
HALF WHEELING TO THE SHIELD, HALF TO THE SPEAR. 4 785
BACK STEPT THOSE TWO FAIRE ANGELS HALF AMAZ'D 4 820
DISDAINFULLY HALF SMILING THUS REPLI'D. 4 903
BEST IMAGE OF MY SELF AND DEARER HALF, 5 95
GO THEREFORE, HALF THIS DAY AS FRIEND WITH FRIEND 5 229
HATH FINISHT HALF HIS JOURNEY, AND SCARCE BEGINS 5 559
HIS OTHER HALF IN THE GREAT ZONE OF HEAV'N. 5 560
FORTH STEPPING OPPOSITE, HALF WAY HE MET 6 128
HALF SUNK WITH ALL HIS PINES. AMAZEMENT SEIS'D 6 198
DESCENDING, AND IN HALF CUT SHEERE, NOR STAID, 6 325
CHARIOTS OF GOD, HALF ON EACH HAND WERE SEEN: 6 770
YET HALF HIS STRENGTH HE PUT NOT FORTH, BUT CHECK'D 6 853
HALF YET REMAINES UNSUNG BUT NARROWER BOUND 7 21
THE GRASSIE CLODS NOW CALV'D, NOW HALF APPEER'D 7 463
TO WHOM THUS HALF ABASH'T ADAM REPLI'D. 8 595
FROM SERVITUDE INGLORIOUS WELNIGH HALF 9 141
HALF SPI'D, SO THICK THE ROSES BUSHING ROUND 9 426
HALF WHAT IN THEE IS FAIR, ONE MAN EXCEPT, 9 545
UNNAM'D, UNDREADED, AND THY SELF HALF STARV'D? 10 595

HALF-RAIS'D
LEANING HALF-RAIS'D, WITH LOOKS OF CORDIAL LOVE 5 12

HALF-ROUNDING
THE WESTERN POINT, WHERE THOSE HALF-ROUNDING GUARDS 4 862

HALL
AND PORCHES WIDE, BUT CHIEF THE SPACIOUS HALL 1 762
THOUGH WITHOUT NUMBER STILL AMIDST THE HALL 1 791
SERV'D UP IN HALL WITH SEWERS, AND SENESHALS; 9 38
OF THAT PLUTONIAN HALL, INVISIBLE 10 444
OF HISSING THROUGH THE HALL, THICK SWARMING NOW 10 522
WITH TERROR THROUGH THE DARK AEREAL HALL. 10 667

HALLELUIA
SUNG HALLELUIA, AS THE SOUND OF SEAS, 10 642

HALLELUIAH'S
FORC'T HALLELUIAH'S; WHILE HE LORDLY SITS 2 243

HALLELUIAHS
UNFAINED HALLELUIAHS TO THEE SING, 6 744
WITH HALLELUIAHS: THUS WAS SABBATH KEPT. 7 634

HALLOW
WHICH INTO HALLOW ENGINS LONG AND ROUND 6 484

HALLOWD
THAT WASH THY HALLOWD FEET, AND WARBLING FLOW, 3 31
WITHIN THESE HALLOWD LIMITS THOU APPEER, 4 964
TO WHOM THUS EVE. ADAM, EARTHS HALLOWD MOULD, 5 321
NOW RESTING, BLESS'D AND HALLOWD THE SEAV'NTH DAY, 7 592
FROM HALLOWD GROUND TH' UNHOLIE, AND DENOUNCE 11 106

HAMATH
FROM HAMATH NORTHWARD TO THE DESERT SOUTH 12 139

HAND
HIS MIGHTY STATURE; ON EACH HAND THE FLAMES 1 222
AND SOME THE ARCHITECT: HIS HAND WAS KNOWN 1 732
OR WHERE THE GORGEOUS EAST WITH RICHEST HAND 2 3
HIS RED RIGHT HAND TO PLAGUE US? WHAT IF ALL 2 174
MAY PROVE THIR FOE, AND WITH REPENTING HAND 2 369
HE SCOURS THE RIGHT HAND COAST, SOM TIMES THE LEFT, 2 633
SATAN WAS NOW AT HAND, AND FROM HIS SEAT 2 674
O FATHER, WHAT INTENDS THY HAND, SHE CRY'D, 2 727
THOU INTERPOSEST, THAT MY SUDDEN HAND 2 738
INTO MY HAND WAS GIV'N, WITH CHARGE TO KEEP 2 775
AT THY RIGHT HAND VOLUPTUOUS, AS BESEEMS 2 869
THEE FROM MY BOSOM AND RIGHT HAND, TO SAVE, 3 279
ALL TH' UNACCOMPLISHT WORKS OF NATURES HAND, 3 455
STARS DISTANT, BUT NIGH HAND SEEMD OTHER WORLDS, 3 566
SO HAND IN HAND THEY PASSD, THE LOVLIEST PAIR 4 321
THE HAND THAT FORMD THEM ON THIR SHAPE HATH POURD, 4 365
IN ALL THIS HAPPINESS, WHO AT HIS HAND 4 417
MY OTHER HALF: WITH THAT THY GENTLE HAND 4 488
TH' UNARMED YOUTH OF HEAV'N, BUT NIGH AT HAND 4 552
THUS TALKING HAND IN HAND ALONE THEY PASS'D 4 689
HER HAND SOFT TOUCHING, WHISPERD THUS. AWAKE 5 17
ON EACH HAND PARTING, TO HIS SPEED GAVE WAY 5 252
HEAPS WITH UNSPARING HAND; FOR DRINK THE GRAPE 5 344
DANC'D HAND IN HAND. A WHILE DISCOURSE THEY HOLD; 5 395
AT MY RIGHT HAND; YOUR HEAD I HIM APPOINT; 5 606
WITH COPIOUS HAND, REJOYCING IN THIR JOY. 5 641
OUR PUISSANCE IS OUR OWN, OUR OWN RIGHT HAND 5 864

HAND (CONTINUED)
WAK'T BY THE CIRCLING HOURS, WITH ROSIE HAND 6 3
THY FOLLY; OR WITH SOLITARIE HAND 6 139
OF THIS RIGHT HAND PROVOK'T, SINCE FIRST THAT TONGUE 6 154
A NUMEROUS HOST, IN STRENGTH EACH ARMED HAND 6 231
IN HORROR; FROM EACH HAND WITH SPEED RETIR'D 6 307
ARME, WARRIOURS, ARME FOR FIGHT, THE FOE AT HAND, 6 537
A SERAPH STOOD, AND IN HIS HAND A REED 6 579
AND IN WHOSE HAND WHAT BY DECREE I DOE, 6 683
FROM THE RIGHT HAND OF GLORIE WHERE HE SATE, 6 747
ASCENDED, AT HIS RIGHT HAND VICTORIE 6 762
CHARIOTS OF GOD, HALF ON EACH HAND WERE SEEN: 6 770
TO ALL HIS HOST ON EITHER HAND THUS SPAKE. 6 800
THE PUNISHMENT TO OTHER HAND BELONGS, 6 807
AMONG THEM HE ARRIV'D; IN HIS RIGHT HAND 6 835
WHERE NOW HE SITS AT THE RIGHT HAND OF BLISS. 6 892
AGAINST A SOLEMN DAY, HARNEST AT HAND, 7 202
THEN STAID THE FERVID WHEELES, AND IN HIS HAND 7 224
HER MOTIONS, AS THE GREAT FIRST-MOVERS HAND 7 500
SUCH DISPROPORTIONS, WITH SUPERFLUOUS HAND 8 27
A LOWER FLIGHT, AND SPEAK OF THINGS AT HAND 8 199
SO SAYING, BY THE HAND HE TOOK ME RAIS'D, 8 300
BY SLY ASSAULT; AND SOMWHERE NIGH AT HAND 9 256
OF GOD ORDAIN'D THEM, HIS CREATING HAND 9 344
THUS SAYING, FROM HER HUSBANDS HAND HER HAND 9 385
IMBORDERD ON EACH BANK, THE HAND OF EVE: 9 438
SO SAYING, HER RASH HAND IN EVIL HOUR 9 780
SCARSE FROM THE TREE RETURNING; IN HER HAND 9 850
FROM HIS SLACK HAND THE GARLAND WREATH'D FOR EVE 9 892
WITH LIBERAL HAND: HE SCRUPL'D NOT TO EAT 9 997
HER HAND HE SEIS'D, AND TO A SHADIE BANK, 9 1037
TOWARD THE RIGHT HAND HIS GLORIE, ON THE SON 10 64
THAT FROM HER HAND I COULD SUSPECT NO ILL, 10 140
AND OF THIS WORLD, AND ON THE LEFT HAND HELL 10 322
CONGRATULANT APPROACH'D HIM, WHO WITH HAND 10 458
HIS HAND TO EXECUTE WHAT HIS DECREE 10 772
WHICH HIS OWN HAND MANURING ALL THE TREES 11 28
SELF-LEFT. LEAST THEREFORE HIS NOW BOLDER HAND 11 93
SATANS DIRE DREAD, AND IN HIS HAND THE SPEAR. 11 248
AT EEV'N, WHICH I BRED UP WITH TENDER HAND 11 276
THOU LEAD'ST ME, AND TO THE HAND OF HEAV'N SUBMIT, 11 372
BUT HIM THE GENTLE ANGEL BY THE HAND 11 421
UNCULL'D, AS CAME TO HAND; A SHEPHERD NEXT 11 436
ON EACH HAND SLAUGHTER AND GIGANTIC DEEDS. 11 659
HIS SEAT AT GODS RIGHT HAND, EXALTED HIGH 12 457
IN EITHER HAND THE HASTNING ANGEL CAUGHT 12 637
THEY HAND IN HAND WITH WANDRING STEPS AND SLOW, 12 648

HANDED
HANDED THEY WENT; AND EAS'D THE PUTTING OFF 4 739
SQUADRONS AT ONCE, WITH HUGE TWO-HANDED SWAY 6 251

HANDS
MAIM'D HIS BRUTE IMAGE, HEAD AND HANDS LOPT OFF 1 459
RANSACK'D THE CENTER, AND WITH IMPIOUS HANDS 1 686
AND HANDS INNUMERABLE SCARCE PERFORM. 1 699
LEVEL'D HIS DEADLY AIME; THIR FATALL HANDS 2 712
WITH HEAD, HANDS, WINGS OR FEET PURSUES HIS WAY, 2 949
MORE HANDS THEN OURS TO LOP THIR WANTON GROWTH: 4 629
THIR PAMPERD BOUGHES, AND NEEDED HANDS TO CHECK 5 214
OF SECONDARIE HANDS, BY TASK TRANSFERD 5 854
WHICH ALL SUBDUES, AND MAKES REMISS THE HANDS 6 458
NONE ARGUING STOOD, INNUMERABLE HANDS 6 508
UP LIFTING BORE THEM IN THIR HANDS: AMAZE, 6 646
SO AMPLY, AND WITH HANDS SO LIBERAL 8 362
THE RIB HE FORMD AND FASHOND WITH HIS HANDS; 8 469
UNDER HIS FORMING HANDS A CREATURE GREW, 8 470
THE HANDS DISPATCH OF TWO GARDNING SO WIDE. 9 203
OUR PLEASANT TASK ENJOYN'D, BUT TILL MORE HANDS 9 207
THESE PATHS & BOWERS DOUBT NOT BUT OUR JOYNT HANDS 9 244
AS WE NEED WALK, TILL YOUNGER HANDS ERE LONG 9 246
GROW UP TO THIR PROVISION, AND MORE HANDS 9 623
WHAT THY HANDS BUILDED NOT, THY WISDOM GAIN'D 10 373
WITH OUR OWN HANDS HIS OFFICE ON OUR SELVES; 10 1002
HATH UNBESAUGHT PROVIDED, AND HIS HANDS 10 1058
EXPLODED AND HAD SEIZ'D WITH VIOLENT HANDS, 11 669
THEN WITH UPLIFTED HANDS, AND EYES DEVOUT, 11 863

HANG
AND THY FAIR FRUIT LET HANG, AS TO NO END 9 798

HANGING
AND FAST BY HANGING IN A GOLDEN CHAIN 2 1051
STILL HANGING INCORRUPTIBLE, TILL MEN 9 622

HANGS
HANGS IN THE CLOUDS, BY AEQUINOCTIAL WINDS 2 637
ALL SEASONS, RIPE FOR USE HANGS ON THE STALK; 5 323

HAP
MIGHT HAP TO MOVE NEW BROILES: BE THIS OR AUGHT 2 837
ON MANS DESTRUCTION, MAUGRE WHAT MIGHT HAP 9 56
IN EVERY BUSH AND BRAKE, WHERE HAP MAY FINDE 9 160
HE SOUGHT THEM BOTH, BUT WISH'D HIS HAP MIGHT FIND 9 421

HAPLESS
THIR OWN HEROIC DEEDS AND HAPLESS FALL 2 549

HAPLESS (CONTINUED)
DETERMIND, AND THY HAPLESS CREW INVOLV'D 5 879
THIS SAW HIS HAPLESS FOES BUT STOOD OBDUR'D, . . . 6 785
O MUCH DECEAV'D, MUCH FAILING, HAPLESS EVE, . . . 9 404
BY NIGHT, AND LISTENING WHERE THE HAPLESS PAIRE . 10 342
AND TO OUR SEED (O HAPLESS SEED.) DERIV'D. . . . 10 965

HAPLY
HIM HAPLY SLUMBRING ON THE NORWAY FOAM 1 203
HAPLY SO SCAP'D HIS MORTAL SNARE; FOR NOW . . . 4 8
HENCEFORTH; MY DWELLING HAPLY MAY NOT PLEASE . . . 4 378
IMPOSSIBLE: YET HAPLY OF THY RACE 6 501
USEFUL, WHENCE HAPLY MENTION MAY ARISE 8 200
US HAPLY TOO SECURE OF OUR DISCHARGE 11 196

HAPPIE
OF MANKIND, IN THE HAPPIE GARDEN PLAC'T, ... 3 66
HAPPIE FOR MAN, SO COMING; HE HER AIDE 3 232
THIR HAPPIE HOURS IN JOY AND HYMNING SPENT. . . . 3 417
TO PARADISE THE HAPPIE SEAT OF MAN, ... 3 632
CREATED THIS NEW HAPPIE RACE OF MEN 3 679
THEN HAPPIE; NO UNBOUNDED HOPE HAD RAIS'D 4 60
SPIRIT OF HAPPIE SORT: HIS GESTURES FIERCE . . . 4 128
FAIR COUPLE, LINKT IN HAPPIE NUPTIAL LEAGUE, . . . 4 339
HAPPIE, BUT FOR SO HAPPIE ILL SECUR'D 4 370
BY IGNORANCE, IS THAT THIR HAPPIE STATE, ... 4 519
YET HAPPIE PAIR; ENJOY, TILL I RETURN, ... 4 534
CHARGE AND STRICT WATCH THAT TO THIS HAPPIE PLACE 4 562
HAVE FINISHT HAPPIE IN OUR MUTUAL HELP 4 727
HERE, HAPPIE CREATURE, FAIR ANGELIC EVE, ... 5 74
PARTAKE THOU ALSO; HAPPIE THOUGH THOU ART, ... 5 75
OF PARADISE AND EDENS HAPPIE PLAINS, ... 5 143
AS MAY ADVISE HIM OF HIS HAPPIE STATE, ... 5 234
THOSE HAPPIE PLACES THOU HAST DEIGND A WHILE . . . 5 364
YOUR FILL WHAT HAPPINESS THIS HAPPIE STATE 5 504
ATTEND: THAT THOU ART HAPPIE, OWE TO GOD; 5 520
IN SIGHT OF GOD ENTHRON'D, OUR HAPPIE STATE . . . 5 536
FOR EVER HAPPIE: HIM WHO DISOBEYES 5 611
OUR HAPPIE STATE UNDER ONE HEAD MORE NEER 5 830
THOUGH NOT DESTROY, THIR HAPPIE NATIVE SEAT; . . . 6 226
THIR PLEASANT DWELLING PLACE. THRICE HAPPIE MEN, 7 625
HOLY AND JUST: THRICE HAPPIE IF THEY KNOW 7 631
THIS HAPPIE LIGHT, WHEN ANSWER NONE RETURN'D, . . 8 285
FROM THAT DAY MORTAL, AND THIS HAPPIE STATE . . . 8 331
AND HAPPIE CONSTELLATIONS ON THAT HOURE 8 512
US HAPPIE, AND WITHOUT LOVE NO HAPPINESS. 8 621
BE STRONG, LIVE HAPPIE, AND LOVE, BUT FIRST OF ALL 8 633
HOW ARE WE HAPPIE, STILL IN FEAR OF HARM? 9 326
LET US NOT THEN SUSPECT OUR HAPPIE STATE 9 337
OR AUGHT THAT MIGHT HIS HAPPIE STATE SECURE, . . . 9 347
THIS HAPPIE TRIAL OF THY LOVE, WHICH ELSE 9 975
REMAIND STILL HAPPIE, NOT AS NOW, DESPOILD . . . 9 1138
MADE HAPPIE: HIM BY FRAUD I HAVE SEDUC'D 10 485
O MISERABLE OF HAPPIE. IS THIS THE END 10 720
I HAD PERSISTED HAPPIE, HAD NOT THY PRIDE 10 874
THEE NATIVE SOILE, THESE HAPPIE WALKS AND SHADES, 11 270
WITH MEDITATION ON THE HAPPIE END. 12 605
OF PARADISE, SO LATE THIR HAPPIE SEAT, ... 12 642

HAPPIER
YIELDED WITH FULL CONSENT. THE HAPPIER STATE . . . 2 24
TO NOTHING THIS ESSENTIAL, HAPPIER FARR 2 97
SO FARR THE HAPPIER LOT, ENJOYING THEE 4 446
THE HAPPIER EDEN, SHALL ENJOY THIR FILL 4 507
NO HAPPIER STATE, AND KNOW TO KNOW NO MORE. . . . 4 775
HAPPIER THOU MAYST BE, WORTHIER CANST NOT BE; . . 5 76
THEE ALSO HAPPIER, SHALL NOT BE WITHHELD 7 117
AND FEEL THAT I AM HAPPIER THEN I KNOW, ... 8 282
TO HAPPIER LIFE, KNOWLEDGE OF GOOD AND EVIL; . . . 9 697
IN OTHER WORLDS, AND HAPPIER SEAT PROVIDES . . . 10 237
HAPPIER, HAD IT SUFFIC'D HIM TO HAVE KNOWN . . . 11 88
SHALL ALL BE PARADISE, FAR HAPPIER PLACE 12 464
THEN THIS OF EDEN, AND FAR HAPPIER DAIES. 12 465
A PARADISE WITHIN THEE, HAPPIER FARR. 12 587

HAPPIEST
AND BANISHT FROM MANS LIFE HIS HAPPIEST LIFE, . . . 4 317
IS WOMANS HAPPIEST KNOWLEDGE AND HER PRAISE. . . . 4 638
BLEST PAIR; AND O YET HAPPIEST IF YE SEEK 4 774
BY PARENTS, OR HIS HAPPIEST CHOICE TOO LATE . . . 10 904

HAPPINESS
BOTH OF LOST HAPPINESS AND LASTING PAIN 1 55
OF HAPPINESS AND FINAL MISERY, ... 2 563
OR HAPPINESS IN THIS OR TH' OTHER LIFE; 3 450
IN ALL THIS HAPPINESS, WHO AT HIS HAND 4 417
HAPPINESS IN HIS POWER LEFT FREE TO WILL, ... 5 235
YOUR FILL WHAT HAPPINESS THIS HAPPIE STATE 5 504
WHOM TO OBEY IS HAPPINESS ENTIRE. 6 741
BEREAVD OF HAPPINESS THOU MAIST PARTAKE 6 903
THIR HAPPINESS, AND PERSEVERE UPRIGHT. 7 632
WHAT HAPPINESS, WHO CAN ENJOY ALONE, ... 8 365
A NICE AND SUTTLE HAPPINESS I SEE 8 399
OF HAPPINESS, OR NOT? WHO AM ALONE 8 405
US HAPPIE, AND WITHOUT LOVE NO HAPPINESS. 8 621
ENVYING OUR HAPPINESS, AND OF HIS OWN 9 254
FRAILE IS OUR HAPPINESS, IF THIS BE SO, ... 9 340
FULL HAPPINESS WITH MEE, OR RATHER NOT, ... 9 819

HAPPINESS (CONTINUED)
OF HAPPINESS: YET WELL, IF HERE WOULD END 10 725
CREATED HIM ENDOWD, WITH HAPPINESS 11 58

HAPP'ND
BUT MIGHT AS ILL HAVE HAPP'ND THOU BEING BY, . . . 9 1147

HAPPY
MOV'D OUR GRAND PARENTS IN THAT HAPPY STATE, . . . 1 29
FROM HIM, WHO IN THE HAPPY REALMS OF LIGHT 1 85
THOUGH ALL OUR GLORY EXTINCT, AND HAPPY STATE . . 1 141
ABOVE HIS EQUALS. FAREWEL HAPPY FIELDS 1 249
FOR HAPPY THOUGH BUT ILL, FOR ILL NOT WORST, . . . 2 224
ERR NOT) ANOTHER WORLD, THE HAPPY SEAT 2 347
THE HAPPY ILE; WHAT STRENGTH, WHAT ART CAN THEN . 2 410
BY WHICH, TO VISIT OFT THOSE HAPPY TRIBES, ... 3 532
OR OTHER WORLDS THEY SEEMD, OR HAPPY ILES, . . . 3 567
THRICE HAPPY ILES, BUT WHO DWELT HAPPY THERE . . . 3 570
A HAPPY RURAL SEAT OF VARIOUS VIEW; 4 247
DEPARTURE FROM THIS HAPPY PLACE, OUR SWEET . . . 11 303
SUCH HAPPY INTERVIEW AND FAIR EVENT 11 593
WITH LENGTH OF HAPPY DAYES THE RACE OF MAN; . . . 11 782

HARALDS
MEAN WHILE THE WINGED HARALDS BY COMMAND 1 752
BY HARALDS VOICE EXPLAIN'D; THE HOLLOW ABYSS . . 2 518
IN OTHER PART THE SCEPTER'D HARALDS CALL 11 660

HARAN
TO HARAN, AFTER HIM A CUMBROUS TRAIN 12 131

HARANGUES
ASSEMBLE, AND HARANGUES ARE HEARD, BUT SOON . . . 11 663

HARBINGER
DEATHS HARBINGER; SAD TASK, YET ARGUMENT 9 13
LOVES HARBINGER APPEERD; THEN ALL IN HEAT 11 589

HARBOUR
THERE REST, IF ANY REST CAN HARBOUR THERE, ... 1 185
YET EVIL WHENCE? IN THEE CAN HARBOUR NONE, . . . 5 99
THOUGHTS, WHICH HOW FOUND THEY HARBOUR IN THY BREST 9 288

HARD
OF MOLOCH HOMICIDE, LUST HARD BY HATE; 1 417
HARD LIBERTY BEFORE THE EASIE YOKE 2 256
AND HARD, THAT OUT OF HELL LEADS UP TO LIGHT; . . 2 433
THEN UNKNOWN DANGERS AND AS HARD ESCAPE. 2 444
SO HE WITH DIFFICULTY AND LABOUR HARD 2 1021
THOUGH HARD AND RARE: THEE I [illegible]
BUT HARD BE HARD'ND, BLIND BE BLINDED MORE, . . . 3 200
BY CENTER, OR ECCENTRIC, HARD TO TELL, ... 3 575
UPBRAIDED NONE; NOR WAS HIS SERVICE HARD. 4 45
EARTH, AIRE, AND SEA. THEN LET US NOT THINK HARD 4 432
ON PURPOSE, HARD THOU KNOWST IT TO EXCLUDE 4 584
FROM HARD ASSAIES AND ILL SUCCESSES PAST 4 932
SAD TASK AND HARD, FOR HOW SHALL I RELATE 5 564
ENJOYMENT OF OUR RIGHT AS GODS; YET HARD 6 452
THINK NOTHING HARD, MUCH LESS TO BE DESPAIRD. . . 6 495
OF HARD CONTENTS, AND FULL OF FORCE URG'D HOME, . 6 622
IS HARD; FOR WHO HIMSELF BEGINNING KNEW? 8 251
LITTLE INFERIOUR, BY MY ADVENTURE HARD 10 468
A GROVE HARD BY, SPRUNG UP WITH THIS THIR CHANGE, 10 548
THY TERMS TOO HARD, BY WHICH I WAS TO HOLD . . . 10 751
BUT IF THOU JUDGE IT HARD AND DIFFICULT, ... 10 992
HARD TO BELIEF MAY SEEM; YET THIS WILL PRAYER, . . 11 146

HARDER
ENVIRON'D WINS HIS WAY; HARDER BESET 2 1016

HARDIE
SO HARDIE AS TO PROFFER OR ACCEPT 2 425
LESS HARDIE TO ENDURE? COURAGEOUS CHIEF, ... 4 920

HARDLY
THE ENEMIE, THOUGH BOLD, WILL HARDLY DARE, ... 9 304

HARD'ND
BUT HARD BE HARD'ND, BLIND BE BLINDED MORE, . . . 3 200
THEY HARD'ND MORE BY WHAT MIGHT MOST RECLAME, . . 6 791
MORE HARD'ND AFTER THAW, TILL IN HIS RAGE 12 194

HARDNING
DISTENDS WITH PRIDE, AND HARDNING IN HIS STRENGTH 1 572

HARK'N
FOR MAN WILL HARK'N TO HIS GLOZING LYES, ... 3 93

HARLOT-LAP
HERCULEAN SAMSON FROM THE HARLOT-LAP 9 1060

HARLOTS
OF HARLOTS, LOVELESS, JOYLESS, UNINDEARD, ... 4 766

HARM
THIS PLACE INVIOLABLE, AND THESE FROM HARM. . . . 4 843
THIR ARMOR HELP'D THIR HARM, CRUSH'T IN AND BRUIS'D 6 656
BUT OTHER DOUBT POSSESSES ME, LEAST HARM 9 251

HAUNT (CONTINUED)
THE HAUNT OF SEALES AND ORCS, AND SEA-MEWS CLANG. 11 835

HAUNTED
NOR FAUNUS HAUNTED. HERE IN CLOSE RECESS 4 708

HAUTIE
BUT LIKE A PROUD STEED REIND, WENT HAUTIE ON, 4 858
AND STRENGTH, OF COURAGE HAUTIE, AND OF LIMB 9 484

HAVOC
SORE TOILD, HIS RIV'N ARMES TO HAVOC HEWN, 6 449
WITH LONG AND TEDIOUS HAVOC FABL'D KNIGHTS 9 30
TO WASTE AND HAVOC YONDER WORLD, WHICH I 10 617

HAVOCK
HAVOCK AND SPOIL AND RUIN ARE MY GAIN. 2 1009

HAZARD
AND HAZARD IN THE GLORIOUS ENTERPRIZE, 1 89
OF HAZARD AS OF HONOUR, DUE ALIKE 2 453
OF HAZARD MORE, AS HE ABOVE THE REST 2 455
WHICH HE THROUGH HAZARD HUGE MUST EARN. BUT THEY 2 473
A FAITHFUL LEADER, NOT TO HAZARD ALL 4 933
LET US ADVISE, AND TO THIS HAZARD DRAW 5 729
WITHOUT OUR HAZARD, LABOUR, OR ALLARME, 10 491

HEAD
WITH HEAD UP-LIFT ABOVE THE WAVE, AND EYES 1 193
HAD RIS'N OR HEAV'D HIS HEAD, BUT THAT THE WILL 1 211
MAIM'D HIS BRUTE IMAGE, HEAD AND HANDS LOPT OFF 1 459
OR DREAMS HE SEES, WHILE OVER-HEAD THE MOON 1 784
AND SHOOK A DREADFUL DART; WHAT SEEM'D HIS HEAD 2 672
SHAKES PESTILENCE AND WARR. EACH AT THE HEAD 2 711
AGAINST THY FATHERS HEAD? AND KNOW'ST FOR WHOM; 2 730
IN DARKNESS, WHILE THY HEAD FLAMES THICK AND FAST 2 754
OUT OF THY HEAD I SPRUNG: AMAZEMENT SEIS'D 2 758
WITH HEAD, HANDS, WINGS OR FEET PURSUES HIS WAY, 2 949
MADE HEAD AGAINST HEAV'NS KING, THOUGH OVERTHROWN, 2 992
UPON HIS OWN REBELLIOUS HEAD. AND NOW 3 86
AFFECTING GOD-HEAD, AND SO LOOSING ALL, 3 206
MUCH LESS THAT DURST UPON HIS OWN HEAD DRAW 3 220
THE HEAD OF ALL MANKIND, THOUGH ADAMS SON. 3 286
THY MERITS; UNDER THEE AS HEAD SUPREAM 3 319
CIRCL'D HIS HEAD, NOR LESS HIS LOCKS BEHIND 3 626
AS WITH A RURAL MOUND THE CHAMPAIN HEAD 4 134
ACCESS DENI'D; AND OVER HEAD UP GREW 4 137
BY NILUS HEAD, ENCLOSD WITH SHINING ROCK, 4 283
AND HEAD, WHAT THOU HAST SAID IS JUST AND RIGHT. 4 443
HERE WATCHING AT THE HEAD OF THESE THAT SLEEP? 4 826
ARMIE OF FIENDS, FIT BODY TO FIT HEAD; 4 953
AT MY RIGHT HAND; YOUR HEAD I HIM APPOINT; 5 606
OUR HAPPIE STATE UNDER ONE HEAD MORE NEER 5 830
BUT MORE ILLUSTRIOUS MADE, SINCE HE THE HEAD 5 842
HIS THUNDER ON THY HEAD, DEVOURING FIRE. 5 893
OF CONFLICT; OVER HEAD THE DISMAL HISS 6 212
IN ENTRAILES, HEART OR HEAD, LIVER OR REINES; 6 346
ALL HEART THEY LIVE, ALL HEAD, ALL EYE, ALL EARE, 6 350
A WHILE, BUT SUDDENLY AT HEAD APPEERD 6 556
HAD NEED FROM HEAD TO FOOT WELL UNDERSTAND; 6 625
UNDER THIR HEAD IMBODIED ALL IN ONE. 6 779
BORE UP HIS BRANCHING HEAD: SCARSE FROM HIS MOULD 7 470
WHEN SUDDENLY STOOD AT MY HEAD A DREAM, 8 292
THE MORE SHE WILL ACKNOWLEDGE THEE HER HEAD, 8 574
HIS HEAD THE MIDST, WELL STOR'D WITH SUTTLE WILES: 9 184
IN HEART OR HEAD, POSSESSING SOON INSPIR'D 9 189
EACH FLOUR OF SLENDER STALK, WHOSE HEAD THOUGH GAY 9 428
FOULD ABOVE FOULD A SURGING MAZE, HIS HEAD 9 499
OF KNOWLEDG, NOR WAS GOD-HEAD FROM HER THOUGHT. 9 790
BEING AS I AM, WHY DIDST NOT THOU THE HEAD 9 1155
LEAST ON MY HEAD BOTH SIN AND PUNISHMENT, 10 133
HER SEED SHALL BRUSE THY HEAD, THOU BRUISE HIS
HEEL. 10 181
AT LAST AS FROM A CLOUD HIS FULGENT HEAD 10 449
HIS SEED, WHEN IS NOT SET, SHALL BRUISE MY HEAD: 10 499
WITH COMPLICATED MONSTERS HEAD AND TAILE, 10 523
OR MULTIPLIE, BUT CURSES ON MY HEAD? 10 732
MY HEAD, ILL FARE OUR ANCESTOR IMPURE, 10 735
ON MY DEFENSLESS HEAD; BOTH DEATH AND I 10 815
THE SENTENCE FROM THY HEAD REMOV'D MAY LIGHT 10 934
THAT ON MY HEAD ALL MIGHT BE VISITED, 10 955
THE SERPENTS HEAD; PITEOUS AMENDS, UNLESS 10 1032
AGAINST US THIS DECEIT: TO CRUSH HIS HEAD 10 1035
TILL MANY YEARS OVER THY HEAD RETURN: 11 534
GRATEFUL TO HEAV'N, OVER HIS HEAD BEHOLDS 11 864
THE SERPENTS HEAD; WHEREOF TO THEE ANON 12 150
OF HEAD OR HEEL: NOT THEREFORE JOYNES THE SON 12 388
MANHOOD TO GOD-HEAD, WITH MORE STRENGTH TO FOIL 12 389
SHALL BRUISE THE HEAD OF SATAN, CRUSH HIS STRENGTH 12 430
AND FIX FARR DEEPER IN HIS HEAD THIR STINGS 12 432

HEADED
GREY-HEADED MEN AND GRAVE, WITH WARRIOURS MIXT, 11 662

HEADLONG
HURLD HEADLONG FLAMING FROM TH' ETHEREAL SKIE 1 45
BY ALL HIS ENGINS, BUT WAS HEADLONG SENT 1 750
HURL'D HEADLONG TO PARTAKE WITH US, SHALL CURSE 2 374

HEADLONG (CONTINUED)
DRIV'N HEADLONG FROM THE PITCH OF HEAVEN, DOWN 2 772
URG'D THEM BEHIND; HEADLONG THEMSELVES THEY THREW 6 864

HEADS
THE HEADS AND LEADERS THITHER HAST WHERE STOOD 1 357
TO BESTIAL GODS; FOR WHICH THIR HEADS AS LOW 1 435
ONE DAY UPON OUR HEADS; WHILE WE PERHAPS 2 178
HIDE THIR DIMINISHT HEADS; TO THEE I CALL, 4 35
REAR'D HIGH THIR FLOURISHT HEADS BETWEEN, AND
WROUGHT 4 699
THEMSELVES INVADED NEXT, AND ON THIR HEADS 6 653
OVER THIR HEADS A CHRYSTAL FIRMAMENT, 6 757
O'RE SHIELDS AND HELMES, AND HELMED HEADS HE RODE 6 840
INSTEAD SHALL DOUBLE OURS UPON OUR HEADS. 10 1040

HEAL
TO HEAL THE SCARR OF THESE CORROSIVE FIRES 2 401

HEAL'D
YET SOON HE HEAL'D; FOR SPIRITS THAT LIVE
THROUGHOUT 6 344
SOON CLOSING, AND BY NATIVE VIGOUR HEAL'D. 6 436
BUT SUDDENLY WITH FLESH FILL'D UP AND HEAL'D: 8 468

HEALING
TO WHOM WITH HEALING WORDS ADAM REPLYD. 9 290

HEALTHFUL
WHILE THEY PERVERT PURE NATURES HEALTHFUL RULES 11 523

HEAP
HEAP ON HIMSELF DAMNATION, WHILE HE SOUGHT 1 215
THAWS NOT, BUT GATHERS HEAP, AND RUIN SEEMS 2 590
THIS WORLDS MATERIAL MOULD, CAME TO A HEAP: 3 709
LIGHTS ON A HEAP OF NITROUS POWDER, LAID 4 815
WITH SHIVERD ARMOUR STROW'N, AND ON A HEAP 6 389

HEAP'D
HAVE HEAP'D THIS TABLE. RAIS'D OF GRASSIE TERF 5 391

HEAPS
HEAPS WITH UNSPARING HAND; FOR DRINK THE GRAPE 5 344
BUT ON THY ROULD IN HEAPS, AND UP THE TREES 10 558

HEAPT
HEAPT ON HIM THERE, NOR YET THE MAIN ABYSS 3 83
TO THIS UPROAR; HORRID CONFUSION HEAPT 6 668
HEAPT TO THE POPULAR SUMME, WILL SO INCENSE 12 338

HEAR
IF ONCE THEY HEAR THAT VOYCE, THIR LIVELIEST PLEDGE 1 274
OF HIS ALMIGHTY ENGIN HE SHALL HEAR 2 65
GRINND HORRIBLE A GASTLY SMILE, TO HEAR 2 846
THE REST SHALL HEAR ME CALL, AND OFT BE WARND 3 185
MY UMPIRE CONSCIENCE, WHOM IF THEY WILL HEAR, 3 195
CONTENTED WITH REPORT HEAR ONELY IN HEAV'N: 3 701
TURND HIM ALL EARE TO HEAR NEW UTTERANCE FLOW. 4 410
O FRIENDS, I HEAR THE TREAD OF NIMBLE FEET 4 866
OF SENSE, WHEREBY THEY HEAR, SEE, SMELL, TOUCH,
TASTE, 5 411
BUT MORE DESIRE TO HEAR, IF THOU CONSENT, 5 555
HEAR ALL YE ANGELS, PROGENIE OF LIGHT, 5 600
HEAR MY DECREE, WHICH UNREVOK'T SHALL STAND. 5 602
WORDS WHICH NO EARE EVER TO HEAR IN HEAV'N 5 810
WHAT WE PROPOUND, AND LOUD THAT ALL MAY HEAR. 6 567
THOUGHT HIM STILL SPEAKING, STILL STOOD FIXT TO
HEAR; 8 3
ERE MY REMEMBRANCE: NOW HEAR MEE RELATE 8 204
INVITING THEE TO HEAR WHILE I RELATE, 8 208
MAY TEMPT IT, I EXPECTED NOT TO HEAR. 9 281
TH' ETHEREAL PEOPLE RAN, TO HEAR AND KNOW 10 27
EXPECT TO HEAR, SUPERNAL GRACE CONTENDING 11 359
AND HEAR THE DIN; THUS WAS THE BUILDING LEFT 12 61
OF SQUADROND ANGELS HEAR HIS CAROL SUNG. 12 367

HEARD
OF HOPE IN FEARS AND DANGERS, HEARD SO OFT 1 275
THEY HEARD, AND WERE ABASHT, AND UP THEY SPRUNG 1 331
AFTER THE TEMPEST; SUCH APPLAUSE WAS HEARD 2 290
OF THUNDER HEARD REMOTE. TOWARDS HIM THEY BEND 2 477
HEARD FARR AND WIDE, AND ALL THE HOST OF HELL 2 519
HEARD ON THE RUFUL STREAM; FIERCE PHLEGETON 2 580
I SAW AND HEARD, FOR SUCH A NUMEROUS HOST 2 993
CONFUSION HEARD HIS VOICE, AND WILDE UPROAR 3 710
TH' APOCALYPS, HEARD CRY IN HEAVEN ALOUD, 4 2
OF ECHOING HILL OR THICKET HAVE WE HEARD 4 681
DIVINE INSTRUCTER, I HAVE HEARD, THEN WHEN 5 546
WORTHY OF SACRED SILENCE TO BE HEARD; 5 557
IS HEARD NO MORE IN HEAV'N; HE OF THE FIRST, 5 659
FROM MIDST A GOLDEN CLOUD THUS MILDE WAS HEARD. 6 28
AND CLAMOUR SUCH AS HEARD IN HEAV'N TILL NOW 6 208
SATAN; AND THUS WAS HEARD COMMANDING LOUD. 6 557
IF OUR PROPOSALS ONCE AGAIN WERE HEARD 6 618
AND TWENTIE THOUSAND (I THIR NUMBER HEARD) 6 769
EACH TO HIS PLACE, THEY HEARD HIS VOICE AND WENT 6 782
THE OVERTHROWN HE RAIS'D, AND AS A HEARD 6 856
HELL HEARD TH' UNSUFFERABLE NOISE, HELL SAW 6 867

HEARD (CONTINUED)
THY WEAKER; LET IT PROFIT THEE TO HAVE HEARD . . 6 909
THE STORIE HEARD ATTENTIVE, AND WAS FILL'D . . . 7 51
WHOSE LIQUID MURMUR HEARD NEW THIRST EXCITES, . . 7 68
WHEN SUCH WAS HEARD DECLAR'D THE ALMIGHTIE'S WILL; 7 181
FOR CHAOS HEARD HIS VOICE: HIM ALL HIS TRAINE . . 7 221
OF TRUMPET (FOR OF ARMIES THOU HAST HEARD) . . . 7 296
THINGS ELSE BY ME UNSEARCHABLE, NOW HEARD . . . 8 10
THEE I HAVE HEARD RELATING WHAT WAS DON . . . 8 203
MY STORIE, WHICH PERHAPS THOU HAST NOT HEARD; . . 8 205
BUT LONG ERE OUR APPROACHING HEARD WITHIN . . . 8 242
HEE ENDED, OR I HEARD NO MORE, FOR NOW . . . 8 452
SHE HEARD ME THUS, AND THOUGH DIVINELY BROUGHT, . 8 500
AND FROM THE PARTING ANGEL OVER-HEARD 9 276
TO LURE HER EYE; SHEE BUSIED HEARD THE SOUND . . 9 518
ON TH' OTHER SIDE, ADAM, SOON AS HE HEARD . . . 9 888
HEARD NOT HER LORE, BOTH IN SUBJECTION NOW . . . 9 1128
ALL WERE WHO HEARD, DIM SADNESS DID NOT SPARE . . 10 23
TO SENTENCE MAN: THE VOICE OF GOD THEY HEARD . . 10 97
BROUGHT TO THIR EARS, WHILE DAY DECLIN'D, THEY
HEARD, ... 10 99
I HEARD THEE IN THE GARDEN, AND OF THY VOICE . . 10 116
MY VOICE THOU OFT HAST HEARD, AND HAST NOT FEAR'D, 10 119
WHICH WHEN THE LORD GOD HEARD, WITHOUT DELAY . . 10 163
IS PROPAGATED CURSE. O VOICE ONCE HEARD . . . 10 729
WOULD SPEED BEFORE THEE, AND BE LOUDER HEARD, . . 10 954
AND GRACIOUS TEMPER HE BOTH HEARD AND JUDG'D . . 10 1047
HIS TRUMPET, HEARD IN OREB SINCE PERHAPS . . . 11 74
THAT I WAS HEARD WITH FAVOUR; PEACE RETURND . . 11 153
SUFFICIENT THAT THY PRAYERS ARE HEARD, AND DEATH, 11 252
YET ALL HAD HEARD, WITH AUDIBLE LAMENT 11 266
I HEARD, HERE WITH HIM AT THIS FOUNTAIN TALK'D: . 11 322
WAS HEARD, OF HARP AND ORGAN; AND WHO MOOVD . . 11 560
ASSEMBLE, AND HARANGUES ARE HEARD, BUT SOON . . 11 663
DON TO HIS FATHER, HEARD THIS HEAVIE CURSE, . . 12 103
WHO AGAINST FAITH AND CONSCIENCE CAN BE HEARD . . 12 529
LET HER WITH THEE PARTAKE WHAT THOU HAST HEARD, . 12 598
SO SPAKE OUR MOTHER EVE, AND ADAM HEARD 12 624

HEARDS
OR FLOCKS, OR HEARDS, OR HUMAN FACE DIVINE; . . 3 44

HEARDST
RESOUNDED, (THOU REMEMBER'ST, FOR THOU HEARDST) . 7 561

HEARE
WITH ADMIRATION, AND DEEP MUSE TO HEARE 7 52
AND LONGER WILL DELAY TO HEARE THEE TELL . . . 7 101
HATH BIN THE CAUSE, AND WONDERFUL TO HEARE: . . 9 862
AND GLADLY OF OUR UNION HEARE THEE SPEAK, . . . 9 966
NOW DEATH TO HEARE. FOR WHAT CAN I ENCREASE . . 10 731
TO SUPPLICATION, HEARE HIS SIGHS THOUGH MUTE; . . 11 31

HEARES
HELD BY THY VOICE, THY POTENT VOICE HE HEARES, . 7 100

HEARING
THY HEARING, SUCH COMMISSION FROM ABOVE 7 118

HEARK'ND
WOULD THOU HADST HEARK'ND TO MY WORDS, AND STAI'D 9 1134
BECAUSE THOU HAST HEARK'ND TO THE VOICE OF THY
WIFE, ... 10 198

HEARS
TO FILL HIS EARE, WHEN CONTRARY HE HEARS . . . 10 506

HEAR'ST
OR HEAR'ST THOU RATHER PURE ETHEREAL STREAM, . . 3 7
RAPHAEL, SAID HEE, THOU HEAR'ST WHAT STIR ON EARTH 5 224

HEART
BEFORE ALL TEMPLES TH' UPRIGHT HEART AND PURE, . 1 18
HERE IN THE HEART OF HELL TO WORK IN FIRE, . . . 1 151
AUDACIOUS NEIGHBOURHOOD, THE WISEST HEART . . . 1 400
BY THAT UXORIOUS KING, WHOSE HEART THOUGH LARGE, . 1 444
THIR NUMBER LAST HE SUMMS. AND NOW HIS HEART . . 1 571
AT ONCE WITH JOY AND FEAR HIS HEART REBOUNDS. . . 1 788
MEETS HIS APPROACH, AND TO THE HEART INSPIRES . . 4 154
OUT OF MY SIDE TO THEE, NEEREST MY HEART . . . 4 484
HIS HEART, NOT ELSE DISMAI'D. NOW DREW THEY NIGH 4 861
AND THUS HIS OWN UNDAUNTED HEART EXPLORES. . . . 6 113
IN ENTRAILES, HEART OR HEAD, LIVER OR REINES; . . 6 346
ALL HEART THEY LIVE, ALL HEAD, ALL EYE, ALL EARE, 6 350
THE DOUBTS THAT IN HIS HEART AROSE: AND NOW . . 7 60
OR HEART OF MAN SUFFICE TO COMPREHEND? 7 114
BUT LEAST HIS HEART EXALT HIM IN THE HARME . . . 7 150
OF FUTURE, IN SMALL ROOM LARGE HEART ENCLOS'D, . 7 486
DESCENDS, THITHER WITH HEART AND VOICE AND EYES . 7 513
WITH FRAGRANCE AND WITH JOY MY HEART OREFLOW'D. . 8 266
EATE FREELY WITH GLAD HEART; FEAR HERE NO DEARTH: 8 322
SWEETNESS INTO MY HEART, UNFELT BEFORE, ... 8 475
AND THEY SHALL BE ONE FLESH, ONE HEART, ONE SOULE. 8 499
THE THOUGHTS, AND HEART ENLARGES, HATH HIS SEAT . 8 590
IN HEART OR HEAD, POSSESSING SOON INSPIR'D . . . 9 189
INTO THE HEART OF EVE HIS WORDS MADE WAY, . . . 9 550
INTO HER HEART TOO EASIE ENTRANCE WON: 9 734
YET OFT HIS HEART, DIVINE OF SOMTHING ILL, . . . 9 845

HEART (CONTINUED)
DIMM ERST, DILATED SPIRITS, AMPLER HEART, . . . 9 876
WOULD NEVER FROM MY HEART; NO NO, I FEEL . . . 9 913
SO FORCIBLE WITHIN MY HEART I FEEL 9 955
ONE HEART, ONE SOUL IN BOTH; WHEREOF GOOD PROOFF . 9 967
OF GOD ALL-SEEING, OR DECEAVE HIS HEART 10 6
FOR I NO SOONER IN MY HEART DIVIN'D, ... 10 357
MY HEART, WHICH BY A SECRET HARMONIE 10 358
WHAT LOVE SINCERE, AND REVERENCE IN MY HEART . . 10 915
COMMISERATION; SOON HIS HEART RELENTED 10 940
TO WHOM THUS EVE, RECOVERING HEART, REPLI'D. . . 10 966
THY LOVE, THE SOLE CONTENTMENT OF MY HEART . . . 10 973
BE OPEN, AND HIS HEART TO PITIE INCLINE, . . . 10 1061
SOW'N WITH CONTRITION IN HIS HEART, THEN THOSE . 11 27
HIS HEART I KNOW, HOW VARIABLE AND VAIN 11 92
KNEEL'D AND BEFORE HIM HUMBL'D ALL MY HEART, . . 11 150
WHAT JUSTLY THOU HAST LOST; NOR SET THY HEART, . 11 288
MUCH AT THAT SIGHT WAS ADAM IN HIS HEART . . . 11 448
SIGHT SO DEFORM WHAT HEART OF ROCK COULD LONG . . 11 494
AND CHARMING SYMPHONIES ATTACH'D THE HEART . . . 11 595
WHEREAT THE HEART OF ADAM ERST SO SAD 11 868
GRIEV'D AT HIS HEART, WHEN LOOKING DOWN HE SAW . 11 887
OF PROUD AMBITIOUS HEART, WHO NOT CONTENT . . . 12 25
HUMBLES HIS STUBBORN HEART, BUT STILL AS ICE . . 12 193
MINE EYES TRUE OP'NING, AND MY HEART MUCH EAS'D, . 12 274
SHALL ON THE HEART ENGRAVE. WHAT WILL THEY THEN . 12 524

HEARTS
WHAT MAY SUFFICE, AND SOFT'N STONIE HEARTS . . . 3 189
ENAMOUR'D AT THAT SIGHT; BUT IN THOSE HEARTS . . 5 448
CAN HEARTS, NOT FREE, BE TRI'D WHETHER THEY SERVE 5 532
THY WISH EXACTLY TO THY HEARTS DESIRE. 8 451
FREQUENTING, SENT FROM HEARTS CONTRITE, IN SIGN . 10 1091
FREQUENTING, SENT FROM HEARTS CONTRITE, IN SIGN . 10 1103
THE STONIE FROM THIR HEARTS, & MADE NEW FLESH . . 11 4
WORKING THROUGH LOVE, UPON THIR HEARTS SHALL WRITE, 12 489
PRESAGING, SINCE WITH SORROW AND HEARTS DISTRESS . 12 613

HEART-SICK
OF HEART-SICK AGONIE, ALL FEAVOROUS KINDS, . . . 11 482

HEART-STROOK
HEART-STROOK WITH CHILLING GRIPE OF SORROW STOOD, 11 264

HEAT
INFECTED SIONS DAUGHTERS WITH LIKE HEAT, . . . 1 453
FAMILIAR THE FIERCE HEAT, AND VOID OF PAIN; . . 2 219
THOU FIND'ST HIM FROM THE HEAT OF NOON RETIR'D, . 5 231
TO SIT AND TASTE, TILL THIS MERIDIAN HEAT . . . 5 369
SEE WITH WHAT HEAT THESE DOGS OF HELL ADVANCE . . 10 616
AS MIGHT AFFECT THE EARTH WITH COLD AND HEAT . . 10 653
SOLSTITIAL SUMMERS HEAT. TO THE BLANC MOONE . . 10 656
OR HEAT SHOULD INJURE US, HIS TIMELY CARE . . . 10 1057
AND SENDS A COMFORTABLE HEAT FROM FARR, . . . 10 1077
LOVES HARBINGER APPEERD; THEN ALL IN HEAT . . . 11 589
SEED TIME AND HARVEST, HEAT AND HOARY FROST . . . 11 899
FIERCE AS A COMET; WHICH WITH TORRID HEAT, . . . 12 634

HEATE
NOT ONLY ENLIGHTEN, BUT WITH KINDLY HEATE . . . 4 668
OF REAL HUNGER, AND CONCOCTIVE HEATE 5 437
THERE OFT THE INDIAN HERDSMAN SHUNNING HEATE . . 9 1108
AVOIDED PINCHING COLD AND SCORCHING HEATE? . . . 10 691

HEATH
STANDS ON THE BLASTED HEATH. HE NOW PREPAR'D . . 1 615

HEATHEN
AND VARIOUS IDOLS THROUGH THE HEATHEN WORLD. . . 1 375
AMONG THE HEATHEN OF THIR PURCHASE GOT, ... 10 579

HEAV'D
HAD RIS'N OR HEAV'D HIS HEAD, BUT THAT THE WILL . 1 211
SO HIGH AS HEAV'D THE TUMID HILLS, SO LOW . . . 7 288

HEAVE
BROKE UP, SHALL HEAVE THE OCEAN TO USURP . . . 11 827

HEAVEN
AND HIGH PERMISSION OF ALL-RULING HEAVEN . . . 1 212
AND POWERS THAT EARST IN HEAVEN SAT ON THRONES; . 1 360
FELL NOT FROM HEAVEN, OR MORE GROSS TO LOVE . . 1 491
SHOULD FAVOUR EQUAL TO THE SONS OF HEAVEN: . . . 1 654
DRIV'N HEADLONG FROM THE PITCH OF HEAVEN, DOWN . 2 772
NOW LATELY HEAVEN AND EARTH, ANOTHER WORLD . . . 2 1004
ABOUT HIM ALL THE SANCTITIES OF HEAVEN 3 60
DWELS IN ALL HEAVEN CHARITIE SO DEARE? 3 216
PLEAS'D, OUT OF HEAVEN SHALT LOOK DOWN AND SMILE, 3 257
SHALL ENTER HEAVEN LONG ABSENT, AND RETURNE, . . 3 261
IN HEAVEN, OR EARTH, OR UNDER EARTH IN HELL; . . 3 322
UP TO THE WALL OF HEAVEN A STRUCTURE HIGH, . . . 3 503
SUCH WONDER SEIS'D, THOUGH AFTER HEAVEN SEEN, . . 3 552
THE GOLDEN SUN IN SPLENDOR LIKEST HEAVEN . . . 3 572
AS TO SUPERIOR SPIRITS IS WONT IN HEAVEN, . . . 3 737
TH' APOCALYPS, HEARD CRY IN HEAVEN ALOUD, . . . 4 2
DIVIDE THE NIGHT, AND LIFT OUR THOUGHTS TO HEAVEN. 4 688
THAT SINGING UP TO HEAVEN GATE ASCEND, ... 5 198
AS MAY COMPARE WITH HEAVEN; AND TO TASTE . . . 5 432

HEAVEN (CONTINUED)

TH' ARCH-ANGEL TRUMPET; THROUGH THE VAST OF HEAVEN	6	203
BUT THAT I DOUBT, HOWEVER WITNESS HEAVEN,	6	563
APOSTASIE, BY WHAT BEFELL IN HEAVEN	7	43
TO NONE COMMUNICABLE IN EARTH OR HEAVEN:	7	124
HIGH IN TH' EXPANSE OF HEAVEN TO DIVIDE	7	340
FROM HEAVEN GATE NOT FARR, FOUNDED IN VIEW	7	618
WITH WHAT ALL EARTH OR HEAVEN COULD BESTOW	8	483
FROM EARTH ARRIV'D AT HEAVEN GATE, DISPLEAS'D	10	22
ACCOMPANIED TO HEAVEN GATE, FROM WHENCE	10	88
AS LORDS, A SPACIOUS WORLD, TO OUR NATIVE HEAVEN	10	467
ALIKE IS HELL, OR PARADISE, OR HEAVEN,	10	598
THERE WITH MY CRIES IMPORTUNE HEAVEN, THAT ALL	10	933

HEAVENLY

OF HEAVENLY GRACE: AND GOD PROCLAIMING PEACE,	2	499
GO HEAVENLY GUEST, ETHEREAL MESSENGER,	8	646

HEAVENS

ON HEAVENS AZURE, AND THE TORRID CLIME	1	297
THIR GLORY WITHERD. AS WHEN HEAVENS FIRE	1	612
BEFORE THE HEAVENS THOU WERT, AND AT THE VOICE	3	9
HEE HEAV'N OF HEAVENS AND ALL THE POWERS THEREIN	3	390
FROM MY PREVAILING ARME, THOUGH HEAVENS KING	4	973
UNSPEAKABLE, WHO FIRST ABOVE THESE HEAVENS	5	156
WHAT HEAVENS LORD HAD POWERFULLEST TO SEND	6	425

HEAVIE

NOT DISTANT FAR WITH HEAVIE PACE THE FOE	6	551
HEAVIE, THOUGH IN THIR PLACE. O FLEETING JOYES	10	741
DON TO HIS FATHER, HEARD THIS HEAVIE CURSE,	12	103
WHENCE HEAVIE PERSECUTION SHALL ARISE	12	531

HEAVIER

OR PROUD RETURN THOUGH TO HIS HEAVIER DOOM,	3	159
AND HEAVIER FALL: SO SHOULD I PURCHASE DEARE	4	101
FARR HEAVIER LOAD THY SELF EXPECT TO FEEL	4	972
OF HEAVIER ON HIMSELF, FEARLESS RETURN'D.	9	57
THAT BURDEN HEAVIER THEN THE EARTH TO BEAR	10	835
THEN ALL THE WORLD MUCH HEAVIER, THOUGH DIVIDED	10	836

HEAVIEST

THOUGH HEAVIEST BY JUST MEASURE ON THY SELF	6	265

HEAV'N

SAY FIRST, FOR HEAV'N HIDES NOTHING FROM THY VIEW	1	27
FAVOUR'D OF HEAV'N SO HIGHLY, TO FALL OFF	1	30
HAD CAST HIM OUT FROM HEAV'N, WITH ALL HIS HOST	1	37
RAIS'D IMPIOUS WAR IN HEAV'N AND BATTEL PROUD	1	43
AS FAR REMOV'D FROM GOD AND LIGHT OF HEAV'N	1	73
AND THENCE IN HEAV'N CALL'D SATAN, WITH BOLD WORDS	1	82
IN DUBIOUS BATTEL ON THE PLAINS OF HEAV'N,	1	104
SOLE REIGNING HOLDS THE TYRANNY OF HEAV'N.	1	124
HATH LOST US HEAV'N, AND ALL THIS MIGHTY HOST	1	136
BACK TO THE GATES OF HEAV'N: THE SULPHUROUS HAIL	1	171
OF HEAV'N RECEIV'D US FALLING, AND THE THUNDER,	1	174
THAT WE MUST CHANGE FOR HEAV'N, THIS MOURNFUL GLOOM	1	244
CAN MAKE A HEAV'N OF HELL, A HELL OF HEAV'N.	1	255
BETTER TO REIGN IN HELL, THEN SERVE IN HEAV'N.	1	263
REGAIND IN HEAV'N, OR WHAT MORE LOST IN HELL?	1	270
WARRIERS, THE FLOWR OF HEAV'N, ONCE YOURS, NOW LOST,	1	316
TO SLUMBER HERE, AS IN THE VALES OF HEAV'N?	1	321
HIS SWIFT PURSUERS FROM HEAV'N GATES DISCERN	1	326
ASTARTE, QUEEN OF HEAV'N, WITH CRESCENT HORNS;	1	439
GODS, YET CONFEST LATER THEN HEAV'N AND EARTH	1	509
THIR HIGHEST HEAV'N; OR ON THE DELPHIAN CLIFF,	1	517
OF HEAV'N, AND FROM ETERNAL SPLENDORS FLUNG	1	610
HATH EMPTIED HEAV'N, SHALL FAIL TO RE-ASCEND	1	633
FOR MEE BE WITNESS ALL THE HOST OF HEAV'N,	1	635
MONARCH IN HEAV'N, TILL THEN AS ONE SECURE	1	638
THERE WENT A FAME IN HEAV'N THAT HE ERE LONG	1	651
HURLING DEFIANCE TOWARD THE VAULT OF HEAV'N.	1	669
FROM HEAV'N, FOR EV'N IN HEAV'N HIS LOOKS AND THOUGHTS	1	680
IN HEAV'N BY MANY A TOWRED STRUCTURE HIGH,	1	733
FROM HEAV'N, THEY FABL'D, THROWN BY ANGRY JOVE	1	741
TO HAVE BUILT IN HEAV'N HIGH TOWRS; NOR DID HE SCAPE	1	749
VAIN WARR WITH HEAV'N, AND BY SUCCESS UNTAUGHT	2	9
POWERS AND DOMINIONS, DEITIES OF HEAV'N,	2	11
I GIVE NOT HEAV'N FOR LOST. FROM THIS DESCENT	2	14
MEE THOUGH JUST RIGHT, AND THE FIXT LAWS OF HEAV'N	2	18
IN HEAV'N, WHICH FOLLOWS DIGNITY, MIGHT DRAW	2	25
MORE THEN CAN BE IN HEAV'N, WE NOW RETURN	2	37
THAT FOUGHT IN HEAV'N; NOW FIERCER BY DESPAIR:	2	45
OUR POWER SUFFICIENT TO DISTURB HIS HEAV'N,	2	102
A FAIRER PERSON LOST NOT HEAV'N; HE SEEMD	2	110
FIRST, WHAT REVENGE? THE TOWRS OF HEAV'N ARE FILL'D	2	129
SHALL WE THEN LIVE THUS VILE, THE RACE OF HEAV'N	2	194
EITHER TO DISINTHRONE THE KING OF HEAV'N	2	229
IN HEAV'N THIS OUR DELIGHT; HOW WEARISOM	2	247
UNACCEPTABLE, THOUGH IN HEAV'N, OUR STATE	2	251
MUST'RING THIR RAGE, AND HEAV'N RESEMBLES HELL?	2	268
MAGNIFICENCE; AND WHAT CAN HEAV'N SHEW MORE?	2	273
IN EMULATION OPPOSITE TO HEAV'N.	2	298
THRONES AND IMPERIAL POWERS, OFF-SPRING OF HEAV'N	2	310

HEAV'N (CONTINUED)

AND KNOW NOT THAT THE KING OF HEAV'N HATH DOOM'D	2	316
US HERE, AS WITH HIS GOLDEN THOSE IN HEAV'N.	2	328
HEAV'N, WHOSE HIGH WALLS FEAR NO ASSAULT OR SIEGE,	2	343
(IF ANCIENT AND PROPHETIC FAME IN HEAV'N	2	346
BY FORCE OR SUTTLETY: THOUGH HEAV'N BE SHUT,	2	358
RE-ENTER HEAV'N; OR ELSE IN SOME MILDE ZONE	2	397
O PROGENY OF HEAV'N, EMPYREAL THRONES,	2	430
TERROR OF HEAV'N, THOUGH FALL'N; INTEND AT HOME,	2	457
EXTOLL HIM EQUAL TO THE HIGHEST IN HEAV'N:	2	479
ALONE TH' ANTAGONIST OF HEAV'N, NOR LESS	2	509
FROM EITHER END OF HEAV'N THE WELKIN BURNS.	2	538
HELL-BORN, NOT TO CONTEND WITH SPIRITS OF HEAV'N.	2	687
WHO FIRST BROKE PEACE IN HEAV'N AND FAITH, TILL THEN	2	690
AND RECK'N'ST THOU THY SELF WITH SPIRITS OF HEAV'N,	2	696
IN HEAV'N, WHEN AT TH' ASSEMBLY, AND IN SIGHT	2	749
ALL TH' HOST OF HEAV'N; BACK THEY RECOILD AFFRAID	2	759
AND FIELDS WERE FOUGHT IN HEAV'N; WHEREIN REMAIND	2	768
OF DALLIANCE HAD WITH THEE IN HEAV'N, AND JOYS	2	819
IN THE POURLIEUES OF HEAV'N, AND THEREIN PLAC'T	2	833
LEAST HEAV'N SURCHARG'D WITH POTENT MULTITUDE	2	836
INHABITANT OF HEAV'N, AND HEAV'NLIE-BORN,	2	860
OF HEAV'N WERE FALLING, AND THESE ELEMENTS	2	925
CONFINE WITH HEAV'N; OR IF SOM OTHER PLACE	2	977
CONFUSION WORSE CONFOUNDED; AND HEAV'N GATES	2	996
TO THAT SIDE HEAV'N FROM WHENCE YOUR LEGIONS FELL:	2	1006
FOLLOWING HIS TRACK, SUCH WAS THE WILL OF HEAV'N,	2	1025
OF LIGHT APPEARS, AND FROM THE WALLS OF HEAV'N	2	1035
FARR OFF TH' EMPYREAL HEAV'N, EXTENDED WIDE	2	1047
HAIL HOLY LIGHT, OFSPRING OF HEAV'N FIRST-BORN,	3	1
COASTING THE WALL OF HEAV'N ON THIS SIDE NIGHT	3	71
NOT FARR OFF HEAV'N, IN THE PRECINCTS OF LIGHT,	3	88
THROUGH HEAV'N AND EARTH, SO SHALL MY GLORIE EXCEL,	3	133
ALL HEAV'N, AND IN THE BLESSED SPIRITS ELECT	3	136
FOR WHICH BOTH HEAV'N AND EARTH SHALL HIGH EXTOLL	3	146
AGAINST THE HIGH SUPREMACIE OF HEAV'N,	3	205
AND SILENCE WAS IN HEAV'N: ON MANS BEHALF	3	218
ALL HEAV'N, WHAT THIS MIGHT MEAN, AND WHITHER TEND	3	272
O THOU IN HEAV'N AND EARTH THE ONLY PEACE	3	274
WHEN THOU ATTENDED GLORIOUSLY FROM HEAV'N	3	323
NEW HEAV'N AND EARTH, WHEREIN THE JUST SHALL DWELL,	3	335
AS FROM BLEST VOICES, UTTERING JOY, HEAV'N RUNG	3	347
TO HEAV'N REMOV'D WHERE FIRST IT GREW, THERE GROWS,	3	356
MELODIOUS PART, SUCH CONCORD IS IN HEAV'N.	3	371
YET DAZLE HEAV'N, THAT BRIGHTEST SERAPHIM	3	381
HEE HEAV'N OF HEAVENS AND ALL THE POWERS THEREIN	3	390
THUS THEY IN HEAV'N, ABOVE THE STARRY SPHEAR,	3	416
SAVE ON THAT SIDE WHICH FROM THE WALL OF HEAV'N	3	427
IN GOLGOTHA HIM DEAD, WHO LIVES IN HEAV'N;	3	477
AND WAKING CRI'D, THIS IS THE GATE OF HEAV'N	3	515
THERE ALWAYES, BUT DRAWN UP TO HEAV'N SOMTIMES	3	517
THAT SCAL'D BY STEPS OF GOLD TO HEAV'N GATE	3	541
INTERPRETER THROUGH HIGHEST HEAV'N TO BRING,	3	657
BY HIS PERMISSIVE WILL, THROUGH HEAV'N AND EARTH:	3	685
THE SHARPEST SIGHTED SPIRIT OF ALL IN HEAV'N;	3	691
CONTENTED WITH REPORT HEAR ONELY IN HEAV'N:	3	701
AND THIS ETHEREAL QUINTESSENCE OF HEAV'N	3	716
STILL ENDING, STILL RENEWING, THROUGH MID HEAV'N;	3	729
SOMETIMES TOWARDS HEAV'N AND THE FULL-BLAZING SUN,	4	29
WARRING IN HEAV'N AGAINST HEAV'NS MATCHLESS KING:	4	41
TO WHICH THE HELL I SUFFER SEEMS A HEAV'N.	4	78
A HEAV'N ON EARTH, FOR BLISSFUL PARADISE	4	208
OF HEAV'N THE STARRS THAT USHER EVENING ROSE:	4	355
LONG TO CONTINUE, AND THIS HIGH SEAT YOUR HEAV'N	4	371
ILL SENC'T FOR HEAV'N TO KEEP OUT SUCH A FOE	4	372
PURE AS TH' EXPANSE OF HEAV'N; I THITHER WENT	4	456
SOME WANDRING SPIRIT OF HEAV'N, BY FOUNTAIN SIDE,	4	531
MEAN WHILE IN UTMOST LONGITUDE, WHERE HEAV'N	4	539
TH' UNARMED YOUTH OF HEAV'N, BUT NIGH AT HAND	4	552
ALIEN FROM HEAV'N, WITH PASSIONS FOUL OBSCUR'D:	4	571
WELL KNOWN FROM HEAV'N; AND SINCE MERIDIAN HOUR	4	581
AND THE REGARD OF HEAV'N ON ALL HIS WAIES;	4	620
AND THESE THE GEMMS OF HEAV'N, HER STARRIE TRAIN:	4	649
THAT HEAV'N WOULD WANT SPECTATORS, GOD WANT PRAISE;	4	676
THE GOD THAT MADE BOTH SKIE, AIR, EARTH AND HEAV'N	4	722
AS WHEN THOU STOODST IN HEAV'N UPRIGHT AND PURE;	4	837
GABRIEL, THOU HADST IN HEAV'N TH' ESTEEM OF WISE,	4	886
O LOSS OF ONE IN HEAV'N TO JUDGE OF WISE,	4	904
HIGH UP IN HEAV'N, WITH SONGS TO HYMNE HIS THRONE,	4	944
IN PROGRESS THROUGH THE RODE OF HEAV'N STAR-PAV'D.	4	976
OF HEAV'N PERHAPS, OR ALL THE ELEMENTS	4	993
HUNG FORTH IN HEAV'N HIS GOLDEN SCALES, YET SEEN	4	997
THEN HEAV'N PERMITS, NOR MINE, THOUGH DOUBLD NOW	4	1009
IF NONE REGARD; HEAV'N WAKES WITH ALL HIS EYES,	5	44
ONE SHAPD AND WING'D LIKE ONE OF THOSE FROM HEAV'N	5	55
ASCEND TO HEAV'N, BY MERIT THINE, AND SEE	5	80
CIRCLE HIS THRONE REJOYCING, YEE IN HEAV'N,	5	163
LATE FALLN HIMSELF FROM HEAV'N, IS PLOTTING NOW	5	240
FLEW THROUGH THE MIDST OF HEAV'N; TH' ANGELIC QUIRES	5	251
OF HEAV'N ARRIV'D, THE GATE SELF-OPEND WIDE	5	254
AND COLOURS DIPT IN HEAV'N; THE THIRD HIS FEET	5	283
RIS'N ON MID-NOON; SOM GREAT BEHEST FROM HEAV'N	5	311
GOD HATH DISPENST HIS BOUNTIES AS IN HEAV'N.	5	330
THUS SAID. NATIVE OF HEAV'N, FOR OTHER PLACE	5	361
NONE CAN THEN HEAV'N SUCH GLORIOUS SHAPE CONTAIN;	5	362
AS MAY NOT OFT INVITE, THOUGH SPIRITS OF HEAV'N	5	374

HEAV'N (CONTINUED)

STOOD TO ENTERTAIN HER GUEST FROM HEAV'N; NO VAILE 5 383
SUPS WITH THE OCEAN: THOUGH IN HEAV'N THE TREES 5 426
WHO DWELL IN HEAV'N, WHOSE EXCELLENCE HE SAW 5 456
TO WHOM THE ANGEL. SON OF HEAV'N AND EARTH, 5 519
AND SO FROM HEAV'N TO DEEPEST HELL; O FALL 5 542
HATH PAST IN HEAV'N, SOM DOUBT WITHIN ME MOVE, 5 554
HIS OTHER HALF IN THE GREAT ZONE OF HEAV'N. 5 560
BE BUT THE SHADDOW OF HEAV'N, AND THINGS THEREIN 5 575
FORTHWITH FROM ALL THE ENDS OF HEAV'N APPEERD 5 586
ALL KNEES IN HEAV'N, AND SHALL CONFESS HIM LORD: 5 608
FRUIT OF DELICIOUS VINES, THE GROWTH OF HEAV'N. 5 635
SPRING BOTH, THE FACE OF BRIGHTEST HEAV'N HAD CHANGD 5 644
IS HEARD NO MORE IN HEAV'N; HE OF THE FIRST, 5 659
NOW ERE DIM NIGHT HAD DISINCUMBERD HEAV'N, 5 700
HIS NAME, AND HIGH WAS HIS DEGREE IN HEAV'N; 5 707
THY REBELS, OR BE FOUND THE WORST IN HEAV'N. 5 742
MESSIAH WAS DECLAR'D IN SIGHT OF HEAV'N, 5 765
NATIVES AND SONS OF HEAV'N POSSEST BEFORE 5 790
WORDS WHICH NO EARE EVER TO HEAR IN HEAV'N 5 810
WITH REGAL SCEPTER, EVERY SOULE IN HEAV'N 5 816
THEE WHAT THOU ART, AND FORMD THE POW'RS OF HEAV'N 5 824
ALL THINGS, EV'N THEE, AND ALL THE SPIRITS OF HEAV'N 5 837
OF THIS OUR NATIVE HEAV'N, ETHEREAL SONS. 5 863
LODGE AND DISLODGE BY TURNS, WHICH MAKES THROUGH HEAV'N 6 7
TO VEILE THE HEAV'N, THOUGH DARKNESS THERE MIGHT WELL 6 11
SUCH AS IN HIGHEST HEAV'N, ARRAYD IN GOLD 6 13
FEARLESS ASSAULT, AND TO THE BROW OF HEAV'N 6 51
THAT STOOD FOR HEAV'N, IN MIGHTY QUADRATE JOYN'D 6 62
OF HEAV'N THEY MARCH'D, AND MANY A PROVINCE WIDE 6 77
O HEAV'N. THAT SUCH RESEMBLANCE OF THE HIGHEST 6 114
AT FIRST I THOUGHT THAT LIBERTIE AND HEAV'N 6 164
SUCH HAST THOU ARM'D, THE MINSTRELSIE OF HEAV'N, 6 168
IN HEAV'N GOD EVER BLEST, AND HIS DIVINE 6 184
AND CLAMOUR SUCH AS HEARD IN HEAV'N TILL NOW 6 208
AND INEXTINGUISHABLE RAGE; ALL HEAV'N 6 217
FROM HIS STRONG HOLD OF HEAV'N HIGH OVER-RUL'D 6 228
INTESTINE WAR IN HEAV'N, THE ARCH FOE SUBDU'D 6 259
UNNAM'D IN HEAV'N, NOW PLENTEOUS, AS THOU SEEST 6 263
TO TROUBLE HOLY REST; HEAV'N CASTS THEE OUT 6 272
FROM ALL HER CONFINES. HEAV'N THE SEAT OF BLISS 6 273
OR TURN THIS HEAV'N IT SELF INTO THE HELL 6 291
FIT TO DECIDE THE EMPIRE OF GREAT HEAV'N. 6 303
THREATN'D, NOR FROM THE HOLIE ONE OF HEAV'N 6 359
ANGELS CONTENTED WITH THIR FAME IN HEAV'N 6 375
CANCELD FROM HEAV'N AND SACRED MEMORIE, 6 379
NOW NIGHT HER COURSE BEGAN, AND OVER HEAV'N 6 406
THIS CONTINENT OF SPACIOUS HEAV'N, ADORND 6 474
NOW WHEN FAIR MORN ORIENT IN HEAV'N APPEERD 6 524
HEAV'N WITNESS THOU ANON, WHILE WE DISCHARGE 6 564
BUT SOON OBSCUR'D WITH SMOAK, ALL HEAV'N APPEERD, 6 585
(FOR EARTH HATH THIS VARIETY FROM HEAV'N 6 640
UPON CONFUSION ROSE: AND NOW ALL HEAV'N 6 669
SHRIN'D IN HIS SANCTUARIE OF HEAV'N SECURE, 6 672
TWO DAYES, AS WE COMPUTE THE DAYES OF HEAV'N, 6 685
WILD WORK IN HEAV'N, AND DANGEROUS TO THE MAINE. 6 698
IN HEAV'N AND HELL THY POWER ABOVE COMPARE, 6 705
ARMD WITH THY MIGHT, RID HEAV'N OF THESE REBELL'D, 6 737
DAWNING THROUGH HEAV'N: FORTH RUSH'D WITH WHIRLWIND SOUND 6 749
ALOFT BY ANGELS BORN, HIS SIGN IN HEAV'N: 6 776
OBSEQUIOUS, HEAV'N HIS WONTED FACE RENEWD, 6 783
BECAUSE THE FATHER, T' WHOM IN HEAV'N SUPREAM 6 814
NOT TO DESTROY, BUT ROOT THEM OUT OF HEAV'N: 6 855
AND CHRYSTAL WALL OF HEAV'N, WHICH OP'NING WIDE, 6 860
DOWN FROM THE VERGE OF HEAV'N, ETERNAL WRAUTH 6 865
HEAV'N RUINING FROM HEAV'N AND WOULD HAVE FLED 6 868
DISBURD'ND HEAV'N REJOIC'D, AND SOON REPAIRD 6 878
TRIUMPHANT THROUGH MID HEAV'N, INTO THE COURTS 6 889
THUS MEASURING THINGS IN HEAV'N BY THINGS ON EARTH 6 893
THE DISCORD WHICH BEFEL, AND WARR IN HEAV'N 6 897
DESCEND FROM HEAV'N URANIA, BY THAT NAME 7 1
INTO THE HEAV'N OF HEAV'NS I HAVE PRESUM'D, 7 13
SO UNIMAGINABLE AS HATE IN HEAV'N, 7 54
OF HEAV'N AND EARTH CONSPICIOUS FIRST BEGAN, 7 63
HOW FIRST BEGAN THIS HEAV'N WHICH WE BEHOLD 7 86
MUCH OF HIS RACE THOUGH STEEP, SUSPENS IN HEAV'N 7 99
KNOW THEN, THAT AFTER LUCIFER FROM HEAV'N 7 131
THIR STATION, HEAV'N YET POPULOUS RETAINES 7 146
ALREADY DONE, TO HAVE DISPEOPL'D HEAV'N 7 151
AND EARTH BE CHANG'D TO HEAV'N, & HEAV'N TO EARTH, 7 160
MEAN WHILE INHABIT LAXE, YE POWERS OF HEAV'N, 7 162
WITHIN APPOINTED BOUNDS BE HEAV'N AND EARTH, 7 167
GREAT TRIUMPH AND REJOYCING WAS IN HEAV'N 7 180
ATTENDANT ON THIR LORD: HEAV'N OP'ND WIDE 7 205
THUS GOD THE HEAV'N CREATED, THUS THE EARTH, 7 232
BIRTH-DAY OF HEAV'N AND EARTH; WITH JOY AND SHOUT 7 256
AND HEAV'N HE NAM'D THE FIRMAMENT: SO EEV'N 7 274
BE GATHER'D NOW YE WATERS UNDER HEAV'N 7 283
SEEMD LIKE TO HEAV'N, A SEAT WHERE GODS MIGHT DWELL, 7 329
THIR OFFICE IN THE FIRMAMENT OF HEAV'N 7 344
AND SET THEM IN THE FIRMAMENT OF HEAV'N 7 349
AND SOWD WITH STARRS THE HEAV'N THICK AS A FIELD: 7 358

HEAV'N (CONTINUED)

DISPLAYD ON THE OP'N FIRMAMENT OF HEAV'N. 7 390
NOW HEAV'N IN ALL HER GLORIE SHON, AND ROWLD 7 499
MAGNANIMOUS TO CORRESPOND WITH HEAV'N, 7 511
UP TO THE HEAV'N OF HEAV'NS HIS HIGH ABODE, 7 553
THE GLORIOUS TRAIN ASCENDING: HE THROUGH HEAV'N, 7 574
WITNESS THIS NEW-MADE WORLD, ANOTHER HEAV'N 7 617
OF HEAV'N AND EARTH CONSISTING, AND COMPUTE, 8 16
TO ASK OR SEARCH I BLAME THEE NOT, FOR HEAV'N 8 66
THIS TO ATTAIN, WHETHER HEAV'N MOVE OR EARTH, 8 70
HEREAFTER, WHEN THEY COME TO MODEL HEAV'N 8 79
THE LESS NOT BRIGHT, NOR HEAV'N SUCH JOURNIES RUN, 8 88
THOUGH, IN COMPARISON OF HEAV'N, SO SMALL, 8 92
WHO SINCE THE MORNING HOUR SET OUT FROM HEAV'N 8 111
PLAC'D HEAV'N FROM EARTH SO FARR, THAT EARTHLY SIGHT, 8 120
WHETHER THE SUN PREDOMINANT IN HEAV'N 8 160
AND THY FAIRE EVE; HEAV'N IS FOR THEE TOO HIGH 8 172
NOT OF EARTH ONELY BUT OF HIGHEST HEAV'N. 8 178
INTELLIGENCE OF HEAV'N, ANGEL SERENE, 8 181
FOR WHILE I SIT WITH THEE, I SEEM IN HEAV'N, 8 210
NOR LESS THINK WEE IN HEAV'N OF THEE ON EARTH 8 224
STRAIT TOWARD HEAV'N MY WONDRING EYES I TURND, 8 257
GRACE WAS IN ALL HER STEPS, HEAV'N IN HER EYE, 8 488
I LED HER BLUSHING LIKE THE MORN: ALL HEAV'N, 8 511
LEADS UP TO HEAV'N, IS BOTH THE WAY AND GUIDE; 8 613
SO PARTED THEY, THE ANGEL UP TO HEAV'N 8 652
AND DISOBEDIENCE: ON THE PART OF HEAV'N 9 8
O EARTH, HOW LIKE TO HEAV'N, IF NOT PREFERR'D 9 99
TERRESTRIAL HEAV'N, DANC'T ROUND BY OTHER HEAV'NS 9 103
OF SACRED INFLUENCE: AS GOD IN HEAV'N 9 107
BANE, AND IN HEAV'N MUCH WORSE WOULD BE MY STATE. 9 123
BUT NEITHER HERE SEEK I, NO NOR IN HEAV'N 9 124
OF HEAV'N, THIS MAN OF CLAY, SON OF DESPITE, 9 176
OFSPRING OF HEAV'N AND EARTH, AND ALL EARTHS LORD, 9 273
FAVOUR FROM HEAV'N, OUR WITNESS FROM TH' EVENT. 9 334
THOUGH IN MID HEAV'N, SOON ENDED HIS DELIGHT, 9 468
INFEEBL'D ME, TO WHAT I WAS IN HEAV'N. 9 488
THY LOOKS, THE HEAV'N OF MILDNESS, WITH DISDAIN, 9 534
CONSIDERD ALL THINGS VISIBLE IN HEAV'N, 9 604
AND I PERHAPS AM SECRET; HEAV'N IS HIGH, 9 811
WAS KNOWN IN HEAV'N; FOR WHAT CAN SCAPE THE EYE 10 5
UP INTO HEAV'N FROM PARADISE IN HASTE 10 17
ALL JUDGEMENT, WHETHER IN HEAV'N, OR EARTH, OR HELL. 10 57
MINE BOTH IN HEAV'N AND EARTH TO DO THY WILL 10 69
O HEAV'N. IN EVIL STRAIT THIS DAY I STAND 10 125
SAW SATAN FALL LIKE LIGHTNING DOWN FROM HEAV'N, 10 184
THE CONFINES MET OF EMPYREAN HEAV'N 10 321
OUR FOILE IN HEAV'N; HERE THOU SHALT MONARCH REIGN, 10 375
THE NEW CREATED WORLD, WHICH FAME IN HEAV'N 10 481
THEN HEAV'N AND EARTH RENEWD SHALL BE MADE PURE 10 638
NEW HEAV'N AND EARTH SHALL TO THE AGES RISE, 10 647
OR DOWN FROM HEAV'N DESCEND. SUCH WAS THIR SONG, 10 648
CREATOR WISE, THAT PEOPL'D HIGHEST HEAV'N 10 889
FORSAKE ME NOT THUS, ADAM, WITNESS HEAV'N 10 914
INSPIR'D, AND WING'D FOR HEAV'N WITH SPEEDIER FLIGHT 11 7
OF THEMIS STOOD DEVOUT. TO HEAV'N THIR PRAYERS 11 14
RESIGNES HIM UP WITH HEAV'N AND EARTH RENEWD. 11 66
THE GOOD WHICH WE ENJOY, FROM HEAV'N DESCENDS; 11 142
BUT THAT FROM US OUGHT SHOULD ASCEND TO HEAV'N 11 143
WHICH HEAV'N BY THESE MUTE SIGNS IN NATURE SHEWS 11 194
ADAM, THOU KNOW'ST HEAV'N HIS, AND ALL THE EARTH, 11 335
THOU LEAD'ST ME, AND TO THE HAND OF HEAV'N SUBMIT, 11 372
HIS OFFRING SOON PROPITIOUS FIRE FROM HEAV'N 11 441
FROM HEAV'N ACCEPTANCE; BUT THE BLOODIE FACT 11 457
LIVE WELL, HOW LONG OR SHORT PERMIT TO HEAV'N: 11 554
BUT WHO WAS THAT JUST MAN, WHOM HAD NOT HEAV'N 11 681
FROM UNDER HEAV'N; THE HILLS TO THEIR SUPPLIE 11 740
OF HEAV'N SET OPEN ON THE EARTH SHALL POWRE 11 825
HIS SLUCES, AS THE HEAV'N HIS WINDOWS SHUT. 11 849
GRATEFUL TO HEAV'N, OVER HIS HEAD BEHOLDS 11 864
BOTH HEAV'N AND EARTH, WHEREIN THE JUST SHALL DWELL. 11 901
BEFORE THE LORD, AS IN DESPITE OF HEAV'N, 12 34
OR FROM HEAV'N CLAMING SECOND SOVRANTIE; 12 35
A CITIE AND TOWRE, WHOSE TOP MAY REACH TO HEAV'N; 12 44
OBSTRUCT HEAV'N TOWRS, AND IN DERISION SETS 12 52
AS MOCKT THEY STORM; GREAT LAUGHTER WAS IN HEAV'N 12 59
OR HOW THE SUN SHALL IN MID HEAV'N STAND STILL 12 263
HERE ADAM INTERPOS'D. O SENT FROM HEAV'N, 12 270
TO DAVID, STABLISHT AS THE DAYES OF HEAV'N. 12 347
UNSEEN BEFORE IN HEAV'N PROCLAIMS HIM COM, 12 361
HIGH IN THE LOVE OF HEAV'N, YET FROM MY LOYNES 12 380
SATAN, WHOSE FALL FROM HEAV'N, A DEADLIER BRUISE, 12 391
THEN TO THE HEAV'N OF HEAV'NS HE SHALL ASCEND 12 451
ABOVE ALL NAMES IN HEAV'N; AND THENCE SHALL COME, 12 458
WHETHER IN HEAV'N OR EARTH, FOR THEN THE EARTH 12 463
BUT SAY, IF OUR DELIVERER UP TO HEAV'N 12 479
BE SURE THEY WILL, SAID TH' ANGEL; BUT FROM HEAV'N 12 485
WITH JOY THE TIDINGS BROUGHT FROM HEAV'N: AT LENGTH 12 504
WHO ALL THE SACRED MYSTERIES OF HEAV'N 12 509
LAST IN THE CLOUDS FROM HEAV'N TO BE REVEALD 12 545
OR WORKS OF GOD IN HEAV'N, AIRE, EARTH, OR SEA, 12 579
ART ALL THINGS UNDER HEAV'N, ALL PLACES THOU, 12 618

HEAVN
AND WHERE THE RIVER OF BLISS THROUGH MIDST OF HEAVN 3 358
BUT SAY, WHAT MEAN THOSE COLOURD STREAKS IN HEAVN, 11 879

HEAV'N-BANISHT
HEAV'N-BANISHT HOST, LEFT DESERT UTMOST HELL . . 10 437

HEAV'N-FALL'N
HEAV'N-FALL'N, IN STATION STOOD OR JUST ARRAY, . 10 535

HEAV'NLIE
OF OLD OLYMPUS DWELL'ST, BUT HEAV'NLIE BORNE, . . 7 7
FOR THOU ART HEAV'NLIE, SHEE AN EMPTY DREAME. . . 7 39

HEAV'NLIE-BORN
INHABITANT OF HEAV'N, AND HEAV'NLIE-BORN, ... 2 860

HEAV'NLY
SING HEAV'NLY MUSE, THAT ON THE SECRET TOP . . . 1 6
AS FAR AS GODS AND HEAV'NLY ESSENCES 1 138
THOUGH OF THIR NAMES IN HEAV'NLY RECORDS NOW . . 1 361
THEN SHINING HEAV'NLY FAIR, A GODDESS ARM'D . . 2 757
THOUGH TEMPER'D HEAV'NLY, FOR THAT MORTAL DINT, . 2 813
BOTH HIM AND THEE, AND ALL THE HEAV'NLY HOST . 2 824
TAUGHT BY THE HEAV'NLY MUSE TO VENTURE DOWN . . 3 19
SAY HEAV'NLY POWERS, WHERE SHALL WE FIND SUCH LOVE, 3 213
HE ASK'D, BUT ALL THE HEAV'NLY QUIRE STOOD MUTE, . 3 217
SO HEAV'NLY LOVE SHALL OUTDOO HELLISH HATE . . . 3 298
FOR HEAV'NLY MINDES FROM SUCH DISTEMPERS FOULE . 4 118
NOT SPIRITS, YET TO HEAV'NLY SPIRITS BRIGHT . . 4 361
WITH HEAV'NLY TOUCH OF INSTRUMENTAL SOUNDS . . . 4 686
AND HEAV'NLY QUIRES THE HYMENAEAN SUNG, ... 4 711
AND SHOOK HIS PLUMES, THAT HEAV'NLY FRAGRANCE FILLD 5 286
OUR HEAV'NLY STRANGER; WELL WE MAY AFFORD . . 5 316
OUR AUTHOUR. HEAV'NLY STRANGER, PLEASE TO TASTE . 5 397
HERE OR IN HEAV'NLY PARADISES DWELL; 5 500
TO HEAV'NLY SOULES HAD BIN ALL ONE; BUT NOW . . 6 165
O FATHER, O SUPREAM OF HEAV'NLY THRONES, . . . 6 723
IN HEAV'NLY SPIRITS COULD SUCH PERVERSENESS DWELL? 6 788
PROCEEDED THUS TO ASK HIS HEAV'NLY GUEST. . . . 7 69
ON HEAV'NLY GROUND THEY STOOD, AND FROM THE SHORE 7 210
TO WHOM THUS RAPHAEL ANSWER'D HEAV'NLY MEEK. . . 8 217
AND TO THE HEAV'NLY VISION THUS PRESUM'D. . . . 8 356
LET NOT MY WORDS OFFEND THEE, HEAV'NLY POWER, . . 8 379
MY EARTHLY BY HIS HEAV'NLY OVERPOWERD, ... 8 453
LED BY HER HEAV'NLY MAKER, THOUGH UNSEEN, . . . 8 485
BY WHICH TO HEAV'NLY LOVE THOU MAIST ASCEND, . . 8 592
LOVE NOT THE HEAV'NLY SPIRITS, AND HOW THIR LOVE . 8 615
WITH HEAV'NLY SPOILS, OUR SPOILS: WHAT HE DECREED 9 151
THUS EARLIE, THUS ALONE; HER HEAV'NLY FORME . 9 457
SEMBLANCE, AND IN THY BEAUTIES HEAV'NLY RAY . . 9 607
IN HEAV'NLY BRESTS? THESE, THESE AND MANY MORE . 9 730
AND RAPTURE SO OFT BEHELD? THOSE HEAV'NLY SHAPES 9 1082
A PLACE SO HEAV'NLY, AND CONNIVING SEEM 10 624
HE ENDED, AND THE HEAV'NLY AUDIENCE LOUD . . . 10 641
HENCEFORTH; LEAST THAT TOO HEAV'NLY FORM, PRETENDED 10 872
DIMENTIONLESS THROUGH HEAV'NLY DORES; THEN CLAD . 11 17
AND SLOW DESCENDS, WITH SOMTHING HEAV'NLY FRAUGHT. 11 207
HE ERR'D NOT, FOR BY THIS THE HEAV'NLY BANDS . . 11 208
ONE OF THE HEAV'NLY HOST, AND BY HIS GATE . . . 11 230
AS PRESENT, HEAV'NLY INSTRUCTER, I REVIVE . . . 11 871
THE HEAV'NLY FIRES; OVER THE TENT A CLOUD . . . 12 256

HEAV'NS
IN THE BEGINNING HOW THE HEAV'NS AND EARTH . . . 1 9
FEARLESS, ENDANGER'D HEAV'NS PERPETUAL KING; . . 1 131
THIR BOASTED PARENTS; TITAN HEAV'NS FIRST BORN . 1 510
THE RICHES OF HEAV'NS PAVEMENT, TROD'N GOLD, . . 1 682
HEAV'NS FUGITIVES, AND FOR THIR DWELLING PLACE . 2 57
O'RE HEAV'NS HIGH TOWRS TO FORCE RESISTLESS WAY, . 2 62
HEAV'NS PUREST LIGHT, YET OUR GREAT ENEMY . . . 2 137
WITH HEAV'NS AFFLICTING THUNDER, AND BESOUGHT . . 2 166
VIEWS ALL THINGS AT ONE VIEW? HE FROM HEAV'NS
HIGHTH 2 190
WITHIN HEAV'NS BOUND, UNLESS HEAV'NS LORD SUPREAM 2 236
THICK CLOUDS AND DARK DOTH HEAV'NS ALL-RULING SIRE 2 264
FROM HEAV'NS HIGH JURISDICTION, IN NEW LEAGUE . . 2 319
THAT SHOOK HEAV'NS WHOL CIRCUMFERENCE, CONFIRM'D. 2 353
AND HEAV'NS HIGH ARBITRATOR SIT SECURE 2 359
DWELL NOT UNVISITED OF HEAV'NS FAIR LIGHT . . . 2 398
HEAV'NS CHEARFUL FACE, THE LOWRING ELEMENT . . . 2 490
DREW AFTER HIM THE THIRD PART OF HEAV'NS SONS . . 2 692
WITH HEAV'NS ARTILLERY FRAUGHT, COME RATTLING ON . 2 715
IN BOLD CONSPIRACY AGAINST HEAV'NS KING, . . . 2 751
AND BY COMMAND OF HEAV'NS ALL-POWERFUL KING . . 2 851
MADE HEAD AGAINST HEAV'NS KING, THOUGH OVERTHROWN. 2 992
HEAV'NS EVERLASTING FRAME, WHILE O'RE THE NECKS . 3 395
AND NOW SAINT PETER AT HEAV'NS WICKET SEEMS . . 3 484
OF HEAV'NS ASCENT THEY LIFT THIR FEET, WHEN LOE . 3 486
THAT RUN THROUGH ALL THE HEAV'NS, OR DOWN TO TH'
EARTH 3 651
WARRING IN HEAV'N AGAINST HEAV'NS MATCHLESS KING: 4 41
BUT HEAV'NS FREE LOVE DEALT EQUALLY TO ALL? . . 4 68
DIVIDED EMPIRE WITH HEAV'NS KING I HOLD 4 111
HEAV'NS AWFUL MONARCH? WHEREFORE BUT IN HOPE . . 4 960
HEAV'NS LAST BEST GIFT, MY EVER NEW DELIGHT, . . 5 19
WITH PITTIE HEAV'NS HIGH KING, AND TO HIM CALL'D . 5 220

HEAV'NS (CONTINUED)
AT HEAV'NS HIGH FEASTS TO HAVE FED: YET WHAT
COMPARE? 5 467
REIGND WHERE THESE HEAV'NS NOW ROWL, WHERE EARTH
NOW RESTS 5 578
AS HEAV'NS GREAT YEAR BRINGS FORTH, TH' EMPYREAL
HOST 5 583
OF HEAV'NS ALMIGHTIE. THOU TO ME THY THOUGHTS . 5 676
DREW AFTER HIM THE THIRD PART OF HEAV'NS HOST: . 5 710
THROUGH HEAV'NS WIDE CHAMPAIN HELD HIS WAY, TILL
MORN, ... 6 2
HEAV'NS BLESSED PEACE, AND INTO NATURE BROUGHT . 6 267
WITH HEAV'NS RAY, AND TEMPERD THEY SHOOT FORTH . 6 480
THAT SHAKE HEAV'NS BASIS, BRING FORTH ALL MY WARR, 6 712
FROM ALL HEAV'NS BOUNDS INTO THE UTTER DEEP: . 6 716
INTO THE HEAV'N OF HEAV'NS I HAVE PRESUM'D, . . 7 13
HEAV'NS HIGHTH, AND WITH THE CENTER MIX THE POLE. 7 215
HIS LONGITUDE THROUGH HEAV'NS HIGH RODE: THE GRAY 7 373
REVOLVD ON HEAV'NS GREAT AXLE, AND HER REIGN . 7 381
UP TO THE HEAV'N OF HEAV'NS HIS HIGH ABODE, . . 7 553
THE HEAV'NS AND ALL THE CONSTELLATIONS RUNG, . . 7 562
OPEN, YE HEAV'NS, YOUR LIVING DORES; LET IN . . 7 566
OF HEAV'NS HIGH-SEATED TOP, TH' IMPEREAL THRONE . 7 585
CONJECTURE, HE HIS FABRIC OF THE HEAV'NS . . . 8 76
AND FOR THE HEAV'NS WIDE CIRCUIT, LET IT SPEAK . 8 100
ADMITTING MOTION IN THE HEAV'NS, TO SHEW . . . 8 115
TERRESTRIAL HEAV'N, DANC'T ROUND BY OTHER HEAV'NS 9 103
TO DWELL, UNLESS BY MAISTRING HEAV'NS SUPREAME; . 9 125
ANTAGONIST OF HEAV'NS ALMIGHTIE KING) 10 387
TH' INFERNAL EMPIRE, THAT SO NEER HEAV'NS DORE . 10 389
THESE CHANGES IN THE HEAV'NS, THOUGH SLOW, PRODUC'D 10 692
THROUGH HEAV'NS WIDE BOUNDS; FROM THEM I WILL NOT
HIDE 11 68
ADAM, HEAV'NS HIGH BEHEST NO PREFACE NEEDS: . . 11 251
WITH EARTHS WIDE BOUNDS, HIS GLORY WITH THE
HEAV'NS. 12 371
THEN TO THE HEAV'N OF HEAV'NS HE SHALL ASCEND . . 12 451
NEW HEAV'NS, NEW EARTH, AGES OF ENDLESS DATE . . 12 549

HEAV'N-WARRING
OF THOSE HEAV'N-WARRING CHAMPIONS COULD BE FOUND . 2 424

HEAVY
LIGHT-ARM'D OR HEAVY, SHARP, SMOOTH, SWIFT OR SLOW, 2 902

HEED
GAVE HEED, BUT WAXING MORE IN RAGE REPLI'D. . . 4 969
HIS GREAT COMMAND; TAKE HEED LEAST PASSION SWAY . 8 635
I HAVE IN VIEW, CALLING TO MINDE WITH HEED . . . 10 1030

HEEL
HER SEED SHALL BRUSE THY HEAD, THOU BRUISE HIS
HEEL. 10 181
MEE AND MANKINDE; I AM TO BRUISE HIS HEEL; . . 10 498
THIR FIGHT, WHAT STROKE SHALL BRUISE THE VICTORS
HEEL. 12 385
OF HEAD OR HEEL: NOT THEREFORE JOYNES THE SON . . 12 388
THEN TEMPORAL DEATH SHALL BRUISE THE VICTORS HEEL, 12 433
AND GATHERS GROUND FAST AT THE LABOURERS HEEL . . 12 631

HEELE
SHADDOWD FROM EITHER HEELE WITH FEATHERD MAILE . 5 284

HEELS
BY FORCE, AND AT OUR HEELS ALL HELL SHOULD RISE . 2 135

HEIGHTH
IN HEIGHTH OR DEPTH, STILL FIRST AND LAST WILL
REIGN 2 324

HEIR
IN FULL RESPLENDENCE, HEIR OF ALL MY MIGHT, . . 5 720
TO MANIFEST THEE WORTHIEST TO BE HEIR 6 707
OF ALL THINGS, TO BE HEIR AND TO BE KING . . . 6 708
SON, HEIR, AND LORD, TO HIM DOMINION GIV'N, . . 6 887

HELD
BY ANCIENT TARSUS HELD, OR THAT SEA-BEAST . . . 1 200
TH' IONIAN GODS, OF JAVANS ISSUE HELD 1 508
WITH ALL HIS PEERS: ATTENTION HELD THEM MUTE. . 1 618
WHERE SCEPTER'D ANGELS HELD THIR RESIDENCE, . . 1 734
A SOLEMN COUNCEL FORTHWITH TO BE HELD 1 755
THIS SAID, HE SAT; AND EXPECTATION HELD . . . 2 417
PORTENTOUS HELD ME; BUT FAMILIAR GROWN, . . . 2 761
HIS HABIT FIT FOR SPEED SUCCINCT, AND HELD . . 3 643
URIEL, THOUGH REGENT OF THE SUN, AND HELD . . 3 690
HE HELD IT VAIN; AWE FROM ABOVE HAD QUELLD . . 4 860
AND SUCH I HELD THEE; BUT THIS QUESTION ASKT . 4 887
SO SAYING, HE DREW NIGH, AND TO ME HELD, . . 5 82
EVEN TO MY MOUTH OF THAT SAME FRUIT HELD PART . 5 83
OF COUNTERFETED TRUTH THUS HELD THIR EARS. . . 5 771
THROUGH HEAV'NS WIDE CHAMPAIN HELD HIS WAY, TILL
MORN, ... 6 2
HELD BY THY VOICE, THY POTENT VOICE HE HEARES, . 7 100
LIKE A BLACK MIST LOW CREEPING, HE HELD ON . . 9 180
HELD DALLIANCE WITH HIS FAIRE EGYPTIAN SPOUSE. . 9 443
THIR COURSE THROUGH THICKEST CONSTELLATIONS HELD . 10 411
IMPOSSIBLE IS HELD, AS ARGUMENT 10 800

HELD (CONTINUED)
MAN-SLAUGHTER, SHALL BE HELD THE HIGHEST PITCH . 11 693

HELL
NOR THE DEEP TRACT OF HELL, SAY FIRST WHAT CAUSE . 1 28
HERE IN THE HEART OF HELL TO WORK IN FIRE, ... 1 151
INFERNAL WORLD, AND THOU PROFOUNDEST HELL . . . 1 251
CAN MAKE A HEAV'N OF HELL, A HELL OF HEAV'N. . . 1 255
TO REIGN IS WORTH AMBITION THOUGH IN HELL: . . . 1 262
BETTER TO REIGN IN HELL, THEN SERVE IN HEAV'N. . 1 263
REGAIND IN HEAV'N, OR WHAT MORE LOST IN HELL? . . 1 270
OF HELL RESOUNDED. PRINCES, POTENTATES, . . . 1 315
HOVERING ON WING UNDER THE COPE OF HELL 1 345
THE CHIEF WERE THOSE WHO FROM THE PIT OF HELL . . 1 381
AND BLACK GEHENNA CALL'D THE TYPE OF HELL. . . 1 405
TILL GOOD JOSIAH DROVE THEM THENCE TO HELL. . . 1 418
FAR ROUND ILLUMIN'D HELL: HIGHLY THEY RAG'D . . 1 666
THAT RICHES GROW IN HELL; THAT SOYLE MAY BEST . . 1 691
WITH HIS INDUSTRIOUS CREW TO BUILD IN HELL. . . 1 751
FROM FACTION; FOR NONE SURE WILL CLAIM IN HELL . 2 32
WENT ALL HIS FEAR: OF GOD, OR HELL, OR WORSE . . 2 49
ARM'D WITH HELL FLAMES AND FURY ALL AT ONCE . . 2 61
TO OUR DESTRUCTION: IF THERE BE IN HELL 2 84
BY FORCE, AND AT OUR HEELS ALL HELL SHOULD RISE . 2 135
THE DEEP TO SHELTER US? THIS HELL THEN SEEM'D . 2 167
OF HELL SHOULD SPOUT HER CATARACTS OF FIRE, . . 2 176
MUST'RING THIR RAGE, AND HEAV'N RESEMBLES HELL? . 2 268
THEY DREADED WORSE THEN HELL: SO MUCH THE FEAR . 2 293
PRINCES OF HELL? FOR SO THE POPULAR VOTE . . . 2 313
BY OUR REVOLT, BUT OVER HELL EXTEND 2 326
BY SUDDEN ONSET, EITHER WITH HELL FIRE . . . 2 364
OF MANKIND IN ONE ROOT, AND EARTH WITH HELL . . 2 383
AND HARD, THAT OUT OF HELL LEADS UP TO LIGHT; . . 2 433
THE PRESENT MISERY, AND RENDER HELL 2 459
HEARD FARR AND WIDE, AND ALL THE HOST OF HELL . . 2 519
IN WHIRLWIND; HELL SCARCE HOLDS THE WILDE UPROAR. 2 541
SUSPENDED HELL, AND TOOK WITH RAVISHMENT . . . 2 554
PUTS ON SWIFT WINGS, AND TOWARDS THE GATES OF HELL 2 631
HELL BOUNDS HIGH REACHING TO THE HORRID ROOF, . . 2 644
A CRY OF HELL HOUNDS NEVER CEASING BARK'D . . . 2 654
FIERCE AS TEN FURIES, TERRIBLE AS HELL, ... 2 671
WITH HORRID STRIDES, HELL TREMBLED AS HE STRODE. . 2 676
SO FROWND THE MIGHTY COMBATANTS, THAT HELL . . . 2 719
HAD BEEN ACHIEV'D, WHEREOF ALL HELL HAD RUNG, . . 2 723
FAST BY HELL GATE, AND KEPT THE FATAL KEY, . . . 2 725
T' WHOM THUS THE PORTRESS OF HELL GATE REPLY'D; . 2 746
HELL TREMBL'D AT THE HIDEOUS NAME, AND SIGH'D . . 2 788
STOOD ON THE BRINK OF HELL AND LOOK'D A WHILE, . 2 918
WEAKNING THE SCEPTER OF OLD NIGHT: FIRST HELL . . 2 1002
FROM HELL CONTINU'D REACHING TH' UTMOST ORBE . . 2 1029
HELL AND THE GULF BETWEEN, AND SATAN THERE . . . 3 70
PRESCRIB'D, NO BARRS OF HELL, NOR ALL THE CHAINS . 3 82
YET WITH REVENGE ACCOMPLISH'T AND TO HELL . . . 3 160
MUST HAVE BIN LOST, ADJUDG'D TO DEATH AND HELL . 3 223
SHALL LEAD HELL CAPTIVE MAUGRE HELL, AND SHOW . . 3 255
IN HEAVEN, OR EARTH, OR UNDER EARTH IN HELL; . . 3 322
BENEATH THY SENTENCE; HELL HER NUMBERS FULL . . 3 332
TO DEEPEST HELL, AND TO REPAIR THAT LOSS . . . 3 678
OF THAT FIRST BATTEL, AND HIS FLIGHT TO HELL: . . 4 12
THE HELL WITHIN HIM, FOR WITHIN HIM HELL . . . 4 20
HE BRINGS, AND ROUND ABOUT HIM, NOR FROM HELL . . 4 21
WHICH WAY I FLIE IS HELL; MY SELF AM HELL; . . . 4 75
TO WHICH THE HELL I SUFFER SEEMS A HEAV'N. . . . 4 78
WHILE THEY ADORE ME ON THE THRONE OF HELL, . . . 4 89
O HELL. WHAT DOE MINE EYES WITH GRIEF BEHOLD, . 4 358
WHICH I AS FREELY GIVE; HELL SHALL UNFOLD, . . . 4 381
OF BLISS ON BLISS, WHILE I TO HELL AM THRUST, . . 4 508
THE BARRS OF HELL, ON ERRAND BAD NO DOUBT: . . . 4 795
WHICH OF THOSE REBELL SPIRITS ADJUDG'D TO HELL . . 4 823
AND FIERCE DEMEANOUR SEEMS THE PRINCE OF HELL, . 4 871
WHO WOULD NOT, FINDING WAY, BREAK LOOSE FROM HELL, 4 889
UNLICENC'T FROM HIS BOUNDS IN HELL PRESCRIB'D; . 4 909
SEAVENFOLD, AND SCOURGE THAT WISDOM BACK TO HELL, 4 914
CAME NOT ALL HELL BROKE LOOSE? IS PAIN TO THEM . 4 918
THIS NEW CREATED WORLD, WHEREOF IN HELL 4 937
THE FACIL GATES OF HELL TOO SLIGHTLY BARRD. . . 4 967
SATAN FROM HELL SCAP'T THROUGH THE DARKSOM GULF . 5 225
WAS UNDERSTOOD, THE INJUR'D LOVERS HELL. . . . 5 450
AND SO FROM HEAV'N TO DEEPEST HELL; O FALL . . . 5 542
REIGN THOU IN HELL THY KINGDOM, LET MEE SERVE . . 6 183
YET CHAINS IN HELL, NOT REALMS EXPECT: MEAN WHILE 6 186
THY OFSPRING, TO THE PLACE OF EVIL, HELL, . . . 6 276
OR TURN THIS HEAV'N IT SELF INTO THE HELL . . . 6 291
IN HEAV'N AND HELL THY POWER ABOVE COMPARE, . . 6 705
HELL HEARD TH' UNSUFFERABLE NOISE, HELL SAW . . 6 867
INCUMBERD HIM WITH RUIN: HELL AT LAST . . . 6 874
HELL THIR FIT HABITATION FRAUGHT WITH FIRE . . . 6 876
FARR ON EXCURSION TOWARD THE GATES OF HELL; . . 8 231
BUT THE HOT HELL THAT ALWAYES IN HIM BURNES, . . 9 467
OF PARADISE FOR HELL, HOPE HERE TO TASTE . . . 9 476
I NOT; SO MUCH HATH HELL DEBAS'D, AND PAINE . . 9 487
WHEN FIRST THIS TEMPTER CROSS'D THE GULF FROM HELL. 10 39
ALL JUDGEMENT, WHETHER IN HEAV'N, OR EARTH, OR
HELL. 10 57
WITHIN THE GATES OF HELL SATE SIN AND DEATH, . . 10 230
OVER THIS MAINE FROM HELL TO THAT NEW WORLD . . 10 257
THEN BOTH FROM OUT HELL GATES INTO THE WASTE . . 10 282
FROM EACH SIDE SHOALING TOWARDS THE MOUTH OF HELL. 10 288

HELL (CONTINUED)
DEEP TO THE ROOTS OF HELL THE GATHER'D BEACH . . 10 299
SMOOTH, EASIE, INOFFENSIVE DOWN TO HELL. . . . 10 305
AND OF THIS WORLD, AND ON THE LEFT HAND HELL . . 10 322
AND TIDINGS FRAUGHT, TO HELL HE NOW RETURN'D, . . 10 346
HELL COULD NO LONGER HOLD US IN HER BOUNDS, . . 10 365
WITHIN HELL GATES TILL NOW, THOU US IMPOW'RD . . 10 369
HELL AND THIS WORLD, ONE REALM, ONE CONTINENT . . 10 392
IF YOUR JOYNT POWER PREVAILES, TH' AFFAIRES OF HELL 10 408
THE CAUSEY TO HELL GATE; ON EITHER SIDE 10 415
HEAV'N-BANISHT HOST, LEFT DESERT UTMOST HELL . . 10 437
ALIKE IS HELL, OR PARADISE, OR HEAVEN, ... 10 598
SEE WITH WHAT HEAT THESE DOGS OF HELL ADVANCE . . 10 616
FOLLY TO MEE, SO DOTH THE PRINCE OF HELL . . . 10 621
THROUGH CHAOS HURLD, OBSTRUCT THE MOUTH OF HELL . 10 636
BOILES OUT FROM UNDER GROUND, THE MOUTH OF HELL; . 12 42

HELL-BORN
HELL-BORN, NOT TO CONTEND WITH SPIRITS OF HEAV'N. 2 687

HELL-DOOM'D
HELL-DOOM'D, AND BREATH'ST DEFIANCE HERE AND SCORN 2 697

HELLESPONT
CAME TO THE SEA, AND OVER HELLESPONT 10 309

HELL-HOUNDS
MY HELL-HOUNDS, TO LICK UP THE DRAFF AND FILTH . 10 630

HELLISH
MAN HAD NOT HELLISH FOES ANOW BESIDES, ... 2 504
SHE SPAKE, AND AT HER WORDS THE HELLISH PEST . . . 2 735
SO HEAV'NLY LOVE SHALL OUTDOO HELLISH HATE 3 298
SO DEARLY TO REDEEM WHAT HELLISH HATE 3 300
AGAINST SUCH HELLISH MISCHIEF FIT TO OPPOSE. . . 6 636
WAITED WITH HELLISH RANCOUR IMMINENT 9 409
MEAN WHILE IN PARADISE THE HELLISH PAIR 10 585
TO HELLISH FALSHOOD, SNARE THEM. BUT FOR THEE . 10 873

HELLS
A SHOUT THAT TORE HELLS CONCAVE, AND BEYOND . . 1 542
THAN HELLS DREAD EMPEROUR WITH POMP SUPREAM, . . 2 510

HELME
FIT WELL HIS HELME, GRIPE FAST HIS ORBED SHIELD, . 6 543
HIS STARRIE HELME UNBUCKL'D SHEW'D HIM PRIME . . 11 245

HELMED
O'RE SHIELDS AND HELMES, AND HELMED HEADS HE RODE 6 840

HELMES
CELESTIAL ARMOURIE, SHIELDS, HELMES, AND SPEARES, 4 553
O'RE SHIELDS AND HELMES, AND HELMED HEADS HE RODE 6 840

HELMETS
OF RIGID SPEARS, AND HELMETS THRONG'D, AND SHIELDS 6 83

HELMS
A FORREST HUGE OF SPEARS: AND THRONGING HELMS . . 1 547

HELP
HAVE FINISHT HAPPIE IN OUR MUTUAL HELP 4 727
BY CONVERSATION WITH HIS LIKE TO HELP, ... 8 418
THY LIKENESS, THY FIT HELP, THY OTHER SELF, . . 8 450
ALONE, WITHOUT EXTERIOR HELP SUSTAIND? 9 336
HELP TO DISBURDEN NATURE OF HER BEARTH. 9 624
THIS WOMAN WHOM THOU MAD'ST TO BE MY HELP, . . . 10 137
A HELP, BECAME THY SNARE; TO MEE REPROACH . . . 11 165

HELP'D
THIR ARMOR HELP'D THIR HARM, CRUSH'T IN AND BRUIS'D 6 656

HELS
THEN STIL AT HELS DARK THRESHOLD TO HAVE SATE
WATCH, ... 10 594

HEMISPHERE
HIS DAY, WHICH ELSE AS TH' OTHER HEMISPHERE . . 3 725
AND LIGHT FROM DARKNESS BY THE HEMISPHERE . . . 7 250
SPANGLING THE HEMISPHERE: THEN FIRST ADORND . . 7 384
NIGHTS HEMISPHERE HAD VEILD THE HORIZON ROUND: . 9 52
THE HEMISPHERE OF EARTH IN CLEEREST KEN 11 379

HEMM
THIR PHALANX, AND BEGAN TO HEMM HIM ROUND . . . 4 979

HENCE
HERE FOR HIS ENVY, WILL NOT DRIVE US HENCE: . . 1 260
SATAN FROM HENCE NOW ON THE LOWER STAIR 3 540
WITH LIGHT FROM HENCE, THOUGH BUT REFLECTED,
SHINES; 3 723
HENCE FILLS AND EMPTIES TO ENLIGHTEN TH' EARTH, . 3 731
THIR RUINE. HENCE I WILL EXCITE THIR MINDS . . 4 522
NOT LIKELY TO PART HENCE WITHOUT CONTEST; . . . 4 872
FROM HENCE, NO CLOUD, OR, TO OBSTRUCT HIS SIGHT, . 5 257
HENCE THEN, AND EVIL GO WITH THEE ALONG 6 275
TO CHASE ME HENCE? ERRE NOT THAT SO SHALL END . 6 288
AND HENCE THE MORNING PLANET GUILDS HER HORNS; . 7 366

HIDEOUS (CONTINUED)

IMPENDENT HORRORS, THREATNING HIDEOUS FALL	2	177
A HIDEOUS PEAL: YET, WHEN THEY LIST, WOULD CREEP,	2	656
RIS'N, AND WITH HIDEOUS OUTCRY RUSH'D BETWEEN.	2	726
HELL TREMBL'D AT THE HIDEOUS NAME, AND SIGH'D	2	788
OF HIDEOUS LENGTH: BEFORE THE CLOUDIE VAN,	6	107
THE ADVERSE LEGIONS, NOR LESS HIDEOUS JOYN'D	6	206
WITH HIDEOUS ORIFICE GAP'T ON US WIDE,	6	577
FORTHWITH A HIDEOUS GABBLE RISES LOUD	12	56

HIDES

SAY FIRST, FOR HEAV'N HIDES NOTHING FROM THY VIEW	1	27

HIERARCH

TO WHOM THE WINGED HIERARCH REPLI'D.	5	468
WARR UNPROCLAM'D. THE PRINCELY HIERARCH	11	220

HIERARCHAL

THE GREAT HIERARCHAL STANDARD WAS TO MOVE;	5	701

HIERARCHIE

EACH IN HIS HIERARCHIE, THE ORDERS BRIGHT.	1	737

HIERARCHIES

OF HIERARCHIES, OF ORDERS, AND DEGREES;	5	591
WHO SPEEDILY THROUGH ALL THE HIERARCHIES	5	692
SO SANG THE HIERARCHIES: MEAN WHILE THE SON	7	192

HIERARCHS

UNDER THIR HIERARCHS IN ORDERS BRIGHT	5	587

HIES

ACCURST, AND IN A CURSED HOUR HE HIES.	2	1055

HIGH

HE TRUSTED TO HAVE EQUAL'D THE MOST HIGH,	1	40
AND HIGH DISDAIN, FROM SENCE OF INJUR'D MERIT,	1	98
AND PUT TO PROOF HIS HIGH SUPREMACY,	1	132
AS BEING THE CONTRARY TO HIS HIGH WILL	1	161
AND HIGH PERMISSION OF ALL-RULING HEAVEN	1	212
HIGH OVERARCH'T IMBOWR; OR SCATTERD SEDGE	1	304
THROUGH GODS HIGH SUFFERANCE FOR THE TRYAL OF MAN,	1	366
AND DOWNWARD FISH: YET HAD HIS TEMPLE HIGH	1	463
SOON RECOLLECTING, WITH HIGH WORDS, THAT BORE	1	528
TH' IMPERIAL ENSIGN, WHICH FULL HIGH ADVANC'T	1	536
IN HEAV'N BY MANY A TOWRED STRUCTURE HIGH,	1	733
TO HAVE BUILT IN HEAV'N HIGH TOWRS; NOR DID HE SCAPE	1	749
AT PANDAEMONIUM, THE HIGH CAPITAL	1	756
HIGH ON A THRONE OF ROYAL STATE, WHICH FAR	2	1
THUS HIGH UPLIFTED BEYOND HOPE, ASPIRES	2	7
BEYOND THUS HIGH, INSATIATE TO PURSUE	2	8
O'RE HEAV'NS HIGH TOWRS TO FORCE RESISTLESS WAY,	2	62
FOR DIGNITY COMPOS'D AND HIGH EXPLOIT:	2	111
FROM HEAV'NS HIGH JURISDICTION, IN NEW LEAGUE	2	319
HEAV'N, WHOSE HIGH WALLS FEAR NO ASSAULT OR SIEGE,	2	343
AND HEAV'NS HIGH ARBITRATOR SIT SECURE	2	359
HIGH HONOURD SITS? GO THEREFORE MIGHTY POWERS,	2	456
HIS RIVALS, WINNING CHEAP THE HIGH REPUTE	2	472
IN THOUGHTS MORE ELEVATE, AND REASON'D HIGH	2	558
UP TO THE FIERY CONCAVE TOURING HIGH.	2	635
HELL BOUNDS HIGH REACHING TO THE HORRID ROOF,	2	644
FELL WITH US FROM ON HIGH: FROM THEM I GO	2	826
FORTHWITH THE HUGE PORCULLIS HIGH UP DREW,	2	874
BY WHICH HE REIGNS: NEXT HIM HIGH ARBITER	2	909
HIGH THRON'D ABOVE ALL HIGHTH, BENT DOWN HIS EYE,	3	58
HIM GOD BEHOLDING FROM HIS PROSPECT HIGH,	3	77
OR HIGH FOREKNOWLEDGE; THEY THEMSELVES DECREED	3	116
THIR NATURE, AND REVOKE THE HIGH DECREE	3	126
FOR WHICH BOTH HEAV'N AND EARTH SHALL HIGH EXTOLL	3	146
AGAINST THE HIGH SUPREMACIE OF HEAV'N,	3	205
I THROUGH THE AMPLE AIR IN TRIUMPH HIGH	3	254
FARR MORE THEN GREAT OR HIGH; BECAUSE IN THEE	3	311
THIR SACRED SONG, AND WAKEN RAPTURES HIGH;	3	369
UP TO THE WALL OF HEAVEN A STRUCTURE HIGH,	3	503
ON HIGH BEHESTS HIS ANGELS TO AND FRO	3	533
SO HIGH ABOVE THE CIRCLING CANOPIE	3	556
IN SIGHT OF GOD'S HIGH THRONE, GLORIOUSLY BRIGHT,	3	655
WHICH NOW SAT HIGH IN HIS MERIDIAN TOWRE:	4	30
AND WROUGHT BUT MALICE; LIFTED UP SO HIGH	4	49
WITH DIADEM AND SCEPTER HIGH ADVANC'D	4	90
WOULD HIGTH RECAL HIGH THOUGHTS, HOW SOON UNSAY	4	95
AT ONE SLIGHT BOUND HIGH OVER LEAP'D ALL BOUND	4	181
HIGH EMINENT, BLOOMING AMBROSIAL FRUIT	4	219
THAT MOUNTAIN AS HIS GARDEN MOULD HIGH RAIS'D	4	226
A WHOLE DAYS JOURNY HIGH, BUT WIDE REMOTE	4	284
INTO OUR ROOM OF BLISS THUS HIGH ADVANC'T	4	359
LONG TO CONTINUE, AND THIS HIGH SEAT YOUR HEAV'N	4	371
THEN FROM HIS LOFTIE STAND ON THAT HIGH TREE	4	395
ACCESSIBLE FROM EARTH, ONE ENTRANCE HIGH;	4	546
HUNG HIGH WITH DIAMOND FLAMING, AND WITH GOLD.	4	554
REAR'D HIGH THIR FLOURISHT HEADS BETWEEN, AND WROUGHT	4	699
BLOWN UP WITH HIGH CONCEITS INGENDRING PRIDE.	4	809
HIGH UP IN HEAV'N, WITH SONGS TO HYMNE HIS THRONE,	4	944
TO THIS HIGH EXALTATION; SUDDENLY	5	90
AND WHEN HIGH NOON HAST GAIND, AND WHEN THOU FALLST.	5	174
WITH PITTIE HEAV'NS HIGH KING, AND TO HIM CALL'D	5	220
AND TO HIS MESSAGE HIGH IN HONOUR RISE;	5	289
FOR ON SOM MESSAGE HIGH THEY GUESSD HIM BOUND.	5	290
DIVINE EFFULGENCE, WHOSE HIGH POWER SO FAR	5	458
AT HEAV'NS HIGH FEASTS TO HAVE FED: YET WHAT COMPARE?	5	467
FROM WHAT HIGH STATE OF BLISS INTO WHAT WOE.	5	543
HIGH MATTER THOU INJOINST ME, O PRIME OF MEN,	5	563
TEN THOUSAND THOUSAND ENSIGNES HIGH ADVANC'D,	5	588
FROM THAT HIGH MOUNT OF GOD, WHENCE LIGHT & SHADE	5	643
THAT THE MOST HIGH COMMANDING, NOW ERE NIGHT,	5	699
HIS NAME, AND HIGH WAS HIS DEGREE IN HEAV'N;	5	707
WERE BANDED TO OPPOSE HIS HIGH DECREE;	5	717
THIS OUR HIGH PLACE, OUR SANCTUARIE, OUR HILL.	5	732
HIGH ON A HILL, FAR BLAZING, AS A MOUNT	5	757
IN PLACE THY SELF SO HIGH ABOVE THY PEERES.	5	812
THEY LED HIM HIGH APPLAUDED, AND PRESENT	6	26
ETHEREAL TRUMPET FROM ON HIGH GAN BLOW:	6	60
THIR PERFET RANKS; FOR HIGH ABOVE THE GROUND	6	71
HIGH IN THE MIDST EXALTED AS A GOD	6	99
SO SAYING, A NOBLE STROKE HE LIFTED HIGH,	6	189
FROM HIS STRONG HOLD OF HEAV'N HIGH OVER-RUL'D	6	228
SUCH HIGH ADVANTAGES THIR INNOCENCE	6	401
BORN EEVN OR HIGH, FOR THIS DAY WILL POUR DOWN,	6	544
HYMNS OF HIGH PRAISE, AND I AMONG THEM CHIEF.	6	745
ON HIGH: WHO INTO GLORIE HIM RECEAV'D,	6	891
OF THOSE TOO HIGH ASPIRING, WHO REBELLD	6	899
AS A DESPITE DON AGAINST THE MOST HIGH,	6	906
OF THINGS SO HIGH AND STRANGE, THINGS TO THIR THOUGHT	7	53
DISTANT SO HIGH, WITH MOVING FIRES ADORND	7	87
THIS INACCESSIBLE HIGH STRENGTH, THE SEAT	7	141
THOUGH WIDE, AND THIS HIGH TEMPLE TO FREQUENT	7	148
GLORIE THEY SUNG TO THE MOST HIGH, GOOD WILL	7	182
SO HIGH AS HEAV'D THE TUMID HILLS, SO LOW	7	288
THIR BLOSSOMS; WITH HIGH WOODS THE HILLS WERE CROWND,	7	326
HIGH IN TH' EXPANSE OF HEAVEN TO DIVIDE	7	340
HIS LONGITUDE THROUGH HEAV'NS HIGH RODE: THE GRAY	7	373
THIR AIERIE CARAVAN HIGH OVER SEA'S	7	428
UP TO THE HEAV'N OF HEAV'NS HIS HIGH ABODE,	7	553
WITH GLORIE ATTRIBUTED TO THE HIGH	8	12
OF WHAT WAS HIGH: SUCH PLEASURE SHE RESERV'D,	8	50
GRATEFUL DIGRESSIONS, AND SOLVE HIGH DISPUTE	8	55
THE MAKERS HIGH MAGNIFICENCE, WHO BUILT	8	101
IF IT PRESUME, MIGHT ERRE IN THINGS TOO HIGH,	8	121
THIR WANDRING COURSE NOW HIGH, NOW LOW, THEN HID,	8	126
AND THY FAIRE EVE; HEAV'N IS FOR THEE TOO HIGH	8	172
THEREFORE FROM THIS HIGH PITCH LET US DESCEND	8	198
BUT US HE SENDS UPON HIS HIGH BEHESTS	8	238
A WOODIE MOUNTAIN; WHOSE HIGH TOP WAS PLAINE,	8	303
AS HIGH HE SOARD, OBNOXIOUS FIRST OR LAST	9	170
OR SEX, AND APPREHENDED NOTHING HIGH:	9	574
FOR HIGH FROM GROUND THE BRANCHES WOULD REQUIRE	9	590
THENCEFORTH TO SPECULATIONS HIGH OR DEEP	9	602
OR FANSIED SO, THROUGH EXPECTATION HIGH	9	789
AND I PERHAPS AM SECRET; HEAV'N IS HIGH,	9	811
HIGH AND REMOTE TO SEE FROM THENCE DISTINCT	9	812
US HIS PRIME CREATURES, DIGNIFI'D SO HIGH,	9	940
ILLUSTRIOUS EVIDENCE, EXAMPLE HIGH.	9	962
HIGH OVERARCH'T, AND ECHOING WALKS BETWEEN;	9	1107
RAIND AT THIR EYES, BUT HIGH WINDS WORSE WITHIN	9	1122
BEGAN TO RISE, HIGH PASSIONS, ANGER, HATE,	9	1123
THE HIGH INJUNCTION NOT TO TASTE THAT FRUIT,	10	13
AND EASILY APPROV'D; WHEN THE MOST HIGH	10	31
OF HIGH COLLATERAL GLORIE: HIM THRONES AND POWERS,	10	86
OF MERIT HIGH TO ALL TH' INFERNAL HOST,	10	259
OVER THE FOAMING DEEP HIGH ARCHT, A BRIDGE	10	301
FROM SUSA HIS MEMNONIAN PALACE HIGH	10	308
HIGH PROOF YE NOW HAVE GIV'N TO BE THE RACE	10	385
ASCENDED HIS HIGH THRONE, WHICH UNDER STATE	10	445
THIR UNIVERSAL SHOUT AND HIGH APPLAUSE	10	505
OF HIGH OLYMPUS, THENCE BY SATURN DRIV'N	10	583
COULD ALTER HIGH DECREES, I TO THAT PLACE	10	953
HE ENDED, AND THE SON GAVE SIGNAL HIGH	11	72
HASTED, RESORTING TO THE SUMMONS HIGH,	11	81
ADAM, HEAV'NS HIGH BEHEST NO PREFACE NEEDS:	11	251
INSTINCT THROUGH ALL PROPORTIONS LOW AND HIGH	11	562
FROM THE HIGH NEIGHBOURING HILLS, WHICH WAS THIR SEAT,	11	575
SUCH WERE THESE GIANTS, MEN OF HIGH RENOWN;	11	688
TO JUDGE THEM WITH HIS SAINTS: HIM THE MOST HIGH	11	705
HIGH IN SALVATION AND THE CLIMES OF BLISS,	11	708
FAME IN THE WORLD, HIGH TITLES, AND RICH PREY,	11	793
FAST ON THE TOP OF SOM HIGH MOUNTAIN FIXT.	11	851
FOR GODS. YET HIM GOD THE MOST HIGH VOUTSAFES	12	120
WITHOUT MEDIATOR, WHOSE HIGH OFFICE NOW	12	240
TO THAT PROUD CITIE, WHOSE HIGH WALLS THOU SAW'ST	12	342
THE POWER OF THE MOST HIGH; HE SHALL ASCEND	12	369
HIGH IN THE LOVE OF HEAV'N, YET FROM MY LOYNES	12	380
OF GOD MOST HIGH; SO GOD WITH MAN UNITES.	12	382
SO ONELY CAN HIGH JUSTICE REST APPAID.	12	401
HIS SEAT AT GODS RIGHT HAND, EXALTED HIGH	12	457
HOMEWARD RETURNING. HIGH IN FRONT ADVANC'T,	12	632

HIGH-BLEST

OF GOD HIGH-BLEST, OR TO INCLINE HIS WILL,	11	145

HIGH-CLIMBING
OBTAINS THE BROW OF SOME HIGH-CLIMBING HILL, . . . 3 546

HIGHER
WITH UPRIGHT WING AGAINST A HIGHER FOE. 2 72
SATAN EXCEPT, NONE HIGHER SAT, WITH GRAVE . . . 2 300
I SDEIND SUBJECTION, AND THOUGHT ONE STEP HIGHER . 4 50
OF STATELIEST VIEW. YET HIGHER THEN THIR TOPS . 4 142
AND HIGHER THEN THAT WALL A CIRCLING ROW . . . 4 146
LAUREL AND MIRTLE, AND WHAT HIGHER GREW 4 694
FROM HER MOIST CONTINENT TO HIGHER ORBES. . . . 5 422
ABOVE MANKINDE, OR AUGHT THEN MANKINDE HIGHER, . 8 358
ALL HIGHER KNOWLEDGE IN HER PRESENCE FALLS . . . 8 551
WHAT HIGHER IN HER SOCIETIE THOU FINDST 8 586
(THOUGH HIGHER OF THE GENIAL BED BY FAR, . . . 8 598
NOR SKILLD NOR STUDIOUS, HIGHER ARGUMENT . . . 9 42
SINCE HIGHER I FALL SHORT, ON HIM WHO NEXT . . . 9 174
WHOSE HIGHER INTELLECTUAL MORE I SHUN, . . . 9 483
MEANT MEE, BY VENTRING HIGHER THEN MY LOT. . . . 9 690
HIGHER DEGREE OF LIFE, INDUCEMENT STRONG . . . 9 934
NOT HIGHER THAT HILL NOR WIDER LOOKING ROUND, . . 11 381
OF WISDOME; HOPE NO HIGHER, THOUGH ALL THE STARRS 12 576

HIGHEST
THIR HIGHEST HEAV'N; OR ON THE DELPHIAN CLIFF, . 1 517
AGAINST THE HIGHEST, AND FIERCE WITH GRASPED ARMS 1 667
WILL ENVY WHOM THE HIGHEST PLACE EXPOSES . . . 2 27
CONSCIOUS OF HIGHEST WORTH, UNMOV'D THUS SPAKE. . 2 429
EXTOLL HIM EQUAL TO THE HIGHEST IN HEAV'N: . . . 2 479
SATAN WITH THOUGHTS INFLAM'D OF HIGHEST DESIGN, . 2 630
CONJUR'D AGAINST THE HIGHEST, FOR WHICH BOTH THOU 2 693
BECAUSE THOU HAST, THOUGH THRON'D IN HIGHEST BLISS 3 305
INTERPRETER THROUGH HIGHEST HEAV'N TO BRING, . . 3 657
WOULD SET ME HIGHEST, AND IN A MOMENT QUIT . . . 4 51
OF HILL OR HIGHEST WALL, AND SHEER WITHIN . . . 4 182
THE MIDDLE TREE AND HIGHEST THERE THAT GREW, . . 4 195
SHALL TEACH US HIGHEST DEEDS, BY PROOF TO TRY . . 5 865
SUCH AS IN HIGHEST HEAV'N, ARRAYD IN GOLD . . . 6 13
AMONG THE MIGHTIEST, BENT ON HIGHEST DEEDS, . . . 6 112
O HEAV'N, THAT SUCH RESEMBLANCE OF THE HIGHEST . 6 114
HOSANNA TO THE HIGHEST: NOR STOOD AT GAZE . . . 6 205
FIRST, HIGHEST, HOLIEST, BEST, THOU ALWAYES SEEKST 6 724
OUR KNOWING, AS TO HIGHEST WISDOM SEEMD, . . . 7 83
NOT OF EARTH ONELY BUT OF HIGHEST HEAV'N. . . . 8 178
WITH GODS TO SIT THE HIGHEST, AM NOW CONSTRAIND . 9 164
OF HIGHEST AGENTS, DEEMD HOWEVER WISE. 9 683
OBSCUR'D, WHERE HIGHEST WOODS IMPENETRABLE . . . 9 1086
CREATOR WISE, THAT PEOPL'D HIGHEST HEAV'N . . . 10 889
OF CONTUMACIE WILL PROVOKE THE HIGHEST 10 1027
OF THEM THE HIGHEST, FOR SUCH OF SHAPE MAY SEEM . 11 297
OF PARADISE THE HIGHEST, FROM WHOSE TOP 11 378
MAN-SLAUGHTER, SHALL BE HELD THE HIGHEST PITCH . 11 693
ABOVE THE HIGHEST HILLS: THEN SHALL THIS MOUNT . 11 829
IS FORTITUDE TO HIGHEST VICTORIE, ... 12 570

HIGHLY
FAVOUR'D OF HEAV'N SO HIGHLY, TO FALL OFF . . . 1 30
FAR ROUND ILLUMIN'D HELL: HIGHLY THEY RAG'D . . 1 666
PLEAS'D HIGHLY THOSE INFERNAL STATES, AND JOY . . 2 387
HE CEAS'D, FOR BOTH SEEMD HIGHLY PLEASD, AND DEATH 2 845
WHO HIGHLY THUS TO ENTITLE ME VOUTSAF'ST, . . . 11 170
HIGHLY BELOV'D, BEING BUT THE MINISTER 12 308

HIGH-SEATED
OF HEAV'NS HIGH-SEATED TOP, TH' IMPEREAL THRONE . 7 585

HIGHT
TO HIGHT OF NOBLEST TEMPER HERO'S OLD 1 552
THAT TO THE HIGHT OF DEITIE ASPIR'D; 9 167

HIGHTH
THAT TO THE HIGHTH OF THIS GREAT ARGUMENT . . . 1 24
FROM WHAT HIGHTH FALL'N, SO MUCH THE STRONGER
PROV'D 1 92
NO WONDER, FALL'N SUCH A PERNICIOUS HIGHTH. . . 1 282
STOOD FIXT HER STATELY HIGHTH, AND STRAIT THE DORES 1 723
HIS UTMOST IRE? WHICH TO THE HIGHTH ENRAG'D, . . 2 95
VIEWS ALL THINGS AT ONE VIEW? HE FROM HEAV'NS
HIGHTH 2 190
WITHOUT DIMENSION, WHERE LENGTH, BREADTH, & HIGHTH, 2 893
HIGH THRON'D ABOVE ALL HIGHTH, BENT DOWN HIS EYE, 3 58
INSUPERABLE HIGHTH OF LOFTIEST SHADE, ... 4 138
THIS DAY AT HIGHTH OF NOON CAME TO MY SPHEARE . . 4 564
THE HIGHTH OF THY ASPIRING UNOPPOS'D, ... 6 132
HUMAN IMAGINATION TO SUCH HIGHTH 6 300
TOOK ENVIE, AND ASPIRING TO HIS HIGHTH, ... 6 793
HEAV'NS HIGHTH, AND WITH THE CENTER MIX THE POLE. 7 215
THE HIGHTH AND DEPTH OF THY ETERNAL WAYES . . . 8 413
CANST RAISE THY CREATURE TO WHAT HIGHTH THOU WILT 8 430
WHICH IT HAD LONG STOOD UNDER, STREIND TO THE
HIGHTH 8 454
SCIPIO THE HIGHTH OF ROME. WITH TRACT OBLIQUE . 9 510
SOMTIMES IN HIGHTH BEGAN, AS NO DELAY 9 675
SO STANDING, MOVING, OR TO HIGHTH UPGROWN . . . 9 677
OF GOD, WHOM TO BEHOLD WAS THEN MY HIGHTH . . . 10 724
MEASUR'D BY CUBIT, LENGTH, AND BREADTH, AND HIGHTH, 11 730

HIGHTHN'D
STOOD SCOFFING, HIGHTHN'D IN THIR THOUGHTS BEYOND 6 629

HIGHT'ND
AND HIGHT'ND AS WITH WINE, JOCOND AND BOON, . . . 9 793

HIGTH
WOULD HIGTH RECAL HIGH THOUGHTS, HOW SOON UNSAY . 4 95

HILL
ROSE OUT OF CHAOS: OR IF SION HILL 1 10
OF SUBTERRANEAN WIND TRANSPORTS A HILL 1 231
ON THAT OPPROBRIOUS HILL, AND MADE HIS GROVE . . 1 403
EVEN TO THAT HILL OF SCANDAL, BY THE GROVE . . 1 416
THERE STOOD A HILL NOT FAR WHOSE GRIESLY TOP . . 1 670
OP'ND INTO THE HILL A SPACIOUS WOUND 1 689
ATTEST THIR JOY, THAT HILL AND VALLEY RINGS. . . 2 495
OTHERS APART SAT ON A HILL RETIR'D, ... 2 557
WITH WINGED COURSE ORE HILL OR MOARIE DALE, . . 2 944
CLEER SPRING, OR SHADIE GROVE, OR SUNNIE HILL, . 3 28
OBTAINS THE BROW OF SOME HIGH-CLIMBING HILL, . . 3 546
NOW TO TH' ASCENT OF THAT STEEP SAVAGE HILL . . 4 172
OF HILL OR HIGHEST WALL, AND SHEER WITHIN . . . 4 182
NOR CHANG'D HIS COURSE, BUT THROUGH THE SHAGGIE
HILL 4 224
POWRD FORTH PROFUSE ON HILL AND DALE AND PLAINE, . 4 243
THROUGH WOOD, THROUGH WASTE, O'RE HILL, O'RE DALE
HIS ROAM. 4 538
OF ECHOING HILL OR THICKET HAVE WE HEARD . . . 4 681
HALF WAY UP HILL THIS VAST SUBLUNAR VAULT, . . . 4 777
FROM HILL OR STEAMING LAKE, DUSKIE OR GREY, . . 5 186
TO HILL, OR VALLEY, FOUNTAIN, OR FRESH SHADE . . 5 203
MY ONELY SON, AND ON THIS HOLY HILL 5 604
IN SONG AND DANCE ABOUT THE SACRED HILL, . . . 5 619
THIS OUR HIGH PLACE, OUR SANCTUARIE, OUR HILL. . 5 732
HIGH ON A HILL, FAR BLAZING, AS A MOUNT 5 757
RETURND NOT LOST: ON TO THE SACRED HILL 6 25
TO DARKEN ALL THE HILL, AND SMOAK TO ROWL . . . 6 57
INDISSOLUBLY FIRM; NOR OBVIOUS HILL, ... 6 69
OF PLEASURE SITUATE IN HILL AND DALE) 6 641
AND WITH FRESH FLOURETS HILL AND VALLEY SMIL'D. . 6 784
FOLLOWING, ABOVE TH' OLYMPIAN HILL I SOARE, . . 7 3
SOFT-EBBING; NOR WITHSTOOD THEM ROCK OR HILL, . . 7 300
HILL, DALE, AND SHADIE WOODS, AND SUNNIE PLAINES, 8 262
GAVE SIGN OF GRATULATION, AND EACH HILL; . . . 8 514
ON HIS HILL TOP, TO LIGHT THE BRIDAL LAMP. . . . 8 520
OF HILL, AND VALLIE, RIVERS, WOODS AND PLAINES, . 9 116
DOWN FROM A HILL THE BEAST THAT REIGNS IN WOODS, . 11 187
IN PARADISE, AND ON A HILL MADE ALT, ... 11 210
FROM YONDER BLAZING CLOUD THAT VEILS THE HILL . . 11 229
THIS HILL; LET EVE (FOR I HAVE DRENCHT HER EYES) . 11 367
IN THE VISIONS OF GOD: IT WAS A HILL 11 377
NOT HIGHER THAT HILL NOR WIDER LOOKING ROUND, . . 11 381
BY MEE ENCAMPT ON YONDER HILL, EXPECT 12 591
HE ENDED, AND THEY BOTH DESCEND THE HILL; . . . 12 606
TH' ARCHANGEL STOOD, AND FROM THE OTHER HILL . . 12 626

HILLOC
OR PALMIE HILLOC, OR THE FLOURIE LAP 4 254

HILLOCKS
IN HILLOCKS; THE SWIFT STAG FROM UNDER GROUND . . 7 469
O WOODS, O FOUNTAINS, HILLOCKS, DALES AND BOWRS, . 10 860

HILLS
HEWN ON NORWEGIAN HILLS, TO BE THE MAST 1 293
REND UP BOTH ROCKS AND HILLS, AND RIDE THE AIR . 2 540
ON HILLS WHERE FLOCKS ARE FED, FLIES TOWARD THE
SPRINGS 3 435
DOWN THE SLOPE HILLS, DISPERST, OR IN A LAKE, . . 4 261
ABOVE ALL HILLS. AS WHEN BY NIGHT THE GLASS . . 5 261
CHERUBIC SONGS BY NIGHT FROM NEIGHBOURING HILLS . 5 547
SOON BANDED; OTHERS FROM THE DAWNING HILLS . . . 6 528
THIR ARMS AWAY THEY THREW, AND TO THE HILLS . . 6 639
THEY PLUCKT THE SEATED HILLS WITH ALL THIR LOAD, . 6 644
BETOOK THEM, AND THE NEIGHBOURING HILLS UPTORE; . 6 663
SO HILLS AMID THE AIR ENCOUNTERD HILLS 6 664
AT HIS COMMAND THE UPROOTED HILLS RETIR'D . . . 6 781
BEFORE THE HILLS APPEERD, OR FOUNTAIN FLOW'D, . . 7 8
SO HIGH AS HEAV'D THE TUMID HILLS, SO LOW . . . 7 288
THIR BLOSSOMS; WITH HIGH WOODS THE HILLS WERE
CROWND, ... 7 326
YE HILLS AND DALES, YE RIVERS, WOODS, AND PLAINES, 8 275
FROM THE HIGH NEIGHBOURING HILLS, WHICH WAS THIR
SEAT, ... 11 575
FROM UNDER HEAV'N; THE HILLS TO THEIR SUPPLIE . . 11 740
ABOVE THE HIGHEST HILLS: THEN SHALL THIS MOUNT . 11 829
AND NOW THE TOPS OF HILLS AS ROCKS APPEER; . . . 11 852
SHALL DWELL TO SENIR, THAT LONG RIDGE OF HILLS. . 12 146

HINDE
GOODLIEST OF ALL THE FORREST, HART AND HINDE; . . 11 189

HINDER
HIS HINDER PARTS, THEN SPRINGS AS BROKE FROM BONDS, 7 465

HINDER'D
HINDER'D NOT SATAN TO ATTEMPT THE MINDE 10 8

HINDERS
OF VERTUE TO MAKE WISE: WHAT HINDERS THEN 9 778

HINGES
TH' INFERNAL DORES, AND ON THIR HINGES GRATE . . 2 881
ON GOLDEN HINGES TURNING, AS BY WORK 5 255
ON GOLDEN HINGES MOVING, TO LET FORTH 7 207

HINNOM
THE PLEASANT VALLY OF HINNOM, TOPHET THENCE . . 1 404

HIRELINGS
SO SINCE INTO HIS CHURCH LEWD HIRELINGS CLIMBE. . 4 193

HISPAHAN
IN HISPAHAN, OR WHERE THE RUSSIAN KSAR 11 394

HISS
BRUSHT WITH THE HISS OF RUSSLING WINGS. AS BEES . 1 768
OF CONFLICT; OVER HEAD THE DISMAL HISS 6 212
A DISMAL UNIVERSAL HISS, THE SOUND 10 508
BUT HISS FOR HISS RETURND WITH FORKED TONGUE . . 10 518
AND THE DIRE HISS RENEW'D, AND THE DIRE FORM . . 10 543
TURND TO EXPLODING HISS, TRIUMPH TO SHAME . . . 10 546
AND WORN WITH FAMIN, LONG AND CEASLESS HISS, . . 10 573

HISSING
OF HISSING THROUGH THE HALL, THICK SWARMING NOW . 10 522

HIT
THAT WHOM THEY HIT, NONE ON THIR FEET MIGHT STAND, 6 592

HITHER
WHO HATES ME, AND HATH HITHER THRUST ME DOWN . . 2 857
UP HITHER LIKE AEREAL VAPOURS FLEW 3 445
DISSOLVD ON EARTH, FLEET HITHER, AND IN VAIN, . . 3 457
HITHER OF ILL-JOYND SONS AND DAUGHTERS BORN . . 3 463
THE MORE IT SEEMS EXCESS, THAT LED THEE HITHER . 3 698
LOOK DOWNWARD ON THAT GLOBE WHOSE HITHER SIDE . . 3 722
SUCH WHERE YE FIND, SEISE FAST, AND HITHER BRING. 4 796
OR NOT, WHO ASK WHAT BOLDNESS BROUGHT HIM HITHER . 4 908
HASTE HITHER EVE, AND WORTH THY SIGHT BEHOLD . . 5 308
UP HITHER, UNDER LONG OBEDIENCE TRI'D, ... 7 159
HITHER AS TO THIR FOUNTAIN OTHER STARRS 7 364
UP HITHER, FROM AMONG THE TREES APPEER'D 8 313
NOT HITHER SUMMOND, SINCE THEY CANNOT CHANGE . . 8 347
WHAT HITHER BROUGHT US, HATE, NOT LOVE, NOR HOPE . 9 475
SERPENT, WE MIGHT HAVE SPAR'D OUR COMING HITHER, . 9 647
ALL GENERATIONS, AND HAD HITHER COME 11 344

HITHERTO
WARRS, HITHERTO THE ONELY ARGUMENT 9 28
TO SAPIENCE, HITHERTO OBSCUR'D, INFAM'D, ... 9 797

HITHERWARD
HITHERWARD BENT (WHO COULD HAVE THOUGHT?) ESCAP'D 4 794

HIVE
POUR FORTH THIR POPULOUS YOUTH ABOUT THE HIVE . . 1 770

HOARCE
CALABRIA FROM THE HOARCE TRINACRIAN SHORE: . . . 2 661
HOARCE MURMUR ECHO'D TO HIS WORDS APPLAUSE . . . 5 873
TO HOARCE OR MUTE, THOUGH FALL'N ON EVIL DAYES, . 7 25

HOARIE
THE SECRETS OF THE HOARIE DEEP, A DARK 2 891

HOARSE
HAD ROUS'D THE SEA, NOW WITH HOARSE CADENCE LULL . 2 287
NOT UNDERSTOOD, TILL HOARSE, AND ALL IN RAGE, . . 12 58

HOARY
SEED TIME AND HARVEST, HEAT AND HOARY FROST . . 11 899

HOLD
FOR THIS INFERNAL PIT SHALL NEVER HOLD 1 657
FOR SINCE NO DEEP WITHIN HER GULF CAN HOLD . . . 2 12
TO THEIR DEFENCE WHO HOLD IT: HERE PERHAPS . . . 2 362
AND CHAOS, ANCESTORS OF NATURE, HOLD 2 895
WIDE INTERRUPT CAN HOLD; SO BENT HE SEEMS . . . 3 84
TRANSLATED SAINTS, OR MIDDLE SPIRITS HOLD . . . 3 461
DIVIDED EMPIRE WITH HEAV'NS KING I HOLD 4 111
GRAVELY IN DOUBT WHETHER TO HOLD THEM WISE . . . 4 907
SHE TEMPERS DULCET CREAMS, NOR THESE TO HOLD . . 5 347
DANC'D HAND IN HAND. A WHILE DISCOURSE THEY HOLD; 5 395
HOLD, AS YOU YOURS, WHILE OUR OBEDIENCE HOLDS; . 5 537
WE MEAN TO HOLD WHAT ANCIENTLY WE CLAIM 5 723
FROM HIS STRONG HOLD OF HEAV'N HIGH OVER-RUL'D . 6 228
SUBDUE IT, AND THROUGHOUT DOMINION HOLD 7 532
HOW HAVE I THEN WITH WHOM TO HOLD CONVERSE . . . 8 408
DEVOLV'D; THOUGH SHOULD I HOLD MY PEACE, YET THOU 10 135
HELL COULD NO LONGER HOLD US IN HER BOUNDS, . . 10 365
MY HOLD OF THIS NEW KINGDOM ALL DEPENDS, . . . 10 406
THY TERMS TOO HARD, BY WHICH I WAS TO HOLD . . . 10 751
SAID TH' ANGEL, WHO SHOULD BETTER HOLD HIS PLACE . 11 635
SHALL HOLD THIR COURSE, TILL FIRE PURGE ALL THINGS NEW, ... 11 900

HOLD (CONTINUED)
DOMINION ABSOLUTE; THAT RIGHT WE HOLD 12 68

HOLDS
SOLE REIGNING HOLDS THE TYRANNY OF HEAV'N. . . . 1 124
FIRM CONCORD HOLDS, MEN ONELY DISAGREE 2 497
IN WHIRLWIND; HELL SCARCE HOLDS THE WILDE UPROAR. 2 541
AND LIKE A WEATHER-BEATEN VESSEL HOLDS 2 1043
HER CHRYSTAL MIRROR HOLDS, UNITE THIR STREAMS. . 4 263
HER OFFICE HOLDS; OF ALL EXTERNAL THINGS, . . . 5 103
CAN TURN, OR HOLDS IT POSSIBLE TO TURN 5 441
HOLD, AS YOU YOURS, WHILE OUR OBEDIENCE HOLDS; . 5 537
WITH THOUSAND LESSER LIGHTS DIVIDUAL HOLDS, . . 7 382
HOLDS ON THE SAME, FROM WOMAN TO BEGIN. 11 633

HOLE
COULD ONCE HAVE MOV'D; THEN IN THE KEY-HOLE TURNS 2 876

HOLIE
THREATN'D, NOR FROM THE HOLIE ONE OF HEAV'N . . 6 359
HOLIE AND PURE, CONFORMITIE DIVINE. 11 606

HOLIEST
OR THINK THEE UNBEFITTING HOLIEST PLACE, ... 4 759
FIRST, HIGHEST, HOLIEST, BEST, THOU ALWAYES SEEKST 6 724

HOLLOW
HE CALL'D SO LOUD, THAT ALL THE HOLLOW DEEP . . 1 314
BY STRANGE CONVEYANCE FILL'D EACH HOLLOW NOOK, . 1 707
BUT ALL WAS FALSE AND HOLLOW; THOUGH HIS TONGUE . 2 112
TH' ASSEMBLY, AS WHEN HOLLOW ROCKS RETAIN . . . 2 285
BY HARALDS VOICE EXPLAIN'D: THE HOLLOW ABYSS . . 2 518
BORN THROUGH THE HOLLOW DARK ASSAULTS HIS EARE . 2 953
APPROACHING GROSS AND HUGE; IN HOLLOW CUBE . . . 6 552
PORTENDING HOLLOW TRUCE; AT EACH BEHIND 6 578
THE HOLLOW UNIVERSAL ORB THEY FILL'D, ... 7 257
DOWN SUNK A HOLLOW BOTTOM BROAD AND DEEP, . . . 7 289

HOLLOW'D
OR HOLLOW'D BODIES MADE OF OAK OR FIRR 6 574

HOLY
HIS HOLY RITES, AND SOLEMN FEASTS PROFAN'D, . . 1 390
THEN AUGHT DIVINE OR HOLY ELSE ENJOY'D 1 683
HAIL HOLY LIGHT, OFSPRING OF HEAV'N FIRST-BORN, . 3 1
TO BEERSABA, WHERE THE HOLY LAND 3 536
NOR HOLY RAPTURE WANTED THEY TO PRAISE 5 147
BESTOWD, THE HOLY SALUTATION US'D 5 386
HOLY MEMORIALS, ACTS OF ZEALE AND LOVE 5 593
MY ONELY SON, AND ON THIS HOLY HILL 5 604
ABSTRUSEST THOUGHTS, FROM FORTH HIS HOLY MOUNT . 5 712
TO TROUBLE HOLY REST; HEAV'N CASTS THEE OUT . . 6 272
FARR SEPARATE, CIRCLING THY HOLY MOUNT 6 743
MOV'D THE CREATOR IN HIS HOLY REST 7 91
FORERUNNING NIGHT; WHEN AT THE HOLY MOUNT . . . 7 584
BUT NOT IN SILENCE HOLY KEPT; THE HARP 7 594
HOLY AND JUST: THRICE HAPPIE IF THEY KNOW . . . 7 631
HOLY, DIVINE, GOOD, AMIABLE, OR SWEET. 9 899
HIS HOLY EYES; RESOLVING FROM THENCEFORTH . . . 12 109
THE HOLY ONE WITH MORTAL MEN TO DWELL: 12 248
THIR CITIE, HIS TEMPLE, AND HIS HOLY ARK . . . 12 340

HOME
TERROR OF HEAV'N, THOUGH FALL'N; INTEND AT HOME, . 2 457
WHILE HERE SHALL BE OUR HOME, WHAT BEST MAY EASE . 2 458
OF HARD CONTENTS, AND FULL OF FORCE URG'D HOME, . 6 622
IN DUST, OUR FINAL REST AND NATIVE HOME. . . . 10 1085
HOME TO MY BREST, AND TO MY MEMORIE 11 154
NATIONS, AND BRING HOME SPOILS WITH INFINITE . . 11 692

HOMELY
NO HOMELY MORSELS, AND WHATEVER THING 10 605

HOMEWARD
HOMEWARD WITH FLYING MARCH WHERE WE POSSESS . . 5 688
HOMEWARD RETURNING. HIGH IN FRONT ADVANC'T, . . 12 632

HOMICIDE
OF MOLOCH HOMICIDE, LUST HARD BY HATE; 1 417

HONEY
WITH HONEY STOR'D: THE REST ARE NUMBERLESS, . . 7 492

HONOR
OF NATURES WORKS, HONOR DISHONORABLE, ... 4 314

HONOUR
HIS MIGHTY STANDARD; THAT PROUD HONOUR CLAIM'D . 1 533
OF HAZARD AS OF HONOUR, DUE ALIKE 2 453
ADORE THE SON, AND HONOUR HIM AS MEE. 3 343
LIKE HONOUR TO OBTAIN, AND AS HIS EYE 3 660
WHERE HONOUR DUE AND REVERENCE NONE NEGLECTS, . . 3 738
GODLIKE ERECT, WITH NATIVE HONOUR CLAD 4 289
HONOUR AND EMPIRE WITH REVENGE ENLARG'D, ... 4 390
IN HONOUR TO THE WORLDS GREAT AUTHOR RISE, . . . 5 188
AND TO HIS MESSAGE HIGH IN HONOUR RISE; 5 289
ABUNDANCE, FIT TO HONOUR AND RECEIVE 5 315
TO WANT, AND HONOUR THESE, VOUTSAFE WITH US . . 5 365

HORSES
OF HORSES LED, AND GROOMS BESMEARD WITH GOLD 5 356

HOSANNA
HOSANNA TO THE HIGHEST: NOR STOOD AT GAZE 6 205

HOSANNA'S
WITH JUBILEE, AND LOUD HOSANNA'S FILLD 3 348

HOSPITABLE
IN GIBEAH, WHEN THE HOSPITABLE DOOR 1 504
SHE TURNS, ON HOSPITABLE THOUGHTS INTENT 5 332

HOST
HAD CAST HIM OUT FROM HEAV'N, WITH ALL HIS HOST 1 37
HATH LOST US HEAV'N, AND ALL THIS MIGHTY HOST 1 136
AT WHICH THE UNIVERSAL HOST UPSENT 1 541
FOR MEE BE WITNESS ALL THE HOST OF HEAV'N, 1 635
AND TRUMPETS SOUND THROUGHOUT THE HOST PROCLAIM 1 754
HEARD FARR AND WIDE, AND ALL THE HOST OF HELL 2 519
ALL TH' HOST OF HEAV'N; BACK THEY RECOILD AFFRAID 2 759
BOTH HIM AND THEE, AND ALL THE HEAV'NLY HOST 2 824
THAT WITH EXTENDED WINGS A BANNERD HOST 2 885
I SAW AND HEARD, FOR SUCH A NUMEROUS HOST 2 993
THE STARRIE HOST, RODE BRIGHTEST, TILL THE MOON 4 606
TO THY DESERTED HOST THIS CAUSE OF FLIGHT, 4 922
MY SELF AND ALL TH' ANGELIC HOST THAT STAND 5 535
AS HEAV'NS GREAT YEAR BRINGS FORTH, TH' EMPYREAL HOST 5 583
DREW AFTER HIM THE THIRD PART OF HEAV'NS HOST: 5 710
FAR WAS ADVANC'T ON WINGED SPEED, AN HOST 5 744
THROUGH THE INFINITE HOST, NOR LESS FOR THAT 5 874
REMAINS THEE, AIDED BY THIS HOST OF FRIENDS, 6 38
'TWIXT HOST AND HOST BUT NARROW SPACE WAS LEFT, 6 104
AND FLYING VAULTED EITHER HOST WITH FIRE. 6 214
A NUMEROUS HOST, IN STRENGTH EACH ARMED HAND 6 231
OREWEARIED, THROUGH THE FAINT SATANIC HOST 6 392
OF GOLDEN PANOPLIE, REFULGENT HOST, 6 527
OF IRON GLOBES, WHICH ON THE VICTOR HOST 6 590
AND ALL HIS HOST DERIDED, WHILE THEY STOOD 6 633
BE SURE, AND TERROUR SEIS'D THE REBEL HOST, 6 647
TO ALL HIS HOST ON EITHER HAND THUS SPAKE. 6 800
OF TORRENT FLOODS, OR OF A NUMEROUS HOST. 6 830
(SO CALL HIM, BRIGHTER ONCE AMIDST THE HOST 7 132
ALCINOUS, HOST OF OLD LAERTES SON, 9 441
OF MERIT HIGH TO ALL TH' INFERNAL HOST, 10 259
HEAV'N-BANISHT HOST, LEFT DESERT UTMOST HELL 10 437
ONE OF THE HEAV'NLY HOST, AND BY HIS GATE 11 230
SWALLOWS HIM WITH HIS HOST, BUT THEM LETS PASS 12 196
GOD LOOKING FORTH WILL TROUBLE ALL HIS HOST 12 209

HOSTIL
RAISE OUT OF FRIENDSHIP HOSTIL DEEDS IN PEACE. 11 796

HOSTILE
WITH TUMULT LESS AND WITH LESS HOSTILE DIN, 2 1040
LONG WAY THROUGH HOSTILE SCORN, WHICH HE SUSTEIND 5 904
REBELLIOUS, THEM WITH FIRE AND HOSTILE ARMS 6 50
OR CAPTIVE DRAG'D IN CHAINS, WITH HOSTILE FROWN 6 260
WITH WARR AND HOSTILE SNARE SUCH AS REFUSE 12 31

HOSTILITY
BUT TO OUR POWER HOSTILITY AND HATE, 2 336

HOSTING
AND IN FIERCE HOSTING MEET, WHO WONT TO MEET 6 93

HOT
FOR HOT, COLD, MOIST, AND DRY, FOUR CHAMPIONS FIERCE 2 898
BUT THE HOT HELL THAT ALWAYES IN HIM BURNES, 9 467
VAPOUR, AND MIST, AND EXHALATION HOT, 10 694
DOWN TO THE VEINS OF EARTH, THENCE GLIDING HOT 11 568
GAZ'D HOT, AND OF THE FRESH WAVE LARGELY DREW, 11 845

HOUNDS
A CRY OF HELL HOUNDS NEVER CEASING BARK'D 2 654
MY HELL-HOUNDS, TO LICK UP THE DRAFF AND FILTH 10 630

HOUR
BY SPIRITS REPROBATE, AND IN AN HOUR 1 697
INEXORABLY, AND THE TORTURING HOUR 2 91
DESTIN'D TO THAT GOOD HOUR: NO LESS REJOYC'D 2 848
TEN THOUSAND FADOM DEEP, AND TO THIS HOUR 2 934
ACCURST, AND IN A CURSED HOUR HE HIES. 2 1055
WELL KNOWN FROM HEAV'N; AND SINCE MERIDIAN HOUR 4 581
WHEN ADAM THUS TO EVE: FAIR CONSORT, TH' HOUR 4 610
FORTH ISSUING AT TH' ACCUSTOMD HOUR STOOD ARMD 4 779
WHILE DAY ARISES, THAT SWEET HOUR OF PRIME. 5 170
AND EVE WITHIN, DUE AT HER HOUR PREPAR'D 5 303
BY SIN OF DISOBEDIENCE, TILL THAT HOUR 6 396
WHO SINCE THE MORNING HOUR SET OUT FROM HEAV'N 8 111
EARLY, AND TH' HOUR OF SUPPER COMES UNEARN'D. 9 225
I SPAR'D NOT, FOR SUCH PLEASURE TILL THAT HOUR 9 596
MEAN WHILE THE HOUR OF NOON DREW ON, AND WAK'D 9 739
SO SAYING, HER RASH HAND IN EVIL HOUR 9 780
O EVE, IN EVIL HOUR THOU DIDST GIVE EARE 9 1067
FROM NOON, AND GENTLE AIRES DUE AT THIR HOUR 10 93

HOUR (CONTINUED)
EACH HOUR THEIR GREAT ADVENTURER FROM THE SEARCH 10 440
O WELCOM HOUR WHENEVER. WHY DELAYES 10 771
WHILE YET WE LIVE, SCARSE ONE SHORT HOUR PERHAPS, 10 923
ONE WAY THE SELF-SAME HOUR? WHY IN THE EAST 11 203
OF SPECULATION; FOR THE HOUR PRECISE 12 589

HOURE
FLIE THITHER WHENCE THOU FLEDST: IF FROM THIS HOURE 4 963
SOON AS MIDNIGHT BROUGHT ON THE DUSKIE HOURE 5 667
OBSEQUIOUS DARKNESS ENTERS, TILL HER HOURE 6 10
THUS ANSWERD. ILL FOR THEE, BUT IN WISHT HOURE 6 150
AND HUNGER BOTH, FROM LABOUR, AT THE HOURE 8 213
AND HAPPIE CONSTELLATIONS ON THAT HOURE 8 512
THOU NEVER FROM THAT HOURE IN PARADISE 9 406

HOURLY
SURROUND ME, AS THOU SAWST, HOURLY CONCEIV'D 2 796
AND HOURLY BORN, WITH SORROW INFINITE 2 797

HOURS
THE IRKSOM HOURS, TILL THIS GREAT CHIEF RETURN. 2 527
THIR HAPPIE HOURS IN JOY AND HYMNING SPENT. 3 417
KNIT WITH THE GRACES AND THE HOURS IN DANCE 4 267
ORESHADES; FOR THESE MID-HOURS, TILL EEVNING RISE 5 376
WAK'T BY THE CIRCLING HOURS, WITH ROSIE HAND 6 3
THE SILENT HOURS, AND TH' OTHER WHOSE GAY TRAINE 7 444
HIS SEASONS, HOURS, OR DAYES, OR MONTHS, OR YEARES: 8 69
THE FRUITLESS HOURS, BUT NEITHER SELF-CONDEMNING, 9 1188

HOUSE
HE ALSO AGAINST THE HOUSE OF GOD WAS BOLD: 1 470
WITH LUST AND VIOLENCE THE HOUSE OF GOD. 1 496
FROM OUT THIS DARK AND DISMAL HOUSE OF PAIN, 2 823
UNQUENCHABLE, THE HOUSE OF WOE AND PAINE. 6 877
TO GODS ETERNAL HOUSE DIRECT THE WAY, 7 576
ABOMINABLE, ACCURST, THE HOUSE OF WOE, 10 465
A LAZAR-HOUSE IT SEEMD, WHEREIN WERE LAID 11 479
TO CALL BY VISION FROM HIS FATHERS HOUSE, 12 121
THIR LORDS, WHOM GOD DISPOS'D, THE HOUSE OF GOD 12 349

HOUSES
WHERE HOUSES THICK AND SEWERS ANNOY THE AIRE, 9 446

HOUSHOLD
IN WOMAN, THEN TO STUDIE HOUSHOLD GOOD, 9 233
TO HUMANE LIFE, AND HOUSHOLD PEACE CONFOUND. 10 908
TO SAVE HIMSELF AND HOUSHOLD FROM AMIDST 11 820

HOVERING
HOVERING ON WING UNDER THE COPE OF HELL 1 345
HOVERING AND BLAZING WITH DELUSIVE LIGHT, 9 639
HOVERING UPON THE WATERS; WHAT THEY MET 10 285
WIDE HOVERING, ALL THE CLOUDS TOGETHER DROVE 11 739

HOV'RING
HOV'RING A SPACE, TILL WINDS THE SIGNAL BLOW 2 717
WITH WHEELS YET HOV'RING O'RE THE OCEAN BRIM, 5 140

HOWEVER
HOWEVER, AND TO SCAPE HIS PUNISHMENT. 4 911
STARR INTERPOS'D, HOWEVER SMALL HE SEES, 5 258
THOU FABLEST, HERE HOWEVER TO DWELL FREE, 6 292
BUT THAT I DOUBT, HOWEVER WITNESS HEAVEN, 6 563
OF HIGHEST AGENTS, DEEMD HOWEVER WISE. 9 683
HOWEVER I WITH THEE HAVE FIXT MY LOT, 9 952
HOWEVER INSUPPORTABLE, BE ALL 10 134
HOWEVER SOME TRADITION THEY DISPERS'D 10 578
HOWEVER CHAST'NING, TO THE EVIL TURNE 11 373

HOWL'D
AND KENNEL THERE, YET THERE STILL BARK'D AND HOWL'D, 2 658

HOWLE
THAT BRED THEM THEY RETURN, AND HOWLE AND GNAW 2 799

HUBBUB
AT LENGTH A UNIVERSAL HUBBUB WILDE 2 951
AND LOOKING DOWN, TO SEE THE HUBBUB STRANGE 12 60

HUE
AND SUCH APPEAR'D IN HUE, AS WHEN THE FORCE 1 230
LIKE DOUBTFUL HUE: BUT HE HIS WONTED PRIDE 1 527
BLOSSOMS AND FRUITS AT ONCE OF GOLDEN HUE 4 148
FLOURS OF ALL HUE, AND WITHOUT THORN THE ROSE: 4 256
ADORNS HIM, COLOUR'D WITH THE FLORID HUE 7 445
CELESTIAL ROSIE RED, LOVES PROPER HUE, 8 619
WERE TENTS OF VARIOUS HUE; BY SOME WERE HERDS 11 557

HUES
IRIS ALL HUES, ROSES, AND GESSAMIN 4 698

HUGE
THAT WITNESS'D HUGE AFFLICTION AND DISMAY 1 57
LAY FLOATING MANY A ROOD, IN BULK AS HUGE 1 196
SO STRETCHT OUT HUGE IN LENGTH THE ARCH-FIEND LAY 1 209
A FORREST HUGE OF SPEARS; AND THRONGING HELMS 1 547

HUGE (CONTINUED)
ANON OUT OF THE EARTH A FABRICK HUGE 1 710
OUR PRISON STRONG, THIS HUGE CONVEX OF FIRE, 2 434
WHICH HE THROUGH HAZARD HUGE MUST EARN. BUT THEY 2 473
THAT FIRES THE LENGTH OF OPHIUCUS HUGE 2 709
FORTHWITH THE HUGE PORCULLIS HIGH UP DREW, 2 874
SUCH RUIN INTERCEPT: TEN PACES HUGE 6 193
SQUADRONS AT ONCE, WITH HUGE TWO-HANDED SWAY 6 251
THOUGH HUGE, AND IN A ROCK OF DIAMOND ARMD, 6 364
APPROACHING GROSS AND HUGE; IN HOLLOW CUBE 6 552
THROUGH HIS WILDE ANARCHIE, SO HUGE A ROUT 6 873
IMMEDIATELY THE MOUNTAINS HUGE APPEER 7 285
AND BENDED DOLPHINS PLAY: PART HUGE OF BULK 7 410
OF HUGE EXTENT SOMTIMES, WITH BRAZEN EYES 7 496
HUGE PYTHON, AND HIS POWER NO LESS HE SEEM'D 10 531
BEGAN TO BUILD A VESSEL OF HUGE BULK, 11 729

HUGEST
CREATED HUGEST THAT SWIM TH' OCEAN STREAM: 1 202
HUGEST OF LIVING CREATURES, ON THE DEEP 7 413

HULL
HE LOOKD, AND SAW THE ARK HULL ON THE FLOUD, 11 840

HUMAN
EXCELLING HUMAN, PRINCELY DIGNITIES, 1 359
OF HUMAN SACRIFICE, AND PARENTS TEARS, 1 393
RATHER THEN HUMAN. NOR DID ISRAEL SCAPE 1 482
OR FLOCKS, OR HEARDS, OR HUMAN FACE DIVINE; 3 44
BETWIXT TH' ANGELICAL AND HUMAN KINDE: 3 462
TO ALL DELIGHT OF HUMAN SENSE EXPOS'D 4 206
MOTHER OF HUMAN RACE: WHAT COULD I DOE, 4 475
OF HUMAN OFSSPRING, SOLE PROPRIETIE, 4 751
THIS NIGHT THE HUMAN PAIR, HOW HE DESIGNES 5 227
EXCEEDED HUMAN, AND HIS WARY SPEECH 5 459
HUMAN DESIRES CAN SEEK OR APPREHEND? 5 518
TO HUMAN SENSE TH' INVISIBLE EXPLOITS 5 565
OF HUMAN SENSE, I SHALL DELINEATE SO, 5 572
HUMAN IMAGINATION TO SUCH HIGHTH 6 300
WHAT MIGHT HAVE ELSE TO HUMAN RACE BIN HID; 6 896
UNKNOWN, WHICH HUMAN KNOWLEDG COULD NOT REACH: 7 75
THEN TIME OR MOTION, BUT TO HUMAN EARS 7 177
THIR SMALL PECULIAR, THOUGH FROM HUMAN SIGHT 7 368
AUGHT, NOT SURPASSING HUMAN MEASURE, SAY. 7 640
GOD TO REMOVE HIS WAYES FROM HUMAN SENSE, 8 119
FOR MAN TO TELL HOW HUMAN LIFE BEGAN 8 250
CANNOT BE HUMAN CONSORT; THEY REJOYCE 8 392
ALL HUMAN THOUGHTS COME SHORT, SUPREAM OF THINGS; 8 414
ATTRACTIVE, HUMAN, RATIONAL, LOVE STILL; 8 587
WITH GRATEFUL SMELL, FORTH CAME THE HUMAN PAIR 9 197
LOVE NOT THE LOWEST END OF HUMAN LIFE. 9 241
BY TONGUE OF BRUTE, AND HUMAN SENSE EXPREST? 9 554
I KNEW, BUT NOT WITH HUMAN VOICE ENDU'D; 9 561
I OF BRUTE HUMAN, YEE OF HUMAN GODS. 9 712
HUMAN, TO PUT ON GODS, DEATH TO BE WISHT, 9 714
ENDU'D WITH HUMAN VOICE AND HUMAN SENSE, 9 871
OF HUMAN GLORIE, AND FOR GLORIE DONE 11 694
MUST NEEDS IMPAIRE AND WEARIE HUMAN SENSE: 12 10
RESERVING, HUMAN LEFT FROM HUMAN FREE. 12 71

HUMANE
BELIAL, IN ACT MORE GRACEFUL AND HUMANE; 2 109
GODDESS HUMANE, REACH THEN, AND FREELY TASTE. 9 732
THE DOUBT, SINCE HUMANE REACH NO FURTHER KNOWS. 10 793
TO HUMANE LIFE, AND HOUSHOLD PEACE CONFOUND. 10 908
OR ONE SHORT SIGH OF HUMANE BREATH, UP-BORNE 11 147

HUMBL'D
HUMBL'D BY SUCH REBUKE, SO FARR BENEATH 6 342
KNEEL'D AND BEFORE HIM HUMBL'D ALL MY HEART, 11 150
SO SPAKE, SO WISH'D MUCH-HUMBL'D EVE, BUT FATE 11 181

HUMBLE
STAND IN HIS PRESENCE HUMBLE, AND RECEIVE 2 240
EMBATTELL'D IN HER FIELD: AND THE HUMBLE SHRUB, 7 322
AND HUMBLE DEPRECATION THUS REPLI'D. 8 378
FELL HUMBLE, AND IMBRACING THEM, BESAUGHT 10 912
TO MICHAEL THUS HIS HUMBLE WORDS ADDRESSD. 11 295

HUMBLES
HUMBLES HIS STUBBORN HEART, BUT STILL AS ICE 12 193

HUMBLING
THIS ANNUAL HUMBLING CERTAIN NUMBER'D DAYS, 10 576

HUMBLY
HUMBLY OUR FAULTS, AND PARDON BEG, WITH TEARS 10 1089
HUMBLY THIR FAULTS, AND PARDON BEG'D, WITH TEARS 10 1101

HUMID
THEN IN FAIR EVENING CLOUD, OR HUMID BOW, 4 151
IN HUMID EXHALATIONS, AND AT EVEN 5 425
STREAM, AND PERPETUAL DRAW THIR HUMID TRAINE. 7 306
IN EDEN ON THE HUMID FLOURS, THAT BREATHD 9 193

HUMILIATION
THEREFORE THY HUMILIATION SHALL EXALT 3 313
OF SORROW UNFEIGN'D, AND HUMILIATION MEEK. 10 1092

HUMILIATION (CONTINUED)
OF SORROW UNFEIGN'D, AND HUMILIATION MEEK. 10 1104

HUMOR
PRODUCES WITH TERRESTRIAL HUMOR MIXT 3 610
A STREAM OF NECTAROUS HUMOR ISSUING FLOW'D 6 332

HUMOUR
PROLIFIC HUMOUR SOFT'NING ALL HER GLOBE, 7 280

HUNDERDS
WITH HUNDERDS AND WITH THOUSANDS TROOPING CAME 1 760

HUNG
HUNG ON HIS SHOULDERS LIKE THE MOON, WHOSE ORB 1 287
THAT ORE THE REALM OF IMPIOUS PHARAOH HUNG 1 342
WHEN THE FIERCE FOE HUNG ON OUR BROK'N REAR 2 78
HUNG ORE MY REALM, LINK'D IN A GOLDEN CHAIN 2 1005
LIKE QUIVERS HUNG, AND WITH PRAEAMBLE SWEET 3 367
HUNG AMIABLE, HESPERIAN FABLES TRUE, 4 250
ROUND FROM HIS PARTED FORELOCK MANLY HUNG 4 302
HUNG HIGH WITH DIAMOND FLAMING, AND WITH GOLD. 4 554
HUNG FORTH IN HEAV'N HIS GOLDEN SCALES, YET SEEN 4 997
HUNG OVER HER ENAMOUR'D, AND BEHELD 5 13
WHICH HUNG NOT, BUT SO SWIFT WITH TEMPEST FELL 6 190
THE BATTEL HUNG; TILL SATAN, WHO THAT DAY 6 246
SATE EAGLE-WING'D, BESIDE HIM HUNG HIS BOW 6 763
AND EARTH SELF BALLANC'T ON HER CENTER HUNG. 7 242
THIR BRANCHES HUNG WITH COPIOUS FRUIT; OR GEMM'D 7 325
LOAD'N WITH FAIREST FRUIT THAT HUNG TO THE EYE 8 307
HUNG DROOPING UNSUSTAIND, THEM SHE UPSTAIES 9 430
AMID THE TREE NOW GOT, WHERE PLENTY HUNG 9 594
AS IN A GLISTERING ZODIAC HUNG THE SWORD, 11 247

HUNGER
WHOM HUNGER DRIVES TO SEEK NEW HAUNT FOR PREY, 4 184
OF REAL HUNGER, AND CONCOCTIVE HEATE 5 437
AND HUNGER BOTH, FROM LABOUR, AT THE HOURE 8 213
NOT TO DEFERR; HUNGER AND THIRST AT ONCE, 9 586
YET PARCHT WITH SCALDING THURST AND HUNGER FIERCE, 10 556
HUNGER AND THIRST CONSTRAINING, DRUGD AS OFT, 10 568

HUNTER
FIRST HUNTER THEN, PURSU'D A GENTLE BRACE, 11 188
A MIGHTIE HUNTER THENCE HE SHALL BE STYL'D 12 33

HUNTING
HUNTING (AND MEN NOT BEASTS SHALL BE HIS GAME) 12 30

HURDL'D
IN HURDL'D COTES AMID THE FIELD SECURE, 4 186

HURL'D
CAUGHT IN A FIERIE TEMPEST SHALL BE HURL'D 2 180
HURL'D HEADLONG TO PARTAKE WITH US, SHALL CURSE 2 374
HURL'D TO AND FRO WITH JACULATION DIRE, 6 665

HURLD
HURLD HEADLONG FLAMING FROM TH' ETHEREAL SKIE 1 45
THROUGH CHAOS HURLD, OBSTRUCT THE MOUTH OF HELL 10 636

HURLING
HURLING DEFIANCE TOWARD THE VAULT OF HEAV'N. 1 669

HURRIED
PERIODS OF TIME, THENCE HURRIED BACK TO FIRE. 2 603
INSTINCT WITH FIRE AND NITRE HURRIED HIM 2 937
OF MIDNIGHT MARCH, AND HURRIED MEETING HERE, 5 778

HURT
GOD THEREFORE CANNOT HURT YE, AND BE JUST; 9 700
WHAT CAN YOUR KNOWLEDGE HURT HIM, OR THIS TREE 9 727
NEVER TO HURT THEM MORE WHO RIGHTLY TRUST 12 418

HURTFUL
USEFUL OF HURTFUL, PROSPEROUS OF ADVERSE 2 259

HUSBAND
THE FEMALE BEE THAT FEEDS HER HUSBAND DRONE 7 490
HER HUSBAND THE RELATER SHE PREFERR'D 8 52
AND EVE FIRST TO HER HUSBAND THUS BEGAN. 9 204
AND GOOD WORKES IN HER HUSBAND TO PROMOTE. 9 234
SAFEST AND SEEMLIEST BY HER HUSBAND STAIES, 9 268
HER HUSBAND, FOR I VIEW FAR ROUND, NOT NIGH, 9 482
HER HUSBAND SHEE, TO TASTE THE FATALL FRUIT, 10 4
UPON HER HUSBAND, SAW THIR SHAME THAT SOUGHT 10 336
THY HUSBAND, HIM TO FOLLOW THOU ART BOUND; 11 291

HUSBANDS
THUS SAYING, FROM HER HUSBANDS HAND HER HAND 9 385
IN SORROW FORTH, AND TO THY HUSBANDS WILL 10 195

HUSK
ROUGH, OR SMOOTH RIN'D, OR BEARDED HUSK, OR SHELL 5 342

HYACINTH
CROCUS, AND HYACINTH WITH RICH INLAY 4 701
AND HYACINTH, EARTHS FRESHEST SOFTEST LAP. 9 1041

ILLUSTRATE
- JUSTICE WITH MERCIE, AS MAY ILLUSTRATE MOST 10 78

ILLUSTRATES
- ILLUSTRATES, WHEN THEY SEE ALL REGAL POWER 5 739

ILLUSTRIOUS
- ILLUSTRIOUS ON HIS SHOULDERS FLEDGE WITH WINGS 3 627
- BUT MORE ILLUSTRIOUS MADE, SINCE HE THE HEAD 5 842
- ILLUSTRIOUS FARR AND WIDE, BUT BY HIS OWN 6 773
- THUS ADAM HIS ILLUSTRIOUS GUEST BESOUGHT: 7 109
- ILLUSTRIOUS EVIDENCE, EXAMPLE HIGH. 9 962
- DETAIN FROM FOLLOWING THY ILLUSTRIOUS TRACK. 10 367

ILLYRIA
- LOVELIER, NOT THOSE THAT IN ILLYRIA CHANG'D 9 505

IMAGE
- OFT TO THE IMAGE OF A BRUTE, ADORN'D 1 371
- TO WHOSE BRIGHT IMAGE NIGHTLY BY THE MOON 1 440
- MAIM'D HIS BRUTE IMAGE, HEAD AND HANDS LOPT OFF 1 459
- THY SELF IN ME THY PERFECT IMAGE VIEWING 2 764
- THE RADIANT IMAGE OF HIS GLORY SAT, 3 63
- THE IMAGE OF THIR GLORIOUS MAKER SHON, 4 292
- WHOSE IMAGE THOU ART, HIM THOU SHALL ENJOY 4 472
- THEN THAT SMOOTH WATRY IMAGE; BACK I TURND, 4 480
- GODS LATEST IMAGE: I DESCRIB'D HIS WAY 4 567
- BEST IMAGE OF MY SELF AND DEARER HALF, 5 95
- TO ONE AND TO HIS IMAGE NOW PROCLAIM'D? 5 784
- IMAGE OF THEE IN ALL THINGS; AND SHALL SOON, 6 736
- LET US MAKE NOW MAN IN OUR IMAGE, MAN 7 519
- THE BREATH OF LIFE; IN HIS OWN IMAGE HEE 7 526
- CREATED THEE, IN THE IMAGE OF GOD 7 527
- CREATED IN HIS IMAGE, THERE TO DWELL 7 627
- INWARD AND OUTWARD BOTH, HIS IMAGE FAIRE: 8 221
- LIKE OF HIS LIKE, HIS IMAGE MULTIPLI'D, 8 424
- MY IMAGE, NOT IMPARTED TO THE BRUTE, 8 441
- HIS IMAGE WHO MADE BOTH, AND LESS EXPRESSING 8 544
- TH' IMAGE OF GOD IN MAN CREATED ONCE 11 508
- AND FOR HIS MAKERS IMAGE SAKE EXEMPT? 11 514
- THIR MAKERS IMAGE, ANSWERD MICHAEL, THEN 11 515
- HIS IMAGE WHOM THEY SERV'D, A BRUTISH VICE, 11 518
- GODS IMAGE DID NOT REVERENCE IN THEMSELVES. 11 525

IMAGINATION
- HUMAN IMAGINATION TO SUCH HIGHTH 6 300

IMAGINATIONS
- HIS PROUD IMAGINATIONS THUS DISPLAID. 2 10
- SHE FORMS IMAGINATIONS, AERIE SHAPES, 5 105

IMAGIN'D
- MOUNTAINS OF ICE, THAT STOP TH' IMAGIN'D WAY 10 291
- TO TRUST THEE FROM MY SIDE, IMAGIN'D WISE, 10 881

IMAGIND
- IMAGIND RATHER OFT THEN ELSEWHERE SEEN, 3 599
- IMAGIND LANDS AND REGIONS IN THE MOON: 5 263

IMAGINING
- THIR EARNEST EYES THEY FIX'D, IMAGINING 10 553

IMAUS
- AS WHEN A VULTUR ON IMAUS BRED, 3 431

IMBALM'D
- WING SILENTLY THE BUXOM AIR, IMBALM'D 2 842

IMBALMD
- LEUCOTHEA WAK'D, AND WITH FRESH DEWS IMBALMD 11 135

IMBARK'T
- ALL LEFT, IN ONE SMALL BOTTOM SWUM IMBARK'T. 11 753

IMBATTELLD
- THAT LED TH' IMBATTELLD SERAPHIM TO WARR 1 129
- ON THIR IMBATTELLD RANKS THE WAVES RETURN, 12 213

IMBELLISHT
- IMBELLISHT, THICK WITH SPARKLING ORIENT GEMMES 3 507

IMBLAZ'D
- WITH GEMMS AND GOLDEN LUSTRE RICH IMBLAZ'D, 1 538
- OR IN THIR GLITTERING TISSUES BEAR IMBLAZ'D 5 592

IMBLAZONRIE
- WITH BRIGHT IMBLAZONRIE, AND HORRENT ARMS. 2 513

IMBODIED
- MET SUCH IMBODIED FORCE, AS NAM'D WITH THESE 1 574
- UNDER THIR HEAD IMBODIED ALL IN ONE. 6 779

IMBORDERD
- IMBORDERD ON EACH BANK, THE HAND OF EVE: 9 438

IMBOSOM'D
- FIRM LAND IMBOSOM'D WITHOUT FIRMAMENT, 3 75
- BY WHOM IN BLISS IMBOSOM'D SAT THE SON, 5 597

IMBOSS
- BOTCHES AND BLAINES MUST ALL HIS FLESH IMBOSS, 12 180

IMBOWR
- HIGH OVERARCH'T IMBOWR; OR SCATTERD SEDGE 1 304

IMBOWR'D
- THICK OVERHEAD WITH VERDANT ROOF IMBOWR'D 9 1038

IMBRACE
- NEGLECT NOT, AND THE BENEFIT IMBRACE 12 426

IMBRACEING
- THESE LULLD BY NIGHTINGALES IMBRACEING SLEPT, 4 771

IMBRACES
- THAT EVER SINCE IN LOVES IMBRACES MET, 4 322
- THY COMING, AND THY SOFT IMBRACES, HEE 4 471
- FRUITLESS IMBRACES: OR THEY LED THE VINE 5 215
- FROM LOVES DUE RITES, NUPTIAL IMBRACES SWEET, 10 994

IMBRACING
- AND MEEK SURRENDER, HALF IMBRACING LEAND 4 494
- ON ADAM, WHOM IMBRACING, THUS SHE SPAKE. 5 27
- IMBRACING ROUND THIS FLORID EARTH, WHAT CAUSE 7 90
- FELL HUMBLE, AND IMBRACING THEM, BESAUGHT 10 912

IMBROILD
- AND TUMULT AND CONFUSION ALL IMBROILD, 2 966

IMBROILES
- AND BY DECISION MORE IMBROILES THE FRAY 2 908

IMBROUND
- IMBROUND THE NOONTIDE BOWRS: THUS WAS THIS PLACE, 4 246

IMBRUTE
- THIS ESSENCE TO INCARNATE AND IMBRUTE, 9 166

IMBU'D
- IMBU'D, BRING TO THIR SWEETNESS NO SATIETIE. 8 216

IMITATE
- IMITATE WHEN WE PLEASE? THIS DESART SOILE 2 270
- TO IMITATE HER; BUT MISJOYNING SHAPES, 5 111

IMITATED
- AND GOD-LIKE IMITATED STATE; HIM ROUND 2 511

IMITATION
- IN IMITATION OF THAT MOUNT WHEREON 5 764
- THE REST IN IMITATION TO LIKE ARMES 6 662

IMMATURE
- OF WATERS, EMBRYON IMMATURE INVOLV'D, 7 277

IMMEASURABLE
- OF DEPTH IMMEASURABLE: ANON THEY MOVE 1 549
- THEY VIEW'D THE VAST IMMEASURABLE ABYSS 7 211

IMMEASURABLY
- IMMEASURABLY, ALL THINGS SHALL BE YOUR PREY. 2 844

IMMEDIATE
- MAIN REASON TO PERSWADE IMMEDIATE WARR, 2 121
- WITH NICEST TOUCH. IMMEDIATE IN A FLAME, 6 584
- IMMEDIATE ARE THE ACTS OF GOD, MORE SWIFT 7 176
- IRRADIANCE, VIRTUAL OR IMMEDIATE TOUCH? 8 617
- BY SOME IMMEDIATE STROAK; BUT SOON SHALL FIND 10 52
- IMMEDIATE DISSOLUTION, WHICH WE THOUGHT 10 1049

IMMEDIATELY
- IMMEDIATELY THE MOUNTAINS HUGE APPEER 7 285
- SHALL BRING ON MEN. IMMEDIATELY A PLACE 11 477
- IMMEDIATELY INORDINATE DESIRES 12 87

IMMENSE
- REDUC'D THIR SHAPES IMMENSE, AND WERE AT LARGE, 1 790
- TH' UNFOUNDED DEEP, AND THROUGH THE VOID IMMENSE 2 829
- THE DEBT IMMENSE OF ENDLESS GRATITUDE, 4 52
- THE EARTH OUTSTRETCHT IMMENSE, A PROSPECT WIDE 5 88
- IMMENSE I HAVE TRANSFUS'D, THAT ALL MAY KNOW 6 704
- IMMENSE, AND ALL HIS FATHER IN HIM SHON. 7 196
- OF AMPLITUDE ALMOST IMMENSE, WITH STARR'S 7 620
- THEY FASTEN'D, AND THE MOLE IMMENSE WRAUGHT ON 10 300
- O GOODNESS INFINITE, GOODNESS IMMENSE. 12 469

IMMINENT
- UPLIFTED IMMINENT ONE STROKE THEY AIM'D 6 317
- WAITED WITH HELLISH RANCOUR IMMINENT 9 409
- IN PRISON UNDER JUDGEMENTS IMMINENT: 11 725

IMMORTAL
- CONFOUNDED THOUGH IMMORTAL: BUT HIS DOOM 1 53
- AND STUDY OF REVENGE, IMMORTAL HATE, 1 107
- FROM MORTAL OR IMMORTAL MINDS. THUS THEY 1 559
- O MYRIADS OF IMMORTAL SPIRITS, O POWERS 1 622
- IMMORTAL VIGOR, THOUGH OPPREST AND FALL'N, 2 1

IMPLOY
WITH SPEED WHAT FORCE IS LEFT, AND ALL IMPLOY 5 730

IMPLOY'D
LAY WAVING ROUND; ON SOM GREAT CHARGE IMPLOY'D 3 628

IMPLOYD
WHICH WE IN OUR APPOINTED WORK IMPLOYD 4 726
WELL HAST THOU MOTION'D, WELL THY THOUGHTS IMPLOYD 9 229

IMPLOYMENTS
AND LET US TO OUR FRESH IMPLOYMENTS RISE 5 125

IMPORT
CAUSES IMPORT YOUR NEED OF THIS FAIR FRUIT, 9 731

IMPORTANT
NOT OF MEAN SUITERS, NOR IMPORTANT LESS 11 9

IMPORTS
IMPORTS NOT, IF THOU RECK'N RIGHT, THE REST 8 71

IMPORTUNE
MEE THUS, THOUGH IMPORTUNE PERHAPS, TO COME 9 610
THERE WITH MY CRIES IMPORTUNE HEAVEN, THAT ALL 10 933

IMPOS'D
STRICT LAWS IMPOS'D, TO CELEBRATE HIS THRONE 2 241
THY SLEEP DISSENT? NEW LAWS THOU SEEST IMPOS'D; 5 679
INDUCING DARKNESS, GRATEFUL TRUCE IMPOS'D, 6 407
DEATH IS THE PENALTIE IMPOS'D, BEWARE, 7 545
YET NOT SO STRICTLY HATH OUR LORD IMPOS'D 9 235
TO LABOUR CALLS US NOW WITH SWEAT IMPOS'D, 11 172
OBEDIENCE TO THE LAW OF GOD, IMPOS'D 12 397

IMPOSE
HAD TO IMPOSE: HE THROUGH THE ARMED FILES 1 567
FOR AUGHT APPEERS, AND ON THIR ORBS IMPOSE 8 30
OF US WILL SOON DETERMIN, OR IMPOSE 11 227

IMPOSITION
FROM IMPOSITION OF STRICT LAWS, TO FREE 12 304

IMPOSSIBLE
BY FORCE IMPOSSIBLE, BY LEAVE OBTAIN'D 2 250
STILL AS IT ROSE, IMPOSSIBLE TO CLIMBE, 4 548
IMPOSSIBLE: YET HAPLY OF THY RACE 6 501
FROM WHOM IT SPRUNG, IMPOSSIBLE TO MIX 7 58
IMPOSSIBLE IS HELD, AS ARGUMENT 10 800

IMPOSSIBLY
SINCE REASON NOT IMPOSSIBLY MAY MEET 9 360

IMPOSTOR
WHO TO THE FRAUDULENT IMPOSTOR FOULE 3 692

IMPOTENCE
BELIKE THROUGH IMPOTENCE, OR UNAWARE, 2 156

IMPOW'RD
WITHIN HELL GATES TILL NOW, THOU US IMPOW'RD 10 369

IMPREGNABLE
IMPREGNABLE; OFT ON THE BORDERING DEEP 2 131

IMPREGN'D
YET RUNG OF HIS PERSWASIVE WORDS, IMPREGN'D 9 737

IMPREGNS
ON JUNO SMILES, WHEN HE IMPREGNS THE CLOUDS 4 500

IMPRESES
IMPRESES QUAINT, CAPARISONS AND STEEDS; 9 35

IMPRESS
IMPRESS THE AIR, AND SHEWS THE MARINER 4 558

IMPRESS'D
ON WHICH THE SUN MORE GLAD IMPRESS'D HIS BEAMS 4 150
FOR HASTE; SUCH FLIGHT THE GREAT COMMAND IMPRESS'D 7 294

IMPRESST
IMPRESST THE EFFULGENCE OF HIS GLORIE ABIDES, 3 388

IMPREST
SUBSCRIB'D NOT; NATURE FIRST GAVE SIGNS, IMPREST 11. 182

IMPROV'D
IMPROV'D BY TRACT OF TIME, AND WINGD ASCEND 5 498
OF GABRIEL OUT OF EDEN, NOW IMPROV'D 9 54

IMPRUDENCE
ABHOR TO JOYN; AND BY IMPRUDENCE MIXT, 11 686

IMPULSE
SO WITHOUT LEAST IMPULSE OR SHADOW OF FATE, 3 120
ORGANIC, OR IMPULSE OF VOCAL AIR, 9 530
OR TOUCH WITH LIGHTEST MOMENT OF IMPULSE 10 45

IMPURE
GLAD WAS THE SPIRIT IMPURE AS NOW IN HOPE 3 630
DEFAMING AS IMPURE WHAT GOD DECLARES 4 746
THEN SHALL THY SAINTS UNMIXT, AND FROM TH' IMPURE 6 742
MY HEAD, ILL FARE OUR ANCESTOR IMPURE, 10 735

IMPURPL'D
IMPURPL'D WITH CELESTIAL ROSES SMIL'D, 3 364

IMPUTE
LET IN THESE WASTFUL FURIES, WHO IMPUTE 10 620

IMPUTED
IMPUTED SHALL ABSOLVE THEM WHO RENOUNCE 3 291
TO THEM BY FAITH IMPUTED, THEY MAY FINDE 12 295
IMPUTED BECOMES THEIRS BY FAITH, HIS MERITS 12 409

IMPUT'ST
IMPUT'ST THOU THAT TO MY DEFAULT, OR WILL 9 1145

INABSTINENCE
WHAT MISERIE TH' INABSTINENCE OF EVE 11 476

INACCESSIBLE
THOUGH INACCESSIBLE, HIS FATAL THRONE: 2 104
THRON'D INACCESSIBLE, BUT WHEN THOU SHAD'ST 3 377
THIS INACCESSIBLE HIGH STRENGTH, THE SEAT 7 141

INBRED
TRANSFORM'D: BUT HE MY INBRED ENEMIE 2 785

INCAPABLE
INCAPABLE OF STAIN WOULD SOON EXPEL 2 140
CAN COMPREHEND, INCAPABLE OF MORE, 5 505
INCAPABLE OF MORTAL INJURIE 6 434

INCARNATE
HERE SHALT THOU SIT INCARNATE, HERE SHALT REIGN 3 315
THIS ESSENCE TO INCARNATE AND IMBRUTE, 9 166

INCENC'T
INCENC'T WITH INDIGNATION SATAN STOOD 2 707

INCENSE
WHAT FEAR WE THEN? WHAT DOUBT WE TO INCENSE 2 94
CHORAL OR UNISON: OF INCENSE CLOUDS 7 599
THIR MORNING INCENSE, WHEN ALL THINGS THAT BREATH, 9 194
IS OPEN? OR WILL GOD INCENSE HIS IRE 9 692
WITH INCENSE, WHERE THE GOLDEN ALTAR FUM'D, 11 18
WITH INCENSE, I THY PRIEST BEFORE THEE BRING, 11 25
THE INWARDS AND THIR FAT, WITH INCENSE STREW'D, 11 439
HEAPT TO THE POPULAR SUMME, WILL SO INCENSE 12 338
HIS PLACE, TO OFFER INCENSE, MYRRH, AND GOLD; 12 363

INCENSED
TH' INCENSED DEITIE, WHILE OFFERD GRACE 3 187
TH' INCENSED FATHER, AND TH' INCENSED SON, 5 847

INCENS'T
INCENS'T, AND THUS SECURELY HIM DEFI'D, 6 130

INCENST
LEAST HEE INCENST AT SUCH ERUPTION BOLD, 8 235
TO WHOM THEN FIRST INCENST ADAM REPLI'D, 9 1162

INCENTIVE
OF MISSIVE RUIN; PART INCENTIVE REED 6 519

INCESSANT
WHAT IN AN AGE THEY WITH INCESSANT TOYLE 1 698
HAVE RAIS'D INCESSANT ARMIES TO DEFEAT 6 138
INCESSANT I COULD HOPE TO CHANGE THE WILL 11 308

INCESTUOUS
TO WHOM TH' INCESTUOUS MOTHER THUS REPLI'D, 10 602

INCHANTING
INCHANTING DAUGHTER, THUS THE SILENCE BROKE, 10 353

INCITED
INCITED, DANCE ABOUT HIM VARIOUS ROUNDS? 8 125

INCLEMENT
OF CHAOS BLUSTRING ROUND, INCLEMENT SKIE; 3 426
TH' INCLEMENT SEASONS, RAIN, ICE, HAIL AND SNOW, 10 1063

INCLINABLE
INCLINABLE NOW GROWN TO TOUCH OR TASTE, 9 742

INCLINATION
PURSUES, AS INCLINATION OR SAD CHOICE 2 524
GOE WHITHER FATE AND INCLINATION STRONG 10 265

INCLIN'D
INCLIN'D NOT, BUT HIS COMING THUS DECLAR'D, 11 250

INCLINE
BE OPEN, AND HIS HEART TO PITIE INCLINE, 10 1061

INEVITABLY
TRANSGREST, INEVITABLY THOU SHALT DYE; 8 330

INEXORABLY
INEXORABLY, AND THE TORTURING HOUR 2 91

INEXPERIENCE
ARGUE THY INEXPERIENCE WHAT BEHOOVES 4 931

INEXPERT
WARR TERRIFIE THEM INEXPERT, AND FEARE 12 218

INEXPLICABLE
THE SENSE OF ENDLESS WOES? INEXPLICABLE 10 754

INEXPRESSIBLE
OF CIRCUIT INEXPRESSIBLE THEY STOOD, ... 5 595
IN EDEN, DISTANCE INEXPRESSIBLE 8 113

INEXTINGUISHABLE
AND INEXTINGUISHABLE RAGE; ALL HEAV'N 6 217

INEXTRICABLE
INEXTRICABLE, OR STRICT NECESSITY; 5 528

INFALLIBLE
INFALLIBLE? YET MANY WILL PRESUME: 12 530

INFAM'D
TO SAPIENCE, HITHERTO OBSCUR'D, INFAM'D, ... 9 797

INFAMIE
VAIN GLORIOUS, AND THROUGH INFAMIE SEEKS FAME: . 6 384

INFANT
LUR'D WITH THE SMELL OF INFANT BLOOD, TO DANCE . 2 664
INHOSPITABLY, AND KILLS THIR INFANT MALES: . . . 12 168

INFANTRY
COULD MERIT MORE THEN THAT SMALL INFANTRY 1 575

INFECT
HIS THOUGHTS, HIS LOOKS, WORDS, ACTIONS ALL INFECT, 10 608

INFECTED
INFECTED SIONS DAUGHTERS WITH LIKE HEAT, ... 1 453

INFECTION
TH' INFECTION WHEN THIR BORROW'D GOLD COMPOS'D . 1 483

INFEEBL'D
INFEEBL'D ME, TO WHAT I WAS IN HEAV'N. 9 488

INFERIOR
ENVY FROM EACH INFERIOR; BUT WHO HERE 2 26
THE LUMINOUS INFERIOR ORBS, ENCLOS'D 3 420
LITTLE INFERIOR; WHOM MY THOUGHTS PURSUE 4 362
SUPERIOR; FOR INFERIOR WHO IS FREE? 9 825

INFERIOUR
ME SOME INFERIOUR ANGEL, I HAD STOOD 4 59
AND THESE INFERIOUR FARR BENEATH ME SET? 8 382
TO ME INFERIOUR, INFINITE DESCENTS 8 410
OF NATURE HER TH' INFERIOUR, IN THE MIND 8 541
LITTLE INFERIOUR, BY MY ADVENTURE HARD 10 468

INFERNAL
TH' INFERNAL SERPENT; HE IT WAS, WHOSE GUILE . . . 1 34
INFERNAL WORLD, AND THOU PROFOUNDEST HELL 1 251
FOR THIS INFERNAL PIT SHALL NEVER HOLD 1 657
OF THAT INFERNAL COURT. BUT FAR WITHIN 1 792
INFERNAL THUNDER, AND FOR LIGHTNING SEE 2 66
PLEAS'D HIGHLY THOSE INFERNAL STATES, AND JOY . . 2 387
IN ORDER CAME THE GRAND INFERNAL PEERS, ... 2 507
OF FOUR INFERNAL RIVERS THAT DISGORGE 2 575
IN THIS INFERNAL VAILE FIRST MET THOU CALL'ST . . 2 742
THE KEY OF THIS INFERNAL PIT BY DUE, ... 2 850
TH' INFERNAL DORES, AND ON THIR HINGES GRATE . . 2 881
WHO TELLS OF SOM INFERNAL SPIRIT SEEN . . . 4 793
BACK TO TH' INFERNAL PIT I DRAG THEE CHAIND, . . 4 965
SHALL YIELD US PREGNANT WITH INFERNAL FLAME, . . 6 483
INFERNAL NOISE; WARR SEEM'D A CIVIL GAME . . . 6 667
THE BLACK TARTAREOUS COLD INFERNAL DREGS . . . 7 238
THE INFERNAL POWERS, IN ONE DAY TO HAVE MARR'D . 9 136
OF MERIT HIGH TO ALL TH' INFERNAL HOST, ... 10 259
TH' INFERNAL EMPIRE, THAT SO NEER HEAV'NS DORE . 10 389
TRIUMPHANT OUT OF THIS INFERNAL PIT 10 464

INFERR
TO GLORIFIE THE MAKER, AND INFERR 7 116

INFERRS
OR BRIGHT INFERRS NOT EXCELLENCE: THE EARTH . . 8 91
HIS FRAUD IS THEN THY FEAR, WHICH PLAIN INFERRS . 9 285
COMMENDS THEE MORE, WHILE IT INFERRS THE GOOD . . 9 754

INFIDEL
AND ALL WHO SINCE, BAPTIZ'D OR INFIDEL 1 582

INFINITE
INFINITE GOODNESS, GRACE AND MERCY SHEWN 1 218
THE DARK UNBOTTOM'D INFINITE ABYSS 2 405
AND HOURLY BORN, WITH SORROW INFINITE 2 797
WON FROM THE VOID AND FORMLESS INFINITE. 3 12
IMMUTABLE, IMMORTAL, INFINITE, ... 3 373
THIR NUMBER, OR THE WISDOM INFINITE 3 706
INFINITE WRAUTH, AND INFINITE DESPAIRE? 4 74
AS LIBERAL AND FREE AS INFINITE, ... 4 415
THY GOODNESS INFINITE, BOTH WHEN WE WAKE, ... 4 734
CAN EQUAL ANGER INFINITE PROVOK'T. 4 916
ORB WITHIN ORB, THE FATHER INFINITE, ... 5 596
THROUGH THE INFINITE HOST, NOR LESS FOR THAT . . 5 874
WERE DON, BUT INFINITE: FOR WIDE WAS SPRED . . . 6 241
HIS GOOD TO WORLDS AND AGES INFINITE. 7 191
GREAT ARE THY WORKS, JEHOVAH, INFINITE 7 602
TO ME INFERIOUR, INFINITE DESCENTS 8 410
SHOULDST PROPAGAT, ALREADY INFINITE; 8 420
FOR THOUGH THE LORD OF ALL BE INFINITE, ... 10 794
FOR ANGERS SAKE, FINITE TO INFINITE 10 802
WHICH INFINITE CALAMITIE SHALL CAUSE 10 907
BUT INFINITE IN PARDON WAS MY JUDGE, ... 11 167
NATIONS, AND BRING HOME SPOILS WITH INFINITE . . 11 692
O GOODNESS INFINITE, GOODNESS IMMENSE. 12 469

INFINITLY
BE INFINITLY GOOD, AND OF HIS GOOD 4 414
FOR WHICH TO THE INFINITLY GOOD WE OWE 7 76

INFINITUDE
STOOD RUL'D, STOOD VAST INFINITUDE CONFIN'D; . . 3 711
INFINITUDE, NOR VACUOUS THE SPACE. 7 169

INFIRME
SHEE NEEDED, VERTUE-PROOF, NO THOUGHT INFIRME . . 5 384

INFIRMER
THY FRAILTIE AND INFIRMER SEX FORGIV'N, ... 10 956

INFIX'D
BEFORE HIM, SUCH AS IN THIR SOULES INFIX'D . . . 6 837

INFIXT
IMMOVABLE, INFIXT, AND FROZEN ROUND, ... 2 602

INFLAM'D
SATAN WITH THOUGHTS INFLAM'D OF HIGHEST DESIGN, . 2 630
INFLAM'D WITH LUST THEN RAGE) AND SWIFTER FAR, . 2 791
SATAN, NOW FIRST INFLAM'D WITH RAGE, CAME DOWN, . 4 9

INFLAME
WHOSE WAVES OF TORRENT FIRE INFLAME WITH RAGE. . 2 581

INFLAMED
OF THAT INFLAMED SEA, HE STOOD AND CALL'D . . . 1 300

INFLAMES
WITH SUDDEN BLAZE DIFFUS'D, INFLAMES THE AIRE: . 4 818

INFLICT
CAN ELSE INFLICT, DO I REPENT OR CHANGE, ... 1 96
MIGHT SUDDENLY INFLICT; THAT PAST, RETURN'D . . 10 341

INFLICTED
INFLICTED? AND WHAT PEACE CAN WE RETURN, ... 2 335
BECAUSE NOT YET INFLICTED, AS HE FEAR'D, . . . 10 51

INFLUENCE
BUT NOW AT LAST THE SACRED INFLUENCE 2 1034
FOREKNOWLEDGE HAD NO INFLUENCE ON THEIR FAULT, . 3 118
OF VARIOUS INFLUENCE FOMENT AND WARME, ... 4 669
BAD INFLUENCE INTO TH' UNWARIE BREST 5 695
SHEDDING SWEET INFLUENCE: LESS BRIGHT THE MOON, . 7 375
SHED THIR SELECTEST INFLUENCE; THE EARTH . . . 8 513
OF SACRED INFLUENCE: AS GOD IN HEAV'N 9 107
I FROM THE INFLUENCE OF THY LOOKS RECEAVE . . . 9 309
THIR INFLUENCE MALIGNANT WHEN TO SHOWRE, . . . 10 662

INFORMD
NOT ALL PARTS LIKE, BUT ALL ALIKE INFORMD . . . 3 593
INFORMD BY THEE MIGHT KNOW; IF ELSE THOU SEEKST . 7 639
OUR RUIN, BOTH BY THEE INFORMD I LEARNE, . . . 9 275

INFORMIDABLE
FOE NOT INFORMIDABLE, EXEMPT FROM WOUND, . . . 9 486

INFORMING
OF SACRIFICE, INFORMING THEM, BY TYPES 12 232

INFURIATE
DILATED AND INFURIATE SHALL SEND FORTH 6 486

INFUS'D
SO SPAKE THE FALSE ARCH-ANGEL, AND INFUS'D . . . 5 694
AND VITAL VERTUE INFUS'D, AND VITAL WARMTH . . . 7 236
AND IN HER LOOKS, WHICH FROM THAT TIME INFUS'D . 8 474
THAT DWELT WITHIN, WHOSE PRESENCE HAD INFUS'D . . 9 836

INGAG'D
WAS THIS YOUR DISCIPLINE AND FAITH INGAG'D, 4 954

INGAGING
INGAGING ME TO EMULATE, BUT SHORT 9 963

INGENDERD
INGENDERD IN THE PYTHIAN VALE ON SLIME, 10 530

INGENDRING
INGENDRING WITH ME, OF THAT RAPE BEGOT 2 794
BLOWN UP WITH HIGH CONCEITS INGENDRING PRIDE. 4 809

INGLORIOUS
WAS NOT INGLORIOUS, THOUGH TH' EVENT WAS DIRE, 1 624
INGLORIOUS, OF HIS MORTALL STING DISARM'D. 3 253
FROM SERVITUDE INGLORIOUS WELNIGH HALF 9 141
INGLORIOUS LIFE WITH SERVITUDE; FOR LIFE 12 220

INGORG'D
GREEDILY SHE INGORG'D WITHOUT RESTRAINT, 9 791

INGRAFT
GOOD OR NOT GOOD INGRAFT, MY MERIT THOSE 11 35

INGRATE
WHOSE BUT HIS OWN? INGRATE, HE HAD OF MEE 3 97
EXPECTED, LEAST OF ALL FROM THEE, INGRATE 5 811

INGRATEFUL
NO INGRATEFUL FOOD: AND FOOD ALIKE THOSE PURE 5 407
OF MINE TO THEE, INGRATEFUL EVE, EXPREST 9 1164

INGREDIENTS
SO DEEP THE POWER OF THESE INGREDIENTS PIERC'D, 11 417

INGROSS'T
ANOTHER NOW HATH TO HIMSELF INGROSS'T 5 775

INGULFT
PASS'D UNDERNEATH INGULFT, FOR GOD HAD THROWN 4 225
INTO UTTER DARKNESS, DEEP INGULFT, HIS PLACE 5 614

INHABIT
WHAT CREATURES THERE INHABIT, OF WHAT MOULD, 2 355
MEAN WHILE INHABIT LAXE, YE POWERS OF HEAV'N, 7 162

INHABITANT
INHABITANT OF HEAV'N, AND HEAV'NLIE-BORN, 2 860
INHABITANT WITH GOD, NOW KNOW I WELL 5 461

INHABITANTS
WO TO THE INHABITANTS ON EARTH. THAT NOW, 4 5
FEILDS AND INHABITANTS: HER SPOTS THOU SEEST 8 145

INHABITED
INHABITED, THOUGH SINLESS, MORE THEN NOW, 10 690

INHERITANCE
TO CLAIM OUR JUST INHERITANCE OF OLD, 2 38

INHOSPITABLE
INHOSPITABLE APPEER AND DESOLATE, 11 306

INHOSPITABLY
INHOSPITABLY, AND KILLS THIR INFANT MALES: 12 168

INHUMAN
UNDER INHUMAN PAINS? WHY SHOULD NOT MAN, 11 511

INHUMANLY
INHUMANLY TO MEN, AND MULTIPLY 11 677

INIMITABLE
THE PORTAL SHON, INIMITABLE ON EARTH 3 508

INIQUITIES
WEARIED WITH THEIR INIQUITIES, WITHDRAW 12 107

INJOINST
HIGH MATTER THOU INJOINST ME, O PRIME OF MEN, 5 563

INJUNCTION
THE HIGH INJUNCTION NOT TO TASTE THAT FRUIT, 10 13

INJUR'D
AND HIGH DISDAIN, FROM SENCE OF INJUR'D MERIT, 1 98
WAS UNDERSTOOD, THE INJUR'D LOVERS HELL. 5 450

INJURE
OR HEAT SHOULD INJURE US, HIS TIMELY CARE 10 1057

INJURIE
INCAPABLE OF MORTAL INJURIE 6 434

INJURIES
AS JOYN'D IN INJURIES, ONE ENMITIE 10 925

INJURY
AND INJURY AND OUTRAGE: AND WHEN NIGHT 1 500

INLAID
WHEREON A SAPHIR THRONE, INLAID WITH PURE 6 758

INLAND
FARR TO THE INLAND RETIR'D, ABOUT THE WALLS 10 423

INLAY
CROCUS, AND HYACINTH WITH RICH INLAY 4 701

INLIE
WHEREAT HEE INLIE RAG'D, AND AS THY TALK'D, 11 444

INMATE
IN SERPENT, INMATE BAD, AND TOWARD EVE 9 495
TO STOP THIR OVERGROWTH, AS INMATE GUESTS 12 166

INMOST
HIS INMOST COUNSELS FROM THIR DESTIND AIM. 1 168
WHICH GOD LIKES BEST, INTO THIR INMOST BOWRE 4 738
EARTHS INMOST WOMB, MORE WARMTH THEN ADAM NEEDS; 5 302
ABOUT THIR SPIRITS HAD PLAID, AND INMOST POWERS 9 1048
EEVN TO THE INMOST SEAT OF MENTAL SIGHT, 11 418

INNOCENCE
SIMPLICITIE AND SPOTLESS INNOCENCE. 4 318
AND SHOULD I AT YOUR HARMLESS INNOCENCE 4 388
OF PURITIE AND PLACE AND INNOCENCE, 4 745
WITH PLEASANT LIQUORS CROWN'D: O INNOCENCE 5 445
SUCH HIGH ADVANTAGES THIR INNOCENCE 6 401
YET INNOCENCE AND VIRGIN MODESTIE, 8 501
GO IN THY NATIVE INNOCENCE, RELIE 9 373
DESPOILD OF INNOCENCE, OF FAITH, OF BLISS. 9 411
HER GRACEFUL INNOCENCE, HER EVERY AIRE 9 459
HOW DARK'ND; INNOCENCE, THAT AS A VEILE 9 1054
OF INNOCENCE, OF FAITH, OF PURITIE, 9 1075
FROM INNOCENCE. NOW THEREFORE BEND THINE EARE 11 30

INNOCENT
TO WRECK ON INNOCENT FRAIL MAN HIS LOSS 4 11
SO PRAY'D THEY INNOCENT, AND TO THIR THOUGHTS 5 209

INNUMERABLE
INNUMERABLE FORCE OF SPIRITS ARM'D 1 101
INNUMERABLE. AS WHEN THE POTENT ROD 1 338
AND HANDS INNUMERABLE SCARCE PERFORM. 1 699
THY PRAISES, WITH TH' INNUMERABLE SOUND 3 147
AMONGST INNUMERABLE STARRS, THAT SHON 3 565
INNUMERABLE BEFORE TH' ALMIGHTIES THRONE 5 585
INNUMERABLE AS THE STARRS OF NIGHT, 5 745
AMONG INNUMERABLE FALSE, UNMOV'D, 5 898
BRISTL'D WITH UPRIGHT BEAMS INNUMERABLE 6 82
NONE ARGUING STOOD, INNUMERABLE HANDS 6 508
INNUMERABLE, AND THIS WHICH YEELDS OR FILLS 7 88
OF MEN INNUMERABLE, THERE TO DWELL, 7 156
WITH FRIE INNUMERABLE SWARME, AND SHOALES 7 400
FIRST MAN, OF MEN INNUMERABLE ORDAIN'D 8 297
YE CEDARS, WITH INNUMERABLE BOUGHS 9 1089
OF CARNAGE, PREY INNUMERABLE, AND TASTE 10 268
ON ALL SIDES, FROM INNUMERABLE TONGUES 10 507
AND MORE THAT SHALL BEFALL, INNUMERABLE 10 896

INNUMEROUS
INNUMEROUS LIVING CREATURES, PERFET FORMES, 7 455

INOFFENSIVE
SHE CRUSHES, INOFFENSIVE MOUST, AND MEATHES 5 345
WITH INOFFENSIVE PACE THAT SPINNING SLEEPS 8 164
SMOOTH, EASIE, INOFFENSIVE DOWN TO HELL. 10 305

INORDINATE
VAINE HOPES, VAINE AIMES, INORDINATE DESIRES 4 808
IMMEDIATELY INORDINATE DESIRES 12 87

INQUIRE
THEN OF OUR FELLOW SERVANT, AND INQUIRE 8 225

INROAD
FROM CHAOS AND TH' INROAD OF DARKNESS OLD, 3 421

INRODE
WITH MANY AN INRODE GOR'D; DEFORMED ROUT 6 387

INRODES
AND WITH PERPETUAL INRODES TO ALLARME, 2 103

INROULD
LEFT THEM INROULD, OR WHAT THE SPIRIT WITHIN 12 523

INSATIATE
BEYOND THUS HIGH, INSATIATE TO PURSUE 2 8
INSATIATE, I THUS SINGLE, NOR HAVE FEARD 9 536

INSECT
BEAST, BIRD, INSECT, OR WORM DURST ENTER NONE; 4 704
INSECT OR WORME; THOSE WAV'D THIR LIMBER FANS 7 476

INTENT (CONTINUED)
INTENT NOW WHOLLY ON HER TASTE, NAUGHT ELSE . . . 9 786
OF AMOROUS INTENT, WELL UNDERSTOOD 9 1035

INTERCEDE
PRESENTING, THUS TO INTERCEDE BEGAN. 11 21

INTERCEPT
AND FLY, ERE EVIL INTERCEPT THY FLIGHT. 5 871
SUCH RUIN INTERCEPT: TEN PACES HUGE 6 193
TO INTERCEPT THY WAY, OR SEND THEE BACK 9 410
MIGHT INTERCEPT THIR EMPEROUR SENT, SO HEE 10 429

INTERCESSION
RECOUNTED, MIXING INTERCESSION SWEET. 10 228

INTERCESSOR
PATRON OR INTERCESSOR NONE APPEERD, ... 3 219
CAME THE MILD JUDGE AND INTERCESSOR BOTH . . . 10 96
BY THIR GREAT INTERCESSOR, CAME IN SIGHT . . . 11 19

INTERCHANGE
IF I COULD JOY IN AUGHT, SWEET INTERCHANGE 9 115

INTERCOURSE
WITH EASIE INTERCOURSE PASS TO AND FRO 2 1031
DELIGHTED, AND WITH FREQUENT INTERCOURSE 7 571
FOOD OF THE MIND, OR THIS SWEET INTERCOURSE . . . 9 238
EASING THIR PASSAGE HENCE, FOR INTERCOURSE, . . . 10 260

INTERDICTED
OF INTERDICTED KNOWLEDGE: FAIR IT SEEM'D, ... 5 52
CHARG'D NOT TO TOUCH THE INTERDICTED TREE, ... 7 46

INTERDICTION
THE RIGID INTERDICTION, WHICH RESOUNDS 8 334

INTERFUS'D
ALL SPACE, THE AMBIENT AIRE WIDE INTERFUS'D . . . 7 89

INTERMISSION
THAT REST OR INTERMISSION NONE I FIND. 2 802
SHORT INTERMISSION BOUGHT WITH DOUBLE SMART. . . . 4 102

INTERMIT
OF THIS ILL MANSION: INTERMIT NO WATCH 2 462

INTERMITS
CASUAL DISCOURSE DRAW ON, WHICH INTERMITS 9 223

INTERMITTED
SHOULD INTERMITTED VENGEANCE ARM AGAIN 2 173
SPEECH INTERMITTED THUS TO EVE RENEWD. 9 1133

INTERMIX
CHOSE RATHER; HEE, SHE KNEW WOULD INTERMIX 8 54
AS I SHALL THEE ENLIGHTEN, INTERMIX 11 115

INTERMIXT
TEMPER'D SOFT TUNINGS, INTERMIXT WITH VOICE . . . 7 598
IN YONDER SPRING OF ROSES INTERMIXT 9 218

INTERNAL
OF FANCIE MY INTERNAL SIGHT, BY WHICH 8 461
INTERNAL MAN, IS BUT PROPORTION MEET, ... 9 711

INTERPOS'D
GRASING THE TENDER HERB, WERE INTERPOS'D, ... 4 253
STARR INTERPOS'D, HOWEVER SMALL HE SEES, ... 5 258
BY ANGELS MANY AND STRONG, WHO INTERPOS'D 6 336
WITH LONG REACH INTERPOS'D; THREE SEV'RAL WAYES . 10 323
HERE ADAM INTERPOS'D. O SENT FROM HEAV'N, ... 12 270

INTERPOSE
DEATH READY STANDS TO INTERPOSE HIS DART, ... 2 854
IF ADAM AUGHT PERHAPS MIGHT INTERPOSE; 12 4

INTERPOSES
TIMELY INTERPOSES, AND HER MONTHLY ROUND 3 728

INTERPOSEST
THOU INTERPOSEST, THAT MY SUDDEN HAND 2 738

INTERPRET
INTERPRET FOR HIM, MEE HIS ADVOCATE 11 33

INTERPRETED
INTERPRETED) WHICH NOT LONG AFTER, HE 5 762

INTERPRETER
INTERPRETER THROUGH HIGHEST HEAV'N TO BRING, . . . 3 657
DIVINE INTERPRETER, BY FAVOUR SENT 7 72

INTERRUPT
COMMON REVENGE, AND INTERRUPT HIS JOY 2 371
WIDE INTERRUPT CAN HOLD; SO BENT HE SEEMS 3 84
TO INTERRUPT THE SWEET OF LIFE, FROM WHICH 8 184
TO INTERRUPT, SIDE-LONG HE WORKS HIS WAY. 9 512

INTERRUPT (CONTINUED)
NATIONAL INTERRUPT THIR PUBLIC PEACE, ... 12 317

INTERRUPTED
WHOM THUS THE ANGEL INTERRUPTED MILDE. 11 286

INTERVALL
A DREADFUL INTERVALL, AND FRONT TO FRONT 6 105

INTERVENE
LOOKS INTERVENE AND SMILES, OR OBJECT NEW 9 222

INTERVIEW
TO HIDE THE FRAUD. AT INTERVIEW BOTH STOOD . . . 6 555
SUCH HAPPY INTERVIEW AND FAIR EVENT 11 593

INTERVOLV'D
ECCENTRIC, INTERVOLV'D, YET REGULAR 5 623

INTERWOVE
WORDS INTERWOVE WITH SIGHS FOUND OUT THIR WAY. . . 1 621

INTESTIN
INTESTIN STONE AND ULCER, COLIC PANGS, ... 11 484

INTESTINE
ENCROACHT ON STILL THROUGH OUR INTESTINE BROILES . 2 1001
INTESTINE WAR IN HEAV'N, THE ARCH FOE SUBDU'D . . 6 259

INTIRE
HAVE LEFT US THIS OUR SPIRIT AND STRENGTH INTIRE . 1 146

INTOXICATED
AS WITH NEW WINE INTOXICATED BOTH 9 1008

INTRANS'T
HIS LEGIONS, ANGEL FORMS, WHO LAY INTRANS'T . . . 1 301

INTRANST
SUNK DOWN AND ALL HIS SPIRITS BECAME INTRANST: . . 11 420

INTRENCHT
DEEP SCARS OF THUNDER HAD INTRENCHT, AND CARE . . 1 601

INTRICACIES
AND FREED FROM INTRICACIES, TAUGHT TO LIVE, . . . 8 182

INTRICATE
TH' INTRICATE WARDS, AND EVERY BOLT AND BAR . . . 2 877
RESEMBLES NEAREST, MAZES INTRICATE, ... 5 622
IN TANGLES, AND MADE INTRICATE SEEM STRAIT, . . . 9 632

INTRODUC'D
DEATH INTRODUC'D THROUGH FIERCE ANTIPATHIE: . . . 10 709

INTRODUCE
OF CHARMING SYMPHONIE THEY INTRODUCE 3 368
IN FREEDOME EQUAL? OR CAN INTRODUCE 5 797
MOSES IN FIGURE BEARES, TO INTRODUCE 12 241

INTRUSION
WITH LOATH'D INTRUSION, AND FILL ALL THE LAND; . . 12 178

INTUITIVE
DISCURSIVE, OR INTUITIVE; DISCOURSE 5 488

INUNDATION
BEYOND ALL BOUNDS, TILL INUNDATION RISE 11 828

INUTTERABLE
ABOMINABLE, INUTTERABLE, AND WORSE 2 626

INVADE
WITH DANGEROUS EXPEDITION TO INVADE 2 342
NIGHT WOULD INVADE, BUT THERE THE NEIGHBOURING MOON 3 726
OR IN BEHALF OF MAN, OR TO INVADE 11 102

INVADED
THEMSELVES INVADED NEXT, AND ON THIR HEADS . . . 6 653

INVADERS
AGAINST INVADERS; THEREFORE COOLD IN ZEALE . . . 11 801

INVALID
INVALID THAT WHICH THEE TO DOUBT IT MOV'D; . . . 8 116

INVENT
ALL PATIENCE. HE WHO THEREFORE CAN INVENT . . . 6 464

INVENTED
HIS OWN INVENTED TORMENTS. BUT PERHAPS 2 70
ENVIOUS COMMANDS, INVENTED WITH DESIGNE 4 524
WAS DEATH INVENTED? OR TO US DENI'D 9 767

INVENTER
TO BE TH' INVENTER MISS'D, SO EASIE IT SEEMD . . 6 499

JOUSTED
JOUSTED IN ASPRAMONT OR MONTALBAN, 1 583

JOVE
TITANIAN, OR EARTH-BORN, THAT WARR'D ON JOVE, 1 198
BY YOUNGER SATURN, HE FROM MIGHTIER JOVE 1 512
SO JOVE USURPING REIGN'D: THESE FIRST IN CREET 1 514
FROM HEAV'N, THEY FABL'D, THROWN BY ANGRY JOVE 1 741
WHOM GENTILES AMMON CALL AND LYBIAN JOVE, 4 277
YET VIRGIN OF PROSERPINA FROM JOVE. 9 396
AMMONIAN JOVE, OR CAPITOLINE WAS SEEN, 9 508
AND OPS, ERE YET DICTAEAN JOVE WAS BORN. 10 584
THE BIRD OF JOVE, STOOPT FROM HIS AERIE TOUR, 11 185

JOVES
ON HIM WHO HAD STOLE JOVES AUTHENTIC FIRE. 4 719

JOY
WHO NOW TRIUMPHS, AND IN TH' EXCESS OF JOY 1 123
WHERE JOY FOR EVER DWELLS: HAIL HORROURS, HAIL 1 250
OBSCURE SOME GLIMPS OF JOY, TO HAVE FOUND THIR CHIEF 1 524
AT ONCE WITH JOY AND FEAR HIS HEART REBOUNDS. 1 788
COMMON REVENGE, AND INTERRUPT HIS JOY 2 371
IN OUR CONFUSION, AND OUR JOY UPRAISE 2 372
PLEAS'D HIGHLY THOSE INFERNAL STATES, AND JOY 2 387
ATTEST THIR JOY, THAT HILL AND VALLEY RINGS. 2 495
FORGETS BOTH JOY AND GRIEF, PLEASURE AND PAIN. 2 586
BECAM'ST ENAMOUR'D, AND SUCH JOY THOU TOOK'ST 2 765
REAPING IMMORTAL FRUITS OF JOY AND LOVE, 3 67
UNINTERRUPTED JOY, UNRIVALD LOVE 3 68
SENSE OF NEW JOY INEFFABLE DIFFUS'D: 3 137
THENCEFORTH, BUT IN THY PRESENCE JOY ENTIRE. 3 265
WITH JOY AND LOVE TRIUMPHING, AND FAIR TRUTH. 3 338
AS FROM BLEST VOICES, UTTERING JOY, HEAV'N RUNG 3 347
THIR HAPPIE HOURS IN JOY AND HYMNING SPENT. 3 417
IN MISERIE; SUCH JOY AMBITION FINDES. 4 92
VERNAL DELIGHT AND JOY, ABLE TO DRIVE 4 155
MORE WOE, THE MORE YOUR TASTE IS NOW OF JOY; 4 369
WHERE NEITHER JOY NOR LOVE, BUT FIERCE DESIRE, 4 509
IN WHOSE SIGHT ALL THINGS JOY, WITH RAVISHMENT 5 46
QUAFF IMMORTALITIE AND JOY, SECURE 5 638
WITH COPIOUS HAND, REJOYCING IN THIR JOY. 5 641
WITH JOY AND ACCLAMATIONS LOUD, THAT ONE 6 23
SO OFT IN FESTIVALS OF JOY AND LOVE 6 94
THUS FOIL'D THIR MIGHTIEST, OURS JOY FILLD, AND SHOUT, 6 200
FOR JOY OF OFFERD PEACE: BUT I SUPPOSE 6 617
FIRST SEEN, THEM UNEXPECTED JOY SURPRIZ'D, 6 774
ONE KINGDOM, JOY AND UNION WITHOUT END. 7 161
BIRTH-DAY OF HEAV'N AND EARTH; WITH JOY AND SHOUT 7 256
WHEREVER PLAC'T, LET HIM DISPOSE: JOY THOU 8 170
WITH FRAGRANCE AND WITH JOY MY HEART OREFLOW'D. 8 266
IF I COULD JOY IN AUGHT, SWEET INTERCHANGE 9 115
SAVE WHAT IS IN DESTROYING, OTHER JOY 9 478
TO MISCHIEF SWIFT. HOPE ELEVATES, AND JOY 9 633
HATH TASTED, ENVIES NOT, BUT BRINGS WITH JOY 9 770
GREAT JOY HE PROMIS'D TO HIS THOUGHTS, AND NEW 9 843
MAY JOYNE US, EQUAL JOY, AS EQUAL LOVE; 9 882
SO SAYING, SHE EMBRAC'D HIM, AND FOR JOY 9 990
HENCEFORTH OF GOD OR ANGEL, EARST WITH JOY 9 1081
WHERE ART THOU ADAM, WONT WITH JOY TO MEET 10 103
NOT INSTANT, BUT OF FUTURE TIME. WITH JOY 10 345
GREAT JOY WAS AT THIR MEETING, AND AT SIGHT 10 350
OF THAT STUPENDIOUS BRIDGE HIS JOY ENCREAS'D. 10 351
RAIS'D FROM THIR DARK DIVAN, AND WITH LIKE JOY 10 457
TO DASH THIR PRIDE, AND JOY FOR MAN SEDUC'T. 10 577
AND BRINGING FORTH, SOON RECOMPENC'T WITH JOY, 10 1052
ALL MY REDEEMD MAY DWELL IN JOY AND BLISS, 11 43
IN FELLOWSHIPS OF JOY: THE SONS OF LIGHT 11 80
OUT OF DESPAIRE, JOY, BUT WITH FEAR YET LINKT; 11 139
TRUE PATIENCE, AND TO TEMPER JOY WITH FEAR 11 361
OF THESE FAIR ATHEISTS, AND NOW SWIM IN JOY, 11 625
TO WHOM THUS ADAM OF SHORT JOY BEREFT. 11 628
GREATLY REJOYC'D, AND THUS HIS JOY BROKE FORTH. 11 869
SHAL SPEND THIR DAYES IN JOY UNBLAM'D, AND DWELL 12 22
HE CEAS'D, DISCERNING ADAM WITH SUCH JOY 12 372
REPLETE WITH JOY AND WONDER THUS REPLI'D. 12 468
WITH JOY THE TIDINGS BROUGHT FROM HEAV'N: AT LENGTH 12 504
TO BRING FORTH FRUITS JOY AND ETERNAL BLISS. 12 551

JOYD
WHO MIGHT HAVE LIV'D AND JOYD IMMORTAL BLISS, 9 1166

JOYES
SOLE PARTNER AND SOLE PART OF ALL THESE JOYES, 4 411
AUGMENTED, OP'ND EYES, NEW HOPES, NEW JOYES, 9 985
HEAVIE, THOUGH IN THIR PLACE. O FLEETING JOYES 10 741

JOYLESS
OF HARLOTS, LOVELESS, JOYLESS, UNINDEARD, 4 766

JOYN
TO JOYN THIR DARK ENCOUNTER IN MID AIR: 2 718
THIR NATURE ALSO TO THY NATURE JOYN; 3 282
ON EARTH JOYN ALL YE CREATURES TO EXTOLL 5 164
JOYN VOICES ALL YE LIVING SOULS, YE BIRDS, 5 197
ABHOR TO JOYN; AND BY IMPRUDENCE MIXT, 11 686

JOYN'D
OF PHLEGRA WITH TH' HEROIC RACE WERE JOYN'D 1 577
THAT STOOD FOR HEAV'N, IN MIGHTY QUADRATE JOYN'D 6 62
ON THE ROUGH EDGE OF BATTEL ERE IT JOYN'D, 6 108
THE ADVERSE LEGIONS, NOR LESS HIDEOUS JOYN'D 6 206
SUCH PAIRS, IN LOVE AND MUTUAL HONOUR JOYN'D? 8 58
HE MADE US, AND DELIGHT TO REASON JOYN'D. 9 243
THY SWEET CONVERSE AND LOVE SO DEARLY JOYN'D, 9 909
BRIDGING HIS WAY, EUROPE WITH ASIA JOYN'D, 10 310
AS JOYN'D IN INJURIES, ONE ENMITIE 10 925

JOYND
JOYND WITH ME ONCE, NOW MISERY HATH JOYND 1 90
FALL CIRCUMVENTED THUS BY FRAUD, THOUGH JOYND 3 152
HITHER OF ILL-JOYND SONS AND DAUGHTERS BORN 3 463
TASTES, NOT WELL JOYND, INELEGANT, BUT BRING 5 335
HOPELESS TO CIRCUMVENT US JOYND, WHERE EACH 9 259

JOYNE
MAY JOYNE US, EQUAL JOY, AS EQUAL LOVE; 9 882
OF NOXIOUS EFFICACIE, AND WHEN TO JOYNE 10 660

JOYNES
OF HEAD OR HEEL: NOT THEREFORE JOYNES THE SON 12 388

JOYNING
WHICH REASON JOYNING OR DISJOYNING, FRAMES 5 106
OF LENGTH PRODIGIOUS JOYNING TO THE WALL 10 302
BETWEEN US TWO LET THERE BE PEACE, BOTH JOYNING, 10 924

JOYNS
HEE WITH A CREW, WHOM LIKE AMBITION JOYNS 12 38

JOYNT
NOT TI'D OR MANACL'D WITH JOYNT OR LIMB, 1 426
DISTINGUISHABLE IN MEMBER, JOYNT, OR LIMB, 2 668
OF MEMBRANE, JOYNT, OR LIMB, EXCLUSIVE BARRS: 8 625
THESE PATHS & BOWERS DOUBT NOT BUT OUR JOYNT HANDS 9 244
ISSUING FROM MEE: ON YOUR JOYNT VIGOR NOW 10 405
IF YOUR JOYNT POWER PREVAILES, TH' AFFAIRES OF HELL 10 408

JOYNTS
RAN THROUGH HIS VEINS, AND ALL HIS JOYNTS RELAX'D; 9 891

JOYOUS
JOYOUS THE BIRDS; FRESH GALES AND GENTLE AIRES 8 515

JOYS
OF DALLIANCE HAD WITH THEE IN HEAV'N, AND JOYS 2 819

JUBILANT
WHILE THE BRIGHT POMP ASCENDED JUBILANT. 7 564

JUBILEE
WITH JUBILEE, AND LOUD HOSANNA'S FILLD 3 348

JUBILIE
WITH JUBILIE ADVANC'D; AND AS THEY WENT, 6 884

JUCIEST
EACH PLANT AND JUCIEST GOURD WILL PLUCK SUCH CHOICE 5 327

JUDAH
OF ALIENATED JUDAH. NEXT CAME ONE 1 457

JUDG
THAT FARR BE FROM THEE, FATHER, WHO ART JUDG 3 154
TO WHOM THUS MICHAEL. JUDG NOT WHAT IS BEST 11 603

JUDG'D
WELL HAVE YE JUDG'D, WELL ENDED LONG DEBATE, 2 390
AND JUDG'D OF PUBLIC MOMENT, IN THE SHAPE 2 448
SHALL SATISFIE FOR MAN, BE JUDG'D AND DIE, 3 295
NONE SECONDED, AS OUT OF SEASON JUDG'D, 5 850
JUDG'D THEE PERVERSE: THE EASIER CONQUEST NOW 6 37
AGAINST US FROM ABOUT HIS THRONE, AND JUDG'D 6 426
WHOEVER JUDG'D, THE WORST ON MEE MUST LIGHT, 10 73
ARE TO BEHOLD THE JUDGMENT, BUT THE JUDG'D, 10 81
THOUGH IN MYSTERIOUS TERMS, JUDG'D AS THEN BEST: 10 173
SO JUDG'D HE MAN, BOTH JUDGE AND SAVIOUR SENT, 10 209
MEANWHILE ERE THUS WAS SIN'D AND JUDG'D ON EARTH, 10 229
TRUE IS, MEE ALSO HE HATH JUDG'D, OR RATHER 10 494
AND GRACIOUS TEMPER HE BOTH HEARD AND JUDG'D 10 1047
CLOATH'D US UNWORTHIE, PITYING WHILE HE JUDG'D; 10 1059
REPAIRING WHERE HE JUDG'D US, PROSTRATE FALL 10 1087
REPAIRING WHERE HE JUDG'D THEM PROSTRATE FELL 10 1099
SEIS'D ON BY FORCE, JUDG'D, AND TO DEATH CONDEMND 12 412

JUDGE
TO FICKLE CHANCE, AND CHAOS JUDGE THE STRIFE: 2 233
BOTH WHAT THEY JUDGE AND WHAT THEY CHOOSE; FOR SO 3 123
THEN ALL THY SAINTS ASSEMBL'D, THOU SHALT JUDGE 3 330
O LOSS OF ONE IN HEAV'N TO JUDGE OF WISE, 4 904
SO JUDGE THOU STILL, PRESUMPTUOUS, TILL THE WRAUTH, 4 912
TO SEE HOW THOU COULD'ST JUDGE OF FIT AND MEET: 8 448
BUT WHOM SEND I TO JUDGE THEM? WHOM BUT THEE 10 55
AND DESTIN'D MAN HIMSELF TO JUDGE MAN FALL'N. 10 62
MAYST EVER REST WELL PLEAS'D. I GO TO JUDGE 10 71

JUDGE (CONTINUED)

CAME THE MILD JUDGE AND INTERCESSOR BOTH 10 96
THE GRACIOUS JUDGE WITHOUT REVILE REPLI'D. 10 118
BEFORE MY JUDGE, EITHER TO UNDERGOE 10 126
CONFESSING SOON, YET NOT BEFORE HER JUDGE . . . 10 160
SO JUDG'D HE MAN, BOTH JUDGE AND SAVIOUR SENT, . 10 209
THE SON OF GOD TO JUDGE THEM TERRIFI'D 10 338
BUT IF THOU JUDGE IT HARD AND DIFFICULT, . . . 10 992
BUT INFINITE IN PARDON WAS MY JUDGE, ... 11 167
TO JUDGE THEM WITH HIS SAINTS: HIM THE MOST HIGH . 11 705
WITH GLORY AND POWER TO JUDGE BOTH QUICK AND DEAD, 12 460
TO JUDGE TH' UNFAITHFUL DEAD, BUT TO REWARD . . 12 461

JUDGEMENT

THY JUDGEMENT TO DO AUGHT, WHICH ELSE FREE WILL . 8 636
ANGER AND JUST REBUKE, AND JUDGEMENT GIV'N, . . 9 10
ALL JUDGEMENT, WHETHER IN HEAV'N, OR EARTH, OR HELL. 10 57
TO JUDGEMENT HE PROCEEDED ON TH' ACCUS'D . . . 10 164
ON ADAM LAST THUS JUDGEMENT HE PRONOUNC'D. . . 10 197
AND WHILE THE DREAD OF JUDGEMENT PAST REMAINS . . 12 14
OVER FREE REASON, GOD IN JUDGEMENT JUST 12 92

JUDGEMENTS

IN PRISON UNDER JUDGEMENTS IMMINENT: 11 725
MUST BE COMPELLD BY SIGNES AND JUDGEMENTS DIRE; . 12 175

JUDGES

SO WISE HE JUDGES IT TO FLY FROM PAIN 4 910
BY JUDGES FIRST, THEN UNDER KINGS; OF WHOM . . . 12 320

JUDGEST

OF ALL THINGS MADE, AND JUDGEST ONELY RIGHT. . . 3 155

JUDGMENT

ARE TO BEHOLD THE JUDGMENT, BUT THE JUDG'D, . . 10 81
AND TO THE PLACE OF JUDGMENT WILL RETURN, . . . 10 932
AND JUDGMENT FROM ABOVE: HIM OLD AND YOUNG . . . 11 668

JUDGMENTS

MY JUDGMENTS, HOW WITH MANKIND I PROCEED, . . . 11 69

JUDICIOUS

IN REASON, AND IS JUDICIOUS, IS THE SCALE . . . 8 591
AND PALATE CALL JUDICIOUS; I THE PRAISE 9 1020

JUNO

ON JUNO SMILES, WHEN HE IMPREGNS THE CLOUDS . . 4 500

JUNO'S

OR NEPTUN'S IRE OR JUNO'S, THAT SO LONG 9 18

JUPITER

SMIL'D WITH SUPERIOR LOVE, AS JUPITER 4 499

JURISDICTION

FROM HEAV'NS HIGH JURISDICTION, IN NEW LEAGUE . . 2 319

JUST

MEE THOUGH JUST RIGHT, AND THE FIXT LAWS OF HEAV'N 2 18
TO CLAIM OUR JUST INHERITANCE OF OLD, ... 2 38
OF SPIRITS THAT IN OUR JUST PRETENSES ARM'D . . 2 825
ALL HE COULD HAVE; I MADE HIM JUST AND RIGHT, . . 3 98
MANS MORTAL CRIME, AND JUST TH' UNJUST TO SAVE, . 3 215
RECEIVE NEW LIFE. SO MAN, AS IS MOST JUST, . . 3 294
NEW HEAV'N AND EARTH, WHEREIN THE JUST SHALL DWELL, 3 335
JUST O'RE THE BLISSFUL SEAT OF PARADISE, . . . 3 527
MELT, AS I DOE, YET PUBLIC REASON JUST, . . . 4 389
AND HEAD, WHAT THOU HAST SAID IS JUST AND RIGHT. . 4 443
AS I BENT DOWN TO LOOK, JUST OPPOSITE, ... 4 460
FOUNDED IN REASON, LOYAL, JUST, AND PURE, . . . 4 755
JUST MET, AND CLOSING STOOD IN SQUADRON JOIND . . 4 863
SINGLE, IS YET SO JUST, MY CONSTANT THOUGHTS . . 5 552
THE JUST DECREE OF GOD, PRONOUNC'T AND SWORN, . . 5 814
UNSOUND AND FALSE; NOR IS IT AUGHT BUT JUST, . . 6 121
THOUGH HEAVIEST BY JUST MEASURE ON THY SELF . . 6 265
FOR STRENGTH FROM TRUTH DIVIDED AND FROM JUST, . 6 381
AS IS MOST JUST; THIS I MY GLORIE ACCOUNT, . . . 6 726
THAT FROM THY JUST OBEDIENCE COULD REVOLT, . . . 6 740
GLORIE TO HIM WHOSE JUST AVENGING IRE 7 184
AND TH' HABITATIONS OF THE JUST; TO HIM . . . 7 186
THIS BE THY JUST CIRCUMFERENCE, O WORLD. . . . 7 231
PATTERN OF JUST EQUALITIE PERHAPS 7 487
TO VISIT OFT THE DWELLINGS OF JUST MEN . . . 7 570
HOLY AND JUST: THRICE HAPPIE IF THEY KNOW . . . 7 631
THEN SELF ESTEEM, GROUNDED ON JUST AND RIGHT . . 8 572
ANGER AND JUST REBUKE, AND JUDGEMENT GIV'N, . . 9 10
JUST THEN RETURND AT SHUT OF EVENING FLOURS. . . 9 278
OF GOOD, HOW JUST? OF EVIL, IF WHAT IS EVIL . . 9 698
GOD THEREFORE CANNOT HURT YE, AND BE JUST; . . . 9 700
NOT JUST, NOT GOD; NOT FEARD THEN, NOR OBEYD: . . 9 701
JUST CONFIDENCE, AND NATIVE RIGHTEOUSNESS . . . 9 1056
OMNISCIENT, WHO IN ALL THINGS WISE AND JUST, . . 10 7
HEAV'N-FALL'N, IN STATION STOOD OR JUST ARRAY, . . 10 535
THROUGH MULTITUDE THAT SUNG: JUST ARE THY WAYS, . 10 643
JUSTICE DIVINE NOT HAST'N TO BE JUST? 10 857
TO MY JUST NUMBER FOUND. O WHY DID GOD, . . . 10 888
MEE MEE ONELY JUST OBJECT OF HIS IRE. 10 936

JUST (CONTINUED)

FOUND SO ERRONEOUS, THENCE BY JUST EVENT . . . 10 969
RELUCTANCE AGAINST GOD AND HIS JUST YOKE . . . 10 1045
WAK'T IN THE RENOVATION OF THE JUST, ... 11 65
OUT OF THY LOYNS; TH' UNJUST THE JUST HATH SLAIN, 11 455
I YIELD IT JUST, SAID ADAM, AND SUBMIT. . . . 11 526
JUST MEN THEY SEEMD, AND ALL THIR STUDY BENT . . 11 577
BUT WHO WAS THAT JUST MAN, WHOM HAD NOT HEAV'N . 11 681
WITH FOES FOR DARING SINGLE TO BE JUST, . . . 11 703
THE ONE JUST MAN ALIVE; BY HIS COMMAND . . . 11 818
FOR ONE MAN FOUND SO PERFET AND SO JUST, . . . 11 876
SUCH GRACE SHALL ONE JUST MAN FIND IN HIS SIGHT, . 11 890
BOTH HEAV'N AND EARTH, WHEREIN THE JUST SHALL DWELL. 11 901
WITH SOME REGARD TO WHAT IS JUST AND RIGHT . . 12 16
OVER FREE REASON, GOD IN JUDGEMENT JUST . . . 12 92
JUST ABRAHAM AND HIS SEED: NOW FIRST I FINDE . . 12 273
JUST FOR UNJUST, THAT IN SUCH RIGHTEOUSNESS . . 12 294
APPEER OF RESPIRATION TO THE JUST, ... 12 540

JUSTICE

SUCH PLACE ETERNAL JUSTICE HAD PREPAR'D 1 70
WHAT E'RE HIS WRATH, WHICH HE CALLS JUSTICE, BIDS, 2 733
THE OTHER NONE: IN MERCY AND JUSTICE BOTH, . . . 3 132
DYE HEE OR JUSTICE MUST; UNLESS FOR HIM . . . 3 210
OF MERCY AND JUSTICE IN THY FACE DISCERN'D, . . 3 407
ALL JUSTICE: NOR DELAID THE WINGED SAINT . . . 5 247
JUSTICE SHALL NOT RETURN AS BOUNTIE SCORN'D. . . 10 54
MERCIE COLLEGUE WITH JUSTICE, SENDING THEE . . 10 59
JUSTICE WITH MERCIE, AS MAY ILLUSTRATE MOST . . 10 78
THY JUSTICE SEEMS; YET TO SAY TRUTH, TOO LATE, . 10 755
JUSTICE DIVINE NOT HAST'N TO BE JUST? . . . 10 857
BUT DEATH COMES NOT AT CALL, JUSTICE DIVINE . . 10 858
OF JUSTICE, OF RELIGION, TRUTH AND PEACE, . . . 11 667
JUSTICE AND TEMPERANCE, TRUTH AND FAITH FORGOT; . 11 807
BUT JUSTICE, AND SOME FATAL CURSE ANNEXT . . . 12 99
TO CIVIL JUSTICE, PART RELIGIOUS RITES 12 231
SO ONELY CAN HIGH JUSTICE REST APPAID. 12 401

JUSTIFICATION

JUSTIFICATION TOWARDS GOD, AND PEACE 12 296

JUSTIFIE

AND JUSTIFIE THE WAYES OF GOD TO MEN. 1 26
HER DOING SEEM'D TO JUSTIFIE THE DEED; 10 142

JUSTLING

THROUGH BOSPORUS BETWIXT THE JUSTLING ROCKS: . . 2 1018
JUSTLING OR PUSHT WITH WINDS RUDE IN THIR SHOCK . 10 1074

JUSTLY

SO WERE CREATED, NOR CAN JUSTLY ACCUSE 3 112
WHO JUSTLY HATH DRIVN OUT HIS REBELL FOES . . . 3 677
CHOSE FREELY WHAT IT NOW SO JUSTLY RUES. . . . 4 72
JUSTLY HAST IN DERISION, AND SECURE 5 736
NOT THAT WHICH JUSTLY GIVES HEROIC NAME 9 40
MORE JUSTLY, SEAT WORTHIER OF GODS, AS BUILT . . 9 100
OF HIS CREATION; JUSTLY THEN ACCURST, ... 10 168
THY PUNISHMENT THEN JUSTLY IS AT HIS WILL. . . . 10 768
WHAT JUSTLY THOU HAST LOST; NOR SET THY HEART, . 11 288
TO WHOM THUS MICHAEL. JUSTLY THOU ABHORR'ST . . 12 79

KEEN

OF THEOLOGIANS, BUT WITH KEEN DISPATCH 5 436
WAS GIV'N HIM TEMPERD SO, THAT NEITHER KEEN . . 6 322
BLOW MOIST AND KEEN, SHATTERING THE GRACEFUL LOCKS 10 1066
DRIVN BY A KEEN NORTH-WINDE, THAT BLOWING DRIE . 11 842

KEENE

OF THAT ALLURING FRUIT, URG'D ME SO KEENE. . . . 9 588

KEEP

INTO MY HAND WAS GIV'N, WITH CHARGE TO KEEP . . 2 775
I KEEP, BY HIM FORBIDDEN TO UNLOCK 2 852
KEEP RESIDENCE; IF ALL I CAN WILL SERVE, . . . 2 999
THAT FROM HIS LORDLY EYE KEEP DISTANCE DUE, . . 3 578
ILL SENC'T FOR HEAV'N TO KEEP OUT SUCH A FOE . . 4 372
FROM US NO OTHER SERVICE THEN TO KEEP 4 420
TO KEEP THEM LOW WHOM KNOWLEDGE MIGHT EXALT . . 4 525
WHILE THEY KEEP WATCH, OR NIGHTLY ROUNDING WALK . 4 685
TO HIM WHO SENT US, WHOSE CHARGE IS TO KEEP . . 4 842
TO TILL AND KEEP, AND OF THE FRUIT TO EATE: . . 8 320
HIM WHOM TO LOVE IS TO OBEY, AND KEEP 8 634
WILL KEEP FROM WILDERNESS WITH EASE, AS WIDE . . 9 245
WHY BUT TO KEEP YE LOW AND IGNORANT, ... 9 704
BUT KEEP THE ODDS OF KNOWLEDGE IN MY POWER . . 9 820
TO END ME? SHALL TRUTH FAIL TO KEEP HER WORD, . 10 856
WHICH I MUST KEEP TILL MY APPOINTED DAY . . . 11 550

KEEPES

IN THAT ASPECT, AND STILL THAT DISTANCE KEEPES . 7 379

KEEPING

NOT KEEPING STRICTEST WATCH, AS SHE WAS WARND. . 9 363
TO SIMPLE SHEPHERDS, KEEPING WATCH BY NIGHT; . . 12 365

KEN

THE HEMISPHERE OF EARTH IN CLEEREST KEN 11 379

KINGS (CONTINUED)
ERCOCO AND THE LESS MARITIM KINGS 11 398
HOW MANY KINGS DESTROYD, AND KINGDOMS WON, 12 262
BY JUDGES FIRST, THEN UNDER KINGS; OF WHOM 12 320
ALL NATIONS, AND TO KINGS FORETOLD, OF KINGS 12 329
RETURND FROM BABYLON BY LEAVE OF KINGS 12 348

KISS'D
KISS'D AS THE GRACIOUS SIGNS OF SWEET REMORSE 5 134

KISSES
WITH KISSES PURE: ASIDE THE DEVIL TURND 4 502

KNEE
WITH SUPPLIANT KNEE, AND DEIFIE HIS POWER, 1 112
THE SUPPLE KNEE? YE WILL NOT, IF I TRUST 5 788
SHALL BEND THE KNEE, AND IN THAT HONOUR DUE 5 817
HE BACK RECOILD; THE TENTH ON BENDED KNEE 6 194

KNEEL'D
KNEEL'D AND BEFORE HIM HUMBL'D ALL MY HEART, 11 150

KNEES
ALL KNEES TO THEE SHALL BOW, OF THEM THAT BIDE 3 321
ALL KNEES IN HEAV'N, AND SHALL CONFESS HIM LORD: 5 608
I BEG, AND CLASP THY KNEES; BEREAVE ME NOT, 10 918

KNEE-TRIBUTE
KNEE-TRIBUTE YET UNPAID, PROSTRATION VILE, 5 782

KNEW
HE WITH HIS THUNDER: AND TILL THEN WHO KNEW 1 93
KNOW YE NOT MEE? YE KNEW ME ONCE NO MATE 4 828
IF THOU RESIST. THE FIEND LOOKT UP AND KNEW 4 1013
KNEW NEVER TILL THIS IRKSOM NIGHT; METHOUGHT 5 35
THE CIRCUIT WIDE. STRAIT KNEW HIM ALL THE BANDS 5 287
AEREAL MUSIC SEND: NOR KNEW I NOT 5 548
ALL HIS RIGHT SIDE; THEN SATAN FIRST KNEW PAIN, 6 327
CHOSE RATHER; HEE, SHE KNEW WOULD INTERMIX 8 54
IS HARD; FOR WHO HIMSELF BEGINNING KNEW? 8 251
KNEW NOT; TO SPEAK I TRI'D, AND FORTHWITH SPAKE, 8 271
WHILE THUS I CALL'D, AND STRAY'D I KNEW NOT
WHITHER. 8 283
KNEW IT NOT GOOD FOR MAN TO BE ALONE, 8 445
I FOLLOW'D HER, SHE WHAT WAS HONOUR KNEW, 8 508
I KNEW, BUT NOT WITH HUMAN VOICE ENDU'D; 9 561
AND KNEW NOT EATING DEATH: SATIATE AT LENGTH, 9 792
FOR STILL THEY KNEW, AND OUGHT TO HAVE STILL
REMEMBER'D 10 12
FOR MAN, FOR OF HIS STATE BY THIS THEY KNEW, 10 19
CONCERN'D NOT MAN (SINCE HE NO FURTHER KNEW) 10 170
OBTRUDED ON US THUS? WHO IF WE KNEW 11 504

KNEWST
THOU KNEWST BY NAME, AND ALL TH' ETHEREAL POWERS, 12 577

KNIGHTS
BEGIRT WITH BRITISH AND ARMORIC KNIGHTS; 1 581
PRICK FORTH THE AERIE KNIGHTS, AND COUCH THIR
SPEARS 2 536
WITH LONG AND TEDIOUS HAVOC FABL'D KNIGHTS 9 30
BASES AND TINSEL TRAPPINGS, GORGIOUS KNIGHTS 9 36

KNIT
KNIT WITH THE GRACES AND THE HOURS IN DANCE 4 267

KNOTS
IN BEDS AND CURIOUS KNOTS, BUT NATURE BOON 4 242

KNOW
AS STOOD LIKE THESE, COULD EVER KNOW REPULSE? 1 630
HENCEFORTH HIS MIGHT WE KNOW, AND KNOW OUR OWN 1 643
WHAT YET THEY KNOW MUST FOLLOW, TO ENDURE 2 206
AND KNOW NOT THAT THE KING OF HEAV'N HATH DOOM'D 2 316
WHAT IT INTENDS; TILL FIRST I KNOW OF THEE, 2 740
I KNOW THEE NOT, NOR EVER SAW TILL NOW 2 744
BEFALLN US UNFORESEEN, UNTHOUGHT OF, KNOW 2 821
TO KNOW, AND THIS ONCE KNOWN, SHALL SOON RETURN, 2 839
ANSWER'D. I KNOW THEE, STRANGER, WHO THOU ART, 2 990
BY ME UPHELD, THAT HE MAY KNOW HOW FRAIL 3 180
UNSPEAKABLE DESIRE TO SEE, AND KNOW 3 662
FAIR ANGEL, THY DESIRE WHICH TENDS TO KNOW 3 694
PLEASANT TO KNOW, AND WORTHIEST TO BE ALL 3 703
TH' OMNIPOTENT. AY ME, THEY LITTLE KNOW 4 86
AS MAN ERE LONG, AND THIS NEW WORLD SHALL KNOW. 4 113
ENVIE THEM THAT? CAN IT BE SIN TO KNOW, 4 517
WITH MORE DESIRE TO KNOW, AND TO REJECT 4 523
A SPIRIT, ZEALOUS, AS HE SEEM'D, TO KNOW 4 565
THOU TELLST, BY MORROW DAWNING I SHALL KNOW. 4 588
GOD IS THY LAW, THOU MINE: TO KNOW NO MORE 4 637
NO HAPPIER STATE, AND KNOW TO KNOW NO MORE. 4 775
KNOW YE NOT THEN SAID SATAN, FILL'D WITH SCORN, 4 827
KNOW YE NOT MEE? YE KNEW ME ONCE NO MATE 4 828
NOT TO KNOW MEE ARGUES YOUR SELVES UNKNOWN, 4 830
THE LOWEST OF YOUR THRONG; OR IF YE KNOW, 4 831
SATAN, I KNOW THY STRENGTH, AND THOU KNOWST MINE, 4 1006
CREATED PURE. BUT KNOW THAT IN THE SOULE 5 100
BUT BY DECEIT AND LIES; THIS LET HIM KNOW, 5 243

KNOW (CONTINUED)
TO SPIRITUAL NATURES; ONLY THIS I KNOW, 5 402
FOR KNOW, WHATEVER WAS CREATED, NEEDS 5 414
GIVEN HIM BY THIS GREAT CONFERENCE TO KNOW 5 454
INHABITANT WITH GOD, NOW KNOW I WELL 5 461
KNOW WHETHER I BE DEXTROUS TO SUBDUE 5 741
TO KNOW YE RIGHT, OR IF YE KNOW YOUR SELVES 5 789
YET BY EXPERIENCE TAUGHT WE KNOW HOW GOOD, 5 826
DOCTRIN WHICH WE WOULD KNOW WHENCE LEARNT: WHO SAW 5 856
WE KNOW NO TIME WHEN WE WERE NOT AS NOW; 5 859
KNOW NONE BEFORE US, SELF-BEGOT, SELF-RAIS'D 5 860
WHEN WHO CAN UNCREATE THEE THOU SHALT KNOW. 5 895
HOW FEW SOMTIMES MAY KNOW, WHEN THOUSANDS ERR. 6 148
(UNANSWERD LEAST THOU BOAST) TO LET THEE KNOW; 6 163
IMMENSE I HAVE TRANSFUS'D, THAT ALL MAY KNOW 6 704
LED ON, YET SINLESS, WITH DESIRE TO KNOW 7 61
TO MAGNIFIE HIS WORKS, THE MORE WE KNOW. 7 97
ANOUGH IS LEFT BESIDES TO SEARCH AND KNOW. 7 125
HER TEMPERANCE OVER APPETITE, TO KNOW 7 127
KNOW THEN, THAT AFTER LUCIFER FROM HEAV'N 7 131
HOLY AND JUST: THRICE HAPPIE IF THEY KNOW 7 631
INFORMD BY THEE MIGHT KNOW; IF ELSE THOU SEEKST 7 639
THAT MAN MAY KNOW HE DWELLS NOT IN HIS OWN; 8 103
TO KNOW WHAT PASSES THERE; BE LOWLIE WISE: 8 173
THAT NOT TO KNOW AT LARGE OF THINGS REMOTE 8 191
FROM USE, OBSCURE AND SUTTLE, BUT TO KNOW 8 192
TELL ME, HOW MAY I KNOW HIM, HOW ADORE, 8 280
AND FEEL THAT I AM HAPPIER THEN I KNOW, 8 282
AND SHUN THE BITTER CONSEQUENCE: FOR KNOW, 8 328
THIR LANGUAGE AND THIR WAYES, THEY ALSO KNOW, 8 373
FROM ALL ETERNITIE, FOR NONE I KNOW 8 406
AND IN HER SELF COMPLEAT, SO WELL TO KNOW 8 548
FIRST THY OBEDIENCE; TH' OTHER WHO CAN KNOW, 9 368
KNOWING BOTH GOOD AND EVIL AS THEY KNOW. 9 709
TH' OFFENCE, THAT MAN SHOULD THUS ATTAIN TO KNOW? 9 726
IN PLAIN THEN, WHAT FORBIDS HE BUT TO KNOW, 9 758
WHAT FEAR I THEN, RATHER WHAT KNOW TO FEARE 9 773
IN KNOWLEDGE, AS THE GODS WHO ALL THINGS KNOW; 9 804
OP'ND WE FIND INDEED, AND FIND WE KNOW 9 1071
BAD FRUIT OF KNOWLEDGE, IF THIS BE TO KNOW, 9 1073
I KNOW NOT WHENCE POSSESSD THEE; WE HAD THEN 9 1137
TH' ETHEREAL PEOPLE RAN, TO HEAR AND KNOW 10 27
AS VITIATED IN NATURE: MORE TO KNOW 10 169
OUT OF THE GROUND WAST TAKEN, KNOW THY BIRTH, 10 207
AND KNOW NOT THAT I CALL'D AND DREW THEM THITHER 10 629
ADAM, BY SAD EXPERIMENT I KNOW 10 967
THOSE PURE IMMORTAL ELEMENTS THAT KNOW 11 50
TO KNOW BOTH GOOD AND EVIL, SINCE HIS TASTE 11 85
HIS HEART I KNOW, HOW VARIABLE AND VAIN 11 92
ERE THOU FROM HENCE DEPART, KNOW I AM SENT 11 356
BEFORE THEE SHALL APPEAR; THAT THOU MAYST KNOW 11 475
TO WORSHIP GOD ARIGHT, AND KNOW HIS WORKS 11 578
RATIONAL LIBERTIE; YET KNOW WITHALL, 12 82
TO KNOW THIR GOD, OR MESSAGE TO REGARD, 12 174
CHIEFLY WHAT MAY CONCERN HER FAITH TO KNOW, 12 599
WHENCE THOU RETURNST, AND WHITHER WENTST, I KNOW; 12 610

KNOWING
KNOWLEDGE OF GOOD BOUGHT DEAR BY KNOWING ILL. 4 222
OUR KNOWING, AS TO HIGHEST WISDOM SEEMD, 7 83
GOVERN THE REST, SELF-KNOWING, AND FROM THENCE 7 510
AND FINDE THEE KNOWING NOT OF BEASTS ALONE, 8 438
KNOWING BOTH GOOD AND EVIL AS THEY KNOW. 9 709
HAD SHADOW'D THEM FROM KNOWING ILL, WAS GON, 9 1055
ALL, THOUGH ALL-KNOWING, WHAT HAD PAST WITH MAN 10 227
NOR KNOWING US NOR KNOWN: AND IF BY PRAYER 11 307
NOT KNOWING TO WHAT LAND, YET FIRM BELIEVES: 12 127

KNOWLEDG
CUT OFF, AND FOR THE BOOK OF KNOWLEDG FAIR 3 47
UNKNOWN, WHICH HUMAN KNOWLEDG COULD NOT REACH: 7 75
KNOWLEDG OF GOOD AND ILL, WHICH I HAVE SET 8 324
THIR NATURE, WITH SUCH KNOWLEDG GOD ENDU'D 8 353
OF KNOWLEDG, NOR WAS GOD-HEAD FROM HER THOUGHT. 9 790

KNOWLEDGE
OF KNOWLEDGE PAST OR PRESENT, COULD HAVE FEAR'D, 1 628
OUR DEATH THE TREE OF KNOWLEDGE GREW FAST BY, 4 221
KNOWLEDGE OF GOOD BOUGHT DEAR BY KNOWING ILL. 4 222
OF KNOWLEDGE, PLANTED BY THE TREE OF LIFE, 4 424
ONE FATAL TREE THERE STANDS OF KNOWLEDGE CALL'D, 4 514
FORBIDDEN THEM TO TASTE: KNOWLEDGE FORBIDD'N? 4 515
TO KEEP THEM LOW WHOM KNOWLEDGE MIGHT EXALT 4 525
IS WOMANS HAPPIEST KNOWLEDGE AND HER PRAISE. 4 638
OF INTERDICTED KNOWLEDGE: FAIR IT SEEM'D, 5 52
NOR GOD, NOR MAN; IS KNOWLEDGE SO DESPIS'D? 5 60
OUR KNOWLEDGE OR OPINION; THEN RETIRES 5 108
OUR KNOWLEDGE, AND THE SCALE OF NATURE SET 5 509
OF KNOWLEDGE WITHIN BOUNDS; BEYOND ABSTAIN 7 120
BUT KNOWLEDGE IS AS FOOD, AND NEEDS NO LESS 7 126
WHICH TASTED WORKS KNOWLEDGE OF GOOD AND EVIL, 7 543
THE THIRST I HAD OF KNOWLEDGE, AND VOUTSAF'T 8 8
ALL HIGHER KNOWLEDGE IN HER PRESENCE FALLS 8 551
TO KNOWLEDGE? BY THE THREATNER, LOOK ON MEE, 9 687
TO HAPPIER LIFE, KNOWLEDGE OF GOOD AND EVIL; 9 697
KNOWLEDGE OF GOOD AND EVIL IN THIS TREE, 9 723
WHAT CAN YOUR KNOWLEDGE HURT HIM, OR THIS TREE 9 727
OF KNOWLEDGE, KNOWLEDGE BOTH OF GOOD AND EVIL; 9 752

KNOWLEDGE (CONTINUED)
IN KNOWLEDGE, AS THE GODS WHO ALL THINGS KNOW; 9 804
BUT KEEP THE ODDS OF KNOWLEDGE IN MY POWER 9 820
OF KNOWLEDGE HE MUST PASS, THERE HE HER MET, 9 849
AGAINST HIS BETTER KNOWLEDGE, NOT DECEAV'D, 9 998
BAD FRUIT OF KNOWLEDGE, IF THIS BE TO KNOW, 9 1073
HIS KNOWLEDGE OF GOOD LOST, AND EVIL GOT, 11 87
FORBIDD'N KNOWLEDGE BY FORBIDD'N MEANS. 12 279
OF KNOWLEDGE, WHAT THIS VESSEL CAN CONTAINE; 12 559
DEEDS TO THY KNOWLEDGE ANSWERABLE, ADD FAITH, 12 582

KNOWN
LONG AFTER KNOWN IN PALESTINE, AND NAM'D 1 80
THEN WERE THEY KNOWN TO MEN BY VARIOUS NAMES, 1 374
SAY, MUSE, THIR NAMES THEN KNOWN, WHO FIRST, WHO LAST, 1 376
AND IDA KNOWN, THENCE ON THE SNOWY TOP 1 515
AND SOME THE ARCHITECT: HIS HAND WAS KNOWN 1 732
TO KNOW, AND THIS ONCE KNOWN, SHALL SOON RETURN, 2 839
ADMONISHT BY HIS EAR, AND STRAIT WAS KNOWN 3 647
WELL KNOWN FROM HEAV'N; AND SINCE MERIDIAN HOUR 4 581
OF FATHER, SON, AND BROTHER FIRST WERE KNOWN. 4 757
OR UNDIMINISHT BRIGHTNESS, TO BE KNOWN 4 836
ALREADY KNOWN WHAT HE FOR NEWS HAD THOUGHT 6 20
O NOW IN DANGER TRI'D, NOW KNOWN IN ARMES 6 418
TILL NOW NOT KNOWN, BUT KNOWN AS SOON CONTEMND, 6 432
WHAT MAY NO LESS PERHAPS AVAILE US KNOWN, 7 85
ORDAIN'D FOR USES TO HIS LORD BEST KNOWN. 8 106
NOT IN THEMSELVES, ALL THIR KNOWN VERTUE APPEERS 9 110
BE REAL, WHY NOT KNOWN, SINCE EASIER SHUNND? 9 699
SHALL I APPEER? SHALL I TO HIM MAKE KNOWN 9 817
SO EMINENTLY NEVER HAD BIN KNOWN. 9 976
FROM THIS DELIGHTFUL FRUIT, NOR KNOWN TILL NOW 9 1023
BUT SUCH AS AT THIS DAY TO INDIANS KNOWN 9 1102
NO GROUND OF ENMITIE BETWEEN US KNOWN, 9 1151
WAS KNOWN IN HEAV'N; FOR WHAT CAN SCAPE THE EYE 10 5
AND PERSON, HAD'ST THOU KNOWN THY SELF ARIGHT, 10 156
HAD ROUNDED STILL TH' HORIZON, AND NOT KNOWN 10 684
HAPPIER, HAD IT SUFFIC'D HIM TO HAVE KNOWN 11 88
NOR KNOWING US NOR KNOWN: AND IF BY PRAYER 11 307
NOW AMPLIER KNOWN THY SAVIOUR AND THY LORD, 12 544

KNOWS
DEVOID OF SENSE AND MOTION? AND WHO KNOWS, 2 151
FOR WANT OF OTHER PREY, BUT THAT HE KNOWS 2 806
HIS END WITH MINE INVOLVD; AND KNOWS THAT I 2 807
THIS KNOWS MY PUNISHER; THEREFORE AS FARR 4 103
OF IMMORTALITY. SO LITTLE KNOWS 4 201
DREW MANY, WHOM THIR PLACE KNOWS HERE NO MORE; 7 144
CONTINU'D MAKING, AND WHO KNOWS HOW LONG 9 138
HIS WORSHIPPERS; HE KNOWS THAT IN THE DAY 9 705
AND KNOWS, AND SPEAKS, AND REASONS, AND DISCERNS, 9 765
OF WANDRING, AS THOU CALL'ST IT, WHICH WHO KNOWS 9 1146
OR IN SOME OTHER DISMAL PLACE WHO KNOWS 10 787
THE DOUBT, SINCE HUMANE REACH NO FURTHER KNOWS. 10 793
WHO KNOWS, OR MORE THEN THIS, THAT WE ARE DUST, 11 199

KNOW'ST
INSTRUCT ME, FOR THOU KNOW'ST; THOU FROM THE FIRST 1 19
AGAINST THY FATHERS HEAD? AND KNOW'ST FOR WHOM; 2 730
MY SOLE COMPLACENCE. WELL THOU KNOW'ST HOW DEAR, 3 276
AND THOU THIR NATURES KNOW'ST, & GAV'ST THEM NAMES, 7 493
IS YET DISTINCT BY NAME, THENCE, AS THOU KNOW'ST 7 536
OF DESTIND HABITATION; BUT THOU KNOW'ST 7 622
TO COME AND PLAY BEFORE THEE, KNOW'ST THOU NOT 8 372
WELL MANAG'D; OF THAT SKILL THE MORE THOU KNOW'ST, 8 573
ANSWER'D. LET IT SUFFICE THEE THAT THOU KNOW'ST 8 620
ADAM, THOU KNOW'ST HEAV'N HIS, AND ALL THE EARTH. 11 335

KNOWST
SOM DREADFUL THING NO DOUBT; FOR WELL THOU KNOWST 4 426
ON PURPOSE, HARD THOU KNOWST IT TO EXCLUDE 4 584
TO THEE NO REASON; WHO KNOWST ONLY GOOD, 4 895
INSULTING ANGEL, WELL THOU KNOWST I STOOD 4 926
SATAN, I KNOW THY STRENGTH, AND THOU KNOWST MINE, 4 1006
FOR TO THEMSELVES I LEFT THEM, AND THOU KNOWST, 6 689
BEFALL THEE SEVER'D FROM ME; FOR THOU KNOWST 9 252
ON EARTH THESE THY TRANSGRESSORS, BUT THOU KNOWST, 10 72
SO NOW OF WHAT THOU KNOWST NOT, WHO DESIR'ST 10 948

KSAR
IN HISPAHAN, OR WHERE THE RUSSIAN KSAR 11 394

LABOR'D
TUNES SWEETEST HIS LOVE-LABOR'D SONG; NOW REIGNES 5 41

LABORIOUS
WITH WHAT COMPULSION AND LABORIOUS FLIGHT 2 80
LABORIOUS, TILL DAY DROOP; WHILE HERE WE DWELL, 11 178

LABOUR
OUR LABOUR MUST BE TO PERVERT THAT END, 1 164
THROUGH LABOUR AND INDURANCE. THIS DEEP WORLD 2 262
SO HE WITH DIFFICULTY AND LABOUR HARD 2 1021
MOV'D ON, WITH DIFFICULTY AND LABOUR HEE; 2 1022
OF THIR SWEET GARDNING LABOUR THEN SUFFIC'D 4 328
LABOUR AND REST, AS DAY AND NIGHT TO MEN 4 613
AND AT OUR PLEASANT LABOUR, TO REFORM 4 625

LABOUR (CONTINUED)
TO RESPIT HIS DAY-LABOUR WITH REPAST, 5 232
NOR LONG SHALL BE OUR LABOUR, YET ERE DAWNE, 6 492
OR SAVE THE SUN HIS LABOUR, AND THAT SWIFT 8 133
AND HUNGER BOTH, FROM LABOUR, AT THE HOURE 8 213
ADAM, WELL MAY WE LABOUR STILL TO DRESS 9 205
AID US, THE WORK UNDER OUR LABOUR GROWS, 9 208
LABOUR, AS TO DEBARR US WHEN WE NEED 9 236
IF SUCH AFFRONT I LABOUR TO AVERT 9 302
BE FRUSTRATE, DO, UNDO, AND LABOUR LOOSE, 9 944
WITHOUT OUR HAZARD, LABOUR, OR ALLARME, 10 491
FROM THE SUNS AXLE; THEY WITH LABOUR PUSH'D 10 670
GLANC'D ON THE GROUND, WITH LABOUR I MUST EARNE 10 1054
MY LABOUR WILL SUSTAIN ME; AND LEAST COLD 10 1056
TO LABOUR CALLS US NOW WITH SWEAT IMPOS'D, 11 172
BY SUFFERING, AND EARNE REST FROM LABOUR WON, 11 375

LABOURERS
AND GATHERS GROUND FAST AT THE LABOURERS HEEL 12 631

LABOURING
WITH LAPLAND WITCHES, WHILE THE LABOURING MOON 2 665
LABOURING HAD RAIS'D, AND THUS TO EVE REPLI'D. 10 1012
LABOURING, TWO MASSIE CLODS OF IRON AND BRASS 11 565
LABOURING THE SOILE, AND REAPING PLENTEOUS CROP, 12 18

LABOURS
LET US DIVIDE OUR LABOURS, THOU WHERE CHOICE 9 214
HER TRESSES, AND HER RURAL LABOURS CROWN, 9 841

LABYRINTH
HER WATRIE LABYRINTH, WHEREOF WHO DRINKS, 2 584
IN LABYRINTH OF MANY A ROUND SELF-ROWLD, 9 183

LADEN
THIR PENANCE, LADEN WITH FRUIT LIKE THAT 10 550

LAERTES
ALCINOUS, HOST OF OLD LAERTES SON, 9 441

LAG
LEADS THEE, I SHALL NOT LAG BEHINDE, NOR ERRE 10 266

LAHOR
TO AGRA AND LAHOR OF GREAT MOGUL 11 391

LAID
IN HORRIBLE DESTRUCTION LAID THUS LOW, 1 137
SHOT AFTER US IN STORM, OREBLOWN HATH LAID 1 172
WITH UNEXPERIENC'T THOUGHT, AND LAID ME DOWNE 4 457
O FAIR FOUNDATION LAID WHEREON TO BUILD 4 521
STRAIT SIDE BY SIDE WERE LAID, NOR TURND I WEENE 4 741
NOW LAID PERHAPS ASLEEP SECURE OF HARME. 4 791
LIGHTS ON A HEAP OF NITROUS POWDER, LAID 4 815
FROM OFF THE FILES OF WARR; THERE THEY HIM LAID 6 339
A TRIPLE MOUNTED ROW OF PILLARS LAID 6 572
SOFT ON THE FLOURIE HERB I FOUND ME LAID 8 254
LAID ON OUR NECKS. REMEMBER WITH WHAT MILD 10 1046
CHOICEST AND BEST; THEN SACRIFICING, LAID 11 438
A LAZAR-HOUSE IT SEEMD, WHEREIN WERE LAID 11 479
CONTRIV'D, AND OF PROVISIONS LAID IN LARGE 11 732

LAIRE
AS FROM HIS LAIRE THE WILDE BEAST WHERE HE WONNS 7 457

LAKE
CHAIN'D ON THE BURNING LAKE, NOR EVER THENCE 1 210
WITH SOLID, AS THE LAKE WITH LIQUID FIRE; 1 229
GROVELING AND PROSTRATE ON YON LAKE OF FIRE, 1 280
SLUC'D FROM THE LAKE, A SECOND MULTITUDE 1 702
OF THAT FORGETFUL LAKE BENUMM NOT STILL, 2 74
CHAIN'D ON THE BURNING LAKE? THAT SURE WAS WORSE. 2 169
INTO THE BURNING LAKE THIR BALEFUL STREAMS; 2 576
WAFTED BY ANGELS, OR FLEW O'RE THE LAKE 3 521
DOWN THE SLOPE HILLS, DISPERST, OR IN A LAKE, 4 261
SMOOTH LAKE, THAT TO ME SEEMD ANOTHER SKIE. 4 459
FROM HILL OR STEAMING LAKE, DUSKIE OR GREY, 5 186
NEER THAT BITUMINOUS LAKE WHERE SODOM FLAM'D; 10 562
FROM STANDING LAKE TO TRIPPING EBBE, THAT STOLE 11 847

LAKES
ROCKS, CAVE, LAKES, FENS, BOGS, DENS, AND SHADES OF DEATH, 2 621
AND LAKES AND RUNNING STREAMS THE WATERS FILL; 7 397
OTHERS ON SILVER LAKES AND RIVERS BATH'D 7 437

LAMB
UNSUCKT OF LAMB OR KID, THAT TEND THIR PLAY. 9 583
OFT SACRIFICING BULLOCK, LAMB, OR KID, 12 20

LAMBS
TO GORGE THE FLESH OF LAMBS OR YEANLING KIDS 3 434
EWES AND THIR BLEATING LAMBS OVER THE PLAINE, 11 649

LAMENT
THE SYRIAN DAMSELS TO LAMENT HIS FATE 1 448
TORMENT, AND LOUD LAMENT, AND FURIOUS RAGE. 8 244
YET ALL HAD HEARD, WITH AUDIBLE LAMENT 11 266

LAMENT (CONTINUED)
- LAMENT NOT EVE, BUT PATIENTLY RESIGNE 11 287
- FARR LESS I NOW LAMENT FOR ONE WHOLE WORLD 11 874

LAMENTABLE
- VIEW'D FIRST THIR LAMENTABLE LOT, AND FOUND 2 617

LAMENTATION
- COCYTUS, NAM'D OF LAMENTATION LOUD 2 579

LAMENTED
- THUS ADAM TO HIMSELF LAMENTED LOUD 10 845

LAMENTING
- THEN WHO CREATED THEE LAMENTING LEARNE, 5 894
- LAMENTING TURND FULL SAD; O WHAT ARE THESE, 11 675

LAMP
- AND FEEL THY SOVRAN VITAL LAMP; BUT THOU 3 22
- DAYS, MONTHS, & YEARS, TOWARDS HIS ALL-CHEARING LAMP 3 581
- HIS CONSTANT LAMP, AND WAVES HIS PURPLE WINGS, 4 764
- FIRST IN HIS EAST THE GLORIOUS LAMP WAS SEEN, 7 370
- ON HIS HILL TOP, TO LIGHT THE BRIDAL LAMP. 8 520

LAMPS
- OF STARRY LAMPS AND BLAZING CRESSETS FED 1 728
- AND FROM WITHIN THE GOLDEN LAMPS THAT BURNE 5 713
- THAT SHINE, YET BEAR THIR BRIGHT OFFICIOUS LAMPS, 9 104
- SEAVEN LAMPS AS IN A ZODIAC REPRESENTING 12 255

LANCE
- TO MORTAL COMBAT OR CARREER WITH LANCE) 1 766

LAND
- THAT FELT UNUSUAL WEIGHT, TILL ON DRY LAND 1 227
- HE LIGHTS, IF IT WERE LAND THAT EVER BURN'D 1 228
- LIKE NIGHT, AND DARKEN'D ALL THE LAND OF NILE: 1 343
- OF DORIC LAND; OR WHO WITH SATURN OLD 1 519
- IN ANCIENT GREECE; AND IN AUSONIAN LAND 1 739
- OF WHIRLWIND AND DIRE HAIL, WHICH ON FIRM LAND 2 589
- NOR GOOD DRY LAND: NIGH FOUNDERD ON HE FARES, 2 940
- FIRM LAND IMBOSOM'D WITHOUT FIRMAMENT, 3 75
- SO ON THIS WINDIE SEA OF LAND, THE FIEND 3 440
- OVER THE PROMIS'D LAND TO GOD SO DEAR, 3 531
- TO BEERSABA, WHERE THE HOLY LAND 3 536
- THE GOODLY PROSPECT OF SOME FOREIN LAND 3 548
- O'RE SEA AND LAND: HIM SATAN THUS ACCOSTES; 3 653
- WHEN FIRST ON THIS DELIGHTFUL LAND HE SPREADS 4 643
- ON THIS DELIGHTFUL LAND, NOR HERB, FRUIT, FLOURE, 4 652
- BY MORROW EEVNING, AND FROM LAND TO LAND 4 662
- INTO ONE PLACE, AND LET DRY LAND APPEER. 7 284
- THE DRY LAND, EARTH, AND THE GREAT RECEPTACLE 7 307
- AND SEEMS A MOVING LAND, AND AT HIS GILLES 7 415
- AS PLANTS: AMBIGUOUS BETWEEN SEA AND LAND 7 473
- THIS EARTH? RECIPROCAL, IF LAND BE THERE, 8 144
- WHERE TO LIE HID; SEA HE HAD SEARCHT AND LAND 9 76
- AT DARIEN, THENCE TO THE LAND WHERE FLOWES 9 81
- NOW LAND, NOW SEA, AND SHORES WITH FORREST CROWND, 9 117
- LIKE CHANGE ON SEA AND LAND, SIDERAL BLAST, 10 693
- LAND, SEA, AND AIRE, AND EVERY KINDE THAT LIVES, 11 337
- HIS KINDRED AND FALSE GODS, INTO A LAND 12 122
- NOT KNOWING TO WHAT LAND, YET FIRM BELIEVES: 12 127
- WITH GOD, WHO CALL'D HIM, IN A LAND UNKNOWN. 12 134
- GIFT TO HIS PROGENIE OF ALL THAT LAND; 12 138
- FROM CANAAN, TO A LAND HEREAFTER CALL'D 12 156
- INTO THE SEA: TO SOJOURN IN THAT LAND 12 159
- WITH GLORY AND SPOILE BACK TO THIR PROMIS'D LAND. 12 172
- WITH LOATH'D INTRUSION, AND FILL ALL THE LAND; 12 178
- AS ON DRIE LAND BETWEEN TWO CHRISTAL WALLS, 12 197
- CONDUCTED BY HIS ANGEL TO THE LAND 12 259
- GOD, AS TO LEAVE THEM, AND EXPOSE THIR LAND, 12 339

LANDED
- FIRST LIGHTED FROM HIS WING, AND LANDED SAFE 10 316

LAND-MARK
- ITH' MIDST AN ALTAR AS THE LAND-MARK STOOD 11 432

LANDS
- OR IN VALDARNO, TO DESCRY NEW LANDS, 1 290
- THERE LANDS THE FIEND, A SPOT LIKE WHICH PERHAPS 3 588
- IMAGIND LANDS AND REGIONS IN THE MOON: 5 263
- FLYING, AND OVER LANDS WITH MUTUAL WING 7 429
- IN FORAIGN LANDS THIR MEMORIE BE LOST 12 46

LANGUAGE
- THIR LANGUAGE AND THIR WAYES, THEY ALSO KNOW, 8 373
- WHAT MAY THIS MEAN? LANGUAGE OF MAN PRONOUNC'T 9 553
- QUITE OUT THIR NATIVE LANGUAGE, AND INSTEAD 12 54

LANGUISH
- AND WITH DESIRE TO LANGUISH WITHOUT HOPE, 10 995

LANGUISHING
- BEFORE THE PRESENT OBJECT LANGUISHING 10 996

LANGUISHT
- ENLIGHTN'D, AND THIR LANGUISHT HOPE REVIV'D. 6 497

LANTSKIP
- SCOWLS ORE THE DARK'ND LANTSKIP SNOW, OR SHOWRE; 2 491
- THAT LANTSKIP: AND OF PURE NOW PURER AIRE 4 153
- DISCOVERING IN WIDE LANTSKIP ALL THE EAST 5 142

LAP
- OR PALMIE HILLOC, OR THE FLOURIE LAP 4 254
- AND HYACINTH, EARTHS FRESHEST SOFTEST LAP. 9 1041
- HERCULEAN SAMSON FROM THE HARLOT-LAP 9 1060
- AS IN MY MOTHERS LAP? THERE I SHOULD REST 10 778
- INTO THY MOTHERS LAP, OR BE WITH EASE 11 536

LAPLAND
- WITH LAPLAND WITCHES, WHILE THE LABOURING MOON 2 665

LAPSE
- AND LIQUID LAPSE OF MURMURING STREAMS; BY THESE, 8 263
- SINCE THY ORIGINAL LAPSE, TRUE LIBERTIE 12 83

LAPSED
- HIS LAPSED POWERS, THOUGH FORFEIT AND ENTHRALL'D 3 176

LAPST
- WHOM THEY TRIUMPH'D ONCE LAPST. THUS WERE THEY PLAGU'D 10 572

LARBORD
- OR WHEN ULYSSES ON THE LARBORD SHUNND 2 1019

LARGE
- PRONE ON THE FLOOD, EXTENDED LONG AND LARGE 1 195
- LEFT HIM AT LARGE TO HIS OWN DARK DESIGNS, 1 213
- ETHEREAL TEMPER, MASSY, LARGE AND ROUND, 1 285
- BY THAT UXORIOUS KING, WHOSE HEART THOUGH LARGE, 1 444
- REDUC'D THIR SHAPES IMMENSE, AND WERE AT LARGE, 1 790
- HERE WALK'D THE FIEND AT LARGE IN SPACIOUS FIELD. 3 430
- INTO A LIMBO LARGE AND BROAD, SINCE CALLD 3 495
- OVER MOUNT SION, AND, THOUGH THAT WERE LARGE, 3 530
- WHICH TO OUR GENERAL SIRE GAVE PROSPECT LARGE 4 144
- SOUTHWARD THROUGH EDEN WENT A RIVER LARGE, 4 223
- HIS FAIR LARGE FRONT AND EYE SUBLIME DECLAR'D 4 300
- FREE LEAVE SO LARGE TO ALL THINGS ELSE, AND CHOICE 4 434
- FOR US TOO LARGE, WHERE THY ABUNDANCE WANTS 4 730
- OUR GIVERS THIR OWN GIFTS, AND LARGE BESTOW 5 317
- FROM LARGE BESTOWD, WHERE NATURE MULTIPLIES 5 318
- SHE GATHERS, TRIBUTE LARGE, AND ON THE BOARD 5 343
- AND WE HAVE YET LARGE DAY, FOR SCARCE THE SUN 5 558
- AND LEFT LARGE FIELD, UNSAFE WITHIN THE WIND 6 309
- OF FUTURE, IN SMALL ROOM LARGE HEART ENCLOS'D, 7 486
- AN EDIFICE TOO LARGE FOR HIM TO FILL, 8 104
- THAT NOT TO KNOW AT LARGE OF THINGS REMOTE 8 191
- FIND PASTIME, AND BEARE RULE; THY REALM IS LARGE. 8 375
- WINGS GROWING, AND DOMINION GIV'N ME LARGE 10 244
- (ERELONG TO SWIM AT LARGE) AND LAUGH; FOR WHICH 11 626
- CONTRIV'D, AND OF PROVISIONS LAID IN LARGE 11 732
- WITH LARGE WINE-OFFERINGS POUR'D, AND SACRED FEAST, 12 21
- ACCEPTANCE OF LARGE GRACE, FROM SERVIL FEAR 12 305

LARGELY
- HYSTORIAN, WHO THUS LARGELY HAST ALLAYD 8 7
- TOOK LARGELY, OF THIR MUTUAL GUILT THE SEALE, 9 1043
- GAZ'D HOT, AND OF THE FRESH WAVE LARGELY DREW, 11 845

LARGER
- NOW DRAGON GROWN, LARGER THEN WHOM THE SUN 10 529

LASCIVIOUS
- BEGAN TO CAST LASCIVIOUS EYES, SHE HIM 9 1014

LAST
- SAY, MUSE, THIR NAMES THEN KNOWN, WHO FIRST, WHO LAST, 1 376
- BELIAL CAME LAST, THEN WHOM A SPIRIT MORE LEWD 1 490
- THIR NUMBER LAST HE SUMMS. AND NOW HIS HEART 1 571
- TEARS SUCH AS ANGELS WEEP, BURST FORTH: AT LAST 1 620
- IN HEIGHTH OR DEPTH, STILL FIRST AND LAST WILL REIGN 2 324
- THE WEIGHT OF ALL AND OUR LAST HOPE RELIES. 2 416
- ALONE THE DREADFUL VOYAGE; TILL AT LAST 2 426
- FARR OFF THE FLYING FIEND: AT LAST APPEER 2 643
- AT LAST THIS ODIOUS OFFSPRING WHOM THOU SEEST 2 781
- THE STEDFAST EARTH. AT LAST HIS SAIL-BROAD VANNES 2 927
- BUT NOW AT LAST THE SACRED INFLUENCE 2 1034
- BUT MERCY FIRST AND LAST SHALL BRIGHTEST SHINE. 3 134
- DEATH LAST, AND WITH HIS CARCASS GLUT THE GRAVE: 3 259
- THOUGH LAST CREATED, THAT FOR HIM I SPARE 3 278
- AND LONG HE WANDERD, TILL AT LAST A GLEAME 3 499
- ALL NIGHT; AT LAST BY BREAK OF CHEARFUL DAWNE 3 545
- O THEN AT LAST RELENT: IS THERE NO PLACE 4 79
- HEAV'NS LAST BEST GIFT, MY EVER NEW DELIGHT, 5 19
- OF OUR LAST EEVNINGS TALK, IN THIS THY DREAM, 5 115
- HIM FIRST, HIM LAST, HIM MIDST, AND WITHOUT END. 5 165
- FAIREST OF STARRS, LAST IN THE TRAIN OF NIGHT, 5 166
- MORE AERIE, LAST THE BRIGHT CONSUMMATE FLOURE 5 481
- YOUR BODIES MAY AT LAST TURN ALL TO SPIRIT, 5 497

LAST (CONTINUED)
AND PERFET WHILE THEY STOOD; HOW LAST UNFOULD 5 568
TENFOLD THE LENGTH OF THIS TERRENE: AT LAST 6 78
WHENCE IN PERPETUAL FIGHT THEY NEEDS MUST LAST 6 693
IN UNIVERSAL RUIN LAST, AND NOW 6 797
INCUMBERD HIM WITH RUIN: HELL AT LAST 6 874
AND BUSH WITH FRIZL'D HAIR IMPLICIT: LAST 7 323
THE SIXT, AND OF CREATION LAST AROSE 7 449
SMOOTH SLIDING WITHOUT STEP, LAST LED ME UP 8 302
AS HIGH HE SOARD, OBNOXIOUS FIRST OR LAST 9 170
PERSISTED, YET SUBMISS, THOUGH LAST, REPLI'D. 9 377
CHIEFLY BY WHAT THY OWN LAST REASONING WORDS 9 379
O FAIREST OF CREATION, LAST AND BEST 9 896
EVEN SHAME, THE LAST OF EVILS; OF THE FIRST 9 1079
NOR ALTER'D HIS OFFENCE; YET GOD AT LAST 10 171
WHOM HE SHALL TREAD AT LAST UNDER OUR FEET; 10 190
ON ADAM LAST THUS JUDGEMENT HE PRONOUNC'D. 10 197
AT LAST AS FROM A CLOUD HIS FULGENT HEAD 10 449
AND SEASON HIM THY LAST AND SWEETEST PREY. 10 609
BOTH SIN, AND DEATH, AND YAWNING GRAVE AT LAST 10 635
BOTH IN ME, AND WITHOUT ME, AND SO LAST 10 812
BUT TO MY OWN CONVICTION: FIRST AND LAST 10 831
WITH SPIRITS MASCULINE, CREATE AT LAST 10 890
BY DEATH AT LAST, AND MISERABLE IT IS 10 981
THAT AFTER WRETCHED LIFE MUST BE AT LAST 10 985
MY EARLY VISITATION, AND MY LAST 11 275
TO WEIGH THY SPIRITS DOWN, AND LAST CONSUME 11 545
NOT HID, NOR THOSE THINGS LAST WHICH MIGHT PRESERVE 11 579
IN FACTIOUS OPPOSITION, TILL AT LAST 11 664
THIR ORDER: LAST THE SIRE, AND HIS THREE SONS 11 736
BY TH' ANGEL, ON THY FEET THOU STOODST AT LAST, 11 759
FAMIN AND ANGUISH WILL AT LAST CONSUME 11 778
TO WHOM THUS MICHAEL. THOSE WHOM LAST THOU SAWST 11 787
AT THIS LAST SIGHT, ASSUR'D THAT MAN SHALL LIVE 11 872
STILL TEND FROM BAD TO WORSE, TILL GOD AT LAST 12 106
LAST WITH ONE MIDNIGHT STROKE ALL THE FIRST-BORN 12 189
THE LAST, FOR OF HIS REIGN SHALL BE NO END. 12 330
UPON THE TEMPLE IT SELF: AT LAST THEY SEISE 12 356
LAST IN THE CLOUDS FROM HEAV'N TO BE REVEALD 12 545
HE ENDED; AND THUS ADAM LAST REPLY'D. 12 552
TO WHOM THUS ALSO TH' ANGEL LAST REPLI'D: 12 574

LASTING
BOTH OF LOST HAPPINESS AND LASTING PAIN 1 55
BUILT THIR FOND HOPES OF GLORIE OR LASTING FAME, 3 449
OF PARADISE, DEARE BOUGHT WITH LASTING WOES. 10 742

LASTLY
FREELY PUT OFF, AND FOR HIM LASTLY DYE 3 240
HIM FIRST MAKE SURE YOUR THRALL, AND LASTLY KILL. 10 402
THEE LASTLY NUPTIAL BOWRE, BY MEE ADORND 11 280

LATE
WHO FROM THE TERROUR OF THIS ARM SO LATE 1 113
TO US IS ADVERSE. WHO BUT FELT OF LATE 2 77
THAT MIGHTY LEADING ANGEL, WHO OF LATE 2 991
THY CREATURE LATE SO LOV'D, THY YOUNGEST SON 3 151
ILL MATCHING WORDS AND DEEDS LONG PAST OR LATE. 5 113
LATE FALLN HIMSELF FROM HEAV'N, IS PLOTTING NOW 5 240
OF YESTERDAY, SO LATE HATH PAST THE LIPS 5 675
FROM ALL: MY SECT THOU SEEST, NOW LEARN TOO LATE 6 147
THROUGH ALL ETERNITIE SO LATE TO BUILD 7 92
PLEAS'D ME LONG CHOOSING, AND BEGINNING LATE; 9 26
THAT NAME, UNLESS AN AGE TOO LATE, OR COLD 9 44
WHEN SATAN WHO LATE FLED BEFORE THE THREATS 9 53
DISJOYNE US, AND I THEN TOO LATE RENOUNCE 9 884
REMARKABLY SO LATE OF THY SO TRUE, 9 982
TO THAT FIRST NAKED GLORIE. SUCH OF LATE 9 1115
TO TAURIS OR CASBEEN. SO THESE THE LATE 10 436
OF THIS NEW GLORIOUS WORLD, AND MEE SO LATE 10 721
THY JUSTICE SEEMS; YET TO SAY TRUTH, TOO LATE, 10 755
WITH OTHER ECHO LATE I TAUGHT YOUR SHADES 10 861
BY PARENTS, OR HIS HAPPIEST CHOICE TOO LATE 10 904
TOWARDS HER, HIS LIFE SO LATE AND SOLE DELIGHT, 10 941
THE AIR ATTRITE TO FIRE, AS LATE THE CLOUDS 10 1073
AS HOW WITH PECCANT ANGELS LATE THEY SAW; 11 70
WHERE CATTLE PASTUR'D LATE, NOW SCATTERD LIES 11 653
WHERE LUXURIE LATE REIGN'D, SEA-MONSTERS WHELP'D 11 751
AND STABL'D; OF MANKIND, SO NUMEROUS LATE, 11 752
THOUGH LATE REPENTING HIM OF MAN DEPRAV'D, 11 886
PURSUING WHOM HE LATE DISMISSD, THE SEA 12 195
OF PARADISE, SO LATE THIR HAPPIE SEAT, 12 642

LATELY
POSSESSES LATELY, THITHER TO ARRIVE 2 979
NOW LATELY HEAVEN AND EARTH, ANOTHER WORLD 2 1004
FORETOLD SO LATELY WHAT WOULD COME TO PASS, 10 38
OF HIM SO LATELY PROMIS'D TO THY AID 12 542

LATER
GODS, YET CONFEST LATER THEN HEAV'N AND EARTH 1 509
SOONER OR LATER; WHICH TH' ALMIGHTIE SEEING, 10 613

LATERAL
EURUS AND ZEPHIR WITH THIR LATERAL NOISE, 10 705

LATEST
GODS LATEST IMAGE: I DESCRIB'D HIS WAY 4 567

LATEST (CONTINUED)
MY FAIREST, MY ESPOUS'D, MY LATEST FOUND, 5 18

LATTER
THE LATTER: FOR WHAT PLACE CAN BE FOR US 2 235
THE LATTER QUICK UP FLEW, AND KICKT THE BEAM; 4 1004
IS OFTEST YOURS, THE LATTER MOST IS OURS, 5 489
THE LATTER I DEMURRE, FOR IN THIR LOOKS 9 558
THUS WILL THIS LATTER, AS THE FORMER WORLD, 12 105

LAUGH
I LAUGH, WHEN THOSE WHO AT THE SPEAR ARE BOLD 2 204
THAT LAUGH, AS IF TRANSPORTED WITH SOME FIT 10 626
(ERELONG TO SWIM AT LARGE) AND LAUGH; FOR WHICH 11 626

LAUGHS
FOR HIM WHO SITS ABOVE AND LAUGHS THE WHILE 2 731

LAUGH'ST
LAUGH'ST AT THIR VAIN DESIGNES AND TUMULTS VAIN, 5 737

LAUGHTER
AND TO THIR FOES A LAUGHTER; FOR IN VIEW 6 603
HIS LAUGHTER AT THIR QUAINT OPINIONS WIDE 8 78
OFFENDED, WORTH YOUR LAUGHTER, HATH GIV'N UP 10 488
AS MOCKT THEY STORM; GREAT LAUGHTER WAS IN HEAV'N 12 59

LAUREL
LAUREL AND MIRTLE, AND WHAT HIGHER GREW 4 694

LAVINIA
OF TURNUS FOR LAVINIA DISESPOUS'D, 9 17

LAW
OUR STRENGTH IS EQUAL, NOR THE LAW UNJUST 2 200
GOD IS THY LAW, THOU MINE: TO KNOW NO MORE 4 637
HAILE WEDDED LOVE, MYSTERIOUS LAW, TRUE SOURCE 4 750
LAW AND EDICT ON US, WHO WITHOUT LAW 5 798
SHALT THOU GIVE LAW TO GOD, SHALT THOU DISPUTE 5 822
BY FORCE, WHO REASON FOR THIR LAW REFUSE, 6 41
RIGHT REASON FOR THIR LAW, AND FOR THIR KING 6 42
LAW TO OUR SELVES, OUR REASON IS OUR LAW. 9 654
OF GOD OR DEATH, OF LAW OR PENALTIE? 9 775
CONVICT BY FLIGHT, AND REBEL TO ALL LAW 10 83
HIS SENTENCE BEYOND DUST AND NATURES LAW, 10 805
THE LAW I GAVE TO NATURE HIM FORBIDS; 11 49
PROCEEDED, AND OPPRESSION, AND SWORD-LAW 11 672
CONCORD AND LAW OF NATURE FROM THE EARTH, 12 29
AND THEREFORE WAS LAW GIVEN THEM TO EVINCE 12 287
SIN AGAINST LAW TO FIGHT; THAT WHEN THEY SEE 12 289
LAW CAN DISCOVER SIN, BUT NOT REMOVE, 12 290
OF CONSCIENCE, WHICH THE LAW BY CEREMONIES 12 297
SO LAW APPEARS IMPERFET, AND BUT GIV'N 12 300
TO FILIAL, WORKS OF LAW TO WORKS OF FAITH. 12 306
OF LAW, HIS PEOPLE INTO CANAAN LEAD; 12 309
OBEDIENCE TO THE LAW OF GOD, IMPOS'D 12 397
THE LAW OF GOD EXACT HE SHALL FULFILL 12 402
ALONE FULFILL THE LAW; THY PUNISHMENT 12 404
THE LAW THAT IS AGAINST THEE, AND THE SINS 12 416
HIS SPIRIT WITHIN THEM, AND THE LAW OF FAITH 12 488

LAWES
ORDAINE THEM LAWES; PART SUCH AS APPERTAINE 12 230
SPIRITUAL LAWES BY CARNAL POWER SHALL FORCE 12 521

LAWFUL
NOT LAWFUL TO REVEAL? YET FOR THY GOOD 5 570
BEAR WITH ME THEN, IF LAWFUL WHAT I ASK; 8 614

LAWLESS
BUT FIRST THE LAWLESS TYRANT, WHO DENIES 12 173

LAWNS
BETWIXT THEM LAWNS, OR LEVEL DOWNS, AND FLOCKS 4 252

LAWS
MEE THOUGH JUST RIGHT, AND THE FIXT LAWS OF HEAV'N 2 18
STRICT LAWS IMPOS'D, TO CELEBRATE HIS THRONE 2 241
THY SLEEP DISSENT? NEW LAWS THOU SEEST IMPOS'D; 5 679
NEW LAWS FROM HIM WHO REIGNS, NEW MINDS MAY RAISE 5 680
INTENDS TO PASS TRIUMPHANT, AND GIVE LAWS. 5 693
FLATLY UNJUST, TO BINDE WITH LAWS THE FREE, 5 819
HIS LAWS OUR LAWS, ALL HONOUR TO HIM DONE 5 844
OF GODS MESSIAH; THOSE INDULGENT LAWS 5 883
NEW LAWS TO BE OBSERV'D; FOR I DESCRIE 11 228
THROUGH THE TWELVE TRIBES, TO RULE BY LAWS ORDAIND: 12 226
OF GREAT MESSIAH SHALL SING. THUS LAWS AND RITES 12 244
SO MANY AND SO VARIOUS LAWS ARE GIV'N; 12 282
SO MANY LAWS ARGUE SO MANY SINS 12 283
FROM IMPOSITION OF STRICT LAWS, TO FREE 12 304
ON EVERY CONSCIENCE; LAWS WHICH NONE SHALL FINDE 12 522

LAXE
MEAN WHILE INHABIT LAXE, YE POWERS OF HEAV'N, 7 162

LAY
LAY VANQUISHT, ROWLING IN THE FIERY GULFE 1 52
LAY FLOATING MANY A ROOD, IN BULK AS HUGE 1 196

LAY (CONTINUED)
SO STRETCHT OUT HUGE IN LENGTH THE ARCH-FIEND LAY 1 209
HIS LEGIONS, ANGEL FORMS, WHO LAY INTRANS'T 1 301
ABJECT AND LOST LAY THESE, COVERING THE FLOOD, 1 312
A REFUGE FROM THOSE WOUNDS: OR WHEN WE LAY 2 168
THEN THOU THY REGAL SCEPTER SHALT LAY BY, 3 339
LAY WAVING ROUND; ON SOM GREAT CHARGE IMPLOY'D 3 628
LAY PLEASANT, HIS GRIEVD LOOK HE FIXES SAD, 4 28
AS ONELY IN HIS ARM THE MOMENT LAY 6 239
CHARIOT AND CHARIOTER LAY OVERTURND 6 390
THOUGH SLEEPING, WHERE I LAY, AND SAW THE SHAPE 8 463
OF GROVE OR GARDEN-PLOT MORE PLEASANT LAY, 9 418
THAT LAY IN WAIT; BEYOND THIS HAD BIN FORCE, 9 1173
EDEN AND ALL THE COAST IN PROSPECT LAY. 10 89
INSENSIBLE, HOW GLAD WOULD LAY ME DOWN 10 777
OUTSTRETCHT HE LAY, ON THE COLD GROUND, AND OFT 10 851
STRETCHT OUT TO THE AMPLEST REACH OF PROSPECT LAY. 11 380
LIFE OFFER'D, OR SOON BEG TO LAY IT DOWN, 11 506
LAY SEIGE, ENCAMPT; BY BATTERIE, SCALE, AND MINE, 11 656
LAY SLEEPING RAN BEFORE, BUT FOUND HER WAK'T; 12 608

LAYES
LAYES FORTH HER PURPLE GRAPE, AND GENTLY CREEPS 4 259
CEAS'D WARBLING, BUT ALL NIGHT TUN'D HER SOFT LAYES: 7 436

LAZAR-HOUSE
A LAZAR-HOUSE IT SEEMD, WHEREIN WERE LAID 11 479

LEAD
SHALL LEAD HELL CAPTIVE MAUGRE HELL, AND SHOW 3 255
WHICH WOULD BUT LEAD ME TO A WORSE RELAPSE 4 100
A CHANCE BUT CHANCE MAY LEAD WHERE I MAY MEET 4 530
TO VISIT THEE; LEAD ON THEN WHERE THY BOWRE 5 375
OF ALL THOSE MYRIADS WHICH WE LEAD THE CHIEF; 5 684
GABRIEL, LEAD FORTH TO BATTEL THESE MY SONS 6 46
INVINCIBLE, LEAD FORTH MY ARMED SAINTS 6 47
WHO ART TO LEAD THY OFSPRING, AND SUPPOSEST 8 86
LEAD THEN, SAID EVE. HEE LEADING SWIFTLY ROWLD 9 631
OR TRANSMIGRATION, AS THIR LOT SHALL LEAD. 10 261
SUCCESSFUL BEYOND HOPE, TO LEAD YE FORTH 10 463
AND REASONINGS, THOUGH THROUGH MAZES, LEAD ME STILL 10 830
PROSPEROUS OR ADVERSE: SO SHALT THOU LEAD 11 364
OF DEATH, AND MANY ARE THE WAYES THAT LEAD 11 468
SHALL LEAD THIR LIVES, AND MULTIPLIE APACE, 12 17
OF LAW, HIS PEOPLE INTO CANAAN LEAD; 12 309
WEARIED I FELL ASLEEP: BUT NOW LEAD ON; 12 614

LEADE
DETERRD NOT FROM ATCHIEVING WHAT MIGHT LEADE 9 696

LEADER
THUS ANSWER'D. LEADER OF THOSE ARMIES BRIGHT, 1 272
DID FIRST CREATE YOUR LEADER, NEXT FREE CHOICE, 2 19
A FAITHFUL LEADER, NOT TO HAZARD ALL 4 933
ARGUES NO LEADER BUT A LYAR TRAC'T, 4 949
A LEGION; LED IN FIGHT, YET LEADER SEEMD 6 232
DELIVERER FROM NEW LORDS, LEADER TO FREE 6 451
LEADER, THE TERMS WE SENT WERE TERMS OF WEIGHT, 6 621

LEADERS
THE HEADS AND LEADERS THITHER HAST WHERE STOOD 1 357
UNDER THIR GOD-LIKE LEADERS, IN THE CAUSE 6 67

LEADING
THAT MIGHTY LEADING ANGEL, WHO OF LATE 2 991
LEAD THEN, SAID EVE. HEE LEADING SWIFTLY ROWLD 9 631
THE WAY, THOU LEADING, SUCH A SENT I DRAW 10 267

LEADS
AND HARD, THAT OUT OF HELL LEADS UP TO LIGHT; 2 433
LEADS HIM PERPLEXT, WHERE HE MAY LIKELIEST FIND 2 525
WHAT READIEST PATH LEADS WHERE YOUR GLOOMIE BOUNDS 2 976
THE GREAT WORK-MAISTER, LEADS TO NO EXCESS 3 696
LEADS UP TO HEAV'N, IS BOTH THE WAY AND GUIDE; 8 613
LEADS THEE, OR WHERE MOST NEEDS, WHETHER TO WIND 9 215
LEADS THEE, I SHALL NOT LAG BEHINDE, NOR ERRE 10 266
UNTRAIND IN ARMES, WHERE RASHNESS LEADS NOT ON. 12 222

LEAD'ST
THOU LEAD'ST ME, AND TO THE HAND OF HEAV'N SUBMIT, 11 372

LEAF
OF FIRM AND FRAGRANT LEAF; ON EITHER SIDE 4 695
IMPEARLS ON EVERY LEAF AND EVERY FLOUER. 5 747
THEN HERBS OF EVERY LEAF, THAT SUDDEN FLOUR'D 7 317

LEAFE
AN OLIVE LEAFE HE BRINGS, PACIFIC SIGNE: 11 860

LEAGU'D
BEFITS THEE WITH HIM LEAGU'D, THY SELF AS FALSE 10 868

LEAGUE
MYRIADS THOUGH BRIGHT: IF HE WHOM MUTUAL LEAGUE, 1 87
FROM HEAV'NS HIGH JURISDICTION, IN NEW LEAGUE 2 319
UPLIFTED SPURNS THE GROUND, THENCE MANY A LEAGUE 2 929

LEAGUE (CONTINUED)
WELL PLEAS'D THEY SLACK THIR COURSE, AND MANY A LEAGUE 4 164
FAIR COUPLE, LINKT IN HAPPIE NUPTIAL LEAGUE, 4 339
THOUGH I UNPITTIED: LEAGUE WITH YOU I SEEK, 4 375
OF RAVENOUS FOWL, THOUGH MANY A LEAGUE REMOTE, 10 274
MANY A DARK LEAGUE, REDUC'T IN CAREFUL WATCH 10 438

LEAGUES
BLOWS THEM TRANSVERSE TEN THOUSAND LEAGUES AWRY 3 488

LEAND
AND MEEK SURRENDER, HALF IMBRACING LEAND 4 494

LEANING
LEANING HALF-RAIS'D, WITH LOOKS OF CORDIAL LOVE 5 12

LEAP'D
A GOD, LEAP'D FONDLY INTO AETNA FLAMES, 3 470
PLATO'S ELYSIUM, LEAP'D INTO THE SEA, 3 472
AT ONE SLIGHT BOUND HIGH OVER LEAP'D ALL BOUND 4 181

LEAPS
LEAPS O'RE THE FENCE WITH EASE INTO THE FOULD: 4 187

LEARN
LEARN HOW THIR GREATEST MONUMENTS OF FAME, 1 695
THITHER LET US BEND ALL OUR THOUGHTS, TO LEARN 2 354
RETIRE, OR TASTE THY FOLLY, AND LEARN BY PROOF, 2 686
TO MARK WHAT OF THIR STATE HE MORE MIGHT LEARN 4 400
FROM ALL: MY SECT THOU SEEST, NOW LEARN TOO LATE 6 147
THERE LET THEM LEARN, AS LIKES THEM, TO DESPISE 6 717
WITH SINFULNESS OF MEN; THEREBY TO LEARN 11 360

LEARN'D
TO TEACH ALL NATIONS WHAT OF HIM THEY LEARN'D 12 440

LEARND
SOON LEARND, NOW MILDER, AND THUS ANSWERD SMOOTH. 2 816
DISDAIN'D, BUT MEANER THOUGHTS LEARND IN THIR FLIGHT, 6 367

LEARNE
THEN WHO CREATED THEE LAMENTING LEARNE, 5 894
WHEREIN TO READ HIS WONDROUS WORKS, AND LEARNE 8 68
TILL WARN'D, OR BY EXPERIENCE TAUGHT, SHE LEARNE, 8 190
OUR RUIN, BOTH BY THEE INFORMD I LEARNE, 9 275
HENCEFORTH I LEARNE, THAT TO OBEY IS BEST, 12 561

LEARNT
WHAT FURTHER WOULD BE LEARNT. LIVE WHILE YE MAY, 4 533
DOCTRIN WHICH WE WOULD KNOW WHENCE LEARNT: WHO SAW 5 856
THIS HAVING LEARNT, THOU HAST ATTAIND THE SUMME 12 575

LEAST
WHOM THUNDER HATH MADE GREATER? HERE AT LEAST 1 258
MAMMON, THE LEAST ERECTED SPIRIT THAT FELL 1 679
THUS FARR AT LEAST RECOVER'D, HATH MUCH MORE 2 22
YET EVER PLOTTING HOW THE CONQUEROR LEAST 2 338
MAY REAP HIS CONQUEST, AND MAY LEAST REJOYCE 2 339
PRUDENT, LEAST FROM HIS RESOLUTION RAIS'D 2 468
LOOSE ALL HER VIRTUE; LEAST BAD MEN SHOULD BOAST 2 483
LEAST WITH A WHIP OF SCORPIONS I PURSUE 2 701
LEAST HEAV'N SURCHARG'D WITH POTENT MULTITUDE 2 836
SO WITHOUT LEAST IMPULSE OR SHADOW OF FATE, 3 120
TO ME ARE ALL MY WORKS, NOR MAN THE LEAST 3 277
EVIL BE THOU MY GOOD; BY THEE AT LEAST 4 110
AMONG OUR OTHER TORMENTS NOT THE LEAST, 4 510
LEAST TOTAL DARKNESS SHOULD BY NIGHT REGAINE 4 665
AT LEAST DISTEMPERD, DISCONTENTED THOUGHTS, 4 807
WILL SAVE US TRIAL WHAT THE LEAST CAN DOE 4 855
LEAST ON THE THRESHING FLOORE HIS HOPEFUL SHEAVES 4 984
AT LEAST HAD GON TO RACK, DISTURBD AND TORNE 4 994
LEAST WILFULLY TRANSGRESSING HE PRETEND 5 244
EXPECTED, LEAST OF ALL FROM THEE, INGRATE 5 811
THESE WICKED TENTS DEVOTED, LEAST THE WRAUTH 5 890
(UNANSWERD LEAST THOU BOAST) TO LET THEE KNOW; 6 163
ON EITHER SIDE, THE LEAST OF WHOM COULD WEILD 6 221
THOU CANST NOT. HAST THOU TURND THE LEAST OF THESE 6 284
LEAST FROM THIS FLYING STEED UNREIN'D, (AS ONCE 7 17
TO THOSE APOSTATES, LEAST THE LIKE BEFALL 7 44
AT LEAST OUR ENVIOUS FOE HATH FAIL'D, WHO THOUGHT 7 139
BUT LEAST HIS HEART EXALT HIM IN THE HARME 7 150
OF CHAOS FARR REMOV'D, LEAST FIERCE EXTREAMES 7 272
AND GOVERN WELL THY APPETITE, LEAST SIN 7 546
HER END WITHOUT LEAST MOTION, AND RECEAVES, 8 35
LEAST HEE INCENST AT SUCH ERUPTION BOLD, 8 235
WORS THEN CAN MAN WITH BEAST, AND LEAST OF ALL. 8 397
MORE THEN ENOUGH; AT LEAST ON HER BESTOW'D 8 537
THY MATE, WHO SEES WHEN THOU ART SEEN LEAST WISE. 8 578
HIS GREAT COMMAND; TAKE HEED LEAST PASSION SWAY 8 635
MORE ANGELS TO CREATE, IF THEY AT LEAST 9 146
BUT OTHER DOUBT POSSESSES ME, LEAST HARM 9 251
FOR HEE WHO TEMPTS, THOUGH IN VAIN, AT LEAST ASPERSES 9 296
LEAST BY SOME FAIRE APPEERING GOOD SURPRIS'D 9 354
TOUCHD ONELY, THAT OUR TRIAL, WHEN LEAST SOUGHT, 9 380
THEREOF, NOR SHALL YE TOUCH IT, LEAST YE DIE. 9 663

LEAST (CONTINUED)
LEAST THOU NOT TASTING, DIFFERENT DEGREE 9 883
US TO ABOLISH, LEAST THE ADVERSARY 9 947
LEAST ON MY HEAD BOTH SIN AND PUNISHMENT, 10 133
BUT LEAST THE DIFFICULTIE OF PASSING BACK 10 252
PURSUES ME STILL, LEAST ALL I CANNOT DIE, 10 783
LEAST THAT PURE BREATH OF LIFE, THE SPIRIT OF MAN 10 784
HENCEFORTH; LEAST THAT TOO HEAV'NLY FORM, PRETENDED 10 872
TO BE FORESTALL'D; MUCH MORE I FEAR LEAST DEATH 10 1024
MY LABOUR WILL SUSTAIN ME; AND LEAST COLD 10 1056
BEFORE THEE RECONCIL'D, AT LEAST HIS DAYS 11 39
SELF-LEFT. LEAST THEREFORE HIS NOW BOLDER HAND 11 93
AND LIVE FOR EVER, DREAM AT LEAST TO LIVE 11 95
THY CHOICE OF FLAMING WARRIOURS, LEAST THE FIEND 11 101
PERPETUAL BANISHMENT. YET LEAST THEY FAINT 11 108
LEAST PARADISE A RECEPTACLE PROVE 11 123
LEAST IT AGAIN DISSOLVE AND SHOWR THE EARTH? 11 883
AND GET THEMSELVES A NAME, LEAST FAR DISPERST 12 45
LEAST ENTRING ON THE CANAANITE ALLARMD 12 217

LEASURE
WEIGHS HIS SPREAD WINGS, AT LEASURE TO BEHOLD 2 1046
HAD LEASURE, WONDRING AT HIMSELF NOW MORE; 10 510

LEAVE
IN BILLOWS, LEAVE I' TH' MIDST A HORRID VALE. 1 224
AND LEAVE A SINGED BOTTOM ALL INVOLV'D 1 236
BY FORCE IMPOSSIBLE, BY LEAVE OBTAIN'D 2 250
THAT BE ASSUR'D, WITHOUT LEAVE ASKT OF THEE: 2 685
ACCOUNT MEE MAN; I FOR HIS SAKE WILL LEAVE 3 238
THOU WILT NOT LEAVE ME IN THE LOATHSOM GRAVE 3 247
TOOK LEAVE, AND TOWARD THE COAST OF EARTH BENEATH, 3 739
FREE LEAVE SO LARGE TO ALL THINGS ELSE, AND CHOICE 4 434
THIS GARDEN, AND NO CORNER LEAVE UNSPI'D; 4 529
SEARCH THROUGH THIS GARDEN, LEAVE UNSEARCHT NO NOOK, 4 789
MAY COME AND GO, SO UNAPPROV'D, AND LEAVE 5 118
WITH ALL HIS LEGIONS TO DISLODGE, AND LEAVE 5 669
LEAVE THEM TO GOD ABOVE, HIM SERVE AND FEARE; 8 168
NOT THAT THEY DURST WITHOUT HIS LEAVE ATTEMPT, 8 237
SO ORDERING. I WITH LEAVE OF SPEECH IMPLOR'D, 8 377
OR THIS, OR WORSE, LEAVE NOT THE FAITHFUL SIDE 9 265
WISDOM WITHOUT THEIR LEAVE? AND WHEREIN LIES 9 725
MADE THEE WITHOUT THY LEAVE, WHAT IF THY SON 10 760
THAT I MUST LEAVE YE, SONS; O WERE I ABLE 10 819
TO WASTE IT ALL MY SELF, AND LEAVE YE NONE. 10 820
LEAVE COLD THE NIGHT, HOW WE HIS GATHER'D BEAMS 10 1070
MUST I THUS LEAVE THEE PARADISE? THUS LEAVE 11 269
SHALL LEAVE THEM TO ENJOY; FOR TH' EARTH SHALL BEAR 11 804
TO LEAVE THEM TO THIR OWN POLLUTED WAYES; 12 110
MUST EAT, AND ON THE GROUND LEAVE NOTHING GREEN; 12 186
GOD, AS TO LEAVE THEM, AND EXPOSE THIR LAND, 12 339
RETURND FROM BABYLON BY LEAVE OF KINGS 12 348
STILL FOLLOW'D HIM; TO THEM SHALL LEAVE IN CHARGE 12 439
THROUGH ALL HIS REALME, AND THERE CONFOUNDED LEAVE; 12 455
TO LEAVE THIS PARADISE, BUT SHALT POSSESS 12 586

LEAVES
THICK AS AUTUMNAL LEAVES THAT STROW THE BROOKS 1 302
THE TREMBLING LEAVES, WHILE UNIVERSAL PAN 4 266
PURE, AND COMMANDS TO SOM, LEAVES FREE TO ALL. 4 747
OF LEAVES AND FUMING RILLS, AURORA'S FAN, 5 6
HIS BARREN LEAVES. THEM THUS IMPLOID BEHELD 5 219
SPRINGS LIGHTER THE GREEN STALK, FROM THENCE THE LEAVES 5 480
OF RUSLING LEAVES, BUT MINDED NOT, AS US'D 9 519
SERPENT, THY OVERPRAISING LEAVES IN DOUBT 9 615
AS LEAVES A GREATER STORE OF FRUIT UNTOUCHT, 9 621
WHICH LEAVES US NAKED THUS, OF HONOUR VOID, 9 1074
SOME TREE WHOSE BROAD SMOOTH LEAVES TOGETHER SOWD, 9 1095
AT LOOPHOLES CUT THROUGH THICKEST SHADE: THOSE LEAVES 9 1110
OF TURKISH CRESCENT, LEAVES ALL WASTE BEYOND 10 434
HE LEAVES HIS GODS, HIS FRIENDS, AND NATIVE SOILE 12 129
A SON, AND OF HIS SON A GRAND-CHILDE LEAVES, 12 153
OF PHARAO: THERE HE DIES, AND LEAVES HIS RACE 12 163

LEAVING
AND FISH WITH FISH; TO GRAZE THE HERB ALL LEAVING, 10 711

LEBANON
WHOSE ANNUAL WOUND IN LEBANON ALLUR'D 1 447

LED
THAT LED TH' IMBATTELLD SERAPHIM TO WARR 1 129
OF SOLOMON HE LED BY FRAUD TO BUILD 1 401
EZEKIEL SAW, WHEN BY THE VISION LED 1 455
OR CAST A RAMPART. MAMMON LED THEM ON, 1 678
THE MORE IT SEEMS EXCESS, THAT LED THEE HITHER 3 698
LED ON TH' ETERNAL SPRING. NOT THAT FAIRE FIELD 4 268
BUT FOLLOW STRAIT, INVISIBLY THUS LED? 4 476
WITH LIVING SAPHIRS: HESPERUS THAT LED 4 605
SO SAYING, ON HE LED HIS RADIANT FILES, 4 797
FRUITLESS IMBRACES: OR THEY LED THE VINE 5 215
OF HORSES LED, AND GROOMS BESMEARD WITH GOLD 5 356
THEY LED HIM HIGH APPLAUDED, AND PRESENT 6 26
A LEGION; LED IN FIGHT, YET LEADER SEEMD 6 232
WITH THY CELESTIAL SONG. UP LED BY THEE 7 12

LED (CONTINUED)
LED ON, YET SINLESS, WITH DESIRE TO KNOW 7 61
THAT OPEN'D WIDE HER BLAZING PORTALS, LED 7 575
WITH SUPPLE JOINTS, AND LIVELY VIGOUR LED: 8 269
SMOOTH SLIDING WITHOUT STEP, LAST LED ME UP 8 302
LED BY HER HEAV'NLY MAKER, THOUGH UNSEEN, 8 485
I LED HER BLUSHING LIKE THE MORN: ALL HEAV'N, 8 511
THOUGHTS, WHITHER HAVE YE LED ME, WITH WHAT SWEET 9 473
LED EVE OUR CREDULOUS MOTHER, TO THE TREE 9 644
HE LED HER NOTHING LOATH; FLOURS WERE THE COUCH, 9 1039
CAPTIVITY LED CAPTIVE THROUGH THE AIRE, 10 188
IN SIGHT, TO EACH OF THESE THREE PLACES LED. 10 324
LED THEM DIRECT, AND DOWN THE CLIFF AS FAST 12 639

LEE
MOORS BY HIS SIDE UNDER THE LEE, WHILE NIGHT 1 207

LEER
FOR ENVIE, YET WITH JEALOUS LEER MALIGNE 4 503

LEFT
HAVE LEFT US THIS OUR SPIRIT AND STRENGTH INTIRE 1 146
LEFT HIM AT LARGE TO HIS OWN DARK DESIGNS, 1 213
THIR LIVING STRENGTH, AND UNFREQUENTED LEFT 1 433
THE UTMOST BORDER OF HIS KINGDOM, LEFT 2 361
HE SCOURS THE RIGHT HAND COAST, SOM TIMES THE LEFT, 2 633
THREW FORTH, TILL ON THE LEFT SIDE OP'NING WIDE, 2 755
THAT LITTLE WHICH IS LEFT SO TO DEFEND, 2 1000
TO EXPIATE HIS TREASON HATH NAUGHT LEFT, 3 207
LEFT FOR REPENTANCE, NONE FOR PARDON LEFT? 4 80
NONE LEFT BUT BY SUBMISSION; AND THAT WORD 4 81
THE ONLY SIGN OF OUR OBEDIENCE LEFT 4 428
BY SHORTER FLIGHT TO TH' EAST, HAD LEFT HIM THERE 4 595
HAPPINESS IN HIS POWER LEFT FREE TO WILL, 5 235
LEFT TO HIS OWN FREE WILL, HIS WILL THOUGH FREE, 5 236
HE LEFT IT IN THY POWER, ORDAIND THY WILL 5 526
WITH SPEED WHAT FORCE IS LEFT, AND ALL IMPLOY 5 730
IN OUR DEFENCE, LEFT UNAWARES WE LOSE 5 731
'TWIXT HOST AND HOST BUT NARROW SPACE WAS LEFT, 6 104
AND LEFT LARGE FIELD, UNSAFE WITHIN THE WIND 6 309
LEFT THEM SUPERIOUR, WHILE WE CAN PRESERVE 6 443
VANGUARD, TO RIGHT AND LEFT THE FRONT UNFOULD; 6 558
HAD ENDED; WHEN TO RIGHT AND LEFT THE FRONT 6 569
FOR TO THEMSELVES I LEFT THEM, AND THOU KNOWST, 6 689
AND OF THIR WONTED VIGOUR LEFT THEM DRAIND, 6 851
ANOUGH IS LEFT BESIDES TO SEARCH AND KNOW. 7 125
SO CHARMING LEFT HIS VOICE, THAT HE A WHILE 8 2
HATH LEFT TO THIR DISPUTES, PERHAPS TO MOVE 8 77
MINE EYES HE CLOS'D, BUT OP'N LEFT THE CELL 8 460
WHO STOOPING OP'ND MY LEFT SIDE, AND TOOK 8 465
SHEE DISAPPEERD, AND LEFT ME DARK, I WAK'D 8 478
OR NATURE FAILD IN MEE, AND LEFT SOME PART 8 534
TH' ANGELIC NAME, AND THINNER LEFT THE THRONG 9 142
LEFT SO IMPERFET BY THE MAKER WISE, 9 338
NOTHING IMPERFET OR DEFICIENT LEFT 9 345
BUT GOD LEFT FREE THE WILL, FOR WHAT OBEYES 9 351
GOD SO COMMANDED, AND LEFT THAT COMMAND 9 652
ENCUMBERD, NOW HAD LEFT THEM, UP THEY ROSE 9 1051
AND HONOUR FROM ABOUT THEM, NAKED LEFT 9 1057
AND LEFT TO HER SELF, IF EVIL THENCE ENSUE, 9 1185
HIS FREE WILL, TO HER OWN INCLINING LEFT 10 46
AND OF THIS WORLD, AND ON THE LEFT HAND HELL 10 322
APPOINTED TO SIT THERE, HAD LEFT THIR CHARGE, 10 421
HEAV'N-BANISHT HOST, LEFT DESERT UTMOST HELL 10 437
WAS LEFT HIM, OR FALSE GLITTER: ALL AMAZ'D 10 452
WHERE ALL YET LEFT OF THAT REVOLTED ROUT 10 534
SELF-LEFT. LEAST THEREFORE HIS NOW BOLDER HAND 11 93
IN THIR BRIGHT STAND, THERE LEFT HIS POWERS TO SEISE 11 221
RECESS, AND ONELY CONSOLATION LEFT 11 304
ALL LEFT, IN ONE SMALL BOTTOM SWUM IMBARK'T, 11 753
AND HEAR THE DIN; THUS WAS THE BUILDING LEFT 12 61
RESERVING, HUMAN LEFT FROM HUMAN FREE. 12 71
LEFT IN CONFUSION, BABYLON THENCE CALL'D. 12 343
HIS FAITHFUL, LEFT AMONG TH' UNFAITHFUL HERD, 12 481
THIR DOCTRINE AND THIR STORY WRITTEN LEFT, 12 506
LEFT ONELY IN THOSE WRITTEN RECORDS PURE, 12 513
LEFT THEM INROULD, OR WHAT THE SPIRIT WITHIN 12 523

LEGAL
TO SAVE THEM, NOT THIR OWN, THOUGH LEGAL WORKS. 12 410

LEGGS
HIS ARMES CLUNG TO HIS RIBS, HIS LEGGS ENTWINING 10 512

LEGION
AS EACH DIVIDED LEGION MIGHT HAVE SEEMD 6 230
A LEGION; LED IN FIGHT, YET LEADER SEEMD 6 232
SQUAR'D IN FULL LEGION (SUCH COMMAND WE HAD) 8 232

LEGIONS
HIS LEGIONS, ANGEL FORMS, WHO LAY INTRANS'T 1 301
THAT ALL THESE PUISSANT LEGIONS, WHOSE EXILE 1 632
ENCAMP THIR LEGIONS, OR WITH OBSCURE WING 2 132
TILL THICKEST LEGIONS CLOSE; WITH FEATS OF ARMS 2 537
TO THAT SIDE HEAV'N FROM WHENCE YOUR LEGIONS FELL: 2 1006
WHAT THOU AND THY GAY LEGIONS DARE AGAINST; 4 942
WITH ALL HIS LEGIONS TO DISLODGE, AND LEAVE 5 669

LEGIONS (CONTINUED)
IN SILENCE THIR BRIGHT LEGIONS, TO THE SOUND 6 64
THY LEGIONS UNDER DARKNESS; BUT THOU SEEST 6 142
THE ADVERSE LEGIONS, NOR LESS HIDEOUS JOYN'D 6 206
CAME SHADOWING, AND OPPREST WHOLE LEGIONS ARM'D, 6 655
FELL WITH HIS FLAMING LEGIONS THROUGH THE DEEP 7 134
THERE KEPT THIR WATCH THE LEGIONS, WHILE THE GRAND 10 427

LEMNOS
ON LEMNOS TH' AEGAEAN ILE: THUS THEY RELATE, 1 746

LEND
TO OTHER SPEEDIE AIDE MIGHT LEND AT NEED; 9 260
SUCH WONDROUS POWER GOD TO HIS SAINT WILL LEND, 12 200

LENGTH
SO STRETCHT OUT HUGE IN LENGTH THE ARCH-FIEND LAY 1 209
OF DREADFUL LENGTH AND DAZLING ARMS, IN GUISE 1 564
AT LENGTH FROM US MAY FIND, WHO OVERCOMES 1 648
OR CHANG'D AT LENGTH, AND TO THE PLACE CONFORMD 2 217
OUR TORMENTS ALSO MAY IN LENGTH OF TIME 2 274
THAT FIRES THE LENGTH OF OPHIUCUS HUGE 2 709
WITHOUT DIMENSION, WHERE LENGTH, BREADTH, & HIGHTH, 2 893
AT LENGTH A UNIVERSAL HUBBUB WILDE 2 951
TAMELY ENDUR'D A BRIDGE OF WONDROUS LENGTH 2 1028
SCARCE THUS AT LENGTH FAILD SPEECH RECOVERD SAD. 4 357
RISING IN CLOUDED MAJESTIE, AT LENGTH 4 607
AT LENGTH INTO THE LIMITS OF THE NORTH 5 755
TENFOLD THE LENGTH OF THIS TERRENE: AT LAST 6 78
OF HIDEOUS LENGTH: BEFORE THE CLOUDIE VAN, 6 107
OF FIGHTING SERAPHIM CONFUS'D, AT LENGTH 6 249
RAGE PROMPTED THEM AT LENGTH, AND FOUND THEM ARMS 6 635
WEENING TO PROSPER, AND AT LENGTH PREVAILE 6 795
THEY OPEN TO THEMSELVES AT LENGTH THE WAY 7 158
WONDROUS IN LENGTH AND CORPULENCE INVOLV'D 7 483
DOWNWARD AS FARR ANTARTIC; AND IN LENGTH 9 79
HIS GENTLE DUMB EXPRESSION TURND AT LENGTH 9 527
THOUGH AT THE VOICE MUCH MARVELING; AT LENGTH 9 551
SATED AT LENGTH, ERE LONG I MIGHT PERCEAVE 9 598
AND KNEW NOT EATING DEATH: SATIATE AT LENGTH, 9 792
SPEECHLESS HE STOOD AND PALE, TILL THUS AT LENGTH 9 894
AT LENGTH GAVE UTTERANCE TO THESE WORDS CONSTRAIND. 9 1066
OF LENGTH PRODIGIOUS JOYNING TO THE WALL 10 302
AT LENGTH A REVEREND SIRE AMONG THEM CAME, 11 719
MEASUR'D BY CUBIT, LENGTH, AND BREADTH, AND HIGHTH, 11 730
WITH LENGTH OF HAPPY DAYES THE RACE OF MAN; 11 782
THE RIVER-DRAGON TAM'D AT LENGTH SUBMITS 12 191
SAVE WHEN THEY JOURNIE, AND AT LENGTH THEY COME, 12 258
WITH JOY THE TIDINGS BROUGHT FROM HEAV'N: AT LENGTH 12 504

LENGTH'ND
WHY AM I MOCKT WITH DEATH, AND LENGTH'ND OUT 10 774

LENT
HIS FLESH, HIS BONE; TO GIVE THEE BEING I LENT 4 483

LEO
BY LEO AND THE VIRGIN AND THE SCALES, 10 676

LEPER
A LEPER ONCE HE LOST AND GAIN'D A KING, 1 471

LESS
OF FORCE BELIEVE ALMIGHTY, SINCE NO LESS 1 144
AND WHAT I SHOULD BE, ALL BUT LESS THEN HE 1 257
LESS THEN ARCH ANGEL RUIND, AND TH' EXCESS 1 593
WHAT FORCE EFFECTED NOT: THAT HE NO LESS 1 647
NOW LESS THEN SMALLEST DWARFS, IN NARROW ROOM 1 779
EQUAL IN STRENGTH, AND RATHER THEN BE LESS 2 47
TO LESS THEN GODS. ON TH' OTHER SIDE UP ROSE 2 108
WROUGHT STILL WITHIN THEM; AND NO LESS DESIRE 2 295
TO BE CREATED LIKE TO US, THOUGH LESS 2 349
ALL CIRCUMSPECTION, AND WE NOW NO LESS 2 414
OR UNKNOWN REGION, WHAT REMAINS HIM LESS 2 443
ALONE TH' ANTAGONIST OF HEAV'N, NOR LESS 2 509
(WHAT COULD IT LESS WHEN SPIRITS IMMORTAL SING?) 2 553
WITHIN UNSEEN. FARR LESS ABHORRD THAN THESE 2 659
DESTIN'D TO THAT GOOD HOUR: NO LESS REJOYC'D 2 848
HE HAD TO CROSS. NOR WAS HIS EARE LESS PEAL'D 2 920
SOM CAPITAL CITY; OR LESS THEN IF THIS FRAME 2 924
WITH TUMULT LESS AND WITH LESS HOSTILE DIN, 2 1040
THAT SATAN WITH LESS TOIL, AND NOW WITH EASE 2 1041
WHICH HAD NO LESS PROV'D CERTAIN UNFOREKNOWN. 3 119
MUCH LESS THAT DURST UPON HIS OWN HEAD DRAW 3 220
LOVE NO WHERE TO BE FOUND LESS THEN DIVINE. 3 411
OF GLIMMERING AIR LESS VEXT WITH TEMPEST LOUD: 3 429
CIRCL'D HIS HEAD, NOR LESS HIS LOCKS BEHIND 3 626
WHAT COULD BE LESS THEN TO AFFORD HIM PRAISE, 4 46
UNDER A PLATAN, YET METHOUGHT LESS FAIRE, 4 478
LESS WINNING SOFT, LESS AMIABLIE MILDE, 4 479
DIURNAL, OR THIS LESS VOLUBIL EARTH 4 594
ROVE IDLE UNIMPLOID, AND LESS NEED REST; 4 617
OR LESS BE LOST. THY FEAR, SAID ZEPHON BOLD, 4 854
LESS PAIN, LESS TO BE FLED, OR THOU THEN THEY 4 919
LESS HARDIE TO ENDURE? COURAGEOUS CHIEF, 4 920
NOT THAT I LESS ENDURE, OR SHRINK FROM PAIN, 4 925
OF GALILEO, LESS ASSUR'D, OBSERVES 5 262
HIS EQUALS, IF IN POWER AND SPLENDOR LESS, 5 796

LESS (CONTINUED)
ERRE NOT, MUCH LESS FOR THIS TO BE OUR LORD, 5 799
TO MAKE US LESS, BENT RATHER TO EXALT 5 829
THROUGH THE INFINITE HOST, NOR LESS FOR THAT 5 874
OF WRAUTH AWAK'T: NOR WITH LESS DREAD THE LOUD 6 59
NOR MOTION OF SWIFT THOUGHT, LESS COULD HIS SHIELD 6 192
THE ADVERSE LEGIONS, NOR LESS HIDEOUS JOYN'D 6 206
TWO POTENT THRONES, THAT TO BE LESS THEN GODS 6 366
NOR OF RENOWN LESS EAGER, YET BY DOOME 6 378
OMNISCIENT THOUGHT. TRUE IS, LESS FIRMLY ARM'D, 6 430
NO LESS THEN FOR DELIVERANCE WHAT WE OWE. 6 468
THINK NOTHING HARD, MUCH LESS TO BE DESPAIRD. 6 495
NOR LESS ON EITHER SIDE TEMPESTUOUS FELL 6 844
WHAT MAY NO LESS PERHAPS AVAILE US KNOWN, 7 85
BUT KNOWLEDGE IS AS FOOD, AND NEEDS NO LESS 7 126
THE LESS BY NIGHT ALTERNE: AND MADE THE STARRS, 7 348
SHEDDING SWEET INFLUENCE: LESS BRIGHT THE MOON, 7 375
THAT BETTER MIGHT WITH FARR LESS COMPASS MOVE, 8 33
THE LESS NOT BRIGHT, NOR HEAV'N SUCH JOURNIES RUN, 8 88
NOR LESS THINK WEE IN HEAV'N OF THEE ON EARTH 8 224
PLEAS'D WITH THY WORDS NO LESS THEN THOU WITH MINE. 8 248
MUCH LESS CAN BIRD WITH BEAST, OR FISH WITH FOWLE 8 395
SECOND TO ME OR LIKE, EQUAL MUCH LESS. 8 407
ELABORATE, OF INWARD LESS EXACT. 8 539
IN OUTWARD ALSO HER RESEMBLING LESS 8 543
HIS IMAGE WHO MADE BOTH, AND LESS EXPRESSING 8 544
LESS EXCELLENT, AS THOU THY SELF PERCEAV'ST. 8 566
NOT LESS BUT MORE HEROIC THEN THE WRAUTH 9 14
NOR HOPE TO BE MY SELF LESS MISERABLE 9 126
LESS ATTRIBUTED TO HER FAITH SINCERE, 9 320
OF ALL THAT HE CREATED, MUCH LESS MAN, 9 346
MAY FINDE US BOTH PERHAPS FARR LESS PREPAR'D, 9 381
THOU CANST, WHO ART SOLE WONDER, MUCH LESS ARM 9 533
TILL ADAM, THOUGH NOT LESS THEN EVE ABASH'T, 9 1065
INCURR'D, WHAT COULD THEY LESS, THE PENALTIE, 10 15
OR COME I LESS CONSPICUOUS, OR WHAT CHANGE 10 107
HUGE PYTHON, AND HIS POWER NO LESS HE SEEM'D 10 531
AND TORMENT LESS THEN NONE OF WHAT WE DREAD, 10 998
FELT LESS REMORSE; THEY FORTHWITH TO THE PLACE 10 1098
NOT OF MEAN SUITERS, NOR IMPORTANT LESS 11 9
IN FABLES OLD, LESS ANCIENT YET THEN THESE, 11 11
LESS PURE, ACCUSTOMD TO IMMORTAL FRUITS? 11 285
ERCOCO AND THE LESS MARITIM KINGS 11 398
AND HEE THE FUTURE EVIL SHALL NO LESS 11 774
PEACE TO CORRUPT NO LESS THEN WARR TO WASTE. 11 784
FARR LESS I NOW LAMENT FOR ONE WHOLE WORLD 11 874

LESSEN
TO LESSEN THEE, AGAINST HIS PURPOSE SERVES 7 614

LESSER
ARE MANY LESSER FACULTIES THAT SERVE 5 101
WITH THOUSAND LESSER LIGHTS DIVIDUAL HOLDS, 7 382

LESS'N
MANS NATURE, LESS'N OR DEGRADE THINE OWNE. 3 304

LEST
NO FEAR LEST DINNER COOLE; WHEN THUS BEGAN 5 396
OF GESTURE OR LEST ACTION OVERAWD 9 460
THE FIRST AT LEST OF THESE I THOUGHT DENID 9 555
AND WANDRING VANITIE, WHEN LEST WAS SAFE, 10 875
HIS FULL WRAUTH WHOSE THOU FEELST AS YET LEST PART, 10 951

LET
LET US NOT SLIP TH' OCCASION, WHETHER SCORN, 1 178
CASTS PALE AND DREADFUL? THITHER LET US TEND 1 183
BUT WHEREFORE LET WE THEN OUR FAITHFUL FRIENDS, 1 264
AND DIG'D OUT RIBS OF GOLD. LET NONE ADMIRE 1 690
DESERVE THE PRECIOUS BANE. AND HERE LET THOSE 1 692
MORE UNEXPERT, I BOAST NOT: THEM LET THOSE 2 52
BY OUR DELAY? NO, LET US RATHER CHOOSE 2 60
LET SUCH BETHINK THEM, IF THE SLEEPY DRENCH 2 73
LET THIS BE GOOD, WHETHER OUR ANGRY FOE 2 152
WILL HE, SO WISE, LET LOOSE AT ONCE HIS IRE, 2 155
TO WHOM WE HATE. LET US NOT THEN PURSUE 2 249
THITHER LET US BEND ALL OUR THOUGHTS, TO LEARN 2 354
I OFFER, ON MEE LET THINE ANGER FALL; 3 237
WELL PLEAS'D, ON ME LET DEATH WRECK ALL HIS RAGE; 3 241
THE STAIRS WERE THEN LET DOWN, WHETHER TO DARE 3 523
EARTH, AIRE, AND SEA. THEN LET US NOT THINK HARD 4 432
BUT LET US EVER PRAISE HIM, AND EXTOLL 4 436
YET LET ME NOT FORGET WHAT I HAVE GAIN'D 4 512
HIS WILL WHO BOUND US? LET HIM SURER BARR 4 897
AND LET US TO OUR FRESH IMPLOYMENTS RISE 5 125
BUT SILENTLY A GENTLE TEAR LET FALL 5 130
AND NOURISH ALL THINGS, LET YOUR CEASLESS CHANGE 5 183
BUT BY DECEIT AND LIES; THIS LET HIM KNOW, 5 243
IN ADAM, NOT TO LET TH' OCCASION PASS 5 453
LET US ADVISE, AND TO THIS HAZARD DRAW 5 729
AND EQUAL OVER EQUALS TO LET REIGNE, 5 820
(UNANSWERD LEAST THOU BOAST) TO LET THEE KNOW; 6 163
REIGN THOU IN HELL THY KINGDOM, LET MEE SERVE 6 183
NAMELESS IN DARK OBLIVION LET THEM DWELL. 6 380
SAD RESOLUTION AND SECURE; LET EACH 6 541
AND TO DISORDER'D RAGE LET LOOSE THE REINES, 6 696
THERE LET THEM LEARN, AS LIKES THEM, TO DESPISE 6 717
THY WEAKER; LET IT PROFIT THEE TO HAVE HEARD 6 909

LIFE (CONTINUED)

WHAT LIFE THE GODS LIVE THERE, AND SUCH LIVE THOU.	5	81
OF LIFE AMBROSIAL FRUTAGE BEAR, AND VINES	5	427
OF SUBSTANCE, AND IN THINGS THAT LIVE, OF LIFE;	5	474
TO INTELLECTUAL, GIVE BOTH LIFE AND SENSE,	5	485
BY LIVING STREAMS AMONG THE TREES OF LIFE,	5	652
SPARE OUT OF LIFE PERHAPS, AND NOT REPINE,	6	460
BUT LIVE CONTENT, WHICH IS THE CALMEST LIFE:	6	461
ADVERSE TO LIFE: THEN FOUNDED, THEN CONGLOB'D	7	239
THE BREATH OF LIFE; IN HIS OWN IMAGE HEE	7	526
TO INTERRUPT THE SWEET OF LIFE, FROM WHICH	8	184
THAT WHICH BEFORE US LIES IN DAILY LIFE,	8	193
FOR MAN TO TELL HOW HUMAN LIFE BEGAN	8	250
AMID THE GARDEN BY THE TREE OF LIFE,	8	326
ROSE UP A FOUNTAIN BY THE TREE OF LIFE;	9	73
OF CREATURES ANIMATE WITH GRADUAL LIFE	9	112
LOVE NOT THE LOWEST END OF HUMAN LIFE.	9	241
HOW SHOULD YE? BY THE FRUIT? IT GIVES YOU LIFE	9	686
AND LIFE MORE PERFET HAVE ATTAIND THEN FATE	9	689
TO HAPPIER LIFE, KNOWLEDGE OF GOOD AND EVIL;	9	697
I COULD ENDURE, WITHOUT HIM LIVE NO LIFE.	9	833
HIGHER DEGREE OF LIFE, INDUCEMENT STRONG	9	934
CONSORT WITH THEE, DEATH IS TO MEE AS LIFE;	9	954
FARR OTHERWISE TH' EVENT, NOT DEATH, BUT LIFE	9	984
MY OTHER SELF, THE PARTNER OF MY LIFE;	10	128
AND DUST SHALT EAT ALL THE DAYES OF THY LIFE.	10	178
SHALT EATE THEREOF ALL THE DAYS OF THY LIFE;	10	202
LEAST THAT PURE BREATH OF LIFE, THE SPIRIT OF MAN	10	784
OF LIFE THAT SINN'D; WHAT DIES BUT WHAT HAD LIFE	10	790
TO HUMANE LIFE, AND HOUSHOLD PEACE CONFOUND.	10	908
TOWARDS HER, HIS LIFE SO LATE AND SOLE DELIGHT,	10	941
THAT AFTER WRETCHED LIFE MUST BE AT LAST	10	985
EVE, THY CONTEMPT OF LIFE AND PLEASURE SEEMS	10	1013
FOR LOSS OF LIFE AND PLEASURE OVERLOV'D.	10	1019
TO PASS COMMODIOUSLY THIS LIFE, SUSTAIN'D	10	1083
TO BETTER LIFE SHALL YEELD HIM, WHERE WITH MEE	11	42
HIS FINAL REMEDIE, AND AFTER LIFE	11	62
BY FAITH AND FAITHFUL WORKS, TO SECOND LIFE,	11	64
BY THE WATERS OF LIFE, WHERE ERE THEY SATE	11	79
REACH ALSO OF THE TREE OF LIFE, AND EAT,	11	94
AND GUARD ALL PASSAGE TO THE TREE OF LIFE:	11	122
THE SOURSE OF LIFE; NEXT FAVOURABLE THOU,	11	169
SOME DAYS; HOW LONG, AND WHAT TILL THEN OUR LIFE,	11	198
TO LIFE PROLONGD AND PROMISD RACE, I NOW	11	331
SAFEST THY LIFE, AND BEST PREPAR'D ENDURE	11	365
AS ONCE THOU SLEPST, WHILE SHEE TO LIFE WAS FORMD.	11	369
AND FROM THE WELL OF LIFE THREE DROPS INSTILL'D.	11	416
THAT BEAT OUT LIFE; HE FELL, AND DEADLY PALE	11	446
BETTER END HEER UNBORN. WHY IS LIFE GIV'N	11	502
LIFE OFFER'D, OR SOON BEG TO LAY IT DOWN,	11	506
THE BALME OF LIFE. TO WHOM OUR ANCESTOR.	11	546
LIFE MUCH, BENT RATHER HOW I MAY BE QUIT	11	548
NOR LOVE THY LIFE, NOR HATE; BUT WHAT THOU LIVST	11	553
OF ARTS THAT POLISH LIFE, INVENTERS RARE,	11	610
THIR BOOTIE; SCARCE WITH LIFE THE SHEPHERDS FLYE,	11	650
SELECT FOR LIFE SHALL IN THE ARK BE LODG'D,	11	823
INGLORIOUS LIFE WITH SERVITUDE; FOR LIFE	12	220
TO A REPROACHFUL LIFE AND CURSED DEATH,	12	406
PROCLAIMING LIFE TO ALL WHO SHALL BELIEVE	12	407
BY HIS OWN NATION, SLAINE FOR BRINGING LIFE;	12	414
HIS DEATH FOR MAN, AS MANY AS OFFERD LIFE	12	425
IN SIN FOR EVER LOST FROM LIFE; THIS ACT	12	429
A GENTLE WAFTING TO IMMORTAL LIFE.	12	435
TO HIS DISCIPLES, MEN WHO IN HIS LIFE	12	438
OF WASHING THEM FROM GUILT OF SIN TO LIFE	12	443
AND TO THE FAITHFUL DEATH THE GATE OF LIFE;	12	571

LIFE-BLOOD

AND LIFE-BLOOD STREAMING FRESH; WIDE WAS THE WOUND,	8	467

LIFE-GIVING

OF THAT LIFE-GIVING PLANT, BUT ONLY US'D	4	199

LIFT

WITH HEAD UP-LIFT ABOVE THE WAVE, AND EYES	1	193
WILL ONCE MORE LIFT US UP, IN SPIGHT OF FATE,	2	393
OF HEAV'NS ASCENT THEY LIFT THIR FEET, WHEN LOE	3	486
DIVIDE THE NIGHT, AND LIFT OUR THOUGHTS TO HEAVEN.	4	688
LIKEN ON EARTH CONSPICUOUS, THAT MAY LIFT	6	299

LIFTED

AND WROUGHT BUT MALICE; LIFTED UP SO HIGH	4	49
SO SAYING, A NOBLE STROKE HE LIFTED HIGH,	6	189
CONSPICUOUS WITH THREE LIFTED COLOURS GAY,	11	866

LIFTING

UP LIFTING BORE THEM IN THIR HANDS: AMAZE,	6	646

LIGHT

NO LIGHT, BUT RATHER DARKNESS VISIBLE	1	63
AS FAR REMOV'D FROM GOD AND LIGHT OF HEAV'N	1	73
FROM HIM, WHO IN THE HAPPY REALMS OF LIGHT	1	85
THE SEAT OF DESOLATION, VOYD OF LIGHT,	1	181
FOR THAT CELESTIAL LIGHT? BE IT SO, SINCE HE	1	245
THIR COURSE, IN EVEN BALLANCE DOWN THEY LIGHT	1	349
AND WITH THIR DARKNESS DURST AFFRONT HIS LIGHT.	1	391
WITH NAPHTHA AND ASPHALTUS YEILDED LIGHT	1	729
HEAV'NS PUREST LIGHT, YET OUR GREAT ENEMY	2	137

LIGHT (CONTINUED)

THIS HORROR WILL GROW MILDE, THIS DARKNESS LIGHT,	2	220
AS HE OUR DARKNESS, CANNOT WE HIS LIGHT	2	269
DWELL NOT UNVISITED OF HEAV'NS FAIR LIGHT	2	398
AND HARD, THAT OUT OF HELL LEADS UP TO LIGHT;	2	433
TO THAT NEW WORLD OF LIGHT AND BLISS, AMONG	2	867
BORDERING ON LIGHT; WHEN STRAIT BEHOLD THE THRONE	2	959
LIES THROUGH YOUR SPACIOUS EMPIRE UP TO LIGHT,	2	974
OF LIGHT APPEARS, AND FROM THE WALLS OF HEAV'N	2	1035
WAFTS ON THE CALMER WAVE BY DUBIOUS LIGHT	2	1042
HAIL HOLY LIGHT, OFSPRING OF HEAV'N FIRST-BORN,	3	1
MAY I EXPRESS THEE UNBLAM'D? SINCE GOD IS LIGHT,	3	3
AND NEVER BUT IN UNAPPROACHED LIGHT	3	4
SO MUCH THE RATHER THOU CELESTIAL LIGHT	3	51
NOT FARR OFF HEAV'N, IN THE PRECINCTS OF LIGHT,	3	88
LIGHT AFTER LIGHT WELL US'D THEY SHALL ATTAIN,	3	196
FOUNTAIN OF LIGHT, THY SELF INVISIBLE	3	375
WITH SAILS AND WIND THIR CANIE WAGGONS LIGHT:	3	439
OF DAWNING LIGHT TURND THITHER-WARD IN HASTE	3	500
DISPENSES LIGHT FROM FARR; THEY AS THEY MOVE	3	579
WITH RADIANT LIGHT, AS GLOWING IRON WITH FIRE;	3	594
LIGHT SHON, AND ORDER FROM DISORDER SPRUNG:	3	713
WITH LIGHT FROM HENCE, THOUGH BUT REFLECTED, SHINES;	3	723
THAT PLACE IS EARTH THE SEAT OF MAN, THAT LIGHT	3	724
WITH BORROWD LIGHT HER COUNTENANCE TRIFORM	3	730
APPARENT QUEEN UNVAILD HER PEERLESS LIGHT,	4	608
WITH FIRST APPROACH OF LIGHT, WE MUST BE RIS'N,	4	624
OR GLITTERING STARR-LIGHT WITHOUT THEE IS SWEET.	4	656
MINISTRING LIGHT PREPAR'D, THEY SET AND RISE;	4	664
WHERE THOU ART WEIGH'D, AND SHOWN HOW LIGHT, HOW WEAK,	4	1012
WAS AERIE LIGHT FROM PURE DIGESTION BRED,	5	4
FULL ORB'D THE MOON, AND WITH MORE PLEASING LIGHT	5	42
SPEAK YEE WHO BEST CAN TELL, YE SONS OF LIGHT,	5	160
HIS PRAISE, WHO OUT OF DARKNESS CALL'D UP LIGHT.	5	179
DISPERSE IT, AS NOW LIGHT DISPELS THE DARK.	5	208
VAILD WITH HIS GORGEOUS WINGS, UPSPRINGING LIGHT	5	250
THE SUN THAT LIGHT IMPARTS TO ALL, RECEIVES	5	423
NO INCONVENIENT DIET, NOR TOO LIGHT FARE;	5	495
HEAR ALL YE ANGELS, PROGENIE OF LIGHT,	5	600
FROM THAT HIGH MOUNT OF GOD, WHENCE LIGHT & SHADE	5	643
NIGHTLY BEFORE HIM, SAW WITHOUT THIR LIGHT	5	714
UNBARR'D THE GATES OF LIGHT. THERE IS A CAVE	6	4
WHERE LIGHT AND DARKNESS IN PERPETUAL ROUND	6	6
LIGHT ISSUES FORTH, AND AT THE OTHER DORE	6	9
SO BEAUTEOUS, OP'NING TO THE AMBIENT LIGHT.	6	481
LIGHT AS THE LIGHTNING GLIMPS THEY RAN, THEY FLEW,	6	642
OUT OF SUCH PRISON, THOUGH SPIRITS OF PUREST LIGHT,	6	660
AND THE GREAT LIGHT OF DAY YET WANTS TO RUN	7	98
LET THER BE LIGHT, SAID GOD, AND FORTHWITH LIGHT	7	243
SOJOURN'D THE WHILE. GOD SAW THE LIGHT WAS GOOD;	7	249
AND LIGHT FROM DARKNESS BY THE HEMISPHERE	7	250
DIVIDED: LIGHT THE DAY, AND DARKNESS NIGHT	7	251
BY THE CELESTIAL QUIRES, WHEN ORIENT LIGHT	7	254
TO GIVE LIGHT ON THE EARTH; AND IT WAS SO.	7	345
AND LIGHT FROM DARKNESS TO DIVIDE. GOD SAW,	7	352
OF LIGHT BY FARR THE GREATER PART HE TOOK,	7	359
AND DRINK THE LIQUID LIGHT, FIRM TO RETAINE	7	362
HER GATHER'D BEAMS, GREAT PALACE NOW OF LIGHT.	7	363
REPAIRING, IN THIR GOLD'N URNS DRAW LIGHT,	7	365
HIS MIRROR, WITH FULL FACE BORROWING HER LIGHT	7	377
FROM HIM, FOR OTHER LIGHT SHE NEEDED NONE	7	378
DIURNAL) MEERLY TO OFFICIATE LIGHT	8	22
OF INCORPOREAL SPEED, HER WARMTH AND LIGHT;	8	37
STILL LUMINOUS BY HIS RAY. WHAT IF THAT LIGHT	8	140
COMMUNICATING MALE AND FEMAL LIGHT,	8	150
EACH ORB A GLIMPS OF LIGHT, CONVEYD SO FARR	8	156
LIGHT BACK TO THEM, IS OBVIOUS TO DISPUTE.	8	158
GLAD WE RETURN'D UP TO THE COASTS OF LIGHT	8	245
WHAT E'RE I SAW. THOU SUN, SAID I, FAIRE LIGHT,	8	273
THIS HAPPIE LIGHT, WHEN ANSWER NONE RETURN'D,	8	285
ON HIS HILL TOP, TO LIGHT THE BRIDAL LAMP.	8	520
LIGHT ABOVE LIGHT, FOR THEE ALONE, AS SEEMS,	9	105
LET IT; I RECK NOT, SO IT LIGHT WELL AIM'D,	9	173
NOW WHEN AS SACRED LIGHT BEGAN TO DAWNE	9	192
OR DARING, FIRST ON MEE TH' ASSAULT SHALL LIGHT.	9	305
SOFT SHE WITHDREW, AND LIKE A WOOD-NYMPH LIGHT	9	386
HOVERING AND BLAZING WITH DELUSIVE LIGHT,	9	639
TO STARR OR SUN-LIGHT, SPREAD THIR UMBRAGE BROAD	9	1087
WHOEVER JUDG'D, THE WORST ON MEE MUST LIGHT,	10	73
ON MEE AS ON THIR NATURAL CENTER LIGHT	10	740
THE SENTENCE FROM THY HEAD REMOV'D MAY LIGHT	10	934
IN FELLOWSHIPS OF JOY: THE SONS OF LIGHT	11	80
TO RESALUTE THE WORLD WITH SACRED LIGHT	11	134
DARKNESS ERE DAYES MID-COURSE, AND MORNING LIGHT	11	204
THEY LIGHT THE NUPTIAL TORCH, AND BID INVOKE	11	590
THE BURD'N OF MANY AGES, ON ME LIGHT	11	767
ONE MAN EXCEPT, THE ONELY SON OF LIGHT	11	808
GREEN TREE OR GROUND WHEREON HIS FOOT MAY LIGHT;	11	858
SHALL LONG USURP; ERE THE THIRD DAWNING LIGHT	12	421
OUT OF HIS GRAVE, FRESH AS THE DAWNING LIGHT,	12	423
LIGHT OUT OF DARKNESS. FULL OF DOUBT I STAND.	12	473

LIGHT-ARM'D

LIGHT-ARM'D OR HEAVY, SHARP, SMOOTH, SWIFT OR SLOW,	2	902

LIGHT-ARMED
LOOKD ROUND, AND SCOUTS EACH COAST LIGHT-ARMED SCOURE, 6 529

LIGHTED
WHERE HE FIRST LIGHTED, SOON DISCERND HIS LOOKS 4 570
THEN LIGHTED FROM HIS GORGEOUS THRONE, FOR NOW 6 103
FIRST LIGHTED FROM HIS WING, AND LANDED SAFE 10 316
DOWN FROM A SKIE OF JASPER LIGHTED NOW 11 209

LIGHTER
THIR LIGHTER WINGS. TO WHOM THESE MOST ADHERE, 2 906
SPRINGS LIGHTER THE GREEN STALK, FROM THENCE THE LEAVES 5 480

LIGHTEST
OR TOUCH WITH LIGHTEST MOMENT OF IMPULSE 10 45

LIGHTLY
TOUCH'D LIGHTLY; FOR NO FALSHOOD CAN ENDURE 4 811
LIGHTLY DISPERS'D, AND THE SHRILL MATIN SONG 5 7

LIGHT'N
IN OFFICES OF LOVE, HOW WE MAY LIGHT'N 10 960

LIGHT'NING
LIGHT'NING DIVINE, INEFFABLE, SERENE, 5 734

LIGHTNING
WING'D WITH RED LIGHTNING AND IMPETUOUS RAGE, 1 175
INFERNAL THUNDER, AND FOR LIGHTNING SEE 2 66
LIGHT AS THE LIGHTNING GLIMPS THEY RAN, THEY FLEW, 6 642
GLAR'D LIGHTNING, AND SHOT FORTH PERNICIOUS FIRE 6 849
SAW SATAN FALL LIKE LIGHTNING DOWN FROM HEAV'N, 10 184
TINE THE SLANT LIGHTNING, WHOSE THWART FLAME DRIV'N DOWN 10 1075
IN THUNDER LIGHTNING AND LOUD TRUMPETS SOUND 12 229

LIGHTS
HE LIGHTS, IF IT WERE LAND THAT EVER BURN'D 1 228
BUT IN HIS WAY LIGHTS ON THE BARREN PLAINES 3 437
NOR STAID, TILL ON NIPHATES TOP HE LIGHTS. 3 742
LIGHTS ON HIS FEET. AS WHEN A PROWLING WOLFE, 4 183
HERE LOVE HIS GOLDEN SHAFTS IMPLOIES, HERE LIGHTS 4 763
LIGHTS ON A HEAP OF NITROUS POWDER, LAID 4 815
HE LIGHTS, AND TO HIS PROPER SHAPE RETURNS 5 276
AGAIN TH' ALMIGHTIE SPAKE: LET THERE BE LIGHTS 7 339
AND LET THEM BE FOR LIGHTS AS I ORDAINE 7 343
AND GOD MADE TWO GREAT LIGHTS, GREAT FOR THIR USE 7 346
WITH THOUSAND LESSER LIGHTS DIVIDUAL HOLDS, 7 382
OF ALL CORRUPTION, ALL THE BLAME LIGHTS DUE; 10 833

LIK'D
FAST CAUGHT, THEY LIK'D, AND EACH HIS LIKING CHOSE; 11 587

LIKE
DOVE-LIKE SATST BROODING ON THE VAST ABYSS 1 21
HUNG ON HIS SHOULDERS LIKE THE MOON, WHOSE ORB 1 287
OVER THE BURNING MARLE, NOT LIKE THOSE STEPS 1 296
LIKE NIGHT, AND DARKEN'D ALL THE LAND OF NILE: 1 343
A MULTITUDE, LIKE WHICH THE POPULOUS NORTH 1 351
CAME LIKE A DELUGE ON THE SOUTH, AND SPREAD 1 354
LIKE CUMBROUS FLESH; BUT IN WHAT SHAPE THEY CHOOSE 1 428
INFECTED SIONS DAUGHTERS WITH LIKE HEAT, 1 453
HIS OWN AND RHEA'S SON LIKE MEASURE FOUND; 1 513
LIKE DOUBTFUL HUE: BUT HE HIS WONTED PRIDE 1 527
SHON LIKE A METEOR STREAMING TO THE WIND 1 537
STOOD LIKE A TOWR; HIS FORM HAD YET NOT LOST 1 591
AS STOOD LIKE THESE, COULD EVER KNOW REPULSE? 1 630
ROSE LIKE AN EXHALATION, WITH THE SOUND 1 711
BUILT LIKE A TEMPLE, WHERE PILASTERS ROUND 1 713
DROPT FROM THE ZENITH LIKE A FALLING STAR, 1 745
(THOUGH LIKE A COVER'D FIELD, WHERE CHAMPIONS BOLD 1 763
THRONG NUMBERLESS, LIKE THAT PIGMEAN RACE 1 780
AND IN THIR OWN DIMENSIONS LIKE THEMSELVES 1 793
TO BE CREATED LIKE TO US, THOUGH LESS 2 349
SYNOD OF GODS, AND LIKE TO WHAT YE ARE, 2 391
AND GOD-LIKE IMITATED STATE; HIM ROUND 2 511
UNTERRIFI'D, AND LIKE A COMET BURN'D, 2 708
FOR NEVER BUT ONCE MORE WAS EITHER LIKE 2 721
SO WIDE THEY STOOD, AND LIKE A FURNACE MOUTH 2 888
SPRINGS UPWARD LIKE A PYRAMID OF FIRE 2 1013
AND LIKE A WEATHER-BEATEN VESSEL HOLDS 2 1043
GOD-LIKE FRUITION, QUITTED ALL TO SAVE 3 307
PAVEMENT THAT LIKE A SEA OF JASPER SHON 3 363
LIKE QUIVERS HUNG, AND WITH PRAEAMBLE SWEET 3 367
DRAWN ROUND ABOUT THEE LIKE A RADIANT SHRINE, 3 379
UP HITHER LIKE AEREAL VAPOURS FLEW 3 445
LIKE THOSE HESPERIAN GARDENS FAM'D OF OLD, 3 568
THERE LANDS THE FIEND, A SPOT LIKE WHICH PERHAPS 3 588
NOT ALL PARTS LIKE, BUT ALL ALIKE INFORMD 3 593
THAT STONE, OR LIKE TO THAT WHICH HERE BELOW 3 600
LIKE HONOUR TO OBTAIN, AND AS HIS EYE 3 660
AND LIKE A DEVILLISH ENGINE BACK RECOILES 4 17
LOOK'ST FROM THY SOLE DOMINION LIKE THE GOD 4 33
SAT LIKE A CORMORANT; YET NOT TRUE LIFE 4 196
LIKE THIS FAIR PARADISE, YOUR SENSE, YET SUCH 4 379
NOT LIKE THESE NARROW LIMITS, TO RECEIVE 4 384

LIKE (CONTINUED)
LIKE CONSORT TO THY SELF CANST NO WHERE FIND. 4 448
MULTITUDES LIKE THY SELF, AND THENCE BE CALL'D 4 474
MIND US OF LIKE REPOSE, SINCE GOD HATH SET 4 612
ENDOWD WITH ALL THIR GIFTS, AND O TOO LIKE 4 715
SQUAT LIKE A TOAD, CLOSE AT THE EARE OF EVE; 4 800
LIKE GENTLE BREATHS FROM RIVERS PURE, THENCE RAISE 4 806
WHY SATST THOU LIKE AN ENEMIE IN WAITE 4 825
YOUR MESSAGE, LIKE TO END AS MUCH IN VAIN? 4 833
BUT LIKE A PROUD STEED REIND, WENT HAUTIE ON, 4 858
LIKE TENERIFF OR ATLAS UNREMOV'D: 4 987
ONE SHAPD AND WING'D LIKE ONE OF THOSE FROM HEAV'N 5 55
AFFECTS ME EQUALLY; NOR CAN I LIKE 5 97
THE FALL OF OTHERS FROM LIKE STATE OF BLISS; 5 241
GIRT LIKE A STARRIE ZONE HIS WASTE, AND ROUND 5 281
SKIE-TINCTUR'D GRAIN. LIKE MAIA'S SON HE STOOD, 5 285
HIS GOD-LIKE GUEST, WALKS FORTH, WITHOUT MORE TRAIN 5 351
THEY CAME, THAT LIKE POMONA'S ARBOUR SMIL'D 5 378
EACH TO OTHER LIKE, MORE THEN ON EARTH IS THOUGHT? 5 576
GRATEFUL VICISSITUDE, LIKE DAY AND NIGHT; 6 8
UNDER THIR GOD-LIKE LEADERS, IN THE CAUSE 6 67
MEAN WHILE IN OTHER PARTS LIKE DEEDS DESERVD 6 354
OUR SELVES WITH LIKE DEFENCE, TO ME DESERVES 6 467
LIKE INSTRUMENT TO PLAGUE THE SONS OF MEN 6 505
STAND READIE TO RECEIVE THEM, IF THEY LIKE 6 561
ON WHEELS (FOR LIKE TO PILLARS MOST THEY SEEM'D 6 573
TO WHOM THUS BELIAL IN LIKE GAMESOM MOOD, 6 620
THE REST IN IMITATION TO LIKE ARMES 6 662
THY TEMPRING; WITH LIKE SAFETIE GUIDED DOWN 7 15
TO THOSE APOSTATES, LEAST THE LIKE BEFALL 7 44
ALL LIKE HIMSELF REBELLIOUS, BY WHOSE AID 7 140
LIKE THINGS TO LIKE, THE REST TO SEVERAL PLACE 7 240
SEEMD LIKE TO HEAV'N, A SEAT WHERE GODS MIGHT DWELL, 7 329
STRETCHT LIKE A PROMONTORIE SLEEPS OR SWIMMES, 7 414
WITH GODDESS-LIKE DEMEANOUR FORTH SHE WENT; 8 59
SECOND TO ME OR LIKE, EQUAL MUCH LESS. 8 407
BY CONVERSATION WITH HIS LIKE TO HELP, 8 418
LIKE OF HIS LIKE, HIS IMAGE MULTIPLI'D, 8 424
I LED HER BLUSHING LIKE THE MORN: ALL HEAV'N, 8 511
LOOSES DISCOUNT'NANC'T, AND LIKE FOLLY SHEWES; 8 553
O EARTH, HOW LIKE TO HEAV'N, IF NOT PREFERR'D 9 99
LIKE A BLACK MIST LOW CREEPING, HE HELD ON 9 180
WHY SHOULDST NOT THOU LIKE SENSE WITHIN THEE FEEL 9 315
SINGLE WITH LIKE DEFENCE, WHEREVER MET, 9 325
SOFT SHE WITHDREW, AND LIKE A WOOD-NYMPH LIGHT 9 386
IN GATE SURPASS'D AND GODDESS-LIKE DEPORT, 9 389
ALL OTHER BEASTS THAT SAW, WITH LIKE DESIRE 9 592
AS THEY, PARTICIPATING GOD-LIKE FOOD? 9 717
CERTAIN TO UNDERGOE LIKE DOOM, IF DEATH 9 953
SAW SATAN FALL LIKE LIGHTNING DOWN FROM HEAV'N, 10 184
BY HIS AVENGERS, SINCE NO PLACE LIKE THIS 10 241
WITH SECRET AMITY THINGS OF LIKE KINDE 10 248
RAIS'D FROM THIR DARK DIVAN, AND WITH LIKE JOY 10 457
CATCHT BY CONTAGION, LIKE IN PUNISHMENT, 10 544
THIR PENANCE, LADEN WITH FRUIT LIKE THAT 10 550
THE FRUTAGE FAIR TO SIGHT, LIKE THAT WHICH GREW 10 561
LIKE DISTANT BREADTH TO TAURUS WITH THE SEAV'N 10 673
LIKE CHANGE ON SEA AND LAND, SIDERAL BLAST, 10 693
TO SATAN ONLY LIKE BOTH CRIME AND DOOM. 10 841
LIKE HIS, AND COLOUR SERPENTINE MAY SHEW 10 870
WITH LIKE DESIRE, WHICH WOULD BE MESERIE 10 997
O SONS, LIKE ONE OF US MAN IS BECOME 11 84
HAD, LIKE A DOUBLE JANUS, ALL THIR SHAPE 11 129
ONE MAN, ASSASSIN-LIKE HAD LEVIED WARR, 11 219
SO MAIST THOU LIVE, TILL LIKE RIPE FRUIT THOU DROP 11 535
LIKE A DARK CEELING STOOD; DOWN RUSH'D THE RAIN 11 743
HEE WITH A CREW, WHOM LIKE AMBITION JOYNS 12 38
LIKE HIM IN FAITH, IN WISDOM, AND RENOWN; 12 154
FOR EVER SHALL ENDURE; THE LIKE SHALL SING 12 324
SURCHARG'D, AS HAD LIKE GRIEF BIN DEW'D IN TEARS, 12 373
BY FAITH NOT VOID OF WORKES: THIS GOD-LIKE ACT 12 427
OR THEIRS WHOM HE REDEEMS, A DEATH LIKE SLEEP, 12 434
FOR DEATH, LIKE THAT WHICH THE REDEEMER DY'D. 12 445

LIKELIE
WERE BETTER, AND MOST LIKELIE IF FROM MEE 9 365

LIKELIER
THEY TASTE AND DIE: WHAT LIKELIER CAN ENSUE? 4 527

LIKELIEST
LEADS HIM PERPLEXT, WHERE HE MAY LIKELIEST FIND 2 525
AND HERE ART LIKELIEST BY SUPREAM DECREE 3 659
AS LIKELIEST WAS, WHEN TWO SUCH FOES MET ARM'D; 6 688
LIKELIEST SHE SEEMD, POMONA WHEN SHE FLED 9 394
AND ON HIS QUEST, WHERE LIKELIEST HE MIGHT FINDE 9 414

LIKELY
THOSE ARGENT FIELDS MORE LIKELY HABITANTS, 3 460
NOT LIKELY TO PART HENCE WITHOUT CONTEST; 4 872
TO US, AS LIKELY TASTING TO ATTAINE 9 935

LIKEN
LIKEN ON EARTH CONSPICUOUS, THAT MAY LIFT 6 299

LIKENESS
THE LIKENESS OF A KINGLY CROWN HAD ON. 2 673

LIKENESS (CONTINUED)
- OF FORCE TO ITS OWN LIKENESS: UP HE STARTS 4 813
- THY LIKENESS, THY FIT HELP, THY OTHER SELF, 8 450
- SATAN IN LIKENESS OF AN ANGEL BRIGHT 10 327
- DISFIGURING NOT GODS LIKENESS, BUT THIR OWN, 11 521
- OR IF HIS LIKENESS, BY THEMSELVES DEFAC'T 11 522

LIKES
- WHICH GOD LIKES BEST, INTO THIR INMOST BOWRE 4 738
- ASSUME, AS LIKES THEM BEST, CONDENSE OR RARE. 6 353
- THERE LET THEM LEARN, AS LIKES THEM, TO DESPISE 6 717

LIKEST
- LIKEST TO THEE IN SHAPE AND COUNT'NANCE BRIGHT, 2 756
- THE GOLDEN SUN IN SPLENDOR LIKEST HEAVEN 3 572
- OF GODLIKE POWER: FOR LIKEST GODS THEY SEEMD, 6 301

LIKING
- FAST CAUGHT, THEY LIK'D, AND EACH HIS LIKING CHOSE; 11 587

LIK'NING
- LIK'NING HIS MAKER TO THE GRAZED OX, 1 486
- BY LIK'NING SPIRITUAL TO CORPORAL FORMS, 5 573

LIMB
- NOT TI'D OR MANACL'D WITH JOYNT OR LIMB, 1 426
- DISTINGUISHABLE IN MEMBER, JOYNT, OR LIMB, 2 668
- YOUTH SMIL'D CELESTIAL, AND TO EVERY LIMB 3 638
- THEY LIMB THEMSELVES, AND COLOUR, SHAPE OR SIZE 6 352
- MY SELF I THEN PERUS'D, AND LIMB BY LIMB 8 267
- OF MEMBRANE, JOYNT, OR LIMB, EXCLUSIVE BARRS: 8 625
- AND STRENGTH, OF COURAGE HAUTIE, AND OF LIMB 9 484

LIMB'D
- LIMB'D AND FULL GROWN: OUT OF THE GROUND UP ROSE 7 456

LIMBEC
- DRAIND THROUGH A LIMBEC TO HIS NATIVE FORME. 3 605

LIMBER
- INSECT OR WORME; THOSE WAV'D THIR LIMBER FANS 7 476

LIMBO
- INTO A LIMBO LARGE AND BROAD, SINCE CALLD 3 495

LIMBS
- AND ON THIR NAKED LIMBS THE FLOURIE ROOF 4 772
- OUR LIMBS BENUMM'D, ERE THIS DIURNAL STARR 10 1069

LIMIT
- REACHING BEYOND ALL LIMIT AT ONE BLOW 6 140
- JORDAN, TRUE LIMIT EASTWARD; BUT HIS SONS 12 145

LIMITARIE
- PROUD LIMITARIE CHERUBE, BUT ERE THEN 4 971

LIMITED
- AND LIMITED THIR MIGHT; THOUGH NUMBERD SUCH 6 229

LIMITS
- NOT LIKE THESE NARROW LIMITS, TO RECEIVE 4 384
- WITHIN THESE HALLOWD LIMITS THOU APPEER, 4 964
- AT LENGTH INTO THE LIMITS OF THE NORTH 5 755

LINE
- OF EDEN PLANTED; EDEN STRETCHED HER LINE 4 210
- TRUE PARADISE UNDER THE ETHIOP LINE 4 282
- THESE AS A LINE THIR LONG DIMENSION DREW, 7 480
- SO SPACIOUS, AND HIS LINE STRETCHT OUT SO FARR; 8 102
- WITH DARKNESS, THRICE THE EQUINOCTIAL LINE 9 64

LINEAMENTS
- HIS LINEAMENTS DIVINE; THE PAIR THAT CLAD 5 278
- FOR WINGS, AND SMALLEST LINEAMENTS EXACT 7 477

LINGRING
- THE SIGNAL TO ASCEND, SIT LINGRING HERE 2 56
- THY LINGRING, OR WITH ONE STROKE OF THIS DART 2 702
- OUR LINGRING PARENTS, AND TO TH' EASTERN GATE 12 638

LINK
- THE LINK OF NATURE DRAW ME: FLESH OF FLESH, 9 914

LINK'D
- HUNG ORE MY REALM, LINK'D IN A GOLDEN CHAIN 2 1005

LINKED
- THUS DROOPING, OR WITH LINKED THUNDERBOLTS 1 328

LINKT
- FAIR COUPLE, LINKT IN HAPPIE NUPTIAL LEAGUE, 4 339
- FOLLOW, AS TO HIM LINKT IN WEAL OR WOE, 9 133
- SHALL SEPARATE US, LINKT IN LOVE SO DEARE, 9 970
- SHALL MEET, ALREADIE LINKT AND WEDLOCK-BOUND 10 905
- OUT OF DESPAIRE, JOY, BUT WITH FEAR YET LINKT; 11 139

LION
- SPORTING THE LION RAMPD, AND IN HIS PAW 4 343

LION (CONTINUED)
- A LION NOW HE STALKES WITH FIERIE GLARE, 4 402
- THE TAWNIE LION, PAWING TO GET FREE 7 464
- EACH WITH THIR KINDE, LION WITH LIONESS; 8 393

LIONESS
- EACH WITH THIR KINDE, LION WITH LIONESS; 8 393

LIP
- THE LIP OF TANTALUS. THUS ROVING ON 2 614
- THAT SHED MAY FLOWERS; AND PRESS'D HER MATRON LIP 4 501
- WITH CONJUGAL CARESSES, FROM HIS LIP 8 56

LIPS
- FLOWD FROM THIR LIPS, IN PROSE OR NUMEROUS VERSE, 5 150
- OF YESTERDAY, SO LATE HATH PAST THE LIPS 5 675
- NOR ARE THY LIPS UNGRACEFUL, SIRE OF MEN, 8 218
- WHAT WORDS HAVE PAST THY LIPS, ADAM SEVERE, 9 1144

LIQUID
- WITH SOLID, AS THE LAKE WITH LIQUID FIRE; 1 229
- THAT UNDERNEATH HAD VEINS OF LIQUID FIRE 1 701
- OF JASPER, OR OF LIQUID PEARLE, WHEREON 3 519
- INTO A LIQUID PLAIN, THEN STOOD UNMOV'D 4 455
- SITS ON THE BLOOM EXTRACTING LIQUID SWEET. 5 25
- NOR IN THIR LIQUID TEXTURE MORTAL WOUND 6 348
- WHOSE LIQUID MURMUR HEARD NEW THIRST EXCITES, 7 68
- THE FIRMAMENT, EXPANSE OF LIQUID, PURE, 7 264
- AND DRINK THE LIQUID LIGHT, FIRM TO RETAINE 7 362
- AND LIQUID LAPSE OF MURMURING STREAMS; BY THESE, 8 263
- FROM UNDERGROUND) THE LIQUID ORE HE DREIND 11 570

LIQUORS
- WITH PLEASANT LIQUORS CROWN'D; O INNOCENCE 5 445

LIST
- A HIDEOUS PEAL: YET, WHEN THEY LIST, WOULD CREEP, 2 656
- TO ME, FOR WHEN THEY LIST INTO THE WOMB 2 798
- ILLUSIONS AS HE LIST, PHANTASMS AND DREAMS, 4 803
- RATHER ADMIRE; OR IF THEY LIST TO TRY 8 75

LISTENING
- BY NIGHT, AND LISTENING WHERE THE HAPLESS PAIRE 10 342

LISTENS
- LISTENS DELIGHTED. EEVNING NOW APPROACH'D 5 627

LIST'N
- BUT LIST'N NOT TO HIS TEMPTATIONS, WARNE 6 908

LIST'NING
- THE PLANETS IN THIR STATION LIST'NING STOOD, 7 563

LISTNING
- SILENCE, AND SLEEP LISTNING TO THEE WILL WATCH, 7 106

LITHE
- HIS LITHE PROBOSCIS; CLOSE THE SERPENT SLY 4 347

LITTLE
- THAT LITTLE WHICH IS LEFT SO TO DEFEND, 2 1000
- TH' OMNIPOTENT. AY ME, THEY LITTLE KNOW 4 86
- OF IMMORTALITY. SO LITTLE KNOWS 4 201
- LITTLE INFERIOR; WHOM MY THOUGHTS PURSUE 4 362
- AH GENTLE PAIR, YEE LITTLE THINK HOW NIGH 4 366
- OUR DAYES WORK BROUGHT TO LITTLE, THOUGH BEGUN 9 224
- AND DURABLE; AND NOW IN LITTLE SPACE 10 320
- LITTLE INFERIOUR, BY MY ADVENTURE HARD 10 468
- WHICH HERE, THOUGH PLENTEOUS, ALL TO LITTLE SEEMS 10 600
- HOW LITTLE WEIGHT MY WORDS WITH THEE CAN FINDE, 10 968

LIV'D
- TO THEM WHO LIV'D; NOR ON THE VERTUE THOUGHT 4 198
- WHO MIGHT HAVE LIV'D AND JOYD IMMORTAL BLISS, 9 1166
- LIV'D IGNORANT OF FUTURE, SO HAD BORNE 11 764
- WHILE YET THE PATRIARK LIV'D, WHO SCAP'D THE FLOOD, 12 117

LIVD
- SPONTANEOUS, FOR WITHIN THEM SPIRIT LIVD, 7 204
- CREATURES THAT LIVD, AND MOVD, AND WALK'D, OR FLEW, 8 264
- AND LIVD: ONE CAME, METHOUGHT, OF SHAPE DIVINE, 8 295

LIVE
- SHALL WE THEN LIVE THUS VILE, THE RACE OF HEAV'N 2 194
- LIVE TO OUR SELVES, THOUGH IN THIS VAST RECESS, 2 254
- BEYOND HIS POTENT ARM, TO LIVE EXEMPT 2 318
- YET LIVE IN HATRED, ENMITY, AND STRIFE 2 500
- THE GODS WHO LIVE AT EASE, WHERE I SHALL REIGN 2 868
- LIFE IN MY SELF FOR EVER, BY THEE I LIVE, 3 244
- AND LIVE IN THEE TRANSPLANTED, AND FROM THEE 3 293
- WHAT FURTHER WOULD BE LEARNT. LIVE WHILE YE MAY, 4 533
- WHAT LIFE THE GODS LIVE THERE, AND SUCH LIVE THOU. 5 81
- OF SUBSTANCE, AND IN THINGS THAT LIVE, OF LIFE; 5 474
- MONARCHIE OVER SUCH AS LIVE BY RIGHT 5 795
- YET SOON HE HEAL'D; FOR SPIRITS THAT LIVE THROUGHOUT 6 344
- ALL HEART THEY LIVE, ALL HEAD, ALL EYE, ALL EARE, 6 350
- BUT LIVE CONTENT, WHICH IS THE CALMEST LIFE: 6 461

LIVE (CONTINUED)
STOR'D IN EACH ORB PERHAPS WITH SOME THAT LIVE. 8 152
LIVE, IN WHAT STATE, CONDITION OR DEGREE, 8 176
AND FREED FROM INTRICACIES, TAUGHT TO LIVE, 8 182
AND YE THAT LIVE AND MOVE, FAIR CREATURES, TELL, 8 276
FROM WHOM I HAVE THAT THUS I MOVE AND LIVE, 8 281
POSSESS IT, AND ALL THINGS THAT THEREIN LIVE, 8 340
OR LIVE IN SEA, OR AIRE, BEAST, FISH, AND FOWLE. 8 341
BE STRONG, LIVE HAPPIE, AND LOVE, BUT FIRST OF ALL 8 633
SOLE DAUGHTER OF HIS VOICE; THE REST, WE LIVE 9 653
MEE WHO HAVE TOUCH'D AND TASTED, YET BOTH LIVE, 9 688
SHALL LIVE WITH HER ENJOYING, I EXTINCT; 9 829
I COULD ENDURE, WITHOUT HIM LIVE NO LIFE. 9 833
HOW CAN I LIVE WITHOUT THEE, HOW FORGOE 9 908
TO LIVE AGAIN IN THESE WILDE WOODS FORLORN? 9 910
LIVES, AS THOU SAIDST, AND GAINES TO LIVE AS MAN 9 933
IN SOLITUDE LIVE SAVAGE, IN SOME GLADE 9 1085
THE SAVOUR OF DEATH FROM ALL THINGS THERE THAT
LIVE: 10 269
WHEREON I LIVE, THY GENTLE LOOKS, THY AID, 10 919
WHILE YET WE LIVE, SCARSE ONE SHORT HOUR PERHAPS, 10 923
TO MAKE DEATH IN US LIVE: THEN LET US SEEK 10 1028
THE SMELL OF PEACE TOWARD MANKINDE, LET HIM LIVE 11 38
AND LIVE FOR EVER, DREAM AT LEAST TO LIVE 11 95
IS PAST, AND WE SHALL LIVE. WHENCE HAILE TO THEE, 11 158
MAN IS TO LIVE, AND ALL THINGS LIVE FOR MAN. 11 161
HERE LET US LIVE, THOUGH IN FALL'N STATE, CONTENT. 11 180
SO MAIST THOU LIVE, TILL LIKE RIPE FRUIT THOU DROP 11 535
LIVE WELL, HOW LONG OR SHORT PERMIT TO HEAV'N: 11 554
O PITTIE AND SHAME, THAT THEY WHO TO LIVE WELL 11 629
THENCEFORTH SHALL PRACTICE HOW TO LIVE SECURE, 11 802
AT THIS LAST SIGHT, ASSUR'D THAT MAN SHALL LIVE 11 872
PERFORM, AND NOT PERFORMING CANNOT LIVE. 12 299
IN MEAN ESTATE LIVE MODERATE, TILL GROWN 12 351
FOR THIS HE SHALL LIVE HATED, BE BLASPHEM'D, 12 411
THAT YE MAY LIVE, WHICH WILL BE MANY DAYES, 12 602

LIVELESS
LIVING OR LIVELESS TO BE FOUND WAS NONE, 3 443
AS GOOD HAVE GROWN THERE STILL A LIVELESS RIB. 9 1154
OUTRAGE FROM LIVELESS THINGS; BUT DISCORD FIRST 10 707

LIVELIER
LIVELIER THEN MELIBOEAN, OR THE GRAINE 11 242

LIVELIEST
IF ONCE THEY HEAR THAT VOYCE, THIR LIVELIEST PLEDGE 1 274

LIVELY
WITH WONDER, AND COULD LOVE, SO LIVELY SHINES 4 363
WITH SUPPLE JOINTS, AND LIVELY VIGOUR LED: 8 269
HAD LIVELY SHADOWD: HERE HAD NEW BEGUN 8 311

LIVER
IN ENTRAILES, HEART OR HEAD, LIVER OR REINES; 6 346

LIVERIE
HAD IN HER SOBER LIVERIE ALL THINGS CLAD; 4 599

LIVERIES
IN ALL THE LIVERIES DECT OF SUMMERS PRIDE 7 478

LIVES
WHERE ALL LIFE DIES, DEATH LIVES, AND NATURE
BREEDS, 2 624
IN GOLGOTHA HIM DEAD, WHO LIVES IN HEAV'N; 3 477
PUTS ME IN DOUBT. LIVES THER WHO LOVES HIS PAIN? 4 888
HOW DIES THE SERPENT? HEE HATH EAT'N AND LIVES, 9 764
NOR YET ON HIM FOUND DEADLY, HE YET LIVES, 9 932
LIVES, AS THOU SAIDST, AND GAINES TO LIVE AS MAN 9 933
LAND, SEA, AND AIRE, AND EVERY KINDE THAT LIVES, 11 337
TO THESE THAT SOBER RACE OF MEN, WHOSE LIVES 11 621
SHALL LEAD THIR LIVES, AND MULTIPLIE APACE, 12 17

LIVID
SAVE WHAT THE GLIMMERING OF THESE LIVID FLAMES 1 182

LIVING
THIR LIVING STRENGTH, AND UNFREQUENTED LEFT 1 433
ALL TASTE OF LIVING WIGHT, AS ONCE IT FLED 2 613
FEARLESS TO BE O'RMATCHT BY LIVING MIGHT. 2 855
OF LIVING SAPHIRE, ONCE HIS NATIVE SEAT; 2 1050
THE LIVING, AND FORTHWITH THE CITED DEAD 3 327
LIVING OR LIVELESS TO BE FOUND WAS NONE, 3 443
OF LIVING CREATURES NEW TO SIGHT AND STRANGE: 4 287
WITH LIVING SAPHIRS: HESPERUS THAT LED 4 605
JOYN VOICES ALL YE LIVING SOULS, YE BIRDS, 5 197
BY LIVING STREAMS AMONG THE TREES OF LIFE, 5 652
DISTINCT WITH EYES, AND FROM THE LIVING WHEELS 6 846
REPTIL WITH SPAWN ABUNDANT, LIVING SOULE: 7 388
SOUL LIVING, EACH THAT CREPT, WHICH PLENTEOUSLY 7 392
HUGEST OF LIVING CREATURES, ON THE DEEP 7 413
LET TH' EARTH BRING FORTH FOUL LIVING IN HER KINDE, 7 451
INNUMEROUS LIVING CREATURES, PERFET FORMES, 7 455
EXPRESS, AND THOU BECAM'ST A LIVING SOUL. 7 528
AND EVERY LIVING THING THAT MOVES ON THE EARTH. 7 534
OPEN, YE HEAV'NS, YOUR LIVING DORES; LET IN 7 566
BY LIVING SOULE, DESERT AND DESOLATE, 8 154

LIVING (CONTINUED)
WITH VARIOUS LIVING CREATURES, AND THE AIRE 8 370
COMPARE ABOVE ALL LIVING CREATURES DEARE, 9 228
THEE ALL THINGS LIVING GAZE ON, ALL THINGS THINE 9 539
WITH SENT OF LIVING CARCASSES DESIGN'D 10 277
BUT I SHALL DIE A LIVING DEATH? O THOUGHT 10 788
LIVING OR DYING, FROM THEE I WILL NOT HIDE 10 974
MOTHER OF ALL THINGS LIVING, SINCE BY THEE 11 160
AS TO FORSAKE THE LIVING GOD, AND FALL 12 118
HIS LIVING TEMPLES, BUILT BY FAITH TO STAND, 12 527

LIVST
NOR LOVE THY LIFE, NOR HATE; BUT WHAT THOU LIVST 11 553

LO
WAS MEANT BY DEATH THAT DAY, WHEN LO, TO THEE 10 1050

LOAD
FARR HEAVIER LOAD THY SELF EXPECT TO FEEL 4 972
DEIGNS NONE TO EASE THY LOAD AND TASTE THY SWEET, 5 59
THEY PLUCKT THE SEATED HILLS WITH ALL THIR LOAD, 6 644

LOADEN
OF GOODLIEST TREES LOADEN WITH FAIREST FRUIT, 4 147
LOADEN WITH FRUIT OF FAIREST COLOURS MIXT, 9 577

LOAD'N
LOAD'N WITH FAIREST FRUIT THAT HUNG TO THE EYE 8 307

LOATH
THANK HIM WHO PUTS ME LOATH TO THIS REVENGE 4 386
CREATION COULD REPEATE, YET WOULD BE LOATH 9 946
HE LED HER NOTHING LOATH; FLOURS WERE THE COUCH, 9 1039
OF ALL THE REST: THEN WILT THOU NOT BE LOATH 12 585

LOATH'D
WITH LOATH'D INTRUSION, AND FILL ALL THE LAND; 12 178

LOATHSOM
THOU WILT NOT LEAVE ME IN THE LOATHSOM GRAVE 3 247
TO LOATHSOM SICKNESS, WORTHILY, SINCE THEY 11 524

LOCAL
AS OF A DUEL, OR THE LOCAL WOUNDS 12 387

LOCKS
BIND THIR RESPLENDENT LOCKS INWREATH'D WITH BEAMS, 3 361
CIRCL'D HIS HEAD, NOR LESS HIS LOCKS BEHIND 3 626
ABSOLUTE RULE; AND HYACINTHIN LOCKS 4 301
BY US OFT SEEN; HIS DEWIE LOCKS DISTILL'D 5 56
CLIMBING, SAT THICKER THEN THE SNAKIE LOCKS 10 559
BLOW MOIST AND KEEN, SHATTERING THE GRACEFUL LOCKS 10 1066

LOCUSTS
OF LOCUSTS, WARPING ON THE EASTERN WIND, 1 341
A DARKSOM CLOUD OF LOCUSTS SWARMING DOWN 12 185

LODG'D
WHERE LODG'D, OR WHITHER FLED, OR IF FOR FIGHT, 6 531
MYRIADS BETWEEN TWO BRAZEN MOUNTAINS LODG'D 7 201
LODG'D IN A SMALL PARTITION, AND THE REST 8 105
SELECT FOR LIFE SHALL IN THE ARK BE LODG'D, 11 823

LODGE
THUS AT THIR SHADIE LODGE ARRIV'D, BOTH STOOD 4 720
BUT CHIEFLY WHERE THOSE TWO FAIR CREATURES LODGE, 4 790
I HAVE AT WILL. SO TO THE SILVAN LODGE 5 377
LODGE AND DISLODGE BY TURNS, WHICH MAKES THROUGH
HEAV'N 6 7

LOE
OF HEAV'NS ASCENT THEY LIFT THIR FEET, WHEN LOE 3 486
FOR MAN AND BEAST: WHEN LOE A WONDER STRANGE, 11 733

LOFTIE
ADAMS ABODE, THOSE LOFTIE SHADES HIS BOWRE. 3 734
THEN FROM HIS LOFTIE STAND ON THAT HIGH TREE 4 395

LOFTIEST
OF RIOT ASCENDS ABOVE THEIR LOFTIEST TOWRS, 1 499
INSUPERABLE HIGHTH OF LOFTIEST SHADE, 4 138

LOFTY
CITIES OF MEN WITH LOFTY GATES AND TOWRS, 11 640

LOINES
SKIRTED HIS LOINES AND THIGHES WITH DOWNIE GOLD 5 282
OUR OWN BEGOTTEN, AND OF OUR LOINES TO BRING 10 983
NOT ONELY TO THE SONS OF ABRAHAMS LOINES 12 447

LONELY
MY SELF EXPOSE, WITH LONELY STEPS TO TREAD 2 828
THY GOING IS NOT LONELY, WITH THEE GOES 11 290

LONG
LONG AFTER KNOWN IN PALESTINE, AND NAM'D 1 80
PRONE ON THE FLOOD, EXTENDED LONG AND LARGE 1 195
THIR SEATS LONG AFTER NEXT THE SEAT OF GOD, 1 383

LONG (CONTINUED)

THE REST WERE LONG TO TELL, THOUGH FAR RENOWN'D, 1 507
THERE WENT A FAME IN HEAV'N THAT HE ERE LONG 1 651
LONG UNDER DARKNESS COVER. BUT THESE THOUGHTS 1 659
FELL LONG BEFORE; NOR AUGHT AVAIL'D HIM NOW 1 748
THE SOUND OF BLUSTRING WINDS, WHICH ALL NIGHT LONG 2 286
BY POLLICY, AND LONG PROCESS OF TIME, 2 297
WELL HAVE YE JUDG'D, WELL ENDED LONG DEBATE, 2 390
SEIS'D US, THOUGH UNDISMAID: LONG IS THE WAY 2 432
ALONE, BUT LONG I SAT NOT, TILL MY WOMB 2 778
ESCAP'T THE STYGIAN POOL, THOUGH LONG DETAIN'D 3 14
THIS MY LONG SUFFERANCE AND MY DAY OF GRACE 3 198
UNDER HIS GLOOMIE POWER I SHALL NOT LONG 3 242
SHALL ENTER HEAVEN LONG ABSENT, AND RETURNE, 3 261
AND AFTER ALL THIR TRIBULATIONS LONG 3 336
CLEOMBROTUS, AND MANY MORE TOO LONG, 3 473
LONG AFTER, NOW UNPEOPL'D, AND UNTROD; 3 497
AND LONG HE WANDERD, TILL AT LAST A GLEAME 3 499
PHILOSOPHERS IN VAIN SO LONG HAVE SOUGHT, 3 601
AS MAN ERE LONG, AND THIS NEW WORLD SHALL KNOW. 4 113
OR WHERE THE SONS OF EDEN LONG BEFORE 4 213
YIELDED THEM, SIDE-LONG AS THEY SAT RECLINE 4 333
LONG TO CONTINUE, AND THIS HIGH SEAT YOUR HEAV'N 4 371
SHORT PLEASURES, FOR LONG WOES ARE TO SUCCEED. 4 535
SHE ALL NIGHT LONG HER AMOROUS DESCANT SUNG; 4 603
OUR EYE-LIDS; OTHER CREATURES ALL DAY LONG 4 616
BUT WHEREFORE ALL NIGHT LONG SHINE THESE, FOR WHOM 4 657
ILL MATCHING WORDS AND DEEDS LONG PAST OR LATE. 5 113
ON PRINCES, WHEN THIR RICH RETINUE LONG 5 355
LONG AFTER TO BLEST MARIE, SECOND EVE. 5 387
ALTERNATE ALL NIGHT LONG: BUT NOT SO WAK'D 5 657
INTERPRETED) WHICH NOT LONG AFTER, HE 5 762
LONG WAY THROUGH HOSTILE SCORN, WHICH HE SUSTEIND 5 904
CONFLICTING FIRE: LONG TIME IN EEVEN SCALE 6 245
NOT LONG DIVISIBLE, AND FROM THE GASH 6 331
WHICH INTO HALLOW ENGINS LONG AND ROUND 6 484
NOR LONG SHALL BE OUR LABOUR, YET ERE DAWNE, 6 492
WHOM FLED WE THOUGHT, WILL SAVE US LONG PURSUIT 6 538
NOT LONG, FOR SUDDEN ALL AT ONCE THIR REEDS 6 582
A WHILE IN TROUBLE; BUT THEY STOOD NOT LONG, 6 634
LONG STRUGLING UNDERNEATH, ERE THEY COULD WIND 6 659
UP HITHER, UNDER LONG OBEDIENCE TRI'D, 7 159
WITH BORDERS LONG THE RIVERS. THAT EARTH NOW 7 328
THESE AS A LINE THIR LONG DIMENSION DREW, 7 480
BUT LONG ERE OUR APPROACHING HEARD WITHIN 8 242
WHICH IT HAD LONG STOOD UNDER, STREIND TO THE
    HIGHTH 8 454
OR NEPTUN'S IRE OR JUNO'S, THAT SO LONG 9 18
PLEAS'D ME LONG CHOOSING, AND BEGINNING LATE; 9 26
WITH LONG AND TEDIOUS HAVOC FABL'D KNIGHTS 9 30
HIM AFTER LONG DEBATE, IRRESOLUTE 9 87
CONTINU'D MAKING, AND WHO KNOWS HOW LONG 9 138
BITTER ERE LONG BACK ON IT SELF RECOILES; 9 172
AS WE NEED WALK, TILL YOUNGER HANDS ERE LONG 9 246
HER LONG WITH ARDENT LOOK HIS EYE PURSU'D 9 397
AS ONE WHO LONG IN POPULOUS CITY PENT, 9 445
TO INTERRUPT, SIDE-LONG HE WORKS HIS WAY. 9 512
SATED AT LENGTH, ERE LONG I MIGHT PERCEAVE 9 598
WANTED NOT LONG, THOUGH TO THIS SHAPE RETAIN'D. 9 601
EMPRESS, THE WAY IS READIE, AND NOT LONG, 9 626
WHOSE TASTE, TOO LONG FORBORN, AT FIRST ASSAY 9 747
SOLACE IN HER RETURN, SO LONG DELAY'D; 9 844
THEE I HAVE MISST, AND THOUGHT IT LONG, DEPRIV'D 9 857
MOST FAVORS, WHO CAN PLEASE HIM LONG; MEE FIRST 9 949
CONFOUNDED LONG THEY SATE, AS STRUCK'N MUTE, 9 1064
BRAUNCHING SO BROAD AND LONG, THAT IN THE GROUND 9 1104
WHENCE ADAM FAULTRING LONG, THUS ANSWER'D BRIEF. 10 115
THE REALM IT SELF OF SATAN LONG USURPT, 10 189
WITH LONG REACH INTERPOS'D; THREE SEV'RAL WAYES 10 323
LONG HEE ADMIRING STOOD, TILL SIN, HIS FAIRE 10 352
WITH PERIL GREAT ATCHIEV'D. LONG WERE TO TELL 10 469
LONG HAD FORETOLD, A FABRICK WONDERFUL 10 482
OF PUBLIC SCORN; HE WONDERD, BUT NOT LONG 10 509
AND WORN WITH FAMIN, LONG AND CEASLESS HISS, 10 573
A LONG DAYS DYING TO AUGMENT OUR PAINE, 10 964
SOME DAYS; HOW LONG, AND WHAT TILL THEN OUR LIFE, 11 198
SIGHT SO DEFORM WHAT HEART OF ROCK COULD LONG 11 494
LIVE WELL, HOW LONG OR SHORT PERMIT TO HEAV'N; 11 554
LONG HAD NOT WALKT, WHEN FROM THE TENTS BEHOLD 11 581
LONG TIME IN PEACE BY FAMILIES AND TRIBES 12 23
SHALL DWELL TO SENIR, THAT LONG RIDGE OF HILLS. 12 146
WERE LONG TO TELL, HOW MANY BATTELS FOUGHT, 12 261
THROUGH THE WORLDS WILDERNESS LONG WANDERD MAN 12 313
LONG TIME SHALL DWELL AND PROSPER, BUT WHEN SINS 12 316
BUT FIRST A LONG SUCCESSION MUST ENSUE, 12 331
SHALL LONG USURP; ERE THE THIRD DAWNING LIGHT 12 421

LONGER

HE VIEWS IN BREDTH, AND WITHOUT LONGER PAUSE 3 561
LONGER THY OFFERD GOOD, WHY ELSE SET HERE? 5 63
AND LONGER WILL DELAY TO HEARE THEE TELL 7 101
DESIRE WITH THEE STILL LONGER TO CONVERSE 8 252
NOT LONGER THEN SINCE I IN ONE NIGHT FREED 9 140
HELL COULD NO LONGER HOLD US IN HER BOUNDS, 10 365
WHY STAND WE LONGER SHIVERING UNDER FEARES, 10 1003
BUT LONGER IN THAT PARADISE TO DWELL, 11 48
MY MOTIONS IN HIM, LONGER THEN THEY MOVE, 11 91
BUT LONGER IN THIS PARADISE TO DWELL 11 259

LONGER (CONTINUED)

PART GOOD, PART BAD, OF BAD THE LONGER SCROWLE, 12 336
LONGER ON EARTH THEN CERTAINE TIMES TO APPEER 12 437
WE MAY NO LONGER STAY: GO, WAKEN EVE; 12 594

LONGING

MILLIONS THAT STAND IN ARMS, AND LONGING WAIT 2 55
STILL UNFULFILL'D WITH PAIN OF LONGING PINES; 4 511
LONGING AND ENVYING STOOD, BUT COULD NOT REACH. 9 593
SOLLICITED HER LONGING EYE; YET FIRST 9 743
NOT TO BE TRUSTED, LONGING TO BE SEEN 10 877

LONGITUDE

OR LONGITUDE, WHERE THE GREAT LUMINARIE 3 576
MEAN WHILE IN UTMOST LONGITUDE, WHERE HEAV'N 4 539
STRETCHT INTO LONGITUDE; WHICH HAVING PASS'D 5 754
HIS LONGITUDE THROUGH HEAV'NS HIGH RODE: THE GRAY 7 373

LOOK

HE ENDED FROWNING, AND HIS LOOK DENOUNC'D 2 106
THE WEIGHT OF MIGHTIEST MONARCHIES; HIS LOOK 2 307
HIS LOOK SUSPENCE, AWAITING WHO APPEER'D 2 418
AND WITH DISDAINFUL LOOK THUS FIRST BEGAN. 2 680
PLEAS'D, OUT OF HEAVEN SHALT LOOK DOWN AND SMILE, 3 257
LOOK DOWNWARD ON THAT GLOBE WHOSE HITHER SIDE 3 722
LAY PLEASANT, HIS GRIEVD LOOK HE FIXES SAD, 4 28
ON THE GREEN BANK, TO LOOK INTO THE CLEER 4 458
AS I BENT DOWN TO LOOK, JUST OPPOSITE, 4 460
BENDING TO LOOK ON ME, I STARTED BACK, 4 462
STAND FIRM, FOR IN HIS LOOK DEFIANCE LOURS. 4 873
TO TRAMPLE THEE AS MIRE: FOR PROOF LOOK UP, 4 1010
AND LOOK FOR ADORATION TO TH' ABUSE 5 800
WHERETO WITH LOOK COMPOS'D SATAN REPLI'D. 6 469
HER LONG WITH ARDENT LOOK HIS EYE PURSU'D 9 397
SHE MOST, AND IN HER LOOK SUMMS ALL DELIGHT. 9 454
TO KNOWLEDGE? BY THE THREATNER, LOOK ON MEE, 9 687
ADAM, ESTRANG'D IN LOOK AND ALTERD STILE, 9 1132
AS DELOS FLOATING ONCE; THE REST HIS LOOK 10 296
FROM HIS DISPLEASURE; IN WHOSE LOOK SERENE, 10 1094
HIS TRIPLE-COLOUR'D BOW, WHEREON TO LOOK 11 897

LOOK'D

STOOD ON THE BRINK OF HELL AND LOOK'D A WHILE, 2 918
ONE GATE THERE ONLY WAS, AND THAT LOOK'D EAST 4 178
HE LOOK'D, AND SAW THE FACE OF THINGS QUITE
    CHANG'D, 11 712

LOOKD

LOOKD ROUND, AND SCOUTS EACH COAST LIGHT-ARMED
    SCOURE, 6 529
HE LOOKD AND SAW A SPACIOUS PLAINE, WHEREON 11 556
HE LOOKD AND SAW WIDE TERRITORIE SPRED 11 638
HE LOOKD, AND SAW THE ARK HULL ON THE FLOUD, 11 840

LOOKING

OF OUTWARD STRENGTH; WHILE SHAME, THOU LOOKING ON, 9 312
CONVERSING, LOOKING, LOVING, TO ABSTAIN 10 993
NOT HIGHER THAT HILL NOR WIDER LOOKING ROUND, 11 381
GRIEV'D AT HIS HEART, WHEN LOOKING DOWN HE SAW 11 887
AND LOOKING DOWN, TO SEE THE HUBBUB STRANGE 12 60
GOD LOOKING FORTH WILL TROUBLE ALL HIS HOST 12 209
THEY LOOKING BACK, ALL TH' EASTERN SIDE BEHELD 12 641

LOOKS

ALL THESE AND MORE CAME FLOCKING; BUT WITH LOOKS 1 522
LOOKS THROUGH THE HORIZONTAL MISTY AIR 1 595
FROM HEAV'N, FOR EV'N IN HEAV'N HIS LOOKS AND
    THOUGHTS 1 680
LOOKS DOWN WITH WONDER AT THE SUDDEN VIEW 3 542
AND WORTHIE SEEMD, FOR IN THIR LOOKS DIVINE 4 291
PLEAS'D IT RETURND AS SOON WITH ANSWERING LOOKS 4 464
WHERE HE FIRST LIGHTED, SOON DISCERND HIS LOOKS 4 570
MANKIND WITH HER FAIRE LOOKS, TO BE AVENGD 4 718
LEANING HALF-RAIS'D, WITH LOOKS OF CORDIAL LOVE 5 12
BE NOT DISHEART'ND THEN, NOR CLOUD THOSE LOOKS 5 122
SO SAYING, WITH DISPATCHFUL LOOKS IN HASTE 5 331
AND IN HER LOOKS, WHICH FROM THAT TIME INFUS'D 8 474
EXPRESS THEY, BY LOOKS ONELY, OR DO THEY MIX 8 616
LOOKS INTERVENE AND SMILES, OR OBJECT NEW 9 222
OF LOOKS AND SMILES, FOR SMILES FROM REASON FLOW, 9 239
I FROM THE INFLUENCE OF THY LOOKS RECEAVE 9 309
THY LOOKS, THE HEAV'N OF MILDNESS, WITH DISDAIN, 9 534
THE LATTER I DEMURRE, FOR IN THIR LOOKS 9 558
LOVE WAS NOT IN THIR LOOKS, EITHER TO GOD 10 111
THAT THOU ON EARTH HADST PROSPER'D, WHICH THY LOOKS 10 360
HIS THOUGHTS, HIS LOOKS, WORDS, ACTIONS ALL INFECT, 10 608
WHEREON I LIVE, THY GENTLE LOOKS, THY AID, 10 919

LOOK'ST

LOOK'ST FROM THY SOLE DOMINION LIKE THE GOD 4 33

LOOKT

IF THOU RESIST. THE FIEND LOOKT UP AND KNEW 4 1013
AND AS I WONDRING LOOKT, BESIDE IT STOOD 5 54
SPREADING THIR BANE; THE BLASTED STARRS LOOKT WAN, 10 412

LOOPHOLES

AT LOOPHOLES CUT THROUGH THICKEST SHADE: THOSE LEAVES	9	1110

LOOSE

TO BE NO MORE; SAD CURE; FOR WHO WOULD LOOSE,	2	146
WILL HE, SO WISE, LET LOOSE AT ONCE HIS IRE,	2	155
SOLE KING, AND OF HIS KINGDOM LOOSE NO PART	2	325
LOOSE ALL HER VIRTUE; LEAST BAD MEN SHOULD BOAST	2	483
THE TEMPTING STREAM, WITH ONE SMALL DROP TO LOOSE	2	607
WITH HORSE AND CHARIOTS RANKT IN LOOSE ARRAY;	2	887
THROUGH ALL RESTRAINT BROKE LOOSE HE WINGS HIS WAY	3	87
NOW IN LOOSE GARLANDS THICK THROWN OFF, THE BRIGHT	3	362
OF HER LOOSE TRESSES HID: HE IN DELIGHT	4	497
WHO WOULD NOT, FINDING WAY, BREAK LOOSE FROM HELL,	4	889
CAME NOT ALL HELL BROKE LOOSE? IS PAIN TO THEM	4	918
AND TO DISORDER'D RAGE LET LOOSE THE REINES,	6	696
SHALT LOOSE, EXPELL'D FROM HENCE INTO A WORLD	8	332
BE FRUSTRATE, DO, UNDO, AND LABOUR LOOSE,	9	944
ONE FLESH; TO LOOSE THEE WERE TO LOOSE MY SELF.	9	959
LOOSE NO REWARD, THOUGH HERE THOU SEE HIM DIE,	11	459
SHALL WITH THIR FREEDOM LOST ALL VERTU LOOSE	11	798
THEN LOOSE IT TO A STRANGER, THAT THE TRUE	12	358

LOOSES

LOOSES DISCOUNT'NANC'T, AND LIKE FOLLY SHEWES;	8	553

LOOSING

AFFECTING GOD-HEAD, AND SO LOOSING ALL,	3	206
BY LOOSING THEE A WHILE, THE WHOLE RACE LOST.	3	280

LOOSLY

PART LOOSLY WING THE REGION, PART MORE WISE	7	425

LOOSNING

FROM THIR FOUNDATIONS LOOSNING TO AND FRO	6	643

LOP

MORE HANDS THEN OURS TO LOP THIR WANTON GROWTH:	4	629
LOP OVERGROWN, OR PRUNE, OR PROP, OR BIND,	9	210

LOPT

MAIM'D HIS BRUTE IMAGE, HEAD AND HANDS LOPT OFF	1	459
WITH BRANCHES LOPT, IN WOOD OR MOUNTAIN FELL'D)	6	575

LOQUACIOUS

BOLD OR LOQUACIOUS, THUS ABASHT REPLI'D.	10	161

LORD

WITHIN HEAV'NS BOUND, UNLESS HEAV'NS LORD SUPREAM	2	236
THY KING AND LORD? BACK TO THY PUNISHMENT,	2	699
SUSPICIOUS, REASONLESS. WHY SHOULD THIR LORD	4	516
WHOSE EASIER BUSINESS WERE TO SERVE THIR LORD	4	943
HAIL UNIVERSAL LORD, BE BOUNTEOUS STILL	5	205
ALL KNEES IN HEAV'N, AND SHALL CONFESS HIM LORD:	5	608
ERRE NOT, MUCH LESS FOR THIS TO BE OUR LORD,	5	799
WHAT HEAVENS LORD HAD POWERFULLEST TO SEND	6	425
SON, HEIR, AND LORD, TO HIM DOMINION GIV'N,	6	887
ATTENDANT ON THIR LORD: HEAV'N OP'ND WIDE	7	205
ORDAIN'D FOR USES TO HIS LORD BEST KNOWN.	8	106
SO SPAKE THE UNIVERSAL LORD, AND SEEM'D	8	376
HIM LORD PRONOUNC'D, AND, O INDIGNITIE.	9	154
YET NOT SO STRICTLY HATH OUR LORD IMPOS'D	9	235
OFSPRING OF HEAV'N AND EARTH, AND ALL EARTHS LORD,	9	273
WHICH WHEN THE LORD GOD HEARD, WITHOUT DELAY	10	163
CHIEFLY ON MAN, SOLE LORD OF ALL DECLAR'D,	10	401
FOR THOUGH THE LORD OF ALL BE INFINITE,	10	794
MAYST COVER: WELL MAY THEN THY LORD APPEAS'D	11	257
BEFORE THE LORD, AS IN DESPITE OF HEAV'N,	12	34
HE MADE NOT LORD; SUCH TITLE TO HIMSELF	12	70
AS DID THIR LORD BEFORE THEM. THUS THEY WIN	12	502
NOW AMPLIER KNOWN THY SAVIOUR AND THY LORD,	12	544

LORDLY

FORC'T HALLELUIAH'S; WHILE HE LORDLY SITS	2	243
THAT FROM HIS LORDLY EYE KEEP DISTANCE DUE,	3	578

LORDS

FOR ONE RESTRAINT, LORDS OF THE WORLD BESIDES?	1	32
THE GREAT SERAPHIC LORDS AND CHERUBIM	1	794
IN NAKED MAJESTIE SEEMD LORDS OF ALL,	4	290
DELIVERER FROM NEW LORDS, LEADER TO FREE	6	451
TO THEE AND TO THY RACE I GIVE; AS LORDS	8	339
YET LORDS DECLAR'D OF ALL IN EARTH OR AIRE?	9	658
AS LORDS, A SPACIOUS WORLD, TO OUR NATIVE HEAVEN	10	467
WORLDLIE OR DISSOLUTE, ON WHAT THIR LORDS	11	803
SUBJECTS HIM FROM WITHOUT TO VIOLENT LORDS;	12	93
THIR LORDS, WHOM GOD DISPOS'D, THE HOUSE OF GOD	12	349

LORE

SHE FINISH'D, AND THE SUTTLE FIEND HIS LORE	2	815
HEARD NOT HER LORE, BOTH IN SUBJECTION NOW	9	1128

LOSE

CALLS US, WE LOSE THE PRIME, TO MARK HOW SPRING	5	21
IN OUR DEFENCE, LEFT UNAWARES WE LOSE	5	731
THAT DETRIMENT, IF SUCH IT BE TO LOSE	7	153

LOSS

WITH LOSS OF EDEN, TILL ONE GREATER MAN	1	4
OUR ENEMY, OUR OWN LOSS HOW REPAIR,	1	188
TH' ASSOCIATES AND COPARTNERS OF OUR LOSS	1	265
IN LOSS IT SELF; WHICH ON HIS COUNT'NANCE CAST	1	526
FOR WHO CAN YET BELEEVE, THOUGH AFTER LOSS,	1	631
HATH BIN ACHIEVD OF MERIT, YET THIS LOSS	2	21
WARR HATH DETERMIN'D US, AND FOILD WITH LOSS	2	330
WIDE GAPING, AND WITH UTTER LOSS OF BEING	2	440
CLEER VICTORY, TO OUR PART LOSS AND ROUT	2	770
A WORLD FROM UTTER LOSS, AND HAST BEEN FOUND	3	308
TO DEEPEST HELL, AND TO REPAIR THAT LOSS	3	678
TO WRECK ON INNOCENT FRAIL MAN HIS LOSS	4	11
HIS LOSS; BUT CHIEFLY TO FIND HERE OBSERVD	4	849
O LOSS OF ONE IN HEAV'N TO JUDGE OF WISE,	4	904
US TIMELY OF WHAT MIGHT ELSE HAVE BIN OUR LOSS,	7	74
HER LOSS, AND OTHER PLEASURES ALL ABJURE:	8	480
OR WON TO WHAT MAY WORK HIS UTTER LOSS,	9	131
ANOTHER RIB AFFORD, YET LOSS OF THEE	9	912
THE GOOD I SOUGHT NOT. TO THE LOSS OF THAT,	10	752
FOR LOSS OF LIFE AND PLEASURE OVERLOV'D.	10	1019

LOST

BOTH OF LOST HAPPINESS AND LASTING PAIN	1	55
AND SHOOK HIS THRONE. WHAT THOUGH THE FIELD BE LOST?	1	105
ALL IS NOT LOST; THE UNCONQUERABLE WILL,	1	106
HATH LOST US HEAV'N, AND ALL THIS MIGHTY HOST	1	136
SAID THEN THE LOST ARCH-ANGEL, THIS THE SEAT	1	243
REGAIND IN HEAV'N, OR WHAT MORE LOST IN HELL?	1	270
ABJECT AND LOST LAY THESE, COVERING THE FLOOD,	1	312
WARRIERS, THE FLOWR OF HEAV'N, ONCE YOURS, NOW LOST,	1	316
A LEPER ONCE HE LOST AND GAIN'D A KING,	1	471
NOT IN DESPAIR, TO HAVE FOUND THEMSELVES NOT LOST	1	525
STOOD LIKE A TOWR; HIS FORM HAD YET NOT LOST	1	591
BY ME, HAVE LOST OUR HOPES. BUT HE WHO REIGNS	1	637
I GIVE NOT HEAV'N FOR LOST. FROM THIS DESCENT	2	14
CAR'D NOT TO BE AT ALL; WITH THAT CARE LOST	2	48
A FAIRER PERSON LOST NOT HEAV'N; HE SEEMD	2	110
TO PERISH RATHER, SWALLOWD UP AND LOST	2	149
OUR OWN RIGHT LOST: HIM TO UNTHRONE WE THEN	2	231
AND FOUND NO END, IN WANDRING MAZES LOST.	2	561
AND TIME AND PLACE ARE LOST; WHERE ELDEST NIGHT	2	894
ALONE, AND WITHOUT GUIDE, HALF LOST, I SEEK	2	975
TO YOUR BEHOOF, IF I THAT REGION LOST,	2	982
FOR SHOULD MAN FINALLY BE LOST, SHOULD MAN	3	150
MAN SHALL NOT QUITE BE LOST, BUT SAV'D WHO WILL,	3	173
MUST HAVE BIN LOST, ADJUDG'D TO DEATH AND HELL	3	223
CAN NEVER SEEK, ONCE DEAD IN SINS AND LOST;	3	233
BY LOOSING THEE A WHILE, THE WHOLE RACE LOST.	3	280
FARWEL REMORSE: ALL GOOD TO ME IS LOST;	4	109
LOST SIGHT OF HIM; ONE OF THE BANISHT CREW	4	573
OR LESS BE LOST. THY FEAR, SAID ZEPHON BOLD,	4	854
RETURND NOT LOST: ON TO THE SACRED HILL	6	25
PLAGUES; THEY ASTONISHT ALL RESISTANCE LOST,	6	838
SELF-LOST, AND IN A MOMENT WILL CREATE	7	154
TO ME IS LOST. THEN LET ME NOT LET PASS	9	479
THERE SWALLOW'D UP AND LOST, FROM SUCCOUR FARR.	9	642
THAT ALL WAS LOST. BACK TO THE THICKET SLUNK	9	784
HOW ART THOU LOST, HOW ON A SUDDEN LOST,	9	900
MUCH PLEASURE WE HAVE LOST, WHILE WE ABSTAIN'D	9	1022
BOTH GOOD AND EVIL, GOOD LOST, AND EVIL GOT,	9	1072
IMMUTABLE WHEN THOU WERT LOST, NOT I,	9	1165
WITH ODDS WHAT WARR HATH LOST, AND FULLY AVENG'D	10	374
TILL THIR LOST SHAPE, PERMITTED, THEY RESUM'D,	10	574
ON ME ALREADIE LOST, MEE THEN THY SELF	10	929
AS ONE DISARM'D, HIS ANGER ALL HE LOST,	10	945
WOULD BE REVENGE INDEED; WHICH WILL BE LOST	10	1036
AND IMMORTALITIE: THAT FONDLY LOST,	11	59
HIS KNOWLEDGE OF GOOD LOST, AND EVIL GOT,	11	87
WHAT JUSTLY THOU HAST LOST; NOR SET THY HEART,	11	288
BUT THIS PRAEEMINENCE THOU HAST LOST, BROUGHT DOWN	11	347
OF LOVE AND YOUTH NOT LOST, SONGS, GARLANDS, FLOURS,	11	594
RESCU'D, HAD IN HIS RIGHTEOUSNESS BIN LOST?	11	682
SHALL WITH THIR FREEDOM LOST ALL VERTU LOOSE	11	798
IN FORAIGN LANDS THIR MEMORIE BE LOST	12	46
IS LOST, WHICH ALWAYES WITH RIGHT REASON DWELLS	12	84
THIR INWARD LOST; WITNESS TH' IRREVERENT SON	12	101
IN SIN FOR EVER LOST FROM LIFE; THIS ACT	12	429
I CARRY HENCE; THOUGH ALL BY MEE IS LOST,	12	621

LOT

FOR EVER NOW TO HAVE THIR LOT IN PAIN,	1	608
WORTH WAITING, SINCE OUR PRESENT LOT APPEERS	2	223
VIEW'D FIRST THIR LAMENTABLE LOT, AND FOUND	2	617
SO FARR THE HAPPIER LOT, ENJOYING THEE	4	446
GABRIEL, TO THEE THY COURSE BY LOT HATH GIV'N	4	561
AND READ THY LOT IN YON CELESTIAL SIGN	4	1011
MEANT MEE, BY VENTRING HIGHER THEN MY LOT.	9	690
THOU THEREFORE ALSO TASTE, THAT EQUAL LOT	9	881
HOWEVER I WITH THEE HAVE FIXT MY LOT,	9	952
OR TRANSMIGRATION, AS THIR LOT SHALL LEAD.	10	261
MY PART OF EVIL ONELY, EACH DAYES LOT	11	765

LOTH

HE CAME, AND WITH HIM EVE, MORE LOTH, THOUGH FIRST	10	109

LOUD
HE CALL'D SO LOUD, THAT ALL THE HOLLOW DEEP 1 314
THOUGH FOR THE NOYSE OF DRUMS AND TIMBRELS LOUD 1 394
OF TRUMPETS LOUD AND CLARIONS BE UPREARD 1 532
WITH DEAFNING SHOUT, RETURN'D THEM LOUD ACCLAIM. 2 520
COCYTUS, NAM'D OF LAMENTATION LOUD 2 579
WITH WIDE CERBERIAN MOUTHS FULL LOUD, AND RUNG 2 655
WITH NOISES LOUD AND RUINOUS (TO COMPARE 2 921
LOUD AS FROM NUMBERS WITHOUT NUMBER, SWEET 3 346
WITH JUBILEE, AND LOUD HOSANNA'S FILLD 3 348
BACK FROM PURSUIT THY POWERS WITH LOUD ACCLAIME 3 397
OF GLIMMERING AIR LESS VEXT WITH TEMPEST LOUD: 3 429
BREATHE SOFT OR LOUD; AND WAVE YOUR TOPS, YE PINES, 5 193
WITH JOY AND ACCLAMATIONS LOUD, THAT ONE 6 23
OF WRAUTH AWAK'T: NOR WITH LESS DREAD THE LOUD 6 59
SATAN: AND THUS WAS HEARD COMMANDING LOUD. 6 557
WHAT WE PROPOUND, AND LOUD THAT ALL MAY HEAR. 6 567
CRYSTALLIN OCEAN, AND THE LOUD MISRULE 7 271
TORMENT, AND LOUD LAMENT, AND FURIOUS RAGE. 8 244
THIR MIGHTY CHIEF RETURND: LOUD WAS TH' ACCLAIME: 10 455
HE ENDED, AND THE HEAV'NLY AUDIENCE LOUD 10 641
BOREAS AND CAECIAS AND ARGESTES LOUD 10 699
THUS ADAM TO HIMSELF LAMENTED LOUD 10 845
FORTHWITH A HIDEOUS GABBLE RISES LOUD 12 56
IN THUNDER LIGHTNING AND LOUD TRUMPETS SOUND 12 229

LOUDER
WOULD SPEED BEFORE THEE, AND BE LOUDER HEARD, 10 954

LOUDEST
WITH LOUDEST VEHEMENCE: THITHER HE PLYES, 2 954
THEN LOUDEST ORATORIE: YET THIR PORT 11 8

LOURS
STAND FIRM, FOR IN HIS LOOK DEFIANCE LOURS. 4 873

LOV'D
THY CREATURE LATE SO LOV'D, THY YOUNGEST SON 3 151
HIM WITH HER LOV'D SOCIETIE, THAT NOW 9 1007

LOVE
AND WORKS OF LOVE OR ENMITY FULFILL. 1 431
FELL NOT FROM HEAVEN, OR MORE GROSS TO LOVE 1 491
SMIT WITH THE LOVE OF SACRED SONG; BUT CHIEF 3 29
REAPING IMMORTAL FRUITS OF JOY AND LOVE, 3 67
UNINTERRUPTED JOY, UNRIVALD LOVE 3 68
OF TRUE ALLEGIANCE, CONSTANT FAITH OR LOVE, 3 104
LOVE WITHOUT END, AND WITHOUT MEASURE GRACE, 3 142
SAY HEAV'NLY POWERS, WHERE SHALL WE FIND SUCH LOVE, 3 213
IN WHOM THE FULNESS DWELS OF LOVE DIVINE, 3 225
SILENT YET SPAKE, AND BREATH'D IMMORTAL LOVE 3 267
SO HEAV'NLY LOVE SHALL OUTDOO HELLISH HATE 3 298
LOVE HATH ABOUNDED MORE THEN GLORY ABOUNDS, 3 312
WITH JOY AND LOVE TRIUMPHING, AND FAIR TRUTH. 3 338
FOR MANS OFFENCE. O UNEXAMPL'D LOVE, 3 410
LOVE NO WHERE TO BE FOUND LESS THEN DIVINE. 3 411
BUT HEAV'NS FREE LOVE DEALT EQUALLY TO ALL? 4 68
BE THEN HIS LOVE ACCURST, SINCE LOVE OR HATE, 4 69
WITH WONDER, AND COULD LOVE, SO LIVELY SHINES 4 363
OF SYMPATHIE AND LOVE; THERE I HAD FIXT 4 465
SMIL'D WITH SUPERIOR LOVE, AS JUPITER 4 499
WHERE NEITHER JOY NOR LOVE, BUT FIERCE DESIRE, 4 509
AND MUTUAL LOVE, THE CROWN OF ALL OUR BLISS 4 728
MYSTERIOUS OF CONNUBIAL LOVE REFUS'D: 4 743
HAILE WEDDED LOVE, MYSTERIOUS LAW, TRUE SOURCE 4 750
HERE LOVE HIS GOLDEN SHAFTS IMPLOIES, HERE LIGHTS 4 763
LEANING HALF-RAIS'D, WITH LOOKS OF CORDIAL LOVE 5 12
LOVE UNLIBIDINOUS REIGN'D, NOR JEALOUSIE 5 449
UNALTERABLY FIRM HIS LOVE ENTIRE 5 502
TO HIM, OR POSSIBLY HIS LOVE DESERT 5 515
BECAUSE WEE FREELY LOVE, AS IN OUR WILL 5 539
TO LOVE OR NOT; IN THIS WE STAND OR FALL: 5 540
YET THAT WE NEVER SHALL FORGET TO LOVE 5 550
HOLY MEMORIALS, ACTS OF ZEALE AND LOVE 5 593
HIS LOYALTIE HE KEPT, HIS LOVE, HIS ZEALE; 5 900
SO OFT IN FESTIVALS OF JOY AND LOVE 6 94
OF MAJESTIE DIVINE, SAPIENCE AND LOVE 7 195
OR WANDER WITH DELIGHT, AND LOVE TO HAUNT 7 330
SUCH PAIRS, IN LOVE AND MUTUAL HONOUR JOYN'D? 8 58
ON MAN HIS EQUAL LOVE: SAY THEREFORE ON; 8 228
COLLATERAL LOVE, AND DEEREST AMITIE. 8 426
THE SPIRIT OF LOVE AND AMOROUS DELIGHT. 8 477
IN EVERY GESTURE DIGNITIE AND LOVE. 8 489
THY CHERISHING, THY HONOURING, AND THY LOVE, 8 569
SO AWFUL, THAT WITH HONOUR THOU MAIST LOVE 8 577
ATTRACTIVE, HUMAN, RATIONAL, LOVE STILL; 8 587
WHEREIN TRUE LOVE CONSISTS NOT; LOVE REFINES 8 589
BY WHICH TO HEAV'NLY LOVE THOU MAIST ASCEND, 8 592
FROM ALL HER WORDS AND ACTIONS MIXT WITH LOVE 8 602
TO LOVE THOU BLAM'ST ME NOT, FOR LOVE THOU SAIST 8 612
LOVE NOT THE HEAV'NLY SPIRITS, AND HOW THIR LOVE 8 615
US HAPPIE, AND WITHOUT LOVE NO HAPPINESS. 8 621
BE STRONG, LIVE HAPPIE, AND LOVE, BUT FIRST OF ALL 8 633
HIM WHOM TO LOVE IS TO OBEY, AND KEEP 8 634
TO BRUTE DENI'D, AND ARE OF LOVE THE FOOD, 9 240
LOVE NOT THE LOWEST END OF HUMAN LIFE. 9 241
CONJUGAL LOVE, THEN WHICH PERHAPS NO BLISS 9 263
THY EQUAL FEAR THAT MY FIRM FAITH AND LOVE 9 286

LOVE (CONTINUED)
AND MATRIMONIAL LOVE; BUT EVE, WHO THOUGHT 9 319
AND WHAT IS FAITH, LOVE, VERTUE UNASSAID 9 335
NOT THEN MISTRUST, BUT TENDER LOVE ENJOYNES, 9 357
WHAT HITHER BROUGHT US, HATE, NOT LOVE, NOR HOPE 9 475
SHEE FAIR, DIVINELY FAIR, FIT LOVE FOR GODS, 9 489
NOT TERRIBLE, THOUGH TERROUR BE IN LOVE 9 490
HATE STRONGER, UNDER SHEW OF LOVE WELL FEIGN'D, 9 492
THE TEMPTER, BUT WITH SHEW OF ZEALE AND LOVE 9 665
IN FEMAL SEX, THE MORE TO DRAW HIS LOVE, 9 822
SO DEAR I LOVE HIM THAT WITH HIM ALL DEATHS 9 832
THY PRESENCE, AGONIE OF LOVE TILL NOW 9 858
MAY JOYNE US, EQUAL JOY, AS EQUAL LOVE; 9 882
THY SWEET CONVERSE AND LOVE SO DEARLY JOYN'D, 9 909
O GLORIOUS TRIAL OF EXCEEDING LOVE, 9 961
SHALL SEPARATE US, LINKT IN LOVE SO DEARE, 9 970
THIS HAPPIE TRIAL OF THY LOVE, WHICH ELSE 9 975
SO FAITHFUL LOVE UNEQUALD; BUT I FEEL 9 983
TENDERLY WEPT, MUCH WON THAT HE HIS LOVE 9 991
THERE THEY THIR FILL OF LOVE AND LOVES DISPORT 9 1042
IS THIS THE LOVE, IS THIS THE RECOMPENCE 9 1163
LOVE WAS NOT IN THIR LOOKS, EITHER TO GOD 10 111
THY LOVE, NOT THY SUBJECTION, AND HER GIFTS 10 153
BY A FARR WORSE, OR IF SHE LOVE, WITHHELD 10 903
WHAT LOVE SINCERE, AND REVERENCE IN MY HEART 10 915
IN OFFICES OF LOVE, HOW WE MAY LIGHT'N 10 960
THY LOVE, THE SOLE CONTENTMENT OF MY HEART 10 973
WITH GOODNESS AND PATERNAL LOVE, HIS FACE 11 353
NOR LOVE THY LIFE, NOR HATE; BUT WHAT THOU LIVST 11 553
AND NOW OF LOVE THEY TREAT TILL TH' EEVNING STAR 11 588
OF LOVE AND YOUTH NOT LOST, SONGS, GARLANDS,
FLOURS, 11 594
HIGH IN THE LOVE OF HEAV'N, YET FROM MY LOYNES 12 380
BOTH BY OBEDIENCE AND BY LOVE, THOUGH LOVE 12 403
WORKING THROUGH LOVE, UPON THIR HEARTS SHALL WRITE, 12 489
FOUNDED IN RIGHTEOUSNESS AND PEACE AND LOVE 12 550
AND LOVE WITH FEAR THE ONELY GOD, TO WALK 12 562
ADD VERTUE, PATIENCE, TEMPERANCE, ADD LOVE, 12 583

LOVE-LABOR'D
TUNES SWEETEST HIS LOVE-LABOR'D SONG; NOW REIGNES 5 41

LOVELESS
OF HARLOTS, LOVELESS, JOYLESS, UNINDEARD, 4 766

LOVELIER
UNPRAIS'D: FOR NOTHING LOVELIER CAN BE FOUND 9 232
LOVELIER, NOT THOSE THAT IN ILLYRIA CHANG'D 9 505

LOVELIEST
BUILD IN HER LOVELIEST, AND CREATE AN AWE 8 558

LOVELINESS
HER LOVELINESS, SO ABSOLUTE SHE SEEMS 8 547

LOVELY
WHEN GOD HATH SHOWRD THE EARTH; SO LOVELY SEEMD 4 152
MORE LOVELY THEN PANDORA, WHOM THE GODS 4 714
UNDECKT, SAVE WITH HER SELF MORE LOVELY FAIR 5 380
AND LOVELY, NEVER SINCE OF SERPENT KIND 9 504
SHEE WAS INDEED, AND LOVELY TO ATTRACT 10 152

LOVER
OR SERENATE, WHICH THE STARV'D LOVER SINGS 4 769

LOVERS
WAS UNDERSTOOD, THE INJUR'D LOVERS HELL. 5 450

LOVES
THAT EVER SINCE IN LOVES IMBRACES MET, 4 322
PUTS ME IN DOUBT. LIVES THER WHO LOVES HIS PAIN? 4 888
CELESTIAL ROSIE RED, LOVES PROPER HUE, 8 619
AS ONE WHO LOVES, AND SOME UNKINDNESS MEETS, 9 271
THERE THEY THIR FILL OF LOVE AND LOVES DISPORT 9 1042
FROM LOVES DUE RITES, NUPTIAL IMBRACES SWEET, 10 994
LOVES HARBINGER APPEERD; THEN ALL IN HEAT 11 589

LOVE-TALE
OF THAMMUZ YEARLY WOUNDED: THE LOVE-TALE 1 452

LOVING
IN LOVING THOU DOST WELL, IN PASSION NOT, 8 588
CONVERSING, LOOKING, LOVING, TO ABSTAIN 10 993

LOVLIEST
SO HAND IN HAND THEY PASSD, THE LOVLIEST PAIR 4 321

LOVLY
VERTUE IN HER SHAPE HOW LOVLY, SAW, AND PIN'D 4 848
CONSUMMATE LOVLY SMIL'D; AIRE, WATER, EARTH, 7 502
MANLIKE, BUT DIFFERENT SEX, SO LOVLY FAIRE, 8 471

LOV'ST
FOR EVER, AND IN MEE ALL WHOM THOU LOV'ST: 6 733

LOW
ILLUMIN, WHAT IS LOW RAISE AND SUPPORT; 1 23
DOUBTED HIS EMPIRE, THAT WERE LOW INDEED, 1 114

LOW (CONTINUED)
IN HORRIBLE DESTRUCTION LAID THUS LOW, 1 137
TO BESTIAL GODS; FOR WHICH THIR HEADS AS LOW 1 435
WE SUNK THUS LOW? TH' ASCENT IS EASIE THEN; 2 81
MATUREST COUNSELS: FOR HIS THOUGHTS WERE LOW; 2 115
THUS SAID, HE TURND, AND SATAN BOWING LOW, 3 736
TO KEEP THEM LOW WHOM KNOWLEDGE MIGHT EXALT 4 525
AS TO A SUPERIOR NATURE, BOWING LOW, 5 360
SO HIGH AS HEAV'D THE TUMID HILLS, SO LOW 7 288
THIR WANDRING COURSE NOW HIGH, NOW LOW, THEN HID, 8 126
WITH LOW SUBJECTION; UNDERSTAND THE SAME 8 345
APPROACHING TWO AND TWO, THESE COWRING LOW 8 350
DESCEND TO? WHO ASPIRES MUST DOWN AS LOW 9 169
LIKE A BLACK MIST LOW CREEPING, HE HELD ON 9 180
THE TRODDEN HERB, OF ABJECT THOUGHTS AND LOW, 9 572
WHY BUT TO KEEP YE LOW AND IGNORANT, 9 704
BUT FIRST LOW REVERENCE DON, AS TO THE POWER 9 835
NOW WAS THE SUN IN WESTERN CADENCE LOW 10 92
HAD UNBENIGHTED SHON, WHILE THE LOW SUN 10 682
ADAM BOWD LOW, HEE KINGLY FROM HIS STATE 11 249
INSTINCT THROUGH ALL PROPORTIONS LOW AND HIGH 11 562
YET SOMTIMES NATIONS WILL DECLINE SO LOW 12 97

LOWER
SATAN FROM HENCE NOW ON THE LOWER STAIR 3 540
AND IN THE LOWEST DEEP A LOWER DEEP 4 76
THE LOWER STILL I FALL, ONELY SUPREAM 4 91
WITHIN THEM EVERY LOWER FACULTIE 5 410
BELLEROPHON, THOUGH FROM A LOWER CLIME) 7 18
DEIGN TO DESCEND NOW LOWER, AND RELATE 7 84
A LOWER FLIGHT, AND SPEAK OF THINGS AT HAND 8 199
INTO A LOWER WORLD, TO THIS OBSCURE 11 283

LOWEST
GREAT THINGS RESOLV'D, WHICH FROM THE LOWEST DEEP 2 392
HARSH THUNDER, THAT THE LOWEST BOTTOM SHOOK 2 882
AND IN THE LOWEST DEEP A LOWER DEEP 4 76
THE LOWEST OF YOUR THRONG; OR IF YE KNOW, 4 831
IN THESE THY LOWEST WORKS, YET THESE DECLARE 5 158
ETHEREAL, AND AS LOWEST FIRST THE MOON; 5 418
LOVE NOT THE LOWEST END OF HUMAN LIFE. 9 241
OF LOWEST ORDER, PAST; AND FROM THE DORE 10 443

LOWLIE
TO KNOW WHAT PASSES THERE; BE LOWLIE WISE: 8 173
SHE ENDED WEEPING, AND HER LOWLIE PLIGHT, 10 937

LOWLIEST
THUS THEY IN LOWLIEST PLIGHT REPENTANT STOOD 11 1

LOWLINESS
WITH LOWLINESS MAJESTIC FROM HER SEAT, 8 42

LOWLY
HIS RIGHTEOUS ALTAR, BOWING LOWLY DOWN 1 434
TH' ETERNAL REGIONS: LOWLY REVERENT 3 349
LOWLY THEY BOW'D ADORING, AND BEGAN 5 144
THE EARTH, AND STATELY TREAD, OR LOWLY CREEP; 5 201
UNDER WHOSE LOWLY ROOF THOU HAST VOUTSAF'T 5 463
HE CEAS'D, I LOWLY ANSWER'D. TO ATTAINE 8 412

LOWR'D
SKIE LOWR'D AND MUTTERING THUNDER, SOM SAD DROPS 9 1002

LOWRING
HEAV'NS CHEARFUL FACE, THE LOWRING ELEMENT 2 490

LOYAL
FOUNDED IN REASON, LOYAL, JUST, AND PURE, 4 755

LOYALTIE
HIS LOYALTIE HE KEPT, HIS LOVE, HIS ZEALE; 5 900

LOYNES
HIGH IN THE LOVE OF HEAV'N, YET FROM MY LOYNES 12 380

LOYNS
POUR'D NEVER FROM HER FROZEN LOYNS, TO PASS 1 352
AND GIRDED ON OUR LOYNS, MAY COVER ROUND 9 1096
OUT OF THY LOYNS; TH' UNJUST THE JUST HATH SLAIN, 11 455

LUCENT
ASTRONOMER IN THE SUN'S LUCENT ORBE 3 589

LUCID
OF ABBANA AND PHARPHAR, LUCID STREAMS. 1 469
CLAD TO MEET MAN; OVER HIS LUCID ARMES 11 240

LUCIFER
THE PALACE OF GREAT LUCIFER, (SO CALL 5 760
KNOW THEN, THAT AFTER LUCIFER FROM HEAV'N 7 131
OF LUCIFER, SO BY ALLUSION CALLD, 10 425

LUCRE
OF LUCRE AND AMBITION, AND THE TRUTH 12 511

LULL
HAD ROUS'D THE SEA, NOW WITH HOARSE CADENCE LULL 2 287

LULLD
THESE LULLD BY NIGHTINGALES IMBRACEING SLEPT, 4 771

LUMINARIE
OR LONGITUDE, WHERE THE GREAT LUMINARIE 3 576

LUMINARIES
WITH THIR BRIGHT LUMINARIES THAT SET AND ROSE, 7 385
YET NOT TO EARTH ARE THOSE BRIGHT LUMINARIES 8 98

LUMINOUS
THE LUMINOUS INFERIOR ORBS, ENCLOS'D 3 420
STILL LUMINOUS BY HIS RAY. WHAT IF THAT LIGHT 8 140

LUR'D
LUR'D WITH THE SMELL OF INFANT BLOOD, TO DANCE 2 664
WHERE ARMIES LIE ENCAMPT, COME FLYING, LUR'D 10 276

LURE
TO LURE HER EYE; SHEE BUSIED HEARD THE SOUND 9 518

LURK
IN WHATSOEVER SHAPE HE LURK, OF WHOM 4 587

LURKING
THE DANGER, AND THE LURKING ENEMIE 9 1172

LURKS
THE WIFE, WHERE DANGER OR DISHONOUR LURKS, 9 267

LUST
OF MOLOCH HOMICIDE, LUST HARD BY HATE; 1 417
WITH LUST AND VIOLENCE THE HOUSE OF GOD. 1 496
INFLAM'D WITH LUST THEN RAGE) AND SWIFTER FAR, 2 791
BY THEE ADULTEROUS LUST WAS DRIV'N FROM MEN 4 753
AS WANTONLY REPAID; IN LUST THEY BURNE: 9 1015
SURFET, AND LUST, TILL WANTONNESS AND PRIDE 11 795

LUSTFUL
YET THENCE HIS LUSTFUL ORGIES HE ENLARG'D 1 415
OF LUSTFUL APPETENCE, TO SING, TO DANCE, 11 619

LUSTRE
THOUGH CHANG'D IN OUTWARD LUSTRE; THAT FIXT MIND 1 97
WITH GEMMS AND GOLDEN LUSTRE RICH IMBLAZ'D, 1 538
WANTS NOT HER HIDDEN LUSTRE, GEMMS AND GOLD; 2 271
HIS LUSTRE VISIBLY IMPAR'D; YET SEEMD 4 850
WAS PLAC'T IN REGAL LUSTRE. DOWN A WHILE 10 447
OF LUSTRE FROM THE BROOK, IN MEMORIE, 11 325

LUTE
MORE TUNEABLE THEN NEEDED LUTE OR HARP 5 151

LUXURIANT
LUXURIANT; MEAN WHILE MURMURING WATERS FALL 4 260

LUXURIE
IN WEALTH AND LUXURIE. TH' ASCENDING PILE 1 722
TO LUXURIE AND RIOT, FEAST AND DANCE, 11 715
WHERE LUXURIE LATE REIGN'D, SEA-MONSTERS WHELP'D 11 751

LUXURIOUS
AND IN LUXURIOUS CITIES, WHERE THE NOYSE 1 498
LUXURIOUS BY RESTRAINT; WHAT WE BY DAY 9 209
IN TRIUMPH AND LUXURIOUS WEALTH, ARE THEY 11 788

LUZ
TO PADAN-ARAM IN THE FIELD OF LUZ, 3 513

LYAR
ARGUES NO LEADER BUT A LYAR TRAC'T, 4 949

LYBIAN
BENEATH GIBRALTER TO THE LYBIAN SANDS. 1 355
WHOM GENTILES AMMON CALL AND LYBIAN JOVE, 4 277

LYE
LYE THUS ASTONISHT ON TH' OBLIVIOUS POOL, 1 266
NEW COURAGE AND REVIVE, THOUGH NOW THEY LYE 1 279
IN HIS OWN STRENGTH, THIS PLACE MAY LYE EXPOS'D 2 360

LYES
BY FALSITIES AND LYES THE GREATEST PART 1 367
WHICH WAY THE NEEREST COAST OF DARKNESS LYES 2 958
FOR MAN WILL HARK'N TO HIS GLOZING LYES, 3 93
THE STARRIE FLOCK, ALLUR'D THEM, AND WITH LYES 5 709

LYRE
WITH OTHER NOTES THEN TO TH' ORPHEAN LYRE 3 17

MACE
DEATH WITH HIS MACE PETRIFIC, COLD AND DRY, 10 294

MACHINATION
WITH DEV'LISH MACHINATION MIGHT DEVISE 6 504

MAD
HE MARKD AND MAD DEMEANOUR, THEN ALONE, 4 129

MADDING
HORRIBLE DISCORD, AND THE MADDING WHEELES . . . 6 210

MADE
WHOM REASON HATH EQUALD, FORCE HATH MADE SUPREAM . 1 248
WHOM THUNDER HATH MADE GREATER? HERE AT LEAST . 1 258
GLORY OF HIM THAT MADE THEM, TO TRANSFORM . . . 1 370
ON THAT OPPROBRIOUS HILL, AND MADE HIS GROVE . . 1 403
AND PUBLISH GRACE TO ALL, ON PROMISE MADE . . 2 238
MADE TO DESTROY: I FLED, AND CRY'D OUT DEATH; . . 2 787
MADE HEAD AGAINST HEAV'NS KING, THOUGH OVERTHROWN. 2 992
ALL HE COULD HAVE; I MADE HIM JUST AND RIGHT, . . 3 98
MADE PASSIVE BOTH, HAD SERVD NECESSITIE, . . 3 110
OF ALL THINGS MADE, AND JUDGEST ONELY RIGHT. . . 3 155
FOR HIM, WHAT FOR THY GLORIE THOU HAST MADE? . . 3 164
MADE FLESH, WHEN TIME SHALL BE, OF VIRGIN SEED, . 3 284
MADE VISIBLE, TH' ALMIGHTY FATHER SHINES, . . . 3 386
VOWS MADE IN PAIN, AS VIOLENT AND VOID. 4 97
TO RECOMMEND COOLE ZEPHYR, AND MADE EASE . . . 4 329
THAT MADE US, AND FOR US THIS AMPLE WORLD . . . 4 413
ON EARTH, MADE HEREBY APTER TO RECEIVE 4 672
THE GOD THAT MADE BOTH SKIE, AIR, EARTH AND HEAV'N 4 722
THY BLASTING VOLIED THUNDER MADE ALL SPEED . . 4 928
MADE VOCAL BY MY SONG, AND TAUGHT HIS PRAISE. . . 5 204
GOD MADE THEE PERFET, NOT IMMUTABLE; 5 524
AND GOOD HE MADE THEE, BUT TO PERSEVERE 5 525
THUS ADAM MADE REQUEST, AND RAPHAEL 5 561
BRIGHTNESS HAD MADE INVISIBLE, THUS SPAKE. . . . 5 599
MADE ANSWER. MIGHTIE FATHER, THOU THY FOES . . 5 735
WITH HIM THE POINTS OF LIBERTIE, WHO MADE . . . 5 823
AS BY HIS WORD THE MIGHTY FATHER MADE 5 836
BUT MORE ILLUSTRIOUS MADE, SINCE HE THE HEAD . . 5 842
MADE HORRID CIRCLES; TWO BROAD SUNS THIR SHIELDS . 6 305
OR EQUAL WHAT BETWEEN US MADE THE ODDS, ... 6 441
OR HOLLOW'D BODIES MADE OF OAK OR FIRR 6 574
SO EASIE, AND OF HIS THUNDER MADE A SCORN, . . . 6 632
THE WATERS FROM THE WATERS: AND GOD MADE . . . 7 263
OP'NING THIR VARIOUS COLOURS, AND MADE GAY . . . 7 318
GOD MADE, AND EVERY HERB, BEFORE IT GREW . . . 7 336
AND GOD MADE TWO GREAT LIGHTS, GREAT FOR THIR USE 7 346
THE LESS BY NIGHT ALTERNE: AND MADE THE STARRS, . 7 348
IN THE SUNS ORB, MADE POROUS TO RECEIVE 7 361
AND WORSHIP GOD SUPREAM, WHO MADE HIM CHIEF . . 7 515
HERE FINISH'D HEE, AND ALL THAT HE HAD MADE . . 7 548
WITNESS THIS NEW-MADE WORLD, ANOTHER HEAV'N . . 7 617
HAST THOU NOT MADE ME HERE THY SUBSTITUTE, . . . 8 381
SAVE WITH THE CREATURES WHICH I MADE, AND THOSE . 8 409
THIS TURN HATH MADE AMENDS; THOU HAST FULFILL'D . 8 491
HIS IMAGE WHO MADE BOTH, AND LESS EXPRESSING . . 8 544
AS ONE INTENDED FIRST, NOT AFTER MADE 8 555
MADE SO ADORN FOR THY DELIGHT THE MORE, ... 8 576
TO THEM MADE COMMON AND DIVULG'D, IF AUGHT . . . 8 583
FOR WHOM ALL THIS WAS MADE, ALL THIS WILL SOON . 9 132
HE EFFECTED; MAN HE MADE, AND FOR HIM BUILT . . 9 152
HE MADE US, AND DELIGHT TO REASON JOYN'D. . . . 9 243
REASON, IS FREE, AND REASON HE MADE RIGHT, . . . 9 352
INTO THE HEART OF EVE HIS WORDS MADE WAY, . . . 9 550
IN TANGLES, AND MADE INTRICATE SEEM STRAIT, . . 9 632
THE TONGUE NOT MADE FOR SPEECH TO SPEAK THY PRAISE: 9 749
MADE COMMON AND UNHALLOWD ERE OUR TASTE; . . . 9 931
DEPENDENT MADE; SO GOD SHALL UNCREATE, ... 9 943
MADE ERRE, WAS NOW EXHAL'D, AND GROSSER SLEEP . . 9 1049
ACCOUNTABLE MADE HASTE TO MAKE APPEAR 10 29
BEFORE HIS VOICE, OR WAS SHEE MADE THY GUIDE, . . 10 146
WHEREIN GOD SET THEE ABOVE HER MADE OF THEE, . . 10 149
THE GUILT ON HIM WHO MADE HIM INSTRUMENT . . . 10 166
AND CHAINS THEY MADE ALL FAST, TOO FAST THEY MADE 10 319
MINE WITH THIS GLORIOUS WORK, AND MADE ONE REALM . 10 391
MADE HAPPIE: HIM BY FRAUD I HAVE SEDUC'D . . . 10 485
THEN HEAV'N AND EARTH RENEWD SHALL BE MADE PURE . 10 638
MADE THEE WITHOUT THY LEAVE, WHAT IF THY SON . . 10 760
GOD MADE THEE OF CHOICE HIS OWN, AND OF HIS OWN . 10 766
THE STONIE FROM THIR HEARTS, & MADE NEW FLESH . . 11 4
MADE ONE WITH ME AS I WITH THEE AM ONE. 11 44
IN PARADISE, AND ON A HILL MADE ALT, ... 11 210
OF INSTRUMENTS THAT MADE MELODIOUS CHIME . . . 11 559
WITH THIR FOUR WIVES; AND GOD MADE FAST THE DORE. 11 737
AS AFTER THIRST, WHICH MADE THIR FLOWING SHRINK . 11 846
HE MADE NOT LORD; SUCH TITLE TO HIMSELF 12 70

MADNESS
AND MOON-STRUCK MADNESS, PINING ATROPHIE, ... 11 486

MAD'ST
AND MAD'ST IT PREGNANT: WHAT IN ME IS DARK . . . 1 22
AND STARRIE POLE: THOU ALSO MAD'ST THE NIGHT, . . 4 724
THIS WOMAN WHOM THOU MAD'ST TO BE MY HELP, . . . 10 137

MAEONIDES
BLIND THAMYRIS AND BLIND MAEONIDES, ... 3 35

MAEOTIS
MAEOTIS, UP BEYOND THE RIVER OB; 9 78

MAGAZIN
FIT FOR THE TUN SOM MAGAZIN TO STORE 4 816

MAGELLAN
BENEATH MAGELLAN. AT THAT TASTED FRUIT 10 687

MAGIC
PENDANT BY SUTTLE MAGIC MANY A ROW 1 727

MAGNANIMOUS
MAGNANIMOUS TO CORRESPOND WITH HEAV'N, ... 7 511

MAGNETIC
BY HIS MAGNETIC BEAM, THAT GENTLY WARMS 3 583

MAGNIFIC
IF THESE MAGNIFIC TITLES YET REMAIN 5 773
O PARENT, THESE ARE THY MAGNIFIC DEEDS, ... 10 354

MAGNIFICENCE
NOR GREAT ALCAIRO SUCH MAGNIFICENCE 1 718
MAGNIFICENCE; AND WHAT CAN HEAV'N SHEW MORE? . . 2 273
THE MAKERS HIGH MAGNIFICENCE, WHO BUILT 8 101

MAGNIFICENT
ASCENDING BY DEGREES MAGNIFICENT 3 502
MAGNIFICENT, HIS SIX DAYS WORK, A WORLD; 7 568
MAGNIFICENT THIS WORLD, AND EARTH HIS SEAT, . . . 9 153

MAGNIFI'D
THY THUNDERS MAGNIFI'D; BUT TO CREATE 7 606

MAGNIFIE
TO MAGNIFIE HIS WORKS, THE MORE WE KNOW. 7 97

MAGNITUDE
OF SMALLEST MAGNITUDE CLOSE BY THE MOON. 2 1053
GLOBOSE, AND EVERY MAGNITUDE OF STARRS, ... 7 357

MAGNITUDES
THIR MAGNITUDES, THIS EARTH A SPOT, A GRAINE, . . . 8 17

MAHANAIM
JACOB IN MAHANAIM, WHERE HE SAW 11 214

MAIA'S
SKIE-TINCTUR'D GRAIN. LIKE MAIA'S SON HE STOOD, . . 5 285

MAID
HIS MARRIAGE WITH THE SEAVENTIMES-WEDDED MAID. . . 5 223

MAILE
SHADDOWD FROM EITHER HEELE WITH FEATHERD MAILE . 5 284
MANGL'D WITH GASTLY WOUNDS THROUGH PLATE AND MAILE, 6 368

MAIM'D
MAIM'D HIS BRUTE IMAGE, HEAD AND HANDS LOPT OFF . 1 459

MAIN
MAIN REASON TO PERSWADE IMMEDIATE WARR, ... 2 121
HEAPT ON HIM THERE, NOR YET THE MAIN ABYSS . . . 3 83
AND NOW DIVIDED INTO FOUR MAIN STREAMS, ... 4 233
A STANDING FIGHT, THEN SOARING ON MAIN WING . . 6 243
BELIEVST SO MAIN TO OUR SUCCESS, I BRING; . . . 6 471
MAIN PROMONTORIES FLUNG, WHICH IN THE AIR . . . 6 654
MAIN OCEAN FLOW'D, NOT IDLE, BUT WITH WARME . . 7 279
AND RAMPANT SHAKES HIS BRINDED MAIN; THE OUNCE, . 7 466
AND HAIRIE MAIN TERRIFIC, THOUGH TO THEE . . . 7 497

MAINE
BOTH BATTELS MAINE, WITH RUINOUS ASSAULT . . . 6 216
WILD WORK IN HEAV'N, AND DANGEROUS TO THE MAINE. . 6 698
OVER THIS MAINE FROM HELL TO THAT NEW WORLD . . 10 257
DEFEATING SIN AND DEATH, HIS TWO MAINE ARMES, . . 12 431

MAINLY
INDUCTIVE MAINLY TO THE SIN OF EVE. 11 519

MAINTAIND
THE BETTER FIGHT, WHO SINGLE HAST MAINTAIND . . 6 30

MAISTER
THE GREAT WORK-MAISTER, LEADS TO NO EXCESS . . . 3 696

MAISTRIE
STRIVE HERE FOR MAISTRIE, AND TO BATTEL BRING . . 2 899
HEROIC DEEM'D, CHIEF MAISTRIE TO DISSECT . . . 9 29

MAISTRING
TO DWELL, UNLESS BY MAISTRING HEAV'NS SUPREAME; . 9 125

MAJESTIC
WITH LOWLINESS MAJESTIC FROM HER SEAT, ... 8 42

MAJESTICK
MAJESTICK THOUGH IN RUIN: SAGE HE STOOD 2 305

MAJESTIE
IN NAKED MAJESTIE SEEMD LORDS OF ALL, ... 4 290
RISING IN CLOUDED MAJESTIE, AT LENGTH 4 607
IDOL OF MAJESTIE DIVINE, ENCLOS'D 6 101

MAJESTIE (CONTINUED)
OF MAJESTIE DIVINE, SAPIENCE AND LOVE 7 195
AND WITH OBSEQUIOUS MAJESTIE APPROV'D 8 509
TO WHOM THE VIRGIN MAJESTIE OF EVE, ... 9 270
OR OF THE THRONES ABOVE, SUCH MAJESTIE 11 232

MAJESTY
AND WITH THE MAJESTY OF DARKNESS ROUND 2 266

MAKE
CAN MAKE A HEAV'N OF HELL, A HELL OF HEAV'N. . . . 1 255
DROPT MANNA, AND COULD MAKE THE WORSE APPEAR . . 2 113
TO MAKE THEM MIRTH US'D ALL HIS MIGHT, AND WREATHD 4 346
FOR GOD'S, YET ABLE TO MAKE GODS OF MEN: 5 70
TO MAKE US LESS, BENT RATHER TO EXALT 5 829
LET US MAKE NOW MAN IN OUR IMAGE, MAN 7 519
TO MAKE HER AMIABLE: ON SHE CAME, ... 8 484
BY WHAT I SEEK, BUT OTHERS TO MAKE SUCH 9 127
OF VERTUE TO MAKE WISE: WHAT HINDERS THEN . . . 9 778
SHALL I APPEER? SHALL I TO HIM MAKE KNOWN . . . 9 817
TO OPEN EYES, AND MAKE THEM GODS WHO TASTE; . . . 9 866
ACCOUNTABLE MADE HASTE TO MAKE APPEAR 10 29
HIM FIRST MAKE SURE YOUR THRALL, AND LASTLY KILL. 10 402
BOTH TO DESTROY, OR UNIMMORTAL MAKE 10 611
CAN HE MAKE DEATHLESS DEATH? THAT WERE TO MAKE . 10 798
FROM WHAT WE FEAR FOR BOTH, LET US MAKE SHORT, . 10 1000
TO MAKE DEATH IN US LIVE: THEN LET US SEEK . . . 10 1028
MAKE THEY BUT OF THIR BRETHREN, MEN OF MEN? . . . 11 680

MAKER
LIK'NING HIS MAKER TO THE GRAZED OX, ... 1 486
UNLESS TH' ALMIGHTY MAKER THEM ORDAIN 2 915
THIR MAKER, OR THIR MAKING, OR THIR FATE, ... 3 113
THE UNIVERSAL MAKER WE MAY PRAISE; 3 676
THE IMAGE OF THIR GLORIOUS MAKER SHON, ... 4 292
MAKER OMNIPOTENT, AND THOU THE DAY, ... 4 725
OUR MAKER BIDS INCREASE, WHO BIDS ABSTAIN . . . 4 748
THIR MAKER, IN FIT STRAINS PRONOUNC'T OR SUNG . . 5 148
VARIE TO OUR GREAT MAKER STILL NEW PRAISE. . . . 5 184
OUR MAKER, AND OBEY HIM WHOSE COMMAND 5 551
THY MAKING, WHILE THE MAKER GAVE THEE BEING? . . 5 858
TO GLORIFIE THE MAKER, AND INFERR 7 116
NOT OF MY SELF; BY SOME GREAT MAKER THEN, . . . 8 278
MY MAKER, BE PROPITIOUS WHILE I SPEAK. 8 380
LED BY HER HEAV'NLY MAKER, THOUGH UNSEEN, . . . 8 485
WHOM US THE MORE TO SPITE HIS MAKER RAIS'D . . . 9 177
LEFT SO IMPERFET BY THE MAKER WISE, ... 9 338
FAIREST RESEMBLANCE OF THY MAKER FAIRE, ... 9 538
AGAINST HIS MAKER; NO DECREE OF MINE 10 43
DID I REQUEST THEE, MAKER, FROM MY CLAY . . . 10 743
UNMINDFUL OF THIR MAKER, THOUGH HIS SPIRIT . . . 11 611

MAKERS
ACCEPT YOUR MAKERS WORK; HE GAVE IT ME, ... 4 380
THE MAKERS HIGH MAGNIFICENCE, WHO BUILT 8 101
AND FOR HIS MAKERS IMAGE SAKE EXEMPT? 11 514
THIR MAKERS IMAGE, ANSWERD MICHAEL, THEN . . . 11 515

MAKES
HIS CRIME MAKES GUILTIE ALL HIS SONS, THY MERIT . 3 290
LODGE AND DISLODGE BY TURNS, WHICH MAKES THROUGH
HEAV'N 6 7
WHICH ALL SUBDUES, AND MAKES REMISS THE HANDS . 6 458
WITH MOUNTAINS AS WITH WEAPONS ARM'D, WHICH MAKES 6 697
BUT CALL IN AIDE, WHICH MAKES A BLOODY FRAY; . . 11 651
AND MAKES A COVENANT NEVER TO DESTROY 11 892
TOO NUMEROUS; WHENCE OF GUESTS HE MAKES THEM SLAVES 12 167

MAKING
THIR MAKER, OR THIR MAKING, OR THIR FATE, . . . 3 113
THY MAKING, WHILE THE MAKER GAVE THEE BEING? . . 5 858
CONTINU'D MAKING, AND WHO KNOWS HOW LONG . . . 9 138

MALABAR
IN MALABAR OR DECAN SPREDS HER ARMES 9 1103

MALADIES
NUMBERS OF ALL DISEAS'D, ALL MALADIES 11 480

MALE
OF BAALIM AND ASHTAROTH, THOSE MALE, ... 1 422
MALE HE CREATED THEE, BUT THY CONSORT 7 529
COMMUNICATING MALE AND FEMAL LIGHT, ... 8 150

MALES
INHOSPITABLY, AND KILLS THIR INFANT MALES: . . . 12 168

MALICE
HOW ALL HIS MALICE SERV'D BUT TO BRING FORTH . . 1 217
SO DEEP A MALICE, TO CONFOUND THE RACE 2 382
HIS MALICE, AND THY GOODNESS BRING TO NAUGHT, . . 3 158
NOT SO ON MAN; HIM THROUGH THEIR MALICE FALL'N, . 3 400
AND WROUGHT BUT MALICE; LIFTED UP SO HIGH . . . 4 49
DEEP MALICE TO CONCEALE, COUCH'T WITH REVENGE: . 4 123
DEEP MALICE THENCE CONCEIVING AND DISDAIN, . . . 5 666
THY MALICE INTO THOUSANDS, ONCE UPRIGHT 6 270
IN FUTURE DAYES, IF MALICE SHOULD ABOUND, . . . 6 502
IN MEDITATED FRAUD AND MALICE, BENT 9 55

MALICE (CONTINUED)
NOR THOU HIS MALICE AND FALSE GUILE CONTEMN; . . 9 306
HIS MALICE, AND WITH RAPINE SWEET BEREAV'D . . . 9 461

MALICIOUS
WHAT HATH BIN WARN'D US, WHAT MALICIOUS FOE . . 9 253

MALIGNANT
THIR INFLUENCE MALIGNANT WHEN TO SHOWRE, . . . 10 662
TO GOOD MALIGNANT, TO BAD MEN BENIGNE, ... 12 538

MALIGNE
THE SPIRIT MALIGNE, BUT MUCH MORE ENVY SEIS'D . . 3 553
FOR ENVIE, YET WITH JEALOUS LEER MALIGNE . . . 4 503
TWO PLANETS RUSHING FROM ASPECT MALIGNE 6 313
OF SPIRITS MALIGNE A BETTER RACE TO BRING . . . 7 189

MAMMON
OR CAST A RAMPART. MAMMON LED THEM ON, ... 1 678
MAMMON, THE LEAST ERECTED SPIRIT THAT FELL . . . 1 679
NOT PEACE: AND AFTER HIM THUS MAMMON SPAKE. . . 2 228
AS MAMMON ENDED, AND HIS SENTENCE PLEAS'D, . . . 2 291

MAN
WITH LOSS OF EDEN, TILL ONE GREATER MAN 1 4
ON MAN BY HIM SEDUC'T, BUT ON HIMSELF 1 219
THROUGH GODS HIGH SUFFERANCE FOR THE TRYAL OF MAN, 1 366
DAGON HIS NAME, SEA MONSTER, UPWARD MAN 1 462
GLORIES: FOR NEVER SINCE CREATED MAN, ... 1 573
OF SOME NEW RACE CALL'D MAN, ABOUT THIS TIME . . 2 348
MAN HAD NOT HELLISH FOES ANOW BESIDES, ... 2 504
MEAN WHILE THE ADVERSARY OF GOD AND MAN, . . . 2 629
BUT HEE ONCE PAST, SOON AFTER WHEN MAN FELL, . . 2 1023
AND MAN THERE PLAC'T, WITH PURPOSE TO ASSAY . . 3 90
FOR MAN WILL HARK'N TO HIS GLOZING LYES, . . . 3 93
SELF-TEMPTED, SELF-DEPRAV'D; MAN FALLS DECEIV'D . 3 130
BY THE OTHER FIRST; MAN THEREFORE SHALL FIND GRACE, 3 131
THY SOVRAN SENTENCE, THAT MAN SHOULD FIND GRACE; . 3 145
FOR SHOULD MAN FINALLY BE LOST, SHOULD MAN . . 3 150
MAN SHALL NOT QUITE BE LOST, BUT SAV'D WHO WILL, . 3 173
BUT YET ALL IS NOT DON; MAN DISOBEYING, ... 3 203
FATHER, THY WORD IS PAST, MAN SHALL FIND GRACE; . 3 227
HAPPIE FOR MAN, SO COMING; HE HER AIDE 3 232
ACCOUNT MEE MAN; I FOR HIS SAKE WILL LEAVE . . . 3 238
TO ME ARE ALL MY WORKS, NOR MAN THE LEAST . . . 3 277
AND BE THY SELF MAN AMONG MEN ON EARTH, ... 3 283
RECEIVE NEW LIFE. SO MAN, AS IS MOST JUST, . . . 3 294
SHALL SATISFIE FOR MAN, BE JUDG'D AND DIE, . . . 3 295
BOTH GOD AND MAN, SON BOTH OF GOD AND MAN, . . . 3 316
NOT SO ON MAN; HIM THROUGH THEIR MALICE FALL'N, . 3 400
PERCEIVE THEE PURPOS'D NOT TO DOOM FRAIL MAN . . 3 404
TO PARADISE THE HAPPIE SEAT OF MAN, ... 3 632
ALL THESE HIS WONDROUS WORKS, BUT CHIEFLY MAN, . 3 663
IN WHICH OF ALL THESE SHINING ORBES HATH MAN . . 3 668
FOR NEITHER MAN NOR ANGEL CAN DISCERN 3 682
THAT PLACE IS EARTH THE SEAT OF MAN, THAT LIGHT . 3 724
TO WRECK ON INNOCENT FRAIL MAN HIS LOSS 4 11
AS MAN ERE LONG, AND THIS NEW WORLD SHALL KNOW. . 4 113
ALL PATH OF MAN OR BEAST THAT PAST THAT WAY: . . 4 177
ADAM THE GOODLIEST MAN OF MEN SINCE BORNE . . . 4 323
MORE OF TH' ALMIGHTIES WORKS, AND CHIEFLY MAN . . 4 566
MAN HATH HIS DAILY WORK OF BODY OR MIND 4 618
DAUGHTER OF GOD AND MAN, ACCOMPLISHT EVE, . . . 4 660
SUCH WAS THIR AWE OF MAN. IN SHADIE BOWER . . . 4 705
BUT OUR DESTROYER, FOE TO GOD AND MAN? 4 749
NOR GOD, NOR MAN; IS KNOWLEDGE SO DESPIS'D? . . . 5 60
EVIL INTO THE MIND OF GOD OR MAN 5 117
(WHOSE PRAISE BE EVER SUNG) TO MAN IN PART . . . 5 405
THY FAVOUR, IN THIS HONOUR DONE TO MAN, ... 5 462
VITAL IN EVERY PART, NOT AS FRAIL MAN 6 345
OR HEART OF MAN SUFFICE TO COMPREHEND? 7 114
ANOTHER WORLD, OUT OF ONE MAN A RACE 7 155
UPON THE EARTH, AND MAN TO TILL THE GROUND . . . 7 332
TO MAN, THE GREATER TO HAVE RULE BY DAY, ... 7 347
LET US MAKE NOW MAN IN OUR IMAGE, MAN 7 519
THIS SAID, HE FORMD THEE, ADAM, THEE O MAN . . . 7 524
FROM MAN OR ANGEL THE GREAT ARCHITECT 8 72
THAT MAN MAY KNOW HE DWELLS NOT IN HIS OWN; . . . 8 103
GLADLY INTO THE WAYES OF GOD WITH MAN: 8 226
ON MAN HIS EQUAL LOVE: SAY THEREFORE ON; 8 228
FOR MAN TO TELL HOW HUMAN LIFE BEGAN 8 250
FIRST MAN, OF MEN INNUMERABLE ORDAIN'D 8 297
AND ALL THIS GOOD TO MAN, FOR WHOSE WELL BEING . 8 361
WORS THEN CAN MAN WITH BEAST, AND LEAST OF ALL. . 8 397
IS NO DEFICIENCE FOUND; NOT SO IS MAN, ... 8 416
BUT MAN BY NUMBER IS TO MANIFEST 8 422
KNEW IT NOT GOOD FOR MAN TO BE ALONE, ... 8 445
BEFORE ME; WOMAN IS HER NAME, OF MAN 8 496
THE SOULE OF MAN, OR PASSION IN HIM MOVE. . . . 8 585
WITH MAN, AS WITH HIS FRIEND, FAMILIAR US'D . . . 9 2
DISLOYAL ON THE PART OF MAN, REVOLT, ... 9 7
OF GROWTH, SENSE, REASON, ALL SUMM'D UP IN MAN. . 9 113
HE EFFECTED; MAN HE MADE, AND FOR HIM BUILT . . . 9 152
OF HEAV'N, THIS MAN OF CLAY, SON OF DESPITE, . . 9 176
DAUGHTER OF GOD AND MAN, IMMORTAL EVE, ... 9 291
OF ALL THAT HE CREATED, MUCH LESS MAN, ... 9 346
HALF WHAT IN THEE IS FAIR, ONE MAN EXCEPT, . . . 9 545
WHAT MAY THIS MEAN? LANGUAGE OF MAN PRONOUNC'T . 9 553

MAN (CONTINUED)

TO MAN, AND INDIGNATION AT HIS WRONG, 9 666
SHALL THAT BE SHUT TO MAN, WHICH TO THE BEAST 9 691
THAT YE SHOULD BE AS GODS, SINCE I AS MAN, 9 710
INTERNAL MAN, IS BUT PROPORTION MEET, 9 711
AND WHAT ARE GODS THAT MAN MAY NOT BECOME 9 716
TH' OFFENCE, THAT MAN SHOULD THUS ATTAIN TO KNOW? 9 726
THOUGH KEPT FROM MAN, AND WORTHY TO BE ADMIR'D, 9 746
FRIENDLY TO MAN, FARR FROM DECEIT OR GUILE. 9 772
LIVES, AS THOU SAIDST, AND GAINES TO LIVE AS MAN 9 933
OF MAN, WITH STRENGTH ENTIRE, AND FREE WILL ARM'D, 10 9
FOR MAN, FOR OF HIS STATE BY THIS THEY KNEW, 10 19
ON HIS BAD ERRAND, MAN SHOULD BE SEDUC'T 10 41
AND DESTIN'D MAN HIMSELF TO JUDGE MAN FALL'N. 10 62
TO SENTENCE MAN: THE VOICE OF GOD THEY HEARD 10 97
THE THICKEST TREES, BOTH MAN AND WIFE, TILL GOD 10 101
CONCERN'D NOT MAN (SINCE HE NO FURTHER KNEW) 10 170
SO JUDG'D HE MAN, BOTH JUDGE AND SAVIOUR SENT, 10 209
ALL, THOUGH ALL-KNOWING, WHAT HAD PAST WITH MAN 10 227
CHIEFLY ON MAN, SOLE LORD OF ALL DECLAR'D, 10 401
OF ABSOLUTE PERFECTION, THEREIN MAN 10 483
BOTH HIS BELOVED MAN AND ALL HIS WORLD, 10 489
TO RANGE IN, AND TO DWELL, AND OVER MAN 10 492
MAN I DECEAV'D: THAT WHICH TO MEE BELONGS, 10 496
INTO THE SAME ILLUSION, NOT AS MAN 10 571
TO DASH THIR PRIDE, AND JOY FOR MAN SEDUC'T. 10 577
TILL I IN MAN RESIDING THROUGH THE RACE, 10 607
KEPT IN THAT STATE, HAD NOT THE FOLLY OF MAN 10 619
OF MAN, BUT FLED HIM, OR WITH COUNT'NANCE GRIM 10 713
TO MOULD ME MAN, DID I SOLLICITE THEE 10 744
LEAST THAT PURE BREATH OF LIFE, THE SPIRIT OF MAN 10 784
IS HIS WRAUTH ALSO? BE IT, MAN IS NOT SO, 10 795
WRATH WITHOUT END ON MAN WHOM DEATH MUST END? 10 797
IN PUNISHT MAN, TO SATISFIE HIS RIGOUR 10 803
THROUGH THE STILL NIGHT, NOT NOW, AS ERE MAN FELL, 10 846
FROM THY IMPLANTED GRACE IN MAN, THESE SIGHS 11 23
ALL THY REQUEST FOR MAN, ACCEPTED SON, 11 46
O SONS, LIKE ONE OF US MAN IS BECOME 11 84
OR IN BEHALF OF MAN, OR TO INVADE 11 102
WITH WHOSE STOL'N FRUIT MAN ONCE MORE TO DELUDE. 11 125
MAN IS TO LIVE, AND ALL THINGS LIVE FOR MAN. 11 161
ONE MAN, ASSASSIN-LIKE HAD LEVIED WARR, 11 219
NOT IN HIS SHAPE CELESTIAL, BUT AS MAN 11 239
CLAD TO MEET MAN; OVER HIS LUCID ARMES 11 240
TO THAT MEEK MAN, WHO WELL HAD SACRIFIC'D; 11 451
IN HIS FIRST SHAPE ON MAN; BUT MANY SHAPES 11 467
HIS BEST OF MAN, AND GAVE HIM UP TO TEARS 11 497
TH' IMAGE OF GOD IN MAN CREATED ONCE 11 508
UNDER INHUMAN PAINS? WHY SHOULD NOT MAN, 11 511
BUT WHO WAS THAT JUST MAN, WHOM HAD NOT HEAV'N 11 681
FOR MAN AND BEAST: WHEN LOE A WONDER STRANGE, 11 733
WITH THOUGHT THAT THEY MUST BE. LET NO MAN SEEK 11 770
MAN IS NOT WHOM TO WARNE: THOSE FEW ESCAP'T 11 777
WITH LENGTH OF HAPPY DAYES THE RACE OF MAN; 11 782
AND WHETHER HERE THE RACE OF MAN WILL END 11 786
ONE MAN EXCEPT, THE ONELY SON OF LIGHT 11 808
THE ONE JUST MAN ALIVE; BY HIS COMMAND 11 818
NO SOONER HEE WITH THEM OF MAN AND BEAST 11 822
AT THIS LAST SIGHT, ASSUR'D THAT MAN SHALL LIVE 11 872
FOR ONE MAN FOUND SO PERFET AND SO JUST, 11 876
THOUGH LATE REPENTING HIM OF MAN DEPRAV'D, 11 886
SUCH GRACE SHALL ONE JUST MAN FIND IN HIS SIGHT, 11 890
WITH MAN THEREIN OR BEAST; BUT WHEN HE BRINGS 11 895
AND MAN AS FROM A SECOND STOCK PROCEED. 12 7
BY HIS DONATION; BUT MAN OVER MEN 12 69
STAYES NOT ON MAN; TO GOD HIS TOWER INTENDS 12 73
SIEGE AND DEFIANCE: WRETCHED MAN. WHAT FOOD 12 74
REASON IN MAN OBSCUR'D, OR NOT OBEYD, 12 86
MAN TILL THEN FREE. THEREFORE SINCE HEE PERMITS 12 90
A NATION FROM ONE FAITHFUL MAN TO SPRING: 12 113
SOME BLOUD MORE PRECIOUS MUST BE PAID FOR MAN, 12 293
CANNOT APPEASE, NOR MAN THE MORAL PART 12 298
THROUGH THE WORLDS WILDERNESS LONG WANDERD MAN 12 313
OF GOD MOST HIGH; SO GOD WITH MAN UNITES. 12 382
THY RANSOM PAID, WHICH MAN FROM DEATH REDEEMS, 12 424
HIS DEATH FOR MAN, AS MANY AS OFFERD LIFE 12 425
WHAT MAN CAN DO AGAINST THEM, NOT AFFRAID, 12 493

MANACL'D

NOT TI'D OR MANACL'D WITH JOYNT OR LIMB, 1 426

MANAG'D

WELL MANAG'D; OF THAT SKILL THE MORE THOU KNOW'ST, 8 573

MANGL'D

MANGL'D WITH GASTLY WOUNDS THROUGH PLATE AND MAILE, 6 368

MANHOOD

WITH THEE THY MANHOOD ALSO TO THIS THRONE; 3 314
THOU DID'ST RESIGNE THY MANHOOD, AND THE PLACE 10 148
IN MANHOOD WHERE YOUTH ENDED; BY HIS SIDE 11 246
MANHOOD TO GOD-HEAD, WITH MORE STRENGTH TO FOIL 12 389

MANIFEST

TO MANIFEST THEE WORTHIEST TO BE HEIR 6 707
TO MANIFEST THE MORE THY MIGHT: HIS EVIL 7 615
BUT MAN BY NUMBER IS TO MANIFEST 8 422
RESPLENDENT ALL HIS FATHER MANIFEST 10 66

MANIFOLD

UNLIMITED OF MANIFOLD DELIGHTS: 4 435
GREATER SO MANIFOLD TO THIS ONE USE, 8 29
AND MANIFOLD IN SIN, DESERV'D TO FALL. 10 16

MAN-KIND

THE TEMPTER ERE TH' ACCUSER OF MAN-KIND, 4 10

MANKIND

THE MOTHER OF MANKIND, WHAT TIME HIS PRIDE 1 36
OF MANKIND THEY CORRUPTED TO FORSAKE 1 368
OF MANKIND IN ONE ROOT, AND EARTH WITH HELL 2 383
OF MANKIND, IN THE HAPPIE GARDEN PLAC'T, 3 66
DRAW AFTER HIM THE WHOLE RACE OF MANKIND, 3 161
AND NOW WITHOUT REDEMPTION ALL MANKIND 3 222
FOUND OUT FOR MANKIND UNDER WRAUTH, O THOU 3 275
THE HEAD OF ALL MANKIND, THOUGH ADAMS SON. 3 286
MANKIND CREATED, AND FOR HIM THIS WORLD. 4 107
SIN-BRED, HOW HAVE YE TROUBL'D ALL MANKIND 4 315
MANKIND WITH HER FAIRE LOOKS, TO BE AVENGD 4 718
IN THEM AT ONCE TO RUIN ALL MANKIND. 5 228
HAILE MOTHER OF MANKIND, WHOSE FRUITFUL WOMB 5 388
TO WHOM THE PATRIARCH OF MANKIND REPLI'D, 5 506
BUT IF THE SENSE OF TOUCH WHEREBY MANKIND 8 579
WITH GRATEFUL MEMORIE: THOU TO MANKIND 8 650
SO SPAKE THE ENEMIE OF MANKIND, ENCLOS'D 9 494
HE RUIND, NOW MANKIND; WHOM WILL HE NEXT? 9 950
DESTIN'D RESTORER OF MANKIND, BY WHOM 10 646
ME NOW YOUR CURSE. AH, WHY SHOULD ALL MANKIND 10 822
MANKIND? THIS MISCHIEF HAD NOT THEN BEFALL'N, 10 895
THE RACE OF MANKIND DROWND, BEFORE THE SHRINE 11 13
MY JUDGMENTS, HOW WITH MANKIND I PROCEED, 11 69
EVE RIGHTLY CALL'D, MOTHER OF ALL MANKIND, 11 159
O MISERABLE MANKIND, TO WHAT FALL 11 500
PATRONS OF MANKIND, GODS, AND SONS OF GODS, 11 696
AND STABL'D; OF MANKIND, SO NUMEROUS LATE, 11 752
THAT HE RELENTS, NOT TO BLOT OUT MANKIND, 11 891
OF MEE AND ALL MANKIND; BUT NOW I SEE 12 276
(FOR BY THE WOMANS SEED) ON ALL MANKIND. 12 601

MANKINDE

FEMALE FOR RACE; THEN BLESS'D MANKINDE, AND SAID, 7 530
ABOVE MANKINDE, OR AUGHT THEN MANKINDE HIGHER, 8 358
SO SPAKE THE PATRIARCH OF MANKINDE, BUT EVE 9 376
THE ONELY TWO OF MANKINDE, BUT IN THEM 9 415
MEE AND MANKINDE; I AM TO BRUISE HIS HEEL; 10 498
THE SMELL OF PEACE TOWARD MANKINDE, LET HIM LIVE 11 38
OF ALL MANKINDE, WITH HIM THERE CRUCIFI'D, 12 417

MANKINDS

MANKINDS DELIVERANCE. BUT THE VOICE OF GOD 12 235

MANLIKE

MANLIKE, BUT DIFFERENT SEX, SO LOVLY FAIRE, 8 471

MANLY

ROUND FROM HIS PARTED FORELOCK MANLY HUNG 4 302
HOW BEAUTY IS EXCELLD BY MANLY GRACE 4 490

MANNA

DROPT MANNA, AND COULD MAKE THE WORSE APPEAR 2 113

MANS

OF MANS FIRST DISOBEDIENCE, AND THE FRUIT 1 1
MANS MORTAL CRIME, AND JUST TH' UNJUST TO SAVE, 3 215
AND SILENCE WAS IN HEAV'N: ON MANS BEHALF 3 218
MANS NATURE, LESS'N OR DEGRADE THINE OWNE. 3 304
BEGAN TO BLOOM, BUT SOON FOR MANS OFFENCE 3 355
FOR MANS OFFENCE. O UNEXAMPL'D LOVE, 3 410
AND BANISHT FROM MANS LIFE HIS HAPPIEST LIFE, 4 317
ALL THINGS TO MANS DELIGHTFUL USE; THE ROOFE 4 692
MANS NOURISHMENT, BY GRADUAL SCALE SUBLIM'D 5 483
ON MANS DESTRUCTION, MAUGRE WHAT MIGHT HAP 9 56
TO COUNTERFET MANS VOICE, TRUE IN OUR FALL, 9 1069
MANS FRIEND, HIS MEDIATOR, HIS DESIGN'D 10 60
WHICH MANS POLLUTING SIN WITH TAINT HATH SHED 10 631
FOR ONE MANS FAULT THUS GUILTLESS BE CONDEMN'D, 10 823
BUT STILL I SEE THE TENOR OF MANS WOE 11 632
FROM MANS EFFEMINATE SLACKNESS IT BEGINS, 11 634
MANS VOICE COMMANDING, SUN IN GIBEON STAND, 12 265

MANSION

IN THIS UNHAPPY MANSION, OR ONCE MORE 1 268
OF THIS ILL MANSION: INTERMIT NO WATCH 2 462
FROM THY EMPYREAL MANSION THUS ALONE, 3 699
TO THIR PREPAR'D ILL MANSION DRIVEN DOWN 6 738
AND SAID, THY MANSION WANTS THEE, ADAM, RISE, 8 296

MAN-SLAUGHTER

MAN-SLAUGHTER, SHALL BE HELD THE HIGHEST PITCH 11 693

MANTLE

OF GOD, AS WITH A MANTLE DIDST INVEST 3 10
AND O'RE THE DARK HER SILVER MANTLE THREW. 4 609

MANTLING

OF COOLE RECESS, O'RE WHICH THE MANTLING VINE 4 258
EACH SHOULDER BROAD, CAME MANTLING O'RE HIS BREST 5 279

MANTLING (CONTINUED)
BETWEEN HER WHITE WINGS MANTLING PROUDLY, ROWES . 7 439

MANURING
THAT MOCK OUR SCANT MANURING, AND REQUIRE 4 628
WHICH HIS OWN HAND MANURING ALL THE TREES . . . 11 28

MANY
O PRINCE, O CHIEF OF MANY THRONED POWERS, ... 1 128
LAY FLOATING MANY A ROOD, IN BULK AS HUGE . . . 1 196
NIGH ON THE PLAIN IN MANY CELLS PREPAR'D, . . . 1 700
TO MANY A ROW OF PIPES THE SOUND-BOARD BREATHS. . 1 709
PENDANT BY SUTTLE MAGIC MANY A ROW 1 727
IN HEAV'N BY MANY A TOWRED STRUCTURE HIGH, . . . 1 733
WITH NOTES ANGELICAL TO MANY A HARP 2 548
NO REST: THROUGH MANY A DARK AND DREARIE VAILE . 2 618
THEY PASS'D, AND MANY A REGION DOLOROUS, . . . 2 619
O'RE MANY A FROZEN, MANY A FIERIE ALPE, ... 2 620
BUT ENDED FOUL IN MANY A SCALY FOULD 2 651
UPLIFTED SPURNS THE GROUND, THENCE MANY A LEAGUE . 2 929
AS MANY MILES ALOFT: THAT FURIE STAY'D, ... 2 938
AS MANY AS ARE RESTOR'D, WITHOUT THEE NONE. . . 3 289
WITH MANY A VAIN EXPLOIT, THOUGH THEN RENOWND: . 3 465
CLEOMBROTUS, AND MANY MORE TOO LONG, ... 3 473
HERE IN THE DARK SO MANY PRECIOUS THINGS . . . 3 611
OF MANY A COLOURD PLUME SPRINKL'D WITH GOLD, . . 3 642
THROWS HIS STEEP FLIGHT IN MANY AN AERIE WHEELE, . 3 741
WELL PLEAS'D THEY SLACK THIR COURSE, AND MANY A
LEAGUE 4 164
ROSE A FRESH FOUNTAIN, AND WITH MANY A RILL . . 4 229
RUNS DIVERS, WANDRING MANY A FAMOUS REALME . . . 4 234
AMONG SO MANY SIGNES OF POWER AND RULE 4 429
ARE MANY LESSER FACULTIES THAT SERVE 5 101
FROM MANY A BERRIE, AND FROM SWEET KERNELS PREST . 5 346
THE RUIN OF SO MANY GLORIOUS ONCE 5 567
THAT OF SO MANY MYRIADS FALL'N, YET ONE 6 24
THIR NAMES OF THEE; SO OVER MANY A TRACT . . . 6 76
OF HEAV'N THEY MARCH'D, AND MANY A PROVINCE WIDE . 6 77
BY ANGELS MANY AND STRONG, WHO INTERPOS'D . . . 6 336
WITH MANY AN INRODE GOR'D; DEFORMED ROUT . . . 6 387
AND STUMBL'D MANY, WHO RECEIVES THEM RIGHT, . . 6 624
IMPLACABLE, AND MANY A DOLOROUS GROAN, ... 6 658
DREW MANY, WHOM THIR PLACE KNOWS HERE NO MORE; . 7 144
SO MANY NOBLER BODIES TO CREATE, ... 8 28
IN LABYRINTH OF MANY A ROUND SELF-ROWLD, . . . 9 183
NEERER HE DREW, AND MANY A WALK TRAVERS'D . . . 9 434
CURLD MANY A WANTON WREATH IN SIGHT OF EVE, . . 9 517
FOR MANY ARE THE TREES OF GOD THAT GROW 9 618
IN HEAV'NLY BRESTS? THESE, THESE AND MANY MORE . 9 730
OF RAVENOUS FOWL, THOUGH MANY A LEAGUE REMOTE, . 10 274
AND SCOURG'D WITH MANY A STROAK TH' INDIGNANT
WAVES. 10 311
MANY A DARK LEAGUE, REDUC'T IN CAREFUL WATCH . . 10 438
OF MANY WAYS TO DIE THE SHORTEST CHOOSING, . . . 10 1005
BY HIM WITH MANY COMFORTS, TILL WE END 10 1084
DEFEATED OF HIS SEISURE MANY DAYES 11 254
AND ONE BAD ACT WITH MANY DEEDS WELL DONE . . . 11 256
SO MANY GRATEFUL ALTARS I WOULD REARE 11 323
PRESENT, AND OF HIS PRESENCE MANY A SIGNE . . . 11 351
IN HIS FIRST SHAPE ON MAN; BUT MANY SHAPES . . . 11 467
OF DEATH, AND MANY ARE THE WAYES THAT LEAD . . . 11 468
TILL MANY YEARS OVER THY HEAD RETURN: 11 534
THE BURD'N OF MANY AGES, ON ME LIGHT 11 767
WERE LONG TO TELL, HOW MANY BATTELS FOUGHT, . . 12 261
HOW MANY KINGS DESTROYD, AND KINGDOMS WON, . . . 12 262
SO MANY AND SO VARIOUS LAWS ARE GIV'N; 12 282
SO MANY LAWS ARGUE SO MANY SINS 12 283
HIS DEATH FOR MAN, AS MANY AS OFFERD LIFE . . . 12 425
INFALLIBLE? YET MANY WILL PRESUME: 12 530
THAT YE MAY LIVE, WHICH WILL BE MANY DAYES, . . 12 602

MARASMUS
MARASMUS, AND WIDE-WASTING PESTILENCE, ... 11 487

MARBLE
THROUGH THE PURE MARBLE AIR HIS OBLIQUE WAY . . . 3 564

MARCH
ISRAEL IN SITTIM ON THIR MARCH FROM NILE 1 413
FOUR WAYS THIR FLYING MARCH, ALONG THE BANKS . . 2 574
IN CONFUS'D MARCH FORLORN, TH' ADVENTROUS BANDS . 2 615
HOMEWARD WITH FLYING MARCH WHERE WE POSSESS . . 5 688
OF MIDNIGHT MARCH, AND HURRIED MEETING HERE, . . 5 778
THIR MARCH WAS, AND THE PASSIVE AIR UPBORE . . . 6 72
TO EXPEDITE YOUR GLORIOUS MARCH; BUT I 10 474

MARCH'D
OF HEAV'N THEY MARCH'D, AND MANY A PROVINCE WIDE . 6 77

MARCHING
FROM EGYPT MARCHING, EQUAL'D WITH ONE STROKE . . 1 488
UNDER SPREAD ENSIGNS MARCHING MIGHT PASS THROUGH . 2 886
MARCHING FROM EDEN TOWARDS THE WEST, SHALL FINDE . 12 40

MARIAGEABLE
HER MARIAGEABLE ARMS, AND WITH HER BRINGS 5 217

MARIE
LONG AFTER TO BLEST MARIE, SECOND EVE. 5 387

MARINER
IMPRESS THE AIR, AND SHEWS THE MARINER 4 558

MARISH
RIS'N FROM A RIVER O'RE THE MARISH GLIDES, ... 12 630

MARITIM
ERCOCO AND THE LESS MARITIM KINGS 11 398

MARK
TO MARK WHAT OF THIR STATE HE MORE MIGHT LEARN . 4 400
BUT MARK WHAT I ARREEDE THEE NOW, AVANT; . . . 4 962
CALLS US, WE LOSE THE PRIME, TO MARK HOW SPRING . 5 21
WHATEVER FLEIGHTS NONE WOULD SUSPICIOUS MARK, . . 9 92
THE EYE OF EVE TO MARK HIS PLAY; HE GLAD . . . 9 528
ITH' MIDST AN ALTAR AS THE LAND-MARK STOOD . . 11 432
TO MARK THIR DOINGS, THEM BEHOLDING SOON, . . . 12 50

MARKD
HE MARKD AND MAD DEMEANOUR, THEN ALONE, ... 4 129

MARKT
BY WORD OR ACTION MARKT: ABOUT THEM ROUND . . . 4 401
BENT ALL ON SPEED, AND MARKT HIS AERIE GATE; . . 4 568

MARLE
OVER THE BURNING MARLE, NOT LIKE THOSE STEPS . . 1 296

MAROCCO
DAMASCO, OR MAROCCO, OR TREBISOND, ... 1 584
MAROCCO AND ALGIERS, AND TREMISEN; 11 404

MARR'D
THE INFERNAL POWERS, IN ONE DAY TO HAVE MARR'D . 9 136

MARRD
WHICH MARRD HIS BORROW'D VISAGE, AND BETRAID . . 4 116

MARRIAGE
HIS MARRIAGE WITH THE SEAVENTIMES-WEDDED MAID. . 5 223
OF NUPTIAL SANCTITIE AND MARRIAGE RITES: . . . 8 487
HYMEN, THEN FIRST TO MARRIAGE RITES INVOK'T; . . 11 591

MARRIAGES
OF THOSE ILL MATED MARRIAGES THOU SAW'ST: 11 684

MARRYING
MARRYING OR PROSTITUTING, AS BEFELL, ... 11 716

MARSHAL'D
AT JOUST AND TORNEAMENT; THEN MARSHAL'D FEAST . . 9 37

MARTIAL
SONOROUS METTAL BLOWING MARTIAL SOUNDS: 1 540

MARTYRDOM
OF PATIENCE AND HEROIC MARTYRDOM 9 32

MARVELING
THOUGH AT THE VOICE MUCH MARVELING; AT LENGTH . . 9 551

MARY
WHEN JESUS SON OF MARY SECOND EVE, ... 10 183

MASCULINE
WITH SPIRITS MASCULINE, CREATE AT LAST 10 890

MASK
MIXT DANCE, OR WANTON MASK, OR MIDNIGHT BAL, . . . 4 768

MASS
I SAW WHEN AT HIS WORD THE FORMLESS MASS, . . . 3 708
THROUGHOUT THE FLUID MASS, BUT DOWNWARD PURG'D . 7 237
FROM THE CONFLAGRANT MASS, PURG'D AND REFIN'D, . 12 548

MASSACHER
HIS BROTHER; FOR OF WHOM SUCH MASSACHER 11 679

MASSIE
WITH WOND'ROUS ART FOUND OUT THE MASSIE ORE, . . 1 703
OF MASSIE IRON OR SOLLID ROCK WITH EASE 2 878
IN PEARL, IN DIAMOND, AND MASSIE GOLD, ... 5 634
HIS MASSIE SPEAR UPSTAID; AS IF ON EARTH . . . 6 195
LABOURING, TWO MASSIE CLODS OF IRON AND BRASS . 11 565

MASSY
ETHEREAL TEMPER, MASSY, LARGE AND ROUND, ... 1 285

MAST
HEWN ON NORWEGIAN HILLS, TO BE THE MAST 1 293

MASTER
THERE WANTED YET THE MASTER WORK, THE END 7 505

MATCH
TO MATCH WITH THIR INVENTIONS THEY PRESUM'D 6 631

MATCHING
ILL MATCHING WORDS AND DEEDS LONG PAST OR LATE. 5 113

MATCHLESS
MATCHLESS, BUT WITH TH' ALMIGHTY, AND THAT STRIFE 1 623
ENDED REJOYCING IN THIR MATCHLESS CHIEF: 2 487
WARRING IN HEAV'N AGAINST HEAV'NS MATCHLESS KING: 4 41
TO FIND HIMSELF NOT MATCHLESS, AND HIS PRIDE 6 341
VALOUR OR STRENGTH, THOUGH MATCHLESS, QUELLD WITH PAIN 6 457
PLENIPOTENT ON EARTH, OF MATCHLESS MIGHT 10 404

MATCHT
GREW DARKER AT THIR FROWN, SO MATCHT THEY STOOD; 2 720
WHERE GOOD WITH BAD WERE MATCHT, WHO OF THEMSELVES 11 685

MATE
THUS SATAN TALKING TO HIS NEEREST MATE 1 192
OF UNBLEST FEET. HIM FOLLOWED HIS NEXT MATE, 1 238
KNOW YE NOT MEE? YE KNEW ME ONCE NO MATE 4 828
BANK THE MID SEA: PART SINGLE OR WITH MATE 7 403
THY MATE, WHO SEES WHEN THOU ART SEEN LEAST WISE. 8 578
AMONG THE BEASTS NO MATE FOR THEE WAS FOUND. 8 594
HE NEVER SHALL FIND OUT FIT MATE, BUT SUCH 10 899

MATED
OF THOSE ILL MATED MARRIAGES THOU SAW'ST: 11 684

MATERIAL
THIS WORLDS MATERIAL MOULD, CAME TO A HEAP: 3 709

MATERIALS
HIS DARK MATERIALS TO CREATE MORE WORLDS, 2 916
DEEP UNDER GROUND, MATERIALS DARK AND CRUDE, 6 478

MATES
AND TO HIS MATES THUS IN DERISION CALL'D. 6 608

MATIN
LIGHTLY DISPERS'D, AND THE SHRILL MATIN SONG 5 7
THE MATIN TRUMPET SUNG: IN ARMS THEY STOOD 6 526

MATRIMONIAL
AND MATRIMONIAL LOVE; BUT EVE, WHO THOUGHT 9 319

MATRON
EXPOS'D A MATRON TO AVOID WORSE RAPE. 1 505
THAT SHED MAY FLOWERS; AND PRESS'D HER MATRON LIP 4 501
THE EARTH, WHEN ADAM AND FIRST MATRON EVE 11 136

MATTER
WHAT MATTER WHERE, IF I BE STILL THE SAME, 1 256
SHALL BE THE COPIOUS MATTER OF MY SONG 3 413
HERE MATTER NEW TO GAZE THE DEVIL MET 3 613
SUCH TO PERFECTION, ONE FIRST MATTER ALL, 5 472
HIGH MATTER THOU INJOINST ME, O PRIME OF MEN, 5 563
MATTER TO MEE OF GLORY, WHOM THIR HATE 5 738
MATTER UNFORM'D AND VOID: DARKNESS PROFOUND 7 233
RAIS'D, AS OF SOM GREAT MATTER TO BEGIN. 9 669
MATTER OF SCORNE, NOT TO BE GIVEN THE FOE, 9 951
MATTER OF GLORIOUS TRIAL; AND PERHAPS 9 1177
TO THE RECEPTION OF THIR MATTER ACT, 10 807
REFLECTED, MAY WITH MATTER SERE FOMENT, 10 1071

MATTERS
SOLLICIT NOT THY THOUGHTS WITH MATTERS HID, 8 167

MATTIN
WITH EEVNING HARPS AND MATTIN, WHEN GOD SAID, 7 450

MATURE
FULL COUNSEL MUST MATURE: PEACE IS DESPAIRD, 1 660
HAD CIRCL'D HIS FULL ORBE, THE BIRTH MATURE 5 862
TILL DIETED BY THEE I GROW MATURE 9 803
ALL KINDS, AND FOR DESTRUCTION TO MATURE 10 612
CONSTANT, MATURE, PROOF AGAINST ALL ASSAULTS, 10 882
GATHERD, NOT HARSHLY PLUCKT, FOR DEATH MATURE: 11 537

MATUREST
MATUREST COUNSELS: FOR HIS THOUGHTS WERE LOW; 2 115

MAUGRE
SHALL LEAD HELL CAPTIVE MAUGRE HELL, AND SHOW 3 255
ON MANS DESTRUCTION, MAUGRE WHAT MIGHT HAP 9 56

MAW
TO STUFF THIS MAW, THIS VAST UNHIDE-BOUND CORPS. 10 601
BE FORC'D TO SATISFIE HIS RAV'NOUS MAW. 10 991

MAWE
HIS FAMINE SHOULD BE FILL'D, AND BLEST HIS MAWE 2 847

MAY
THAT SHED MAY FLOWERS; AND PRESS'D HER MATRON LIP 4 501

MAZE
FOULD ABOVE FOULD A SURGING MAZE, HIS HEAD 9 499

MAZES
AND FOUND NO END, IN WANDRING MAZES LOST. 2 561
RESEMBLES NEAREST, MAZES INTRICATE, 5 622
AND REASONINGS, THOUGH THROUGH MAZES, LEAD ME STILL 10 830

MAZIE
WITH MAZIE ERROR UNDER PENDANT SHADES 4 239
THE SERPENT SLEEPING, IN WHOSE MAZIE FOULDS 9 161

MEAGER
WHOM THUS THE MEAGER SHADOW ANSWERD SOON. 10 264

MEAN
TO YONDER GATES? THROUGH THEM I MEAN TO PASS, 2 684
DIRECTED NO MEAN RECOMPENCE IT BRINGS 2 981
ALL HEAV'N, WHAT THIS MIGHT MEAN, AND WHITHER TEND 3 272
AS GREAT MIGHT HAVE ASPIR'D, AND ME THOUGH MEAN 4 62
ASK RIDDANCE, IF WE MEAN TO TREAD WITH EASE; 4 632
WE MEAN TO HOLD WHAT ANCIENTLY WE CLAIM 5 723
I MEAN TO TRY, WHOSE REASON I HAVE TRI'D 6 120
THE STRIFE OF GLORIE: WHICH WE MEAN TO WIN, 6 290
TOO MEAN PRETENSE, BUT WHAT WE MORE AFFECT, 6 421
MEAN, OR IN HER SUMMD UP, IN HER CONTAIND 8 473
I MEAN OF TASTE, SIGHT, SMELL, HERBS, FRUITS, AND FLOURS, 8 527
THE SKILL OF ARTIFICE OR OFFICE MEAN, 9 39
WHAT MAY THIS MEAN? LANGUAGE OF MAN PRONOUNC'T 9 553
MEAN I TO TRIE, WHAT RASH UNTRI'D I SOUGHT, 9 860
WHY HEE SHOULD MEAN ME ILL, OR SEEK TO HARME. 9 1152
NOT OF MEAN SUITERS, NOR IMPORTANT LESS 11 9
BUT SAY, WHAT MEAN THOSE COLOURD STREAKS IN HEAVN, 11 879
IN MEAN ESTATE LIVE MODERATE, TILL GROWN 12 351

MEANER
DISDAIN'D, BUT MEANER THOUGHTS LEARND IN THIR FLIGHT, 6 367

MEANEST
TO WORST ABUSE, OR TO THIR MEANEST USE. 4 204
NONE OF THE MEANEST, SOME GREAT POTENTATE 11 231

MEANING
THE MEANING, NOT THE NAME I CALL: FOR THOU 7 5
SINCE TO EACH MEANING SAVOUR ME APPLY, 9 1019

MEANS
AND OUT OF GOOD STILL TO FIND MEANS OF EVIL; 1 165
AND SHALL GRACE NOT FIND MEANS, THAT FINDS HER WAY, 3 228
AND TEACH US FURTHER BY WHAT MEANS TO SHUN 10 1062
THE SERPENT, BY WHAT MEANS HE SHALL ACHIEVE 12 234
FORBIDD'N KNOWLEDGE BY FORBIDD'N MEANS. 12 279

MEANT
EACH STAIR MYSTERIOUSLY WAS MEANT, NOR STOOD 3 516
WHAT MEANT THAT CAUTION JOIND, IF YE BE FOUND 5 513
HIS THUNDER IN MID VOLIE, FOR HE MEANT 6 854
MEANT MEE, BY VENTRING HIGHER THEN MY LOT, 9 690
AS IN THIR CRIME. THUS WAS TH' APPLAUSE THEY MEANT, 10 545
BE MEANT, WHOM I CONJECTURE, OUR GRAND FOE 10 1033
WAS MEANT BY DEATH THAT DAY, WHEN LO, TO THEE 10 1050
IS MEANT THY GREAT DELIVERER, WHO SHALL BRUISE 12 149

MEAN WHILE
MEAN WHILE THE WINGED HARALDS BY COMMAND 1 752
MEAN WHILE THE ADVERSARY OF GOD AND MAN, 2 629
A GROWING BURDEN. MEAN WHILE WARR AROSE, 2 767
THENCEFORTH SHALL BE FOR EVER SHUT. MEAN WHILE 3 333
MEAN WHILE UPON THE FIRM OPACOUS GLOBE 3 418
LUXURIANT; MEAN WHILE MURMURING WATERS FALL 4 260
MEAN WHILE IN UTMOST LONGITUDE, WHERE HEAV'N 4 539
MEAN WHILE, AS NATURE WILLS, NIGHT BIDS US REST, 4 633
MEAN WHILE OUR PRIMITIVE GREAT SIRE, TO MEET 5 350
AS FROM THE MINE. MEAN WHILE AT TABLE EVE 5 443
WHOSE PROGENIE YOU ARE. MEAN WHILE ENJOY 5 503
MEAN WHILE TH' ETERNAL EYE, WHOSE SIGHT DISCERNES 5 711
YET CHAINS IN HELL, NOT REALMS EXPECT: MEAN WHILE 6 186
IF NOT TO REIGN: MEAN WHILE THY UTMOST FORCE, 6 293
MEAN WHILE IN OTHER PARTS LIKE DEEDS DESERVD 6 354
EFFECT SHALL END OUR WISH. MEAN WHILE REVIVE; 6 493
MEAN WHILE INHABIT LAXE, YE POWERS OF HEAV'N, 7 162
SO SANG THE HIERARCHIES: MEAN WHILE THE SON 7 192
MEAN WHILE THE TEPID CAVES, AND FENS AND SHOARES 7 417
MEAN WHILE THE HOUR OF NOON DREW ON, AND WAK'D 9 739
MEAN WHILE IN PARADISE THE HELLISH PAIR 10 585
OF HERMES, OR HIS OPIATE ROD. MEAN WHILE 11 133

MEANWHILE
MEANWHILE THE HAINOUS AND DESPIGHTFULL ACT 10 1
MEANWHILE ERE THUS WAS SIN'D AND JUDG'D ON EARTH, 10 229
MEANWHILE THE SOUTHWIND ROSE, AND WITH BLACK WINGS 11 738
MEANWHILE THEY IN THIR EARTHLY CANAAN PLAC'T 12 315

MEASUR'D
NOW HAD NIGHT MEASUR'D WITH HER SHADDOWIE CONE 4 776

MEN (CONTINUED)
SEA-FARING MEN OREWATCHT, WHOSE BARK BY CHANCE 2 288
LOOSE ALL HER VIRTUE; LEAST BAD MEN SHOULD BOAST 2 483
O SHAME TO MEN. DEVIL WITH DEVIL DAMN'D 2 496
FIRM CONCORD HOLDS, MEN ONELY DISAGREE 2 497
SURROUNDS ME, FROM THE CHEARFUL WAYES OF MEN 3 46
TO MORTAL MEN, ABOVE WHICH ONLY SHON 3 268
AND BE THY SELF MAN AMONG MEN ON EARTH, 3 283
AS IN HIM PERISH ALL MEN, SO IN THEE 3 287
BAD MEN AND ANGELS, THEY ARRAIGND SHALL SINK 3 331
HAIL SON OF GOD, SAVIOUR OF MEN, THY NAME 3 412
WITH VANITY HAD FILLD THE WORKS OF MEN: 3 447
NAUGHT SEEKING BUT THE PRAISE OF MEN, HERE FIND 3 453
CREATED THIS NEW HAPPIE RACE OF MEN 3 679
CAME FURIOUS DOWN TO BE REVENG'D ON MEN, 4 4
WHENCE TRUE AUTORITIE IN MEN; THOUGH BOTH 4 295
ADAM THE GOODLIEST MAN OF MEN SINCE BORNE 4 323
GRIP'T IN EACH PAW: WHEN ADAM FIRST OF MEN 4 408
LABOUR AND REST, AS DAY AND NIGHT TO MEN 4 613
SHINE NOT IN VAIN, NOR THINK, THOUGH MEN WERE NONE, 4 675
BY THEE ADULTEROUS LUST WAS DRIV'N FROM MEN 4 753
FOR GOD'S, YET ABLE TO MAKE GODS OF MEN: 5 70
AND WHY NOT GODS OF MEN, SINCE GOOD, THE MORE 5 71
TO PROPER SUBSTANCE; TIME MAY COME WHEN MEN 5 493
HIGH MATTER THOU INJOINST ME, O PRIME OF MEN, 5 563
THAT STRUCTURE IN THE DIALECT OF MEN 5 761
SEEK NOT THE PRAISE OF MEN: THE OTHER SORT 6 376
LIKE INSTRUMENT TO PLAGUE THE SONS OF MEN 6 505
OF MEN INNUMERABLE, THERE TO DWELL, 7 156
TO FUTURE MEN, AND IN THIR DWELLINGS PEACE: 7 183
TO VISIT OFT THE DWELLINGS OF JUST MEN 7 570
THIR SEASONS: AMONG THESE THE SEAT OF MEN, 7 623
THIR PLEASANT DWELLING PLACE. THRICE HAPPIE MEN, 7 625
AND SONS OF MEN, WHOM GOD HATH THUS ADVANC'T, 7 626
NOR ARE THY LIPS UNGRACEFUL, SIRE OF MEN, 8 218
FIRST MAN, OF MEN INNUMERABLE ORDAIN'D 8 297
STILL HANGING INCORRUPTIBLE, TILL MEN 9 622
WITH MEN AS ANGELS WITHOUT FEMININE, 10 893
WITH SINFULNESS OF MEN; THEREBY TO LEARN 11 360
SHALL BRING ON MEN. IMMEDIATELY A PLACE 11 477
JUST MEN THEY SEEMD, AND ALL THIR STUDY BENT 11 577
FREEDOM AND PEACE TO MEN: THEY ON THE PLAIN 11 580
THE MEN THOUGH GRAVE, EY'D THEM, AND LET THIR EYES 11 585
TO THESE THAT SOBER RACE OF MEN, WHOSE LIVES 11 621
CITIES OF MEN WITH LOFTY GATES AND TOWRS, 11 640
GREY-HEADED MEN AND GRAVE, WITH WARRIOURS MIXT, 11 662
DEATHS MINISTERS, NOT MEN, WHO THUS DEAL DEATH 11 676
INHUMANLY TO MEN, AND MULTIPLY 11 677
MAKE THEY BUT OF THIR BRETHREN, MEN OF MEN? 11 680
SUCH WERE THESE GIANTS, MEN OF HIGH RENOWN; 11 688
DESTROYERS RIGHTLIER CALL'D AND PLAGUES OF MEN. 11 697
BY MEN WHO THERE FREQUENT, OR THEREIN DWELL. 11 838
THIS SECOND SOURS OF MEN, WHILE YET BUT FEW; 12 13
HUNTING (AND MEN NOT BEASTS SHALL BE HIS GAME) 12 30
BUT GOD WHO OFT DESCENDS TO VISIT MEN 12 48
BY HIS DONATION; BUT MAN OVER MEN 12 69
THAT SON, WHO ON THE QUIET STATE OF MEN 12 80
BRED UP IN IDOL-WORSHIP; O THAT MEN 12 115
ESTABLISHT, SUCH DELIGHT HATH GOD IN MEN 12 245
THE HOLY ONE WITH MORTAL MEN TO DWELL: 12 248
MEN WHO ATTEND THE ALTAR, AND SHOULD MOST 12 354
TO HIS DISCIPLES, MEN WHO IN HIS LIFE 12 438
TO GOD MORE GLORY, MORE GOOD WILL TO MEN 12 477
TO GOOD MALIGNANT, TO BAD MEN BENIGNE, 12 538

MENAC'T
WERE IT I THOUGHT DEATH MENAC'T WOULD ENSUE 9 977

MENDS
MENDS NOT HER SLOWEST PACE FOR PRAYERS OR CRIES. 10 859

MENTAL
EEVN TO THE INMOST SEAT OF MENTAL SIGHT, 11 418

MENTION
THEN SWEET, NOW SAD TO MENTION, THROUGH DIRE CHANGE 2 820
USEFUL, WHENCE HAPLY MENTION MAY ARISE 8 200

MENTION'D
NO MORE BE MENTION'D THEN OF VIOLENCE 10 1041

MERCHANTS
OF TERNATE AND TIDORE, WHENCE MERCHANTS BRING 2 639

MERCIE
FATHER OF MERCIE AND GRACE, THOU DIDST NOT DOOME 3 401
MERCIE COLLEGUE WITH JUSTICE, SENDING THEE 10 59
JUSTICE WITH MERCIE, AS MAY ILLUSTRATE MOST 10 78
WHAT ELSE BUT FAVOR, GRACE, AND MERCIE SHON? 10 1096
REMEMBRING MERCIE, AND HIS COV'NANT SWORN 12 346

MERCIE-SEAT
PRAYING, FOR FROM THE MERCIE-SEAT ABOVE 11 2
A MERCIE-SEAT OF GOLD BETWEEN THE WINGS 12 253

MERCIFULL
MERCIFULL OVER ALL HIS WORKS, WITH GOOD 12 565

MERCY
INFINITE GOODNESS, GRACE AND MERCY SHEWN 1 218
THE OTHER NONE: IN MERCY AND JUSTICE BOTH, 3 132
BUT MERCY FIRST AND LAST SHALL BRIGHTEST SHINE. 3 134
AND NONE BUT SUCH FROM MERCY I EXCLUDE. 3 202
OF MERCY AND JUSTICE IN THY FACE DISCERN'D, 3 407

MERIDIAN
WHICH NOW SAT HIGH IN HIS MERIDIAN TOWRE: 4 30
WELL KNOWN FROM HEAV'N; AND SINCE MERIDIAN HOUR 4 581
TO SIT AND TASTE, TILL THIS MERIDIAN HEAT 5 369

MERIT
AND HIGH DISDAIN, FROM SENCE OF INJUR'D MERIT, 1 98
COULD MERIT MORE THEN THAT SMALL INFANTRY 1 575
SATAN EXALTED SAT, BY MERIT RAIS'D 2 5
HATH BIN ACHIEVD OF MERIT, YET THIS LOSS 2 21
HIS CRIME MAKES GUILTIE ALL HIS SONS, THY MERIT 3 290
BY MERIT MORE THEN BIRTHRIGHT SON OF GOD, 3 309
ASCEND TO HEAV'N, BY MERIT THINE, AND SEE 5 80
MESSIAH, WHO BY RIGHT OF MERIT REIGNS. 6 43
NOT HERE, TILL BY DEGREES OF MERIT RAIS'D 7 157
OF MERIT HIGH TO ALL TH' INFERNAL HOST, 10 259
GOOD OR NOT GOOD INGRAFT, MY MERIT THOSE 11 35

MERITED
HAVE NOTHING MERITED, NOR CAN PERFORME 4 418
THY MERITED REWARD, THE FIRST ASSAY 6 153
AMPLY HAVE MERITED OF ME, OF ALL 10 388

MERITS
THY MERITS; UNDER THEE AS HEAD SUPREAM 3 319
THAT REACHES BLAME, BUT RATHER MERITS PRAISE 3 697
ILLAUDABLE, NAUGHT MERITS BUT DISPRAISE 6 382
SUCH RECOMPENCE BEST MERITS) FROM THE BOUGH 9 995
AND WHAT MOST MERITS FAME IN SILENCE HID. 11 699
IMPUTED BECOMES THEIRS BY FAITH, HIS MERITS 12 409

MESERIE
WITH LIKE DESIRE, WHICH WOULD BE MESERIE 10 997

MESSAGE
YOUR MESSAGE, LIKE TO END AS MUCH IN VAIN? 4 833
AND TO HIS MESSAGE HIGH IN HONOUR RISE; 5 289
FOR ON SOM MESSAGE HIGH THEY GUESSD HIM BOUND. 5 290
THY MESSAGE, WHICH MIGHT ELSE IN TELLING WOUND, 11 299
TO KNOW THIR GOD, OR MESSAGE TO REGARD, 12 174

MESSENGER
GO HEAVENLY GUEST, ETHEREAL MESSENGER, 8 646
AND AFTER HIM, THE SURER MESSENGER, 11 856

MESSENGERS
THE SPEEDIEST OF THY WINGED MESSENGERS, 3 229
THITHER WILL SEND HIS WINGED MESSENGERS 7 572

MESSIAH
MESSIAH KING ANOINTED, COULD NOT BEARE 5 664
THE GREAT MESSIAH, AND HIS NEW COMMANDS, 5 691
MESSIAH WAS DECLAR'D IN SIGHT OF HEAV'N, 5 765
OF GODS MESSIAH; THOSE INDULGENT LAWS 5 883
MESSIAH, WHO BY RIGHT OF MERIT REIGNS. 6 43
OF GOD AND HIS MESSIAH. ON THEY MOVE 6 68
GOD AND MESSIAH HIS ANOINTED KING. 6 718
WHEN THE GREAT ENSIGN OF MESSIAH BLAZ'D 6 775
AGAINST GOD AND MESSIAH, OR TO FALL 6 796
MESSIAH HIS TRIUMPHAL CHARIOT TURND: 6 881
OF GREAT MESSIAH SHALL SING. THUS LAWS AND RITES 12 244
ANOINTED KING MESSIAH MIGHT BE BORN 12 359

MET
MET SUCH IMBODIED FORCE, AS NAM'D WITH THESE 1 574
IN THIS INFERNAL VAILE FIRST MET THOU CALL'ST 2 742
HERE MATTER NEW TO GAZE THE DEVIL MET 3 613
DOWN THE STEEP GLADE, AND MET THE NEATHER FLOOD, 4 231
THAT EVER SINCE IN LOVES IMBRACES MET, 4 322
NAKED MET HIS UNDER THE FLOWING GOLD 4 496
JUST MET, AND CLOSING STOOD IN SQUADRON JOIND 4 863
REFLECTING BLAZE ON BLAZE, FIRST MET HIS VIEW: 6 18
FORTH STEPPING OPPOSITE, HALF WAY HE MET 6 128
PROUD, ART THOU MET? THY HOPE WAS TO HAVE REACHT 6 131
A THIRD PART OF THE GODS, IN SYNOD MET 6 156
PRODIGIOUS POWER HAD SHEWN, AND MET IN ARMES 6 247
NOR SOLID MIGHT RESIST THAT EDGE: IT MET 6 323
IN MOTION OR IN ALT: HIM SOON THEY MET 6 532
AS LIKELIEST WAS, WHEN TWO SUCH FOES MET ARM'D; 6 688
SINGLE WITH LIKE DEFENCE, WHEREVER MET, 9 325
ADJOYND, FROM EACH THING MET CONCEAVES DELIGHT, 9 449
OF KNOWLEDGE HE MUST PASS, THERE HE HER MET, 9 849
HOVERING UPON THE WATERS; WHAT THEY MET 10 285
THE CONFINES MET OF EMPYREAN HEAV'N 10 321
MET WHO TO MEET HIM CAME, HIS OFSPRING DEAR. 10 349
TRIUMPHAL WITH TRIUMPHAL ACT HAVE MET, 10 390
NOT THAT MORE GLORIOUS, WHEN THE ANGELS MET 11 213
FREQUENTED THIR ASSEMBLIES, WHERESO MET, 11 722

METALLIC
THAT IN HIS WOMB WAS HID METALLIC ORE, 1 673

MIGHT (CONTINUED)

THAT HIS GREAT PURPOSE HE MIGHT SO FULFILL, 6 675
GO THEN THOU MIGHTIEST IN THY FATHERS MIGHT, 6 710
ARMD WITH THY MIGHT, RID HEAV'N OF THESE REBELL'D, 6 737
THEY HARD'ND MORE BY WHAT MIGHT MOST RECLAME, 6 791
THAT WISHT THE MOUNTAINS NOW MIGHT BE AGAIN 6 842
WHAT MIGHT HAVE ELSE TO HUMAN RACE BIN HID; 6 896
OF DISOBEDIENCE; FIRM THEY MIGHT HAVE STOOD, 6 911
WHAT NEERER MIGHT CONCERN HIM, HOW THIS WORLD 7 62
US TIMELY OF WHAT MIGHT ELSE HAVE BIN OUR LOSS, 7 74
MY OVERSHADOWING SPIRIT AND MIGHT WITH THEE 7 165
CREATION, AND THE WONDERS OF HIS MIGHT. 7 223
CONTIGUOUS MIGHT DISTEMPER THE WHOLE FRAME: 7 273
SEEMD LIKE TO HEAV'N, A SEAT WHERE GODS MIGHT DWELL, 7 329
WITH SANCTITIE OF REASON, MIGHT ERECT 7 508
TO MANIFEST THE MORE THY MIGHT: HIS EVIL 7 615
INFORMD BY THEE MIGHT KNOW; IF ELSE THOU SEEKST 7 639
THAT BETTER MIGHT WITH FARR LESS COMPASS MOVE, 8 33
IF IT PRESUME, MIGHT ERRE IN THINGS TOO HIGH, 8 121
DESTRUCTION WITH CREATION MIGHT HAVE MIXT. 8 236
ON MANS DESTRUCTION, MAUGRE WHAT MIGHT HAP 9 56
MOST OPPORTUNE MIGHT SERVE HIS WILES, AND FOUND 9 85
DOUBT MIGHT BEGET OF DIABOLIC POW'R 9 95
HIS MIDNIGHT SEARCH, WHERE SOONEST HE MIGHT FINDE 9 181
HOW WE MIGHT BEST FULFILL THE WORK WHICH HERE 9 230
TO OTHER SPEEDIE AIDE MIGHT LEND AT NEED; 9 260
OR AUGHT THAT MIGHT HIS HAPPIE STATE SECURE, 9 347
AND ON HIS QUEST, WHERE LIKELIEST HE MIGHT FINDE 9 414
HE SOUGHT THEM BOTH, BUT WISH'D HIS HAP MIGHT FIND 9 421
SATED AT LENGTH, ERE LONG I MIGHT PERCEAVE 9 598
SERPENT, WE MIGHT HAVE SPAR'D OUR COMING HITHER, 9 647
DETERRD NOT FROM ATCHIEVING WHAT MIGHT LEADE 9 696
MIGHT TEMPT ALONE, AND IN HER EARS THE SOUND 9 736
THE GUILTIE SERPENT, AND WELL MIGHT, FOR EVE 9 785
IN THINGS TO US FORBIDDEN, IT MIGHT BE WISH'D, 9 1025
INSUFFERABLY BRIGHT. O MIGHT I HERE 9 1084
BUT MIGHT AS ILL HAVE HAPP'ND THOU BEING BY, 9 1147
WHO MIGHT HAVE LIV'D AND JOYD IMMORTAL BLISS, 9 1166
EASIE IT MIGHT BE SEEN THAT I INTEND 10 58
MIGHT SUDDENLY INFLICT; THAT PAST, RETURN'D 10 341
PLENIPOTENT ON EARTH, OF MATCHLESS MIGHT 10 404
MIGHT INTERCEPT THIR EMPEROUR SENT, SO HEE 10 429
AS MIGHT AFFECT THE EARTH WITH COLD AND HEAT 10 653
SO MIGHT THE WRAUTH. FOND WISH. COULDST THOU SUPPORT 10 834
THAT ON MY HEAD ALL MIGHT BE VISITED, 10 955
WHICH MIGHT SUPPLIE THE SUN: SUCH FIRE TO USE, 10 1078
THY MESSAGE, WHICH MIGHT ELSE IN TELLING WOUND, 11 299
HIS EYE MIGHT THERE COMMAND WHEREVER STOOD 11 385
FIRST HIS OWN TOOLES; THEN, WHAT MIGHT ELSE BE WROUGHT 11 572
NOT HID, NOR THOSE THINGS LAST WHICH MIGHT PRESERVE 11 579
FOR IN THOSE DAYES MIGHT ONELY SHALL BE ADMIR'D, 11 689
OF PARADISE BY MIGHT OF WAVES BE MOOVD 11 830
IF ADAM AUGHT PERHAPS MIGHT INTERPOSE; 12 4
THAT MOSES MIGHT REPORT TO THEM HIS WILL, 12 237
ANOINTED KING MESSIAH MIGHT BE BORN 12 359

MIGHTIE

MADE ANSWER. MIGHTIE FATHER, THOU THY FOES 5 735
REGIONS THEY PASS'D, THE MIGHTIE REGENCIES 5 748
AND TEMPLE OF HIS MIGHTIE FATHER THRON'D 6 890
A MIGHTIE SPHEARE HE FRAM'D, UNLIGHTSOM FIRST, 7 355
THE MIGHTIE FRAME, HOW BUILD, UNBUILD, CONTRIVE 8 81
HIS MIGHTIE ANGELS GAVE THEM SEVERAL CHARGE, 10 650
GIANTS OF MIGHTIE BONE, AND BOULD EMPRISE; 11 642
A MIGHTIE HUNTER THENCE HE SHALL BE STYL'D 12 33
A MIGHTIE NATION, AND UPON HIM SHOWRE 12 124

MIGHTIER

OR DO HIM MIGHTIER SERVICE AS HIS THRALLS 1 149
BY YOUNGER SATURN, HE FROM MIGHTIER JOVE 1 512
OF TRUTH, IN WORD MIGHTIER THEN THEY IN ARMES; 6 32

MIGHTIEST

THAT WITH THE MIGHTIEST RAIS'D ME TO CONTEND, 1 99
THE WEIGHT OF MIGHTIEST MONARCHIES; HIS LOOK 2 307
AMONG THE MIGHTIEST, BENT ON HIGHEST DEEDS, 6 112
THUS FOIL'D THIR MIGHTIEST, OURS JOY FILLD, AND SHOUT, 6 200
AND NOW THIR MIGHTIEST QUELLD, THE BATTEL SWERV'D, 6 386
OF MIGHTIEST. SENSE OF PLEASURE WE MAY WELL 6 459
GO THEN THOU MIGHTIEST IN THY FATHERS MIGHT, 6 710
OF MIGHTIEST EMPIRE, FROM THE DESTIND WALLS 11 387

MIGHTY

WAST PRESENT, AND WITH MIGHTY WINGS OUTSPREAD 1 20
HATH LOST US HEAV'N, AND ALL THIS MIGHTY HOST 1 136
HIS MIGHTY STATURE; ON EACH HAND THE FLAMES 1 222
HIS MIGHTY STANDARD; THAT PROUD HONOUR CLAIM'D 1 533
AWAITING WHAT COMMAND THIR MIGHTY CHIEF 1 566
OF MIGHTY CHERUBIM; THE SUDDEN BLAZE 1 665
HIGH HONOURD SITS? GO THEREFORE MIGHTY POWERS, 2 456
MIDST CAME THIR MIGHTY PARAMOUNT, AND SEEMD 2 508
SO FROWND THE MIGHTY COMBATANTS, THAT HELL 2 719
THAT MIGHTY LEADING ANGEL, WHO OF LATE 2 991
AS BY HIS WORD THE MIGHTY FATHER MADE 5 836

MIGHTY (CONTINUED)

THAT STOOD FOR HEAV'N, IN MIGHTY QUADRATE JOYN'D 6 62
WHICH GOD HATH IN HIS MIGHTY ANGELS PLAC'D) 6 638
OF THRONES AND MIGHTY SERAPHIM PROSTRATE, 6 841
WHO CAN IMPAIR THEE, MIGHTY KING, OR BOUND 7 608
THIR MIGHTY CHIEF RETURND: LOUD WAS TH' ACCLAIME: 10 455

MILD

NOR GRATEFUL EEVNING MILD, NOR SILENT NIGHT 4 654
TO WHOM MILD ANSWER ADAM THUS RETURN'D. 9 226
CAME THE MILD JUDGE AND INTERCESSOR BOTH 10 96
WHOLSOM AND COOL, AND MILD, BUT WITH BLACK AIR 10 847
LAID ON OUR NECKS. REMEMBER WITH WHAT MILD 10 1046
METHOUGHT I SAW HIM PLACABLE AND MILD, 11 151
THAT I SHOULD FEAR, NOR SOCIABLY MILD, 11 234

MILDE

THIS HORROR WILL GROW MILDE, THIS DARKNESS LIGHT, 2 220
RE-ENTER HEAV'N; OR ELSE IN SOME MILDE ZONE 2 397
INTO TH' EUBOIC SEA. OTHERS MORE MILDE, 2 546
LESS WINNING SOFT, LESS AMIABLIE MILDE, 4 479
OF GRATEFUL EEVNING MILDE, THEN SILENT NIGHT 4 647
MILDE, AS WHEN ZEPHYRUS ON FLORA BREATHES, 5 16
WHOM THUS THE ANGELIC VERTUE ANSWERD MILDE. 5 371
FROM MIDST A GOLDEN CLOUD THUS MILDE WAS HEARD. 6 28
AND THUS THE GODLIKE ANGEL ANSWERD MILDE. 7 110
EXPRESS'D, AND THUS DIVINELY ANSWER'D MILDE. 10 67
WHOM THUS THE ANGEL INTERRUPTED MILDE. 11 286

MILDELY

SAID MILDELY, AUTHOR OF ALL THIS THOU SEEST 8 317

MILDER

SOON LEARND, NOW MILDER, AND THUS ANSWERD SMOOTH. 2 816
OF ONSET ENDED SOON EACH MILDER THOUGHT, 6 98

MILDNESS

THY TERRORS, AS I PUT THY MILDNESS ON, 6 735
THY LOOKS, THE HEAV'N OF MILDNESS, WITH DISDAIN, 9 534

MILES

AS MANY MILES ALOFT: THAT FURIE STAY'D, 2 938

MILITANT

AT WHICH COMMAND THE POWERS MILITANT, 6 61
IN SHEW PLEBEIAN ANGEL MILITANT 10 442

MILITARIE

A MILITARIE VEST OF PURPLE FLOWD 11 241

MILITARY

YOUR MILITARY OBEDIENCE, TO DISSOLVE 4 955
AND THOU IN MILITARY PROWESS NEXT 6 45

MILK

OF EWE OR GOAT DROPPING WITH MILK AT EEVN, 9 582

MILKIE

OF NECTAROUS DRAUGHTS BETWEEN, FROM MILKIE STREAM, 5 306
SEEN IN THE GALAXIE, THAT MILKIE WAY 7 579

MILLIONS

MILLIONS OF SPIRITS FOR HIS FAULT AMERC'T 1 609
MILLIONS OF FLAMING SWORDS, DRAWN FROM THE THIGHS 1 664
MILLIONS THAT STAND IN ARMS, AND LONGING WAIT 2 55
POURD OUT BY MILLIONS HER VICTORIOUS BANDS 2 997
MILLIONS OF SPIRITUAL CREATURES WALK THE EARTH 4 677
BY THOUSANDS AND BY MILLIONS RANG'D FOR FIGHT; 6 48
MILLIONS OF FIERCE ENCOUNTRING ANGELS FOUGHT 6 220

MIMIC

OFT IN HER ABSENCE MIMIC FANSIE WAKES 5 110

MIND

THOUGH CHANG'D IN OUTWARD LUSTRE; THAT FIXT MIND 1 97
CAN PERISH: FOR THE MIND AND SPIRIT REMAINS 1 139
A MIND NOT TO BE CHANG'D BY PLACE OR TIME. 1 253
THE MIND IS ITS OWN PLACE, AND IN IT SELF 1 254
HATEFUL TO UTTER: BUT WHAT POWER OF MIND 1 626
OF PRESENT PAIN, THAT WITH AMBITIOUS MIND 2 34
WITH HIM, OR WHO DECEIVE HIS MIND, WHOSE EYE 2 189
NOT MIND US NOT OFFENDING, SATISFI'D 2 212
SHINE INWARD, AND THE MIND THROUGH ALL HER POWERS 3 52
BUT WHAT CREATED MIND CAN COMPREHEND 3 705
AND UNDERSTOOD NOT THAT A GRATEFUL MIND 4 55
MIND US OF LIKE REPOSE, SINCE GOD HATH SET 4 612
MAN HATH HIS DAILY WORK OF BODY OR MIND 4 618
BUT OF OFFENCE AND TROUBLE, WHICH MY MIND 5 34
EVIL INTO THE MIND OF GOD OR MAN 5 117
NOT BURD'ND NATURE, SUDDEN MIND AROSE 5 452
TO SWERVE FROM TRUTH, OR CHANGE HIS CONSTANT MIND 5 902
THESE THINGS, AS NOT TO MIND FROM WHENCE THEY GROW 6 477
IN MEASURE WHAT THE MIND MAY WELL CONTAIN, 7 128
BUT APT THE MIND OR FANCIE IS TO ROAVE 8 188
AS US'D OR NOT, WORKS IN THE MIND NO CHANGE, 8 525
OF NATURE HER TH' INFERIOUR, IN THE MIND 8 541
GREATNESS OF MIND AND NOBLENESS THIR SEAT 8 557
UNION OF MIND, OR IN US BOTH ONE SOULE; 8 604

MIND (CONTINUED)
FOOD OF THE MIND, OR THIS SWEET INTERCOURSE . . 9 238
THAT I SHOULD MIND THEE OFT, AND MIND THOU ME. . 9 358
I TURND MY THOUGHTS, AND WITH CAPACIOUS MIND . . 9 603
TO REACH, AND FEED AT ONCE BOTH BODIE AND MIND? . 9 779
COVERD, BUT NOT AT REST OR EASE OF MIND, . . . 9 1120
THIR INWARD STATE OF MIND, CALM REGION ONCE . . 9 1125
BUT ALL CORRUPT, BOTH MIND AND WILL DEPRAV'D, . . 10 825
SO PREVALENT AS TO CONCERNE THE MIND 11 144
PRODUCE PRODIGIOUS BIRTHS OF BODIE OR MIND. . . 11 687
AND CALL TO MIND HIS COV'NANT: DAY AND NIGHT, . . 11 898
PURE, AND IN MIND PREPAR'D, IF SO BEFALL, . . . 12 444

MINDE
OR BEAR WHAT TO MY MINDE FIRST THOUGHTS PRESENT, . 9 213
HINDER'D NOT SATAN TO ATTEMPT THE MINDE 10 8
TO BETTER HOPES HIS MORE ATTENTIVE MINDE . . . 10 1011
AND EXCELLENT THEN WHAT THY MINDE CONTEMNES; . . 10 1015
I HAVE IN VIEW, CALLING TO MINDE WITH HEED . . . 10 1030

MINDED
SO MINDED, HAVE ORELEAPT THESE EARTHIE BOUNDS . . 4 583
AND BE SO MINDED STILL; I, ERE THOU SPAK'ST, . . 8 444
OF RUSLING LEAVES, BUT MINDED NOT, AS US'D . . 9 519
WHICH THEN NOT MINDED IN DISMAY, YET NOW . . . 11 156

MINDES
FOR HEAV'NLY MINDES FROM SUCH DISTEMPERS FOULE . 4 118
UNHURT OUR MINDES, AND UNDERSTANDING SOUND, . . 6 444
FRESH IN THIR MINDES, FEARING THE DEITIE, . . . 12 15

MINDLESS
GENTLY WITH MIRTLE BAND, MINDLESS THE WHILE, . . 9 431

MINDS
FROM MORTAL OR IMMORTAL MINDS. THUS THEY . . . 1 559
THENCE MORE AT EASE THIR MINDS AND SOMWHAT RAIS'D 2 521
THIR RUINE. HENCE I WILL EXCITE THIR MINDS . 4 522
NEW LAWS FROM HIM WHO REIGNS, NEW MINDS MAY RAISE 5 680
OUR MINDS AND TEACH US TO CAST OFF THIS YOKE? . . 5 786
OF COMPOSITION, STRAIT THEY CHANG'D THIR MINDS, . 6 613
SOON FOUND THIR EYES HOW OP'ND, AND THIR MINDS . 9 1053

MINERAL
SUBLIM'D WITH MINERAL FURY, AID THE WINDS, . . . 1 235
ENTRAILS UNLIKE) OF MINERAL AND STONE, ... 6 517

MINGL'D
THEY FOUND, THEY MINGL'D, AND WITH SUTTLE ART, . 6 513

MINGLE
TO MINGLE AND INVOLVE, DONE ALL TO SPITE . . . 2 384
THOU AND THY WICKED CREW; THERE MINGLE BROILES, . 6 277

MINIMS
MINIMS OF NATURE; SOME OF SERPENT KINDE 7 482

MINISTER
THUS TO TH' EMPYREAL MINISTER HE FRAM'D. . . . 5 460
TO THE BRIGHT MINISTER THAT WATCHD, HEE BLEW . . 11 73
HIGHLY BELOV'D, BEING BUT THE MINISTER 12 308

MINISTERD
MINISTERD NAKED, AND THIR FLOWING CUPS 5 444

MINISTERIES
WITH MINISTERIES DUE AND SOLEMN RITES: 7 149

MINISTERS
HIS MINISTERS OF VENGEANCE AND PURSUIT 1 170
AND FLAMING MINISTERS TO WATCH AND TEND 9 156
DEATHS MINISTERS, NOT MEN, WHO THUS DEAL DEATH . 11 676

MINISTRANT
PRINCEDOMS, AND DOMINATIONS MINISTRANT 10 87

MINISTRING
MINISTRING LIGHT PREPAR'D, THEY SET AND RISE; . . 4 664
MINISTRING SPIRITS, TRAIND UP IN FEAST AND SONG; . 6 167
YET LEUDLY DAR'ST OUR MINISTRING UPBRAID. . . . 6 182

MINISTRY
THIR MINISTRY PERFORM'D, AND RACE WELL RUN, . . . 12 505

MINSTRELSIE
SUCH HAST THOU ARM'D, THE MINSTRELSIE OF HEAV'N, . 6 168

MINUTES
TIME COUNTS NOT, THOUGH WITH SWIFTEST MINUTES
WING'D. 10 91

MIRACLE
REDOUBLE THEN THIS MIRACLE, AND SAY, ... 9 562

MIRACLES
TO SPEAK ALL TONGUES, AND DO ALL MIRACLES, ... 12 501

MIRE
TO TRAMPLE THEE AS MIRE: FOR PROOF LOOK UP, . . . 4 1010

MIRES
TO BOGGS AND MIRES, AND OFT THROUGH POND OR POOLE, 9 641

MIRROR
HER CHRYSTAL MIRROR HOLDS, UNITE THIR STREAMS. . 4 263
HIS MIRROR, WITH FULL FACE BORROWING HER LIGHT . 7 377

MIRTH
WHEELS HER PALE COURSE, THEY ON THIR MIRTH AND
DANCE 1 786
TO MAKE THEM MIRTH US'D ALL HIS MIGHT, AND WREATHD 4 346
THEY SWIM IN MIRTH, AND FANSIE THAT THEY FEEL . . 9 1009

MIRTLE
LAUREL AND MIRTLE, AND WHAT HIGHER GREW 4 694
GENTLY WITH MIRTLE BAND, MINDLESS THE WHILE, . . . 9 431

MISCHIEF
HER MISCHIEF, AND PURGE OFF THE BASER FIRE . . . 2 141
SUCH IMPLEMENTS OF MISCHIEF AS SHALL DASH . . . 6 488
SOME ONE INTENT ON MISCHIEF, OR INSPIR'D . . . 6 503
AGAINST SUCH HELLISH MISCHIEF FIT TO OPPOSE. . . 6 636
OF MISCHIEF, GRATULATING, THUS EXCITES. 9 472
TO MISCHIEF SWIFT. HOPE ELEVATES, AND JOY . . . 9 633
OF MISCHIEF, AND POLLUTED FROM THE END 10 167
MANKIND? THIS MISCHIEF HAD NOT THEN BEFALL'N, . 10 895
O TEACHER, SOME GREAT MISCHIEF HATH BEFALL'N . . 11 450

MISCHIEVOUS
THITHER FULL FRAUGHT WITH MISCHIEVOUS REVENGE, . 2 1054

MISCREATED
THY MISCREATED FRONT ATHWART MY WAY 2 683

MISDEEDS
TO EVILS WHICH OUR OWN MISDEEDS HAVE WROUGHT, . . 10 1080

MISDEEM
THOUGH INEFFECTUAL FOUND: MISDEEM NOT THEN, . . 9 301

MISERABLE
FALL'N CHERUBE, TO BE WEAK IS MISERABLE 1 157
THEN MISERABLE TO HAVE ETERNAL BEING: 2 98
ALL ON A SUDDEN MISERABLE PAIN 2 752
ME MISERABLE. WHICH WAY SHALL I FLIE 4 73
NOR HOPE TO BE MY SELF LESS MISERABLE 9 126
OF ALL OUR GOOD, SHAM'D, NAKED, MISERABLE. . . . 9 1139
O MISERABLE OF HAPPIE. IS THIS THE END 10 720
OF REFUGE, AND CONCLUDES THEE MISERABLE 10 839
MORE MISERABLE; BOTH HAVE SIN'D, BUT THOU . . . 10 930
BY DEATH AT LAST, AND MISERABLE IT IS 10 981
O MISERABLE MANKIND, TO WHAT FALL 11 500

MISERIE
IN MISERIE; SUCH JOY AMBITION FINDES. 4 92
MISERIE, UNCREATED TILL THE CRIME 6 268
BUT PAIN IS PERFET MISERIE, THE WORST 6 462
HIS PUNISHMENT, ETERNAL MISERIE; 6 904
SINNE AND HER SHADOW DEATH, AND MISERIE 9 12
THE MISERIE, I DESERV'D IT, AND WOULD BEARE . . 10 726
BEREAVING SENSE, BUT ENDLESS MISERIE 10 810
THY HATRED FOR THIS MISERIE BEFALL'N, ... 10 928
OF MISERIE, SO THINKING TO EVADE 10 1021
WHAT MISERIE TH' INABSTINENCE OF EVE 11 476

MISERIES
THE GROWING MISERIES, WHICH ADAM SAW 10 715

MISERY
JOYND WITH ME ONCE, NOW MISERY HATH JOYND . . . 1 90
HERE SWALLOW'D UP IN ENDLESS MISERY. 1 142
THE PRESENT MISERY, AND RENDER HELL 2 459
OF HAPPINESS AND FINAL MISERY, ... 2 563
TO BE TO OTHERS CAUSE OF MISERY, ... 10 982

MISFORTUNE
AS SOME MISFORTUNE BRINGS HIM, OR MISTAKE, . . . 10 900

MISGAVE
MISGAVE HIM; HEE THE FAULTRING MEASURE FELT; . . 9 846

MISHAP
BUT THAT SUCCESS ATTENDS HIM; IF MISHAP, . . . 10 239

MISJOYNING
TO IMITATE HER; BUT MISJOYNING SHAPES, ... 5 111

MISLEADS
MISLEADS TH' AMAZ'D NIGHT-WANDERER FROM HIS WAY . 9 640

MISRULE
CRYSTALLIN OCEAN, AND THE LOUD MISRULE 7 271
AT RANDOM YIELDED UP TO THEIR MISRULE; 10 628

MISS
THY WAY THOU CANST NOT MISS, ME MINE REQUIRES. 3 735
MY COMING SEEN FAR OFF? I MISS THEE HERE, 10 104
NOR CAN I MISS THE WAY, SO STRONGLY DRAWN 10 262

MISS'D
TO BE TH' INVENTER MISS'D, SO EASIE IT SEEMD 6 499

MISSD
FLEW UP, NOR MISSD THE WAY, BY ENVIOUS WINDES 11 15

MISSINFORME
SHE DICTATE FALSE, AND MISSINFORME THE WILL 9 355

MISSIVE
OF MISSIVE RUIN; PART INCENTIVE REED 6 519

MISST
THEE I HAVE MISST, AND THOUGHT IT LONG, DEPRIV'D 9 857

MISSTHOUGHT
ADAM, MISSTHOUGHT OF HER TO THEE SO DEAR? 9 289

MIST
IRRADIATE, THERE PLANT EYES, ALL MIST FROM THENCE 3 53
THE ANGEL, NOR IN MIST, THE COMMON GLOSS 5 435
NONE WAS, BUT FROM THE EARTH A DEWIE MIST 7 333
SATAN INVOLV'D IN RISING MIST, THEN SOUGHT 9 75
I DREAD, AND TO ELUDE, THUS WRAPT IN MIST 9 158
LIKE A BLACK MIST LOW CREEPING, HE HELD ON 9 180
VAPOUR, AND MIST, AND EXHALATION HOT, 10 694
GLIDING METEOROUS, AS EV'NING MIST 12 629

MISTAKE
AS SOME MISFORTUNE BRINGS HIM, OR MISTAKE, 10 900

MISTRESS
WONDER NOT, SOVRAN MISTRESS, IF PERHAPS 9 532

MISTRUST
NOT THEN MISTRUST, BUT TENDER LOVE ENJOYNES, 9 357
MISTRUST, SUSPICION, DISCORD, AND SHOOK SORE 9 1124

MISTRUSTFUL
MISTRUSTFUL, GROUNDS HIS COURAGE ON DESPAIR 2 126

MISTS
YE MISTS AND EXHALATIONS THAT NOW RISE 5 185

MISTY
LOOKS THROUGH THE HORIZONTAL MISTY AIR 1 595

MITIGATE
NOR WANTING POWER TO MITIGATE AND SWAGE 1 556
OF RIGHT, THAT I MAY MITIGATE THIR DOOM 10 76
TO MITIGATE THUS PLEAD, NOT TO REVERSE) 11 41

MIX
PERPETUAL CIRCLE, MULTIFORM; AND MIX 5 182
WHAT ORDER, SO CONTRIV'D AS NOT TO MIX 5 334
FROM WHOM IT SPRUNG, IMPOSSIBLE TO MIX 7 58
HEAV'NS HIGHTH, AND WITH THE CENTER MIX THE POLE. 7 215
EXPRESS THEY, BY LOOKS ONELY, OR DO THEY MIX 8 616
TOTAL THEY MIX, UNION OF PURE WITH PURE 8 627
AS FLESH TO MIX WITH FLESH, OR SOUL WITH SOUL. 8 629
TO DEATH, AND MIX WITH OUR CONNATURAL DUST? 11 529

MIXING
RECOUNTED, MIXING INTERCESSION SWEET. 10 228

MIXT
MIXT WITH OBDURATE PRIDE AND STEDFAST HATE: 1 58
MIXT WITH AUXILIAR GODS; AND WHAT RESOUNDS 1 579
MIXT WITH TARTAREAN SULPHUR, AND STRANGE FIRE, 2 69
BUT ALL THESE IN THIR PREGNANT CAUSES MIXT 2 913
ABORTIVE, MONSTROUS, OR UNKINDLY MIXT, 3 456
PRODUCES WITH TERRESTRIAL HUMOR MIXT 3 610
APPEERD, WITH GAY ENAMELD COLOURS MIXT: 4 149
MIXT DANCE, OR WANTON MASK, OR MIDNIGHT BAL, 4 768
TO HAVE REPORTED: GLADLY THEN HE MIXT 6 21
DESTRUCTION WITH CREATION MIGHT HAVE MIXT. 8 236
FROM ALL HER WORDS AND ACTIONS MIXT WITH LOVE 8 602
INTO A BEAST, AND MIXT WITH BESTIAL SLIME, 9 165
LOADEN WITH FRUIT OF FAIREST COLOURS MIXT, 9 577
THAT TIME CELESTIAL VISAGES, YET MIXT 10 24
AND PRAYERS, WHICH IN THIS GOLDEN CENSER, MIXT 11 24
GREY-HEADED MEN AND GRAVE, WITH WARRIOURS MIXT, 11 662
ABHOR TO JOYN; AND BY IMPRUDENCE MIXT, 11 686
AND ALL HIS PEOPLE; THUNDER MIXT WITH HAILE, 12 181
HAILE MIXT WITH FIRE MUST REND TH' EGYPTIAN SKIE 12 182

MIXTURE
NO GROSS, NO UNHARMONEOUS MIXTURE FOULE, 11 51

MOABS
NEXT CHEMOS, TH' OBSCENE DREAD OF MOABS SONS, 1 406

MOALE
THE LIBBARD, AND THE TYGER, AS THE MOALE 7 467

MOAPING
DAEMONIAC PHRENZIE, MOAPING MELANCHOLIE 11 485

MOARIE
WITH WINGED COURSE ORE HILL OR MOARIE DALE, 2 944

MOCK
THAT MOCK OUR SCANT MANURING, AND REQUIRE 4 628

MOCKT
WHY AM I MOCKT WITH DEATH, AND LENGTH'ND OUT 10 774
AS MOCKT THEY STORM; GREAT LAUGHTER WAS IN HEAV'N 12 59

MODE
FOR ONE OF SYRIAN MODE, WHEREON TO BURN 1 474

MODEL
BY MODEL, OR BY SHADING PENCIL DRAWN. 3 509
HEREAFTER, WHEN THEY COME TO MODEL HEAV'N 8 79

MODERATE
IN MEAN ESTATE LIVE MODERATE, TILL GROWN 12 351

MODERATION
BY MODERATION EITHER STATE TO BEARE, 11 363

MODERN
CITY OF OLD OR MODERN FAME, THE SEAT 11 386

MODEST
YIELDED WITH COY SUBMISSION, MODEST PRIDE, 4 310

MODESTIE
YET INNOCENCE AND VIRGIN MODESTIE, 8 501

MOGUL
TO AGRA AND LAHOR OF GREAT MOGUL 11 391

MOIST
FOR HOT, COLD, MOIST, AND DRY, FOUR CHAMPIONS FIERCE 2 898
BEAR HIS SWIFT ERRANDS OVER MOIST AND DRY, 3 652
TO NOURISH, AND SUPERFLUOUS MOIST CONSUMES: 5 325
FROM HER MOIST CONTINENT TO HIGHER ORBES. 5 422
MOIST NUTRIMENT, OR UNDER ROCKS THIR FOOD 7 408
BLOW MOIST AND KEEN, SHATTERING THE GRACEFUL LOCKS 10 1066
VAPOUR, AND EXHALATION DUSK AND MOIST, 11 741

MOISTURE
SATIATE WITH GENIAL MOISTURE, WHEN GOD SAID 7 282
SOON DRI'D, AND ON THE REAKING MOISTURE FED. 8 256

MOLE
THEY FASTEN'D, AND THE MOLE IMMENSE WRAUGHT ON 10 300

MOLEST
AND NOT MOLEST US, UNLESS WE OUR SELVES 8 186

MOLOC
HE CEAS'D, AND NEXT HIM MOLOC, SCEPTER'D KING 2 43
OF MOLOC FURIOUS KING, WHO HIM DEFI'D, 6 357

MOLOCH
FIRST MOLOCH, HORRID KING BESMEAR'D WITH BLOOD 1 392
OF MOLOCH HOMICIDE, LUST HARD BY HATE; 1 417

MOMBAZA
MOMBAZA, AND QUILOA, AND MELIND, 11 399

MOMENT
ALL IN A MOMENT THROUGH THE GLOOM WERE SEEN 1 544
AND JUDG'D OF PUBLIC MOMENT, IN THE SHAPE 2 448
ALL IN ONE MOMENT, AND SO NEER THE BRINK; 2 609
HEE RULES A MOMENT; CHAOS UMPIRE SITS, 2 907
WOULD SET ME HIGHEST, AND IN A MOMENT QUIT 4 51
AS ONELY IN HIS ARM THE MOMENT LAY 6 239
WERE READY, IN A MOMENT UP THEY TURND 6 509
SELF-LOST, AND IN A MOMENT WILL CREATE 7 154
OR TOUCH WITH LIGHTEST MOMENT OF IMPULSE 10 45

MONARCH
MONARCH IN HEAV'N, TILL THEN AS ONE SECURE 1 638
THE MONARCH, AND PREVENTED ALL REPLY, 2 467
HEAV'NS AWFUL MONARCH? WHEREFORE BUT IN HOPE 4 960
THAT EQUAL OVER EQUALS MONARCH REIGNE: 5 832
OUR FOILE IN HEAV'N; HERE THOU SHALT MONARCH REIGN, 10 375

MONARCHAL
ABOVE HIS FELLOWS, WITH MONARCHAL PRIDE 2 428

MONARCHIE
MONARCHIE OVER SUCH AS LIVE BY RIGHT 5 795
AND HENCEFORTH MONARCHIE WITH THEE DIVIDE 10 379

MONARCHIES
THE WEIGHT OF MIGHTIEST MONARCHIES; HIS LOOK . . . 2 307

MONARCHS
PERPLEXES MONARCHS. DARK'N'D SO, YET SHON 1 599

MONARCHY
AGAINST THE THRONE AND MONARCHY OF GOD 1 42

MONSTER
DAGON HIS NAME, SEA MONSTER, UPWARD MAN 1 462
THE MONSTER MOVING ONWARD CAME AS FAST 2 675
WHOM THUS THE SIN-BORN MONSTER ANSWERD SOON. . . 10 596
FOOD FOR SO FOULE A MONSTER, IN THY POWER . . . 10 986

MONSTERS
THESE YELLING MONSTERS THAT WITH CEASLESS CRY . . 2 795
WITH COMPLICATED MONSTERS HEAD AND TAILE, . . . 10 523
WHERE LUXURIE LATE REIGN'D, SEA-MONSTERS WHELP'D . 11 751

MONSTROUS
AS WHOM THE FABLES NAME OF MONSTROUS SIZE, ... 1 197
WITH MONSTROUS SHAPES AND SORCERIES ABUS'D 1 479
PERVERSE, ALL MONSTROUS, ALL PRODIGIOUS THINGS, . 2 625
ABORTIVE, MONSTROUS, OR UNKINDLY MIXT, ... 3 456
INTO THE WASTFUL DEEP; THE MONSTROUS SIGHT 6 862
A MONSTROUS SERPENT ON HIS BELLY PRONE, ... 10 514
DISEASES DIRE, OF WHICH A MONSTROUS CREW 11 474

MONTALBAN
JOUSTED IN ASPRAMONT OR MONTALBAN, ... 1 583

MONTHLY
TIMELY INTERPOSES, AND HER MONTHLY ROUND 3 728

MONTHS
DAYS, MONTHS, & YEARS, TOWARDS HIS ALL-CHEARING
LAMP 3 581
HIS SEASONS, HOURS, OR DAYES, OR MONTHS, OR YEARES: 8 69

MONUMENT
WHERE SATAN NOW PREVAILES, A MONUMENT 10 258
OR MONUMENT TO AGES, AND THEREON 11 326

MONUMENTS
LEARN HOW THIR GREATEST MONUMENTS OF FAME, ... 1 695

MOOD
IN PERFECT PHALANX TO THE DORIAN MOOD 1 550
TO WHOM THUS BELIAL IN LIKE GAMESOM MOOD, ... 6 620
THUS IN CALM MOOD HIS WORDS TO EVE HE TURND. . . . 9 920

MOON
HUNG ON HIS SHOULDERS LIKE THE MOON, WHOSE ORB . 1 287
TO WHOSE BRIGHT IMAGE NIGHTLY BY THE MOON 1 440
SHORN OF HIS BEAMS, OR FROM BEHIND THE MOON . . . 1 596
OR DREAMS HE SEES, WHILE OVER-HEAD THE MOON . . . 1 784
WITH LAPLAND WITCHES, WHILE THE LABOURING MOON . 2 665
OF SMALLEST MAGNITUDE CLOSE BY THE MOON. 2 1053
NOT IN THE NEIGHBOURING MOON, AS SOME HAVE DREAMD; 3 459
NIGHT WOULD INVADE, BUT THERE THE NEIGHBOURING MOON 3 726
THE STARRIE HOST, RODE BRIGHTEST, TILL THE MOON . 4 606
WITH THIS HER SOLEMN BIRD AND THIS FAIR MOON, . . 4 648
WITH THIS HER SOLEMN BIRD, NOR WALK BY MOON, . . 4 655
DAZ'LING THE MOON; THESE TO THE BOWER DIRECT . . 4 798
FULL ORB'D THE MOON, AND WITH MORE PLEASING LIGHT 5 42
MOON, THAT NOW MEETST THE ORIENT SUN, NOW FLI'ST . 5 175
IMAGIND LANDS AND REGIONS IN THE MOON: 5 263
ETHEREAL, AND AS LOWEST FIRST THE MOON; 5 418
NOR DOTH THE MOON NO NOURISHMENT EXHALE 5 421
OR IF THE STARR OF EEVNING AND THE MOON 7 104
THOUGH OF ETHEREAL MOULD: THEN FORM'D THE MOON . 7 356
SHEDDING SWEET INFLUENCE: LESS BRIGHT THE MOON, . 7 375
TO THE TERRESTRIAL MOON BE AS A STARR 8 142
AND THOU MOON IN THE VALE OF AIALON, ... 12 266

MOONE
SOLSTITIAL SUMMERS HEAT. TO THE BLANC MOONE . . 10 656

MOONED
TURND FIERIE RED, SHARPNING IN MOONED HORNES . . . 4 978

MOONS
WHICH THEY BEHELD, THE MOONS RESPLENDENT GLOBE . 4 723
WITH THIR ATTENDANT MOONS THOU WILT DESCRIE . . . 8 149

MOON-STRUCK
AND MOON-STRUCK MADNESS, PINING ATROPHIE, ... 11 486

MOORS
MOORS BY HIS SIDE UNDER THE LEE, WHILE NIGHT . . . 1 207

MOOVD
WAS HEARD, OF HARP AND ORGAN; AND WHO MOOVD . . . 11 560
OF PARADISE BY MIGHT OF WAVES BE MOOVD 11 830

MORAL
CANNOT APPEASE, NOR MAN THE MORAL PART 12 298

MORE
DELIGHT THEE MORE, AND SILOA'S BROOK THAT FLOW'D . 1 11
RESERV'D HIM TO MORE WRATH; FOR NOW THE THOUGHT . 1 54
WE MAY WITH MORE SUCCESSFUL HOPE RESOLVE 1 120
IN THIS UNHAPPY MANSION, OR ONCE MORE 1 268
REGAIND IN HEAV'N, OR WHAT MORE LOST IN HELL? . . 1 270
BELIAL CAME LAST, THEN WHOM A SPIRIT MORE LEWD . 1 490
FELL NOT FROM HEAVEN, OR MORE GROSS TO LOVE . . 1 491
OR ALTAR SMOAK'D; YET WHO MORE OFT THEN HEE . . 1 493
ALL THESE AND MORE CAME FLOCKING; BUT WITH LOOKS . 1 522
COULD MERIT MORE THEN THAT SMALL INFANTRY 1 575
WERE ALWAYS DOWNWARD BENT, ADMIRING MORE 1 681
MORE GLORIOUS AND MORE DREAD THEN FROM NO FALL, . 2 16
THUS FARR AT LEAST RECOVER'D, HATH MUCH MORE . . 2 22
WILL COVET MORE. WITH THIS ADVANTAGE THEN . . . 2 35
MORE THEN CAN BE IN HEAV'N, WE NOW RETURN . . . 2 37
MORE UNEXPERT, I BOAST NOT: THEM LET THOSE . . . 2 52
CALLS US TO PENANCE? MORE DESTROY'D THEN THUS . 2 92
BELIAL, IN ACT MORE GRACEFUL AND HUMANE; . . . 2 109
TO BE NO MORE; SAD CURE; FOR WHO WOULD LOOSE, . . 2 146
WHATEVER DOING, WHAT CAN WE SUFFER MORE, . . . 2 162
NOT MORE ALMIGHTY TO RESIST OUR MIGHT 2 192
IF WE PROCURE NOT TO OUR SELVES MORE WOE. . . . 2 225
MAGNIFICENCE; AND WHAT CAN HEAV'N SHEW MORE? . . 2 273
IN POWER AND EXCELLENCE, BUT FAVOUR'D MORE . . 2 350
WILL ONCE MORE LIFT US UP, IN SPIGHT OF FATE, . . 2 393
OF HAZARD MORE, AS HE ABOVE THE REST 2 455
MORE TOLLERABLE; IF THERE BE CURE OR CHARM . . 2 460
DREADED NOT MORE TH' ADVENTURE THEN HIS VOICE . . 2 474
THENCE MORE AT EASE THIR MINDS AND SOMWHAT RAIS'D 2 521
OTHERS WITH VAST TYPHOEAN RAGE MORE FELL 2 539
INTO TH' EUBOIC SEA. OTHERS MORE MILDE, ... 2 546
THE THRONGING AUDIENCE. IN DISCOURSE MORE SWEET . 2 555
IN THOUGHTS MORE ELEVATE, AND REASON'D HIGH . . 2 558
OF FIERCE EXTREAMS, EXTREAMS BY CHANGE MORE FIERCE, 2 599
WHERE I REIGN KING, AND TO ENRAGE THEE MORE, . . 2 698
MORE DREADFUL AND DEFORM: ON TH' OTHER SIDE . . 2 706
FOR NEVER BUT ONCE MORE WAS EITHER LIKE 2 721
SIGHT MORE DETESTABLE THEN HIM AND THEE. . . . 2 745
I FLED, BUT HE PURSU'D (THOUGH MORE, IT SEEMS, . 2 790
PERHAPS OUR VACANT ROOM, THOUGH MORE REMOV'D, . . 2 835
THEN THIS MORE SECRET NOW DESIGN'D, I HASTE . . 2 838
AND BY DECISION MORE IMBROILES THE FRAY 2 908
HIS DARK MATERIALS TO CREATE MORE WORLDS, . . . 2 916
(WHICH IS MY PRESENT JOURNEY) AND ONCE MORE . . 2 985
AND MORE ENDANGER'D, THEN WHEN ARGO PASS'D . . . 2 1017
OR DIM SUFFUSION VEILD. YET NOT THE MORE . . . 3 26
FREELY VOUTSAFT; ONCE MORE I WILL RENEW 3 175
UPHELD BY ME, YET ONCE MORE HE SHALL STAND . . . 3 178
BUT HARD BE HARD'ND, BLIND BE BLINDED MORE, . . 3 200
AND RECONCILEMENT; WRAUTH SHALL BE NO MORE . . . 3 264
BY MERIT MORE THEN BIRTHRIGHT SON OF GOD, . . . 3 309
FARR MORE THEN GREAT OR HIGH; BECAUSE IN THEE . . 3 311
LOVE HATH ABOUNDED MORE THEN GLORY ABOUNDS, . . 3 312
FOR REGAL SCEPTER THEN NO MORE SHALL NEED, . . 3 340
SO STRICTLY, BUT MUCH MORE TO PITIE ENCLINE: . . 3 402
SO STRICTLY, BUT MUCH MORE TO PITIE ENCLIN'D, . 3 405
THOSE ARGENT FIELDS MORE LIKELY HABITANTS, . . . 3 460
CLEOMBROTUS, AND MANY MORE TOO LONG, ... 3 473
AT TOP WHEREOF, BUT FARR MORE RICH APPEERD . . . 3 504
THE SPIRIT MALIGNE, BUT MUCH MORE ENVY SEIS'D . . 3 553
THE MORE IT SEEMS EXCESS, THAT LED THEE HITHER . 3 698
ONE STEP NO MORE THEN FROM HIMSELF CAN FLY . . . 4 22
BY THEE, AND MORE THEN HALF PERHAPS WILL REIGNE; . 4 112
SAW HIM DISFIGUR'D, MORE THEN COULD BEFALL . . . 4 127
ON WHICH THE SUN MORE GLAD IMPRESS'D HIS BEAMS . 4 150
IN NARROW ROOM NATURES WHOLE WEALTH, YEA MORE, . 4 207
HIS FARR MORE PLEASANT GARDEN GOD ORDAIND; . . . 4 215
THEY SAT THEM DOWN, AND AFTER NO MORE TOIL . . . 4 327
MORE EASIE, WHOLSOM THIRST AND APPETITE 4 330
MORE GRATEFUL, TO THIR SUPPER FRUITS THEY FELL, . 4 331
MORE WOE, THE MORE YOUR TASTE IS NOW OF JOY; . . 4 369
TO MARK WHAT OF THIR STATE HE MORE MIGHT LEARN . 4 400
WITH MORE DESIRE TO KNOW, AND TO REJECT 4 523
MORE OF TH' ALMIGHTIES WORKS, AND CHIEFLY MAN . . 4 566
MORE HANDS THEN OURS TO LOP THIR WANTON GROWTH: . 4 629
GOD IS THY LAW, THOU MINE: TO KNOW NO MORE . . . 4 637
PERFECTION FROM THE SUNS MORE POTENT RAY. . . . 4 673
BROIDERD THE GROUND, MORE COLOUR'D THEN WITH STONE 4 702
MORE SACRED AND SEQUESTERD, THOUGH BUT FEIGND, . 4 706
BROUGHT HER IN NAKED BEAUTY MORE ADORN'D, . . . 4 713
MORE LOVELY THEN PANDORA, WHOM THE GODS 4 714
NO HAPPIER STATE, AND KNOW TO KNOW NO MORE. . . 4 775
THAT GLORIE THEN, WHEN THOU NO MORE WAST GOOD, . 4 838
OR ALL AT ONCE; MORE GLORIE WILL BE WONN, . . . 4 853
THOUGH FOR POSSESSION PUT TO TRY ONCE MORE . . . 4 941
PATRON OF LIBERTY, WHO MORE THEN THOU 4 958
GAVE HEED, BUT WAXING MORE IN RAGE REPLI'D. . . 4 969
TO BOAST WHAT ARMS CAN DOE, SINCE THINE NO MORE . 4 1008
HIS MOUNTED SCALE ALOFT: NOR MORE; BUT FLED . . 4 1014
OF BIRDS ON EVERY BOUGH; SO MUCH THE MORE . . . 5 8
FULL ORB'D THE MOON, AND WITH MORE PLEASING LIGHT 5 42
SWEET OF THY SELF, BUT MUCH MORE SWEET THUS CROPT, 5 68
AND WHY NOT GODS OF MEN, SINCE GOOD, THE MORE . . 5 71
COMMUNICATED, MORE ABUNDANT GROWES, ... 5 72
THE AUTHOR NOT IMPAIR'D, BUT HONOURD MORE? . . . 5 73
THAT WONT TO BE MORE CHEARFUL AND SERENE . . . 5 123
MORE TUNEABLE THEN NEEDED LUTE OR HARP 5 151

MORE (CONTINUED)

TO ADD MORE SWEETNESS, AND THEY THUS BEGAN.	5	152
HER VIRGIN FANCIES, POURING FORTH MORE SWEET,	5	296
EARTHS INMOST WOMB, MORE WARMTH THEN ADAM NEEDS;	5	302
MORE FRUITFUL, WHICH INSTRUCTS US NOT TO SPARE.	5	320
HIS GOD-LIKE GUEST, WALKS FORTH, WITHOUT MORE TRAIN	5	351
MORE SOLEMN THEN THE TEDIOUS POMP THAT WAITS	5	354
BE OVER, AND THE SUN MORE COOLE DECLINE.	5	370
UNDECKT, SAVE WITH HER SELF MORE LOVELY FAIR	5	380
SHALL FILL THE WORLD MORE NUMEROUS WITH THY SONS	5	389
AS THAT MORE WILLINGLY THOU COULDST NOT SEEM	5	466
BUT MORE REFIN'D, MORE SPIRITOUS, AND PURE,	5	475
MORE AERIE, LAST THE BRIGHT CONSUMMATE FLOURE	5	481
CAN COMPREHEND, INCAPABLE OF MORE.	5	505
ATTENTIVE, AND WITH MORE DELIGHTED EARE,	5	545
BUT MORE DESIRE TO HEAR, IF THOU CONSENT,	5	555
EACH TO OTHER LIKE, MORE THEN ON EARTH IS THOUGHT?	5	576
IS HEARD NO MORE IN HEAV'N; HE OF THE FIRST,	5	659
WHAT DOUBTFUL MAY ENSUE, MORE IN THIS PLACE	5	682
ALL THY DOMINION, ADAM, IS NO MORE	5	751
ABDIEL, THEN WHOM NONE WITH MORE ZEALE ADOR'D	5	805
OUR HAPPIE STATE UNDER ONE HEAD MORE NEER	5	830
BUT MORE ILLUSTRIOUS MADE, SINCE HE THE HEAD	5	842
TH' APOSTAT, AND MORE HAUGHTY THUS REPLI'D.	5	852
NO MORE BE TROUBL'D HOW TO QUIT THE YOKE	5	882
BACK ON THY FOES MORE GLORIOUS TO RETURN	6	39
HIS DARING FOE, AT THIS PREVENTION MORE	6	129
OF ALL THIR REGIONS: HOW MUCH MORE OF POWER	6	223
OR SOM MORE SUDDEN VENGEANCE WING'D FROM GOD	6	279
RECEIVE, NO MORE THEN CAN THE FLUID AIRE:	6	349
TOO MEAN PRETENSE, BUT WHAT WE MORE AFFECT,	6	421
THE REMEDIE; PERHAPS MORE VALID ARMES,	6	438
WEAPONS MORE VIOLENT, WHEN NEXT WE MEET,	6	439
WITH WHAT MORE FORCIBLE WE MAY OFFEND	6	465
DOUBL'D, WOULD RENDER THEM YET MORE DESPIS'D,	6	602
AND BREST, (WHAT COULD WE MORE?) PROPOUNDED TERMS	6	612
THEY HARD'ND MORE BY WHAT MIGHT MOST RECLAME,	6	791
MORE SAFE I SING WITH MORTAL VOICE, UNCHANG'D	7	24
OF HIS ETERNAL EMPIRE, BUT THE MORE	7	96
TO MAGNIFIE HIS WORKS, THE MORE WE KNOW.	7	97
DREW MANY, WHOM THIR PLACE KNOWS HERE NO MORE;	7	144
IMMEDIATE ARE THE ACTS OF GOD, MORE SWIFT	7	176
PART LOOSLY WING THE REGION, PART MORE WISE	7	425
TO MANIFEST THE MORE THY MIGHT: HIS EVIL	7	615
THOU USEST, AND FROM THENCE CREAT'ST MORE GOOD.	7	616
SERV'D BY MORE NOBLE THEN HER SELF, ATTAINES	8	34
MORE PLENTY THEN THE SUN THAT BARREN SHINES,	8	94
IS THE PRIME WISDOM, WHAT IS MORE, IS FUME,	8	194
AS WITH A SMILE MORE BRIGHT'ND, THUS REPLI'D.	8	368
HEE ENDED, OR I HEARD NO MORE, FOR NOW	8	452
THE MORE DESIRABLE, OR TO SAY ALL,	8	505
MORE THEN ENOUGH; AT LEAST ON HER BESTOW'D	8	537
THEN VALUE: OFT TIMES NOTHING PROFITS MORE	8	571
WELL MANAG'D; OF THAT SKILL THE MORE THOU KNOW'ST,	8	573
THE MORE SHE WILL ACKNOWLEDGE THEE HER HEAD,	8	574
MADE SO ADORN FOR THY DELIGHT THE MORE,	8	576
MORE GRATEFUL THEN HARMONIOUS SOUND TO THE EARE.	8	606
BUT I CAN NOW NO MORE; THE PARTING SUN	8	630
NO MORE OF TALK WHERE GOD OR ANGEL GUEST	9	1
NOT LESS BUT MORE HEROIC THEN THE WRAUTH	9	14
MORE JUSTLY, SEAT WORTHIER OF GODS, AS BUILT	9	100
FIND PLACE OR REFUGE; AND THE MORE I SEE	9	119
PLEASURES ABOUT ME, SO MUCH MORE I FEEL	9	120
MORE ANGELS TO CREATE, IF THEY AT LEAST	9	146
ARE HIS CREATED, OR TO SPITE US MORE,	9	147
WHOM US THE MORE TO SPITE HIS MAKER RAIS'D	9	177
OUR PLEASANT TASK ENJOYN'D, BUT TILL MORE HANDS	9	207
ENJOY'D BY US EXCITES HIS ENVIE MORE;	9	264
MORE WISE, MORE WATCHFUL, STRONGER, IF NEED WERE	9	311
GO; FOR THY STAY, NOT FREE, ABSENTS THEE MORE;	9	372
SO BENT, THE MORE SHALL SHAME HIM HIS REPULSE.	9	384
DELIGHTED, BUT DESIRING MORE HER STAY.	9	398
OF GROVE OR GARDEN-PLOT MORE PLEASANT LAY,	9	418
SPOT MORE DELICIOUS THEN THOSE GARDENS FEIGN'D	9	439
MUCH HEE THE PLACE ADMIR'D, THE PERSON MORE.	9	444
WHAT PLEASING SEEMD, FOR HER NOW PLEASES MORE,	9	453
ANGELIC, BUT MORE SOFT, AND FEMININE,	9	458
AND TORTURES HIM NOW MORE, THE MORE HE SEES	9	469
WHOSE HIGHER INTELLECTUAL MORE I SHUN,	9	483
FROM EVERY BEAST, MORE DUTEOUS AT HER CALL,	9	521
THY AWFUL BROW, MORE AWFUL THUS RETIR'D.	9	537
GRATEFUL TO APPETITE, MORE PLEAS'D MY SENSE	9	580
YET MORE AMAZ'D UNWARIE THUS REPLY'D.	9	614
GROW UP TO THIR PROVISION, AND MORE HANDS	9	623
SHE SCARSE HAD SAID, THOUGH BRIEF, WHEN NOW MORE BOLD	9	664
AND LIFE MORE PERFET HAVE ATTAIND THEN FATE	9	689
IN HEAV'NLY BRESTS? THESE, THESE AND MANY MORE	9	730
COMMENDS THEE MORE, WHILE IT INFERRS THE GOOD	9	754
IN FEMAL SEX, THE MORE TO DRAW HIS LOVE,	9	822
AND RENDER ME MORE EQUAL, AND PERHAPS,	9	823
AND DEATH ENSUE? THEN I SHALL BE NO MORE,	9	827
NOT FELT, NOR SHALL BE TWICE, FOR NEVER MORE	9	859
MUCH MORE TO TASTE IT UNDER BANNE TO TOUCH.	9	925
RATHER THEN DEATH OR AUGHT THEN DEATH MORE DREAD	9	969
HER FORMER TRESPASS FEAR'D, THE MORE TO SOOTHE	9	1006
UNCOVER'D MORE, SO ROSE THE DANITE STRONG	9	1059
HIDE ME, WHERE I MAY NEVER SEE THEM MORE.	9	1090
IT SEEMS, IN THY RESTRAINT: WHAT COULD I MORE?	9	1170
THE EEVNING COOLE WHEN HE FROM WRAUTH MORE COOLE	10	95
HE CAME, AND WITH HIM EVE, MORE LOTH, THOUGH FIRST	10	109
AS VITIATED IN NATURE: MORE TO KNOW	10	169
OF BEASTS, BUT INWARD NAKEDNESS, MUCH MORE	10	221
OR TRIE THEE NOW MORE DANG'ROUS TO HIS THRONE.	10	382
FROM HIS CREATOR, AND THE MORE TO INCREASE	10	486
OR MUCH MORE GRIEVOUS PAIN? YE HAVE TH' ACCOUNT	10	501
HAD LEASURE, WONDRING AT HIMSELF NOW MORE;	10	510
THIS MORE DELUSIVE, NOT THE TOUCH, BUT TASTE	10	563
THE POLES OF EARTH TWICE TEN DEGREES AND MORE	10	669
INHABITED, THOUGH SINLESS, MORE THEN NOW,	10	690
AND SLEEP SECURE; HIS DREADFUL VOICE NO MORE	10	779
MORE TO THE PART SINISTER FROM ME DRAWN,	10	886
AND MORE THAT SHALL BEFALL, INNUMERABLE	10	896
MORE MISERABLE; BOTH HAVE SIN'D, BUT THOU	10	930
BUT RISE, LET US NO MORE CONTEND, NOR BLAME	10	958
TO BETTER HOPES HIS MORE ATTENTIVE MINDE	10	1011
TO ARGUE IN THEE SOMTHING MORE SUBLIME	10	1014
TO BE FORESTALL'D; MUCH MORE I FEAR LEAST DEATH	10	1024
NO MORE BE MENTION'D THEN OF VIOLENCE	10	1041
HOW MUCH MORE, IF WE PRAY HIM, WILL HIS EAR	10	1060
FRUITS OF MORE PLEASING SAVOUR FROM THY SEED	11	26
AND IN THIR STATE, THOUGH FIRM, STOOD MORE CONFIRMD.	11	71
WHEN GOD DESCENDED, AND PERHAPS ONCE MORE	11	75
WITH WHOSE STOL'N FRUIT MAN ONCE MORE TO DELUDE.	11	125
SPANGL'D WITH EYES MORE NUMEROUS THEN THOSE	11	130
OF ARGUS, AND MORE WAKEFUL THEN TO DROUZE,	11	131
WHO KNOWS, OR MORE THEN THIS, THAT WE ARE DUST,	11	199
AND THITHER MUST RETURN AND BE NO MORE.	11	200
MORE ORIENT IN YON WESTERN CLOUD THAT DRAWS	11	205
NOT THAT MORE GLORIOUS, WHEN THE ANGELS MET	11	213
NO MORE AVAILES THEN BREATH AGAINST THE WINDE,	11	312
CORRUPTION TO BRING FORTH MORE VIOLENT DEEDS.	11	428
MORE MEEK CAME WITH THE FIRSTLINGS OF HIS FLOCK	11	437
MORE TERRIBLE AT TH' ENTRANCE THEN WITHIN.	11	470
BY FIRE, FLOOD, FAMIN, BY INTEMPERANCE MORE	11	472
MUCH BETTER SEEMS THIS VISION, AND MORE HOPE	11	599
NO MORE WAS SEEN; THE FLOATING VESSEL SWUM	11	745
MORE THEN ANOUGH, THAT TEMPERANCE MAY BE TRI'D:	11	805
THE PATHS OF RIGHTEOUSNESS, HOW MUCH MORE SAFE,	11	814
THE ARK NO MORE NOW FLOTES, BUT SEEMS ON GROUND	11	850
MORE HARD'ND AFTER THAW, TILL IN HIS RAGE	12	194
MOSES ONCE MORE HIS POTENT ROD EXTENDS	12	211
TO NOBLE AND IGNOBLE IS MORE SWEET	12	221
SOME BLOUD MORE PRECIOUS MUST BE PAID FOR MAN,	12	293
MANHOOD TO GOD-HEAD, WITH MORE STRENGTH TO FOIL	12	389
NEVER TO HURT THEM MORE WHO RIGHTLY TRUST	12	418
AND EVIL TURN TO GOOD; MORE WONDERFUL	12	471
MUCH MORE, THAT MUCH MORE GOOD THEREOF SHALL SPRING,	12	476
TO GOD MORE GLORY, MORE GOOD WILL TO MEN	12	477
WITH CAUSE FOR EVILS PAST, YET MUCH MORE CHEER'D	12	604

MOREB

OF MOREB; THERE BY PROMISE HE RECEAVES	12	137

MORN

INVESTS THE SEA, AND WISHED MORN DELAYES:	1	208
SHEER O'RE THE CHRYSTAL BATTLEMENTS; FROM MORN	1	742
DAY, OR THE SWEET APPROACH OF EV'N OR MORN,	3	42
SWEET IS THE BREATH OF MORN, HER RISING SWEET,	4	641
BUT NEITHER BREATH OF MORN WHEN SHE ASCENDS	4	650
SHOWRD ROSES, WHICH THE MORN REPAIR'D. SLEEP ON	4	773
NOW MORN HER ROSIE STEPS IN TH' EASTERN CLIME	5	1
THY FACE, AND MORN RETURN'D, FOR I THIS NIGHT,	5	30
SURE PLEDGE OF DAY, THAT CROWNST THE SMILING MORN	5	168
WITNESS IF I BE SILENT, MORN OR EEVEN,	5	202
COMES THIS WAY MOVING; SEEMS ANOTHER MORN	5	310
YIELD NECTAR, THOUGH FROM OFF THE BOUGHS EACH MORN	5	428
(FOR WEE HAVE ALSO OUR EEVNING AND OUR MORN,	5	628
AMONG THE SONS OF MORN, WHAT MULTITUDES	5	716
THROUGH HEAV'NS WIDE CHAMPAIN HELD HIS WAY, TILL MORN,	6	2
SEEM TWILIGHT HERE; AND NOW WENT FORTH THE MORN	6	12
NOW WHEN FAIR MORN ORIENT IN HEAV'N APPEERD	6	524
AND THE THIRD SACRED MORN BEGAN TO SHINE	6	748
VISIT'ST MY SLUMBERS NIGHTLY, OR WHEN MORN	7	29
HE NAM'D. THUS WAS THE FIRST DAY EEV'N AND MORN:	7	252
BOTH WHEN FIRST EEVNING WAS, AND WHEN FIRST MORN.	7	260
SO EEV'N AND MORN RECORDED THE THIRD DAY.	7	338
GLAD EEVNING AND GLAD MORN CROWND THE FOURTH DAY.	7	386
EV'NING AND MORN SOLEMNIZ'D THE FIFT DAY.	7	448
SO EV'N AND MORN ACCOMPLISH'D THE SIXT DAY:	7	550
I LED HER BLUSHING LIKE THE MORN: ALL HEAV'N,	8	511
DISTURBD NOT, WAITING CLOSE TH' APPROACH OF MORN.	9	191
FORTH ISSUING ON A SUMMERS MORN TO BREATHE	9	447
THAT MORN WHEN FIRST THEY PARTED; BY THE TREE	9	848
DESIRE OF WANDRING THIS UNHAPPIE MORN,	9	1136
THOUGH AFTER SLEEPLESS NIGHT; FOR SEE THE MORN,	11	173
AFTER SHORT BLUSH OF MORN; NIGH IN HER SIGHT	11	184
RETURNE, THE STARRES OF MORN SHALL SEE HIM RISE	12	422

MORNING

BOTH WHERE THE MORNING SUN FIRST WARMLY SMOTE	4	244
TO MORROW ERE FRESH MORNING STREAK THE EAST	4	623

MORNING (CONTINUED)
AWAKE, THE MORNING SHINES, AND THE FRESH FIELD 5 20
THEN WHEN FAIR MORNING FIRST SMILES ON THE WORLD, 5 124
THIR ORISONS, EACH MORNING DULY PAID 5 145
HIS COUNT'NANCE, AS THE MORNING STARR THAT GUIDES 5 708
OR STARRS OF MORNING, DEW-DROPS, WHICH THE SUN 5 746
END, AND DISMISS THEE ERE THE MORNING SHINE, 7 108
AND MORNING CHORUS SUNG THE SECOND DAY. 7 275
AND HENCE THE MORNING PLANET GUILDS HER HORNS; 7 366
WHO SINCE THE MORNING HOUR SET OUT FROM HEAV'N 8 111
THIR MORNING INCENSE, WHEN ALL THINGS THAT BREATH, 9 194
NOT WITHOUT SONG, EACH MORNING, AND DUE PRAISE 9 800
DARKNESS ERE DAYES MID-COURSE, AND MORNING LIGHT 11 204
DARKNESS DEFENDS BETWEEN TILL MORNING WATCH; 12 207

MORNINGS
ON TO THIR MORNINGS RURAL WORK THEY HASTE 5 211

MORROW
THOU TELLST, BY MORROW DAWNING I SHALL KNOW. 4 588
BY MORROW EEVNING, AND FROM LAND TO LAND 4 662

MORROWS
WORKS OF DAY PASS'T, OR MORROWS NEXT DESIGNE, 5 33

MORSEL
SHOULD PROVE A BITTER MORSEL, AND HIS BANE, 2 808

MORSELS
NO HOMELY MORSELS, AND WHATEVER THING 10 605

MORTAL
OF THAT FORBIDDEN TREE, WHOSE MORTAL TAST 1 2
TO MORTAL MEN, HE WITH HIS HORRID CREW 1 51
FROM MORTAL OR IMMORTAL MINDS. THUS THEY 1 559
COMPARE OF MORTAL PROWESS, YET OBSERV'D 1 588
WHO BOAST IN MORTAL THINGS, AND WOND'RING TELL 1 693
TO MORTAL COMBAT OR CARREER WITH LANCE) 1 766
WITH MORTAL STING: ABOUT HER MIDDLE ROUND 2 653
POSSESSES THEE TO BEND THAT MORTAL DART 2 729
THOUGH TEMPER'D HEAV'NLY, FOR THAT MORTAL DINT, 2 813
OF THINGS INVISIBLE TO MORTAL SIGHT. 3 55
ON EVEN GROUND AGAINST HIS MORTAL FOE, 3 179
WHICH OF YE WILL BE MORTAL TO REDEEM 3 214
MANS MORTAL CRIME, AND JUST TH' UNJUST TO SAVE, 3 215
TO MORTAL MEN, ABOVE WHICH ONLY SHON 3 268
HAPLY SO SCAP'D HIS MORTAL SNARE; FOR NOW 4 8
NOR IN THIR LIQUID TEXTURE MORTAL WOUND 6 348
INCAPABLE OF MORTAL INJURIE 6 434
MORE SAFE I SING WITH MORTAL VOICE, UNCHANG'D 7 24
FROM THAT DAY MORTAL, AND THIS HAPPIE STATE 8 331
WEPT AT COMPLEATING OF THE MORTAL SIN 9 1003
WHAT RESTS BUT THAT THE MORTAL SENTENCE PASS 10 48
OF MORTAL CHANGE ON EARTH. AS WHEN A FLOCK 10 273
BUT MORTAL DOOM'D. HOW CAN HE EXERCISE 10 796
AND MORTAL FOOD, AS MAY DISPOSE HIM BEST 11 54
THAT MUST BE MORTAL TO US BOTH. O FLOURS, 11 273
THY MORTAL PASSAGE WHEN IT COMES. ASCEND 11 366
THY MORTAL SIGHT TO FAILE; OBJECTS DIVINE 12 9
TO MORTAL EARE IS DREADFUL; THEY BESEECH 12 236
THE HOLY ONE WITH MORTAL MEN TO DWELL; 12 248
EXPECT WITH MORTAL PAINE: SAY WHERE AND WHEN 12 384

MORTALITIE
MORTALITIE MY SENTENCE, AND BE EARTH 10 776

MORTALL
INGLORIOUS, OF HIS MORTALL STING DISARM'D. 3 253

MORTALS
TO TEMPT OR PUNISH MORTALS, EXCEPT WHOM 2 1032

MOSAIC
MOSAIC; UNDERFOOT THE VIOLET, 4 700

MOSCO
IN MOSCO, OR THE SULTAN IN BIZANCE, 11 395

MOSES
MOSES AND AARON) SENT FROM GOD TO CLAIME 12 170
AW'D BY THE ROD OF MOSES SO TO STAND 12 198
MOSES ONCE MORE HIS POTENT ROD EXTENDS 12 211
THAT MOSES MIGHT REPORT TO THEM HIS WILL, 12 237
MOSES IN FIGURE BEARES, TO INTRODUCE 12 241
AND THEREFORE SHALL NOT MOSES, THOUGH OF GOD 12 307

MOSSIE
THIR TABLE WAS, AND MOSSIE SEATS HAD ROUND, 5 392
ABOUT THE MOSSIE TRUNK I WOUND ME SOON, 9 589

MOST
HE TRUSTED TO HAVE EQUAL'D THE MOST HIGH, 1 40
CONSULT HOW WE MAY HENCEFORTH MOST OFFEND 1 187
DID NOT DISSWADE ME MOST, AND SEEM TO CAST 2 122
WHEN HE WHO MOST EXCELS IN FACT OF ARMS, 2 124
THEN MOST CONSPICUOUS, WHEN GREAT THINGS OF SMALL, 2 258
IN DOING WHAT WE MOST IN SUFFERING FEEL? 2 340
THE MOST AVERSE, THEE CHIEFLY, WHO FULL OFT 2 763

MOST (CONTINUED)
THIR LIGHTER WINGS. TO WHOM THESE MOST ADHERE, 2 906
MOST GLORIOUS, IN HIM ALL HIS FATHER SHON 3 139
RECEIVE NEW LIFE. SO MAN, AS IS MOST JUST, 3 294
IF STONE, CARBUNCLE MOST OR CHRYSOLITE, 3 596
WILDE WORK PRODUCES OFT, AND MOST IN DREAMS, 5 112
IS OFTEST YOURS, THE LATTER MOST IS OURS, 5 489
THEN MOST, WHEN MOST IRREGULAR THEY SEEM, 5 624
THAT THE MOST HIGH COMMANDING, NOW ERE NIGHT, 5 699
MOST REASON IS THAT REASON OVERCOME. 6 126
I SEE THAT MOST THROUGH SLOTH HAD RATHER SERVE, 6 166
ONCE FOUND, WHICH YET UNFOUND MOST WOULD HAVE
THOUGHT 6 500
ON WHEELS (FOR LIKE TO PILLARS MOST THEY SEEM'D 6 573
AS IS MOST JUST; THIS I MY GLORIE ACCOUNT, 6 726
THEY HARD'ND MORE BY WHAT MIGHT MOST RECLAME, 6 791
AS A DESPITE DON AGAINST THE MOST HIGH, 6 906
GLORIE THEY SUNG TO THE MOST HIGH, GOOD WILL 7 182
AND RENDERS US IN THINGS THAT MOST CONCERNE 8 196
AND INWARD FACULTIES, WHICH MOST EXCELL, 8 542
DISMISS NOT HER, WHEN MOST THOU NEEDST HER NIGH, 8 564
MOST OPPORTUNE MIGHT SERVE HIS WILES, AND FOUND 9 85
LEADS THEE, OR WHERE MOST NEEDS, WHETHER TO WIND 9 215
WERE BETTER, AND MOST LIKELIE IF FROM MEE 9 365
SHE MOST, AND IN HER LOOK SUMMS ALL DELIGHT. 9 454
MOST FAVORS, WHO CAN PLEASE HIM LONG; MEE FIRST 9 949
THE PARTS OF EACH FOR OTHER, THAT SEEM MOST 9 1093
AND EASILY APPROV'D; WHEN THE MOST HIGH 10 31
JUSTICE WITH MERCIE, AS MAY ILLUSTRATE MOST 10 78
THERE BEST, WHERE MOST WITH RAVIN I MAY MEET; 10 599
OR WHOM HE WISHES MOST SHALL SELDOM GAIN 10 901
IF CARE OF OUR DESCENT PERPLEX US MOST, 10 979
WHEN ANGRY MOST HE SEEM'D AND MOST SEVERE, 10 1095
THIS MOST AFFLICTS ME, THAT DEPARTING HENCE, 11 315
AND WHAT MOST MERITS FAME IN SILENCE HID. 11 699
TO JUDGE THEM WITH HIS SAINTS: HIM THE MOST HIGH 11 705
FOR GODS. YET HIM GOD THE MOST HIGH VOUTSAFES 12 120
MEN WHO ATTEND THE ALTAR, AND SHOULD MOST 12 354
THE POWER OF THE MOST HIGH; HE SHALL ASCEND 12 369
OF GOD MOST HIGH; SO GOD WITH MAN UNITES. 12 382

MOTEZUME
RICH MEXICO THE SEAT OF MOTEZUME, 11 407

MOTHER
THE MOTHER OF MANKIND, WHAT TIME HIS PRIDE 1 36
RIFL'D THE BOWELS OF THIR MOTHER EARTH 1 687
MEE OVERTOOK HIS MOTHER ALL DISMAID, 2 792
HIS MOTHER BAD, AND THUS BESPAKE HER SIRE. 2 849
MOTHER OF HUMAN RACE: WHAT COULD I DOE, 4 475
SO SPAKE OUR GENERAL MOTHER, AND WITH EYES 4 492
WHATEVER EARTH ALL-BEARING MOTHER YIELDS 5 338
HAILE MOTHER OF MANKIND, WHOSE FRUITFUL WOMB 5 388
FERMENTED THE GREAT MOTHER TO CONCEAVE, 7 281
FATHER AND MOTHER, AND TO HIS WIFE ADHERE; 8 498
LED EVE OUR CREDULOUS MOTHER, TO THE TREE 9 644
MOTHER OF SCIENCE, NOW I FEEL THY POWER 9 680
ABOUT THE MOTHER TREE, A PILLARD SHADE 9 1106
TO WHOM TH' INCESTUOUS MOTHER THUS REPLI'D. 10 602
EVE RIGHTLY CALL'D, MOTHER OF ALL MANKIND, 11 159
MOTHER OF ALL THINGS LIVING, SINCE BY THEE 11 160
A VIRGIN IS HIS MOTHER, BUT HIS SIRE 12 368
THE SEED OF WOMAN: VIRGIN MOTHER, HAILE, 12 379
SO SPAKE OUR MOTHER EVE, AND ADAM HEARD 12 624

MOTHERS
AS IN MY MOTHERS LAP? THERE I SHOULD REST 10 778
INTO THY MOTHERS LAP, OR BE WITH EASE 11 536

MOTION
THAT IN OUR PROPER MOTION WE ASCEND 2 75
DEVOID OF SENSE AND MOTION? AND WHO KNOWS, 2 151
PRODIGIOUS MOTION FELT AND RUEFUL THROES. 2 780
TO MOTION, MEASURES ALL THINGS DURABLE 5 581
NOR MOTION OF SWIFT THOUGHT, LESS COULD HIS SHIELD 6 192
STOOD THEY OR MOV'D, IN STATURE, MOTION, ARMS 6 302
IN MOTION OR IN ALT: HIM SOON THEY MET 6 532
THEN TIME OR MOTION, BUT TO HUMAN EARS 7 177
HER END WITHOUT LEAST MOTION, AND RECEAVES, 8 35
ADMITTING MOTION IN THE HEAV'NS, TO SHEW 8 115
ATTENDS THEE, AND EACH WORD, EACH MOTION FORMES, 8 223
BY QUICK INSTINCTIVE MOTION UP I SPRUNG, 8 259
MOTION, EACH ACT WON AUDIENCE ERE THE TONGUE, 9 674
THIR MOTION, AT WHOSE FRONT A FLAMING SWORD, 12 592

MOTION'D
WELL HAST THOU MOTION'D, WELL THY THOUGHTS IMPLOYD 9 229

MOTIONS
ALL THESE OUR MOTIONS VAIN, SEES AND DERIDES; 2 191
TURN SWIFT THIR VARIOUS MOTIONS, OR ARE TURND 3 582
AND IN THIR MOTIONS HARMONIE DIVINE 5 625
HER MOTIONS, AS THE GREAT FIRST-MOVERS HAND 7 500
INSENSIBLY THREE DIFFERENT MOTIONS MOVE? 8 130
THIR PLANETARIE MOTIONS AND ASPECTS 10 658
MY MOTIONS IN HIM, LONGER THEN THEY MOVE, 11 91

MOULD
A VARIOUS MOULD, AND FROM THE BOYLING CELLS . . 1 706
SIT UNPOLLUTED, AND TH' ETHEREAL MOULD 2 139
WHAT CREATURES THERE INHABIT, OF WHAT MOULD, . . 2 355
THIS WORLDS MATERIAL MOULD, CAME TO A HEAP: . . 3 709
THAT MOUNTAIN AS HIS GARDEN MOULD HIGH RAIS'D . 4 226
CREATURES OF OTHER MOULD, EARTH-BORN PERHAPS, . 4 360
TO WHOM THUS EVE. ADAM, EARTHS HALLOWD MOULD, . 5 321
OF THIS ETHEREOUS MOULD WHEREON WE STAND, . . 6 473
BRASS, IRON, STONIE MOULD, HAD NOT THIR MOUTHES . 6 576
THOUGH OF ETHEREAL MOULD: THEN FORM'D THE MOON . 7 356
BORE UP HIS BRANCHING HEAD: SCARSE FROM HIS MOULD 7 470
HEROIC BUILT, THOUGH OF TERRESTRIAL MOULD, . . . 9 485
TO MOULD ME MAN, DID I SOLLICITE THEE 10 744

MOULDS
INTO FIT MOULDS PREPAR'D; FROM WHICH HE FORMD . . 11 571

MOUND
AS WITH A RURAL MOUND THE CHAMPAIN HEAD 4 134

MOUNT
ABOVE TH' AONIAN MOUNT, WHILE IT PURSUES . . . 1 15
BEYOND THE INDIAN MOUNT, OR FAERIE ELVES, . . . 1 781
BETWIXT DAMIATA AND MOUNT CASIUS OLD, . . . 2 593
OVER MOUNT SION, AND, THOUGH THAT WERE LARGE, . . 3 530
THE WAY HE WENT, AND ON TH' ASSYRIAN MOUNT . . 4 126
MOUNT AMARA, THOUGH THIS BY SOM SUPPOS'D . . 4 281
BUT IN THE MOUNT THAT LIES FROM EDEN NORTH, . . 4 569
OF THREE THAT IN MOUNT IDA NAKED STROVE, . . . 5 382
AMIDST AS FROM A FLAMING MOUNT, WHOSE TOP . . 5 598
FROM THAT HIGH MOUNT OF GOD, WHENCE LIGHT & SHADE 5 643
ABSTRUSEST THOUGHTS, FROM FORTH HIS HOLY MOUNT . 5 712
HIGH ON A HILL, FAR BLAZING, AS A MOUNT 5 757
RAIS'D ON A MOUNT, WITH PYRAMIDS AND TOWRS . . 5 758
IN IMITATION OF THAT MOUNT WHEREON 5 764
WITHIN THE MOUNT OF GOD, FAST BY HIS THRONE, . . 6 5
TO WIN THE MOUNT OF GOD, AND ON HIS THRONE . . 6 88
FARR SEPARATE, CIRCLING THY HOLY MOUNT 6 743
FORERUNNING NIGHT; WHEN AT THE HOLY MOUNT . . . 7 584
FUMING FROM GOLDEN CENSERS HID THE MOUNT. . . . 7 600
NOR THAT WHICH ON THE FLAMING MOUNT APPEERD . . 11 216
ON THIS MOUNT HE APPEERD, UNDER THIS TREE . . 11 320
OR THENCE FROM NIGER FLOOD TO ATLAS MOUNT . . 11 402
ABOVE THE HIGHEST HILLS: THEN SHALL THIS MOUNT . 11 829
MOUNT HERMON, YONDER SEA, EACH PLACE BEHOLD . . 12 142
MOUNT CARMEL; HERE THE DOUBLE-FOUNTED STREAM . . 12 144
GOD FROM THE MOUNT OF SINAI, WHOSE GRAY TOP . . 12 227

MOUNTAIN
HER TEMPLE ON TH' OFFENSIVE MOUNTAIN, BUILT . . 1 443
HATH SCATH'D THE FORREST OAKS, OR MOUNTAIN PINES, 1 613
AS WHEN FROM MOUNTAIN TOPS THE DUSKY CLOUDS . . 2 488
THAT MOUNTAIN AS HIS GARDEN MOULD HIGH RAIS'D . 4 226
THE MOUNTAIN OF THE CONGREGATION CALL'D; . . . 5 766
SIDELONG, HAD PUSH'T A MOUNTAIN FROM HIS SEAT . 6 197
WITH BRANCHES LOPT, IN WOOD OR MOUNTAIN FELL'D) 6 575
A WOODIE MOUNTAIN; WHOSE HIGH TOP WAS PLAINE, . 8 303
TO SHEW US IN THIS MOUNTAIN, WHILE THE WINDS . 10 1065
HAD WASTED WOODS ON MOUNTAIN OR IN VALE, . . . 11 567
THEN FROM THE MOUNTAIN HEWING TIMBER TALL, . . 11 728
FAST ON THE TOP OF SOM HIGH MOUNTAIN FIXT. . . 11 851

MOUNTAINS
RIVERS OR MOUNTAINS IN HER SPOTTY GLOBE. . . . 1 291
THE BOTTOM OF THE MOUNTAINS UPWARD TURN'D, . . . 6 649
UNDER THE WEIGHT OF MOUNTAINS BURIED DEEP, . . 6 652
WITH MOUNTAINS AS WITH WEAPONS ARM'D, WHICH MAKES 6 697
THAT WISHT THE MOUNTAINS NOW MIGHT BE AGAIN . . 6 842
MYRIADS BETWEEN TWO BRAZEN MOUNTAINS LODG'D . . 7 201
AND SURGING WAVES, AS MOUNTAINS TO ASSAULT . . 7 214
IMMEDIATELY THE MOUNTAINS HUGE APPEER 7 285
MOUNTAINS OF ICE, THAT STOP TH' IMAGIN'D WAY . . 10 291

MOUNTED
HIS MOUNTED SCALE ALOFT: NOR MORE; BUT FLED . . 4 1014
OF HIS COOLE BOWRE, WHILE NOW THE MOUNTED SUN . . 5 300
A TRIPLE MOUNTED ROW OF PILLARS LAID 6 572
CLOSE FOLLOWING PACE FOR PACE, NOT MOUNTED YET . 10 589

MOURN'D
WHO MOURN'D IN EARNEST, WHEN THE CAPTIVE ARK . . 1 458

MOURNFUL
THAT WE MUST CHANGE FOR HEAV'N, THIS MOURNFUL GLOOM 1 244

MOURNS
THOUGH COMFORTLESS, AS WHEN A FATHER MOURNS . . 11 760

MOUST
SHE CRUSHES, INOFFENSIVE MOUST, AND MEATHES . . 5 345

MOUTH
SO WIDE THEY STOOD, AND LIKE A FURNACE MOUTH . . 2 888
EVEN TO MY MOUTH OF THAT SAME FRUIT HELD PART . . 5 83
FEARLESS UNFEARD HE SLEPT: IN AT HIS MOUTH . . 9 187
NIGH RIVERS MOUTH OR FORELAND, WHERE THE WIND . . 9 514
FROM EACH SIDE SHOALING TOWARDS THE MOUTH OF HELL. 10 288

MOUTH (CONTINUED)
THROUGH CHAOS HURLD, OBSTRUCT THE MOUTH OF HELL . 10 636
TO SOM CAVES MOUTH, OR WHETHER WASHT BY STREAM . 11 569
BOILES OUT FROM UNDER GROUND, THE MOUTH OF HELL; . 12 42

MOUTHES
BRASS, IRON, STONIE MOULD, HAD NOT THIR MOUTHES . 6 576
SEE WHERE IT FLOWS, DISGORGING AT SEAVEN MOUTHES . 12 158

MOUTHS
PUT TO THIR MOUTHS THE SOUNDING ALCHYMIE . . . 2 517
WITH WIDE CERBERIAN MOUTHS FULL LOUD, AND RUNG . 2 655
AND DISCORD WITH A THOUSAND VARIOUS MOUTHS. . . 2 967
FROM THIR OWN MOUTHS; ALL IS NOT THEIRS IT SEEMS: 4 513
CAST ON THEMSELVES FROM THIR OWN MOUTHS. THERE
STOOD 10 547

MOV'D
MOV'D OUR GRAND PARENTS IN THAT HAPPY STATE, . . 1 29
MOV'D ON IN SILENCE TO SOFT PIPES THAT CHARM'D . 1 561
COULD ONCE HAVE MOV'D; THEN IN THE KEY-HOLE TURNS 2 876
MOV'D ON, WITH DIFFICULTY AND LABOUR HEE; . . . 2 1022
THE TREPIDATION TALKT, AND THAT FIRST MOV'D; . . 3 483
THUS HE IN SCORN. THE WARLIKE ANGEL MOV'D, . . 4 902
OF UNION IRRESISTIBLE, MOV'D ON 6 63
STOOD THEY OR MOV'D, IN STATURE, MOTION, ARMS . . 6 302
BY WOUND, THOUGH FROM THIR PLACE BY VIOLENCE MOV'D. 6 405
MOV'D THE CREATOR IN HIS HOLY REST 7 91
INVALID THAT WHICH THEE TO DOUBT IT MOV'D; . . . 8 116
MOV'D CONTRARIE WITH THWART OBLIQUITIES, . . . 8 132
WHOSE INWARD APPARITION GENTLY MOV'D 8 293
NEW PART PUTS ON, AND AS TO PASSION MOV'D, . . . 9 667
TO WHOM SOON MOV'D WITH TOUCH OF BLAME THUS EVE. . 9 1143
T' WHOM MICHAEL THUS, HEE ALSO MOV'D, REPLI'D. . 11 453

MOVD
CREATURES THAT LIVD, AND MOVD, AND WALK'D, OR FLEW, 8 264

MOVE
OF DEPTH IMMEASURABLE: ANON THEY MOVE 1 549
MIGHT HAP TO MOVE NEW BROILES: BE THIS OR AUGHT . 2 837
THEN FEED ON THOUGHTS, THAT VOLUNTARIE MOVE . . 3 37
DISPENSES LIGHT FROM FARR; THEY AS THEY MOVE . . 3 579
NUMBERLESS, AS THOU SEEST, AND HOW THEY MOVE; . . 3 719
AND YEE FIVE OTHER WANDRING FIRES THAT MOVE . . 5 177
HATH PAST IN HEAV'N, SOM DOUBT WITHIN ME MOVE, . . 5 554
THE GREAT HIERARCHAL STANDARD WAS TO MOVE; . . . 5 701
OF GOD AND HIS MESSIAH. ON THEY MOVE 6 68
AND ONWARD MOVE EMBATTELLD; WHEN BEHOLD 6 550
OR WONDERS MOVE TH' OBDURATE TO RELENT? 6 790
THAT BETTER MIGHT WITH FARR LESS COMPASS MOVE, . . 8 33
THIS TO ATTAIN, WHETHER HEAV'N MOVE OR EARTH, . . 8 70
HATH LEFT TO THIR DISPUTES, PERHAPS TO MOVE . . 8 77
INSENSIBLY THREE DIFFERENT MOTIONS MOVE? . . . 8 130
AND YE THAT LIVE AND MOVE, FAIR CREATURES, TELL, . 8 276
FROM WHOM I HAVE THAT THUS I MOVE AND LIVE, . . 8 281
THE SOULE OF MAN, OR PASSION IN HIM MOVE. . . . 8 585
TILL ADAM THUS 'GAN EVE TO DALLIANCE MOVE, . . . 9 1016
BOUND WITH GORGONIAN RIGOR NOT TO MOVE, ... 10 297
HAD FIRST HIS PRECEPT SO TO MOVE, SO SHINE, . . 10 652
MY MOTIONS IN HIM, LONGER THEN THEY MOVE, . . . 11 91

MOVERS
HER MOTIONS, AS THE GREAT FIRST-MOVERS HAND . . 7 500

MOVES
AND EVERY LIVING THING THAT MOVES ON THE EARTH. . 7 534
STILL MOVES WITH THINE, JOIN'D IN CONNEXION SWEET, 10 359

MOVING
WAS MOVING TOWARD THE SHOAR; HIS PONDEROUS SHIELD 1 284
THE MONSTER MOVING ONWARD CAME AS FAST 2 675
TO FIRST OF WOMEN EVE THUS MOVING SPEECH, . . . 4 409
COMES THIS WAY MOVING; SEEMS ANOTHER MORN . . . 5 310
UNDER SPRED ENSIGNES MOVING NIGH, IN SLOW . . . 6 533
DISTANT SO HIGH, WITH MOVING FIRES ADORND . . . 7 87
ON GOLDEN HINGES MOVING, TO LET FORTH 7 207
AND SEEMS A MOVING LAND, AND AT HIS GILLES . . . 7 415
SO STANDING, MOVING, OR TO HIGHTH UPGROWN . . . 9 677

MOWES
THE SITHE OF TIME MOWES DOWN, DEVOUR UNSPAR'D, . 10 606

MOZAMBIC
MOZAMBIC, OFF AT SEA NORTH-EAST WINDES BLOW . . 4 161

MUCH
FROM WHAT HIGHTH FALL'N, SO MUCH THE STRONGER
PROV'D 1 92
IN ARMS NOT WORSE, IN FORESIGHT MUCH ADVANC'T, . 1 119
THUS FARR AT LEAST RECOVER'D, HATH MUCH MORE . . 2 22
I SHOULD BE MUCH FOR OPEN WARR, O PEERS, . . . 2 119
OUR SUPREAM FOE IN TIME MAY MUCH REMIT 2 210
THEY DREADED WORSE THEN HELL: SO MUCH THE FEAR . 2 293
TO HIM WHO REIGNS, AND SO MUCH TO HIM DUE . . . 2 454
NOR FAIL'D THEY TO EXPRESS HOW MUCH THEY PRAIS'D, 2 480
OF GOOD AND EVIL MUCH THEY ARGU'D THEN, ... 2 562
SO MUCH THE NEERER DANGER; GO AND SPEED; . . . 2 1008

MUCH (CONTINUED)
SO MUCH THE RATHER THOU CELESTIAL LIGHT 3 51
MUCH LESS THAT DURST UPON HIS OWN HEAD DRAW 3 220
SO STRICTLY, BUT MUCH MORE TO PITIE ENCLINE: 3 402
SO STRICTLY, BUT MUCH MORE TO PITIE ENCLIN'D, 3 405
THE SPIRIT MALIGNE, BUT MUCH MORE ENVY SEIS'D 3 553
THEN MUCH REVOLVING, THUS IN SIGHS BEGAN. 4 31
PRAEEMINENT BY SO MUCH ODDS, WHILE THOU 4 447
UNDER A SHADE OF FLOURS, MUCH WONDRING WHERE 4 451
YOUR MESSAGE, LIKE TO END AS MUCH IN VAIN? 4 833
IN THAT DARK DURANCE: THUS MUCH WHAT WAS ASKT. 4 899
OF BIRDS ON EVERY BOUGH; SO MUCH THE MORE 5 8
MUCH FAIRER TO MY FANCIE THEN BY DAY: 5 53
SWEET OF THY SELF, BUT MUCH MORE SWEET THUS CROPT, 5 68
TOO MUCH TO ONE, BUT DOUBLE HOW ENDUR'D, 5 783
ERRE NOT, MUCH LESS FOR THIS TO BE OUR LORD, 5 799
OF ALL THIR REGIONS: HOW MUCH MORE OF POWER 6 223
THINK NOTHING HARD, MUCH LESS TO BE DESPAIRD. 6 495
MUCH OF HIS RACE THOUGH STEEP, SUSPENS IN HEAV'N 7 99
MUCH LESS CAN BIRD WITH BEAST, OR FISH WITH FOWLE 8 395
SECOND TO ME OR LIKE, EQUAL MUCH LESS. 8 407
TOO MUCH OF ORNAMENT, IN OUTWARD SHEW 8 538
SO MUCH DELIGHTS ME AS THOSE GRACEFUL ACTS, 8 600
DEPREST, AND MUCH THEY MAY, IF ALL BE MINE, 9 46
PLEASURES ABOUT ME, SO MUCH MORE I FEEL 9 120
BANE, AND IN HEAV'N MUCH WORSE WOULD BE MY STATE. 9 123
THIR GROWING WORK: FOR MUCH THIR WORK OUTGREW 9 202
ASSIST US: BUT IF MUCH CONVERSE PERHAPS 9 247
OF ALL THAT HE CREATED, MUCH LESS MAN, 9 346
THE WILLINGER I GOE, NOR MUCH EXPECT 9 382
O MUCH DECEAV'D, MUCH FAILING, HAPLESS EVE, 9 404
MUCH HEE THE PLACE ADMIR'D, THE PERSON MORE. 9 444
I NOT; SO MUCH HATH HELL DEBAS'D, AND PAINE 9 487
THOU CANST, WHO ART SOLE WONDER, MUCH LESS ARM 9 533
THOUGH AT THE VOICE MUCH MARVELING; AT LENGTH 9 551
MUCH REASON, AND IN THIR ACTIONS OFT APPEERS. 9 559
MUCH MORE TO TASTE IT UNDER BANNE TO TOUCH. 9 925
TENDERLY WEPT, MUCH WON THAT HE HIS LOVE 9 991
MUCH PLEASURE WE HAVE LOST, WHILE WE ABSTAIN'D 9 1022
TOO FACIL THEN THOU DIDST NOT MUCH GAINSAY, 9 1158
MUCH WONDRING HOW THE SUTTLE FIEND HAD STOLN 10 20
AND THOUGHT NOT MUCH TO CLOATH HIS ENEMIES: 10 219
OF BEASTS, BUT INWARD NAKEDNESS, MUCH MORE 10 221
OR MUCH MORE GRIEVOUS PAIN? YE HAVE TH' ACCOUNT 10 501
AND HIS ADHERENTS, THAT WITH SO MUCH EASE 10 622
DEVOURD EACH OTHER; NOR STOOD MUCH IN AWE 10 712
THEN ALL THE WORLD MUCH HEAVIER, THOUGH DIVIDED 10 836
BROKE OFF THE REST; SO MUCH OF DEATH HER THOUGHTS 10 1008
TO BE FORESTALL'D; MUCH MORE I FEAR LEAST DEATH 10 1024
HOW MUCH MORE, IF WE PRAY HIM, WILL HIS EAR 10 1060
AS RAPHAEL, THAT I SHOULD MUCH CONFIDE, 11 235
THE VISUAL NERVE, FOR HE HAD MUCH TO SEE; 11 415
MUCH AT THAT SIGHT WAS ADAM IN HIS HEART 11 448
THE RULE OF NOT TOO MUCH, BY TEMPERANCE TAUGHT 11 531
LIFE MUCH, BENT RATHER HOW I MAY BE QUIT 11 548
MUCH BETTER SEEMS THIS VISION, AND MORE HOPE 11 599
THOSE WERE OF HATE AND DEATH, OR PAIN MUCH WORSE, 11 601
IN WISE DEPORT, SPAKE MUCH OF RIGHT AND WRONG, 11 666
WHO HAVING SPILT MUCH BLOOD, AND DON MUCH WASTE 11 791
THE PATHS OF RIGHTEOUSNESS, HOW MUCH MORE SAFE, 11 814
MUCH THOU HAST YET TO SEE, BUT I PERCEAVE 12 8
MINE EYES TRUE OP'NING, AND MY HEART MUCH EAS'D, 12 274
MUCH MORE, THAT MUCH MORE GOOD THEREOF SHALL
SPRING, 12 476
WITH CAUSE FOR EVILS PAST, YET MUCH MORE CHEER'D 12 604

MUCH-HUMBL'D
SO SPAKE, SO WISH'D MUCH-HUMBL'D EVE, BUT FATE 11 181

MULCIBER
MEN CALL'D HIM MULCIBER; AND HOW HE FELL 1 740

MULTIFORM
PERPETUAL CIRCLE, MULTIFORM; AND MIX 5 182

MULTIPLI'D
LIKE OF HIS LIKE, HIS IMAGE MULTIPLI'D, 8 424

MULTIPLIE
BE FRUITFUL, MULTIPLIE, AND FILL THE EARTH, 7 531
THY SORROW I WILL GREATLY MULTIPLIE 10 193
OR MULTIPLIE, BUT CURSES ON MY HEAD? 10 732
SHALL LEAD THIR LIVES, AND MULTIPLIE APACE, 12 17

MULTIPLIES
FROM LARGE BESTOWD, WHERE NATURE MULTIPLIES 5 318

MULTIPLY
BE FRUITFUL, MULTIPLY, AND IN THE SEAS 7 396
AND MULTIPLY A RACE OF WORSHIPPERS 7 630
DELIGHTFULLY, ENCREASE AND MULTIPLY, 10 730
INHUMANLY TO MEN, AND MULTIPLY 11 677

MULTIPLY'D
AND LET THE FOWLE BE MULTIPLY'D ON THE EARTH. 7 398

MULTITUDE
A MULTITUDE, LIKE WHICH THE POPULOUS NORTH 1 351

MULTITUDE (CONTINUED)
SLUC'D FROM THE LAKE, A SECOND MULTITUDE 1 702
AS FROM A SKY. THE HASTY MULTITUDE 1 730
HIS CAPTIVE MULTITUDE: FOR HE, BE SURE 2 323
LEAST HEAV'N SURCHARG'D WITH POTENT MULTITUDE 2 836
THEN WITH THE MULTITUDE OF MY REDEEMD 3 260
THE MULTITUDE OF ANGELS WITH A SHOUT 3 345
NOR MULTITUDE, STAND ONELY AND BEHOLD 6 810
DISTINCT ALIKE WITH MULTITUDE OF EYES, 6 847
THIR MULTITUDE, AND TO HIS SON THUS SPAKE. 7 138
FOR ONE FORBIDDEN TREE A MULTITUDE 10 554
THROUGH MULTITUDE THAT SUNG: JUST ARE THY WAYS, 10 643
IN WEALTH AND MULTITUDE, FACTIOUS THEY GROW; 12 352

MULTITUDES
MULTITUDES LIKE THY SELF, AND THENCE BE CALL'D 4 474
AMONG THE SONS OF MORN, WHAT MULTITUDES 5 716
AGAINST REVOLTED MULTITUDES THE CAUSE 6 31
ABOUT THE NEW-ARRIV'D, IN MULTITUDES 10 26

MURAL
HER MURAL BREACH, RETURNING WHENCE IT ROWLD. 6 879

MURKIE
HIS NOSTRIL WIDE INTO THE MURKIE AIR, 10 280

MURMUR
HE SCARCE HAD FINISHT, WHEN SUCH MURMUR FILLD 2 284
HOARCE MURMUR ECHO'D TO HIS WORDS APPLAUSE 5 873
WHOSE LIQUID MURMUR HEARD NEW THIRST EXCITES, 7 68

MURMURING
LUXURIANT; MEAN WHILE MURMURING WATERS FALL 4 260
NOT DISTANT FAR FROM THENCE A MURMURING SOUND 4 453
MURMURING, AND WITH HIM FLED THE SHADES OF NIGHT. 4 1015
AND LIQUID LAPSE OF MURMURING STREAMS; BY THESE, 8 263

MURMURS
MELODIOUS MURMURS, WARBLING TUNE HIS PRAISE. 5 196

MURREN
HIS CATTEL MUST OF ROT AND MURREN DIE. 12 179

MUS'D
PAUSING A WHILE, THUS TO HER SELF SHE MUS'D. 9 744

MUSE
SING HEAV'NLY MUSE, THAT ON THE SECRET TOP 1 6
SAY, MUSE, THIR NAMES THEN KNOWN, WHO FIRST, WHO
LAST, 1 376
TAUGHT BY THE HEAV'NLY MUSE TO VENTURE DOWN 3 19
BOTH HARP AND VOICE; NOR COULD THE MUSE DEFEND 7 37
WITH ADMIRATION, AND DEEP MUSE TO HEARE 7 52

MUSES
CEASE I TO WANDER WHERE THE MUSES HAUNT 3 27
NOR OF THE MUSES NINE, NOR ON THE TOP 7 6

MUSIC
INTENT, WITH JOCOND MUSIC CHARM HIS EAR; 1 787
AEREAL MUSIC SEND: NOR KNEW I NOT 5 548

MUSICK
WITH FEAST AND MUSICK ALL THE TENTS RESOUND. 11 592

MUST'RING
MUST'RING THIR RAGE, AND HEAV'N RESEMBLES HELL? 2 268

MUSTRING
BOTH HORSE AND FOOT, NOR IDELY MUSTRING STOOD; 11 645

MUTABLE
YET MUTABLE; WHENCE WARNE HIM TO BEWARE 5 237

MUTE
WITH ALL HIS PEERS: ATTENTION HELD THEM MUTE. 1 618
THE PERILOUS ATTEMPT: BUT ALL SAT MUTE, 2 420
HE ASK'D, BUT ALL THE HEAV'NLY QUIRE STOOD MUTE, 3 217
TO HOARCE OR MUTE, THOUGH FALL'N ON EVIL DAYES, 7 25
SPEAKING OR MUTE ALL COMLINESS AND GRACE 8 222
CREATED MUTE TO ALL ARTICULAT SOUND; 9 557
HOW CAM'ST THOU SPEAKABLE OF MUTE, AND HOW 9 563
FLOURISHD, SINCE MUTE, TO SOM GREAT CAUSE ADDREST, 9 672
GAVE ELOCUTION TO THE MUTE, AND TAUGHT 9 748
CONFOUNDED LONG THEY SATE, AS STRUCK'N MUTE, 9 1064
TH' ANGELIC GUARDS ASCENDED, MUTE AND SAD 10 18
TO SUPPLICATION, HEARE HIS SIGHS THOUGH MUTE; 11 31
WHICH HEAV'N BY THESE MUTE SIGNS IN NATURE SHEWS 11 194

MUTINIE
IN MUTINIE HAD FROM HER AXLE TORN 2 926

MUTTERING
SKIE LOWR'D AND MUTTERING THUNDER, SOM SAD DROPS 9 1002

MUTUAL
MYRIADS THOUGH BRIGHT: IF HE WHOM MUTUAL LEAGUE, 1 87
AND MUTUAL AMITIE SO STREIGHT, SO CLOSE, 4 376

MUTUAL (CONTINUED)
HAVE FINISHT HAPPIE IN OUR MUTUAL HELP 4 727
AND MUTUAL LOVE, THE CROWN OF ALL OUR BLISS . . 4 728
FOR SIN, ON WARR AND MUTUAL SLAUGHTER BENT. . . 6 506
FLYING, AND OVER LANDS WITH MUTUAL WING . . . 7 429
SUCH PAIRS, IN LOVE AND MUTUAL HONOUR JOYN'D? . . 8 58
WHICH MUST BE MUTUAL, IN PROPORTION DUE . . . 8 385
TOOK LARGELY, OF THIR MUTUAL GUILT THE SEALE, . . 9 1043
THUS THEY IN MUTUAL ACCUSATION SPENT 9 1187

MYRIADS
MYRIADS THOUGH BRIGHT: IF HE WHOM MUTUAL LEAGUE, . 1 87
O MYRIADS OF IMMORTAL SPIRITS, O POWERS 1 622
OF ALL THOSE MYRIADS WHICH WE LEAD THE CHIEF; . . 5 684
THAT OF SO MANY MYRIADS FALL'N, YET ONE 6 24
MYRIADS BETWEEN TWO BRAZEN MOUNTAINS LODG'D . . 7 201

MYRRH
OF BLOWING MYRRH AND BALME; IF THOU ACCEPT . . . 9 629
HIS PLACE, TO OFFER INCENSE, MYRRH, AND GOLD; . . 12 363

MYRRHE
WHAT DROPS THE MYRRHE, AND WHAT THE BALMIE REED, . 5 23
INTO THE BLISSFUL FIELD, THROUGH GROVES OF MYRRHE, 5 292

MYRTLE
THAT TO THE FRINGED BANK WITH MYRTLE CROWND, . . 4 262
WITH MYRTLE, FIND WHAT TO REDRESS TILL NOON: . . 9 219

MYRTLES
BEYOND A ROW OF MYRTLES, ON A FLAT, ... 9 627

MYSTERIES
WHO ALL THE SACRED MYSTERIES OF HEAV'N 12 509

MYSTERIOUS
NOR THOSE MYSTERIOUS PARTS WERE THEN CONCEALD, . 4 312
MYSTERIOUS OF CONNUBIAL LOVE REFUS'D: 4 743
HAILE WEDDED LOVE, MYSTERIOUS LAW, TRUE SOURCE . 4 750
AND WITH MYSTERIOUS REVERENCE I DEEM) 8 599
THOUGH IN MYSTERIOUS TERMS, JUDG'D AS THEN BEST: . 10 173

MYSTERIOUSLY
EACH STAIR MYSTERIOUSLY WAS MEANT, NOR STOOD . . 3 516

MYSTIC
IN MYSTIC DANCE NOT WITHOUT SONG, RESOUND . . . 5 178
OR THAT, NOT MYSTIC, WHERE THE SAPIENT KING . . 9 442

MYSTICAL
MYSTICAL DANCE, WHICH YONDER STARRIE SPHEARE . . 5 620

NAILD
A SHAMEFUL AND ACCURST, NAILD TO THE CROSS . . . 12 413

NAILES
BUT TO THE CROSS HE NAILES THY ENEMIES, ... 12 415

NAKED
IN NAKED MAJESTIE SEEMD LORDS OF ALL, ... 4 290
SO PASSD THEY NAKED ON, NOR SHUND THE SIGHT . . 4 319
NAKED MET HIS UNDER THE FLOWING GOLD 4 496
BROUGHT HER IN NAKED BEAUTY MORE ADORN'D, . . . 4 713
AND ON THIR NAKED LIMBS THE FLOURIE ROOF . . . 4 772
OF THREE THAT IN MOUNT IDA NAKED STROVE, . . . 5 382
MINISTERD NAKED, AND THIR FLOWING CUPS 5 444
AND HONOUR FROM ABOUT THEM, NAKED LEFT . . . 9 1057
WHICH LEAVES US NAKED THUS, OF HONOUR VOID, . . 9 1074
TO THAT FIRST NAKED GLORIE. SUCH OF LATE . . . 9 1115
WITH FEATHERD CINCTURE, NAKED ELSE AND WILDE . . 9 1117
OF ALL OUR GOOD, SHAM'D, NAKED, MISERABLE, . . . 9 1139
AFFRAID, BEING NAKED, HID MY SELF. TO WHOM . . 10 117
SO DREADFUL TO THEE? THAT THOU ART NAKED, WHO . 10 121
BEFORE HIM NAKED TO THE AIRE, THAT NOW 10 212

NAKEDNESS
THIR NAKEDNESS WITH SKINS OF BEASTS, OR SLAIN, . 10 217
OF BEASTS, BUT INWARD NAKEDNESS, MUCH MORE . . . 10 221

NAM'D
LONG AFTER KNOWN IN PALESTINE, AND NAM'D 1 80
MET SUCH IMBODIED FORCE, AS NAM'D WITH THESE . . 1 574
COCYTUS, NAM'D OF LAMENTATION LOUD 2 579
CROWND THEM WITH GLORY, AND TO THIR GLORY NAM'D . 5 839
AND JOIN HIM NAM'D ALMIGHTY TO THY AID, ... 6 294
HE NAM'D. THUS WAS THE FIRST DAY EEV'N AND MORN: 7 252
AND HEAV'N HE NAM'D THE FIRMAMENT: SO EEV'N . . 7 274
I NAM'D THEM, AS THEY PASS'D, AND UNDERSTOOD . . 8 352
WHICH THOU HAST RIGHTLY NAM'D, BUT OF THY SELF, . 8 439
CELESTIAL, WHETHER AMONG THE THRONES, OR NAM'D . 11 296
RIDICULOUS, AND THE WORK CONFUSION NAM'D. . . . 12 62

NAME
AS WHOM THE FABLES NAME OF MONSTROUS SIZE, ... 1 197
PEOR HIS OTHER NAME, WHEN HE ENTIC'D 1 412
DAGON HIS NAME, SEA MONSTER, UPWARD MAN 1 462
NOR WAS HIS NAME UNHEARD OR UNADOR'D 1 738
HELL TREMBL'D AT THE HIDEOUS NAME, AND SIGH'D . . 2 788

NAME (CONTINUED)
ORCUS AND ADES, AND THE DREADED NAME 2 964
HAIL SON OF GOD, SAVIOUR OF MEN, THY NAME . . . 3 412
BUT WITH NO FRIENDLY VOICE, AND ADD THY NAME . . 4 36
SATAN, AND COULDST THOU FAITHFUL ADD? O NAME, . 4 950
O SACRED NAME OF FAITHFULNESS PROFAN'D. 4 951
SATAN, SO CALL HIM NOW, HIS FORMER NAME 5 658
HIS NAME, AND HIGH WAS HIS DEGREE IN HEAV'N; . . 5 707
ALL POWER, AND US ECLIPST UNDER THE NAME . . . 5 776
UNJUSTLY THOU DEPRAV'ST IT WITH THE NAME . . . 6 174
DESCEND FROM HEAV'N URANIA, BY THAT NAME . . . 7 1
THE MEANING, NOT THE NAME I CALL: FOR THOU . . . 7 5
IS YET DISTINCT BY NAME, THENCE, AS THOU KNOW'ST . 7 536
BY NUMBERS THAT HAVE NAME. BUT THIS I URGE, . . 8 114
MY TONGUE OBEY'D AND READILY COULD NAME 8 272
O BY WHAT NAME, FOR THOU ABOVE ALL THESE, . . . 8 357
BEFORE ME; WOMAN IS HER NAME, OF MAN 8 496
NOT THAT WHICH JUSTLY GIVES HEROIC NAME 9 40
THAT NAME, UNLESS AN AGE TOO LATE, OR COLD . . . 9 44
TH' ANGELIC NAME, AND THINNER LEFT THE THRONG . . 9 142
OF SATAN (FOR I GLORIE IN THE NAME, ... 10 386
WHILE THE CREATOR CALLING FORTH BY NAME 10 649
OUT OF MY SIGHT, THOU SERPENT, THAT NAME BEST . . 10 867
FARR OTHER NAME DESERVING. BUT THE FIELD . . . 11 171
AND FROM REBELLION SHALL DERIVE HIS NAME, . . . 12 36
AND GET THEMSELVES A NAME, LEAST FAR DISPERST . . 12 45
HIS NAME AND OFFICE BEARING, WHO SHALL QUELL . . 12 311
OF DAVID (SO I NAME THIS KING) SHALL RISE . . . 12 326
THOU KNEWST BY NAME, AND ALL TH' ETHEREAL POWERS, 12 577
BY NAME TO COME CALL'D CHARITIE, THE SOUL . . . 12 584

NAMELESS
NAMELESS IN DARK OBLIVION LET THEM DWELL. . . . 6 380

NAMES
THOUGH OF THIR NAMES IN HEAV'NLY RECORDS NOW . . 1 361
GOT THEM NEW NAMES, TILL WANDRING ORE THE EARTH, . 1 365
THEN WERE THEY KNOWN TO MEN BY VARIOUS NAMES, . . 1 374
SAY, MUSE, THIR NAMES THEN KNOWN, WHO FIRST, WHO LAST, ... 1 376
EGYPT FROM SYRIAN GROUND, HAD GENERAL NAMES . . 1 421
A CREW WHO UNDER NAMES OF OLD RENOWN, ... 1 477
THIR NAMES OF THEE; SO OVER MANY A TRACT . . . 6 76
I MIGHT RELATE OF THOUSANDS, AND THIR NAMES . . 6 373
AND THOU THIR NATURES KNOW'ST, & GAV'ST THEM NAMES, 7 493
FROM THEE THIR NAMES, AND PAY THEE FEALTIE . . . 8 344
FROM THE FIRST OP'NING BUD, AND GAVE YE NAMES, . 11 277
(THINGS BY THIR NAMES I CALL, THOUGH YET UNNAM'D) 12 140
ABOVE ALL NAMES IN HEAV'N; AND THENCE SHALL COME, 12 458
THEN SHALL THEY SEEK TO AVAIL THEMSELVES OF NAMES, 12 515

NAMING
SURPASSEST FARR MY NAMING, HOW MAY I 8 359
CONCEALES NOT FROM US, NAMING THEE THE TREE . . 9 751

NAPHTHA
WITH NAPHTHA AND ASPHALTUS YEILDED LIGHT 1 729

NARD
AND FLOURING ODOURS, CASSIA, NARD, AND BALME; . . 5 293

NARROW
NOW LESS THEN SMALLEST DWARFS, IN NARROW ROOM . . 1 779
PONDERING HIS VOYAGE; FOR NO NARROW FRITH . . . 2 919
IN NARROW ROOM NATURES WHOLE WEALTH, YEA MORE, . 4 207
NOT LIKE THESE NARROW LIMITS, TO RECEIVE . . . 4 384
BUT FIRST WITH NARROW SEARCH I MUST WALK ROUND . 4 528
'TWIXT HOST AND HOST BUT NARROW SPACE WAS LEFT, . 6 104
PUT FORTH, AND TO A NARROW VENT APPLI'D 6 583
WITH NARROW SEARCH; AND WITH INSPECTION DEEP . . 9 83
IN NARROW CIRCUIT STRAIT'ND BY A FOE, ... 9 323
HIS PRESENCE TO THESE NARROW BOUNDS CONFIN'D . . 11 341

NARROWER
HALF YET REMAINES UNSUNG BUT NARROWER BOUND . . 7 21

NATHLESS
NATHLESS HE SO ENDUR'D, TILL ON THE BEACH . . . 1 299

NATION
AND ONE PECULIAR NATION TO SELECT 12 111
A NATION FROM ONE FAITHFUL MAN TO SPRING: . . . 12 113
A MIGHTIE NATION, AND UPON HIM SHOWRE 12 124
GROWING INTO A NATION, AND NOW GROWN 12 164
BY HIS OWN NATION, SLAINE FOR BRINGING LIFE; . . 12 414
GREAT NUMBERS OF EACH NATION TO RECEAVE 12 503

NATIONAL
NATIONAL INTERRUPT THIR PUBLIC PEACE, ... 12 317

NATIONS
AMONG THE NATIONS ROUND, AND DURST ABIDE 1 385
ON HALF THE NATIONS, AND WITH FEAR OF CHANGE . . 1 598
IN ORDER, THOUGH TO NATIONS YET UNBORN, ... 4 663
NATIONS, AND BRING HOME SPOILS WITH INFINITE . . 11 692
SUBDUING NATIONS, AND ACHIEVD THEREBY 11 792
YET SOMTIMES NATIONS WILL DECLINE SO LOW . . . 12 97
ALL NATIONS SHALL BE BLEST; HE STRAIGHT OBEYS, . 12 126

NEED (CONTINUED)
MORE WISE, MORE WATCHFUL, STRONGER, IF NEED WERE 9 311
CAUSES IMPORT YOUR NEED OF THIS FAIR FRUIT. 9 731
ATTENDANCE NONE SHALL NEED, NOR TRAIN, WHERE NONE 10 80
NO DETRIMENT NEED FEARE, GOE AND BE STRONG. 10 409
BESEECHING HIM, SO AS WE NEED NOT FEAR 10 1082

NEEDED
MORE TUNEABLE THEN NEEDED LUTE OR HARP 5 151
THIR PAMPERD BOUGHES, AND NEEDED HANDS TO CHECK 5 214
SHEE NEEDED, VERTUE-PROOF, NO THOUGHT INFIRME 5 384
FROM HIM, FOR OTHER LIGHT SHE NEEDED NONE 7 378

NEEDLESS
LET NONE HENCEFORTH SEEK NEEDLESS CAUSE TO APPROVE 9 1140

NEEDLEST
NEEDLEST TO THEE REPEATED; NOR UNKNOWN 7 494

NEEDS
INTO THEIR TEMPER; WHICH MUST NEEDS REMOVE 2 277
WHERE ONELY WHAT THEY NEEDS MUST DO, APPEARD, 3 105
AND COUNTRY WHEREOF HERE NEEDS NO ACCOUNT, 4 235
DEARER THY SELF THEN ALL; NEEDS MUST THE POWER 4 412
EARTHS INMOST WOMB, MORE WARMTH THEN ADAM NEEDS; 5 302
FOR KNOW, WHATEVER WAS CREATED, NEEDS 5 414
THE FULL RELATION, WHICH MUST NEEDS BE STRANGE, 5 556
RUIN MUST NEEDS ENSUE; FOR WHAT AVAILES 6 456
WHENCE IN PERPETUAL FIGHT THEY NEEDS MUST LAST 6 693
BUT KNOWLEDGE IS AS FOOD, AND NEEDS NO LESS 7 126
OF DAY AND NIGHT; WHICH NEEDS NOT THY BELEEFE, 8 136
LEADS THEE, OR WHERE MOST NEEDS, WHETHER TO WIND 9 215
SUTTLE HE NEEDS MUST BE, WHO COULD SEDUCE 9 307
FOR US CREATED, NEEDS WITH US MUST FAILE, 9 942
ADAM, HEAV'NS HIGH BEHEST NO PREFACE NEEDS: 11 251
MUST NEEDS IMPAIRE AND WEARIE HUMAN SENSE: 12 10
NEEDS MUST THE SERPENT NOW HIS CAPITAL BRUISE 12 383

NEEDST
DISMISS NOT HER, WHEN MOST THOU NEEDST HER NIGH, 8 564

NEER
ALL IN ONE MOMENT, AND SO NEER THE BRINK; 2 609
SO NEER GROWS DEATH TO LIFE, WHAT ERE DEATH IS, 4 425
THAT NEER HIM STOOD, AND GAVE THEM THUS IN CHARGE. 4 787
OUR HAPPIE STATE UNDER ONE HEAD MORE NEER 5 830
AND WARR SO NEER THE PEACE OF GOD IN BLISS 7 55
AND AT THE BRINK OF CHAOS, NEER THE FOOT 10 347
TH' INFERNAL EMPIRE, THAT SO NEER HEAV'NS DORE 10 389
NEER THAT BITUMINOUS LAKE WHERE SODOM FLAM'D; 10 562

NEERER
SITS ARBITRESS, AND NEERER TO THE EARTH 1 785
NEERER OUR ANCIENT SEAT; PERHAPS IN VIEW 2 394
SO MUCH THE NEERER DANGER; GO AND SPEED; 2 1008
NEERER TO VIEW HIS PREY, AND UNESPI'D 4 399
NEERER HIS PRESENCE ADAM THOUGH NOT AWD, 5 358
AS NEERER TO HIM PLAC'T OR NEERER TENDING 5 476
IN BATTAILOUS ASPECT, AND NEERER VIEW 6 81
WHAT NEERER MIGHT CONCERN HIM, HOW THIS WORLD 7 62
NEERER HE DREW, AND MANY A WALK TRAVERS'D 9 434

NEEREST
THUS SATAN TALKING TO HIS NEEREST MATE 1 192
WHICH WAY THE NEEREST COAST OF DARKNESS LYES 2 958
WHO IN GODS PRESENCE, NEEREST TO HIS THRONE 3 649
OUT OF MY SIDE TO THEE, NEEREST MY HEART 4 484

NEERLY
NEERLY IT NOW CONCERNES US TO BE SURE 5 721

NEGLECT
THEY WHO NEGLECT AND SCORN, SHALL NEVER TASTE; 3 199
NEGLECT NOT, AND THE BENEFIT IMBRACE 12 426

NEGLECTS
WHERE HONOUR DUE AND REVERENCE NONE NEGLECTS, 3 738

NEGUS
TH' EMPIRE OF NEGUS TO HIS UTMOST PORT 11 397

NEIGHBOURHOOD
AUDACIOUS NEIGHBOURHOOD, THE WISEST HEART 1 400

NEIGHBOURING
OF THOSE BRIGHT CONFINES, WHENCE WITH NEIGHBOURING
ARMS 2 395
NOT IN THE NEIGHBOURING MOON, AS SOME HAVE DREAMD; 3 459
NIGHT WOULD INVADE, BUT THERE THE NEIGHBOURING MOON 3 726
INTO HIS NEATHER EMPIRE NEIGHBOURING ROUND. 4 145
CHERUBIC SONGS BY NIGHT FROM NEIGHBOURING HILLS 5 547
BETOOK THEM, AND THE NEIGHBOURING HILLS UPTORE; 6 663
FROM THE HIGH NEIGHBOURING HILLS, WHICH WAS THIR
SEAT, 11 575
PITCHT ABOUT SECHEM, AND THE NEIGHBOURING PLAINE 12 136

NEPTUN'S
OR NEPTUN'S IRE OR JUNO'S, THAT SO LONG 9 18

NERVE
THE VISUAL NERVE, FOR HE HAD MUCH TO SEE; 11 415

NESTS
THEY TO THIR GRASSIE COUCH, THESE TO THIR NESTS 4 601

NET
ROVE WITHOUT REIN, TILL IN THE AMOROUS NET 11 586

NETHER
'TWIXT UPPER, NETHER, AND SURROUNDING FIRES; 1 346
TO FOUND THIS NETHER EMPIRE, WHICH MIGHT RISE 2 296
DISTORTED, ALL MY NETHER SHAPE THUS GREW 2 784
EARTH WITH HER NETHER OCEAN CIRCUMFUS'D, 7 624
IN YONDER NETHER WORLD WHERE SHALL I SEEK 11 328

NETHERMOST
OR SPIRIT OF THE NETHERMOST ABYSS 2 956
AND SPIRITS OF THIS NETHERMOST ABYSS, 2 969

NEVER
AND REST CAN NEVER DWELL, HOPE NEVER COMES 1 66
AND COURAGE NEVER TO SUBMIT OR YIELD: 1 108
THAT GLORY NEVER SHALL HIS WRATH OR MIGHT 1 110
TO DO OUGHT GOOD NEVER WILL BE OUR TASK, 1 159
POUR'D NEVER FROM HER FROZEN LOYNS, TO PASS 1 352
GLORIES: FOR NEVER SINCE CREATED MAN, 1 573
FOR THIS INFERNAL PIT SHALL NEVER HOLD 1 657
IS DOUBTFUL; THAT HE NEVER WILL IS SURE. 2 154
A CRY OF HELL HOUNDS NEVER CEASING BARK'D 2 654
FOR NEVER BUT ONCE MORE WAS EITHER LIKE 2 721
AND NEVER BUT IN UNAPPROACHED LIGHT 3 4
THEY WHO NEGLECT AND SCORN, SHALL NEVER TASTE; 3 199
CAN NEVER SEEK, ONCE DEAD IN SINS AND LOST; 3 233
WITH THESE THAT NEVER FADE THE SPIRITS ELECT 3 360
HENCEFORTH, AND NEVER SHALL MY HARP THY PRAISE 3 414
THROUGH HIS GLAZ'D OPTIC TUBE YET NEVER SAW. 3 590
FOR NEVER CAN TRUE RECONCILEMENT GROW 4 98
PAN OR SILVANUS NEVER SLEPT, NOR NYMPH, 4 707
SUCH NIGHT TILL THIS I NEVER PASS'D, HAVE DREAM'D, 5 31
KNEW NEVER TILL THIS IRKSOM NIGHT; METHOUGHT 5 35
WAKING THOU NEVER WILT CONSENT TO DO. 5 121
YET THAT WE NEVER SHALL FORGET TO LOVE 5 550
WAS NEVER, ARMS ON ARMOUR CLASHING BRAY'D 6 209
THOU NEVER FROM THAT HOURE IN PARADISE 9 406
AND LOVELY, NEVER SINCE OF SERPENT KIND 9 504
AT FEED OR FOUNTAIN NEVER HAD I FOUND. 9 597
IN FRUIT SHE NEVER TASTED, WHETHER TRUE 9 788
NOT FELT, NOR SHALL BE TWICE, FOR NEVER MORE 9 859
WOULD NEVER FROM MY HEART; NO NO, I FEEL 9 913
MINE NEVER SHALL BE PARTED, BLISS OR WOE. 9 916
SO EMINENTLY NEVER HAD BIN KNOWN. 9 976
FOR NEVER DID THY BEAUTIE SINCE THE DAY 9 1029
HIDE ME, WHERE I MAY NEVER SEE THEM MORE. 9 1090
WAS I TO HAVE NEVER PARTED FROM THY SIDE? 9 1153
SATISFI'D NEVER; THAT WERE TO EXTEND 10 804
HE NEVER SHALL FIND OUT FIT MATE, BUT SUCH 10 899
I NEVER FROM THY SIDE HENCEFORTH TO STRAY, 11 176
THAT NEVER WILL IN OTHER CLIMATE GROW, 11 274
IN SOME TO SPRING FROM THEE, WHO NEVER TOUCH'D 11 425
AND MAKES A COVENANT NEVER TO DESTROY 11 892
NEVER TO HURT THEM MORE WHO RIGHTLY TRUST 12 418

NEVER-ENDING
BESIDES WHAT HOPE THE NEVER-ENDING FLIGHT 2 221

NEVERTHELESS
FOUND SO UNFORTUNATE; NEVERTHELESS, 10 970

NEW
RECEIVE THY NEW POSSESSOR: ONE WHO BRINGS 1 252
NEW COURAGE AND REVIVE, THOUGH NOW THEY LYE 1 279
OR IN VALDARNO, TO DESCRY NEW LANDS, 1 290
GOT THEM NEW NAMES, TILL WANDRING ORE THE EARTH, 1 365
OF GLORY OBSCUR'D: AS WHEN THE SUN NEW RIS'N 1 594
NEW WARR, PROVOK'T; OUR BETTER PART REMAINS 1 645
SPACE MAY PRODUCE NEW WORLDS; WHEREOF SO RIFE 1 650
NEW RUB'D WITH BAUM, EXPATIATE AND CONFER 1 774
OF NEW SUBJECTION; WITH WHAT EYES COULD WE 2 239
FROM HEAV'NS HIGH JURISDICTION, IN NEW LEAGUE 2 319
OF SOME NEW RACE CALL'D MAN, ABOUT THIS TIME 2 348
IN SEARCH OF THIS NEW WORLD, WHOM SHALL WE FIND 2 403
MIGHT HAP TO MOVE NEW BROILES: BE THIS OR AUGHT 2 837
TO THAT NEW WORLD OF LIGHT AND BLISS, AMONG 2 867
DIRECTLY TOWARDS THE NEW CREATED WORLD, 3 89
SENSE OF NEW JOY INEFFABLE DIFFUS'D: 3 137
RECEIVE NEW LIFE. SO MAN, AS IS MOST JUST, 3 294
NEW HEAV'N AND EARTH, WHEREIN THE JUST SHALL DWELL, 3 335
NEW BABELS, HAD THEY WHEREWITHALL, WOULD BUILD: 3 468
HERE MATTER NEW TO GAZE THE DEVIL MET 3 613
TO VISIT OFT THIS NEW CREATION ROUND; 3 661
CREATED THIS NEW HAPPIE RACE OF MEN 3 679
OF THIS NEW WORLD; AT WHOSE SIGHT ALL THE STARRS 4 34
OF US OUT-CAST, EXIL'D, HIS NEW DELIGHT, 4 106
AS MAN ERE LONG, AND THIS NEW WORLD SHALL KNOW. 4 113
WHOM HUNGER DRIVES TO SEEK NEW HAUNT FOR PREY, 4 184
BENEATH HIM WITH NEW WONDER NOW HE VIEWS 4 205
OF LIVING CREATURES NEW TO SIGHT AND STRANGE: 4 287

NEW (CONTINUED)
BY CONQUERING THIS NEW WORLD, COMPELS ME NOW 4 391
TURND HIM ALL EARE TO HEAR NEW UTTERANCE FLOW. 4 410
NEW TROUBLES; HIM THY CARE MUST BE TO FIND. 4 575
THIS NEW CREATED WORLD, WHEREOF IN HELL 4 937
HEAV'NS LAST BEST GIFT, MY EVER NEW DELIGHT, 5 19
VARIE TO OUR GREAT MAKER STILL NEW PRAISE. 5 184
VARIED HIS BOUNTY SO WITH NEW DELIGHTS. 5 431
THY SLEEP DISSENT? NEW LAWS THOU SEEST IMPOS'D; 5 679
NEW LAWS FROM HIM WHO REIGNS, NEW MINDS MAY RAISE 5 680
IN US WHO SERVE, NEW COUNSELS, TO DEBATE 5 681
THE GREAT MESSIAH, AND HIS NEW COMMANDS, 5 691
WITH WHAT MAY BE DEVIS'D OF HONOURS NEW 5 780
FROM FATHER TO HIS SON? STRANGE POINT AND NEW. 5 855
DELIVERER FROM NEW LORDS, LEADER TO FREE 6 451
WHICH TO OUR EYES DISCOVERD NEW AND STRANGE, 6 571
WHOSE LIQUID MURMUR HEARD NEW THIRST EXCITES, 7 68
AND SPIRIT COMING TO CREATE NEW WORLDS. 7 209
THENCE TO BEHOLD THIS NEW CREATED WORLD 7 554
THEN AS NEW WAK'T THUS GRATEFULLY REPLI'D. 8 4
INDUC'D ME. AS NEW WAK'T FROM SOUNDEST SLEEP 8 253
HAD LIVELY SHADOWD: HERE HAD NEW BEGUN 8 311
PROVOKES MY ENVIE, THIS NEW FAVORITE 9 175
LOOKS INTERVENE AND SMILES, OR OBJECT NEW 9 222
NEW PART PUTS ON, AND AS TO PASSION MOV'D, 9 667
GREAT JOY HE PROMIS'D TO HIS THOUGHTS, AND NEW 9 843
NEW GATHERD, AND AMBROSIAL SMELL DIFFUS'D. 9 852
AUGMENTED, OP'ND EYES, NEW HOPES, NEW JOYES, 9 985
AS WITH NEW WINE INTOXICATED BOTH 9 1008
THOSE MIDDLE PARTS, THAT THIS NEW COMMER, SHAME, 9 1097
METHINKS I FEEL NEW STRENGTH WITHIN ME RISE, 10 243
OVER THIS MAINE FROM HELL TO THAT NEW WORLD 10 257
BY THIS NEW FELT ATTRACTION AND INSTINCT. 10 263
OF THIS NEW WONDROUS PONTIFICE, UNHOP'T 10 348
AS BATTEL HATH ADJUDG'D, FROM THIS NEW WORLD 10 377
MY HOLD OF THIS NEW KINGDOM ALL DEPENDS, 10 406
THE NEW CREATED WORLD, WHICH FAME IN HEAV'N 10 481
NEW HEAV'N AND EARTH SHALL TO THE AGES RISE, 10 647
OF THIS NEW GLORIOUS WORLD, AND MEE SO LATE 10 721
OF NEW ACCEPTANCE, HOPEFUL TO REGAINE 10 972
THE STONIE FROM THIR HEARTS, & MADE NEW FLESH 11 4
VACANT POSSESSION SOM NEW TROUBLE RAISE: 11 103
STRENGTH ADDED FROM ABOVE, NEW HOPE TO SPRING 11 138
NEW LAWS TO BE OBSERV'D; FOR I DESCRIE 11 228
NEW REAPT, THE OTHER PART SHEEP-WALKS AND FOULDS; 11 431
BETOK'NING PEACE FROM GOD, AND COV'NANT NEW. 11 867
SHALL HOLD THIR COURSE, TILL FIRE PURGE ALL THINGS NEW, 11 900
THEN WITH TRANSITION SWEET NEW SPEECH RESUMES. 12 5
NEW HEAV'NS, NEW EARTH, AGES OF ENDLESS DATE 12 549

NEW-ARRIV'D
ABOUT THE NEW-ARRIV'D, IN MULTITUDES 10 26

NEWES
HE ADDED NOT, FOR ADAM AT THE NEWES 11 263

NEW-MADE
WITNESS THIS NEW-MADE WORLD, ANOTHER HEAV'N 7 617

NEWS
ALREADY KNOWN WHAT HE FOR NEWS HAD THOUGHT 6 20
ENTRANCE UNSEEN. SOON AS TH' UNWELCOME NEWS 10 21

NEXT
ONE NEXT HIMSELF IN POWER, AND NEXT IN CRIME, 1 79
OF UNBLEST FEET. HIM FOLLOWED HIS NEXT MATE, 1 238
AT THIR GREAT EMPERORS CALL, AS NEXT IN WORTH 1 378
THIR SEATS LONG AFTER NEXT THE SEAT OF GOD, 1 383
NEXT CHEMOS, TH' OBSCENE DREAD OF MOABS SONS, 1 406
TO IDOLS FOUL. THAMMUZ CAME NEXT BEHIND, 1 446
OF ALIENATED JUDAH. NEXT CAME ONE 1 457
DID FIRST CREATE YOUR LEADER, NEXT FREE CHOICE, 2 19
HE CEAS'D, AND NEXT HIM MOLOC, SCEPTER'D KING 2 43
OF UNESSENTIAL NIGHT RECEIVES HIM NEXT 2 439
BY WHICH HE REIGNS: NEXT HIM HIGH ARBITER 2 909
OF DEMOGORGON; RUMOR NEXT AND CHANCE, 2 965
THY BOSOM, AND THIS GLORIE NEXT TO THEE 3 239
THEE NEXT THEY SANG OF ALL CREATION FIRST, 3 383
THE BUILDERS NEXT OF BABEL ON THE PLAIN 3 466
OF VEGETABLE GOLD; AND NEXT TO LIFE 4 220
WHEN GABRIEL TO HIS NEXT IN POWER THUS SPAKE. 4 781
AWAITING NEXT COMMAND. TO WHOM THIR CHIEF 4 864
WISE TO FLIE PAIN, PROFESSING NEXT THE SPIE, 4 948
WORKS OF DAY PASS'T, OR MORROWS NEXT DESIGNE, 5 33
REASON AS CHIEF; AMONG THESE FANSIE NEXT 5 102
CONTEMPTUOUS, AND HIS NEXT SUBORDINATE 5 671
AND THOU IN MILITARY PROWESS NEXT 6 45
TOGETHER BOTH WITH NEXT TO ALMIGHTIE ARME, 6 316
WEAPONS MORE VIOLENT, WHEN NEXT WE MEET, 6 439
HE SAT; AND IN TH' ASSEMBLY NEXT UPSTOOD 6 446
THEMSELVES INVADED NEXT, AND ON THIR HEADS 6 653
OF COMMONALTIE: SWARMING NEXT APPEER'D 7 489
WHAT NEXT I BRING SHALL PLEASE THEE, BE ASSUR'D, 8 449
SINCE HIGHER I FALL SHORT, ON HIM WHO NEXT 9 174
THUS GROWN. EXPERIENCE, NEXT TO THEE I OWE, 9 807
HE RUIND, NOW MANKIND; WHOM WILL HE NEXT? 9 950

NEXT (CONTINUED)
FEED FIRST, ON EACH BEAST NEXT, AND FISH, AND FOWLE, 10 604
WHO CAN EXTENUATE THEE? NEXT, TO THE SON, 10 645
THE SOURSE OF LIFE; NEXT FAVOURABLE THOU, 11 169
UNCULL'D, AS CAME TO HAND; A SHEPHERD NEXT 11 436
AND HIS NEXT SON FOR WEALTH AND WISDOM FAM'D, 12 332

NICE
FLOURS WORTHY OF PARADISE WHICH NOT NICE ART 4 241
THINK NOT I SHALL BE NICE. SO DOWN THEY SAT, 5 433
A NICE AND SUTTLE HAPPINESS I SEE 8 399

NICEST
WITH NICEST TOUCH. IMMEDIATE IN A FLAME, 6 584

NIGER
OR THENCE FROM NIGER FLOOD TO ATLAS MOUNT 11 402

NIGH
NIGH ON THE PLAIN IN MANY CELLS PREPAR'D, 1 700
NOR GOOD DRY LAND: NIGH FOUNDERD ON HE FARES, 2 940
STARS DISTANT, BUT NIGH HAND SEEMD OTHER WORLDS, 3 566
HE DREW NOT NIGH UNHEARD, THE ANGEL BRIGHT, 3 645
ERE HE DREW NIGH, HIS RADIANT VISAGE TURND, 3 646
BEGINS HIS DIRE ATTEMPT, WHICH NIGH THE BIRTH 4 15
AH GENTLE PAIR, YEE LITTLE THINK HOW NIGH 4 366
TH' UNARMED YOUTH OF HEAV'N, BUT NIGH AT HAND 4 552
HIS HEART, NOT ELSE DISMAI'D. NOW DREW THEY NIGH 4 861
SO SAYING, HE DREW NIGH, AND TO ME HELD, 5 82
I FLIE NOT, BUT HAVE SOUGHT THEE FARR AND NIGH. 6 295
UNDER SPRED ENSIGNES MOVING NIGH, IN SLOW 6 533
DISMISS NOT HER, WHEN MOST THOU NEEDST HER NIGH, 8 564
BY SLY ASSAULT; AND SOMWHERE NIGH AT HAND 9 256
FROM HER BEST PROP SO FARR, AND STORM SO NIGH. 9 433
HER HUSBAND, FOR I VIEW FAR ROUND, NOT NIGH, 9 482
NIGH RIVERS MOUTH OR FORELAND, WHERE THE WIND 9 514
TEMPTING SO NIGH, TO PLUCK AND EAT MY FILL 9 595
TO WHOM SAD EVE WITH SHAME NIGH OVERWHELM'D, 10 159
ON WHAT WAS PURE, TILL CRAMM'D AND GORG'D, NIGH BURST 10 632
DESOLATE WHERE SHE SATE, APPROACHING NIGH, 10 864
AFTER SHORT BLUSH OF MORN; NIGH IN HER SIGHT 11 184
O EVE, SOME FURDER CHANGE AWAITS US NIGH, 11 193
HE ENDED; AND TH' ARCH-ANGEL SOON DREW NIGH, 11 238
WELL PLEAS'D, BUT ANSWER'D NOT; FOR NOW TOO NIGH 12 625

NIGHT
NINE TIMES THE SPACE THAT MEASURES DAY AND NIGHT 1 50
MOORS BY HIS SIDE UNDER THE LEE, WHILE NIGHT 1 207
LIKE NIGHT, AND DARKEN'D ALL THE LAND OF NILE: 1 343
JEHOVAH, WHO IN ONE NIGHT WHEN HE PASS'D 1 487
AND INJURY AND OUTRAGE: AND WHEN NIGHT 1 500
WITNESS THE STREETS OF SODOM, AND THAT NIGHT 1 503
FRIGHTED THE REIGN OF CHAOS AND OLD NIGHT. 1 543
SCOUT FARR AND WIDE INTO THE REALM OF NIGHT, 2 133
IN THE WIDE WOMB OF UNCREATED NIGHT, 2 150
THE SOUND OF BLUSTRING WINDS, WHICH ALL NIGHT LONG 2 286
DREW AUDIENCE AND ATTENTION STILL AS NIGHT 2 308
OF UNESSENTIAL NIGHT RECEIVES HIM NEXT 2 439
THAT DAY AND NIGHT FOR HIS DESTRUCTION WAITE. 2 505
FOR EACH SEEM'D EITHER; BLACK IT STOOD AS NIGHT, 2 670
AND TIME AND PLACE ARE LOST; WHERE ELDEST NIGHT 2 894
SAT SABLE-VESTED NIGHT, ELDEST OF THINGS, 2 962
CHAOS AND ANCIENT NIGHT, I COME NO SPY, 2 970
ERECT THE STANDARD THERE OF ANCIENT NIGHT; 2 986
WEAKNING THE SCEPTER OF OLD NIGHT: FIRST HELL 2 1002
SHOOTS FARR INTO THE BOSOM OF DIM NIGHT 2 1036
I SUNG OF CHAOS AND ETERNAL NIGHT, 3 18
COASTING THE WALL OF HEAV'N ON THIS SIDE NIGHT 3 71
DARK, WASTE, AND WILD, UNDER THE FROWN OF NIGHT 3 424
DREAMING BY NIGHT UNDER THE OPEN SKIE, 3 514
ALL NIGHT; AT LAST BY BREAK OF CHEARFUL DAWNE 3 545
NIGHT WOULD INVADE, BUT THERE THE NEIGHBOURING MOON 3 726
AND IN HER PALE DOMINION CHECKS THE NIGHT. 3 732
CHIEF OF TH' ANGELIC GUARDS, AWAITING NIGHT; 4 550
IN AUTUMN THWARTS THE NIGHT, WHEN VAPORS FIR'D 4 557
SHE ALL NIGHT LONG HER AMOROUS DESCANT SUNG; 4 603
OF NIGHT, AND ALL THINGS NOW RETIR'D TO REST 4 611
LABOUR AND REST, AS DAY AND NIGHT TO MEN 4 613
MEAN WHILE, AS NATURE WILLS, NIGHT BIDS US REST. 4 633
OF GRATEFUL EEVNING MILDE, THEN SILENT NIGHT 4 647
NOR GRATEFUL EEVNING MILD, NOR SILENT NIGHT 4 654
BUT WHEREFORE ALL NIGHT LONG SHINE THESE, FOR WHOM 4 657
LEAST TOTAL DARKNESS SHOULD BY NIGHT REGAINE 4 665
THESE THEN, THOUGH UNBEHELD IN DEEP OF NIGHT, 4 674
BOTH DAY AND NIGHT; HOW OFTEN FROM THE STEEP 4 680
DIVIDE THE NIGHT, AND LIFT OUR THOUGHTS TO HEAVEN. 4 688
AND STARRIE POLE: THOU ALSO MAD'ST THE NIGHT, 4 724
NOW HAD NIGHT MEASUR'D WITH HER SHADDOWIE CONE 4 776
TO THIR NIGHT WATCHES IN WARLIKE PARADE, 4 780
MURMURING, AND WITH HIM FLED THE SHADES OF NIGHT. 4 1015
THY FACE, AND MORN RETURN'D, FOR I THIS NIGHT, 5 30
SUCH NIGHT TILL THIS I NEVER PASS'D, HAVE DREAM'D, 5 31
KNEW NEVER TILL THIS IRKSOM NIGHT; METHOUGHT 5 35
TO FIND THIS BUT A DREAM. THUS EVE HER NIGHT 5 93
THE TROUBLE OF THY THOUGHTS THIS NIGHT IN SLEEP 5 96
RESERVD FROM NIGHT, AND KEPT FOR THEE IN STORE. 5 128

NIGHT (CONTINUED)

AND CHORAL SYMPHONIES, DAY WITHOUT NIGHT, 5 162
FAIREST OF STARRS, LAST IN THE TRAIN OF NIGHT, 5 166
TO GIVE US ONELY GOOD; AND IF THE NIGHT 5 206
THIS NIGHT THE HUMAN PAIR, HOW HE DESIGNES 5 227
ABOVE ALL HILLS. AS WHEN BY NIGHT THE GLASS 5 261
CHERUBIC SONGS BY NIGHT FROM NEIGHBOURING HILLS 5 547
NOW WHEN AMBROSIAL NIGHT WITH CLOUDS EXHAL'D 5 642
TO GRATEFUL TWILIGHT (FOR NIGHT COMES NOT THERE 5 645
ALTERNATE ALL NIGHT LONG: BUT NOT SO WAK'D 5 657
TELL THEM THAT BY COMMAND, ERE YET DIM NIGHT 5 685
THAT THE MOST HIGH COMMANDING, NOW ERE NIGHT, 5 699
NOW ERE DIM NIGHT HAD DISINCUMBERD HEAV'N, 5 700
INNUMERABLE AS THE STARRS OF NIGHT, 5 745
ALL NIGHT THE DREADLESS ANGEL UNPURSU'D 6 1
GRATEFUL VICISSITUDE, LIKE DAY AND NIGHT; 6 8
EMPYREAL, FROM BEFORE HER VANISHT NIGHT, 6 14
NOW NIGHT HER COURSE BEGAN, AND OVER HEAV'N 6 406
HIS POTENTATES TO COUNCEL CALL'D BY NIGHT; 6 416
SO ALL ERE DAY-SPRING, UNDER CONSCIOUS NIGHT 6 521
GLOOMIE AS NIGHT; UNDER HIS BURNING WHEELES 6 832
HASTE TO THY AUDIENCE, NIGHT WITH HER WILL BRING 7 105
ONELY OMNISCIENT, HATH SUPPREST IN NIGHT, 7 123
DIVIDED: LIGHT THE DAY, AND DARKNESS NIGHT 7 251
THE DAY FROM NIGHT; AND LET THEM BE FOR SIGNES, 7 341
THE LESS BY NIGHT ALTERNE: AND MADE THE STARRS, 7 348
IN THIR VICISSITUDE, AND RULE THE NIGHT, 7 351
TILL NIGHT, THEN IN THE EAST HER TURN SHE SHINES, 7 380
CEAS'D WARBLING, BUT ALL NIGHT TUN'D HER SOFT LAYES; 7 436
FORERUNNING NIGHT; WHEN AT THE HOLY MOUNT 7 584
ONE DAY AND NIGHT; IN ALL THIR VAST SURVEY 8 24
OF DAY AND NIGHT; WHICH NEEDS NOT THY BELEEFE, 8 136
FROM THE SUNS BEAM MEET NIGHT, HER OTHER PART 8 139
ENLIGHTNING HER BY DAY, AS SHE BY NIGHT 8 143
DISPORTING, TILL THE AMOROUS BIRD OF NIGHT 8 518
TWIXT DAY AND NIGHT, AND NOW FROM END TO END 9 51
BY NIGHT HE FLED, AND AT MIDNIGHT RETURN'D 9 58
HE CIRCL'D, FOUR TIMES CROSS'D THE CARR OF NIGHT 9 65
NOT LONGER THEN SINCE I IN ONE NIGHT FREED 9 140
ONE NIGHT OR TWO WITH WANTON GROWTH DERIDES 9 211
COMPACT OF UNCTUOUS VAPOR, WHICH THE NIGHT 9 635
BY NIGHT, AND LISTENING WHERE THE HAPLESS PAIRE 10 342
OF UNORIGINAL NIGHT AND CHAOS WILDE, 10 477
THROUGH THE STILL NIGHT, NOT NOW, AS ERE MAN FELL, 10 846
LEAVE COLD THE NIGHT, HOW WE HIS GATHER'D BEAMS 10 1070
THOUGH AFTER SLEEPLESS NIGHT; FOR SEE THE MORN, 11 173
RAINE DAY AND NIGHT, ALL FOUNTAINS OF THE DEEP 11 826
AND CALL TO MIND HIS COV'NANT: DAY AND NIGHT, 11 898
BY DAY A CLOUD, BY NIGHT A PILLAR OF FIRE, 12 203
ALL NIGHT HE WILL PURSUE, BUT HIS APPROACH 12 206
SHALL REST BY DAY, A FIERY GLEAME BY NIGHT, 12 257
TO SIMPLE SHEPHERDS, KEEPING WATCH BY NIGHT; 12 365

NIGHT-FOUNDER'D

THE PILOT OF SOME SMALL NIGHT-FOUNDER'D SKIFF, 1 204

NIGHT-HAG

NOR UGLIER FOLLOW THE NIGHT-HAG, WHEN CALL'D 2 662

NIGHTINGAL

TILL EV'N, NOR THEN THE SOLEMN NIGHTINGAL 7 435

NIGHTINGALE

WERE SLUNK, ALL BUT THE WAKEFUL NIGHTINGALE; 4 602

NIGHTINGALES

THESE LULLD BY NIGHTINGALES IMBRACEING SLEPT, 4 771

NIGHTLY

TO WHOSE BRIGHT IMAGE NIGHTLY BY THE MOON 1 440
PLY STEMMING NIGHTLY TOWARD THE POLE. SO SEEM'D 2 642
NIGHTLY I VISIT: NOR SOMTIMES FORGET 3 32
WHILE THEY KEEP WATCH, OR NIGHTLY ROUNDING WALK 4 685
NIGHTLY BEFORE HIM, SAW WITHOUT THIR LIGHT 5 714
VISIT'ST MY SLUMBERS NIGHTLY, OR WHEN MORN 7 29
WHICH NIGHTLY AS A CIRCLING ZONE THOU SEEST 7 580
HER NIGHTLY VISITATION UNIMPLOR'D, 9 22
NOT HERS WHO BRINGS IT NIGHTLY TO MY EAR. 9 47

NIGHTS

OF NIGHTS EXTENDED SHADE; FROM EASTERN POINT 3 557
NIGHTS HEMISPHERE HAD VEILD THE HORIZON ROUND: 9 52
THE SPACE OF SEVEN CONTINU'D NIGHTS HE RODE 9 63
WHAT HE ALMIGHTIE STYL'D, FIX NIGHTS AND DAYS 9 137
EQUAL IN DAYS AND NIGHTS, EXCEPT TO THOSE 10 680
A DAY ENTIRE, AND NIGHTS DUE COURSE ADJOURNE, 12 264

NIGHT-WANDERER

MISLEADS TH' AMAZ'D NIGHT-WANDERER FROM HIS WAY 9 640

NIGHT-WARBLING

TO THE NIGHT-WARBLING BIRD, THAT NOW AWAKE 5 40

NILE

LIKE NIGHT, AND DARKEN'D ALL THE LAND OF NILE: 1 343
ISRAEL IN SITTIM ON THIR MARCH FROM NILE 1 413
EGYPT, DIVIDED BY THE RIVER NILE; 12 157

NILUS

BY NILUS HEAD, ENCLOSD WITH SHINING ROCK, 4 283

NIMBLE

O FRIENDS, I HEAR THE TREAD OF NIMBLE FEET 4 866
THIR NIMBLE TREAD, AS WHEN THE TOTAL KIND 6 73
CONSUM'D WITH NIMBLE GLANCE, AND GRATEFUL STEAME; 11 442

NINE

NINE TIMES THE SPACE THAT MEASURES DAY AND NIGHT 1 50
NINE DAYES THEY FELL; CONFOUNDED CHAOS ROARD, 6 871
NOR OF THE MUSES NINE, NOR ON THE TOP 7 6

NINEFOLD

NINEFOLD, AND GATES OF BURNING ADAMANT 2 436

NIPHATES

NOR STAID, TILL ON NIPHATES TOP HE LIGHTS. 3 742

NISROC

NISROC, OF PRINCIPALITIES THE PRIME; 6 447

NITRE

INSTINCT WITH FIRE AND NITRE HURRIED HIM 2 937

NITROUS

LIGHTS ON A HEAP OF NITROUS POWDER, LAID 4 815
CONCEPTION; SULPHUROUS AND NITROUS FOAME 6 512

NOBLE

SO SAYING, A NOBLE STROKE HE LIFTED HIGH, 6 189
SERV'D BY MORE NOBLE THEN HER SELF, ATTAINES 8 34
TO NOBLE AND IGNOBLE IS MORE SWEET 12 221

NOBLENESS

GREATNESS OF MIND AND NOBLENESS THIR SEAT 8 557

NOBLER

TO VICE INDUSTRIOUS, BUT TO NOBLER DEEDS 2 116
TWO OF FAR NOBLER SHAPE ERECT AND TALL, 4 288
SO MANY NOBLER BODIES TO CREATE, 8 28
PRODUCTIVE IN HERB, PLANT, AND NOBLER BIRTH 9 111
CALL EL DORADO: BUT TO NOBLER SIGHTS 11 411
CREATED, AS THOU ART, TO NOBLER END 11 605

NOBLEST

TO HIGHT OF NOBLEST TEMPER HERO'S OLD 1 552
ALL TREES OF NOBLEST KIND FOR SIGHT, SMELL, TASTE; 4 217

NOCENT

NOR NOCENT YET, BUT ON THE GRASSIE HERBE 9 186

NOCTURNAL

TUNES HER NOCTURNAL NOTE. THUS WITH THE YEAR 3 40
NOCTURNAL AND DIURNAL RHOMB SUPPOS'D, 8 134

NOISE

AGAINST THE TORTURER; WHEN TO MEET THE NOISE 2 64
ETERNAL ANARCHIE, AMIDST THE NOISE 2 896
MIGHT IN THAT NOISE RESIDE, OF WHOM TO ASK 2 957
OF BRAZEN CHARIOTS RAG'D; DIRE WAS THE NOISE 6 211
FROM FAR WITH THUNDRING NOISE AMONG OUR FOES 6 487
EMBOWELD WITH OUTRAGIOUS NOISE THE AIR, 6 587
INFERNAL NOISE; WARR SEEM'D A CIVIL GAME 6 667
HELL HEARD TH' UNSUFFERABLE NOISE, HELL SAW 6 867
NOISE, OTHER THEN THE SOUND OF DANCE OR SONG, 8 243
WITH SPATTERING NOISE REJECTED: OFT THEY ASSAYD, 10 567
EURUS AND ZEPHIR WITH THIR LATERAL NOISE, 10 705
TO SOW A JANGLING NOISE OF WORDS UNKNOWN: 12 55

NOISES

WITH NOISES LOUD AND RUINOUS (TO COMPARE 2 921

NONE

WHICH BUT TH' OMNIPOTENT NONE COULD HAVE FOYLD, 1 273
AND DIG'D OUT RIBS OF GOLD. LET NONE ADMIRE 1 690
FROM FACTION; FOR NONE SURE WILL CLAIM IN HELL 2 32
PRECEDENCE, NONE, WHOSE PORTION IS SO SMALL 2 33
FREE, AND TO NONE ACCOUNTABLE, PREFERRING 2 255
SATAN EXCEPT, NONE HIGHER SAT, WITH GRAVE 2 300
IRREPARABLE; TEARMS OF PEACE YET NONE 2 331
ASTONISHT: NONE AMONG THE CHOICE AND PRIME 2 423
NONE SHALL PARTAKE WITH ME. THUS SAYING ROSE 2 466
IF SHAPE IT MIGHT BE CALL'D THAT SHAPE HAD NONE 2 667
THESE GATES FOR EVER SHUT, WHICH NONE CAN PASS 2 776
THAT REST OR INTERMISSION NONE I FIND. 2 802
SAVE HE WHO REIGNS ABOVE, NONE CAN RESIST. 2 814
THE OTHER NONE: IN MERCY AND JUSTICE BOTH, 3 132
ALL HIS DELIV'RANCE, AND TO NONE BUT ME. 3 182
AND NONE BUT SUCH FROM MERCY I EXCLUDE. 3 202
PATRON OR INTERCESSOR NONE APPEERD, 3 219
INDEBTED AND UNDON, HATH NONE TO BRING: 3 235
AS MANY AS ARE RESTOR'D, WITHOUT THEE NONE. 3 289
LIVING OR LIVELESS TO BE FOUND WAS NONE, 3 443
NONE YET, BUT STORE HEREAFTER FROM THE EARTH 3 444
HIS FIXED SEAT, OR FIXED SEAT HATH NONE, 3 669
WHERE HONOUR DUE AND REVERENCE NONE NEGLECTS, 3 738
UPBRAIDED NONE; NOR WAS HIS SERVICE HARD. 4 45

NONE (CONTINUED)
LEFT FOR REPENTANCE, NONE FOR PARDON LEFT? 4 80
NONE LEFT BUT BY SUBMISSION; AND THAT WORD 4 81
BUT FURTHER WAY FOUND NONE, SO THICK ENTWIN'D, 4 174
SEE FARR AND WIDE: IN AT THIS GATE NONE PASS 4 579
SHINE NOT IN VAIN, NOR THINK, THOUGH MEN WERE NONE, 4 675
BEAST, BIRD, INSECT, OR WORM DURST ENTER NONE; 4 704
OBSERVING NONE, BUT ADORATION PURE 4 737
IF NONE REGARD; HEAV'N WAKES WITH ALL HIS EYES, 5 44
DEIGNS NONE TO EASE THY LOAD AND TASTE THY SWEET, 5 59
FORBID WHO WILL, NONE SHALL FROM ME WITHHOLD 5 62
YET EVIL WHENCE? IN THEE CAN HARBOUR NONE, 5 99
NONE CAN THEN HEAV'N SUCH GLORIOUS SHAPE CONTAIN; 5 362
ON OTHER SURETY NONE; FREELY WE SERVE, 5 538
BY NONE, AND IF NOT EQUAL ALL, YET FREE, 5 791
ABDIEL, THEN WHOM NONE WITH MORE ZEALE ADOR'D 5 805
NONE SECONDED, AS OUT OF SEASON JUDG'D, 5 850
KNOW NONE BEFORE US, SELF-BEGOT, SELF-RAIS'D 5 860
OMNIPOTENCE TO NONE. BUT WELL THOU COMST 6 159
NONE OF RETREAT, NO UNBECOMING DEED 6 237
IN NATURE NONE: IF OTHER HIDDEN CAUSE 6 442
NONE ARGUING STOOD, INNUMERABLE HANDS 6 508
THAT WHOM THEY HIT, NONE ON THIR FEET MIGHT STAND, 6 592
OF ENDING THIS GREAT WARR, SINCE NONE BUT THOU 6 702
TO NONE COMMUNICABLE IN EARTH OR HEAVEN: 7 124
NONE WAS, BUT FROM THE EARTH A DEWIE MIST 7 333
FROM HIM, FOR OTHER LIGHT SHE NEEDED NONE 7 378
TO SEE THAT NONE THENCE ISSU'D FORTH A SPIE, 8 233
THIS HAPPIE LIGHT, WHEN ANSWER NONE RETURN'D, 8 285
FROM ALL ETERNITIE, FOR NONE I KNOW 8 406
IN EMINENCE, AND OBSTACLE FIND NONE 8 624
WHATEVER FLEIGHTS NONE WOULD SUSPICIOUS MARK, 9 92
ROCKS, DENS, AND CAVES; BUT I IN NONE OF THESE 9 118
LET NONE HENCEFORTH SEEK NEEDLESS CAUSE TO APPROVE 9 1140
ATTENDANCE NONE SHALL NEED, NOR TRAIN, WHERE NONE 10 80
CONVICTION TO THE SERPENT NONE BELONGS. 10 84
TO WASTE IT ALL MY SELF, AND LEAVE YE NONE. 10 820
AND TORMENT LESS THEN NONE OF WHAT WE DREAD, 10 998
NONE OF THE MEANEST, SOME GREAT POTENTATE 11 231
TAUGHT THEM, BUT THEY HIS GIFTS ACKNOWLEDG'D NONE. 11 612
THROUGH ALL THE PLAIN, AND REFUGE NONE WAS FOUND. 11 673
NO SANCTITIE, IF NONE BE THITHER BROUGHT 11 837
ON EVERY CONSCIENCE; LAWS WHICH NONE SHALL FINDE 12 522

NOOK
BY STRANGE CONVEYANCE FILL'D EACH HOLLOW NOOK, 1 707
SEARCH THROUGH THIS GARDEN, LEAVE UNSEARCHT NO NOOK, 4 789
AS IN A SHADIE NOOK I STOOD BEHIND, 9 277

NOON
TO NOON HE FELL, FROM NOON TO DEWY EVE, 1 743
BUT ALL SUN-SHINE, AS WHEN HIS BEAMS AT NOON 3 616
THIS DAY AT HIGHTH OF NOON CAME TO MY SPHEARE 4 564
OUR WALK AT NOON, WITH BRANCHES OVERGROWN, 4 627
AND WHEN HIGH NOON HAST GAIND, AND WHEN THOU FALLST. 5 174
THOU FIND'ST HIM FROM THE HEAT OF NOON RETIR'D, 5 231
RIS'N ON MID-NOON; SOM GREAT BEHEST FROM HEAV'N 5 311
WITH MYRTLE, FIND WHAT TO REDRESS TILL NOON: 9 219
TO BE RETURND BY NOON AMID THE BOWRE, 9 401
MEAN WHILE THE HOUR OF NOON DREW ON, AND WAK'D 9 739
FROM NOON, AND GENTLE AIRES DUE AT THIR HOUR 10 93

NOONE
AS ONE WHO IN HIS JOURNEY BATES AT NOONE, 12 1

NOON-TIDE
OR SUMMERS NOON-TIDE AIR, WHILE THUS HE SPAKE. 2 309

NOONTIDE
IMBROUND THE NOONTIDE BOWRS: THUS WAS THIS PLACE, 4 246
NOONTIDE REPAST, OR AFTERNOONS REPOSE. 9 403

NORTH
A MULTITUDE, LIKE WHICH THE POPULOUS NORTH 1 351
ASCENDING, WHILE THE NORTH WIND SLEEPS, O'RESPREAD 2 489
BUT IN THE MOUNT THAT LIES FROM EDEN NORTH, 4 569
WITH STRICTEST WATCH; THESE OTHER WHEEL THE NORTH, 4 783
THE QUARTERS OF THE NORTH, THERE TO PREPARE 5 689
EQUAL TO OURS, THROUGHOUT THE SPACIOUS NORTH; 5 726
AT LENGTH INTO THE LIMITS OF THE NORTH 5 755
FARR IN TH' HORIZON TO THE NORTH APPEER'D 6 79
SCARCE TOLLERABLE, AND FROM THE NORTH TO CALL 10 654
CORRUPT AND PESTILENT: NOW FROM THE NORTH 10 695

NORTH-EAST
MOZAMBIC, OFF AT SEA NORTH-EAST WINDES BLOW 4 161

NORTHWARD
FROM HAMATH NORTHWARD TO THE DESERT SOUTH 12 139

NORTH-WINDE
DRIVN BY A KEEN NORTH-WINDE, THAT BLOWING DRIE 11 842

NORUMBEGA
OF NORUMBEGA, AND THE SAMOED SHOAR 10 696

NORWAY
HIM HAPLY SLUMBRING ON THE NORWAY FOAM 1 203

NORWEGIAN
HEWN ON NORWEGIAN HILLS, TO BE THE MAST 1 293

NOSTRIL
HIS NOSTRIL WIDE INTO THE MURKIE AIR, 10 280

NOSTRILS
DUST OF THE GROUND, AND IN THY NOSTRILS BREATH'D 7 525
TO THE CREATOR, AND HIS NOSTRILS FILL 9 196

NOTE
TUNES HER NOCTURNAL NOTE. THUS WITH THE YEAR 3 40
SOLE, OR RESPONSIVE EACH TO OTHERS NOTE 4 683

NOTES
THE BIRDS THIR NOTES RENEW, AND BLEATING HERDS 2 494
WITH NOTES ANGELICAL TO MANY A HARP 2 548
WITH OTHER NOTES THEN TO TH' ORPHEAN LYRE 3 17
BEAR ON YOUR WINGS AND IN YOUR NOTES HIS PRAISE; 5 199
THOSE NOTES TO TRAGIC; FOUL DISTRUST, AND BREACH 9 6

NOTHING
SAY FIRST, FOR HEAV'N HIDES NOTHING FROM THY VIEW 1 27
TO NOTHING THIS ESSENTIAL, HAPPIER FARR 2 97
ON THIS SIDE NOTHING; AND BY PROOF WE FEEL 2 101
HAVE NOTHING MERITED, NOR CAN PERFORME 4 418
THINK NOTHING HARD, MUCH LESS TO BE DESPAIRD. 6 495
THEN VALUE: OFT TIMES NOTHING PROFITS MORE 8 571
UNPRAIS'D: FOR NOTHING LOVELIER CAN BE FOUND 9 232
NOTHING IMPERFET OR DEFICIENT LEFT 9 345
OR SEX, AND APPREHENDED NOTHING HIGH: 9 574
THEM NOTHING: IF THEY ALL THINGS, WHO ENCLOS'D 9 722
HE LED HER NOTHING LOATH; FLOURS WERE THE COUCH, 9 1039
AND HATEFUL; NOTHING WANTS, BUT THAT THY SHAPE, 10 869
BUT ADAM WITH SUCH COUNSEL NOTHING SWAY'D, 10 1010
MUST EAT, AND ON THE GROUND LEAVE NOTHING GREEN; 12 186

NOTION
SO TOLD AS EARTHLY NOTION CAN RECEAVE. 7 179

NOTIONS
SEEK THEM WITH WANDRING THOUGHTS, AND NOTIONS VAIN. 8 187

NOTUS
NOTUS AND AFER BLACK WITH THUNDROUS CLOUDS 10 702

NOURISH
TEMPER OR NOURISH, OR IN PART SHED DOWN 4 670
AND NOURISH ALL THINGS, LET YOUR CEASLESS CHANGE 5 183
TO NOURISH, AND SUPERFLUOUS MOIST CONSUMES: 5 325

NOURISHER
THESE BOUNTIES WHICH OUR NOURISHER, FROM WHOM 5 398

NOURISHMENT
NOR DOTH THE MOON NO NOURISHMENT EXHALE 5 421
MANS NOURISHMENT, BY GRADUAL SCALE SUBLIM'D 5 483
WISDOM TO FOLLY, AS NOURISHMENT TO WINDE. 7 130
DUE NOURISHMENT, NOT GLUTTONOUS DELIGHT, 11 533

NOVELTIE
THIS NOVELTIE ON EARTH, THIS FAIR DEFECT 10 891

NO WHERE
LOVE NO WHERE TO BE FOUND LESS THEN DIVINE. 3 411
NO WHERE SO CLEER, SHARP'ND HIS VISUAL RAY 3 620
LIKE CONSORT TO THY SELF CANST NO WHERE FIND. 4 448

NOXIOUS
THIR NOXIOUS VAPOUR, OR ENUR'D NOT FEEL, 2 216
NOT NOXIOUS, BUT OBEDIENT AT THY CALL. 7 498
OF NOXIOUS EFFICACIE, AND WHEN TO JOYNE 10 660

NOYSE
THOUGH FOR THE NOYSE OF DRUMS AND TIMBRELS LOUD 1 394
AND IN LUXURIOUS CITIES, WHERE THE NOYSE 1 498
IF AUGHT DISTURB'D THIR NOYSE, INTO HER WOOMB, 2 657

NOYSOM
BEFORE HIS EYES APPEARD, SAD, NOYSOM, DARK, 11 478

NUMBER
THIR NUMBER LAST HE SUMMS. AND NOW HIS HEART 1 571
THOUGH WITHOUT NUMBER STILL AMIDST THE HALL 1 791
LOUD AS FROM NUMBERS WITHOUT NUMBER, SWEET 3 346
THIR NUMBER, OR THE WISDOM INFINITE 3 706
IN FULL HARMONIC NUMBER JOIND, THIR SONGS 4 687
ONE OF OUR NUMBER THUS REDUC'T BECOMES, 5 843
NOR NUMBER, NOR EXAMPLE WITH HIM WROUGHT 5 901
EQUAL IN NUMBER TO THAT GODLESS CREW 6 49
AND TWENTIE THOUSAND (I THIR NUMBER HEARD) 6 769
NUMBER TO THIS DAYES WORK IS NOT ORDAIN'D 6 809
NUMBER SUFFICIENT TO POSSESS HER REALMES 7 147
THE NUMBER OF THY WORSHIPPERS. WHO SEEKES 7 613
SPEED, TO DESCRIBE WHOSE SWIFTNESS NUMBER FAILES. 8 38

NUMBER (CONTINUED)
BUT MAN BY NUMBER IS TO MANIFEST 8 422
TO MY JUST NUMBER FOUND. O WHY DID GOD, . . . 10 888

NUMBER'D
THIS ANNUAL HUMBLING CERTAIN NUMBER'D DAYS, . . 10 576

NUMBERD
AND LIMITED THIR MIGHT; THOUGH NUMBERD SUCH . . . 6 229
AND ALL HER NUMBERD STARRS, THAT SEEM TO ROWLE . 8 19
NUMBERD, THOUGH SAD, TILL DEATH, HIS DOOM (WHICH I 11 40

NUMBERLESS
SO NUMBERLESS WERE THOSE BAD ANGELS SEEN 1 344
THRONG NUMBERLESS, LIKE THAT PIGMEAN RACE 1 780
NUMBERLESS, AS THOU SEEST, AND HOW THEY MOVE; . . 3 719
PAVILIONS NUMBERLESS, AND SUDDEN REARD, ... 5 653
ARMIE AGAINST ARMIE NUMBERLESS TO RAISE 6 224
ABOUT HIS CHARIOT NUMBERLESS WERE POUR'D . . . 7 197
WITH HONEY STOR'D: THE REST ARE NUMBERLESS, . . . 7 492
THOUGH NUMBERLESS, TO HIS OMNIPOTENCE, ... 8 108
BY ANGELS NUMBERLESS, THY DAILY TRAIN. 9 548

NUMBERS
HARMONIOUS NUMBERS; AS THE WAKEFUL BIRD 3 38
BENEATH THY SENTENCE; HELL HER NUMBERS FULL . . . 3 332
LOUD AS FROM NUMBERS WITHOUT NUMBER, SWEET . . . 3 346
THIR STARRY DANCE IN NUMBERS THAT COMPUTE . . . 3 580
BY NUMBERS THAT HAVE NAME. BUT THIS I URGE, . . . 8 114
AND THROUGH ALL NUMBERS ABSOLUTE, THOUGH ONE; . . . 8 421
AND TO REPAIRE HIS NUMBERS THUS IMPAIR'D, ... 9 144
NUMBERS OF ALL DISEAS'D, ALL MALADIES 11 480
GREAT NUMBERS OF EACH NATION TO RECEAVE 12 503

NUMEROUS
A NUMEROUS BRIGAD HASTEN'D. AS WHEN BANDS 1 675
I SAW AND HEARD, FOR SUCH A NUMEROUS HOST 2 993
YOUR NUMEROUS OFSPRING; IF NO BETTER PLACE, . . . 4 385
FLOWD FROM THIR LIPS, IN PROSE OR NUMEROUS VERSE, 5 150
SHALL FILL THE WORLD MORE NUMEROUS WITH THY SONS . 5 389
A NUMEROUS HOST, IN STRENGTH EACH ARMED HAND . . 6 231
OF TORRENT FLOODS, OR OF A NUMEROUS HOST. . . . 6 830
THIR BROOD AS NUMEROUS HATCH, FROM THE EGG THAT SOON 7 418
NUMEROUS, AND EVERY STARR PERHAPS A WORLD . . . 7 621
YOU TWO THIS WAY, AMONG THESE NUMEROUS ORBS . . 10 397
SPANGL'D WITH EYES MORE NUMEROUS THEN THOSE . . 11 130
AND STABL'D; OF MANKIND, SO NUMEROUS LATE, . . . 11 752
OF HERDS AND FLOCKS, AND NUMEROUS SERVITUDE; . . 12 132
TOO NUMEROUS; WHENCE OF GUESTS HE MAKES THEM SLAVES 12 167

NUPTIAL
FAIR COUPLE, LINKT IN HAPPIE NUPTIAL LEAGUE, . . . 4 339
ESPOUSED EVE DECKT FIRST HER NUPTIAL BED, ... 4 710
OF NUPTIAL SANCTITIE AND MARRIAGE RITES: 8 487
MY PLEADED REASON. TO THE NUPTIAL BOWRE 8 510
FROM LOVES DUE RITES, NUPTIAL IMBRACES SWEET, . . 10 994
THEE LASTLY NUPTIAL BOWRE, BY MEE ADORND . . . 11 280
THEY LIGHT THE NUPTIAL TORCH, AND BID INVOKE . . 11 590

NURSERIE
HER NURSERIE; THEY AT HER COMING SPRUNG 8 46

NUTRIMENT
MOIST NUTRIMENT, OR UNDER ROCKS THIR FOOD 7 408

NUTRIMENTS
AND FROM THESE CORPORAL NUTRIMENTS PERHAPS 5 496

NYMPH
PAN OR SILVANUS NEVER SLEPT, NOR NYMPH, ... 4 707
THEN WOOD-NYMPH, OR THE FAIREST GODDESS FEIGN'D . 5 381
SOFT SHE WITHDREW, AND LIKE A WOOD-NYMPH LIGHT . 9 386

NYMPHLIKE
IF CHANCE WITH NYMPHLIKE STEP FAIR VIRGIN PASS, . 9 452

NYSEIAN
OF EDEN STRIVE; NOR THAT NYSEIAN ILE 4 275

O
AND CHIEFLY THOU, O SPIRIT, THAT DOST PREFER . . . 1 17
O HOW UNLIKE THE PLACE FROM WHENCE THEY FELL. . . 1 75
IF THOU BEEST HE; BUT O HOW FALL'N. HOW CHANG'D . 1 84
O PRINCE, O CHIEF OF MANY THRONED POWERS, . . . 1 128
O MYRIADS OF IMMORTAL SPIRITS, O POWERS 1 622
I SHOULD BE MUCH FOR OPEN WARR, O PEERS, . . . 2 119
O PROGENY OF HEAV'N, EMPYREAL THRONES, ... 2 430
BUT I SHOULD ILL BECOME THIS THRONE, O PEERS, . . 2 445
O SHAME TO MEN. DEVIL WITH DEVIL DAMN'D . . . 2 496
O FATHER, WHAT INTENDS THY HAND, SHE CRY'D, . . 2 727
AGAINST THY ONLY SON? WHAT FURY O SON, ... 2 728
BUT THOU O FATHER, I FOREWARN THEE, SHUN . . . 2 810
O FATHER, GRACIOUS WAS THAT WORD WHICH CLOS'D . . 3 144
O SON, IN WHOM MY SOUL HATH CHIEF DELIGHT, . . . 3 168
O THOU IN HEAV'N AND EARTH THE ONLY PEACE . . . 3 274
FOUND OUT FOR MANKIND UNDER WRAUTH, O THOU . . . 3 275
FOR MANS OFFENCE. O UNEXAMPL'D LOVE, ... 3 410

O (CONTINUED)
O FOR THAT WARNING VOICE, WHICH HE WHO SAW 4 1
O THOU THAT WITH SURPASSING GLORY CROWND, ... 4 32
O SUN, TO TELL THEE HOW I HATE THY BEAMS 4 37
O HAD HIS POWERFUL DESTINY ORDAIND 4 58
O THEN AT LAST RELENT: IS THERE NO PLACE . . . 4 79
O HELL. WHAT DOE MINE EYES WITH GRIEF BEHOLD, . 4 358
TO WHOM THUS EVE REPLI'D. O THOU FOR WHOM . . . 4 440
O FAIR FOUNDATION LAID WHEREON TO BUILD 4 521
ENDOWD WITH ALL THIR GIFTS, AND O TOO LIKE . . . 4 715
BLEST PAIR; AND O YET HAPPIEST IF YE SEEK . . . 4 774
O FRIENDS, I HEAR THE TREAD OF NIMBLE FEET . . . 4 866
O LOSS OF ONE IN HEAV'N TO JUDGE OF WISE, . . . 4 904
SATAN, AND COULDST THOU FAITHFUL ADD? O NAME, . 4 950
O SACRED NAME OF FAITHFULNESS PROFAN'D. 4 951
O SOLE IN WHOM MY THOUGHTS FIND ALL REPOSE, . . . 5 28
AND O FAIR PLANT, SAID HE, WITH FRUIT SURCHARG'D, 5 58
BUT HE THUS OVERJOY'D, O FRUIT DIVINE, ... 5 67
AND FELL ASLEEP; BUT O HOW GLAD I WAK'D 5 92
WITH PLEASANT LIQUORS CROWN'D: O INNOCENCE . . . 5 445
O ADAM, ONE ALMIGHTIE IS, FROM WHOM 5 469
O FAVOURABLE SPIRIT, PROPITIOUS GUEST, ... 5 507
AND SO FROM HEAV'N TO DEEPEST HELL; O FALL . . . 5 542
HIGH MATTER THOU INJOINST ME, O PRIME OF MEN, . . 5 563
O ARGUMENT BLASPHEMOUS, FALSE AND PROUD. . . . 5 809
O ALIENATE FROM GOD, O SPIRIT ACCURST, ... 5 877
O HEAV'N. THAT SUCH RESEMBLANCE OF THE HIGHEST . 6 114
O NOW IN DANGER TRI'D, NOW KNOWN IN ARMES . . . 6 418
O FRIENDS, WHY COME NOT ON THESE VICTORS PROUD? . 6 609
O FATHER, O SUPREAM OF HEAV'NLY THRONES, ... 6 723
THIS BE THY JUST CIRCUMFERENCE, O WORLD. . . . 7 231
THIS SAID, HE FORMD THEE, ADAM, THEE O MAN . . . 7 524
NOT WORDS ALONE PLEAS'D HER. O WHEN MEET NOW . . 8 57
O BY WHAT NAME, FOR THOU ABOVE ALL THESE, . . . 8 357
O EARTH, HOW LIKE TO HEAV'N, IF NOT PREFERR'D . . 9 99
HIM LORD PRONOUNC'D, AND, O INDIGNITIE. 9 154
O FOUL DESCENT. THAT I WHO ERST CONTENDED . . . 9 163
O WOMAN, BEST ARE ALL THINGS AS THE WILL . . . 9 343
O MUCH DECEAV'D, MUCH FAILING, HAPLESS EVE, . . . 9 404
O SACRED, WISE, AND WISDOM-GIVING PLANT, ... 9 679
O SOVRAN, VERTUOUS, PRECIOUS OF ALL TREES . . . 9 795
O FAIREST OF CREATION, LAST AND BEST 9 896
O GLORIOUS TRIAL OF EXCEEDING LOVE, ... 9 961
O EVE, IN EVIL HOUR THOU DIDST GIVE EARE 9 1067
INSUFFERABLY BRIGHT. O MIGHT I HERE 9 1084
THIR GUILT AND DREADED SHAME; O HOW UNLIKE . . . 9 1114
O HEAV'N. IN EVIL STRAIT THIS DAY I STAND . . . 10 125
O SON, WHY SIT WE HERE EACH OTHER VIEWING . . . 10 235
O PARENT, THESE ARE THY MAGNIFIC DEEDS, ... 10 354
O MISERABLE OF HAPPIE. IS THIS THE END 10 720
IS PROPAGATED CURSE. O VOICE ONCE HEARD 10 729
HEAVIE, THOUGH IN THIR PLACE. O FLEETING JOYES . 10 741
O WELCOM HOUR WHENEVER. WHY DELAYES 10 771
BUT I SHALL DIE A LIVING DEATH? O THOUGHT . . . 10 788
THAT I MUST LEAVE YE, SONS; O WERE I ABLE . . . 10 819
O CONSCIENCE, INTO WHAT ABYSS OF FEARS 10 842
O WOODS, O FOUNTAINS, HILLOCKS, DALES AND BOWRS, . 10 860
TO MY JUST NUMBER FOUND. O WHY DID GOD, ... 10 888
AND TO OUR SEED (O HAPLESS SEED.) DERIV'D. . . . 10 965
O SONS, LIKE ONE OF US MAN IS BECOME 11 84
O EVE, SOME FURDER CHANGE AWAITS US NIGH, . . . 11 193
O UNEXPECTED STROKE, WORSE THEN OF DEATH. . . . 11 268
THAT MUST BE MORTAL TO US BOTH. O FLOURS, . . . 11 273
O TEACHER, SOME GREAT MISCHIEF HATH BEFALL'N . . 11 450
I MUST RETURN TO NATIVE DUST? O SIGHT 11 463
O MISERABLE MANKIND, TO WHAT FALL 11 500
O PITTIE AND SHAME, THAT THEY WHO TO LIVE WELL . 11 629
LAMENTING TURND FULL SAD; O WHAT ARE THESE, . . 11 675
O VISIONS ILL FORESEEN. BETTER HAD I 11 763
O THOU WHO FUTURE THINGS CANST REPRESENT 11 870
O EXECRABLE SON SO TO ASPIRE 12 64
BRED UP IN IDOL-WORSHIP; O THAT MEN 12 115
HERE ADAM INTERPOS'D. O SENT FROM HEAV'N, . . . 12 270
O PROPHET OF GLAD TIDINGS, FINISHER 12 375
O GOODNESS INFINITE, GOODNESS IMMENSE. 12 469

OAK
OR HOLLOW'D BODIES MADE OF OAK OR FIRR 6 574

OAKS
HATH SCATH'D THE FORREST OAKS, OR MOUNTAIN PINES, 1 613

OARE
HALF FLYING; BEHOVES HIM NOW BOTH OARE AND SAILE. 2 942

OARIE
HER STATE WITH OARIE FEET: YET OFT THEY QUIT . . 7 440

OATH
PRONOUNC'D AMONG THE GODS, AND BY AN OATH, . . . 2 352

OB
MAEOTIS, UP BEYOND THE RIVER OB; 9 78

OBDURAT
BEHINDE THEM, WHILE TH' OBDURAT KING PURSUES: . . 12 205

OBDURATE
MIXT WITH OBDURATE PRIDE AND STEDFAST HATE: 1 58
OR WONDERS MOVE TH' OBDURATE TO RELENT? 6 790

OBDUR'D
THIS SAW HIS HAPLESS FOES BUT STOOD OBDUR'D, 6 785

OBDURED
FALLACIOUS HOPE, OR ARM TH' OBDURED BREST 2 568

OBEDIENCE
SOLE PLEDGE OF HIS OBEDIENCE: SO WILL FALL, 3 95
WHAT PLEASURE I FROM SUCH OBEDIENCE PAID, 3 107
TO PRAY, REPENT, AND BRING OBEDIENCE DUE. 3 190
TO PRAYER, REPENTANCE, AND OBEDIENCE DUE, 3 191
FILIAL OBEDIENCE: AS A SACRIFICE 3 269
THE ONLY SIGN OF OUR OBEDIENCE LEFT 4 428
THE PROOF OF THIR OBEDIENCE AND THIR FAITH? 4 520
YOUR MILITARY OBEDIENCE, TO DISSOLVE 4 955
OBEDIENT? CAN WE WANT OBEDIENCE THEN 5 514
THAT IS, TO THY OBEDIENCE; THEREIN STAND. 5 522
HOLD, AS YOU YOURS, WHILE OUR OBEDIENCE HOLDS; 5 537
THAT FROM THY JUST OBEDIENCE COULD REVOLT, 6 740
THEE ALSO FROM OBEDIENCE, THAT WITH HIM 6 902
UP HITHER, UNDER LONG OBEDIENCE TRI'D, 7 159
OUR PROMPT OBEDIENCE. FAST WE FOUND, FAST SHUT 8 240
THE PLEDGE OF THY OBEDIENCE AND THY FAITH, 8 325
FIRST THY OBEDIENCE; TH' OTHER WHO CAN KNOW, 9 368
OBEDIENCE TO THE LAW OF GOD, IMPOS'D 12 397
BOTH BY OBEDIENCE AND BY LOVE, THOUGH LOVE 12 403
IN HIS REDEMPTION, AND THAT HIS OBEDIENCE 12 408

OBEDIENT
IF YE BE FOUND OBEDIENT, AND RETAIN 5 501
OBEDIENT? CAN WE WANT OBEDIENCE THEN 5 514
NOT NOXIOUS, BUT OBEDIENT AT THY CALL. 7 498
OBEDIENT TO HIS WILL, THAT HE VOUTSAFES 12 246

OBEI'D
THE DEITIE, AND DIVINE COMMANDS OBEI'D, 5 806

OBEY
MY BEING GAV'ST ME; WHOM SHOULD I OBEY 2 865
UNARGU'D I OBEY; SO GOD ORDAINS, 4 636
OUR MAKER, AND OBEY HIM WHOSE COMMAND 5 551
BEHESTS OBEY, WORTHIEST TO BE OBEY'D, 6 185
WHOM TO OBEY IS HAPPINESS ENTIRE. 6 741
HIM WHOM TO LOVE IS TO OBEY, AND KEEP 8 634
WAS SHEE THY GOD, THAT HER THOU DIDST OBEY 10 145
IF PATIENTLY THY BIDDING THEY OBEY, 11 112
HENCEFORTH I LEARNE, THAT TO OBEY IS BEST, 12 561

OBEY'D
OR TAINT INTEGRITIE; BUT ALL OBEY'D 5 704
BEHESTS OBEY, WORTHIEST TO BE OBEY'D, 6 185
EACH IN THEIR KINDE. THE EARTH OBEY'D, AND STRAIT 7 453
MY TONGUE OBEY'D AND READILY COULD NAME 8 272

OBEYD
YET TO THIR GENERALS VOYCE THEY SOON OBEYD 1 337
SO EASILY OBEYD AMID THE CHOICE 7 48
WHAT THOU COMMANDST, AND RIGHT THOU SHOULDST BE
OBEYD: 9 570
NOT JUST, NOT GOD; NOT FEARD THEN, NOR OBEYD: 9 701
REASON IN MAN OBSCUR'D, OR NOT OBEYD, 12 86

OBEYES
BUT GOD LEFT FREE THE WILL, FOR WHAT OBEYES 9 351

OBEYING
OR NOT RESTRAIND AS WEE, OR NOT OBEYING, 9 868
WHOEVER TEMPTED; WHICH THEY NOT OBEYING, 10 14

OBEYS
ALL NATIONS SHALL BE BLEST; HE STRAIGHT OBEYS, 12 126
OVER THE SEA; THE SEA HIS ROD OBEYS; 12 212

OBJECT
BUT EVIL HAST NOT TRI'D: AND WILT OBJECT 4 896
AS WITH AN OBJECT THAT EXCELS THE SENSE, 8 456
NOT PROOF ENOUGH SUCH OBJECT TO SUSTAIN, 8 535
LOOKS INTERVENE AND SMILES, OR OBJECT NEW 9 222
SOME SPECIOUS OBJECT BY THE FOE SUBORND, 9 361
MEE MEE ONELY JUST OBJECT OF HIS IRE. 10 936
BEFORE THE PRESENT OBJECT LANGUISHING 10 996
WHY ELSE THIS DOUBLE OBJECT IN OUR SIGHT 11 201

OBJECTS
TO OBJECTS DISTANT FARR, WHEREBY HE SOON 3 621
WHO MEET WITH VARIOUS OBJECTS, FROM THE SENSE 8 609
THY MORTAL SIGHT TO FAILE; OBJECTS DIVINE 12 9

OBLIGE
DESERTED, THEN OBLIGE THEE WITH A FACT 9 980

OBLIQUE
THROUGH THE PURE MARBLE AIR HIS OBLIQUE WAY 3 564
SCIPIO THE HIGHTH OF ROME. WITH TRACT OBLIQUE 9 510

OBLIQUE (CONTINUED)
OBLIQUE THE CENTRIC GLOBE: SOM SAY THE SUN 10 671

OBLIQUITIES
MOV'D CONTRARIE WITH THWART OBLIQUITIES, 8 132

OBLIVION
LETHE THE RIVER OF OBLIVION ROULES 2 583
NAMELESS IN DARK OBLIVION LET THEM DWELL. 6 380

OBLIVIOUS
LYE THUS ASTONISHT ON TH' OBLIVIOUS POOL, 1 266

OBLOQUIE
CANST THOU WITH IMPIOUS OBLOQUIE CONDEMNE 5 813

OBNOXIOUS
AS HIGH HE SOARD, OBNOXIOUS FIRST OR LAST 9 170
TO SHAME OBNOXIOUS, AND UNSEEMLIEST SEEN, 9 1094

OBSCENE
NEXT CHEMOS, TH' OBSCENE DREAD OF MOABS SONS, 1 406

OBSCUR'D
OF GLORY OBSCUR'D: AS WHEN THE SUN NEW RIS'N 1 594
ALIEN FROM HEAV'N, WITH PASSIONS FOUL OBSCUR'D: 4 571
ESSENTIAL POWERS, NOR BY HIS REIGN OBSCUR'D, 5 841
BUT SOON OBSCUR'D WITH SMOAK, ALL HEAV'N APPEERD, 6 585
TO SAPIENCE, HITHERTO OBSCUR'D, INFAM'D, 9 797
OBSCUR'D, WHERE HIGHEST WOODS IMPENETRABLE 9 1086
REASON IN MAN OBSCUR'D, OR NOT OBEYD, 12 86

OBSCURE
DILATED OR CONDENS'T, BRIGHT OR OBSCURE, 1 429
OBSCURE SOME GLIMPS OF JOY, TO HAVE FOUND THIR
CHIEF 1 524
ENCAMP THIR LEGIONS, OR WITH OBSCURE WING 2 132
AND THROUGH THE PALPABLE OBSCURE FIND OUT 2 406
IN THAT OBSCURE SOJOURN, WHILE IN MY FLIGHT 3 15
THY SIN AND PLACE OF DOOM OBSCURE AND FOULE. 4 840
ROUND THROUGH THE VAST PROFUNDITIE OBSCURE, 7 229
FROM USE, OBSCURE AND SUTTLE, BUT TO KNOW 8 192
BOUND ON A VOYAGE UNCOUTH AND OBSCURE, 8 230
OF MIDNIGHT VAPOR GLIDE OBSCURE, AND PRIE 9 159
NOR THIS UNVOYAGEABLE GULF OBSCURE 10 366
INTO A LOWER WORLD, TO THIS OBSCURE 11 283

OBSCURELY
THE WOMANS SEED, OBSCURELY THEN FORETOLD, 12 543

OBSEQUIOUS
OBSEQUIOUS DARKNESS ENTERS, TILL HER HOURE 6 10
OBSEQUIOUS, HEAV'N HIS WONTED FACE RENEWD, 6 783
AND WITH OBSEQUIOUS MAJESTIE APPROV'D 8 509

OBSERV'D
COMPARE OF MORTAL PROWESS, YET OBSERV'D 1 588
PROCEEDING, WHICH IN OTHER BEASTS OBSERV'D 9 94
DEPARTING GAVE COMMAND, AND THEY OBSERV'D. 10 430
ADAM OBSERV'D, AND WITH HIS EYE THE CHASE 11 191
NEW LAWS TO BE OBSERV'D; FOR I DESCRIE 11 228

OBSERVD
HIS LOSS; BUT CHIEFLY TO FIND HERE OBSERVD 4 849
OF THEM DERIDED, BUT OF GOD OBSERVD 11 817

OBSERVE
RECEAVE WITH SOLEMNE PURPOSE TO OBSERVE 7 78
TO OBSERVE THE SEQUEL, SAW HIS GUILEFUL ACT 10 334
THERE IS, SAID MICHAEL, IF THOU WELL OBSERVE 11 530
AS IN HIS PRESENCE, EVER TO OBSERVE 12 563

OBSERVES
OF GALILEO, LESS ASSUR'D, OBSERVES 5 262

OBSERVING
OBSERVING NONE, BUT ADORATION PURE 4 737

OBSTACLE
FOR SIGHT NO OBSTACLE FOUND HERE, NOR SHADE, 3 615
IN EMINENCE, AND OBSTACLE FIND NONE 8 624

OBSTINACIE
ANGER, AND OBSTINACIE, AND HATE, AND GUILE. 10 114

OBSTRUCT
FROM HENCE, NO CLOUD, OR, TO OBSTRUCT HIS SIGHT, 5 257
THROUGH CHAOS HURLD, OBSTRUCT THE MOUTH OF HELL 10 636
OBSTRUCT HEAV'N TOWRS, AND IN DERISION SETS 12 52

OBTAIN
OR SHALL THE ADVERSARIE THUS OBTAIN 3 156
LIKE HONOUR TO OBTAIN, AND AS HIS EYE 3 660
OBTAIN, ALL THY REQUEST WAS MY DECREE: 11 47

OBTAIN'D
BY FORCE IMPOSSIBLE, BY LEAVE OBTAIN'D 2 250
IMMOVEABLE TILL PEACE OBTAIN'D FROM FAULT 10 938

OBTAINE
BUT SAY I COULD REPENT AND COULD OBTAINE 4 93
OBTAINE: THOUGH TO RECOUNT ALMIGHTIE WORKS 7 112
IF ANSWERABLE STYLE I CAN OBTAINE 9 20
BEFORE THEE; AND NOT REPENTING, THIS OBTAINE . . 10 75

OBTAINS
OBTAINS THE BROW OF SOME HIGH-CLIMBING HILL, . . . 3 546

OBTRUDED
OBTRUDED ON US THUS? WHO IF WE KNEW 11 504

OBTRUSIVE
NOT OBVIOUS, NOT OBTRUSIVE, BUT RETIR'D, . . . 8 504

OBTUSE
OBTUSE, ALL TASTE OF PLEASURE MUST FORGOE, ... 11 541

OBVIOUS
INDISSOLUBLY FIRM; NOR OBVIOUS HILL, ... 6 69
LIGHT BACK TO THEM, IS OBVIOUS TO DISPUTE. 8 158
NOT OBVIOUS, NOT OBTRUSIVE, BUT RETIR'D, ... 8 504
WHERE OBVIOUS DUTIE EREWHILE APPEAR'D UNSAUGHT: . 10 106
MY OBVIOUS BREAST, ARMING TO OVERCOM 11 374

OCCASION
LET US NOT SLIP TH' OCCASION, WHETHER SCORN, . . . 1 178
NOR WILL OCCASION WANT, NOR SHALL WE NEED 2 341
IN ADAM, NOT TO LET TH' OCCASION PASS 5 453
OCCASION WHICH NOW SMILES, BEHOLD ALONE 9 480
DIRECT, OR BY OCCASION HATH PRESENTED 9 974

OCCASIONALLY
OCCASIONALLY; AND TO CONSUMMATE ALL, ... 8 556

OCCASIOND
BY MEE DONE AND OCCASIOND, OR REJOYCE 12 475

OCEAN
CREATED HUGEST THAT SWIM TH' OCEAN STREAM: 1 202
UNDER YON BOYLING OCEAN, WRAPT IN CHAINS; 2 183
ILLIMITABLE OCEAN WITHOUT BOUND, ... 2 892
UNCERTAIN WHICH, IN OCEAN OR IN AIR, ... 3 76
TO DARKNESS, SUCH AS BOUND THE OCEAN WAVE. 3 539
CHEAR'D WITH THE GRATEFUL SMELL OLD OCEAN SMILES. 4 165
TO TH' OCEAN ILES, AND IN TH' ASCENDING SCALE . . 4 354
WITH EARTH AND OCEAN MEETS, THE SETTING SUN . . . 4 540
WITH WHEELS YET HOV'RING O'RE THE OCEAN BRIM, . . 5 140
SUPS WITH THE OCEAN: THOUGH IN HEAV'N THE TREES . 5 426
CRYSTALLIN OCEAN, AND THE LOUD MISRULE 7 271
MAIN OCEAN FLOW'D, NOT IDLE, BUT WITH WARME . . . 7 279
TEMPEST THE OCEAN: THERE LEVIATHAN 7 412
EARTH WITH HER NETHER OCEAN CIRCUMFUS'D, ... 7 624
WEST FROM ORONTES TO THE OCEAN BARR'D 9 80
BROKE UP, SHALL HEAVE THE OCEAN TO USURP 11 827

ODDS
PRAEEMINENT BY SO MUCH ODDS, WHILE THOU 4 447
AS NOT OF POWER, AT ONCE; NOR ODDS APPEERD 6 319
OR EQUAL WHAT BETWEEN US MADE THE ODDS, ... 6 441
BUT KEEP THE ODDS OF KNOWLEDGE IN MY POWER 9 820
WITH ODDS WHAT WARR HATH LOST, AND FULLY AVENG'D . 10 374

ODIOUS
HIS ODIOUS OFFRINGS, AND ADORE THE GODS 1 475
AT LAST THIS ODIOUS OFFSPRING WHOM THOU SEEST . . 2 781
AND SILENCE ON THE ODIOUS DINN OF WARR; 6 408
TEDIOUS, UNSHAR'D WITH THEE, AND ODIOUS SOON. . . 9 880
AND UTTER ODIOUS TRUTH, THAT GOD WOULD COME . . . 11 704

ODORIFEROUS
FANNING THIR ODORIFEROUS WINGS DISPENSE 4 157

ODOROUS
SO ENTERTAIND THOSE ODOROUS SWEETS THE FIEND . . . 4 166
GROVES WHOSE RICH TREES WEPT ODOROUS GUMMS AND BALME, ... 4 248
ACANTHUS, AND EACH ODOROUS BUSHIE SHRUB 4 696
SPIRITS ODOROUS BREATHES: FLOURS AND THIR FRUIT . 5 482

ODOUR
WHEN FROM THE BOUGHES A SAVORIE ODOUR BLOW'N, . . . 9 579

ODOURS
AMBROSIAL ODOURS AND AMBROSIAL FLOWERS, ... 2 245
WITH ODOURS; THERE YE SHALL BE FED AND FILL'D . . 2 843
SABEAN ODOURS FROM THE SPICIE SHOARE 4 162
AND FLOURING ODOURS, CASSIA, NARD, AND BALME; . . 5 293
WITH ROSE AND ODOURS FROM THE SHRUB UNFUM'D. . . 5 349
FLUNG ROSE, FLUNG ODOURS FROM THE SPICIE SHRUB, . 8 517

OECHALIA
AS WHEN ALCIDES FROM OECHALIA CROWN'D 2 542

OETA
AND LICHAS FROM THE TOP OF OETA THREW 2 545

OFF
FAVOUR'D OF HEAV'N SO HIGHLY, TO FALL OFF 1 30
FROM OFF THE TOSSING OF THESE FIERY WAVES, ... 1 184
FORTHWITH UPRIGHT HE REARS FROM OFF THE POOL . . 1 221
MAIM'D HIS BRUTE IMAGE, HEAD AND HANDS LOPT OFF . 1 459
HER MISCHIEF, AND PURGE OFF THE BASER FIRE . . . 2 141
PURGE OFF THIS GLOOM; THE SOFT DELICIOUS AIR, . . 2 400
FARR OFF FROM THESE A SLOW AND SILENT STREAM, . . 2 582
AS WHEN FARR OFF AT SEA A FLEET DESCRI'D . . . 2 636
FARR OFF THE FLYING FIEND: AT LAST APPEER . . . 2 643
FARR OFF TH' EMPYREAL HEAV'N, EXTENDED WIDE . . 2 1047
CUT OFF, AND FOR THE BOOK OF KNOWLEDG FAIR . . . 3 47
NOT FARR OFF HEAV'N, IN THE PRECINCTS OF LIGHT, . 3 88
FREELY PUT OFF, AND FOR HIM LASTLY DYE 3 240
NOW IN LOOSE GARLANDS THICK THROWN OFF, THE BRIGHT 3 362
SATAN ALIGHTED WALKS: A GLOBE FARR OFF 3 422
FLY O'RE THE BACKSIDE OF THE WORLD FARR OFF . . 3 494
ANDROMEDA FARR OFF ATLANTIC SEAS 3 559
FAR OFF AND FEARLESS, NOR WITH CAUSE TO BOAST, . 4 14
MOZAMBIC, OFF AT SEA NORTH-EAST WINDES BLOW . . 4 161
HANDED THEY WENT; AND EAS'D THE PUTTING OFF . . 4 739
UZZIEL, HALF THESE DRAW OFF, AND COAST THE SOUTH . 4 782
SHADOWIE SETS OFF THE FACE OF THINGS; IN VAIN, . 5 43
YIELD NECTAR, THOUGH FROM OFF THE BOUGHS EACH MORN 5 428
OUR MINDS AND TEACH US TO CAST OFF THIS YOKE? . . 5 786
FROM OFF THE FILES OF WARR; THERE THEY HIM LAID . 6 339
FLEW OFF, AND INTO STRANGE VAGARIES FELL, . . . 6 614
HE ONWARD CAME, FARR OFF HIS COMING SHON, . . . 6 768
BUT DRIVE FARR OFF THE BARBAROUS DISSONANCE . . 7 32
GOD HATH BID DWELL FARR OFF ALL ANXIOUS CARES, . 8 185
WHEN OUT OF HOPE, BEHOLD HER, NOT FARR OFF, . . 8 481
SO YE SHALL DIE PERHAPS, BY PUTTING OFF 9 713
MY COMING SEEN FAR OFF? I MISS THEE HERE, . . . 10 104
REMOV'D FARR OFF; THEN PITTYING HOW THEY STOOD . 10 211
BROKE OFF THE REST; SO MUCH OF DEATH HER THOUGHTS 10 1008
THAT CUTS US OFF FROM HOPE, AND FAVOURS ONELY . . 10 1043
EJECT HIM TAINTED NOW, AND PURGE HIM OFF . . . 11 52
WIDE WAVING, ALL APPROACH FARR OFF TO FRIGHT, . . 11 121
OF GLORY, AND FARR OFF HIS STEPS ADORE. 11 333
CONTENDING, AND REMOV'D HIS TENTS FARR OFF; . . 11 727

OFFAL
WITH SUCKT AND GLUTTED OFFAL, AT ONE FLING . . . 10 633

OFFENCE
BEGAN TO BLOOM, BUT SOON FOR MANS OFFENCE . . . 3 355
FOR MANS OFFENCE. O UNEXAMPL'D LOVE, ... 3 410
BUT OF OFFENCE AND TROUBLE, WHICH MY MIND . . . 5 34
TH' OFFENCE, THAT MAN SHOULD THUS ATTAIN TO KNOW? 9 726
NOR ALTER'D HIS OFFENCE; YET GOD AT LAST . . . 10 171
THE DAY OF HIS OFFENCE. WHY COMES NOT DEATH, . . 10 854

OFFEND
CONSULT HOW WE MAY HENCEFORTH MOST OFFEND . . . 1 187
WITH WHAT MORE FORCIBLE WE MAY OFFEND 6 465
LET NOT MY WORDS OFFEND THEE, HEAV'NLY POWER, . . 8 379
TO OFFEND, DISCOUNT'NANC'T BOTH, AND DISCOMPOS'D; 10 110
BUT SOLEMN AND SUBLIME, WHOM NOT TO OFFEND, . . 11 236

OFFENDED
AND PIOUS AWE, THAT FEARD TO HAVE OFFENDED. . . 5 135
OFFENDED, WORTH YOUR LAUGHTER, HATH GIV'N UP . . 10 488
CHEWD BITTER ASHES, WHICH TH' OFFENDED TASTE . . 10 566
I BEARE THEE, AND UNWEETING HAVE OFFENDED, . . . 10 916
BY PRAYER TH' OFFENDED DEITIE TO APPEASE, . . . 11 149
OFFENDED; FEARLESS OF REPROACH AND SCORN, . . . 11 811

OFFENDING
NOT MIND US NOT OFFENDING, SATISFI'D 2 212

OFFENSIVE
HER TEMPLE ON TH' OFFENSIVE MOUNTAIN, BUILT . . . 1 443

OFFER
OTHERS AMONG THE CHIEF MIGHT OFFER NOW 2 469
I OFFER, ON MEE LET THINE ANGER FALL; 3 237
OFFER SWEET SMELLING GUMMS AND FRUITS AND FLOURS: 11 327
HIS PLACE, TO OFFER INCENSE, MYRRH, AND GOLD; . . 12 363

OFFER'D
GLAD TO BE OFFER'D, HE ATTENDS THE WILL 3 270
AND ANGER WOULDST RESENT THE OFFER'D WRONG, . . 9 300
OF THY FULL BRANCHES OFFER'D FREE TO ALL; . . . 9 802
LIFE OFFER'D, OR SOON BEG TO LAY IT DOWN, . . . 11 506

OFFERD
TH' INCENSED DEITIE, WHILE OFFERD GRACE 3 187
SECOND TO THEE, OFFERD HIMSELF TO DIE 3 409
LONGER THY OFFERD GOOD, WHY ELSE SET HERE? . . . 5 63
FOR JOY OF OFFERD PEACE: BUT I SUPPOSE 6 617
HIS DEATH FOR MAN, AS MANY AS OFFERD LIFE . . . 12 425

OFFERING
ATTONEMENT FOR HIMSELF OR OFFERING MEET, . . . 3 234
FOR ENVIE THAT HIS BROTHERS OFFERING FOUND . . . 11 456

OFFERINGS
OUR SERVILE OFFERINGS. THIS MUST BE OUR TASK . . 2 246

OMNIPRESENCE

HATH OMNIPRESENCE) AND THE WORK ORDAIN'D, 7 590
NOT THIS ROCK ONELY; HIS OMNIPRESENCE FILLS 11 336

OMNISCIENT

OMNISCIENT THOUGHT. TRUE IS, LESS FIRMLY ARM'D, 6 430
ONELY OMNISCIENT, HATH SUPPREST IN NIGHT, 7 123
OMNISCIENT, WHO IN ALL THINGS WISE AND JUST, 10 7

ONCE

AT ONCE AS FAR AS ANGELS KENN HE VIEWS 1 59
JOYND WITH ME ONCE, NOW MISERY HATH JOYND 1 90
IN THIS UNHAPPY MANSION, OR ONCE MORE 1 268
IF ONCE THEY HEAR THAT VOYCE, THIR LIVELIEST PLEDGE 1 274
WARRIERS, THE FLOWR OF HEAV'N, ONCE YOURS, NOW LOST, 1 316
A LEPER ONCE HE LOST AND GAIN'D A KING, 1 471
(FAR OTHER ONCE BEHELD IN BLISS) CONDEMN'D 1 607
AT ONCE WITH JOY AND FEAR HIS HEART REBOUNDS. 1 788
ARM'D WITH HELL FLAMES AND FURY ALL AT ONCE 2 61
WILL HE, SO WISE, LET LOOSE AT ONCE HIS IRE, 2 155
WILL ONCE MORE LIFT US UP, IN SPIGHT OF FATE, 2 393
FORBIDDING; AND AT ONCE WITH HIM THEY ROSE; 2 475
THIR RISING ALL AT ONCE WAS AS THE SOUND 2 476
ALL TASTE OF LIVING WIGHT, AS ONCE IT FLED 2 613
FOR NEVER BUT ONCE MORE WAS EITHER LIKE 2 721
NOW IN THINE EYE SO FOUL, ONCE DEEMD SO FAIR 2 748
TO KNOW, AND THIS ONCE KNOWN, SHALL SOON RETURN, 2 839
COULD ONCE HAVE MOV'D; THEN IN THE KEY-HOLE TURNS 2 876
(WHICH IS MY PRESENT JOURNEY) AND ONCE MORE 2 985
BUT HEE ONCE PAST, SOON AFTER WHEN MAN FELL, 2 1023
OF LIVING SAPHIRE, ONCE HIS NATIVE SEAT; 2 1050
HIS OWN WORKS AND THEIR WORKS AT ONCE TO VIEW: 3 59
FREELY VOUTSAFT; ONCE MORE I WILL RENEW 3 175
UPHELD BY ME, YET ONCE MORE HE SHALL STAND 3 178
CAN NEVER SEEK, ONCE DEAD IN SINS AND LOST; 3 233
IMMORTAL AMARANT, A FLOUR WHICH ONCE 3 353
OF ALL THIS WORLD AT ONCE. AS WHEN A SCOUT 3 543
WHERE NO ILL SEEMS: WHICH NOW FOR ONCE BEGUIL'D 3 689
I FELL, HOW GLORIOUS ONCE ABOVE THY SPHEARE; 4 39
BY OWING OWES NOT, BUT STILL PAYS, AT ONCE 4 56
URIEL ONCE WARND; WHOSE EYE PURSU'D HIM DOWN 4 125
BLOSSOMS AND FRUITS AT ONCE OF GOLDEN HUE 4 148
KNOW YE NOT MEE? YE KNEW ME ONCE NO MATE 4 828
OR ALL AT ONCE; MORE GLORIE WILL BE WONN, 4 853
THOUGH FOR POSSESSION PUT TO TRY ONCE MORE 4 941
ONCE FAWN'D, AND CRING'D, AND SERVILLY ADOR'D 4 959
IN THEM AT ONCE TO RUIN ALL MANKIND. 5 228
AT ONCE ON TH' EASTERN CLIFF OF PARADISE 5 275
THE RUIN OF SO MANY GLORIOUS ONCE 5 567
SQUADRONS AT ONCE, WITH HUGE TWO-HANDED SWAY 6 251
THY MALICE INTO THOUSANDS, ONCE UPRIGHT 6 270
AS NOT OF POWER, AT ONCE; NOR ODDS APPEERD 6 319
ONCE FOUND, WHICH YET UNFOUND MOST WOULD HAVE THOUGHT 6 500
NOT LONG, FOR SUDDEN ALL AT ONCE THIR REEDS 6 582
IF OUR PROPOSALS ONCE AGAIN WERE HEARD 6 618
AT ONCE THE FOUR SPRED OUT THIR STARRIE WINGS 6 827
THEE ONCE TO GAINE COMPANION OF HIS WOE. 6 907
LEAST FROM THIS FLYING STEED UNREIN'D, (AS ONCE 7 17
(SO CALL HIM, BRIGHTER ONCE AMIDST THE HOST 7 132
PASTURING AT ONCE, AND IN BROAD HERDS UPSPRUNG. 7 462
AT ONCE CAME FORTH WHATEVER CREEPS THE GROUND, 7 475
FROM THEE ALONE, WHICH ON US BOTH AT ONCE 9 303
NOT TO DEFERR; HUNGER AND THIRST AT ONCE, 9 586
TO REACH, AND FEED AT ONCE BOTH BODIE AND MIND? 9 779
THIR INWARD STATE OF MIND, CALM REGION ONCE 9 1125
AS DELOS FLOATING ONCE; THE REST HIS LOOK 10 296
AND DIPSAS (NOT SO THICK SWARM'D ONCE THE SOIL 10 526
WHOM THEY TRIUMPH'D ONCE LAPST. THUS WERE THEY PLAGU'D 10 572
ONCE ACTUAL, NOW IN BODY, AND TO DWELL 10 587
IS PROPAGATED CURSE. O VOICE ONCE HEARD 10 729
OF NATURE, AND NOT FILL THE WORLD AT ONCE 10 892
THEN BOTH OUR SELVES AND SEED AT ONCE TO FREE 10 999
WHEN GOD DESCENDED, AND PERHAPS ONCE MORE 11 75
WITH WHOSE STOL'N FRUIT MAN ONCE MORE TO DELUDE. 11 125
AS ONCE THOU SLEPST, WHILE SHEE TO LIFE WAS FORMD. 11 369
TH' IMAGE OF GOD IN MAN CREATED ONCE 11 508
HIS CHILDREN, ALL IN VIEW DESTROYD AT ONCE; 11 761
AT ONCE, BY MY FOREKNOWLEDGE GAINING BIRTH 11 768
A DOVE SENT FORTH ONCE AND AGEN TO SPIE 11 857
MOSES ONCE MORE HIS POTENT ROD EXTENDS 12 211

ONE

WITH LOSS OF EDEN, TILL ONE GREATER MAN 1 4
FOR ONE RESTRAINT, LORDS OF THE WORLD BESIDES? 1 32
AS ONE GREAT FURNACE FLAM'D, YET FROM THOSE FLAMES 1 62
ONE NEXT HIMSELF IN POWER, AND NEXT IN CRIME, 1 79
RECEIVE THY NEW POSSESSOR: ONE WHO BRINGS 1 252
OF ALIENATED JUDAH. NEXT CAME ONE 1 457
FOR ONE OF SYRIAN MODE, WHEREON TO BURN 1 474
JEHOVAH, WHO IN ONE NIGHT WHEN HE PASS'D 1 487
FROM EGYPT MARCHING, EQUAL'D WITH ONE STROKE 1 488
MONARCH IN HEAV'N, TILL THEN AS ONE SECURE 1 638
AS IN AN ORGAN FROM ONE BLAST OF WIND 1 708
ONE DAY UPON OUR HEADS; WHILE WE PERHAPS 2 178

ONE (CONTINUED)

VIEWS ALL THINGS AT ONE VIEW? HE FROM HEAV'NS HIGHTH 2 190
OF MANKIND IN ONE ROOT, AND EARTH WITH HELL 2 383
THE TEMPTING STREAM, WITH ONE SMALL DROP TO LOOSE 2 607
ALL IN ONE MOMENT, AND SO NEER THE BRINK; 2 609
THE ONE SEEM'D WOMAN TO THE WASTE, AND FAIR, 2 650
THY LINGRING, OR WITH ONE STROKE OF THIS DART 2 702
HIS WRATH WHICH ONE DAY WILL DESTROY YE BOTH. 2 734
THIS UNCOUTH ERRAND SOLE, AND ONE FOR ALL 2 827
AND WISDOME AT ONE ENTRANCE QUITE SHUT OUT. 3 50
POTABLE GOLD, WHEN WITH ONE VERTUOUS TOUCH 3 608
TH' ARCH-ANGEL URIEL, ONE OF THE SEAV'N 3 648
ONE STEP NO MORE THEN FROM HIMSELF CAN FLY 4 22
I SDEIND SUBJECTION, AND THOUGHT ONE STEP HIGHER 4 50
AS ONE CONTINU'D BRAKE, THE UNDERGROWTH 4 175
ONE GATE THERE ONLY WAS, AND THAT LOOK'D EAST 4 178
AT ONE SLIGHT BOUND HIGH OVER LEAP'D ALL BOUND 4 181
OF THOSE FOURFOOTED KINDES, HIMSELF NOW ONE, 4 397
HIS COUCHANT WATCH, AS ONE WHO CHOSE HIS GROUND 4 406
THIS ONE, THIS EASIE CHARGE, OF ALL THE TREES 4 421
ONE EASIE PROHIBITION, WHO ENJOY 4 433
IMPARADIS'T IN ONE ANOTHERS ARMS 4 506
ONE FATAL TREE THERE STANDS OF KNOWLEDGE CALL'D, 4 514
CONSPICUOUS FARR, WINDING WITH ONE ASCENT 4 545
ACCESSIBLE FROM EARTH, ONE ENTRANCE HIGH; 4 546
LOST SIGHT OF HIM; ONE OF THE BANISHT CREW 4 573
O LOSS OF ONE IN HEAV'N TO JUDGE OF WISE, 4 904
CLOSE AT MINE EAR ONE CALL'D ME FORTH TO WALK 5 36
ONE SHAPD AND WING'D LIKE ONE OF THOSE FROM HEAV'N 5 55
THAT ONE CELESTIAL FATHER GIVES TO ALL. 5 403
O ADAM, ONE ALMIGHTIE IS, FROM WHOM 5 469
SUCH TO PERFECTION, ONE FIRST MATTER ALL, 5 472
UNITED AS ONE INDIVIDUAL SOULE 5 610
BOTH WAKING WE WERE ONE; HOW THEN CAN NOW 5 678
OR SEVERAL ONE BY ONE, THE REGENT POWERS, 5 697
AND ALL THE SEA, FROM ONE ENTIRE GLOBOSE 5 753
TOO MUCH TO ONE, BUT DOUBLE HOW ENDUR'D, 5 783
TO ONE AND TO HIS IMAGE NOW PROCLAIM'D? 5 784
ONE OVER ALL WITH UNSUCCEEDED POWER. 5 821
OUR HAPPIE STATE UNDER ONE HEAD MORE NEER 5 830
OR ALL ANGELIC NATURE JOIND IN ONE, 5 834
ONE OF OUR NUMBER THUS REDUC'T BECOMES, 5 843
WITH JOY AND ACCLAMATIONS LOUD, THAT ONE 6 23
THAT OF SO MANY MYRIADS FALL'N, YET ONE 6 24
UNANIMOUS, AS SONS OF ONE GREAT SIRE 6 95
REACHING BEYOND ALL LIMIT AT ONE BLOW 6 140
TO HEAV'NLY SOULES HAD BIN ALL ONE; BUT NOW 6 165
UPLIFTED IMMINENT ONE STROKE THEY AIM'D 6 317
THREATN'D, NOR FROM THE HOLIE ONE OF HEAV'N 6 359
WHO HAVE SUSTAIND ONE DAY IN DOUBTFUL FIGHT 6 423
(AND IF ONE DAY, WHY NOT ETERNAL DAYES?) 6 424
AS ONE HE STOOD ESCAP'T FROM CRUEL FIGHT, 6 448
SOME ONE INTENT ON MISCHIEF, OR INSPIR'D 6 503
PROVIDE, PERNICIOUS WITH ONE TOUCH TO FIRE. 6 520
UNDER THIR HEAD IMBODIED ALL IN ONE. 6 779
ONE SPIRIT IN THEM RUL'D, AND EVERY EYE 6 848
BEFORE HIS MEMORIE, AS ONE WHOSE DROUTH 7 66
ANOTHER WORLD, OUT OF ONE MAN A RACE 7 155
ONE KINGDOM, JOY AND UNION WITHOUT END. 7 161
ONE FOOT HE CENTER'D, AND THE OTHER TURN'D 7 228
INTO ONE PLACE, AND LET DRY LAND APPEER. 7 284
WAS SET, AND TWILIGHT FROM THE EAST CAME ONE, 7 583
ONE DAY AND NIGHT; IN ALL THIR VAST SURVEY 8 24
GREATER SO MANIFOLD TO THIS ONE USE, 8 29
AND LIVD: ONE CAME, METHOUGHT, OF SHAPE DIVINE, 8 295
THE ONE INTENSE, THE OTHER STILL REMISS 8 387
AND THROUGH ALL NUMBERS ABSOLUTE, THOUGH ONE; 8 421
AND THEY SHALL BE ONE FLESH, ONE HEART, ONE SOULE. 8 499
AS ONE INTENDED FIRST, NOT AFTER MADE 8 555
UNION OF MIND, OR IN US BOTH ONE SOULE; 8 604
THE INFERNAL POWERS, IN ONE DAY TO HAVE MARR'D 9 136
NOT LONGER THEN SINCE I IN ONE NIGHT FREED 9 140
ONE NIGHT OR TWO WITH WANTON GROWTH DERIDES 9 211
AS ONE WHO LOVES, AND SOME UNKINDNESS MEETS, 9 271
AS ONE WHO LONG IN POPULOUS CITY PENT, 9 445
THAT SPACE THE EVIL ONE ABSTRACTED STOOD 9 463
AT FIRST, AS ONE WHO SOUGHT ACCESS, BUT FEARD 9 511
HALF WHAT IN THEE IS FAIR, ONE MAN EXCEPT, 9 545
WHO SEES THEE? (AND WHAT IS ONE?) WHO SHOULDST BE SEEN 9 546
FAST BY A FOUNTAIN, ONE SMALL THICKET PAST 9 628
FOR BEASTS IT SEEMS: YET THAT ONE BEAST WHICH FIRST 9 769
SO HAVING SAID, AS ONE FROM SAD DISMAY 9 917
OUR STATE CANNOT BE SEVERD, WE ARE ONE, 9 958
ONE FLESH; TO LOOSE THEE WERE TO LOOSE MY SELF. 9 959
ONE HEART, ONE SOUL IN BOTH; WHEREOF GOOD PROOFF 9 967
TO UNDERGOE WITH MEE ONE GUILT, ONE CRIME, 9 971
FOR THIS ONE TREE HAD BIN FORBIDDEN TEN. 9 1026
MINE WITH THIS GLORIOUS WORK, AND MADE ONE REALM 10 391
HELL AND THIS WORLD, ONE REALM, ONE CONTINENT 10 392
FOR ONE FORBIDDEN TREE A MULTITUDE 10 554
WITH SUCKT AND GLUTTED OFFAL, AT ONE FLING 10 633
WITH CRUEL EXPECTATION. YET ONE DOUBT 10 782
THAT DEATH BE NOT ONE STROAK, AS I SUPPOS'D, 10 809
FOR ONE MANS FAULT THUS GUILTLESS BE CONDEMN'D, 10 823
SAID HEE, WITH ONE THRICE ACCEPTABLE STROKE 10 855
WHILE YET WE LIVE, SCARSE ONE SHORT HOUR PERHAPS, 10 923

ONE (CONTINUED)

AS JOYN'D IN INJURIES, ONE ENMITIE	10	925
AS ONE DISARM'D, HIS ANGER ALL HE LOST,	10	945
MADE ONE WITH ME AS I WITH THEE AM ONE.	11	44
O SONS, LIKE ONE OF US MAN IS BECOME	11	84
OR ONE SHORT SIGH OF HUMANE BREATH, UP-BORNE	11	147
ONE WAY THE SELF-SAME HOUR? WHY IN THE EAST	11	203
ONE MAN, ASSASSIN-LIKE HAD LEVIED WARR,	11	219
ONE OF THE HEAV'NLY HOST, AND BY HIS GATE	11	230
AND ONE BAD ACT WITH MANY DEEDS WELL DONE	11	256
IN OTHER PART STOOD ONE WHO AT THE FORGE	11	564
ONE WAY A BAND SELECT FROM FORAGE DRIVES	11	646
OF MIDDLE AGE ONE RISING, EMINENT	11	665
ALL LEFT, IN ONE SMALL BOTTOM SWUM IMBARK'T.	11	753
ONE MAN EXCEPT, THE ONELY SON OF LIGHT	11	808
THE ONE JUST MAN ALIVE; BY HIS COMMAND	11	818
FARR LESS I NOW LAMENT FOR ONE WHOLE WORLD	11	874
FOR ONE MAN FOUND SO PERFET AND SO JUST,	11	876
SUCH GRACE SHALL ONE JUST MAN FIND IN HIS SIGHT,	11	890
AS ONE WHO IN HIS JOURNEY BATES AT NOONE,	12	1
THUS THOU HAST SEEN ONE WORLD BEGIN AND END;	12	6
UNDER PATERNAL RULE; TILL ONE SHALL RISE	12	24
AND ONE PECULIAR NATION TO SELECT	12	111
A NATION FROM ONE FAITHFUL MAN TO SPRING:	12	113
LAST WITH ONE MIDNIGHT STROKE ALL THE FIRST-BORN	12	189
ONE GREATER, OF WHOSE DAY HE SHALL FORETELL,	12	242
THE HOLY ONE WITH MORTAL MEN TO DWELL:	12	248
AND ALL THE RULE, ONE EMPIRE; ONELY ADD	12	581
BOTH IN ONE FAITH UNANIMOUS THOUGH SAD,	12	603

ONELY

SERV'D ONELY TO DISCOVER SIGHTS OF WOE,	1	64
FIRM CONCORD HOLDS, MEN ONELY DISAGREE	2	497
HIS ONELY SON; ON EARTH HE FIRST BEHELD	3	64
OUR TWO FIRST PARENTS, YET THE ONELY TWO	3	65
THUS TO HIS ONELY SON FORESEEING SPAKE.	3	79
ONELY BEGOTTEN SON, SEEST THOU WHAT RAGE	3	80
WHERE ONELY WHAT THEY NEEDS MUST DO, APPEARD,	3	105
OF ALL THINGS MADE, AND JUDGEST ONELY RIGHT.	3	155
NO SOONER DID THY DEAR AND ONELY SON	3	403
HYPOCRISIE, THE ONELY EVIL THAT WALKS	3	683
CONTENTED WITH REPORT HEAR ONELY IN HEAV'N:	3	701
THE LOWER STILL I FALL, ONELY SUPREAM	4	91
SO VARIOUS, NOT TO TASTE THAT ONELY TREE	4	423
CAN IT BE DEATH? AND DO THEY ONELY STAND	4	518
MIGHT HAVE ENSU'D, NOR ONELY PARADISE	4	991
FORBIDD'N HERE, IT SEEMS, AS ONELY FIT	5	69
TO GIVE US ONELY GOOD; AND IF THE NIGHT	5	206
TWO ONELY, WHO YET BY SOV'RAN GIFT POSSESS	5	366
MY ONELY SON, AND ON THIS HOLY HILL	5	604
OF SURFET WHERE FULL MEASURE ONELY BOUNDS	5	639
AND SMILING TO HIS ONELY SON THUS SAID.	5	718
THIS ONELY TO CONSULT HOW WE MAY BEST	5	779
AS ONELY IN HIS ARM THE MOMENT LAY	6	239
NOR MULTITUDE, STAND ONELY AND BEHOLD	6	810
ONELY OMNISCIENT, HATH SUPPREST IN NIGHT,	7	123
WHICH ONELY THY SOLUTION CAN RESOLVE.	8	14
ONELY TO SHINE, YET SCARCE TO CONTRIBUTE	8	155
THINK ONELY WHAT CONCERNES THEE AND THY BEING;	8	174
NOT OF EARTH ONELY BUT OF HIGHEST HEAV'N.	8	178
NOT ONELY THESE FAIR BOUNDS, BUT ALL THE EARTH	8	338
INTENDED THEE, FOR TRIAL ONELY BROUGHT,	8	447
SUPERIOUR AND UNMOV'D, HERE ONELY WEAKE	8	532
EXPRESS THEY, BY LOOKS ONELY, OR DO THEY MIX	8	616
WARRS, HITHERTO THE ONELY ARGUMENT	9	28
FOR ONELY IN DESTROYING I FIND EASE	9	129
BUT HARM PRECEDES NOT SIN; ONELY OUR FOE	9	327
TOUCHD ONELY, THAT OUR TRIAL, WHEN LEAST SOUGHT,	9	380
THE ONELY TWO OF MANKINDE, BUT IN THEM	9	415
WITHIN ME CLEERE, NOT ONELY TO DISCERNE	9	681
HAD IT BEEN ONELY COVETING TO EYE	9	923
THEY SATE THEM DOWN TO WEEP, NOR ONELY TEARES	9	1121
NOR HEE THIR OUTWARD ONELY WITH THE SKINS	10	220
FOR IN POSSESSION SUCH, NOT ONELY OF RIGHT,	10	461
NOT TO DO ONELY, BUT TO WILL THE SAME	10	826
ON MEE, MEE ONELY, AS THE SOURSE AND SPRING	10	832
MY ONELY STRENGTH AND STAY: FORLORN OF THEE,	10	921
AGAINST GOD ONELY, I AGAINST GOD AND THEE,	10	931
MEE MEE ONELY JUST OBJECT OF HIS IRE.	10	936
THAT CUTS US OFF FROM HOPE, AND FAVOURS ONELY	10	1043
PAINS ONELY IN CHILD-BEARING WERE FORETOLD,	10	1051
RECESS, AND ONELY CONSOLATION LEFT	11	304
NOT THIS ROCK ONELY; HIS OMNIPRESENCE FILLS	11	336
BRED ONELY AND COMPLETED TO THE TASTE	11	618
FOR IN THOSE DAYES MIGHT ONELY SHALL BE ADMIR'D,	11	689
THE ONELY RIGHTEOUS IN A WORLD PERVERSE,	11	701
MY PART OF EVIL ONELY, EACH DAYES LOT	11	765
ONE MAN EXCEPT, THE ONELY SON OF LIGHT	11	808
HE GAVE US ONELY OVER BEAST, FISH, FOWL	12	67
SO ONELY CAN HIGH JUSTICE REST APPAID.	12	401
NOT ONELY TO THE SONS OF ABRAHAMS LOINES	12	447
LEFT ONELY IN THOSE WRITTEN RECORDS PURE,	12	513
AND LOVE WITH FEAR THE ONELY GOD, TO WALK	12	562
AND ALL THE RULE, ONE EMPIRE; ONELY ADD	12	581

ONLY

CREATED EVIL, FOR EVIL ONLY GOOD,	2	623
AGAINST THY ONLY SON? WHAT FURY O SON,	2	728

ONLY (CONTINUED)

TO MORTAL MEN, ABOVE WHICH ONLY SHON	3	268
O THOU IN HEAV'N AND EARTH THE ONLY PEACE	3	274
THOU THEREFORE WHOM THOU ONLY CANST REDEEM,	3	281
THEE ONLY EXTOLL'D, SON OF THY FATHERS MIGHT,	3	398
ONE GATE THERE ONLY WAS, AND THAT LOOK'D EAST	4	178
OF THAT LIFE-GIVING PLANT, BUT ONLY US'D	4	199
IF TRUE, HERE ONLY, AND OF DELICIOUS TASTE:	4	251
HEE FOR GOD ONLY, SHEE FOR GOD IN HIM:	4	299
THE ONLY SIGN OF OUR OBEDIENCE LEFT	4	428
NOT ONLY ENLIGHTEN, BUT WITH KINDLY HEATE	4	668
TO THEE NO REASON; WHO KNOWST ONLY GOOD,	4	895
AND TEMPERAT VAPORS BLAND, WHICH TH' ONLY SOUND	5	5
TO SPIRITUAL NATURES; ONLY THIS I KNOW,	5	402
THAT TO HIS ONLY SON BY RIGHT ENDU'D	5	815
AMONG THE FAITHLESS, FAITHFUL ONLY HEE;	5	897
THE THUNDERER OF HIS ONLY DREADED BOLT.	6	491
TO SATAN ONLY LIKE BOTH CRIME AND DOOM.	10	841

ONSET

BY SUDDEN ONSET, EITHER WITH HELL FIRE	2	364
OF ONSET ENDED SOON EACH MILDER THOUGHT.	6	98

ONWARD

THE MONSTER MOVING ONWARD CAME AS FAST	2	675
HIM THROUGH THE SPICIE FORREST ONWARD COM	5	298
AND ONWARD MOVE EMBATTELLD; WHEN BEHOLD	6	550
HE ONWARD CAME, FARR OFF HIS COMING SHON,	6	768
HEE ON HIS IMPIOUS FOES RIGHT ONWARD DROVE,	6	831
FROM THIS DAY ONWARD, WHICH I FEEL BEGUN	10	811

OOSE

AND ON THE WASHIE OOSE DEEP CHANNELS WORE;	7	303

OPACOUS

MEAN WHILE UPON THE FIRM OPACOUS GLOBE	3	418
ROUND THIS OPACOUS EARTH, THIS PUNCTUAL SPOT,	8	23

OPAL

WITH OPAL TOWRS AND BATTLEMENTS ADORN'D	2	1049

OPAQUE

SHADOW FROM BODY OPAQUE CAN FALL, AND THE AIRE,	3	619

OPE

ADAM, NOW OPE THINE EYES, AND FIRST BEHOLD	11	423

OPEN

OPEN OR UNDERSTOOD MUST BE RESOLV'D.	1	662
WHETHER OF OPEN WARR OR COVERT GUILE,	2	41
MY SENTENCE IS FOR OPEN WARR: OF WILES,	2	51
I SHOULD BE MUCH FOR OPEN WARR, O PEERS,	2	119
WARR THEREFORE, OPEN OR CONCEAL'D, ALIKE	2	187
DREAMING BY NIGHT UNDER THE OPEN SKIE,	3	514
OR OPEN ADMIRATION HIM BEHOLD	3	672
THE OPEN FIELD, AND WHERE THE UNPIERC'T SHADE	4	245
THAT OPEN NOW THIR CHOICEST BOSOM'D SMELLS	5	127
SOON AS THEY FORTH WERE COME TO OPEN SIGHT	5	138
OF BATTEL, OPEN WHEN, AND WHEN TO CLOSE	6	235
PEACE AND COMPOSURE, AND WITH OPEN BREST	6	560
TO ENTERTAIN THEM FAIR WITH OPEN FRONT	6	611
THEY OPEN TO THEMSELVES AT LENGTH THE WAY	7	158
OPEN, YE EVERLASTING GATES, THEY SUNG,	7	565
OPEN, YE HEAV'NS, YOUR LIVING DORES; LET IN	7	566
OPEN, AND HENCEFORTH OFT; FOR GOD WILL DEIGNE	7	569
IS OPEN? OR WILL GOD INCENSE HIS IRE	9	692
TO OPEN EYES, AND MAKE THEM GODS WHO TASTE;	9	866
IN OPEN SHEW, AND WITH ASCENTION BRIGHT	10	187
STOOD OPEN WIDE, BELCHING OUTRAGEOUS FLAME	10	232
WIDE OPEN AND UNGUARDED, SATAN PASS'D,	10	419
HIM FOLLOW'D ISSUING FORTH TO TH' OPEN FIELD,	10	533
BE OPEN, AND HIS HEART TO PITIE INCLINE,	10	1061
OF HEAV'N SET OPEN ON THE EARTH SHALL POWRE	11	825

OPEN'D

HER STORES WERE OPEN'D, AND THIS FIRMAMENT	2	175
THAT OPEN'D WIDE HER BLAZING PORTALS, LED	7	575

OPEND

OF HEAV'N ARRIV'D, THE GATE SELF-OPEND WIDE	5	254

OPENER

TH' EFFECTS TO CORRESPOND, OPENER MINE EYES,	9	875
TRUE OPENER OF MINE EYES, PRIME ANGEL BLEST,	11	598

OPENING

SIN OPENING, WHO THUS NOW TO DEATH BEGAN.	10	234

OPENS

STILL THREATNING TO DEVOUR ME OPENS WIDE,	4	77
OF TARTARUS, WHICH READY OPENS WIDE	6	54

OPERATION

BUT OF THE TREE WHOSE OPERATION BRINGS	8	323
IN PARADISE, OF OPERATION BLEST	9	796
FARR OTHER OPERATION FIRST DISPLAID,	9	1012

OPHION
OPHION WITH EURYNOME, THE WIDE- 10 581

OPHIR
AND SOFALA THOUGHT OPHIR, TO THE REALME 11 400

OPHIUCUS
THAT FIRES THE LENGTH OF OPHIUCUS HUGE 2 709

OPHIUSA
OPHIUSA) BUT STILL GREATEST HEE THE MIDST, 10 528

OPIATE
OF HERMES, OR HIS OPIATE ROD. MEAN WHILE 11 133

OPINION
AND SO REFUS'D MIGHT IN OPINION STAND 2 471
OUR KNOWLEDGE OR OPINION; THEN RETIRES 5 108

OPINIONS
HIS LAUGHTER AT THIR QUAINT OPINIONS WIDE 8 78

OP'N
UNFAST'NS: ON A SUDDEN OP'N FLIE 2 879
EXCEL'D HER POWER; THE GATES WIDE OP'N STOOD, 2 884
BOTH TURND, AND UNDER OP'N SKIE ADOR'D 4 721
DISPLAYD ON THE OP'N FIRMAMENT OF HEAV'N. 7 390
MINE EYES HE CLOS'D, BUT OP'N LEFT THE CELL 8 460

OP'ND
OP'ND INTO THE HILL A SPACIOUS WOUND 1 689
OF EREBUS. SHE OP'ND, BUT TO SHUT 2 883
DIRECT AGAINST WHICH OP'ND FROM BENEATH, 3 526
ATTENDANT ON THIR LORD: HEAV'N OP'ND WIDE 7 205
WHO STOOPING OP'ND MY LEFT SIDE, AND TOOK 8 465
OP'ND AND CLEERD, AND YE SHALL BE AS GODS, 9 708
AUGMENTED, OP'ND EYES, NEW HOPES, NEW JOYES, 9 985
SOON FOUND THIR EYES HOW OP'ND, AND THIR MINDS 9 1053
OP'ND WE FIND INDEED, AND FIND WE KNOW 9 1071
HIS EYES HE OP'ND, AND BEHELD A FIELD, 11 429

OP'NING
OP'NING THIR BRAZEN FOULDS DISCOVER WIDE 1 724
THREW FORTH, TILL ON THE LEFT SIDE OP'NING WIDE, 2 755
WITHOUT MY OP'NING. PENSIVE HERE I SAT 2 777
SO WIDE THE OP'NING SEEMD, WHERE BOUNDS WERE SET 3 538
SO BEAUTEOUS, OP'NING TO THE AMBIENT LIGHT. 6 481
AND CHRYSTAL WALL OF HEAV'N, WHICH OP'NING WIDE, 6 860
OP'NING THIR VARIOUS COLOURS, AND MADE GAY 7 318
OP'NING HER FERTIL WOOMB TEEM'D AT A BIRTH 7 454
OP'NING THE WAY, BUT OF DIVINE EFFECT 9 865
FROM THE FIRST OP'NING BUD, AND GAVE YE NAMES, 11 277
DOWN THE GREAT RIVER TO THE OP'NING GULF, 11 833
MINE EYES TRUE OP'NING, AND MY HEART MUCH EAS'D, 12 274

OP'NST
IN IGNORANCE, THOU OP'NST WISDOMS WAY, 9 809

OPPORTUNE
AND OPPORTUNE EXCURSION WE MAY CHANCE 2 396
MOST OPPORTUNE MIGHT SERVE HIS WILES, AND FOUND 9 85
THE WOMAN, OPPORTUNE TO ALL ATTEMPTS, 9 481

OPPOS'D
IF HE OPPOS'D; AND WITH AMBITIOUS AIM 1 41
HIS UTMOST POWER WITH ADVERSE POWER OPPOS'D 1 103
THE CURRENT OF HIS FURY THUS OPPOS'D. 5 808
HE HASTED, AND OPPOS'D THE ROCKIE ORB 6 254
THAT JEALOUS OF THIR SECRETS FIERCELY OPPOS'D 10 478

OPPOSE
TO SECOND, OR OPPOSE, OR UNDERTAKE 2 419
BUT FATE WITHSTANDS, AND TO OPPOSE TH' ATTEMPT 2 610
WERE BANDED TO OPPOSE HIS HIGH DECREE; 5 717
INSPIR'D WITH CONTRADICTION DURST OPPOSE 6 155
AGAINST SUCH HELLISH MISCHIEF FIT TO OPPOSE. 6 636

OPPOSITE
IN EMULATION OPPOSITE TO HEAV'N. 2 298
(SO CALL THAT OPPOSITE FAIR STARR) HER AIDE 3 727
AS I BENT DOWN TO LOOK, JUST OPPOSITE, 4 460
FORTH STEPPING OPPOSITE, HALF WAY HE MET 6 128
BLAZ'D OPPOSITE, WHILE EXPECTATION STOOD 6 306
BUT OPPOSITE IN LEVELD WEST WAS SET 7 376
IN SEXTILE, SQUARE, AND TRINE, AND OPPOSITE, 10 659

OPPOSITION
BEFORE MINE EYES IN OPPOSITION SITS 2 803
OF FIERCEST OPPOSITION IN MID SKIE, 6 314
IN FACTIOUS OPPOSITION, TILL AT LAST 11 664

OPPRESS'D
OPPRESS'D THEM, WEARIED WITH THIR AMOROUS PLAY. 9 1045

OPPRESSES
OPPRESSES ELSE WITH SURFET, AND SOON TURNS 7 129

OPPRESSION
FIRST FOUND ME, AND WITH SOFT OPPRESSION SEIS'D 8 288
PROCEEDED, AND OPPRESSION, AND SWORD-LAW 11 672

OPPREST
IMMORTAL VIGOR, THOUGH OPPREST AND FALL'N, 2 13
CAME SHADOWING, AND OPPREST WHOLE LEGIONS ARM'D, 6 655

OPPROBRIOUS
ON THAT OPPROBRIOUS HILL, AND MADE HIS GROVE 1 403
ACCEPT THIS DARK OPPROBRIOUS DEN OF SHAME, 2 58
OPPROBRIOUS, WITH HIS ROBE OF RIGHTEOUSNESS, 10 222

OPS
AND OPS, ERE YET DICTAEAN JOVE WAS BORN, 10 584

OPTIC
THROUGH OPTIC GLASS THE TUSCAN ARTIST VIEWS 1 288
THROUGH HIS GLAZ'D OPTIC TUBE YET NEVER SAW, 3 590

ORACLE
FAST BY THE ORACLE OF GOD; I THENCE 1 12
SO SPAKE THIS ORACLE, THEN VERIFI'D 10 182

ORATOR
AS WHEN OF OLD SOM ORATOR RENOUND 9 670

ORATORIE
THEN LOUDEST ORATORIE: YET THIR PORT 11 8

ORB
HUNG ON HIS SHOULDERS LIKE THE MOON, WHOSE ORB 1 287
BENEATH TH' AZORES; WHITHER THE PRIME ORB, 4 592
WITH THE FIXT STARRS, FIXT IN THIR ORB THAT FLIES, 5 176
ORB WITHIN ORB, THE FATHER INFINITE, 5 596
HE HASTED, AND OPPOS'D THE ROCKIE ORB 6 254
THE HOLLOW UNIVERSAL ORB THEY FILL'D, 7 257
IN THE SUNS ORB, MADE POROUS TO RECEIVE 7 361
CYCLE AND EPICYCLE, ORB IN ORB: 8 84
STOR'D IN EACH ORB PERHAPS WITH SOME THAT LIVE. 8 152
EACH ORB A GLIMPS OF LIGHT, CONVEYD SO FARR 8 156
GANGES AND INDUS: THUS THE ORB HE ROAM'D 9 82

ORB'D
FULL ORB'D THE MOON, AND WITH MORE PLEASING LIGHT 5 42

ORBE
FROM HELL CONTINU'D REACHING TH' UTMOST ORBE 2 1029
ASTRONOMER IN THE SUN'S LUCENT ORBE 3 589
HAD CIRCL'D HIS FULL ORBE, THE BIRTH MATURE 5 862

ORBED
FIT WELL HIS HELME, GRIPE FAST HIS ORBED SHIELD, 6 543

ORBES
IN WHICH OF ALL THESE SHINING ORBES HATH MAN 3 668
BUT ALL THESE SHINING ORBES HIS CHOICE TO DWELL; 3 670
FROM HER MOIST CONTINENT TO HIGHER ORBES. 5 422
RECORDED EMINENT. THUS WHEN IN ORBES 5 594
WITH DREADFUL SHADE CONTIGUOUS, AND THE ORBES 6 828

ORBICULAR
THAT ROWLD ORBICULAR, AND TURND TO STARRS 3 718
HIS QUADRATURE, FROM THY ORBICULAR WORLD, 10 381

ORBS
SO THICK A DROP SERENE HATH QUENCHT THIR ORBS, 3 25
THE LUMINOUS INFERIOR ORBS, ENCLOS'D 3 420
FOR AUGHT APPEERS, AND ON THIR ORBS IMPOSE 8 30
CENTRING RECEAV'ST FROM ALL THOSE ORBS; IN THEE, 9 109
YOU TWO THIS WAY, AMONG THESE NUMEROUS ORBS 10 397

ORCS
THE HAUNT OF SEALES AND ORCS, AND SEA-MEWS CLANG. 11 835

ORCUS
ORCUS AND ADES, AND THE DREADED NAME 2 964

ORDAIN
UNLESS TH' ALMIGHTY MAKER THEM ORDAIN 2 915

ORDAIN'D
FOR THOSE REBELLIOUS, HERE THEIR PRISON ORDAIN'D 1 71
AT THEE ORDAIN'D HIS DRUDGE, TO EXECUTE 2 732
UNCHANGEABLE, ETERNAL, WHICH ORDAIN'D 3 127
THIR FREEDOM, THEY THEMSELVES ORDAIN'D THIR FALL. 3 128
OUR BEING ORDAIN'D TO GOVERN, NOT TO SERVE? 5 802
FOR THEE I HAVE ORDAIN'D IT, AND THUS FARR 6 700
NUMBER TO THIS DAYES WORK IS NOT ORDAIN'D 6 809
GLORIE AND PRAISE, WHOSE WISDOM HAD ORDAIN'D 7 187
HATH OMNIPRESENCE) AND THE WORK ORDAIN'D, 7 590
ORDAIN'D FOR USES TO HIS LORD BEST KNOWN. 8 106
FIRST MAN, OF MEN INNUMERABLE ORDAIN'D 8 297
OF GOD ORDAIN'D THEM, HIS CREATING HAND 9 344
OF PLEASURE NOT FOR HIM ORDAIN'D: THEN SOON 9 470
SHALL SCAPE HIS PUNISHMENT ORDAIN'D, AND WEE 10 1039

ORDAIND
ALL THESE HIS WORKS SO WONDROUS HE ORDAIND, 3 665
O HAD HIS POWERFUL DESTINY ORDAIND 4 58
HIS FARR MORE PLEASANT GARDEN GOD ORDAIND; 4 215
ORDAIND BY THEE, AND THIS DELICIOUS PLACE 4 729
HE LEFT IT IN THY POWER, ORDAIND THY WILL 5 526
ORDAIND WITHOUT REDEMPTION, WITHOUT END. 5 615
TO ME TRANSGRESSOUR, WHO FOR THEE ORDAIND 11 164
THROUGH THE TWELVE TRIBES, TO RULE BY LAWS ORDAIND: 12 226

ORDAINE
AND LET THEM BE FOR LIGHTS AS I ORDAINE 7 343
ORDAINE THEM LAWES; PART SUCH AS APPERTAINE 12 230

ORDAINS
THAT SO ORDAINS: THIS WAS AT FIRST RESOLV'D, 2 201
UNARGU'D I OBEY; SO GOD ORDAINS, 4 636
OF SERVITUDE TO SERVE WHOM GOD ORDAINS, 6 175

ORDER
THESE WERE THE PRIME IN ORDER AND IN MIGHT; 1 506
THE WHOLE BATTALION VIEWS, THIR ORDER DUE, 1 569
OF ORDER, HOW IN SAFETY BEST WE MAY 2 280
IN ORDER CAME THE GRAND INFERNAL PEERS, 2 507
LIGHT SHON, AND ORDER FROM DISORDER SPRUNG: 3 713
IN ORDER, THOUGH TO NATIONS YET UNBORN, 4 663
WHAT ORDER, SO CONTRIV'D AS NOT TO MIX 5 334
SECRET THEY FINISH'D, AND IN ORDER SET, 6 522
IN ORDER, QUIT OF ALL IMPEDIMENT; 6 548
SHADED WITH BRANCHING PALME, EACH ORDER BRIGHT, 6 885
AND ALL THINGS IN BEST ORDER TO INVITE 9 402
OF LOWEST ORDER, PAST; AND FROM THE DORE 10 443
THIR ORDER: LAST THE SIRE, AND HIS THREE SONS 11 736

ORDER'D
OF WARRIERS OLD WITH ORDER'D SPEAR AND SHIELD, 1 565

ORDERING
SO ORDERING. I WITH LEAVE OF SPEECH IMPLOR'D, 8 377

ORDERLY
OF BIRDS IN ORDERLY ARRAY ON WING 6 74

ORDERS
EACH IN HIS HIERARCHIE, THE ORDERS BRIGHT. 1 737
UNDER THIR HIERARCHS IN ORDERS BRIGHT 5 587
OF HIERARCHIES, OF ORDERS, AND DEGREES; 5 591
EQUALLY FREE; FOR ORDERS AND DEGREES 5 792
TO THOSE BRIGHT ORDERS UTTERD THUS HIS VOICE. 10 615

O'RE
THIR PAINFUL STEPS O'RE THE BURNT SOYLE; AND NOW 1 562
WITHIN, HER AMPLE SPACES, O'RE THE SMOOTH 1 725
SHEER O'RE THE CHRYSTAL BATTLEMENTS; FROM MORN 1 742
O'RE HEAV'NS HIGH TOWRS TO FORCE RESISTLESS WAY, 2 62
OR CLOS AMBITION VARNISHT O'RE WITH ZEAL. 2 485
O'RE MANY A FROZEN, MANY A FIERIE ALPE, 2 620
ROWLS O'RE ELISIAN FLOURS HER AMBER STREAM; 3 359
HEAV'NS EVERLASTING FRAME, WHILE O'RE THE NECKS 3 395
FLY O'RE THE BACKSIDE OF THE WORLD FARR OFF 3 494
WAFTED BY ANGELS, OR FLEW O'RE THE LAKE 3 521
JUST O'RE THE BLISSFUL SEAT OF PARADISE, 3 527
O'RE SEA AND LAND; HIM SATAN THUS ACCOSTES; 3 653
LEAPS O'RE THE FENCE WITH EASE INTO THE FOULD: 4 187
IN AT THE WINDOW CLIMBS, OR O'RE THE TILES; 4 191
OF COOLE RECESS, O'RE WHICH THE MANTLING VINE 4 258
THROUGH WOOD, THROUGH WASTE, O'RE HILL, O'RE DALE
HIS ROAM. 4 538
AND O'RE THE DARK HER SILVER MANTLE THREW. 4 609
WITH WHEELS YET HOV'RING O'RE THE OCEAN BRIM, 5 140
EACH SHOULDER BROAD, CAME MANTLING O'RE HIS BREST 5 279
SO SAID, HE O'RE HIS SCEPTER BOWING, ROSE 6 746
O'RE SHIELDS AND HELMES, AND HELMED HEADS HE RODE 6 840
WITH CENTRIC AND ECCENTRIC SCRIBL'D O'RE, 8 83
O'RE OTHER CREATURES; YET WHEN I APPROACH 8 546
O'RE THE BLEW FIRMAMENT A RADIANT WHITE, 11 206
RODE TILTING O'RE THE WAVES, ALL DWELLINGS ELSE 11 747
RIS'N FROM A RIVER O'RE THE MARISH GLIDES, 12 630

ORE
THAT ORE THE REALM OF IMPIOUS PHARAOH HUNG 1 342
GOT THEM NEW NAMES, TILL WANDRING ORE THE EARTH, 1 365
AND ORE THE CELTIC ROAM'D THE UTMOST ISLES. 1 521
THAT IN HIS WOMB WAS HID METALLIC ORE, 1 673
WITH WOND'ROUS ART FOUND OUT THE MASSIE ORE, 1 703
SCOWLS ORE THE DARK'ND LANTSKIP SNOW, OR SHOWRE; 2 491
WITH WINGED COURSE ORE HILL OR MOARIE DALE, 2 944
ORE BOG OR STEEP, THROUGH STRAIT, ROUGH, DENSE, OR
RARE, 2 948
HUNG ORE MY REALM, LINK'D IN A GOLDEN CHAIN 2 1005
METALS OF DROSSIEST ORE TO PERFET GOLD 5 442
OF FLIGHT PURSU'D IN TH' AIR AND ORE THE GROUND 11 202
FROM UNDERGROUND) THE LIQUID ORE HE DREIND 11 570

OREAD
OREAD OR DRYAD, OR OF DELIA'S TRAINE, 9 387

OREB
OF OREB, OR OF SINAI, DIDST INSPIRE 1 7
THE CALF IN OREB: AND THE REBEL KING 1 484
HIS TRUMPET, HEARD IN OREB SINCE PERHAPS 11 74

OREBLOWN
SHOT AFTER US IN STORM, OREBLOWN HATH LAID 1 172

OREFLOW'D
WITH FRAGRANCE AND WITH JOY MY HEART OREFLOW'D. 8 266

ORELEAPT
SO MINDED, HAVE ORELEAPT THESE EARTHIE BOUNDS 4 583

OREPOW'RD
THEN SUCH COULD HAV OREPOW'RD SUCH FORCE AS OURS) 1 145

ORESHADES
ORESHADES; FOR THESE MID-HOURS, TILL EEVNING RISE 5 376

O'RESPREAD
ASCENDING, WHILE THE NORTH WIND SLEEPS, O'RESPREAD 2 489

ORETHREW
HATH VEXT THE RED-SEA COAST, WHOSE WAVES ORETHREW 1 306

OREWATCHT
SEA-FARING MEN OREWATCHT, WHOSE BARK BY CHANCE 2 288

OREWEARIED
OREWEARIED, THROUGH THE FAINT SATANIC HOST 6 392

OREWHELM
TO PIECES, AND OREWHELM WHATEVER STANDS 6 489

O'REWHELM'D
THERE THE COMPANIONS OF HIS FALL, O'REWHELM'D 1 76

ORGAN
AS IN AN ORGAN FROM ONE BLAST OF WIND 1 708
WAS HEARD, OF HARP AND ORGAN; AND WHO MOOVD 11 560

ORGANIC
ORGANIC, OR IMPULSE OF VOCAL AIR, 9 530

ORGANS
THE ORGANS OF HER FANCIE, AND WITH THEM FORGE 4 802
AND DULCIMER, ALL ORGANS OF SWEET STOP, 7 596

ORGIES
YET THENCE HIS LUSTFUL ORGIES HE ENLARG'D 1 415

ORIENT
WITH ORIENT COLOURS WAVING: WITH THEM ROSE 1 546
SECURE, AND AT THE BRIGHTNING ORIENT BEAM 2 399
IMBELLISHT, THICK WITH SPARKLING ORIENT GEMMES 3 507
ROWLING ON ORIENT PEARL AND SANDS OF GOLD, 4 238
HIS ORIENT BEAMS, ON HERB, TREE, FRUIT, AND FLOUR, 4 644
ADVANCING, SOW'D THE EARTH WITH ORIENT PEARLE, 5 2
MOON, THAT NOW MEETST THE ORIENT SUN, NOW FLI'ST 5 175
SHOT THROUGH WITH ORIENT BEAMS; WHEN ALL THE PLAIN 6 15
NOW WHEN FAIR MORN ORIENT IN HEAV'N APPEERD 6 524
BY THE CELESTIAL QUIRES, WHEN ORIENT LIGHT 7 254
MORE ORIENT IN YON WESTERN CLOUD THAT DRAWS 11 205

ORIFICE
WITH HIDEOUS ORIFICE GAP'T ON US WIDE, 6 577

ORIGINAL
ALL HER ORIGINAL BRIGHTNESS, NOR APPEAR'D 1 592
THIR FRAIL ORIGINAL, AND FADED BLISS, 2 375
TO HER ORIGINAL DARKNESS AND YOUR SWAY 2 984
EXALTED FROM SO BASE ORIGINAL, 9 150
ORIGINAL; WHILE ADAM TOOK NO THOUGHT, 9 1004
TH' EFFECTS WHICH THY ORIGINAL CRIME HATH WROUGHT 11 424
SINCE THY ORIGINAL LAPSE, TRUE LIBERTIE 12 83

ORIGINALS
TH' ORIGINALS OF NATURE IN THIR CRUDE 6 511

ORION
AFLOAT, WHEN WITH FIERCE WINDS ORION ARM'D 1 305

ORISONS
THIR ORISONS, EACH MORNING DULY PAID 5 145
HAD ENDED NOW THIR ORISONS, AND FOUND 11 137

O'RMATCHT
FEARLESS TO BE O'RMATCHT BY LIVING MIGHT. 2 855

ORMUS
OUTSHON THE WEALTH OF ORMUS AND OF IND, 2 2

ORNAMENT
WITH REGAL ORNAMENT; THE MIDDLE PAIR 5 280
TOO MUCH OF ORNAMENT, IN OUTWARD SHEW 8 538

ORNAMENTS
OUR WONTED ORNAMENTS NOW SOILD AND STAIND, 9 1076

ORONTES
OF DAPHNE BY ORONTES, AND TH' INSPIR'D 4 273
WEST FROM ORONTES TO THE OCEAN BARR'D 9 80

ORPHEAN
WITH OTHER NOTES THEN TO TH' ORPHEAN LYRE 3 17

ORUS
OSIRIS, ISIS, ORUS AND THEIR TRAIN 1 478

OSIRIS
OSIRIS, ISIS, ORUS AND THEIR TRAIN 1 478

OTHER
THAT SPARKLING BLAZ'D, HIS OTHER PARTS BESIDES 1 194
PEOR HIS OTHER NAME, WHEN HE ENTIC'D 1 412
(FAR OTHER ONCE BEHELD IN BLISS) CONDEMN'D 1 607
TO LESS THEN GODS. ON TH' OTHER SIDE UP ROSE 2 108
WASTING THE EARTH, EACH OTHER TO DESTROY: 2 502
ECLIPSES AT THIR CHARMS. THE OTHER SHAPE, 2 666
MORE DREADFUL AND DEFORM: ON TH' OTHER SIDE 2 706
EACH CAST AT TH' OTHER, AS WHEN TWO BLACK CLOUDS 2 714
FOR WANT OF OTHER PREY, BUT THAT HE KNOWS 2 806
CONFINE WITH HEAV'N; OR IF SOM OTHER PLACE 2 977
CHARYBDIS, AND BY TH' OTHER WHIRLPOOL STEARD. 2 1020
WITH OTHER NOTES THEN TO TH' ORPHEAN LYRE 3 17
THOSE OTHER TWO EQUAL'D WITH ME IN FATE, 3 33
BY THE OTHER FIRST: MAN THEREFORE SHALL FIND GRACE, 3 131
THE OTHER NONE: IN MERCY AND JUSTICE BOTH, 3 132
SOM OTHER ABLE, AND AS WILLING, PAY 3 211
ALONE, FOR OTHER CREATURE IN THIS PLACE 3 442
OR HAPPINESS IN THIS OR TH' OTHER LIFE; 3 450
STARS DISTANT, BUT NIGH HAND SEEMD OTHER WORLDS, 3 566
OR OTHER WORLDS THEY SEEMD, OR HAPPY ILES, 3 567
HIS DAY, WHICH ELSE AS TH' OTHER HEMISPHERE 3 725
AMBITION. YET WHY NOT? SOM OTHER POWER 4 61
DRAWN TO HIS PART; BUT OTHER POWERS AS GREAT 4 63
WITH OTHER PROMISES AND OTHER VAUNTS 4 84
ON TH' OTHER SIDE: WHICH WHEN TH' ARCH-FELLON SAW 4 179
CREATURES OF OTHER MOULD, EARTH-BORN PERHAPS, 4 360
NOW OTHER, AS THIR SHAPE SERVD BEST HIS END 4 398
FROM US NO OTHER SERVICE THEN TO KEEP 4 420
OVER ALL OTHER CREATURES THAT POSSESS 4 431
MY OTHER HALF: WITH THAT THY GENTLE HAND 4 488
AMONG OUR OTHER TORMENTS NOT THE LEAST, 4 510
NO CREATURE THENCE: IF SPIRIT OF OTHER SORT, 4 582
OUR EYE-LIDS; OTHER CREATURES ALL DAY LONG 4 616
WHILE OTHER ANIMALS UNACTIVE RANGE, 4 621
OF COSTLIEST EMBLEM: OTHER CREATURE HERE 4 703
THIS SAID UNANIMOUS, AND OTHER RITES 4 736
WITH STRICTEST WATCH; THESE OTHER WHEEL THE NORTH, 4 783
PROVE CHAFF. ON TH' OTHER SIDE SATAN ALLARM'D 4 985
TWO OTHER PRECIOUS DROPS THAT READY STOOD, 5 132
AND YEE FIVE OTHER WANDRING FIRES THAT MOVE 5 177
NOT UNCONFORM TO OTHER SHINING GLOBES, 5 259
THUS SAID. NATIVE OF HEAV'N, FOR OTHER PLACE 5 361
BY DESTINIE, AND CAN NO OTHER CHOOSE? 5 534
ON OTHER SURETY NONE; FREELY WE SERVE, 5 538
HIS OTHER HALF IN THE GREAT ZONE OF HEAV'N, 5 560
EACH TO OTHER LIKE, MORE THEN ON EARTH IS THOUGHT? 5 576
THAT DAY, AS OTHER SOLEMN DAYES, THEY SPENT 5 618
WILL NOT BE NOW VOUTSAF'T, OTHER DECREES 5 884
LIGHT ISSUES FORTH, AND AT THE OTHER DORE 6 9
MEAN WHILE IN OTHER PARTS LIKE DEEDS DESERVD 6 354
SEEK NOT THE PRAISE OF MEN: THE OTHER SORT 6 376
CHERUBIC WAVING FIRES: ON TH' OTHER PART 6 413
IN NATURE NONE: IF OTHER HIDDEN CAUSE 6 442
THICK-RAMMD, AT TH' OTHER BORE WITH TOUCH OF FIRE 6 485
THE PUNISHMENT TO OTHER HAND BELONGS, 6 807
THEY MEASURE ALL, OF OTHER EXCELLENCE 6 821
NOR OTHER STRIFE WITH THEM DO I VOUTSAFE. 6 823
ONE FOOT HE CENTER'D, AND THE OTHER TURN'D 7 228
HITHER AS TO THIR FOUNTAIN OTHER STARRS 7 364
FROM HIM, FOR OTHER LIGHT SHE NEEDED NONE 7 378
THE SILENT HOURS, AND TH' OTHER WHOSE GAY TRAINE 7 444
AND BRUTE AS OTHER CREATURES, BUT ENDU'D 7 507
BE CENTER TO THE WORLD, AND OTHER STARRS 8 123
FROM THE SUNS BEAM MEET NIGHT, HER OTHER PART 8 139
ALLOTTED THERE; AND OTHER SUNS PERHAPS 8 148
OF OTHER CREATURES, AS HIM PLEASES BEST, 8 169
DREAM NOT OF OTHER WORLDS, WHAT CREATURES THERE 8 175
NOISE, OTHER THEN THE SOUND OF DANCE OR SONG, 8 243
THE ONE INTENSE, THE OTHER STILL REMISS 8 387
BENEATH WHAT OTHER CREATURES ARE TO THEE? 8 411
THY LIKENESS, THY FIT HELP, THY OTHER SELF, 8 450
HER LOSS, AND OTHER PLEASURES ALL ABJURE: 8 480
O'RE OTHER CREATURES; YET WHEN I APPROACH 8 546
BEYOND ALL OTHER, THINK THE SAME VOUTSAF'T 8 581
PROCEEDING, WHICH IN OTHER BEASTS OBSERV'D 9 94
TERRESTRIAL HEAV'N, DANC'T ROUND BY OTHER HEAV'NS 9 103
FOR WHILE SO NEAR EACH OTHER THUS ALL DAY 9 220
BUT OTHER DOUBT POSSESSES ME, LEAST HARM 9 251
TO OTHER SPEEDIE AIDE MIGHT LEND AT NEED; 9 260
FIRST THY OBEDIENCE; TH' OTHER WHO CAN KNOW, 9 368
SAVE WHAT IS IN DESTROYING, OTHER JOY 9 478

OTHER (CONTINUED)
I WAS AT FIRST AS OTHER BEASTS THAT GRAZE 9 571
ALL OTHER BEASTS THAT SAW, WITH LIKE DESIRE 9 592
EACH THING ON EARTH; AND OTHER CARE PERHAPS 9 813
ON TH' OTHER SIDE, ADAM, SOON AS HE HEARD 9 888
FARR OTHER OPERATION FIRST DISPLAID, 9 1012
AS FROM UNREST, AND EACH THE OTHER VIEWING, 9 1052
THE PARTS OF EACH FOR OTHER, THAT SEEM MOST 9 1093
OR TO EACH OTHER, BUT APPARENT GUILT, 10 112
MY OTHER SELF, THE PARTNER OF MY LIFE; 10 128
O SON, WHY SIT WE HERE EACH OTHER VIEWING 10 235
IN OTHER WORLDS, AND HAPPIER SEAT PROVIDES 10 237
THEN SUFFERD. TH' OTHER WAY SATAN WENT DOWN 10 414
EACH OTHER, TILL SUPPLANTED DOWN HE FELL 10 513
THEY SAW, BUT OTHER SIGHT INSTEAD, A CROWD 10 538
HER OFFICE THEY PRESCRIB'D, TO TH' OTHER FIVE 10 657
DEVOURD EACH OTHER; NOR STOOD MUCH IN AWE 10 712
OR IN SOME OTHER DISMAL PLACE WHO KNOWS 10 787
WITH OTHER ECHO LATE I TAUGHT YOUR SHADES 10 861
TO ANSWER, AND RESOUND FARR OTHER SONG. 10 862
OR FIND SOME OTHER WAY TO GENERATE 10 894
EACH OTHER, BLAM'D ENOUGH ELSEWHERE, BUT STRIVE 10 959
THIS OTHER SERV'D BUT TO ETERNIZE WOE; 11 60
FARR OTHER NAME DESERVING. BUT THE FIELD 11 171
THAT NEVER WILL IN OTHER CLIMATE GROW, 11 274
AND WILDE, HOW SHALL WE BREATH IN OTHER AIRE 11 284
NEW REAPT, THE OTHER PART SHEEP-WALKS AND FOULDS; 11 431
BUT IS THERE YET NO OTHER WAY, BESIDES 11 527
IN OTHER PART STOOD ONE WHO AT THE FORGE 11 564
IN OTHER PART THE SCEPTER'D HARALDS CALL 11 660
AMONG THE BUILDERS; EACH TO OTHER CALLS 12 57
WHOSE FOUL IDOLATRIES, AND OTHER FAULTS 12 337
TH' ARCHANGEL STOOD, AND FROM THE OTHER HILL 12 626

OTHERS
EVIL TO OTHERS, AND ENRAG'D MIGHT SEE 1 216
IN OTHERS COUNT'NANCE READ HIS OWN DISMAY 2 422
OTHERS AMONG THE CHIEF MIGHT OFFER NOW 2 469
OTHERS WITH VAST TYPHOEAN RAGE MORE FELL 2 539
INTO TH' EUBOIC SEA. OTHERS MORE MILDE, 2 546
OTHERS APART SAT ON A HILL RETIR'D, 2 557
OTHERS CAME SINGLE; HE WHO TO BE DEEMD 3 469
OTHERS WHOSE FRUIT BURNISHT WITH GOLDEN RINDE 4 249
GAVE PROOF UNHEEDED; OTHERS ON THE GRASS 4 350
SOLE, OR RESPONSIVE EACH TO OTHERS NOTE 4 683
OF OTHERS, WHO APPROVE NOT TO TRANSGRESS 4 880
THE FALL OF OTHERS FROM LIKE STATE OF BLISS; 5 241
DEFENCE, WHILE OTHERS BORE HIM ON THIR SHIELDS 6 337
SOON BANDED; OTHERS FROM THE DAWNING HILLS 6 528
OTHERS ON SILVER LAKES AND RIVERS BATH'D 7 437
THE MID AEREAL SKIE: OTHERS ON GROUND 7 442
BY WHAT I SEEK, BUT OTHERS TO MAKE SUCH 9 127
ANGELS, NOR THINK SUPERFLUOUS OTHERS AID. 9 308
THOUGH OTHERS ENVIE WHAT THEY CANNOT GIVE; 9 805
EACH OTHERS BURDEN IN OUR SHARE OF WOE; 10 961
TO BE TO OTHERS CAUSE OF MISERY, 10 982
THE OTHERS NOT, FOR HIS WAS NOT SINCERE; 11 443
WILL BE AVENG'D, AND TH' OTHERS FAITH APPROV'D 11 458
OF CATTEL GRAZING: OTHERS, WHENCE THE SOUND 11 558
DESERTED: OTHERS TO A CITIE STRONG 11 655
ASSAULTING; OTHERS FROM THE WALL DEFEND 11 657
THOUGH OF REBELLION OTHERS HE ACCUSE. 12 37

OTHERWISE
FAR OTHERWISE TH' INVIOLABLE SAINTS 6 398
FARR OTHERWISE, TRANSPORTED I BEHOLD, 8 529
FARR OTHERWISE TH' EVENT, NOT DEATH, BUT LIFE 9 984

OUGHT
TO DO OUGHT GOOD NEVER WILL BE OUR TASK, 1 159
HIS SECRETS TO BE SCANN'D BY THEM WHO OUGHT 8 74
FOR STILL THEY KNEW, AND OUGHT TO HAVE STILL REMEMBER'D 10 12
SINCE THIS DAYS DEATH DENOUNC'T, IF OUGHT I SEE, 10 962
BUT THAT FROM US OUGHT SHOULD ASCEND TO HEAV'N 11 143

OUNCE
AND RAMPANT SHAKES HIS BRINDED MAIN; THE OUNCE, 7 466

OUNCES
DANDL'D THE KID; BEARS, TYGERS, OUNCES, PARDS, 4 344

OUT
ROSE OUT OF CHAOS: OR IF SION HILL 1 10
HAD CAST HIM OUT FROM HEAV'N, WITH ALL HIS HOST 1 37
OUT OF OUR EVIL SEEK TO BRING FORTH GOOD, 1 163
AND OUT OF GOOD STILL TO FIND MEANS OF EVIL; 1 165
SO STRETCHT OUT HUGE IN LENGTH THE ARCH-FIEND LAY 1 209
BE NO MEMORIAL BLOTTED OUT AND RAS'D 1 362
JEHOVAH THUNDRING OUT OF SION, THRON'D 1 386
WORDS INTERWOVE WITH SIGHS FOUND OUT THIR WAY. 1 621
AND DIG'D OUT RIBS OF GOLD. LET NONE ADMIRE 1 690
WITH WOND'ROUS ART FOUND OUT THE MASSIE ORE, 1 703
ANON OUT OF THE EARTH A FABRICK HUGE 1 710
THEN TO DWELL HERE, DRIV'N OUT FROM BLISS, CONDEMN'D 2 86
THRIVE UNDER EVIL, AND WORK EASE OUT OF PAIN 2 261
AND THROUGH THE PALPABLE OBSCURE FIND OUT 2 406

OUT (CONTINUED)
AND HARD, THAT OUT OF HELL LEADS UP TO LIGHT; 2 433
OUT OF THY HEAD I SPRUNG: AMAZEMENT SEIS'D 2 758
MADE TO DESTROY: I FLED, AND CRY'D OUT DEATH; 2 787
FROM OUT THIS DARK AND DISMAL HOUSE OF PAIN, 2 823
POURD OUT BY MILLIONS HER VICTORIOUS BANDS 2 997
AND WISDOME AT ONE ENTRANCE QUITE SHUT OUT. 3 50
PLEAS'D, OUT OF HEAVEN SHALT LOOK DOWN AND SMILE, 3 257
FOUND OUT FOR MANKIND UNDER WRAUTH, O THOU 3 275
WHO JUSTLY HATH DRIVN OUT HIS REBELL FOES 3 677
OUT OF THE FERTIL GROUND HE CAUS'D TO GROW 4 216
ILL SENC'T FOR HEAV'N TO KEEP OUT SUCH A FOE 4 372
OUT OF MY SIDE TO THEE, NEEREST MY HEART 4 484
HIS PRAISE, WHO OUT OF DARKNESS CALL'D UP LIGHT. 5 179
ALL PERFET GOOD UNMEASUR'D OUT, DESCENDS, 5 399
CAST OUT FROM GOD AND BLESSED VISION, FALLS 5 613
THEN ALL THIS GLOBOUS EARTH IN PLAIN OUT SPRED, 5 649
NONE SECONDED, AS OUT OF SEASON JUDG'D, 5 850
PURSUING DRIVE THEM OUT FROM GOD AND BLISS, 6 52
WHO OUT OF SMALLEST THINGS COULD WITHOUT END 6 137
TO TROUBLE HOLY REST; HEAV'N CASTS THEE OUT 6 272
SPARE OUT OF LIFE PERHAPS, AND NOT REPINE, 6 460
OUT OF SUCH PRISON, THOUGH SPIRITS OF PUREST LIGHT, 6 660
PURSUE THESE SONS OF DARKNESS, DRIVE THEM OUT 6 715
AT ONCE THE FOUR SPRED OUT THIR STARRIE WINGS 6 827
NOT TO DESTROY, BUT ROOT THEM OUT OF HEAV'N: 6 855
ANOTHER WORLD, OUT OF ONE MAN A RACE 7 155
HAD DRIVEN OUT TH' UNGODLY FROM HIS SIGHT 7 185
GOOD OUT OF EVIL TO CREATE, IN STEAD 7 188
DISPARTED, AND BETWEEN SPUN OUT THE AIR, 7 241
DRAWS IN, AND AT HIS TRUNCK SPOUTS OUT A SEA. 7 416
LIMB'D AND FULL GROWN: OUT OF THE GROUND UP ROSE 7 456
SO SPACIOUS, AND HIS LINE STRETCHT OUT SO FARR; 8 102
WHO SINCE THE MORNING HOUR SET OUT FROM HEAV'N 8 111
WHEN OUT OF HOPE, BEHOLD HER, NOT FARR OFF, 8 481
OF GABRIEL OUT OF EDEN, NOW IMPROV'D 9 54
AND FLATTER'D OUT OF ALL, BELIEVING LIES 10 42
OUT OF THE GROUND WAST TAKEN, KNOW THY BIRTH, 10 207
THEN BOTH FROM OUT HELL GATES INTO THE WASTE 10 282
FROM OUT OF CHAOS TO THE OUT SIDE BARE 10 317
TRIUMPHANT OUT OF THIS INFERNAL PIT 10 464
TOILD OUT MY UNCOUTH PASSAGE, FORC'T TO RIDE 10 475
WHY AM I MOCKT WITH DEATH, AND LENGTH'ND OUT 10 774
OF WEAKNESS, NOT OF POWER. WILL HE, DRAW OUT, 10 801
AND HORRORS HAST THOU DRIV'N ME; OUT OF WHICH 10 843
OUT OF MY SIGHT, THOU SERPENT, THAT NAME BEST 10 867
WELL IF THROWN OUT, AS SUPERNUMERARIE 10 887
HE NEVER SHALL FIND OUT FIT MATE, BUT SUCH 10 899
WITHOUT REMORSE DRIVE OUT THE SINFUL PAIR, 11 105
OUT OF DESPAIRE, JOY, BUT WITH FEAR YET LINKT; 11 139
STRETCHT OUT TO THE AMPLEST REACH OF PROSPECT LAY, 11 380
THAT BEAT OUT LIFE; HE FELL, AND DEADLY PALE 11 446
GROAND OUT HIS SOUL WITH GUSHING BLOUD EFFUS'D. 11 447
OUT OF THY LOYNS; TH' UNJUST THE JUST HATH SLAIN, 11 455
RAISE OUT OF FRIENDSHIP HOSTIL DEEDS IN PEACE. 11 796
OUT OF HIS PLACE, PUSHD BY THE HORNED FLOUD, 11 831
FORTHWITH FROM OUT THE ARKE A RAVEN FLIES, 11 855
THAT HE RELENTS, NOT TO BLOT OUT MANKIND, 11 891
BOILES OUT FROM UNDER GROUND, THE MOUTH OF HELL; 12 42
QUITE OUT THIR NATIVE LANGUAGE, AND INSTEAD 12 54
PALPABLE DARKNESS, AND BLOT OUT THREE DAYES; 12 188
AND DUE TO THEIRS WHICH OUT OF THINE WILL GROW: 12 400
OUT OF HIS GRAVE, FRESH AS THE DAWNING LIGHT, 12 423
LIGHT OUT OF DARKNESS. FULL OF DOUBT I STAND, 12 473

OUTCAST
AND THEY OUTCAST FROM GOD, ARE HERE CONDEMN'D 2 694

OUT-CAST
OF US OUT-CAST, EXIL'D, HIS NEW DELIGHT, 4 106

OUTCRY
RIS'N, AND WITH HIDEOUS OUTCRY RUSH'D BETWEEN. 2 726
SO STRANGE THY OUTCRY, AND THY WORDS SO STRANGE 2 737

OUT-DONE
AND STRENGTH AND ART ARE EASILY OUT-DONE 1 696

OUTDOO
SO HEAV'NLY LOVE SHALL OUTDOO HELLISH HATE 3 298

OUT-FLEW
HE SPAKE: AND TO CONFIRM HIS WORDS, OUT-FLEW 1 663

OUTGREW
THIR GROWING WORK: FOR MUCH THIR WORK OUTGREW 9 202

OUTLIVE
THIS IS OLD AGE; BUT THEN THOU MUST OUTLIVE 11 538

OUTMOST
AS FROM HER OUTMOST WORKS A BROK'D FOE 2 1039

OUTRAGE
AND INJURY AND OUTRAGE: AND WHEN NIGHT 1 500
OUTRAGE FROM LIVELESS THINGS; BUT DISCORD FIRST 10 707

OUTRAGEOUS
OUTRAGEOUS TO DEVOUR, IMMURES US ROUND 2 435
OUTRAGEOUS AS A SEA, DARK, WASTEFUL, WILDE, 7 212
STOOD OPEN WIDE, BELCHING OUTRAGEOUS FLAME 10 232

OUTRAGIOUS
EMBOWELD WITH OUTRAGIOUS NOISE THE AIR, 6 587

OUT-SHINE
CLOTH'D WITH TRANSCENDENT BRIGHTNESS DIDST
OUT-SHINE 1 86

OUTSHON
OUTSHON THE WEALTH OF ORMUS AND OF IND, 2 2

OUT SIDE
FROM OUT OF CHAOS TO THE OUT SIDE BARE 10 317

OUT-SIDE
NEITHER HER OUT-SIDE FORMD SO FAIR, NOR AUGHT 8 596

OUTSIDE
ON THE BARE OUTSIDE OF THIS WORLD, THAT SEEM'D 3 74
AN OUTSIDE? FAIR NO DOUBT, AND WORTHY WELL 8 568

OUTSPREAD
WAST PRESENT, AND WITH MIGHTY WINGS OUTSPREAD 1 20

OUTSPRED
HIS BROODING WINGS THE SPIRIT OF GOD OUTSPRED, 7 235

OUTSTRETCHT
THE EARTH OUTSTRETCHT IMMENSE, A PROSPECT WIDE 5 88
OUTSTRETCHT HE LAY, ON THE COLD GROUND, AND OFT 10 851

OUTWARD
THOUGH CHANG'D IN OUTWARD LUSTRE; THAT FIXT MIND 1 97
EACH PERTURBATION SMOOTH'D WITH OUTWARD CALME, 4 120
INWARD AND OUTWARD BOTH, HIS IMAGE FAIRE: 8 221
TOO MUCH OF ORNAMENT, IN OUTWARD SHEW 8 538
IN OUTWARD ALSO HER RESEMBLING LESS 8 543
PERFET WITHIN, NO OUTWARD AID REQUIRE; 8 642
OF OUTWARD STRENGTH; WHILE SHAME, THOU LOOKING ON, 9 312
SECURE FROM OUTWARD FORCE; WITHIN HIMSELF 9 348
NOR HEE THIR OUTWARD ONELY WITH THE SKINS 10 220
HIS OUTWARD FREEDOM: TYRANNIE MUST BE, 12 95
DEPRIVES THEM OF THIR OUTWARD LIBERTIE, 12 100
WELL DEEM IN OUTWARD RITES AND SPECIOUS FORMES 12 534

OVER
OVER THE BURNING MARLE, NOT LIKE THOSE STEPS 1 296
FLED OVER ADRIA TO TH' HESPERIAN FIELDS, 1 520
BY OUR REVOLT, BUT OVER HELL EXTEND 2 326
OVER THE VAST ABRUPT, ERE HE ARRIVE 2 409
BARR'D OVER US PROHIBIT ALL EGRESS. 2 437
THEY FERRY OVER THIS LETHEAN SOUND 2 604
OVER THE CASPIAN, THEN STAND FRONT TO FRONT 2 716
OVER THE DARK ABYSS, WHOSE BOILING GULF 2 1027
OVER MOUNT SION, AND, THOUGH THAT WERE LARGE, 3 530
OVER THE PROMIS'D LAND TO GOD SO DEAR, 3 531
BEAR HIS SWIFT ERRANDS OVER MOIST AND DRY, 3 652
ACCESS DENI'D; AND OVER HEAD UP GREW 4 137
AT ONE SLIGHT BOUND HIGH OVER LEAP'D ALL BOUND 4 181
OVER ALL OTHER CREATURES THAT POSSESS 4 431
HUNG OVER HER ENAMOUR'D, AND BEHELD 5 13
BE OVER, AND THE SUN MORE COOLE DECLINE. 5 370
WIDE OVER ALL THE PLAIN, AND WIDER FARR 5 648
MONARCHIE OVER SUCH AS LIVE BY RIGHT 5 795
AND EQUAL OVER EQUALS TO LET REIGNE, 5 820
ONE OVER ALL WITH UNSUCCEEDED POWER. 5 821
THAT EQUAL OVER EQUALS MONARCH REIGNE: 5 832
CAME SUMMOND OVER EDEN TO RECEIVE 6 75
THIR NAMES OF THEE; SO OVER MANY A TRACT 6 76
OF CONFLICT; OVER HEAD THE DISMAL HISS 6 212
NOW NIGHT HER COURSE BEGAN, AND OVER HEAV'N 6 406
OVER THIR HEADS A CHRYSTAL FIRMAMENT, 6 757
HER TEMPERANCE OVER APPETITE, TO KNOW 7 127
APPEER'D NOT: OVER ALL THE FACE OF EARTH 7 278
THIR AIERIE CARAVAN HIGH OVER SEA'S 7 428
FLYING, AND OVER LANDS WITH MUTUAL WING 7 429
OVER THE FISH AND FOWLE OF SEA AND AIRE, 7 521
BEAST OF THE FIELD, AND OVER ALL THE EARTH, 7 522
OVER FISH OF THE SEA, AND FOWLE OF THE AIRE, 7 533
OVER HIS WORKS, ON EARTH, IN SEA, OR AIR, 7 629
AND OVER FIELDS AND WATERS, AS IN AIRE 8 301
FROM EDEN OVER PONTUS, AND THE POOLE 9 77
SET OVER ALL HIS WORKS, WHICH IN OUR FALL, 9 941
USURPING OVER SOVRAN REASON CLAIMD 9 1130
THINE SHALL SUBMIT, HEE OVER THEE SHALL RULE. 10 196
STAY HIS RETURN PERHAPS OVER THIS GULFE 10 253
OVER THIS MAINE FROM HELL TO THAT NEW WORLD 10 257
OVER THE FOAMING DEEP HIGH ARCHT, A BRIDGE 10 301
CAME TO THE SEA, AND OVER HELLESPONT 10 309
OVER THE VEXT ABYSS, FOLLOWING THE TRACK 10 314
BY ASTRACAN OVER THE SNOWIE PLAINES 10 432
OF HORRIBLE CONFUSION, OVER WHICH 10 472
TO RANGE IN, AND TO DWELL, AND OVER MAN 10 492
TO RULE, AS OVER ALL HE SHOULD HAVE RUL'D. 10 493

OVER (CONTINUED)
CLAD TO MEET MAN; OVER HIS LUCID ARMES 11 240
AND OVER THEM TRIUMPHANT DEATH HIS DART 11 491
TILL MANY YEARS OVER THY HEAD RETURN: 11 534
EWES AND THIR BLEATING LAMBS OVER THE PLAINE, . . 11 649
GRATEFUL TO HEAV'N, OVER HIS HEAD BEHOLDS . . . 11 864
OVER THE EARTH A CLOUD, WILL THEREIN SET . . . 11 896
OVER HIS BRETHREN, AND QUITE DISPOSSESS 12 28
HE GAVE US ONELY OVER BEAST, FISH, FOWL 12 67
BY HIS DONATION; BUT MAN OVER MEN 12 69
OVER FREE REASON, GOD IN JUDGEMENT JUST 12 92
OVER THE SEA; THE SEA HIS ROD OBEYS; 12 212
THE RECORDS OF HIS COV'NANT, OVER THESE 12 252
THE HEAV'NLY FIRES; OVER THE TENT A CLOUD . . . 12 256
BUT SOON REVIVES, DEATH OVER HIM NO POWER . . . 12 420
OVER HIS FOES AND THINE; THERE SHALL SURPRISE . . 12 453
FROM GOD, AND OVER WRAUTH GRACE SHALL ABOUND. . . 12 478
MERCIFULL OVER ALL HIS WORKS, WITH GOOD 12 565
WAV'D OVER BY THAT FLAMING BRAND, THE GATE . . . 12 643

OVERARCH'T
HIGH OVERARCH'T IMBOWR; OR SCATTERD SEDGE 1 304
HIGH OVERARCH'T, AND ECHOING WALKS BETWEEN; . . . 9 1107

OVERAWD
OF GESTURE OR LEST ACTION OVERAWD 9 460

OVERBUILT
DISPARTED CHAOS OVERBUILT EXCLAIMD, ... 10 416

OVERCOM
MY OBVIOUS BREAST, ARMING TO OVERCOM 11 374

OVERCOME
AND WHAT IS ELSE NOT TO BE OVERCOME? 1 109
HOW OVERCOME THIS DIRE CALAMITY, ... 1 189
BY FORCE, HATH OVERCOME BUT HALF HIS FOE. 1 649
OUR PURER ESSENCE THEN WILL OVERCOME 2 215
THE FIEND REPLI'D NOT, OVERCOME WITH RAGE; 4 857
MOST REASON IS THAT REASON OVERCOME. 6 126
SHAME TO BE OVERCOME OR OVER-REACHT 9 313
BUT FONDLY OVERCOME WITH FEMAL CHARM. 9 999
TO OVERCOME IN BATTLE, AND SUBDUE 11 691
TILL ISRAEL OVERCOME; SO CALL THE THIRD 12 267
THY ENEMIE; NOR SO IS OVERCOME 12 390

OVERCOMES
AT LENGTH FROM US MAY FIND, WHO OVERCOMES 1 648

OVERCOMING
STILL OVERCOMING EVIL, AND BY SMALL 12 566

OVER-FOND
THUS OVER-FOND, ON THAT WHICH IS NOT THINE; . . . 11 289

OVERGROWN
WITH THICKET OVERGROWN, GOTTESQUE AND WILDE, . . . 4 136
OUR WALK AT NOON, WITH BRANCHES OVERGROWN, ... 4 627
LOP OVERGROWN, OR PRUNE, OR PROP, OR BIND, ... 9 210

OVERGROWTH
TO STOP THIR OVERGROWTH, AS INMATE GUESTS 12 166

OVERHEAD
THICK OVERHEAD WITH VERDANT ROOF IMBOWR'D 9 1038

OVER-HEAD
OR DREAMS HE SEES, WHILE OVER-HEAD THE MOON . . . 1 784

OVER-HEARD
AND FROM THE PARTING ANGEL OVER-HEARD 9 276

OVERHUNG
THE REST WAS CRAGGIE CLIFF, THAT OVERHUNG 4 547

OVERJOY'D
BUT HE THUS OVERJOY'D, O FRUIT DIVINE, ... 5 67

OVERJOYD
I OVERJOYD COULD NOT FORBEAR ALOUD. 8 490

OVERLAID
WERE SET, AND DORIC PILLARS OVERLAID 1 714
OF CEDAR, OVERLAID WITH GOLD, THEREIN 12 250

OVERLAY
TO FORTIFIE THUS FARR, AND OVERLAY 10 370

OVERLIVE
FIXD ON THIS DAY? WHY DO I OVERLIVE, ... 10 773

OVERLOV'D
FOR LOSS OF LIFE AND PLEASURE OVERLOV'D. 10 1019

OVERMUCH
BY ATTRIBUTING OVERMUCH TO THINGS 8 565
I ALSO ERR'D IN OVERMUCH ADMIRING 9 1178

OVERPOWER
WE OVERPOWER? SUPPOSE HE SHOULD RELENT 2 237

OVERPOWERD
NOT TO BE OVERPOWERD, COMPANIONS DEARE, ... 6 419
MY EARTHLY BY HIS HEAV'NLY OVERPOWERD, ... 8 453

OVERPRAISING
SERPENT, THY OVERPRAISING LEAVES IN DOUBT 9 615

OVER-REACH
TO OVER-REACH, BUT WITH THE SERPENT MEETING . . . 10 879

OVER-REACHT
SHAME TO BE OVERCOME OR OVER-REACHT 9 313

OVER-RUL'D
AS IF PREDESTINATION OVER-RUL'D 3 114
BY NATURE FREE, NOT OVER-RUL'D BY FATE 5 527
FROM HIS STRONG HOLD OF HEAV'N HIGH OVER-RUL'D . . 6 228

OVERSHADOW
DARKNESS MUST OVERSHADOW ALL HIS BOUNDS, ... 12 187

OVERSHADOWING
MY OVERSHADOWING SPIRIT AND MIGHT WITH THEE . . . 7 165

OVERSPRED
HAD GON TO WRACK, WITH RUIN OVERSPRED, ... 6 670

OVERTHREW
SINCE SATAN FELL, WHOM FOLLIE OVERTHREW, ... 4 905
OF RAMIEL SCORCHT AND BLASTED OVERTHREW. 6 372

OVERTHROW
THAT WITH SAD OVERTHROW AND FOUL DEFEAT 1 135
REPEATED, AND INDECENT OVERTHROW 6 601

OVERTHROWN
MADE HEAD AGAINST HEAV'NS KING, THOUGH OVERTHROWN. 2 992
THE OVERTHROWN HE RAIS'D, AND AS A HEARD 6 856

OVERTOOK
MEE OVERTOOK HIS MOTHER ALL DISMAID, ... 2 792

OVERTRUSTING
HIM WHO TO WORTH IN WOMEN OVERTRUSTING 9 1183

OVERTURE
OUR OVERTURE, AND TURN NOT BACK PERVERSE; 6 562

OVERTURND
CHARIOT AND CHARIOTER LAY OVERTURND 6 390

OVERTURNES
OF EVILS, AND EXCESSIVE, OVERTURNES 6 463

OVERWEENING
THOUGH BY THE DEVIL HIMSELF, HIM OVERWEENING . . . 10 878

OVERWHELM
AND OVERWHELM THIR WARR: THE RACE ELECT 12 214

OVERWHELM'D
TO WHOM SAD EVE WITH SHAME NIGH OVERWHELM'D, . . . 10 159

OVERWHELMD
FLOOD OVERWHELMD, AND THEM WITH ALL THIR POMP . . . 11 748

OVERWOODIE
OF FRUIT-TREES OVERWOODIE REACHD TOO FARR 5 213

OW
BUT WHAT OW I TO HIS COMMANDS ABOVE 2 856
HIS FALL'N CONDITION IS, AND TO ME OW 3 181
SO BURTHENSOME STILL PAYING, STILL TO OW; 4 53

OWE
FOR WEE TO HIM INDEED ALL PRAISES OWE, ... 4 444
ATTEND: THAT THOU ART HAPPIE, OWE TO GOD; 5 520
THAT THOU CONTINU'ST SUCH, OWE TO THY SELF, . . . 5 521
NO LESS THEN FOR DELIVERANCE WHAT WE OWE. 6 468
FOR WHICH TO THE INFINITLY GOOD WE OWE 7 76
THUS GROWN. EXPERIENCE, NEXT TO THEE I OWE, . . . 9 807
THE FAITH THEY OWE; WHEN EARNESTLY THEY SEEK . . . 9 1141

OWES
BY OWING OWES NOT, BUT STILL PAYS, AT ONCE . . . 4 56

OWING
BY OWING OWES NOT, BUT STILL PAYS, AT ONCE . . . 4 56

OWN
OUR ENEMY, OUR OWN LOSS HOW REPAIR, ... 1 188
LEFT HIM AT LARGE TO HIS OWN DARK DESIGNS, ... 1 213
AS GODS, AND BY THIR OWN RECOVER'D STRENGTH, . . . 1 240
THE MIND IS ITS OWN PLACE, AND IN IT SELF 1 254
IN HIS OWN TEMPLE, ON THE GRUNSEL EDGE, ... 1 460

PAINT
TILL THE SUN PAINT YOUR FLEECIE SKIRTS WITH GOLD, 5 187

PAINTED
SOLAC'D THE WOODS, AND SPRED THIR PAINTED WINGS 7 434

PAINTS
HOW NATURE PAINTS HER COLOURS, HOW THE BEE 5 24

PAIR
SO HAND IN HAND THEY PASSD, THE LOVLIEST PAIR 4 321
AH GENTLE PAIR, YEE LITTLE THINK HOW NIGH 4 366
YET HAPPIE PAIR; ENJOY, TILL I RETURN, 4 534
BLEST PAIR; AND O YET HAPPIEST IF YE SEEK 4 774
THIS NIGHT THE HUMAN PAIR, HOW HE DESIGNES 5 227
HIS LINEAMENTS DIVINE; THE PAIR THAT CLAD 5 278
WITH REGAL ORNAMENT; THE MIDDLE PAIR 5 280
HARMONIE TO BEHOLD IN WEDDED PAIR 8 605
WITH GRATEFUL SMELL, FORTH CAME THE HUMAN PAIR 9 197
MEAN WHILE IN PARADISE THE HELLISH PAIR 10 585
SEEM'D THIR PETITION, THEN WHEN TH' ANCIENT PAIR 11 10
WITHOUT REMORSE DRIVE OUT THE SINFUL PAIR, 11 105

PAIRE
BY NIGHT, AND LISTENING WHERE THE HAPLESS PAIRE 10 342

PAIRS
AMONG THE TREES IN PAIRS THEY ROSE, THEY WALK'D: 7 459
SUCH PAIRS, IN LOVE AND MUTUAL HONOUR JOYN'D? 8 58
SO FITLY THEM IN PAIRS THOU HAST COMBIN'D; 8 394
CAME SEAVENS, AND PAIRS, AND ENTERD IN, AS TAUGHT 11 735

PALACE
THE WORK AS OF A KINGLY PALACE GATE 3 505
THE PALACE OF GREAT LUCIFER, (SO CALL 5 760
HER GATHER'D BEAMS, GREAT PALACE NOW OF LIGHT. 7 363
FROM SUSA HIS MEMNONIAN PALACE HIGH 10 308
FROGS, LICE AND FLIES MUST ALL HIS PALACE FILL 12 177

PALACES
IN COURTS AND PALACES HE ALSO REIGNS 1 497
SEA WITHOUT SHOAR; AND IN THIR PALACES 11 750

PALATE
AND PALATE CALL JUDICIOUS; I THE PRAISE 9 1020

PALE
CASTS PALE AND DREADFUL? THITHER LET US TEND 1 183
WHEELS HER PALE COURSE, THEY ON THIR MIRTH AND DANCE 1 786
WITH SHUDDRING HORROR PALE, AND EYES AGAST 2 616
AND IN HER PALE DOMINION CHECKS THE NIGHT. 3 732
THRICE CHANG'D WITH PALE, IRE, ENVIE AND DESPAIR, 4 115
DEFENSIVE SCARSE, OR WITH PALE FEAR SURPRIS'D, 6 393
SPEECHLESS HE STOOD AND PALE, TILL THUS AT LENGTH 9 894
ON HIS PALE HORSE: TO WHOM SIN THUS BEGAN. 10 590
HAD ENTERTAIND, AS DI'D HER CHEEKS WITH PALE. 10 1009
THAT BEAT OUT LIFE; HE FELL, AND DEADLY PALE 11 446

PALES
TO PALES, OR POMONA THUS ADORND, 9 393

PALESTINE
LONG AFTER KNOWN IN PALESTINE, AND NAM'D 1 80
OF PALESTINE, IN GATH AND ASCALON 1 465

PALM
CEDAR, AND PINE, AND FIRR, AND BRANCHING PALM, 4 139

PALME
SHADED WITH BRANCHING PALME, EACH ORDER BRIGHT, 6 885
OF STATELIEST COVERT, CEDAR, PINE, OR PALME, 9 435

PALMIE
OR PALMIE HILLOC, OR THE FLOURIE LAP 4 254

PALM-TREE
THEN FRUITS OF PALM-TREE PLEASANTEST TO THIRST 8 212

PALPABLE
AND THROUGH THE PALPABLE OBSCURE FIND OUT 2 406
PALPABLE DARKNESS, AND BLOT OUT THREE DAYES; 12 188

PAMPERD
THIR PAMPERD BOUGHES, AND NEEDED HANDS TO CHECK 5 214

PAN
THE TREMBLING LEAVES, WHILE UNIVERSAL PAN 4 266
PAN OR SILVANUS NEVER SLEPT, NOR NYMPH, 4 707

PANDAEMONIUM
AT PANDAEMONIUM, THE HIGH CAPITAL 1 756
OF PANDAEMONIUM, CITIE AND PROUD SEATE 10 424

PANDORA
MORE LOVELY THEN PANDORA, WHOM THE GODS 4 714

PANEAS
FROM PANEAS THE FOUNT OF JORDANS FLOOD 3 535

PANGS
STRANGE HORROR SEISE THEE, AND PANGS UNFELT BEFORE. 2 703
IN PANGS, AND NATURE GAVE A SECOND GROAN, 9 1001
INTESTIN STONE AND ULCER, COLIC PANGS, 11 484

PANIM
DEFI'D THE BEST OF PANIM CHIVALRY 1 765

PANOPLIE
OF GOLDEN PANOPLIE, REFULGENT HOST, 6 527
HEE IN CELESTIAL PANOPLIE ALL ARMD 6 760

PANSIES
PANSIES, AND VIOLETS, AND ASPHODEL, 9 1040

PAQUIN
TO PAQUIN OF SINAEAN KINGS, AND THENCE 11 390

PARADE
TO THIR NIGHT WATCHES IN WARLIKE PARADE, 4 780

PARADISE
IN PARADISE, FAST BY THE TREE OF LIFE 3 354
AND THEY WHO TO BE SURE OF PARADISE 3 478
THE PARADISE OF FOOLS, TO FEW UNKNOWN 3 496
JUST O'RE THE BLISSFUL SEAT OF PARADISE, 3 527
TO PARADISE THE HAPPIE SEAT OF MAN, 3 632
THAT SPOT TO WHICH I POINT IS PARADISE, 3 733
OF EDEN, WHERE DELICIOUS PARADISE, 4 132
THE VERDUROUS WALL OF PARADISE UP SPRUNG: 4 143
A HEAV'N ON EARTH, FOR BLISSFUL PARADISE 4 208
FLOURS WORTHY OF PARADISE WHICH NOT NICE ART 4 241
CASTALIAN SPRING, MIGHT WITH THIS PARADISE 4 274
TRUE PARADISE UNDER THE ETHIOP LINE 4 282
LIKE THIS FAIR PARADISE, YOUR SENSE, YET SUCH 4 379
IN PARADISE THAT BEAR DELICIOUS FRUIT 4 422
AGAINST THE EASTERN GATE OF PARADISE 4 542
IN PARADISE OF ALL THINGS COMMON ELSE. 4 752
MIGHT HAVE ENSU'D, NOR ONELY PARADISE 4 991
OF PARADISE AND EDENS HAPPIE PLAINS, 5 143
HATH RAISD IN PARADISE, AND HOW DISTURBD 5 226
AT ONCE ON TH' EASTERN CLIFF OF PARADISE 5 275
DESERVING PARADISE. IF EVER, THEN, 5 446
IN PARADISE TO ADAM OR HIS RACE, 7 45
IN WHAT HE GIVES TO THEE, THIS PARADISE 8 171
THIS PARADISE I GIVE THEE, COUNT IT THINE 8 319
WHERE TIGRIS AT THE FOOT OF PARADISE 9 71
THOU NEVER FROM THAT HOURE IN PARADISE 9 406
OF PARADISE FOR HELL, HOPE HERE TO TASTE 9 476
IN PARADISE, AND VARIOUS, YET UNKNOWN 9 619
IN PARADISE, OF OPERATION BLEST 9 796
OF SATAN DONE IN PARADISE, AND HOW 10 2
UP INTO HEAV'N FROM PARADISE IN HASTE 10 17
TO PARADISE FIRST TENDING, WHEN BEHOLD 10 326
ALL YOURS, RIGHT DOWN TO PARADISE DESCEND; 10 398
PLAC'T IN A PARADISE, BY OUR EXILE 10 484
WHICH GREW IN PARADISE, THE BAIT OF EVE 10 551
MEAN WHILE IN PARADISE THE HELLISH PAIR 10 585
ALIKE IS HELL, OR PARADISE, OR HEAVEN, 10 598
OF PARADISE, DEARE BOUGHT WITH LASTING WOES. 10 742
OF PARADISE COULD HAVE PRODUC'T, ERE FALL'N 11 29
BUT LONGER IN THAT PARADISE TO DWELL, 11 48
HAST THEE, AND FROM THE PARADISE OF GOD 11 104
LEAST PARADISE A RECEPTACLE PROVE 11 123
IN PARADISE, AND ON A HILL MADE ALT, 11 210
BUT LONGER IN THIS PARADISE TO DWELL 11 259
MUST I THUS LEAVE THEE PARADISE? THUS LEAVE 11 269
OF PARADISE OR EDEN: THIS HAD BEEN 11 342
OF PARADISE THE HIGHEST, FROM WHOSE TOP 11 378
OF PARADISE BY MIGHT OF WAVES BE MOOVD 11 830
SAFE TO ETERNAL PARADISE OF REST. 12 314
SHALL ALL BE PARADISE, FAR HAPPIER PLACE 12 464
TO LEAVE THIS PARADISE, BUT SHALT POSSESS 12 586
A PARADISE WITHIN THEE, HAPPIER FARR. 12 587
OF PARADISE, SO LATE THIR HAPPIE SEAT, 12 642

PARADISES
HERE OR IN HEAV'NLY PARADISES DWELL; 5 500

PARAGOND
OF THAT BRIGHT STARR TO SATAN PARAGOND. 10 426

PARALEL
SHOT PARALEL TO THE EARTH HIS DEWIE RAY, 5 141

PARAMOUNT
MIDST CAME THIR MIGHTY PARAMOUNT, AND SEEMD 2 508

PARCH
BEGAN TO PARCH THAT TEMPERATE CLIME; WHEREAT 12 636

PARCHING
WHERE ARMIES WHOLE HAVE SUNK: THE PARCHING AIR 2 594

PARCHT
YET PARCHT WITH SCALDING THURST AND HUNGER FIERCE, 10 556

PARDON
LEFT FOR REPENTANCE, NONE FOR PARDON LEFT? 4 80
WHILE PARDON MAY BE FOUND IN TIME BESOUGHT. 5 848
HUMBLY OUR FAULTS, AND PARDON BEG, WITH TEARS 10 1089
HUMBLY THIR FAULTS, AND PARDON BEG'D, WITH TEARS 10 1101
BUT INFINITE IN PARDON WAS MY JUDGE, 11 167

PARDONS
INDULGENCES, DISPENSES, PARDONS, BULLS, 3 492

PARDS
DANDL'D THE KID; BEARS, TYGERS, OUNCES, PARDS, 4 344

PARENT
AND ME HIS PARENT WOULD FULL SOON DEVOUR 2 805
THESE ARE THY GLORIOUS WORKS, PARENT OF GOOD, 5 153
THIR PARENT SOON DISCERN'D, THOUGH IN DISGUISE. 10 331
O PARENT, THESE ARE THY MAGNIFIC DEEDS, 10 354

PARENTS
MOV'D OUR GRAND PARENTS IN THAT HAPPY STATE, 1 29
OF HUMAN SACRIFICE, AND PARENTS TEARS, 1 393
THIR BOASTED PARENTS; TITAN HEAV'NS FIRST BORN 1 510
OUR TWO FIRST PARENTS, YET THE ONELY TWO 3 65
WHILE TIME WAS, OUR FIRST-PARENTS HAD BIN WARND 4 6
BY PARENTS, OR HIS HAPPIEST CHOICE TOO LATE 10 904
OUR LINGRING PARENTS, AND TO TH' EASTERN GATE 12 638

PARLE
THEY ENDED PARLE, AND BOTH ADDREST FOR FIGHT 6 296

PARSIMONIOUS
THE PARSIMONIOUS EMMET, PROVIDENT 7 485

PART
AND CALL THEM NOT TO SHARE WITH US THEIR PART 1 267
BY FALSITIES AND LYES THE GREATEST PART 1 367
NEW WARR, PROVOK'T; OUR BETTER PART REMAINS 1 645
SOLE KING, AND OF HIS KINGDOM LOOSE NO PART 2 325
BY SATAN, AND IN PART PROPOS'D: FOR WHENCE, 2 380
PART ON THE PLAIN, OR IN THE AIR SUBLIME 2 528
PART CURB THIR FIERIE STEEDS, OR SHUN THE GOAL 2 531
ANOTHER PART IN SQUADRONS AND GROSS BANDS, 2 570
DREW AFTER HIM THE THIRD PART OF HEAV'NS SONS 2 692
CLEER VICTORY, TO OUR PART LOSS AND ROUT 2 770
MELODIOUS PART, SUCH CONCORD IS IN HEAV'N. 3 371
THE UNIVERS, AND TO EACH INWARD PART 3 584
IF METTAL, PART SEEMD GOLD, PART SILVER CLEER; 3 595
DRAWN TO HIS PART; BUT OTHER POWERS AS GREAT 4 63
SOLE PARTNER AND SOLE PART OF ALL THESE JOYES, 4 411
PART OF MY SOUL I SEEK THEE, AND THEE CLAIM 4 487
TEMPER OR NOURISH, OR IN PART SHED DOWN 4 670
OUR CIRCUIT MEETS FULL WEST. AS FLAME THEY PART 4 784
NOT LIKELY TO PART HENCE WITHOUT CONTEST; 4 872
EVEN TO MY MOUTH OF THAT SAME FRUIT HELD PART 5 83
(WHOSE PRAISE BE EVER SUNG) TO MAN IN PART 5 405
DREW AFTER HIM THE THIRD PART OF HEAV'NS HOST: 5 710
A THIRD PART OF THE GODS, IN SYNOD MET 6 156
VITAL IN EVERY PART, NOT AS FRAIL MAN 6 345
CHERUBIC WAVING FIRES: ON TH' OTHER PART 6 413
PART HIDD'N VEINS DIGGD UP (NOR HATH THIS EARTH 6 516
OF MISSIVE RUIN; PART INCENTIVE REED 6 519
FREELY OUR PART; YEE WHO APPOINTED STAND 6 565
YET FARR THE GREATER PART HAVE KEPT, I SEE, 7 145
PART RISE IN CRYSTAL WALL, OR RIDGE DIRECT, 7 293
OF LIGHT BY FARR THE GREATER PART HE TOOK, 7 359
BANK THE MID SEA: PART SINGLE OR WITH MATE 7 403
AND BENDED DOLPHINS PLAY: PART HUGE OF BULK 7 410
PART LOOSLY WING THE REGION, PART MORE WISE 7 425
TRAVELLING EAST, AND WITH HER PART AVERSE 8 138
FROM THE SUNS BEAM MEET NIGHT, HER OTHER PART 8 139
OR NATURE FAILD IN MEE, AND LEFT SOME PART 8 534
ACCUSE NOT NATURE, SHE HATH DON HER PART; 8 561
FOLLOW'D WITH BENEDICTION. SINCE TO PART, 8 645
DISLOYAL ON THE PART OF MAN, REVOLT, 9 7
AND DISOBEDIENCE: ON THE PART OF HEAV'N 9 8
INTO A GULF SHOT UNDER GROUND, TILL PART 9 72
FOR GOD TOWARDS THEE HATH DONE HIS PART, DO THINE, 9 375
NEW PART PUTS ON, AND AS TO PASSION MOV'D, 9 667
STOOD IN HIMSELF COLLECTED, WHILE EACH PART, 9 673
FOR BLISS, AS THOU HAST PART, TO ME IS BLISS, 9 879
AND ELEGANT, OF SAPIENCE NO SMALL PART, 9 1018
THUS FENC'T, AND AS THEY THOUGHT, THIR SHAME IN PART 9 1119
UNSEEMLY TO BEARE RULE, WHICH WAS THY PART 10 155
ALREADIE IN PART, THOUGH HID IN GLOOMIEST SHADE, 10 716
NOR I ON MY PART SINGLE, IN MEE ALL 10 817
MORE TO THE PART SINISTER FROM ME DRAWN, 10 886
HIS FULL WRAUTH WHOSE THOU FEELST AS YET LEST PART, 10 951
PART OF OUR SENTENCE, THAT THY SEED SHALL BRUISE 10 1031
HOW SHALL I PART, AND WHITHER WANDER DOWN 11 282
PART ARABLE AND TILTH, WHEREON WERE SHEAVES 11 430
NEW REAPT, THE OTHER PART SHEEP-WALKS AND FOULDS; 11 431
IN PART, FROM SUCH DEFORMITIES BE FREE, 11 513
IN OTHER PART STOOD ONE WHO AT THE FORGE 11 564

PART (CONTINUED)
PART WIELD THIR ARMS, PART COURB THE FOAMING STEED, 11 643
IN OTHER PART THE SCEPTER'D HARALDS CALL 11 660
MY PART OF EVIL ONELY, EACH DAYES LOT 11 765
ORDAINE THEM LAWES; PART SUCH AS APPERTAINE 12 230
TO CIVIL JUSTICE, PART RELIGIOUS RITES 12 231
CANNOT APPEASE, NOR MAN THE MORAL PART 12 298
PART GOOD, PART BAD, OF BAD THE LONGER SCROWLE, 12 336
OF SPIRIT AND TRUTH; THE REST, FARR GREATER PART, 12 533

PARTAKE
HURL'D HEADLONG TO PARTAKE WITH US, SHALL CURSE 2 374
NONE SHALL PARTAKE WITH ME. THUS SAYING ROSE 2 466
PARTAKE THOU ALSO; HAPPIE THOUGH THOU ART, 5 75
BEREAVD OF HAPPINESS THOU MAIST PARTAKE 6 903
TO SIT INDULGENT, AND WITH HIM PARTAKE 9 3
OF CREATURES WANTING VOICE, THAT DONE, PARTAKE 9 199
AS YET MY CHANGE, AND GIVE HIM TO PARTAKE 9 818
LET HER WITH THEE PARTAKE WHAT THOU HAST HEARD, 12 598

PARTAKERS
PARTAKERS, AND UNCROPT FALLS TO THE GROUND. 4 731

PARTAKES
I SEE NOT WHO PARTAKES. IN SOLITUDE 8 364

PARTED
ROUND FROM HIS PARTED FORELOCK MANLY HUNG 4 302
SO PARTED THEY, THE ANGEL UP TO HEAV'N 8 652
THAT MORN WHEN FIRST THEY PARTED; BY THE TREE 9 848
MINE NEVER SHALL BE PARTED, BLISS OR WOE. 9 916
WAS I TO HAVE NEVER PARTED FROM THY SIDE? 9 1153
OF ALL THINGS PARTED BY TH' EMPYREAL BOUNDS, 10 380

PARTIAL
THIR SONG WAS PARTIAL, BUT THE HARMONY 2 552

PARTICIPATE
WITH ANGELS MAY PARTICIPATE, AND FIND 5 494
SUCH AS I SEEK, FIT TO PARTICIPATE 8 390

PARTICIPATING
AS THEY, PARTICIPATING GOD-LIKE FOOD? 9 717

PARTING
THE SEQUEL EACH OF PARTING AND OF FIGHT; 4 1003
ON EACH HAND PARTING, TO HIS SPEED GAVE WAY 5 252
BUT I CAN NOW NO MORE; THE PARTING SUN 8 630
AND FROM THE PARTING ANGEL OVER-HEARD 9 276
EXACTS OUR PARTING HENCE; AND SEE THE GUARDS, 12 590

PARTITION
OF THIS GREAT ROUND: PARTITION FIRM AND SURE, 7 267
LODG'D IN A SMALL PARTITION, AND THE REST 8 105

PARTNER
SOLE PARTNER AND SOLE PART OF ALL THESE JOYES, 4 411
MY OTHER SELF, THE PARTNER OF MY LIFE; 10 128

PARTS
THAT SPARKLING BLAZ'D, HIS OTHER PARTS BESIDES 1 194
OF OLD EUPHRATES TO THE BROOK THAT PARTS 1 420
VEX'D SCYLLA BATHING IN THE SEA THAT PARTS 2 660
NOT ALL PARTS LIKE, BUT ALL ALIKE INFORMD 3 593
NOR THOSE MYSTERIOUS PARTS WERE THEN CONCEALD, 4 312
MEAN WHILE IN OTHER PARTS LIKE DEEDS DESERVD 6 354
HIS HINDER PARTS, THEN SPRINGS AS BROKE FROM BONDS, 7 465
THE PARTS OF EACH FOR OTHER, THAT SEEM MOST 9 1093
THOSE MIDDLE PARTS, THAT THIS NEW COMMER, SHAME, 9 1097

PARTY
SEDUCE THEM TO OUR PARTY, THAT THIR GOD 2 368

PASS
POUR'D NEVER FROM HER FROZEN LOYNS, TO PASS 1 352
THESE PAST, IF ANY PASS, THE VOID PROFOUND 2 438
AND WISH AND STRUGGLE, AS THEY PASS, TO REACH 2 606
TO YONDER GATES? THROUGH THEM I MEAN TO PASS, 2 684
THESE GATES FOR EVER SHUT, WHICH NONE CAN PASS 2 776
UNDER SPREAD ENSIGNS MARCHING MIGHT PASS THROUGH 2 886
WITH EASIE INTERCOURSE PASS TO AND FRO 2 1031
OR IN FRANCISCAN THINK TO PASS DISGUIS'D; 3 480
THEY PASS THE PLANETS SEVEN, AND PASS THE FIXT, 3 481
SEE FARR AND WIDE: IN AT THIS GATE NONE PASS 4 579
IN ADAM, NOT TO LET TH' OCCASION PASS 5 453
INTENDS TO PASS TRIUMPHANT, AND GIVE LAWS. 5 693
FLOATS, AS THEY PASS, FANN'D WITH UNNUMBER'D PLUMES: 7 432
GOD HATH ASSIGN'D US, NOR OF ME SHALT PASS 9 231
IF CHANCE WITH NYMPHLIKE STEP FAIR VIRGIN PASS, 9 452
TO ME IS LOST. THEN LET ME NOT LET PASS 9 479
OF KNOWLEDGE HE MUST PASS, THERE HE HER MET, 9 849
FORETOLD SO LATELY WHAT WOULD COME TO PASS, 10 38
WHAT RESTS BUT THAT THE MORTAL SENTENCE PASS 10 48
TO PASS COMMODIOUSLY THIS LIFE, SUSTAIN'D 10 1083
SWALLOWS HIM WITH HIS HOST, BUT THEM LETS PASS 12 196

PASSAGE		
A PASSAGE DOWN TO TH' EARTH, A PASSAGE WIDE,	3	528
WHICH FROM HIS DARKSOM PASSAGE NOW APPEERS,	4	232
EASING THIR PASSAGE HENCE, FOR INTERCOURSE,	10	260
FORFEIT TO DEATH; FROM HENCE A PASSAGE BROAD,	10	304
TOILD OUT MY UNCOUTH PASSAGE, FORC'T TO RIDE	10	475
AND GUARD ALL PASSAGE TO THE TREE OF LIFE:	11	122
THY MORTAL PASSAGE WHEN IT COMES. ASCEND	11	366
PASSAGES		
THESE PAINFUL PASSAGES, HOW WE MAY COME	11	528
PASS'D		
JEHOVAH, WHO IN ONE NIGHT WHEN HE PASS'D	1	487
THEY PASS'D, AND MANY A REGION DOLOROUS,	2	619
AND MORE ENDANGER'D, THEN WHEN ARGO PASS'D	2	1017
ALL THIS DARK GLOBE THE FIEND FOUND AS HE PASS'D,	3	498
PASS'D FREQUENT, AND HIS EYE WITH CHOICE REGARD	3	534
PASS'D UNDERNEATH INGULFT, FOR GOD HAD THROWN	4	225
THUS TALKING HAND IN HAND ALONE THEY PASS'D	4	689
SUCH NIGHT TILL THIS I NEVER PASS'D, HAVE DREAM'D,	5	31
AND ON, METHOUGHT, ALONE I PASS'D THROUGH WAYS	5	50
REGIONS THEY PASS'D, THE MIGHTIE REGENCIES	5	748
STRETCHT INTO LONGITUDE; WHICH HAVING PASS'D	5	754
PASS'D THROUGH HIM, BUT TH' ETHEREAL SUBSTANCE CLOS'D	6	330
I NAM'D THEM, AS THEY PASS'D, AND UNDERSTOOD	8	352
FARR INTO CHAOS, SINCE THE FIEND PASS'D THROUGH,	10	233
WIDE OPEN AND UNGUARDED, SATAN PASS'D,	10	419
PASSD		
SO PASSD THEY NAKED ON, NOR SHUND THE SIGHT	4	319
SO HAND IN HAND THEY PASSD, THE LOVLIEST PAIR	4	321
THIR GLITTERING TENTS HE PASSD, AND NOW IS COME	5	291
THOUGH SINGLE. FROM AMIDST THEM FORTH HE PASSD,	5	903
BLOW'N VAGABOND OR FRUSTRATE: IN THEY PASSD	11	16
PASSES		
TO KNOW WHAT PASSES THERE; BE LOWLIE WISE:	8	173
PASSING		
I THEN WAS PASSING TO MY FORMER STATE	8	290
BUT LEAST THE DIFFICULTIE OF PASSING BACK	10	252
GLAR'D ON HIM PASSING: THESE WERE FROM WITHOUT	10	714
RAPE OR ADULTERIE, WHERE PASSING FAIRE	11	717
UR OF CHALDAEA, PASSING NOW THE FORD	12	130
PASSION		
SIGNS OF REMORSE AND PASSION TO BEHOLD	1	605
PASSION AND APATHIE, AND GLORY AND SHAME,	2	564
THUS WHILE HE SPAKE, EACH PASSION DIMM'D HIS FACE	4	114
TRANSPORTED TOUCH; HERE PASSION FIRST I FELT,	8	530
THE SOULE OF MAN, OR PASSION IN HIM MOVE.	8	585
IN LOVING THOU DOST WELL, IN PASSION NOT,	8	588
HIS GREAT COMMAND; TAKE HEED LEAST PASSION SWAY	8	635
HIS BURSTING PASSION INTO PLAINTS THUS POUR'D:	9	98
NEW PART PUTS ON, AND AS TO PASSION MOV'D,	9	667
OF PASSION, I TO THEM HAD QUITTED ALL,	10	627
AND IN A TROUBL'D SEA OF PASSION TOST,	10	718
SOFT WORDS TO HIS FIERCE PASSION SHE ASSAY'D:	10	865
PASSIONS		
WHOSE WANTON PASSIONS IN THE SACRED PORCH	1	454
ALIEN FROM HEAV'N, WITH PASSIONS FOUL OBSCUR'D:	4	571
BEGAN TO RISE, HIGH PASSIONS, ANGER, HATE,	9	1123
AND UPSTART PASSIONS CATCH THE GOVERNMENT	12	88
PASSIVE		
MADE PASSIVE BOTH, HAD SERVD NECESSITIE,	3	110
THIR MARCH WAS, AND THE PASSIVE AIR UPBORE	6	72
PASS'T		
WORKS OF DAY PASS'T, OR MORROWS NEXT DESIGNE,	5	33
PAST		
THIR CHILDRENS CRIES UNHEARD, THAT PAST THROUGH FIRE	1	395
OF KNOWLEDGE PAST OR PRESENT, COULD HAVE FEAR'D,	1	628
THESE PAST, IF ANY PASS, THE VOID PROFOUND	2	438
BUT HEE ONCE PAST, SOON AFTER WHEN MAN FELL,	2	1023
BEATITUDE PAST UTTERANCE; ON HIS RIGHT	3	62
WHEREIN PAST, PRESENT, FUTURE HE BEHOLDS,	3	78
FATHER, THY WORD IS PAST, MAN SHALL FIND GRACE;	3	227
OF ALL PAST AGES TO THE GENERAL DOOM	3	328
BEYOND THE CAPE OF HOPE, AND NOW ARE PAST	4	160
ALL PATH OF MAN OR BEAST THAT PAST THAT WAY:	4	177
PRESENT, OR PAST, AS SAINTS AND PATRIARCHS US'D.	4	762
FROM HARD ASSAIES AND ILL SUCCESSES PAST	4	932
ILL MATCHING WORDS AND DEEDS LONG PAST OR LATE.	5	113
HATH PAST IN HEAV'N, SOM DOUBT WITHIN ME MOVE,	5	554
BY PRESENT, PAST, AND FUTURE) ON SUCH DAY	5	582
OF YESTERDAY, SO LATE HATH PAST THE LIPS	5	675
SECOND OMNIPOTENCE, TWO DAYES ARE PAST,	6	684
TWO DAYES ARE THEREFORE PAST, THE THIRD IS THINE;	6	699
BY WHAT IS PAST, TO THEE I HAVE REVEAL'D	6	895
NOR PAST UNCELEBRATED, NOR UNSUNG	7	253
FAST BY A FOUNTAIN, ONE SMALL THICKET PAST	9	628
BUT PAST WHO CAN RECALL, OR DON UNDOE?	9	926
PAST (CONTINUED)		
WHAT WORDS HAVE PAST THY LIPS, ADAM SEVERE,	9	1144
ALL, THOUGH ALL-KNOWING, WHAT HAD PAST WITH MAN	10	227
MIGHT SUDDENLY INFLICT; THAT PAST, RETURN'D	10	341
OF LOWEST ORDER, PAST; AND FROM THE DORE	10	443
BEYOND ALL PAST EXAMPLE AND FUTURE,	10	840
IS PAST, AND WE SHALL LIVE. WHENCE HAILE TO THEE,	11	158
OF PEACEFUL DAYES PORTENDS, THEN THOSE TWO PAST;	11	600
GRIEVOUS TO BEAR: BUT THAT CARE NOW IS PAST,	11	776
AND WHILE THE DREAD OF JUDGEMENT PAST REMAINS	12	14
WITH CAUSE FOR EVILS PAST, YET MUCH MORE CHEER'D	12	604
PASTIME		
FIND PASTIME, AND BEARE RULE; THY REALM IS LARGE.	8	375
PASTORAL		
CHARM'D WITH ARCADIAN PIPE, THE PASTORAL REED	11	132
PASTUR'D		
WHERE CATTLE PASTUR'D LATE, NOW SCATTERD LIES	11	653
PASTURE		
COUCHT, AND NOW FILD WITH PASTURE GAZING SAT,	4	351
GRAZE THE SEA WEED THIR PASTURE, AND THROUGH GROVES	7	404
PASTURING		
PASTURING AT ONCE, AND IN BROAD HERDS UPSPRUNG.	7	462
SHELTERS IN COOLE, AND TENDS HIS PASTURING HERDS	9	1109
PATERNAL		
THE CHARIOT OF PATERNAL DEITIE,	6	750
UPLIFTED, IN PATERNAL GLORIE RODE	7	219
WITH GOODNESS AND PATERNAL LOVE, HIS FACE	11	353
UNDER PATERNAL RULE; TILL ONE SHALL RISE	12	24
PATH		
WHAT READIEST PATH LEADS WHERE YOUR GLOOMIE BOUNDS	2	976
ALL PATH OF MAN OR BEAST THAT PAST THAT WAY:	4	177
OF ERRING, FROM THE PATH OF TRUTH REMOTE:	6	173
NOT UNAGREEABLE, TO FOUND A PATH	10	256
ASCEND, I FOLLOW THEE, SAFE GUIDE, THE PATH	11	371
PATHS		
THESE PATHS & BOWERS DOUBT NOT BUT OUR JOYNT HANDS	9	244
PATHS INDIRECT, OR IN THE MID WAY FAINT.	11	631
THE PATHS OF RIGHTEOUSNESS, HOW MUCH MORE SAFE,	11	814
PATIENCE		
WITH STUBBORN PATIENCE AS WITH TRIPLE STEEL.	2	569
ALL PATIENCE. HE WHO THEREFORE CAN INVENT	6	464
OF PATIENCE AND HEROIC MARTYRDOM	9	32
TRUE PATIENCE, AND TO TEMPER JOY WITH FEAR	11	361
ADD VERTUE, PATIENCE, TEMPERANCE, ADD LOVE,	12	583
PATIENTLY		
IF PATIENTLY THY BIDDING THEY OBEY,	11	112
LAMENT NOT EVE, BUT PATIENTLY RESIGNE	11	287
OF RENDRING UP, AND PATIENTLY ATTEND	11	551
PATRIARCH		
TO WHOM THE PATRIARCH OF MANKIND REPLI'D,	5	506
SO SPAKE THE PATRIARCH OF MANKINDE, BUT EVE	9	376
PLAINLIER SHALL BE REVEALD. THIS PATRIARCH BLEST,	12	151
PATRIARCHS		
PRESENT, OR PAST, AS SAINTS AND PATRIARCHS US'D.	4	762
PATRIARK		
WHILE YET THE PATRIARK LIV'D, WHO SCAP'D THE FLOOD,	12	117
PATRIMONIE		
POSTERITIE STANDS CURST: FAIR PATRIMONIE	10	818
PATRON		
PATRON OR INTERCESSOR NONE APPEERD,	3	219
PATRON OF LIBERTY, WHO MORE THEN THOU	4	958
PATRONESS		
OF MY CELESTIAL PATRONESS, WHO DEIGNES	9	21
PATRONS		
PATRONS OF MANKIND, GODS, AND SONS OF GODS,	11	696
PATTERN		
PATTERN OF JUST EQUALITIE PERHAPS	7	487
PAUS'D		
THIS SAID HE PAUS'D NOT, BUT WITH VENTROUS ARME	5	64
THOUGH BENT ON SPEED, SO HEER THE ARCHANGEL PAUS'D	12	2
SO SPAKE TH' ARCHANGEL MICHAEL, THEN PAUS'D,	12	466
PAUSE		
HE VIEWS IN BREDTH, AND WITHOUT LONGER PAUSE	3	561
AFTER SHORT PAUSE ASSENTING, THUS BEGAN.	5	562
DESTRUCTION TO THE REST: THIS PAUSE BETWEEN	6	162
PAUSING		
PAUSING A WHILE, THUS TO HER SELF SHE MUS'D.	9	744

PAV'D
- PAV'D AFTER HIM A BROAD AND BEAT'N WAY 2 1026
- IN PROGRESS THROUGH THE RODE OF HEAV'N STAR-PAV'D. 4 976
- BY SIN AND DEATH A BROAD WAY NOW IS PAV'D 10 473

PAVEMENT
- THE RICHES OF HEAV'NS PAVEMENT, TROD'N GOLD, 1 682
- AND LEVEL PAVEMENT: FROM THE ARCHED ROOF 1 726
- PAVEMENT THAT LIKE A SEA OF JASPER SHON 3 363
- AND PAVEMENT STARRS, AS STARRS TO THEE APPEER, 7 578

PAVILION
- OF CHAOS, AND HIS DARK PAVILION SPREAD 2 960

PAVILION'D
- THE FIELD PAVILION'D WITH HIS GUARDIANS BRIGHT; 11 215

PAVILIONS
- PAVILIONS NUMBERLESS, AND SUDDEN REARD, 5 653

PAW
- SPORTING THE LION RAMPD, AND IN HIS PAW 4 343
- GRIP'T IN EACH PAW: WHEN ADAM FIRST OF MEN 4 408

PAWING
- THE TAWNIE LION, PAWING TO GET FREE 7 464

PAY
- SOM OTHER ABLE, AND AS WILLING, PAY 3 211
- THE EASIEST RECOMPENCE, AND PAY HIM THANKS, 4 47
- FROM THEE THIR NAMES, AND PAY THEE FEALTIE 8 344
- WE ARE BY DOOM TO PAY; RATHER SUCH ACTS 10 1026
- SHALL PERFET, AND FOR THESE MY DEATH SHALL PAY. 11 36

PAYING
- SO BURTHENSOME STILL PAYING, STILL TO OW; 4 53

PAYS
- BY OWING OWES NOT, BUT STILL PAYS, AT ONCE 4 56

PEACE
- REGIONS OF SORROW, DOLEFUL SHADES, WHERE PEACE 1 65
- FULL COUNSEL MUST MATURE: PEACE IS DESPAIRD, 1 660
- NOT PEACE: AND AFTER HIM THUS MAMMON SPAKE. 2 228
- ADVISING PEACE: FOR SUCH ANOTHER FIELD 2 292
- WHAT SIT WE THEN PROJECTING PEACE AND WARR? 2 329
- IRREPARABLE; TEARMS OF PEACE YET NONE 2 331
- VOUTSAF'T OR SOUGHT; FOR WHAT PEACE WILL BE GIV'N 2 332
- INFLICTED? AND WHAT PEACE CAN WE RETURN, 2 335
- OF HEAVENLY GRACE: AND GOD PROCLAIMING PEACE, 2 499
- WHO FIRST BROKE PEACE IN HEAV'N AND FAITH, TILL THEN 2 690
- OF ANGER SHALL REMAIN, BUT PEACE ASSUR'D, 3 263
- O THOU IN HEAV'N AND EARTH THE ONLY PEACE 3 274
- FROM GRANTING HEE, AS I FROM BEGGING PEACE: 4 104
- FIRM PEACE RECOVERD SOON AND WONTED CALM. 5 210
- HEAV'NS BLESSED PEACE, AND INTO NATURE BROUGHT 6 267
- PEACE AND COMPOSURE, AND WITH OPEN BREST 6 560
- FOR JOY OF OFFERD PEACE: BUT I SUPPOSE 6 617
- AND WARR SO NEER THE PEACE OF GOD IN BLISS 7 55
- TO FUTURE MEN, AND IN THIR DWELLINGS PEACE: 7 183
- SILENCE, YE TROUBL'D WAVES, AND THOU DEEP, PEACE, 7 216
- FROM HIS SURMISE PROV'D FALSE, FIND PEACE WITHIN, 9 333
- PERNICIOUS TO THY PEACE, CHIEFLY ASSUR'D 9 981
- AND FULL OF PEACE, NOW TOST AND TURBULENT: 9 1126
- DEVOLV'D; THOUGH SHOULD I HOLD MY PEACE, YET THOU 10 135
- TO HUMANE LIFE, AND HOUSHOLD PEACE CONFOUND. 10 908
- HIS PEACE, AND THUS PROCEEDED IN HER PLAINT. 10 913
- BETWEEN US TWO LET THERE BE PEACE, BOTH JOYNING, 10 924
- IMMOVEABLE TILL PEACE OBTAIN'D FROM FAULT 10 938
- THE SMELL OF PEACE TOWARD MANKINDE, LET HIM LIVE 11 38
- SO SEND THEM FORTH, THOUGH SORROWING, YET IN PEACE: 11 117
- THAT I WAS HEARD WITH FAVOUR; PEACE RETURND 11 153
- GLAD TO BE SO DISMIST IN PEACE. CAN THUS 11 507
- FREEDOM AND PEACE TO MEN: THEY ON THE PLAIN 11 580
- OF JUSTICE, OF RELIGION, TRUTH AND PEACE, 11 667
- ALL WOULD HAVE THEN GON WELL, PEACE WOULD HAVE CROWND 11 781
- PEACE TO CORRUPT NO LESS THEN WARR TO WASTE. 11 784
- RAISE OUT OF FRIENDSHIP HOSTIL DEEDS IN PEACE. 11 796
- AND FULL OF PEACE, DENOUNCING WRAUTH TO COME 11 815
- BETOK'NING PEACE FROM GOD, AND COV'NANT NEW. 11 867
- LONG TIME IN PEACE BY FAMILIES AND TRIBES 12 23
- JUSTIFICATION TOWARDS GOD, AND PEACE 12 296
- NATIONAL INTERRUPT THIR PUBLIC PEACE, 12 317
- ENDEAVOUR PEACE: THIR STRIFE POLLUTION BRINGS 12 355
- FOUNDED IN RIGHTEOUSNESS AND PEACE AND LOVE 12 550
- GREATLY IN PEACE OF THOUGHT, AND HAVE MY FILL 12 558

PEACEFUL
- COUNSEL'D IGNOBLE EASE, AND PEACEFUL SLOATH, 2 227
- TO PEACEFUL COUNSELS, AND THE SETTL'D STATE 2 279
- AND THUS WITH PEACEFUL WORDS UPRAIS'D HER SOON. 10 946
- OF PEACEFUL DAYES PORTENDS, THEN THOSE TWO PAST; 11 600

PEAL
- A HIDEOUS PEAL: YET, WHEN THEY LIST, WOULD CREEP, 2 656
- SHALL HAST'N, SUCH A PEAL SHALL ROUSE THIR SLEEP. 3 329

PEAL'D
- HE HAD TO CROSS. NOR WAS HIS EARE LESS PEAL'D 2 920

PEARL
- SHOWRS ON HER KINGS BARBARIC PEARL AND GOLD, 2 4
- ROWLING ON ORIENT PEARL AND SANDS OF GOLD, 4 238
- IN PEARL, IN DIAMOND, AND MASSIE GOLD, 5 634

PEARLE
- OF JASPER, OR OF LIQUID PEARLE, WHEREON 3 519
- ADVANCING, SOW'D THE EARTH WITH ORIENT PEARLE, 5 2

PEARLIE
- OR IN THIR PEARLIE SHELLS AT EASE, ATTEND 7 407

PEARLY
- COVER'D WITH PEARLY GRAIN: YET GOD HATH HERE 5 430

PEASANT
- OR FOUNTAIN SOME BELATED PEASANT SEES, 1 783

PECCANT
- AS HOW WITH PECCANT ANGELS LATE THEY SAW; 11 70

PECULIAR
- SOME I HAVE CHOSEN OF PECULIAR GRACE 3 183
- SHOT FORTH PECULIAR GRACES; THEN WITH VOICE 5 15
- THIR SMALL PECULIAR, THOUGH FROM HUMAN SIGHT 7 368
- AND ONE PECULIAR NATION TO SELECT 12 111

PEERAGE
- WHEN CHARLEMAIN WITH ALL HIS PEERAGE FELL 1 586

PEERES
- IN PLACE THY SELF SO HIGH ABOVE THY PEERES. 5 812

PEERLESS
- APPARENT QUEEN UNVAILD HER PEERLESS LIGHT, 4 608

PEERS
- TO SET HIMSELF IN GLORY ABOVE HIS PEERS, 1 39
- WITH ALL HIS PEERS: ATTENTION HELD THEM MUTE. 1 618
- OF SATAN AND HIS PEERS: THIR SUMMONS CALL'D 1 757
- I SHOULD BE MUCH FOR OPEN WARR, O PEERS, 2 119
- BUT I SHOULD ILL BECOME THIS THRONE, O PEERS, 2 445
- IN ORDER CAME THE GRAND INFERNAL PEERS, 2 507
- SO PONDERING, AND FROM HIS ARMED PEERS 6 127
- FORTH RUSH'D IN HASTE THE GREAT CONSULTING PEERS, 10 456

PEGASEAN
- ABOVE THE FLIGHT OF PEGASEAN WING. 7 4

PEIRC'D
- WHERE WOUNDS OF DEADLY HATE HAVE PEIRC'D SO DEEP: 4 99
- IMPERISHABLE, AND THOUGH PEIRC'D WITH WOUND, 6 435

PELORUS
- TORN FROM PELORUS, OR THE SHATTER'D SIDE 1 232

PEN
- WATCHING WHERE SHEPHERDS PEN THIR FLOCKS AT EEVE 4 185

PENAL
- IN ADAMANTINE CHAINS AND PENAL FIRE, 1 48

PENALTIE
- DEATH IS THE PENALTIE IMPOS'D, BEWARE, 7 545
- OF GOD OR DEATH, OF LAW OR PENALTIE? 9 775
- INCURR'D, WHAT COULD THEY LESS, THE PENALTIE, 10 15
- SUFFICIENT PENALTIE, WHY HAST THOU ADDED 10 753
- THE PENALTIE PRONOUNC'T, DOUBT NOT BUT GOD 10 1022
- FROM PENALTIE, BECAUSE FROM DEATH RELEAST 11 197
- ON PENALTIE OF DEATH, AND SUFFERING DEATH, 12 398
- THE PENALTIE TO THY TRANSGRESSION DUE, 12 399

PENANCE
- CALLS US TO PENANCE? MORE DESTROY'D THEN THUS 2 92
- THIR PENANCE, LADEN WITH FRUIT LIKE THAT 10 550

PENCIL
- BY MODEL, OR BY SHADING PENCIL DRAWN. 3 509

PENDANT
- PENDANT BY SUTTLE MAGIC MANY A ROW 1 727
- THIS PENDANT WORLD, IN BIGNESS AS A STARR 2 1052
- WITH MAZIE ERROR UNDER PENDANT SHADES 4 239

PENDENT
- PONTIFICAL, A RIDGE OF PENDENT ROCK 10 313

PENDULOUS
- THE PENDULOUS ROUND EARTH WITH BALLANC'T AIRE 4 1000

PENETRATION
- WITH GENTLE PENETRATION, THOUGH UNSEEN, 3 585

PENITENT
- SO SPAKE OUR FATHER PENITENT, NOR EVE 10 1097

PENITENT (CONTINUED)
FROM WHOM AS OFT HE SAVES THEM PENITENT 12 319

PENNONS
FLUTTRING HIS PENNONS VAIN PLUMB DOWN HE DROPS 2 933
THE DANK, AND RISING ON STIFF PENNONS, TOWRE 7 441

PENNS
THEY SUMM'D THIR PENNS, AND SOARING TH' AIR SUBLIME 7 421

PENSIVE
WITHOUT MY OP'NING. PENSIVE HERE I SAT 2 777
SATAN HAD JOURNIED ON, PENSIVE AND SLOW; 4 173
PENSIVE I SATE ME DOWN; THERE GENTLE SLEEP 8 287

PENT
INTO THIR SUBSTANCE PENT, WHICH WROUGHT THEM PAIN 6 657
AS ONE WHO LONG IN POPULOUS CITY PENT, 9 445

PEOPL'D
CREATOR WISE, THAT PEOPL'D HIGHEST HEAV'N 10 889

PEOPLE
TH' ETHEREAL PEOPLE RAN, TO HEAR AND KNOW 10 27
HIS PEOPLE FROM ENTHRALMENT, THEY RETURN 12 171
AND ALL HIS PEOPLE; THUNDER MIXT WITH HAILE, 12 181
OF LAW, HIS PEOPLE INTO CANAAN LEAD; 12 309
HIS PEOPLE, WHO DEFEND? WILL THEY NOT DEALE 12 483

PEOR
PEOR HIS OTHER NAME, WHEN HE ENTIC'D 1 412

PERCEAV'D
WARR HE PERCEAV'D, WARR IN PROCINCT, AND FOUND 6 19

PERCEAVE
NOR DID THEY NOT PERCEAVE THE EVIL PLIGHT 1 335
SATED AT LENGTH, ERE LONG I MIGHT PERCEAVE 9 598
MUCH THOU HAST YET TO SEE, BUT I PERCEAVE 12 8

PERCEAVING
PERCEAVING WHERE SHE SAT RETIR'D IN SIGHT, 8 41

PERCEAV'ST
LESS EXCELLENT, AS THOU THY SELF PERCEAV'ST. 8 566

PERCEIV'D
WHICH WHEN BEELZEBUB PERCEIV'D, THEN WHOM, 2 299

PERCEIVE
PERCEIVE THEE PURPOS'D NOT TO DOOM FRAIL MAN 3 404
SUCH AS WE MIGHT PERCEIVE AMUS'D THEM ALL, 6 623

PERDITION
TO BOTTOMLESS PERDITION, THERE TO DWELL 1 47

PERFECT
IN PERFECT PHALANX TO THE DORIAN MOOD 1 550
THY SELF IN ME THY PERFECT IMAGE VIEWING 2 764

PERFECTION
PERFECTION FROM THE SUNS MORE POTENT RAY. 4 673
MY GLORIE, MY PERFECTION, GLAD I SEE 5 29
SUCH TO PERFECTION, ONE FIRST MATTER ALL, 5 472
OF THY PERFECTION, HOW SHALL I ATTAINE, 9 964
AND FOR THEE, WHOSE PERFECTION FARR EXCELL'D 10 150
OF ABSOLUTE PERFECTION, THEREIN MAN 10 483

PERFECTIONS
PERFECTIONS, IN HIMSELF WAS ALL HIS STATE, 5 353
WITH ALL PERFECTIONS, SO ENFLAME MY SENSE 9 1031

PERFET
URIEL, NO WONDER IF THY PERFET SIGHT, 4 577
TO WHOM THUS EVE WITH PERFET BEAUTY ADORND. 4 634
ALL PERFET GOOD UNMEASUR'D OUT, DESCENDS, 5 399
METALS OF DROSSIEST ORE TO PERFET GOLD 5 442
GOD MADE THEE PERFET, NOT IMMUTABLE; 5 524
AND PERFET WHILE THEY STOOD; HOW LAST UNFOULD 5 568
THIR PERFET RANKS; FOR HIGH ABOVE THE GROUND 6 71
BUT PAIN IS PERFET MISERIE, THE WORST 6 462
INNUMEROUS LIVING CREATURES, PERFET FORMES, 7 455
THOU IN THY SELF ART PERFET, AND IN THEE 8 415
PERFET WITHIN, NO OUTWARD AID REQUIRE; 8 642
AND LIFE MORE PERFET HAVE ATTAIND THEN FATE 9 689
WHAT SEEMD IN THEE SO PERFET, THAT I THOUGHT 9 1179
AND GAV'ST ME AS THY PERFET GIFT, SO GOOD, 10 138
SHALL PERFET, AND FOR THESE MY DEATH SHALL PAY. 11 36
FOR ONE MAN FOUND SO PERFET AND SO JUST, 11 876

PERFETLY
YET ARE BUT DIM, SHALL PERFETLY BE THEN 9 707

PERFIDIOUS
WHILE WITH PERFIDIOUS HATRED THEY PURSU'D 1 308
IN THIS PERFIDIOUS FRAUD, CONTAGION SPRED 5 880

PERFORM
AND HANDS INNUMERABLE SCARCE PERFORM. 1 699
THIS I PERFORM, SPEAK THOU, AND BE IT DON: 7 164
PERFORM, AND NOT PERFORMING CANNOT LIVE. 12 299

PERFORMANCE
OF MY PERFORMANCE: WHAT REMAINS, YE GODS, 10 502

PERFORM'D
WARR WEARIED HATH PERFORM'D WHAT WARR CAN DO, 6 695
ON THE CLEFT WOOD, AND ALL DUE RITES PERFORM'D, 11 440
THIR MINISTRY PERFORM'D, AND RACE WELL RUN, 12 505

PERFORME
HAVE NOTHING MERITED, NOR CAN PERFORME 4 418
ALL I RECEAV'D, UNABLE TO PERFORME 10 750

PERFORMING
AND IN PERFORMING END US; WHAT BESIDES 11 300
PERFORM, AND NOT PERFORMING CANNOT LIVE. 12 299

PERFORMS
BURNS FRORE, AND COLD PERFORMS TH' EFFECT OF FIRE. 2 595

PERFUMES
NATIVE PERFUMES, AND WHISPER WHENCE THEY STOLE 4 158

PERHAPS
WHICH OFT TIMES MAY SUCCEED, SO AS PERHAPS 1 166
PERHAPS HATH SPENT HIS SHAFTS, AND CEASES NOW 1 176
THITHER, IF BUT TO PRY, SHALL BE PERHAPS 1 655
HIS OWN INVENTED TORMENTS. BUT PERHAPS 2 70
ONE DAY UPON OUR HEADS; WHILE WE PERHAPS 2 178
HIS ANGER, AND PERHAPS THUS FARR REMOV'D 2 211
TO THEIR DEFENCE WHO HOLD IT: HERE PERHAPS 2 362
NEERER OUR ANCIENT SEAT; PERHAPS IN VIEW 2 394
THAT DISMAL WORLD, IF ANY CLIME PERHAPS 2 572
PERHAPS OUR VACANT ROOM, THOUGH MORE REMOV'D, 2 835
THE WOMB OF NATURE AND PERHAPS HER GRAVE, 2 911
THERE LANDS THE FIEND, A SPOT LIKE WHICH PERHAPS 3 588
TO WITNESS WITH THINE EYES WHAT SOME PERHAPS 3 700
BY THEE, AND MORE THEN HALF PERHAPS WILL REIGNE; 4 112
CREATURES OF OTHER MOULD, EARTH-BORN PERHAPS, 4 360
NOW LAID PERHAPS ASLEEP SECURE OF HARME. 4 791
OF HEAV'N PERHAPS, OR ALL THE ELEMENTS 4 993
TO US PERHAPS HE BRINGS, AND WILL VOUTSAFE 5 312
THE EARTH TO YIELD; UNSAVOURIE FOOD PERHAPS 5 401
AND FROM THESE CORPORAL NUTRIMENTS PERHAPS 5 496
THE SECRETS OF ANOTHER WORLD, PERHAPS 5 569
THE REMEDIE; PERHAPS MORE VALID ARMES, 6 438
SPARE OUT OF LIFE PERHAPS, AND NOT REPINE, 6 460
SOMEWHAT EXTRAVAGANT AND WILDE, PERHAPS 6 616
WHAT MAY NO LESS PERHAPS AVAILE US KNOWN, 7 85
PATTERN OF JUST EQUALITIE PERHAPS 7 487
NUMEROUS, AND EVERY STARR PERHAPS A WORLD 7 621
HATH LEFT TO THIR DISPUTES, PERHAPS TO MOVE 8 77
ALLOTTED THERE; AND OTHER SUNS PERHAPS 8 148
STOR'D IN EACH ORB PERHAPS WITH SOME THAT LIVE. 8 152
MY STORIE, WHICH PERHAPS THOU HAST NOT HEARD; 8 205
OR FROM MY SIDE SUBDUCTING, TOOK PERHAPS 8 536
BEFORE HAD BIN CONTRIVING, THOUGH PERHAPS 9 139
ASSIST US: BUT IF MUCH CONVERSE PERHAPS 9 247
CONJUGAL LOVE, THEN WHICH PERHAPS NO BLISS 9 263
MAY FINDE US BOTH PERHAPS FARR LESS PREPAR'D, 9 381
WONDER NOT, SOVRAN MISTRESS, IF PERHAPS 9 532
MEE THUS, THOUGH IMPORTUNE PERHAPS, TO COME 9 610
SO YE SHALL DIE PERHAPS, BY PUTTING OFF 9 713
AND I PERHAPS AM SECRET; HEAV'N IS HIGH, 9 811
EACH THING ON EARTH; AND OTHER CARE PERHAPS 9 813
AND RENDER ME MORE EQUAL, AND PERHAPS, 9 823
PERHAPS THOU SHALT NOT DIE, PERHAPS THE FACT 9 928
OR TO THY SELF PERHAPS: HADST THOU BEEN THERE, 9 1148
MATTER OF GLORIOUS TRIAL; AND PERHAPS 9 1177
STAY HIS RETURN PERHAPS OVER THIS GULFE 10 253
ENCROACHING EVE PERHAPS, HAD FIRST THE RULE 10 582
WHILE YET WE LIVE, SCARSE ONE SHORT HOUR PERHAPS, 10 923
HIS TRUMPET, HEARD IN OREB SINCE PERHAPS 11 74
WHEN GOD DESCENDED, AND PERHAPS ONCE MORE 11 75
EVE, NOW EXPECT GREAT TIDINGS, WHICH PERHAPS 11 226
PERHAPS THY CAPITAL SEATE, FROM WHENCE HAD SPRED 11 343
THE WORLD: IN SPIRIT PERHAPS HE ALSO SAW 11 406
IF ADAM AUGHT PERHAPS MIGHT INTERPOSE; 12 4

PERIL
THROUGH DARK AND DESART WAYES WITH PERIL GONE 3 544
AND PERIL GREAT PROVOK'T, WHO THUS HATH DAR'D 9 922
WITH PERIL GREAT ATCHIEV'D. LONG WERE TO TELL 10 469

PERILOUS
IN WORST EXTREAMS, AND ON THE PERILOUS EDGE 1 276
THE PERILOUS ATTEMPT: BUT ALL SAT MUTE, 2 420

PERIOD
AS AT THE WORLDS GREAT PERIOD; AND OUR SIRE 12 467

PERIODS
PERIODS OF TIME, THENCE HURRIED BACK TO FIRE. 2 603

PERISH
CAN PERISH; FOR THE MIND AND SPIRIT REMAINS 1 139
TO PERISH RATHER, SWALLOWD UP AND LOST 2 149
AS IN HIM PERISH ALL MEN, SO IN THEE 3 287
WHICH GOD INSPIR'D, CANNOT TOGETHER PERISH 10 785

PERMISSION
AND HIGH PERMISSION OF ALL-RULING HEAVEN 1 212
WITH THY PERMISSION THEN, AND THUS FOREWARND 9 378

PERMISSIVE
BY HIS PERMISSIVE WILL, THROUGH HEAV'N AND EARTH: 3 685
PERMISSIVE, AND ACCEPTANCE FOUND, WHICH GAIN'D 8 435
WITH WHAT PERMISSIVE GLORY SINCE HIS FALL 10 451

PERMIT
DEITIE FOR THEE, WHEN FATE WILL NOT PERMIT. 9 885
NAY DIDST PERMIT, APPROVE, AND FAIR DISMISS. 9 1159
LIVE WELL, HOW LONG OR SHORT PERMIT TO HEAV'N: 11 554

PERMITS
THEN HEAV'N PERMITS, NOR MINE, THOUGH DOUBLD NOW 4 1009
PERMITS NOT; TO REMOVE THEE I AM COME, 11 260
MAN TILL THEN FREE. THEREFORE SINCE HEE PERMITS 12 90

PERMITTED
THIS TUMULT, AND PERMITTED ALL, ADVIS'D: 6 674
TILL THIR LOST SHAPE, PERMITTED, THEY RESUM'D, 10 574

PERMITTING
RURAL REPAST, PERMITTING HIM THE WHILE 9 4

PERNICIOUS
NO WONDER, FALL'N SUCH A PERNICIOUS HIGHTH. 1 282
PROVIDE, PERNICIOUS WITH ONE TOUCH TO FIRE. 6 520
GLAR'D LIGHTNING, AND SHOT FORTH PERNICIOUS FIRE 6 849
PERNICIOUS TO THY PEACE, CHIEFLY ASSUR'D 9 981

PERPETUAL
FEARLESS, ENDANGER'D HEAV'NS PERPETUAL KING; 1 131
AND WITH PERPETUAL INRODES TO ALLARME, 2 103
LIES DARK AND WILDE, BEAT WITH PERPETUAL STORMS 2 588
HERE IN PERPETUAL AGONIE AND PAIN, 2 861
PERPETUAL FOUNTAIN OF DOMESTIC SWEETS, 4 760
PERPETUAL CIRCLE, MULTIFORM; AND MIX 5 182
WHERE LIGHT AND DARKNESS IN PERPETUAL ROUND 6 6
WHENCE IN PERPETUAL FIGHT THEY NEEDS MUST LAST 6 693
STREAM, AND PERPETUAL DRAW THIR HUMID TRAINE. 7 306
PERPETUAL SMIL'D ON EARTH WITH VERNANT FLOURS, 10 679
PERPETUAL BANISHMENT. YET LEAST THEY FAINT 11 108

PERPETUITIE
TO PERPETUITIE; AY ME, THAT FEAR 10 813

PERPLEX
THE BETTER REASON, TO PERPLEX AND DASH 2 114
IF CARE OF OUR DESCENT PERPLEX US MOST, 10 979

PERPLEX'D
PERPLEX'D THE GREEK AND CYTHEREA'S SON; 9 19

PERPLEXES
PERPLEXES MONARCHS. DARK'N'D SO, YET SHON 1 599

PERPLEXING
THE EASIEST WAY, NOR WITH PERPLEXING THOUGHTS 8 183

PERPLEXT
LEADS HIM PERPLEXT, WHERE HE MAY LIKELIEST FIND 2 525
OF SHRUBS AND TANGLING BUSHES HAD PERPLEXT 4 176
ERWHILE PERPLEXT WITH THOUGHTS WHAT WOULD BECOM 12 275

PERSECUTERS
THIR PROUDEST PERSECUTERS: FOR THE SPIRIT 12 497

PERSECUTION
WHENCE HEAVIE PERSECUTION SHALL ARISE 12 531

PERSEVERE
AND GOOD HE MADE THEE, BUT TO PERSEVERE 5 525
THIR HAPPINESS, AND PERSEVERE UPRIGHT. 7 632
ON ALL WHO IN THE WORSHIP PERSEVERE 12 532

PERSEVERING
I IN THY PERSEVERING SHALL REJOYCE, 8 639

PERSIAN
THE PERSIAN IN ECBATAN SATE, OR SINCE 11 393

PERSISTED
PERSISTED, YET SUBMISS, THOUGH LAST, REPLI'D. 9 377
I HAD PERSISTED HAPPIE, HAD NOT THY PRIDE 10 874

PERSISTING
AND TO THE END PERSISTING, SAFE ARRIVE. 3 197

PERSON
A FAIRER PERSON LOST NOT HEAV'N; HE SEEMD 2 110

PERSON (CONTINUED)
TO PERSON OR TO POEM. MEE OF THESE 9 41
MUCH HEE THE PLACE ADMIR'D, THE PERSON MORE. 9 444
AND PERSON, HAD'ST THOU KNOWN THY SELF ARIGHT. 10 156

PERSWADE
MAIN REASON TO PERSWADE IMMEDIATE WARR, 2 121
THE WORST, AND NOT PERSWADE THEE RATHER DIE 9 979

PERSWADERS
POWERFUL PERSWADERS, QUICK'ND AT THE SCENT 9 587

PERSWASION
BENDING HIS EARE; PERSWASION IN ME GREW 11 152

PERSWASIVE
AND WITH PERSWASIVE ACCENT THUS BEGAN. 2 118
YET RUNG OF HIS PERSWASIVE WORDS, IMPREGN'D 9 737

PERSWASIVELY
PERSWASIVELY HATH SO PREVAILD, THAT I 9 873

PERTURBATION
EACH PERTURBATION SMOOTH'D WITH OUTWARD CALME, 4 120
AND SHAME, AND PERTURBATION, AND DESPAIRE, 10 113

PERU
AND CUSCO IN PERU, THE RICHER SEAT 11 408

PERUS'D
MY SELF I THEN PERUS'D, AND LIMB BY LIMB 8 267

PERVERSE
PERVERSE, ALL MONSTROUS, ALL PRODIGIOUS THINGS, 2 625
OF THIS FRAIL WORLD; BY WHICH THE SPIRITS PERVERSE 2 1030
JUDG'D THEE PERVERSE: THE EASIER CONQUEST NOW 6 37
OUR OVERTURE, AND TURN NOT BACK PERVERSE; 6 562
AND THIS PERVERSE COMMOTION GOVERND THUS, 6 706
OF THY PRESUM'D RETURN. EVENT PERVERSE. 9 405
THE ONELY RIGHTEOUS IN A WORLD PERVERSE, 11 701

PERVERSENESS
IN HEAV'NLY SPIRITS COULD SUCH PERVERSENESS DWELL? 6 788

PERVERSNESS
THROUGH HER PERVERSNESS, BUT SHALL SEE HER GAIND 10 902

PERVERT
OUR LABOUR MUST BE TO PERVERT THAT END, 1 164
BY SOME FALSE GUILE PERVERT; AND SHALL PERVERT 3 92
WHILE THEY PERVERT PURE NATURES HEALTHFUL RULES 11 523

PERVERTED
HEE IN THE SERPENT, HAD PERVERTED EVE, 10 3
SATAN WITH HIS PERVERTED WORLD, THEN RAISE 12 547

PERVERTS
THE GOOD BEFORE HIM, BUT PERVERTS BEST THINGS 4 203

PEST
SHE SPAKE, AND AT HER WORDS THE HELLISH PEST 2 735

PESTILENCE
SHAKES PESTILENCE AND WARR. EACH AT THE HEAD 2 711
MARASMUS, AND WIDE-WASTING PESTILENCE, 11 487

PESTILENT
CORRUPT AND PESTILENT: NOW FROM THE NORTH 10 695

PETER
AND NOW SAINT PETER AT HEAV'NS WICKET SEEMS 3 484

PETITION
SEEM'D THIR PETITION, THEN WHEN TH' ANCIENT PAIR 11 10

PETRIFIC
DEATH WITH HIS MACE PETRIFIC, COLD AND DRY, 10 294

PETSORA
BEYOND PETSORA EASTWARD, TO THE RICH 10 292

PETTY
FOR SUCH A PETTY TRESPASS, AND NOT PRAISE 9 693

PHALANX
IN PERFECT PHALANX TO THE DORIAN MOOD 1 550
THIR PHALANX, AND BEGAN TO HEMM HIM ROUND 4 979
IN CUBIC PHALANX FIRM ADVANC'T ENTIRE, 6 399

PHANTASMS
ILLUSIONS AS HE LIST, PHANTASMS AND DREAMS, 4 803

PHARAO
OF PHARAO: THERE HE DIES, AND LEAVES HIS RACE 12 163

PHARAOH
THAT ORE THE REALM OF IMPIOUS PHARAOH HUNG 1 342

PLACE (CONTINUED)
O HOW UNLIKE THE PLACE FROM WHENCE THEY FELL. 1 75
A MIND NOT TO BE CHANG'D BY PLACE OR TIME. 1 253
THE MIND IS ITS OWN PLACE, AND IN IT SELF 1 254
ETERNAL SPIRITS; OR HAVE YE CHOS'N THIS PLACE 1 318
AS THIS PLACE TESTIFIES, AND THIS DIRE CHANGE 1 625
BY PLACE OR CHOICE THE WORTHIEST; THEY ANON 1 759
WILL ENVY WHOM THE HIGHEST PLACE EXPOSES 2 27
HEAV'NS FUGITIVES, AND FOR THIR DWELLING PLACE 2 57
OR CHANG'D AT LENGTH, AND TO THE PLACE CONFORMD 2 217
THE LATTER: FOR WHAT PLACE CAN BE FOR US 2 235
WE CAN CREATE, AND IN WHAT PLACE SO E'RE 2 260
THIS PLACE OUR DUNGEON, NOT OUR SAFE RETREAT 2 317
SOME EASIER ENTERPRIZE? THERE IS A PLACE 2 345
IN HIS OWN STRENGTH, THIS PLACE MAY LYE EXPOS'D 2 360
TO SEARCH WITH WANDRING QUEST A PLACE FORETOLD 2 830
CREATED VAST AND ROUND, A PLACE OF BLISS 2 832
AND BRING YE TO THE PLACE WHERE THOU AND DEATH 2 840
AND TIME AND PLACE ARE LOST; WHERE ELDEST NIGHT 2 894
CONFINE WITH HEAV'N; OR IF SOM OTHER PLACE 2 977
AND I WILL PLACE WITHIN THEM AS A GUIDE 3 194
ALONE, FOR OTHER CREATURE IN THIS PLACE 3 442
THE PLACE HE FOUND BEYOND EXPRESSION BRIGHT, 3 591
EACH HAD HIS PLACE APPOINTED, EACH HIS COURSE, 3 720
THAT PLACE IS EARTH THE SEAT OF MAN, THAT LIGHT 3 724
BY CHANGE OF PLACE: NOW CONSCIENCE WAKES DESPAIR 4 23
O THEN AT LAST RELENT: IS THERE NO PLACE 4 79
IMBROUND THE NOONTIDE BOWRS: THUS WAS THIS PLACE, 4 246
YOUR NUMEROUS OFSPRING; IF NO BETTER PLACE, 4 385
CHARGE AND STRICT WATCH THAT TO THIS HAPPIE PLACE 4 562
ON TO THIR BLISSFUL BOWER; IT WAS A PLACE 4 690
ORDAIND BY THEE, AND THIS DELICIOUS PLACE 4 729
OF PURITIE AND PLACE AND INNOCENCE, 4 745
OR THINK THEE UNBEFITTING HOLIEST PLACE, 4 759
THY SIN AND PLACE OF DOOM OBSCURE AND FOULE. 4 840
THIS PLACE INVIOLABLE, AND THESE FROM HARM. 4 843
TO QUESTION THY BOLD ENTRANCE ON THIS PLACE; 4 882
AND BOLDLY VENTURE TO WHATEVER PLACE 4 891
DOLE WITH DELIGHT, WHICH IN THIS PLACE I SOUGHT; 4 894
THUS SAID. NATIVE OF HEAV'N, FOR OTHER PLACE 5 361
CREATED, OR SUCH PLACE HAST HERE TO DWELL. 5 373
INTO UTTER DARKNESS, DEEP INGULFT, HIS PLACE 5 614
WHAT DOUBTFUL MAY ENSUE, MORE IN THIS PLACE 5 682
THIS OUR HIGH PLACE, OUR SANCTUARIE, OUR HILL. 5 732
IN PLACE THY SELF SO HIGH ABOVE THY PEERES. 5 812
INTO THIR PLACE OF PUNISHMENT, THE GULF 6 53
THY OFSPRING, TO THE PLACE OF EVIL, HELL, 6 276
BY WOUND, THOUGH FROM THIR PLACE BY VIOLENCE MOV'D. 6 405
EACH TO HIS PLACE, THEY HEARD HIS VOICE AND WENT 6 782
INTO HIS PLACE, AND THE GREAT SON RETURND 7 135
DREW MANY, WHOM THIR PLACE KNOWS HERE NO MORE; 7 144
LIKE THINGS TO LIKE, THE REST TO SEVERAL PLACE 7 240
INTO ONE PLACE, AND LET DRY LAND APPEER. 7 284
WHEREVER THUS CREATED, FOR NO PLACE 7 535
THIR PLEASANT DWELLING PLACE. THRICE HAPPIE MEN, 7 625
FOUND UNSUSPECTED WAY. THERE WAS A PLACE, 9 69
FIND PLACE OR REFUGE; AND THE MORE I SEE 9 119
MUCH HEE THE PLACE ADMIR'D, THE PERSON MORE. 9 444
AND FORCE UPON FREE WILL HATH HERE NO PLACE. 9 1174
THOU DID'ST RESIGNE THY MANHOOD, AND THE PLACE 10 148
BY HIS AVENGERS, SINCE NO PLACE LIKE THIS 10 241
OF SATAN, TO THE SELF SAME PLACE WHERE HEE 10 315
A PLACE SO HEAV'NLY, AND CONNIVING SEEM 10 624
HEAVIE, THOUGH IN THIR PLACE. O FLEETING JOYES 10 741
FROM DARKNESS TO PROMOTE ME, OR HERE PLACE 10 745
OR IN SOME OTHER DISMAL PLACE WHO KNOWS 10 787
AND TO THE PLACE OF JUDGMENT WILL RETURN, 10 932
COULD ALTER HIGH DECREES, I TO THAT PLACE 10 953
RESTOR'D BY THEE, VILE AS I AM, TO THE PLACE 10 971
WHAT BETTER CAN WE DO, THEN TO THE PLACE 10 1086
FELT LESS REMORSE: THEY FORTHWITH TO THE PLACE 10 1098
AND ON THE EAST SIDE OF THE GARDEN PLACE, 11 118
DISCOVER'D SOON THE PLACE OF HER RETIRE. 11 267
DEPARTURE FROM THIS HAPPY PLACE, OUR SWEET 11 303
WITH WORSHIP, PLACE BY PLACE WHERE HE VOUTSAF'D 11 318
SHALL BRING ON MEN. IMMEDIATELY A PLACE 11 477
SAID TH' ANGEL, WHO SHOULD BETTER HOLD HIS PLACE 11 635
OUT OF HIS PLACE, PUSHD BY THE HORNED FLOUD, 11 831
TO TEACH THEE THAT GOD ATTRIBUTES TO PLACE 11 836
MOUNT HERMON, YONDER SEA, EACH PLACE BEHOLD 12 142
HIS PLACE, TO OFFER INCENSE, MYRRH, AND GOLD; 12 363
HIS PLACE OF BIRTH A SOLEMN ANGEL TELLS 12 364
SHALL ALL BE PARADISE, FAR HAPPIER PLACE 12 464
THIR PLACE OF REST, AND PROVIDENCE THIR GUIDE: 12 647

PLACES
THOSE HAPPIE PLACES THOU HAST DEIGND A WHILE 5 364
IN SIGHT, TO EACH OF THESE THREE PLACES LED. 10 324
FAMILIAR TO OUR EYES, ALL PLACES ELSE 11 305
PLACES AND TITLES, AND WITH THESE TO JOINE 12 516
ART ALL THINGS UNDER HEAV'N, ALL PLACES THOU, 12 618

PLAC'T
IN THE POURLIEUES OF HEAV'N, AND THEREIN PLAC'T 2 833
OF MANKIND, IN THE HAPPIE GARDEN PLAC'T, 3 66
AND MAN THERE PLAC'T, WITH PURPOSE TO ASSAY 3 90
SEVERE BUT IN TRUE FILIAL FREEDOM PLAC'T; 4 294
THAT RAIS'D US FROM THE DUST AND PLAC'T US HERE 4 416

PLAC'T (CONTINUED)
THE VIGILANCE HERE PLAC'T, BUT SUCH AS COME 4 580
AS NEERER TO HIM PLAC'T OR NEERER TENDING 5 476
WHEREVER PLAC'T, LET HIM DISPOSE: JOY THOU 8 170
ABOUT HER, AS A GUARD ANGELIC PLAC'T. 8 559
THE WEAL OR WOE IN THEE IS PLAC'T; BEWARE. 8 638
WAS PLAC'T IN REGAL LUSTRE. DOWN A WHILE 10 447
PLAC'T IN A PARADISE, BY OUR EXILE 10 484
MEANWHILE THEY IN THIR EARTHLY CANAAN PLAC'T 12 315

PLAGU'D
WHOM THEY TRIUMPH'D ONCE LAPST. THUS WERE THEY
PLAGU'D 10 572

PLAGUE
HIS RED RIGHT HAND TO PLAGUE US? WHAT IF ALL 2 174
LIKE INSTRUMENT TO PLAGUE THE SONS OF MEN 6 505

PLAGUES
PLAGUES; THEY ASTONISHT ALL RESISTANCE LOST, 6 838
DESTROYERS RIGHTLIER CALL'D AND PLAGUES OF MEN. 11 697

PLAID
IN CURLES ON EITHER CHEEK PLAID, WINGS HE WORE 3 641
WANTOND AS IN HER PRIME, AND PLAID AT WILL 5 295
ABOUT THIR SPIRITS HAD PLAID, AND INMOST POWERS 9 1048

PLAIN
SEEST THOU YON DREARY PLAIN, FORLORN AND WILDE, 1 180
ON THE FIRM BRIMSTONE, AND FILL ALL THE PLAIN; 1 350
WORSHIPT IN RABBA AND HER WATRY PLAIN, 1 397
NIGH ON THE PLAIN IN MANY CELLS PREPAR'D, 1 700
PART ON THE PLAIN, OR IN THE AIR SUBLIME 2 528
THE BUILDERS NEXT OF BABEL ON THE PLAIN 3 466
INTO A LIQUID PLAIN, THEN STOOD UNMOV'D 4 455
WIDE OVER ALL THE PLAIN, AND WIDER FARR 5 648
THEN ALL THIS GLOBOUS EARTH IN PLAIN OUT SPRED, 5 649
SHOT THROUGH WITH ORIENT BEAMS: WHEN ALL THE PLAIN 6 15
HIS FRAUD IS THEN THY FEAR, WHICH PLAIN INFERRS 9 285
IN PLAIN THEN, WHAT FORBIDS HE BUT TO KNOW, 9 758
DOWN TO THE PLAIN DESCENDED; BY THIR GUISE 11 576
FREEDOM AND PEACE TO MEN: THEY ON THE PLAIN 11 580
THROUGH ALL THE PLAIN, AND REFUGE NONE WAS FOUND. 11 673
THE PLAIN, WHEREIN A BLACK BITUMINOUS GURGE 12 41

PLAIND
EY'D THEM ASKANCE, AND TO HIMSELF THUS PLAIND. 4 504

PLAINE
POWRD FORTH PROFUSE ON HILL AND DALE AND PLAINE, 4 243
IF STEEP, WITH TORRENT RAPTURE, IF THROUGH PLAINE, 7 299
A WOODIE MOUNTAIN; WHOSE HIGH TOP WAS PLAINE, 8 303
YET DOUBT NOT BUT IN VALLIE AND IN PLAINE 11 349
HE LOOKD AND SAW A SPACIOUS PLAINE, WHEREON 11 556
EWES AND THIR BLEATING LAMBS OVER THE PLAINE, 11 649
PITCHT ABOUT SECHEM, AND THE NEIGHBOURING PLAINE 12 136
TO THE SUBJECTED PLAINE; THEN DISAPPEER'D. 12 640

PLAINES
BUT IN HIS WAY LIGHTS ON THE BARREN PLAINES 3 437
HILL, DALE, AND SHADIE WOODS, AND SUNNIE PLAINES, 8 262
YE HILLS AND DALES, YE RIVERS, WOODS, AND PLAINES, 8 275
OF HILL, AND VALLIE, RIVERS, WOODS AND PLAINES, 9 116
BY ASTRACAN OVER THE SNOWIE PLAINES 10 432

PLAINLIER
PLAINLIER SHALL BE REVEALD. THIS PATRIARCH BLEST, 12 151

PLAINS
IN DUBIOUS BATTEL ON THE PLAINS OF HEAV'N, 1 104
OF PARADISE AND EDENS HAPPIE PLAINS, 5 143

PLAINT
SATE IN THIR SAD DISCOURSE, AND VARIOUS PLAINT, 10 343
HIS PEACE, AND THUS PROCEEDED IN HER PLAINT. 10 913
AND SCARCE RECOVERING WORDS HIS PLAINT RENEW'D. 11 499
AND SCARCE TO TH' ANGEL UTTERDST THUS THY PLAINT. 11 762

PLAINTS
HIS BURSTING PASSION INTO PLAINTS THUS POUR'D: 9 98

PLANET
AND HENCE THE MORNING PLANET GUILDS HER HORNS; 7 366
THE PLANET EARTH, SO STEDFAST THOUGH SHE SEEM, 8 129

PLANETARIE
THIR PLANETARIE MOTIONS AND ASPECTS 10 658

PLANETS
THEY PASS THE PLANETS SEVEN, AND PASS THE FIXT, 3 481
OF PLANETS AND OF FIXT IN ALL HER WHEELES 5 621
TWO PLANETS RUSHING FROM ASPECT MALIGNE 6 313
THE PLANETS IN THIR STATION LIST'NING STOOD, 7 563
AND PLANETS, PLANET-STROOK, REAL ECLIPS 10 413

PLANET-STROOK
AND PLANETS, PLANET-STROOK, REAL ECLIPS 10 413

PLEIADES
DAWN, AND THE PLEIADES BEFORE HIM DANC'D 7 374

PLENIPOTENT
PLENIPOTENT ON EARTH, OF MATCHLESS MIGHT 10 404

PLENTEOUS
UNNAM'D IN HEAV'N, NOW PLENTEOUS, AS THOU SEEST . 6 263
WHICH HERE, THOUGH PLENTEOUS, ALL TO LITTLE SEEMS 10 600
LABOURING THE SOILE, AND REAPING PLENTEOUS CROP, . 12 18

PLENTEOUSLY
SOUL LIVING, EACH THAT CREPT, WHICH PLENTEOUSLY . 7 392

PLENTY
MORE PLENTY THEN THE SUN THAT BARREN SHINES, . . 8 94
AMID THE TREE NOW GOT, WHERE PLENTY HUNG . . . 9 594

PLIGHT
NOR DID THEY NOT PERCEAVE THE EVIL PLIGHT . . . 1 335
THEY WORSE ABHORR'D. SATAN BEHELD THIR PLIGHT, . 6 607
BUT LET US NOW, AS IN BAD PLIGHT, DEVISE . . . 9 1091
SHE ENDED WEEPING, AND HER LOWLIE PLIGHT, . . . 10 937
THUS THEY IN LOWLIEST PLIGHT REPENTANT STOOD . . 11 1

PLOT
OF GROVE OR GARDEN-PLOT MORE PLEASANT LAY, . . . 9 418

PLOTS
THEN WISE TO FRUSTRATE ALL OUR PLOTS AND WILES. . 2 193

PLOTTING
YET EVER PLOTTING HOW THE CONQUEROR LEAST . . . 2 338
LATE FALLN HIMSELF FROM HEAV'N, IS PLOTTING NOW . 5 240
WHO NOW IS PLOTTING HOW HE MAY SEDUCE 6 901

PLOWMAN
SWAYES THEM; THE CAREFUL PLOWMAN DOUBTING STANDS . 4 983

PLUCK
EACH PLANT AND JUCIEST GOURD WILL PLUCK SUCH CHOICE 5 327
TO PLUCK AND EATE; WHEREAT I WAK'D, AND FOUND . . 8 309
TEMPTING SO NIGH, TO PLUCK AND EAT MY FILL . . . 9 595

PLUCK'D
FORTH REACHING TO THE FRUIT, SHE PLUCK'D, SHE EAT: 9 781
THAT CURLD MEGARA: GREEDILY THEY PLUCK'D . . . 10 560

PLUCKT
HE PLUCKT, HE TASTED; MEE DAMP HORROR CHIL'D . . 5 65
WHICH HE HAD PLUCKT; THE PLEASANT SAVOURIE SMELL . 5 84
THEY PLUCKT THE SEATED HILLS WITH ALL THIR LOAD, . 6 644
GATHERD, NOT HARSHLY PLUCKT, FOR DEATH MATURE: . 11 537

PLUMB
FLUTTRING HIS PENNONS VAIN PLUMB DOWN HE DROPS . 2 933

PLUM'D
SAT HORROR PLUM'D; NOR WANTED IN HIS GRASPE . . 4 989

PLUME
OF MANY A COLOURD PLUME SPRINKL'D WITH GOLD, . . 3 642
FROM ME SOM PLUME, THAT THY SUCCESS MAY SHOW . . 6 161
TWO BIRDS OF GAYEST PLUME BEFORE HIM DROVE: . . 11 186

PLUMES
AND SHOOK HIS PLUMES, THAT HEAV'NLY FRAGRANCE FILLD 5 286
FLOATS, AS THEY PASS, FANN'D WITH UNNUMBER'D
PLUMES: 7 432

PLUNG'D
THREATENS HIM, PLUNG'D IN THAT ABORTIVE GULF. . . 2 441
TH' UNTRACTABLE ABYSSE, PLUNG'D IN THE WOMB . . 10 476
I FIND NO WAY, FROM DEEP TO DEEPER PLUNG'D. . . 10 844

PLUNGE
AND PLUNGE US IN THE FLAMES? OR FROM ABOVE . . 2 172

PLUTONIAN
OF THAT PLUTONIAN HALL, INVISIBLE 10 444

PLY
PLY STEMMING NIGHTLY TOWARD THE POLE. SO SEEM'D . 2 642
THEN COMMUNE HOW THAT DAY THEY BEST MAY PLY . . 9 201

PLYES
WITH LOUDEST VEHEMENCE: THITHER HE PLYES, . . . 2 954

POEM
TO PERSON OR TO POEM. MEE OF THESE 9 41

POINT
OF NIGHTS EXTENDED SHADE; FROM EASTERN POINT . . 3 557
THAT SPOT TO WHICH I POINT IS PARADISE, ... 3 733
FROM WHAT POINT OF HIS COMPASS TO BEWARE . . . 4 559
RETURND ON THAT BRIGHT BEAM, WHOSE POINT NOW RAISD 4 590
THE WESTERN POINT, WHERE THOSE HALF-ROUNDING GUARDS 4 862
FROM FATHER TO HIS SON? STRANGE POINT AND NEW. . 5 855

POINT (CONTINUED)
IN PROSPECT, AS I POINT THEM; ON THE SHOARE . . 12 143

POINTING
DRIVN BACKWARD SLOPE THIR POINTING SPIRES, AND
ROWLD 1 223

POINTS
WITH HIM THE POINTS OF LIBERTIE, WHO MADE . . . 5 823

POIS'D
UPON HER CENTER POIS'D, WHEN ON A DAY 5 579

POISE
LEVIED TO SIDE WITH WARRING WINDS, AND POISE . . 2 905

POLAR
NOW ON THE POLAR WINDES, THEN WITH QUICK FANN . . 5 269
AS WHEN TWO POLAR WINDS BLOWING ADVERSE 10 289
BEYOND THE POLAR CIRCLES; TO THEM DAY 10 681

POLE
AS FROM THE CENTER THRICE TO TH' UTMOST POLE. . . 1 74
PLY STEMMING NIGHTLY TOWARD THE POLE. SO SEEM'D . 2 642
BEYOND TH' HORIZON; THEN FROM POLE TO POLE . . . 3 560
AND STARRIE POLE: THOU ALSO MAD'ST THE NIGHT, . . 4 724
STANDING ON EARTH, NOT RAPT ABOVE THE POLE, . . 7 23
HEAV'NS HIGHTH, AND WITH THE CENTER MIX THE POLE. 7 215
FROM POLE TO POLE, TRAVERSING EACH COLURE; . . . 9 66

POLES
THE POLES OF EARTH TWICE TEN DEGREES AND MORE . . 10 669

POLISH
OF ARTS THAT POLISH LIFE, INVENTERS RARE, . . . 11 610

POLLICY
BY POLLICY, AND LONG PROCESS OF TIME, ... 2 297

POLLUTED
OF MISCHIEF, AND POLLUTED FROM THE END 10 167
TO LEAVE THEM TO THIR OWN POLLUTED WAYES; . . . 12 110

POLLUTING
WHICH MANS POLLUTING SIN WITH TAINT HATH SHED . . 10 631

POLLUTION
ENDEAVOUR PEACE: THIR STRIFE POLLUTION BRINGS . . 12 355

POMONA
TO PALES, OR POMONA THUS ADORND, ... 9 393
LIKELIEST SHE SEEMD, POMONA WHEN SHE FLED . . . 9 394

POMONA'S
THEY CAME, THAT LIKE POMONA'S ARBOUR SMIL'D . . 5 378

POMP
WITH GAY RELIGIONS FULL OF POMP AND GOLD, . . . 1 372
OF SERVILE POMP. OUR GREATNESS WILL APPEER . . 2 257
THAN HELLS DREAD EMPEROUR WITH POMP SUPREAM, . . 2 510
MORE SOLEMN THEN THE TEDIOUS POMP THAT WAITS . . 5 354
WHILE THE BRIGHT POMP ASCENDED JUBILANT. . . . 7 564
A POMP OF WINNING GRACES WAITED STILL, ... 8 61
FLOOD OVERWHELMD, AND THEM WITH ALL THIR POMP . . 11 748

POND
TO BOGGS AND MIRES, AND OFT THROUGH POND OR POOLE, 9 641

PONDER
THIS PONDER, THAT ALL NATIONS OF THE EARTH . . . 12 147

PONDERING
PONDERING THE DANGER WITH DEEP THOUGHTS; AND EACH 2 421
PONDERING HIS VOYAGE; FOR NO NARROW FRITH . . . 2 919
SO PONDERING, AND FROM HIS ARMED PEERS 6 127

PONDEROUS
WAS MOVING TOWARD THE SHOAR; HIS PONDEROUS SHIELD 1 284

PONDERS
IN COUNTERPOISE, NOW PONDERS ALL EVENTS, . . . 4 1001

PONENT
FORTH RUSH THE LEVANT AND THE PONENT WINDES . . 10 704

PONTIFICAL
PONTIFICAL, A RIDGE OF PENDENT ROCK 10 313

PONTIFICE
OF THIS NEW WONDROUS PONTIFICE, UNHOP'T 10 348

PONTUS
IN PONTUS OR THE PUNIC COAST, OR WHERE 5 340
FROM EDEN OVER PONTUS, AND THE POOLE 9 77

POOL
FORTHWITH UPRIGHT HE REARS FROM OFF THE POOL . . 1 221
LYE THUS ASTONISHT ON TH' OBLIVIOUS POOL, . . . 1 266

POOL (CONTINUED)
AND ELEALE TO TH' ASPHALTICK POOL. 1 411
ESCAP'T THE STYGIAN POOL, THOUGH LONG DETAIN'D 3 14

POOLE
FROM EDEN OVER PONTUS, AND THE POOLE 9 77
TO BOGGS AND MIRES, AND OFT THROUGH POND OR POOLE, 9 641

POOR
NOT WANDRING POOR, BUT TRUSTING ALL HIS WEALTH 12 133

POPULAR
PRINCES OF HELL? FOR SO THE POPULAR VOTE 2 313
HEREAFTER, JOIN'D IN HER POPULAR TRIBES 7 488
HEAPT TO THE POPULAR SUMME, WILL SO INCENSE 12 338

POPULOUS
A MULTITUDE, LIKE WHICH THE POPULOUS NORTH 1 351
POUR FORTH THIR POPULOUS YOUTH ABOUT THE HIVE 1 770
SWARM POPULOUS, UNNUMBER'D AS THE SANDS 2 903
THIR STATION, HEAV'N YET POPULOUS RETAINES 7 146
AS ONE WHO LONG IN POPULOUS CITY PENT, 9 445

PORCH
WHOSE WANTON PASSIONS IN THE SACRED PORCH 1 454

PORCHES
AND PORCHES WIDE, BUT CHIEF THE SPACIOUS HALL 1 762

PORCULLIS
FORTHWITH THE HUGE PORCULLIS HIGH UP DREW, 2 874

POROUS
OF POROUS EARTH WITH KINDLY THIRST UP DRAWN, 4 228
IN THE SUNS ORB, MADE POROUS TO RECEIVE 7 361

PORT
GLADLY THE PORT, THOUGH SHROUDS AND TACKLE TORN; 2 1044
AND FROM THIR IVORIE PORT THE CHERUBIM 4 778
AND WITH THEM COMES A THIRD OF REGAL PORT, 4 869
THEN LOUDEST ORATORIE: YET THIR PORT 11 8
TH' EMPIRE OF NEGUS TO HIS UTMOST PORT 11 397

PORTAL
THE PORTAL SHON, INIMITABLE ON EARTH 3 508

PORTALS
THAT OPEN'D WIDE HER BLAZING PORTALS, LED 7 575

PORTED
WITH PORTED SPEARS, AS THICK AS WHEN A FIELD 4 980

PORTENDING
PORTENDING HOLLOW TRUCE; AT EACH BEHIND 6 578
PORTENDING GOOD, AND ALL HER SPIRITS COMPOS'D 12 596

PORTENDS
OF PEACEFUL DAYES PORTENDS, THEN THOSE TWO PAST; 11 600

PORTENTOUS
PORTENTOUS HELD ME; BUT FAMILIAR GROWN, 2 761
WITH THIS PORTENTOUS BRIDGE THE DARK ABYSS. 10 371

PORTION
IN UTTER DARKNESS, AND THIR PORTION SET 1 72
PRECEDENCE, NONE, WHOSE PORTION IS SO SMALL 2 33

PORTRAID
VARIOUS, WITH BOASTFUL ARGUMENT PORTRAID, 6 84

PORTRESS
T' WHOM THUS THE PORTRESS OF HELL GATE REPLY'D; 2 746

POSSESS
TO WASTE HIS WHOLE CREATION, OR POSSESS 2 365
LIE VANQUISHT; THOU HAST GIVN ME TO POSSESS 3 243
OVER ALL OTHER CREATURES THAT POSSESS 4 431
TWO ONELY, WHO YET BY SOV'RAN GIFT POSSESS 5 366
HOMEWARD WITH FLYING MARCH WHERE WE POSSESS 5 688
NUMBER SUFFICIENT TO POSSESS HER REALMES 7 147
POSSESS IT, AND ALL THINGS THAT THEREIN LIVE, 8 340
AND DUNGEON OF OUR TYRANT: NOW POSSESS, 10 466
I SUFFER THEM TO ENTER AND POSSESS 10 623
ALL TH' EARTH HE GAVE THEE TO POSSESS AND RULE, 11 339
TO LEAVE THIS PARADISE, BUT SHALT POSSESS 12 586

POSSESSD
I KNOW NOT WHENCE POSSESSD THEE; WE HAD THEN 9 1137

POSSESSES
POSSESSES THEE TO BEND THAT MORTAL DART 2 729
POSSESSES LATELY, THITHER TO ARRIVE 2 979
BUT OTHER DOUBT POSSESSES ME, LEAST HARM 9 251

POSSESSING
IN HEART OR HEAD, POSSESSING SOON INSPIR'D 9 189

POSSESSION
HER OLD POSSESSION, AND EXTINGUISH LIFE 4 666
THOUGH FOR POSSESSION PUT TO TRY ONCE MORE 4 941
FOR IN POSSESSION SUCH, NOT ONELY OF RIGHT, 10 461
VACANT POSSESSION SOM NEW TROUBLE RAISE: 11 103
POSSESSION OF THE GARDEN; HEE ALONE, 11 222

POSSESSOR
RECEIVE THY NEW POSSESSOR: ONE WHO BRINGS 1 252

POSSEST
NATIVES AND SONS OF HEAV'N POSSEST BEFORE 5 790
SEEM I TO THEE SUFFICIENTLY POSSEST 8 404

POSSIBLE
CAN TURN, OR HOLDS IT POSSIBLE TO TURN 5 441
FIRM WE SUBSIST, YET POSSIBLE TO SWERVE, 9 359

POSSIBLY
TO HIM, OR POSSIBLY HIS LOVE DESERT 5 515

POST
FROM MEDIA POST TO AEGYPT, THERE FAST BOUND. 4 171

POSTERITIE
HE WITH HIS WHOLE POSTERITIE MUST DYE, 3 209
FROM THE BEGINNING, THAT POSTERITIE 7 638
POSTERITIE STANDS CURST: FAIR PATRIMONIE 10 818

POSTURE
OR IN THIS ABJECT POSTURE HAVE YE SWORN 1 322
HOW BUSIED, IN WHAT FORM AND POSTURE COUCHT. 4 876
IN POSTURE TO DISPLODE THIR SECOND TIRE 6 605

POTABLE
POTABLE GOLD, WHEN WITH ONE VERTUOUS TOUCH 3 608

POTENT
NOR WHAT THE POTENT VICTOR IN HIS RAGE 1 95
INNUMERABLE. AS WHEN THE POTENT ROD 1 338
BEYOND HIS POTENT ARM, TO LIVE EXEMPT 2 318
LEAST HEAV'N SURCHARG'D WITH POTENT MULTITUDE 2 836
PERFECTION FROM THE SUNS MORE POTENT RAY. 4 673
OR POTENT TONGUE; FOOL, NOT TO THINK HOW VAIN 6 135
TWO POTENT THRONES, THAT TO BE LESS THEN GODS 6 366
HELD BY THY VOICE, THY POTENT VOICE HE HEARES, 7 100
MOSES ONCE MORE HIS POTENT ROD EXTENDS 12 211

POTENTATE
OF THIR GREAT POTENTATE; FOR GREAT INDEED 5 706
NONE OF THE MEANEST, SOME GREAT POTENTATE 11 231

POTENTATES
OF HELL RESOUNDED. PRINCES, POTENTATES, 1 315
OF SERAPHIM AND POTENTATES AND THRONES 5 749
HIS POTENTATES TO COUNCEL CALL'D BY NIGHT; 6 416
CHERUB AND SERAPH, POTENTATES AND THRONES, 7 198

POUDERD
POUDERD WITH STARRS. AND NOW ON EARTH THE SEVENTH 7 581

POUR
POUR FORTH THIR POPULOUS YOUTH ABOUT THE HIVE 1 770
BORN EEVN OR HIGH, FOR THIS DAY WILL POUR DOWN, 6 544

POUR'D
TREBLE CONFUSION, WRATH AND VENGEANCE POUR'D. 1 220
POUR'D NEVER FROM HER FROZEN LOYNS, TO PASS 1 352
ABOUT HIS CHARIOT NUMBERLESS WERE POUR'D 7 197
ABUNDANTLY HIS GIFTS HATH ALSO POUR'D 8 220
HIS BURSTING PASSION INTO PLAINTS THUS POUR'D: 9 98
WITH LARGE WINE-OFFERINGS POUR'D, AND SACRED FEAST, 12 21

POURD
POURD OUT BY MILLIONS HER VICTORIOUS BANDS 2 997
THE HAND THAT FORMD THEM ON THIR SHAPE HATH POURD. 4 365
GODS INDIGNATION ON THESE GODLESS POURD 6 811

POURE
AND WHAT THY STORES CONTAIN, BRING FORTH AND POURE 5 314

POURING
HER VIRGIN FANCIES, POURING FORTH MORE SWEET, 5 296

POURLIEUES
IN THE POURLIEUES OF HEAV'N, AND THEREIN PLAC'T 2 833

POWDER
LIGHTS ON A HEAP OF NITROUS POWDER, LAID 4 815

POWER
WITH VAIN ATTEMPT. HIM THE ALMIGHTY POWER 1 44
ONE NEXT HIMSELF IN POWER, AND NEXT IN CRIME, 1 79
HIS UTMOST POWER WITH ADVERSE POWER OPPOS'D 1 103
WITH SUPPLIANT KNEE, AND DEIFIE HIS POWER, 1 112
NOT BY THE SUFFERANCE OF SUPERNAL POWER. 1 241
NOR WANTING POWER TO MITIGATE AND SWAGE 1 556
HATEFUL TO UTTER: BUT WHAT POWER OF MIND 1 626

POWER (CONTINUED)
EXALTED TO SUCH POWER, AND GAVE TO RULE, 1 736
OF SOVRAN POWER, WITH AWFUL CEREMONY 1 753
OUR POWER SUFFICIENT TO DISTURB HIS HEAV'N, 2 102
BUT TO OUR POWER HOSTILITY AND HATE, 2 336
IN POWER AND EXCELLENCE, BUT FAVOUR'D MORE 2 350
OR SUBSTANCE, HOW ENDU'D, AND WHAT THIR POWER, 2 356
WITH SPLENDOR, ARM'D WITH POWER, IF AUGHT PROPOS'D 2 447
EXCEL'D HER POWER; THE GATES WIDE OP'N STOOD, 2 884
UNDAUNTED TO MEET THERE WHAT EVER POWER 2 955
UNDER HIS GLOOMIE POWER I SHALL NOT LONG 3 242
ANOINTED UNIVERSAL KING; ALL POWER 3 317
AMBITION. YET WHY NOT? SOM OTHER POWER 4 61
HADST THOU THE SAME FREE WILL AND POWER TO STAND? 4 66
DEARER THY SELF THEN ALL; NEEDS MUST THE POWER 4 412
AMONG SO MANY SIGNES OF POWER AND RULE 4 429
WHEN GABRIEL TO HIS NEXT IN POWER THUS SPAKE. 4 781
BY THY EXAMPLE, BUT HAVE POWER AND RIGHT 4 881
ALLEGEANCE TO TH' ACKNOWLDG'D POWER SUPREAM? 4 956
THY GOODNESS BEYOND THOUGHT, AND POWER DIVINE: 5 159
HAPPINESS IN HIS POWER LEFT FREE TO WILL, 5 235
DIVINE EFFULGENCE, WHOSE HIGH POWER SO FAR 5 458
HE LEFT IT IN THY POWER, ORDAIND THY WILL 5 526
IF NOT THE FIRST ARCH-ANGEL, GREAT IN POWER, 5 660
IN BATTEL, WHAT OUR POWER IS, OR OUR RIGHT. 5 728
ILLUSTRATES, WHEN THEY SEE ALL REGAL POWER 5 739
ALL POWER, AND US ECLIPST UNDER THE NAME 5 776
HIS EQUALS, IF IN POWER AND SPLENDOR LESS, 5 796
ONE OVER ALL WITH UNSUCCEEDED POWER. 5 821
BY OUR OWN QUICK'NING POWER, WHEN FATAL COURSE 5 861
ABANDOND AT THE TERROR OF THY POWER 6 134
OF ALL THIR REGIONS: HOW MUCH MORE OF POWER 6 223
PRODIGIOUS POWER HAD SHEWN, AND MET IN ARMES 6 247
OF GODLIKE POWER: FOR LIKEST GODS THEY SEEMD, 6 301
AS NOT OF POWER, AT ONCE; NOR ODDS APPEERD 6 319
HIS CONFIDENCE TO EQUAL GOD IN POWER. 6 343
FORTHWITH (BEHOLD THE EXCELLENCE, THE POWER 6 637
ALL POWER ON HIM TRANSFERR'D: WHENCE TO HIS SON 6 678
IN HEAV'N AND HELL THY POWER ABOVE COMPARE, 6 705
SCEPTER AND POWER, THY GIVING, I ASSUME, 6 730
BEFORE HIM POWER DIVINE HIS WAY PREPAR'D; 6 780
KINGDOM AND POWER AND GLORIE APPERTAINS, 6 815
THE FILIAL POWER ARRIV'D, AND SATE HIM DOWN 7 587
THY POWER; WHAT THOUGHT CAN MEASURE THEE OR TONGUE 7 603
SO SPAKE THE GODLIKE POWER, AND THUS OUR SIRE. 8 249
IN GOODNESS AND IN POWER PRAEEMINENT; 8 279
LET NOT MY WORDS OFFEND THEE, HEAV'NLY POWER, 8 379
THE DANGER LIES, YET LIES WITHIN HIS POWER: 9 349
MOTHER OF SCIENCE, NOW I FEEL THY POWER 9 680
BUT KEEP THE ODDS OF KNOWLEDGE IN MY POWER 9 820
BUT FIRST LOW REVERENCE DON, AS TO THE POWER 9 835
NOT WELL CONCEAV'D OF GOD, WHO THOUGH HIS POWER 9 945
FOR DEATH FROM SIN NO POWER CAN SEPARATE. 10 251
ADVENTROUS WORK, YET TO THY POWER AND MINE 10 255
FLEW DIVERS, AND WITH POWER (THIR POWER WAS GREAT) 10 284
IF YOUR JOYNT POWER PREVAILES, TH' AFFAIRES OF HELL 10 408
RELUCTANT, BUT IN VAINE, A GREATER POWER 10 515
HUGE PYTHON, AND HIS POWER NO LESS HE SEEM'D 10 531
TOO SOON ARRIV'D, SIN THERE IN POWER BEFORE, 10 586
OF WEAKNESS, NOT OF POWER. WILL HE, DRAW OUT, 10 801
FOOD FOR SO FOULE A MONSTER, IN THY POWER 10 986
THAT SHEW NO END BUT DEATH, AND HAVE THE POWER, 10 1004
HE CEAS'D; AND TH' ARCHANGELIC POWER PREPAR'D 11 126
FOMENTED BY HIS VIRTUAL POWER AND WARMD: 11 338
SO DEEP THE POWER OF THESE INGREDIENTS PIERC'D, 11 417
SUCH WONDROUS POWER GOD TO HIS SAINT WILL LEND, 12 200
THE POWER OF THE MOST HIGH; HE SHALL ASCEND 12 369
BUT SOON REVIVES, DEATH OVER HIM NO POWER 12 420
WITH GLORY AND POWER TO JUDGE BOTH QUICK AND DEAD, 12 460
SECULAR POWER, THOUGH FEIGNING STILL TO ACT 12 517
SPIRITUAL LAWES BY CARNAL POWER SHALL FORCE 12 521

POWERFUL
I ALSO; AT WHICH TIME THIS POWERFUL KEY 2 774
AND BY COMMAND OF HEAV'NS ALL-POWERFUL KING 2 851
IN VAIN, THOUGH BY THIR POWERFUL ART THEY BINDE 3 602
O HAD HIS POWERFUL DESTINY ORDAIND 4 58
THE KING OF GLORIE IN HIS POWERFUL WORD 7 208
AGAINST THE CHARM OF BEAUTIES POWERFUL GLANCE. 8 533
POWERFUL PERSWADERS, QUICK'ND AT THE SCENT 9 587
POWERFUL AT GREATEST DISTANCE TO UNITE 10 247

POWERFULLEST
WHAT HEAVENS LORD HAD POWERFULLEST TO SEND 6 425

POWERS
O PRINCE, O CHIEF OF MANY THRONED POWERS, 1 128
AND REASSEMBLING OUR AFFLICTED POWERS, 1 186
AND POWERS THAT EARST IN HEAVEN SAT ON THRONES; 1 360
O MYRIADS OF IMMORTAL SPIRITS, O POWERS 1 622
POWERS AND DOMINIONS, DEITIES OF HEAV'N, 2 11
THRONES AND IMPERIAL POWERS, OFF-SPRING OF HEAV'N 2 310
HIGH HONOURD SITS? GO THEREFORE MIGHTY POWERS, 2 456
BY FALSE PRESUMPTUOUS HOPE, THE RANGED POWERS 2 522
WHICH BUT HER SELF NOT ALL THE STYGIAN POWERS 2 875
T' WHOM SATAN TURNING BOLDLY, THUS. YE POWERS 2 968
SHINE INWARD, AND THE MIND THROUGH ALL HER POWERS 3 52
SUCH I CREATED ALL TH' ETHEREAL POWERS 3 100

POWERS (CONTINUED)
HIS LAPSED POWERS, THOUGH FORFEIT AND ENTHRALL'D 3 176
SAY HEAV'NLY POWERS, WHERE SHALL WE FIND SUCH LOVE, 3 213
THE POWERS OF DARKNESS BOUND. THOU AT THE SIGHT 3 256
THRONES, PRINCEDOMS, POWERS, DOMINIONS I REDUCE: 3 320
HEE HEAV'N OF HEAVENS AND ALL THE POWERS THEREIN 3 390
BACK FROM PURSUIT THY POWERS WITH LOUD ACCLAIME 3 397
DRAWN TO HIS PART; BUT OTHER POWERS AS GREAT 4 63
BETTER ABODE, AND MY AFFLICTED POWERS 4 939
THRONES, DOMINATIONS, PRINCEDOMS, VERTUES, POWERS, 5 601
OR SEVERAL ONE BY ONE, THE REGENT POWERS, 5 697
SO SPAKE THE SON, BUT SATAN WITH HIS POWERS 5 743
THRONES, DOMINATIONS, PRINCEDOMES, VERTUES, POWERS, 5 772
THRONES, DOMINATIONS, PRINCEDOMS, VERTUES, POWERS, 5 840
ESSENTIAL POWERS, NOR BY HIS REIGN OBSCUR'D, 5 841
AMONG THOSE FRIENDLY POWERS WHO HIM RECEAV'D 6 22
AT WHICH COMMAND THE POWERS MILITANT, 6 61
THE BANDED POWERS OF SATAN HASTING ON 6 85
SINCE MICHAEL AND HIS POWERS WENT FORTH TO TAME 6 686
AND TO REBELLIOUS FIGHT RALLIED THIR POWERS 6 786
AMONG TH' ANGELIC POWERS, AND THE DEEP FALL 6 898
MEAN WHILE INHABIT LAXE, YE POWERS OF HEAV'N, 7 162
THE INFERNAL POWERS, IN ONE DAY TO HAVE MARR'D 9 136
OF REASON IN MY INWARD POWERS, AND SPEECH 9 600
ABOUT THIR SPIRITS HAD PLAID, AND INMOST POWERS 9 1048
ASSEMBL'D ANGELS, AND YE POWERS RETURN'D 10 34
OF HIGH COLLATERAL GLORIE: HIM THRONES AND POWERS, 10 86
SPOILD PRINCIPALITIES AND POWERS, TRIUMPHT 10 186
TO MY ASSOCIATE POWERS, THEM TO ACQUAINT 10 395
THRONES, DOMINATIONS, PRINCEDOMS, VERTUES, POWERS, 10 460
IN THIR BRIGHT STAND, THERE LEFT HIS POWERS TO
SEISE 11 221
WITHIN HIMSELF UNWORTHIE POWERS TO REIGN 12 91
THOU KNEWST BY NAME, AND ALL TH' ETHEREAL POWERS, 12 577

POW'R
DOUBT MIGHT BEGET OF DIABOLIC POW'R 9 95

POWRD
WORLDS, AND ON WHOM HATH ALL THESE GRACES POWRD; 3 674
POWRD FORTH PROFUSE ON HILL AND DALE AND PLAINE, 4 243
POWRD FIRST ON HIS APOSTLES, WHOM HE SENDS 12 498

POWRE
OF HEAV'N SET OPEN ON THE EARTH SHALL POWRE 11 825

POW'RS
THEE WHAT THOU ART, AND FORMD THE POW'RS OF HEAV'N 5 824

PRACTICE
THENCEFORTH SHALL PRACTICE HOW TO LIVE SECURE, 11 802

PRACTIS'D
AND PRACTIS'D DISTANCES TO CRINGE, NOT FIGHT. 4 945

PRACTISD
THAT PRACTISD FALSHOOD UNDER SAINTLY SHEW, 4 122
YET NOT ANOUGH HAD PRACTISD TO DECEIVE 4 124

PRAEAMBLE
LIKE QUIVERS HUNG, AND WITH PRAEAMBLE SWEET 3 367

PRAEEMINENCE
IN FAVOUR AND PRAEEMINENCE, YET FRAUGHT 5 661
BUT THIS PRAEEMINENCE THOU HAST LOST, BROUGHT DOWN 11 347

PRAEEMINENT
PRAEEMINENT BY SO MUCH ODDS, WHILE THOU 4 447
IN GOODNESS AND IN POWER PRAEEMINENT; 8 279

PRAIS'D
NOR FAIL'D THEY TO EXPRESS HOW MUCH THEY PRAIS'D, 2 480
AND TOUCH'T THIR GOLDEN HARPS, AND HYMNING PRAIS'D 7 258

PRAISE
ADMIRING ENTER'D, AND THE WORK SOME PRAISE 1 731
NOT WHAT THEY WOULD? WHAT PRAISE COULD THEY
RECEIVE? 3 106
HENCEFORTH, AND NEVER SHALL MY HARP THY PRAISE 3 414
FORGET, NOR FROM THY FATHERS PRAISE DISJOINE. 3 415
NAUGHT SEEKING BUT THE PRAISE OF MEN, HERE FIND 3 453
THE UNIVERSAL MAKER WE MAY PRAISE; 3 676
THAT REACHES BLAME, BUT RATHER MERITS PRAISE 3 697
WHAT COULD BE LESS THEN TO AFFORD HIM PRAISE, 4 46
BUT LET US EVER PRAISE HIM, AND EXTOLL 4 436
IS WOMANS HAPPIEST KNOWLEDGE AND HER PRAISE. 4 638
THAT HEAV'N WOULD WANT SPECTATORS, GOD WANT PRAISE; 4 676
ALL THESE WITH CEASLESS PRAISE HIS WORKS BEHOLD 4 679
NOR HOLY RAPTURE WANTED THEY TO PRAISE 5 147
WITH THY BRIGHT CIRCLET, PRAISE HIM IN THY SPHEARE 5 169
ACKNOWLEDGE HIM THY GREATER, SOUND HIS PRAISE 5 172
HIS PRAISE, WHO OUT OF DARKNESS CALL'D UP LIGHT. 5 179
VARIE TO OUR GREAT MAKER STILL NEW PRAISE. 5 184
RISING OR FALLING STILL ADVANCE HIS PRAISE. 5 191
HIS PRAISE YE WINDS, THAT FROM FOUR QUARTERS BLOW, 5 192
MELODIOUS MURMURS, WARBLING TUNE HIS PRAISE. 5 196
BEAR ON YOUR WINGS AND IN YOUR NOTES HIS PRAISE; 5 199
MADE VOCAL BY MY SONG, AND TAUGHT HIS PRAISE. 5 204

PRAISE (CONTINUED)
(WHOSE PRAISE BE EVER SUNG) TO MAN IN PART 5 405
SEEK NOT THE PRAISE OF MEN: THE OTHER SORT 6 376
HYMNS OF HIGH PRAISE, AND I AMONG THEM CHIEF. 6 745
GLORIE AND PRAISE, WHOSE WISDOM HAD ORDAIN'D 7 187
FROM TH' EARTHS GREAT ALTAR SEND UP SILENT PRAISE 9 195
FOR SUCH A PETTY TRESPASS, AND NOT PRAISE 9 693
THE TONGUE NOT MADE FOR SPEECH TO SPEAK THY PRAISE: 9 749
THY PRAISE HEE ALSO WHO FORBIDS THY USE, 9 750
NOT WITHOUT SONG, EACH MORNING, AND DUE PRAISE 9 800
AND PALATE CALL JUDICIOUS; I THE PRAISE 9 1020
WOMANS DOMESTIC HONOUR AND CHIEF PRAISE; 11 617

PRAISES
THY PRAISES, WITH TH' INNUMERABLE SOUND 3 147
FOR WEE TO HIM INDEED ALL PRAISES OWE, 4 444

PRAVITIE
THIR NATURAL PRAVITIE, BY STIRRING UP 12 288

PRAY
TO PRAY, REPENT, AND BRING OBEDIENCE DUE. 3 190
HOW MUCH MORE, IF WE PRAY HIM, WILL HIS EAR 10 1060
UNSKILFUL WITH WHAT WORDS TO PRAY, LET MEE 11 32

PRAY'D
SO PRAY'D THEY INNOCENT, AND TO THIR THOUGHTS 5 209

PRAYER
TO PRAYER, REPENTANCE, AND OBEDIENCE DUE, 3 191
UNUTTERABLE, WHICH THE SPIRIT OF PRAYER 11 6
HARD TO BELIEF MAY SEEM; YET THIS WILL PRAYER, 11 146
BY PRAYER TH' OFFENDED DEITIE TO APPEASE, 11 149
NOR KNOWING US NOR KNOWN: AND IF BY PRAYER 11 307
BUT PRAYER AGAINST HIS ABSOLUTE DECREE 11 311

PRAYERS
MENDS NOT HER SLOWEST PACE FOR PRAYERS OR CRIES. 10 859
AND MY DISPLEASURE BEARST SO ILL. IF PRAYERS 10 952
OF THEMIS STOOD DEVOUT. TO HEAV'N THIR PRAYERS 11 14
AND PRAYERS, WHICH IN THIS GOLDEN CENSER, MIXT 11 24
SUFFICIENT THAT THY PRAYERS ARE HEARD, AND DEATH, 11 252

PRAYES
HE SORROWS NOW, REPENTS, AND PRAYES CONTRITE, 11 90

PRAYING
HEE WILL INSTRUCT US PRAYING, AND OF GRACE 10 1081
PRAYING, FOR FROM THE MERCIE-SEAT ABOVE 11 2

PREACHD
TRIUMPHS OR FESTIVALS, AND TO THEM PREACHD 11 723

PREACHT
SALVATION SHALL BE PREACHT, BUT TO THE SONS 12 448

PRECEDENCE
PRECEDENCE, NONE, WHOSE PORTION IS SO SMALL 2 33

PRECEDES
BUT HARM PRECEDES NOT SIN: ONELY OUR FOE 9 327
TILL THEN THE CURSE PRONOUNC'T ON BOTH PRECEDES. 10 640

PRECEPT
HAD FIRST HIS PRECEPT SO TO MOVE, SO SHINE, 10 652

PRECINCTS
NOT FARR OFF HEAV'N, IN THE PRECINCTS OF LIGHT, 3 88

PRECIOUS
DESERVE THE PRECIOUS BANE. AND HERE LET THOSE 1 692
HERE IN THE DARK SO MANY PRECIOUS THINGS 3 611
TWO OTHER PRECIOUS DROPS THAT READY STOOD, 5 132
IN THEE CONCENTRING ALL THIR PRECIOUS BEAMS 9 106
O SOVRAN, VERTUOUS, PRECIOUS OF ALL TREES 9 795
SOME BLOUD MORE PRECIOUS MUST BE PAID FOR MAN, 12 293

PRECIPICE
THE FIERY SURGE, THAT FROM THE PRECIPICE 1 173

PRECIPITANCE
HASTED WITH GLAD PRECIPITANCE, UPROWLD 7 291

PRECIPITANT
HIS FLIGHT PRECIPITANT, AND WINDES WITH EASE 3 563

PRECIPITATE
PRECIPITATE THEE WITH AUGMENTED PAINE. 6 280

PRECISE
OF SPECULATION; FOR THE HOUR PRECISE 12 589

PREDESTINATION
AS IF PREDESTINATION OVER-RUL'D 3 114

PREDICTION
HOW SOON HATH THY PREDICTION, SEER BLEST, 12 553

PREDOMINANT
WHETHER THE SUN PREDOMINANT IN HEAV'N 8 160

PREFACE
OF PREFACE BROOKING THROUGH HIS ZEAL OF RIGHT. 9 676
ADAM, HEAV'NS HIGH BEHEST NO PREFACE NEEDS: 11 251

PREFER
AND CHIEFLY THOU, O SPIRIT, THAT DOST PREFER 1 17
PREFER, AND PIETIE TO GOD, THOUGH THEN 6 144

PREFERR'D
HER HUSBAND THE RELATER SHE PREFERR'D 8 52
O EARTH, HOW LIKE TO HEAV'N, IF NOT PREFERR'D 9 99

PREFERRING
THAT DURST DISLIKE HIS REIGN, AND ME PREFERRING, 1 102
FREE, AND TO NONE ACCOUNTABLE, PREFERRING 2 255

PREGNANT
AND MAD'ST IT PREGNANT: WHAT IN ME IS DARK 1 22
PREGNANT BY THEE, AND NOW EXCESSIVE GROWN 2 779
BUT ALL THESE IN THIR PREGNANT CAUSES MIXT 2 913
SHALL YIELD US PREGNANT WITH INFERNAL FLAME, 6 483

PREPAR'D
SUCH PLACE ETERNAL JUSTICE HAD PREPAR'D 1 70
STANDS ON THE BLASTED HEATH. HE NOW PREPAR'D 1 615
NIGH ON THE PLAIN IN MANY CELLS PREPAR'D, 1 700
MINISTRING LIGHT PREPAR'D, THEY SET AND RISE; 4 664
AND EVE WITHIN, DUE AT HER HOUR PREPAR'D 5 303
TO THIR PREPAR'D ILL MANSION DRIVEN DOWN 6 738
BEFORE HIM POWER DIVINE HIS WAY PREPAR'D; 6 780
HE TOOK THE GOLDEN COMPASSES, PREPAR'D 7 225
TO THE GARDEN OF BLISS, THY SEAT PREPAR'D. 8 299
MAY FINDE US BOTH PERHAPS FARR LESS PREPAR'D, 9 381
HE CEAS'D; AND TH' ARCHANGELIC POWER PREPAR'D 11 126
SAFEST THY LIFE, AND BEST PREPAR'D ENDURE 11 365
INTO FIT MOULDS PREPAR'D; FROM WHICH HE FORMD 11 571
PURE, AND IN MIND PREPAR'D, IF SO BEFALL, 12 444

PREPARE
THE QUARTERS OF THE NORTH, THERE TO PREPARE 5 689
AND NOW PREPARE THEE FOR ANOTHER SIGHT. 11 555
BUT NOW PREPARE THEE FOR ANOTHER SCENE. 11 637

PRESAGE
PRESAGE OF VICTORIE AND FIERCE DESIRE 6 201

PRESAGING
FORESEEING OR PRESAGING, FROM THE DEPTH 1 627
PRESAGING, SINCE WITH SORROW AND HEARTS DISTRESS 12 613

PRESCRIB'D
PRESCRIB'D, NO BARRS OF HELL, NOR ALL THE CHAINS 3 82
WHY HAST THOU, SATAN, BROKE THE BOUNDS PRESCRIB'D 4 878
UNLICENC'T FROM HIS BOUNDS IN HELL PRESCRIB'D; 4 909
HER OFFICE THEY PRESCRIB'D, TO TH' OTHER FIVE 10 657

PRESCRIPT
BY HIS PRESCRIPT A SANCTUARY IS FRAM'D 12 249

PRESENCE
STAND IN HIS PRESENCE HUMBLE, AND RECEIVE 2 240
THENCEFORTH, BUT IN THY PRESENCE JOY ENTIRE. 3 265
WHO IN GODS PRESENCE, NEEREST TO HIS THRONE 3 649
NEERER HIS PRESENCE ADAM THOUGH NOT AWD, 5 358
IN PRESENCE OF TH' ALMIGHTIE FATHER, PLEAS'D 7 11
PRESENCE DIVINE. REJOYCING, BUT WITH AW 8 314
ALL HIGHER KNOWLEDGE IN HER PRESENCE FALLS 8 551
THAT DWELT WITHIN, WHOSE PRESENCE HAD INFUS'D 9 836
THY PRESENCE, AGONIE OF LOVE TILL NOW 9 858
AND FROM HIS PRESENCE HID THEMSELVES AMONG 10 100
TO WHOM THE SOVRAN PRESENCE THUS REPLI'D. 10 144
PRESENCE DIVINE, AND TO MY SONS RELATE; 11 319
HIS PRESENCE TO THESE NARROW BOUNDS CONFIN'D 11 341
PRESENT, AND OF HIS PRESENCE MANY A SIGNE 11 351
HIS PRESENCE FROM AMONG THEM, AND AVERT 12 108
AS IN HIS PRESENCE, EVER TO OBSERVE 12 563

PRESENT
WAST PRESENT, AND WITH MIGHTY WINGS OUTSPREAD 1 20
OF KNOWLEDGE PAST OR PRESENT, COULD HAVE FEAR'D, 1 628
OF PRESENT PAIN, THAT WITH AMBITIOUS MIND 2 34
WORTH WAITING, SINCE OUR PRESENT LOT APPEERS 2 223
COMPOSE OUR PRESENT EVILS, WITH REGARD 2 281
THE PRESENT MISERY, AND RENDER HELL 2 459
(WHICH IS MY PRESENT JOURNEY) AND ONCE MORE 2 985
WHEREIN PAST, PRESENT, FUTURE HE BEHOLDS, 3 78
PRESENT, OR PAST, AS SAINTS AND PATRIARCHS US'D. 4 762
BY PRESENT, PAST, AND FUTURE) ON SUCH DAY 5 582
THEY LED HIM HIGH APPLAUDED, AND PRESENT 6 26
PRESENT) THUS TO HIS SON AUDIBLY SPAKE. 7 518
OR BEAR WHAT TO MY MINDE FIRST THOUGHTS PRESENT, 9 213
WHEN I AM PRESENT, AND THY TRIAL CHOOSE 9 316
WHAT BEST MAY FROM THE PRESENT SERVE TO HIDE 9 1092
THE PRESENT, FEARING GUILTIE WHAT HIS WRAUTH 10 340
AS SORTED BEST WITH PRESENT THINGS. THE SUN 10 651

PRINCELY (CONTINUED)
AND PRINCELY COUNSEL IN HIS FACE YET SHON, ... 2 304
WARR UNPROCLAM'D, THE PRINCELY HIERARCH . . . 11 220

PRINCES
OF HELL RESOUNDED. PRINCES, POTENTATES, . . . 1 315
AND SAT AS PRINCES, WHOM THE SUPREME KING . . . 1 735
PRINCES OF HELL? FOR SO THE POPULAR VOTE . . . 2 313
ON PRINCES, WHEN THIR RICH RETINUE LONG 5 355
PRINCE ABOVE PRINCES, GENTLY HAST THOU TOULD . . 11 298

PRINCIPALITIES
NISROC, OF PRINCIPALITIES THE PRIME; 6 447
SPOILD PRINCIPALITIES AND POWERS, TRIUMPHT . . . 10 186

PRISON
FOR THOSE REBELLIOUS, HERE THEIR PRISON ORDAIN'D . 1 71
THE PRISON OF HIS TYRANNY WHO REIGNS 2 59
OUR PRISON STRONG, THIS HUGE CONVEX OF FIRE, . . 2 434
COM'ST THOU, ESCAP'D THY PRISON, AND TRANSFORM'D, 4 824
AND NOW RETURNS HIM FROM HIS PRISON SCAP'T, . . 4 906
OUT OF SUCH PRISON, THOUGH SPIRITS OF PUREST LIGHT, 6 660
IN PRISON UNDER JUDGEMENTS IMMINENT: 11 725

PRIVATE
INTO HER PRIVATE CELL WHEN NATURE RESTS. 5 109

PRIVILEDGE
INVISIBLE, YET STAID (SUCH PRIVILEDGE 7 589

PROBOSCIS
HIS LITHE PROBOSCIS; CLOSE THE SERPENT SLY 4 347

PROCEED
ALL THINGS PROCEED, AND UP TO HIM RETURN, ... 5 470
IF GUILTLESS? BUT FROM ME WHAT CAN PROCEED, . . 10 824
MY JUDGMENTS, HOW WITH MANKIND I PROCEED, . . . 11 69
AND MAN AS FROM A SECOND STOCK PROCEED. 12 7
THOU SHALT PROCEED, AND FROM THY WOMB THE SON . . 12 381

PROCEEDED
PROCEEDED THUS TO ASK HIS HEAV'NLY GUEST. 7 69
TO JUDGEMENT HE PROCEEDED ON TH' ACCUS'D . . . 10 164
HIS PEACE, AND THUS PROCEEDED IN HER PLAINT. . . 10 913
PROCEEDED, AND OPPRESSION, AND SWORD-LAW . . . 11 672

PROCEEDING
PROCEEDING, WHICH IN OTHER BEASTS OBSERV'D 9 94

PROCEEDS
ON OUR BELIEF, THAT ALL FROM THEM PROCEEDS; . . . 9 719
WHOSE VERTUE, FOR OF GOOD STILL GOOD PROCEEDS, . 9 973

PROCESS
BY POLLICY, AND LONG PROCESS OF TIME, ... 2 297
CANNOT WITHOUT PROCESS OF SPEECH BE TOLD, ... 7 178

PROCESSION
FOLLOW'D IN BRIGHT PROCESSION TO BEHOLD 7 222

PROCINCT
WARR HE PERCEAV'D, WARR IN PROCINCT, AND FOUND . 6 19

PROCLAIM
AND TRUMPETS SOUND THROUGHOUT THE HOST PROCLAIM . 1 754

PROCLAIM'D
TO ONE AND TO HIS IMAGE NOW PROCLAIM'D? 5 784

PROCLAIMD
HONOURD BY HIS GREAT FATHER, AND PROCLAIMD 5 663

PROCLAIME
THE SUMMONING ARCH-ANGELS TO PROCLAIME 3 325

PROCLAIMING
OF HEAVENLY GRACE: AND GOD PROCLAIMING PEACE, . . . 2 499
PROCLAIMING LIFE TO ALL WHO SHALL BELIEVE . . . 12 407

PROCLAIMS
UNSEEN BEFORE IN HEAV'N PROCLAIMS HIM COM, . . . 12 361

PROCREATION
IN PROCREATION COMMON TO ALL KINDES 8 597

PROCURE
IF WE PROCURE NOT TO OUR SELVES MORE WOE. 2 225

PRODIGIOUS
PERVERSE, ALL MONSTROUS, ALL PRODIGIOUS THINGS, . 2 625
PRODIGIOUS MOTION FELT AND RUEFUL THROES. . . . 2 780
PRODIGIOUS POWER HAD SHEWN, AND MET IN ARMES . . 6 247
OF LENGTH PRODIGIOUS JOYNING TO THE WALL . . . 10 302
PRODUCE PRODIGIOUS BIRTHS OF BODIE OR MIND. . . 11 687

PRODUC'D
THESE CHANGES IN THE HEAV'NS, THOUGH SLOW, PRODUC'D 10 692

PRODUCE
SPACE MAY PRODUCE NEW WORLDS; WHEREOF SO RIFE . . 1 650
AS CLOUDS, AND CLOUDS MAY RAIN, AND RAIN PRODUCE . 8 146
PRODUCE PRODIGIOUS BIRTHS OF BODIE OR MIND. . . 11 687
THAT ALL THIS GOOD OF EVIL SHALL PRODUCE, . . . 12 470

PRODUCES
PRODUCES WITH TERRESTRIAL HUMOR MIXT 3 610
WILDE WORK PRODUCES OFT, AND MOST IN DREAMS, . . 5 112

PRODUCING
WARM'D BY THE SUN, PRODUCING EVERY KIND, ... 9 721

PRODUC'T
OF PARADISE COULD HAVE PRODUC'T, ERE FALL'N . . 11 29

PRODUCT
TO WHOM THUS MICHAEL. THESE ARE THE PRODUCT . . 11 683

PRODUCTIVE
PRODUCTIVE IN HERB, PLANT, AND NOBLER BIRTH . . 9 111

PROEM
SO GLOZ'D THE TEMPTER, AND HIS PROEM TUN'D; . . 9 549

PROFAN'D
HIS HOLY RITES, AND SOLEMN FEASTS PROFAN'D, . . 1 390
O SACRED NAME OF FAITHFULNESS PROFAN'D. 4 951
PROFAN'D FIRST BY THE SERPENT, BY HIM FIRST . . 9 930

PROFESSING
WISE TO FLIE PAIN, PROFESSING NEXT THE SPIE, . . 4 948

PROFFER
SO HARDIE AS TO PROFFER OR ACCEPT 2 425

PROFIT
THY WEAKER; LET IT PROFIT THEE TO HAVE HEARD . . 6 909

PROFITS
THEN VALUE: OFT TIMES NOTHING PROFITS MORE . . . 8 571
BIND US WITH AFTER-BANDS, WHAT PROFITS THEN . . 9 761

PROFLUENT
BAPTIZING IN THE PROFLUENT STREAM, THE SIGNE . . 12 442

PROFOUND
THESE PAST, IF ANY PASS, THE VOID PROFOUND . . . 2 438
A GULF PROFOUND AS THAT SERBONIAN BOG 2 592
INTO THIS GLOOM OF TARTARUS PROFOUND, ... 2 858
I TRAVEL THIS PROFOUND, DIRECT MY COURSE; . . . 2 980
MATTER UNFORM'D AND VOID: DARKNESS PROFOUND . . 7 233

PROFOUNDEST
INFERNAL WORLD, AND THOU PROFOUNDEST HELL . . . 1 251

PROFUNDITIE
ROUND THROUGH THE VAST PROFUNDITIE OBSCURE, . . 7 229

PROFUSE
POWRD FORTH PROFUSE ON HILL AND DALE AND PLAINE, . 4 243
ON A GREEN SHADIE BANK PROFUSE OF FLOURS . . . 8 286

PROGENIE
HEE AND HIS FAITHLESS PROGENIE: WHOSE FAULT? . . 3 96
WHOSE PROGENIE YOU ARE. MEAN WHILE ENJOY . . . 5 503
HEAR ALL YE ANGELS, PROGENIE OF LIGHT, ... 5 600
TO THEM AND TO THIR PROGENIE FROM THENCE . . . 11 107
GIFT TO HIS PROGENIE OF ALL THAT LAND; 12 138

PROGENITOR
TO WHOM OUR GREAT PROGENITOR. THY WORDS . . . 5 544
AND REVERENCE THEE THIR GREAT PROGENITOR. . . . 11 346

PROGENY
O PROGENY OF HEAV'N, EMPYREAL THRONES, ... 2 430

PROGRESS
IN PROGRESS THROUGH THE RODE OF HEAV'N STAR-PAV'D. 4 976
HER ROSIE PROGRESS SMILING; LET US FORTH, . . . 11 175

PROGRESSIVE
PROGRESSIVE, RETROGRADE, OR STANDING STILL, . . 8 127

PROHIBIT
BARR'D OVER US PROHIBIT ALL EGRESS. 2 437

PROHIBITION
ONE EASIE PROHIBITION, WHO ENJOY 4 433
OF PROHIBITION, ROOT OF ALL OUR WOE; 9 645

PROHIBITIONS
SUCH PROHIBITIONS BINDE NOT. BUT IF DEATH . . . 9 760

PROJECTING
WHAT SIT WE THEN PROJECTING PEACE AND WARR? . . 2 329

PROLIFIC
PROLIFIC HUMOUR SOFT'NING ALL HER GLOBE, 7 280

PROLOGUE
CAME PROLOGUE, AND APOLOGIE TO PROMPT, 9 854

PROLONG
HENCEFORTH I FLIE NOT DEATH, NOR WOULD PROLONG 11 547

PROLONGD
TO LIFE PROLONGD AND PROMISD RACE, I NOW 11 331

PROMISCUOUS
WHILE THE PROMISCUOUS CROUD STOOD YET ALOOF? 1 380

PROMIS'D
OVER THE PROMIS'D LAND TO GOD SO DEAR, 3 531
SO PROMIS'D HEE, AND URIEL TO HIS CHARGE 4 589
BUT THOU HAST PROMIS'D FROM US TWO A RACE 4 732
GREAT JOY HE PROMIS'D TO HIS THOUGHTS, AND NEW 9 843
FALSE IN OUR PROMIS'D RISING; SINCE OUR EYES 9 1070
WHICH THAT FALSE FRUIT THAT PROMIS'D CLEARER SIGHT 11 413
WITH GLORY AND SPOILE BACK TO THIR PROMIS'D LAND. 12 172
OF HIM SO LATELY PROMIS'D TO THY AID 12 542
BY MEE THE PROMIS'D SEED SHALL ALL RESTORE. 12 623

PROMISD
TO LIFE PROLONGD AND PROMISD RACE, I NOW 11 331
PROMISD TO ABRAHAM AND HIS SEED: THE REST 12 260
THE SPIRIT OF GOD, PROMISD ALIKE AND GIV'N 12 519

PROMISE
AND PUBLISH GRACE TO ALL, ON PROMISE MADE 2 238
HIS PROMISE, THAT THY SEED SHALL BRUISE OUR FOE; 11 155
OF MOREB; THERE BY PROMISE HE RECEAVES 12 137
AND PUISSANT DEEDS, A PROMISE SHALL RECEIVE 12 322
THE PROMISE OF THE FATHER, WHO SHALL DWELL 12 487

PROMISES
WITH OTHER PROMISES AND OTHER VAUNTS 4 84

PROMONTORIE
STRETCHT LIKE A PROMONTORIE SLEEPS OR SWIMMES, 7 414

PROMONTORIES
MAIN PROMONTORIES FLUNG, WHICH IN THE AIR 6 654

PROMOTE
AND GOOD WORKES IN HER HUSBAND TO PROMOTE. 9 234
FROM DARKNESS TO PROMOTE ME, OR HERE PLACE 10 745

PROMPT
UNMEDITATED, SUCH PROMPT ELOQUENCE 5 149
OUR PROMPT OBEDIENCE. FAST WE FOUND, FAST SHUT 8 240
CAME PROLOGUE, AND APOLOGIE TO PROMPT, 9 854

PROMPTED
RAGE PROMPTED THEM AT LENGTH, AND FOUND THEM ARMS 6 635

PRONE
PRONE ON THE FLOOD, EXTENDED LONG AND LARGE 1 195
WITH AWFUL REVERENCE PRONE; AND AS A GOD 2 478
DECLIN'D WAS HASTING NOW WITH PRONE CARREER 4 353
A CLOUDY SPOT. DOWN THITHER PRONE IN FLIGHT 5 266
OF ALL YET DON; A CREATURE WHO NOT PRONE 7 506
FROM PRONE, NOR IN THIR WAYES COMPLACENCE FIND. 8 433
PRONE ON THE GROUND, AS SINCE, BUT ON HIS REARE, 9 497
A MONSTROUS SERPENT ON HIS BELLY PRONE, 10 514

PRONOUNC'D
PRONOUNC'D AMONG THE GODS, AND BY AN OATH, 2 352
WHEN EVER THAT SHALL BE; SO FATE PRONOUNC'D. 2 809
OF WOE AND SORROW. STERNLY HE PRONOUNC'D 8 333
HIM LORD PRONOUNC'D, AND, O INDIGNITIE. 9 154
ON ADAM LAST THUS JUDGEMENT HE PRONOUNC'D. 10 197

PRONOUNCD
TH' ALMIGHTY THUS PRONOUNCD HIS SOVRAN WILL. 11 83

PRONOUNC'T
GOD HATH PRONOUNC'T IT DEATH TO TASTE THAT TREE, 4 427
WHOSE BED IS UNDEFIL'D AND CHASTE PRONOUNC'T, 4 761
THIR MAKER, IN FIT STRAINS PRONOUNC'T OR SUNG 5 148
THE JUST DECREE OF GOD, PRONOUNC'T AND SWORN, 5 814
WHAT MAY THIS MEAN? LANGUAGE OF MAN PRONOUNC'T 9 553
TILL THEN THE CURSE PRONOUNC'T ON BOTH PRECEDES. 10 640
THE PENALTIE PRONOUNC'T, DOUBT NOT BUT GOD 10 1022

PROOF
AND PUT TO PROOF HIS HIGH SUPREMACY, 1 132
ON THIS SIDE NOTHING; AND BY PROOF WE FEEL 2 101
RETIRE, OR TASTE THY FOLLY, AND LEARN BY PROOF, 2 686
NOT FREE, WHAT PROOF COULD THEY HAVE GIVN SINCERE 3 103
GAVE PROOF UNHEEDED; OTHERS ON THE GRASS 4 350
THE PROOF OF THIR OBEDIENCE AND THIR FAITH? 4 520
TO TRAMPLE THEE AS MIRE: FOR PROOF LOOK UP, 4 1010
SHEE NEEDED, VERTUE-PROOF, NO THOUGHT INFIRME 5 384
SHALL TEACH US HIGHEST DEEDS, BY PROOF TO TRY 5 865

PROOF (CONTINUED)
NOT PROOF ENOUGH SUCH OBJECT TO SUSTAIN, 8 535
SUCH PROOF, CONCLUDE, THEY THEN BEGIN TO FAILE. 9 1142
HIGH PROOF YE NOW HAVE GIV'N TO BE THE RACE 10 385
CONSTANT, MATURE, PROOF AGAINST ALL ASSAULTS, 10 882

PROOFF
NOT INCORRUPTIBLE OF FAITH, NOT PROOFF 9 298
ONE HEART, ONE SOUL IN BOTH; WHEREOF GOOD PROOFF 9 967

PROP
LOP OVERGROWN, OR PRUNE, OR PROP, OR BIND, 9 210
FROM HER BEST PROP SO FARR, AND STORM SO NIGH. 9 433

PROPAGAT
SHOULDST PROPAGAT, ALREADY INFINITE; 8 420

PROPAGATED
IS PROPAGATED SEEM SUCH DEAR DELIGHT 8 580
IS PROPAGATED CURSE. O VOICE ONCE HEARD 10 729

PROPER
THAT IN OUR PROPER MOTION WE ASCEND 2 75
BUT FIRST HE CASTS TO CHANGE HIS PROPER SHAPE, 3 634
HE LIGHTS, AND TO HIS PROPER SHAPE RETURNS 5 276
TO PROPER SUBSTANCE; TIME MAY COME WHEN MEN 5 493
CELESTIAL ROSIE RED, LOVES PROPER HUE, 8 619

PROPERLY
AND SIN? THE BODIE PROPERLY HATH NEITHER. 10 791

PROPHECIE
ALL PROPHECIE, THAT OF THE ROYAL STOCK 12 325

PROPHET
O PROPHET OF GLAD TIDINGS, FINISHER 12 375

PROPHETIC
(IF ANCIENT AND PROPHETIC FAME IN HEAV'N 2 346

PROPHETS
AND TIRESIAS AND PHINEUS PROPHETS OLD. 3 36
AND ALL THE PROPHETS IN THIR AGE THE TIMES 12 243

PROPITIATION
AND PROPITIATION, ALL HIS WORKS ON MEE 11 34

PROPITIOUS
O FAVOURABLE SPIRIT, PROPITIOUS GUEST, 5 507
MY MAKER, BE PROPITIOUS WHILE I SPEAK. 8 380
HIS OFFRING SOON PROPITIOUS FIRE FROM HEAV'N 11 441
WHICH HE HATH SENT PROPITIOUS, SOME GREAT GOOD 12 612

PROPORTION
WHICH MUST BE MUTUAL, IN PROPORTION DUE 8 385
INTERNAL MAN, IS BUT PROPORTION MEET, 9 711

PROPORTIONAL
PROPORTIONAL ASCENT, WHICH CANNOT BE 9 936

PROPORTIOND
PROPORTIOND TO EACH KIND. SO FROM THE ROOT 5 479

PROPORTIONS
INSTINCT THROUGH ALL PROPORTIONS LOW AND HIGH 11 562

PROPOSALS
IF OUR PROPOSALS ONCE AGAIN WERE HEARD 6 618

PROPOS'D
BY SATAN, AND IN PART PROPOS'D: FOR WHENCE, 2 380
WITH SPLENDOR, ARM'D WITH POWER, IF AUGHT PROPOS'D 2 447
AND RAPHAEL NOW TO ADAM'S DOUBT PROPOS'D 8 64
THOSE TERMS WHATEVER, WHEN THEY WERE PROPOS'D; 10 757

PROPOSEST
THOU TO THY SELF PROPOSEST, IN THE CHOICE 8 400
RESOLV'D, AS THOU PROPOSEST; SO OUR FOE 10 1038

PROPOUND
WHAT WE PROPOUND, AND LOUD THAT ALL MAY HEAR. 6 567

PROPOUNDED
AND BREST, (WHAT COULD WE MORE?) PROPOUNDED TERMS 6 612

PROPRIETIE
OF HUMAN OFSSPRING, SOLE PROPRIETIE, 4 751

PROSE
THINGS UNATTEMPTED YET IN PROSE OR RHIME. 1 16
FLOWD FROM THIR LIPS, IN PROSE OR NUMEROUS VERSE, 5 150

PROSERPIN
OF ENNA, WHERE PROSERPIN GATHERING FLOURS 4 269

PROSERPINA
YET VIRGIN OF PROSERPINA FROM JOVE. 9 396

PROSPECT
HIM GOD BEHOLDING FROM HIS PROSPECT HIGH, ... 3 77
THE GOODLY PROSPECT OF SOME FOREIN LAND 3 548
WHICH TO OUR GENERAL SIRE GAVE PROSPECT LARGE . . 4 144
FOR PROSPECT, WHAT WELL US'D HAD BIN THE PLEDGE . 4 200
THE EARTH OUTSTRETCHT IMMENSE, A PROSPECT WIDE . 5 88
IN PROSPECT; THERE THE EAGLE AND THE STORK . . . 7 423
IN PROSPECT FROM HIS THRONE, HOW GOOD, HOW FAIRE, 7 556
EDEN AND ALL THE COAST IN PROSPECT LAY. 10 89
US'D BY THE TEMPTER: ON THAT PROSPECT STRANGE . . 10 552
STRETCHT OUT TO THE AMPLEST REACH OF PROSPECT LAY. 11 380
IN PROSPECT, AS I POINT THEM; ON THE SHOARE . . 12 143

PROSPER
SURER TO PROSPER THEN PROSPERITY 2 39
WEENING TO PROSPER, AND AT LENGTH PREVAILE . . . 6 795
LONG TIME SHALL DWELL AND PROSPER, BUT WHEN SINS . 12 316

PROSPER'D
TO VISIT HOW THEY PROSPER'D, BUD AND BLOOM, . . . 8 45
THAT THOU ON EARTH HADST PROSPER'D, WHICH THY LOOKS 10 360

PROSPERITY
SURER TO PROSPER THEN PROSPERITY 2 39

PROSPEROUS
USEFUL OF HURTFUL, PROSPEROUS OF ADVERSE 2 259
PROSPEROUS OR ADVERSE: SO SHALT THOU LEAD . . . 11 364

PROSTITUTING
MARRYING OR PROSTITUTING, AS BEFELL, ... 11 716

PROSTRATE
GROVELING AND PROSTRATE ON YON LAKE OF FIRE, . . . 1 280
OF THRONES AND MIGHTY SERAPHIM PROSTRATE, ... 6 841
REPAIRING WHERE HE JUDG'D US, PROSTRATE FALL . . 10 1087
REPAIRING WHERE HE JUDG'D THEM PROSTRATE FELL . . 10 1099

PROSTRATION
KNEE-TRIBUTE YET UNPAID, PROSTRATION VILE, ... 5 782

PROTECTS
THAT GAVE THEE BEING, STILL SHADES THEE AND
PROTECTS. 9 266

PROTESTING
PROTESTING FATE SUPREAME; THENCE HOW I FOUND . . 10 480

PROTEUS
IN VARIOUS SHAPES OLD PROTEUS FROM THE SEA, . . . 3 604

PROUD
RAIS'D IMPIOUS WAR IN HEAV'N AND BATTEL PROUD . . 1 43
HIS MIGHTY STANDARD; THAT PROUD HONOUR CLAIM'D . 1 533
HIS PROUD IMAGINATIONS THUS DISPLAID. 2 10
AS WHEN TO WARN PROUD CITIES WARR APPEARS . . . 2 533
UNBROK'N, AND IN PROUD REBELLIOUS ARMS 2 691
OR PROUD RETURN THOUGH TO HIS HEAVIER DOOM, . . 3 159
SO SAYING, HIS PROUD STEP HE SCORNFUL TURN'D, . . 4 536
TO HIS PROUD FAIR, BEST QUITTED WITH DISDAIN. . . 4 770
BUT LIKE A PROUD STEED REIND, WENT HAUTIE ON, . . 4 858
PROUD LIMITARIE CHERUBE, BUT ERE THEN 4 971
O ARGUMENT BLASPHEMOUS, FALSE AND PROUD. . . . 5 809
ON THOSE PROUD TOWRS TO SWIFT DESTRUCTION DOOM'D. 5 907
TO SET THE ENVIER OF HIS STATE, THE PROUD . . . 6 89
PROUD, ART THOU MET? THY HOPE WAS TO HAVE REACHT 6 131
ON THE PROUD CREST OF SATAN, THAT NO SIGHT, . . 6 191
O FRIENDS, WHY COME NOT ON THESE VICTORS PROUD? . 6 609
BUT TO CONVINCE THE PROUD WHAT SIGNS AVAILE, . . 6 789
THY EMPIRE? EASILY THE PROUD ATTEMPT 7 609
A FOE SO PROUD WILL FIRST THE WEAKER SEEK, . . . 9 383
OF PANDAEMONIUM, CITIE AND PROUD SEATE 10 424
THAT PROUD EXCUSE? YET HIM NOT THY ELECTION, . . 10 764
OF PROUD AMBITIOUS HEART, WHO NOT CONTENT . . . 12 25
BUT THIS USURPER HIS ENCROACHMENT PROUD 12 72
TO THAT PROUD CITIE, WHOSE HIGH WALLS THOU SAW'ST 12 342

PROUDEST
THIR PROUDEST PERSECUTERS: FOR THE SPIRIT . . . 12 497

PROUDLY
IN SHAPE AND GESTURE PROUDLY EMINENT 1 590
BETWEEN HER WHITE WINGS MANTLING PROUDLY, ROWES . 7 439

PROV'D
FROM WHAT HIGHTH FALL'N, SO MUCH THE STRONGER
PROV'D 1 92
WHICH HAD NO LESS PROV'D CERTAIN UNFOREKNOWN. . . 3 119
HOW DUE. YET ALL HIS GOOD PROV'D ILL IN ME, . . 4 48
ASPIRER, BUT THIR THOUGHTS PROV'D FOND AND VAIN . 6 90
AND FAITHFUL, NOW PROV'D FALSE. BUT THINK NOT HERE 6 271
FROM HIS SURMISE PROV'D FALSE, FIND PEACE WITHIN, 9 333
THE VERTUE OF THAT FRUIT, IN THEE FIRST PROV'D: . 9 616

PROVE
MAY PROVE THIR FOE, AND WITH REPENTING HAND . . 2 369
SHOULD PROVE A BITTER MORSEL, AND HIS BANE, . . 2 808
PROVE CHAFF. ON TH' OTHER SIDE SATAN ALLARM'D . 4 985

PROVE (CONTINUED)
THERE FAIL WHERE VERTUE FAILS, OR WEAKEST PROVE . 6 117
AS BOTH THIR DEEDS COMPAR'D THIS DAY SHALL PROVE. 6 170
CANNOT WELL SUITE WITH EITHER, BUT SOON PROVE . . 8 388
SHOULD PROVE TEMPESTUOUS: TO THE WINDS THEY SET . 10 664
PROVE DISOBEDIENT, AND REPROV'D, RETORT, . . . 10 761
WILL PROVE NO SUDDEN, BUT A SLOW-PAC'T EVILL, . . 10 963
LEAST PARADISE A RECEPTACLE PROVE 11 123

PROVES
BUT PROVES NOT SO: THEN FALLIBLE, IT SEEMS, . . 6 428
IN BATTEL WHICH THE STRONGER PROVES, THEY ALL, . 6 819

PROVIDE
PROVIDE, PERNICIOUS WITH ONE TOUCH TO FIRE. . . 6 520

PROVIDED
THOU HAST PROVIDED ALL THINGS: BUT WITH MEE . . 8 363
HATH UNBESAUGHT PROVIDED, AND HIS HANDS 10 1058
TILL I PROVIDED DEATH; SO DEATH BECOMES 11 61

PROVIDENCE
I MAY ASSERT ETERNAL PROVIDENCE, ... 1 25
WHOM WE RESIST. IF THEN HIS PROVIDENCE 1 162
OF PROVIDENCE, FOREKNOWLEDGE, WILL AND FATE, . . . 2 559
HIS PROVIDENCE, AND ON HIM SOLE DEPEND, ... 12 564
THIR PLACE OF REST, AND PROVIDENCE THIR GUIDE: . 12 647

PROVIDENT
HOW PROVIDENT HE IS, HOW FARR FROM THOUGHT . . . 5 828
THE PARSIMONIOUS EMMET, PROVIDENT 7 485

PROVIDES
IN OTHER WORLDS, AND HAPPIER SEAT PROVIDES . . . 10 237

PROVINCE
OF HEAV'N THEY MARCH'D, AND MANY A PROVINCE WIDE . 6 77

PROVISION
GROW UP TO THIR PROVISION, AND MORE HANDS . . . 9 623

PROVISIONS
CONTRIV'D, AND OF PROVISIONS LAID IN LARGE . . . 11 732

PROVOKE
SO AS NOT EITHER TO PROVOKE, OR DREAD 1 644
TH' EVENT IS FEAR'D; SHOULD WE AGAIN PROVOKE . . 2 82
OF CONTUMACIE WILL PROVOKE THE HIGHEST 10 1027

PROVOKES
PROVOKES MY ENVIE, THIS NEW FAVORITE 9 175

PROVOKING
PROVOKING GOD TO RAISE THEM ENEMIES: 12 318

PROVOK'T
NEW WARR, PROVOK'T; OUR BETTER PART REMAINS . . 1 645
CAN EQUAL ANGER INFINITE PROVOK'T. 4 916
OF THIS RIGHT HAND PROVOK'T, SINCE FIRST THAT
TONGUE 6 154
AND PERIL GREAT PROVOK'T, WHO THUS HATH DAR'D . . 9 922

PROW
UPLIFTED; AND SECURE WITH BEAKED PROW 11 746

PROWESS
COMPARE OF MORTAL PROWESS, YET OBSERV'D 1 588
AND THOU IN MILITARY PROWESS NEXT 6 45
FIRST SEEN IN ACTS OF PROWESS EMINENT 11 789

PROWLING
LIGHTS ON HIS FEET. AS WHEN A PROWLING WOLFE, . 4 183

PRUDENT
PRUDENT, LEAST FROM HIS RESOLUTION RAIS'D . . . 2 468
EASING THIR FLIGHT; SO STEARS THE PRUDENT CRANE . 7 430

PRUNE
TO PRUNE THESE GROWING PLANTS, AND TEND THESE
FLOURS, ... 4 438
LOP OVERGROWN, OR PRUNE, OR PROP, OR BIND, . . . 9 210

PRY
THITHER, IF BUT TO PRY, SHALL BE PERHAPS . . . 1 655

PUBLIC
DELIBERATION SAT AND PUBLIC CARE; 2 303
AND JUDG'D OF PUBLIC MOMENT, IN THE SHAPE . . . 2 448
MELT, AS I DOE, YET PUBLIC REASON JUST, ... 4 389
OF PUBLIC SCORN; HE WONDERD, BUT NOT LONG . . . 10 509
NATIONAL INTERRUPT THIR PUBLIC PEACE, ... 12 317

PUBLISH
AND PUBLISH GRACE TO ALL, ON PROMISE MADE . . . 2 238

PUISSANCE
OUR PUISSANCE IS OUR OWN, OUR OWN RIGHT HAND . . 5 864
HIS PUISSANCE, TRUSTING IN TH' ALMIGHTIE'S AIDE, . 6 119

PUISSANT
THAT ALL THESE PUISSANT LEGIONS, WHOSE EXILE 1 632
GIRD ON, AND SWORD UPON THY PUISSANT THIGH; 6 714
AND PUISSANT DEEDS, A PROMISE SHALL RECEIVE 12 322

PULP
THE SAVOURIE PULP THEY CHEW, AND IN THE RINDE 4 335

PUNCTUAL
ROUND THIS OPACOUS EARTH, THIS PUNCTUAL SPOT, 8 23

PUNIC
IN PONTUS OR THE PUNIC COAST, OR WHERE 5 340

PUNIE
THE PUNIE HABITANTS, OR IF NOT DRIVE, 2 367

PUNISH
TO PUNISH ENDLESS? WHEREFORE CEASE WE THEN? 2 159
TO TEMPT OR PUNISH MORTALS, EXCEPT WHOM 2 1032

PUNISHER
THIS KNOWS MY PUNISHER; THEREFORE AS FARR 4 103

PUNISHMENT
TO UNDERGO ETERNAL PUNISHMENT? 1 155
AND STRIPES, AND ARBITRARY PUNISHMENT 2 334
THY KING AND LORD? BACK TO THY PUNISHMENT, 2 699
HOWEVER, AND TO SCAPE HIS PUNISHMENT. 4 911
BOTH OF THY CRIME AND PUNISHMENT: HENCEFORTH 5 881
INTO THIR PLACE OF PUNISHMENT, THE GULF 6 53
THE PUNISHMENT TO OTHER HAND BELONGS, 6 807
HIS PUNISHMENT, ETERNAL MISERIE; 6 904
LEAST ON MY HEAD BOTH SIN AND PUNISHMENT, 10 133
CAN FIT HIS PUNISHMENT, OR THEIR REVENGE. 10 242
CATCHT BY CONTAGION, LIKE IN PUNISHMENT, 10 544
THY PUNISHMENT THEN JUSTLY IS AT HIS WILL. 10 768
THE PUNISHMENT ALL ON THY SELF; ALAS, 10 949
SHALL SCAPE HIS PUNISHMENT ORDAIN'D, AND WEE 10 1039
THEREFORE SO ABJECT IS THIR PUNISHMENT, 11 520
AWAITS THE GOOD, THE REST WHAT PUNISHMENT? 11 710
ALONE FULFILL THE LAW; THY PUNISHMENT 12 404

PUNISH'T
WITH WHAT IS PUNISH'T; WHENCE THESE RAGING FIRES 2 213

PUNISHT
NOW RUL'D HIM, PUNISHT IN THE SHAPE HE SIN'D, 10 516
IN PUNISHT MAN, TO SATISFIE HIS RIGOUR 10 803

PURCHASE
AND HEAVIER FALL: SO SHOULD I PURCHASE DEARE 4 101
A WORLD WHO WOULD NOT PURCHASE WITH A BRUISE, 10 500
AMONG THE HEATHEN OF THIR PURCHASE GOT, 10 579

PURE
BEFORE ALL TEMPLES TH' UPRIGHT HEART AND PURE, 1 18
AND UNCOMPOUNDED IS THIR ESSENCE PURE, 1 425
OR HEAR'ST THOU RATHER PURE ETHEREAL STREAM, 3 7
FROM THE PURE EMPYREAN WHERE HE SITS 3 57
THROUGH THE PURE MARBLE AIR HIS OBLIQUE WAY 3 564
BREATHE FORTH ELIXIR PURE, AND RIVERS RUN 3 607
THAT LANTSKIP: AND OF PURE NOW PURER AIRE 4 153
TRUTH, WISDOME, SANCTITUDE SEVERE AND PURE, 4 293
WITH SHEWS INSTEAD, MEER SHEWS OF SEEMING PURE, 4 316
PURE AS TH' EXPANSE OF HEAV'N; I THITHER WENT 4 456
WITH KISSES PURE: ASIDE THE DEVIL TURND 4 502
OBSERVING NONE, BUT ADORATION PURE 4 737
PURE, AND COMMANDS TO SOM, LEAVES FREE TO ALL. 4 747
FOUNDED IN REASON, LOYAL, JUST, AND PURE, 4 755
TH' ANIMAL SPIRITS THAT FROM PURE BLOOD ARISE 4 805
LIKE GENTLE BREATHS FROM RIVERS PURE, THENCE RAISE 4 806
AS WHEN THOU STOODST IN HEAV'N UPRIGHT AND PURE; 4 837
WAS AERIE LIGHT FROM PURE DIGESTION BRED, 5 4
CREATED PURE. BUT KNOW THAT IN THE SOULE 5 100
WANTS HER FIT VESSELS PURE, THEN STREWS THE GROUND 5 348
NO INGRATEFUL FOOD: AND FOOD ALIKE THOSE PURE 5 407
BUT MORE REFIN'D, MORE SPIRITOUS, AND PURE, 5 475
WHEREON A SAPHIR THRONE, INLAID WITH PURE 6 758
ETHEREAL, FIRST OF THINGS, QUINTESSENCE PURE 7 244
THE FIRMAMENT, EXPANSE OF LIQUID, PURE, 7 264
HOW FULLY HAST THOU SATISFI'D MEE, PURE 8 180
NATURE HER SELF, THOUGH PURE OF SINFUL THOUGHT, 8 506
WHATEVER PURE THOU IN THE BODY ENJOY'ST 8 622
(AND PURE THOU WERT CREATED) WE ENJOY 8 623
TOTAL THEY MIX, UNION OF PURE WITH PURE 8 627
ON WHAT WAS PURE, TILL CRAMM'D AND GORG'D, NIGH
BURST 10 632
THEN HEAV'N AND EARTH RENEWD SHALL BE MADE PURE 10 638
LEAST THAT PURE BREATH OF LIFE, THE SPIRIT OF MAN 10 784
THOSE PURE IMMORTAL ELEMENTS THAT KNOW 11 50
LESS PURE, ACCUSTOMD TO IMMORTAL FRUITS? 11 285
IS PIETIE THUS AND PURE DEVOTION PAID? 11 452
WHILE THEY PERVERT PURE NATURES HEALTHFUL RULES 11 523
HOLIE AND PURE, CONFORMITIE DIVINE. 11 606
PURE, AND IN MIND PREPAR'D, IF SO BEFALL, 12 444
LEFT ONELY IN THOSE WRITTEN RECORDS PURE, 12 513

PURER
OUR PURER ESSENCE THEN WILL OVERCOME 2 215
THAT LANTSKIP: AND OF PURE NOW PURER AIRE 4 153
THE GROSSER FEEDS THE PURER, EARTH THE SEA, 5 416

PUREST
HEAV'NS PUREST LIGHT, YET OUR GREAT ENEMY 2 137
SPIRITUAL, MAY OF PUREST SPIRITS BE FOUND 5 406
OUT OF SUCH PRISON, THOUGH SPIRITS OF PUREST LIGHT, 6 660
PUREST AT FIRST, NOW GROSS BY SINNING GROWN. 6 661

PURG'D
THROUGHOUT THE FLUID MASS, BUT DOWNWARD PURG'D 7 237
HAD BRED; THEN PURG'D WITH EUPHRASIE AND RUE 11 414
FROM THE CONFLAGRANT MASS, PURG'D AND REFIN'D, 12 548

PURGE
HER MISCHIEF, AND PURGE OFF THE BASER FIRE 2 141
PURGE OFF THIS GLOOM; THE SOFT DELICIOUS AIR, 2 400
PURGE AND DISPERSE, THAT I MAY SEE AND TELL 3 54
EJECT HIM TAINTED NOW, AND PURGE HIM OFF 11 52
SHALL HOLD THIR COURSE, TILL FIRE PURGE ALL THINGS
NEW, 11 900

PURITIE
OF PURITIE AND PLACE AND INNOCENCE, 4 745
OF INNOCENCE, OF FAITH, OF PURITIE, 9 1075

PURLIEU
IN SOME PURLIEU TWO GENTLE FAWNES AT PLAY, 4 404

PURLOIND
HAD FROM HIS WAKEFUL CUSTODY PURLOIND 2 946

PURPLE
RAN PURPLE TO THE SEA, SUPPOS'D WITH BLOOD 1 451
LAYES FORTH HER PURPLE GRAPE, AND GENTLY CREEPS 4 259
ARRAYING WITH REFLECTED PURPLE AND GOLD 4 596
HIS CONSTANT LAMP, AND WAVES HIS PURPLE WINGS, 4 764
WITH SPOTS OF GOLD AND PURPLE, AZURE AND GREEN; 7 479
CARNATION, PURPLE, AZURE, OR SPECT WITH GOLD, 9 429
A MILITARIE VEST OF PURPLE FLOWD 11 241

PURPLES
PURPLES THE EAST: STILL GOVERN THOU MY SONG, 7 30

PURPOS'D
PERCEIVE THEE PURPOS'D NOT TO DOOM FRAIL MAN 3 404
AS NOW IS ENTERD; YET NO PURPOS'D FOE 4 373

PURPOSD
THE WHOLE INCLUDED RACE, HIS PURPOSD PREY. 9 416

PURPOSE
WITH PURPOSE TO EXPLORE OR TO DISTURB 2 971
AND MAN THERE PLAC'T, WITH PURPOSE TO ASSAY 3 90
AS MY ETERNAL PURPOSE HATH DECREED; 3 172
NOR GENTLE PURPOSE, NOR ENDEARING SMILES 4 337
ON PURPOSE, HARD THOU KNOWST IT TO EXCLUDE 4 584
THAT HIS GREAT PURPOSE HE MIGHT SO FULFILL, 6 675
RECEAVE WITH SOLEMNE PURPOSE TO OBSERVE 7 78
TO LESSEN THEE, AGAINST HIS PURPOSE SERVES 7 614
RETURN'D AND GRACIOUS PURPOSE THUS RENEW'D. 8 337
FORERUNNERS OF HIS PURPOSE, OR TO WARN 11 195
WITH PURPOSE TO RESIGN THEM IN FULL TIME 12 301

PURPOSES
CAN EXECUTE THIR AERIE PURPOSES, 1 430

PURSU'D
WHILE WITH PERFIDIOUS HATRED THEY PURSU'D 1 308
INSULTING, AND PURSU'D US THROUGH THE DEEP, 2 79
WHAT WHEN WE FLED AMAIN, PURSU'D AND STROOK 2 165
I FLED, BUT HE PURSU'D (THOUGH MORE, IT SEEMS, 2 790
URIEL ONCE WARND; WHOSE EYE PURSU'D HIM DOWN 4 125
MINE EYE PURSU'D HIM STILL, BUT UNDER SHADE 4 572
DROVE THEM BEFORE HIM THUNDER-STRUCK, PURSU'D 6 858
OF STERN ACHILLES ON HIS FOE PURSU'D 9 15
HER LONG WITH ARDENT LOOK HIS EYE PURSU'D 9 397
FIRST HUNTER THEN, PURSU'D A GENTLE BRACE, 11 188
OF FLIGHT PURSU'D IN TH' AIR AND ORE THE GROUND 11 202
FLED AND PURSU'D TRANSVERSE THE RESONANT FUGUE. 11 563

PURSUE
BEYOND THUS HIGH, INSATIATE TO PURSUE 2 8
TO WHOM WE HATE. LET US NOT THEN PURSUE 2 249
LEAST WITH A WHIP OF SCORPIONS I PURSUE 2 701
LITTLE INFERIOR; WHOM MY THOUGHTS PURSUE 4 362
PURSUE THESE SONS OF DARKNESS, DRIVE THEM OUT 6 715
ALL NIGHT HE WILL PURSUE, BUT HIS APPROACH 12 206

PURSUERS
HIS SWIFT PURSUERS FROM HEAV'N GATES DISCERN 1 326

PURSUES
ABOVE TH' AONIAN MOUNT, WHILE IT PURSUES 1 15
PURSUES, AS INCLINATION OR SAD CHOICE 2 524
PURSUES THE ARIMASPIAN, WHO BY STELTH 2 945

PURSUES (CONTINUED)
WITH HEAD, HANDS, WINGS OR FEET PURSUES HIS WAY, . 2 949
PURSUES ME STILL, LEAST ALL I CANNOT DIE, . . . 10 783
BEHINDE THEM, WHILE TH' OBDURAT KING PURSUES; . . 12 205

PURSUING
PURSUING, I UPON MY FRONTIERES HERE 2 998
PURSUING DRIVE THEM OUT FROM GOD AND BLISS, . . 6 52
PURSUING, NOT UNMOV'D TO EVE THUS SPAKE. . . . 11 192
PURSUING WHOM HE LATE DISMISSD, THE SEA 12 195

PURSUIT
HIS MINISTERS OF VENGEANCE AND PURSUIT 1 170
BACK FROM PURSUIT THY POWERS WITH LOUD ACCLAIME . 3 397
WHOM FLED WE THOUGHT, WILL SAVE US LONG PURSUIT . 6 538

PURVEY'D
YEILD THEE, SO WELL THIS DAY THOU HAST PURVEY'D. . 9 1021

PUSH'D
FROM THE SUNS AXLE; THEY WITH LABOUR PUSH'D . . 10 670

PUSHD
OUT OF HIS PLACE, PUSHD BY THE HORNED FLOUD, . . 11 831

PUSH'T
SIDELONG, HAD PUSH'T A MOUNTAIN FROM HIS SEAT . . 6 197

PUSHT
JUSTLING OR PUSHT WITH WINDS RUDE IN THIR SHOCK . 10 1074

PUT
AND PUT TO PROOF HIS HIGH SUPREMACY, ... 1 132
PUT FORTH AT FULL, BUT STILL HIS STRENGTH
CONCEAL'D, ... 1 641
PUT TO THIR MOUTHS THE SOUNDING ALCHYMIE . . . 2 517
FREELY PUT OFF, AND FOR HIM LASTLY DYE 3 240
DYING PUT ON THE WEEDS OF DOMINIC, ... 3 479
THEN WHEN THE DRAGON, PUT TO SECOND ROUT, . . . 4 3
THOUGH FOR POSSESSION PUT TO TRY ONCE MORE . . . 4 941
BATTELS AND REALMS: IN THESE HE PUT TWO WEIGHTS . 4 1002
PUT FORTH, AND TO A NARROW VENT APPLI'D 6 583
BUT WHOM THOU HAT'ST, I HATE, AND CAN PUT ON . . 6 734
THY TERRORS, AS I PUT THY MILDNESS ON, ... 6 735
YET HALF HIS STRENGTH HE PUT NOT FORTH, BUT CHECK'D 6 853
AND PUT NOT FORTH MY GOODNESS, WHICH IS FREE . . 7 171
PUT FORTH THE VERDANT GRASS, HERB YIELDING SEED, . 7 310
HUMAN, TO PUT ON GODS, DEATH TO BE WISHT, . . . 9 714
BETWEEN THEE AND THE WOMAN I WILL PUT 10 179
IS ENMITY, WHICH HE WILL PUT BETWEEN 10 497

PUTS
PUTS ON SWIFT WINGS, AND TOWARDS THE GATES OF HELL 2 631
THANK HIM WHO PUTS ME LOATH TO THIS REVENGE . . 4 386
PUTS ME IN DOUBT. LIVES THER WHO LOVES HIS PAIN? 4 888
NEW PART PUTS ON, AND AS TO PASSION MOV'D, . . . 9 667

PUTTING
HANDED THEY WENT; AND EAS'D THE PUTTING OFF . . 4 739
SO YE SHALL DIE PERHAPS, BY PUTTING OFF 9 713

PYRAMID
SPRINGS UPWARD LIKE A PYRAMID OF FIRE 2 1013

PYRAMIDS
RAIS'D ON A MOUNT, WITH PYRAMIDS AND TOWRS . . . 5 758

PYRRHA
DEUCALION AND CHASTE PYRRHA TO RESTORE 11 12

PYTHIAN
AS AT TH' OLYMPIAN GAMES OR PYTHIAN FIELDS; . . . 2 530
INGENDERD IN THE PYTHIAN VALE ON SLIME, ... 10 530

PYTHON
HUGE PYTHON, AND HIS POWER NO LESS HE SEEM'D . . 10 531

QUADRATE
THAT STOOD FOR HEAV'N, IN MIGHTY QUADRATE JOYN'D . 6 62

QUADRATURE
HIS QUADRATURE, FROM THY ORBICULAR WORLD, . . . 10 381

QUAFF
QUAFF IMMORTALITIE AND JOY, SECURE 5 638

QUAINT
HIS LAUGHTER AT THIR QUAINT OPINIONS WIDE 8 78
IMPRESES QUAINT, CAPARISONS AND STEEDS; 9 35

QUALMES
OF GASTLY SPASM, OR RACKING TORTURE, QUALMES . . 11 481

QUARRIES
FROM DIAMOND QUARRIES HEW'N, AND ROCKS OF GOLD, . 5 759

QUARRY
SAGACIOUS OF HIS QUARRY FROM SO FARR. 10 281

QUARTER
EACH QUARTER, TO DESCRIE THE DISTANT FOE, ... 6 530

QUARTERS
SWIFT TO THIR SEVERAL QUARTERS HASTED THEN . . . 3 714
HIS PRAISE YE WINDS, THAT FROM FOUR QUARTERS BLOW, 5 192
THE QUARTERS OF THE NORTH, THERE TO PREPARE . . 5 689

QUATERNION
OF NATURES WOMB, THAT IN QUATERNION RUN 5 181

QUEEN
ASTARTE, QUEEN OF HEAV'N, WITH CRESCENT HORNS; . 1 439
APPARENT QUEEN UNVAILD HER PEERLESS LIGHT, . . . 4 608
NOT UNATTENDED, FOR ON HER AS QUEEN 8 60
QUEEN OF THIS UNIVERSE, DOE NOT BELIEVE 9 684
AS REAPERS OFT ARE WONT THIR HARVEST QUEEN, . . 9 842

QUELL
GIV'N ME TO QUELL THIR PRIDE, AND IN EVENT . . . 5 740
HIS NAME AND OFFICE BEARING, WHO SHALL QUELL . . 12 311

QUELL'D
THOUGH NOT OF WOMAN BORN; COMPASSION QUELL'D . . 11 496

QUELLD
HE HELD IT VAIN; AWE FROM ABOVE HAD QUELLD . . . 4 860
AND NOW THIR MIGHTIEST QUELLD, THE BATTEL SWERV'D, 6 386
VALOUR OR STRENGTH, THOUGH MATCHLESS, QUELLD WITH
PAIN 6 457

QUENCH
SATANS ASSAULTS, AND QUENCH HIS FIERIE DARTS, . . 12 492

QUENCHT
QUENCHT IN A BOGGIE SYRTIS, NEITHER SEA, . . . 2 939
SO THICK A DROP SERENE HATH QUENCHT THIR ORBS, . 3 25

QUEST
TO SEARCH WITH WANDRING QUEST A PLACE FORETOLD . 2 830
AND ON HIS QUEST, WHERE LIKELIEST HE MIGHT FINDE . 9 414

QUESTION
TO QUESTION THY BOLD ENTRANCE ON THIS PLACE; . . 4 882
AND SUCH I HELD THEE; BUT THIS QUESTION ASKT . . 4 887
I QUESTION IT, FOR THIS FAIR EARTH I SEE, . . . 9 720

QUESTIOND
BE QUESTIOND AND BLASPHEAM'D WITHOUT DEFENCE. . . 3 166

QUICK
THE LATTER QUICK UP FLEW, AND KICKT THE BEAM; . . 4 1004
NOW ON THE POLAR WINDES, THEN WITH QUICK FANN . . 5 269
BY QUICK CONTRACTION OR REMOVE; BUT NOW . . . 6 597
WE SHOULD COMPEL THEM TO A QUICK RESULT. . . . 6 619
OF CORAL STRAY, OR SPORTING WITH QUICK GLANCE . . 7 405
BY QUICK INSTINCTIVE MOTION UP I SPRUNG, . . . 8 259
OFT HE TO HER HIS CHARGE OF QUICK RETURNE . . . 9 399
WITH GLORY AND POWER TO JUDGE BOTH QUICK AND DEAD, 12 460

QUICK'ND
SO QUICK'ND APPETITE, THAT I, METHOUGHT, . . . 5 85
POWERFUL PERSWADERS, QUICK'ND AT THE SCENT . . . 9 587

QUICK'NING
BY OUR OWN QUICK'NING POWER, WHEN FATAL COURSE . 5 861

QUIET
QUIET THOUGH SAD, THE RESPIT OF THAT DAY . . . 11 272
THAT SON, WHO ON THE QUIET STATE OF MEN 12 80

QUILOA
MOMBAZA, AND QUILOA, AND MELIND, ... 11 399

QUINTESSENCE
AND THIS ETHEREAL QUINTESSENCE OF HEAV'N . . . 3 716
ETHEREAL, FIRST OF THINGS, QUINTESSENCE PURE . . 7 244

QUIRE
HE ASK'D, BUT ALL THE HEAV'NLY QUIRE STOOD MUTE, . 3 217
THE BIRDS THIR QUIRE APPLY; AIRES, VERNAL AIRES, . 4 264
AND JOIND THIR VOCAL WORSHIP TO THE QUIRE . . . 9 198
THEY GLADLY THITHER HASTE, AND BY A QUIRE . . . 12 366

QUIRES
HATH BROUGHT ME FROM THE QUIRES OF CHERUBIM . . 3 666
AND HEAV'NLY QUIRES THE HYMENAEAN SUNG, ... 4 711
FLEW THROUGH THE MIDST OF HEAV'N; TH' ANGELIC
QUIRES 5 251
BY THE CELESTIAL QUIRES, WHEN ORIENT LIGHT . . . 7 254

QUIT
WOULD SET ME HIGHEST, AND IN A MOMENT QUIT . . . 4 51
NO MORE BE TROUBL'D HOW TO QUIT THE YOKE . . . 5 882
IN ORDER, QUIT OF ALL IMPEDIMENT; 6 548
HER STATE WITH OARIE FEET: YET OFT THEY QUIT . . 7 440
LIFE MUCH, BENT RATHER HOW I MAY BE QUIT . . . 11 548

QUITE
WE SHOULD BE QUITE ABOLISHT AND EXPIRE. 2 93
WILL EITHER QUITE CONSUME US, AND REDUCE 2 96
OF WHAT WE ARE AND WERE, DISMISSING QUITE 2 282
AND WISDOME AT ONE ENTRANCE QUITE SHUT OUT. 3 50
MAN SHALL NOT QUITE BE LOST, BUT SAV'D WHO WILL, 3 173
REDEEM THEE QUITE FROM DEATHS RAPACIOUS CLAIME; 11 258
HE LOOK'D, AND SAW THE FACE OF THINGS QUITE CHANG'D, 11 712
OVER HIS BRETHREN, AND QUITE DISPOSSESS 12 28
QUITE OUT THIR NATIVE LANGUAGE, AND INSTEAD 12 54

QUITTED
GOD-LIKE FRUITION, QUITTED ALL TO SAVE 3 307
TO HIS PROUD FAIR, BEST QUITTED WITH DISDAIN. 4 770
OF PASSION, I TO THEM HAD QUITTED ALL, 10 627

QUIVER
AND QUIVER WITH THREE-BOLTED THUNDER STOR'D, 6 764
THOUGH NOT AS SHEE WITH BOW AND QUIVER ARMD, 9 390

QUIVERS
LIKE QUIVERS HUNG, AND WITH PRAEAMBLE SWEET 3 367

RABBA
WORSHIPT IN RABBA AND HER WATRY PLAIN, 1 397

RACE
FOR THOSE THE RACE OF ISRAEL OFT FORSOOK 1 432
OF PHLEGRA WITH TH' HEROIC RACE WERE JOYN'D 1 577
THRONG NUMBERLESS, LIKE THAT PIGMEAN RACE 1 780
SHALL WE THEN LIVE THUS VILE, THE RACE OF HEAV'N 2 194
OF SOME NEW RACE CALL'D MAN, ABOUT THIS TIME 2 348
SO DEEP A MALICE, TO CONFOUND THE RACE 2 382
UPON THE WING, OR IN SWIFT RACE CONTEND, 2 529
A RACE OF UPSTART CREATURES, TO SUPPLY 2 834
DRAW AFTER HIM THE WHOLE RACE OF MANKIND, 3 161
BY LOOSING THEE A WHILE, THE WHOLE RACE LOST. 3 280
CREATED THIS NEW HAPPIE RACE OF MEN 3 679
MOTHER OF HUMAN RACE: WHAT COULD I DOE, 4 475
BUT THOU HAST PROMIS'D FROM US TWO A RACE 4 732
IMPOSSIBLE: YET HAPLY OF THY RACE 6 501
WHAT MIGHT HAVE ELSE TO HUMAN RACE BIN HID; 6 896
OF BACCHUS AND HIS REVELLERS, THE RACE 7 33
IN PARADISE TO ADAM OR HIS RACE, 7 45
MUCH OF HIS RACE THOUGH STEEP, SUSPENS IN HEAV'N 7 99
ANOTHER WORLD, OUT OF ONE MAN A RACE 7 155
OF SPIRITS MALIGNE A BETTER RACE TO BRING 7 189
FEMALE FOR RACE; THEN BLESS'D MANKINDE, AND SAID, 7 530
AND MULTIPLY A RACE OF WORSHIPPERS 7 630
TO THEE AND TO THY RACE I GIVE; AS LORDS 8 339
THE WHOLE INCLUDED RACE, HIS PURPOSD PREY. 9 416
HIGH PROOF YE NOW HAVE GIV'N TO BE THE RACE 10 385
TILL I IN MAN RESIDING THROUGH THE RACE, 10 607
INTO THIS CURSED WORLD A WOFUL RACE, 10 984
THE RACE UNBLEST, TO BEING YET UNBEGOT. 10 988
THE RACE OF MANKIND DROWND, BEFORE THE SHRINE 11 13
TO LIFE PROLONGD AND PROMISD RACE, I NOW 11 331
OF WICKEDNESS, WHEREIN SHALL DWELL HIS RACE 11 608
TO THESE THAT SOBER RACE OF MEN, WHOSE LIVES 11 621
WITH LENGTH OF HAPPY DAYES THE RACE OF MAN; 11 782
AND WHETHER HERE THE RACE OF MAN WILL END 11 786
SERVANT OF SERVANTS, ON HIS VITIOUS RACE. 12 104
OF PHARAO: THERE HE DIES, AND LEAVES HIS RACE 12 163
AND OVERWHELM THIR WARR: THE RACE ELECT 12 214
THIR MINISTRY PERFORM'D, AND RACE WELL RUN, 12 505
MEASUR'D THIS TRANSIENT WORLD, THE RACE OF TIME, 12 554

RACES
UNSUNG; OR TO DESCRIBE RACES AND GAMES, 9 33

RACK
AT LEAST HAD GON TO RACK, DISTURBD AND TORNE 4 994
A WORLD DEVOTE TO UNIVERSAL RACK. 11 821

RACKING
OF RACKING WHIRLWINDS, OR FOR EVER SUNK 2 182
OF GASTLY SPASM, OR RACKING TORTURE, QUALMES 11 481
DROPSIES, AND ASTHMA'S, AND JOINT-RACKING RHEUMS. 11 488

RACKT
VAUNTING ALOUD, BUT RACKT WITH DEEP DESPARE: 1 126

RADIANCE
GIRT WITH OMNIPOTENCE, WITH RADIANCE CROWN'D 7 194

RADIANT
IF CHANCE THE RADIANT SUN WITH FAREWELL SWEET 2 492
THE RADIANT IMAGE OF HIS GLORY SAT, 3 63
DRAWN ROUND ABOUT THEE LIKE A RADIANT SHRINE, 3 379
WITH RADIANT LIGHT, AS GLOWING IRON WITH FIRE; 3 594
ERE HE DREW NIGH, HIS RADIANT VISAGE TURND, 3 646
SO SAYING, ON HE LED HIS RADIANT FILES, 4 797
TRANSCEND HIS OWN SO FARR, WHOSE RADIANT FORMS 5 457
OF RADIANT URIM, WORK DIVINELY WROUGHT, 6 761
SPHEAR'D IN A RADIANT CLOUD, FOR YET THE SUN 7 247
THUS SAYING, FROM HIS RADIANT SEAT HE ROSE 10 85
O'RE THE BLEW FIRMAMENT A RADIANT WHITE, 11 206

RAG'D
OF BATTEL WHEN IT RAG'D, IN ALL ASSAULTS 1 277
FAR ROUND ILLUMIN'D HELL: HIGHLY THEY RAG'D 1 666
OF BRAZEN CHARIOTS RAG'D; DIRE WAS THE NOISE 6 211
WHEREAT HEE INLIE RAG'D, AND AS THY TALK'D, 11 444

RAGE
NOR WHAT THE POTENT VICTOR IN HIS RAGE 1 95
WING'D WITH RED LIGHTNING AND IMPETUOUS RAGE, 1 175
ARMING TO BATTEL, AND IN STEAD OF RAGE 1 553
BLACK FIRE AND HORROR SHOT WITH EQUAL RAGE 2 67
TH' ALMIGHTY VICTOR TO SPEND ALL HIS RAGE, 2 144
AWAK'D SHOULD BLOW THEM INTO SEVENFOLD RAGE 2 171
MUST'RING THIR RAGE, AND HEAV'N RESEMBLES HELL? 2 268
OTHERS WITH VAST TYPHOEAN RAGE MORE FELL 2 539
WHOSE WAVES OF TORRENT FIRE INFLAME WITH RAGE. 2 581
INFLAM'D WITH LUST THEN RAGE) AND SWIFTER FAR, 2 791
ONELY BEGOTTEN SON, SEEST THOU WHAT RAGE 3 80
WELL PLEAS'D, ON ME LET DEATH WRECK ALL HIS RAGE; 3 241
SATAN, NOW FIRST INFLAM'D WITH RAGE, CAME DOWN, 4 9
THE FIEND REPLI'D NOT, OVERCOME WITH RAGE; 4 857
GAVE HEED, BUT WAXING MORE IN RAGE REPLI'D. 4 969
RETURNS OUR OWN. CEASE THEN THIS IMPIOUS RAGE, 5 845
THE REBEL THRONES, BUT GREATER RAGE TO SEE 6 199
AND INEXTINGUISHABLE RAGE; ALL HEAV'N 6 217
RAGE PROMPTED THEM AT LENGTH, AND FOUND THEM ARMS 6 635
AND TO DISORDER'D RAGE LET LOOSE THE REINES, 6 696
YET ENVIED; AGAINST MEE IS ALL THIR RAGE, 6 813
TORMENT, AND LOUD LAMENT, AND FURIOUS RAGE. 8 244
THRICE FUGITIVE ABOUT TROY WALL; OR RAGE 9 16
NOT UNDERSTOOD, TILL HOARSE, AND ALL IN RAGE, 12 58
MORE HARD'ND AFTER THAW, TILL IN HIS RAGE 12 194

RAGGS
AND FLUTTERD INTO RAGGS, THEN RELIQUES, BEADS, 3 491

RAGING
WITH WHAT IS PUNISH'T; WHENCE THESE RAGING FIRES 2 213
FROM BEDS OF RAGING FIRE TO STARVE IN ICE 2 600
IMPENDENT, RAGING INTO SUDDEN FLAME 5 891
SOLID OR SLIMIE, AS IN RAGING SEA 10 286

RAIES
OF BEAMING SUNNIE RAIES, A GOLDEN TIAR 3 625
SHOT DOWN DIRECT HIS FERVID RAIES TO WARME 5 301

RAIN
AS CLOUDS, AND CLOUDS MAY RAIN, AND RAIN PRODUCE 8 146
TH' INCLEMENT SEASONS, RAIN, ICE, HAIL AND SNOW, 10 1063
LIKE A DARK CEELING STOOD; DOWN RUSH'D THE RAIN 11 743
SURPASS HIS BOUNDS, NOR RAIN TO DROWN THE WORLD 11 894

RAINBOWS
OF RAINBOWS AND STARRIE EYES. THE WATERS THUS 7 446

RAIN'D
HER SACRED SHADES: THOUGH GOD HAD YET NOT RAIN'D 7 331

RAIND
RAIND AT THIR EYES, BUT HIGH WINDS WORSE WITHIN 9 1122

RAINE
RAINE DAY AND NIGHT, ALL FOUNTAINS OF THE DEEP 11 826

RAIS'D
RAIS'D IMPIOUS WAR IN HEAV'N AND BATTEL PROUD 1 43
THAT WITH THE MIGHTIEST RAIS'D ME TO CONTEND, 1 99
SEMBLANCE OF WORTH, NOT SUBSTANCE, GENTLY RAIS'D 1 529
OF FLUTES AND SOFT RECORDERS; SUCH AS RAIS'D 1 551
SELF-RAIS'D, AND REPOSSESS THIR NATIVE SEAT? 1 634
SATAN EXALTED SAT, BY MERIT RAIS'D 2 5
SATAN, WHOM NOW TRANSCENDENT GLORY RAIS'D 2 427
PRUDENT, LEAST FROM HIS RESOLUTION RAIS'D 2 468
THENCE MORE AT EASE THIR MINDS AND SOMWHAT RAIS'D 2 521
WHILE BY THEE RAIS'D I RUIN ALL MY FOES, 3 258
THEN HAPPIE; NO UNBOUNDED HOPE HAD RAIS'D 4 60
THAT MOUNTAIN AS HIS GARDEN MOULD HIGH RAIS'D 4 226
THAT RAIS'D US FROM THE DUST AND PLAC'T US HERE 4 416
LEANING HALF-RAIS'D, WITH LOOKS OF CORDIAL LOVE 5 12
HAVE HEAP'D THIS TABLE. RAIS'D OF GRASSIE TERF 5 391
RAIS'D ON A MOUNT, WITH PYRAMIDS AND TOWRS 5 758
KNOW NONE BEFORE US, SELF-BEGOT, SELF-RAIS'D 5 860
HAVE RAIS'D INCESSANT ARMIES TO DEFEAT 6 138
THE OVERTHROWN HE RAIS'D, AND AS A HEARD 6 856
NOT HERE, TILL BY DEGREES OF MERIT RAIS'D 7 157
AND GAZ'D A WHILE THE AMPLE SKIE, TILL RAIS'D 8 258
SO SAYING, BY THE HAND HE TOOK ME RAIS'D, 8 300
WHOM US THE MORE TO SPITE HIS MAKER RAIS'D 9 177
WOULD UTMOST VIGOR RAISE, AND RAIS'D UNITE. 9 314
RAIS'D, AS OF SOM GREAT MATTER TO BEGIN. 9 669
AN EAGER APPETITE, RAIS'D BY THE SMELL 9 740
RAIS'D FROM THIR DARK DIVAN, AND WITH LIKE JOY 10 457
LABOURING HAD RAIS'D, AND THUS TO EVE REPLI'D. 10 1012
SOON RAIS'D, AND HIS ATTENTION THUS RECALL'D. 11 422

RAISD
RETURND ON THAT BRIGHT BEAM, WHOSE POINT NOW RAISD 4 590
HATH RAISD IN PARADISE, AND HOW DISTURBD 5 226

RAISE
ILLUMIN, WHAT IS LOW RAISE AND SUPPORT; 1 23
NOR WANT WE SKILL OR ART, FROM WHENCE TO RAISE 2 272
AND DYING RISE, AND RISING WITH HIM RAISE 3 296
I FEAR, HATH VENTUR'D FROM THE DEEP, TO RAISE 4 574
LIKE GENTLE BREATHS FROM RIVERS PURE, THENCE RAISE 4 806
NEW LAWS FROM HIM WHO REIGNS, NEW MINDS MAY RAISE 5 680
ARMIE AGAINST ARMIE NUMBERLESS TO RAISE 6 224
CANST RAISE THY CREATURE TO WHAT HIGHTH THOU WILT 8 430
REMAINES, SUFFICIENT OF IT SELF TO RAISE 9 43
WOULD UTMOST VIGOR RAISE, AND RAIS'D UNITE. 9 314
VACANT POSSESSION SOM NEW TROUBLE RAISE: 11 103
RAISE OUT OF FRIENDSHIP HOSTIL DEEDS IN PEACE. 11 796
THAT GOD VOUTSAFES TO RAISE ANOTHER WORLD 11 877
WHICH HE WILL SHEW HIM, AND FROM HIM WILL RAISE 12 123
RAISE HIM TO BE THE SECOND IN THAT REALME 12 162
PROVOKING GOD TO RAISE THEM ENEMIES: 12 318
SATAN WITH HIS PERVERTED WORLD, THEN RAISE 12 547

RALLIED
WITH RALLIED ARMS TO TRY WHAT MAY BE YET 1 269
AND TO REBELLIOUS FIGHT RALLIED THIR POWERS 6 786

RAMIEL
OF RAMIEL SCORCHT AND BLASTED OVERTHREW. 6 372

RAMMD
THICK-RAMMD, AT TH' OTHER BORE WITH TOUCH OF FIRE 6 485

RAMPANT
AND RAMPANT SHAKES HIS BRINDED MAIN; THE OUNCE, 7 466

RAMPART
OR CAST A RAMPART. MAMMON LED THEM ON, 1 678

RAMPD
SPORTING THE LION RAMPD, AND IN HIS PAW 4 343

RAN
RAN PURPLE TO THE SEA, SUPPOS'D WITH BLOOD 1 451
RAN NECTAR, VISITING EACH PLANT, AND FED 4 240
LIGHT AS THE LIGHTNING GLIMPS THEY RAN, THEY FLEW, 6 642
SURVEY'D, AND SOMETIMES WENT, AND SOMETIMES RAN 8 268
RAN THROUGH HIS VEINS, AND ALL HIS JOYNTS RELAX'D; 9 891
TH' ETHEREAL PEOPLE RAN, TO HEAR AND KNOW 10 27
LAY SLEEPING RAN BEFORE, BUT FOUND HER WAK'T; 12 608

RANCOR
RANCOR AND PRIDE, IMPATIENCE AND DESPITE, 10 1044

RANCOUR
WAITED WITH HELLISH RANCOUR IMMINENT 9 409

RANDOM
BUT STILL THY WORDS AT RANDOM, AS BEFORE, 4 930
AT RANDOM YIELDED UP TO THEIR MISRULE; 10 628

RANG'D
BY THOUSANDS AND BY MILLIONS RANG'D FOR FIGHT; 6 48
IN COMMON, RANG'D IN FIGURE WEDGE THIR WAY, 7 426
SINGLE OR IN ARRAY OF BATTEL RANG'D 11 644

RANGE
WHILE OTHER ANIMALS UNACTIVE RANGE, 4 621
IN WO THEN; THAT DESTRUCTION WIDE MAY RANGE: 9 134
TO RANGE IN, AND TO DWELL, AND OVER MAN 10 492

RANGED
BY FALSE PRESUMPTUOUS HOPE, THE RANGED POWERS 2 522

RANKE
WHO NOW SHALL REARE YE TO THE SUN, OR RANKE 11 278

RANKS
TO SPEAK; WHEREAT THIR DOUBL'D RANKS THEY BEND 1 616
A SILVAN SCENE, AND AS THE RANKS ASCEND 4 140
THIR PERFET RANKS; FOR HIGH ABOVE THE GROUND 6 71
ON THIR IMBATTELLD RANKS THE WAVES RETURN, 12 213

RANKT
WITH HORSE AND CHARIOTS RANKT IN LOOSE ARRAY; 2 887
STOOD RANKT OF SERAPHIM ANOTHER ROW 6 604

RANSACK'D
RANSACK'D THE CENTER, AND WITH IMPIOUS HANDS 1 686

RANSOM
THE DEADLY FORFEITURE, AND RANSOM SET. 3 221
BOTH RANSOM AND REDEEMER VOLUNTARIE, 10 61
THY RANSOM PAID, WHICH MAN FROM DEATH REDEEMS, 12 424

RANSOMD
HIS BRETHREN, RANSOMD WITH HIS OWN DEAR LIFE. 3 297

RAPACIOUS
REDEEM THEE QUITE FROM DEATHS RAPACIOUS CLAIME; 11 258

RAPE
EXPOS'D A MATRON TO AVOID WORSE RAPE. 1 505
INGENDRING WITH ME, OF THAT RAPE BEGOT 2 794
RAPE OR ADULTERIE, WHERE PASSING FAIRE 11 717

RAPHAEL
RAPHAEL, THE SOCIABLE SPIRIT, THAT DEIGN'D 5 221
RAPHAEL, SAID HEE, THOU HEAR'ST WHAT STIR ON EARTH 5 224
THUS ADAM MADE REQUEST, AND RAPHAEL 5 561
URIEL AND RAPHAEL HIS VAUNTING FOE, 6 363
SAY GODDESS, WHAT ENSU'D WHEN RAPHAEL, 7 40
AND RAPHAEL NOW TO ADAM'S DOUBT PROPOS'D 8 64
TO WHOM THUS RAPHAEL ANSWER'D HEAV'NLY MEEK. 8 217
AS RAPHAEL, THAT I SHOULD MUCH CONFIDE, 11 235

RAPID
WITH RAPID WHEELS, OR FRONTED BRIGADS FORM. 2 532
UPON THE RAPID CURRENT, WHICH THROUGH VEINS 4 227
ASCEND MY CHARIOT, GUIDE THE RAPID WHEELES 6 711
WITH CLAMOR THENCE THE RAPID CURRENTS DRIVE 11 853

RAPINE
HIS MALICE, AND WITH RAPINE SWEET BEREAV'D 9 461

RAPT
RAPT IN A CHARIOT DRAWN BY FIERY STEEDS. 3 522
STANDING ON EARTH, NOT RAPT ABOVE THE POLE, 7 23
RAPT IN A BALMIE CLOUD WITH WINGED STEEDS 11 706

RAPTURE
NOR HOLY RAPTURE WANTED THEY TO PRAISE 5 147
TO RAPTURE, TILL THE SAVAGE CLAMOR DROUND 7 36
IF STEEP, WITH TORRENT RAPTURE, IF THROUGH PLAINE, 7 299
AND RAPTURE SO OFT BEHELD? THOSE HEAV'NLY SHAPES 9 1082

RAPTURES
THIR SACRED SONG, AND WAKEN RAPTURES HIGH; 3 369

RARE
ORE BOG OR STEEP, THROUGH STRAIT, ROUGH, DENSE, OR
RARE, 2 948
THOUGH HARD AND RARE: THEE I REVISIT SAFE, 3 21
OF COLOUR GLORIOUS AND EFFECT SO RARE? 3 612
ASSUME, AS LIKES THEM BEST, CONDENSE OR RARE. 6 353
THOSE RARE AND SOLITARIE, THESE IN FLOCKS 7 461
OF ARTS THAT POLISH LIFE, INVENTERS RARE, 11 610

RARELY
RARELY BE FOUND: SO SHALL THE WORLD GOE ON, 12 537

RAS'D
BE NO MEMORIAL BLOTTED OUT AND RAS'D 1 362
OF NATURES WORKS TO MEE EXPUNG'D AND RAS'D, 3 49

RASE
WITH ALL HER BATTERING ENGINES BENT TO RASE 2 923
UPON THIR TONGUES A VARIOUS SPIRIT TO RASE 12 53

RASH
OR SINGULAR AND RASH, WHEREAT REJOIC'D 5 851
SO SAYING, HER RASH HAND IN EVIL HOUR 9 780
MEAN I TO TRIE, WHAT RASH UNTRI'D I SOUGHT, 9 860
HIMSELF AND HIS RASH ARMIE, WHERE THIN AIRE 12 76

RASHNESS
UNTRAIND IN ARMES, WHERE RASHNESS LEADS NOT ON. 12 222

RATHER
NO LIGHT, BUT RATHER DARKNESS VISIBLE 1 63
RATHER THEN HUMAN. NOR DID ISRAEL SCAPE 1 482
THE FELLOWS OF HIS CRIME, THE FOLLOWERS RATHER 1 606
EQUAL IN STRENGTH, AND RATHER THEN BE LESS 2 47
BY OUR DELAY? NO, LET US RATHER CHOOSE 2 60
TO PERISH RATHER, SWALLOWD UP AND LOST 2 149
OF SPLENDID VASSALAGE, BUT RATHER SEEK 2 252
OR HEAR'ST THOU RATHER PURE ETHEREAL STREAM, 3 7
SO MUCH THE RATHER THOU CELESTIAL LIGHT 3 51
IMAGIND RATHER OFT THEN ELSEWHERE SEEN, 3 599
THAT REACHES BLAME, BUT RATHER MERITS PRAISE 3 697
BUT RATHER TO TELL HOW, IF ART COULD TELL, 4 236
TO MAKE US LESS, BENT RATHER TO EXALT 5 829
I SEE THAT MOST THROUGH SLOTH HAD RATHER SERVE, 6 166
CHOSE RATHER; HEE, SHE KNEW WOULD INTERMIX 8 54
RATHER ADMIRE; OR IF THEY LIST TO TRY 8 75
BY US? WHO RATHER DOUBLE HONOUR GAINE 9 332
RATHER YOUR DAUNTLESS VERTUE, WHOM THE PAIN 9 694
WHAT FEAR I THEN, RATHER WHAT KNOW TO FEARE 9 773
FULL HAPPINESS WITH MEE, OR RATHER NOT, 9 819
RATHER HOW HAST THOU YEELDED TO TRANSGRESS 9 902
RATHER THEN DEATH OR AUGHT THEN DEATH MORE DREAD 9 969
THE WORST, AND NOT PERSWADE THEE RATHER DIE 9 979
YET WILLINGLY CHOSE RATHER DEATH WITH THEE: 9 1167
TRUE IS, MEE ALSO HE HATH JUDG'D, OR RATHER 10 494
RATHER THEN SOLID VERTU, ALL BUT A RIB 10 884
WE ARE BY DOOM TO PAY; RATHER SUCH ACTS 10 1026
RATHER BELONGS, DISTRUST AND ALL DISPRAISE: 11 166
TO BE THUS WRESTED FROM US? RATHER WHY 11 503
LIFE MUCH, BENT RATHER HOW I MAY BE QUIT 11 548

RE-ASCEND
HATH EMPTIED HEAV'N, SHALL FAIL TO RE-ASCEND 1 633

REASON
WHOM REASON HATH EQUALD, FORCE HATH MADE SUPREAM 1 248
THE BETTER REASON, TO PERPLEX AND DASH 2 114
MAIN REASON TO PERSWADE IMMEDIATE WARR, 2 121
WITH REASON HATH DEEP SILENCE AND DEMURR 2 431
WHEN WILL AND REASON (REASON ALSO IS CHOICE) 3 108
MELT, AS I DOE, YET PUBLIC REASON JUST, 4 389
FOUNDED IN REASON, LOYAL, JUST, AND PURE, 4 755
TO THEE NO REASON; WHO KNOWST ONLY GOOD, 4 895
REASON AS CHIEF; AMONG THESE FANSIE NEXT 5 102
WHICH REASON JOYNING OR DISJOYNING, FRAMES 5 106
REASON RECEIVES, AND REASON IS HER BEING, 5 487
WHO CAN IN REASON THEN OR RIGHT ASSUME 5 794
BY FORCE, WHO REASON FOR THIR LAW REFUSE, 6 41
RIGHT REASON FOR THIR LAW, AND FOR THIR KING 6 42
I MEAN TO TRY, WHOSE REASON I HAVE TRI'D 6 120
WHEN REASON HATH TO DEAL WITH FORCE, YET SO 6 125
MOST REASON IS THAT REASON OVERCOME. 6 126
WITH SANCTITIE OF REASON, MIGHT ERECT 7 508
AND REASON NOT CONTEMPTIBLY; WITH THESE 8 374
GOOD REASON WAS THOU FREELY SHOULDST DISLIKE, 8 443
MY PLEADED REASON. TO THE NUPTIAL BOWRE 8 510
AUTHORITY AND REASON ON HER WAITE, 8 554
IN REASON, AND IS JUDICIOUS, IS THE SCALE 8 591
OF GROWTH, SENSE, REASON, ALL SUMM'D UP IN MAN. 9 113
OF LOOKS AND SMILES, FOR SMILES FROM REASON FLOW, 9 239
HE MADE US, AND DELIGHT TO REASON JOYN'D. 9 243
REASON, IS FREE, AND REASON HE MADE RIGHT, 9 352
SINCE REASON NOT IMPOSSIBLY MAY MEET 9 360
MUCH REASON, AND IN THIR ACTIONS OFT APPEERS. 9 559
OF REASON IN MY INWARD POWERS, AND SPEECH 9 600
LAW TO OUR SELVES, OUR REASON IS OUR LAW. 9 654
WITH REASON, TO HER SEEMING, AND WITH TRUTH; 9 738
USURPING OVER SOVRAN REASON CLAIMD 9 1130
IS LOST, WHICH ALWAYES WITH RIGHT REASON DWELLS 12 84
REASON IN MAN OBSCUR'D, OR NOT OBEYD, 12 86
FROM REASON, AND TO SERVITUDE REDUCE 12 89
OVER FREE REASON, GOD IN JUDGEMENT JUST 12 92
FROM VERTUE, WHICH IS REASON, THAT NO WRONG, 12 98

REASON'D
IN THOUGHTS MORE ELEVATE, AND REASON'D HIGH 2 558

REASONING
USELESS BESIDES, REASONING I OFT ADMIRE, 8 25
ALREADIE BY THY REASONING THIS I GUESS, 8 85
CHIEFLY BY WHAT THY OWN LAST REASONING WORDS 9 379
REASONING TO ADMIRATION, AND WITH MEE 9 872

REASONINGS
AND REASONINGS, THOUGH THROUGH MAZES, LEAD ME STILL 10 830

REASONLESS
SUSPICIOUS, REASONLESS. WHY SHOULD THIR LORD 4 516

REASONS
THUS BELIAL WITH WORDS CLOATH'D IN REASONS GARB 2 226
AND KNOWS, AND SPEAKS, AND REASONS, AND DISCERNS, 9 765

REASSEMBLING
AND REASSEMBLING OUR AFFLICTED POWERS, 1 186

REASSUM'D
INTO HIS BLISSFUL BOSOM REASSUM'D 10 225

REBEL
OF REBEL ANGELS, BY WHOSE AID ASPIRING 1 38
THE CALF IN OREB: AND THE REBEL KING 1 484
THE REBEL THRONES, BUT GREATER RAGE TO SEE 6 199
BE SURE, AND TERROUR SEIS'D THE REBEL HOST, 6 647
CONVICT BY FLIGHT, AND REBEL TO ALL LAW 10 83

REBELL
WHO JUSTLY HATH DRIVN OUT HIS REBELL FOES 3 677
WHICH OF THOSE REBELL SPIRITS ADJUDG'D TO HELL 4 823

REBELL'D
ARMD WITH THY MIGHT, RID HEAV'N OF THESE REBELL'D, 6 737

REBELLD
TO SERVE TH' UNWISE, OR HIM WHO HATH REBELLD 6 179
OF THOSE TOO HIGH ASPIRING, WHO REBELLD 6 899

REBELLION
BY THIR REBELLION, FROM THE BOOKS OF LIFE. 1 363
REBELLION RISING, SAW IN WHOM, HOW SPRED 5 715
OF THY REBELLION? HOW HAST THOU INSTILL'D 6 269
AND FROM REBELLION SHALL DERIVE HIS NAME, 12 36
THOUGH OF REBELLION OTHERS HE ACCUSE. 12 37

REBELLIOUS
FOR THOSE REBELLIOUS, HERE THEIR PRISON ORDAIN'D 1 71
ERRING; FOR HE WITH THIS REBELLIOUS ROUT 1 747
UNBROK'N, AND IN PROUD REBELLIOUS ARMS 2 691
UPON HIS OWN REBELLIOUS HEAD. AND NOW 3 86

REBELLIOUS (CONTINUED)
FAITHFUL TO WHOM? TO THY REBELLIOUS CREW? 4 952
REBELLIOUS, THEM WITH FIRE AND HOSTILE ARMS 6 50
SATAN WITH HIS REBELLIOUS DISAPPEERD, 6 414
AND TO REBELLIOUS FIGHT RALLIED THIR POWERS 6 786
ALL LIKE HIMSELF REBELLIOUS, BY WHOSE AID 7 140

REBELS
THY REBELS, OR BE FOUND THE WORST IN HEAV'N. 5 742

REBOUNDING
AND WITH REBOUNDING SURGE THE BARRS ASSAILD, 10 417

REBOUNDS
AT ONCE WITH JOY AND FEAR HIS HEART REBOUNDS. 1 788

REBUFF
THE STRONG REBUFF OF SOM TUMULTUOUS CLOUD 2 936

REBUKE
SO SPAKE THE CHERUBE, AND HIS GRAVE REBUKE 4 844
HUMBL'D BY SUCH REBUKE, SO FARR BENEATH 6 342
ANGER AND JUST REBUKE, AND JUDGEMENT GIV'N, 9 10

RECAL
WOULD HIGTH RECAL HIGH THOUGHTS, HOW SOON UNSAY 4 95

RECALL
AGAINST THEE ARE GON FORTH WITHOUT RECALL; 5 885
BUT PAST WHO CAN RECALL, OR DON UNDOE? 9 926

RECALL'D
BUT SEE THE ANGRY VICTOR HATH RECALL'D 1 169
FOR THOUGH I FLED HIM ANGRIE, YET RECALL'D 11 330
SOON RAIS'D, AND HIS ATTENTION THUS RECALL'D. 11 422

RECANT
WHAT FEIGN'D SUBMISSION SWORE: EASE WOULD RECANT 4 96

RECEAV'D
AMONG THOSE FRIENDLY POWERS WHO HIM RECEAV'D 6 22
ON HIGH: WHO INTO GLORIE HIM RECEAV'D, 6 891
I HAVE RECEAV'D, TO ANSWER THY DESIRE 7 119
ALL I RECEAV'D, UNABLE TO PERFORME 10 750
BY WISDOME, AND SUPERIOUR GIFTS RECEAV'D. 11 636
AND THUS WITH WORDS NOT SAD SHE HIM RECEAV'D. 12 609

RECEAVD
YAWNING RECEAVD THEM WHOLE, AND ON THEM CLOS'D, 6 875
BUT IN THE FRUITFUL EARTH; THERE FIRST RECEAVD 8 96

RECEAVE
HIS FIERY CHAOS TO RECEAVE THIR FALL. 6 55
FROM FLIGHT, SEDITIOUS ANGEL, TO RECEAVE 6 152
RECEAVE WITH SOLEMNE PURPOSE TO OBSERVE 7 78
SO TOLD AS EARTHLY NOTION CAN RECEAVE. 7 179
AFTER THIR KINDES; I BRING THEM TO RECEAVE 8 343
CAN EITHER NOT RECEAVE, OR CAN REPELL. 9 284
I FROM THE INFLUENCE OF THY LOOKS RECEAVE 9 309
AGAINST HIS WILL HE CAN RECEAVE NO HARME. 9 350
ACCEPT ME, AND IN MEE FROM THESE RECEAVE 11 37
DID, AS THOU SAWST, RECEAVE, TO WALK WITH GOD 11 707
HIS FAITHFUL, AND RECEAVE THEM INTO BLISS, 12 462
GREAT NUMBERS OF EACH NATION TO RECEAVE 12 503

RECEAVES
HER END WITHOUT LEAST MOTION, AND RECEAVES, 8 35
EARTH SITTING STILL, WHEN SHE ALONE RECEAVES 8 89
OF MOREB; THERE BY PROMISE HE RECEAVES 12 137

RECEAV'ST
CENTRING RECEAV'ST FROM ALL THOSE ORBS; IN THEE, 9 109

RECEIV'D
OF HEAV'N RECEIV'D US FALLING, AND THE THUNDER, 1 174
STOOD THICK AS STARRS, AND FROM HIS SIGHT RECEIV'D 3 61
INEFFABLY INTO HIS FACE RECEIV'D, 6 721
GIV'N AND RECEIV'D; BUT IN DISPARITIE 8 386

RECEIVD
FORGETFUL WHAT FROM HIM I STILL RECEIVD, 4 54
AND BY HER YIELDED, BY HIM BEST RECEIVD, 4 309
AFTER HIS CHARGE RECEIVD; BUT FROM AMONG 5 248
AND AS YE HAVE RECEIVD, SO HAVE YE DON 6 805

RECEIVE
RECEIVE THY NEW POSSESSOR: ONE WHO BRINGS 1 252
IN TEMPER AND IN NATURE, WILL RECEIVE 2 218
STAND IN HIS PRESENCE HUMBLE, AND RECEIVE 2 240
NOT WHAT THEY WOULD? WHAT PRAISE COULD THEY
RECEIVE? 3 106
DEATH HIS DEATHS WOUND SHALL THEN RECEIVE, AND
STOOP 3 252
RECEIVE NEW LIFE. SO MAN, AS IS MOST JUST, 3 294
NOT LIKE THESE NARROW LIMITS, TO RECEIVE 4 384
ON EARTH, MADE HEREBY APTER TO RECEIVE 4 672
ABUNDANCE, FIT TO HONOUR AND RECEIVE 5 315
FIT ENTERTAINMENT TO RECEIVE OUR KING 5 690

RECEIVE (CONTINUED)
RECEIVE HIM COMING TO RECEIVE FROM US 5 781
CAME SUMMOND OVER EDEN TO RECEIVE 6 75
THIS GREETING ON THY IMPIOUS CREST RECEIVE. . . 6 188
RECEIVE, NO MORE THEN CAN THE FLUID AIRE: . . . 6 349
STAND READIE TO RECEIVE THEM, IF THEY LIKE . . . 6 561
IN THE SUNS ORB, MADE POROUS TO RECEIVE 7 361
TO SANCTITIE THAT SHALL RECEIVE NO STAINE: . . . 10 639
WHAT WE RECEIVE, WOULD EITHER NOT ACCEPT . . . 11 505
AND PUISSANT DEEDS, A PROMISE SHALL RECEIVE . . 12 322

RECEIVES
OF UNESSENTIAL NIGHT RECEIVES HIM NEXT 2 439
THE SUN THAT LIGHT IMPARTS TO ALL, RECEIVES . . . 5 423
REASON RECEIVES, AND REASON IS HER BEING, ... 5 487
AND STUMBL'D MANY, WHO RECEIVES THEM RIGHT, . . . 6 624

RECEPTACLE
THE DRY LAND, EARTH, AND THE GREAT RECEPTACLE . . 7 307
LEAST PARADISE A RECEPTACLE PROVE 11 123

RECEPTION
ABOUT THE GREAT RECEPTION OF THIR KING, ... 5 769
TO THE RECEPTION OF THIR MATTER ACT, ... 10 807

RECESS
IN CLOSE RECESS AND SECRET CONCLAVE SAT 1 795
LIVE TO OUR SELVES, THOUGH IN THIS VAST RECESS, . 2 254
OF COOLE RECESS, O'RE WHICH THE MANTLING VINE . . 4 258
NOR FAUNUS HAUNTED. HERE IN CLOSE RECESS 4 708
THIS FLOURIE PLAT, THE SWEET RECESS OF EVE . . . 9 456
RECESS, AND ONELY CONSOLATION LEFT 11 304

RECIPROCAL
THIS EARTH? RECIPROCAL, IF LAND BE THERE, ... 8 144

RECK
LET IT; I RECK NOT, SO IT LIGHT WELL AIM'D, . . . 9 173

RECK'D
HE RECK'D NOT, AND THESE WORDS THEREAFTER SPAKE. . 2 50

RECK'N
IMPORTS NOT, IF THOU RECK'N RIGHT, THE REST . . . 8 71

RECK'N'ST
AND RECK'N'ST THOU THY SELF WITH SPIRITS OF HEAV'N, 2 696

RECLAME
THEY HARD'ND MORE BY WHAT MIGHT MOST RECLAME, . . . 6 791

RECLINE
YIELDED THEM, SIDE-LONG AS THEY SAT RECLINE . . . 4 333

RECOILD
ALL TH' HOST OF HEAV'N; BACK THEY RECOILD AFFRAID 2 759
HE BACK RECOILD; THE TENTH ON BENDED KNEE . . . 6 194

RECOILE
WITH IMPETUOUS RECOILE AND JARRING SOUND 2 880

RECOILES
AND LIKE A DEVILLISH ENGINE BACK RECOILES 4 17
BITTER ERE LONG BACK ON IT SELF RECOILES; 9 172

RECOLLECTING
SOON RECOLLECTING, WITH HIGH WORDS, THAT BORE . . . 1 528

RECOLLECTS
FIERCE HATE HE RECOLLECTS, AND ALL HIS THOUGHTS . 9 471

RECOMFORTED
RECOMFORTED, AND AFTER THOUGHTS DISTURBD 9 918

RECOMMEND
TO RECOMMEND COOLE ZEPHYR, AND MADE EASE 4 329

RECOMPENCE
DIRECTED NO MEAN RECOMPENCE IT BRINGS 2 981
THE EASIEST RECOMPENCE, AND PAY HIM THANKS, . . . 4 47
TORMENT WITH EASE, AND SOONEST RECOMPENCE 4 893
FROM ALL HIS ALIMENTAL RECOMPENCE 5 424
WHAT THANKS SUFFICIENT, OR WHAT RECOMPENCE 8 5
IN RECOMPENCE (FOR SUCH COMPLIANCE BAD 9 994
SUCH RECOMPENCE BEST MERITS) FROM THE BOUGH . . . 9 995
IS THIS THE LOVE, IS THIS THE RECOMPENCE 9 1163
TO RECOMPENCE HIS DISTANCE, IN THIR SIGHT . . . 10 683

RECOMPENC'T
AND BRINGING FORTH, SOON RECOMPENC'T WITH JOY, . 10 1052
WITH INWARD CONSOLATIONS RECOMPENC'T, ... 12 495

RECONCIL'D
BEFORE THEE RECONCIL'D, AT LEAST HIS DAYS . . . 11 39

RECONCILEMENT
AND RECONCILEMENT; WRAUTH SHALL BE NO MORE 3 264
FOR NEVER CAN TRUE RECONCILEMENT GROW 4 98

RECONCILEMENT (CONTINUED)
CREATURE SO FAIRE HIS RECONCILEMENT SEEKING, . . 10 943

RECORDED
RECORDED EMINENT. THUS WHEN IN ORBES 5 594
SO EEV'N AND MORN RECORDED THE THIRD DAY. . . . 7 338

RECORDERS
OF FLUTES AND SOFT RECORDERS; SUCH AS RAIS'D . . 1 551

RECORDS
THOUGH OF THIR NAMES IN HEAV'NLY RECORDS NOW . . 1 361
THE RECORDS OF HIS COV'NANT, OVER THESE 12 252
LEFT ONELY IN THOSE WRITTEN RECORDS PURE, . . . 12 513

RECOUNT
OBTAINE; THOUGH TO RECOUNT ALMIGHTIE WORKS . . . 7 112

RECOUNTED
RECOUNTED, MIXING INTERCESSION SWEET. 10 228

RECOVER'D
AS GODS, AND BY THIR OWN RECOVER'D STRENGTH, . . 1 240
THUS FARR AT LEAST RECOVER'D, HATH MUCH MORE . . 2 22

RECOVERD
SCARCE THUS AT LENGTH FAILD SPEECH RECOVERD SAD. . 4 357
FIRM PEACE RECOVERD SOON AND WONTED CALM. . . . 5 210

RECOVERING
TO WHOM THUS EVE, RECOVERING HEART, REPLI'D. . . 10 966
RECOVERING, AND HIS SCATTERD SPIRITS RETURND, . 11 294
AND SCARCE RECOVERING WORDS HIS PLAINT RENEW'D. . 11 499

RECOYLD
AND FIERIE FOAMING STEEDS; WHAT STOOD, RECOYLD . 6 391

RECURE
WHICH HEE, WHO COMES THY SAVIOUR, SHALL RECURE, . 12 393

RED
WING'D WITH RED LIGHTNING AND IMPETUOUS RAGE, . . 1 175
HIS RED RIGHT HAND TO PLAGUE US? WHAT IF ALL . . 2 174
TURND FIERIE RED, SHARPNING IN MOONED HORNES . . 4 978
CELESTIAL ROSIE RED, LOVES PROPER HUE, ... 8 619

REDEEM
WHICH OF YE WILL BE MORTAL TO REDEEM 3 214
THOU THEREFORE WHOM THOU ONLY CANST REDEEM, . . 3 281
SO DEARLY TO REDEEM WHAT HELLISH HATE 3 300
REDEEM THEE QUITE FROM DEATHS RAPACIOUS CLAIME; . 11 258

REDEEMD
THEN WITH THE MULTITUDE OF MY REDEEMD 3 260
ALL MY REDEEMD MAY DWELL IN JOY AND BLISS, . . . 11 43

REDEEME
GIVING TO DEATH, AND DYING TO REDEEME, ... 3 299

REDEEMER
BOTH RANSOM AND REDEEMER VOLUNTARIE, ... 10 61
FOR DEATH, LIKE THAT WHICH THE REDEEMER DY'D. . . 12 445
ACKNOWLEDGE MY REDEEMER EVER BLEST. 12 573

REDEEMS
THY RANSOM PAID, WHICH MAN FROM DEATH REDEEMS, . 12 424
OR THEIRS WHOM HE REDEEMS, A DEATH LIKE SLEEP, . 12 434

REDEMPTION
AND NOW WITHOUT REDEMPTION ALL MANKIND 3 222
ORDAIND WITHOUT REDEMPTION, WITHOUT END. 5 615
IN HIS REDEMPTION, AND THAT HIS OBEDIENCE . . . 12 408

REDOUBL'D
THE ATHEIST CREW, BUT WITH REDOUBL'D BLOW 6 370

REDOUBLE
REDOUBLE THEN THIS MIRACLE, AND SAY, ... 9 562

REDOUND
ON DESPARATE REVENG, THAT SHALL REDOUND 3 85
AS I, THOUGH THEREBY WORSE TO ME REDOUND: 9 128
SHALL WITH A FIERCE REFLUX ON MEE REDOUND, . . . 10 739

REDOUNDED
DRIV'N BACK REDOUNDED AS A FLOOD ON THOSE . . . 7 57

REDOUNDING
CAST FORTH REDOUNDING SMOAK AND RUDDY FLAME. . . 2 889

REDOUNDS
TO TRANSUBSTANTIATE; WHAT REDOUNDS, TRANSPIRES . 5 438

REDRESS
WITH MYRTLE, FIND WHAT TO REDRESS TILL NOON: . . 9 219

RED-SEA
HATH VEXT THE RED-SEA COAST, WHOSE WAVES ORETHREW 1 306

REDUC'D
REDUC'D THIR SHAPES IMMENSE, AND WERE AT LARGE, 1 790
CONCOCTED AND ADUSTED THEY REDUC'D 6 514
UNDER WHOSE CONDUCT MICHAEL SOON REDUC'D 6 777

REDUCE
WILL EITHER QUITE CONSUME US, AND REDUCE 2 96
ALL USURPATION THENCE EXPELL'D, REDUCE 2 983
THRONES, PRINCEDOMS, POWERS, DOMINIONS I REDUCE: 3 320
AND EQUAL TO REDUCE ME TO MY DUST, 10 748
FROM REASON, AND TO SERVITUDE REDUCE 12 89

REDUC'T
ONE OF OUR NUMBER THUS REDUC'T BECOMES, 5 843
MANY A DARK LEAGUE, REDUC'T IN CAREFUL WATCH 10 438

REDUNDANT
FLOTED REDUNDANT: PLEASING WAS HIS SHAPE, 9 503

REED
WHAT DROPS THE MYRRHE, AND WHAT THE BALMIE REED, 5 23
OF MISSIVE RUIN; PART INCENTIVE REED 6 519
A SERAPH STOOD, AND IN HIS HAND A REED 6 579
THE SMELLING GOURD, UP STOOD THE CORNIE REED 7 321
CHARM'D WITH ARCADIAN PIPE, THE PASTORAL REED 11 132

RE-EDIFIE
THEY FIRST RE-EDIFIE, AND FOR A WHILE 12 350

REEDS
NOT LONG, FOR SUDDEN ALL AT ONCE THIR REEDS 6 582

RE-ENTER
RE-ENTER HEAV'N; OR ELSE IN SOME MILDE ZONE 2 397

REFIN'D
BUT MORE REFIN'D, MORE SPIRITOUS, AND PURE, 5 475
TRI'D IN SHARP TRIBULATION, AND REFIN'D 11 63
FROM THE CONFLAGRANT MASS, PURG'D AND REFIN'D, 12 548

REFINES
WHEREIN TRUE LOVE CONSISTS NOT; LOVE REFINES 8 589

REFLECTED
WITH LIGHT FROM HENCE, THOUGH BUT REFLECTED,
SHINES; 3 723
ARRAYING WITH REFLECTED PURPLE AND GOLD 4 596
REFLECTED, MAY WITH MATTER SERE FOMENT, 10 1071

REFLECTING
REFLECTING BLAZE ON BLAZE, FIRST MET HIS VIEW; 6 18

REFLECTION
THOUGH DISTANT FARR SOM SMALL REFLECTION GAINES 3 428
BY TINCTURE OR REFLECTION THEY AUGMENT 7 367

REFLUX
SHALL WITH A FIERCE REFLUX ON MEE REDOUND, 10 739

REFORM
AND AT OUR PLEASANT LABOUR, TO REFORM 4 625

REFORMING
WITH SECOND THOUGHTS, REFORMING WHAT WAS OLD. 9 101

REFREIN'D
REFREIN'D HIS TONGUE BLASPHEMOUS; BUT ANON 6 360

REFRESHMENT
REFRESHMENT, WHETHER FOOD, OR TALK BETWEEN, 9 237

REFRESH'T
BUT COME, SO WELL REFRESH'T, NOW LET US PLAY, 9 1027

REFUGE
A REFUGE FROM THOSE WOUNDS: OR WHEN WE LAY 2 168
FIND PLACE OR REFUGE; AND THE MORE I SEE 9 119
OF REFUGE, AND CONCLUDES THEE MISERABLE 10 839
THROUGH ALL THE PLAIN, AND REFUGE NONE WAS FOUND. 11 673

REFULGENT
OF GOLDEN PANOPLIE, REFULGENT HOST, 6 527

REFUS'D
(CERTAIN TO BE REFUS'D) WHAT ERST THEY FEARD; 2 470
AND SO REFUS'D MIGHT IN OPINION STAND 2 471
MYSTERIOUS OF CONNUBIAL LOVE REFUS'D: 4 743

REFUSD
I THUS CONTEST; THEN SHOULD HAVE BEEN REFUSD 10 756

REFUSE
THESE ROYALTIES, AND NOT REFUSE TO REIGN, 2 451
IF I REFUSE NOT, BUT CONVERT, AS YOU, 5 492
BY FORCE, WHO REASON FOR THIR LAW REFUSE, 6 41
WITH WARR AND HOSTILE SNARE SUCH AS REFUSE 12 31

REFUSING
REFUSING TO ACCEPT AS GREAT A SHARE 2 452

REFUTES
BUT SELF-DESTRUCTION THEREFORE SAUGHT, REFUTES 10 1016

REGAIN
RESTORE US, AND REGAIN THE BLISSFUL SEAT, 1 5
WE WARR, IF WARR BE BEST, OR TO REGAIN 2 230

REGAIND
REGAIND IN HEAV'N, OR WHAT MORE LOST IN HELL? 1 270
THEREBY REGAIND, BUT SAT DEVISING DEATH 4 197

REGAINE
LEAST TOTAL DARKNESS SHOULD BY NIGHT REGAINE 4 665
OF NEW ACCEPTANCE, HOPEFUL TO REGAINE 10 972

REGAL
CONSENT OR CUSTOME, AND HIS REGAL STATE 1 640
WITH TRUMPETS REGAL SOUND THE GREAT RESULT: 2 515
THEN THOU THY REGAL SCEPTER SHALT LAY BY, 3 339
FOR REGAL SCEPTER THEN NO MORE SHALL NEED, 3 340
AND WITH THEM COMES A THIRD OF REGAL PORT, 4 869
WITH REGAL ORNAMENT; THE MIDDLE PAIR 5 280
ILLUSTRATES, WHEN THEY SEE ALL REGAL POWER 5 739
WITH REGAL SCEPTER, EVERY SOULE IN HEAV'N 5 816
WAS PLAC'T IN REGAL LUSTRE. DOWN A WHILE 10 447
IRREVOCABLE, THAT HIS REGAL THRONE 12 323

REGARD
A GENERATION, WHOM HIS CHOICE REGARD 1 653
COMPOSE OUR PRESENT EVILS, WITH REGARD 2 281
PASS'D FREQUENT, AND HIS EYE WITH CHOICE REGARD 3 534
AND THE REGARD OF HEAV'N ON ALL HIS WAIES; 4 620
TO WHOM WITH STERN REGARD THUS GABRIEL SPAKE. 4 877
IF NONE REGARD; HEAV'N WAKES WITH ALL HIS EYES, 5 44
BUT HER WITH STERN REGARD HE THUS REPELL'D. 10 866
TO WHOM THUS MICHAEL WITH REGARD BENIGNE. 11 334
WITH SOME REGARD TO WHAT IS JUST AND RIGHT 12 16
TO KNOW THIR GOD, OR MESSAGE TO REGARD, 12 174
THE SCEPTER, AND REGARD NOT DAVIDS SONS, 12 357

REGARDED
REGARDED, SUCH DELIGHT TILL THEN, AS SEEMD, 9 787

REGARDLESS
REGARDLESS OF THE BLISS WHEREIN HEE SAT 3 408
REGARDLESS WHETHER GOOD OR EVIL FAME. 12 47

REGENCIES
REGIONS THEY PASS'D, THE MIGHTIE REGENCIES 5 748

REGENERATE
REGENERATE GROW INSTEAD, THAT SIGHS NOW BREATH'D 11 5

REGENT
URIEL, THOUGH REGENT OF THE SUN, AND HELD 3 690
OR SEVERAL ONE BY ONE, THE REGENT POWERS, 5 697
UNDER HIM REGENT, TELLS, AS HE WAS TAUGHT, 5 698
REGENT OF DAY, AND ALL TH' HORIZON ROUND 7 371
SINCE URIEL REGENT OF THE SUN DESCRI'D 9 60

REGIMENT
FROM EVERY BAND AND SQUARED REGIMENT 1 758

REGION
IS THIS THE REGION, THIS THE SOIL, THE CLIME, 1 242
OR UNKNOWN REGION, WHAT REMAINS HIM LESS 2 443
THEY PASS'D, AND MANY A REGION DOLOROUS, 2 619
TO YOUR BEHOOF, IF I THAT REGION LOST, 2 982
DISLODGING FROM A REGION SCARCE OF PREY 3 433
DOWN RIGHT INTO THE WORLDS FIRST REGION THROWS 3 562
FROM SKIRT TO SKIRT A FIERIE REGION, STRETCHT 6 80
PART LOOSLY WING THE REGION, PART MORE WISE 7 425
THIR INWARD STATE OF MIND, CALM REGION ONCE 9 1125

REGIONS
REGIONS OF SORROW, DOLEFUL SHADES, WHERE PEACE 1 65
TH' ETERNAL REGIONS: LOWLY REVERENT 3 349
WHAT WONDER THEN IF FIELDS AND REGIONS HERE 3 606
IMAGIND LANDS AND REGIONS IN THE MOON: 5 263
REGIONS THEY PASS'D, THE MIGHTIE REGENCIES 5 748
IN THIR TRIPLE DEGREES, REGIONS TO WHICH 5 750
OF ALL THIR REGIONS; HOW MUCH MORE OF POWER 6 223
FILLD ALL THE REGIONS: FROM THIR BLISSFUL BOWRS 11 77

REGISTERD
SUCH FOLLOW HIM, AS SHALL BE REGISTERD 12 335

REGRET
NOT THY CONTEMPT, BUT ANGUISH AND REGRET 10 1018

REGULAR
ECCENTRIC, INTERVOLV'D, YET REGULAR 5 623

REIGN
THAT DURST DISLIKE HIS REIGN, AND ME PREFERRING, 1 102

REIGN (CONTINUED)
HERE WE MAY REIGN SECURE, AND IN MY CHOYCE 1 261
TO REIGN IS WORTH AMBITION THOUGH IN HELL: 1 262
BETTER TO REIGN IN HELL, THEN SERVE IN HEAV'N. 1 263
FRIGHTED THE REIGN OF CHAOS AND OLD NIGHT. 1 543
IN HEIGHTH OR DEPTH, STILL FIRST AND LAST WILL REIGN 2 324
THESE ROYALTIES, AND NOT REFUSE TO REIGN, 2 451
WHERE I REIGN KING, AND TO ENRAGE THEE MORE, 2 698
THE GODS WHO LIVE AT EASE, WHERE I SHALL REIGN 2 868
THE CONSORT OF HIS REIGN; AND BY THEM STOOD 2 963
HERE SHALT THOU SIT INCARNATE, HERE SHALT REIGN 3 315
I GIVE THEE, REIGN FOR EVER, AND ASSUME 3 318
UNDER HIS GREAT VICE-GERENT REIGN ABIDE 5 609
ESSENTIAL POWERS, NOR BY HIS REIGN OBSCUR'D, 5 841
REIGN THOU IN HELL THY KINGDOM, LET MEE SERVE 6 183
IF NOT TO REIGN: MEAN WHILE THY UTMOST FORCE, 6 293
WORTHIEST TO REIGN: HE CELEBRATED RODE 6 888
REVOLVD ON HEAV'NS GREAT AXLE, AND HER REIGN 7 381
OUR FOILE IN HEAV'N; HERE THOU SHALT MONARCH REIGN, 10 375
THERE DWELL AND REIGN IN BLISS, THENCE ON THE EARTH 10 399
WITHIN HIMSELF UNWORTHIE POWERS TO REIGN 12 91
WILL REIGN AMONG THEM, AS OF THEE BEGOT; 12 286
THE LAST, FOR OF HIS REIGN SHALL BE NO END. 12 330
THE THRONE HEREDITARIE, AND BOUND HIS REIGN 12 370

REIGN'D
SO JOVE USURPING REIGN'D: THESE FIRST IN CREET 1 514
ALCINOUS REIGN'D, FRUIT OF ALL KINDES, IN COATE, 5 341
LOVE UNLIBIDINOUS REIGN'D, NOR JEALOUSIE 5 449
WHERE LUXURIE LATE REIGN'D, SEA-MONSTERS WHELP'D 11 751

REIGND
REIGND WHERE THESE HEAV'NS NOW ROWL, WHERE EARTH NOW RESTS 5 578

REIGNE
BY THEE, AND MORE THEN HALF PERHAPS WILL REIGNE; 4 112
TO DISPOSSESS HIM, AND THY SELF TO REIGNE? 4 961
AND EQUAL OVER EQUALS TO LET REIGNE, 5 820
THAT EQUAL OVER EQUALS MONARCH REIGNE: 5 832
HOPEFUL AND CHEERFUL, IN THY BLOOD WILL REIGNE 11 543

REIGNES
TUNES SWEETEST HIS LOVE-LABOR'D SONG; NOW REIGNES 5 41

REIGNING
SOLE REIGNING HOLDS THE TYRANNY OF HEAV'N. 1 124

REIGNS
IN COURTS AND PALACES HE ALSO REIGNS 1 497
BY ME, HAVE LOST OUR HOPES. BUT HE WHO REIGNS 1 637
THE PRISON OF HIS TYRANNY WHO REIGNS 2 59
TO HIM WHO REIGNS, AND SO MUCH TO HIM DUE 2 454
SAVE HE WHO REIGNS ABOVE, NONE CAN RESIST. 2 814
BY WHICH HE REIGNS: NEXT HIM HIGH ARBITER 2 909
REIGNS HERE AND REVELS; NOT IN THE BOUGHT SMILE 4 765
NEW LAWS FROM HIM WHO REIGNS, NEW MINDS MAY RAISE 5 680
MESSIAH, WHO BY RIGHT OF MERIT REIGNS. 6 43
HIS WILL WHO REIGNS ABOVE, TO AGGRAVATE 10 549
DOWN FROM A HILL THE BEAST THAT REIGNS IN WOODS, 11 187

REIMBATTELL'D
STOOD REIMBATTELL'D FIERCE, BY FORCE OR FRAUD 6 794

REIN
ROVE WITHOUT REIN, TILL IN THE AMOROUS NET 11 586

REIND
BUT LIKE A PROUD STEED REIND, WENT HAUTIE ON, 4 858

REINES
IN ENTRAILES, HEART OR HEAD, LIVER OR REINES; 6 346
AND TO DISORDER'D RAGE LET LOOSE THE REINES, 6 696
WAS BID TURN REINES FROM TH' EQUINOCTIAL RODE 10 672

REINFORCEMENT
WHAT REINFORCEMENT WE MAY GAIN FROM HOPE, 1 190

REITERATED
THAT WITH REITERATED CRIMES HE MIGHT 1 214

REJECT
WITH MORE DESIRE TO KNOW, AND TO REJECT 4 523
THAT GOLDEN SCEPTER WHICH THOU DIDST REJECT 5 886

REJECTED
WITH SPATTERING NOISE REJECTED: OFT THEY ASSAYD, 10 567
REJECTED MY FOREWARNING, AND DISDAIN'D 10 876

REJOIC'D
OR SINGULAR AND RASH, WHEREAT REJOIC'D 5 851
DISBURD'ND HEAV'N REJOIC'D, AND SOON REPAIRD 6 878

REJOYC'D
DESTIN'D TO THAT GOOD HOUR: NO LESS REJOYC'D 2 848
GREATLY REJOYC'D, AND THUS HIS JOY BROKE FORTH. 11 869

REJOYCE
MAY REAP HIS CONQUEST, AND MAY LEAST REJOYCE 2 339
CANNOT BE HUMAN CONSORT; THEY REJOYCE 8 392
I IN THY PERSEVERING SHALL REJOYCE, 8 639
WITH THESE SUCCESSES, AND WITH THEM REJOYCE, 10 396
OF WICKED SONS DESTROYD, THEN I REJOYCE 11 875
BY MEE DONE AND OCCASIOND, OR REJOYCE 12 475

REJOYCING
ENDED REJOYCING IN THIR MATCHLESS CHIEF: 2 487
YET NOT REJOYCING IN HIS SPEED, THOUGH BOLD, 4 13
CIRCLE HIS THRONE REJOYCING, YEE IN HEAV'N, 5 163
WITH COPIOUS HAND, REJOYCING IN THIR JOY. 5 641
GREAT TRIUMPH AND REJOYCING WAS IN HEAV'N 7 180
PRESENCE DIVINE. REJOYCING, BUT WITH AW 8 314

REJOYC'T
BUT STILL REJOYC'T, HOW IS IT NOW BECOME 10 120

RELAPSE
WHICH WOULD BUT LEAD ME TO A WORSE RELAPSE 4 100

RELATE
ON LEMNOS TH' AEGAEAN ILE: THUS THEY RELATE, 1 746
SAD TASK AND HARD, FOR HOW SHALL I RELATE 5 564
OF ANGELS, CAN RELATE, OR TO WHAT THINGS 6 298
I MIGHT RELATE OF THOUSANDS, AND THIR NAMES 6 373
DEIGN TO DESCEND NOW LOWER, AND RELATE 7 84
RELATE THEE; GREATER NOW IN THY RETURN 7 604
THIS FRIENDLY CONDESCENTION TO RELATE 8 9
ERE MY REMEMBRANCE: NOW HEAR MEE RELATE 8 204
INVITING THEE TO HEAR WHILE I RELATE, 8 208
PRESENCE DIVINE, AND TO MY SONS RELATE; 11 319
HENCEFORTH WHAT IS TO COM I WILL RELATE, 12 11

RELATED
AND BRIEF RELATED WHOM THEY BROUGHT, WHERE FOUND, 4 875
RELATED, AND THUS ADAM ANSWERD SAD. 5 94

RELATER
HER HUSBAND THE RELATER SHE PREFERR'D 8 52

RELATING
ADAM RELATING, THE SOLE AUDITRESS; 8 51
THEE I HAVE HEARD RELATING WHAT WAS DON 8 203

RELATION
THE FULL RELATION, WHICH MUST NEEDS BE STRANGE, 5 556
BUT THY RELATION NOW; FOR I ATTEND, 8 247

RELATIONS
RELATIONS DEAR, AND ALL THE CHARITIES 4 756

RELAX
NOR SERV'D IT TO RELAX THIR SERRIED FILES. 6 599

RELAX'D
RAN THROUGH HIS VEINS, AND ALL HIS JOYNTS RELAX'D; 9 891

RELEAST
FROM PENALTIE, BECAUSE FROM DEATH RELEAST 11 197

RELENT
WE OVERPOWER? SUPPOSE HE SHOULD RELENT 2 237
O THEN AT LAST RELENT: IS THERE NO PLACE 4 79
OR WONDERS MOVE TH' OBDURATE TO RELENT? 6 790
UNDOUBTEDLY HE WILL RELENT AND TURN 10 1093

RELENTED
COMMISERATION; SOON HIS HEART RELENTED 10 940

RELENTLESS
TO MY RELENTLESS THOUGHTS; AND HIM DESTROYD, 9 130

RELENTS
THAT HE RELENTS, NOT TO BLOT OUT MANKIND, 11 891

RELI'D
THAT ARGU'D FEAR; EACH ON HIMSELF RELI'D, 6 238

RELIE
GO IN THY NATIVE INNOCENCE, RELIE 9 373

RELIEF
TENDING TO SOME RELIEF OF OUR EXTREMES, 10 976

RELIES
THE WEIGHT OF ALL AND OUR LAST HOPE RELIES. 2 416

RELIGION
OF JUSTICE, OF RELIGION, TRUTH AND PEACE, 11 667
RELIGION SATISFI'D; TRUTH SHALL RETIRE 12 535

RELIGIONS
WITH GAY RELIGIONS FULL OF POMP AND GOLD, 1 372

RELIGIOUS
RELIGIOUS TITL'D THEM THE SONS OF GOD, 11 622

RELIGIOUS (CONTINUED)
TO CIVIL JUSTICE, PART RELIGIOUS RITES 12 231

RELIQUES
AND FLUTTERD INTO RAGGS, THEN RELIQUES, BEADS, 3 491
WHEN TO ENSHRINE HIS RELIQUES IN THE SUN'S 5 273

RELISH
TRUE RELISH, TASTING; IF SUCH PLEASURE BE 9 1024

RELUCTANCE
UNTAM'D RELUCTANCE, AND REVENGE THOUGH SLOW, 2 337
RELUCTANCE AGAINST GOD AND HIS JUST YOKE 10 1045

RELUCTANT
AND SWEET RELUCTANT AMOROUS DELAY. 4 311
IN DUSKIE WREATHES, RELUCTANT FLAMES, THE SIGNE 6 58
RELUCTANT, BUT IN VAINE, A GREATER POWER 10 515

REMAIN
I FORMD THEM FREE, AND FREE THEY MUST REMAIN, 3 124
OF ANGER SHALL REMAIN, BUT PEACE ASSUR'D, 3 263
IF THESE MAGNIFIC TITLES YET REMAIN 5 773
SHOULD YET REMAIN, WHERE FAITH AND REALTIE 6 115
REMAIN NOT; WHEREFORE SHOULD NOT STRENGTH AND MIGHT 6 116

REMAIN'D
FREQUENT; AND OF THE SIXT DAY YET REMAIN'D; 7 504

REMAIND
AND FIELDS WERE FOUGHT IN HEAV'N; WHEREIN REMAIND 2 768
FROM HIS OWN EVIL, AND FOR THE TIME REMAIND 9 464
BEST GUIDE; NOT FOLLOWING THEE, I HAD REMAIND 9 808
REMAIND STILL HAPPIE, NOT AS NOW, DESPOILD 9 1138

REMAINE
BANDED AGAINST HIS THRONE, BUT TO REMAINE 2 320
CHILDLESS THOU ART, CHILDLESS REMAINE; 10 989

REMAINES
HALF YET REMAINES UNSUNG BUT NARROWER BOUND 7 21
CREATOR; SOMETHING YET OF DOUBT REMAINES, 8 13
REMAINES, SUFFICIENT OF IT SELF TO RAISE 9 43
WHOSE FAILING, WHILE HER FAITH TO ME REMAINES, 10 129

REMAINS
CAN PERISH: FOR THE MIND AND SPIRIT REMAINS 1 139
NEW WARR, PROVOK'T; OUR BETTER PART REMAINS 1 645
OR UNKNOWN REGION, WHAT REMAINS HIM LESS 2 443
REMAINS THEE, AIDED BY THIS HOST OF FRIENDS, 6 38
OF MY PERFORMANCE: WHAT REMAINS, YE GODS, 10 502
AND WHILE THE DREAD OF JUDGEMENT PAST REMAINS 12 14

REMARKABLY
REMARKABLY SO LATE OF THY SO TRUE, 9 982

REMEDIE
THE REMEDIE; PERHAPS MORE VALID ARMES, 6 438
AND WHAT MAY ELSE BE REMEDIE OR CURE 10 1079
HIS FINAL REMEDIE, AND AFTER LIFE 11 62

REMEDILESS
SUBMITTING TO WHAT SEEMD REMEDILESS, 9 919

REMEMBER
THAT DAY I OFT REMEMBER, WHEN FROM SLEEP 4 449
YET FELL; REMEMBER, AND FEAR TO TRANSGRESS. 6 912
REMEMBER WHAT I WARNE THEE, SHUN TO TASTE, 8 327
LAID ON OUR NECKS. REMEMBER WITH WHAT MILD 10 1046

REMEMBER'D
FOR STILL THEY KNEW, AND OUGHT TO HAVE STILL
REMEMBER'D 10 12

REMEMBER'ST
RESOUNDED, (THOU REMEMBER'ST, FOR THOU HEARDST) 7 561

REMEMBERST
WHEN THIS CREATION WAS? REMEMBERST THOU 5 857

REMEMBRANCE
HAD IN REMEMBRANCE ALWAYES WITH DELIGHT; 3 704
THAT BRING TO MY REMEMBRANCE FROM WHAT STATE 4 38
ERE MY REMEMBRANCE: NOW HEAR MEE RELATE 8 204

REMEMBREST
THY EYE-LIDS? AND REMEMBREST WHAT DECREE 5 674

REMEMBRING
REMEMBRING MERCIE, AND HIS COV'NANT SWORN 12 346

REMISS
WHICH ALL SUBDUES, AND MAKES REMISS THE HANDS 6 458
THE ONE INTENSE, THE OTHER STILL REMISS 8 387

REMIT
OUR SUPREAM FOE IN TIME MAY MUCH REMIT 2 210
SO WILLINGLY DOTH GOD REMIT HIS IRE, 11 885

REMOOV'D
CORRUPTING EACH THIR WAY; YET THOSE REMOOV'D, 11 889

REMORSE
SIGNS OF REMORSE AND PASSION TO BEHOLD 1 605
FARWEL REMORSE: ALL GOOD TO ME IS LOST; 4 109
KISS'D AS THE GRACIOUS SIGNS OF SWEET REMORSE 5 134
OF WARRING SPIRITS; HOW WITHOUT REMORSE 5 566
FELT LESS REMORSE: THEY FORTHWITH TO THE PLACE 10 1098
WITHOUT REMORSE DRIVE OUT THE SINFUL PAIR, 11 105

REMOTE
OF THUNDER HEARD REMOTE. TOWARDS HIM THEY BEND 2 477
TH' ARCH-CHIMIC SUN SO FARR FROM US REMOTE 3 609
A WHOLE DAYS JOURNY HIGH, BUT WIDE REMOTE 4 284
OF ERRING, FROM THE PATH OF TRUTH REMOTE: 6 173
SO FARR REMOTE, WITH DIMINUTION SEEN, 7 369
THAT NOT TO KNOW AT LARGE OF THINGS REMOTE 8 191
HIGH AND REMOTE TO SEE FROM THENCE DISTINCT 9 812
OF RAVENOUS FOWL, THOUGH MANY A LEAGUE REMOTE, 10 274

REMOV'D
AS FAR REMOV'D FROM GOD AND LIGHT OF HEAV'N 1 73
HIS ANGER, AND PERHAPS THUS FARR REMOV'D 2 211
IN STRICTEST BONDAGE, THOUGH THUS FAR REMOV'D, 2 321
PERHAPS OUR VACANT ROOM, THOUGH MORE REMOV'D, 2 835
TO HEAV'N REMOV'D WHERE FIRST IT GREW, THERE GROWS, 3 356
OF CHAOS FARR REMOV'D, LEAST FIERCE EXTREAMES 7 272
REMOV'D FARR OFF; THEN PITTYING HOW THEY STOOD 10 211
THE SENTENCE FROM THY HEAD REMOV'D MAY LIGHT 10 934
PREVENIENT GRACE DESCENDING HAD REMOV'D 11 3
MICHAEL FROM ADAMS EYES THE FILME REMOV'D 11 412
CONTENDING, AND REMOV'D HIS TENTS FARR OFF; 11 727

REMOVE
INTO THEIR TEMPER; WHICH MUST NEEDS REMOVE 2 277
BY QUICK CONTRACTION OR REMOVE; BUT NOW 6 597
GOD TO REMOVE HIS WAYES FROM HUMAN SENSE, 8 119
FOR EVER, TO REMOVE HIM I DECREE, 11 96
PERMITS NOT; TO REMOVE THEE I AM COME, 11 260
TO GUIDE THEM IN THIR JOURNEY, AND REMOVE 12 204
LAW CAN DISCOVER SIN, BUT NOT REMOVE, 12 290
IN SIGNAL OF REMOVE, WAVES FIERCELY ROUND; 12 593

REMOVES
YOUR FEARE IT SELF OF DEATH REMOVES THE FEARE. 9 702

REND
REND UP BOTH ROCKS AND HILLS, AND RIDE THE AIR 2 540
AND THRASCIAS REND THE WOODS AND SEAS UPTURN; 10 700
HAILE MIXT WITH FIRE MUST REND TH' EGYPTIAN SKIE 12 182

RENDER
WITH ARMED WATCH, THAT RENDER ALL ACCESS 2 130
THE PRESENT MISERY, AND RENDER HELL 2 459
DOUBL'D, WOULD RENDER THEM YET MORE DESPIS'D, 6 602
EQUAL HAVE I TO RENDER THEE, DIVINE 8 6
AND RENDER ME MORE EQUAL, AND PERHAPS, 9 823
DESIROUS TO RESIGNE, AND RENDER BACK 10 749

RENDERS
AND RENDERS US IN THINGS THAT MOST CONCERNE 8 196

RENDRING
OF RENDRING UP, AND PATIENTLY ATTEND 11 551

RENEW
THE BIRDS THIR NOTES RENEW, AND BLEATING HERDS 2 494
FREELY VOUTSAFT; ONCE MORE I WILL RENEW 3 175

RENEW'D
WITH FRESH ALACRITIE AND FORCE RENEW'D 2 1012
RETURN'D AND GRACIOUS PURPOSE THUS RENEW'D. 8 337
AND THE DIRE HISS RENEW'D, AND THE DIRE FORM 10 543
AND SCARCE RECOVERING WORDS HIS PLAINT RENEW'D. 11 499

RENEWD
HIS DEAREST MEDIATION THUS RENEWD. 3 226
OBSEQUIOUS, HEAV'N HIS WONTED FACE RENEWD, 6 783
THUS HER REPLY WITH ACCENT SWEET RENEWD. 9 321
SPEECH INTERMITTED THUS TO EVE RENEWD. 9 1133
THEN HEAV'N AND EARTH RENEWD SHALL BE MADE PURE 10 638
RESIGNES HIM UP WITH HEAV'N AND EARTH RENEWD. 11 66
MY COV'NANT IN THE WOMANS SEED RENEWD; 11 116
WHICH THUS TO EVE HIS WELCOME WORDS RENEWD. 11 140

RENEWING
STILL ENDING, STILL RENEWING, THROUGH MID HEAV'N; 3 729

RENEWS
THEY VOTE: WHEREAT HIS SPEECH HE THUS RENEWS. 2 389

RENOUNCE
MUST WE RENOUNCE, AND CHANGING STILE BE CALL'D 2 312
IMPUTED SHALL ABSOLVE THEM WHO RENOUNCE 3 291
DISJOYNE US, AND I THEN TOO LATE RENOUNCE 9 884

RENOUND
AS WHEN OF OLD SOM ORATOR RENOUND 9 670

RENOVATION
WAK'T IN THE RENOVATION OF THE JUST, 11 65

RENOWN
A CREW WHO UNDER NAMES OF OLD RENOWN, 1 477
SO WERE I EQUAL'D WITH THEM IN RENOWN, 3 34
NOR OF RENOWN LESS EAGER, YET BY DOOME 6 378
SUCH WERE THESE GIANTS, MEN OF HIGH RENOWN; 11 688
THUS FAME SHALL BE ATCHIEV'D, RENOWN ON EARTH, 11 698
LIKE HIM IN FAITH, IN WISDOM, AND RENOWN; 12 154

RENOWN'D
THE REST WERE LONG TO TELL, THOUGH FAR RENOWN'D, 1 507
FIRST-SEEN, OR SOME RENOWN'D METROPOLIS 3 549
THE FIGTREE, NOT THAT KIND FOR FRUIT RENOWN'D, 9 1101

RENOWND
WITH MANY A VAIN EXPLOIT, THOUGH THEN RENOWND: 3 465
OR OF REVIV'D ADONIS, OR RENOWND 9 440
THE SECOND, BOTH FOR PIETIE RENOWND 12 321

RENOWNE
HONOUR, DOMINION, GLORIE, AND RENOWNE, 6 422

REPAID
FROM DUST: SPITE THEN WITH SPITE IS BEST REPAID. 9 178
AS WANTONLY REPAID; IN LUST THEY BURNE: 9 1015
OR AS THE SNAKE WITH YOUTHFUL COATE REPAID; 10 218

REPAIR
OUR ENEMY, OUR OWN LOSS HOW REPAIR, 1 188
TO DEEPEST HELL, AND TO REPAIR THAT LOSS 3 678
DAZL'D AND SPENT, SUNK DOWN, AND SOUGHT REPAIR 8 457

REPAIR'D
SHOWRD ROSES, WHICH THE MORN REPAIR'D. SLEEP ON 4 773

REPAIRD
DISBURD'ND HEAV'N REJOIC'D, AND SOON REPAIRD 6 878

REPAIRE
MY DAMAGE FONDLY DEEM'D, I CAN REPAIRE 7 152
AND TO REPAIRE HIS NUMBERS THUS IMPAIR'D, 9 144

REPAIRING
REPAIRING, IN THIR GOLD'N URNS DRAW LIGHT, 7 365
REPAIRING WHERE HE JUDG'D US, PROSTRATE FALL 10 1087
REPAIRING WHERE HE JUDG'D THEM PROSTRATE FELL 10 1099

REPAST
MY BOWELS, THIR REPAST; THEN BURSTING FORTH 2 800
TO RESPIT HIS DAY-LABOUR WITH REPAST, 5 232
FORTHWITH FROM DANCE TO SWEET REPAST THEY TURN 5 630
OF SWEET REPAST; THEY SATIATE, AND SOON FILL, 8 214
RURAL REPAST, PERMITTING HIM THE WHILE 9 4
NOONTIDE REPAST, OR AFTERNOONS REPOSE. 9 403
FOUNDST EITHER SWEET REPAST, OR SOUND REPOSE; 9 407

REPEAL'D
WITH BLESSEDNESS. WHENCE ADAM SOON REPEAL'D 7 59

REPEATE
THAT MIGHT DETERMINE, AND NOT NEED REPEATE, 6 318
CREATION COULD REPEATE, YET WOULD BE LOATH 9 946

REPEATED
REPEATED, AND INDECENT OVERTHROW 6 601
NEEDLEST TO THEE REPEATED; NOR UNKNOWN 7 494
REPEATED, WHILE THE SEDENTARIE EARTH, 8 32
REPEATED, SHEE TO HIM AS OFT ENGAG'D 9 400

REPEL
AND ALL TEMPTATION TO TRANSGRESS REPEL. 8 643

REPELD
THOU HAST REPELD, WHILE IMPIOUSLY THEY THOUGHT 7 611

REPELL
CAN EITHER NOT RECEAVE, OR CAN REPELL. 9 284

REPELL'D
BUT HER WITH STERN REGARD HE THUS REPELL'D. 10 866

REPENT
CAN ELSE INFLICT, DO I REPENT OR CHANGE, 1 96
TO PRAY, REPENT, AND BRING OBEDIENCE DUE. 3 190
BUT SAY I COULD REPENT AND COULD OBTAINE 4 93
GIV'N THEE OF GRACE, WHEREIN THOU MAY'ST REPENT, 11 255
WHETHER I SHOULD REPENT ME NOW OF SIN 12 474

REPENTANCE
TO PRAYER, REPENTANCE, AND OBEDIENCE DUE, 3 191
LEFT FOR REPENTANCE, NONE FOR PARDON LEFT? 4 80
CONVERSION AND REPENTANCE, AS TO SOULS 11 724

REPENTANT
THUS THEY IN LOWLIEST PLIGHT REPENTANT STOOD 11

REPENTING
MAY PROVE THIR FOE, AND WITH REPENTING HAND 2 36
BEFORE THEE; AND NOT REPENTING, THIS OBTAINE 10 7
THOUGH LATE REPENTING HIM OF MAN DEPRAV'D, 11 88

REPENTS
HE SORROWS NOW, REPENTS, AND PRAYES CONTRITE, 11 9

REPINE
SPARE OUT OF LIFE PERHAPS, AND NOT REPINE, 6 46

REPLENISHT
WITH FISH REPLENISHT, AND THE AIRE WITH FOWLE, 7 44
REPLENISHT, AND ALL THESE AT THY COMMAND 8 37

REPLETE
HE ENDED, AND HIS WORDS REPLETE WITH GUILE 9 73
REPLETE WITH JOY AND WONDER THUS REPLI'D. 12 46

REPLI'D
TO WHOM THUS EVE REPLI'D. O THOU FOR WHOM 4 44
TO WHOM OUR GENERAL ANCESTOR REPLI'D. 4 65
THE FIEND REPLI'D NOT, OVERCOME WITH RAGE; 4 85
DISDAINFULLY HALF SMILING THUS REPLI'D. 4 90
TO WHOM THE WARRIOUR ANGEL, SOON REPLI'D. 4 94
GAVE HEED, BUT WAXING MORE IN RAGE REPLI'D. 4 96
TO WHOM THE WINGED HIERARCH REPLI'D. 5 46
TO WHOM THE PATRIARCH OF MANKIND REPLI'D, 5 50
TH' APOSTAT, AND MORE HAUGHTY THUS REPLI'D. 5 85
TO WHOM IN BRIEF THUS ABDIEL STERN REPLI'D. 6 17
WHERETO WITH LOOK COMPOS'D SATAN REPLI'D. 6 46
THEN AS NEW WAK'T THUS GRATEFULLY REPLI'D. 8
BENEVOLENT AND FACIL THUS REPLI'D. 8 6
TO WHOM THUS ADAM CLEERD OF DOUBT, REPLI'D. 8 17
AS WITH A SMILE MORE BRIGHT'ND, THUS REPLI'D. 8 36
AND HUMBLE DEPRECATION THUS REPLI'D. 8 37
TO WHOM THUS HALF ABASH'T ADAM REPLI'D. 8 59
TO WHOM THUS ADAM FERVENTLY REPLI'D. 9 34
PERSISTED, YET SUBMISS, THOUGH LAST, REPLI'D. 9 37
TO WHOM THE TEMPTER GUILEFULLY REPLI'D. 9 65
SO ADAM, AND THUS EVE TO HIM REPLI'D. 9 96
TO WHOM THEN FIRST INCENST ADAM REPLI'D, 9 116
THE GRACIOUS JUDGE WITHOUT REVILE REPLI'D. 10 11
TO WHOM THUS ADAM SORE BESET REPLI'D. 10 12
TO WHOM THE SOVRAN PRESENCE THUS REPLI'D. 10 14
BOLD OR LOQUACIOUS, THUS ABASHT REPLI'D. 10 16
TO WHOM TH' INCESTUOUS MOTHER THUS REPLI'D. 10 60
TO WHOM THUS EVE, RECOVERING HEART, REPLI'D. 10 96
LABOURING HAD RAIS'D, AND THUS TO EVE REPLI'D. 10 101
TO WHOM THUS ADAM GRATEFULLY REPLI'D. 11 37
T' WHOM MICHAEL THUS, HEE ALSO MOV'D, REPLI'D. 11 45
MY DISSOLUTION. MICHAEL REPLI'D, 11 55
REPLETE WITH JOY AND WONDER THUS REPLI'D. 12 46
TO WHOM THUS ALSO TH' ANGEL LAST REPLI'D: 12 57

REPLY
THE MONARCH, AND PREVENTED ALL REPLY, 2 46
HE CEAS'D; AND SATAN STAID NOT TO REPLY, 2 101
FOND, WERE IT NOT IN HOPE OF THY REPLY: 8 20
THUS HER REPLY WITH ACCENT SWEET RENEWD. 9 32

REPLY'D
WHERETO WITH SPEEDY WORDS TH' ARCH-FIEND REPLY'D. 1 15
TO WHOM THE GOBLIN FULL OF WRAUTH REPLY'D, 2 68
T' WHOM THUS THE PORTRESS OF HELL GATE REPLY'D; 2 74
TO WHOM THE GREAT CREATOUR THUS REPLY'D. 3 16
WONDRING; BUT SOON TH' ALMIGHTY THUS REPLY'D: 3 27
WITH SWEET AUSTEER COMPOSURE THUS REPLY'D, 9 27
TO WHOM THE GUILEFUL TEMPTER THUS REPLY'D. 9 56
YET MORE AMAZ'D UNWARIE THUS REPLY'D. 9 61
HE ENDED; AND THUS ADAM LAST REPLY'D. 12 55

REPLYD
TO WHOM WITH HEALING WORDS ADAM REPLYD. 9 29

REPORT
CONTENTED WITH REPORT HEAR ONELY IN HEAV'N: 3 70
BESEECHING OR BESIEGING. THIS REPORT, 5 86
THAT MOSES MIGHT REPORT TO THEM HIS WILL, 12 23

REPORTED
TO HAVE REPORTED: GLADLY THEN HE MIXT 6 2

REPOS'D
I FIRST AWAK'T, AND FOUND MY SELF REPOS'D 4 45
ON FLOURS REPOS'D, AND WITH FRESH FLOURETS CROWND, 5 63

REPOSE
AFTER THE TOYL OF BATTEL TO REPOSE 1 31
MIND US OF LIKE REPOSE, SINCE GOD HATH SET 4 61
O SOLE IN WHOM MY THOUGHTS FIND ALL REPOSE, 5 2
OR WITH REPOSE; AND SUCH DISCOURSE BRING ON, 5 23
NOONTIDE REPAST, OR AFTERNOONS REPOSE. 9 40
FOUNDST EITHER SWEET REPAST, OR SOUND REPOSE; 9 40

RESOUND
- ENCOMPASS'D SHALL RESOUND THEE EVER BLEST. 3 149
- IN MYSTIC DANCE NOT WITHOUT SONG, RESOUND 5 178
- TO ANSWER, AND RESOUND FARR OTHER SONG. 10 862
- WITH FEAST AND MUSICK ALL THE TENTS RESOUND. 11 592

RESOUNDED
- OF HELL RESOUNDED. PRINCES, POTENTATES, 1 315
- FROM ALL HER CAVES, AND BACK RESOUNDED DEATH. 2 789
- RESOUNDED, AND HAD EARTH BIN THEN, ALL EARTH 6 218
- RESOUNDED, (THOU REMEMBER'ST, FOR THOU HEARDST) 7 561

RESOUNDS
- MIXT WITH AUXILIAR GODS; AND WHAT RESOUNDS 1 579
- THE RIGID INTERDICTION, WHICH RESOUNDS 8 334

RESPIRATION
- APPEER OF RESPIRATION TO THE JUST, 12 540

RESPIT
- TO RESPIT HIS DAY-LABOUR WITH REPAST, 5 232
- QUIET THOUGH SAD, THE RESPIT OF THAT DAY 11 272

RESPITE
- TO RESPITE OR DECEIVE, OR SLACK THE PAIN 2 461

RESPLENDENCE
- IN FULL RESPLENDENCE, HEIR OF ALL MY MIGHT, 5 720

RESPLENDENT
- BIND THIR RESPLENDENT LOCKS INWREATH'D WITH BEAMS, 3 361
- WHICH THEY BEHELD, THE MOONS RESPLENDENT GLOBE 4 723
- EMPRESS OF THIS FAIR WORLD, RESPLENDENT EVE, 9 568
- RESPLENDENT ALL HIS FATHER MANIFEST 10 66

RESPONSIVE
- SOLE, OR RESPONSIVE EACH TO OTHERS NOTE 4 683

REST
- AND REST CAN NEVER DWELL, HOPE NEVER COMES 1 66
- THERE REST, IF ANY REST CAN HARBOUR THERE, 1 185
- THE REST WERE LONG TO TELL, THOUGH FAR RENOWN'D, 1 507
- THIR DREAD COMMANDER: HE ABOVE THE REST 1 589
- BELCH'D FIRE AND ROWLING SMOAK; THE REST ENTIRE 1 671
- FOR WHILE THEY SIT CONTRIVING, SHALL THE REST 2 54
- OF HAZARD MORE, AS HE ABOVE THE REST 2 455
- NO REST: THROUGH MANY A DARK AND DREARIE VAILE 2 618
- THAT REST OR INTERMISSION NONE I FIND. 2 802
- ELECT ABOVE THE REST; SO IS MY WILL: 3 184
- THE REST SHALL HEAR ME CALL, AND OFT BE WARND 3 185
- THE REST IN CIRCUIT WALLES THIS UNIVERSE. 3 721
- THE REST WAS CRAGGIE CLIFF, THAT OVERHUNG 4 547
- OF NIGHT, AND ALL THINGS NOW RETIR'D TO REST 4 611
- LABOUR AND REST, AS DAY AND NIGHT TO MEN 4 613
- ROVE IDLE UNIMPLOID, AND LESS NEED REST; 4 617
- MEAN WHILE, AS NATURE WILLS, NIGHT BIDS US REST. 4 633
- THE REST IS TRUE, THEY FOUND ME WHERE THEY SAY; 4 900
- AS THROUGH UNQUIET REST: HE ON HIS SIDE 5 11
- TO REST, AND WHAT THE GARDEN CHOICEST BEARS 5 368
- ALL BUT THE UNSLEEPING EYES OF GOD TO REST, 5 647
- DESTRUCTION TO THE REST: THIS PAUSE BETWEEN 6 162
- TO TROUBLE HOLY REST; HEAV'N CASTS THEE OUT 6 272
- FAR IN THE DARK DISLODG'D, AND VOID OF REST, 6 415
- THE REST IN IMITATION TO LIKE ARMES 6 662
- YE ANGELS ARM'D, THIS DAY FROM BATTEL REST; 6 802
- MOV'D THE CREATOR IN HIS HOLY REST 7 91
- LIKE THINGS TO LIKE, THE REST TO SEVERAL PLACE 7 240
- WITH HONEY STOR'D: THE REST ARE NUMBERLESS, 7 492
- GOVERN THE REST, SELF-KNOWING, AND FROM THENCE 7 510
- IMPORTS NOT, IF THOU RECK'N RIGHT, THE REST 8 71
- LODG'D IN A SMALL PARTITION, AND THE REST 8 105
- TO ME SO FRIENDLY GROWN ABOVE THE REST 9 564
- THE CREDIT OF WHOSE VERTUE REST WITH THEE, 9 649
- SOLE DAUGHTER OF HIS VOICE; THE REST, WE LIVE 9 653
- COVERD, BUT NOT AT REST OR EASE OF MIND, 9 1120
- MAYST EVER REST WELL PLEAS'D. I GO TO JUDGE 10 71
- AS DELOS FLOATING ONCE; THE REST HIS LOOK 10 296
- FLOWN TO THE UPPER WORLD; THE REST WERE ALL 10 422
- ABOVE THE REST STILL TO RETAIN; THEY ALL 10 532
- AS IN MY MOTHERS LAP? THERE I SHOULD REST 10 778
- BROKE OFF THE REST; SO MUCH OF DEATH HER THOUGHTS 10 1008
- IN DUST, OUR FINAL REST AND NATIVE HOME. 10 1085
- BY SUFFERING, AND EARNE REST FROM LABOUR WON, 11 375
- AWAITS THE GOOD, THE REST WHAT PUNISHMENT? 11 710
- FROM ALL THE REST, OF WHOM TO BE INVOK'D, 12 112
- SHALL REST BY DAY, A FIERY GLEAME BY NIGHT, 12 257
- PROMISD TO ABRAHAM AND HIS SEED: THE REST 12 260
- SAFE TO ETERNAL PARADISE OF REST. 12 314
- SO ONELY CAN HIGH JUSTICE REST APPAID. 12 401
- OF SPIRIT AND TRUTH; THE REST, FARR GREATER PART, 12 533
- OF ALL THE REST: THEN WILT THOU NOT BE LOATH 12 585
- THIR PLACE OF REST, AND PROVIDENCE THIR GUIDE: 12 647

RESTED
- HAD WORK AND RESTED NOT, THE SOLEMN PIPE, 7 595

RESTING
- WITH STENCH AND SMOAK: SUCH RESTING FOUND THE SOLE 1 237

RESTING (CONTINUED)
- NOW RESTING, BLESS'D AND HALLOWD THE SEAV'NTH DAY, 7 592
- AS RESTING ON THAT DAY FROM ALL HIS WORK, 7 593

RESTLESS
- TRUCE TO HIS RESTLESS THOUGHTS, AND ENTERTAIN 2 526
- SUCH RESTLESS REVOLUTION DAY BY DAY 8 31

RESTOR'D
- AS FROM A SECOND ROOT SHALL BE RESTOR'D, 3 288
- AS MANY AS ARE RESTOR'D, WITHOUT THEE NONE. 3 289
- RESTOR'D BY THEE, VILE AS I AM, TO PLACE 10 971
- BETWIXT THE WORLD DESTROY'D AND WORLD RESTOR'D, 12 3

RESTORE
- RESTORE US, AND REGAIN THE BLISSFUL SEAT, 1 5
- DEUCALION AND CHASTE PYRRHA TO RESTORE 11 12
- BY MEE THE PROMIS'D SEED SHALL ALL RESTORE. 12 623

RESTORER
- DESTIN'D RESTORER OF MANKIND, BY WHOM 10 646

RESTRAIN'D
- DESIRING; NOR RESTRAIN'D CONVEYANCE NEED 8 628

RESTRAIND
- OR NOT RESTRAIND AS WEE, OR NOT OBEYING, 9 868
- A SPACE, TILL FIRMER THOUGHTS RESTRAIND EXCESS, 11 498

RESTRAINT
- FOR ONE RESTRAINT, LORDS OF THE WORLD BESIDES? 1 32
- THROUGH ALL RESTRAINT BROKE LOOSE HE WINGS HIS WAY 3 87
- LUXURIOUS BY RESTRAINT; WHAT WE BY DAY 9 209
- GREEDILY SHE INGORG'D WITHOUT RESTRAINT, 9 791
- IT SEEMS, IN THY RESTRAINT: WHAT COULD I MORE? 9 1170
- LETS HER WILL RULE; RESTRAINT SHE WILL NOT BROOK, 9 1184

RESTS
- TRANSFUS'D ON THEE HIS AMPLE SPIRIT RESTS. 3 389
- INTO HER PRIVATE CELL WHEN NATURE RESTS. 5 109
- REIGND WHERE THESE HEAV'NS NOW ROWL, WHERE EARTH NOW RESTS 5 578
- WHAT RESTS BUT THAT THE MORTAL SENTENCE PASS 10 48

RESULT
- WITH TRUMPETS REGAL SOUND THE GREAT RESULT: 2 515
- WE SHOULD COMPEL THEM TO A QUICK RESULT. 6 619

RESUM'D
- TILL THIR LOST SHAPE, PERMITTED, THEY RESUM'D, 10 574

RESUME
- THIR SUREST SIGNAL, THEY WILL SOON RESUME 1 278
- THEN ENTER INTO GLORY, AND RESUME 12 456

RESUMES
- THEN WITH TRANSITION SWEET NEW SPEECH RESUMES. 12 5

RESURRECTION
- NOR AFTER RESURRECTION SHALL HE STAY 12 436

RETAIN
- TH' ASSEMBLY, AS WHEN HOLLOW ROCKS RETAIN 2 285
- IF YE BE FOUND OBEDIENT, AND RETAIN 5 501
- ABOVE THE REST STILL TO RETAIN; THEY ALL 10 532

RETAIN'D
- WANTED NOT LONG, THOUGH TO THIS SHAPE RETAIN'D. 9 601

RETAINE
- AND DRINK THE LIQUID LIGHT, FIRM TO RETAINE 7 362

RETAINES
- THIR STATION, HEAV'N YET POPULOUS RETAINES 7 146

RETAINING
- RETAINING STILL DIVINE SIMILITUDE 11 512

RETINUE
- ON PRINCES, WHEN THIR RICH RETINUE LONG 5 355

RETIR'D
- OTHERS APART SAT ON A HILL RETIR'D, 2 557
- OR IN THICK SHADE RETIR'D, FROM HIM TO DRAW 4 532
- OF NIGHT, AND ALL THINGS NOW RETIR'D TO REST 4 611
- THOU FIND'ST HIM FROM THE HEAT OF NOON RETIR'D, 5 231
- IN HORROR; FROM EACH HAND WITH SPEED RETIR'D 6 307
- BACK TO HIS CHARIOT; WHERE IT STOOD RETIR'D 6 338
- UNDER HER CLOUDIE COVERT BOTH RETIR'D, 6 409
- DIVIDED, AND TO EITHER FLANK RETIR'D. 6 570
- AT HIS COMMAND THE UPROOTED HILLS RETIR'D 6 781
- PERCEAVING WHERE SHE SAT RETIR'D IN SIGHT, 8 41
- NOT OBVIOUS, NOT OBTRUSIVE, BUT RETIR'D, 8 504
- THY AWFUL BROW, MORE AWFUL THUS RETIR'D. 9 537
- FARR TO THE INLAND RETIR'D, ABOUT THE WALLS 10 423

RETIRE
- RETIRE, OR TASTE THY FOLLY, AND LEARN BY PROOF, 2 686

RETIRE (CONTINUED)
HER FARDEST VERGE, AND CHAOS TO RETIRE 2 1038
THOUGH I UNCIRCUMSCRIB'D MY SELF RETIRE, 7 170
AND GIV'ST ACCESS, THOUGH SECRET SHE RETIRE. 9 810
WITH REVERENCE I MUST MEET, AND THOU RETIRE. 11 237
DISCOVER'D SOON THE PLACE OF HER RETIRE. 11 267
RELIGION SATISFI'D; TRUTH SHALL RETIRE 12 535

RETIREMENT
AND SHORT RETIREMENT URGES SWEET RETURNE. 9 250

RETIRES
OUR KNOWLEDGE OR OPINION; THEN RETIRES 5 108
RETIRES, OR BACTRIAN SOPHI FROM THE HORNES 10 433

RETIRING
RETIRING, BY HIS OWN DOOM ALIENATED, 10 378

RETORT
PROVE DISOBEDIENT, AND REPROV'D, RETORT, 10 761

RETORTED
AND WITH RETORTED SCORN HIS BACK HE TURN'D 5 906

RETREAT
WITH DREAD OF DEATH TO FLIGHT OR FOUL RETREAT, 1 555
THIS PLACE OUR DUNGEON, NOT OUR SAFE RETREAT 2 317
NONE OF RETREAT, NO UNBECOMING DEED 6 237
OR FAINT RETREAT; WHEN THE GREAT SON OF GOD 6 799

RETREATE
THE REALM OF ALADULE, IN HIS RETREATE 10 435

RETREATED
RETREATED IN A SILENT VALLEY, SING 2 547

RETREATING
TOWARDS THE RETREATING SEA THIR FURIOUS TYDE. 11 854

RETRIBUTION
FIT RETRIBUTION, EMPTIE AS THIR DEEDS; 3 454

RETROGRADE
PROGRESSIVE, RETROGRADE, OR STANDING STILL, 8 127

RETURN
MORE THEN CAN BE IN HEAV'N, WE NOW RETURN 2 37
INFLICTED? AND WHAT PEACE CAN WE RETURN, 2 335
THE IRKSOM HOURS, TILL THIS GREAT CHIEF RETURN. 2 527
THAT BRED THEM THEY RETURN, AND HOWLE AND GNAW 2 799
TO KNOW, AND THIS ONCE KNOWN, SHALL SOON RETURN, 2 839
SEASONS RETURN, BUT NOT TO ME RETURNS 3 41
OR PROUD RETURN THOUGH TO HIS HEAVIER DOOM, 3 159
AH WHEREFORE. HE DESERVD NO SUCH RETURN 4 42
THOU FOLLOWING CRYD'ST ALOUD, RETURN FAIRE EVE; 4 481
YET HAPPIE PAIR; ENJOY, TILL I RETURN, 4 534
ALL THINGS PROCEED, AND UP TO HIM RETURN, 5 470
BACK ON THY FOES MORE GLORIOUS TO RETURN 6 39
OF THUNDER: BACK DEFEATED TO RETURN 6 606
RETURN ME TO MY NATIVE ELEMENT: 7 16
RELATE THEE; GREATER NOW IN THY RETURN 7 604
THIR DISTANCE ARGUES AND THIR SWIFT RETURN 8 21
BE GOOD AND FRIENDLY STILL, AND OFT RETURN. 8 651
OF THY PRESUM'D RETURN. EVENT PERVERSE. 9 405
WAITING DESIROUS HER RETURN, HAD WOVE 9 839
SOLACE IN HER RETURN, SO LONG DELAY'D; 9 844
JUSTICE SHALL NOT RETURN AS BOUNTIE SCORN'D. 10 54
TILL THOU RETURN UNTO THE GROUND, FOR THOU 10 206
STAY HIS RETURN PERHAPS OVER THIS GULFE 10 253
AND TO THE PLACE OF JUDGMENT WILL RETURN, 10 932
AND THITHER MUST RETURN AND BE NO MORE. 11 200
I MUST RETURN TO NATIVE DUST? O SIGHT 11 463
TILL MANY YEARS OVER THY HEAD RETURN: 11 534
HIS PEOPLE FROM ENTHRALMENT, THEY RETURN 12 171
ON THIR IMBATTELLD RANKS THE WAVES RETURN, 12 213
RETURN THEM BACK TO EGYPT, CHOOSING RATHER 12 219
AND VENGEANCE TO THE WICKED, AT RETURN 12 541

RETURN'D
WITH DEAFNING SHOUT, RETURN'D THEM LOUD ACCLAIM. 2 520
FORBORE, THEN THESE TO HER SATAN RETURN'D: 2 736
THY FACE, AND MORN RETURN'D, FOR I THIS NIGHT, 5 30
GLAD WE RETURN'D UP TO THE COASTS OF LIGHT 8 245
THIS HAPPIE LIGHT, WHEN ANSWER NONE RETURN'D, 8 285
RETURN'D AND GRACIOUS PURPOSE THUS RENEW'D. 8 337
OF HEAVIER ON HIMSELF, FEARLESS RETURN'D. 9 57
BY NIGHT HE FLED, AND AT MIDNIGHT RETURN'D 9 58
ON THE EIGHTH RETURN'D, AND ON THE COAST AVERSE 9 67
TO WHOM MILD ANSWER ADAM THUS RETURN'D. 9 226
ASSEMBL'D ANGELS, AND YE POWERS RETURN'D 10 34
ERE THIS HE HAD RETURN'D, WITH FURY DRIV'N 10 240
MIGHT SUDDENLY INFLICT; THAT PAST, RETURN'D 10 341
AND TIDINGS FRAUGHT, TO HELL HE NOW RETURN'D, 10 346

RETURND
IN HIS UPRIGHTNESS ANSWER THUS RETURND. 3 693
IT STARTED BACK, BUT PLEAS'D I SOON RETURND, 4 463
PLEAS'D IT RETURND AS SOON WITH ANSWERING LOOKS 4 464

RETURND (CONTINUED)
TO WHOM THE WINGED WARRIOUR THUS RETURND: 4 576
RETURND ON THAT BRIGHT BEAM, WHOSE POINT NOW RAISD 4 590
RETURND NOT LOST: ON TO THE SACRED HILL 6 25
FROM MEE RETURND, AS ERST THOU SAIDST, FROM FLIGHT, 6 187
INTO HIS PLACE, AND THE GREAT SON RETURND 7 135
DESISTING, THOUGH UNWEARIED, UP RETURND 7 552
THE GREAT CREATOR FROM HIS WORK RETURND 7 567
JUST THEN RETURND AT SHUT OF EVENING FLOURS. 9 278
TO BE RETURND BY NOON AMID THE BOWRE, 9 401
TO HIM WITH SWIFT ASCENT HE UP RETURND, 10 224
THIR MIGHTY CHIEF RETURND: LOUD WAS TH' ACCLAIME: 10 455
I CALL YE AND DECLARE YE NOW, RETURND 10 462
BUT HISS FOR HISS RETURND WITH FORKED TONGUE 10 518
THAT I WAS HEARD WITH FAVOUR; PEACE RETURND 11 153
RECOVERING, AND HIS SCATTERD SPIRITS RETURND, 11 294
RETURND FROM BABYLON BY LEAVE OF KINGS 12 348

RETURNE
SHALL ENTER HEAVEN LONG ABSENT, AND RETURNE, 3 261
AND SHORT RETIREMENT URGES SWEET RETURNE. 9 250
OFT HE TO HER HIS CHARGE OF QUICK RETURNE 9 399
FOR DUST THOU ART, AND SHALT TO DUST RETURNE. 10 208
THAT DUST I AM, AND SHALL TO DUST RETURNE: 10 770
ON THIR IMPENITENCE; AND SHALL RETURNE 11 816
RETURNE, THE STARRES OF MORN SHALL SEE HIM RISE 12 422

RETURNES
DOWN TO THIS HABITABLE, WHICH RETURNES 8 157

RETURNING
HER MURAL BREACH, RETURNING WHENCE IT ROWLD. 6 879
SCARSE FROM THE TREE RETURNING; IN HER HAND 9 850
THE SECOND TIME RETURNING, IN HIS BILL 11 859
HOMEWARD RETURNING. HIGH IN FRONT ADVANC'T, 12 632

RETURNS
INVINCIBLE, AND VIGOUR SOON RETURNS, 1 140
SEASONS RETURN, BUT NOT TO ME RETURNS 3 41
TOUCH OF CELESTIAL TEMPER, BUT RETURNS 4 812
AND NOW RETURNS HIM FROM HIS PRISON SCAP'T, 4 906
HE LIGHTS, AND TO HIS PROPER SHAPE RETURNS 5 276
RETURNS OUR OWN. CEASE THEN THIS IMPIOUS RAGE, 5 845

RETURNST
OF MY REVENGE, FIRST SOUGHT FOR THOU RETURNST 6 151
WHENCE THOU RETURNST, AND WHITHER WENTST, I KNOW; 12 610

REVEAL
NOT LAWFUL TO REVEAL? YET FOR THY GOOD 5 570

REVEAL'D
BY WHAT IS PAST, TO THEE I HAVE REVEAL'D 6 895
FARR DIFFERING FROM THIS WORLD, THOU HAST REVEAL'D 7 71
THINGS NOT REVEAL'D, WHICH TH' INVISIBLE KING, 7 122
CONTENTED THAT THUS FARR HATH BEEN REVEAL'D 8 177

REVEALD
PLAINLIER SHALL BE REVEALD. THIS PATRIARCH BLEST, 12 151
THOU HAST REVEALD, THOSE CHIEFLY WHICH CONCERNE 12 272
LAST IN THE CLOUDS FROM HEAV'N TO BE REVEALD 12 545

REVEALE
DISMISS THEM NOT DISCONSOLATE; REVEALE 11 113

REVELLERS
OF BACCHUS AND HIS REVELLERS, THE RACE 7 33

REVELS
WHOSE MIDNIGHT REVELS, BY A FORREST SIDE 1 782
REIGNS HERE AND REVELS; NOT IN THE BOUGHT SMILE 4 765

REVENG
ON DESPARATE REVENG, THAT SHALL REDOUND 3 85

REVENG'D
CAME FURIOUS DOWN TO BE REVENG'D ON MEN, 4 4

REVENGE
STIRD UP WITH ENVY AND REVENGE, DECEIV'D 1 35
AND STUDY OF REVENGE, IMMORTAL HATE, 1 107
WAITING REVENGE: CRUEL HIS EYE, BUT CAST 1 604
WHICH IF NOT VICTORY IS YET REVENGE. 2 105
DESPERATE REVENGE, AND BATTEL DANGEROUS 2 107
OF ALL HIS AIM, AFTER SOME DIRE REVENGE. 2 128
FIRST, WHAT REVENGE? THE TOWRS OF HEAV'N ARE FILL'D 2 129
UNTAM'D RELUCTANCE, AND REVENGE THOUGH SLOW, 2 337
COMMON REVENGE, AND INTERRUPT HIS JOY 2 371
YOURS BE TH' ADVANTAGE ALL, MINE THE REVENGE. 2 987
THITHER FULL FRAUGHT WITH MISCHIEVOUS REVENGE, 2 1054
YET WITH REVENGE ACCOMPLISH'T AND TO HELL 3 160
DEEP MALICE TO CONCEALE, COUCH'T WITH REVENGE: 4 123
THANK HIM WHO PUTS ME LOATH TO THIS REVENGE 4 386
HONOUR AND EMPIRE WITH REVENGE ENLARG'D, 4 390
OF MY REVENGE, FIRST SOUGHT FOR THOU RETURNST 6 151
WHICH WOULD BE ALL HIS SOLACE AND REVENGE, 6 905
BUT WHAT WILL NOT AMBITION AND REVENGE 9 168

REVENGE (CONTINUED)
TO BASEST THINGS. REVENGE, AT FIRST THOUGH SWEET, 9 171
OF GUILE, OF HATE, OF ENVIE, OF REVENGE; 9 466
CAN FIT HIS PUNISHMENT, OR THEIR REVENGE. 10 242
WOULD BE REVENGE INDEED; WHICH WILL BE LOST 10 1036

REVERENCE
WITH AWFUL REVERENCE PRONE; AND AS A GOD 2 478
WHERE HONOUR DUE AND REVERENCE NONE NEGLECTS, 3 738
YET WITH SUBMISS APPROACH AND REVERENCE MEEK, 5 359
AND WITH MYSTERIOUS REVERENCE I DEEM) 8 599
BUT FIRST LOW REVERENCE DON, AS TO THE POWER 9 835
WHAT LOVE SINCERE, AND REVERENCE IN MY HEART 10 915
WITH REVERENCE I MUST MEET, AND THOU RETIRE. 11 237
AND REVERENCE THEE THIR GREAT PROGENITOR. 11 346
GODS IMAGE DID NOT REVERENCE IN THEMSELVES. 11 525

REVEREND
AT LENGTH A REVEREND SIRE AMONG THEM CAME, 11 719

REVERENT
TH' ETERNAL REGIONS: LOWLY REVERENT 3 349
BEFORE HIM REVERENT, AND THERE CONFESS 10 1088
BEFORE HIM REVERENT, AND BOTH CONFESS'D 10 1100

REVERSE
BUT WITH SWIFT WHEELE REVERSE, DEEP ENTRING SHAR'D 6 326
TO MITIGATE THUS PLEAD, NOT TO REVERSE) 11 41

REVILE
THE GRACIOUS JUDGE WITHOUT REVILE REPLI'D. 10 118

REVILING
WITHOUT WRAUTH OR REVILING; WEE EXPECTED 10 1048

RE-VISIT
THEE I RE-VISIT NOW WITH BOLDER WING, 3 13

REVISIT
THOUGH HARD AND RARE: THEE I REVISIT SAFE, 3 21

REVISIT'ST
REVISIT'ST NOT THESE EYES, THAT ROWLE IN VAIN 3 23

REVIV'D
ENLIGHTN'D, AND THIR LANGUISHT HOPE REVIV'D. 6 497
OR OF REVIV'D ADONIS, OR RENOWND 9 440

REVIVE
NEW COURAGE AND REVIVE, THOUGH NOW THEY LYE 1 279
EXTEND HIS EV'NING BEAM, THE FIELDS REVIVE, 2 493
EFFECT SHALL END OUR WISH. MEAN WHILE REVIVE; 6 493
AS PRESENT, HEAV'NLY INSTRUCTER, I REVIVE 11 871

REVIVES
BUT SOON REVIVES, DEATH OVER HIM NO POWER 12 420

REVOKE
THIR NATURE, AND REVOKE THE HIGH DECREE 3 126

REVOLT
WHO FIRST SEDUC'D THEM TO THAT FOUL REVOLT? 1 33
FOR HIS REVOLT, YET FAITHFULL HOW THEY STOOD, 1 611
BY OUR REVOLT, BUT OVER HELL EXTEND 2 326
THIR OWN REVOLT, NOT I: IF I FOREKNEW, 3 117
AUTHOR OF EVIL, UNKNOWN TILL THY REVOLT, 6 262
THAT FROM THY JUST OBEDIENCE COULD REVOLT, 6 740
DISLOYAL ON THE PART OF MAN, REVOLT, 9 7

REVOLTED
THINK NOT, REVOLTED SPIRIT, THY SHAPE THE SAME, 4 835
AGAINST REVOLTED MULTITUDES THE CAUSE 6 31
WHERE ALL YET LEFT OF THAT REVOLTED ROUT 10 534

REVOLUTION
SUCH RESTLESS REVOLUTION DAY BY DAY 8 31
COMES THUNDRING BACK WITH DREADFUL REVOLUTION 10 814

REVOLUTIONS
AT CERTAIN REVOLUTIONS ALL THE DAMN'D 2 597

REVOLV'D
OF THOUGHTS REVOLV'D, HIS FINAL SENTENCE CHOSE 9 88

REVOLVD
REVOLVD ON HEAV'NS GREAT AXLE, AND HER REIGN 7 381

REVOLVING
THEN MUCH REVOLVING, THUS IN SIGHS BEGAN. 4 31

REWARD
ALL WHO HAVE THIR REWARD ON EARTH, THE FRUITS 3 451
THY MERITED REWARD, THE FIRST ASSAY 6 153
BY TERRIBLE EXAMPLE THE REWARD 6 910
AND WORSHIP HIM, AND IN REWARD TO RULE 7 628
TO SERVE HIM, THY REWARD WAS OF HIS GRACE, 10 767
LOOSE NO REWARD, THOUGH HERE THOU SEE HIM DIE, 11 459
EXEMPT FROM DEATH; TO SHEW THEE WHAT REWARD 11 709

REWARD (CONTINUED)
TO JUDGE TH' UNFAITHFUL DEAD, BUT TO REWARD 12 461

RHEA'S
HIS OWN AND RHEA'S SON LIKE MEASURE FOUND; 1 513
YOUNG BACCHUS FROM HIS STEPDAME RHEA'S EYE; 4 279

RHENE
RHENE OR THE DANAW, WHEN HER BARBAROUS SONS 1 353

RHEUMS
DROPSIES, AND ASTHMA'S, AND JOINT-RACKING RHEUMS. 11 488

RHIME
THINGS UNATTEMPTED YET IN PROSE OR RHIME. 1 16

RHODOPE
IN RHODOPE, WHERE WOODS AND ROCKS HAD EARES 7 35

RHOMB
NOCTURNAL AND DIURNAL RHOMB SUPPOS'D, 8 134

RIB
FROM THENCE A RIB, WITH CORDIAL SPIRITS WARME; 8 466
THE RIB HE FORMD AND FASHOND WITH HIS HANDS; 8 469
ANOTHER RIB AFFORD, YET LOSS OF THEE 9 912
AS GOOD HAVE GROWN THERE STILL A LIVELESS RIB. 9 1154
RATHER THEN SOLID VERTU, ALL BUT A RIB 10 884

RIBS
AND DIG'D OUT RIBS OF GOLD. LET NONE ADMIRE 1 690
HIS ARMES CLUNG TO HIS RIBS, HIS LEGGS ENTWINING 10 512

RICH
WITH GEMMS AND GOLDEN LUSTRE RICH IMBLAZ'D, 1 538
AT TOP WHEREOF, BUT FARR MORE RICH APPEERD 3 504
OF SOME RICH BURGHER, WHOSE SUBSTANTIAL DORES, 4 189
GROVES WHOSE RICH TREES WEPT ODOROUS GUMMS AND
BALME, 4 248
CROCUS, AND HYACINTH WITH RICH INLAY 4 701
ON PRINCES, WHEN THIR RICH RETINUE LONG 5 355
FIRST WHEELD THIR COURSE; EARTH IN HER RICH ATTIRE 7 501
BEYOND PETSORA EASTWARD, TO THE RICH 10 292
RICH MEXICO THE SEAT OF MOTEZUME, 11 407
FAME IN THE WORLD, HIGH TITLES, AND RICH PREY, 11 793

RICHER
AND CUSCO IN PERU, THE RICHER SEAT 11 408

RICHES
THE RICHES OF HEAV'NS PAVEMENT, TROD'N GOLD, 1 682
THAT RICHES GROW IN HELL; THAT SOYLE MAY BEST 1 691
AND ALL THE RICHES OF THIS WORLD ENJOYDST, 12 580

RICHEST
OR WHERE THE GORGEOUS EAST WITH RICHEST HAND 2 3
OF RICHEST TEXTURE SPRED, AT TH' UPPER END 10 446

RICHLY
A BEAVIE OF FAIR WOMEN, RICHLY GAY 11 582

RID
ARMD WITH THY MIGHT, RID HEAV'N OF THESE REBELL'D, 6 737

RIDDANCE
ASK RIDDANCE, IF WE MEAN TO TREAD WITH EASE; 4 632

RIDE
WONT RIDE IN ARM'D, AND AT THE SOLDANS CHAIR 1 764
REND UP BOTH ROCKS AND HILLS, AND RIDE THE AIR 2 540
RIDE ON THY WINGS, AND THOU WITH THY COMPEERS, 4 974
I SEND ALONG, RIDE FORTH, AND BID THE DEEP 7 166
TOILD OUT MY UNCOUTH PASSAGE, FORC'T TO RIDE 10 475

RIDES
IN SPRING TIME, WHEN THE SUN WITH TAURUS RIDES, 1 769
AS IN A CLOUDY CHAIR ASCENDING RIDES 2 930

RIDGE
WHOSE SNOWIE RIDGE THE ROVING TARTAR BOUNDS, 3 432
PART RISE IN CRYSTAL WALL, OR RIDGE DIRECT, 7 293
PONTIFICAL, A RIDGE OF PENDENT ROCK 10 313
SHALL DWELL TO SENIR, THAT LONG RIDGE OF HILLS. 12 146

RIDGES
THE RIDGES OF GRIM WARR; NO THOUGHT OF FLIGHT, 6 236

RIDICULOUS
RIDICULOUS, AND THE WORK CONFUSION NAM'D. 12 62

RIDING
IN SECRET, RIDING THROUGH THE AIR SHE COMES 2 663

RIFE
SPACE MAY PRODUCE NEW WORLDS; WHEREOF SO RIFE 1 650

RIFL'D
RIFL'D THE BOWELS OF THIR MOTHER EARTH 1 687

RIGHT
BY RIGHT OF WARR, WHAT E'RE HIS BUSINESS BE . . . 1 150
WHAT SHALL BE RIGHT: FARDEST FROM HIM IS BEST . . 1 247
HIS TEMPLE RIGHT AGAINST THE TEMPLE OF GOD . . . 1 402
AZAZEL AS HIS RIGHT, A CHERUBE TALL: 1 534
MEE THOUGH JUST RIGHT, AND THE FIXT LAWS OF HEAV'N 2 18
HIS RED RIGHT HAND TO PLAGUE US? WHAT IF ALL . . 2 174
OUR OWN RIGHT LOST: HIM TO UNTHRONE WE THEN . . 2 231
HE SCOURS THE RIGHT HAND COAST, SOM TIMES THE LEFT, 2 633
AT THY RIGHT HAND VOLUPTUOUS, AS BESEEMS . . . 2 869
BEATITUDE PAST UTTERANCE; ON HIS RIGHT 3 62
ALL HE COULD HAVE; I MADE HIM JUST AND RIGHT, . . 3 98
NOT MEE. THEY THEREFORE AS TO RIGHT BELONGD, . . 3 111
OF ALL THINGS MADE, AND JUDGEST ONELY RIGHT. . . 3 155
THEE FROM MY BOSOM AND RIGHT HAND, TO SAVE, . . 3 279
DOWN RIGHT INTO THE WORLDS FIRST REGION THROWS . 3 562
ANY, BUT GOD ALONE, TO VALUE RIGHT 4 202
AND HEAD, WHAT THOU HAST SAID IS JUST AND RIGHT. . 4 443
SLOWLY DESCENDED, AND WITH RIGHT ASPECT 4 541
BY THY EXAMPLE, BUT HAVE POWER AND RIGHT . . . 4 881
AT MY RIGHT HAND; YOUR HEAD I HIM APPOINT; . . . 5 606
IN BATTEL, WHAT OUR POWER IS, OR OUR RIGHT. . . 5 728
TO KNOW YE RIGHT, OR IF YE KNOW YOUR SELVES . . 5 789
WHO CAN IN REASON THEN OR RIGHT ASSUME 5 794
MONARCHIE OVER SUCH AS LIVE BY RIGHT 5 795
THAT TO HIS ONLY SON BY RIGHT ENDU'D 5 815
OUR PUISSANCE IS OUR OWN, OUR OWN RIGHT HAND . . 5 864
RIGHT REASON FOR THIR LAW, AND FOR THIR KING . . 6 42
MESSIAH, WHO BY RIGHT OF MERIT REIGNS. 6 43
OF THIS RIGHT HAND PROVOK'T, SINCE FIRST THAT
TONGUE 6 154
ALL HIS RIGHT SIDE; THEN SATAN FIRST KNEW PAIN, . 6 327
ENJOYMENT OF OUR RIGHT AS GODS; YET HARD . . . 6 452
VANGUARD, TO RIGHT AND LEFT THE FRONT UNFOULD; . 6 558
HAD ENDED; WHEN TO RIGHT AND LEFT THE FRONT . . 6 569
AND STUMBL'D MANY, WHO RECEIVES THEM RIGHT, . . 6 624
BY SACRED UNCTION, THY DESERVED RIGHT. 6 709
FROM THE RIGHT HAND OF GLORIE WHERE HE SATE, . . 6 747
ASCENDED, AT HIS RIGHT HAND VICTORIE 6 762
HEE ON HIS IMPIOUS FOES RIGHT ONWARD DROVE, . . 6 831
AMONG THEM HE ARRIV'D; IN HIS RIGHT HAND . . . 6 835
WHERE NOW HE SITS AT THE RIGHT HAND OF BLISS. . . 6 892
IMPORTS NOT, IF THOU RECK'N RIGHT, THE REST . . 8 71
THEN SELF ESTEEM, GROUNDED ON JUST AND RIGHT . . 8 572
REASON, IS FREE, AND REASON HE MADE RIGHT, . . . 9 352
WHAT THOU COMMANDST, AND RIGHT THOU SHOULDST BE
OBEYD: 9 570
AND GAZE, AND WORSHIP THEE OF RIGHT DECLAR'D . . 9 611
OF PREFACE BROOKING THROUGH HIS ZEAL OF RIGHT. . 9 676
TOWARD THE RIGHT HAND HIS GLORIE, ON THE SON . . 10 64
OF RIGHT, THAT I MAY MITIGATE THIR DOOM 10 76
ALL YOURS, RIGHT DOWN TO PARADISE DESCEND; . . . 10 398
FOR IN POSSESSION SUCH, NOT ONELY OF RIGHT, . . . 10 461
CONCURD NOT TO MY BEING, IT WERE BUT RIGHT . . . 10 747
IN WISE DEPORT, SPAKE MUCH OF RIGHT AND WRONG, . . 11 666
WITH SOME REGARD TO WHAT IS JUST AND RIGHT . . . 12 16
DOMINION ABSOLUTE; THAT RIGHT WE HOLD 12 68
IS LOST, WHICH ALWAYES WITH RIGHT REASON DWELLS . 12 84
BARR'D OF HIS RIGHT; YET AT HIS BIRTH A STARR . . 12 360
HIS SEAT AT GODS RIGHT HAND, EXALTED HIGH . . . 12 457

RIGHTEOUS
HIS RIGHTEOUS ALTAR, BOWING LOWLY DOWN 1 434
THIR OWN BOTH RIGHTEOUS AND UNRIGHTEOUS DEEDS, . . 3 292
ACCEPTED, FEARLESS IN HIS RIGHTEOUS CAUSE, . . . 6 804
WITH RIGHTEOUS PLEA, THIR UTMOST VIGILANCE, . . . 10 30
RIGHTEOUS ARE THY DECREES ON ALL THY WORKS; . . . 10 644
THE ONELY RIGHTEOUS IN A WORLD PERVERSE, ... 11 701

RIGHTEOUSNESS
JUST CONFIDENCE, AND NATIVE RIGHTEOUSNESS 9 1056
OPPROBRIOUS, WITH HIS ROBE OF RIGHTEOUSNESS, . . . 10 222
RESCU'D, HAD IN HIS RIGHTEOUSNESS BIN LOST? . . . 11 682
THE PATHS OF RIGHTEOUSNESS, HOW MUCH MORE SAFE, . . 11 814
JUST FOR UNJUST, THAT IN SUCH RIGHTEOUSNESS . . . 12 294
FOUNDED IN RIGHTEOUSNESS AND PEACE AND LOVE . . . 12 550

RIGHTFUL
CONFESS HIM RIGHTFUL KING? UNJUST THOU SAIST . . 5 818

RIGHTLIER
DESTROYERS RIGHTLIER CALL'D AND PLAGUES OF MEN. . 11 697

RIGHTLY
IF RIGHTLY THOU ART CALL'D, WHOSE VOICE DIVINE . 7 2
WHICH THOU HAST RIGHTLY NAM'D, BUT OF THY SELF, . 8 439
EVE RIGHTLY CALL'D, MOTHER OF ALL MANKIND, . . . 11 159
NEVER TO HURT THEM MORE WHO RIGHTLY TRUST . . . 12 418

RIGID
THE RIGID SATISFACTION, DEATH FOR DEATH. 3 212
OF RIGID SPEARS, AND HELMETS THRONG'D, AND SHIELDS 6 83
THE RIGID INTERDICTION, WHICH RESOUNDS 8 334
THOSE RIGID THREATS OF DEATH; YE SHALL NOT DIE: . 9 685

RIGOR
BOUND WITH GORGONIAN RIGOR NOT TO MOVE, ... 10 297

RIGOROUSLY
AT THE SAD SENTENCE RIGOROUSLY URG'D, ... 11 109

RIGOUR
IN PUNISHT MAN, TO SATISFIE HIS RIGOUR 10 803

RILL
ROSE A FRESH FOUNTAIN, AND WITH MANY A RILL . . 4 229

RILLS
OF LEAVES AND FUMING RILLS, AURORA'S FAN, . . . 5 6

RIMMON
HIM FOLLOW'D RIMMON, WHOSE DELIGHTFUL SEAT . . . 1 467

RIN'D
ROUGH, OR SMOOTH RIN'D, OR BEARDED HUSK, OR SHELL 5 342

RIND
WITH FIXED ANCHOR IN HIS SKALY RIND 1 206

RINDE
OTHERS WHOSE FRUIT BURNISHT WITH GOLDEN RINDE . . 4 249
THE SAVOURIE PULP THEY CHEW, AND IN THE RINDE . . 4 335

RINGLETS
DISHEVELD, BUT IN WANTON RINGLETS WAV'D 4 306

RINGS
ATTEST THIR JOY, THAT HILL AND VALLEY RINGS. . . 2 495

RIOT
OF RIOT ASCENDS ABOVE THEIR LOFTIEST TOWRS, . . . 1 499
TO HIS BOLD RIOT: DREADFUL WAS THE DIN 10 521
TO LUXURIE AND RIOT, FEAST AND DANCE, ... 11 715

RIPE
OF CERES RIPE FOR HARVEST WAVING BENDS 4 981
ALL SEASONS, RIPE FOR USE HANGS ON THE STALK; . . 5 323
SO MAIST THOU LIVE, TILL LIKE RIPE FRUIT THOU DROP 11 535
WHEN THIS WORLDS DISOLUTION SHALL BE RIPE, . . . 12 459

RISE
TEN THOUSAND BANNERS RISE INTO THE AIR 1 545
BY FORCE, AND AT OUR HEELS ALL HELL SHOULD RISE . 2 135
TO FOUND THIS NETHER EMPIRE, WHICH MIGHT RISE . . 2 296
BUT I SHALL RISE VICTORIOUS, AND SUBDUE 3 250
AND DYING RISE, AND RISING WITH HIM RAISE . . . 3 296
MINISTRING LIGHT PREPAR'D, THEY SET AND RISE; . . 4 664
AND LET US TO OUR FRESH IMPLOYMENTS RISE . . . 5 125
YE MISTS AND EXHALATIONS THAT NOW RISE 5 185
IN HONOUR TO THE WORLDS GREAT AUTHOR RISE, . . . 5 188
AND TO HIS MESSAGE HIGH IN HONOUR RISE; 5 289
ORESHADES; FOR THESE MID-HOURS, TILL EEVNING RISE 5 376
AGAINST TH' OMNIPOTENT TO RISE IN ARMS; 6 136
TO FLIGHT, OR IF TO FALL, BUT THAT THEY RISE . . 6 285
PART RISE IN CRYSTAL WALL, OR RIDGE DIRECT, . . 7 293
RISE ON THE EARTH, OR EARTH RISE ON THE SUN, . . 8 161
AND SAID, THY MANSION WANTS THEE, ADAM, RISE, . . 8 296
BEGAN TO RISE, HIGH PASSIONS, ANGER, HATE, . . . 9 1123
METHINKS I FEEL NEW STRENGTH WITHIN ME RISE, . . 10 243
NEW HEAV'N AND EARTH SHALL TO THE AGES RISE, . . 10 647
BUT RISE, LET US NO MORE CONTEND, NOR BLAME . . 10 958
BEYOND ALL BOUNDS, TILL INUNDATION RISE 11 828
UNDER PATERNAL RULE; TILL ONE SHALL RISE . . . 12 24
OF DAVID (SO I NAME THIS KING) SHALL RISE . . . 12 326
RETURNE, THE STARRES OF MORN SHALL SEE HIM RISE . 12 422

RISEN
OF DAY-SPRING, AND THE SUN, WHO SCARCE UP RISEN . 5 139

RISES
FORTHWITH A HIDEOUS GABBLE RISES LOUD 12 56

RISING
CELESTIAL VERTUES RISING, WILL APPEAR 2 15
ASPECT HE ROSE, AND IN HIS RISING SEEM'D . . . 2 301
THIR RISING ALL AT ONCE WAS AS THE SOUND . . . 2 476
THE RISING WORLD OF WATERS DARK AND DEEP, . . . 3 11
AND DYING RISE, AND RISING WITH HIM RAISE . . . 3 296
WHICH NOW THE RISING SUN GUILDS WITH HIS BEAMS. . 3 551
STRAIT COUCHES CLOSE, THEN RISING CHANGES OFT . . 4 405
RISING IN CLOUDED MAJESTIE, AT LENGTH 4 607
SWEET IS THE BREATH OF MORN, HER RISING SWEET, . . 4 641
WITH CHARM OF EARLIEST BIRDS, NOR RISING SUN . . 4 651
RISING OR FALLING STILL ADVANCE HIS PRAISE. . . 5 191
REBELLION RISING, SAW IN WHOM, HOW SPRED . . . 5 715
IS RISING, WHO INTENDS TO ERECT HIS THRONE . . . 5 725
HIS GENERATION, AND THE RISING BIRTH 7 102
THE DANK, AND RISING ON STIFF PENNONS, TOWRE . . 7 441
RISING, THE CRUMBL'D EARTH ABOVE THEM THREW . . 7 468
SATAN INVOLV'D IN RISING MIST, THEN SOUGHT . . . 9 75
CIRCULAR BASE OF RISING FOULDS, THAT TOUR'D . . 9 498
FALSE IN OUR PROMIS'D RISING; SINCE OUR EYES . . 9 1070
PRINCE OF THE AIRE; THEN RISING FROM HIS GRAVE . . 10 185
WHICH OF THEM RISING WITH THE SUN, OR FALLING, . . 10 663
OF MIDDLE AGE ONE RISING, EMINENT 11 665

RIS'N
HAD RIS'N OR HEAV'D HIS HEAD, BUT THAT THE WILL . 1 211
OF GLORY OBSCUR'D: AS WHEN THE SUN NEW RIS'N . . 1 594
RIS'N, AND WITH HIDEOUS OUTCRY RUSH'D BETWEEN. . 2 726
WITH FIRST APPROACH OF LIGHT, WE MUST BE RIS'N, . 4 624
RIS'N ON MID-NOON; SOM GREAT BEHEST FROM HEAV'N . 5 311
NOW RIS'N, TO WORK THEM FURDER WOE OR SHAME; . . 10 555
WHAT THOUGHTS IN MY UNQUIET BREST ARE RIS'N, . . 10 975
RIS'N FROM A RIVER O'RE THE MARISH GLIDES, . . . 12 630

RITES
HIS HOLY RITES, AND SOLEMN FEASTS PROFAN'D, . . . 1 390
TO DO HIM WANTON RITES, WHICH COST THEM WOE. . . 1 414
THIS SAID UNANIMOUS, AND OTHER RITES 4 736
ADAM FROM HIS FAIR SPOUSE, NOR EVE THE RITES . . 4 742
WITH MINISTERIES DUE AND SOLEMN RITES: 7 149
OF NUPTIAL SANCTITIE AND MARRIAGE RITES: . . . 8 487
FROM LOVES DUE RITES, NUPTIAL IMBRACES SWEET, . 10 994
ON THE CLEFT WOOD, AND ALL DUE RITES PERFORM'D. . 11 440
HYMEN, THEN FIRST TO MARRIAGE RITES INVOK'T; . . 11 591
TO CIVIL JUSTICE, PART RELIGIOUS RITES 12 231
OF GREAT MESSIAH SHALL SING. THUS LAWS AND RITES 12 244
WELL DEEM IN OUTWARD RITES AND SPECIOUS FORMES . 12 534

RIVALS
HIS RIVALS, WINNING CHEAP THE HIGH REPUTE 2 472

RIVER
LETHE THE RIVER OF OBLIVION ROULES 2 583
AND WHERE THE RIVER OF BLISS THROUGH MIDST OF HEAVN 3 358
SOUTHWARD THROUGH EDEN WENT A RIVER LARGE, . . . 4 223
GIRT WITH THE RIVER TRITON, WHERE OLD CHAM, . . 4 276
THE RIVER HORSE AND SCALIE CROCODILE. 7 474
IN WITH THE RIVER SUNK, AND WITH IT ROSE . . . 9 74
MAEOTIS, UP BEYOND THE RIVER OB; 9 78
DOWN THE GREAT RIVER TO THE OP'NING GULF, . . . 11 833
EGYPT, DIVIDED BY THE RIVER NILE; 12 157
RIS'N FROM A RIVER O'RE THE MARISH GLIDES, . . . 12 630

RIVER-DRAGON
THE RIVER-DRAGON TAM'D AT LENGTH SUBMITS 12 191

RIVERS
RIVERS OR MOUNTAINS IN HER SPOTTY GLOBE. . . . 1 291
OF FOUR INFERNAL RIVERS THAT DISGORGE 2 575
BREATHE FORTH ELIXIR PURE, AND RIVERS RUN . . . 3 607
LIKE GENTLE BREATHS FROM RIVERS PURE, THENCE RAISE 4 806
ALL BUT WITHIN THOSE BANKS, WHERE RIVERS NOW . . 7 305
WITH BORDERS LONG THE RIVERS. THAT EARTH NOW . . 7 328
OTHERS ON SILVER LAKES AND RIVERS BATH'D . . . 7 437
YE HILLS AND DALES, YE RIVERS, WOODS, AND PLAINES, 8 275
OF HILL, AND VALLIE, RIVERS, WOODS AND PLAINES, . 9 116
NIGH RIVERS MOUTH OR FORELAND, WHERE THE WIND . . 9 514
TO BLOOD UNSHED THE RIVERS MUST BE TURND, . . . 12 176

RIV'N
SORE TOILD, HIS RIV'N ARMES TO HAVOC HEWN, ... 6 449

RIVULET
BY FOUNTAIN OR BY SHADIE RIVULET 9 420

ROAD
THROUGH ALL TH' EMPYREAL ROAD; TILL AT THE GATE . 5 253

ROAM
HERE PILGRIMS ROAM, THAT STRAY'D SO FARR TO SEEK . 3 476
THROUGH WOOD, THROUGH WASTE, O'RE HILL, O'RE DALE HIS ROAM. 4 538

ROAM'D
AND ORE THE CELTIC ROAM'D THE UTMOST ISLES. . . 1 521
GANGES AND INDUS: THUS THE ORB HE ROAM'D 9 82

ROAMING
ROAMING TO SEEK THIR PREY ON EARTH, DURST FIX . . 1 382

ROAR
COVERS HIS THRONE; FROM WHENCE DEEP THUNDERS ROAR 2 267
FROM THOSE DEEP THROATED ENGINS BELCHT, WHOSE ROAR 6 586
THE BRAZEN THROAT OF WARR HAD CEAST TO ROAR, . . 11 713

ROARD
NINE DAYES THEY FELL; CONFOUNDED CHAOS ROARD, . . 6 871

ROAVE
BUT APT THE MIND OR FANCIE IS TO ROAVE 8 188

ROAVING
UNCHECKT, AND OF HER ROAVING IS NO END; 8 189
TILL ON A DAY ROAVING THE FIELD, I CHANC'D . . . 9 575

ROBE
WITH CONQUEST, FELT TH' ENVENOM'D ROBE, AND TORE . 2 543
TO GUILTIE SHAME HEE COVER'D, BUT HIS ROBE . . . 9 1058
OPPROBRIOUS, WITH HIS ROBE OF RIGHTEOUSNESS, . . 10 222

ROCK
WHILE SMOOTH ADONIS FROM HIS NATIVE ROCK 1 450

ROCK (CONTINUED)
EACH ON HIS ROCK TRANSFIXT, THE SPORT AND PREY . 2 181
THREE IRON, THREE OF ADAMANTINE ROCK, ... 2 646
OF MASSIE IRON OR SOLLID ROCK WITH EASE 2 878
BY NILUS HEAD, ENCLOSD WITH SHINING ROCK, . . . 4 283
LEVELD HIS EEVNING RAYES: IT WAS A ROCK 4 543
THOUGH HUGE, AND IN A ROCK OF DIAMOND ARMD, . . 6 364
SOFT-EBBING; NOR WITHSTOOD THEM ROCK OR HILL, . . 7 300
PONTIFICAL, A RIDGE OF PENDENT ROCK 10 313
NOT THIS ROCK ONELY; HIS OMNIPRESENCE FILLS . . 11 336
SIGHT SO DEFORM WHAT HEART OF ROCK COULD LONG . . 11 494

ROCKIE
BETWIXT THESE ROCKIE PILLARS GABRIEL SAT 4 549
HE HASTED, AND OPPOS'D THE ROCKIE ORB 6 254

ROCKS
TH' ASSEMBLY, AS WHEN HOLLOW ROCKS RETAIN 2 285
REND UP BOTH ROCKS AND HILLS, AND RIDE THE AIR . 2 540
ROCKS, CAVE, LAKES, FENS, BOGS, DENS, AND SHADES OF DEATH, ... 2 621
THROUGH BOSPORUS BETWIXT THE JUSTLING ROCKS: . . 2 1018
FROM DIAMOND QUARRIES HEW'N, AND ROCKS OF GOLD, . 5 759
THOUGH STANDING ELSE AS ROCKS, BUT DOWN THEY FELL 6 593
ROCKS, WATERS, WOODS, AND BY THE SHAGGIE TOPS . . 6 645
IN RHODOPE, WHERE WOODS AND ROCKS HAD EARES . . 7 35
MOIST NUTRIMENT, OR UNDER ROCKS THIR FOOD . . . 7 408
ROCKS, DENS, AND CAVES; BUT I IN NONE OF THESE . 9 118
AND NOW THE TOPS OF HILLS AS ROCKS APPEER; . . . 11 852

ROD
INNUMERABLE. AS WHEN THE POTENT ROD 1 338
IS NOW AN IRON ROD TO BRUISE AND BREAKE 5 887
OF HERMES, OR HIS OPIATE ROD. MEAN WHILE . . . 11 133
AW'D BY THE ROD OF MOSES SO TO STAND 12 198
MOSES ONCE MORE HIS POTENT ROD EXTENDS 12 211
OVER THE SEA; THE SEA HIS ROD OBEYS; 12 212

RODE
THE STARRIE HOST, RODE BRIGHTEST, TILL THE MOON . 4 606
IN PROGRESS THROUGH THE RODE OF HEAV'N STAR-PAV'D. 4 976
HEE ON THE WINGS OF CHERUB RODE SUBLIME 6 771
O'RE SHIELDS AND HELMES, AND HELMED HEADS HE RODE 6 840
WORTHIEST TO REIGN; HE CELEBRATED RODE 6 888
UPLIFTED, IN PATERNAL GLORIE RODE 7 219
HIS LONGITUDE THROUGH HEAV'NS HIGH RODE: THE GRAY 7 373
ANSWERING HIS GREAT IDEA. UP HE RODE 7 557
A BROAD AND AMPLE RODE, WHOSE DUST IS GOLD . . . 7 577
HEE FROM THE EAST HIS FLAMING RODE BEGIN, . . . 8 162
THE SPACE OF SEVEN CONTINU'D NIGHTS HE RODE . . . 9 63
DESCEND THROUGH DARKNESS, ON YOUR RODE WITH EASE . 10 394
WAS BID TURN REINES FROM TH' EQUINOCTIAL RODE . . 10 672
RODE TILTING O'RE THE WAVES, ALL DWELLINGS ELSE . 11 747

ROMANCE
IN FABLE OR ROMANCE OF UTHERS SON 1 580

ROME
SCIPIO THE HIGHTH OF ROME. WITH TRACT OBLIQUE . . 9 510
IN ATHENS OR FREE ROME, WHERE ELOQUENCE 9 671
ON EUROPE THENCE, AND WHERE ROME WAS TO SWAY . . 11 405

ROOD
LAY FLOATING MANY A ROOD, IN BULK AS HUGE 1 196

ROOF
THE ROOF WAS FRETTED GOLD. NOT BABILON, ... 1 717
AND LEVEL PAVEMENT: FROM THE ARCHED ROOF 1 726
HELL BOUNDS HIGH REACHING TO THE HORRID ROOF, . . 2 644
AND ON THIR NAKED LIMBS THE FLOURIE ROOF 4 772
BUT FIRST FROM UNDER SHADIE ARBOROUS ROOF, . . . 5 137
UNDER WHOSE LOWLY ROOF THOU HAST VOUTSAF'T . . . 5 463
THICK OVERHEAD WITH VERDANT ROOF IMBOWR'D 9 1038

ROOFE
ALL THINGS TO MANS DELIGHTFUL USE; THE ROOFE . . 4 692

ROOM
NOW LESS THEN SMALLEST DWARFS, IN NARROW ROOM . . 1 779
PERHAPS OUR VACANT ROOM, THOUGH MORE REMOV'D, . . 2 835
BY WONDROUS BIRTH: BE THOU IN ADAMS ROOM . . . 3 285
IN NARROW ROOM NATURES WHOLE WEALTH, YEA MORE, . 4 207
INTO OUR ROOM OF BLISS THUS HIGH ADVANC'T . . . 4 359
AND SEND FORTH ALL HER KINGS; THERE WILL BE ROOM, 4 383
INTO THIR VACANT ROOM, AND THENCE DIFFUSE . . . 7 190
OF FUTURE, IN SMALL ROOM LARGE HEART ENCLOS'D, . 7 486
FOR SUCH VAST ROOM IN NATURE UNPOSSEST 8 153
DETERMIN'D TO ADVANCE INTO OUR ROOM 9 148
THEY DIE; BUT IN THIR ROOM, AS THEY FOREWARNE, . 12 507

ROOT
OF MANKIND IN ONE ROOT, AND EARTH WITH HELL . . . 2 383
AS FROM A SECOND ROOT SHALL BE RESTOR'D, . . . 3 288
PROPORTIOND TO EACH KIND. SO FROM THE ROOT . . 5 479
NOT TO DESTROY, BUT ROOT THEM OUT OF HEAV'N: . . 6 855
OF PROHIBITION, ROOT OF ALL OUR WOE; 9 645
THE BENDED TWIGS TAKE ROOT, AND DAUGHTERS GROW . 9 1105
AND THERE TAKE ROOT AN ILAND SALT AND BARE, . . 11 834

ROOTS
THROUGH PAIN UP BY THE ROOTS THESSALIAN PINES, 2 544
DEEP TO THE ROOTS OF HELL THE GATHER'D BEACH 10 299

ROSE
ROSE OUT OF CHAOS: OR IF SION HILL 1 10
WITH ORIENT COLOURS WAVING: WITH THEM ROSE 1 546
ROSE LIKE AN EXHALATION, WITH THE SOUND 1 711
TO LESS THEN GODS. ON TH' OTHER SIDE UP ROSE 2 108
ASPECT HE ROSE, AND IN HIS RISING SEEM'D 2 301
NONE SHALL PARTAKE WITH ME. THUS SAYING ROSE 2 466
FORBIDDING; AND AT ONCE WITH HIM THEY ROSE; 2 475
OR SIGHT OF VERNAL BLOOM, OR SUMMERS ROSE, 3 43
ROSE A FRESH FOUNTAIN, AND WITH MANY A RILL 4 229
FLOURS OF ALL HUE, AND WITHOUT THORN THE ROSE: 4 256
OF HEAV'N THE STARRS THAT USHER EVENING ROSE: 4 355
STILL AS IT ROSE, IMPOSSIBLE TO CLIMBE, 4 548
I ROSE AS AT THY CALL, BUT FOUND THEE NOT; 5 48
WITH ROSE AND ODOURS FROM THE SHRUB UNFUM'D. 5 349
THE HORRID SHOCK: NOW STORMING FURIE ROSE, 6 207
UP ROSE THE VICTOR ANGELS, AND TO ARMS 6 525
UPON CONFUSION ROSE: AND NOW ALL HEAV'N 6 669
SO SAID, HE O'RE HIS SCEPTER BOWING, ROSE 6 746
ROSE AS IN DANCE THE STATELY TREES, AND SPRED 7 324
WITH THIR BRIGHT LUMINARIES THAT SET AND ROSE, 7 385
LIMB'D AND FULL GROWN: OUT OF THE GROUND UP ROSE 7 456
AMONG THE TREES IN PAIRS THEY ROSE, THEY WALK'D: 7 459
HIS VASTNESS: FLEEC'T THE FLOCKS AND BLEATING ROSE, 7 472
ROSE, AND WENT FORTH AMONG HER FRUITS AND FLOURS, 8 44
FLUNG ROSE, FLUNG ODOURS FROM THE SPICIE SHRUB, 8 517
ROSE UP A FOUNTAIN BY THE TREE OF LIFE; 9 73
IN WITH THE RIVER SUNK, AND WITH IT ROSE 9 74
ENCUMBERD, NOW HAD LEFT THEM, UP THEY ROSE 9 1051
UNCOVER'D MORE, SO ROSE THE DANITE STRONG 9 1059
THUS SAYING, FROM HIS RADIANT SEAT HE ROSE 10 85
HIS ZENITH, WHILE THE SUN IN ARIES ROSE: 10 329
MEANWHILE THE SOUTHWIND ROSE, AND WITH BLACK WINGS 11 738

ROSEAT
IN DARKER VEILE) AND ROSEAT DEWS DISPOS'D 5 646

ROSES
IMPURPL'D WITH CELESTIAL ROSES SMIL'D. 3 364
IRIS ALL HUES, ROSES, AND GESSAMIN 4 698
SHOWRD ROSES, WHICH THE MORN REPAIR'D. SLEEP ON 4 773
IN YONDER SPRING OF ROSES INTERMIXT 9 218
HALF SPI'D, SO THICK THE ROSES BUSHING ROUND 9 426
DOWN DROP'D, AND ALL THE FADED ROSES SHED: 9 893

ROSIE
NOW MORN HER ROSIE STEPS IN TH' EASTERN CLIME 5 1
WAK'T BY THE CIRCLING HOURS, WITH ROSIE HAND 6 3
CELESTIAL ROSIE RED, LOVES PROPER HUE, 8 619
HER ROSIE PROGRESS SMILING; LET US FORTH, 11 175

ROT
HIS CATTEL MUST OF ROT AND MURREN DIE, 12 179

ROUGH
ORE BOG OR STEEP, THROUGH STRAIT, ROUGH, DENSE, OR
RARE, 2 948
ROUGH, OR SMOOTH RIN'D, OR BEARDED HUSK, OR SHELL 5 342
ON THE ROUGH EDGE OF BATTEL ERE IT JOYN'D, 6 108

ROULD
BUT ON THY ROULD IN HEAPS, AND UP THE TREES 10 558
DEEP UNDER WATER ROULD; SEA COVER'D SEA, 11 749

ROULE
TO DRESS, AND TROULE THE TONGUE, AND ROULE THE EYE. 11 620

ROULES
LETHE THE RIVER OF OBLIVION ROULES 2 583

ROULING
AND TOWARDS THE GATE ROULING HER BESTIAL TRAIN, 2 873

ROULS
AND WHEEL ON TH' EARTH, DEVOURING WHERE IT ROULS; 12 183

ROUND
TORMENTS HIM; ROUND HE THROWS HIS BALEFUL EYES 1 56
A DUNGEON HORRIBLE, ON ALL SIDES ROUND 1 61
ETHEREAL TEMPER, MASSY, LARGE AND ROUND, 1 285
WAV'D ROUND THE COAST, UP CALL'D A PITCHY CLOUD 1 340
AMONG THE NATIONS ROUND, AND DURST ABIDE 1 385
FROM WING TO WING, AND HALF ENCLOSE HIM ROUND 1 617
FAR ROUND ILLUMIN'D HELL: HIGHLY THEY RAG'D 1 666
BUILT LIKE A TEMPLE, WHERE PILASTERS ROUND 1 713
AND WITH THE MAJESTY OF DARKNESS ROUND 2 266
OF ANGELS WATCHING ROUND? HERE HE HAD NEED 2 413
OUTRAGEOUS TO DEVOUR, IMMURES US ROUND 2 435
AND GOD-LIKE IMITATED STATE; HIM ROUND 2 511
IMMOVABLE, INFIXT, AND FROZEN ROUND, 2 602
WITH MORTAL STING: ABOUT HER MIDDLE ROUND 2 653
AFRESH WITH CONSCIOUS TERROURS VEX ME ROUND, 2 801
CREATED VAST AND ROUND, A PLACE OF BLISS 2 832
WITH TERRORS AND WITH CLAMORS COMPASST ROUND 2 862

ROUND (CONTINUED)
OF FIGHTING ELEMENTS, ON ALL SIDES ROUND 2 1015
IN CIRCUIT, UNDETERMIND SQUARE OR ROUND, 2 1048
DRAWN ROUND ABOUT THEE LIKE A RADIANT SHRINE, 3 379
OF THIS ROUND WORLD, WHOSE FIRST CONVEX DIVIDES 3 419
OF CHAOS BLUSTRING ROUND, INCLEMENT SKIE; 3 426
ROUND HE SURVEYS, AND WELL MIGHT, WHERE HE STOOD 3 555
SHOT UPWARD STILL DIRECT, WHENCE NO WAY ROUND 3 618
LAY WAVING ROUND; ON SOM GREAT CHARGE IMPLOY'D 3 628
TO VISIT OFT THIS NEW CREATION ROUND; 3 661
TIMELY INTERPOSES, AND HER MONTHLY ROUND 3 728
HE BRINGS, AND ROUND ABOUT HIM, NOR FROM HELL 4 21
INTO HIS NEATHER EMPIRE NEIGHBOURING ROUND. 4 145
ROUND FROM HIS PARTED FORELOCK MANLY HUNG 4 302
BY WORD OR ACTION MARKT: ABOUT THEM ROUND 4 401
BUT FIRST WITH NARROW SEARCH I MUST WALK ROUND 4 528
THOSE HAVE THIR COURSE TO FINISH, ROUND THE EARTH, 4 661
THIR PHALANX, AND BEGAN TO HEMM HIM ROUND 4 979
THE PENDULOUS ROUND EARTH WITH BALLANC'T AIRE 4 1000
GIRT LIKE A STARRIE ZONE HIS WASTE, AND ROUND 5 281
THIR TABLE WAS, AND MOSSIE SEATS HAD ROUND, 5 392
WHENCE IN HER VISAGE ROUND THOSE SPOTS, UNPURG'D 5 419
ENCOMPASS'D ROUND WITH FOES, THUS ANSWERD BOLD. 5 876
WHERE LIGHT AND DARKNESS IN PERPETUAL ROUND 6 6
ENCAMPING, PLAC'D IN GUARD THIR WATCHES ROUND, 6 412
WHICH INTO HALLOW ENGINS LONG AND ROUND 6 484
LOOKD ROUND, AND SCOUTS EACH COAST LIGHT-ARMED
SCOURE, 6 529
IN DARKNESS, AND WITH DANGERS COMPAST ROUND, 7 27
IMBRACING ROUND THIS FLORID EARTH, WHAT CAUSE 7 90
ROUND THROUGH THE VAST PROFUNDITIE OBSCURE, 7 229
OF THIS GREAT ROUND: PARTITION FIRM AND SURE, 7 267
REGENT OF DAY, AND ALL TH' HORIZON ROUND 7 371
ROUND THIS OPACOUS EARTH, THIS PUNCTUAL SPOT, 8 23
STOOD ON MY FEET; ABOUT ME ROUND I SAW 8 261
ABOVE, OR ROUND ABOUT THEE OR BENEATH. 8 318
NIGHTS HEMISPHERE HAD VEILD THE HORIZON ROUND: 9 52
TERRESTRIAL HEAV'N, DANC'T ROUND BY OTHER HEAV'NS 9 103
WITH WHAT DELIGHT COULD I HAVE WALKT THEE ROUND, 9 114
IN LABYRINTH OF MANY A ROUND SELF-ROWLD, 9 183
THE WOODBINE ROUND THIS ARBOUR, OR DIRECT 9 216
HALF SPI'D, SO THICK THE ROSES BUSHING ROUND 9 426
HER HUSBAND, FOR I VIEW FAR ROUND, NOT NIGH, 9 482
THY UTMOST REACH OR ADAMS: ROUND THE TREE 9 591
CONDENSES, AND THE COLD INVIRONS ROUND, 9 636
AND GIRDED ON OUR LOYNS, MAY COVER ROUND 9 1096
OF THIS ROUND WORLD: WITH PINNS OF ADAMANT 10 318
ROUND THIR METROPOLIS, AND NOW EXPECTING 10 439
HE SATE, AND ROUND ABOUT HIM SAW UNSEEN: 10 448
STILL FOLLOWING THEE, STILL COMPASSING THEE ROUND 11 352
NOT HIGHER THAT HILL NOR WIDER LOOKING ROUND, 11 381
SMEARD ROUND WITH PITCH, AND IN THE SIDE A DORE 11 731
AND SHELTERD ROUND, BUT ALL THE CATARACTS 11 824
IN SIGNAL OF REMOVE, WAVES FIERCELY ROUND; 12 593

ROUNDED
HAD ROUNDED STILL TH' HORIZON, AND NOT KNOWN 10 684

ROUNDING
WHILE THEY KEEP WATCH, OR NIGHTLY ROUNDING WALK 4 685
THE WESTERN POINT, WHERE THOSE HALF-ROUNDING GUARDS 4 862

ROUNDS
INCITED, DANCE ABOUT HIM VARIOUS ROUNDS? 8 125

ROUS'D
ROUS'D FROM THE SLUMBER, ON THAT FIERY COUCH, 1 377
HAD ROUS'D THE SEA, NOW WITH HOARSE CADENCE LULL 2 287

ROUSE
ROUSE AND BESTIR THEMSELVES ERE WELL AWAKE. 1 334
SHALL HAST'N, SUCH A PEAL SHALL ROUSE THIR SLEEP. 3 329

ROUT
ERRING; FOR HE WITH THIS REBELLIOUS ROUT 1 747
CLEER VICTORY, TO OUR PART LOSS AND ROUT 2 770
WITH RUIN UPON RUIN, ROUT ON ROUT, 2 995
THEN WHEN THE DRAGON, PUT TO SECOND ROUT, 4 3
WITH MANY AN INRODE GOR'D; DEFORMED ROUT 6 387
FOULE DISSIPATION FOLLOW'D AND FORC'T ROUT; 6 598
THROUGH HIS WILDE ANARCHIE, SO HUGE A ROUT 6 873
OF THAT WILDE ROUT THAT TORE THE THRACIAN BARD 7 34
WHERE ALL YET LEFT OF THAT REVOLTED ROUT 10 534

ROVE
ROVE IDLE UNIMPLOID, AND LESS NEED REST; 4 617
ROVE WITHOUT REIN, TILL IN THE AMOROUS NET 11 586

ROVING
THE LIP OF TANTALUS. THUS ROVING ON 2 614
WHOSE SNOWIE RIDGE THE ROVING TARTAR BOUNDS, 3 432

ROW
TO MANY A ROW OF PIPES THE SOUND-BOARD BREATHS. 1 709
PENDANT BY SUTTLE MAGIC MANY A ROW 1 727
AND HIGHER THEN THAT WALL A CIRCLING ROW 4 146
AMONG SWEET DEWES AND FLOURS; WHERE ANY ROW 5 212
A TRIPLE MOUNTED ROW OF PILLARS LAID 6 572

ROW (CONTINUED)
STOOD RANKT OF SERAPHIM ANOTHER ROW 6 604
TILL ON THOSE CURSED ENGINS TRIPLE-ROW 6 650
BEYOND A ROW OF MYRTLES, ON A FLAT, 9 627

ROWES
BETWEEN HER WHITE WINGS MANTLING PROUDLY, ROWES 7 439

ROWL
REIGND WHERE THESE HEAV'NS NOW ROWL, WHERE EARTH NOW RESTS 5 578
TO DARKEN ALL THE HILL, AND SMOAK TO ROWL 6 57

ROWL'D
INCREDIBLE HOW SWIFT, HAD THITHER ROWL'D 4 593
BY THOUSANDS, ANGEL ON ARCH-ANGEL ROWL'D; 6 594

ROWLD
DRIVN BACKWARD SLOPE THIR POINTING SPIRES, AND ROWLD 1 223
THAT ROWLD ORBICULAR, AND TURND TO STARRS 3 718
AND FROM ABOUT HIM FIERCE EFFUSION ROWLD 6 765
OF HIS FIERCE CHARIOT ROWLD, AS WITH THE SOUND 6 829
ROWLD INWARD, AND A SPACIOUS GAP DISCLOS'D 6 861
HER MURAL BREACH, RETURNING WHENCE IT ROWLD. 6 879
NOW HEAV'N IN ALL HER GLORIE SHON, AND ROWLD 7 499
IN LABYRINTH OF MANY A ROUND SELF-ROWLD, 9 183
LEAD THEN, SAID EVE. HEE LEADING SWIFTLY ROWLD 9 631

ROWLE
REVISIT'ST NOT THESE EYES, THAT ROWLE IN VAIN 3 23
AND ALL HER NUMBERD STARRS, THAT SEEM TO ROWLE 8 19
SEA, AIRE, AND SHOAR, THE THUNDER WHEN TO ROWLE 10 666

ROWLING
LAY VANQUISHT, ROWLING IN THE FIERY GULFE 1 52
CHERUBE AND SERAPH ROWLING IN THE FLOOD 1 324
BELCH'D FIRE AND ROWLING SMOAK; THE REST ENTIRE 1 671
NOW ROWLING, BOILES IN HIS TUMULTUOUS BREST, 4 16
ROWLING ON ORIENT PEARL AND SANDS OF GOLD, 4 238
WAVE ROWLING AFTER WAVE, WHERE WAY THEY FOUND, 7 298
ROWLING IN DUST AND GORE. TO WHICH OUR SIRE. 11 460

ROWLS
ROWLS O'RE ELISIAN FLOURS HER AMBER STREAM; 3 359

ROYAL
FORERUN THE ROYAL CAMP, TO TRENCH A FIELD, 1 677
HIGH ON A THRONE OF ROYAL STATE, WHICH FAR 2 1
FROM AURAN EASTWARD TO THE ROYAL TOWRS 4 211
THEY CAME, AND SATAN TO HIS ROYAL SEAT 5 756
ALL PROPHECIE, THAT OF THE ROYAL STOCK 12 325

ROYALTIES
THESE ROYALTIES, AND NOT REFUSE TO REIGN, 2 451

RUB'D
NEW RUB'D WITH BAUM, EXPATIATE AND CONFER 1 774

RUBIE
RUBIE OR TOPAZ, TO THE TWELVE THAT SHON 3 597

RUBIED
WITH ANGELS FOOD, AND RUBIED NECTAR FLOWS 5 633

RUDDIE
RUDDIE AND GOLD: I NEARER DREW TO GAZE; 9 578

RUDDY
CAST FORTH REDOUNDING SMOAK AND RUDDY FLAME. 2 889

RUDE
BUT WITH SUCH GARDNING TOOLS AS ART YET RUDE, 9 391
BEHOLDERS RUDE, AND SHALLOW TO DISCERNE 9 544
JUSTLING OR PUSHT WITH WINDS RUDE IN THIR SHOCK 10 1074

RUE
TOO WELL I SEE AND RUE THE DIRE EVENT, 1 134
NO EVIL DURST ATTEMPT THEE, BUT I RUE 9 1180
HAD BRED; THEN PURG'D WITH EUPHRASIE AND RUE 11 414

RUEFUL
PRODIGIOUS MOTION FELT AND RUEFUL THROES. 2 780

RUES
CHOSE FREELY WHAT IT NOW SO JUSTLY RUES. 4 72

RUFUL
HEARD ON THE RUFUL STREAM; FIERCE PHLEGETON 2 580

RUIN
IN EQUAL RUIN: INTO WHAT PIT THOU SEEST 1 91
MAJESTICK THOUGH IN RUIN: SAGE HE STOOD 2 305
THAWS NOT, BUT GATHERS HEAP, AND RUIN SEEMS 2 590
WITH RUIN UPON RUIN, ROUT ON ROUT, 2 995
HAVOCK AND SPOIL AND RUIN ARE MY GAIN. 2 1009
WHILE BY THEE RAIS'D I RUIN ALL MY FOES, 3 258
IN THEM AT ONCE TO RUIN ALL MANKIND. 5 228

RUIN (CONTINUED)
THE RUIN OF SO MANY GLORIOUS ONCE 5 567
SUCH RUIN INTERCEPT: TEN PACES HUGE 6 193
RUIN MUST NEEDS ENSUE; FOR WHAT AVAILES 6 456
OF MISSIVE RUIN; PART INCENTIVE REED 6 519
HAD GON TO WRACK, WITH RUIN OVERSPRED, 6 670
IN UNIVERSAL RUIN LAST, AND NOW 6 797
INCUMBERD HIM WITH RUIN: HELL AT LAST 6 874
OUR RUIN, BOTH BY THEE INFORMD I LEARNE, 9 275
THE WAY WHICH TO HER RUIN NOW I TEND. 9 493

RUIND
LESS THEN ARCH ANGEL RUIND, AND TH' EXCESS 1 593
AND MEE WITH THEE HATH RUIND, FOR WITH THEE 9 906
HE RUIND, NOW MANKIND; WHOM WILL HE NEXT? 9 950

RUINE
WITH HIDEOUS RUINE AND COMBUSTION DOWN 1 46
THIR RUINE. HENCE I WILL EXCITE THIR MINDS 4 522

RUINING
HEAV'N RUINING FROM HEAV'N AND WOULD HAVE FLED 6 868

RUINOUS
WITH NOISES LOUD AND RUINOUS (TO COMPARE 2 921
BOTH BATTELS MAINE, WITH RUINOUS ASSAULT 6 216

RUL'D
OF COLD OLYMPUS RUL'D THE MIDDLE AIR 1 516
AS IF PREDESTINATION OVER-RUL'D 3 114
STOOD RUL'D, STOOD VAST INFINITUDE CONFIN'D; 3 711
BY NATURE FREE, NOT OVER-RUL'D BY FATE 5 527
FROM HIS STRONG HOLD OF HEAV'N HIGH OVER-RUL'D 6 228
ONE SPIRIT IN THEM RUL'D, AND EVERY EYE 6 848
FOR UNDERSTANDING RUL'D NOT, AND THE WILL 9 1127
TO RULE, AS OVER ALL HE SHOULD HAVE RUL'D. 10 493
NOW RUL'D HIM, PUNISHT IN THE SHAPE HE SIN'D, 10 516

RULE
EXALTED TO SUCH POWER, AND GAVE TO RULE, 1 736
HIS EMPIRE, AND WITH IRON SCEPTER RULE 2 327
ABSOLUTE RULE; AND HYACINTHIN LOCKS 4 301
AMONG SO MANY SIGNES OF POWER AND RULE 4 429
WILDE ABOVE RULE OR ART; ENORMOUS BLISS. 5 297
TO MAN, THE GREATER TO HAVE RULE BY DAY, 7 347
TO ILLUMINATE THE EARTH, AND RULE THE DAY 7 350
IN THIR VICISSITUDE, AND RULE THE NIGHT, 7 351
IN OUR SIMILITUDE, AND LET THEM RULE 7 520
AND WORSHIP HIM, AND IN REWARD TO RULE 7 628
FIND PASTIME, AND BEARE RULE; THY REALM IS LARGE. 8 375
LETS HER WILL RULE; RESTRAINT SHE WILL NOT BROOK, 9 1184
UNSEEMLY TO BEARE RULE, WHICH WAS THY PART 10 155
THINE SHALL SUBMIT, HEE OVER THEE SHALL RULE. 10 196
TO RULE, AS OVER ALL HE SHOULD HAVE RUL'D. 10 493
ENCROACHING EVE PERHAPS, HAD FIRST THE RULE 10 582
ALL TH' EARTH HE GAVE THEE TO POSSESS AND RULE, 11 339
THE RULE OF NOT TOO MUCH, BY TEMPERANCE TAUGHT 11 531
UNDER PATERNAL RULE; TILL ONE SHALL RISE 12 24
THROUGH THE TWELVE TRIBES, TO RULE BY LAWS ORDAIND: 12 226
AND ALL THE RULE, ONE EMPIRE; ONELY ADD 12 581

RULES
OF HIM WHO RULES ABOVE; SO WAS HIS WILL 2 351
HEE RULES A MOMENT; CHAOS UMPIRE SITS, 2 907
WHEN HE WHO RULES IS WORTHIEST, AND EXCELLS 6 177
WHILE THEY PERVERT PURE NATURES HEALTHFUL RULES 11 523

RULING
AND HIGH PERMISSION OF ALL-RULING HEAVEN 1 212
THICK CLOUDS AND DARK DOTH HEAV'NS ALL-RULING SIRE 2 264

RUMINATING
OR BEDWARD RUMINATING: FOR THE SUN 4 352

RUMOR
OF DEMOGORGON; RUMOR NEXT AND CHANCE, 2 965

RUMORD
AGAINST A RUMORD WARR, THE SMUTTIE GRAINE 4 817

RUN
BREATHE FORTH ELIXIR PURE, AND RIVERS RUN 3 607
THAT RUN THROUGH ALL THE HEAV'NS, OR DOWN TO TH' EARTH 3 651
OF NATURES WOMB, THAT IN QUATERNION RUN 5 181
FORTHWITH ON ALL SIDES TO HIS AIDE WAS RUN 6 335
AND THE GREAT LIGHT OF DAY YET WANTS TO RUN 7 98
INVESTED WITH BRIGHT RAYES, JOCOND TO RUN 7 372
THE LESS NOT BRIGHT, NOR HEAV'N SUCH JOURNIES RUN, 8 88
THIR MINISTRY PERFORM'D, AND RACE WELL RUN, 12 505

RUNG
WITH WIDE CERBERIAN MOUTHS FULL LOUD, AND RUNG 2 655
HAD BEEN ACHIEV'D, WHEREOF ALL HELL HAD RUNG, 2 723
AS FROM BLEST VOICES, UTTERING JOY, HEAV'N RUNG 3 347
IT SOUNDED, AND THE FAITHFUL ARMIES RUNG 6 204
THE HEAV'NS AND ALL THE CONSTELLATIONS RUNG, 7 562
SO SUNG THEY, AND THE EMPYREAN RUNG, 7 633

RUNG (CONTINUED)
YET RUNG OF HIS PERSWASIVE WORDS, IMPREGN'D 9 737

RUNNING
AND LAKES AND RUNNING STREAMS THE WATERS FILL; 7 397

RUNS
RUNS DIVERS, WANDRING MANY A FAMOUS REALME 4 234

RUPTURE
BURSTING WITH KINDLY RUPTURE FORTH DISCLOS'D 7 419

RURAL
AS WITH A RURAL MOUND THE CHAMPAIN HEAD 4 134
A HAPPY RURAL SEAT OF VARIOUS VIEW; 4 247
ON TO THIR MORNINGS RURAL WORK THEY HASTE 5 211
RURAL REPAST, PERMITTING HIM THE WHILE 9 4
OR DAIRIE, EACH RURAL SIGHT, EACH RURAL SOUND; 9 451
HER TRESSES, AND HER RURAL LABOURS CROWN, 9 841
BEFORE HIM, TOWNS, AND RURAL WORKS BETWEEN, 11 639

RUSH
WAG'D IN THE TROUBL'D SKIE, AND ARMIES RUSH 2 534
FORTH RUSH THE LEVANT AND THE PONENT WINDES 10 704

RUSH'D
RIS'N, AND WITH HIDEOUS OUTCRY RUSH'D BETWEEN. 2 726
SO UNDER FIERIE COPE TOGETHER RUSH'D 6 215
DAWNING THROUGH HEAV'N: FORTH RUSH'D WITH WHIRLWIND SOUND 6 749
FORTH RUSH'D IN HASTE THE GREAT CONSULTING PEERS, 10 456
LIKE A DARK CEELING STOOD; DOWN RUSH'D THE RAIN 11 743

RUSHING
WHENCE RUSHING HE MIGHT SUREST SEIZE THEM BOTH 4 407
OF BATTEL NOW BEGAN, AND RUSHING SOUND 6 97
TWO PLANETS RUSHING FROM ASPECT MALIGNE 6 313

RUSHT
WHAT SHOULD THEY DO? IF ON THEY RUSHT, REPULSE 6 600

RUSLING
OF RUSLING LEAVES, BUT MINDED NOT, AS US'D 9 519

RUSSIAN
AS WHEN THE TARTAR FROM HIS RUSSIAN FOE 10 431
IN HISPAHAN, OR WHERE THE RUSSIAN KSAR 11 394

RUSSLING
BRUSHT WITH THE HISS OF RUSSLING WINGS. AS BEES 1 768

RUSTIC
RUSTIC, OF GRASSIE SORD; THITHER ANON 11 433

SABBATH
WITH HALLELUIAHS: THUS WAS SABBATH KEPT. 7 634
ERE SABBATH EEV'NING: SO WE HAD IN CHARGE. 8 246

SABEAN
SABEAN ODOURS FROM THE SPICIE SHOARE 4 162

SABLE-VESTED
SAT SABLE-VESTED NIGHT, ELDEST OF THINGS, 2 962

SACRED
WHOSE WANTON PASSIONS IN THE SACRED PORCH 1 454
BUT NOW AT LAST THE SACRED INFLUENCE 2 1034
SMIT WITH THE LOVE OF SACRED SONG; BUT CHIEF 3 29
OF HYMNS AND SACRED SONGS, WHEREWITH THY THRONE 3 148
BUT TO DESTRUCTION SACRED AND DEVOTE, 3 208
THIR SACRED SONG, AND WAKEN RAPTURES HIGH; 3 369
MORE SACRED AND SEQUESTERD, THOUGH BUT FEIGND, 4 706
O SACRED NAME OF FAITHFULNESS PROFAN'D. 4 951
WORTHY OF SACRED SILENCE TO BE HEARD; 5 557
IN SONG AND DANCE ABOUT THE SACRED HILL, 5 619
RETURND NOT LOST: ON TO THE SACRED HILL 6 25
CANCELD FROM HEAV'N AND SACRED MEMORIE, 6 379
BY SACRED UNCTION, THY DESERVED RIGHT. 6 709
AND THE THIRD SACRED MORN BEGAN TO SHINE 6 748
HER SACRED SHADES: THOUGH GOD HAD YET NOT RAIN'D 7 331
OF SACRED INFLUENCE: AS GOD IN HEAV'N 9 107
NOW WHEN AS SACRED LIGHT BEGAN TO DAWNE 9 192
O SACRED, WISE, AND WISDOM-GIVING PLANT, 9 679
THE SACRED FRUIT FORBIDD'N. SOM CURSED FRAUD 9 904
THAT SACRED FRUIT, SACRED TO ABSTINENCE, 9 924
TO RESALUTE THE WORLD WITH SACRED LIGHT 11 134
WITH LARGE WINE-OFFERINGS POUR'D, AND SACRED FEAST, 12 21
WITH ALL HIS SACRED THINGS, A SCORN AND PREY 12 341
WHO ALL THE SACRED MYSTERIES OF HEAV'N 12 509

SACRIFIC'D
TO THAT MEEK MAN, WHO WELL HAD SACRIFIC'D; 11 451

SACRIFICE
OF HUMAN SACRIFICE, AND PARENTS TEARS, 1 393
FILIAL OBEDIENCE: AS A SACRIFICE 3 269
OF SACRIFICE, INFORMING THEM, BY TYPES 12 232

SACRIFICING
CHOICEST AND BEST; THEN SACRIFICING, LAID 11 438
OFT SACRIFICING BULLOCK, LAMB, OR KID, 12 20

SAD
THAT WITH SAD OVERTHROW AND FOUL DEFEAT 1 135
TO BE NO MORE; SAD CURE; FOR WHO WOULD LOOSE, 2 146
PURSUES, AS INCLINATION OR SAD CHOICE 2 524
SAD ACHERON OF SORROW, BLACK AND DEEP; 2 578
THEN SWEET, NOW SAD TO MENTION, THROUGH DIRE CHANGE 2 820
SAD INSTRUMENT OF ALL OUR WOE, SHE TOOK; 2 872
HIS SAD EXCLUSION FROM THE DORES OF BLISS. 3 525
LAY PLEASANT, HIS GRIEVD LOOK HE FIXES SAD, 4 28
SCARCE THUS AT LENGTH FAILD SPEECH RECOVERD SAD. 4 357
IN SAD EVENT, WHEN TO THE UNWISER SON 4 716
RELATED, AND THUS ADAM ANSWERD SAD. 5 94
BUT WITH ADDITION STRANGE; YET BE NOT SAD. 5 116
SAD TASK AND HARD, FOR HOW SHALL I RELATE 5 564
SAD RESOLUTION AND SECURE: LET EACH 6 541
DEATHS HARBINGER: SAD TASK, YET ARGUMENT 9 13
SO HAVING SAID, AS ONE FROM SAD DISMAY 9 917
SKIE LOWR'D AND MUTTERING THUNDER, SOM SAD DROPS 9 1002
TH' ANGELIC GUARDS ASCENDED, MUTE AND SAD 10 18
TO WHOM SAD EVE WITH SHAME NIGH OVERWHELM'D, 10 159
SATE IN THIR SAD DISCOURSE, AND VARIOUS PLAINT, 10 343
THUS TO DISBURD'N SOUGHT WITH SAD COMPLAINT. 10 719
WHOM THUS AFFLICTED WHEN SAD EVE BEHELD, 10 863
ADAM, BY SAD EXPERIMENT I KNOW 10 967
OR END, THOUGH SHARP AND SAD, YET TOLERABLE, 10 977
NUMBERD, THOUGH SAD, TILL DEATH, HIS DOOM (WHICH I 11 40
AT THE SAD SENTENCE RIGOROUSLY URG'D, 11 109
TO WHOM THUS EVE WITH SAD DEMEANOUR MEEK. 11 162
QUIET THOUGH SAD, THE RESPIT OF THAT DAY 11 272
BEFORE HIS EYES APPEARD, SAD, NOYSOM, DARK, 11 478
LAMENTING TURND FULL SAD; O WHAT ARE THESE, 11 675
THE END OF ALL THY OFSPRING, END SO SAD, 11 755
WHEREAT THE HEART OF ADAM ERST SO SAD 11 868
BOTH IN ONE FAITH UNANIMOUS THOUGH SAD, 12 603
AND THUS WITH WORDS NOT SAD SHE HIM RECEAV'D. 12 609

SADNESS
ALL SADNESS BUT DESPAIR: NOW GENTLE GALES 4 156
ALL WERE WHO HEARD, DIM SADNESS DID NOT SPARE 10 23

SAFE
FROM THE SAFE SHORE THIR FLOATING CARKASES 1 310
ESTABLISHT IN A SAFE UNENVIED THRONE 2 23
THIS PLACE OUR DUNGEON, NOT OUR SAFE RETREAT 2 317
SUFFICE, OR WHAT EVASION BEAR HIM SAFE 2 411
THOUGH HARD AND RARE: THEE I REVISIT SAFE, 3 21
AND TO THE END PERSISTING, SAFE ARRIVE. 3 197
TO UTTER IS NOT SAFE. ASSEMBLE THOU 5 683
MORE SAFE I SING WITH MORTAL VOICE, UNCHANG'D 7 24
OUR GREAT FORBIDDER, SAFE WITH ALL HIS SPIES 9 815
FIRST LIGHTED FROM HIS WING, AND LANDED SAFE 10 316
AND WANDRING VANITIE, WHEN LEST WAS SAFE, 10 875
ASCEND, I FOLLOW THEE, SAFE GUIDE, THE PATH 11 371
THE PATHS OF RIGHTEOUSNESS, HOW MUCH MORE SAFE, 11 814
SAFE TOWARDS CANAAN FROM THE SHOAR ADVANCE 12 215
SAFE TO ETERNAL PARADISE OF REST. 12 314

SAFER
SOME SAFER RESOLUTION, WHICH METHINKS 10 1029

SAFEST
SAFEST AND SEEMLIEST BY HER HUSBAND STAIES, 9 268
SAFEST THY LIFE, AND BEST PREPAR'D ENDURE 11 365

SAFETIE
THY TEMPRING; WITH LIKE SAFETIE GUIDED DOWN 7 15

SAFETY
OF ORDER, HOW IN SAFETY BEST WE MAY 2 280
THAT FOR THE GENERAL SAFETY HE DESPIS'D 2 481

SAGACIOUS
SAGACIOUS OF HIS QUARRY FROM SO FARR, 10 281

SAGE
MAJESTICK THOUGH IN RUIN: SAGE HE STOOD 2 305

SAGES
AND GUIDES THE EASTERN SAGES, WHO ENQUIRE 12 362

SAID
SAID THEN THE LOST ARCH-ANGEL, THIS THE SEAT 1 243
THIS SAID, HE SAT; AND EXPECTATION HELD 2 417
THUS SAID, HE TURND, AND SATAN BOWING LOW, 3 736
AND HEAD, WHAT THOU HAST SAID IS JUST AND RIGHT. 4 443
THIS SAID UNANIMOUS, AND OTHER RITES 4 736
KNOW YE NOT THEN SAID SATAN, FILL'D WITH SCORN, 4 827
UNDAUNTED. IF I MUST CONTEND, SAID HE, 4 851
OR LESS BE LOST. THY FEAR, SAID ZEPHON BOLD, 4 854
WITH GENTLE VOICE, I THOUGHT IT THINE; IT SAID, 5 37
AND O FAIR PLANT, SAID HE, WITH FRUIT SURCHARG'D, 5 58
THIS SAID HE PAUS'D NOT, BUT WITH VENTROUS ARME 5 64
RAPHAEL, SAID HEE, THOU HEAR'ST WHAT STIR ON EARTH 5 224
THUS SAID, NATIVE OF HEAV'N, FOR OTHER PLACE 5 361

SAID (CONTINUED)
AND SMILING TO HIS ONELY SON THUS SAID. 5 718
HE SAID, AND AS THE SOUND OF WATERS DEEP 5 872
HE SAID, AND ON HIS SON WITH RAYES DIRECT 6 719
SO SAID, HE O'RE HIS SCEPTER BOWING, ROSE 6 746
SAID THEN TH' OMNIFIC WORD, YOUR DISCORD END: 7 217
AND SAID, THUS FARR EXTEND, THUS FARR THY BOUNDS, 7 230
LET THER BE LIGHT, SAID GOD, AND FORTHWITH LIGHT 7 243
AGAIN, GOD SAID, LET THER BE FIRMAMENT 7 261
SATIATE WITH GENIAL MOISTURE, WHEN GOD SAID 7 282
AND SAW THAT IT WAS GOOD, AND SAID, LET TH' EARTH 7 309
HE SCARCE HAD SAID, WHEN THE BARE EARTH, TILL THEN 7 313
AND GOD SAID, LET THE WATERS GENERATE 7 387
WITH EEVNING HARPS AND MATTIN, WHEN GOD SAID, 7 450
THIS SAID, HE FORMD THEE, ADAM, THEE O MAN 7 524
FEMALE FOR RACE; THEN BLESS'D MANKINDE, AND SAID, 7 530
WHAT E'RE I SAW. THOU SUN, SAID I, FAIRE LIGHT, 8 273
AND SAID, THY MANSION WANTS THEE, ADAM, RISE, 8 296
SAID MILDELY, AUTHOR OF ALL THIS THOU SEEST 8 317
LEAD THEN, SAID EVE. HEE LEADING SWIFTLY ROWLD 9 631
INDEED? HATH GOD THEN SAID THAT OF THE FRUIT 9 656
THE GARDEN, GOD HATH SAID, YE SHALL NOT EATE 9 662
SHE SCARSE HAD SAID, THOUGH BRIEF, WHEN NOW MORE BOLD 9 664
SO HAVING SAID, AS ONE FROM SAD DISMAY 9 917
SO SAID HE, AND FORBORE NOT GLANCE OR TOY 9 1034
SO HAVING SAID, HE THUS TO EVE IN FEW: 10 157
SO HAVING SAID, A WHILE HE STOOD, EXPECTING 10 504
THIS SAID, THEY BOTH BETOOK THEM SEVERAL WAYES, 10 610
SAID HEE, WITH ONE THRICE ACCEPTABLE STROKE 10 855
I YIELD IT JUST, SAID ADAM, AND SUBMIT. 11 526
THERE IS, SAID MICHAEL, IF THOU WELL OBSERVE 11 530
SAID TH' ANGEL, WHO SHOULD BETTER HOLD HIS PLACE 11 635
BE SURE THEY WILL, SAID TH' ANGEL; BUT FROM HEAV'N 12 485

SAIDST
FROM MEE RETURND, AS ERST THOU SAIDST, FROM FLIGHT, 6 187
LIVES, AS THOU SAIDST, AND GAINES TO LIVE AS MAN 9 933
GOING INTO SUCH DANGER AS THOU SAIDST? 9 1157

SAIL
BUT FIRM BATTALION; BACK WITH SPEEDIEST SAIL 6 534

SAIL-BROAD
THE STEDFAST EARTH. AT LAST HIS SAIL-BROAD VANNES 2 927

SAILE
HALF FLYING; BEHOVES HIM NOW BOTH OARE AND SAILE. 2 942
THOSE BALMIE SPOILES. AS WHEN TO THEM WHO SAILE 4 159
VERES OFT, AS OFT SO STEERS, AND SHIFTS HER SAILE; 9 515

SAILES
SAILES BETWEEN WORLDS AND WORLDS, WITH STEDDIE WING 5 268

SAILING
CLOSE SAILING FROM BENGALA, OR THE ILES 2 638

SAILS
WITH SAILS AND WIND THIR CANIE WAGGONS LIGHT: 3 439

SAINT
AND NOW SAINT PETER AT HEAV'NS WICKET SEEMS 3 484
ALL JUSTICE: NOR DELAID THE WINGED SAINT 5 247
SUCH WONDROUS POWER GOD TO HIS SAINT WILL LEND, 12 200

SAINTLY
THAT PRACTISD FALSHOOD UNDER SAINTLY SHEW, 4 122

SAINTS
THEN ALL THY SAINTS ASSEMBL'D, THOU SHALT JUDGE 3 330
TRANSLATED SAINTS, OR MIDDLE SPIRITS HOLD 3 461
PRESENT, OR PAST, AS SAINTS AND PATRIARCHS US'D. 4 762
INVINCIBLE, LEAD FORTH MY ARMED SAINTS 6 47
FAR OTHERWISE TH' INVIOLABLE SAINTS 6 398
THEN SHALL THY SAINTS UNMIXT, AND FROM TH' IMPURE 6 742
ATTENDED WITH TEN THOUSAND THOUSAND SAINTS, 6 767
STAND STILL IN BRIGHT ARRAY YE SAINTS, HERE STAND 6 801
TO MEET HIM ALL HIS SAINTS, WHO SILENT STOOD 6 882
VICTORIOUS WITH HIS SAINTS, TH' OMNIPOTENT 7 136
FROM HIS TRANSCENDENT SEAT THE SAINTS AMONG, 10 614
TO JUDGE THEM WITH HIS SAINTS: HIM THE MOST HIGH 11 705

SAIST
CONFESS HIM RIGHTFUL KING? UNJUST THOU SAIST 5 818
THAT WE WERE FORMD THEN SAIST THOU? AND THE WORK 5 853
TO LOVE THOU BLAM'ST ME NOT, FOR LOVE THOU SAIST 8 612

SAKE
ACCOUNT MEE MAN; I FOR HIS SAKE WILL LEAVE 3 238
DIVINE DISPLEASURE FOR HER SAKE, OR DEATH. 9 993
CURS'D IS THE GROUND FOR THY SAKE, THOU IN SORROW 10 201
FOR ANGERS SAKE, FINITE TO INFINITE 10 802
AND FOR HIS MAKERS IMAGE SAKE EXEMPT? 11 514
BY SIMPLY MEEK; THAT SUFFERING FOR TRUTHS SAKE 12 569

SALT
AND THERE TAKE ROOT AN ILAND SALT AND BARE, 11 834

SALUTATION
BESTOWD, THE HOLY SALUTATION US'D 5 386

SALVATION
HIGH IN SALVATION AND THE CLIMES OF BLISS, 11 708
AND HIS SALVATION, THEM WHO SHALL BELEEVE 12 441
SALVATION SHALL BE PREACHT, BUT TO THE SONS 12 448

SAMARCHAND
AND SAMARCHAND BY OXUS, TEMIRS THRONE, 11 389

SAME
WHAT MATTER WHERE, IF I BE STILL THE SAME, 1 256
THE SAME WHOM JOHN SAW ALSO IN THE SUN: 3 623
HADST THOU THE SAME FREE WILL AND POWER TO STAND? 4 66
THINK NOT, REVOLTED SPIRIT, THY SHAPE THE SAME, 4 835
EVEN TO MY MOUTH OF THAT SAME FRUIT HELD PART 5 83
DIFFERING BUT IN DEGREE, OF KIND THE SAME. 5 490
THAT SELF SAME DAY BY FIGHT, OR BY SURPRIZE 6 87
OR NATURE; GOD AND NATURE BID THE SAME, 6 176
WITH LOW SUBJECTION; UNDERSTAND THE SAME 8 345
BEYOND ALL OTHER, THINK THE SAME VOUTSAF'T 8 581
OF SATAN, TO THE SELF SAME PLACE WHERE HEE 10 315
INTO THE SAME ILLUSION, NOT AS MAN 10 571
NOT TO DO ONELY, BUT TO WILL THE SAME 10 826
ONE WAY THE SELF-SAME HOUR? WHY IN THE EAST 11 203
HOLDS ON THE SAME, FROM WOMAN TO BEGIN. 11 633
THE FLUID SKIRTS OF THAT SAME WATRIE CLOUD, 11 882

SAMOED
OF NORUMBEGA, AND THE SAMOED SHOAR 10 696

SAMOS
DELOS OR SAMOS FIRST APPEERING KENNS 5 265

SAMSON
HERCULEAN SAMSON FROM THE HARLOT-LAP 9 1060

SANCTITIE
WITH SANCTITIE OF REASON, MIGHT ERECT 7 508
OF NUPTIAL SANCTITIE AND MARRIAGE RITES: 8 487
TO SANCTITIE THAT SHALL RECEIVE NO STAINE: 10 639
NO SANCTITIE, IF NONE BE THITHER BROUGHT 11 837

SANCTITIES
ABOUT HIM ALL THE SANCTITIES OF HEAVEN 3 60

SANCTITUDE
TRUTH, WISDOME, SANCTITUDE SEVERE AND PURE, 4 293

SANCTUARIE
THIS OUR HIGH PLACE, OUR SANCTUARIE, OUR HILL. 5 732
SHRIN'D IN HIS SANCTUARIE OF HEAV'N SECURE, 6 672

SANCTUARY
WITHIN HIS SANCTUARY IT SELF THIR SHRINES, 1 388
BY HIS PRESCRIPT A SANCTUARY IS FRAM'D 12 249

SANDS
BENEATH GIBRALTER TO THE LYBIAN SANDS. 1 355
SWARM POPULOUS, UNNUMBER'D AS THE SANDS 2 903
ROWLING ON ORIENT PEARL AND SANDS OF GOLD, 4 238

SANG
THEE NEXT THEY SANG OF ALL CREATION FIRST, 3 383
SO SANG THE HIERARCHIES: MEAN WHILE THE SON 7 192

SANGUIN
SANGUIN, SUCH AS CELESTIAL SPIRITS MAY BLEED, 6 333

SAP
INTO THE PLANT SCIENTIAL SAP, DERIV'D 9 837

SAPHIR
WHEREON A SAPHIR THRONE, INLAID WITH PURE 6 758
ON THE CHRYSTALLIN SKIE, IN SAPHIR THRON'D. 6 772

SAPHIRE
OF LIVING SAPHIRE, ONCE HIS NATIVE SEAT; 2 1050
HOW FROM THAT SAPHIRE FOUNT THE CRISPED BROOKS, 4 237

SAPHIRS
WITH LIVING SAPHIRS: HESPERUS THAT LED 4 605

SAPIENCE
OF MAJESTIE DIVINE, SAPIENCE AND LOVE 7 195
TO SAPIENCE, HITHERTO OBSCUR'D, INFAM'D, 9 797
AND ELEGANT, OF SAPIENCE NO SMALL PART, 9 1018

SAPIENT
OR THAT, NOT MYSTIC, WHERE THE SAPIENT KING 9 442

SARRA
OF SARRA, WORN BY KINGS AND HERO'S OLD 11 243

SAT
AND POWERS THAT EARST IN HEAVEN SAT ON THRONES; 1 360
SAT ON HIS FADED CHEEK, BUT UNDER BROWES 1 602

SAT (CONTINUED)
SAT ON HIS THRONE, UPHELD BY OLD REPUTE, 1 639
AND SAT AS PRINCES, WHOM THE SUPREME KING 1 735
IN CLOSE RECESS AND SECRET CONCLAVE SAT 1 795
SATAN EXALTED SAT, BY MERIT RAIS'D 2 5
SATAN EXCEPT, NONE HIGHER SAT, WITH GRAVE 2 300
DELIBERATION SAT AND PUBLIC CARE; 2 303
THIS SAID, HE SAT; AND EXPECTATION HELD 2 417
THE PERILOUS ATTEMPT: BUT ALL SAT MUTE, 2 420
OTHERS APART SAT ON A HILL RETIR'D, 2 557
YET UNCONSUM'D. BEFORE THE GATES THERE SAT 2 648
HAD NOT THE SNAKIE SORCERESS THAT SAT 2 724
WITHOUT MY OP'NING. PENSIVE HERE I SAT 2 777
ALONE, BUT LONG I SAT NOT, TILL MY WOMB 2 778
SAT SABLE-VESTED NIGHT, ELDEST OF THINGS, 2 962
THE RADIANT IMAGE OF HIS GLORY SAT, 3 63
REGARDLESS OF THE BLISS WHEREIN HEE SAT 3 408
WHICH NOW SAT HIGH IN HIS MERIDIAN TOWRE: 4 30
SAT LIKE A CORMORANT; YET NOT TRUE LIFE 4 196
THEREBY REGAIND, BUT SAT DEVISING DEATH 4 197
THEY SAT THEM DOWN, AND AFTER NO MORE TOIL 4 327
YIELDED THEM, SIDE-LONG AS THEY SAT RECLINE 4 333
COUCHT, AND NOW FILD WITH PASTURE GAZING SAT, 4 351
BETWIXT THESE ROCKIE PILLARS GABRIEL SAT 4 549
SAT HORROR PLUM'D; NOR WANTED IN HIS GRASPE 4 989
ADAM DISCERND, AS IN THE DORE HE SAT 5 299
THINK NOT I SHALL BE NICE. SO DOWN THEY SAT, 5 433
BY WHOM IN BLISS IMBOSOM'D SAT THE SON, 5 597
HE SAT; AND IN TH' ASSEMBLY NEXT UPSTOOD 6 446
PERCEAVING WHERE SHE SAT RETIR'D IN SIGHT, 8 41
CLIMBING, SAT THICKER THEN THE SNAKIE LOCKS 10 559

SATAN
AND THENCE IN HEAV'N CALL'D SATAN, WITH BOLD WORDS 1 82
THUS SATAN TALKING TO HIS NEEREST MATE 1 192
SO SATAN SPAKE, AND HIM BEELZEBUB 1 271
OF SATAN AND HIS PEERS: THIR SUMMONS CALL'D 1 757
SATAN EXALTED SAT, BY MERIT RAIS'D 2 5
SATAN EXCEPT, NONE HIGHER SAT, WITH GRAVE 2 300
BY SATAN, AND IN PART PROPOS'D: FOR WHENCE, 2 380
SATAN, WHOM NOW TRANSCENDENT GLORY RAIS'D 2 427
SATAN WITH THOUGHTS INFLAM'D OF HIGHEST DESIGN, 2 630
SATAN WAS NOW AT HAND, AND FROM HIS SEAT 2 674
INCENC'T WITH INDIGNATION SATAN STOOD 2 707
FORBORE, THEN THESE TO HER SATAN RETURN'D: 2 736
T' WHOM SATAN TURNING BOLDLY, THUS. YE POWERS 2 968
THUS SATAN; AND HIM THUS THE ANARCH OLD 2 988
HE CEAS'D; AND SATAN STAID NOT TO REPLY, 2 1010
THAT SATAN WITH LESS TOIL, AND NOW WITH EASE 2 1041
HELL AND THE GULF BETWEEN, AND SATAN THERE 3 70
SATAN ALIGHTED WALKS: A GLOBE FARR OFF 3 422
SATAN FROM HENCE NOW ON THE LOWER STAIR 3 540
O'RE SEA AND LAND: HIM SATAN THUS ACCOSTES; 3 653
THUS SAID, HE TURND, AND SATAN BOWING LOW, 3 736
SATAN, NOW FIRST INFLAM'D WITH RAGE, CAME DOWN, 4 9
SATAN HAD JOURNIED ON, PENSIVE AND SLOW; 4 173
WHEN SATAN STILL IN GAZE, AS FIRST HE STOOD, 4 356
KNOW YE NOT THEN SAID SATAN, FILL'D WITH SCORN, 4 827
WHY HAST THOU, SATAN, BROKE THE BOUNDS PRESCRIB'D 4 878
TO WHOM THUS SATAN, WITH CONTEMPTUOUS BROW. 4 885
SINCE SATAN FELL, WHOM FOLLIE OVERTHREW, 4 905
SATAN, AND COULDST THOU FAITHFUL ADD? O NAME, 4 950
SO THREATN'D HEE, BUT SATAN TO NO THREATS 4 968
PROVE CHAFF. ON TH' OTHER SIDE SATAN ALLARM'D 4 985
SATAN, I KNOW THY STRENGTH, AND THOU KNOWST MINE, 4 1006
SATAN FROM HELL SCAP'T THROUGH THE DARKSOM GULF 5 225
SATAN, SO CALL HIM NOW, HIS FORMER NAME 5 658
SO SPAKE THE SON, BUT SATAN WITH HIS POWERS 5 743
THEY CAME, AND SATAN TO HIS ROYAL SEAT 5 756
THE BANDED POWERS OF SATAN HASTING ON 6 85
SATAN WITH VAST AND HAUGHTIE STRIDES ADVANC'T, 6 109
ON THE PROUD CREST OF SATAN, THAT NO SIGHT, 6 191
THE BATTEL HUNG; TILL SATAN, WHO THAT DAY 6 246
THE SWORD OF SATAN WITH STEEP FORCE TO SMITE 6 324
ALL HIS RIGHT SIDE; THEN SATAN FIRST KNEW PAIN, 6 327
SATAN WITH HIS REBELLIOUS DISAPPEERD, 6 414
WHERETO WITH LOOK COMPOS'D SATAN REPLI'D. 6 469
SATAN: AND THUS WAS HEARD COMMANDING LOUD. 6 557
THEY WORSE ABHORR'D. SATAN BEHELD THIR PLIGHT, 6 607
WITH SATAN, HEE WHO ENVIES NOW THY STATE, 6 900
WHEN SATAN WHO LATE FLED BEFORE THE THREATS 9 53
SATAN INVOLV'D IN RISING MIST, THEN SOUGHT 9 75
OF SATAN DONE IN PARADISE, AND HOW 10 2
HINDER'D NOT SATAN TO ATTEMPT THE MINDE 10 8
TO SATAN FIRST IN SIN HIS DOOM APPLY'D, 10 172
SAW SATAN FALL LIKE LIGHTNING DOWN FROM HEAV'N, 10 184
THE REALM IT SELF OF SATAN LONG USURPT, 10 189
IDLELY, WHILE SATAN OUR GREAT AUTHOR THRIVES 10 236
WHERE SATAN NOW PREVAILES, A MONUMENT 10 258
OF SATAN, TO THE SELF SAME PLACE WHERE HEE 10 315
SATAN IN LIKENESS OF AN ANGEL BRIGHT 10 327
OF SATAN (FOR I GLORIE IN THE NAME, 10 386
THEN SUFFERD. TH' OTHER WAY SATAN WENT DOWN 10 414
WIDE OPEN AND UNGUARDED, SATAN PASS'D, 10 419
OF THAT BRIGHT STARR TO SATAN PARAGOND. 10 426
SECOND OF SATAN SPRUNG, ALL CONQUERING DEATH, 10 591
TO SATAN ONLY LIKE BOTH CRIME AND DOOM. 10 841
SATAN, WHO IN THE SERPENT HATH CONTRIV'D 10 1034

SATAN (CONTINUED)
SATAN, WHOSE FALL FROM HEAV'N, A DEADLIER BRUISE, 12 391
NOT BY DESTROYING SATAN, BUT HIS WORKS 12 394
SHALL BRUISE THE HEAD OF SATAN, CRUSH HIS STRENGTH 12 430
SATAN WITH HIS PERVERTED WORLD, THEN RAISE 12 547

SATANIC
OREWEARIED, THROUGH THE FAINT SATANIC HOST 6 392

SATANS
SATANS DIRE DREAD, AND IN HIS HAND THE SPEAR. 11 248
SATANS ASSAULTS, AND QUENCH HIS FIERIE DARTS, 12 492

SATE
TH' APOSTAT IN HIS SUN-BRIGHT CHARIOT SATE 6 100
FROM THE RIGHT HAND OF GLORIE WHERE HE SATE, 6 747
SATE EAGLE-WING'D, BESIDE HIM HUNG HIS BOW 6 763
THE FILIAL POWER ARRIV'D, AND SATE HIM DOWN 7 587
PENSIVE I SATE ME DOWN; THERE GENTLE SLEEP 8 287
CONFOUNDED LONG THEY SATE, AS STRUCK'N MUTE, 9 1064
THEY SATE THEM DOWN TO WEEP, NOR ONELY TEARES 9 1121
WITHIN THE GATES OF HELL SATE SIN AND DEATH, 10 230
SATE IN THIR SAD DISCOURSE, AND VARIOUS PLAINT, 10 343
IN COUNCIL SATE, SOLLICITOUS WHAT CHANCE 10 428
HE SATE, AND ROUND ABOUT HIM SAW UNSEEN: 10 448
THEN STIL AT HELS DARK THRESHOLD TO HAVE SATE WATCH, 10 594
DESOLATE WHERE SHE SATE, APPROACHING NIGH, 10 864
BY THE WATERS OF LIFE, WHERE ERE THEY SATE 11 79
THE PERSIAN IN ECBATAN SATE, OR SINCE 11 393

SATED
SATED AT LENGTH, ERE LONG I MIGHT PERCEAVE 9 598

SATIATE
OR SATIATE FURY YIELD IT FROM OUR FOE. 1 179
SATIATE WITH GENIAL MOISTURE, WHEN GOD SAID 7 282
OF SWEET REPAST; THEY SATIATE, AND SOON FILL, 8 214
THEE SATIATE, TO SHORT ABSENCE I COULD YIELD. 9 248
AND KNEW NOT EATING DEATH: SATIATE AT LENGTH, 9 792

SATIETIE
IMBU'D, BRING TO THIR SWEETNESS NO SATIETIE. 8 216

SATISFACTION
THE RIGID SATISFACTION, DEATH FOR DEATH. 3 212
IN THIS HIS SATISFACTION; SO HE DIES, 12 419

SATISFI'D
NOT MIND US NOT OFFENDING, SATISFI'D 2 212
HOW FULLY HAST THOU SATISFI'D MEE, PURE 8 180
SATISFI'D NEVER; THAT WERE TO EXTEND 10 804
RELIGION SATISFI'D; TRUTH SHALL RETIRE 12 535

SATISFIE
SHALL SATISFIE FOR MAN, BE JUDG'D AND DIE, 3 295
TO SATISFIE THE SHARP DESIRE I HAD 9 584
IN PUNISHT MAN, TO SATISFIE HIS RIGOUR 10 803
BE FORC'D TO SATISFIE HIS RAV'NOUS MAW. 10 991

SATISFIED
THEM FULLY SATISFIED, AND THEE APPEASE. 10 79

SATST
DOVE-LIKE SATST BROODING ON THE VAST ABYSS 1 21
WHY SATST THOU LIKE AN ENEMIE IN WAITE 4 825

SATURN
BY YOUNGER SATURN, HE FROM MIGHTIER JOVE 1 512
OF DORIC LAND; OR WHO WITH SATURN OLD 1 519
OF HIGH OLYMPUS, THENCE BY SATURN DRIV'N 10 583

SAUGHT
BUT SELF-DESTRUCTION THEREFORE SAUGHT, REFUTES 10 1016
EV'N TO THE SEAT OF GOD. FOR SINCE I SAUGHT 11 148

SAVAGE
NOW TO TH' ASCENT OF THAT STEEP SAVAGE HILL 4 172
TO RAPTURE, TILL THE SAVAGE CLAMOR DROUND 7 36
IN SOLITUDE LIVE SAVAGE, IN SOME GLADE 9 1085

SAV'D
MAN SHALL NOT QUITE BE LOST, BUT SAV'D WHO WILL, 3 173

SAVE
SAVE WHAT THE GLIMMERING OF THESE LIVID FLAMES 1 182
SAVE HE WHO REIGNS ABOVE, NONE CAN RESIST. 2 814
MANS MORTAL CRIME, AND JUST TH' UNJUST TO SAVE, 3 215
THEE FROM MY BOSOM AND RIGHT HAND, TO SAVE, 3 279
GOD-LIKE FRUITION, QUITTED ALL TO SAVE 3 307
SAVE ON THAT SIDE WHICH FROM THE WALL OF HEAV'N 3 427
WILL SAVE US TRIAL WHAT THE LEAST CAN DOE 4 855
THE COOL, THE SILENT, SAVE WHERE SILENCE YIELDS 5 39
SAVE WHAT BY FRUGAL STORING FIRMNESS GAINS 5 324
UNDECKT, SAVE WITH HER SELF MORE LOVELY FAIR 5 380
FANND WITH COOLE WINDS, SAVE THOSE WHO IN THIR COURSE 5 655
WHOM FLED WE THOUGHT, WILL SAVE US LONG PURSUIT 6 538

SAVE (CONTINUED)

SAVE WHAT SIN HATH IMPAIRD, WHICH YET HATH WROUGHT 6 691
TO SAVE APPEARANCES, HOW GIRD THE SPHEAR 8 82
OR SAVE THE SUN HIS LABOUR, AND THAT SWIFT 8 133
SAVE WITH THE CREATURES WHICH I MADE, AND THOSE 8 409
SAVE WHAT IS IN DESTROYING, OTHER JOY 9 478
TO SAVE HIMSELF AND HOUSHOLD FROM AMIDST 11 820
SAVE WHEN THEY JOURNIE, AND AT LENGTH THEY COME, 12 258
SAVE BY THOSE SHADOWIE EXPIATIONS WEAK, 12 291
TO SAVE THEM, NOT THIR OWN, THOUGH LEGAL WORKS. 12 410

SAVES

THEM IN HIS ANGER, WHOM HIS ANGER SAVES 2 158
FROM WHOM AS OFT HE SAVES THEM PENITENT 12 319

SAVIOUR

HAIL SON OF GOD, SAVIOUR OF MEN, THY NAME 3 412
SO JUDG'D HE MAN, BOTH JUDGE AND SAVIOUR SENT, 10 209
WHICH HEE, WHO COMES THY SAVIOUR, SHALL RECURE, 12 393
NOW AMPLIER KNOWN THY SAVIOUR AND THY LORD, 12 544

SAVORIE

WHEN FROM THE BOUGHES A SAVORIE ODOUR BLOW'N, 9 579
SO SAVORIE OF THAT FRUIT, WHICH WITH DESIRE, 9 741

SAVOUR

SINCE TO EACH MEANING SAVOUR ME APPLY, 9 1019
THE SAVOUR OF DEATH FROM ALL THINGS THERE THAT LIVE: 10 269
FRUITS OF MORE PLEASING SAVOUR FROM THY SEED 11 26

SAVOURIE

THE SAVOURIE PULP THEY CHEW, AND IN THE RINDE 4 335
WHICH HE HAD PLUCKT; THE PLEASANT SAVOURIE SMELL 5 84
FOR DINNER SAVOURIE FRUITS, OF TASTE TO PLEASE 5 304

SAW

EZEKIEL SAW, WHEN BY THE VISION LED 1 455
I KNOW THEE NOT, NOR EVER SAW TILL NOW 2 744
I SAW AND HEARD, FOR SUCH A NUMEROUS HOST 2 993
THE STAIRS WERE SUCH AS WHEREON JACOB SAW 3 510
THROUGH HIS GLAZ'D OPTIC TUBE YET NEVER SAW. 3 590
SAW WITHIN KENN A GLORIOUS ANGEL STAND, 3 622
THE SAME WHOM JOHN SAW ALSO IN THE SUN; 3 623
I SAW WHEN AT HIS WORD THE FORMLESS MASS, 3 708
O FOR THAT WARNING VOICE, WHICH HE WHO SAW 4 1
SAW HIM DISFIGUR'D, MORE THEN COULD BEFALL 4 127
ON TH' OTHER SIDE: WHICH WHEN TH' ARCH-FELLON SAW 4 179
SAW UNDELIGHTED ALL DELIGHT, ALL KIND 4 286
AND FELT HOW AWFUL GOODNESS IS, AND SAW 4 847
VERTUE IN HER SHAPE HOW LOVLY, SAW, AND PIN'D 4 848
WHO DWELL IN HEAV'N, WHOSE EXCELLENCE HE SAW 5 456
WONDER NOT THEN, WHAT GOD FOR YOU SAW GOOD 5 491
NIGHTLY BEFORE HIM, SAW WITHOUT THIR LIGHT 5 714
REBELLION RISING, SAW IN WHOM, HOW SPRED 5 715
DOCTRIN WHICH WE WOULD KNOW WHENCE LEARNT: WHO SAW 5 856
SAW WHERE THE SWORD OF MICHAEL SMOTE, AND FELL'D 6 250
WIDE THE CELESTIAL SOILE, AND SAW BENEATH 6 510
WHEN COMING TOWARDS THEM SO DREAD THEY SAW 6 648
THEY SAW THEM WHELM'D, AND ALL THIR CONFIDENCE 6 651
THIS SAW HIS HAPLESS FOES BUT STOOD OBDUR'D, 6 785
HELL HEARD TH' UNSUFFERABLE NOISE, HELL SAW 6 867
SOJOURN'D THE WHILE. GOD SAW THE LIGHT WAS GOOD; 7 249
AND SAW THAT IT WAS GOOD, AND SAID, LET TH' EARTH 7 309
ON THE GREEN STEMM; GOD SAW THAT IT WAS GOOD. 7 337
AND LIGHT FROM DARKNESS TO DIVIDE. GOD SAW, 7 352
AND SAW THAT IT WAS GOOD, AND BLESS'D THEM, SAYING, 7 395
AND GRACE THAT WON WHO SAW TO WISH HER STAY, 8 43
STOOD ON MY FEET; ABOUT ME ROUND I SAW 8 261
WHAT E'RE I SAW. THOU SUN, SAID I, FAIRE LIGHT, 8 273
TELL, IF YE SAW, HOW CAME I THUS, HOW HERE? 8 277
PLANTED, WITH WALKS, AND BOWERS, THAT WHAT I SAW 8 305
ABSTRACT AS IN A TRANSE METHOUGHT I SAW, 8 462
THOUGH SLEEPING, WHERE I LAY, AND SAW THE SHAPE 8 463
SUCH AS I SAW HER IN MY DREAM, ADORND 8 482
ALL OTHER BEASTS THAT SAW, WITH LIKE DESIRE 9 592
WHICH WHEN SHE SAW, THUS TO HER GUIDE SHE SPAKE. 9 646
I SAW THEE FIRST AND WEDDED THEE, ADORN'D 9 1030
SAW SATAN FALL LIKE LIGHTNING DOWN FROM HEAV'N, 10 184
TO OBSERVE THE SEQUEL, SAW HIS GUILEFUL ACT 10 334
UPON HER HUSBAND, SAW THIR SHAME THAT SOUGHT 10 336
VAIN COVERTURES; BUT WHEN HE SAW DESCEND 10 337
HE SATE, AND ROUND ABOUT HIM SAW UNSEEN: 10 448
THEY SAW, BUT OTHER SIGHT INSTEAD, A CROWD 10 538
AND HORRID SYMPATHIE; FOR WHAT THEY SAW, 10 540
THE GROWING MISERIES, WHICH ADAM SAW 10 715
AS HOW WITH PECCANT ANGELS LATE THEY SAW; 11 70
METHOUGHT I SAW HIM PLACABLE AND MILD, 11 151
JACOB IN MAHANAIM, WHERE HE SAW 11 214
THE WORLD: IN SPIRIT PERHAPS HE ALSO SAW 11 406
HE LOOKD AND SAW A SPACIOUS PLAINE, WHEREON 11 556
HE LOOKD AND SAW WIDE TERRITORIE SPRED 11 638
HE LOOK'D, AND SAW THE FACE OF THINGS QUITE CHANG'D, 11 712
BUT ALL IN VAIN: WHICH WHEN HE SAW, HE CEAS'D 11 726
HE LOOKD, AND SAW THE ARK HULL ON THE FLOUD, 11 840
GRIEV'D AT HIS HEART, WHEN LOOKING DOWN HE SAW 11 887

SAW'ST

AND NO SUCH COMPANIE AS THEN THOU SAW'ST 8 446
SOME, AS THOU SAW'ST, BY VIOLENT STROKE SHALL DIE, 11 471
OF THOSE ILL MATED MARRIAGES THOU SAW'ST: 11 684
TO THAT PROUD CITIE, WHOSE HIGH WALLS THOU SAW'ST 12 342

SAWST

SURROUND ME, AS THOU SAWST, HOURLY CONCEIV'D 2 796
THOSE TENTS THOU SAWST SO PLEASANT, WERE THE TENTS 11 607
FOR THAT FAIR FEMAL TROOP THOU SAWST, THAT SEEMD 11 614
DID, AS THOU SAWST, RECEAVE, TO WALK WITH GOD 11 707
TO WHOM THUS MICHAEL. THOSE WHOM LAST THOU SAWST 11 787

SAY

SAY FIRST, FOR HEAV'N HIDES NOTHING FROM THY VIEW 1 27
NOR THE DEEP TRACT OF HELL, SAY FIRST WHAT CAUSE 1 28
SAY, MUSE, THIR NAMES THEN KNOWN, WHO FIRST, WHO LAST, 1 376
SAY THEY WHO COUNSEL WARR, WE ARE DECREED, 2 160
SAY HEAV'NLY POWERS, WHERE SHALL WE FIND SUCH LOVE, 3 213
BUT SAY I COULD REPENT AND COULD OBTAINE 4 93
THE REST IS TRUE, THEY FOUND ME WHERE THEY SAY; 4 900
TO SAY AND STRAIT UNSAY, PRETENDING FIRST 4 947
BY STEPS WE MAY ASCEND TO GOD. BUT SAY, 5 512
SAY GODDESS, WHAT ENSU'D WHEN RAPHAEL, 7 40
AUGHT, NOT SURPASSING HUMAN MEASURE, SAY. 7 640
ON MAN HIS EQUAL LOVE: SAY THEREFORE ON; 8 228
THE MORE DESIRABLE, OR TO SAY ALL, 8 505
HER OWN, THAT WHAT SHE WILLS TO DO OR SAY, 8 549
REDOUBLE THEN THIS MIRACLE, AND SAY, 9 562
SAY, FOR SUCH WONDER CLAIMS ATTENTION DUE. 9 566
BUT SAY, WHERE GROWN THE TREE, FROM HENCE HOW FAR? 9 617
WHICH OFT, THEY SAY, SOME EVIL SPIRIT ATTENDS 9 638
TRIUMPH AND SAY; FICKLE THEIR STATE WHOM GOD 9 948
SAY WOMAN, WHAT IS THIS WHICH THOU HAST DONE? 10 158
YEARLY ENJOYND, SOME SAY, TO UNDERGO 10 575
SOME SAY HE BID HIS ANGELS TURNE ASCANSE 10 668
OBLIQUE THE CENTRIC GLOBE: SOM SAY THE SUN 10 671
THY JUSTICE SEEMS; YET TO SAY TRUTH, TOO LATE, 10 755
NOT TO TH' EXTENT OF THIR OWN SPHEARE. BUT SAY 10 808
BUT SAY, WHAT MEAN THOSE COLOURD STREAKS IN HEAVN, 11 879
EXPECT WITH MORTAL PAINE: SAY WHERE AND WHEN 12 384
BUT SAY, IF OUR DELIVERER UP TO HEAV'N 12 479

SAYING

NONE SHALL PARTAKE WITH ME. THUS SAYING ROSE 2 466
THUS SAYING, FROM HER SIDE THE FATAL KEY, 2 871
SO SAYING, HIS PROUD STEP HE SCORNFUL TURN'D, 4 536
SO SAYING, ON HE LED HIS RADIANT FILES, 4 797
SO SAYING, HE DREW NIGH, AND TO ME HELD, 5 82
SO SAYING, WITH DISPATCHFUL LOOKS IN HASTE 5 331
SO SAYING, A NOBLE STROKE HE LIFTED HIGH, 6 189
AND SAW THAT IT WAS GOOD, AND BLESS'D THEM, SAYING, 7 395
SO SAYING, BY THE HAND HE TOOK ME RAIS'D, 8 300
SO SAYING, HE AROSE; WHOM ADAM THUS 8 644
SO SAYING, THROUGH EACH THICKET DANCK OR DRIE, 9 179
THUS SAYING, FROM HER HUSBANDS HAND HER HAND 9 385
SO SAYING, HER RASH HAND IN EVIL HOUR 9 780
SO SAYING, FROM THE TREE HER STEP SHE TURND, 9 834
SO SAYING, SHE EMBRAC'D HIM, AND FOR JOY 9 990
THUS SAYING, FROM HIS RADIANT SEAT HE ROSE 10 85
I CHARG'D THEE, SAYING: THOU SHALT NOT EATE THEREOF, 10 200
SO SAYING, WITH DELIGHT HE SNUFF'D THE SMELL 10 272
SO SAYING HE DISMISS'D THEM, THEY WITH SPEED 10 410

SAYLING

WHO AFTER CAME FROM EARTH, SAYLING ARRIV'D, 3 520

SCAL'D

THAT SCAL'D BY STEPS OF GOLD TO HEAV'N GATE 3 541

SCALDING

YET PARCHT WITH SCALDING THURST AND HUNGER FIERCE, 10 556

SCALE

THE WAY SEEMS DIFFICULT AND STEEP TO SCALE 2 71
TO TH' OCEAN ILES, AND IN TH' ASCENDING SCALE 4 354
HIS MOUNTED SCALE ALOFT: NOR MORE; BUT FLED 4 1014
MANS NOURISHMENT, BY GRADUAL SCALE SUBLIM'D 5 483
OUR KNOWLEDGE, AND THE SCALE OF NATURE SET 5 509
CONFLICTING FIRE: LONG TIME IN EEVEN SCALE 6 245
IN REASON, AND IS JUDICIOUS, IS THE SCALE 8 591
IN EEVN SCALE. BUT FALL'N HE IS, AND NOW 10 47
LAY SEIGE, ENCAMPT; BY BATTERIE, SCALE, AND MINE, 11 656

SCALES

HUNG FORTH IN HEAV'N HIS GOLDEN SCALES, YET SEEN 4 997
OF FISH THAT WITH THIR FINNS AND SHINING SCALES 7 401
BY LEO AND THE VIRGIN AND THE SCALES, 10 676

SCALIE

THE RIVER HORSE AND SCALIE CROCODILE. 7 474

SCALY

BUT ENDED FOUL IN MANY A SCALY FOULD 2 651

SCANDAL
EVEN TO THAT HILL OF SCANDAL, BY THE GROVE 1 416

SCANN'D
HIS SECRETS TO BE SCANN'D BY THEM WHO OUGHT 8 74

SCANT
THAT MOCK OUR SCANT MANURING, AND REQUIRE 4 628

SCAP'D
THE COMING OF THIR SECRET FOE, AND SCAP'D 4 7
HAPLY SO SCAP'D HIS MORTAL SNARE; FOR NOW 4 8
WHILE YET THE PATRIARK LIV'D, WHO SCAP'D THE FLOOD, 12 117

SCAPE
RATHER THEN HUMAN. NOR DID ISRAEL SCAPE 1 482
TO HAVE BUILT IN HEAV'N HIGH TOWRS; NOR DID HE SCAPE 1 749
IF THENCE HE SCAPE INTO WHAT EVER WORLD, 2 442
HOWEVER, AND TO SCAPE HIS PUNISHMENT. 4 911
WAS KNOWN IN HEAV'N; FOR WHAT CAN SCAPE THE EYE 10 5
SHALL SCAPE HIS PUNISHMENT ORDAIN'D, AND WEE 10 1039

SCAP'T
BOTH GLORYING TO HAVE SCAP'T THE STYGIAN FLOOD 1 239
AND NOW RETURNS HIM FROM HIS PRISON SCAP'T, 4 906
SATAN FROM HELL SCAP'T THROUGH THE DARKSOM GULF 5 225

SCARCE
HE SCARCE HAD CEAS'T WHEN THE SUPERIOUR FIEND 1 283
AND HANDS INNUMERABLE SCARCE PERFORM. 1 699
HE SCARCE HAD FINISHT, WHEN SUCH MURMUR FILLD 2 284
IN WHIRLWIND; HELL SCARCE HOLDS THE WILDE UPROAR. 2 541
DISLODGING FROM A REGION SCARCE OF PREY 3 433
SCARCE THUS AT LENGTH FAILD SPEECH RECOVERD SAD. 4 357
HE SCARCE HAD ENDED, WHEN THOSE TWO APPROACHD 4 874
OF DAY-SPRING, AND THE SUN, WHO SCARCE UP RISEN 5 139
AND WE HAVE YET LARGE DAY, FOR SCARCE THE SUN 5 558
HATH FINISHT HALF HIS JOURNEY, AND SCARCE BEGINS 5 559
SO SCOFFING IN AMBIGUOUS WORDS HE SCARCE, 6 568
YET SCARCE ALLAY'D STILL EYES THE CURRENT STREAME, 7 67
HE SCARCE HAD SAID, WHEN THE BARE EARTH, TILL THEN 7 313
HER BOSOM SMELLING SWEET: AND THESE SCARCE BLOWN, 7 319
ONELY TO SHINE, YET SCARCE TO CONTRIBUTE 8 155
OF EARTH BEFORE SCARCE PLEASANT SEEMD. EACH TREE 8 306
SCARCE TOLLERABLE, AND FROM THE NORTH TO CALL 10 654
AND SCARCE RECOVERING WORDS HIS PLAINT RENEW'D. 11 499
THIR BOOTIE; SCARCE WITH LIFE THE SHEPHERDS FLYE, 11 650
AND SCARCE TO TH' ANGEL UTTERDST THUS THY PLAINT. 11 762

SCARR
TO HEAL THE SCARR OF THESE CORROSIVE FIRES 2 401

SCARS
DEEP SCARS OF THUNDER HAD INTRENCHT, AND CARE 1 601

SCARSE
DEFENSIVE SCARSE, OR WITH PALE FEAR SURPRIS'D, 6 393
BORE UP HIS BRANCHING HEAD: SCARSE FROM HIS MOULD 7 470
SHE SCARSE HAD SAID, THOUGH BRIEF, WHEN NOW MORE BOLD 9 664
SCARSE FROM THE TREE RETURNING; IN HER HAND 9 850
WHILE YET WE LIVE, SCARSE ONE SHORT HOUR PERHAPS, 10 923

SCATH'D
HATH SCATH'D THE FORREST OAKS, OR MOUNTAIN PINES, 1 613

SCATTER'D
WITH SCATTER'D ARMS AND ENSIGNS, TILL ANON 1 325

SCATTERD
HIGH OVERARCH'T IMBOWR; OR SCATTERD SEDGE 1 304
RECOVERING, AND HIS SCATTERD SPIRITS RETURND, 11 294
WHERE CATTLE PASTUR'D LATE, NOW SCATTERD LIES 11 653

SCENE
A SILVAN SCENE, AND AS THE RANKS ASCEND 4 140
BUT NOW PREPARE THEE FOR ANOTHER SCENE. 11 637

SCENT
POWERFUL PERSWADERS, QUICK'ND AT THE SCENT 9 587

SCEPTER
HIS EMPIRE, AND WITH IRON SCEPTER RULE 2 327
WEAKNING THE SCEPTER OF OLD NIGHT: FIRST HELL 2 1002
THEN THOU THY REGAL SCEPTER SHALT LAY BY, 3 339
FOR REGAL SCEPTER THEN NO MORE SHALL NEED, 3 340
WITH DIADEM AND SCEPTER HIGH ADVANC'D 4 90
WITH REGAL SCEPTER, EVERY SOULE IN HEAV'N 5 816
THAT GOLDEN SCEPTER WHICH THOU DIDST REJECT 5 886
SCEPTER AND POWER, THY GIVING, I ASSUME, 6 730
SO SAID, HE O'RE HIS SCEPTER BOWING, ROSE 6 746
THE SCEPTER, AND REGARD NOT DAVIDS SONS, 12 357

SCEPTER'D
WHERE SCEPTER'D ANGELS HELD THIR RESIDENCE, 1 734
HE CEAS'D, AND NEXT HIM MOLOC, SCEPTER'D KING 2 43
IN OTHER PART THE SCEPTER'D HARALDS CALL 11 660

SCIENCE
MOTHER OF SCIENCE, NOW I FEEL THY POWER 9 680

SCIENTIAL
INTO THE PLANT SCIENTIAL SAP, DERIV'D 9 837

SCIPIO
SCIPIO THE HIGHTH OF ROME. WITH TRACT OBLIQUE 9 510

SCOFFING
SO SCOFFING IN AMBIGUOUS WORDS HE SCARCE, 6 568
STOOD SCOFFING, HIGHTHN'D IN THIR THOUGHTS BEYOND 6 629

SCOOP
STILL AS THEY THIRSTED SCOOP THE BRIMMING STREAM; 4 336

SCOPE
AND UTTER DISSOLUTION, AS THE SCOPE 2 127

SCORCHING
AVOIDED PINCHING COLD AND SCORCHING HEATE? 10 691

SCORCHT
OF RAMIEL SCORCHT AND BLASTED OVERTHREW. 6 372

SCORN
LET US NOT SLIP TH' OCCASION, WHETHER SCORN, 1 178
THRICE HE ASSAYD, AND THRICE IN SPIGHT OF SCORN, 1 619
HELL-DOOM'D, AND BREATH'ST DEFIANCE HERE AND SCORN 2 697
THEY WHO NEGLECT AND SCORN, SHALL NEVER TASTE; 3 199
KNOW YE NOT THEN SAID SATAN, FILL'D WITH SCORN, 4 827
TO WHOM THUS ZEPHON, ANSWERING SCORN WITH SCORN. 4 834
THUS HE IN SCORN. THE WARLIKE ANGEL MOV'D, 4 902
LONG WAY THROUGH HOSTILE SCORN, WHICH HE SUSTEIND 5 904
AND WITH RETORTED SCORN HIS BACK HE TURN'D 5 906
SO EASIE, AND OF HIS THUNDER MADE A SCORN, 6 632
OF PUBLIC SCORN; HE WONDERD, BUT NOT LONG 10 509
OFFENDED; FEARLESS OF REPROACH AND SCORN, 11 811
WITH ALL HIS SACRED THINGS, A SCORN AND PREY 12 341

SCORN'D
JUSTICE SHALL NOT RETURN AS BOUNTIE SCORN'D. 10 54
THAT SCORN'D HIS INDIGNATION; THROUGH THE GATE, 10 418

SCORND
THEN SCORND THOU DIDST DEPART, AND TO SUBDUE 6 40

SCORNE
AND SEALE THEE SO, AS HENCEFORTH NOT TO SCORNE 4 966
AGAINST TEMPTATION: THOU THY SELF WITH SCORNE 9 299
MATTER OF SCORNE, NOT TO BE GIVEN THE FOE, 9 951
WHEREWITH TO SCORNE THE EARTH: BUT THAT FALSE FRUIT 9 1011

SCORNFUL
SO SAYING, HIS PROUD STEP HE SCORNFUL TURN'D, 4 536
WHOM THE GRAND FOE WITH SCORNFUL EYE ASKANCE 6 149
TO GRATIFIE MY SCORNFUL ENEMIES, 10 625

SCORNING
SCORNING SURPRIZE. OR COULD WE BREAK OUR WAY 2 134

SCORPION
BETWIXT ASTREA AND THE SCORPION SIGNE, 4 998
BETWIXT THE CENTAURE AND THE SCORPION STEARING 10 328
SCORPION AND ASP, AND AMPHISBAENA DIRE, 10 524

SCORPIONS
LEAST WITH A WHIP OF SCORPIONS I PURSUE 2 701

SCOURE
LOOKD ROUND, AND SCOUTS EACH COAST LIGHT-ARMED SCOURE, 6 529

SCOURG'D
AND SCOURG'D WITH MANY A STROAK TH' INDIGNANT WAVES. 10 311

SCOURGE
THE VASSALS OF HIS ANGER, WHEN THE SCOURGE 2 90
SEAVENFOLD, AND SCOURGE THAT WISDOM BACK TO HELL, 4 914

SCOURS
HE SCOURS THE RIGHT HAND COAST, SOM TIMES THE LEFT, 2 633

SCOUT
SCOUT FARR AND WIDE INTO THE REALM OF NIGHT, 2 133
OF ALL THIS WORLD AT ONCE. AS WHEN A SCOUT 3 543

SCOUTS
LOOKD ROUND, AND SCOUTS EACH COAST LIGHT-ARMED SCOURE, 6 529

SCOWLS
SCOWLS ORE THE DARK'ND LANTSKIP SNOW, OR SHOWRE; 2 491

SCRIBL'D
WITH CENTRIC AND ECCENTRIC SCRIBL'D O'RE, 8 83

SCROWLE
PART GOOD, PART BAD, OF BAD THE LONGER SCROWLE, . 12 336

SCRUPL'D
WITH LIBERAL HAND: HE SCRUPL'D NOT TO EAT 9 997

SCULLES
GLIDE UNDER THE GREEN WAVE, IN SCULLES THAT OFT . 7 402

SCULPTURES
CORNICE OR FREEZE, WITH BOSSY SCULPTURES GRAV'N, . 1 716

SCUM'D
SEVERING EACH KIND, AND SCUM'D THE BULLION DROSS: 1 704

SCURFF
SHON WITH A GLOSSIE SCURFF, UNDOUBTED SIGN 1 672

SCYLLA
VEX'D SCYLLA BATHING IN THE SEA THAT PARTS 2 660

SDEIND
I SDEIND SUBJECTION, AND THOUGHT ONE STEP HIGHER . 4 50

SEA
INVESTS THE SEA, AND WISHED MORN DELAYES: 1 208
OF THAT INFLAMED SEA, HE STOOD AND CALL'D . . . 1 300
HATH VEXT THE RED-SEA COAST, WHOSE WAVES ORETHREW 1 306
RAN PURPLE TO THE SEA, SUPPOS'D WITH BLOOD 1 451
DAGON HIS NAME, SEA MONSTER, UPWARD MAN 1 462
HAD ROUS'D THE SEA, NOW WITH HOARSE CADENCE LULL . 2 287
INTO TH' EUBOIC SEA. OTHERS MORE MILDE, . . . 2 546
AS WHEN FARR OFF AT SEA A FLEET DESCRI'D . . . 2 636
VEX'D SCYLLA BATHING IN THE SEA THAT PARTS . . . 2 660
OF NEITHER SEA, NOR SHORE, NOR AIR, NOR FIRE, . . 2 912
QUENCHT IN A BOGGIE SYRTIS, NEITHER SEA, . . . 2 939
BUT GLAD THAT NOW HIS SEA SHOULD FIND A SHORE, . 2 1011
PAVEMENT THAT LIKE A SEA OF JASPER SHON 3 363
SO ON THIS WINDIE SEA OF LAND, THE FIEND . . . 3 440
PLATO'S ELYSIUM, LEAP'D INTO THE SEA, . . . 3 472
VIEWLESS, AND UNDERNEATH A BRIGHT SEA FLOW'D . . 3 518
IN VARIOUS SHAPES OLD PROTEUS FROM THE SEA, . . 3 604
O'RE SEA AND LAND; HIM SATAN THUS ACCOSTES; . . 3 653
MOZAMBIC, OFF AT SEA NORTH-EAST WINDES BLOW . . 4 161
EARTH, AIRE, AND SEA. THEN LET US NOT THINK HARD 4 432
THE GROSSER FEEDS THE PURER, EARTH THE SEA, . . 5 416
EARTH AND THE SEA FEED AIR, THE AIR THOSE FIRES . 5 417
AND ALL THE SEA, FROM ONE ENTIRE GLOBOSE . . . 5 753
OUTRAGEOUS AS A SEA, DARK, WASTEFUL, WILDE, . . 7 212
BANK THE MID SEA: PART SINGLE OR WITH MATE . . . 7 403
GRAZE THE SEA WEED THIR PASTURE, AND THROUGH GROVES 7 404
DRAWS IN, AND AT HIS TRUNCK SPOUTS OUT A SEA. . . 7 416
AS PLANTS: AMBIGUOUS BETWEEN SEA AND LAND . . . 7 473
OVER THE FISH AND FOWLE OF SEA AND AIRE, . . . 7 521
OVER FISH OF THE SEA, AND FOWLE OF THE AIRE, . . 7 533
ON THE CLEER HYALINE, THE GLASSIE SEA; 7 619
OVER HIS WORKS, ON EARTH, IN SEA, OR AIR, . . . 7 629
OR LIVE IN SEA, OR AIRE, BEAST, FISH, AND FOWLE. . 8 341
WHERE TO LIE HID; SEA HE HAD SEARCHT AND LAND . . 9 76
NOW LAND, NOW SEA, AND SHORES WITH FORREST CROWND, 9 117
SOLID OR SLIMIE, AS IN RAGING SEA 10 286
UPON THE CRONIAN SEA, TOGETHER DRIVE 10 290
CAME TO THE SEA, AND OVER HELLESPONT 10 309
SEA, AIRE, AND SHOAR, THE THUNDER WHEN TO ROWLE . 10 666
LIKE CHANGE ON SEA AND LAND, SIDERAL BLAST, . . 10 693
AND IN A TROUBL'D SEA OF PASSION TOST, ... 10 718
LAND, SEA, AND AIRE, AND EVERY KINDE THAT LIVES, . 11 337
DEEP UNDER WATER ROULD; SEA COVER'D SEA, . . . 11 749
SEA WITHOUT SHOAR; AND IN THIR PALACES 11 750
TOWARDS THE RETREATING SEA THIR FURIOUS TYDE. . . 11 854
THE EARTH AGAIN BY FLOOD, NOR LET THE SEA . . . 11 893
FROM HERMON EAST TO THE GREAT WESTERN SEA, . . . 12 141
MOUNT HERMON, YONDER SEA, EACH PLACE BEHOLD . . 12 142
INTO THE SEA: TO SOJOURN IN THAT LAND 12 159
PURSUING WHOM HE LATE DISMISSD, THE SEA 12 195
OVER THE SEA; THE SEA HIS ROD OBEYS; 12 212
OR WORKS OF GOD IN HEAV'N, AIRE, EARTH, OR SEA, . 12 579

SEA-BEAST
BY ANCIENT TARSUS HELD, OR THAT SEA-BEAST 1 200

SEA-FARING
SEA-FARING MEN OREWATCHT, WHOSE BARK BY CHANCE . 2 288

SEAL
FOR EVER, AND SEAL UP HIS RAVENOUS JAWES. 10 637

SEALE
AND SEALE THEE SO, AS HENCEFORTH NOT TO SCORNE . 4 966
IN JOINTED ARMOUR WATCH: ON SMOOTH THE SEALE, . . 7 409
TOOK LARGELY, OF THIR MUTUAL GUILT THE SEALE, . . 9 1043

SEALES
THE HAUNT OF SEALES AND ORCS, AND SEA-MEWS CLANG. 11 835

SEA-MEN
DEEMING SOME ISLAND, OFT, AS SEA-MEN TELL, ... 1 205

SEA-MEWS
THE HAUNT OF SEALES AND ORCS, AND SEA-MEWS CLANG. 11 835

SEA-MONSTERS
WHERE LUXURIE LATE REIGN'D, SEA-MONSTERS WHELP'D . 11 751

SEARCH
IN SEARCH OF THIS NEW WORLD, WHOM SHALL WE FIND . 2 403
TO SEARCH WITH WANDRING QUEST A PLACE FORETOLD . 2 830
BUT FIRST WITH NARROW SEARCH I MUST WALK ROUND . 4 528
SEARCH THROUGH THIS GARDEN, LEAVE UNSEARCHT NO NOOK, ... 4 789
IN SEARCH OF WHOM THEY SOUGHT: HIM THERE THEY FOUND 4 799
DUE SEARCH AND CONSULTATION WILL DISCLOSE. . . . 6 445
ANOUGH IS LEFT BESIDES TO SEARCH AND KNOW. . . . 7 125
TO ASK OR SEARCH I BLAME THEE NOT, FOR HEAV'N . . 8 66
WITH NARROW SEARCH; AND WITH INSPECTION DEEP . . 9 83
HIS MIDNIGHT SEARCH, WHERE SOONEST HE MIGHT FINDE 9 181
EACH HOUR THEIR GREAT ADVENTURER FROM THE SEARCH . 10 440

SEARCHT
WHERE TO LIE HID; SEA HE HAD SEARCHT AND LAND . . 9 76
WHAT OFT MY STEDDIEST THOUGHTS HAVE SEARCHT IN VAIN, ... 12 377

SEA'S
THIR AIERIE CARAVAN HIGH OVER SEA'S 7 428

SEAS
ANDROMEDA FARR OFF ATLANTIC SEAS 3 559
OF CONGREGATED WATERS HE CALL'D SEAS: 7 308
BE FRUITFUL, MULTIPLY, AND IN THE SEAS 7 396
FORTHWITH THE SOUNDS AND SEAS, EACH CREEK AND BAY 7 399
SUNG HALLELUIA, AS THE SOUND OF SEAS, ... 10 642
AND THRASCIAS REND THE WOODS AND SEAS UPTURN; . 10 700

SEASON
NONE SECONDED, AS OUT OF SEASON JUDG'D, ... 5 850
THE SEASON, PRIME FOR SWEETEST SENTS AND AIRES: . 9 200
AND SEASON HIM THY LAST AND SWEETEST PREY. . . . 10 609
TO MEEK SUBMISSION: THOU AT SEASON FIT 12 597

SEASONS
SEASONS RETURN, BUT NOT TO ME RETURNS 3 41
ALL SEASONS AND THIR CHANGE, ALL PLEASE ALIKE. . 4 640
ALL SEASONS, RIPE FOR USE HANGS ON THE STALK; . . 5 323
FOR SEASONS, AND FOR DAYES, AND CIRCLING YEARS, . 7 342
INTELLIGENT OF SEASONS, AND SET FORTH 7 427
THIR SEASONS: AMONG THESE THE SEAT OF MEN, . . 7 623
HIS SEASONS, HOURS, OR DAYES, OR MONTHS, OR YEARES: 8 69
OF SEASONS TO EACH CLIME; ELSE HAD THE SPRING . . 10 678
TH' INCLEMENT SEASONS, RAIN, ICE, HAIL AND SNOW, . 10 1063

SEAT
RESTORE US, AND REGAIN THE BLISSFUL SEAT, ... 1 5
THE SEAT OF DESOLATION, VOYD OF LIGHT, ... 1 181
SAID THEN THE LOST ARCH-ANGEL, THIS THE SEAT . . 1 243
THIR SEATS LONG AFTER NEXT THE SEAT OF GOD, . . 1 383
HIM FOLLOW'D RIMMON, WHOSE DELIGHTFUL SEAT . . 1 467
SELF-RAIS'D, AND REPOSSESS THIR NATIVE SEAT? . . 1 634
BELUS OR SERAPIS THIR GODS, OR SEAT 1 720
UP TO OUR NATIVE SEAT: DESCENT AND FALL . . . 2 76
ERR NOT) ANOTHER WORLD, THE HAPPY SEAT . . . 2 347
NEERER OUR ANCIENT SEAT; PERHAPS IN VIEW . . . 2 394
SATAN WAS NOW AT HAND, AND FROM HIS SEAT . . . 2 674
AUDACIOUS, BUT THAT SEAT SOON FAILING, MEETS . . 2 931
OF LIVING SAPHIRE, ONCE HIS NATIVE SEAT; . . . 2 1050
JUST O'RE THE BLISSFUL SEAT OF PARADISE, . . . 3 527
TO PARADISE THE HAPPIE SEAT OF MAN, ... 3 632
HIS FIXED SEAT, OR FIXED SEAT HATH NONE, . . . 3 669
THAT PLACE IS EARTH THE SEAT OF MAN, THAT LIGHT . 3 724
A HAPPY RURAL SEAT OF VARIOUS VIEW; 4 247
LONG TO CONTINUE, AND THIS HIGH SEAT YOUR HEAV'N . 4 371
THEY CAME, AND SATAN TO HIS ROYAL SEAT 5 756
BEFORE THE SEAT SUPREAM; FROM WHENCE A VOICE . . 6 27
SIDELONG, HAD PUSH'T A MOUNTAIN FROM HIS SEAT . . 6 197
THOUGH NOT DESTROY, THIR HAPPIE NATIVE SEAT; . . 6 226
FROM ALL HER CONFINES. HEAV'N THE SEAT OF BLISS . 6 273
THIS INACCESSIBLE HIGH STRENGTH, THE SEAT . . . 7 141
SEEMD LIKE TO HEAV'N, A SEAT WHERE GODS MIGHT DWELL, ... 7 329
THIR SEASONS: AMONG THESE THE SEAT OF MEN, . . . 7 623
WITH LOWLINESS MAJESTIC FROM HER SEAT, ... 8 42
TO THE GARDEN OF BLISS, THY SEAT PREPAR'D. . . . 8 299
GREATNESS OF MIND AND NOBLENESS THIR SEAT . . . 8 557
THE THOUGHTS, AND HEART ENLARGES, HATH HIS SEAT . 8 590
MORE JUSTLY, SEAT WORTHIER OF GODS, AS BUILT . . 9 100
MAGNIFICENT THIS WORLD, AND EARTH HIS SEAT, . . 9 153
EARTH FELT THE WOUND, AND NATURE FROM HER SEAT . 9 782
THUS SAYING, FROM HIS RADIANT SEAT HE ROSE . . . 10 85
IN OTHER WORLDS, AND HAPPIER SEAT PROVIDES . . . 10 237
FROM HIS TRANSCENDENT SEAT THE SAINTS AMONG, . . 10 614
PRAYING, FOR FROM THE MERCIE-SEAT ABOVE 11 2
EV'N TO THE SEAT OF GOD. FOR SINCE I SAUGHT . . 11 148
CITY OF OLD OR MODERN FAME, THE SEAT 11 386
OF CAMBALU, SEAT OF CATHAIAN CAN 11 388
RICH MEXICO THE SEAT OF MOTEZUME, ... 11 407
AND CUSCO IN PERU, THE RICHER SEAT ; 11 408

SEAT (CONTINUED)
EEVN TO THE INMOST SEAT OF MENTAL SIGHT, 11 418
FROM THE HIGH NEIGHBOURING HILLS, WHICH WAS THIR SEAT, 11 575
A MERCIE-SEAT OF GOLD BETWEEN THE WINGS 12 253
HIS SEAT AT GODS RIGHT HAND, EXALTED HIGH 12 457
OF PARADISE, SO LATE THIR HAPPIE SEAT, 12 642

SEATE
OF PANDAEMONIUM, CITIE AND PROUD SEATE 10 424
PERHAPS THY CAPITAL SEATE, FROM WHENCE HAD SPRED 11 343

SEATED
THEY PLUCKT THE SEATED HILLS WITH ALL THIR LOAD, 6 644
OF HEAV'NS HIGH-SEATED TOP, TH' IMPEREAL THRONE 7 585

SEAT'S
A THOUSAND DEMY-GODS ON GOLDEN SEAT'S, 1 796

SEATS
THIR SEATS LONG AFTER NEXT THE SEAT OF GOD, 1 383
THIR TABLE WAS, AND MOSSIE SEATS HAD ROUND, 5 392
AND TOOK THIR SEATS; TILL FROM HIS THRONE SUPREAM 11 82

SEAVEN
SEE WHERE IT FLOWS, DISGORGING AT SEAVEN MOUTHES 12 158
SEAVEN LAMPS AS IN A ZODIAC REPRESENTING 12 255

SEAVENFOLD
SEAVENFOLD, AND SCOURGE THAT WISDOM BACK TO HELL, 4 914

SEAVENS
CAME SEAVENS, AND PAIRS, AND ENTERD IN, AS TAUGHT 11 735

SEAVENTIMES-WEDDED
HIS MARRIAGE WITH THE SEAVENTIMES-WEDDED MAID. 5 223

SEAV'N
TH' ARCH-ANGEL URIEL, ONE OF THE SEAV'N 3 648
URIEL, FOR THOU OF THOSE SEAV'N SPIRITS THAT STAND 3 654
LIKE DISTANT BREADTH TO TAURUS WITH THE SEAV'N 10 673

SEAV'NTH
NOW RESTING, BLESS'D AND HALLOWD THE SEAV'NTH DAY, 7 592

SECHEM
PITCHT ABOUT SECHEM, AND THE NEIGHBOURING PLAINE 12 136

SECOND
SLUC'D FROM THE LAKE, A SECOND MULTITUDE 1 702
AND TRUST THEMSELVES TO FEAR NO SECOND FATE: 2 17
TO SECOND, OR OPPOSE, OR UNDERTAKE 2 419
NO SECOND STROKE INTEND, AND SUCH A FROWN 2 713
AS FROM A SECOND ROOT SHALL BE RESTOR'D, 3 288
SECOND TO THEE, OFFERD HIMSELF TO DIE 3 409
TILL AT HIS SECOND BIDDING DARKNESS FLED, 3 712
THEN WHEN THE DRAGON, PUT TO SECOND ROUT, 4 3
LONG AFTER TO BLEST MARIE, SECOND EVE. 5 387
IN POSTURE TO DISPLODE THIR SECOND TIRE 6 605
SECOND OMNIPOTENCE, TWO DAYES ARE PAST, 6 684
AND MORNING CHORUS SUNG THE SECOND DAY. 7 275
SECOND TO ME OR LIKE, EQUAL MUCH LESS. 8 407
WITH SECOND THOUGHTS, REFORMING WHAT WAS OLD. 9 101
EQUIVALENT OR SECOND, WHICH COMPEL'D 9 609
IN PANGS, AND NATURE GAVE A SECOND GROAN, 9 1001
WHEN JESUS SON OF MARY SECOND EVE, 10 183
SECOND OF SATAN SPRUNG, ALL CONQUERING DEATH, 10 591
BY FAITH AND FAITHFUL WORKS, TO SECOND LIFE, 11 64
OUR SECOND ADAM IN THE WILDERNESS, 11 383
THE SECOND TIME RETURNING, IN HIS BILL 11 859
AND MAN AS FROM A SECOND STOCK PROCEED. 12 7
THIS SECOND SOURS OF MEN, WHILE YET BUT FEW; 12 13
OR FROM HEAV'N CLAMING SECOND SOVRANTIE; 12 35
RAISE HIM TO BE THE SECOND IN THAT REALME 12 162
THE SECOND, BOTH FOR PIETIE RENOWND 12 321

SECONDARIE
OF SECONDARIE HANDS, BY TASK TRANSFERD 5 854

SECONDED
AND SECONDED THY ELSE NOT DREADED SPEAR. 4 929
NONE SECONDED, AS OUT OF SEASON JUDG'D, 5 850
BY EVE, THOUGH ALL UNWEETING, SECONDED 10 335

SECRESIE
THOU IN THY SECRESIE ALTHOUGH ALONE, 8 427

SECRET
SING HEAV'NLY MUSE, THAT ON THE SECRET TOP 1 6
IN CLOSE RECESS AND SECRET CONCLAVE SAT 1 795
IN SECRET, RIDING THROUGH THE AIR SHE COMES 2 663
WITH ME IN SECRET, THAT MY WOMB CONCEIV'D 2 766
THEN THIS MORE SECRET NOW DESIGN'D, I HASTE 2 838
THAT I MAY FIND HIM, AND WITH SECRET GAZE, 3 671
THE COMING OF THIR SECRET FOE, AND SCAP'D 4 7
AWAK'NING, THUS TO HIM IN SECRET SPAKE. 5 672
SECRET THEY FINISH'D, AND IN ORDER SET, 6 522
AND GIV'ST ACCESS, THOUGH SECRET SHE RETIRE. 9 810

SECRET (CONTINUED)
AND I PERHAPS AM SECRET; HEAV'N IS HIGH, 9 811
ETERNAL FATHER FROM HIS SECRET CLOUD, 10 32
WITH SECRET AMITY THINGS OF LIKE KINDE 10 248
MY HEART, WHICH BY A SECRET HARMONIE 10 358

SECRETEST
BY SECRETEST CONVEYANCE. THOU MY SHADE 10 249

SECRETS
THE SECRETS OF THE HOARIE DEEP, A DARK 2 891
THE SECRETS OF YOUR REALM, BUT BY CONSTRAINT 2 972
THE SECRETS OF ANOTHER WORLD, PERHAPS 5 569
WHAT WEE, NOT TO EXPLORE THE SECRETS ASKE 7 95
HIS SECRETS TO BE SCANN'D BY THEM WHO OUGHT 8 74
THAT JEALOUS OF THIR SECRETS FIERCELY OPPOS'D 10 478
ALL SECRETS OF THE DEEP, ALL NATURES WORKS, 12 578

SECT
FROM ALL: MY SECT THOU SEEST, NOW LEARN TOO LATE 6 147

SECULAR
SECULAR POWER, THOUGH FEIGNING STILL TO ACT 12 517

SECUR'D
HAPPIE, BUT FOR SO HAPPIE ILL SECUR'D 4 370
TO TRAVEL WITH TOBIAS, AND SECUR'D 5 222

SECURE
HERE WE MAY REIGN SECURE, AND IN MY CHOYCE 1 261
MONARCH IN HEAV'N, TILL THEN AS ONE SECURE 1 638
AND HEAV'NS HIGH ARBITRATOR SIT SECURE 2 359
SECURE, AND AT THE BRIGHTNING ORIENT BEAM 2 399
IN HURDL'D COTES AMID THE FIELD SECURE, 4 186
NOW LAID PERHAPS ASLEEP SECURE OF HARME. 4 791
HE SWERVE NOT TOO SECURE: TELL HIM WITHALL 5 238
QUAFF IMMORTALITIE AND JOY, SECURE 5 638
JUSTLY HAST IN DERISION, AND SECURE 5 736
SAD RESOLUTION AND SECURE: LET EACH 6 541
SHRIN'D IN HIS SANCTUARIE OF HEAV'N SECURE, 6 672
AS NOT SECURE TO SINGLE OR COMBIN'D. 9 339
OR AUGHT THAT MIGHT HIS HAPPIE STATE SECURE, 9 347
SECURE FROM OUTWARD FORCE; WITHIN HIMSELF 9 348
BUT CONFIDENCE THEN BORE THEE ON, SECURE 9 1175
AND SLEEP SECURE; HIS DREADFUL VOICE NO MORE 10 779
US HAPLY TOO SECURE OF OUR DISCHARGE 11 196
UPLIFTED; AND SECURE WITH BEAKED PROW 11 746
THENCEFORTH SHALL PRACTICE HOW TO LIVE SECURE, 11 802
THIS FURTHER CONSOLATION YET SECURE 12 620

SECURELY
INCENS'T, AND THUS SECURELY HIM DEFI'D. 6 130

SECURER
US BOTH SECURER THEN THUS WARND THOU SEEMST, 9 371

SEDENTARIE
REPEATED, WHILE THE SEDENTARIE EARTH, 8 32

SEDGE
HIGH OVERARCH'T IMBOWR; OR SCATTERD SEDGE 1 304

SEDITIOUS
FROM FLIGHT, SEDITIOUS ANGEL, TO RECEAVE 6 152

SEDUC'D
WHO FIRST SEDUC'D THEM TO THAT FOUL REVOLT? 1 33
AMONG THE SPIRITS BENEATH, WHOM I SEDUC'D 4 83
MADE HAPPIE: HIM BY FRAUD I HAVE SEDUC'D 10 485

SEDUCE
SEDUCE THEM TO OUR PARTY, THAT THIR GOD 2 368
WHO NOW IS PLOTTING HOW HE MAY SEDUCE 6 901
SUTTLE HE NEEDS MUST BE, WHO COULD SEDUCE 9 307

SEDUC'T
ON MAN BY HIM SEDUC'T, BUT ON HIMSELF 1 219
CAN BY HIS FRAUD BE SHAK'N OR SEDUC'T; 9 287
ON HIS BAD ERRAND, MAN SHOULD BE SEDUC'T 10 41
HEE AFTER EVE SEDUC'T, UNMINDED SLUNK 10 332
TO DASH THIR PRIDE, AND JOY FOR MAN SEDUC'T. 10 577

SEDULOUS
NOT SEDULOUS BY NATURE TO INDITE 9 27

SEE
TOO WELL I SEE AND RUE THE DIRE EVENT, 1 134
BUT SEE THE ANGRY VICTOR HATH RECALL'D 1 169
EVIL TO OTHERS, AND ENRAG'D MIGHT SEE 1 216
INFERNAL THUNDER, AND FOR LIGHTNING SEE 2 66
PURGE AND DISPERSE, THAT I MAY SEE AND TELL 3 54
FATHER, TO SEE THY FACE, WHEREIN NO CLOUD 3 262
SEE GOLDEN DAYS, FRUITFUL OF GOLDEN DEEDS, 3 337
INTO THE DEVIOUS AIR; THEN MIGHT YE SEE 3 489
UNSPEAKABLE DESIRE TO SEE, AND KNOW 3 662
SEISD MINE, I YIELDED, AND FROM THAT TIME SEE 4 489
SEE FARR AND WIDE: IN AT THIS GATE NONE PASS 4 579
MY GLORIE, MY PERFECTION, GLAD I SEE 5 29

SEE (CONTINUED)

ASCEND TO HEAV'N, BY MERIT THINE, AND SEE 5 80
OF SENSE, WHEREBY THEY HEAR, SEE, SMELL, TOUCH, TASTE. 5 411
ILLUSTRATES, WHEN THEY SEE ALL REGAL POWER 5 739
FORSAK'N OF ALL GOOD; I SEE THY FALL 5 878
I SEE THAT MOST THROUGH SLOTH HAD RATHER SERVE, 6 166
THE REBEL THRONES, BUT GREATER RAGE TO SEE 6 199
HE COMES, AND SETTL'D IN HIS FACE I SEE 6 540
THAT ALL MAY SEE WHO HATE US, HOW WE SEEK 6 559
GRIEVING TO SEE HIS GLORIE, AT THE SIGHT 6 792
YET FARR THE GREATER PART HAVE KEPT, I SEE, 7 145
FOR GOD WE SEE HATH HONOUR'D THEE, AND SET 8 227
TO SEE THAT NONE THENCE ISSU'D FORTH A SPIE, 8 233
I SEE NOT WHO PARTAKES. IN SOLITUDE 8 364
A NICE AND SUTTLE HAPPINESS I SEE 8 399
TO SEE HOW THOU COULD'ST JUDGE OF FIT AND MEET: 8 448
OF ALL THY GIFTS, NOR ENVIEST. I NOW SEE 8 494
FIND PLACE OR REFUGE; AND THE MORE I SEE 9 119
I QUESTION IT, FOR THIS FAIR EARTH I SEE, 9 720
HIGH AND REMOTE TO SEE FROM THENCE DISTINCT 9 812
EVE, NOW I SEE THOU ART EXACT OF TASTE, 9 1017
HIDE ME, WHERE I MAY NEVER SEE THEM MORE. 9 1090
SUBLIME WITH EXPECTATION WHEN TO SEE 10 536
SEE WITH WHAT HEAT THESE DOGS OF HELL ADVANCE 10 616
THROUGH HER PERVERSNESS, BUT SHALL SEE HER GAIND 10 902
SINCE THIS DAYS DEATH DENOUNC'T, IF OUGHT I SEE, 10 962
SEE FATHER, WHAT FIRST FRUITS ON EARTH ARE SPRUNG 11 22
THOUGH AFTER SLEEPLESS NIGHT; FOR SEE THE MORN, 11 173
THE VISUAL NERVE, FOR HE HAD MUCH TO SEE; 11 415
LOOSE NO REWARD, THOUGH HERE THOU SEE HIM DIE, 11 459
BUT STILL I SEE THE TENOR OF MANS WOE 11 632
BUT I WAS FARR DECEAV'D; FOR NOW I SEE 11 783
MUCH THOU HAST YET TO SEE, BUT I PERCEAVE 12 8
COMES DOWN TO SEE THIR CITIE, ERE THE TOWER 12 51
AND LOOKING DOWN, TO SEE THE HUBBUB STRANGE 12 60
I SEE HIM, BUT THOU CANST NOT, WITH WHAT FAITH 12 128
CANAAN HE NOW ATTAINS, I SEE HIS TENTS 12 135
SEE WHERE IT FLOWS, DISGORGING AT SEAVEN MOUTHES 12 158
OF MEE AND ALL MANKIND; BUT NOW I SEE 12 276
SIN AGAINST LAW TO FIGHT; THAT WHEN THEY SEE 12 289
RETURNE, THE STARRES OF MORN SHALL SEE HIM RISE 12 422
EXACTS OUR PARTING HENCE; AND SEE THE GUARDS, 12 590

SEED

THAT SHEPHERD, WHO FIRST TAUGHT THE CHOSEN SEED, 1 8
MADE FLESH, WHEN TIME SHALL BE, OF VIRGIN SEED, 3 284
PUT FORTH THE VERDANT GRASS, HERB YIELDING SEED, 7 310
WHOSE SEED IS IN HER SELF UPON THE EARTH. 7 312
ENMITIE, AND BETWEEN THINE AND HER SEED; 10 180
HER SEED SHALL BRUSE THY HEAD, THOU BRUISE HIS HEEL. 10 181
HIS SEED, WHEN IS NOT SET, SHALL BRUISE MY HEAD: 10 499
AND TO OUR SEED (O HAPLESS SEED.) DERIV'D. 10 965
THEN BOTH OUR SELVES AND SEED AT ONCE TO FREE 10 999
PART OF OUR SENTENCE, THAT THY SEED SHALL BRUISE 10 1031
FRUITS OF MORE PLEASING SAVOUR FROM THY SEED 11 26
MY COV'NANT IN THE WOMANS SEED RENEWD; 11 116
HIS PROMISE, THAT THY SEED SHALL BRUISE OUR FOE; 11 155
WITH ALL THE CREATURES, AND THIR SEED PRESERVE. 11 873
SEED TIME AND HARVEST, HEAT AND HOARY FROST 11 899
HIS BENEDICTION SO, THAT IN HIS SEED 12 125
SHALL IN HIS SEED BE BLESSED; BY THAT SEED 12 148
AND SHADOWS, OF THAT DESTIND SEED TO BRUISE 12 233
PROMISD TO ABRAHAM AND HIS SEED: THE REST 12 260
JUST ABRAHAM AND HIS SEED: NOW FIRST I FINDE 12 273
A SON, THE WOMANS SEED TO THEE FORETOLD, 12 327
THE SEED OF WOMAN: VIRGIN MOTHER, HAILE, 12 379
IN THEE AND IN THY SEED: NOR CAN THIS BE, 12 395
SO IN HIS SEED ALL NATIONS SHALL BE BLEST. 12 450
THE WOMANS SEED, OBSCURELY THEN FORETOLD, 12 543
THE GREAT DELIVERANCE BY HER SEED TO COME 12 600
(FOR BY THE WOMANS SEED) ON ALL MANKIND. 12 601
BY MEE THE PROMIS'D SEED SHALL ALL RESTORE. 12 623

SEEING

WROUGHT IN HER SO, THAT SEEING ME, SHE TURN'D; 8 507
NOT SEEING THEE ATTEMPTED, WHO ATTEST? 9 369
OF GOD ALL-SEEING, OR DECEAVE HIS HEART 10 6
SOONER OR LATER; WHICH TH' ALMIGHTIE SEEING, 10 613

SEEK

OUT OF OUR EVIL SEEK TO BRING FORTH GOOD, 1 163
ROAMING TO SEEK THIR PREY ON EARTH, DURST FIX 1 382
FANATIC EGYPT AND HER PRIESTS, TO SEEK 1 480
OF SPLENDID VASSALAGE, BUT RATHER SEEK 2 252
THROUGH ALL THE COASTS OF DARK DESTRUCTION SEEK 2 464
ALONE, AND WITHOUT GUIDE, HALF LOST, I SEEK 2 975
CAN NEVER SEEK, ONCE DEAD IN SINS AND LOST; 3 233
HERE PILGRIMS ROAM, THAT STRAY'D SO FARR TO SEEK 3 476
WHOM HUNGER DRIVES TO SEEK NEW HAUNT FOR PREY, 4 184
TO SEEK HER THROUGH THE WORLD; NOR THAT SWEET GROVE 4 272
THOUGH I UNPITTIED: LEAGUE WITH YOU I SEEK, 4 375
PART OF MY SOUL I SEEK THEE, AND THEE CLAIM 4 487
AND WHEN WE SEEK, AS NOW, THY GIFT OF SLEEP. 4 735
BLEST PAIR; AND O YET HAPPIEST IF YE SEEK 4 774
HUMAN DESIRES CAN SEEK OR APPREHEND? 5 518
SEEK NOT THE PRAISE OF MEN: THE OTHER SORT 6 376

SEEK (CONTINUED)

THAT ALL MAY SEE WHO HATE US, HOW WE SEEK 6 559
SEEK THEM WITH WANDRING THOUGHTS, AND NOTIONS VAIN. 8 187
UNPRACTIS'D, UNPREPAR'D, AND STILL TO SEEK. 8 197
SUCH AS I SEEK, FIT TO PARTICIPATE 8 390
BUT NEITHER HERE SEEK I, NO NOR IN HEAV'N 9 124
BY WHAT I SEEK, BUT OTHERS TO MAKE SUCH 9 127
SEEK NOT TEMPTATION THEN, WHICH TO AVOIDE 9 364
A FOE SO PROUD WILL FIRST THE WEAKER SEEK, 9 383
LET NONE HENCEFORTH SEEK NEEDLESS CAUSE TO APPROVE 9 1140
THE FAITH THEY OWE; WHEN EARNESTLY THEY SEEK 9 1141
WHY HEE SHOULD MEAN ME ILL, OR SEEK TO HARME. 9 1152
LET US SEEK DEATH, OR HE NOT FOUND, SUPPLY 10 1001
TO MAKE DEATH IN US LIVE: THEN LET US SEEK 10 1028
OF THESE FAIR SPREADING TREES; WHICH BIDS US SEEK 10 1067
IN YONDER NETHER WORLD WHERE SHALL I SEEK 11 328
WITH THOUGHT THAT THEY MUST BE. LET NO MAN SEEK 11 770
THEN SHALL THEY SEEK TO AVAIL THEMSELVES OF NAMES, 12 515

SEEKES

THE NUMBER OF THY WORSHIPPERS. WHO SEEKES 7 613

SEEKING

NAUGHT SEEKING BUT THE PRAISE OF MEN, HERE FIND 3 453
CREATURE SO FAIRE HIS RECONCILEMENT SEEKING, 10 943
IN WHAT THOU EATST AND DRINKST, SEEKING FROM THENCE 11 532

SEEKS

VAIN GLORIOUS, AND THROUGH INFAMIE SEEKS FAME: 6 384
DESPAIRING, SEEKS TO WORK US WOE AND SHAME 9 255
THAT SUCH AN ENEMIE WE HAVE, WHO SEEKS 9 274
SUSPECTED TO A SEQUENT KING, WHO SEEKS 12 165

SEEK'ST

BEST WITH THY SELF ACCOMPANIED, SEEK'ST NOT 8 428

SEEKST

FIRST, HIGHEST, HOLIEST, BEST, THOU ALWAYES SEEKST 6 724
INFORMD BY THEE MIGHT KNOW; IF ELSE THOU SEEKST 7 639

SEEM

DID NOT DISSWADE ME MOST, AND SEEM TO CAST 2 122
HAST THOU FORGOT ME THEN, AND DO I SEEM 2 747
AND THOU SLY HYPOCRITE, WHO NOW WOULDST SEEM 4 957
AS THAT MORE WILLINGLY THOU COULDST NOT SEEM 5 466
THEN MOST, WHEN MOST IRREGULAR THEY SEEM, 5 624
SEEM TWILIGHT HERE; AND NOW WENT FORTH THE MORN 6 12
AND ALL HER NUMBERD STARRS, THAT SEEM TO ROWLE 8 19
NOT THAT I SO AFFIRM, THOUGH SO IT SEEM 8 117
THE PLANET EARTH, SO STEDFAST THOUGH SHE SEEM, 8 129
FOR WHILE I SIT WITH THEE, I SEEM IN HEAV'N, 8 210
SEEM I TO THEE SUFFICIENTLY POSSEST 8 404
IS PROPAGATED SEEM SUCH DEAR DELIGHT 8 580
IN TANGLES, AND MADE INTRICATE SEEM STRAIT, 9 632
YE EATE THEREOF, YOUR EYES THAT SEEM SO CLEERE, 9 706
THE PARTS OF EACH FOR OTHER, THAT SEEM MOST 9 1093
A PLACE SO HEAV'NLY, AND CONNIVING SEEM 10 624
HARD TO BELIEF MAY SEEM; YET THIS WILL PRAYER, 11 146
OF THEM THE HIGHEST, FOR SUCH OF SHAPE MAY SEEM 11 297

SEEM'D

THE DEEP TO SHELTER US? THIS HELL THEN SEEM'D 2 167
ASPECT HE ROSE, AND IN HIS RISING SEEM'D 2 301
PLY STEMMING NIGHTLY TOWARD THE POLE. SO SEEM'D 2 642
THE ONE SEEM'D WOMAN TO THE WASTE, AND FAIR, 2 650
OR SUBSTANCE MIGHT BE CALL'D THAT SHADOW SEEM'D, 2 669
FOR EACH SEEM'D EITHER; BLACK IT STOOD AS NIGHT, 2 670
AND SHOOK A DREADFUL DART; WHAT SEEM'D HIS HEAD 2 672
ON THE BARE OUTSIDE OF THIS WORLD, THAT SEEM'D 3 74
IT SEEM'D, NOW SEEMS A BOUNDLESS CONTINENT 3 423
A SPIRIT, ZEALOUS, AS HE SEEM'D, TO KNOW 4 565
OF INTERDICTED KNOWLEDGE: FAIR IT SEEM'D, 5 52
ALL SEEMD WELL PLEAS'D, ALL SEEM'D, BUT WERE NOT ALL 5 617
ON WHEELS (FOR LIKE TO PILLARS MOST THEY SEEM'D 6 573
INFERNAL NOISE; WARR SEEM'D A CIVIL GAME 6 667
SO SPAKE THE UNIVERSAL LORD, AND SEEM'D 8 376
HER DOING SEEM'D TO JUSTIFIE THE DEED; 10 142
WERE SUCH AS UNDER GOVERNMENT WELL SEEM'D, 10 154
HUGE PYTHON, AND HIS POWER NO LESS HE SEEM'D 10 531
WHEN ANGRY MOST HE SEEM'D AND MOST SEVERE, 10 1095
SEEM'D THIR PETITION, THEN WHEN TH' ANCIENT PAIR 11 10

SEEMD

BEHOLD A WONDER. THEY BUT NOW WHO SEEMD 1 777
A FAIRER PERSON LOST NOT HEAV'N; HE SEEMD 2 110
MIDST CAME THIR MIGHTY PARAMOUNT, AND SEEMD 2 508
HE CEAS'D, FOR BOTH SEEMD HIGHLY PLEASD, AND DEATH 2 845
SO WIDE THE OP'NING SEEMD, WHERE BOUNDS WERE SET 3 538
STARS DISTANT, BUT NIGH HAND SEEMD OTHER WORLDS, 3 566
OR OTHER WORLDS THEY SEEMD, OR HAPPY ILES, 3 567
IF METTAL, PART SEEMD GOLD, PART SILVER CLEER; 3 595
HE SEEMD, OR FIXT IN COGITATION DEEP. 3 629
WHEN GOD HATH SHOWRD THE EARTH; SO LOVELY SEEMD 4 152
IN NAKED MAJESTIE SEEMD LORDS OF ALL, 4 290
AND WORTHIE SEEMD, FOR IN THIR LOOKS DIVINE 4 291
NOT EQUAL, AS THIR SEX NOT EQUAL SEEMD; 4 296
SMOOTH LAKE, THAT TO ME SEEMD ANOTHER SKIE. 4 459

SEEMD (CONTINUED)
HIS LUSTRE VISIBLY IMPAR'D; YET SEEMD 4 850
WHAT SEEMD BOTH SPEAR AND SHIELD; NOW DREADFUL DEEDS 4 990
ALL SEEMD WELL PLEAS'D, ALL SEEM'D, BUT WERE NOT ALL 5 617
IN THE MID WAY: THOUGH STRANGE TO US IT SEEMD 6 91
SEEMD IN THY WORLD ERRONEOUS TO DISSENT 6 146
AS EACH DIVIDED LEGION MIGHT HAVE SEEMD 6 230
A LEGION; LED IN FIGHT, YET LEADER SEEMD 6 232
TORMENTED ALL THE AIR; ALL AIR SEEMD THEN 6 244
OF GODLIKE POWER: FOR LIKEST GODS THEY SEEMD, 6 301
TO BE TH' INVENTER MISS'D, SO EASIE IT SEEMD 6 499
AS THEY WOULD DANCE, YET FOR A DANCE THEY SEEMD 6 615
OUR KNOWING, AS TO HIGHEST WISDOM SEEMD, 7 83
SEEMD LIKE TO HEAV'N, A SEAT WHERE GODS MIGHT DWELL, 7 329
SO SPAKE OUR SIRE, AND BY HIS COUNT'NANCE SEEMD 8 39
OF EARTH BEFORE SCARCE PLEASANT SEEMD. EACH TREE 8 306
THAT WHAT SEEMD FAIR IN ALL THE WORLD, SEEMD NOW 8 472
LIKELIEST SHE SEEMD, POMONA WHEN SHE FLED 9 394
WHAT PLEASING SEEMD, FOR HER NOW PLEASES MORE, 9 453
REGARDED, SUCH DELIGHT TILL THEN, AS SEEMD, 9 787
SUBMITTING TO WHAT SEEMD REMEDILESS, 9 919
WHAT SEEMD IN THEE SO PERFET, THAT I THOUGHT 9 1179
A LAZAR-HOUSE IT SEEMD, WHEREIN WERE LAID 11 479
JUST MEN THEY SEEMD, AND ALL THIR STUDY BENT 11 577
FOR THAT FAIR FEMAL TROOP THOU SAWST, THAT SEEMD 11 614

SEEMING
WITH SHEWS INSTEAD, MEER SHEWS OF SEEMING PURE, 4 316
WITH REASON, TO HER SEEMING, AND WITH TRUTH; 9 738
WHATEVER WILES OF FOE OR SEEMING FRIEND. 10 11
BY PLEASURE, THOUGH TO NATURE SEEMING MEET, 11 604

SEEMINGLY
AND TO THIR VIANDS FELL, NOR SEEMINGLY 5 434

SEEMLIEST
SAFEST AND SEEMLIEST BY HER HUSBAND STAIES, 9 268

SEEMS
THE WAY SEEMS DIFFICULT AND STEEP TO SCALE 2 71
THAWS NOT, BUT GATHERS HEAP, AND RUIN SEEMS 2 590
I FLED, BUT HE PURSU'D (THOUGH MORE, IT SEEMS, 2 790
WIDE INTERRUPT CAN HOLD; SO BENT HE SEEMS 3 84
IT SEEM'D, NOW SEEMS A BOUNDLESS CONTINENT 3 423
AND NOW SAINT PETER AT HEAV'NS WICKET SEEMS 3 484
WHERE NO ILL SEEMS: WHICH NOW FOR ONCE BEGUIL'D 3 689
THE MORE IT SEEMS EXCESS, THAT LED THEE HITHER 3 698
TO WHICH THE HELL I SUFFER SEEMS A HEAV'N. 4 78
FROM THIR OWN MOUTHS; ALL IS NOT THEIRS IT SEEMS: 4 513
AND FIERCE DEMEANOUR SEEMS THE PRINCE OF HELL, 4 871
IMPLOI'D IT SEEMS TO VIOLATE SLEEP, AND THOSE 4 883
FORBIDD'N HERE, IT SEEMS, AS ONELY FIT 5 69
OF TOWRING EAGLES, TO ALL THE FOWLES HE SEEMS 5 271
COMES THIS WAY MOVING; SEEMS ANOTHER MORN 5 310
BUT PROVES NOT SO: THEN FALLIBLE, IT SEEMS, 6 428
AND SEEMS A MOVING LAND, AND AT HIS GILLES 7 415
HER LOVELINESS, SO ABSOLUTE SHE SEEMS 8 547
SEEMS WISEST, VERTUOUSEST, DISCREETEST, BEST; 8 550
LIGHT ABOVE LIGHT, FOR THEE ALONE, AS SEEMS, 9 105
FOR BEASTS IT SEEMS: YET THAT ONE BEAST WHICH FIRST 9 769
HATH TOUCHT MY SENSE, FLAT SEEMS TO THIS, AND HARSH. 9 987
IT SEEMS, IN THY RESTRAINT: WHAT COULD I MORE? 9 1170
WHICH HERE, THOUGH PLENTEOUS, ALL TO LITTLE SEEMS 10 600
THY JUSTICE SEEMS; YET TO SAY TRUTH, TOO LATE, 10 755
EVE, THY CONTEMPT OF LIFE AND PLEASURE SEEMS 10 1013
MUCH BETTER SEEMS THIS VISION, AND MORE HOPE 11 599
HERE NATURE SEEMS FULFILLD IN ALL HER ENDS. 11 602
THE ARK NO MORE NOW FLOTES, BUT SEEMS ON GROUND 11 850

SEEMST
US BOTH SECURER THEN THUS WARND THOU SEEMST, 9 371

SEEN
SO NUMBERLESS WERE THOSE BAD ANGELS SEEN 1 344
ALL IN A MOMENT THROUGH THE GLOOM WERE SEEN 1 544
BEYOND COMPARE THE SON OF GOD WAS SEEN 3 138
FIRST-SEEN, OR SOME RENOWN'D METROPOLIS 3 549
SUCH WONDER SEIS'D, THOUGH AFTER HEAVEN SEEN, 3 552
IMAGIND RATHER OFT THEN ELSEWHERE SEEN, 3 599
WHO TELLS OF SOM INFERNAL SPIRIT SEEN 4 793
HUNG FORTH IN HEAV'N HIS GOLDEN SCALES, YET SEEN 4 997
BY US OFT SEEN; HIS DEWIE LOCKS DISTILL'D 5 56
TO US INVISIBLE OR DIMLY SEEN 5 157
CHARIOTS OF GOD, HALF ON EACH HAND WERE SEEN; 6 770
FIRST SEEN, THEM UNEXPECTED JOY SURPRIZ'D, 6 774
SO FARR REMOTE, WITH DIMINUTION SEEN. 7 369
FIRST IN HIS EAST THE GLORIOUS LAMP WAS SEEN, 7 370
SEEN IN THE GALAXIE, THAT MILKIE WAY 7 579
THY MATE, WHO SEES WHEN THOU ART SEEN LEAST WISE. 8 578
THEN VOLUBLE AND BOLD, NOW HID, NOW SEEN 9 436
AMMONIAN JOVE, OR CAPITOLINE WAS SEEN, 9 508
WHO SEES THEE? (AND WHAT IS ONE?) WHO SHOULDST BE SEEN 9 546
THIS MAY BE WELL: BUT WHAT IF GOD HAVE SEEN, 9 826

SEEN (CONTINUED)
TO SHAME OBNOXIOUS, AND UNSEEMLIEST SEEN, 9 1094
EASIE IT MIGHT BE SEEN THAT I INTEND 10 58
MY COMING SEEN FAR OFF? I MISS THEE HERE, 10 104
NOT TO BE TRUSTED, LONGING TO BE SEEN 10 877
BUT HAVE I NOW SEEN DEATH? IS THIS THE WAY 11 462
TO WHOM THUS MICHAEL. DEATH THOU HAST SEEN 11 466
THIR STOPS AND CHORDS WAS SEEN: HIS VOLANT TOUCH 11 561
NO MORE WAS SEEN; THE FLOATING VESSEL SWUM 11 745
FIRST SEEN IN ACTS OF PROWESS EMINENT 11 789
THUS THOU HAST SEEN ONE WORLD BEGIN AND END; 12 6

SEER
HOW SOON HATH THY PREDICTION, SEER BLEST, 12 553

SEES
OR FOUNTAIN SOME BELATED PEASANT SEES, 1 783
OR DREAMS HE SEES, WHILE OVER-HEAD THE MOON 1 784
ALL THESE OUR MOTIONS VAIN, SEES AND DERIDES; 2 191
STARR INTERPOS'D, HOWEVER SMALL HE SEES, 5 258
THY MATE, WHO SEES WHEN THOU ART SEEN LEAST WISE. 8 578
AND TORTURES HIM NOW MORE, THE MORE HE SEES 9 469
WHO SEES THEE? (AND WHAT IS ONE?) WHO SHOULDST BE SEEN 9 546

SEEST
IN EQUAL RUIN: INTO WHAT PIT THOU SEEST 1 91
SEEST THOU YON DREARY PLAIN, FORLORN AND WILDE, 1 180
AT LAST THIS ODIOUS OFFSPRING WHOM THOU SEEST 2 781
ONELY BEGOTTEN SON, SEEST THOU WHAT RAGE 3 80
NUMBERLESS, AS THOU SEEST, AND HOW THEY MOVE; 3 719
HAD NOT A VOICE THUS WARND ME, WHAT THOU SEEST, 4 467
WHAT THERE THOU SEEST FAIR CREATURE IS THY SELF, 4 468
THY SLEEP DISSENT? NEW LAWS THOU SEEST IMPOS'D; 5 679
THY LEGIONS UNDER DARKNESS; BUT THOU SEEST 6 142
FROM ALL: MY SECT THOU SEEST, NOW LEARN TOO LATE 6 147
UNNAM'D IN HEAV'N, NOW PLENTEOUS, AS THOU SEEST 6 263
WHICH NIGHTLY AS A CIRCLING ZONE THOU SEEST 7 580
IN SIX THOU SEEST, AND WHAT IF SEV'NTH TO THESE 8 128
FEILDS AND INHABITANTS: HER SPOTS THOU SEEST 8 145
AND DAY IS YET NOT SPENT; TILL THEN THOU SEEST 8 206
SAID MILDELY, AUTHOR OF ALL THIS THOU SEEST 8 317

SEIGE
LAY SEIGE, ENCAMPT; BY BATTERIE, SCALE, AND MINE, 11 656

SEIS'D
WITH HIS ENORMOUS BROOD, AND BIRTHRIGHT SEIS'D 1 511
SEIS'D US, THOUGH UNDISMAID: LONG IS THE WAY 2 432
OUT OF THY HEAD I SPRUNG: AMAZEMENT SEIS'D 2 758
OF HIS GREAT FATHER. ADMIRATION SEIS'D 3 271
SUCH WONDER SEIS'D, THOUGH AFTER HEAVEN SEEN, 3 552
THE SPIRIT MALIGNE, BUT MUCH MORE ENVY SEIS'D 3 553
HALF SUNK WITH ALL HIS PINES. AMAZEMENT SEIS'D 6 198
BE SURE, AND TERROUR SEIS'D THE REBEL HOST, 6 647
HE TRUSTED TO HAVE SEIS'D, AND INTO FRAUD 7 143
FIRST FOUND ME, AND WITH SOFT OPPRESSION SEIS'D 8 288
HER HAND HE SEIS'D, AND TO A SHADIE BANK, 9 1037
SEIS'D ON BY FORCE, JUDG'D, AND TO DEATH CONDEMND 12 412

SEISD
SEISD MINE, I YIELDED, AND FROM THAT TIME SEE 4 489

SEISE
STRANGE HORROR SEISE THEE, AND PANGS UNFELT BEFORE. 2 703
SUCH WHERE YE FIND, SEISE FAST, AND HITHER BRING. 4 796
IN THIR BRIGHT STAND, THERE LEFT HIS POWERS TO SEISE 11 221
UPON THE TEMPLE IT SELF: AT LAST THEY SEISE 12 356

SEISURE
DEFEATED OF HIS SEISURE MANY DAYES 11 254

SEIZ'D
EXPLODED AND HAD SEIZ'D WITH VIOLENT HANDS, 11 669

SEIZE
WHENCE RUSHING HE MIGHT SUREST SEIZE THEM BOTH 4 407

SELDOM
OF WHAT SO SELDOM CHANC'D, WHEN TO HIS WISH, 9 423
OR WHOM HE WISHES MOST SHALL SELDOM GAIN 10 901

SELECT
ONE WAY A BAND SELECT FROM FORAGE DRIVES 11 646
SELECT FOR LIFE SHALL IN THE ARK BE LODG'D, 11 823
AND ONE PECULIAR NATION TO SELECT 12 111

SELECTEST
SHED THIR SELECTEST INFLUENCE; THE EARTH 8 513

SELEUCIA
OF GREAT SELEUCIA, BUILT BY GRECIAN KINGS, 4 212

SELF
THAT SELF SAME DAY BY FIGHT, OR BY SURPRIZE 6 87
AND EARTH SELF BALLANC'T ON HER CENTER HUNG. 7 242
THY LIKENESS, THY FIT HELP, THY OTHER SELF, 8 450

SELF (CONTINUED)
THEN SELF ESTEEM, GROUNDED ON JUST AND RIGHT 8 572
BETOOK HER TO THE GROVES, BUT DELIA'S SELF 9 388
MY OTHER SELF, THE PARTNER OF MY LIFE; 10 128
OF SATAN, TO THE SELF SAME PLACE WHERE HEE 10 315

SELF-BEGOT
KNOW NONE BEFORE US, SELF-BEGOT, SELF-RAIS'D 5 860

SELF-CONDEMNING
THE FRUITLESS HOURS, BUT NEITHER SELF-CONDEMNING, 9 1188

SELF-DEPRAV'D
SELF-TEMPTED, SELF-DEPRAV'D: MAN FALLS DECEIV'D 3 130

SELF-DESTRUCTION
BUT SELF-DESTRUCTION THEREFORE SAUGHT, REFUTES 10 1016

SELF-KNOWING
GOVERN THE REST, SELF-KNOWING, AND FROM THENCE 7 510

SELF-LEFT
SELF-LEFT. LEAST THEREFORE HIS NOW BOLDER HAND 11 93

SELF-LOST
SELF-LOST, AND IN A MOMENT WILL CREATE 7 154

SELF-OPEND
OF HEAV'N ARRIV'D, THE GATE SELF-OPEND WIDE 5 254

SELF-RAIS'D
SELF-RAIS'D, AND REPOSSESS THIR NATIVE SEAT? 1 634
KNOW NONE BEFORE US, SELF-BEGOT, SELF-RAIS'D 5 860

SELF-ROWLD
IN LABYRINTH OF MANY A ROUND SELF-ROWLD, 9 183

SELF-SAME
ONE WAY THE SELF-SAME HOUR? WHY IN THE EAST 11 203

SELF-TEMPTED
SELF-TEMPTED, SELF-DEPRAV'D: MAN FALLS DECEIV'D 3 130

SEMBLANCE
SEMBLANCE OF WORTH, NOT SUBSTANCE, GENTLY RAIS'D 1 529
SEMBLANCE, AND IN THY BEAUTIES HEAV'NLY RAY 9 607

SENATE
THIR GOVERNMENT, AND THIR GREAT SENATE CHOOSE 12 225

SENCE
AND HIGH DISDAIN, FROM SENCE OF INJUR'D MERIT, 1 98

SENC'T
ILL SENC'T FOR HEAV'N TO KEEP OUT SUCH A FOE 4 372

SEND
SHALL BREATHE HER BALME. BUT FIRST WHOM SHALL WE SEND 2 402
CHOICE IN OUR SUFFRAGE; FOR ON WHOM WE SEND, 2 415
SHALT IN THE SKY APPEER, AND FROM THEE SEND 3 324
AND SEND FORTH ALL HER KINGS; THERE WILL BE ROOM, 4 383
AEREAL MUSIC SEND: NOR KNEW I NOT 5 548
WHAT HEAVENS LORD HAD POWERFULLEST TO SEND 6 425
DILATED AND INFURIATE SHALL SEND FORTH 6 486
I SEND ALONG, RIDE FORTH, AND BID THE DEEP 7 166
THITHER WILL SEND HIS WINGED MESSENGERS 7 572
FROM TH' EARTHS GREAT ALTAR SEND UP SILENT PRAISE 9 195
TO INTERCEPT THY WAY, OR SEND THEE BACK 9 410
BUT WHOM SEND I TO JUDGE THEM? WHOM BUT THEE 10 55
MY SUBSTITUTES I SEND YE, AND CREATE 10 403
AND SEND HIM FROM THE GARDEN FORTH TO TILL 11 97
SO SEND THEM FORTH, THOUGH SORROWING, YET IN PEACE: 11 117
AND SEND THEE FROM THE GARDEN FORTH TO TILL 11 261
HEE TO HIS OWN A COMFORTER WILL SEND, 12 486

SENDER
BEST WITH THE BEST, THE SENDER NOT THE SENT, 4 852

SENDING
MERCIE COLLEGUE WITH JUSTICE, SENDING THEE 10 59

SENDS
BUT US HE SENDS UPON HIS HIGH BEHESTS 8 238
AND SENDS A COMFORTABLE HEAT FROM FARR, 10 1077
POWRD FIRST ON HIS APOSTLES, WHOM HE SENDS 12 498

SENESHALS
SERV'D UP IN HALL WITH SEWERS, AND SENESHALS; 9 38

SENIR
SHALL DWELL TO SENIR, THAT LONG RIDGE OF HILLS, 12 146

SENNAAR
OF SENNAAR, AND STILL WITH VAIN DESIGNE 3 467

SENSE
DEVOID OF SENSE AND MOTION? AND WHO KNOWS, 2 151

SENSE (CONTINUED)
(FOR ELOQUENCE THE SOUL, SONG CHARMS THE SENSE,) 2 556
SENSE OF NEW JOY INEFFABLE DIFFUS'D: 3 137
TO ALL DELIGHT OF HUMAN SENSE EXPOS'D 4 206
LIKE THIS FAIR PARADISE, YOUR SENSE, YET SUCH 4 379
OF SENSE, WHEREBY THEY HEAR, SEE, SMELL, TOUCH, TASTE, 5 411
TO INTELLECTUAL, GIVE BOTH LIFE AND SENSE, 5 485
TO HUMAN SENSE TH' INVISIBLE EXPLOITS 5 565
OF HUMAN SENSE, I SHALL DELINEATE SO, 5 572
ALL INTELLECT, ALL SENSE, AND AS THEY PLEASE, 6 351
THEN FIRST WITH FEAR SURPRIS'D AND SENSE OF PAINE 6 394
OF MIGHTIEST. SENSE OF PLEASURE WE MAY WELL 6 459
GOD TO REMOVE HIS WAYES FROM HUMAN SENSE, 8 119
MY DROUSED SENSE, UNTROUBL'D, THOUGH I THOUGHT 8 289
AS WITH AN OBJECT THAT EXCELS THE SENSE, 8 456
BUT IF THE SENSE OF TOUCH WHEREBY MANKIND 8 579
WHO MEET WITH VARIOUS OBJECTS, FROM THE SENSE 8 609
ACTIVE WITHIN BEYOND THE SENSE OF BRUTE, 9 96
OF GROWTH, SENSE, REASON, ALL SUMM'D UP IN MAN, 9 113
THE DEVIL ENTERD, AND HIS BRUTAL SENSE, 9 188
WHY SHOULDST NOT THOU LIKE SENSE WITHIN THEE FEEL 9 315
BY TONGUE OF BRUTE, AND HUMAN SENSE EXPREST? 9 554
GRATEFUL TO APPETITE, MORE PLEAS'D MY SENSE 9 580
ENDU'D WITH HUMAN VOICE AND HUMAN SENSE, 9 871
HATH TOUCHT MY SENSE, FLAT SEEMS TO THIS, AND HARSH. 9 987
WITH ALL PERFECTIONS, SO ENFLAME MY SENSE 9 1031
THE SENSE OF ENDLESS WOES? INEXPLICABLE 10 754
BEREAVING SENSE, BUT ENDLESS MISERIE 10 810
TO HIS GRIM CAVE, ALL DISMAL; YET TO SENSE 11 469
MUST NEEDS IMPAIRE AND WEARIE HUMAN SENSE: 12 10

SENSES
INVITES; FOR I WILL CLEER THIR SENSES DARK, 3 188
WHICH THE FIVE WATCHFUL SENSES REPRESENT, 5 104
THAT ALL HIS SENSES BOUND; EVE, WHO UNSEEN 11 265
TO WITHERD WEAK AND GRAY; THY SENSES THEN 11 540

SENSIBLE
THE SENSIBLE OF PAIN. ALL THINGS INVITE 2 278

SENSUAL
TO SENSUAL APPETITE, WHO FROM BENEATHE 9 1129

SENT
OR WHOM BISERTA SENT FROM AFRIC SHORE 1 585
BY ALL HIS ENGINS, BUT WAS HEADLONG SENT 1 750
OF TOBITS SON, AND WITH A VENGEANCE SENT 4 170
TO HIM WHO SENT US, WHOSE CHARGE IS TO KEEP 4 842
BEST WITH THE BEST, THE SENDER NOT THE SENT, 4 852
LEADER, THE TERMS WE SENT WERE TERMS OF WEIGHT, 6 621
GRASPING TEN THOUSAND THUNDERS, WHICH HE SENT 6 836
DIVINE INTERPRETER, BY FAVOUR SENT 7 72
SENT FROM HER THROUGH THE WIDE TRANSPICUOUS AIRE, 8 141
SENT FROM WHOSE SOVRAN GOODNESS I ADORE. 8 647
SO JUDG'D HE MAN, BOTH JUDGE AND SAVIOUR SENT, 10 209
THE WAY, THOU LEADING, SUCH A SENT I DRAW 10 267
WITH SENT OF LIVING CARCASSES DESIGN'D 10 277
MIGHT INTERCEPT THIR EMPEROUR SENT, SO HEE 10 429
THOUGH TO DELUDE THEM SENT, COULD NOT ABSTAIN, 10 557
FREQUENTING, SENT FROM HEARTS CONTRITE, IN SIGN 10 1091
FREQUENTING, SENT FROM HEARTS CONTRITE, IN SIGN 10 1103
ERE THOU FROM HENCE DEPART, KNOW I AM SENT 11 356
SENT UP AMAIN; AND NOW THE THICK'ND SKIE 11 742
A DOVE SENT FORTH ONCE AND AGEN TO SPIE 11 857
MOSES AND AARON) SENT FROM GOD TO CLAIME 12 170
HERE ADAM INTERPOS'D. O SENT FROM HEAV'N, 12 270
WHICH HE HATH SENT PROPITIOUS, SOME GREAT GOOD 12 612

SENTED
SO SENTED THE GRIM FEATURE, AND UPTURN'D 10 279

SENTENCE
MY SENTENCE IS FOR OPEN WARR: OF WILES, 2 51
THE SENTENCE OF THIR CONQUEROUR: THIS IS NOW 2 208
AS MAMMON ENDED, AND HIS SENTENCE PLEAS'D, 2 291
THY SOVRAN SENTENCE, THAT MAN SHOULD FIND GRACE; 3 145
BENEATH THY SENTENCE; HELL HER NUMBERS FULL 3 332
OF THOUGHTS REVOLV'D, HIS FINAL SENTENCE CHOSE 9 88
WHAT RESTS BUT THAT THE MORTAL SENTENCE PASS 10 48
TO SENTENCE MAN: THE VOICE OF GOD THEY HEARD 10 97
AND TO THE WOMAN THUS HIS SENTENCE TURN'D. 10 192
MORTALITIE MY SENTENCE, AND BE EARTH 10 776
HIS SENTENCE BEYOND DUST AND NATURES LAW, 10 805
THE SENTENCE FROM THY HEAD REMOV'D MAY LIGHT 10 934
PART OF OUR SENTENCE, THAT THY SEED SHALL BRUISE 10 1031
AT THE SAD SENTENCE RIGOROUSLY URG'D, 11 109
THEN DUE BY SENTENCE WHEN THOU DIDST TRANSGRESS, 11 253

SENTERIES
THROUGH THE STRICT SENTERIES AND STATIONS THICK 2 412

SENTS
THE SEASON, PRIME FOR SWEETEST SENTS AND AIRES; 9 200

SEONS
AND HORONAIM, SEONS REALM, BEYOND 1 409

SEPARATE
- FARR SEPARATE, CIRCLING THY HOLY MOUNT 6 743
- EVE SEPARATE, HE WISH'D, BUT NOT WITH HOPE 9 422
- BEYOND HIS HOPE, EVE SEPARATE HE SPIES, 9 424
- SHALL SEPARATE US, LINKT IN LOVE SO DEARE, 9 970
- FOR DEATH FROM SIN NO POWER CAN SEPARATE. 10 251

SEQUEL
- THE SEQUEL EACH OF PARTING AND OF FIGHT; 4 1003
- TO OBSERVE THE SEQUEL, SAW HIS GUILEFUL ACT 10 334

SEQUENT
- SUSPECTED TO A SEQUENT KING, WHO SEEKS 12 165

SEQUESTERD
- MORE SACRED AND SEQUESTERD, THOUGH BUT FEIGND, 4 706

SERAPH
- CHERUBE AND SERAPH ROWLING IN THE FLOOD 1 324
- ALONE THUS WANDRING. BRIGHTEST SERAPH TELL 3 667
- A SERAPH WINGD; SIX WINGS HE WORE, TO SHADE 5 277
- THE FLAMING SERAPH FEARLESS, THOUGH ALONE 5 875
- SO SPAKE THE SERAPH ABDIEL FAITHFUL FOUND, 5 896
- A SERAPH STOOD, AND IN HIS HAND A REED 6 579
- WHAT WORDS OR TONGUE OF SERAPH CAN SUFFICE, 7 113
- CHERUB AND SERAPH, POTENTATES AND THRONES, 7 198

SERAPHIC
- SERAPHIC ARMS AND TROPHIES: ALL THE WHILE 1 539
- THE GREAT SERAPHIC LORDS AND CHERUBIM 1 794

SERAPHIM
- THAT LED TH' IMBATTELLD SERAPHIM TO WARR 1 129
- A GLOBE OF FIERIE SERAPHIM INCLOS'D 2 512
- OF ALL THE SERAPHIM WITH THEE COMBIN'D 2 750
- YET DAZLE HEAV'N, THAT BRIGHTEST SERAPHIM 3 381
- OF SERAPHIM AND POTENTATES AND THRONES 5 749
- HAD AUDIENCE, WHEN AMONG THE SERAPHIM 5 804
- OF FIGHTING SERAPHIM CONFUS'D, AT LENGTH 6 249
- STOOD RANKT OF SERAPHIM ANOTHER ROW 6 604
- OF THRONES AND MIGHTY SERAPHIM PROSTRATE, 6 841

SERAPIS
- BELUS OR SERAPIS THIR GODS, OR SEAT 1 720

SERBONIAN
- A GULF PROFOUND AS THAT SERBONIAN BOG 2 592

SERE
- REFLECTED, MAY WITH MATTER SERE FOMENT, 10 1071

SERENATE
- OR SERENATE, WHICH THE STARV'D LOVER SINGS 4 769

SERENE
- SO THICK A DROP SERENE HATH QUENCHT THIR ORBS, 3 25
- THAT WONT TO BE MORE CHEARFUL AND SERENE 5 123
- LIGHT'NING DIVINE, INEFFABLE, SERENE, 5 734
- HIS STATURE, AND UPRIGHT WITH FRONT SERENE 7 509
- INTELLIGENCE OF HEAV'N, ANGEL SERENE, 8 181
- FROM HIS DISPLEASURE; IN WHOSE LOOK SERENE, 10 1094
- TO WHOM THE FATHER, WITHOUT CLOUD, SERENE. 11 45

SERICANA
- OF SERICANA, WHERE CHINESES DRIVE 3 438

SERPENT
- TH' INFERNAL SERPENT; HE IT WAS, WHOSE GUILE 1 34
- VOLUMINOUS AND VAST, A SERPENT ARM'D 2 652
- HIS LITHE PROBOSCIS; CLOSE THE SERPENT SLY 4 347
- WITH SERPENT ERROUR WANDRING, FOUND THIR WAY, 7 302
- MINIMS OF NATURE; SOME OF SERPENT KINDE 7 482
- THE SERPENT SUTTL'ST BEAST OF ALL THE FIELD, 7 495
- THE SERPENT SUTTLEST BEAST OF ALL THE FIELD. 9 86
- THE SERPENT SLEEPING, IN WHOSE MAZIE FOULDS 9 161
- THE SERPENT: HIM FAST SLEEPING SOON HE FOUND 9 182
- MEER SERPENT IN APPEARANCE, FORTH WAS COME, 9 413
- SUCH PLEASURE TOOK THE SERPENT TO BEHOLD 9 455
- IN SERPENT, INMATE BAD, AND TOWARD EVE 9 495
- AND LOVELY, NEVER SINCE OF SERPENT KIND 9 504
- OF HER ATTENTION GAIND, WITH SERPENT TONGUE 9 529
- THEE, SERPENT, SUTTLEST BEAST OF ALL THE FIELD 9 560
- SERPENT, THY OVERPRAISING LEAVES IN DOUBT 9 615
- SERPENT, WE MIGHT HAVE SPAR'D OUR COMING HITHER, 9 647
- HOW DIES THE SERPENT? HEE HATH EAT'N AND LIVES, 9 764
- THE GUILTIE SERPENT, AND WELL MIGHT, FOR EVE 9 785
- AND HATH BIN TASTED SUCH; THE SERPENT WISE, 9 867
- PROFAN'D FIRST BY THE SERPENT, BY HIM FIRST 9 930
- FRAUD IN THE SERPENT, SPEAKING AS HE SPAKE; 9 1150
- HEE IN THE SERPENT, HAD PERVERTED EVE, 10 3
- CONVICTION TO THE SERPENT NONE BELONGS. 10 84
- THE SERPENT ME BEGUIL'D AND I DID EATE. 10 162
- SERPENT THOUGH BRUTE, UNABLE TO TRANSFERRE 10 165
- AND ON THE SERPENT THUS HIS CURSE LET FALL. 10 174
- MEE NOT, BUT THE BRUTE SERPENT IN WHOSE SHAPE 10 495
- A MONSTROUS SERPENT ON HIS BELLY PRONE, 10 514
- AND FABL'D HOW THE SERPENT, WHOM THEY CALLD 10 580
- OUT OF MY SIGHT, THOU SERPENT, THAT NAME BEST 10 867

SERPENT (CONTINUED)
- TO OVER-REACH, BUT WITH THE SERPENT MEETING 10 879
- THAT CRUEL SERPENT; ON ME EXERCISE NOT 10 927
- SATAN, WHO IN THE SERPENT HATH CONTRIV'D 10 1034
- THE SERPENT, BY WHAT MEANS HE SHALL ACHIEVE 12 234
- THE ADVERSARIE SERPENT, AND BRING BACK 12 312
- NEEDS MUST THE SERPENT NOW HIS CAPITAL BRUISE 12 383
- THE SERPENT, PRINCE OF AIRE, AND DRAG IN CHAINES 12 454

SERPENTINE
- LIKE HIS, AND COLOUR SERPENTINE MAY SHEW 10 870

SERPENTS
- ALIKE, TO SERPENTS ALL AS ACCESSORIES 10 520
- OF UGLY SERPENTS; HORROR ON THEM FELL, 10 539
- THE SERPENTS HEAD; PITEOUS AMENDS, UNLESS 10 1032
- THE SERPENTS HEAD; WHEREOF TO THEE ANON 12 150

SERRALIONA
- FROM SERRALIONA; THWART OF THESE AS FIERCE 10 703

SERRIED
- APPEAR'D, AND SERRIED SHIELDS IN THICK ARRAY 1 548
- NOR SERV'D IT TO RELAX THIR SERRIED FILES. 6 599

SERVANT
- SERVANT OF GOD, WELL DONE, WELL HAST THOU FOUGHT 6 29
- THEN OF OUR FELLOW SERVANT, AND INQUIRE 8 225
- THENCEFORTH THE FORM OF SERVANT TO ASSUME, 10 214
- SERVANT OF SERVANTS, ON HIS VITIOUS RACE. 12 104

SERVANTS
- AS WHEN HE WASH'D HIS SERVANTS FEET SO NOW 10 215
- SERVANT OF SERVANTS, ON HIS VITIOUS RACE. 12 104

SERV'D
- SERV'D ONELY TO DISCOVER SIGHTS OF WOE, 1 64
- HOW ALL HIS MALICE SERV'D BUT TO BRING FORTH 1 217
- NOR SERV'D IT TO RELAX THIR SERRIED FILES. 6 599
- SERV'D BY MORE NOBLE THEN HER SELF, ATTAINES 8 34
- SERV'D UP IN HALL WITH SEWERS, AND SENESHALS; 9 38
- A GODDESS AMONG GODS, ADOR'D AND SERV'D 9 547
- THIS OTHER SERV'D BUT TO ETERNIZE WOE; 11 60
- HIS IMAGE WHOM THEY SERV'D, A BRUTISH VICE, 11 518

SERVD
- MADE PASSIVE BOTH, HAD SERVD NECESSITIE, 3 110
- NOW OTHER, AS THIR SHAPE SERVD BEST HIS END 4 398

SERVE
- BETTER TO REIGN IN HELL, THEN SERVE IN HEAV'N. 1 263
- KEEP RESIDENCE; IF ALL I CAN WILL SERVE, 2 999
- TO SERVE HIM BETTER: WISE ARE ALL HIS WAYES, 3 680
- WHOSE EASIER BUSINESS WERE TO SERVE THIR LORD 4 943
- ARE MANY LESSER FACULTIES THAT SERVE 5 101
- OF GOD INSPIR'D, SMALL STORE WILL SERVE, WHERE STORE, 5 322
- CAN HEARTS, NOT FREE, BE TRI'D WHETHER THEY SERVE 5 532
- ON OTHER SURETY NONE; FREELY WE SERVE, 5 538
- STREAME IN THE AIRE, AND FOR DISTINCTION SERVE 5 590
- IN US WHO SERVE, NEW COUNSELS, TO DEBATE 5 681
- OUR BEING ORDAIN'D TO GOVERN, NOT TO SERVE? 5 802
- I SEE THAT MOST THROUGH SLOTH HAD RATHER SERVE, 6 166
- OF SERVITUDE TO SERVE WHOM GOD ORDAINS, 6 175
- TO SERVE TH' UNWISE, OR HIM WHO HATH REBELLD 6 179
- AGAINST HIS WORTHIER, AS THINE NOW SERVE THEE, 6 180
- REIGN THOU IN HELL THY KINGDOM, LET MEE SERVE 6 183
- MAY SERVE TO BETTER US, AND WORSE OUR FOES, 6 440
- YET WHAT THOU CANST ATTAIN, WHICH BEST MAY SERVE 7 115
- THAT BODIES BRIGHT AND GREATER SHOULD NOT SERVE 8 87
- LEAVE THEM TO GOD ABOVE, HIM SERVE AND FEARE; 8 168
- MOST OPPORTUNE MIGHT SERVE HIS WILES, AND FOUND 9 85
- WHAT BEST MAY FROM THE PRESENT SERVE TO HIDE 9 1092
- MY OWN DESERVINGS; BUT THIS WILL NOT SERVE; 10 727
- TO SERVE HIM, THY REWARD WAS OF HIS GRACE, 10 767
- TO SERVE UNGOVERN'D APPETITE, AND TOOK 11 517
- OR SERVE THEY AS A FLOURIE VERGE TO BINDE 11 881

SERVES
- THE GREAT CREATOUR? BUT THIR SPITE STILL SERVES 2 385
- TO LESSEN THEE, AGAINST HIS PURPOSE SERVES 7 614

SERVICE
- OR DO HIM MIGHTIER SERVICE AS HIS THRALLS 1 149
- UPBRAIDED NONE; NOR WAS HIS SERVICE HARD, 4 45
- FROM US NO OTHER SERVICE THEN TO KEEP 4 420
- OUR VOLUNTARIE SERVICE HE REQUIRES, 5 529
- SUBJECTED TO HIS SERVICE ANGEL WINGS, 9 155

SERVIL
- ACCEPTANCE OF LARGE GRACE, FROM SERVIL FEAR 12 305

SERVILE
- OUR SERVILE OFFERINGS. THIS MUST BE OUR TASK 2 246
- OF SERVILE POMP. OUR GREATNESS WILL APPEER 2 257

SERVILITIE
- SERVILITIE WITH FREEDOM TO CONTEND, 6 169

SERVILLY
ONCE FAWN'D, AND CRING'D, AND SERVILLY ADOR'D 4 959

SERVITUDE
OF SERVITUDE TO SERVE WHOM GOD ORDAINS, 6 175
THEM WHOM HE GOVERNS. THIS IS SERVITUDE, 6 178
FROM SERVITUDE INGLORIOUS WELNIGH HALF 9 141
FROM REASON, AND TO SERVITUDE REDUCE 12 89
OF HERDS AND FLOCKS, AND NUMEROUS SERVITUDE; 12 132
INGLORIOUS LIFE WITH SERVITUDE; FOR LIFE 12 220

SESSION
THEN OF THIR SESSION ENDED THEY BID CRY 2 514

SET
TO SET HIMSELF IN GLORY ABOVE HIS PEERS, 1 39
IN UTTER DARKNESS, AND THIR PORTION SET 1 72
WERE SET, AND DORIC PILLARS OVERLAID 1 714
I COME NO ENEMIE, BUT TO SET FREE 2 822
THE DEADLY FORFEITURE, AND RANSOM SET. 3 221
SO WIDE THE OP'NING SEEMD, WHERE BOUNDS WERE SET 3 538
SO WONDROUSLY WAS SET HIS STATION BRIGHT. 3 587
WOULD SET ME HIGHEST, AND IN A MOMENT QUIT 4 51
MIND US OF LIKE REPOSE, SINCE GOD HATH SET 4 612
MINISTRING LIGHT PREPAR'D, THEY SET AND RISE; 4 664
LONGER THY OFFERD GOOD, WHY ELSE SET HERE? 5 63
OUR KNOWLEDGE, AND THE SCALE OF NATURE SET 5 509
TABLES ARE SET, AND ON A SUDDEN PIL'D 5 632
TO SET THE ENVIER OF HIS STATE, THE PROUD 6 89
OF SUCH COMMOTION, SUCH AS TO SET FORTH 6 310
SECRET THEY FINISH'D, AND IN ORDER SET, 6 522
AND WINGS WERE SET WITH EYES, WITH EYES THE WHEELS 6 755
AND SET THEM IN THE FIRMAMENT OF HEAV'N 7 349
BUT OPPOSITE IN LEVELD WEST WAS SET 7 376
WITH THIR BRIGHT LUMINARIES THAT SET AND ROSE, 7 385
INTELLIGENT OF SEASONS, AND SET FORTH 7 427
WAS SET, AND TWILIGHT FROM THE EAST CAME ONE, 7 583
IS AS THE BOOK OF GOD BEFORE THEE SET, 8 67
WHO SINCE THE MORNING HOUR SET OUT FROM HEAV'N 8 111
FOR GOD WE SEE HATH HONOUR'D THEE, AND SET 8 227
KNOWLEDG OF GOOD AND ILL, WHICH I HAVE SET 8 324
AND THESE INFERIOUR FARR BENEATH ME SET? 8 382
SET OVER ALL HIS WORKS, WHICH IN OUR FALL, 9 941
WHEREIN GOD SET THEE ABOVE HER MADE OF THEE, 10 149
HIS SEED, WHEN IS NOT SET, SHALL BRUISE MY HEAD: 10 499
SHOULD PROVE TEMPESTUOUS: TO THE WINDS THEY SET 10 664
WHAT JUSTLY THOU HAST LOST; NOR SET THY HEART, 11 288
WHEREON FOR DIFFERENT CAUSE THE TEMPTER SET 11 382
SHALL THEM ADMONISH, AND BEFORE THEM SET 11 813
OF HEAV'N SET OPEN ON THE EARTH SHALL POWRE 11 825
OVER THE EARTH A CLOUD, WILL THEREIN SET 11 896
AMONG THEM TO SET UP HIS TABERNACLE, 12 247

SETS
GRIM DEATH MY SON AND FOE, WHO SETS THEM ON, 2 804
SHADOWIE SETS OFF THE FACE OF THINGS; IN VAIN, 5 43
DAZLES THE CROUD, AND SETS THEM ALL AGAPE. 5 357
HESPEREAN SETS, MY SIGNAL TO DEPART. 8 632
OBSTRUCT HEAV'N TOWRS, AND IN DERISION SETS 12 52

SETTING
A SUMMERS DAY; AND WITH THE SETTING SUN 1 744
WITH EARTH AND OCEAN MEETS, THE SETTING SUN 4 540

SETTL'D
TO PEACEFUL COUNSELS, AND THE SETTL'D STATE 2 279
HE COMES, AND SETTL'D IN HIS FACE I SEE 6 540

SETTLE
TO SETTLE HERE ON EARTH, OR IN MID AIRE; 4 940

SEVEN
THEY PASS THE PLANETS SEVEN, AND PASS THE FIXT, 3 481
THE SPACE OF SEVEN CONTINU'D NIGHTS HE RODE 9 63

SEVENFOLD
AWAK'D SHOULD BLOW THEM INTO SEVENFOLD RAGE 2 171

SEVENTH
POUDERD WITH STARRS. AND NOW ON EARTH THE SEVENTH 7 581
BUT HEE THE SEVENTH FROM THEE, WHOM THOU BEHELDST 11 700

SEVENTIE
THE SPACE OF SEVENTIE YEARS, THEN BRINGS THEM BACK, 12 345

SEVER
THOU SEVER NOT: TRIAL WILL COME UNSOUGHT. 9 366

SEVERAL
DISBAND, AND WANDRING, EACH HIS SEVERAL WAY 2 523
OF EACH HIS FACTION, IN THIR SEVERAL CLANNS, 2 901
SWIFT TO THIR SEVERAL QUARTERS HASTED THEN 3 714
EACH IN THIR SEVERAL ACTIVE SPHEARS ASSIGND, 5 477
OR SEVERAL ONE BY ONE, THE REGENT POWERS, 5 697
LIKE THINGS TO LIKE, THE REST TO SEVERAL PLACE 7 240
WHICH ELSE TO SEVERAL SPHEARS THOU MUST ASCRIBE, 8 131
THIS SAID, THEY BOTH BETOOK THEM SEVERAL WAYES, 10 610
HIS MIGHTIE ANGELS GAVE THEM SEVERAL CHARGE, 10 650

SEVER'D
BEFALL THEE SEVER'D FROM ME; FOR THOU KNOWST 9 252

SEVERD
OUR STATE CANNOT BE SEVERD, WE ARE ONE, 9 958

SEVERE
AS SOFT AS NOW SEVERE, OUR TEMPER CHANG'D 2 276
TO US ENSLAV'D, BUT CUSTODY SEVERE, 2 333
BY DOOM SEVERE, HAD NOT THE SON OF GOD, 3 224
TRUTH, WISDOME, SANCTITUDE SEVERE AND PURE, 4 293
SEVERE BUT IN TRUE FILIAL FREEDOM PLAC'T; 4 294
SEVERE IN YOUTHFUL BEAUTIE, ADDED GRACE 4 845
STOOD UP, AND IN A FLAME OF ZEALE SEVERE 5 807
HIS COUNT'NANCE TOO SEVERE TO BE BEHELD 6 825
WHAT WORDS HAVE PAST THY LIPS, ADAM SEVERE, 9 1144
OF THY TRANSGRESSING? NOT ENOUGH SEVERE, 9 1169
WHEN ANGRY MOST HE SEEM'D AND MOST SEVERE, 10 1095

SEVERING
SEVERING EACH KIND, AND SCUM'D THE BULLION DROSS: 1 704

SEV'NTH
IN SIX THOU SEEST, AND WHAT IF SEV'NTH TO THESE 8 128

SEV'RAL
WITH LONG REACH INTERPOS'D; THREE SEV'RAL WAYES 10 323

SEWERS
SERV'D UP IN HALL WITH SEWERS, AND SENESHALS; 9 38
WHERE HOUSES THICK AND SEWERS ANNOY THE AIRE, 9 446

SEX
CAN EITHER SEX ASSUME, OR BOTH; SO SOFT 1 424
NOT EQUAL, AS THIR SEX NOT EQUAL SEEMD; 4 296
MANLIKE, BUT DIFFERENT SEX, SO LOVLY FAIRE, 8 471
OR SEX, AND APPREHENDED NOTHING HIGH: 9 574
IN FEMAL SEX, THE MORE TO DRAW HIS LOVE, 9 822
AND STRAIGHT CONJUNCTION WITH THIS SEX: FOR EITHER 10 898
THY FRAILTIE AND INFIRMER SEX FORGIV'N, 10 956

SEXES
WHICH TWO GREAT SEXES ANIMATE THE WORLD, 8 151

SEXTILE
IN SEXTILE, SQUARE, AND TRINE, AND OPPOSITE, 10 659

SHADDOW
BE BUT THE SHADDOW OF HEAV'N, AND THINGS THEREIN 5 575

SHADDOWD
SHADDOWD FROM EITHER HEELE WITH FEATHERD MAILE 5 284

SHADDOWIE
NOW HAD NIGHT MEASUR'D WITH HER SHADDOWIE CONE 4 776

SHADDOWING
ON EVERY SIDE WITH SHADDOWING SQUADRONS DEEP, 6 554

SHADE
OF NIGHTS EXTENDED SHADE; FROM EASTERN POINT 3 557
FOR SIGHT NO OBSTACLE FOUND HERE, NOR SHADE, 3 615
INSUPERABLE HIGHTH OF LOFTIEST SHADE, 4 138
SHADE ABOVE SHADE, A WOODIE THEATRE 4 141
THE OPEN FIELD, AND WHERE THE UNPIERC'T SHADE 4 245
UNDER A TUFT OF SHADE THAT ON A GREEN 4 325
UNDER A SHADE OF FLOURS, MUCH WONDRING WHERE 4 451
OR IN THICK SHADE RETIR'D, FROM HIM TO DRAW 4 532
MINE EYE PURSU'D HIM STILL, BUT UNDER SHADE 4 572
OF THICKEST COVERT WAS INWOVEN SHADE 4 693
ITHURIEL AND ZEPHON THROUGH THE SHADE, 4 868
TO HILL, OR VALLEY, FOUNTAIN, OR FRESH SHADE 5 203
CONVERSE WITH ADAM, IN WHAT BOWRE OR SHADE 5 230
A SERAPH WINGD; SIX WINGS HE WORE, TO SHADE 5 277
FROM THAT HIGH MOUNT OF GOD, WHENCE LIGHT & SHADE 5 643
THAT UNDER GROUND, THEY FOUGHT IN DISMAL SHADE; 6 666
WITH DREADFUL SHADE CONTIGUOUS, AND THE ORBES 6 828
FROM THE THICK SHADE, AND ADAM TO HIS BOWRE. 8 653
NOT YET IN HORRID SHADE OR DISMAL DEN, 9 185
ABOUT THE MOTHER TREE, A PILLARD SHADE 9 1106
AT LOOPHOLES CUT THROUGH THICKEST SHADE: THOSE LEAVES 9 1110
BY SECRETEST CONVEYANCE. THOU MY SHADE 10 249
ALREADIE IN PART, THOUGH HID IN GLOOMIEST SHADE, 10 716
OF AMARANTIN SHADE, FOUNTAIN OR SPRING, 11 78

SHADED
SHADED WITH BRANCHING PALME, EACH ORDER BRIGHT, 6 885

SHADES
REGIONS OF SORROW, DOLEFUL SHADES, WHERE PEACE 1 65
IN VALLOMBROSA, WHERE TH' ETRURIAN SHADES 1 303
ROCKS, CAVE, LAKES, FENS, BOGS, DENS, AND SHADES OF DEATH, 2 621
ADAMS ABODE, THOSE LOFTIE SHADES HIS BOWRE. 3 734
WITH MAZIE ERROR UNDER PENDANT SHADES 4 239
MURMURING, AND WITH HIM FLED THE SHADES OF NIGHT. 4 1015
HER SACRED SHADES: THOUGH GOD HAD YET NOT RAIN'D 7 331

SHATTERD
DOWN CLOV'N TO THE WASTE, WITH SHATTERD ARMES 6 361

SHATTERING
BLOW MOIST AND KEEN, SHATTERING THE GRACEFUL LOCKS 10 1066

SHAVES
NOW SHAVES WITH LEVEL WING THE DEEP, THEN SOARES 2 634

SHEAF
FIRST FRUITS, THE GREEN EARE, AND THE YELLOW SHEAF, 11 435

SHEAVES
LEAST ON THE THRESHING FLOORE HIS HOPEFUL SHEAVES 4 984
PART ARABLE AND TILTH, WHEREON WERE SHEAVES 11 430

SHED
THAT SHED MAY FLOWERS; AND PRESS'D HER MATRON LIP 4 501
TEMPER OR NOURISH, OR IN PART SHED DOWN 4 670
SHED THIR SELECTEST INFLUENCE; THE EARTH 8 513
DOWN DROP'D, AND ALL THE FADED ROSES SHED: 9 893
WHICH MANS POLLUTING SIN WITH TAINT HATH SHED 10 631

SHEDDING
SHEDDING SWEET INFLUENCE: LESS BRIGHT THE MOON, 7 375

SHEDS
IN DIM ECLIPS DISASTROUS TWILIGHT SHEDS 1 597

SHEEP-WALKS
NEW REAPT, THE OTHER PART SHEEP-WALKS AND FOULDS; 11 431

SHEER
SHEER O'RE THE CHRYSTAL BATTLEMENTS; FROM MORN 1 742
OF HILL OR HIGHEST WALL, AND SHEER WITHIN 4 182

SHEERE
DESCENDING, AND IN HALF CUT SHEERE, NOR STAID, 6 325

SHELL
ROUGH, OR SMOOTH RIN'D, OR BEARDED HUSK, OR SHELL 5 342

SHELLS
OR IN THIR PEARLIE SHELLS AT EASE, ATTEND 7 407

SHELTER
THE DEEP TO SHELTER US? THIS HELL THEN SEEM'D 2 167
THROWN ON THEM AS A SHELTER FROM HIS IRE. 6 843

SHELTERD
TO FIND WHERE ADAM SHELTERD, TOOK HIS WAY, 11 223
AND SHELTERD ROUND, BUT ALL THE CATARACTS 11 824

SHELTERS
SHELTERS IN COOLE, AND TENDS HIS PASTURING HERDS 9 1109

SHEPHERD
THAT SHEPHERD, WHO FIRST TAUGHT THE CHOSEN SEED, 1 8
UNCULL'D, AS CAME TO HAND; A SHEPHERD NEXT 11 436

SHEPHERDS
WATCHING WHERE SHEPHERDS PEN THIR FLOCKS AT EEVE 4 185
THIR BOOTIE; SCARCE WITH LIFE THE SHEPHERDS FLYE, 11 650
TO SIMPLE SHEPHERDS, KEEPING WATCH BY NIGHT; 12 365

SHEW
MAGNIFICENCE; AND WHAT CAN HEAV'N SHEW MORE? 2 273
THAT PRACTISD FALSHOOD UNDER SAINTLY SHEW, 4 122
THEY SHEW US WHEN OUR FOES WALK NOT UPRIGHT. 6 627
ADMITTING MOTION IN THE HEAV'NS, TO SHEW 8 115
TOO MUCH OF ORNAMENT, IN OUTWARD SHEW 8 538
HATE STRONGER, UNDER SHEW OF LOVE WELL FEIGN'D, 9 492
THE TEMPTER, BUT WITH SHEW OF ZEALE AND LOVE 9 665
IN OPEN SHEW, AND WITH ASCENTION BRIGHT 10 187
IN SHEW PLEBEIAN ANGEL MILITANT 10 442
LIKE HIS, AND COLOUR SERPENTINE MAY SHEW 10 870
AND UNDERSTOOD NOT ALL WAS BUT A SHEW 10 883
THAT SHEW NO END BUT DEATH, AND HAVE THE POWER, 10 1004
TO SHEW US IN THIS MOUNTAIN, WHILE THE WINDS 10 1065
TO SHEW THEE WHAT SHALL COME IN FUTURE DAYES 11 357
TO SHEW HIM ALL EARTHS KINGDOMES AND THIR GLORY, 11 384
EXEMPT FROM DEATH; TO SHEW THEE WHAT REWARD 11 709
WHICH HE WILL SHEW HIM, AND FROM HIM WILL RAISE 12 123

SHEW'D
TH' ADDITION OF HIS EMPIRE, HOW IT SHEW'D 7 555
HIS STARRIE HELME UNBUCKL'D SHEW'D HIM PRIME 11 245

SHEWES
LOOSES DISCOUNT'NANC'T, AND LIKE FOLLY SHEWES; 8 553

SHEWN
INFINITE GOODNESS, GRACE AND MERCY SHEWN 1 218
PRODIGIOUS POWER HAD SHEWN, AND MET IN ARMES 6 247

SHEWS
WITH SHEWS INSTEAD, MEER SHEWS OF SEEMING PURE, 4 316
IMPRESS THE AIR, AND SHEWS THE MARINER 4 558

SHEWS (CONTINUED)
WHICH HEAV'N BY THESE MUTE SIGNS IN NATURE SHEWS 11 194

SHIELD
WAS MOVING TOWARD THE SHOAR; HIS PONDEROUS SHIELD 1 284
OF WARRIERS OLD WITH ORDER'D SPEAR AND SHIELD, 1 565
HALF WHEELING TO THE SHIELD, HALF TO THE SPEAR. 4 785
WHAT SEEMD BOTH SPEAR AND SHIELD; NOW DREADFUL DEEDS 4 990
NOR MOTION OF SWIFT THOUGHT, LESS COULD HIS SHIELD 6 192
OF TENFOLD ADAMANT, HIS AMPLE SHIELD 6 255
FIT WELL HIS HELME, GRIPE FAST HIS ORBED SHIELD, 6 543
DOWN FELL BOTH SPEAR AND SHIELD, DOWN THEY AS FAST, 10 542

SHIELDS
APPEAR'D, AND SERRIED SHIELDS IN THICK ARRAY 1 548
CLASH'D ON THIR SOUNDING SHIELDS THE DIN OF WAR, 1 668
CELESTIAL ARMOURIE, SHIELDS, HELMES, AND SPEARES, 4 553
OF RIGID SPEARS, AND HELMETS THRONG'D, AND SHIELDS 6 83
WITH FLAMING CHERUBIM, AND GOLDEN SHIELDS; 6 102
MADE HORRID CIRCLES; TWO BROAD SUNS THIR SHIELDS 6 305
DEFENCE, WHILE OTHERS BORE HIM ON THIR SHIELDS 6 337
O'RE SHIELDS AND HELMES, AND HELMED HEADS HE RODE 6 840
OR TILTING FURNITURE, EMBLAZON'D SHIELDS, 9 34

SHIFTS
VERES OFT, AS OFT SO STEERS, AND SHIFTS HER SAILE; 9 515

SHINE
CLOTH'D WITH TRANSCENDENT BRIGHTNESS DIDST OUT-SHINE 1 86
SHINE INWARD, AND THE MIND THROUGH ALL HER POWERS 3 52
BUT MERCY FIRST AND LAST SHALL BRIGHTEST SHINE. 3 134
BUT ALL SUN-SHINE, AS WHEN HIS BEAMS AT NOON 3 616
BUT WHEREFORE ALL NIGHT LONG SHINE THESE, FOR WHOM 4 657
SHINE NOT IN VAIN, NOR THINK, THOUGH MEN WERE NONE, 4 675
AND THE THIRD SACRED MORN BEGAN TO SHINE 6 748
END, AND DISMISS THEE ERE THE MORNING SHINE. 7 108
ONELY TO SHINE, YET SCARCE TO CONTRIBUTE 8 155
THAT SHINE, YET BEAR THIR BRIGHT OFFICIOUS LAMPS, 9 104
HAD FIRST HIS PRECEPT SO TO MOVE, SO SHINE, 10 652

SHINES
MADE VISIBLE, TH' ALMIGHTY FATHER SHINES, 3 386
WITH LIGHT FROM HENCE, THOUGH BUT REFLECTED, SHINES; 3 723
WITH WONDER, AND COULD LOVE, SO LIVELY SHINES 4 363
AWAKE, THE MORNING SHINES, AND THE FRESH FIELD 5 20
TILL NIGHT, THEN IN THE EAST HER TURN SHE SHINES, 7 380
MORE PLENTY THEN THE SUN THAT BARREN SHINES, 8 94

SHINING
THEN SHINING HEAV'NLY FAIR, A GODDESS ARM'D 2 757
IN WHICH OF ALL THESE SHINING ORBES HATH MAN 3 668
BUT ALL THESE SHINING ORBES HIS CHOICE TO DWELL; 3 670
BY NILUS HEAD, ENCLOSD WITH SHINING ROCK, 4 283
NOT UNCONFORM TO OTHER SHINING GLOBES, 5 259
OF FISH THAT WITH THIR FINNS AND SHINING SCALES 7 401

SHIP
AS WHEN A SHIP BY SKILFUL STEARSMAN WROUGHT 9 513

SHIVERD
WITH SHIVERD ARMOUR STROW'N, AND ON A HEAP 6 389

SHIVERING
WHY STAND WE LONGER SHIVERING UNDER FEARES, 10 1003

SHOALES
WITH FRIE INNUMERABLE SWARME, AND SHOALES 7 400

SHOALING
FROM EACH SIDE SHOALING TOWARDS THE MOUTH OF HELL. 10 288

SHOAR
WAS MOVING TOWARD THE SHOAR; HIS PONDEROUS SHIELD 1 284
SEA, AIRE, AND SHOAR, THE THUNDER WHEN TO ROWLE 10 666
OF NORUMBEGA, AND THE SAMOED SHOAR 10 696
SEA WITHOUT SHOAR; AND IN THIR PALACES 11 750
DIVIDED, TILL HIS RESCU'D GAIN THIR SHOAR; 12 199
SAFE TOWARDS CANAAN FROM THE SHOAR ADVANCE 12 215

SHOARE
BORDERS ON AEGYPT AND THE ARABIAN SHOARE; 3 537
SABEAN ODOURS FROM THE SPICIE SHOARE 4 162
IN INDIA EAST OR WEST, OR MIDDLE SHOARE 5 339
IN PROSPECT, AS I POINT THEM; ON THE SHOARE 12 143

SHOARES
MEAN WHILE THE TEPID CAVES, AND FENS AND SHOARES 7 417

SHOCK
INTO THE WILDE EXPANSE, AND THROUGH THE SHOCK 2 1014
THE HORRID SHOCK: NOW STORMING FURIE ROSE, 6 207
JUSTLING OR PUSHT WITH WINDS RUDE IN THIR SHOCK 10 1074

SHON
SHON LIKE A METEOR STREAMING TO THE WIND 1 537

SHON (CONTINUED)
PERPLEXES MONARCHS. DARK'N'D SO, YET SHON 1 599
SHON WITH A GLOSSIE SCURFF, UNDOUBTED SIGN 1 672
AND PRINCELY COUNSEL IN HIS FACE YET SHON, 2 304
MOST GLORIOUS, IN HIM ALL HIS FATHER SHON 3 139
TO MORTAL MEN, ABOVE WHICH ONLY SHON 3 268
PAVEMENT THAT LIKE A SEA OF JASPER SHON 3 363
THE PORTAL SHON, INIMITABLE ON EARTH 3 508
AMONGST INNUMERABLE STARRS, THAT SHON 3 565
RUBIE OR TOPAZ, TO THE TWELVE THAT SHON 3 597
LIGHT SHON, AND ORDER FROM DISORDER SPRUNG: 3 713
THE IMAGE OF THIR GLORIOUS MAKER SHON, 4 292
SHON FULL, HE ALL HIS FATHER FULL EXPREST 6 720
HE ONWARD CAME, FARR OFF HIS COMING SHON, 6 768
IMMENSE, AND ALL HIS FATHER IN HIM SHON. 7 196
NOW HEAV'N IN ALL HER GLORIE SHON, AND ROWLD 7 499
HAD UNBENIGHTED SHON, WHILE THE LOW SUN 10 682
WHAT ELSE BUT FAVOR, GRACE, AND MERCIE SHON? 10 1096

SHOOK
AND SHOOK HIS THRONE. WHAT THOUGH THE FIELD BE
LOST? 1 105
THAT SHOOK HEAV'NS WHOL CIRCUMFERENCE, CONFIRM'D. 2 353
AND SHOOK A DREADFUL DART; WHAT SEEM'D HIS HEAD 2 672
HARSH THUNDER, THAT THE LOWEST BOTTOM SHOOK 2 882
NOR STOP THY FLAMING CHARIOT WHEELS, THAT SHOOK 3 394
AND SHOOK HIS PLUMES, THAT HEAV'NLY FRAGRANCE FILLD 5 286
HAD TO HER CENTER SHOOK. WHAT WONDER? WHEN 6 219
THE STEDFAST EMPYREAN SHOOK THROUGHOUT, 6 833
MISTRUST, SUSPICION, DISCORD, AND SHOOK SORE 9 1124
SHOOK, BUT DELAID TO STRIKE, THOUGH OFT INVOK'T 11 492

SHOOT
WITH HEAV'NS RAY, AND TEMPERD THEY SHOOT FORTH 6 480

SHOOTING
ON A SUN BEAM, SWIFT AS A SHOOTING STARR 4 556

SHOOTS
SHOOTS FARR INTO THE BOSOM OF DIM NIGHT 2 1036
SHOOTS INVISIBLE VERTUE EVEN TO THE DEEP: 3 586

SHORE
FROM THE SAFE SHORE THIR FLOATING CARKASES 1 310
OR WHOM BISERTA SENT FROM AFRIC SHORE 1 585
CALABRIA FROM THE HOARCE TRINACRIAN SHORE: 2 661
OF NEITHER SEA, NOR SHORE, NOR AIR, NOR FIRE, 2 912
BUT GLAD THAT NOW HIS SEA SHOULD FIND A SHORE, 2 1011
ON HEAV'NLY GROUND THEY STOOD, AND FROM THE SHORE 7 210

SHORES
NOW LAND, NOW SEA, AND SHORES WITH FORREST CROWND, 9 117
AMONG THE TREES ON ILES AND WOODIE SHORES. 9 1118

SHORN
SHORN OF HIS BEAMS, OR FROM BEHIND THE MOON 1 596
SHORN OF HIS STRENGTH, THEY DESTITUTE AND BARE 9 1062

SHORT
FREQUENT AND FULL. AFTER SHORT SILENCE THEN 1 797
SHORT INTERMISSION BOUGHT WITH DOUBLE SMART. 4 102
SHORT PLEASURES, FOR LONG WOES ARE TO SUCCEED. 4 535
AFTER SHORT PAUSE ASSENTING, THUS BEGAN. 5 562
ALL HUMAN THOUGHTS COME SHORT, SUPREAM OF THINGS; 8 414
TWILIGHT UPON THE EARTH, SHORT ARBITER 9 50
SINCE HIGHER I FALL SHORT, ON HIM WHO NEXT 9 174
THEE SATIATE, TO SHORT ABSENCE I COULD YIELD. 9 248
AND SHORT RETIREMENT URGES SWEET RETURNE. 9 250
INGAGING ME TO EMULATE, BUT SHORT 9 963
WHILE YET WE LIVE, SCARSE ONE SHORT HOUR PERHAPS, 10 923
FROM WHAT WE FEAR FOR BOTH, LET US MAKE SHORT, 10 1000
OR ONE SHORT SIGH OF HUMANE BREATH, UP-BORNE 11 147
AFTER SHORT BLUSH OF MORN; NIGH IN HER SIGHT 11 184
LIVE WELL, HOW LONG OR SHORT PERMIT TO HEAV'N: 11 554
TO WHOM THUS ADAM OF SHORT JOY BEREFT. 11 628

SHORTER
BY SHORTER FLIGHT TO TH' EAST, HAD LEFT HIM THERE 4 595

SHORTEST
OF MANY WAYS TO DIE THE SHORTEST CHOOSING, 10 1005

SHOT
SHOT AFTER US IN STORM, OREBLOWN HATH LAID 1 172
BLACK FIRE AND HORROR SHOT WITH EQUAL RAGE 2 67
SHOT UPWARD STILL DIRECT, WHENCE NO WAY ROUND 3 618
SHOT FORTH PECULIAR GRACES; THEN WITH VOICE 5 15
SHOT PARALEL TO THE EARTH HIS DEWIE RAY, 5 141
SHOT DOWN DIRECT HIS FERVID RAIES TO WARME 5 301
SHOT THROUGH WITH ORIENT BEAMS; WHEN ALL THE PLAIN 6 15
GLAR'D LIGHTNING, AND SHOT FORTH PERNICIOUS FIRE 6 849
AND FROM ABOUT HER SHOT DARTS OF DESIRE 8 62
INTO A GULF SHOT UNDER GROUND, TILL PART 9 72

SHOULDER
EACH SHOULDER BROAD, CAME MANTLING O'RE HIS BREST 5 279

SHOULDERS
HUNG ON HIS SHOULDERS LIKE THE MOON, WHOSE ORB 1 287
WITH ATLANTEAN SHOULDERS FIT TO BEAR 2 306
ILLUSTRIOUS ON HIS SHOULDERS FLEDGE WITH WINGS 3 627
CLUSTRING, BUT NOT BENEATH HIS SHOULDERS BROAD: 4 303

SHOUT
A SHOUT THAT TORE HELLS CONCAVE, AND BEYOND 1 542
WITH DEAFNING SHOUT, RETURN'D THEM LOUD ACCLAIM. 2 520
THE MULTITUDE OF ANGELS WITH A SHOUT 3 345
HYMNING TH' ETERNAL FATHER: BUT THE SHOUT 6 96
THUS FOIL'D THIR MIGHTIEST, OURS JOY FILLD, AND
SHOUT, 6 200
BIRTH-DAY OF HEAV'N AND EARTH; WITH JOY AND SHOUT 7 256
THIR UNIVERSAL SHOUT AND HIGH APPLAUSE 10 505

SHOW
SHALL LEAD HELL CAPTIVE MAUGRE HELL, AND SHOW 3 255
FROM ME SOM PLUME, THAT THY SUCCESS MAY SHOW 6 161
SHOW TO THE SUN THIR WAV'D COATS DROPT WITH GOLD, 7 406

SHOWERS
AFTER SOFT SHOWERS; AND SWEET THE COMING ON 4 646
GLISTRING WITH DEW, NOR FRAGRANCE AFTER SHOWERS, 4 653
OR WET THE THIRSTIE EARTH WITH FALLING SHOWERS, 5 190

SHOWN
WHERE THOU ART WEIGH'D, AND SHOWN HOW LIGHT, HOW
WEAK, 4 1012

SHOWR
IF I CONJECTURE AUGHT, NO DRIZLING SHOWR, 6 545
LEAST IT AGAIN DISSOLVE AND SHOWR THE EARTH? 11 883

SHOWRD
WHEN GOD HATH SHOWRD THE EARTH; SO LOVELY SEEMD 4 152
SHOWRD ROSES, WHICH THE MORN REPAIR'D. SLEEP ON 4 773
EXCESS, BEFORE TH' ALL BOUNTEOUS KING, WHO SHOWRD 5 640

SHOWRE
SCOWLS ORE THE DARK'ND LANTSKIP SNOW, OR SHOWRE; 2 491
THIR INFLUENCE MALIGNANT WHEN TO SHOWRE, 10 662
A MIGHTIE NATION, AND UPON HIM SHOWRE 12 124

SHOWRIE
AMBER, AND COLOURS OF THE SHOWRIE ARCH. 6 759

SHOWRS
SHOWRS ON HER KINGS BARBARIC PEARL AND GOLD, 2 4

SHOWS
AND TO REALITIES YIELD ALL HER SHOWS: 8 575

SHOWST
AND MY FAIR SON HERE SHOWST ME, THE DEAR PLEDGE 2 818

SHRILL
LIGHTLY DISPERS'D, AND THE SHRILL MATIN SONG 5 7

SHRIN'D
SHRIN'D IN HIS SANCTUARIE OF HEAV'N SECURE, 6 672

SHRINE
DRAWN ROUND ABOUT THEE LIKE A RADIANT SHRINE, 3 379
TRANSPLANTED FROM HER CLOUDIE SHRINE, AND PLAC'D 7 360
THE RACE OF MANKIND DROWND, BEFORE THE SHRINE 11 13

SHRINES
WITHIN HIS SANCTUARY IT SELF THIR SHRINES, 1 388

SHRINK
AND VENT'ROUS, IF THAT FAIL THEM, SHRINK AND FEAR 2 205
NOT THAT I LESS ENDURE, OR SHRINK FROM PAIN, 4 925
AS AFTER THIRST, WHICH MADE THIR FLOWING SHRINK 11 846

SHROUD
SOM BETTER SHROUD, SOM BETTER WARMTH TO CHERISH 10 1068

SHROUDS
GLADLY THE PORT, THOUGH SHROUDS AND TACKLE TORN; 2 1044

SHRUB
ACANTHUS, AND EACH ODOROUS BUSHIE SHRUB 4 696
WITH ROSE AND ODOURS FROM THE SHRUB UNFUM'D. 5 349
EMBATTELL'D IN HER FIELD: AND THE HUMBLE SHRUB, 7 322
FLUNG ROSE, FLUNG ODOURS FROM THE SPICIE SHRUB, 8 517

SHRUBS
OF SHRUBS AND TANGLING BUSHES HAD PERPLEXT 4 176

SHUDDRING
WITH SHUDDRING HORROR PALE, AND EYES AGAST 2 616

SHUN
PART CURB THIR FIERIE STEEDS, OR SHUN THE GOAL 2 531
BUT THOU O FATHER, I FOREWARN THEE, SHUN 2 810
REMEMBER WHAT I WARNE THEE, SHUN TO TASTE, 8 327
AND SHUN THE BITTER CONSEQUENCE: FOR KNOW, 8 328

SIGHT (CONTINUED)
GREAT JOY WAS AT THIR MEETING, AND AT SIGHT . . 10 350
THEY SAW, BUT OTHER SIGHT INSTEAD, A CROWD . . 10 538
THE FRUTAGE FAIR TO SIGHT, LIKE THAT WHICH GREW . 10 561
TO RECOMPENCE HIS DISTANCE, IN THIR SIGHT . . 10 683
IN SIGHT OF GOD? HIM AFTER ALL DISPUTES . . 10 828
OUT OF MY SIGHT, THOU SERPENT, THAT NAME BEST . 10 867
BY THIR GREAT INTERCESSOR, CAME IN SIGHT . . 11 19
AFTER SHORT BLUSH OF MORN; NIGH IN HER SIGHT . 11 184
WHY ELSE THIS DOUBLE OBJECT IN OUR SIGHT . . 11 201
WITH WHAT TO SIGHT OR SMELL WAS SWEET; FROM THEE . 11 281
WHICH THAT FALSE FRUIT THAT PROMIS'D CLEARER SIGHT 11 413
EEVN TO THE INMOST SEAT OF MENTAL SIGHT, . . . 11 418
MUCH AT THAT SIGHT WAS ADAM IN HIS HEART . . . 11 448
I MUST RETURN TO NATIVE DUST? O SIGHT . . . 11 463
SIGHT SO DEFORM WHAT HEART OF ROCK COULD LONG . 11 494
AND NOW PREPARE THEE FOR ANOTHER SIGHT. . . . 11 555
AT THIS LAST SIGHT, ASSUR'D THAT MAN SHALL LIVE . 11 872
SUCH GRACE SHALL ONE JUST MAN FIND IN HIS SIGHT, . 11 890
THY MORTAL SIGHT TO FAILE; OBJECTS DIVINE . . 12 9

SIGHTED
THE SHARPEST SIGHTED SPIRIT OF ALL IN HEAV'N; . . 3 691

SIGHTS
SERV'D ONELY TO DISCOVER SIGHTS OF WOE, ... 1 64
CALL EL DORADO: BUT TO NOBLER SIGHTS 11 411

SIGN
SHON WITH A GLOSSIE SCURFF, UNDOUBTED SIGN . . . 1 672
AT FIRST, AND CALL'D ME SIN, AND FOR A SIGN . . 2 760
THE ONLY SIGN OF OUR OBEDIENCE LEFT 4 428
AND READ THY LOT IN YON CELESTIAL SIGN . . . 4 1011
WITH EVERY PLANT, IN SIGN OF WORSHIP WAVE. . . 5 194
ALOFT BY ANGELS BORN, HIS SIGN IN HEAV'N: . . 6 776
GAVE SIGN OF GRATULATION, AND EACH HILL; . . 8 514
FREQUENTING, SENT FROM HEARTS CONTRITE, IN SIGN . 10 1091
FREQUENTING, SENT FROM HEARTS CONTRITE, IN SIGN . 10 1103

SIGNAL
THIR SUREST SIGNAL, THEY WILL SOON RESUME . . . 1 278
TILL, AS A SIGNAL GIV'N, TH' UPLIFTED SPEAR . . 1 347
SWARM'D AND WERE STRAITN'D; TILL THE SIGNAL GIV'N. 1 776
THE SIGNAL TO ASCEND, SIT LINGRING HERE 2 56
HOV'RING A SPACE, TILL WINDS THE SIGNAL BLOW . . 2 717
THE WONTED SIGNAL, AND SUPERIOR VOICE 5 705
HESPEREAN SETS, MY SIGNAL TO DEPART. 8 632
HE ENDED, AND THE SON GAVE SIGNAL HIGH . . . 11 72
IN SIGNAL OF REMOVE, WAVES FIERCELY ROUND; . . 12 593

SIGNE
BETWIXT ASTREA AND THE SCORPION SIGNE, ... 4 998
IN DUSKIE WREATHES, RELUCTANT FLAMES, THE SIGNE . 6 58
IN SIGNE WHEREOF EACH BIRD AND BEAST BEHOLD . . 8 342
PRESENT, AND OF HIS PRESENCE MANY A SIGNE . . 11 351
AN OLIVE LEAFE HE BRINGS, PACIFIC SIGNE: . . 11 860
BAPTIZING IN THE PROFLUENT STREAM, THE SIGNE . . 12 442

SIGNES
AMONG SO MANY SIGNES OF POWER AND RULE 4 429
THE DAY FROM NIGHT; AND LET THEM BE FOR SIGNES, . 7 341
AND IN OUR FACES EVIDENT THE SIGNES 9 1077
MUST BE COMPELLD BY SIGNES AND JUDGEMENTS DIRE; . 12 175

SIGNS
SIGNS OF REMORSE AND PASSION TO BEHOLD 1 605
SHOULD BE, AND, BY CONCURRING SIGNS, ERE NOW . . 2 831
KISS'D AS THE GRACIOUS SIGNS OF SWEET REMORSE . . 5 134
BUT TO CONVINCE THE PROUD WHAT SIGNS AVAILE, . . 6 789
SIGHING THROUGH ALL HER WORKS GAVE SIGNS OF WOE, . 9 783
SUBSCRIB'D NOT; NATURE FIRST GAVE SIGNS, IMPREST . 11 182
WHICH HEAV'N BY THESE MUTE SIGNS IN NATURE SHEWS . 11 194

SILENCE
BREAKING THE HORRID SILENCE THUS BEGAN. 1 83
MOV'D ON IN SILENCE TO SOFT PIPES THAT CHARM'D . 1 561
FREQUENT AND FULL. AFTER SHORT SILENCE THEN . 1 797
WITH REASON HATH DEEP SILENCE AND DEMURR . . 2 431
FLED NOT IN SILENCE THROUGH THE FRIGHTED DEEP . 2 994
AND SILENCE WAS IN HEAV'N: ON MANS BEHALF . . 3 218
SILENCE ACCOMPANIED, FOR BEAST AND BIRD, . . 4 600
SILENCE WAS PLEAS'D: NOW GLOW'D THE FIRMAMENT . 4 604
THE COOL, THE SILENT, SAVE WHERE SILENCE YIELDS . 5 39
WORTHY OF SACRED SILENCE TO BE HEARD; . . . 5 557
FRIENDLIEST TO SLEEP AND SILENCE, HE RESOLV'D . 5 668
IN SILENCE THIR BRIGHT LEGIONS, TO THE SOUND . 6 64
THEREFORE ETERNAL SILENCE BE THIR DOOME. . . 6 385
AND SILENCE ON THE ODIOUS DINN OF WARR; . . 6 408
SILENCE, AND SLEEP LISTNING TO THEE WILL WATCH, . 7 106
SILENCE, YE TROUBL'D WAVES, AND THOU DEEP, PEACE, 7 216
BUT NOT IN SILENCE HOLY KEPT; THE HARP . . . 7 594
FIRST TO HIMSELF HE INWARD SILENCE BROKE. . . 9 895
INCHANTING DAUGHTER, THUS THE SILENCE BROKE. . 10 353
SILENCE, AND WITH THESE WORDS ATTENTION WON. . 10 459
AND WHAT MOST MERITS FAME IN SILENCE HID. . . 11 699

SILENT
RETREATED IN A SILENT VALLEY, SING 2 547

SILENT (CONTINUED)
FARR OFF FROM THESE A SLOW AND SILENT STREAM, . . 2 582
SILENT YET SPAKE, AND BREATH'D IMMORTAL LOVE . . 3 267
OF GRATEFUL EEVNING MILDE, THEN SILENT NIGHT . . 4 647
NOR GRATEFUL EEVNING MILD, NOR SILENT NIGHT . . 4 654
FAME IS NOT SILENT, HERE IN HOPE TO FIND . . . 4 938
THE COOL, THE SILENT, SAVE WHERE SILENCE YIELDS . 5 39
WITNESS IF I BE SILENT, MORN OR EEVEN, ... 5 202
WITH SILENT CIRCUMSPECTION UNESPI'D. 6 523
TO MEET HIM ALL HIS SAINTS, WHO SILENT STOOD . . 6 882
THE SILENT HOURS, AND TH' OTHER WHOSE GAY TRAINE . 7 444
OR SHEE FROM WEST HER SILENT COURSE ADVANCE . . 8 163
FROM TH' EARTHS GREAT ALTAR SEND UP SILENT PRAISE 9 195
OF ALL THIR VERTUE: SILENT, AND IN FACE 9 1063

SILENTLY
WING SILENTLY THE BUXOM AIR, IMBALM'D 2 842
BUT SILENTLY A GENTLE TEAR LET FALL 5 130

SILOA'S
DELIGHT THEE MORE, AND SILOA'S BROOK THAT FLOW'D . 1 11

SILVAN
A SILVAN SCENE, AND AS THE RANKS ASCEND 4 140
I HAVE AT WILL. SO TO THE SILVAN LODGE 5 377

SILVANUS
PAN OR SILVANUS NEVER SLEPT, NOR NYMPH, ... 4 707

SILVER
IF METTAL, PART SEEMD GOLD, PART SILVER CLEER; . 3 595
BEFORE HIS DECENT STEPS A SILVER WAND. 3 644
AND O'RE THE DARK HER SILVER MANTLE THREW. . . 4 609
OTHERS ON SILVER LAKES AND RIVERS BATH'D . . . 7 437

SIMILITUDE
BEGOTTEN SON, DIVINE SIMILITUDE, ... 3 384
IN OUR SIMILITUDE, AND LET THEM RULE 7 520
RETAINING STILL DIVINE SIMILITUDE 11 512

SIMPLE
TO SIMPLE SHEPHERDS, KEEPING WATCH BY NIGHT; . . 12 365

SIMPLICITIE
AT WISDOMS GATE, AND TO SIMPLICITIE 3 687
SIMPLICITIE AND SPOTLESS INNOCENCE. 4 318

SIMPLY
BY SIMPLY MEEK; THAT SUFFERING FOR TRUTHS SAKE . 12 569

SIN
DOUBL'D THAT SIN IN BETHEL AND IN DAN, ... 1 485
AT FIRST, AND CALL'D ME SIN, AND FOR A SIGN . . 2 760
STRANGE ALTERATION. SIN AND DEATH AMAIN . . . 2 1024
BY SIN TO FOUL EXORBITANT DESIRES; 3 177
OF ALL THINGS TRANSITORIE AND VAIN, WHEN SIN . . 3 446
ENVIE THEM THAT? CAN IT BE SIN TO KNOW, . . . 4 517
FARR BE IT, THAT I SHOULD WRITE THEE SIN OR BLAME, 4 758
THY SIN AND PLACE OF DOOM OBSCURE AND FOULE. . . 4 840
BY SIN OF DISOBEDIENCE, TILL THAT HOUR . . . 6 396
FOR SIN, ON WARR AND MUTUAL SLAUGHTER BENT. . . 6 506
SAVE WHAT SIN HATH IMPAIRD, WHICH YET HATH WROUGHT 6 691
AND GOVERN WELL THY APPETITE, LEAST SIN . . . 7 546
NOW NOT, THOUGH SIN, NOT TIME, FIRST WRAUGHT THE
CHANGE, ... 9 70
FOR SUCH THOU ART, FROM SIN AND BLAME ENTIRE: . 9 292
BUT HARM PRECEDES NOT SIN: ONELY OUR FOE . . 9 327
WEPT AT COMPLEATING OF THE MORTAL SIN . . . 9 1003
THE SOLACE OF THIR SIN, TILL DEWIE SLEEP . . 9 1044
AND MANIFOLD IN SIN, DESERV'D TO FALL. . . . 10 16
LEAST ON MY HEAD BOTH SIN AND PUNISHMENT, . . 10 133
TO SATAN FIRST IN SIN HIS DOOM APPLY'D, . . 10 172
WITHIN THE GATES OF HELL SATE SIN AND DEATH, . 10 230
SIN OPENING, WHO THUS NOW TO DEATH BEGAN. . . 10 234
FOR DEATH FROM SIN NO POWER CAN SEPARATE. . . 10 251
LONG HEE ADMIRING STOOD, TILL SIN, HIS FAIRE . 10 352
THROUGH SIN TO DEATH EXPOS'D BY MY EXPLOIT. . 10 407
BY SIN AND DEATH A BROAD WAY NOW IS PAV'D . . 10 473
TO SIN AND DEATH A PREY, AND SO TO US, . . . 10 490
TOO SOON ARRIV'D, SIN THERE IN POWER BEFORE, . 10 586
ON HIS PALE HORSE: TO WHOM SIN THUS BEGAN. . . 10 590
WHICH MANS POLLUTING SIN WITH TAINT HATH SHED . 10 631
BOTH SIN, AND DEATH, AND YAWNING GRAVE AT LAST . 10 635
DAUGHTER OF SIN, AMONG TH' IRRATIONAL, . . . 10 708
AND SIN? THE BODIE PROPERLY HATH NEITHER. . . 10 791
FOR DISSOLUTION WROUGHT BY SIN, THAT FIRST . . 11 55
NOR SINN'D THY SIN, YET FROM THAT DERIVE . . . 11 427
INDUCTIVE MAINLY TO THE SIN OF EVE. 11 519
TEN THOUSANDFOULD THE SIN OF HIM WHO SLEW . . 11 678
TO WHOM THUS MICHAEL. DOUBT NOT BUT THAT SIN . 12 285
SIN AGAINST LAW TO FIGHT; THAT WHEN THEY SEE . 12 289
LAW CAN DISCOVER SIN, BUT NOT REMOVE, . . . 12 290
IN SIN FOR EVER LOST FROM LIFE; THIS ACT . . 12 429
DEFEATING SIN AND DEATH, HIS TWO MAINE ARMES, . 12 431
OF WASHING THEM FROM GUILT OF SIN TO LIFE . . 12 443
WHETHER I SHOULD REPENT ME NOW OF SIN 12 474

SINAEAN
TO PAQUIN OF SINAEAN KINGS, AND THENCE 11 390

SINAI
OF OREB, OR OF SINAI, DIDST INSPIRE 1 7
GOD FROM THE MOUNT OF SINAI, WHOSE GRAY TOP . . 12 227

SIN-BORN
WHOM THUS THE SIN-BORN MONSTER ANSWERD SOON. . . 10 596

SIN-BRED
SIN-BRED, HOW HAVE YE TROUBL'D ALL MANKIND . . . 4 315

SINCE
THIS DOWNFALL; SINCE BY FATE THE STRENGTH OF GODS 1 116
SINCE THROUGH EXPERIENCE OF THIS GREAT EVENT . . 1 118
OF FORCE BELIEVE ALMIGHTY, SINCE NO LESS . . . 1 144
FOR THAT CELESTIAL LIGHT? BE IT SO, SINCE HE . . 1 245
GLORIES: FOR NEVER SINCE CREATED MAN, ... 1 573
AND ALL WHO SINCE, BAPTIZ'D OR INFIDEL 1 582
FOR SINCE NO DEEP WITHIN HER GULF CAN HOLD . . . 2 12
BY MY ADVICE; SINCE FATE INEVITABLE 2 197
WORTH WAITING, SINCE OUR PRESENT LOT APPEERS . . 2 223
DEAR DAUGHTER, SINCE THOU CLAIM'ST ME FOR THY SIRE, 2 817
MAY I EXPRESS THEE UNBLAM'D? SINCE GOD IS LIGHT, 3 3
INTO A LIMBO LARGE AND BROAD, SINCE CALLD . . . 3 495
BE THEN HIS LOVE ACCURST, SINCE LOVE OR HATE, . . 4 69
NAY CURS'D BE THOU; SINCE AGAINST HIS THY WILL . 4 71
SO SINCE INTO HIS CHURCH LEWD HIRELINGS CLIMBE. . 4 193
THAT EVER SINCE IN LOVES IMBRACES MET, . . . 4 322
ADAM THE GOODLIEST MAN OF MEN SINCE BORNE . . . 4 323
ALL BEASTS OF TH' EARTH, SINCE WILDE, AND OF ALL CHASE 4 341
WELL KNOWN FROM HEAV'N; AND SINCE MERIDIAN HOUR . 4 581
MIND US OF LIKE REPOSE, SINCE GOD HATH SET . . . 4 612
SINCE SATAN FELL, WHOM FOLLIE OVERTHREW, . . . 4 905
TO BOAST WHAT ARMS CAN DOE, SINCE THINE NO MORE 4 1008
AND WHY NOT GODS OF MEN, SINCE GOOD, THE MORE . . 5 71
SINCE BY DESCENDING FROM THE THRONES ABOVE, . . 5 363
NOT MEERLY TITULAR, SINCE BY DECREE 5 774
BUT MORE ILLUSTRIOUS MADE, SINCE HE THE HEAD . . 5 842
OF THIS RIGHT HAND PROVOK'T, SINCE FIRST THAT TONGUE 6 154
SINCE NOW WE FIND THIS OUR EMPYREAL FORM . . . 6 433
SINCE MICHAEL AND HIS POWERS WENT FORTH TO TAME . 6 686
OF ENDING THIS GREAT WARR, SINCE NONE BUT THOU . 6 702
OR I ALONE AGAINST THEM, SINCE BY STRENGTH . . . 6 820
OF WHAT WE ARE. BUT SINCE THOU HAST VOUTSAF'T . 7 80
WHO SINCE THE MORNING HOUR SET OUT FROM HEAV'N . 8 111
NOT HITHER SUMMOND, SINCE THEY CANNOT CHANGE . . 8 347
FOLLOW'D WITH BENEDICTION. SINCE TO PART, . . . 8 645
SINCE FIRST THIS SUBJECT FOR HEROIC SONG . . . 9 25
SINCE URIEL REGENT OF THE SUN DESCRI'D . . . 9 60
NOT LONGER THEN SINCE I IN ONE NIGHT FREED . . . 9 140
SINCE HIGHER I FALL SHORT, ON HIM WHO NEXT . . . 9 174
SINCE REASON NOT IMPOSSIBLY MAY MEET 9 360
FOR NOW, AND SINCE FIRST BREAK OF DAWNE THE FIEND, 9 412
PRONE ON THE GROUND, AS SINCE, BUT ON HIS REARE, . 9 497
AND LOVELY, NEVER SINCE OF SERPENT KIND . . . 9 504
FLOURISHD, SINCE MUTE, TO SOM GREAT CAUSE ADDREST, 9 672
BE REAL, WHY NOT KNOWN, SINCE EASIER SHUNND? . . 9 699
THAT YE SHOULD BE AS GODS, SINCE I AS MAN, . . 9 710
SINCE TO EACH MEANING SAVOUR ME APPLY, ... 9 1019
FOR NEVER DID THY BEAUTIE SINCE THE DAY . . . 9 1029
FALSE IN OUR PROMIS'D RISING; SINCE OUR EYES . . 9 1070
CONCERN'D NOT MAN (SINCE HE NO FURTHER KNEW) . . 10 170
FARR INTO CHAOS, SINCE THE FIEND PASS'D THROUGH, . 10 233
BY HIS AVENGERS, SINCE NO PLACE LIKE THIS . . . 10 241
WITH WHAT PERMISSIVE GLORY SINCE HIS FALL . . . 10 451
THE DOUBT, SINCE HUMANE REACH NO FURTHER KNOWS. . 10 793
OF TARDIE EXECUTION, SINCE DENOUNC'T 10 853
SINCE THIS DAYS DEATH DENOUNC'T, IF OUGHT I SEE, . 10 962
HIS TRUMPET, HEARD IN OREB SINCE PERHAPS . . . 11 74
TO KNOW BOTH GOOD AND EVIL, SINCE HIS TASTE . . 11 85
EV'N TO THE SEAT OF GOD. FOR SINCE I SAUGHT . . 11 148
MOTHER OF ALL THINGS LIVING, SINCE BY THEE . . . 11 160
THE PERSIAN IN ECBATAN SATE, OR SINCE 11 393
SO GOODLY AND ERECT, THOUGH FAULTIE SINCE, . . . 11 509
TO LOATHSOM SICKNESS, WORTHILY, SINCE THEY . . . 11 524
SINCE THY ORIGINAL LAPSE, TRUE LIBERTIE 12 83
MAN TILL THEN FREE. THEREFORE SINCE HEE PERMITS . 12 90
PRESAGING, SINCE WITH SORROW AND HEARTS DISTRESS . 12 613

SINCERE
NOT FREE, WHAT PROOF COULD THEY HAVE GIVN SINCERE 3 103
THOUGH BUT ENDEVORD WITH SINCERE INTENT, ... 3 192
LESS ATTRIBUTED TO HER FAITH SINCERE, ... 9 320
WHAT LOVE SINCERE, AND REVERENCE IN MY HEART . . 10 915
THE OTHERS NOT, FOR HIS WAS NOT SINCERE; . . . 11 443

SINCEREST
WHICH YOUR SINCEREST CARE COULD NOT PREVENT, . . . 10 37

SIN'D
MEANWHILE ERE THUS WAS SIN'D AND JUDG'D ON EARTH, 10 229
NOW RUL'D HIM, PUNISHT IN THE SHAPE HE SIN'D, . . 10 516
MORE MISERABLE; BOTH HAVE SIN'D, BUT THOU . . . 10 930

SINFUL
THIR SINFUL STATE, AND TO APPEASE BETIMES . . . 3 186
NATURE HER SELF, THOUGH PURE OF SINFUL THOUGHT, . 8 506
WITHOUT REMORSE DRIVE OUT THE SINFUL PAIR, . . . 11 105

SINFULNESS
WITH SINFULNESS OF MEN; THEREBY TO LEARN . . . 11 360

SING
SING HEAV'NLY MUSE, THAT ON THE SECRET TOP . . . 1 6
WITH WARBL'D HYMNS, AND TO HIS GODHEAD SING . . 2 242
RETREATED IN A SILENT VALLEY, SING 2 547
(WHAT COULD IT LESS WHEN SPIRITS IMMORTAL SING?) . 2 553
UNFAINED HALLELUIAHS TO THEE SING, ... 6 744
MORE SAFE I SING WITH MORTAL VOICE, UNCHANG'D . . 7 24
OF LUSTFUL APPETENCE, TO SING, TO DANCE, . . . 11 619
OF GREAT MESSIAH SHALL SING. THUS LAWS AND RITES 12 244
FOR EVER SHALL ENDURE; THE LIKE SHALL SING . . 12 324

SINGED
AND LEAVE A SINGED BOTTOM ALL INVOLV'D 1 236
WITH SINGED TOP THIR STATELY GROWTH THOUGH BARE . 1 614

SINGING
SINGING THIR GREAT CREATOR: OFT IN BANDS . . . 4 684
THAT SINGING UP TO HEAVEN GATE ASCEND, ... 5 198

SINGLE
OTHERS CAME SINGLE; HE WHO TO BE DEEMD 3 469
SINGLE AGAINST THEE WICKED, AND THENCE WEAK, . . 4 856
SINGLE, IS YET SO JUST, MY CONSTANT THOUGHTS . . 5 552
THOUGH SINGLE. FROM AMIDST THEM FORTH HE PASSD, . 5 903
THE BETTER FIGHT, WHO SINGLE HAST MAINTAIND . . 6 30
EACH WARRIOUR SINGLE AS IN CHIEF, EXPERT . . . 6 233
BANK THE MID SEA: PART SINGLE OR WITH MATE . . . 7 403
HIS SINGLE IMPERFECTION, AND BEGET 8 423
SINGLE WITH LIKE DEFENCE, WHEREVER MET, ... 9 325
AS NOT SECURE TO SINGLE OR COMBIN'D. 9 339
INSATIATE, I THUS SINGLE, NOR HAVE FEARD . . . 9 536
NOR I ON MY PART SINGLE, IN MEE ALL 10 817
SINGLE OR IN ARRAY OF BATTEL RANG'D 11 644
WITH FOES FOR DARING SINGLE TO BE JUST, . . . 11 703

SINGLY
CAME SINGLY WHERE HE STOOD ON THE BARE STRAND, . 1 379

SINGS
SINGS DARKLING, AND IN SHADIEST COVERT HID . . . 3 39
OR SERENATE, WHICH THE STARV'D LOVER SINGS . . . 4 769

SINGULAR
OR SINGULAR AND RASH, WHEREAT REJOIC'D 5 851

SINISTER
MORE TO THE PART SINISTER FROM ME DRAWN, . . . 10 886

SINK
BAD MEN AND ANGELS, THEY ARRAIGND SHALL SINK . . 3 331

SINKS
AND SWIMS OR SINKS, OR WADES, OR CREEPS, OR FLYES: 2 950

SINLESS
LED ON, YET SINLESS, WITH DESIRE TO KNOW . . . 7 61
TO WHOM THUS EVE YET SINLESS. OF THE FRUIT . . 9 659
INHABITED, THOUGH SINLESS, MORE THEN NOW, . . . 10 690

SINN'D
OF LIFE THAT SINN'D; WHAT DIES BUT WHAT HAD LIFE . 10 790
NOR SINN'D THY SIN, YET FROM THAT DERIVE . . . 11 427

SINND
GAVE THEM ABOVE THIR FOES, NOT TO HAVE SINND, . . 6 402

SINNE
SINNE AND HER SHADOW DEATH, AND MISERIE 9 12

SINNING
PUREST AT FIRST, NOW GROSS BY SINNING GROWN. . . 6 661

SINNS
DISLOYAL BREAKS HIS FEALTIE, AND SINNS 3 204

SINS
CAN NEVER SEEK, ONCE DEAD IN SINS AND LOST; . . 3 233
SO MANY LAWS ARGUE SO MANY SINS 12 283
LONG TIME SHALL DWELL AND PROSPER, BUT WHEN SINS . 12 316
THE LAW THAT IS AGAINST THEE, AND THE SINS . . 12 416

SINUOUS
STREAKING THE GROUND WITH SINUOUS TRACE; NOT ALL . 7 481

SION
ROSE OUT OF CHAOS: OR IF SION HILL 1 10
JEHOVAH THUNDRING OUT OF SION, THRON'D 1 386
IN SION ALSO NOT UNSUNG, WHERE STOOD 1 442
THEE SION AND THE FLOWRIE BROOKS BENEATH . . . 3 30
OVER MOUNT SION, AND, THOUGH THAT WERE LARGE, . . 3 530

SLEEK
HIS TURRET CREST, AND SLEEK ENAMEL'D NECK, 9 525

SLEEP
SHALL HAST'N, SUCH A PEAL SHALL ROUSE THIR SLEEP. 3 329
THAT DAY I OFT REMEMBER, WHEN FROM SLEEP 4 449
SUCCESSIVE, AND THE TIMELY DEW OF SLEEP 4 614
THIS GLORIOUS SIGHT, WHEN SLEEP HATH SHUT ALL EYES? 4 658
UNSEEN, BOTH WHEN WE WAKE, AND WHEN WE SLEEP: 4 678
AND WHEN WE SEEK, AS NOW, THY GIFT OF SLEEP. 4 735
SHOWRD ROSES, WHICH THE MORN REPAIR'D. SLEEP ON 4 773
HERE WATCHING AT THE HEAD OF THESE THAT SLEEP? 4 826
IMPLOI'D IT SEEMS TO VIOLATE SLEEP, AND THOSE 4 883
WHEN ADAM WAK'T, SO CUSTOMD, FOR HIS SLEEP 5 3
THE TROUBLE OF THY THOUGHTS THIS NIGHT IN SLEEP 5 96
THAT WHAT IN SLEEP THOU DIDST ABHORR TO DREAM, 5 120
FRIENDLIEST TO SLEEP AND SILENCE, HE RESOLV'D 5 668
SLEEPST THOU COMPANION DEAR, WHAT SLEEP CAN CLOSE 5 673
THY SLEEP DISSENT? NEW LAWS THOU SEEST IMPOS'D; 5 679
SILENCE, AND SLEEP LISTNING TO THEE WILL WATCH, 7 106
INDUC'D ME. AS NEW WAK'T FROM SOUNDEST SLEEP 8 253
PENSIVE I SATE ME DOWN; THERE GENTLE SLEEP 8 287
OF SLEEP, WHICH INSTANTLY FELL ON ME, CALL'D 8 458
WITH ACT INTELLIGENTIAL; BUT HIS SLEEP 9 190
THE SOLACE OF THIR SIN, TILL DEWIE SLEEP 9 1044
MADE ERRE, WAS NOW EXHAL'D, AND GROSSER SLEEP 9 1049
AND SLEEP SECURE; HIS DREADFUL VOICE NO MORE 10 779
HERE SLEEP BELOW WHILE THOU TO FORESIGHT WAK'ST, 11 368
OR THEIRS WHOM HE REDEEMS, A DEATH LIKE SLEEP, 12 434
FOR GOD IS ALSO IN SLEEP, AND DREAMS ADVISE, 12 611

SLEEPING
ON DUTY, SLEEPING FOUND BY WHOM THEY DREAD, 1 333
THOUGH SLEEPING, WHERE I LAY, AND SAW THE SHAPE 8 463
THE SERPENT SLEEPING, IN WHOSE MAZIE FOULDS 9 161
THE SERPENT: HIM FAST SLEEPING SOON HE FOUND 9 182
LAY SLEEPING RAN BEFORE, BUT FOUND HER WAK'T; 12 608

SLEEPLESS
THOUGH AFTER SLEEPLESS NIGHT; FOR SEE THE MORN, 11 173

SLEEPS
ASCENDING, WHILE THE NORTH WIND SLEEPS, O'RESPREAD 2 489
AND OFT THOUGH WISDOM WAKE, SUSPICION SLEEPS 3 686
STRETCHT LIKE A PROMONTORIE SLEEPS OR SWIMMES, 7 414
WITH INOFFENSIVE PACE THAT SPINNING SLEEPS 8 164

SLEEPST
WHY SLEEPST THOU EVE? NOW IS THE PLEASANT TIME, 5 38
SLEEPST THOU COMPANION DEAR, WHAT SLEEP CAN CLOSE 5 673

SLEEPY
LET SUCH BETHINK THEM, IF THE SLEEPY DRENCH 2 73

SLENDER
SHEE AS A VAIL DOWN TO THE SLENDER WASTE 4 304
EACH FLOUR OF SLENDER STALK, WHOSE HEAD THOUGH GAY 9 428

SLEPST
AS ONCE THOU SLEPST, WHILE SHEE TO LIFE WAS FORMD. 11 369

SLEPT
PAN OR SILVANUS NEVER SLEPT, NOR NYMPH, 4 707
THESE LULLD BY NIGHTINGALES IMBRACEING SLEPT, 4 771
CELESTIAL TABERNACLES, WHERE THEY SLEPT 5 654
FEARLESS UNFEARD HE SLEPT: IN AT HIS MOUTH 9 187

SLEW
WHO SLEW HIS BROTHER; STUDIOUS THEY APPERE 11 609
TEN THOUSANDFOULD THE SIN OF HIM WHO SLEW 11 678

SLIDING
SMOOTH SLIDING WITHOUT STEP, LAST LED ME UP 8 302

SLIGHT
AT ONE SLIGHT BOUND HIGH OVER LEAP'D ALL BOUND 4 181
IF THEY TRANSGRESS, AND SLIGHT THAT SOLE COMMAND, 7 47

SLIGHTLY
THE FACIL GATES OF HELL TOO SLIGHTLY BARRD. 4 967

SLIME
INTO A BEAST, AND MIXT WITH BESTIAL SLIME, 9 165
AND WITH ASPHALTIC SLIME; BROAD AS THE GATE, 10 298
INGENDERD IN THE PYTHIAN VALE ON SLIME, 10 530

SLIMIE
SOLID OR SLIMIE, AS IN RAGING SEA 10 286

SLIP
LET US NOT SLIP TH' OCCASION, WHETHER SCORN, 1 178

SLOATH
COUNSEL'D IGNOBLE EASE, AND PEACEFUL SLOATH, 2 227

SLOPE
DRIVN BACKWARD SLOPE THIR POINTING SPIRES, AND
ROWLD 1 223

SLOPE (CONTINUED)
DOWN THE SLOPE HILLS, DISPERST, OR IN A LAKE, 4 261
BORE HIM SLOPE DOWNWARD TO THE SUN NOW FALL'N 4 591

SLOTH
I SEE THAT MOST THROUGH SLOTH HAD RATHER SERVE, 6 166
SHALL CHANGE THIR COURSE TO PLEASURE, EASE, AND
SLOTH, 11 794

SLOTHFUL
TIMOROUS AND SLOTHFUL: YET HE PLEAS'D THE EAR, 2 117

SLOW
UNTAM'D RELUCTANCE, AND REVENGE THOUGH SLOW, 2 337
FARR OFF FROM THESE A SLOW AND SILENT STREAM, 2 582
LIGHT-ARM'D OR HEAVY, SHARP, SMOOTH, SWIFT OR SLOW, 2 902
MINE EAR SHALL NOT BE SLOW, MINE EYE NOT SHUT. 3 193
SATAN HAD JOURNIED ON, PENSIVE AND SLOW; 4 173
UNDER SPRED ENSIGNES MOVING NIGH, IN SLOW 6 533
SPEED ALMOST SPIRITUAL; MEE THOU THINKST NOT SLOW, 8 110
THESE CHANGES IN THE HEAV'NS, THOUGH SLOW, PRODUC'D 10 692
AND SLOW DESCENDS, WITH SOMTHING HEAV'NLY FRAUGHT. 11 207
THEY HAND IN HAND WITH WANDRING STEPS AND SLOW, 12 648

SLOWEST
MENDS NOT HER SLOWEST PACE FOR PRAYERS OR CRIES. 10 859

SLOWLY
SLOWLY DESCENDED, AND WITH RIGHT ASPECT 4 541

SLOW-PAC'T
WILL PROVE NO SUDDEN, BUT A SLOW-PAC'T EVILL, 10 963

SLUC'D
SLUC'D FROM THE LAKE, A SECOND MULTITUDE 1 702

SLUCE
EACH IN THIR CHRYSTAL SLUCE, HEE ERE THEY FELL 5 133

SLUCES
HIS SLUCES, AS THE HEAV'N HIS WINDOWS SHUT. 11 849

SLUMBER
TO SLUMBER HERE, AS IN THE VALES OF HEAV'N? 1 321
ROUS'D FROM THE SLUMBER, ON THAT FIERY COUCH, 1 377

SLUMBERD
THAT SLUMBERD, WAKES THE BITTER MEMORIE 4 24

SLUMBERS
VISIT'ST MY SLUMBERS NIGHTLY, OR WHEN MORN 7 29

SLUMBRING
HIM HAPLY SLUMBRING ON THE NORWAY FOAM 1 203
AND DICTATES TO ME SLUMBRING, OR INSPIRES 9 23

SLUMBROUS
NOW FALLING WITH SOFT SLUMBROUS WEIGHT INCLINES 4 615

SLUNK
WERE SLUNK, ALL BUT THE WAKEFUL NIGHTINGALE; 4 602
THAT ALL WAS LOST. BACK TO THE THICKET SLUNK 9 784
HEE AFTER EVE SEDUC'T, UNMINDED SLUNK 10 332

SLY
HIS LITHE PROBOSCIS; CLOSE THE SERPENT SLY 4 347
BUT WITH SLY CIRCUMSPECTION, AND BEGAN 4 537
AND THOU SLY HYPOCRITE, WHO NOW WOULDST SEEM 4 957
BY SLY ASSAULT; AND SOMWHERE NIGH AT HAND 9 256
SO TALK'D THE SPIRITED SLY SNAKE; AND EVE 9 613

SMALL
THE PILOT OF SOME SMALL NIGHT-FOUNDER'D SKIFF, 1 204
COULD MERIT MORE THEN THAT SMALL INFANTRY 1 575
PRECEDENCE, NONE, WHOSE PORTION IS SO SMALL 2 33
THEN MOST CONSPICUOUS, WHEN GREAT THINGS OF SMALL, 2 258
THE TEMPTING STREAM, WITH ONE SMALL DROP TO LOOSE 2 607
GREAT THINGS WITH SMALL) THEN WHEN BELLONA STORMS, 2 922
THOUGH DISTANT FARR SOM SMALL REFLECTION GAINES 3 428
STARR INTERPOS'D, HOWEVER SMALL HE SEES, 5 258
OF GOD INSPIR'D, SMALL STORE WILL SERVE, WHERE
STORE, 5 322
GREAT THINGS BY SMALL, IF NATURES CONCORD BROKE, 6 311
OF EVIL THEN SO SMALL AS EASIE THINK 6 437
THIR SMALL PECULIAR, THOUGH FROM HUMAN SIGHT 7 368
OF FUTURE, IN SMALL ROOM LARGE HEART ENCLOS'D, 7 486
THOUGH, IN COMPARISON OF HEAV'N, SO SMALL, 8 92
LODG'D IN A SMALL PARTITION, AND THE REST 8 105
FAST BY A FOUNTAIN, ONE SMALL THICKET PAST 9 628
AND ELEGANT, OF SAPIENCE NO SMALL PART, 9 1018
SO, IF GREAT THINGS TO SMALL MAY BE COMPAR'D, 10 306
OF EVERY BEAST, AND BIRD, AND INSECT SMALL 11 734
ALL LEFT, IN ONE SMALL BOTTOM SWUM IMBARK'T. 11 753
STILL OVERCOMING EVIL, AND BY SMALL 12 566

SMALLER
FROM BRANCH TO BRANCH THE SMALLER BIRDS WITH SONG 7 433

SMALLEST
NOW LESS THEN SMALLEST DWARFS, IN NARROW ROOM 1 779
THUS INCORPOREAL SPIRITS TO SMALLEST FORMS 1 789
OF SMALLEST MAGNITUDE CLOSE BY THE MOON. 2 1053
WHO OUT OF SMALLEST THINGS COULD WITHOUT END 6 137
FOR WINGS, AND SMALLEST LINEAMENTS EXACT 7 477

SMART
SHORT INTERMISSION BOUGHT WITH DOUBLE SMART. 4 102

SMEARD
SMEARD ROUND WITH PITCH, AND IN THE SIDE A DORE 11 731

SMELL
LUR'D WITH THE SMELL OF INFANT BLOOD, TO DANCE 2 664
CHEAR'D WITH THE GRATEFUL SMELL OLD OCEAN SMILES. 4 165
ALL TREES OF NOBLEST KIND FOR SIGHT, SMELL, TASTE; 4 217
BREATHING THE SMELL OF FIELD AND GROVE, ATTUNE 4 265
WHICH HE HAD PLUCKT; THE PLEASANT SAVOURIE SMELL 5 84
OF SENSE, WHEREBY THEY HEAR, SEE, SMELL, TOUCH, TASTE, 5 411
I MEAN OF TASTE, SIGHT, SMELL, HERBS, FRUITS, AND FLOURS, 8 527
WITH GRATEFUL SMELL, FORTH CAME THE HUMAN PAIR 9 197
THE SMELL OF GRAIN, OR TEDDED GRASS, OR KINE, 9 450
THEN SMELL OF SWEETEST FENEL OR THE TEATS 9 581
AN EAGER APPETITE, RAIS'D BY THE SMELL 9 740
NEW GATHERD, AND AMBROSIAL SMELL DIFFUS'D. 9 852
SO SAYING, WITH DELIGHT HE SNUFF'D THE SMELL 10 272
THE SMELL OF PEACE TOWARD MANKINDE, LET HIM LIVE 11 38
WITH WHAT TO SIGHT OR SMELL WAS SWEET; FROM THEE 11 281

SMELLING
WITH FLOWERS, GARLANDS, AND SWEET-SMELLING HERBS 4 709
HER BOSOM SMELLING SWEET: AND THESE SCARCE BLOWN, 7 319
THE SMELLING GOURD, UP STOOD THE CORNIE REED 7 321
OFFER SWEET SMELLING GUMMS AND FRUITS AND FLOURS: 11 327

SMELLS
THAT OPEN NOW THIR CHOICEST BOSOM'D SMELLS 5 127
WITH FLOURETS DECK'T AND FRAGRANT SMELLS; BUT EVE 5 379

SMIL'D
IMPURPL'D WITH CELESTIAL ROSES SMIL'D. 3 364
YOUTH SMIL'D CELESTIAL, AND TO EVERY LIMB 3 638
SMIL'D WITH SUPERIOR LOVE, AS JUPITER 4 499
THEY CAME, THAT LIKE POMONA'S ARBOUR SMIL'D 5 378
AND WITH FRESH FLOURETS HILL AND VALLEY SMIL'D. 6 784
CONSUMMATE LOVLY SMIL'D; AIRE, WATER, EARTH, 7 502
BIRDS ON THE BRANCHES WARBLING; ALL THINGS SMIL'D, 8 265
A BOUGH OF FAIREST FRUIT THAT DOWNIE SMIL'D, 9 851
PERPETUAL SMIL'D ON EARTH WITH VERNANT FLOURS, 10 679

SMILE
GRINND HORRIBLE A GASTLY SMILE, TO HEAR 2 846
PLEAS'D, OUT OF HEAVEN SHALT LOOK DOWN AND SMILE, 3 257
REIGNS HERE AND REVELS; NOT IN THE BOUGHT SMILE 4 765
AS WITH A SMILE MORE BRIGHT'ND, THUS REPLI'D. 8 368
TO WHOM THE ANGEL WITH A SMILE THAT GLOW'D 8 618

SMILES
CHEAR'D WITH THE GRATEFUL SMELL OLD OCEAN SMILES. 4 165
NOR GENTLE PURPOSE, NOR ENDEARING SMILES 4 337
ON JUNO SMILES, WHEN HE IMPREGNS THE CLOUDS 4 500
THEN WHEN FAIR MORNING FIRST SMILES ON THE WORLD, 5 124
LOOKS INTERVENE AND SMILES, OR OBJECT NEW 9 222
OF LOOKS AND SMILES, FOR SMILES FROM REASON FLOW, 9 239
OCCASION WHICH NOW SMILES, BEHOLD ALONE 9 480
IGNOBLY, TO THE TRAINES AND TO THE SMILES 11 624

SMILING
DISDAINFULLY HALF SMILING THUS REPLI'D. 4 903
SURE PLEDGE OF DAY, THAT CROWNST THE SMILING MORN 5 168
AND SMILING TO HIS ONELY SON THUS SAID. 5 718
HER ROSIE PROGRESS SMILING; LET US FORTH, 11 175

SMIT
SMIT WITH THE LOVE OF SACRED SONG; BUT CHIEF 3 29

SMITE
THE SWORD OF SATAN WITH STEEP FORCE TO SMITE 6 324

SMOAK
WITH STENCH AND SMOAK: SUCH RESTING FOUND THE SOLE 1 237
BELCH'D FIRE AND ROWLING SMOAK; THE REST ENTIRE 1 671
CAST FORTH REDOUNDING SMOAK AND RUDDY FLAME. 2 889
HE SPREADS FOR FLIGHT, AND IN THE SURGING SMOAK 2 928
TO DARKEN ALL THE HILL, AND SMOAK TO ROWL 6 57
BUT SOON OBSCUR'D WITH SMOAK, ALL HEAV'N APPEERD, 6 585
OF SMOAK AND BICKERING FLAME, AND SPARKLES DIRE; 6 766

SMOAK'D
OR ALTAR SMOAK'D; YET WHO MORE OFT THEN HEE 1 493

SMOOTH
WHILE SMOOTH ADONIS FROM HIS NATIVE ROCK 1 450
WITHIN, HER AMPLE SPACES, O'RE THE SMOOTH 1 725
SOON LEARND, NOW MILDER, AND THUS ANSWERD SMOOTH. 2 816

SMOOTH (CONTINUED)
LIGHT-ARM'D OR HEAVY, SHARP, SMOOTH, SWIFT OR SLOW, 2 902
SMOOTH LAKE, THAT TO ME SEEMD ANOTHER SKIE. 4 459
THEN THAT SMOOTH WATRY IMAGE; BACK I TURND, 4 480
ROUGH, OR SMOOTH RIN'D, OR BEARDED HUSK, OR SHELL 5 342
IN JOINTED ARMOUR WATCH: ON SMOOTH THE SEALE, 7 409
AND BEARES THEE SOFT WITH THE SMOOTH AIR ALONG, 8 166
SMOOTH SLIDING WITHOUT STEP, LAST LED ME UP 8 302
SOME TREE WHOSE BROAD SMOOTH LEAVES TOGETHER SOWD, 9 1095
SMOOTH, EASIE, INOFFENSIVE DOWN TO HELL. 10 305
OF GODDESSES, SO BLITHE, SO SMOOTH, SO GAY, 11 615

SMOOTH'D
EACH PERTURBATION SMOOTH'D WITH OUTWARD CALME, 4 120

SMOOTHED
FLIE TO AND FRO, OR ON THE SMOOTHED PLANK, 1 772

SMOOTHS
SO SMOOTHS HER CHARMING TONES, THAT GODS OWN EAR 5 626

SMOTE
SMOTE ON HIM SORE BESIDES, VAULTED WITH FIRE; 1 298
BOTH WHERE THE MORNING SUN FIRST WARMLY SMOTE 4 244
SAW WHERE THE SWORD OF MICHAEL SMOTE, AND FELL'D 6 250
LEVEL'D, WITH SUCH IMPETUOUS FURIE SMOTE, 6 591
AS WITH A TRIDENT SMOTE, AND FIX'T AS FIRM 10 295
SMOTE HIM INTO THE MIDRIFF WITH A STONE 11 445

SMUTTIE
AGAINST A RUMORD WARR, THE SMUTTIE GRAINE 4 817

SNAKE
FROM SHARPEST SIGHT: FOR IN THE WILIE SNAKE, 9 91
SO TALK'D THE SPIRITED SLY SNAKE; AND EVE 9 613
SO GLISTER'D THE DIRE SNAKE, AND INTO FRAUD 9 643
OR AS THE SNAKE WITH YOUTHFUL COATE REPAID; 10 218
TH' EXCEPTED TREE, NOR WITH THE SNAKE CONSPIR'D, 11 426

SNAKIE
HAD NOT THE SNAKIE SORCERESS THAT SAT 2 724
THIR SNAKIE FOULDS, AND ADDED WINGS. FIRST CREPT 7 484
CLIMBING, SAT THICKER THEN THE SNAKIE LOCKS 10 559

SNARE
HAPLY SO SCAP'D HIS MORTAL SNARE; FOR NOW 4 8
TO HELLISH FALSHOOD, SNARE THEM. BUT FOR THEE 10 873
A HELP, BECAME THY SNARE; TO MEE REPROACH 11 165
WITH WARR AND HOSTILE SNARE SUCH AS REFUSE 12 31

SNARES
DISTURBANCES ON EARTH THROUGH FEMAL SNARES, 10 897

SNATCH'D
HAD NOT A CLOUD DESCENDING SNATCH'D HIM THENCE 11 670

SNATCHT
SO SNATCHT WILL NOT EXEMPT US FROM THE PAINE 10 1025

SNOW
SCOWLS ORE THE DARK'ND LANTSKIP SNOW, OR SHOWRE; 2 491
OF ANCIENT PILE; ALL ELSE DEEP SNOW AND ICE, 2 591
OR EAST OR WEST, WHICH HAD FORBID THE SNOW 10 685
AND SNOW AND HAILE AND STORMIE GUST AND FLAW, 10 698
TH' INCLEMENT SEASONS, RAIN, ICE, HAIL AND SNOW, 10 1063

SNOWIE
WHOSE SNOWIE RIDGE THE ROVING TARTAR BOUNDS, 3 432
BY ASTRACAN OVER THE SNOWIE PLAINES 10 432

SNOWY
AND IDA KNOWN, THENCE ON THE SNOWY TOP 1 515

SNUFF'D
SO SAYING, WITH DELIGHT HE SNUFF'D THE SMELL 10 272

SOAR
THAT WITH NO MIDDLE FLIGHT INTENDS TO SOAR 1 14

SOARD
AS HIGH HE SOARD, OBNOXIOUS FIRST OR LAST 9 170

SOARE
FOR YOU, THERE SITTING WHERE YE DURST NOT SOARE; 4 829
WINNOWS THE BUXOM AIR; TILL WITHIN SOARE 5 270
FOLLOWING, ABOVE TH' OLYMPIAN HILL I SOARE, 7 3

SOARES
NOW SHAVES WITH LEVEL WING THE DEEP, THEN SOARES 2 634

SOARING
A STANDING FIGHT, THEN SOARING ON MAIN WING 6 243
THEY SUMM'D THIR PENNS, AND SOARING TH' AIR SUBLIME 7 421

SOBER
HAD IN HER SOBER LIVERIE ALL THINGS CLAD; 4 599
TO THESE THAT SOBER RACE OF MEN, WHOSE LIVES 11 621

SOCIABLE
RAPHAEL, THE SOCIABLE SPIRIT, THAT DEIGN'D 5 221

SOCIABLY
THAT I SHOULD FEAR, NOR SOCIABLY MILD, 11 234

SOCIAL
SOCIAL COMMUNICATION, YET SO PLEAS'D, 8 429

SOCIETIE
AMONG UNEQUALS WHAT SOCIETIE 8 383
WHAT HIGHER IN HER SOCIETIE THOU FINDST 8 586
FOR SOLITUDE SOMTIMES IS BEST SOCIETIE, 9 249
HIM WITH HER LOV'D SOCIETIE, THAT NOW 9 1007

SODOM
WITNESS THE STREETS OF SODOM, AND THAT NIGHT 1 503
NEER THAT BITUMINOUS LAKE WHERE SODOM FLAM'D; 10 562

SOFALA
AND SOFALA THOUGHT OPHIR, TO THE REALME 11 400

SOFT
CAN EITHER SEX ASSUME, OR BOTH; SO SOFT 1 424
OF FLUTES AND SOFT RECORDERS; SUCH AS RAIS'D 1 551
MOV'D ON IN SILENCE TO SOFT PIPES THAT CHARM'D 1 561
AS SOFT AS NOW SEVERE, OUR TEMPER CHANG'D 2 276
PURGE OFF THIS GLOOM; THE SOFT DELICIOUS AIR, 2 400
THIR SOFT ETHEREAL WARMTH, AND THERE TO PINE 2 601
STOOD WHISPERING SOFT, BY A FRESH FOUNTAIN SIDE 4 326
ON THE SOFT DOWNIE BANK DAMASKT WITH FLOURS: 4 334
THY COMING, AND THY SOFT IMBRACES, HEE 4 471
LESS WINNING SOFT, LESS AMIABLIE MILDE, 4 479
NOW FALLING WITH SOFT SLUMBROUS WEIGHT INCLINES 4 615
AFTER SOFT SHOWERS; AND SWEET THE COMING ON 4 646
IN NATURE AND ALL THINGS, WHICH THESE SOFT FIRES 4 667
HER HAND SOFT TOUCHING, WHISPERD THUS. AWAKE 5 17
BREATHE SOFT OR LOUD; AND WAVE YOUR TOPS, YE PINES, 5 193
CEAS'D WARBLING, BUT ALL NIGHT TUN'D HER SOFT
LAYES: 7 436
TEMPER'D SOFT TUNINGS, INTERMIXT WITH VOICE 7 598
ON HER SOFT AXLE, WHILE SHE PACES EEV'N, 8 165
AND BEARES THEE SOFT WITH THE SMOOTH AIR ALONG, 8 166
SOFT ON THE FLOURIE HERB I FOUND ME LAID 8 254
FIRST FOUND ME, AND WITH SOFT OPPRESSION SEIS'D 8 288
SOFT SHE WITHDREW, AND LIKE A WOOD-NYMPH LIGHT 9 386
ANGELIC, BUT MORE SOFT, AND FEMININE, 9 458
NOW WALKING IN THE GARDEN, BY SOFT WINDES 10 98
SOFT WORDS TO HIS FIERCE PASSION SHE ASSAY'D: 10 865
SOFT AMOROUS DITTIES, AND IN DANCE CAME ON: 11 584
WITH SOFT FOOT TOWARDS THE DEEP, WHO NOW HAD STOPT 11 848

SOFT-EBBING
SOFT-EBBING; NOR WITHSTOOD THEM ROCK OR HILL, 7 300

SOFTEST
AND HYACINTH, EARTHS FRESHEST SOFTEST LAP. 9 1041

SOFT'N
WHAT MAY SUFFICE, AND SOFT'N STONIE HEARTS 3 189

SOFT'ND
FRUITS IN HER SOFT'ND SOILE, FOR SOME TO EATE 8 147

SOFTN'D
FOR I BEHOLD THEM SOFTN'D AND WITH TEARS 11 110

SOFTNESS
FOR SOFTNESS SHEE AND SWEET ATTRACTIVE GRACE, 4 298

SOFT'NING
PROLIFIC HUMOUR SOFT'NING ALL HER GLOBE, 7 280

SOIL
IS THIS THE REGION, THIS THE SOIL, THE CLIME, 1 242
OF BARCA OR CYRENE'S TORRID SOIL, 2 904
AND DIPSAS (NOT SO THICK SWARM'D ONCE THE SOIL 10 526

SOILD
OUR WONTED ORNAMENTS NOW SOILD AND STAIND, 9 1076

SOILE
IMITATE WHEN WE PLEASE? THIS DESART SOILE 2 270
DWELT IN TELASSAR: IN THIS PLEASANT SOILE 4 214
WIDE THE CELESTIAL SOILE, AND SAW BENEATH 6 510
FRUITS IN HER SOFT'ND SOILE, FOR SOME TO EATE 8 147
THE GROUND WHENCE HE WAS TAKEN, FITTER SOILE. 11 98
THE GROUND WHENCE THOU WAST TAK'N, FITTER SOILE. 11 262
THEE NATIVE SOILE, THESE HAPPIE WALKS AND SHADES, 11 270
WHERE HE ABIDES, THINK THERE THY NATIVE SOILE. 11 292
LABOURING THE SOILE, AND REAPING PLENTEOUS CROP, 12 18
HE LEAVES HIS GODS, HIS FRIENDS, AND NATIVE SOILE 12 129

SOJOURN
IN THAT OBSCURE SOJOURN, WHILE IN MY FLIGHT 3 15
INTO THE SEA: TO SOJOURN IN THAT LAND 12 159

SOJOURN'D
SOJOURN'D THE WHILE. GOD SAW THE LIGHT WAS GOOD; 7 249

SOJOURNERS
THE SOJOURNERS OF GOSHEN, WHO BEHELD 1 309
TO LET HIS SOJOURNERS DEPART, AND OFT 12 192

SOLAC'D
SOLAC'D THE WOODS, AND SPRED THIR PAINTED WINGS 7 434

SOLACE
HENCEFORTH AN INDIVIDUAL SOLACE DEAR; 4 486
WHICH WOULD BE ALL HIS SOLACE AND REVENGE, 6 905
OR SOLACE HIS DEFECTS. NO NEED THAT THOU 8 419
SOLACE IN HER RETURN, SO LONG DELAY'D; 9 844
THE SOLACE OF THIR SIN, TILL DEWIE SLEEP 9 1044

SOLDANS
WONT RIDE IN ARM'D, AND AT THE SOLDANS CHAIR 1 764

SOLE
SOLE REIGNING HOLDS THE TYRANNY OF HEAV'N. 1 124
BUT EVER TO DO ILL OUR SOLE DELIGHT, 1 160
WITH STENCH AND SMOAK; SUCH RESTING FOUND THE SOLE 1 237
SOLE KING, AND OF HIS KINGDOM LOOSE NO PART 2 325
THIS UNCOUTH ERRAND SOLE, AND ONE FOR ALL 2 827
AND EASILY TRANSGRESS THE SOLE COMMAND, 3 94
SOLE PLEDGE OF HIS OBEDIENCE: SO WILL FALL, 3 95
MY SOLE COMPLACENCE. WELL THOU KNOW'ST HOW DEAR, 3 276
LOOK'ST FROM THY SOLE DOMINION LIKE THE GOD 4 33
SOLE PARTNER AND SOLE PART OF ALL THESE JOYES, 4 411
SOLE, OR RESPONSIVE EACH TO OTHERS NOTE 4 683
OF HUMAN OFSSPRING, SOLE PROPRIETIE, 4 751
THOU SURELY HADST NOT COME SOLE FUGITIVE. 4 923
O SOLE IN WHOM MY THOUGHTS FIND ALL REPOSE, 5 28
A PHOENIX, GAZ'D BY ALL, AS THAT SOLE BIRD 5 272
VENGEANCE IS HIS, OR WHOSE HE SOLE APPOINTS; 6 808
SOLE VICTOR FROM TH' EXPULSION OF HIS FOES 6 880
IF THEY TRANSGRESS, AND SLIGHT THAT SOLE COMMAND, 7 47
ADAM RELATING, THE SOLE AUDITRESS; 8 51
THE DAY THOU EAT'ST THEREOF, MY SOLE COMMAND 8 329
TO MEE SHALL BE THE GLORIE SOLE AMONG 9 135
SOLE EVE, ASSOCIATE SOLE, TO ME BEYOND 9 227
THOU CANST, WHO ART SOLE WONDER, MUCH LESS ARM 9 533
SOLE DAUGHTER OF HIS VOICE; THE REST, WE LIVE 9 653
CHIEFLY ON MAN, SOLE LORD OF ALL DECLAR'D, 10 401
ON ME, SOLE CAUSE TO THEE OF ALL THIS WOE, 10 935
TOWARDS HER, HIS LIFE SO LATE AND SOLE DELIGHT, 10 941
THY LOVE, THE SOLE CONTENTMENT OF MY HEART 10 973
HIS PROVIDENCE, AND ON HIM SOLE DEPEND, 12 564

SOLEMN
HIS HOLY RITES, AND SOLEMN FEASTS PROFAN'D, 1 390
WITH SOLEMN TOUCHES, TROUBL'D THOUGHTS, AND CHASE 1 557
A SOLEMN COUNCEL FORTHWITH TO BE HELD 1 755
WITH SOLEMN ADORATION DOWN THEY CAST 3 351
WITH THIS HER SOLEMN BIRD AND THIS FAIR MOON, 4 648
WITH THIS HER SOLEMN BIRD, NOR WALK BY MOON, 4 655
MORE SOLEMN THEN THE TEDIOUS POMP THAT WAITS 5 354
THAT DAY, AS OTHER SOLEMN DAYES, THEY SPENT 5 618
WITH MINISTERIES DUE AND SOLEMN RITES: 7 149
AGAINST A SOLEMN DAY, HARNEST AT HAND, 7 202
TILL EV'N, NOR THEN THE SOLEMN NIGHTINGAL 7 435
HAD WORK AND RESTED NOT, THE SOLEMN PIPE, 7 595
BUT SOLEMN AND SUBLIME, WHOM NOT TO OFFEND, 11 236
HIS PLACE OF BIRTH A SOLEMN ANGEL TELLS 12 364

SOLEMNE
RECEAVE WITH SOLEMNE PURPOSE TO OBSERVE 7 78

SOLEMNIZ'D
EV'NING AND MORN SOLEMNIZ'D THE FIFT DAY. 7 448

SOLID
WITH SOLID, AS THE LAKE WITH LIQUID FIRE; 1 229
NOR SOLID MIGHT RESIST THAT EDGE: IT MET 6 323
NOR GLISTERING, MAY OF SOLID GOOD CONTAINE 8 93
SOLID OR SLIMIE, AS IN RAGING SEA 10 286
RATHER THEN SOLID VERTU, ALL BUT A RIB 10 884

SOLITARIE
THY FOLLY; OR WITH SOLITARIE HAND 6 139
THOSE RARE AND SOLITARIE, THESE IN FLOCKS 7 461
NO PLEASURE, THOUGH IN PLEASURE, SOLITARIE. 8 402
THROUGH EDEN TOOK THIR SOLITARIE WAY. 12 649

SOLITARY
EXPLORES HIS SOLITARY FLIGHT; SOM TIMES 2 632

SOLITUDE
IN BLISSFUL SOLITUDE; HE THEN SURVEY'D 3 69
AND SOLITUDE; YET NOT ALONE, WHILE THOU 7 28
I SEE NOT WHO PARTAKES. IN SOLITUDE 8 364
WHAT CALL'ST THOU SOLITUDE, IS NOT THE EARTH 8 369
FOR SOLITUDE SOMTIMES IS BEST SOCIETIE, 9 249
IN SOLITUDE LIVE SAVAGE, IN SOME GLADE 9 1085
NOT PLEAS'D, THUS ENTERTAIND WITH SOLITUDE, 10 105

SOLLICIT
SOLLICIT NOT THY THOUGHTS WITH MATTERS HID, 8 167

SOLLICITE
TO MOULD ME MAN, DID I SOLLICITE THEE 10 744

SOLLICITED
SOLLICITED HER LONGING EYE; YET FIRST 9 743

SOLLICITOUS
IN COUNCIL SATE, SOLLICITOUS WHAT CHANCE 10 428

SOLLID
OF MASSIE IRON OR SOLLID ROCK WITH EASE 2 878

SOLOMON
OF SOLOMON HE LED BY FRAUD TO BUILD 1 401

SOLSTITIAL
SOLSTITIAL SUMMERS HEAT. TO THE BLANC MOONE 10 656

SOLUTION
ENDLESS, AND NO SOLUTION WILL BE FOUND: 6 694
WHICH ONELY THY SOLUTION CAN RESOLVE. 8 14

SOLVE
GRATEFUL DIGRESSIONS, AND SOLVE HIGH DISPUTE 8 55

SOM
SOM ADVANTAGIOUS ACT MAY BE ACHIEV'D 2 363
EXPLORES HIS SOLITARY FLIGHT; SOM TIMES 2 632
HE SCOURS THE RIGHT HAND COAST, SOM TIMES THE LEFT, 2 633
SOM CAPITAL CITY; OR LESS THEN IF THIS FRAME 2 924
THE STRONG REBUFF OF SOM TUMULTUOUS CLOUD 2 936
CONFINE WITH HEAV'N; OR IF SOM OTHER PLACE 2 977
SOM OTHER ABLE, AND AS WILLING, PAY 3 211
THOUGH DISTANT FARR SOM SMALL REFLECTION GAINES 3 428
LAY WAVING ROUND; ON SOM GREAT CHARGE IMPLOY'D 3 628
AMBITION. YET WHY NOT? SOM OTHER POWER 4 61
OF SOM IRRIGUOUS VALLEY SPRED HER STORE, 4 255
MOUNT AMARA, THOUGH THIS BY SOM SUPPOS'D 4 281
SOM DREADFUL THING NO DOUBT; FOR WELL THOU KNOWST 4 426
PURE, AND COMMANDS TO SOM, LEAVES FREE TO ALL. 4 747
WHO TELLS OF SOM INFERNAL SPIRIT SEEN 4 793
FIT FOR THE TUN SOM MAGAZIN TO STORE 4 816
SOM SUCH RESEMBLANCES METHINKS I FIND 5 114
FOR ON SOM MESSAGE HIGH THEY GUESSD HIM BOUND. 5 290
RIS'N ON MID-NOON; SOM GREAT BEHEST FROM HEAV'N 5 311
AND SOM ARE FALL'N, TO DISOBEDIENCE FALL'N, 5 541
HATH PAST IN HEAV'N, SOM DOUBT WITHIN ME MOVE, 5 554
FROM ME SOM PLUME, THAT THY SUCCESS MAY SHOW 6 161
OR SOM MORE SUDDEN VENGEANCE WING'D FROM GOD 6 279
RAIS'D, AS OF SOM GREAT MATTER TO BEGIN. 9 669
AS WHEN OF OLD SOM ORATOR RENOUND 9 670
FLOURISHD, SINCE MUTE, TO SOM GREAT CAUSE ADDREST, 9 672
THE SACRED FRUIT FORBIDD'N. SOM CURSED FRAUD 9 904
SKIE LOWR'D AND MUTTERING THUNDER, SOM SAD DROPS 9 1002
OR SYMPATHIE, OR SOM CONNATURAL FORCE 10 246
OBLIQUE THE CENTRIC GLOBE: SOM SAY THE SUN 10 671
SOM BETTER SHROUD, SOM BETTER WARMTH TO CHERISH 10 1068
VACANT POSSESSION SOM NEW TROUBLE RAISE: 11 103
TO SOM CAVES MOUTH, OR WHETHER WASHT BY STREAM 11 569
FAST ON THE TOP OF SOM HIGH MOUNTAIN FIXT. 11 851
SOM NATURAL TEARS THEY DROP'D, BUT WIP'D THEM SOON; 12 645

SOME
THE PILOT OF SOME SMALL NIGHT-FOUNDER'D SKIFF, 1 204
DEEMING SOME ISLAND, OFT, AS SEA-MEN TELL, 1 205
OF SOME GREAT AMMIRAL, WERE BUT A WAND, 1 294
OBSCURE SOME GLIMPS OF JOY, TO HAVE FOUND THIR CHIEF 1 524
ADMIRING ENTER'D, AND THE WORK SOME PRAISE 1 731
AND SOME THE ARCHITECT: HIS HAND WAS KNOWN 1 732
OR FOUNTAIN SOME BELATED PEASANT SEES, 1 783
OUR STRONGER, SOME WORSE WAY HIS WRATH MAY FIND 2 83
OF ALL HIS AIM, AFTER SOME DIRE REVENGE. 2 128
SOME EASIER ENTERPRIZE? THERE IS A PLACE 2 345
OF SOME NEW RACE CALL'D MAN, ABOUT THIS TIME 2 348
RE-ENTER HEAV'N; OR ELSE IN SOME MILDE ZONE 2 397
BY SOME FALSE GUILE PERVERT; AND SHALL PERVERT 3 92
SOME I HAVE CHOSEN OF PECULIAR GRACE 3 183
NOT IN THE NEIGHBOURING MOON, AS SOME HAVE DREAMD; 3 459
OBTAINS THE BROW OF SOME HIGH-CLIMBING HILL, 3 546
THE GOODLY PROSPECT OF SOME FOREIN LAND 3 548
FIRST-SEEN, OR SOME RENOWN'D METROPOLIS 3 549
TO WITNESS WITH THINE EYES WHAT SOME PERHAPS 3 700
ME SOME INFERIOUR ANGEL, I HAD STOOD 4 59
OF SOME RICH BURGHER, WHOSE SUBSTANTIAL DORES, 4 189
IN SOME PURLIEU TWO GENTLE FAWNES AT PLAY, 4 404
SOME WANDRING SPIRIT OF HEAV'N, BY FOUNTAIN SIDE, 4 531
SOME DISADVANTAGE WE ENDUR'D AND PAINE, 6 431
SOME ONE INTENT ON MISCHIEF, OR INSPIR'D 6 503
MINIMS OF NATURE; SOME OF SERPENT KINDE 7 482
FRUITS IN HER SOFT'ND SOILE, FOR SOME TO EATE 8 147
STOR'D IN EACH ORB PERHAPS WITH SOME THAT LIVE. 8 152
NOT OF MY SELF; BY SOME GREAT MAKER THEN, 8 278
OR NATURE FAILD IN MEE, AND LEFT SOME PART 8 534
AS ONE WHO LOVES, AND SOME UNKINDNESS MEETS, 9 271

SOME (CONTINUED)
LEAST BY SOME FAIRE APPEERING GOOD SURPRIS'D 9 354
SOME SPECIOUS OBJECT BY THE FOE SUBORND, 9 361
WHICH OFT, THEY SAY, SOME EVIL SPIRIT ATTENDS 9 638
IN SOLITUDE LIVE SAVAGE, IN SOME GLADE 9 1085
SOME TREE WHOSE BROAD SMOOTH LEAVES TOGETHER SOWD, 9 1095
BY SOME IMMEDIATE STROAK; BUT SOON SHALL FIND 10 52
YEARLY ENJOYND, SOME SAY, TO UNDERGO 10 575
HOWEVER SOME TRADITION THEY DISPERS'D 10 578
THAT LAUGH, AS IF TRANSPORTED WITH SOME FIT 10 626
SOME SAY HE BID HIS ANGELS TURNE ASCANSE 10 668
OR IN SOME OTHER DISMAL PLACE WHO KNOWS 10 787
OR FIND SOME OTHER WAY TO GENERATE 10 894
AS SOME MISFORTUNE BRINGS HIM, OR MISTAKE, 10 900
TENDING TO SOME RELIEF OF OUR EXTREMES, 10 976
SOME SAFER RESOLUTION, WHICH METHINKS 10 1029
O EVE, SOME FURDER CHANGE AWAITS US NIGH, 11 193
SOME DAYS; HOW LONG, AND WHAT TILL THEN OUR LIFE, 11 198
NONE OF THE MEANEST, SOME GREAT POTENTATE 11 231
IN SOME TO SPRING FROM THEE, WHO NEVER TOUCH'D 11 425
O TEACHER, SOME GREAT MISCHIEF HATH BEFALL'N 11 450
SOME, AS THOU SAW'ST, BY VIOLENT STROKE SHALL DIE, 11 471
WERE TENTS OF VARIOUS HUE; BY SOME WERE HERDS 11 557
WITH SOME REGARD TO WHAT IS JUST AND RIGHT 12 16
BUT JUSTICE, AND SOME FATAL CURSE ANNEXT 12 99
SOME BLOUD MORE PRECIOUS MUST BE PAID FOR MAN, 12 293
WHICH HE HATH SENT PROPITIOUS, SOME GREAT GOOD 12 612

SOMETHING
CREATOR; SOMETHING YET OF DOUBT REMAINES, 8 13

SOMETIMES
SOMETIMES TOWARDS EDEN WHICH NOW IN HIS VIEW 4 27
SOMETIMES TOWARDS HEAV'N AND THE FULL-BLAZING SUN, 4 29
SURVEY'D, AND SOMETIMES WENT, AND SOMETIMES RAN 8 268

SOMEWHAT
SOMEWHAT EXTRAVAGANT AND WILDE, PERHAPS 6 616

SOMTHING
OF SOMTHING NOT UNSEASONABLE TO ASK 8 201
YET OFT HIS HEART, DIVINE OF SOMTHING ILL, 9 845
TO ARGUE IN THEE SOMTHING MORE SUBLIME 10 1014
AND SLOW DESCENDS, WITH SOMTHING HEAV'NLY FRAUGHT. 11 207

SOMTIME
A THING NOT UNDESIREABLE, SOMTIME 9 824

SOMTIMES
NIGHTLY I VISIT: NOR SOMTIMES FORGET 3 32
THERE ALWAYES, BUT DRAWN UP TO HEAV'N SOMTIMES 3 517
BUT SOMTIMES IN THE AIR, AS WEE, SOMTIMES 5 79
HOW FEW SOMTIMES MAY KNOW, WHEN THOUSANDS ERR. 6 148
THAT WARR AND VARIOUS; SOMTIMES ON FIRM GROUND 6 242
OF HUGE EXTENT SOMTIMES, WITH BRAZEN EYES 7 496
FOR SOLITUDE SOMTIMES IS BEST SOCIETIE, 9 249
SOMTIMES IN HIGHTH BEGAN, AS NO DELAY 9 675
YET SOMTIMES NATIONS WILL DECLINE SO LOW 12 97

SOMWHAT
THENCE MORE AT EASE THIR MINDS AND SOMWHAT RAIS'D 2 521

SOMWHERE
BY SLY ASSAULT; AND SOMWHERE NIGH AT HAND 9 256

SON
OF AMRAMS SON IN EGYPTS EVILL DAY 1 339
HIS OWN AND RHEA'S SON LIKE MEASURE FOUND; 1 513
IN FABLE OR ROMANCE OF UTHERS SON 1 580
ADMIR'D, NOT FEAR'D; GOD AND HIS SON EXCEPT, 2 678
AGAINST THY ONLY SON? WHAT FURY O SON, 2 728
ME FATHER, AND THAT FANTASM CALL'ST MY SON? 2 743
GRIM DEATH MY SON AND FOE, WHO SETS THEM ON, 2 804
AND MY FAIR SON HERE SHOWST ME, THE DEAR PLEDGE 2 818
HIS ONELY SON; ON EARTH HE FIRST BEHELD 3 64
THUS TO HIS ONELY SON FORESEEING SPAKE. 3 79
ONELY BEGOTTEN SON, SEEST THOU WHAT RAGE 3 80
BEYOND COMPARE THE SON OF GOD WAS SEEN 3 138
THY CREATURE LATE SO LOV'D, THY YOUNGEST SON 3 151
O SON, IN WHOM MY SOUL HATH CHIEF DELIGHT, 3 168
SON OF MY BOSOM, SON WHO ART ALONE 3 169
BY DOOM SEVERE, HAD NOT THE SON OF GOD, 3 224
THE HEAD OF ALL MANKIND, THOUGH ADAMS SON. 3 286
BY MERIT MORE THEN BIRTHRIGHT SON OF GOD, 3 309
BOTH GOD AND MAN, SON BOTH OF GOD AND MAN, 3 316
ADORE THE SON, AND HONOUR HIM AS MEE. 3 343
BEGOTTEN SON, DIVINE SIMILITUDE, 3 384
THEE ONLY EXTOLL'D, SON OF THY FATHERS MIGHT, 3 398
NO SOONER DID THY DEAR AND ONELY SON 3 403
HAIL SON OF GOD, SAVIOUR OF MEN, THY NAME 3 412
OF TOBITS SON, AND WITH A VENGEANCE SENT 4 170
HID AMALTHEA AND HER FLORID SON 4 278
IN SAD EVENT, WHEN TO THE UNWISER SON 4 716
OF FATHER, SON, AND BROTHER FIRST WERE KNOWN. 4 757
SKIE-TINCTUR'D GRAIN. LIKE MAIA'S SON HE STOOD, 5 285
TO WHOM THE ANGEL. SON OF HEAV'N AND EARTH, 5 519
BY WHOM IN BLISS IMBOSOM'D SAT THE SON, 5 597
MY ONELY SON, AND ON THIS HOLY HILL 5 604

SON (CONTINUED)

WITH ENVIE AGAINST THE SON OF GOD, THAT DAY	5	662
AND SMILING TO HIS ONELY SON THUS SAID.	5	718
SON, THOU IN WHOM MY GLORY I BEHOLD	5	719
TO WHOM THE SON WITH CALM ASPECT AND CLEER	5	733
SO SPAKE THE SON, BUT SATAN WITH HIS POWERS	5	743
THAT TO HIS ONLY SON BY RIGHT ENDU'D	5	815
EQUAL TO HIM BEGOTTEN SON, BY WHOM	5	835
TH' INCENSED FATHER, AND TH' INCENSED SON,	5	847
FROM FATHER TO HIS SON? STRANGE POINT AND NEW.	5	855
TO HONOUR HIS ANOINTED SON AVENG'D	6	676
ALL POWER ON HIM TRANSFERR'D: WHENCE TO HIS SON	6	678
EFFULGENCE OF MY GLORIE, SON BELOV'D,	6	680
SON IN WHOSE FACE INVISIBLE IS BEHELD	6	681
HE SAID, AND ON HIS SON WITH RAYES DIRECT	6	719
TO GLORIFIE THY SON, I ALWAYES THEE,	6	725
OR FAINT RETREAT; WHEN THE GREAT SON OF GOD	6	799
SO SPAKE THE SON, AND INTO TERROUR CHANG'D	6	824
SON, HEIR, AND LORD, TO HIM DOMINION GIV'N,	6	887
HER SON. SO FAIL NOT THOU, WHO THEE IMPLORES:	7	38
INTO HIS PLACE, AND THE GREAT SON RETURND	7	135
THIR MULTITUDE, AND TO HIS SON THUS SPAKE.	7	138
AND THOU MY WORD, BEGOTTEN SON, BY THEE	7	163
SO SANG THE HIERARCHIES: MEAN WHILE THE SON	7	192
PRESENT) THUS TO HIS SON AUDIBLY SPAKE.	7	518
PERPLEX'D THE GREEK AND CYTHEREA'S SON;	9	19
OF HEAV'N, THIS MAN OF CLAY, SON OF DESPITE,	9	176
ALCINOUS, HOST OF OLD LAERTES SON,	9	441
VICEGERENT SON, TO THEE I HAVE TRANSFERR'D	10	56
TOWARD THE RIGHT HAND HIS GLORIE, ON THE SON	10	64
SUPREAM, THAT THOU IN MEE THY SON BELOV'D	10	70
WHEN JESUS SON OF MARY SECOND EVE,	10	183
O SON, WHY SIT WE HERE EACH OTHER VIEWING	10	235
THE SON OF GOD TO JUDGE THEM TERRIFI'D	10	338
THAT I MUST AFTER THEE WITH THIS THY SON;	10	363
FAIR DAUGHTER, AND THOU SON AND GRANDCHILD BOTH,	10	384
OF THY VICTORIOUS ARM, WELL-PLEASING SON,	10	634
WHO CAN EXTENUATE THEE? NEXT, TO THE SON,	10	645
MADE THEE WITHOUT THY LEAVE, WHAT IF THY SON	10	760
BEFORE THE FATHERS THRONE: THEM THE GLAD SON	11	20
ALL THY REQUEST FOR MAN, ACCEPTED SON,	11	46
HE ENDED, AND THE SON GAVE SIGNAL HIGH	11	72
ONE MAN EXCEPT, THE ONELY SON OF LIGHT	11	808
O EXECRABLE SON SO TO ASPIRE	12	64
THAT SON, WHO ON THE QUIET STATE OF MEN	12	80
THIR INWARD LOST: WITNESS TH' IRREVERENT SON	12	101
A SON, AND OF HIS SON A GRAND-CHILDE LEAVES,	12	153
HE COMES INVITED BY A YONGER SON	12	160
IN TIME OF DEARTH, A SON WHOSE WORTHY DEEDS	12	161
FROM ABRAHAM, SON OF ISAAC, AND FROM HIM	12	268
A SON, THE WOMANS SEED TO THEE FORETOLD,	12	327
AND HIS NEXT SON FOR WEALTH AND WISDOM FAM'D,	12	332
THOU SHALT PROCEED, AND FROM THY WOMB THE SON	12	381
OF HEAD OR HEEL: NOT THEREFORE JOYNES THE SON	12	388

SONG

INVOKE THY AID TO MY ADVENTROUS SONG,	1	13
THIR SONG WAS PARTIAL, BUT THE HARMONY	2	552
(FOR ELOQUENCE THE SOUL, SONG CHARMS THE SENSE,)	2	556
SMIT WITH THE LOVE OF SACRED SONG; BUT CHIEF	3	29
THIR SACRED SONG, AND WAKEN RAPTURES HIGH;	3	369
SHALL BE THE COPIOUS MATTER OF MY SONG	3	413
LIGHTLY DISPERS'D, AND THE SHRILL MATIN SONG	5	7
TUNES SWEETEST HIS LOVE-LABOR'D SONG; NOW REIGNES	5	41
IN MYSTIC DANCE NOT WITHOUT SONG, RESOUND	5	178
MADE VOCAL BY MY SONG, AND TAUGHT HIS PRAISE.	5	204
IN SONG AND DANCE ABOUT THE SACRED HILL,	5	619
MINISTRING SPIRITS, TRAIND UP IN FEAST AND SONG;	6	167
WITH THY CELESTIAL SONG. UP LED BY THEE	7	12
PURPLES THE EAST: STILL GOVERN THOU MY SONG,	7	30
OR WE CAN BID HIS ABSENCE, TILL THY SONG	7	107
FROM BRANCH TO BRANCH THE SMALLER BIRDS WITH SONG	7	433
NOISE, OTHER THEN THE SOUND OF DANCE OR SONG,	8	243
SINCE FIRST THIS SUBJECT FOR HEROIC SONG	9	25
NOT WITHOUT SONG, EACH MORNING, AND DUE PRAISE	9	800
OR DOWN FROM HEAV'N DESCEND. SUCH WAS THIR SONG,	10	648
TO ANSWER, AND RESOUND FARR OTHER SONG.	10	862

SONGS

SIDONIAN VIRGINS PAID THIR VOWS AND SONGS,	1	441
OF HYMNS AND SACRED SONGS, WHEREWITH THY THRONE	3	148
IN FULL HARMONIC NUMBER JOIND, THIR SONGS	4	687
HIGH UP IN HEAV'N, WITH SONGS TO HYMNE HIS THRONE,	4	944
ANGELS, FOR YEE BEHOLD HIM, AND WITH SONGS	5	161
CHERUBIC SONGS BY NIGHT FROM NEIGHBOURING HILLS	5	547
OF LOVE AND YOUTH NOT LOST, SONGS, GARLANDS, FLOURS.	11	594

SONOROUS

SONOROUS METTAL BLOWING MARTIAL SOUNDS:	1	540

SONS

RHENE OR THE DANAW, WHEN HER BARBAROUS SONS	1	353
NOR HAD THEY YET AMONG THE SONS OF EVE	1	364
NEXT CHEMOS, TH' OBSCENE DREAD OF MOABS SONS,	1	406
TURNS ATHEIST, AS DID ELY'S SONS, WHO FILL'D	1	495
DARKENS THE STREETS, THEN WANDER FORTH THE SONS	1	501
SHOULD FAVOUR EQUAL TO THE SONS OF HEAVEN:	1	654

SONS (CONTINUED)

IN BIGNESS TO SURPASS EARTHS GIANT SONS	1	778
IN HIS DISTURBANCE; WHEN HIS DARLING SONS	2	373
DREW AFTER HIM THE THIRD PART OF HEAV'NS SONS	2	692
HIS CRIME MAKES GUILTIE ALL HIS SONS, THY MERIT	3	290
HITHER OF ILL-JOYND SONS AND DAUGHTERS BORN	3	463
WHERE ALL HIS SONS THY EMBASSIE ATTEND;	3	658
OR WHERE THE SONS OF EDEN LONG BEFORE	4	213
HIS SONS, THE FAIREST OF HER DAUGHTERS EVE.	4	324
SPEAK YEE WHO BEST CAN TELL, YE SONS OF LIGHT,	5	160
SHALL FILL THE WORLD MORE NUMEROUS WITH THY SONS	5	389
THEN HAD THE SONS OF GOD EXCUSE TO HAVE BIN	5	447
AMONG THE SONS OF MORN, WHAT MULTITUDES	5	716
NATIVES AND SONS OF HEAV'N POSSEST BEFORE	5	790
OF THIS OUR NATIVE HEAV'N, ETHEREAL SONS.	5	863
GABRIEL, LEAD FORTH TO BATTEL THESE MY SONS	6	46
UNANIMOUS, AS SONS OF ONE GREAT SIRE	6	95
LIKE INSTRUMENT TO PLAGUE THE SONS OF MEN	6	505
PURSUE THESE SONS OF DARKNESS, DRIVE THEM OUT	6	715
AND SONS OF MEN, WHOM GOD HATH THUS ADVANC'T,	7	626
WOULD NOT ADMIT; THINE AND OF ALL THY SONS	8	637
THAT I MUST LEAVE YE, SONS; O WERE I ABLE	10	819
IN FELLOWSHIPS OF JOY: THE SONS OF LIGHT	11	80
O SONS, LIKE ONE OF US MAN IS BECOME	11	84
PRESENCE DIVINE, AND TO MY SONS RELATE;	11	319
TO DWELL ON EEVEN GROUND NOW WITH THY SONS:	11	348
GUIANA, WHOSE GREAT CITIE GERYONS SONS	11	410
RELIGIOUS TITL'D THEM THE SONS OF GOD,	11	622
PATRONS OF MANKIND, GODS, AND SONS OF GODS,	11	696
THIR ORDER: LAST THE SIRE, AND HIS THREE SONS	11	736
AND SUNK THEE AS THY SONS; TILL GENTLY REARD	11	758
OF WICKED SONS DESTROYD, THEN I REJOYCE	11	875
JORDAN, TRUE LIMIT EASTWARD; BUT HIS SONS	12	145
THE GRANDCHILDE WITH TWELVE SONS INCREAST, DEPARTS	12	155
THE SCEPTER, AND REGARD NOT DAVIDS SONS,	12	357
NOT ONELY TO THE SONS OF ABRAHAMS LOINES	12	447
SALVATION SHALL BE PREACHT, BUT TO THE SONS	12	448

SOON

HE SOON DISCERNS, AND WELTRING BY HIS SIDE	1	78
AND HIM THUS ANSWER'D SOON HIS BOLD COMPEER.	1	127
INVINCIBLE, AND VIGOUR SOON RETURNS,	1	140
THIR SUREST SIGNAL, THEY WILL SOON RESUME	1	278
YET TO THIR GENERALS VOYCE THEY SOON OBEYD	1	337
SOON RECOLLECTING, WITH HIGH WORDS, THAT BORE	1	528
DARTS HIS EXPERIENC'T EYE, AND SOON TRAVERSE	1	568
FOR TREASURES BETTER HID. SOON HAD HIS CREW	1	688
A THIRD AS SOON HAD FORM'D WITHIN THE GROUND	1	705
INCAPABLE OF STAIN WOULD SOON EXPEL	2	140
FADED SO SOON. ADVISE IF THIS BE WORTH	2	376
AND ME HIS PARENT WOULD FULL SOON DEVOUR	2	805
SOON LEARND, NOW MILDER, AND THUS ANSWERD SMOOTH.	2	816
TO KNOW, AND THIS ONCE KNOWN, SHALL SOON RETURN,	2	839
BUT THEE, WHOM FOLLOW? THOU WILT BRING ME SOON	2	866
AUDACIOUS, BUT THAT SEAT SOON FAILING, MEETS	2	931
BUT HEE ONCE PAST, SOON AFTER WHEN MAN FELL,	2	1023
WONDRING; BUT SOON TH' ALMIGHTY THUS REPLY'D:	3	273
BEGAN TO BLOOM, BUT SOON FOR MANS OFFENCE	3	355
TO OBJECTS DISTANT FARR, WHEREBY HE SOON	3	621
BY ACT OF GRACE MY FORMER STATE; HOW SOON	4	94
WOULD HIGTH RECAL HIGH THOUGHTS, HOW SOON UNSAY	4	95
ARE EVER CLEER. WHEREOF HEE SOON AWARE,	4	119
IT STARTED BACK, BUT PLEAS'D I SOON RETURND,	4	463
PLEAS'D IT RETURND AS SOON WITH ANSWERING LOOKS	4	464
WHERE HE FIRST LIGHTED, SOON DISCERND HIS LOOKS	4	570
YET THUS, UNMOVD WITH FEAR, ACCOST HIM SOON.	4	822
TO WHOM THE WARRIOUR ANGEL, SOON REPLI'D.	4	946
WITH VIOLENCE OF THIS CONFLICT, HAD NOT SOON	4	995
SOON AS THEY FORTH WERE COME TO OPEN SIGHT	5	138
FIRM PEACE RECOVERD SOON AND WONTED CALM.	5	210
SOON AS MIDNIGHT BROUGHT ON THE DUSKIE HOURE	5	667
DISTINGUISH NOT; FOR SOON EXPECT TO FEEL	5	892
OF ONSET ENDED SOON EACH MILDER THOUGHT.	6	98
YET SOON HE HEAL'D; FOR SPIRITS THAT LIVE THROUGHOUT	6	344
TILL NOW NOT KNOWN, BUT KNOWN AS SOON CONTEMND,	6	432
SOON CLOSING, AND BY NATIVE VIGOUR HEAL'D.	6	436
SOON BANDED; OTHERS FROM THE DAWNING HILLS	6	528
IN MOTION OR IN ALT: HIM SOON THEY MET	6	532
SO WARND HE THEM AWARE THEMSELVES, AND SOON	6	547
BUT SOON OBSCUR'D WITH SMOAK, ALL HEAV'N APPEERD,	6	585
IMAGE OF THEE IN ALL THINGS; AND SHALL SOON,	6	736
UNDER WHOSE CONDUCT MICHAEL SOON REDUC'D	6	777
ALL BUT THE THRONE IT SELF OF GOD. FULL SOON	6	834
DISBURD'ND HEAV'N REJOIC'D, AND SOON REPAIRD	6	878
WITH SUCH CONFUSION: BUT THE EVIL SOON	7	56
WITH BLESSEDNESS. WHENCE ADAM SOON REPEAL'D	7	59
IN CHAOS, AND THE WORK BEGUN, HOW SOON	7	93
OPPRESSES ELSE WITH SURFET, AND SOON TURNS	7	129
THIR BROOD AS NUMEROUS HATCH, FROM THE EGG THAT SOON	7	418
THIR CALLOW YOUNG, BUT FEATHERD SOON AND FLEDGE	7	420
OF SWEET REPAST; THEY SATIATE, AND SOON FILL,	8	214
SOON DRI'D, AND ON THE REAKING MOISTURE FED.	8	256
NOT TO INCUR; BUT SOON HIS CLEER ASPECT	8	336
CANNOT WELL SUITE WITH EITHER, BUT SOON PROVE	8	388
FOR WHOM ALL THIS WAS MADE, ALL THIS WILL SOON	9	132
THE SERPENT: HIM FAST SLEEPING SOON HE FOUND	9	182

SOON (CONTINUED)
IN HEART OR HEAD, POSSESSING SOON INSPIR'D 9 189
THOUGH IN MID HEAV'N, SOON ENDED HIS DELIGHT, 9 468
OF PLEASURE NOT FOR HIM ORDAIN'D: THEN SOON 9 470
ABOUT THE MOSSIE TRUNK I WOUND ME SOON, 9 589
MY CONDUCT, I CAN BRING THEE THITHER SOON. 9 630
TEDIOUS, UNSHAR'D WITH THEE, AND ODIOUS SOON. 9 880
ON TH' OTHER SIDE, ADAM, SOON AS HE HEARD 9 888
SOON AS THE FORCE OF THAT FALLACIOUS FRUIT, 9 1046
SOON FOUND THIR EYES HOW OP'ND, AND THIR MINDS 9 1053
INTO THE THICKEST WOOD, THERE SOON THEY CHOSE 9 1100
TO WHOM SOON MOV'D WITH TOUCH OF BLAME THUS EVE. 9 1143
ENTRANCE UNSEEN. SOON AS TH' UNWELCOME NEWS 10 21
BY SOME IMMEDIATE STROAK; BUT SOON SHALL FIND 10 52
CONFESSING SOON, YET NOT BEFORE HER JUDGE 10 160
WHOM THUS THE MEAGER SHADOW ANSWERED SOON. 10 264
THIR PARENT SOON DISCERN'D, THOUGH IN DISGUISE. 10 331
TOO SOON ARRIV'D, SIN THERE IN POWER BEFORE, 10 586
WHOM THUS THE SIN-BORN MONSTER ANSWERD SOON. 10 596
COMMISERATION; SOON HIS HEART RELENTED 10 940
AND THUS WITH PEACEFUL WORDS UPRAIS'D HER SOON. 10 946
AND BRINGING FORTH, SOON RECOMPENC'T WITH JOY, 10 1052
OF US WILL SOON DETERMIN, OR IMPOSE 11 227
HE ENDED; AND TH' ARCH-ANGEL SOON DREW NIGH, 11 238
DISCOVER'D SOON THE PLACE OF HER RETIRE. 11 267
SOON RAIS'D, AND HIS ATTENTION THUS RECALL'D. 11 422
HIS OFFRING SOON PROPITIOUS FIRE FROM HEAV'N 11 441
LIFE OFFER'D, OR SOON BEG TO LAY IT DOWN, 11 506
OF ADAM, SOON ENCLIN'D TO ADMIT DELIGHT, 11 596
ASSEMBLE, AND HARANGUES ARE HEARD, BUT SOON 11 663
WHICH NOW DIRECT THINE EYES AND SOON BEHOLD. 11 711
TO MARK THIR DOINGS, THEM BEHOLDING SOON, 12 50
BUT SOON REVIVES, DEATH OVER HIM NO POWER 12 420
HOW SOON HATH THY PREDICTION, SEER BLEST, 12 553
SOM NATURAL TEARS THEY DROP'D, BUT WIP'D THEM SOON; 12 645

SOONER
NO SOONER HAD TH' ALMIGHTY CEAS'T, BUT ALL 3 344
NO SOONER DID THY DEAR AND ONELY SON 3 403
THE SOONER FOR THIR ARMS, UNARM'D THEY MIGHT 6 595
FOR I NO SOONER IN MY HEART DIVIN'D, 10 357
SOONER OR LATER; WHICH TH' ALMIGHTIE SEEING, 10 613
NO SOONER HEE WITH THEM OF MAN AND BEAST 11 822

SOONEST
TORMENT WITH EASE, AND SOONEST RECOMPENCE 4 893
HIS MIDNIGHT SEARCH, WHERE SOONEST HE MIGHT FINDE 9 181

SOOT
WITH SOOT AND CINDERS FILL'D; SO OFT THEY FELL 10 570

SOOTHE
HER FORMER TRESPASS FEAR'D, THE MORE TO SOOTHE 9 1006

SOOTY
OF SOOTY COAL THE EMPIRIC ALCHIMIST 5 440

SOPHI
RETIRES, OR BACTRIAN SOPHI FROM THE HORNES 10 433

SORCERESS
HAD NOT THE SNAKIE SORCERESS THAT SAT 2 724

SORCERIE
YET WITH A PLEASING SORCERIE COULD CHARM 2 566

SORCERIES
WITH MONSTROUS SHAPES AND SORCERIES ABUS'D 1 479

SORD
RUSTIC, OF GRASSIE SORD; THITHER ANON 11 433

SORE
SMOTE ON HIM SORE BESIDES, VAULTED WITH FIRE; 1 298
AND WRITH'D HIM TO AND FRO CONVOLV'D; SO SORE 6 328
SORE TOILD, HIS RIV'N ARMES TO HAVOC HEWN, 6 449
THESE DISOBEDIENT; SORE HATH BEEN THIR FIGHT, 6 687
MISTRUST, SUSPICION, DISCORD, AND SHOOK SORE 9 1124
TO WHOM THUS ADAM SORE BESET REPLI'D. 10 124

SORROW
REGIONS OF SORROW, DOLEFUL SHADES, WHERE PEACE 1 65
ANGUISH AND DOUBT AND FEAR AND SORROW AND PAIN 1 558
SAD ACHERON OF SORROW, BLACK AND DEEP; 2 578
BOTH TO AND FRO, THIR SORROW TO AUGMENT, 2 605
AND HOURLY BORN, WITH SORROW INFINITE 2 797
OF WOE AND SORROW. STERNLY HE PRONOUNC'D 8 333
THY SORROW I WILL GREATLY MULTIPLIE 10 193
IN SORROW FORTH, AND TO THY HUSBANDS WILL 10 195
CURS'D IS THE GROUND FOR THY SAKE, THOU IN SORROW 10 201
TO SORROW ABANDOND, BUT WORSE FELT WITHIN, 10 717
OF SORROW UNFEIGN'D, AND HUMILIATION MEEK. 10 1092
OF SORROW UNFEIGN'D, AND HUMILIATION MEEK. 10 1104
HEART-STROOK WITH CHILLING GRIPE OF SORROW STOOD, 11 264
OF SORROW AND DEJECTION AND DESPAIR 11 301
AND PIOUS SORROW, EQUALLY ENUR'D 11 362
OF TEARS AND SORROW A FLOUD THEE ALSO DROWN'D, 11 757
PRESAGING, SINCE WITH SORROW AND HEARTS DISTRESS 12 613

SORROWING
SO SEND THEM FORTH, THOUGH SORROWING, YET IN PEACE: 11 117

SORROWS
HE SORROWS NOW, REPENTS, AND PRAYES CONTRITE, 11 90

SORT
THE FIRST SORT BY THIR OWN SUGGESTION FELL, 3 129
SPIRIT OF HAPPIE SORT: HIS GESTURES FIERCE 4 128
NO CREATURE THENCE: IF SPIRIT OF OTHER SORT, 4 582
SEEK NOT THE PRAISE OF MEN; THE OTHER SORT 6 376
CAN SORT, WHAT HARMONIE OR TRUE DELIGHT? 8 384
ABOUT HIM. BUT TO ADAM IN WHAT SORT 9 816
BUT ON THE HETHER SIDE A DIFFERENT SORT 11 574

SORTED
AS SORTED BEST WITH PRESENT THINGS. THE SUN 10 651

SORTS
GAVE THEE, ALL SORTS ARE HERE THAT ALL TH' EARTH YIELDS, 7 541

SOTTISH
AHAZ HIS SOTTISH CONQUEROUR, WHOM HE DREW 1 472

SOUGHT
HEAP ON HIMSELF DAMNATION, WHILE HE SOUGHT 1 215
VOUTSAF'T OR SOUGHT; FOR WHAT PEACE WILL BE GIV'N 2 332
PHILOSOPHERS IN VAIN SO LONG HAVE SOUGHT, 3 601
IN SEARCH OF WHOM THEY SOUGHT: HIM THERE THEY FOUND 4 799
DOLE WITH DELIGHT, WHICH IN THIS PLACE I SOUGHT; 4 894
OF MY REVENGE, FIRST SOUGHT FOR THOU RETURNST 6 151
I FLIE NOT, BUT HAVE SOUGHT THEE FARR AND NIGH. 6 295
DAZL'D AND SPENT, SUNK DOWN, AND SOUGHT REPAIR 8 457
SATAN INVOLV'D IN RISING MIST, THEN SOUGHT 9 75
TOUCHD ONELY, THAT OUR TRIAL, WHEN LEAST SOUGHT, 9 380
IN BOWRE AND FIELD HE SOUGHT, WHERE ANY TUFT 9 417
HE SOUGHT THEM BOTH, BUT WISH'D HIS HAP MIGHT FIND 9 421
AT FIRST, AS ONE WHO SOUGHT ACCESS, BUT FEARD 9 511
MEAN I TO TRIE, WHAT RASH UNTRI'D I SOUGHT, 9 860
CHIEFLY I SOUGHT, WITHOUT THEE CAN DESPISE. 9 878
UPON HER HUSBAND, SAW THIR SHAME THAT SOUGHT 10 336
THUS TO DISBURD'N SOUGHT WITH SAD COMPLAINT. 10 719
THE GOOD I SOUGHT NOT. TO THE LOSS OF THAT, 10 752
WHEREFORE DIDST THOU BEGET ME? I SOUGHT IT NOT 10 762
FAVOUR UNMERITED BY ME, WHO SOUGHT 12 278

SOUGHTST
SUBMISS: HE REAR'D ME, AND WHOM THOU SOUGHTST I AM, 8 316

SOUL
(FOR ELOQUENCE THE SOUL, SONG CHARMS THE SENSE,) 2 556
O SON, IN WHOM MY SOUL HATH CHIEF DELIGHT, 3 168
PART OF MY SOUL I SEEK THEE, AND THEE CLAIM 4 487
SOUL LIVING, EACH THAT CREPT, WHICH PLENTEOUSLY 7 392
EXPRESS, AND THOU BECAM'ST A LIVING SOUL. 7 528
AS FLESH TO MIX WITH FLESH, OR SOUL WITH SOUL. 8 629
ONE HEART, ONE SOUL IN BOTH; WHEREOF GOOD PROOFF 9 967
GROAND OUT HIS SOUL WITH GUSHING BLOUD EFFUS'D. 11 447
BY NAME TO COME CALL'D CHARITIE, THE SOUL 12 584

SOULE
HIS PREY, NOR SUFFER MY UNSPOTTED SOULE 3 248
CREATED PURE. BUT KNOW THAT IN THE SOULE 5 100
THOU SUN, OF THIS GREAT WORLD BOTH EYE AND SOULE, 5 171
FANSIE AND UNDERSTANDING, WHENCE THE SOULE 5 486
UNITED AS ONE INDIVIDUAL SOULE 5 610
WITH REGAL SCEPTER, EVERY SOULE IN HEAV'N 5 816
REPTIL WITH SPAWN ABUNDANT, LIVING SOULE: 7 388
BY LIVING SOULE, DESERT AND DESOLATE, 8 154
AND THEY SHALL BE ONE FLESH, ONE HEART, ONE SOULE. 8 499
THE SOULE OF MAN, OR PASSION IN HIM MOVE. 8 585
UNION OF MIND, OR IN US BOTH ONE SOULE; 8 604

SOULES
TO HEAV'NLY SOULES HAD BIN ALL ONE; BUT NOW 6 165
BEFORE HIM, SUCH AS IN THIR SOULES INFIX'D 6 837

SOULS
JOYN VOICES ALL YE LIVING SOULS, YE BIRDS, 5 197
CONVERSION AND REPENTANCE, AS TO SOULS 11 724

SOUND
THEN STRAIT COMMANDS THAT AT THE WARLIKE SOUND 1 531
ROSE LIKE AN EXHALATION, WITH THE SOUND 1 711
AND TRUMPETS SOUND THROUGHOUT THE HOST PROCLAIM 1 754
THE SOUND OF BLUSTRING WINDS, WHICH ALL NIGHT LONG 2 286
THIR RISING ALL AT ONCE WAS AS THE SOUND 2 476
WITH TRUMPETS REGAL SOUND THE GREAT RESULT: 2 515
THEY FERRY OVER THIS LETHEAN SOUND 2 604
WITH IMPETUOUS RECOILE AND JARRING SOUND 2 880
THY PRAISES, WITH TH' INNUMERABLE SOUND 3 147
NOT DISTANT FAR FROM THENCE A MURMURING SOUND 4 453
AND TEMPERAT VAPORS BLAND, WHICH TH' ONLY SOUND 5 5
ACKNOWLEDGE HIM THY GREATER, SOUND HIS PRAISE 5 172
AMBIGUOUS WORDS AND JEALOUSIES, TO SOUND 5 703
HE SAID, AND AS THE SOUND OF WATERS DEEP 5 872
IN SILENCE THIR BRIGHT LEGIONS, TO THE SOUND 6 64

SOUND (CONTINUED)
OF BATTEL NOW BEGAN, AND RUSHING SOUND 6 97
OF BATTEL: WHEREAT MICHAEL BID SOUND 6 202
UNHURT OUR MINDES, AND UNDERSTANDING SOUND, . . . 6 444
DAWNING THROUGH HEAV'N: FORTH RUSH'D WITH WHIRLWIND SOUND 6 749
OF HIS FIERCE CHARIOT ROWLD, AS WITH THE SOUND . 6 829
HER EVER DURING GATES, HARMONIOUS SOUND 7 206
FOLLOWD WITH ACCLAMATION AND THE SOUND 7 558
NOISE, OTHER THEN THE SOUND OF DANCE OR SONG, . . 8 243
MORE GRATEFUL THEN HARMONIOUS SOUND TO THE EARE. . 8 606
FOUNDST EITHER SWEET REPAST, OR SOUND REPOSE; . . 9 407
OR DAIRIE, EACH RURAL SIGHT, EACH RURAL SOUND; . . 9 451
TO LURE HER EYE; SHEE BUSIED HEARD THE SOUND . . 9 518
CREATED MUTE TO ALL ARTICULAT SOUND; 9 557
MIGHT TEMPT ALONE, AND IN HER EARS THE SOUND . . 9 736
A DISMAL UNIVERSAL HISS, THE SOUND 10 508
SUNG HALLELUIA, AS THE SOUND OF SEAS, ... 10 642
TO SOUND AT GENERAL DOOM. TH' ANGELIC BLAST . . 11 76
OF CATTEL GRAZING: OTHERS, WHENCE THE SOUND . . 11 558
IN THUNDER LIGHTNING AND LOUD TRUMPETS SOUND . . 12 229

SOUND-BOARD
TO MANY A ROW OF PIPES THE SOUND-BOARD BREATHS. . 1 709

SOUNDED
IT SOUNDED, AND THE FAITHFUL ARMIES RUNG 6 204

SOUNDEST
INDUC'D ME. AS NEW WAK'T FROM SOUNDEST SLEEP . . 8 253

SOUNDING
CLASH'D ON THIR SOUNDING SHIELDS THE DIN OF WAR, . 1 668
PUT TO THIR MOUTHS THE SOUNDING ALCHYMIE . . . 2 517

SOUNDS
SONOROUS METTAL BLOWING MARTIAL SOUNDS: 1 540
OF STUNNING SOUNDS AND VOICES ALL CONFUS'D . . . 2 952
WITH HEAV'NLY TOUCH OF INSTRUMENTAL SOUNDS . . . 4 686
FORTHWITH THE SOUNDS AND SEAS, EACH CREEK AND BAY 7 399
WALK'D FIRM; THE CRESTED COCK WHOSE CLARION SOUNDS 7 443
ALL SOUNDS ON FRET BY STRING OR GOLDEN WIRE . . 7 597

SOURCE
HAILE WEDDED LOVE, MYSTERIOUS LAW, TRUE SOURCE . 4 750

SOURS
THIS SECOND SOURS OF MEN, WHILE YET BUT FEW; . . 12 13

SOURSE
ON MEE, MEE ONELY, AS THE SOURSE AND SPRING . . 10 832
THE SOURSE OF LIFE; NEXT FAVOURABLE THOU, . . . 11 169

SOUTH
CAME LIKE A DELUGE ON THE SOUTH, AND SPREAD . . 1 354
UZZIEL, HALF THESE DRAW OFF, AND COAST THE SOUTH . 4 782
DECREPIT WINTER, FROM THE SOUTH TO BRING . . . 10 655
FROM COLD ESTOTILAND, AND SOUTH AS FARR 10 686
WITH ADVERSE BLAST UP-TURNS THEM FROM THE SOUTH . 10 701
OF CONGO, AND ANGOLA FARDEST SOUTH; 11 401
FROM HAMATH NORTHWARD TO THE DESERT SOUTH . . . 12 139

SOUTHMOST
OF SOUTHMOST ABARIM; IN HESEBON 1 408

SOUTHWARD
SOUTHWARD THROUGH EDEN WENT A RIVER LARGE, . . . 4 223

SOUTHWIND
MEANWHILE THE SOUTHWIND ROSE, AND WITH BLACK WINGS 11 738

SOV'RAN
DIVINE THE SOV'RAN ARCHITECT HAD FRAM'D. . . . 5 256
TWO ONELY, WHO YET BY SOV'RAN GIFT POSSESS . . . 5 366

SOVRAN
WHO NOW IS SOVRAN CAN DISPOSE AND BID 1 246
OF SOVRAN POWER, WITH AWFUL CEREMONY 1 753
OUR ENVIED SOVRAN, AND HIS ALTAR BREATHES . . . 2 244
AND FEEL THY SOVRAN VITAL LAMP; BUT THOU . . . 3 22
THY SOVRAN SENTENCE, THAT MAN SHOULD FIND GRACE; . 3 145
CHOS'N BY THE SOVRAN PLANTER, WHEN HE FRAM'D . . 4 691
MELODIOUS HYMNS ABOUT THE SOVRAN THRONE 5 656
SO SPAKE THE SOVRAN VOICE, AND CLOUDS BEGAN . . 6 56
IMMUTABLY HIS SOVRAN WILL, THE END 7 79
FOR STATE, AS SOVRAN KING, AND TO ENURE 8 239
SENT FROM WHOSE SOVRAN GOODNESS I ADORE. 8 647
WONDER NOT, SOVRAN MISTRESS, IF PERHAPS 9 532
SOVRAN OF CREATURES, UNIVERSAL DAME. 9 612
O SOVRAN, VERTUOUS, PRECIOUS OF ALL TREES . . . 9 795
USURPING OVER SOVRAN REASON CLAIMD 9 1130
TO WHOM THE SOVRAN PRESENCE THUS REPLI'D. . . . 10 144
TH' ALMIGHTY THUS PRONOUNCD HIS SOVRAN WILL. . . 11 83

SOVRANTIE
OR FROM HEAV'N CLAMING SECOND SOVRANTIE; 12 35

SOV'RANTY
AND THIS IMPERIAL SOV'RANTY, ADORN'D 2 446

SOW
TO SOW A JANGLING NOISE OF WORDS UNKNOWN: . . . 12 55

SOW'D
ADVANCING, SOW'D THE EARTH WITH ORIENT PEARLE, . 5 2

SOWD
AND SOWD WITH STARRS THE HEAV'N THICK AS A FIELD: 7 358
SOME TREE WHOSE BROAD SMOOTH LEAVES TOGETHER SOWD, 9 1095
AND WITH WHAT SKILL THEY HAD, TOGETHER SOWD, . . 9 1112

SOW'N
SOW'N WITH CONTRITION IN HIS HEART, THEN THOSE . 11 27

SOYLE
THIR PAINFUL STEPS O'RE THE BURNT SOYLE; AND NOW . 1 562
THAT RICHES GROW IN HELL; THAT SOYLE MAY BEST . . 1 691
CATHAIAN COAST. THE AGGREGATED SOYLE 10 293

SPACE
NINE TIMES THE SPACE THAT MEASURES DAY AND NIGHT . 1 50
SPACE MAY PRODUCE NEW WORLDS; WHEREOF SO RIFE . . 1 650
HOV'RING A SPACE, TILL WINDS THE SIGNAL BLOW . . 2 717
'TWIXT HOST AND HOST BUT NARROW SPACE WAS LEFT, . 6 104
ALL SPACE, THE AMBIENT AIRE WIDE INTERFUS'D . . 7 89
INFINITUDE, NOR VACUOUS THE SPACE. 7 169
THE SPACE OF SEVEN CONTINU'D NIGHTS HE RODE . . 9 63
THAT SPACE THE EVIL ONE ABSTRACTED STOOD . . . 9 463
AND DURABLE; AND NOW IN LITTLE SPACE 10 320
A SPACE, TILL FIRMER THOUGHTS RESTRAIND EXCESS, . 11 498
THE SPACE OF SEVENTIE YEARS, THEN BRINGS THEM BACK, 12 345

SPACES
WITHIN, HER AMPLE SPACES, O'RE THE SMOOTH . . . 1 725
SPACES INCOMPREHENSIBLE (FOR SUCH 8 20

SPACIOUS
OP'ND INTO THE HILL A SPACIOUS WOUND 1 689
AND PORCHES WIDE, BUT CHIEF THE SPACIOUS HALL . . 1 762
LIES THROUGH YOUR SPACIOUS EMPIRE UP TO LIGHT, . 2 974
HERE WALK'D THE FIEND AT LARGE IN SPACIOUS FIELD. 3 430
THIS SPACIOUS GROUND, IN YONDER SHADIE BOWRE . . 5 367
EQUAL TO OURS, THROUGHOUT THE SPACIOUS NORTH; . . 5 726
THIS CONTINENT OF SPACIOUS HEAV'N, ADORND . . . 6 474
ROWLD INWARD, AND A SPACIOUS GAP DISCLOS'D . . . 6 861
SO SPACIOUS, AND HIS LINE STRETCHT OUT SO FARR; . 8 102
AS LORDS, A SPACIOUS WORLD, TO OUR NATIVE HEAVEN . 10 467
HE LOOKD AND SAW A SPACIOUS PLAINE, WHEREON . . 11 556

SPADE
OF PIONERS WITH SPADE AND PICKAX ARM'D 1 676

SPAKE
SO SPAKE TH' APOSTATE ANGEL, THOUGH IN PAIN, . . 1 125
SO SATAN SPAKE, AND HIM BEELZEBUB 1 271
HE SPAKE: AND TO CONFIRM HIS WORDS, OUT-FLEW . . 1 663
HE RECK'D NOT, AND THESE WORDS THEREAFTER SPAKE. . 2 50
NOT PEACE: AND AFTER HIM THUS MAMMON SPAKE. . . 2 228
OR SUMMERS NOON-TIDE AIR, WHILE THUS HE SPAKE. . 2 309
CONSCIOUS OF HIGHEST WORTH, UNMOV'D THUS SPAKE. . 2 429
SO SPAKE THE GRIESLIE TERROUR, AND IN SHAPE, . . 2 704
SHE SPAKE, AND AT HER WORDS THE HELLISH PEST . . 2 735
THUS TO HIS ONELY SON FORESEEING SPAKE. 3 79
THUS WHILE GOD SPAKE, AMBROSIAL FRAGRANCE FILL'D . 3 135
WHICH UTTERING THUS HE TO HIS FATHER SPAKE. . . 3 143
SILENT YET SPAKE, AND BREATH'D IMMORTAL LOVE . . 3 267
SO SPAKE THE FALSE DISSEMBLER UNPERCEIVD; . . . 3 681
THUS WHILE HE SPAKE, EACH PASSION DIMM'D HIS FACE 4 114
SO SPAKE THE FIEND, AND WITH NECESSITIE, . . . 4 393
SO SPAKE OUR GENERAL MOTHER, AND WITH EYES . . . 4 492
WHEN GABRIEL TO HIS NEXT IN POWER THUS SPAKE. . . 4 781
SO SPAKE THE CHERUBE, AND HIS GRAVE REBUKE . . . 4 844
TO WHOM WITH STERN REGARD THUS GABRIEL SPAKE. . . 4 877
WHILE THUS HE SPAKE, TH' ANGELIC SQUADRON BRIGHT . 4 977
ON ADAM, WHOM IMBRACING, THUS SHE SPAKE. . . . 5 27
SO SPAKE TH' ETERNAL FATHER, AND FULFILLD . . . 5 246
BRIGHTNESS HAD MADE INVISIBLE, THUS SPAKE. . . . 5 599
SO SPAKE TH' OMNIPOTENT, AND WITH HIS WORDS . . 5 616
AWAK'NING, THUS TO HIM IN SECRET SPAKE. 5 672
SO SPAKE THE FALSE ARCH-ANGEL, AND INFUS'D . . . 5 694
SO SPAKE THE SON, BUT SATAN WITH HIS POWERS . . 5 743
SO SPAKE THE FERVENT ANGEL, BUT HIS ZEALE . . . 5 849
SO SPAKE THE SERAPH ABDIEL FAITHFUL FOUND, . . . 5 896
SO SPAKE THE SOVRAN VOICE, AND CLOUDS BEGAN . . 6 56
SO SPAKE THE PRINCE OF ANGELS; TO WHOM THUS . . 6 281
AND CLOUDIE IN ASPECT THUS ANSWERING SPAKE. . . 6 450
AND THUS THE FILIAL GODHEAD ANSWERING SPAKE. . . 6 722
TO ALL HIS HOST ON EITHER HAND THUS SPAKE. . . . 6 800
SO SPAKE THE SON, AND INTO TERROUR CHANG'D . . . 6 824
THIR MULTITUDE, AND TO HIS SON THUS SPAKE. . . . 7 138
SO SPAKE TH' ALMIGHTIE, AND TO WHAT HE SPAKE . . 7 174
AGAIN TH' ALMIGHTIE SPAKE: LET THERE BE LIGHTS . 7 339
PRESENT) THUS TO HIS SON AUDIBLY SPAKE. 7 518
SO SPAKE OUR SIRE, AND BY HIS COUNT'NANCE SEEMD . 8 39
SO SPAKE THE GODLIKE POWER, AND THUS OUR SIRE. . 8 249

SPEEDILY
- WHO SPEEDILY THROUGH ALL THE HIERARCHIES 5 692

SPEEDS
- HE SPEEDS, AND THROUGH THE VAST ETHEREAL SKIE 5 267

SPEEDY
- WHERETO WITH SPEEDY WORDS TH' ARCH-FIEND REPLY'D, 1 156
- TOWARD THE FOUR WINDS FOUR SPEEDY CHERUBIM 2 516

SPEND
- TH' ALMIGHTY VICTOR TO SPEND ALL HIS RAGE, 2 144
- FIT HAUNT OF GODS? WHERE I HAD HOPE TO SPEND, 11 271
- SHAL SPEND THIR DAYES IN JOY UNBLAM'D, AND DWELL 12 22

SPENT
- PERHAPS HATH SPENT HIS SHAFTS, AND CEASES NOW 1 176
- ETERNITY SO SPENT IN WORSHIP PAID 2 248
- THIR HAPPIE HOURS IN JOY AND HYMNING SPENT, 3 417
- THAT DAY, AS OTHER SOLEMN DAYES, THEY SPENT 5 618
- AND DAY IS YET NOT SPENT; TILL THEN THOU SEEST 8 206
- DAZL'D AND SPENT, SUNK DOWN, AND SOUGHT REPAIR 8 457
- WHETHER SUCH VERTUE SPENT OF OLD NOW FAILD 9 145
- THUS THEY IN MUTUAL ACCUSATION SPENT 9 1187

SPHEAR
- THUS THEY IN HEAV'N, ABOVE THE STARRY SPHEAR, 3 416
- AND THAT CRYSTALLINE SPHEAR WHOSE BALLANCE WEIGHS 3 482
- TO SAVE APPEERANCES, HOW GIRD THE SPHEAR 8 82

SPHEAR'D
- SPHEAR'D IN A RADIANT CLOUD, FOR YET THE SUN 7 247

SPHEARE
- I FELL, HOW GLORIOUS ONCE ABOVE THY SPHEARE; 4 39
- THIS DAY AT HIGHTH OF NOON CAME TO MY SPHEARE 4 564
- WITH THY BRIGHT CIRCLET, PRAISE HIM IN THY SPHEARE 5 169
- MYSTICAL DANCE, WHICH YONDER STARRIE SPHEARE 5 620
- WITHIN THE VISIBLE DIURNAL SPHEARE; 7 22
- A MIGHTIE SPHEARE HE FRAM'D, UNLIGHTSOM FIRST, 7 355
- NOT TO TH' EXTENT OF THIR OWN SPHEARE. BUT SAY 10 808

SPHEARS
- EACH IN THIR SEVERAL ACTIVE SPHEARS ASSIGND, 5 477
- SHOULD COMBAT, AND THIR JARRING SPHEARS CONFOUND. 6 315
- WHICH ELSE TO SEVERAL SPHEARS THOU MUST ASCRIBE, 8 131

SPICIE
- THIR SPICIE DRUGS: THEY ON THE TRADING FLOOD 2 640
- SABEAN ODOURS FROM THE SPICIE SHOARE 4 162
- HIM THROUGH THE SPICIE FORREST ONWARD COM 5 298
- FLUNG ROSE, FLUNG ODOURS FROM THE SPICIE SHRUB, 8 517

SPI'D
- THEN AS A TYGER, WHO BY CHANCE HATH SPI'D 4 403
- HALF SPI'D, SO THICK THE ROSES BUSHING ROUND 9 426

SPIE
- TO WING THE DESOLATE ABYSS, AND SPIE 4 936
- WISE TO FLIE PAIN, PROFESSING NEXT THE SPIE, 4 948
- TO SEE THAT NONE THENCE ISSU'D FORTH A SPIE, 8 233
- A DOVE SENT FORTH ONCE AND AGEN TO SPIE 11 857

SPIES
- BEYOND HIS HOPE, EVE SEPARATE HE SPIES, 9 424
- OUR GREAT FORBIDDER, SAFE WITH ALL HIS SPIES 9 815

SPIGHT
- THRICE HE ASSAYD, AND THRICE IN SPIGHT OF SCORN, 1 619
- WILL ONCE MORE LIFT US UP, IN SPIGHT OF FATE, 2 393

SPILT
- WHO HAVING SPILT MUCH BLOOD, AND DON MUCH WASTE 11 791

SPINNING
- WITH INOFFENSIVE PACE THAT SPINNING SLEEPS 8 164

SPIRES
- DRIVN BACKWARD SLOPE THIR POINTING SPIRES, AND ROWLD 1 223
- WITH GLISTERING SPIRES AND PINNACLES ADORND, 3 550
- AMIDST HIS CIRCLING SPIRES, THAT ON THE GRASS 9 502

SPIRIT
- AND CHIEFLY THOU, O SPIRIT, THAT DOST PREFER 1 17
- CAN PERISH: FOR THE MIND AND SPIRIT REMAINS 1 139
- HAVE LEFT US THIS OUR SPIRIT AND STRENGTH INTIRE 1 146
- BELIAL CAME LAST, THEN WHOM A SPIRIT MORE LEWD 1 490
- MAMMON, THE LEAST ERECTED SPIRIT THAT FELL 1 679
- STOOD UP, THE STRONGEST AND THE FIERCEST SPIRIT 2 44
- OR SPIRIT OF THE NETHERMOST ABYSS 2 956
- TRANSFUS'D ON THEE HIS AMPLE SPIRIT RESTS. 3 389
- THE SPIRIT MALIGNE, BUT MUCH MORE ENVY SEIS'D 3 553
- GLAD WAS THE SPIRIT IMPURE AS NOW IN HOPE 3 630
- THE SHARPEST SIGHTED SPIRIT OF ALL IN HEAV'N; 3 691
- SPIRIT OF HAPPIE SORT: HIS GESTURES FIERCE 4 128
- SOME WANDRING SPIRIT OF HEAV'N, BY FOUNTAIN SIDE, 4 531
- A SPIRIT, ZEALOUS, AS HE SEEM'D, TO KNOW 4 565

SPIRIT (CONTINUED)
- NO CREATURE THENCE: IF SPIRIT OF OTHER SORT, 4 582
- WHO TELLS OF SOM INFERNAL SPIRIT SEEN 4 793
- THINK NOT, REVOLTED SPIRIT, THY SHAPE THE SAME, 4 835
- RAPHAEL, THE SOCIABLE SPIRIT, THAT DEIGN'D 5 221
- TILL BODY UP TO SPIRIT WORK, IN BOUNDS 5 478
- YOUR BODIES MAY AT LAST TURN ALL TO SPIRIT, 5 497
- O FAVOURABLE SPIRIT, PROPITIOUS GUEST, 5 507
- O ALIENATE FROM GOD, O SPIRIT ACCURST, 5 877
- IT SELF INSTINCT WITH SPIRIT, BUT CONVOYD 6 752
- ONE SPIRIT IN THEM RUL'D, AND EVERY EYE 6 848
- MY OVERSHADOWING SPIRIT AND MIGHT WITH THEE 7 165
- SPONTANEOUS, FOR WITHIN THEM SPIRIT LIVD, 7 204
- AND SPIRIT COMING TO CREATE NEW WORLDS. 7 209
- HIS BROODING WINGS THE SPIRIT OF GOD OUTSPRED, 7 235
- EXPRESSING WELL THE SPIRIT WITHIN THEE FREE, 8 440
- THE SPIRIT OF LOVE AND AMOROUS DELIGHT. 8 477
- WHICH OFT, THEY SAY, SOME EVIL SPIRIT ATTENDS 9 638
- LEAST THAT PURE BREATH OF LIFE, THE SPIRIT OF MAN 10 784
- UNUTTERABLE, WHICH THE SPIRIT OF PRAYER 11 6
- THE WORLD: IN SPIRIT PERHAPS HE ALSO SAW 11 406
- UNMINDFUL OF THIR MAKER, THOUGH HIS SPIRIT 11 611
- UPON THIR TONGUES A VARIOUS SPIRIT TO RASE 12 53
- FROM SHADOWIE TYPES TO TRUTH, FROM FLESH TO SPIRIT, 12 303
- HIS SPIRIT WITHIN THEM, AND THE LAW OF FAITH 12 488
- THIR PROUDEST PERSECUTERS: FOR THE SPIRIT 12 497
- THOUGH NOT BUT BY THE SPIRIT UNDERSTOOD, 12 514
- THE SPIRIT OF GOD, PROMISD ALIKE AND GIV'N 12 519
- LEFT THEM INROULD, OR WHAT THE SPIRIT WITHIN 12 523
- BUT FORCE THE SPIRIT OF GRACE IT SELF, AND BINDE 12 525
- OF SPIRIT AND TRUTH; THE REST, FARR GREATER PART, 12 533

SPIRITED
- FLEW UPWARD, SPIRITED WITH VARIOUS FORMS, 3 717
- SO TALK'D THE SPIRITED SLY SNAKE; AND EVE 9 613

SPIRITLESS
- EXHAUSTED, SPIRITLESS, AFFLICTED, FALL'N. 6 852

SPIRITOUS
- BUT MORE REFIN'D, MORE SPIRITOUS, AND PURE, 5 475
- OF SPIRITOUS AND FIERIE SPUME, TILL TOUCHT 6 479

SPIRITS
- INNUMERABLE FORCE OF SPIRITS ARM'D 1 101
- ETERNAL SPIRITS; OR HAVE YE CHOS'N THIS PLACE 1 318
- THESE FEMININE. FOR SPIRITS WHEN THEY PLEASE 1 423
- MILLIONS OF SPIRITS FOR HIS FAULT AMERC'T 1 609
- O MYRIADS OF IMMORTAL SPIRITS, O POWERS 1 622
- CAELESTIAL SPIRITS IN BONDAGE, NOR TH' ABYSS 1 658
- BY SPIRITS REPROBATE, AND IN AN HOUR 1 697
- THUS INCORPOREAL SPIRITS TO SMALLEST FORMS 1 789
- HIS OWN: FOR NEITHER DO THE SPIRITS DAMN'D 2 482
- (WHAT COULD IT LESS WHEN SPIRITS IMMORTAL SING?) 2 553
- HELL-BORN, NOT TO CONTEND WITH SPIRITS OF HEAV'N. 2 687
- AND RECK'N'ST THOU THY SELF WITH SPIRITS OF HEAV'N, 2 696
- OF SPIRITS THAT IN OUR JUST PRETENSES ARM'D 2 825
- AND SPIRITS OF THIS NETHERMOST ABYSS, 2 969
- OF THIS FRAIL WORLD; BY WHICH THE SPIRITS PERVERSE 2 1030
- AND SPIRITS, BOTH THEM WHO STOOD AND THEM WHO FAILD; 3 101
- ALL HEAV'N, AND IN THE BLESSED SPIRITS ELECT 3 136
- WITH THESE THAT NEVER FADE THE SPIRITS ELECT 3 360
- TRANSLATED SAINTS, OR MIDDLE SPIRITS HOLD 3 461
- URIEL, FOR THOU OF THOSE SEAV'N SPIRITS THAT STAND 3 654
- AS TO SUPERIOR SPIRITS IS WONT IN HEAVEN, 3 737
- AMONG THE SPIRITS BENEATH, WHOM I SEDUC'D 4 83
- NOT SPIRITS, YET TO HEAV'NLY SPIRITS BRIGHT 4 361
- FROM THESE, TWO STRONG AND SUTTLE SPIRITS HE CALLD 4 786
- TH' ANIMAL SPIRITS THAT FROM PURE BLOOD ARISE 4 805
- WHICH OF THOSE REBELL SPIRITS ADJUDG'D TO HELL 4 823
- AS MAY NOT OFT INVITE, THOUGH SPIRITS OF HEAV'N 5 374
- SPIRITUAL, MAY OF PUREST SPIRITS BE FOUND 5 406
- THROUGH SPIRITS WITH EASE; NOR WONDER; IF BY FIRE 5 439
- SPIRITS ODOROUS BREATHES: FLOURS AND THIR FRUIT 5 482
- TO VITAL SPIRITS ASPIRE, TO ANIMAL, 5 484
- OF WARRING SPIRITS; HOW WITHOUT REMORSE 5 566
- ALL THINGS, EV'N THEE, AND ALL THE SPIRITS OF HEAV'N 5 837
- MINISTRING SPIRITS, TRAIND UP IN FEAST AND SONG; 6 167
- SANGUIN, SUCH AS CELESTIAL SPIRITS MAY BLEED, 6 333
- YET SOON HE HEAL'D; FOR SPIRITS THAT LIVE THROUGHOUT 6 344
- HAVE EASILY AS SPIRITS EVADED SWIFT 6 596
- OUT OF SUCH PRISON, THOUGH SPIRITS OF PUREST LIGHT, 6 660
- IN HEAV'NLY SPIRITS COULD SUCH PERVERSENESS DWELL? 6 788
- OF SPIRITS MALIGNE A BETTER RACE TO BRING 7 189
- AND VERTUES, WINGED SPIRITS, AND CHARIOTS WING'D, 7 199
- OF SPIRITS APOSTAT AND THIR COUNSELS VAINE 7 610
- FROM THENCE A RIB, WITH CORDIAL SPIRITS WARME; 8 466
- LOVE NOT THE HEAV'NLY SPIRITS, AND HOW THIR LOVE 8 615
- EASIER THEN AIR WITH AIR, IF SPIRITS EMBRACE, 8 626
- DIMM ERST, DILATED SPIRITS, AMPLER HEART, 9 876
- ABOUT THIR SPIRITS HAD PLAID, AND INMOST POWERS 9 1048
- WITH SPIRITS MASCULINE, CREATE AT LAST 10 890
- TO SPIRITS FOULE, AND ALL MY TREES THIR PREY, 11 124
- RECOVERING, AND HIS SCATTERD SPIRITS RETURND, 11 294
- SUNK DOWN AND ALL HIS SPIRITS BECAME INTRANST: 11 420

SPIRITS (CONTINUED)
TO WEIGH THY SPIRITS DOWN, AND LAST CONSUME . . 11 545
PORTENDING GOOD, AND ALL HER SPIRITS COMPOS'D . . 12 596

SPIRITUAL
SPIRITUAL SUBSTANCE WITH CORPOREAL BARR. 4 585
MILLIONS OF SPIRITUAL CREATURES WALK THE EARTH . 4 677
TO SPIRITUAL NATURES; ONLY THIS I KNOW, ... 5 402
SPIRITUAL, MAY OF PUREST SPIRITS BE FOUND . . . 5 406
BY LIK'NING SPIRITUAL TO CORPORAL FORMS, . . . 5 573
SPEED ALMOST SPIRITUAL; MEE THOU THINKST NOT SLOW, 8 110
WITH SPIRITUAL ARMOUR, ABLE TO RESIST 12 491
BY SPIRITUAL, TO THEMSELVES APPROPRIATING . . . 12 518
SPIRITUAL LAWES BY CARNAL POWER SHALL FORCE . . 12 521

SPITE
TO MINGLE AND INVOLVE, DONE ALL TO SPITE . . . 2 384
THE GREAT CREATOUR? BUT THIR SPITE STILL SERVES . 2 385
ARE HIS CREATED, OR TO SPITE US MORE, . . . 9 147
WHOM US THE MORE TO SPITE HIS MAKER RAIS'D . . . 9 177
FROM DUST: SPITE THEN WITH SPITE IS BEST REPAID. . 9 178

SPLENDID
OF SPLENDID VASSALAGE, BUT RATHER SEEK 2 252

SPLENDOR
WITH SPLENDOR, ARM'D WITH POWER, IF AUGHT PROPOS'D 2 447
THE GOLDEN SUN IN SPLENDOR LIKEST HEAVEN . . . 3 572
BUT FADED SPLENDOR WAN; WHO BY HIS GATE 4 870
HIS EQUALS, IF IN POWER AND SPLENDOR LESS, . . . 5 796

SPLENDORS
OF HEAV'N, AND FROM ETERNAL SPLENDORS FLUNG . . 1 610

SPOIL
HAVOCK AND SPOIL AND RUIN ARE MY GAIN. 2 1009

SPOIL'D
WITH ALL HIS VERDURE SPOIL'D, AND TREES ADRIFT . 11 832

SPOILD
MY VANQUISHER, SPOILD OF HIS VANTED SPOILE; . . 3 251
SPOILD PRINCIPALITIES AND POWERS, TRIUMPHT . . . 10 186

SPOILE
MY VANQUISHER, SPOILD OF HIS VANTED SPOILE; . . 3 251
WITH GLORY AND SPOILE BACK TO THIR PROMIS'D LAND. 12 172

SPOILES
THOSE BALMIE SPOILES. AS WHEN TO THEM WHO SAILE . 4 159

SPOILS
WITH HEAV'NLY SPOILS, OUR SPOILS: WHAT HE DECREED 9 151
NATIONS, AND BRING HOME SPOILS WITH INFINITE . . 11 692

SPOKE
ACCORDING TO HIS DOOM: HE WOULD HAVE SPOKE, . . 10 517

SPOK'N
ALL HAST THOU SPOK'N AS MY THOUGHTS ARE, ALL . . 3 171

SPONTANEOUS
SPONTANEOUS, FOR WITHIN THEM SPIRIT LIVD, . . . 7 204

SPORT
EACH ON HIS ROCK TRANSFIXT, THE SPORT AND PREY . 2 181
THE SPORT OF WINDS: ALL THESE UPWHIRLD ALOFT . . 3 493

SPORTFUL
DOWN HE ALIGHTS AMONG THE SPORTFUL HERD 4 396

SPORTING
SPORTING THE LION RAMPD, AND IN HIS PAW 4 343
OF CORAL STRAY, OR SPORTING WITH QUICK GLANCE . . 7 405

SPOT
THERE LANDS THE FIEND, A SPOT LIKE WHICH PERHAPS . 3 588
THAT SPOT TO WHICH I POINT IS PARADISE, ... 3 733
NO SPOT OR BLAME BEHIND: WHICH GIVES ME HOPE . . 5 119
A CLOUDY SPOT. DOWN THITHER PRONE IN FLIGHT . . 5 266
THIR MAGNITUDES, THIS EARTH A SPOT, A GRAINE, . . 8 17
ROUND THIS OPACOUS EARTH, THIS PUNCTUAL SPOT, . . 8 23
SPOT MORE DELICIOUS THEN THOSE GARDENS FEIGN'D . 9 439

SPOTLESS
SIMPLICITIE AND SPOTLESS INNOCENCE. 4 318

SPOTS
WHENCE IN HER VISAGE ROUND THOSE SPOTS, UNPURG'D . 5 419
WITH SPOTS OF GOLD AND PURPLE, AZURE AND GREEN; . 7 479
FEILDS AND INHABITANTS: HER SPOTS THOU SEEST . . 8 145

SPOTTY
RIVERS OR MOUNTAINS IN HER SPOTTY GLOBE. . . . 1 291

SPOUSAL
SUNG SPOUSAL, AND BID HASTE THE EEVNING STARR . . 8 519

SPOUS'D
TO WED HER ELM; SHE SPOUS'D ABOUT HIM TWINES . . 5 216

SPOUSE
THAT DROVE HIM, THOUGH ENAMOURD, FROM THE SPOUSE . 4 169
ADAM FROM HIS FAIR SPOUSE, NOR EVE THE RITES . . 4 742
SO CHEARD HE HIS FAIR SPOUSE, AND SHE WAS CHEARD, 5 129
HELD DALLIANCE WITH HIS FAIRE EGYPTIAN SPOUSE. . 9 443

SPOUT
OF HELL SHOULD SPOUT HER CATARACTS OF FIRE, . . 2 176

SPOUTS
DRAWS IN, AND AT HIS TRUNCK SPOUTS OUT A SEA. . . 7 416

SPREAD
CAME LIKE A DELUGE ON THE SOUTH, AND SPREAD . . 1 354
HIS UNCOUTH WAY, OR SPREAD HIS AERIE FLIGHT . . 2 407
UNDER SPREAD ENSIGNS MARCHING MIGHT PASS THROUGH . 2 886
OF CHAOS, AND HIS DARK PAVILION SPREAD 2 960
WEIGHS HIS SPREAD WINGS, AT LEASURE TO BEHOLD . . 2 1046
OF WATERS ISSU'D FROM A CAVE AND SPREAD 4 454
TO STARR OR SUN-LIGHT, SPREAD THIR UMBRAGE BROAD . 9 1087

SPREADING
SPREADING THIR BANE; THE BLASTED STARRS LOOKT WAN, 10 412
OF THESE FAIR SPREADING TREES; WHICH BIDS US SEEK 10 1067

SPREADS
HE SPREADS FOR FLIGHT, AND IN THE SURGING SMOAK . 2 928
WHEN FIRST ON THIS DELIGHTFUL LAND HE SPREADS . . 4 643

SPRED
OF SOM IRRIGUOUS VALLEY SPRED HER STORE, . . . 4 255
THEN ALL THIS GLOBOUS EARTH IN PLAIN OUT SPRED, . 5 649
REBELLION RISING, SAW IN WHOM, HOW SPRED . . . 5 715
IN THIS PERFIDIOUS FRAUD, CONTAGION SPRED . . . 5 880
WERE DON, BUT INFINITE: FOR WIDE WAS SPRED . . . 6 241
UNDER SPRED ENSIGNES MOVING NIGH, IN SLOW . . . 6 533
AT ONCE THE FOUR SPRED OUT THIR STARRIE WINGS . . 6 827
ROSE AS IN DANCE THE STATELY TREES, AND SPRED . . 7 324
SOLAC'D THE WOODS, AND SPRED THIR PAINTED WINGS . 7 434
OF RICHEST TEXTURE SPRED, AT TH' UPPER END . . . 10 446
PERHAPS THY CAPITAL SEATE, FROM WHENCE HAD SPRED . 11 343
HE LOOKD AND SAW WIDE TERRITORIE SPRED 11 638

SPREDS
IN MALABAR OR DECAN SPREDS HER ARMES 9 1103

SPRING
IN SPRING TIME, WHEN THE SUN WITH TAURUS RIDES, . 1 769
THRONES AND IMPERIAL POWERS, OFF-SPRING OF HEAV'N 2 310
BUT FROM THE AUTHOR OF ALL ILL COULD SPRING . . 2 381
CLEER SPRING, OR SHADIE GROVE, OR SUNNIE HILL, . 3 28
THE WORLD SHALL BURN, AND FROM HER ASHES SPRING . 3 334
LED ON TH' ETERNAL SPRING. NOT THAT FAIRE FIELD . 4 268
CASTALIAN SPRING, MIGHT WITH THIS PARADISE . . . 4 274
CALLS US, WE LOSE THE PRIME, TO MARK HOW SPRING . 5 21
OF DAY-SPRING, AND THE SUN, WHO SCARCE UP RISEN . 5 139
ALL AUTUMN PIL'D, THOUGH SPRING AND AUTUMN HERE . 5 394
SPRING BOTH, THE FACE OF BRIGHTEST HEAV'N HAD
CHANGD 5 644
SO ALL ERE DAY-SPRING, UNDER CONSCIOUS NIGHT . . 6 521
IN YONDER SPRING OF ROSES INTERMIXT 9 218
OF SEASONS TO EACH CLIME; ELSE HAD THE SPRING . . 10 678
ON MEE, MEE ONELY, AS THE SOURSE AND SPRING . . 10 832
OF AMARANTIN SHADE, FOUNTAIN OR SPRING, ... 11 78
STRENGTH ADDED FROM ABOVE, NEW HOPE TO SPRING . . 11 138
IN SOME TO SPRING FROM THEE, WHO NEVER TOUCH'D . 11 425
A NATION FROM ONE FAITHFUL MAN TO SPRING; . . . 12 113
MUCH MORE, THAT MUCH MORE GOOD THEREOF SHALL
SPRING, ... 12 476

SPRINGS
SPRINGS UPWARD LIKE A PYRAMID OF FIRE 2 1013
ON HILLS WHERE FLOCKS ARE FED, FLIES TOWARD THE
SPRINGS 3 435
SPRINGS LIGHTER THE GREEN STALK, FROM THENCE THE
LEAVES 5 480
HIS HINDER PARTS, THEN SPRINGS AS BROKE FROM BONDS, 7 465
BUT FIRST AMONG THE PRIESTS DISSENSION SPRINGS, . 12 353

SPRINKL'D
OF MANY A COLOURD PLUME SPRINKL'D WITH GOLD, . . 3 642

SPRUNG
THEY HEARD, AND WERE ABASHT, AND UP THEY SPRUNG . 1 331
OUT OF THY HEAD I SPRUNG: AMAZEMENT SEIS'D . . . 2 758
LIGHT SHON, AND ORDER FROM DISORDER SPRUNG; . . 3 713
THE VERDUROUS WALL OF PARADISE UP SPRUNG; . . . 4 143
THIS UNCOUTH DREAM, OF EVIL SPRUNG I FEAR; . . . 5 98
AMONG THE CONSTELLATIONS WARR WERE SPRUNG, . . . 6 312
FROM WHOM IT SPRUNG, IMPOSSIBLE TO MIX 7 58
SPRUNG FROM THE DEEP, AND FROM HER NATIVE EAST . 7 245
HER NURSERIE; THEY AT HER COMING SPRUNG 8 46
BY QUICK INSTINCTIVE MOTION UP I SPRUNG, . . . 8 259
ADAM, FROM WHOSE DEARE SIDE I BOAST ME SPRUNG, . 9 965
A GROVE HARD BY, SPRUNG UP WITH THIS THIR CHANGE, 10 548

SPRUNG (CONTINUED)
SECOND OF SATAN SPRUNG, ALL CONQUERING DEATH, 10 591
SEE FATHER, WHAT FIRST FRUITS ON EARTH ARE SPRUNG 11 22

SPUME
OF SPIRITOUS AND FIERIE SPUME, TILL TOUCHT 6 479

SPUN
DISPARTED, AND BETWEEN SPUN OUT THE AIR, 7 241

SPURNS
UPLIFTED SPURNS THE GROUND, THENCE MANY A LEAGUE 2 929

SPY
CHAOS AND ANCIENT NIGHT, I COME NO SPY, 2 970

SPYING
WHICH GABRIEL SPYING, THUS BESPAKE THE FIEND. 4 1005

SQUADRON
FORTHWITH FROM EVERY SQUADRON AND EACH BAND 1 356
JUST MET, AND CLOSING STOOD IN SQUADRON JOIND 4 863
WHILE THUS HE SPAKE, TH' ANGELIC SQUADRON BRIGHT 4 977

SQUADROND
OF SQUADROND ANGELS HEAR HIS CAROL SUNG. 12 367

SQUADRONS
ANOTHER PART IN SQUADRONS AND GROSS BANDS, 2 570
COVERD WITH THICK EMBATTELD SQUADRONS BRIGHT, 6 16
SQUADRONS AT ONCE, WITH HUGE TWO-HANDED SWAY 6 251
ON EVERY SIDE WITH SHADDOWING SQUADRONS DEEP, 6 554
WITH CRUEL TOURNAMENT THE SQUADRONS JOINE; 11 652

SQUAR'D
SQUAR'D IN FULL LEGION (SUCH COMMAND WE HAD) 8 232

SQUARE
IN CIRCUIT, UNDETERMIND SQUARE OR ROUND, 2 1048
AND ON HER AMPLE SQUARE FROM SIDE TO SIDE 5 393
IN SEXTILE, SQUARE, AND TRINE, AND OPPOSITE, 10 659

SQUARED
FROM EVERY BAND AND SQUARED REGIMENT 1 758

SQUAT
SQUAT LIKE A TOAD, CLOSE AT THE EARE OF EVE; 4 800

STABL'D
AND STABL'D; OF MANKIND, SO NUMEROUS LATE, 11 752

STABLISHT
TO DAVID, STABLISHT AS THE DAYES OF HEAV'N. 12 347

STAFF
WHO FORTHWITH FROM THE GLITTERING STAFF UNFURLD 1 535

STAG
IN HILLOCKS; THE SWIFT STAG FROM UNDER GROUND 7 469

STAI'D
WOULD THOU HADST HEARK'ND TO MY WORDS, AND STAI'D 9 1134

STAID
HE CEAS'D; AND SATAN STAID NOT TO REPLY, 2 1010
NOR STAID, TILL ON NIPHATES TOP HE LIGHTS. 3 742
DESCENDING, AND IN HALF CUT SHEERE, NOR STAID, 6 325
NOR STAID, BUT ON THE WINGS OF CHERUBIM 7 218
THEN STAID THE FERVID WHEELES, AND IN HIS HAND 7 224
INVISIBLE, YET STAID (SUCH PRIVILEDGE 7 589

STAIES
AND I WILL BRING THEE WHERE NO SHADOW STAIES 4 470
SAFEST AND SEEMLIEST BY HER HUSBAND STAIES, 9 268

STAIN
INCAPABLE OF STAIN WOULD SOON EXPEL 2 140

STAIND
AND ALL HIS ARMOUR STAIND ERE WHILE SO BRIGHT. 6 334
OUR WONTED ORNAMENTS NOW SOILD AND STAIND, 9 1076

STAINE
TO SANCTITIE THAT SHALL RECEIVE NO STAINE: 10 639

STAIR
EACH STAIR MYSTERIOUSLY WAS MEANT, NOR STOOD 3 516
SATAN FROM HENCE NOW ON THE LOWER STAIR 3 540

STAIRS
THE STAIRS WERE SUCH AS WHEREON JACOB SAW 3 510
THE STAIRS WERE THEN LET DOWN, WHETHER TO DARE 3 523

STALK
ALL SEASONS, RIPE FOR USE HANGS ON THE STALK; 5 323
BESTIRS HER THEN, AND FROM EACH TENDER STALK 5 337
SPRINGS LIGHTER THE GREEN STALK, FROM THENCE THE LEAVES 5 480

STALK (CONTINUED)
EACH FLOUR OF SLENDER STALK, WHOSE HEAD THOUGH GAY 9 428

STALKES
A LION NOW HE STALKES WITH FIERIE GLARE, 4 402

STAND
ADVANC'T IN VIEW, THEY STAND, A HORRID FRONT 1 563
FORMOST TO STAND AGAINST THE THUNDERERS AIM 2 28
MILLIONS THAT STAND IN ARMS, AND LONGING WAIT 2 55
STAND IN HIS PRESENCE HUMBLE, AND RECEIVE 2 240
AND SO REFUS'D MIGHT IN OPINION STAND 2 471
OVER THE CASPIAN, THEN STAND FRONT TO FRONT 2 716
OF ENDLESS WARRS, AND BY CONFUSION STAND. 2 897
UPHELD BY ME, YET ONCE MORE HE SHALL STAND 3 178
SAW WITHIN KENN A GLORIOUS ANGEL STAND, 3 622
STAND READY AT COMMAND, AND ARE HIS EYES 3 650
URIEL, FOR THOU OF THOSE SEAV'N SPIRITS THAT STAND 3 654
FELL NOT, BUT STAND UNSHAK'N, FROM WITHIN 4 64
HADST THOU THE SAME FREE WILL AND POWER TO STAND? 4 66
THEN FROM HIS LOFTIE STAND ON THAT HIGH TREE 4 395
CAN IT BE DEATH? AND DO THEY ONELY STAND 4 518
STAND FIRM, FOR IN HIS LOOK DEFIANCE LOURS. 4 873
THAT IS, TO THY OBEDIENCE; THEREIN STAND. 5 522
MY SELF AND ALL TH' ANGELIC HOST THAT STAND 5 535
TO LOVE OR NOT; IN THIS WE STAND OR FALL: 5 540
HEAR MY DECREE, WHICH UNREVOK'T SHALL STAND. 5 602
TO STAND APPROV'D IN SIGHT OF GOD, THOUGH WORLDS 6 36
WHEN TO ADVANCE, OR STAND, OR TURN THE SWAY 6 234
OF THIS ETHEREOUS MOULD WHEREON WE STAND, 6 473
STAND READIE TO RECEIVE THEM, IF THEY LIKE 6 561
FREELY OUR PART; YEE WHO APPOINTED STAND 6 565
THAT WHOM THEY HIT, NONE ON THIR FEET MIGHT STAND, 6 592
STAND STILL IN BRIGHT ARRAY YE SAINTS, HERE STAND 6 801
NOR MULTITUDE, STAND ONELY AND BEHOLD 6 810
FROM THE ARMOURY OF GOD, WHERE STAND OF OLD 7 200
AND ALL THE BLEST: STAND FAST; TO STAND OR FALL 8 640
O HEAV'N. IN EVIL STRAIT THIS DAY I STAND 10 125
WITH ME? HOW CAN THEY THEN ACQUITTED STAND 10 827
WHY STAND WE LONGER SHIVERING UNDER FEARES, 10 1003
IN THIR BRIGHT STAND, THERE LEFT HIS POWERS TO SEISE 11 221
AW'D BY THE ROD OF MOSES SO TO STAND 12 198
OR HOW THE SUN SHALL IN MID HEAV'N STAND STILL 12 263
MANS VOICE COMMANDING, SUN IN GIBEON STAND, 12 265
LIGHT OUT OF DARKNESS. FULL OF DOUBT I STAND. 12 473
HIS LIVING TEMPLES, BUILT BY FAITH TO STAND, 12 527
TILL TIME STAND FIXT: BEYOND IS ALL ABYSS, 12 555

STANDARD
HIS MIGHTY STANDARD; THAT PROUD HONOUR CLAIM'D 1 533
ERECT THE STANDARD THERE OF ANCIENT NIGHT; 2 986
THE GREAT HIERARCHAL STANDARD WAS TO MOVE; 5 701
TROOP TO THIR STANDARD, SO THE WATRIE THRONG, 7 297

STANDARDS
STANDARDS, AND GONFALONS TWIXT VAN AND REARE 5 589

STANDING
A STANDING FIGHT, THEN SOARING ON MAIN WING 6 243
THOUGH STANDING ELSE AS ROCKS, BUT DOWN THEY FELL 6 593
STANDING ON EARTH, NOT RAPT ABOVE THE POLE, 7 23
PROGRESSIVE, RETROGRADE, OR STANDING STILL, 8 127
SO STANDING, MOVING, OR TO HIGHTH UPGROWN 9 677
FROM STANDING LAKE TO TRIPPING EBBE, THAT STOLE 11 847

STANDS
STANDS ON THE BLASTED HEATH. HE NOW PREPAR'D 1 615
DEATH READY STANDS TO INTERPOSE HIS DART, 2 854
ONE FATAL TREE THERE STANDS OF KNOWLEDGE CALL'D, 4 514
SWAYES THEM; THE CAREFUL PLOWMAN DOUBTING STANDS 4 983
TO PIECES, AND OREWHELM WHATEVER STANDS 6 489
POSTERITIE STANDS CURST: FAIR PATRIMONIE 10 818

STAR
DROPT FROM THE ZENITH LIKE A FALLING STAR, 1 745
AND NOW OF LOVE THEY TREAT TILL TH' EEVNING STAR 11 588

STARLESS
STARLESS EXPOS'D, AND EVER-THREATNING STORMS 3 425

STAR-PAV'D
IN PROGRESS THROUGH THE RODE OF HEAV'N STAR-PAV'D. 4 976

STARR
THIS PENDANT WORLD, IN BIGNESS AS A STARR 2 1052
OF LIBRA TO THE FLEECIE STARR THAT BEARS 3 558
(SO CALL THAT OPPOSITE FAIR STARR) HER AIDE 3 727
ON A SUN BEAM, SWIFT AS A SHOOTING STARR 4 556
STARR INTERPOS'D, HOWEVER SMALL HE SEES, 5 258
HIS COUNT'NANCE, AS THE MORNING STARR THAT GUIDES 5 708
OR IF THE STARR OF EEVNING AND THE MOON 7 104
OF ANGELS, THEN THAT STARR THE STARRS AMONG) 7 133
NUMEROUS, AND EVERY STARR PERHAPS A WORLD 7 621
TO THE TERRESTRIAL MOON BE AS A STARR 8 142
SUNG SPOUSAL, AND BID HASTE THE EEVNING STARR 8 519
THE SUN WAS SUNK, AND AFTER HIM THE STARR 9 48
TO STARR OR SUN-LIGHT, SPREAD THIR UMBRAGE BROAD 9 1087

STARR (CONTINUED)
OF THAT BRIGHT STARR TO SATAN PARAGOND. 10 426
AND SHAPE STARR BRIGHT APPEER'D, OR BRIGHTER, CLAD 10 450
OUR LIMBS BENUMM'D, ERE THIS DIURNAL STARR 10 1069
BARR'D OF HIS RIGHT; YET AT HIS BIRTH A STARR 12 360

STARRES
WITH THOUSAND THOUSAND STARRES, THAT THEN APPEER'D 7 383
RETURNE, THE STARRES OF MORN SHALL SEE HIM RISE 12 422

STARRIE
THE STARRIE HOST, RODE BRIGHTEST, TILL THE MOON 4 606
AND THESE THE GEMMS OF HEAV'N, HER STARRIE TRAIN: 4 649
AND STARRIE POLE: THOU ALSO MAD'ST THE NIGHT, 4 724
IN THIS COMMOTION, BUT THE STARRIE COPE 4 992
GIRT LIKE A STARRIE ZONE HIS WASTE, AND ROUND 5 281
MYSTICAL DANCE, WHICH YONDER STARRIE SPHEARE 5 620
THE STARRIE FLOCK, ALLUR'D THEM, AND WITH LYES 5 709
AT ONCE THE FOUR SPRED OUT THIR STARRIE WINGS 6 827
OF RAINBOWS AND STARRIE EYES. THE WATERS THUS 7 446
HIS STARRIE HELME UNBUCKL'D SHEW'D HIM PRIME 11 245

STARR-LIGHT
OR GLITTERING STARR-LIGHT WITHOUT THEE IS SWEET. 4 656

STARR'S
OF AMPLITUDE ALMOST IMMENSE, WITH STARR'S 7 620

STARRS
STOOD THICK AS STARRS, AND FROM HIS SIGHT RECEIV'D 3 61
AMONGST INNUMERABLE STARRS, THAT SHON 3 565
THAT ROWLD ORBICULAR, AND TURND TO STARRS 3 718
OF THIS NEW WORLD; AT WHOSE SIGHT ALL THE STARRS 4 34
OF HEAV'N THE STARRS THAT USHER EVENING ROSE: 4 355
FAIREST OF STARRS, LAST IN THE TRAIN OF NIGHT, 5 166
WITH THE FIXT STARRS, FIXT IN THIR ORB THAT FLIES, 5 176
INNUMERABLE AS THE STARRS OF NIGHT, 5 745
OR STARRS OF MORNING, DEW-DROPS, WHICH THE SUN 5 746
HAD WONDROUS, AS WITH STARRS THIR BODIES ALL 6 754
OF ANGELS, THEN THAT STARR THE STARRS AMONG) 7 133
THE LESS BY NIGHT ALTERNE: AND MADE THE STARRS, 7 348
GLOBOSE, AND EVERY MAGNITUDE OF STARRS, 7 357
AND SOWD WITH STARRS THE HEAV'N THICK AS A FIELD: 7 358
HITHER AS TO THIR FOUNTAIN OTHER STARRS 7 364
AND PAVEMENT STARRS, AS STARRS TO THEE APPEER, 7 578
POUDERD WITH STARRS. AND NOW ON EARTH THE SEVENTH 7 581
AND ALL HER NUMBERD STARRS, THAT SEEM TO ROWLE 8 19
AND CALCULATE THE STARRS, HOW THEY WILL WEILD 8 80
BE CENTER TO THE WORLD, AND OTHER STARRS 8 123
INVISIBLE ELSE ABOVE ALL STARRS, THE WHEELE 8 135
SPREADING THIR BANE; THE BLASTED STARRS LOOKT WAN, 10 412
OF WISDOME; HOPE NO HIGHER, THOUGH ALL THE STARRS 12 576

STARRY
OF STARRY LAMPS AND BLAZING CRESSETS FED 1 728
THUS THEY IN HEAV'N, ABOVE THE STARRY SPHEAR, 3 416
THIR STARRY DANCE IN NUMBERS THAT COMPUTE 3 580

STARS
STARS DISTANT, BUT NIGH HAND SEEMD OTHER WORLDS, 3 566

STARTED
BENDING TO LOOK ON ME, I STARTED BACK, 4 462
IT STARTED BACK, BUT PLEAS'D I SOON RETURND, 4 463
SO STARTED UP IN HIS OWN SHAPE THE FIEND. 4 819

STARTL'D
SUCH WHISPERING WAK'D HER, BUT WITH STARTL'D EYE 5 26

STARTS
OF FORCE TO ITS OWN LIKENESS: UP HE STARTS 4 813

STARV'D
OR SERENATE, WHICH THE STARV'D LOVER SINGS 4 769
UNNAM'D, UNDREADED, AND THY SELF HALF STARV'D? 10 595

STARVE
FROM BEDS OF RAGING FIRE TO STARVE IN ICE 2 600

STATE
MOV'D OUR GRAND PARENTS IN THAT HAPPY STATE, 1 29
THOUGH ALL OUR GLORY EXTINCT, AND HAPPY STATE 1 141
CONSENT OR CUSTOME, AND HIS REGAL STATE 1 640
THIR STATE AFFAIRS. SO THICK THE AERIE CROWD 1 775
HIGH ON A THRONE OF ROYAL STATE, WHICH FAR 2 1
YIELDED WITH FULL CONSENT. THE HAPPIER STATE 2 24
UNACCEPTABLE, THOUGH IN HEAV'N, OUR STATE 2 251
TO PEACEFUL COUNSELS, AND THE SETTL'D STATE 2 279
A PILLAR OF STATE; DEEP ON HIS FRONT ENGRAVEN 2 302
AND GOD-LIKE IMITATED STATE; HIM ROUND 2 511
FORTHWITH HIS FORMER STATE AND BEING FORGETS, 2 585
THIR SINFUL STATE, AND TO APPEASE BETIMES 3 186
THAT BRING TO MY REMEMBRANCE FROM WHAT STATE 4 38
BY ACT OF GRACE MY FORMER STATE; HOW SOON 4 94
TO MARK WHAT OF THIR STATE HE MORE MIGHT LEARN 4 400
BY IGNORANCE, IS THAT THIR HAPPIE STATE, 4 519
NO HAPPIER STATE, AND KNOW TO KNOW NO MORE. 4 775
AS MAY ADVISE HIM OF HIS HAPPIE STATE, 5 234

STATE (CONTINUED)
THE FALL OF OTHERS FROM LIKE STATE OF BLISS; 5 241
OF ANGELS UNDER WATCH; AND TO HIS STATE, 5 288
PERFECTIONS, IN HIMSELF WAS ALL HIS STATE, 5 353
YOUR FILL WHAT HAPPINESS THIS HAPPIE STATE 5 504
IN SIGHT OF GOD ENTHRON'D, OUR HAPPIE STATE 5 536
FROM WHAT HIGH STATE OF BLISS INTO WHAT WOE. 5 543
OUR HAPPIE STATE UNDER ONE HEAD MORE NEER 5 830
TO SET THE ENVIER OF HIS STATE, THE PROUD 6 89
WITH SATAN, HEE WHO ENVIES NOW THY STATE, 6 900
HER STATE WITH OARIE FEET: YET OFT THEY QUIT 7 440
LIVE, IN WHAT STATE, CONDITION OR DEGREE, 8 176
FOR STATE, AS SOVRAN KING, AND TO ENURE 8 239
I THEN WAS PASSING TO MY FORMER STATE 8 290
FROM THAT DAY MORTAL, AND THIS HAPPIE STATE 8 331
WHAT THINKST THOU THEN OF MEE, AND THIS MY STATE, 8 403
THUS I HAVE TOLD THEE ALL MY STATE, AND BROUGHT 8 521
BANE, AND IN HEAV'N MUCH WORSE WOULD BE MY STATE. 9 123
LET US NOT THEN SUSPECT OUR HAPPIE STATE 9 337
OR AUGHT THAT MIGHT HIS HAPPIE STATE SECURE, 9 347
BONE OF MY BONE THOU ART, AND FROM THY STATE 9 915
TRIUMPH AND SAY; FICKLE THEIR STATE WHOM GOD 9 948
OUR STATE CANNOT BE SEVERD, WE ARE ONE, 9 958
THIR INWARD STATE OF MIND, CALM REGION ONCE 9 1125
FOR MAN, FOR OF HIS STATE BY THIS THEY KNEW, 10 19
ASCENDED HIS HIGH THRONE, WHICH UNDER STATE 10 445
KEPT IN THAT STATE, HAD NOT THE FOLLY OF MAN 10 619
AND IN THIR STATE, THOUGH FIRM, STOOD MORE CONFIRMD. 11 71
HERE LET US LIVE, THOUGH IN FALL'N STATE, CONTENT. 11 180
ADAM BOWD LOW, HEE KINGLY FROM HIS STATE 11 249
BY MODERATION EITHER STATE TO BEARE, 11 363
DEGRADED, TO WHAT WRETCHED STATE RESERV'D, 11 501
WITH FAIR EQUALITIE, FRATERNAL STATE, 12 26
THAT SON, WHO ON THE QUIET STATE OF MEN 12 80

STATELIEST
OF STATELIEST VIEW. YET HIGHER THEN THIR TOPS 4 142
OF STATELIEST COVERT, CEDAR, PINE, OR PALME, 9 435

STATELY
WITH SINGED TOP THIR STATELY GROWTH THOUGH BARE 1 614
STOOD FIXT HER STATELY HIGHTH, AND STRAIT THE DORES 1 723
THE EARTH, AND STATELY TREAD, OR LOWLY CREEP; 5 201
ROSE AS IN DANCE THE STATELY TREES, AND SPRED 7 324

STATES
PLEAS'D HIGHLY THOSE INFERNAL STATES, AND JOY 2 387

STATION
SO WONDROUSLY WAS SET HIS STATION BRIGHT. 3 587
THIR STATION, HEAV'N YET POPULOUS RETAINES 7 146
THE PLANETS IN THIR STATION LIST'NING STOOD, 7 563
HEAV'N-FALL'N, IN STATION STOOD OR JUST ARRAY, 10 535
TO THIR FIXT STATION, ALL IN BRIGHT ARRAY 12 627

STATIONS
THROUGH THE STRICT SENTERIES AND STATIONS THICK 2 412

STATURE
HIS MIGHTY STATURE; ON EACH HAND THE FLAMES 1 222
THIR VISAGES AND STATURE AS OF GODS, 1 570
HIS STATURE REACHT THE SKIE, AND ON HIS CREST 4 988
STOOD THEY OR MOV'D, IN STATURE, MOTION, ARMS 6 302
HIS STATURE, AND UPRIGHT WITH FRONT SERENE 7 509

STAY
HIS IRON GATES, IF HE INTENDS OUR STAY 4 898
AND GRACE THAT WON WHO SAW TO WISH HER STAY, 8 43
GO; FOR THY STAY, NOT FREE, ABSENTS THEE MORE; 9 372
DELIGHTED, BUT DESIRING MORE HER STAY. 9 398
HAST THOU NOT WONDERD, ADAM, AT MY STAY? 9 856
STAY HIS RETURN PERHAPS OVER THIS GULFE 10 253
MY ONELY STRENGTH AND STAY: FORLORN OF THEE, 10 921
NOR AFTER RESURRECTION SHALL HE STAY 12 436
WE MAY NO LONGER STAY: GO, WAKEN EVE; 12 594
IS TO STAY HERE; WITHOUT THEE HERE TO STAY, 12 616

STAY'D
AS MANY MILES ALOFT: THAT FURIE STAY'D, 2 938

STAYD
HE STAYD NOT TO ENQUIRE: ABOVE THEM ALL 3 571

STAYES
STAYES NOT ON MAN; TO GOD HIS TOWER INTENDS 12 73

STEALTH
FROM ENTRANCE OR CHERUBIC WATCH, BY STEALTH 9 68

STEAME
CONSUM'D WITH NIMBLE GLANCE, AND GRATEFUL STEAME; 11 442

STEAMING
FROM HILL OR STEAMING LAKE, DUSKIE OR GREY, 5 186

STEARD
CHARYBDIS, AND BY TH' OTHER WHIRLPOOL STEARD. 2 1020

STEARING
BETWIXT THE CENTAURE AND THE SCORPION STEARING 10 328

STEARS
THEN WITH EXPANDED WINGS HE STEARS HIS FLIGHT 1 225
EASING THIR FLIGHT; SO STEARS THE PRUDENT CRANE 7 430

STEARSMAN
AS WHEN A SHIP BY SKILFUL STEARSMAN WROUGHT 9 513

STEDDIE
SAILES BETWEEN WORLDS AND WORLDS, WITH STEDDIE WING 5 268

STEDDIEST
WHAT OFT MY STEDDIEST THOUGHTS HAVE SEARCHT IN VAIN, 12 377

STEDFAST
MIXT WITH OBDURATE PRIDE AND STEDFAST HATE: 1 58
THE STEDFAST EARTH. AT LAST HIS SAIL-BROAD VANNES 2 927
THE STEDFAST EMPYREAN SHOOK THROUGHOUT, 6 833
THE PLANET EARTH, SO STEDFAST THOUGH SHE SEEM, 8 129

STEED
BUT LIKE A PROUD STEED REIND, WENT HAUTIE ON, 4 858
LEAST FROM THIS FLYING STEED UNREIN'D, (AS ONCE 7 17
PART WIELD THIR ARMS, PART COURB THE FOAMING STEED, 11 643

STEEDS
PART CURB THIR FIERIE STEEDS, OR SHUN THE GOAL 2 531
RAPT IN A CHARIOT DRAWN BY FIERY STEEDS. 3 522
CHARIOTS AND FLAMING ARMES, AND FIERIE STEEDS 6 17
AND FIERIE FOAMING STEEDS; WHAT STOOD, RECOYLD 6 391
IMPRESES QUAINT, CAPARISONS AND STEEDS; 9 35
RAPT IN A BALMIE CLOUD WITH WINGED STEEDS 11 706

STEEL
WITH STUBBORN PATIENCE AS WITH TRIPLE STEEL. 2 569

STEEP
THE WAY SEEMS DIFFICULT AND STEEP TO SCALE 2 71
ORE BOG OR STEEP, THROUGH STRAIT, ROUGH, DENSE, OR RARE, 2 948
THROWS HIS STEEP FLIGHT IN MANY AN AERIE WHEELE, 3 741
OF A STEEP WILDERNESS, WHOSE HAIRIE SIDES 4 135
NOW TO TH' ASCENT OF THAT STEEP SAVAGE HILL 4 172
DOWN THE STEEP GLADE, AND MET THE NEATHER FLOOD, 4 231
BOTH DAY AND NIGHT; HOW OFTEN FROM THE STEEP 4 680
THE SWORD OF SATAN WITH STEEP FORCE TO SMITE 6 324
MUCH OF HIS RACE THOUGH STEEP, SUSPENS IN HEAV'N 7 99
IF STEEP, WITH TORRENT RAPTURE, IF THROUGH PLAINE, 7 299

STEERS
VERES OFT, AS OFT SO STEERS, AND SHIFTS HER SAILE; 9 515

STELLAR
THIR STELLAR VERTUE ON ALL KINDS THAT GROW 4 671

STELTH
PURSUES THE ARIMASPIAN, WHO BY STELTH 2 945

STEMM
ON THE GREEN STEMM; GOD SAW THAT IT WAS GOOD. 7 337

STEMMING
PLY STEMMING NIGHTLY TOWARD THE POLE. SO SEEM'D 2 642

STENCH
WITH STENCH AND SMOAK: SUCH RESTING FOUND THE SOLE 1 237

STEP
ONE STEP NO MORE THEN FROM HIMSELF CAN FLY 4 22
I SDEIND SUBJECTION, AND THOUGHT ONE STEP HIGHER 4 50
SO SAYING, HIS PROUD STEP HE SCORNFUL TURN'D, 4 536
SMOOTH SLIDING WITHOUT STEP, LAST LED ME UP 8 302
IF CHANCE WITH NYMPHLIKE STEP FAIR VIRGIN PASS, 9 452
SO SAYING, FROM THE TREE HER STEP SHE TURND, 9 834

STEPDAME
YOUNG BACCHUS FROM HIS STEPDAME RHEA'S EYE; 4 279

STEPPING
FORTH STEPPING OPPOSITE, HALF WAY HE MET 6 128

STEPS
HE WALKT WITH TO SUPPORT UNEASIE STEPS 1 295
OVER THE BURNING MARLE, NOT LIKE THOSE STEPS 1 296
THIR PAINFUL STEPS O'RE THE BURNT SOYLE; AND NOW 1 562
MY SELF EXPOSE, WITH LONELY STEPS TO TREAD 2 828
HIS TRAVELL'D STEPS; FARR DISTANT HE DESCRIES 3 501
THAT SCAL'D BY STEPS OF GOLD TO HEAV'N GATE 3 541
BEFORE HIS DECENT STEPS A SILVER WAND. 3 644
NOW MORN HER ROSIE STEPS IN TH' EASTERN CLIME 5 1
BY STEPS WE MAY ASCEND TO GOD. BUT SAY, 5 512
GRACE WAS IN ALL HER STEPS, HEAV'N IN HER EYE, 8 488
OF GLORY, AND FARR OFF HIS STEPS ADORE. 11 333
EXPRESS, AND OF HIS STEPS THE TRACK DIVINE. 11 354
THEY HAND IN HAND WITH WANDRING STEPS AND SLOW, 12 648

STEPT
BACK STEPT THOSE TWO FAIRE ANGELS HALF AMAZ'D 4 820

STEP-TRACE
HIS BRIGHT APPEARANCES, OR FOOT STEP-TRACE? 11 329

STERN
TO WHOM WITH STERN REGARD THUS GABRIEL SPAKE. 4 877
TO WHICH THE FIEND THUS ANSWERD FROWNING STERN. 4 924
TO WHOM IN BRIEF THUS ABDIEL STERN REPLI'D. 6 171
OF STERN ACHILLES ON HIS FOE PURSU'D 9 15
BUT HER WITH STERN REGARD HE THUS REPELL'D. 10 866

STERNLY
OF WOE AND SORROW. STERNLY HE PRONOUNC'D 8 333

STICKS
STICKS NO DISHONOR ON OUR FRONT, BUT TURNS 9 330

STIFF
THE DANK, AND RISING ON STIFF PENNONS, TOWRE 7 441

STIFLING
BLOWN STIFLING BACK ON HIM THAT BREATHS IT FORTH: 11 313

STIL
THEN STIL AT HELS DARK THRESHOLD TO HAVE SATE WATCH, 10 594

STILE
MUST WE RENOUNCE, AND CHANGING STILE BE CALL'D 2 312
ADAM, ESTRANG'D IN LOOK AND ALTERD STILE, 9 1132

STILL
STILL URGES, AND A FIERY DELUGE, FED 1 68
AND OUT OF GOOD STILL TO FIND MEANS OF EVIL; 1 165
WHAT MATTER WHERE, IF I BE STILL THE SAME, 1 256
PUT FORTH AT FULL, BUT STILL HIS STRENGTH CONCEAL'D, 1 641
THOUGH WITHOUT NUMBER STILL AMIDST THE HALL 1 791
OF THAT FORGETFUL LAKE BENUMM NOT STILL, 2 74
WROUGHT STILL WITHIN THEM; AND NO LESS DESIRE 2 295
DREW AUDIENCE AND ATTENTION STILL AS NIGHT 2 308
IN HEIGHTH OR DEPTH, STILL FIRST AND LAST WILL REIGN 2 324
THE GREAT CREATOUR? BUT THIR SPITE STILL SERVES 2 385
AND KENNEL THERE, YET THERE STILL BARK'D AND HOWL'D, 2 658
ENCROACHT ON STILL THROUGH OUR INTESTINE BROILES 2 1001
SO EASILY DESTROY'D, AND STILL DESTROYES 3 301
OF SENNAAR, AND STILL WITH VAIN DESIGNE 3 467
SHOT UPWARD STILL DIRECT, WHENCE NO WAY ROUND 3 618
STILL ENDING, STILL RENEWING, THROUGH MID HEAV'N; 3 729
SO BURTHENSOME STILL PAYING, STILL TO OW; 4 53
FORGETFUL WHAT FROM HIM I STILL RECEIVD, 4 54
BY OWING OWES NOT, BUT STILL PAYS, AT ONCE 4 56
STILL THREATNING TO DEVOUR ME OPENS WIDE, 4 77
THE LOWER STILL I FALL, ONELY SUPREAM 4 91
STILL AS THEY THIRSTED SCOOP THE BRIMMING STREAM; 4 336
WHEN SATAN STILL IN GAZE, AS FIRST HE STOOD, 4 356
STILL UNFULFILL'D WITH PAIN OF LONGING PINES; 4 511
STILL AS IT ROSE, IMPOSSIBLE TO CLIMBE. 4 548
MINE EYE PURSU'D HIM STILL, BUT UNDER SHADE 4 572
NOW CAME STILL EEVNING ON, AND TWILIGHT GRAY 4 598
SO JUDGE THOU STILL, PRESUMPTUOUS, TILL THE WRAUTH, 4 912
BUT STILL THY WORDS AT RANDOM, AS BEFORE, 4 930
ATTRACTED BY THY BEAUTY STILL TO GAZE. 5 47
VARIE TO OUR GREAT MAKER STILL NEW PRAISE. 5 184
RISING OR FALLING STILL ADVANCE HIS PRAISE. 5 191
HAIL UNIVERSAL LORD, BE BOUNTEOUS STILL 5 205
ASSUR'D ME, AND STILL ASSURE: THOUGH WHAT THOU TELLST 5 553
APOSTAT, STILL THOU ERRST, NOR END WILT FIND 6 172
STAND STILL IN BRIGHT ARRAY YE SAINTS, HERE STAND 6 801
PURPLES THE EAST; STILL GOVERN THOU MY SONG, 7 30
YET SCARCE ALLAY'D STILL EYES THE CURRENT STREAME, 7 67
IN THAT ASPECT, AND STILL THAT DISTANCE KEEPES 7 379
THOUGHT HIM STILL SPEAKING, STILL STOOD FIXT TO HEAR; 8 3
A POMP OF WINNING GRACES WAITED STILL, 8 61
INTO ALL EYES TO WISH HER STILL IN SIGHT. 8 63
EARTH SITTING STILL, WHEN SHE ALONE RECEAVES 8 89
PROGRESSIVE, RETROGRADE, OR STANDING STILL, 8 127
STILL LUMINOUS BY HIS RAY. WHAT IF THAT LIGHT 8 140
UNPRACTIS'D, UNPREPAR'D, AND STILL TO SEEK. 8 197
DESIRE WITH THEE STILL LONGER TO CONVERSE 8 252
I FOUND NOT WHAT ME THOUGHT I WANTED STILL; 8 355
THE ONE INTENSE, THE OTHER STILL REMISS 8 387
AND BE SO MINDED STILL; I, ERE THOU SPAK'ST, 8 444
STILL GLORIOUS BEFORE WHOM AWAKE I STOOD; 8 464
ATTRACTIVE, HUMAN, RATIONAL, LOVE STILL; 8 587
VARIOUSLY REPRESENTING; YET STILL FREE 8 610
BE GOOD AND FRIENDLY STILL, AND OFT RETURN. 8 651
ADAM, WELL MAY WE LABOUR STILL TO DRESS 9 205
THIS GARDEN, STILL TO TEND PLANT, HERB AND FLOUR, 9 206
THAT GAVE THEE BEING, STILL SHADES THEE AND PROTECTS. 9 266
HOW ARE WE HAPPIE, STILL IN FEAR OF HARM? 9 326

STILL (CONTINUED)

BUT BID HER WELL BEWARE, AND STILL ERECT, ... 9 353
STILL HANGING INCORRUPTIBLE, TILL MEN 9 622
WHOSE VERTUE, FOR OF GOOD STILL GOOD PROCEEDS, . 9 973
REMAIND STILL HAPPIE, NOT AS NOW, DESPOILD . . . 9 1138
AS GOOD HAVE GROWN THERE STILL A LIVELESS RIB. . 9 1154
FOR STILL THEY KNEW, AND OUGHT TO HAVE STILL REMEMBER'D 10 12
BUT STILL REJOYC'T, HOW IS IT NOW BECOME . . . 10 120
STILL MOVES WITH THINE, JOIN'D IN CONNEXION SWEET, 10 359
THERE DIDST NOT; THERE LET HIM STILL VICTOR SWAY, 10 376
OPHIUSA) BUT STILL GREATEST HEE THE MIDST, . . . 10 528
ABOVE THE REST STILL TO RETAIN; THEY ALL . . . 10 532
SO FAIR AND GOOD CREATED, AND HAD STILL . . . 10 618
HAD ROUNDED STILL TH' HORIZON, AND NOT KNOWN . . 10 684
PURSUES ME STILL, LEAST ALL I CANNOT DIE, . . . 10 783
BY WHICH ALL CAUSES ELSE ACCORDING STILL . . . 10 806
AND REASONINGS, THOUGH THROUGH MAZES, LEAD ME STILL 10 830
THROUGH THE STILL NIGHT, NOT NOW, AS ERE MAN FELL, 10 846
STILL FOLLOWING THEE, STILL COMPASSING THEE ROUND 11 352
RETAINING STILL DIVINE SIMILITUDE 11 512
BUT STILL I SEE THE TENOR OF MANS WOE 11 632
STILL TEND FROM BAD TO WORSE, TILL GOD AT LAST . 12 106
HUMBLES HIS STUBBORN HEART, BUT STILL AS ICE . . 12 193
OR HOW THE SUN SHALL IN MID HEAV'N STAND STILL . 12 263
STILL FOLLOW'D HIM; TO THEM SHALL LEAVE IN CHARGE 12 439
SECULAR POWER, THOUGH FEIGNING STILL TO ACT . . 12 517
STILL OVERCOMING EVIL, AND BY SMALL 12 566

STING

WITH MORTAL STING: ABOUT HER MIDDLE ROUND . . . 2 653
INGLORIOUS, OF HIS MORTALL STING DISARM'D. . . . 3 253

STINGS

AND FIX FARR DEEPER IN HIS HEAD THIR STINGS . . 12 432

STIR

WILL SLACK'N, IF HIS BREATH STIR NOT THIR FLAMES. 2 214
RAPHAEL, SAID HEE, THOU HEAR'ST WHAT STIR ON EARTH 5 224

STIRD

STIRD UP WITH ENVY AND REVENGE, DECEIV'D . . . 1 35

STIRR

HIS TROUBL'D THOUGHTS, AND FROM THE BOTTOM STIRR . 4 19

STIRR'D

TEMPTING, STIRR'D IN ME SUDDEN APPETITE 8 308

STIRRING

THIR NATURAL PRAVITIE, BY STIRRING UP 12 288

STOCK

AND MAN AS FROM A SECOND STOCK PROCEED. 12 7
ALL PROPHECIE, THAT OF THE ROYAL STOCK 12 325

STOLE

NATIVE PERFUMES, AND WHISPER WHENCE THEY STOLE . 4 158
ON HIM WHO HAD STOLE JOVES AUTHENTIC FIRE. . . . 4 719
FROM STANDING LAKE TO TRIPPING EBBE, THAT STOLE . 11 847

STOL'N

WITH WHOSE STOL'N FRUIT MAN ONCE MORE TO DELUDE. . 11 125

STOLN

MUCH WONDRING HOW THE SUTTLE FIEND HAD STOLN . . 10 20

STONE

COMPAR'D WITH AUGHT ON EARTH, MEDAL OR STONE; . . 3 592
IF STONE, CARBUNCLE MOST OR CHRYSOLITE, ... 3 596
IN AARONS BREST-PLATE, AND A STONE BESIDES . . . 3 598
THAT STONE, OR LIKE TO THAT WHICH HERE BELOW . . 3 600
BROIDERD THE GROUND, MORE COLOUR'D THEN WITH STONE 4 702
ENTRAILS UNLIKE) OF MINERAL AND STONE, ... 6 517
OF GRASSIE TERFE, AND PILE UP EVERY STONE . . . 11 324
SMOTE HIM INTO THE MIDRIFF WITH A STONE . . . 11 445
INTESTIN STONE AND ULCER, COLIC PANGS, . . . 11 484
TO WORSHIP THIR OWN WORK IN WOOD AND STONE . . . 12 119

STONES

WITH DART AND JAV'LIN, STONES AND SULFUROUS FIRE; 11 658

STONIE

WHAT MAY SUFFICE, AND SOFT'N STONIE HEARTS . . . 3 189
BRASS, IRON, STONIE MOULD, HAD NOT THIR MOUTHES . 6 576
THE STONIE FROM THIR HEARTS, & MADE NEW FLESH . . 11 4

STOOD

OF THAT INFLAMED SEA, HE STOOD AND CALL'D . . . 1 300
THE HEADS AND LEADERS THITHER HAST WHERE STOOD . 1 357
CAME SINGLY WHERE HE STOOD ON THE BARE STRAND, . 1 379
WHILE THE PROMISCUOUS CROUD STOOD YET ALOOF? . . 1 380
IN SION ALSO NOT UNSUNG, WHERE STOOD 1 442
VICE FOR IT SELF; TO HIM NO TEMPLE STOOD . . . 1 492
STOOD LIKE A TOWR; HIS FORM HAD YET NOT LOST . . 1 591
FOR HIS REVOLT, YET FAITHFULL HOW THEY STOOD, . . 1 611
AS STOOD LIKE THESE, COULD EVER KNOW REPULSE? . . 1 630
THERE STOOD A HILL NOT FAR WHOSE GRIESLY TOP . . 1 670

STOOD (CONTINUED)

STOOD FIXT HER STATELY HIGHTH, AND STRAIT THE DORES 1 723
STOOD UP, THE STRONGEST AND THE FIERCEST SPIRIT . 2 44
MAJESTICK THOUGH IN RUIN: SAGE HE STOOD . . . 2 305
FOR EACH SEEM'D EITHER; BLACK IT STOOD AS NIGHT, . 2 670
INCENC'T WITH INDIGNATION SATAN STOOD 2 707
GREW DARKER AT THIR FROWN, SO MATCHT THEY STOOD; . 2 720
EXCEL'D HER POWER; THE GATES WIDE OP'N STOOD, . . 2 884
SO WIDE THEY STOOD, AND LIKE A FURNACE MOUTH . . 2 888
STOOD ON THE BRINK OF HELL AND LOOK'D A WHILE, . 2 918
THE CONSORT OF HIS REIGN; AND BY THEM STOOD . . 2 963
STOOD THICK AS STARRS, AND FROM HIS SIGHT RECEIV'D 3 61
SUFFICIENT TO HAVE STOOD, THOUGH FREE TO FALL. . 3 99
AND SPIRITS, BOTH THEM WHO STOOD AND THEM WHO FAILD; 3 101
FREELY THEY STOOD WHO STOOD, AND FELL WHO FELL. . 3 102
HE ASK'D, BUT ALL THE HEAV'NLY QUIRE STOOD MUTE, . 3 217
EACH STAIR MYSTERIOUSLY WAS MEANT, NOR STOOD . . 3 516
ROUND HE SURVEYS, AND WELL MIGHT, WHERE HE STOOD . 3 555
STOOD RUL'D, STOOD VAST INFINITUDE CONFIN'D; . . 3 711
ME SOME INFERIOUR ANGEL, I HAD STOOD 4 59
AND ALL AMID THEM STOOD THE TREE OF LIFE, . . . 4 218
STOOD WHISPERING SOFT, BY A FRESH FOUNTAIN SIDE . 4 326
WHEN SATAN STILL IN GAZE, AS FIRST HE STOOD, . . 4 356
INTO A LIQUID PLAIN, THEN STOOD UNMOV'D . . . 4 455
THUS AT THIR SHADIE LODGE ARRIV'D, BOTH STOOD . . 4 720
FORTH ISSUING AT TH' ACCUSTOMD HOUR STOOD ARMD . 4 779
THAT NEER HIM STOOD, AND GAVE THEM THUS IN CHARGE. 4 787
INVINCIBLE: ABASHT THE DEVIL STOOD, ... 4 846
JUST MET, AND CLOSING STOOD IN SQUADRON JOIND . 4 863
INSULTING ANGEL, WELL THOU KNOWST I STOOD . . . 4 926
COLLECTING ALL HIS MIGHT DILATED STOOD, ... 4 986
AND AS I WONDRING LOOKT, BESIDE IT STOOD . . . 5 54
TWO OTHER PRECIOUS DROPS THAT READY STOOD, . . . 5 132
THOUSAND CELESTIAL ARDORS, WHERE HE STOOD . . . 5 249
SKIE-TINCTUR'D GRAIN. LIKE MAIA'S SON HE STOOD, . 5 285
STOOD TO ENTERTAIN HER GUEST FROM HEAV'N; NO VAILE 5 383
AND PERFET WHILE THEY STOOD; HOW LAST UNFOULD . . 5 568
OF CIRCUIT INEXPRESSIBLE THEY STOOD, ... 5 595
DESIROUS; ALL IN CIRCLES AS THEY STOOD, ... 5 631
STOOD UP, AND IN A FLAME OF ZEALE SEVERE . . . 5 807
THAT STOOD FOR HEAV'N, IN MIGHTY QUADRATE JOYN'D . 6 62
PRESENTED STOOD IN TERRIBLE ARRAY 6 106
ABDIEL THAT SIGHT ENDUR'D NOT, WHERE HE STOOD . . 6 111
HOSANNA TO THE HIGHEST: NOR STOOD AT GAZE . . . 6 205
STOOD THEY OR MOV'D, IN STATURE, MOTION, ARMS . . 6 302
BLAZ'D OPPOSITE, WHILE EXPECTATION STOOD . . . 6 306
BACK TO HIS CHARIOT; WHERE IT STOOD RETIR'D . . 6 338
NOR STOOD UNMINDFUL ABDIEL TO ANNOY 6 369
AND FIERIE FOAMING STEEDS; WHAT STOOD, RECOYLD . 6 391
NOT TO HAVE DISOBEI'D; IN FIGHT THEY STOOD . . . 6 403
AS ONE HE STOOD ESCAP'T FROM CRUEL FIGHT, . . . 6 448
NONE ARGUING STOOD, INNUMERABLE HANDS 6 508
THE MATIN TRUMPET SUNG: IN ARMS THEY STOOD . . . 6 526
TO HIDE THE FRAUD. AT INTERVIEW BOTH STOOD . . . 6 555
A SERAPH STOOD, AND IN HIS HAND A REED 6 579
STOOD WAVING TIPT WITH FIRE; WHILE WE SUSPENSE, . 6 580
COLLECTED STOOD WITHIN OUR THOUGHTS AMUS'D, . . 6 581
STOOD RANKT OF SERAPHIM ANOTHER ROW 6 604
STOOD SCOFFING, HIGHTHN'D IN THIR THOUGHTS BEYOND 6 629
AND ALL HIS HOST DERIDED, WHILE THEY STOOD . . . 6 633
A WHILE IN TROUBLE; BUT THEY STOOD NOT LONG, . . 6 634
THIS SAW HIS HAPLESS FOES BUT STOOD OBDUR'D, . . 6 785
STOOD REIMBATTELL'D FIERCE, BY FORCE OR FRAUD . . 6 794
TO MEET HIM ALL HIS SAINTS, WHO SILENT STOOD . . 6 882
OF DISOBEDIENCE; FIRM THEY MIGHT HAVE STOOD, . . 6 911
ON HEAV'NLY GROUND THEY STOOD, AND FROM THE SHORE 7 210
THE SMELLING GOURD, UP STOOD THE CORNIE REED . . 7 321
THE PLANETS IN THIR STATION LIST'NING STOOD, . . 7 563
THOUGHT HIM STILL SPEAKING, STILL STOOD FIXT TO HEAR; 8 3
STOOD ON MY FEET; ABOUT ME ROUND I SAW 8 261
WHEN SUDDENLY STOOD AT MY HEAD A DREAM, ... 8 292
WHICH IT HAD LONG STOOD UNDER, STREIND TO THE HIGHTH 8 454
STILL GLORIOUS BEFORE WHOM AWAKE I STOOD; . . . 8 464
AS IN A SHADIE NOOK I STOOD BEHIND, ... 9 277
VEILD IN A CLOUD OF FRAGRANCE, WHERE SHE STOOD, . 9 425
THAT SPACE THE EVIL ONE ABSTRACTED STOOD . . . 9 463
HEE BOULDER NOW, UNCALL'D BEFORE HER STOOD; . . 9 523
LONGING AND ENVYING STOOD, BUT COULD NOT REACH. . 9 593
STOOD IN HIMSELF COLLECTED, WHILE EACH PART, . . 9 673
ASTONIED STOOD AND BLANK, WHILE HORROR CHILL . . 9 890
SPEECHLESS HE STOOD AND PALE, TILL THUS AT LENGTH 9 894
REMOV'D FARR OFF; THEN PITTYING HOW THEY STOOD . 10 211
STOOD OPEN WIDE, BELCHING OUTRAGEOUS FLAME . . . 10 232
LONG HEE ADMIRING STOOD, TILL SIN, HIS FAIRE . . 10 352
SO HAVING SAID, A WHILE HE STOOD, EXPECTING . . 10 504
HEAV'N-FALL'N, IN STATION STOOD OR JUST ARRAY, . 10 535
CAST ON THEMSELVES FROM THIR OWN MOUTHS. THERE STOOD 10 547
DEVOURD EACH OTHER; NOR STOOD MUCH IN AWE . . . 10 712
THUS THEY IN LOWLIEST PLIGHT REPENTANT STOOD . . 11 1
OF THEMIS STOOD DEVOUT. TO HEAV'N THIR PRAYERS . 11 14
AND IN THIR STATE, THOUGH FIRM, STOOD MORE CONFIRMD. 11 71
HEART-STROOK WITH CHILLING GRIPE OF SORROW STOOD. 11 264
STOOD VISIBLE, AMONG THESE PINES HIS VOICE . . . 11 321

STOOD (CONTINUED)
HIS EYE MIGHT THERE COMMAND WHEREVER STOOD 11 385
ITH' MIDST AN ALTAR AS THE LAND-MARK STOOD 11 432
IN OTHER PART STOOD ONE WHO AT THE FORGE 11 564
BOTH HORSE AND FOOT, NOR IDELY MUSTRING STOOD; 11 645
LIKE A DARK CEELING STOOD; DOWN RUSH'D THE RAIN 11 743
TH' ARCHANGEL STOOD, AND FROM THE OTHER HILL 12 626

STOODST
AS WHEN THOU STOODST IN HEAV'N UPRIGHT AND PURE; 4 837
BY TH' ANGEL, ON THY FEET THOU STOODST AT LAST, 11 759

STOOP
TO STOOP WITH WEARIED WINGS, AND WILLING FEET 3 73
DEATH HIS DEATHS WOUND SHALL THEN RECEIVE, AND STOOP 3 252

STOOP'D
WITH BLANDISHMENT, EACH BIRD STOOP'D ON HIS WING. 8 351

STOOPING
WHO STOOPING OP'ND MY LEFT SIDE, AND TOOK 8 465
ABOUT HER GLOWD, OFT STOOPING TO SUPPORT 9 427

STOOPT
THE BIRD OF JOVE, STOOPT FROM HIS AERIE TOUR, 11 185

STOP
NOR STOP THY FLAMING CHARIOT WHEELS, THAT SHOOK 3 394
AND DULCIMER, ALL ORGANS OF SWEET STOP, 7 596
MOUNTAINS OF ICE, THAT STOP TH' IMAGIN'D WAY 10 291
TO STOP THIR OVERGROWTH, AS INMATE GUESTS 12 166

STOPS
THIR STOPS AND CHORDS WAS SEEN: HIS VOLANT TOUCH 11 561

STOPT
WITH SOFT FOOT TOWARDS THE DEEP, WHO NOW HAD STOPT 11 848

STOR'D
AND QUIVER WITH THREE-BOLTED THUNDER STOR'D, 6 764
WITH HONEY STOR'D: THE REST ARE NUMBERLESS, 7 492
STOR'D IN EACH ORB PERHAPS WITH SOME THAT LIVE. 8 152
HIS HEAD THE MIDST, WELL STOR'D WITH SUTTLE WILES: 9 184

STORE
NONE YET, BUT STORE HEREAFTER FROM THE EARTH 3 444
OF SOM IRRIGUOUS VALLEY SPRED HER STORE, 4 255
FIT FOR THE TUN SOM MAGAZIN TO STORE 4 816
RESERVD FROM NIGHT, AND KEPT FOR THEE IN STORE. 5 128
OF GOD INSPIR'D, SMALL STORE WILL SERVE, WHERE STORE, 5 322
TO BLACKEST GRAIN, AND INTO STORE CONVEY'D: 6 515
IN GODS ETERNAL STORE, TO CIRCUMSCRIBE 7 226
AS LEAVES A GREATER STORE OF FRUIT UNTOUCHT, 9 621
OF FOUL CONCUPISCENCE; WHENCE EVIL STORE; 9 1078

STORES
HER STORES WERE OPEN'D, AND THIS FIRMAMENT 2 175
AND WHAT THY STORES CONTAIN, BRING FORTH AND POURE 5 314

STORIE
THE STORIE HEARD ATTENTIVE, AND WAS FILL'D 7 51
MY STORIE, WHICH PERHAPS THOU HAST NOT HEARD; 8 205
MY STORIE TO THE SUM OF EARTHLY BLISS 8 522
THUS EVE WITH COUNTNANCE BLITHE HER STORIE TOLD; 9 886

STORING
SAVE WHAT BY FRUGAL STORING FIRMNESS GAINS 5 324

STORK
IN PROSPECT; THERE THE EAGLE AND THE STORK 7 423

STORM
SHOT AFTER US IN STORM, OREBLOWN HATH LAID 1 172
BUT RATLING STORM OF ARROWS BARBD WITH FIRE. 6 546
FROM HER BEST PROP SO FARR, AND STORM SO NIGH. 9 433
AS MOCKT THEY STORM; GREAT LAUGHTER WAS IN HEAV'N 12 59

STORMIE
AND SNOW AND HAILE AND STORMIE GUST AND FLAW, 10 698

STORMING
THE HORRID SHOCK: NOW STORMING FURIE ROSE, 6 207

STORMS
LIES DARK AND WILDE, BEAT WITH PERPETUAL STORMS 2 588
GREAT THINGS WITH SMALL) THEN WHEN BELLONA STORMS, 2 922
STARLESS EXPOS'D, AND EVER-THREATNING STORMS 3 425

STORY
THIR DOCTRINE AND THIR STORY WRITTEN LEFT, 12 506

STRAIGHT
NOW ALSO EVIDENCE, BUT STRAIGHT I FELT 10 361
AND STRAIGHT CONJUNCTION WITH THIS SEX: FOR EITHER 10 898
ALL NATIONS SHALL BE BLEST; HE STRAIGHT OBEYS, 12 126

STRAINS
THIR MAKER, IN FIT STRAINS PRONOUNC'T OR SUNG 5 148

STRAIT
THEN STRAIT COMMANDS THAT AT THE WARLIKE SOUND 1 531
STOOD FIXT HER STATELY HIGHTH, AND STRAIT THE DORES 1 723
ORE BOG OR STEEP, THROUGH STRAIT, ROUGH, DENSE, OR RARE, 2 948
BORDERING ON LIGHT; WHEN STRAIT BEHOLD THE THRONE 2 959
ADMONISHT BY HIS EAR, AND STRAIT WAS KNOWN 3 647
STRAIT COUCHES CLOSE, THEN RISING CHANGES OFT 4 405
BUT FOLLOW STRAIT, INVISIBLY THUS LED? 4 476
STRAIT SIDE BY SIDE WERE LAID, NOR TURND I WEENE 4 741
TO SAY AND STRAIT UNSAY, PRETENDING FIRST 4 947
THE CIRCUIT WIDE. STRAIT KNEW HIM ALL THE BANDS 5 287
OF COMPOSITION, STRAIT THEY CHANG'D THIR MINDS, 6 613
EACH IN THEIR KINDE. THE EARTH OBEY'D, AND STRAIT 7 453
STRAIT TOWARD HEAV'N MY WONDRING EYES I TURND, 8 257
IN TANGLES, AND MADE INTRICATE SEEM STRAIT, 9 632
DOWN HE DESCENDED STRAIT; THE SPEED OF GODS 10 90
O HEAV'N, IN EVIL STRAIT THIS DAY I STAND 10 125

STRAIT'ND
IN NARROW CIRCUIT STRAIT'ND BY A FOE, 9 323

STRAITN'D
SWARM'D AND WERE STRAITN'D; TILL THE SIGNAL GIV'N. 1 776

STRAND
CAME SINGLY WHERE HE STOOD ON THE BARE STRAND, 1 379

STRANGE
BY STRANGE CONVEYANCE FILL'D EACH HOLLOW NOOK, 1 707
MIXT WITH TARTAREAN SULPHUR, AND STRANGE FIRE, 2 69
STRANGE HORROR SEISE THEE, AND PANGS UNFELT BEFORE. 2 703
SO STRANGE THY OUTCRY, AND THY WORDS SO STRANGE 2 737
STRANGE ALTERATION. SIN AND DEATH AMAIN 2 1024
OF LIVING CREATURES NEW TO SIGHT AND STRANGE: 4 287
BUT WITH ADDITION STRANGE; YET BE NOT SAD. 5 116
THE FULL RELATION, WHICH MUST NEEDS BE STRANGE, 5 556
FROM FATHER TO HIS SON? STRANGE POINT AND NEW. 5 855
IN THE MID WAY: THOUGH STRANGE TO US IT SEEMD 6 91
WHICH TO OUR EYES DISCOVERD NEW AND STRANGE, 6 571
FLEW OFF, AND INTO STRANGE VAGARIES FELL, 6 614
OF THINGS SO HIGH AND STRANGE, THINGS TO THIR THOUGHT 7 53
COMMOTION STRANGE, IN ALL ENJOYMENTS ELSE 8 531
STRANGE ALTERATION IN ME, TO DEGREE 9 599
THE PAIN OF ABSENCE FROM THY SIGHT. BUT STRANGE 9 861
WITH ME, AS I BESOUGHT THEE, WHEN THAT STRANGE 9 1135
MY JOURNEY STRANGE, WITH CLAMOROUS UPROARE 10 479
US'D BY THE TEMPTER: ON THAT PROSPECT STRANGE 10 552
STRANGE CONTRADICTION, WHICH TO GOD HIMSELF 10 799
FOR MAN AND BEAST: WHEN LOE A WONDER STRANGE. 11 733
AND LOOKING DOWN, TO SEE THE HUBBUB STRANGE 12 60

STRANGER
ANSWER'D. I KNOW THEE, STRANGER, WHO THOU ART, 2 990
OUR HEAV'NLY STRANGER; WELL WE MAY AFFORD 5 316
OUR AUTHOUR. HEAV'NLY STRANGER, PLEASE TO TASTE 5 397
THEN LOOSE IT TO A STRANGER, THAT THE TRUE 12 358

STRAW-BUILT
THE SUBURB OF THIR STRAW-BUILT CITTADEL, 1 773

STRAY
OF CORAL STRAY, OR SPORTING WITH QUICK GLANCE 7 405
I NEVER FROM THY SIDE HENCEFORTH TO STRAY, 11 176

STRAY'D
HERE PILGRIMS ROAM, THAT STRAY'D SO FARR TO SEEK 3 476
WHILE THUS I CALL'D, AND STRAY'D I KNEW NOT WHITHER. 8 283

STREAK
TO MORROW ERE FRESH MORNING STREAK THE EAST 4 623

STREAKING
STREAKING THE GROUND WITH SINUOUS TRACE; NOT ALL 7 481

STREAKS
BUT SAY, WHAT MEAN THOSE COLOURD STREAKS IN HEAVN, 11 879

STREAM
CREATED HUGEST THAT SWIM TH' OCEAN STREAM: 1 202
IN ARGOB AND IN BASAN, TO THE STREAM 1 398
HEARD ON THE RUFUL STREAM; FIERCE PHLEGETON 2 580
FARR OFF FROM THESE A SLOW AND SILENT STREAM, 2 582
THE TEMPTING STREAM, WITH ONE SMALL DROP TO LOOSE 2 607
OR HEAR'ST THOU RATHER PURE ETHEREAL STREAM, 3 7
ROWLS O'RE ELISIAN FLOURS HER AMBER STREAM; 3 359
STILL AS THEY THIRSTED SCOOP THE BRIMMING STREAM; 4 336
OF NECTAROUS DRAUGHTS BETWEEN, FROM MILKIE STREAM, 5 306
NOR STREIT'NING VALE, NOR WOOD, NOR STREAM DIVIDES 6 70
A STREAM OF NECTAROUS HUMOR ISSUING FLOW'D 6 332
STREAM, AND PERPETUAL DRAW THIR HUMID TRAINE. 7 306
TO SOM CAVES MOUTH, OR WHETHER WASHT BY-STREAM 11 569
MOUNT CARMEL; HERE THE DOUBLE-FOUNTED STREAM 12 144

STRONGEST
STOOD UP, THE STRONGEST AND THE FIERCEST SPIRIT . 2 44

STRONGLY
STRONGLY TO SUFFER AND SUPPORT OUR PAINS, ... 1 147
NOR CAN I MISS THE WAY, SO STRONGLY DRAWN 10 262

STROOK
WHAT WHEN WE FLED AMAIN, PURSU'D AND STROOK . . 2 165
STROOK THEM WITH HORROR BACKWARD, BUT FAR WORSE . 6 863
AND PLANETS, PLANET-STROOK, REAL ECLIPS 10 413
HEART-STROOK WITH CHILLING GRIPE OF SORROW STOOD, 11 264

STROVE
THIR KINGS, WHEN AEGYPT WITH ASSYRIA STROVE . . 1 721
OF THREE THAT IN MOUNT IDA NAKED STROVE, . . . 5 382

STROW
THICK AS AUTUMNAL LEAVES THAT STROW THE BROOKS . 1 302

STROW'N
WITH SHIVERD ARMOUR STROW'N, AND ON A HEAP . . . 6 389

STRUCK
DROVE THEM BEFORE HIM THUNDER-STRUCK, PURSU'D . . 6 858
AND MOON-STRUCK MADNESS, PINING ATROPHIE, . . . 11 486

STRUCK'N
CONFOUNDED LONG THEY SATE, AS STRUCK'N MUTE, . . 9 1064

STRUCTURE
IN HEAV'N BY MANY A TOWRED STRUCTURE HIGH, . . . 1 733
UP TO THE WALL OF HEAVEN A STRUCTURE HIGH, . . . 3 503
THAT STRUCTURE IN THE DIALECT OF MEN 5 761

STRUGGLE
AND WISH AND STRUGGLE, AS THEY PASS, TO REACH . . 2 606

STRUGLING
LONG STRUGLING UNDERNEATH, ERE THEY COULD WIND . 6 659

STUBBORN
WITH STUBBORN PATIENCE AS WITH TRIPLE STEEL. . . 2 569
HUMBLES HIS STUBBORN HEART, BUT STILL AS ICE . . 12 193

STUDIE
IN WOMAN, THEN TO STUDIE HOUSHOLD GOOD, ... 9 233

STUDIOUS
ENTRING ON STUDIOUS THOUGHTS ABSTRUSE, WHICH EVE . 8 40
NOR SKILLD NOR STUDIOUS, HIGHER ARGUMENT . . . 9 42
WHO SLEW HIS BROTHER; STUDIOUS THEY APPERE . . . 11 609

STUDY
AND STUDY OF REVENGE, IMMORTAL HATE, ... 1 107
JUST MEN THEY SEEMD, AND ALL THIR STUDY BENT . . 11 577

STUFF
TO STUFF THIS MAW, THIS VAST UNHIDE-BOUND CORPS. . 10 601
OF BRICK, AND OF THAT STUFF THEY CAST TO BUILD . 12 43

STUMBL'D
AND STUMBL'D MANY, WHO RECEIVES THEM RIGHT, . . . 6 624

STUMBLE
THAT THEY MAY STUMBLE ON, AND DEEPER FALL; 3 201

STUNNING
OF STUNNING SOUNDS AND VOICES ALL CONFUS'D 2 952

STUPENDIOUS
OF THAT STUPENDIOUS BRIDGE HIS JOY ENCREAS'D, . . 10 351

STUPID
(CANST THOU BELIEVE?) SHOULD BE SO STUPID GROWN, . 12 116

STUPIDLY
STUPIDLY GOOD, OF ENMITIE DISARM'D, ... 9 465

STYGIAN
BOTH GLORYING TO HAVE SCAP'T THE STYGIAN FLOOD . 1 239
THE STYGIAN COUNSEL THUS DISSOLV'D; AND FORTH . . 2 506
WHICH BUT HER SELF NOT ALL THE STYGIAN POWERS . . 2 875
ESCAP'T THE STYGIAN POOL, THOUGH LONG DETAIN'D . 3 14
AT THAT SO SUDDEN BLAZE THE STYGIAN THRONG . . . 10 453

STYL'D
WHAT HE ALMIGHTIE STYL'D, FIX NIGHTS AND DAYS . . 9 137
OF TRIUMPH, TO BE STYL'D GREAT CONQUEROURS, . . 11 695
A MIGHTIE HUNTER THENCE HE SHALL BE STYL'D . . . 12 33

STYLE
IN VARIOUS STYLE, FOR NEITHER VARIOUS STYLE . . 5 146
THE STRIFE WHICH THOU CALL'ST EVIL, BUT WEE STYLE 6 289
IF ANSWERABLE STYLE I CAN OBTAINE 9 20

STYX
ABHORRED STYX THE FLOOD OF DEADLY HATE, ... 2 577

SUBDUCTING
OR FROM MY SIDE SUBDUCTING, TOOK PERHAPS 8 536

SUBDU'D
INTESTINE WAR IN HEAV'N, THE ARCH FOE SUBDU'D . . 6 259

SUBDUE
BUT I SHALL RISE VICTORIOUS, AND SUBDUE 3 250
THEN TO SUBMIT, BOASTING I COULD SUBDUE 4 85
KNOW WHETHER I BE DEXTROUS TO SUBDUE 5 741
THEN SCORND THOU DIDST DEPART, AND TO SUBDUE . . 6 40
SUFFICIENT TO SUBDUE US TO HIS WILL, ... 6 427
SUBDUE IT, AND THROUGHOUT DOMINION HOLD 7 532
THEREIN ENJOY'D WERE WORTHY TO SUBDUE 8 584
TO OVERCOME IN BATTLE, AND SUBDUE 11 691
SUCH TROUBLE BROUGHT, AFFECTING TO SUBDUE . . . 12 81

SUBDUES
SUBDUES US, AND OMNIPOTENT DECREE, ... 2 198
WHICH ALL SUBDUES, AND MAKES REMISS THE HANDS . . 6 458
SUBDUES ME, AND CALAMITOUS CONSTRAINT 10 132

SUBDUING
SUBDUING NATIONS, AND ACHIEVD THEREBY 11 792

SUBJECT
YET THESE SUBJECT NOT; I TO THEE DISCLOSE . . . 8 607
SINCE FIRST THIS SUBJECT FOR HEROIC SONG . . . 9 25

SUBJECTED
SUBJECTED TO HIS SERVICE ANGEL WINGS, ... 9 155
TO THE SUBJECTED PLAINE; THEN DISAPPEER'D. . . . 12 640

SUBJECTION
OF NEW SUBJECTION; WITH WHAT EYES COULD WE . . . 2 239
I SDEIND SUBJECTION, AND THOUGHT ONE STEP HIGHER . 4 50
SUBJECTION, BUT REQUIR'D WITH GENTLE SWAY, . . . 4 308
WITH LOW SUBJECTION; UNDERSTAND THE SAME . . . 8 345
NOT THY SUBJECTION: WEIGH WITH HER THY SELF; . . 8 570
HEARD NOT HER LORE, BOTH IN SUBJECTION NOW . . . 9 1128
THY LOVE, NOT THY SUBJECTION, AND HER GIFTS . . 10 153
SUBJECTION TO HIS EMPIRE TYRANNOUS: 12 32

SUBJECTS
SUBJECTS HIM FROM WITHOUT TO VIOLENT LORDS; . . 12 93

SUBLIM'D
SUBLIM'D WITH MINERAL FURY, AID THE WINDS, ... 1 235
MANS NOURISHMENT, BY GRADUAL SCALE SUBLIM'D . . 5 483

SUBLIME
PART ON THE PLAIN, OR IN THE AIR SUBLIME . . . 2 528
IN THE DUN AIR SUBLIME, AND READY NOW 3 72
HIS FAIR LARGE FRONT AND EYE SUBLIME DECLAR'D . . 4 300
HEE ON THE WINGS OF CHERUB RODE SUBLIME 6 771
THEY SUMM'D THIR PENNS, AND SOARING TH' AIR SUBLIME 7 421
IN THAT CELESTIAL COLLOQUIE SUBLIME, ... 8 455
SUBLIME WITH EXPECTATION WHEN TO SEE 10 536
TO ARGUE IN THEE SOMTHING MORE SUBLIME 10 1014
BUT SOLEMN AND SUBLIME, WHOM NOT TO OFFEND, . . 11 236

SUBLUNAR
HALF WAY UP HILL THIS VAST SUBLUNAR VAULT, ... 4 777

SUBMISS
YET WITH SUBMISS APPROACH AND REVERENCE MEEK, . . 5 359
SUBMISS: HE REAR'D ME, AND WHOM THOU SOUGHTST I AM, 8 316
PERSISTED, YET SUBMISS, THOUGH LAST, REPLI'D. . . 9 377

SUBMISSION
FOR WHO CAN THINK SUBMISSION? WARR THEN, WARR . 1 661
NONE LEFT BUT BY SUBMISSION; AND THAT WORD . . . 4 81
WHAT FEIGN'D SUBMISSION SWORE: EASE WOULD RECANT . 4 96
YIELDED WITH COY SUBMISSION, MODEST PRIDE, . . . 4 310
TO MEEK SUBMISSION: THOU AT SEASON FIT 12 597

SUBMISSIVE
BOTH OF HER BEAUTY AND SUBMISSIVE CHARMS . . . 4 498
NOW AT HIS FEET SUBMISSIVE IN DISTRESS, ... 10 942

SUBMIT
AND COURAGE NEVER TO SUBMIT OR YIELD: 1 108
THEN TO SUBMIT, BOASTING I COULD SUBDUE 4 85
WILL YE SUBMIT YOUR NECKS, AND CHUSE TO BEND . . 5 787
THINE SHALL SUBMIT, HEE OVER THEE SHALL RULE. . . 10 196
BE IT SO, FOR I SUBMIT, HIS DOOM IS FAIR, . . . 10 769
THEREFORE TO HIS GREAT BIDDING I SUBMIT. . . . 11 314
THOU LEAD'ST ME, AND TO THE HAND OF HEAV'N SUBMIT, 11 372
I YIELD IT JUST, SAID ADAM, AND SUBMIT. 11 526

SUBMITS
THE RIVER-DRAGON TAM'D AT LENGTH SUBMITS . . . 12 191

SUBMITTING
SUBMITTING TO WHAT SEEMD REMEDILESS, ... 9 919

SUBORDINATE
CONTEMPTUOUS, AND HIS NEXT SUBORDINATE 5 671

SUBORND
SOME SPECIOUS OBJECT BY THE FOE SUBORND, 9 361

SUBSCRIB'D
SUBSCRIB'D NOT; NATURE FIRST GAVE SIGNS, IMPREST 11 182

SUBSIST
FIRM WE SUBSIST, YET POSSIBLE TO SWERVE, 9 359
WHITHER SHALL I BETAKE ME, WHERE SUBSIST? 10 922

SUBSTANCE
AND THIS EMPYREAL SUBSTANCE CANNOT FAIL, 1 117
SEMBLANCE OF WORTH, NOT SUBSTANCE, GENTLY RAIS'D 1 529
OR IF OUR SUBSTANCE BE INDEED DIVINE, 2 99
OR SUBSTANCE, HOW ENDU'D, AND WHAT THIR POWER, 2 356
OR SUBSTANCE MIGHT BE CALL'D THAT SHADOW SEEM'D, 2 669
SPIRITUAL SUBSTANCE WITH CORPOREAL BARR. 4 585
VAPOURS NOT YET INTO HER SUBSTANCE TURND. 5 420
OF SUBSTANCE, AND IN THINGS THAT LIVE, OF LIFE; 5 474
TO PROPER SUBSTANCE; TIME MAY COME WHEN MEN 5 493
PASS'D THROUGH HIM, BUT TH' ETHEREAL SUBSTANCE CLOS'D 6 330
INTO THIR SUBSTANCE PENT, WHICH WROUGHT THEM PAIN 6 657
IN APPREHENSION THEN IN SUBSTANCE FEEL 11 775

SUBSTANCES
INTELLIGENTIAL SUBSTANCES REQUIRE 5 408
THAT TO CORPOREAL SUBSTANCES COULD ADDE 8 109

SUBSTANTIAL
OF SOME RICH BURGHER, WHOSE SUBSTANTIAL DORES, 4 189
SUBSTANTIAL LIFE, TO HAVE THEE BY MY SIDE 4 485

SUBSTANTIALLY
SUBSTANTIALLY EXPRESS'D, AND IN HIS FACE 3 140

SUBSTITUTE
HAST THOU NOT MADE ME HERE THY SUBSTITUTE, 8 381

SUBSTITUTES
MY SUBSTITUTES I SEND YE, AND CREATE 10 403

SUBTERRANEAN
OF SUBTERRANEAN WIND TRANSPORTS A HILL 1 231

SUBURB
THE SUBURB OF THIR STRAW-BUILT CITTADEL, 1 773

SUBVERTING
SUBVERTING WORLDLY STRONG, AND WORLDLY WISE 12 568

SUCCEED
WHICH OFT TIMES MAY SUCCEED, SO AS PERHAPS 1 166
SHORT PLEASURES, FOR LONG WOES ARE TO SUCCEED. 4 535
WHO OF ALL AGES TO SUCCEED, BUT FEELING 10 733
WOLVES SHALL SUCCEED FOR TEACHERS, GRIEVOUS WOLVES, 12 508

SUCCESS
VAIN WARR WITH HEAV'N, AND BY SUCCESS UNTAUGHT 2 9
OMINOUS CONJECTURE ON THE WHOLE SUCCESS: 2 123
DOWN FROM TH' ECLIPTIC, SPED WITH HOP'D SUCCESS, 3 740
FROM ME SOM PLUME, THAT THY SUCCESS MAY SHOW 6 161
BELIEVST SO MAIN TO OUR SUCCESS, I BRING; 6 471
BUT THAT SUCCESS ATTENDS HIM; IF MISHAP, 10 239

SUCCESSES
FROM HARD ASSAIES AND ILL SUCCESSES PAST 4 932
WITH THESE SUCCESSES, AND WITH THEM REJOYCE, 10 396

SUCCESSFUL
WE MAY WITH MORE SUCCESSFUL HOPE RESOLVE 1 120
SUCCESSFUL BEYOND HOPE, TO LEAD YE FORTH 10 463

SUCCESSION
BUT FIRST A LONG SUCCESSION MUST ENSUE, 12 331

SUCCESSIVE
SUCCESSIVE, AND THE TIMELY DEW OF SLEEP 4 614

SUCCINCT
HIS HABIT FIT FOR SPEED SUCCINCT, AND HELD 3 643

SUCCOUR
THERE SWALLOW'D UP AND LOST, FROM SUCCOUR FARR. 9 642

SUCH
SUCH PLACE ETERNAL JUSTICE HAD PREPAR'D 1 70
THEN SUCH COULD HAV OREPOW'RD SUCH FORCE AS OURS) 1 145
AND SUCH APPEAR'D IN HUE, AS WHEN THE FORCE 1 230
WITH STENCH AND SMOAK: SUCH RESTING FOUND THE SOLE 1 237
NO WONDER, FALL'N SUCH A PERNICIOUS HIGHTH. 1 282
IF SUCH ASTONISHMENT AS THIS CAN SIEZE 1 317
OF UTMOST ARNON. NOR CONTENT WITH SUCH 1 399
DOWN CAST AND DAMP, YET SUCH WHEREIN APPEAR'D 1 523
OF FLUTES AND SOFT RECORDERS; SUCH AS RAIS'D 1 551
MET SUCH IMBODIED FORCE, AS NAM'D WITH THESE 1 574
TEARS SUCH AS ANGELS WEEP, BURST FORTH: AT LAST 1 620
HOW SUCH UNITED FORCE OF GODS, HOW SUCH 1 629

SUCH (CONTINUED)
NOR GREAT ALCAIRO SUCH MAGNIFICENCE 1 718
EXALTED TO SUCH POWER, AND GAVE TO RULE, 1 736
LET SUCH BETHINK THEM, IF THE SLEEPY DRENCH 2 73
HE SCARCE HAD FINISHT, WHEN SUCH MURMUR FILLD 2 284
AFTER THE TEMPEST: SUCH APPLAUSE WAS HEARD 2 290
ADVISING PEACE: FOR SUCH ANOTHER FIELD 2 292
NO SECOND STROKE INTEND, AND SUCH A FROWN 2 713
BECAM'ST ENAMOUR'D, AND SUCH JOY THOU TOOK'ST 2 765
I SAW AND HEARD, FOR SUCH A NUMEROUS HOST 2 993
FOLLOWING HIS TRACK, SUCH WAS THE WILL OF HEAV'N, 2 1025
SUCH I CREATED ALL TH' ETHEREAL POWERS 3 100
WHAT PLEASURE I FROM SUCH OBEDIENCE PAID, 3 107
AND NONE BUT SUCH FROM MERCY I EXCLUDE. 3 202
SAY HEAV'NLY POWERS, WHERE SHALL WE FIND SUCH LOVE, 3 213
SHALL HAST'N, SUCH A PEAL SHALL ROUSE THIR SLEEP. 3 329
MELODIOUS PART, SUCH CONCORD IS IN HEAV'N. 3 371
THE STAIRS WERE SUCH AS WHEREON JACOB SAW 3 510
TO DARKNESS, SUCH AS BOUND THE OCEAN WAVE. 3 539
SUCH WONDER SEIS'D, THOUGH AFTER HEAVEN SEEN, 3 552
NOT OF THE PRIME, YET SUCH AS IN HIS FACE 3 637
AH WHEREFORE. HE DESERVD NO SUCH RETURN 4 42
IN MISERIE; SUCH JOY AMBITION FINDES. 4 92
FOR HEAV'NLY MINDES FROM SUCH DISTEMPERS FOULE 4 118
OF ARABIE THE BLEST, WITH SUCH DELAY 4 163
IN THEM DIVINE RESEMBLANCE, AND SUCH GRACE 4 364
ILL SENC'T FOR HEAV'N TO KEEP OUT SUCH A FOE 4 372
LIKE THIS FAIR PARADISE, YOUR SENSE, YET SUCH 4 379
EQUAL WITH GODS; ASPIRING TO BE SUCH, 4 526
THE VIGILANCE HERE PLAC'T, BUT SUCH AS COME 4 580
SUCH WAS THIR AWE OF MAN. IN SHADIE BOWER 4 705
SUCH WHERE YE FIND, SEISE FAST, AND HITHER BRING. 4 796
AND SUCH I HELD THEE; BUT THIS QUESTION ASKT 4 887
TH' ETERNAL TO PREVENT SUCH HORRID FRAY 4 996
SUCH WHISPERING WAK'D HER, BUT WITH STARTL'D EYE 5 26
SUCH NIGHT TILL THIS I NEVER PASS'D, HAVE DREAM'D, 5 31
AT SUCH BOLD WORDS VOUCHT WITH A DEED SO BOLD: 5 66
WHAT LIFE THE GODS LIVE THERE, AND SUCH LIVE THOU. 5 81
SOM SUCH RESEMBLANCES METHINKS I FIND 5 114
UNMEDITATED, SUCH PROMPT ELOQUENCE 5 149
OR WITH REPOSE; AND SUCH DISCOURSE BRING ON, 5 233
EACH PLANT AND JUCIEST GOURD WILL PLUCK SUCH CHOICE 5 327
NONE CAN THEN HEAV'N SUCH GLORIOUS SHAPE CONTAIN; 5 362
ADAM, I THEREFORE CAME, NOR ART THOU SUCH 5 372
CREATED, OR SUCH PLACE HAST HERE TO DWELL, 5 373
SUCH TO PERFECTION, ONE FIRST MATTER ALL, 5 472
THAT THOU CONTINU'ST SUCH, OWE TO THY SELF, 5 521
NOT OUR NECESSITATED, SUCH WITH HIM 5 530
BY PRESENT, PAST, AND FUTURE) ON SUCH DAY 5 582
(SUCH ARE THE COURTS OF GOD) TH' ANGELIC THRONG 5 650
OF DEITIE OR EMPIRE, SUCH A FOE 5 724
MONARCHIE OVER SUCH AS LIVE BY RIGHT 5 795
SUCH AS HE PLEASD, AND CIRCUMSCRIB'D THIR BEING? 5 825
SUCH AS IN HIGHEST HEAV'N, ARRAYD IN GOLD 6 13
O HEAV'N. THAT SUCH RESEMBLANCE OF THE HIGHEST 6 114
SUCH HAST THOU ARM'D, THE MINSTRELSIE OF HEAV'N, 6 168
SUCH RUIN INTERCEPT: TEN PACES HUGE 6 193
AND CLAMOUR SUCH AS HEARD IN HEAV'N TILL NOW 6 208
AND LIMITED THIR MIGHT; THOUGH NUMBERD SUCH 6 229
WIDE WASTING; SUCH DESTRUCTION TO WITHSTAND 6 253
HUMAN IMAGINATION TO SUCH HIGHTH 6 300
OF SUCH COMMOTION, SUCH AS TO SET FORTH 6 310
SANGUIN, SUCH AS CELESTIAL SPIRITS MAY BLEED, 6 333
HUMBL'D BY SUCH REBUKE, SO FARR BENEATH 6 342
FLED IGNOMINIOUS, TO SUCH EVIL BROUGHT 6 395
SUCH HIGH ADVANTAGES THIR INNOCENCE 6 401
SUCH IMPLEMENTS OF MISCHIEF AS SHALL DASH 6 488
LEVEL'D, WITH SUCH IMPETUOUS FURIE SMOTE, 6 591
SUCH AS WE MIGHT PERCEIVE AMUS'D THEM ALL, 6 623
AGAINST SUCH HELLISH MISCHIEF FIT TO OPPOSE. 6 636
OUT OF SUCH PRISON, THOUGH SPIRITS OF PUREST LIGHT, 6 660
AS LIKELIEST WAS, WHEN TWO SUCH FOES MET ARM'D; 6 688
CAN END IT. INTO THEE SUCH VERTUE AND GRACE 6 703
IN HEAV'NLY SPIRITS COULD SUCH PERVERSENESS DWELL? 6 788
BEFORE HIM, SUCH AS IN THIR SOULES INFIX'D 6 837
WITH SUCH CONFUSION: BUT THE EVIL SOON 7 56
THY HEARING, SUCH COMMISSION FROM ABOVE 7 118
THAT DETRIMENT, IF SUCH IT BE TO LOSE 7 153
WHEN SUCH WAS HEARD DECLAR'D THE ALMIGHTIE'S WILL; 7 181
FOR HASTE; SUCH FLIGHT THE GREAT COMMAND IMPRESS'D 7 294
INVISIBLE, YET STAID (SUCH PRIVILEDGE 7 589
SPACES INCOMPREHENSIBLE (FOR SUCH 8 20
SUCH DISPROPORTIONS, WITH SUPERFLUOUS HAND 8 27
SUCH RESTLESS REVOLUTION DAY BY DAY 8 31
AS TRIBUTE SUCH A SUMLESS JOURNEY BROUGHT 8 36
YET WENT SHE NOT, AS NOT WITH SUCH DISCOURSE 8 48
OF WHAT WAS HIGH: SUCH PLEASURE SHE RESERV'D, 8 50
SUCH PAIRS, IN LOVE AND MUTUAL HONOUR JOYN'D? 8 58
THE LESS NOT BRIGHT, NOR HEAV'N SUCH JOURNIES RUN, 8 88
FOR SUCH VAST ROOM IN NATURE UNPOSSEST 8 153
SQUAR'D IN FULL LEGION (SUCH COMMAND WE HAD) 8 232
LEAST HEE INCENST AT SUCH ERUPTION BOLD, 8 235
THIR NATURE, WITH SUCH KNOWLEDG GOD ENDU'D 8 353
SUCH AS I SEEK, FIT TO PARTICIPATE 8 390
AND NO SUCH COMPANIE AS THEN THOU SAW'ST 8 446
SUCH AS I SAW HER IN MY DREAM, ADORND 8 482
IN ALL THINGS ELSE DELIGHT INDEED, BUT SUCH 8 524
NOT PROOF ENOUGH SUCH OBJECT TO SUSTAIN, 8 535

SUCH (CONTINUED)
IS PROPAGATED SEEM SUCH DEAR DELIGHT 8 580
BY WHAT I SEEK, BUT OTHERS TO MAKE SUCH 9 127
WHETHER SUCH VERTUE SPENT OF OLD NOW FAILD 9 145
THAT SUCH AN ENEMIE WE HAVE, WHO SEEKS 9 274
HIS VIOLENCE THOU FEARST NOT, BEING SUCH, 9 282
FOR SUCH THOU ART, FROM SIN AND BLAME ENTIRE: 9 292
IF SUCH AFFRONT I LABOUR TO AVERT 9 302
BUT WITH SUCH GARDNING TOOLS AS ART YET RUDE, 9 391
SUCH AMBUSH HID AMONG SWEET FLOURS AND SHADES 9 408
SUCH PLEASURE TOOK THE SERPENT TO BEHOLD 9 455
TO SUCH DISPORT BEFORE HER THROUGH THE FIELD, 9 520
SAY, FOR SUCH WONDER CLAIMS ATTENTION DUE. 9 566
I SPAR'D NOT, FOR SUCH PLEASURE TILL THAT HOUR 9 596
TO US, IN SUCH ABOUNDANCE LIES OUR CHOICE, 9 620
WONDROUS INDEED, IF CAUSE OF SUCH EFFECTS. 9 650
FOR SUCH A PETTY TRESPASS, AND NOT PRAISE 9 693
SUCH PROHIBITIONS BINDE NOT. BUT IF DEATH 9 760
REGARDED, SUCH DELIGHT TILL THEN, AS SEEMD, 9 787
AND HATH BIN TASTED SUCH: THE SERPENT WISE, 9 867
IN RECOMPENCE (FOR SUCH COMPLIANCE BAD 9 994
SUCH RECOMPENCE BEST MERITS) FROM THE BOUGH 9 995
TRUE RELISH, TASTING; IF SUCH PLEASURE BE 9 1024
AS MEET IS, AFTER SUCH DELICIOUS FARE; 9 1028
BUT SUCH AS AT THIS DAY TO INDIANS KNOWN 9 1102
TO THAT FIRST NAKED GLORIE. SUCH OF LATE 9 1115
SUCH PROOF, CONCLUDE, THEY THEN BEGIN TO FAILE. 9 1142
GOING INTO SUCH DANGER AS THOU SAIDST? 9 1157
WERE SUCH AS UNDER GOVERNMENT WELL SEEM'D, 10 154
THE WAY, THOU LEADING, SUCH A SENT I DRAW 10 267
SUCH FATAL CONSEQUENCE UNITES US THREE: 10 364
FOR IN POSSESSION SUCH, NOT ONELY OF RIGHT, 10 461
OR DOWN FROM HEAV'N DESCEND. SUCH WAS THIR SONG, 10 648
HE NEVER SHALL FIND OUT FIT MATE, BUT SUCH 10 899
BUT ADAM WITH SUCH COUNSEL NOTHING SWAY'D, 10 1010
WE ARE BY DOOM TO PAY; RATHER SUCH ACTS 10 1026
WHICH MIGHT SUPPLIE THE SUN: SUCH FIRE TO USE, 10 1078
ILL WORTHIE I SUCH TITLE SHOULD BELONG 11 163
OR OF THE THRONES ABOVE, SUCH MAJESTIE 11 232
OF THEM THE HIGHEST, FOR SUCH OF SHAPE MAY SEEM 11 297
TO SUCH UNSIGHTLY SUFFERINGS BE DEBAS'T 11 510
IN PART, FROM SUCH DEFORMITIES BE FREE, 11 513
SUCH HAPPY INTERVIEW AND FAIR EVENT 11 593
HIS BROTHER; FOR OF WHOM SUCH MASSACHER 11 679
SUCH WERE THESE GIANTS, MEN OF HIGH RENOWN; 11 688
SUCH GRACE SHALL ONE JUST MAN FIND IN HIS SIGHT, 11 890
WITH WARR AND HOSTILE SNARE SUCH AS REFUSE 12 31
HE MADE NOT LORD; SUCH TITLE TO HIMSELF 12 70
SUCH TROUBLE BROUGHT, AFFECTING TO SUBDUE 12 81
SUCH WONDROUS POWER GOD TO HIS SAINT WILL LEND, 12 200
ORDAINE THEM LAWES; PART SUCH AS APPERTAINE 12 230
ESTABLISHT, SUCH DELIGHT HATH GOD IN MEN 12 245
AMONG THEM; HOW CAN GOD WITH SUCH RESIDE? 12 284
JUST FOR UNJUST, THAT IN SUCH RIGHTEOUSNESS 12 294
SUCH FOLLOW HIM, AS SHALL BE REGISTERD 12 335
HE CEAS'D, DISCERNING ADAM WITH SUCH JOY 12 372
THOUGH TO THE DEATH, AGAINST SUCH CRUELTIES 12 494
SUCH FAVOUR I UNWORTHIE AM VOUTSAFT, 12 622

SUCKT
WITH SUCKT AND GLUTTED OFFAL, AT ONE FLING 10 633

SUDDEN
OF MIGHTY CHERUBIM; THE SUDDEN BLAZE 1 665
BY SUDDEN ONSET, EITHER WITH HELL FIRE 2 364
THOU INTERPOSEST, THAT MY SUDDEN HAND 2 738
ALL ON A SUDDEN MISERABLE PAIN 2 752
UNFAST'NS: ON A SUDDEN OP'N FLIE 2 879
BEFORE THIR EYES IN SUDDEN VIEW APPEAR 2 890
LOOKS DOWN WITH WONDER AT THE SUDDEN VIEW 3 542
WITH SUDDEN BLAZE DIFFUS'D, INFLAMES THE AIRE: 4 818
SO SUDDEN TO BEHOLD THE GRIESLIE KING; 4 821
THAT BROUGHT ME ON A SUDDEN TO THE TREE 5 51
NOT BURD'ND NATURE, SUDDEN MIND AROSE 5 452
TABLES ARE SET, AND ON A SUDDEN PIL'D 5 632
PAVILIONS NUMBERLESS, AND SUDDEN REARD, 5 653
IMPENDENT, RAGING INTO SUDDEN FLAME 5 891
OR SOM MORE SUDDEN VENGEANCE WING'D FROM GOD 6 279
NOT LONG, FOR SUDDEN ALL AT ONCE THIR REEDS 6 582
THEN HERBS OF EVERY LEAF, THAT SUDDEN FLOUR'D 7 317
TEMPTING, STIRR'D IN ME SUDDEN APPETITE 8 308
MY SUDDEN APPREHENSION: BUT IN THESE 8 354
HOW ART THOU LOST, HOW ON A SUDDEN LOST, 9 900
AT THAT SO SUDDEN BLAZE THE STYGIAN THRONG 10 453
WILL PROVE NO SUDDEN, BUT A SLOW-PAC'T EVILL, 10 963
ADAM BY THIS FROM THE COLD SUDDEN DAMP 11 293

SUDDENLY
TO THIS HIGH EXALTATION; SUDDENLY 5 90
A WHILE, BUT SUDDENLY AT HEAD APPEERD 6 556
WHEN SUDDENLY STOOD AT MY HEAD A DREAM, 8 292
BUT SUDDENLY WITH FLESH FILL'D UP AND HEAL'D: 8 468
MIGHT SUDDENLY INFLICT; THAT PAST, RETURN'D 10 341
ON BIRD, BEAST, AIRE, AIRE SUDDENLY ECLIPS'D 11 183

SUE
EXTORT FROM ME. TO BOW AND SUE FOR GRACE 1 111

SUFFER
STRONGLY TO SUFFER AND SUPPORT OUR PAINS, 1 147
WHATEVER DOING, WHAT CAN WE SUFFER MORE, 2 162
WHAT CAN WE SUFFER WORSE? IS THIS THEN WORST, 2 163
THUS TRAMPL'D, THUS EXPELL'D TO SUFFER HERE 2 195
THE VICTORS WILL. TO SUFFER, AS TO DOE, 2 199
HIS PREY, NOR SUFFER MY UNSPOTTED SOULE 3 248
TO WHICH THE HELL I SUFFER SEEMS A HEAV'N. 4 78
MUST SUFFER CHANGE, DISDAIN'D NOT TO BEGIN 10 213
I SUFFER THEM TO ENTER AND POSSESS 10 623

SUFFERANCE
NOT BY THE SUFFERANCE OF SUPERNAL POWER. 1 241
THROUGH GODS HIGH SUFFERANCE FOR THE TRYAL OF MAN, 1 366
THIS MY LONG SUFFERANCE AND MY DAY OF GRACE 3 198
BY SUFFERANCE, AND THY WONTED FAVOUR DEIGN'D. 8 202

SUFFERD
HAVE SUFFERD, THAT THE GLORIE MAY BE THINE 6 701
THEN SUFFERD. TH' OTHER WAY SATAN WENT DOWN 10 414
WHAT I HAVE DON, WHAT SUFFERD, WITH WHAT PAINE 10 470

SUFFERING
DOING OR SUFFERING: BUT OF THIS BE SURE, 1 158
IN DOING WHAT WE MOST IN SUFFERING FEEL? 2 340
BY SUFFERING, AND EARNE REST FROM LABOUR WON, 11 375
ON PENALTIE OF DEATH, AND SUFFERING DEATH, 12 398
BY SIMPLY MEEK; THAT SUFFERING FOR TRUTHS SAKE 12 569

SUFFERINGS
WORSE; OF WORSE DEEDS WORSE SUFFERINGS MUST ENSUE. 4 26
TO SUCH UNSIGHTLY SUFFERINGS BE DEBAS'T 11 510

SUFFIC'D
OF THIR SWEET GARDNING LABOUR THEN SUFFIC'D 4 328
THUS WHEN WITH MEATS AND DRINKS THEY HAD SUFFIC'D, 5 451
HAPPIER, HAD IT SUFFIC'D HIM TO HAVE KNOWN 11 88

SUFFICE
THAT WE MAY SO SUFFICE HIS VENGEFUL IRE, 1 148
SUFFICE, OR WHAT EVASION BEAR HIM SAFE 2 411
WHAT MAY SUFFICE, AND SOFT'N STONIE HEARTS 3 189
WHAT WORDS OR TONGUE OF SERAPH CAN SUFFICE, 7 113
OR HEART OF MAN SUFFICE TO COMPREHEND? 7 114
ANSWER'D. LET IT SUFFICE THEE THAT THOU KNOW'ST 8 620

SUFFICIENT
OUR POWER SUFFICIENT TO DISTURB HIS HEAV'N, 2 102
SUFFICIENT? WHO SHALL TEMPT WITH WANDRING FEET 2 404
SUFFICIENT TO HAVE STOOD, THOUGH FREE TO FALL. 3 99
SUFFICIENT TO SUBDUE US TO HIS WILL, 6 427
NUMBER SUFFICIENT TO POSSESS HER REALMES 7 147
WHAT THANKS SUFFICIENT, OR WHAT RECOMPENCE 8 5
REMAINES, SUFFICIENT OF IT SELF TO RAISE 9 43
SUFFICIENT PENALTIE, WHY HAST THOU ADDED 10 753
SUFFICIENT THAT THY PRAYERS ARE HEARD, AND DEATH, 11 252

SUFFICIENTLY
SEEM I TO THEE SUFFICIENTLY POSSEST 8 404

SUFFRAGE
CHOICE IN OUR SUFFRAGE; FOR ON WHOM WE SEND, 2 415

SUFFUSION
OR DIM SUFFUSION VEILD. YET NOT THE MORE 3 26

SUGGESTED
TELLS THE SUGGESTED CAUSE, AND CASTS BETWEEN 5 702

SUGGESTION
MEN ALSO, AND BY HIS SUGGESTION TAUGHT, 1 685
THE FIRST SORT BY THIR OWN SUGGESTION FELL, 3 129

SUGGESTIONS
TO ENTER, AND HIS DARK SUGGESTIONS HIDE 9 90

SUITE
CANNOT WELL SUITE WITH EITHER, BUT SOON PROVE 8 388

SUITERS
NOT OF MEAN SUITERS, NOR IMPORTANT LESS 11 9

SULFUROUS
WITH DART AND JAV'LIN, STONES AND SULFUROUS FIRE; 11 658

SULPHUR
WITH EVER-BURNING SULPHUR UNCONSUM'D: 1 69
THE WORK OF SULPHUR. THITHER WING'D WITH SPEED 1 674
MIXT WITH TARTAREAN SULPHUR, AND STRANGE FIRE, 2 69

SULPHUROUS
BACK TO THE GATES OF HEAV'N: THE SULPHUROUS HAIL 1 171
CONCEPTION; SULPHUROUS AND NITROUS FOAME 6 512

SULTAN
OF THIR GREAT SULTAN WAVING TO DIRECT 1 348
IN MOSCO, OR THE SULTAN IN BIZANCE, 11 395

SUM
- CONSULTING ON THE SUM OF THINGS, FORESEEN 6 673
- MY STORIE TO THE SUM OF EARTHLY BLISS 8 522

SUMLESS
- AS TRIBUTE SUCH A SUMLESS JOURNEY BROUGHT 8 36

SUMM'D
- THEY SUMM'D THIR PENNS, AND SOARING TH' AIR SUBLIME 7 421
- OF GROWTH, SENSE, REASON, ALL SUMM'D UP IN MAN. 9 113

SUMMD
- MEAN, OR IN HER SUMMD UP, IN HER CONTAIND 8 473

SUMME
- HEAPT TO THE POPULAR SUMME, WILL SO INCENSE 12 338
- THIS HAVING LEARNT, THOU HAST ATTAIND THE SUMME 12 575

SUMMERS
- IN AMOROUS DITTYES ALL A SUMMERS DAY, 1 449
- A SUMMERS DAY; AND WITH THE SETTING SUN 1 744
- OR SUMMERS NOON-TIDE AIR, WHILE THUS HE SPAKE. 2 309
- OR SIGHT OF VERNAL BLOOM, OR SUMMERS ROSE, 3 43
- IN ALL THE LIVERIES DECT OF SUMMERS PRIDE 7 478
- FORTH ISSUING ON A SUMMERS MORN TO BREATHE 9 447
- SOLSTITIAL SUMMERS HEAT. TO THE BLANC MOONE 10 656

SUMMON
- ON WHAT THOU HAST OF VERTUE, SUMMON ALL, 9 374

SUMMOND
- CAME SUMMOND OVER EDEN TO RECEIVE 6 75
- NOT HITHER SUMMOND, SINCE THEY CANNOT CHANGE 8 347

SUMMONING
- THE SUMMONING ARCH-ANGELS TO PROCLAIME 3 325

SUMMONS
- OF SATAN AND HIS PEERS: THIR SUMMONS CALL'D 1 757
- AND SUMMONS READ, THE GREAT CONSULT BEGAN. 1 798
- OF ANGELS BY IMPERIAL SUMMONS CALL'D, 5 584
- HASTED, RESORTING TO THE SUMMONS HIGH, 11 81

SUMMS
- THIR NUMBER LAST HE SUMMS. AND NOW HIS HEART 1 571
- SHE MOST, AND IN HER LOOK SUMMS ALL DELIGHT. 9 454

SUN
- OF GLORY OBSCUR'D: AS WHEN THE SUN NEW RIS'N 1 594
- A SUMMERS DAY; AND WITH THE SETTING SUN 1 744
- IN SPRING TIME, WHEN THE SUN WITH TAURUS RIDES, 1 769
- IF CHANCE THE RADIANT SUN WITH FAREWELL SWEET 2 492
- WHOSE FOUNTAIN WHO SHALL TELL? BEFORE THE SUN, 3 8
- WHICH NOW THE RISING SUN GUILDS WITH HIS BEAMS. 3 551
- THE GOLDEN SUN IN SPLENDOR LIKEST HEAVEN 3 572
- TH' ARCH-CHIMIC SUN SO FARR FROM US REMOTE 3 609
- THE SAME WHOM JOHN SAW ALSO IN THE SUN: 3 623
- URIEL, THOUGH REGENT OF THE SUN, AND HELD 3 690
- SOMETIMES TOWARDS HEAV'N AND THE FULL-BLAZING SUN, 4 29
- O SUN, TO TELL THEE HOW I HATE THY BEAMS 4 37
- ON WHICH THE SUN MORE GLAD IMPRESS'D HIS BEAMS 4 150
- BOTH WHERE THE MORNING SUN FIRST WARMLY SMOTE 4 244
- OR BEDWARD RUMINATING: FOR THE SUN 4 352
- WITH EARTH AND OCEAN MEETS, THE SETTING SUN 4 540
- ON A SUN BEAM, SWIFT AS A SHOOTING STARR 4 556
- BORE HIM SLOPE DOWNWARD TO THE SUN NOW FALL'N 4 591
- WITH CHARM OF EARLIEST BIRDS; PLEASANT THE SUN 4 642
- WITH CHARM OF EARLIEST BIRDS, NOR RISING SUN 4 651
- OF DAY-SPRING, AND THE SUN, WHO SCARCE UP RISEN 5 139
- THOU SUN, OF THIS GREAT WORLD BOTH EYE AND SOULE, 5 171
- MOON, THAT NOW MEETST THE ORIENT SUN, NOW FLI'ST 5 175
- TILL THE SUN PAINT YOUR FLEECIE SKIRTS WITH GOLD, 5 187
- OF HIS COOLE BOWRE, WHILE NOW THE MOUNTED SUN 5 300
- BE OVER, AND THE SUN MORE COOLE DECLINE. 5 370
- THE SUN THAT LIGHT IMPARTS TO ALL, RECEIVES 5 423
- AND WE HAVE YET LARGE DAY, FOR SCARCE THE SUN 5 558
- OR STARRS OF MORNING, DEW-DROPS, WHICH THE SUN 5 746
- SPHEAR'D IN A RADIANT CLOUD, FOR YET THE SUN 7 247
- FOR OF CELESTIAL BODIES FIRST THE SUN 7 354
- SHOW TO THE SUN THIR WAV'D COATS DROPT WITH GOLD, 7 406
- EEV'NING AROSE IN EDEN, FOR THE SUN 7 582
- MORE PLENTY THEN THE SUN THAT BARREN SHINES, 8 94
- AND NO ADVANTAGE GAINE. WHAT IF THE SUN 8 122
- OR SAVE THE SUN HIS LABOUR, AND THAT SWIFT 8 133
- WHETHER THE SUN PREDOMINANT IN HEAV'N 8 160
- RISE ON THE EARTH, OR EARTH RISE ON THE SUN, 8 161
- IN BALMIE SWEAT, WHICH WITH HIS BEAMES THE SUN 8 255
- WHAT E'RE I SAW. THOU SUN, SAID I, FAIRE LIGHT, 8 273
- BUT I CAN NOW NO MORE; THE PARTING SUN 8 630
- THE SUN WAS SUNK, AND AFTER HIM THE STARR 9 48
- SINCE URIEL REGENT OF THE SUN DESCRI'D 9 60
- WARM'D BY THE SUN, PRODUCING EVERY KIND, 9 721
- NOW WAS THE SUN IN WESTERN CADENCE LOW 10 92
- HIS ZENITH, WHILE THE SUN IN ARIES ROSE: 10 329
- NOW DRAGON GROWN, LARGER THEN WHOM THE SUN 10 529
- AS SORTED BEST WITH PRESENT THINGS. THE SUN 10 651
- WHICH OF THEM RISING WITH THE SUN, OR FALLING, 10 663
- OBLIQUE THE CENTRIC GLOBE: SOM SAY THE SUN 10 671

SUN (CONTINUED)
- HAD UNBENIGHTED SHON, WHILE THE LOW SUN 10 682
- THE SUN, AS FROM THYESTEAN BANQUET, TURN'D 10 688
- WHICH MIGHT SUPPLIE THE SUN: SUCH FIRE TO USE, 10 1078
- WHO NOW SHALL REARE YE TO THE SUN, OR RANKE 11 278
- AND THE CLEER SUN ON HIS WIDE WATRIE GLASS 11 844
- OR HOW THE SUN SHALL IN MID HEAV'N STAND STILL 12 263
- MANS VOICE COMMANDING, SUN IN GIBEON STAND, 12 265

SUN-BRIGHT
- TH' APOSTAT IN HIS SUN-BRIGHT CHARIOT SATE 6 100

SUNG
- I SUNG OF CHAOS AND ETERNAL NIGHT, 3 18
- THEE FATHER FIRST THEY SUNG OMNIPOTENT, 3 372
- SHE ALL NIGHT LONG HER AMOROUS DESCANT SUNG; 4 603
- AND HEAV'NLY QUIRES THE HYMENAEAN SUNG, 4 711
- THIR MAKER, IN FIT STRAINS PRONOUNC'T OR SUNG 5 148
- (WHOSE PRAISE BE EVER SUNG) TO MAN IN PART 5 405
- THE MATIN TRUMPET SUNG: IN ARMS THEY STOOD 6 526
- SUNG TRIUMPH, AND HIM SUNG VICTORIOUS KING, 6 886
- GLORIE THEY SUNG TO THE MOST HIGH, GOOD WILL 7 182
- GOD AND HIS WORKS, CREATOUR HIM THEY SUNG, 7 259
- AND MORNING CHORUS SUNG THE SECOND DAY. 7 275
- OPEN, YE EVERLASTING GATES, THEY SUNG, 7 565
- ON ERRANDS OF SUPERNAL GRACE. SO SUNG 7 573
- CREATION AND THE SIX DAYES ACTS THEY SUNG, 7 601
- SO SUNG THEY, AND THE EMPYREAN RUNG, 7 633
- SUNG SPOUSAL, AND BID HASTE THE EEVNING STARR 8 519
- SUNG HALLELUIA, AS THE SOUND OF SEAS, 10 642
- THROUGH MULTITUDE THAT SUNG: JUST ARE THY WAYS, 10 643
- IN GEMS AND WANTON DRESS; TO THE HARP THEY SUNG 11 583
- OF SQUADROND ANGELS HEAR HIS CAROL SUNG. 12 367

SUNK
- BOW'D DOWN IN BATTEL, SUNK BEFORE THE SPEAR 1 436
- WE SUNK THUS LOW? TH' ASCENT IS EASIE THEN; 2 81
- OF RACKING WHIRLWINDS, OR FOR EVER SUNK 2 182
- WHERE ARMIES WHOLE HAVE SUNK: THE PARCHING AIR 2 594
- MY GUIDE WAS GON, AND I, ME THOUGHT, SUNK DOWN, 5 91
- HALF SUNK WITH ALL HIS PINES. AMAZEMENT SEIS'D 6 198
- DOWN SUNK A HOLLOW BOTTOM BROAD AND DEEP, 7 289
- DAZL'D AND SPENT, SUNK DOWN, AND SOUGHT REPAIR 8 457
- NOT SUNK IN CARNAL PLEASURE, FOR WHICH CAUSE 8 593
- THE SUN WAS SUNK, AND AFTER HIM THE STARR 9 48
- IN WITH THE RIVER SUNK, AND WITH IT ROSE 9 74
- SUNK DOWN AND ALL HIS SPIRITS BECAME INTRANST: 11 420
- AND SUNK THEE AS THY SONS; TILL GENTLY REARD 11 758

SUN-LIGHT
- TO STARR OR SUN-LIGHT, SPREAD THIR UMBRAGE BROAD 9 1087

SUNNIE
- CLEER SPRING, OR SHADIE GROVE, OR SUNNIE HILL, 3 28
- OF BEAMING SUNNIE RAIES, A GOLDEN TIAR 3 625
- HILL, DALE, AND SHADIE WOODS, AND SUNNIE PLAINES, 8 262

SUN'S
- ASTRONOMER IN THE SUN'S LUCENT ORBE 3 589
- THIS EEVNING FROM THE SUN'S DECLINE ARRIV'D 4 792
- WHEN TO ENSHRINE HIS RELIQUES IN THE SUN'S 5 273

SUNS
- AMID THE SUNS BRIGHT CIRCLE WHERE THOU SITST, 4 578
- PERFECTION FROM THE SUNS MORE POTENT RAY. 4 673
- MADE HORRID CIRCLES; TWO BROAD SUNS THIR SHIELDS 6 305
- IN THE SUNS ORB, MADE POROUS TO RECEIVE 7 361
- FROM THE SUNS BEAM MEET NIGHT, HER OTHER PART 8 139
- ALLOTTED THERE; AND OTHER SUNS PERHAPS 8 148
- FROM THE SUNS AXLE; THEY WITH LABOUR PUSH'D 10 670

SUN-SHINE
- BUT ALL SUN-SHINE, AS WHEN HIS BEAMS AT NOON 3 616

SUPERFICIALLY
- WHOSE EYE SO SUPERFICIALLY SURVEYES 6 476

SUPERFLUOUS
- WHY ASK YE, AND SUPERFLUOUS BEGIN 4 832
- TO NOURISH, AND SUPERFLUOUS MOIST CONSUMES: 5 325
- SUCH DISPROPORTIONS, WITH SUPERFLUOUS HAND 8 27
- ANGELS, NOR THINK SUPERFLUOUS OTHERS AID. 9 308

SUPERIOR
- AS TO SUPERIOR SPIRITS IS WONT IN HEAVEN, 3 737
- SMIL'D WITH SUPERIOR LOVE, AS JUPITER 4 499
- AS TO A SUPERIOR NATURE, BOWING LOW, 5 360
- THE WONTED SIGNAL, AND SUPERIOR VOICE 5 705
- SUPERIOR, NOR OF VIOLENCE FEAR'D AUGHT; 5 905
- SUPERIOR; FOR INFERIOR WHO IS FREE? 9 825
- SUPERIOR SWAY; FROM THUS DISTEMPERD BREST, 9 1131
- SUPERIOR, OR BUT EQUAL, THAT TO HER 10 147

SUPERIOUR
- HE SCARCE HAD CEAS'T WHEN THE SUPERIOUR FIEND 1 283
- LEFT THEM SUPERIOUR, WHILE WE CAN PRESERVE 6 443
- SUPERIOUR AND UNMOV'D, HERE ONELY WEAKE 8 532
- BY WISDOME, AND SUPERIOUR GIFTS RECEAV'D. 11 636

SUPERNAL
NOT BY THE SUFFERANCE OF SUPERNAL POWER. 1 241
ON ERRANDS OF SUPERNAL GRACE. SO SUNG 7 573
EXPECT TO HEAR, SUPERNAL GRACE CONTENDING 11 359

SUPERNUMERARIE
WELL IF THROWN OUT, AS SUPERNUMERARIE 10 887

SUPERSTITION
OF PAINFUL SUPERSTITION AND BLIND ZEAL, 3 452

SUPERSTITIONS
WITH SUPERSTITIONS AND TRADITIONS TAINT, 12 512

SUPPER
MORE GRATEFUL, TO THIR SUPPER FRUITS THEY FELL, 4 331
EARLY, AND TH' HOUR OF SUPPER COMES UNEARN'D. 9 225

SUPPLANTED
EACH OTHER, TILL SUPPLANTED DOWN HE FELL 10 513

SUPPLE
THE SUPPLE KNEE? YE WILL NOT, IF I TRUST 5 788
WITH SUPPLE JOINTS, AND LIVELY VIGOUR LED: 8 269

SUPPLIANT
WITH SUPPLIANT KNEE, AND DEIFIE HIS POWER, 1 112
UNHAPPILIE DECEAV'D; THY SUPPLIANT 10 917

SUPPLICATION
WHETHER BY SUPPLICATION WE INTEND 5 867
TO SUPPLICATION, HEARE HIS SIGHS THOUGH MUTE; 11 31

SUPPLIE
WHICH MIGHT SUPPLIE THE SUN: SUCH FIRE TO USE, 10 1078
FROM UNDER HEAV'N; THE HILLS TO THEIR SUPPLIE 11 740

SUPPLY
A RACE OF UPSTART CREATURES, TO SUPPLY 2 834
LET US SEEK DEATH, OR HE NOT FOUND, SUPPLY 10 1001

SUPPORT
ILLUMIN, WHAT IS LOW RAISE AND SUPPORT; 1 23
STRONGLY TO SUFFER AND SUPPORT OUR PAINS, 1 147
HE WALKT WITH TO SUPPORT UNEASIE STEPS 1 295
ABOUT HER GLOWD, OFT STOOPING TO SUPPORT 9 427
SO MIGHT THE WRAUTH. FOND WISH. COULDST THOU
SUPPORT 10 834

SUPPORTED
AND OFT SUPPORTED SO AS SHALL AMAZE 12 496

SUPPOS'D
RAN PURPLE TO THE SEA, SUPPOS'D WITH BLOOD 1 451
AS HE SUPPOS'D, ALL UNOBSERV'D, UNSEEN. 4 130
MOUNT AMARA, THOUGH THIS BY SOM SUPPOS'D 4 281
NOCTURNAL AND DIURNAL RHOMB SUPPOS'D, 8 134
THE TEMPTED WITH DISHONOUR FOUL, SUPPOS'D 9 297
THAT DEATH BE NOT ONE STROAK, AS I SUPPOS'D, 10 809

SUPPOSE
WE OVERPOWER? SUPPOSE HE SHOULD RELENT 2 237
FOR JOY OF OFFERD PEACE: BUT I SUPPOSE 6 617

SUPPOSEST
WHO ART TO LEAD THY OFSPRING, AND SUPPOSEST 8 86

SUPPREST
ONELY OMNISCIENT, HATH SUPPREST IN NIGHT, 7 123

SUPREAM
WHOM REASON HATH EQUALD, FORCE HATH MADE SUPREAM 1 248
OUR SUPREAM FOE IN TIME MAY MUCH REMIT 2 210
WITHIN HEAV'NS BOUND, UNLESS HEAV'NS LORD SUPREAM 2 236
THAN HELLS DREAD EMPEROUR WITH POMP SUPREAM, 2 510
THY MERITS; UNDER THEE AS HEAD SUPREAM 3 319
AND HERE ART LIKELIEST BY SUPREAM DECREE 3 659
THE LOWER STILL I FALL, ONELY SUPREAM 4 91
ALLEGEANCE TO TH' ACKNOWLDG'D POWER SUPREAM? 4 956
UNWORSHIPT, UNOBEY'D THE THRONE SUPREAM 5 670
BEFORE THE SEAT SUPREAM; FROM WHENCE A VOICE 6 27
O FATHER, O SUPREAM OF HEAV'NLY THRONES, 6 723
BECAUSE THE FATHER, T' WHOM IN HEAV'N SUPREAM 6 814
OF DEITIE SUPREAM, US DISPOSSEST, 7 142
AND WORSHIP GOD SUPREAM, WHO MADE HIM CHIEF 7 515
ALL HUMAN THOUGHTS COME SHORT, SUPREAM OF THINGS; 8 414
HOW ALL BEFELL: THEY TOWARDS THE THRONE SUPREAM 10 28
SUPREAM, THAT THOU IN MEE THY SON BELOV'D 10 70
AND TOOK THIR SEATS; TILL FROM HIS THRONE SUPREAM 11 82

SUPREAME
TO DWELL, UNLESS BY MAISTRING HEAV'NS SUPREAME; 9 125
PROTESTING FATE SUPREAME; THENCE HOW I FOUND 10 480

SUPREMACIE
AGAINST THE HIGH SUPREMACIE OF HEAV'N, 3 205

SUPREMACY
AND PUT TO PROOF HIS HIGH SUPREMACY, 1 132

SUPREME
AND SAT AS PRINCES, WHOM THE SUPREME KING 1 735

SUPS
SUPS WITH THE OCEAN: THOUGH IN HEAV'N THE TREES 5 426

SURCEAS'D
SURCEAS'D, AND GLAD AS HOPING HERE TO END 6 258

SURCHARG'D
LEAST HEAV'N SURCHARG'D WITH POTENT MULTITUDE 2 836
AND O FAIR PLANT, SAID HE, WITH FRUIT SURCHARG'D, 5 58
SURCHARG'D, AS HAD LIKE GRIEF BIN DEW'D IN TEARS, 12 373

SURE
DOING OR SUFFERING: BUT OF THIS BE SURE, 1 158
FROM FACTION; FOR NONE SURE WILL CLAIM IN HELL 2 32
IS DOUBTFUL; THAT HE NEVER WILL IS SURE. 2 154
CHAIN'D ON THE BURNING LAKE? THAT SURE WAS WORSE. 2 169
HIS CAPTIVE MULTITUDE: FOR HE, BE SURE 2 323
AND THEY WHO TO BE SURE OF PARADISE 3 478
BUT COME, FOR THOU, BE SURE, SHALT GIVE ACCOUNT 4 841
SURE PLEDGE OF DAY, THAT CROWNST THE SMILING MORN 5 168
NEERLY IT NOW CONCERNES US TO BE SURE 5 721
BE SURE, AND TERROUR SEIS'D THE REBEL HOST, 6 647
OF THIS GREAT ROUND: PARTITION FIRM AND SURE, 7 267
OF GODHEAD, FIXT FOR EVER FIRM AND SURE, 7 586
FOR GOOD UNKNOWN, SURE IS NOT HAD, OR HAD 9 756
BE SURE THEN. HOW SHALL I BEHOLD THE FACE 9 1080
HIM FIRST MAKE SURE YOUR THRALL, AND LASTLY KILL. 10 402
HIM OR HIS CHILDERN, EVIL HE MAY BE SURE, 11 772
BE SURE THEY WILL, SAID TH' ANGEL; BUT FROM HEAV'N 12 485

SURELY
THOU SURELY HADST NOT COME SOLE FUGITIVE. 4 923

SURER
SURER TO PROSPER THEN PROSPERITY 2 39
HIS WILL WHO BOUND US? LET HIM SURER BARR 4 897
AND AFTER HIM, THE SURER MESSENGER, 11 856

SUREST
THIR SUREST SIGNAL, THEY WILL SOON RESUME 1 278
WHENCE RUSHING HE MIGHT SUREST SEIZE THEM BOTH 4 407

SURETY
ON OTHER SURETY NONE; FREELY WE SERVE, 5 538

SURFACE
WHICH OF US WHO BEHOLDS THE BRIGHT SURFACE 6 472

SURFET
OF SURFET WHERE FULL MEASURE ONELY BOUNDS 5 639
OPPRESSES ELSE WITH SURFET, AND SOON TURNS 7 129
SURFET, AND LUST, TILL WANTONNESS AND PRIDE 11 795

SURGE
THE FIERY SURGE, THAT FROM THE PRECIPICE 1 173
AND WITH REBOUNDING SURGE THE BARRS ASSAILD, 10 417

SURGING
HE SPREADS FOR FLIGHT, AND IN THE SURGING SMOAK 2 928
AND SURGING WAVES, AS MOUNTAINS TO ASSAULT 7 214
FOULD ABOVE FOULD A SURGING MAZE, HIS HEAD 9 499

SURMISE
FROM HIS SURMISE PROV'D FALSE, FIND PEACE WITHIN, 9 333
NO DESPICABLE GIFT; SURMISE NOT THEN 11 340

SURMOUNTS
THIS IS DISPENC'T, AND WHAT SURMOUNTS THE REACH 5 571

SURPASS
IN BIGNESS TO SURPASS EARTHS GIANT SONS 1 778
ABOLISH HIS OWN WORKS. THIS WOULD SURPASS 2 370
SURPASS HIS BOUNDS, NOR RAIN TO DROWN THE WORLD 11 894

SURPASS'D
IN GATE SURPASS'D AND GODDESS-LIKE DEPORT, 9 389

SURPASSEST
SURPASSEST FARR MY NAMING, HOW MAY I 8 359

SURPASSING
O THOU THAT WITH SURPASSING GLORY CROWND, 4 32
AUGHT, NOT SURPASSING HUMAN MEASURE, SAY. 7 640

SURPRISAL
SURPRISAL, UNADMONISHT, UNFOREWARND. 5 245

SURPRIS'D
SURPRIS'D THEE, DIM THINE EYES, AND DIZZIE SWUMM 2 753
DEFENSIVE SCARSE, OR WITH PALE FEAR SURPRIS'D, 6 393
THEN FIRST WITH FEAR SURPRIS'D AND SENSE OF PAINE 6 394
LEAST BY SOME FAIRE APPEERING GOOD SURPRIS'D 9 354

SURPRISE
SURPRISE THEE, AND HER BLACK ATTENDANT DEATH. 7 547
OVER HIS FOES AND THINE; THERE SHALL SURPRISE 12 453

SURPRIZ'D
DISCOVERD AND SURPRIZ'D. AS WHEN A SPARK 4 814
FIRST SEEN, THEM UNEXPECTED JOY SURPRIZ'D, 6 774

SURPRIZE
SCORNING SURPRIZE. OR COULD WE BREAK OUR WAY 2 134
THAT SELF SAME DAY BY FIGHT, OR BY SURPRIZE 6 87
AGAINST THE SYRIAN KING, WHO TO SURPRIZE 11 218

SURRENDER
AND MEEK SURRENDER, HALF IMBRACING LEAND 4 494

SURROUND
SURROUND ME, AS THOU SAWST, HOURLY CONCEIV'D 2 796

SURROUNDING
'TWIXT UPPER, NETHER, AND SURROUNDING FIRES; 1 346

SURROUNDS
SURROUNDS ME, FROM THE CHEARFUL WAYES OF MEN 3 46

SURVAY'D
HIS EYE SURVAY'D THE DARK IDOLATRIES 1 456

SURVEY
ONE DAY AND NIGHT; IN ALL THIR VAST SURVEY 8 24

SURVEY'D
IN BLISSFUL SOLITUDE; HE THEN SURVEY'D 3 69
SURVEY'D, AND SOMETIMES WENT, AND SOMETIMES RAN 8 268

SURVEYES
WHOSE EYE SO SUPERFICIALLY SURVEYES 6 476

SURVEYING
SURVEYING HIS GREAT WORK, THAT IT WAS GOOD: 7 353

SURVEYS
ROUND HE SURVEYS, AND WELL MIGHT, WHERE HE STOOD 3 555

SUS
THE KINGDOMS OF ALMANSOR, FEZ AND SUS, 11 403

SUSA
FROM SUSA HIS MEMNONIAN PALACE HIGH 10 308

SUSPECT
LET US NOT THEN SUSPECT OUR HAPPIE STATE 9 337
THAT FROM HER HAND I COULD SUSPECT NO ILL, 10 140

SUSPECTED
SUSPECTED TO A SEQUENT KING, WHO SEEKS 12 165

SUSPENCE
HIS LOOK SUSPENCE, AWAITING WHO APPEER'D 2 418

SUSPEND
INSENSIBLY, FOR I SUSPEND THIR DOOM; 6 692

SUSPENDED
SUSPENDED HELL, AND TOOK WITH RAVISHMENT 2 554

SUSPENS
MUCH OF HIS RACE THOUGH STEEP, SUSPENS IN HEAV'N 7 99

SUSPENSE
STOOD WAVING TIPT WITH FIRE; WHILE WE SUSPENSE, 6 580

SUSPICION
AND OFT THOUGH WISDOM WAKE, SUSPICION SLEEPS 3 686
MISTRUST, SUSPICION, DISCORD, AND SHOOK SORE 9 1124

SUSPICIOUS
SUSPICIOUS, REASONLESS. WHY SHOULD THIR LORD 4 516
WHATEVER FLEIGHTS NONE WOULD SUSPICIOUS MARK, 9 92

SUSTAIN
OUR DOOM; WHICH IF WE CAN SUSTAIN AND BEAR, 2 209
NOT PROOF ENOUGH SUCH OBJECT TO SUSTAIN, 8 535
THIS MY ATTEMPT, I WOULD SUSTAIN ALONE 9 978
MY LABOUR WILL SUSTAIN ME; AND LEAST COLD 10 1056
OUR FRAILTIE CAN SUSTAIN, THY TIDINGS BRING, 11 302
WILL HE CONVEY UP THITHER TO SUSTAIN 12 75

SUSTAIN'D
TO PASS COMMODIOUSLY THIS LIFE, SUSTAIN'D 10 1083

SUSTAIND
TO BE SUSTAIND AND FED; OF ELEMENTS 5 415
WHO HAVE SUSTAIND ONE DAY IN DOUBTFUL FIGHT 6 423
ALONE, WITHOUT EXTERIOR HELP SUSTAIND? 9 336

SUSTAINE
BEARE THINE OWN FIRST, ILL ABLE TO SUSTAINE 10 950

SUSTEIND
LONG WAY THROUGH HOSTILE SCORN, WHICH HE SUSTEIND 5 904

SUTABLE
SUTABLE GRACE DIFFUS'D, SO WELL HE FEIGND; 3 639

SUTTLE
PENDANT BY SUTTLE MAGIC MANY A ROW 1 727
SHE FINISH'D, AND THE SUTTLE FIEND HIS LORE 2 815
FROM THESE, TWO STRONG AND SUTTLE SPIRITS HE CALLD 4 786
THEY FOUND, THEY MINGL'D, AND WITH SUTTLE ART, 6 513
FROM USE, OBSCURE AND SUTTLE, BUT TO KNOW 8 192
A NICE AND SUTTLE HAPPINESS I SEE 8 399
HIS HEAD THE MIDST, WELL STOR'D WITH SUTTLE WILES: 9 184
SUTTLE HE NEEDS MUST BE, WHO COULD SEDUCE 9 307
SUTTLE OR VIOLENT, WE NOT ENDU'D 9 324
MUCH WONDRING HOW THE SUTTLE FIEND HAD STOLN 10 20

SUTTLEST
THE SERPENT SUTTLEST BEAST OF ALL THE FIELD. 9 86
THEE, SERPENT, SUTTLEST BEAST OF ALL THE FIELD 9 560

SUTTLETIE
AS FROM HIS WIT AND NATIVE SUTTLETIE 9 93

SUTTLETY
BY FORCE OR SUTTLETY: THOUGH HEAV'N BE SHUT, 2 358

SUTTL'ST
THE SERPENT SUTTL'ST BEAST OF ALL THE FIELD, 7 495

SUTTLY
HOW SUTTLY TO DETAINE THEE I DEVISE, 8 207

SWAGE
NOR WANTING POWER TO MITIGATE AND SWAGE 1 556

SWALLOW'D
HERE SWALLOW'D UP IN ENDLESS MISERY. 1 142
THERE SWALLOW'D UP AND LOST, FROM SUCCOUR FARR. 9 642

SWALLOWD
TO PERISH RATHER, SWALLOWD UP AND LOST 2 149

SWALLOWS
SWALLOWS HIM WITH HIS HOST, BUT THEM LETS PASS 12 196

SWAN
THIR DOWNIE BREST; THE SWAN WITH ARCHED NECK 7 438

SWARM
SWARM POPULOUS, UNNUMBER'D AS THE SANDS 2 903

SWARM'D
THICK SWARM'D, BOTH ON THE GROUND AND IN THE AIR, 1 767
SWARM'D AND WERE STRAITN'D; TILL THE SIGNAL GIV'N, 1 776
AND DIPSAS (NOT SO THICK SWARM'D ONCE THE SOIL 10 526

SWARME
WITH FRIE INNUMERABLE SWARME, AND SHOALES 7 400

SWARMING
OF COMMONALTIE: SWARMING NEXT APPEER'D 7 489
OF HISSING THROUGH THE HALL, THICK SWARMING NOW 10 522
A DARKSOM CLOUD OF LOCUSTS SWARMING DOWN 12 185

SWAY
TO HER ORIGINAL DARKNESS AND YOUR SWAY 2 984
SUBJECTION, BUT REQUIR'D WITH GENTLE SWAY, 4 308
WHEN TO ADVANCE, OR STAND, OR TURN THE SWAY 6 234
SQUADRONS AT ONCE, WITH HUGE TWO-HANDED SWAY 6 251
HIS GREAT COMMAND; TAKE HEED LEAST PASSION SWAY 8 635
SUPERIOR SWAY: FROM THUS DISTEMPERD BREST, 9 1131
THERE DIDST NOT; THERE LET HIM STILL VICTOR SWAY, 10 376
ON EUROPE THENCE, AND WHERE ROME WAS TO SWAY 11 405

SWAY'D
BUT ADAM WITH SUCH COUNSEL NOTHING SWAY'D, 10 1010

SWAYES
SWAYES THEM; THE CAREFUL PLOWMAN DOUBTING STANDS 4 983

SWEAT
IN BALMIE SWEAT, WHICH WITH HIS BEAMES THE SUN 8 255
IN THE SWEAT OF THY FACE SHALT THOU EAT BREAD, 10 205
TO LABOUR CALLS US NOW WITH SWEAT IMPOS'D, 11 172

SWEATIE
A SWEATIE REAPER FROM HIS TILLAGE BROUGHT 11 434

SWEET
OF DULCET SYMPHONIES AND VOICES SWEET, 1 712
IF CHANCE THE RADIANT SUN WITH FAREWELL SWEET 2 492
THE THRONGING AUDIENCE. IN DISCOURSE MORE SWEET 2 555
IN SWEET FORGETFULNESS ALL PAIN AND WOE, 2 608
THEN SWEET, NOW SAD TO MENTION, THROUGH DIRE CHANGE 2 820
DAY, OR THE SWEET APPROACH OF EV'N OR MORN, 3 42
LOUD AS FROM NUMBERS WITHOUT NUMBER, SWEET 3 346

SYRIAN
EGYPT FROM SYRIAN GROUND, HAD GENERAL NAMES . . . 1 421
THE SYRIAN DAMSELS TO LAMENT HIS FATE 1 448
FOR ONE OF SYRIAN MODE, WHEREON TO BURN 1 474
AGAINST THE SYRIAN KING, WHO TO SURPRIZE . . . 11 218

SYRTIS
QUENCHT IN A BOGGIE SYRTIS, NEITHER SEA, ... 2 939

TABERNACLE
WAS NOT; SHEE IN A CLOUDIE TABERNACLE 7 248
AMONG THEM TO SET UP HIS TABERNACLE, ... 12 247

TABERNACLES
CELESTIAL TABERNACLES, WHERE THEY SLEPT 5 654

TABLE
HAVE HEAP'D THIS TABLE. RAIS'D OF GRASSIE TERF . 5 391
THIR TABLE WAS, AND MOSSIE SEATS HAD ROUND, . . 5 392
AS FROM THE MINE. MEAN WHILE AT TABLE EVE . . . 5 443

TABLES
TABLES ARE SET, AND ON A SUDDEN PIL'D 5 632

TACKLE
GLADLY THE PORT, THOUGH SHROUDS AND TACKLE TORN; . 2 1044

TAILE
WITH COMPLICATED MONSTERS HEAD AND TAILE, ... 10 523

TAINT
OR IF, INSPIRING VENOM, HE MIGHT TAINT 4 804
OR TAINT INTEGRITIE; BUT ALL OBEY'D 5 704
WHICH MANS POLLUTING SIN WITH TAINT HATH SHED . . 10 631
WITH SUPERSTITIONS AND TRADITIONS TAINT, . . . 12 512

TAINTED
EJECT HIM TAINTED NOW, AND PURGE HIM OFF 11 52

TAKE
HIS GREAT COMMAND; TAKE HEED LEAST PASSION SWAY . 8 635
THE BENDED TWIGS TAKE ROOT, AND DAUGHTERS GROW . 9 1105
TAKE TO THEE FROM AMONG THE CHERUBIM 11 100
AND THERE TAKE ROOT AN ILAND SALT AND BARE, . . 11 834

TAKEN
OUT OF THE GROUND WAST TAKEN, KNOW THY BIRTH, . . 10 207
THE GROUND WHENCE HE WAS TAKEN, FITTER SOILE. . . 11 98

TAKES
AND OF THIR DOINGS GOD TAKES NO ACCOUNT. 4 622

TAK'N
THE GROUND WHENCE THOU WAST TAK'N, FITTER SOILE. . 11 262

TALE
OF THAMMUZ YEARLY WOUNDED: THE LOVE-TALE 1 452

TALK
WHATEVER HYPOCRITES AUSTERELY TALK 4 744
THEN WHEN I AM THY CAPTIVE TALK OF CHAINES, . . . 4 970
OF OUR LAST EEVNINGS TALK, IN THIS THY DREAM, . . 5 115
NO MORE OF TALK WHERE GOD OR ANGEL GUEST 9 1
REFRESHMENT, WHETHER FOOD, OR TALK BETWEEN, . . . 9 237

TALK'D
SO TALK'D THE SPIRITED SLY SNAKE; AND EVE 9 613
I HEARD, HERE WITH HIM AT THIS FOUNTAIN TALK'D: . 11 322
WHEREAT HEE INLIE RAG'D, AND AS THY TALK'D, . . 11 444

TALKING
THUS SATAN TALKING TO HIS NEEREST MATE 1 192
THUS TALKING HAND IN HAND ALONE THEY PASS'D . . . 4 689

TALKT
THE TREPIDATION TALKT, AND THAT FIRST MOV'D; . . . 3 483

TALL
AZAZEL AS HIS RIGHT, A CHERUBE TALL: 1 534
TWO OF FAR NOBLER SHAPE ERECT AND TALL, ... 4 288
TILL I ESPI'D THEE, FAIR INDEED AND TALL, ... 4 477
THEN FROM THE MOUNTAIN HEWING TIMBER TALL, . . . 11 728

TALLEST
HIS SPEAR, TO EQUAL WHICH THE TALLEST PINE 1 292

TAM'D
THE RIVER-DRAGON TAM'D AT LENGTH SUBMITS 12 191

TAME
SINCE MICHAEL AND HIS POWERS WENT FORTH TO TAME . 6 686

TAMELY
TAMELY ENDUR'D A BRIDGE OF WONDROUS LENGTH 2 1028

TANGLES
IN TANGLES, AND MADE INTRICATE SEEM STRAIT, . . . 9 632

TANGLING
OF SHRUBS AND TANGLING BUSHES HAD PERPLEXT 4 176

TANTALUS
THE LIP OF TANTALUS. THUS ROVING ON 2 614

TARDIE
OF TARDIE EXECUTION, SINCE DENOUNC'T 10 853

TARGE
THEY GATHERD, BROAD AS AMAZONIAN TARGE, ... 9 1111

TARSUS
BY ANCIENT TARSUS HELD, OR THAT SEA-BEAST 1 200

TARTAR*
WHOSE SNOWIE RIDGE THE ROVING TARTAR BOUNDS, . . . 3 432
AS WHEN THE TARTAR FROM HIS RUSSIAN FOE 10 431

TARTAREAN
MIXT WITH TARTAREAN SULPHUR, AND STRANGE FIRE, . 2 69

TARTAREOUS
THE BLACK TARTAREOUS COLD INFERNAL DREGS 7 238

TARTARUS
INTO THIS GLOOM OF TARTARUS PROFOUND, ... 2 858
OF TARTARUS, WHICH READY OPENS WIDE 6 54

TASK
TO DO OUGHT GOOD NEVER WILL BE OUR TASK, ... 1 159
OUR SERVILE OFFERINGS. THIS MUST BE OUR TASK . . 2 246
HIS BOUNTIE, FOLLOWING OUR DELIGHTFUL TASK . . . 4 437
SAD TASK AND HARD, FOR HOW SHALL I RELATE . . . 5 564
OF SECONDARIE HANDS, BY TASK TRANSFERD 5 854
DEATHS HARBINGER: SAD TASK, YET ARGUMENT . . . 9 13
OUR PLEASANT TASK ENJOYN'D, BUT TILL MORE HANDS . 9 207

TASKE
OUR TASKE WE CHOOSE, WHAT WONDER IF SO NEAR . . . 9 221

TAST
OF THAT FORBIDDEN TREE, WHOSE MORTAL TAST 1 2

TASTE
ALL TASTE OF LIVING WIGHT, AS ONCE IT FLED . . . 2 613
RETIRE, OR TASTE THY FOLLY, AND LEARN BY PROOF, . 2 686
THEY WHO NEGLECT AND SCORN, SHALL NEVER TASTE; . 3 199
ALL TREES OF NOBLEST KIND FOR SIGHT, SMELL, TASTE; 4 217
IF TRUE, HERE ONLY, AND OF DELICIOUS TASTE: . . 4 251
MORE WOE, THE MORE YOUR TASTE IS NOW OF JOY; . . 4 369
SO VARIOUS, NOT TO TASTE THAT ONELY TREE . . . 4 423
GOD HATH PRONOUNC'T IT DEATH TO TASTE THAT TREE, . 4 427
FORBIDDEN THEM TO TASTE: KNOWLEDGE FORBIDD'N? . . 4 515
THEY TASTE AND DIE: WHAT LIKELIER CAN ENSUE? . . 4 527
DEIGNS NONE TO EASE THY LOAD AND TASTE THY SWEET, 5 59
OR ENVIE, OR WHAT RESERVE FORBIDS TO TASTE? . . 5 61
TASTE THIS, AND BE HENCEFORTH AMONG THE GODS . . 5 77
COULD NOT BUT TASTE. FORTHWITH UP TO THE CLOUDS . 5 86
FOR DINNER SAVOURIE FRUITS, OF TASTE TO PLEASE . 5 304
TASTE AFTER TASTE UPHELD WITH KINDLIEST CHANGE, . 5 336
TO SIT AND TASTE, TILL THIS MERIDIAN HEAT . . . 5 369
OUR AUTHOUR. HEAV'NLY STRANGER, PLEASE TO TASTE . 5 397
OF SENSE, WHEREBY THEY HEAR, SEE, SMELL, TOUCH,
TASTE, ... 5 411
AS MAY COMPARE WITH HEAVEN; AND TO TASTE . . . 5 432
TO ENTER, AND THESE EARTHLY FRUITS TO TASTE, . . 5 464
DELECTABLE BOTH TO BEHOLD AND TASTE; 7 539
REMEMBER WHAT I WARNE THEE, SHUN TO TASTE, . . . 8 327
OF THY ASSOCIATES, ADAM, AND WILT TASTE 8 401
I MEAN OF TASTE, SIGHT, SMELL, HERBS, FRUITS, AND
FLOURS, ... 8 527
OF PARADISE FOR HELL, HOPE HERE TO TASTE . . . 9 476
BUT OF THIS TREE WE MAY NOT TASTE NOR TOUCH; . . 9 651
GODDESS HUMANE, REACH THEN, AND FREELY TASTE. . . 9 732
INCLINABLE NOW GROWN TO TOUCH OR TASTE, ... 9 742
WHOSE TASTE, TOO LONG FORBORN, AT FIRST ASSAY . . 9 747
FORBIDS US THEN TO TASTE, BUT HIS FORBIDDING . . 9 753
FAIR TO THE EYE, INVITING TO THE TASTE, ... 9 777
INTENT NOW WHOLLY ON HER TASTE, NAUGHT ELSE . . . 9 786
TO OPEN EYES, AND MAKE THEM GODS WHO TASTE; . . . 9 866
THOU THEREFORE ALSO TASTE, THAT EQUAL LOT . . . 9 881
MUCH MORE TO TASTE IT UNDER BANNE TO TOUCH. . . . 9 925
MADE COMMON AND UNHALLOWD ERE OUR TASTE; 9 931
TASTE SO DIVINE, THAT WHAT OF SWEET BEFORE . . . 9 986
ON MY EXPERIENCE, ADAM, FREELY TASTE, ... 9 988
EVE, NOW I SEE THOU ART EXACT OF TASTE, ... 9 1017
HER HUSBAND SHEE, TO TASTE THE FATALL FRUIT, . . 10 4
THE HIGH INJUNCTION NOT TO TASTE THAT FRUIT, . . 10 13
OF CARNAGE, PREY INNUMERABLE, AND TASTE 10 268
THIS MORE DELUSIVE, NOT THE TOUCH, BUT TASTE . . 10 563
CHEWD BITTER ASHES, WHICH TH' OFFENDED TASTE . . 10 566
TO KNOW BOTH GOOD AND EVIL, SINCE HIS TASTE . . 11 85
OBTUSE, ALL TASTE OF PLEASURE MUST FORGOE, . . . 11 541
BRED ONELY AND COMPLETED TO THE TASTE 11 618

TASTED
HE PLUCKT, HE TASTED; MEE DAMP HORROR CHIL'D . . . 5 65

TASTED (CONTINUED)
WHICH TASTED WORKS KNOWLEDGE OF GOOD AND EVIL, 7 543
MEE WHO HAVE TOUCH'D AND TASTED, YET BOTH LIVE, 9 688
HATH TASTED, ENVIES NOT, BUT BRINGS WITH JOY 9 770
IN FRUIT SHE NEVER TASTED, WHETHER TRUE 9 788
OF DANGER TASTED, NOR TO EVIL UNKNOWN 9 864
AND HATH BIN TASTED SUCH: THE SERPENT WISE, 9 867
HAVE ALSO TASTED, AND HAVE ALSO FOUND 9 874
BENEATH MAGELLAN. AT THAT TASTED FRUIT 10 687

TASTES
TASTES, NOT WELL JOYND, INELEGANT, BUT BRING 5 335
OF ALL TASTES ELSE TO PLEASE THIR APPETITE, 7 49

TASTING
TASTING CONCOCT, DIGEST, ASSIMILATE, 5 412
OF TASTING THOSE FAIR APPLES, I RESOLV'D 9 585
LEAST THOU NOT TASTING, DIFFERENT DEGREE 9 883
TO US, AS LIKELY TASTING TO ATTAINE 9 935
IF ANY BE, OF TASTING THIS FAIR FRUIT, 9 972
TRUE RELISH, TASTING; IF SUCH PLEASURE BE 9 1024

TAUGHT
THAT SHEPHERD, WHO FIRST TAUGHT THE CHOSEN SEED, 1 8
MEN ALSO, AND BY HIS SUGGESTION TAUGHT, 1 685
TAUGHT BY THE HEAV'NLY MUSE TO VENTURE DOWN 3 19
WHICH TAUGHT THEE YET NO BETTER, THAT NO PAIN 4 915
MADE VOCAL BY MY SONG, AND TAUGHT HIS PRAISE. 5 204
WELL HAST THOU TAUGHT THE WAY THAT MIGHT DIRECT 5 508
UNDER HIM REGENT, TELLS, AS HE WAS TAUGHT, 5 698
YET BY EXPERIENCE TAUGHT WE KNOW HOW GOOD, 5 826
AND FREED FROM INTRICACIES, TAUGHT TO LIVE, 8 182
TILL WARN'D, OR BY EXPERIENCE TAUGHT, SHE LEARNE, 8 190
GAVE ELOCUTION TO THE MUTE, AND TAUGHT 9 748
TO THAT FALSE WORM, OF WHOMSOEVER TAUGHT 9 1068
IN SYNOD UNBENIGNE, AND TAUGHT THE FIXT 10 661
WITH OTHER ECHO LATE I TAUGHT YOUR SHADES 10 861
THE RULE OF NOT TOO MUCH, BY TEMPERANCE TAUGHT 11 531
TAUGHT THEM, BUT THEY HIS GIFTS ACKNOWLEDG'D NONE, 11 612
CAME SEAVENS, AND PAIRS, AND ENTERD IN, AS TAUGHT 11 735
TAUGHT THIS BY HIS EXAMPLE WHOM I NOW 12 572

TAURIS
TO TAURIS OR CASBEEN. SO THESE THE LATE 10 436

TAURUS
IN SPRING TIME, WHEN THE SUN WITH TAURUS RIDES, 1 769
LIKE DISTANT BREADTH TO TAURUS WITH THE SEAV'N 10 673

TAWNIE
THE TAWNIE LION, PAWING TO GET FREE 7 464

TEACH
OUR MINDS AND TEACH US TO CAST OFF THIS YOKE? 5 786
SHALL TEACH US HIGHEST DEEDS, BY PROOF TO TRY 5 865
AND TEACH US FURTHER BY WHAT MEANS TO SHUN 10 1062
TO TEACH THEE THAT GOD ATTRIBUTES TO PLACE 11 836
TO TEACH ALL NATIONS WHAT OF HIM THEY LEARN'D 12 440
ALL NATIONS THEY SHALL TEACH; FOR FROM THAT DAY 12 446

TEACHER
O TEACHER, SOME GREAT MISCHIEF HATH BEFALL'N 11 450

TEACHERS
WOLVES SHALL SUCCEED FOR TEACHERS, GRIEVOUS WOLVES, 12 508

TEAR
BUT SILENTLY A GENTLE TEAR LET FALL 5 130

TEARES
THEY SATE THEM DOWN TO WEEP, NOR ONELY TEARES 9 1121

TEARMS
IRREPARABLE; TEARMS OF PEACE YET NONE 2 331

TEARS
OF HUMAN SACRIFICE, AND PARENTS TEARS, 1 393
TEARS SUCH AS ANGELS WEEP, BURST FORTH: AT LAST 1 620
NOT SO REPULST, WITH TEARS THAT CEAS'D NOT FLOWING, 10 910
HUMBLY OUR FAULTS, AND PARDON BEG, WITH TEARS 10 1089
HUMBLY THIR FAULTS, AND PARDON BEG'D, WITH TEARS 10 1101
FOR I BEHOLD THEM SOFTN'D AND WITH TEARS 11 110
HIS BEST OF MAN, AND GAVE HIM UP TO TEARS 11 497
THE WORLD ERELONG A WORLD OF TEARS MUST WEEPE. 11 627
ADAM WAS ALL IN TEARS, AND TO HIS GUIDE 11 674
OF TEARS AND SORROW A FLOUD THEE ALSO DROWN'D, 11 757
SURCHARG'D, AS HAD LIKE GRIEF BIN DEW'D IN TEARS, 12 373
SOM NATURAL TEARS THEY DROP'D, BUT WIP'D THEM SOON; 12 645

TEATS
THEN SMELL OF SWEETEST FENEL OR THE TEATS 9 581

TEDDED
THE SMELL OF GRAIN, OR TEDDED GRASS, OR KINE, 9 450

TEDIOUS
MORE SOLEMN THEN THE TEDIOUS POMP THAT WAITS 5 354
TEDIOUS ALIKE: OF FELLOWSHIP I SPEAK 8 389

TEDIOUS (CONTINUED)
WITH LONG AND TEDIOUS HAVOC FABL'D KNIGHTS 9 30
TEDIOUS, UNSHAR'D WITH THEE, AND ODIOUS SOON. 9 880

TEEM'D
OP'NING HER FERTIL WOOMB TEEM'D AT A BIRTH 7 454

TELASSAR
DWELT IN TELASSAR: IN THIS PLEASANT SOILE 4 214

TELL
DEEMING SOME ISLAND, OFT, AS SEA-MEN TELL, 1 205
THE REST WERE LONG TO TELL, THOUGH FAR RENOWN'D, 1 507
WHO BOAST IN MORTAL THINGS, AND WOND'RING TELL 1 693
PREVENTED SPARES TO TELL THEE YET BY DEEDS 2 739
WHOSE FOUNTAIN WHO SHALL TELL? BEFORE THE SUN, 3 8
PURGE AND DISPERSE, THAT I MAY SEE AND TELL 3 54
BY CENTER, OR ECCENTRIC, HARD TO TELL, 3 575
ALONE THUS WANDRING. BRIGHTEST SERAPH TELL 3 667
O SUN, TO TELL THEE HOW I HATE THY BEAMS 4 37
BUT RATHER TO TELL HOW, IF ART COULD TELL, 4 236
SPEAK YEE WHO BEST CAN TELL, YE SONS OF LIGHT, 5 160
HE SWERVE NOT TOO SECURE: TELL HIM WITHALL 5 238
TELL THEM THAT BY COMMAND, ERE YET DIM NIGHT 5 685
AND LONGER WILL DELAY TO HEARE THEE TELL 7 101
FOR MAN TO TELL HOW HUMAN LIFE BEGAN 8 250
AND YE THAT LIVE AND MOVE, FAIR CREATURES, TELL, 8 276
TELL, IF YE SAW, HOW CAME I THUS, HOW HERE? 8 277
TELL ME, HOW MAY I KNOW HIM, HOW ADORE, 8 280
EASIE TO MEE IT IS TO TELL THEE ALL 9 569
WITH PERIL GREAT ATCHIEV'D. LONG WERE TO TELL 10 469
WERE LONG TO TELL, HOW MANY BATTELS FOUGHT, 12 261

TELLING
THY MESSAGE, WHICH MIGHT ELSE IN TELLING WOUND, 11 299

TELLS
WHO TELLS OF SOM INFERNAL SPIRIT SEEN 4 793
UNDER HIM REGENT, TELLS, AS HE WAS TAUGHT, 5 698
TELLS THE SUGGESTED CAUSE, AND CASTS BETWEEN 5 702
HIS PLACE OF BIRTH A SOLEMN ANGEL TELLS 12 364

TELLST
THOU TELLST, BY MORROW DAWNING I SHALL KNOW. 4 588
ASSUR'D ME, AND STILL ASSURE: THOUGH WHAT THOU
TELLST 5 553

TEMIRS
AND SAMARCHAND BY OXUS, TEMIRS THRONE, 11 389

TEMPER
ETHEREAL TEMPER, MASSY, LARGE AND ROUND, 1 285
TO HIGHT OF NOBLEST TEMPER HERO'S OLD 1 552
IN TEMPER AND IN NATURE, WILL RECEIVE 2 218
AS SOFT AS NOW SEVERE, OUR TEMPER CHANG'D 2 276
INTO THEIR TEMPER; WHICH MUST NEEDS REMOVE 2 277
TEMPER OR NOURISH, OR IN PART SHED DOWN 4 670
TOUCH OF CELESTIAL TEMPER, BUT RETURNS 4 812
ON ME DERIV'D, YET I SHALL TEMPER SO 10 77
AND GRACIOUS TEMPER HE BOTH HEARD AND JUDG'D 10 1047
TRUE PATIENCE, AND TO TEMPER JOY WITH FEAR 11 361

TEMPERANCE
HER TEMPERANCE OVER APPETITE, TO KNOW 7 127
THE RULE OF NOT TOO MUCH, BY TEMPERANCE TAUGHT 11 531
MORE THEN ANOUGH, THAT TEMPERANCE MAY BE TRI'D: 11 805
JUSTICE AND TEMPERANCE, TRUTH AND FAITH FORGOT; 11 807
ADD VERTUE, PATIENCE, TEMPERANCE, ADD LOVE, 12 583

TEMPERAT
AND TEMPERAT VAPORS BLAND, WHICH TH' ONLY SOUND 5 5

TEMPERATE
BEGAN TO PARCH THAT TEMPERATE CLIME; WHEREAT 12 636

TEMPER'D
THOUGH TEMPER'D HEAV'NLY, FOR THAT MORTAL DINT, 2 813
TEMPER'D SOFT TUNINGS, INTERMIXT WITH VOICE 7 598

TEMPERD
WAS GIV'N HIM TEMPERD SO, THAT NEITHER KEEN 6 322
WITH HEAV'NS RAY, AND TEMPERD THEY SHOOT FORTH 6 480

TEMPERS
SHE TEMPERS DULCET CREAMS, NOR THESE TO HOLD 5 347

TEMPEST
CAUGHT IN A FIERIE TEMPEST SHALL BE HURL'D 2 180
AFTER THE TEMPEST; SUCH APPLAUSE WAS HEARD 2 290
OF GLIMMERING AIR LESS VEXT WITH TEMPEST LOUD: 3 429
WHICH HUNG NOT, BUT SO SWIFT WITH TEMPEST FELL 6 190
TEMPEST THE OCEAN: THERE LEVIATHAN 7 412

TEMPESTUOUS
WITH FLOODS AND WHIRLWINDS OF TEMPESTUOUS FIRE, 1 77
NOR LESS ON EITHER SIDE TEMPESTUOUS FELL 6 844
SHOULD PROVE TEMPESTUOUS: TO THE WINDS THEY SET 10 664

TEMPLE
HIS TEMPLE RIGHT AGAINST THE TEMPLE OF GOD 1 402
HER TEMPLE ON TH' OFFENSIVE MOUNTAIN, BUILT 1 443
IN HIS OWN TEMPLE, ON THE GRUNSEL EDGE, 1 460
AND DOWNWARD FISH: YET HAD HIS TEMPLE HIGH 1 463
VICE FOR IT SELF: TO HIM NO TEMPLE STOOD 1 492
BUILT LIKE A TEMPLE, WHERE PILASTERS ROUND 1 713
BRIGHT TEMPLE, TO AEGYPTIAN THEB'S HE FLIES. 5 274
AND TEMPLE OF HIS MIGHTIE FATHER THRON'D 6 890
THOUGH WIDE, AND THIS HIGH TEMPLE TO FREQUENT 7 148
WANDRING, SHALL IN A GLORIOUS TEMPLE ENSHRINE. 12 334
THIR CITIE, HIS TEMPLE, AND HIS HOLY ARK 12 340
UPON THE TEMPLE IT SELF: AT LAST THEY SEISE 12 356

TEMPLES
BEFORE ALL TEMPLES TH' UPRIGHT HEART AND PURE, 1 18
IN TEMPLES AND AT ALTARS, WHEN THE PRIEST 1 494
HIS LIVING TEMPLES, BUILT BY FAITH TO STAND, 12 527

TEMPORAL
THEN TEMPORAL DEATH SHALL BRUISE THE VICTORS HEEL, 12 433

TEMPRING
THY TEMPRING; WITH LIKE SAFETIE GUIDED DOWN 7 15

TEMPT
SUFFICIENT? WHO SHALL TEMPT WITH WANDRING FEET 2 404
TO TEMPT OR PUNISH MORTALS, EXCEPT WHOM 2 1032
AND TEMPT NOT THESE; BUT HAST'N TO APPEASE 5 846
MAY TEMPT IT, I EXPECTED NOT TO HEAR. 9 281
MIGHT TEMPT ALONE, AND IN HER EARS THE SOUND 9 736

TEMPTATION
AND ALL TEMPTATION TO TRANSGRESS REPEL. 8 643
AGAINST TEMPTATION: THOU THY SELF WITH SCORNE 9 299
SEEK NOT TEMPTATION THEN, WHICH TO AVOIDE 9 364
HIS FRAUDULENT TEMPTATION THUS BEGAN. 9 531

TEMPTATIONS
OR FROM WITHOUT, TO ALL TEMPTATIONS ARM'D. 4 65
BUT LIST'N NOT TO HIS TEMPTATIONS, WARNE 6 908

TEMPTED
WHICH TEMPTED OUR ATTEMPT, AND WROUGHT OUR FALL. 1 642
SELF-TEMPTED, SELF-DEPRAV'D: MAN FALLS DECEIV'D 3 130
THE TEMPTED WITH DISHONOUR FOUL, SUPPOS'D 9 297
WHOEVER TEMPTED; WHICH THEY NOT OBEYING, 10 14

TEMPTER
THE TEMPTER ERE TH' ACCUSER OF MAN-KIND, 4 10
SO GLOZ'D THE TEMPTER, AND HIS PROEM TUN'D; 9 549
TO WHOM THE GUILEFUL TEMPTER THUS REPLY'D. 9 567
TO WHOM THE TEMPTER GUILEFULLY REPLI'D. 9 655
THE TEMPTER, BUT WITH SHEW OF ZEALE AND LOVE 9 665
THE TEMPTER ALL IMPASSIOND THUS BEGAN. 9 678
WHEN FIRST THIS TEMPTER CROSS'D THE GULF FROM HELL. 10 39
US'D BY THE TEMPTER: ON THAT PROSPECT STRANGE 10 552
WHEREON FOR DIFFERENT CAUSE THE TEMPTER SET 11 382

TEMPTING
THE TEMPTING STREAM, WITH ONE SMALL DROP TO LOOSE 2 607
TEMPTING, STIRR'D IN ME SUDDEN APPETITE 8 308
TEMPTING AFFRONTS US WITH HIS FOUL ESTEEM 9 328
TEMPTING SO NIGH, TO PLUCK AND EAT MY FILL 9 595

TEMPTS
FOR HEE WHO TEMPTS, THOUGH IN VAIN, AT LEAST
ASPERSES 9 296

TEN
TEN THOUSAND BANNERS RISE INTO THE AIR 1 545
FIERCE AS TEN FURIES, TERRIBLE AS HELL, 2 671
TEN THOUSAND FADOM DEEP, AND TO THIS HOUR 2 934
BLOWS THEM TRANSVERSE TEN THOUSAND LEAGUES AWRY 3 488
TEN THOUSAND THOUSAND ENSIGNES HIGH ADVANC'D, 5 588
SUCH RUIN INTERCEPT: TEN PACES HUGE 6 193
ATTENDED WITH TEN THOUSAND THOUSAND SAINTS, 6 767
GRASPING TEN THOUSAND THUNDERS, WHICH HE SENT 6 836
SYMPHONIOUS OF TEN THOUSAND HARPES THAT TUN'D 7 559
FOR THIS ONE TREE HAD BIN FORBIDDEN TEN. 9 1026
THE POLES OF EARTH TWICE TEN DEGREES AND MORE 10 669
TEN THOUSANDFOULD THE SIN OF HIM WHO SLEW 11 678
OF EGYPT MUST LIE DEAD, THUS WITH TEN WOUNDS 12 190

TEND
CASTS PALE AND DREADFUL? THITHER LET US TEND 1 183
ALL HEAV'N, WHAT THIS MIGHT MEAN, AND WHITHER TEND 3 272
TO PRUNE THESE GROWING PLANTS, AND TEND THESE
FLOURS, 4 438
AND FLAMING MINISTERS TO WATCH AND TEND 9 156
THIS GARDEN, STILL TO TEND PLANT, HERB AND FLOUR, 9 206
THE WAY WHICH TO HER RUIN NOW I TEND. 9 493
UNSUCKT OF LAMB OR KID, THAT TEND THIR PLAY. 9 583
SHALL TEND THEE, AND THE FERTIL BURDEN EASE 9 801
STILL TEND FROM BAD TO WORSE, TILL GOD AT LAST 12 106

TENDANCE
AND TOUCHT BY HER FAIR TENDANCE GLADLIER GREW. 8 47

TENDANCE (CONTINUED)
THIR TENDANCE OR PLANTATION FOR DELIGHT, 9 419

TENDED
OUR TENDED PLANTS, HOW BLOWS THE CITRON GROVE, 5 22
TENDED THE SICK BUSIEST FROM COUCH TO COUCH; 11 490

TENDER
GRASING THE TENDER HERB, WERE INTERPOS'D, 4 253
BESTIRS HER THEN, AND FROM EACH TENDER STALK 5 337
BROUGHT FORTH THE TENDER GRASS, WHOSE VERDURE CLAD 7 315
NOT THEN MISTRUST, BUT TENDER LOVE ENJOYNES, 9 357
AT EEV'N, WHICH I BRED UP WITH TENDER HAND 11 276

TENDERLY
TENDERLY WEPT, MUCH WON THAT HE HIS LOVE 9 991

TENDING
AS NEERER TO HIM PLAC'T OR NEERER TENDING 5 476
TENDING TO WILDE. THOU THEREFORE NOW ADVISE 9 212
TO PARADISE FIRST TENDING, WHEN BEHOLD 10 326
TENDING TO SOME RELIEF OF OUR EXTREMES, 10 976

TENDRILS
AS THE VINE CURLES HER TENDRILS, WHICH IMPLI'D 4 307

TENDS
FAIR ANGEL, THY DESIRE WHICH TENDS TO KNOW 3 694
SHELTERS IN COOLE, AND TENDS HIS PASTURING HERDS 9 1109

TENERIFF
LIKE TENERIFF OR ATLAS UNREMOV'D: 4 987

TENFOLD
SO SPEAKING AND SO THREATNING, GREW TENFOLD 2 705
TENFOLD THE LENGTH OF THIS TERRENE: AT LAST 6 78
OF TENFOLD ADAMANT, HIS AMPLE SHIELD 6 255
AND FELT TENFOLD CONFUSION IN THIR FALL 6 872

TENOR
BUT STILL I SEE THE TENOR OF MANS WOE 11 632

TENT
THE HEAV'NLY FIRES; OVER THE TENT A CLOUD 12 256

TENTH
HE BACK RECOILD; THE TENTH ON BENDED KNEE 6 194

TENTS
THIR GLITTERING TENTS HE PASSD, AND NOW IS COME 5 291
THESE WICKED TENTS DEVOTED, LEAST THE WRAUTH 5 890
WERE TENTS OF VARIOUS HUE; BY SOME WERE HERDS 11 557
LONG HAD NOT WALKT, WHEN FROM THE TENTS BEHOLD 11 581
WITH FEAST AND MUSICK ALL THE TENTS RESOUND. 11 592
THOSE TENTS THOU SAWST SO PLEASANT, WERE THE TENTS 11 607
CONTENDING, AND REMOV'D HIS TENTS FARR OFF; 11 727
CANAAN HE NOW ATTAINS, I SEE HIS TENTS 12 135
THE CLOUDED ARK OF GOD TILL THEN IN TENTS 12 333

TEPID
MEAN WHILE THE TEPID CAVES, AND FENS AND SHOARES 7 417

TERF
HAVE HEAP'D THIS TABLE, RAIS'D OF GRASSIE TERF 5 391

TERFE
OF GRASSIE TERFE, AND PILE UP EVERY STONE 11 324

TERMS
AND BREST, (WHAT COULD WE MORE?) PROPOUNDED TERMS 6 612
LEADER, THE TERMS WE SENT WERE TERMS OF WEIGHT, 6 621
THOUGH IN MYSTERIOUS TERMS, JUDG'D AS THEN BEST: 10 173
THY TERMS TOO HARD, BY WHICH I WAS TO HOLD 10 751
THOSE TERMS WHATEVER, WHEN THEY WERE PROPOS'D: 10 757

TERNATE
OF TERNATE AND TIDORE, WHENCE MERCHANTS BRING 2 639

TERRENE
TENFOLD THE LENGTH OF THIS TERRENE: AT LAST 6 78

TERRESTRIAL
PRODUCES WITH TERRESTRIAL HUMOR MIXT 3 610
TO THE TERRESTRIAL MOON BE AS A STARR 8 142
TERRESTRIAL HEAV'N, DANC'T ROUND BY OTHER HEAV'NS 9 103
HEROIC BUILT, THOUGH OF TERRESTRIAL MOULD, 9 485

TERRIBLE
FIERCE AS TEN FURIES, TERRIBLE AS HELL, 2 671
THAT DAR'ST, THOUGH GRIM AND TERRIBLE, ADVANCE 2 682
PRESENTED STOOD IN TERRIBLE ARRAY 6 106
BY TERRIBLE EXAMPLE THE REWARD 6 910
NOT TERRIBLE, THOUGH TERROUR BE IN LOVE 9 490
INVESTS HIM COMING? YET NOT TERRIBLE, 11 233
MORE TERRIBLE AT TH' ENTRANCE THEN WITHIN. 11 470

TERRIFIC
AND HAIRIE MAIN TERRIFIC, THOUGH TO THEE 7 497

TERRIFI'D
THE SON OF GOD TO JUDGE THEM TERRIFI'D 10 338

TERRIFIE
WARR TERRIFIE THEM INEXPERT, AND FEARE 12 218

TERRITORIE
HE LOOKD AND SAW WIDE TERRITORIE SPRED 11 638

TERROR
TERROR OF HEAV'N, THOUGH FALL'N; INTEND AT HOME, . 2 457
MEDUSA WITH GORGONIAN TERROR GUARDS 2 611
ABANDOND AT THE TERROR OF THY POWER 6 134
WITH TERROR THROUGH THE DARK AEREAL HALL. . . . 10 667
ALL THINGS WITH DOUBLE TERROR: ON THE GROUND . . 10 850
BEWAILING THIR EXCESS, ALL TERROR HIDE. 11 111
AND TERROR CEASE; HE GRANTS WHAT THEY BESAUGHT . 12 238

TERRORS
WITH TERRORS AND WITH CLAMORS COMPASST ROUND . . . 2 862
THY TERRORS, AS I PUT THY MILDNESS ON, ... 6 735
WITH TERRORS AND WITH FURIES TO THE BOUNDS . . . 6 859

TERROUR
WHO FROM THE TERROUR OF THIS ARM SO LATE 1 113
SO SPAKE THE GRIESLIE TERROUR, AND IN SHAPE, . . . 2 704
BE SURE, AND TERROUR SEIS'D THE REBEL HOST, . . . 6 647
SO SPAKE THE SON, AND INTO TERROUR CHANG'D . . . 6 824
NOT TERRIBLE, THOUGH TERROUR BE IN LOVE 9 490
OF TERROUR, FOUL AND UGLY TO BEHOLD, ... 11 464

TERROURS
AFRESH WITH CONSCIOUS TERROURS VEX ME ROUND, . . . 2 801

TESTIFI'D
AND TESTIFI'D AGAINST THIR WAYES; HEE OFT . . . 11 721

TESTIFIES
AS THIS PLACE TESTIFIES, AND THIS DIRE CHANGE . . 1 625

TESTIMONIE
AND FOR THE TESTIMONIE OF TRUTH HAST BORN 6 33

TESTIMONY
AN ARK, AND IN THE ARK HIS TESTIMONY, ... 12 251

TEXTURE
NOR IN THIR LIQUID TEXTURE MORTAL WOUND 6 348
OF RICHEST TEXTURE SPRED, AT TH' UPPER END . . . 10 446

THAMMUZ
TO IDOLS FOUL. THAMMUZ CAME NEXT BEHIND, ... 1 446
OF THAMMUZ YEARLY WOUNDED: THE LOVE-TALE 1 452

THAMYRIS
BLIND THAMYRIS AND BLIND MAEONIDES, ... 3 35

THAN
THAN HELLS DREAD EMPEROUR WITH POMP SUPREAM, . . . 2 510
THAN FABLES YET HAVE FEIGN'D, OR FEAR CONCEIV'D, . 2 627
WITHIN UNSEEN. FARR LESS ABHORRD THAN THESE . . . 2 659

THANK
THANK HIM WHO PUTS ME LOATH TO THIS REVENGE . . . 4 386
FOR THIS WE MAY THANK ADAM; BUT HIS THANKS . . . 10 736

THANKS
THE EASIEST RECOMPENCE, AND PAY HIM THANKS, . . . 4 47
AND DAILY THANKS, I CHIEFLY WHO ENJOY 4 445
IMMORTAL THANKS, AND HIS ADMONISHMENT 7 77
WHAT THANKS SUFFICIENT, OR WHAT RECOMPENCE 8 5
FOR THIS WE MAY THANK ADAM; BUT HIS THANKS . . . 10 736

THAW
MORE HARD'ND AFTER THAW, TILL IN HIS RAGE 12 194

THAWS
THAWS NOT, BUT GATHERS HEAP, AND RUIN SEEMS . . . 2 590

THEATRE
SHADE ABOVE SHADE, A WOODIE THEATRE 4 141

THEB'S
THAT FOUGHT AT THEB'S AND ILIUM, ON EACH SIDE . . 1 578
BRIGHT TEMPLE, TO AEGYPTIAN THEB'S HE FLIES. . . 5 274

THEMIS
OF THEMIS STOOD DEVOUT. TO HEAV'N THIR PRAYERS . 11 14

THEN
HE WITH HIS THUNDER: AND TILL THEN WHO KNEW . . . 1 93
THEN SUCH COULD HAV OREPOW'RD SUCH FORCE AS OURS) 1 145
WHAT CAN IT THEN AVAIL THOUGH YET WE FEEL . . . 1 153
WHOM WE RESIST. IF THEN HIS PROVIDENCE 1 162
THEN WITH EXPANDED WINGS HE STEARS HIS FLIGHT . . 1 225
SAID THEN THE LOST ARCH-ANGEL, THIS THE SEAT . . 1 243
AND WHAT I SHOULD BE, ALL BUT LESS THEN HE . . . 1 257
BETTER TO REIGN IN HELL, THEN SERVE IN HEAV'N. . 1 263

THEN (CONTINUED)
BUT WHEREFORE LET WE THEN OUR FAITHFUL FRIENDS, . 1 264
THEN WERE THEY KNOWN TO MEN BY VARIOUS NAMES, . . 1 374
SAY, MUSE, THIR NAMES THEN KNOWN, WHO FIRST, WHO LAST, ... 1 376
RATHER THEN HUMAN. NOR DID ISRAEL SCAPE . . . 1 482
BELIAL CAME LAST, THEN WHOM A SPIRIT MORE LEWD . 1 490
OR ALTAR SMOAK'D; YET WHO MORE OFT THEN HEE . . 1 493
DARKENS THE STREETS, THEN WANDER FORTH THE SONS . 1 501
GODS, YET CONFEST LATER THEN HEAV'N AND EARTH . . 1 509
THEN STRAIT COMMANDS THAT AT THE WARLIKE SOUND . 1 531
COULD MERIT MORE THEN THAT SMALL INFANTRY . . . 1 575
LESS THEN ARCH ANGEL RUIND, AND TH' EXCESS . . . 1 593
MONARCH IN HEAV'N, TILL THEN AS ONE SECURE . . . 1 638
FOR WHO CAN THINK SUBMISSION? WARR THEN, WARR . 1 661
THEN AUGHT DIVINE OR HOLY ELSE ENJOY'D 1 683
NOW LESS THEN SMALLEST DWARFS, IN NARROW ROOM . . 1 779
FREQUENT AND FULL. AFTER SHORT SILENCE THEN . . 1 797
MORE GLORIOUS AND MORE DREAD THEN FROM NO FALL, . 2 16
OF ENDLESS PAIN? WHERE THERE IS THEN NO GOOD . . 2 30
WILL COVET MORE. WITH THIS ADVANTAGE THEN . . . 2 35
MORE THEN CAN BE IN HEAV'N, WE NOW RETURN . . . 2 37
SURER TO PROSPER THEN PROSPERITY 2 39
EQUAL IN STRENGTH, AND RATHER THEN BE LESS . . . 2 47
WE SUNK THUS LOW? TH' ASCENT IS EASIE THEN; . . 2 81
THEN TO DWELL HERE, DRIV'N OUT FROM BLISS, CONDEMN'D 2 86
CALLS US TO PENANCE? MORE DESTROY'D THEN THUS . 2 92
WHAT FEAR WE THEN? WHAT DOUBT WE TO INCENSE . . 2 94
THEN MISERABLE TO HAVE ETERNAL BEING: 2 98
TO LESS THEN GODS. ON TH' OTHER SIDE UP ROSE . . 2 108
TO PUNISH ENDLESS? WHEREFORE CEASE WE THEN? . . 2 159
WHAT CAN WE SUFFER WORSE? IS THIS THEN WORST, . 2 163
THE DEEP TO SHELTER US? THIS HELL THEN SEEM'D . 2 167
THEN WISE TO FRUSTRATE ALL OUR PLOTS AND WILES. . 2 193
SHALL WE THEN LIVE THUS VILE, THE RACE OF HEAV'N . 2 194
CHAINS AND THESE TORMENTS? BETTER THESE THEN WORSE 2 196
OUR PURER ESSENCE THEN WILL OVERCOME 2 215
OUR OWN RIGHT LOST: HIM TO UNTHRONE WE THEN . . 2 231
TO WHOM WE HATE. LET US NOT THEN PURSUE . . . 2 249
THEN MOST CONSPICUOUS, WHEN GREAT THINGS OF SMALL, 2 258
THEY DREADED WORSE THEN HELL: SO MUCH THE FEAR . 2 293
WHICH WHEN BEELZEBUB PERCEIV'D, THEN WHOM, . . . 2 299
WHAT SIT WE THEN PROJECTING PEACE AND WARR? . . 2 329
THE HAPPY ILE; WHAT STRENGTH, WHAT ART CAN THEN . 2 410
THEN UNKNOWN DANGERS AND AS HARD ESCAPE. . . . 2 444
DREADED NOT MORE TH' ADVENTURE THEN HIS VOICE . . 2 474
THEN OF THIR SESSION ENDED THEY BID CRY 2 514
OF GOOD AND EVIL MUCH THEY ARGU'D THEN, ... 2 562
NOW SHAVES WITH LEVEL WING THE DEEP, THEN SOARES . 2 634
WHO FIRST BROKE PEACE IN HEAV'N AND FAITH, TILL THEN 2 690
OVER THE CASPIAN, THEN STAND FRONT TO FRONT . . . 2 716
FORBORE, THEN THESE TO HER SATAN RETURN'D: . . . 2 736
SIGHT MORE DETESTABLE THEN HIM AND THEE. . . . 2 745
HAST THOU FORGOT ME THEN, AND DO I SEEM 2 747
THEN SHINING HEAV'NLY FAIR, A GODDESS ARM'D . . . 2 757
INFLAM'D WITH LUST THEN RAGE) AND SWIFTER FAR, . 2 791
MY BOWELS, THIR REPAST; THEN BURSTING FORTH . . 2 800
THEN SWEET, NOW SAD TO MENTION, THROUGH DIRE CHANGE 2 820
THEN THIS MORE SECRET NOW DESIGN'D, I HASTE . . 2 838
COULD ONCE HAVE MOV'D; THEN IN THE KEY-HOLE TURNS 2 876
GREAT THINGS WITH SMALL) THEN WHEN BELLONA STORMS, 2 922
SOM CAPITAL CITY; OR LESS THEN IF THIS FRAME . . 2 924
AND MORE ENDANGER'D, THEN WHEN ARGO PASS'D . . . 2 1017
DWELT FROM ETERNITIE, DWELT THEN IN THEE, . . . 3 5
WITH OTHER NOTES THEN TO TH' ORPHEAN LYRE . . . 3 17
THEN FEED ON THOUGHTS, THAT VOLUNTARIE MOVE . . 3 37
IN BLISSFUL SOLITUDE; HE THEN SURVEY'D 3 69
BEHOLD MEE THEN, MEE FOR HIM, LIFE FOR LIFE . . 3 236
DEATH HIS DEATHS WOUND SHALL THEN RECEIVE, AND STOOP 3 252
THEN WITH THE MULTITUDE OF MY REDEEMD 3 260
BY MERIT MORE THEN BIRTHRIGHT SON OF GOD, . . . 3 309
FARR MORE THEN GREAT OR HIGH; BECAUSE IN THEE . . 3 311
LOVE HATH ABOUNDED MORE THEN GLORY ABOUNDS, . . 3 312
THEN ALL THY SAINTS ASSEMBL'D, THOU SHALT JUDGE . 3 330
THEN THOU THY REGAL SCEPTER SHALT LAY BY, . . . 3 339
FOR REGAL SCEPTER THEN NO MORE SHALL NEED, . . . 3 340
THEN CROWN'D AGAIN THIR GOLD'N HARPS THEY TOOK, . 3 365
LOVE NO WHERE TO BE FOUND LESS THEN DIVINE. . . 3 411
WITH MANY A VAIN EXPLOIT, THOUGH THEN RENOWND: . 3 465
INTO THE DEVIOUS AIR; THEN MIGHT YE SEE 3 489
AND FLUTTERD INTO RAGGS, THEN RELIQUES, BEADS, . 3 491
THE STAIRS WERE THEN LET DOWN, WHETHER TO DARE . 3 523
WIDER BY FARR THEN THAT OF AFTER-TIMES 3 529
BEYOND TH' HORIZON; THEN FROM POLE TO POLE . . . 3 560
IMAGIND RATHER OFT THEN ELSEWHERE SEEN, ... 3 599
WHAT WONDER THEN IF FIELDS AND REGIONS HERE . . 3 606
SWIFT TO THIR SEVERAL QUARTERS HASTED THEN . . . 3 714
THEN WHEN THE DRAGON, PUT TO SECOND ROUT, . . . 4 3
ONE STEP NO MORE THEN FROM HIMSELF CAN FLY . . . 4 22
THEN MUCH REVOLVING, THUS IN SIGHS BEGAN. . . . 4 31
WHAT COULD BE LESS THEN TO AFFORD HIM PRAISE, . . 4 46
INDEBTED AND DISCHARGD; WHAT BURDEN THEN? . . . 4 57
THEN HAPPIE; NO UNBOUNDED HOPE HAD RAIS'D . . . 4 60
THOU HADST; WHOM HAST THOU THEN OR WHAT TO ACCUSE, 4 67
BE THEN HIS LOVE ACCURST, SINCE LOVE OR HATE, . . 4 69

THEN (CONTINUED)

O THEN AT LAST RELENT: IS THERE NO PLACE	4	79
THEN TO SUBMIT, BOASTING I COULD SUBDUE	4	85
BY THEE, AND MORE THEN HALF PERHAPS WILL REIGNE;	4	112
SAW HIM DISFIGUR'D, MORE THEN COULD BEFALL	4	127
HE MARKD AND MAD DEMEANOUR, THEN ALONE,	4	129
OF STATELIEST VIEW. YET HIGHER THEN THIR TOPS	4	142
AND HIGHER THEN THAT WALL A CIRCLING ROW	4	146
THEN IN FAIR EVENING CLOUD, OR HUMID BOW,	4	151
THEN ASMODEUS WITH THE FISHIE FUME,	4	168
NOR THOSE MYSTERIOUS PARTS WERE THEN CONCEALD,	4	312
THEN WAS NOT GUILTIE SHAME, DISHONEST SHAME	4	313
OF THIR SWEET GARDNING LABOUR THEN SUFFIC'D	4	328
THEN FROM HIS LOFTIE STAND ON THAT HIGH TREE	4	395
THEN AS A TYGER, WHO BY CHANCE HATH SPI'D	4	403
STRAIT COUCHES CLOSE, THEN RISING CHANGES OFT	4	405
DEARER THY SELF THEN ALL; NEEDS MUST THE POWER	4	412
FROM US NO OTHER SERVICE THEN TO KEEP	4	420
EARTH, AIRE, AND SEA. THEN LET US NOT THINK HARD	4	432
INTO A LIQUID PLAIN, THEN STOOD UNMOV'D	4	455
THEN THAT SMOOTH WATRY IMAGE; BACK I TURND,	4	480
MORE HANDS THEN OURS TO LOP THIR WANTON GROWTH:	4	629
OF GRATEFUL EEVNING MILDE, THEN SILENT NIGHT	4	647
THESE THEN, THOUGH UNBEHELD IN DEEP OF NIGHT,	4	674
BROIDERD THE GROUND, MORE COLOUR'D THEN WITH STONE	4	702
MORE LOVELY THEN PANDORA, WHOM THE GODS	4	714
KNOW YE NOT THEN SAID SATAN, FILL'D WITH SCORN,	4	827
THAT GLORIE THEN, WHEN THOU NO MORE WAST GOOD,	4	838
LESS PAIN, LESS TO BE FLED, OR THOU THEN THEY	4	919
PATRON OF LIBERTY, WHO MORE THEN THOU	4	958
THEN WHEN I AM THY CAPTIVE TALK OF CHAINES,	4	970
PROUD LIMITARIE CHERUBE, BUT ERE THEN	4	971
NEITHER OUR OWN BUT GIV'N; WHAT FOLLIE THEN	4	1007
THEN HEAV'N PERMITS, NOR MINE, THOUGH DOUBLD NOW	4	1009
SHOT FORTH PECULIAR GRACES; THEN WITH VOICE	5	15
TO FIND THEE I DIRECTED THEN MY WALK;	5	49
MUCH FAIRER TO MY FANCIE THEN BY DAY:	5	53
OUR KNOWLEDGE OR OPINION; THEN RETIRES	5	108
BE NOT DISHEART'ND THEN, NOR CLOUD THOSE LOOKS	5	122
THEN WHEN FAIR MORNING FIRST SMILES ON THE WORLD,	5	124
MORE TUNEABLE THEN NEEDED LUTE OR HARP	5	151
THUS WONDROUS FAIR; THY SELF HOW WONDROUS THEN.	5	155
NOW ON THE POLAR WINDES, THEN WITH QUICK FANN	5	269
EARTHS INMOST WOMB, MORE WARMTH THEN ADAM NEEDS;	5	302
BESTIRS HER THEN, AND FROM EACH TENDER STALK	5	337
WANTS HER FIT VESSELS PURE, THEN STREWS THE GROUND	5	348
ACCOMPANI'D THEN WITH HIS OWN COMPLEAT	5	352
MORE SOLEMN THEN THE TEDIOUS POMP THAT WAITS	5	354
NONE CAN THEN HEAV'N SUCH GLORIOUS SHAPE CONTAIN;	5	362
TO VISIT THEE; LEAD ON THEN WHERE THY BOWRE	5	375
THEN WOOD-NYMPH, OR THE FAIREST GODDESS FEIGN'D	5	381
THEN WITH THESE VARIOUS FRUITS THE TREES OF GOD	5	390
DESERVING PARADISE. IF EVER, THEN,	5	446
THEN HAD THE SONS OF GOD EXCUSE TO HAVE BIN	5	447
WONDER NOT THEN, WHAT GOD FOR YOU SAW GOOD	5	491
OBEDIENT? CAN WE WANT OBEDIENCE THEN	5	514
DIVINE INSTRUCTER, I HAVE HEARD, THEN WHEN	5	546
EACH TO OTHER LIKE, MORE THEN ON EARTH IS THOUGHT?	5	576
THEN MOST, WHEN MOST IRREGULAR THEY SEEM,	5	624
THEN ALL THIS GLOBOUS EARTH IN PLAIN OUT SPRED,	5	649
BOTH WAKING WE WERE ONE; HOW THEN CAN NOW	5	678
THEN WHAT THIS GARDEN IS TO ALL THE EARTH,	5	752
WHO CAN IN REASON THEN OR RIGHT ASSUME	5	794
ABDIEL, THEN WHOM NONE WITH MORE ZEALE ADOR'D	5	805
RETURNS OUR OWN. CEASE THEN THIS IMPIOUS RAGE,	5	845
THAT WE WERE FORMD THEN SAIST THOU? AND THE WORK	5	853
WHO IS OUR EQUAL: THEN THOU SHALT BEHOLD	5	866
THEN WHO CREATED THEE LAMENTING LEARNE,	5	894
TO HAVE REPORTED: GLADLY THEN HE MIXT	6	21
OF TRUTH, IN WORD MIGHTIER THEN THEY IN ARMES;	6	32
THEN VIOLENCE: FOR THIS WAS ALL THY CARE	6	35
THEN SCORND THOU DIDST DEPART, AND TO SUBDUE	6	40
THEN LIGHTED FROM HIS GORGEOUS THRONE, FOR NOW	6	103
PREFER, AND PIETIE TO GOD, THOUGH THEN	6	144
RESOUNDED, AND HAD EARTH BIN THEN, ALL EARTH	6	218
A STANDING FIGHT, THEN SOARING ON MAIN WING	6	243
TORMENTED ALL THE AIR; ALL AIR SEEMD THEN	6	244
HENCE THEN, AND EVIL GO WITH THEE ALONG	6	275
ALL HIS RIGHT SIDE; THEN SATAN FIRST KNEW PAIN,	6	327
RECEIVE, NO MORE THEN CAN THE FLUID AIRE:	6	349
TWO POTENT THRONES, THAT TO BE LESS THEN GODS	6	366
THEN FIRST WITH FEAR SURPRIS'D AND SENSE OF PAINE	6	394
BUT PROVES NOT SO: THEN FALLIBLE, IT SEEMS,	6	428
OF EVIL THEN SO SMALL AS EASIE THINK	6	437
NO LESS THEN FOR DELIVERANCE WHAT WE OWE.	6	468
GO THEN THOU MIGHTIEST IN THY FATHERS MIGHT,	6	710
THEN SHALL THY SAINTS UNMIXT, AND FROM TH' IMPURE	6	742
KNOW THEN, THAT AFTER LUCIFER FROM HEAV'N	7	131
OF ANGELS, THEN THAT STARR THE STARRS AMONG)	7	133
THEN TIME OR MOTION, BUT TO HUMAN EARS	7	177
SAID THEN TH' OMNIFIC WORD, YOUR DISCORD END:	7	217
THEN STAID THE FERVID WHEELES, AND IN HIS HAND	7	224
ADVERSE TO LIFE: THEN FOUNDED, THEN CONGLOB'D	7	239
HE SCARCE HAD SAID, WHEN THE BARE EARTH, TILL THEN	7	313
THEN HERBS OF EVERY LEAF, THAT SUDDEN FLOUR'D	7	317
THOUGH OF ETHEREAL MOULD: THEN FORM'D THE MOON	7	356
TILL NIGHT, THEN IN THE EAST HER TURN SHE SHINES,	7	380
WITH THOUSAND THOUSAND STARRES, THAT THEN APPEER'D	7	383

THEN (CONTINUED)

SPANGLING THE HEMISPHERE: THEN FIRST ADORND	7	384
TILL EV'N, NOR THEN THE SOLEMN NIGHTINGAL	7	435
HIS HINDER PARTS, THEN SPRINGS AS BROKE FROM BONDS,	7	465
FEMALE FOR RACE; THEN BLESS'D MANKINDE, AND SAID,	7	530
THEN FROM THE GIANT ANGELS; THEE THAT DAY	7	605
IS GREATER THEN CREATED TO DESTROY.	7	607
THEN AS NEW WAK'T THUS GRATEFULLY REPLI'D.	8	4
SERV'D BY MORE NOBLE THEN HER SELF, ATTAINES	8	34
MORE PLENTY THEN THE SUN THAT BARREN SHINES,	8	94
THIR WANDRING COURSE NOW HIGH, NOW LOW, THEN HID,	8	126
AND DAY IS YET NOT SPENT; TILL THEN THOU SEEST	8	206
THEN FRUITS OF PALM-TREE PLEASANTEST TO THIRST	8	212
THEN OF OUR FELLOW SERVANT, AND INQUIRE	8	225
NOISE, OTHER THEN THE SOUND OF DANCE OR SONG,	8	243
PLEAS'D WITH THY WORDS NO LESS THEN THOU WITH MINE.	8	248
MY SELF I THEN PERUS'D, AND LIMB BY LIMB	8	267
NOT OF MY SELF; BY SOME GREAT MAKER THEN,	8	278
AND FEEL THAT I AM HAPPIER THEN I KNOW.	8	282
I THEN WAS PASSING TO MY FORMER STATE	8	290
ABOVE MANKINDE, OR AUGHT THEN MANKINDE HIGHER,	8	358
WORS THEN CAN MAN WITH BEAST, AND LEAST OF ALL.	8	397
WHAT THINKST THOU THEN OF MEE, AND THIS MY STATE,	8	403
HOW HAVE I THEN WITH WHOM TO HOLD CONVERSE	8	408
AND NO SUCH COMPANIE AS THEN THOU SAW'ST	8	446
MORE THEN ENOUGH; AT LEAST ON HER BESTOW'D	8	537
THEN VALUE: OFT TIMES NOTHING PROFITS MORE	8	571
THEN SELF ESTEEM, GROUNDED ON JUST AND RIGHT	8	572
MORE GRATEFUL THEN HARMONIOUS SOUND TO THE EARE.	8	606
BEAR WITH ME THEN, IF LAWFUL WHAT I ASK;	8	614
EASIER THEN AIR WITH AIR, IF SPIRITS EMBRACE,	8	626
NOT LESS BUT MORE HEROIC THEN THE WRAUTH	9	14
AT JOUST AND TORNEAMENT; THEN MARSHAL'D FEAST	9	37
SATAN INVOLV'D IN RISING MIST, THEN SOUGHT	9	75
IN WO THEN; THAT DESTRUCTION WIDE MAY RANGE:	9	134
NOT LONGER THEN SINCE I IN ONE NIGHT FREED	9	140
FROM DUST: SPITE THEN WITH SPITE IS BEST REPAID.	9	178
THEN COMMUNE HOW THAT DAY THEY BEST MAY PLY	9	201
IN WOMAN, THEN TO STUDIE HOUSHOLD GOOD,	9	233
CONJUGAL LOVE, THEN WHICH PERHAPS NO BLISS	9	263
JUST THEN RETURND AT SHUT OF EVENING FLOURS.	9	278
HIS FRAUD IS THEN THY FEAR, WHICH PLAIN INFERRS	9	285
THOUGH INEFFECTUAL FOUND: MISDEEM NOT THEN,	9	301
FOUL ON HIMSELF; THEN WHEREFORE SHUND OR FEARD	9	331
LET US NOT THEN SUSPECT OUR HAPPIE STATE	9	337
NOT THEN MISTRUST, BUT TENDER LOVE ENJOYNES,	9	357
SEEK NOT TEMPTATION THEN, WHICH TO AVOIDE	9	364
US BOTH SECURER THEN THUS WARND THOU SEEMST,	9	371
WITH THY PERMISSION THEN, AND THUS FOREWARND	9	378
THEN VOLUBLE AND BOLD, NOW HID, NOW SEEN	9	436
SPOT MORE DELICIOUS THEN THOSE GARDENS FEIGN'D	9	439
OF PLEASURE NOT FOR HIM ORDAIN'D; THEN SOON	9	470
TO ME IS LOST. THEN LET ME NOT LET PASS	9	479
THEN AT CIRCEAN CALL THE HERD DISGUIS'D.	9	522
REDOUBLE THEN THIS MIRACLE, AND SAY,	9	562
THEN SMELL OF SWEETEST FENEL OR THE TEATS	9	581
LEAD THEN, SAID EVE. HEE LEADING SWIFTLY ROWLD	9	631
INDEED? HATH GOD THEN SAID THAT OF THE FRUIT	9	656
AND LIFE MORE PERFET HAVE ATTAIND THEN FATE	9	689
MEANT MEE, BY VENTRING HIGHER THEN MY LOT.	9	690
NOT JUST, NOT GOD; NOT FEARD THEN, NOR OBEYD:	9	701
WHY THEN WAS THIS FORBID? WHY BUT TO AWE,	9	703
YET ARE BUT DIM, SHALL PERFETLY BE THEN	9	707
THOUGH THREAT'ND, WHICH NO WORSE THEN THIS CAN BRING.	9	715
GODDESS HUMANE, REACH THEN, AND FREELY TASTE.	9	732
FORBIDS US THEN TO TASTE, BUT HIS FORBIDDING	9	753
IN PLAIN THEN, WHAT FORBIDS HE BUT TO KNOW,	9	758
BIND US WITH AFTER-BANDS, WHAT PROFITS THEN	9	761
IRRATIONAL TILL THEN. FOR US ALONE	9	766
WHAT FEAR I THEN, RATHER WHAT KNOW TO FEARE	9	773
OF VERTUE TO MAKE WISE: WHAT HINDERS THEN	9	778
REGARDED, SUCH DELIGHT TILL THEN, AS SEEMD,	9	787
AND DEATH ENSUE? THEN I SHALL BE NO MORE,	9	827
A DEATH TO THINK. CONFIRM'D THEN I RESOLVE,	9	830
DISJOYNE US, AND I THEN TOO LATE RENOUNCE	9	884
RATHER THEN DEATH OR AUGHT THEN DEATH MORE DREAD	9	969
DESERTED, THEN OBLIGE THEE WITH A FACT	9	980
THEN EVER, BOUNTIE OF THIS VERTUOUS TREE.	9	1033
TILL ADAM, THOUGH NOT LESS THEN EVE ABASH'T,	9	1065
BE SURE THEN. HOW SHALL I BEHOLD THE FACE	9	1080
I KNOW NOT WHENCE POSSESSD THEE; WE HAD THEN	9	1137
SUCH PROOF, CONCLUDE, THEY THEN BEGIN TO FAILE.	9	1142
TOO FACIL THEN THOU DIDST NOT MUCH GAINSAY,	9	1158
TO WHOM THEN FIRST INCENST ADAM REPLI'D,	9	1162
BUT CONFIDENCE THEN BORE THEE ON, SECURE	9	1175
I TOLD YE THEN HE SHOULD PREVAIL AND SPEED	10	40
OF HIS CREATION; JUSTLY THEN ACCURST,	10	168
THOUGH IN MYSTERIOUS TERMS, JUDG'D AS THEN BEST:	10	173
SO SPAKE THIS ORACLE, THEN VERIFI'D	10	182
PRINCE OF THE AIRE; THEN RISING FROM HIS GRAVE	10	185
REMOV'D FARR OFF; THEN PITTYING HOW THEY STOOD	10	211
THEN BOTH FROM OUT HELL GATES INTO THE WASTE	10	282
THEN SUFFERD. TH' OTHER WAY SATAN WENT DOWN	10	414
NOW DRAGON GROWN, LARGER THEN WHOM THE SUN	10	529
CLIMBING, SAT THICKER THEN THE SNAKIE LOCKS	10	559
THEN STIL AT HELS DARK THRESHOLD TO HAVE SATE WATCH,	10	594

THEN (CONTINUED)

THEN HEAV'N AND EARTH RENEWD SHALL BE MADE PURE 10 638
TILL THEN THE CURSE PRONOUNC'T ON BOTH PRECEDES. 10 640
INHABITED, THOUGH SINLESS, MORE THEN NOW, 10 690
OF GOD, WHOM TO BEHOLD WAS THEN MY HIGHTH 10 724
I THUS CONTEST; THEN SHOULD HAVE BEEN REFUSD 10 756
THEN CAVIL THE CONDITIONS? AND THOUGH GOD 10 759
THY PUNISHMENT THEN JUSTLY IS AT HIS WILL. 10 768
WITH THIS CORPOREAL CLOD; THEN IN THE GRAVE, 10 786
ALL OF ME THEN SHALL DIE: LET THIS APPEASE 10 792
WITH ME? HOW CAN THEY THEN ACQUITTED STAND 10 827
THAT BURDEN HEAVIER THEN THE EARTH TO BEAR 10 835
THEN ALL THE WORLD MUCH HEAVIER, THOUGH DIVIDED 10 836
RATHER THEN SOLID VERTU, ALL BUT A RIB 10 884
MANKIND? THIS MISCHIEF HAD NOT THEN BEFALL'N, 10 895
ON ME ALREADIE LOST, MEE THEN THY SELF 10 929
AND TORMENT LESS THEN NONE OF WHAT WE DREAD, 10 998
THEN BOTH OUR SELVES AND SEED AT ONCE TO FREE 10 999
AND EXCELLENT THEN WHAT THY MINDE CONTEMNES; 10 1015
HATH WISELIER ARM'D HIS VENGEFUL IRE THEN SO 10 1023
TO MAKE DEATH IN US LIVE: THEN LET US SEEK 10 1028
NO MORE BE MENTION'D THEN OF VIOLENCE 10 1041
WHAT BETTER CAN WE DO, THEN TO THE PLACE 10 1086
THEN LOUDEST ORATORIE: YET THIR PORT 11 8
SEEM'D THIR PETITION, THEN WHEN TH' ANCIENT PAIR 11 10
IN FABLES OLD, LESS ANCIENT YET THEN THESE, 11 11
DIMENTIONLESS THROUGH HEAV'NLY DORES; THEN CLAD 11 17
SOW'N WITH CONTRITION IN HIS HEART, THEN THOSE 11 27
MY MOTIONS IN HIM, LONGER THEN THEY MOVE, 11 91
SPANGL'D WITH EYES MORE NUMEROUS THEN THOSE 11 130
OF ARGUS, AND MORE WAKEFUL THEN TO DROUZE, 11 131
WHICH THEN NOT MINDED IN DISMAY, YET NOW 11 156
FIRST HUNTER THEN, PURSU'D A GENTLE BRACE, 11 188
SOME DAYS; HOW LONG, AND WHAT TILL THEN OUR LIFE, 11 198
WHO KNOWS, OR MORE THEN THIS, THAT WE ARE DUST, 11 199
LIVELIER THEN MELIBOEAN, OR THE GRAINE 11 242
THEN DUE BY SENTENCE WHEN THOU DIDST TRANSGRESS, 11 253
MAYST COVER: WELL MAY THEN THY LORD APPEAS'D 11 257
O UNEXPECTED STROKE, WORSE THEN OF DEATH. 11 268
NO MORE AVAILES THEN BREATH AGAINST THE WINDE, 11 312
NO DESPICABLE GIFT; SURMISE NOT THEN 11 340
HAD BRED; THEN PURG'D WITH EUPHRASIE AND RUE 11 414
CHOICEST AND BEST; THEN SACRIFICING, LAID 11 438
MORE TERRIBLE AT TH' ENTRANCE THEN WITHIN. 11 470
THIR MAKERS IMAGE, ANSWERD MICHAEL, THEN 11 515
THIS IS OLD AGE; BUT THEN THOU MUST OUTLIVE 11 538
TO WITHERD WEAK AND GRAY; THY SENSES THEN 11 540
FIRST HIS OWN TOOLES; THEN, WHAT MIGHT ELSE BE
WROUGHT 11 572
LOVES HARBINGER APPEERD; THEN ALL IN HEAT 11 589
HYMEN, THEN FIRST TO MARRIAGE RITES INVOK'T; 11 591
OF PEACEFUL DAYES PORTENDS, THEN THOSE TWO PAST; 11 600
THEN FROM THE MOUNTAIN HEWING TIMBER TALL, 11 728
HOW DIDST THOU GRIEVE THEN, ADAM, TO BEHOLD 11 754
IN APPREHENSION THEN IN SUBSTANCE FEEL 11 775
ALL WOULD HAVE THEN GON WELL, PEACE WOULD HAVE
CROWND 11 781
PEACE TO CORRUPT NO LESS THEN WARR TO WASTE. 11 784
MORE THEN ANOUGH, THAT TEMPERANCE MAY BE TRI'D: 11 805
ABOVE THE HIGHEST HILLS: THEN SHALL THIS MOUNT 11 829
THEN WITH UPLIFTED HANDS, AND EYES DEVOUT, 11 863
OF WICKED SONS DESTROYD, THEN I REJOYCE 11 875
THEN WITH TRANSITION SWEET NEW SPEECH RESUMES. 12 5
MAN TILL THEN FREE. THEREFORE SINCE HEE PERMITS 12 90
THEN THROUGH THE FIREY PILLAR AND THE CLOUD 12 208
BY JUDGES FIRST, THEN UNDER KINGS; OF WHOM 12 320
THE CLOUDED ARK OF GOD TILL THEN IN TENTS 12 333
THE SPACE OF SEVENTIE YEARS, THEN BRINGS THEM BACK, 12 345
THEN LOOSE IT TO A STRANGER, THAT THE TRUE 12 358
THEN TEMPORAL DEATH SHALL BRUISE THE VICTORS HEEL, 12 433
LONGER ON EARTH THEN CERTAINE TIMES TO APPEER 12 437
THEN TO THE HEAV'N OF HEAV'NS HE SHALL ASCEND 12 451
THEN ENTER INTO GLORY, AND RESUME 12 456
WHETHER IN HEAV'N OR EARTH, FOR THEN THE EARTH 12 463
THEN THIS OF EDEN, AND FAR HAPPIER DAIES. 12 465
SO SPAKE TH' ARCHANGEL MICHAEL, THEN PAUS'D, 12 466
THEN THAT WHICH BY CREATION FIRST BROUGHT FORTH 12 472
THE ENEMIES OF TRUTH; WHO THEN SHALL GUIDE 12 482
WORS WITH HIS FOLLOWERS THEN WITH HIM THEY DEALT? 12 484
TO EVANGELIZE THE NATIONS, THEN ON ALL 12 499
THEN SHALL THEY SEEK TO AVAIL THEMSELVES OF NAMES, 12 515
SHALL ON THE HEART ENGRAVE. WHAT WILL THEY THEN 12 524
THE WOMANS SEED, OBSCURELY THEN FORETOLD, 12 543
SATAN WITH HIS PERVERTED WORLD, THEN RAISE 12 547
OF ALL THE REST: THEN WILT THOU NOT BE LOATH 12 585
TO THE SUBJECTED PLAINE; THEN DISAPPEER'D. 12 640

THENCE

FAST BY THE ORACLE OF GOD; I THENCE 1 12
AND THENCE IN HEAV'N CALL'D SATAN, WITH BOLD WORDS 1 82
CHAIN'D ON THE BURNING LAKE, NOR EVER THENCE 1 210
AND FEWEL'D ENTRALS THENCE CONCEIVING FIRE, 1 234
THE PLEASANT VALLY OF HINNOM, TOPHET THENCE 1 404
YET THENCE HIS LUSTFUL ORGIES HE ENLARG'D 1 415
TILL GOOD JOSIAH DROVE THEM THENCE TO HELL. 1 418
AND IDA KNOWN, THENCE ON THE SNOWY TOP 1 515
IF THENCE HE SCAPE INTO WHAT EVER WORLD, 2 442
THENCE MORE AT EASE THIR MINDS AND SOMWHAT RAIS'D 2 521

THENCE (CONTINUED)

PERIODS OF TIME, THENCE HURRIED BACK TO FIRE. 2 603
UPLIFTED SPURNS THE GROUND, THENCE MANY A LEAGUE 2 929
ALL USURPATION THENCE EXPELL'D, REDUCE 2 983
IRRADIATE, THERE PLANT EYES, ALL MIST FROM THENCE 3 53
THENCE UP HE FLEW, AND ON THE TREE OF LIFE 4 194
WATERD THE GARDEN; THENCE UNITED FELL 4 230
NOT DISTANT FAR FROM THENCE A MURMURING SOUND 4 453
MULTITUDES LIKE THY SELF, AND THENCE BE CALL'D 4 474
NO CREATURE THENCE: IF SPIRIT OF OTHER SORT, 4 582
LIKE GENTLE BREATHS FROM RIVERS PURE, THENCE RAISE 4 806
SINGLE AGAINST THEE WICKED, AND THENCE WEAK. 4 856
SPRINGS LIGHTER THE GREEN STALK, FROM THENCE THE
LEAVES 5 480
DEEP MALICE THENCE CONCEIVING AND DISDAIN, 5 666
INTO THIR VACANT ROOM, AND THENCE DIFFUSE 7 190
GOVERN THE REST, SELF-KNOWING, AND FROM THENCE 7 510
IS YET DISTINCT BY NAME, THENCE, AS THOU KNOW'ST 7 536
THENCE TO BEHOLD THIS NEW CREATED WORLD 7 554
THOU USEST, AND FROM THENCE CREAT'ST MORE GOOD. 7 616
TO SEE THAT NONE THENCE ISSU'D FORTH A SPIE, 8 233
FROM THENCE A RIB, WITH CORDIAL SPIRITS WARME; 8 466
WHAT INWARD THENCE I FEEL, NOT THEREFORE FOILD, 8 608
THAT KEPT THIR WATCH; THENCE FULL OF ANGUISH
DRIV'N, 9 62
AT DARIEN, THENCE TO THE LAND WHERE FLOWES 9 81
HIGH AND REMOTE TO SEE FROM THENCE DISTINCT 9 812
AND LEFT TO HER SELF, IF EVIL THENCE ENSUE, 9 1185
THENCE GATHERD HIS OWN DOOM, WHICH UNDERSTOOD 10 344
THERE DWELL AND REIGN IN BLISS, THENCE ON THE EARTH 10 399
PROTESTING FATE SUPREAME; THENCE HOW I FOUND 10 480
OF HIGH OLYMPUS, THENCE BY SATURN DRIV'N 10 583
UP TO THE TROPIC CRAB; THENCE DOWN AMAINE 10 675
FOUND SO ERRONEOUS, THENCE BY JUST EVENT 10 969
TO THEM AND TO THIR PROGENIE FROM THENCE 11 107
TO PAQUIN OF SINAEAN KINGS, AND THENCE 11 390
OR THENCE FROM NIGER FLOOD TO ATLAS MOUNT 11 402
ON EUROPE THENCE, AND WHERE ROME WAS TO SWAY 11 405
IN WHAT THOU EATST AND DRINKST, SEEKING FROM THENCE 11 532
DOWN TO THE VEINS OF EARTH, THENCE GLIDING HOT 11 568
HAD NOT A CLOUD DESCENDING SNATCH'D HIM THENCE 11 670
ALLURD THEM; THENCE FROM CUPS TO CIVIL BROILES. 11 718
WITH CLAMOR THENCE THE RAPID CURRENTS DRIVE 11 853
A MIGHTIE HUNTER THENCE HE SHALL BE STYL'D 12 33
LEFT IN CONFUSION, BABYLON THENCE CALL'D. 12 343
ABOVE ALL NAMES IN HEAV'N; AND THENCE SHALL COME, 12 458

THENCEFORTH

THENCEFORTH, BUT IN THY PRESENCE JOY ENTIRE. 3 265
THENCEFORTH SHALL BE FOR EVER SHUT. MEAN WHILE 3 333
THENCEFORTH TO SPECULATIONS HIGH OR DEEP 9 602
NOT DEAD, AS WE ARE THREATN'D, BUT THENCEFORTH 9 870
THENCEFORTH THE FORM OF SERVANT TO ASSUME, 10 214
THENCEFORTH SHALL PRACTICE HOW TO LIVE SECURE, 11 802
HIS HOLY EYES; RESOLVING FROM THENCEFORTH 12 109

THEOLOGIANS

OF THEOLOGIANS, BUT WITH KEEN DISPATCH 5 436

THEREAFTER

HE RECK'D NOT, AND THESE WORDS THEREAFTER SPAKE. 2 50

THEREAT

YOUR WONDER, WITH AN APPLE; HE THEREAT 10 487

THEREBY

THE WORKS OF GOD, THEREBY TO GLORIFIE 3 695
THEREBY REGAIND, BUT SAT DEVISING DEATH 4 197
AS I, THOUGH THEREBY WORSE TO ME REDOUND; 9 128
WITH SINFULNESS OF MEN; THEREBY TO LEARN 11 360
SUBDUING NATIONS, AND ACHIEVD THEREBY 11 792
THOUGH TO THE TYRANT THEREBY NO EXCUSE. 12 96

THEREFORE

WARR THEREFORE, OPEN OR CONCEAL'D, ALIKE 2 187
HIGH HONOURD SITS? GO THEREFORE MIGHTY POWERS, 2 456
NOT MEE. THEY THEREFORE AS TO RIGHT BELONGD, 3 111
BY THE OTHER FIRST: MAN THEREFORE SHALL FIND GRACE, 3 131
THOU THEREFORE WHOM THOU ONLY CANST REDEEM, 3 281
THEREFORE THY HUMILIATION SHALL EXALT 3 313
THIS KNOWS MY PUNISHER; THEREFORE AS FARR 4 103
I THEREFORE, I ALONE FIRST UNDERTOOK 4 935
GO THEREFORE, HALF THIS DAY AS FRIEND WITH FRIEND 5 229
ADAM, I THEREFORE CAME, NOR ART THOU SUCH 5 372
TO WHOM THE ANGEL. THEREFORE WHAT HE GIVES 5 404
THEREFORE ETERNAL SILENCE BE THIR DOOME. 6 385
ALL PATIENCE. HE WHO THEREFORE CAN INVENT 6 464
TWO DAYES ARE THEREFORE PAST, THE THIRD IS THINE; 6 699
THEREFORE TO MEE THIR DOOM HE HATH ASSIG'N'D; 6 817
OF ALL HIS WORKS: THEREFORE THE OMNIPOTENT 7 516
THEREFORE FROM THIS HIGH PITCH LET US DESCEND 8 198
ON MAN HIS EQUAL LOVE: SAY THEREFORE ON; 8 228
WHOSE FELLOWSHIP THEREFORE UNMEET FOR THEE 8 442
WHAT INWARD THENCE I FEEL, NOT THEREFORE FOILD, 8 608
TENDING TO WILDE. THOU THEREFORE NOW ADVISE 9 212
BUT THAT THOU SHOULDST MY FIRMNESS THEREFORE DOUBT 9 279
GOD THEREFORE CANNOT HURT YE, AND BE JUST; 9 700
THOU THEREFORE ALSO TASTE, THAT EQUAL LOT 9 881

THEREFORE (CONTINUED)
OF EASIE THOROUGH-FARE. THEREFORE WHILE I 10 393
THOU THEREFORE ON THESE HERBS, AND FRUITS, AND FLOURS 10 603
BUT SELF-DESTRUCTION THEREFORE SAUGHT, REFUTES 10 1016
FROM INNOCENCE. NOW THEREFORE BEND THINE EARE 11 30
SELF-LEFT. LEAST THEREFORE HIS NOW BOLDER HAND 11 93
THEREFORE TO HIS GREAT BIDDING I SUBMIT. 11 314
THEREFORE SO ABJECT IS THIR PUNISHMENT, 11 520
AND THEREFORE HATED, THEREFORE SO BESET 11 702
AGAINST INVADERS; THEREFORE COOLD IN ZEALE 11 801
THOU THEREFORE GIVE DUE AUDIENCE, AND ATTEND. 12 12
MAN TILL THEN FREE. THEREFORE SINCE HEE PERMITS 12 90
AND THEREFORE WAS LAW GIVEN THEM TO EVINCE 12 287
AND THEREFORE SHALL NOT MOSES, THOUGH OF GOD 12 307
OF HEAD OR HEEL: NOT THEREFORE JOYNES THE SON 12 388
LET US DESCEND NOW THEREFORE FROM THIS TOP 12 588

THEREIN
INTENDED TO CREATE, AND THEREIN PLANT 1 652
IN THE POURLIEUES OF HEAV'N, AND THEREIN PLAC'T 2 833
HEE HEAV'N OF HEAVENS AND ALL THE POWERS THEREIN 3 390
THAT IS, TO THY OBEDIENCE; THEREIN STAND. 5 522
BE BUT THE SHADDOW OF HEAV'N, AND THINGS THEREIN 5 575
POSSESS IT, AND ALL THINGS THAT THEREIN LIVE, 8 340
THEREIN ENJOY'D WERE WORTHY TO SUBDUE 8 584
OF ABSOLUTE PERFECTION, THEREIN MAN 10 483
BY MEN WHO THERE FREQUENT, OR THEREIN DWELL. 11 838
WITH MAN THEREIN OR BEAST; BUT WHEN HE BRINGS 11 895
OVER THE EARTH A CLOUD, WILL THEREIN SET 11 896
OF CEDAR, OVERLAID WITH GOLD, THEREIN 12 250

THEREOF
THE DAY THOU EAT'ST THEREOF, MY SOLE COMMAND 8 329
THEREOF, NOR SHALL YE TOUCH IT, LEAST YE DIE. 9 663
YE EATE THEREOF, YOUR EYES THAT SEEM SO CLEERE, 9 706
THAT WHOSO EATS THEREOF, FORTHWITH ATTAINS 9 724
I CHARG'D THEE, SAYING: THOU SHALT NOT EATE THEREOF, 10 200
SHALT EATE THEREOF ALL THE DAYS OF THY LIFE; 10 202
MUCH MORE, THAT MUCH MORE GOOD THEREOF SHALL SPRING, 12 476

THEREON
OR MONUMENT TO AGES, AND THEREON 11 326

THESSALIAN
THROUGH PAIN UP BY THE ROOTS THESSALIAN PINES, 2 544

THICK
THICK AS AUTUMNAL LEAVES THAT STROW THE BROOKS 1 302
AND BROKEN CHARIOT WHEELS, SO THICK BESTROWN 1 311
APPEAR'D, AND SERRIED SHIELDS IN THICK ARRAY 1 548
THICK SWARM'D, BOTH ON THE GROUND AND IN THE AIR, 1 767
THIR STATE AFFAIRS. SO THICK THE AERIE CROWD 1 775
THICK CLOUDS AND DARK DOTH HEAV'NS ALL-RULING SIRE 2 264
THROUGH THE STRICT SENTERIES AND STATIONS THICK 2 412
IN DARKNESS, WHILE THY HEAD FLAMES THICK AND FAST 2 754
SO THICK A DROP SERENE HATH QUENCHT THIR ORBS, 3 25
STOOD THICK AS STARRS, AND FROM HIS SIGHT RECEIV'D 3 61
NOW IN LOOSE GARLANDS THICK THROWN OFF, THE BRIGHT 3 362
IMBELLISHT, THICK WITH SPARKLING ORIENT GEMMES 3 507
ALOOFF THE VULGAR CONSTELLATIONS THICK, 3 577
BUT FURTHER WAY FOUND NONE, SO THICK ENTWIN'D, 4 174
OR IN THICK SHADE RETIR'D, FROM HIM TO DRAW 4 532
WITH PORTED SPEARS, AS THICK AS WHEN A FIELD 4 980
COVERD WITH THICK EMBATTELD SQUADRONS BRIGHT, 6 16
THIS DAY, FEAR NOT HIS FLIGHT; SO THICK A CLOUD 6 539
FLASHING THICK FLAMES, WHEELE WITHIN WHEELE UNDRAWN, 6 751
FORTH FLOURISH'T THICK THE CLUSTRING VINE, FORTH CREPT 7 320
AND SOWD WITH STARRS THE HEAV'N THICK AS A FIELD: 7 358
FROM THE THICK SHADE, AND ADAM TO HIS BOWRE. 8 653
HALF SPI'D, SO THICK THE ROSES BUSHING ROUND 9 426
WHERE HOUSES THICK AND SEWERS ANNOY THE AIRE, 9 446
THICK OVERHEAD WITH VERDANT ROOF IMBOWR'D 9 1038
OF HISSING THROUGH THE HALL, THICK SWARMING NOW 10 522
AND DIPSAS (NOT SO THICK SWARM'D ONCE THE SOIL 10 526

THICKER
CLIMBING, SAT THICKER THEN THE SNAKIE LOCKS 10 559

THICKEST
TILL THICKEST LEGIONS CLOSE; WITH FEATS OF ARMS 2 537
OF THICKEST COVERT WAS INWOVEN SHADE 4 693
WHERE ERST WAS THICKEST FIGHT, TH' ANGELIC THRONG, 6 308
INTO THE THICKEST WOOD, THERE SOON THEY CHOSE 9 1100
AT LOOPHOLES CUT THROUGH THICKEST SHADE: THOSE LEAVES 9 1110
THE THICKEST TREES, BOTH MAN AND WIFE, TILL GOD 10 101
THIR COURSE THROUGH THICKEST CONSTELLATIONS HELD 10 411

THICKET
WITH THICKET OVERGROWN, GOTTESQUE AND WILDE, 4 136
OF ECHOING HILL OR THICKET HAVE WE HEARD 4 681
IN FORREST WILDE, IN THICKET, BRAKE, OR DEN; 7 458
SO SAYING, THROUGH EACH THICKET DANCK OR DRIE, 9 179

THICKET (CONTINUED)
FAST BY A FOUNTAIN, ONE SMALL THICKET PAST 9 628
THAT ALL WAS LOST. BACK TO THE THICKET SLUNK 9 784

THICK'ND
SENT UP AMAIN; AND NOW THE THICK'ND SKIE 11 742

THICK-RAMMD
THICK-RAMMD, AT TH' OTHER BORE WITH TOUCH OF FIRE 6 485

THICK-WOV'N
AMONG THICK-WOV'N ARBORETS AND FLOURS 9 437

THIEF
OR AS A THIEF BENT TO UNHOORD THE CASH 4 188
SO CLOMB THIS FIRST GRAND THIEF INTO GODS FOULD: 4 192

THIGH
GIRD ON, AND SWORD UPON THY PUISSANT THIGH; 6 714

THIGHES
SKIRTED HIS LOINES AND THIGHES WITH DOWNIE GOLD 5 282

THIGHS
MILLIONS OF FLAMING SWORDS, DRAWN FROM THE THIGHS 1 664

THIN
HIMSELF AND HIS RASH ARMIE, WHERE THIN AIRE 12 76

THING
CREATED THING NAUGHT VALU'D HE NOR SHUN'D; 2 679
WHAT THING THOU ART, THUS DOUBLE-FORM'D, AND WHY 2 741
SOM DREADFUL THING NO DOUBT; FOR WELL THOU KNOWST 4 426
NO EVIL THING APPROACH OR ENTER IN; 4 563
AND EVERY CREEPING THING THAT CREEPS THE GROUND. 7 523
AND EVERY LIVING THING THAT MOVES ON THE EARTH. 7 534
ADJOYND, FROM EACH THING MET CONCEAVES DELIGHT, 9 449
OF DEATH DENOUNC'T, WHATEVER THING DEATH BE, 9 695
EACH THING ON EARTH; AND OTHER CARE PERHAPS 9 813
A THING NOT UNDESIREABLE, SOMTIME 9 824
NO HOMELY MORSELS, AND WHATEVER THING 10 605

THINGS
THINGS UNATTEMPTED YET IN PROSE OR RHIME. 1 16
ABOMINATIONS; AND WITH CURSED THINGS 1 389
WHO BOAST IN MORTAL THINGS, AND WOND'RING TELL 1 693
VIEWS ALL THINGS AT ONE VIEW? HE FROM HEAV'NS HIGHTH 2 190
THEN MOST CONSPICUOUS, WHEN GREAT THINGS OF SMALL, 2 258
THE SENSIBLE OF PAIN. ALL THINGS INVITE 2 278
GREAT THINGS RESOLV'D, WHICH FROM THE LOWEST DEEP 2 392
PERVERSE, ALL MONSTROUS, ALL PRODIGIOUS THINGS, 2 625
IMMEASURABLY, ALL THINGS SHALL BE YOUR PREY. 2 844
GREAT THINGS WITH SMALL) THEN WHEN BELLONA STORMS, 2 922
SAT SABLE-VESTED NIGHT, ELDEST OF THINGS, 2 962
OF THINGS INVISIBLE TO MORTAL SIGHT. 3 55
OF ALL THINGS MADE, AND JUDGEST ONELY RIGHT. 3 155
OF ALL THINGS TRANSITORIE AND VAIN, WHEN SIN 3 446
BOTH ALL THINGS VAIN, AND ALL WHO IN VAIN THINGS 3 448
HERE IN THE DARK SO MANY PRECIOUS THINGS 3 611
THAT BOTH IN HIM AND ALL THINGS, AS IS MEET, 3 675
THE GOOD BEFORE HIM, BUT PERVERTS BEST THINGS 4 203
FREE LEAVE SO LARGE TO ALL THINGS ELSE, AND CHOICE 4 434
HAD IN HER SOBER LIVERIE ALL THINGS CLAD; 4 599
OF NIGHT, AND ALL THINGS NOW RETIR'D TO REST 4 611
IN NATURE AND ALL THINGS, WHICH THESE SOFT FIRES 4 667
ALL THINGS TO MANS DELIGHTFUL USE; THE ROOFE 4 692
IN PARADISE OF ALL THINGS COMMON ELSE. 4 752
WHEREIN ALL THINGS CREATED FIRST HE WEIGHD, 4 999
SHADOWIE SETS OFF THE FACE OF THINGS; IN VAIN, 5 43
IN WHOSE SIGHT ALL THINGS JOY, WITH RAVISHMENT 5 46
HER OFFICE HOLDS; OF ALL EXTERNAL THINGS, 5 103
AND NOURISH ALL THINGS, LET YOUR CEASLESS CHANGE 5 183
OF THINGS ABOVE HIS WORLD, AND OF THIR BEING 5 455
ALL THINGS PROCEED, AND UP TO HIM RETURN, 5 470
OF SUBSTANCE, AND IN THINGS THAT LIVE, OF LIFE; 5 474
IN CONTEMPLATION OF CREATED THINGS 5 511
BE BUT THE SHADDOW OF HEAV'N, AND THINGS THEREIN 5 575
TO MOTION, MEASURES ALL THINGS DURABLE 5 581
ALL THINGS, EV'N THEE, AND ALL THE SPIRITS OF HEAV'N 5 837
WHO OUT OF SMALLEST THINGS COULD WITHOUT END 6 137
OF ANGELS, CAN RELATE, OR TO WHAT THINGS 6 298
GREAT THINGS BY SMALL, IF NATURES CONCORD BROKE, 6 311
THESE THINGS, AS NOT TO MIND FROM WHENCE THEY GROW 6 477
CONSULTING ON THE SUM OF THINGS, FORESEEN 6 673
OF ALL THINGS, TO BE HEIR AND TO BE KING 6 708
IMAGE OF THEE IN ALL THINGS; AND SHALL SOON, 6 736
THUS MEASURING THINGS IN HEAV'N BY THINGS ON EARTH 6 893
OF THINGS SO HIGH AND STRANGE, THINGS TO THIR THOUGHT 7 53
GREAT THINGS, AND FULL OF WONDER IN OUR EARES, 7 70
THINGS ABOVE EARTHLY THOUGHT, WHICH YET CONCERND 7 82
THINGS NOT REVEAL'D, WHICH TH' INVISIBLE KING, 7 122
THIS UNIVERSE, AND ALL CREATED THINGS: 7 227
LIKE THINGS TO LIKE, THE REST TO SEVERAL PLACE 7 240
ETHEREAL, FIRST OF THINGS, QUINTESSENCE PURE 7 244
CATTEL AND CREEPING THINGS, AND BEAST OF THE EARTH, 7 452

THINGS (CONTINUED)

AUTHOR AND END OF ALL THINGS, AND FROM WORK 7 591
HOW FIRST THIS WORLD AND FACE OF THINGS BEGAN, 7 636
THINGS ELSE BY ME UNSEARCHABLE, NOW HEARD 8 10
IF IT PRESUME, MIGHT ERRE IN THINGS TOO HIGH, 8 121
BUT WHETHER THUS THESE THINGS, OR WHETHER NOT, 8 159
THAT NOT TO KNOW AT LARGE OF THINGS REMOTE 8 191
AND RENDERS US IN THINGS THAT MOST CONCERNE 8 196
A LOWER FLIGHT, AND SPEAK OF THINGS AT HAND 8 199
BIRDS ON THE BRANCHES WARBLING; ALL THINGS SMIL'D, 8 265
POSSESS IT, AND ALL THINGS THAT THEREIN LIVE, 8 340
THOU HAST PROVIDED ALL THINGS: BUT WITH MEE 8 363
ALL HUMAN THOUGHTS COME SHORT, SUPREAM OF THINGS; 8 414
AND INTO ALL THINGS FROM HER AIRE INSPIR'D 8 476
GIVER OF ALL THINGS FAIRE, BUT FAIREST THIS 8 493
IN ALL THINGS ELSE DELIGHT INDEED, BUT SUCH 8 524
BY ATTRIBUTING OVERMUCH TO THINGS 8 565
TO BASEST THINGS. REVENGE, AT FIRST THOUGH SWEET, 9 171
THIR MORNING INCENSE, WHEN ALL THINGS THAT BREATH, 9 194
O WOMAN, BEST ARE ALL THINGS AS THE WILL 9 343
AND ALL THINGS IN BEST ORDER TO INVITE 9 402
THEE ALL THINGS LIVING GAZE ON, ALL THINGS THINE 9 539
CONSIDERD ALL THINGS VISIBLE IN HEAV'N, 9 604
OR EARTH, OR MIDDLE, ALL THINGS FAIR AND GOOD; 9 605
THINGS IN THIR CAUSES, BUT TO TRACE THE WAYES 9 682
THEM NOTHING: IF THEY ALL THINGS, WHO ENCLOS'D 9 722
IN KNOWLEDGE, AS THE GODS WHO ALL THINGS KNOW; 9 804
IN THINGS TO US FORBIDDEN, IT MIGHT BE WISH'D, 9 1025
OMNISCIENT, WHO IN ALL THINGS WISE AND JUST, 10 7
WITH SECRET AMITY THINGS OF LIKE KINDE 10 248
THE SAVOUR OF DEATH FROM ALL THINGS THERE THAT LIVE: 10 269
SO, IF GREAT THINGS TO SMALL MAY BE COMPAR'D, 10 306
OF ALL THINGS PARTED BY TH' EMPYREAL BOUNDS, 10 380
AS SORTED BEST WITH PRESENT THINGS. THE SUN 10 651
OUTRAGE FROM LIVELESS THINGS; BUT DISCORD FIRST 10 707
ALL THINGS WITH DOUBLE TERROR: ON THE GROUND 10 850
DISTEMPERD ALL THINGS, AND OF INCORRUPT 11 56
MOTHER OF ALL THINGS LIVING, SINCE BY THEE 11 160
MAN IS TO LIVE, AND ALL THINGS LIVE FOR MAN. 11 161
OF HIM WHO ALL THINGS CAN, I WOULD NOT CEASE 11 309
NOT HID, NOR THOSE THINGS LAST WHICH MIGHT PRESERVE 11 579
HE LOOK'D, AND SAW THE FACE OF THINGS QUITE CHANG'D, 11 712
O THOU WHO FUTURE THINGS CANST REPRESENT 11 870
SHALL HOLD THIR COURSE, TILL FIRE PURGE ALL THINGS NEW, 11 900
(THINGS BY THIR NAMES I CALL, THOUGH YET UNNAM'D) 12 140
ENLIGHTNER OF MY DARKNESS, GRACIOUS THINGS 12 271
WITH ALL HIS SACRED THINGS, A SCORN AND PREY 12 341
ACCOMPLISHING GREAT THINGS, BY THINGS DEEMD WEAK 12 567
ART ALL THINGS UNDER HEAV'N, ALL PLACES THOU, 12 618

THINK

FOR WHO CAN THINK SUBMISSION? WARR THEN, WARR 1 661
OR IN FRANCISCAN THINK TO PASS DISGUIS'D; 3 480
AH GENTLE PAIR, YEE LITTLE THINK HOW NIGH 4 366
EARTH, AIRE, AND SEA. THEN LET US NOT THINK HARD 4 432
SHINE NOT IN VAIN, NOR THINK, THOUGH MEN WERE NONE, 4 675
OR THINK THEE UNBEFITTING HOLIEST PLACE, 4 759
THINK NOT, REVOLTED SPIRIT, THY SHAPE THE SAME, 4 835
THINK NOT I SHALL BE NICE. SO DOWN THEY SAT, 5 433
OR POTENT TONGUE; FOOL, NOT TO THINK HOW VAIN 6 135
AND FAITHFUL, NOW PROV'D FALSE. BUT THINK NOT HERE 6 271
THE ADVERSARIE. NOR THINK THOU WITH WIND 6 282
OF EVIL THEN SO SMALL AS EASIE THINK 6 437
THINK NOTHING HARD, MUCH LESS TO BE DESPAIRD. 6 495
AND THY REQUEST THINK NOW FULFILL'D, THAT ASK'D 7 635
THINK ONELY WHAT CONCERNES THEE AND THY BEING; 8 174
NOR LESS THINK WEE IN HEAV'N OF THEE ON EARTH 8 224
BEYOND ALL OTHER, THINK THE SAME VOUTSAF'T 8 581
ANGELS, NOR THINK SUPERFLUOUS OTHERS AID. 9 308
BUT IF THOU THINK, TRIAL UNSOUGHT MAY FINDE 9 370
A DEATH TO THINK. CONFIRM'D THEN I RESOLVE, 9 830
NOR CAN I THINK THAT GOD, CREATOR WISE, 9 938
WHERE HE ABIDES, THINK THERE THY NATIVE SOILE. 11 292
HORRID TO THINK, HOW HORRIBLE TO FEEL. 11 465

THINKING

DECEAV'D; THEY FONDLY THINKING TO ALLAY 10 564
OF MISERIE, SO THINKING TO EVADE 10 1021

THINKS

RESIGNS HER CHARGE, WHILE GOODNESS THINKS NO ILL 3 688

THINKST

SPEED ALMOST SPIRITUAL; MEE THOU THINKST NOT SLOW, 8 110
WHAT THINKST THOU THEN OF MEE, AND THIS MY STATE, 8 403
WHAT THINKST THOU OF OUR EMPIRE NOW, THOUGH EARND 10 592

THINNER

THIR ELEMENT TO DRAW THE THINNER AIRE. 8 348
TH' ANGELIC NAME, AND THINNER LEFT THE THRONG 9 142

THIRD

A THIRD AS SOON HAD FORM'D WITHIN THE GROUND 1 705
DREW AFTER HIM THE THIRD PART OF HEAV'NS SONS 2 692
AND WITH THEM COMES A THIRD OF REGAL PORT, 4 869

THIRD (CONTINUED)

AND COLOURS DIPT IN HEAV'N; THE THIRD HIS FEET 5 283
DREW AFTER HIM THE THIRD PART OF HEAV'NS HOST: 5 710
A THIRD PART OF THE GODS, IN SYNOD MET 6 156
TWO DAYES ARE THEREFORE PAST, THE THIRD IS THINE; 6 699
AND THE THIRD SACRED MORN BEGAN TO SHINE 6 748
SO EEV'N AND MORN RECORDED THE THIRD DAY. 7 338
THOSE TWO; THE THIRD BEST ABSENT IS CONDEMN'D, 10 82
TILL ISRAEL OVERCOME; SO CALL THE THIRD 12 267
SHALL LONG USURP; ERE THE THIRD DAWNING LIGHT 12 421

THIRST

OF POROUS EARTH WITH KINDLY THIRST UP DRAWN, 4 228
MORE EASIE, WHOLSOM THIRST AND APPETITE 4 330
TRUE APPETITE, AND NOT DISRELISH THIRST 5 305
WHOSE LIQUID MURMUR HEARD NEW THIRST EXCITES, 7 68
THE THIRST I HAD OF KNOWLEDGE, AND VOUTSAF'T 8 8
THEN FRUITS OF PALM-TREE PLEASANTEST TO THIRST 8 212
NOT TO DEFERR; HUNGER AND THIRST AT ONCE, 9 586
HUNGER AND THIRST CONSTRAINING, DRUGD AS OFT, 10 568
AS AFTER THIRST, WHICH MADE THIR FLOWING SHRINK 11 846

THIRSTED

STILL AS THEY THIRSTED SCOOP THE BRIMMING STREAM; 4 336

THIRSTIE

OR WET THE THIRSTIE EARTH WITH FALLING SHOWERS, 5 190

THISTLES

THORNS ALSO AND THISTLES IT SHALL BRING THEE FORTH 10 203

THITHER

CASTS PALE AND DREADFUL? THITHER LET US TEND 1 183
THE HEADS AND LEADERS THITHER HAST WHERE STOOD 1 357
THITHER, IF BUT TO PRY, SHALL BE PERHAPS 1 655
OUR FIRST ERUPTION, THITHER OR ELSEWHERE: 1 656
THE WORK OF SULPHUR. THITHER WING'D WITH SPEED 1 674
THITHER LET US BEND ALL OUR THOUGHTS, TO LEARN 2 354
THITHER BY HARPY-FOOTED FURIES HAIL'D, 2 596
WITH LOUDEST VEHEMENCE: THITHER HE PLYES, 2 954
POSSESSES LATELY, THITHER TO ARRIVE 2 979
THITHER FULL FRAUGHT WITH MISCHIEVOUS REVENGE, 2 1054
ALLUR'D HIS EYE: THITHER HIS COURSE HE BENDS 3 573
AND WHAT I WAS, WHENCE THITHER BROUGHT, AND HOW. 4 452
PURE AS TH' EXPANSE OF HEAV'N; I THITHER WENT 4 456
THITHER CAME URIEL, GLIDING THROUGH THE EEVEN 4 555
INCREDIBLE HOW SWIFT, HAD THITHER ROWL'D 4 593
THOUGH THITHER DOOMD? THOU WOULDST THY SELF, NO DOUBT, 4 890
FLIE THITHER WHENCE THOU FLEDST: IF FROM THIS HOURE 4 963
A CLOUDY SPOT. DOWN THITHER PRONE IN FLIGHT 5 266
FOR THITHER HE ASSEMBL'D ALL HIS TRAIN, 5 767
THITHER TO COME, AND WITH CALUMNIOUS ART 5 770
CAPACIOUS BED OF WATERS: THITHER THEY 7 290
DESCENDS, THITHER WITH HEART AND VOICE AND EYES 7 513
THITHER WILL SEND HIS WINGED MESSENGERS 7 572
MY CONDUCT, I CAN BRING THEE THITHER SOON. 9 630
AND KNOW NOT THAT I CALL'D AND DREW THEM THITHER 10 629
AND THITHER MUST RETURN AND BE NO MORE. 11 200
RUSTIC, OF GRASSIE SORD; THITHER ANON 11 433
NO SANCTITIE, IF NONE BE THITHER BROUGHT 11 837
WILL HE CONVEY UP THITHER TO SUSTAIN 12 75
THEY GLADLY THITHER HASTE, AND BY A QUIRE 12 366

THITHER-WARD

OF DAWNING LIGHT TURND THITHER-WARD IN HASTE 3 500

THITHERWARD

AS THITHERWARD ENDEVORING, AND UPRIGHT 8 260

THORN

FLOURS OF ALL HUE, AND WITHOUT THORN THE ROSE: 4 256

THORNS

THORNS ALSO AND THISTLES IT SHALL BRING THEE FORTH 10 203

THOROUGH-FARE

OF EASIE THOROUGH-FARE. THEREFORE WHILE I 10 393

THOUGHT

RESERV'D HIM TO MORE WRATH; FOR NOW THE THOUGHT 1 54
BREATHING UNITED FORCE WITH FIXED THOUGHT 1 560
I SDEIND SUBJECTION, AND THOUGHT ONE STEP HIGHER 4 50
TO THEM WHO LIV'D; NOR ON THE VERTUE THOUGHT 4 198
OF GOD OR ANGEL, FOR THEY THOUGHT NO ILL: 4 320
WITH UNEXPERIENC'T THOUGHT, AND LAID ME DOWNE 4 457
HITHERWARD BENT (WHO COULD HAVE THOUGHT?) ESCAP'D 4 794
WITH GENTLE VOICE, I THOUGHT IT THINE; IT SAID, 5 37
THY GOODNESS BEYOND THOUGHT, AND POWER DIVINE: 5 159
SHEE NEEDED, VERTUE-PROOF, NO THOUGHT INFIRME 5 384
EACH TO OTHER LIKE, MORE THEN ON EARTH IS THOUGHT? 5 576
THROUGH PRIDE THAT SIGHT, & THOUGHT HIMSELF IMPAIRD. 5 665
NOR SO CONTENT, HATH IN HIS THOUGHT TO TRY 5 727
HOW PROVIDENT HE IS, HOW FARR FROM THOUGHT 5 828
ALREADY KNOWN WHAT HE FOR NEWS HAD THOUGHT 6 20
OF ONSET ENDED SOON EACH MILDER THOUGHT, 6 98
AT FIRST I THOUGHT THAT LIBERTIE AND HEAV'N 6 164

THOUGHT (CONTINUED)
NOR MOTION OF SWIFT THOUGHT, LESS COULD HIS SHIELD 6 192
THE RIDGES OF GRIM WARR; NO THOUGHT OF FLIGHT, 6 236
OMNISCIENT THOUGHT. TRUE IS, LESS FIRMLY ARM'D, 6 430
ONCE FOUND, WHICH YET UNFOUND MOST WOULD HAVE THOUGHT 6 500
WHOM FLED WE THOUGHT, WILL SAVE US LONG PURSUIT 6 538
OF THINGS SO HIGH AND STRANGE, THINGS TO THIR THOUGHT 7 53
THINGS ABOVE EARTHLY THOUGHT, WHICH YET CONCERND 7 82
AT LEAST OUR ENVIOUS FOE HATH FAIL'D, WHO THOUGHT 7 139
THY POWER; WHAT THOUGHT CAN MEASURE THEE OR TONGUE 7 603
THOU HAST REPELD, WHILE IMPIOUSLY THEY THOUGHT 7 611
THOUGHT HIM STILL SPEAKING, STILL STOOD FIXT TO HEAR; 8 3
MY DROUSED SENSE, UNTROUBL'D, THOUGH I THOUGHT 8 289
NATURE HER SELF, THOUGH PURE OF SINFUL THOUGHT, 8 506
AND MATRIMONIAL LOVE; BUT EVE, WHO THOUGHT 9 319
THE FIRST AT LEST OF THESE I THOUGHT DENID 9 555
OF KNOWLEDG, NOR WAS GOD-HEAD FROM HER THOUGHT. 9 790
THEE I HAVE MISST, AND THOUGHT IT LONG, DEPRIV'D 9 857
WHATEVER CAN TO SIGHT OR THOUGHT BE FORMD, 9 898
WERE IT I THOUGHT DEATH MENAC'T WOULD ENSUE 9 977
ORIGINAL; WHILE ADAM TOOK NO THOUGHT, 9 1004
THUS FENC'T, AND AS THEY THOUGHT, THIR SHAME IN PART 9 1119
WHAT SEEMD IN THEE SO PERFET, THAT I THOUGHT 9 1179
AND THOUGHT NOT MUCH TO CLOATH HIS ENEMIES: 10 219
BUT I SHALL DIE A LIVING DEATH? O THOUGHT 10 788
THAT EXCELLENCE THOUGHT IN THEE, AND IMPLIES, 10 1017
IMMEDIATE DISSOLUTION, WHICH WE THOUGHT 10 1049
AND SOFALA THOUGHT OPHIR, TO THE REALME 11 400
WITH THOUGHT THAT THEY MUST BE. LET NO MAN SEEK 11 770
GREATLY IN PEACE OF THOUGHT, AND HAVE MY FILL 12 558

THOUGHTS
UNITED THOUGHTS AND COUNSELS, EQUAL HOPE 1 88
WITH SOLEMN TOUCHES, TROUBL'D THOUGHTS, AND CHASE 1 557
LONG UNDER DARKNESS COVER. BUT THESE THOUGHTS 1 659
FROM HEAV'N, FOR EV'N IN HEAV'N HIS LOOKS AND THOUGHTS 1 680
MATUREST COUNSELS: FOR HIS THOUGHTS WERE LOW; 2 115
THOSE THOUGHTS THAT WANDER THROUGH ETERNITY, 2 148
ALL THOUGHTS OF WARR: YE HAVE WHAT I ADVISE. 2 283
THITHER LET US BEND ALL OUR THOUGHTS, TO LEARN 2 354
PONDERING THE DANGER WITH DEEP THOUGHTS; AND EACH 2 421
TRUCE TO HIS RESTLESS THOUGHTS, AND ENTERTAIN 2 526
IN THOUGHTS MORE ELEVATE, AND REASON'D HIGH 2 558
SATAN WITH THOUGHTS INFLAM'D OF HIGHEST DESIGN, 2 630
THEN FEED ON THOUGHTS, THAT VOLUNTARIE MOVE 3 37
ALL HAST THOU SPOK'N AS MY THOUGHTS ARE, ALL 3 171
HIS TROUBL'D THOUGHTS, AND FROM THE BOTTOM STIRR 4 19
WOULD HIGTH RECAL HIGH THOUGHTS, HOW SOON UNSAY 4 95
LITTLE INFERIOR; WHOM MY THOUGHTS PURSUE 4 362
DIVIDE THE NIGHT, AND LIFT OUR THOUGHTS TO HEAVEN. 4 688
AT LEAST DISTEMPERD, DISCONTENTED THOUGHTS, 4 807
O SOLE IN WHOM MY THOUGHTS FIND ALL REPOSE, 5 28
THE TROUBLE OF THY THOUGHTS THIS NIGHT IN SLEEP 5 96
SO PRAY'D THEY INNOCENT, AND TO THIR THOUGHTS 5 209
SHE TURNS, ON HOSPITABLE THOUGHTS INTENT 5 332
SINGLE, IS YET SO JUST, MY CONSTANT THOUGHTS 5 552
OF HEAV'NS ALMIGHTIE. THOU TO ME THY THOUGHTS 5 676
ABSTRUSEST THOUGHTS, FROM FORTH HIS HOLY MOUNT 5 712
ASPIRER, BUT THIR THOUGHTS PROV'D FOND AND VAIN 6 90
DISDAIN'D, BUT MEANER THOUGHTS LEARND IN THIR FLIGHT, 6 367
COLLECTED STOOD WITHIN OUR THOUGHTS AMUS'D, 6 581
STOOD SCOFFING, HIGHTHN'D IN THIR THOUGHTS BEYOND 6 629
ENTRING ON STUDIOUS THOUGHTS ABSTRUSE, WHICH EVE 8 40
SOLLICIT NOT THY THOUGHTS WITH MATTERS HID, 8 167
THE EASIEST WAY, NOR WITH PERPLEXING THOUGHTS 8 183
SEEK THEM WITH WANDRING THOUGHTS, AND NOTIONS VAIN. 8 187
ALL HUMAN THOUGHTS COME SHORT, SUPREAM OF THINGS; 8 414
THE THOUGHTS, AND HEART ENLARGES, HATH HIS SEAT 8 590
OF THOUGHTS REVOLV'D, HIS FINAL SENTENCE CHOSE 9 88
WITH SECOND THOUGHTS, REFORMING WHAT WAS OLD. 9 101
TO MY RELENTLESS THOUGHTS; AND HIM DESTROYD, 9 130
OR BEAR WHAT TO MY MINDE FIRST THOUGHTS PRESENT, 9 213
WELL HAST THOU MOTION'D, WELL THY THOUGHTS IMPLOYD 9 229
THOUGHTS, WHICH HOW FOUND THEY HARBOUR IN THY BREST 9 288
FIERCE HATE HE RECOLLECTS, AND ALL HIS THOUGHTS 9 471
THOUGHTS, WHITHER HAVE YE LED ME, WITH WHAT SWEET 9 473
THE TRODDEN HERB, OF ABJECT THOUGHTS AND LOW, 9 572
I TURND MY THOUGHTS, AND WITH CAPACIOUS MIND 9 603
GREAT JOY HE PROMIS'D TO HIS THOUGHTS, AND NEW 9 843
RECOMFORTED, AND AFTER THOUGHTS DISTURBD 9 918
HIS THOUGHTS, HIS LOOKS, WORDS, ACTIONS ALL INFECT, 10 608
WHAT THOUGHTS IN MY UNQUIET BREST ARE RIS'N, 10 975
BROKE OFF THE REST; SO MUCH OF DEATH HER THOUGHTS 10 1008
A SPACE, TILL FIRMER THOUGHTS RESTRAIND EXCESS, 11 498
ERWHILE PERPLEXT WITH THOUGHTS WHAT WOULD BECOM 12 275
WHAT OFT MY STEDDIEST THOUGHTS HAVE SEARCHT IN VAIN, 12 377

THOUSAND
TEN THOUSAND BANNERS RISE INTO THE AIR 1 545
A THOUSAND DEMY-GODS ON GOLDEN SEAT'S, 1 796
TEN THOUSAND FADOM DEEP, AND TO THIS HOUR 2 934

THOUSAND (CONTINUED)
AND DISCORD WITH A THOUSAND VARIOUS MOUTHS. 2 967
BLOWS THEM TRANSVERSE TEN THOUSAND LEAGUES AWRY 3 488
THOUSAND CELESTIAL ARDORS, WHERE HE STOOD 5 249
TEN THOUSAND THOUSAND ENSIGNES HIGH ADVANC'D, 5 588
ATTENDED WITH TEN THOUSAND THOUSAND SAINTS, 6 767
AND TWENTIE THOUSAND (I THIR NUMBER HEARD) 6 769
GRASPING TEN THOUSAND THUNDERS, WHICH HE SENT 6 836
WITH THOUSAND LESSER LIGHTS DIVIDUAL HOLDS, 7 382
WITH THOUSAND THOUSAND STARRES, THAT THEN APPEER'D 7 383
SYMPHONIOUS OF TEN THOUSAND HARPES THAT TUN'D 7 559
THOSE THOUSAND DECENCIES THAT DAILY FLOW 8 601

THOUSANDFOULD
TEN THOUSANDFOULD THE SIN OF HIM WHO SLEW 11 678

THOUSANDS
WITH HUNDERDS AND WITH THOUSANDS TROOPING CAME 1 760
BY THOUSANDS AND BY MILLIONS RANG'D FOR FIGHT; 6 48
HOW FEW SOMTIMES MAY KNOW, WHEN THOUSANDS ERR. 6 148
THY MALICE INTO THOUSANDS, ONCE UPRIGHT 6 270
I MIGHT RELATE OF THOUSANDS, AND THIR NAMES 6 373
BY THOUSANDS, ANGEL ON ARCH-ANGEL ROWL'D; 6 594

THRACIAN
OF THAT WILDE ROUT THAT TORE THE THRACIAN BARD 7 34

THRALL
HIM FIRST MAKE SURE YOUR THRALL, AND LASTLY KILL. 10 402

THRALLS
OR DO HIM MIGHTIER SERVICE AS HIS THRALLS 1 149

THRASCIAS
AND THRASCIAS REND THE WOODS AND SEAS UPTURN; 10 700

THREATENS
THREATENS HIM, PLUNG'D IN THAT ABORTIVE GULF. 2 441

THREAT'ND
THOUGH THREAT'ND, WHICH NO WORSE THEN THIS CAN BRING. 9 715

THREATN'D
SO THREATN'D HEE, BUT SATAN TO NO THREATS 4 968
THREATN'D, NOR FROM THE HOLIE ONE OF HEAV'N 6 359
NOT DEAD, AS WE ARE THREATN'D, BUT THENCEFORTH 9 870

THREATNER
TO KNOWLEDGE? BY THE THREATNER, LOOK ON MEE, 9 687

THREATNING
IMPENDENT HORRORS, THREATNING HIDEOUS FALL 2 177
SO SPEAKING AND SO THREATNING, GREW TENFOLD 2 705
STARLESS EXPOS'D, AND EVER-THREATNING STORMS 3 425
STILL THREATNING TO DEVOUR ME OPENS WIDE, 4 77
THOUGH THREATNING, WILL IN EARNEST SO DESTROY 9 939
CONCOURS IN ARMS, FIERCE FACES THREATNING WARR, 11 641

THREATS
SO THREATN'D HEE, BUT SATAN TO NO THREATS 4 968
YET NOT FOR THY ADVISE OR THREATS I FLY 5 889
OF AIRIE THREATS TO AW WHOM YET WITH DEEDS 6 283
THAT THOU SHOULDST HOPE, IMPERIOUS, AND WITH THREATS 6 287
WHEN SATAN WHO LATE FLED BEFORE THE THREATS 9 53
THOSE RIGID THREATS OF DEATH; YE SHALL NOT DIE: 9 685

THREE
AND THRICE THREEFOLD THE GATES; THREE FOLDS WERE BRASS, 2 645
THREE IRON, THREE OF ADAMANTINE ROCK, 2 646
OF THREE THAT IN MOUNT IDA NAKED STROVE, 5 382
INSENSIBLY THREE DIFFERENT MOTIONS MOVE? 8 130
WITH LONG REACH INTERPOS'D; THREE SEV'RAL WAYES 10 323
IN SIGHT, TO EACH OF THESE THREE PLACES LED. 10 324
SUCH FATAL CONSEQUENCE UNITES US THREE: 10 364
AND FROM THE WELL OF LIFE THREE DROPS INSTILL'D. 11 416
THIR ORDER: LAST THE SIRE, AND HIS THREE SONS 11 736
CONSPICUOUS WITH THREE LIFTED COLOURS GAY, 11 866
PALPABLE DARKNESS, AND BLOT OUT THREE DAYES; 12 188

THREE-BOLTED
AND QUIVER WITH THREE-BOLTED THUNDER STOR'D, 6 764

THREEFOLD
AND THRICE THREEFOLD THE GATES; THREE FOLDS WERE BRASS, 2 645

THRESHING
LEAST ON THE THRESHING FLOORE HIS HOPEFUL SHEAVES 4 984

THRESHOLD
THEN STIL AT HELS DARK THRESHOLD TO HAVE SATE WATCH, 10 594

THREW
AND LICHAS FROM THE TOP OF OETA THREW 2 545

THUNDERERS
FORMOST TO STAND AGAINST THE THUNDERERS AIM 2 28

THUNDERS
COVERS HIS THRONE; FROM WHENCE DEEP THUNDERS ROAR 2 267
GRASPING TEN THOUSAND THUNDERS, WHICH HE SENT 6 836
THY THUNDERS MAGNIFI'D; BUT TO CREATE 7 606

THUNDER-STRUCK
DROVE THEM BEFORE HIM THUNDER-STRUCK, PURSU'D 6 858

THUNDRING
OF THUNDRING AETNA, WHOSE COMBUSTIBLE 1 233
JEHOVAH THUNDRING OUT OF SION, THRON'D 1 386
FROM FAR WITH THUNDRING NOISE AMONG OUR FOES 6 487
COMES THUNDRING BACK WITH DREADFUL REVOLUTION 10 814

THUNDROUS
NOTUS AND AFER BLACK WITH THUNDROUS CLOUDS 10 702

THURST
YET PARCHT WITH SCALDING THURST AND HUNGER FIERCE, 10 556

THWART
MOV'D CONTRARIE WITH THWART OBLIQUITIES, 8 132
FROM SERRALIONA; THWART OF THESE AS FIERCE 10 703
TINE THE SLANT LIGHTNING, WHOSE THWART FLAME DRIV'N DOWN 10 1075

THWARTS
IN AUTUMN THWARTS THE NIGHT, WHEN VAPORS FIR'D 4 557

THYESTEAN
THE SUN, AS FROM THYESTEAN BANQUET, TURN'D 10 688

TIAR
OF BEAMING SUNNIE RAIES, A GOLDEN TIAR 3 625

TI'D
NOT TI'D OR MANACL'D WITH JOYNT OR LIMB, 1 426

TIDE
OR SUMMERS NOON-TIDE AIR, WHILE THUS HE SPAKE. 2 309

TIDINGS
THESE TIDINGS CARRIE TO TH' ANOINTED KING; 5 870
NOR TROUBL'D AT THESE TIDINGS FROM THE EARTH, 10 36
AND TIDINGS FRAUGHT, TO HELL HE NOW RETURN'D, 10 346
EVE, NOW EXPECT GREAT TIDINGS, WHICH PERHAPS 11 226
OUR FRAILTIE CAN SUSTAIN, THY TIDINGS BRING, 11 302
O PROPHET OF GLAD TIDINGS, FINISHER 12 375
WITH JOY THE TIDINGS BROUGHT FROM HEAV'N: AT LENGTH 12 504

TIDORE
OF TERNATE AND TIDORE, WHENCE MERCHANTS BRING 2 639

TIGRIS
WHERE TIGRIS AT THE FOOT OF PARADISE 9 71

TILES
IN AT THE WINDOW CLIMBS, OR O'RE THE TILES; 4 191

TILL
WITH LOSS OF EDEN, TILL ONE GREATER MAN 1 4
HE WITH HIS THUNDER: AND TILL THEN WHO KNEW 1 93
THAT FELT UNUSUAL WEIGHT, TILL ON DRY LAND 1 227
NATHLESS HE SO ENDUR'D, TILL ON THE BEACH 1 299
WITH SCATTER'D ARMS AND ENSIGNS, TILL ANON 1 325
TILL, AS A SIGNAL GIV'N, TH' UPLIFTED SPEAR 1 347
GOT THEM NEW NAMES, TILL WANDRING ORE THE EARTH, 1 365
TILL GOOD JOSIAH DROVE THEM THENCE TO HELL. 1 418
MONARCH IN HEAV'N, TILL THEN AS ONE SECURE 1 638
SWARM'D AND WERE STRAITN'D; TILL THE SIGNAL GIV'N, 1 776
ALONE THE DREADFUL VOYAGE; TILL AT LAST 2 426
THE IRKSOM HOURS, TILL THIS GREAT CHIEF RETURN. 2 527
TILL THICKEST LEGIONS CLOSE; WITH FEATS OF ARMS 2 537
WHO FIRST BROKE PEACE IN HEAV'N AND FAITH, TILL THEN 2 690
HOV'RING A SPACE, TILL WINDS THE SIGNAL BLOW 2 717
WHAT IT INTENDS; TILL FIRST I KNOW OF THEE, 2 740
I KNOW THEE NOT, NOR EVER SAW TILL NOW 2 744
THREW FORTH, TILL ON THE LEFT SIDE OP'NING WIDE, 2 755
ALONE, BUT LONG I SAT NOT, TILL MY WOMB 2 778
TILL THEY ENTHRALL THEMSELVES: I ELSE MUST CHANGE 3 125
TILL FINAL DISSOLUTION, WANDER HERE, 3 458
AND LONG HE WANDERD, TILL AT LAST A GLEAME 3 499
TILL AT HIS SECOND BIDDING DARKNESS FLED, 3 712
NOR STAID, TILL ON NIPHATES TOP HE LIGHTS. 3 742
TILL PRIDE AND WORSE AMBITION THREW ME DOWN 4 40
MINE EYES TILL NOW, AND PIN'D WITH VAIN DESIRE, 4 466
TILL I ESPI'D THEE, FAIR INDEED AND TALL, 4 477
YET HAPPIE PAIR; ENJOY, TILL I RETURN, 4 534
THE STARRIE HOST, RODE BRIGHTEST, TILL THE MOON 4 606
SO JUDGE THOU STILL, PRESUMPTUOUS, TILL THE WRAUTH, 4 912
SUCH NIGHT TILL THIS I NEVER PASS'D, HAVE DREAM'D, 5 31
KNEW NEVER TILL THIS IRKSOM NIGHT; METHOUGHT 5 35
TILL THE SUN PAINT YOUR FLEECIE SKIRTS WITH GOLD, 5 187
THROUGH ALL TH' EMPYREAL ROAD; TILL AT THE GATE 5 253

TILL (CONTINUED)
WINNOWS THE BUXOM AIR; TILL WITHIN SOARE 5 270
TO SIT AND TASTE, TILL THIS MERIDIAN HEAT 5 369
ORESHADES; FOR THESE MID-HOURS, TILL EEVNING RISE 5 376
TILL BODY UP TO SPIRIT WORK, IN BOUNDS 5 478
THROUGH HEAV'NS WIDE CHAMPAIN HELD HIS WAY, TILL MORN, 6 2
OBSEQUIOUS DARKNESS ENTERS, TILL HER HOURE 6 10
AND CLAMOUR SUCH AS HEARD IN HEAV'N TILL NOW 6 208
THE BATTEL HUNG; TILL SATAN, WHO THAT DAY 6 246
AUTHOR OF EVIL, UNKNOWN TILL THY REVOLT, 6 262
MISERIE, UNCREATED TILL THE CRIME 6 268
BY SIN OF DISOBEDIENCE, TILL THAT HOUR 6 396
OF FUTURE WE MAY DEEM HIM, THOUGH TILL NOW 6 429
TILL NOW NOT KNOWN, BUT KNOWN AS SOON CONTEMND, 6 432
OF SPIRITOUS AND FIERIE SPUME, TILL TOUCHT 6 479
TILL ON THOSE CURSED ENGINS TRIPLE-ROW 6 650
TO RAPTURE, TILL THE SAVAGE CLAMOR DROUND 7 36
OR WE CAN BID HIS ABSENCE, TILL THY SONG 7 107
NOT HERE, TILL BY DEGREES OF MERIT RAIS'D 7 157
HE SCARCE HAD SAID, WHEN THE BARE EARTH, TILL THEN 7 313
UPON THE EARTH, AND MAN TO TILL THE GROUND 7 332
TILL NIGHT, THEN IN THE EAST HER TURN SHE SHINES, 7 380
TILL EV'N, NOR THEN THE SOLEMN NIGHTINGAL 7 435
YET NOT TILL THE CREATOR FROM HIS WORK 7 551
TILL WARN'D, OR BY EXPERIENCE TAUGHT, SHE LEARNE, 8 190
AND DAY IS YET NOT SPENT; TILL THEN THOU SEEST 8 206
AND GAZ'D A WHILE THE AMPLE SKIE, TILL RAIS'D 8 258
TO TILL AND KEEP, AND OF THE FRUIT TO EATE: 8 320
DISPORTING, TILL THE AMOROUS BIRD OF NIGHT 8 518
INTO A GULF SHOT UNDER GROUND, TILL PART 9 72
OUR PLEASANT TASK ENJOYN'D, BUT TILL MORE HANDS 9 207
WITH MYRTLE, FIND WHAT TO REDRESS TILL NOON: 9 219
AS WE NEED WALK, TILL YOUNGER HANDS ERE LONG 9 246
TILL ON A DAY ROAVING THE FIELD, I CHANC'D 9 575
I SPAR'D NOT, FOR SUCH PLEASURE TILL THAT HOUR 9 596
STILL HANGING INCORRUPTIBLE, TILL MEN 9 622
IRRATIONAL TILL THEN. FOR US ALONE 9 766
REGARDED, SUCH DELIGHT TILL THEN, AS SEEMD, 9 787
TILL DIETED BY THEE I GROW MATURE 9 803
THY PRESENCE, AGONIE OF LOVE TILL NOW 9 858
SPEECHLESS HE STOOD AND PALE, TILL THUS AT LENGTH 9 894
TILL ADAM THUS 'GAN EVE TO DALLIANCE MOVE, 9 1016
FROM THIS DELIGHTFUL FRUIT, NOR KNOWN TILL NOW 9 1023
THE SOLACE OF THIR SIN, TILL DEWIE SLEEP 9 1044
TILL ADAM, THOUGH NOT LESS THEN EVE ABASH'T, 9 1065
THE THICKEST TREES, BOTH MAN AND WIFE, TILL GOD 10 101
TILL THOU RETURN UNTO THE GROUND, FOR THOU 10 206
LONG HEE ADMIRING STOOD, TILL SIN, HIS FAIRE 10 352
WITHIN HELL GATES TILL NOW, THOU US IMPOW'RD 10 369
EACH OTHER, TILL SUPPLANTED DOWN HE FELL 10 513
TILL THIR LOST SHAPE, PERMITTED, THEY RESUM'D, 10 574
TILL I IN MAN RESIDING THROUGH THE RACE, 10 607
ON WHAT WAS PURE, TILL CRAMM'D AND GORG'D, NIGH BURST 10 632
TILL THEN THE CURSE PRONOUNC'T ON BOTH PRECEDES. 10 640
IMMOVEABLE TILL PEACE OBTAIN'D FROM FAULT 10 938
BY HIM WITH MANY COMFORTS, TILL WE END 10 1084
NUMBERD, THOUGH SAD, TILL DEATH, HIS DOOM (WHICH I 11 40
TILL I PROVIDED DEATH; SO DEATH BECOMES 11 61
AND TOOK THIR SEATS; TILL FROM HIS THRONE SUPREAM 11 82
AND SEND HIM FROM THE GARDEN FORTH TO TILL 11 97
LABORIOUS, TILL DAY DROOP; WHILE HERE WE DWELL, 11 178
SOME DAYS; HOW LONG, AND WHAT TILL THEN OUR LIFE, 11 198
AND SEND THEE FROM THE GARDEN FORTH TO TILL 11 261
A SPACE, TILL FIRMER THOUGHTS RESTRAIND EXCESS, 11 498
TILL MANY YEARS OVER THY HEAD RETURN: 11 534
SO MAIST THOU LIVE, TILL LIKE RIPE FRUIT THOU DROP 11 535
WHICH I MUST KEEP TILL MY APPOINTED DAY 11 550
ROVE WITHOUT REIN, TILL IN THE AMOROUS NET 11 586
AND NOW OF LOVE THEY TREAT TILL TH' EEVNING STAR 11 588
IN FACTIOUS OPPOSITION, TILL AT LAST 11 664
IMPETUOUS, AND CONTINU'D TILL THE EARTH 11 744
AND SUNK THEE AS THY SONS; TILL GENTLY REARD 11 758
SURFET, AND LUST, TILL WANTONNESS AND PRIDE 11 795
BEYOND ALL BOUNDS, TILL INUNDATION RISE 11 828
SHALL HOLD THIR COURSE, TILL FIRE PURGE ALL THINGS NEW, 11 900
UNDER PATERNAL RULE; TILL ONE SHALL RISE 12 24
NOT UNDERSTOOD, TILL HOARSE, AND ALL IN RAGE, 12 58
MAN TILL THEN FREE. THEREFORE SINCE HEE PERMITS 12 90
STILL TEND FROM BAD TO WORSE, TILL GOD AT LAST 12 106
TILL BY TWO BRETHREN (THOSE TWO BRETHREN CALL 12 169
MORE HARD'ND AFTER THAW, TILL IN HIS RAGE 12 194
DIVIDED, TILL HIS RESCU'D GAIN THIR SHOAR: 12 199
DARKNESS DEFENDS BETWEEN TILL MORNING WATCH; 12 207
TILL ISRAEL OVERCOME; SO CALL THE THIRD 12 267
THE CLOUDED ARK OF GOD TILL THEN IN TENTS 12 333
IN MEAN ESTATE LIVE MODERATE, TILL GROWN 12 351
UNDER HER OWN WAIGHT GROANING TILL THE DAY 12 539
TILL TIME STAND FIXT: BEYOND IS ALL ABYSS, 12 555

TILLAGE
A SWEATIE REAPER FROM HIS TILLAGE BROUGHT 11 434

TILTH
PART ARABLE AND TILTH, WHEREON WERE SHEAVES 11 430

TONGUE (CONTINUED)
BY TONGUE OF BRUTE, AND HUMAN SENSE EXPREST? 9 554
MOTION, EACH ACT WON AUDIENCE ERE THE TONGUE, 9 674
THE TONGUE NOT MADE FOR SPEECH TO SPEAK THY PRAISE: 9 749
BUT HISS FOR HISS RETURND WITH FORKED TONGUE 10 518
TO FORKED TONGUE, FOR NOW WERE ALL TRANSFORM'D 10 519
TO DRESS, AND TROULE THE TONGUE, AND ROULE THE EYE. 11 620

TONGUES
ON EVIL DAYES THOUGH FALL'N, AND EVIL TONGUES; 7 26
ON ALL SIDES, FROM INNUMERABLE TONGUES 10 507
UPON THIR TONGUES A VARIOUS SPIRIT TO RASE 12 53
TO SPEAK ALL TONGUES, AND DO ALL MIRACLES, 12 501

TOOK
SUSPENDED HELL, AND TOOK WITH RAVISHMENT 2 554
SAD INSTRUMENT OF ALL OUR WOE, SHE TOOK; 2 872
THEN CROWN'D AGAIN THIR GOLD'N HARPS THEY TOOK, 3 365
TOOK LEAVE, AND TOWARD THE COAST OF EARTH BENEATH, 3 739
INSTANT WITHOUT DISTURB THEY TOOK ALLARM, 6 549
TOOK ENVIE, AND ASPIRING TO HIS HIGHTH, 6 793
HE TOOK THE GOLDEN COMPASSES, PREPAR'D 7 225
OF LIGHT BY FARR THE GREATER PART HE TOOK, 7 359
SO SAYING, BY THE HAND HE TOOK ME RAIS'D, 8 300
WHO STOOPING OP'ND MY LEFT SIDE, AND TOOK 8 465
OR FROM MY SIDE SUBDUCTING, TOOK PERHAPS 8 536
SUCH PLEASURE TOOK THE SERPENT TO BEHOLD 9 455
AND FORTH TO MEET HER WENT, THE WAY SHE TOOK 9 847
ORIGINAL; WHILE ADAM TOOK NO THOUGHT, 9 1004
TOOK LARGELY, OF THIR MUTUAL GUILT THE SEALE, 9 1043
AND TOOK THIR SEATS; TILL FROM HIS THRONE SUPREAM 11 82
TO FIND WHERE ADAM SHELTERD, TOOK HIS WAY, 11 223
TO SERVE UNGOVERN'D APPETITE, AND TOOK 11 517
THROUGH EDEN TOOK THIR SOLITARIE WAY. 12 649

TOOK'ST
BECAM'ST ENAMOUR'D, AND SUCH JOY THOU TOOK'ST 2 765

TOOLES
FIRST HIS OWN TOOLES; THEN, WHAT MIGHT ELSE BE WROUGHT 11 572

TOOLS
BUT WITH SUCH GARDNING TOOLS AS ART YET RUDE, 9 391

TOP
SING HEAV'NLY MUSE, THAT ON THE SECRET TOP 1 6
AT EV'NING FROM THE TOP OF FESOLE, 1 289
AND IDA KNOWN, THENCE ON THE SNOWY TOP 1 515
WITH SINGED TOP THIR STATELY GROWTH THOUGH BARE 1 614
THERE STOOD A HILL NOT FAR WHOSE GRIESLY TOP 1 670
AND LICHAS FROM THE TOP OF OETA THREW 2 545
AT TOP WHEREOF, BUT FARR MORE RICH APPEERD 3 504
NOR STAID, TILL ON NIPHATES TOP HE LIGHTS. 3 742
AMIDST AS FROM A FLAMING MOUNT, WHOSE TOP 5 598
NOR OF THE MUSES NINE, NOR ON THE TOP 7 6
OF HEAV'NS HIGH-SEATED TOP, TH' IMPEREAL THRONE 7 585
A WOODIE MOUNTAIN; WHOSE HIGH TOP WAS PLAINE, 8 303
ON HIS HILL TOP, TO LIGHT THE BRIDAL LAMP. 8 520
OF PARADISE THE HIGHEST, FROM WHOSE TOP 11 378
FAST ON THE TOP OF SOM HIGH MOUNTAIN FIXT. 11 851
A CITIE AND TOWRE, WHOSE TOP MAY REACH TO HEAV'N; 12 44
GOD FROM THE MOUNT OF SINAI, WHOSE GRAY TOP 12 227
LET US DESCEND NOW THEREFORE FROM THIS TOP 12 588

TOPAZ
RUBIE OR TOPAZ, TO THE TWELVE THAT SHON 3 597

TOPHET
THE PLEASANT VALLY OF HINNOM, TOPHET THENCE 1 404

TOPS
AS WHEN FROM MOUNTAIN TOPS THE DUSKY CLOUDS 2 488
OF STATELIEST VIEW. YET HIGHER THEN THIR TOPS 4 142
BREATHE SOFT OR LOUD; AND WAVE YOUR TOPS, YE PINES, 5 193
ROCKS, WATERS, WOODS, AND BY THE SHAGGIE TOPS 6 645
INTO THE CLOUDS, THIR TOPS ASCEND THE SKIE: 7 287
ON CLIFFS AND CEDAR TOPS THIR EYRIES BUILD: 7 424
AND NOW THE TOPS OF HILLS AS ROCKS APPEER; 11 852

TORCH
THEY LIGHT THE NUPTIAL TORCH, AND BID INVOKE 11 590

TORE
A SHOUT THAT TORE HELLS CONCAVE, AND BEYOND 1 542
WITH CONQUEST, FELT TH' ENVENOM'D ROBE, AND TORE 2 543
TORE THROUGH MY ENTRAILS, THAT WITH FEAR AND PAIN 2 783
AND ALL HER ENTRAILS TORE, DISGORGING FOULE 6 588
OF THAT WILDE ROUT THAT TORE THE THRACIAN BARD 7 34

TORMENT
TORMENT WITH EASE, AND SOONEST RECOMPENCE 4 893
TORMENT, AND LOUD LAMENT, AND FURIOUS RAGE. 8 244
TORMENT WITHIN ME, AS FROM THE HATEFUL SIEGE 9 121
TO MEE AND TO MY OFSPRING WOULD TORMENT ME 10 781
AND TORMENT LESS THEN NONE OF WHAT WE DREAD, 10 998
ABORTIVE, TO TORMENT ME ERE THIR BEING, 11 769

TORMENTED
TORMENTED ALL THE AIR; ALL AIR SEEMD THEN 6 244

TORMENTING
SIGHT HATEFUL, SIGHT TORMENTING. THUS THESE TWO 4 505

TORMENTS
TORMENTS HIM; ROUND HE THROWS HIS BALEFUL EYES 1 56
HIS OWN INVENTED TORMENTS. BUT PERHAPS 2 70
CHAINS AND THESE TORMENTS? BETTER THESE THEN WORSE 2 196
OUR TORMENTS ALSO MAY IN LENGTH OF TIME 2 274
UNDER WHAT TORMENTS INWARDLY I GROANE; 4 88
AMONG OUR OTHER TORMENTS NOT THE LEAST, 4 510

TORN
TORN FROM PELORUS, OR THE SHATTER'D SIDE 1 232
IN MUTINIE HAD FROM HER AXLE TORN 2 926
GLADLY THE PORT, THOUGH SHROUDS AND TACKLE TORN; 2 1044

TORNE
AT LEAST HAD GON TO RACK, DISTURBD AND TORNE 4 994

TORNEAMENT
AT JOUST AND TORNEAMENT; THEN MARSHAL'D FEAST 9 37

TORRENT
WHOSE WAVES OF TORRENT FIRE INFLAME WITH RAGE. 2 581
OF TORRENT FLOODS, OR OF A NUMEROUS HOST. 6 830
IF STEEP, WITH TORRENT RAPTURE, IF THROUGH PLAINE, 7 299

TORRID
ON HEAVENS AZURE, AND THE TORRID CLIME 1 297
OF BARCA OR CYRENE'S TORRID SOIL, 2 904
FIERCE AS A COMET; WHICH WITH TORRID HEAT, 12 634

TORTUOUS
SO VARIED HEE, AND OF HIS TORTUOUS TRAINE 9 516

TORTURE
THAT COMES TO ALL; BUT TORTURE WITHOUT END 1 67
OF GASTLY SPASM, OR RACKING TORTURE, QUALMES 11 481

TORTURER
AGAINST THE TORTURER; WHEN TO MEET THE NOISE 2 64

TORTURES
TURNING OUR TORTURES INTO HORRID ARMS 2 63
AND TORTURES HIM NOW MORE, THE MORE HE SEES 9 469

TORTURING
INEXORABLY, AND THE TORTURING HOUR 2 91

TOSSING
FROM OFF THE TOSSING OF THESE FIERY WAVES, 1 184
DIRE WAS THE TOSSING, DEEP THE GROANS, DESPAIR 11 489

TOST
COWLES, HOODS AND HABITS WITH THIR WEARERS TOST 3 490
AND FULL OF PEACE, NOW TOST AND TURBULENT: 9 1126
TOST UP AND DOWN, TOGETHER CROWDED DROVE 10 287
AND IN A TROUBL'D SEA OF PASSION TOST, 10 718

TOTAL
LEAST TOTAL DARKNESS SHOULD BY NIGHT REGAINE 4 665
THIR NIMBLE TREAD, AS WHEN THE TOTAL KIND 6 73
TOTAL THEY MIX, UNION OF PURE WITH PURE 8 627
MY SELF THE TOTAL CRIME, OR TO ACCUSE 10 127

TOUCH
POTABLE GOLD, WHEN WITH ONE VERTUOUS TOUCH 3 608
WITH HEAV'NLY TOUCH OF INSTRUMENTAL SOUNDS 4 686
TOUCH OF CELESTIAL TEMPER, BUT RETURNS 4 812
OF SENSE, WHEREBY THEY HEAR, SEE, SMELL, TOUCH, TASTE, 5 411
THICK-RAMMD, AT TH' OTHER BORE WITH TOUCH OF FIRE 6 485
PROVIDE, PERNICIOUS WITH ONE TOUCH TO FIRE. 6 520
DO AS YOU HAVE IN CHARGE, AND BRIEFLY TOUCH 6 566
WITH NICEST TOUCH. IMMEDIATE IN A FLAME, 6 584
CHARG'D NOT TO TOUCH THE INTERDICTED TREE, 7 46
TRANSPORTED TOUCH; HERE PASSION FIRST I FELT, 8 530
BUT IF THE SENSE OF TOUCH WHEREBY MANKIND 8 579
IRRADIANCE, VIRTUAL OR IMMEDIATE TOUCH? 8 617
BUT OF THIS TREE WE MAY NOT TASTE NOR TOUCH; 9 651
THEREOF, NOR SHALL YE TOUCH IT, LEAST YE DIE. 9 663
INCLINABLE NOW GROWN TO TOUCH OR TASTE, 9 742
MUCH MORE TO TASTE IT UNDER BANNE TO TOUCH. 9 925
TO WHOM SOON MOV'D WITH TOUCH OF BLAME THUS EVE. 9 1143
OR TOUCH WITH LIGHTEST MOMENT OF IMPULSE 10 45
THIS MORE DELUSIVE, NOT THE TOUCH, BUT TASTE 10 563
THIR STOPS AND CHORDS WAS SEEN: HIS VOLANT TOUCH 11 561

TOUCH'D
TOUCH'D LIGHTLY; FOR NO FALSHOOD CAN ENDURE 4 811
MEE WHO HAVE TOUCH'D AND TASTED, YET BOTH LIVE, 9 688
IN SOME TO SPRING FROM THEE, WHO NEVER TOUCH'D 11 425

TOUCHD
TOUCHD ONELY, THAT OUR TRIAL, WHEN LEAST SOUGHT, 9 380

TREE (CONTINUED)

BUT OF THIS TREE WE MAY NOT TASTE NOR TOUCH; 9 651
OF EACH TREE IN THE GARDEN WE MAY EATE, 9 660
BUT OF THE FRUIT OF THIS FAIR TREE AMIDST 9 661
KNOWLEDGE OF GOOD AND EVIL IN THIS TREE, 9 723
WHAT CAN YOUR KNOWLEDGE HURT HIM, OR THIS TREE 9 727
CONCEALES NOT FROM US, NAMING THEE THE TREE 9 751
SO SAYING, FROM THE TREE HER STEP SHE TURND, 9 834
THAT MORN WHEN FIRST THEY PARTED; BY THE TREE 9 848
SCARSE FROM THE TREE RETURNING; IN HER HAND 9 850
THIS TREE IS NOT AS WE ARE TOLD, A TREE 9 863
FOR THIS ONE TREE HAD BIN FORBIDDEN TEN, 9 1026
THEN EVER, BOUNTIE OF THIS VERTUOUS TREE. 9 1033
SOME TREE WHOSE BROAD SMOOTH LEAVES TOGETHER SOWD, 9 1095
ABOUT THE MOTHER TREE, A PILLARD SHADE 9 1106
HATH TOLD THEE? HAST THOU EATEN OF THE TREE 10 122
SHEE GAVE ME OF THE TREE, AND I DID EATE. 10 143
AND EATEN OF THE TREE CONCERNING WHICH 10 199
FOR ONE FORBIDDEN TREE A MULTITUDE 10 554
REACH ALSO OF THE TREE OF LIFE, AND EAT, 11 94
AND GUARD ALL PASSAGE TO THE TREE OF LIFE: 11 122
ON THIS MOUNT HE APPEERD, UNDER THIS TREE 11 320
TH' EXCEPTED TREE, NOR WITH THE SNAKE CONSPIR'D, 11 426
GREEN TREE OR GROUND WHEREON HIS FOOT MAY LIGHT; 11 858

TREES

OF GOODLIEST TREES LOADEN WITH FAIREST FRUIT, 4 147
ALL TREES OF NOBLEST KIND FOR SIGHT, SMELL, TASTE; 4 217
GROVES WHOSE RICH TREES WEPT ODOROUS GUMMS AND BALME, 4 248
THIS ONE, THIS EASIE CHARGE, OF ALL THE TREES 4 421
OF FRUIT-TREES OVERWOODIE REACHD TOO FARR 5 213
EASTWARD AMONG THOSE TREES, WHAT GLORIOUS SHAPE 5 309
THEN WITH THESE VARIOUS FRUITS THE TREES OF GOD 5 390
SUPS WITH THE OCEAN: THOUGH IN HEAV'N THE TREES 5 426
BY LIVING STREAMS AMONG THE TREES OF LIFE, 5 652
ROSE AS IN DANCE THE STATELY TREES, AND SPRED 7 324
AMONG THE TREES IN PAIRS THEY ROSE, THEY WALK'D: 7 459
THIS GARDEN, PLANTED WITH THE TREES OF GOD, 7 538
A CIRCUIT WIDE, ENCLOS'D, WITH GOODLIEST TREES 8 304
UP HITHER, FROM AMONG THE TREES APPEER'D 8 313
FOR MANY ARE THE TREES OF GOD THAT GROW 9 618
OF ALL THESE GARDEN TREES YE SHALL NOT EATE, 9 657
O SOVRAN, VERTUOUS, PRECIOUS OF ALL TREES 9 795
AMONG THE TREES ON ILES AND WOODIE SHORES. 9 1118
THE THICKEST TREES, BOTH MAN AND WIFE, TILL GOD 10 101
BUT ON THY ROULD IN HEAPS, AND UP THE TREES 10 558
OF THESE FAIR SPREADING TREES; WHICH BIDS US SEEK 10 1067
WHICH HIS OWN HAND MANURING ALL THE TREES 11 28
TO SPIRITS FOULE, AND ALL MY TREES THIR PREY, 11 124
WITH ALL HIS VERDURE SPOIL'D, AND TREES ADRIFT 11 832

TREMBL'D

HELL TREMBL'D AT THE HIDEOUS NAME, AND SIGH'D 2 788
EARTH TREMBL'D FROM HER ENTRAILS, AS AGAIN 9 1000

TREMBLE

SHALL TREMBLE, HE DESCENDING, WILL HIMSELF 12 228

TREMBLED

WITH HORRID STRIDES, HELL TREMBLED AS HE STRODE. 2 676

TREMBLING

THE TREMBLING LEAVES, WHILE UNIVERSAL PAN 4 266

TREMISEN

MAROCCO AND ALGIERS, AND TREMISEN; 11 404

TRENCH

FORERUN THE ROYAL CAMP, TO TRENCH A FIELD, 1 677

TREPIDATION

THE TREPIDATION TALKT, AND THAT FIRST MOV'D; 3 483

TRESPASS

THEY TRESPASS, AUTHORS TO THEMSELVES IN ALL 3 122
FOR SUCH A PETTY TRESPASS, AND NOT PRAISE 9 693
THE FATAL TRESPASS DON BY EVE, AMAZ'D, 9 889
HER FORMER TRESPASS FEAR'D, THE MORE TO SOOTHE 9 1006

TRESSES

HER UNADORNED GOLDEN TRESSES WORE 4 305
OF HER LOOSE TRESSES HID; HE IN DELIGHT 4 497
WITH TRESSES DISCOMPOS'D, AND GLOWING CHEEK, 5 10
HER TRESSES, AND HER RURAL LABOURS CROWN, 9 841
AND TRESSES ALL DISORDERD, AT HIS FEET 10 911

TRIAL

WILL SAVE US TRIAL WHAT THE LEAST CAN DOE 4 855
INTENDED THEE, FOR TRIAL ONELY BROUGHT, 8 447
WHEN I AM PRESENT, AND THY TRIAL CHOOSE 9 316
THOU SEVER NOT: TRIAL WILL COME UNSOUGHT. 9 366
BUT IF THOU THINK, TRIAL UNSOUGHT MAY FINDE 9 370
TOUCHD ONELY, THAT OUR TRIAL, WHEN LEAST SOUGHT, 9 380
O GLORIOUS TRIAL OF EXCEEDING LOVE, 9 961
THIS HAPPIE TRIAL OF THY LOVE, WHICH ELSE 9 975
MATTER OF GLORIOUS TRIAL; AND PERHAPS 9 1177

TRIBES

BY WHICH, TO VISIT OFT THOSE HAPPY TRIBES, 3 532
HEREAFTER, JOIN'D IN HER POPULAR TRIBES 7 488
YOUR TRIBES, AND WATER FROM TH' AMBROSIAL FOUNT? 11 279
LONG TIME IN PEACE BY FAMILIES AND TRIBES 12 23
THROUGH THE TWELVE TRIBES, TO RULE BY LAWS ORDAIND: 12 226

TRIBULATION

TRI'D IN SHARP TRIBULATION, AND REFIN'D 11 63

TRIBULATIONS

AND AFTER ALL THIR TRIBULATIONS LONG 3 336

TRIBUNAL

THY DREAD TRIBUNAL: FORTHWITH FROM ALL WINDES 3 326

TRIBUTE

SHE GATHERS, TRIBUTE LARGE, AND ON THE BOARD 5 343
KNEE-TRIBUTE YET UNPAID, PROSTRATION VILE, 5 782
AS TRIBUTE SUCH A SUMLESS JOURNEY BROUGHT 8 36

TRI'D

BUT EVIL HAST NOT TRI'D: AND WILT OBJECT 4 896
CAN HEARTS, NOT FREE, BE TRI'D WHETHER THEY SERVE 5 532
I MEAN TO TRY, WHOSE REASON I HAVE TRI'D 6 120
O NOW IN DANGER TRI'D, NOW KNOWN IN ARMES 6 418
UP HITHER, UNDER LONG OBEDIENCE TRI'D, 7 159
KNEW NOT; TO SPEAK I TRI'D, AND FORTHWITH SPAKE, 8 271
WITH ME, BEST WITNESS OF THY VERTUE TRI'D. 9 317
TRI'D IN SHARP TRIBULATION, AND REFIN'D 11 63
MORE THEN ANOUGH, THAT TEMPERANCE MAY BE TRI'D: 11 805

TRIDENT

AS WITH A TRIDENT SMOTE, AND FIX'T AS FIRM 10 295

TRIE

THAT THEY MAY HAVE THIR WISH, TO TRIE WITH MEE 6 818
MEAN I TO TRIE, WHAT RASH UNTRI'D I SOUGHT, 9 860
OR TRIE THEE NOW MORE DANG'ROUS TO HIS THRONE. 10 382

TRIFORM

WITH BORROWD LIGHT HER COUNTENANCE TRIFORM 3 730

TRINACRIAN

CALABRIA FROM THE HOARCE TRINACRIAN SHORE: 2 661

TRINE

IN SEXTILE, SQUARE, AND TRINE, AND OPPOSITE, 10 659

TRIPLE

WITH STUBBORN PATIENCE AS WITH TRIPLE STEEL. 2 569
IN THIR TRIPLE DEGREES, REGIONS TO WHICH 5 750
A TRIPLE MOUNTED ROW OF PILLARS LAID 6 572

TRIPLE-COLOUR'D

HIS TRIPLE-COLOUR'D BOW, WHEREON TO LOOK 11 897

TRIPLE-ROW

TILL ON THOSE CURSED ENGINS TRIPLE-ROW 6 650

TRIPPING

FROM STANDING LAKE TO TRIPPING EBBE, THAT STOLE 11 847

TRITON

GIRT WITH THE RIVER TRITON, WHERE OLD CHAM, 4 276

TRIUMPH

I THROUGH THE AMPLE AIR IN TRIUMPH HIGH 3 254
SUNG TRIUMPH, AND HIM SUNG VICTORIOUS KING, 6 886
GREAT TRIUMPH AND REJOYCING WAS IN HEAV'N 7 180
TRIUMPH AND SAY; FICKLE THEIR STATE WHOM GOD 9 948
IN TRIUMPH ISSUING FORTH THIR GLORIOUS CHIEF; 10 537
TURND TO EXPLODING HISS, TRIUMPH TO SHAME 10 546
OF TRIUMPH, TO BE STYL'D GREAT CONQUEROURS, 11 695
IN TRIUMPH AND LUXURIOUS WEALTH, ARE THEY 11 788

TRIUMPHAL

MESSIAH HIS TRIUMPHAL CHARIOT TURND: 6 881
TRIUMPHAL WITH TRIUMPHAL ACT HAVE MET, 10 390

TRIUMPHANT

US'D TO THE YOAK, DRAW'ST HIS TRIUMPHANT WHEELS 4 975
INTENDS TO PASS TRIUMPHANT, AND GIVE LAWS. 5 693
TRIUMPHANT THROUGH MID HEAV'N, INTO THE COURTS 6 889
TRIUMPHANT OUT OF THIS INFERNAL PIT 10 464
AND OVER THEM TRIUMPHANT DEATH HIS DART 11 491

TRIUMPH'D

WHOM THEY TRIUMPH'D ONCE LAPST. THUS WERE THEY PLAGU'D 10 572

TRIUMPHING

WITH JOY AND LOVE TRIUMPHING, AND FAIR TRUTH. 3 338
WITH VICTORY, TRIUMPHING THROUGH THE AIRE 12 452

TRIUMPHS

WHO NOW TRIUMPHS, AND IN TH' EXCESS OF JOY 1 123
TRIUMPHS OR FESTIVALS, AND TO THEM PREACHD 11 723

UNBLAM'D
- MAY I EXPRESS THEE UNBLAM'D? SINCE GOD IS LIGHT, 3 3
- VENIAL DISCOURSE UNBLAM'D: I NOW MUST CHANGE 9 5
- SHAL SPEND THIR DAYES IN JOY UNBLAM'D, AND DWELL 12 22

UNBLEST
- OF UNBLEST FEET. HIM FOLLOWED HIS NEXT MATE, 1 238
- THE RACE UNBLEST, TO BEING YET UNBEGOT. 10 988

UNBORN
- IN ORDER, THOUGH TO NATIONS YET UNBORN, 4 663
- FARR INTO CHAOS, AND THE WORLD UNBORN; 7 220
- BETTER END HEER UNBORN. WHY IS LIFE GIV'N 11 502

UNBOTTOM'D
- THE DARK UNBOTTOM'D INFINITE ABYSS 2 405

UNBOUND
- VOLATIL HERMES, AND CALL UP UNBOUND 3 603

UNBOUNDED
- THEN HAPPIE; NO UNBOUNDED HOPE HAD RAIS'D 4 60
- VOYAG'D TH' UNREAL, VAST, UNBOUNDED DEEP 10 471

UNBROK'N
- UNBROK'N, AND IN PROUD REBELLIOUS ARMS 2 691

UNBUCKL'D
- HIS STARRIE HELME UNBUCKL'D SHEW'D HIM PRIME 11 245

UNBUILD
- THE MIGHTIE FRAME, HOW BUILD, UNBUILD, CONTRIVE 8 81
- HIS CONSORT LIBERTIE; WHAT, BUT UNBUILD 12 526

UNCALL'D
- HEE BOULDER NOW, UNCALL'D BEFORE HER STOOD; 9 523

UNCELEBRATED
- NOR PAST UNCELEBRATED, NOR UNSUNG 7 253

UNCERTAIN
- UNCERTAIN WHICH, IN OCEAN OR IN AIR. 3 76

UNCHANG'D
- MORE SAFE I SING WITH MORTAL VOICE, UNCHANG'D 7 24

UNCHANGEABLE
- UNCHANGEABLE, ETERNAL, WHICH ORDAIN'D 3 127

UNCHECKT
- UNCHECKT, AND OF HER ROAVING IS NO END; 8 189

UNCIRCUMSCRIB'D
- THOUGH I UNCIRCUMSCRIB'D MY SELF RETIRE, 7 170

UNCLEAN
- THERE SIT NOT, AND REPROACH US AS UNCLEAN, 9 1098

UNCLOUDED
- BLAZ'D FORTH UNCLOUDED DEITIE; HE FULL 10 65

UNCOLOURD
- WHETHER TO DECK WITH CLOUDS THE UNCOLOURD SKIE, 5 189

UNCOMPOUNDED
- AND UNCOMPOUNDED IS THIR ESSENCE PURE, 1 425

UNCONCERN'D
- ALL UNCONCERN'D WITH OUR UNREST, BEGINS 11 174

UNCONFORM
- NOT UNCONFORM TO OTHER SHINING GLOBES, 5 259

UNCONQUERABLE
- ALL IS NOT LOST; THE UNCONQUERABLE WILL, 1 106
- WHERE BOLDEST; THOUGH TO SIGHT UNCONQUERABLE? 6 118

UNCONSUM'D
- WITH EVER-BURNING SULPHUR UNCONSUM'D: 1 69
- YET UNCONSUM'D. BEFORE THE GATES THERE SAT 2 648

UNCOUTH
- HIS UNCOUTH WAY, OR SPREAD HIS AERIE FLIGHT 2 407
- THIS UNCOUTH ERRAND SOLE, AND ONE FOR ALL 2 827
- THIS UNCOUTH DREAM, OF EVIL SPRUNG I FEAR; 5 98
- AND UNCOUTH PAINE FLED BELLOWING. ON EACH WING 6 362
- BOUND ON A VOYAGE UNCOUTH AND OBSCURE, 8 230
- TOILD OUT MY UNCOUTH PASSAGE, FORC'T TO RIDE 10 475

UNCOVER'D
- UNCOVER'D MORE, SO ROSE THE DANITE STRONG 9 1059

UNCREATE
- WHEN WHO CAN UNCREATE THEE THOU SHALT KNOW. 5 895
- DEPENDENT MADE; SO GOD SHALL UNCREATE, 9 943

UNCREATED
- IN THE WIDE WOMB OF UNCREATED NIGHT, 2 150

UNCREATED (CONTINUED)
- MISERIE, UNCREATED TILL THE CRIME 6 268

UNCROPT
- PARTAKERS, AND UNCROPT FALLS TO THE GROUND. 4 731

UNCTION
- BY SACRED UNCTION, THY DESERVED RIGHT. 6 709

UNCTUOUS
- COMPACT OF UNCTUOUS VAPOR, WHICH THE NIGHT 9 635

UNCULL'D
- UNCULL'D, AS CAME TO HAND; A SHEPHERD NEXT 11 436

UNDAUNTED
- TH' UNDAUNTED FIEND WHAT THIS MIGHT BE ADMIR'D, 2 677
- UNDAUNTED TO MEET THERE WHAT EVER POWER 2 955
- UNDAUNTED. IF I MUST CONTEND, SAID HE, 4 851
- AND THUS HIS OWN UNDAUNTED HEART EXPLORES. 6 113

UNDAZL'D
- UNDAZL'D, FARR AND WIDE HIS EYE COMMANDS, 3 614

UNDECKT
- UNDECKT, SAVE WITH HER SELF MORE LOVELY FAIR 5 380

UNDEFIL'D
- WHOSE BED IS UNDEFIL'D AND CHASTE PRONOUNC'T, 4 761

UNDELIGHTED
- SAW UNDELIGHTED ALL DELIGHT, ALL KIND 4 286

UNDER
- UNDER THY CONDUCT, AND IN DREADFUL DEEDS 1 130
- MOORS BY HIS SIDE UNDER THE LEE, WHILE NIGHT 1 207
- UNDER AMAZEMENT OF THIR HIDEOUS CHANGE. 1 313
- HOVERING ON WING UNDER THE COPE OF HELL 1 345
- A CREW WHO UNDER NAMES OF OLD RENOWN, 1 477
- SAT ON HIS FADED CHEEK, BUT UNDER BROWES 1 602
- LONG UNDER DARKNESS COVER. BUT THESE THOUGHTS 1 659
- UNDER YON BOYLING OCEAN, WRAPT IN CHAINS; 2 183
- THRIVE UNDER EVIL, AND WORK EASE OUT OF PAIN 2 261
- UNDER TH' INEVITABLE CURB, RESERV'D 2 322
- OF CREATURES RATIONAL, THOUGH UNDER HOPE 2 498
- UNDER SPREAD ENSIGNS MARCHING MIGHT PASS THROUGH 2 886
- UNDER HIS GLOOMIE POWER I SHALL NOT LONG 3 242
- FOUND OUT FOR MANKIND UNDER WRAUTH, O THOU 3 275
- THY MERITS; UNDER THEE AS HEAD SUPREAM 3 319
- IN HEAVEN, OR EARTH, OR UNDER EARTH IN HELL; 3 322
- DARK, WASTE, AND WILD, UNDER THE FROWN OF NIGHT 3 424
- DREAMING BY NIGHT UNDER THE OPEN SKIE, 3 514
- UNDER A CORONET HIS FLOWING HAIRE 3 640
- UNDER WHAT TORMENTS INWARDLY I GROANE; 4 88
- THAT PRACTISD FALSHOOD UNDER SAINTLY SHEW, 4 122
- WITH MAZIE ERROR UNDER PENDANT SHADES 4 239
- TRUE PARADISE UNDER THE ETHIOP LINE 4 282
- UNDER A TUFT OF SHADE THAT ON A GREEN 4 325
- UNDER A SHADE OF FLOURS, MUCH WONDRING WHERE 4 451
- UNDER A PLATAN, YET METHOUGHT LESS FAIRE, 4 478
- NAKED MET HIS UNDER THE FLOWING GOLD 4 496
- MINE EYE PURSU'D HIM STILL, BUT UNDER SHADE 4 572
- BOTH TURND, AND UNDER OP'N SKIE ADOR'D 4 721
- BUT FIRST FROM UNDER SHADIE ARBOROUS ROOF, 5 137
- OF ANGELS UNDER WATCH; AND TO HIS STATE, 5 288
- UNDER WHOSE LOWLY ROOF THOU HAST VOUTSAF'T 5 463
- UNDER THIR HIERARCHS IN ORDERS BRIGHT 5 587
- UNDER HIS GREAT VICE-GERENT REIGN ABIDE 5 609
- AND ALL WHO UNDER ME THIR BANNERS WAVE, 5 687
- UNDER HIM REGENT, TELLS, AS HE WAS TAUGHT, 5 698
- ALL POWER, AND US ECLIPST UNDER THE NAME 5 776
- OUR HAPPIE STATE UNDER ONE HEAD MORE NEER 5 830
- UNDER THIR GOD-LIKE LEADERS, IN THE CAUSE 6 67
- THY LEGIONS UNDER DARKNESS; BUT THOU SEEST 6 142
- WINDS UNDER GROUND OR WATERS FORCING WAY 6 196
- SO UNDER FIERIE COPE TOGETHER RUSH'D 6 215
- UNDER HER CLOUDIE COVERT BOTH RETIR'D, 6 409
- DEEP UNDER GROUND, MATERIALS DARK AND CRUDE, 6 478
- SO ALL ERE DAY-SPRING, UNDER CONSCIOUS NIGHT 6 521
- UNDER SPRED ENSIGNES MOVING NIGH, IN SLOW 6 533
- UNDER THE WEIGHT OF MOUNTAINS BURIED DEEP, 6 652
- THAT UNDER GROUND, THEY FOUGHT IN DISMAL SHADE; 6 666
- UNDER WHOSE CONDUCT MICHAEL SOON REDUC'D 6 777
- UNDER THIR HEAD IMBODIED ALL IN ONE. 6 779
- GLOOMIE AS NIGHT; UNDER HIS BURNING WHEELES 6 832
- UP HITHER, UNDER LONG OBEDIENCE TRI'D, 7 159
- BE GATHER'D NOW YE WATERS UNDER HEAV'N 7 283
- BUT THEY, OR UNDER GROUND, OR CIRCUIT WIDE 7 301
- GLIDE UNDER THE GREEN WAVE, IN SCULLES THAT OFT 7 402
- MOIST NUTRIMENT, OR UNDER ROCKS THIR FOOD 7 408
- WITH CLANG DESPIS'D THE GROUND, UNDER A CLOUD 7 422
- IN HILLOCKS; THE SWIFT STAG FROM UNDER GROUND 7 469
- WHICH IT HAD LONG STOOD UNDER, STREIND TO THE HIGHTH 8 454
- UNDER HIS FORMING HANDS A CREATURE GREW, 8 470
- INTO A GULF SHOT UNDER GROUND, TILL PART 9 72
- AID US, THE WORK UNDER OUR LABOUR GROWS, 9 208
- HATE STRONGER, UNDER SHEW OF LOVE WELL FEIGN'D, 9 492

UNDER (CONTINUED)
UNDER THIS IGNORANCE OF GOOD AND EVIL, 9 774
MUCH MORE TO TASTE IT UNDER BANNE TO TOUCH. 9 925
WERE SUCH AS UNDER GOVERNMENT WELL SEEM'D, 10 154
WHOM HE SHALL TREAD AT LAST UNDER OUR FEET; 10 190
ASCENDED HIS HIGH THRONE, WHICH UNDER STATE 10 445
WHY STAND WE LONGER SHIVERING UNDER FEARES, 10 1003
ON THIS MOUNT HE APPEERD, UNDER THIS TREE 11 320
UNDER INHUMAN PAINS? WHY SHOULD NOT MAN, 11 511
IN PRISON UNDER JUDGEMENTS IMMINENT: 11 725
FROM UNDER HEAV'N; THE HILLS TO THEIR SUPPLIE 11 740
DEEP UNDER WATER ROULD; SEA COVER'D SEA, 11 749
UNDER PATERNAL RULE; TILL ONE SHALL RISE 12 24
WITH HIM OR UNDER HIM TO TYRANNIZE, 12 39
BOILES OUT FROM UNDER GROUND, THE MOUTH OF HELL; 12 42
BY JUDGES FIRST, THEN UNDER KINGS; OF WHOM 12 320
UNDER HER OWN WAIGHT GROANING TILL THE DAY 12 539
ART ALL THINGS UNDER HEAV'N, ALL PLACES THOU, 12 618

UNDERFOOT
MOSAIC; UNDERFOOT THE VIOLET, 4 700

UNDERGO
TO UNDERGO ETERNAL PUNISHMENT? 1 155
YEARLY ENJOYND, SOME SAY, TO UNDERGO 10 575

UNDERGOE
CERTAIN TO UNDERGOE LIKE DOOM, IF DEATH 9 953
TO UNDERGOE WITH MEE ONE GUILT, ONE CRIME, 9 971
BEFORE MY JUDGE, EITHER TO UNDERGOE 10 126

UNDERGROUND
FROM UNDERGROUND) THE LIQUID ORE HE DREIND 11 570

UNDERGROWTH
AS ONE CONTINU'D BRAKE, THE UNDERGROWTH 4 175

UNDERNEATH
THAT UNDERNEATH HAD VEINS OF LIQUID FIRE 1 701
VIEWLESS, AND UNDERNEATH A BRIGHT SEA FLOW'D 3 518
PASS'D UNDERNEATH INGULFT, FOR GOD HAD THROWN 4 225
WITH HIM I FLEW, AND UNDERNEATH BEHELD 5 87
LONG STRUGLING UNDERNEATH, ERE THEY COULD WIND 6 659
THE WATERS UNDERNEATH FROM THOSE ABOVE 7 268

UNDERSTAND
HAD NEED FROM HEAD TO FOOT WELL UNDERSTAND; 6 625
WITH LOW SUBJECTION; UNDERSTAND THE SAME 8 345
FOR WELL I UNDERSTAND IN THE PRIME END 8 540
OF UTMOST HOPE. NOW CLEAR I UNDERSTAND 12 376

UNDERSTANDING
FANSIE AND UNDERSTANDING, WHENCE THE SOULE 5 486
UNHURT OUR MINDES, AND UNDERSTANDING SOUND, 6 444
FOR UNDERSTANDING RUL'D NOT, AND THE WILL 9 1127

UNDERSTOOD
OPEN OR UNDERSTOOD MUST BE RESOLV'D. 1 662
AND UNDERSTOOD NOT THAT A GRATEFUL MIND 4 55
WAS UNDERSTOOD, THE INJUR'D LOVERS HELL. 5 450
NOT UNDERSTOOD, THIS GIFT THEY HAVE BESIDES, 6 626
I NAM'D THEM, AS THEY PASS'D, AND UNDERSTOOD 8 352
OF AMOROUS INTENT, WELL UNDERSTOOD 9 1035
THENCE GATHERD HIS OWN DOOM, WHICH UNDERSTOOD 10 344
AND UNDERSTOOD NOT ALL WAS BUT A SHEW 10 883
NOT UNDERSTOOD, TILL HOARSE, AND ALL IN RAGE, 12 58
THOUGH NOT BUT BY THE SPIRIT UNDERSTOOD. 12 514

UNDERTAKE
TO SECOND, OR OPPOSE, OR UNDERTAKE 2 419

UNDERTOOK
I THEREFORE, I ALONE FIRST UNDERTOOK 4 935
WHEN TIME SHALL BE, FOR SO I UNDERTOOK 10 74

UNDESERV'D
WILL ARROGATE DOMINION UNDESERV'D 12 27

UNDESERVEDLY
WHO OFT AS UNDESERVEDLY ENTHRALL 12 94

UNDESIREABLE
A THING NOT UNDESIREABLE, SOMTIME 9 824

UNDETERMIND
IN CIRCUIT, UNDETERMIND SQUARE OR ROUND, 2 1048

UNDIMINISHT
STRENGTH UNDIMINISHT, OR ETERNAL BEING 1 154
OR UNDIMINISHT BRIGHTNESS, TO BE KNOWN 4 836

UNDISMAI'D
AND IN THE MIDST THUS UNDISMAI'D BEGAN. 6 417

UNDISMAID
SEIS'D US, THOUGH UNDISMAID: LONG IS THE WAY 2 432

UNDO
BE FRUSTRATE, DO, UNDO, AND LABOUR LOOSE, 9 944

UNDOE
BUT PAST WHO CAN RECALL, OR DON UNDOE? 9 926

UNDON
INDEBTED AND UNDON, HATH NONE TO BRING: 3 235

UNDOUBTED
SHON WITH A GLOSSIE SCURFF, UNDOUBTED SIGN 1 672

UNDOUBTEDLY
UNDOUBTEDLY HE WILL RELENT AND TURN 10 1093

UNDRAWN
FLASHING THICK FLAMES, WHEELE WITHIN WHEELE
UNDRAWN, 6 751

UNDREADED
UNNAM'D, UNDREADED, AND THY SELF HALF STARV'D? 10 595

UNDYING
TO CHAINS OF DARKNESS, AND TH' UNDYING WORM, 6 739

UNEARN'D
EARLY, AND TH' HOUR OF SUPPER COMES UNEARN'D. 9 225

UNEASIE
HE WALKT WITH TO SUPPORT UNEASIE STEPS 1 295

UNENVIED
ESTABLISHT IN A SAFE UNENVIED THRONE 2 23

UNEQUAL
FOR GODS, AND TOO UNEQUAL WORK WE FIND 6 453
AGAINST UNEQUAL ARMES TO FIGHT IN PAINE, 6 454

UNEQUALD
SO FAITHFUL LOVE UNEQUALD; BUT I FEEL 9 983

UNEQUALS
AMONG UNEQUALS WHAT SOCIETIE 8 383

UNESPI'D
NEERER TO VIEW HIS PREY, AND UNESPI'D 4 399
WITH SILENT CIRCUMSPECTION UNESPI'D. 6 523

UNESSENTIAL
OF UNESSENTIAL NIGHT RECEIVES HIM NEXT 2 439

UNEXAMPL'D
FOR MANS OFFENCE. O UNEXAMPL'D LOVE, 3 410

UNEXPECTED
FIRST SEEN, THEM UNEXPECTED JOY SURPRIZ'D, 6 774
O UNEXPECTED STROKE, WORSE THEN OF DEATH. 11 268

UNEXPERIENC'T
WITH UNEXPERIENC'T THOUGHT, AND LAID ME DOWNE 4 457

UNEXPERT
MORE UNEXPERT, I BOAST NOT: THEM LET THOSE 2 52

UNEXTINGUISHABLE
WHERE PAIN OF UNEXTINGUISHABLE FIRE 2 88

UNFAINED
UNFAINED HALLELUIAHS TO THEE SING, 6 744

UNFAITHFUL
TO JUDGE TH' UNFAITHFUL DEAD, BUT TO REWARD 12 461
HIS FAITHFUL, LEFT AMONG TH' UNFAITHFUL HERD, 12 481

UNFAST'NS
UNFAST'NS: ON A SUDDEN OP'N FLIE 2 879

UNFEARD
FEARLESS UNFEARD HE SLEPT: IN AT HIS MOUTH 9 187

UNFEIGN'D
AND SWEET COMPLIANCE, WHICH DECLARE UNFEIGN'D 8 603
OF SORROW UNFEIGN'D, AND HUMILIATION MEEK. 10 1092
OF SORROW UNFEIGN'D, AND HUMILIATION MEEK. 10 1104

UNFELT
STRANGE HORROR SEISE THEE, AND PANGS UNFELT BEFORE. 2 703
SWEETNESS INTO MY HEART, UNFELT BEFORE, 8 475

UNFOLD
WHICH I AS FREELY GIVE; HELL SHALL UNFOLD, 4 381

UNFORBID
ABSOLV'D, IF UNFORBID THOU MAIST UNFOULD 7 94

UNFOREKNOWN
WHICH HAD NO LESS PROV'D CERTAIN UNFOREKNOWN. 3 119

UNFORESEEN
- BEFALLN US UNFORESEEN, UNTHOUGHT OF, KNOW — 2 821

UNFOREWARND
- SURPRISAL, UNADMONISHT, UNFOREWARND. — 5 245

UNFORM'D
- MATTER UNFORM'D AND VOID: DARKNESS PROFOUND — 7 233

UNFORTUNATE
- FOUND SO UNFORTUNATE; NEVERTHELESS, — 10 970

UNFOULD
- AND PERFET WHILE THEY STOOD; HOW LAST UNFOULD — 5 568
- VANGUARD, TO RIGHT AND LEFT THE FRONT UNFOULD; — 6 558
- ABSOLV'D, IF UNFORBID THOU MAIST UNFOULD — 7 94
- HOW COMES IT THUS? UNFOULD, CELESTIAL GUIDE, — 11 785

UNFOULDING
- SO SPAKE THE FATHER, AND UNFOULDING BRIGHT — 10 63

UNFOUND
- ONCE FOUND, WHICH YET UNFOUND MOST WOULD HAVE THOUGHT — 6 500

UNFOUNDED
- TH' UNFOUNDED DEEP, AND THROUGH THE VOID IMMENSE — 2 829

UNFREQUENTED
- THIR LIVING STRENGTH, AND UNFREQUENTED LEFT — 1 433

UNFULFILL'D
- STILL UNFULFILL'D WITH PAIN OF LONGING PINES; — 4 511

UNFUM'D
- WITH ROSE AND ODOURS FROM THE SHRUB UNFUM'D. — 5 349

UNFURLD
- WHO FORTHWITH FROM THE GLITTERING STAFF UNFURLD — 1 535

UNGODLY
- HAD DRIVEN OUT TH' UNGODLY FROM HIS SIGHT — 7 185

UNGOVERN'D
- TO SERVE UNGOVERN'D APPETITE, AND TOOK — 11 517

UNGRACEFUL
- NOR ARE THY LIPS UNGRACEFUL, SIRE OF MEN, — 8 218

UNGUARDED
- THE THRONE OF GOD UNGUARDED, AND HIS SIDE — 6 133
- WIDE OPEN AND UNGUARDED, SATAN PASS'D, — 10 419

UNHALLOWD
- MADE COMMON AND UNHALLOWD ERE OUR TASTE; — 9 931

UNHAPPIE
- DESIRE OF WANDRING THIS UNHAPPIE MORN, — 9 1136

UNHAPPILIE
- UNHAPPILIE DECEAV'D; THY SUPPLIANT — 10 917

UNHAPPY
- IN THIS UNHAPPY MANSION, OR ONCE MORE — 1 268

UNHARMONEOUS
- NO GROSS, NO UNHARMONEOUS MIXTURE FOULE, — 11 51

UNHEARD
- THIR CHILDRENS CRIES UNHEARD, THAT PAST THROUGH FIRE — 1 395
- NOR WAS HIS NAME UNHEARD OR UNADOR'D — 1 738
- HE DREW NOT NIGH UNHEARD, THE ANGEL BRIGHT, — 3 645

UNHEEDED
- GAVE PROOF UNHEEDED; OTHERS ON THE GRASS — 4 350

UNHIDE-BOUND
- TO STUFF THIS MAW, THIS VAST UNHIDE-BOUND CORPS. — 10 601

UNHOLIE
- FROM HALLOWD GROUND TH' UNHOLIE, AND DENOUNCE — 11 106

UNHOORD
- OR AS A THIEF BENT TO UNHOORD THE CASH — 4 188

UNHOP'T
- OF THIS NEW WONDROUS PONTIFICE, UNHOP'T — 10 348

UNHURT
- UNHURT OUR MINDES, AND UNDERSTANDING SOUND, — 6 444

UNIMAGINABLE
- SO UNIMAGINABLE AS HATE IN HEAV'N, — 7 54

UNIMMORTAL
- BOTH TO DESTROY, OR UNIMMORTAL MAKE — 10 611

UNIMPLOID
- ROVE IDLE UNIMPLOID, AND LESS NEED REST; — 4 617

UNIMPLOR'D
- COMES UNPREVENTED, UNIMPLOR'D, UNSOUGHT, — 3 231
- HER NIGHTLY VISITATION UNIMPLOR'D, — 9 22

UNINDEARD
- OF HARLOTS, LOVELESS, JOYLESS, UNINDEARD, — 4 766

UNINFORMD
- AND GUIDED BY HIS VOICE, NOR UNINFORMD — 8 486

UNINTERRUPTED
- UNINTERRUPTED JOY, UNRIVALD LOVE — 3 68

UNINVENTED
- NOT UNINVENTED THAT, WHICH THOU ARIGHT — 6 470

UNION
- TO UNION, AND FIRM FAITH, AND FIRM ACCORD, — 2 36
- MEE DISOBEYES, BREAKS UNION, AND THAT DAY — 5 612
- OF UNION IRRESISTIBLE, MOV'D ON — 6 63
- ONE KINGDOM, JOY AND UNION WITHOUT END. — 7 161
- OF UNION OR COMMUNION, DEIFI'D; — 8 431
- UNION OF MIND, OR IN US BOTH ONE SOULE; — 8 604
- TOTAL THEY MIX, UNION OF PURE WITH PURE — 8 627
- AND GLADLY OF OUR UNION HEARE THEE SPEAK, — 9 966

UNISON
- CHORAL OR UNISON: OF INCENSE CLOUDS — 7 599

UNITE
- HER CHRYSTAL MIRROR HOLDS, UNITE THIR STREAMS. — 4 263
- WOULD UTMOST VIGOR RAISE, AND RAIS'D UNITE. — 9 314
- POWERFUL AT GREATEST DISTANCE TO UNITE — 10 247

UNITED
- UNITED THOUGHTS AND COUNSELS, EQUAL HOPE — 1 88
- BREATHING UNITED FORCE WITH FIXED THOUGHT — 1 560
- HOW SUCH UNITED FORCE OF GODS, HOW SUCH — 1 629
- WATERD THE GARDEN; THENCE UNITED FELL — 4 230
- UNITED AS ONE INDIVIDUAL SOULE — 5 610
- UNITED. BUT TO GRANT IT THEE UNJUST, — 5 831
- UNITED I BEHELD; NO FAIR TO THINE — 9 608

UNITES
- SUCH FATAL CONSEQUENCE UNITES US THREE: — 10 364
- OF GOD MOST HIGH; SO GOD WITH MAN UNITES. — 12 382

UNITIE
- IN UNITIE DEFECTIVE, WHICH REQUIRES — 8 425

UNIVERS
- THE UNIVERS, AND TO EACH INWARD PART — 3 584

UNIVERSAL
- AT WHICH THE UNIVERSAL HOST UPSENT — 1 541
- AT LENGTH A UNIVERSAL HUBBUB WILDE — 2 951
- PRESENTED WITH A UNIVERSAL BLANC — 3 48
- ANOINTED UNIVERSAL KING; ALL POWER — 3 317
- THE UNIVERSAL MAKER WE MAY PRAISE; — 3 676
- THE TREMBLING LEAVES, WHILE UNIVERSAL PAN — 4 266
- ALMIGHTIE, THINE THIS UNIVERSAL FRAME, — 5 154
- HAIL UNIVERSAL LORD, BE BOUNTEOUS STILL — 5 205
- UNIVERSAL REPROACH, FAR WORSE TO BEARE — 6 34
- IN UNIVERSAL RUIN LAST, AND NOW — 6 797
- THE HOLLOW UNIVERSAL ORB THEY FILL'D, — 7 257
- HER UNIVERSAL FACE WITH PLEASANT GREEN, — 7 316
- SO SPAKE THE UNIVERSAL LORD, AND SEEM'D — 8 376
- SOVRAN OF CREATURES, UNIVERSAL DAME. — 9 612
- THIR UNIVERSAL SHOUT AND HIGH APPLAUSE — 10 505
- A DISMAL UNIVERSAL HISS, THE SOUND — 10 508
- A WORLD DEVOTE TO UNIVERSAL RACK. — 11 821

UNIVERSALLY
- WHERE UNIVERSALLY ADMIR'D; BUT HERE — 9 542

UNIVERSE
- A UNIVERSE OF DEATH, WHICH GOD BY CURSE — 2 622
- THE REST IN CIRCUIT WALLES THIS UNIVERSE. — 3 721
- THIS UNIVERSE, AND ALL CREATED THINGS: — 7 227
- ADORE THEE, AUTHOR OF THIS UNIVERSE, — 8 360
- QUEEN OF THIS UNIVERSE, DOE NOT BELIEVE — 9 684

UNJUST
- OUR STRENGTH IS EQUAL, NOR THE LAW UNJUST — 2 200
- MANS MORTAL CRIME, AND JUST TH' UNJUST TO SAVE, — 3 215
- CONFESS HIM RIGHTFUL KING? UNJUST THOU SAIST — 5 818
- FLATLY UNJUST, TO BINDE WITH LAWS THE FREE, — 5 819
- UNITED. BUT TO GRANT IT THEE UNJUST, — 5 831
- OUT OF THY LOYNS; TH' UNJUST THE JUST HATH SLAIN, — 11 455
- JUST FOR UNJUST, THAT IN SUCH RIGHTEOUSNESS — 12 294

UNJUSTLY
- UNJUSTLY THOU DEPRAV'ST IT WITH THE NAME — 6 174

UNKINDLY
ABORTIVE, MONSTROUS, OR UNKINDLY MIXT, ... 3 456
BRED OF UNKINDLY FUMES, WITH CONSCIOUS DREAMS . . 9 1050

UNKINDNESS
AS ONE WHO LOVES, AND SOME UNKINDNESS MEETS, . . . 9 271

UNKNOWN
OR UNKNOWN REGION, WHAT REMAINS HIM LESS 2 443
THEN UNKNOWN DANGERS AND AS HARD ESCAPE. 2 444
THE PARADISE OF FOOLS, TO FEW UNKNOWN 3 496
NOT TO KNOW MEE ARGUES YOUR SELVES UNKNOWN, . . . 4 830
AUTHOR OF EVIL, UNKNOWN TILL THY REVOLT, ... 6 262
UNKNOWN, WHICH HUMAN KNOWLEDG COULD NOT REACH: . . 7 75
NEEDLEST TO THEE REPEATED; NOR UNKNOWN 7 494
IN PARADISE, AND VARIOUS, YET UNKNOWN 9 619
FOR GOOD UNKNOWN, SURE IS NOT HAD, OR HAD 9 756
AND YET UNKNOWN, IS AS NOT HAD AT ALL. 9 757
OF DANGER TASTED, NOR TO EVIL UNKNOWN 9 864
OF ENEMIE HATH BEGUIL'D THEE, YET UNKNOWN, ... 9 905
TO SOW A JANGLING NOISE OF WORDS UNKNOWN: . . . 12 55
WITH GOD, WHO CALL'D HIM, IN A LAND UNKNOWN. . . 12 134

UNLESS
WITHIN HEAV'NS BOUND, UNLESS HEAV'NS LORD SUPREAM 2 236
UNLESS TH' ALMIGHTY MAKER THEM ORDAIN 2 915
DYE HEE OR JUSTICE MUST; UNLESS FOR HIM 3 210
AND NOT MOLEST US, UNLESS WE OUR SELVES 8 186
THAT NAME, UNLESS AN AGE TOO LATE, OR COLD . . . 9 44
TO DWELL, UNLESS BY MAISTRING HEAV'NS SUPREAME; . 9 125
THE SERPENTS HEAD; PITEOUS AMENDS, UNLESS . . . 10 1032

UNLIBIDINOUS
LOVE UNLIBIDINOUS REIGN'D, NOR JEALOUSIE 5 449

UNLICENC'T
UNLICENC'T FROM HIS BOUNDS IN HELL PRESCRIB'D; . 4 909

UNLIGHTSOM
A MIGHTIE SPHEARE HE FRAM'D, UNLIGHTSOM FIRST, . 7 355

UNLIKE
O HOW UNLIKE THE PLACE FROM WHENCE THEY FELL. . . 1 75
ENTRAILS UNLIKE) OF MINERAL AND STONE, ... 6 517
THIR GUILT AND DREADED SHAME; O HOW UNLIKE . . . 9 1114

UNLIMITED
UNLIMITED OF MANIFOLD DELIGHTS: 4 435

UNLOCK
I KEEP, BY HIM FORBIDDEN TO UNLOCK 2 852

UNMAKE
ABOLISH THY CREATION, AND UNMAKE, ... 3 163

UNMARKT
OF FORREIN WORLDS: HE THROUGH THE MIDST UNMARKT, . 10 441

UNMEASUR'D
ALL PERFET GOOD UNMEASUR'D OUT, DESCENDS, ... 5 399

UNMEDITATED
UNMEDITATED, SUCH PROMPT ELOQUENCE 5 149

UNMEET
WHOSE FELLOWSHIP THEREFORE UNMEET FOR THEE 8 442

UNMERITED
FAVOUR UNMERITED BY ME, WHO SOUGHT 12 278

UNMINDED
HEE AFTER EVE SEDUC'T, UNMINDED SLUNK 10 332

UNMINDFUL
NOR STOOD UNMINDFUL ABDIEL TO ANNOY 6 369
UNMINDFUL OF THIR MAKER, THOUGH HIS SPIRIT . . . 11 611

UNMIXT
THEN SHALL THY SAINTS UNMIXT, AND FROM TH' IMPURE 6 742

UNMOV'D
DELIBERATE VALOUR BREATH'D, FIRM AND UNMOV'D . . 1 554
CONSCIOUS OF HIGHEST WORTH, UNMOV'D THUS SPAKE. . 2 429
INTO A LIQUID PLAIN, THEN STOOD UNMOV'D 4 455
AMONG INNUMERABLE FALSE, UNMOV'D, ... 5 898
SUPERIOUR AND UNMOV'D, HERE ONELY WEAKE 8 532
PURSUING, NOT UNMOV'D TO EVE THUS SPAKE. . . . 11 192

UNMOVD
YET THUS, UNMOVD WITH FEAR, ACCOST HIM SOON. . . . 4 822

UNNAM'D
UNNAM'D IN HEAV'N, NOW PLENTEOUS, AS THOU SEEST . 6 263
UNNAM'D, UNDREADED, AND THY SELF HALF STARV'D? . 10 595
(THINGS BY THIR NAMES I CALL, THOUGH YET UNNAM'D) 12 140

UNNUMBER'D
SWARM POPULOUS, UNNUMBER'D AS THE SANDS 2 903

UNNUMBER'D (CONTINUED)
FLOATS, AS THEY PASS, FANN'D WITH UNNUMBER'D PLUMES: 7 432

UNOBEY'D
UNWORSHIPT, UNOBEY'D THE THRONE SUPREAM 5 670

UNOBNOXIOUS
UNWEARIED, UNOBNOXIOUS TO BE PAIN'D 6 404

UNOBSCUR'D
CHOOSE TO RESIDE, HIS GLORY UNOBSCUR'D, ... 2 265

UNOBSERV'D
AS HE SUPPOS'D, ALL UNOBSERV'D, UNSEEN. 4 130

UNOPPOS'D
THE HIGHTH OF THY ASPIRING UNOPPOS'D, ... 6 132

UNORIGINAL
OF UNORIGINAL NIGHT AND CHAOS WILDE, ... 10 477

UNPAID
KNEE-TRIBUTE YET UNPAID, PROSTRATION VILE, ... 5 782

UNPAIND
AGAINST UNPAIND, IMPASSIVE; FROM WHICH EVIL . . . 6 455

UNPEOPL'D
LONG AFTER, NOW UNPEOPL'D, AND UNTROD; 3 497

UNPERCEAV'D
NOT UNPERCEAV'D OF ADAM, WHO TO EVE, ... 11 224

UNPERCEIVD
SO SPAKE THE FALSE DISSEMBLER UNPERCEIVD; 3 681

UNPIERC'T
THE OPEN FIELD, AND WHERE THE UNPIERC'T SHADE . . 4 245

UNPITIED
UNRESPITED, UNPITIED, UNREPREEVD, ... 2 185

UNPITTIED
THOUGH I UNPITTIED: LEAGUE WITH YOU I SEEK, . . . 4 375

UNPOLLUTED
SIT UNPOLLUTED, AND TH' ETHEREAL MOULD 2 139

UNPOSSEST
FOR SUCH VAST ROOM IN NATURE UNPOSSEST 8 153

UNPRACTIS'D
UNPRACTIS'D, UNPREPAR'D, AND STILL TO SEEK. . . . 8 197

UNPRAIS'D
UNPRAIS'D: FOR NOTHING LOVELIER CAN BE FOUND . . 9 232

UNPREMEDITATED
EASIE MY UNPREMEDITATED VERSE: 9 24

UNPREPAR'D
UNPRACTIS'D, UNPREPAR'D, AND STILL TO SEEK. . . . 8 197

UNPREVENTED
COMES UNPREVENTED, UNIMPLOR'D, UNSOUGHT, ... 3 231

UNPROCLAM'D
WARR UNPROCLAM'D. THE PRINCELY HIERARCH 11 220

UNPURG'D
WHENCE IN HER VISAGE ROUND THOSE SPOTS, UNPURG'D . 5 419

UNPURSU'D
ALL NIGHT THE DREADLESS ANGEL UNPURSU'D 6 1

UNQUENCHABLE
UNQUENCHABLE, THE HOUSE OF WOE AND PAINE. 6 877

UNQUIET
AS THROUGH UNQUIET REST: HE ON HIS SIDE 5 11
WHAT THOUGHTS IN MY UNQUIET BREST ARE RIS'N, . . 10 975

UNREAL
VOYAG'D TH' UNREAL, VAST, UNBOUNDED DEEP 10 471

UNREIN'D
LEAST FROM THIS FLYING STEED UNREIN'D, (AS ONCE . 7 17

UNREMOV'D
LIKE TENERIFF OR ATLAS UNREMOV'D: 4 987

UNREPREEVD
UNRESPITED, UNPITIED, UNREPREEVD, ... 2 185

UNREPROV'D
OF CONJUGAL ATTRACTION UNREPROV'D, ... 4 493

UNRESPITED
UNRESPITED, UNPITIED, UNREPREEVD, 2 185

UNREST
AS FROM UNREST, AND EACH THE OTHER VIEWING, 9 1052
ALL UNCONCERN'D WITH OUR UNREST, BEGINS 11 174

UNREVOK'T
HEAR MY DECREE, WHICH UNREVOK'T SHALL STAND. 5 602

UNRIGHTEOUS
THIR OWN BOTH RIGHTEOUS AND UNRIGHTEOUS DEEDS, 3 292

UNRIVALD
UNINTERRUPTED JOY, UNRIVALD LOVE 3 68

UNSAFE
AND LEFT LARGE FIELD, UNSAFE WITHIN THE WIND 6 309

UNSAUGHT
WHERE OBVIOUS DUTIE EREWHILE APPEAR'D UNSAUGHT: 10 106

UNSAVOURIE
THE EARTH TO YIELD; UNSAVOURIE FOOD PERHAPS 5 401

UNSAY
WOULD HIGTH RECAL HIGH THOUGHTS, HOW SOON UNSAY 4 95
TO SAY AND STRAIT UNSAY, PRETENDING FIRST 4 947

UNSEARCHABLE
THINGS ELSE BY ME UNSEARCHABLE, NOW HEARD 8 10

UNSEARCHT
SEARCH THROUGH THIS GARDEN, LEAVE UNSEARCHT NO NOOK, 4 789

UNSEASONABLE
OF SOMTHING NOT UNSEASONABLE TO ASK 8 201

UNSEDUC'D
UNSHAK'N, UNSEDUC'D, UNTERRIFI'D 5 899

UNSEEMLIEST
TO SHAME OBNOXIOUS, AND UNSEEMLIEST SEEN, 9 1094

UNSEEMLY
UNSEEMLY TO BEARE RULE, WHICH WAS THY PART 10 155

UNSEEN
WITHIN UNSEEN. FARR LESS ABHORRD THAN THESE 2 659
SHALL DWELL AT EASE, AND UP AND DOWN UNSEEN 2 841
WITH GENTLE PENETRATION, THOUGH UNSEEN, 3 585
AS HE SUPPOS'D, ALL UNOBSERV'D, UNSEEN. 4 130
UNSEEN, BOTH WHEN WE WAKE, AND WHEN WE SLEEP: 4 678
LED BY HER HEAV'NLY MAKER, THOUGH UNSEEN, 8 485
ENTRANCE UNSEEN. SOON AS TH' UNWELCOME NEWS 10 21
HE SATE, AND ROUND ABOUT HIM SAW UNSEEN: 10 448
THAT ALL HIS SENSES BOUND; EVE, WHO UNSEEN 11 265
UNSEEN AMID THE THRONG: SO VIOLENCE 11 671
UNSEEN, AND THROUGH THIR HABITATIONS WALKS 12 49
UNSEEN BEFORE IN HEAV'N PROCLAIMS HIM COM, 12 361

UNSHAK'N
FELL NOT, BUT STAND UNSHAK'N, FROM WITHIN 4 64
UNSHAK'N, UNSEDUC'D, UNTERRIFI'D 5 899

UNSHAR'D
TEDIOUS, UNSHAR'D WITH THEE, AND ODIOUS SOON. 9 880

UNSHED
TO BLOOD UNSHED THE RIVERS MUST BE TURND, 12 176

UNSIGHTLY
THAT LIE BESTROWNE UNSIGHTLY AND UNSMOOTH, 4 631
DESERT AND BARE, UNSIGHTLY, UNADORND, 7 314
TO SUCH UNSIGHTLY SUFFERINGS BE DEBAS'T 11 510

UNSKILFUL
UNSKILFUL WITH WHAT WORDS TO PRAY, LET MEE 11 32

UNSLEEPING
ALL BUT THE UNSLEEPING EYES OF GOD TO REST, 5 647

UNSMOOTH
THAT LIE BESTROWNE UNSIGHTLY AND UNSMOOTH, 4 631

UNSOUGHT
COMES UNPREVENTED, UNIMPLOR'D, UNSOUGHT, 3 231
THAT WOULD BE WOO'D, AND NOT UNSOUGHT BE WON, 8 503
THOU SEVER NOT: TRIAL WILL COME UNSOUGHT. 9 366
BUT IF THOU THINK, TRIAL UNSOUGHT MAY FINDE 9 370

UNSOUND
UNSOUND AND FALSE; NOR IS IT AUGHT BUT JUST, 6 121

UNSPAR'D
THE SITHE OF TIME MOWES DOWN, DEVOUR UNSPAR'D, 10 606

UNSPARING
HEAPS WITH UNSPARING HAND; FOR DRINK THE GRAPE 5 344

UNSPEAKABLE
UNSPEAKABLE DESIRE TO SEE, AND KNOW 3 662
UNSPEAKABLE, WHO FIRST ABOVE THESE HEAVENS 5 156
UNSPEAKABLE; FOR WHO, THOUGH WITH THE TONGUE 6 297

UNSPI'D
THIS GARDEN, AND NO CORNER LEAVE UNSPI'D; 4 529

UNSPOIL'D
OF ATABALIPA, AND YET UNSPOIL'D 11 409

UNSPOTTED
HIS PREY, NOR SUFFER MY UNSPOTTED SOULE 3 248

UNSUCCEEDED
ONE OVER ALL WITH UNSUCCEEDED POWER. 5 821

UNSUCCESSFUL
FROM UNSUCCESSFUL CHARGE, BE NOT DISMAID, 10 35

UNSUCKT
UNSUCKT OF LAMB OR KID, THAT TEND THIR PLAY. 9 583

UNSUFFERABLE
HELL HEARD TH' UNSUFFERABLE NOISE, HELL SAW 6 867

UNSUNG
IN SION ALSO NOT UNSUNG, WHERE STOOD 1 442
HALF YET REMAINES UNSUNG BUT NARROWER BOUND 7 21
NOR PAST UNCELEBRATED, NOR UNSUNG 7 253
UNSUNG; OR TO DESCRIBE RACES AND GAMES, 9 33

UNSUPPORTED
HER SELF, THOUGH FAIREST UNSUPPORTED FLOUR, 9 432

UNSUSPECT
THE GOOD BEFALL'N HIM, AUTHOR UNSUSPECT, 9 771

UNSUSPECTED
FOUND UNSUSPECTED WAY. THERE WAS A PLACE, 9 69

UNSUSTAIND
HUNG DROOPING UNSUSTAIND, THEM SHE UPSTAIES 9 430

UNTAM'D
UNTAM'D RELUCTANCE, AND REVENGE THOUGH SLOW, 2 337

UNTAUGHT
VAIN WARR WITH HEAV'N, AND BY SUCCESS UNTAUGHT 2 9

UNTERRIFI'D
UNTERRIFI'D, AND LIKE A COMET BURN'D, 2 708
UNSHAK'N, UNSEDUC'D, UNTERRIFI'D 5 899

UNTHOUGHT
BEFALLN US UNFORESEEN, UNTHOUGHT OF, KNOW 2 821

UNTHRONE
OUR OWN RIGHT LOST: HIM TO UNTHRONE WE THEN 2 231

UNTO
TILL THOU RETURN UNTO THE GROUND, FOR THOU 10 206

UNTOUCHT
AS LEAVES A GREATER STORE OF FRUIT UNTOUCHT, 9 621

UNTRACTABLE
TH' UNTRACTABLE ABYSSE, PLUNG'D IN THE WOMB 10 476

UNTRAIND
UNTRAIND IN ARMES, WHERE RASHNESS LEADS NOT ON. 12 222

UNTRI'D
THROUGH WAYES OF DANGER BY HIMSELF UNTRI'D, 4 934
MEAN I TO TRIE, WHAT RASH UNTRI'D I SOUGHT, 9 860

UNTROD
LONG AFTER, NOW UNPEOPL'D, AND UNTROD; 3 497

UNTROUBL'D
MY DROUSED SENSE, UNTROUBL'D, THOUGH I THOUGHT 8 289

UNUSUAL
THAT FELT UNUSUAL WEIGHT, TILL ON DRY LAND 1 227

UNUTTERABLE
UNUTTERABLE, WHICH THE SPIRIT OF PRAYER 11 6

UNVAILD
APPARENT QUEEN UNVAILD HER PEERLESS LIGHT, 4 608

UNVANQUISHT
UNVANQUISHT, EASIER TO TRANSACT WITH MEE 6 286

UNVISITED
DWELL NOT UNVISITED OF HEAV'NS FAIR LIGHT 2 398

UNVOYAGEABLE
NOR THIS UNVOYAGEABLE GULF OBSCURE 10 366

UNWAK'ND
HIS WONDER WAS TO FIND UNWAK'ND EVE 5 9

UNWARIE
BAD INFLUENCE INTO TH' UNWARIE BREST 5 695
YET MORE AMAZ'D UNWARIE THUS REPLY'D. 9 614
UNWARIE, AND TOO DESIROUS, AS BEFORE, 10 947

UNWEARIED
UNWEARIED, UNOBNOXIOUS TO BE PAIN'D 6 404
DESISTING, THOUGH UNWEARIED, UP RETURND 7 552

UNWEETING
BY EVE, THOUGH ALL UNWEETING, SECONDED 10 335
I BEARE THEE, AND UNWEETING HAVE OFFENDED, 10 916

UNWEILDIE
WALLOWING UNWEILDIE, ENORMOUS IN THIR GATE 7 411

UNWELCOME
ENTRANCE UNSEEN. SOON AS TH' UNWELCOME NEWS 10 21

UNWIELDY
GAMBOLD BEFORE THEM, TH' UNWIELDY ELEPHANT 4 345

UNWILLING
IS TO GO HENCE UNWILLING; THOU TO MEE 12 617

UNWISE
TO SERVE TH' UNWISE, OR HIM WHO HATH REBELLD 6 179

UNWISER
IN SAD EVENT, WHEN TO THE UNWISER SON 4 716

UNWORSHIPT
UNWORSHIPT, UNOBEY'D THE THRONE SUPREAM 5 670

UNWORTHIE
CLOATH'D US UNWORTHIE, PITYING WHILE HE JUDG'D; 10 1059
WITHIN HIMSELF UNWORTHIE POWERS TO REIGN 12 91
SUCH FAVOUR I UNWORTHIE AM VOUTSAFT, 12 622

UNWOUNDED
OUR YET UNWOUNDED ENEMIES, OR ARME 6 466

UP
STIRD UP WITH ENVY AND REVENGE, DECEIV'D 1 35
HERE SWALLOW'D UP IN ENDLESS MISERY. 1 142
THEY HEARD, AND WERE ABASHT, AND UP THEY SPRUNG 1 331
WAV'D ROUND THE COAST, UP CALL'D A PITCHY CLOUD 1 340
FOR WHICH TO STRIVE, NO STRIFE CAN GROW UP THERE 2 31
STOOD UP, THE STRONGEST AND THE FIERCEST SPIRIT 2 44
UP TO OUR NATIVE SEAT: DESCENT AND FALL 2 76
TO LESS THEN GODS. ON TH' OTHER SIDE UP ROSE 2 108
TO PERISH RATHER, SWALLOWD UP AND LOST 2 149
INCLINES, HERE TO CONTINUE, AND BUILD UP HERE 2 314
WILL ONCE MORE LIFT US UP, IN SPIGHT OF FATE, 2 393
AND HARD, THAT OUT OF HELL LEADS UP TO LIGHT; 2 433
REND UP BOTH ROCKS AND HILLS, AND RIDE THE AIR 2 540
THROUGH PAIN UP BY THE ROOTS THESSALIAN PINES, 2 544
UP TO THE FIERY CONCAVE TOURING HIGH. 2 635
SHALL DWELL AT EASE, AND UP AND DOWN UNSEEN 2 841
FORTHWITH THE HUGE PORCULLIS HIGH UP DREW, 2 874
LIES THROUGH YOUR SPACIOUS EMPIRE UP TO LIGHT, 2 974
THE DARK DESCENT, AND UP TO REASCEND, 3 20
WALK'D UP AND DOWN ALONE BENT ON HIS PREY, 3 441
UP HITHER LIKE AEREAL VAPOURS FLEW 3 445
UP TO THE WALL OF HEAVEN A STRUCTURE HIGH, 3 503
THERE ALWAYES, BUT DRAWN UP TO HEAV'N SOMTIMES 3 517
THROUGH THE CALM FIRMAMENT; BUT UP OR DOWNE 3 574
VOLATIL HERMES, AND CALL UP UNBOUND 3 603
AND WROUGHT BUT MALICE; LIFTED UP SO HIGH 4 49
ACCESS DENI'D; AND OVER HEAD UP GREW 4 137
THE VERDUROUS WALL OF PARADISE UP SPRUNG: 4 143
THENCE UP HE FLEW, AND ON THE TREE OF LIFE 4 194
OF POROUS EARTH WITH KINDLY THIRST UP DRAWN, 4 228
OF ALABLASTER, PIL'D UP TO THE CLOUDS, 4 544
FENC'D UP THE VERDANT WALL; EACH BEAUTEOUS FLOUR, 4 697
HALF WAY UP HILL THIS VAST SUBLUNAR VAULT, 4 777
BLOWN UP WITH HIGH CONCEITS INGENDRING PRIDE. 4 809
OF FORCE TO ITS OWN LIKENESS: UP HE STARTS 4 813
SO STARTED UP IN HIS OWN SHAPE THE FIEND. 4 819
HIGH UP IN HEAV'N, WITH SONGS TO HYMNE HIS THRONE, 4 944
THE LATTER QUICK UP FLEW, AND KICKT THE BEAM; 4 1004
TO TRAMPLE THEE AS MIRE; FOR PROOF LOOK UP, 4 1010
IF THOU RESIST. THE FIEND LOOKT UP AND KNEW 4 1013
COULD NOT BUT TASTE. FORTHWITH UP TO THE CLOUDS 5 86
OF DAY-SPRING, AND THE SUN, WHO SCARCE UP RISEN 5 139
HIS PRAISE, WHO OUT OF DARKNESS CALL'D UP LIGHT. 5 179
THAT SINGING UP TO HEAVEN GATE ASCEND, 5 198
ALL THINGS PROCEED, AND UP TO HIM RETURN, 5 470
TILL BODY UP TO SPIRIT WORK, IN BOUNDS 5 478

UP (CONTINUED)
STOOD UP, AND IN A FLAME OF ZEALE SEVERE 5 807
MINISTRING SPIRITS, TRAIND UP IN FEAST AND SONG; 6 167
WERE READY, IN A MOMENT UP THEY TURND 6 509
PART HIDD'N VEINS DIGGD UP (NOR HATH THIS EARTH 6 516
UP ROSE THE VICTOR ANGELS, AND TO ARMS 6 525
UP LIFTING BORE THEM IN THIR HANDS: AMAZE, 6 646
WITH THY CELESTIAL SONG. UP LED BY THEE 7 12
UP HITHER, UNDER LONG OBEDIENCE TRI'D, 7 159
UP FROM THE BOTTOM TURN'D BY FURIOUS WINDES 7 213
THE SMELLING GOURD, UP STOOD THE CORNIE REED 7 321
WENT UP AND WATERD ALL THE GROUND, AND EACH 7 334
LIMB'D AND FULL GROWN: OUT OF THE GROUND UP ROSE 7 456
BORE UP HIS BRANCHING HEAD: SCARSE FROM HIS MOULD 7 470
DESISTING, THOUGH UNWEARIED, UP RETURND 7 552
UP TO THE HEAV'N OF HEAV'NS HIS HIGH ABODE, 7 553
ANSWERING HIS GREAT IDEA. UP HE RODE 7 557
GLAD WE RETURN'D UP TO THE COASTS OF LIGHT 8 245
BY QUICK INSTINCTIVE MOTION UP I SPRUNG, 8 259
SMOOTH SLIDING WITHOUT STEP, LAST LED ME UP 8 302
UP HITHER, FROM AMONG THE TREES APPEER'D 8 313
BUT SUDDENLY WITH FLESH FILL'D UP AND HEAL'D: 8 468
MEAN, OR IN HER SUMMD UP, IN HER CONTAIND 8 473
LEADS UP TO HEAV'N, IS BOTH THE WAY AND GUIDE; 8 613
SO PARTED THEY, THE ANGEL UP TO HEAV'N 8 652
SERV'D UP IN HALL WITH SEWERS, AND SENESHALS; 9 38
ROSE UP A FOUNTAIN BY THE TREE OF LIFE; 9 73
MAEOTIS, UP BEYOND THE RIVER OB; 9 78
OF GROWTH, SENSE, REASON, ALL SUMM'D UP IN MAN, 9 113
FROM TH' EARTHS GREAT ALTAR SEND UP SILENT PRAISE 9 195
GROW UP TO THIR PROVISION, AND MORE HANDS 9 623
THERE SWALLOW'D UP AND LOST, FROM SUCCOUR FARR, 9 642
AND GROWING UP TO GODHEAD; WHICH FOR THEE 9 877
ENCUMBERD, NOW HAD LEFT THEM, UP THEY ROSE 9 1051
UP INTO HEAV'N FROM PARADISE IN HASTE 10 17
TO HIM WITH SWIFT ASCENT HE UP RETURND, 10 224
TOST UP AND DOWN, TOGETHER CROWDED DROVE 10 287
OFFENDED, WORTH YOUR LAUGHTER, HATH GIV'N UP 10 488
BUT UP AND ENTER NOW INTO FULL BLISS. 10 503
A GROVE HARD BY, SPRUNG UP WITH THIS THIR CHANGE, 10 548
BUT ON THEY ROULD IN HEAPS, AND UP THE TREES 10 558
AT RANDOM YIELDED UP TO THEIR MISRULE; 10 628
MY HELL-HOUNDS, TO LICK UP THE DRAFF AND FILTH 10 630
FOR EVER, AND SEAL UP HIS RAVENOUS JAWES. 10 637
UP TO THE TROPIC CRAB; THENCE DOWN AMAINE 10 675
FLEW UP, NOR MISSD THE WAY, BY ENVIOUS WINDES 11 15
RESIGNES HIM UP WITH HEAV'N AND EARTH RENEWD. 11 66
WHERE ENTRANCE UP FROM EDEN EASIEST CLIMBES, 11 119
AT EEV'N, WHICH I BRED UP WITH TENDER HAND 11 276
OF GRASSIE TERFE, AND PILE UP EVERY STONE 11 324
HIS BEST OF MAN, AND GAVE HIM UP TO TEARS 11 497
OF RENDRING UP, AND PATIENTLY ATTEND 11 551
SHALL YIELD UP ALL THIR VERTUE, ALL THIR FAME 11 623
SENT UP AMAIN; AND NOW THE THICK'ND SKIE 11 742
BROKE UP, SHALL HEAVE THE OCEAN TO USURP 11 827
WILL HE CONVEY UP THITHER TO SUSTAIN 12 75
BRED UP IN IDOL-WORSHIP; O THAT MEN 12 115
AMONG THEM TO SET UP HIS TABERNACLE, 12 247
THIR NATURAL PRAVITIE, BY STIRRING UP 12 288
UP TO A BETTER COV'NANT, DISCIPLIN'D 12 302
BUT SAY, IF OUR DELIVERER UP TO HEAV'N 12 479

UPBORE
THIR MARCH WAS, AND THE PASSIVE AIR UPBORE 6 72

UPBORN
UPBORN WITH INDEFATIGABLE WINGS 2 408

UP-BORNE
OR ONE SHORT SIGH OF HUMANE BREATH, UP-BORNE 11 147

UPBRAID
YET LEUDLY DAR'ST OUR MINISTRING UPBRAID. 6 182

UPBRAIDED
UPBRAIDED NONE; NOR WAS HIS SERVICE HARD. 4 45
AND AM I NOW UPBRAIDED, AS THE CAUSE 9 1168

UPGROWN
SO STANDING, MOVING, OR TO HIGHTH UPGROWN 9 677

UPHEAV'D
BEHEMOTH BIGGEST BORN OF EARTH UPHEAV'D 7 471

UPHEAVE
EMERGENT, AND THIR BROAD BARE BACKS UPHEAVE 7 286

UPHELD
WHETHER UPHELD BY STRENGTH, OR CHANCE, OR FATE, 1 133
SAT ON HIS THRONE, UPHELD BY OLD REPUTE, 1 639
UPHELD BY ME, YET ONCE MORE HE SHALL STAND 3 178
BY ME UPHELD, THAT HE MAY KNOW HOW FRAIL 3 180
TASTE AFTER TASTE UPHELD WITH KINDLIEST CHANGE, 5 336

UP-LIFT
WITH HEAD UP-LIFT ABOVE THE WAVE, AND EYES 1 193

UPLIFTED
TILL, AS A SIGNAL GIV'N, TH' UPLIFTED SPEAR 1 347
THUS HIGH UPLIFTED BEYOND HOPE, ASPIRES 2 7
UPLIFTED SPURNS THE GROUND, THENCE MANY A LEAGUE 2 929
UPLIFTED IMMINENT ONE STROKE THEY AIM'D 6 317
UPLIFTED, IN PATERNAL GLORIE RODE 7 219
UPLIFTED; AND SECURE WITH BEAKED PROW 11 746
THEN WITH UPLIFTED HANDS, AND EYES DEVOUT, 11 863

UPON
UPON THE WING, AS WHEN MEN WONT TO WATCH 1 332
ONE DAY UPON OUR HEADS; WHILE WE PERHAPS 2 178
UPON THE WING, OR IN SWIFT RACE CONTEND, 2 529
WITH RUIN UPON RUIN, ROUT ON ROUT, 2 995
PURSUING. I UPON MY FRONTIERES HERE 2 998
UPON HIS OWN REBELLIOUS HEAD. AND NOW 3 86
MUCH LESS THAT DURST UPON HIS OWN HEAD DRAW 3 220
MEAN WHILE UPON THE FIRM OPACOUS GLOBE 3 418
UPON HIMSELF; HORROR AND DOUBT DISTRACT 4 18
UPON THE RAPID CURRENT, WHICH THROUGH VEINS 4 227
CONFERRD UPON US, AND DOMINION GIV'N 4 430
UPON HER CENTER POIS'D, WHEN ON A DAY 5 579
UPON CONFUSION ROSE: AND NOW ALL HEAV'N 6 669
UPON HIS ENEMIES, AND TO DECLARE 6 677
GIRD ON, AND SWORD UPON THY PUISSANT THIGH; 6 714
WHOSE SEED IS IN HER SELF UPON THE EARTH. 7 312
UPON THE EARTH, AND MAN TO TILL THE GROUND 7 332
BUT US HE SENDS UPON HIS HIGH BEHESTS 8 238
TWILIGHT UPON THE EARTH, SHORT ARBITER 9 50
AND FORCE UPON FREE WILL HATH HERE NO PLACE. 9 1174
UPON THY BELLY GROVELING THOU SHALT GOE, 10 177
HOVERING UPON THE WATERS; WHAT THEY MET 10 285
UPON THE CRONIAN SEA, TOGETHER DRIVE 10 290
UPON HER HUSBAND, SAW THIR SHAME THAT SOUGHT 10 336
MINE OWN THAT BIDE UPON ME, ALL FROM MEE 10 738
INSTEAD SHALL DOUBLE OURS UPON OUR HEADS. 10 1040
UPON THIR TONGUES A VARIOUS SPIRIT TO RASE 12 53
A MIGHTIE NATION, AND UPON HIM SHOWRE 12 124
UPON THE TEMPLE IT SELF: AT LAST THEY SEISE 12 356
WORKING THROUGH LOVE, UPON THIR HEARTS SHALL WRITE, 12 489

UPPER
'TWIXT UPPER, NETHER, AND SURROUNDING FIRES; 1 346
FLOWN TO THE UPPER WORLD; THE REST WERE ALL 10 422
OF RICHEST TEXTURE SPRED, AT TH' UPPER END 10 446

UPRAIS'D
AND THUS WITH PEACEFUL WORDS UPRAIS'D HER SOON. 10 946

UPRAISE
IN OUR CONFUSION, AND OUR JOY UPRAISE 2 372

UPREARD
OF TRUMPETS LOUD AND CLARIONS BE UPREARD 1 532

UPRIGHT
BEFORE ALL TEMPLES TH' UPRIGHT HEART AND PURE, 1 18
FORTHWITH UPRIGHT HE REARS FROM OFF THE POOL 1 221
WITH UPRIGHT WING AGAINST A HIGHER FOE. 2 72
AS WHEN THOU STOODST IN HEAV'N UPRIGHT AND PURE; 4 837
BRISTL'D WITH UPRIGHT BEAMS INNUMERABLE 6 82
THY MALICE INTO THOUSANDS, ONCE UPRIGHT 6 270
THEY SHEW US WHEN OUR FOES WALK NOT UPRIGHT. 6 627
HIS STATURE, AND UPRIGHT WITH FRONT SERENE 7 509
THIR HAPPINESS, AND PERSEVERE UPRIGHT. 7 632
AS THITHERWARD ENDEVORING, AND UPRIGHT 8 260

UPRIGHTNESS
IN HIS UPRIGHTNESS ANSWER THUS RETURND. 3 693

UPROAR
IN WHIRLWIND; HELL SCARCE HOLDS THE WILDE UPROAR. 2 541
CONFUSION HEARD HIS VOICE, AND WILDE UPROAR 3 710
TO THIS UPROAR; HORRID CONFUSION HEAPT 6 668

UPROARE
MY JOURNEY STRANGE, WITH CLAMOROUS UPROARE 10 479

UPROOTED
AT HIS COMMAND THE UPROOTED HILLS RETIR'D 6 781

UPROWLD
HASTED WITH GLAD PRECIPITANCE, UPROWLD 7 291

UPSENT
AT WHICH THE UNIVERSAL HOST UPSENT 1 541

UPSPRINGING
VAILD WITH HIS GORGEOUS WINGS, UPSPRINGING LIGHT 5 250

UPSPRUNG
PASTURING AT ONCE, AND IN BROAD HERDS UPSPRUNG. 7 462

UPSTAID
HIS MASSIE SPEAR UPSTAID; AS IF ON EARTH 6 195

UPSTAIES
HUNG DROOPING UNSUSTAIND, THEM SHE UPSTAIES 9 430

UPSTART
A RACE OF UPSTART CREATURES, TO SUPPLY 2 834
AND UPSTART PASSIONS CATCH THE GOVERNMENT 12 88

UPSTOOD
HE SAT; AND IN TH' ASSEMBLY NEXT UPSTOOD 6 446

UPTORE
BETOOK THEM, AND THE NEIGHBOURING HILLS UPTORE; 6 663

UPTURN
AND THRASCIAS REND THE WOODS AND SEAS UPTURN; 10 700

UPTURN'D
SO SENTED THE GRIM FEATURE, AND UPTURN'D 10 279

UP-TURNS
WITH ADVERSE BLAST UP-TURNS THEM FROM THE SOUTH 10 701

UPWARD
DAGON HIS NAME, SEA MONSTER, UPWARD MAN 1 462
SPRINGS UPWARD LIKE A PYRAMID OF FIRE 2 1013
SHOT UPWARD STILL DIRECT, WHENCE NO WAY ROUND 3 618
FLEW UPWARD, SPIRITED WITH VARIOUS FORMS, 3 717
THE BOTTOM OF THE MOUNTAINS UPWARD TURN'D, 6 649

UPWHIRLD
THE SPORT OF WINDS: ALL THESE UPWHIRLD ALOFT 3 493

UR
UR OF CHALDAEA, PASSING NOW THE FORD 12 130

URANIA
DESCEND FROM HEAV'N URANIA, BY THAT NAME 7 1
URANIA, AND FIT AUDIENCE FIND, THOUGH FEW. 7 31

URG'D
AS NOT BEHIND IN HATE; IF WHAT WAS URG'D 2 120
OF HARD CONTENTS, AND FULL OF FORCE URG'D HOME, 6 622
URG'D THEM BEHIND; HEADLONG THEMSELVES THEY THREW 6 864
OF THAT ALLURING FRUIT, URG'D ME SO KEENE. 9 588
AT THE SAD SENTENCE RIGOROUSLY URG'D, 11 109

URGE
BY NUMBERS THAT HAVE NAME. BUT THIS I URGE, 8 114

URGES
STILL URGES, AND A FIERY DELUGE, FED 1 68
AND SHORT RETIREMENT URGES SWEET RETURNE. 9 250

URIEL
TH' ARCH-ANGEL URIEL, ONE OF THE SEAV'N 3 648
URIEL, FOR THOU OF THOSE SEAV'N SPIRITS THAT STAND 3 654
URIEL, THOUGH REGENT OF THE SUN, AND HELD 3 690
URIEL ONCE WARND; WHOSE EYE PURSU'D HIM DOWN 4 125
THITHER CAME URIEL, GLIDING THROUGH THE EEVEN 4 555
URIEL, NO WONDER IF THY PERFET SIGHT, 4 577
SO PROMIS'D HEE, AND URIEL TO HIS CHARGE 4 589
URIEL AND RAPHAEL HIS VAUNTING FOE, 6 363
SINCE URIEL REGENT OF THE SUN DESCRI'D 9 60

URIM
OF RADIANT URIM, WORK DIVINELY WROUGHT, 6 761

URNS
REPAIRING, IN THIR GOLD'N URNS DRAW LIGHT, 7 365

US'D
LIGHT AFTER LIGHT WELL US'D THEY SHALL ATTAIN, 3 196
OF THAT LIFE-GIVING PLANT, BUT ONLY US'D 4 199
FOR PROSPECT, WHAT WELL US'D HAD BIN THE PLEDGE 4 200
TO MAKE THEM MIRTH US'D ALL HIS MIGHT, AND WREATHD 4 346
PRESENT, OR PAST, AS SAINTS AND PATRIARCHS US'D, 4 762
US'D TO THE YOAK, DRAW'ST HIS TRIUMPHANT WHEELS 4 975
BESTOWD, THE HOLY SALUTATION US'D 5 386
THUS I EMBOLD'ND SPAKE, AND FREEDOM US'D 8 434
AS US'D OR NOT, WORKS IN THE MIND NO CHANGE, 8 525
WITH MAN, AS WITH HIS FRIEND, FAMILIAR US'D 9 2
OF RUSLING LEAVES, BUT MINDED NOT, AS US'D 9 519
US'D BY THE TEMPTER: ON THAT PROSPECT STRANGE 10 552

USE
TO WORST ABUSE, OR TO THIR MEANEST USE. 4 204
ALL THINGS TO MANS DELIGHTFUL USE; THE ROOFE 4 692
ALL SEASONS, RIPE FOR USE HANGS ON THE STALK; 5 323
AND GOD MADE TWO GREAT LIGHTS, GREAT FOR THIR USE 7 346
GREATER SO MANIFOLD TO THIS ONE USE, 8 29
FROM USE, OBSCURE AND SUTTLE, BUT TO KNOW 8 192
THE GODS ARE FIRST, AND THAT ADVANTAGE USE 9 718
THY PRAISE HEE ALSO WHO FORBIDS THY USE, 9 750
WHICH MIGHT SUPPLIE THE SUN: SUCH FIRE TO USE, 10 1078

USEFUL
USEFUL OF HURTFUL, PROSPEROUS OF ADVERSE 2 259
USEFUL, WHENCE HAPLY MENTION MAY ARISE 8 200

USELESS
USELESS AND VAIN, OF FREEDOM BOTH DESPOILD, 3 109

VALLIE
- OF HILL, AND VALLIE, RIVERS, WOODS AND PLAINES, 9 116
- YET DOUBT NOT BUT IN VALLIE AND IN PLAINE 11 349

VALLIES
- WITH TUFTS THE VALLIES AND EACH FOUNTAIN SIDE, 7 327

VALLOMBROSA
- IN VALLOMBROSA, WHERE TH' ETRURIAN SHADES 1 303

VALLY
- THE PLEASANT VALLY OF HINNOM, TOPHET THENCE 1 404

VALOUR
- DELIBERATE VALOUR BREATH'D, FIRM AND UNMOV'D 1 554
- FOR CONTEMPLATION HEE AND VALOUR FORMD, 4 297
- VALOUR OR STRENGTH, THOUGH MATCHLESS, QUELLD WITH PAIN 6 457
- AND VALOUR AND HEROIC VERTU CALL'D; 11 690

VALU'D
- CREATED THING NAUGHT VALU'D HE NOR SHUN'D; 2 679

VALUE
- ANY, BUT GOD ALONE, TO VALUE RIGHT 4 202
- THEN VALUE: OFT TIMES NOTHING PROFITS MORE 8 571

VAN
- TO BATTEL IN THE CLOUDS, BEFORE EACH VAN 2 535
- STANDARDS, AND GONFALONS TWIXT VAN AND REARE 5 589
- OF HIDEOUS LENGTH: BEFORE THE CLOUDIE VAN, 6 107

VANGUARD
- VANGUARD, TO RIGHT AND LEFT THE FRONT UNFOULD; 6 558

VANISH
- WILL VANISH AND DELIVER YE TO WOE, 4 368

VANISHT
- EMPYREAL, FROM BEFORE HER VANISHT NIGHT, 6 14

VANITIE
- AND WANDRING VANITIE, WHEN LEST WAS SAFE, 10 875

VANITY
- WITH VANITY HAD FILLD THE WORKS OF MEN: 3 447

VANNES
- THE STEDFAST EARTH. AT LAST HIS SAIL-BROAD VANNES 2 927

VANQUISH'D
- VANQUISH'D ADRAMELEC, AND ASMADAI, 6 365

VANQUISHER
- MY VANQUISHER, SPOILD OF HIS VANTED SPOILE; 3 251

VANQUISHT
- LAY VANQUISHT, ROWLING IN THE FIERY GULFE 1 52
- WHOM HE HAD VANQUISHT. AFTER THESE APPEAR'D 1 476
- LIE VANQUISHT; THOU HAST GIVN ME TO POSSESS 3 243
- VICTOR AND VANQUISHT: ON THE FOUGHTEN FIELD 6 410

VANTED
- MY VANQUISHER, SPOILD OF HIS VANTED SPOILE; 3 251

VAPOR
- OF MIDNIGHT VAPOR GLIDE OBSCURE, AND PRIE 9 159
- COMPACT OF UNCTUOUS VAPOR, WHICH THE NIGHT 9 635

VAPORS
- IN AUTUMN THWARTS THE NIGHT, WHEN VAPORS FIR'D 4 557
- AND TEMPERAT VAPORS BLAND, WHICH TH' ONLY SOUND 5 5

VAPOUR
- THIR NOXIOUS VAPOUR, OR ENUR'D NOT FEEL, 2 216
- THAT WITH EXHILERATING VAPOUR BLAND 9 1047
- VAPOUR, AND MIST, AND EXHALATION HOT, 10 694
- VAPOUR, AND EXHALATION DUSK AND MOIST, 11 741
- AND VAPOUR AS THE LIBYAN AIR ADUST, 12 635

VAPOURS
- UP HITHER LIKE AEREAL VAPOURS FLEW 3 445
- VAPOURS NOT YET INTO HER SUBSTANCE TURND. 5 420

VARIABLE
- HIS HEART I KNOW, HOW VARIABLE AND VAIN 11 92

VARIE
- VARIE TO OUR GREAT MAKER STILL NEW PRAISE. 5 184

VARIED
- VARIED HIS BOUNTY SO WITH NEW DELIGHTS, 5 431
- SO VARIED HEE, AND OF HIS TORTUOUS TRAINE 9 516

VARIETIE
- VARIETIE WITHOUT END; BUT OF THE TREE 7 542

VARIETY
- (FOR EARTH HATH THIS VARIETY FROM HEAV'N 6 640

VARIOUS
- THEN WERE THEY KNOWN TO MEN BY VARIOUS NAMES, 1 374
- AND VARIOUS IDOLS THROUGH THE HEATHEN WORLD. 1 375
- A VARIOUS MOULD, AND FROM THE BOYLING CELLS 1 706
- AND DISCORD WITH A THOUSAND VARIOUS MOUTHS. 2 967
- TURN SWIFT THIR VARIOUS MOTIONS, OR ARE TURND 3 582
- IN VARIOUS SHAPES OLD PROTEUS FROM THE SEA, 3 604
- FLEW UPWARD, SPIRITED WITH VARIOUS FORMS, 3 717
- A HAPPY RURAL SEAT OF VARIOUS VIEW; 4 247
- SO VARIOUS, NOT TO TASTE THAT ONELY TREE 4 423
- OF VARIOUS INFLUENCE FOMENT AND WARME, 4 669
- AND VARIOUS: WONDRING AT MY FLIGHT AND CHANGE 5 89
- IN VARIOUS STYLE, FOR NEITHER VARIOUS STYLE 5 146
- THEN WITH THESE VARIOUS FRUITS THE TREES OF GOD 5 390
- INDU'D WITH VARIOUS FORMS VARIOUS DEGREES 5 473
- VARIOUS, WITH BOASTFUL ARGUMENT PORTRAID, 6 84
- THAT WARR AND VARIOUS; SOMTIMES ON FIRM GROUND 6 242
- OP'NING THIR VARIOUS COLOURS, AND MADE GAY 7 318
- INCITED, DANCE ABOUT HIM VARIOUS ROUNDS? 8 125
- WITH VARIOUS LIVING CREATURES, AND THE AIRE 8 370
- WHO MEET WITH VARIOUS OBJECTS, FROM THE SENSE 8 609
- IN PARADISE, AND VARIOUS, YET UNKNOWN 9 619
- SATE IN THIR SAD DISCOURSE, AND VARIOUS PLAINT, 10 343
- WHICH NOW THE SKIE WITH VARIOUS FACE BEGINS 10 1064
- WERE TENTS OF VARIOUS HUE; BY SOME WERE HERDS 11 557
- UPON THIR TONGUES A VARIOUS SPIRIT TO RASE 12 53
- SO MANY AND SO VARIOUS LAWS ARE GIV'N; 12 282

VARIOUSLY
- VARIOUSLY REPRESENTING; YET STILL FREE 8 610

VARNISHT
- OR CLOS AMBITION VARNISHT O'RE WITH ZEAL. 2 485

VASSALAGE
- OF SPLENDID VASSALAGE, BUT RATHER SEEK 2 252

VASSALS
- THE VASSALS OF HIS ANGER, WHEN THE SCOURGE 2 90

VAST
- DOVE-LIKE SATST BROODING ON THE VAST ABYSS 1 21
- TO BELLOW THROUGH THE VAST AND BOUNDLESS DEEP. 1 177
- LIVE TO OUR SELVES, THOUGH IN THIS VAST RECESS, 2 254
- OVER THE VAST ABRUPT, ERE HE ARRIVE 2 409
- OTHERS WITH VAST TYPHOEAN RAGE MORE FELL 2 539
- VOLUMINOUS AND VAST, A SERPENT ARM'D 2 652
- CREATED VAST AND ROUND, A PLACE OF BLISS 2 832
- A VAST VACUITIE: ALL UNAWARES 2 932
- STOOD RUL'D, STOOD VAST INFINITUDE CONFIN'D; 3 711
- HALF WAY UP HILL THIS VAST SUBLUNAR VAULT, 4 777
- HE SPEEDS, AND THROUGH THE VAST ETHEREAL SKIE 5 267
- SATAN WITH VAST AND HAUGHTIE STRIDES ADVANC'T, 6 109
- TH' ARCH-ANGEL TRUMPET; THROUGH THE VAST OF HEAVEN 6 203
- A VAST CIRCUMFERENCE: AT HIS APPROACH 6 256
- THEY VIEW'D THE VAST IMMEASURABLE ABYSS 7 211
- ROUND THROUGH THE VAST PROFUNDITIE OBSCURE, 7 229
- ONE DAY AND NIGHT; IN ALL THIR VAST SURVEY 8 24
- FOR SUCH VAST ROOM IN NATURE UNPOSSEST 8 153
- VOYAG'D TH' UNREAL, VAST, UNBOUNDED DEEP 10 471
- TO STUFF THIS MAW, THIS VAST UNHIDE-BOUND CORPS. 10 601

VASTNESS
- HIS VASTNESS: FLEEC'T THE FLOCKS AND BLEATING ROSE, 7 472

VAULT
- HURLING DEFIANCE TOWARD THE VAULT OF HEAV'N. 1 669
- HALF WAY UP HILL THIS VAST SUBLUNAR VAULT, 4 777

VAULTED
- SMOTE ON HIM SORE BESIDES, VAULTED WITH FIRE; 1 298
- AND FLYING VAULTED EITHER HOST WITH FIRE. 6 214

VAUNTING
- VAUNTING ALOUD, BUT RACKT WITH DEEP DESPARE: 1 126
- URIEL AND RAPHAEL HIS VAUNTING FOE, 6 363

VAUNTS
- WITH OTHER PROMISES AND OTHER VAUNTS 4 84

VEGETABLE
- OF VEGETABLE GOLD; AND NEXT TO LIFE 4 220

VEHEMENCE
- WITH LOUDEST VEHEMENCE: THITHER HE PLYES, 2 954

VEHEMENT
- NOR VEHEMENT DESIRE, THESE DELICACIES 8 526
- SHE ENDED HEER, OR VEHEMENT DESPAIRE 10 1007

VEIL
- APPROACH NOT, BUT WITH BOTH WINGS VEIL THIR EYES. 3 382

VEILD
- OR DIM SUFFUSION VEILD. YET NOT THE MORE 3 26

VEILD (CONTINUED)
NIGHTS HEMISPHERE HAD VEILD THE HORIZON ROUND: . 9 52
VEILD IN A CLOUD OF FRAGRANCE, WHERE SHE STOOD, . 9 425

VEILE
IN DARKER VEILE) AND ROSEAT DEWS DISPOS'D . . . 5 646
TO VEILE THE HEAV'N, THOUGH DARKNESS THERE MIGHT
WELL 6 11
HOW DARK'ND; INNOCENCE, THAT AS A VEILE 9 1054

VEILS
FROM YONDER BLAZING CLOUD THAT VEILS THE HILL . . 11 229

VEINE
SO THEY AMONG THEMSELVES IN PLEASANT VEINE . . . 6 628

VEINS
THAT UNDERNEATH HAD VEINS OF LIQUID FIRE . . . 1 701
UPON THE RAPID CURRENT, WHICH THROUGH VEINS . . 4 227
PART HIDD'N VEINS DIGGD UP (NOR HATH THIS EARTH . 6 516
RAN THROUGH HIS VEINS, AND ALL HIS JOYNTS RELAX'D; 9 891
DOWN TO THE VEINS OF EARTH, THENCE GLIDING HOT . 11 568

VENGEANCE
HIS MINISTERS OF VENGEANCE AND PURSUIT 1 170
TREBLE CONFUSION, WRATH AND VENGEANCE POUR'D. . . 1 220
SHOULD INTERMITTED VENGEANCE ARM AGAIN 2 173
TO EXECUTE FIERCE VENGEANCE ON HIS FOES, . . . 3 399
OF TOBITS SON, AND WITH A VENGEANCE SENT . . . 4 170
OR SOM MORE SUDDEN VENGEANCE WING'D FROM GOD . . 6 279
VENGEANCE IS HIS, OR WHOSE HE SOLE APPOINTS; . . 6 808
AND VENGEANCE TO THE WICKED, AT RETURN 12 541

VENGEFUL
THAT WE MAY SO SUFFICE HIS VENGEFUL IRE, . . . 1 148
HATH WISELIER ARM'D HIS VENGEFUL IRE THEN SO . . 10 1023

VENIAL
VENIAL DISCOURSE UNBLAM'D: I NOW MUST CHANGE . . 9 5

VENOM
OR IF, INSPIRING VENOM, HE MIGHT TAINT 4 804

VENT
PUT FORTH, AND TO A NARROW VENT APPLI'D 6 583
WITHOUT THE VENT OF WORDS, WHICH THESE HE BREATHD. 12 374

VENTRING
MEANT MEE, BY VENTRING HIGHER THEN MY LOT. . . . 9 690

VENT'ROUS
AND VENT'ROUS, IF THAT FAIL THEM, SHRINK AND FEAR 2 205

VENTROUS
THIS SAID HE PAUS'D NOT, BUT WITH VENTROUS ARME . 5 64

VENTUR'D
I FEAR, HATH VENTUR'D FROM THE DEEP, TO RAISE . . 4 574

VENTURE
TAUGHT BY THE HEAV'NLY MUSE TO VENTURE DOWN . . 3 19
AND BOLDLY VENTURE TO WHATEVER PLACE 4 891

VERDANT
FENC'D UP THE VERDANT WALL; EACH BEAUTEOUS FLOUR, 4 697
PUT FORTH THE VERDANT GRASS, HERB YIELDING SEED, . 7 310
BEYOND THE EARTHS GREEN CAPE AND VERDANT ISLES . 8 631
WITH BURNISHT NECK OF VERDANT GOLD, ERECT . . . 9 501
THICK OVERHEAD WITH VERDANT ROOF IMBOWR'D . . . 9 1038

VERDURE
BROUGHT FORTH THE TENDER GRASS, WHOSE VERDURE CLAD 7 315
WITH ALL HIS VERDURE SPOIL'D, AND TREES ADRIFT . 11 832

VERDUROUS
THE VERDUROUS WALL OF PARADISE UP SPRUNG: . . . 4 143

VERES
VERES OFT, AS OFT SO STEERS, AND SHIFTS HER SAILE; 9 515

VERGE
HER FARDEST VERGE, AND CHAOS TO RETIRE 2 1038
DOWN FROM THE VERGE OF HEAV'N, ETERNAL WRAUTH . . 6 865
OR SERVE THEY AS A FLOURIE VERGE TO BINDE . . . 11 881

VERIFI'D
SO SPAKE THIS ORACLE, THEN VERIFI'D 10 182

VERNAL
OR SIGHT OF VERNAL BLOOM, OR SUMMERS ROSE, . . . 3 43
VERNAL DELIGHT AND JOY, ABLE TO DRIVE 4 155
THE BIRDS THIR QUIRE APPLY; AIRES, VERNAL AIRES, . 4 264

VERNANT
PERPETUAL SMIL'D ON EARTH WITH VERNANT FLOURS, . 10 679

VERSE
FLOWD FROM THIR LIPS, IN PROSE OR NUMEROUS VERSE, 5 150

VERSE (CONTINUED)
EASIE MY UNPREMEDITATED VERSE: 9 24

VERTU
RATHER THEN SOLID VERTU, ALL BUT A RIB 10 884
AND VALOUR AND HEROIC VERTU CALL'D; 11 690
AND GREAT EXPLOITS, BUT OF TRUE VERTU VOID; . . 11 790
SHALL WITH THIR FREEDOM LOST ALL VERTU LOOSE . . 11 798

VERTUE
YOUR WEARIED VERTUE, FOR THE EASE YOU FIND . . . 1 320
FREE VERTUE SHOULD ENTHRALL TO FORCE OR CHANCE. . 2 551
SHOOTS INVISIBLE VERTUE EVEN TO THE DEEP: . . . 3 586
TO THEM WHO LIV'D; NOR ON THE VERTUE THOUGHT . . 4 198
THIR STELLAR VERTUE ON ALL KINDS THAT GROW . . . 4 671
VERTUE IN HER SHAPE HOW LOVLY, SAW, AND PIN'D . . 4 848
WHOM THUS THE ANGELIC VERTUE ANSWERD MILDE. . . 5 371
THERE FAIL WHERE VERTUE FAILS, OR WEAKEST PROVE . 6 117
CAN END IT. INTO THEE SUCH VERTUE AND GRACE . . 6 703
AND VITAL VERTUE INFUS'D, AND VITAL WARMTH . . . 7 236
WHOSE VERTUE ON IT SELF WORKES NO EFFECT, . . . 8 95
BY HIS ATTRACTIVE VERTUE AND THIR OWN 8 124
HER VERTUE AND THE CONSCIENCE OF HER WORTH, . . 8 502
NOT IN THEMSELVES, ALL THIR KNOWN VERTUE APPEARS . 9 110
WHETHER SUCH VERTUE SPENT OF OLD NOW FAILD . . . 9 145
ACCESS IN EVERY VERTUE, IN THY SIGHT 9 310
WITH ME, BEST WITNESS OF THY VERTUE TRI'D. . . . 9 317
AND WHAT IS FAITH, LOVE, VERTUE UNASSAID . . . 9 335
ON WHAT THOU HAST OF VERTUE, SUMMON ALL, . . . 9 374
THE VERTUE OF THAT FRUIT, IN THEE FIRST PROV'D: . 9 616
THE CREDIT OF WHOSE VERTUE REST WITH THEE, . . . 9 649
RATHER YOUR DAUNTLESS VERTUE, WHOM THE PAIN . . 9 694
OF VERTUE TO MAKE WISE: WHAT HINDERS THEN . . . 9 778
WHOSE VERTUE, FOR OF GOOD STILL GOOD PROCEEDS, . 9 973
OF ALL THIR VERTUE: SILENT, AND IN FACE 9 1063
THINE NOW IS ALL THIS WORLD, THY VERTUE HATH WON . 10 372
SHALL YIELD UP ALL THIR VERTUE, ALL THIR FAME . . 11 623
FROM VERTUE, WHICH IS REASON, THAT NO WRONG, . . 12 98
ADD VERTUE, PATIENCE, TEMPERANCE, ADD LOVE, . . 12 583

VERTUE-PROOF
SHEE NEEDED, VERTUE-PROOF, NO THOUGHT INFIRME . . 5 384

VERTUES
CELESTIAL VERTUES RISING, WILL APPEAR 2 15
ETHEREAL VERTUES; OR THESE TITLES NOW 2 311
THRONES, DOMINATIONS, PRINCEDOMS, VERTUES, POWERS, 5 601
THRONES, DOMINATIONS, PRINCEDOMES, VERTUES, POWERS, 5 772
THRONES, DOMINATIONS, PRINCEDOMS, VERTUES, POWERS, 5 840
AND VERTUES, WINGED SPIRITS, AND CHARIOTS WING'D, 7 199
GREAT ARE THY VERTUES, DOUBTLESS, BEST OF FRUITS. 9 745
THRONES, DOMINATIONS, PRINCEDOMS, VERTUES, POWERS, 10 460

VERTUMNUS
VERTUMNUS, OR TO CERES IN HER PRIME, ... 9 395

VERTUOUS
POTABLE GOLD, WHEN WITH ONE VERTUOUS TOUCH . . . 3 608
O SOVRAN, VERTUOUS, PRECIOUS OF ALL TREES . . . 9 795
THEN EVER, BOUNTIE OF THIS VERTUOUS TREE. . . . 9 1033

VERTUOUSEST
SEEMS WISEST, VERTUOUSEST, DISCREETEST, BEST; . . 8 550

VESSEL
AND LIKE A WEATHER-BEATEN VESSEL HOLDS 2 1043
FIT VESSEL, FITTEST IMP OF FRAUD, IN WHOM . . . 9 89
BEGAN TO BUILD A VESSEL OF HUGE BULK, ... 11 729
NO MORE WAS SEEN; THE FLOATING VESSEL SWUM . . . 11 745
OF KNOWLEDGE, WHAT THIS VESSEL CAN CONTAINE; . . 12 559

VESSELS
WANTS HER FIT VESSELS PURE, THEN STREWS THE GROUND 5 348

VEST
A MILITARIE VEST OF PURPLE FLOWD 11 241

VESTED
SAT SABLE-VESTED NIGHT, ELDEST OF THINGS, . . . 2 962

VEX
AFRESH WITH CONSCIOUS TERROURS VEX ME ROUND, . . 2 801

VEX'D
VEX'D SCYLLA BATHING IN THE SEA THAT PARTS . . . 2 660

VEXT
HATH VEXT THE RED-SEA COAST, WHOSE WAVES ORETHREW 1 306
OF GLIMMERING AIR LESS VEXT WITH TEMPEST LOUD: . 3 429
OVER THE VEXT ABYSS, FOLLOWING THE TRACK . . . 10 314

VIANDS
AND TO THIR VIANDS FELL, NOR SEEMINGLY 5 434

VICE
VICE FOR IT SELF: TO HIM NO TEMPLE STOOD . . . 1 492
TO VICE INDUSTRIOUS, BUT TO NOBLER DEEDS . . . 2 116
HIS IMAGE WHOM THEY SERV'D, A BRUTISH VICE, . . 11 518

VICEGERENT
VICEGERENT SON, TO THEE I HAVE TRANSFERR'D 10 56

VICE-GERENT
UNDER HIS GREAT VICE-GERENT REIGN ABIDE 5 609

VICISSITUDE
GRATEFUL VICISSITUDE, LIKE DAY AND NIGHT; 6 8
IN THIR VICISSITUDE, AND RULE THE NIGHT, 7 351

VICTOR
NOR WHAT THE POTENT VICTOR IN HIS RAGE 1 95
BUT SEE THE ANGRY VICTOR HATH RECALL'D 1 169
TH' ALMIGHTY VICTOR TO SPEND ALL HIS RAGE, 2 144
VICTOR; THOUGH BRUTISH THAT CONTEST AND FOULE, 6 124
VICTOR AND VANQUISHT: ON THE FOUGHTEN FIELD 6 410
UP ROSE THE VICTOR ANGELS, AND TO ARMS 6 525
OF IRON GLOBES, WHICH ON THE VICTOR HOST 6 590
SOLE VICTOR FROM TH' EXPULSION OF HIS FOES 6 880
THERE DIDST NOT; THERE LET HIM STILL VICTOR SWAY, 10 376

VICTORIE
PRESAGE OF VICTORIE AND FIERCE DESIRE 6 201
OF VICTORIE; DEEDS OF ETERNAL FAME 6 240
ALL DOUBT OF VICTORIE, ETERNAL MIGHT 6 630
ASCENDED, AT HIS RIGHT HAND VICTORIE 6 762
IS FORTITUDE TO HIGHEST VICTORIE, 12 570

VICTORIOUS
VICTORIOUS. THUS REPULS'D, OUR FINAL HOPE 2 142
POURD OUT BY MILLIONS HER VICTORIOUS BANDS 2 997
BUT I SHALL RISE VICTORIOUS, AND SUBDUE 3 250
SUNG TRIUMPH, AND HIM SUNG VICTORIOUS KING, 6 886
VICTORIOUS WITH HIS SAINTS, TH' OMNIPOTENT 7 136
OF THY VICTORIOUS ARM, WELL-PLEASING SON, 10 634

VICTORS
THE VICTORS WILL. TO SUFFER, AS TO DOE, 2 199
O FRIENDS, WHY COME NOT ON THESE VICTORS PROUD? 6 609
THIR FIGHT, WHAT STROKE SHALL BRUISE THE VICTORS HEEL. 12 385
THEN TEMPORAL DEATH SHALL BRUISE THE VICTORS HEEL, 12 433

VICTORY
WHICH IF NOT VICTORY IS YET REVENGE. 2 105
CLEER VICTORY, TO OUR PART LOSS AND ROUT 2 770
WITH VICTORY, TRIUMPHING THROUGH THE AIRE 12 452

VIEW
SAY FIRST, FOR HEAV'N HIDES NOTHING FROM THY VIEW 1 27
ADVANC'T IN VIEW, THEY STAND, A HORRID FRONT 1 563
VIEWS ALL THINGS AT ONE VIEW? HE FROM HEAV'NS HIGHTH 2 190
NEERER OUR ANCIENT SEAT; PERHAPS IN VIEW 2 394
BEFORE THIR EYES IN SUDDEN VIEW APPEAR 2 890
HIS OWN WORKS AND THEIR WORKS AT ONCE TO VIEW: 3 59
LOOKS DOWN WITH WONDER AT THE SUDDEN VIEW 3 542
SOMETIMES TOWARDS EDEN WHICH NOW IN HIS VIEW 4 27
OF STATELIEST VIEW. YET HIGHER THEN THIR TOPS 4 142
A HAPPY RURAL SEAT OF VARIOUS VIEW; 4 247
NEERER TO VIEW HIS PREY, AND UNESPI'D 4 399
REFLECTING BLAZE ON BLAZE, FIRST MET HIS VIEW: 6 18
IN BATTAILOUS ASPECT, AND NEERER VIEW 6 81
AND TO THIR FOES A LAUGHTER; FOR IN VIEW 6 603
FROM HEAVEN GATE NOT FARR, FOUNDED IN VIEW 7 618
HER HUSBAND, FOR I VIEW FAR ROUND, NOT NIGH, 9 482
I HAVE IN VIEW, CALLING TO MINDE WITH HEED 10 1030
HIS CHILDREN, ALL IN VIEW DESTROYD AT ONCE; 11 761

VIEW'D
VIEW'D FIRST THIR LAMENTABLE LOT, AND FOUND 2 617
THEY VIEW'D THE VAST IMMEASURABLE ABYSS 7 211
VIEW'D, AND BEHOLD ALL WAS ENTIRELY GOOD; 7 549

VIEWING
THY SELF IN ME THY PERFECT IMAGE VIEWING 2 764
AS FROM UNREST, AND EACH THE OTHER VIEWING, 9 1052
O SON, WHY SIT WE HERE EACH OTHER VIEWING 10 235

VIEWLESS
VIEWLESS, AND UNDERNEATH A BRIGHT SEA FLOW'D 3 518

VIEWS
AT ONCE AS FAR AS ANGELS KENN HE VIEWS 1 59
THROUGH OPTIC GLASS THE TUSCAN ARTIST VIEWS 1 288
THE WHOLE BATTALION VIEWS, THIR ORDER DUE, 1 569
VIEWS ALL THINGS AT ONE VIEW? HE FROM HEAV'NS HIGHTH 2 190
HE VIEWS IN BREDTH, AND WITHOUT LONGER PAUSE 3 561
BENEATH HIM WITH NEW WONDER NOW HE VIEWS 4 205

VIEW'ST
THY TROPHIES, WHICH THOU VIEW'ST AS NOT THINE OWN, 10 355

VIGILANCE
THE VIGILANCE HERE PLAC'T, BUT SUCH AS COME 4 580
THIR EARTHY CHARGE: OF THESE THE VIGILANCE 9 157
WITH RIGHTEOUS PLEA, THIR UTMOST VIGILANCE, 10 30

VIGOR
IMMORTAL VIGOR, THOUGH OPPREST AND FALL'N, 2 13
WOULD UTMOST VIGOR RAISE, AND RAIS'D UNITE. 9 314
ISSUING FROM MEE: ON YOUR JOYNT VIGOR NOW 10 405

VIGOUR
INVINCIBLE, AND VIGOUR SOON RETURNS, 1 140
VIGOUR DIVINE WITHIN THEM, CAN ALLOW 6 158
SOON CLOSING, AND BY NATIVE VIGOUR HEAL'D. 6 436
AND OF THIR WONTED VIGOUR LEFT THEM DRAIND, 6 851
HIS BEAMS, UNACTIVE ELSE, THIR VIGOUR FIND. 8 97
WITH SUPPLE JOINTS, AND LIVELY VIGOUR LED: 8 269

VILE
SHALL WE THEN LIVE THUS VILE, THE RACE OF HEAV'N 2 194
KNEE-TRIBUTE YET UNPAID, PROSTRATION VILE, 5 782
RESTOR'D BY THEE, VILE AS I AM, TO PLACE 10 971
TO THIR OWN VILE ADVANTAGES SHALL TURNE 12 510

VILLAGES
AMONG THE PLEASANT VILLAGES AND FARMES 9 448

VILLIFI'D
FORSOOK THEM, WHEN THEMSELVES THEY VILLIFI'D 11 516

VINE
OF COOLE RECESS, O'RE WHICH THE MANTLING VINE 4 258
AS THE VINE CURLES HER TENDRILS, WHICH IMPLI'D 4 307
FRUITLESS IMBRACES: OR THEY LED THE VINE 5 215
FORTH FLOURISH'T THICK THE CLUSTRING VINE, FORTH CREPT 7 320

VINES
THE FLOWRY DALE OF SIBMA CLAD WITH VINES, 1 410
OF LIFE AMBROSIAL FRUTAGE BEAR, AND VINES 5 427
FRUIT OF DELICIOUS VINES, THE GROWTH OF HEAV'N. 5 635

VIOLATE
IMPLOI'D IT SEEMS TO VIOLATE SLEEP, AND THOSE 4 883
THE STRICT FORBIDDANCE, HOW TO VIOLATE 9 903

VIOLATED
WITH PITIE, VIOLATED NOT THIR BLISS. 10 25

VIOLENCE
WITH LUST AND VIOLENCE THE HOUSE OF GOD. 1 496
BUT THAT IMPLIES NOT VIOLENCE OR HARME. 4 901
WITH VIOLENCE OF THIS CONFLICT, HAD NOT SOON 4 995
BY VIOLENCE, NO, FOR THAT SHALL BE WITHSTOOD, 5 242
SUPERIOR, NOR OF VIOLENCE FEAR'D AUGHT; 5 905
THEN VIOLENCE: FOR THIS WAS ALL THY CARE 6 35
BROOKS NOT THE WORKS OF VIOLENCE AND WARR. 6 274
ARIEL AND ARIOC, AND THE VIOLENCE 6 371
BY WOUND, THOUGH FROM THIR PLACE BY VIOLENCE MOV'D. 6 405
HIS VIOLENCE THOU FEARST NOT, BEING SUCH, 9 282
NO MORE BE MENTION'D THEN OF VIOLENCE 10 1041
UNSEEN AMID THE THRONG; SO VIOLENCE 11 671
WHEN VIOLENCE WAS CEAS'T, AND WARR ON EARTH, 11 780
OR VIOLENCE, HEE OF THIR WICKED WAYES 11 812
THE WHOLE EARTH FILL'D WITH VIOLENCE, AND ALL FLESH 11 888

VIOLENT
THINE OWN BEGOTTEN, BREAKING VIOLENT WAY 2 782
A VIOLENT CROSS WIND FROM EITHER COAST 3 487
VOWS MADE IN PAIN, AS VIOLENT AND VOID. 4 97
WEAPONS MORE VIOLENT, WHEN NEXT WE MEET, 6 439
SUTTLE OR VIOLENT, WE NOT ENDU'D 9 324
CORRUPTION TO BRING FORTH MORE VIOLENT DEEDS. 11 428
SOME, AS THOU SAW'ST, BY VIOLENT STROKE SHALL DIE, 11 471
EXPLODED AND HAD SEIZ'D WITH VIOLENT HANDS, 11 669
SUBJECTS HIM FROM WITHOUT TO VIOLENT LORDS; 12 93

VIOLET
MOSAIC; UNDERFOOT THE VIOLET, 4 700

VIOLETS
PANSIES, AND VIOLETS, AND ASPHODEL, 9 1040

VIRGIN
MADE FLESH, WHEN TIME SHALL BE, OF VIRGIN SEED, 3 284
HER VIRGIN FANCIES, POURING FORTH MORE SWEET, 5 296
YET INNOCENCE AND VIRGIN MODESTIE, 8 501
TO WHOM THE VIRGIN MAJESTIE OF EVE, 9 270
YET VIRGIN OF PROSERPINA FROM JOVE. 9 396
IF CHANCE WITH NYMPHLIKE STEP FAIR VIRGIN PASS, 9 452
BY LEO AND THE VIRGIN AND THE SCALES, 10 676
A VIRGIN IS HIS MOTHER, BUT HIS SIRE 12 368
THE SEED OF WOMAN: VIRGIN MOTHER, HAILE, 12 379

VIRGINS
SIDONIAN VIRGINS PAID THIR VOWS AND SONGS, 1 441

VIRTUAL
IRRADIANCE, VIRTUAL OR IMMEDIATE TOUCH? 8 617
FOMENTED BY HIS VIRTUAL POWER AND WARMD: 11 338

VIRTUE
LOOSE ALL HER VIRTUE; LEAST BAD MEN SHOULD BOAST 2 483

VISAG'D
HIS ARROWS, FROM THE FOURFOLD-VISAG'D FOURE, 6 845

VISAGE
WITH FAULTRING SPEECH AND VISAGE INCOMPOS'D 2 989
ERE HE DREW NIGH, HIS RADIANT VISAGE TURND, 3 646
WHICH MARRD HIS BORROW'D VISAGE, AND BETRAID 4 116
WHENCE IN HER VISAGE ROUND THOSE SPOTS, UNPURG'D 5 419
AND VISAGE ALL ENFLAM'D FIRST THUS BEGAN. 6 261
HIS VISAGE DRAWN HE FELT TO SHARP AND SPARE, 10 511

VISAGES
THIR VISAGES AND STATURE AS OF GODS, 1 570
THAT TIME CELESTIAL VISAGES, YET MIXT 10 24

VISIBLE
NO LIGHT, BUT RATHER DARKNESS VISIBLE 1 63
MADE VISIBLE, TH' ALMIGHTY FATHER SHINES, 3 386
TO THEE NOT VISIBLE, WHEN I ALONE 6 145
WITHIN THE VISIBLE DIURNAL SPHEARE; 7 22
CONSIDERD ALL THINGS VISIBLE IN HEAV'N, 9 604
STOOD VISIBLE, AMONG THESE PINES HIS VOICE 11 321

VISIBLY
DIVINE COMPASSION VISIBLY APPEERD, 3 141
HIS LUSTRE VISIBLY IMPAR'D; YET SEEMD 4 850
VISIBLY, WHAT BY DEITIE I AM, 6 682

VISION
EZEKIEL SAW, WHEN BY THE VISION LED 1 455
IN VISION BEATIFIC: BY HIM FIRST 1 684
CAST OUT FROM GOD AND BLESSED VISION, FALLS 5 613
AND TO THE HEAV'NLY VISION THUS PRESUM'D. 8 356
THUS I PRESUMPTUOUS; AND THE VISION BRIGHT, 8 367
MUCH BETTER SEEMS THIS VISION, AND MORE HOPE 11 599
TO CALL BY VISION FROM HIS FATHERS HOUSE, 12 121

VISIONS
IN THE VISIONS OF GOD: IT WAS A HILL 11 377
O VISIONS ILL FORESEEN. BETTER HAD I 11 763

VISIT
THEE I RE-VISIT NOW WITH BOLDER WING, 3 13
NIGHTLY I VISIT: NOR SOMTIMES FORGET 3 32
TO VISIT ALL THY CREATURES, AND TO ALL 3 230
BY WHICH, TO VISIT OFT THOSE HAPPY TRIBES, 3 532
TO VISIT OFT THIS NEW CREATION ROUND; 3 661
TO VISIT THEE; LEAD ON THEN WHERE THY BOWRE 5 375
TO VISIT OFT THE DWELLINGS OF JUST MEN 7 570
TO VISIT HOW THEY PROSPER'D, BUD AND BLOOM, 8 45
BUT GOD WHO OFT DESCENDS TO VISIT MEN 12 48

VISITANT
WHILE THE GREAT VISITANT APPROACHD, THUS SPAKE. 11 225

VISITATION
HER NIGHTLY VISITATION UNIMPLOR'D, 9 22
MY EARLY VISITATION, AND MY LAST 11 275

VISITED
THAT ON MY HEAD ALL MIGHT BE VISITED, 10 955

VISITING
RAN NECTAR, VISITING EACH PLANT, AND FED 4 240

VISIT'ST
VISIT'ST MY SLUMBERS NIGHTLY, OR WHEN MORN 7 29

VISUAL
NO WHERE SO CLEER, SHARP'ND HIS VISUAL RAY 3 620
THE VISUAL NERVE, FOR HE HAD MUCH TO SEE; 11 415

VITAL
AND FEEL THY SOVRAN VITAL LAMP; BUT THOU 3 22
TO VITAL SPIRITS ASPIRE, TO ANIMAL, 5 484
VITAL IN EVERY PART, NOT AS FRAIL MAN 6 345
AND VITAL VERTUE INFUS'D, AND VITAL WARMTH 7 236

VITIATED
AS VITIATED IN NATURE: MORE TO KNOW 10 169

VITIOUS
SERVANT OF SERVANTS, ON HIS VITIOUS RACE. 12 104

VOCAL
MADE VOCAL BY MY SONG, AND TAUGHT HIS PRAISE. 5 204
AND JOIND THIR VOCAL WORSHIP TO THE QUIRE 9 198
ORGANIC, OR IMPULSE OF VOCAL AIR, 9 530

VOIAGE
HER ANNUAL VOIAGE, BORN ON WINDES; THE AIRE 7 431

VOICE
MY VOICE DISSWADES; FOR WHAT CAN FORCE OR GUILE 2 188
DREADED NOT MORE TH' ADVENTURE THEN HIS VOICE 2 474
BY HARALDS VOICE EXPLAIN'D: THE HOLLOW ABYSS 2 518
BEFORE THE HEAVENS THOU WERT, AND AT THE VOICE 3 9
NO VOICE EXEMPT, NO VOICE BUT WELL COULD JOINE 3 370

VOICE (CONTINUED)
CONFUSION HEARD HIS VOICE, AND WILDE UPROAR 3 710
O FOR THAT WARNING VOICE, WHICH HE WHO SAW 4 1
BUT WITH NO FRIENDLY VOICE, AND ADD THY NAME 4 36
HAD NOT A VOICE THUS WARND ME, WHAT THOU SEEST, 4 467
SHOT FORTH PECULIAR GRACES; THEN WITH VOICE 5 15
WITH GENTLE VOICE, I THOUGHT IT THINE; IT SAID, 5 37
THE WONTED SIGNAL, AND SUPERIOR VOICE 5 705
BEFORE THE SEAT SUPREAM; FROM WHENCE A VOICE 6 27
SO SPAKE THE SOVRAN VOICE, AND CLOUDS BEGAN 6 56
EACH TO HIS PLACE, THEY HEARD HIS VOICE AND WENT 6 782
IF RIGHTLY THOU ART CALL'D, WHOSE VOICE DIVINE 7 2
MORE SAFE I SING WITH MORTAL VOICE, UNCHANG'D 7 24
BOTH HARP AND VOICE; NOR COULD THE MUSE DEFEND 7 37
HELD BY THY VOICE, THY POTENT VOICE HE HEARES, 7 100
FOR CHAOS HEARD HIS VOICE; HIM ALL HIS TRAINE 7 221
DESCENDS, THITHER WITH HEART AND VOICE AND EYES 7 513
TEMPER'D SOFT TUNINGS, INTERMIXT WITH VOICE 7 598
SO CHARMING LEFT HIS VOICE, THAT HE A WHILE 8 2
THIS ANSWER FROM THE GRATIOUS VOICE DIVINE. 8 436
AND GUIDED BY HIS VOICE, NOR UNINFORMD 8 486
OF CREATURES WANTING VOICE, THAT DONE, PARTAKE 9 199
THOUGH AT THE VOICE MUCH MARVELING; AT LENGTH 9 551
I KNEW, BUT NOT WITH HUMAN VOICE ENDU'D; 9 561
SOLE DAUGHTER OF HIS VOICE; THE REST, WE LIVE 9 653
ENDU'D WITH HUMAN VOICE AND HUMAN SENSE, 9 871
TO COUNTERFET MANS VOICE, TRUE IN OUR FALL, 9 1069
AMIDST IN THUNDER UTTER'D THUS HIS VOICE. 10 33
TO SENTENCE MAN: THE VOICE OF GOD THEY HEARD 10 97
I HEARD THEE IN THE GARDEN, AND OF THY VOICE 10 116
MY VOICE THOU OFT HAST HEARD, AND HAST NOT FEAR'D, 10 119
BEFORE HIS VOICE, OR WAS SHEE MADE THY GUIDE, 10 146
BECAUSE THOU HAST HEARK'ND TO THE VOICE OF THY WIFE, 10 198
TO THOSE BRIGHT ORDERS UTTERD THUS HIS VOICE. 10 615
IS PROPAGATED CURSE. O VOICE ONCE HEARD 10 729
AND SLEEP SECURE; HIS DREADFUL VOICE NO MORE 10 779
STOOD VISIBLE, AMONG THESE PINES HIS VOICE 11 321
MANKINDS DELIVERANCE. BUT THE VOICE OF GOD 12 235
MANS VOICE COMMANDING, SUN IN GIBEON STAND, 12 265

VOICES
OF DULCET SYMPHONIES AND VOICES SWEET, 1 712
OF STUNNING SOUNDS AND VOICES ALL CONFUS'D 2 952
AS FROM BLEST VOICES, UTTERING JOY, HEAV'N RUNG 3 347
CELESTIAL VOICES TO THE MIDNIGHT AIR, 4 682
JOYN VOICES ALL YE LIVING SOULS, YE BIRDS, 5 197

VOID
FAMILIAR THE FIERCE HEAT, AND VOID OF PAIN; 2 219
THESE PAST, IF ANY PASS, THE VOID PROFOUND 2 438
TH' UNFOUNDED DEEP, AND THROUGH THE VOID IMMENSE 2 829
WON FROM THE VOID AND FORMLESS INFINITE. 3 12
VOWS MADE IN PAIN, AS VIOLENT AND VOID. 4 97
FAR IN THE DARK DISLODG'D, AND VOID OF REST, 6 415
MATTER UNFORM'D AND VOID: DARKNESS PROFOUND 7 233
WHICH LEAVES US NAKED THUS, OF HONOUR VOID, 9 1074
WHICH HE PRESUMES ALREADY VAIN AND VOID, 10 50
AND GREAT EXPLOITS, BUT OF TRUE VERTU VOID; 11 790
BY FAITH NOT VOID OF WORKES: THIS GOD-LIKE ACT 12 427

VOLANT
THIR STOPS AND CHORDS WAS SEEN: HIS VOLANT TOUCH 11 561

VOLATIL
VOLATIL HERMES, AND CALL UP UNBOUND 3 603

VOLIE
HIS THUNDER IN MID VOLIE, FOR HE MEANT 6 854

VOLIED
THY BLASTING VOLIED THUNDER MADE ALL SPEED 4 928

VOLIES
OF FIERY DARTS IN FLAMING VOLIES FLEW, 6 213

VOLUBIL
DIURNAL, OR THIS LESS VOLUBIL EARTH 4 594

VOLUBLE
THEN VOLUBLE AND BOLD, NOW HID, NOW SEEN 9 436

VOLUMINOUS
VOLUMINOUS AND VAST, A SERPENT ARM'D 2 652

VOLUNTARIE
THEN FEED ON THOUGHTS, THAT VOLUNTARIE MOVE 3 37
OUR VOLUNTARIE SERVICE HE REQUIRES, 5 529
BOTH RANSOM AND REDEEMER VOLUNTARIE, 10 61

VOLUPTUOUS
AT THY RIGHT HAND VOLUPTUOUS, AS BESEEMS 2 869

VOTE
PRINCES OF HELL? FOR SO THE POPULAR VOTE 2 313
THEY VOTE: WHEREAT HIS SPEECH HE THUS RENEWS. 2 389

VOUCHT
AT SUCH BOLD WORDS VOUCHT WITH A DEED SO BOLD: 5 66

VOUTSAF'D
WITH WORSHIP, PLACE BY PLACE WHERE HE VOUTSAF'D 11 318

VOUTSAFE
TO US PERHAPS HE BRINGS, AND WILL VOUTSAFE 5 312
TO WANT, AND HONOUR THESE, VOUTSAFE WITH US 5 365
NOR OTHER STRIFE WITH THEM DO I VOUTSAFE. 6 823

VOUTSAFES
THAT GOD VOUTSAFES TO RAISE ANOTHER WORLD 11 877
FOR GODS. YET HIM GOD THE MOST HIGH VOUTSAFES 12 120
OBEDIENT TO HIS WILL, THAT HE VOUTSAFES 12 246

VOUTSAF'ST
WHO HIGHLY THUS TO ENTITLE ME VOUTSAF'ST, 11 170

VOUTSAF'T
VOUTSAF'T OR SOUGHT; FOR WHAT PEACE WILL BE GIV'N 2 332
UNDER WHOSE LOWLY ROOF THOU HAST VOUTSAF'T 5 463
WILL NOT BE NOW VOUTSAF'T, OTHER DECREES 5 884
OF WHAT WE ARE. BUT SINCE THOU HAST VOUTSAF'T 7 80
THE THIRST I HAD OF KNOWLEDGE, AND VOUTSAF'T 8 8
BEYOND ALL OTHER, THINK THE SAME VOUTSAF'T 8 581

VOUTSAFT
FREELY VOUTSAFT; ONCE MORE I WILL RENEW 3 175
SUCH FAVOUR I UNWORTHIE AM VOUTSAFT, 12 622

VOWS
SIDONIAN VIRGINS PAID THIR VOWS AND SONGS, 1 441
VOWS MADE IN PAIN, AS VIOLENT AND VOID. 4 97
WITH VOWS, AS THIR CHIEF GOOD, AND FINAL HOPE. 11 493

VOYAG'D
VOYAG'D TH' UNREAL, VAST, UNBOUNDED DEEP 10 471

VOYAGE
ALONE THE DREADFUL VOYAGE; TILL AT LAST 2 426
PONDERING HIS VOYAGE; FOR NO NARROW FRITH 2 919
BOUND ON A VOYAGE UNCOUTH AND OBSCURE, 8 230

VOYCE
IF ONCE THEY HEAR THAT VOYCE, THIR LIVELIEST PLEDGE 1 274
YET TO THIR GENERALS VOYCE THEY SOON OBEYD 1 337

VOYD
THE SEAT OF DESOLATION, VOYD OF LIGHT, 1 181

VULGAR
ALOOFF THE VULGAR CONSTELLATIONS THICK, 3 577

VULTUR
AS WHEN A VULTUR ON IMAUS BRED, 3 431

WADES
AND SWIMS OR SINKS, OR WADES, OR CREEPS, OR FLYES: 2 950

WAFTED
WAFTED BY ANGELS, OR FLEW O'RE THE LAKE 3 521

WAFTING
A GENTLE WAFTING TO IMMORTAL LIFE. 12 435

WAFTS
WAFTS ON THE CALMER WAVE BY DUBIOUS LIGHT 2 1042

WAG'D
WAG'D IN THE TROUBL'D SKIE, AND ARMIES RUSH 2 534

WAGE
TO WAGE BY FORCE OR GUILE ETERNAL WARR 1 121

WAGGONS
WITH SAILS AND WIND THIR CANIE WAGGONS LIGHT: 3 439

WAIES
AND THE REGARD OF HEAV'N ON ALL HIS WAIES; 4 620

WAIGHT
UNDER HER OWN WAIGHT GROANING TILL THE DAY 12 539

WAIT
MILLIONS THAT STAND IN ARMS, AND LONGING WAIT 2 55
TO WAIT THEM WITH HIS KEYS, AND NOW AT FOOT 3 485
THAT LAY IN WAIT; BEYOND THIS HAD BIN FORCE, 9 1173

WAITE
THAT DAY AND NIGHT FOR HIS DESTRUCTION WAITE. 2 505
WHY SATST THOU LIKE AN ENEMIE IN WAITE 4 825
AUTHORITY AND REASON ON HER WAITE, 8 554

WAITED
A POMP OF WINNING GRACES WAITED STILL, 8 61
WAITED WITH HELLISH RANCOUR IMMINENT 9 409

WAITING
WAITING REVENGE: CRUEL HIS EYE, BUT CAST 1 604
WORTH WAITING, SINCE OUR PRESENT LOT APPEERS 2 223
DISTURBD NOT, WAITING CLOSE TH' APPROACH OF MORN. 9 191
WAITING DESIROUS HER RETURN, HAD WOVE 9 839

WAITS
MORE SOLEMN THEN THE TEDIOUS POMP THAT WAITS 5 354

WAK'D
SUCH WHISPERING WAK'D HER, BUT WITH STARTL'D EYE 5 26
AND FELL ASLEEP; BUT O HOW GLAD I WAK'D 5 92
ALTERNATE ALL NIGHT LONG: BUT NOT SO WAK'D 5 657
TO PLUCK AND EATE; WHEREAT I WAK'D, AND FOUND 8 309
SHEE DISAPPEERD, AND LEFT ME DARK, I WAK'D 8 478
MEAN WHILE THE HOUR OF NOON DREW ON, AND WAK'D 9 739
OF PHILISTEAN DALILAH, AND WAK'D 9 1061
TO FAN THE EARTH NOW WAK'D, AND USHER IN 10 94
LEUCOTHEA WAK'D, AND WITH FRESH DEWS IMBALMD 11 135

WAKE
AND OFT THOUGH WISDOM WAKE, SUSPICION SLEEPS 3 686
UNSEEN, BOTH WHEN WE WAKE, AND WHEN WE SLEEP: 4 678
THY GOODNESS INFINITE, BOTH WHEN WE WAKE, 4 734

WAKEFUL
AGAINST A WAKEFUL FOE, WHILE I ABROAD 2 463
HAD FROM HIS WAKEFUL CUSTODY PURLOIND 2 946
HARMONIOUS NUMBERS; AS THE WAKEFUL BIRD 3 38
WERE SLUNK, ALL BUT THE WAKEFUL NIGHTINGALE; 4 602
OF ARGUS, AND MORE WAKEFUL THEN TO DROUZE, 11 131

WAKEN
THIR SACRED SONG, AND WAKEN RAPTURES HIGH; 3 369
WE MAY NO LONGER STAY: GO, WAKEN EVE; 12 594

WAKES
BY CHANGE OF PLACE; NOW CONSCIENCE WAKES DESPAIR 4 23
THAT SLUMBERD, WAKES THE BITTER MEMORIE 4 24
IF NONE REGARD; HEAV'N WAKES WITH ALL HIS EYES, 5 44
OFT IN HER ABSENCE MIMIC FANSIE WAKES 5 110

WAKING
AND WAKING CRI'D, THIS IS THE GATE OF HEAV'N 3 515
BEAUTIE, WHICH WHETHER WAKING OR ASLEEP, 5 14
WAKING THOU NEVER WILT CONSENT TO DO. 5 121
BOTH WAKING WE WERE ONE; HOW THEN CAN NOW 5 678

WAK'ST
HERE SLEEP BELOW WHILE THOU TO FORESIGHT WAK'ST, 11 368

WAK'T
WHEN ADAM WAK'T, SO CUSTOMD, FOR HIS SLEEP 5 3
WAK'T BY THE CIRCLING HOURS, WITH ROSIE HAND 6 3
THEN AS NEW WAK'T THUS GRATEFULLY REPLI'D. 8 4
INDUC'D ME. AS NEW WAK'T FROM SOUNDEST SLEEP 8 253
WAK'T IN THE RENOVATION OF THE JUST, 11 65
LAY SLEEPING RAN BEFORE, BUT FOUND HER WAK'T; 12 608

WALK
IF THAT WAY BE YOUR WALK, YOU HAVE NOT FARR; 2 1007
BUT FIRST WITH NARROW SEARCH I MUST WALK ROUND 4 528
OUR WALK AT NOON, WITH BRANCHES OVERGROWN, 4 627
WITH THIS HER SOLEMN BIRD, NOR WALK BY MOON, 4 655
MILLIONS OF SPIRITUAL CREATURES WALK THE EARTH 4 677
WHILE THEY KEEP WATCH, OR NIGHTLY ROUNDING WALK 4 685
CLOSE AT MINE EAR ONE CALL'D ME FORTH TO WALK 5 36
TO FIND THEE I DIRECTED THEN MY WALK; 5 49
YEE THAT IN WATERS GLIDE, AND YEE THAT WALK 5 200
THEY SHEW US WHEN OUR FOES WALK NOT UPRIGHT. 6 627
AS WE NEED WALK, TILL YOUNGER HANDS ERE LONG 9 246
NEERER HE DREW, AND MANY A WALK TRAVERS'D 9 434
DID, AS THOU SAWST, RECEAVE, TO WALK WITH GOD 11 707
AND LOVE WITH FEAR THE ONELY GOD, TO WALK 12 562

WALK'D
HERE WALK'D THE FIEND AT LARGE IN SPACIOUS FIELD. 3 430
WALK'D UP AND DOWN ALONE BENT ON HIS PREY, 3 441
WALK'D FIRM; THE CRESTED COCK WHOSE CLARION SOUNDS 7 443
AMONG THE TREES IN PAIRS THEY ROSE, THEY WALK'D; 7 459
CREATURES THAT LIVD, AND MOVD, AND WALK'D, OR FLEW, 8 264

WALKES
WHAT CAN BE TOILSOM IN THESE PLEASANT WALKES? 11 179

WALKING
NOW WALKING IN THE GARDEN, BY SOFT WINDES 10 98

WALKS
SATAN ALIGHTED WALKS; A GLOBE FARR OFF 3 422
HYPOCRISIE, THE ONELY EVIL THAT WALKS 3 683
BUT IF WITHIN THE CIRCUIT OF THESE WALKS, 4 586
HIS GOD-LIKE GUEST, WALKS FORTH, WITHOUT MORE TRAIN 5 351
PLANTED, WITH WALKS, AND BOWERS, THAT WHAT I SAW 8 305
WALKS, AND THE MELODIE OF BIRDS; BUT HERE 8 528
HIGH OVERARCH'T, AND ECHOING WALKS BETWEEN; 9 1107
THEE NATIVE SOILE, THESE HAPPIE WALKS AND SHADES, 11 270
NEW REAPT, THE OTHER PART SHEEP-WALKS AND FOULDS; 11 431

WALKS (CONTINUED)
UNSEEN, AND THROUGH THIR HABITATIONS WALKS 12 49

WALKT
HE WALKT WITH TO SUPPORT UNEASIE STEPS 1 295
BY FOWL, FISH, BEAST, WAS FLOWN, WAS SWUM, WAS WALKT 7 503
WITH WHAT DELIGHT COULD I HAVE WALKT THEE ROUND, . 9 114
LONG HAD NOT WALKT, WHEN FROM THE TENTS BEHOLD . 11 581

WALL
COASTING THE WALL OF HEAV'N ON THIS SIDE NIGHT . 3 71
SAVE ON THAT SIDE WHICH FROM THE WALL OF HEAV'N . 3 427
UP TO THE WALL OF HEAVEN A STRUCTURE HIGH, . . . 3 503
THE VERDUROUS WALL OF PARADISE UP SPRUNG: . . . 4 143
AND HIGHER THEN THAT WALL A CIRCLING ROW . . . 4 146
OF HILL OR HIGHEST WALL, AND SHEER WITHIN . . . 4 182
FENC'D UP THE VERDANT WALL; EACH BEAUTEOUS FLOUR, 4 697
AND CHRYSTAL WALL OF HEAV'N, WHICH OP'NING WIDE, . 6 860
PART RISE IN CRYSTAL WALL, OR RIDGE DIRECT, . . 7 293
THRICE FUGITIVE ABOUT TROY WALL; OR RAGE . . . 9 16
OF LENGTH PRODIGIOUS JOYNING TO THE WALL 10 302
ASSAULTING; OTHERS FROM THE WALL DEFEND 11 657

WALLES
THE REST IN CIRCUIT WALLES THIS UNIVERSE. 3 721

WALLOWING
WALLOWING UNWEILDIE, ENORMOUS IN THIR GATE . . . 7 411

WALLS
HEAV'N, WHOSE HIGH WALLS FEAR NO ASSAULT OR SIEGE, 2 343
OF LIGHT APPEARS, AND FROM THE WALLS OF HEAV'N . 2 1035
FARR TO THE INLAND RETIR'D, ABOUT THE WALLS . . 10 423
OF MIGHTIEST EMPIRE, FROM THE DESTIND WALLS . . 11 387
AS ON DRIE LAND BETWEEN TWO CHRISTAL WALLS, . . 12 197
TO THAT PROUD CITIE, WHOSE HIGH WALLS THOU SAW'ST 12 342

WAN
BUT FADED SPLENDOR WAN; WHO BY HIS GATE 4 870
SPREADING THIR BANE; THE BLASTED STARRS LOOKT WAN, 10 412

WAND
OF SOME GREAT AMMIRAL, WERE BUT A WAND, ... 1 294
BEFORE HIS DECENT STEPS A SILVER WAND. 3 644

WANDER
DARKENS THE STREETS, THEN WANDER FORTH THE SONS . 1 501
THOSE THOUGHTS THAT WANDER THROUGH ETERNITY, . . 2 148
CEASE I TO WANDER WHERE THE MUSES HAUNT 3 27
TILL FINAL DISSOLUTION, WANDER HERE, ... 3 458
ERRONEOUS THERE TO WANDER AND FORLORNE. 7 20
OR WANDER WITH DELIGHT, AND LOVE TO HAUNT . . . 7 330
HOW SHALL I PART, AND WHITHER WANDER DOWN . . . 11 282

WANDERD
AND LONG HE WANDERD, TILL AT LAST A GLEAME . . . 3 499
THROUGH THE WORLDS WILDERNESS LONG WANDERD MAN . 12 313

WANDERER
MISLEADS TH' AMAZ'D NIGHT-WANDERER FROM HIS WAY . 9 640

WANDRING
GOT THEM NEW NAMES, TILL WANDRING ORE THE EARTH, . 1 365
THIR WANDRING GODS DISGUIS'D IN BRUTISH FORMS . . 1 481
SUFFICIENT? WHO SHALL TEMPT WITH WANDRING FEET . 2 404
DISBAND, AND WANDRING, EACH HIS SEVERAL WAY . . 2 523
AND FOUND NO END, IN WANDRING MAZES LOST. . . . 2 561
TO SEARCH WITH WANDRING QUEST A PLACE FORETOLD . 2 830
WANDRING THIS DARKSOME DESART, AS MY WAY, . . . 2 973
TO FIND WHO MIGHT DIRECT HIS WANDRING FLIGHT . . 3 631
ALONE THUS WANDRING. BRIGHTEST SERAPH TELL . . . 3 667
RUNS DIVERS, WANDRING MANY A FAMOUS REALME . . . 4 234
SOME WANDRING SPIRIT OF HEAV'N, BY FOUNTAIN SIDE, 4 531
AND YEE FIVE OTHER WANDRING FIRES THAT MOVE . . 5 177
THOUGH WANDRING. HE WITH HIS CONSORTED EVE . . 7 50
WITH SERPENT ERROUR WANDRING, FOUND THIR WAY, . . 7 302
THIR WANDRING COURSE NOW HIGH, NOW LOW, THEN HID, 8 126
SEEK THEM WITH WANDRING THOUGHTS, AND NOTIONS VAIN. 8 187
MY WANDRING, HAD NOT HEE WHO WAS MY GUIDE . . . 8 312
BRIGHT'NS HIS CREST, AS WHEN A WANDRING FIRE, . . 9 634
DESIRE OF WANDRING THIS UNHAPPIE MORN, ... 9 1136
OF WANDRING, AS THOU CALL'ST IT, WHICH WHO KNOWS 9 1146
AND WANDRING VANITIE, WHEN LEST WAS SAFE, . . . 10 875
WANDRING THAT WATRIE DESERT: I HAD HOPE 11 779
NOT WANDRING POOR, BUT TRUSTING ALL HIS WEALTH . 12 133
WANDRING, SHALL IN A GLORIOUS TEMPLE ENSHRINE. . 12 334
THEY HAND IN HAND WITH WANDRING STEPS AND SLOW, . 12 648

WANT
WITH GOLDEN ARCHITRAVE; NOR DID THERE WANT . . . 1 715
NOR WANT WE SKILL OR ART, FROM WHENCE TO RAISE . 2 272
NOR WILL OCCASION WANT, NOR SHALL WE NEED . . . 2 341
FOR WANT OF OTHER PREY, BUT THAT HE KNOWS . . . 2 806
THAT HEAV'N WOULD WANT SPECTATORS, GOD WANT PRAISE; 4 676
TO WANT, AND HONOUR THESE, VOUTSAFE WITH US . . 5 365
OBEDIENT? CAN WE WANT OBEDIENCE THEN 5 514
BY THEE COMMUNICATED, AND OUR WANT: 9 755

WANT (CONTINUED)
BUT BY FULFILLING THAT WHICH THOU DIDST WANT, . . 12 396

WANTED
WANTED, NOR YOUTHFUL DALLIANCE AS BESEEMS . . . 4 338
SAT HORROR PLUM'D; NOR WANTED IN HIS GRASPE . . 4 989
NOR HOLY RAPTURE WANTED THEY TO PRAISE 5 147
THERE WANTED YET THE MASTER WORK, THE END . . . 7 505
I FOUND NOT WHAT ME THOUGHT I WANTED STILL; . . 8 355
WANTED NOT LONG, THOUGH TO THIS SHAPE RETAIN'D. . 9 601

WANTING
NOR WANTING POWER TO MITIGATE AND SWAGE 1 556
OF CREATURES WANTING VOICE, THAT DONE, PARTAKE . 9 199
BE WANTING, BUT AFFORD THEE EQUAL AID, ... 10 271

WANTON
TO DO HIM WANTON RITES, WHICH COST THEM WOE. . . 1 414
WHOSE WANTON PASSIONS IN THE SACRED PORCH . . . 1 454
DISHEVELD, BUT IN WANTON RINGLETS WAV'D 4 306
MORE HANDS THEN OURS TO LOP THIR WANTON GROWTH: . 4 629
MIXT DANCE, OR WANTON MASK, OR MIDNIGHT BAL, . . 4 768
ONE NIGHT OR TWO WITH WANTON GROWTH DERIDES . . 9 211
CURLD MANY A WANTON WREATH IN SIGHT OF EVE, . . 9 517
IN GEMS AND WANTON DRESS; TO THE HARP THEY SUNG . 11 583

WANTOND
WANTOND AS IN HER PRIME, AND PLAID AT WILL . . . 5 295

WANTONLY
AS WANTONLY REPAID; IN LUST THEY BURNE: 9 1015

WANTONNESS
SURFET, AND LUST, TILL WANTONNESS AND PRIDE . . 11 795

WANTS
WANTS NOT HER HIDDEN LUSTRE, GEMMS AND GOLD; . . 2 271
FOR US TOO LARGE, WHERE THY ABUNDANCE WANTS . . 4 730
WANTS HER FIT VESSELS PURE, THEN STREWS THE GROUND 5 348
AND THE GREAT LIGHT OF DAY YET WANTS TO RUN . . 7 98
AND SAID, THY MANSION WANTS THEE, ADAM, RISE, . . 8 296
WITHOUT COPARTNER? SO TO ADD WHAT WANTS . . 9 821
AND HATEFUL; NOTHING WANTS, BUT THAT THY SHAPE, . 10 869

WAR
RAIS'D IMPIOUS WAR IN HEAV'N AND BATTEL PROUD . . 1 43
CLASH'D ON THIR SOUNDING SHIELDS THE DIN OF WAR, . 1 668
INTESTINE WAR IN HEAV'N, THE ARCH FOE SUBDU'D . . 6 259
BEAST NOW WITH BEAST GAN WAR, AND FOWLE WITH FOWLE, 10 710

WARBL'D
WITH WARBL'D HYMNS, AND TO HIS GODHEAD SING . . 2 242

WARBLE
FOUNTAINS AND YEE, THAT WARBLE, AS YE FLOW, . . 5 195

WARBLING
THAT WASH THY HALLOWD FEET, AND WARBLING FLOW, . 3 31
TO THE NIGHT-WARBLING BIRD, THAT NOW AWAKE . . . 5 40
MELODIOUS MURMURS, WARBLING TUNE HIS PRAISE. . . 5 196
CEAS'D WARBLING, BUT ALL NIGHT TUN'D HER SOFT LAYES: 7 436
BIRDS ON THE BRANCHES WARBLING; ALL THINGS SMIL'D, 8 265

WARD
OF DAWNING LIGHT TURND THITHER-WARD IN HASTE . . 3 500

WARDS
TH' INTRICATE WARDS, AND EVERY BOLT AND BAR . . 2 877

WARFARE
FAITHFUL HATH BEEN YOUR WARFARE, AND OF GOD . . 6 803

WARIE
INTO THIS WILD ABYSS THE WARIE FIEND 2 917

WARLIKE
THEN STRAIT COMMANDS THAT AT THE WARLIKE SOUND . 1 531
TO THIR NIGHT WATCHES IN WARLIKE PARADE, . . . 4 780
THUS HE IN SCORN. THE WARLIKE ANGEL MOV'D, . . 4 902
THE GREAT ARCH-ANGEL FROM HIS WARLIKE TOILE . . 6 257

WARM'D
WARM'D BY THE SUN, PRODUCING EVERY KIND, ... 9 721

WARMD
FOMENTED BY HIS VIRTUAL POWER AND WARMD: . . . 11 338

WARME
OF VARIOUS INFLUENCE FOMENT AND WARME, ... 4 669
SHOT DOWN DIRECT HIS FERVID RAIES TO WARME . . . 5 301
MAIN OCEAN FLOW'D, NOT IDLE, BUT WITH WARME . . 7 279
FROM THENCE A RIB, WITH CORDIAL SPIRITS WARME; . 8 466

WARMLY
BOTH WHERE THE MORNING SUN FIRST WARMLY SMOTE . . 4 244

WATCH (CONTINUED)
THERE KEPT THIR WATCH THE LEGIONS, WHILE THE GRAND 10 427
MANY A DARK LEAGUE, REDUC'T IN CAREFUL WATCH . . 10 438
THEN STIL AT HELS DARK THRESHOLD TO HAVE SATE WATCH, ... 10 594
CHERUBIC WATCH, AND OF A SWORD THE FLAME . . 11 120
DARKNESS DEFENDS BETWEEN TILL MORNING WATCH; . . 12 207
TO SIMPLE SHEPHERDS, KEEPING WATCH BY NIGHT; . . 12 365

WATCHD
TO THE BRIGHT MINISTER THAT WATCHD, HEE BLEW . . 11 73

WATCHES
TO THIR NIGHT WATCHES IN WARLIKE PARADE, . . . 4 780
ENCAMPING, PLAC'D IN GUARD THIR WATCHES ROUND, . 6 412
WATCHES, NO DOUBT, WITH GREEDY HOPE TO FIND . . 9 257

WATCHFUL
WHICH THE FIVE WATCHFUL SENSES REPRESENT, . . . 5 104
MORE WISE, MORE WATCHFUL, STRONGER, IF NEED WERE . 9 311
OF WATCHFUL CHERUBIM; FOUR FACES EACH 11 128

WATCHING
OF ANGELS WATCHING ROUND? HERE HE HAD NEED . . 2 413
WATCHING WHERE SHEPHERDS PEN THIR FLOCKS AT EEVE . 4 185
HERE WATCHING AT THE HEAD OF THESE THAT SLEEP? . 4 826

WATER
THE FORD, AND OF IT SELF THE WATER FLIES . . . 2 612
CONSUMMATE LOVLY SMIL'D; AIRE, WATER, EARTH, . . 7 502
YOUR TRIBES, AND WATER FROM TH' AMBROSIAL FOUNT? . 11 279
DEEP UNDER WATER ROULD; SEA COVER'D SEA, . . . 11 749

WATERD
WATERD THE GARDEN; THENCE UNITED FELL 4 230
WENT UP AND WATERD ALL THE GROUND, AND EACH . . 7 334

WATERING
WATERING THE GROUND, AND WITH OUR SIGHS THE AIR . 10 1090
WATERING THE GROUND, AND WITH THIR SIGHS THE AIR . 10 1102

WATERS
THE RISING WORLD OF WATERS DARK AND DEEP, . . . 3 11
LUXURIANT; MEAN WHILE MURMURING WATERS FALL . . 4 260
OF WATERS ISSU'D FROM A CAVE AND SPREAD 4 454
YEE THAT IN WATERS GLIDE, AND YEE THAT WALK . . 5 200
HE SAID, AND AS THE SOUND OF WATERS DEEP . . . 5 872
WINDS UNDER GROUND OR WATERS FORCING WAY . . . 6 196
ROCKS, WATERS, WOODS, AND BY THE SHAGGIE TOPS . . 6 645
AMID THE WATERS, AND LET IT DIVIDE 7 262
THE WATERS FROM THE WATERS: AND GOD MADE . . . 7 263
THE WATERS UNDERNEATH FROM THOSE ABOVE 7 268
BUILT ON CIRCUMFLUOUS WATERS CALME, IN WIDE . . 7 270
OF WATERS, EMBRYON IMMATURE INVOLV'D, ... 7 277
BE GATHER'D NOW YE WATERS UNDER HEAV'N 7 283
CAPACIOUS BED OF WATERS: THITHER THEY 7 290
OF CONGREGATED WATERS HE CALL'D SEAS: 7 308
AND GOD SAID, LET THE WATERS GENERATE 7 387
THE WATERS GENERATED BY THIR KINDES, ... 7 393
AND LAKES AND RUNNING STREAMS THE WATERS FILL; . . 7 397
OF RAINBOWS AND STARRIE EYES. THE WATERS THUS . 7 446
AND OVER FIELDS AND WATERS, AS IN AIRE 8 301
HOVERING UPON THE WATERS; WHAT THEY MET 10 285
BY THE WATERS OF LIFE, WHERE ERE THEY SATE . . . 11 79

WATRIE
HER WATRIE LABYRINTH, WHEREOF WHO DRINKS, . . . 2 584
COVER'D TH' ABYSS: BUT ON THE WATRIE CALME . . . 7 234
TROOP TO THIR STANDARD, SO THE WATRIE THRONG, . . 7 297
WANDRING THAT WATRIE DESERT: I HAD HOPE . . . 11 779
AND THE CLEER SUN ON HIS WIDE WATRIE GLASS . . . 11 844
THE FLUID SKIRTS OF THAT SAME WATRIE CLOUD, . . . 11 882

WATRY
WORSHIPT IN RABBA AND HER WATRY PLAIN, ... 1 397
A SHAPE WITHIN THE WATRY GLEAM APPEERD 4 461
THEN THAT SMOOTH WATRY IMAGE; BACK I TURND, . . 4 480
OF FISH WITHIN THIR WATRY RESIDENCE, ... 8 346

WAV'D
WAV'D ROUND THE COAST, UP CALL'D A PITCHY CLOUD . 1 340
DISHEVELD, BUT IN WANTON RINGLETS WAV'D 4 306
NOW WAV'D THIR FIERIE SWORDS, AND IN THE AIRE . . 6 304
SHOW TO THE SUN THIR WAV'D COATS DROPT WITH GOLD, 7 406
INSECT OR WORME; THOSE WAV'D THIR LIMBER FANS . . 7 476
WAV'D OVER BY THAT FLAMING BRAND, THE GATE . . . 12 643

WAVE
WITH HEAD UP-LIFT ABOVE THE WAVE, AND EYES . . . 1 193
WAFTS ON THE CALMER WAVE BY DUBIOUS LIGHT . . . 2 1042
TO DARKNESS, SUCH AS BOUND THE OCEAN WAVE. . . . 3 539
BREATHE SOFT OR LOUD; AND WAVE YOUR TOPS, YE PINES, 5 193
WITH EVERY PLANT, IN SIGN OF WORSHIP WAVE. . . . 5 194
AND ALL WHO UNDER ME THIR BANNERS WAVE, ... 5 687
WAVE ROWLING AFTER WAVE, WHERE WAY THEY FOUND, . 7 298
GLIDE UNDER THE GREEN WAVE, IN SCULLES THAT OFT . 7 402
ADDRESS'D HIS WAY, NOT WITH INDENTED WAVE, . . . 9 496
GAZ'D HOT, AND OF THE FRESH WAVE LARGELY DREW, . 11 845

WAVES
FROM OFF THE TOSSING OF THESE FIERY WAVES, . . . 1 184
HATH VEXT THE RED-SEA COAST, WHOSE WAVES ORETHREW 1 306
WHOSE WAVES OF TORRENT FIRE INFLAME WITH RAGE. . 2 581
HIS CONSTANT LAMP, AND WAVES HIS PURPLE WINGS, . 4 764
AND SURGING WAVES, AS MOUNTAINS TO ASSAULT . . . 7 214
SILENCE, YE TROUBL'D WAVES, AND THOU DEEP, PEACE, 7 216
AND SCOURG'D WITH MANY A STROAK TH' INDIGNANT WAVES. 10 311
RODE TILTING O'RE THE WAVES, ALL DWELLINGS ELSE . 11 747
OF PARADISE BY MIGHT OF WAVES BE MOOVD 11 830
ON THIR IMBATTELLD RANKS THE WAVES RETURN, . . . 12 213
IN SIGNAL OF REMOVE, WAVES FIERCELY ROUND; . . . 12 593

WAVING
OF THIR GREAT SULTAN WAVING TO DIRECT 1 348
WITH ORIENT COLOURS WAVING: WITH THEM ROSE . . . 1 546
LAY WAVING ROUND; ON SOM GREAT CHARGE IMPLOY'D . 3 628
OF CERES RIPE FOR HARVEST WAVING BENDS 4 981
CHERUBIC WAVING FIRES: ON TH' OTHER PART . . . 6 413
STOOD WAVING TIPT WITH FIRE; WHILE WE SUSPENSE, . 6 580
WIDE WAVING, ALL APPROACH FARR OFF TO FRIGHT, . . 11 121

WAXEN
DELICIOUSLY, AND BUILDS HER WAXEN CELLS 7 491

WAXING
GAVE HEED, BUT WAXING MORE IN RAGE REPLI'D. . . 4 969

WAY
WORDS INTERWOVE WITH SIGHS FOUND OUT THIR WAY. . 1 621
COULD HAVE ASSUR'D US; AND BY WHAT BEST WAY, . . 2 40
O'RE HEAV'NS HIGH TOWRS TO FORCE RESISTLESS WAY, . 2 62
THE WAY SEEMS DIFFICULT AND STEEP TO SCALE . . . 2 71
OUR STRONGER, SOME WORSE WAY HIS WRATH MAY FIND . 2 83
SCORNING SURPRIZE. OR COULD WE BREAK OUR WAY . . 2 134
HIS UNCOUTH WAY, OR SPREAD HIS AERIE FLIGHT . . 2 407
SEIS'D US, THOUGH UNDISMAID: LONG IS THE WAY . . 2 432
DISBAND, AND WANDRING, EACH HIS SEVERAL WAY . . 2 523
THY MISCREATED FRONT ATHWART MY WAY 2 683
THINE OWN BEGOTTEN, BREAKING VIOLENT WAY . . . 2 782
WITH HEAD, HANDS, WINGS OR FEET PURSUES HIS WAY, . 2 949
WHICH WAY THE NEEREST COAST OF DARKNESS LYES . . 2 958
WANDRING THIS DARKSOME DESART, AS MY WAY, . . . 2 973
IF THAT WAY BE YOUR WALK, YOU HAVE NOT FARR; . . 2 1007
ENVIRON'D WINS HIS WAY; HARDER BESET 2 1016
PAV'D AFTER HIM A BROAD AND BEAT'N WAY 2 1026
THROUGH ALL RESTRAINT BROKE LOOSE HE WINGS HIS WAY 3 87
AND SHALL GRACE NOT FIND MEANS, THAT FINDS HER WAY, 3 228
BUT IN HIS WAY LIGHTS ON THE BARREN PLAINES . . 3 437
THROUGH THE PURE MARBLE AIR HIS OBLIQUE WAY . . 3 564
SHOT UPWARD STILL DIRECT, WHENCE NO WAY ROUND . . 3 618
THY WAY THOU CANST NOT MISS, ME MINE REQUIRES. . 3 735
ME MISERABLE. WHICH WAY SHALL I FLIE 4 73
WHICH WAY I FLIE IS HELL; MY SELF AM HELL; . . . 4 75
THE WAY HE WENT, AND ON TH' ASSYRIAN MOUNT . . . 4 126
BUT FURTHER WAY FOUND NONE, SO THICK ENTWIN'D, . 4 174
ALL PATH OF MAN OR BEAST THAT PAST THAT WAY: . . 4 177
GODS LATEST IMAGE: I DESCRIB'D HIS WAY 4 567
HALF WAY UP HILL THIS VAST SUBLUNAR VAULT, . . . 4 777
HASTING THIS WAY, AND NOW BY GLIMPS DISCERNE . . 4 867
WHO WOULD NOT, FINDING WAY, BREAK LOOSE FROM HELL, 4 889
HER BEARDED GROVE OF EARS, WHICH WAY THE WIND . . 4 982
ON EACH HAND PARTING, TO HIS SPEED GAVE WAY . . 5 252
COMES THIS WAY MOVING; SEEMS ANOTHER MORN . . . 5 310
WELL HAST THOU TAUGHT THE WAY THAT MIGHT DIRECT . 5 508
LONG WAY THROUGH HOSTILE SCORN, WHICH HE SUSTEIND 5 904
THROUGH HEAV'NS WIDE CHAMPAIN HELD HIS WAY, TILL MORN, ... 6 2
IN THE MID WAY: THOUGH STRANGE TO US IT SEEMD . . 6 91
FORTH STEPPING OPPOSITE, HALF WAY HE MET . . . 6 128
WINDS UNDER GROUND OR WATERS FORCING WAY . . . 6 196
BEFORE HIM POWER DIVINE HIS WAY PREPAR'D; . . . 6 780
THEY OPEN TO THEMSELVES AT LENGTH THE WAY . . . 7 158
WAVE ROWLING AFTER WAVE, WHERE WAY THEY FOUND, . 7 298
WITH SERPENT ERROUR WANDRING, FOUND THIR WAY, . . 7 302
IN COMMON, RANG'D IN FIGURE WEDGE THIR WAY, . . 7 426
TO GODS ETERNAL HOUSE DIRECT THE WAY, ... 7 576
SEEN IN THE GALAXIE, THAT MILKIE WAY 7 579
THE EASIEST WAY, NOR WITH PERPLEXING THOUGHTS . 8 183
LEADS UP TO HEAV'N, IS BOTH THE WAY AND GUIDE; . 8 613
FOUND UNSUSPECTED WAY. THERE WAS A PLACE, . . . 9 69
TO INTERCEPT THY WAY, OR SEND THEE BACK 9 410
THE WAY WHICH TO HER RUIN NOW I TEND. 9 493
ADDRESS'D HIS WAY, NOT WITH INDENTED WAVE, . . . 9 496
TO INTERRUPT, SIDE-LONG HE WORKS HIS WAY. . . . 9 512
INTO THE HEART OF EVE HIS WORDS MADE WAY, . . . 9 550
EMPRESS, THE WAY IS READIE, AND NOT LONG, . . . 9 626
MISLEADS TH' AMAZ'D NIGHT-WANDERER FROM HIS WAY . 9 640
IN IGNORANCE, THOU OP'NST WISDOMS WAY, ... 9 809
AND FORTH TO MEET HER WENT, THE WAY SHE TOOK . . 9 847
OP'NING THE WAY, BUT OF DIVINE EFFECT 9 865
NOR CAN I MISS THE WAY, SO STRONGLY DRAWN . . . 10 262
THE WAY, THOU LEADING, SUCH A SENT I DRAW . . . 10 267
MOUNTAINS OF ICE, THAT STOP TH' IMAGIN'D WAY . . 10 291
BRIDGING HIS WAY, EUROPE WITH ASIA JOYN'D, . . . 10 310
AND NOW THIR WAY TO EARTH THEY HAD DESCRI'D, . . 10 325
YOU TWO THIS WAY, AMONG THESE NUMEROUS ORBS . . 10 397

WAY (CONTINUED)
THEN SUFFERD. TH' OTHER WAY SATAN WENT DOWN 10 414
BY SIN AND DEATH A BROAD WAY NOW IS PAV'D 10 473
I FIND NO WAY, FROM DEEP TO DEEPER PLUNG'D. 10 844
OR FIND SOME OTHER WAY TO GENERATE 10 894
FLEW UP, NOR MISSD THE WAY, BY ENVIOUS WINDES 11 15
ONE WAY THE SELF-SAME HOUR? WHY IN THE EAST 11 203
TO FIND WHERE ADAM SHELTERD, TOOK HIS WAY, 11 223
BUT HAVE I NOW SEEN DEATH? IS THIS THE WAY 11 462
BUT IS THERE YET NO OTHER WAY, BESIDES 11 527
PATHS INDIRECT, OR IN THE MID WAY FAINT. 11 631
ONE WAY A BAND SELECT FROM FORAGE DRIVES 11 646
CORRUPTING EACH THIR WAY; YET THOSE REMOOV'D, 11 889
THROUGH THE WILDE DESERT, NOT THE READIEST WAY, 12 216
THROUGH EDEN TOOK THIR SOLITARIE WAY. 12 649

WAYES
AND JUSTIFIE THE WAYES OF GOD TO MEN. 1 26
SURROUNDS ME, FROM THE CHEARFUL WAYES OF MEN 3 46
THROUGH DARK AND DESART WAYES WITH PERIL GONE 3 544
TO SERVE HIM BETTER: WISE ARE ALL HIS WAYES. 3 680
THROUGH WAYES OF DANGER BY HIMSELF UNTRI'D, 4 934
GOD TO REMOVE HIS WAYES FROM HUMAN SENSE, 8 119
GLADLY INTO THE WAYES OF GOD WITH MAN: 8 226
THIR LANGUAGE AND THIR WAYES, THEY ALSO KNOW, 8 373
THE HIGHTH AND DEPTH OF THY ETERNAL WAYES 8 413
FROM PRONE, NOR IN THIR WAYES COMPLACENCE FIND. 8 433
THINGS IN THIR CAUSES, BUT TO TRACE THE WAYES 9 682
WITH LONG REACH INTERPOS'D; THREE SEV'RAL WAYES 10 323
THIS SAID, THEY BOTH BETOOK THEM SEVERAL WAYES, 10 610
OF DEATH, AND MANY ARE THE WAYES THAT LEAD 11 468
AND TESTIFI'D AGAINST THIR WAYES; HEE OFT 11 721
OR VIOLENCE, HEE OF THIR WICKED WAYES 11 812
TO LEAVE THEM TO THIR OWN POLLUTED WAYES; 12 110

WAYS
FOUR WAYS THIR FLYING MARCH, ALONG THE BANKS 2 574
AND ON, METHOUGHT, ALONE I PASS'D THROUGH WAYS 5 50
THROUGH MULTITUDE THAT SUNG: JUST ARE THY WAYS, 10 643
OF MANY WAYS TO DIE THE SHORTEST CHOOSING, 10 1005

WEAK
FALL'N CHERUBE, TO BE WEAK IS MISERABLE 1 157
SINGLE AGAINST THEE WICKED, AND THENCE WEAK. 4 856
WHERE THOU ART WEIGH'D, AND SHOWN HOW LIGHT, HOW WEAK, 4 1012
SHEE FIRST HIS WEAK INDULGENCE WILL ACCUSE. 9 1186
TO WITHERD WEAK AND GRAY; THY SENSES THEN 11 540
SAVE BY THOSE SHADOWIE EXPIATIONS WEAK, 12 291
ACCOMPLISHING GREAT THINGS, BY THINGS DEEMD WEAK 12 567

WEAKE
SUPERIOUR AND UNMOV'D, HERE ONELY WEAKE 8 532

WEAKER
THY WEAKER; LET IT PROFIT THEE TO HAVE HEARD 6 909
A FOE SO PROUD WILL FIRST THE WEAKER SEEK, 9 383

WEAKEST
THERE FAIL WHERE VERTUE FAILS, OR WEAKEST PROVE 6 117

WEAKNESS
AND WHERE THIR WEAKNESS, HOW ATTEMPTED BEST, 2 357
OF WEAKNESS, NOT OF POWER. WILL HE, DRAW OUT, 10 801

WEAKNING
WEAKNING THE SCEPTER OF OLD NIGHT: FIRST HELL 2 1002

WEAL
THE WEAL OR WOE IN THEE IS PLAC'T; BEWARE. 8 638
FOLLOW, AS TO HIM LINKT IN WEAL OR WOE, 9 133

WEALTH
IN WEALTH AND LUXURIE. TH' ASCENDING PILE 1 722
OUTSHON THE WEALTH OF ORMUS AND OF IND, 2 2
IN NARROW ROOM NATURES WHOLE WEALTH, YEA MORE, 4 207
IN TRIUMPH AND LUXURIOUS WEALTH, ARE THEY 11 788
NOT WANDRING POOR, BUT TRUSTING ALL HIS WEALTH 12 133
AND HIS NEXT SON FOR WEALTH AND WISDOM FAM'D, 12 332
IN WEALTH AND MULTITUDE, FACTIOUS THEY GROW; 12 352

WEAPONS
WEAPONS MORE VIOLENT, WHEN NEXT WE MEET, 6 439
WITH MOUNTAINS AS WITH WEAPONS ARM'D, WHICH MAKES 6 697
ALL COURAGE; DOWN THIR IDLE WEAPONS DROP'D; 6 839

WEAR
THESE TROUBLESOM DISGUISES WHICH WEE WEAR, 4 740

WEARERS
COWLES, HOODS AND HABITS WITH THIR WEARERS TOST 3 490

WEARIE
TO WEARIE HIM WITH MY ASSIDUOUS CRIES: 11 310
MUST NEEDS IMPAIRE AND WEARIE HUMAN SENSE: 12 10

WEARIED
YOUR WEARIED VERTUE, FOR THE EASE YOU FIND 1 320

WEARIED (CONTINUED)
TO STOOP WITH WEARIED WINGS, AND WILLING FEET 3 73
WARR WEARIED HATH PERFORM'D WHAT WARR CAN DO, 6 695
OPPRESS'D THEM, WEARIED WITH THIR AMOROUS PLAY. 9 1045
WEARIED WITH THEIR INIQUITIES, WITHDRAW 12 107
WEARIED I FELL ASLEEP: BUT NOW LEAD ON; 12 614

WEARISOM
IN HEAV'N THIS OUR DELIGHT; HOW WEARISOM 2 247

WEATHER-BEATEN
AND LIKE A WEATHER-BEATEN VESSEL HOLDS 2 1043

WED
TO WED HER ELM; SHE SPOUS'D ABOUT HIM TWINES 5 216

WEDDED
HAILE WEDDED LOVE, MYSTERIOUS LAW, TRUE SOURCE 4 750
HIS MARRIAGE WITH THE SEAVENTIMES-WEDDED MAID. 5 223
HARMONIE TO BEHOLD IN WEDDED PAIR 8 605
AND ADAM WEDDED TO ANOTHER EVE, 9 828
I SAW THEE FIRST AND WEDDED THEE, ADORN'D 9 1030

WEDGE
IN COMMON, RANG'D IN FIGURE WEDGE THIR WAY, 7 426

WEDLOCK-BOUND
SHALL MEET, ALREADIE LINKT AND WEDLOCK-BOUND 10 905

WEED
GRAZE THE SEA WEED THIR PASTURE, AND THROUGH GROVES 7 404

WEEDS
DYING PUT ON THE WEEDS OF DOMINIC, 3 479

WEEND
WITH FURIOUS EXPEDITION; FOR THEY WEEND 6 86

WEENE
STRAIT SIDE BY SIDE WERE LAID, NOR TURND I WEENE 4 741

WEENING
WEENING TO PROSPER, AND AT LENGTH PREVAILE 6 795

WEEP
TEARS SUCH AS ANGELS WEEP, BURST FORTH: AT LAST 1 620
THEY SATE THEM DOWN TO WEEP, NOR ONELY TEARES 9 1121

WEEPE
THE WORLD ERELONG A WORLD OF TEARS MUST WEEPE. 11 627

WEEPING
SHE ENDED WEEPING, AND HER LOWLIE PLIGHT, 10 937

WEIGH
NOT THY SUBJECTION; WEIGH WITH HER THY SELF; 8 570
TO WEIGH THY SPIRITS DOWN, AND LAST CONSUME 11 545

WEIGH'D
WHERE THOU ART WEIGH'D, AND SHOWN HOW LIGHT, HOW WEAK, 4 1012

WEIGHD
WHEREIN ALL THINGS CREATED FIRST HE WEIGHD, 4 999

WEIGHS
WEIGHS HIS SPREAD WINGS, AT LEASURE TO BEHOLD 2 1046
AND THAT CRYSTALLINE SPHEAR WHOSE BALLANCE WEIGHS 3 482

WEIGHT
THAT FELT UNUSUAL WEIGHT, TILL ON DRY LAND 1 227
THE WEIGHT OF MIGHTIEST MONARCHIES; HIS LOOK 2 307
THE WEIGHT OF ALL AND OUR LAST HOPE RELIES. 2 416
NOW FALLING WITH SOFT SLUMBROUS WEIGHT INCLINES 4 615
LEADER, THE TERMS WE SENT WERE TERMS OF WEIGHT, 6 621
UNDER THE WEIGHT OF MOUNTAINS BURIED DEEP, 6 652
HOW LITTLE WEIGHT MY WORDS WITH THEE CAN FINDE, 10 968

WEIGHTS
BATTELS AND REALMS: IN THESE HE PUT TWO WEIGHTS 4 1002

WEILD
ON EITHER SIDE, THE LEAST OF WHOM COULD WEILD 6 221
AND CALCULATE THE STARRS, HOW THEY WILL WEILD 8 80

WELCOM
O WELCOM HOUR WHENEVER. WHY DELAYES 10 771

WELCOME
WHICH THUS TO EVE HIS WELCOME WORDS RENEWD. 11 140

WELKIN
FROM EITHER END OF HEAV'N THE WELKIN BURNS. 2 538

WELL
TOO WELL I SEE AND RUE THE DIRE EVENT, 1 134
ROUSE AND BESTIR THEMSELVES ERE WELL AWAKE. 1 334
WELL HAVE YE JUDG'D, WELL ENDED LONG DEBATE, 2 390

WELL (CONTINUED)

LIGHT AFTER LIGHT WELL US'D THEY SHALL ATTAIN, 3 196
WELL PLEAS'D, ON ME LET DEATH WRECK ALL HIS RAGE; 3 241
MY SOLE COMPLACENCE. WELL THOU KNOW'ST HOW DEAR, 3 276
NO VOICE EXEMPT, NO VOICE BUT WELL COULD JOINE 3 370
ROUND HE SURVEYS, AND WELL MIGHT, WHERE HE STOOD 3 555
SUTABLE GRACE DIFFUS'D, SO WELL HE FEIGND; 3 639
WELL PLEAS'D THEY SLACK THIR COURSE, AND MANY A LEAGUE 4 164
FOR PROSPECT, WHAT WELL US'D HAD BIN THE PLEDGE 4 200
SOM DREADFUL THING NO DOUBT; FOR WELL THOU KNOWST 4 426
WELL KNOWN FROM HEAV'N; AND SINCE MERIDIAN HOUR 4 581
INSULTING ANGEL, WELL THOU KNOWST I STOOD 4 926
OUR HEAV'NLY STRANGER; WELL WE MAY AFFORD 5 316
TASTES, NOT WELL JOYND, INELEGANT, BUT BRING 5 335
INHABITANT WITH GOD, NOW KNOW I WELL 5 461
WELL HAST THOU TAUGHT THE WAY THAT MIGHT DIRECT 5 508
ALL SEEMD WELL PLEAS'D, ALL SEEM'D, BUT WERE NOT ALL 5 617
JARR NOT WITH LIBERTY, BUT WELL CONSIST. 5 793
THY DISOBEDIENCE. WELL THOU DIDST ADVISE, 5 888
TO VEILE THE HEAV'N, THOUGH DARKNESS THERE MIGHT WELL 6 11
SERVANT OF GOD, WELL DONE, WELL HAST THOU FOUGHT 6 29
OMNIPOTENCE TO NONE. BUT WELL THOU COMST 6 159
OF MIGHTIEST. SENSE OF PLEASURE WE MAY WELL 6 459
HIS ADAMANTINE COAT GIRD WELL, AND EACH 6 542
FIT WELL HIS HELME, GRIPE FAST HIS ORBED SHIELD, 6 543
HAD NEED FROM HEAD TO FOOT WELL UNDERSTAND; 6 625
THAT THOU IN ME WELL PLEAS'D, DECLARST THY WILL 6 728
IN MEASURE WHAT THE MIND MAY WELL CONTAIN, 7 128
AND GOVERN WELL THY APPETITE, LEAST SIN 7 546
AND ALL THIS GOOD TO MAN, FOR WHOSE WELL BEING 8 361
CANNOT WELL SUITE WITH EITHER, BUT SOON PROVE 8 388
SO WELL CONVERSE, NOR WITH THE OX THE APE; 8 396
EXPRESSING WELL THE SPIRIT WITHIN THEE FREE, 8 440
FOR WELL I UNDERSTAND IN THE PRIME END 8 540
AND IN HER SELF COMPLEAT, SO WELL TO KNOW 8 548
AN OUTSIDE? FAIR NO DOUBT, AND WORTHY WELL 8 568
WELL MANAG'D; OF THAT SKILL THE MORE THOU KNOW'ST, 8 573
IN LOVING THOU DOST WELL, IN PASSION NOT, 8 588
LET IT; I RECK NOT, SO IT LIGHT WELL AIM'D, 9 173
HIS HEAD THE MIDST, WELL STOR'D WITH SUTTLE WILES: 9 184
ADAM, WELL MAY WE LABOUR STILL TO DRESS 9 205
WELL HAST THOU MOTION'D, WELL THY THOUGHTS IMPLOYD 9 229
BUT BID HER WELL BEWARE, AND STILL ERECT, 9 353
HATE STRONGER, UNDER SHEW OF LOVE WELL FEIGN'D, 9 492
THE GUILTIE SERPENT, AND WELL MIGHT, FOR EVE 9 785
THIS MAY BE WELL: BUT WHAT IF GOD HAVE SEEN, 9 826
NOT WELL CONCEAV'D OF GOD, WHO THOUGH HIS POWER 9 945
YEILD THEE, SO WELL THIS DAY THOU HAST PURVEY'D, 9 1021
BUT COME, SO WELL REFRESH'T, NOW LET US PLAY, 9 1027
OF AMOROUS INTENT, WELL UNDERSTOOD 9 1035
MAYST EVER REST WELL PLEAS'D. I GO TO JUDGE 10 71
WERE SUCH AS UNDER GOVERNMENT WELL SEEM'D, 10 154
OF HAPPINESS; YET WELL, IF HERE WOULD END 10 725
WELL IF THROWN OUT, AS SUPERNUMERARIE 10 887
AND ONE BAD ACT WITH MANY DEEDS WELL DONE 11 256
MAYST COVER: WELL MAY THEN THY LORD APPEAS'D 11 257
AND FROM THE WELL OF LIFE THREE DROPS INSTILL'D. 11 416
TO THAT MEEK MAN, WHO WELL HAD SACRIFIC'D; 11 451
THERE IS, SAID MICHAEL, IF THOU WELL OBSERVE 11 530
LIVE WELL, HOW LONG OR SHORT PERMIT TO HEAV'N: 11 554
O PITTIE AND SHAME, THAT THEY WHO TO LIVE WELL 11 629
ALL WOULD HAVE THEN GON WELL, PEACE WOULD HAVE CROWND 11 781
THIR MINISTRY PERFORM'D, AND RACE WELL RUN, 12 505
WELL DEEM IN OUTWARD RITES AND SPECIOUS FORMES 12 534
WELL PLEAS'D, BUT ANSWER'D NOT; FOR NOW TOO NIGH 12 625

WELL-PLEASING

OF THY VICTORIOUS ARM, WELL-PLEASING SON, 10 634

WELNIGH

FROM SERVITUDE INGLORIOUS WELNIGH HALF 9 141

WELTRING

HE SOON DISCERNS, AND WELTRING BY HIS SIDE 1 78

WENT

THERE WENT A FAME IN HEAV'N THAT HE ERE LONG 1 651
WENT ALL HIS FEAR: OF GOD, OR HELL, OR WORSE 2 49
THE WAY HE WENT, AND ON TH' ASSYRIAN MOUNT 4 126
SOUTHWARD THROUGH EDEN WENT A RIVER LARGE, 4 223
PURE AS TH' EXPANSE OF HEAV'N; I THITHER WENT 4 456
HANDED THEY WENT; AND EAS'D THE PUTTING OFF 4 739
BUT LIKE A PROUD STEED REIND, WENT HAUTIE ON, 4 858
SEEM TWILIGHT HERE; AND NOW WENT FORTH THE MORN 6 12
SINCE MICHAEL AND HIS POWERS WENT FORTH TO TAME 6 686
EACH TO HIS PLACE, THEY HEARD HIS VOICE AND WENT 6 782
WITH JUBILIE ADVANC'D; AND AS THEY WENT, 6 884
WENT UP AND WATERD ALL THE GROUND, AND EACH 7 334
WITH HIS GREAT FATHER (FOR HE ALSO WENT 7 588
ROSE, AND WENT FORTH AMONG HER FRUITS AND FLOURS, 8 44
YET WENT SHE NOT, AS NOT WITH SUCH DISCOURSE 8 48
WITH GODDESS-LIKE DEMEANOUR FORTH SHE WENT; 8 59
SURVEY'D, AND SOMETIMES WENT, AND SOMETIMES RAN 8 268
AND FORTH TO MEET HER WENT, THE WAY SHE TOOK 9 847

WENT (CONTINUED)

SO COUNSEL'D HEE, AND BOTH TOGETHER WENT 9 1099
THEN SUFFERD. TH' OTHER WAY SATAN WENT DOWN 10 414

WENTST

WHENCE THOU RETURNST, AND WHITHER WENTST, I KNOW; 12 610

WEPT

GROVES WHOSE RICH TREES WEPT ODOROUS GUMMS AND BALME, 4 248
TENDERLY WEPT, MUCH WON THAT HE HIS LOVE 9 991
WEPT AT COMPLEATING OF THE MORTAL SIN 9 1003
DRIE-EY'D BEHOLD? ADAM COULD NOT, BUT WEPT, 11 495

WEST

OUR CIRCUIT MEETS FULL WEST. AS FLAME THEY PART 4 784
IN INDIA EAST OR WEST, OR MIDDLE SHOARE 5 339
BUT OPPOSITE IN LEVELD WEST WAS SET 7 376
OR SHEE FROM WEST HER SILENT COURSE ADVANCE 8 163
WEST FROM ORONTES TO THE OCEAN BARR'D 9 80
OR EAST OR WEST, WHICH HAD FORBID THE SNOW 10 685
MARCHING FROM EDEN TOWARDS THE WEST, SHALL FINDE 12 40

WESTERN

THE CLOUDS THAT ON HIS WESTERN THRONE ATTEND: 4 597
THE WESTERN POINT, WHERE THOSE HALF-ROUNDING GUARDS 4 862
NOW WAS THE SUN IN WESTERN CADENCE LOW 10 92
MORE ORIENT IN YON WESTERN CLOUD THAT DRAWS 11 205
FROM HERMON EAST TO THE GREAT WESTERN SEA, 12 141

WET

OR WET THE THIRSTIE EARTH WITH FALLING SHOWERS, 5 190

WHALES

AND GOD CREATED THE GREAT WHALES, AND EACH 7 391

WHAT E'RE

BY RIGHT OF WARR, WHAT E'RE HIS BUSINESS BE 1 150
WHAT E'RE HIS WRATH, WHICH HE CALLS JUSTICE, BIDS, 2 733
WHAT E'RE I SAW. THOU SUN, SAID I, FAIRE LIGHT, 8 273

WHAT ERE

SO NEER GROWS DEATH TO LIFE, WHAT ERE DEATH IS, 4 425

WHAT EVER

IF THENCE HE SCAPE INTO WHAT EVER WORLD, 2 442
UNDAUNTED TO MEET THERE WHAT EVER POWER 2 955

WHATEVER

WHATEVER DOING, WHAT CAN WE SUFFER MORE, 2 162
WHATEVER HYPOCRITES AUSTERELY TALK 4 744
AND BOLDLY VENTURE TO WHATEVER PLACE 4 891
WHATEVER EARTH ALL-BEARING MOTHER YIELDS 5 338
FOR KNOW, WHATEVER WAS CREATED, NEEDS 5 414
TO PIECES, AND OREWHELM WHATEVER STANDS 6 489
AT ONCE CAME FORTH WHATEVER CREEPS THE GROUND, 7 475
WHATEVER PURE THOU IN THE BODY ENJOY'ST 8 622
WHATEVER FLEIGHTS NONE WOULD SUSPICIOUS MARK, 9 92
OF DEATH DENOUNC'T, WHATEVER THING DEATH BE, 9 695
WHATEVER CAN TO SIGHT OR THOUGHT BE FORMD, 9 898
WHATEVER WILES OF FOE OR SEEMING FRIEND. 10 11
AND WHAT SHE DID, WHATEVER IN IT SELF, 10 141
BEYOND THIS DEEP; WHATEVER DRAWES ME ON, 10 245
NO HOMELY MORSELS, AND WHATEVER THING 10 605
THOSE TERMS WHATEVER, WHEN THEY WERE PROPOS'D: 10 757

WHATSOEVER

IN WHATSOEVER SHAPE HE LURK, OF WHOM 4 587

WHEEL

WITH STRICTEST WATCH; THESE OTHER WHEEL THE NORTH, 4 783
AND WHEEL ON TH' EARTH, DEVOURING WHERE IT ROULS; 12 183

WHEELD

FIRST WHEELD THIR COURSE; EARTH IN HER RICH ATTIRE 7 501

WHEELE

THROWS HIS STEEP FLIGHT IN MANY AN AERIE WHEELE, 3 741
BUT WITH SWIFT WHEELE REVERSE, DEEP ENTRING SHAR'D 6 326
FLASHING THICK FLAMES, WHEELE WITHIN WHEELE UNDRAWN, 6 751
INVISIBLE ELSE ABOVE ALL STARRS, THE WHEELE 8 135

WHEELES

OF PLANETS AND OF FIXT IN ALL HER WHEELES 5 621
HORRIBLE DISCORD, AND THE MADDING WHEELES 6 210
AND AT HIS CHARIOT WHEELES TO DRAG HIM BOUND 6 358
ASCEND MY CHARIOT, GUIDE THE RAPID WHEELES 6 711
GLOOMIE AS NIGHT; UNDER HIS BURNING WHEELES 6 832
THEN STAID THE FERVID WHEELES, AND IN HIS HAND 7 224

WHEELING

HALF WHEELING TO THE SHIELD, HALF TO THE SPEAR. 4 785

WHEELS

AND BROKEN CHARIOT WHEELS, SO THICK BESTROWN 1 311
WHEELS HER PALE COURSE, THEY ON THIR MIRTH AND DANCE 1 786

WHEELS (CONTINUED)
WITH RAPID WHEELS, OR FRONTED BRIGADS FORM. 2 532
NOR STOP THY FLAMING CHARIOT WHEELS, THAT SHOOK 3 394
US'D TO THE YOAK, DRAW'ST HIS TRIUMPHANT WHEELS 4 975
WITH WHEELS YET HOV'RING O'RE THE OCEAN BRIM, 5 140
ON WHEELS (FOR LIKE TO PILLARS MOST THEY SEEM'D 6 573
AND WINGS WERE SET WITH EYES, WITH EYES THE WHEELS 6 755
DISTINCT WITH EYES, AND FROM THE LIVING WHEELS 6 846
AND CRAZE THIR CHARIOT WHEELS: WHEN BY COMMAND 12 210

WHELM'D
THEY SAW THEM WHELM'D, AND ALL THIR CONFIDENCE 6 651

WHELMD
UNAIDED COULD HAVE FINISHT THEE, AND WHELMD 6 141

WHELP'D
WHERE LUXURIE LATE REIGN'D, SEA-MONSTERS WHELP'D 11 751

WHENCE
O HOW UNLIKE THE PLACE FROM WHENCE THEY FELL. 1 75
WITH WHAT IS PUNISH'T; WHENCE THESE RAGING FIRES 2 213
COVERS HIS THRONE; FROM WHENCE DEEP THUNDERS ROAR 2 267
NOR WANT WE SKILL OR ART, FROM WHENCE TO RAISE 2 272
BY SATAN, AND IN PART PROPOS'D: FOR WHENCE, 2 380
OF THOSE BRIGHT CONFINES, WHENCE WITH NEIGHBOURING ARMS 2 395
OF TERNATE AND TIDORE, WHENCE MERCHANTS BRING 2 639
WHENCE AND WHAT ART THOU, EXECRABLE SHAPE, 2 681
TO THAT SIDE HEAV'N FROM WHENCE YOUR LEGIONS FELL: 2 1006
SHOT UPWARD STILL DIRECT, WHENCE NO WAY ROUND 3 618
NATIVE PERFUMES, AND WHISPER WHENCE THEY STOLE 4 158
WHENCE TRUE AUTORITIE IN MEN; THOUGH BOTH 4 295
WHENCE RUSHING HE MIGHT SUREST SEIZE THEM BOTH 4 407
AND WHAT I WAS, WHENCE THITHER BROUGHT, AND HOW. 4 452
FLIE THITHER WHENCE THOU FLEDST: IF FROM THIS HOURE 4 963
YET EVIL WHENCE? IN THEE CAN HARBOUR NONE, 5 99
YET MUTABLE; WHENCE WARNE HIM TO BEWARE 5 237
WHENCE IN HER VISAGE ROUND THOSE SPOTS, UNPURG'D 5 419
FANSIE AND UNDERSTANDING, WHENCE THE SOULE 5 486
FROM THAT HIGH MOUNT OF GOD, WHENCE LIGHT & SHADE 5 643
DOCTRIN WHICH WE WOULD KNOW WHENCE LEARNT: WHO SAW 5 856
BEFORE THE SEAT SUPREAM; FROM WHENCE A VOICE 6 27
THESE THINGS, AS NOT TO MIND FROM WHENCE THEY GROW 6 477
ALL POWER ON HIM TRANSFERR'D: WHENCE TO HIS SON 6 678
WHENCE IN PERPETUAL FIGHT THEY NEEDS MUST LAST 6 693
HER MURAL BREACH, RETURNING WHENCE IT ROWLD. 6 879
WITH BLESSEDNESS. WHENCE ADAM SOON REPEAL'D 7 59
BUT GRATEFUL TO ACKNOWLEDGE WHENCE HIS GOOD 7 512
USEFUL, WHENCE HAPLY MENTION MAY ARISE 8 200
OF FOUL CONCUPISCENCE; WHENCE EVIL STORE; 9 1078
I KNOW NOT WHENCE POSSESSD THEE; WE HAD THEN 9 1137
ACCOMPANIED TO HEAVEN GATE, FROM WHENCE 10 88
WHENCE ADAM FAULTRING LONG, THUS ANSWER'D BRIEF. 10 115
THE GROUND WHENCE HE WAS TAKEN, FITTER SOILE. 11 98
IS PAST, AND WE SHALL LIVE. WHENCE HAILE TO THEE, 11 158
THE GROUND WHENCE THOU WAST TAK'N, FITTER SOILE. 11 262
PERHAPS THY CAPITAL SEATE, FROM WHENCE HAD SPRED 11 343
OF CATTEL GRAZING: OTHERS, WHENCE THE SOUND 11 558
TOO NUMEROUS; WHENCE OF GUESTS HE MAKES THEM SLAVES 12 167
WHENCE HEAVIE PERSECUTION SHALL ARISE 12 531
WHENCE THOU RETURNST, AND WHITHER WENTST, I KNOW; 12 610

WHEN EVER
WHEN EVER THAT SHALL BE; SO FATE PRONOUNC'D. 2 809

WHENEVER
O WELCOM HOUR WHENEVER. WHY DELAYES 10 771

WHEREAT
TO SPEAK; WHEREAT THIR DOUBL'D RANKS THEY BEND 1 616
THEY VOTE: WHEREAT HIS SPEECH HE THUS RENEWS. 2 389
OR SINGULAR AND RASH, WHEREAT REJOIC'D 5 851
OF BATTEL: WHEREAT MICHAEL BID SOUND 6 202
TO PLUCK AND EATE; WHEREAT I WAK'D, AND FOUND 8 309
WHEREAT HEE INLIE RAG'D, AND AS THY TALK'D, 11 444
WHEREAT THE HEART OF ADAM ERST SO SAD 11 868
BEGAN TO PARCH THAT TEMPERATE CLIME; WHEREAT 12 636

WHEREBY
TO OBJECTS DISTANT FARR, WHEREBY HE SOON 3 621
OF SENSE, WHEREBY THEY HEAR, SEE, SMELL, TOUCH, TASTE, 5 411
BUT IF THE SENSE OF TOUCH WHEREBY MANKIND 8 579

WHERE ERE
BY THE WATERS OF LIFE, WHERE ERE THEY SATE 11 79

WHEREFORE
BUT WHEREFORE LET WE THEN OUR FAITHFUL FRIENDS, 1 264
TO PUNISH ENDLESS? WHEREFORE CEASE WE THEN? 2 159
ME FROM ATTEMPTING. WHEREFORE DO I ASSUME 2 450
AH WHEREFORE. HE DESERVD NO SUCH RETURN 4 42
BUT WHEREFORE ALL NIGHT LONG SHINE THESE, FOR WHOM 4 657
BUT WHEREFORE THOU ALONE? WHEREFORE WITH THEE 4 917
HEAV'NS AWFUL MONARCH? WHEREFORE BUT IN HOPE 4 960
REMAIN NOT; WHEREFORE SHOULD NOT STRENGTH AND MIGHT 6 116
FOUL ON HIMSELF; THEN WHEREFORE SHUND OR FEARD 9 331

WHEREFORE (CONTINUED)
WHEREFORE DIDST THOU BEGET ME? I SOUGHT IT NOT 10 762

WHEREIN
DOWN CAST AND DAMP, YET SUCH WHEREIN APPEAR'D 1 523
AND FIELDS WERE FOUGHT IN HEAV'N; WHEREIN REMAIND 2 768
WHEREIN PAST, PRESENT, FUTURE HE BEHOLDS, 3 78
FATHER, TO SEE THY FACE, WHEREIN NO CLOUD 3 262
NEW HEAV'N AND EARTH, WHEREIN THE JUST SHALL DWELL, 3 335
REGARDLESS OF THE BLISS WHEREIN HEE SAT 3 408
WHEREIN ALL THINGS CREATED FIRST HE WEIGHD, 4 999
WHEREIN TO READ HIS WONDROUS WORKS, AND LEARNE 8 68
ALL RATIONAL DELIGHT, WHEREIN THE BRUTE 8 391
WHEREIN TRUE LOVE CONSISTS NOT; LOVE REFINES 8 589
WISDOM WITHOUT THEIR LEAVE? AND WHEREIN LIES 9 725
WHEREIN GOD SET THEE ABOVE HER MADE OF THEE, 10 149
GIV'N THEE OF GRACE, WHEREIN THOU MAY'ST REPENT, 11 255
A LAZAR-HOUSE IT SEEMD, WHEREIN WERE LAID 11 479
OF WICKEDNESS, WHEREIN SHALL DWELL HIS RACE 11 608
YET EMPTY OF ALL GOOD WHEREIN CONSISTS 11 616
BOTH HEAV'N AND EARTH, WHEREIN THE JUST SHALL DWELL. 11 901
THE PLAIN, WHEREIN A BLACK BITUMINOUS GURGE 12 41

WHEREOF
SPACE MAY PRODUCE NEW WORLDS; WHEREOF SO RIFE 1 650
HER WATRIE LABYRINTH, WHEREOF WHO DRINKS, 2 584
HAD BEEN ACHIEV'D, WHEREOF ALL HELL HAD RUNG, 2 723
AT TOP WHEREOF, BUT FARR MORE RICH APPEERD 3 504
ARE EVER CLEER. WHEREOF HEE SOON AWARE, 4 119
AND COUNTRY WHEREOF HERE NEEDS NO ACCOUNT, 4 235
AUGHT WHEREOF HEE HATH NEED, HEE WHO REQUIRES 4 419
THIS NEW CREATED WORLD, WHEREOF IN HELL 4 937
WHEREOF TO FOUND THIR ENGINS AND THIR BALLS 6 518
WHEN, AND WHEREOF CREATED, FOR WHAT CAUSE, 7 64
IN SIGNE WHEREOF EACH BIRD AND BEAST BEHOLD 8 342
ONE HEART, ONE SOUL IN BOTH; WHEREOF GOOD PROOFF 9 967
WHEREOF I GAVE THEE CHARGE THOU SHOULDST NOT EAT? 10 123
THE SERPENTS HEAD; WHEREOF TO THEE ANON 12 150

WHEREON
FOR ONE OF SYRIAN MODE, WHEREON TO BURN 1 474
THE STAIRS WERE SUCH AS WHEREON JACOB SAW 3 510
OF JASPER, OR OF LIQUID PEARLE, WHEREON 3 519
O FAIR FOUNDATION LAID WHEREON TO BUILD 4 521
FROM CENTER TO CIRCUMFERENCE, WHEREON 5 510
IN IMITATION OF THAT MOUNT WHEREON 5 764
OF THIS ETHEREOUS MOULD WHEREON WE STAND, 6 473
WHEREON A SAPHIR THRONE, INLAID WITH PURE 6 758
FAWNING, AND LICK'D THE GROUND WHEREON SHE TROD. 9 526
WHEREON I LIVE, THY GENTLE LOOKS, THY AID, 10 919
WHEREON FOR DIFFERENT CAUSE THE TEMPTER SET 11 382
PART ARABLE AND TILTH, WHEREON WERE SHEAVES 11 430
HE LOOKD AND SAW A SPACIOUS PLAINE, WHEREON 11 556
GREEN TREE OR GROUND WHEREON HIS FOOT MAY LIGHT; 11 858
HIS TRIPLE-COLOUR'D BOW, WHEREON TO LOOK 11 897

WHERERE
WHERERE OUR DAYS WORK LIES, THOUGH NOW ENJOIND 11 177

WHERESO
FREQUENTED THIR ASSEMBLIES, WHERESO MET, 11 722

WHERETO
WHERETO WITH SPEEDY WORDS TH' ARCH-FIEND REPLY'D. 1 156
WHERETO WITH LOOK COMPOS'D SATAN REPLI'D. 6 469
WHERETO TH' ALMIGHTY ANSWER'D, NOT DISPLEAS'D. 8 398
WHERETO THUS ADAM FATHERLY DISPLEAS'D. 12 63

WHEREVER
WHEREVER THUS CREATED, FOR NO PLACE 7 535
WHEREVER PLAC'T, LET HIM DISPOSE: JOY THOU 8 170
SINGLE WITH LIKE DEFENCE, WHEREVER MET, 9 325
HIS EYE MIGHT THERE COMMAND WHEREVER STOOD 11 385
OF ABRAHAMS FAITH WHEREVER THROUGH THE WORLD; 12 449

WHEREWITH
OF HYMNS AND SACRED SONGS, WHEREWITH THY THRONE 3 148
WHEREWITH TO SCORNE THE EARTH: BUT THAT FALSE FRUIT 9 1011

WHEREWITHALL
NEW BABELS, HAD THEY WHEREWITHALL, WOULD BUILD: 3 468

WHICH E'RE
PLANT OF THE FIELD, WHICH E'RE IT WAS IN THE EARTH 7 335

WHILE
ABOVE TH' AONIAN MOUNT, WHILE IT PURSUES 1 15
MOORS BY HIS SIDE UNDER THE LEE, WHILE NIGHT 1 207
HEAP ON HIMSELF DAMNATION, WHILE HE SOUGHT 1 215
WHILE WITH PERFIDIOUS HATRED THEY PURSU'D 1 308
WHILE THE PROMISCUOUS CROUD STOOD YET ALOOF? 1 380
WHILE SMOOTH ADONIS FROM HIS NATIVE ROCK 1 450
SERAPHIC ARMS AND TROPHIES: ALL THE WHILE 1 539
OR DREAMS HE SEES, WHILE OVER-HEAD THE MOON 1 784
FOR WHILE THEY SIT CONTRIVING, SHALL THE REST 2 54
ONE DAY UPON OUR HEADS; WHILE WE PERHAPS 2 178
FORC'T HALLELUIAH'S; WHILE HE LORDLY SITS 2 243

WHILE (CONTINUED)

OR SUMMERS NOON-TIDE AIR, WHILE THUS HE SPAKE. 2 309
A GROWING EMPIRE; DOUBTLESS; WHILE WE DREAM, 2 315
WHILE HERE SHALL BE OUR HOME, WHAT BEST MAY EASE 2 458
AGAINST A WAKEFUL FOE, WHILE I ABROAD 2 463
ASCENDING, WHILE THE NORTH WIND SLEEPS, O'RESPREAD 2 489
PAIN FOR A WHILE OR ANGUISH, AND EXCITE 2 567
WITH LAPLAND WITCHES, WHILE THE LABOURING MOON 2 665
FOR HIM WHO SITS ABOVE AND LAUGHS THE WHILE 2 731
IN DARKNESS, WHILE THY HEAD FLAMES THICK AND FAST 2 754
STOOD ON THE BRINK OF HELL AND LOOK'D A WHILE, 2 918
IN THAT OBSCURE SOJOURN, WHILE IN MY FLIGHT 3 15
THUS WHILE GOD SPAKE, AMBROSIAL FRAGRANCE FILL'D 3 135
TH' INCENSED DEITIE, WHILE OFFERD GRACE 3 187
WHILE BY THEE RAIS'D I RUIN ALL MY FOES, 3 258
BY LOOSING THEE A WHILE, THE WHOLE RACE LOST. 3 280
HEAV'NS EVERLASTING FRAME, WHILE O'RE THE NECKS 3 395
RESIGNS HER CHARGE, WHILE GOODNESS THINKS NO ILL 3 688
WHILE TIME WAS, OUR FIRST-PARENTS HAD BIN WARND 4 6
WHILE THEY ADORE ME ON THE THRONE OF HELL, 4 89
THUS WHILE HE SPAKE, EACH PASSION DIMM'D HIS FACE 4 114
THE TREMBLING LEAVES, WHILE UNIVERSAL PAN 4 266
PRAEEMINENT BY SO MUCH ODDS, WHILE THOU 4 447
OF BLISS ON BLISS, WHILE I TO HELL AM THRUST, 4 508
WHAT FURTHER WOULD BE LEARNT. LIVE WHILE YE MAY, 4 533
WHILE OTHER ANIMALS UNACTIVE RANGE, 4 621
WHILE THEY KEEP WATCH, OR NIGHTLY ROUNDING WALK 4 685
WHILE THUS HE SPAKE, TH' ANGELIC SQUADRON BRIGHT 4 977
WHILE DAY ARISES, THAT SWEET HOUR OF PRIME. 5 170
OF HIS COOLE BOWRE, WHILE NOW THE MOUNTED SUN 5 300
THOSE HAPPIE PLACES THOU HAST DEIGND A WHILE 5 364
DANC'D HAND IN HAND. A WHILE DISCOURSE THEY HOLD; 5 395
HOLD, AS YOU YOURS, WHILE OUR OBEDIENCE HOLDS; 5 537
AND PERFET WHILE THEY STOOD; HOW LAST UNFOULD 5 568
WHILE PARDON MAY BE FOUND IN TIME BESOUGHT. 5 848
THY MAKING, WHILE THE MAKER GAVE THEE BEING? 5 858
THIR DEITIES TO ASSERT, WHO WHILE THEY FEEL 6 157
BLAZ'D OPPOSITE, WHILE EXPECTATION STOOD 6 306
AND ALL HIS ARMOUR STAIND ERE WHILE SO BRIGHT. 6 334
DEFENCE, WHILE OTHERS BORE HIM ON THIR SHIELDS 6 337
LEFT THEM SUPERIOUR, WHILE WE CAN PRESERVE 6 443
A WHILE, BUT SUDDENLY AT HEAD APPEERD 6 556
HEAV'N WITNESS THOU ANON, WHILE WE DISCHARGE 6 564
STOOD WAVING TIPT WITH FIRE; WHILE WE SUSPENSE, 6 580
ERE WHILE THEY FIERCE WERE COMING, AND WHEN WEE, 6 610
AND ALL HIS HOST DERIDED, WHILE THEY STOOD 6 633
A WHILE IN TROUBLE; BUT THEY STOOD NOT LONG, 6 634
AND SOLITUDE; YET NOT ALONE, WHILE THOU 7 28
SOJOURN'D THE WHILE. GOD SAW THE LIGHT WAS GOOD; 7 249
WHILE THE BRIGHT POMP ASCENDED JUBILANT. 7 564
THOU HAST REPELD, WHILE IMPIOUSLY THEY THOUGHT 7 611
SO CHARMING LEFT HIS VOICE, THAT HE A WHILE 8 2
REPEATED, WHILE THE SEDENTARIE EARTH, 8 32
ON HER SOFT AXLE, WHILE SHE PACES EEV'N, 8 165
INVITING THEE TO HEAR WHILE I RELATE, 8 208
FOR WHILE I SIT WITH THEE, I SEEM IN HEAV'N, 8 210
OR ENEMIE, WHILE GOD WAS IN HIS WORK, 8 234
AND GAZ'D A WHILE THE AMPLE SKIE, TILL RAIS'D 8 258
WHILE THUS I CALL'D, AND STRAY'D I KNEW NOT
WHITHER. 8 283
MY MAKER, BE PROPITIOUS WHILE I SPEAK. 8 380
RURAL REPAST, PERMITTING HIM THE WHILE 9 4
THE CLASPING IVIE WHERE TO CLIMB, WHILE I 9 217
FOR WHILE SO NEAR EACH OTHER THUS ALL DAY 9 220
OF OUTWARD STRENGTH; WHILE SHAME, THOU LOOKING ON, 9 312
GENTLY WITH MIRTLE BAND, MINDLESS THE WHILE, 9 431
STOOD IN HIMSELF COLLECTED, WHILE EACH PART, 9 673
PAUSING A WHILE, THUS TO HER SELF SHE MUS'D. 9 744
COMMENDS THEE MORE, WHILE IT INFERRS THE GOOD 9 754
FROM NECTAR, DRINK OF GODS. ADAM THE WHILE 9 838
ASTONIED STOOD AND BLANK, WHILE HORROR CHILL 9 890
ORIGINAL; WHILE ADAM TOOK NO THOUGHT, 9 1004
MUCH PLEASURE WE HAVE LOST, WHILE WE ABSTAIN'D 9 1022
BROUGHT TO THIR EARS, WHILE DAY DECLIN'D, THEY
HEARD, 10 99
WHOSE FAILING, WHILE HER FAITH TO ME REMAINES, 10 129
IDLELY, WHILE SATAN OUR GREAT AUTHOR THRIVES 10 236
HIS ZENITH, WHILE THE SUN IN ARIES ROSE: 10 329
OF EASIE THOROUGH-FARE. THEREFORE WHILE I 10 393
THERE KEPT THIR WATCH THE LEGIONS, WHILE THE GRAND 10 427
WAS PLAC'T IN REGAL LUSTRE. DOWN A WHILE 10 447
SO HAVING SAID, A WHILE HE STOOD, EXPECTING 10 504
WHILE THE CREATOR CALLING FORTH BY NAME 10 649
HAD UNBENIGHTED SHON, WHILE THE LOW SUN 10 682
WHILE YET WE LIVE, SCARSE ONE SHORT HOUR PERHAPS, 10 923
CLOATH'D US UNWORTHIE, PITYING WHILE HE JUDG'D; 10 1059
TO SHEW US IN THIS MOUNTAIN, WHILE THE WINDS 10 1065
LABORIOUS, TILL DAY DROOP; WHILE HERE WE DWELL, 11 178
WHILE THE GREAT VISITANT APPROACHD, THUS SPAKE. 11 225
HERE SLEEP BELOW WHILE THOU TO FORESIGHT WAK'ST, 11 368
AS ONCE THOU SLEPST, WHILE SHEE TO LIFE WAS FORMD. 11 369
WHILE THEY PERVERT PURE NATURES HEALTHFUL RULES 11 523
THIS SECOND SOURS OF MEN, WHILE YET BUT FEW; 12 13
AND WHILE THE DREAD OF JUDGEMENT PAST REMAINS 12 14
WHILE YET THE PATRIARK LIV'D, WHO SCAP'D THE FLOOD, 12 117
BEHINDE THEM, WHILE TH' OBDURAT KING PURSUES: 12 205
THEY FIRST RE-EDIFIE, AND FOR A WHILE 12 350

WHIP

LEAST WITH A WHIP OF SCORPIONS I PURSUE 2 701

WHIRLPOOL

CHARYBDIS, AND BY TH' OTHER WHIRLPOOL STEARD. 2 1020

WHIRLWIND

IN WHIRLWIND; HELL SCARCE HOLDS THE WILDE UPROAR. 2 541
OF WHIRLWIND AND DIRE HAIL, WHICH ON FIRM LAND 2 589
DAWNING THROUGH HEAV'N: FORTH RUSH'D WITH WHIRLWIND
SOUND 6 749

WHIRLWINDS

WITH FLOODS AND WHIRLWINDS OF TEMPESTUOUS FIRE, 1 77
OF RACKING WHIRLWINDS, OR FOR EVER SUNK 2 182

WHISPER

NATIVE PERFUMES, AND WHISPER WHENCE THEY STOLE 4 158

WHISPER'D

WHISPER'D IT TO THE WOODS, AND FROM THIR WINGS 8 516

WHISPERD

HER HAND SOFT TOUCHING, WHISPERD THUS. AWAKE 5 17

WHISPERING

STOOD WHISPERING SOFT, BY A FRESH FOUNTAIN SIDE 4 326
SUCH WHISPERING WAK'D HER, BUT WITH STARTL'D EYE 5 26

WHITE

WHITE, BLACK AND GREY, WITH ALL THIR TRUMPERIE. 3 475
BETWEEN HER WHITE WINGS MANTLING PROUDLY, ROWES 7 439
O'RE THE BLEW FIRMAMENT A RADIANT WHITE, 11 206

WHITHER

ALL HEAV'N, WHAT THIS MIGHT MEAN, AND WHITHER TEND 3 272
BENEATH TH' AZORES; WHITHER THE PRIME ORB, 4 592
WHERE LODG'D, OR WHITHER FLED, OR IF FOR FIGHT, 6 531
WHILE THUS I CALL'D, AND STRAY'D I KNEW NOT
WHITHER. 8 283
THOUGHTS, WHITHER HAVE YE LED ME, WITH WHAT SWEET 9 473
GOE WHITHER FATE AND INCLINATION STRONG 10 265
WHITHER SHALL I BETAKE ME, WHERE SUBSIST? 10 922
HOW SHALL I PART, AND WHITHER WANDER DOWN 11 282
WHENCE THOU RETURNST, AND WHITHER WENTST, I KNOW; 12 610

WHOEVER

WHOEVER TEMPTED; WHICH THEY NOT OBEYING, 10 14
WHOEVER JUDG'D, THE WORST ON MEE MUST LIGHT, 10 73

WHOL

THAT SHOOK HEAV'NS WHOL CIRCUMFERENCE, CONFIRM'D. 2 353

WHOLE

THE WHOLE BATTALION VIEWS, THIR ORDER DUE, 1 569
OMINOUS CONJECTURE ON THE WHOLE SUCCESS: 2 123
TO WASTE HIS WHOLE CREATION, OR POSSESS 2 365
WHERE ARMIES WHOLE HAVE SUNK: THE PARCHING AIR 2 594
DRAW AFTER HIM THE WHOLE RACE OF MANKIND, 3 161
HE WITH HIS WHOLE POSTERITIE MUST DYE, 3 209
BY LOOSING THEE A WHILE, THE WHOLE RACE LOST. 3 280
IN NARROW ROOM NATURES WHOLE WEALTH, YEA MORE, 4 207
A WHOLE DAYS JOURNY HIGH, BUT WIDE REMOTE 4 284
CAME SHADOWING, AND OPPREST WHOLE LEGIONS ARM'D, 6 655
MY EXALTATION, AND MY WHOLE DELIGHT, 6 727
YAWNING RECEAVD THEM WHOLE, AND ON THEM CLOS'D, 6 875
CONTIGUOUS MIGHT DISTEMPER THE WHOLE FRAME: 7 273
THE WHOLE INCLUDED RACE, HIS PURPOSD PREY. 9 416
FARR LESS I NOW LAMENT FOR ONE WHOLE WORLD 11 874
THE WHOLE EARTH FILL'D WITH VIOLENCE, AND ALL FLESH 11 888
HIS WHOLE DESCENT, WHO THUS SHALL CANAAN WIN. 12 269

WHOLLY

INTENT NOW WHOLLY ON HER TASTE, NAUGHT ELSE 9 786

WHOLSOM

MORE EASIE, WHOLSOM THIRST AND APPETITE 4 330
WHOLSOM AND COOL, AND MILD, BUT WITH BLACK AIR 10 847

WHOMSOEVER

TO THAT FALSE WORM, OF WHOMSOEVER TAUGHT 9 1068

WHOSO

THAT WHOSO EATS THEREOF, FORTHWITH ATTAINS 9 724

WICKED

SINGLE AGAINST THEE WICKED, AND THENCE WEAK. 4 856
THESE WICKED TENTS DEVOTED, LEAST THE WRAUTH 5 890
THOU AND THY WICKED CREW; THERE MINGLE BROILES, 6 277
OR VIOLENCE, HEE OF THIR WICKED WAYES 11 812
OF WICKED SONS DESTROYD, THEN I REJOYCE 11 875
AND VENGEANCE TO THE WICKED, AT RETURN 12 541

WICKEDNESS

OF WICKEDNESS, WHEREIN SHALL DWELL HIS RACE 11 608

WICKET

AND NOW SAINT PETER AT HEAV'NS WICKET SEEMS 3 484

WIDE

OP'NING THIR BRAZEN FOULDS DISCOVER WIDE 1 724
AND PORCHES WIDE, BUT CHIEF THE SPACIOUS HALL 1 762
SCOUT FARR AND WIDE INTO THE REALM OF NIGHT, 2 133
IN THE WIDE WOMB OF UNCREATED NIGHT, 2 150
WIDE GAPING, AND WITH UTTER LOSS OF BEING 2 440
HEARD FARR AND WIDE, AND ALL THE HOST OF HELL 2 519
ON BOLD ADVENTURE TO DISCOVER WIDE 2 571
THROUGH THE WIDE ETHIOPIAN TO THE CAPE 2 641
WITH WIDE CERBERIAN MOUTHS FULL LOUD, AND RUNG 2 655
THREW FORTH, TILL ON THE LEFT SIDE OP'NING WIDE, 2 755
EXCEL'D HER POWER; THE GATES WIDE OP'N STOOD, 2 884
SO WIDE THEY STOOD, AND LIKE A FURNACE MOUTH 2 888
WIDE ON THE WASTEFUL DEEP; WITH HIM ENTHRON'D 2 961
YOUR DUNGEON STRETCHING FAR AND WIDE BENEATH; 2 1003
FARR OFF TH' EMPYREAL HEAV'N, EXTENDED WIDE 2 1047
WIDE INTERRUPT CAN HOLD; SO BENT HE SEEMS 3 84
A PASSAGE DOWN TO TH' EARTH, A PASSAGE WIDE, 3 528
SO WIDE THE OP'NING SEEMD, WHERE BOUNDS WERE SET 3 538
UNDAZL'D, FARR AND WIDE HIS EYE COMMANDS, 3 614
STILL THREATNING TO DEVOUR ME OPENS WIDE, 4 77
A WHOLE DAYS JOURNY HIGH, BUT WIDE REMOTE 4 284
SEE FARR AND WIDE: IN AT THIS GATE NONE PASS 4 579
THE EARTH OUTSTRETCHT IMMENSE, A PROSPECT WIDE 5 88
DISCOVERING IN WIDE LANTSKIP ALL THE EAST 5 142
OF HEAV'N ARRIV'D, THE GATE SELF-OPEND WIDE 5 254
THE CIRCUIT WIDE. STRAIT KNEW HIM ALL THE BANDS 5 287
WIDE OVER ALL THE PLAIN, AND WIDER FARR 5 648
THROUGH HEAV'NS WIDE CHAMPAIN HELD HIS WAY, TILL MORN, 6 2
OF TARTARUS, WHICH READY OPENS WIDE 6 54
OF HEAV'N THEY MARCH'D, AND MANY A PROVINCE WIDE 6 77
WERE DON, BUT INFINITE: FOR WIDE WAS SPRED 6 241
WIDE WASTING; SUCH DESTRUCTION TO WITHSTAND 6 253
WIDE THE CELESTIAL SOILE, AND SAW BENEATH 6 510
WITH HIDEOUS ORIFICE GAP'T ON US WIDE, 6 577
ILLUSTRIOUS FARR AND WIDE, BUT BY HIS OWN 6 773
AND CHRYSTAL WALL OF HEAV'N, WHICH OP'NING WIDE, 6 860
ALL SPACE, THE AMBIENT AIRE WIDE INTERFUS'D 7 89
THOUGH WIDE, AND THIS HIGH TEMPLE TO FREQUENT 7 148
ATTENDANT ON THIR LORD: HEAV'N OP'ND WIDE 7 205
BUILT ON CIRCUMFLUOUS WATERS CALME, IN WIDE 7 270
BUT THEY, OR UNDER GROUND, OR CIRCUIT WIDE 7 301
THAT OPEN'D WIDE HER BLAZING PORTALS, LED 7 575
HIS LAUGHTER AT THIR QUAINT OPINIONS WIDE 8 78
AND FOR THE HEAV'NS WIDE CIRCUIT, LET IT SPEAK 8 100
SENT FROM HER THROUGH THE WIDE TRANSPICUOUS AIRE, 8 141
A CIRCUIT WIDE, ENCLOS'D, WITH GOODLIEST TREES 8 304
AND LIFE-BLOOD STREAMING FRESH; WIDE WAS THE WOUND, 8 467
IN WO THEN; THAT DESTRUCTION WIDE MAY RANGE: 9 134
THE HANDS DISPATCH OF TWO GARDNING SO WIDE. 9 203
WILL KEEP FROM WILDERNESS WITH EASE, AS WIDE 9 245
STOOD OPEN WIDE, BELCHING OUTRAGEOUS FLAME 10 232
HIS NOSTRIL WIDE INTO THE MURKIE AIR, 10 280
WIDE ANARCHIE OF CHAOS DAMP AND DARK 10 283
WIDE OPEN AND UNGUARDED, SATAN PASS'D, 10 419
OPHION WITH EURYNOME, THE WIDE- 10 581
THROUGH HEAV'NS WIDE BOUNDS; FROM THEM I WILL NOT HIDE 11 68
WIDE WAVING, ALL APPROACH FARR OFF TO FRIGHT, 11 121
HE LOOKD AND SAW WIDE TERRITORIE SPRED 11 638
WIDE HOVERING, ALL THE CLOUDS TOGETHER DROVE 11 739
AND THE CLEER SUN ON HIS WIDE WATRIE GLASS 11 844
IN THE WIDE WILDERNESS, THERE THEY SHALL FOUND 12 224
WITH EARTHS WIDE BOUNDS, HIS GLORY WITH THE HEAV'NS. 12 371

WIDER

WIDER BY FARR THEN THAT OF AFTER-TIMES 3 529
WIDE OVER ALL THE PLAIN, AND WIDER FARR 5 648
NOT HIGHER THAT HILL NOR WIDER LOOKING ROUND, 11 381

WIDEST

TO ENTERTAIN YOU TWO, HER WIDEST GATES, 4 382

WIDE-WASTING

MARASMUS, AND WIDE-WASTING PESTILENCE, 11 487

WIELD

PART WIELD THIR ARMS, PART COURB THE FOAMING STEED, 11 643

WIFE

FATHER AND MOTHER, AND TO HIS WIFE ADHERE; 8 498
THE WIFE, WHERE DANGER OR DISHONOUR LURKS, 9 267
THE THICKEST TREES, BOTH MAN AND WIFE, TILL GOD 10 101
BECAUSE THOU HAST HEARK'ND TO THE VOICE OF THY WIFE, 10 198

WIGHT

ALL TASTE OF LIVING WIGHT, AS ONCE IT FLED 2 613

WILD

FROM AROAR TO NEBO, AND THE WILD 1 407
INTO THIS WILD ABYSS THE WARIE FIEND 2 917
DARK, WASTE, AND WILD, UNDER THE FROWN OF NIGHT 3 424
WILD WORK IN HEAV'N, AND DANGEROUS TO THE MAINE. 6 698
IN THIS ENCLOSURE WILD, THESE BEASTS AMONG, 9 543

WILDE

THE DISMAL SITUATION WASTE AND WILDE, 1 60
SEEST THOU YON DREARY PLAIN, FORLORN AND WILDE, 1 180
IN WHIRLWIND; HELL SCARCE HOLDS THE WILDE UPROAR. 2 541
LIES DARK AND WILDE, BEAT WITH PERPETUAL STORMS 2 588
CHANCE GOVERNS ALL. INTO THIS WILDE ABYSS, 2 910
AT LENGTH A UNIVERSAL HUBBUB WILDE 2 951
INTO THE WILDE EXPANSE, AND THROUGH THE SHOCK 2 1014
CONFUSION HEARD HIS VOICE, AND WILDE UPROAR 3 710
WITH THICKET OVERGROWN, GOTTESQUE AND WILDE, 4 136
ALL BEASTS OF TH' EARTH, SINCE WILDE, AND OF ALL CHASE 4 341
WILDE WORK PRODUCES OFT, AND MOST IN DREAMS, 5 112
WILDE ABOVE RULE OR ART; ENORMOUS BLISS. 5 297
AS YET THIS WORLD WAS NOT, AND CHAOS WILDE 5 577
SOMEWHAT EXTRAVAGANT AND WILDE, PERHAPS 6 616
THROUGH HIS WILDE ANARCHIE, SO HUGE A ROUT 6 873
OF THAT WILDE ROUT THAT TORE THE THRACIAN BARD 7 34
OUTRAGEOUS AS A SEA, DARK, WASTEFUL, WILDE, 7 212
AS FROM HIS LAIRE THE WILDE BEAST WHERE HE WONNS 7 457
IN FORREST WILDE, IN THICKET, BRAKE, OR DEN; 7 458
TENDING TO WILDE. THOU THEREFORE NOW ADVISE 9 212
TO LIVE AGAIN IN THESE WILDE WOODS FORLORN? 9 910
WITH FEATHERD CINCTURE, NAKED ELSE AND WILDE 9 1117
OF UNORIGINAL NIGHT AND CHAOS WILDE, 10 477
AND WILDE, HOW SHALL WE BREATH IN OTHER AIRE 11 284
THROUGH THE WILDE DESERT, NOT THE READIEST WAY, 12 216

WILDERNESS

AS WHEN A GRYFON THROUGH THE WILDERNESS 2 943
OF A STEEP WILDERNESS, WHOSE HAIRIE SIDES 4 135
IN WOOD OR WILDERNESS, FORREST OR DEN; 4 342
A WILDERNESS OF SWEETS; FOR NATURE HERE 5 294
WILL KEEP FROM WILDERNESS WITH EASE, AS WIDE 9 245
OUR SECOND ADAM IN THE WILDERNESS, 11 383
IN THE WIDE WILDERNESS, THERE THEY SHALL FOUND 12 224
THROUGH THE WORLDS WILDERNESS LONG WANDERD MAN 12 313

WILES

MY SENTENCE IS FOR OPEN WARR; OF WILES, 2 51
THEN WISE TO FRUSTRATE ALL OUR PLOTS AND WILES. 2 193
MOST OPPORTUNE MIGHT SERVE HIS WILES, AND FOUND 9 85
HIS HEAD THE MIDST, WELL STOR'D WITH SUTTLE WILES: 9 184
WHATEVER WILES OF FOE OR SEEMING FRIEND. 10 11

WILFUL

AGAINST OUR SELVES, AND WILFUL BARRENNESS, 10 1042
WHO FOR MY WILFUL CRIME ART BANISHT HENCE. 12 619

WILFULLY

LEAST WILFULLY TRANSGRESSING HE PRETEND 5 244

WILIE

FROM SHARPEST SIGHT: FOR IN THE WILIE SNAKE, 9 91
TO WHOM THE WILIE ADDER, BLITHE AND GLAD. 9 625

WILL

FROM THIR CREATOR, AND TRANSGRESS HIS WILL 1 31
ALL IS NOT LOST; THE UNCONQUERABLE WILL, 1 106
TO DO OUGHT GOOD NEVER WILL BE OUR TASK, 1 159
AS BEING THE CONTRARY TO HIS HIGH WILL 1 161
HAD RIS'N OR HEAV'D HIS HEAD, BUT THAT THE WILL 1 211
HERE FOR HIS ENVY, WILL NOT DRIVE US HENCE: 1 260
THIR SUREST SIGNAL, THEY WILL SOON RESUME 1 278
CELESTIAL VERTUES RISING, WILL APPEAR 2 15
WILL ENVY WHOM THE HIGHEST PLACE EXPOSES 2 27
FROM FACTION; FOR NONE SURE WILL CLAIM IN HELL 2 32
WILL COVET MORE. WITH THIS ADVANTAGE THEN 2 35
WILL EITHER QUITE CONSUME US, AND REDUCE 2 96
CAN GIVE IT, OR WILL EVER? HOW HE CAN 2 153
IS DOUBTFUL; THAT HE NEVER WILL IS SURE. 2 154
WILL HE, SO WISE, LET LOOSE AT ONCE HIS IRE, 2 155
THE VICTORS WILL. TO SUFFER, AS TO DOE, 2 199
WILL SLACK'N, IF HIS BREATH STIR NOT THIR FLAMES. 2 214
OUR PURER ESSENCE THEN WILL OVERCOME 2 215
IN TEMPER AND IN NATURE, WILL RECEIVE 2 218
THIS HORROR WILL GROW MILDE, THIS DARKNESS LIGHT, 2 220
OF SERVILE POMP. OUR GREATNESS WILL APPEER 2 257
IN HEIGHTH OR DEPTH, STILL FIRST AND LAST WILL REIGN 2 324
VOUTSAF'T OR SOUGHT; FOR WHAT PEACE WILL BE GIV'N 2 332
NOR WILL OCCASION WANT, NOR SHALL WE NEED 2 341
OF HIM WHO RULES ABOVE; SO WAS HIS WILL 2 351
WILL ONCE MORE LIFT US UP, IN SPIGHT OF FATE, 2 393
OF PROVIDENCE, FOREKNOWLEDGE, WILL AND FATE, 2 559
FIXT FATE, FREE WILL, FOREKNOWLEDG ABSOLUTE, 2 560
HIS WRATH WHICH ONE DAY WILL DESTROY YE BOTH. 2 734
KEEP RESIDENCE; IF ALL I CAN WILL SERVE, 2 999
FOLLOWING HIS TRACK, SUCH WAS THE WILL OF HEAV'N, 2 1025
FOR MAN WILL HARK'N TO HIS GLOZING LYES, 3 93
SOLE PLEDGE OF HIS OBEDIENCE: SO WILL FALL, 3 95
WHEN WILL AND REASON (REASON ALSO IS CHOICE) 3 108
THIR WILL, DISPOS'D BY ABSOLUTE DECREE 3 115
MAN SHALL NOT QUITE BE LOST, BUT SAV'D WHO WILL, 3 173
YET NOT OF WILL IN HIM, BUT GRACE IN ME 3 174
FREELY VOUTSAFT; ONCE MORE I WILL RENEW 3 175
ELECT ABOVE THE REST; SO IS MY WILL: 3 184
INVITES; FOR I WILL CLEER THIR SENSES DARK, 3 188

WILL (CONTINUED)
AND I WILL PLACE WITHIN THEM AS A GUIDE 3 194
MY UMPIRE CONSCIENCE, WHOM IF THEY WILL HEAR, 3 195
WHICH OF YE WILL BE MORTAL TO REDEEM 3 214
ACCOUNT MEE MAN; I FOR HIS SAKE WILL LEAVE 3 238
GLAD TO BE OFFER'D, HE ATTENDS THE WILL 3 270
THE FIRST ART WONT HIS GREAT AUTHENTIC WILL 3 656
BY HIS PERMISSIVE WILL, THROUGH HEAV'N AND EARTH: 3 685
HADST THOU THE SAME FREE WILL AND POWER TO STAND? 4 66
NAY CURS'D BE THOU; SINCE AGAINST HIS THY WILL 4 71
BY THEE, AND MORE THEN HALF PERHAPS WILL REIGNE; 4 112
WILL VANISH AND DELIVER YE TO WOE, 4 368
AND SEND FORTH ALL HER KINGS; THERE WILL BE ROOM, 4 383
AND I WILL BRING THEE WHERE NO SHADOW STAIES 4 470
THIR RUINE. HENCE I WILL EXCITE THIR MINDS 4 522
OR ALL AT ONCE; MORE GLORIE WILL BE WONN, 4 853
WILL SAVE US TRIAL WHAT THE LEAST CAN DOE 4 855
HIS WILL WHO BOUND US? LET HIM SURER BARR 4 897
FORBID WHO WILL, NONE SHALL FROM ME WITHHOLD 5 62
HAPPINESS IN HIS POWER LEFT FREE TO WILL, 5 235
LEFT TO HIS OWN FREE WILL, HIS WILL THOUGH FREE, 5 236
WANTOND AS IN HER PRIME, AND PLAID AT WILL 5 295
TO US PERHAPS HE BRINGS, AND WILL VOUTSAFE 5 312
OF GOD INSPIR'D, SMALL STORE WILL SERVE, WHERE STORE, 5 322
BUT I WILL HASTE AND FROM EACH BOUGH AND BREAK, 5 326
EACH PLANT AND JUCIEST GOURD WILL PLUCK SUCH CHOICE 5 327
I HAVE AT WILL. SO TO THE SILVAN LODGE 5 377
HE LEFT IT IN THY POWER, ORDAIND THY WILL 5 526
WILLING OR NO, WHO WILL BUT WHAT THEY MUST 5 533
BECAUSE WEE FREELY LOVE, AS IN OUR WILL 5 539
TO BE BOTH WILL AND DEED CREATED FREE; 5 549
WILL YE SUBMIT YOUR NECKS, AND CHUSE TO BEND 5 787
THE SUPPLE KNEE? YE WILL NOT, IF I TRUST 5 788
WILL NOT BE NOW VOUTSAF'T, OTHER DECREES 5 884
SUFFICIENT TO SUBDUE US TO HIS WILL, 6 427
DUE SEARCH AND CONSULTATION WILL DISCLOSE. 6 445
WHOM FLED WE THOUGHT, WILL SAVE US LONG PURSUIT 6 538
BORN EEVN OR HIGH, FOR THIS DAY WILL POUR DOWN, 6 544
ENDLESS, AND NO SOLUTION WILL BE FOUND: 6 694
THAT THOU IN ME WELL PLEAS'D, DECLARST THY WILL 6 728
HATH HONOURD ME ACCORDING TO HIS WILL. 6 816
IMMUTABLY HIS SOVRAN WILL, THE END 7 79
AND LONGER WILL DELAY TO HEARE THEE TELL 7 101
HASTE TO THY AUDIENCE, NIGHT WITH HER WILL BRING 7 105
SILENCE, AND SLEEP LISTNING TO THEE WILL WATCH, 7 106
SELF-LOST, AND IN A MOMENT WILL CREATE 7 154
APPROACH NOT MEE, AND WHAT I WILL IS FATE. 7 173
WHEN SUCH WAS HEARD DECLAR'D THE ALMIGHTIE'S WILL; 7 181
GLORIE THEY SUNG TO THE MOST HIGH, GOOD WILL 7 182
OPEN, AND HENCEFORTH OFT; FOR GOD WILL DEIGNE 7 569
THITHER WILL SEND HIS WINGED MESSENGERS 7 572
AND CALCULATE THE STARRS, HOW THEY WILL WEILD 8 80
THE MORE SHE WILL ACKNOWLEDGE THEE HER HEAD, 8 574
THY JUDGEMENT TO DO AUGHT, WHICH ELSE FREE WILL 8 636
FOR WHOM ALL THIS WAS MADE, ALL THIS WILL SOON 9 132
BUT WHAT WILL NOT AMBITION AND REVENGE 9 168
WILL KEEP FROM WILDERNESS WITH EASE, AS WIDE 9 245
THE ENEMIE, THOUGH BOLD, WILL HARDLY DARE, 9 304
O WOMAN, BEST ARE ALL THINGS AS THE WILL 9 343
AGAINST HIS WILL HE CAN RECEAVE NO HARME. 9 350
BUT GOD LEFT FREE THE WILL, FOR WHAT OBEYES 9 351
SHE DICTATE FALSE, AND MISSINFORME THE WILL 9 355
THOU SEVER NOT: TRIAL WILL COME UNSOUGHT. 9 366
A FOE SO PROUD WILL FIRST THE WEAKER SEEK, 9 383
IS OPEN? OR WILL GOD INCENSE HIS IRE 9 692
IMPART AGAINST HIS WILL IF ALL BE HIS? 9 728
WHICH WITH BLAND WORDS AT WILL SHE THUS ADDREST. 9 855
DEITIE FOR THEE, WHEN FATE WILL NOT PERMIT. 9 885
THOUGH THREATNING, WILL IN EARNEST SO DESTROY 9 939
HE RUIND, NOW MANKIND; WHOM WILL HE NEXT? 9 950
WILL DAZLE NOW THIS EARTHLY, WITH THIR BLAZE 9 1083
FOR UNDERSTANDING RUL'D NOT, AND THE WILL 9 1127
IMPUT'ST THOU THAT TO MY DEFAULT, OR WILL 9 1145
AND FORCE UPON FREE WILL HATH HERE NO PLACE. 9 1174
LETS HER WILL RULE; RESTRAINT SHE WILL NOT BROOK, 9 1184
SHEE FIRST HIS WEAK INDULGENCE WILL ACCUSE. 9 1186
OF MAN, WITH STRENGTH ENTIRE, AND FREE WILL ARM'D, 10 9
HIS FREE WILL, TO HER OWN INCLINING LEFT 10 46
MINE BOTH IN HEAV'N AND EARTH TO DO THY WILL 10 69
BETWEEN THEE AND THE WOMAN I WILL PUT 10 179
THY SORROW I WILL GREATLY MULTIPLIE 10 193
IN SORROW FORTH, AND TO THY HUSBANDS WILL 10 195
IS ENMITY, WHICH HE WILL PUT BETWEEN 10 497
HIS WILL WHO REIGNS ABOVE, TO AGGRAVATE 10 549
MY OWN DESERVINGS; BUT THIS WILL NOT SERVE; 10 727
THE EVIL ON HIM BROUGHT BY ME, WILL CURSE 10 734
IN THIS DELICIOUS GARDEN? AS MY WILL 10 746
THY PUNISHMENT THEN JUSTLY IS AT HIS WILL. 10 768
OF WEAKNESS, NOT OF POWER. WILL HE, DRAW OUT, 10 801
BUT ALL CORRUPT, BOTH MIND AND WILL DEPRAV'D, 10 825
NOT TO DO ONELY, BUT TO WILL THE SAME 10 826
AND TO THE PLACE OF JUDGMENT WILL RETURN, 10 932
WILL PROVE NO SUDDEN, BUT A SLOW-PAC'T EVILL, 10 963
LIVING OR DYING, FROM THEE I WILL NOT HIDE 10 974
SO SNATCHT WILL NOT EXEMPT US FROM THE PAINE 10 1025
OF CONTUMACIE WILL PROVOKE THE HIGHEST 10 1027
WOULD BE REVENGE INDEED; WHICH WILL BE LOST 10 1036

WILL (CONTINUED)
MY LABOUR WILL SUSTAIN ME; AND LEAST COLD 10 1056
HOW MUCH MORE, IF WE PRAY HIM, WILL HIS EAR 10 1060
HEE WILL INSTRUCT US PRAYING, AND OF GRACE 10 1081
UNDOUBTEDLY HE WILL RELENT AND TURN 10 1093
THROUGH HEAV'NS WIDE BOUNDS; FROM THEM I WILL NOT HIDE 11 68
TH' ALMIGHTY THUS PRONOUNCD HIS SOVRAN WILL. 11 83
OF GOD HIGH-BLEST, OR TO INCLINE HIS WILL, 11 145
HARD TO BELIEF MAY SEEM; YET THIS WILL PRAYER, 11 146
OF US WILL SOON DETERMIN, OR IMPOSE 11 227
THAT NEVER WILL IN OTHER CLIMATE GROW, 11 274
INCESSANT I COULD HOPE TO CHANGE THE WILL 11 308
GOD IS AS HERE, AND WILL BE FOUND ALIKE 11 350
WILL BE AVENG'D, AND TH' OTHERS FAITH APPROV'D 11 458
THY YOUTH, THY STRENGTH, THY BEAUTY, WHICH WILL CHANGE 11 539
HOPEFUL AND CHEERFUL, IN THY BLOOD WILL REIGNE 11 543
FAMIN AND ANGUISH WILL AT LAST CONSUME 11 778
AND WHETHER HERE THE RACE OF MAN WILL END 11 786
OVER THE EARTH A CLOUD, WILL THEREIN SET 11 896
HENCEFORTH WHAT IS TO COM I WILL RELATE, 12 11
WILL ARROGATE DOMINION UNDESERV'D 12 27
WILL HE CONVEY UP THITHER TO SUSTAIN 12 75
ABOVE THE CLOUDS WILL PINE HIS ENTRAILS GROSS, 12 77
YET SOMTIMES NATIONS WILL DECLINE SO LOW 12 97
THUS WILL THIS LATTER, AS THE FORMER WORLD, 12 105
WHICH HE WILL SHEW HIM, AND FROM HIM WILL RAISE 12 123
SUCH WONDROUS POWER GOD TO HIS SAINT WILL LEND, 12 200
ALL NIGHT HE WILL PURSUE, BUT HIS APPROACH 12 206
GOD LOOKING FORTH WILL TROUBLE ALL HIS HOST 12 209
SHALL TREMBLE, HE DESCENDING, WILL HIMSELF 12 228
THAT MOSES MIGHT REPORT TO THEM HIS WILL, 12 237
OBEDIENT TO HIS WILL, THAT HE VOUTSAFES 12 246
AMONG WHOM GOD WILL DEIGNE TO DWELL ON EARTH 12 281
WILL REIGN AMONG THEM, AS OF THEE BEGOT; 12 286
HEAPT TO THE POPULAR SUMME, WILL SO INCENSE 12 338
AND DUE TO THEIRS WHICH OUT OF THINE WILL GROW: 12 400
TO GOD MORE GLORY, MORE GOOD WILL TO MEN 12 477
MUST REASCEND, WHAT WILL BETIDE THE FEW 12 480
HIS PEOPLE, WHO DEFEND? WILL THEY NOT DEALE 12 483
BE SURE THEY WILL, SAID TH' ANGEL; BUT FROM HEAV'N 12 485
HEE TO HIS OWN A COMFORTER WILL SEND, 12 486
SHALL ON THE HEART ENGRAVE. WHAT WILL THEY THEN 12 524
INFALLIBLE? YET MANY WILL PRESUME: 12 530
THAT YE MAY LIVE, WHICH WILL BE MANY DAYES, 12 602

WILLING
TO STOOP WITH WEARIED WINGS, AND WILLING FEET 3 73
SOM OTHER ABLE, AND AS WILLING, PAY 3 211
WILLING OR NO, WHO WILL BUT WHAT THEY MUST 5 533

WILLINGER
THE WILLINGER I GOE, NOR MUCH EXPECT 9 382

WILLINGLY
AS THAT MORE WILLINGLY THOU COULDST NOT SEEM 5 466
YET WILLINGLY CHOSE RATHER DEATH WITH THEE: 9 1167
SO WILLINGLY DOTH GOD REMIT HIS IRE, 11 885

WILLS
MEAN WHILE, AS NATURE WILLS, NIGHT BIDS US REST. 4 633
HER OWN, THAT WHAT SHE WILLS TO DO OR SAY, 8 549

WILT
BUT THEE, WHOM FOLLOW? THOU WILT BRING ME SOON 2 866
BY HIM CORRUPTED? OR WILT THOU THY SELF 3 162
THOU WILT NOT LEAVE ME IN THE LOATHSOM GRAVE 3 247
BUT EVIL HAST NOT TRI'D: AND WILT OBJECT 4 896
WAKING THOU NEVER WILT CONSENT TO DO. 5 121
APOSTAT, STILL THOU ERRST, NOR END WILT FIND 6 172
WITH THIR ATTENDANT MOONS THOU WILT DESCRIE 8 149
OF THY ASSOCIATES, ADAM, AND WILT TASTE 8 401
CANST RAISE THY CREATURE TO WHAT HIGHTH THOU WILT 8 430
THOU DIDST ACCEPT THEM; WILT THOU ENJOY THE GOOD, 10 758
OF ALL THE REST: THEN WILT THOU NOT BE LOATH 12 585

WIN
TO WIN THE MOUNT OF GOD, AND ON HIS THRONE 6 88
SHOULD WIN IN ARMS, IN BOTH DISPUTES ALIKE 6 123
BEFORE THY FELLOWS, AMBITIOUS TO WIN 6 160
THE STRIFE OF GLORIE: WHICH WE MEAN TO WIN, 6 290
HIS WHOLE DESCENT, WHO THUS SHALL CANAAN WIN. 12 269
AS DID THIR LORD BEFORE THEM. THUS THEY WIN 12 502

WIND
OF SUBTERRANEAN WIND TRANSPORTS A HILL 1 231
OF LOCUSTS, WARPING ON THE EASTERN WIND, 1 341
SHON LIKE A METEOR STREAMING TO THE WIND 1 537
AS IN AN ORGAN FROM ONE BLAST OF WIND 1 708
ASCENDING, WHILE THE NORTH WIND SLEEPS, O'RESPREAD 2 489
WITH SAILS AND WIND THIR CANIE WAGGONS LIGHT: 3 439
A VIOLENT CROSS WIND FROM EITHER COAST 3 487
HER BEARDED GROVE OF EARS, WHICH WAY THE WIND 4 982
THE ADVERSARIE. NOR THINK THOU WITH WIND 6 282
AND LEFT LARGE FIELD, UNSAFE WITHIN THE WIND 6 309
LONG STRUGLING UNDERNEATH, ERE THEY COULD WIND 6 659
LEADS THEE, OR WHERE MOST NEEDS, WHETHER TO WIND 9 215

WIND (CONTINUED)
NIGH RIVERS MOUTH OR FORELAND, WHERE THE WIND 9 514

WINDE
WISDOM TO FOLLY, AS NOURISHMENT TO WINDE. 7 130
NO MORE AVAILES THEN BREATH AGAINST THE WINDE, 11 312
DRIVN BY A KEEN NORTH-WINDE, THAT BLOWING DRIE 11 842

WINDES
THY DREAD TRIBUNAL: FORTHWITH FROM ALL WINDES 3 326
HIS FLIGHT PRECIPITANT, AND WINDES WITH EASE 3 563
MOZAMBIC, OFF AT SEA NORTH-EAST WINDES BLOW 4 161
NOW ON THE POLAR WINDES, THEN WITH QUICK FANN 5 269
UP FROM THE BOTTOM TURN'D BY FURIOUS WINDES 7 213
HER ANNUAL VOIAGE, BORN ON WINDES; THE AIRE 7 431
AND FEAR OF DEATH DELIVER TO THE WINDES. 9 989
NOW WALKING IN THE GARDEN, BY SOFT WINDES 10 98
FORTH RUSH THE LEVANT AND THE PONENT WINDES 10 704
FLEW UP, NOR MISSD THE WAY, BY ENVIOUS WINDES 11 15

WINDIE
SO ON THIS WINDIE SEA OF LAND, THE FIEND 3 440

WINDING
CONSPICUOUS FARR, WINDING WITH ONE ASCENT 4 545

WINDOW
IN AT THE WINDOW CLIMBS, OR O'RE THE TILES; 4 191

WINDOWS
HIS SLUCES, AS THE HEAV'N HIS WINDOWS SHUT. 11 849

WINDS
SUBLIM'D WITH MINERAL FURY, AID THE WINDS, 1 235
AFLOAT, WHEN WITH FIERCE WINDS ORION ARM'D 1 305
THE SOUND OF BLUSTRING WINDS, WHICH ALL NIGHT LONG 2 286
TOWARD THE FOUR WINDS FOUR SPEEDY CHERUBIM 2 516
HANGS IN THE CLOUDS, BY AEQUINOCTIAL WINDS 2 637
HOV'RING A SPACE, TILL WINDS THE SIGNAL BLOW 2 717
LEVIED TO SIDE WITH WARRING WINDS, AND POISE 2 905
THE SPORT OF WINDS: ALL THESE UPWHIRLD ALOFT 3 493
IMPETUOUS WINDS: HE THUS BEGAN IN HASTE. 4 560
HIS PRAISE YE WINDS, THAT FROM FOUR QUARTERS BLOW, 5 192
FANND WITH COOLE WINDS, SAVE THOSE WHO IN THIR COURSE 5 655
WINDS UNDER GROUND OR WATERS FORCING WAY 6 196
RAIND AT THIR EYES, BUT HIGH WINDS WORSE WITHIN 9 1122
AS WHEN TWO POLAR WINDS BLOWING ADVERSE 10 289
SHOULD PROVE TEMPESTUOUS; TO THE WINDS THEY SET 10 664
TO SHEW US IN THIS MOUNTAIN, WHILE THE WINDS 10 1065
JUSTLING OR PUSHT WITH WINDS RUDE IN THIR SHOCK 10 1074

WINE
OF BELIAL, FLOWN WITH INSOLENCE AND WINE. 1 502
AND HIGHT'ND AS WITH WINE, JOCOND AND BOON, 9 793
AS WITH NEW WINE INTOXICATED BOTH 9 1008
CORN WINE AND OYLE; AND FROM THE HERD OR FLOCK, 12 19

WINE-OFFERINGS
WITH LARGE WINE-OFFERINGS POUR'D, AND SACRED FEAST, 12 21

WING
UPON THE WING, AS WHEN MEN WONT TO WATCH 1 332
HOVERING ON WING UNDER THE COPE OF HELL 1 345
FROM WING TO WING, AND HALF ENCLOSE HIM ROUND 1 617
WITH UPRIGHT WING AGAINST A HIGHER FOE. 2 72
ENCAMP THIR LEGIONS, OR WITH OBSCURE WING 2 132
UPON THE WING, OR IN SWIFT RACE CONTEND, 2 529
NOW SHAVES WITH LEVEL WING THE DEEP, THEN SOARES 2 634
WING SILENTLY THE BUXOM AIR, IMBALM'D 2 842
THEE I RE-VISIT NOW WITH BOLDER WING, 3 13
TO WING THE DESOLATE ABYSS, AND SPIE 4 936
SAILES BETWEEN WORLDS AND WORLDS, WITH STEDDIE WING 5 268
OF BIRDS IN ORDERLY ARRAY ON WING 6 74
A STANDING FIGHT, THEN SOARING ON MAIN WING 6 243
AND UNCOUTH PAINE FLED BELLOWING. ON EACH WING 6 362
ZOPHIEL, OF CHERUBIM THE SWIFTEST WING, 6 535
HIS ARMIE, CIRCUMFUS'D ON EITHER WING, 6 778
ABOVE THE FLIGHT OF PEGASEAN WING. 7 4
AND EVERY BIRD OF WING AFTER HIS KINDE; 7 394
PART LOOSLY WING THE REGION, PART MORE WISE 7 425
FLYING, AND OVER LANDS WITH MUTUAL WING 7 429
WITH BLANDISHMENT, EACH BIRD STOOP'D ON HIS WING. 8 351
CLIMAT, OR YEARS DAMP MY INTENDED WING 9 45
FIRST LIGHTED FROM HIS WING, AND LANDED SAFE 10 316

WING'D
WING'D WITH RED LIGHTNING AND IMPETUOUS RAGE, 1 175
THE WORK OF SULPHUR. THITHER WING'D WITH SPEED 1 674
ONE SHAPD AND WING'D LIKE ONE OF THOSE FROM HEAV'N 5 55
OR SOM MORE SUDDEN VENGEANCE WING'D FROM GOD 6 279
SATE EAGLE-WING'D, BESIDE HIM HUNG HIS BOW 6 763
AND VERTUES, WINGED SPIRITS, AND CHARIOTS WING'D, 7 199
TIME COUNTS NOT, THOUGH WITH SWIFTEST MINUTES WING'D. 10 91
INSPIR'D, AND WING'D FOR HEAV'N WITH SPEEDIER FLIGHT 11 7

WINGD
ITHURIEL AND ZEPHON, WITH WINGD SPEED 4 788
A SERAPH WINGD; SIX WINGS HE WORE, TO SHADE 5 277
IMPROV'D BY TRACT OF TIME, AND WINGD ASCEND 5 498

WINGED
MEAN WHILE THE WINGED HARALDS BY COMMAND 1 752
WITH WINGED COURSE ORE HILL OR MOARIE DALE, 2 944
THE SPEEDIEST OF THY WINGED MESSENGERS, 3 229
TO WHOM THE WINGED WARRIOUR THUS RETURND: 4 576
ALL JUSTICE: NOR DELAID THE WINGED SAINT 5 247
TO WHOM THE WINGED HIERARCH REPLI'D. 5 468
FAR WAS ADVANC'T ON WINGED SPEED, AN HOST 5 744
AND VERTUES, WINGED SPIRITS, AND CHARIOTS WING'D, 7 199
THITHER WILL SEND HIS WINGED MESSENGERS 7 572
RAPT IN A BALMIE CLOUD WITH WINGED STEEDS 11 706

WINGS
WAST PRESENT, AND WITH MIGHTY WINGS OUTSPREAD 1 20
THEN WITH EXPANDED WINGS HE STEARS HIS FLIGHT 1 225
BRUSHT WITH THE HISS OF RUSSLING WINGS. AS BEES 1 768
UPBORN WITH INDEFATIGABLE WINGS 2 408
PUTS ON SWIFT WINGS, AND TOWARDS THE GATES OF HELL 2 631
FALSE FUGITIVE, AND TO THY SPEED ADD WINGS, 2 700
THAT WITH EXTENDED WINGS A BANNERD HOST 2 885
THIR LIGHTER WINGS. TO WHOM THESE MOST ADHERE, 2 906
WITH HEAD, HANDS, WINGS OR FEET PURSUES HIS WAY, 2 949
WEIGHS HIS SPREAD WINGS, AT LEASURE TO BEHOLD 2 1046
TO STOOP WITH WEARIED WINGS, AND WILLING FEET 3 73
THROUGH ALL RESTRAINT BROKE LOOSE HE WINGS HIS WAY 3 87
APPROACH NOT, BUT WITH BOTH WINGS VEIL THIR EYES. 3 382
ILLUSTRIOUS ON HIS SHOULDERS FLEDGE WITH WINGS 3 627
IN CURLES ON EITHER CHEEK PLAID, WINGS HE WORE 3 641
FANNING THIR ODORIFEROUS WINGS DISPENSE 4 157
HIS CONSTANT LAMP, AND WAVES HIS PURPLE WINGS, 4 764
RIDE ON THY WINGS, AND THOU WITH THY COMPEERS, 4 974
BEAR ON YOUR WINGS AND IN YOUR NOTES HIS PRAISE; 5 199
VAILD WITH HIS GORGEOUS WINGS, UPSPRINGING LIGHT 5 250
A SERAPH WINGD; SIX WINGS HE WORE, TO SHADE 5 277
AND WINGS WERE SET WITH EYES, WITH EYES THE WHEELS 6 755
HEE ON THE WINGS OF CHERUB RODE SUBLIME 6 771
AT ONCE THE FOUR SPRED OUT THIR STARRIE WINGS 6 827
NOR STAID, BUT ON THE WINGS OF CHERUBIM 7 218
HIS BROODING WINGS THE SPIRIT OF GOD OUTSPRED, 7 235
AND LET FOWLE FLIE ABOVE THE EARTH, WITH WINGS 7 389
SOLAC'D THE WOODS, AND SPRED THIR PAINTED WINGS 7 434
BETWEEN HER WHITE WINGS MANTLING PROUDLY, ROWES 7 439
FOR WINGS, AND SMALLEST LINEAMENTS EXACT 7 477
THIR SNAKIE FOULDS, AND ADDED WINGS. FIRST CREPT 7 484
WHISPER'D IT TO THE WOODS, AND FROM THIR WINGS 8 516
SUBJECTED TO HIS SERVICE ANGEL WINGS, 9 155
DIVINITIE WITHIN THEM BREEDING WINGS 9 1010
WINGS GROWING, AND DOMINION GIV'N ME LARGE 10 244
MEANWHILE THE SOUTHWIND ROSE, AND WITH BLACK WINGS 11 738
A MERCIE-SEAT OF GOLD BETWEEN THE WINGS 12 253

WINNING
HIS RIVALS, WINNING CHEAP THE HIGH REPUTE 2 472
LESS WINNING SOFT, LESS AMIABLIE MILDE, 4 479
A POMP OF WINNING GRACES WAITED STILL, 8 61

WINNOWS
WINNOWS THE BUXOM AIR; TILL WITHIN SOARE 5 270

WINS
ENVIRON'D WINS HIS WAY; HARDER BESET 2 1016

WINTER
DECREPIT WINTER, FROM THE SOUTH TO BRING 10 655

WIP'D
FROM EITHER EYE, AND WIP'D THEM WITH HER HAIRE; 5 131
SOM NATURAL TEARS THEY DROP'D, BUT WIP'D THEM SOON; 12 645

WIRE
ALL SOUNDS ON FRET BY STRING OR GOLDEN WIRE 7 597

WISDOM
VAIN WISDOM ALL, AND FALSE PHILOSOPHIE: 2 565
MY WORD, MY WISDOM, AND EFFECTUAL MIGHT, 3 170
AND OFT THOUGH WISDOM WAKE, SUSPICION SLEEPS 3 686
THIR NUMBER, OR THE WISDOM INFINITE 3 706
AND WISDOM, WHICH ALONE IS TRULY FAIR. 4 491
SEAVENFOLD, AND SCOURGE THAT WISDOM BACK TO HELL, 4 914
THOU WITH ETERNAL WISDOM DIDST CONVERSE, 7 9
WISDOM THY SISTER, AND WITH HER DIDST PLAY 7 10
OUR KNOWING, AS TO HIGHEST WISDOM SEEMD, 7 83
WISDOM TO FOLLY, AS NOURISHMENT TO WINDE. 7 130
GLORIE AND PRAISE, WHOSE WISDOM HAD ORDAIN'D 7 187
IS THE PRIME WISDOM, WHAT IS MORE, IS FUME, 8 194
DEGRADED, WISDOM IN DISCOURSE WITH HER 8 552
OF WISDOM, SHE DESERTS THEE NOT, IF THOU 8 563
WISDOM WITHOUT THEIR LEAVE? AND WHEREIN LIES 9 725
WHAT THY HANDS BUILDED NOT, THY WISDOM GAIN'D 10 373
LIKE HIM IN FAITH, IN WISDOM, AND RENOWN; 12 154
AND HIS NEXT SON FOR WEALTH AND WISDOM FAM'D, 12 332

WISDOME
AND WISDOME AT ONE ENTRANCE QUITE SHUT OUT. 3 50
TRUTH, WISDOME, SANCTITUDE SEVERE AND PURE, 4 293
BY WISDOME, AND SUPERIOUR GIFTS RECEAV'D. 11 636
OF WISDOME; HOPE NO HIGHER, THOUGH ALL THE STARRS 12 576

WISDOM-GIVING
O SACRED, WISE, AND WISDOM-GIVING PLANT, 9 679

WISDOMS
AT WISDOMS GATE, AND TO SIMPLICITIE 3 687
IN IGNORANCE, THOU OP'NST WISDOMS WAY, 9 809

WISE
WILL HE, SO WISE, LET LOOSE AT ONCE HIS IRE, 2 155
THEN WISE TO FRUSTRATE ALL OUR PLOTS AND WILES. 2 193
IF WE WERE WISE, AGAINST SO GREAT A FOE 2 202
TO SERVE HIM BETTER: WISE ARE ALL HIS WAYES. 3 680
GABRIEL, THOU HADST IN HEAV'N TH' ESTEEM OF WISE, 4 886
O LOSS OF ONE IN HEAV'N TO JUDGE OF WISE, 4 904
GRAVELY IN DOUBT WHETHER TO HOLD THEM WISE 4 907
SO WISE HE JUDGES IT TO FLY FROM PAIN 4 910
WISE TO FLIE PAIN, PROFESSING NEXT THE SPIE, 4 948
PART LOOSLY WING THE REGION, PART MORE WISE 7 425
HOW NATURE WISE AND FRUGAL COULD COMMIT 8 26
TO KNOW WHAT PASSES THERE; BE LOWLIE WISE: 8 173
THY MATE, WHO SEES WHEN THOU ART SEEN LEAST WISE. 8 578
MORE WISE, MORE WATCHFUL, STRONGER, IF NEED WERE 9 311
LEFT SO IMPERFET BY THE MAKER WISE, 9 338
O SACRED, WISE, AND WISDOM-GIVING PLANT, 9 679
OF HIGHEST AGENTS, DEEMD HOWEVER WISE. 9 683
FORBIDS US GOOD, FORBIDS US TO BE WISE? 9 759
OF VERTUE TO MAKE WISE: WHAT HINDERS THEN 9 778
AND HATH BIN TASTED SUCH: THE SERPENT WISE, 9 867
NOR CAN I THINK THAT GOD, CREATOR WISE, 9 938
OMNISCIENT, WHO IN ALL THINGS WISE AND JUST, 10 7
TO TRUST THEE FROM MY SIDE, IMAGIN'D WISE, 10 881
CREATOR WISE, THAT PEOPL'D HIGHEST HEAV'N 10 889
IN WISE DEPORT, SPAKE MUCH OF RIGHT AND WRONG, 11 666
SUBVERTING WORLDLY STRONG, AND WORLDLY WISE 12 568

WISELIER
HATH WISELIER ARM'D HIS VENGEFUL IRE THEN SO 10 1023

WISELY
DID WISELY TO CONCEAL, AND NOT DIVULGE 8 73

WISEST
AUDACIOUS NEIGHBOURHOOD, THE WISEST HEART 1 400
SEEMS WISEST, VERTUOUSEST, DISCREETEST, BEST; 8 550

WISH
TO GIVE HIS ENEMIES THIR WISH, AND END 2 157
AND WISH AND STRUGGLE, AS THEY PASS, TO REACH 2 606
EFFECT SHALL END OUR WISH. MEAN WHILE REVIVE; 6 493
THAT THEY MAY HAVE THIR WISH, TO TRIE WITH MEE 6 818
AND GRACE THAT WON WHO SAW TO WISH HER STAY, 8 43
INTO ALL EYES TO WISH HER STILL IN SIGHT. 8 63
THY WISH EXACTLY TO THY HEARTS DESIRE. 8 451
HIS WISH AND BEST ADVANTAGE, US ASUNDER, 9 258
OF WHAT SO SELDOM CHANC'D, WHEN TO HIS WISH, 9 423
SO MIGHT THE WRAUTH. FOND WISH. COULDST THOU
SUPPORT 10 834

WISH'D
HE SOUGHT THEM BOTH, BUT WISH'D HIS HAP MIGHT FIND 9 421
EVE SEPARATE, HE WISH'D, BUT NOT WITH HOPE 9 422
IN THINGS TO US FORBIDDEN, IT MIGHT BE WISH'D, 9 1025
BENT THIR ASPECT, AND WHOM THEY WISH'D BEHELD, 10 454
SO SPAKE, SO WISH'D MUCH-HUMBL'D EVE, BUT FATE 11 181

WISHED
INVESTS THE SEA, AND WISHED MORN DELAYES: 1 208

WISHES
OR WHOM HE WISHES MOST SHALL SELDOM GAIN 10 901

WISHT
THUS ANSWERD. ILL FOR THEE, BUT IN WISHT HOURE 6 150
THAT WISHT THE MOUNTAINS NOW MIGHT BE AGAIN 6 842
HUMAN, TO PUT ON GODS, DEATH TO BE WISHT, 9 714

WIT
AS FROM HIS WIT AND NATIVE SUTTLETIE 9 93

WITCHES
WITH LAPLAND WITCHES, WHILE THE LABOURING MOON 2 665

WITHALL
HE SWERVE NOT TOO SECURE: TELL HIM WITHALL 5 238
RATIONAL LIBERTIE; YET KNOW WITHALL, 12 82

WITHDRAW
THEE TO DIMINISH, AND FROM THEE WITHDRAW 7 612
WHETHER HIS FIRST DESIGN BE TO WITHDRAW 9 261
WEARIED WITH THEIR INIQUITIES, WITHDRAW 12 107

WITHDRAWS
HER SHADOWIE CLOUD WITHDRAWS, I AM TO HASTE, 5 686

WITHDREW
SOFT SHE WITHDREW, AND LIKE A WOOD-NYMPH LIGHT 9 386

WITHERD
THIR GLORY WITHERD. AS WHEN HEAVENS FIRE 1 612
AMONG TH' ACCURST, THAT WITHERD ALL THIR STRENGTH, 6 850
TO WITHERD WEAK AND GRAY; THY SENSES THEN 11 540

WITHHELD
THEE ALSO HAPPIER, SHALL NOT BE WITHHELD 7 117
BY A FARR WORSE, OR IF SHE LOVE, WITHHELD 10 903

WITHHOLD
FORBID WHO WILL, NONE SHALL FROM ME WITHHOLD 5 62

WITHIN
WITHIN HIS SANCTUARY IT SELF THIR SHRINES, 1 388
A THIRD AS SOON HAD FORM'D WITHIN THE GROUND 1 705
WITHIN, HER AMPLE SPACES, O'RE THE SMOOTH 1 725
OF THAT INFERNAL COURT. BUT FAR WITHIN 1 792
FOR SINCE NO DEEP WITHIN HER GULF CAN HOLD 2 12
WITHIN HEAV'NS BOUND, UNLESS HEAV'NS LORD SUPREAM 2 236
WROUGHT STILL WITHIN THEM; AND NO LESS DESIRE 2 295
WITHIN UNSEEN. FARR LESS ABHORRD THAN THESE 2 659
AND I WILL PLACE WITHIN THEM AS A GUIDE 3 194
SAW WITHIN KENN A GLORIOUS ANGEL STAND, 3 622
THE HELL WITHIN HIM, FOR WITHIN HIM HELL 4 20
FELL NOT, BUT STAND UNSHAK'N, FROM WITHIN 4 64
OF HILL OR HIGHEST WALL, AND SHEER WITHIN 4 182
A SHAPE WITHIN THE WATRY GLEAM APPEERD 4 461
BUT IF WITHIN THE CIRCUIT OF THESE WALKS, 4 586
WITHIN THESE HALLOWD LIMITS THOU APPEER, 4 964
WINNOWS THE BUXOM AIR; TILL WITHIN SOARE 5 270
AND EVE WITHIN, DUE AT HER HOUR PREPAR'D 5 303
WITHIN THEM EVERY LOWER FACULTIE 5 410
HATH PAST IN HEAV'N, SOM DOUBT WITHIN ME MOVE, 5 554
ORB WITHIN ORB, THE FATHER INFINITE, 5 596
AND FROM WITHIN THE GOLDEN LAMPS THAT BURNE 5 713
WITHIN THE MOUNT OF GOD, FAST BY HIS THRONE, 6 5
VIGOUR DIVINE WITHIN THEM, CAN ALLOW 6 158
AND LEFT LARGE FIELD, UNSAFE WITHIN THE WIND 6 309
COLLECTED STOOD WITHIN OUR THOUGHTS AMUS'D, 6 581
FLASHING THICK FLAMES, WHEELE WITHIN WHEELE
UNDRAWN, 6 751
WITHIN THE VISIBLE DIURNAL SPHEARE; 7 22
WHAT WITHIN EDEN OR WITHOUT WAS DONE 7 65
OF KNOWLEDGE WITHIN BOUNDS; BEYOND ABSTAIN 7 120
WITHIN APPOINTED BOUNDS BE HEAV'N AND EARTH, 7 167
SPONTANEOUS, FOR WITHIN THEM SPIRIT LIVD, 7 204
ALL BUT WITHIN THOSE BANKS, WHERE RIVERS NOW 7 305
BUT LONG ERE OUR APPROACHING HEARD WITHIN 8 242
OF FISH WITHIN THIR WATRY RESIDENCE, 8 346
EXPRESSING WELL THE SPIRIT WITHIN THEE FREE, 8 440
PERFET WITHIN, NO OUTWARD AID REQUIRE; 8 642
ACTIVE WITHIN BEYOND THE SENSE OF BRUTE. 9 96
TORMENT WITHIN ME, AS FROM THE HATEFUL SIEGE 9 121
WHY SHOULDST NOT THOU LIKE SENSE WITHIN THEE FEEL 9 315
FROM HIS SURMISE PROV'D FALSE, FIND PEACE WITHIN, 9 333
SECURE FROM OUTWARD FORCE; WITHIN HIMSELF 9 348
THE DANGER LIES, YET LIES WITHIN HIS POWER: 9 349
WITHIN ME CLEERE, NOT ONELY TO DISCERNE 9 681
THAT DWELT WITHIN, WHOSE PRESENCE HAD INFUS'D 9 836
SO FORCIBLE WITHIN MY HEART I FEEL 9 955
DIVINITIE WITHIN THEM BREEDING WINGS 9 1010
RAIND AT THIR EYES, BUT HIGH WINDS WORSE WITHIN 9 1122
WITHIN THE GATES OF HELL SATE SIN AND DEATH, 10 230
IN COUNTERVIEW WITHIN THE GATES, THAT NOW 10 231
METHINKS I FEEL NEW STRENGTH WITHIN ME RISE, 10 243
WITHIN HELL GATES TILL NOW, THOU US IMPOW'RD 10 369
TO SORROW ABANDOND, BUT WORSE FELT WITHIN, 10 717
MORE TERRIBLE AT TH' ENTRANCE THEN WITHIN. 11 470
WITHIN HIMSELF UNWORTHIE POWERS TO REIGN 12 91
HIS SPIRIT WITHIN THEM, AND THE LAW OF FAITH 12 488
LEFT THEM INROULD, OR WHAT THE SPIRIT WITHIN 12 523
A PARADISE WITHIN THEE, HAPPIER FARR. 12 587

WITHOUT
THAT COMES TO ALL; BUT TORTURE WITHOUT END 1 67
THOUGH WITHOUT NUMBER STILL AMIDST THE HALL 1 791
MUST EXERCISE US WITHOUT HOPE OF END 2 89
THAT BE ASSUR'D, WITHOUT LEAVE ASKT OF THEE: 2 685
WITHOUT MY OP'NING. PENSIVE HERE I SAT 2 777
THY DAUGHTER AND THY DARLING, WITHOUT END. 2 870
ILLIMITABLE OCEAN WITHOUT BOUND, 2 892
WITHOUT DIMENSION, WHERE LENGTH, BREADTH, & HIGHTH, 2 893
ALONE, AND WITHOUT GUIDE, HALF LOST, I SEEK 2 975
FIRM LAND IMBOSOM'D WITHOUT FIRMAMENT, 3 75
SO WITHOUT LEAST IMPULSE OR SHADOW OF FATE, 3 120
LOVE WITHOUT END, AND WITHOUT MEASURE GRACE, 3 142
BE QUESTIOND AND BLASPHEAM'D WITHOUT DEFENCE. 3 166
AND NOW WITHOUT REDEMPTION ALL MANKIND 3 222
AS MANY AS ARE RESTOR'D, WITHOUT THEE NONE. 3 289
LOUD AS FROM NUMBERS WITHOUT NUMBER, SWEET 3 346
IN WHOSE CONSPICUOUS COUNT'NANCE, WITHOUT CLOUD 3 385
HE VIEWS IN BREDTH, AND WITHOUT LONGER PAUSE 3 561

WONDER
NO WONDER, FALL'N SUCH A PERNICIOUS HIGHTH. 1 282
BEHOLD A WONDER. THEY BUT NOW WHO SEEMD 1 777
LOOKS DOWN WITH WONDER AT THE SUDDEN VIEW 3 542
SUCH WONDER SEIS'D, THOUGH AFTER HEAVEN SEEN, 3 552
WHAT WONDER THEN IF FIELDS AND REGIONS HERE 3 606
BENEATH HIM WITH NEW WONDER NOW HE VIEWS 4 205
WITH WONDER, AND COULD LOVE, SO LIVELY SHINES 4 363
URIEL, NO WONDER IF THY PERFET SIGHT, 4 577
HIS WONDER WAS TO FIND UNWAK'ND EVE 5 9
THROUGH SPIRITS WITH EASE; NOR WONDER; IF BY FIRE 5 439
WONDER NOT THEN, WHAT GOD FOR YOU SAW GOOD 5 491
HAD TO HER CENTER SHOOK. WHAT WONDER? WHEN 6 219
GREAT THINGS, AND FULL OF WONDER IN OUR EARES, 7 70
WITH WONDER, BUT DELIGHT, AND, AS IS DUE, 8 11
OUR TASKE WE CHOOSE, WHAT WONDER IF SO NEAR 9 221
WONDER NOT, SOVRAN MISTRESS, IF PERHAPS 9 532
THOU CANST, WHO ART SOLE WONDER, MUCH LESS ARM 9 533
SAY, FOR SUCH WONDER CLAIMS ATTENTION DUE. 9 566
YOUR WONDER, WITH AN APPLE; HE THEREAT 10 487
FOR MAN AND BEAST: WHEN LOE A WONDER STRANGE, 11 733
REPLETE WITH JOY AND WONDER THUS REPLI'D. 12 468

WONDERD
HAST THOU NOT WONDERD, ADAM, AT MY STAY? 9 856
OF PUBLIC SCORN; HE WONDERD, BUT NOT LONG 10 509

WONDERFUL
FOR WONDERFUL INDEED ARE ALL HIS WORKS, 3 702
HATH BIN THE CAUSE, AND WONDERFUL TO HEARE: 9 862
LONG HAD FORETOLD, A FABRICK WONDERFUL 10 482
AND EVIL TURN TO GOOD; MORE WONDERFUL 12 471

WONDERS
OR WONDERS MOVE TH' OBDURATE TO RELENT? 6 790
CREATION, AND THE WONDERS OF HIS MIGHT. 7 223

WOND'RING
WHO BOAST IN MORTAL THINGS, AND WOND'RING TELL 1 693

WONDRING
WONDRING; BUT SOON TH' ALMIGHTY THUS REPLY'D: 3 273
UNDER A SHADE OF FLOURS, MUCH WONDRING WHERE 4 451
AND AS I WONDRING LOOKT, BESIDE IT STOOD 5 54
AND VARIOUS: WONDRING AT MY FLIGHT AND CHANGE 5 89
STRAIT TOWARD HEAV'N MY WONDRING EYES I TURND, 8 257
MUCH WONDRING HOW THE SUTTLE FIEND HAD STOLN 10 20
HAD LEASURE, WONDRING AT HIMSELF NOW MORE; 10 510

WOND'ROUS
WITH WOND'ROUS ART FOUND OUT THE MASSIE ORE, 1 703

WONDROUS
TAMELY ENDUR'D A BRIDGE OF WONDROUS LENGTH 2 1028
BY WONDROUS BIRTH: BE THOU IN ADAMS ROOM 3 285
ALL THESE HIS WONDROUS WORKS, BUT CHIEFLY MAN, 3 663
ALL THESE HIS WORKS SO WONDROUS HE ORDAIND, 3 665
THUS WONDROUS FAIR; THY SELF HOW WONDROUS THEN. 5 155
IN MIGHT THOUGH WONDROUS AND IN ACTS OF WARR, 6 377
HAD WONDROUS, AS WITH STARRS THIR BODIES ALL 6 754
WONDROUS IN LENGTH AND CORPULENCE INVOLV'D 7 483
WHEREIN TO READ HIS WONDROUS WORKS, AND LEARNE 8 68
WONDROUS INDEED, IF CAUSE OF SUCH EFFECTS. 9 650
NOW HAD THEY BROUGHT THE WORK BY WONDROUS ART 10 312
OF THIS NEW WONDROUS PONTIFICE, UNHOP'T 10 348
SHALL BUILD A WONDROUS ARK, AS THOU BEHELDST, 11 819
SUCH WONDROUS POWER GOD TO HIS SAINT WILL LEND, 12 200
BAPTIZ'D, SHALL THEM WITH WONDROUS GIFTS ENDUE 12 500

WONDROUSLY
SO WONDROUSLY WAS SET HIS STATION BRIGHT. 3 587

WONN
OR ALL AT ONCE; MORE GLORIE WILL BE WONN, 4 853

WONNS
AS FROM HIS LAIRE THE WILDE BEAST WHERE HE WONNS 7 457

WONT
UPON THE WING, AS WHEN MEN WONT TO WATCH 1 332
WONT RIDE IN ARM'D, AND AT THE SOLDANS CHAIR 1 764
THE FIRST ART WONT HIS GREAT AUTHENTIC WILL 3 656
AS TO SUPERIOR SPIRITS IS WONT IN HEAVEN, 3 737
IF DREAM'D, NOT AS I OFT AM WONT, OF THEE, 5 32
THAT WONT TO BE MORE CHEARFUL AND SERENE 5 123
WAST WONT, I MINE TO THEE WAS WONT TO IMPART; 5 677
AND IN FIERCE HOSTING MEET, WHO WONT TO MEET 6 93
AS REAPERS OFT ARE WONT THIR HARVEST QUEEN. 9 842
WHERE ART THOU ADAM, WONT WITH JOY TO MEET 10 103

WONTED
LIKE DOUBTFUL HUE: BUT HE HIS WONTED PRIDE 1 527
FIRM PEACE RECOVERD SOON AND WONTED CALM. 5 210
THE WONTED SIGNAL, AND SUPERIOR VOICE 5 705
OBSEQUIOUS, HEAV'N HIS WONTED FACE RENEWD, 6 783
AND OF THIR WONTED VIGOUR LEFT THEM DRAIND, 6 851
BY SUFFERANCE, AND THY WONTED FAVOUR DEIGN'D. 8 202
OUR WONTED ORNAMENTS NOW SOILD AND STAIND, 9 1076

WOO'D
THAT WOULD BE WOO'D, AND NOT UNSOUGHT BE WON, 8 503

WOOD
IN WOOD OR WILDERNESS, FORREST OR DEN; 4 342
THROUGH WOOD, THROUGH WASTE, O'RE HILL, O'RE DALE HIS ROAM. 4 538
NOR STREIT'NING VALE, NOR WOOD, NOR STREAM DIVIDES 6 70
WITH BRANCHES LOPT, IN WOOD OR MOUNTAIN FELL'D) 6 575
INTO THE THICKEST WOOD, THERE SOON THEY CHOSE 9 1100
INTO THE WOOD FAST BY, AND CHANGING SHAPE 10 333
ON THE CLEFT WOOD, AND ALL DUE RITES PERFORM'D. 11 440
TO WORSHIP THIR OWN WORK IN WOOD AND STONE 12 119

WOODBINE
THE WOODBINE ROUND THIS ARBOUR, OR DIRECT 9 216

WOODIE
SHADE ABOVE SHADE, A WOODIE THEATRE 4 141
A WOODIE MOUNTAIN; WHOSE HIGH TOP WAS PLAINE, 8 303
AMONG THE TREES ON ILES AND WOODIE SHORES. 9 1118

WOOD-NYMPH
THEN WOOD-NYMPH, OR THE FAIREST GODDESS FEIGN'D 5 381
SOFT SHE WITHDREW, AND LIKE A WOOD-NYMPH LIGHT 9 386

WOODS
ROCKS, WATERS, WOODS, AND BY THE SHAGGIE TOPS 6 645
IN RHODOPE, WHERE WOODS AND ROCKS HAD EARES 7 35
THIR BLOSSOMS: WITH HIGH WOODS THE HILLS WERE CROWND, 7 326
SOLAC'D THE WOODS, AND SPRED THIR PAINTED WINGS 7 434
HILL, DALE, AND SHADIE WOODS, AND SUNNIE PLAINES, 8 262
YE HILLS AND DALES, YE RIVERS, WOODS, AND PLAINES, 8 275
WHISPER'D IT TO THE WOODS, AND FROM THIR WINGS 8 516
OF HILL, AND VALLIE, RIVERS, WOODS AND PLAINES, 9 116
TO LIVE AGAIN IN THESE WILDE WOODS FORLORN? 9 910
OBSCUR'D, WHERE HIGHEST WOODS IMPENETRABLE 9 1086
AND THRASCIAS REND THE WOODS AND SEAS UPTURN; 10 700
O WOODS, O FOUNTAINS, HILLOCKS, DALES AND BOWRS, 10 860
DOWN FROM A HILL THE BEAST THAT REIGNS IN WOODS, 11 187
HAD WASTED WOODS ON MOUNTAIN OR IN VALE, 11 567

WOOFF
IN TIME OF TRUCE; IRIS HAD DIPT THE WOOFF; 11 244

WOOMB
IF AUGHT DISTURB'D THIR NOYSE, INTO HER WOOMB, 2 657
OP'NING HER FERTIL WOOMB TEEM'D AT A BIRTH 7 454

WORD
O FATHER, GRACIOUS WAS THAT WORD WHICH CLOS'D 3 144
MY WORD, MY WISDOM, AND EFFECTUAL MIGHT, 3 170
FATHER, THY WORD IS PAST, MAN SHALL FIND GRACE; 3 227
I SAW WHEN AT HIS WORD THE FORMLESS MASS, 3 708
NONE LEFT BUT BY SUBMISSION; AND THAT WORD 4 81
BY WORD OR ACTION MARKT: ABOUT THEM ROUND 4 401
AS BY HIS WORD THE MIGHTY FATHER MADE 5 836
OF TRUTH, IN WORD MIGHTIER THEN THEY IN ARMES; 6 32
AND THOU MY WORD, BEGOTTEN SON, BY THEE 7 163
HIS WORD, THE FILIAL GODHEAD, GAVE EFFECT. 7 175
THE KING OF GLORIE IN HIS POWERFUL WORD 7 208
SAID THEN TH' OMNIFIC WORD, YOUR DISCORD END: 7 217
ATTENDS THEE, AND EACH WORD, EACH MOTION FORMES, 8 223
TO END ME? SHALL TRUTH FAIL TO KEEP HER WORD, 10 856

WORDS
AND THENCE IN HEAV'N CALL'D SATAN, WITH BOLD WORDS 1 82
WHERETO WITH SPEEDY WORDS TH' ARCH-FIEND REPLY'D. 1 156
SOON RECOLLECTING, WITH HIGH WORDS, THAT BORE 1 528
WORDS INTERWOVE WITH SIGHS FOUND OUT THIR WAY. 1 621
HE SPAKE: AND TO CONFIRM HIS WORDS, OUT-FLEW 1 663
HE RECK'D NOT, AND THESE WORDS THEREAFTER SPAKE. 2 50
THUS BELIAL WITH WORDS CLOATH'D IN REASONS GARB 2 226
SHE SPAKE, AND AT HER WORDS THE HELLISH PEST 2 735
SO STRANGE THY OUTCRY, AND THY WORDS SO STRANGE 2 737
HIS WORDS HERE ENDED, BUT HIS MEEK ASPECT 3 266
BUT STILL THY WORDS AT RANDOM, AS BEFORE, 4 930
AT SUCH BOLD WORDS VOUCHT WITH A DEED SO BOLD: 5 66
ILL MATCHING WORDS AND DEEDS LONG PAST OR LATE. 5 113
TO WHOM OUR GREAT PROGENITOR. THY WORDS 5 544
SO SPAKE TH' OMNIPOTENT, AND WITH HIS WORDS 5 616
AMBIGUOUS WORDS AND JEALOUSIES, TO SOUND 5 703
WORDS WHICH NO EARE EVER TO HEAR IN HEAV'N 5 810
HOARCE MURMUR ECHO'D TO HIS WORDS APPLAUSE 5 873
HE ENDED, AND HIS WORDS THIR DROOPING CHERE 6 496
SO SCOFFING IN AMBIGUOUS WORDS HE SCARCE, 6 568
WHAT WORDS OR TONGUE OF SERAPH CAN SUFFICE, 7 113
NOT WORDS ALONE PLEAS'D HER. O WHEN MEET NOW 8 57
THOUGH PLEASANT, BUT THY WORDS WITH GRACE DIVINE 8 215
PLEAS'D WITH THY WORDS NO LESS THEN THOU WITH MINE. 8 248
LET NOT MY WORDS OFFEND THEE, HEAV'NLY POWER, 8 379
THY WORDS, CREATOR BOUNTEOUS AND BENIGNE, 8 492
FROM ALL HER WORDS AND ACTIONS MIXT WITH LOVE 8 602
TO WHOM WITH HEALING WORDS ADAM REPLYD. 9 290
CHIEFLY BY WHAT THY OWN LAST REASONING WORDS 9 379
INTO THE HEART OF EVE HIS WORDS MADE WAY, 9 550
HE ENDED, AND HIS WORDS REPLETE WITH GUILE 9 733

WORDS (CONTINUED)
YET RUNG OF HIS PERSWASIVE WORDS, IMPREGN'D 9 737
WHICH WITH BLAND WORDS AT WILL SHE THUS ADDREST. 9 855
THUS IN CALM MOOD HIS WORDS TO EVE HE TURND. 9 920
AT LENGTH GAVE UTTERANCE TO THESE WORDS CONSTRAIND. 9 1066
WOULD THOU HADST HEARK'ND TO MY WORDS, AND STAI'D 9 1134
WHAT WORDS HAVE PAST THY LIPS, ADAM SEVERE, 9 1144
SILENCE, AND WITH THESE WORDS ATTENTION WON. 10 459
HIS THOUGHTS, HIS LOOKS, WORDS, ACTIONS ALL INFECT, 10 608
SOFT WORDS TO HIS FIERCE PASSION SHE ASSAY'D: 10 865
AND THUS WITH PEACEFUL WORDS UPRAIS'D HER SOON. 10 946
HOW LITTLE WEIGHT MY WORDS WITH THEE CAN FINDE, 10 968
UNSKILFUL WITH WHAT WORDS TO PRAY, LET MEE 11 32
WHICH THUS TO EVE HIS WELCOME WORDS RENEWD. 11 140
TO MICHAEL THUS HIS HUMBLE WORDS ADDRESSD. 11 295
AND SCARCE RECOVERING WORDS HIS PLAINT RENEW'D. 11 499
TO SOW A JANGLING NOISE OF WORDS UNKNOWN: 12 55
WITHOUT THE VENT OF WORDS, WHICH THESE HE BREATHD. 12 374
AND THUS WITH WORDS NOT SAD SHE HIM RECEAV'D. 12 609

WORE
IN CURLES ON EITHER CHEEK PLAID, WINGS HE WORE 3 641
HER UNADORNED GOLDEN TRESSES WORE 4 305
A SERAPH WINGD; SIX WINGS HE WORE, TO SHADE 5 277
AND ON THE WASHIE OOSE DEEP CHANNELS WORE; 7 303

WORK
HERE IN THE HEART OF HELL TO WORK IN FIRE, 1 151
TO WORK IN CLOSE DESIGN, BY FRAUD OR GUILE 1 646
THE WORK OF SULPHUR. THITHER WING'D WITH SPEED 1 674
ADMIRING ENTER'D, AND THE WORK SOME PRAISE 1 731
THRIVE UNDER EVIL, AND WORK EASE OUT OF PAIN 2 261
THE WORK AS OF A KINGLY PALACE GATE 3 505
WHICH ELSE MIGHT WORK HIM DANGER OR DELAY: 3 635
ACCEPT YOUR MAKERS WORK; HE GAVE IT ME, 4 380
MAN HATH HIS DAILY WORK OF BODY OR MIND 4 618
WHICH WE IN OUR APPOINTED WORK IMPLOYD 4 726
WILDE WORK PRODUCES OFT, AND MOST IN DREAMS, 5 112
ON TO THIR MORNINGS RURAL WORK THEY HASTE 5 211
ON GOLDEN HINGES TURNING, AS BY WORK 5 255
TILL BODY UP TO SPIRIT WORK, IN BOUNDS 5 478
THAT WE WERE FORMD THEN SAIST THOU? AND THE WORK 5 853
FOR GODS, AND TOO UNEQUAL WORK WE FIND 6 453
FORTHWITH FROM COUNCEL TO THE WORK THEY FLEW, 6 507
WILD WORK IN HEAV'N, AND DANGEROUS TO THE MAINE. 6 698
OF RADIANT URIM, WORK DIVINELY WROUGHT, 6 761
NUMBER TO THIS DAYES WORK IS NOT ORDAIN'D 6 809
IN CHAOS, AND THE WORK BEGUN, HOW SOON 7 93
SURVEYING HIS GREAT WORK, THAT IT WAS GOOD: 7 353
THERE WANTED YET THE MASTER WORK, THE END 7 505
YET NOT TILL THE CREATOR FROM HIS WORK 7 551
THE GREAT CREATOR FROM HIS WORK RETURND 7 567
MAGNIFICENT, HIS SIX DAYS WORK, A WORLD; 7 568
HATH OMNIPRESENCE) AND THE WORK ORDAIN'D, 7 590
AUTHOR AND END OF ALL THINGS, AND FROM WORK 7 591
AS RESTING ON THAT DAY FROM ALL HIS WORK, 7 593
HAD WORK AND RESTED NOT, THE SOLEMN PIPE, 7 595
OR ENEMIE, WHILE GOD WAS IN HIS WORK, 8 234
OR WON TO WHAT MAY WORK HIS UTTER LOSS, 9 131
THIR GROWING WORK; FOR MUCH THIR WORK OUTGREW 9 202
AID US, THE WORK UNDER OUR LABOUR GROWS, 9 208
OUR DAYES WORK BROUGHT TO LITTLE, THOUGH BEGUN 9 224
HOW WE MIGHT BEST FULFILL THE WORK WHICH HERE 9 230
DESPAIRING, SEEKS TO WORK US WOE AND SHAME 9 255
ADVENTROUS WORK, YET TO THY POWER AND MINE 10 255
NOR SHALL I TO THE WORK THOU ENTERPRISEST 10 270
NOW HAD THEY BROUGHT THE WORK BY WONDROUS ART 10 312
MINE WITH THIS GLORIOUS WORK, AND MADE ONE REALM 10 391
NOW RIS'N, TO WORK THEM FURDER WOE OR SHAME; 10 555
WHERERE OUR DAYS WORK LIES, THOUGH NOW ENJOIND 11 177
RIDICULOUS, AND THE WORK CONFUSION NAM'D. 12 62
TO WORSHIP THIR OWN WORK IN WOOD AND STONE 12 119

WORKES
WHOSE VERTUE ON IT SELF WORKES NO EFFECT, 8 95
AND GOOD WORKES IN HER HUSBAND TO PROMOTE. 9 234
BY FAITH NOT VOID OF WORKES: THIS GOD-LIKE ACT 12 427

WORKING
WORKING THROUGH LOVE, UPON THIR HEARTS SHALL WRITE, 12 489

WORK-MAISTER
THE GREAT WORK-MAISTER, LEADS TO NO EXCESS 3 696

WORKS
LEVIATHAN, WHICH GOD OF ALL HIS WORKS 1 201
AND WORKS OF LOVE OR ENMITY FULFILL. 1 431
OF BABEL, AND THE WORKS OF MEMPHIAN KINGS 1 694
ABOLISH HIS OWN WORKS. THIS WOULD SURPASS 2 370
AS FROM HER OUTMOST WORKS A BROK'D FOE 2 1039
OF NATURES WORKS TO MEE EXPUNG'D AND RAS'D, 3 49
HIS OWN WORKS AND THEIR WORKS AT ONCE TO VIEW: 3 59
TO ME ARE ALL MY WORKS, NOR MAN THE LEAST 3 277
WITH VANITY HAD FILLD THE WORKS OF MEN: 3 447
ALL TH' UNACCOMPLISHT WORKS OF NATURES HAND, 3 455
ALL THESE HIS WONDROUS WORKS, BUT CHIEFLY MAN, 3 663
ALL THESE HIS WORKS SO WONDROUS HE ORDAIND, 3 665
THE WORKS OF GOD, THEREBY TO GLORIFIE 3 695

WORKS (CONTINUED)
FOR WONDERFUL INDEED ARE ALL HIS WORKS, 3 702
OF NATURES WORKS, HONOR DISHONORABLE, 4 314
MORE OF TH' ALMIGHTIES WORKS, AND CHIEFLY MAN 4 566
ALL THESE WITH CEASLESS PRAISE HIS WORKS BEHOLD 4 679
WORKS OF DAY PASS'T, OR MORROWS NEXT DESIGNE, 5 33
THESE ARE THY GLORIOUS WORKS, PARENT OF GOOD, 5 153
IN THESE THY LOWEST WORKS, YET THESE DECLARE 5 158
BROOKS NOT THE WORKS OF VIOLENCE AND WARR. 6 274
TO MAGNIFIE HIS WORKS, THE MORE WE KNOW. 7 97
OBTAINE: THOUGH TO RECOUNT ALMIGHTIE WORKS 7 112
GOD AND HIS WORKS, CREATOUR HIM THEY SUNG, 7 259
OF ALL HIS WORKS: THEREFORE THE OMNIPOTENT 7 516
WHICH TASTED WORKS KNOWLEDGE OF GOOD AND EVIL, 7 543
GREAT ARE THY WORKS, JEHOVAH, INFINITE 7 602
OVER HIS WORKS, ON EARTH, IN SEA, OR AIR, 7 629
WHEREIN TO READ HIS WONDROUS WORKS, AND LEARNE 8 68
AS US'D OR NOT, WORKS IN THE MIND NO CHANGE, 8 525
TO INTERRUPT, SIDE-LONG HE WORKS HIS WAY. 9 512
SIGHING THROUGH ALL HER WORKS GAVE SIGNS OF WOE, 9 783
OF ALL GODS WORKS, CREATURE IN WHOM EXCELL'D 9 897
SET OVER ALL HIS WORKS, WHICH IN OUR FALL, 9 941
RIGHTEOUS ARE THY DECREES ON ALL THY WORKS; 10 644
AND PROPITIATION, ALL HIS WORKS ON MEE 11 34
BY FAITH AND FAITHFUL WORKS, TO SECOND LIFE, 11 64
TO WORSHIP GOD ARIGHT, AND KNOW HIS WORKS 11 578
BEFORE HIM, TOWNS, AND RURAL WORKS BETWEEN, 11 639
TO FILIAL, WORKS OF LAW TO WORKS OF FAITH. 12 306
NOT BY DESTROYING SATAN, BUT HIS WORKS 12 394
TO SAVE THEM, NOT THIR OWN, THOUGH LEGAL WORKS. 12 410
BESTUCK WITH SLANDROUS DARTS, AND WORKS OF FAITH 12 536
MERCIFULL OVER ALL HIS WORKS, WITH GOOD 12 565
ALL SECRETS OF THE DEEP, ALL NATURES WORKS, 12 578
OR WORKS OF GOD IN HEAV'N, AIRE, EARTH, OR SEA, 12 579

WORLD
BROUGHT DEATH INTO THE WORLD, AND ALL OUR WOE, 1 3
FOR ONE RESTRAINT, LORDS OF THE WORLD BESIDES? 1 32
INFERNAL WORLD, AND THOU PROFOUNDEST HELL 1 251
AND VARIOUS IDOLS THROUGH THE HEATHEN WORLD. 1 375
THROUGH LABOUR AND INDURANCE. THIS DEEP WORLD 2 262
ERR NOT) ANOTHER WORLD, THE HAPPY SEAT 2 347
IN SEARCH OF THIS NEW WORLD, WHOM SHALL WE FIND 2 403
IF THENCE HE SCAPE INTO WHAT EVER WORLD, 2 442
THAT DISMAL WORLD, IF ANY CLIME PERHAPS 2 572
TO THAT NEW WORLD OF LIGHT AND BLISS, AMONG 2 867
NOW LATELY HEAVEN AND EARTH, ANOTHER WORLD 2 1004
OF THIS FRAIL WORLD; BY WHICH THE SPIRITS PERVERSE 2 1030
THIS PENDANT WORLD, IN BIGNESS AS A STARR 2 1052
THE RISING WORLD OF WATERS DARK AND DEEP, 3 11
ON THE BARE OUTSIDE OF THIS WORLD, THAT SEEM'D 3 74
DIRECTLY TOWARDS THE NEW CREATED WORLD, 3 89
A WORLD FROM UTTER LOSS, AND HAST BEEN FOUND 3 308
THE WORLD SHALL BURN, AND FROM HER ASHES SPRING 3 334
OF THIS ROUND WORLD, WHOSE FIRST CONVEX DIVIDES 3 419
FIRST FROM THE ANCIENT WORLD THOSE GIANTS CAME 3 464
FLY O'RE THE BACKSIDE OF THE WORLD FARR OFF 3 494
OF ALL THIS WORLD AT ONCE. AS WHEN A SCOUT 3 543
AT SIGHT OF ALL THIS WORLD BEHELD SO FAIRE. 3 554
OF THIS NEW WORLD; AT WHOSE SIGHT ALL THE STARRS 4 34
MANKIND CREATED, AND FOR HIM THIS WORLD. 4 107
AS MAN ERE LONG, AND THIS NEW WORLD SHALL KNOW. 4 113
TO SEEK HER THROUGH THE WORLD; NOR THAT SWEET GROVE 4 272
BY CONQUERING THIS NEW WORLD, COMPELS ME NOW 4 391
THAT MADE US, AND FOR US THIS AMPLE WORLD 4 413
THIS NEW CREATED WORLD, WHEREOF IN HELL 4 937
THEN WHEN FAIR MORNING FIRST SMILES ON THE WORLD, 5 124
THOU SUN, OF THIS GREAT WORLD BOTH EYE AND SOULE, 5 171
SHALL FILL THE WORLD MORE NUMEROUS WITH THY SONS 5 389
OF THINGS ABOVE HIS WORLD, AND OF THIR BEING 5 455
THE SECRETS OF ANOTHER WORLD, PERHAPS 5 569
AS YET THIS WORLD WAS NOT, AND CHAOS WILDE 5 577
SEEMD IN THY WORLD ERRONEOUS TO DISSENT 6 146
WHAT NEERER MIGHT CONCERN HIM, HOW THIS WORLD 7 62
FARR DIFFERING FROM THIS WORLD, THOU HAST REVEAL'D 7 71
ANOTHER WORLD, OUT OF ONE MAN A RACE 7 155
FARR INTO CHAOS, AND THE WORLD UNBORN; 7 220
THIS BE THY JUST CIRCUMFERENCE, O WORLD. 7 231
DIVIDING: FOR AS EARTH, SO HE THE WORLD 7 269
THENCE TO BEHOLD THIS NEW CREATED WORLD 7 554
MAGNIFICENT, HIS SIX DAYS WORK, A WORLD; 7 568
WITNESS THIS NEW-MADE WORLD, ANOTHER HEAV'N 7 617
NUMEROUS, AND EVERY STARR PERHAPS A WORLD 7 621
HOW FIRST THIS WORLD AND FACE OF THINGS BEGAN, 7 636
WHEN I BEHOLD THIS GOODLY FRAME, THIS WORLD 8 15
BE CENTER TO THE WORLD, AND OTHER STARRS 8 123
WHICH TWO GREAT SEXES ANIMATE THE WORLD, 8 151
SHALT LOOSE, EXPELL'D FROM HENCE INTO A WORLD 8 332
THAT WHAT SEEMD FAIR IN ALL THE WORLD, SEEMD NOW 8 472
THAT BROUGHT INTO THIS WORLD A WORLD OF WOE, 9 11
MAGNIFICENT THIS WORLD, AND EARTH HIS SEAT, 9 153
EMPRESS OF THIS FAIR WORLD, RESPLENDENT EVE, 9 568
OVER THIS MAINE FROM HELL TO THAT NEW WORLD 10 257
IMMOVABLE OF THIS NOW FENCELESS WORLD 10 303
OF THIS ROUND WORLD; WITH PINNS OF ADAMANT 10 318
AND OF THIS WORLD, AND ON THE LEFT HAND HELL 10 322
THINE NOW IS ALL THIS WORLD, THY VERTUE HATH WON 10 372
AS BATTEL HATH ADJUDG'D, FROM THIS NEW WORLD 10 377

WORLD (CONTINUED)
HIS QUADRATURE, FROM THY ORBICULAR WORLD, ... 10 381
HELL AND THIS WORLD, ONE REALM, ONE CONTINENT . . 10 392
FLOWN TO THE UPPER WORLD; THE REST WERE ALL . . 10 422
AS LORDS, A SPACIOUS WORLD, TO OUR NATIVE HEAVEN . 10 467
THE NEW CREATED WORLD, WHICH FAME IN HEAV'N . . 10 481
BOTH HIS BELOVED MAN AND ALL HIS WORLD, ... 10 489
A WORLD WHO WOULD NOT PURCHASE WITH A BRUISE, . . 10 500
TO WASTE AND HAVOC YONDER WORLD, WHICH I . . . 10 617
HIS COURSE INTENDED; ELSE HOW HAD THE WORLD . . 10 689
OF THIS NEW GLORIOUS WORLD, AND MEE SO LATE . . 10 721
THEN ALL THE WORLD MUCH HEAVIER, THOUGH DIVIDED . 10 836
OF NATURE, AND NOT FILL THE WORLD AT ONCE . . 10 892
INTO THIS CURSED WORLD A WOFUL RACE, ... 10 984
TO RESALUTE THE WORLD WITH SACRED LIGHT . . . 11 134
INTO A LOWER WORLD, TO THIS OBSCURE 11 283
IN YONDER NETHER WORLD WHERE SHALL I SEEK . . 11 328
THE WORLD: IN SPIRIT PERHAPS HE ALSO SAW . . . 11 406
THE WORLD ERELONG A WORLD OF TEARS MUST WEEPE. . 11 627
THE ONELY RIGHTEOUS IN A WORLD PERVERSE, . . . 11 701
FAME IN THE WORLD, HIGH TITLES, AND RICH PREY, . 11 793
AGAINST ALLUREMENT, CUSTOM, AND A WORLD . . . 11 810
A WORLD DEVOTE TO UNIVERSAL RACK. 11 821
FARR LESS I NOW LAMENT FOR ONE WHOLE WORLD . . 11 874
THAT GOD VOUTSAFES TO RAISE ANOTHER WORLD . . 11 877
SURPASS HIS BOUNDS, NOR RAIN TO DROWN THE WORLD . 11 894
BETWIXT THE WORLD DESTROY'D AND WORLD RESTOR'D, . 12 3
THUS THOU HAST SEEN ONE WORLD BEGIN AND END; . . 12 6
THUS WILL THIS LATTER, AS THE FORMER WORLD, . . 12 105
OF ABRAHAMS FAITH WHEREVER THROUGH THE WORLD; . 12 449
RARELY BE FOUND: SO SHALL THE WORLD GOE ON, . . 12 537
SATAN WITH HIS PERVERTED WORLD, THEN RAISE . . 12 547
MEASUR'D THIS TRANSIENT WORLD, THE RACE OF TIME, . 12 554
AND ALL THE RICHES OF THIS WORLD ENJOYDST, . . 12 580
THE WORLD WAS ALL BEFORE THEM, WHERE TO CHOOSE . 12 646

WORLDLIE
WORLDLIE OR DISSOLUTE, ON WHAT THIR LORDS 11 803

WORLDLY
SUBVERTING WORLDLY STRONG, AND WORLDLY WISE . . 12 568

WORLDS
SPACE MAY PRODUCE NEW WORLDS; WHEREOF SO RIFE . . 1 650
HIS DARK MATERIALS TO CREATE MORE WORLDS, . . . 2 916
DOWN RIGHT INTO THE WORLDS FIRST REGION THROWS . 3 562
STARS DISTANT, BUT NIGH HAND SEEMD OTHER WORLDS, . 3 566
OR OTHER WORLDS THEY SEEMD, OR HAPPY ILES, . . 3 567
WORLDS, AND ON WHOM HATH ALL THESE GRACES POWRD; . 3 674
THIS WORLDS MATERIAL MOULD, CAME TO A HEAP: . . 3 709
IN HONOUR TO THE WORLDS GREAT AUTHOR RISE, . . . 5 188
SAILES BETWEEN WORLDS AND WORLDS, WITH STEDDIE WING 5 268
TO STAND APPROV'D IN SIGHT OF GOD, THOUGH WORLDS . 6 36
HIS GOOD TO WORLDS AND AGES INFINITE. 7 191
AND SPIRIT COMING TO CREATE NEW WORLDS. 7 209
DREAM NOT OF OTHER WORLDS, WHAT CREATURES THERE . 8 175
IN OTHER WORLDS, AND HAPPIER SEAT PROVIDES . . . 10 237
THOUGH DISTANT FROM THEE WORLDS BETWEEN, YET FELT 10 362
OF FORREIN WORLDS: HE THROUGH THE MIDST UNMARKT, . 10 441
THROUGH THE WORLDS WILDERNESS LONG WANDERD MAN . 12 313
WHEN THIS WORLDS DISOLUTION SHALL BE RIPE, . . 12 459
AS AT THE WORLDS GREAT PERIOD; AND OUR SIRE . . 12 467

WORM
BEAST, BIRD, INSECT, OR WORM DURST ENTER NONE; . 4 704
TO CHAINS OF DARKNESS, AND TH' UNDYING WORM, . . 6 739
TO THAT FALSE WORM, OF WHOMSOEVER TAUGHT . . . 9 1068

WORME
INSECT OR WORME; THOSE WAV'D THIR LIMBER FANS . . 7 476

WORN
AND WORN WITH FAMIN, LONG AND CEASLESS HISS, . . 10 573
OF SARRA, WORN BY KINGS AND HERO'S OLD 11 243

WORS
WORS THEN CAN MAN WITH BEAST, AND LEAST OF ALL. . 8 397
WORS WITH HIS FOLLOWERS THEN WITH HIM THEY DEALT? 12 484

WORSE
IN ARMS NOT WORSE, IN FORESIGHT MUCH ADVANC'T, . 1 119
EXPOS'D A MATRON TO AVOID WORSE RAPE. 1 505
WENT ALL HIS FEAR: OF GOD, OR HELL, OR WORSE . . 2 49
OUR STRONGER, SOME WORSE WAY HIS WRATH MAY FIND . 2 83
FEAR TO BE WORSE DESTROY'D: WHAT CAN BE WORSE . 2 85
DROPT MANNA, AND COULD MAKE THE WORSE APPEAR . . 2 113
WHAT CAN WE SUFFER WORSE? IS THIS THEN WORST, . 2 163
CHAIN'D ON THE BURNING LAKE? THAT SURE WAS WORSE. 2 169
AGES OF HOPELESS END; THIS WOULD BE WORSE. . . 2 186
CHAINS AND THESE TORMENTS? BETTER THESE THEN WORSE 2 196
THEY DREADED WORSE THEN HELL: SO MUCH THE FEAR . 2 293
ABOMINABLE, INUTTERABLE, AND WORSE 2 626
CONFUSION WORSE CONFOUNDED; AND HEAV'N GATES . . 2 996
IF HIM BY FORCE HE CAN DESTROY, OR WORSE, . . . 3 91
WORSE; OF WORSE DEEDS WORSE SUFFERINGS MUST ENSUE. 4 26
TILL PRIDE AND WORSE AMBITION THREW ME DOWN . . 4 40
WHICH WOULD BUT LEAD ME TO A WORSE RELAPSE . . . 4 100
UNIVERSAL REPROACH, FAR WORSE TO BEARE 6 34

WORSE (CONTINUED)
MAY SERVE TO BETTER US, AND WORSE OUR FOES, . . 6 440
THEY WORSE ABHORR'D. SATAN BEHELD THIR PLIGHT, . 6 607
STROOK THEM WITH HORROR BACKWARD, BUT FAR WORSE . 6 863
FOR WHAT GOD AFTER BETTER WORSE WOULD BUILD? . . 9 102
BANE, AND IN HEAV'N MUCH WORSE WOULD BE MY STATE. 9 123
AS I, THOUGH THEREBY WORSE TO ME REDOUND: . . . 9 128
OR THIS, OR WORSE, LEAVE NOT THE FAITHFUL SIDE . 9 265
THOUGH THREAT'ND, WHICH NO WORSE THEN THIS CAN
BRING. 9 715
RAIND AT THIR EYES, BUT HIGH WINDS WORSE WITHIN . 9 1122
TO SORROW ABANDOND, BUT WORSE FELT WITHIN, . . . 10 717
WOULD THUNDER IN MY EARS, NO FEAR OF WORSE . . 10 780
BY A FARR WORSE, OR IF SHE LOVE, WITHHELD . . 10 903
MY BREAD; WHAT HARM? IDLENESS HAD BIN WORSE; . 10 1055
O UNEXPECTED STROKE, WORSE THEN OF DEATH. . . 11 268
THOSE WERE OF HATE AND DEATH, OR PAIN MUCH WORSE, 11 601
STILL TEND FROM BAD TO WORSE, TILL GOD AT LAST . 12 106

WORSHIP
ETERNITY SO SPENT IN WORSHIP PAID 2 248
WITH EVERY PLANT, IN SIGN OF WORSHIP WAVE. . . . 5 194
AND WORSHIP GOD SUPREAM, WHO MADE HIM CHIEF . . 7 515
AND WORSHIP HIM, AND IN REWARD TO RULE 7 628
AND JOIND THIR VOCAL WORSHIP TO THE QUIRE . . . 9 198
AND GAZE, AND WORSHIP THEE OF RIGHT DECLAR'D . . 9 611
WITH WORSHIP, PLACE BY PLACE WHERE HE VOUTSAF'D . 11 318
TO WORSHIP GOD ARIGHT, AND KNOW HIS WORKS . . 11 578
BRED UP IN IDOL-WORSHIP; O THAT MEN 12 115
TO WORSHIP THIR OWN WORK IN WOOD AND STONE . . 12 119
ON ALL WHO IN THE WORSHIP PERSEVERE 12 532

WORSHIPERS
WHERE HE FELL FLAT, AND SHAM'D HIS WORSHIPERS: . 1 461

WORSHIPPERS
THE NUMBER OF THY WORSHIPPERS. WHO SEEKES . . . 7 613
AND MULTIPLY A RACE OF WORSHIPPERS 7 630
HIS WORSHIPPERS; HE KNOWS THAT IN THE DAY . . . 9 705

WORSHIPT
WORSHIPT IN RABBA AND HER WATRY PLAIN, ... 1 397

WORST
IN WORST EXTREAMS, AND ON THE PERILOUS EDGE . . 1 276
AND CANNOT CEASE TO BE, WE ARE AT WORST 2 100
WHAT CAN WE SUFFER WORSE? IS THIS THEN WORST, . 2 163
FOR HAPPY THOUGH BUT ILL, FOR ILL NOT WORST, . . 2 224
TO WORST ABUSE, OR TO THIR MEANEST USE. . . . 4 204
THY REBELS, OR BE FOUND THE WORST IN HEAV'N. . . 5 742
BUT PAIN IS PERFET MISERIE, THE WORST 6 462
WHO GUARDS HER, OR WITH HER THE WORST ENDURES. . 9 269
THE WORST, AND NOT PERSWADE THEE RATHER DIE . . 9 979
WHOEVER JUDG'D, THE WORST ON MEE MUST LIGHT, . . 10 73

WORTH
TO REIGN IS WORTH AMBITION THOUGH IN HELL: . . . 1 262
AT THIR GREAT EMPERORS CALL, AS NEXT IN WORTH . . 1 378
SEMBLANCE OF WORTH, NOT SUBSTANCE, GENTLY RAIS'D . 1 529
WORTH WAITING, SINCE OUR PRESENT LOT APPEERS . . 2 223
FADED SO SOON. ADVISE IF THIS BE WORTH 2 376
CONSCIOUS OF HIGHEST WORTH, UNMOV'D THUS SPAKE. . 2 429
HASTE HITHER EVE, AND WORTH THY SIGHT BEHOLD . . 5 308
HER VERTUE AND THE CONSCIENCE OF HER WORTH, . . 8 502
HIM WHO TO WORTH IN WOMEN OVERTRUSTING 9 1183
OFFENDED, WORTH YOUR LAUGHTER, HATH GIV'N UP . . 10 488

WORTHIE
AND WORTHIE SEEMD, FOR IN THIR LOOKS DIVINE . . 4 291
ILL WORTHIE I SUCH TITLE SHOULD BELONG 11 163

WORTHIER
HAPPIER THOU MAYST BE, WORTHIER CANST NOT BE: . . 5 76
AGAINST HIS WORTHIER, AS THINE NOW SERVE THEE, . 6 180
MORE JUSTLY, SEAT WORTHIER OF GODS, AS BUILT . . 9 100

WORTHIEST
BY PLACE OR CHOICE THE WORTHIEST; THEY ANON . . 1 759
FOUND WORTHIEST TO BE SO BY BEING GOOD, ... 3 310
PLEASANT TO KNOW, AND WORTHIEST TO BE ALL . . . 3 703
WHEN HE WHO RULES IS WORTHIEST, AND EXCELLS . . 6 177
BEHESTS OBEY, WORTHIEST TO BE OBEY'D, . . . 6 185
TO MANIFEST THEE WORTHIEST TO BE HEIR 6 707
WORTHIEST TO REIGN: HE CELEBRATED RODE 6 888

WORTHILY
TO LOATHSOM SICKNESS, WORTHILY, SINCE THEY . . . 11 524

WORTHY
FLOURS WORTHY OF PARADISE WHICH NOT NICE ART . . 4 241
WORTHY OF SACRED SILENCE TO BE HEARD; 5 557
FOUND WORTHY NOT OF LIBERTIE ALONE, ... 6 420
AN OUTSIDE? FAIR NO DOUBT, AND WORTHY WELL . . 8 568
THEREIN ENJOY'D WERE WORTHY TO SUBDUE 8 584
THOUGH KEPT FROM MAN, AND WORTHY TO BE ADMIR'D, . 9 746
IN TIME OF DEARTH, A SON WHOSE WORTHY DEEDS . . 12 161

WOUND
WHOSE ANNUAL WOUND IN LEBANON ALLUR'D 1 447
OP'ND INTO THE HILL A SPACIOUS WOUND 1 689
DEATH HIS DEATHS WOUND SHALL THEN RECEIVE, AND STOOP 3 252
THE GRIDING SWORD WITH DISCONTINUOUS WOUND . . . 6 329
NOR IN THIR LIQUID TEXTURE MORTAL WOUND 6 348
BY WOUND, THOUGH FROM THIR PLACE BY VIOLENCE MOV'D, 6 405
IMPERISHABLE, AND THOUGH PEIRC'D WITH WOUND, . . 6 435
AND LIFE-BLOOD STREAMING FRESH; WIDE WAS THE WOUND, 8 467
FOE NOT INFORMIDABLE, EXEMPT FROM WOUND, . . . 9 486
ABOUT THE MOSSIE TRUNK I WOUND ME SOON, ... 9 589
EARTH FELT THE WOUND, AND NATURE FROM HER SEAT . 9 782
THY MESSAGE, WHICH MIGHT ELSE IN TELLING WOUND, . 11 299
DISABL'D NOT TO GIVE THEE THY DEATHS WOUND: . . 12 392

WOUNDED
OF THAMMUZ YEARLY WOUNDED: THE LOVE-TALE 1 452

WOUNDS
A REFUGE FROM THOSE WOUNDS: OR WHEN WE LAY . . . 2 168
WHERE WOUNDS OF DEADLY HATE HAVE PEIRC'D SO DEEP: 4 99
MANGL'D WITH GASTLY WOUNDS THROUGH PLATE AND MAILE, 6 368
OF EGYPT MUST LIE DEAD. THUS WITH TEN WOUNDS . . 12 190
AS OF A DUEL, OR THE LOCAL WOUNDS 12 387

WOVE
INSINUATING, WOVE WITH GORDIAN TWINE 4 348
WAITING DESIROUS HER RETURN, HAD WOVE 9 839

WOV'N
AMONG THICK-WOV'N ARBORETS AND FLOURS 9 437

WRACK
HAD GON TO WRACK, WITH RUIN OVERSPRED, ... 6 670

WRAPT
UNDER YON BOYLING OCEAN, WRAPT IN CHAINS; . . . 2 183
I DREAD, AND TO ELUDE, THUS WRAPT IN MIST . . . 9 158

WRATH
RESERV'D HIM TO MORE WRATH; FOR NOW THE THOUGHT . 1 54
THAT GLORY NEVER SHALL HIS WRATH OR MIGHT . . . 1 110
TREBLE CONFUSION, WRATH AND VENGEANCE POUR'D. . . 1 220
OUR STRONGER, SOME WORSE WAY HIS WRATH MAY FIND . 2 83
WHAT E'RE HIS WRATH, WHICH HE CALLS JUSTICE, BIDS, 2 733
HIS WRATH WHICH ONE DAY WILL DESTROY YE BOTH. . . 2 734
WRATH WITHOUT END ON MAN WHOM DEATH MUST END? . . 10 797

WRAUGHT
NOW NOT, THOUGH SIN, NOT TIME, FIRST WRAUGHT THE CHANGE, ... 9 70
THEY FASTEN'D, AND THE MOLE IMMENSE WRAUGHT ON . 10 300
ACKNOWLEDG'D AND DEPLOR'D, IN ADAM WRAUGHT . . . 10 939

WRAUTH
TO WHOM THE GOBLIN FULL OF WRAUTH REPLY'D, . . . 2 688
AND RECONCILEMENT; WRAUTH SHALL BE NO MORE . . . 3 264
FOUND OUT FOR MANKIND UNDER WRAUTH, O THOU . . . 3 275
HE TO APPEASE THY WRAUTH, AND END THE STRIFE . . 3 406
INFINITE WRAUTH, AND INFINITE DESPAIRE? 4 74
SO JUDGE THOU STILL, PRESUMPTUOUS, TILL THE WRAUTH, 4 912
THESE WICKED TENTS DEVOTED, LEAST THE WRAUTH . . 5 890
OF WRAUTH AWAK'T: NOR WITH LESS DREAD THE LOUD . 6 59
AND FULL OF WRAUTH BENT ON HIS ENEMIES. 6 826
DOWN FROM THE VERGE OF HEAV'N, ETERNAL WRAUTH . . 6 865
NOT LESS BUT MORE HEROIC THEN THE WRAUTH . . . 9 14
THE EEVNING COOLE WHEN HE FROM WRAUTH MORE COOLE . 10 95
THE PRESENT, FEARING GUILTIE WHAT HIS WRAUTH . . 10 340
IS HIS WRAUTH ALSO? BE IT, MAN IS NOT SO, . . . 10 795
SO MIGHT THE WRAUTH. FOND WISH. COULDST THOU SUPPORT 10 834
HIS FULL WRAUTH WHOSE THOU FEELST AS YET LEST PART, 10 951
WITHOUT WRAUTH OR REVILING; WEE EXPECTED . . . 10 1048
AND FULL OF PEACE, DENOUNCING WRAUTH TO COME . . 11 815
FROM GOD, AND OVER WRAUTH GRACE SHALL ABOUND. . . 12 478

WREATH
CURLD MANY A WANTON WREATH IN SIGHT OF EVE, . . . 9 517

WREATH'D
FROM HIS SLACK HAND THE GARLAND WREATH'D FOR EVE . 9 892

WREATHD
TO MAKE THEM MIRTH US'D ALL HIS MIGHT, AND WREATHD 4 346

WREATHES
IN DUSKIE WREATHES, RELUCTANT FLAMES, THE SIGNE . 6 58

WRECK
WELL PLEAS'D, ON ME LET DEATH WRECK ALL HIS RAGE; 3 241
TO WRECK ON INNOCENT FRAIL MAN HIS LOSS 4 11

WRESTED
TO BE THUS WRESTED FROM US? RATHER WHY 11 503

WRETCHED
THAT AFTER WRETCHED LIFE MUST BE AT LAST . . . 10 985

WRETCHED (CONTINUED)
DEGRADED, TO WHAT WRETCHED STATE RESERV'D. . . . 11 501
SIEGE AND DEFIANCE: WRETCHED MAN, WHAT FOOD . . 12 74

WRINKL'D
WRINKL'D THE FACE OF DELUGE, AS DECAI'D; . . . 11 843

WRITE
FARR BE IT, THAT I SHOULD WRITE THEE SIN OR BLAME, 4 758
WORKING THROUGH LOVE, UPON THIR HEARTS SHALL WRITE, 12 489

WRITH'D
AND WRITH'D HIM TO AND FRO CONVOLV'D; SO SORE . . 6 328
WITH HATEFULLEST DISRELISH WRITH'D THIR JAWS . . 10 569

WRITTEN
THIR DOCTRINE AND THIR STORY WRITTEN LEFT, . . . 12 506
LEFT ONELY IN THOSE WRITTEN RECORDS PURE, . . . 12 513

WRONG
ON YOU WHO WRONG ME NOT FOR HIM WHO WRONGD. . . 4 387
AND ANGER WOULDST RESENT THE OFFER'D WRONG, . . 9 300
TO MAN, AND INDIGNATION AT HIS WRONG, ... 9 666
IN WISE DEPORT, SPAKE MUCH OF RIGHT AND WRONG, . 11 666
FROM VERTUE, WHICH IS REASON, THAT NO WRONG, . . 12 98

WRONGD
ON YOU WHO WRONG ME NOT FOR HIM WHO WRONGD. . . 4 387

WROUGHT
WHICH TEMPTED OUR ATTEMPT, AND WROUGHT OUR FALL. . 1 642
WROUGHT STILL WITHIN THEM; AND NO LESS DESIRE . . 2 295
AND WROUGHT BUT MALICE; LIFTED UP SO HIGH . . . 4 49
REAR'D HIGH THIR FLOURISHT HEADS BETWEEN, AND WROUGHT 4 699
NOR NUMBER, NOR EXAMPLE WITH HIM WROUGHT . . . 5 901
INTO THIR SUBSTANCE PENT, WHICH WROUGHT THEM PAIN 6 657
SAVE WHAT SIN HATH IMPAIRD, WHICH YET HATH WROUGHT 6 691
OF RADIANT URIM, WORK DIVINELY WROUGHT, ... 6 761
WROUGHT IN HER SO, THAT SEEING ME, SHE TURN'D; . 8 507
AS WHEN A SHIP BY SKILFUL STEARSMAN WROUGHT . . 9 513
TO EVILS WHICH OUR OWN MISDEEDS HAVE WROUGHT, . . 10 1080
FOR DISSOLUTION WROUGHT BY SIN, THAT FIRST . . . 11 55
TH' EFFECTS WHICH THY ORIGINAL CRIME HATH WROUGHT 11 424
FIRST HIS OWN TOOLES; THEN, WHAT MIGHT ELSE BE WROUGHT 11 572

XERXES
XERXES, THE LIBERTIE OF GREECE TO YOKE, ... 10 307

YAWNING
YAWNING RECEAVD THEM WHOLE, AND ON THEM CLOS'D, . 6 875
BOTH SIN, AND DEATH, AND YAWNING GRAVE AT LAST . 10 635

YEA
BETWEEN THE CHERUBIM; YEA, OFTEN PLAC'D 1 387
IN NARROW ROOM NATURES WHOLE WEALTH, YEA MORE, . 4 207

YEANLING
TO GORGE THE FLESH OF LAMBS OR YEANLING KIDS . . 3 434

YEAR
TUNES HER NOCTURNAL NOTE. THUS WITH THE YEAR . . 3 40
AS HEAV'NS GREAT YEAR BRINGS FORTH, TH' EMPYREAL HOST 5 583

YEARES
HIS SEASONS, HOURS, OR DAYES, OR MONTHS, OR YEARES: 8 69

YEARLY
OF THAMMUZ YEARLY WOUNDED: THE LOVE-TALE . . . 1 452
YEARLY ENJOYND, SOME SAY, TO UNDERGO 10 575

YEARS
DAYS, MONTHS, & YEARS, TOWARDS HIS ALL-CHEARING LAMP 3 581
FOR SEASONS, AND FOR DAYES, AND CIRCLING YEARS, . 7 342
CLIMAT, OR YEARS DAMP MY INTENDED WING 9 45
TILL MANY YEARS OVER THY HEAD RETURN: 11 534
THE SPACE OF SEVENTIE YEARS, THEN BRINGS THEM BACK, 12 345

YEELD
TO BETTER LIFE SHALL YEELD HIM, WHERE WITH MEE . 11 42

YEELDED
RATHER HOW HAST THOU YEELDED TO TRANSGRESS . . . 9 902

YEELDS
INNUMERABLE, AND THIS WHICH YEELDS OR FILLS . . 7 88

YEILD
MAY HOPE WHEN EVERLASTING FATE SHALL YEILD . . . 2 232
YEILD THEE, SO WELL THIS DAY THOU HAST PURVEY'D. . 9 1021

YEILDED
WITH NAPHTHA AND ASPHALTUS YEILDED LIGHT . . . 1 729

YELLING
THESE YELLING MONSTERS THAT WITH CEASLESS CRY 2 795

YELLOW
FIRST FRUITS, THE GREEN EARE, AND THE YELLOW SHEAF, 11 435

YESTERDAY
OF YESTERDAY, SO LATE HATH PAST THE LIPS 5 675

YET
THINGS UNATTEMPTED YET IN PROSE OR RHIME. 1 16
AS ONE GREAT FURNACE FLAM'D, YET FROM THOSE FLAMES 1 62
THE FORCE OF THOSE DIRE ARMS? YET NOT FOR THOSE, 1 94
WHAT CAN IT THEN AVAIL THOUGH YET WE FEEL 1 153
WITH RALLIED ARMS TO TRY WHAT MAY BE YET 1 269
YET TO THIR GENERALS VOYCE THEY SOON OBEYD 1 337
NOR HAD THEY YET AMONG THE SONS OF EVE 1 364
WHILE THE PROMISCUOUS CROUD STOOD YET ALOOF? 1 380
YET THENCE HIS LUSTFUL ORGIES HE ENLARG'D 1 415
AND DOWNWARD FISH: YET HAD HIS TEMPLE HIGH 1 463
OR ALTAR SMOAK'D; YET WHO MORE OFT THEN HEE 1 493
GODS, YET CONFEST LATER THEN HEAV'N AND EARTH 1 509
DOWN CAST AND DAMP, YET SUCH WHEREIN APPEAR'D 1 523
COMPARE OF MORTAL PROWESS, YET OBSERV'D 1 588
STOOD LIKE A TOWR; HIS FORM HAD YET NOT LOST 1 591
PERPLEXES MONARCHS. DARK'N'D SO, YET SHON 1 599
FOR HIS REVOLT, YET FAITHFULL HOW THEY STOOD, 1 611
FOR WHO CAN YET BELEEVE, THOUGH AFTER LOSS, 1 631
HATH BIN ACHIEVD OF MERIT, YET THIS LOSS 2 21
WHICH IF NOT VICTORY IS YET REVENGE. 2 105
TIMOROUS AND SLOTHFUL: YET HE PLEAS'D THE EAR, 2 117
HEAV'NS PUREST LIGHT, YET OUR GREAT ENEMY 2 137
WHAT YET THEY KNOW MUST FOLLOW, TO ENDURE 2 206
AND PRINCELY COUNSEL IN HIS FACE YET SHON, 2 304
IRREPARABLE; TEARMS OF PEACE YET NONE 2 331
YET EVER PLOTTING HOW THE CONQUEROR LEAST 2 338
YET LIVE IN HATRED, ENMITY, AND STRIFE 2 500
YET WITH A PLEASING SORCERIE COULD CHARM 2 566
THAN FABLES YET HAVE FEIGN'D, OR FEAR CONCEIV'D, 2 627
YET UNCONSUM'D. BEFORE THE GATES THERE SAT 2 648
A HIDEOUS PEAL: YET, WHEN THEY LIST, WOULD CREEP, 2 656
AND KENNEL THERE, YET THERE STILL BARK'D AND HOWL'D, 2 658
PREVENTED SPARES TO TELL THEE YET BY DEEDS 2 739
OR DIM SUFFUSION VEILD. YET NOT THE MORE 3 26
OUR TWO FIRST PARENTS, YET THE ONELY TWO 3 65
HEAPT ON HIM THERE, NOR YET THE MAIN ABYSS 3 83
YET WITH REVENGE ACCOMPLISH'T AND TO HELL 3 160
YET NOT OF WILL IN HIM, BUT GRACE IN ME 3 174
UPHELD BY ME, YET ONCE MORE HE SHALL STAND 3 178
BUT YET ALL IS NOT DON; MAN DISOBEYING, 3 203
ALL THAT OF ME CAN DIE, YET THAT DEBT PAID, 3 246
SILENT YET SPAKE, AND BREATH'D IMMORTAL LOVE 3 267
YET DAZLE HEAV'N, THAT BRIGHTEST SERAPHIM 3 381
NONE YET, BUT STORE HEREAFTER FROM THE EARTH 3 444
THROUGH HIS GLAZ'D OPTIC TUBE YET NEVER SAW. 3 590
NOT OF THE PRIME, YET SUCH AS IN HIS FACE 3 637
YET NOT REJOYCING IN HIS SPEED, THOUGH BOLD, 4 13
HOW DUE. YET ALL HIS GOOD PROV'D ILL IN ME, 4 48
AMBITION. YET WHY NOT? SOM OTHER POWER 4 61
YET NOT ANOUGH HAD PRACTISD TO DECEIVE 4 124
OF STATELIEST VIEW. YET HIGHER THEN THIR TOPS 4 142
SAT LIKE A CORMORANT; YET NOT TRUE LIFE 4 196
NOT SPIRITS, YET TO HEAV'NLY SPIRITS BRIGHT 4 361
AS NOW IS ENTERD; YET NO PURPOS'D FOE 4 373
LIKE THIS FAIR PARADISE, YOUR SENSE, YET SUCH 4 379
MELT, AS I DOE, YET PUBLIC REASON JUST, 4 389
WHICH WERE IT TOILSOM, YET WITH THEE WERE SWEET. 4 439
UNDER A PLATAN, YET METHOUGHT LESS FAIRE, 4 478
FOR ENVIE, YET WITH JEALOUS LEER MALIGNE 4 503
YET LET ME NOT FORGET WHAT I HAVE GAIN'D 4 512
YET HAPPIE PAIR; ENJOY, TILL I RETURN, 4 534
IN ORDER, THOUGH TO NATIONS YET UNBORN, 4 663
BLEST PAIR; AND O YET HAPPIEST IF YE SEEK 4 774
YET THUS, UNMOVD WITH FEAR, ACCOST HIM SOON. 4 822
HIS LUSTRE VISIBLY IMPAR'D; YET SEEMD 4 850
WHICH TAUGHT THEE YET NO BETTER, THAT NO PAIN 4 915
HUNG FORTH IN HEAV'N HIS GOLDEN SCALES, YET SEEN 4 997
FOR GOD'S, YET ABLE TO MAKE GODS OF MEN: 5 70
YET EVIL WHENCE? IN THEE CAN HARBOUR NONE, 5 99
BUT WITH ADDITION STRANGE; YET BE NOT SAD. 5 116
WITH WHEELS YET HOV'RING O'RE THE OCEAN BRIM, 5 140
IN THESE THY LOWEST WORKS, YET THESE DECLARE 5 158
YET MUTABLE; WHENCE WARNE HIM TO BEWARE 5 237
YET WITH SUBMISS APPROACH AND REVERENCE MEEK, 5 359
TWO ONELY, WHO YET BY SOV'RAN GIFT POSSESS 5 366
VAPOURS NOT YET INTO HER SUBSTANCE TURND. 5 420
COVER'D WITH PEARLY GRAIN: YET GOD HATH HERE 5 430
FOOD NOT OF ANGELS, YET ACCEPTED SO, 5 465
AT HEAV'NS HIGH FEASTS TO HAVE FED: YET WHAT COMPARE? 5 467
YET THAT WE NEVER SHALL FORGET TO LOVE 5 550
SINGLE, IS YET SO JUST, MY CONSTANT THOUGHTS 5 552
AND WE HAVE YET LARGE DAY, FOR SCARCE THE SUN 5 558
NOT LAWFUL TO REVEAL? YET FOR THY GOOD 5 570
AS YET THIS WORLD WAS NOT, AND CHAOS WILDE 5 577
ECCENTRIC, INTERVOLV'D, YET REGULAR 5 623
IN FAVOUR AND PRAEEMINENCE, YET FRAUGHT 5 661

YET (CONTINUED)
TELL THEM THAT BY COMMAND, ERE YET DIM NIGHT 5 685
IF THESE MAGNIFIC TITLES YET REMAIN 5 773
KNEE-TRIBUTE YET UNPAID, PROSTRATION VILE, 5 782
BY NONE, AND IF NOT EQUAL ALL, YET FREE, 5 791
YET BY EXPERIENCE TAUGHT WE KNOW HOW GOOD, 5 826
YET NOT FOR THY ADVISE OR THREATS I FLY 5 889
THAT OF SO MANY MYRIADS FALL'N, YET ONE 6 24
SHOULD YET REMAIN, WHERE FAITH AND REALTIE 6 115
WHEN REASON HATH TO DEAL WITH FORCE, YET SO 6 125
YET LEUDLY DAR'ST OUR MINISTRING UPBRAID. 6 182
YET CHAINS IN HELL, NOT REALMS EXPECT: MEAN WHILE 6 186
A LEGION; LED IN FIGHT, YET LEADER SEEMD 6 232
OF AIRIE THREATS TO AW WHOM YET WITH DEEDS 6 283
YET SOON HE HEAL'D; FOR SPIRITS THAT LIVE THROUGHOUT 6 344
NOR OF RENOWN LESS EAGER, YET BY DOOME 6 378
AND IGNOMINIE, YET TO GLORIE ASPIRES 6 383
ENJOYMENT OF OUR RIGHT AS GODS; YET HARD 6 452
OUR YET UNWOUNDED ENEMIES, OR ARME 6 466
NOR LONG SHALL BE OUR LABOUR, YET ERE DAWNE, 6 492
ONCE FOUND, WHICH YET UNFOUND MOST WOULD HAVE THOUGHT 6 500
IMPOSSIBLE: YET HAPLY OF THY RACE 6 501
DOUBL'D, WOULD RENDER THEM YET MORE DESPIS'D, 6 602
AS THEY WOULD DANCE, YET FOR A DANCE THEY SEEMD 6 615
SAVE WHAT SIN HATH IMPAIRD, WHICH YET HATH WROUGHT 6 691
YET ENVIED; AGAINST MEE IS ALL THIR RAGE, 6 813
YET HALF HIS STRENGTH HE PUT NOT FORTH, BUT CHECK'D 6 853
YET FELL; REMEMBER, AND FEAR TO TRANSGRESS. 6 912
HALF YET REMAINES UNSUNG BUT NARROWER BOUND 7 21
AND SOLITUDE; YET NOT ALONE, WHILE THOU 7 28
LED ON, YET SINLESS, WITH DESIRE TO KNOW 7 61
YET SCARCE ALLAY'D STILL EYES THE CURRENT STREAME, 7 67
THINGS ABOVE EARTHLY THOUGHT, WHICH YET CONCERND 7 82
AND THE GREAT LIGHT OF DAY YET WANTS TO RUN 7 98
YET WHAT THOU CANST ATTAIN, WHICH BEST MAY SERVE 7 115
YET FARR THE GREATER PART HAVE KEPT, I SEE, 7 145
THIR STATION, HEAV'N YET POPULOUS RETAINES 7 146
SPHEAR'D IN A RADIANT CLOUD, FOR YET THE SUN 7 247
THE EARTH WAS FORM'D, BUT IN THE WOMB AS YET 7 276
HER SACRED SHADES: THOUGH GOD HAD YET NOT RAIN'D 7 331
HER STATE WITH OARIE FEET: YET OFT THEY QUIT 7 440
FREQUENT; AND OF THE SIXT DAY YET REMAIN'D; 7 504
THERE WANTED YET THE MASTER WORK, THE END 7 505
OF ALL YET DON; A CREATURE WHO NOT PRONE 7 506
IS YET DISTINCT BY NAME, THENCE, AS THOU KNOW'ST 7 536
YET NOT TILL THE CREATOR FROM HIS WORK 7 551
INVISIBLE, YET STAID (SUCH PRIVILEDGE 7 589
CREATOR; SOMETHING YET OF DOUBT REMAINES, 8 13
YET WENT SHE NOT, AS NOT WITH SUCH DISCOURSE 8 48
YET NOT TO EARTH ARE THOSE BRIGHT LUMINARIES 8 98
ONELY TO SHINE, YET SCARCE TO CONTRIBUTE 8 155
AND DAY IS YET NOT SPENT; TILL THEN THOU SEEST 8 206
MY FANCY TO BELIEVE I YET HAD BEING, 8 294
YET DREADFUL IN MINE EARE, THOUGH IN MY CHOICE 8 335
SOCIAL COMMUNICATION, YET SO PLEAS'D, 8 429
YET INNOCENCE AND VIRGIN MODESTIE, 8 501
O'RE OTHER CREATURES; YET WHEN I APPROACH 8 546
YET THESE SUBJECT NOT; I TO THEE DISCLOSE 8 607
VARIOUSLY REPRESENTING; YET STILL FREE 8 610
DEATHS HARBINGER: SAD TASK, YET ARGUMENT 9 13
THAT SHINE, YET BEAR THIR BRIGHT OFFICIOUS LAMPS, 9 104
IS CENTER, YET EXTENDS TO ALL, SO THOU 9 108
NOT YET IN HORRID SHADE OR DISMAL DEN, 9 185
NOR NOCENT YET, BUT ON THE GRASSIE HERBE 9 186
YET NOT SO STRICTLY HATH OUR LORD IMPOS'D 9 235
THE DANGER LIES, YET LIES WITHIN HIS POWER: 9 349
FIRM WE SUBSIST, YET POSSIBLE TO SWERVE, 9 359
PERSISTED, YET SUBMISS, THOUGH LAST, REPLI'D. 9 377
BUT WITH SUCH GARDNING TOOLS AS ART YET RUDE, 9 391
YET VIRGIN OF PROSERPINA FROM JOVE. 9 396
YET MORE AMAZ'D UNWARIE THUS REPLY'D. 9 614
IN PARADISE, AND VARIOUS, YET UNKNOWN 9 619
YET LORDS DECLAR'D OF ALL IN EARTH OR AIRE? 9 658
TO WHOM THUS EVE YET SINLESS. OF THE FRUIT 9 659
FLUCTUATS DISTURBD, YET COMELY AND IN ACT 9 668
MEE WHO HAVE TOUCH'D AND TASTED, YET BOTH LIVE, 9 688
YET ARE BUT DIM, SHALL PERFETLY BE THEN 9 707
YET RUNG OF HIS PERSWASIVE WORDS, IMPREGN'D 9 737
SOLLICITED HER LONGING EYE; YET FIRST 9 743
AND YET UNKNOWN, IS AS NOT HAD AT ALL. 9 757
FOR BEASTS IT SEEMS; YET THAT ONE BEAST WHICH FIRST 9 769
AS YET MY CHANGE, AND GIVE HIM TO PARTAKE 9 818
YET OFT HIS HEART, DIVINE OF SOMTHING ILL, 9 845
OF ENEMIE HATH BEGUIL'D THEE, YET UNKNOWN, 9 905
ANOTHER RIB AFFORD, YET LOSS OF THEE 9 912
NOT GOD OMNIPOTENT, NOR FATE, YET SO 9 927
NOR YET ON HIM FOUND DEADLY, HE YET LIVES, 9 932
CREATION COULD REPEATE, YET WOULD BE LOATH 9 946
YET WILLINGLY CHOSE RATHER DEATH WITH THEE: 9 1167
THAT TIME CELESTIAL VISAGES, YET MIXT 10 24
BECAUSE NOT YET INFLICTED, AS HE FEAR'D, 10 51
ON ME DERIV'D, YET I SHALL TEMPER SO 10 77
DEVOLV'D; THOUGH SHOULD I HOLD MY PEACE, YET THOU 10 135
CONFESSING SOON, YET NOT BEFORE HER JUDGE 10 160
NOR ALTER'D HIS OFFENCE; YET GOD AT LAST 10 171
ADVENTROUS WORK, YET TO THY POWER AND MINE 10 255

YET (CONTINUED)

THOUGH DISTANT FROM THEE WORLDS BETWEEN, YET FELT 10 362
WHERE ALL YET LEFT OF THAT REVOLTED ROUT 10 534
YET PARCHT WITH SCALDING THURST AND HUNGER FIERCE, 10 556
AND OPS, ERE YET DICTAEAN JOVE WAS BORN. 10 584
CLOSE FOLLOWING PACE FOR PACE, NOT MOUNTED YET 10 589
OF HAPPINESS: YET WELL, IF HERE WOULD END 10 725
THY JUSTICE SEEMS; YET TO SAY TRUTH, TOO LATE, 10 755
THAT PROUD EXCUSE? YET HIM NOT THY ELECTION, 10 764
WITH CRUEL EXPECTATION. YET ONE DOUBT 10 782
HORRID, IF TRUE. YET WHY? IT WAS BUT BREATH 10 789
WHILE YET WE LIVE, SCARSE ONE SHORT HOUR PERHAPS, 10 923
HIS FULL WRAUTH WHOSE THOU FEELST AS YET LEST PART, 10 951
OR END, THOUGH SHARP AND SAD, YET TOLERABLE, 10 977
IT LIES, YET ERE CONCEPTION TO PREVENT 10 987
THE RACE UNBLEST, TO BEING YET UNBEGOT. 10 988
THEN LOUDEST ORATORIE: YET THIR PORT 11 8
IN FABLES OLD, LESS ANCIENT YET THEN THESE, 11 11
PERPETUAL BANISHMENT. YET LEAST THEY FAINT 11 108
SO SEND THEM FORTH, THOUGH SORROWING, YET IN PEACE: 11 117
OUT OF DESPAIRE, JOY, BUT WITH FEAR YET LINKT; 11 139
HARD TO BELIEF MAY SEEM; YET THIS WILL PRAYER, 11 146
WHICH THEN NOT MINDED IN DISMAY, YET NOW 11 156
INVESTS HIM COMING? YET NOT TERRIBLE, 11 233
YET ALL HAD HEARD, WITH AUDIBLE LAMENT 11 266
FOR THOUGH I FLED HIM ANGRIE, YET RECALL'D 11 330
YET DOUBT NOT BUT IN VALLIE AND IN PLAINE 11 349
OF ATABALIPA, AND YET UNSPOIL'D 11 409
NOR SINN'D THY SIN, YET FROM THAT DERIVE 11 427
TO HIS GRIM CAVE, ALL DISMAL; YET TO SENSE 11 469
BUT IS THERE YET NO OTHER WAY, BESIDES 11 527
YET THEY A BEAUTEOUS OFSPRING SHALL BEGET; 11 613
YET EMPTY OF ALL GOOD WHEREIN CONSISTS 11 616
CORRUPTING EACH THIR WAY; YET THOSE REMOOV'D, 11 889
MUCH THOU HAST YET TO SEE, BUT I PERCEAVE 12 8
THIS SECOND SOURS OF MEN, WHILE YET BUT FEW; 12 13
RATIONAL LIBERTIE; YET KNOW WITHALL, 12 82
YET SOMTIMES NATIONS WILL DECLINE SO LOW 12 97
HIM ON THIS SIDE EUPHRATES YET RESIDING, 12 114
WHILE YET THE PATRIARK LIV'D, WHO SCAP'D THE FLOOD, 12 117
FOR GODS. YET HIM GOD THE MOST HIGH VOUTSAFES 12 120
NOT KNOWING TO WHAT LAND, YET FIRM BELIEVES: 12 127
(THINGS BY THIR NAMES I CALL, THOUGH YET UNNAM'D) 12 140
THIS YET I APPREHEND NOT, WHY TO THOSE 12 280
BARR'D OF HIS RIGHT; YET AT HIS BIRTH A STARR 12 360
HIGH IN THE LOVE OF HEAV'N, YET FROM MY LOYNES 12 380
INFALLIBLE? YET MANY WILL PRESUME: 12 530
WITH CAUSE FOR EVILS PAST, YET MUCH MORE CHEER'D 12 604
THIS FURTHER CONSOLATION YET SECURE 12 620

YIELD

AND COURAGE NEVER TO SUBMIT OR YIELD: 1 108
OR SATIATE FURY YIELD IT FROM OUR FOE. 1 179
MIGHT YIELD THEM EASIER HABITATION, BEND 2 573
THOUGH NOW TO DEATH I YIELD, AND AM HIS DUE 3 245
THE EARTH TO YIELD; UNSAVOURIE FOOD PERHAPS 5 401
YIELD NECTAR, THOUGH FROM OFF THE BOUGHS EACH MORN 5 428
SHALL YIELD US PREGNANT WITH INFERNAL FLAME, 6 483
AND TO REALITIES YIELD ALL HER SHOWS: 8 575
THEE SATIATE, TO SHORT ABSENCE I COULD YIELD. 9 248
I YIELD IT JUST, SAID ADAM, AND SUBMIT. 11 526
SHALL YIELD UP ALL THIR VERTUE, ALL THIR FAME 11 623

YIELDED

YIELDED WITH FULL CONSENT. THE HAPPIER STATE 2 24
AND BY HER YIELDED, BY HIM BEST RECEIVD, 4 309
YIELDED WITH COY SUBMISSION, MODEST PRIDE, 4 310
YIELDED THEM, SIDE-LONG AS THEY SAT RECLINE 4 333
SEISD MINE, I YIELDED, AND FROM THAT TIME SEE 4 489
AT RANDOM YIELDED UP TO THEIR MISRULE; 10 628

YIELDING

PUT FORTH THE VERDANT GRASS, HERB YIELDING SEED, 7 310
AND FRUIT TREE YIELDING FRUIT AFTER HER KIND; 7 311

YIELDS

THE COOL, THE SILENT, SAVE WHERE SILENCE YIELDS 5 39
WHATEVER EARTH ALL-BEARING MOTHER YIELDS 5 338
GAVE THEE, ALL SORTS ARE HERE THAT ALL TH' EARTH YIELDS, 7 541

YOAK

US'D TO THE YOAK, DRAW'ST HIS TRIUMPHANT WHEELS 4 975

YOKE

HARD LIBERTY BEFORE THE EASIE YOKE 2 256
OUR MINDS AND TEACH US TO CAST OFF THIS YOKE? 5 786
NO MORE BE TROUBL'D HOW TO QUIT THE YOKE 5 882
XERXES, THE LIBERTIE OF GREECE TO YOKE, 10 307
RELUCTANCE AGAINST GOD AND HIS JUST YOKE 10 1045

YON

SEEST THOU YON DREARY PLAIN, FORLORN AND WILDE, 1 180
GROVELING AND PROSTRATE ON YON LAKE OF FIRE, 1 280
UNDER YON BOYLING OCEAN, WRAPT IN CHAINS; 2 183

YON (CONTINUED)

YON FLOURIE ARBORS, YONDER ALLIES GREEN, 4 626
AND READ THY LOT IN YON CELESTIAL SIGN 4 1011
MORE ORIENT IN YON WESTERN CLOUD THAT DRAWS 11 205

YONDER

TO YONDER GATES? THROUGH THEM I MEAN TO PASS, 2 684
YON FLOURIE ARBORS, YONDER ALLIES GREEN, 4 626
THIS SPACIOUS GROUND, IN YONDER SHADIE BOWRE 5 367
MYSTICAL DANCE, WHICH YONDER STARRIE SPHEARE 5 620
IN YONDER SPRING OF ROSES INTERMIXT 9 218
TO WASTE AND HAVOC YONDER WORLD, WHICH I 10 617
FROM YONDER BLAZING CLOUD THAT VEILS THE HILL 11 229
IN YONDER NETHER WORLD WHERE SHALL I SEEK 11 328
MOUNT HERMON, YONDER SEA, EACH PLACE BEHOLD 12 142
BY MEE ENCAMPT ON YONDER HILL, EXPECT 12 591

YONGER

HE COMES INVITED BY A YONGER SON 12 160

YOUNG

YOUNG BACCHUS FROM HIS STEPDAME RHEA'S EYE; 4 279
THIR CALLOW YOUNG, BUT FEATHERD SOON AND FLEDGE 7 420
AND JUDGMENT FROM ABOVE: HIM OLD AND YOUNG 11 668

YOUNGER

BY YOUNGER SATURN, HE FROM MIGHTIER JOVE 1 512
AS WE NEED WALK, TILL YOUNGER HANDS ERE LONG 9 246

YOUNGEST

THY CREATURE LATE SO LOV'D, THY YOUNGEST SON 3 151

YOUTH

POUR FORTH THIR POPULOUS YOUTH ABOUT THE HIVE 1 770
YOUTH SMIL'D CELESTIAL, AND TO EVERY LIMB 3 638
TH' UNARMED YOUTH OF HEAV'N, BUT NIGH AT HAND 4 552
IN MANHOOD WHERE YOUTH ENDED; BY HIS SIDE 11 246
THY YOUTH, THY STRENGTH, THY BEAUTY, WHICH WILL CHANGE 11 539
TO WHAT THOU HAST, AND FOR THE AIRE OF YOUTH 11 542
OF LOVE AND YOUTH NOT LOST, SONGS, GARLANDS, FLOURS, 11 594

YOUTHFUL

WANTED, NOR YOUTHFUL DALLIANCE AS BESEEMS 4 338
SEVERE IN YOUTHFUL BEAUTIE, ADDED GRACE 4 845
OR AS THE SNAKE WITH YOUTHFUL COATE REPAID; 10 218

ZEAL

OR CLOS AMBITION VARNISHT O'RE WITH ZEAL. 2 485
OF PAINFUL SUPERSTITION AND BLIND ZEAL, 3 452
OF PREFACE BROOKING THROUGH HIS ZEAL OF RIGHT. 9 676

ZEALE

HOLY MEMORIALS, ACTS OF ZEALE AND LOVE 5 593
ABDIEL, THEN WHOM NONE WITH MORE ZEALE ADOR'D 5 805
STOOD UP, AND IN A FLAME OF ZEALE SEVERE 5 807
SO SPAKE THE FERVENT ANGEL, BUT HIS ZEALE 5 849
HIS LOYALTIE HE KEPT, HIS LOVE, HIS ZEALE; 5 900
THE TEMPTER, BUT WITH SHEW OF ZEALE AND LOVE 9 665
AGAINST INVADERS; THEREFORE COOLD IN ZEALE 11 801

ZEALOUS

A SPIRIT, ZEALOUS, AS HE SEEM'D, TO KNOW 4 565

ZENITH

DROPT FROM THE ZENITH LIKE A FALLING STAR, 1 745
HIS ZENITH, WHILE THE SUN IN ARIES ROSE: 10 329

ZEPHIR

EURUS AND ZEPHIR WITH THIR LATERAL NOISE, 10 705

ZEPHON

ITHURIEL AND ZEPHON, WITH WINGD SPEED 4 788
TO WHOM THUS ZEPHON, ANSWERING SCORN WITH SCORN. 4 834
OR LESS BE LOST. THY FEAR, SAID ZEPHON BOLD, 4 854
ITHURIEL AND ZEPHON THROUGH THE SHADE, 4 868

ZEPHYR

TO RECOMMEND COOLE ZEPHYR, AND MADE EASE 4 329

ZEPHYRUS

MILDE, AS WHEN ZEPHYRUS ON FLORA BREATHES, 5 16

ZODIAC

AS IN A GLISTERING ZODIAC HUNG THE SWORD, 11 247
SEAVEN LAMPS AS IN A ZODIAC REPRESENTING 12 255

ZONE

RE-ENTER HEAV'N; OR ELSE IN SOME MILDE ZONE 2 397
GIRT LIKE A STARRIE ZONE HIS WASTE, AND ROUND 5 281
HIS OTHER HALF IN THE GREAT ZONE OF HEAV'N. 5 560
WHICH NIGHTLY AS A CIRCLING ZONE THOU SEEST 7 580

ZOPHIEL

ZOPHIEL, OF CHERUBIM THE SWIFTEST WING, 6 535

Table of Words in Text by Frequency

**Indicates word not indexed in concordance*

3,393
*AND

2,754
*THE

2,227
*TO

2,054
*OF

1,363
*IN

1,177
*HIS

1,161
*WITH

714
*OR

703
*THAT

693
ALL

686
*FROM

629
*NOT

592
*I

588
*BUT

576
*THIR

562
AS

538
*A

535
*ON

517
*BY

471
*HE

449
*FOR

447
*SO

436
*THOU

424
*THIS

422
*THY

393
*WHAT

380
*THEY

378
THEN

362
*THEE

351
*HIM

339
*BE

330
HEAV'N

327
*HER

325
*NOW

319
*THUS

309
*WHICH

293
*WHO

284
*SHALL

280
*TH'

274
*OUR

272
*AT

258
*MY

252
MORE

240
GOD

232
*IS

230
YET

228
*THEM

224
*WHEN

219
*THOUGH

209
*WHOM

206
*NOR

205
EARTH

201
*ME

198
*WAS

194
*NO

185
*HAD
*US

182
WILL

178
*IF

177
*WE

172
FIRST

169
SUCH

166
*WHERE

159
*THESE

155
MAN

153
*HOW

150
HIGH

147
*HAVE

143
ONE

142
*THROUGH

138
*IT

129
*CAN

126
*MAY

123
GREAT

121
DEATH
TILL

116
LIKE

115
*HATH

114
OTHER

113
HELL
*HERE

111
*BOTH

110
DAY
*EACH
STOOD

108
MIGHT
*WHOSE

106
GOOD
*THOSE
UP

105
*INTO
THINGS
WHILE

102
LIGHT

102 (CONT.)
*THERE

101
NIGHT

99
WORLD

98
LOVE

97
EVE
FARR

96
O

94
ADAM

91
SOON

89
DOWN
STILL
*WERE

88
SON

87
LET
LIFE
LONG

86
KNOW

85
FORTH
*MEE
PLACE

83
LESS
*YE

81
WAY

80
OWN
UNDER

79
NEW
POWER

78
FOUND
HAND

77
*HEE
OUT

76
BEFORE
DEEP
MADE
MUCH
*SHE

74
*MUST

71
MEN
PART
WITHOUT

70
*ARE
FAIR
ONCE
WELL

69
GODS
ROUND
SATAN
SIGHT

67
AGAINST
*COULD
NONE

66
AMONG
OVER
SINCE

64
END
*HAST
*SHOULD

63
ABOVE
ANGEL
EVIL
HEAV'NS
LAST
ONELY

62
MANY
SPAKE
WIDE

61
BRIGHT
HEAD

60
FRUIT

60 (CONT.)
JOY
LEAST

59
FIND
GROUND
OFT
SAW
WITHIN

58
*WOULD

57
EYES
HEARD
LEFT
LOST
RIGHT
SOME
SUN

56
JUST
SWEET

55
BEST
PERHAPS

54
FIRE
REST
SEA
SPIRITS
THOUGHTS

53
AFTER
CAME
PARADISE
SEE
SIDE
THENCE
*YOUR

52
ART
HOPE
NATURE
TREE
WARR

51
HEART
LIVE
STATE

50
FATHER

49
AIR
BEHOLD
SEAT
TASTE
WORDS

48
FREE
WORKS

47
ANGELS
DARK
KING
MOST
TWO

46
CREATED
THOUGHT
THRONE
WORK

45
AIRE
DIVINE
ERE
ETERNAL
FEAR
PEACE
SAID
VOICE

44
FALL
FELL

44 (CONT.)
FOE
HEAV'NLY
HILL
POWERS
SIN
SPIRIT

43
DARKNESS
EYE
FULL
HAPPIE
PAIN

42
BRING
ELSE
NEVER
REASON
SONS
STAND

41
ALSO
PURE
WHENCE

40
ALONE
BLISS
DWELL
THEREFORE
TIME

39
BEGAN
CALL'D
GRACE
OFF
RACE
SEEMD

38
FORCE
LAND
NEXT
SERPENT
SHAPE
VAIN

37
EQUAL
GOLD
HUMAN
SET
WINGS
WORSE

36
ARMS
BROUGHT
COME
DELIGHT
FLIGHT
HOST
MIND
SOM
*THINE
*TOO

35
BACK
CHANGE
FAITH
FIELD
*HIMSELF
*MINE
*WHY

34
ABOUT
BEYOND
FIERCE
NAME
REPLI'D
SAD
SOUND
STRENGTH
*THY SELF

33
LENGTH
MORN
PRAISE
SEEK

32
BEAST

32 (CONT.)
CALL
*DO
*EITHER
EVERY
FAR
GLORIE
HALF
KNOWLEDGE
PAST
ROSE
SAT
WOE

31
BETTER
CLOUD
HEAVEN
LEAVE
RATHER
RETURN
SOLE

30
DUE
FACE
GLORY
HIGHEST
ILL
MANKIND
MORTAL
OLD
SEED
SEEN
SENSE
*SHALT
THITHER
UPON

29
CREATURES
DAYES
DOUBT
GAVE
GLORIOUS
GOLDEN
KNOWN
LATE
LIVING
MEET
RAIS'D
SEEMS
VERTUE

28
*AN
BEING
CELESTIAL
DEEDS
FIT
GATE
LAW
SAY
VARIOUS
*WHETHER

27
*AM
BATTEL
FAST
FIRM
LARGE
O'RE
OTHERS
SOFT
THICK
TRUE

26
BETWEEN
BOUNDS
EASE
FLOURS
GATES
HATE
LED
MOUNT
SECOND
SERVE
SHAME
SLEEP
*THEMSELVES
WISE

25
CAUSE
CHAOS
EDEN
ENDED

25 (CONT.)
FIEND
GARDEN
IMAGE
NIGH
OPEN
RAGE
RISE
SACRED
SHADE
WANDRING
WILDE

24
CHIEF
DOOM
EVER
FATE
FIGHT
FLED
HANDS
INFINITE
LOUD
MET
MICHAEL
PROUD
REIGN
STARRS
TREES
TURND
WING

23
AUGHT
BEHELD
CHOICE
COURSE
DESIRE
DIRE
FEEL
GIV'N
HONOUR
HOUR
LORD
LOW
NATIVE
PLEAS'D
SENT
STRANGE
SUDDEN
SWIFT
THINK
THUNDER
WATERS

22
BENT
BOLD
BORN
CLOUDS
COMMAND
*DIDST
FORTHWITH
HARD
HEAR
HIGHTH
HILLS
HOLD
LABOUR
LOOKS
MEAN WHILE
MOON
MOVE
PASS
REVENGE
RISING
TELL

21
*BIN
CHARGE
FAIRE
FALL'N
FALSE
HELD
HENCE
LAY
LOOK
MAKER
PLEASANT
PRESENT
RULE
SAVE
SILENCE
SMALL
SONG
SPEED
SUNG
TRUTH

21 (CONT.)
WATCH
WONDER

20
ARM'D
BAD
BOUND
*DID
DIE
DREADFUL
ETHEREAL
FLESH
FRUITS
GENTLE
HID
INFERNAL
JUDGE
LOSS
NEED
OBEDIENCE
PLEASURE
RECEIVE
SCARCE
SECURE
SEEM'D
SKIE
SOUGHT
SPRING
TOUCH
VAST
WENT
WORLDS

19
ANOTHER
DREW
EAST
EMPIRE
FILL
FIXT
FOES
FOOD
FOUL
GIVE
GLAD
HENCEFORTH
HOLY
HUGE
HUNG
*IT SELF
KNEW
LOOSE
MAKE
MIXT
MOTHER
ONLY
RETURND
SAYING
*SHEE
TOOK
WRAUTH

18
BLEST
BROAD
*CANNOT
COMES
DUST
EARE
FEET
FOR EVER
GUIDE
HAPPINESS
HASTE
HIGHER
HORRID
INNUMERABLE
MEAN
SEEM
SHON
SUPREAM
TAUGHT
*THEIR
THRONES
TOP
TOWARDS
UTMOST
VIEW
WHEREIN
WISDOM

17
ABYSS
ALMIGHTY
ASCEND
BENEATH
CAST
CHANCE

17 (CONT.)
DANCE
DREAD
EASIE
FAITHFUL
FELT
FLOOD
FOUNTAIN
FRAUD
FRESH
GRATEFUL
INWARD
JUDG'D
JUSTICE
LEAD
MANS
NEEDS
PRIDE
PRIME
PUNISHMENT
PUT
RAISE
RUIN
SEND
SHEW
SORROW
SOVRAN
STARR
SURE
THOUSAND
UNIVERSAL
WASTE
WAYES
WHOLE
WINDS
*YOU

16
ANGELIC
BIRD
CLOSE
DECREE
DIRECT
EEVNING
FLAMING
FRONT
HITHER
IMMORTAL
KEEP
LAWS
LEAVES
MIGHTY
MOV'D
*MY SELF
*NEITHER
OCEAN
PERFET
PLAIN
PRESENCE
PREY
SAME
SEEST
SHORT
SIRE
STRAIT
TONGUE
TURN
WHATEVER
WONDROUS

15
ACT
ARMES
BRUISE
COLD
COMING
CREATION
DEAR
DESTRUCTION
*DON
*DONE
DRAW
EATE
FAME
FLEW
GO
GREATER
GREEN
GROW
HAPPY
MORNING
NAKED
NUMBER
PASS'D
REACH
SAFE
SATE
SENTENCE
SIT

15 (CONT.)
SMELL
STREAM
VIOLENCE
*WEE
WHEREON

14
ALIKE
ALMIGHTIE
APPEERD
BEAMS
BEAR
BRINGS
BUILT
CHERUBIM
CREATE
CREATOR
CREATURE
DANGER
DAYS
ENJOY
FIERIE
FORMD
FUTURE
GREW
HAPPIER
KINGS
LAID
LIES
MOTION
NAMES
NATIONS
NOTHING
NUMEROUS
ORDAIN'D
PREPAR'D
RETURN'D
RODE
SCORN
SECRET
SILENT
SINGLE
SOLEMN
SPRUNG
UNKNOWN
WALK
WHEREOF
WON
WOODS
WORD
WROUGHT

13
ANGER
APPEER
APPROACH
AUTHOR
BEASTS
BESIDES
BID
BLACK
BUILD
CARE
CHARIOT
CHIEFLY
COAST
CONFUSION
CREW
CRIME
DOMINION
ENVIE
FAIREST
FIRES
FIRMAMENT
FISH
FOUR
FREELY
GOODNESS
GROWN
INVISIBLE
KNOWS
LAKE
LEGIONS
LONGER
MID
MOULD
MULTITUDE
MUTE
ORB
ORDER
PAINE
PLAC'T
PLANT
PROOF
RETIR'D
SMOOTH
STEPS
STRONG

13 (CONT.)
SUNK
TEMPLE
TEN
TRAIN
WIND
WOMAN
WOMB
WOUND

12
ADORE
AMIDST
APPETITE
ATTEMPT
BIRDS
BOWRE
BREATH
*CANST
CHANG'D
DESTROY
FILL'D
FINDE
GUILE
HEAT
HERB
*HER SELF
INDEED
INNOCENCE
KIND
LIGHTS
MALICE
MATTER
MESSIAH
MIDST
MOUNTAIN
NATURES
NOISE
NOON
OBSCURE
OMNIPOTENT
OP'NING
ORE
OUTWARD
PAIR
PASSION
PURSU'D
RECEAVE
RITES
SAINTS
SEIS'D
SPEAK
SPEAR
SPRED
SUBSTANCE
TEARS
THEREIN
THIRD
THREE
UNSEEN
US'D
UTTER
WALL

11
AGAIN
AID
ANCIENT
ANSWERD
*BEEN
BIRTH
BREST
BROKE
BRUTE
CENTER
CIRCUIT
CLEER
DEITIE
DESPAIR
DISCOURSE
DISTANT
DRAWN
DREAM
DRIVE
DURST
EMPYREAL
ENEMIE
EVENT
FATAL
FLAME
FORETOLD
GRAVE
GULF
HEROIC
HIDE
HORROR
IRE
LIQUID
LOT

11 (CONT.)
MEEK
MERIT
MIDDLE
MILDE
MISERABLE
NAM'D
OFSPRING
ORIENT
OVERCOME
PERPETUAL
POSSESS
PROSPECT
PURPOSE
RADIANT
REGARD
REIGNS
RELATE
REMOV'D
RIVERS
ROCK
ROCKS
ROOM
SEARCH
SEVERE
SHADES
SHINE
SHUT
SOULE
SPACE
SPACIOUS
SPEECH
STAY
STROKE
SWORD
THING
THRICE
TOGETHER
TOWARD
VOID
WAVE
WAVES
WHEREFORE
WILT
WITNESS
WONT
WORSHIP
YIELD

10
AERIE
AIDE
AMID
ANON
ANSWER'D
APPEER'D
ARK
ARRIV'D
ASK
ASPECT
BANDS
BEARE
*BECAUSE
BEHIND
BOW
COUNSEL
CURSE
DELICIOUS
DESCEND
DISMAL
EARTHS
ENTRANCE
ERECT
FAVOUR
FIELDS
FIERY
FLAMES
FLIE
FLYING
FOLLOW
FOLLOWING
FOOT
FOULE
FOWLE
GABRIEL
GAY
GAZE
GROVE
GUEST
HIDEOUS
HOLDS
HOLLOW
IRON
JUSTLY
KEPT
KNOW'ST
LITTLE
LORDS
MEASURE

10 (CONT.)
MISERIE
MUTUAL
NARROW
NEERER
NORTH
OP'ND
*OUR SELVES
PALE
PLEASE
PROVE
REALM
REGAL
RICH
RIVER
ROUT
SCEPTER
SHADIE
SHOOK
SHOT
SITS
SLOW
SOILE
SOMTIMES
SOUL
STARRIE
STEEP
STONE
STORE
STRIFE
SUTTLE
TEMPER
TENTS
TOWRS
TURN'D
UNDERSTOOD
UPRIGHT
WALKS
WANT
WHEELS
WINDES
WINGED
WISH
WORST
WORTH
*YEE
YONDER

9
*&
ACCEPT
ACCURST
ACTS
ADD
ADORND
ADVANC'T
ADVERSE
ADVISE
ALTAR
AMBROSIAL
AMOROUS
ARCH-ANGEL
ARMIES
ARRAY
BARE
BLAME
BLOOD
BOAST
BRED
CEAS'D
CHOOSE
CLAD
COOLE
COUNSELS
COUNT'NANCE
CROWND
DELAY
DIVIDED
DRIV'N
EASILY
EASTERN
EAT
ELEMENTS
ENDLESS
ENEMIES
ENSUE
ENTER
ENTIRE
FEARLESS
FORMS
FREEDOM
GIFT
GIFTS
GLOBE
HAIL
HEADS
HEARTS
HOUSE
HOWEVER

9 (CONT.)
HUSBAND
IMMENSE
INCENSE
INFLUENCE
INTENT
JOVE
JOYN'D
KNOWING
KNOWST
LIBERTIE
LIVES
MAIN
MIDNIGHT
MIGHTIE
MISCHIEF
MOMENT
MOUNTAINS
MOVING
NIGHTLY
NUMBERLESS
NUMBERS
OBEY
OFFICE
PARTS
POLE
POTENT
PRINCE
PROMIS'D
QUITE
REBELLIOUS
RECOMPENCE
REGION
REPLY'D
REVERENCE
ROWLD
RUL'D
SCALE
SEASONS
SERAPHIM
SEVERAL
SHAPES
SHIELDS
*SHOULDST
SIGN
SIGNAL
SING
SMIL'D
SMILES
SPIRITUAL
SUBDUE
SUBLIME
SUFFER
SUFFICIENT
TASTED
TEMPTER
TEND
THIRST
TIMES
TRIAL
TRI'D
URIEL
USE
VICTOR
VIOLENT
VIRGIN
VISIT
WAK'D
WHITHER

8
ABSOLUTE
AGES
ALOFT
AMBITION
AMPLE
ANOINTED
ANSWER
ANY
ARM
ASSUME
ASSUR'D
ATTEND
AUDIENCE
BEAM
BEGIN
BEND
BETWIXT
BLISSFUL
BLOW
BORE
BOTTOM
CHAINS
CIRCLING
CITIE
COLOURS
CONSCIENCE
CONVERSE
DAUGHTER

8 (CONT.)
DEARE
DECLAR'D
DEGREES
DESCENDING
DIM
DOE
DRY
EAR
EARTHLY
EASIER
ENDURE
EXAMPLE
EXCESS
EXPECT
FALLING
FATHERS
FED
FINAL
FOLLY
FORBIDS
FORREST
FOUGHT
GENERAL
GENTLY
GOE
GRIM
GROSS
GROWING
*HADST
HAILE
HELLISH
HISS
HOURS
INSPIR'D
KINDE
LEADS
LEAGUE
LIMB
LOWER
LOWEST
MANKINDE
MEANT
MEMORIE
MIGHTIEST
MIST
MIX
MOUTH
NEER
NEIGHBOURING
OBJECT
ORDAIND
PAID
PARTAKE
PASSAGE
PEERS
PENALTIE
PLAINE
PLAY
POWERFUL
PRONE
QUICK
RAPHAEL
REGIONS
REMOTE
REMOVE
RENEWD
REWARD
RIS'N
ROW
RUN
RURAL
SERAPH
SERV'D
SHIELD
SPENT
STREAMS
STRICT
SUBJECTION
SUBMIT
SUPERIOR
SWAY
THREW
THRONG
TRANSGRESS
TREAD
TRIUMPH
TROUBL'D
TRY
TURNS
UNION
VENGEANCE
VERTUES
WANTON
WHEREAT
WILDERNESS
WING'D
WOOD

7
ACCESS
ADAMS
ADMIR'D
ADVANCE
ALOUD
APPEASE
APPEERS
APPOINTED
APPROVE
ARGUMENT
ARMD
ARME
ASCENDING
ASCENT
ASSAULT
AWFUL
BANK
BECOME
BEFALL
BEWARE
BLAZE
BODIES
BRETHREN
BURNING
CERTAIN
CHARM
CHOSE
CLIME
COMMANDS
COMMON
COMPARE
CONSORT
COURAGE
COVER'D
CURSED
DART
DEAD
DEADLY
DECEAV'D
DEGREE
DESCENT
DESERT
DEVIL
DISTANCE
DOUBLE
DREADED
DROPS
DROVE
ENDU'D
EVEN
EXCEPT
EXPOS'D
EXPRESS
FAIL
FEAR'D
FEIGN'D
FEW
FLOCKS
FLOUR
FLOURIE
FOLLOW'D
FORGET
FORM
FORMER
FREQUENT
FRO
FURTHER
GLADLY
GRAND
HARP
HATEFUL
HAZARD
HEAVENS
HELP
HOURE
HUE
IMPIOUS
IMPOS'D
INTENDS
JUDGEMENT
LEADER
LEARN
LIGHTNING
LOOKING
LOVES
MAJESTIE
MAKES
MARCH
MARK
MATE
METHOUGHT
MILD
MILLIONS
MINDS
MOIST
MONSTROUS
MOTIONS
NUPTIAL

7 (CONT.)
OBSCUR'D
OPPOSITE
ORIGINAL
*OURS
OWE
PARENTS
PERVERSE
PINE
PINES
PIT
POINT
POMP
PRISON
PRONOUNC'T
PROV'D
PURPLE
RAN
RAY
REPAST
REQUEST
RESOLV'D
RETIRE
RETURNE
REVOLT
ROOF
ROOT
ROWLING
RUNG
SECRETS
SEES
SELF
SERENE
SEX
SHOUT
SHUN
SIGHS
SIGNS
SMOAK
SOLITUDE
SONGS
SORT
SOUTH
SPHEARE
SPOT
SPREAD
SUMMERS
SUNS
TASK
TERRIBLE
TERROR
THENCEFORTH
THEREOF
THICKEST
TIDINGS
TOLD
TOPS
TROUBLE
UNITED
UNJUST
UNLESS
UPLIFTED
VISION
WANDER
WANTS
WARND
WAVING
WEAK
WEALTH
WEIGHT
WEST
WONDRING
WONTED
WORTHIEST
WORTHY
WRATH
YOUTH
ZEALE

6
ABLE
ACCOUNT
ACCUSE
ADDED
ADVANTAGE
AGE
ALONG
ALWAYES
AMAZ'D
ANGUISH
APPEAR'D
ARMED
AROSE
ASPIRING
ATTENTION
AWAKE
AWE
BEAUTY
BEGINS

6 (CONT.)
BEGOTTEN
BITTER
BLAZING
BLESSED
BODY
BONE
BOSOM
BRANCHES
BRAZEN
BRIGHTNESS
BROW
CALLS
CANAAN
CAPTIVE
CEASE
CHERUBE
CONSPICUOUS
CONTEND
COUCH
COV'NANT
CRUEL
DAILY
DALE
DAMP
DAWNING
DEATHS
DEED
DEFENCE
DELIGHTFUL
DESCENDED
DESCENDS
DIES
DIFFERENT
DISCORD
DISOBEDIENCE
DISTURB
DISTURBD
DIVIDE
DOMINATIONS
DORE
DORES
DOUBTFUL
DOWNWARD
DREAMS
DRIE
EARS
EFFECT
EGYPT
EMPYREAN
ENCLOS'D
ERST
EVILS
EV'N
EXCELLENCE
EXEMPT
EXPECTATION
FEARD
FEARE
FEED
FERTIL
FILIAL
FILLD
FLIES
FLOCK
FOND
FORBIDDEN
FORM'D
FRAIL
FRAME
FRAUGHT
FRIENDLY
FRUITFUL
FULFILL
FURIOUS
FURY
GIVES
GLOOM
GODDESS
GOD-LIKE
GON
GRACIOUS
GRASSIE
GROVES
GROWTH
GUARDS
GUILT
HALL
HAPLESS
HAPLY
HARM
*HAVING
HEARE
HEAVIER
HEEL
HERDS
HIGHLY
HOME
HORRIBLE

6 (CONT.)
HUNGER
ICE
ILLUSTRIOUS
IMMEDIATE
INSTEAD
INTENDED
ISSUING
JOIND
JOURNEY
JOYND
JOYNT
KINGDOM
LIKENESS
LOCKS
LOWLY
LUST
LUSTRE
*MAIST
MATCHLESS
MATURE
MERITS
MOSES
NATION
NAUGHT
NIGHTS
NOBLER
ODOURS
OFFENCE
OFFENDED
ONWARD
PARTED
PERFECTION
PLAC'D
PLEASING
PLEDGE
POUR'D
PRAYER
PRECIOUS
PURSUE
PURSUES
RARE
READY
RECEAV'D
RECESS
REJOYCE
REJOYCING
REMAINS
REMORSE
RENDER
RENOWN
REPOSE
RESERV'D
RESIST
RESTRAINT
RETURNS
RIGHTEOUS
RIGHTEOUSNESS
ROD
ROSES
SAKE
SCAPE
SEAS
SERVITUDE
SHADOW
SHARP
SHINES
SHINING
SHOAR
SHORE
SIGNE
SMOTE
SOONER
SORE
SOUNDS
SPARE
SPITE
STAID
STANDING
STANDS
STEEDS
STEP
STRETCHT
STRONGER
SUCCESS
SUDDENLY
SUFFICE
SUPPOS'D
SUSTAIN
TASTING
TEACH
TERMS
TERROUR
THEREBY
THICKET
THOUSANDS
THREATNING
THREATS
THRON'D

6 (CONT.)
THROUGHOUT
TORMENT
TORMENTS
TRUST
TWILIGHT
UNCOUTH
UNDERNEATH
UNMOV'D
VICTORIOUS
VIEWS
VIGOUR
VISAGE
VISIBLE
VOUTSAF'T
WAK'T
WALLS
WANTED
WARRING
WATRIE
WAV'D
WEARIED
WHEELES
WICKED
WIN
WOMANS
*WOULDST
YIELDED
YON

5
ABDIEL
ABRAHAM
ABSENCE
ACCEPTANCE
ADMIRING
ADOR'D
ADORN'D
ADVERSARIE
AIRES
ANSWERING
APPEAR
APPROACHING
ARMIE
ARMOUR
ATTAIN
BALME
BANE
BEAUTIE
BEGET
BEGINNING
BEGOT
BEGUIL'D
BELIAL
BELIEVE
BIDS
BINDE
BLAZ'D
BORNE
BREAK
BREATH'D
BRIGHTEST
BURDEN
CALLD
CALL'ST
CALM
CATTEL
CAUSES
CAVES
CHARIOTS
CHEEK
CHERUBIC
CHRYSTAL
CIRCUMFERENCE
CLOS'D
CLOUDIE
CONDEMN'D
CONFESS
CONFOUND
CONFOUNDED
CONSTANT
CONSTELLATIONS
CONTENT
CONTEST
CONTINENT
CONTINU'D
COVERT
CREST
CURE
DARTS
DEBATE
DECLARE
DELIGHTED
DEN
DENOUNC'T
DEPART
DEPRAV'D
DESOLATE
DESPIS'D

5 (CONT.)
DESPITE
DEVILISH
DEWIE
DIAMOND
DIFFUS'D
DISDAIN
DISPLEAS'D
DISSOLUTION
DIURNAL
*DOTH
DRINK
DUNGEON
DWELLING
DWELT
DYING
EDGE
EEV'N
EEVN
ELECT
EMINENT
ENDUR'D
ENGINS
ENTERTAIN
ENTRAILS
ENVY
EQUAL'D
EQUALLY
ERRE
ETERNITIE
EXALTED
EXPERIENCE
EXTEND
EXTOLL
FACES
FADED
FAULT
FEAST
FEMAL
FILES
FLOW
FLOW'D
FLOWING
FLY
FONDLY
FORBIDD'N
FOULD
FOULDS
FOUNDED
FRAGRANCE
FRAM'D
FRIEND
FRIENDS
GAIN
GATHERD
GAZ'D
GLITTERING
GODHEAD
GODLIKE
GOT
GRACES
GRASS
GREATEST
GROWS
GUARD
GUILTIE
HALLOWD
HARME
HARMONIE
HASTED
HAUNT
HEADLONG
HEAP
HEMISPHERE
HERD
HOPES
HORIZON
HOSTILE
HOT
HUMANE
HUMBLE
ILES
IMPERIAL
IMPETUOUS
IMPOSSIBLE
INFERIOUR
INMOST
INTERPOS'D
INTERRUPT
INVOLV'D
JOYN
KINDES
KNOWLEDG
LAMENT
LAMP
LANDS
LAP
LATTER
LEARNE

5 (CONT.)
LEST
LIE
LIFT
LIKELIEST
LINE
LINKT
LONGING
LOVELY
MANSION
MASSIE
*MAYST
MEANS
MEETS
MERCIE
MERCY
MESSAGE
MINDE
MISERY
MONARCH
MOUTHS
MUSE
MYRIADS
MYSTERIOUS
NETHER
NOTES
OBEYD
OBSERV'D
OBVIOUS
OCCASION
ODDS
ODIOUS
OFFEND
OFFERD
OMNIPOTENCE
OP'N
OPPOS'D
OPPOSE
ORBES
ORBS
ORDERS
OUGHT
PACE
PALACE
PARDON
PARTING
PASSD
PASSING
PATH
PATIENCE
PAY
PEOPLE
PLACES
PLAINES
PLANETS
PLANTED
PLIGHT
POPULOUS
PORT
POSSESSION
PRAYERS
PRESUM'D
PRINCEDOMS
PRINCES
PROCEED
PRODIGIOUS
PROFOUND
PROGENIE
PROMISE
PRONOUNC'D
PROPER
PROVIDENCE
PUBLIC
PURGE
QUEEN
QUIT
RAIN
RATIONAL
REAL
REBEL
REBELLION
REDUCE
REED
REGENT
REIGNE
REMAIN
REPENT
RESOLUTION
RIB
RIDE
ROYAL
RUSH'D
SATIATE
SAWST
SCARSE
SEDUC'T
SEPARATE
SERVICE
SETS

5 (CONT.)
SHARE
SHED
SIDES
SINCERE
SION
SLEEPING
SLY
SMALLEST
SMILE
SNAKE
SNOW
SOLACE
SOLID
SPRINGS
SQUADRONS
STATION
STATURE
STERN
STRIVE
STYGIAN
SUBMISSION
SUFFERING
SUPPORT
TALK
TEMPERANCE
TEMPEST
TEMPT
TENDER
THANKS
*THEIRS
THROWN
TITLES
TORE
TRAINE
TRESSES
TRIBES
TRIUMPHANT
TRUMPET
UNIVERSE
UPHELD
UPWARD
URG'D
VAINE
VALE
VALLEY
VAPOUR
VEINS
VERDANT
VESSEL
VICTORIE
VITAL
VOICES
WAKEFUL
WALK'D
WARBLING
WARMTH
*WAST
WEDDED
WESTERN
WHEELE
WHEREVER
WILD
WILES
WISH'D
WOUNDS
WRONG
YEARS
YOKE
*YOURS

4
ABJECT
ABSTAIN
ACCOMPANIED
ACKNOWLEDGE
ADAMANT
ADAMANTINE
ADMIRATION
ADMIT
ADORATION
ADVENTROUS
AEREAL
AFFLICTED
AFFORD
AIM
ALREADIE
ALREADY
AMBITIOUS
ANGRY
ANOUGH
APOSTAT
APPEARS
APPLAUSE
APPROV'D
ARCH
ARCHANGEL
ARCHITECT
ARGUES

4 (CONT.)
ARISE
ASCENDED
ASKT
ASLEEP
ASSAULTS
ATTENDS
ATTRACTIVE
AUGMENT
AVENG'D
AWAITING
AXLE
BALMIE
BAND
BANDED
BANISHT
BARRS
BATTELS
BECOMES
BED
BEELZEBUB
BEFALL'N
BEFELL
BEGUN
BEHOLDS
BELONGS
BESOUGHT
BESTIAL
BLAST
BLEATING
BLIND
BLOOM
BLOWING
BOUGH
BOUGHT
BOWING
BREATHE
BRIDGE
BRIEF
BROILES
BROOD
BROOK
BROOKS
BURSTING
CAPITAL
CARNAL
CASTS
CAVE
CEASLESS
CEDAR
CHARMING
CHASE
CHEARFUL
CHOICEST
CIRCLES
CLAIM
CLIFF
COMMOTION
COMPAR'D
COMPOS'D
CONCORD
CONFIDENCE
CONFIN'D
CONJECTURE
CONQUEROUR
CONSCIOUS
CONSENT
CONSULT
CONTAIN
CONTEMPT
CORPOREAL
*COULDST
COVER
CREEPS
CRIES
CROSS
CROWN'D
CRY
DALLIANCE
DAUGHTERS
DAWN
DAWNE
DECREED
DEEMD
DEFEND
DEFIANCE
DELIGHTS
DELIVERANCE
DEMEANOUR
DEPTH
DESIGN
DESIRES
DESIROUS
DESPAIRE
DESTIN'D
DESTIND
DESTROY'D
DESTROYD
DEVOUR

4 (CONT.)
DIGNITIE
DILATED
DIN
DISCOVER
DISGUIS'D
DISMAY
DISMISS
DISSOLVE
DISTINCT
DIVINELY
DOING
DOOM'D
DOOME
DOWNIE
DYE
EASIEST
EASTWARD
EEVEN
ENJOYING
ENMITIE
ENOUGH
ENTERD
EQUALS
ESSENCE
EVENING
EVERLASTING
EV'NING
EXACT
EXALT
EXCITES
EXCUSE
EXECUTE
EXERCISE
EXPANSE
EXTENDED
FABLES
FACT
FAILD
FAINT
FAIRER
FALLS
FAMILIAR
FAMIN
FANCIE
FANSIE
FARE
FINISHT
FIXED
FLAT
FLOATING
FLOUD
FLOWERS
FLUNG
FORBID
FORC'T
FOREKNOWLEDGE
FORLORN
FOUNT
FOUNTAINS
FROWN
FROZEN
FRUSTRATE
FURIES
GAIN'D
GATHER'D
GEMMS
GIRD
GIRT
GIVING
GLANCE
GLIMPS
GLOOMIE
GOODLIEST
GOODLY
GOVERN
GRACEFUL
GRAIN
GRAINE
GRAY
GREATLY
HAP
HAPPIEST
HARPS
HEATE
HEAVIE
HEIR
HERBS
HEREAFTER
HONOURD
HORSE
HOVERING
HUMID
HYMNS
IMBRACES
IMBRACING
IMPURE
INDIGNATION
INFERIOR

4 (CONT.)
INFUS'D
INGLORIOUS
IN STEAD
INSTINCT
INTELLECTUAL
INTEND
INTERCEPT
INTERCOURSE
ISRAEL
KEEN
KEY
KNEE
KNIGHTS
LABOURING
LAMPS
LATELY
LAUGHTER
LIGHTED
LION
LIPS
LIST
LIV'D
LOATH
LODG'D
LODGE
LONGITUDE
LOOKD
LYES
MAINE
MAKERS
MALIGNE
MAMMON
MANHOOD
MANIFEST
MEANWHILE
MELODIOUS
MINDED
MONSTER
MOUNTED
MULTIPLIE
MULTIPLY
MULTITUDES
MURMURING
NATURAL
NECESSITIE
NECTAR
NEEDED
NEEREST
NOURISHMENT
OBEDIENT
OBEY'D
OBSERVE
OBTAINE
ODOROUS
OFFER
OFFER'D
PAINS
PAIRS
PARENT
PASSIONS
PATERNAL
PAVEMENT
PEACEFUL
PECULIAR
PERISH
PERNICIOUS
PERSON
PERVERT
PIETIE
PILLAR
PILLARS
PITCH
PITIE
PLAINT
PLUCKT
POOL
POTENTATES
PREGNANT
PRESCRIB'D
PREVENT
PROCEEDED
PRODUCE
PROPITIOUS
PROPOS'D
PROSTRATE
PROVOK'T
PUREST
PURSUING
PUTS
QUIRE
QUIRES
RAG'D
RAGING
RANKS
RAPID
RAPTURE
RASH
REACHING

4 (CONT.)
READ
REALME
REARE
REASONING
RECEIV'D
RECEIVD
RECEIVES
RED
REDEEM
REFUGE
REFUSE
REIGN'D
RELENT
REMAIND
REMAINES
REMEMBER
RENEW'D
REPEATED
REPLY
REPROACH
REQUIRE
REQUIRES
RESOUND
RESOUNDED
RESPLENDENT
RESTOR'D
RESTS
RETREAT
RETURNING
REVEAL'D
REVIVE
RIDGE
RIGHTLY
RIGID
RIPE
ROSIE
RULES
SANCTITIE
SATISFI'D
SATISFIE
SAVIOUR
SAW'ST
SCORNE
SEASON
SEEING
SEEKS
SEEMING
SEISE
SENSES
SERPENTS
SERVANT
SHADOWIE
SHEWS
SHOARE
SHOULDERS
SHRUB
SIGNES
SILVER
SINS
SIX
SKILL
SKIRTS
SLEEPS
SLEPT
SMELLING
SMILING
SNARE
SOCIETIE
SOLITARIE
SOMETIMES
SOMTHING
SPEAKING
SPEARS
SPICIE
SPIE
SPLENDOR
SPOUSE
STALK
STANDARD
STATELY
STEDFAST
STOP
STOR'D
STORIE
STORM
STRANGER
STROOK
STYLE
SUCCEED
SUFFERANCE
SUMMONS
SUPERFLUOUS
SUPERIOUR
SURPRIS'D
SWEETEST
SWIM
SWORN
SYNOD

4 (CONT.)
SYRIAN
*T'
TAINT
TAKE
TALL
TEDIOUS
TELLS
TEMPTATION
TEMPTED
TEMPTING
TENDING
TENFOLD
TERRESTRIAL
THUNDRING
TIMELY
TONGUES
TOST
TOTAL
TRACK
TRACT
TRANSPORTED
TRESPASS
TRUCE
TRUMPETS
TUN'D
UNDAUNTED
UNDERSTAND
UNFOULD
UNSOUGHT
UNSUNG
VALOUR
VANQUISHT
VERTU
VICTORS
VILE
VINE
WAITING
WAKES
WAKING
WALKT
WAR
WARLIKE
WARME
WARNE
WATER
WATRY
WAYS
WEPT
WHERETO
WIFE
WINE
WISDOME
WONDERFUL
WORE
ZEPHON
ZONE

3
ABASHT
ABIDE
ABODE
ABOLISH
ABORTIVE
ABSENT
ACCEPTED
ACCORDING
ACTIONS
ADDREST
ADJUDG'D
ADMIRE
ADVANC'D
ADVENTURE
AEGYPT
AFFECTING
AFFRAID
AGONIE
AH
ALIENATED
ALLUR'D
ALTARS
AMAIN
AMAZEMENT
AMBIGUOUS
AMIABLE
ANARCHIE
ANCESTOR
ANNUAL
APPEAS'D
ARGUE
ARIGHT
ARRIVE
ASPIRE
ASPIRES
ASSAY
ASSEMBL'D
ASSEMBLY
ASSERT
ASSOCIATE

3 (CONT.)
ASTONISHT
ATCHIEV'D
ATTAINE
ATTENDANT
ATTENDED
ATTENTIVE
AUTUMN
AVERSE
AZURE
BANKS
BARR'D
BARREN
BEARING
BEARS
BEAUTEOUS
BEG
BEHEST
BEHESTS
BEHOLDING
BELEEVE
BELOV'D
BENDED
BENIGNE
BESET
BESTOWD
BETOOK
BIDDING
BIND
BLAND
BLASTED
BLESS'D
BLITHE
BLOSSOMS
BLOUD
BLOWN
BODIE
BOUGHES
BOUNDLESS
BOUNTEOUS
BOUNTIE
BOWELS
BOWER
BOWRS
BRAKE
BRANCHING
BRASS
BREAD
BREADTH
BREATHES
BREATHS
BRINK
BROTHER
BRUTISH
BULK
BURN
CALME
CAMP
CAPE
CASUAL
CAUGHT
CAUTION
CEAS'T
CELLS
CERES
CHAMPIONS
CHANGING
CHARMS
CHILDLESS
CHILDREN
CHOOSING
CIRCL'D
CIRCLE
CIRCUMSPECTION
CITIES
CITY
CIVIL
COLOUR
COLOUR'D
COM
COMBIN'D
COMMANDING
COMPASS
COMPREHEND
COMPUTE
CONCEIV'D
CONCEIVING
CONCEPTION
CONCERNE
CONDITION
CONDUCT
CONFINES
CONFUS'D
CONJUGAL
CONQUEST
CONSULTING
CONSUME
CONSUMMATE
CONTENDING

3 (CONT.)
CONTENTED
CONTRITE
CONTRIV'D
CONVERSING
CONVEX
CONVEYANCE
COPE
COPIOUS
CORRUPT
CORRUPTED
CORRUPTION
COUNCEL
COURTS
CREATOUR
CREEPING
CREPT
CRI'D
CROWN
CRUDE
CUMBROUS
CURB
CURRENT
CURS'D
CUT
DAMN'D
DANGEROUS
DANGERS
DARE
DARING
DARKSOM
DASH
DEARLY
DECEIT
DECEIVE
DECLINE
DECREES
DEEM
DEEM'D
DEEPER
DEFI'D
DEITIES
DELIVERER
DELUGE
DENI'D
DERISION
DERIV'D
DESART
DESCRI'D
DESCRIE
DESERTED
DESIGN'D
DESIGNE
DESPOILD
DESTROYING
DEVISE
DEVOTE
DEW
DEWS
DIFFICULT
DIFFICULTY
DIRECTED
DISARM'D
DISCERN'D
DISCERND
DISCERNE
DISDAIN'D
DISLIKE
DISPERST
DISPLEASURE
DISPOS'D
DISPOSE
DISPUTE
DISPUTES
DISSENT
DISTEMPER
DISTEMPERD
DISTRESS
DOINGS
*DOST
DOUBL'D
DRAG
DRAGON
DRESS
DRINKS
DRIVEN
DRIVN
DROOPING
DROP
DROP'D
DROPT
DUSKIE
DWELLINGS
DWELLS
EARLY
EARNEST
ECCENTRIC
EFFECTS
EFFULGENCE

3 (CONT.)
ELDEST
ELEMENT
ELOQUENCE
ELSEWHERE
EMINENCE
ENAMOUR'D
ENCAMPT
ENDING
ENDS
ENEMY
ENJOY'D
ENLIGHTEN
ENMITY
ENORMOUS
ENSIGNES
ENTERPRIZE
ENTERTAIND
ENTHRALL
ENTRING
ENVIOUS
ERRAND
ERRANDS
ERRONEOUS
ESCAP'T
ESTEEM
EXCELS
EXCESSIVE
EXHALATION
EXILE
EXPECTED
EXPEDITION
EXPELL'D
EXPLOIT
EXPOSE
EXPRESS'D
EXPREST
EXTREAMS
EY'D
FABL'D
FACIL
FAILE
FAILING
FALSHOOD
FARDEST
FARWEL
FAULTRING
FAULTS
FEALTIE
FEARS
FEATHERD
FELLOWS
FEMININE
FIERCEST
FILLS
FINISH'D
FIRR
FIVE
FIX
FLI'ST
FLORID
FLOURE
FLOURETS
FLOWN
FLUID
FOAMING
FORCIBLE
FORESEEN
FORGOE
FORMES
FORSAKE
FOWL
FRAGRANT
FRAY
FRUITLESS
FUGITIVE
FULFILL'D
FULLY
FURIE
GAIND
GAINE
GAME
GAMES
GARDNING
GARLANDS
GASTLY
GATHERS
GAV'ST
GENIAL
GESTURE
GIANT
GIANTS
GIVEN
GLASS
GLIDE
GLIDING
GLIMMERING
GLISTERING
GLORIFIE

3 (CONT.)
GLUT
GOD-HEAD
GORGEOUS
GOVERNMENT
GRAPE
GRAZE
GREATNESS
GRIEF
GRIEVOUS
GUILTLESS
GULFE
GUMMS
HABITATION
HARALDS
HARBOUR
HARD'ND
HARMONIOUS
HARVEST
HASTING
HAST'N
HATRED
HAVOC
HEAL'D
HEAPT
HEED
*HEER
HERMES
HESPERIAN
HIERARCHIES
HINGES
HOARCE
HOPEFUL
HOUSHOLD
HUMBL'D
HUMILIATION
HURL'D
HURRIED
HURT
HYMNING
IDLE
IGNORANCE
ILE
IMMEDIATELY
IMMINENT
IMMUTABLE
IMPART
IMPERFET
IMPOSE
IMPULSE
IMPUTED
INACCESSIBLE
INCAPABLE
INCENSED
INCESSANT
INCORPOREAL
INCORRUPTIBLE
INDIAN
INDUSTRIOUS
INFERRS
INFLAM'D
INFORMD
INOFFENSIVE
INSECT
INSTANT
INSTRUMENT
INTERCESSOR
INTRICATE
INTRODUCE
INVADE
INVENTED
INVINCIBLE
INVITE
IRKSOM
ISSU'D
ITHURIEL
JASPER
JEHOVAH
JOCOND
JOINE
JOYES
JOYNING
JUDGMENT
KID
KINDLY
KINDS
KINGLY
KNEES
LAKES
LANGUAGE
LANTSKIP
LARGELY
LASTING
LASTLY
LAUGH
LEADING
LEAF
LEAP'D
LEARNT

3 (CONT.)
LEGION
LETS
LEVEL
LIBERAL
LIBERTY
LIFTED
LIKELY
LIKES
LIKEST
LIMITS
LINGRING
LIP
LIVD
LIVELESS
LIVELY
LOAD
LOINES
LOOK'D
LOOKT
LOSE
LOVLY
LOYNS
LUCIFER
LUXURIE
LUXURIOUS
LYE
MAD'ST
MAGNIFICENCE
MAGNIFICENT
MAKING
MALE
MANIFOLD
MANTLING
MARCHING
MARRIAGE
MASS
MATRON
MAZES
MEASUR'D
MEETING
MERIDIAN
MERITED
METHINKS
MIGHTIER
MINDES
MINISTER
MINISTERS
MINISTRING
MIRTH
MISS
MITIGATE
MONSTERS
MOOD
MURMUR
NECK
NECKS
NICE
NILE
NIMBLE
NINE
NOBLE
NOOK
NOURISH
NO WHERE
NOXIOUS
NOYSE
NUMBERD
NYMPH
OBJECTS
OBLIQUE
OBSEQUIOUS
OBSTRUCT
OBTAIN
OLYMPUS
OMNISCIENT
OPERATION
OPPORTUNE
OPPOSITION
OPPROBRIOUS
ORBE
ORDAINS
OREB
OTHERWISE
OUTRAGEOUS
OVERGROWN
OVER-RUL'D
OW
PAINFUL
PANGS
PATHS
PATIENTLY
PATRIARCH
PAUS'D
PAUSE
PAV'D
PEARL
PENDANT
PENSIVE

3 (CONT.)
PERCEAVE
PERFORM
PERFORM'D
PERIL
PERMISSIVE
PERMIT
PERMITS
PERPLEXT
PERSEVERE
PHALANX
PIL'D
PILE
PITTIE
PLAID
PLANTS
PLEASURES
PLENTEOUS
PLOTTING
PLUCK
PLUME
PLUNG'D
POLAR
PONDERING
POPULAR
POSSESSES
POSTERITIE
POSTURE
POURD
POWRD
PRAY
PREPARE
PRESENTED
PRESERVE
PRESUMPTUOUS
PRINCELY
PROFAN'D
PROMISD
PROMPT
PROSPER
PROVIDED
PROVOKE
PROWESS
PUISSANT
PURCHASE
PURER
PURG'D
PURSUIT
QUARTERS
QUELLD
QUESTION
QUITTED
RACKING
RANG'D
RANGE
RANSOM
RAPE
RAPT
RAVISHMENT
RAYES
REACHT
REALMS
REAR'D
REBUKE
RECALL'D
RECEAVES
RECONCILEMENT
RECORDS
RECOVERING
REDEEMER
REDEMPTION
REDOUND
REDUC'D
REFIN'D
REFLECTED
REFUS'D
REINES
RELUCTANT
REMEDIE
REMEMBRANCE
REND
RENOUNCE
RENOWN'D
RENOWND
REPAID
REPAIR
REPAIRING
REPENTANCE
REPENTING
REPORT
REPULSE
RESEMBLANCE
RESIDE
RESIDENCE
RESIGNE
RESOLVE
RESTING
RESTORE
RETAIN

3 (CONT.)
REVEALD
REVERENT
REVOLTED
RICHES
RIOT
ROAR
ROBE
ROME
ROUGH
ROWLE
RUDE
RUE
RUIND
RUSHING
SACRIFICE
SAIDST
SAILE
SAINT
SAIST
SALVATION
SANDS
SAPIENCE
SATURN
SAVAGE
SAVOUR
SAVOURIE
SCALES
SCAP'D
SCAP'T
SCATTERD
SCEPTER'D
SCORNFUL
SCORPION
SEALE
SEATS
SEAV'N
SECONDED
SEDUC'D
SEDUCE
SEEKING
SELECT
SENDS
SHEPHERDS
SHOCK
SHOW
SHOWERS
SHOWRD
SHOWRE
SHRINE
SHRINK
SIEGE
SIMILITUDE
SIN'D
SINFUL
SINLESS
SITTING
SIXT
SKY
SLACK
SLAUGHTER
SLIME
SLOPE
SLUNK
SNAKIE
SOARE
SOIL
SOWD
SOYLE
SPECIOUS
SPEND
SPHEAR
SPHEARS
SPIRES
SPOILS
SPOTS
SQUADRON
SQUARE
STARRY
STARTED
STEED
STOLE
STONIE
STORMS
STRAIGHT
STRICTEST
STRICTLY
STROAK
STRUCTURE
STUDIOUS
STYL'D
SUBDUES
SUBMISS
SUFFERD
SUFFIC'D
SULPHUR
SUNNIE
SUN'S
SUPERNAL

3 (CONT.)
SURCHARG'D
SURER
SURFET
SURGING
SURPASS
SURPRIZE
SUSTAIND
SWARM'D
SWARMING
SWEAT
SWEETNESS
SWEETS
SWERVE
SWUM
SYMPATHIE
SYMPHONIES
TABLE
TALK'D
TEMPESTUOUS
TEMPLES
TERRORS
THAN
*THER
THINKST
THREATN'D
THRONG'D
THROWS
THUNDERS
THWART
TORN
TORRENT
TORRID
TOUCH'D
TOUCHT
TOWRE
TRACE
TRANSCENDENT
TRANSFORM'D
TRANSPORTS
TRIBUTE
TRIE
TRIPLE
TRIUMPHAL
TROOP
TRUSTED
TUMULT
TURNE
TURNING
TWELVE
TYRANT
UNANIMOUS
UNAWARE
UNBLAM'D
UNBORN
UNDERGOE
UNDERSTANDING
UNFEIGN'D
UNHEARD
UNITE
UNLIKE
UNNAM'D
UNSIGHTLY
UNSPEAKABLE
UNWARIE
UNWORTHIE
UPPER
UPROAR
UTTERANCE
VACANT
VAILE
VAN
VEILD
VEILE
VERGE
VERNAL
VERTUOUS
VEXT
VICE
VICTORY
VIEW'D
VIEWING
VIGILANCE
VIGOR
VINES
VISIBLY
VOCAL
VOLUNTARIE
VOUTSAFE
VOUTSAFES
VOWS
VOYAGE
WAIT
WAITE
WAKE
WANTING
WARN
WARN'D
WARRIOUR

3 (CONT.)
WARRIOURS
WASTING
WATCHES
WATCHFUL
WATCHING
WEAPONS
*WERT
WHAT E'RE
WHEREBY
WHIRLWIND
WHITE
WIDER
WILLING
WILLINGLY
WINDE
WINGD
WINNING
WISHT
WITHDRAW
WITHERD
WOES
WOMEN
WOODIE
WORKES
WORM
WORSHIPPERS
WORTHIER
WRAUGHT
WRETCHED
YIELDS
YOUNG
YOUTHFUL
ZEAL

2
ABANDOND
ABASH'T
ABHORRED
ABIDES
ABOMINABLE
ABOUND
ABRAHAMS
ABSENTS
ABSOLVE
ABUNDANCE
ABUNDANT
ABUSE
ACCENT
ACCEPTABLE
ACCLAIME
ACCORD
ACCOUNTABLE
ACCUS'D
ACCUSER
ACCUSTOMD
ACHIEV'D
ACHIEVD
ACKNOWLEDG'D
ACTION
ACTIVE
ADDITION
ADHERE
ADHERENTS
ADONIS
ADORN
ADVANTAGES
ADVERSARY
ADVIS'D
AETNA
AFFABLE
AFFECT
AFFIRM
AFFRONT
AGGRAVATE
AIM'D
AIRIE
ALAS
ALCINOUS
ALLARME
ALL-RULING
ALMIGHTIE'S
ALMIGHTIES
ALMOST
ALT
ALTERATION
ALTERD
AMARANT
AMAZE
AMBER
AMBIENT
AMBUSH
AMENDS
AMITIE
AMPLY
AMUS'D
ANGELICAL
ANIMAL
ANIMATE

2 (CONT.)
ANNOY
ANOTHERS
ANSWERABLE
ANTAGONIST
APPARENT
APPARITION
APPEARD
APPEERING
APPLI'D
APPLY
APPREHEND
APPREHENSION
APPROACH'D
APPROACHD
ARBITER
ARBOUR
ARCHED
ARCH-FIEND
ARDOR
ARGU'D
ARKE
ARMING
ARROWS
ASCENDS
ASHES
ASIDE
ASKANCE
ASK'D
ASPIR'D
ASSAYD
ASSEMBLE
ASSIGN'D
ASSOCIATES
ASSYRIAN
ATHEIST
ATLAS
ATTAIND
ATTAINS
ATTEMPTED
ATTEMPTING
ATTEST
ATTRACTION
ATTRIBUTED
AUDACIOUS
AUGMENTED
AUTHENTIC
AVAIL
AVAILE
AVAILES
AVENGING
AVERT
AVOID
AW
AWAITS
AWAK'T
AWARE
AY
BABEL
BABYLON
BACCHUS
BACKWARD
BALEFUL
BALLANCE
BALLANC'T
BANNERS
BAPTIZ'D
BARBAROUS
BARK
BARK'D
BARR
BARRD
BASE
BATTALION
BATTLEMENTS
BAY
BEACH
BEARDED
BEARES
BEAT
BEAUTIES
BECAME
BECAM'ST
BECOM
BEDS
BEE
BEGIRT
BEHALF
BEHELDST
BEHINDE
BELIEF
BELLY
BELONG
BELOW
BENDING
BENDS
BENEDICTION
BENEFIT
BERRIE

2 (CONT.)
BESAUGHT
BESEECHING
BESEEMS
BESIDE
BESPAKE
BESTOW
BIDE
BIGNESS
BIRTHRIGHT
BITUMINOUS
BLACKEST
BLANC
BLASPHEMOUS
BLEW
BLOODIE
BLOT
BLOW'N
BLOWS
BLUSTRING
BOARD
BOG
BOILES
BOLDER
BOLDLY
BOLT
BOLTED
BONDAGE
BONDS
BOOK
BOON
BORDER
BORDERING
BORDERS
BORROW'D
BOTTOMLESS
BOUGHS
BOUNTIES
BOW'D
BOWD
BOWERS
BOYLING
BRANCH
BRANDISHT
BREACH
BREAKING
BREAKS
BREAST
BREATHD
BREATHING
BRIGHTER
BRINGING
BROODING
BRUTAL
BUD
BUILDERS
BULLS
BURN'D
BURNE
BURNISHT
BURNS
BURNT
BURST
BUSH
BUSIED
BUSINESS
BUXOM
CADENCE
CALLING
CAPABLE
CAPACIOUS
CARBUNCLE
CARCASSES
CAREFUL
CARREER
CATARACTS
CATHAIAN
CATTLE
CAUS'D
CEDARS
CELEBRATE
CELL
CENTRIC
CHAIN
CHAIN'D
CHAIND
CHAINES
CHAIR
CHAMPAIN
CHANC'D
CHANGES
CHARG'D
CHARITIE
CHARM'D
CHASTE
CHEARD
CHERUB
CHIVALRY
CHORAL

2 (CONT.)
CHOSEN
CHOS'N
CHUSE
CIRCUMFUS'D
CLAIME
CLAMOR
CLANG
CLAY
CLEERD
CLEERE
CLIMBE
CLIMBING
CLOATH'D
CLODS
CLOSING
CLOUDED
CLOUDY
CLUSTERS
CLUSTRING
COASTS
COATE
COLLATERAL
COLLECTED
COLOURD
COMBAT
COMBUSTION
COMET
COMMANDED
COMMANDER
COMMUNICATED
COMMUNION
COMPANION
COMPANIONS
COMPASSING
COMPASSION
COMPLACENCE
COMPLAINT
COMPLEAT
COMPLIANCE
COMPOSURE
COMPULSION
CONCAVE
CONCEAL
CONCEAL'D
CONCEALD
CONCEALE
CONCERN
CONCERNES
CONCLUDE
CONCURRING
CONFIRM'D
CONFIRMD
CONFLICT
CONNATURAL
CONQUERING
CONSEQUENCE
CONSISTS
CONSOLATION
CONSTRAIND
CONSTRAINT
CONTAGION
CONTAINE
CONTEMPLATION
CONTEMPTUOUS
CONTENTMENT
CONTIGUOUS
CONTINUE
CONTRADICTION
CONTRARY
CONTRIVE
CONTRIVING
CONVICTION
COOL
CORDIAL
CORPORAL
CORRESPOND
COST
COUCHT
COUNCIL
COUNSEL'D
COUNT
COUNTERFET
COURT
COVERD
COVERING
COVET
CREEP
CRESCENT
CRESTED
CROSS'D
CROUD
CROWD
CROWNS
CRUSH
CRY'D
CUPS
CURLD
CURLES

2 (CONT.)
CUSTODY
DAIES
DALES
DANC'D
DARKER
DARK'ND
DARLING
DAR'ST
DAUNTLESS
DAVID
DAY-SPRING
DAZLE
DEAL
DEALT
DEARER
DEARTH
DEATHLESS
DEBT
DECEIV'D
DECLARES
DECLIN'D
DEEPEST
DEFAC'T
DEFEAT
DEFEATED
DEFORM
DEGRADED
DEIGN'D
DEIGNE
DELAID
DELAYES
DELECTABLE
DELIA'S
DELIVER
DELOS
DELUDE
DELUSIVE
DENS
DEPARTING
DEPORT
DERIDED
DERIDES
DERIVE
DESCRIBE
DESERV'D
DESERVD
DESERVING
DESIGNES
DESIRING
DESIR'ST
DESPAIRD
DESPARE
DESPICABLE
DESPISE
DESTROYES
DETERMIN'D
DETRIMENT
DEVIS'D
DEVOTION
DEVOURD
DEVOURING
DEVOUT
DEWES
DIFFERING
DIFFIDENT
DIGNITY
DIMENSION
DIMM'D
DINNER
DIPT
DISAPPEERD
DISCERN
DISCERNS
DISCHARGE
DISCLOS'D
DISCLOSE
DISCOMPOS'D
DISCOUNT'NANC'T
DISCOVER'D
DISCOVERD
DISGORGING
DISHONOUR
DISLODGE
DISLOYAL
DISMAI'D
DISMAID
DISOBEDIENT
DISOBEYES
DISORDER
DISPARTED
DISPATCH
DISPENSES
DISPENST
DISPERS'D
DISPERSE
DISPLAID
DISPORT
DISPOSSESS

2 (CONT.)
DISPRAISE
DISRELISH
DISTRUST
DISTURB'D
DIVERS
DIVIDES
DIVIDUAL
DOLOROUS
DOMESTIC
DOMINIONS
DORIC
DOUBTLESS
DOWNE
DRAIND
DRAWS
DREAM'D
DRIVES
DROPPING
DUBIOUS
DULCET
DURABLE
DURING
DUSKY
DWELS
DY'D
EAGER
EARES
EARLIEST
EARNE
EARST
EARTH-BORN
EAS'D
EASING
EATEN
EATING
EAT'N
EAT'ST
ECHOING
ECLIPS
EEV'NING
EFFECTED
EGYPTIAN
EMBRYON
EMPEROUR
EMPRESS
EMPTY
ENCLIN'D
ENCLOSURE
ENCOMPASS'D
ENCREASE
ENDANGER'D
ENDOWD
ENLARG'D
ENQUIRE
ENRAG'D
ENSHRINE
ENSIGN
ENSIGNS
ENSLAV'D
ENSU'D
ENTER'D
ENTHRALL'D
ENTHRON'D
ENUR'D
ENVIED
ENVIES
ENVYING
EQUALITIE
EQUINOCTIAL
E'RE
ERELONG
EREWHILE
ERR
ERR'D
ERRING
ERROUR
ERUPTION
ESCAP'D
ESCAPE
ESSENTIAL
ESTABLISHT
ETERNITY
ETERNIZE
EUPHRATES
EUROPE
EVIDENCE
EVILL
EXALTATION
EXCELL'D
EXCELLENT
EXCELLS
EXCITE
EXCLUDE
EXCURSION
EXECRABLE
EXHALATIONS
EXHAL'D
EXPECTING

2 (CONT.)
EXPLOITS
EXPLORE
EXPLORES
EXPRESSING
EXPRESSION
EXTENDS
EXTENT
EXTINCT
EYE-LIDS
FABRICK
FACTION
FACTIOUS
FACULTIES
FAIL'D
FAITHLESS
FALLACIOUS
FAM'D
FAN
FARES
FAT
FATALL
FAVOURABLE
FAVOUR'D
FEARING
FEARST
FEASTS
FEEDS
FEIGND
FELL'D
FELLOWSHIP
FEMALE
FENS
FERVID
FESTIVALS
FICKLE
FIERCELY
FIGHTING
FIGURE
FINDES
FIRMNESS
FIRST-BORN
FITTER
FLAM'D
FLEDGE
FLEECIE
FLEET
FLOODS
FLOWD
FLOWS
FOILD
FOLLIE
FOLLOWERS
FOMENT
FORBIDDING
FORBORE
FORD
FORESEEING
FORESIGHT
FOREWARND
FOREWARNE
FORFEIT
FORGE
FORGETFUL
FORGETS
FORGOT
FORKED
FORLORNE
FORME
FORMLESS
FORSOOK
FORTITUDE
FOUNDATIONS
FRAILTIE
FRAUDULENT
FREED
FREQUENTING
FRIGHTED
FROWNING
FRUGAL
FRUITION
FRUTAGE
FULFIL
FULFILLD
FUME
FUMING
FURDER
FURNACE
GAINES
GALES
GAN
GANGES
GARDENS
GARLAND
GENERATE
GENERATION
GENTILES
GET
GIVN

2 (CONT.)
GLADE
GLADLIER
GLAR'D
GLEAME
GLISTRING
GLOBES
GLOBOSE
GLORIES
GLORIOUSLY
GLOW'D
GLOWD
GLOWING
GOATS
GODDESS-LIKE
GODLESS
GOD'S
GOES
GOING
GOLD'N
GORGONIAN
GOURD
GOVERNS
GRADUAL
GRATEFULLY
GRAV'N
GREECE
GREEDILY
GREY
GRIESLIE
GRIEVE
GRIPE
GROAN
GROANS
GROSSER
GROVELING
GROWES
GUARDIANS
GUESTS
GUIDED
GUIDES
GUILDS
GUILEFUL
GUISE
GUST
HABITANT
HABITANTS
HABITATIONS
HAD'ST
HAINOUS
HAIR
HAIRE
HAIRIE
HALLELUIAHS
HANDED
HANGING
HANGS
HARBINGER
HARDIE
HARSH
HATED
HAUTIE
HEAPS
HEARK'ND
HEAR'ST
HEATHEN
HEAV'D
HEAVENLY
HEAVN
HEAV'NLIE
HELLS
HELME
HELMES
HERMON
HERO'S
*HERS
HESPERUS
HEWN
HIDDEN
HIERARCH
HIGHT
HILLOCKS
HITHERTO
HOARSE
HOLIE
HOLIEST
HOMEWARD
HONOUR'D
HOPELESS
HOPING
HORNES
HORNS
HORRORS
HOSPITABLE
HOUNDS
HOURLY
HOV'RING
HUBBUB
HUGEST

2 (CONT.)
HUMBLY
HUMOR
HUNTER
HURLD
HUSBANDS
HYACINTH
IDA
IDOL
IDOLATRIES
IDOLS
IGNOBLE
IGNOMINY
IGNORANT
IMAGINATIONS
IMAGIN'D
IMAGIND
IMBATTELLD
IMBLAZ'D
IMBODIED
IMBOSOM'D
IMITATE
IMITATION
IMMEASURABLE
IMMORTALITIE
IMMOVABLE
IMPAIR'D
IMPAIRD
IMPAL'D
IMPENDENT
IMPENETRABLE
IMPLIES
IMPLOYD
IMPORTUNE
IMPRESS'D
IMPROV'D
INCARNATE
INCENST
INCLEMENT
INCLINATION
INCLINE
INCLINES
INCREASE
INDEBTED
INDIVIDUAL
INDULGENT
INEFFABLE
INEVITABLE
INEXPRESSIBLE
INFANT
INFINITLY
INFINITUDE
INFLICT
INFLICTED
INGENDRING
INGRATE
INGRATEFUL
INGULFT
INHABIT
INHABITANT
INHABITANTS
INJUR'D
INMATE
INNOCENT
INORDINATE
INSATIATE
INSENSIBLE
INSENSIBLY
INSPIRES
INSTILL'D
INSTRUCT
INSTRUCTED
INSTRUCTER
INSTRUMENTAL
INSULTING
INTEGRITIE
INTELLIGENTIAL
INTERDICTED
INTERMISSION
INTERMITTED
INTERMIX
INTERMIXT
INTERNAL
INTERPOSE
INTERPRETER
INTERVIEW
INTESTINE
INVENTIONS
INVESTS
INVIOLABLE
INVITING
INVOKE
INVOK'T
INVULNERABLE
IRIS
IRRATIONAL
ISLES
ISSUE
*ITS

2 (CONT.)
JACOB
JARRING
JEALOUS
JESUS
JOIN'D
JOURNIE
JOURNIES
JOYNE
JUDG
JUDGEMENTS
JUDGES
JUDICIOUS
JUSTIFIE
JUSTLING
KEEPING
KEN
KENN
KINDL'D
KINE
KINGDOMS
LABORIOUS
LABOURS
LABYRINTH
LAMB
LAMBS
LAMENTING
LAPSE
LATER
LATEST
LAWES
LAWFUL
LAYES
LEADERS
LEARND
LEASURE
LEND
LESSER
LEVEL'D
LEVELD
LEVIATHAN
LEVIED
LEWD
LIDS
LIGHTER
LIGHTLY
LIK'NING
LIMBS
LIMIT
LINEAMENTS
LOADEN
LOATHSOM
LOCUSTS
LOE
LOFTIE
LOFTIEST
LONELY
LOOSING
LOP
LOPT
LORDLY
LORE
LOUDEST
LOV'D
LOVELIER
LOVING
LOWLIE
LUCID
LUMINARIES
LUMINOUS
LUR'D
LUSTFUL
LYBIAN
MAGNIFIC
MAGNITUDE
MAILE
MAISTRIE
MALIGNANT
MANLY
MANTLE
MANURING
MARKT
MAROCCO
MATCHT
MATERIALS
MATIN
MAUGRE
MAW
MAZIE
MEANEST
MEANING
MEASURES
MEATS
MEDIATOR
MEER
MEERLY
MEMORIAL
MEMPHIAN
MENTION

2 (CONT.)
MERCIE-SEAT
MESSENGER
MESSENGERS
ME THOUGHT
METROPOLIS
METTAL
MILDER
MILDNESS
MILITANT
MILITARY
MILKIE
MINERAL
MINGLE
MIRROR
MIRTLE
MISRULE
MISTRUST
MOCKT
MODEL
MOISTURE
MOLOC
MOLOCH
MONARCHIE
MONTHS
MONUMENT
MOONS
MOOVD
MORROW
MOSSIE
MOTHERS
MOUTHES
MOVES
MUSES
MUSIC
MYRRH
MYRRHE
MYRTLE
MYSTIC
NAKEDNESS
NAMING
NAY
NEAR
NEARER
NEATHER
NECESSITY
NECTAROUS
NEGLECT
NETHERMOST
NEWS
NITROUS
NOBLEST
NOCTURNAL
NOONTIDE
NOSTRILS
NOTE
OBDURATE
OBEYING
OBEYS
OBLIVION
OBNOXIOUS
OBSERVD
OBSTACLE
OBTAIN'D
OFFERING
OFFERINGS
OFFICIOUS
OFTEN
OLYMPIAN
OMNIPRESENCE
ONSET
OPACOUS
OPEN'D
OPENER
OPENS
OPINION
OPPRESSION
OPPREST
OPTIC
ORACLE
ORBICULAR
ORDAINE
ORGAN
ORGANS
ORISONS
ORNAMENT
ORONTES
OUTCRY
OUTRAGE
OUTSIDE
OUTSTRETCHT
OVERARCH'T
OVERLAID
OVERMUCH
OVERPOWERD
OVERTHREW
OVERTHROW
OVERTHROWN
OWNE

2 (CONT.)
OX
PACES
PALACES
PALESTINE
PALME
PALPABLE
PAN
PANDAEMONIUM
PANOPLIE
PARTICIPATE
PARTITION
PARTNER
PASSIVE
PASTURE
PASTURING
PATRON
PAW
PEAL
PEARLE
PEIRC'D
PENANCE
PENITENT
PENNONS
PENT
PERCEIVE
PERFECT
PERFECTIONS
PERFIDIOUS
PERFORME
PERFORMING
PERILOUS
PERMISSION
PERMITTED
PERPLEX
PERSISTED
PERSWADE
PERSWASIVE
PERTURBATION
PERVERTED
PESTILENCE
PIERC'D
PIERCING
PILOT
PIN'D
PIOUS
PIPE
PIPES
PLAGUE
PLAGUES
PLAINS
PLANET
PLATE
PLEA
PLEADED
PLEASD
PLEASES
PLENTY
PLUCK'D
PLUMES
PLY
POLLUTED
POMONA
PONTUS
POOLE
POROUS
PORTENDING
PORTENTOUS
PORTION
POSSEST
POSSIBLE
POTENTATE
POUR
PRACTISD
PRAEEMINENCE
PRAEEMINENT
PRAIS'D
PRAISES
PRAYING
PRECEDES
PREFACE
PREFER
PREFERR'D
PREFERRING
PRESAGING
PRESUME
PRETENDING
PRETENSE
PREVAILES
PREVALENT
PREVENTED
PREVENTION
PRIEST
PRIESTS
PRINCIPALITIES
PROCEEDS
PROCESS
PROCLAIMING
PRODUCES

2 (CONT.)
PROFITS
PROFUSE
PROGENITOR
PROGRESS
PROHIBITION
PROMOTE
PROOFF
PROP
PROPAGATED
PROPHETS
PROPORTION
PROPOSEST
PROSE
PROSPER'D
PROSPEROUS
PROUDLY
PROVES
PROVIDENT
PRUDENT
PRUNE
PUISSANCE
PUNISH
PUNISHT
PURITIE
PURPOS'D
PUTTING
PYTHIAN
QUAINT
QUELL
QUENCHT
QUEST
QUICK'ND
QUIET
QUINTESSENCE
QUIVER
RACK
RAIES
RAISD
RALLIED
RANDOM
RANKT
RAS'D
RASE
RAVENOUS
READIE
READIEST
REAPING
REARD
REASCEND
REASONS
REBELL
REBELLD
RECALL
RECEAVD
RECEPTACLE
RECEPTION
RECOILD
RECOILES
RECOMPENC'T
RECORDED
RECOVER'D
RECOVERD
REDEEMD
REDEEMS
REDUC'T
REFLECTION
REGAIN
REGAIND
REGAINE
REGARDLESS
REJECT
REJECTED
REJOIC'D
REJOYC'D
RELATED
RELATING
RELATION
RELIGION
RELIGIOUS
RELIQUES
RELUCTANCE
REMAINE
REMISS
REMIT
RENEW
REPAIRE
REPEATE
REPLENISHT
REPLETE
REPOS'D
REPRESENT
REPRESENTING
REPULST
REPUTE
RESCU'D
RESEMBLES
RESEMBLING
RESIDING

2 (CONT.)
RESIGN
RESOUNDS
RESPIT
RESTLESS
RESTRAIND
RESULT
RESUME
RETIRES
RETURNST
REVELS
REVERSE
REVIV'D
REVOLUTION
RHEA'S
RIBS
RICHEST
RIDES
RINDE
ROAM
ROAM'D
ROAVING
ROCKIE
ROOTS
ROULD
ROUNDING
ROUS'D
ROUSE
ROVE
ROVING
ROWL
ROWL'D
RUINE
RUINOUS
RULING
RUSH
RUSSIAN
SABBATH
SACRIFICING
SADNESS
SAFEST
SAFETY
SANCTUARIE
SANCTUARY
SANG
SAPHIR
SAPHIRE
SATANS
SATISFACTION
SATST
SAUGHT
SAVES
SAVORIE
SCENE
SCOFFING
SCORN'D
SCOURGE
SCOUT
SEARCHT
SEATE
SEATED
SEAVEN
SECUR'D
SEEKST
SELDOM
SELF-RAIS'D
SEMBLANCE
SEQUEL
SERAPHIC
SERRIED
SERVANTS
SERVD
SERVES
SERVILE
SETTING
SETTL'D
SEVEN
SEVENTH
SEWERS
SHADING
SHAFTS
SHAGGIE
SHAKES
SHAM'D
SHARPEST
SHEAVES
SHEER
SHELTER
SHELTERD
SHEPHERD
SHEW'D
SHEWN
SHOOTS
SHORES
SHORN
SHOWR
SHUN'D
SHUND
SHUNND

2 (CONT.)
SICK
SIDE-LONG
SIGHTS
SILENTLY
SILVAN
SIMPLICITIE
SINAI
SINGED
SINGING
SINGS
SINN'D
SIZE
SKINS
SKIRT
SLAIN
SLEEPST
SLENDER
SLEW
SLIGHT
SLOTH
SLUMBER
SLUMBRING
SMELLS
SNOWIE
SOARING
SOBER
SODOM
SOJOURN
SOJOURNERS
SOLUTION
SOONEST
SOULES
SOULS
SOUNDING
SOURSE
SOV'RAN
SPACES
SPAR'D
SPARKLING
SPEEDIEST
SPEEDY
SPI'D
SPIES
SPIGHT
SPIRITED
SPIRITOUS
SPOILD
SPOILE
SPORT
SPORTING
SPREADING
SPREADS
STAIES
STAIND
STAIR
STAIRS
STAR
STARRES
STARV'D
STATELIEST
STEARS
STILE
STING
STIR
STOCK
STOODST
STOOP
STOOPING
STORES
STRAY
STRAY'D
STREAME
STREAMING
STREETS
STRIDES
STRONGLY
STROVE
STRUCK
STUBBORN
STUDY
STUFF
SUBJECT
SUBJECTED
SUBLIM'D
SUBMISSIVE
SUBSIST
SUBSTANCES
SUBSTANTIAL
SUCCESSES
SUCCESSFUL
SUFFERINGS
SUGGESTION
SULPHUROUS
SULTAN
SUM
SUMM'D
SUMME
SUMMOND

2 (CONT.)
SUMMS
SUPPER
SUPPLE
SUPPLIANT
SUPPLICATION
SUPPLIE
SUPPLY
SUPPOSE
SUPREAME
SUREST
SURGE
SURMISE
SURPASSING
SURPRISE
SURPRIZ'D
SURVEY'D
SUSPECT
SUSPICION
SUSPICIOUS
SUTTLEST
SWALLOW'D
SWIFTEST
SWIFTNESS
SWORDS
TABERNACLE
TAKEN
TALKING
TARTAR
TARTARUS
TASTES
TAURUS
TELLST
TEMPER'D
TEMPERD
TEMPTATIONS
TENDANCE
TENDED
TENDS
TEXTURE
THAMMUZ
THANK
THEB'S
THIEF
THINKING
THINNER
THRONGING
THRUST
THUNDERBOLTS
TILTING
TITLE
TOIL
TOILD
TOILE
TOILSOM
TOLLERABLE
TORTURE
TORTURES
TOSSING
TOWER
TOWRING
TRANSFERR'D
TRANSFUS'D
TRANSGRESSING
TRANSGRESSION
TRANSPLANTED
TRANSVERSE
TRAVEL
TREMBL'D
TRIUMPHING
TRIUMPHS
TROPHIES
TRUSTING
TUFT
TUMULTUOUS
TUNES
TWICE
'TWIXT
TWIXT
TYGER
TYPES
TYRANNY
UGLY
UMPIRE
UNABLE
UNACTIVE
UNAWARES
UNBLEST
UNBOUNDED
UNBUILD
UNCONQUERABLE
UNCONSUM'D
UNCREATE
UNCREATED
UNDERGO
UNDERTOOK
UNDIMINISHT
UNEQUAL
UNESPI'D

2 (CONT.)
UNEXPECTED
UNFAITHFUL
UNFELT
UNGUARDED
UNIMPLOR'D
UNITES
UNKINDLY
UNMINDFUL
UNNUMBER'D
UNQUIET
UNREST
UNSAY
UNSHAK'N
UNTERRIFI'D
UNTRI'D
UNWEARIED
UNWEETING
UPBRAIDED
UPSTART
URANIA
URGES
USEFUL
USELESS
USHER
USURP
USURPING
USURPT
UTTERING
UTTERMOST
VALES
VALLIE
VALUE
VAPOR
VAPORS
VAPOURS
VARIED
VAULT
VAULTED
VAUNTING
VEHEMENT
VENGEFUL
VENT
VENTURE
VERDURE
VERSE
VICISSITUDE
VIOLATE
VIRTUAL
VISAGES
VISIONS
VISITATION
VISUAL
VOTE
VOUTSAFT
VOYCE
WAITED
WAKEN
WAN
WAND
WANDERD
WARR'D
WARRIERS
WARRS
WASTEFUL
WASTFUL
WATERD
WATERING
WEAKER
WEAKNESS
WEAL
WEARIE
WEEP
WEIGH
WEIGHS
WEILD
WHAT EVER
WHEEL
WHEREWITH
WHIRLWINDS
WHISPERING
WHOEVER
WHOLSOM
WILFUL
WILIE
WILLS
WIP'D
WISDOMS
WISEST
WITHALL
WITHHELD
WITHSTOOD
WO
WOLVES
WONDERD
WONDERS
WOOD-NYMPH
WOOMB
WORLDLY

2 (CONT.)
WORN
WORS
WORTHIE
WOVE
WRAPT
WRECK
WRITE
WRITH'D
WRITTEN
YAWNING
YEA
YEAR
YEARLY
YEILD
YIELDING
YOUNGER
*YOUR SELVES
ZENITH
ZODIAC

1
AARON
AARONS
ABANDON
ABARIM
ABASSIN
ABATED
ABBANA
ABHOR
ABHORR
ABHORR'D
ABHORRD
ABHORRE
ABHORR'ST
ABJURE
ABOLISHT
ABOMINATIONS
ABOUNDANCE
ABOUNDED
ABOUNDS
ABROAD
ABRUPT
ABSOLUTELY
ABSOLV'D
ABSTAIN'D
ABSTINENCE
ABSTRACT
ABSTRACTED
ABSTRUSE
ABSTRUSEST
ABUNDANTLY
ABUS'D
ABYSSE
ACANTHUS
ACCARON
ACCESSIBLE
ACCESSORIES
ACCLAIM
ACCLAMATION
ACCLAMATIONS
ACCOMPANI'D
ACCOMPLISH'D
ACCOMPLISHING
ACCOMPLISH'T
ACCOMPLISHT
ACCOST
ACCOSTES
ACCUSATION
ACHERON
ACHIEVE
ACHILLES
ACKNOWLDG'D
ACQUAINT
ACQUITTANCE
ACQUITTED
ACTUAL
ADAM'S
ADDE
ADDER
ADDRESS
ADDRESS'D
ADDRESSD
ADES
ADJOURNE
ADJOYND
ADMIR'ST
ADMITTING
ADMONISH
ADMONISH'D
ADMONISHMENT
ADMONISHT
ADOPTED
ADORERS
ADORING
ADORNE
ADORNS
ADRAMELEC
ADRIA

1 (CONT.)
ADRIFT
ADULTERIE
ADULTEROUS
ADUST
ADUSTED
ADVANCING
ADVANTAGIOUS
ADVENT'ROUS
ADVENTURER
ADVICE
ADVISING
ADVOCATE
AEGAEAN
AEGYPTIAN
AEQUATOR
AEQUINOCTIAL
AFER
AFFAIRES
AFFAIRS
AFFECTS
AFFLICTING
AFFLICTION
AFFLICTS
AFFORDS
AFFRIGHTED
AFFRONTS
AFLOAT
AFRESH
AFRIC
AFTER-BANDS
AFTERNOONS
AFTER-TIMES
AGAPE
AGAST
AGEN
AGENTS
AGGREGATED
AGITATION
AGRA
AHAZ
AIALON
AIDED
AIERIE
AIME
AIMES
AIM'ST
ALABLASTER
ALACRITIE
ALADULE
ALCAIRO
ALCHIMIST
ALCHYMIE
ALCIDES
ALEIAN
ALGIERS
ALIEN
ALIENATE
ALIGHTED
ALIGHTS
ALIMENTAL
ALIVE
ALLARM
ALLARM'D
ALLARMD
ALLAY
ALLAY'D
ALLAYD
ALL-BEARING
ALL-CHEARING
ALLEDG'D
ALLEGEANCE
ALLEGIANCE
ALLIES
ALL-KNOWING
ALLOTTED
ALLOW
ALL-POWERFUL
ALL-SEEING
ALLURD
ALLUREMENT
ALLURING
ALLUSION
ALMANSOR
ALOOF
ALOOFF
ALPE
ALTER
ALTER'D
ALTERNATE
ALTERNE
ALTHOUGH
ALWAYS
AMAINE
AMALTHEA
AMARA
AMARANTIN
AMAZONIAN
AMBROSIA

1 (CONT.)
AMERC'T
AMERICAN
AMIABLIE
AMITY
AMMIRAL
AMMON
AMMONIAN
AMMONITE
AMONGST
AMOURS
AMPHISBAENA
AMPLER
AMPLEST
AMPLIER
AMPLITUDE
AMRAMS
ANARCH
ANCESTORS
ANCHOR
ANCHORS
ANCIENTLY
ANDROMEDA
ANGERS
ANGOLA
ANGRIE
ANIMALS
ANNEXT
ANNIHILATING
ANNULS
ANOW
ANTARTIC
ANTIPATHIE
ANXIOUS
AONIAN
APACE
APART
APATHIE
APE
APOCALYPS
APOLOGIE
APOSTASIE
APOSTATE
APOSTATES
APOSTLES
APPAID
APPEARANCE
APPEARANCES
APPEERANCES
APPERE
APPERTAINE
APPERTAINS
APPETENCE
APPLAUDED
APPLE
APPLES
APPLY'D
APPOINT
APPOINTS
APPREHENDED
APPROACHES
APPROACHT
APPROPRIATING
APT
APTER
ARABIAN
ARABIE
ARABLE
ARAM
ARAYING
ARBITRARY
ARBITRATOR
ARBITREMENT
ARBITRESS
ARBORETS
ARBOROUS
ARBORS
ARCADIAN
ARCHANGELIC
ARCH-ANGELS
ARCH-CHIMIC
ARCH-ENEMY
ARCH-FELLON
ARCHITRAVE
ARCHT
ARDENT
ARDORS
ARGENT
ARGESTES
ARGO
ARGOB
ARGUING
ARGUS
ARIEL
ARIES
ARIMASPIAN
ARIOC
ARISES
ARMOR

1 (CONT.)
ARMORIC
ARMORIE
ARMOURIE
ARMOURY
ARNON
AROAR
AROUND
ARRAIGND
ARRAYD
ARRAYING
ARREEDE
ARROGATE
ARROW
ARTICK
ARTICULAT
ARTIFICE
ARTIFICER
ARTILLERY
ARTIST
ARTS
ASCALON
ASCANSE
ASCENTION
ASCRIBE
ASHTAROTH
ASIA
ASKE
ASLOPE
ASMADAI
ASMODEUS
ASP
ASPECTS
ASPERSES
ASPHALTIC
ASPHALTICK
ASPHALTUS
ASPHODEL
ASPIRER
ASPRAMONT
ASSAIES
ASSAILD
ASSASSIN-LIKE
ASSAULTING
ASSAY'D
ASSAYING
ASSEMBLIES
ASSENT
ASSENTING
ASSESSOR
ASSIDUOUS
ASSIG'N'D
ASSIGND
ASSIMILATE
ASSIST
ASSUMING
ASSURE
ASSURES
ASSYRIA
ASTARTE
ASTHMA'S
ASTONIED
ASTONISHMENT
ASTORETH
ASTOUNDED
ASTRACAN
ASTREA
ASTRONOMER
ASUNDER
ATABALIPA
ATCHIEVING
ATHEISTS
ATHENS
ATHWART
ATLANTEAN
ATLANTIC
ATLANTICK
ATOM
ATOMS
ATROPHIE
ATTACH'D
ATTACK
ATTAINES
ATTEMPTS
ATTENDANCE
ATTIRE
ATTONEMENT
ATTRACT
ATTRACTED
ATTRIBUTE
ATTRIBUTES
ATTRIBUTING
ATTRITE
ATTUNE
AUDIBLE
AUDIBLY
AUDITRESS
AURAN
AURORA'S

1 (CONT.)
AUSONIAN
AUSTEER
AUSTERELY
AUTHORITIE
AUTHORITY
AUTHORS
AUTHOUR
AUTORITIE
AUTUMNAL
AUXILIAR
AVAIL'D
AVANT
AVENGD
AVENGERS
AVOIDE
AVOIDED
AWAK'D
AWAK'NING
AWAY
AW'D
AWD
AWRY
AZAZEL
AZORES
AZOTUS
BAALIM
BABELS
BABILON
BACKS
BACKSIDE
BACTRIAN
BAIT
BAL
BALLS
BANISHMENT
BANNE
BANNERD
BANQUET
BAPTIZING
BAR
BARBARIC
BARBD
BARCA
BARD
BARRENNESS
BARRICADO'D
BASAN
BASER
BASES
BASEST
BASIS
BATES
BATH'D
BATHING
BATTAILOUS
BATTERIE
BATTERING
BATTLE
BAUM
BEADS
BEAKED
BEAMES
BEAMING
BEARST
BEARTH
BEATEN
BEATIFIC
BEATITUDE
BEAT'N
BEAVIE
BEDROPT
BEDWARD
BEERSABA
BEES
*BEEST
BEEVES
BEFALLN
BEFEL
BEFITS
BEG'D
BEGGING
BEHEMOTH
BEHOLDERS
BEHOOF
BEHOOVES
BEHOVES
BELATED
BELCH'D
BELCHING
BELCHT
BELEEFE
BELEEVERS
BELIEVES
BELIEVING
BELIEVST
BELIKE
BELLEROPHON
BELLONA

1 (CONT.)
BELLOW
BELLOWING
BELONGD
BELOVED
BELUS
BENEATHE
BENEVOLENT
BENGALA
BENUMM
BENUMM'D
BEREAV'D
BEREAVD
BEREAVE
BEREAVING
BEREFT
BERIL
BESEECH
BESIEGING
BESMEAR'D
BESMEARD
BESTIR
BESTIRS
BESTOW'D
BESTROWN
BESTROWNE
BESTUCK
BETAKE
BETHEL
BETHINK
BETIDE
BETIMES
BETOK'NING
BETRAID
BEWAILING
BICKERING
BIDST
BIGGEST
BILL
BILLOWS
BIRTH-DAY
BIRTHS
BISERTA
BITTERNESS
BIZANCE
BLAINES
BLAM'D
BLAM'ST
BLANDISHMENT
BLANK
BLASPHEAM'D
BLASPHEM'D
BLASTING
BLEED
BLESS
BLESSEDNESS
BLINDED
BLOODY
BLOOMING
BLOTTED
BLUSH
BLUSHING
BLUSTER
BOASTED
BOASTFUL
BOASTING
BOGGIE
BOGGS
BOGS
BOILING
BOLDEST
BOLDNESS
BOND
BONES
BOOKS
BOOTIE
BORDRING
BOREAS
BORROWD
BORROWING
BOSOM'D
BOSPORUS
BOSSY
BOTCHES
BOULD
BOULDER
BOUNTY
BRACE
BRAND
BRANDISHING
BRAUNCHING
BRAY'D
BREADED
BREAKE
BREATH'ST
BREDTH
BREEDING
BREEDS
BREST-PLATE

1 (CONT.)
BRESTS
BRIAREOS
BRICK
BRIDAL
BRIDGING
BRIEFLY
BRIGAD
BRIGADS
BRIGHT'ND
BRIGHTNING
BRIGHT'NS
BRIM
BRIMMING
BRIMSTONE
BRINDED
BRISTL'D
BRITISH
BRITTLE
BROIDERD
BROK'D
BROKEN
BROK'N
BROOKING
BROTHERS
BROWES
BROWN
BRUIS'D
BRUSE
BRUSH
BRUSHT
BUILDED
BUILDING
BUILDS
BULLION
BULLOCK
BULWARK
BURD'N
BURD'ND
BURGHER
BURIED
BURNES
BURTHENSOME
BUSHES
BUSHIE
BUSHING
BUSIEST
BUSIRIS
CADMUS
CAECIAS
CAELESTIAL
CALABRIA
CALAMITIE
CALAMITOUS
CALAMITY
CALCULATE
CALF
CALLOW
CALM'D
CALMER
CALMEST
CALUMNIOUS
CALV'D
CAMBALU
CAM'ST
CANAANITE
CANCELD
CANIE
CANOPIE
CAPARISONS
CAPITOLINE
CAPRICORNE
CAPTIVITIE
CAPTIVITY
CARAVAN
CARCASS
CAR'D
CAREERING
CARES
CARESSES
CARKASES
CARMEL
CARNAGE
CARNATION
CAROL
CARR
CARRIE
CARRY
CASBEEN
CASH
CASIUS
CASPIAN
CASSIA
CASTALIAN
CATARRHS
CATCH
CATCHT
CAUSEY
CAUTIOUS

1 (CONT.)
CAVIL
CEASES
CEASING
CEAST
CEELING
CELEBRATED
CELTIC
CENSER
CENSERS
CENTAURE
CENTER'D
CENTRING
CERASTES
CERBERIAN
CEREMONIES
CEREMONY
CERTAINE
CHAFF
CHALDAEA
CHAM
CHANGD
CHANNELS
CHARACTER
CHARIOTER
CHARITIES
CHARLEMAIN
CHARYBDIS
CHAST'NING
CHAUMPING
CHEAP
CHEAR'D
CHEARING
CHECK
CHECK'D
CHECKS
CHEEKS
CHEER'D
CHEERFUL
CHEMOS
CHERE
CHERISH
CHERISHING
CHERSONESE
CHEW
CHEWD
CHIL'D
CHILD-BEARING
CHILDE
CHILDERN
CHILDRENS
CHILL
CHILLING
CHIME
CHIMERA'S
CHIMIC
CHINESES
CHORDS
CHORUS
CHOYCE
CHRISTAL
CHRYSOLITE
CHRYSTALLIN
CHURCH
CINCTURE
CINDERS
CIRCEAN
CIRCLET
CIRCULAR
CIRCUMFLUOUS
CIRCUMSCRIB'D
CIRCUMSCRIBE
CIRCUMVENT
CIRCUMVENTED
CITED
CITRON
CITTADEL
CLAIM'D
CLAIMD
CLAIMS
CLAIM'ST
CLAMING
CLAMOROUS
CLAMORS
CLAMOUR
CLANNS
CLARION
CLARIONS
CLASH'D
CLASHING
CLASP
CLASPING
CLEAR
CLEARD
CLEARER
CLEEREST
CLEFT
CLEOMBROTUS
CLIFFS

1 (CONT.)
CLIMAT
CLIMATE
CLIMB
CLIMBES
CLIMBS
CLIMBST
CLIMES
CLOATH
CLOD
CLOMB
CLOS
CLOTH'D
CLOV'N
CLUNG
COAL
COASTING
COAT
COATS
COCK
COCYTUS
COETERNAL
COGITATION
COHORT
COLIC
COLLECTING
COLLEGUE
COLLISION
COLLOQUIE
COLUMBUS
COLURE
COMBATANTS
COMBROUS
COMBUSTIBLE
COMELY
COMFORTABLE
COMFORTER
COMFORTLESS
COMFORTS
COMLINESS
COMMANDST
COMMENDS
COMMER
COMMISERATION
COMMISSION
COMMIT
COMMITTED
COMMODIOUSLY
COMMONALTIE
COMMUNE
COMMUNICABLE
COMMUNICATING
COMMUNICATION
COMPACT
COMPANIE
COMPARISON
COMPASSES
COMPASST
COMPAST
COMPEER
COMPEERS
COMPEL
COMPEL'D
COMPELLD
COMPELS
COMPLAIN
COMPLEATING
COMPLETE
COMPLETED
COMPLIANT
COMPLICATED
COMPOSE
COMPOSITION
COM'ST
COMST
CONCEALES
CONCEAV'D
CONCEAVE
CONCEAVES
CONCEITS
CONCENTRING
CONCERN'D
CONCERND
CONCERNING
CONCLAVE
CONCLUDES
CONCOCT
CONCOCTED
CONCOCTIVE
CONCOURS
CONCUPISCENCE
CONCURD
CONDEMND
CONDEMNE
CONDEMNING
CONDEMNS
CONDENSE
CONDENSES
CONDENS'T

1 (CONT.)
CONDESCENSION
CONDESCENTION
CONDITIONS
CONDUCTED
CONE
CONFER
CONFERENCE
CONFERRD
CONFESS'D
CONFESSING
CONFEST
CONFIDE
CONFIND
CONFINE
CONFIRM
CONFLAGRANT
CONFLICTING
CONFORMD
CONFORMITIE
CONFUS'DLY
CONGLOB'D
CONGLOBING
CONGO
CONGRATULANT
CONGREGATED
CONGREGATION
CONJUNCTION
CONJUR'D
CONNEXION
CONNIVING
CONNUBIAL
CONQUERD
CONQUEROR
CONQUEROURS
CONSIDER
CONSIDERATE
CONSIDER'D
CONSIDERD
CONSIST
CONSISTENCE
CONSISTING
CONSOLATIONS
CONSORTED
CONSPICIOUS
CONSPIRACY
CONSPIR'D
CONSTANCIE
CONSTRAINING
CONSULTATION
CONSULTATIONS
CONSUM'D
CONSUMES
CONTAGIOUS
CONTAIND
CONTEMN
CONTEMND
CONTEMNES
CONTEMPTIBLY
CONTENDED
CONTENTION
CONTENTS
CONTINUAL
CONTINU'ST
CONTRACTED
CONTRACTION
CONTRARIE
CONTRARIES
CONTRIBUTE
CONTRITION
CONTROULE
CONTUMACIE
CONVERSATION
CONVERSION
CONVERT
CONVEY
CONVEY'D
CONVEYD
CONVICT
CONVINCE
CONVOLV'D
CONVOYD
CONVULSIONS
COOLD
COPARTNER
COPARTNERS
CORAL
CORMORANT
CORN
CORNER
CORNERS
CORNICE
CORNIE
CORONET
CORPS
CORPULENCE
CORROSIVE
CORRUPTING
COSTLIEST

1 (CONT.)
COTES
COUCHANT
COUCHES
COUCH'T
*COULD'ST
COUNTENANCE
COUNTERFETED
COUNTERPOISE
COUNTERVIEW
COUNTNANCE
COUNTRY
COUNTS
COUPLE
COURAGEOUS
COURB
COVENANT
COVERS
COVERTURES
COVETING
COWLES
COWRING
COY
CRAB
CRAGGIE
CRAGGY
CRAMM'D
CRANE
CRANES
CRAZE
CREAMS
CREATING
CREATION-DAY
CREAT'ST
CREDIT
CREDULOUS
CREEK
CREET
CRESSETS
CRIMES
CRING'D
CRINGE
CRISPED
CROCODILE
CROCUS
CRONIAN
CROOKED
CROP
CROPT
CROSS-BARRD
CROWDED
CROWNST
CRUCIFI'D
CRUELTIES
CRUMBL'D
CRUSHES
CRUSH'T
CRYD'ST
CRYSTAL
CRYSTALLIN
CRYSTALLINE
CUBE
CUBIC
CUBIT
CULMINATE
CURIOUS
CURRENTS
CURSES
CURST
CUSCO
CUSTOM
CUSTOMD
CUSTOME
CUTS
CYCLADES
CYCLE
CYRENE'S
CYTHEREA'S
DAEMONIAC
DAGON
DAIRIE
DALILAH
DAMAGE
DAMASCO
DAMASCUS
DAMASKT
DAME
DAMIATA
DAMNATION
DAMND
DAMPS
DAMSELS
DAN
DANAW
DANCK
DANC'T
DANDL'D
DANG'ROUS
DANITE

1 (CONT.)
DANK
DAPHNE
DAR'D
DARIEN
DARKEN
DARKEN'D
DARKENS
DARKLING
DARK'N'D
DARKSOME
DARTED
DATE
DAVIDS
DAY-LABOUR
DAZL'D
DAZLES
DAZ'LING
DAZLING
DEADLIER
DEAFNING
DEALE
DEALS
DEAREST
DEBARR
DEBAS'D
DEBAS'T
DECAI'D
DECAN
DECEAVE
DECENCIES
DECENT
DECEPTION
DECIDE
DECISION
DECK
DECK'T
DECKT
DECLARING
DECLARST
DECREPIT
DECT
DEEMING
DEEREST
DEFAMING
DEFAULT
DEFEATING
DEFECT
DEFECTIVE
DEFECTS
DEFENDED
DEFENDS
DEFENSIVE
DEFENSLESS
DEFERR
DEFICIENCE
DEFICIENT
DEFIE
DEFLOURD
DEFORMED
DEFORMITIES
DEGENERATE
DEGRADE
DEIFI'D
DEIFIE
DEIGN
DEIGND
DEIGNES
DEIGNS
DEJECTION
DELAY'D •
DELIBERATE
DELIBERATION
DELICACIE
DELICACIES
DELICIOUSLY
DELIGHTFULLY
DELINEATE
DELIV'RANCE
DELPHIAN
DEMI-GODS
DEMOGORGON
DEMURR
DEMURRE
DEMY-GODS
DENID
DENIES
DENOUNC'D
DENOUNCE
DENOUNCING
DENSE
DENY
DEPARTED
DEPARTS
DEPARTURE
DEPEND
DEPENDENT
DEPENDS
DEPLOR'D

1 (CONT.)
DEPLORE
DEPOPULATION
DEPRAV'ST
DEPRECATION
DEPREST
DEPRIV'D
DEPRIVD
DEPRIVES
DESCANT
DESCENTS
DESCRIB'D
DESCRIES
DESCRY
DESERTS
DESERVE
DESERVED
DESERVES
DESERVINGS
DESIGNING
DESIGNS
DESIRABLE
DESISTING
DESOLATION
DESPAIRING
DESPARATE
DESPERATE
DESPIGHTFULL
DESTINIE
DESTINY
DESTITUTE
DESTROYER
DESTROYERS
DETAIN
DETAIN'D
DETAINE
DETAINS
DETECT
DETERMIN
DETERMIND
DETERMINE
DETERR
DETERRD
DETESTABLE
DEUCALION
DEVILLISH
DEVILS
DEVIOUS
DEVISING
DEV'LISH
DEVOID
DEVOLV'D
DEVOTED
DEVOURS
DEW'D
DEW-DROPS
DEWY
DEXTROUS
DEXTROUSLY
DIABOLIC
DIADEM
DIALECT
DICTAEAN
DICTATE
DICTATES
DI'D
DID'ST
DIET
DIETED
DIFFICULTIE
DIFFUSE
DIG'D
DIGEST
DIGESTION
DIGGD
DIGNIFI'D
DIGNITIES
DIGRESSIONS
DIMENSIONS
DIMENTIONLESS
DIMINISH
DIMINISHT
DIMINUTION
DIMLY
DIMM
DINN
DINT
DIPSAS
DIRECTLY
DIS
DISABL'D
DISADVANTAGE
DISAGREE
DISAPPEER'D
DISARMD
DISARRAID
DISASTROUS
DISBAND
DISBURDEN

1 (CONT.)
DISBURD'N
DISBURD'ND
DISBURD'NING
DISCERNES
DISCERNING
DISCHARGD
DISCIPLES
DISCIPLIN'D
DISCIPLINE
DISCONSOLATE
DISCONTENTED
DISCONTINUOUS
DISCOVERING
DISCOVERS
DISCREETEST
DISCURSIVE
DISDAIND
DISDAINFUL
DISDAINFULLY
DISDAINING
DISEAS'D
DISEASES
DISESPOUS'D
DISFIGUR'D
DISFIGURING
DISGORGE
DISGUISE
DISGUISES
DISHEART'ND
DISHEVELD
DISHONEST
DISHONOR
DISHONORABLE
DISINCUMBERD
DISINHERITED
DISINTHRONE
DISJOINE
DISJOYNE
DISJOYNING
DISLODG'D
DISLODGING
DISMISS'D
DISMISSD
DISMISSING
DISMIST
DISMOUNTED
DISOBEI'D
DISOBEYING
DISOLUTION
DISORDER'D
DISORDERD
DISPARAGE
DISPARITIE
DISPATCHFUL
DISPEL'D
DISPELS
DISPENC'T
DISPENSE
DISPEOPL'D
DISPLACE
DISPLAYD
DISPLODE
DISPORTING
DISPOSER
DISPOSSEST
DISPROPORTIONS
DISSECT
DISSEMBLER
DISSENSION
DISSIPATION
DISSOLUTE
DISSOLV'D
DISSOLVD
DISSONANCE
DISSUADE
DISSWADE
DISSWADES
DI'ST
DISTANCES
DISTASTE
DISTEMPERS
DISTENDED
DISTENDS
DISTILL'D
DISTINCTION
DISTINGUISH
DISTINGUISHABLE
DISTORTED
DISTRACT
DISTURBANCE
DISTURBANCES
DITTIES
DITTYES
DIVAN
DIVERTED
DIVIDING
DIVIN'D
DIVINITIE

1 (CONT.)
DIVISIBLE
DIVULG'D
DIVULGE
DIZZIE
DOCTRIN
DOCTRINE
DODONA
DOGS
DOLE
DOLEFUL
DOLPHINS
DOMESTICK
DOMINIC
DONATION
DOOMD
DOOR
DORIAN
DOTHAN
DOUBLD
DOUBLE-FORM'D
DOUBLE-FOUNTED
DOUBTED
DOUBTING
DOUBTS
DOVE
DOVE-LIKE
DOWNFALL
DOWNS
DOWR
DRAFF
DRAG'D
DRAUGHTS
DRAWES
DRAW'ST
DREADLESS
DREAMD
DREAME
DREAMING
DREAR
DREARIE
DREARY
DREGS
DREIND
DRENCH
DRENCHT
DRI'D
DRIE-EY'D
DRINKST
DRIZLING
DRONE
DROOP
DROPSIES
DROSS
DROSSIEST
DROUND
DROUSED
DROUTH
DROUZE
DROV'ST
DROWN
DROWN'D
DROWND
DRUDGE
DRUGD
DRUGS
DRUMS
DRYAD
DUEL
DULCIMER
DULY
DUMB
DUN
DURANCE
DUSK
DUTEOUS
DUTIE
DUTY
DWARFS
DWELL'ST
EAGERLY
EAGLE
EAGLES
EAGLE-WING'D
EARLIE
EARN
EARND
EARNESTLY
EARTHIE
EARTHLIE
EARTHY
EATS
EATST
EBBE
EBBING
ECBATAN
ECHO
ECHO'D
ECLIPS'D

1 (CONT.)
ECLIPSES
ECLIPST
ECLIPTIC
EDENS
EDICT
EDIFICE
EDIFIE
EEVE
EEVNINGS
EFFECTUAL
EFFEMINATE
EFFICACIE
EFFLUENCE
EFFUS'D
EFFUSION
EGG
EGRESS
EGYPTS
EIGHTH
EJECT
ELABORATE
EL DORADO
ELEALE
ELECTION
ELEGANT
ELEMENTAL
ELEPHANT
ELEVATE
ELEVATES
ELISIAN
ELIXIR
ELLOPS
ELM
ELOCUTION
ELUDE
ELVES
ELY'S
ELYSIUM
EMBASSIE
EMBATTELD
EMBATTELL'D
EMBATTELLD
EMBLAZON'D
EMBLEM
EMBOLD'ND
EMBOWELD
EMBRAC'D
EMBRACE
EMBRACES
EMBRYO'S
EMERGENT
EMINENTLY
EMMET
EMPEDOCLES
EMPERORS
EMPIRES
EMPIRIC
EMPRISE
EMPTIE
EMPTIED
EMPTIER
EMPTIES
EMPTINESS
EMULATE
EMULATION
EMULOUS
ENAMEL'D
ENAMELD
ENAMOURD
ENCAMP
ENCAMPING
ENCLINE
ENCLOSD
ENCLOSE
ENCOUNTER
ENCOUNTERD
ENCOUNTRING
ENCREAS'D
ENCROACHING
ENCROACHMENT
ENCROACHT
ENCUMBERD
ENDEARING
ENDEAVOUR
ENDEVORD
ENDEVORING
ENDOW
ENDUE
ENDURES
ENFLAM'D
ENFLAME
ENFLAMING
ENFORC'T
ENGAG'D
ENGIN
ENGINE
ENGINES
ENGINRIE

1 (CONT.)
ENGRAVE
ENGRAVEN
ENJOIND
ENJOYDST
ENJOYMENT
ENJOYMENTS
ENJOYN'D
ENJOYND
ENJOYNES
ENJOY'ST
ENLARGES
ENLIGHT'ND
ENLIGHTN'D
ENLIGHTNER
ENLIGHTNING
ENNA
ENOBL'D
ENRAGE
ENSANGUIND
ENSNAR'D
ENTERPRISEST
ENTERS
ENTERTAINMENT
ENTHRALMENT
ENTIC'D
ENTICING
ENTIRELY
ENTITLE
ENTRAILES
ENTRALS
ENTWIN'D
ENTWINING
ENURE
ENVENOM'D
ENVIER
ENVIEST
ENVIRON'D
EPICYCLE
EPIDAURUS
EPILEPSIES
EQUALD
EQUALITY
EQUIPAGE
EQUIVALENT
ERCOCO
EREBUS
ERECTED
EREMITS
ERROR
ERRST
ERWHILE
ESAU
ESPI'D
ESPOUS'D
ESPOUSED
ESSENCES
ESTATE
ESTEEME
ESTOTILAND
ESTRANG'D
ETHEREOUS
ETHIOP
ETHIOPIAN
ETRURIAN
EUBOIC
EUPHRASIE
EURUS
EURYNOME
EVADE
EVADED
EVANGELIZE
EVASION
EVASIONS
EVENTS
EVER-BURNING
EVER-DURING
EVER-THREATNING
EVIDENT
EVINCE
EWE
EWES
EXACTLY
EXACTS
EXASPERATE
EXCEEDED
EXCEEDING
EXCEL
EXCEL'D
EXCELL
EXCELLD
EXCELLING
EXCEPTED
EXCLAIMD
EXCLUDED
EXCLUSION
EXCLUSIVE
EXCUS'D
EXECRATION

1 (CONT.)
EXECUTION
EXERCIS'D
EXHALE
EXHALING
EXHAUSTED
EXHILERATING
EXHORTING
EXIL'D
EXORBITANT
EXPANDED
EXPATIATE
EXPEDITE
EXPEL
EXPERIENC'T
EXPERIMENT
EXPERT
EXPIATE
EXPIATIONS
EXPIRE
EXPLAIN'D
EXPLODED
EXPLODING
EXPOSES
EXPRESLY
EXPULSION
EXPUNG'D
EXTENUATE
EXTERIOR
EXTERNAL
EXTINGUISH
EXTOLL'D
EXTORT
EXTRACTED
EXTRACTING
EXTRAVAGANT
EXTREAMES
EXTREMES
EYRIES
EZEKIEL
FABLE
FABLEST
FABRIC
FACULTIE
FADE
FADOM
FAERIE
FAILES
FAILS
FAITHFULL
FAITHFULNESS
FALLIBLE
FALLN
FALLST
FALSITIES
FAMILIE
FAMILIES
FAMINE
FAMISH
FAMOUS
FANATIC
FANCIES
FANCY
FANN
FANN'D
FANND
FANNING
FANS
FANSIED
FANTASM
FANTING
FAREWEL
FAREWELL
FARING
FARMES
FARTHEST
FASHOND
FASTEN'D
FATHERLY
FAULTIE
FAUNUS
FAVOR
FAVORITE
FAVORS
FAVOURS
FAWN'D
FAWNES
FAWNING
FEARES
FEATS
FEATURE
FEAVOROUS
FEELING
FEELST
FEIGNING
FEILDS
FELLON
FELLOW
FELLOWSHIPS

1 (CONT.)
FENC'D
FENCE
FENCELESS
FENC'T
FENEL
FERMENTED
FERRY
FERVENT
FERVENTLY
FESOLE
FETCH
FEWEL'D
FEZ
FIENDS
FIERCENESS
FIERCER
FIFT
FIGTREE
FILD
FILME
FILTH
FINALLY
FINDING
FINDS
FIND'ST
FINDST
FINISH
FINISHER
FINITE
FINNS
FIR'D
FIREY
FIRMER
FIRMLY
FIRSTLINGS
FIRST-MOVERS
FIRST-PARENTS
FIRST-SEEN
FISHIE
FITLY
FITTEST
FIX'D
FIXD
FIXES
FIX'T
FLAG
FLANK
FLASHING
FLATLY
FLATTER'D
FLAW
FLEDST
FLEEC'T
FLEECY
FLEETING
FLEIGHTS
FLING
FLOATS
FLOCKING
FLOORE
FLORA
FLOTED
FLOTES
FLOUDS
FLOUER
FLOUR'D
FLOURING
FLOURISHD
FLOURISH'T
FLOURISHT
FLOWES
FLOWR
FLOWRIE
FLOWRY
FLUCTUATS
FLUSHING
FLUTES
FLUTTERD
FLUTTRING
FLYE
FLYES
FOAM
FOAME
FOIL
FOIL'D
FOILE
FOLDS
FOLLOWD
FOLLOWED
FOLLOWS
FOMENTED
FONTARABBIA
FOOL
FOOL'D
FOOLS
FOOTED
FORAGE
FORAIGN

1 (CONT.)
FORBEAR
FORBEARANCE
FORBIDDANCE
FORBIDDER
FORBORN
FORC'D
FORCING
FOREIN
FOREKNEW
FOREKNOWING
FOREKNOWLEDG
FORELAND
FORELOCK
FORERUN
FORERUNNERS
FORERUNNING
FORESTALL'D
FORETASTED
FORETELL
FOREWARN
FOREWARN'D
FOREWARNING
FORFEITURE
FORGETFULNESS
FORGIV'N
FORMIDABLE
FORMING
FORMOST
FORREIN
FORSAK'N
FORTIFIE
FORTUNATE
FOUGHTEN
FOUNDATION
FOUNDER'D
FOUNDERD
FOUNDST
FOUNTED
FOURE
FOURFOLD-VISAG'D
FOURFOOTED
FOURTH
FOWLES
FOYLD
FRAILE
FRAMES
FRANCISCAN
FRATERNAL
FREEDOME
FREEZE
FREQUENTED
FRESHEST
FRET
FRETTED
FRIE
FRIENDLIEST
FRIENDSHIP
FRIERS
FRIGHT
FRINGED
FRISKING
FRITH
FRIZL'D
FROGS
FRONTED
FRONTIER
FRONTIERES
FRONTISPICE
FRORE
FROST
FROWND
FRUIT-TREES
FUGITIVES
FUGUE
FULFILLING
FULGENT
FULL-BLAZING
FULNESS
FUM'D
FUMES
FURNITURE
GABBLE
GAINING
GAINS
GAINSAY
GALAXIE
GALILEO
GAMBOLD
GAMESOM
'GAN
GAP
GAPING
GAP'T
GARB
GARDEN-PLOT
GARD'N
GASH
GATH

1 (CONT.)
GATHERED
GATHERING
GAYEST
GAZA'S
GAZING
GEHENNA
GEMM'D
GEMMES
GEMS
GENERALS
GENERATED
GENERATIONS
GERENT
GERYONS
GESSAMIN
GESTURES
GIBEAH
GIBEON
GIBRALTER
GIGANTIC
GILLES
GIRDED
GIVER
GIVERS
GIV'ST
GLANC'D
GLARE
GLASSIE
GLAZ'D
GLEAM
GLIDES
GLISTER'D
GLITTER
GLOBOUS
GLOOMIEST
GLOOMY
GLORYING
GLOSS
GLOSSIE
GLOZ'D
GLOZING
GLUTTED
GLUTTONOUS
GNASHING
GNAW
GOAL
GOAT
GOBLIN
GODDESSES
GOLGOTHA
GONE
GONFALONS
GOR'D
GORDIAN
GORE
GORG'D
GORGE
GORGIOUS
GORGON
GORGONS
GOSHEN
GOTTESQUE
GOVERND
GRAC'T
GRANDCHILD
GRANDCHILDE
GRAND-CHILDE
GRANT
GRANTING
GRANTS
GRASING
GRASPE
GRASPED
GRASPING
GRATE
GRATIFIE
GRATIOUS
GRATITUDE
GRATULATING
GRATULATION
GRAVELY
GRAZED
GRAZING
GRECIAN
GREEDY
GREEK
GREETING
GREY-HEADED
GRIDING
GRIEFE
GRIESLY
GRIEV'D
GRIEVD
GRIEVING
GRINDE
GRINND
GRIP'T
GROAND

1 (CONT.)
GROANE
GROANING
GROOMS
GROTS
GROUNDED
GROUNDS
GRUNSEL
GRYFON
GUARDED
GUESS
GUESSD
GUIANA
GUILEFULLY
GUMMIE
GURGE
GUSHING
HABIT
HABITABLE
HABITS
HABITUAL
HAG
HAIL'D.
HALF-RAIS'D
HALF-ROUNDING
HALLELUIA
HALLELUIAH'S
HALLOW
HAMATH
HANG
HAPP'ND
HARAN
HARANGUES
HARDER
HARDLY
HARDNING
HARK'N
HARLOT-LAP
HARLOTS
HARMLESS
HARMONIC
HARMONIES
HARMONY
HARNEST
HARPES
HARPY-FOOTED
HARSHLY
HART
HAST
HASTEN'D
HASTNING
HASTY
HATCH
HATCHING
HATEFULLEST
HATES
HAT'ST
HAUGHTIE
HAUGHTY
HAUNTED
*HAV
HAVOCK
HEADED
HEAL
HEALING
HEALTHFUL
HEAP'D
HEARDS
HEARDST
HEARES
HEARING
HEARS
HEART-SICK
HEART-STROOK
HEATH
HEAVE
HEAVIEST
HEAV'N-BANISHT
HEAV'N-FALL'N
HEAV'NLIE-BORN
HEAV'N-WARRING
HEAVY
HEELE
HEELS
HEIGHTH
HELL-BORN
HELL-DOOM'D
HELLESPONT
HELL-HOUNDS
HELMED
HELMETS
HELMS
HELP'D
HELS
HEMM
HERBE
HERCULEAN
HERDSMAN
HEREBY

1 (CONT.)
HEREDITARIE
HERMIONE
HESEBON
HESPEREAN
HETHER
HEWING
HEW'N
HIDD'N
HIDES
HIERARCHAL
HIERARCHIE
HIERARCHS
HIES
HIGH-BLEST
HIGH-CLIMBING
HIGH-SEATED
HIGHTHN'D
HIGHT'ND
HIGTH
HILLOC
HINDE
HINDER
HINDER'D
HINDERS
HINNOM
HIRELINGS
HISPAHAN
HISSING
HIT
HITHERWARD
HIVE
HOARIE
HOARY
HOLE
HOLLOW'D
HOMELY
HOMICIDE
HONEY
HONOR
HONOURING
HONOURS
HOODS
HOP'D
HORIZONTAL
HORND
HORNED
HORONAIM
HORRENT
HORROURS
HORSES
HOSANNA
HOSANNA'S
HOSTIL
HOSTILITY
HOSTING
HOUSES
HOWL'D
HOWLE
HUES
HULL
HUMBLES
HUMBLING
HUMOUR
HUNDERDS
HUNTING
HURDL'D
HURLING
HURTFUL
HUSK
HYACINTHIN
HYALINE
HYDASPES
HYDRA'S
HYDRUS
HYMEN
HYMENAEAN
HYMNE
HYPOCRISIE
HYPOCRITE
HYPOCRITES
HYSTORIAN
*I'
IDEA
IDELY
IDIOTS
IDLELY
IDLENESS
IDOLATRESSES
IDOL-WORSHIP
IGNOBLY
IGNOMINIE
IGNOMINIOUS
ILAND
ILIUM
ILLAUDABLE
ILLIMITABLE
ILL-JOYND
ILLUMIN

1 (CONT.)
ILLUMINATE
ILLUMIN'D
ILLUSION
ILLUSIONS
ILLUSTRATE
ILLUSTRATES
ILLYRIA
IMAGINATION
IMAGINING
IMAUS
IMBALM'D
IMBALMD
IMBARK'T
IMBELLISHT
IMBLAZONRIE
IMBORDERD
IMBOSS
IMBOWR
IMBOWR'D
IMBRACE
IMBRACEING
IMBROILD
IMBROILES
IMBROUND
IMBRUTE
IMBU'D
IMITATED
IMMATURE
IMMEASURABLY
IMMORTALITY
IMMOVEABLE
IMMURES
IMMUTABLIE
IMMUTABLY
IMP
IMPAIR
IMPAIRE
IMPARADIS'T
IMPAR'D
IMPARTED
IMPARTS
IMPASSABLE
IMPASSIOND
IMPASSIVE
IMPATIENCE
IMPEARLS
IMPEDIMENT
IMPENITENCE
IMPENITRABLY
IMPEREAL
IMPERFECTION
IMPERIOUS
IMPERISHABLE
IMPERTINENCE
IMPERVIOUS
IMPIOUSLY
IMPLACABLE
IMPLANTED
IMPLEMENTS
IMPLICIT
IMPLI'D
IMPLOI'D
IMPLOID
IMPLOIES
IMPLOR'D
IMPLORES
IMPLOY
IMPLOY'D
IMPLOYMENTS
IMPORT
IMPORTANT
IMPORTS
IMPOSITION
IMPOSSIBLY
IMPOSTOR
IMPOTENCE
IMPOW'RD
IMPREGNABLE
IMPREGN'D
IMPREGNS
IMPRESES
IMPRESS
IMPRESST
IMPREST
IMPRUDENCE
IMPURPL'D
IMPUTE
IMPUT'ST
INABSTINENCE
INBRED
INCENC'T
INCENS'T
INCENTIVE
INCESTUOUS
INCHANTING
INCITED
INCLINABLE
INCLIN'D

1 (CONT.)
INCLINING
INCLOS'D
INCLUDED
INCOMPOS'D
INCOMPREHENSIBLE
INCONVENIENT
INCORPORATE
INCORRUPT
INCREAST
INCREATE
INCREDIBLE
INCUMBENT
INCUMBERD
INCUR
INCURR
INCURR'D
INCURR'ST
IND
INDECENT
INDEFATIGABLE
INDENTED
INDIA
INDIANS
INDIGNANT
INDIGNITIE
INDIRECT
INDISSOLUBLY
INDITE
INDUC'D
INDUCE
INDUCEMENT
INDUCING
INDUCTIVE
INDU'D
INDULGENCE
INDULGENCES
INDURANCE
INDUS
INEFFABLY
INEFFECTUAL
INELEGANT
INELOQUENT
INEVITABLY
INEXORABLY
INEXPERIENCE
INEXPFRT
INEXPLICABLE
INEXTINGUISHABLE
INEXTRICABLE
INFALLIBLE
INFAM'D
INFAMIE
INFANTRY
INFECT
INFECTED
INFECTION
INFEEBL'D
INFERR
INFIDEL
INFIRME
INFIRMER
INFIX'D
INFIXT
INFLAME
INFLAMED
INFLAMES
INFORMIDABLE
INFORMING
INFURIATE
INGAG'D
INGAGING
INGENDERD
INGORG'D
INGRAFT
INGREDIENTS
INGROSS'T
INHABITED
INHERITANCE
INHOSPITABLE
INHOSPITABLY
INHUMAN
INHUMANLY
INIMITABLE
INIQUITIES
INJOINST
INJUNCTION
INJURE
INJURIE
INJURIES
INJURY
INLAID
INLAND
INLAY
INLIE
INNUMEROUS
INQUIRE
INROAD
INRODE

1 (CONT.)
INRODES
INROULD
INSENSATE
INSEPARABLE
INSEPARABLIE
INSHRINE
INSINUATING
INSOLENCE
INSPECTION
INSPIRE
INSPIRING
INSTANTLY
INSTINCTIVE
INSTRUCTION
INSTRUCTS
INSTRUMENTS
INSUFFERABLY
INSUPERABLE
INSUPPORTABLE
INSURRECTION
INTELLECT
INTELLIGENCE
INTELLIGENT
INTEMPERANCE
INTENSE
INTERCEDE
INTERCESSION
INTERCHANGE
INTERDICTION
INTERFUS'D
INTERMIT
INTERMITS
INTERPOSES
INTERPOSEST
INTERPRET
INTERPRETED
INTERRUPTED
INTERVALL
INTERVENE
INTERVOLV'D
INTERWOVE
INTESTIN
INTIRE
INTOXICATED
INTRANS'T
INTRANST
INTRENCHT
INTRICACIES
INTRODUC'D
INTRUSION
INTUITIVE
INUNDATION
INUTTERABLE
INVADED
INVADERS
INVALID
INVENT
INVENTER
INVENTERS
INVENTION
INVEST
INVESTED
INVINCIBLY
INVIRONS
INVISIBLY
INVITED
INVITES
INVOK'D
INVOLVD
INVOLVE
INWARDLY
INWARDS
INWOVE
INWOVEN
INWREATH'D
IONIAN
IRRADIANCE
IRRADIATE
IRRECONCILEABLE
IRREGULAR
IRREPARABLE
IRRESISTIBLE
IRRESOLUTE
IRREVERENT
IRREVOCABLE
IRRIGUOUS
ISAAC
ISIS
ISLAND
ISLE
ISSUES
ITERATE
*ITH'
IVIE
IVORIE
JACULATION
JANGLING
JANUS

1 (CONT.)
JAPHET
JARR
JAVANS
JAV'LIN
JAWES
JAWS
JEALOUSIE
JEALOUSIES
JOHN
JOIN
JOINTED
JOINT-RACKING
JOINTS
JOLLITIE
JORDAN
JORDANS
JOSHUA
JOSIAH
JOURNIED
JOURNY
JOUST
JOUSTED
JOVES
JOYD
JOYLESS
JOYNES
JOYNS
JOYNTS
JOYOUS
JOYS
JUBILANT
JUBILEE
JUBILIE
JUCIEST
JUDAH
JUDGEST
JUDGMENTS
JUNO
JUNO'S
JUPITER
JURISDICTION
JUSTIFICATION
KEENE
KEEPES
KENNEL
KENNS
KERNELS
KEY-HOLE
KEYS
KICKT
KIDS
KILL
KILLS
KINDLES
KINDLIEST
KINDRED
KINGDOMES
KISS'D
KISSES
KNEEL'D
KNEE-TRIBUTE
KNEWST
KNIT
KNOTS
KSAR
LABOR'D
LABOURERS
LADEN
LAERTES
LAG
LAHOR
LAIRE
LAMENTABLE
LAMENTATION
LAMENTED
LANCE
LANDED
LAND-MARK
LANGUISH
LANGUISHING
LANGUISHT
LAPLAND
LAPSED
LAPST
LARBORD
LARGER
LASCIVIOUS
LATERAL
LAUGHS
LAUGH'ST
LAUREL
LAVINIA
LAWLESS
LAWNS
LAXE
LAZAR-HOUSE
LEADE
LEAD'ST

1 (CONT.)
LEAFE
LEAGU'D
LEAGUES
LEAND
LEANING
LEAPS
LEARN'D
LEAVING
LEBANON
LEE
LEER
LEGAL
LEGGS
LEMNOS
LENGTH'ND
LENT
LEO
LEPER
LESSEN
LESS'N
LETHE
LETHEAN
LEUCOTHEA
LEUDLY
LEVANT
LEVIE
LIABLE
LIBBARD
LIBECCHIO
LIBRA
LIBYAN
LICE
LICHAS
LICK
LICK'D
LIFE-BLOOD
LIFE-GIVING
LIFTING
LIGHT-ARM'D
LIGHT-ARMED
LIGHTEST
LIGHT'N
LIGHT'NING
LIK'D
LIKELIE
LIKELIFR
LIKEN
LIKING
LIMB'D
LIMBEC
LIMBER
LIMBO
LIMITARIE
LIMITED
LINK
LINK'D
LINKED
LIONESS
LIQUORS
LISTENING
LISTENS
LIST'N
LIST'NING
LISTNING
LITHE
LIVELIER
LIVELIEST
LIVER
LIVERIE
LIVERIES
LIVID
LIVST
LO
LOAD'N
LOATH'D
LOCAL
LOFTY
LOOK'ST
LOOPHOLES
LOOSES
LOOSLY
LOOSNING
LOQUACIOUS
LOTH
LOUDER
LOURS
LOVE-LABOR'D
LOVELESS
LOVELIEST
LOVELINESS
LOVER
LOVERS
LOVE-TALE
LOVLIEST
LOV'ST
LOWLIEST
LOWLINESS
LOWR'D

1 (CONT.)
LOWRING
LOYAL
LOYALTIE
LOYNES
LUCENT
LUCRE
LULL
LULLD
LUMINARIE
LURE
LURK
LURKING
LURKS
LUTE
LUXURIANT
LUZ
LYAR
LYRE
MACE
MACHINATION
MAD
MADDING
MADNESS
MAEONIDES
MAEOTIS
MAGAZIN
MAGELLAN
MAGIC
MAGNANIMOUS
MAGNETIC
MAGNIFI'D
MAGNIFIE
MAGNITUDES
MAHANAIM
MAIA'S
MAID
MAIM'D
MAINLY
MAINTAIND
*MAI'ST
MAISTER
MAISTRING
MAJESTIC
MAJESTICK
MAJESTY
MALABAR
MALADIES
MALES
MALICIOUS
MANACL'D
MANAG'D
MANGL'D
MAN-KIND
MANKINDS
MANLIKE
MANNA
MAN-SLAUGHTER
MARASMUS
MARBLE
MARCH'D
MARIAGEABLE
MARIE
MARINER
MARISH
MARITIM
MARKD
MARLE
MARR'D
MARRD
MARRIAGES
MARRYING
MARSHAL'D
MARTIAL
MARTYRDOM
MARVELING
MARY
MASCULINE
MASK
MASSACHER
MASSY '
MAST
MASTER
MATCH
MATCHING
MATED
MATERIAL
MATES
MATRIMONIAL
MATTERS
MATTIN
MATUREST
MAWE
MAY
*MAY'ST
MAZE
MEAGER
MEANER
MEASURING

1 (CONT.)
MEATHES
MEDAL
MEDDOW
MEDDOWES
MEDIA
MEDIATION
MEDITATED
MEDITATION
MEDUSA
MEETST
MEGARA
MELANCHOLIE
MELANCHOLLY
MELIBOEAN
MELIND
MELLIFLUOUS
MELODIE
MELT
MELTED
MEMBER
MEMBRANE
MEMNONIAN
MEMORIALS
MENAC'T
MENDS
MENTAL
MENTION'D
MERCHANTS
MERCIFULL
MESERIE
METALLIC
METALS
METEOR
METEOROUS
METTLE
MEWS
MEXICO
MID-COURSE
MID-DAY
MID-HOURS
MID-NOON
MIDRIFF
*MIGHTST
MILDELY
MILES
MILITARIE
MILK
MIMIC
MINDLESS
MINGL'D
MINIMS
MINISTERD
MINISTERIES
MINISTRANT
MINISTRY
MINSTRELSIE
MINUTES
MIRACLE
MIRACLES
MIRE
MIRES
MISCHIEVOUS
MISCREATED
MISDEEDS
MISDEEM
MISERIES
MISFORTUNE
MISGAVE
MISHAP
MISJOYNING
MISLEADS
MISS'D
MISSD
MISSINFORME
MISSIVE
MISST
MISSTHOUGHT
MISTAKE
MISTRESS
MISTRUSTFUL
MISTS
MISTY
MIXING
MIXTURE
MOABS
MOALE
MOAPING
MOARIE
MOCK
MODE
MODERATE
MODERATION
MODERN
MODEST
MODESTIE
MOGUL
MOLE
MOLEST

1 (CONT.)
MOMBAZA
MONARCHAL
MONARCHIES
MONARCHS
MONARCHY
MONTALBAN
MONTHLY
MONUMENTS
MOONE
MOONED
MOON-STRUCK
MOORS
MORAL
MOREB
MORNINGS
MORROWS
MORSEL
MORSELS
MORTALITIE
MORTALL
MORTALS
MOSAIC
MOSCO
MOTEZUME
MOTION'D
MOULDS
MOUND
MOURN'D
MOURNFUL
MOURNS
MOUST
MOVD
MOVERS
MOWES
MOZAMBIC
MUCH-HUMBL'D
MULCIBER
MULTIFORM
MULTIPLI'D
MULTIPLIES
MULTIPLY'D
MURAL
MURKIE
MURMURS
MURREN
MUS'D
MUSICK
MUST'RING
MUSTRING
MUTABLE
MUTINIE
MUTTERING
MYRTLES
MYSTERIES
MYSTERIOUSLY
MYSTICAL
NAILD
NAILES
NAMELESS
NAPHTHA
NARD
NARROWER
NATHLESS
NATIONAL
NATIVES
NATIVITIE
NEAREST
NEBO
NECESSITATE
NECESSITATED
NECTARINE
NEEDLESS
NEEDLEST
NEEDST
NEERLY
NEGLECTS
NEGUS
NEIGHBOURHOOD
NEPTUN'S
NERVE
NESTS
NET
NEVER-ENDING
NEVERTHELESS
NEW-ARRIV'D
NEWES
NEW-MADE
NICEST
NIGER
NIGHT-FOUNDER'D
NIGHT-HAG
NIGHTINGAL
NIGHTINGALE
NIGHTINGALES
NIGHT-WANDERER
NIGHT-WARBLING
NILUS
NINEFOLD

1 (CONT.)
NIPHATES
NISROC
NITRE
NOBLENESS
NOCENT
NOISES
NOONE
NOON-TIDE
NORTH-EAST
NORTHWARD
NORTH-WINDE
NORUMBEGA
NORWAY
NORWEGIAN
NOSTRIL
NOTION
NOTIONS
NOTUS
NOURISHER
NOVELTIE
NOYSOM
NUMBER'D
NURSERIE
NUTRIMENT
NUTRIMENTS
NYMPHLIKE
NYSEIAN
OAK
OAKS
OARE
OARIE
OATH
OB
OBDURAT
OBDUR'D
OBDURED
OBEI'D
OBEYES
OBLIGE
OBLIQUITIES
OBLIVIOUS
OBLOQUIE
OBSCENE
OBSCURELY
OBSERVES
OBSERVING
OBSTINACIE
OBTAINS
OBTRUDED
OBTRUSIVE
OBTUSE
OCCASIONALLY
OCCASIOND
ODORIFEROUS
ODOUR
OECHALIA
OETA
OFFAL
OFFENDING
OFFENSIVE
OFFICES
OFFICIATE
OFFRING
OFFRINGS
OFF-SPRING
OFFSPRING
OFSSPRING
OFTEST
OLIVE
OLYMPIAS
OMINOUS
OMNIFIC
OOSE
OPAL
OPAQUE
OPE
OPEND
OPENING
OPHION
OPHIR
OPHIUCUS
OPHIUSA
OPIATE
OPINIONS
OP'NST
OPPRESS'D
OPPRESSES
OPS
ORATOR
ORATORIE
ORB'D
ORBED
ORCS
ORCUS
ORDAIN
ORDER'D
ORDERING
ORDERLY

1 (CONT.)
OREAD
OREBLOWN
OREFLOW'D
ORELEAPT
OREPOW'RD
ORESHADES
O'RESPREAD
ORETHREW
OREWATCHT
OREWEARIED
OREWHELM
O'REWHELM'D
ORGANIC
ORGIES
ORIFICE
ORIGINALS
ORION
O'RMATCHT
ORMUS
ORNAMENTS
ORPHEAN
ORUS
OSIRIS
OUNCE
OUNCES
OUTCAST
OUT-CAST
OUT-DONE
OUTDOO
OUT-FLEW
OUTGREW
OUTLIVE
OUTMOST
OUTRAGIOUS
OUT-SHINE
OUTSHON
OUT SIDE
OUT-SIDE
OUTSPREAD
OUTSPRED
OVERAWD
OVERBUILT
OVERCOM
OVERCOMES
OVERCOMING
OVER-FOND
OVERGROWTH
OVERHEAD
OVER-HEAD
OVER-HEARD
OVERHUNG
OVERJOY'D
OVERJOYD
OVERLAY
OVERLIVE
OVERLOV'D
OVERPOWER
OVERPRAISING
OVER-REACH
OVER-REACHT
OVERSHADOW
OVERSHADOWING
OVERSPRED
OVERTOOK
OVERTRUSTING
OVERTURE
OVERTURND
OVERTURNES
OVERWEENING
OVERWHELM
OVERWHELM'D
OVERWHELMD
OVERWOODIE
OWES
OWING
OXEN
OXUS
OYLE
PACIFIC
PAC'T
PADAN-ARAM
PAIN'D
PAINT
PAINTED
PAINTS
PAIRE
PALATE
PALES
PALM
PALMIE
PALM-TREE
PAMPERD
PANDORA
PANEAS
PANIM
PANSIES
PAQUIN
PARADE

1 (CONT.)
PARADISES
PARAGOND
PARALEL
PARAMOUNT
PARCH
PARCHING
PARCHT
PARDONS
PARDS
PARLE
PARSIMONIOUS
PARTAKERS
PARTAKES
PARTIAL
PARTICIPATING
PARTY
PASSAGES
PASSES
PASS'T
PASTIME
PASTORAL
PASTUR'D
PATRIARCHS
PATRIARK
PATRIMONIE
PATRONESS
PATRONS
PATTERN
PAUSING
PAVILION
PAVILION'D
PAVILIONS
PAWING
PAYING
PAYS
PEAL'D
PEARLIE
PEARLY
PEASANT
PECCANT
PEERAGE
PEERES
PEERLESS
PEGASEAN
PELORUS
PEN
PENAL
PENCIL
PENDENT
PENDULOUS
PENETRATION
PENNS
PEOPL'D
PEOR
PERCEAV'D
PERCEAVING
PERCEAV'ST
PERCEIV'D
PERDITION
PERFETLY
PERFORMANCE
PERFORMS
PERFUMES
PERIOD
PERIODS
PERMITTING
PERPETUITIE
PERPLEX'D
PERPLEXES
PERPLEXING
PERSECUTERS
PERSECUTION
PERSEVERING
PERSIAN
PERSISTING
PERSWADERS
PERSWASION
PERSWASIVELY
PERU
PERUS'D
PERVERSENESS
PERVERSNESS
PERVERTS
PEST
PESTILENT
PETER
PETITION
PETRIFIC
PETSORA
PETTY
PHANTASMS
PHARAO
PHARAOH
PHARPHAR
PHILISTEAN
PHILOSOPHERS
PHILOSOPHIE
PHINEUS

1 (CONT.)
PHLEGETON
PHLEGRA
PHOENICIANS
PHOENIX
PHRENZIE
PICKAX
PIECES
PIGMEAN
PILASTERS
PILGRIMS
PILLARD
PINCHING
PINING
PINNACE
PINNACLES
PINNS
PIONERS
PITCHT
PITCHY
PITEOUS
PITTYING
PITYING
PLACABLE
PLAGU'D
PLAIND
PLAINLIER
PLAINTS
PLANETARIE
PLANET-STROOK
PLANK
PLANTATION
PLANTER
PLAT
PLATAN
PLATO'S
PLAYD
PLEAD
PLEASANTEST
PLEASINGLY
PLEBEIAN
PLEIADES
PLENIPOTENT
PLENTEOUSLY
PLOT
PLOTS
PLOWMAN
PLUMB
PLUM'D
PLUNGE
PLUTONIAN
PLYES
POEM
POINTING
POINTS
POIS'D
POISE
POLES
POLISH
POLLICY
POLLUTING
POLLUTION
POMONA'S
POND
PONDER
PONDEROUS
PONDERS
PONENT
PONTIFICAL
PONTIFICE
POOR
PORCH
PORCHES
PORCULLIS
PORTAL
PORTALS
PORTED
PORTENDS
PORTRAID
PORTRESS
POSSESSD
POSSESSING
POSSESSOR
POSSIBLY
POST
POTABLE
POUDERD
POURE
POURING
POURLIEUES
POWDER
POWERFULLEST
POW'R
POWRE
POW'RS
PRACTICE
PRACTIS'D
PRAEAMBLE
PRAVITIE

1 (CONT.)
PRAY'D
PRAYES
PREACHD
PREACHT
PRECEDENCE
PRECEPT
PRECINCTS
PRECIPICE
PRECIPITANCE
PRECIPITANT
PRECIPITATE
PRECISE
PREDESTINATION
PREDICTION
PREDOMINANT
PRESAGE
PRESCRIPT
PRESENTING
PRESS'D
PREST
PRESUMES
PRETEND
PRETENDED
PRETENSES
PREVAIL
PREVAILD
PREVAILE
PREVAILING
PREVENIENT
PRICK
PRIE
PRIMITIVE
PRINCEDOMES
PRIVATE
PRIVILEDGE
PROBOSCIS
PROCEEDING
PROCESSION
PROCINCT
PROCLAIM
PROCLAIM'D
PROCLAIMD
PROCLAIME
PROCLAIMS
PROCREATION
PROCURE
PRODUC'D
PRODUCING
PRODUC'T
PRODUCT
PRODUCTIVE
PROEM
PROFESSING
PROFFER
PROFIT
PROFLUENT
PROFOUNDEST
PROFUNDITIE
PROGENY
PROGRESSIVE
PROHIBIT
PROHIBITIONS
PROJECTING
PROLIFIC
PROLOGUE
PROLONG
PROLONGD
PROMISCUOUS
PROMISES
PROMONTORIE
PROMONTORIES
PROMPTED
PRONOUNCD
PROPAGAT
PROPERLY
PROPHECIE
PROPHET
PROPHETIC
PROPITIATION
PROPORTIONAL
PROPORTIOND
PROPORTIONS
PROPOSALS
PROPOUND
PROPOUNDED
PROPRIETIE
PROSERPIN
PROSERPINA
PROSPERITY
PROSTITUTING
PROSTRATION
PROTECTS
PROTESTING
PROTEUS
PROUDEST
PROVIDE
PROVIDES
PROVINCE

1 (CONT.)
PROVISION
PROVISIONS
PROVOKES
PROVOKING
PROW
PROWLING
PRY
PUBLISH
PULP
PUNCTUAL
PUNIC
PUNIE
PUNISHER
PUNISH'T
PURLIEU
PURLOIND
PURPLES
PURPOSD
PURPOSES
PURSUERS
PURVEY'D
PUSH'D
PUSHD
PUSH'T
PUSHT
PYRAMID
PYRAMIDS
PYRRHA
PYTHON
QUADRATE
QUADRATURE
QUAFF
QUALMES
QUARRIES
QUARRY
QUARTER
QUATERNION
QUELL'D
QUENCH
QUESTIOND
QUICK'NING
QUILOA
QUIVERS
RABBA
RACES
RACKT
RADIANCE
RAGGS
RAINBOWS
RAIN'D
RAIND
RAINE
RAMIEL
RAMMD
RAMPANT
RAMPART
RAMPD
RANCOR
RANCOUR
RANGED
RANKE
RANSACK'D
RANSOMD
RAPACIOUS
RAPINE
RAPTURES
RARELY
RASHNESS
RATLING
RATTLING
RAUNGE
RAUNGING
RAVEN
RAVIN
RAV'NOUS
REACHD
REACHES
READILY
REAKING
REALITIES
REALMES
REALTIE
REAP
REAPER
REAPERS
REAPT
REAR
REARS
RE-ASCEND
REASON'D
REASONINGS
REASONLESS
REASSEMBLING
REASSUM'D
REBELL'D
REBELS
REBOUNDING
REBOUNDS

1 (CONT.)
REBUFF
RECAL
RECANT
RECEAV'ST
RECIPROCAL
RECK
RECK'D
RECK'N
RECK'N'ST
RECLAME
RECLINE
RECOILE
RECOLLECTING
RECOLLECTS
RECOMFORTED
RECOMMEND
RECONCIL'D
RECORDERS
RECOUNT
RECOUNTED
RECOYLD
RECURE
REDEEME
REDOUBL'D
REDOUBLE
REDOUNDED
REDOUNDING
REDOUNDS
REDRESS
RED-SEA
REDUNDANT
RE-EDIFIE
REEDS
RE-ENTER
REFINES
REFLECTING
REFLUX
REFORM
REFORMING
REFREIN'D
REFRESHMENT
REFRESH'T
REFULGENT
REFUSD
REFUSING
REFUTES
REGARDED
REGENCIES
REGENERATE
REGIMENT
REGISTERD
REGRET
REGULAR
REIGND
REIGNES
REIGNING
REIMBATTELL'D
REIN
REIND
REINFORCEMENT
REITERATED
REJOYC'T
RELAPSE
RELATER
RELATIONS
RELAX
RELAX'D
RELEAST
RELENTED
RELENTLESS
RELENTS
RELI'D
RELIE
RELIEF
RELIES
RELIGIONS
RELISH
REMAIN'D
REMARKABLY
REMEDILESS
REMEMBER'D
REMEMBER'ST
REMEMBERST
REMEMBREST
REMEMBRING
REMOOV'D
REMOVES
RENDERS
RENDRING
RENEWING
RENEWS
RENOUND
RENOVATION
RENOWNE
REPAIR'D
REPAIRD
REPEAL'D
REPEL

1 (CONT.)
REPELD
REPELL
REPELL'D
REPENTANT
REPENTS
REPINE
REPLYD
REPORTED
REPOSSESS
REPRESENTED
REPROACHFUL
REPROBATE
REPROV'D
REPTIL
REPULS'D
REQUIR'D
RESALUTE
RESEMBLANCES
RESEMBL'ST
RESENT
RESERVD
RESERVE
RESERVING
RESIDES
RESIGNES
RESIGNS
RESISTANCE
RESISTLESS
RESOLVD
RESOLVING
RESONANT
RESORTING
RESPIRATION
RESPITE
RESPLENDENCE
RESPONSIVE
RESTED
RESTORER
RESTRAIN'D
RESUM'D
RESUMES
RESURRECTION
RETAIN'D
RETAINE
RETAINES
RETAINING
RETINUE
RETIREMENT
RETIRING
RETORT
RETORTED
RETREATE
RETREATED
RETREATING
RETRIBUTION
RETROGRADE
RETURNES
REVEAL
REVEALE
REVELLERS
REVENG
REVENG'D
REVEREND
REVILE
REVILING
RE-VISIT
REVISIT
REVISIT'ST
REVIVES
REVOKE
REVOLUTIONS
REVOLV'D
REVOLVD
REVOLVING
RHENE
RHEUMS
RHIME
RHODOPE
RHOMB
RICHER
RICHLY
RID
RIDDANCE
RIDGES
RIDICULOUS
RIDING
RIFE
RIFL'D
RIGHTFUL
RIGHTLIER
RIGOR
RIGOROUSLY
RIGOUR
RILL
RILLS
RIMMON
RIN'D
RIND

1 (CONT.)
RINGLETS
RINGS
RISEN
RISES
RIVALS
RIVER-DRAGON
RIV'N
RIVULET
ROAD
ROAMING
ROARD
ROAVE
ROMANCE
ROOD
ROOFE
ROSEAT
ROT
ROULE
ROULES
ROULING
ROULS
ROUNDED
ROUNDS
ROWES
ROWLS
ROYALTIES
RUB'D
RUBIE
RUBIED
RUDDIE
RUDDY
RUEFUL
RUES
RUFUL
RUINING
RUMINATING
RUMOR
RUMORD
RUNNING
RUNS
RUPTURE
RUSHT
RUSLING
RUSSLING
RUSTIC
SABEAN
SABLE-VESTED
SACRIFIC'D
SAFER
SAFETIE
SAGACIOUS
SAGE
SAGES
SAIL
SAIL-BROAD
SAILES
SAILING
SAILS
SAINTLY
SALT
SALUTATION
SAMARCHAND
SAMOED
SAMOS
SAMSON
SANCTITIES
SANCTITUDE
SANGUIN
SAP
SAPHIRS
SAPIENT
SARRA
SATANIC
SATED
SATIETIE
SATISFIED
SAV'D
SAYLING
SCAL'D
SCALDING
SCALIE
SCALY
SCANDAL
SCANN'D
SCANT
SCARR
SCARS
SCATH'D
SCATTER'D
SCENT
SCIENCE
SCIENTIAL
SCIPIO
SCOOP
SCOPE
SCORCHING
SCORCHT
SCORND

1 (CONT.)
SCORNING
SCORPIONS
SCOURE
SCOURG'D
SCOURS
SCOUTS
SCOWLS
SCRIBL'D
SCROWLE
SCRUPL'D
SCULLES
SCULPTURES
SCUM'D
SCURFF
SCYLLA
SDEIND
SEA-BEAST
SEA-FARING
SEAL
SEALES
SEA-MEN
SEA-MEWS
SEA-MONSTERS
SEA'S
SEAT'S
SEAVENFOLD
SEAVENS
SEAVENTIMES-WEDDED
SEAV'NTH
SECHEM
SECONDARIE
SECRESIE
SECRETEST
SECT
SECULAR
SECURELY
SECURER
SEDENTARIE
SEDGE
SEDITIOUS
SEDULOUS
SEEKES
SEEK'ST
SEEMINGLY
SEEMLIEST
SEEMST
SEER
SEIGE
SEISD
SEISURE
SEIZ'D
SEIZE
SELECTEST
SELEUCIA
SELF-BEGOT
SELF-CONDEMNING
SELF-DEPRAV'D
SELF-DESTRUCTION
SELF-KNOWING
SELF-LEFT
SELF-LOST
SELF-OPEND
SELF-ROWLD
SELF-SAME
SELF-TEMPTED
SENATE
SENCE
SENC'T
SENDER
SENDING
SENESHALS
SENIR
SENNAAR
SENSIBLE
SENSUAL
SENTED
SENTERIES
SENTS
SEONS
SEQUENT
SEQUESTERD
SERAPIS
SERBONIAN
SERE
SERENATE
SERICANA
SERPENTINE
SERRALIONA
SERVIL
SERVILITIE
SERVILLY
SESSION
SETTLE
SEVENFOLD
SEVENTIE
SEVER
SEVER'D
SEVERD

1 (CONT.)
SEVERING
SEV'NTH
SEV'RAL
SEXES
SEXTILE
SHADDOW
SHADDOWD
SHADDOWIE
SHADDOWING
SHADED
SHADIEST
SHADOW'D
SHADOWD
SHADOWING
SHADOWS
SHAD'ST
SHAKE
SHAK'N
*SHAL
SHALLOW
SHAMEFUL
SHAPD
SHAR'D
SHARP'ND
SHARPNING
SHATTER'D
SHATTERD
SHATTERING
SHAVES
SHEAF
SHEDDING
SHEDS
SHEEP-WALKS
SHEERE
SHELL
SHELLS
SHELTERS
SHEWES
SHIFTS
SHIP
SHIVERD
SHIVERING
SHOALES
SHOALING
SHOARES
SHOOT
SHOOTING
SHORTER
SHORTEST
SHOULDER
SHOWN
SHOWRIE
SHOWRS
SHOWS
SHOWST
SHRILL
SHRIN'D
SHRINES
SHROUD
SHROUDS
SHRUBS
SHUDDRING
SHUNNING
SIBMA
SICKNESS
SIDELONG
SIDERAL
SIDONIAN
SIEZE
SIGH
SIGH'D
SIGHING
SIGHTED
SILOA'S
SILVANUS
SIMPLE
SIMPLY
SINAEAN
SIN-BORN
SIN-BRED
SINCEREST
SINFULNESS
SINGLY
SINGULAR
SINISTER
SINK
SINKS
SINND
SINNE
SINNING
SINNS
SINUOUS
SIONS
SIROCCO
SISTER
SISTERS
SITHE
SIT'ST

1 (CONT.)
SITST
SITTIM
SITUATE
SITUATION
SKALY
SKIE-TINCTUR'D
SKIFF
SKILFUL
SKILLD
SKIRTED
SLACK'N
SLACKNESS
SLAINE
SLANDROUS
SLANT
SLAVES
SLEEK
SLEEPLESS
SLEEPY
SLEPST
SLIDING
SLIGHTLY
SLIMIE
SLIP
SLOATH
SLOTHFUL
SLOWEST
SLOWLY
SLOW-PAC'T
SLUC'D
SLUCE
SLUCES
SLUMBERD
SLUMBERS
SLUMBROUS
SMALLER
SMART
SMEARD
SMIT
SMITE
SMOAK'D
SMOOTH'D
SMOOTHED
SMOOTHS
SMUTTIE
SNARES
SNATCH'D
SNATCHT
SNOWY
SNUFF'D
SOAR
SOARD
SOARES
SOCIABLE
SOCIABLY
SOCIAL
SOFALA
SOFT-EBBING
SOFTEST
SOFT'N
SOFT'ND
SOFTN'D
SOFTNESS
SOFT'NING
SOILD
SOJOURN'D
SOLAC'D
SOLDANS
SOLEMNE
SOLEMNIZ'D
SOLITARY
SOLLICIT
SOLLICITE
SOLLICITED
SOLLICITOUS
SOLLID
SOLOMON
SOLSTITIAL
SOLVE
SOMETHING
SOMEWHAT
SOMTIME
SOMWHAT
SOMWHERE
SONOROUS
SOOT
SOOTHE
SOOTY
SOPHI
SORCERESS
SORCERIE
SORCERIES
SORD
SORROWING
SORROWS
SORTED
SORTS
SOTTISH

1 (CONT.)
SOUGHTST
SOUND-BOARD
SOUNDED
SOUNDEST
SOURCE
SOURS
SOUTHMOST
SOUTHWARD
SOUTHWIND
SOVRANTIE
SOV'RANTY
SOW
SOW'D
SOW'N
SPADE
SPAK'ST
SPANGL'D
SPANGLING
SPARES
SPARK
SPARKL'D
SPARKLES
SPARTAN
SPASM
SPATTERING
SPAWN
SPEAKABLE
SPEAKS
SPEARES
SPECIAL
SPECT
SPECTATORS
SPECULATION
SPECULATIONS
SPED
SPEECHLESS
SPEEDIE
SPEEDIER
SPEEDILY
SPEEDS
SPHEAR'D
SPILT
SPINNING
SPIRITLESS
SPLENDID
SPLENDORS
SPOIL
SPOIL'D
SPOILES
SPOKE
SPOK'N
SPONTANEOUS
SPORTFUL
SPOTLESS
SPOTTY
SPOUSAL
SPOUS'D
SPOUT
SPOUTS
SPREDS
SPRINKL'D
SPUME
SPUN
SPURNS
SPY
SPYING
SQUADROND
SQUAR'D
SQUARED
SQUAT
STABL'D
STABLISHT
STAFF
STAG
STAI'D
STAIN
STAINE
STALKES
STANDARDS
STARLESS
STAR-PAV'D
STARR-LIGHT
STARR'S
STARS
STARTL'D
STARTS
STARVE
STATES
STATIONS
STAY'D
STAYD
STAYES
STEALTH
STEAME
STEAMING
STEARD
STEARING
STEARSMAN

1 (CONT.)
STEDDIE
STEDDIEST
STEEL
STEERS
STELLAR
STELTH
STEMM
STEMMING
STENCH
STEPDAME
STEPPING
STEPT
STEP-TRACE
STERNLY
STICKS
STIFF
STIFLING
STIL
STINGS
STIRD
STIRR
STIRR'D
STIRRING
STOL'N
STOLN
STONES
STOOP'D
STOOPT
STOPS
STOPT
STORING
STORK
STORMIE
STORMING
STORY
STRAINS
STRAIT'ND
STRAITN'D
STRAND
STRAW-BUILT
STREAK
STREAKING
STREAKS
STREIGHT
STREIND
STREIT'NING
STRETCHED
STRETCHING
STREW'D
STREWS
STRIKE
STRING
STRIPES
STRIPLING
STRODE
STRONGEST
STROW
STROW'N
STRUCK'N
STRUGGLE
STRUGLING
STUDIE
STUMBL'D
STUMBLE
STUNNING
STUPENDIOUS
STUPID
STUPIDLY
STYX
SUBDUCTING
SUBDU'D
SUBDUING
SUBJECTS
SUBLUNAR
SUBMITS
SUBMITTING
SUBORDINATE
SUBORND
SUBSCRIB'D
SUBSTANTIALLY
SUBSTITUTE
SUBSTITUTES
SUBTERRANEAN
SUBURB
SUBVERTING
SUCCESSION
SUCCESSIVE
SUCCINCT
SUCCOUR
SUCKT
SUE
SUFFICIENTLY
SUFFRAGE
SUFFUSION
SUGGESTED
SUGGESTIONS
SUITE
SUITERS

1 (CONT.)
SULFUROUS
SUMLESS
SUMMD
SUMMON
SUMMONING
SUN-BRIGHT
SUN-LIGHT
SUN-SHINE
SUPERFICIALLY
SUPERNUMERARIE
SUPERSTITION
SUPERSTITIONS
SUPPLANTED
SUPPORTED
SUPPOSEST
SUPPREST
SUPREMACIE
SUPREMACY
SUPREME
SUPS
SURCEAS'D
SURELY
SURETY
SURFACE
SURMOUNTS
SURPASS'D
SURPASSEST
SURPRISAL
SURRENDER
SURROUND
SURROUNDING
SURROUNDS
SURVAY'D
SURVEY
SURVEYES
SURVEYING
SURVEYS
SUS
SUSA
SUSPECTED
SUSPENCE
SUSPEND
SUSPENDED
SUSPENS
SUSPENSE
SUSTAIN'D
SUSTAINE
SUSTEIND
SUTABLE
SUTTLETIE
SUTTLETY
SUTTL'ST
SUTTLY
SWAGE
SWALLOWD
SWALLOWS
SWAN
SWARM
SWARME
SWAY'D
SWAYES
SWEATIE
SWEETER
SWEET-SMELLING
SWELLING
SWERV'D
SWIFTER
SWIFTLY
SWIMMES
SWIMS
SWORD-LAW
SWORE
SWUMM
SYMPHONIE
SYMPHONIOUS
SYRTIS
TABERNACLES
TABLES
TACKLE
TAILE
TAINTED
TAKES
TAK'N
TALE
TALKT
TALLEST
TAM'D
TAME
TAMELY
TANGLES
TANGLING
TANTALUS
TARDIE
TARGE
TARSUS
TARTAREAN
TARTAREOUS
TASKE

1 (CONT.)
TAST
TAURIS
TAWNIE
TEACHER
TEACHERS
TEAR
TEARES
TEARMS
TEATS
TEDDED
TEEM'D
TELASSAR
TELLING
TEMIRS
TEMPERAT
TEMPERATE
TEMPERS
TEMPORAL
TEMPRING
TEMPTS
TENDERLY
TENDRILS
TENERIFF
TENOR
TENT
TENTH
TEPID
TERF
TERFE
TERNATE
TERRENE
TERRIFIC
TERRIFI'D
TERRIFIE
TERRITORIE
TERROURS
TESTIFI'D
TESTIFIES
TESTIMONIE
TESTIMONY
THAMYRIS
THAW
THAWS
THEATRE
THEMIS
*THEMSELVS
THEOLOGIANS
THEREAFTER
THEREAT
THEREON
THESSALIAN
THICKER
THICK'ND
THICK-RAMMD
THICK-WOV'N
THIGH
THIGHES
THIGHS
THIN
THINKS
THIRSTED
THIRSTIE
THISTLES
THITHER-WARD
THITHERWARD
THORN
THORNS
THOROUGH-FARE
THOUSANDFOULD
THRACIAN
THRALL
THRALLS
THRASCIAS
THREATENS
THREAT'ND
THREATNER
THREE-BOLTED
THREEFOLD
THRESHING
THRESHOLD
THRIVE
THRIVES
THROAT
THROATED
THROES
THRONED
THRONGD
THUNDERER
THUNDERERS
THUNDER-STRUCK
THUNDROUS
THURST
THWARTS
THYESTEAN
TIAR
TI'D
TIDE
TIDORE

1 (CONT.)
TIGRIS
TILES
TILLAGE
TILTH
TIMBER
TIMBRELS
TIMEROUS
TIMOROUS
TINCTUR'D
TINCTURE
TINE
TINSEL
TIPT
TIRE
TIRESIAS
TISSUES
TITAN
TITANIAN
TITL'D
TITULAR
TOAD
TOBIAS
TOBITS
TOLERABLE
TO MORROW
TONES
TOOK'ST
TOOLES
TOOLS
TOPAZ
TOPHET
TORCH
TORMENTED
TORMENTING
TORNE
TORNEAMENT
TORTUOUS
TORTURER
TORTURING
TOUCHD
TOUCHES
TOUCHING
TOUCH'T
TOULD
TOUR
TOUR'D
TOURING
TOURNAMENT
TOWNS
TOWR
TOWRED
TOY
TOYL
TOYLE
TRAC'T
TRADING
TRADITION
TRADITIONS
TRAGIC
TRAIND
TRAINES
TRAINING
TRAITOR
TRAMPL'D
TRAMPLE
TRANSACT
TRANSCEND
TRANSE
TRANSFERD
TRANSFERRE
TRANSFIX
TRANSFIXT
TRANSFORM
TRANSFORMD
TRANSGRESS'D
TRANSGRESSIONS
TRANSGRESSORS
TRANSGRESSOUR
TRANSGREST
TRANSIENT
TRANSITION
TRANSITORIE
TRANSLATED
TRANSMIGRATION
TRANSPARENT
TRANSPICUOUS
TRANSPIRES
TRANSUBSTANTIATE
TRAPPINGS
TRAVAIL
TRAVELL'D
TRAVELLING
TRAVERS'D
TRAVERSE
TRAVERSING
TREADING
TREASON
TREASURES

1 (CONT.)
TREAT
TREBISOND
TREBLE
TREMBLE
TREMBLED
TREMBLING
TREMISEN
TRENCH
TREPIDATION
TRIBULATION
TRIBULATIONS
TRIBUNAL
TRIDENT
TRIFORM
TRINACRIAN
TRINE
TRIPLE-COLOUR'D
TRIPLE-ROW
TRIPPING
TRITON
TRIUMPH'D
TRIUMPHT
TROD
TRODDEN
TROD'N
TROOPING
TROPIC
TROUBLES
TROUBLESOM
TROULE
TROY
TRULY
TRUMPERIE
TRUNCK
TRUNK
TRUTHS
TRYAL
TUBE
TUFTS
TUMID
TUMULTS
TUN
TUNE
TUNEABLE
TUNINGS
TURBULENT
TURCHESTAN-BORN
TURKISH
TURNUS
TURRET
TUSCAN
TWENTIE
TWIGS
TWINE
TWINES
TWINN'D
TWINS
TWO-HANDED
TYDE
TYGERS
TYPE
TYPHOEAN
TYPHOON
TYRANNIE
TYRANNIZE
TYRANNOUS
TYRANTS
UGLIER
ULCER
ULYSSES
UMBRAGE
UMBRAGEOUS
UNACCEPTABLE
UNACCOMPLISHT
UNADMONISHT
UNADOR'D
UNADORND
UNADORNED
UNAGREEABLE
UNAIDED
UNALTERABLY
UNAMAZ'D
UNANSWERD
UNAPPARENT
UNAPPROACHED
UNAPPROV'D
UNARGU'D
UNARM'D
UNARMED
UNASSAID
UNATTEMPTED
UNATTENDED
UNBARR'D
UNBECOMING
UNBEFITTING
UNBEGOT
UNBEHELD
UNBENIGHTED

1 (CONT.)
UNBENIGNE
UNBESAUGHT
UNBID
UNBOTTOM'D
UNBOUND
UNBROK'N
UNBUCKL'D
UNCALL'D
UNCELEBRATED
UNCERTAIN
UNCHANG'D
UNCHANGEABLE
UNCHECKT
UNCIRCUMSCRIB'D
UNCLEAN
UNCLOUDED
UNCOLOURD
UNCOMPOUNDED
UNCONCERN'D
UNCONFORM
UNCOVER'D
UNCROPT
UNCTION
UNCTUOUS
UNCULL'D
UNDAZL'D
UNDECKT
UNDEFIL'D
UNDELIGHTED
UNDERFOOT
UNDERGROUND
UNDERGROWTH
UNDERTAKE
UNDESERV'D
UNDESERVEDLY
UNDESIREABLE
UNDETERMIND
UNDISMAI'D
UNDISMAID
UNDO
UNDOE
UNDON
UNDOUBTED
UNDOUBTEDLY
UNDRAWN
UNDREADED
UNDYING
UNEARN'D
UNEASIE
UNENVIED
UNEQUALD
UNEQUALS
UNESSENTIAL
UNEXAMPL'D
UNEXPERIENC'T
UNEXPERT
UNEXTINGUISHABLE
UNFAINED
UNFAST'NS
UNFEARD
UNFOLD
UNFORBID
UNFOREKNOWN
UNFORESEEN
UNFOREWARND
UNFORM'D
UNFORTUNATE
UNFOULDING
UNFOUND
UNFOUNDED
UNFREQUENTED
UNFULFILL'D
UNFUM'D
UNFURLD
UNGODLY
UNGOVERN'D
UNGRACEFUL
UNHALLOWD
UNHAPPIE
UNHAPPILIE
UNHAPPY
UNHARMONEOUS
UNHEEDED
UNHIDE-BOUND
UNHOLIE
UNHOORD
UNHOP'T
UNHURT
UNIMAGINABLE
UNIMMORTAL
UNIMPLOID
UNINDEARD
UNINFORMD
UNINTERRUPTED
UNINVENTED
UNISON
UNITIE
UNIVERS

1 (CONT.)
UNIVERSALLY
UNJUSTLY
UNKINDNESS
UNLIBIDINOUS
UNLICENC'T
UNLIGHTSOM
UNLIMITED
UNLOCK
UNMAKE
UNMARKT
UNMEASUR'D
UNMEDITATED
UNMEET
UNMERITED
UNMINDED
UNMIXT
UNMOVD
UNOBEY'D
UNOBNOXIOUS
UNOBSCUR'D
UNOBSERV'D
UNOPPOS'D
UNORIGINAL
UNPAID
UNPAIND
UNPEOPL'D
UNPERCEAV'D
UNPERCEIVD
UNPIERC'T
UNPITIED
UNPITTIED
UNPOLLUTED
UNPOSSEST
UNPRACTIS'D
UNPRAIS'D
UNPREMEDITATED
UNPREPAR'D
UNPREVENTED
UNPROCLAM'D
UNPURG'D
UNPURSU'D
UNQUENCHABLE
UNREAL
UNREIN'D
UNREMOV'D
UNREPREEVD
UNREPROV'D
UNRESPITED
UNREVOK'T
UNRIGHTEOUS
UNRIVALD
UNSAFE
UNSAUGHT
UNSAVOURIE
UNSEARCHABLE
UNSEARCHT
UNSEASONABLE
UNSEDUC'D
UNSEEMLIEST
UNSEEMLY
UNSHAR'D
UNSHED
UNSKILFUL
UNSLEEPING
UNSMOOTH
UNSOUND
UNSPAR'D
UNSPARING
UNSPI'D
UNSPOIL'D
UNSPOTTED
UNSUCCEEDED
UNSUCCESSFUL
UNSUCKT
UNSUFFERABLE
UNSUPPORTED
UNSUSPECT
UNSUSPECTED
UNSUSTAIND
UNTAM'D
UNTAUGHT
UNTHOUGHT
UNTHRONE
UNTO
UNTOUCHT
UNTRACTABLE
UNTRAIND
UNTROD
UNTROUBL'D
UNUSUAL
UNUTTERABLE
UNVAILD
UNVANQUISHT
UNVISITED
UNVOYAGEABLE
UNWAK'ND
UNWEILDIE
UNWELCOME

1 (CONT.)
UNWIELDY
UNWILLING
UNWISE
UNWISER
UNWORSHIPT
UNWOUNDED
UPBORE
UPBORN
UP-BORNE
UPBRAID
UPGROWN
UPHEAV'D
UPHEAVE
UP-LIFT
UPRAIS'D
UPRAISE
UPREARD
UPRIGHTNESS
UPROARE
UPROOTED
UPROWLD
UPSENT
UPSPRINGING
UPSPRUNG
UPSTAID
UPSTAIES
UPSTOOD
UPTORE
UPTURN
UPTURN'D
UP-TURNS
UPWHIRLD
UR
URGE
URIM
URNS
USES
USEST
USURPATION
USURPER
UTHERS
UTTER'D
UTTERD
UTTERDST
UXORIOUS
UZZIEL
VACUITIE
VACUOUS
VAGABOND
VAGARIES
VAIL
VAILD
VAINLY
VALDARNO
VALID
VALLIES
VALLOMBROSA
VALLY
VALU'D
VANGUARD
VANISH
VANISHT
VANITIE
VANITY
VANNES
VANQUISH'D
VANQUISHER
VANTED
VARIABLE
VARIE
VARIETIE
VARIETY
VARIOUSLY
VARNISHT
VASSALAGE
VASSALS
VASTNESS
VAUNTS
VEGETABLE
VEHEMENCE
VEIL
VEILS
VEINE
VENIAL
VENOM
VENTRING
VENT'ROUS
VENTROUS
VENTUR'D
VERDUROUS
VERES
VERIFI'D
VERNANT
VERTUE-PROOF
VERTUMNUS
VERTUOUSEST
VESSELS
VEST

1 (CONT.)
VESTED
VEX
VEX'D
VIANDS
VICEGERENT
VICE-GERENT
VIEWLESS
VIEW'ST
VILLAGES
VILLIFI'D
VIOLATED
VIOLET
VIOLETS
VIRGINS
VIRTUE
VISAG'D
VISITANT
VISITED
VISITING
VISIT'ST
VITIATED
VITIOUS
VOIAGE
VOLANT
VOLATIL
VOLIE
VOLIED
VOLIES
VOLUBIL
VOLUBLE
VOLUMINOUS
VOLUPTUOUS
VOUCHT
VOUTSAF'D
VOUTSAF'ST

1 (CONT.)
VOYAG'D
VOYD
VULGAR
VULTUR
WADES
WAFTED
WAFTING
WAFTS
WAG'D
WAGE
WAGGONS
WAIES
WAIGHT
WAITS
WAK'ST
WALKES
WALKING
WALLES
WALLOWING
WANDERER
WANTOND
WANTONLY
WANTONNESS
WARBL'D
WARBLE
WARD
WARDS
WARFARE
WARIE
WARM'D
WARMD
WARMLY
WARMS
WARNING
WARPING

1 (CONT.)
WARRES
WARY
WASH
WASH'D
WASHIE
WASHING
WASHT
WASTED
WATCHD
WAXEN
WAXING
WEAKE
WEAKEST
WEAKNING
WEAR
WEARERS
WEARISOM
WEATHER-BEATEN
WED
WEDGE
WEDLOCK-BOUND
WEED
WEEDS
WEEND
WEENE
WEENING
WEEPE
WEEPING
WEIGH'D
WEIGHD
WEIGHTS
WELCOM
WELCOME
WELKIN
WELL-PLEASING

1 (CONT.)
WELNIGH
WELTRING
WENTST
WET
WHALES
WHAT ERE
WHATSOEVER
WHEELD
WHEELING
WHELM'D
WHELMD
WHELP'D
WHEN EVER
WHENEVER
WHERE ERE
WHERERE
WHERESO
WHEREWITHALL
WHICH E'RE
WHIP
WHIRLPOOL
WHISPER
WHISPER'D
WHISPERD
WHOL
WHOLLY
WHOMSOEVER
WHOSO
WICKEDNESS
WICKET
WIDEST
WIDE-WASTING
WIELD
WIGHT
WILFULLY

1 (CONT.)
WILLINGER
WINDIE
WINDING
WINDOW
WINDOWS
WINE-OFFERINGS
WINNOWS
WINS
WINTER
WIRE
WISDOM-GIVING
WISELIER
WISELY
WISHED
WISHES
WIT
WITCHES
WITHDRAWS
WITHDREW
WITHHOLD
WITHSTAND
WITHSTANDS
WITNESS'D
WITNESSES
WIVES
WOFUL
WOLFE
WOND'RING
WOND'ROUS
WONDROUSLY
WONN
WONNS
WOO'D
WOODBINE
WOOFF

1 (CONT.)
WORKING
WORK-MAISTER
WORLDLIE
WORME
WORSHIPERS
WORSHIPT
WORTHILY
WOUNDED
WOV'N
WRACK
WREATH
WREATH'D
WREATHD
WREATHES
WRESTED
WRINKL'D
WRONGD
XERXES
YEANLING
YEARES
YEELD
YEELDED
YEELDS
YEILDED
YELLING
YELLOW
YESTERDAY
YOAK
YONGER
YOUNGEST
ZEALOUS
ZEPHIR
ZEPHYR
ZEPHYRUS

[redacted]